ATHLETICS 2004

THE INTERNATIONAL TRACK AND FIELD ANNUAL

ASSOCIATION OF TRACK & FIELD STATISTICIANS

BY PETER MATTHEWS

SPORTSBOOKS

Published by SportsBooks Ltd

SportsBooks Limited
PO Box 422
Cheltenham
GL50 2YN
United Kingdom
Tel: 08700 713 965
Fax: 08700 750 888
e-mail randall@sportsbooks.ltd.uk
Website www.sportsbooks.ltd.uk

This publication incorporates the ATFS Annual.

Photographs supplied by Mark Shearman, 22 Grovelands Road, Purley, Surrey, CR8 4LA.
Tel: 0208-660-0156 Fax: 0208-660-3437

British Library Cataloguing in Publication Data

Athletics: the international track and
field annual – 2004
1. Athletics. Track & Field events –
Serials
1. International athletics annual (London)
796.4'2'05

ISBN 1899807 21 7

Cover design: Katherine Northam

Printed by Compass Press.

CONTENTS

INTRODUCTION

Olympic Year. In the spring of any such year the thoughts of all athletics enthusiasts are, of course, focused on the Games to come. In this Annual Bill Mallon take a look back at the Olympic Games held a century ago in St Louis – and how vastly different the world of sport is today. The Olympics grew rapidly in importance during the 20th century, and while there are now a lot of major international events, the staging of the Olympic Games remains all the more special for being just every four years, exciting the ambitions of athletes to maximum effect.

Arguably the supreme male and female athletes of our age are Hicham El Guerrouj and Paula Radcliffe, but neither has yet won an Olympic gold medal. For them Athens 2004 has long been the ultimate goal and we hope that they, as well as other top athletes, stay clear of injuries and reach prime form at the right time. We hope, too, that despite considerable worries in advance, that the staging of the Games in Athens is successful and that the weather is kind.

This Annual, with its considerable detail of the performances of the last year, is once again the indispensable guide to our sport. Such features as records, results, biographies (with a further increase in the number included), reviews and the deep world all-time and year lists remain substantially the same as in previous editions, enabling you, the reader, to have a huge array of facts at your fingertips. I always try to add in some extra miscellaneous items each year if I can without exceeding my page limitations, and also, as ever the book is as up-to-date as I can make it, with results of the 2004 World Indoor and Cross Country Championships, 2004 World Indoor lists and such details incorporated in the athlete biographies.

This year is the 50th anniversary of the running of the first sub 4-minute-mile by Roger Bannister at Oxford on 6 May 1954 and Bob Phillips writes about the build up to a feat that captured the imagination of the world in a way unparalleled by any other single performance in history. The accompanying statistics show the immense improvements in standards in the decades from the 1950s at the mile, a trend that was reflected across the whole range of athletic activity.

One of the other great barrier breakers of that age, Charles Dumas, the first seven-foot high jumper, died in January 2004, and within a few weeks, two of the greatest women athletes of all-time had also passed away – Fanny Blankers-Koen and Shirley Strickland – and we pay tribute to their brilliant feats with their career details in the Obituaries section.

Sadly, at the time of going to press, uncertainty remains over the allocation of several of the medals at the 2003 World Championships. The fight against drugs and the cheats who try to use illegal performance-enhancing substances goes on – but with large sums of money at stake and the need to ensure fair play for all, the processing of evidence is protracted and surely has taken far too long in these high-profile cases from last summer. In particular we have the discovery of THG, allegedly a tailor-made steroid, and the curious incidence of the use of Modafinil, a drug used to treat narcolepsy, by a group of athletes. The production of the former has taken the debate deep into the heart of American sport, and that could be good news for track and field athletics, which has for too long borne an unfair share of accusations about drug using while far worse abuse has been largely ignored in the major US pro sports.

Let us hope, perhaps against realistic expectations, that there are no major scandals this year over drugs, and in particular that the Olympics provide a supreme celebration of sporting excellence and that mix of drama, upsets, thrilling races and sustained brilliance that regularly renews our enthusiasm for the sport.

Peter Matthews
2 April 2004

Please send me information, results, corrections etc. to 10 Madgeways Close, Great Amwell, Ware, Herts SG12 9RU, England. Fax 44 1920-877392.
Email: pmatthews@macunlimited.net

Information or requests re sales, distribution, publication etc. to our publisher, Randall Northam, SportsBooks Ltd, 1 Evelyn Court, Cheltenham GL50 2JP. Fax 44 (0)1242 254326.
Email: randall@sportsbooks.ltd.uk

ABBREVIATIONS

Meeting Abbreviations

The following abbreviations have been used for meetings with, in parentheses, the first year that they were held.

AAA	(GBR) Amateur Athletic Association Champs (1880)
AAU	(USA) Amateur Athletic Union Champs (1888) (now TAC)
Af-AsG	Afro-Asian Games (2003)
AfCh	African Champs (1979)
AfG	African Games (1965)
Af-J	African Junior Champs
AmCp	America's Cup (World Cup Trial)
APM	Adriaan Paulen Memorial, Hengelo
AsiC	Asian Champs (1973)
AsiG	Asian Games (1951)
Asi-J	Asian Junior Champs
ASV	Weltklasse in Köln, ASV club meeting (1934)
Athl	Athletissima, Lausanne (1976)
Balk	Balkan Games (1929), C - Champs
Barr	(Cuba) Barrientos Memorial (1950)
BGP	Budapest Grand Prix (1978)
Bisl	Bislett Games, Oslo (1965)
BrGP	British Grand Prix
CAC	Central American and Caribbean Champs (1967)
CAG	Central American and Caribbean Games (1926)
CalR	California Relays (1942)
C.Asian	Central Asian Champs
CAU	Inter-counties, GBR (1934)
CISM	International Military Champs (1946)
CG	Commonwealth Games (1930)
DNG	DN Galan, Stockholm (1966)
Drake	Drake Relays (1910)
Drz	Druzhba/Friendship Games
EAsG	East Asian Games
EC	European Champs (1934)
ECCp	European Clubs Cup (1975)
EChall	European Challenge (10,000m) (1997, Throws 2001))
ECp	European Cup - track & field (1965), multi-events (1973)
EI	European Indoor Champs (1970, Games 1966-9)
EICp	European Indoor Cup (2003)EJ
	European Junior Champs (1970)
EU23	European Under-23 Champs (1997) and European Under-23 Cup (1992-4)
FBK	Fanny Blankers-Koen Games, Hengelo (formerly APM)
FlaR	Florida Relays (1939)
FOT	(USA) Final Olympic Trials (1920)
Franc	Francophone Games
Gaz	Gaz de France meeting, Paris, Lille or Villeneuve d'Ascq (was BNP) (1968)
GGala	Golden Gala, Roma (from 1980), Verona (1988), Pescara (1989), Bologna (1990)
GNR	Great North Run – Newcastle to South Shields, GBR (1981)
GO	Golden Oval, Dresden
GP	Grand Prix
GPF	IAAF Grand Prix Final (1985)
GS	Golden Spike, Ostrava (1969)
Gugl	Zipfer Gugl Grand Prix, Linz (1988)
GWG	Goodwill Games (1986)
Herc	Herculis, Monte Carlo, Monaco (1987)
IAAF	International Amateur Athletic Federation
IAAFg	IAAF Golden events (1978)
IAC	IAC meeting (1968), formerly Coca-Cola
IAU	International Association of Ultrarunners
IbAm	Ibero-American Champs (1983)
ISTAF	Internationales Stadionfest, Berlin (1921)
Izv	(URS) Izvestia Cup
Jen	Bruce Jenner Classic, San Jose (1979)
Jerome	Harry Jerome Track Classic (1984)
JUCO	Junior Colleges Champs, USA
KansR	Kansas Relays, Lawrence (1923)
King	Martin Luther King Games (1969)
Kuso	Janusz Kusocinski Memorial (1954)
Kuts	Vladimir Kuts Memorial
LAT	Los Angeles Times indoors (1960, from 1968 at Inglewood)
Macc	Maccabiah Games, Israel
MAI	Malmö AI Galan, Sweden (formerly Idag) (1958)
Mal	Malinowski Memorial, Poland
Mast	Masters pole vault, Grenoble (1987)
McD	McDonald's Games, Sheffield or London (1992)
MedG	Mediterranean Games (1951)
Mill	Millrose Games, New York indoors (1908)
ModR	Modesto Relays
MSR	Mt. San Antonio College Relays (1959)
NA	Night of Athletics, Heusden (2000) formerly Hechtel
NC	National Champs
NC-w	National Winter Champs
NCAA	National Collegiate Athletic Association Champs, USA (1921)
NCp	National Cup
NG	National Games
Nik	Nikaïa, Nice (1976)
NM	Narodna Mladezhe, Sofia (1955)
N.Sch	National Schools
Nurmi	Paavo Nurmi Games (1957)
NYG	New York Games (1989)
OD	Olympischer Tag (Olympic Day)
OG	Olympic Games (1896)
OT	Olympic Trials
Owens	Jesse Owens Memorial (1981)
PAm	Pan American Games (1951)
PArab	Pan Arab Champs (G- Games)
PennR	Pennsylvania Relays (1895)
Pepsi	Pepsi Cola Invitational
PG	Peugeot (Talbot) Games (1980), Royal Mail Parcels Games 1989-90, Parcelforce Games 1991
Prav	(URS) Pravda Cup
PTS	Pravda Televízia Slovnaft, Bratislava (1957) (now GPB)

Pre	Steve Prefontaine Memorial (1976)
RdVin	Route du Vin Half Marathon, Luxembourg
RomIC	Romanian International Champs (1948)
Ros	Evzen Rosicky Memorial, Praha (1947)
R-W	Rot-Weiss meeting, Koblenz
SACh	South American Champs (1919)
SEAG	South East Asia Games
SEC	Southeast Conference Champs
SGP	Softeland Grand Prix (walking)
Slovn	Slovnaft, Bratislava (formerly PTS) (1990)
Spark	Sparkassen Cup, Stuttgart (indoor) (1987)
Spart	(URS) Spartakiad (1956)
Stra	Stramilano Half marathon, Milan
TAC	(USA) The Athletics Congress Champs (1980-91)
TexR	Texas Relays (1925)
Toto	Toto International Super Meet, Tokyo
USOF	US Olympic Festival
VD	Ivo Van Damme Memorial, Brussels (1977)
Veniz	Venizelia, Haniá, Crete
WAAA	(GBR) Women's Amateur Athletic Association Champs (1922-91)
WAC	Western Athletic Conference Champs
WAF	World Athletics Finals, Monaco (2003)
WAfC	West African Champs
WAsG	West Asian Games
WCh	World Champs (1983)
WCp	World Cup - track & field (1977), marathon (1985) Walking – Lugano Trophy – men (1961), Eschborn Cup – women (1979)
WCT	World Champs Trial
WG	World Games, Helsinki (1961)
WI	World Indoor Champs (1987), World Indoor Games (1985)
WJ	World Junior Champs (1986)
WK	Weltklasse, Zürich (1962)
WMilG	World Military Games
WUG	World University Games (1923)
WY	World Youth Champs (1999)
Zat	Emil Zátopek Classic, Melbourne
Znam	Znamenskiy Brothers Memorial (1958)

-j, -y, -23 Junior, Youth or under-23

Dual and triangular matches are indicated by "v" (versus) followed by the name(s) of the opposition. Quadrangular and larger inter-nation matches are denoted by the number of nations and -N; viz 8-N designates an 8-nation meeting.

Events

CC	cross-country
Dec	decathlon
DT	discus
h	hurdles
Hep	heptathlon
HJ	high jump
HMar	half marathon
HT	hammer
JT	javelin
LJ	long jump
Mar	marathon
Pen	pentathlon
PV	pole vault
R	relay
SP	shot
St	steeplechase
TJ	triple jump
W	walk
Wt	weight

Miscellaneous abbreviations

+	Intermediate time in longer race
=	Tie (ex-aequo)
A	Made at an altitude of 1000m or higher
b	date of birth
D	Made in decathlon competition
dnf	did not finish
dnq	did not qualify
dns	did not start
exh	exhibition
h	heat
H	Made in heptathlon competition
hr	hour
i	indoors
kg	kilograms
km	kilometres
m	metres
M	mile
m/s	metres per second
mx	Made in mixed men's and women's race
O	Made in octathlon
P	Made in pentathlon
pb	personal best
Q	Made in qualifying round
qf	quarter final (or q in lists)
r	Race number in a series of races
sf	semi final (or s in lists)
w	wind assisted
WR	world record or best
WIR	world indoor record
y	yards
*	Converted time from yards to metres: For 200m: 220 yards less 0.11 second For 400m: 440 yards less 0.26 second For 110mh: 120yh plus 0.03 second

Countries

(IAAF membership reached 211 in 2003)

After the 2000 Olympic Games, the IAAF determined to align their abbreviations with those of the IOC, so we switched also. Former IAAF abbreviations are shown in brackets in this list.

AFG	Afghanistan
AHO	Netherlands Antilles
AIA	Anguilla (ANG)
ALB	Albania
ALG	Algeria
AND	Andorra
ANG	Angola (ANO)
ANT	Antigua & Barbuda
ARG	Argentina
ARM	Armenia
ARU	Aruba
ASA	American Samoa (AMS)
AUS	Australia
AUT	Austria
AZE	Azerbaijan
BAH	Bahamas
BAN	Bangladesh
BAR	Barbados
BDI	Burundi (BUR)
BEL	Belgium
BEN	Benin
BER	Bermuda

BHU	Bhutan
BIH	Bosnia Herzegovina (BSH)
BIZ	Belize
BLR	Belarus
BOL	Bolivia
BOT	Botswana
BRA	Brazil
BRK	Burkina Faso
BRN	Bahrain (BHR)
BRU	Brunei
BUL	Bulgaria
BUR	Burkina Faso (BKF)
CAF	Central African Republic
CAM	Cambodia
CAN	Canada
CAY	Cayman Islands
CGO	Congo
CHA	Chad
CHI	Chile
CHN	People's Republic of China
CIV	Côte d'Ivoire (Ivory Coast)
CMR	Cameroon
COD	Democratic Republic of Congo (ex ZAI Zaïre)
COK	Cook Islands (CKI)
COL	Colombia
COM	Comoros
CPV	Cape Verde Islands (CVD)
CRC	Costa Rica
CRO	Croatia
CUB	Cuba
CYP	Cyprus
CZE	Czech Republic
DEN	Denmark
DJI	Djibouti
DMA	Dominica (DMN)
DOM	Dominican Republic
ECU	Ecuador
EGY	Egypt
ENG	England
ERI	Eritrea
ESA	El Salvador
ESP	Spain
EST	Estonia
ETH	Ethiopia
FIJ	Fiji
FIN	Finland
FRA	France
FRG	Federal Republic of Germany (1948-90)
FSM	Micronesia
GAB	Gabon
GAM	The Gambia
GBR	United Kingdom of Great Britain & Northern Ireland
GBS	Guinea-Bissau
GDR	German Democratic Republic (1948-90)
GEO	Georgia
GEQ	Equatorial Guinea
GER	Germany (pre 1948 and from 1991)
GHA	Ghana
GIB	Gibraltar
GRE	Greece
GRN	Grenada
GUA	Guatemala
GUI	Guinea
GUM	Guam
GUY	Guyana
HAI	Haiti
HKG	Hong Kong, China
HON	Honduras
HUN	Hungary
INA	Indonesia
IND	India
IRI	Iran (IRN)
IRL	Ireland
IRQ	Iraq
ISL	Iceland
ISR	Israel
ISV	US Virgin Islands
ITA	Italy
IVB	British Virgin Islands (BVI)
JAM	Jamaica
JOR	Jordan
JPN	Japan
KAZ	Kazakhstan (KZK)
KEN	Kenya
KGZ	Kirgizstan
KIR	Kiribati
KOR	Korea
KSA	Saudi Arabia (from SAU)
KUW	Kuwait
LAO	Laos
LAT	Latvia
LBA	Libya
LBR	Liberia
LCA	St Lucia (STL)
LES	Lesotho
LIB	Lebanon
LIE	Liechtenstein
LTU	Lithuania (LIT)
LUX	Luxembourg
MAC	Macao
MAD	Madagascar
MAR	Morocco
MAS	Malaysia
MAW	Malawi
MDA	Moldova (MOL)
MDV	Maldives (MLD)
MEX	Mexico
MGL	Mongolia
MKD	Former Yugoslav Republic of Macedonia
MLI	Mali
MLT	Malta
MNT	Montserrat
MON	Monaco
MOZ	Mozambique
MRI	Mauritius
MSH	Marshall Islands
MTN	Mauritania
MYA	Myanmar (formerly BIR Burma)
NAM	Namibia
NCA	Nicaragua
NED	Netherlands (HOL)
NEP	Nepal
NFI	Norfolk Islands
NGR	Nigeria
NGU	Papua New Guinea (PNG)
NI	Northern Ireland
NIG	Niger
NMA	Northern Marianas Islands.
NOR	Norway
NRU	Nauru (NAU)
NZL	New Zealand
OMN	Oman
PAK	Pakistan
PAN	Panama
PAR	Paraguay
PER	Peru
PHI	Philippines
PLE	Palestine (PAL)
PLW	Palau
PNG	Papua New Guinea
POL	Poland
POR	Portugal
PRK	North Korea (DPR Korea)
PUR	Puerto Rico
PYF	French Polynesia
QAT	Qatar
ROM	Romania
RSA	South Africa
RUS	Russia
RWA	Rwanda
SAM	Western Samoa
SCG	Serbia & Montenegro (Crna Gora)
SCO	Scotland
SEN	Sénégal
SEY	Seychelles
SIN	Singapore
SKN	St Kitts & Nevis (STK)
SLE	Sierra Leone
SLO	Slovenia
SMR	San Marino
SOL	Solomon Islands
SOM	Somalia
SRI	Sri Lanka
STP	São Tomé & Principé
SUD	Sudan
SUI	Switzerland
SUR	Surinam
SVK	Slovakia
SWE	Sweden
SWZ	Swaziland
SYR	Syria
TAH	Tahiti
TAN	Tanzania
TCH	Czechoslovakia (to 1991)
TGA	Tonga (TON)
THA	Thailand
TJK	Tadjikistan
TKM	Turkmenistan
TKS	Turks & Caicos Islands
TLS	East Timor
TOG	Togo
TPE	Taiwan (Chinese Taipeih)
TRI	Trinidad & Tobago
TUN	Tunisia
TUR	Turkey
UAE	United Arab Emirates
UGA	Uganda
UKR	Ukraine
URS	Soviet Union (to 1991)
URU	Uruguay
USA	United States
UZB	Uzbekistan
VAN	Vanuatu
VEN	Venezuela
VIE	Vietnam
VIN	St Vincent & the Grenadines (STV)
WAL	Wales
YEM	Republic of Yemen
YUG	Yugoslavia (to 2002)
ZAM	Zambia
ZIM	Zimbabwe

ACKNOWLEDGEMENTS

My thanks, as always, go to the worldwide collection of experts have helped me to make this book the supreme compilation of information on our sport.
Firstly I would like to think the ATFS members who have contributed most to the annual world lists: Mirko Jalava, Jirí Havlín and Richard Hymans and to Milan Skocovsky for juniors. Then to such specialist contributors as Carlos Fernández for middle and long-distance events, Dr. David E Martin, marathons, Emmerich Götze, walks and relays, and Winfried Kramer for national records and widespread probing for results. Throughout the year the area specialists contribute invaluable work: *Africa*: Yves Pinaud, *Asia*: Heinrich Hubbeling, *Central and South America*: Eduardo Biscayart and Luis Vinker, *Europe*: Nejat Kök.
The following specialists supplied information for their respective areas of interest and countries:
Records Martin Rix, *Ultrarunning* Andy Milroy, *Indoors* Ed Gordon, *Men's middle and long distance* Ian Smith, *Multi events:* Hans van Kuijen, Enrique Tré, Enn Endjärv and Vaclav Klvana.
Albania: Luigi Mengoni; *Australia*: Paul Jenes and David Tarbotton; *Austria*: Dr Karl Graf; *Belgium*: André de Hooghe and Alain Monet; *Bulgaria*: Alexander Vangelov; *Caribbean*: Bernard Linley and Néstor Calixto; *Canada*: Cecil Smith; *China*: Mirko Jalava and Shen Xinsheng; *Cuba*: Roberto Ávila, Basilio Fuentes, Alberto Sánchez and Eddy Nápoles; *Czech Republic*: Milan Skocovsky, Jirí Havlín and Milan Urban; *Denmark*: Erik Laursen; *Estonia*: Erlend Teemägi; *Finland*: Juhani Jalava, Mirko Jalava and Matti Hannus; *France*: Alain Bouillé, Jean Gilbert and Yves Pinaud; *Germany*: Sven Kuus and Klaus Amrhein; *Greece*: Thomas Konstas; *Hungary*: György Csiki; *Iceland*: Fridrik Oskarsson; *India*: R Murali Krishnan; *Ireland*: Liam Hennessy and Pierce O'Callaghan; *Israel*: David Eiger; *Italy*: Raul Leoni; *Jamaica*: Richard Ashenheim; *Japan*: Yoshimasa Noguchi, Akihiro Onishi, Isao Sugawara and Ken Nakamura; *Kenya*: Phil Minshull; *Latvia*: Andris Stagis; *Lithuania*: Stepas Misiunas; *Luxembourg*: Georges Klepper; *Netherlands*: Wilmar Kortleever and Remko Riebeek; *New Zealand*: Peter Heidenstrom; *Norway*: Tore Johansen and Børre Lilloe; *Pacific Islands*: Tony Isaacs; *Poland*: Zbigniew Jonik, Janusz Rozum, Tadeusz Wolejko and Henryk Paskal; *Portugal:* Manuel Arons Carvalho; *Romania*: Alexandru Boriga; *Russia*: Sergey Tikhonov; *San Marino:* Dr Giorgio Rizzoli; *Serbia & CG*: Ozren Karamata; *Slovakia*: Alfons Juck; *Slovenia*: Zdravko Peternelj; *South Africa:* Gert le Roux and Riël Haumann; *Spain*: José Luis Hernández, Carles Baronet and the AEEA team; *Sweden*: A.Lennart Julin, Owe Fröberg, Peter Larsson and Birger Fält; *Switzerland*: Alberto Bordoli and Antonin Hejda; *Syria and Arab world*: Fouad Habbash; *Turkey* Nejat Kök; *Ukraine*: Oleg Cherkasenko and Leonid Epshteyn; *UK*: Peter Matthews and Ian Hodge; *USA*: FAST and Track Newsletter.
Also various national federation lists and to those who post results or ranking lists to various web sites.
Also to Marco Buccellato, Mark Butler, Malcolm Campbell, Ottavio Castellini (IAAF), Eric Cowe, José Maria García, Arild Gjerde, Stan Greenberg, Norbert Heinrich, Raymundt Herdt, Ove Karlsson, Alan Lindop, Rooney Magnusson, Bill Mallon, Pino Mappa, David Martin, Tony Miller, Walt Murphy, Lionel Peters, Bob Phillips, Chris Turner, Pierre-Jean Vazel and Ken Young. And, as ever, to Rob Whittingham for his computer expertise and advice.
My apologies to anybody whose name I may have missed or who have corresponded with other key ATFS personnel, but all help, however small, is deeply appreciated.

Keep the results flowing

During the year Mel Watman and I publish all marks that we know about to ATFS standards in *Athletics International*, of which there are 30 issues per year. This serves as a base from which the lists in this book can be compiled, together with information from the major magazines that are published around the world, such as *Track & Field News* (USA) with its email results spin-off *Track Newsletter*, and *Leichtathletik* (Germany) and the newsletters with particular spheres of interest such as Yves Pinaud's *Lettre de l'Athlétisme, Atletismo en España* by Francisco J Ascorbe and José Luis Hernández, and Luis Vinker's *South America Bulletin*,.
Many of the national contributors to *Athletics International* are included in the list above. In order to ensure that the record of 2004 is as complete as possible I urge results contribution worldwide to AI, and then in turn our lists in *Athletics 2005* will be as comprehensive as we can make them.

Peter Matthews

THE ASSOCIATION OF TRACK & FIELD STATISTICIANS

The ATFS was founded in Brussels (at the European Championships) in 1950 and ever since has built upon the work of such key founding members as Roberto Quercetani, Don Potts and Fulvio Regli to produce authoritative ranking lists in the International Athletics Annual and elsewhere.

Current Executive Committee

President
Paul Jenes AUS
Vice-President
A.Lennart Julin SWE
Secretary General
Scott Davis USA
Treasurer
Rob Whittingham GBR
Past Presidents
Rooney Magnusson SWE
Dr Roberto Quercetani ITA
Bob Sparks GBR
Committee
Jír]í Havlín CZE
Nejat Kök TUR
Gert le Roux RSA
Bernard Linley TRI
Peter J Matthews GBR
Yves Pinaud FRA
Tatsumi Senda JPN
Luis R Vinker ARG

For details of ATFS Membership, which is open to keen statisticians, apply to the secretary:
Scott Davis, 4432 Snowbird Circle, Cerritos, California 90703, USA.
EMail address: ssd@aol.com

Internet – Web sites

Sites of international and national federations or other comprehensive sites for athletics: (all start – http://)

IAAF	www.iaaf.org
CAC Confederation	www.athlecac.org
European AA	www.european-athletics.org
World Mountain Running Association	www.wmra.info
World Masters Athletics	www.world-masters-athletics.org
Africa	www.africathle.com
Andorra	www.faa.ad
Argentina	www.cada-atletismo.org
Australia	www.athletics.org.au
Austria	www.oelv.at
Bahamas	www.bahamastrack.com
Belgium	www.val.be www.lbfa.be
Bermuda	www.bermudatracknfield.com
Bolivia	www.atle-bolivia.com
Brazil	www.cbat.org.br
Bulgaria	www.athletics.netbg.com
Canada	www.athleticscanada.com
Caribbean	www.cac-athletics.org
Chile	www.fedachi.cl
China	www.chinaaa.net
Croatia	www.has.hr
Czech Republic	www.atletika.cz
Denmark	www.dansk-atletik.dk
Estonia	www.ekjl.ee
Finland	www.sul.fi
France	www.athle.org
Georgia	www.geo-athletic.de
Germany	www.leichtathletik.de
Great Britain	www.ukathletics.net
deeper statistics	www.britishathletics.info
Greece	www.segas.gr
also for results	www.athletix.org
Hong Kong	www.hkaaa.com
Hungary	www.masz.hu
Iceland	www.fri.is
India	www.aafindia.com
Ireland	www.athleticsireland.ie
Israel	www.iaa.co.il http://members.tripod.com/~eiger
Italy	www.fidal.it
Jamaica	www.jaaa.org.jm
Japan	www.rikuren.or.jp
Kenya	www.athleticskenya.org
Korea	www.kaaf.or.kr
Kuwait	www.kaaf.net/home.htm
Latvia	www.lat-athletics.lv
Lithuania	www.laf.lt
Luxembourg	www.fla.lu
Macedonia	www.asm.org.mk
Malta	www.global.net.mt/maaa
Mauritius	www.maaa.intnet.mu
Monaco	www.fma.mc
Netherlands	www.knau.nl
New Zealand	www.athletics.org.nz
Nigeria	www.afn.org.ng
Northern Ireland	www.niathletics.org
Norway	www.friidrett.no
Poland	www.pzla.pl
Portugal	www.fpatletismo.pt
Puerto Rico	www.fapur.net
Romania	www.fra.ro
Russia	www.rusathletics.ru www.russian-athletics.org
San Marino	www.omniway.sm/cons
Saudi Arabia	www.saaaf.com
Scotland	www.saf.or.uk
Serbia & Montenegro	www.asj.org.yu
Singapore	www.singaporeathletics.org.sg
Slovakia	www.saz.sk
Slovenia	www.atletska-zveza.si
South Africa	www.athletics.org.za
Spain	www.sportec.es/rfea/
Sweden	www.friidrott.se
Switzerland	www.swiss-athletics.ch
Turkey	www.taf.org.tr
USA	www.usatf.org
Venezuela	www.mipagina.cantv.net/feveatletismo
US Virgin Islands	www.virginislandspace.org
Wales	www.welshathletics.org

Other recommended sites for statistics and results

AIMS	www.aims-association.org
ARRS	www.arrs.net
Mirko Jalava	www.tilastopaja.com
Martin Rix site	www.gbrathletics.com
Running Stats	www.runningstats.com
Runners World	www.runnersworld.com
Track & Field News	www.trackandfieldnews.com
Ultramarathon news	www.ultramarathonworld.com
US colleges	www.fansonly.com
World junior news	www.wjan.org

DIARY OF 2003

by Peter Matthews

A chronological survey of highlights in major events in the world of track and field athletics during the year

January

6 **San Giorgio Su Legnano**, Italy. Sergey Lebed had a fine win over top African opposition in the 47th edition of the Campaccio international cross-country race, near Milan

12/19 **Elgóibar/Seville**, Spain. Kenenisa Bekele had his 11th and 12th successive cross-country victories, unbeaten since losing by inches to Haile Gebrselassie in December 2001.

30 **Moscow**, Russia. Irina Privalova was third in a 400m race in 53.88 in her first race since her Sydney Olympic 400mh victory in 53.02, a serious knee injury and the birth of a daughter in December 2001.

26 **Osaka**, Japan. Five women broke 2:24 in the annual international women's marathon, Mizuki Noguchi, in her second marathon moved to eighth on the world all-time list with 2:21:18 and was followed home by Masako Chiba 2:21:45 and Naoko Sakamoto 2:21:51; these three were later to be 2-3-4 in the World Champs.

February

1 **Boston (Roxbury)**, USA. 39 year-old Regina Jacobs broke 4 minutes for the first time in her long career in setting a world indoor record of 3:59.98 at the adidas Boston Indoor Games. She went out fast early, running splits of 62.3 for 400, 2:06.2 for 800, 2:38.8 at 1000 and 3:12.0 for 1200m. Stacy Dragila added 1cm her American pole vault record with 4.71.

2 **Glasgow**, GBR. After five world indoor vault records in 2002, Svetlana Feofanova produced her sixth successive one centimetre addition to the record with a first-time clearance at 4.76. Britain was the winning team in the Norwich Union International with 59 from Russia 58, European Select 56, Sweden 42 and Italy 39. Colin Jackson celebrated his record 70th international appearance for Britain by winning the 60m hurdles in 7.55.

2 **Stuttgart**, Germany. Berhane Adere ran the second-fastest ever indoor 3000m with 8:31.73 at the 17th Sparkassen Cup meeting. Svetlana Feofanova vaulted 4.71 to add a centimetre to Stacy Dragila's best and, despite complete inexperience of indoor running, cut almost four seconds off Gabriela Szabo's year-old 3000m mark with 8:29.15 (leading from 2000m in 5:41.80).

5 **Dortmund**, Germany. Berhane Adere just missed Gabriela Szabo's 14:47.35 world indoor record for 5000m with an African record 14:48.21.

7 **Millrose Games**, New York, USA. 36-year-old Gail Devers broke Jackie Joyner-Kersee's 14 year-old American record with 7.78 for 60m hurdles at the 96th edition of this famous indoor meeting; her previous best was 7.85 in 1994. Stacy Dragila added another centimetre to her US vault record.

8 **Arnstadt**, Germany. Stefan Holm jumped a personal best and world-leading 2.36 to win the 27th High Jump with Music competition, and Yaroslav Rybakov's 2.34 for second was also a personal best. Marina Kuptsova won the women's event from Kajsa Bergqvist on count-back, both jumping 2.02

9 **Gent**, Belgium. Alberto García's 13:11.39 took the European indoor 5000m record of 13:20.8 set by Emile Puttemanns back in 1975. This was the first of the four Energizer Euroseries meetings staged over two weeks – to come: Stockholm, Birmingham and Liévin.

15 **Fayetteville**, USA. Terrence Trammell achieved the fastest ever one-day double with 6.46 for 60m and 7.42 for 60mh at the Tyson Invitational.

15 **European Indoor Cup**, Leipzig, Germany. Highlight of this inaugural event staged in the new 42 million Euro state-of-the-art Arena Leipzig was the pole vaulting of Svetlana Feofanova, who won at 4.65 and took three unsuccessful attempts at a world record 4.77. Her win helped Russia to a clear-cut women's team victory. Spain won the men's title. *See Championships section for winners.*

16 **Donetsk**, Ukraine. Tim Lobinger won the Zepter Pole Vault Stars meeting with 5.81. In 4th place at the 14th edition of this annual competition founded by the great Sergey Bubka, was Artyom Kuptsov with a world junior indoor best 5.66.

16 **Kumamoto**, Japan. Takayuki Matsumiya ran a world 30km road best of 1:28:36.

18 **Stockholm**, Sweden. Yuriy Borzakovskiy won a superb 800m in 1:44.37 from Wilson Kipketer 1:44.68, Mehdi Baala 1:44.82 and Wilfred Bungei 1:45.08. Kajsa Bergqvist delighted her home crowd with a Swedish high jump record at 2.03.

21 **Birmingham**, GBR. Svetlana Feofanova cleared 4.77 for another world indoor

pole vault record and Haile Gebrselassie ran a world indoor best for 2 miles of 8:04.69. His 400m splits were approx 60.0, 2:01.2, 3:01.7, 4:01.6 and 5:01.5 as he followed Graham Hood (59.49, 2:00.82, 2:31.08, 3:01.29, 4:01.42) and Gert-Jan Liefers (4:03.1 mile, 5:01.37 2000) and he maintained that formidable pace to the finish – 2400 in 6:01.86, 2800 in 7:02.85 and 3000 in 7:32.81, a time only he and Daniel Komen have ever bettered indoors. Jonathan Edwards won the triple jump with 17.44 and Christian Olsson was only 4th with 16.92 after 27 successive meetings over 17m.

22 **Seville**, Spain. Alberto García set his second European record of the winter with 7:32.98 for 3000m.

23 **Liévin**, France. Hicham El Guerrouj's 8:06.61 2 miles would have been a world best until two days earlier. Overall winners of the Energizer mini-Grand Prix were James Davis (400m), Coby Miller (60m), Christian Olsson (TJ) and Muriel Hurtis (60m).

23 **San Juan**, Puerto Rico. Despite warm, humid weather and a hilly course, Paula Radcliffe began 2003 just as she had in 2002 with an astonishing run to win the 'World's Best 10k Road Race' in 30:21,which was ratified as the inaugural world record for the event by the IAAF at the end of the year. She won $120,000 including a $100k WR bonus. Men's winner was Hendrick Ramaala in 28:16.

23 **Yokohama**, Japan. The Russian women's team won the 21st edition of the oldest international Ekiden by six seconds from Ethiopia in 2:15:10.

25-27 **Russian Indoor Championships**, Moscow. For the first time ever, indoors or out, four women high jumped 2m or higher in the same competition. Winner was Yelena Yelesina 2.02 from Anna Chicherova 2.02, Marina Kuptsova 2.00 and Svetlana Lapina 2.00. There was a world best at the rarely contested women's indoor 3000m steeplechase from Gulnara Samitova (9:29.54). Natalya Gorelova moved to third on the indoor world all-time list for 1500m with her Russian record 4:00.75.

28 **Karlsruhe**, Germany. Haile Gebrselassie won the 3000m in 7:28.29, the world's top mark of the season and Yamilé Aldama the women's triple jump with 14.88.

28-2 Mar **US Indoor Championships**, Boston (Roxbury). Stacy Dragila regained her world indoor pole vault record with her second attempt at 4.78 and Gail Devers improved her US 60m hurdles record to 7.74 in a heat. There were 2003 world bests from Allen Johnson, 7.39 for 60mh, and Justin Gatlin, 6.45 for 60m, with Terrence Trammell second in both in.7.43 and 6.48. Regina Jacobs won the 1500m and 3000m to take her to 24 US national titles at all events.

March

1-2 **3rd EAA Winter Throws Challenge**, Gioia Tauro, Italy. The top mark came from Manuela Montebrun with 72.18 in the women's hammer. *See Championships section for leading results.*

8-9 **Tijuana**, Mexico. The first stage of the new IAAF Race Walking Challenge included a great three-way clash at 20km, in which Bernardo Segura prevailed in 1:19:06 from Francisco Fernández 1:19:08 and Robert Korzeniowski 1:19:11.

14-15 **NCAA Indoor Championships**, Fayetteville, Arkansas. Arkansas took their 17th men's title and LSU, headed by Muna Lee's 60m/200m double, their 10th women's title. Carl Myerscough took the Commonwealth shot record with 21.49.

14-16 **World Indoor Championships**, Birmingham, GBR. Top performance of a highly successful meeting was Svetlana Feofanova's world pole vault record of 4.80, winning her a $50,000 bonus on top of the $40,000 first prize. Championship records also fell in the women's 1500m (Regina Jacobs 4:01.67), 60m hurdles (Gail Devers 7.80), shot (Irina Korzhanenko 20.55) and pentathlon (Carolina Klüft 4933). Klüft, one of four Swedes to win gold medals, gave thrilling demonstration of individual brilliance (8.19, 1.89, 14.48, 6.61, 2:15.58) for the second best ever score and Maria Mutola won her fifth world indoor title at 800m (tying the record of Stefka Kostadinova if one includes the World Indoor Games of 1985). World-leading marks for 2003 were set in ten events and a total of 55 national records (six of them area records) were established. Most successful nation was the USA with 10 gold, 3 silver and 4 bronze medals from Russia 5-4-3. Two of their stars were Justin Gatlin, whose win in 6.46 to Kim Collins 6.53 was the biggest margin at 60m in the nine championships, and Michelle Collins who ran the fastest indoor 200m since 1995 with a US record 22.18. *For leading results see Athletics 2003 p.607.*

16 **Lisbon**, Portugal. As usual there was a top quality field in the annul half marathon (69m downhill overall). Martin Lel won in 60:10, with Derartu Tulu 69:20 the first woman.

22 **Sydney**, Australia. Jana Pittman smashed her pb to win the 400m in 50.43 and end the 24 race winning streak (1999-2003) at 400m of Cathy Freeman, second in 51.81. Freeman won the Australian title in 51.66 but later declared her retirement.

29-30 **World Cross-Country Championships**, La Broye region, Switzerland. Kenenisa Bekele repeated his amazing feat of 2003 by winning both short and long course titles. He won a total of $60,000 for his individual wins plus a share of $32,000 awarded to the Ethiopian team for their two second places behind the Kenyans, who won the 12km team award for the 18th consecutive year. Africans took the first 22 places in the men's junior race, with Eliud Kipchoge leading Kenya to their 15th junior team title in 16 years. Worknesh Kidane outkicked Deena Drossin to win the women's s 8km title but was just beaten by Edith Masai in the 4km race. Kenya won the women's 4km team title and Ethiopia the 12km and junior women's, in which Tirunesh Dibaba was the individual champion. *For details see Athletics 2003 p.608.*

April

4 **Pretoria**, South Africa. Shaun Crawford had a brilliant sprint double, 10.07 and 20.08, in the second of three Engen Grand Prix meetings.

6 **Paris Marathon**, France. Four men beat 2:07 in the 27th edition of this race: Mike Rotich won in 2:06:33 from Benoit Zwierchiewski ,who equalled the European record of 2:06:36, Wilson Onsare, the fastest ever marathon debut 2:0-6:47, and Driss El Himer 2:06:48.

12 **European Challenge 10,000m**, Athens (Ellinikó), Greece. Ismaïl Sghyr and Fernanda Ribeiro had clear wins. *See Championships section for medallists.*

13 **London Marathon**, GBR. Paul Radcliffe left even her great runs of 2002 behind with a wonderful win which depleted all available superlatives as she took another 1:53 off the world record with 2:15:25 and set world bests en route at 30km (1:36:36, compared to the initial IAAF mark of 1:39:02, but slightly downhill to this stage) and 20 miles (1:43:33). She went through 10km in 32:01 and reached halfway in 68:02, before a second half marathon of 67:23, which was equal to the best that any other woman managed for a half marathon alone in 2003!. There was controversy over the fact that she was accompanied for most of the way by two Kenyan men, Samson Loywapet and Christopher Kandie, but a look at the split times shows that she dictated the pace throughout and it is unlikely that her companions made any significant difference to her performance. She won a total of $255,000 ($55,000 for first place, $50,000 for breaking 2:22, $25,000 for a course record and $125,000 world record bonus), and it has been estimated that together with appearance fees and sponsors' bonuses she earned some $600,000 from the race. Way behind Radcliffe, Catherine Ndereba was second in 2:19:55 and Deena Drossin third in a US record 2:21:16.

Just 14 seconds separated the top seven men, and winner Gezahegne Abera and runner-up Stefano Baldini both ran 2:07:56 with Joseph Ngolepus third at 2:07:57 and Paul Tergat fourth in 2:07:59.

Paula's mile splits: 5:10, 10:18 (5:08), 15:15 (4:57), 20:22 (5:07), 25:32 (5:10), 30:54 (5:22), 36:06 (5:12), 41:17 (5:11), 46:35 (5:18), 51:48 (5:13), 56:58 (5:10), 1:02:14 (5:16), 1:07:30 (5:16), 1:12:38 (5:08), 1:17:48 (5:10), 1:23:01 (5:13), 1:28:08 (5:07), 1:33:19 (5:11), 1:38:26 (5:07), 1:43:33 (5:07), 1:48:44 (5:11), 1:53:50 (5:06), 1:59:03 (5:13), 2:04:06 (5:03), 25M-2:09:14 (5:08).

13 **Rotterdam Marathon**, Netherlands. William Kiplagat beat his former schoolmate Josephat Kiprono 2:07:42 to 2:07:53 and the women's winner was Olivera Jevtic in a national record 2:25:23.

17-19 **Mt SAC Relays**, Walnut, California, USA. As ever there was great depth of competition at this meeting and fast sprinting captured the headlines. Maurice Greene was an impressive winner over Coby Miller 20.16 to 20.59 in his first outdoor race of the season, Kelli White ran a pb of 10.97 in the 100m and 17 year-old high school student Allyson Felix set a US junior record of 22.51.

18-19 **Kansas Relays**, Lawrence, USA. Kevin Toth's shot mark of 22.67 was the best throw in the world since 1990.

19 **European 100km Challenge**, Chernogolovka, Russia. *See Championships section for medallists.*

21 **Boston Marathon**, USA. Kenyans dominated the men's race as usual with Robert K Cheruiyot winning in 2:10:11, but Svetlana Zakharova was the women's winner in 2:25:20.

26 **Fort-de-France**, Martinique. Top performances at the GP II meeting came from Allen Johnson, 13.21w at 110mh, and Maurice Greene, 20.31 at 200m.

May

1 **Sesto San Giovanni**, Italy. 20km winners at this IAAF Walking Challenge event were Francisco Fernández 1:19:25 and Gillian O'Sullivan in an Irish record 1:27:22.

3 **Mexico City**. Ana Guevara broke Kathy Cook's 1984 world best of 35.46 with an altitude-assisted time of 35.30 for 300m (although Marita Koch was timed at 34.1 en route to her world 400m record of 47.60 in 1985). Allyson Felix broke the world junior 200m record, held since 1980 by Natalya Bochina of Russia at 22.19, with 22.11.

4 **Belém**, Brazil. This IAAF Grand Prix I meeting attracted the largest ever crowd (41,215) for a track and field event in South America. Maurren Maggi starred with a 6.80 long jump win.

5 **Mito**, Japan. Patrick Johnson, who had run 9.88w in Perth on 8 February, ran the year's fastest wind-legal 100m time of 9.93, an Oceania record.

10 **62nd Modesto Relays**, USA. Top marks included a 2.34 high jump by Matt Hemingway.

10 **Osaka** GP, Japan. Tim Montgomery just beat Patrick Johnson 10.04 to 10.05 at

100m at this IAAF Grand Prix meeting. Koji Murofushi was a popular hammer winner with 82.95.

17 **Oregon Track Classic** (Portland Grand Prix), Gresham, USA. In cold and wet conditions, John Capel, in his first outdoor 200m since the Sydney Olympics, won in 20.38 by inches from Darvis Patton.

18 **European Cup of Race Walking**, Cheboksary, Russia. Russia dominated, with three of the five team titles, and individual senior winners in German Skurygin, 50km 3:47:50, and Yelena Nikolayeva, women's 20km 1:26:22. Francisco Fernández won the 20km in 1:19:48. 245 walkers from 27 nations took part in races wtached by large crowds. *See Championships section for details.*

24 **Halle**, Germany. Lars Riedel, 69.50 discus, and Jan Zelezny, 87.92, were in top form at the annual throwers' meeting, and Natalya Sadova's discus throw of 69.38 remained the world's top mark of 2003.

24 **28th Prefontaine Classic**, Eugene, USA. Ana Guevara, who ran 49.34 in her first 400m of the season and Brigitte Foster, 12.45 for 100mh, a Jamaican and CAC record just 0.01 outside the Commonwealth record, were amongst ten world-leading marks,

24-25 **European Champion Clubs Cup**, Valencia, Spain. As in 2001, Sports Club Luch of Moscow won the men's title for the sixth time in seven years and the women's for the seventh successive year. No new meeting records were set and top marks included 85.53 javelin by Aleksandr Ivanov and a 200m/400m double in 22.58w and 51.46 by Anastasiya Kapachinskaya. *See Championships section for details.*

28 **Hyderabad**, India. The first of a new series of Asian Grand Prix meetings with 13 individual events at each meeting which continued in Colombo SRI on 1 June, Bangkok THA on 5 June and Manila PHI on 9 June.

30 **Dessau**, Germany. The one 90m javelin throw of the year, Sergey Makarov 90.11, came at the 'Anhalt 2003' meeting.

30-31 **NCAA Regionals**. A new US Collegiate system of having four regional qualifying meetings for the NCAAs came into force this year. The top 5 individuals (and top 3 relays) in each automatically qualified for the Nationals. Meetings were: Mideast at Columbus, Ohio, East at Fairfax, Virginia, Midwest at Lincoln, Nebraska, and West at Stanford.

31 **Barrientos Memorial**, Havana, Cuba. Yipsi Moreno set her 18th CAC women's hammer record with 74.07.

31- June 1 **Götzis**, Austria. In a near repeat of the 2002 result, Roman Sebrle won the decathlon with 8807 from Tom Pappas 8585. Carolina Klüft continued her relentless progress by winning the women's heptathlon by 389 points in a Swedish record 6602..

June

1 **Carson**, USA. Maurice Greene ran 9.94 for 100m at the Home Depot Invitational in this Los Angeles suburb, the site for the 2006 World Cup. Kelli White took the women's race in a windy 10.79.

1 **Hengelo**, Netherlands. Kenenisa Bekele covered the last 1km in 2:30.5 to outkick his hero Haile Gebrselassie, 26:53.70 to 26:54.58 and in third place Sileshi Sihine ran 26:58.76 in the 10,000m at the Fanny Blankers-Koen Games (IAAF GP meeting). There were also there were world-leading marks by Wilfred Bungei, 800m 1:43.05, Paul Koech, 3000m St 8:06.68, and Marina Kuptsova, 2.02 high jump and James Kwalia took 0.02 off the world junior mile record with 3:50.39.

3 **Milan**, Italy (IAAF GP II). Maurren Maggi, whose great grandfather emigrated from Italy to Brazil, long jumped a world-leading 7.06. She tested positive for steroids eleven days later.

6 **Turin**, Italy (IAAF GP II). Hicham El Guerrouj opened his season with a 7:30.23 3000m and Cuban-born Magdelin Martinez set an Italian triple jump record of 14.77 at the Memorial Primo Nebiolo.

6 **Warstein**, Germany. Tegla Loroupe set a world record for the very rarely run 30,000m, but her time 1:45:50:00 is far inferior to many road race times..

7 **La Coruña**, Spain. 20km winners at this IAAF Walking Challenge event were Robert Korzeniowski 1:19:56 and Yelena Nikolayeva in 1:27:25.

7 **Seville**, Spain (IAAF GP). Róbert Fazekas had a clear discus win over Virgilijus Alekna, 69.62 to 66.21, and Wilfred Bungei beat Yuriy Borzakovskiy, 1:43.62 to 1:43.93 at 800m.

7 **US Open**, Stanford, USA (IAAF GP II). Miesha McKelvy starred with a 12.60 win at 100mh and a record four Americans, headed by Amy Acuff 1.9,7 cleared 1.97 in the women's high jump.

7-8 **Arles**, France. Eunice Barber totalled 6694 in her first heptathlon for two years.

7-8 **35th South American Junior Championships**, Guayaquil, Ecuador. *See Championships section for winners.*

7-8 **Znamenskiy Memorial**, Tula, Russia. Natalya Khrushchelyova, 800m 1:58.05, and Olga Kuzenkova, hammer 71.38, were amongst the top performers at a meeting which had IAAF GP II status, but is now almost exclusively domestic.

9 **Rehlingen**, Germany. Boris Henry, javelin 88.10, was the top performer at the 39th Internationales Pfingstsportfest.

10 **Bratislava**, Slovakia. IAAF GP II meeting.

11-14 **NCAA Championships**, Sacramento, USA. Arkansas and LSU repeated their indoor triumphs with outdoor wins number 10 and 13 respectively. The fastest 400m times of the year were run by the first three at 400m: Adam Steele 44.57, Otis Harris 44.57 and Mitch Potter 44.58, and Carl Myerscough threw 21.92 in the last round of the shot to come from behind Christian Cantwell's 21.56 and break the 22 year-old British record of Geoff Capes. Daniel Lincoln won his third steeplechase title and had a unique double by also winning at 10,000m. Aileen Bailey had an upset sprint double over Muna Lee, in each race coming from well behind. The precocious Sanya Richards improved her American junior record to 50.58 and there were women's collegiate records from Sheena Johnson, 400m hurdles 54.24 and Candice Scott, hammer 69.79. *See USA section for winners.*

12 **Ostrava**, Czech Republic. The 42nd edition of the Golden Spike meeting was elevated to Super Grand Prix status, triumphantly justified as meeting records were set in 14 of the 18 events on the main programme with ten world-leading marks for the 2003 outdoor season. Hicham El Guerrouj made his senior debut at 5000 metres in the Emil Zátopek Trophy race and ran 12:50.24 but was defeated by Stephen Cherono, who improved from 13:11,55 to 12:48.81. Alesya Turova ran the second fastest ever women's steeplechase, 9:20.28, Cornelius Chirchir won the 1500m in 3:31.17 and Wilfred Bungei's 1:43.24 ran his third 1:43 winning time of the year at 800m. Stanislav Olijar 13.15 and Felix Sánchez 48.10 impressed in the hurdles, local favourite Jan Zelezny threw 88.99 to win the javelin and there was the first women's 15m triple jump of the outdoor season as Yamilé Aldama achieved exactly that.

13 **Kassel**, Germany. Tim Lobinger, pole vault 5.86, and Sergey Makarov, javelin 88.61, produced the top marks at the Internationales Askina Sportfest.

16 **Villeneuve d'Ascq**, France. Svetlana Feofanova won the pole vault at 4.72 and Manuela Montebrun extended her French hammer record to 74.50.

19-22 **US Championships**, Stanford. Tyree Washington's 44.33 for 400m was the best mark of 2003 and the 8784 decathlon by Tom Pappas was the second best. Regina Jacobs (12th in all at 1500m), Gail Devers (ninth at 100mh) and Stacy Dragila won their fifth successive titles, Allen Johnson and Breaux Greer their fourth. Kelly White won an impressive sprint double in 10.93 and 22.21, both personal bests. *See USA section for winners.*

20-22 **South American Championships**, Barquisimeto, Venezuela. *See Championships section for medallists.*

21-22 **European Cup Super League**, Florence, Italy. The French men's team won the European Cup for the first time with a solid team effort and just two individual victories – from Ladji Doucouré at 110m hurdles and Romain Mesnil at pole vault – while Russia were clear women's winners for the seventh successive year. Manuela Montebrun was a brilliant winner of the women's hammer, with all her four throws, capped with 74.43, better than the world record setters Manuela Melinte and Olga Kuzenkova. *See Championships section for details.*

21-22 **European Cup First Leagues**. Held at Lappeenranta, Finland where Sweden's men and Poland's women won promotion, and Velenje, Slovenia, where the winners were Netherlands (men) and Ukraine (women). *See Championships section for details.*

21-22 **European Cup Second Leagues**. Held at Århus, Denmark and Istanbul, Turkey. *See Championships section for details.*

24 **Tríkala**, Greece. The IAAF Super GP meeting was transferred from Athens while the Olympic Stadium is being renovated. In hot and practically windless conditions there was a high standard throughout, winners including Felix Sánchez, 400mh 48.07, Dwight Phillips, LJ 8.44 pb and Yamilé Aldama, TJ 15.00. Deji Aliu beat Dwain Chambers 10.00 to 10.03 in the 100m.

27 **Bislett Games**, Oslo, Norway. The first Golden League meeting of the year became the last meeting before the Bislett Stadium is rebuilt. Berhane Adere just missed the world record for 5000m with an African record 14:29.32 from her compatriots Worknesh Kidane 14:33.04 and Tirunesh Dibaba, whose 14:39.94 smashed the world junior record. Another came in the men's 5000m where Eliud Kipchoge, also the world junior CC champion, improved his best by 18.4 secs to 12:52.61 for third place in a race of great quality won by Kenenisa Bekele, who improved his pb by an even greater margin, 21.07 secs to 12:52.26, narrowly from Sammy Kipketer 12:52.33. Abraham Chebii was 4th in 12:52.99. Yamilé Aldama won the triple jump with 15.11 to make it five CAC records in five outdoor competitions.

28-29 **German Championships**, Ulm. Top marks came from pole vaulters, Tim Lobinger 5.75 and Yvonne Buschbaum 4.70. *See Germany section for winners.*

29 **Glasgow**, GBR. The USA were again winners at this mini-international with 137 points to Russia 113 and GBR 109. Strong winds helped two women long jumpers over 6.90 – Grace Upshaw 6.99w and Tatyana Kotova 6.94w.

29 **Odlozil Memorial**, Prague, Czech Republic. Koji Murofushi moved to third on the world all-time hammer list with 84.86, his 18th Japanese record from 1998, beating Adrián Annus 82.73 in this GP II meeting.

July

1 **Athletissima, Lausanne**, Switzerland. World leading marks for the year were set at the rain-lashed IAAF Super Grand Prix meeting by Allen Johnson, 110mh 13.06 from Stanislav Olijar's Latvian record 13.08, Felix Sánchez, 400mh 47.80, and Maria Mutola, 800m 1:56.57. But the most eye-catching performance came from Kenenisa Bekele's spectacular 52.64 last lap to win the 5000m in 13:06.05. Coby Miller won the 200m in 20.04, the fastest ever run in lane 1.

2-13 **World Masters Championships**, Carolina, Puerto Rico. Some 2600 athletes from 78 nations took part.

4 **Saint-Denis**, France. Of the 13 Golden League event winners from Oslo, just two won again at the Meeting Gaz de France Paris Saint-Denis. Chandra Sturrup again beat Kelli White at 100m, and Maria Mutola powered to yet another big 800m win. Top mark was Allen Johnson's 12.97 for 110m hurdles, his eighth win in eight meetings in 2003 and the world's fastest time for three years. Other world-leading marks came from Gail Devers, 100mh 12.49, Mehdi Baala, 1500m French record 3:30.97, Gabriela Szabo, 3000m 8:34.09, and Tatyana Lebedeva, triple jump 15.12 ahead of Yamilé Aldama 15.08. Haile Gebrselassie ran his first 5000m race since 2000 but his 16 successive wins at the distance was ended by a scintillating burst of speed (25.0 for last 200m) from Abraham Chebii to win in 12:53.37 to Geb's 12:54.36. Jan Zelezny beat Sergey Makarov 89.06 to 87.69 in the javelin.

4-6 **Central American and Caribbean Championships**, Saint George's, Grenada. Lavern Eve, javelin, became the first 5-time winner of a CAC individual event. *See Championships section for winners.*

5-6 **European Cup for Combined Events**. France won the decathlon and Russia the heptathlon at the Super League in Bressanone, Italy, but higher individual scores came at the First League held at Tallinn, Estonia from Erki Nool 8281, and Carolina Klüft, who set three individual events pbs en route to 6692, her fifth successive Swedish record. The Second League was held at Maribor, Slovenia. *See Championships section for details.*

6 **European Mountain Running Championships**, Trento, Italy. *See Championships section for medallists.*

7 **Rethímno**, Greece. Top performances came at discus: Róbert Fazekas winning the men's event with 70.00 and Vera Pospisílová the women's with 67.71 from Franka Dietzsch 66.00.

8 **Zagreb**, Croatia. Blanka Vlasic lost on count-back to Hestrie Cloete but thrilled the local crowd at this IAAF Grand Prix meeting by tying the Croatian high jump record of 2.00.

9-13 **World Youth Championships**, Sherbrooke, Canada. Usain Bolt, 200m 20.40, and Cristine Spîtaru, LJ/TJ 6.41/13.86, were the top athletes with 3 of the 22 meeting records at the third edition of this event for under-18s. Ronald Kipchumba Rutto, only 15, broke a world youth 2000m steeplechase best which had stood for almost 20 years when he ran 5:30.27. Elizaveta Ryshich became, at 14 years 299 days, the youngest ever gold medallist when she won the pole vault with 4.05. A total of 158 countries were represented, of which 36 won medals. The winners came from 21 nations with the USA topping the medal table with 6 gold, 4 silver and 4 bronze. *See Championships section for medallists.*

11 **Belarus Championships**, Minsk. Ivan Tikhon won the hammer with 83.64 from Igor Astapkovich, who set a world masters record of 81.35; it is his 19th successive year exceeding 80m. *See Belarus section for winners.*

11 **Golden Gala**, Roma, Italy. Both Maria Mutola, who held off Jolanda Ceplak to score her 12th successive win at 800m, and Chandra Sturrup, an impressive winner of the 100m in 10.89, maintained their Golden League jackpot chase. Sturrup's time was one of eight world-leading marks set on a warm, calm evening. The stateless Yamilé Aldama's final-round 15.29 represented her sixth CAC triple jump record of 2003 and her fifth successive meeting at 15m or more. Hicham El Guerrouj flowed smoothly away from a top quality field to a 1500m time of 3:29.76, the first sub-3:30 time of 2003, and there was superb depth in the women's 1500m won by Olga Yegorova in 4:01.00, as 17 of the 18 finishers (all under 4:08.5) ran seasonal bests with eight personal bests. John Capel continued his impressive comeback to beat Bernard Williams 10.04 to 10.06 in the 100m, but Williams came back to shade Shawn Crawford 20.10 to 20.02 for the year's fastest times at 200m. Giuseppe Gibilisco thrilled the crowd by adding a centimetre to his personal best at 5.72 and going on to Italian records at 5.77 and 5.82, but Romain Mesnil topping that by winning the pole vault with 5.92. That was a year's best, as was the 2.35 high jump clearance by Jacques Freitag, showing that he was back after his serious injury over a year earlier. Abraham Chebii ran his third successive sub-13 5000m time to sprint to victory over Kenenisa Bekele,. 12:57.14 to 12:57.34.

12-13 **Balkan Championships**, Thiva, Greece. Mihaela Melinte won the women's hammer with 71.75. *See Championships section for winners.*

13 **Gateshead**, GBR. Some while after the conclusion of the track events at this IAAF Super Grand Prix meeting, Yelena Isinbayeva set a world pole vault record at her second attempt at 4.82. Christian Olsson won a thrilling triple jump clash with Jonathan Edwards 17.92w to 17.61.

17-20 **European U23 Championships**, Bydgoszcz, Poland. The best of 16 championship records came in the high jump where Aleksander Walerianczyk improved from 2.32 to the world's top mark of the year, 2.36. Another major breakthrough came from triple jumper Dmitriy Valyukevich, who improved his pb by 2cm with 16.83 in qualifying, then 17.16, 17.51 and 17.57 in the final. Carolina Klüft won the long jump with a pb 6.86 and Yelena Isinbayeva won the pole vault with 4,65, taking just one try at a WR height of 4.85. Russia topped the medals table with 20 (7 gold, 7 silver, 6 bronze), followed by Poland 16 (5-5-6), Germany 13 (3-6-4) and Britain 10 (5-3-2). *See Championships section for medallists.*

18-20 **Pan-American Junior Championships**, Bridgetown, Barbados. Still a month short of his 17th birthday, the gigantic and precocious Jamaican sprinter, Usain Bolt, took 200m title in windless conditions in 20.13, equalling the world junior record. The USA, fielding a team of over 80, dominated the event with 20 gold, 18 silver and 10 bronze medals, but 21 nations won at least one medal. *See Championships section for winners.*

19 **Madrid**, Spain. Maria Mutola ran the fastest women's 800m of 2003 in 1:55.55 and Alex Averbukh set a world leading mark of 5.93 to win the pole vault in this Super GP meeting.

24-26 **French Championships**, Narbonne. Women were the stars with women. Christine Arron and Muriel Hurtis clocking wind-aided 100m times of 10.95 and 10.97, Vanessa Boslak raising the national pole vault record to 4.50, Patricia Girard winning her seventh French 100m hurdles title in 12.74 and Manuela Montebrun the hammer with 70.89. *See France section for winners.*

25-26 **Kenyan Trials**, Nairobi. Japheth Kimutai ran the fastest ever 800m time in Kenya of 1:43.71 and John Cheruiyot Korir ran an exceptional high-altitude time of 27:59.18 to win the 10,000m. Ezra Sambu won the 400m in 44.43.

24-27 **European U20 Championships**, Tampere, Finland. A world junior and youth record of 6:21.78 in the 2000m steeplechase by Catalina Oprea was the most notable mark and Ivet Lalova impressed with a 100m/200m double in 11.43 and 22.88, but standards have fallen drastically in this meeting over the last 20 years. Germany topped the medals table with 10 gold, 10 silver, 7 bronze from Russia (9-8-7). Local fans were thrilled with a Finnish 1-2-3 in the men's javelin. *See Championships section for medallists.*

25-27 **AAA Championships**, Birmingham. The star was Yamilé Aldama, winner of the women's triple jump with 14.98; it seemed that she could not obtain a British passport until November 2004 (later she gave up and in January 2004 was accepted as able to compete for Sudan). The 10.08 by Dwain Chambers to win the 100m was most impressive given that he had a 1.8 m/s headwind and Carl Myerscough set a championship record of 21.55 in the shot. *See UK section for winners.*

26-27 **Eberstadt**, Germany. Kajsa Bergqvist moved to the top of the world list with a Swedish record 2.06 at the 25th annual high jump competition. Jacques Freitag was the men's winner at 2.30.

31 **Linz**, Austria. Frank Fredericks won a sprint double in 10.14 and 20.38 in cool and wet conditions at this IAAF Grand Prix meeting.

31- 3 Aug **African Junior Championships**, Garoua, Cameroon. Boniface Kiprop starred by winning both 5000m and 10,000m. *See Championships section for winners.*

August

2 **Heusden-Zolder**, Belgium. Isaac Songok, sill a junior, won the 1500m at the KBC Night of Athletics (IAAF Grand Prix II) meeting in his fastest time of 3:31.54

3 **Lappeenranta**, Finland. Françoise Mbango improved her African triple jump record to 15.03.

3 **Leverkusen**, Germany. Amongst the top performances at the 9th Bayer Meeting was an 8.27 long jump by James Beckford.

5 **DN Galan**, Stockholm, Sweden. The 37th edition of the IAAF Super Grand Prix meeting included a 2.01 high jump by Hestrie Cloete beating home star Kajsa Bergqvist into 4th place at 1.95, and world leading marks by Stephen Cherono, 3000m steeplechase 8:04.75, and Maria Mutola, 1000m 2:33.15. Yelena Isinbayeva beat all her leading rivals in the pole vault at 4.63 as a record five women cleared 4.58 or higher.

5-9 **Pan-American Games**, Santo Domingo, Dominican Republic. Felix Sánchez became the first ever gold medallist for his nation he took the 400m hurdles title on home soil in 48.19. A record number of 22 nations won least one medal. The top individual performance was 74.25 in the hammer by Yipsi Moreno. Adriana Fernández won both 5000m and 10,000m to tie the record of four individual Pan-Am gold medals and a 100m bronze took Liliana Allen to eight medals, tying the record. *See Championships section for medallists.*

6 **Castres**, France. Romain Mesnil achieved the best pole vault of 2003 with 5.95.

7-10 **Russian Championships**, Tula. Yuliya Pechonkina smashed the world record for 400m hurdles, taking 0.27 off Kim Batten's 1995 figures with 52.34. This was the first women's world record in an Olympic track event since Jiang Bo's 5000m in October 1997 and another world record came in the 3000m steeplechase when Gulnara Samitova ran 9:08.33, a big improvement on Alesya Turova's 9:16.51. There were world-leading marks from Svetlana Krivelyova (20.77 shot) and Tatyana Shikolenko (66.00 javelin) and excellent hammer wins from Ilya Konovalov 82.28 and Olga Kuzenkova 74.98. There was a surprise in the pole vault as the world's top three, Yelena Isinbayeva (3= 4.40), Svetlana Feofanova (2nd 4.60) and Tatyana Polnova (3= 4.40), were all defeated by Yelena Belyakova's pb 4.60. *See Russia section for winners.*

8 **London Grand Prix**, (CP), GBR (IAAF Super Grand Prix). A faulty timing system delayed the start of the 100m for 20 minutes and when the race was eventually run the winner first came up on the scoreboard as Dwain Chambers 9.53 WR; in fact the system failed again and back-up hand timing had to be used, with the first four men given 10.0. As this was proper timekeeping there was not the stupid fast times that appertain elsewhere in the world and video analysis later showed probable auto times of: Chambers 9.96, Kim Collins 9.98, Deji Aliu 10.00, Bernard Williams 10.05, Justin Gatlin 10.05, Darren Campbell 10.08. Jonathan Edwards, trailing 17.19 to the 17.40 by Leevan Sands, had a sad end to his British career as he was stretchered off after veering too much to his right on his fifth round jump,. He landed his step on the concrete border of the runway, twisting his right ankle and collapsing in a heap in the pit. Yamilé Aldama jumped UK all-comers records of 15.12 and 15.27 in the women's event and the 50th Emsley Carr Mile was won by Paul Korir in 3:48.17.

10 **ISTAF**, Berlin, Germany. Hestrie Cloete (African and Commonwealth high jump record 2.05) and Süreyya Ayhan (1500m 3:59.58) produced the top performances of the IAAF Golden League meeting held for the second successive year in the Friedrich-Ludwig-Jahn Sportpark while the Olympic Stadium is renovated. Maria Mutola was left as the sole contender for the Golden Jackpot of $1 million as she won the 800m, but although Chandra Sturrup ran 10.88w for 100m, she was beaten by Kelli White 10.84w and Chryste Gaines 10.86w. The US 4x100m team ran 37.77, the fastest time in the world for nearly three years. Yamilé Aldama's winning run at the triple jump ended as she was 4th with 14.52 in a competition won by Tatyana Lebedeva 14.89. *See Championships section for all Golden League event winners.*

10 **San Sebastián**, Spain.

12 **Malmö**, Sweden. Stefan Holm was very close at 2.37 after winning the high jump with 2.32.

15 **Weltklasse**, Zürich, Switzerland. Süreyya Ayhan won the 1500m in 3:55.60, a Turkish record and the fastest time in the world since October 1997. She was led by Yuliya Kosenkova led through 400m in 60.35 and 800m in 2:05.92, then took over through 1200m in 3:11.54 and had the strength to run the last lap in 59.5. Yekaterina Rozenberg, Tatyana Tomashova and Hayley Tullett, 2-4, ran personal bests of just outside four minutes. Maria Mutola maintained her jackpot chase with her 11th successive win in Zürich. The two Kenyans who received Qatari passports (and a guaranteed $1000 a month for life) six days earlier both set Asian records. Saïf Saaeed Shaheen (formerly Stephen Cherono) just beat the Kenyan champion Ezekiel Kemboi in a great eyeballs-out race in the 3000m steeplechase, 8:02.48 to 8:02.49 and Ahmad Hassan Abdullah (formerly Albert Chepkurui) ran 13:04.65 for seventh in the 5000m won by John Kibowen in 13:01.01. World-leading marks also came from Chryste Gaines, 100m 10.89, Ana Guevara, 49.11 her third CAC400m record, Gabriela Szabo, 3000m 8:33.95, and Hicham El Guerrouj, 1500m 3:29.13. John Capel and Justin Gatlin tied for first at 100m in 9.97 ahead of Kim Collins 9.99 and a record four women cleared 2.01 in the high jump, with Hestrie Cloete then jumping 2.03 to win.

18 **Helsinki**, Finland. IAAF GP II.

23-31 **World Championships**, Saint-Denis, France. There were more close and exciting finishes in the Stade de France than in any of the eight previous editions of the event, even if overall standards were not exceptional. There were two world records – in both the men's walks – from Jefferson Pérez 1:17:21 for 20km and Robert Korzeniowski 3:36:03 for 50km, both men receiving $100,000 bonuses for their exploits. Other stars included Hicham El Guerrouj (1500m) and Allen Johnson (110m hurdles), who won their fourth World titles, Felix Sánchez (400m hurdles) and Ana Guevara (400m), a class apart at their events, and the ebullient Swedish heptathlon winner Carolina Klüft. The crowds were kept waiting for French success, but revelled in two gold medals on the penultimate day, from Eunice Barber in the long jump and their women's sprint relay team. Drug issues involving two celebrated American athletes, Kevin Young and Kelli White, together with the truculent behaviour of a third, Jon Drummond, who for long refused to accept his disqualification for false starting in his quarter-final of the 100m, cast a shadow over what were otherwise a joyous nine days of great competition. *See Championships section for details.*

25-30 **World University Games**, Daegu, Korea. Two World champions, the Belarus throwers Andrey Mikhnevich and Ivan Tikhon, collected golds here as well. Tatyana Polnova matched her best by winning the women's pole vault with 4.70. Russia was the most successful team with 30 medals (8-12-10), followed by China 13 (7-4-2), Ukraine 9 (7-1-1) and Poland 9 (3-4-2). A total of 34 countries produced at least one medallist, but the USA was not represented. *See Championships section for medallists.*

15-25 **European Veterans Championships,** Potsdam, Germany. 4385 competitors contested 586 titles. One of the most notable marks was a world M50 record of 66.62 with the 6kg hammer by Chris Black GBR.

27 **Naimette-Xhovémont**, Belgium. Maria Mutola came agonisingly close to Ana Quirot's 1:22.63 world best at 600m with 1:22.87 after going through 400m in 53.92. The men's event also produced the second fastest ever, Joseph Mutua 1:13.49.

September

5-6 **Finland v Sweden**, Helsinki, Finland. A combined audience of 57,440 over the two days saw the Finns, in a nail biting finish, win the men's match 205-203 after being 12 points down after the first day, while Sweden took the women's match 208.5-201.5. Christian Olsson won the triple jump with 17.51 and also the long jump with a lifetime best of 7.84w. Carolina Klüft participated in five events; she won the long jump and was on the winning 4x100m relay team, placed second in the 200m and 100m hurdles, and third in the 100m with a pb of 11.53.

6 **Van Damme Memorial**, Brussels, Belgium. Maria Mutola won the 800m in 1:57.78 to become the first solo winner of the greatest prize in track and field history, the IAAF Golden League jackpot of $1 million, for winning at all six meetings in the 2003 series. Five world leading marks in distance races emphasised the quality once again of this great meeting watched by a 47,000 crowd. The men's 10,000m fully lived up its history as Haile Gebrselassie had a great victory in 26:29.22 from Nicholas Kemboi, who ran 26:30.03 after just 28:19.77 in his previous 10,000m for sixth in Hengelo in June. Third was Abdullah Ahmad Hassan, with the eighth fastest ever 10,000m of 26:38.76 and his fourth Asian record in four races as a Qatari. There were best ever marks for places 2-3 and 8-16, and 13 men ran under 27:30 compared to the previous best of ten (Brussels 2002). Saif Saaeed Shaheen ran his second Asian record since gaining his Qatari passport with 8:00.06 for the 3000m steeplechase, holding off a strong Kenyan challenge from Paul Koech, whose 8:00.42 was a 4.86 sec improvement in his pb. Hicham El Guerrouj ran a world-leading 3:28.40 and his 78th win in his last 81 1500m/1M races and in second place Mehdi Baala regained the French record with 3:28.98. Wilfred Bungei, who had to miss the Worlds, improved his own world-leading 800m mark of 1:43.05 to 1:42.52 with season's bests behind him for the next six,, as six under 1:44 equalled the record for any race. The final world-leading mark came from Süreyya Ayhan who won the 1500m easily in a Turkish record 3:55.33.

6-9 **13th Arab Championships**, Amman, Jordan. Fawzi Al-Shammari starred with Kuwaiti records for 200m 20.41 and 400m 44.93. Athletes from Morocco and Tunisia did not compete. *See Championships section for winners.*

7 **Rieti**, Italy. Hicham El Guerrouj the mile in 3:50.20 at the final IAAF Grand Prix meeting of the season from 18 year-old Alex Kipchirchir whose time of 3:50.25 shaved 0.14 off the world junior record. Sandra Glover just beat Yuliya Pechonkina, 53.34 to 53.43.

7 **Szombathely**, Hungary. As they could not be held in Monaco's Louis II stadium the hammer events of the World Athletics Final were held here and local hero Adrián Annus won the men's event with 82.10 and Yipsi Moreno the women's with 73.42.

13-14 **IAAF World Athletics Final**, Monaco. The meeting replaced the former Grand Prix Finals with a two-day meeting which included the full range of track and field events instead of just those on the year's GP schedule. The IAAF Athletes of the Year, announced at the conclusion of this meeting, were for the first time those ranked top of their World Rankings – Hicham El Guerrouj and Hestrie Cloete, the South African high jumper. El Guerrouj did not compete here but Cloete added $30,000 for winning the high jump at 2.01 to add to her $100,000 prize. Saif Saaeed Shaheen won the steeplechase in 7:57.38, an Asian record and the fifth fastest ever, from Paul Koech 7:57.42, the two sub-8 minute times of 2003. Chryste Gaines ran a personal best of 10.86 to win the 100m on 33rd birthday, Gail Devers tied the 2003 world best with 12.45 for 100m hurdles and Eunice Barber improved the French long jump record to 7.05. *See Championships section for details.*

19-21 **World Mountain Running Trophy**, Girdwood, near Anchorage, Alaska. Marco De Gasperi had a record fourth win. Italy took the senior men's team title for the 11th successive year and the senior women's for the third year in a row, *See Championships section for medallists*

20 **Moscow Challenge**, Russia. Justin Gatlin was scheduled to receive $500,000 for winning the 100m in 10.05 clearly from Dwain Chambers and Tim Montgomery. Tatyana Lebedeva contested the long jump for the first time for a couple of years, and jumped 6.82, compared to her previous best of 6.71 indoors, and beat Eunice Barber 6.72 and Tatyana Kotova 6.63.

20-21 **Talence**, France. Contesting his fifth decathlon of the year, Laurent Hernu added one point to the total which brought him fifth place in the World Champs by scoring 8219 for victory in a somewhat depleted Decastar meeting. Yelena Prokhorova won the heptathlon with 6254 points.

20-23 **15th Asian Championships**, Manila. Philippines. The ex-Kenyans brought medals to their new nation of Qatar as Abdullah

Ahmad Hassan won the 10,000m and Saif Saaeed Shaheen was second at both 1500m and 5000m. Two other Qataris won their fourth titles: Mubarak Al-Nubi at 400m hurdles and Bilal Saad Mubarak at shot (both won previously in 1995, 1998 and 2002); and there were third successive titles for Gu Yuan, women's hammer, and Khamis Seif Abdullah at 3000m steeplechase (he also won once at 5000m). *See Championships section for medallists.*

21 **Great North Run**, Newcastle to South Shields, GBR. The route is point to point with the finish more than 30% of the distance away from the start and the course drops 30.5m, which is more than the permitted maximum of one metre per kilometre, so world records cannot be set here. Nonetheless Paula Radcliffe's superb win in 65:40 goes into the lists as the fastest half marathon ever run by a woman. She ran away from the field, as Berhane Adere was second in 67:32, to average c.5:01 for 13 consecutive miles. Her slowest mile was 5:18 on a particularly tough uphill stretch between 8 and 9 miles, while her fastest was a fantastic 4:44 for the preceding downhill section. Her 5k splits were 15:26, 15:52 (31:18), 15:23 (world best of 46:41 for 15k) and 15:40 (world best of an estimated 62:21 for 20k She also ran the fastest ever 10 miles time of 50:01 en route. Hendrick Ramaala 60:01 beat Jackson Koech 60:05 to take the men's race.

23 **Yokohama**, Japan. Koji Murofushi beat world champion Ivan Tikhon 80.44 to 77.52 in the hammer at the annual Super meet. Felix Sánchez ended his second successive unbeaten season at 400mh with a win in 48.86 and there were fine 2000m wins for Shawn Crawford 20.19w and Chryste Gaines pb 22.67.

21-22 **San Giovanni Lupatoto**, Italy. Norimi Sakurai set a world women's track record for 100 kilometres of 7:14:05.8; she went through 50k in 3:33:20.3 and 50M in 5:48:12.

28 **Berlin Marathon**, Germany. Paul Tergat took 43 seconds off the world record with his 2:04:55. Yet he still won by only 1 second from Sammy Korir, who had done much of the pacing, with a third Kenyan Titus Munji an isolated third in 2:06:15. This was Tergat's first ever marathon win, following his debut at London in 2001 and a series of great times, sub-2:09 in all five races, but had no wins until now. The pacemakers reached halfway in 63:01 (Tergat 63:04) and it was after the 25k mark that Tergat himself pushed the pace for the first time and he covered the second half in 61:51. His intermediate times: 5k-15:01, 10k-29:58, 15k-44:48, 20k-59:45, 25k-1:14:43, 30k-1:29:25, 35k-1:44:00, 40k-1:58:38. His fastest 10k stretch was 29:13 between 30 and 40k.

October

4 **World Half Marathon Championships**, Vilamoura, Portugal. Martin Lel won the final sprint to snatch individual gold for Kenya in the men's race in 60:49 while Tanzania, with Fabian Joseph 2nd and Martin Sulle 3rd and John Yuda battling on despite injury to fifth, won its first ever team gold. Paula Radcliffe won a third women's title in four years and her winning margin of 1 min 27 sec was the greatest ever in the 12 year history of the event, but hot weather slowed her to 67:35. Defending champion Berhane Adere was runner-up in 69:02, and Benita Johnson took the bronze in 69:26 on her debut at the event. Good packing with 4th, 6th and 7th finishers brought Russia the team honours. *See Championships section for details.*

5 **Mountain Running Grand Prix Final**, Bergen, Norway. Jonathan Wyatt (NZL) and Antonella Contenella (ITA) won the final races of the season and the series titles for men and women.

11-12 **IAU European 24 Hours Challenge**, Uden, Netherlands. *See Championships section for medallists.*

11-16 **8th All-Africa Games**, Abuja, Nigeria. Nigerians dominated the athletics at the multi-sport Games, claiming 13 titles to seven by South Africa and five by Ethiopia. Deji Aliu improved his 100m best to 9.95 just ahead of Uchenna Emedolu 9.97. Mary Onyali retired after winning a sprint treble (100m, 200m, 4x100m); she won a record 23 medals (14 individual) at African Games and Championships and her 12 individual gold medals is a women's record. *See Championships section for medallists.*

12 **Chicago Marathon**, USA. Evans Rutto ran the world's fastest ever debut marathon when he won the LaSalle Bank Marathon in 2:05:50 with halves of 63:34 and 62:16; he earned a total of $225,000 ($100,000 for winning and $125,000 for breaking 2:06). Another debutant, Paul Koech, was second in 2:07:07 and the women's winner was Svetlana Zakharova in 2:23:07.

19 **Amsterdam Marathon**, Netherlands. William Kipsang won in a course record of 2:06:39.

19 **Beijing Marathon**, China. Sun Yingjie set an Asian women's record of 2:19:39, while the men's winner was Ian Syster in 2:07:49 despite being impeded by a bus near the finish.

19 **Scanzorosciate**, Italy. Men's and women's winners both recorded the third fastest ever recorded at the distance: Viktor Ginko 8:44:28 and Anita Liepina 10:23:47.

23-27 **Chinese Inter-City Games**, Changsha. Contested by athletes born in 1983 or later, there was a world junior record of 1:29:32.4 for women's 20,000m track walk from Song Hongjuan and 17 year-old Xue Juan first set a world youth record with 61.06 in qualifying and then a world junior record 62.93 in the final of the women's javelin. Zhang Wenxiu fell just

38cm short of her world youth record in winning the hammer with 70.22.

28 **New York Marathon**, USA. Despite uncomfortably warm conditions Margaret Okayo smashed her own course record of 2:24:21 with an impressive 2:22:31 (halves of 72:04 and 70:27). Catherine Ndereba was second in 2:23:04 and Lornah Kiplagat third in a Dutch record 2:23:43. In contrast the men's winning time of 2:10:30 by Martin Lel was the slowest for eight years. There were a record 35,286 starters & 34,662 finishers.

28-30 **1st Afro-Asian Games**, Hyderabad, India. Ethiopian distance runners concluded a most impressive championships season in 2003, taking men's and women's 5000m and 10000m titles. *See Championships section for medallists.*

November

7-12 **South East Asia Games**, Hanoi, Vietnam. Loo Kum Zee of Malaysia won a fifth successive SEAG title. *See Championships section for winners.*

16 **IAU World Cup 100km**, Tainan, Taiwan. A hilly course and very hot and humid conditions slowed times considerably. *See Championships section for medallists.*

16 **Tokyo Women's Marathon**, Japan. Elfenesh Alemu caused an upset by beating Naoko Takahashi 2:24:47 to 2:27:21.

24 **Chiba Ekiden Relays**, Japan. There were world bests over the marathon distance by both Ethiopian teams, bath winning by huge margins. The men's time was 1:55:59 (Berhane Dejene 10k 27:18, Hailu Mekonnen 5k 13:43, Gebre Gebremariam 10k 27:35, Markos Geneti 5k 13:29, Sileshi Sihine 12.195k 33:54) with Kenya 2nd in 1:58:56 and Japan 3rd in 2:01.53. The women's time was 2:11:22 (Berhane Adere 10k 30:12, Tirunesh Dibaba 5k 15:14, Eyerusalem Kuma 10k 32:16, Ejigayehu Dibaba 5k 15:11, Meseret Defar 4.767k 15:43, Worknesh Kidane 7.428k: 22:46) with Kenya 2nd in 2:15:37 and Japan 3rd in 2:15:40. Paula Radcliffe, affected by illness, was beaten into third place on the opening leg, her first loss in any race since August 2002 (at 3000m on the track in Monaco).

December

6-8 **3rd World Military Games**, Catania and Palermo Italy. *See Championships section for winners.*

7 **Fukuoka**, Japan. Tomoaki Kunichika won the 58th annual International Marathon in 2:07:52, a personal best by over two minutes.

14 **European Cross-country Championships**, Edinburgh, GBR. Sergey Lebed and Paula Radcliffe were convincing winners of the senior races and the twins Yevgeniy and Anatoliy Rybakov repeated their 2002 feat of filling the top two places in the men's junior race, with Inna Polushkina winning the women's junior race by 25 secs. Britain won both women's team titles with France and Russia taking senior and junior men. The event commemorated the first ever International CC Championship held nearby in Scotland at Hamilton in 1903. *See Cross-country section for details.*

Quotes of the Year

Amy Acuff, questioned in Glasgow after winning the high jump with 1.98: "... and with regard to the wind, it didn't bother me today; back in Texas I have seen small animals float by in practice".

Kelli White at the press conference at the World Championships after the disclosure of her positive test for Modafinil – when pushed as to why she did not disclose its use "...You know, we take so many things these days it is impossible to remember them all..."

IAAF Council Decisions

At the IAAF Council meeting in Dakar, Senegal in April

• It was agreed that the "new" false start rule had worked well in practice but that a new line would be added to the rule to ensure there would not be a repetition of an incident at the World Indoor Championships, where British sprinter Allyn Condon competed "under protest" despite being disqualified. Council proposed adding a clause to the new rule to clarify that protests should NOT be allowed in competitions where there is automatic recall equipment which clearly indicates false starts.

• Council discussed the new rule related to the length of the supporting pegs in the pole vault and agreed that no changes were necessary, despite complaints from a group of elite athletes.

At the IAAF Congress in Paris in August

Official Road World Records

• It was agreed by Congress that official IAAF Road World Records would be accepted, under the same conditions as current IAAF World Bests at: 10k, 15k, 20k, Half Marathon, 25k, 30k, Marathon, 100k and Road Relay (with stages of 5-10-5-10-5-7.195k); also race walking events on the road: Men: 20k and 50k, Women: 20k.

• The IAAF agreed that it should be known as the World Governing Body not only for track and field athletics, road running, race walking and cross country running but also for mountain running.

• Congress decided to accept the World Anti-Doping code as the basis for the fight against doping and that existing IAAF rules will be adapted if necessary. It was also agreed that the IAAF Anti-doping Commission and the Medical Committee would be merged.

• World Athletics Plan. IAAF President Lamine

Diack launched a far reaching plan, designed to help the sport develop and grow up to and beyond the centenary of the IAAF in 2012.

President Diack reminded the Congress of the challenges that the sport now faced in the ever more competitive sporting environment and stated that his vision for the sport was "To remain the number one sport for individuals in a changing world". In order to achieve this vision, the sport has now set itself a number of objectives, which include improving the quality and appeal of its events, providing everyone with the greatest opportunities to participate in the sport and making athletics, once again, the number one participatory sport in schools. The IAAF is also determined to use training programmes to increase the levels of competence amongst the sports' administrators and officials and to improve access in all countries for people to utilise athletics facilities and equipment. The sport has also set itself an objective of improving the quality and quantity of its media coverage and to work more closely with its commercial partners.

Some of the actions to be taken in the next couple of years include:

• A full review of the format of athletics competition.
• The development of a participation and development programme for schools, "a plan for everyone to take to their Minister of Sports".
• The establishment of a clear and coherent international competition calendar.
• A much stronger role in the administration of the sport for the six Area Associations.
• Greatly improved communications between all the sports' stakeholders.

New IAAF Council

President: Lamine Diack SEN. Vice-Presidents: Dapeng Lou CHN, Amadeo Francis PUR, Helmut Digel GER, Arne Ljungqvist SWE. Honorary Treasurer: Jean Poczobut FRA. Area Representatives elected by Area Association and confirmed by Congress: Leonard Chuene RSA, Africa; Suresh Kalmadi IND, Asia; Hansjorg Wirz SUI, Europe; Neville McCook JAM, NACAC; Bill Bailey AUS, Oceania; Roberto Gesta de Melo BRA, South America. Female Members: Nawal El Moutawakel MAR, Abby Hoffman CAN. Individual Members: Sergey Bubka UKR, Taizo Watanabe JPN, Minos Kyriakou GRE, Alberto Juantorena CUB, Park Jung-ki KOR, Dahlan Al-Hamad QAT, Cásar Moreno Bravo MEX, Robert Hersh USA, Sebastian Coe GBR, Jamel Simohamed ALG, Isaiah Kiplagat KEN, Jose-María Odriozola ESP, Ilkka Kanerva FIN. István Gyulai HUN, General Secretary, is Ex-Officio Member of the Council. Elected as Honorary Life Vice President: Robert Stinson GBR.

IAAF Athletes Commission. Elected following a procedure in which more than a thousand athletes voted for their peers: Haile Gebrselassie 733 votes, Hicham El Guerrouj 654, Debbie Ferguson 633, Stéphane Diagana 611, Felix Sánchez 610, Paul Tergat 575, Deon Hemmings 553, Irina Privalova 482, Jolanda Ceplak & Sonia O'Sullivan 475, Paula Radcliffe 465, Faraj Ibrahim Ismail 460.

IAAF Council in Paris August 2004

Following examination of the results from the last World Indoor Champs in Birmingham, it was clear that top performances depended solely on the lane draw. In the great majority of cases, winner and runner up came from lanes 5 and 6. Council agreed, following a recommendation of the Commission, that the 200m event be cancelled from the World Indoor Championships' programme from 2006.

IAAF Council – Athens March 2004

Pending discussions with the Athletes' Commission and Women's Committee it was proposed to change the format of the World Cross Country Championships from 2007. This would be reduced, ideally, to a single day format with the short races dropped from the programme: Senior Men 12km (9 runners per team, 6 to score); Senior Women 8 or 10 or 12km (9 or 6 runners per team, 6 or 4 to score); Junior Men 8km (6 runners per team, 4 to score); Junior Women 6km (6 runners per team, 4 to score).

The future of the World Half Marathon Champs was also discussed, and a number of possibilities were considered, including a new IAAF World Road Running Champs to be held over two days, possibly every second year, and possibly including 10km or other distances as well as Half Marathon. Another possibility would be to link the competition with existing mass participation races in an effort to increase public acceptance and media coverage. It was agreed that the IAAF's Marketing experts would study possibilities in the coming months in an effort to develop a new solution following the 2005 edition which had already been awarded to Edmonton under the old format.

Council agreed that the starting age for Men Master athletes could be changed to 35 instead of 40 years of age at the next Congress. This is a way of encouraging more older athletes to stay in the sport and to reinforce the idea that athletics can be a "sport for life". Women Master athletes were already accepted from the age of 35.

The IAAF has announced that TDK Corporation has agreed to extend its long standing sponsor partnership until 2009. TDK will continue to be Bib Partner at the next three editions of the IAAF World Championships in 2005-09 and will be the title sponsor for the IAAF Golden League for 2004 and 2005.

ATHLETES OF 2003

By Peter Matthews

THERE WAS no clear-choice for male Athlete of the Year in 2003, a year in which the only world records by men went on the roads – to the race walkers Jefferson Pérez and Robert Korzeniowski at the World Championships and to Paul Tergat in the Berlin Marathon. Hicham El Guerrouj, Male Athlete of the Year in 2001 and 2002, was again a strong contender. He was again undefeated at 1500m or 1 mile to add to his extraordinary record of having won 80 of his 83 races at 1500m or 1 mile from 1996 to 2003. Felix Sánchez was undefeated for the second successive year at 400m hurdles, and Saïf Saeed Shaheeen and Christian Olsson had great years. But my choice as Athlete of the Year is the 21 year-old World 10,000m champion, Kenenisa Bekele, whose form on the track is backed by his great achievements at cross-country at which to the end of 2003 he has a run of 15 successive victories.

100 Metres

AFTER 26 wind-legal auto times under 10 seconds in 2002 by 11 athletes there were just nine in 2003, the least in any year since 1995, although video evidence showed two more (Dwain Chambers 9.96 and Kim Collins 9.98) in the London GP where the auto-timing failed. The only man to run two of those nine times was Deji Aliu, both in Nigeria, at his national championships and, at the end of the season, in the African Games. He was one of several men who at one part of the season or another could lay claim to being the world's best. Aliu had some good wins in June, and in Lausanne on 1 July had an important win over US champion Bernard Williams, with Maurice Greene, who had earlier run 9.94, third. Both Aliu and Williams slipped in important races thereafter in Europe, although Williams returned to his best with a win at the World Athletics Finals (WAF).

By August, Chambers looked to be the best, winning at the London GP from Collins, Aliu, Williams and Justin Gatlin, but he could not recapture his 2002 form and just missed a medal at the Worlds, where Collins took gold, 18 year-old Darrel Brown silver and Darren Campbell bronze, with world record-holder Tim Montgomery fifth, Williams sixth (and just 0.06 between 1-6), Aliu seventh and Uchenna Emedolu eighth. Collins and Brown were also 1-2 at the CAC Championships. Greene exited in the World semis through injury and Asafa Powell, with Jon Drummond, was disqualified for a false start in his quarterfinal after running the fastest time (10.05) in the heats. Powell showed what might have been with big wins at Brussels and Rieti in September, but was only 8th at the WAF, where John Capel was 2nd, Emedolu 3rd, Chambers 4th and Justin Gatlin 5th and Collins only 6th and Aliu 7th. Emedolu was second at the African Games in 9.97 behind Aliu 9.95. Capel ran the 200m at the Worlds and Gatlin, so impressive in winning the World Indoor 60m, went out in the US Champs heats after missing several months through injury; on win-loss these two men were 2-2 with one tie, that being in Zürich where they ran 9.97 from Collins 9.99. But Collins, who won six of his 14 competitions at 100m, is perhaps the safest choice for top ranking.

Win-loss records in an exceptionally closely matched leading group included: Collins 4-2 v Williams; Williams 5-3 v Chambers and Aliu;

Kenenisa Bekele in 2003

4 Jan		Newcastle	8.8k CC	1	29:12
12 Jan		Elgóibar	10.13k CC	1	30:58
19 Jan		Sevilla	10.8k CC	1	31:31
29 Mar	WCh	La Broye	4.03k CC	1	11:01
30 Mar	WCh	La Broye	12.355k CC	1	35:56
10 May	NC	Addis Ababa	5000m	2	13:47.3A
1 Jun	FBK	Hengelo	10000m	1	26:53.70
27 Jun	Bisl	Oslo	5000m	1	12:52.26
1 Jul	Athl	Lausanne	5000m	1	13:06.05
11 Jul	GGala	Roma	5000m	2	12:57.34
24 Aug	WCh	Saint-Denis	10000m	1	26:49.57
26 Aug	WCh	Saint-Denis	5000m	1h1	13:38.03
30 Aug	WCh	Saint-Denis	5000m	3	12:53.12
13 Sep	WAF	Monaco	3000m	1	7:36.98
28 Sep		Scicli	10k road	1	28:50
15 Oct	AfG	Abuja	5000m	1	13:26.16
16 Nov	Oeiras	10k CC		1	27:22

Bekele first came to the fore in 1999 when he won a silver medal at the World Youth Championships and in past three years has won one World Junior and five World senior gold medals.

Male Athlete of the Year

My selection of the top 10 athletes of 2003 together with the list compiled by international experts polled by Track & Field News and those of Athletics International readers is as follows:

	PJM	*T&FN*	*AI*
Kenenisa Bekele	1	6	3
Hicham El Guerrouj	2	2	1
Felix Sánchez	3	1	2
Saif Saaeed Shaheen	4	3	5
Robert Korzeniowski	5	8	7
Allen Johnson	6	5	8
Christian Olsson	7	4	4
Tom Pappas	8	9	10
Paul Tergat	9	7	6
Jefferson Pérez	10		9
Sergey Makarov	-	10	-

Note that T&FN rankings do not consider cross-country or road running (other than marathons). AI readers voted for top five only.

The EAA European Athlete of the Year was Christian Olsson from Robert Korzeniowski and Giuseppe Gibilisco.

Capel 5-3 v Williams, 3-1 v Collins, 3-2 v Chambers; Gatlin 3-1 v Collins, 3-3 v Williams, 2-2 v Chambers; Montgomery 3-0 v Aliu, Chambers 4-3 v Aliu.

Campbell, 6th in London, had little to back his great World champs form and Brown, who ran a world junior record 10.01 in his Worlds quarter-final, also did not get the chance to meet the top men on other occasions. Heading the world list at 9.93 at Mito in May was Patrick Johnson, who also ran 9.88w and 9.90w in Perth, but who faded after a good start in Europe.

Most times at 10.05 or faster: Aliu 8*, Collins 4*+2w, Capel 4, Gatlin & Williams 3*+1w, Montgomery 3, P Johnson 3+2w, Chambers 3* (* inc. video-time at London GP).

1. Collins, 2. Capel, 3. Williams, 4. Gatlin, (5. Chambers), 6. Montgomery, 7. Aliu, 8. Brown, 9. Powell, 10. Greene, 11. J J Johnson

200 Metres

JOHN CAPEL, after missing 2001 and 2002 while trying out for American football, won four of his seven outdoor competitions, including taking the World title by 0.01 from Darvis Patton with Shingo Suetsugu third, and was also US indoor champion. Capel was beaten at Stanford by J.J.Johnson and at the US Champs by Patton (20.15 to 20.17, Capel's fastest of the year, 12th on the world list). The Olympic champion Konstadínos Kedéris was undefeated but had just two races, European Cup and Tríkala, and did not defend his World crown through injury. Shawn Crawford, only 6th in the US Championships, came through to produce the best set of times and was 2-2 with Patton, although he was beaten 20.01 to 20.02 in the year's fastest race at Rome by Bernard Williams and indeed Crawford allegedly ran out of his lane in this race; Crawford was also beaten 3-1 by J.J.Johnson, who won the WAF race. Third equal on the world list at 20.03 were Patton in his World semi and Suetsugu at the Japanese Championships, his only 200m competition in 2003 apart from the Worlds.

Darren Campbell was 4th at the Worlds, but no better than third in his other five 200m races outdoors, and was beaten 4-1 by his compatriot Christian Malcolm. More solid seasons were those of World 5-6-7, Stéphane Buckland, Johnson and Frank Fredericks (beaten by Uchenna Emedolu for the African title). Tying for fifth on the world's list at 20.04 were Coby Miller, a fine win in Lausanne over Patton, Ramon Clay and Buckland, but mostly disappointing otherwise, and Justin Gatlin, who had an important win in Brussels in 20.04 over Williams, Crawford and Patton, but with a dnf in Mexico City as his only other 200m.

Undoubtedly the most exciting young talent was 16 year-old Usain Bolt, who was undefeated and ran his best of 20.13 to win the Pan-American Junior title after taking the World Youth title; he was Jamaican senior champion but did not meet any of the world elite.

Most times at 20.30 or better: Capel 7, Crawford 6+1w, Johnson 6, Fredericks & Patton 5, Bolt & Buckland 3.

1. Capel, 2. Patton, 3. Johnson, 4. Crawford, 5. Buckland, 6. Suetsugu, 7. Fredericks, 8. Williams, 9. Bolt, 10. Malcolm.

400 Metres

JEROME YOUNG ended the year with clear wins in both World Championships and World Athletics Finals, but his record before then was five wins from ten finals, and top ranking goes to Tyree Washington, beaten 44.77 to 44.50 by Young in Saint-Denis, but undefeated to then in three indoor (inc. US & Worlds) and seven outdoor finals; he ran the year's fastest time of 44.33 to win the US title (Young 2nd 44.79) and beat Young 4-1. It was a fine return for Washington, who had sustained a hamstring injury at the 2001 US Championships and missed the whole of the 2002 season. Jamaican champion Michael Blackwood was beaten by Marc Raquil for the World bronze medal but came back for second in the WAF, where behind him came Alleyne Francique (World 8th), Eric Milazar (World 7th), David Canal and Raquil. Blackwood was 5-0 v Francique, who was 2-1 v Milazar, in turn 5-1 v Raquil. Leslie Djhone added to French joy with a splendid 5th in the Worlds after winning the European U23 title and the B race in Zürich, but otherwise had few chances against the top men. Similarly lightly-raced was Calvin Harrison, but with 2nd in the US and 6th in the Worlds.

Rankings may be changed by decisions on apparent positive drugs tests pending hearings.

Eric Sambu was the world's second fastest in 2003, but his 44.43 was at high altitude in Nairobi, and although he went on to win African and Afro-Asian titles, he went out in the heats of the Worlds. Taking positions 4-6 on the world list were the 1-2-3 at the NCAA Championships, Adam Steele 44.57, Otis Harris 44.57 and Mitch Potter 44.58. Harris ended his season there, Potter and Steele were 5th and 6th at the US Champs (Derrick Brew 4th), and Potter won the Pan-American title from Yeimar López, Francique and Steele.

Amazingly Blackwood (top) is the only one of the 2002 top ten to retain his place in the rankings.

Most sub-45.00 times: Washington 8, Blackwood 6, Young 5, Raquil 4, Francique, C Harrison & Potter 3.

1.Washington, 2. Young, 3. Blackwood,
4. Francique, 5. Milazar, 6. Raquil, 7. Djhone,
8. C Harrison, 9. Brew, 10. Potter

800 Metres

A BOUT of malaria prevented Wilfred Bungei from running at the Kenyan Trials and thus of competing at the Worlds. However, he is a clear choice for top ranking with seven wins in major races, including the WAF. The top six places on the 2003 world lists came from the Brussels Golden League race, won by Bungei in 1:42.52 from Mbulaeni Mulaudzi 1:42.89, Hezekiél Sepeng 1:43.12, Wilson Kipketer 1:43.28, Joseph Mutua 1:43.52 and Yuriy Borzakovskiy 1:43.68, with André Bucher 7th and Bram Som 8th. After modest form Djabir Saïd Guerni won the B race in Zürich in his season's fastest of 1:44.60 and then surprised to take the gold medal at the Worlds, taking advantage of tactical errors by his rivals, with Borzakovskiy and Mulaudzi the other medallists and Kipketer fourth, as he was also at the WAF. Mutua was 2nd and Bucher 3rd in the WAF race, but Mutua, although Kenyan champion, was 4th in a fast Kenyan trials race won by Japheth Kimutai in 1:43.71. Kimutai and his team-mate Nicholas Wachira went out, however, in the World semis, and more consistent was Justus Koech, second in the three big Kenyan races and sixth at the Worlds.

David Krummenacker was only sixth in his semi at the Worlds but won US titles indoors and out and the World Indoors. In that race Kipketer and Bungei were the other medallists and Antonio Reina and Som 4th and 5th. Outdoors Som beat Krummenacker 4-1, Mutua 3-2 and Kimutai 3-1 and was 2-2 with Reina who beat Krummenacker 3-1. Other win-loss records included: Sepeng (7th Worlds, 6th WAF) 4-1 v Mutua, Bucher 4-3 v Sepeng and 2-3 v Mutua. Mehdi Baala ran 1:44.17 to win at the Lille GP and was 4th in Zürich in 1:44.46, but this was insufficient form to justify a ranking at this event.

Most times sub-1:45: Bungei 10+1i, Mulaudzi 9, Sepeng 8, Mutua 7, Borzakovskiy 6+1i, Som 5, Bucher & Kimutai 4, Reina & Wachira 3.

1. Bungei, 2. Mulaudzi, 3. Borzakovskiy,
4. Kipketer, 5. Saïd Guerni, 6. Sepeng, 7. Mutua,
8. Bucher, 9. Som, 10. Reina

1500 Metres

HICHAM EL GUERROUJ is top for the seventh successive year and again he was unbeaten (in seven races) and a class apart. Mehdi Baala came in about six metres down in second place at both the World Champs and Brussels, where he improved the French record to 3:28.98, having set one in his only other 1500m race at 3:30.77 when he won at the Paris Golden League. Bernard Lagat had to miss the Worlds after allegedly failing a test for EPO, a verdict later rescinded; he was third at the Kenyan Trials behind Paul Korir and Isaac Songok, but beat both Korir and Ivan Heshko, who were 4th and 3rd at the Worlds, 2-1. Korir was 3-3 in clashes with Heshko, who from a previous best of 3:37.07 set Ukrainian records in his first three outdoor 1500m races of the year within ten days in June, but Korir won at the WAF from Alex Kipchirchir and Heshko, and Kipchirchir beat Heshko 4-2. Korir was also the one man to run a mile in under 3:50 in 2003, winning the Emsley Carr Mile in London in 3:48.17. Remarkably two juniors make the rankings – Kipchirchir and Songok (Kenyan champion and 10th in the Worlds) – and Cornelius Chirchir, beaten 3-2 by Kipchirchir, turned 20 in June. Europeans took places 5-9 in the Worlds (until Fouad Chouki was disqualified from 8th), with Rui Silva 5th, Reyes Estévez 6th, Gert-Jan Liefers 7th and Vyacheslav Shabunin 9th. While Estévez had little to back that up apart from a good 3rd in Rome, Silva has positive win-loss records against Kenyan ranking contenders (there were 11 Kenyans in the world top 20), the two Chirchirs, Laban Rotich and Songok and was 3-3 v Robert Rono. Songok was 4-1 v Rono and 2-1 v William Chirchir, who beat Rono 4-3 and Rotich 3-2.

Most times sub-3:34 or 3:51M: El Guerrouj, Kipchirchir & Korir 6, Heshko 5, Lagat, Rono, Rotich, Silva & Songok 4, Baala, Benjamin Kipkurui, C Chirchir, W Chirchir 3.

1. El Guerrouj, 2. Baala, 3. Lagat, 4. Korir,
5. Kipchirchir, 6. Heshko, 7. Silva, 8. C Chirchir,
9. Songok, 10. W Chirchir.

3000 Metres/2 Miles

THE FASTEST times came indoors, as Haile Gebrselassie set a world indoor 2 miles best of 8:04.69 in Birmingham and 7:28.29 for 3000m at

Karlsruhe before winning his third World Indoor title. Hicham El Guerrouj just missed that 2 miles indoor record two days later with 8:06.61 at Liévin and he ran the fastest 3000m outdoors with 7:30.23 on his season's opener at Turin in June. The next five best times came at Brussels, where Ali Saïdi-Sief won in 7:30.79 from Eliud Kipchoge, John Kibowen, Benjamin Limo and James Kwalia. Luke Kipkosgei was 6th in this race, and he was much the most prolific racer at this distance with four meetings indoors, including 2nd in the Birmingham 2 miles and 3rd in the World Indoors, and seven outdoor 3000m races. He was, however, only 7th at the WAF, a race won by Kenenisa Bekele (his only 3000m of the year) from Kibowen, Abraham Chebii, Leonard Mucheru, Kwalia and Ben Limo. Saïdi-Sief was second to Paul Koech at Rieti with Kibowen third. Having set a European indoor record of 7:32.98 in Seville, Alberto García came second in the World Indoor 3000m, but received a two-year drugs ban for a positive test for EPO at this meeting.

5000 Metres

A RECORD 13 men (all Africans) broke 13 minutes in 2003 and again there was remarkably little to choose between them. The year's fastest time came when the then Stephen Cherono ran 12:48.81 in Ostrava in June, outsprinting Hicham El Guerrouj, who ran 12:50.24 in his first 5000m since his World Junior bronze in 1992. Cherono had just two other (slow) 5000m races, winning at the European Clubs and taking the Asian silver medal at the end of the year, by when he was named Saif Saaeed Shaheen, but El Guerrouj went on to attempt an audacious 1500m/5000m double at the Worlds. He just failed as his 12:52.83 was 0.04 behind the World Junior CC champion, Eliud Kipchoge, with Kenenisa Bekele, Abraham Chebii and Gebre Gebremariam breaking 13 minutes in 3rd to 6th and defending champion Richard Limo just outside in 7th place. Bekele, Sammy Kipketer, Kipchoge and Chebii had finished 1-4, all running 12:52s in a great race in Oslo, where James Kwalia, like Kipchoge still a junior, and Albert Chepkurui were also under 13 minutes. Chebii, who had earlier wins in Osaka and Eugene, went on to produce exciting sprint finishes in Golden League races to beat Haile Gebrselassie, Ben Limo and Kipchoge in Paris and Bekele and Gebrselassie in Rome, with Gebremariam 4th and 6th in those races. But, after winning the Kenyan Trial from Kibowen, Kipchoge and Kipketer (who thus missed the Worlds), Chebii slipped a little to 6th in Zürich (where Kibowen, Nicholas Kemboi and Kipketer were 1-2-3) and to 5th in the Worlds. Gebrselassie beat Kipketer and Kibowen at the London GP, another race in which three men beat 13 minutes. Kipchoge, after wins also in Milan and Stockholm, made it 4/7 and just enough to take top ranking with a win in a slowly-run race at the WAF, where he was followed home by Richard Limo, Gebremariam and Kipketer. Christian Belz, 26th at 13:12.16, was the highest ranked non-African-born athlete.

Most times sub 13:10: Chebii 6, Bekele, Chepkurui (later Hassan), Kipchoge & Kipketer 4; Gebremariam, Gebrselassie, Kibowen, Kwalia & Leonard Mucheru 3.

1. Kipchoge, 2. El Guerrouj, 3. Bekele, 4. Chebii, 5. Gebrselassie, 6. Kibowen, 7. Kipketer, 8. Shaheen, 9. B Limo, 10. Gebremariam

10,000 Metres

TWO RACES dominate considerations for the world rankings – the Worlds and Brussels. Kenenisa Bekele ran the second 5000m at the Worlds in an astonishing 12:57.24 in his 26:49.57, 1.2 ahead of the great Haile Gebrselassie with Sileshi Sihine an isolated third in 27:01.44 and Abdullah Ahmad Hassan (formerly Albert Chepkurui of Kenya) who set an Asian record 27:18.28 in his first race in Qatari colours. Three Kenyans followed: John Cheruiyot Korir, Wilberforce Talel and Charles Kamathi; Korir had won all three major Kenyan races with Talel second, Gilbert Okari (who did not have the World qualifying time) and Chepkurui 4th at the Kenyan Trials. The 10,000m in Brussels was run in a very different way from that in the Stade de France, as 5000m as reached in 13:15.58 compared to 13:52.33 at the Worlds. Even so, the second half was still faster, as Gebrselassie won in 26:29.22, the third fastest ever time for the distance. There were the best ever marks for 2-3 and 8-16 and 13 men ran under 27:30 compared to the previous best of ten (Brussels 2002). Nicholas Kemboi, just 19 years old, was second in 26:30.03, having run 28:19.77 in his only previous 10,000 when sixth at Hengelo, and Hassan smashed his Asian record with 26:38.76 in third. Fourth was Richard Limo in 26:56.63, and 5-10, all under 27:20, were John Yuda (World 12th), Sammy Kipketer, Moses Mosop, Berhanu Dejene, Boniface Kiprop and Korir. In all there were nine sub-27 minute times in 2003, with three more having come at Hengelo, won by Bekele from Gebrselassie and Sihine, with Gebre Gebremariam and Limo in 5th and 6th. At the end of the year Sihine and Gebremariam were 1-2 at both African Games (with Dejene 3rd, Kiprop 4th, Mosop 5th and Kipketer 6th) and at the Afro-Asian Games. Hassan won the Asian title.

1. Bekele, 2. Gebrselassie, 3. Sihine, 4. Hassan, 5. Korir, 6. Kemboi, 7. R Limo, 8. Talel, 9. Gebremariam, 10. Yuda

Half Marathon

MARTIN LEL gave early notice of a breakthrough in 2003 by winning the always-competitive, slightly downhill Lisbon race in March in 60:10, and also at Virginia Beach before completing an unbeaten season at the event by taking the World title in 60:49 from the Tanzanians Fabian Joseph and Martin Sulle, with John Cheruiyot Korir and John Yuda, despite hamstring cramps, fifth. Earlier Yuda had won the Stramilano in Milan in 60:25 from Patrick Ivuti, Sulle and Joseph. The latter two were also 6th and 3rd respectively at Vitry-sur-Seine behind John Kwalo and Paul Kirui (also a winner in Berlin). Hendrick Ramaala produced the year's fastest time on another slightly downhill course, as he won the Great North Run in 60:01 from Jackson Koech 60:05. Ramaala had been second in the March Lisbon race (3. Robert Cheruiyot, 4, Nicholas Kemboi, 5. Christopher Cheboiboch, 6. Rodgers Rop, 7. Paul Tergat all under 61 minutes), and won on a flat course there just a week after his GNR triumph, with Korir second. Koech had two good wins in Mexico and was 8th in the Worlds. Another fast time came from Zakayo Ngatho who won at Marugame in Japan in 60:21.

1. Lel, 2. Ramaala, 3. Yuda, 4. Joseph, 5. Sulle, 6. Korir, 7. Koech, 8. Kirui, 9. Ivuti, 10. Ngatho

Marathon

FROM HIS marathon debut at London in 2001, Paul Tergat had strung together a series of great times, running sub-2:09 in all five races, but had no wins until Berlin 2003. There he took 43 seconds off the world record with his 2:04:55. Yet he still won by only 1 second from Sammy Korir with Titus Munji an isolated third in 2:06:15. In their previous races in 2003, Tergat was fourth in a very tight finish in London, where just seven seconds covered the top six. behind Gezahegne Abera 2:07:56, Stefano Baldini and Joseph Ngolepus, with Samson Ramadhani 5th and Abdelkader El Mouaziz 6th. Korir had been 2nd at Xiamen 2:10:44 and 4th at San Diego 2:11:36. Four early-season marathons were faster: Paris, won by Michael Rotich 2:06:33 with Benoit Zwierzchiewski, Wilson Onsare and Driss El Himer all under 2:06:50, Hamburg, won by Julio Rey 2:07:27, Otsu, won by Japhet Kosgei 2:07:39, and Rotterdam, won by William Kiplagat 2:07:42 from Josephat Kiprono 2:07:53. Abera, reigning World and Olympic champion, was the favourite at the Worlds, but he had to drop out with an Achilles injury, and there was a surprise winner in 2:08:31: Jaouad Gharib, who had been sixth in Rotterdam on his marathon debut. Rey and Baldini confirmed their form by taking the other medals, with Alberto Chaíça a surprise fourth and Shigeru Aburaya (earlier second in Tokyo) fifth. Seventh was Ian Syster (9th London, 1st Beijing), 8th Rotich and 15th Ramadhani (also 1st Beppu). Kiplagat was a non-finisher, but in September came fourth at Amsterdam, over a minute behind the first two, William Kipsang 2:06:39 and Felix Limo 2:06:41. Third there was Benjamin Kimutai, who had been second at Boston to Robert K.Cheruiyot. Kipsang made a vast improvement from his 2:12:34 for 12th in Paris and Limo would have been the fastest ever debutant, except that a week earlier Evans Rutto had won in Chicago in 2:05:50 from Paul Koech 2:07:07.

1. Tergat, 2. Rey, 3. Baldini, 4. Gharib, 5. Korir, 6. Rutto, 7. Rotich, 8. Abera, 9. Kipsang, 10. Aburaya

3000 Metres Steeplechase

STEPHEN CHERONO, by now Saif Saaeed Shaheen, ran an extraordinary race to win the world title, slowing drastically after setting off at world record pace, getting caught by Ezekiel Kemboi, and then sprinting home for victory. That confirmed an eyeballs-out race between these two men eleven days earlier in Zürich, when with 8:02.48 and 8:02.49 they posted the fastest times of the year to date. Shaheen went on complete an unbeaten season of eight steeplechase competitions, improving to 8:00.06 in Brussels and 7:57.38 at the WAF, with Kemboi, who had earlier won both Kenyan Champs and Trials, 5th and 3rd in these races, and the main challenge to Shaheen came from Paul Koech, second in both after fifth at the Kenyan Trials and third in Zürich. Kemboi sealed second ranking by coming back to beat Koech at the African Games and with a 5-3 win-loss advantage. The WAF brought together the top men as 4-5-6 were Julius Nyamu, Bob Tahri and Eliseo Martín. Nyamu had a 4-0 record against E Martín and 2-0 v Tahri, who were 4th and 3rd respectively at the Worlds. 2-6 at the vital Kenyan Trials were Abraham Cherono, Michael Kipyego, Kipkirui Misoi, Koech and Wilson Boit Kipketer, and Cherono went on to 5th at the Worlds and 5-4 v Misoi overall. Final placings in the rankings are taken by Luis Miguel Martín and Simon Vroemen, 6th and 7th at the Worlds and 8th and 9th at the WAF, where A Cherono was 10th and Boit Kipketer was 11th. Vroeman ranks higher than Martín on his faster times, especially his third at Brussels in 8:09.18.

Most times under 8:15: Kemboi 10, Koech 9, Nyamu 8, Shaheen 7, Tahri 5, Misoi 4, A Cherono 3.

1. Shaheen, 2. Kemboi, 3. Koech, 4. Nyamu, 5. Tahri, 6. E Martín, 7. A Cherono, 8. Misoi, 9. Vroemen, 10. L M Martín

110 Metres Hurdles

ALLEN JOHNSON won 14 of his 15 finals and, in his ninth successive season running under 13.05, returned to the top ranking he held in 1996-8 and 2001, while the man who has been his top rival in recent years, Anier García had injury problems and dropped out of contention with a season's best of 13.57. Johnson ran a season's best 12.97 in the Golden League meeting at Saint-Denis, won his fourth World title in 13.12 and the WAF in 13.11 and also took his sixth US title; his one loss was to Stanislav Olijar and Duane Ross in Berlin. Terrence Trammell was second to Johnson in US, Worlds and WAF, although his form was modest otherwise. Olijar was unfortunate to restrain a hamstring and pull up in his heats at the Worlds, as he had looked the man most likely to challenge Johnson and was the year's second fastest at 13.08 (behind Johnson's 13.06 in Lausanne); he was third at the WAF and beat the World bronze medallist Liu Xiang 5-1. Liu in turn had a clear 5-0 record over World fourth placer Larry Wade. The US Champs 1-2-3-4 finished in that order at the Worlds where Chris Phillips (later to test positive for Modafinil) was 6th, and Ron Bramlett, 5th in the US Champs, and Ross, a non-finisher there, had strong seasons, with Ross 3-4 v Wade, 9-6 v Bramlett and 7-6 v Phillips; Phillips 11-6 v Bramlett and 4-3 v Wade. Maurice Wignall could not compete at the Worlds through injury but had faster times than the World 6-8, Marcio de Souza, Shi Dongpeng and Yoel Hernández, as did Ladji Doucouré, who was fifth in his semi, having won at the European Cup and European U23s. Yoel Hernández had but one other meeting, while his namesake Yuniel Hernández won the Cuban and Pan-American titles, with Wade 2nd and Souza 3rd in the latter.

Most times under 13.30: Olijar 9+1w, Liu Xiang 9, Johnson 7+3w, Ross 6+2w, Wade 5, Phillips 4, Doucouré & Trammell 2.

1. Johnson, 2. Olijar, 3. Trammell, 4. Liu, 5. Ross, 6. Wade, 7. Phillips, 8. Bramlett, 9. Doucouré, 10. Wignall, 11. Yuniel Hernández

400 Metres Hurdles

FELIX SÁNCHEZ ranks top for the third successive year, and took his win-streak to 33 races including heats from his loss to Dai Tamesue on 2 July 2001. He won all his 11 finals in 2003 and his superiority was amazing. His average winning margin was 0.60 and the closest that anyone came to him was the 0.35 secs by which he beat Llewellyn Herbert in Rome. Sánchez won the World title in 47.25, his third CAC record and the world's fastest for five years, from Joey Woody, Periklís Iakovákis and Danny McFarlane. The fifth placer, Kamel Thompson, had however a better record than the World 2-3-4 as he beat Woody 5-1, Iakovákis 3-1 and was 2-2 with his compatriot McFarlane, who excelled in his debut season at the event. At the WAF the order was Sánchez, Thompson, McFarlane, Woody, Dean Griffiths and Iakovákis. Chris Rawlinson was 6th at the Worlds and had solid form during the year, including winning at the European Cup, but he tailed off to 8th in the WAF, a place behind Eric Thomas, who like Griffiths (NCAA champion and 3rd Jamaican Champs) went out in the semis at the Worlds. 20 year-old Bershawn Jackson was 2nd to Thomas (with Woody third) at the US Champs, but was disqualified in his heat for a trailing-leg violation at the Worlds. Mubarak Al-Nubi was 7th in the Worlds after no preliminary races, but followed that with wins at the Arab, Asian and Gulf Championships. Herbert was heading for second in the Worlds but fell at the final hurdle and slots into the rankings a place behind Rawlinson who beat him 2-1 and ahead of Griffiths and Thomas whom he beat 2-1. Marek Plawgo was the world's eighth fastest of the year, winning the European U23 title in 48.45, but his only other competition was when he won the Polish title.

Most times under 49.00: Sánchez 14, Thompson 13, Woody 11, McFarlane & Rawlinson 8, Thomas 7, Griffiths, Herbert, Iakovákis & Jackson 6, Jirí Muzík & Ian Weakley 5.

1. Sanchez, 2. Thompson, 3. Woody, 4. Iakovákis, 5. McFarlane, 6. Rawlinson, 7. Herbert. 8. Griffiths, 9. Thomas, 10. Jackson

High Jump

JACQUES FREITAG topped the world list in 2002 with 2.37, but lost much of that season through injury. He was a clear choice for top ranking on 2003 outdoor form and had a couple of competitions at 2.35, one of which was to win the World title. Stefan Holm won all eight indoor competitions with a best of 2.36 and 2.35 to take the World Indoor title; outdoors he had a best of 2.34 and was second at the Worlds and WAF, won by Yaroslav Rybakov (World Indoor 2nd, but 9th at the Worlds). Freitag beat Holm 4-2, and Holm was 6-2 (and 4-0 indoors) v Rybakov. The top outdoor mark of the year was 2.36 by Aleksander Walerianczyk to win the European U23s from a previous best of 2.32 when he won the Polish title, but he did not otherwise exceed 2.27 and was 19th at the Worlds. Germaine Mason and James Nieto were 1-2 at the Pan-Am Games and Mason was 5th Worlds and 4= (with Freitag) at the WAF, and Nieto (in a busy breakthrough season) was 7th Worlds and 3rd WAF, with Mark Boswell 3rd and 7th at these events. Mason was 2-2 (0-1 indoors) v Boswell, 4-2 (1-2) v Nieto and 4-1 (1-2) v Rybakov; Rybakov 4-2 (1-0) v Boswell, Nieto 6-1 v Boswell, 3-1 (1-0, 1T) v Rybakov. Andrey Sokolovskiy, 8th Worlds and 6th WAF, was 2-2 (0-2) v Boswell. Matt Hemingway (12th Worlds and 8th WAF) was second to Nieto at the US Champs and two other men to fare well at the Worlds were Mikhayil Tsvetkov 4th and Grzegorz Sposób 6th. Further top placings at the World Indoors: 3. Gennadiy Moroz (2.27 best outdoors), 4. Dragutin Topic, 5. Boswell... 8, Sokolovskiy.

Most competitions over 2.30m: Holm 10+7i, Mason 7+1i, Rybakov 5+4i, Nieto 5+1i, Freitag 5, Sokolovskiy 4+3i, Topic 3+3i, Jaroslav Bába 2+5i, Boswell 2+1i, Moroz 1+3i, Staffan Strand 3i.

1. Freitag, 2. Holm, 3. Mason, 4. Rybakov, 5. Nieto, 6. Boswell, 7. Sokolovskiy, 8. Sposób, 9. Tsvetkov, 10. Walerianczyk. – Moroz (10). (including indoors).

Pole Vault

GIUSEPPE GIBILISCO excelled to set two Italian records (5.77 and 5.82) at the Rome Golden League meeting and repeated the feat (5.85 and 5.90) to take the World gold medal. But his record in other Golden League meetings did not match this: 10= Berlin, 11 Zürich, 7= Brussels. Tim Lobinger was, as ever, the most prolific jumper, with 10 indoor and 16 outdoor competitions at 5.70 or better and he produced a season's best 5.91 to win at the World Athletics Finals, also taking the World Indoor gold. But the man with the best record on win-loss against his opponents was Okkert Brits, second at both Worlds and WAF; after a no height at the World Indoors he beat Gibilisco 4-2, Lobinger (5th Worlds) 4-1, and Dmitriy Markov (4th/3rd) 6-2. These men were behind Romain Mesnil 5.95 and Aleksandr Averbukh 5.93 on the world list. Mesnil cleared 5.92 to win at the Paris GL, but failed to clear a height in World qualifying and was 7th at the WAF, and Averbukh was beaten 3-2 by Gibilisco and was 4-4 with Markov. Patrik Kristiansson took the World bronze medal with a pb 5.85, but lost 2-1 to both Mesnil and Derek Miles, who was beaten by Jeff Hartwig for the US title (Miles won indoors) but fared better, 6th equal (with Tim Mack and Denys Yurchenko) to Hartwig's non-qualifying at the Worlds. Miles beat Hartwig 4-0 indoors, but was 4-5 down outdoors. Mack was third at the US Champs both indoors and out.

Most competitions over 5.80m: Brits 8, Lobinger 5+5i, Averbukh & Gibilisco 4, Markov 3, Mesnil 2+1i.

1. Brits, 2. Lobinger, 3. Gibilisco, 4. Markov, 5. Kristiansson (6), 6. Averbukh (8), 7. Mesnil, 8. Miles (5), 9. Yurchenko, 10. Hartwig. (Including indoors).

Long Jump

DWIGHT PHILLIPS won World titles indoors and out, and he also won at the WAF. His overall record was 3 wins in 6 competitions indoors and 6 in 8 outdoors; he won the US title outdoors but indoors was second to Miguel Pate. Pate was third at the World Indoors but is hard to rank on outdoor form as he had just three competitions before injury, but those were excellent wins: 8.25 at the Drake Relays, 8.46A in Mexico City well ahead of Kareem Streete-Thompson and Savante Stringfellow, and a 8.27–8.23 win over Phillips at Eugene. Yago Lamela took two World medals, silver indoors and bronze outdoors, and had the world's top mark with 8.53 at Castellón in August, while James Beckford was the World silver medallist. The man who made the most progress was Ignisious Gaisah, who set five Ghanaian records outdoors from 8.15 to 8.30, the last at the African Games.

Gaisah was 4th in the Worlds and third at the WAF. He was beaten 3-1 by Beckford, but had a 2-1 advantage over Hussein Al-Sabee, 5th Worlds, Arab and Asian champion and 2nd WAF. Stringfellow jumped 8.46 in April but failed to qualify for the World final, although he returned for WAF 4th, a place ahead of Lamela. Vladimir Zyuskov was second to Louis Tsátoumas (12th Worlds, 8th WAF) at the European U23s and was 6th at both Worlds and WAF, and Walter Davis, although contesting only five long jumps, was 2nd to Phillips and ahead of Stringfellow at the US Champs and was 7th in the Worlds. The great Iván Pedroso had no jumps in qualifying at the Worlds, but had a best of 8.31 and won the Pan-Ams with 8.23.

Most competitions over 8.15m: Lamela 8+1w/5i, Gaisah 8+1w, Stringfellow 6/1i, Phillips 5/3i, Zyuskov 5/1i, Beckford 4+1w/2i, Pate 3/3i, Al-Sabee 3+1w, Streete-Thompson & Tsátoumas 3, Joan Lino Martínez 1+2w.

1. Phillips, 2. Lamela, 3. Beckford (4), 4. Gaisah (6), 5. Al-Sabee (7), 6. Stringfellow (5), 7. Zyuskov (8), 8. Davis (9), 9. Pate (3), 10. Pedroso. (Including indoors).

Triple Jump

JONATHAN EDWARDS bowed out in disappointing fashion at the World Championships, but it was a surprise that he was able to compete after what looked a serious injury at the London GP just 17 days earlier. He had jumped over 17m four times indoors including 4th at the World Indoors and three times outdoors, including a sensational start to the season, when he jumped 17.61 at Gateshead. Even that, however, was not enough to defeat his successor as world number one, Christian Olsson, who jumped 17.92w and 17.74 there. Olsson had a superb year, winning 6/8 indoors to a best of 17.70 to take the World Indoor title and all 15 outdoors when he was over 17m on 52 of his 64 valid jumps, but the competitive situation behind him was confused. Martin Oprea (8th World Indoors) had perhaps the best outdoor record with eight wins and two second places until the Worlds, where he was just 17th in qualifying a place behind the man who beaten him for the European U23 title, Dmitriy Valyukevich (17.57).

Although ninth on the world lists with 17.28, Yoandri Betanzos did that to take the World silver medal and was also Cuban and Pan-American champion with a season's record of six firsts and two seconds. Leevan Sands won the CAC title and was third at the Worlds, but was 7th at the WAF and was beaten 2-1 by South American champion Jadel Gregório (2nd Pan-Am, 5th Worlds, 4th WAF) and 5-4 by US champion Kenta Bell (6th Worlds, 3rd WAF). World Indoor silver medallist Walter Davis was beaten outdoors by Bell for the US title and was another to fail to make the World final (15th), but he returned for 2nd at the WAF and in Moscow, and beat Gregório 2-1. David Giralt was fourth at the Worlds and won the Pan-American Juniors. Tim Rusan beat Davis and Bell to win the US indoor title and was 5th at the World Indoors, outdoors he was third at the US Championships but unable to compete at the Worlds.

Most competitions over 17m: Olsson 16/7i, Oprea 10/3i, Bell 8/2i, Betanzos 5, Gregório 4+2w/3, Edwards 4/3i, Rusan 4/1i, Giralt & Sands 4, Valyukevich 3, Davis 2+1w/4i, Allen Simms 2/1i.

1. Olsson, 2. Oprea (4), 3. Betanzos (5),
4. Edwards (2), 5. Davis (3), 6. Gregório (6),
7. Bell, 8. Sands, 9. Valyukevich (10),
10. Giralt (-), – Rusan (9). (Including indoors).

Shot

ANDREY MIKHNEVICH came straight off a two-year drugs ban with a 21.66 in Belarus and 21.69 to take the World title. He then won the World Universities title but was third at the WAF behind Christian Cantwell and Yuriy Belonog. Is that enough for the world top ranking? – well maybe as nobody established a clear-cut case. The world list indoors and out was headed by Kevin Toth at 21.70 and 22.67 (the world's best since 1990) and he did better than usual in the championships as he won US titles indoors and out and was 4th at the Worlds, but 7th at the WAF. Ahead of him in both these two major meetings were Yuriy Belonog 3rd and 2nd and Adam Nelson 2nd and 5th. Belonog was, as usual, consistent and won his six other outdoor competitions, while Nelson, only 4th at the US Champs, came into form when it mattered. Surprisingly John Godina (US 2nd indoors and out) was only 9th at the Worlds after leading the qualifiers.

Two big favourites who did not even make the final were Carl Myerscough, NCAA champion indoors and out with British records of 21.49 and 21.92, and Manuel Martínez. Myerscough beat Cantwell (5th US Champs) 2-1 both indoors and out and had wins in Britain at 21.55 and 21.50 just before the Worlds, but managed only 19.51 in Saint-Denis, where Justin Anlezark, Ralf Bartels, Teppa Reinikainen and Ville Tiisanoja were 5-8, but none bettered 21m in 2003. Martínez beat Myerscough 2-1, including at the European Cup, and was 4-1 v Bartels and 3-2 v Cantwell outdoors. Reese Hoffa was 3rd in the US Champs and won the Pan-Am title with a pb 20.95, but fouled out in qualifying at the Worlds. The order at the World Indoor Championships was 1. Martínez, 2, Godina, 3. Belonog, 4. Arsi Harju, 5. Anlezark, 6, Reinikainen, but Toth, later to test positive for THG, was only 12th, distracted by a small sector.

Competitions over 21.00: Toth 6+3i, Belonog 5+2i, Cantwell 5, Myerscough 4+1i, Nelson 3, Mikhnevich 2, Godina & Martínez 1+1i, Yuriy Belov 1, Harju & Dan Taylor 1i.

1. Mikhnevich (2), 2. Belonog (1), 3. Nelson,
4. Toth, 5. Godina, 6. Martínez, 7. Myerscough,
8. Cantwell, 9. Anlezark, 10. Hoffa,
11. Reinikainen. (Including indoors).

Discus

OF THE top 20 performances in 2003, Virgilijus Alekna had 10, Róbert Fazekas 8 and Lars Riedel 2. Alekna won 11 of his 16 competitions and Fazekas won 11 of his 13, but although Fazekas beat Alekna 3-2, those two losses were at the Worlds and WAF. Vasiliy Kaptyukh was 3rd, Riedel 4th and Michael Möllenbeck 5th at both Worlds and WAF, with Aleksandr Tammert 7th and 6th and Frantz Kruger 6th and 7th. Riedel had an astonishing 10-1 record over Möllenbeck and Tammert beat Kruger 6-3, so ranking was pretty easy.

The Worlds and WAF 8th Mario Pestano did not have other performances as good as the US and Russian champions Carl Brown and Dmitriy Shevchenko, 9th and 10th at the Worlds, and Gerd Kanter, at 24 much the youngest of the top ten, was another with superior marks.

Most competitions over 65m: Alekna 16, Fazekas & Riedel 12, Möllenbeck 9, Kruger 6, Zoltán Kövágó & Tammert 5, Brown, Kanter & Kaptyukh 4, Shevchenko 3.

1. Alekna, 2. Fazekas, 3. Kaptyukh, 4. Riedel,
5. Möllenbeck, 6. Tammert, 7. Kruger, 8. Brown,
9. Shevchenko, 10. Kanter

Hammer

IN COMMON with other Belarus athletes, Ivan Tikhon had a fairly thin season, but won when it mattered, taking BLR, World and World University Games titles, before third place at the WAF behind Adrián Annus and Libor Charfreitag, and second at Yokohama to Koji Murofushi. Tikhon's three competitions over 83m, to one by Annus and two by Murofushi, just gives him the edge for top ranking. Murofushi, world leader at 84.86, won six of eight, but was unfortunate to injure an elbow in a fall just before the Worlds, so fared less well than hoped with 3rd Worlds and 4th WAF, whereas Annus was 2nd and 1st, although earlier beaten three times by Murofushi. Ukrainian champion Andrey Skvaruk and Russian champion Ilya Konovalov went 4&5 and 6&7 at Worlds and WAF, with Promoz Kozmus, who had inferior marks 5&6. Charfreitag just missed a place in the World final but beat Kozmus 3-1 as well as 1-2 down to Konovalov. After leading the qualifying with 79.66, Igor Astapkovich failed to have a valid throw in the World final, but his marks are enough to retain a place in the rankings. German champion Karsten Kobs won at the European Cup from two men who just miss rankings places: Wojciech Kondratowicz and Aléxandros Papadimitríou (World 8th). World 7th Vadim Devyatovskiy otherwise competed only in Belarus. This is the event most domiated by Europeans, with 37 of the world top 40.

Most competitions over 80m: Murofushi 8, Annus 7, Tikhon 6, Charfreitag & Konovalov 4, Astapkovich, Péter Botfa, Kobs & Skvaruk 2.

1. Tikhon, 2. Annus, 3. Murofushi, 4. Skvaruk, 5. Konovalov, 6. Charfreitag, 7. Kozmus, 8. Astapkovich, 9. Kobs, 10. Devyatovskiy

Javelin

SERGEY MAKAROV retains top ranking although without the level of performance he showed in 2002; he had 9 wins in 11 competitions, including Worlds and WAF. Jan Zelezny beat him in Paris and Zürich with Boris Henry also ahead at third in Zürich and these two men were 2nd and 3rd at the WAF, although Zelezny was beaten by Andrus Värnik and Henry into 4th at the Worlds. However, Zelezny beat Henry 5-2, and Henry was 4-1 over the rapidly improving Värnik. Aki Parviainen came back from injury just in time to win the Finnish title and take fifth place at the Worlds, where 6-9 were Christian Nicolau, Miroslav Guzdek, Peter Blank and Steve Backley. The Germans had plenty of competition, with Nicolay ahead of Blank 9-4 and Raymond Hecht 7-3. Blank, who set a world masters record of 84.08, when 3rd at the German Champs, was 4-4 v Hecht. These men, and Backley, all had clear win-loss advantage over Aleksandr Ivanov, who tailed off (including World 12th) after 88.90 in June. Another to fall away was Eriks Rags after 86.32 in April. Standards in general were well down on previous years.

Most competitions over 85m: Makarov 10, Zelezny 5, Henry 4, Ivanov 3, Värnik 2.

1. Makarov, 2. Zelezny, 3. Henry, 4. Värnik, 5. Nicolay, 6. Blank, 7. Hecht, 8. Ivanov, 9. Parviainen, 10. Backley

Decathlon

TOM PAPPAS achieved a World Championships double with the indoor heptathlon gold and outdoor decathlon. He added two points to his pb with 8585 when second to Roman Sebrle (8807) at Götzis and then broke into new territory when winning the US title with 8784 and the Worlds with 8750. Sebrle won at Ratingen with 8606 and took the World silver with 8634. These two men were a long way ahead of the rest as the only other scores over 8300 were Bryan Clay's 8482 for second at the US Champs and Dmitriy Karpov's 8374 for the World bronze. Clay had a win with 8225 at Berkeley but pulled up with a hamstring injury in the 400m when lying third overall at the Worlds. The 22 year-old Karpov improved from 7995 to 8253 when he won at Desenzano, but did not finish at Götzis. There Jón Arnar Magnússon was 3rd with 8222, but, after second at Ratingen, he failed to finish at the Worlds and in Talence.

Tomás Dvorák returned to place fourth at the Worlds with 8242 in his only decathlon of the year, just ahead of Laurent Hernu 8218 and Lev Lobodin 8198. Hernu went on to win at Talence with 8219; he also won the French title with 8184 after being well below 8000 for 10th at Götzis and 5th in the European Cup. Another Frenchman Romain Barras had a most consistent season scoring 7900 or more in his six decathlons, topped by 8196 for the World University Games gold medal. Paul Terek was third at Desenzano and scored 8275 for third at the US Champs; he was deemed to have intentionally pushed over hurdles at the World Championships to be shown as 12th at 7503, but if his hurdles time had counted he would have scored 8253 (and taken fourth place). A non-finisher at the Worlds was Erki Nool, winner of the European Cup 1st League with 8281. Later year I remarked that only 23 men scored over 8000 points in 2002, the lowest number since 1979, and in 2003 there was a further decline – to 22.

1. Pappas, 2. Sebrle, 3. Karpov, 4. Clay, 5. Hernu, 6. Dvorák, 7. Barras, 8. Terek, 9. Nool, 10. Lobodin

20 Kilometres Walk

FRANCISCO FERNÁNDEZ went to the World Championships as favourite after second (to Bernardo Segura) at Tijuana and wins at Sesto San Giovanni, European Cup and Spanish Champs, but although he recorded 1:18:00, his fourth sub 1:20 time of 2003, in Saint-Denis, he had to yield to the world best 1:17:21 walked by Jefferson Pérez, who had been only 14th at Tijuana and 3rd at Sesto, but who won the Pan-American Cup and Games races. So these men swapped rankings from 2002. Robert Korzeniowski contested the 50km at the Worlds, but had been 3rd at Tijuana, 2nd at Sesto and 3rd at La Coruña, all races included in the newly introduced IAAF Race Walking Challenge .The other race in the series, at Rio Maior, was won by Aigars Fadejevs, also 4th at Sesto and 5th at La Coruña. Third and fourth in the latter were Ivan Trotskiy and Noé Hernández, who went on to 6th and 4th respectively in the Worlds, where Roman Rasszazov returned from injury to take the bronze medal and Luke Adams excelled to place fifth after 6th at Sesto and 12th at La Coruña. Segura was disqualified at La Coruña and Worlds, but was second at the Pan-Ams with Alejandro López (World 10th) third. Just missing rankings are two men who had European Cup/Worlds placings as follows: David Márquez 6th/7th, José David Domínguez 7th/9th, but Ilya Markov 5th/8th also had a good win at the Russian Winter Champs.

1. Pérez, 2. Fernández, 3. Korzeniowski, 4. Rasskazov, 5. Hernández, 6. Trotskiy, 7. Segura, 8. Fadejevs, 9. Adams, 10. Markov.

50 Kilometres Walk

KORZENIOWSKI, surely the world's greatest ever walker, repeated his 2002 formula of contesting just one 50k and winning in a world best time. He was pushed, however, to his 3:36:03 at the Worlds as five men bettered 3:40 compared to the previous record of three at the 1988 Olympic Games. German Skurygin accelerated from 67 seconds down on Korzeniowski at 30k to 6 seconds at 45k, but the Polish master stretched away to a 39 seconds win at the finish. Skurygin won the European Cup in his other race. while the Worlds' 3-4-5 were Andreas Erm, also winner at Naumberg, Aleksey Voyevodin, also 2nd the European Cup, and Denis Nizhegorodov, also Russian champion. The World sixth placer Jesús Angel García won at Tijuana after second to Mikel Odriozola (World 14th) at the Spanish Championships. Roman Madziarczyk was 7th at the Worlds, followed by Trond Nymark and Sergey Korepanov, who were 3rd and 4th respectively at Naumberg, where Aigars Fadejevs (dq Worlds) was second. Yu Chaohong was disqualified at the Worlds but won the Chinese Championships and Games races in fast times and Nathan Deakes returned at the end of the year with 3:39:43.

1. Korzeniowski, 2. Skurygin, 3. Èrm, 4. Voyevodin, 5. Nizhegorodov, 6. García, 7. Madziarczyk, 8. Nymark, 9. Odriozola, 10. Korepanov

WOMEN ATHLETES OF 2002

PAULA RADCLIFFE missed the track season through illness and injury, but in Spring and Autumn had a series of road races that fully maintained her supremacy amongst women distance runners. Indeed she is the phenomenon of our age. She had taken 1 minute 29 seconds off the world record for the marathon with 2:17:18 in Chicago 2002, but then took another 1 minute 53 seconds off the record with 2:15:25 in London six months later. She started 2003 in even better form than she had started 2002, as she set a world record for 10km on the roads with a superb win in San Juan, Puerto Rico in 30:21. Her London Marathon win then depleted all available superlatives as she set world bests en route at 30km (1:36:36, compared to the initial IAAF mark of 1:39:02) and 20 miles (1:43:33). She went through 10km in 32:01 and halfway in 68:02, before a second half marathon of 67:23. There was controversy over the fact that she was accompanied for most of the way by two Kenyan men, but a look at the split times shows that she dictated the pace throughout, and what a pace! I do not believe that the 'pacing' made any significant difference to her performance.

Having been a woman who had struggled gallantly but failed to win track titles until her step up in class in 2002, we looked forward to her gaining records and titles on the track in 2003, but sadly a leg injury followed by bronchitis and tonsillitis prevented her competing in the summer.

She returned in superb form in the Autumn with world bests at 5km and, more importantly, in the Great North Run, where her 65:40 for half marathon won by 1 minute 52 seconds from World 10,000m champion Berhane Adere and other top-class women were left far behind. The Newcastle to South Shields course, being point-to-point and very slightly downhill, does not meet IAAF or ARRS standards for records.

When she won the World Half marathon title for the third time it was almost an anti-climax that she did not set a world record in so doing, but even she has to yield to the conditions from time to time and she still left Adere trailing 1 min 27 seconds behind in second place.

Her winning run, which dated back to a track 3000m in Monaco on 19 July 2002 was ended when she was third for Britain on the opening leg of the Chiba Ekiden road relay on 24 November, as although she ran 30:42 for her 10k leg she was passed by Berhane Adere and Lucy Wangui.

Paula Radcliffe in 2003

23 Feb		San Juan	10k road	1	30:21	world best
13 Apr		London	Mar	1	2:15:25	WR
7 Sep		Richmond Park	10km Rd	1	30:51	
14 Sep		London (HP)	5km Rd	1	14:51	world best
21 Sep	GNR	South Shields	HMar	1	65:40	world best
4 Oct	WCh	Vilamoura	HMar	1	67:35	
24 Nov		Chiba	10k relay	3	30:42	

100 Metres

UNTIL NEWS came through of a positive test for the stimulant Modafinil, Kelli White was clearly the top woman sprinter of the year. Her record at 100m was nine wins and four seconds before she ended with 4th at the WAF and 3rd in Moscow. She ran a world-leading time 10.85 to take the World title and, after sitting out the World 4x100m after news of her positive test, came back to win at Brussels in 10.87. Just 0.01 behind in that race was Chryste Gaines, the winner of four World and Olympic relay golds, who had been only fifth in the US Champs, but who came through to six successive sub-11 second times in August and September and a pb 10.86 on her 33rd birthday in the World Athletics Finals where she won in 10.86. However she too was later revealed to have tested posititive for Modafinil. Gaines had a 5-2 record against Torri Edwards, who was second to White in US Champs and Worlds and 3rd at Brussels and WAF, and 4-3 against Chandra Sturrup, who won the first three Golden League races, at Oslo, Paris and Rome, and went on to 4th Worlds and Brussels and 5th WAF.

Zhanna Block took the World bronze medal and was 5th in Brussels and 7th WAF, where Christine Arron was 2nd. Arron, 6th in the Worlds, had a 4-1 advantage over Block. Muriel Hurtis ran just the 200m at the Worlds, but was 6th in the WAF race and was well ahead of the World 7th placer Aleen Bailey (also NCAA and Jamaican champion) in their one meeting, in Zürich. Ekateríni Thánou had a season that was thin even by modern Greek standards; she was fifth in the World 100m, but her only other race was an 11.71 win in Athens, and the other World finalist Gail Devers (8th) had just two other 100ms, 3rd in US Champs and 2nd in Glasgow. Worlds semi-finalists, Debbie Ferguson (0-2 v Bailey) and Marina Kislova had many more major races.

Most times under 11.10: White 14+4w, Sturrup 10+1w, Arron 9+2w, Gaines 9+1w, Edwards 5+4w, Block & Thánou 3, Hurtis 1+3w.

1. White, 2. Gaines, 3. Edwards, 4. Sturrup, 5. Arron, 6. Block, 7. Hurtis, 8. Bailey, 9. Thánou, 10. Ferguson

Female Athlete of the Year

My selection of the top 10 athletes of 2003 together with the list compiled by international experts polled by *Track & Field News* and those of *Athletics International* readers (who only voted for 1-2-3) is as follows:

	PJM	*T&FN*	*AI*
Paul Radcliffe	1	-	1
Carolina Klüft	2	3	2
Maria Mutola	3	1	3
Ana Guevara	4	2	5
Eunice Barber	5	9	8
Hestrie Cloete	6	4	4
Berhane Adere	7	5	6
Svetlana Feofanova	8	8	9
Kelli White	9	6	-
Yipsi Moreno	10	10	-
Süreyya Ayhan	-	7	7
Yelena Isinbayeva	-	-	10

Note that Track and Field News has a curious policy of debarring cross-country and road performances, except for the marathon, and did not include Radcliffe on their list of contenders. AI readers voted for top five only.

The EAA European Athlete of the Year was Carolina Klüft from Paula Radcliffe and Eunice Barber.

200 Metres

WHITE WON her three biggest races: US and World Champs and WAF and ran the year's fastest time of 22.05 at the Worlds where the other medals were won by Anastasiya Kapachinskaya and Torri Edwards, and they were followed by Muriel Hurtis, Zhanna Block, Beverly McDonald, Natalya Safronnikova and Anzhela Kravchenko. Hurtis had been runner-up to Michelle Collins (who did not run outdoors) at the World Indoors with Kapachinskaya third and Juliet Campbell, Cydonie Mothersill and Safronnikova taking places 4-6. Outdoors Hurtis took a little while to find top form, and was beaten by Kapachinskaya and Ionela Tîrlea in the European Cup, but she ended well with 2nd at the WAF, with Kapachinskaya 3rd, Edwards 4th, Kim Gevaert (5th in semi at Worlds) 5th, and Safronnikova, McDonald and Mothersill completing the field. After the top four there was little to choose between a dozen or so women.

Aleen Bailey won NCAA and Jamaican titles but did not finish in her World quarter-final, Debbie Ferguson also went out at that stage and Chryste Gaines ran just two 200m races, but beat McDonald in Helsinki and Hurtis and Block in Yokohama. Block's only other 200m was her 2nd to Hurtis at Heusden, but ahead of Gevaert. Second and fourth on the world lists came at the high altitude of Mexico City, when Allyson Felix ran the fastest ever time by a junior, 22.11, and LaTasha Jenkins 22.31 ahead of White 22.33. Felix was 3rd and Jenkins 4th at the US Champs and Felix later took the Pan-American bronze behind Roxana Díaz and Mothersill, but ran only 23.33 at the Worlds (qf). Mary Onyali finished a distinguished career with a 100m/200m/4x100m treble at the African Games to take her to a record eleven gold medals at the quadrennial event; she had just missed a place in the World final.

Most times under 22.80: White 9, Kapachinskaya 7+1w/2i, Hurtis 7/6i, Edwards 7, Felix 5+1w, Jenkins 4, Gevaert 3+1w, Block & Ferguson 3, Collins 3i, Mothersill & Onyali 2+1w.

1. White, 2. Kapachinskaya, 3. Edwards, 4. Hurtis, 5. Block, 6. Gevaert, 7. McDonald, 8. Safronnikova, 9. Onyali, 10. Mothersill. Including indoors: 5. Collins, rest down a place.

400 Metres

ANA GUEVARA started her season with a world best of 35.30 for 300m in Mexico City and took her winning run to 23 successive 400m finals from the 2001 World Championships, by winning all eight in 2003 and took her CAC record to 49.11 at Zürich and 48.89 at the Worlds. Like Felix Sánchez in the men's 400mh, her superiority over her rivals was massive, and she won all but two races (when Lorraine Fenton was 0.54 behind her in the Worlds and 0.95 behind at the WAF) by a least a second. Fenton won her other six finals. The other two women to beat 50 seconds in 2003 were the world 3-4, Amy Mbacké

Thiam and Natalya Nazarova. This pair were beaten into 4th and 6th places at the WAF by the World's 5th and 6th Tonique Williams (3rd) and Olesya Zykina (5th). Lee McConnell was 7th and Svetlana Pospelova 8th at both Worlds and WAF, but Pospelova had earlier beaten McConnell three times, including at the European Cup and was 2-2 v Zykina. Three athletes made the world top ten on best times but had only limited competition: Anastasiya Kapachinskaya, Jearl Miles-Clark and Jana Pittman.

The latter ran just two races, 50.43 in Sydney and 50.98 at Lausanne, but that race, won by Fenton, she had Pospelova and Zykina behind her as well as Miles-Clark, who was later 4th in Zürich in 50.53, two places ahead of NCAA and US champion Sanya Richards, a World semi-finalist. Richards takes the final ranking spot with a 2-1 advantage over McConnell. Nazarova ran the three fastest indoor times and won the World Indoor title.

Most times under 51.00: Fenton 10, Guevara 9, Nazarova 6+3i, Williams & Zykina 6, Thiam 5, Pospelova 4.

1. Guevara, 2. Fenton, 3. Thiam, 4. Nazarova, 5. Williams, 6. Zykina, 7. Pospelova, 8. Pittman, 9. Miles Clark, 10. Richards

800 Metres

MARIA MUTOLA has been a world-class runner since 1991, but had her greatest ever year in 2003, when she won her fifth World Indoor title, her third World outdoor title and was the sole winner of the Golden League jackpot of £1 million. She won all her races – 13 outdoor and 2 indoor finals plus three heats (and she also won two races at 1000m and one at 600m). Mutola's new training partner Kelly Holmes ranks second as in the Worlds and WAF despite not contesting the distance outdoors until mid-August. She was 2-2 v Amina Aït-Hammou (4th Worlds and 3rd WAF) and 2-1 v World bronze medallist Natalya Khrushchelyova (7th WAF), who had a fine year after moving up from 400m. Jolanda Ceplak broke 2 minutes in her first nine outdoor races before slipping outside that time when 6th at WAF and in Moscow; after beating Aït-Hammou in their first four clashes, she lost the last three and she was 2-2 v Khrushchelyova.

Ceplak also beat Stephanie Graf in their two clashes outdoors. Graf, who beat Khrushchelyova 2-0 and Holmes 1-0, lost the chance of a higher outdoor rating through a freak accident that caused her withdrawal from the World final. In that race Claudia Gesell was 5th and Diane Cummins 6th. Jearl Miles-Clark ran a couple of 1:58s, including when she won the US title, but then dropped out in Golden League races in Rome and Berlin and went out in her heat at the Worlds and the final ranking spots are taken by a couple of athletes with a good depth of times, Faith Macharia and Larisa Chzhao. Behind Mutola the World Indoor 2-3-4 were Graf, Mayte Martínez and Ceplak.

Most times under 2:00: Mutola 13+3i, Ceplak 9+2i, Aït-Hammou 7, Graf 5+3i, Cummins 5, Holmes 4+1i, Khrushchelyova, Macharia & Chzhao 4.

1. Mutola, 2. Holmes, 3. Aït-Hammou, 4. Ceplak, 5. Graf, 6. Khrushchelyova, 7. Cummins, 8. Macharia, 9. Gesell, 10. Chzhao.

1500 Metres

IT WAS a major surprise when Süreyya Ayhan, having set off as usual to control the race from the start, was caught by Tatyana Tomashova in the World 1500m. However, she came back from that to run the fastest time of the year, 3:55.33 at Brussels and had a clear win in the WAF, so that in all she ran five of the seven sub-4-minute times run in 2003, the other two being by Tomashova and bronze-medallist Hayley Tullett in the Worlds. Tomashova had just one more win, at the Russian Champs, in her seven races at 1500m, coming 7th in the WAF, where Kenyan champion and World 5th, Jackline Maranga was 2nd, Tullett 3rd, Jo Pavey (World 10th) 4th, Judit Varga 5th and Naomi Mugo 6th, the same position that she had been at the Worlds. Maranga beat Tullett 4-1 in all, and Tullett was 3-2 v Yekaterina Rozenburg, who had four runs in the 4:00-4:01 region, including 2nd Zürich, 3rd Russian Champs and Brussels and 4th Worlds, and ran 4:02s when 8th in Rome and WAF.

The first three in that Rome race were Olga Yegorova (9th Brussels), Natalia Rodríguez and Suzy Favor Hamilton. Rodríguez won in the European Cup and Paris Golden League, but was 11th in her semi-final at the Worlds, from which Favor Hamilton had to withdraw after a good series of runs, including 2nd at the US Champs to Regina Jacobs, another to exit the Worlds at the semi-final stage. Yelena Zadorozhnaya had four second places in major races, Oslo (won by Irina Lishchinskaya), Paris GL, Russian Champs and Brussels, but was 8th in the Worlds attempting to double at 5000m (qv) and 9th WAF. Daniela Yordanova was back from tendon surgery to 7th Worlds and 6th Brussels, and Judit Varga, 5th WAF, just missed a ranking place.

Indoors, Jacobs set a world record at 3:59.98 in Boston, and won the world title from Kelly Holmes, Rozenburg, Natalya Gorelova and Lishchinskaya.

Most times under 4:04: Rozenburg 6+2i. Ayhan & Zadorozhnaya 6, Pavey, Tomashova & Tullett 5, Favor Hamilton 4 Maria Cioncan, Lishchinskaya, Maranga, Mugo & Varga 3, Jacobs 2+2i, Gorelova 2+1i.

1. Ayhan, 2. Tomashova, 3. Maranga, 4. Tullett, 5. Rozenburg, 6. Zadorozhnaya, 7. Mugo, 8. Favor Hamilton (9), 9. Pavey (-), 10. Yordanova (-). (Including indoors: 8. Jacobs, 10. Holmes)

3000 Metres

BERHANE ADERE ran the fastest time of the year, 8:31.73 indoors in Stuttgart and won the World Indoor title from Marta Domínguez and Meseret Defar, but outdoors her two 3000m races were 3rd at the Paris GL and 5th at the WAF. Gabriela Szabo ran the two fastest outdoor times, in her wins in Paris 8:34.09 and Zürich 8:33.95. Five women broke 8:40 in the former as 2-5 were Zhor El Kamch, Adere, Olga Yegorova and Werknesh Kidane. Edith Masai won the WAF, her one 3000m race of the year, from Yelena Zadorozhnaya, Jo Pavey, Defar and Adere with El Kamch 7th. Other important races included Lausanne: 1. Zadorozhnaya, 2. Defar, 3. Tatyana Tomashova, 4. Kidane; and Gateshead: 1. El Kamch, 2. Pavey, 3, Benita Johnson (Oceania record 8:38.06), 4. Defar, 5. Sonia O'Sullivan. O'Sullivan was later second in Zürich with Johnson fifth.

5000 Metres

THE THREE fastest times of the year were run at Oslo, where Berhane Adere missed the world record by just 1.23 secs with 14:29.32, Werknesh Kidane was 2nd in 14:33.04 and Tirunesh Dibaba ran a world junior record 14:39.94. Meseret Defar was fourth in this race in 14:43.36 and then won in Rome, where the next six fastest times of the year were run. Following Defar's 14:40.34 were Gabriela Szabo, Ejigayehu Dibaba, T Dibaba, Zhor El Kamch and Adere. Two more important races preceded the worlds: and both were won by Edith Masai (who had won Kenyan Champs and Trial). In Stockholm she won from Isabella Ochichi and Lornah Kiplagat, and in London from Szabo and Derartu Tulu; Zahra Ouaziz was fourth in both races.

Then came the World Championships, in which the heats were sensationally fast, with 13 of the 15 finalists breaking 15 minutes, and the form-book was considerably upset in the final. Sun and Adere were coming back from the very fast 10,000m and were unable to live up to expectations, as they were 9th and 10th and another favourite, Szabo, faded to 11th. Victory went to the junior Tirunesh Dibaba, with that formidable racer Marta Domínguez (who had been 5th in Seville and won the Spanish title in a slow race, but did not finish in Zürich) second and Masai third. Yelena Zadorozhnaya came fourth, later she must have rued mixing the 5000m with the 1500m, as surely she would otherwise have won this race. Her programme was 26th August 5000m heat, 27th 1500m heat, 29th 1500m semi, 30th 5000m final, 31st 1500m final (8th!).

Zadorozhnaya won at the European Cup but was 8th in Rome. Elvan Abeylegasse was 5th in the Worlds and won her four other 5000m races: at Hengelo, European Cup 2B, European U23 and WAF. In the latter she had Tulu, T Dibaba, Kidane, Ochichi (6th Worlds, 2nd Seville) and Benita Johnson (1st Seville, 2nd Hengelo) behind her. More evidence of confused form at this event came at Brussels, where Tulu won from Ochichi and Masai, and in a very slow race at the African Games where Defar won from Docus Inzikuru, Ochichi, T Dibaba, Sentayehu Ejigu and Masai. Defar went out in the heats at the Worlds!

Most times under 15 mins: T Dibaba & Ochichi 5, Adere 4+1i, Masai & Szabo 4, Abeylegasse, Defar, Kidane, Ouaziz, Tulu & Zadorozhnaya 3.

1. T Dibaba, 2. Adere, 3. Masai, 4. Kidane,
5. Defar, 6. Abeylegasse, 7. Tulu,
8. Zadorozhnaya, 9. Ochichi, 10. Szabo

10,000 Metres

ONE DOES not need to look beyond the World Championships to determine rankings at this event, for the race was the greatest in women's 10,000m history and the times from 2 to 16 were the fastest ever for each place. Berhane Adere won in an African record 30:04.18, the third fastest ever by a woman. She ran one other 10,000m in 2003, winning in Marseille in 31:15.95. The form of the rest of the World top ten is backed up by their other races. The second placer Werknesh Kidane was Ethiopian champion, won at Stanford and was second to World ninth placer Ejigayehu Dibaba at the African Games. Dibaba had been 3rd Ethiopian and 2nd Stanford and won the Afro-Asian title at the end of the year. Sun Yingjie was third in the Worlds after making the race with her fast pace and went on to win Chinese and Asian titles, and Lornah Kiplagat, fourth, won her other 10,000m.

Alla Zhilyayeva and Galina Bogomolova, World 5th and 6th, reversed the order in which they had been Russian 1-2. Worlds 8-10 were the 19 year-old Xing Huina, who won at the Chinese National Games, Benita Johnson, 3rd in Stanford in May, a race won by Adriana Fernández in 31:13.75, who went on to win the Pan-American title, and Jelena Prokopcuka, also Latvian champion. The only other women to run faster than Prokopcuka's 31:06.14 was Lidiya Grigoryeva, third in the Russian Champs in 30:57.83, but she was 16th at the Worlds. Fernanda Ribeiro won the European Challenge race in 31:13.42 but was a Worlds non-finisher.

1. Adere, 2. Kidane, 3. Sun, 4. Kiplagat,
5. Zhilyayeva, 6. Bogomolova, 7. Xing,
8. Johnson, 9. E Dibaba, 10. Prokopcuka

Half Marathon

PAULA RADCLIFFE ran the two halves of the London marathon in 68:02 and 67:23, and the latter was equal to the best that any other woman managed for a half marathon alone in 2003! Radcliffe swept aside the opposition as she won the Great North Run (on the slightly downhill course from Newcastle to South Shields) in a world best 65:40 and the World title in less clement conditions in 67:35. Runner-up in both those races was Berhane Adere in 67:32 and 69:06 respectively, and Susan Chepkemei (who also had a win at Bogotá) was 3rd and 8th. Following in the GNR were: 4th Sonia O'Sullivan, 5th Derartu Tulu (also winner of both Lisbon half marathons), 6th Jelena Prokopcuka (also winner in Paris). Following in the Worlds were: 3rd Benita Johnson (on her debut at the distance), 4th Lidiya Grigoryeva, 5th Constantina Tomescu, 6th Alla Zhilyayeva. Margaret Okayo was the woman to match Radcliffe's London second half, when she won at Udine; she also won at Virginia Beach. Other big race winners in good times were Catherine Ndereba, 68:23 at Sapporo and Mizuki Noguchi, 68:29 at Yamaguchi, and the latter went on to two more wins in Japan.

1. Radcliffe, 2. Adere, 3. Okayo, 4. Chepkemei, 5. Tulu, 6. Noguchi, 7. Johnson, 8. Grigoryeva, 9. Ndereba, 10. Tomescu

Marathon

HAVING TAKEN 1:29 off the world marathon record in Chicago 2002, Paula Radcliffe went further into unknown territory for a woman when she won again in London in 2:15:25. It was a sensational piece of running. The controversial part was that in what was otherwise a women's only race, Radcliffe was accompanied by two Kenyan men, Samson Loywapet and Christopher Kandie for much of the way, although one was unable to keep up near the end. The reason for the men being there was that there is no woman pacemaker capable of running with Radcliffe for any substantial distance. Catherine Ndereba, the former world record holder, ran her own race and clocked her third sub-2:20 for second in 2:19:55. Radcliffe ran no more marathons, but Ndereba went on to win the World title in 2:23:55 and was second in New York in 2:23:03 behind Margaret Okayo 2:22:30. One other woman ran a sub 2:20 time in 2003: Sun Yingjie, winner in Beijing in 2:19:30, having earlier won in Tianjin with 2:25:33. The 2-3-4 in the World Championships were Japanese women who had been 1-2-3, running 2:21 times, in Osaka in January: Mizuki Noguchi, Masako Chiba and Naoko Sakamoto.

Fourth in Osaka in 2:22:22 was Lornah Kiplagat who was later third in New York, whose winner Osaka had been 4th in Boston in her other marathon of the year, behind Svetlana Zakharova 2:25:20 (later 9th Worlds, 1st Chicago 2:23:07), Lyubov Denisova (5th New York) and Joyce Chepchumba (7th Worlds, 6th New York). Deena Drossin was third in London, followed by Susan Chepkemei (7th New York), Lyudmila Petrova (4th New York), Constantina Dita-Tomescu (dnf Worlds, 2nd Chicago), Jelena Prokopcuka (3rd Chicago) and Elfenesh Alemu (6th Worlds). Fifth at the Worlds was Ham Bong-sil, who had won in Pyongyang and 8th Olivera Jevtic, the Rotterdam winner. In November Alemu won the Tokyo Marathon in 2:24:47 well clear of Naoko Takahashi.

1. Radcliffe, 2. Ndereba, 3. Noguchi, 4. Chiba, 5. Sakamoto, 6. Sun Yingjie, 7. Okayo, 8. Kiplagat, 9. Zakharova, 10. Petrova

3000 Metres Steeplechase

STANDARDS IN the women's steeplechase continued to advance, and the world record was improved from Alesya Turova's 2002 mark of 9:16.51 to 9:08.33 by Gulnara Samitova at the Russian Championships. Samitova won all her five steeplechases, including a victory over Turova at Rethímno with other top women following: Cristina Casandra, Yekaterina Volkova and Alina Proca. Turova ran the second fastest time of the year, 9:20.28 in beating Docus Inzikuru, Anália Rosa and Casandra at Ostrava, and the third fastest was Lyubov Ivanova, 2nd at the Russian Champs and the European U23 champion from Michaela Mannová, Sigrid Vandenbempt and Proca. Another crucial race was at Tríkala, where Samitova won from Inzikuru, Casandra, Alina Cucerzan, Yekaterina Volkova (4th Rethímno, 3rd Russian), and Proca. Casandra had the greatest depth of times, with six under 9:50 to 5 by Samitova and 3 by Turova, Proca and Kassi Anderson, NCAA champion and 2nd at the US Champs to Brianna Shook. 30 women beat 10 minutes, compared to 26 in 2002, 19 in 2001 and 7 in 2000.

1. Samitova, 2. Turova, 3. Ivanova, 4. Inzikuru, 5. Casandra, 6. Volkova, 7. Mannová, 8. Vandenbempt, 9. Shook, 10. Anderson

100 Metres Hurdles

GAIL DEVERS is again top ranked, with three of the top four times (to 12.50) and winning five of her seven 100mh competitions. She hit the fifth hurdle in her semi and just missed a place in the World finals, but came back to tie Brigitte Foster's world leading mark of 12.45 in winning at the WAF. Devers had a 4-0 advantage over Foster, who was injured and came in last at the WAF, but who had a record of seven wins and four seconds prior to that. One of these seconds was to Perdita Felicien at the Worlds. That was a surprise, but Felicien had been just behind Foster at the Pan-Ams and lost only one other race (to Danielle Carruthers at Walnut) and counted NCAA and Canadian titles in her seven wins in nine finals. Foster, however, had a much better set of times and had the opportunity of running in the major European races, whereas Felicien ran just one before the Worlds, a B race win in Zürich. Miesha McKelvy and Glory Alozie were third and fourth in the Worlds, with McKelvy ahead 4-2 on win-loss although at the WAF Alozie was second, ahead of McKelvy, Jenny Adams (World 6th), Patricia Girard (World 7th), Melissa

Morrison (4th at US Champs) and Lacena Golding-Clarke (World 8th). Aurelia Trywianska was fifth in the Worlds, but was beaten 5-1 by Morrison and 2-1 by Adams, who was 4-4 with Morrison. Donica Merriman fared well on overall record as she was 3-2 v Morrison, 1-0 v Girard, 3-1 v Golding-Clarke and 2-2 v Trywianska.

Most times at 12.80 or faster: Foster 14, Adams 11, McKelvy 10+1w, Felicien 7+1w, Devers & Morrison 7, Alozie 6, Trywianska 5, Merriman 4, Golding-Clarke 3

1. Devers, 2. Foster, 3. Felicien, 4. McKelvy, 5. Alozie, 6. Adams, 7. Morrison, 8. Merriman, 9. Trywianska, 10. Girard

400 Metres Hurdles

WORLD RECORDS are rare these days, and that run by Yuliya Pechonkina was a surprise, because although she had run much the fastest time of 2002 with 53.10, she had then been sidelined by illness. She started the 2003 summer season with two wins in Moscow in July, in 55.34 and 54.27, but then ran 53.52 in her heat and the record 52.34 (to take Kim Batten's 1995 World Champs 52.61) at the Russian Championships. However, 20 days later, having run a 54.01 heat and 53.57 semi, she faded badly, after setting out hell-bent for another world record, in the World final to come in third in 53.71 as the title went to the strong 20 year-old Jana Pittman in 53.22 and silver to the experienced Sandra Glover. Pittman ended her season there having won 7 of her 9 finals; her two losses had been Golden League third places behind Glover and Ionela Tîrlea in both Paris and Zürich, but she beat Glover 4-2 overall and Glover ended 2-1 v Pechonkina, as these two traded wins in Brussels and Rieti.

Tîrlea was fourth at the Worlds and third at the WAF behind Glover and Andrea Blackett, with Tatyana Tereshchuk fifth and fourth in these two big races. That represented a return to top form for Blackett from 3rd in CAC Champs (behind Allison Beckford and Yvonne Harrison) and at the Pan-Ams (behind Joanna Hayes and Daimí Pernía, with Brenda Taylor 4th), to 6th in the Worlds. Raasin McIntosh was 2nd in the NCAAs to Sheena Johnson and then won the US title from Hayes, Glover and Taylor, but did not finish her semi at the Worlds, where the other two finalists were Heike Meissner 7th and Surita Febbraio 8th. Also missing out in the World semis was Natasha Danvers, who had shown good form earlier in the year, improving her best in successive races to 54.91, 54.32 and 54.01, the latter for second to Pittman in Rome, ahead of Glover and Tîrlea.

Most times under 54.0/55.0: Glover 6/21, Pittman 6/11, Pechonkina 6/8, Tîrlea 1/12, Blackett 1/4, Tereshchuk 5, Febbraio & Danvers 4, Hayes & McIntosh 3.

1. Pittman, 2. Glover, 3. Pechonkina, 4. Tîrlea, 5. Tereshchuk, 6. Blackett, 7. McIntosh, 8. Hayes, 9. Taylor, 10. Danvers

High Jump

KAJSA BERGQVIST led the indoor rankings at 2.03 and her World Indoor win was her eighth competition at 2.00m or more in 2003; but outdoors, with modifications to her style, she added only three more, topped however by a joint world-leading 2.06 in Eberstadt and she was third at Worlds and WAF. Ending the year in great style with seven successive (and nine in all) at 2m plus was Hestrie Cloete, who excelled at the Worlds with 2.06 and looked as a contender to at last challenge the world record set by Stefka Kostadinova at 2.09 in the 1987 Worlds. In all Cloete won 21 of 25 competitions in 2003.
Marina Kuptsova was slightly better indoors than out, but hit form when it mattered with the World silver. She was, however, 1-4 down to Vita Palamar, World 5th and WAF 2nd, and was 3-3 v Blanka Vlasic, World 7th and World Indoor and WAF 4th. Palamar beat Bergvist 5-2 outdoors. Others to do better indoors than out were the World Indoor 2-3, Yelena Yelesina and Anna Chicherova, 2nd and 4th at the Russian Champs outdoors and 7th and 8th at the WAF, with Chicherova 6th at the Worlds. Venelina Veneva was 4th at the Worlds followed by a 2.01 win at Rieti. Standards rose with 50 performancees at 2.00 or more from 12 women outdoors and another three indoors (compared to 21 from 7 women in 2002) and, with there was little between many contenders. Amy Acuff beat Inga Babakova 6-3 outdoors (0-1 in) and Babakova (dnq Worlds) was 6-1 v Chicherova and 5-3 v Viktoria Styopina (9= Worlds) outdoors

Most competitions over 2.00m/1.98m (indoors and out): Bergqvist 11/13, Cloete 9/11, Kuptsova 6/13, Chicherova 6/9, Palamar 5/8, Babakova & Vlasic 2/6, Yelesina 2/4, Styopina 1/5, Acuff & Veneva 1/3.

1. Cloete, 2. Bergqvist, 3. Palamar (4), 4. Kuptsova (3), 5. Vlasic (5), 6. Veneva (8), 7. Acuff (9), 8. Babakova (10), 9. Chicherova (6), 10. Styopina (-). – Yelesina (7). (inc. indoors).

Pole Vault

INDOORS Svetlana Feofanova added three world records (4.76 at Glasgow, 4.77 at Birmingham and 4.80 at the Worlds) to the five she set in 2002 and won five of six competitions, the one loss being to Yelena Isinbayeva, who took the World Indoor silver. Outdoors Isinbayeva took Stacy Dragila's world record with 4.82 at Gateshead (all four women's PV world records of 2003 were set in Britain), but it was Feofanova who won the World title outdoors as well from Annika Becker and Isinbayeva. At the Worlds, Dragila and Monika Pyrek (World Indoor 3rd) shared 4th place, Yvonne Buschbaum was 6th, Anna Rogowska 7th and Yelena Belyakova 8th. Missing World Championships both indoors and out was Tatyana Polnova, who ended with major wins at the World University Games and WAF, beating all the top women in the latter. She was beaten 4-2 with one tie outdoors and also at the Russian Champs indoors by Isinbayeva and was 2-2 with Becker outdoors and 2-0 indoors.

Buschbaum had the better top mark (4.70 to win the German Champs) but lost 2-5 (and 0-2 indoors) to Pyrek (4.60), while Dragila, who also set a world indoor record at 4.78 in between Feofanova's records but no-heighted at the World Indoors, had an outdoor best of 4.62 and was 3-2 v Pyrek. Belyakova won the Russian title and beat Czech champion Pavla Hamácková, who missed the end of the season through injury, 3-2. Kellie Suttle takes the last rankings spot, although she was only 5= at the US Champs and 4th at the Pan-Ams, as she was 4-1 (2-2 in) with Pan-Am champion Mel Mueller and had much better marks than other contenders. Suttle was 4th at the World Indoors, with Becker 5th, Tatyana Koleva and Rogowska 6th equal.

Most competitions over 4.50m (outdoors/in): Dragila 12/7, Polnova 11/6, Feofanova 10/6, Isinbayeva 10/3, Buschbaum 10/2, Pyrek 9/3, Becker 7/7, Hamáckova 5/2, Belyakova 4, Suttle 3.

1. Feofanova, 2. Isinbayeva, 3. Polnova, 4. Becker, 5. Dragila, 6. Pyrek, 7. Buschbaum, 8. Belyakova, 9. Hamácková, 10. Suttle.

Long Jump

THE FINAL jump of Eunice Barber that gained her the gold medal was the highlight of the World Championships, at least for the French fans. Barber had earlier won at the European Cup and went on to improve her French record to 7.05 at the WAF. She lost her final competition of the year when she jumped 6.72 in Moscow – and the winner was in her only outdoor long jump competition of the year as top triple jumper Tatyana Lebedeva improved her pb to 6.82 (but insufficient for a ranking). Top in 2002, Tatyana Kotova, had another fine year, including winning World Indoor gold and outdoor silver with second at the WAF. Maurren Maggi, after World Indoor bronze, had six outdoor wins, four over 6.90 and a best of 7.06, but then came news that she had failed a drugs test and received a two-year ban.

Elva Goulbourne won NCAA (indoors and out), Jamaican and CAC titles, but had a bad day with only 6.27 in non-qualifying at the Worlds. She was also only sixth at the WAF, where the US champion Grace Upshaw was third and Russian champion Olga Rublyova fourth, after these two had been 8th and 4th respectively at the Worlds. Anju Bobby George took the World bronze, but although she was consistent and also won the Afro-Asian title, she did not have the marks set by some of her rivals with a best of 6.70, a mark Lyudmila Galkina, 10th at the Worlds, for instance bettered four times. Carolina Klüft contested a few long jump competitions as well as heptathlons, and was unbeaten, winning the European U23s with 6.86 from Irina Simagina, who later won the World Universities title. Jade Johnson exceeded 6.70 only once (with a strong following wind), but was 4th at the Worlds. Tünde Vaszi, World 6th, did not have good enough marks to make the top ten, while Niki Xánthou had the marks but a poor competitive record. Inessa Kravets had only three competitions outdoors, but her three indoors included 2nd at the World Indoors (4, Rublyova, 5. Xánthou, 6. Stilianí Pilátou, 7. George, 8. Vaszi).

Most competitions over 6.70m (outdoors/in): Kotova 6/2, Barber 6, Goulbourne 5+1w/2, (Maggi 4/1), Galkina 4, Xánthou 3+1w/1, Kravets 2/3, Rublyova 2/1.

1. Barber, 2. Kotova, 3. Rublyova, 4. Goulbourne, 5. Klüft (6), 6. Upshaw (7), 7. Galkina (8), 8. Simagina (9), 9. George (10), 10. Johnson. Including indoor form: 5. Kravets.

Triple Jump

THE STATELESS Yamilé Aldama won 3/4 indoors including what would have been CAC indoor records at 14.65 and 14.88 and set five such records outdoors from 14.98 to 15.29. She had seven competitions at 15m plus to five by Tatyana Lebedeva, but was unable to compete at the Worlds. Lebedeva returned from the birth of her son in August 2002, to have a reasonable indoor season, but only two wins (including the Russian Champs) and 9th at the World Indoors, losing twice to Aldama, but started outdoors with 15.00 and progressed steadily winning the Worlds at 15.18 and beating Aldama, with whom she was 4-4 outdoors, in their last three meetings: Berlin, Brussels and WAF.

Ashia Hansen won the World Indoor title with 15.01 from Françoise Mbango 14.88 and Kéné Ndoye 14.72, with Anna Pyatykh, Magdelin Martínez, Carlota Castrejana, Baha Rahouli and Adelina Gavrila 4-8. Hansen also beat Mbango, Aldama, Inessa Kravets and Martínez at the Birmingham GP, but was then unable to compete at all outdoors. Mbango was 2nd/3rd, Martínez 3rd/5th, Pyatykh 4th/4th, Yelena Govorova 7th/6th, Gavrila 9th/7th and Ndoye 10th/8th at the Worlds/WAF. The 20 year-old Cuban, Mabel Gay, won the Pan-American title and was 5th at the Worlds, and another to fare well there was 6th Barbara Lah. 11th placer Rahouli went on to win the Arab title and Ndoye the African. The Russian second placer Yelena Oleynikova was let down by her World 14th.

Most competitions over 14.40m (outdoors/in): Aldama 14/4, Martínez 13/2, Gavrila 11/3, Lebedeva 10/1, Mbango 9/3, Pyatykh 7/1, Ndoye 5/1, Govorova 5, Oleynikova 4, Rahouli 3+1w, Gay 3.

1. Lebedeva, 2. Aldama, 3. Mbango, 4. Martínez,

5. Pyatykh, 6. Govorova (9), 7. Gavrila (8), 8. Ndoye (7), 9. Gay (10), 10. Rahouli (-). – Hansen (6) (inc. indoors).

Shot

JUST FOUR women exceeded 20m in 2003. The rankings were headed by Svetlana Krivelyova's 20.77 to win the Russian title and she was close to that in winning the World title with 20.63. Nadezhda Ostapchuk and Vita Pavlysh were also over 20m in taking World silver and bronze. Irina Korzhanenko was fourth at 19.17 but had thrown 20.17 when second at the Russian Champs and had been the best indoors, winning the World title with 20.55 from Ostapchuk, Astrid Kumbernuss, Pavlysh and Krivelyova. Kumbernuss was the one of these big five to surprisingly fail when only 15th in the World qualifying outdoors at 17.83, but she otherwise won 9 of her 12 outdoor competitions and recovered to WAF 4th behind Pavlysh, Krivelyova and Ostapchuk, with Korzhanenko fifth. Completing the same top six as in 2002, although in a different order, Yumileidi Cumbá, 6th in the World Indoors, won eleven successive competitions outdoors including Cuban and Pan-Am titles, the latter with a season's best 19.31, but was another surprise non-qualifier, missing by just one place, at the Worlds. Still a junior, Valerie Adams excelled to take 5th place in the Worlds, where she was followed by Krystyna Zabawska, Nadine Kleinert, Assunta Legnante and Elisángela Adriano in 6-9.

2003 record		Aldama	Lebedeva
28 Feb	Karlsruhe (i)	1- 14.88	4- 14.24
5 Mar	Tallinn (i)	1- 14.72	2- 14.05
24 Jun	Tríkala	1- 15.00	2- 15.00
27 Jun	Oslo	1- 15.11	3- 14.86
4 Jul	Saint-Denis	2- 15.08	1- 15.12
11 Jul	Rome	1- 15.29	2- 14.86
8 Aug	London (CP)	1- 15.27	2- 14.99
10 Aug	Berlin	4- 14.52	1- 14.89
5 Sep	Brussels	2- 15.00	1- 15.14
13 Sep	WAF (St-D)	2- 14.99	1- 15.13

Most competitions over 19m: Kumbernuss 10+3in, Pavlysh 7+3i, Krivelyova & Ostapchuk 5+2i, Korzhanenko 4+3i, Cumbá 3+1i, Kleinert 1+2i.

1. Krivelyova, 2. Ostapchuk, 3. Pavlysh, 4. Korzhanenko, 5. Kumbernuss, 6. Cumbá, 7. Adams (8), 8. Zabawska (9), 9. Kleinert (7), 10. Olga Ryabinkina. (Including indoors)

Discus

ALTHOUGH SHE was fifth at the Worlds, Vera Pospisilová takes top ranking. She beat World champion Irina Yatchenko 3-1 and World bronze medallist Olga Vóggoli 2-1, had the best depth of marks and crucially was the WAF winner. Yatchenko slipped to 8th in that competition, but Vóggoli (2-1 v Yatchenko) and Yelena Antonova (4th) maintained their World placings. Making up for a dismal 50.79 in qualifying at the Worlds was US and Pan-Am champion Aretha Hill, 2nd at the WAF. Most difficult to rank is the World silver medallist Anastasiá Kelesídou as, although she threw 67.14 there, she had only four other competitions, all of which she won but in which her best was 63.87 and she did not meet any major rivals. Natalya Sadova headed the world list with 69.38 at Halle, was Russian champion, 6th at the Worlds and 5th WAF and beat German champion Franka Dietzsch (6th WAF after 14th in qualifying at the Worlds) 5-1. Suzy Powell was US 2nd and Pan-Am 4th before World 9th; she lost 4-6 to Hill, who was 1-3 down to Dietzsch. Song Aimin was World 7th, but Beatrice Faumuina was a non-qualifying 13th and only 7th at the WAF.

Most competitions over 63m: Pospisilová 10, Hill 8, Faumuina & Vóggoli 7, Yatchenko 6, Sadova 5, Antonova 4, Dietzsch, Kelesídou & Song 3.

1. Pospisilová, 2. Yatchenko, 3. Vóggoli, 4. Antonova, 5. Kelesídou, 6. Sadova, 7. Dietzsch, 8. Hill, 9. Powell, 10. Song.

Hammer

YIPSI MORENO had nine wins, including World and WAF titles, and three seconds with the world best mark of 75.14, her 19th CAC record over five years. Olga Kuzenkova collected yet another silver medal at the Worlds but was beaten overall 3-2 by the bronze medallist Manuela Montebrun. These women, all at 74.50 or better, were clearly the top three, with the next best marks 72.96 by Irina Sekachova and 72.03 by Gu Yuan. Gu did that to win the Chinese title and was also Asian champion and World fourth, but Sekachova, after five meetings over 71m, all in Ukriane except her European Cup 1B win, threw only 61.23 in the World qualifying and was 7th at the WAF, having also started the year with 13th in the European Challenge. Much better competitive records were put together by Mihaela Melinte (6th Worlds, 3rd WAF), Susanne Keil (5th and 5th) and Anna Mahon (7th and 6th). Yuneika Crawford was another non-qualifier at the Worlds but had beaten Moreno twice in Cuba and beat Candice Scott (9th Worlds) and Mahon for the Pan-Am silver behind Moreno. Kamila Skolimowska was European U23 champion and 8th at both Worlds and WAF. The top seven from the 2002 rankings all remain in the top ten. 70 women over 65m was easily a record, compared to 9, 22, 36, 39 and 44 in the years 1998-2002.

Most competitions over 70m/68m: Montebrun 14/16, Moreno 11/12, Melinte 8/16, Kuzenkova 8/12, Keil 6/13, Sekachova 6/7, Gu Yuan 3/3, Crawford 2/8, Skolimowska 2/7, Mahon 2/6, Ester Balassini & Zhang Wenxui 2/5, Bronwyn Eagles 2/3.

1. Moreno, 2. Kuzenkova, 3. Montebrun, 4. Melinte, 5. Gu Yuan, 6. Keil, 7. Crawford, 8. Mahon, 9. Sekachova, 10. Skolimowska

Javelin

MIRELA MANJANI had a typical season of two wins in minor meetings in Greece in May, second in the European Cup (beaten 63.30 to 63.13 by Steffi Nerius) and then a clear win at the World Championships, where she had the best four throws of the final and her 66.52 was 3.24m ahead of silver medallist Tatyana Shikolenko. That was thin, but enough to justify top ranking, as with the event included in only very few GP meetings, there were not many top competitive opportunities and only Nerius, World bronze medallist, had a particularly full season. She came to the Worlds having won all her eleven competitions, but afterwards was runner-up to Shikolenko at both Brussels and WAF. Nikolett Szabó was third in both those events, but had been 12th at the Worlds, where Mikaela Ingberg and Osleidys Menéndez were 4th and 5th. Ingberg was also 5th at the WAF a place behind world 8th Lavern Eve, who had also won the CAC title (her fifth from 1989) and taken Pan-Am silver behind Kim Kreiner and ahead of Menéndez with Sonia Bisset (World 6th) in 5th place. Paula Huhtaniemi had beaten Ingberg 64.90 to 58.93 to win the Finnish title but was only 20th at the Worlds and 8th at the WAF. Claudia Coslovich and Valeriya Zabruskova were 7th and 9th at the Worlds and 6th and 7th at the WAF.

Most competitions over 62m: Nerius 13, Shikolenko 6, Eve 4, Ingberg & Manjani 3.

1. Manjani, 2. Shikolenko, 3. Nerius, 4. Ingberg, 5. Menéndez, 6. Eve, 7. Szabó, 8. Coslovich, 9. Zabruskova, 10. Bisset.

Heptathlon

CAROLINA KLÜFT, top ranked as a junior in 2002, continued her delightful and majestic progress, as she set three Swedish records, taking her best of 6542 to 6602 at Götzis, 6692 in the European Cup 1 and then 7001 at the Worlds for third on the world all-time list, just six points behind Larisa Nikitina's 14 year-old European record. It will be fascinating to see how close she can get to Jackie Joyner-Kersee's 7291 world record in the years to come. Eunice Barber returned with a fine 6694 win at Arles but, although improving to 6755 at the Worlds, had to yield to the 20 year-old Swede, who had a scare with no jumps on her first two long jumps but overcame that in style. Natalya Sazanovich took the World bronze at 6524, her sixth major championships silver or bronze at heptathlon and the World Championships generally determined the ranking positions, with Yelena Prokohorova and Denise Lewis (her first heptathlons since winning the Olympic gold medal in 2000), who were both second in their European Cup events, retaining their 4th and 5th places, although I have reversed the placings of Gertrud Bacher (6th Worlds) and Larisa Netseporuk (8th), and Austra Skujyte moves up a few places from 10th, with 2nd at Götzis, where she beat World 8th Sonja Kesselschläger. Russian champion Natalya Roshchupkina and African champion Margaret Simpson contest tenth ranking.

Lyudmila Blonskaya would have been fourth with three scores over 6300 but was disqualified for drug abuse.

1. Klüft, 2. Barber, 3. Sazanovich, 4. Prokhorova, 5. Lewis, 6. Netseporuk, 7. Skujyte, 8. Bacher, 9. Kesselschläger, 10. Simpson

20 Kilometres Walk

YELENA NIKOLAYEVA was clearly the world's best, winning her three races with the two fastest times: 1:26:22 European Cup and 1:26:52 World Champs and also 1:27:25 at La Coruña. She thus had two wins in the newly introduced IAAF Race Walking Challenge, but, with three races to score, that title (and $30,000) went to Gillian O'Sullivan, who had series wins at Tijuana and Sesto San Giovanni, with second at La Coruña and at the Worlds. The other World Challenge race was Rio Maior, won by Elisabetta Perrone, who was 4th in La Coruña and 6th at Tijuana, but she was third in the Challenge behind Kjersti Plätzer, who was 3rd and 4th in these races after 2nd at Sesto. However, neither Perrone or Plätzer finished at the Worlds, where Valentina Tsybulskaya took the bronze medal after 5th at Sesto and 9th at La Coruña.

Perrone, Maria Vasco and Natalya Fedoskina were 2-3-4 in the fast European Cup race at Cheboksary, where a month later Tatyana Gudkova, later fourth in the Worlds, took the Russian title. There were fast times at the Russian Winter Champs at Adler from Antonina Petrova 1:27:14, Larisa Yemelyanova 1:27:23 and Tatyana Sibileva 1:27:54. The latter later won the World Universities title but the other two were 39th and dnf at the European Cup, their only other 20k. In her only 20k of the year Claudia Stef was fifth in the Worlds, while disqualified there was Song Hongjuan, who was third on the world list with the 1:27:16 with which she won the Chinese title and she later won at the National Games in 1:29:32.4 (track).

Just missing ranking places are Rossella Giordano and Melanie Seeger, respectively 6th and 8th at the Worlds and 12th and 9th in the European Cup, and Nadezhda Ryashkina, who had 2nd Tijuana, 6th Sesto and 8th La Coruña after 5th at Adler.

1. Nikolayeva, 2, O'Sullivan, 3. Plätzer, 4. Perrone, 5. Tsybulskaya, 6. Gudkova, 7. Stef, 8. Song, 9. Vasco, 10. Fedoskina

IAAF WORLD RANKINGS

THE IAAF World Rankings were trailed in 2000 and formally adopted in November 2000. They are now updated and issued every week, with the intention of giving an image of how the leading athletes of our sport are performing.

The IAAF book containing 2003 World Rankings showed those as at 14 September 2003 – and the top ranked athletes were acclaimed on that day as the World Athletes of the Year. However that was for the convenience of combing the IAAF's Annual Gala with the World Athletic Finals and several important championships took place in 2003 after that date. In line with the contents of this Annual here are positions as at the end of 2003 – the top 50 men and women overall and the top 20 for each event.

Full rankings can be viewed at www.iaaf.org

Overall Ranking List - as at 29/12/2003

Note that event shown is main one, but athletes have often gained points at other events as well. e.g. Decathletes also at indoor heptathlon, 5000m at 3000/CC etc.

Men

1	Hicham El Guerrouj	MAR	1450	1500/5000m
2	Saif Saueed Shaheen	QAT	1448	5000m/3kst
3	Kenenisa Bekele	ETH	1441	5/10000m
4	Allen Johnson	USA	1440	110mh
5	Haile Gebrselassie	ETH	1429	5/10000m
6	Felix Sánchez	DOM	1422	400mh
7	Tom Pappas	USA	1408	Dec/Hep i
8	Christian Olsson	SWE	1398	TJ
8	Eliud Kipchoge	KEN	1398	3/5000m
10	Ezekiel Kemboi	KEN	1389	3000mSt
11	Paul Koech	KEN	1383	3000mSt
12	Abraham Chebii	KEN	1379	3/5000m
13	John Capel	USA	1378	100/200m
13	Roman Sebrle	CZE	1378	Dec/Hep i
15	Stanislav Olijar	LAT	1377	110mh
16	Mbulaeni Mulaudzi	RSA	1372	800m
16	Liu Xiang	CHN	1372	110mh
18	Tyree Washington	USA	1370	400m
19	Mehdi Baala	FRA	1367	800/1500m
20	Bernard Williams	USA	1363	100/200m
21	Jerome Young	USA	1362	400m
22	Justin Gatlin	USA	1360	100/200m
23	Róbert Fazekas	HUN	1358	DT
24	Okkert Brits	RSA	1356	PV
25	Wilfred Bungei	KEN	1355	800m
25	Terrence Trammell	USA	1355	110mh
27	Yuriy Borzakovskiy	RUS	1354	800m
28	John Kibowen	KEN	1351	5000m
28	Abdullah Ah.Hassan	QAT	1351	5/10000m
30	Virgilijus Alekna	LTU	1350	DT
30	Duane Ross	USA	1350	110mh
30	Sergey Makarov	RUS	1350	JT
33	Paul Korir	KEN	1349	1500m
34	Dwight Phillips	USA	1348	LJ
34	Tim Lobinger	GER	1348	PV
36	Kim Collins	SKN	1347	100m
37	Joey Woody	USA	1346	400mh
38	Chris Phillips	USA	1344	110mh
38	Kemel Thompson	JAM	1344	400mh
40	Darvis Patton	USA	1340	100/200m
41	Wilson Kipketer	DEN	1337	800m
41	Sammy Kipketer	KEN	1337	5/10000m
43	Jan Zelezny	CZE	1336	JT
44	Stefan Holm	SWE	1335	HJ
45	Hezekiél Sepeng	RSA	1334	800m
45	Ivan Tikhon	BLR	1334	HT
47	Dmitriy Markov	AUS	1333	PV
47	Periklís Iakovákis	GRE	1333	400mh
47	Larry Wade	USA	1333	110mh
50	Bernard Lagat	KEN	1332	1500m

Women

1	Hestrie Cloete	RSA	1437	HJ
2	Carolina Klüft	SWE	1436	Hep/Pen i
3	Kelli White	USA	1429	100/200m
4	Tatyana Lebedeva	RUS	1427	TJ
5	Yamilé Aldama	CUB	1394	TJ
6	Berhane Adere	ETH	1392	5/10000m
7	Sandra Cummings	USA	1390	400mh
7	Maria Mutola	MOZ	1390	800m
9	Ana G Guevara	MEX	1389	400m
10	Jana Pittman	AUS	1387	400mh
11	Werknesh Kidane	ETH	1385	5/10000m
12	Françoise Mbango	CMR	1384	TJ
13	Süreyya Ayhan	TUR	1382	1500m
14	Gail Devers	USA	1381	100mh
15	Torri Edwards	USA	1375	100/200m
15	Svetlana Feofanova	RUS	1375	PV
17	Edith Masai	KEN	1368	5000m
17	Lorraine Fenton	JAM	1368	400m
19	Chandra Sturrup	BAH	1367	100m
20	Kajsa Bergqvist	SWE	1366	HJ
21	Brigitte Foster	JAM	1365	100mh
22	IonelaTîrlea	ROM	1355	400mh
23	Chryste Gaines	USA	1354	100m
24	Eunice Barber	FRA	1351	100mh/LJ/Hep
25	Yuliya Pechonkina	RUS	1350	400mh/400m
25	Yelena Zadorozhnaya	RUS	1350	1500/3/5000m
25	Muriel Hurtis	FRA	1350	200m
28	Vita Palamar	UKR	1349	HJ
28	Zhanna Block	UKR	1349	100/200m
30	Yelena Isinbayeva	RUS	1343	PV
31	Tirunesh Dibaba	ETH	1339	5000m
31	Glory Alozie	ESP	1339	100mh
33	Kelly Holmes	GBR	1338	800/1500m
33	Yekaterina Rozenberg	RUS	1338	1500m
35	Ana. Kapachinskaya	RUS	1336	200m
36	Magdelín Martínez	ITA	1334	TJ
37	Christine Arron	FRA	1330	100m
38	Jolanda Ceplak	SLO	1329	800m
39	Miesha McKelvy	USA	1326	100mh
40	Tatyana Tomashova	RUS	1325	1500/3000m
40	Natalya Nazarova	RUS	1325	400m
40	Amy Mbacké Thiam	SEN	1325	400m
40	Isabella Ochichi	KEN	1325	5000m
40	Perdita Felicien	CAN	1325	100mh
45	Blanka Vlasic	CRO	1323	HJ
46	Hayley Tullett	GBR	1320	1500/3000m
47	Marina Kuptsova	RUS	1319	HJ
48	Andrea Blackett	BAR	1315	400mh
48	Tonique Williams	BAH	1315	400m
48	Inga Babakova	UKR	1315	HJ

Event Ranking Lists
Men

100m (50m - 55m - 60m)

1	Kim Collins	SKN	1347
2	Justin Gatlin	USA	1343
3	Bernard Williams	USA	1340
4	Deji Aliu	NGR	1325
5	John Capel	USA	1323
6	Dwain Chambers	GBR	1320
7	Mark Lewis-Francis	GBR	1282
8	Maurice Greene	USA	1281
8	Uchenna Emedolu	NGR	1281
10	Darrel Brown	TRI	1275
11	Tim Montgomery	USA	1268
12	Darren Campbell	GBR	1265
13	Coby Miller	USA	1263
14	Asafa Powell	JAM	1261
15	Darvis Patton	USA	1252
16	Mickey Grimes	USA	1248
17	Patrick Johnson	AUS	1244
17	Jason Gardener	GBR	1244
19	Aziz Zakari	GHA	1239
19	Shawn Crawford	USA	1239

200m

1	Darvis Patton	USA	1334
2	Shawn Crawford	USA	1322
3	John Capel	USA	1315
4	Stéphane Buckland	MRI	1308
5	Frank Fredericks	NAM	1305
6	Joshua J. Johnson	USA	1291
7	Marlon Devonish	GBR	1283
8	Christian Malcolm	GBR	1250
9	Darren Campbell	GBR	1248
10	Bernard Williams	USA	1244
11	Coby Miller	USA	1241
11	Dominic Demeritte	BAH	1241
13	Shingo Suetsugu	JPN	1239
14	Ramon Clay	USA	1238
15	Uchenna Emedolu	NGR	1237
16	Ricardo Williams	JAM	1227
17	Marcin Jedrusinski	POL	1223
18	Julian Golding	GBR	1222
19	Joseph Batangdon	CMR	1219
20	Usain Bolt	JAM	1207

400m (300m - 500m ind.)

1	Tyree Washington	USA	1370
2	Jerome Young	USA	1362
3	Michael Blackwood	JAM	1321
4	Marc Raquil	FRA	1306
5	Alleyne Francique	GRN	1299
6	Eric Milazar	MRI	1283
7	C. Van Branteghem	BEL	1277
8	Daniel Caines	GBR	1274
9	Brandon Simpson	JAM	1267
10	Calvin Harrison	USA	1258
11	Leslie Djhone	FRA	1256
12	Derrick Brew	USA	1245
13	Avard Moncur	BAH	1239
14	Ezra Sambu	KEN	1238
15	David Canal	ESP	1235
16	Mitch Potter	USA	1231
17	Hamdan O Al Bishi	KSA	1221
18	Clinton Hill	AUS	1220
19	Ingo Schultz	GER	1216
20	Gary Kikaya	COD	1214

800m (1000m)

1	Mbulaeni Mulaudzi	RSA	1372
2	Wilfred Bungei	KEN	1355
3	Yuriy Borzakovskiy	RUS	1354
4	Wilson Kipketer	DEN	1337
5	Hezekiel Sepeng	RSA	1334
6	Joseph Mutua	KEN	1303
7	André Bucher	SUI	1295
8	Bram Som	NED	1293
9	Djabir Saïd-Guerni	ALG	1283
10	David Krummenacker	USA	1276
11	Antonio M Reina	ESP	1261
12	Japheth Kimutai	KEN	1256
13	Nicholas Wachira	KEN	1254
14	Andrea Longo	ITA	1250
15	Michael Rotich	KEN	1249
16	Justus Koech	KEN	1240
17	Osmar dos Santos	BRA	1237
18	Florent Lacasse	FRA	1215
19	Nicolas Aissat	FRA	1212
20	Dmitriy Bogdanov	RUS	1211

1500m (Mile -2000m)

1	Hicham El Guerrouj	MAR	1406
2	Paul Korir	KEN	1349
3	Bernard Lagat	KEN	1332
4	Cornelius Chirchir	KEN	1330
5	Ivan Heshko	UKR	1324
6	Alex Kipchirchir	KEN	1316
7	Rui Silva	POR	1293
8	Benjamin Kipkurui	KEN	1285
9	Robert Rono	KEN	1276
10	Mehdi Baala	FRA	1272
11	William Chirchir	KEN	1270
12	Vyach Shabunin	RUS	1264
13	Laban Rotich	KEN	1260
14	Juan C. Higuero	ESP	1259
15	Fouad Chouki	FRA	1253
15	Isaac Songok	KEN	1253
15	Gert Jan Liefers	NED	1253
15	Abdelkader Hachlaf	MAR	1253
19	Roberto Parra	ESP	1212
20	Hudson de Souza	BRA	1207

5000 -10,000m (3000m - CC)

1	Kenenisa Bekele	ETH	1441
2	Haile Gebrselassie	ETH	1429
3	Eliud Kipchoge	KEN	1398
4	Abraham Chebii	KEN	1379
5	John Kibowen	KEN	1351
5	Abdullah A Hassan	QAT	1351
7	Sammy Kipketer	KEN	1337
8	James Kwalia	KEN	1321
9	Sileshi Sihine	ETH	1317
10	Leonard Mucheru	KEN	1313
11	Geb. Gebremariam	ETH	1310
12	Benjamin Limo	KEN	1309
13	Richard Limo	KEN	1291
14	Nicholas Kemboi	KEN	1275
15	Salah Hissou	MAR	1262
16	Luke Kipkosgei	KEN	1257
17	Dejene Berhanu	ETH	1238
18	Abderrahim Goumri	MAR	1237
19	Moses Mosop	KEN	1234
19	Abiyote Abate	ETH	1234

3000m SC (2000mSt)

1	Saif S Shaheen	QAT	1445
2	Ezekiel Kemboi	KEN	1389
3	Paul Koech	KEN	1383
4	Bouabdallah Tahri	FRA	1326
5	Julius Nyamu	KEN	1325
6	Kipkurui Misoi	KEN	1311
7	Abraham Cherono	KEN	1290
8	Ali Ezzine	MAR	1286
9	Eliseo Martín	ESP	1278
10	Simon Vroemen	NED	1258
11	Luis Miguel Martín	ESP	1237
11	José Luis Blanco	ESP	1237
13	Abel Cheruiyot	KEN	1234
14	Khamis S Abdullah	QAT	1223
15	Wilson Boit Kipketer	KEN	1210
16	Pavel Potapovich	RUS	1208
17	David Chemweno	KEN	1201
17	Jukka Keskisalo	FIN	1201
19	Bostjan Buc	SLO	1195
20	Günther Weidlinger	AUT	1191
20	Martin Pröll	AUT	1191

110mh (50mh - 55mh - 60mh)

1	Allen Johnson	USA	1440
2	Stanislav Olijar	LAT	1377
3	Liu Xiang	CHN	1372
4	Terrence Trammell	USA	1353
5	Duane Ross	USA	1350
6	Chris Phillips	USA	1344
7	Larry Wade	USA	1333
8	Ron Bramlett	USA	1307
9	Maurice Wignall	JAM	1295
10	Ladji Doucouré	FRA	1288
11	Márcio de Souza	BRA	1274
12	Shi Dongpeng	CHN	1261
13	Yoel Hernández	CUB	1258
14	Dudley Dorival	HAI	1256
15	Anier García	CUB	1239
16	Shaun Bownes	RSA	1233
17	Robert Kronberg	SWE	1231
18	Redelén dos Santos	BRA	1230
19	Dawane Wallace	USA	1223
20	Mateus Inocêncio	BRA	1219

400mh

1	Felix Sánchez	DOM	1422
2	Joey Woody	USA	1346
3	Kemel Thompson	JAM	1344
4	Periklís Iakovákis	GRE	1333
5	Chris Rawlinson	GBR	1322
6	Danny McFarlane	JAM	1312
7	Dean Griffiths	JAM	1294
8	Eric Thomas	USA	1292
9	Ian Weakley	JAM	1281
9	Llewellyn Herbert	RSA	1281
11	Jirí Muzík	CZE	1271
12	Bershawn Jackson	USA	1256
13	Boris Gorban	RUS	1245
14	Mubarak Al Nubi	QAT	1231
15	Okkert Cilliers	RSA	1230
16	Yevg. Meleshenko	KAZ	1221
17	Hadi S. Al Somaily	KSA	1220
18	Alwyn Myburgh	RSA	1212
19	Stepán Tesarík	CZE	1205
19	Neil Gardner	JAM	1205

HJ

1	Stefan Holm	SWE	1335
2	Jermaine Mason	JAM	1309
3	Jacques Freitag	RSA	1296
4	Yaroslav Rybakov	RUS	1290
5	Mark Boswell	CAN	1273
6	Jamie Nieto	USA	1272
7	Andriy Sokolovskiy	UKR	1234
8	Matt Hemingway	USA	1232
9	Dragutin Topic	SCG	1225
10	Mikhayil Tsvetkov	RUS	1216

11 Jaroslav Bába CZE 1209
12 Grzegorz Sposób POL 1200
13 Aleks. Walerianczyk POL 1186
14 Gennadiy Moroz BLR 1183
15 Tomás Janku CZE 1179
16 Alessandro Talotti ITA 1178
17 Staffan Strand SWE 1175
18 Stefan Vasilache ROM 1159
19 Pyotr Brayko RUS 1157
19 Andrea Bettinelli ITA 1157

PV

1 Okkert Brits RSA 1356
2 Tim Lobinger GER 1348
3 Dmitriy Markov AUS 1333
4 Giuseppe Gibilisco ITA 1308
5 Derek Miles USA 1300
6 Nick Hysong USA 1299
7 Romain Mesnil FRA 1291
8 Jeff Hartwig USA 1271
9 Aleksandr Averbukh ISR 1263
10 Patrik Kristiansson SWE 1260
11 Timothy Mack USA 1256
12 Denys Yurchenko UKR 1255
13 Lars Börgeling GER 1252
14 Rens Blom NED 1250
15 Vadim Strogalyov RUS 1239
16 Toby Stevenson USA 1227
17 Viktor Chistyakov AUS 1213
18 Richard Spiegelburg GER 1199
19 Adam Ptácek CZE 1188
20 Oscar Jansson SWE 1178

LJ

1 Dwight Phillips USA 1348
2 Yago Lamela ESP 1300
3 Savanté Stringfellow USA 1283
4 Hussein Al Sabee KSA 1280
5 Ignisious Gaisah GHA 1279
6 James Beckford JAM 1249
7 Volodimir Zyuskov UKR 1244
8 Louis Tsatoumas GRE 1225
9 Luis Felipe Méliz CUB 1220
9 Oleksiy Lukashevich UKR 1220
11 K. Streete-Thompson CAY 1217
12 Juan Lino Martínez CUB 1203
13 Dimítrios Serélis GRE 1189
14 Walter Davis USA 1187
15 Bogdan Tarus ROM 1186
16 Salim Sdiri FRA 1179
17 Sinisa Ergotic CRO 1175
18 Younés Moudrik MAR 1174
18 Ruslan Gataullin RUS 1174
18 Valeriy Vasilyev UKR 1174

TJ

1 Christian Olsson SWE 1398
2 Jadel Gregório BRA 1297
3 Kenta Bell USA 1291
4 Marian Oprea ROM 1285
5 Walter Davis USA 1279
6 Jonathan Edwards GBR 1278
7 Leevan Sands BAH 1277
8 Yoandri Betanzos CUB 1266
9 Tim Rusan USA 1247
10 Ivailo Rusenov BUL 1234
11 Yoelbi Quesada CUB 1228
12 Alexander Martínez CUB 1225
13 Dmitriy Valyukevich BLR 1223
14 David Giralt CUB 1213
15 Allen Simms USA 1189

16 Aleksandr Glovatskiy BLR 1187
17 Hrístos Melétoglou GRE 1186
18 Sébastien Pincemail FRA 1177
18 Karl Taillepierre FRA 1177
20 Julien Kapek FRA 1171

SP

1 Yuriy Bilonog UKR 1321
2 Manuel Martínez ESP 1306
3 Kevin Toth USA 1304
4 Christian Cantwell USA 1283
5 Adam Nelson USA 1269
6 Carl Myerscough GBR 1263
7 Justin Anlezark AUS 1252
8 John Godina USA 1243
9 Reese Hoffa USA 1227
10 Tepa Reinikainen FIN 1226
11 Brad Snyder CAN 1218
12 Milan Haborák SVK 1207
13 Ralf Bartels GER 1201
14 Ville Tiisanoja FIN 1190
15 Rutger Smith NED 1187
16 Pavel Chumachenko RUS 1184
17 Daniel Taylor USA 1183
18 Conny Karlsson FIN 1180
19 Marco Antonio Verni CHI 1178
20 Pavel Lyzhin BLR 1177

DT

1 Róbert Fazekas HUN 1358
2 Virgilijus Alekna LTU 1350
3 Lars Riedel GER 1286
4 Michael Möllenbeck GER 1258
5 Vasiliy Kaptyukh BLR 1234
6 Aleksandr Tammert EST 1229
7 Frantz Kruger RSA 1226
8 Carl Brown USA 1202
9 Gerd Kanter EST 1198
10 Dmitriy Shevchenko RUS 1195
11 Jason Tunks CAN 1186
11 Zoltán Kövágó HUN 1186
13 Mario Pestano ESP 1181
14 Gábor Máté HUN 1160
15 Libor Malina CZE 1147
16 Frank Casanas CUB 1143
17 Jo Van Daele BEL 1138
18 Sergiu Ursu ROM 1135
19 Nick Petrucci USA 1133
20 Leonid Cherevko BLR 1131

HT

1 Ivan Tikhon BLR 1334
2 Adrián Annus HUN 1320
3 Koji Murofushi JPN 1318
4 Andriy Skvaruk UKR 1280
5 Ilya Konovalov RUS 1251
6 Libor Charfreitag SVK 1245
7 Primoz Kozmus SLO 1239
8 Aléx. Papadimitríou GRE 1219
9 Karsten Kobs GER 1214
10 Péter Botfa HUN 1206
11 Vadim Devyatovskiy BLR 1197
12 Stuart Rendell AUS 1193
13 Woj. Kondratowicz POL 1192
14 Sergey Kirmasov RUS 1186
15 Oleksiy Krykun UKR 1182
15 Olli-Pekka Karjalainen FIN 1182
17 Christophe Épalle FRA 1181
18 Chris Harmse RSA 1180
18 Aleksey Zagorniy RUS 1180
20 Krisztián Pars HUN 1170

JT

1 Sergey Makarov RUS 1350
2 Jan Zelezny CZE 1336
3 Boris Henry GER 1314
4 Andrus Värnik EST 1232
5 Aleksandr Ivanov RUS 1223
5 Christian Nicolay GER 1223
7 Eriks Rags LAT 1201
8 Peter Blank GER 1199
9 Dariusz Trafas POL 1181
10 Aki Parviainen FIN 1176
11 Andreas Thorkildsen NOR 1175
12 Raymond Hecht GER 1169
13 Voldemars Lusis LAT 1168
14 Steve Backley GBR 1166
14 Peter Esenwein GER 1166
16 Li Rongxiang CHN 1135
17 Breaux Greer USA 1134
18 Miroslav Guzdek CZE 1133
19 Will Hamlyn-Harris AUS 1120
19 Igor Janik POL 1120
19 Gergely Horváth HUN 1120

Decathlon (Indoor Heptathlon)

1 Tom Pappas USA 1408
2 Roman Sebrle CZE 1378
3 Laurent Hernu FRA 1277
4 Dmitriy Karpov KAZ 1248
5 Jón Arnar Magnússon ISL 1233
6 Aleksandr Pogorelov RUS 1196
7 Romain Barras FRA 1187
8 Vitaly Smirnov UZB 1177
8 Stephen Moore USA 1177
10 André Niklaus GER 1176
11 Qi Haifeng CHN 1172
12 Paul Terek USA 1153
13 Nikolay Tishchenko RUS 1130
14 Chiel Warners NED 1127
15 Stephen Harris USA 1126
15 Sergey Nikitin RUS 1126
17 Indrek Turi EST 1120
18 Alek. Parkhomenko BLR 1116
19 Lionel Marceny FRA 1115
19 Pavel Dubitskiy KAZ 1115

Women

100m (50m - 55m - 60m)

1 Kelli White USA 1387
2 Chandra Sturrup BAH 1367
3 Chryste Gaines USA 1354
4 Torri Edwards USA 1346
5 Zhanna Block UKR 1337
6 Christine Arron FRA 1330
7 Muriel Hurtis FRA 1287
8 Angela Williams USA 1272
9 Debbie Ferguson BAH 1270
10 Marina Kislova RUS 1263
10 Aleen Bailey JAM 1263
12 Inger Miller USA 1250
13 Merlene Ottey SLO 1245
14 Karin Mayr-Krifka AUT 1238
15 Gail Devers USA 1223
16 Endurance Ojokolo NGR 1215
16 Joice Maduaka GBR 1215
18 Mary Onyali NGR 1211
19 Kim Gevaert BEL 1208
20 Juliet Campbell JAM 1206

200m

1 Kelli White USA 1360
2 Muriel Hurtis FRA 1350

3	A. Kapachinskaya	RUS	1336
4	Torri Edwards	USA	1314
5	Kim Gevaert	BEL	1287
6	Cydonie Mothersill	CAY	1282
7	Natalya Safronnikova	BLR	1278
8	Beverly McDonald	JAM	1266
9	Allyson Felix	USA	1252
10	Juliet Campbell	JAM	1246
11	Lauren Hewitt	AUS	1228
12	Anzhela Kravchenko	UKR	1225
13	Maryna Maydanova	UKR	1221
14	Zhanna Block	UKR	1219
15	Joice Maduaka	GBR	1216
16	Karin Mayr-Krifka	AUT	1215
17	Latasha Jenkins	USA	1214
18	Mary Onyali	NGR	1211
19	Debbie Ferguson	BAH	1209
20	Johanna Manninen	FIN	1207

400m (300m - 500m ind.)

1	Ana G Guevara	MEX	1389
2	Lorraine Fenton	JAM	1368
3	Natalya Nazarova	RUS	1325
3	Amy Mbacké Thiam	SEN	1325
5	Tonique Williams	BAH	1315
6	Olesya Zykina	RUS	1282
7	Lee McConnell	GBR	1257
7	Svetlana Pospelova	RUS	1257
9	Sanya Richards	USA	1252
10	Christine Amertil	BAH	1236
11	Demetria Washington	USA	1234
12	Monique Hennagan	USA	1225
13	Olabisi Afolabi	NGR	1213
14	Mireille Nguimgo	CMR	1210
15	Hazel-Ann Regis	GRN	1208
16	Heide Quinn	RSA	1206
17	Svetlana Usovich	BLR	1205
18	Aliann Pompey	GUY	1202
19	Fatou Bintou Fall	SEN	1197
20	Ronetta Smith	JAM	1192
20	Claudia Marx	GER	1192

800m (1000m)

1	Maria Mutola	MOZ	1390
2	Jolanda Ceplak	SLO	1329
3	Kelly Holmes	GBR	1313
4	Mina Ait Hammou	MAR	1312
5	Stephanie Graf	AUT	1309
6	N. Khrushchelyova	RUS	1286
7	Diane Cummins	CAN	1276
8	Faith Macharia	KEN	1264
9	Claudia Gesell	GER	1256
10	Larisa Chzhao	RUS	1244
11	María Martínez	ESP	1234
12	Tamsyn Lewis	AUS	1218
13	Brigita Langerholc	SLO	1210
14	Irina Vashentseva	RUS	1209
15	Svetlana Klyuka	RUS	1204
16	Akosua Serwah	GHA	1195
16	Laetitia Vriesde	SUR	1195
18	Maria Cioncan	ROM	1194
19	Monika Gradzki	GER	1193
20	Joanne Fenn	GBR	1191

1500m (Mile - 2000m)

1	Süreyya Ayhan	TUR	1382
2	Yekat. Rozenberg	RUS	1338
3	Hayley Tullett	GBR	1317
4	Tatyana Tomashova	RUS	1314
5	Yel. Zadorozhnaya	RUS	1304
6	Jackline Maranga	KEN	1294
7	Naomi Mugo	KEN	1291
8	Irina Lishchinska	UKR	1288
9	Judit Varga	HUN	1277
10	Joanne Pavey	GBR	1273
11	Regina Jacobs	USA	1258
12	Alesya Turova	BLR	1257
13	Natalya Gorelova	RUS	1249
14	Suzy Favor Hamilton	USA	1240
15	Yuliya Kosenkova	RUS	1234
16	Maria Cioncan	ROM	1231
17	Natalia Rodríguez	ESP	1226
18	Nelya Neporadna	UKR	1213
19	Kutre Dulecha	ETH	1206
20	Johanna Risku	FIN	1196
20	Olga Komyagina	RUS	1196

5000 -10 000m (3000m - CC)

1	Berhane Adere	ETH	1392
2	Werknesh Kidane	ETH	1385
3	Edith Masai	KEN	1368
4	Tirunesh Dibaba	ETH	1339
5	Isabella Ochichi	KEN	1325
6	Gabriela Szabo	ROM	1313
7	Meseret Defar	ETH	1304
8	Benita Johnson	AUS	1303
9	Zahra Ouaziz	MAR	1300
10	Sun Yingjie	CHN	1299
11	Yel. Zadorozhnaya	RUS	1298
12	Elvan Abeylegesse	TUR	1280
13	Marta Domínguez	ESP	1274
14	Zhor El Kamch	MAR	1273
15	Merima Denboba	ETH	1253
16	Alla Zhilyayeva	RUS	1252
17	Deena Drossin	USA	1244
18	Ejagayou Dibaba	ETH	1243
19	Sentayehu Ejigu	ETH	1242
20	Irina Mikitenko	GER	1238

100mh (50mh - 55mh - 60mh)

1	Gail Devers	USA	1381
2	Brigitte Foster	JAM	1365
3	Glory Alozie	ESP	1339
4	Miesha McKelvy	USA	1326
5	Perdita Felicien	CAN	1325
6	Melissa Morrison	USA	1310
7	L. Golding-Clarke	JAM	1309
8	Jenny Adams	USA	1301
9	Aurelia Trywianska	POL	1279
9	Patricia Girard	FRA	1279
11	Vonette Dixon	JAM	1257
12	Susanna Kallur	SWE	1255
13	Irina Lenskiy	ISR	1251
14	Donica Merriman	USA	1246
15	Svetlana Laukhova	RUS	1228
16	Yahumara Neyra	CUB	1220
17	Nat. Shekhodanova	RUS	1217
17	L. Ferga-Khodadin	FRA	1217
19	Aliuska López	ESP	1213
20	Angela Whyte	CAN	1207
20	Angela Atede	NGR	1207

400mh

1	Sandra Glover	USA	1390
2	Jana Pittman	AUS	1387
3	Ionela Tîrlea	ROM	1355
4	Yuliya Pechonkina	RUS	1345
5	Andrea Blackett	BAR	1315
6	Tetyana Tereshchuk	UKR	1314
7	Natasha Danvers	GBR	1304
8	Surita Febbraio	RSA	1280
9	Brenda Taylor	USA	1279
10	Joanna Hayes	USA	1273
11	Yvonne Harrison	PUR	1260
12	Raasin Mcintosh	USA	1256
13	Natalya Torshina	KAZ	1244
14	Heike Meissner	GER	1237
15	Allison Beckford	JAM	1236
16	Monika Niederstätter	ITA	1229
17	Debbie-Ann Parris	JAM	1225
18	Anna Jesien	POL	1219
19	Stephanie Kampf	GER	1215
20	Malgorzata Pskit	POL	1200
20	Cora Olivero	ESP	1200

HJ

1	Hestrie Cloete	RSA	1437
2	Kajsa Bergqvist	SWE	1366
3	Vita Palamar	UKR	1349
4	Blanka Vlasic	CRO	1323
5	Marina Kuptsova	RUS	1319
6	Inga Babakova	UKR	1315
7	Yelena Yelesina	RUS	1300
8	Anna Chicherova	RUS	1299
9	Amy Acuff	USA	1298
10	Viktoriya Styopina	UKR	1269
11	Venelina Veneva	BUL	1260
12	Irina Mikhalchenko	UKR	1243
13	Viktoriya Seryogina	RUS	1234
13	Ruth Beitia	ESP	1234
15	Tisha Waller	USA	1228
16	Yelena Slesarenko	RUS	1210
17	Tatyana Efimenko	KGZ	1207
18	Daniela Rath	GER	1203
19	Svetlana Lapina	RUS	1199
20	Anna Ksok	POL	1182

PV

1	Svetlana Feofanova	RUS	1375
2	Yelena Isinbayeva	RUS	1343
3	Tatyana Polnova	RUS	1293
4	Stacy Dragila	USA	1283
5	Annika Becker	GER	1271
6	Monika Pyrek	POL	1263
7	Yvonne Buschbaum	GER	1212
8	Yelena Belyakova	RUS	1196
9	Pavla Hamácková	CZE	1184
10	Kellie Suttle	USA	1174
11	Anna Rogowska	POL	1158
12	Melissa Mueller	USA	1145
13	Vanessa Boslak	FRA	1135
14	Thórey Elisdóttir	ISL	1127
15	Tanya Koleva	BUL	1118
16	Carolin Hingst	GER	1116
17	Mary Sauer	USA	1115
18	Nataliya Kusch	UKR	1113
19	Jillian Schwartz	USA	1110
20	Becky Holliday	USA	1109

LJ

1	Tatyana Kotova	RUS	1308
2	Eunice Barber	FRA	1269
3	Elva Goulbourne	JAM	1256
4	Maurren Maggi	BRA	1248
5	Olga Rublyova	RUS	1238
6	Grace Upshaw	USA	1222
6	Anju Bobby George	IND	1222
8	Tünde Vaszi	HUN	1209
9	Jade Johnson	GBR	1188
10	Bronwyn Thompson	AUS	1187
11	Concepción Montaner	ESP	1182
12	Niki Xánthou	GRE	1181
13	Irina Simagina	RUS	1174

14	Jacqueline Edwards	BAH	1164
14	Carolina Klüft	SWE	1164
16	Bianca Kappler	GER	1163
17	Lyudmila Galkina	RUS	1158
18	Valentina Gotovska	LAT	1139
19	Maho Hanaoka	JPN	1138
20	Fiona May	ITA	1133

TJ

1	Tatyana Lebedeva	RUS	1427
2	Yamilé Aldama	CUB	1394
3	Françoise Mbango	CMR	1384
4	Magdelín Martínez	ITA	1334
5	Anna Pyatykh	RUS	1313
6	Kéné Ndoye	SEN	1284
7	Olena Govorova	UKR	1275
8	Adelina Gavrila	ROM	1272
9	Yelena Oleynikova	RUS	1243
10	Baya Rahouli	ALG	1233
11	Mabel Gay	CUB	1231
12	Barbara Lah	ITA	1217
13	Carlota Castrejana	ESP	1209
14	Hrisopiyí Devetzí	GRE	1205
15	Heli Koivula-Kruger	FIN	1179
16	Inessa Kravets	UKR	1176
17	Viktoriya Gurova	RUS	1166
18	Huang Qiuyan	CHN	1164
19	Olga Vasdeki	GRE	1163
20	Yuliana Pérez	USA	1160

SP

1	Svetlana Krivelyova	RUS	1287
2	Vita Pavlysh	UKR	1270
3	Nad. Ostapchuk	BLR	1267
4	Irina Korzhanenko	RUS	1251
5	Astrid Kumbernuss	GER	1215
6	Yumileidi Cumbá	CUB	1179
7	Valerie Adams	NZL	1158
8	Nadine Kleinert	GER	1151
9	Elisângela Adriano	BRA	1150
9	Krystyna Zabawska	POL	1150
11	Yanina Korolchik	BLR	1126
12	Assunta Legnante	ITA	1123
13	Lieja Tunks	NED	1122
14	Li Meiju	CHN	1121
15	Olga Ryabinkina	RUS	1112
16	Irina Khudoroshkina	RUS	1111
17	Misleydis González	CUB	1091
18	Iríni Terzoglou	GRE	1088
19	Laura Gerraughty	USA	1087
20	Vivian Chukwuemeka	NGR	1084

DT

1	Véra Pospísilová	CZE	1257
2	Irina Yatchenko	BLR	1231
3	Ekateríni Vóggoli	GRE	1229
4	Aretha Hill	USA	1211
5	Natalya Sadova	RUS	1208
6	Olena Antonova	UKR	1201
7	Franka Dietzsch	GER	1187
8	Beatrice Faumuina	NZL	1161
9	Anastasía Kelesídou	GRE	1156
10	Suzy Powell	USA	1145
11	Song Aimin	CHN	1144
12	Joanna Wisniewska	POL	1115
13	Stilíani Tsikoúna	GRE	1113
14	Teresa Machado	POR	1112
14	Mélina Robert-Michon	FRA	1112
16	Marzena Wysocka	POL	1105
17	Neelam J Singh	IND	1096
17	Yania Ferrales	CUB	1096
19	Anna Söderberg	SWE	1083
20	Nataliya Fokina	UKR	1082

HT

1	Yipsi Moreno	CUB	1293
2	Manuela Montebrun	FRA	1264
3	Olga Kuzenkova	RUS	1252
4	Mihaela Melinte	ROM	1202
5	Susanne Keil	GER	1194
6	Anna Mahon	USA	1173
7	Irina Sekachova	UKR	1167
8	Gu Yuan	CHN	1153
8	Kamila Skolimowska	POL	1153
10	Yunaika Crawford	CUB	1143
11	Candice Scott	TRI	1129
12	Ester Balassini	ITA	1126
13	Bronwyn Eagles	AUS	1117
14	Betty Heidler	GER	1102
15	Zhang Wenxiu	CHN	1101
16	Alla Davydova	RUS	1096
17	Andrea Bunjes	GER	1094
18	Olga Tsander	BLR	1093
19	Dawn Ellerbe	USA	1091
20	Gulya Khanafeyeva	RUS	1088

JT

1	Tatyana Shikolenko	RUS	1266
2	Steffi Nerius	GER	1249
3	Lavern Eve	BAH	1179
4	Mikaela Ingberg	FIN	1177
5	Nikolett Szabó	HUN	1164
6	Valeriya Zabruskova	RUS	1144
7	Claudia Coslovich	ITA	1135
8	Paula Huhtaniemi	FIN	1118
9	Sonia Bisset	CUB	1090
10	Taina Kolkkala	FIN	1089
11	Yekaterina Ivakina	RUS	1084
12	Kim Kreiner	USA	1080
13	Ma Ning	CHN	1079
14	Noraida Bicet	CUB	1072
15	Sarah Walter	FRA	1068
16	Sabina Moya	COL	1058
17	Mercedes Chilla	ESP	1055
18	Oksana Gromova	RUS	1048
19	Savva Lyka	GRE	1041
19	Barbara Madejczyk	POL	1041

Heptathlon (Indoor Pentathlon)

1	Carolina Klüft	SWE	1436
2	Yelena Prokhorova	RUS	1268
3	Sonja Kesselschläger	GER	1234
4	Larisa Netseporuk	EST	1203
5	Gertrud Bacher	ITA	1197
6	Austra Skujyté	LTU	1166
7	Argyió Stratáki	GRE	1158
8	Svetlana Kazanina	KAZ	1155
9	Marie Collonvillé	FRA	1154
10	Margaret Simpson	GHA	1153
11	Tiffany Lott-Hogan	USA	1151
12	Irina Butor	BLR	1150
13	Irina Naumenko	KAZ	1143
14	Nicole Haynes	CAN	1136
15	Katja Keller	GER	1130
16	Tia Hellebaut	BEL	1118
17	Kylie Wheeler	AUS	1114
18	Kim Schiemenz	USA	1112
19	Mag. Szczepanska	POL	1110
20	Kelly Sotherton	GBR	1109

Performance scores are the sum of two components:

a) Result scores calculated using the IAAF Scoring Tables produced by Dr Bojidar Spiriev, modified by wind speeds for relevant events and with bonus points for world records.

b) Placing scores according to nine categories of competition. For the top category of World Championships and Olympic Games athletes score from 300 points for 1st to 70 for 12th. The next category of World Indoor Championships, World Athletics Final and World CC Champs score 200 for 1st to 100 for 8th. Then Golden League, World Cup and African, Asian, European and Pan-American Champs with 170 for 1st to 80 for 8th, etc.

The Ranking score is the average of top six Performance scores (or the top three for combined event).

The IAAF announced that their first Road Running and Race Walking Rankings would be issued on 23 March 2004, thereby upgrading the IAAF World Rankings to better reflect the many and varied disciplines of the sport. The system will be similar to the one currently applied to combined events, in that the Ranking score will be given by the average of the athlete's best three Performance scores, instead of six for individual events.

International Association of Road Racing Statisticians [ARRS]

This Association has been formed with the goals of:

(1) Establishing valid criteria for road record-keeping

(2) Maintaining a list of world road records based on these valid criteria.

(3) Promoting communication and the exchange of information with regards to road racing.

The aim of the road record-keeping criteria will be to encourage and recognise marks made in women-only races which will, in turn, enhance the status of women's road racing. It will also recognise a maximum separation of 30% between the start and finish to ensure that records represent valid achievements.

Further details of the draft ARRS road record list can be found at: http://www.mattoleriver.com/ARRS.htm

CROSS-COUNTRY - NATIONAL CHAMPIONS 2003

	MEN (longer distance)	WOMEN (longer distance)
Australia (Trials)	Brett Cartwright	Benita Johnson
Austria	Günther Weidlinger	Sandra Baumann
Belgium	Tom Van Hooste	Fatima Baouf
Bulgaria	Stanislav Lambev	Milka Mikhaylova
Canada (Nov)	Simon Bairu	Émilie Mondor
Chile	Carlos Jaramillo	Luz Silva
Czech Rep. (Nov)	David Gerych	Jana Biolková
Denmark	Robert K.Andersen	Dorte Vibjerg
Ecuador	Franklin Tenorio	Mónica Amboya
England	Matt Smith	Hayley Yelling
Estonia	Toomas Tarm	Maile Mangusson
Ethiopia	Gebreegziabher Gebremariam	Werknesh Kidane
Finland	Jussi Utriainen	Johanna Risku
France	Mohammed Essaïd	Rodica Moroianu
Germany	André Green	Sabrina Mockenhaupt
Greece	Panayiótis Haramís	María Tsírba
Hungary	Miklós Zatykó	Simona Staicu
Ireland	Martin McCarthy	Ann Keenan Buckley
Israel	Haile Satayin	Eti Einer
Italy	Giuliano Battocletti	Patrizia Tisi
Kenya	John C Korir	Alice Timbilil
Latvia	Ivo Zigadlo	Inna Poluskina
Lithuania	Egidijus Rupsys	Rasa Drazdauskaite
Luxembourg	Vincent Nothum	Pascale Schmoetten
Netherlands	Kamiel Maase	Irma Heeren
New Zealand	Phil Costley	Nyla Carroll
Northern Ireland	Dermot Donnelly IRL	Suzanne McCormick
Norway	Karl Johan Rasmussen	Bente Landøy
Poland	Artur Osman	Grazyna Syrek
Portugal	Domingos Castro	Fernanda Ribeiro
Scotland	Graeme Reid	Susan Partridge
Serbia & Crna Gora	Sreten Ninkovic	Sonja Stolic
Slovakia	Marcel Matanin	Dana Janecková
Slovenia	Bostjan Buc	Sonja Roman
South Africa	Motsehi Moeketsana	Poppy Mlambo
Spain	Fabián Roncero	Maria Abel
Sweden	Erik Sjöqvist	Marie Söderström-Lundberg
Switzerland	Christian Belz	Marie-Luce Romanens
UK	Glyn Tromans	Hayley Yelling
Ukraine	Vitaliy Shafar	Anastasiya Hayeva
Uruguay	Oscar Fernández	Ana Paula Díaz
USA Winter	Alan Culpepper	Deena Drossin
Wales	Chris Davies	Catherine Dugdale
Balkan	Labros Zaraggas GRE	Sonja Stolic SCG
European Clubs	Alberto García ESP	Helena Sampaio POR
Teams	Adidas Zaragoza, ESP	Maratona Maia, POR
Gulf	Ahmad Jouma Jaber QAT (& team: QAT)	
NCAA (Nov)	Dathan Ritzenhein USA	Shalane Flanagan USA
Nordic	Samuli Vasala FIN	Ulla Tuimala FIN
S.American	Javier Guerin COL	Susana Rebolledo CHI

	MEN (short distance)	WOMEN (short distance)
Austria	Günther Weidlinger	–
Belgium	Ridouane Es-Saadi	–
Bulgaria	Ivaylo Ignatov	Rumyana Panovska
Chile	Roberto Echeverría	Luz Silva
Czech Rep. (Nov)	Jirí Miler	–
Denmark	Dennis Jensen	Dorte Vibjerg
Ecuador	Edgar Chancusig	Mónica Amboya

Ethiopia	Haylu Mekonnen	Tirunesh Dibaba
Finland	Jari Matinlauri	–
France	Driss Maazouzi	Ben Thami MAR
Germany	Damien Kallabis	–
Hungary	Olivér Bodor	–
Israel	Gezachw Yossef	–
Italy	Luciano Di Pardo	Silvia Weissteiner
Kenya	John Kibowen	Isabella Ochichi
New Zealand	Phil Costley	Nyla Carroll
Norway	Trond Idland	Susanne Wigene
Poland	Tomasz Pakulski	Grazyna Syrek
Portugal	Rui Silva	Fernanda Ribeiro
Slovakia	Miroslav Vanko	–
South Africa	Johan Cronje	Ronel Thomas
Spain	Yusef El Nasri	Iris Fuentes-Pila
Sweden	Erik Sjöqvist	Malin Ohrn
Switzerland	Philipp Bandi	Anita Weyermann
UK	Steve Vernon	Hayley Yelling
Ukraine	Vadym Slobodenyuk	Olha Lukyanchuk
USA Winter	Robert Gary	Shayne Culpepper
South American	Clodoaldo da Silva BRA	Valeria Rodríguez ARG

10th European Cross-Country Championships 2003

At Edinburgh, GBR 14 December.

Senior Men (10095m)
1. Sergiy Lebid UKR 30:47
2. Juan Carlos de la Ossa ESP 31:08
3. Eduardo Henriques POR 31:15
4. Tom Van Hooste BEL 31:18
5. Yevgeniy Bozhko UKR 31:19
6. Fabián Roncero ESP 31:23
7. Mustapha Essaid FRA 31:26
8. El Hassan Lahssini FRA 31:29
9. Umberto Pusterla ITA 31:32
10. Driss El Himer FRA 31:34
11. Günther Weidlinger AUT 31:35
12. Ivan Hierro ESP 31:35
13. Claes Nyberg SWE 31:36
14. Fernando Silva POR 31:36
15. Tom Compernolle BEL 31:37

67 of 73 finished

Teams: 1. FRA 47, 2. ESP 47, 3. POR 65, 4. ITA 71, 5. BEL 96, 6. RUS 117, 7. GBR 126, 8. SWE 132, 9. GER 143, 10. IRL 181.

Junior Men (6595m)
1. Yevgeniy Rybakov RUS 20:52
2. Anatoliy Rybakov RUS 20:52
3. Aleksey Reunkov RUS 20:53
4. Cosmin Suteu ROM 20:58
5. Marius Ionescu ROM 21:04
6. Mark Christie IRL 21:07
7. Francisco Bachiller ESP 21:09
8. Jéremy Pierrat FRA 21:12
9. Alejandro Fernández ESP 21:15
10. Stefan Patru ROM 21:19

91 of 94 finished

Teams: 1. RUS 20, 2. ROM 31, 3. ESP 44, 4. GBR 92, 5. FRA 108, 6. GER 129, 7. IRL 142, 8. POL 161, 9. HUN 163, 10. POR 178, 11. ITA 183, 12. CZE 210, 13. NED 241, 14. BEL 246, 15. DEN 250, 16. TUR 253

Senior Women (6595m)
1. Paula Radcliffe GBR 22:04
2. Elvan Abeylegesse TUR 22:13
3. Anikó Kalovics HUN 22:26
4. Sonia O'Sullivan IRL 22:36
5. Hayley Yelling GBR 22:44
6. Olivera Jevtic SCG 22:45
7. Justyna Bak POL 22:47
8. Liz Yelling GBR 22:49
9. Patrizia Tisi ITA 22:50
10. Galina Bogomolova RUS 22:54
11. Hayley Tullett GBR 22:59
12. Kathy Butler GBR 23:00
13. Rosemary Ryan IRL 23:00
14. Anália Rosa POR 23:01
15. Sabrina Mockenhaupt GER 23:02

62 of 62 finished

Teams: GBR 25, 2. IRL 78, 3. POR 84, 4. FRA 84, 5. RUS 114, 6. BEL 116, 7. ITA 126, 8. ESP 130, 9. GER 140, 10. TUR 185.

Junior Women (4520m)
1. Inna Polushkina LAT 15:32
2. Snezana Kostic SCG 15:57
3. Charlotte Dale GBR 16:04
4. Volha Minina BLR 16:06
5. Faye Fullerton GBR 16:07
6. Viktoriya Trushenko RUS 16:10
7. Azra Eminovic SCG 16:20
8. Regina Khamzina RUS 16:23
9. Dani Barnes GBR 16:23
10. Binnaz Uslu TUR 16:24

72 of 75 finished

Teams: 1. GBR 32, 2. RUS 53, 3. GER 63, 4. ROM 112, 4. BLR 116, 6. ESP 129, 7. FRA 135, 8. IRL 137, 9. TUR 145, 10. BEL 151, 11. ITA 186, 12. POR 192, 13. NED 259

See ATHLETICS 2003 page 608 for results of the 2003 World Cross-Country Championships.

2003 WORLD ROAD RACE REVIEW

By David E Martin

ROAD RACE participation by the masses continued to increase worldwide, with entry limits often necessary due to the width of the streets. Leading these fitness and participation enthusiasts, elite runners vie for ever-increasing prize-money payouts. A good example is the Peachtree Road Race in Atlanta. At one point near the finish the roadway is only four lanes wide, which limits the field to 55,000 participants for its 10km trek along Atlanta's famed main street. Runners are corralled at the start into nearly a dozen different time groups, defined by past performance achieved over the distance. Each succeeding group is permitted to start after the group in front has begun to run. While this ensures a safe race on a hot humid morning in July, only for the elites is it an event where finish time really matters. The last runners are crossing the start line nearly half an hour after the elites have already finished!

While most road races function independently due to their unique identity, in several nations a union of races to form a circuit has occurred. As just one example, the Peachtree Road Race served as the final event of a USA-based group of four highly competitive international races called the Professional Road Race Organization (PRRO). Again in 2003, Kenyans were victorious, Robert Cheruiyot and Susan Chepkemei each earning $15,000 for their clear victories. Also in the USA, a larger group of nine races for men and seven for women organized under the aegis of its national governing body as the USA Running Circuit (USARC) distributed $437,350 to its winners. Now in its ninth year, and including races over distances from 5 km to the marathon, the 2003 winners were Ryan Shea and Colleen De Reuck.

The demographics of the accompanying list of winners of major road races are quite different as the men represent 21 countries, the women a considerably larger 32 countries. This is primarily due to the somewhat lesser Kenyan domination among the women. Kenyan men won 66% of the men's races and although Kenyan women won about a quarter of the women's races, other nations such as Russia, Ethiopia and the USA also provided many winners.

At the highest competitive level, the most significant road race of 2003 was the IAAF's World Half Marathon Championship, held in warm (22°C), sunny Vilamoura, Portugal in early October, just after the track season had finished. On the women's side, Paula Radcliffe won again – by 1 min 27 secs (her third such title), continuing her year of extraordinary performances. For the men, third-place Boston marathoner Martin Lel took the honours, and later took full advantage of his developing fall fitness to win the New York City marathon.

Radcliffe's performance underscored a dilemma in road running, namely how to categorize her fine (67:35) effort. Because the Vilamoura course is a loop, there is no net downslope or wind aid. Thus, her performance falls within the kind of defined limits that have been established for performances given the status of "records" in the world of track. Indeed, over such a defined course, only Elana Mayer has ever run faster (66:44, Tokyo, 1999). However, neither performance has been technically termed a "world record" because that distinction was reserved for track races.

Two weeks previously, Radcliffe won another half-marathon race in a faster time (65:40), but this was a slightly downhill point-to-point course from Newcastle to South Shields in England. This Great North Run result is thus termed a "world-best aided performance," while Mayer's Tokyo performance is termed a "world best." Clearly, such semantic confusion isn't good for sport promotion. Indeed, discussion has been ongoing worldwide for more than a decade to establish a set of criteria that would identify road-running "world records." Finally, during the 2003 IAAF Congress, such criteria were defined (no more than 50% start/finish separation, no more than 1 m/km downslope on a point-to-point course, proper measurement by certified experts, and with drugs-testing scheduled). From the start of 2004 the IAAF is publishing performance lists for road running similar to those produced for track running. "Road World Records" are thus established for nine different distances: 10 km, 15 km, 20 km, half marathon, 25 km, 30 km, marathon, 100 km, and a 6-stage marathon-distance road relay (Ekiden).

Leading Road Races 2003

5-Jan	Punta del Este 10km	Robert Cheruiyot KEN 28:44	Ednalva da Silva BRA 33:53
5-Jan	Ratingen 10km	Wilson Chemweno KEN 29:23	Restituta Joseph TAN 33:00
6-Jan	Miyazaki HMar	Women only	Masako Chiba JPN 70:06
12-Jan	Egmond aan Zee HMar	Luc Krotwaar NED 63:43	Lornah Kiplagat KEN 72:29
19-Jan	Carlsbad HMar	Michael Kamau KEN 63:30	Jennifer Rhines USA 71:55
24-Jan	Nairobi 30km @	Onesmus Kilonzo KEN 1:30:11	Jackline Torori KEN 1:52:15
25-Jan	Rio de Janeiro 10km	Clodaldo Gomes BRA 28:02	Nadir Sabino BRA 33:12
26-Jan	Best HMar	Luc Krotwaar NED 62:45*	Mounia Aboulahem BEL 74:19*
2-Feb	Kuta, Bali 10km	John Korir KEN 28:32*	Benita Johnson AUS 31:39*
2-Feb	Marugame HMar	Zakayo Ngatho KEN 60:21*	Yasuko Hashimoto JPN 69:32
9-Feb	Karatsu 10M	Kazuhiro Maeda JPN 46:53	Men only
9-Feb	Coamo HMar	Philip Rugut KEN 64:20	Tatyana Khmeleva RUS 78:29
11-Feb	Himeji 10M	Tomoaki Kunichika JPN 46:47	Men only
16-Feb	Kumamoto 30km	Takayuki Matsumiya JPN 1:28:36 WB	
16-Feb	Ome 30km	Kenjiro Jitsui JPN 1:33:23	Tomoe Yokoyama JPN 1:44:36
16-Feb	Schoorl 30km	Kamiel Maase NED 1:30:20*	Irma Heeren NED 1:46:24*
16-Feb	Torrevieja HMar	Oscar Fernández ESP 62:21	Sandra Ruales ECU 75:53
23-Feb	Ostia HMar	Boniface Usisivu KEN 61:13	Gloria Marconi ITA 69:25
23-Feb	Roja HMar	William Kiplagat KEN 63:30	Shitaye Gemechu ETH 72:01
23-Feb	San Juan 10km	Hendrick Ramaala RSA 28:16	Paula Radcliffe GBR 30:21 WB
8-Mar	Jacksonville 15km US Ch	Mebrahtom Keflezighi USA 43:31	Deena Drossin USA 47:15*
9-Mar	Aalphen aan Rijn 20km	Shadrack Hoff RSA 58:33	Joyce Chepchumba KEN 66:58
9-Mar	Kyoto HMar	Khalid Khannouchi USA 62:15	Adriana Fernández MEX 69:28
9-Mar	Paris HMar	Mike Rotich KEN 61:30	Jelena Prokopcuka LAT 69:42
9-Mar	Peterborough HMar	Wilson Kogo KEN 63:07	Jane Omoro KEN 70:36
9-Mar	Piacenza HMar	Charles Tangus KEN 62:34	Maria Cocchetti ITA 75:12
9-Mar	Sendai HMar	Shuichi Fujii JPN 63:27	Naomi Sakashita JPN 72:10
9-Mar	Yamaguchi HMar	Toshinari Takaoka JPN 61:07	Mizuki Noguchi JPN 68:29
15-Mar	Virginia Beach 8km	Linus Maiyo KEN 22:27	Gladys Asiba KEN 25:47
16-Mar	Bath HMar	Huw Lobb GBR 64:51	Deborah Robinson GBR 71:57
16-Mar	Hastings HMar	Johnson Muriuri KEN 63:26	Jane Omoro KEN 71:52
16-Mar	Lisboa HMar	Martin Lel KEN 60:10	Derartu Tulu ETH 69:20
16-Mar	Matsue HMar	Women only	Nozomi Iijima JPN 71:12
22-Mar	Mobile 10km	Linus Maiyo KEN 27:36	Edna Kiplagat KEN 32:12
22-Mar	Praha HMar	Fred Kiprop KEN 62:47	Helena Javornik SLO 71:03*
23-Mar	Dresden 10km	Barnabas Kenduiywo KEN 28:50	Claudia Dreher GER 33:33
23-Mar	La Courneuve 10km	Wilson Onsare KEN 28:02	Leah Malot KEN 32:11
23-Mar	Palma de Mallorca HMar	Samson Kosgei KEN 62:57	Lena Gavelin SWE 74:28
23-Mar	Wilmslow HMar	Julius Kibet KEN 62:23	Yelena Burykina RUS 72:44
29-Mar	Azpeitia HMar	Oscar Fernández ESP 64:13	Yesenia Centeno CUB 69:59
29-Mar	Den Haag HMar	Joseph Ngolepus KEN 60:56	Marleen Renders BEL 69:54
29-Mar	Louisville 10M USA Ch	Chris Graff USA 47:09	Christina Wells USA 57:25
29-Mar	Richmond 10km	Gilbert Koech KEN 28:34	Edna Kiplagat KEN 32:28
30-Mar	Barcelona 10km	David Tuwei KEN 28:32	Marta Domínguez ESP 34:07
30-Mar	Malaga HMar	Samson Kosgei KEN 63:57	Farida Gusi TAN 79:58
5-Apr	Milano HMar	John Yuda TAN 60:25	Men only
5-Apr	New York 8km US Ch	Mebrahtom Keflezighi USA 22:28	Christina Blackmer USA 28:13
6-Apr	Berlin HMar	Paul Kirui KEN 61:05	Magdeline Chemjor KEN 71:12
6-Apr	Brunssum 10km	John Kibowen KEN 27:40	Ann Wambui KEN 34:08
6-Apr	Korschenbroich 10/5km	Wilfried Kigen KEN 28:44	Leah Malot KEN 15:51
6-Apr	Madrid HMar	Cuthbert Nyasango ZIM 62:40	Faustina Maria ESP 75:09
6-Apr	Monterrey HMar	Jackson Koech KEN 61:29	Madai Pérez MEX 71:49
6-Apr	Washington 10M	John Korir KEN 46:56	Olga Romanova RUS 53:43
13 Apr	Carlsbad 5km	Dejene Berhanu ETH 13:19	Berhane Adere ETH 14:54 WB
13-Apr	Vancouver 10km	Paul Koech KEN 28:48	Aster Demissie ETH 33:20
19-Apr	Cape Town HMar	Luwis Masunda ZIM 63:46*	Charne Rademeyer RSA 75:48
19-Apr	New Orleans 10km	John Korir KEN 28:15	Isabellah Ochichi KEN 31:24*
19-Apr	Paderborn 10km	Moses Kipkosgei Kigen KEN 28:18	Irina Mikitenko GER 31:28
19-Apr	Paderborn HMar	Tendai Chimusasa ZIM 62:04	Petra Kaminková CZE 73:17

21-Apr	Dongio 10/5km	John Yuda TAN 28:42	Aiyabei Chepkorir KEN 16:03
21-Apr	Gualtieri 10km	Benson Barus KEN 27:52	Gloria Marconi ITA 32:47
21-Apr	Prato HMar	Philimon Kipkering KEN 62:33	Patrizia Ritondo ITA 76:53
27-Apr	Cleveland 10km	Gilbert Okari KEN 28:18	Lyudmila Biktasheva RUS 33:01
27-Apr	Heillecourt 8.8km/4.7km	Paul Kosgei KEN 24:07	Seloua Ouaziz MAR 14:41
27-Apr	Merano HMar	Philip Manyim KEN 61:15	Rita Jeptoo KEN 73:51
27-Apr	Nice HMar	Benjamin Pseret KEN 62:38	Isabella Ochichi KEN 68:42*
27-Apr	Vitry-sur-Seine HMar	John Kyalo KEN 60:51	Anne Chelagat KEN 72:21
27-Apr	Würzburg 10km	Moses Kipkosgei Kigen KEN 27:48	Caroline Kwambai KEN 32:26
1-May	Marseille 10km	Paul Kosgei KEN 28:22	Irina Mikitenko GER 32:04
1-May	Puy-en-Velay 15km	Nicholas Kemboi KEN 43:56	Isabella Ochichi KEN 48:24
3-May	Indianapolis HMar	Joseph Kariuki KEN 63:43	Albina Ivanova RUS 71:24
4-May	Almere 10km	Valentine Orare KEN 28:27	Christine Chepchunga KEN 33:38
4-May	Berlin 25km	Jason Mbote KEN 1:15:07	Caroline Kwambai KEN 1:24:50
4-May	Setúbal HMar	Samuel Korir KEN 62:16	Fatima Yvelain FRA 73:07
4-May	Spokane 12km	John Korir KEN 34:16	Lyudmila Biktasheva RUS 40:01
4-May	Strasbourg 10km	Wesley Ochoro KEN 28:59	Esther Maina KEN 33:06
4-May	Toronto 10km #	Peter Ntabo KEN 28:02	Nicole Stevenson CAN 33:38
10-May	Balmoral 5M	John Kibowen KEN 22:48	Berhane Adere ETH 25:12
10-May	Bern 10M	Girma Tola ETH 45:43	Helena Javornik SLO 53:46
10-May	Grand Rapids 25km US Ch	Dan Browne USA 1:16:13	Albina Ivanova RUS 1:27:28
10-May	Moskva HMar	Sergey Lukin RUS 64:44	Yelena Burykina RUS 70:21
10-May	Port Elizabeth 10km	Women only	Rene Kalmer RSA 33:03
11-May	Casablanca 10km	Women only	Zhor El Kamch MAR 31:38
11-May	Ottawa 10km	Yevgeniy Bozhko UKR 28:24	Lyudmila Biktasheva RUS 32:17
11-May	Washington 10km	Simon Wangai KEN 28:54	Olga Romanova RUS 32:56
17-May	Göteborg HMar	Benjamin Rotich KEN 63:43	Miriam Wangari KEN 73:27
18-May	Cobán HMar	Enos Keter KEN 62:15*	Ramilya Burangulova RUS 76:08
18-May	Glasgow 10km	Women only	Lornah Kiplagat KEN 31:37
18-May	Milano 10km	Women only	Agata Balsamo ITA 33:07
18-May	San Francisco 12km	James Koskei KEN 35:11	Lyudmila Biktasheva RUS 39:22
24-May	Wheeling 20km	Augustus Kavutu KEN 61:19	Leah Malot KEN 71:01
25-May	Sydney HMar	Roderic de Highden AUS 65:00	Susie Power AUS 71:31
26-May	Boulder 10km@	Dejene Berhanu ETH 28:54	Deena Drossin USA 33:17
26-May	Manchester 10km	Paul Tergat KEN 28:48	Berhane Adere ETH 31:50
31-May	Albany 5km US Ch	Women only	Marla Runyan USA 15:25
31-May	Des Moines 20km	Julius Rotich KEN 63:34	Charne Rademeyer RSA 71:38
31-May	Logrono HMar	James Moiben KEN 62:53	Filomena Chepchirchir KEN 75:26
1-Jun	Valencia HMar	Elhoussine Essemali MAR 62:40	Sandra Ruales ECU 71:10
2-Jun	Dublin 10km	Women only	Sonia O'Sullivan IRL 33:21
6-Jun	Clermond Ferrand 10km	Francis Komu KEN 28:30	Elizabeth Chemweno KEN 33:19
7-Jun	Bellville 10km	Lindikaya Mthangayi RSA 28:49	Theresa du Toit RSA 34:50
7-Jun	New York 10km	Women only	Lornah Kiplagat KEN 31:13
7-Jun	Peoria 4M	Shadrack Kosgei KEN 17:34	Constantina Tomescu ROM 20:16
8-Jun	Coahuila HMar	Jackson Koech KEN 61:39	Madai Pérez MEX 72:48
14-Jun	Green Bay 10km	Albert Chepkurui KEN 28:56	Kathy Butler GBR 32:47
14-Jun	Zwolle HMar	Simon Kiprop KEN 64:00	Emily Kimuria KEN 73:44
15-Jun	Bern 5km	Women only	Leah Malot KEN 15:51
15-Jun	Albacete HMar	Tadesse Zersenay ERI 63:59	Yesenia Centeno CUB 73:23
15-Jun	Langueux 10km NCh	George Morara Choga KEN 28:19	Fatima Yvelain FRA 32:44
21-Jun	Porto 15km	Kipchumba Cherono KEN 43:41	Helena Sampaio POR 51:27
22-Jun	Durban 10km	Poppy Mlambo RSA 32:58	Women only
22-Jun	Fairfield HMar	Simon Wangai KEN 62:40	Jackline Torori KEN 75:09
22-Jun	Suresnes 10km	Francis Komu KEN 28:44	Martha Komu KEN 33:14
22-Jun	Vancouver HMar	Mustapha Bennacer ALG 63:14*	Lyudmila Korchagina RUS 70:50*
25-Jun	Darmstadt 7.535km	Laban Chege KEN 21:50	Catherine Chikwakura MAW 15:25 (4.86km)
29-Jun	Johannesburg 10km @	Shadrack Hoff RSA 29:19*	Zola Pieterse RSA 35:37
4-Jul	Atlanta 10km	Robert Kipkoech Cheruiyot KEN 28:23	Susan Chepkemei KEN 31:13
4-Jul	Cedar Rapids 8km	Simon Sawe KEN 23:24	Atalelech Ketema ETH 27:02
5-Jul	Eerste River 15km	Thembelani Zola RSA 47:18	Elana Meyer RSA 51:49*

5-Jul	Oelde 10km	Hosea Kogo KEN 28:44	Petra Kaminková CZE 32:40
6-Jul	Cali HMar @	Augustus Kavutu KEN 63:04	Lyudmila Korchagina RUS 73:10
6-Jul	Gold Coast HMar	Tomonori Watanabe JPN 63:25	Hiromi Fujii JPN 70:26
6-Jul	Guayaquil HMar	Silvio Guerra ECU 63:59	Adriana Sánchez MEX 75:50
6-Jul	Sapporo HMar	John Kanyi KEN 62:08	Catherine Ndereba KEN 68:23*
12-Jul	Alphen 10km	Richard Yatich KEN 28:17	Grete Koens NED 33:50
13-Jul	Arusha HMar	Martin Hhaway Sulle TAN 62:47*	Neema Deemay TAN 76:47
13-Jul	London (HP) 10km	Albert Chepkurui KEN 28:12	Iulia Olteanu ROM 32:24
13-Jul	Utica 15km	John Korir KEN 43:23	Susan Chepkemei KEN 48:55
19-Jul	Kingsport 8km	Linus Maiyo KEN 22:11	Silviya Skvortsova RUS 26:04
20 Jul	Johannesburg HMar @	Jaouad Gharib MAR 62:24	Galina Aleksandrova RUS 73:40
20-Jul	Mende 22.4km	Paul Kanda FRA 71:58	Elizabeth Chemweno KEN 83:37
23-Jul	Voorthuizen 10km	Stanley Kagora KEN 28:57	Jane Kiptoo KEN 32:07
24 Jul	Salt Lake City @ 10km #	Patrick Nthiwa KEN 27:16	Emily Jameson USA 32:05
26-Jul	Castelbuono 11.5km	Paul Tergat KEN 34:28	Merima Denboba ETH 19:03 (5.75km)
26-Jul	Clarksburg 10km	David Korir KEN 28:40	Rahab Ndungu KEN 32:59=*
26-Jul	Davenport 7M	John Korir KEN 32:34	Catherine Ndereba KEN 37:12
26-Jul	Namakgale HMar	Abner Chipu RSA 62:00	Elana Meyer RSA 75:15
27-Jul	Pombal HMar	Elijah Yator KEN 64:46	Fatima Silva POR 74:10
2-Aug	Cape Elizabeth 10km	Gilbert Okari KEN 27:28	Catherine Ndereba KEN 31:53
3-Aug	Bogotá HMar @	Alirio Carrasco COL 64:23	Susan Chepkemei KEN 70:29*
3-Aug	Navazzo 10M/5M	Vincent Rop KEN 47:42	Tegla Loroupe KEN 26:38
10-Aug	Falmouth 6.999M	John Korir KEN 31:59	Jennifer Rhines USA 37:08
10-Aug	Sydney 14km	Patrick Nyangelo TAN 41:55	Hayley McGregor AUS 47:28
16-Aug	Parkersburg HMar	John Gwako KEN 63:35	Olga Romanova RUS 72:15
17-Aug	Configno 8.5km	Paul Kosgei KEN 23:47	Alice Timbilil KEN 27:46
17-Aug	San Diego HMar	Kazuhiro Masuda JPN 63:57	Silviya Skvortskova RUS 74:24
23-Aug	Flint 10M	John Korir KEN 46:22	Lyudmila Biktasheva RUS 51:52
26-Aug	Zwolle 10km	Richard Yatich KEN 28:17	Caroline Kwambai KEN 33:16
27-Aug	Port Elizabeth 10km	Andrew Limo KEN 28:35	Azwindini Lukhwareni RSA 33:47
30-Aug	Charleston 15M	Hillary Lelei KEN 1:16:16	Silviya Skvortsova RUS 1:31:52
31-Aug	Hamburg 10km	James Kiplagat Koskei KEN 28:44	Dorte Vibjerg DEN 32:42
31-Aug	Rio de Janeiro HMar	Philip Rugut KEN 63:43	Marizete Rezende BRA 72:19
31-Aug	Stockholm 10km	Women only	Kirsi Valasti FIN 33:16
31-Aug	Virginia Beach HMar	Martin Lel KEN 61:27*	Margaret Okayo KEN 69:17
31-Aug	Zevenaar 10km	Jason Mbote KEN 28:09	Caroline Kwambai KEN 32:37
1-Sep	Marietta 10km	Thomas Kiplitan KEN 28:49	Jane Kiptoo KEN 33:31
1-Sep	New Haven 20km US Ch	Mebrahtom Keflezighi USA 58:57*	Marla Runyan USA 65:52*
1-Sep	Park Forest 10M	Patrick Nthiwa KEN 47:48	Alevtina Ivanova RUS 53:18*
6-Sep	Lille HMar	Wilson Onsare KEN 60:52	Magdalene Chemjor KEN 69:39
7-Sep	Bristol HMar	Julius Kibet KEN 62:52	Miriam Wangari KEN 72:22
7 Sep	Düsseldorf 10km	Moses Kipkosgei Kigen KEN 28:22	Anikó Kalovics HUN 32:01
7-Sep	Glasgow HMar	Peter Kiprotich KEN 61:49	Caroline Kwambai KEN 70:56
7-Sep	Maracaibo HMar	Joseph Kahugu KEN 62:11	Emily Samoei KEN 72:27
7-Sep	Pila HMar	Waldemar Glinka POL 63:22	Nataliya Berkut UKR 72:49*
7-Sep	Providence 5km	Thomas Kiplitan KEN 13:29	Marie Davenport IRL 15:24
7-Sep	Richmond Park 10km	Isaac Arusei KEN 29:38	Paula Radclffe GBR 30:51
7-Sep	Tilburg 10M/10km	Luke Kibet KEN 46:18	Susan Chepkemei KEN 32:10
12-Sep	Gouda 10km	Jeroen van Damme NED 28:24	Linda Milo BEL 35:40
14-Sep	London (Hyde Park) 5km	Women only	Paula Radcliffe GBR 14:51WR
21 Sep	Addis Ababa HMar	Dejere Adere ETH 61:59	Teyiba Erkesso ETH 73:09
21-Sep	Philadelphia HMar	Laban Kipkemboi KEN 61:29	Leah Malot KEN 71:20
21-Sep	South Shields HMar	Hendrick Ramaala RSA 60:01	Paula Radcliffe GBR 65:40*
21-Sep	Zaandam 10M	Francis Kibiwott KEN 45:46	Restituta Joseph TAN 52:17
28-Sep	Gargnano HMar	David Cherui KEN 62:28	Stefania Benedetti ITA 73:33
28-Sep	Haarlem HMar	Peter Raburu KEN 62:42	Elive Korir KEN 76:04
28-Sep	Lisboa HMar	Hendrick Ramaala RSA 62:10	Derartu Tulu ETH 71:30
28-Sep	Montbéliard HMar	Denis Ndiso KEN 61:24	Nancy Omwenga KEN 73:42
28-Sep	Toronto HMar	Giitha Macharia KEN 63:51	Lyudmila Korchagina RUS 73:20
28-Sep	Remich HMar	Paul Kanda KEN 62:36	Restituta Joseph TAN 69:42
28-Sep	Scicli 10km	Kenenisa Bekele ETH 28:50	Men only

28-Sep	Udine HMar	James Kwambai KEN 60:38	Margaret Okayo KEN 67:23
28-Sep	Versailles 16.3km	Francis Komu KEN 48:39	Margaret Maury FRA 55:19
5-Oct	Breda HMar	Sammy Kipruto KEN 62:06	Restituta Joseph TAN 71:44
5-Oct	Dublin 10km	Craig Mottram AUS 28:36	Sonia O'Sullivan IRL 32:24
5-Oct	Saint-Denis HMar	Daniel Rono KEN 62:13	Alice Chelangat KEN 70:23
5-Oct	Syracuse 5km	John Itati KEN 13:43	Naomi Wangui KEN 16:32
12-Oct	Boston HMar	Laban Kipkemboi KEN 63:04	Marie Davenport IRL 70:57*
12-Oct	Burnie 10km	Craig Mottram AUS 28:25	Hayley McGregor AUS 32:42
12-Oct	Groningen 4M	Assefa Mezgebu ETH 18:26	Beáta Rakonczai HUN 20:56
12-Oct	Pettinengo 9.5/4km	John Cheruiyot Korir KEN 27:16	Berhane Adere ETH 12:31
12-Oct	Portsmouth 10M	John Yuda TAN 46:35	Sonia O'Sullivan IRL 53:26
13-Oct	Boston 10km USA Ch	Women only	Elva Dryer USA 32:34
19-Oct	Paris 20km	Sammy Chumba KEN 58:26	Mestewat Tufa ETH 66:29
26-Oct	Cassis 20.3km	Paul Biwott KEN 60:01	Teyiba Erkesso ETH 70:07
30-Oct	Fukuroi NG HMar	Nobuhiko Chiba JPN 63:52	Aki Fujikawa JPN 71:08
1 Nov	Arezzo HMar	Vasili Matviychuk UKR 62:15	Rose Chepchumba KEN 71:15
8-Nov	Mobile 10km USA Ch	Bob Kennedy USA 28:35	Elva Dryer USA 32:03
9 Nov	Kobe HMar	Women only	Mizuki Noguchi JPN 69:52
15-Nov	Richmond 8km	Joseph Mwai KEN 23:21	Tatyana Petrova RUS 25:47
16-Nov	Nijmegen 15km	Richard Yatich KEN 42:43	Mestewat Tufa ETH 49:06
16-Nov	Orlando 10km	Boaz Cheboiywo KEN 28:53	Lyudmila Petrova RUS 32:54
23-Nov	Madrid 10km	Juan Carlos Higuero ESP 28:37	Mestewat Tufa ETH 32:24
23-Nov	Philadelphia 8km	Patrick Nthiwa KEN 23:18	Firiya Zhdanova RUS 26:09
24 Nov	Nagoya HMar	James Wainaina KEN 61:41	Megumi Kobayashi JPN 71:48
27-Nov	Manchester 4.75M	Patrick Nthiwa KEN 21:37	Emilie Mondor CAN 23:59
30-Nov	Addis Ababa 10km @	Sileshi Sihine ETH 29:53*	Tirunesh Dibaba ETH 34:49*
7-Dec	Heerenberg 15km	Richard Yatich KEN 43:20	Ayelech Worku ETH 50:58
7-Dec	Okayama HMar	Women only	Mizuki Noguchi JPN 70:04
14-Dec	Kosa 10M	Martin Irungu Mathathi KEN 45:30	Men only
28 Dec	Houilles 10km	Mulugeta Wondimu ETH 28:49	Merima Denboba ETH 32:43
31-Dec	Bolzano 10.05/5.05km	Sergey Lebed UKR 28:37	Berhane Adere ETH 15:50
31-Dec	Madrid 10km?	José Manuel Martínez ESP 28:12	Marta Domínguez ESP 31:35
31-Dec	São Paulo 15km	Marilson dos Santos BRA 43:49	Margaret Okayo KEN 51:24
31 Dec	Trier 8km/5km	Daniel Gachara KEN 23:11	Selena Kurui KEN 15:57

@=altitude > 1000m, WB = world best, *= course record, # downhill

2003 WORLD MARATHON REVIEW

By David Martin

THE MARATHON has a reputation for bringing surprises, and there were plenty in 2003. Who would have predicted that a fine Moroccan track runner, having run only one marathon and finishing last in the 3000m final of the IAAF World Indoor Championships at Birmingham in March, would be victorious over one of the best marathon fields ever assembled for a summertime IAAF World Athletics Championships? Jaouad Gharib took advantage of the first cool, rainy day after weeks of dry heat, racing from the Hotel de Ville in Paris to the Stade de France in Saint-Denis. His time of 2:08:31 and those of the first five behind him were all faster than Rob de Castella's inaugural 2:10:03 run at Helsinki in 1983. The next day Catherine Ndereba had similarly cool weather, and along with two others bettered Rosa Mota's 1987 Rome Championships record. It was her eighth sub-2:24 marathon. The women's racing was of such quality that finish times from 13th through 52nd were all best times for place. Japanese men and women captured the team trophies.

In 2003 the world best marathon performances for both men and women were bettered in spectacular fashion, first by Paula Radcliffe at London, followed by Paul Tergat at Berlin. The circumstances behind these records were quite different – befitting the differing competitive environments characterizing the two sexes. Perusal of a list of 200 fastest performers for 2003 reveals a much larger women's time gap separating fastest from slowest (more than 20 minutes) than for the men (slightly more than 8 minutes). Thus, the depth of women's marathon participation at the top level is less than for the men. But women's marathon racing dates only to the 1970s, whereas the men's marathon originated with the 1896 Olympics.

Radcliffe's record was thus an individual achievement, 4 mins 30 secs in front of her nearest rival, and 2:25 faster than ever run by a woman (herself!). By contrast, Tergat crossed the finish line only one second ahead of Sammy Korir. Not only did those two both better Khalid Khannouchi's previous world best of 2:05:38, but also the combined average time for the top three finishers at Berlin (2:05:22) was 16 seconds faster! As shown in the Table, both athletes broke established time barriers.

Both races were paced but the circumstances were very different. Radcliffe already held the world record for a women's only race and she desired the mixed race record as well. Since pacing is nowadays the norm in the top-end big-city races, this meant finding women who could run with her – there weren't any! So, the London organizers put several Kenyan men in with the elite women in a race which started at 9am – 45 minutes ahead of the mass mixed race. For the record, the male pacemakers were Samson Loywapet, Christopher Kandie, Mark Yatich, Ibrahim Mitei, John Kiprono, Paul Kanda, and Wesley Chelule, with signs on their backs indicating their intended pace. Weather conditions were ideal: temperature ranging from 10 to 16°C, humidity ranging from 75 to 55%, but with noticeable wind (up to 15 mph or 6.7 m/s). Radcliffe's 10km splits were 32:01, 32:27, 32:08 and 31:53, and her two half-marathon splits were 68:02 and 67:23. Her take-home pay was worthy of her achievement: $55,000 for the victory, $25,000 for a course record, $125,000 for a world record bonus, and $50,000 for breaking 2:22:00. If she can remain healthy, she is the favorite for an historic Athens Olympic marathon gold in 2004. She remains under the tutelage of the only coaches in her long career, Alex and Rosemary Stanton.

In contrast to Radcliffe, then 29, who had never lost a marathon, Tergat, at 34, had never won one. Despite his super-star status as winner of five successive world cross country titles, twice Olympic silver medalist at 10,000m, a former world recordholder at that event, and current half-marathon recordholder, his five previous marathons had produced "only" three 2nds and two 4ths (still, an incredible average time of 2:07:27!). After his fourth place in London's spectacular 2003 finish where six crossed the line within 7 seconds averaging 2:07:58, he decided to attack the event with an even more passionate fury. He entered the Berlin race, and contacted two countrymen to train with him: the heralded Sammy Korir (six wins, five sub-2:08:30 performances) and the scarcely known Titus Munji (debut winner at Zürich). Three more joined on race day to complete his pacing team: Joshua Chelanga, Christopher Kandie, and Matthew Sigei. The pacers indeed delivered the intended splits, remaining competitive to the finish line under Brandenburg Gate, pushing Tergat as never before to secure his record. Weather conditions were ideal: temperature ranging from 9 to 12°C, humidity averaging 65%, but with no noticeable wind. The race's lead 10km splits were 29:55, 29:48, 29:41 and 30:12. Tergat's half marathon splits were 63:04 and 61:51. He earned ¤30,000 for his victory, ¤50,000 for his world record, and ¤40,000 for time bonuses. He is the first Kenyan man to hold the world record. Despite Tergat's lowering of the men's world record by 43 seconds, Radcliffe's performance contributed even more to the ever-decreasing time gap between the men's and women's world records in this event, as shown in the Table

Other observations at year's end indicate the global increase in both quality and quantity of marathon activity. For the first time, four marathons had more than 30,000 finishers. Notice that there is a considerably greater percentage of female finishers among North American marathons than in European events. It was routine for smaller races as well to find increased participation. Many races offered computerized on-line application, and several reached capacity months before the event even took place.

An examination of the winners of 150+ marathons around the world again reveals an enormous dominance by Kenyan men on the victory podium. Although the winners represented 31 countries, Kenyan men won 59% of the events. Athletes from five nations each accounted for about 4.5% of the winners listed: BRA, TAN, ITA, RSA, and RUS. For women the winners represented a simi-

Marathon Barrier Breakers

Men				
First under 2:10	Derek Clayton	2:09:37	Fukuoka	3.12.67
First under 2:09	Clayton	2:08:34	Antwerp	30.5.69
First under 2:08	Carlos Lopes	2:07:12	Rotterdam	20.4.85
First under 2:07	Belayneh Densimo	2:06:50	Rotterdam	17.4.88
First under 2:06	Khalid Khannouchi	2:05:42	Chicago	24.10.99
First under 2:05	Paul Tergat	2:04:55	Berlin	28.9.03
Women				
First under 2:22	Ingrid Kristiansen	2:21:06	London	21.4.85
First under 2:21	Tegla Loroupe	2:20:47	Rotterdam	19.4.98
First under 2:20	Naoko Takahashi	2:19:46	Berlin	30.9.01
First under 2:19	Catherine Ndereba	2:18:47	Chicago	7.10.01
First under 2:18	Paula Radcliffe	2:17:18	Chicago	13.10.02
First under 2:17	Paula Radcliffe	2:15:25	London	13.4.03

larly diverse 38 countries, dominated by Russians (21) and Kenyans (16). At ten international races (Paris, Madrid, Praha, Köln, Carpi, Beirut, Reims, Dublin, New York, and Milano), both male and female winners were Kenyans.

This Kenyan dominance can be described in another way. Of the 1054 sub-2:20:00 marathon performances delivered worldwide by men from 64 countries, 35% (368) were by Kenyans (231 different athletes!) – again an increase over the preceding year (343 performances by 215 athletes). Runner-up was Japan (119 performances). Amazingly, the two countries account for 46% (486) of the sub-2:20:00 performances by men, the remaining 567 coming from 62 countries. The significant increase in marathon racing by Kenyan women is also striking. Over the past few years Japanese and Russian women have dominated, but in 2003 Kenyan women matched them in numbers. Kenyan women had the most sub-2:30:00 performances (18 by 11 athletes), followed by Russia (17 sub-2:30s by 12 athletes) and Japan (16 performances by 13 athletes). Whereas the 1000th fastest performance for men in 2003 was 2:19:39, the equivalent for the women was 2:50:24.

Time Gap Between Men's and Women's Marathon World Records

2:27:33	Grete Waitz	1979	18:59
2:25:42	Waitz	1980	17:08
2:25:29	Waitz	1983	17:11
2:22:43	Joan Benoit	1983	14:25
2:21:06	Ingrid Kristiansen	1985	13:54
2:20:47	Tegla Loroupe	1998	13:57
2:20:43	Loroupe	1999	14:38
2:19:46	Naoko Takahashi	2001	14:04
2:18:47	Catherine Ndereba	2001	13:05
2:17:18	Paula Radcliffe	2002	11:40
2:15:25	Radcliffe	2003	9:47

Demographics of Major World Marathon Finishers

Venue	Total	Men (%)	Women (%)
New York	34,729	23,014 (66.3%)	11,715 (33.7%)
Chicago	32,395	18,720 (57.8%)	13,675 (42.2%)
London	32,167	23,893 (74.3%)	8,274 (26.4%)
Berlin	30,709	25,105 (81.8%)	5,604 (18.2%)
Honolulu	22,136	11,614 (52.5%)	10,522 (47.5%)

Leading Marathons 2003

See also Championships section for results in those events.

9-Jan	Tiberias	Moges Taye ETH	2:12:45	Ester Einer ISR	2:51:06
10-Jan	Dubai	Joseph Kahugu KEN	2:09:33	Irina Permitina RUS	2:36:26
19-Jan	Marrakech	Abdelfattah Aitzouri MAR	2:12:15		
26-Jan	Osaka	Women only		Mizuki Noguchi JPN	2:21:18
26-Jan	Port of Spain	Pamenos Ballentyne VIN	2:15:30	Gitte Karlshøj DEN	2:43:17
2-Feb	Beppu	Samson Ramadhani TAN	2:09:24	Men only	
2-Feb	Miami	David Ruto KEN	2:12:22	Volha Yudziankova BLR	2:40:23
2-Feb	Valencia	Samwel Tangus KEN	2:14:43	Mulu Seboka ETH	2:46:33
9-Feb	Tokyo	Zebedayo Bayo TAN	2:09:07	Men only	
11-Feb	Hitachinaka	Minoru Isono JPN	2:19:04	Kiyoko Shimahara JPN	2:28:17
16-Feb	Austin #	Andrzej Krzyscin POL	2:12:41	Silviya Skvortsova RUS	2:37:23
16-Feb	Guadalajara @	Thomas Omwenga KEN	2:17:18	Albina Galliamova RUS	2:38:56
16-Feb	Hong Kong	Tendai Chimusasa ZIM	2:18:11	Sun Weiwei CHN	2:38:55
23-Feb	Nobeoka	Tomohiro Sato JPN	2:13:02	Men only	
23-Feb	Sevilla	Onesmus Mutisya KEN	2:17:24	Beatriz Ros ESP	2:31:09
2-Mar	Genova	Valerio Brignone ITA	2:16:39	Ruth Pickvance GBR	2:45:41
2-Mar	Los Angeles	Mark Yatich KEN	2:09:52	Tatyana Pozdnyakova UKR	2:29:40
2-Mar	Moshi @	Lucian Hombo TAN	2:16:25	Sara Maja TAN	2:51:24
2-Mar	Otsu	Japhet Kosgei KEN	2:07:39	Men only	
2-Mar	Torreón	Francisco Bautista MEX	2:14:28	Albina Galliamova RUS	2:35:48
9-Mar	Brescia	Matthew Sigei KEN	2:09:17	Simona Viola ITA	2:35:23
9-Mar	Nagoya	Women only		Takami Ominami JPN	2:25:03
9-Mar	Napoli	Lukas Cherono KEN	2:13:11	Maura Viceconte ITA	2:33:36
9-Mar	Piacenza	Abraham Maiyo KEN	2:13:29	Galina Zhulyeva UKR	2:38:22
16-Mar	Barcelona	Alberto Juzdado ESP	2:10:53	Kenza Whabi KEN	2:38:36
16-Mar	Casablanca	Benjamin Itok KEN	2:10:58		
16-Mar	Seoul	Gert Thys RSA	2:08:42	Zhang Shujing CHN	2:23:18
23-Mar	Marseille	Patrick Chumba KEN	2:12:06	Tatyana Gladyr UKR	2:37:52
23-Mar	Roma	Frederick Cherono KEN	2:08:47	Gloria Marconi ITA	2:29:35

29-Mar	Ngodwana #	Kenneth Ncgobo RSA	2:16:29	Yolande Maclean RSA	2:50:53
30-Mar	Lyon	Sergey Gorintsev RUS	2:16:55	Yelena Deryabina RUS	2:40:37
30-Mar	Xiamen	Hailu Negussie ETH	2:09:03	Zhou Chunxiu CHN	2:34:16
6-Apr	Linz	Joseph Mereng KEN	2:13:37	Elena Fadeyeva RUS	2:33:03
6-Apr	Paris	Mike Rotich KEN	2:06:33	Beatrice Omwanza KEN	2:27:44
13-Apr	Debno	Waldemar Glinka POL	2:14:48	Grazyna Syrek POL	2:32:09
13-Apr	Kunsan	Cho Keun-hyung KOR	2:17:04	Oh Mi-ja KOR	2:39:41
13-Apr	London	Gezahegne Abera ETH	2:07:56	Paula Radcliffe GBR	2:15:25
13-Apr	Pyongyang	Jong Myong-chol PRK	2:15:05	Ham Bong-sil PRK	2:27:48
13-Apr	Rotterdam	William Kiplagat KEN	2:07:42	Olivera Jevtic SCG	2:25:23
13-Apr	Torino	Daniele Caimmi ITA	2:10:08	Stine Larsen NOR	2:27:12
13-Apr	Vitoria	Kamal Ziani ESP	2:12:57	Winnie Cheruiyot KEN	2:41:09
13-Apr	Zürich	Tesfaye Eticha ETH	2:10:59	Karina Szymanska POL	2:33:28
19-Apr	Tianjin	Wang Xiangfeng CHN	2:22:41	Sun Yingjie CHN	2:25:33
20-Apr	Nagano #	Erick Wainaina KEN	2:12:00	Madina Biktagirova RUS	2:28:23
21-Apr	Boston #	Robert Kip.Cheruiyot KEN	2:10:11	Svetlana Zakharova RUS	2:25:20
21-Apr	De Meern	Luc Krotwaar BEL	2:13:41	Mounia Aboulachem BEL	2:43:09
26-Apr	Nashville	Godwin Jomo Kororia KEN	2:12:56	Irina Bogacheva KGZ	2:28:06
27-Apr	Hamburg	Julio Rey ESP	2:07:27	Hellen Kimutai KEN	2:25:52
27-Apr	La Habana	Aguelmis Rojas CUB	2:15:47	Mariela González CUB	2:38:37
27-Apr	Madrid	Henry Tarus KEN	2:12:42	Ruth Kutol KEN	2:34:41
27-Apr	Padova	Dawit Terefa ETH	2:10:38	Marcella Mancini ITA	2:36:14
27-Apr	Wroclaw	Mihaylo Iveruk UKR	2:17:18	Wioletta Uryga POL	2:39:27
4-May	Hannover	David Simukwo KEN	2:15:27	Tadelesh Birra ETH	2:33:42
4-May	Pittsburgh	Juan Camacho MEX	2:12:05	Lyudmila Korchagina RUS	2:29:53
4-May	Trieste	Ibrahim Mitei Kipkurui KEN	2:11:26	Maria Cocchetti ITA	2:33:50
6-May	Belfast	Lezan Kimutai KEN	2:17:09	Trudi Thomson GBR	2:45:48
11-May	Essen	John Rotich KEN	2:15:55	Dorota Gruca POL	2:34:23
11-May	Mainz	Arthur Miklos ROM	2:18:11	Olena Fadeyeva UKR	2:38:02
11-May	Ottawa	Joseph Nderitu KEN	2:15:30	Sandy Jacobson CAN	2:33:52
11-May	São Paulo	Genilson da Silva BRA	2:16:42	Maria Arruda BRA	2:39:12
18-May	Praha	Willy Cheruiyot KEN	2:11:56	Anne Chelagat KEN	2:31:10
25-May	Enschede	Wilson Kibet KEN	2:11:38	Lidiya Vasilevskaya RUS	2:29:23
25-May	Wien	Joseph Chebet KEN	2:14:49	Lucilla Andreucci ITA	2:35:32
1-Jun	Porto Alegre	Arnaldo Sales de Sa BRA	2:16:13	Rosa Jussara Barbosa BRA	2:42:08
1-Jun	San Diego	Ondoro Osoro KEN	2:09:38	Irina Bogacheva KGZ	2:29:52
14-Jun	Stockholm	Josephat Chemjor KEN	2:18:14	Marie S-Lundberg SWE	2:35:07
15-Jun	Caen	Elijah Mutai KEN	2:19:00	Karina Szymanska POL	2:36:52
21-Jun	Duluth	Joseph Kamau KEN	2:11:22	Firiya Zhdanova RUS	2:27:05
21-Jun	Sankt Peterburg	Nikolay Kerimov RUS	2:11:46	Tatyana Zolotaryova RUS	2:40:21
22-Jun	Mont St. Michel	Nelson Lebo KEN	2:16:08	Corrine Raux FRA	2:37:51
22-Jun	San Luis Potosi	Simon Sawe KEN	2:19:10	Martha Durán MEX	2:45:27
29-Jun	Rio de Janeiro	Alex Januario BRA	2:16:39	Leone Justino da Silva BRA	2:46:54
6-Jul	Southport	Dickson Marwa TAN	2:12:53	Shireen Crumpton NZL	2:40:10
2-Aug	Omsk	Mikhail Khobotov RUS	2:17:40	Anfisa Kosacheva RUS	2:40:16
3-Aug	Arusha @	David Kwino KEN	2:15:50	Fabiola William TAN	2:40:10
31-Aug	Sapporo	Erick Wainaina KEN	2:13:13	Chihiro Tanaka JPN	2:34:11
14-Sep	Florianopolis	Elson Alex Gracioli BRA	2:17:23	Ilda Alves dos Santos BRA	2:39:21
14-Sep	Krems	John Rotich KEN	2:12:32	Olena Rozhko UKR	2:52:48
28-Sep	Berlin	Paul Tergat KEN	2:04:55	Yasuko Hashimoto JPN	2:26:32
28-Sep	Ciudad de México	George Otworo KEN	2:18:11	Dulce María Rodríguez MEX	2:40:58
28-Sep	Toronto	Joseph Nderitu KEN	2:17:50	Lyubov Morgunova RUS	2:36:20
5-Oct	Graz	Charles Cheruiyot KEN	2:15:27	Eva-Maria Gradwohl AUT	2:42:05
5-Oct	Köln	Benjamin Rotich KEN	2:12:03	Tegla Loroupe KEN	2:33:48
5-Oct	Kosice	Grigoriy Andreyev RUS	2:13:24	Yelena Mazovka BLR	2:39:23
5-Oct	Poznan	Andrzej Krzyscin POL	2:17:57	Krystyna Kuta POL	2:38:13
5-Oct	St. Paul	Eddy Hellebuyck USA	2:12:46	Blake Russell USA	2:30:41
11-Oct	Hartford	Michael Mislay TAN	2:17:44	Ramilya Burangulova RUS	2:33:26
12-Oct	Carpi	Philemon Rotich KEN	2:12:13	Jennifer Chesinon KEN	2:31:39
12-Oct	Chicago	Evans Rutto KEN	2:05:50	Svetlana Zakharova RUS	2:23:07
12-Oct	Eindhoven	Willy Cheruiyot KEN	2:09:05	Vivian Ruijters NED	2:36:36

12-Oct	Essen	Carsten Schütz GER	2:14:58	Romy Spitzmüller GER	2:34:57
12-Oct	Melbourne	Magnus Michelsson AUS	2:14:00	Loretta McGrath AUS	2:49:02
12-Oct	Odense	Aleksey Khlokhlov RUS	2:19:33	Gitte Karlshøj DEN	2:34:57
18-Oct	Baltimore	Erickson Kimaiyo KEN	2:18:41	Elvira Kolpakova RUS	2:48:49
18 Oct	Beograd	Benson Ogata KEN	2:14:48	Zana Malykova RUS	2:40:24
19-Oct	Amsterdam	William Kipsang KEN	2:06:39	Helena Sampaio POR	2:28:06
19-Oct	Beijing	Ian Syster RSA	2:07:49	Sun Yingjie CHN	2:19:39
19-Oct	Beirut	Paul Rugut KEN	2:17:04	Jackline Torori KEN	2:42:12
19-Oct	Chunchon	Elijah Mutai KEN	2:13:54	Young Sun-sook KOR	2:34:27
19-Oct	Columbus	Ronald Mogaka RSA	2:14:11	Lyudmila Pushkina RUS	2:28:15
19-Oct	Istanbul	Belaye Wolashe ETH	2:18:29	Rimma Dubovik UKR	2:36:49
19-Oct	Marengo	Rachid Kisri MAR	2:15:39	Stefania Benedetti ITA	2:35:38
26-Oct	Dalian	Gong Ke CHN	2:17:02	Zeng Hong CHN	2:40:17
26-Oct	Frankfurt	Boaz Kimaiyo Kibet KEN	2:09:28	Luminita Zaituc GER	2:29:41
26-Oct	Lausanne	Tesfaye Eticha ETH	2:10:05	Emebet Abossa ETH	2:34:40
26-Oct	Ljubljana	Andrey Naumov RUS	2:13:58	Galina Zhulyeva UKR	2:38:13
26-Oct	Reims	Charles Kibiwott KEN	2:10:20	Beatrice Omwanza KEN	2:32:04
26-Oct	Venezia	El Hassan Lahssini FRA	2:11:01	Anne Chelagat KEN	2:30:17
27-Oct	Dublin	Onesmus Kilonzo KEN	2:17:03	Ruth Kutol KEN	2:27:22
2-Nov	Athína	Zebedayo Bayo TAN	2:16:59	Nadezhda Wijenberg NED	2:43:18
2-Nov	Nairobi @	Philip Kirui KEN	2:15:40	Alice Chelangat KEN	2:41:27
2-Nov	New York	Martin Lel KEN	2:10:30	Margaret Okayo KEN	2:22:31
2-Nov	Seoul	Pavel Loskutov EST	2:09:15	Chung Yun-hee KOR	2:30:50
2-Nov	Soweto @	Elijah Mutandiro ZIM	2:17:19	Charne Rademeyer RSA	2:44:53
15-Nov	Richmond	Elly Rono KEN	2:15:36	Dorota Gruca POL	2:44:22
16-Nov	Curitiba	Rildo Alves dos Santos BRA	2:19:34	Rosa Jussara Barbosa BRA	2:48:07
16-Nov	Tokyo	Women only		Elfenesh Alemu ETH	2:24:47
23-Nov	Firenze	Angelo Carosi ITA	2:15:55	Anna Incerti ITA	2:34:40
23-Nov	San Sebastián	Peter Korir KEN	2:10:46	Remedios Alonso ESP	2:45:04
30-Nov	La Rochelle	Elijah Yator KEN	2:11:34	Helena Javornik SLO	2:31:54
30-Nov	Mazatlan	Juan Camacho MEX	2:14:59	Lucia Subano KEN	2:40:21
30-Nov	Milano	John Birgen KEN	2:09:08	Anne Chelagat KEN	2:29:23
7-Dec	Fukuoka	Tomoaki Kunichika JPN	2:07:52	Men only	
7-Dec	Lisboa	Luís Jesus POR	2:15:31	Madina Biktagirova RUS	2:42:06
7-Dec	Sacramento	Michal Bartoszak POL	2:16:21	Tatiana Titova RUS	2:33:31
7-Dec	Singapore	John Kelai KEN	2:19:02	Wang Yu CHN	2:43:57
12-Dec	Palermo	Francesco Ingargiola ITA	2:14:51	Jo Bun-hui PRK	2:36:54
14-Dec	Dallas	Nephat Kinyaniui KEN	2:16:27	Lyudmila Korchagina RUS	2:37:06
14-Dec	Hofu	Hironori Sato JPN	2:15:04	Men only	
14-Dec	Honolulu	Jimmy Muindi KEN	2:12:59	Eri Hayakawa JPN	2:31:57
14-Dec	Reggio Emilia	Philemon Kipkering KEN	2:15:23	Francesca Zanusso ITA	2:45:51

@ = altitude > 1000m, # = downhill > 1 m/km

Ultra Summary

by Andy Milroy

2003 was yet another uneven year. Although after a break of two years, the men once again broke the 6:30 barrier in the 100km, there was not strength in depth. The winner of the World 100km, Mario Fattore, and the fastest man in the world in 2003, José Aubeso, chose not to run in the European event, as did leading women Elvira Kolpakova (Russia), Tania Hoos-Schäfer (Germany) and Danielle Sanderson (Great Britain). Leading runners from the European 100km and the Comrades Marathon, Farit Ganiyev, Tatyana Zhyrkova and the Nurgalieva twins did not run in the World 100km; neither did the fastest woman in the world in 2003, Norimi Sakurai of Japan.

Therefore the results were at best mixed for anyone who attempted more than two major events for the year. This problem was exacerbated by the overbearing conditions of the World 100km, which produced the personal slowest times recorded by many of the world's top competitors; some of the men ranked in our top 10 were beaten by the top women in that event.

In the inaugural World 24 Hour at Uden, the absence of dominant figure Yiannis Kouros actually made for a more competitive men's race with the greatest field, race, and depth of results in the history of the event.

It is interesting to note that neither the year's fastest man for the 100km (José Aubeso, Spain) nor for the 24 Hours (Valmir Nunes, Brazil) are ranked among the top ten.

Europeans continue to dominate the sport, and in particular Russia have 11 of the 20 in my rankings – attributable this year, in part, to the fact that the fastest 100km race in the world in depth was held in Russia and supported by most of the top native performers. Not a single ultrarunner from the Western Hemisphere is ranked among the top 10 of either sex.

Men

1. Mario Fattore (Italy) won both his 100km races – the hilly Faenza race in 6:54:03 and then he defended his title in the World 100km in Taiwan in 7:04:56.
2. Farit Ganiyev (Russia) won at Chernogolovka (Russia) from Grigoriy Murzin (who took the European title) 6:28:27 to 6:29:41. Ganiyev also headed Murzin in the Torhout (Belgium) race 6:39:32 (2nd) to 6:40:22 (3rd), but lost to Murzin at Santa Cruz de Bezaña (Spain) 6:39:40 (1st) to 7:14:37 (3rd).
3. Grigoriy Murzin (Russia) was second in the World 100km but was twice beaten by Ganiyev.
4. Fusi Nhlapo (South Africa) beat Oleg Kharitonov in the 89.179 km Comrades Marathon (South Africa). His time (5:28:52) on the downhill course (the race alternates uphill and downhill years) was the ninth fastest ever but slower than the first four in 2001 when Andrew Kelehe ran the second fastest ever on the down run.
5. Oleg Kharitonov (Russia) was 5th in the World 100km in 7:22:08, and was 2nd in the Comrades in 5:31:41 for 13th all-time (with the 14th fastest time).
6. Paul Beckers (Belgium) ran 270.087km in 24 hours, the second best distance of the year to win the World and European 24 hours, beating Ryoichi Sekiya. Beckers was beaten by Yiannis Kouros (Greece/Australia) in the longer 48 Hour event at Surgères, 438.813km to 374.574km, but Kouros did not contest the far more competitive 24 Hour World event.
7. Yiannis Kouros (Greece/Australia) covered a greater distance in the first 24 hours at the Surgères 48 hours than Sekiya did in the World 24. He also beat Beckers at 48 hours with a distance bettered only by him on the all-time 2-day event list.
8. Ryoichi Sekiya (Japan) ran 261.640km behind Valmir Nunes (273.828km: world-leading distance for the year) in Taiwan, but Nunes was well beaten (235.094km) by both Beckers and Sekiya (267,223km) in the World event.
9. Mario Ardemagni (Italy) was 3rd in the European 100km and 9th in the World 100km (7:43:28), but he was ahead of Igor Tyazhkorob in the European, at Verona, 6:41:48 (1st) to 6:49:52 (3rd), and in Taiwan, where Yoshiaki Kobayashi (Japan; winner of the Yubetsu/Saroma 100km) wasback in 48th at 9:00:12.
10. Igor Tyazhkorob (Russia) beat Murzin and Ganiyev at Torhout in 6:36:33, was 4th in the European in 6:45:27 and 13th in the World 100km in 8:01:25.

Women

1. Norimi Sakurai (Japan) was unbeaten and ran the fastest 100km time of 2003. She won the Yubetsu/Saroma race in 7:20:02 and at Verona beat Monica Casiraghi (Italy) in the 50km (3:33:23.3 to 3:39:06.6) before setting new world track bests at 50 miles (5:48:12.0), 6 hours (83,200km), and 100km, (7:14:05.8, fifth fastest performance road or track all-time/fourth fastest performer).
2. Monica Casiraghi (Italy) won the World 100km under brutally difficult conditions in 8:04:46, one of eight ultra wins in all including also Faenza (7:59:42) and the Swiss Alpine Marathon (6:47:55), and was beaten in two races, the European 100km (7:28:00) by Zhyrkova and the track 50km at Verona by Sakurai.
3. Tatyiana Zhyrkova (Russia) won the best race in depth, running 7:19:51 (then 5th fastest all-time) at Chernogolovka in the European 100km, beating Casiraghi, but did not run the World event. She also ran the fastest-ever third place (6:17:50) at Comrades.
4. Elena Nurgalieva (Russia) won the 89.179 km Comrades Marathon in 6:07:46, the fourth fastest time ever (behind Van der Merwe, Trason and Bak), and nipped her twin sister for third in the European 100km (7:31:14). Zhyrkova and Elena are 1-1 on race wins, but Zhyrkova won by a bigger margin at 100km over a deeper quality field than Elena did at Comrades.
5. Olesya Nurgalieva (Russia) ran second to her twin sister at Comrades (6:12:07, fifth fastest all-time performer, sixth fastest performance), and finished in an almost virtual tie with her (7:31:14) in the European 100km.
6. Irina Reutovich (Russia) won the World 24 Hour (237.052km), the most competitive long-range race of the year, beating Galina Yeremina (232.050km). She was second to Bérces at the Worschach 24-Hour (231.576km) and the Surgères 48-Hour, and she won at Brno in the second best 48 hour of the year, 366.927km.
7. Edit Bérces (Hungary) ran 228.906km in the first 24 hours of the Surgères 48Hour, 227.777km

to win the Taipei 24-Hour. Her 237.645km at Worschach was the best performance of the year and in the 48-hour at Surgères she covered 369.749km to Reutovich's 358.288km, but she was 4th in the World 24-Hour at Uden with 225.710km.

8. Galina Yeremina (Russia) finished second in the World 24-Hour with the third best distance of the year, 232.050km and won the Russian title with 207.366km.

9. Marina Myshlianova (Russia) finished 5th in 7:33:21 at the European 100km.

10. Nadezhda Karaseva (Russia) finished 6th in 7:35:01 at the European 100km.

Although Paola Sanna finished second in the World 100km in 8:15:12, she otherwise ran some relatively mediocre performances, 8:26:19.4 for 3rd in Verona and 8:31:31.8 for 2nd in Faenza. Thus Myshlianova and Karaseva win the final ranking spots over her by virtue of significantly faster times in what turned out to be the most significant 100km of the year, the European 100km.

Aside from Kouros' top 48 hour mark, John Geesler set a new US mark of 400km for the second best performance at the end of the year. There was a range of good performances by women; in addition to the dominant figures of Bérces and Reutovich, there were also strong road performances from Barbara Szlachetka of Poland (348.915km), Fumie Sata of Japan (346.5km) and 328.222km by Heiki Pawzik of Germany.

The best 6 day marks of the year were made on the road. Claude Hardel of France ran 761.64km in Copenhagen and Dipali Cunningham of AUS/GBR set the best women's mark with 711.330km in New York. The best men's 1000 mile mark was also set in New York by Rainer Koch of Germany at just over 14 hours, with the Swiss Paula Maier setting the best women's mark with 14:12:15:09.

The longest race on a certified course in the world is the 3100 miler in New York, held on a 0.5488 mile loop. It was won by Namitabha Arsic of Yugoslavia in 49:02:24:45 who went on to run 5000km in 49:04:15:13. Women's winner was the experienced American Suprabha Beckjord who covered 5000km in 56:03:00:22.

The London to Brighton was won by Brian Hennessey, for the second time in succession, in a time of 6:24:04 from Ian Bailey (RSA) in 6:26:32 and Miguel Basurko(ESP) in 6:36:31. Ellen McCurtin (USA) was first woman in 7:02:27 well clear of British runners Isobel Partridge 7:33:26 and Christine Costiff 8:12:52.

The Spartathlon from Athens to Sparta was won by the Markus Thalmann (AUT) in 23:28:24, some two hours ahead of Valmir Nunes (BRA), 25:30:35 and Jean-Jacques Moros (FRA) close to an hour further back in 26:26:16. The first two women were Japanese: Akiko Sakamoto 29:07:44 and Sumie Ingaki 29:38:54, with Barbara Szlachetka (POL) third in 31:50:23.

The longest race of the year lasted 64 stages and went from Lisbon in Portugal to Moscow in Russia, and covered 5053km. The winner was Bernard Grojean (FRA) with an elapsed time of 469:32:12 from Robert Wimmer (GER) 480:29:51 and Martin Wagen (SUI) 494:44:52.

Long term developments in the sport are interesting. An analysis of the top 100 runners in the Comrades shows an overwhelming dominance of black African runners, yet this talent did not appear on the world stage since the South African Federation chose not to send a team to the World 100km. Thus the African dominance so apparent in the subultra races is not yet apparent in ultra races.

However Europe's dominance is challenged by runners from Asia. One third of the Spartathlon finishers were from Japan, one of the top three ultra nations at both 100km and 24 hours, and beginning to make itself felt at 48 hours. The changing power balance was also shown by the staging of the World 100km in Taiwan with the improving standards there, the largest 100km in the world held in Hong Kong, uktra races in Korea, Malaysia and Singapore and ultrarunning emerging in India.

IAAF WORLD CHAMPIONSHIPS 2003

9th IAAF World Championships, Saint-Denis 23-31 August

THERE WERE more close and exciting finishes at the Stade de France in Saint-Denis, to the north of Paris, France, than in any of the eight previous editions of the World Championships, even if overall standards were not exceptional. There were two world records – in both the men's walks – from Jefferson Pérez and Robert Korzeniowski, both men receiving $100,000 bonuses for their exploits. Other stars included Hicham El Guerrouj and Allen Johnson, who won their fourth World titles, Felix Sánchez and Ana Guevara (400m), a class apart at their events, and the ebullient Swedish heptathlon winner Carolina Klüft. The crowds were kept waiting for French success, but revelled in two gold medals in 20 minutes on the penultimate day, from Eunice Barber in the long jump and their women's sprint relay team.

The increasing practice of athletes switching nations was brought to the fore by the steeplechase victory of Saïf Saaeed Shaheen of Qatar (Stephen Cherono of Kenya until just days earlier) after a fascinating race against Ezekiel Kemboi of Kenya.

Drug issues involving two celebrated American athletes, Kevin Young and Kelli White, together with the truculent behaviour of a third, Jon Drummond, cast a shadow over what were otherwise a joyous nine days of great competition. As we go to press, the authorities have yet to decide on what action to take in the White affair, as she (and five other Americans) tested positive for Modafinil, a stimulant that was not specifically named on the IAAF list of banned drugs but which should be covered under a clause dealing with "related substances". It was originally classified as a weak stimulant and if the charge is sustained White would forfeit the titles she won at 100m and 200m and the $120,000 prize money involved. It is interesting to note that it was not the first time that White has fallen foul of doping regulations in France. After competing in the Golden League meeting in 2002 the particularly stringent French Anti-Doping Agency banned her from competing in France for six months for testing positive for corticoid, an anti-inflammatory steroid. The IAAF accepted her explanation that she took it for medical reasons but had failed to present a valid medical certificate, and cleared her of any doping offence.

Young, who won gold medals at 400m and 4x400m here, was reported to have tested positive for the steroid nandrolene in 1999 but had been cleared on appeal to an internal inquiry in the USA and went on to win an Olympic gold medal at 4x400m relay in Sydney 2000. The International Olympic Committee proposed a joint inquiry with the World Anti-Doping Agency into this matter, and why Young was allowed to run in Sydney.

With three silver and two (possibly three) bronze medals also, France's medal total was exceeded only by the USA (20) and Russia (19). However, if Kelli White is stripped of the 100m and 200m gold medals, which would mean that Torri Edwards (100) and Anastasiya Kapachinskaya (200) would become champions, while Chandra Sturrup and Muriel Hurtis would step up to bronze, the medal count would become 19-18 in Russia's favour.

Unhappily for the image of athletics, the abiding memory of Paris for countless millions of TV viewers around the world will be of Jon Drummond's antics after being thrown out of his 100m quarter-final for a false start. Whether the new starting rule is fair and effective needs to be the subject of continuing scrutiny, but what is not in dispute is that when an athlete is ruled out he must accept the decision. Drummond's dismay at being disqualified is understandable, but as a professional athlete of immense experience he should not only know the rules but also abide by them.

By his actions, resulting in a long delay, he upset countless other competitors in his and other events and provoked an ugly crowd reaction that should play no part in athletics. The inability of officials to deal with the problem quickly and firmly only exacerbated the situation.

Incredibly, two 18 year-olds (both 2003 World Junior Cross-country champions) won the 5000m titles in Eliud Kipchoge and Tirunesh Dibaba; another 18 year-old, Darrel Brown, came within a whisker of claiming the 100m, and athletes of 20 or 21 struck gold in the 10,000m, steeplechase, high jump, women's 400m hurdles and heptathlon. At the other end of the age spectrum there was the oldest ever women's World champion, first Yelena Nikolayeva and then Irina Yatchenko.

Jan Zelezny became the only man to have competed at eight World Championships. Liliana Allen, Gail Devers, Franka Dietzsch, Jackie Edwards, Lavern Eve, Susana Feitor, Beverly McDonald, Teresa Machado, Fiona May, Jearl Miles Clark, Maria Mutola, Yelena Nikolayeva, Merlene Ottey, Fernanda Robeiro and Letitia Vriesde tied the women's record of seven.

100 Metres (h, qf 24th, sf, F 25th) (0.0)

THIS WAS the first World or Olympic 100m for 20 years to be without a sub-10 time, but just 0.06 separated the top six men in the final and there were faster times in the prelims. The background of the new starting procedures surely affected the event and meant the elimination in the quarter-finals of Asafa Powell, who had run a pb of 10.05 for the fastest time in the 1st round, and John Drummond, who caused chaos by refusing, for a long time, to accept his disqualification after being shown to twitched on his blocks at a reaction time of .052. Fastest in the 2nd round was 10.01, a world junior record, in windless conditions by 18 year-old Brown, Collins ran 10.02, Chambers 10.03 and Montgomery 10.04.

Drummond left the track in tears – only to be directed back without authority by an American official, causing further delay and argument. For far too long no decisive action was taken by the relevant officials, who at last asked all the athletes to leave to enable the next two heats to be run. When they returned, an already damaging situation was made worse when the spectators realised that Drummond and Powell would not be permitted to take part. Certain elements in the crowd created so much noise each time the athletes went to their marks that it would have been impossible to start (unfortunately no proper attempt was made by the announcers to inform the crowd, who had seen an apparently fair start as all the athletes were away together, of the rules). The stalemate continued for so long that the heat eventually got underway some 50 minutes late and was won by an angry Ato Boldon in 10.09. It was ironic that a rule introduced to reduce the amount of time spent on false starts in order to provide a slicker show for spectators and TV should lead to such a long hiatus.

Williams 10.11 and Chambers 10.06 won their semis, and Maurice Greene, challenging for a fourth 100m title, limped in one from last in his race. Collins won the final from lane one, to become the first ever world champion from St Kitts and Nevis, from Brown, Campbell and Chambers.

1. Kim Collins SKN	10.07
2. Darrel Brown TRI-J	10.08
3. Darren Campbell GBR	10.08
4. Dwain Chambers GBR	10.08
5. Tim Montgomery USA	10.11
6. Bernard Williams USA	10.13
7. Deji Aliu NGR	10.21
8. Uchenna Emedolu NGR	10.22

200 Metres (h, qf 27th, sf 28th, F 29th) 0.1)

AFTER NO medals in the 100, there was a 1-2 in the 200 for the USA. Four rounds and cool weather took their toll as all the finalists had run faster in previous rounds and 20.30 was the slowest time to win a global title since Henry Carr won the 1964 Olympic gold on a cinder track in 20.36. Patton was fastest in round 1 at 20.27 and won his semi in 20.03 from Buckland 20.11 and Capel had won his semi in 20.18 from Suetsugu 20.22, while Buckland had run 20.06 in his quarter-final.

1. John Capel USA	20.30
2. Darvis Patton USA	20.31
3. Shingo Suetsugu JPN	20.38
4. Darren Campbell GBR	20.39
5. Stéphane Buckland MRI	20.41
6. Joshua J Johnson USA	20.47
7. Frank Fredericks NAM	20.47
8. Uchenna Emedolu NGR	20.62

400 Metres (h 23rd, sf 24th, F 26th)

WASHINGTON, UNBEATEN in 2003, was the favourite and won his semi in 44.60 after Young had won the first in 44.70 from Harrison 44.71, but in the final Young moved away from the top of the final bend and finished well clear (100m splits 11.2, 21.4 and 32.1). Just 0.06 separated Washington from fifth place as Raquil thrilled the home fans with a great finish (11.7 for his final 100m to 12.2/12.3 for the other top five) that carried him from 7th with 30m to go to third in a French record of 44.79. Nine men broke 45 in the semis, but the standard was far short of 1997, when Washington was third in 44.39 and Young fifth in 44.51, and 1999 when Young placed fourth in 44.36.

1. Jerome Young USA	44.50
2. Tyree Washington USA	44.77
3. Marc Raquil FRA	44.79
4. Michael Blackwood JAM	44.80
5. Leslie Djhone FRA	44.83
6. Calvin Harrison USA	44.96
7. Eric Milazar MRI	45.17
8. Alleyne Francique GRN	45.48

800 Metres (h 28th, sf 29th, F 31st)

JUST 0.09 separated the medallists in the final in which Kipketer led at 200m 24.5 and the bell 52.46. Borzakovskiy (fastest in the semis at 1:45.31), after his usual slow start, surged into the lead before 600 (1:19.5), but surprisingly faltered in the final strides to be passed by Olympic bronze medallist Saïd-Guerni, whose last 200 was 25.2. There was very nearly a sensation in the heats when, for all his experience, Kipketer slackened too soon in a tight finish and only progressed to the next round by 0.01, and title holder Bucher went out in the semis.

1. Djabir Saïd-Guerni ALG	1:44.81
2. Yuriy Borzakovskiy RUS	1:44.84
3. Mbulaeni Mulaudzi RSA	1:44.90
4. Wilson Kipketer DEN	1:45.23
5. Andrea Longo ITA	1:45.43
6. Justus Koech KEN	1:45.63
7.Hezekiél Sepeng RSA	1:45.74
8. Osmar dos Santos BRA	1:46.28

1500 Metres (h28th, F 31st)

EL GUERROUJ won his fourth consecutive

world title. Estévez led at 400m in 57.70, 4m ahead of Korir with El Guerrouj third, but at 700m the pattern of the race became clear when the world record holder moved ahead with Baala in his slipstream. The 800m split was 1:56.29 (58.59 second lap) and at the bell El Guerrouj's time was 2:37.87 with Baala 3m back. The 1200m time was 2:51.28 (third 400 in 54.99) and Baala did well to close the gap slightly by the 200m mark, but El Guerrouj pulled away to win by a safe four metres, having covered the final lap in 53.90, the last 800 in 1:49.7. Estévez and Chouki faded out of contention and Heshko stormed through from way back to snatch the medal from Korir and Silva.

1. Hicham El Guerrouj MAR	3:31.77
2. Mehdi Baala FRA	3:32.31
3. Ivan Heshko UKR	3:33.17
4. Paul Korir KEN	3:33.47
5. Rui Silva POR	3:33.68
6. Reyes Estévez ESP	3:33.84
7. Gert-Jan Liefers NED	3:33.99
8. Vyacheslav Shabunin RUS	3:34.37
9. Isaac Songok KEN-J	3:34.39
10. Roberto Parra ESP	3:35.02
11. Juan Carlos Higuero ESP	3:38.49
drugs dq (8) Fouad Chouki FRA	3:34.05

5000 Metres (31st)

THE FINAL pitted the 10,000m champion Bekele against the 1500m champion El Guerrouj. Both came through the heats impressively; Bekele ran a 54.75 last lap to win his race and El Guerrouj, easing off in fourth place, ran 54.71, but while they took medals in the final they were beaten by the 18 year-old World Junior Cross-country champion Kipchoge.

Bekele led the final at a quick pace through the first three kilometres in 2:31.94, 5:07.27 (2:35.33) and 7:45.44 (2:38.17). At that point Kipchoge moved ahead and the pace slowed to 2:43.02 (10:28.46) to 4k with eight men still in contention. El Guerrouj made a long run for home from 800m out. The 11th lap took 60.19 and at the bell (11:59.27) he was just ahead of Kipchoge, Bekele, Kibowen and Chebii and sped through the next 200m in 26.77, 4m ahead of Kipchoge with Bekele another 2m back, and still led into the finishing straight. A titanic struggle climaxed with Kipchoge getting the better of a dip finish, with Bekele only a stride behind. The time of 12:52.79, was the fastest in any global championship, with a final kilometre of 2:24.33. Kipchoge's last 200 was timed at 26.3, 400 at 53.4, 800 at 1:52.9 and 1600 at 4:02.5.

1. Eliud Kipchoge KEN-J	12:52.79*
2. Hicham El Guerrouj MAR	12:52.83
3. Kenenisa Bekele ETH	12:53.12
4. John Kibowen KEN	12:54.07
5. Abrahim Chebii KEN	12:57.74
6. Gebre Gebremariam ETH-J	12:58.08
7. Richard Limo KEN	13:01.13
8. Zersenay Tadesse ERI	13:05.57
9. Juan Carlos de la Ossa ESP	13:21.04
10. Abderrahim Goumri MAR	13:23.67
11. Abiyote Abate ETH	13:23.81
12. Alejandro Suárez MEX	13:24.51
13. Christian Belz SUI	13:26.02
14. Moukheld Al-Outaibi KSA	13:38.92
15. Jorge Torres USA	13:43.37

10,000 Metres (24th)

IN THIS astonishing race Bekele ran the second 5000m in 12:57.24, a time only bettered for that distance in the last decade. There was a fairly sedate start, with the first four kilometres of 2:52.01, 2:44.75 (Meb Keflezighi), 2:47.96 (Salim Kipsang 8:24.72) and 2:46.05. At that point Gebrselassie, bidding for a fifth world title, went ahead to speed it up and halfway, with Bekele just ahead of team-mates Gebrselassie and Sihine, was reached in 13:52.33 (2:41.56). From then the Ethiopians, led by Gebrselassie, pushed on at a relentless pace. Bekele shared the pacemaking duties while 20 year-old Sihine was always third. The sixth kilometre took just 2:34.52, but defending champion Kamathi, Korir and Hassan remained in contact. Kamathi was there longer than the others but paid the price, eventually finishing seventh nearly a minute behind the winner.

The seventh and eighth kilometres were faster still at 2:38.29 and 2:37.44 and nothing like this had ever been seen before in a 10,000m race. Geb kept the pace boiling with a penultimate km of 2:37.98. Sihine dropped back before the bell (Geb 25:54.54), and as in Hengelo in June it was 21 year-old Bekele who had the stronger kick. He exploded past the master 150m out to complete the last 200 in 26.1, 400 in 55.0, 800 in 1:56.6, 1000 in 2:29.01, 1200 in 2:59.4 and 1600m in 4:02.8! Gebrselassie was a magnificent second with the fifth sub-27 of his career and his fastest ever championship time, with splits of 13:52.4 and 12:58.8. Hassan, he former Kenyan Chepkurui set an Asian record in fourth place ahead of three Kenyans and the first non-African born finishers were 8th and 9th.

1. Kenenisa Bekele ETH	26:49.57*
2. Haile Gebrselassie ETH	26:50.77
3. Sileshi Sihine ETH	27:01.44
4. Abdullah Ahmad Hassan QAT	27:18.28
5. John Cheruiyot Korir KEN	27:19.94
6. Wilberforce Talel KEN	27:33.60
7. Charles Kamathi KEN	27:45.05
8. Kamiel Maase NED	27:45.46
9. Karl Keska GBR	27:47.89
10. Ismaïl Sghyr FRA	27:54.87
11. David Galván MEX	27:55.31
12. John Yuda TAN	27:56.21
13. Fabian Joseph TAN-J	28:06.36
14. Alan Culpepper USA	28:14.92
15. Teodoro Vega MEX	28:31.71

Marathon (30th)

IN COOL and wet conditions, there was a cautious start as 47 of the 89 starters were still together in the lead pack at 20km. Halfway was reached in 64:45 and 30km in 1:32:32, but defending champion and favourite Gezahegne Abera dropped out in the 28th kilometre with an Achilles tendon problem. Gharib, Rotich and Rey broke clear in the 32nd kilometre and the 5k to 35k was covered in 14:44 by Gharib and Rotich, 14:45 by Rey. Rotich was dropped before 37k and Baldini moved into third just before 40k, at which point he was 37 sec behind Gharib and Rey (2:02:05), who had covered that 5k in 14:49. Gharib, in just his second marathon, pulled away on the track at the finish for a 7 sec win. Japan won the World Marathon Cup, in which up to five runners can compete and placings are determined by the aggregate of the top three times.

1. Jaoaud Gharib MAR	2:08:31*
2. Julio Rey ESP	2:08:38
3. Stefano Baldini ITA	2:09:14
4. Alberto Chaiça POR	2:09:25
5. Shigeru Aburaya JPN	2:09:26
6. Daniele Caimmi ITA	2:09:29
7. Ian Syster RSA	2:10:17
8. Michael Rotich KEN	2:10:35
9. Hendrick Ramaala RSA	2:10:37
10. Atsushi Sato JPN	2:10:38
11. Lee Bong-ju KOR	2:10:38
12. Tsuyoshi Ogata JPN	2:10:39
13. Rachid El Ghanmouni MAR	2:10:56
14. Viktor Röthlin SUI	2:11:14
15. Samson Ramadhani TAN	2:11:21

World Cup: 1. JPN 6:30:43, 2. ITA 6:32:19, 3. RSA 6:35:54, 4. MAR 6:36:01, 5. ESP 6:38:43, 6. ETH 6:44:44, 7. AUS 6:44:54, 8. KOR 6:47:45, 9. FRA 6:48:10, 10. USA 6:50:37, 11. COL 7:01:29, 12. QAT 7:04:44

3000 Metres Steeplechase (h 23rd, F 26th)

AN ENTHRALLING and bizarre race was won by the former Kenyan from the current Kenyan top man. Accompanied for a while by fellow Qatari, Abdullah, Shaheen started at a terrific pace, c. 59 sec for the first lap and 2:36.24 at 1km. He realised that he could not keep up this pace and slowed to 2:43.34 for the second kilo, enabling Kemboi to close up astonishingly quickly to within 5m. Kemboi went ahead at the next water jump and then both slowed so drastically, taking turns to lead, that by the bell the three top Europeans were almost with them. The two main contenders had, however, harnessed their strength, and opened up 30m or so during a phenomenal last lap (water jump inside track) of 57.5. Kemboi launched his sprint along the back straight, but Shaheen was ahead with 200 to go. They took the last barrier together, Kemboi edging ahead momentarily before Shaheen summoned one last burst of speed for victory. Shaheen's brother, Abraham Cherono, came fifth, but the usual Kenyan triumph was marred by Michael Kipyego falling at the final water jump in his heat and defending champion Reuben Kosgei failing to finish in the final.

1. Saif Saaeed Shaheen QAT	8:04.39
2. Ezekiel Kemboi KEN	8:05.11
3. Eliseo Martín ESP	8:09.09
4. Bouabdallah Tahri FRA	8:10.65
5. Abraham Cherono KEN	8:13.37
6. Luis Miguel Martín ESP	8:13.52
7. Simon Vroemen NED	8:13.71
8. José Luis Blanco ESP	8:17.16
9. Jukka Keskisalo FIN	8:17.72
10. Ali Ezzine MAR	8:19.15
11. Yoshitaka Iwamizu JPN	8:19.29
12. Khamis S Abdullah QAT	8:28.37
13. Abdelkader Hachlaf MAR	8:35.17
dnf. Reuben Kosgei KEN	–
dns. Luleseged Wale ETH	–

110 Metres Hurdles (h 28th, sf 29th, F 30th) (0.3)

JOHNSON WON a fourth world title by a comfortable 0.08 margin with a delighted Liu Xiang (the first Chinese man to win a running medal) splitting the American four. Phillips was fastest in the heats with a pb of 13.26 and in the semis the fastest time was Johnson's casual 13.19 from Trammell 13.34. One of the favourites, Stanislav Olijar pulled up injured before the third hurdle in his heat.

1. Allen Johnson USA	13.12
2. Terrence Trammell USA	13.20
3. Liu Xiang CHN	13.23
4. Larry Wade USA	13.34
5. Chris Phillips USA	13.36
6. Márcio de Souza BRA	13.48
7. Shi Dongpeng CHN-J	13.55
8. Yoel Hernández CUB	13.57

400 Metres Hurdles (h 26th, sf 27th, F 29th)

THE DAY before his 26th birthday, Sánchez successfully defended his title and maintained his two-year unbeaten run in a brilliant 47.25, a tenth inside his Central American record, the 11th quickest time in history and the world's best for five years. Woody ran his best time of the season for the silver, half a metre ahead of Iakovákis, who had lowered the Greek record to 48.17 to win his semi – Sánchez won the other in 48.16. Just out of the medals in his first season as a 400m hurdles specialist was 31 year-old McFarlane who improved to 48.35 in his semi and 48.30 in the final. Herbert, a renowned strong finisher who was seemingly heading for second place, was unlucky to fall at the final hurdle.

1. Felix Sánchez DOM	47.25
2. Joey Woody USA	48.18
3. Periklís Iakovákis GRE	48.24
4. Danny McFarlane JAM	48.30
5. Kemel Thompson JAM	48.51
6. Chris Rawlinson GBR	48.90
7. Mubarak Al-Nubi QAT	52.64
8. Llewellyn Herbert RSA	72.10

High Jump (Q 23rd, F 25th)

FREITAG BECAME one of the select new breed of champions who have won World Youth (1999),

World Junior (2000) and World Senior titles. Critically he cleared 2.32 first time, Holm at the second try and Boswell (nursing an ankle injury) at the third, and Freitag alone made 2.35, at the second attempt. Eight men cleared the automatic qualifying height of 2.29, and five more advancing from first-time clearances of 2.27; Gennadiy Moroz and and Andrey Chubsa set the highest ever non-qualifying mark at 2.27.

1. Jacques Freitag RSA	2.35
2. Stefan Holm SWE	2.32
3. Mark Boswell CAN	2.32
4. Mikhayil Tsvetkov RUS	2.29
5. Germaine Mason JAM	2.29
6. Grzegorz Sposób POL	2.29
7. James Nieto USA	2.29
8. Andrey Sokolovskiy UKR	2.29
9. Yaroslav Rybakov RUS	2.25
10. Aleksander Walerianczyk POL	2.25
11. Jaroslav Baba CZE-J	2.25
12. Matt Hemingway USA	2.25
13. Roman Fricke GER	2.20

Pole Vault (Q 26th, F28th)

IN ANTICIPATION this event was wide open, and one of the least supported candidates won as Gibilisco improved his Italian record twice with first-time clearances at 5.85 and 5.90, having had a fright when he failed twice at 5.75 only to clear 5.80 with a stiffer pole on his one chance at the height. Brits cleared by 5.85 a massive margin on the second attempt and both Kristiansson (equalling his pb) and Markov on the third, while Lobinger failed. Gibilisco was one of nine men to qualify at 5.70 with two more going through from 5.60 jumps. Alex Averbukh no heighted at 5.60 and world leader Mesnil entered and departed at a ridiculous 5.70.

1. Giuseppe Gibilisco ITA	5.90
2. Okkert Brits RSA	5.85
3. Patrik Kristiansson SWE	5.85
4. Dmitriy Markov AUS	5.85
5. Tim Lobinger GER	5.80
6= Tim Mack USA	5.70
6= Derek Miles USA	5.70
6= Denys Yurchenko UKR	5.70
9= Adam Kolasa POL	5.70
9= Vadim Strogalev RUS	5.70
11. Viktor Chistiakov AUS	5.60
dns Daichi Sawano JPN	

Long Jump (Q 27th, F29th)

WORLD INDOOR champion Phillips held the lead after the first round with 8.09, lost it to Gaisah (8.13) in round two, and regained it in round three with 8.22 after Beckford had briefly gone ahead with 8.16. Lamela jumped 8.16 in the fourth round, but the top action came in the fifth. Lamela seized the lead with 8.22 (8.33 from take off); then Beckford came up with his longest jump for two years with 8.28... only for Phillips to top that with 8.32. It was an exciting contest but, in cool and rainy weather, the winning mark was the shortest in World Champs history. In qualifying just two men exceeded the automatic standard of 8.15: Lamela 8.19 and Tomlinson 8.16, as 7.97 proved enough to advance, but Iván Pedroso pulled out injured after one no-jump and world leader (at 8.46) Stringfellow was 19th with 7.83.

1. Dwight Phillips USA	8.32/0.5
2. James Beckford JAM	8.28/0.1
3. Yago Lamela ESP	8.22/0.5
4. Ignisious Gaisah GHA	8.13/0.0
5. Hussein Al-Sabee KSA	8.10/0.0
6. Vladimir Zyuskov UKR	8.08/-0.2
7. Walter Davis USA	8.02/0.4
8. Osbourne Moxey BAH	7.93/0.5
9. Chris Tomlinson GBR	7.93/0.6
10. Bogdan Tarus ROM	7.84/0.4
11. Luis Felipe Méliz CUB	7.73/0.8
12. Loúis Tsátoumas GRE	7.72/0.1

Triple Jump (Q 23rd, F 25th)

IN THE qualifying round, the 16.95 standard was achieved by five men and 16.71 was 12th. Olsson led with 17.56, the brilliant junior Giralt improved his best to 17.31 and Edwards, just recovered from his horrendous looking injury at Crystal Palace, advanced at 16.94 with 11.2cm to spare on the board. Three men who had exceeded 17.50 in 2003 went out: Walter Davis (15th 16.60), Dmitriy Valyukevich (16th 16.59) and Marian Oprea (17th 16.55). In the final Olsson's first five jumps were better than anybody else: 17.72, 17.52, 17,50, 17.52 and 17.34. Betanzos jumped 17.28 in the first round and Sands 17.26 in the third, although Giralt came close to a medal with his last round 17.23. Edwards collapsed going into the jump phase on his first attempt and his second (16.31) was a very tentative effort. Deciding he wasn't sufficiently fired up to challenge for a medal, he passed up his third attempt, an anti-climactic end to a great career.

1. Christian Olsson SWE	17.72/-0.3
2. Yoandri Betanzos CUB	17.28/0.2
3. Leevan Sands BAH	17.26/-0.4
4. David Giralt CUB-J	17.23/0.1
5. Jadel Gregório BRA	17.11/0.2
6. Kenta Bell USA	17.08/0.0
7. Hristos Melétoglou GRE	16.92/1.2
8. Andrew Owusu GHA	16.86/0.0
9. Yoelbi Quesada CUB	16.84/-0.1
10. Ivaylo Rusenov BUL	16.66/0.1
11. Aleksandr Glavatskiy BLR	16.40/-0.3
12. Jonathan Edwards GBR	16.31/0.3

Shot (Q & F 23rd)

MIKHNEVICH, WHO failed a drugs test after placing tenth in Edmonton and only completed a two year ban on 4 August, opened with 21.24 before effectively ending the contest with a second round 21.69. Nobody came close, or even matched his other three valid throws (21.36, 21.45 and 21.44. In the third round Belonog (21.10) overtook Toth's

20.89 opener (his only valid put), while in the fourth Nelson moved from eighth to second with 21.26, the only spinner to win a medal. Godina missed the cut when his third round effort of well over 20m was called a foul, a ruling with which he strongly disagreed. Just four men, led by Godina 21.08, made the 20.45 automatic qualifying standard, and top men eliminated included Manuel Martínez (15th 19.78) and Carl Myerscough (19th 19.91). Milan Haborák achieved the longest ever non-qualifying mark at 19.95.

1. Andrey Mikhenevich BLR	21.69
2. Adam Nelson USA	21.26
3. Yuriy Belonog UKR	21.10
4. Kevin Toth USA	20.89
5. Justin Anlezark AUS	20.61
6. Ralf Bartels GER 19.41	20.50
7. Tepa Reinikainen FIN	20.45
8. Ville Tiisanoja FIN	20.09
9. John Godina USA	19.84
10. Roman Virastyuk UKR	19.61
11. Brad Snyder CAN	19.38
dns. Joachim Olsen DEN	

Discus (Q 24th, F 26th)

ALEKNA'S 68.29 was the best ever qualifying mark at World Champs and he opened the final with the gold medal throw of 69.69. Fazekas started with 66.86 and 69.01, but that was as close as he was to get. Kaptyukh's first throw of 66.51 took the bronze although Riedel – in his seventh final and seeking a sixth world title in one event to tie Bubka's record – ran him close with two marks of 66.28. Five men made the automatic qualifying standard of 64.50 and 62.46 made the final.

1. Virgilijus Alekna LTU	69.69
2. Róbert Fazekas HUN	69.01
3. Vasiliy Kaptyukh BLR	66.51
4. Lars Riedel GER	66.28
5. Michael Möllenbeck GER	66.23
6. Frantz Kruger RSA	65.26
7. Aleksander Tammert EST	64.50
8. Mario Pestano ESP	64.39
9. Carl Brown USA	62.66
10. Dmitriy Shevchenko RUS	62.28
11. Jason Tunks CAN	62.21
12. Leonid Cherevko BLR	61.90

Hammer (Q 23rd, F 25th)

FROM A circle that was criticised by some as being too slow, Tikhon took the lead with 80.89 in round 2, and improved to 81.77 in the third and 83.05 with the final throw of the contest. Annus and Murofushi had a prolonged battle for second. Murofushi, hampered by an elbow injury after falling in training, started with 79.87 and extended to 79.99 and 80.12, but Annus, after 79.22 in round 3, completed his series with 80.36. Astapkovich, now 40, had the longest qualifying throw of 79.66 (76.56 was enough to qualify) but failed to register a valid mark in the final.

1. Ivan Tikhon BLR	83.05
2. Adrián Annus HUN	80.36
3. Koji Murofushi JPN	80.12
4. Andriy Skvaruk UKR	79.68
5. Primoz Kozmus SLO	79.68
6. Ilya Konovalov RUS	78.55
7. Vadim Devyatovskiy BLR	78.13
8. Alexandros Papadimitríou GRE	77.79
9. Miloslav Konopka SVK	75.86
10. Stuart Rendell AUS	75.72
11. Nicolas Figère FRA	74.06
nt. Igor Astapkovich BLR	-

Javelin (Q 29th, F 31st)

THIS WAS a disappointing contest, with the opening throws by the three medallists not being bettered. Zelezny had his best throw in round 4, and Backley failed to make the cut after three rounds for the first time in 15 finals at World/Olympic/European level. Henry (83.43) led five men over the automatic qualifying standard of 81.00 and 78.48 was enough to make the final.

1. Sergey Makarov RUS	85.44
2. Andrus Värnik EST	85.17
3. Boris Henry GER	84.74
4. Jan Zelezny CZE	84.09
5. Aki Parviainen FIN	83.05
6. Christian Nicolay GER	81.77
7. Miroslav Guzdek CZE	81.40
8. Peter Blank GER	80.34
9. Steve Backley GBR	80.13
10. Li Rongxiang CHN	78.24
11. Andreas Thorkildsen NOR	77.75
12. Aleksandr Ivanov RUS	77.32

Decathlon (26-27th)

PAPPAS HAD only one disappointing event (only 2.09 in the high jump) as he added outdoor gold to follow his indoor heptathlon triumph. Sebrle move up steadily after a slow start and they were well clear of the rest, although Karpov improved his national record from 8253 to 8374 and led at the end of the first day with 4599 from Pappas 4546 and Sebrle 4423. Terek, placed 12th with 7503, scored only for nine events as he was disqualified from the hurdles for deliberately knocking down all ten barriers; his time of 15.85 for that would have given him 8253 points. An appeal, citing an injury and consequent lack of mobility, was rejected. Jon Arnar Magnússon achieved the unenviable record of failing to finish for the fifth Championships and Erki Nool was another of the eight non-finishers.

1. Tom Pappas USA	8750
2. Román Sebrle CZE	8634
3. Dmitriy Karpov KAZ	8374
4. Tomás Dvorák CZE	8242
5. Laurent Hernu FRA	8218
6. Lev Lobodin RUS	8198
7. Qi Haifeng CHN	8126
8. André Niklaus GER	8020

9. Claston Bernard JAM	8000
10. Vitaliy Smirnov UZB	7897
11. Chiel Warners NED	7753
12. Paul Terek USA	7503

20 Kilometres Walk (23rd)

PÉREZ, WHO in 1996 became at 22 the youngest ever Olympic walking champion, opened the World Champs with a fabulous performance. Not only did he enhance his already iconic status in his native land by becoming Ecuador's first world athletics champion but by winning in a world's best time he netted $160,000 for the richest prize ever won by a walker.

Fernández was 6 sec up on Pérez and Andreyev at 5k in 19:29, 32 sec clear of Pérez at halfway in 38:38 and 50 sec up at 12k. However, Pérez pulled away from the pack and covered the third 5k in 19:09 to halve the gap to 16 sec by 15k (58:03-58:19) with Rasskazov third in 58:34. He overtook Fernández in the 17th kilometre and covered the final 5k in 19:02 (last 10k 38:11) to win by 39 sec in 1:17:21, one second inside the Spaniard's world best. In the cool, overcast conditions that morning six of the top ten finishers registered pbs and times for third and fourth were the fastest ever for those positions. Nine of 38 starters were disqualified.

1. Jefferson Pérez ECU	1:17:21*
2. Francisco Fernández ESP	1:18:00
3. Roman Rasskazov RUS	1:18:07
4. Noe Hernández MEX	1:18:14
5. Luke Adams AUS	1:19:35
6. Ivan Trotskiy BLR	1:19:40
7. David Márquez ESP	1:19:46
8. Ilya Markov RUS	1:20:14
9. José David Domínguez ESP	1:20:15
10. Alejandro López MEX	1:20:24
11. Lorenzo Civallero ITA	1:20:34
12. Yevgeniy Misyulya BLR	1:20:38
13. André Hohne GER	1:20:44
14. Hatem Ghoula TUN	1:21:12
15. Yu Chaohong CHN	1:21:18

50 Kilometres Walk (27th)

KORZENIOWSKI ADDED to the performances that have made him the greatest-ever race walker with his finest performance yet in a race that had an unprecedented five men inside 3:40. Voyevodin set a time bettered only three times in history, but failed to gain a medal. At halfway Korzeniowski led in 1:50:14 from Erm 1:50:20, Skurygin & Voyevodin 1:50:44 and Nizhegorodov 1:50:45, before covering the second half in a staggering 1:45:49. Skurygin, stripped of the gold medal at the 1999 World Champs and banned for two years, overtook Erm approaching 40k and closed to within 6 sec of Korzeniowski at 45k, but the master had something in reserve and stretched his lead to 39 sec by the finish. His 3:36:03 took 36 sec off the world best he set when winning the 2002 European title and he thus earned $160,000 like Pérez. Skurygin became second fastest of all time, Erm fifth, Voyevodin sixth and Nizhegorodov eighth. 20 of the 39 starters failed to finish with 15 disqualifications including all three Chinese.

1. Robert Korzeniowski POL	3:36:03* WR
2. German Skurygin RUS	3:36:42
3. Andreas Erm GER	3:37:46
4. Aleksey Voyevodin RUS	3:38:01
5. Denis Nizhegorodov RUS	3:38:23
6. Jesús Angel García ESP	3:43:56
7. Roman Magdziarczyk POL	3:44:53
8. Trond Nymark NOR	3:46:14
9. Sergey Korepanov KAZ	3:47:42
10. Denis Langlois FRA	3:49:05
11. Eddy Riva FRA	3:53:18
12. Germán Sánchez MEX	3:53:24
13. Peter Korcok SVK	3:54:12
14. Mikel Odriozola ESP	3:56:27
15. Fredrik Svensson SWE	3:56:31

4 x 100 Metres (h & sf 30th, F 31st)

THE USA ran 38.28 and 37.99 in the preliminary rounds and the British 38.24 and 28.26. The Americans had lost Greene, Montgomery and Drummond from their squad, and the final looked a golden opportunity for the British. Malcolm, Campbell (in his tenth race of the Worlds) and Devonish (and a poor exchange by the Americans between Williams and Patton), meant that Chambers took the baton a metre up on J J Johnson with Brazil also in close proximity. But Chambers was perhaps too tense (as in the 100m) and Johnson closed all the way and outdipped him. The time was the slowest of any of the USA's seven winning teams in these championships.

1. USA	38.06	(Capel, Williams, Patton, J J Johnson)	
2. GBR	38.08	(Malcolm, Campbell, Devonish, Chambers)	
3. BRA	38.26	(Lima, Ribeiro, A da Silva, Souza)	
4. NED	38.87	5. NGR	38.89
6. POL	38.96	7. JPN	39.05
dnf. JAM	–		

4 x 400 Metres (h 30th, F 31st)

AN INSPIRED French team, for whom Marc Raquil ran the anchor leg in 44.15, almost caught the USA (splits of 45.2, 44.6, 44.75 and 44.31). Avard Moncur ran a splendid 44.6 for the Bahamas on the first leg before Tyree Washington took the USA into a lead that was never lost on the second leg. Davian Clarke of Jamaica ran the fastest split with 44.04 on the third leg for Jamaica. Hurdles champion Félix Sánchez had run a 44.07 final leg for the Dominican Republic in the heats but his team was disqualified.

1. USA 2:58.88 (C Harrison, Washington, Brew, Young)
(gold from running in heats: Potter, Steele)
2. FRA 2:58.96 (Djhone, Keita, Diagana, Raquill) (heat: Douhou)

3. JAM	2:59.60	(Simpson, McFarlane, Clarke, Blackwood (Heats: Campbell, Spence, Clarke)
4. BAH	3:00.53	5. GBR 3:01.00
6. ESP	3:02.50	7. GRE 3:02.56
8. JPN	3:03.15	

Women

100 Metres (h, qf 23rd; sf, F 24th) (0.9)

DESPITE A poor start, White ran her quickest ever wind-free time of 10.85 to win by nearly a metre, but her subsequent positive test for Modafinil left her gold medal in doubt. Edwards improved her best from 11.05 to 10.93 after a brilliant start that meant that she led for the first half and Block was delighted to snatch bronze in a season's best of 10.99. Devers was contesting her eighth World final at 100m or 100mh. Sturrup was fastest in the first round with 11.08 and there were sub-11 second times from White 10.96 and Sturrup 10.98 in the quarters and from White 10.96 in the semis. Merlene Ottey at the age of 43 clocked 11.26 in heat and semi.

1. Kelli White USA	10.85
2. Torri Edwards USA	10.93
3. Zhanna Block UKR	10.99
4. Chandra Sturrup BAH	11.02
5. Ekateríni Thánou GRE	11.03
6. Christine Arron FRA	11.06
7. Aleen Bailey JAM	11.07
8. Gail Devers USA	11.11

200 Metres (h & qf 26th, sf 27th, F 28th) (-0.3)

WHITE COMPLETED the sprint double to emulate Gladisch (1987) and Krabbe (1991), although she could lose her medals later. She ran a very swift bend to build up a commanding lead and won by over three metres in 22.05, the world's fastest of 2003 and a personal best. Edwards looked set for a second silver medal when a clear second at 150m but as fatigue set in she began to overstride and was passed by Kapachinskaya, who moved from fourth to second in the closing stages. Hurtis had run the fastest time in the first round (22.51) and semis (22.41), and Kapachinskaya had lowered her pb to 22.43 in her semi.

1. Kelli White USA	22.05
2. Anastasiya Kapachinskaya RUS	22.38
3. Torri Edwards USA	22.47
4. Muriel Hurtis FRA	22.59
5. Zhanna Block UKR	22.92
6. Beverley McDonald JAM	22.95
7. Natalya Safronnikova BLR	22.98
8. Anzhela Kravchenko UKR	23.00

400 Metres (h 24th, sf 25th, F 27th)

GUEVARA'S Central American record of 48.89 was the world's quickest since the 1996 Olympics to rank eighth on the world all-time list. She and defending champion Thiam were up at 200m (23.2-23.3), with Guevara 2m clear of Fenton at 300 (35.7-35.9, with Thiam 36.0, Nazarova 36.3, Williams 36.4, Zykina 36.6, Pospelova 36.7, McConnell 37.0) and then doubling that advantage in the finishing straight. Fenton ran her season's best of 49.43 for a silver medal to add to those at the 2000 Olympics and 2001 Worlds, while Thiam broke 50 for the first time in two years, just holding off Nazarova for the bronze. Thiam (50.86) was fastest in the first round and Williams (50.43) in the semis.

1. Ana Guevara MEX	48.89
2. Lorraine Fenton JAM	49.43
3. Amy Mbacké Thiam SEN	49.95
4. Natalya Nazarova RUS	49.98
5. Tonique Williams BAH	50.38
6. Olesya Zykina RUS	50.59
7. Lee McConnell GBR	51.07
8. Svetlana Pospelova RUS	51.30

800 Metres (h 23rd, sf 24th, F 26th)

MUTOLA, THE clear favourite, ran the fastest time in the first round (2:00.81) and semis (1:58.45 from her training companion Holmes 1:58.86), and won her third world outdoor title comfortably by controlling the race from the front. She passed 200m in 28.16 before slowing to 61.20 at 400m and 1:32.32 at 600m, when Holmes shot into the lead but was passed by Mutola, who ran the last 200m in 27.57, in the straight. Khrushchelyova tried unavailingly to creep by on the inside. It was the slowest winning time at global level since the 1968 Olympics. Jolanda Ceplak did not contest the event, Jearl Miles Clark was a surprise elimination in the heats (4th 2:04.21) and Graf had an unfortunate accident when, the night after winning her semi in 1:59.26, she apparently cut her foot on a broken bottle.

1. Maria Mutola MOZ	1:59.89
2. Kelly Holmes GBR	2:00.18
3. Natalya Khrushchelyova RUS	2:00.29
4. Amina Aït Hammou MAR	2:01.09
5. Claudia Gesell GER	2:01.84
6. Diane Cummins CAN	2:02.48
7. Akosua Serwaa GHA	2:03.24
dns. Stephanie Graf AUT	

1500 Metres (h 27th, sf 29th, F 31st)

THE CLEAR favourite Ayhan used her usual tactics, zipping through 400 in 60.50 but slowing to 2:06.76 at 800m with Zadorozhnaya and Rozenberg close behind. She passed the bell in 2:56.58 and 1200m in 3:12.61 (65.85), opening up along the back straight so that she was some 6m ahead entering the home straight. But then there was a stunning upset as Tomashova flew past, running the last 200 in 29.7 to Ayhan's 31.3, for a lifetime and Championship best time. In third place, thanks to a 30.9 final 200 was Tullett whose 3:59.95 was a Welsh record. Six women broke 4:10 in the heats and 19 in the semis, with Cioncan fastest at 4:03.40 and many top names went out including Regina Jacobs, Natalia Rodríguez, Alesya Turova, Kutre Dulecha and Irina Lishchinskaya.

1. Tatyana Tomashova RUS	3:58.52*
2. Süreyya Ayhan TUR	3:59.04
3. Hayley Tullett GBR	3:59.95
4. Yekaterina Rozenberg RUS	4:00.59
5. Jackline Maranga KEN	4:01.64
6. Naomi Mugo KEN	4:02.33
7. Daniela Yordanova BUL	4:02.34
8. Yelena Zadorozhnaya RUS	4:02.46
9. Maria Cioncan ROM	4:02.80
10. Joanne Pavey GBR	4:03.03
11. Nelya Neporadna UKR-J	4:04.44
12. Jolanda Ceplak SLO	4:14.18

5000 Metres (h 26th, F 30th)

EIGHTEEN WOMEN ran faster than the previous quickest ever heat time of 15:07.01. The first heat was particularly remarkable with Masai winning in 14:45.35, with four others inside 15 min, and Abeylegesse won the second in a pb of 14:54.95. Szabo only got through as a fastest loser in 14:56.70 and Jane Wanjiku found a pb of 15:04.00 made her the fastest non-qualifier in history, while controversial titleholder Olga Yegorova was 10th in 15:12.41. Tired legs surely affected many finalists and only those placed 4-7 bettered their heat times. Without a willing pacemaker, the race was very slow to 1000m 3:04.25 and 2000m 6:09.88 before Ochichi increased the tempo a little to 3000m 9:08.88 and 4000m 12:06.45. Zadorozhnaya, in her fourth race in four days and due to run the 1500 final next day, went ahead on the penultimate lap to the bell (13:50.01), and Domínguez ran the next 200m in 31.47. She led into the straight ahead of Zadorozhnaya and Masai, but Dibaba produced an inspired finish to pass Domínguez on the outside while Masai tried to creep past on the inside. Dibaba, who became at 18 years 36 days the youngest ever world champion in any individual event, completed her final 200 in 29.7. The final kilometre took 2:45.27.

1. Tirunesh Dibaba ETH-J	14:51.72
2. Marta Domínguez ESP	14:52.26
3. Edith Masai KEN	14:52.30
4. Yelena Zadorozhnaya RUS	14:52.36
5. Elvan Abeylegesse TUR	14:53.56
6. Isabella Ochichi KEN	14:54.08
7. Gulnara Samitova RUS	14:54.38
8. Courtney Babcock CAN	14:54.98
9. Sun Yingjie CHN	14:57.01
10. Berhane Adere ETH	14:58.07
11. Gabriela Szabo ROM	14:59.36
12. Émilie Mondor CAN	15:02.36
13. Zahra Ouaziz MAR	15:16.73
14. Zhor El Kamch MAR	15:29.72
15. Sonia O'Sullivan IRL	15:36.62

10,000 Metres (23rd)

THIS WAS the greatest race in women's 10,000m history. Adere won in an African record and the third fastest time ever, and there were the fastest ever times for places 2-16. Sun and Kiplagat set a tremendous pace for most of the race with kilometre splits of 2:59.62, 6:03.41, 8:59.93, 12:00.16, 15:06.53 and 18:07.25. Adere briefly showed ahead at 7000m (21:08.18) but the pace for the next two kilometres dipped at 3:02.84 and 3:03.04 as the contenders – now down to four – gathered themselves for the final assault. Sun was first to strike, going hard with 700m to run. A penultimate lap of 68.55 took her to the bell in 29:01.03, the other three all within a stride or two. The big kicker proved to be Adere, who raced ahead with about 230m to go and ran a final kilometre of 2:50.12 (29.9 last 200m). Her 5k splits were 15:06.6 and 14:57.6. Kidane just pipped Sun for silver, leaving Kiplagat as the sixth fastest of all time, taking over a minute off her best. Zhilyayeva ran a Russian record, Johnson an Oceanian record, and Xing a world junior record of 30:31.55. 26 runners started and Fernanda Ribeiro and Derartu Tulu did not finish.

1. Berhane Adere ETH	30:04.18*
2. Werknesh Kidane ETH	30:07.15
3. Sun Yingjie CHN	30:07.20
4. Lornah Kiplagat NED	30:12.53
5. Alla Zhilyayeva RUS	30:23.07
6. Galina Bogomolova RUS	30:26.20
7. Xing Huina CHN-J	30:31.55
8. Benita Johnson AUS	30:37.68
9. Ejigayehu Dibaba ETH	31:01.07
10. Jelena Prokopcuka LAT	31:06.14
11. Kayoko Fukushi JPN	31:10.57
12. Deena Drossin USA	31:17.86
13. Mihaela Botezan ROM	31:28.72
14. Yoko Shibui JPN	31:42.01
15. Megumi Tanaka JPN	31:47.00

Marathon (31st)

IN IDEAL conditions 14 runners broke 2:30, a record for the World Champs. Tomescu, who eventually dropped out, possibly costing Romania a set of medals in the World Cup, tried similar tactics to previous championships and was 32 sec ahead at 5k but her lead had shrunk to 12 sec by 10k and she was swallowed up by the pack after 15k. A group of 18 passed halfway in 72:46/72:47 and the crucial move came at around 33k when Ndereba started to exert pressure. She covered the 5k to 35k in 16:46, opening up 4 sec over Noguchi and flew through the next 5k in 15:58 to lead by 20 sec at 40k and win by 19 sec with a second half of 71:08. Japan with 2-3-4 had an overwhelming fourth successive Cup victory. 62 of the 69 starters finished.

1. Catherine Ndereba KEN	2:23:55*
2. Mizuki Noguchi JPN	2:24:14
3. Masako Chiba JPN	2:25:09
4. Naoko Sakamoto JPN	2:25:25
5. Ham Bong-sil PRK	2:25:31

6. Elfenesh Alemu ETH	2:26:29
7. Joyce Chepchumba KEN	2:26:33
8. Olivera Jevtic SCG	2:26:49
9. Svetlana Zakharova RUS	2:26:53
10. Shitaye Gemechu ETH	2:27:26
11. Nuta Olaru ROM	2:28:24
12. Zhang Shujing CHN	2:29:24
13. Beatriz Ros ESP	2:29:25
14. Li Helan CHN	2:29:46
15. Maria Abel ESP	2:30:15

World Cup: 1, JPN 7:14:48; 2, ETH 7:24:56; 3, RUS 7:31:04, 4, PRK 7:31:51; 5, ESP 7:34:17; 6, CHN 7:36:20; 7, ROM 7:38:17; 8, FRA 7:48:17; 9, ITA 7:55:26; 10, USA 7:58:30.

100 Metres Hurdles (h 25th, sf 26th, F 27th) (-0.2)

GAIL DEVERS was in the lead in her semi when she hit the fifth hurdle; she recovered her balance astonishingly quickly to finish in 12.87, but that wasn't quite fast enough to advance to the final. Foster, fastest in heats (12.67) and semis (12.65) was then the obvious favourite but in the final Felicien, the youngest in the field at 22, who had set a pb of 12.68 to win her semi, capitalised on a fast start and improved again to 12.53 as Foster's desperate lunge at the finish fell 0.04 short. There were nine finalists as Girard and Dixon dead-heated for second place in their semi.

1. Perditia Felicien CAN	12.53
2. Brigitte Foster JAM	12.57
3. Miesha McKelvy USA	12.67
4. Glory Alozie ESP	12.75
5. Aurelia Trywianska POL	12.75
6. Jenny Adams USA	12.77
7. Patricia Girard FRA	12.83
8. Lacena Golding-Clarke JAM	12.87
9. Vonette Dixon JAM	12.87

400 Metres Hurdles (h 24th, sf 25th, F 28th)

PECHONKINA HAD set a stunning world record of 52.34 on 8 August and was fastest in the prelims, winning heat in 54.01 and semi in 53.57 by big margins. In the other semi Pittman was close to her best with 53.77 just ahead of Glover. In the final Pechonkina set out looking for the big bonus for setting a world record but faltered at the eighth hurdle and although still 5m up at the ninth and just at the tenth had run out of steam and was left standing on the run-in by Pittman and eventually pipped also by Glover, who at 34 clocked the second quickest time and first medal of her long career. Pittman, still only 20, reduced her best to 53.22, just 0.05 outside the Australian record Debbie Flintoff-King to win the 1988 Olympic gold.

1. Jana Pittman AUS	53.22
2. Sandra Glover USA	53.65
3. Yuliya Pechonkina RUS	53.71
4. Ionela Tîrlea ROM	54.41
5. Tatyana Tereshchuk UKR	54.61
6. Andrea Blackett BAR	54.79
7. Heike Meissner GER	55.60
8. Surita Febbraio RSA	55.90

High Jump (Q 29th, F 31st)

CLOETE DEFENDED her title in brilliant style, clearing every height from 1.85 to a Commonwealth and African record at 2.06 at the first attempt. Kuptsova also cleared 2.00 on the first go but Bergqvist needed two attempts. Ten women cleared the stipulated qualifying height of 1.93.

1. Hestrie Cloete RSA	2.06
2. Marina Kuptsova RUS	2.00
3. Kajsa Bergqvist SWE	2.00
4. Venelina Veneva BUL	1.98
5. Vita Palamar UKR	1.95
6. Anna Chicherova RUS	1.95
7. Blanka Vlasic CRO	1.95
8. Juana Arrendel DOM	1.95
9= Amy Acuff USA	1.90
9= Viktoriya Styopina UKR	1.90
11= Ruth Beitia ESP	1.90
11= Olga Kaliturina RUS	1.90

Pole Vault (Q 23rd, F 25th)

THE FIRST crucial height in the final was 4.55, cleared first time by Feofanova and Isinbayeva, with Pyrek and Dragila over at the third try. Becker and Feofanova went over 4.60 first time and Isinbayeva ensured at least the bronze medal by clearing second time while the other three, including Buschbaum who had passed 4.55, failed. Becker passed 4.65, a height cleared without trouble by the Russian pair. At 4.70 first Becker and then Feofanova made it at the second try, with Isinbayeva – desperately close at her first attempt – failing twice and once at 4.75, at which Feofanova clinched the title by clearing first time, while Becker had two misses at that height and one at 4.80. Seven women cleared 4.40 for the best ever in a qualifying competition, joined in the final by four at 4.35 and one at 4.25.

1. Svetlana Feofanova RUS	4.75*
2. Annika Becker GER	4.70
3. Yelena Isinbayeva RUS	4.65
4= Stacy Dragila USA	4.55
4= Monika Pyrek POL	4.55
6. Yvonne Buschbaum GER	4.50
7. Anna Rogowska POL	4.45
8. Yelena Belyakova RUS	4.45
9. Gao Shuying CHN	4.35
10. Mary Sauer USA	4.35
nh. Thórey Elisdóttir ISL	
nh. Marie Poissonnier FRA	

Long Jump (Q 28th, F30th)

ONLY FOUR women, led by Barber 6.78 and Galkina 6.72, jumped the automatic qualifying standard of 6.65 and a modest 6.53 was enough to make the final. The favourite Kotova had two no jumps and a 6.56, but took the lead in the second round of the final with 6.74, a distance immediately matched by Barber. Kotova then took the lead as her 6.72 in the fifth round was better than Barber's second best of 6.52. All depended on the final jump and Barber had full attention and thunderous roar from the stadium crowd on her run-up and even more so when the distance was revealed – a superb jump of 6.99, 2cm short of her French record, yet with 11cm to spare on the board. George, advised by Mike Powell, became India's first ever World Champs medallist with her fifth round 6.70.

1. Eunice Barber FRA	6.99/0.4
2. Tatyana Kotova RUS	6.74/0.1
3. Anju Bobby George IND	6.70/1.2
4. Jade Johnson GBR	6.63/0.5
5. Olga Rublyova RUS	6.58/-0.2
6. Tünde Vaszi HUN	6.53/0.5
7. Bronwyn Thompson AUS	6.48/-0.3
8. Grace Upshaw USA	6.47/0.1
9. Fiona May ITA	6.46/0.1
10. Lyudmila Galkina RUS	6.45/-1.4
11. Valentina Gotovska LAT	6.43/-0.7
12. Concepción Montaner ESP	6.37/-0.4

Triple Jump (Q 24th, F 26th)

FOURTEEN WOMEN, headed by Martínez 14.73 and Lebedeva 14.62, exceeded the qualifying standard of 14.15, and there was a fine contest in the final with the best ever marks for 7 and 9-11. Defending champion Lebedeva led after the first round at 14.80, and Mbango moved ahead in the second with a new African record of 15.05. But Lebedeva then took over with jumps of 15.16 and 15.18. Mbango fought hard and jumped 15.02 in the fifth round, while ex-Cuban Martínez held third place throughout, adding 1cm to her Italian record with 14.90 in the fifth round with almost 12cm to spare on the board.

1. Tatyana Lebedeva RUS	15.18/-0.2
2. Françoise Mbango CMR	15.05/-0.7
3. Magdelín Martínez ITA	14.90/-0.2
4. Anna Pyatykh RUS	14.72/-0.4
5. Mabel Gay CUB	14.52/0.0
6. Barbara Lah ITA	14.38/0.6
7. Yelena Govorova UKR	14.38/0.1
8. Hrysopiyí Devetzí GRE	14.34/0.5
9. Adelina Gavrila ROM	14.29/0.0
10. Kéné Ndoye SEN	14.29/0.0
11. Baya Rahouli ALG	14.26/-0.1
12. Ólga Vasdéki GRE	14.08/0.3
13. Huang Qiuyan CHN	13.98/-0.6
14. Yelena Oleynikova RUS	13.92/0.2

Shot (Q & F 27th)

AFTER SILVER in 1993 and bronze in 1991 and 1999, 34 year-old Krivelyova took the gold medal. She led throughout, with 19.60, 19.97, 20.30 and 20.63 in the first four rounds. Ostapchuk led the qualifiers with 19.56 and smashed her pb with 20.12 in the fifth round to overtake Pavlysh, who had 20.03 in the third round, improving to 20.08 in the fifth. Three time world champion and 1996 Olympic gold medallist Kumbernuss failed to reach the final, her first ever such failure in 22 international championships, as she managed just 17.83 for 15th.

1. Svetlana Krivelyova RUS	20.63
2. Nadezhda Ostapchuk BLR	20.12
3. Vita Pavlysh UKR	20.08
4. Irina Korzhanenko RUS	19.17
5. Valerie Adams NZL-J	18.65
6. Krystyna Zabawska POL	18.62
7. Nadine Kleinert GER	18.48
8. Assunta Legnante ITA	18.28
9. Elisângela Adriano BRA	18.11
10. Lieja Tunks NED	17.99
11. Li Meiju CHN	17.92
12. Iríni Terzóglou GRE	17.88

Discus (Q 23rd, F 25th)

YELENA NIKOLAYEVA (20km walk) had become the oldest female world champion, but the next day Yatchenko – at 37 years 298 days three months older– produced the performance of her life in her sixth World final. Her opening throw sailed out to 67.32, her longest throw since 1997, and that remained the winner although Kelesídou came very close with 67.13 in the third round and 67.14 with her final effort. 11 women achieved the qualifying standard of 60m. led by Sadova 63.47, and Anna Söderberg was added to the final despite being placed 13th at 59.66 because her appeal that a throw in excess of 60m had been incorrectly measured was allowed.

1. Irina Yatchenko BLR	67.32
2. Anastasia Kelesídou GRE	67.14
3. Ekateríni Vóggoli GRE	66.73
4. Yelena Antonova UKR	65.90
5. Vera Pospísilová CZE	65.55
6. Natalya Sadova RUS	65.22
7. Song Aimin CHN	63.84
8. Anna Söderberg SWE	61.61
9. Suzanne Powell USA	59.86
10. Teresa Machado POR	59.46
11. Melina Robert-Michon FRA	58.52
12. Neelam J Singh IND	57.92
13. Beatrice Faumuina NZL	56.86

Hammer (Q 26th, F 28th)

MORENO LED throughout in the final and was the only 2001 throws champion, male or female, to defend their title. She opened with 71.02 and her second throw of 73.33 (and third of 72.52) was enough for gold. Kuzenkova took her customary silver medal from 71.14 in R2 and 71.71 in R4, while Montebrun (her left knee strapped) displaced Gu Yuan from third place (70.77 in the third round) with her 70.92 in the following round. There were best ever marks for places 4-11, although even better for 10-12 came with 66 women over 66m in the qualifying round. Montebrun, unbeaten all season, had raised hopes of a home victory by leading them with 71.36 and Svetlana Sudak's 65.29 was the longest ever non-qualifying mark; there were 44 competitors in all.

1. Yipsi Moreno CUB	73.33
2. Olga Kuzenkova RUS	71.71
3. Manuela Montebrun FRA	70.92
4. Gu Yuan CHN	70.77
5. Susanne Keil GER	69.43
6. Mihaela Melinte ROM	68.69
7. Anna Mahon USA	68.45
8. Kamila Skolimowska POL	68.39
9. Candice Scott TRI	67.73
10. Lorraine Shaw GBR	65.95
11. Betty Heidler GER	65.81
12. Melissa Price USA	62.34

Javelin (Q 28th, F 30th)

MANJANI OVERTOOK Shikolenko's 62.76 with her opening throw of 64.55 and put the issue beyond doubt with a fourth round 66.52, the world's best mark of the year, but the lowest ever winning mark at the Worlds. Shikolenko, who had led the qualifiers with 63.71, progressed to 62.99 and 63.28 to take the silver ahead of Nerius. 38 year-old Eve made her first final at her sixth Worlds with 62.89 but could not match that in the final.

1. Mirela Manjani GRE	66.52
2. Tatyana Shikolenko RUS	63.28
3. Steffi Nerius GER	62.70
4. Mikaela Ingberg FIN	62.20
5. Osleidys Menéndez CUB	62.19
6. Sonia Bisset CUB	60.17
7. Claudia Coslovich ITA	59.64
8. Lavern Eve BAH	59.60
9. Valeriya Zabruskova RUS	59.51
10. Taina Kolkkala FIN	57.50
11. Ma Ning CHN	57.43
12. Nikolett Szabó HUN	56.98

Heptathlon (23rd/24th)

APART FROM a near-nightmare in the long jump where she had two fouls before a fine 6.68, the 20 year-old Klüft experienced a dream of a competition. She set pbs in five of the seven events and rose to third on the world all-time list and just 6 points off the European record with a score of 7001, adding 309 points to her best. Even Barber, striving to regain the world title before an adoring crowd, was no match for her despite scoring 6755, her best for three years. Barber began with a solid 13.05 hurdles and an excellent 1.91 high jump, but Klüft clocked a pb of 13.18 and then made 1.94. Barber must have realised her chance was slim when she ran the 200m in 23.92 and watched the ebullient Swede cream away from her to finish at 22.98. Her first day score of 4143 has only ever been exceeded by Jackie Joyner-Kersee. Sazanovich added to her imposing list of medals with bronze ahead of defending champion Prokhorova, while Olympic champion Lewis continued her comeback in fifth place.

1. Carolina Klüft SWE	7001
2. Eunice Barber FRA	6755
3. Natalya Sazanovich BLR	6524
4. Yelena Prokhorova RUS	6452
5. Denise Lewis GBR	6254
6. Gertrud Bacher ITA	6166
7. Larisa Netseporuk EST	6154
8. Sonja Kesselschläger GER	6134
9. Sryiró Strатáki GRE	6077
10. Austra Skujyté LTU	6077
11. Svetlana Kazanina KAZ	6047
12. Irina Butor BLR	6035
13. Natalya Roshchupkina RUS	6034
14. Julie Hollman GBR	6018
15. Irina Naumenko KAZ	5971

20 Kilometres Walk (24th)

NIKOLAYEVA, THE 1996 Olympic 10km walk gold medallist, won the world title at her seventh attempt having had five placings between 3rd and 12th. Third at 5k (22:10) just behind O'Sullivan and Perrone (22:09), she had built up a substantial lead by 10k (43:26) from O'Sullivan and Perrone 43:46. By 15k Nikolayeva's lead had grown to 48 sec (1:04:53) from O'Sullivan 1:05:41, Gudkova 1:06:04, Giordano 1:06:06 and Tsybulskaya 1:06:11 after Perrone had dropped out. The defending champion Olga Ivanova retired injured in the 2nd kilometre, one of 14 of 42 starters who did not finish (7 disqualified).

1. Yelena Nikolayeva RUS	1:26:52*
2. Gillian O'Sullivan IRL	1:27:34
3. Valentina Tsybulskaya BLR	1:28:10
4. Tatyana Gudkova RUS	1:28:53
5. Claudia Stef ROM	1:29:09
6. Rossella Giordano ITA	1:29:14
7. Athanasia Tsoumeléka GRE	1:29:34
8. Melanie Seeger GER	1:29:44
9. Susana Feitor POR	1:30:15
10. Elisa Rigaudo ITA	1:30:34
11. Jane Saville AUS	1:30:51
12. Olive Loughnane IRL	1:30:53
13. Xu Aihui CHN	1:31:34
14. Kristina Saltanovic LTU	1:32:13
15. Vera Santos POR	1:32:43

4 x 100 Metres (ht 29th, 30th)

THE AMERICANS prudently dropped Kelly White, under threat of disqualification, from their relay squad, but ran a world-leading 42.03 in heat 1, while a full strength France clocked a national record of 42.04 in heat 3. The US team was strengthened for the final by the inclusion of Torri Edwards on the anchor leg, but even she was unable to withstand the onslaught of Christine Arron on that final stage and the French team raced to a glorious triumph (just 20 minutes after Barber's long jump finale) by half a metre in 41.78, a time which only the GDR, USA and Russia have ever bettered.

1. FRA	41.78	(Girard, Hurtis, S Félix, Arron)
2. USA	41.83	(A Williams, Gaines, Miller, Edwards) (heat: L Williams)

3. RUS 42.66	(Fyodorova, Tabakova, Kislova, Kruglova)	
4. UKR 43.07	5. GER	43.27
6. BEL 43.45	7. BLR	43.47
dnf. JAM –		

4 x 400 Metres (ht 30th, 31st)

DESPITE THE fact that no Americans had got beyond the semis of the 400m, the US came out victorious against Russia, who had three individual finalists. Encouraged by a world-leading heat time of 3:24.57 the American squad produced an inspired performance. Olesya Zykina led on the first leg for Russia (50.8) from Sandie Richards of Jamaica (51.0) and Me'Lisa Barber of the USA (51.1). Russia (Pechonkina 50.6) were still just ahead of Jamaica (Beckford 50.5) at halfway, with the USA (Washington 50.9) some 4m down. But a 50.05 third leg from Jearl Miles Clark, who won her ninth World Champs medal, paved the way for an American victory as she brought her team to within inches of the Russians (Kapachinskaya 50.67) and Sanya Richards (50.28) anchored the USA to victory. Lorraine Fenton, with easily the fastest split of the race (49.38), ran a spectacular leg for Jamaica, failing by just 0.01 to catch Nazarova (50.93). Fastest split in the heats was Guevara's 50.0 but Mexico didn't qualify.

1. USA	3:22.63	(Me'Lisa Barber, Washington, Miles Clark, Richards)	
2. RUS	3:22.91	(Zykina, Pechonkina, Kapachinskaya, Nazarova)	
3. JAM	3:22.92	(Richards, Beckford, Smith, Fenton)	
4. GER	3:26.25	5. POL	3:26.64
6. GBR	3:26.67	7. CMR	3:27.08
dq. SEN	(3:25.87)		

Prize Money awarded by the IAAF

(pending negative doping results)

	Individual	*Relays*	*Marathon Cup*
1	$60,000	$80,000	$20,000
2	$30,000	$40,000	$15,000
3	$20,000	$20,000	$12,000
4	$15,000	$16,000	$10,000
5	$10,000	$12,000	$8,000
6	$6,000	$8,000	$6,000
7	$5,000	$6,000	
8	$4,000	$4,000	

World Championships Points Table

Nation	*1st*	*2nd*	*3rd*	*4th*	*5th*	*6th*	*7th*	*8th*	*Points*	*2001*	*1999*
RUS	6	8	5	9	3	6	1	4	215	181	132
USA	10	8	2	3	2	7	3	2	200	196.5	209
KEN	2	1	1	2	4	4	3	1	74	82	65
FRA	2	3	2	2	2	1	1	1	73	36	42
GER	0	1	3	2	5	3	2	4	72	104.5	148.5
UKR	0	0	4	3	3	2	1	2	61	35	48
BLR	3	1	3	0	0	1	3	0	58	38	11
JAM	0	3	2	2	2	1	1	2	58	55	51.5
GBR	0	2	2	3	2	2	1	0	57	54	66
ETH	3	2	2	0	0	2	0	0	56	69	62
ESP	0	3	2	1	0	4	1	2	54	69	51
GRE	1	1	2	0	1	0	3	2	39	38	46
ITA	1	0	2	0	1	4	1	1	39	44	53
RSA	2	1	1	0	0	1	2	2	38	21	14
JPN	0	1	3	1	1	0	1	1	37	31	28
SWE	2	1	2	0	0	0	0	1	36	23	16
POL	1	0	0	1	2	3	2	1	35	50	29
CUB	1	1	0	1	2	1	0	1	32	61	57
MAR	2	1	0	1	0	0	0	0	28	29	42
CHN	0	0	2	1	0	0	4	0	25	9	29
AUS	1	0	0	1	2	0	1	1	24	29	58
CZE	0	1	0	2	1	0	1	0	23	29	40
BAH	0	0	1	2	1	0	0	2	22	30	16
CAN	1	0	1	0	0	1	0	1	18	8	19.5
HUN	0	2	0	0	0	1	0	0	17	17.5	23
QAT	1	0	0	1	0	0	1	0	14	2	0
NED	0	0	0	2	0	0	2	1	15	2.5	1
BRA	0	0	1	0	1	1	0	1	14	7	25
MEX	1	0	0	1	0	0	0	0	13	15	12
ROM	0	0	0	1	1	1	0	0	12	44.5	38
FIN	0	0	0	1	1	0	1	1	12	22	13

23 nations won gold medals, 42 medals of any colour, and 63 nations placed athletes in the top eight (compared to 21, 42 and 57 in 1999, 23, 42 and 64 in 2001).

2003 CHAMPIONSHIPS

IAAF World Half Marathon Championships 2003

At Vilamoura, Portugal 4 October

Men

1. Martin Lel KEN 60:49
2. Fabian Joseph TAN 60:52
3. Martin Sulle TAN 60:56
4. John Cheruiyot Korir KEN 61:02
5. John Yuda TAN 61:13
6. Yusuf Songoka KEN 61:18
7. Tadesse Zersenay ERI 61:26
8. Jackson Koech KEN 61:28
9. Tesfaye Tola ETH 61:35
10. Ridouane Harroufi MAR 62:46
11. Dereje Adere ETH 62:47
12. Abderrahim Goumri MAR 62:59
13. Paulo Gomes POR 63:00
14. Kazuyuki Maeda JPN 63:07
15. Wilson Busienei UGA 63:08
16. Hailu Mesfin ETH-J 63:12
17. Tariku Jifar ETH-J 63:23
18. Rachid Aït Bensalem MAR 63:37
19. Abdelghani Lahlali FRA 63:37
20. Oscar Fernández ESP 63:41

86 of 97 finished

Team: 1. TAN 3:03:01, 2. KEN 3:03:09, 3. ETH 3:07:34, 4. MAR 3:09:22, 5. ERI 3:09:25, 6. UGA 3:11:46, 7. FRA 3:11:55, 8. JPN 3:12:11, 9. ITA 3:12:51, 10. ESP 3:12:53, 11. ALG 3:14:31, 12. POR 3:16:56, 13. USA 3:17:33, 14. MEX 3:18:00, 15. BEL 3:19:58, 16. ECU 3:27:36, 17. CHN 3:18:51

Women

1. Paula Radcliffe GBR 67:35
2. Berhane Adere ETH 69:02
3. Benita Johnson AUS 69:26
4. Lidiya Grigoryeva RUS 69:32
5. Constantina Tomescu ROM 70:05
6. Alla Zhilyayeva RUS 70:13
7. Lyudmila Biktasheva RUS 70:31
8. Susan Chepkemei KEN 70:35
9. Mikie Takanaka JPN 70:36
10. Alina Ivanova RUS 70:59
11. Helena Javornik SLO 71:17
12. Sylvia Mosqueda USA 71:22
13. Takako Kotorida JPN 71:37
14. Yesenia Centeno ESP 71:53
15. Luminita Talpos ROM 72:02
16. Risa Hagiwara JPN 72:10
17. Galina Bogomolova RUS 72:12
18. Corinne Raux FRA 72:17
19. Yumiko Hara JPN 72:21
20. Bruna Genovese ITA 72:38

68 of 73 finished

Team: 1. RUS 3:30:16, 2. JPN 3:34:23, 3. ROM 3:35:07, 4. ETH 3:36:37, 5. GBR 3:36:44, 6. ESP 3:39:19, 7. FRA 3:40:02, 8. ITA 3:40:40, 9. KEN 3:40:58, 10. USA 3:44:22, 11. MAR 3:44:39, 12. POR 3:52:35, 13. IND 4:18:41

IAAF World Youth Championships

At Sherbrooke (Canada), 9-13 July

Men

100m	1. Yahya Al-Gahes KSA 10.69
(-3.1)	2. Yahya Ibrahim Hassan KSA 10.73
	3. Craig Pickering GBR 10.85
200m	1. Usain Bolt JAM 20.40*
(1.1)	2. Michael Grant USA 21.04
	3. Jamahl Alert-Khan GBR 21.35
400m	1. Nagmeldin El Abubakr SUD 46.10*
	2. Cedric Goodman USA 46.42
	3. Zeljko Vincek CRO 47.45
800m	1. Mohammed Al-Salhi KSA 1:48.79*
	2. Bernard Kiptanui Kiptum KEN 1:49.14
	3. Abraham Kipngetich Ngeno KEN 1:49.17
1500m	1. Benson Marrianyi Esho KEN 3:44.94
	2. Samson Kiplangat KEN 3:45.13
	3. Isaac Mboyaza RSA 3:48.05
3000m	1. Augustine Kiprono Choge KEN 7:52.53 (7:52.34* ht)
	2. Tariku Bekele ETH 7:54.71
	3. Shimelis Girma ETH 7:55.12
2000mSt	1. Ronald Kipchumba Rutto KEN 5:30.27
	2. Justus Kipchirchir Kiprono KEN 5:31.24
	3. Chris Winter CAN 5:44.23
110mh	1. Jason Richardson USA 13.29
(91.4cm)	2. Mubarak Al-Mabadi KSA 13.41
(1.9)	3. Alexander John GER 13.50
400mh	1. Jason Richardson USA 49.91
(84cm)	2. Wouter Le Roux RSA 50.85
	3. Jamaal Charles USA 51.48
HJ	1. Martin Günther GER 2.11
	2. Oleksandr Nartov UKR 2.11
	3. Hikaru Tsuchiya JPN 2.11
PV	1. Germán Chiaraviglio ARG 5.15
	2. Dmitriy Starodubtsev RUS 5.10
	3. Steven Lewis GBR 5.05
LJ	1. Naohiro Shinada JPN 7.61/-2.0
	2. Yves Renaux FRA 7.44/-1.2
	3. Ahmed Al-Sharfa KSA 7.15/-0.3
TJ	1. Denny Fernandez CUB 15.77/1.8
	2. Mousa Qarqaran KSA 15.60/1.9
	3. Mohamed A Darwish UAE 15.55/0.1
SP 5kg	1. Feng Liu CHN 21.45*
	2. Kyle Helf CAN 20.79
	3. Amin Al-Aradi KSA 19.69
DT 1.5kg	1. Ronnie Buckley AUS 64.34*
	2. Wu Jian CHN 63.18
	3. Wang Yao-Hui TPE 60.00
HT 5kg	1. Mikhail Levin RUS 76.41
	2. Kristóf Németh HUN 75.59
	3. Sándor Pálhegyi HUN 75.47
JT 700g	1. Júlio César de Oliveira BRA 81.16*
	2. Robert Oosthuizen RSA 81.07
	3. Raldu Potgieter RSA 75.56
Oct	1. Andrés Silva URU 6456
	2. Andrei Krauchanka BLR 6366
	3. Lukás Patera CZE 6316

10kmW 1. Aleksandr Prokhorov RUS 42:16.16*
2. Makoto Sawada JPN 42:17.62
3. Vyacheslav Golovin RUS 42:37.15

Medley R 1. USA (Cooper, Grant, Charles, Goodman) 1:52.03
2. POL (Kuc, Witkowski, Blocian, Rys) 1:53.08
3. JPN (Saburi, Fujimitsu, Shinada, Tanabe) 1:53.11

Women

100m (1.8) 1. Jessica Onyepunuka USA 11.31*
2. Krystin Lacy USA 11.50
3. Kelly-Ann Baptiste TRI 11.58

200m (-0.4) 1. Anneisha McLaughlin JAM 23.26
2. Courtney Champion USA 23.56
3. Cleo Tyson USA 23.67

400m 1. Natasha Hastings USA 53.41
2. Antonina Krivoshapka RUS 53.54
3. Jaimee-Lee Hoebergen AUS 53.78

800m 1. Maria Chapayeva RUS 2:03.40*
2. Olga Cristea MDA 2:04.30
3. Larisa Arcip ROM 2:04.31

1500m 1. Alem Techale ETH 4:17.41
2. Jelena Stina LAT 4:17.43
3. Joyce Jepkosgei Musungu KEN 4:17.65

3000m 1. Siham Hilali MAR 9:12.70
2. Pasalia Chepkorir Kipkoech KEN 9:13.77
3. Yuko Nohara JPN 9:14.82

100mh (76.2cm) (-1.9) 1. Sally McLellan AUS 13.42
2. Latoya Greaves JAM 13.49
3. Domenique Manning USA 13.60

400mh 1. Zuzana Hejnová CZE 57.54*
2. Yekaterina Kostetskaya RUS 58.37
3. Mackenzie Hill USA 59.15

HJ 1. Iryna Kovalenko UKR 1.92*
2= Svetlana Shkolina RUS 1.86
2= Annett Engel GER 1.86

PV 1. Lisa Ryshich GER 4.05
2. Svetlana Makarevich BLR 4.00
3. Charmaine Lucock AUS 4.00

LJ 1. Cristine Spîtaru ROM 6.41/1.7*
2. Denisa Scerbová CZE 6.40/1.0
3. Ganna Demydova UKR 6.15/0.9

TJ 1. Cristine Spîtaru ROM 13.86/-0.6*
2. Elina Sorsa FIN 12.95/-0.3
3. Alíki Askitopoúlou GRE 12.93/0.2

SP 1. Jiang Limin CHN 15.60
2. Magdalena Sobieszek POL 15.42
3. Marli Knoetze RSA 15.10

DT 1. Lisandra Rodriguez CUB 48.56
2. Julie Bennell AUS 48.32
3. Kristina Gehrig GER 48.31

HT 1. Valentina Srsa CRO 61.18
2. Maria Bespalova RUS 57.81
3. Johanna Hoppe GER 56.46

JT 1. Xue Juan CHN 56.82*
2. Shin Bo-ra KOR 53.74
3. Vivian Zimmer GER 52.20

Hep 1. Marisa de Aniceto FRA 5458
2. Sarah Kern GER 5445
3. Marina Goncharova RUS 5338

5kmW 1. Vera Sokolova RUS 22:50.23
2. Ann Loughnane IRL 23:37.00
3. Noriko Nishide JPN 23:50.69

Medley R 1. USA (Onyepunuka, Anderson, Lacy, Hastings) 2:03.87
2. JAM (Henry, Duncan, Sutherland, McLaughlin) 2:07.05
3. RUS (Kremneva, Khvashevskaya, Shuvalova, Krivoshapka) 2:07.52

Medal and Points Table

	G	*S*	*B*	*Points*
USA	6	4	4	134
RUS	4	5	3	130
KEN	3	4	2	75
CHN	3	1	-	45
KSA	2	3	2	52
GER	2	2	4	89
JAM	2	2	-	42
AUS	2	1	2	58
ROM	2	-	1	33
CUB	2	-	-	23
JPN	1	1	4	64
GBR	-	-	3	56
RSA	-	2	3	42

IAAF Race Walking Challenge 2003

First held in 2003. Events: Tijuana MEX, Rio Maior POR, Sesto San Giovanni ITA, La Coruña ESP, World Championships (Paris, FRA). In 2004 Shanghai may be added. and the Olympic Games is instead of the World Champs

Men

1 Robert Korzeniowski POL 33
2 Francisco Fernández ESP 28
3 Aigars Fadejevs LAT 23
4. Jefferson Pérez ECU 22
5 João Vieira POR 22
6 Ivan Trotskiy BLR 19
7 Jesús Ángel García ESP 15
8 Alejandro López MEX 8

Women

1 Gillian O'Sullivan IRL 29
2 Kjersti Plätzer NOR 24
3 Elisabetta Perrone ITA 22
4 Susana Feitor POR 22
5 Nadezhda Ryashkina RUS 17
6 Valentina Tsybulskaya BLR 17
7 Elisa Rigaudo ITA 6
8 Jane Saville AUS 6

Participation in three events is required. Prize Money 2003 and 2004 for the IAAF World Combined Events and Race Walking Challenges: 1st place $30.000, 2nd $20,000, 3rd $15,000, 4th $10,000, 5th $8000, 6th $7000, 7th $6000, 8th $5000

World University Games 2003

At Daegu, Korea 25-30 August

Men

100m (-1.2) 1. Chris Lambert GBR 10.44
2. Leigh Julius RSA 10.50
3. Dejan Vojnovic CRO 10.58

200m (-0.7) 1. Leigh Julius RSA 20.49
2. Paul Hession IRL 20.89
3. Jirí Vojtik CZE 21.03

400m 1. Andriy Tverdostup UKR 46.08
2. Debis Rypakov KAZ 46.51
3. Rafal Wieruszewski POL 46.53

800m 1. Roman Oravec CZE 1:48.01
2. Ramil Aritkulov RUS 1:48.19
3. Fabiano Pecanha BRA 1:48.20

IAAF World Combined Events Challenge 2003

Events: Multistars (Desenzano del Garda, ITA), Hypo-Meeting (Götzis, AUT), Arles (FRA), 6th Ruhrgas DLV Mehrkampf (Ratingen, GER), US Championships (Stanford, USA), European Cup (several venues), Pan-American Games (Santo Domingo, DOM), World Championships (Saint-Denis, FRA), Decastar (Talence, FRA) and African Games (Abuja, NGR)

Ranking is based on the sum of the best scores achieved by an athlete in any three of these competitions

Men Decathlon

1	Tom Pappas USA	26,119	8585 Götzis	8784 US Ch	8750 Worlds
2	Roman Sebrle CZE	26.047	8807 Götzis	8606 Ratingen	8634 Worlds
3	Laurent Hernu FRA	24.244	7807 Götzis	8218 Worlds	8219 Talence
4	Romain Barras FRA	24,034	7966 Arles	8008 ECp S	8060 Talence
5	Stephen Moore USA	23,786	7967 Götzis	8010 US Ch	7809 Pan Ams
6	Paul Terek USA	23,659	7881 Desenzano	8275 US Ch	7503 Worlds
7	Chiel Warners NED	23,552	7739 Götzis	8060 ECp 1	7753 Worlds
8	Lionel Marceny FRA	23,277	7716 Arles	7788 ECp S	7773 Talence
9	Michal Modelski POL	22,928	7570 Desenzano	7835 ECp 1	7523 Talence
10	Luca Ceglie ITA	22,464	7413 Desenzano	7339 Arles	7712 ECp S

Women Heptathlon

1	Carolina Klüft SWE	20,295	6602 Götzis	6692 ECp 1	7001 Worlds
2	Yelena Prokhorova RUS	19,019	6313 ECp S	6452 Worlds	6254 Talence
3	Larisa Netseporuk EST	18,482	6215 ECp 1	6154 Worlds	6113 Talence
4	Sonja Kesselschläger GER	18,426	6175 Götzis	6117 Ratingen	6134 Worlds
5	Austra Skujyte LTU	18,343	6213 Götzis	6053 ECp 1	6077 Worlds
6	Gertrud Bacher ITA	18,326	6097 Götzis	6166 Worlds	6063 Talence
7	Irina Butor BLR	18,235	5936 Götzis	6264 ECp S	6035 Worlds
8	Margaret Simpson GHA	18,224	5952 Desenzano	6120 Götzis	6152 African G
9	Svetlana Kazanina KAZ	18,126	5996 Arles	6047 Worlds	6083 Talence
10	Kelly Sotherton GBR	17,989	5893 Götzis	6059 ECp 1	6037 Talence

1500m 1. Johan Pretorius RSA 3:42.81
2. Pedro A. Esteso ESP 3:42.82
3. Fabiano Pecanha BRA 3:43.91

5000m 1. Sergiy Lebid UKR 13:50.94
2. Jan Fitschen GER 13:53.06
3. Hicham Bellani MAR 13:53.79

10,000m 1. Jan Fitschen GER 29:39.47
2. Abdellah Bay MAR 29:41.54
3. Ryuichi Hashinokuchi JPN 29:42.07

H Mar 1. Abdellah Bay MAR 64:21
2. Francis Yiga UGA 65:24
3. Iván Sánchez ESP 65:29

3000mSt 1. César Pérez ESP 8:38.52
2. Zouaoui Dandrieux FRA 8:39.24
3. Andrey Olshanskiy RUS 8:39.62

110mh (-1.6) 1. Anselmo Silva BRA 13.68
2. Igor Peremota RUS 13.75
3. Park Tae-kyong KOR 13.78

400mh 1. Thomas Kortbeek NED 48.95
2. Matt Douglas GBR 49.26
3. Hennie Botha RSA 49.51

HJ 1. Emilian Kaszczyk POL 2.26
2. Joan Charmant FRA 2.23
3= Cui Kai CHN 2.20
3= Yiannis Constaninou CYP 2.20
3= Aleksandr Veryutin BLR 2.20

PV 1. Olexandr Korchmyd UKR 5.75
2. Igor Pavlov RUS 5.65
3= Bjorn Otto GER 5.50
3= Tiberiu Agoston ROM 5.50

LJ 1. Valeriy Vasilyev UKR 8.07/0.7
2. Danut Simion ROM 8.04/-0.8
3. Andrey Bragin RUS 8.04/0.8

TJ 1. Gu Junjie CHN 16.90/1.0
2. Viktor Yastrebov UKR 16.88/ 0.1
3. Yevgeniy Plotnir RUS 16.82/-0.2

SP 1. Andrey Mikhnevich BLR 20.76
2. Pavel Lyzhin BLR 20.72
3. Nedzad Mulabegovic CRO 19.99

DT 1. Wu Tao CHN 62.32
2. Andrzej Krawczyk POL 60.70
3. Emeka Udechuku GBR 60.44

HT 1. Ivan Tikhon BLR 82.77
2. Péter Botfa HUN 74.41
3. David Söderberg FIN 72.84

JT 1. Igor Janik POL 76.83
2. Esko Mikkola FIN 75.82
3. Williams Hamlyn-Harris AUS 75.50

Dec 1. Romain Barras FRA 8196
2. Indrek Turi EST 8122
3. Nikolay Tishchenko RUS 7911

20kmW 1. Stepan Yudin RUS 1:23:34
2. Vladimir Potemin RUS 1:23:50
3. Vasiliy Ivanov RUS 1:23:55

4x100m 1. JPN (Ishikura, Takaihira, Yoshino, Arai) 39.45
2. RUS 39.67
3. EST 39.99

4x400m 1. UKR (Demchenko, Zyukov, Gorbenko, Tverdostup) 3:03.15
2. RUS 3:04.78
3. GBR 3:05.54

Women

100m (-0.7) 1. Qin Wangping CHN 11.53
2. Enikó Szabó HUN 11.61
3. Yelena Bolsun RUS 11.65

200m (1.4) 1. Yelena Bolsun RUS 23.39
2. Yekaterina Kondratyeva RUS 23.43
3. Jenice Daley JAM 23.55

400m 1. Tatyana Firova RUS 51.81
2. Mariya Lisnichenko RUS 52.54
3. Estie Wittstock RSA 52.86

800m 1. Liliana Barbulescu ROM 2:00.06

2. Anna Zagórska POL 2:00.11
3. Irina Vashentseva RUS 2:00.77

1500m 1. Natalya Sidorenko UKR 4:11.69
2. Johanna Risku FIN 4:11.88
3. Malindi Elmore CAN 4:12.00

5000m 1. Eloise Poppett AUS 15:47.19
2. Zhang Yuhong CHN 15:47.62
3. Cristina Casandra ROM 15:50.44

10,000m 1. Natalia Cerches MDA 33:37.05
2. Yelena Samokhvalova RUS 33:40.57
3. Anna Incerti ITA 33:49.71

H Mar 1. Machi Tanaka JPN 73:06
2. Jo Bun-hui PRK 73:47
3. Chang Son-ok PRK 73:55

100mh (-0.9) 1. Xu Jia CHN 13.29
2. Yevgeniya Likhuta BLR 13.33
3. Natalya Kresova RUS 13.35

400mh 1. Maren Schott GER 55.28
2. Huang Xiaoxiao CHN 56.10
3. Anastasiya Rabchenyuk UKR 56.30

HJ 1. Dóra Györffy HUN 1.94
2. Anna Ksok POL 1.94
3. Yelena Slesarenko RUS 1.94

PV 1. Tatyana Polnova RUS 4.70
2. Anastasiya Ivanova RUS 4.40
3. Nadine Rohr SUI 4.25

LJ 1. Irina Simagina RUS 6.49/0.0
2. Alina Militaru ROM 6.45/0.4
3. Zita Ajkler HUN 6.38/0.7

TJ 1. Oksana Rogova RUS 14.16/1.0
2. Viktoriya Gurova RUS 14.14/1.1
3. Mariana Solomon ROM 14.09/1.0

SP 1. Li Fengfeng CHN 18.55
2. Lee Myung-sun KOR 17.58
3. Yelena Ivanenko BLR 17.29

DT 1. Natalya Fokina UKR 63.11
2. Li Yanfeng CHN 61.12
3. Xu Shaoyang CHN 58.64

HT 1. Liu Yinghui CHN 69.05
2. Gulfiya Khanafeyeva RUS 65.12
3. Agnieszka Pogroszewska POL 64.27

JT 1. Barbara Madejczyk POL 56.23
2. Christina Scherwin DEN 56.08
3. Mercedes Chilla ESP 55.94

Hep 1. Kylie Wheeler AUS 6031
2. Jane Jamieson AUS 5908
3. Michaela Hejnová CZE 5795

20kmW 1. Tatyana Sibileva RUS 1:34:55
2. Jian Xingli CHN 1:35:52
3. Tatyana Korotkova RUS 1:36:52

4x100m 1. CHN (Chen Lisha, Zhu Juanhong, Ni Xiaoli, Qin Wangping) 44.09
2. FRA 44.68
3. BRA 45.79

4x400m 1. RUS (Kondratyeva, Firova, Lavshuk, Lisnichenko) 3:31.63
2. POL 3:38.17
3. GER 3:38.87

8th All-Africa Games

At Abuja, Nigeria 11-15 October

Men

100m (0.6) 1. Deji Aliu NGR 9.95*
2. Uchenna Emedolu NGR 9.97
3. Leonard Myles-Mills GHA 10.03

200m (-0.9) 1. Uchenna Emedolu NGR 20.42
2. Frank Fredericks NAM 20.43
3. Aziz Zakari GHA 20.51

400m 1. Ezra Sambu KEN 44.98
2. Nagmeldis El Abubakr SUD 45.22
3. Sofiane Labidi TUN 45.42

800m 1. Samuel Mwera TAN 1:46.13
2. Mbulaeni Mulaudzi RSA 1:46.44
3. Justus Koech KEN 1:46.50

1500m 1. Paul Korir KEN 3:37.52
2. Richard Rono KEN 3:38.13
3. Benjamin Kipkurui KEN 3:38.94

5000m 1. Kenenisa Bekele ETH 13:26.16*
2. Hailu Mekonnen ETH 13:26.73
3. John Kibowen KEN 13:29.14

10,000m 1. Sileshi Sihine ETH 27:42.13*
2. Gebregziabher Gebremariam ETH 27:43.12
3. Dejene Berhanu ETH 27:47.19

Mar 1. Johannes Kekana RSA 2:25:01
2. Gashaw Melese ETH 2:26:08
3. Gudisa Shentema ETH 2:27:39

3000mSt 1. Ezekiel Kemboi KEN 8:12.27*
2. Paul Koech KEN 8:14.77
3. Tewodros Shiferaw ETH 8:27.33

110mh (-0.6) 1. Joseph-Berlioz Randriahihaja MAD 13.77
2. Todd Jouda Matthews SUD 13.81
3. Park Tae-kyong KOR 13.83

400mh 1. Osita Okeagbu NGR 50.25
2. Victor Okorie NGR 50.36
3. Ibou Faye SEN 50.89

HJ 1. Kabelo Mmono BOT 2.15
2. Jude Sidonie SEY 2.10
3. Samson Idiata NGR 2.10

PV 1. Bechir Zaghouani TUN 5.20
2. Fanie Jacobs RSA 5.20
3. Karim Sene SEN 5.00

LJ 1. Ignisious Gaisah GHA 8.30/0.1*
2. Ndiss Kaba Badji SEN 7.92/0.8
3. Godfrey Mokoena RSA 7.83/0.2

TJ 1. Andrew Owusu GHA 16.41/0.4
2. Godfrey Mokoena RSA 16.28/0.3
3. Olivier Sanou BUR 16.21/0.2

SP 1. Burger Lambrechts RSA 18.87
2. Chima Ugwu NGR 18.66
3. Yasser Fathi Ibrahim EGY 17.96

DT (1.75kg) 1. Omar El-Ghazaly EGY 63.61 lt
2. Hannes Hopley RSA 62.86 lt
3. Johannes van Wyk RSA 62.43 lt

HT 1. Chris Harmse RSA 75.17*
2. Sabreur Souid TUN 70.81
3. Samir Haouam ALG 68.95

JT 1. Gerhardus Pienaar RSA 76.95
2. Walid Abderrazak Mohamed EGY 73.79
3. Brian Erasmus RSA 72.94

20kmW 1. Hatem Ghoula TUN 1:30:32
2. Moussa Aouanouk ALG 1:30:36
3. Rezki Yahi ALG 1:35:19

4x100m 1. GHA (Boakye, Myles-Mills, Nknasah, Nsiah) 38.63
2. NGR 38.70
3. SEN 39.79

4x400m 1. BOT (Kilego, Kubisa, Molefe, Moseki) 3:02.24
2. NGR 3:04.49
3. ZIM 3:05.62

Women

100m 1. Mary Onyali NGR 11.26

(0.2) 2. Endurance Ojokolo NGR 11.26
3. Vida Anim GHA 11.29
200m 1. Mary Onyali NGR 23.09
(-0.3) 2. Vida Anim GHA 23.17
3. Estie Wittstock RSA 23.46
400m 1. Fatou Binetou Fall SEN 51.38
2. Doris Jacob NGR 51.41
3. Mireille Nguimgo CMR 51.59
800m 1. Grace Ebor NGR 2:02.04
2. Akosua Serwaa GHA 2:02.40
3. Lwiza John TAN 2:02.85
1500m 1. Kutre Dulecha ETH 4:21.63
2. Jackline Maranga KEN 4:22.69
3. Naomi Mugo KEN 4:24.33
5000m 1. Meseret Defar ETH 16:42.0
2. Dorcus Inzikuru UGA 16:42.9
3. Isabela Ochichi KEN 16:43.4
10,000m 1. Ejagayehu Dibaba ETH 32:34.54
2. Werknesh Kidane ETH 32:37.35
3. Leah Malot KEN 32:56.43
Mar 1. Clarisse Rasoarizy MAD 2:46:58
2. Tadelech Birra ETH 2:52:04
3. Leila Aman ETH 2:55:07
100mh 1. Angela Atede NGR 13.01
(-1.5) 2. Damaris Agbugba NGR 13.06
3. Christy Akinremi NGR 13.55
400mh 1. Omolade Akinremi NGR 56.98
2. Kate Obilor NGR 57.53
3. Kaboud Mébam CMR 58.28
HJ 1. Nneka Ukuah NGR 1.84
2. Marizca Gertenbach RSA 1.84
3. Anika Smit RSA 1.80
PV 1. Samantha Dodd RSA 3.90*
2. Annelie van Wyk RSA 3.80
3. Margaretha du Plessis RSA 3.50
LJ 1. Esther Aghatise NGR 6.58/0.2
2. Grace Umelo NGR 6.56/0.0
3. Chinedu Odozor NGR 6.52/-0.9
TJ 1. Kéné Ndoye 14.23/0.2
2. Salamotu Alimi NGR 13.47/0.1
3. Nkechi Mbaoma NGR 13.18/0.2
SP 1. Vivian Chukwuemeka NGR 18.12*
2. Veronica Abrahamse RSA 15.77
3. Wafaa Ismail EGY 15.32
DT 1. Elizna Naude RSA 57.44*
2. Vivian Chukwuemeka NGR 54.83
3. Alifatou Djibril TOG 54.79
HT 1. Marwa Ahmed Hussein EGY 64.28*
2. Olufunke Adoeye NGR 58.86
3. Vivian Chukwuemeka NGR 56.54
JT 1. Aïda Sellam TUN 54.58*
2. Lindy Leveaux SEY 53.23
3. Sunette Viljoen RSA
Hep 1. Margaret Simpson GHA 6152*
2. Justine Robbeson RSA 5697
3. Patience Okoro NGR 5436
20kmW 1. Estlé Viljoen RSA 1:44:29*
2. Amsale Yakob ETH 1:47:42
3. Natalie Fourie RSA 1:48:08
4x100m 1. NGR (Edem, Ojokolo, Odozor, Onyali) 43.04*
2. RSA 44.44
3. SEN 45.42
4x400m 1. NGR 3:27.76
2. CMR 3:31.52

1st Afro-Asian Games

At Hyderabad, India 28-30 October

Men

100m 1. Olusoji Fasula NGR 10.15
(-0.6) 2. Tamunosiki Atorudibo NGR 10.20
3. Shingo Suetsugu JPN 10.36
200m 1. Frank Fredericks NAM 20.57
(-0.8) 2. Gennadiy Chernovol KAZ 20.81
3. Oumar Loum SEN 20.99
400m 1. Ezra Sambu KEN 45.04
2. Nagmeldin El Abubakr SUD 45.44
3. Sugath Thilakaratne SRI 45.99
800m 1. Ahmed Ismail SUD 1:46.92
2. Peter Ashak SUD 1:47.48
3. Samuel Mwera TAN 1:47.98
1500m 1. Abdallah Abdelkadir SUD 3:40.17
2. Peter Ashak SUD 3:40.21
3. Benjamin Cheruiyot KEN 3:40.65
5000m 1. Hailu Mekonnen ETH 13:49.08
2. Markos Geneti ETH 13:49.61
3. Denis Keter KEN 13:50.41
10,000m 1. Sileshi Sihine ETH 27:48.40
2. Gebregziabher Gebremariam ETH 28:08.79
3. Boniface Kiprop UGA 28:12.67
3000mSt 1. John Kemboi KEN 8:56.43
2. Arun D'Souza IND 9:05.97
3. Joel Chelimo KEN 9:24.08
110mh 1. Todd Jouda Matthews SUD 13.68
(-2.2) 2. Masato Naito JPN 13.71
3. Park Tae-kyong KOR 13.83
400mh 1. Yevgeniy Meleshenko KAZ 49.66
2. Ibou Faye SEN 50.08
3. Osita Okeagbu NGR 50.87
HJ 1. Cui Kai CHN 2.18
2. Samson Idiata NGR 2.15
3. Jude Sidonie SEY 2.10
PV 1. Grigoriy Yegorov KAZ 5.25
2. Karim Sene SEN 5.05
3. Rafik Mefti ALG 4.95
LJ 1. Nabil Adamou ALG 7.93/0.0
2. Ndiss Kaba Badji SEN 7.86/0.2
3. Godfrey Mokoena RSA 7.76/-0.4
TJ 1. Takashi Komatsu JPN 16.65/1.8
2. Olivier Sanou BUR 16.16/0.9
3. Godfrey Mokoena RSA 15.92/0.7
SP 1. Shakti Singh IND 19.05
2. Burger Lambrechts RSA 18.97
3. Navpreet Singh IND 18.81
DT 1. Anil Kumar IND 60.68
2. Chima Ugwu NGR 59.87
3. Omar El-Ghazaly EGY 59.77
HT 1. Chris Harmse RSA 75.67
2. Dilchod Nazarov TJK 69.72
3. Samir Haouam ALG 69.37
JT 1. Hardus Pienaar RSA 84.50
2. Li Rongxiang CHN 79.01
3. Jagdish Singh Bishnoi IND 75.34
10kmW 1. Moussa Aouanouk ALG 43:33.58
2. Sita Ram IND 45:09.40
3. Sakchai Samutkoa THA 45:54.04
4x100m 1. Africa 39.07
2. SEN 39.58
3. IND 39.64
4x400m 1. Africa 3:04.61
2. NGR 3:05.09
3. ZIM 3:05.35

Women

100m (-1.8)
1. Endurance Ojokolo NGR 11.45
2. Lyubov Perepelova UZB 11.49
3. Delphine Atangana CMR 11.49

200m (-0.8)
1. Delphine Atangana CMR 23.37
2. Saraswati Saha IND 23.43
3. Geraldine Pillay RSA 23.48

400m
1. Estie Wittstock RSA 52.09
2. Doris Jacob NGR 53.08
3. Vassanee Vinatho THA 53.88

800m
1. Lwiza John TAN 2:01.68
2. Wang Yuanping CHN 2:04.36
3. Birhane Hirpassa ETH 2:05.31

1500m
1. Birhane Hirpassa ETH 4:17.36
2. Kutre Dulecha ETH 4:18.14
3. Madhuri A. Singh IND 4:22.32

5000m
1. Meseret Defar ETH 15:47.69
2. Tirunesh Dibaba ETH 15:48.21
3. Dorcus Inzikuru UGA 16:33.71

10,000m
1. Ejagayehu Dibaba ETH 33:01.12
2. Eyerusalem Kuma ETH 33:20.19
3. Sujeewa Jayasena SRI 35:53.45

100mh (-1.0)
1. Angela Atede NGR 13.18
2. Feng Yun CHN 13.20
3. Damaris Agbugba NGR 13.21

400mh
1. Natalya Torshina KAZ 55.81
2. Yao Yuehua CHN 56.29
3. Vassanee Vinatho THA 57.09

HJ
1. Marina Aitova KAZ 1.88
2. Bobby Aloysius IND 1.88
3. Marizca Gertenbach RSA 1.75

PV
1. Zhang Na CHN 4.10
2. Annelie van Wyk RSA 4.00
3. Qin Xia CHN 3.90

LJ
1. Anju Bobby George IND 6.53/-0.7
2. Lerma Elmira Gabito PHI 6.30/-0.6
3. Esther Aghatise NGR 6.30/-0.7

TJ
1. Huang Qiuyan CHN 13.50/0.6
2. Tatyana Bocharova KAZ 13.34/-0.6
3. Salamotu Alimi NGR 13.00/-0.9

SP
1. Li Meiju CHN 17.61
2. Li Fengfeng CHN 17.21
3. Jutaporn Krasaeyan THA 16.63

DT
1. Neelam Jaswant Singh IND 61.94
2. Li Yanfeng CHN 60.42
3. Song Aimin CHN 58.41

HT
1. Liu Yinghui CHN 68.03
2. Zhao Wei CHN 65.22
3. Marwa Ahmed Hussein EGY 60.60

JT
1. Sunette Viljoen RSA 55.49
2. Gurmeet Kaur IND 53.37
3. Ha Xiaoyan CHN 51.96

Hep
1. J.J. Shobha IND 5884
2. Justine Robbeson RSA 5587
3. Soma Biswas IND 5532

10kmW
1. Bahia Boussad ALG 51:23.70
2. Jasmin Kaur IND 51:36.60
3. Estlé Viljoen RSA 52:01.30

4x100m
1. Africa I 43.75
2. Africa II 43.86
3. THA 43.90

4x400m
1. Africa I 3:29.75
2. Africa II 3:32.16
3. KAZ 3:32.41

Asian Championships

At Manila, Philippines 20-23 September

Men

100m (0.0)
1. Chen Haijian CHN 10.25
2. Gennadiy Chernovol KAZ 10.27
3. Salem Mubarak Al-Yami KSA 10.28

200m (0.4)
1. Fawzi Al-Shammari KUW 20.70
2. Hamed Hamadan Al-Bishi KSA 20.73
3. Yang Yaozu CHN 20.82

400m
1. Fawzi Al-Shammari KUW 45.16
2. Hamdan Odha Al-Bishi KSA 45.39
3. Yuki Yamaguchi JPN 46.18

800m
1. Adam Abdou Adam QAT 1:46.20*
2. Salem Al-Badri QAT 1:46.95
3. Rashid Mohamed BRN 1:47.09

1500m
1. Rachid Ramzi BRN 3:41.66
2. Saif Saeed Shaheen QAT 3:42.79
3. Fumikazu Kobayashi JPN 3:42.96

5000m
1. Abdul Aziz Al-Amri QAT 13:58.89
2. Saif Saaeed Shaheen QAT 13:58.92
3. Nobuya Matsunaga JPN 14:12.73

10,000m
1. Abdullah Ahmad Hassan QAT 28:45.64*
2. Abdulhak Zakaria BRN 30:04.13
3. Eduardo Buenavista PHI 30:06.29

3000mSt
1. Khamis Seif Abdullah QAT 8:51.60
2. Wu Wen-Chien TPE 8:55.38
3. Yasunori Uchitomi JPN 8:56.31

110mh (-0.7)
1. Shi Dongpeng CHN 13.50
2. Park Tae-kyong KOR 13.71
3. Wu Youjia CHN 13.80

400mh
1. Mubarak Al-Nubi QAT 49.19
2. Yevgeniy Meleshenko KAZ 49.55
3. Chen Tien-Wen TPE 50.72

HJ
1. Wang Zhouzhou CHN 2.23
2. Bae Kyung-Ho KOR 2.19
3= Naoyuki Daigo JPN 2.19
3= Loo Kum Zee MAS 2.19

PV
1. Grigoriy Yegorov KAZ 5.40
2. Satoru Yasuda JPN 5.30
3. Yang Mu-Huei TPE 5.10

LJ
1. Hussein Al-Sabee KSA 8.23
2. Zhou Can CHN 8.11
3. Shin-ichi Terano JPN 8.04

TJ
1. Kazuyoshi Ishikawa JPN 16.72/0.7
2. Gu Junjie CHN 16.68/-0.4
3. Wu Ji CHN 16.67/0.7

SP
1. Bilal Saad Mubarak QAT 19.41
2. Shakti Singh IND 19.04
3. Khaled H. Al-Suwaidi QAT 18.57

DT
1. Wu Tao CHN 61.43
2. Abbas Samimi IRI 59.51
3. Anil Kumar IND 59.50

HT
1. Mohamed Al-Zankawi KUW 70.64
2. Hiroaki Doi JPN 70.11
3. Dilchod Nazarov TJK 69.90

JT
1. Li Rongxiang CHN 79.25
2. Yukifumi Murakami JPN 277.04
3. Sergey Voynov UZB 76.09

Dec
1. Vitaliy Smirnov UZB 8021*
2. Pavel Dubitskiy KAZ 7604
3. Pavel Andreyev UZB 27487

20kmW
1. Han Yucheng CHN 1:21:12*
2. Yuki Yamazaki JPN 1:21:54
3. Bai Liansheng CHN 1:22:14

4x100m
1. CHN 39.22

2. THA 39.57
3. JPN 39.59

4x400m 1. SRI 3:03.05
2. JPN 3:03.59
3. QAT 3:04.32

Women

100m (-0.2) 1. Lyubov Perepelova UZB 11.43 (11.24*h)
2. Qin Wangping CHN 11.56
3. Guzel Khubbieva UZB 11.57

200m (0.5) 1. Lyubov Perepelova UZB 23.11
2. Chen Lizha CHN 23.39
3. Guzel Khubbieva UZB 23.63

400m 1. Yin Yin Khine MYA 52.96
2. Bu Fanfang CHN 52.97
3. Svetlana Bodritskaya KAZ 53.19

800m 1. Yin Yin Khine MYA 2:01.96
2. Tatyana Roslanova KAZ 2:02.41
3. Zamira Amirova UZB 2:02.84

1500m 1. Tatyana Borisova KGZ 4:15.97
2. Madhuri A. Singh IND 4:17.87
3. Svetlana Lukashova KAZ 4:23.12

5000m 1. Sun Yingjie CHN 15:48.42
2. Yuko Manabe JPN 15:59.81
3. Hiromi Fujii JPN 16:31.18

10,000m 1. Sun Yingjie CHN 32:37.04
2. Sujeewa Jayasena SRI 34:46.99
3. L. Aruna Devi IND 37:23.28

100mh (-0.2) 1. Su Yiping CHN 13.09
2. Feng Yun CHN 13.25
3. Trecia Roberts THA 13.29

400mh 1. Huang Xiaoxiao CHN 55.66*
2. Natalya Torshina KAZ 55.88
3. Vassanee Vinatho THA 56.40

HJ 1. Bui Thi Nhung VIE 1.88
2. Miyuki Aoyama JPN 1.84
3. Noengrothai Chaipetch THA 1.84

PV 1. Wu Sha CHN 4.20*
2. Takayo Kondo JPN 4.10
3. Desy Margawati INA 3.90

LJ 1. Anastasiya Zhuravlyeva UZB 6.53/0.7
2. Liang Shuyan CHN 6.51/0.2
3. Lerma Gabito PHI 6.50/-0.1

TJ 1. Huang Qiuyan CHN 14.39*
2. Anastasiya Zhuravlyeva UZB 14.21
3. Zhang Hao CHN 13.63

SP 1. Li Meiju CHN 18.45
2. Li Fengfeng CHN 18.07
3. Chinatsu Mori JPN 17.80

DT 1. Li Yanfeng CHN 61.87
2. Neelam Jaswant Singh IND 58.64
3. Xu Shaoyang CHN 58.13

HT 1. Gu Yuan CHN 70.78
2. Liu Yinghui CHN 66.66
3. Masumi Aya JPN 64.04

JT 1. Ma Ning CHN 57.05
2. Jang Jung-Yeon KOR 53.23
3. Anne Maheshi De Silva SRI 150.18

Hep 1. Irina Naumenko KAZ 5845
2. Yuki Nakata JPN 5723
3. Shen Shengfei CHN 5633

20kmW 1. Ha Mingming CHN 1:31:47*
2. Zou Ying CHN 1:32:07
3. Yuan Yufang MAS 1:32:25

4x100m 1. THA 44.25
2. JPN 44.56
3. CHN 44.97

4x400m 1. CHN 3:31.30*
2. KAZ 3:32.82
3. IND 3:35.34

Medal table

Country	*G*	*S*	*B*	*Total*
CHN	19	10	8	37
QAT	6	3	2	11
UZB	4	1	5	10
KUW	3	-	-	3
KAZ	2	6	2	10
MYA	2	-	-	2
JPN	1	10	10	21
KSA	1	2	1	4
THA	1	1	3	5
BRN	1	1	1	3
SWR	1	1	1	3
KGZ	1	-	-	1
VIE	1	-	-	1
IND	-	3	3	6
KOR	-	3	1	4

TPE, MAS, PHI 2 medals; IRI, INA, TAJ 1 medal

European Under-23 Championships

At Bydgoszcz, Poland, July 17-20

Men

100m (1.2) 1. Ronald Pognon FRA 10.19*
2. Argo Golberg EST 10.28
3. Fabrice Calligny FRA 10.34

200m (0.7) 1. Chris Lambert GBR 20.34*
2. Marcin Jedrusinski POL 20.39
3. Johan Wissman SWE 20.43

400m 1. Leslie Djhone FRA 45.04*
2. Tim Benjamin GBR 45.86
3. Rafal Wieruszewski POL 45.87

800m 1. René Herms GER 1:46.26
2. Florent Lacasse FRA 1:46.47
3. Manuel Olmedo ESP 1:46.83

1500m 1. Mounir Yemmouni FRA 3:44.02
2. Xavier Areny ESP 3:44.65
3. Lorenzo Perrone ITA 3:45.05

5000m 1. Chris Thompson GBR 13:58.62
2. Mohammed Farah GBR 13:58.88
3. Robert Connolly IRL 14:03.75

10,000m 1. Ioánnis Kanellópoulos GRE 29:00.78
2. Vasiliy Matviychuk UKR 29:01.29
3. Pawel Ochal POL 29:17.41

3000mSt 1. Martin Pröll AUT 8:25.86*
2. Radoslaw Poplawski POL 8:27.95
3. Jukka Keskisalo FIN 8:28.53

110mh (0.6) 1. Ladji Doucouré FRA 13.25 (13.23* sf)
2. Philip Nossmy SWE 13.50
3. Gregory Sedoc NED 13.55

400mh 1. Marek Plawgo POL 48.45*
2. Christian Duma GER 49.53
3. Thomas Kortbeek NED 49.68

HJ 1. Aleksander Walerianczyk POL 2.36*
2. Andrey Tereshin RUS 2.27
3. Wojciech Borysiewicz POL 2.27

PV 1. Aleksandr Korchmid UKR 5.50
2. Marvin Osei-Tutu GER 5.50
3. Maksim Mazurik UKR 5.45

LJ 1. Louis Tsátoumas GRE 8.24/-0.5

2. Vladimir Zyuskov UKR 8.22/1.7
3. Danut Simion ROM 8.09/0.9

TJ 1. Dmitriy Valyukevich BLR 17.57/0.2*
2. Marian Oprea ROM 17.28/0.1
3. Rudolf Helpling GER 16.66/0.4

SP 1. Pavel Lyzhin BLR 20.43*
2. Pavel Sofin RUS 20.33
3. Rutger Smith NED 20.18

DT 1. Rutger Smith NED 59.90
2. Dmitriy Sivakov BLR 58.00
3. Bogdan Pishchalnikov RUS 56.88

HT 1. Krisztian Pars HUN 77.25
2. Esref Apak TUR 76.52
3. Aleksandr Vashchilo BLR 71.91

JT 1. Aleksandr Ivanov RUS 82.59
2. Igor Janik POL 82.54
3. Tero Pitkämäki FIN 78.84

Dec 1. André Niklaus GER 7983
2. Indrek Turi EST 7864
3. Atis Vaisjuns LAT 7681

20kmW 1. Beniamin Kucinski POL 1:22:07
2. Sergey Lystsov RUS 1:24:04
3. Andrey Talashko BLR 1:24:28

4x100m 1. GBR (Edgar, Lambert, Chin, Grant) 39.31
2. FRA (Adolia, Calligny, Socrier, Djhone) 39.38
3. BEL (Vereecke, Gourmet, Beyens, De Baerdemaker) 39.54

4x400m 1. POL (Wieruszewski, Skalski, Dabrowski, Plawgo) 3:03.32
2. GER (Gatzka, Duma, Sattelmaier, Swillims) 3:03.36
3. RUS (Matveyev, Petrov, Borshchenko, Polukeyev) 3:04.18

Women

100m (1.3) 1. Georgia Kokloni GRE 11.33
2. Daria Onysko POL 11.46
3. Oksana Dragun BLR 11.48

200m (1.0) 1. Marina Maydanova UKR 22.82
2. Maja Nose SLO 23.09
3. Dorota Dydo POL 23.34

400m 1. Helen Karagounis GBR 51.78
2. Solen Désert FRA 52.05
3. Tatyana Firova RUS 52.14

800m 1. Rebecca Lyne GBR 2:04.66
2. Lucia Klocová SVK 2:05.02
3. Esther Desviat ESP 2:05.38

1500m 1. Olesya Chumakova RUS 4:11.75
2. Lisa Dobriskey GBR 4:12.95
3. Ingvill Måkestad NOR 3:13.58
drugs dq (2) Rasa Drazdauskaite LTU 4:12.16

5000m 1. Elvan Abeylegesse TUR 15:16.79*
2. Tatyana Petrova RUS 16:02.79
3. Sonia Bejarano ESP 16:17.81

10,000m 1. Krisztina Papp HUN 33:23.02
2. Valentina Levushkina RUS 33:28.73
3. Louise Damen GBR 33:29.82

3000mSt 1. Lyubov Ivanova RUS 9:41.1*
2. Michaela Mannová CZE 9:42.01
3. Sigrid Vandenbempt BEL 9:42.04

100mh (1.0) 1. Susanna Kallur SWE 12.88*
2. Nadine Hentschke GER 12.89
3. Mariya Koroteyeva RUS 12.95

400mh 1. Oksana Gulumyan RUS 56.23
2. Irena Zauna LAT 56.47
3. Maria Rus ROM 57.01

HJ 1. Blanka Vlasic CRO 1.98*
2. Yelena Slesarenko RUS 1.96
3. Anna Ksok POL 1.92

PV 1. Yelena Isinbayeva RUS 4.65*
2. Vanessa Boslak FRA 4.40
3. Anna Rogowska POL 4.35

LJ 1. Carolina Klüft SWE 6.86/0.5*
2. Irina Simagina RUS 6.70/1.6
3. Ineta Radevica LAT 6.70/1.8

TJ 1. Viktoria Gurova RUS 14.37/1.4
2. Simona La Mantia ITA 14.31/2.0
3. Ineta Radevica LAT 14.04/1.2

SP 1. Natalya Khoroneko BLR 17.66
2. Kathleen Kluge GER 17.09
3. Filiz Kadogan TUR 16.72

DT 1. Natalya Fokina UKR 59.30*
2. Jana Tucholke GER 58.24
3. Olga Chernogorova BLR 56.57

HT 1. Kamila Skolimowska POL 71.38*
2. Oksana Menkova BLR 67.58
3. Gulya Khanafeyeva RUS 66.98

JT 1. Jarmila Klimesová CZE 60.54
2. Irina Kharun UKR 58.28
3. Mariya Yakovenko RUS 57.52

Hep 1. Jennifer Oeser GER 5901
2. Yvonne Wisse NED 5895
3. Vassiliki Delinikola GRE 5863

20km W 1. Athanasia Tsoumeleka GRE 1:33:55
2. Vera Santos POR 1:35:18
3. Sabine Zimmer GER 1:35:56

4x100m 1. UKR (Pigida, Shepetyuk, Chebanu, Maydanova) 44.29
2. POL (Radoszewska, Onysko, Dydo, Flejszar) 44.51
3. GER (Kuckelkorn, Schorr, Wakan, Hentschke) 44.59

4x400m 1. RUS (Gushchina, N Ivanova, Gulumyan, Firova) 3:29.25
2. GBR (Meadows, Halsall, Wall, Karagounis) 3:30.44
3. GER (Müller, Gröb, Kron, Hoffmann) 3:33.59

Medal and Points table

Country	*G*	*S*	*B*	*Total*	*Points*
RUS	7	7	6	20	205
POL	5	5	6	16	160
GER	3	6	4	13	150
GBR	5	3	2	10	124
UKR	4	3	1	8	110
BLR	3	2	4	9	99
FRA	4	4	1	9	95
SWE	2	1	1	4	57
GRE	4	0	1	5	50
ITA	0	1	1	2	50
ESP	0	1	3	4	45
NED	1	1	3	5	42
ROM	0	1	2	3	41
HUN	2	0	0	2	36
LAT	0	1	3	4	33
CZE	1	1	0	2	29.5
TUR	1	1	1	3	29
BEL	0	0	2	2	28
CRO	1	0	0	1	24
SVK	0	1	0	1	24
FIN	0	0	2	2	19.5
EST	0	2	0	2	17

1 gold: AUT; 1 silver: LTU, POR, SLO; 1 bronze: IRL

European Junior (U20) Championships

At Tampere, Finland, July 24-27

Men

100m (-0.2) 1. Leon Baptiste GBR 10.50
2. Till Helmke GER 10.52
3. Monu Miah GBR 10.54

200m (1.0) 1. Sebastian Ernst GER 20.63
2. Roman Smirnov RUS 20.86
3. Till Helmke GER 20.86

400m 1. Dimítrios Grávalos GRE 46.54
2. Kamghe Gaba GER 46.63
3. Piotr Kedzia POL 46.69

800m 1. René Bauschinger GER 1:49.43
2. David Fiegen LUX 1:49.91
3. Ireneusz Sekreterski POL 1:49.97

1500m 1. Bartosz Nowicki POL 3:45.01
2. Tom Lancashire GBR 3:45.60
3. Olle Walleräng SWE 3:46.17

5000m 1. Anatoliy Rybakov RUS 14:13.41
2. Marius Ionescu ROM 14:16.12
3. Cristinel Irimia ROM 14:17.30

10,000m 1. Marius Ionescu ROM 29:40.41
2. Aleksey Reunkov RUS 29:40.80
3. Mohammed Bashir DEN 29:42.42

3000mSt 1. Ruben Schwarz GER 8:46.21
2. Maricel Ionescu ROM 8:53.31
3. Peter Kellie GBR 8:55.69

110mh (0.0) 1. Bano Traore FRA 13.95
2. Andreas Kundert SUI 14.18
3. Kai Doskoczynski GER 14.26

400mh 1. Rhys Williams GBR 51.15
2. Mohamed Atig FRA 51.46
3. Rupert Gardner GBR 51.83

HJ 1. Jaroslav Bába CZE 2.28
2. Aleksey Dmitrik RUS 2.26
3. Linus Thörnblad SWE 2.23

PV 1. Vincent Favretto FRA 5.50
2. Artem Kuptsov RUS 5.50
3. Fabian Schulze GER 5.40

LJ 1. Nelson Évora POR 7.83/0.7
2. Christian Kaczmarek GER 7.81/1.2
3. Tim Riedel GER 7.65/0.4

TJ 1. Nelson Évora POR 16.43/0.4
2. Dmitriy Detsuk BLR 16.13w/2.4
3. Yevgeniy Semenenko UKR 16.04/ -1.9

SP 6kg 1. Magnus Lohse SWE 20.28
2. Anton Lyuboslavskiy RUS 20.10
3. Georgi Ivanov BUL 19.94

DT 1.75kg 1. Erik Cadee NED 60.42
2. Martin Maric CRO 58.59
3. Andreas Porth GER 58.45

HT 6kg 1. Lorenzo Povegliano ITA 72.72
2. Kamilius Bethke GER 72.60
3. Andrey Azarenkov RUS 72.10

JT 1. Teemu Wirkkala FIN 79.90
2. Tero Järvenpää FIN 73.66
3. Antti Ruuskanen FIN 72.87

Dec 1. Nicklas Wiberg SWE 7604
SP (6kg) 2. Aleksey Sysoyev RUS 7531
DT (1.75k) 3. Steffen Willwacher GER 7497

10kmW 1. Vladimir Parvatkin RUS 41:33.55
2. Michal Blazek SVK 41:54.66
3. Francisco Arcilla ESP 42:06.15

4x100m 1. GBR (Matthews, Oboh, Miah, Baptiste) 40.37
2. GER (Lohmann, Doskoczynski, Ernst, Helmke) 40.41
3. FRA (Fagris, Fernandez, Wallard, De Lepine) 40.50

4x400m 1. GER (Förster, Wilelm, Gernand, Gaba) 3:08.31
2. POL (Pryga, Grzegorczyk, Blocian, Kedzia) 3:08.62
3. RUS (Svechkar, Aleksandrenko, Kozhukhar, Shubin) 3:08.81

Women

100m (0.0) 1. Ivet Lalova BUL 11.43
2. Véronique Mang FRA 11.56
3. Jade Lucas-Read GBR 11.60

200m (1.6) 1. Ivet Lalova BUL 22.88
2. Jenny Ljunggren SWE 23.35
3. Virginie Michanol FRA 23.36

400m 1. Mariya Dryakhlova RUS 52.65
2. Joanne Cuddihy IRL 53.62
3. Christine Ohuruogu GBR 54.21

800m 1. Simona Barcau ROM 2:02.76
2. Charlotte Moore GBR 2:03.40
3. Jemma Simpson GBR 2:03.42

1500m 1. Nelya Neporadna UKR 4:12.57
2. Danielle Barnes GBR 4:16.91
3. Corina Dumbravean ROM 4:17.56

3000m 1. Inna Poluskina LAT 9:07.85
2. Binnaz Uslu TUR 9:23.10
3. Adrienne Herzog NED 9:26.01

5000m 1. Silvia La Barbera ITA 15:52.20
2. Inna Poluskina LAT 15:55.69
3. Charlotte Dale GBR 16:07.26

2000mSt 1. Catalina Oprea ROM 6:21.78*
2. Ancufia Bobocel ROM 6:32.03
3. Yekaterina Bespalova RUS 6:35.11

100mh (-0.1) 1. Sophie Krauel GER 13.28
2. Symone Belle GBR 13.53
3. Sabrina Altermatt SUI 13.59

400mh 1. Yekaterina Kostetskaya RUS 57.52
2. Irina Obedina RUS 57.57
3. Zuzana Hejnová CZE 58.30

HJ 1. Ariane Friedrich GER 1.88
2. Aileen Herrmann GER 1.86
3. Emma Green SWE 1.86

PV 1. Silke Spiegelburg GER 4.15
2. Floé Kühnert GER 4.15
3. Aleksandra Kiryashova RUS 4.15

LJ 1. Sophie Krauel GER 6.47/1.8
2. Adina Anton ROM 6.46/1.2
3. Daniela Lincoln-Saavedra SWE 6.35/-1.1

TJ 1. Anastasiya Taranova RUS 13.61/0.3
2. Cristine Spîtaru ROM 13.54/-0.5
3. Svetlana Bolshakova RUS 13.37/-1.4

SP 1. Anna Avdeyeva RUS 16.71
2. Yuliya Leantsyuk BLR 16.29
3. Petra Lammert GER 16.16

DT 1. Ulrike Giesa GER 53.75
2. Nadine Müller GER 53.44
3. Darya Pishchalnikova RUS 52.39

HT 1. Katarzyna Kita POL 66.08
2. Marina Smolyachkova BLR 65.89
3. Berta Castells ESP 65.64

JT 1. Julia Zandt GER 56.96
2. Mareike Rittweg GER 54.74
3. Ilze Gribule LAT 52.76

Hep 1. Olga Levenkova RUS 5748
2. Kathrin Geissler GER 5631
3. Anna Kryazheva RUS 5605

10kmW 1. Irina Petrova RUS 47:12.77
2. Anna Bragina RUS 47:17.56
3. Ana Cabecinha POR 47:36.15

4x100m 1. FRA (Vouaux, Jacques-Sebastien, Kamga, Mang) 44.60
2. GBR (Anyika Onuora, K-A Thomas, Spencer, Lucas Read) 44.81
3. FIN (Pylkkä, Korjansalo, Keskitalo, Hakamäki) 45.00

4x400m 1. RUS (Popova, Kostetskaya, Migounova, Dryakhlova) 3:33.48
2. FRA (Jemaa, Sigere, Ndje, Michanol) 3:37.78
3. GBR (Ohuruogu, Scott, Griffiths, Nicol) 3:38.96

Medal and points table

Country	*G*	*S*	*B*	*Total*	*Points*
GER	10	10	7	27	282.5
RUS	9	8	7	24	210
GBR	3	5	8	16	173.5
FRA	3	3	2	8	106.5
POL	2	1	2	5	92
ROM	3	5	2	10	81
SWE	2	1	4	7	64
UKR	1	0	1	2	59
BLR	0	3	0	3	50.5
ESP	0	0	2	2	45.5
FIN	1	1	2	4	45
ITA	2	0	0	2	42
CZE	1	0	1	2	39
NED	1	0	1	2	31
GRE	1	0	0	1	26
BUL	2	0	1	3	25
POR	2	0	1	3	25
LAT	1	1	1	3	23
SUI	0	1	1	2	20

1 silver: CRO, IRL., LUX, SVK, TUR; 1 bronze: DEN

European Cup 2003

Super-League at Firenze, Italy June 21-22

Men: 1. FRA 109, 2. GER 100.5, 3. GBR 96, 4. RUS 92, 5. ITA 84, 6. POL 83, 7. ESP 80, 8. GRE 74.5

100m (-1.0) 1. Mark Lewis-Francis GBR 10.22
2. Aimé-Issa Nthépé FRA 10.36
3. Aristotélis Gavélas GRE 10.44

200m (-2.3) 1. Konstadínos Kedéris GRE 20.37
2. Christian Malcolm GBR 20.45
3. Marcin Jedrusinski POL 20.53

400m 1. Marc Raquil FRA 44.88
2. Ingo Schultz GER 45.19
3. Iwan Thomas GBR 45.58

800m 1. Antonio M Reina ESP 1:48.13
2. Florent Lacasse FRA 1:48.37
3. René Herms GER 1:49.15

1500m 1. Juan Carlos Higuero ESP 3:49.16
2. Miroslaw Formela POL 3:49.22
3. Michael East GBR 3:49.60

3000m 1. Fouad Chouki FRA 8:22.56
2. Carlos Castillejo ESP 8:22.79
3. Vyacheslav Shabunin RUS 8:23.18

5000m 1. Ismaïl Sghyr FRA 13:43.70
2. Jesús España ESP 13:44.68
3. Dieter Baumann GER 13:45.55

3000mSt 1. Pavel Potapovich RUS 8:26.28
2. Radoslaw Poplawski POL 8:29.70
3. Angelo Iannelli ITA 8:30.40

110mh (-0.2) 1. Ladji Doucouré FRA 13.55
2. Mike Fenner GER 13.58
3. Andrea Giaconi ITA 13.66

400mh 1. Chris Rawlinson GBR 48.45
2. Periklís Iakovákis GRE 49.23 0.160
3. Ruslan Mashchenko RUS 49.43

HJ 1. Yaroslav Rybakov RUS 2.34
2. Alessandro Talotti ITA 2.30
3. Grzegorz Sposób POL 2.27

PV 1. Romain Mesnil FRA 5.75
2. Giuseppe Gibilisco ITA 5.70
3. Lars Börgeling GER 5.70

LJ 1. Louis Tsátoumas GRE 8.06/-0.9
2. Yago Lamela ESP 7.96/-1.3
3. Nils Winter GER 7.85/-0.4

TJ 1, Fabrizio Donato ITA 17.16/0.5
2. Julien Kapek FRA 16.59/0.4
3. Hristos Melétoglou GRE 16.52/0.5

SP 1. Manuel Martínez ESP 21.08
2. Carl Myerscough GBR 20.72
3. Pavel Chumachenko RUS 20.12

DT 1. Dmitriy Shevchenko RUS 65.39
2. Michael Möllenbeck GER 65.26
3. Andrzej Krawczyk POL 61.27

HT 1. Karsten Kobs GER 80.63
2. Wojciech Kondratowicz POL 78.37
3. Aléxandros Papadimitríou GRE 78.11

JT 1. Sergey Makarov RUS 85.86
2. Christian Nicolay GER 81.93
3. Dariusz Trafas POL 79.3

4x100m 1. ITA (Scuderi, Collio, Donati, Cavallero) 38.42
2. POL 38.45
3. GBR 38.60

4x400m 1. GBR (Rawlinson, Benjamin, Baulch, Elias) 3:02.43
2. GRE 3:02.69
3. GER 3:02.83

Women: 1. RUS 130, 2. GER 103, 3. FRA 102, 4. GBR 83, 5. ESP 82, 6. GRE 78.5, 7. ROM 77.5, 8. ITA 62

100m (-1.3) 1. Christine Arron FRA 11.07
2. Marina Kislova RUS 11.19
3. Glory Alozie ESP 11.29

200m (-0.4) 1. Anastasiya Kapachinskaya RUS 22.71
2. Ionela Tîrlea ROM 22.78
3. Nuriel Hurtis FRA 22.89

400m 1. Svetlana Pospelova RUS 50.85
2. Lee McConnell GBR 51.37
3. Hrïsa Goudenoúdi GRE 52.11

800m 1. Claudia Gesell GER 2:00.85
2. Maria Cioncan ROM 2:01.02
3. Mayte Martínez ESP 2:01.63

1500m 1. Natalia Rodríguez ESP 4:07.18
2. Helen Clitheroe GBR 4:08.18
3. Konstadína Efedáki GRE 4:09.06

3000m 1. Olga Yegorova RUS 8:55.73
2. Hayley Tullett GBR 8:57.45
3. Sabrina Mockenhaupt GER 8:57.69

5000m 1. Yelena Zadorozhnaya RUS 15:34.07
2. Jo Pavey GBR 15:35.31
3. Mihaela Botezan ROM 15:39.63

3000mSt 1. Gulnara Samitova RUS 9:40.89*

	2. Cristina Casandra ROM 9:48.47
	3. Elodie Olivares FRA 9:54.51
100mh	1. Glory Alozie 12.86
(-0.1)	2. Svetlana Laukhova RUS 12.88
	3. Patricia Girard FRA 12.95
400mh	1. Ionela Tîrlea ROM 54.47
	2. Natasha Danvers GBR 55.01
	3. Heike Meissner GER 55.22
HJ	1. Daniela Rath GER 2.00
	2. Ruth Beitia ESP 1.95
	3. Marina Kuptsova RUS 1.95
PV	1. Annika Becker GER 4.50
	2. Tatyana Polnova RUS 4.45
	3. Marie Poissonnier FRA 4.35
LJ	1. Eunice Barber FRA 6.76/0.5
	2. Concepción Montaner ESP 6.69/0.6
	3. Fiona May ITA 6.67/1.5
TJ	1. Anna Pyatykh RUS 14.79/-0.7
	2. Magdelin Martinez IYA 14.76 -0.5
	3. Adelina Gavrila ROM 14.45/-0.2
SP	1. Astrid Kumbernuss GER 19.46
	2. Svetlana Krivelyova RUS 18.98
	3. Laurence Manfrédi FRA 17.97
DT	1. Ekateríni Vóggoli GRE 62.11
	2. Melina Robert-Michon FRA 61.67
	3. Natalya Sadova RUS 61.59
HT	1. Manuela Montebrun FRA 74.43
	2. Mihaela Melinte ROM 71.99
	3. Olga Kuzenkova RUS 69.89
JT	1. Steffi Nerius GER 63.30
	2. Mirela Manjani GRE 63.13
	3. Claudia Coslovich ITA 62.70
4x100m	1. FRA (Girard, Hurtis, Dia, Arron) 42.62
	2. GER (Paschke, G Rockmeier, Möller, Wagner) 43.13
	3. RUS (Fedorova, Khabarova, Kislova, Kruglova) 43.23
4x400m	1. RUS (Lavshuk, N Ivanova, Firova, Pospelova) 3:26.02
	2. GBR 3:26.52
	3. FRA 3:28.39

First League Group A *at Lappeenranta FIN, June 21-22*
Men: 1. SWE 125, 2. FIN 113, 3. HUN 104, 4. BEL 89, 5. BLR 83, 6. NOR 77, 7. DEN 67, 8. EST 60. **Winners**: **100m**: Gábor Dobos HUN 10.35, **200m**: Johan Wissman SWE 20.58w, **400m**: Cédric Van Branteghem BEL 45.91, **800m**: Rickard Pell SWE 1:49.13, **1500m/3000mSt**: Jukka Keskisalo FIN 3:44.81.8:26.37, **3000m**: Erik Sjöqvist SWE 7:55.30, **5000m**: Azat Rakipov BLR 13:43.11, **110mh**: Robert Kronberg SWE 13.58, **400mh**: Leonid Vershinin BLR 51.15, **HJ**: Stefan Holm SWE 2.24, **PV**: Patrik Kristiansson SWE 5.55, **LJ**: Tommi Evilä FIN 7.73/0.6, **TJ**: Christian Olsson SWE 17.38, **SP**: Conny Karlsson FIN 19.94, **DT**: Gábor Máté HUN 62.63, **HT**: Péter Botfa HUN 79.61, **JT**: Andreas Thorkildsen NOR 81.42, **4x100m**: SWE 39.47, **4x400m**: BLR 3:06.29
Women: 1. POL 125, 2. FIN 105, 3. SWE 105, 4. HUN 100, 5. BLR 93, 6. BEL 82.5, 7. IRL 59, 8. LTU 48.5 (after Korolchik dq). **Winners**: **100m**: Johanna Manninen FIN 11.26w, **200m**: Kim Gevaert 22.81, **400m**: Svetlana Usovich BLR 52.24, **800m**: Judit Varga HUN 2:04.80, **1500m/3000mSt**: Alesya Turova BLR 4:10.82/9:48.19, **3000m**: Justyna Lesman POL 9:09.87, **5000m**: Anikó Kálovics HUN 15:18.45, **100mh**: Aurelia Trywianska POL 12.84, **400mh**: Anna Jesien POL 55.98, **HJ**: Kajsa Bergqvist SWE 1.96, **PV**: Monika Pyrek POL 4.30, **LJ**: Tünde Vaszi HUN 6.34, **TJ**: Heli Koivula FIN 14.15w, **SP**: Krystyna Zabawska POL 18.12, **DT**: Irina Yatchenko BLR 63.67, **HT**: Sini Pöyry 67.64, **JT**: Nikolett Szabó HUN 56.83, **4x100m**: BEL 43.78, **4x400m**: BLR 3:28.34

First League Group B *at Velenje SLO, June 21-22*
Men: 1. NED 121, 2. UKR 115, 3. CZE 110, 4. POR 100, 5. SLO 82, 6. BUL 67.5, 7. ISR 63, 8. SVK 60.5.
Winners: **100m**: Konstantin Rurak UKR 10.33, **200m**: Francis Obikwelu POR 20.41, **400m**: Jirí Muzík CZE 46.26, **800m**: Bram Som NED 1:47.18, **3000m**: Rui Silva POR 7:57.75, **5000m**: Casiliy Matviychuk UKR 14:09.35, **3000mSt**: Bostjan Buc 8:28.42, **110mh**: Gregory Sedoc NED 13.72, **400mh**: Stepán Tesarík CZE 49.72, **HJ**: Tomás Janku CZE 2.30, **PV**: Rens Blom NED 5.75, **LJ**: Jurgen Cools NED 7.85, **TJ**: Ivailo Rusenov BUL 17.02, **SP**: Rutger Smith NED 20.00, **DT**: Libor Malina CZE 63.92, **HT**: Libor Charfreitag SVK 78.23, **JT**: Vadim Bavikin ISR 79.31, **4x100m**: UKR 39.15, **4x400m**: NED 3:04.16
Women: 1. UKR 125, 2. CZE 104, 3. POR 96, 4. NED 92, 5. BUL 87, 6. SLO 86, 7. SVK 67, 8. SCG 58.
Winners: **100m**: Merlene Ottey 11.25, **200m**: Marina Maydanova UKR 22.70, **400m**: Miriam Hrdlicková SVK 53.13, **800m**: Jolanda Ceplak 1:58.30, **1500m**: Sonja Roman 4:10.50, **3000m**: Andrea Suldesová CZE 9:11.87, **5000m**: Fernanda Ribeiro POR 15:42.29, **3000mSt**: Jana Biolková CZE 9:50.24, **100mh**: Lucie Martincová CZE 13.41, **400mh**: Maria Carmo Tavares POR 57.10, **HJ**: Viktoriya Styopina UKR 1.95, **PV**: Pavla Hamácková CZE 4.60, **LJ**: Katerina Chernyavska UKR 6.45, **TJ**: Yelena Govorova UKR 14.35, **SP**: Lieja Tunks NED 18.52, **DT**: Yelena Antonova UKR 62.65, **HT**: Irina Sekachova UKR 71.73, **JT**: Tatyana Lyakhovich UKR 56.00, **4x100m**: UKR 43.27, **4x400m**: UKR 3:33.97

Second League Group A *at Århus DEN, June 21-22*
Men: 1. SWE 131, 2. AUT 121, 3. IRL 104, 4. LTU 103, 5. LAT 86, 6. LUX 57.5, 7. ISL 53, 8. Small Sates 47.5
Women: 1. SUI 122, 2. LAT 117, 3. AUT 114.5, 4. NOR 111, 5. DEN 101.5, 6. ISL 81, 7. Small States 38, 8. LUX 27

Second League Group B *at Istanbul TUR, June 21-22*
Men: 1. ROM 209, 2. CRO 183, 3. TUR 175.5, 4. CYP 164, 5. SCG 162, 6. MDA 121, 7. BIH 114, 8. AZE 106, 9. ARM 103.5, 10. GEO 103, 11. ALB 75, 12. MKD 15
Women: 1. EST 212.5, 2. TUR 203, 3. ISR 183, 4. CRO 169, 5. CYP 151, 6. MDA 138, 7. GEO 98, 8. BIH 90, 9. ARM 88.5, 10. AZE 76, 11. ALB 74, 12. MKD 15

2004 Matches – all on June 19-20

Spar European Cup, *Bydgoszcz (POL)*: **Men**: FRA, GER, GBR, ITA, NED, POL, RUS, SWE; **Women**: FRA, GER, GBR, GRE, POL, RUS, ESP, UKR
First League Group A, *Plovdiv (BUL)*: **Men**: BLR, BEL, BUL, CRO, CZE, GRE, ROM, UKR; **Women**: BLR, BEL, BUL, CZE, EST, LAT, ROM, SWE
First League Group B, *Istanbul (TUR)*: **Men**: AUT, FIN, HUN, NOR, POR, SLO, ESP, SUI; **Women**: FIN, HUN, ITA, NED, POR, SLO, SUI, TUR
Second League Group A, *Reykjavik (ISL)*: **Men**: AASSE*, CYP, DEN, EST, ISL, IRL, LTU, LUX; **Women**: AASSE*, AUT, CYP, DEN, ISL, IRL, LTU, NOR;
* =Athletic Association of the Small States of Europe
Second League Group B, Belgrade (SCG): **Men**: ALB, ARM, AZE, BIH, MKD, GEO, ISR, LAT, MDA, SCG, SVK, TUR; **Women**: ALB, ARM, AZE, BIH, CRO, CYP, MKD, GEO, ISR, MDA, SCG, SVK

1st European Indoor Cup 2003

At Leipzig, Germany 15 February

Men: 1. ESP 56, 2. GER 56, 3. FRA 49, 4, RUS 49, 5. ITA 47, 6. POL 46, 7, GBR 39, 8, GRE 24. **Winners**: **60m**: Jason Gardener GBR 6.55, **400m**: Marek Plawgo POL 46.76, **800m**: René Herms GER 1:48.65, **1500m**: Juan Carlos Higuero ESP 3:41.64, **3000m**: Yusef El Nasri ESP 8:00.28, **60mh**: Mike Fenner GER 7.68, **HJ**: Alessandro Talotti ITA 2.28, **LJ**: Yago Lamela ESP 8.09, **SP**: Ralf Bartels GER 19.69, **200/400/600/800mR:** FRA 4:14.42

Women: 1. RUS 60, 2. GER 49, 3. GBR 40, 4. FRA 40, 5. POL 40, 6. ESP 37, 7. GRE 32, 8. ROM 31. **Winners**: **60m**: Christine Arron FRA 7.18, **400m**: Grit Breuer GER 51.91, **800m**: Mayte Martínez ESP 2:03.14, **1500m**: Hayley Tullett GBR 4:08.63, **3000m**: Galina Bogomolova RUS 8:55.41, **60mh**: Glorie Alozie ESP 7.94, **PV**: Svetlana Feofanova RUS 4.65, **TJ**: Adelina Gavrila ROM 14.23, **200/400/600/800mR:** RUS 4:41.69

European Cup for Combined Events 2003

Super League at Bressanone ITA, July 5-6

Men Dec: 1. FRA 23,538, 2. RUS 23,357, 3. ITA 22,678, 4. UKR 22,286, 5. GER 22,165, 6. FIN 21,824, 7. CZE 21,134, 8. AUT 19,518. **Ind**: 1. Romain Barras FRA 8008. 2. Aleksandr Pogorelov RUS 7896, 3. Sergey Nikitin RUS 7850

Women Hep: 1. RUS 17,983, 2. BLR 17,982, 3. GRE 17,433, 4. GER 17,249, 5. POL 17,131, 6. CZE 16,663, 7. FRA 16,408, 8. UKR 11,102. **Ind**: 1. Yelena Prokhorova RUS 6313, 2. Inna Butor BLR 6264, 3. Aryiró Stratáki GRE 6064; drugs dq: Lyudmila Blonska UKR 6425

First League *at Tallinn EST, July 5-6*

Men Dec: 1. POL 23,082, 2. EST 22,921, 3. NED 22,637, 4. SUI 22,551, 5. ESP 22,151, 6. GBR 21,830, 7. HUN 21,323, 8. LAT 21,001. **Ind**: 1. Erki Nool EST 8281. 2. Chiel Warners NED 8060. 3. Michal Modelski POL 7835,

Women Hep: 1. GBR 18,239, 2. NED 17,346, 3. ITA 17,197, 4. FIN 17,174, 5. EST 16,958, 6. SWE 16,923, 7. LTU 16,597, 8. POR 13,897. **Ind**: 1. Carolina Klüft SWE 6692. 2. Denise Lewis GBR 6282. 3. Larisa Netseporuk EST 6215

Second League at Maribor SLO, June 29-30

Men Dec: 1. GRE 21,539, 2. SLO 21,080, 3. SWE 20,020, 4. LTU 19,884, 5. SVK 19,039, – CRO;. **Ind**: Georgios Andreou CYP 7711

Women Hep: 1. SUI 16,845, 2. ESP 15,735, 3. AUT 15,577, 4. HUN 15,232, 5. LAT 14,811, 6. DEN 14,044, 7. SLO 13,525. **Ind**: Sylvine Dufour BEL 6033

European Cup of Race Walking 2003

At Cheboksary, Russia 18 May

Men 20km: 1. Francisco Fernández ESP 1:19:48, 2. Alessandro Gandellini ITA 1:20:53, 3. Vladimir Andreyev RUS 1:20:56, 4. João Vieira POR 1:21:01, 5. Ilya Markov RUS 1:21:29, 6. David Marques ESP 1:21:41, 7. David Dominguez ESP 1:21:53, 8. Lorenzo Civallero ITA 1:22:01, 9. Predrag Filipovic SCG 1:22:25, 10. Andrey Stadnichuk RUS 1:22:56. 57 of 67 finished. **Team:** 1. ESP 13, 2. RUS 18, 3. ITA 26, 4. BLR 60, 5. SVK 81, 6. POL 91, 7. FRA 99, 8. LAT 102, 9. GER 111, 10. UKR 134, 11. MDA 144, 12. SUI 154

50km: 1. German Skurygin RUS 3:47:50, 2. Aleksey Voyevodin RUS 3:48:43, 3. Semyon Lovkin RUS 3:51:36, 4. Santiago Pérez ESP 3:52:57, 5. Francisco Pinardo ESP 3:54:01, 6. Stepan Yudin RUS 3:55:26, 7. Mario Avellaneda ESP 3:56:21, 8. Fredrik Svensson SWE 3:56:53, 9. Milos Holusa CZE 3:58:05, 10. Perdo Martins POR 3:58:07. 30 of 45 finished. **Team:** 1. RUS 6, 2. ESP 11, 3. POR 54, 4. UKR 61, 5. HUN 66, 6. GRE 67.

U20 Men 10km: 1. Andrey Yurin UKR 41:32, 2. Aleksandr Prokhorov RUS 41:36, 3. Mikhail Seradovich BLR 41:40. **Team:** 1. RUS 6, 2. ESP 11, 3. BLR 14, 4. UKR 15, 5. ITA 20, 6. SVK 31, 7. POL 33, 8. GER 38, 9. CZE 41, 10. HUN 57, 11. FRA 58, 12. LAT 58, 13. LTU 61, 14. GRE 68

Women 20km: 1. Yelena Nikolayeva RUS 1:26:22, 2. Elisabetta Perrone ITA 1:27:58, 3. Maria Vasco ESP 1:28:10, 4. Natalya Fedoskina RUS 1:28:17, 5. Susana Feitor POR 1:29:08, 6. Kjersti Plätzer NOR 1:29:36, 7. Norica Cîmpean ROM 1:30:27, 8. Olive Loughnane IRL 1:30:29, 9. Melanie Seeger GER 1:30:41, 10. Vera Zozulya UKR 1:30:54. 48 of 54 finished. **Team:** 1. ITA 27, 2. ESP 40, 3. RUS 44, 4. GER 48, 5. POR 56, 6. UKR 62, 7. BLR 70, 8. GRE 72. 9. ROM 82, 10. LTU 83, 11. FRA 96

U20 Women 10km: 1. Irina Petrova RUS 46:54, 2. Vera Sokolova RUS 47:02, 3. Snezhana Yurchenko BLR 47:03. **Team:** 1. RUS 3, 2. BLR 7, 3. GER 14, 4. ESP 18, 5. UKR 27, 6. IRL 27, 7. LTU 29, 8. ITA 31, 9. GBR 41, 10. TUR 45, 11. FRA 46, 12. ARM 55

Pan-American Games 2003

At Santo Domingo, Dominican Republic 5 - 9 August

Men

100m	1. Michael Frater JAM 10.21
(0.7)	2. Mardy Scales USA 10.22
	3. Anson Henry CAN 10.30
	drugs dq (1) Mickey Grimes # USA 10.10
200m	1. Kenny Brokenburr USA 20.42
(0.6)	2. Chris Williams JAM 20.54
	3. André da Silva BRA 20.68
400m	1. Mitch Potter USA 45.11
	2. Yeiman López CUB 45.13
	3. Alleyne Francique GRN 45.51
800m	1. Ashraf Tadili CAN 1:45.05*
	2. Osmar dos Santos BRA 1:45.64
	3. Fabiano Peçanha BRA 1:46.39
1500m	1. Hudson de Souza BRA 3:45.72
	2. Michael Stember USA 3:46.31
	3. Grant Robison USA 3:46.68
5000m	1. Hudson de Souza BRA 13:50.71
	2. David Galván MEX 13:52.92
	3. Marílson dos Santos BRA 13:56.90
10,000m	1. Teodoro Vega MEX 28:49.38
	2. Marílson dos Santos BRA 28:49.48
	3. Dan Browne USA 29:06.23
Mar	1. Vanderlei de Lima BRA 2:19:08
	2. Bruce Deacon CAN 2:20:25
	3. Diego Colorado COL 2:21:48
3000mSt	1. Néstor Nieves VEN 8:34.26
	2. Joël Bourgeois CAN 8:36.78
	3. Anthony Famiglietti USA 8:40.22
110mh	1. Yuniel Hernández CUB 13.35

(-0.2) 2. Larry Wade USA 13.35
3. Márcio de Souza BRA 13.45
400mh 1. Félix Sánchez DOM 48.19
2. Eric Thomas USA 48.74
3. Dean Griffiths JAM 49.35
HJ 1. Germaine Mason JAM 2.34
2. Jamie Nieto USA 2.28
3. Terrance Woods USA 2.22
PV 1. Toby Stevenson USA 5.45
2. Russ Buller USA 5.40
3. Dominic Johnson LCA 5.40
LJ 1. Iván Pedroso CUB 8.23/0.7
2. Luis Méliz CUB 8.20/0.7
3. Víctor Castillo VEN 7.98/1.1
TJ 1. Yoandri Betanzos CUB 17.26/1.1
2. Jadel Gregório BRA 17.03/-1.2
3. Yoelbi Quesada CUB 16.78/-0.4
SP 1. Reese Hoffa USA 20.95
2. Marco Antonio Verni CHI 20.14
3. Brad Snyder CAN 20.10
DT 1. Jason Tunks CAN 63.70
2. Frank Casañas CUB 62.61
3. Loy Maikel Martínez CUB 61.36
HT 1. Juan Cerra ARG 75.53
2. James Parker USA 74.35
3. John McEwen USA 71.49
JT 1. Emeterio González CUB 81.72
2. Isbel Luaces CUB 80.95
3. Breaux Greer USA 79.21
Dec 1. Stephen Moore USA 7809
2. Luiggi Llanos PUR 7704
3. Yonelvis Aguila CUB 7593
4x100m 1. BRA (V de Lima, Ribeiro, A da Silva, Cl. da Silva) 38.44
2. TRI (Alexander, Burns, Boldon, D Brown) 38.53
3. CUB (César, Peña, Reyes, Pita) 39.09
dq. USA (Coleman, Brokenburr, Smoots, Grimes #) 38.27
4x400m 1. JAM (Campbell, Ayre, Spence, Clarke) 3:01.81
2. USA (Potter, Hooker, Steele, James Davis) 3:01.87
3. DOM (Peguero, Santa, Vidal, Sánchez) 3:02.02
20kmW 1. Jefferson Pérez ECU 1:23:06
2. Bernardo Segura MEX 1:23:31
3. Alejandro López MEX 1:24:33
50kmW 1. Germán Sánchez MEX 4:05:18
2. Mário José dos Santos BRA 4:07:37
3. Luis García GUA 4:12:16

Women

100m 1. Lauryn Williams USA 11.12
(1,6) 2. Angela Williams USA 11.15
3. Liliana Allen MEX 11.28
200m 1. Roxana Díaz CUB 22.69
(1.3) 2. Cydonie Mothersill CAY 22.86
3. Allyson Felix USA 22.93
400m 1. Ana Guevara MEX 50.36
2. Hazel-Ann Regis GRN 51.56
3. Aliann Pompey GUY 52.06
800m 1. Adriana Muñoz CUB 2:02.96
2. Marian Burnett GUY 2:03.58
3. Christiane R dos Santos BRA 2:04.37
drugs dq. Letitia Vriesde # SUR 2:02.92
1500m 1. Adriana Muñoz CUB 4:09.57
2. Mary Jayne Harrelson USA 4:09.72
3. Mardrea Hyman JAM 4:10.08
5000m 1. Adriana Fernández MEX 15:30.65
2. Nora Rocha MEX 15:40.98
3. Nicole Jefferson USA 15:42.40
10,000m 1. Adriana Fernández MEX 33:16.05
2. Yudelkis Fernández CUB 33:55.12
3. Bertha Sánchez COL 33:56.17
Mar 1. Márcia Narloch BRA 2:39:54
2. Mariela González CUB 2:42:55
3. Erika Olivera CHI 2:44:52
100mh 1. Brigitte Foster JAM 12.67
(-0.3) 2. Perdita Felicien CAN 12.70
3. Lacena Golding JAM 12.79
400mh 1. Joanna Hayes USA 54.77
2. Daimí Pernía CUB 55.10
3. Andrea Blackett BAR 55.24
HJ 1. Juana Rosario Arrendel DOM 1.94
2. Romary Rifka MEX 1.94
3. Yariannis Argüelles CUB 1.89
PV 1. Mel Mueller USA 4.40
2. Carolina Torres-Maurer CHI 4.30
3. Stephanie McCann CAN 4.20
LJ 1. Alice Falaiye CAN 6.43/0.0
2. Jackie Edwards BAH 6.41/-0.9
3. Yangelis Savigne CUB 6.40/-0.3
TJ 1. Mabel Gay CUB 14.42/0.4
2. Yuliana Pérez USA 13.99/0.6
3. Yusmay Bicet CUB 13.90/0.9
SP 1. Yumileidi Cumbá CUB 19.31
2. Elisângela Adriano BRA 18.48
3. Flor Vásquez DOM 18.14
DT 1. Aretha Hill USA 63.30
2. Ana Elis Fernández CUB 61.26
3. Yania Ferrales CUB 60.03
HT 1. Yipsi Moreno CUB 74.25
2. Yunaika Crawford CUB 69.57
3. Candice Scott TRI 69.06
JT 1. Kim Kreiner USA 60.86
2. Laverne Eve BAH 60.68
3. Osleidis Menéndez CUB 60.20
Hep 1. Tiffany Hogan USA 6064
2. Nicole Haynes CAN 5969
3. Magalys García CUB 5864
4x100m 1. USA (A Williams, C Moore, Daigle, L Williams) 43.06
2. CUB (Pérez, Díaz, Benavides, Lazo) 43.40
3. JAM (Golding-Clarke, Ktson, S Williams, Browning) 43.71
4x400m 1. USA (Me'Lisa Barber, Robinson, Clay, Trotter) 3:26.40
2. JAM (Downer, Burgher, N Williams, Beckford) 3:27.34
3. BRA (Almirão, Tito, Coutinho, Teodoro) 3:28.07
20kmW 1. Victoria Palacios MEX 1:35:16
2. Rosario Sánchez MEX 1:35:21
3. Joanne Dow USA 1:35:48

42nd South American Championships 2003

At Barquisimeto, Venezuela 20-22 June

Men

100m 1. Édson Ribeiro BRA 10.30
(1.2) 2. Heber Viera URU 10.33
3. Jarbas Mascarenhas BRA 10.36
200m 1. Heber Viera URU 20.60
(-0.9) 2. Claudinei da Silva BRA 20.63

3. Jorge Célio Sena BRA 20.71

400m 1. William Hernández VEN 45.81
2. Anderson J dos Santos BRA 46.07
3. Mauricio Mery CHI 46.20

800m 1. Fabiano Peçanha BRA 1:46.32
2. Osmar dos Santos BRA 1:46.92
3. Simoncito Silvera VEN 1:48.31

1500m 1. Fabiano Peçanha BRA 3:39.74
2. Miguel Ángel García VEN 3:41.01
3. Javier Carriqueo ARG 3:42.65

5000m 1. Marílson dos Santos BRA 13:52.15
2. William Naranjo COL 14:03.41
3. Luis Fonseca VEN 14:17.44

10,000m 1. William Naranjo COL 29:37.38
2. Luiz F de Paula BRA 29:49.11
3. Alejandro Semprúm VEN 30:06.03

3000mSt 1. Néstor Nieves VEN 8:46.41
2. Celso Ficagna BRA 8:51.73
3. Richard Arias ECU 8:52.66

110mh (1.5) 1. Redelen dos Santos BRA 13.45*
2. Jackson Quiñónez ECU 13.59
3. Mateus Inocêncio BRA 13.69

400mh 1. Bayano Kamani PAN 50.10
2. Cleverson da Silva BRA 50.35
3. Eronilde de Araújo BRA 50.81

HJ 1. Fabrízio Romero BRA 2.22
2. Jessé de Lima BRA 2.22
3. Alfredo Deza PER 2.16

PV 1. Ricardo Diez VEN 5.20
2. Javier Benítez ARG 5.20
3. Gustavo Rehder BRA 5.10

LJ 1. Víctor Castillo VEN 7.78/0.7
2. Sérgio dos Santos BRA 7.65/0.4
3. Irving Saladino PAN 7.46/0.1

TJ 1. Jadel Gregório BRA 16.76/0.9
2. Anísio Silva BRA 16.22/1.8
3. Jhonny Rodríguez VEN 16.12/-1.5

SP 1. Marco Antonio Verni CHI 20.23*
2. Yojer Medina VEN 19.29
3. Jhonny Rodríguez COL 18.22

DT 1. Marcelo Pugliese ARG 57.44
2. Jorge Balliengo ARG 55.22
3. Héctor Hurtado VEN 54.61

HT 1. Juan Cerra ARG 73.31
2. Adrián Marzo ARG 67.25
3. Aldo Bello VEN 65.27

JT 1. Luiz F da Silva BRA 79.50*
2. Noraldo Palacios COL 76.81
3. Nery Kennedy PAR 75.53

Dec 1. Édson Bindilatti BRA 7254
2. Juan Jaramillo VEN 6763
3. Enrique Aguirre ARG 6585

20kmW 1. Sérgio Galdino BRA 1:25:54.2
2. Freddy Hernández COL 1:26:00.0
3. Cristián Muñoz CHI 1:31:16.1

4x100m 1. BRA (Mascarenhas, Ribeiro, Sousa, Claudinei da Silva) 38.96
2. VEN 39,85
3. CHI 40.04

4x400m 1. BRA (Ambrósio, de Araújo, Godoy, A J dos Santos) 3:05.28
2. VEN 3:09.26
3. COL 3:09.48

Women

100m (0.2) 1. Digna Murillo COL 11.35
2. Lucimar de Moura BRA 11.43
3. Wilmary Álvarez VEN 11.59

200m (0.0) 1. Digna Murillo COL 23.13
2. Lucimar de Moura BRA 23.34
3. Wilmary Álvarez VEN 23.40

400m 1. Geisa Coutinho BRA 51.81
2. Eliana Pacheco VEN 52.43
3. Josiane Tito BRA 52.68

800m 1. Luciana Mendes BRA 2:02.06
2. Christiane R dos Santos BRA 2:02.50
3. Rosibel García COL 2:02.84

1500m 1. Juliana de Azevedo BRA 4:17.54*
2. Niusha Mancilla BOL 4:21.54
3. Ana Cláudia Coimbra BRA 4:21.75

5000m 1. Maria C Rodrigues BRA 16:11.70
2. Erika Olivera CHI 16:23.97
3. Lucélia Peres BRA 16:36.31

10,000m 1. Ednalva da Silva BRA 34:13.50
2. Erika Olivera CHI 34:43.02
3. Luz Silva CHI 35:01.73

3000mSt 1. Mónica Amboya ECU 10:25.90*
2. Silvia Paredes ECU 10:38.22
3. Patrícia Lobo BRA 10:55.88

100mh (-1.5) 1. Gilvaneide Parrela BRA 13.44
2. Maíla Machado BRA 13.63
3. Princesa Oliveros COL 13.77

400mh 1. Lucimar Teodoro BRA 56.86*
2. Raquel da Costa BRA 57.51
3. Princesa Oliveros COL 57.53

HJ 1. Luciane Dambacher BRA 1.82
2. Yetzálida Pérez VEN 1.82
3. Claudia Casals ARG 1.79

PV 1. Alejandra García ARG 4.20
2. Carolina Torres CHI 4.20
3. Milena Agudelo COL 4.00

LJ 1. Keila Costa BRA 6.30/0.2
2. Caterine Ibargüen COL 6.04/-0.4
3. Mónica Falcioni URU 5.94/0.0

TJ 1. Keila Costa BRA 13.62/0.8
2. Luciana dos Santos BRA 13.42w/2.1
3. Caterine Ibargüen COL 13.07/-0.1

SP 1. Elisângela Adriano BRA 18.34
2. Luz Dary Castro COL 16.59
3. Marianne Berndt CHI 16.39

DT 1. Elisângela Adriano BRA 58.37
2. Luz Dary Castro COL 51.73
3. María Cubillán VEN 50.47

HT 1. Katiuscia de Jesus BRA 61.01*
2. Josiane Soares BRA 59.65
3. Adriana Benaventa VEN 58.34

JT 1. Sabina Moya COL 58.30
2. Alessandra Resende BRA 57.01
3. Romina Maggi ARG 52.36

Hep 1. Thaimara Rivas VEN 5622
2. Elizete da Silva BRA 5334
3. Valeria Steffens CHI 5169

20kmW 1. Sandra Zapata COL 1:40:52.6
2. Morelba Useche VEN 1:48:24.9
3. Marcela Pacheco CHI 1:49:50.1

4x100m 1. BRA (Sampaio, de Moura, Coelho Neto, Ignácio) 44.16
2. COL 44.67
3. CHI 45.37

4x400m 1. BRA (Almirão, Tito, Teodoro, Coutinho) 3:28.64*
2. VEN 3:34.30
3. COL 3:41.05

Table

Nation	Men	Women	Points
BRA	239	273	512
VEN	131	101	232
COL	63	110	173
CHI	58	74	132
ARG	77	39	116
ECU	34	25	59
URU	20	9	29
PAN	14	2	16
BOL	2	9	11
PER	6	1	7
GUY	0	5	5
PAR	4	0	4

Points (8-7-6-5-4-3-2-1)

6th African Junior Championships 2003

July 31- August 3, Garoua, Cameroon

Men: **100m**: Emmanuel Ngom Priso CMR 10.50w, **200m**: Saidi Jaysuma GAM 21.23, **400m**: Sammy Rono KEN 46.79, **800m**: Cosmas Rono Kipkorir KEN 1:48.45, **1500m**: Tesfu Bikila ETH 3:42.6, **5000m/10,000m**: Boniface Kiprop UGA 13:48.49/29:08.16, **3000mSt**: Abraham Kebeto ETH 8:39.90, **110mh**: Séléké Samake SEN 14.50, **400mh**: Badr El Amine MAR 51.57, **HJ**: Hamza Labadi ALG 2.06, **PV**: Mohamed Karbib MAR 4.60, **LJ**: Robert Mariey GHA 7.29, **TJ**: Ahmem Ibrahim El Zohbi EGY 15.44, **SP** (6kg): Yasser Ibrahim EGY 18.13, **DT** (1.75kg): Omar El Ghazaly EGY 61.87, **HT** (6kg): Anani Mohsen Mohamed EGY 68.41, **JT**: Elsayed Wahib Abd Elwahab EGY 61.30, **10kmW**: Mohamed Ameur ALG 48:35.02, **4x100m**: CMR 41.24, **4x400m**: KEN 3:11.71, **Women**: **100m/200m**: Delphine Bertille Atangana CMR 11.42/23.40, **400m**: Nina Chigozie NGR 54.06, **800m**: Aminata Sylla SEN 2:15.78, **1500m**: Penina Jepchumba Biwott KEN 4:15.35, **3000m**: Mariem Selsouli Alaoui MAR 9:08.53, **5000m**: Anésie Kwizéra BUR 16:16.57, **2000mSt**: Loice Kiptoo KEN 6:45.71, **100mh**: Gnima Faye SEN 13.59, **400mh**: Joke Odomusu NGR 61.19, **HJ**: Mama Gassama GAM 1.60, **PV**: Nissrin Dinar MAR 3.20, **LJ**: Latifa Ezziraoui MAR 5.76, **TJ**: Latifa Ezziraoui MAR 13.01, **SP**: Carine Meka CMR 14.25, **DT**: Amina Moudden MAR 47.49, **HT**: Yasmin Ashraf EGY 48.62, **Hep**: Laporte SEY 5235, **10kmW**: Ghania Amzal ALG 53'09"0, **4x100m/4x400m**: NGR 46.52/3:43.47

13th Arab Championships 2003

September 7-9, Amman, Jordan

Men: **100m**: Salem Al-Yami KSA 10.18w, **200m/400m**: Fawzi Al-Shammari KUW 20.41/44.93, **800m**: Ahmed Ismail SUD 1:46.76, **1500m**: Rachid Ramzi BRN 3:53.18, **5000m**: Khoudir Aggoune ALG 13:59.2, **10,000m**: Ali Al-Dawoodi Saadoun QAT 31:07.10, **HMar**: Mohamed Abdul Hamed QAT 65:48, **3000mSt**: Khamis Seif Abdullah QAT 8:40.90, **110mh**: Mubarak Ata Mubarak KSA 13.71w, **400mh**: Mubarak Al-Nubi QAT 49.66, **HJ**: Jean-Claude Rabbath LIB 2.21, **PV**: Rafik Mefti ALG 4.95, **LJ**: Hussein Al-Sabee KSA 8.30w, **TJ**: Mohammed Hamdi Awadh QAT 16.55, **SP**: Bilal Saad Mubarak QAT 18.73, **DT**: Omar El Ghazaly EGY 58.30, **HT**: Ali Mohamed Al-Zankawi KUW 72.70, **JT**: Walid Abderrazak EGY 77.30, **Dec**: Ahmad H Moussa QAT 7377, **20kmW**: Walid Ahmed Al-Sahabi QAT 1:31:07, **4x100m**: KSA 39.60, **4x400m**: KSA 3:06.37. **Women**: **100m/200m**: Rakia Al-Gassra BRN 11.61w/24.09w, **400m**: Muna Jabir Adam Ahmed SUD 54.34, **800m/1500m**: Nahida Touhami ALG 2:05.83/4:25.6, **5000m/10,000m**: Souad Ait Salem ALG 16.18.8/34:47.73, **100mh**: Naima Bentahar ALG 14.25w, **400mh**: Diala El Chab LIB 62.81, **HJ**: Amina Lemgherbi ALG 1.66, **PV**: Nesrine Ahmad Imam EGY 2.70, **LJ/TJ**: Baya Rahouli ALG 6.180/14.02, **SP**: Wafaa Ismail El Baghdadi EGY 15.17, **DT**: Hiba Zaghari EGY 51.94, **HT**: Marwa A Hussein EGY 61.74, **JT**: Hanaa Ramadan Omar EGY 54.03, **10kmW**: Bahia Boussad ALG 51:01, **4x100m/4x400m**: ALG 48.18/3:50.42

58th Balkan Championships 2003

July 12-13, Thíva, Greece.

Men: **100m**: Yeóryios-Aléxandros Terzián GRE 10.49, **200m**: Anastásios Goúsis GRE 20.53*, **400m**: Ionut Vieru ROM 46.44, **800m**: Fernet Rigo ROM 1:48.29, **1500m**: Darko Radomirovic SCG 3:48.93, **3000m**: Vasílios PouliópoulosGRE 8:08.96, **5000m**: Goran Stojiljkovic SCG 14:13.76, **3000mSt**: Iaroslav Musinschi MDA 8:48.75, **110mh**: Nenad Loncar SCG 13.71, **400mh**: Panayiótis Andriópoulos GRE 51.66, **HJ**: Stefan Vasilache ROM 2.30, **PV**: Ilian Efremov BUL 5.62, **LJ**: Bogdan Tarus ROM 8.02, **TJ**: Marian Oprea ROM 17.24*, **SP**: Dragan Peric SCG 20.48, **DT**: Sergiu Ursu ROM 62.50, **HT**: Aléxandros Papadimitríou GRE 79.16*, **JT**: Elefthérios Karasmanákis GRE 75.00, **4x100m**: GRE 39.96, **4x400m**: ROM 3:06.19. **Team:** 1. GRE 167, 2. ROM 143, 3. SCG (SCG) 113, 4. BUL 109, 5. BIH 89, 6. TUR 87, 7. ALB 56, 8. MKD 22, 9. MDA 22. **Women**: **100m**: Marína Vasarmídou GRE 11.55, **200m**: Ólga Kaidantzí GRE 23.83, **400m**: Nedialka Nedkova BUL 53.9, **800m/1500m**: Alina Cucerzan ROM 2:04.75/4:40.93, **3000m**: Daniela Petrescu ROM 9.40.68, **5000m**: Natalia Cerches MDA 16:10.81, **3000mSt**: Cristina Casandra ROM 9:51.16, **100mh**: Carmen Zamfir ROM 13.22, **400mh**: Hrísa Goudenoúdi GRE 56.85, **HJ**: Venelina Veneva BUL 1.95, **PV**: Tanya Koleva BUL 4.30*, **LJ**: Déspina Papavasiláki GRE 6.39, **TJ**: Cristina Nicolau ROM 13.86, **SP**: Iríni-Hrisovaládo Terzóglou GRE 18.21, **DT**: Stilianí Tsikoúna GRE 59.02, **HT**: Mihaela Melinte ROM 71.75*, **JT**: Rumiana Karapetrova BUL 53.30, **4x100m**: GRE 44.73, **4x400m**: BUL 3:33.57. **Team:** 1. ROM 155, 2. GRE 148, 3. SCG 111, 4. BUL 94, 5. ALB 65, 6. TUR 58, 7. MKD 36, 8. BIH 29, 9. MDA 15

Road Walks: *6 April at Ruse, Bulgaria.* **Men 20km**: Pregrag Filipovic SCG 1:22:40, **Women 20km**: Veronica Budileanu ROM 1:35:12

19th Central American and Caribbean Championships 2003

July 4-6, Saint George's, Grenada

Men: **100m**: Kim Collins SKN 10.13, **200m**: Dominic Demeritte BAH 20.43, **400m**: Alleyne Francique GRN 45.27, **800m**: Sheridan Kirk TRI 1:49.10, **1500m**: Juan Barrios MEX 3:44.78, **5000m/10,000m**: Eduardo Rojas MEX 14:29.88/29:37.08, **HMar**: Pamenos Ballantyne VIN 69:14, **3000mSt**: Alexander Greaux PUR 8:39.68, **110mh**: Hugh Henry BAR 13.85, **400mh**: Gregory Little JAM 50.04, **HJ**: Lisvany Pérez CUB 2.21, **PV**: Giovanni Lanaro MEX 5.30, **LJ**: Kareem Streete-Thompson CAY 8.12w, **TJ**: Leevan Sands BAH 17.16, **SP**: Yojer Medina VEN 19.17, **DT**: Alfredo Romero PUR 54.09, **HT**: Iosvany

Suárez CUB 69.59, **JT**: Manuel Fuenmayor VEN 72.35, **Dec**: Yonelvis Águila CUB 7337, **4x100m**: TRI (Dillon, Burns, Alexander, Brown) 39.05*, **4x400m**: BAH (Moncur, Oliver, McKinney, Brown) 3:02.56. **20kmW**: Julio Martínez GUA 1:22:07. **Women**: **100m**: Fana Ashby TRI 11.23, **200m**: Cydonie Mothersill CAY 22.45, **400m**: Hazel-Ann Regis GRN 51.56, **800m**: Neisha Bernard-Thomas GRN 2:04.12, **1500m**: Ashley Couper BER 4:27.71, **5000m**: not held, **10,000m**: Yudelkis Martínez CUB 34:29.05, **HMar**: Lourdes Cruz PUR 1:31:50, **100mh**: Delloreen Ennis-London JAM 12.70*, **400mh**: Allison Beckford JAM 55.12*, **HJ**: Desiree Crichlow BAR 1.81, **PV**: Alejandra Meza MEX 4.00*, **LJ**: Elva Goulbourne JAM 6.96w/6.81*, **TJ**: Suzette Lee Lee JAM 13.89w, **SP**: Misleidi González CUB 18.09, **DT**: Yania Ferrales CUB 59.07, **HT**: Violeta Guzmán MEX 55.72. **JT**: Laverne Eve BAH 56.75, **4x100m**: BAH (Clarke, Ferguson, Amertil, Brown) 43.06*, **4x400m**: JAM (Downer, Burgher, Robinson, Beckford) 3:29.75, **10kmW**: Rosario Sánchez MEX 49:06. **Medal Table** Leaders: JAM 6-8-8, MEX 6-3-2, CUB 6-2-1, BAH 5-5-1, PUR 3-3-4, TRI 3-3-4, GRN 3-3-0, VEN 2-4-2, BAR 2-1-4, CAY 2-0-0

5th Central Asian Games 2003

October 16-19, Dushanbe, Tajikistan

Men: **100m/200m**: Gennadiy Chernovoy KZK 10.50/21.04, **400m/400mh**: Yevgeniy Meleshenko KAZ 46.69/52.75, **800m/1500m**: Mikhail Kolganov KAZ 1:49.60/3:56.45, **5000m**: Denis Bagrev KGZ 14:50.86, **10,000m**: Sergey Milyutin KAZ 31:35.44, **3000mSt**: Yevgeniy Stakanov TJK 9:16.05, **110mh**: Andrey Kornienko UZB 14.36, **HJ**: Pavel Dubitskiy 2.05, **LJ**: Rustam Khusnutdinov UZB 7.22, **TJ**: Deniya Sauranbayev KAZ 15.92, **SP**: Sergey Kot UZB 16.95, **DT**: Dmitriy Kondratenko KAZ 50.91, **HT**: Dilshod Nazarov TJK 71.20, **JT**: Renat Tarzumanov UZB 66.37, **4x100m/4x400m**: KAZ 41.15/3:14.88, **20kmW**: Valeriy Borisov UZK 1:29:51.56. **Women**: **100m/200m**: Guzel Khubbieva UZB 11.51/23.72, **400m/800m**: Tatyana Roslanova KAZ 53.03/2:04.47, **1500m**: Svetlana Lukashova KAZ 4:32.87, **5000m**: Tatyana Borisova KGZ 17:06.72, **10,000m**: Marina Gurbina KAZ 38:17.67, **100mh**: Irina Naumenko KAZ 14.30, **400mh**: Natalya Torschina KZK 57.80, **HJ**: Marina Aitova KAZ 1.89, **LJ/TJ**: Anastasiya Zhuravlyeva UZB 6.28/13.55, **SP**: Iolanta Ulyeva KZK 16.14, **DT**: Olga Schukina UZB 46.26, **HT**: Olga Shogoleva UZB 49.50, **JT**: Liliya Dusmetova UZB 50.21, **Hep**: Olga Alekseyev KAZ 5505, **4x100m**: UZB 44.68, **4x400m**: KAZ 3:37.44

3rd European Winter Throws Challenge 2003

At Gioia Tauro, Italya, March1-2

Men: 1. GER 8482, 2. RUS 8296, 3. ITA 8161. **SP**: 1. Rutger Smith NED 20.52, 2. Ivan Yushkov RUS 19.54, 3. Peter Sack GER 19.53; **DT**: 1. Gerd Kanter EST 64.17, 2. Mario Pestano ESP 63.71, 3. Ioan Oprea ROM 62.29; **HT**: 1. Nicola Vizzoni ITA 75.35. 2. Aléxandros Papadimitríou GRE 74.74. 3. Ilya Konovalov RUS 74.73; **JT**: 1. Christian Nicolay GER 83.80, 2. Aleksandr Ivanov RUS 79.24, 3. Dominique Pause FRA 78.60. **Women**: 1. RUS 8238, 2. GER 7885, 3. ITA 7882. **SP**: 1. Irina Khudoroshkina RUS 18.47, 2. Anna Romanova RUS 18.09, 3. Cristiana Checchi ITA 17.91; **DT**: 1. Teresa Machado POR 63.65, 2. Viktoriya Boyko UKR 60.63, 3. Stilianí Tsikouna GRE 59.73; **HT**: 1. Manuela Montebrun FRA 72.18, 2. Doina Melinte ROM 69.24, 3. Olga Kuzenkova RUS 66.25; **JT**: 1. Steffi Nerius GER 62.50, 2. Oana Gromova RUS 61.12, 3. Yekaterina Ivakina RUS 60.42

European 10,000m Challenge 2003

At Athína (Ellinikó), April 12

Men: 1. Ismaïl Sghyr FRA 27:45.14, 2. Eduardo Henriques POR 28:05.09, 3. Juan Carlos de la Ossa ESP 28:07.19; **Team:** 1. POR, 2. ESP, 3. ITA. **Women**: 1. Fernanda Ribeiro POR 31:13.42, 2. Irina Mikitenko GER 31:38.48, 3. Ana Dias POR 31:48.32, **Team:** 1. POR, 2. ESP, 3. GBR

European Champion Clubs Cup 2003

Group A at Valencia, Spain 24-25 May

Men: 1. SC Luch RUS 135, 2. Fiamme Galle ITA 115, 3. Dukla Praha CZE 106, 4. Panellinos GRE 97, 5. Puma Chapin Jerez ESP 93.5, 6. Belgrave H GBR 75.5, 7. CA Montreuil FRA 50, 8. AAC Amsterdam 45; **Women**: 1. SC Luch RUS 123, 2. Valencia Terra I Mar ESP 111, 3. Panellinos GRE 106, 4. Sporting POR 98, 5. Fondiara SAI Atletica ITA 91, 6. USK Praha CZE 69, 7. Sale H Manchester GBR 47, 8. Slavia UK Bratislava SVK 35

Group B at Belgrade. SCG 24-25 May

Men: 1. Sporting POR 106, 2. Crvena Zvezde YUG 84, 3. DEN 70, 4. ISR 62, 5. SVK 60, 6. CYP 36; **Women**: 1. Enkaspor TUR 122, 2. Crvena Zvezde YUG 104, 3. FRA 103, 4. DEN 95, 5. SWE 87, 6. CRO 64.5, 7. ISR 54.5, 8. NED 53

Games of the Small States of Europe 2003

June 3-7, Marsa, Malta

Men: **100m/200m**: Anninos Marcoullides CYP 10.38/20.95, **400m**: Marios Mardas CYP 47.51, **800m**: David Fiegen LUX 1:51.52, **1500m**: Björn Margeirsson ISL 3:48.53, **5000m/10,000m**: Toni Bernado AND 14:29.93/30:57.33, **3000mSt**: Panayiotis Kyprianou CYP 8:56.1, **LJ**: Rachid Chouhal MLT 7.50, **TJ**: Stelios Kapsalis CYP 15.20w, **SP**: George Aresti CYP 15.98, **DT**: Magnus Hallgrimsson ISL 59.01, **JT**: Panayiotis Kalogerou CYP 72.10, **4x100m/4x400m**: CYP 40.08*/3:12.51*. **Women**: **100m/200m**: Marilia Gregogiou CYP 11.67*/23.56*, **400m**: Androulla Sialou CYP 52.66*, **800m/1500m**: Tanya Blake MLT 2:07.21/4:29.01, **5000m**: Frída Thorderdottir ISL 17:10.14, **10,000m**: Carol Galea MLT 36:13.97, **100mh**: Morfo Baourda CYP 13.99/1.2, **LJ**: Ireni Charalambous CYP 6.38*, **TJ**: Maria Diikiti CYP 12.89*, **DT**: Alexandra Klatsia CYP 41.38, **JT**: Si. Fjeldsdóttir ISL 47.80, **4x100m/4x400m**: CYP 47.71/3:44.48

10th Gulf Countries Championships 2003

October 8-10, Al Kuwait, Kuwaiit

Men: **100m**: Salem Al-Yami KSA 10.32, **200m/400m**: Fawzi Al-Shammari KUW 20.64/45.34, **800m**: Rashid Habib Mohamed BRN 1:49.08, **1500m**: Rashid Ramzi BRN 4:09.98, **5000m/3000mSt**: Khamis Seif Abdullah QAT 14:38.84/8:54.62, **10,000m**: Aman Majed Awadh QAT 30:34.72, **HMar**: Mohamed Abdul Hamed QAT

69:25, **110mh**: Mubarak Ata Mubarak KSA 14.03, **400mh**: Mubarak Al-Nubi QAT 49.81, **HJ**: Salem Nasser Bakheet BRN 2.14, **PV**: Fahad Bader Al-Mershad KUW 4.85; **LJ**: Hussein Al-Sabee KSA 8.10/0.7, **TJ**: Salem Al-Ahmadi KSA 16.21, **SP**: Bilal Saad Mubarak QAT 19.19, **DT**: Khaled Al-Suwaidi QAT 55.86, **HT**: Ali Mohamed Al-Zankawi KUW 67.44, **JT**: Mohamed Al-Khalifa QAT 72/93, **Dec**: Mohamed Al-Matroud KSA 7235, **10kmW**: Walid Ahmed Al-Sabahi QAT 52:56.49, **4x100m**: QAT 39.75, **4x400m**: KSA 3:05.54

6th Games of Indian Ocean Islands 2003

September 3-6, Bambous, Mauritius

Men: 100m/200m: Stéphane Buckland MRI 10.60/20.64; **400m**: Éric Milazar MRI 45.78; **800m**: Mahefa Manoa Andrianjafy MAD 1:53.14, **5000m**: Jeetun MRI 15:10.90, **10,000m**: Ménon Ramsamy MRI 30:26.42, **Mar**: Prosper Randriasolaaza MAD 2:23:59, **3000mSt**: Ronnie Marie SEY 8:59.34, **110mh**: Joseph-Berlioz Randriamihaja MAD 14.57; **400mh**: Lensley Juhel MRI 52.02, **HJ**: Perry Prosper MRI 2.10. **LJ**: Arnaud Casquette MRI 7.85w; **TJ**: Stéphane Grezé REU 15.81w, **SP**: Eric Sandanon REU 17.48, **DT**: Stéphane Nativel REU 50.58, **HT**: Nicolas Li Yun Fomg MRI 63.28, **JT**: Dominique Pausé REU 74.73; **4x100m/4x400m**: MRI 39.23/3:10.84, **10kmW**: Kaviraj Mardemootoo MRI 46:01.50. **Women: 100m**: Hanitriaina Rakotondrabe MAD 12.00, **200m**: Ony Paule Rasimbazafy MAD 25.74, **400m**: Rahanitraniriana MAD 55.52, **800m/1500m**: Eliane Saholinirina MAD 2:10.93/4:30.20, **5000m**: Haingo Rakotomalala MAD 17:57.23, **10,000m/Mar**: Clarisse Rasoarizay MAD 36:27.74/2:38:21, **100mh**: Patin Sianpayen REU 14.27, **400mh**: Salhate Djamaladine COM 60.07, **HJ**: Arielle Brette NRI 1.72, **PV**: Denis REU 3.80, **LJ**: Laporte SEY 5.89, **TJ** : Rapitsaravolazandry MAD 13.41w, **SP**: Gaëlle Éléléara REU 14.75, **DT**: Jeanne díArc Momus MRI 44.07, **HT**: Caroline Fournier MRI 56.14, **JT**: Bernadette Ravina MRI 51.70, **Hep**: Rarivorimanana MAD 4678, **4x100m/4x400m**: MAD 45.82/3:40.50, **5kmW**: Yolande Raffin MRI 27:15.20. REU – Réunion (FRA).

Pan-American Junior Championships 2003

July 18-20, Bridgetown, Barbados

Men: **100m**: Churandy Martina AHO 10.33, **200m**: Usain Bolt JAM 20.13*, **400m**: Ashton Collins USA 45.59, **800m**: Thiago Chyaromont BRA 1:48.76, **1500m**: Maurys Castillo CUB 3:47.13, **5000m**: Galen Rupp USA 14:20.29, **10,000m**: Gotcher Brett USA 30:39.51, **3000mSt**: Cristian Patino ECU 9:05.70, **110mh/400mh**: Kenneth Ferguson USA 13.60*/50.07, **HJ**: Keith Moffatt USA 2.20, **PV**: Germán Chiaraviglo ARG 5.15, **LJ**: Wilfredo Martínez CUB 7.70, **TJ**: David Giralt CUB 16.93*, 6kg **SP**: Garrett Johnson USA 19.95*, 1.75kg **DT**: Gustavo de Mendonça BRA 58.76, 6kg **HT**: James Steacy CAN 70.70*, **JT**: Júlio César de Oliveira BRA 68.42, **Dec** (jnr): Donovan Kilmartin USA 7486*, **4x100m**: USA (Moore, Aaron Collins, Ashton Collins, Hordge) 39.29*, **4x400m**: USA (Coleman, Wariner, Ferguson, Ashton Collins) 3:02.88*, **Women 100m/200m**: Shalonda Solomon USA 11.35/22.93*, **400m**: Stephanie Smith USA 52.52, **800/1500m**: Yuneysi Santiusty CUB 2:04.77/4:24.56, **5000m**: Ines Melchor PER 16:53.37, **2000mSt**: Angela Marvin USA 6:37.84, **100mh**: Dawn Harper USA 13.42, **400mh**: Amanda Fontes Dias BRA 58.09, **HJ**: Sharon Day USA 1.85, **PV**: Julene Bailey USA 4.05*, **LJ/TJ**: Yudelkis Fernández CUB 6.46*/13.89, **SP**: Michelle Carter USA 16.23, **DT**: Amarachi Ukabam USA 52.05, **HT**: Jennifer Dahlgren ARG 58.61, **JT**: Emma Gene Evans LCA 49.67*, **Hep**: Juana Castillo DOM 5381, **4x100m**: USA (Owens, Broaddus, Sherman, Solomon) 44.00, **4x400m**: USA (Lee, Perkins, Hastings, Smith) 3:34.08. **Medal Table Leaders:** USA 13G-10S-6B, CUB 3-1-5, BRA 2-1-1, MEX 1-4-0, JAM 1-3-4, CAN 1-1-2, ARG 1-1-2;. 17 nations won medals (9 gold)

South American Junior Championships 2003

June 7-8, Guayaquil, Ecuador

Men: **100m/200m**: Jorge Sena BRA 10.45/21.32, **400m**: Andrés Silva URU 46.54, **800m**: Thiago Chyaromont BRA 1:51.41, **1500m**: Matías Carranza ARG 3:54.3, **5000m**: Gilialdo Koball BRA 14:43.2, **10,000m**: Davis Sánchez VEN 31:21.8, **3000mSt**: Rodolfo Hass BRA 9:02.23, **110mh**: Rodrigo Pereira BRA 14.19*, **400mh**: Ricardo Luiz Silva BRA 52.81, **HJ**: Fábio Baptista BRA 2.09, **PV**: Germán Chiaraviglio ARG 5.16*, **LJ**: Thiago Dias BRA 7.51, **TJ**: Leonardo dos Santos BRA 15.89w, **SP** 5.8Kg: Gustavo de Mendonça BRA 19.67, **DT** 1.75Kg: Gustavo de Mendonça BRA 62.29*, **HT** 6Kg: Leandro Benetti ARG 66.69, **JT**: Julio César de Oliveira BRA 70.94, **Dec** (SP 6kg, DT 1.75kg) Matías López ARG 6749, **4x100m/4x400m**: BRA 41.19/3:14.03, **10kW**: Patricio Ortega ECU 44:07.5, **Women 100m**: Evelyn dos Santos BRA 11.66, **200m**: Wilmary Álvarez VEN 23.68, **400m**: Amanda Dias BRA 54.50, **800m/1500m**: Rejane da Silva BRA 2:11.16/4:32.2, **3000m/5000m**: Inés Melchor PER 9:58.83/16:57.0, **3000mSt**: Zenaide Vieira BRA 10:37.85*, **100mh**: Lucimara da Silva BRA 14.16, **400mh**: Amanda Dias BRA 59.38, **HJ**: Katherine Ibargüen COL 1.80, **PV**: Karla da Silva BRA 3.85*, **LJ**: Macarena Reyes CHI 6.10, **TJ**: Katherine Ibargüen COL 13.05, **SP**: Paola Cheppi ARG 15.11, **DT**: Roberta Argentino BRA 42.36, **HT**: Adriana Benaventa VEN 55.39, **JT**: Mariela Aguer ARG 48.20, **Hep**: Jaílma de Lima BRA 4979, **4x100m**: CHI 46.54, **4x400m**: BRA 3:42.24. **Medal Table Leaders:** BRA 26-21-13, ARG 6-3-6, VEN 4-7-6, CHI 2-6-4, COL 2-6-3, PER 2-1-2, ECU 1-1-3, URU 1-0-2, BOL 0-0-3, PAN 0-0-1

South East Asian Games 2003

November 7-12, Hanoi, Vietnam

Men: **100m/200m**: Nazmizan Muhammad MAS 10.48/21.05w, **400m**: Ernie Candelario PHI 47.06, **800m**: Le Van Duong VIE 1:50.74, **1500m**: John Lozada PHI 3:56.80, **5000m**: Srisung Boonthung THA 14:15.20, **10,000m**: Eduardo Buenavista PHI 29:19.62*, **Mar**: Allan Ballester PHI 2:21:03, **3000mSt**: Rene Herrera PHI 8:50.78, **110mh**: Suphan Wongsriphuck THA 13.92; **400mh**: Apisit Kuttiyawan THA 51.47, **HJ**: Loo Kun Zee MAS 2.15, **PV**: Amnat Kunpadit THA 4.80, **LJ**: Mohd Shahrul Amri Suhaimimas 7.65, **TJ**: Nattaporn Nomkanha THA 15.76, **SP**: Dong Enxin SIN 17.28*, **DT**: James Wong Tuck Yim SIN 56.49, **HT**: Arniel Ferrera PHI 55.28, **JT**. Danilo Fresnido PHI 67.11, **Dec**: Mohd Malik Ahmad Tobias MAS 6668, **4x100m/4x400m**: THA 40.05/3:09.33, **20kmW**: Mohd Shahrulhaizy MAS 1:31:57. **Women**: **100m**: Oranut Klomdee THA 11.51w, **200m/400m**: Nguyen Thi Tinh VIE 23.19w/51.83*, **800m**: Do Thi Bong VIE

2:10.92, **1500m**: Nguyen Lan Anh VIR 4:19.58*, **5000m**: Supriati Sutono INA 16:09.39, **10,000m**: Doan Nu Truc Van VIE 34:48.28, **Mar**: Erni Ulatingsih INA 2:52:28, **100mh**: Trecia Roberts THA 13.45w, **400mh**: Norasheela Mohd Khalid MAS 57.62, **HJ**: Noengruthai Chaipetch THA 1.86, **PV**: Desy Margawati INA 3.95*, **LJ**: Lerma E Gabito 6.21, **TJ**: Wacharee Ritthiwat THA 13.44, **SP**: Du Xianhui SIN 18.20*, **DT**: Zhang Guirong SIN 49.91, **HT**: Yurita Ariyani INA 49.79, **JT**: Buaban Phamang THA 53.23, **Hep**: Nguyen Thi Thu Cuc VIE 5274, **4x100m**: THA 44.82, **4x400m**: VIE 3:38.06, **20kmW**: Yuan Yufang MAS 1:39:25*. **Medals**: THA 13G-14S-12B, VIE 8-16-8, PHI 8-3-5, MAS 8-2-6, INA 4-4-7, SIN 4-4-1, MYA 0-2-4

South Pacific Games 2003

July 7-12, Suva, Fiji

Men: **100m/200m**: Jon Lumkon FIJ 10.8/21.28*, **400m**: Jeffrey Bai PNG 47.20, **800m/1500m**: Isireli Naikelekelevesi FIJ 1:51.06/4:01.15, **5000m**: Neil Weare GUM 14:48.40, **10,000m/HMar**: Georges Richmond PYF 31:54.7/69:53*, **c3400mSt**: Esala Talebula FIJ 11:11.8, **110mh**: Jovesa Naivalu FIJ 14.36/1.6, **400mh**: Mowen Boino PNG 51.93, **HJ**: Sandy Katusele PNG 2.06, **PV**: Jean-Bernard Harper NC 4.50, **LJ**: Eroni Tuivanuavou FIJ 7.82*, **TJ**: Frédéric Erin NC 15.14, **SP**: Daniel Kilama NC 16.57, **DT**: Shaka Solo SAM 50.46, **HT**: Jean-Pierre Totele NC 54.12, **JT**: Gatean Siakinuu:Schmidt NC 70.99, **Dec**: Joseph Rodan FIJ 6161, **20kmW**: Dip Chand FIJ 2:06:19.9, **4x100m/4x400m**: PNG 40.94/3:11.43. **Women**: **100m/200m/400m**: Makelesi Bulikiobo FIJ 11.9/23.68*/52.66*, **800m**: Vasiti Vatureba FIJ 2:18.46, **1500m**: Stéphanie Nonnotte PYF 4:36.13, **5000m/HMar**: Sophie Gardon PYF 18:22.9*/86:51, **100mh/400mh**: Rachel Rogers FIJ 13.97/61.50, **HJ/TJ**: Véronique Boyer PYF 1.70/13.10w, **PV**: Marion Becker NC 2.90*, **LJ**: Laurence Upigit NC 5.94w, **SP**: Ana Po'uhila TGA 15.89*, **DT**: Melehifo Uhi TGA 50.78*, **HT**: Patricia Kolivai NC 44.95 (Siniva Marsters COK 45.83 drugs dq), **JT**: Bina Ramesh NC 54.36*, **Hep**: Rose-Marie Vakie NC 4185, **20kmW**: Dipeeka Chand FIJ 2-47-32.3, **4x100m**: Fiji 44.86*, **4x400m**: New Caledonia 3:59.88 (FIJ 3:40.03* dq). NC = New Caledonia

3rd World Military Championships 2003

December 6-8, Catania. Marathons at Palermo, Dec 7

Men: **100m**: Bruno Pacheco BRA 10.53, **200m**: Evgenios Papadopoúlos 21.76, **400m**: Vincent Mumo KEN 46.39, **800m**: Joseph Mutua KEN 1:48.84, **1500m**: Abdelkader Hachlaf MAR 3:55.12, **5000m**: Sammy Kipketer KEN 13:59.30, **10,000m**: John Cheruiyot Korir KEN 28:38.93, **Mar**: Francesco Ingargiola ITA 2:14:51, **3000mSt**: Abel Yacoob Jowher Salem BRN-J 8:42.97, **110mh**: Artur Kohutek POL 14.17, **400mh**: Ibrahim Al-Hamaidi KSA 51.44, **HJ**: Yuriy Krimarenko UKR 2.18, **PV**: Igor Pavlov RUS 5.45, **LJ**: Ruslan Gataullin RUS 7.81, **TJ**: Aleksandr Sergeyev RUS 16.23, **SP**: Milan Haborák SVK 19.55, **DT**: Diego Fortuna ITA 60.16, **HT**: Miloslav Konopka SVK 75.59, **JT**: Aleksandr Ivanov RUS 78.13, **10kW**: Alessandro Gandellini ITA 39:29.45, **4x100m**: ITA 41.07, **4x400m**: POL 3:11.24. **Women**: **100m/200m**: Yuliya Timofeyeva 12.11/24.70, **400m**: Awatef Ben Hassine TUN 54.37, **800m**: Soltana Aït Hammou MAR 2:06.86, **1500m**: Tatyana Buloychik BLR 4:27.67, **5000m**: Mihaela Botezan ROM 15:10.69, **Mar**: Jo Bun-hui PRK 2:36:54, **400mh**: Irena Zauna LAT 57.35, **HJ**: Anna Chicherova RUS 1.89, **LJ**: Tatyana Ter-Mesrobyan RUS 6.03, **TJ**: Cristina Nicolau ROM 13.45, **HT**: Zhang Wenxiu CHN 69.89, **5kmW**: Yelena Nikolayeva RUS 22:11.69

IAU 100km World Cup 2003

November 16, Tainan County, Taiwan

Men: 1. Mario Fattore ITA 7:04:57, 2. Grigoriy Murzin RUS 7:08:21, 3. Michael Sommer GER 7:15:04. **Team:** 1. ITA 22:04:57, 2. RUS 22:31:55, 3. GER 23:35:36
Women: 1. Monica Casiraghi ITA 8:04:47, 2. Sanna Paola ITA 8:15:13. 3, Elke Hiebl GER 8:23:06. **Team:** 1. ITA 25:52:05, 2. GER 26:29:59, 3. JPN 26:44:27

IAU European 100km Championships 2003

April 19, Chernogolovka, Russia

Men: 1. Farid Ganiyev 6:28:27, 2. Grigoriy Murzin 6:29:41, 3. Mario Ardemagnu ITA 6:33:22
Team: 1. RUS 20:20:00, 2. FRA 21:04:44, 3. ITA 21:11:41.
Women: 1. Tatyana Zbyrkova 7:19:51, 2. Monica Castraghi ITA 7:28:00, 3. Marina Myshlyanova 7:33:21
Team: 1. RUS 22:28:13, 2. FRA 24:11:50, 3. ITA 24:33:48

IAU European and World 24 Hours Challenge 2003

October 11-12, Uden, Netherlands

Men: 1. Paul Beckers BEL 270.087k, 2. Ryochi Sekiya JPN 267.223, 3 (2 Eur). Etienne Van Acker BEL 264.967, 4 (3 Eur). Andrey Kazantsev RUS 258.037; **Team:** 1. BEL 791,901, 2. RUS 739,569, 3. JPN 729,956, 4 (3 EUR) FRA 715.792. **Women**: 1. Irina Reutovich RUS 237.052, 2. Galina Yeremina RUS 232.050, 3. Joëlle Semur FRA 227.279; **Team:** 1. RUS 684,858, 2. FRA 649,303, 3. JPN 628,440, 3 EUR. GER 594.304

2nd European Mountain Running Championships 2003

July 6, Trento-Monte Bondone, Italy

Men (13.5km, 1460m height difference): 1. Marco Gaiardo ITA 66:05, 2. Helmut Schmuck AUT 67:13, 3. Robert Krupicka CZE 67:31. **Team:** 1. ITA 9. 2. SVK 30, 3. CZE 39
Women (8km, 855m height difference): 1. Catherine Lallemand BEL 43:48, 2. Angela Mudge GBR 44:01, 3. Antonella Confortola ITA 44:30. Teams: 1. ITA 19, 2. CZE 39, 3. GBR 39

19th World Mountain Running Trophy 2003

September 20-21, Girdwood, Anchorage, USA

Men (11.7k, 1331m uphill): 1. Marco De Gasperi ITA 50:30, 2. Florian Heinzle AUT 51:16, 3. Marco Gaiardo ITA 51:56, 4. Andrew Jones GBR 52:11, 5. Tim Davies WAL 52:47. **Team:** 1. ITA 24, 2. ENG 48, 3. GER 67
Jnr Men (9.2k, 1044m uphill): Mitja Kosovelj SLO 35:41, **Team:** SLO 23
Women (9.2k, 1044m uphill): 1. Melissa Moon NZL 39:02, 2. Angela Mudge SCO 39:41, 3. Tracey Brindley SCO 39:59, 4. Antonella Confortola ITA 40:27, 5. Izabela Zatorska POL 40:54. **Team:** 1. SCO 23, 2. FRA 29, 3. AUT 34
Jnr Women (3.3k, 334m uphill): Karrissa Hawitt ENG 17:24, **Team:** SLO 7

** = Championships record throughout this section*

IAAF GRAND PRIX

INTRODUCED IN 1985, the IAAF's Grand Prix series linked the world's leading invitational meetings, so that athletes earned points over the season, with a final contested by the leaders in the points tables. Half the standard events are held each year. There was an Individual Event Grand Prix for each event and an Overall Grand Prix for men and women. The Grand Prix Final was replaced in 2003 by the World Athletics Final, which encompassed 35 standard events, with athletes qualifying from their placings on the IAAF World Rankings.

There is now a four-tier structure of IAAF World Outdoor meetings. From 1998 the top GP meetings have constituted the IAAF Golden League, and below them from 1998 to 2002 were Grand Prix I and Grand Prix II meetings. In 2003 the IAAF Competition Circuit was restructured to 38 one-day meetings: Golden League (6), Super Grand Prix (9), Grand Prix (10) and Grand Prix II (replacing the previous IAAF Permit Meetings) (11).

IAAF Golden League

The Golden League was initiated in 1998, bringing together the six leading Grand Prix meetings – Oslo, Zürich, Brussels, Berlin, Monte Carlo and Rome. In 1999 a seventh, Paris, was added. In 1998 and 1999 a jackpot of $1 million was divided amongst any athletes winning all of his or her Golden League events (provided that they also competed at the Grand Prix Final).

The Golden League Jackpot was made easier to win in the Olympic year of 2000, when the 50kg of gold bars was shared among those competitors who won five of the seven Golden League events.

The seven Golden League meets had a revised format in 2001 in a move that organizers hoped would draw larger crowds and TV audiences. The 14 events in each meet were divided into premium events and classic events. The winners of premium events collected 15,000 Euro, with 7500 Euro going to classic event winners. There was no change, however, in the Golden League jackpot payout. Any athlete winning five of the seven meets – in a premium or classic event – collected a share of the end-of-season 50 kilograms of gold.

In 2002 and 2003

Grand Prix meetings 2003 and 2004

2003 date		*Meeting*	*2004 date*
1 Mar	GP II	Telstra A Series, Melbourne, AUS	12 Feb
26 Apr	GP II	Conseil General, Fort-de-France, Martinique	24 Apr
4 May	GP	Grande Premio Brasil de Atletismo, Belém BRA	23 May
10 May	GP	Japan Grand Prix, Osaka, JPN	8 May
15 May	SGP	Qatar Athletic Super Grand Prix, Doha	14 May
	GP II	Grande Premio Rio de Athletismo	16 May
18 May	GP II	adidas Oregon Track Classic, Portland, USA	5 Jun
24 May	GP	Prefontaine Classic, Eugene, Oregon, USA	19 Jun
1 Jun	GP	Thales FBK Games, Hengelo, NED	31 May
3 Jun	GP II	GP Regione Lombardia, Milan, ITA	2 Jun
6 Jun	GP II	Memorial Primo Nebiolo, Turin, Italy	4 Jun
7 Jun	GP	Gran Premio, Seville, ESP	5 Jun
–	GP II	US Open, Palo Alto, California, USA	6 Jun
8 Jun	GP II	Znamenskiy Memorial, Tula, RUS (at Kazan 2004)	8 Jul
10 Jun	GP II	Slovak Gold, Bratislava, SVK	not GP II
12 Jun	SGP	Golden Spike, Ostrava, CZE	8 Jun
15 Jun	GP	Lille Métropole, Villeneuve d'Ascq, FRA	26 Jun
24 Jun	SGP	Tsiklitiria, Athens, GRE (at Tríkala 2003)	26 Jul
27 Jun	GL	Bislett Games, Oslo, NOR (at Bergen 2004)	11 Jul
29 Jun	GP II	Josef Odlozil Memorial, Orague, CZE	29 Jun
1 Jul	SGP	Athletissima, Lausanne, SUI	6 Jul
4 Jul	GL	Gaz de France Paris Saint-Denis, FRA	23 Jul
7 Jul	GP	Grand Prix Zagreb, CRO	29 Jun
11 Jul	GL	Golden Gala, Rome, ITA	2 Jul
13 Jul	SGP	Norwich Union Super League, Gateshead, GBR	27 Jun
19 Jul	SGP	Madrid 2012, ESP	17 Jul
31 Jul	GP	Gugl Meeting, Linz, AUT	2 Aug
2 Aug	GP II	Night of Athletics, Heusden, BEL	31 Jul
3 Aug	GP II	Thessaloniki, Greece	19 Jul
5 Aug	SGP	DN Galan, Stockholm, SWE	27 Jul
8 Aug	SGP	Norwich Union London Grand Prix, (CP), GBR	30 Jul
10 Aug	GL	ISTAF, Berlin, GER	12 Sep
15 Aug	GL	Weltklasse, Zürich, SUI	6 Aug
18 Aug	GP II	Asics GP, Helsinki, FIN	not GP II
5 Sep	GL	Memorial Ivo van Damme, Brussels, BEL	3 Sep
7 Sep	GP	Rieti, ITA	5 Sep
7 Sep		World Athletics Final (HT), Szombathely, HUN	5 Sep
12-13 Sep		World Athletics Final, Monaco, MON	18-19 Sep

GL = Golden League, SGP = Super Grand Prix, GP = Grand Prix, GP II = Grand Prix II

Winners of IAAF Golden League Events 2003

Event	*Oslo 27/6*	*Saint-Denis 4/7*	*Rome 11/7*	*Berlin 10/8*	*Zürich 15/8*	*Brussels 30/8*
Men						
100m	M Lewis-Francis	B Williams	J Capel	Fredericks/Capel	Capel/J Gatlin	A Powell
800m	M Mulaudzi	Y Borzakovskiy	M Mulaudzi	E Sepeng	M Mulaudzi	W Bungei
3/5000m	K Bekele	A Chebii	A Chebii	L Mucheru	J Kibowen	A Saïdi-Sief
110mh	S Olijar	A Johnson	A Johnson	S Olijar	D Ross	A Johnson
PV	N Hysong	D Miles	R Mesnil	D Markov	O Brits	D Yurchenko
JT	S Makarov	J Zelezny	S Makarov	R Hecht	J Zelezny	B Henry
Women						
100m	C Sturrup	C Sturrup	C Sturrup	K White	C Gaines	K White
800m	M Mutola	M Mutola	M Mutola	M Mutola	M Mutola	M Mutola
1500m	I Lishchynska	N Rodriguez	O Yegorova	S Ayhan	S Ayhan	S Ayhan
400mh	J Pittman	S Glover	J Pittman	J Pittman	S Glover	Y Pechonkina
TJ	Y Aldama	T Lebedeva	Y Aldama	T Lebedeva	F Mbango	T Lebedeva

Jackpot winners had to win at all meetings in the series, but the IAAF Council reduced the Golden League to six meetings from 2003 with Monaco now the venue for the World Athletics Finals.

Golden League Jackpot winners:

1998: Marion Jones (women's 100m), Hicham El Guerrouj (1500m), Haile Gebrselassie (3000m/5000m).

1999 Gabriela Szabo (W 3000m/5000m), Wilson Kipketer (800m).

2000 Gail Devers (W 100mh), Trine Hattestad (W JT), Tatyana Kotova (W LJ). Maurice Greene (100m) and Hicham El Guerrouj (1500m/1M) lost their share as they did not compete in the GP Final.

2001 Marion Jones (W 100m), Violeta Szekely (W 1500m), Olga Yegorova (W 3000/5000m), André Bucher (800m), Hicham El Guerrouj (1500m), Allen Johnson (110mh)

2002 Marion Jones (W 100m), Ana Guevara (W 400m), Felix Seanchez (400mh), Hicham El Guerrouj (1500m)

2003 Maria Mutola (W 800m)

Golden League events 2004

Men: 200m, 800m, 1500m, 400mh, TJ, DT; **Women:** 100m, 400m, 1500m, 3000m/5000m, 100mh, HJ

WORLD ATHLETICS FINAL 2003

Prize Money for each event: 1st $30,000, 2nd $20,000, 3rd $12,000, 4th $7000, 5th $5000, 6th $4000, 7th $3000, 8th $2000. Also at 1500m, 5000m, 3000mSt: 9th to 12th each $1000.

100 Metres (1.9)
1. Bernard Williams USA 10.04
2. John Capel USA 10.05
3. Uchenna Emedolu NGR 10.08
4. Dwain Chambers GBR 10.10
5. Justin Gatlin USA 10.12
6. Kim Collins SKN 10.13
7. Deji Aliu NGR 10.18
8. Asafa Powell JAM 10.23

200 Metres (0.1)
1. Joshua J.Johnson USA 20.35
2. Shawn Crawford USA 20.37
3. Stéphane Buckland MRI 20.44
4. Darvis Patton USA 20.46
5. Marlon Devonish GBR 20.70
6. Bernard Williams USA 20.80
7. Ramon Clay USA 21.01

400 Metres
1. Kevin Young USA 45.04
2. Michael Blackwood JAM 45.25
3. Alleyne Francique GRN 45.25
4. Éric Milazar MRI 45.67
5. David Canal ESP 45.82
6. Marc Raquil FRA 45.96
7. Cedric Van Branteghem BEL 46.02
8. Brandon Simpson JAM 46.02

800 Metres
1. Wilfred Bungei KEN 1:45.97
2. Joseph Mutua KEN 1:46.13
3. André Bucher SUI 1:46.28
4. Wilson Kipketer DEN 1:46.40
5. Mbulaeni Mulaudzi RSA 1:46.42
6. Hezekiél Sepeng RSA 1:46.61
7. Andrea Longo ITA 1:47.12
8. Yuriy Borzakovskiy RUS 1:47.42

1500 Metres
1. Paul Korir KEN 3:40.09
2. Alex Kipchirchir KEN-J 3:40.21
3. Ivan Heshko UKR 3:40.72
4. Rui Silva POR 3:41.10
5. Laban Rotich KEN 3:41.12
6. Cornelius Chirchir KEN 3:41.77
7. Robert Rono KEN 3:41.89
8. Benjamin Kipkurui KEN 3:42.27
9. Vyacheslav Shabunin RUS 3:42.72
10. Adrian Blincoe NZL 3:43.28
11. Abdelkader Hachlaf MAR 3:45.48

3000 Metres
1. Kenenisa Bekele ETH 7:36.98
2. John Kibowen KEN 7:38.21
3. Abrahim Chebii KEN 7:39.28
4. Leonard Mucheru KEN 7:40.20
5. James Kwalia KEN-J 7:41.40
6. Bnjamin Limo KEN 7:44.25
7. Luke Kipkosgei KEN 7:44.94

8. Craig Mottram AUS 7:48.76
9. Jesús España ESP 7:57.33
5000 Metres
1. Eliud Kipchoge KEN-J 13:23.34
2. Richard Limo KEN 13:23.95
3. Geb. Gebremariam ETH-J 13:24.13
4. Sammy Kipketer KEN 13:24.19
5. Sileshi Sihine ETH 13:24.61
6. Dejene Berhanu ETH 13:24.88
7. Nicholas Kemboi KEN 13:24.89
8. Charles Kamathi KEN 13:34.65
9. Moses Mosop KEN-J 13:35.51
10. Abdullah Hassan QAT 13:37.44
3000mSt
1. Saif Saaeed Shaheen QAT 7:57.38
2. Paul Koech KEN 7:57.42
3. Ezekiel Kemboi KEN 8:11.79
4. Julius Nyamu KEN 8:14.04
5. Bouabdallah Tahri FRA 8:15.60
6. Eliseo Martín ESP 8:16.38
7. Ali Ezzine MAR 8:18.05
8. Luis Miguel Martín ESP 8:23.66
9. Simon Vroemen NED 8:26.97
10. Abraham Cherono KEN 8:35.67
11. Wilson Boit Kipketer KEN 8:36.52
dnf. Kipkirui Misoi KEN
110 Hurdles (-1.5)
1. Allen Johnson USA 13.11
2. Terrence Trammell USA 13.17
3. Stanislav Olijar LAT 13.25
4. Liu Xiang CHN 13.27
5. Chris Phillips USA 13.33
6. Duane Ross USA 13.46
7. Ron Bramlett USA 13.48
8. Larry Wade USA 14.10
400 Metres Hurdles
1. Felix Sánchez DOM 47.80
2. Kemel Thompson JAM 48.50
3. Danny McFarlane JAM 48.66
4. Joey Woody USA 48.73
5. Dean Griffiths JAM 49.18
6. Periklís Iakovákis GRE 49.25
7. Eric Thomas USA 49.47
8. Chris Rawlinson GBR 50.67
High Jump
1. Yaroslav Rybakov RUS 2.30
2. Stephan Holm SWE 2.30
3. Jamie Nieto USA 2.30
4= Jacques Freitag RSA 2,27
4= Germaine Mason JAM 2.27
6. Andrey Sokolovskiy UKR 2.27
7. Mark Boswell CAN 2.27
8. Matt Hemingway USA 2.23
Pole Vault
1. Tim Lobinger GER 5.91
2. Okkert Brits RSA 5.86
3. Dmitri Markov AUS 5.76
4. Jeff Hartwig USA 5.70
5. Derek Miles USA 5.70
6. Giuseppe Gibilisco ITA 5.60
7. Romain Mesnil FRA 5.45
nh. Nick Hysong USA
Long Jump
1. Dwight Phillips USA 8.31/0.1
2. Hussein Al-Sabee KSA 8.30/0.4
3. Ignisious Gaisah GHA 8.26/0.1
4. Savanté Stringfellow USA 8.17/0.0
5. Yago Lamela ESP 8.00/0.2
6. Vladimir Zyuskov UKR 7.94/0.2
7. James Beckford JAM 7.93/0.1
8. Loúis Tsátoumas GRE 7.22/-0.1
Triple Jump
1. Christian Olsson SWE 17.55/-0.1
2. Walter Davis USA 17.09/-0.7
3. Kenta Bell USA 16.95/0.5
4. Jadel Gregório BRA 16.91/0.5
5. Ivaylo Rusenov BUL 16.70/1.0
6. Alexander Martínez CUB 16.60/-0.2
7. Leevan Sands BAH 16.40/0.0
8. Sébastien Pincemail FRA 16.12/-0.6
Shot
1. Christian Cantwell USA 20.93
2. Yuriy Bilonog UKR 20.53
3. Andrey Mikhnevich BLR 20.51
4. Manuel Martínez ESP 20.32
5. Adam Nelson USA 20.15
6. Justin Anlezark AUS 19.96
7. Kevin Toth USA 19.50
8. Milan Haborák SVK 18.97
Discus
1. Virgilijus Alekna LTU 68.30
2. Róbert Fazekas HUN 66.08
3. Vasiliy Kaptyukh BLR 65.85
4. Lars Riedel GER 65.74
5. Michael Möllenbeck GER 64.36
6. Aleksander Tammert EST 64.02
7. Frantz Kruger RSA 60.05
8. Mario Pestano ESP 59.96
Hammer *(at Szombathely, 7 Sep)*
1. Adrían Annus HUN 82.10
2. Libor Charfreitag SVK 81.22
3. Ivan Tikhon BLR 80.84
4. Koji Murofushi JPN 79.12
5. Andrey Skvaruk UKR 78.76
6. Primoz Kozmus SLO 78.59
7. Ilya Konovalov RUS 78.57
8. Karsten Kobs GER 74.18
Javelin
1. Sergey Makarov RUS 85.66
2. Jan Zelezny CZE 84.33
3. Boris Henry GER 81.00
4. Aleksandr Ivanov RUS 80.58
5. Andrus Värnik EST 80.43
6. Peter Blank GER 77.39
7. Christian Nicolay GER 77.02
8. Eriks Rags LAT 72.20
Women
100 Metres (1.2)
1. Chryste Gaines USA 10.86
2. Christine Arron FRA 11.04
3. Torri Edwards USA 11.06
4. Kelli White USA 11.08
5. Chandra Sturrup BAH 11.12
6. Muriel Hurtis FRA 11.24
7. Zhanna Block UKR 11.27
8. Angela Williams USA 11.38
200 Metres (1.6)
1. Kelli White USA 22.31
2. Muriel Hurtis FRA 22.41
3. Anastasiya Kapachinskaya RUS 22.57
4. Torri Edwards USA 22.58
5. Kim Gevaert BEL 22.95
6. Natalya Safronnikova BLR 22.97
7. Beverly McDonald JAM 23.01
8. Cydonie Mothersill CAY 23.16
400 Metres
1. Ana Guevara MEX 49.34
2. Lorraine Fenton JAM 50.29

3. Tonique Williams BAH 50.87
4. Amy Mbacké Thiam SEN 51.06
5. Olesya Zykina RUS 51.81
6. Natalya Nazarova RUS 51.88
7. Lee McConnell GBR 52.16
8. Svetlana Pospelova RUS 53.72

800 Metres
1. Maria Mutola MOZ 1:59.59
2. Kelly Holmes GBR 1:59.92
3. Amina Aït Hammou MAR 1:59.97
4. Faith Macharia KEN 2:00.44
5. Diane Cummins CAN 2:00.70
6. Jolanda Ceplak SLO 2:00.91
7. Natalya Khrushchelyova RUS 2:00.96
8. Claudia Gesell GER 2:03.66

1500 Metres
1. Süreyya Ayhan TUR 3:57.72
2. Jackline Maranga KEN 4:01.48
3. Hayley Tullett GBR 4:01.60
4. Jo Pavey GBR 4:01.79
5. Judit Varga HUN 4:02.42
6. Naomi Mugo KEN 4:02.63
7. Tatyana Tomashova RUS 4:02.78
8. Yekaterina Rozenberg RUS 4:02.82
9. Yelena Zadorozhnaya RUS 4:03.71
10. Irina Lishchinskaya UKR 4:03.89
11. Alesya Turova BLR 4:04.24
12. Natalya Gorelova RUS 4:04.31

3000 Metres
1. Edith Masai KEN 8:36.82
2. Yelena Zadorozhnaya RUS 8:37.40
3. Jo Pavey GBR 8:37.89
4. Meseret Defar ETH 8:38.31
5. Berhane Adere ETH 8:39.26
6. Zakia Mrisho TAN 8:46.77
7. Zhor El Kamch MAR 8:49.52
8. Irina Poluskina LAT-J 9:04.23
9. Carla Sacramento POR 9:23.14

5000 Metres
1. Elvan Abeylegesse TUR 14:56.25
2. Derartu Tulu ETH 14:56.93
3. Tirunesh Dibaba ETH-J 14:57.87
4. Werknesh Kidane ETH 14:58.13
5. Isabella Ochichi KEN 15:00.04
6. Benita Johnson AUS 15:11.69
7. Sentayehu Ejigu ETH-J 15:25.60
8. Alla Zhilyayeva RUS 15:41.86
9. Ines Chenonge KEN 15:49.14

100 Metres Hurdles (1.3)
1. Gail Devers USA 12.45
2. Glora Alozie ESP 12.66
3. Miesha McKelvy USA 12.69
4. Jenny Adams USA 12.78
5. Patricia Girard FRA 13.00
6. Melissa Morrison USA 13.05
7. Lacena Golding-Clarke JAM 13.10
8. Brigitte Foster JAM 13.26

400 Metres Hurdles
1. Sandra Glover USA 53.65
2. Andrea Blackett BAR 54.28
3. Ionela Tîrlea ROM 54.44
4. Tatyana Tereschuk UKR 54.63
5. Brenda Taylor USA 54.93
6. Natasha Danvers GBR 55.54
7. Monika Niederstatter ITA 56.84

dnf. Surrita Febbraio RSA

High Jump
1. Hestrie Cloete RSA 2.01
2. Vita Palamar UKR 2.01
3. Kajsa Bergqvist SWE 1.99
4. Blanka Vlasic CRO 1:96
5. Inga Babakova UKR 1.96
6. Marina Kuptsova RUS 1.92
7. Yelena Yelesina RUS 1.88
8. Anna Chicherova RUS 1.83

Pole Vault
1. Tatyana Polnova RUS 4.68
2. Svetlana Feofanova RUS 4.60
3. Stacy Dragila USA 4.50
4. Monika Pyrek POL 4.50
5. Yelena Isinbayeva RUS 4.40
6. Annika Becker GER 4.40
7. Vanessa Boslak FRA 4.25

nh. Yvonne Buschbaum GER

Long Jump
1. Eunice Barber FRA 7.05/-0.4
2. Tatyana Kotova RUS 6.92/-0.3
3. Grace Upshaw USA 6.60/-0.3
4. Olga Rublyova RUS 6.57/-0.4
5. Anju Bobby George IND 6.50/-0.9
6. Elva Goulbourne JAM 6.49/-0.4
7. Concepción Montaner ESP 6.45/-0.2

nj. Tünde Vaszi HUN

Triple Jump
1. Tatyana Lebedeva RUS 15.13/0.1
2. Yamilé Aldama CUB 14.99/0.1
3. Françoise Mbango CMR 14.83/0.0
4. Anna Pyatykh RUS 14.55/0.8
5. Magdelín Martínez ITA 14.52/0.1
6. Yelena Govorova UKR 14.46/0.5
7. Adelina Gavrila ROM 14.44/0.7
8. Kéné Ndoye SEN 14.02/-0.3

Shot
1. Vita Pavlysh UKR 19.86
2. Svetlana Krivelyova RUS 19.66
3. Nadezhda Ostapchuk BLR 19.51
4. Astrid Kumbernuss GER 18.89
5. Irina Korzhanenko RUS 18.48
6. Nadine Kleinert GER 18.15
7. Elisângela Adriano BRA 17.92
8. Krystyna Zabawska POL 17.85

Discus
1. Vera Pospísilová CZE 65.42
2. Aretha Hill USA 65.10
3. Ekateríni Vóggoli GRE 63.55
4. Yelena Antonova UKR 63.04
5. Natalya Sadova RUS 62.00
6. Franka Dietzsch GER 61.88
7. Beatrice Faumuina NZL 61.81
8. Irina Yatchenko BLR 60.96

Hammer *(at Szombathely, 7 Sep)*
1. Yipsi Moreno CUB 73.42
2. Olga Kuzenkova RUS 71.16
3. Mihaela Melinte ROM 69.27
4. Manuela Montebrun FRA 68.88
5. Susanna Keil GER 67.78
6. Anna Mahon USA 66.94
7. Irina Sekachova UKR 66.46
8. Kamila Skolimowska POL 61.46

Javelin
1. Tatyana Shikolenko RUS 64.47
2. Steffi Nerius GER 64.25
3. Nikolett Szabó HUN 62.88
4. Lavern Eve BAH 62.10
5. Mikaela Ingberg FIN 61.29
6. Valeriya Zabruskova RUS 60.67
7. Claudia Coslovich ITA 58.61
8. Paula Huhtaniemi FIN 57.36

OLYMPIC GAMES

THE FIRST Olympic Games of the modern era were staged in Athens, Greece from the 6th to 15th April 1896. Those in Athens 2004, the Games of the XXVIII Olympiad, will be the 25th to be staged, including the intercalated Games of 1906.

Just 59 athletes from ten nations contested the athletics events in 1896. In 2000 there was a record participation for a summer Games, at all sports, with 10,651 competitors from 200 nations.

Olympic Games Records after Sydney 2000

Men

100m	9.84	Donovan Bailey CAN 1996
200m	19.32	Michael Johnson USA 1996
400m	43.49	Michael Johnson USA 1996
800m	1:42.58	Vebjørn Rodal NOR 1996
1500m	3:32.07	Noah Ngeny KEN 2000
5000m	13:05.59	Saïd Aouita MAR 1984
10000m	27:07.34	Haile Gebrselassie ETH 1996
Marathon	2hr 09:21	Carlos Lopes POR 1984
3000mSt	8:05.51	Julius Kariuki KEN 1988
110mh	12.95	Allen Johnson USA 1996
400mh	46.78	Kevin Young USA 1992
4x100mR	37.40	USA 1992
4x400mR	2:55.74	USA 1992
20km walk	1hr 18:59	Robert Korzeniowski POL 2000
50km walk	3hr 38:29	Vyacheslav Ivanenko URS 1988
High jump	2.38	Gennadiy Avdeyenko URS 1988
Pole vault	5.92	Jean Galfione FRA 1996
		Igor Trandenkov RUS 1996
		Andrei Tivontchik GER 1996
Long jump	8.90A	Bob Beamon USA 1968
Triple jump	18.17w	Mike Conley USA 1992
	18.09	Kenny Harrison USA 1996
Shot	22.47	Ulf Timmermann GDR 1988
Discus	69.40	Lars Riedel GER 1996
Hammer	84.80	Sergey Litvinov URS 1988
Javelin	90.17	Jan Zelezny CZE 2000
old	94.58	Miklós Németh HUN 1976
Decathlon	8847	Daley Thompson GBR 1984

Women

100m	10.62	Florence Griffith-Joyner USA 1988
	10.54w	Florence Griffith-Joyner USA 1988
200m	21.34	Florence Griffith-Joyner USA 1988
400m	48.25	Marie-José Pérec FRA 1996
800m	1:53.43	Nadezhda Olizarenko URS 1980
1500m	3:53.96	Paula Ivan ROM 1988
3000m	8:26.53	Tatyana Samolenko URS 1988
5000m	14:40.79	Gabriela Szabo ROM 2000
10000m	30:17.49	Derartu Tulu ETH 2000
Marathon	2hr 23:14	Naoko Takahashi JPN 2000
100mh	12.38	Yordanka Donkova BUL 1988
400mh	52.82	Deon Hemmings JAM 1996
4x100mR	41.60	GDR 1980
4x400mR	3:15.17	USSR 1988
10km walk	41:49	Yelena Nikolayeva RUS 1996
20km walk	1:29:05	Wang Liping CHN 2000
High jump	2.05	Stefka Kostadinova BUL 1996
Pole vault	4.60	Stacy Dragila USA 2000
Long jump	7.40	Jackie Joyner-Kersee USA 1988
Triple jump	15.33	Inessa Kravets UKR 1996
Shot	22.41	Ilona Slupianek GDR 1980
Discus	72.30	Martina Hellmann GDR 1988
Hammer	71.16	Kamila Skolimowska POL 2000
Javelin	68.91	Trine Hattestad NOR 2000
old	74.68	Petra Felke GDR 1988
Heptathlon	7291	Jackie Joyner-Kersee USA 1988

** performance made in qualifying round, A at high altitude, Mexico City 2240m*

Most gold medals – all events

Men

10 Raymond Ewry USA StHJ and StLJ 1900-04-06-08, StTJ 1900-04

9 Paavo Nurmi FIN 1500m 1924, 5000m 1924, 10000m 1920-28, 3000mSt 1924, CC 1920-24, CC team 1920-24

9 Carl Lewis USA 100m, 200m, LJ & 4x100mR 1984; 100m, LJ 1988; LJ, 4x100mR 1992; LJ 1996

5 Martin Sheridan USA DT 1904-06-08, SP 1906, DT Greek style 1908

5 Ville Ritola FIN 10000m, 3000mSt, CC team & 3000m team 1924, 5000m 1928

5 Michael Johnson USA 200m 1996, 400m 1996-2000, 4x400m 1992-2000

4 twelve men

Women

4 Fanny Blankers-Koen NED 100m, 200m, 80mh & 4x100mR 1948

4 Betty Cuthbert AUS 100m, 200m, 4x100mR 1956, 400m 1964

4 Bärbel Eckert/Wöckel GDR 200m & 4x100mR 1976-80

4 Evelyn Ashford USA 100m 1984, 4x100mR 1984-88-92

Most medals – all events

G gold, S silver, B bronze

Men

12 Paavo Nurmi FIN 9G as above; 3S 5000m 1920-28, 3000mSt 1928

10 Raymond Ewry USA 10G as above

10 Carl Lewis USA 9G as above; 1S 200m 1988

9 Martin Sheridan USA 5G as above; 3S StHJ, StLJ & Stone 1906; 1B StLJ 1908

8 Ville Ritola FIN 5G as above; 3S 5000m & CC 1924, 10000m 1928

7 Eric Lemming SWE 4G JT 1906-08-12 freestyle 1908, 3B SP, Pen, Tug of War 1906

Women

8 Merlene Ottey JAM 3S 100m, 200m 1996; 4x100mR 2000; 5B 4x100mR 1980, 1996; 100m 1984, 200m 1984-92

7 Shirley Strickland/de la Hunty AUS 3G 80mh

1952-56, 4x100mR 1956; 1S 4x100mR 1948; 3B 100m 1948-52, 80mh 1948 *(later evidence showed that she should also have been awarded the 1948 200m bronze)*

7 Irena Kirszenstein/Szewinska POL 3G 200m 1968, 400m 1976, 4x100mR 1964; 2S 200m & LJ 1964, 2B 100m 1968, 200m 1972

Most gold medals at one Games: Men: 5 Paavo Nurmi FIN 1924; **Women**: 4 Fanny Blankers-Koen NED as above

Most medals at one Games: Men: 6 – 4 gold, 2 silver – Ville Ritola FIN 1924; **Women**: 5 – 3 gold, 2 bronze – Marion Jones 2000

Most Games contested: 6 Lia Manoliu ROM 1952-72 at women's discus, Tessa Sanderson GBR 1976-96 at women's javelin

Most finals or first eight at the same event: 5 Vladimir Golubnichiy URS 20kmW 1960-76: 1-3-1-2-7

Oldests

Men

Winner	42y 23d	Pat McDonald USA 56lb Wt 1920
Medallist	48y 115d	Tebbs Lloyd Johnson GBR 3rd 50kmW 1948
Competitor	52y 199d	Percy Wyer CAN Mar 1936

Women

Winner	39y 315d	Ellian Zvereva BLR DT 2000
Medallist	40y 143d	Merlene Ottey JAM 4x100mR 2000
Competitor	48y 234d	Lourdes Klitzkie GUM 63rd Mar 1984=8

Youngests

Men

Winner	17y 263d	Bob Mathias USA Dec 1948
Medallist	17y 169d	Frank Castleman USA 2nd 200mh 1904
	17y 206d	Pál Simon HUN 3rd Medley relay 1908
	born 1891,	but exact date unknown, 17-206 is oldest possible
Ind. medal	17y 263d	Bob Mathias as above

Women

Winner	15y 123d	Barbara Pearl Jones USA 4x100mR 1952
Ind. winner	16y 123d	Ulrike Meyfarth FRG HJ 1972
Medallist	15y 123d	Barbara Pearl Jones as above
Ind. medal	16y 115d	Dorothy Odam GBR 2nd HJ 1936

y – years, d – days

Medal table of leading nations 1896-2000 including 1906 Games

	Men			Women			Total Medals
Nation	*Gold*	*Silver*	*Bronze*	*Gold*	*Silver*	*Bronze*	
USA	267	197	163	43	25	20	715
USSR/CIS	37	37	42	34	29	35	214
United Kingdom	43	63	43	6	20	16	191
Germany *	12	27	38	17	13	18	125
GDR	14	19	14	25	28	24	124
Finland	48	33	30	1	2	-	114
Sweden	17	25	41	1	-	4	88
Australia	6	10	12	12	11	12	63
France	8	20	18	6	1	4	57
Italy	13	8	20	3	7	3	54
Canada	12	10	16	2	5	7	52
Poland	13	8	5	8	8	7	49
Kenya	15	18	12	-	1	1	47
Hungary	7	13	16	3	1	2	42
Jamaica	4	11	7	1	9	6	38
Romania	-	-	1	10	12	8	31
Greece	4	7	14	1	4	-	30
Cuba	5	8	5	2	2	5	27
Czechoslovakia	8	7	3	3	2	2	25
Ethiopia	9	1	8	3	1	2	24
Russia	1	2	4	5	7	2	21
South Africa	5	5	6	1	3	1	21
Japan	4	5	6	1	2	1	19
New Zealand	7	1	7	1	-	2	18
Bulgaria	-	-	1	5	7	5	18
Norway	4	2	7	1	2	1	17
Netherlands	-	-	5	6	2	1	14
Morocco	3	3	5	1	-	1	13
Brazil	3	3	6	-	-	-	12
China	-	-	1	3	3	4	11
Belgium	2	6	2	-	-	-	10

In all 80 nations have won medals at track and field events

* Germany 1896-1952 and from 1992, Federal Republic of Germany 1956-88. Medals won by the combined German teams of 1956, 1960 and 1964 have been allocated to FRG or GDR according to the athlete's origin. Note that tug of war events, held from 1900 to 1920 have been excluded.

Olympic Games, Sydney 2000 – Medallists

Men

100 Metres
1. Maurice Greene USA 9.87
2. Ato Boldon TRI 9.99
3. Obadele Thompson BAR 10.04

200 Metres
1. Konstadínos Kedéris GRE 20.09
2. Darren Campbell GBR 20.14
3. Ato Boldon TRI 20.20

400 Metres
1. Michael Johnson USA 43.84
2. Alvin Harrison USA 44.40
3. Greg Haughton JAM 44.70

800 Metres
1. Nils Schumann GER 1:45.08
2. Wilson Kipketer DEN 1:45.14
3. Djabir Saïd-Guerni ALG 1:45.16

1500 Metres
1. Noah Ngeny KEN 3:32.07*
2. Hicham El Guerrouj MAR 3:32.32
3. Bernard Lagat KEN 3:32.44

5000 Metres
1. Million Wolde ETH 13:35.49
2. Ali Saïdi-Sief ALG 13:36.20
3. Brahim Lahlafi MAR 13:36.47

10,000 Metres
1. Haile Gebrselassie ETH 27:18.20
2. Paul Tergat KEN 27:18.29
3. Assefa Mezegebu ETH 27:19.75

Marathon
1. Gezahegne Abera ETH 2:10:11
2. Eric Wainaina KEN 2:10:31
3. Tesfaye Tola ETH 2:11:10

3000 Metres Steeplechase
1. Reuben Kosgei KEN 8:21.43
2. Wilson Boit Kipketer KEN 8:21.77
3. Ali Ezzine MAR 8:22.15

110 Metres Hurdles
1. Anier García CUB 13.00
2. Terrence Trammell USA 13.16
3. Mark Crear USA 13.22

400 Metres Hurdles
1. Angelo Taylor USA 47.50
2. Hadi Al-Somaily KSA 47.53
3. Llewellyn Herbert RSA 47.81

High Jump
1. Sergey Klyugin RUS 2.35
2. Javier Sotomayor CUB 2.32
3. Abderahmane Hammad ALG 2.32

Pole Vault
1. Nick Hysong USA 5.90
2. Lawrence Johnson USA 5.90
3. Maksim Tarasov RUS 5.90

Long Jump
1. Iván Pedroso CUB 8.55
2. Jai Taurima AUS 8.49
3. Roman Shchurenko UKR 8.31

Triple Jump
1. Jonathan Edwards GBR 17.71
2. Yoel García CUB 17.47
3. Denis Kapustin RUS 17.46

Shot
1. Arsi Harju FIN 21.29
2. Adam Nelson USA 21.21
3. John Godina USA 21.20

Discus
1. Virgilijus Alekna LTU 69.30
2. Lars Riedel GER 68.50
3. Frantz Kruger RSA 68.19

Hammer
1. Szymon Ziólkowski POL 80.02
2. Nicola Vizzoni ITA 79.64
3. Igor Astapkovich BLR 79.17

Javelin
1. Jan Zelezny CZE 90.17*
2. Steve Backley GBR 89.85
3. Sergey Makarov RUS 88.67

Decathlon
1. Erki Nool EST 8641
2. Roman Sebrle CZE 8606
3. Chris Huffins USA 8595

20 Kilometres Walk
1. Robert Korzeniowski POL 1:18:59*
2. Noe Hernández MEX 1:19:03
3. Vladimir Andreyev RUS 1:19:27

50 Kilometres Walk
1. Robert Korzeniowski POL 3:42:22
2. Aigars Fadejevs LAT 3:43:40
3. Joel Sánchez MEX 3:44:36

4 x 100 Metres
1. USA 37.61
2. BRA 37.90
3. CUB 38.04

4 x 400 Metres
1. USA 2:56.35
2. NGR 2:58.68
3. JAM 2:58.78

Women

100 Metres
1. Marion Jones USA 10.75
2. Ekaterini Thánou GRE 11.12
3. Tanya Lawrence JAM 11.18

200 Metres
1. Marion Jones USA 21.84
2. Pauline Davis-Thompson BAH 22.27
3. Susanthika Jayasinghe SRI 22.28

400 Metres
1. Cathy Freeman AUS 49.11
2. Lorraine Graham JAM 49.58
3. Katharine Merry GBR 49.72

800 Metres
1. Maria Mutola MOZ 1:56.15
2. Stephanie Graf AUT 1:56.64
3. Kelly Holmes GBR 1:56.80

1500 Metres
1. Nouria Mérah-Benida ALG 4:05.10
2. Violeta Szekely ROM 4:05.15
3. Gabriela Szabo ROM 4:05.27

5000 Metres
1. Gabriela Szabo ROM 14:40.79*
2. Sonia O'Sullivan IRL 14:41.02
3. Gete Wami ETH 14:42.23

10,000 Metres
1. Derartu Tulu ETH 30:17.49*
2. Gete Wami ETH 30:22.48
3. Fernanda Ribeiro POR 30:22.88

Marathon
1. Naoko Takahashi JPN 2:23:14*
2. Lidia Simon ROM 2:23:22
3. Joyce Chepchumba KEN 2:24:45

100 Metres Hurdles
1. Olga Shishigina KAZ 12.65
2. Glory Alozie NGR 12.68
3. Melissa Morrison USA 12.76

400 Metres Hurdles
1. Irina Privalova RUS 53.02
2. Deon Hemmings JAM 53.45
3. Nezha Bidouane MAR 53.57

High Jump
1. Yelena Yelesina RUS 2.01
2. Hestrie Cloete RSA 2.01
3= Kajsa Bergqvist SWE 1.99
3= Oana Pantelimon ROM 1.99

Pole Vault
1. Stacy Dragila USA 4.60*
2. Tatiana Grigorieva AUS 4.55
3. Vala Flosadóttir ISL 4.50

Long Jump
1. Heike Drechsler GER 6.99
2. Fiona May ITA 6.92
3. Marion Jones USA 6.92

Triple Jump
1. Tereza Marinova BUL 15.20
2. Tatyana Lebedeva RUS 15.00
3. Yelena Govorova UKR 14.96

Shot
1. Yanina Korolchik BLR 20.56
2. Larisa Peleshenko RUS 19.92
3. Astrid Kumbernuss GER 19.62

Discus
1. Ellina Zvereva BLR 68.40
2. Anastasía Kelesídou GRE 65.71
3. Irina Yatchenko BLR 65.20

Hammer
1. Kamila Skolimowska POL 71.16*
2. Olga Kuzenkova RUS 69.77
3. Kirsten Münchow GER 69.28

Javelin
1. Trine Hattestad NOR 68.91*
2. Miréla Tzelíli GRE 67.51
3. Osleidys Menéndez CUB 66.18

Heptathlon
1. Denise Lewis GBR 6584
2. Yelena Prokhorova RUS 6531
3. Natalya Sazanovich BLR 6527

20 Kilometres Walk
1. Wang Liping CHN 1:29:05*
2. Kjersti Plätzer NOR 1:29:33
3. María Vasco ESP 1:30:23

4 x 100 Metres
1. BAH 41.95
2. JAM 42.12
3. USA 42.20

4 x 400 Metres
1. USA 3:22.62
2. JAM 3:23.25
3. RUS 3:23.46

** Olympic record*

Olympic Qualifying Standards 2004

Achievable from 1 Jan 2003 (marathon from 1 Sep 2002) to 9 Aug 2004.
Many of the original standards were changed (downwards) by the IAAF in October 2003.

Men

	A	B
100m	10.21	10.28
200m	20.59	20.75
400m	45.55	45.95
800m	1:46.00	1:47.00
1500m	3:36.20	3:38.00
5000m	13:21.50	13:25.40
10,000m	27:49.00	28:06.00
Mar	2:15:00	2:18:00
3000mSt	8:24.60	8:32.00
110mh	13.55	13.62
400mh	49.20	49.50
HJ	2.30	2.27
PV	5.65	5.55
LJ	8.19	8.05
TJ	16.95	16.55
SP	20.30	20.00
DT	64.00	62.55
HT	78.65	74.35
JT	81.80	77.80
Dec	8000	7700
20kmW	1:23:00	1:24:30
50kmW	4:00:00	4:07:00
Relays	top 16 teams invited	

Women

	A	B
100m	11.30	11.40
200m	22.97	23.13
400m	51.59	52.30
800m	2:00.00	2:01.30
1500m	4:05.80	4:07.15
5000m	15:08.70	15:20.45
10,000m	31:45.00	32:17.00
Mar	2:37:00	2:42:00
100mh	12.96	13.11
400mh	55.60	56.25
HJ	1.95	1.91
PV	4.40	4.25
LJ	6.70	6.55
TJ	14.20	14.00
SP	18.55	17.15
DT	61.00	57.70
HT	67.50	64.00
JT	60.50	56.00
Hep	6050	5900
20kmW	1:33:30	1:38:00
Relays	top 16 teams invited	

Hand-timed sprints, wind-assisted or performances made in mixed races will not be accepted, but indoor performances for all field events and for races of 200m and longer will be accepted.
The IOC and the IAAF have adopted a new rule so that there is a maximum of 16 qualified teams in each relay event, based on the fastest times achieved by national teams at IAAF recognised international events from 1 January 2002 to 21 July 2004.

ATHENS OLYMPIC SCHEDULE

Both Olympic shot put events will take place in Olympia, site of the ancient Games. The dates will be either Aug 18 or 19 (before the start of the main athletics programme), with both medal ceremonies staged on Aug 20 in the Athens Olympic Stadium.

August 20-29 2004 (Finals in bold)

Fri, Aug 20: (09.00-13.35) **20k Walk**, W Hep 100H, TJ qual, HT qual, W 100 hts, W Hep HJ; (19.30-00.07) W Hep SP, 1500 hts, W DT qual, W 100 qf, HJ qual, W Hep 200, 400 hts, W 800 hts, **10,000m**, W 5000 hts

Sat, Aug 21: (09.00-12.12) DT qual, W Hep LJ, W 400H hts, W 400 hts, 100 hts; (18.30-23.00) W Hep JT, W PV qual, 100 qf, W TJ qual, W 100 sf, W 800 sf, 400 sf, **W Discus, W Heptathlon 800m** (final event), 3000SC hts, **W 100m**

Sun, Aug 22: (18.00) **W Marathon** (ends in Panathinaiko Stadium); (19.30-21.15) W 100H hts, **Hammer, High Jump, Triple Jump**, 100 sf, W 400H sf, 1500 sf, W 400 sf, W 100H qf, **100m**

Mon, Aug 23: (09.00-13.00) **W 20k Walk**, W HT qual, Dec 100, Dec LJ, W 200 hts, Dec SP; (18.30-22.15) Dec HJ, **W Triple Jump**, W 100H sf, 400H hts, **Discus**, W 200 qf, **W 800m, 400m**, Dec 400, **W 5000m**

Tue, Aug 24: (09.00-16.00) Dec 110H, 110H hts, Dec DT, 200 hts, Dec PV; (19.30-23.30) Dec JT, LJ qual, 200 qf, **W Pole Vault**, W 1500 hts, 400H sf, **3000m Steeplechase**, W 200 sf, **W 400m, W 100m Hurdles, Decathlon 1500m** (final event), **1500m**

Wed, Aug 25: (19.30-23.25) W JT qual, PV qual, 5000 hts, W LJ qual, 800 hts, **W 400m Hurdles**, 110H qf, **W Hammer**, 200 sf, **W 200m**

Thu, Aug 26: (19.30-22.30) JT qual, W HJ qual, **Long Jump**, W 1500 sf, 110H sf, 800 sf, W 4x100 hts, **400m Hurdles, 200m**

Fri, Aug 27: (07.00) **50k Walk**; (19.30-22.35) **Pole Vault, W Long Jump**, 4x100 hts, W 4x400 hts, 4x400 hts; **W Javelin, 110m Hurdles, W 10,000m, W 4x100m**

Sat, Aug 28: (19.30-23.00) **W High Jump, Javelin, W 1500m, 800m, 5000m, 4x100m, W 4x400m, 4x400m**

Sun, Aug 29: (18.00) **Marathon** (ends in Panathinaiko Stadium).

Medal table for leading nations 1986-2002

Nation	*1st*	*2nd*	*3rd*				
USA	40	39	27	South Africa	9	6	5
Kenya	38	33	17	Bulgaria	8	4	7
China	27	23	13	Australia	9	14	16
USSR/CIS 86-92	22	18	27	Finland	7	8	12
GDR 1986-90	22	10	18	Poland	6	8	12
FRG/GER	19	22	19	Croatia	5	-	1
Russia (94-)	18	12	13	Spain	4	12	3
GBR	17	18	19	Sweden	4	7	4
Ethiopia	17	14	14	France	3	7	8
Cuba	16	20	13	Hungary	3	5	3
Romania	16	13	11	Ukraine	3	4	1
Jamaica	14	17	15	Netherlands	3	2	4
Nigeria	9	8	7	Trinidad & Tobago	3	1	3
				Mexico	3	1	1

World Records Set in Athens

Men

26 Apr 1906	OG	JT	53.90	Eric Lemming SWE
20 Sep 1969	EC	HT	74.68	Anatoliy Bondarchuk URS
24 Oct 1970		PV	5.49	Hrístos Papanikolaou GRE
7-8 Sep 1982	EC	Dec	8774/8743	Daley Thompson GBR
16 Jun 1999	GP	100m	9.79	Maurice Greene USA

Women

16 Sep 1969	EC	SP	20.10 & 20.43	Nadezhda Chizhova URS
18 Sep 1969	EC	400m	51.7	Nicole Duclos FRA & Colette Besson FRA
19 Sep 1969	EC	4x400m	3:33.9	FRG (in heat 2)
20 Sep 1969	EC	1500m	4:10.77	Jaroslava Jehlicková TCH
20 Sep 1969	EC	4x400m	3:30.8	GBR & FRA
24 Aug 1973	Balkan G	800m	1:57.48	Svetla Zlateva BUL
8 Sep 1982	EC	400m	48.16	Marita Koch GDR
8 Sep 1982	EC	HJ	2.02	Ulrike Meyfarth FRG
11 Sep 1982	EC	4x400m	3:19.04	GDR

Marks in 1969-72 (inc. European Championships 1969 and Balkan Champs 1972) set at Karaskiakis Stadium, Piréas.

WORLD JUNIOR CHAMPIONSHIPS

The 10th IAAF World Junior Championships will be staged at Grosseto, Italy on 12-18 July 2004.

Championship bests after 2002

Men

100m	10.09	Darrel Brown TRI	2002
200m	20.44	Christian Malcolm GBR	1998
400m	44.66	Hamdam Al-Bishi KSA	2000
800m	1:44.77	Benson Koech KEN	1992
1500m	3:37.94	Atoi Boru KEN	1992
5000m	13:28.30	Hillary Chenonge KEN	2002
10,000m	28:03.99	Haile Gebresilasie ETH	1992
20km Road#	59:27	Metaferia Zeleke ETH	1988
2000mSt#	5:28.56	Juan Azkueta ESP	1986
3000mSt	8:16.34	Raymond Yator KEN	2000
110mh	13.44	Colin Jackson GBR	1986
400mh	48.89	Louis van Zyl RSA	2002
HJ	2.37	Dragutin Topic YUG	1990
	2.37	Steve Smith GBR	1992
PV	5.65	István Bagyula HUN	1988
LJ	8.20	James Stallworth USA q	1990
TJ	17.04	Yoelbi Quesada CUB	1992
SP	19.48	Rutger Smith NED	2000
6kg	21.47	Edis Elkasevic CRO	2002
DT	60.60	Vasil Baklarov BUL	1986
1.75kg	64.51	Wu Tao CHN	2002
HT	72.40	Olli-Pekka Karjalainen FIN	1998
6kg	76.43	Werner Smit RSA	2002
JT	79.78	Sergey Voynov UZB	1996
Dec	7897	Dennis Leyckes GER	2000
10kmW	39:55.52	Ilya Markov URS	1990
4x100mR	38.92	USA	2002
	(Ashton Collins, Wes Felix, Ivory Williams, Willie Hordge)		
4x400mR	3:01.90	USA	1986
	(Clifton Campbell, Chip Rish, Percy Waddle, William Reed		

Women

100m	11.12	Veronica Campbell JAM	2000
200m	22.87	Veronica Campbell	2000
	22.80w	Heide Seyerling RSA	1994
400m	50.62	Fatima Yusuf NGR	1990
800m	2:00.67	Birte Bruhns GDR	1988
1500m	4:05.14	Liu Dong CHN	1992
3000m	8:46.86	Zhang Linli CHN	1992
5000m	15:29.65	Yin Lili CHN	1998
10,000m#	32:22.90	Wang Junxia CHN	1992
3000mSt		added for 2004	
100mh	12.96	Aliuska López CUB	sf 1988
	12.81w	Anay Tejeda CUB	2002
400mh	54.70	Lashinda Demus USA	2002
HJ	2.00	Galina Astafei ROM	1988
PV	4.40	Floe Kühnert GER	2002
LJ	6.82	Fiona May GBR	1988
	6.88w	Fiona May	1988
TJ	14.62	Tereza Marinova BUL	1996
SP	18.76	Cheng Xiaoyan CHN	1994
DT	68.24	Ilke Wyludda GDR	1988
HT	65.39	Ivana Brkljajcic CRO	2002
JT	68.17	Osleidys Menéndez CUB	1998
Hep	6470	Carolina Klüft SWE	2002
5kmW	21:05.41	Irina Stankina RUS	1994
10kmW	44:07.74	Lyudmila Yefimkina RUS	2000
4x100mR	43.40	Jamaica	2002
	(Sherone Simpson, Kerron Stewart, Ammesisha McLaughlin, Simone Facey)		
4x400mR	3:28.39	GDR	1988
	(Manuela Deer, Stefanie Fabert, Anke Wöhlk, Grit Breuer		

 # Events no longer contested

Championships have been held:

Venue	*Dates*	*Athletes*	*Nations*
Athens, Greece	16-20 July 1986	1188	143
Sudbury, Canada	27-31 July 1988	1052	122
Plovdiv, Bulgaria	8-12 Aug 1990	1033	86
Seoul, Korea	16-20 Sep 1992	988	90
Lisbon, Portugal	20-24 Jul 1994	1179	143
Sydney, Australia	21-25 Aug 1996	1080	143
Annecy, France	28 Jul- 2 Aug 1998	1184	170
Santiago, Chile	17-22 Oct 2000	1150	157
Kingston, Jamaica	16-21 Jul 2002		

Medals were won by athletes from a record 39 countries in 1994 and 2000.

Most gold medals

Men

4 Chris Nelloms USA 19881990
3 William Obea Moore USA 1996

Women

4 Gillian Russell JAM 1990 & 1992
3 Grit Breuer GDR 1988
3 Nikole Mitchell J1990 & 1992

Most medals

5 Katrin Krabbe 1986 & 1988

Youngest champions

Men

15y 332d Usain Bolt JAM 200m 2002
16yr 215d Jonah Birir KEN 800m 1988
16yr 221d Wilfred Oanda Kirochi KEN 1500m 1986
16yr 284d Robert Kipchumba KEN 10,000m 2000

Women

15yr 102d Wang Yan CHN 5000m walk 1986
15yr 169d Ann Mwangi KEN 3000m 1988
15yr 196d Susana Feitor POR 5000m walk 1990
15yr 245d Diane Smith GBR 200m 1990

Youngest medalist:

Men 15yr 169d Ismael Kirui KEN 2nd 10,000m 1990

Women 14yr 182d Sally Barsosio KEN 3rd 10,000m 1992
14yr 279d Jackline Maranga KEN 2nd 1500m 1992

Most championship bests

7 Ilke Wyludda GDR DT 61.58, 62.26, 62.30, 64.02 1986; 65.78, 67.00, 68.24 1988

MAJOR INTERNATIONAL EVENTS 2004-2010

2004

1st Asian Indoor Championships – Tehran, Iran (6-8 Feb)
IAAF World Indoor Championships – Budapest, Hungary (5-7 Mar)
IAAF World Cross Country Championships – Brussels, Belgium (20-21 Mar)
IAAF World Race Walking Cup – Naumburg, Germany (1-2 May)
Asian Junior Championships, Penang, Malaysia (12=-15 June)
African Championships – Brazzaville, CUD (14-18 July)
European Cup – Super League – Bydgoszcz, Poland (19-20 June)
European Cup for Combined Events (3-4 Jul)
IAAF World Junior Championships – Grosseto, Italy (13-18 Jul)
NACAC - U23 Championships – Sherbrooke, Canada (30 Jul-1 Aug)
Ibero-American Championships – Huelva, Spain (7-8 Aug)
Olympic Games – Athens, Greece (20-29 Aug)
World Mountain Rinning Trophy – Sauze d'Oulx, Italy (4-5 Sep)
IAAF World Athletics Final – Monaco (18-19 Sep)
Asian All-Stars Championships, Singapore (25 Sep)
Pan-Arab Games – Alger, Algeria (25-28 Sep)
IAAF World Half Marathon Championships – New Delhi, India (3 Oct)
European Cross Country Championships – Heringsdorf, Germany (12 Dec)

2005

European Indoor Championships – Madrid, Spain (4-6 Mar)
IAAF World Cross Country Championships – St.Galmier, France (19-20 Mar)
European Cup of Race Walking – Miskolc, Hungary (21 May)
Mediterranean Games – Almeria, Spain (29 June – 2 July)
WMA World Masters Championships – San Sebastián, Spain (7-16 July)
European U23 Championships – Erfurt, Germany (14-17 July)
IAAF World Youth Championships – Marrakesh, Morocco (14-17 July)
World University Games – Izmir, Turkey (16-26 July)
European Junior Championships – Kaurus, Lithuania (21-24 July)
IAAF World Championships – Helsinki, Finland (5-14 Aug)
IAAF World Athletics Final – Monaco (17-18 Sep)
IAAF World Half Marathon Championships – Edmonton, Canada (1 Oct)
Francophone Games – Niamey, Niger (7-17 Dec)
European Cross Country Championships – Tilburg, Netherlands (Dec)

2006

IAAF World Indoor Championships – Moscow, Russia (10-12 Mar)
Commonwealth Games – Melbourne, Australia (20-25 Mar)
IAAF World Cross Country Championships – Fukuoka, Japan (1-2 Apr)
IAAF World Race Walking Cup – La Coruña, Spain
European Championships – Göteborg, Sweden (8-13 Aug)
IAAF World Junior Championships – Beijing, China (15-20 Aug)
IAAF World Cup – Carson, Los Angeles, USA (1-3 Sep)
Asian Games – Doha, Qatar (8-22 Dec)
European Cross Country Championships – San Georgio su Legnano, Italy (Dec)

2007

Pan-American Games – Rio de Janeiro, Brazil (23-29 July)
IAAF World Championships – Osaka, Japan (24 Aug - 2 Sep)
European Cross Country Championships – Toro, Spain (Dec)

2008

IAAF World Indoor Championships
Olympic Games – Beijing (8-24 August)

2009

Mediterranean Games – Pescara, Italy

2010

Commonwealth Games – New Delhi, India

OBITUARY 2003

See Athletics 2003 for biographies of leading figures who died in early 2003: Jean-Luc Assemat, Herma Bauma, Olle Bexell, Avril Bowring, Chris Brasher, Valeriy Brumel, William Cloney, Ignace Heinrich, Peter Martin, Mieke Pullen, Reg Revans, Nobuyoshi Sadanaga, Susumu Sato, Les Steers, Bruno Tabourin, Alastair Wood.

Hans AXMANN (Germany) (b. 8 Jul 1922 Tachau, Sudetenland) on 24 August. A former handball international, he was a leading figure in veteran's athletics, vice-president of the WAVA Council 1979-87.

Robert BART (France) (b. 21 Jun 1930 Merville) on 14 January. French champion at 400mh in 1952 and 1954, he made 22 international appearances for France 1951-5, including at the 1952 Olympics (qf 400mh, 6th 4x400m). Pbs: 400mh 52.6 (1955), 200mh 25.0 (1954), 400m 48.6 (1952).

Dora BLASK (née Voigt) (Germany) (b. 3 Jul 1920 Berlin) on 14 March in Wachtberg-Berkum. She made five international appearances for Germany in 1938-9, including running in the European 200m in 1938. Pbs: 12.0 (1939), 200m 24.8 (1938); she ran on the Brandenburg team that set a world record of 1:45.3 for 4x200m in 1938 and on the SC Charlottenburg Berlin team that ran an unratified 1:44.6 in 1940. She was married to hammer thrower Erwin Blask, who was silver medallist at 1936 Olympics and 1938 Europeans and set a world record with 59.00 in 1938.

Gianni BRANDIZZI (Italy) (b. 20 Oct 1943 Rome) on 13 September. He had a discus pb of 56.64 (1971) and played rugby for Italy. He worked as an architect for the Italian Olympic Committee (CONI) on several projects of sporting facilities and was also an actor, appearing in Pasolini's movie "Medea" with the former WR holder at TJ Giuseppe Gentile.

Yves BROUZET (France) (b. 5 Sep 1948 Béziers) on 8 May of cancer in Grenoble. Holder of the oldest standing French records with his shot put of 20.20 outdoors in 1973, after earlier records at 19.90 and 19.99 in 1972, and indoor 19.88 in 1972. He represented France in 44 internationals and placed 12th in 1972 and 14th in 1976 at the Olympics and 8th in the 1971 Europeans. He was French champion four times outdoors (1972-3, 1975-6) and six times indoors (1972-4, 1976, 1980, 1982). Pb DT 49.00 (1972). A massive man, at 1.98m and 150kg, he became a sports professor and was the national shot coach 1986-93. He had five children – two daughters were French internationals, Anne at shot and Marie at hammer, and his son Olivier is a world-renowned rugby international with 72 caps for France to the end of 2003.

Sir Ralph KILNER BROWN (GBR) (b. 28 Aug 1909, Bankura, India) on 12 June. He ran his best time for 400m hurdles when second in the 1933 World Student Games in 54.8, and he was AAA champion and bronze medallist at 440yh at the Empire Games in 1934. He was the elder brother of Godfrey Brown, who won silver at 400m and gold at 4x400m, and of Audrey, who won a 4x100m silver medal at the Berlin Olympics in 1936. Ralph Kilner Brown was called to the Bar in 1934 and, following war service during which he reached the rank of brigadier, eventually became a High Court judge, retiring from the Bench in 1984. As a candidate for the Liberal Party he unsuccessfully fought four general elections between 1945 and 1964. He was knighted in 1970.

Fernanda BULLANO (Italy) (b. 26 Sep 1914 Torino) on 16 November. She ran on the Italian 4x100m team that was 4th at the 1936 Olympic Games and twice tied the Italian 80m record at 10.4 in 1935, 100m pb 12.8 (1935).

James Alexander "Alec" **BURNS** (GBR) (b. 5 Nov 1907 Newcastle-upon-Tyne) in May. He set a British record of 30:58.2 when fifth in the 1936 Olympic 10,000m, having, three weeks earlier clocked 29:45.0 at the AAA Champs for a British 6 miles record. AAA 4 miles champion in 1931, he finished second eight times at 3M, 6M and 10M between 1932 and 1937. He was seventh in the 1932 Olympic 5000m; his best time being 14:56.0 in 1931 although he had a superior 3M mark of 14:22.0 in 1932. At cross-country he was English champion in 1932 and was second in the International Championship in 1934. The 2001 world rally-driving champion Richard Burns is his grandson.

Erik CASSEL (Sweden) (b. 3 Sep 1922 Gällivare) on 5 April. He ranked 11th on the world list for 3000m steeplechase with 9:14.2 for third in the Swedish Championships in 1950. He made three international appearances.

Rebka CHENASHU (Ethiopia) (b. 23 May 1986) from cerebral malaria on 5 November, aged 17. She was the 400m silver medallist at the East African Youth Champs in May 2003.

Bruce COLLINS (USA) (b. 8 Jan 1951) in Chester, Pennsylvania on 22 January. NCAA 440y hurdles champion in 1972 (in a personal best time of 49.4) and 1974 for University of Pennsylvania. Pb 120yh 13.9 (1972).

Miguel CONSEGAL (Spain) (b. 7 Oct 1943) on 14 August in Barcelona. Spanish indoor champion at pole vault 1962-4 and 1970, he set Spanish records outdoors at 4.21 and 4.23 in 1963 and indoors at 4.35 in 1964 as well as at decathlon in 1969. He made 45 international appearances for Spain 1963-75. His father and mother were both Spanish champions.

Nicholas COSTES (USA) (b. 3 Aug 1926) on 14 March in Lexington, Kentucky. He was the 1955 US marathon champion and placed 20th in the 1956 Olympics. He was 3rd in 1955 in 2:19:57 and 4th in 1956 in 2:17:56 at the Boston Marathon, but the course in those years was considerably short at 25 miles 938 yards. He coached at Troy State for 12 years.

Milos DAJBYCH (Czech Republic) (b. 17 Sep 1923) on 30 November. Head coach of Czechoslovak athletics 1976 -86 an era which included the great performances in Helsinki 1983.

John DAVIES (New Zealand) (b. 25 May 1938 Chingford, London) of cancer on 21 July in Auckland. He was second to Peter Snell in the 1962 Commonwealth Games mile and when he took the 1964 Olympic 1500m bronze in 3:39.6 behind Snell's 3:38.1 off a then unprecedented 52.6 last lap. He had a mile best of 3:56.8 in Auckland a month later behind Snell's world record 3:54.1 and matched that in London in 1965. He possessed good speed (4th ranked in the world over 1000m in 1964 at 2:19.3) and endurance (7:51.0 3000m in 1965 and 13:54.4 5000m in 1966), and did on occasion get the better of Snell. He twice ran 3:39.6 for 1500 in 1964 and in one 4:00.6 mile victory in Oslo was timed at 1:55.5 for the second half. Of Welsh descent (emigrated to New Zealand at age 14), he was coached by Arthur Lydiard. He was forced into retirement by Achilles injury and later became a successful broadcaster and coach, guiding Dick Quax and Anne Audain to world 5000m records and Toni Hodgkinson to NZ records. He was president of the New Zealand Olympic Federation from October 2000.

Annual progression at 1M (/1500m): 1956- 4:48.2, 1957- 4:31.4, 1959- 4:28.2, 1960- 4:25.0, 1961- 4:15.4, 1962- 4:00.2, 1963- 3:58.8, 1964- 3:56.8/3:39.6, 1965- 3:56.8/3:41.5, 1966- 4:02.8. Pb 880y 1:50.1 (1964).

Michel DELAVIER (France) (b. 20 Apr 1930) on 23 February. One international for France 1955 at javelin, pb 63.08 (1958).

Ivars DRIBA (Latvia) (b. 5 Nov 1920) on 13 May. He won 17 Latvian titles at shot and discus and was 2nd in the USSR DT champs 1949. Pb DT 48.97 (1953).

Pål Arne **FAGERNES** (Norway) (b. 8 Jun 1974 Asker) was killed on 4 August in a car accident. An accomplished all-round sportsman, especially at skiing (at which he won 72 national competitions) and cycling, he set eight Norwegian javelin records to a best of 86.74 in 2000 and was national champion in 1996, 1998-9 and 2002; he also won the NCAA title in 1996 for Arizona State University. His best international placings were 4th at the 1999 Worlds and 9th at the 2000 Olympics. A controversial character, he confessed to drug taking in 2001.

Arvid FERNSTRÖM (Sweden) (b. 27 Jan 1911 Spånga) on 23 March. He competed in 13 international matches, the first two as a junior in 1930-1 and won nine medals in Swedish Championships 1931-43 – eight second places at shot and one third at javelin. pbs: SP 15.27 (1938) and extra trial 15.35 (1938), DT 44.78 (1934), JT 60.39 (1932).

John Arthur 'Jack' **GREGORY** (GBR) (b. 22 June 1923 Sea Mills, Bristol) on 15 December in Bristol. He made six international appearances for Britain 1948-52, and won an Olympic silver medal in the 4x100m relay in 1948 and also ran on the teams that were 4th at the 1950 Europeans and 1952 Olympics. Pbs: 100y 9.8 (1950), 100m 10.9 (1952), 220y 21.8 (1951). Educated at Rydal School and St Andrew's College, Dublin, he was Irish champion for three years at 100m/200m while based there, and was then a member of Bristol AC (later its president for many years) and of Bristol Rugby Club; he played one rugby union international for England against Wales as a winger in 1949. he became a sports presenter for HTV and columnist for the Bristol Evening Post.

Mounir HASSAINE (France) (b. 12 May 1936 Morocco) in September. Of Algerian descent, as a long jumper he made seven international appearances for France 1956-8. Pbs: 100m 10.8 (1954), LJ 7.51 (1957).

István HAVASI (Hungary) (b. 21 Dec 1930 Dánszentmiklós) on 16 February in Budapest. He was the winner at the 1963 Lugano Cup in his third Hungarian record for 50km walk of 4:14:24 and won 11 national walks titles, 9 at 50km (1957-9, 1961, 1963-4, 1966, 1968-9), 2 at 20km (1958 and 1963). Also at 50kmW: 19th 1964 Olympics, 6th 1962 and 12th 1966 at Europeans. Pb 20kmW 1:32:59 (1963).

Leo HEINLA (Estonia) (b. 6 May 1933 Kärdla) on 29 October in Tallinn. An ATFS member from 1964, he was a maestro of combined events statistics.

John HERRING (GBR) (b. 10 Apr 1935 Lewisham, London) on 7 October at Lavenham, Suffolk. The Blackheath Harrier made three international appearances for Britain at 5000m, including the 1964 Olympics. Having worked as a Customs & Excise officer, he was assistant director of the Crystal Palace National Sports centre 1970-87. He was heavily involved in the organisation of the London Marathon, as start co-ordinator 1982-93 and as course director 1994-6. Pbs: 1M 4:02.7 (1964), 3000m 8:02.2 (1965), 2M 8:37.6 (1964), 5000m 13:51.4 (1964), 6M 29:26.2 (1966).

Erwin HUBER (Germany) (b. 5 Apr 1907 Karlsruhe-Durlach) on 23 May in München. He was German decathlon champion in 1935 with two second and three third places and made six international appearances 1928-36, including 15th in 1928 and 4th in 1936 at the Olympic Games, when he set a personal best of 7087 points (6649 on current tables). He became a leading coach. Pbs: 100m 10.8 (1934), 110mh 15.0 (1935), HJ 1.82 (1933), PV 3.80 (1931), LJ 7.24 (1933), SP 13.26 (1934), JT 60.95 (1935).

László JESZENSZKY (Hungary) (b. 14 Jul 1927 Ujpest) in Budapest on 10 December. He set seven Hungarian 3000m steeplechase records from 9:11.2 in 1949 to 8:40.8 when winning his fifth and last national title in 1956 (also winning in 1948, 1950-1 and 1953 and at CC 1955-6), breaking 9 minutes for the first time with 8:58,6 in 1953. He went out in the heats at the 1952 and 1956 Olympics and placed 5th in the 1954 Europeans. Pb 10,000m 30:01.0 (1955).

Chantal JOUVHOMME (later Taupin) (France) (b. 7 Jul 1952) in November. French champion at 800m 1971, she made 17 international appearances for France 1970-7, including at 4x200m at the 1973 European Indoors. She ran on two teams that set French records at 4x800m. Pbs: 400m 54.8 (1975), 800m 2:05.5 (1974).

David KIMANI (Kenya) (b. 28 Feb 1978) on 16 April after collapsing while eating lunch at a campus dining hall at the University of Alabama in Tuscaloosa. He won six NCAA titles: 5000m 2002, CC 1999, indoor 3000m & 5000m 2000-01. Pbs, all in 2001: 1500m 3:38.74, 1M 3:56.69, 3000m 7:43.82, 5000m 13:10.29.

Samson KITUR (Kenya) (b. 25 Feb 1966 Moiben) on 25 April in Ziwa; after complaining of a headache, he was dead before reaching hospital. He set a Kenyan record of 44.18 (still standing 11 years later) in his semi-final in Barcelona 1992 before taking the Olympic bronze medal in the final in 44.25. At the World Championships he was 3rd in 1993 (silver in the 4x400 with an anchor leg of 43.75) and was 4th in 1995, and was 2nd at the 1990 Commonwealth Games (gold in relay). He was second in the 1991 World Indoor Champs and was African champion in 1990, 1991 and 1995.

Annual progression at 400m: 1989- 45.2, 1990- 44.88, 1991- 45.23, 1992- 44.18, 1993- 44.34, 1994- 44.32, 1995- 44.36A/44.71, 1996- 44.65. Other pbs: 100m 10.3 (1989), 200m 20.7/21.14 (1990), 800m 1:47.53 (1990).

One of his elder brothers, David, preceded him as Kenyan 400m record holder at 44.73 in 1987; another, Simeon, ran 49.70 for 400m hurdles in 1984.

Joe KLEINERMAN (USA) (b. 12 Jan 1912 Spring Valley NY) on 11 November. He was 10th in the Boston Marathon in 1941 and 1942 and a leading coach. He gave a lifetime of service to running, helping found the New York Road Runners in 1958 and the New York City Marathon in 1970.

Zdzislaw KRZYSZKOWIAK (Poland) (b. 3 Aug 1929 Wielichowo) on 24 March in Warsaw. Despite never caring very much for the event he became one of the greats of steeplechasing, setting world records of 8:31.4 for Poalnd v the Russian Republic in Tula on 26 Jun 1960 and 8:30.4 in Walcz on 10 Aug 1961, and winning the Olympic title in 1960. He was a brilliant performer on the flat too. In 1958 he won the European 5000m and 10,000m (world's fastest that year 28:56.0), while in Olympics he was 4th in 1956 and 7th (in his fastest time of 28:52.4) in 1960 at 10,000m. His long career was peppered with injuries and illness, and he won the Polish steeplechase title only once, in 1953, but he was Polish 5000m champion each year 1955-9 and 10,000m 1960.

Annual progression (position on world list) at 3000mSt: 1949- 9:59.6, 1950- 9:58.4, 1951- 9:50.4, 1952- 9:13.6 (44), 1956- 8:48.29 (15), 1957- 8:48.8 (7=), 1958- 8:33.6 (2), 1959- 8:46.4 (12), 1960- 8:31.3 (1), 1961- 8:30.4 (1), 1962- 8:37.9 (70, 1963- 9:06.4: Other pbs: 1500m 3:44.8 (1960), 3000m 7:58.2 (1957), 5000m 13:51.6 (1960).

Margarete KÜHLMANN (Germany) (b. 9 May 1915 Hamburg) on 21 April in Virginia, USA. Silver medallist at 60m (7.6) and gold at 4x100m at the Women's World Games in 1934. Pbs: 100m 12.1 (1934), 200m 25.4 (1939), JT 40.77 (1935). She lived in the USA from 1963.

Jari KUOPPA (Finland) (b. 25 Jun 1960) on 31 January in Ähtäri. The Finnish shot champion in 1986 and 1990, he also had three other medals, the last of them a surprising silver in 1996. He competed five times against Sweden, winning in 1988. Pb: 20.46 (1986, seventh Finn to exceed 20m).

Michael Denny 'Mike' **LARRABEE** (USA) (b. 2 Dec 1933 Los Angeles) at his home in Santa Maria, California on 22 April. He was seventh fastest in the world at 46.9 for 440y in 1955, but although he improved a little over a period of several years, untimely injuries and illness conspired to deprive him of any substantial success until in 1964 when he was 30, Then, to widespread astonishment, he won his first American title, equalled the world record of 44.9 in the Olympic Trials (splits of 22.4 and 22.5) and won two gold medals in the Tokyo Olympics after having come nowhere near to making the team in 1956 and 1960. He took the 400m in 45.15 (the oldest winner of that title until Michael Johnson in 2000) and contributed a 44.8 leg to the world record-breaking relay team (3:00.7). Although diagnosed with pancreatic cancer two years earlier, he remained active and was skiing only six weeks before his death.

Annual progression (position on world list) at 400m (y = 440y): 1954- 47.8y (22=), 1955- 46.9y (7=), 1956- 47.0y (15=), 1957- 46.5y (2), 1958- 47.7y (62=), 1959- 46.1y (3=), 1960- 46.3y (15=), 1961- 47.6y (81=), 1962- 47.0y (47=), 1963- 46.6y (18=), 1964- 44.9 (1), 1965- 47;0y (52=). Other pbs: 100m 10.5 (1964), 220ySt 20.6w (1959), 20.7 (1957); 220yt 21.0 (1962), 330y 32.4, 660y 1:17.0.

Anna LARSSON (Sweden) (married name Hedlund) (b. 2 Jan 1922 Uøskeviksby) on 13 June. In her first competitive 800m in 1943 she won the first of seven successive Swedish titles in a Swedish record of 2:16.6. Then she set three ratified world records at 800m: 2:15.9 in 1944 and 2:14.8 and 2:13.8 in 1945, and one at 880y: 2:15.6 in 1945. although Yevdokiya Vasilyeva of the USSR, not then a member of the IAAF, had run 2:12.0 in 1940. The lack of races longer than 200m for women on the programme in that era deprived her of any chance of international championship honours. Pb 400m 59.2 (1946).

Annual progression at 800m (position on world list): 1943- 2:16.6 (2), 1944- 2:15.9 (2), 1945- 2:13.8 (1), 1946- 2:15.6 (2), 1947- 2:14.8 (1), 1948- 2:16.3 (2), 1949- 2:20.8 (c.40+).

Gustaf 'Gusti' LAURELL (Finland) (b. 2 Aug 1918 Lapväärtti) on 9 June in Vaasa. He lived in Sweden, where he was a national coach with the Swedish federation, from 1958 to 1985 before returning to his native country, still coaching athletes especially in sprints and hurdles in the SFI (Finnish Swedish-speaking federation) up to his death. He was a coach with the European team at the 1977 World Cup in Düsseldorf. Pb 400mh 56.5 (1947).

Stanley LAY (New Zealand) (b. 27 Jul 1906) on 12 May. He had a long and distinguished career as a javelin thrower and was patron of Athletics New Zealand. He was the first thrower to compete at the Olympic Games for New Zealand (7th in 1928) and won the javelin at the first British Empire Games in 1930, adding a silver at the 1938 Games and placing 6th in 1950. He won 12 NZ titles between 1926 and 1950 (his only loss in 1948) and was Australasian champion in 1926 and 1927 (66.51, then 3rd world all-time) and AAA champion in 1928 (67.89, then 2nd world all-time). He was 2nd in 1928 and 1st in 1930 for the British Empire v USA. Because there were no experienced coaches in NZ, he was self-coached apart from a few days in Britain with F A M Webster, followed by his 67.89. His 66.51 was not allowed as a NZ record when disbelieving officials ruled it "wind-assisted". He was also a notable cricketer, who specialised in running out unwitting batsmen with huge throws from the boundary and right over the stumps. Discus pb 34.70 (1932). He was awarded the MBE.

Leopold LÁZNICKA (Czech Republic) (b. 7 Aug 1920) on 17 March. Bronze medallist at 4x100m, 6th 4x100m and heat 400m at 1946 Europeans. 12 internationals for Czechoslovakia. Pbs: 100y 10.0 (1950), 100m 10.8 (1944), 10.6w (1945); 200m 22.0 (1945), 400m 49.4 (1946), 500m 67.0 (1945).

Raymond LEWIS (Canada) (b. 24 Oct 1912) on 15 November in Hamilton. 'Rapid Ray' was the first Canadian-born black athlete to win an Olympic medal, bronze at 4x400m in 1932, running the first leg for the Canadian team; he was also a quarter-finalist in the 400m. He won a silver medal at 4x440y at the 1934 Empire Games. He briefly attended Marquette University in Milwaukee, returning to Canada to work for over 20 years with the Canadian Pacific Railway. He was awarded the Order of Canada in 2001. Pb 440y 48.8 (1934).

Aleksandrs LINDE (Latvia) (b. 2 Jun 1918) on 31 October. Five times Latvian champion, his 4:10:13 was the world-leading 50km walk mark in 1958, although thought to have been possibly on a short course.

Antal LIPPAY (Hungary) (b. 7 Sep 1923 Peterd) on 24 February in Pécs. He competed in 32 internationals 1947-59 and at 400m hurdles set five Hungarian records from 52.7 in 1952 to 52.2 in 1956. He was 6th in the 1954 Europeans, a semi-finalist at the 1952 Olympics, and Hungarian champion at 110mh 1949 and 400mh 1951-3. Pb 110mh 15.1 (1954).

Olle LJUNGGREN (Sweden) (b. 9 Feb 1921) on 13 February. Fourth at 800m in the 1946 Europeans, Swedish champion in 1947 and an Olympic semi-finalist in 1948. Pbs: 800m 1:50.1 (2nd in world in 1946 and 7= in 1947), 1000m 2:26.4 (1945), 400mh 55.9 (1943). His twin brother Sven set the Swedish 400m record with 47.5 (1943).

André LONLAS (France) (b. 5 Jun 1910) in October. He ran for France in the International Cross-Country Championships of 1936 (4th) and 1937 (9th).

Erk MAASCH (Germany) (b. 21 Jun 1942) on 10 February in Hamburg. He made four international appearances 1970-2 and had pbs: 800m 1:50.0 (1966), 1000m 2:22.8 (1970), 1500m 3:42.4 (1972), 3000m 8:03.7 (1972), 5000m 13:59.8 (1972), 400mh 53.8 (1965).

Duncan McKECHNIE (GBR) (b. 18 Jun 1937) on 23 December. A former editor of the *Scottish Athletics Yearbook*, he was Scottish triple jump champion in 1960 and 1961, with a pb of 14.49 set for Scotland against Ireland in 1960.

Charlie McMULLEN (USA) (b. 23 Jun 1951) on 11 August. From first breaking 4 minutes for the mile in 1973 he move up to the Marathon. pbs: 1500m 3:41.7 (1974), 1M 3:56.9 (1974). 2:15:19 (1978).

Harold 'Hal' **MANNING** (USA) (b. 9 Jan 1909) on 26 January in Wichita, Kansas. He set a world 3000m steeplechase record of 9:08.2 when winning the US Olympic Trial in New York on 12 July 1936. This record lasted only 27 days, for Volmari Iso-Hollo FIN ran 9:03.8 in the Berlin Olympics, where Manning was fifth in 9:11.2. He won the NCAA 2 miles in 1930 for Wichita State University and was US steeplechase champion in 1934 (in a US record 9:13.1) and 1936 (3rd at 1 mile in 1929). Pb 2M 9:18.1 (1930).

Vladimir MARJANOVIC (Yugoslavia) (b. 14 Apr 1931) on 20 November in Belgrade. Secretary-General of the Yugoslav Athletic Federation 1977-93, he was Yugoslav HJ champion 1954-9, Balkan champion 1954, 1956-7 and second at the 1959 Universiade. He was 10th in 1954 and 16th at 1958 at Europeans and, having equalled it at 1.97 in 1954, improved the Yugoslav record to 2.00 and 2.03 (1955) and 2.04 (1957).

Benson MASYA (Kenya) (b. 14 May 1970 Kitui region) on 24 September after some years of alcohol-related problems. Formerly a bantamweight boxer, he forged a notable reputation in road running, excelling at the half marathon distance, winning the Great North Run on a record four occasions: 61:28 in 1991, 60:24 in 1992, a world best time on a certified course when the race was also the first World Half Marathon, 60:02 in 1994 and 61:43 in 1996. He won the Honolulu Marathon three times 1991, 1992 and 1994 and had a best at the distance of 2:12:35 (Boston 1994). Other bests: 10,000m 28:45.5 (1991), 3000mSt 9:13.0 (1991); Road: 10km 28:01 (1994), 15km 42:57 (1994), 10M 45:56 (1995).

Charles MEGNIN (GBR) (b. 1 Apr 1915) on 2 November in Epping, Essex. A woodwork teacher, he won the RWA 50k walk and then took the bronze medal at the European Champs in 1946. His best time was 4:42:01 in 1947 and he won the London to Brighton walk in 1949. A vociferous critic of current walking regulations, he stopped competing regularly at the age of 70 and took up marathons, completing 12 before returning to walk his last 50k at Bradford in 1996 (completing the distance in just over 7 hours at the age of 81), exactly 50 years after he won the race in preparation for his European moment of glory in Oslo.

John C. 'Johnny' **MILES** (Canada) (b. 30 Oct 1905) in Hamilton, Ontario on 15 June aged 97. The Welsh-born runner grew up in Nova Scotia and represented Canada at the Olympics of 1928 (17th) and 1932 (14th) and was the oldest surviving Boston Marathon winner – 1926 (2:25:40.4 on course 176 yards short) and 1929 (pb 2:33:08.6). Received Order of Canada 1983.

Manfred MOLZBERGER (Germany) (b. 27 Jan 1936 Gummersbach) on 1 March in Gummersbach. He was German champion each year 1956-9 and made 28 international appearances 1955-61 at long jump, including 9th at the 1960 Olympic Games, also competing at the 1958 Europeans. Pbs: LJ 7.84 (1960), HJ 1.90 (1957), TJ 14.45 (1961).

Veronika NESZMÉLYI (Hungary) (b. 10 Jun 1939 Budapest) in June in Adelaide (Australia had been her home since 1957). She was 5th in the European 100m in 1954 at age 15 and in 1954-5 she set five Hungarian records at 100m to a European record of 11.5 at the age of 16, and three at 200m to 24.1 in 1955 with a 60m record at 7.7 in 1955. Hungarian champion at 100m 1954-6, 200m 1956.

Toni NETT (Germany) (b. 28 Dec 1912 Mayen/Eifel) on 19 April in Bad Urbach. A former national coach, he was celebrated for his filming of athletes in action. He was the first president of the European Athletics Coaches Association (ELLV) 1959-69. As an athlete he had pbs of 100m 10.9 and LJ 7.28.

Stan NICHOLLS (Australia) (b. 16 Jun 1911) on 19 June. He was 5th in the 3 miles at the 1938 Empire Games in 14:30.0. From Ballarat, he was a very successful cross-country runner but his Olympic ambitions were cut short by World War 2. He served in the army during the war and afterwards became an official and was a timekeeper at the 1956 Melbourne Olympics and also officiated at the 1982 Brisbane Commonwealth Games. He became an active veteran athlete, setting 32 world age records, with a pb marathon of 3:07.00 at age 66. His two children, Graeme and Alison, both became national walk champions.

Gayle OLINEKOVA (Canada) (b. 23 Mar 1953 Toronto), also known as Gayle Olinek, of breast cancer, on 26 November at Duarte, California, USA. She ran 47 marathons with a best of 2:35:12 in Feb 1980, which at the time ranked her fifth fastest of all time.

Arthur W. **PENNY** (GBR) (b. 13 Dec 1907) on 29 November in Kingston, Surrey. At 6 miles, he won for England in 31:00.6 at the 1934 Empire Games and his best AAA placing was 2nd in 1935, but his fastest time was an estimated 30:12.0 when fifth in his race in 1936. He ran three times in the International Cross-country: 9th 1933, 3rd 1934, 18th 1939. He was in his 76th year as a member of Belgrave Harriers. Other pbs: 3M 14:47.2 (1934), 10M 52:52.0 (1938).

Tuto GoGo **PETERS** (Nigeria) (b. 9 Oct 1971) was killed while changing a tyre on Interstate 5 in Portland, Oregon, USA on 15 March. He won eight Big Eight conference titles while at Iowa State University, USA. Pbs: LJ 7.93 (1999), TJ 16.44 (1994).

Gunnar PETERSSON (Sweden) (b. 10 Oct 1915 Chicago, USA) on 4 July. Nicknamed 'Växjö-Pelle' after his home town. At the javelin he made nine international appearances, was 9th at the 1948 Olympics and Swedish champion in 1947 and 1948.

Annual progression (position on world list): 1938- 60.74, 1939- 62.88, 1940- 63.75 (48), 1941- 66.32 (18), 1942- 70.76 (2), 1943- 70.67 (3), 1944- 70.69 (3), 1945- 67.81 (12), 1946- 70.07 (6), 1947- 72.77 (2), 1948- 70.43 (6), 1949- 69.92 (8), 1950- 71.26 (8=), 1951- 68.30 (13), 1952- 65.59 (51), 1953- 62.63, 1954- 64.18, 1955- 61.87, 1956- 58.71, 1957- 58.33, 1958- 58.64, 1959- 56.26, 1960- 58.71, 1961- 62.69.

Eugen PIISANG (Estonia) (b. 4 Jan 1917) on 2 December. An ATFS member from 1958. An 800m international (pb 1:58.1 in 1940), his statistics book 'Kergejöustik arvudes' was published in 1958.

Frederick Douglas 'Fritz' **POLLARD** (USA) (b. 18 Feb 1915) on 14 February. While at the University of North Dakota, he was the Olympic bronze medallist in 14.4 behind Forrest Towns 14.2 and Don Finlay 14.4 at 110mh in 1936 and set a pb of 14.2 two weeks later at Colombes sharing the winning time of Towns for the USA against France and Japan. He had been second to Towns in the US Olympic Trials. That was his only year featuring in the world lists apart from 14.8y in 1937.

Francesco PUTTI (Italy) (b. 14 May 1931) on 26 September. Silver medallist at the 1963 Mediterranean Games with a marathon pb of 2:32:03.45 (1963).

Denise RAMSDEN (Later Mrs Castle) (GBR) (b. 11 Feb 1952 Wakefield) in April. She made her international debut in 1969 at the age of 17 and that year won a 4x100m bronze medal at the European Championships. She also ran on the British 4x100m team at the 1974 Europeans (4th) and 1976 Olympics (8th). A member of the Dorothy Hyman Track Club, she won English Schools 100y titles each year 1967-9 and the WAAA 200m in 1976. Pbs: 100m 11.67/11.4w (1976), 11.6 (1968); 200m 23.48 (1976).

Hermanis RENGA (Latvia) (b. 24 Feb 1932) on 19 May. He had a decathlon best of 6829 (1952 tables, 6946 on current tables) in 1960 and a pentathlon best of 3307 (3594 points on current table) in 1958, and coached top decathletes.

Charles Fraser **RIACH** (GBR) (b. 14 Nov 1928) on 14 May in Glasgow. He was Scottish javelin champion eight times – 1953, 1955, 1957, 1959-60, 1962 and 1964-5, with a best of 61.88 (1960), having earlier set three Scottish native records in 1953. He had a distinguished career on the PE staff at Glasgow University. His sister Nancy Riach (who died at the age of 20) was a top swimmer who won the ASA 100y freestyle title in 1946 and 1947 and won a European bronze medal at 4x100m freestyle relay in 1947, but was pulled from the water at the end of her 100m freestyle race, having contracted polio. She never regained consciousness.

Bertha Helene 'Leni' **RIEFENSTAHL** (Germany) (b. 22 Aug 1902 Berlin) on 8 September in Pockling at the age of 101. Sports fans will recall her as director of the superb Olympia, the great film record of the 1936 Olympic Games, with its innovative techniques. She made her first film in 1926 and the notorious Nazi propaganda film *Triumph des Willens* in 1934.

Jorma RINNE (Finland) (b. 20 Apr 1936 Sauvo) on 25 May in Hämeenlinna. He improved slowly at discus, bettering 40m in 1956, 50m in 1961 and 60m as the second Finn in 1970. He was 8th in the 1971 Europeans in Helsinki and 11th in the 1972 Olympics. Finnish champion in 1972, he also had 15 international dual matches. Pb 63.50 (1973).

Arthur ROWE (GBR) (b. 17 Aug 1937 Barnsley) on 13 September in Barnsley. Commonwealth and European shot champion in 1958, he set 15 British records (from 16.94m in 1958) and six European records (from 18.59 in 1959) to 19.56 in 1961, and he was AAA champion each year 1957-61. He failed to qualify for the Olympic final in 1960. Sadly he ended his amateur athletics career on the edge of greatness at the age of 25 when he signed to play professional rugby league for Oldham. Little came of that, but he enjoyed much success from then until 1970 on the Scottish Highland Games circuit, being proclaimed world caber-tossing champion in 1968. A member of Doncaster Plant Works AC, he had been a blacksmith and founded his own construction company.

Annual progression (position on world list): 1956- 15.62, 1957- 16.94 (17), 1958- 17.96 (5), 1959- 18.59 (5), 1960- 19.11 (4=), 1961- 19.56 (2), 1962- 19.49 (3).

Jacques SAPIN (France) (b. 6 Jul 1921) on 19 February. French champion at 110mh in 1941, pb 15.5 (1942). He became a notable basketball coach.

Karl SCHOLZ (Germany) (b. 17 Jan 1921) on 7 October in Weimar. He was GDR champion at LJ 1948, 1950, 200mh 1952, 400mh 1949-52 and set four GDR records at 400mh to 54.2 (1951) with a later best of 53.9 (1953). Other pbs: 100m 10.8 (1952), 200m 21.9 (1951), 400m 49.6 (1953), 200mh 24.8 (1953), LJ 7.01 (1950).

Seppo SIMOLA (Finland) (b. 27 Jul 1936 Somero) at Valkeakoski on 9 March. Captain of the national team, Simola had two shot putting careers: he was the first Finn over 18m and then, after a lay-off in the late 1960s, the first over 20m with seven Finnish records in all from 18.00 (1963) to his pb of 20.15 (1972). A travelling salesman, Simola had several shots in his car trunk and always found a place to train anywhere around the country, sometimes on a grassy area or a stretch of road. He won five Finnish titles (1963-4 and 1970-2) and put eight times against Sweden, winning in 1964. He competed in the 1972 Olympics and 1969 (11th) and 1971 Europeans.

Jan SLANINA (Czech Republic) (b. 31 Jan 1949) committed suicide in early April at his home in Ostrava. A former sprinter, pbs: 100m 10.5 (1972), 200m 21.4 (1974), he was later a successful coach, notably of Tatiana Kocembová, who became his wife as Slaninová and was second in the 1983 World Champs 400m (48.59). They later divorced and Jan was also the leading force in organising the Ostrava Golden Spike meeting.

Willem 'Wim' **SLIJKHUIS** (Netherlands) (b. 13 Jan 1923) at Badhoevedorp in late June. The stylish runner was European 1500m champion in 1950, having placed second to Sydney Wooderson over 5000m in the 1946 Europeans in a pb of 14:14.0, and was the bronze medallist in both the 1500m and 5000m at the 1948 Olympics. His greatest 1500m came in Antwerp in 1949 when he defeated Belgium's Olympic 5000m champion Gaston Reiff in 3:43.8, only 0.8 sec outside the world record and making him the third quickest of all-time; it was the Dutch record until 1966. Other Dutch records: 1M 4:09.4 (1948) & 4:09.2 indoors (1949), 3000m 8:08.8 (equal fastest in the world for 1946), 2M 8:55.0 (1951), 3M 13:54.2 (1 sec behind Wooderson in an epic AAA championship clash in 1946), 10,000m 30:53.4 (1951), 1 Hr 18,156m (1952). Also pb 800m 1:53.4 (1947).

Annual progression at 1500m, 5000m (position on world list): 1941- 4:05.6, 1942- 15:43.3, 1943- 14:52.0 (26), 1944- 3:55.9 (31), 14:50.0 (20); 1945- 4:06.0, 1946- 3:50.4 (6=), 14:14.0 (2); 1947- 14:58.6, 1948- 3:49.6 (7=), 14:26.8 (5=); 1949- 3:43.8 (1), 1950- 3:47.2 (3=), 15:13.6; 1951- 3:52.2 (32=), 14:51.2; 1952- 3:50.6 (37=), 14:35.2 (41=); 1953- 4:00.2; 1954- 3:53.0 (89=), 14:44.0.

Robin 'Bob' **SPARKS** (GBR) (b. 13 Nov 1937 Huddersfield) in Surrey on 30 April. President of the ATFS 1977-2000, he contributed immensely to the advancement of athletics documentation and statistics and the presentation of athletics in a lifetime of devotion to the sport. A founder member of the NUTS in January 1958 and its chairman 1974-9, he was for many years statistician for the AAA and worked for ITV as their statistician for athletics broadcasts 1971-85. He was British correspondent for *Leichtathletik* for many years and announced at meetings including the 1992 Olympic Games, and three each of World Championships, European Championships and World Cups to 1998.

Pierre SPRÉCHER (France) (b. 9 Nov 1921 Amiens) in November. French champion at javelin in 1942 and 1950 and decathlon 1946 and 1950, he made 27 international appearances for France 1946-52. He set two French records at decathlon – 6316 in 1946 and 6496 (6203 on current tables) when 5th at the 1946 European Championships. Pb JT 61.28 (1948).

Naftali TEMU (Kenya; b.20 Apr 1945 Sotik) on 10 March in Nairobi. He failed to finish in the 10,000m and was 49th in the marathon (2:40:47) on his Olympic debut as a 19 year-old in Tokyo in 1964, but he was 2nd in the African Games 5000m in 1965 and made a huge impact at the 1966 Commonwealth Games in Kingston by running away from world record holder Ron Clarke to take the 6 miles in a Kenyan record of 27:14.6, with 4th at 3M. Two years later, in high altitude Mexico City, he became Kenya's first Olympic gold medallist as he outkicked Mamo Wolde for the 10,000m title in 29:27.40, followed four days later by a bronze medal at 5000m (14:06.41). Another three days after that he was 19th in the marathon in his best time of 2:32:36. He went on to compete without success in the 1970 Commonwealth Games (18th 10,000m) and 1972 Olympic 10,000m (heats). Other pbs: 5000m 13:36.6 and 10,000m 28:21.8, both in 1971.

Alton TERRY (USA) (b. 25 Nov 1912) in Houston on 23 July. He set US javelin records at 67.86 in 1936 and 69.85 in 1937, and in 1936 won the NCAA title (Hardin-Simmons College) and was sixth in the Olympics.

Juha TIAINEN (Finland) (b. 5 Dec 1955 Uukuniemi) from a stroke at his home in Lappeenranta on 28 April. A police constable and member of the Finnish national team for 15 years, he won the 1984 Olympic hammer title in Los Angeles with 78.08 by 10cm from Karl-Hans Riehm after a dramatic tussle. He competed in three Olympics (10th 1980. dnq 18th 1988), two World Championships (9th 1983, 13th 1987) and three Europeans (12th 1982, 18th 1986, 9th 1990). He improved the Finnish record eight times from 71.80 (1996), breaking 80m as the fourth non-Russian thrower in 1983 and with a best of 81.52 in June 1984, a Finnish record until 2002. Alternating year after year with his rival Harri Huhtala, Tiainen won six Finnish titles: 1977, 1979, 1981, 1984, 1987 and 1990. Throwing 14 times against Sweden, he won seven times (1979-84 and 1990).

Annual progression (position on world list): 1972- 40.94, 1973- 49.62, 1974- 51.64, 1975- 65.12, 1976- 71.80 (43), 1977- 72.62 (30), 1978- 71.08 (53), 1979- 74.42 (28), 1980- 75.88 (23), 1981- 76.64 (13), 1982- 78.34 (8), 1983- 81.02 (4), 1984- 81.52 (5), 1985- 78.10 (29), 1986- 79.32 (19), 1987- 77.94 (38), 1988- 78.46 (30), 1989- 77.88 (26), 1990- 77.98 (21).

Dalibor TRPIK (Czech Republic) (b. 22 May

1925) on 16 March. President of Czechoslovak Athletic Federation 1977-88.

Nils WÄSTBERG (Sweden) (b. 29 Dec 1914 Bollnäs) on 25 November. He was the Swedish pole vault champion in 1938 and 1939 and competed in five international matches. Pb 4.10 (1942).

Cliff YOUNG (Australia) (b. 1922 Beech Forest, Victoria) on 2 November in Beerwah, Queensland. He became a national hero when he won the inaugural Sydney to Melbourne ultra-marathon in 1983 at age 61; his time of 5 days 15 hours 6 minutes smashed the record by 36 hours.

Danica ZIVANOV-SLJAPIC (Yugoslavia) (b. 8 Feb 1967) on 21 January in Zrenjanin. She was second in the javelin at the European Juniors 1985 (5th at shot) and also competed at the 1986 Europeans. She won the Yugoslav shot 1985-9 and javelin 1985-6 and 1989 and set four national shot records in 1985-8 with a best of 16.95 (1988). Javelin pb 61.98 (1985). Her career ended prematurely after being disqualified for drugs when third in SP at the 1989 Balkan Championships.

OBITUARY 2004

Josiah BEMBE (South Africa; b. 28 Nov 1974) apparently committed suicide on 12 January. He had a marathon best of 2:11:49 when he won at Seoul in 2001. 8th 2002 Commonwealth Games.

George Alexander **CMELA** (GBR) (b. 15 Aug 1941) on 25 February in Manchester. One international for Britain indoors in 1962. pbs: 60y 6.3i í62, 100y 9.7 '61, 100m 10.6 í60, 10.5w í62; 220y 21.7 í61.

Charles DUMAS (USA) (b. 12 Feb 1937 Tulsa, Oklahoma) on 5 January in Inglewood, Los Angeles. He became the first ever 7ft high jumper officially, a feat he achieved when, at the age of 19, he cleared 7ft 0 5/8 in 2.15m at the US Olympic Trials at Los Angeles in 1956. He went on to win the Olympic title that year in an Olympic record 2.12. He was AAU champion each year 1955-9 and won the Pan-American title in 1959, before finishing sixth at the 1960 Olympics when he suffered from a knee injury. He tried a comeback in 1964 but did not continue after 2.14m in April. He went to the University of Southern California and later coached in high school.

Annual progression (position on world list): 1950- 1.51, 1952- 1.68, 1953- 1.88, 1954- 1.97 (65=), 1955- 2.09 (3), 1956- 2.15 (1), 1957- 2.095 (6), 1958- 2.12 (1=), 1959- 2.134 (1), 1960- 2.14 (5), 1964- 2.14 12=). Pb 120yh 14.1 (1958).

Sunday EMMANUEL (Nigeria) (b. 8 Oct 1978) in Kaduna on 15 January after a bus accident. He won the 100m and 200m at the 1997 African Junior Championships and was West African champion that year in a hand-timed 10.0. He was second in the 200m in his pb time of 20.45 at the 1998 African Championships when he also took a silver medal at 4x100m. He was Nigerian champion in hand-timed 20.3 in 1998. Also pb 100m 10.14 (1999), 10.06dt (1997).

Reginald George **GOSNEY** (GBR) (b. 24 Feb 1910) in January. He was a leading cross-country runner in the immediate post-War era, placing 3rd in the English National CC in 1946 and 1950 and 4th in 1949 and had two top ten finishes in the International CC in four runs 1946-50: 7th 1946 and 10th 1949. He was secretary of Southampton AC 1934-57 and became a senior coach and timekeeper.

Albert **HEPPNER** (USA) (b. 24 Apr 1974 Columbia. Maryland) on 17 February two days after placing fifth in the US Olympic Trials 50km race. He set a pb of 3:58:45 for 2nd in the USA 50km walk in 1999, but was disqualified at the subsequent World Champs. 20km walk best 1:26:50 (1999). He won the US 5km walk title in 2002. He studied at Wisconsin-Parkside before joining the US Army.

Herman KRISTOFERSSON (Sweden) (b. 4 Feb 1918 Smedjebacken) on 7 January. Swedish champion at high jump 1943-4, pb 1.96 (1943) and international at 110mh, at which he was 2nd three times and 3rd four times in the Swedish Champs in an era dominated by Håkan Lidman, pb 14.7 (8= on world list 1945). 11 international matches.

Margaret Oakley **LASBREY** (later **SMITH**) (South Africa) (b. 31 Jul 1918) on 18 January. Having won South African javelin titles in 1939 and 1940, she spent seven years teaching and lecturing and in this time was WAAA javelin champion in 1946, competing with the WAAA team at an international meeting in Strasbourg that year at shot, discus and javelin, and played four times for England at hockey in 1950. She was secretary of the South African Women's Hockey Association 1961-81 and married Denis Smith in 1982.

Owen Guinn **SMITH** (USA) (b. 2 May 1920 McKinney, Texas) died on 24 January in San Francisco. He was tbe last man to win an Olympic pole vault title using a bamboo pole – in 1948 he cleared 4.30 on his final attempt in pouring rain despite a painful knee injury, having set a personal best of 4.47 for second place at the US Trials. He had ranked third in the world with 4.43 in 1941, when he also tied for the NCAA title, but after graduating from Cal/Berkeley in history in 1942 then lost several years of competition due to the War, in which he won the Distinguished Flying Cross as a captain in the army air corps. At the AAU Championships

Fanny BLANKERS-KOEN (Netherlands) (b. Francina Elsje Koen 26 Apr 1918 Baarn) on 25 January. She was the heroine of the 1948 Olympics when she won four gold medals in London, at 100m, 200m, 80m hurdles and sprint relay. At the European Championships she won the same individual events in 1950, but took silver in the relay; having won gold at hurdles and relay in 1946 and bronze at 100m and 200m in 1938.

Her exceptional versatility is shown by the fact that she set 16 world records at eight different events, including two at 100y: 11.0 in 1939 and 10.8 in 1944, three times at 11.5 for 100m 1943-50, 24.0u for 200m in 1950, three at 80m hurdles to 11.0 in 1948, three high jump marks at 1.67, 1.69 and 1.71 in one competition in 1943, long jump 6.25 in 1943 and pentathlon 4692 points in 1951 as well as two at 4x110y relay. She won 58 Dutch titles between 1936 and 1955 at individual events: 13 at 100m, 12 at 200m, 11 at 80m hurdles, 10 high jump, 9 long jump, 2 shot (best 12.52 in 1955) and 1 pentathlon. Her first Dutch record had been 2:29.0 for 800m in 1935 and she also competed at the Olympics in 1936 when she was fifth equal at high jump and fifth at sprint relay, and in 1952. That year she showed that she was in great form, with her fastest ever times for 100y (10.3) and 100m (11.4), both wind-assisted, and for 200m (23.7), but, suffering from a carbuncle on her leg, had to pull up in the final of the 80m hurdles after hitting the first two hurdles.

She married her coach, the Dutch triple jumper Jan Blankers in 1940, and their children were Jantje born in 1941 and Fanneke born in 1945. A statue was erected in her honour in Amsterdam and she was voted by the IAAF its Woman Athlete of the Century at the end of 1999.

Annual progression (position on world list):

Year	*100m*	*200m*	*80mh*	*HJ*	*LJ*	*Also*
1936	12.3 (20=)			1.605 (4)		HJ 1.625u
1937	12.0 (3=)	25.0 (5)		1.58 (7=)	5.48 (22)	100y 11.2, Pen 302 (8)
1938	12.0 (3=)	24.6 (4)		1.60 (5=)		60m 7.5, 100y 11.0
1939	11.9 (1=)	25.0 (4)		1.60 (6=)	5.97 (3)	
1940	12.0/11.9w (1)	25.3 (5=)	12.2 (20=)	1.63 (2=)	5.87 (2=)	
1942	11.7 (1)		11.3 (1)	1.63 (1)	6.00 (2)	
1943	11.5 (1)	24.5/24.4w (1)	11.8 (1=)	1.71 (1)	6.25 (1)	Pen 339 (1)
1944	11.8 (1)	25.0 (2)	11.7 (4)	1.65 (1)	5.82 (2)	60m 7.7, 100y 10.8
1946	12.1/12.0w (3=)	25.0 (2)	11.7/11.4w (1=)	1.60 (7=)	5.74 (3)	
1947	11.8 (1=)	24.7 (1)	11.4 (1)	1.61 (3=)	5.75 (3)	
1948	11.5 (1)	24.2 (1)	11.0 (1)	1.60 (8=)	5.89 (2)	100y 10.8
1949	11.7 (1)	24.3 (2)	11.3 (1=)	1.515		100y 10.8
1950	11.7 (1=)	24.0/23.8w (1)	11.1 (1=)	1.60 (8=)	5.515	
1951	11.9 (4=)	24.4 (1=)	11.1 (1)	1.605 (8)	5.90 (6=)	100y 10.8, Pen 4692 (1)
1952	11.5/11.4w (2)	23.7 (2)	11.1/11.0w (3=)	6.05 (3)	100y 10.3w	
1953	11.7 (1=)		11.1 (1)		5.855 (11)	
1954			11.1 (4=)			

Other pbs: SP 12.08 (1943), DT 36.74 (1943).

he was 2nd in 1941 and 1946 and 3rd in 1947 and 1943, and won the AAU indoor title in 1947. He worked as an investment counsellor.

Annual progression (position on world list): 1938- 3.90, 1939- 4.11 (32=), 1940- 4.38 (4), 1941- 4.43 (3), 1942- 4.36 (6), 1943- 3.96, 1946- 4.31 (2), 1947- 4.45 (1), 1948- 4.47 (1=). Pbs:1.956 (1941), LJ 6.94 (1944), JT 53.62 (1944).

Erik STAI (Norway) (b. 29 Nov 1915) on 4 March. His best high jump was a Norwegian record 2.00 in 1940 and he was national champion in 1938 and 1939. He competed in 12 internationals 1937-51, including the 1938 Europeans, when he was 4th equal.

Lennart STRAND (Sweden) (b. 13 Jun 1921 Malmö), died on 23 January, having suffered severe injuries in a car accident in November. He was European champion in 1946 (dnf 1950) and Olympic silver medallist in 1948 and his career might have been even more notable had he not suffered so much from nerves. Seven international matches, Swedish champion 1500m 1945-7, 1949-50 and 4km CC 1950. He also won the AAU (US) 1500m in 1946.

He set the pace when Gunder Hägg took two seconds off the world record for 1500m with 3:43.0 in 1944 and also for Arne Andersson's WR 4:01.6 mile 11 days later, reaching 800m in 1:56.0 in both these races. Three years later Strand equalled the 3:43.0 WR at Malmö. He ran the fastest leg on two relay world records: 3:50.2 for the third leg on the Malmö AI's 15:38.6 for 4x1500m at Norrköping in 1945, and 1:51.0 for the anchor leg on the Swedish team's 7:29.0 for 4x800m at Stockholm in 1946.

Annual progression at 1500m (position on world list): 1943- 4:04.0, 1944- 3:55.4 (24=), 1945- 3:47.0 (4), 1946- 3:48.0 (1), 1947- 3:43.0 (1), 1948- 3:47.6 (1), 1949- 3:45.2 (2), 1950- 3:47.0 (2),

1951- 3:53.0 (40=), 1952- 3:55.0. Other pbs: 800m 1:51.8 (1949), 1000m 2:23.8 (1946), 1 mile 4:04.8 (1945), 3000m 8:18.8 (1949).

Shirley STRICKLAND (Australia) (b. 18 Jul 1925 Guildford, Western Australia) at her home in Perth on 16 February. The first Australian woman athlete to win a medal at the Olympics, she went on to set an all-time record with seven. Her glittering collection would have been one more if there had been an examination of the photo-finish for the 200m in 1948, when she was actually 3rd rather than the official 4th place. In 1948 she won bronze medals at 100m and 80m hurdles with a sprint relay silver. In 1952 she won the 80m hurdles in 1952 with world records of 11.0 in a heat and 10.9 in the final and took the bronze at 100m, she also ran the opening leg on the Australian team that set a world record of 46.1 in a 4x100m heat, they dropped the baton on the final exchange in the final and came in fifth.

She retained her 80mh title in 1956 and took her final gold on the 4x100m team that set world records in heat (44.9) and final (44.6). She also set a world record for 100m with 11.3 to win the World Universities title in 1955 (also gold at 80mh, bronze at 200m), and ran on three Australian teams that set world records at 4x110y. Her 80mh time of 10.89 in the Olympic semi in 1956 was then the fastest ever on auto timing. At the Empire Games she secured three golds, in the hurdles and two relays, and two silvers, 100y and 220y, in 1950, but missed the 1954 Games after the birth of her son, the first of her four children. Australian champion at 90yh 1948, 80mh 1950, 1952; 440y 1950, 1952, 1956.

Her father had been a champion professional runner. A graduate of the University of Western Australia, she became a teacher and university lecturer in mathematics and physics, and later an athletics manager and coach. She was one of the inaugural six athletes inducted into the Athletics Australia Hall of Fame in February 2000. Awarded the OBE in 1957 and Order of Australia in 2001.

Annual progression at 80mh (position on world list): 1948- 11.3 (3), 1949- 11.4 (2=), 1950- 11.3 (3), 1951- 11.2 (2=), 1952- 10.9 (1), 1954- 11.4 (19=), 1955- 11.0 (4=), 1956- 10.7 (2=). Other bests: 100y 10.6 (1955), 200m 24.1 (1955), 440y 56.8 (1956).

Kerneels UYS (South Africa) (b. 12 Jun 1943) on 18 February in Cape Town. A farmer, he was the second South African to break 14 secs for 110mh with 13.9 in 1966. pb 220yh (half turn) 23.5A (1966).

Add to OBITUARY 2002

Paul BOCKEL (France) (b. 14 Mar 1916) on 1 December. He competed in 15 internationals for France 1945-52 and was French champion at hammer in 1944 and discus in 1947.

Theodore 'Bill' **BRUCE** (Australia) (b. 28 July 1923) on 1 August. He took the silver medal in the long jump at the 1948 Olympics with 7.55 and also ran on the 4x100m team that was third in their heat. His pb was an Australian record 7.59 in 1947 in winning the first of four successive Australian titles and he was also second at high jump in 1949.

Branko DANGUBIC (Yugoslavia) (b. 13 July 1922) on 24 November in Belgrade. He was Yugoslav javelin champion 1949, 1951-2, Balkan champion 1953 and Mediterranean Games winner 1951. He also competed at the 1950 Europeans and his finest result came when he was fifth at the Olympic Games 1952 in a pb 70.55. 17 internationals.

Béla JUHÁSZ (Hungary) (b. 20 Apr 1921 Nagykáta) in June in Budapest. 14th in the 1952 Olympics and dnf 1954 Europeans at 10,000m, Hungarian marathon champion 1955 in 2:31:54. Pbs: 3000m 8:17.4 (1955), 5000m 14:25.8 (1955), 10,000m 29:50.6 (1962 at age 41).

Károly KIRSZT (Hungary) (b. 23 Jul 1969 Komló) in June in Budapest. Pbs: 20kW 1:24:00, 50kW 3:58:01 (to win National title), both in 1992.

Wakaki MAEDA (Japan) (b. 20 Feb 1920) on 21 September. As a 19 year-old he triple jumped 15.28 to rank sixth in the world in 1939. He was an ATFS member from 1952.

Katri 'Kaisa' **PARVIANEN** (Finland) (b. 3 Dec 1914 Muuruvesi) on 21 October in Rauma. A pioneer of Finnish women's athletics, she won the 1948 Olympic javelin silver medal in London with her best ever distance of 43.79; that improved her own national record of 42.06 set 13 years earlier. It was another 36 years before a Finnish woman again got to an Olympic podium (Tiina Lillak, javelin silver 1984). Parviainen won Finnish titles at LJ 1948 and JT 1948 and 1950-1. She also competed in the Helsinki Olympic Games in 1952, finishing 16th with an injured arm. She took part in the first ever international match of Finnish women in Göteborg in 1951. Other pbs: LJ 5.48 (Finnish record 1948), 5.69w (1947), SP 11.62, DT 38.02 (1939.

Died in 2000

John IRWIN (USA) (b. 1913) on 28 February. While at Princeton, Irwin ranked third in the world at 220 yards hurdles in 1936 with 23.2 and 13th at 400mh with 53.1. He then came to Oxford University, winning the 220yh in the Varsity matches of 1938 and 1939. He was a Colonel in the US Army in World War II and, after a career as a lawyer, was US Ambassador to the Philippines and then to France in the 1970s.

DRUGS BANS

The IAAF has a long-standing history in the fight against doping and continues to take a lead in the world of sport, conducting far more tests than any other international federation.

It was agreed in 2002 that the IAAF Council's Doping Review Board should not only have the power to refer cases to the Court of Arbitration in Sport (CAS) but also to suspend athletes pending a CAS hearing. It was also agreed that the prohibited substances list used by the IAAF should be updated so that it is exactly the same as the IOC-WADA list.

The following cases were reported of athletes failing drug tests in 2003

Suspension: Life - life ban, 4y/2y = 4/2 years, 3m = 3 months, W = warning and disqualification, P = pending hearing

Leading athletes

Men

Name	*Date*	
Georgios Andreou CYP	6 Jul	2y
Ambrose Bitok KEN	19 Aug	
Okkert Brits RSA	31 Jan	W
Dwain Chambers USA	1 Aug	2y
Fouad Chouki FRA	27 Aug	18m
François Coertzer RSA	7 Feb	2y
Marco Cuneo ITA	3 Aug	
Stéphane Desaulty FRA	5 Aug	2y
Alberto García ESP	29 Mar	2y
Mickey Grimes USA	6 Aug	W
Calvin Harrison USA	21 Jun	P
John McEwen USA		P
Isaiah Nkuna RSA	14 Feb	2y
Chris Phillips USA		P
Luis Ramos BRA	19 Jan	2y
Eric Thomas USA		P
Kevin Toth USA		P
Innis Viviers RSA	7 Feb	2y
Aleksander Walerianczyk POL	27 Jul	W
Women		
Olga Balayeva RUS	1 Jul	3m
Lyudmila Blonskaya UKR	8 Jun	2y
Cristiana Checchi ITA	2 Mar	W
Pamela Chepchumba KEN	29 Mar	2y
Damu Cherry USA	18 Feb	2y
Martina Danisová SVK	15 May	2y
Rasa Drazdauskaite LTU	17 Jul	2y
Natalia Dziadkova BLR	13 Jun	2y
Florence Ekpo-Umoh GER	24 Jan	2y
Chryste Gaines USA		P
Sandra Glover USA		P
Geraldine Hendricken IRL	10 Feb	2y
Regina Jacobs USA	21 Jun	P
Yanina Korolchik BLR	15 Jun	2y
Asmae Leghzaoui MAR	29 Mar	2y
Maurren Maggi BRA	14 Jun	2y
Aggeliki Makri GRE	16 Mar	W
Elana Meyer RSA	2 Feb	W
Sheryl Morgan JAM	26 Apr	W
Melissa Price USA	19 Jun	P
Maria Tsírba GRE	15 Mar	2y
Kelli White USA		P

Others: 3y: Nathalie Chabran FRA; 2y: Luciene Soares de Deus BRA, Andrew Eggerth USA (9 Feb), Ksenia Kudrevatykh RUS (16 Mar), Soumiya Labani MAR (28 Mar), Valeria Lorena Rodríguez ARG (4 May), Mohamed Aghad MAR (17 May), Daniel Lopez Ferreira BRA (25 May), Diana-Cristina Panait ROM (31 May), El Houssine Essemaali MAR (1 Jun), Maria Schneider BRA (1 Jun), Saman Yanphiboon THA, Eliane Luanda Cardosaper BRA, Stamatis Papadoníou GRE (29 Jun), Olga Stefashina RUS (10 Jul), Eberhard Kliesch GER (2 Aug), Mohamed Zouak ESP (24 Aug & 7 Sep), Rafael Araújo BRA (5 Sep), Alexandra Motone RSA (27 Sep); 3m: Raymond Ejiogu NGR (12 Jun). Public warning & disqualification from event: Trent Blair USA (7 Jun), Matthew Macdonald AUS, Siniva Marsters COK (7 Jul); Suspended sentence: (2yr 10mth) Stéphane Begaud FRA (2.2.03).

Named as failing tests for THG but subject to review: John McEwen USA, Regina Jacobs USA, Eric Thomas USA, Kevin Toth USA

Named as failing tests for Modafinil but subject to review: Chryste Gaines USA, Sandra Glover USA, Calvin Harrison USA, Chris Phillips USA, Eric Thomas USA, Kelli White USA

Add to list of athletes failing drug tests in 2002

Men

Name	*Date*	
Brahim Boulami MAR	15 Aug	2y
Liu Huyuan CHN	5 Jun	2y
Joseph Sitinei KEN	13 Oct	3m
Women		
Lin Na CHN	17 Aug	2y
Myriam Mani CMR	Jun	2+1y*
Elisa Rigaudo ITA	22 Sep	W
Alina Serdyuk BLR	24 Aug	2y
Wei Yanan CHN	3 Oct	2y

Others: 2y: Luigi Venturelli ITA (16 Jun), Warunee Kittihiran THA (29 Aug), Lin Lengmei CHN (27 May), Ramiro Nogueira Filho BRA (1 Sep), Sergey Pavliy RUS (15 Sep), Jagdish Basak IND (Dec), Alapati Kalyani IND (Dec); 6m suspended: Marie-Catherine Blacodon FRA (19 Jul), Patricia Farget FRA (17 Sep); 3m suspended: David Josyfyszyn FRA (31 Aug); Public warning: Cristina Neri ITA (10 Nov), Salah Zereg ALG (24 Nov), Ramandeep Singh, Maha Singh, Sukhjinder Singh, Hridayanand Singh (all IND, Dec); Provisonally suspened: P Udaya Laxmi & Kavita Pandya IND (Dec)

* Myriam Mani was provisonally suspended for a doping offence, but the IAAF reported that she had defied IAAF rules by continuing to compete internationally and will now be required to serve two years from the date of her last competition in May 2003.

Add to list of athletes failing drug tests in 2001

3m: Mark Awere GHA (13 Jun)

THE SUB-FOUR-MINUTE MILE

By Bob Phillips

THE RACE to be the first man to beat four minutes for the mile was popularly regarded in the early 1950s as being exclusively a three-way affair between an Englishman (Roger Bannister), an Australian (John Landy) and an American (Wes Santee). The bare statistical evidence justified the assumption, because by the end of 1953 – when the World record still stood at 4:01.3, set by the Swede, Gunder Hägg, eight years before – Bannister and Landy had both run 4:02.0 and Santee 4:02.4. The contest could hardly have been more delicately poised.

Other names had been bandied about by the experts as prime candidates – Josy Barthel, of Luxemburg, and Bob McMillen, of the USA, the unexpected gold-medallist and silver-medallist from the Helsinki Olympic 1500m of the previous year; Gaston Reiff, of Belgium, the World record-holder at 2000 and 3000m; even Emil Zátopek, the peerless triple Olympic champion in the distance events. But Barthel went down with injury; McMillen was called up for military service; Reiff, at 32, proved to be past his best; and the happy-go-lucky Zátopek was far too busy breaking more World records from 5000m upwards and doubtless never gave the matter of a four-minute mile a moment's thought. Bannister, Landy and Santee had also been competitors at the Helsinki Olympics, but Bannister had failed to match expectations in finishing 4th at 1500m and the other two were still raw novices who made their exit in the heats.

In reality, the idea of a man running a mile in four minutes had been proposed long, long before Bannister, Landy and Santee began their vicarious competition on three different Continents. There is even a reference from 1770 to a man named James Parrot running "exactly a mile" in four minutes through the streets of London, and while the distance may well have been accurate there must be serious reservations regarding the methods of timekeeping. Yet by the 1820s the concept of achieving the four-minute mile – at least in some form or other – seems to have seized public imagination in England and there are accounts of a noted athlete, Curley, known familiarly as "The Brighton Shepherd", achieving under four minutes for the mile in four separate quarter-miles. Frustratingly, for statisticians of the 21st Century, no "split" times have survived, though an army officer named Lieutenant Fairman is known to have run successive "quarters" of 61, 60, 62 and 61sec for a total time of 4min 4sec in 1823.

Less reliably, the outstanding miler of that decade, James Metcalf, was later credited with running a mile in 4min 5sec on a downhill course, though his authenticated best was a rather more credible 4:30. A similar anecdote from the early 1840s concerns an attempt by a Cumbrian runner named Dan Fleming to run a mile in four minutes, again on a downhill stretch of the public highway, but he fell short of his target by 11sec and was then allegedly beaten shortly afterwards by a local farmer named Walker in 4min 2sec. Metcalf and Fleming were professional "pedestrians" who took on such challenges for wagers, and while the circumstances of their competitions were in no way conventional it can be reasonably assumed that the times they achieved were properly recorded. Maybe the most convincing of miling feats at such alfresco venues was another time of 4min 2sec achieved in 1863 by a runner of unquestionable ability, William Lang, along the Cambridge road near Newmarket. Opinion is divided as to how much of a help were the gradients of the surface.

It is no doubt significant that when custom-built tracks had come into use from the 1840s onwards, principally in London and Manchester, and miling had become more rationalised, there seemed to be rather less talk about four minutes. The first performance of note was 4:28 by Charley Westhall on a gravel track of half-a-mile in circumference at the Copenhagen House Grounds, in Islington, North London, in 1852, and from 1857 to 1865 there was a series of marvellous races in Manchester which progressively brought the record down by more than 10 seconds. The culmination was a "Champion Cup" event on the 651-yard cinder track at the Royal Oak Grounds in which William Lang and a Welshman, William Richards, dead-heated in 4:1714, with a Scotsman, Robert McKinstray, only five yards behind and also inside the previous record. This was a carefully-conceived promotion in the best traditions of Oslo's Dream Miles of more than a century later with a noted 440/880 yards runner, James Nuttall, designated as the pacemaker and carrying out his duties to perfection with intermediate times of 60.0 and 2:0512. The third lap was much slower – as was the custom of an age in which it was thought imperative to save energy for the final dash to the tape – and none of the spectators that day, nor those reading of this Victorian "Mile Of The Century" in their newspapers the following morning, could assuredly have conceived of anyone being able to run the distance any faster.

It was not until 1881 that the record was beaten, when another Scot, William Cummings, achieved 4:1615, and before the end of that decade ideas of what could be achieved for the mile had been radically revised by Walter George, who had been the outstanding amateur runner in Britain at all distances from 880 yards to 10 miles, and who turned professional for the specific purpose of challenging Cummings. When they met on a 440-yard track at Lillie Bridge, in West London, in August 1886 George won in a sensational time of 4:1234, but an even more historic achievement of his had been to run a mile time-trial on a track which was found to be slightly over-distance, thus crediting him with a clocking of inside 4min 10sec.

This was to be a characteristic of mile record-breakers for the next three-quarters of a century. Whatever times they were credited with in official competition, there was often strong evidence to suggest that they could have run very much faster. An Irishman, George Tincler, was the outstanding professional of the 1890s, and though he never bettered 4:15 in a race he was said to have accomplished a time of 4:08 in training. There seems no reason to disbelieve this tale because the professionals ran only to win and once they had the beating of their opponents they tended to slow down. As a startlingly early example, the name of a Sheffield runner, Jem Sherdon, appears nowhere in the record-books and yet during a mile race in 1853 which he was winning with ease he stopped to put his overcoat on some 90 yards from the finish, still finished "in a walk" in 4:33, and was said by the reporter for "Bell's Life" magazine that day to have been capable of 4:12 had he kept going!

It was not until 1915 that Walter George's time was marginally improved by an American, Norman Taber, with 4:12.6, and by then the formation of the IAAF had led to formal consideration and ratification of record-breaking applications. Taber's record was beaten by the legendary "Flying Finn", Paavo Nurmi, in 1923, but it has to be said that his time of 4:10.4 was probably no indication of his real ability. Nurmi, like Zátopek, was more interested in longer distances and ran barely a dozen or so races of any consequence at 1500m or the mile during his career. Speculation was rife for very many years after the great man's retirement in 1932 as to what he could have done for the mile, and Nurmi himself was to admit to believing he could have run 4:04. Joe Binks, the AAA mile champion in 1902 in a British amateur record of 4:16.8, and then a newspaper correspondent until the 1950s, saw Nurmi in action on frequent occasions, met and talked at length to him, and firmly believed that he could have run the four-minute mile if he had put his mind to it.

The 4:10 "barrier" was breached in 1931 by a Frenchman, Jules Ladoumègue, who like Nurmi was banned for breaking the draconian rules regarding amateurism, but at this juncture it is worth pointing out that the mile did not have the same obsessive appeal for Continental Europeans as it did for the English-speaking nations, and this was graphically reflected in the standard of the respective records. Ladoumègue earned rather more acclaim from his fellow-countrymen for also being the first man under 3:50 for 1500m in 1930 – when his time of 3:49.2 could be regarded as the equivalent of some three seconds faster than Nurmi's existing mile record. Subsequent miling achievements in the 1930s by Jack Lovelock, Glenn Cunningham and Sydney Wooderson set the balance straight, and an indoor time of 4:04.4 by Cunningham in 1938 – relegated to a footnote in all subsequent ranking-lists – deserves far more recognition than it has ever received as a significant "milestone" along the road to four minutes. Curious correspondence which surfaced in unlikely fashion in the columns of the "British Medical Journal" half-a-century later was to give Lovelock credit for twice breaking four minutes in training, and if the astonishing claims of times of around 3:52 and 3:56 made on Lovelock's behalf by a medical colleague were ever to be verified this entire four-minute business would now be viewed in a very different light! Fortunately for the peace of mind of statisticians and historians of the sport, these secret time-trials of Lovelock's remain in the realms of folk-lore.

Gunder Hägg and his compatriot, Arne Andersson, between them brought the record down in six instalments by more than five seconds from Wooderson's 4:06.4 of 1937, and the intense rivalry between them on those balmy evenings in the tranquillity of their neutral native land would lead one to immediately suppose that they had fulfilled the potential of their talents in the process. Yet they actually met in only three of those races, whereas all but one of their four improvements of the 1500m record from Lovelock's 3:47.8 at the 1936 Olympics to Hägg's 3:43.0 of 1944 involved a head-to-head confrontation between the two majestic runners.

That time of 3:43.0 is worth under 4:01 for a mile, and the view of the experts – most notably, Roberto Quercetani, whose numerous authoritative publications include detailed histories of the mile event in 1973 and 1985 – is that four minutes would have been broken by both Hägg and Andersson within another year or so, but they were then banned for accepting excessive expenses. Each of them claimed that their priority was always beating the other rather than setting any records, and certainly the pattern of their races suggests that the competitive instinct usually prevailed. The authoritative American coach, J.Kenneth Doherty, even went so far as to suggest in 1953 that Hägg had possessed the ability to run in the order of 3:56-to-3:57, and should have done so!

Despite the progress made in Sweden, the ravages elsewhere of the war years from 1939 to 1945 must be regarded as a major factor in slowing the race towards four minutes. Glenn Cunningham's last competitions were in 1940 and he suffered a rare loss to a fellow-American in the AAU Championships 1500m that year when Walter Mehl both won the race and missed the World record by one-tenth of a second in 3:47.9. Mehl, who was a fine indoor runner and two-miler, went into the armed forces soon afterwards and never had another chance to prove his track ability. Over 60 years later, at the age of 87, he was to regretfully recall that he genuinely believed that he could have run a four-minute mile, given the chance, and there were surely several other Americans of the early 1940s who might have nursed the same hopes. Britain's Sydney Wooderson, who came back after the war to win the European 5000m title, could have been bracketed with them, though he was far too modest ever to have suggested as much himself.

Hägg's 1500m record was equalled by another Swede, Lennart Strand, in 1947, but Strand was too highly strung ever to capitalise on that, and though promising young milers such as Bannister had already emerged before the end of the 1940s there was a curious sort of lull in the event for several years. Strand had proved, however fleetingly, that the times of Hägg and Andersson were not invulnerable, and World records were being broken in most other athletic disciplines between 1946 and 1949, including even such related events as 1000, 2000 and 3000m for which the respective records of 2:21.4, 5:07.0 and 7:58.8 represent almost exactly a straight line on a graph, and that line passes through a theoretical time of fractionally over four minutes for the mile! It could thus be reasoned that the lull was caused by the mile record having reached a peak of 4:01.3 in 1945, at which it must stay until given some sort of new impetus. An alternative argument could be that the 1000, 2000 or 3000 were not standard events, and so the mile record really ought to have been better. Yet a third theory to be offered is that Reiff – despite having won the Olympic 5000m in 1948 – was one of those rare characters who was of exceptional ability at "odd" distances, and so his 2000 and 3000 times were above the expected norm.

Happily, though, the progression of track and field achievements is not readily explained by graph-lines but rather by the force and the frailty of human nature. "Four minutes" was a conveniently round figure for speculation by the press and the public, but for the athletes it maybe came to represent a psychological barrier rather than a physical one. John Landy, who frustratingly ran successive mile times largely in isolation of 4:02.1, 4:02.8, 4:02.0, 4:02.4, 4:02.6, and again 4:02.6 between December 1952 and April 1954, reached a point of despair, bemoaning the fact that, in his own words, "Two little seconds is not much, but when you are on the track those 15 yards seem solid and impenetrable, like a cement wall". Roger Bannister, ever the analyst, was to write perceptively in hindsight in his 1955 autobiography; "To say 'Four minutes is only a time' was presumptuous, unless I had an answer for the inevitable follow-up question – 'Well, if it's possible, why don't you do it?' "

As we all now know, it was Bannister, having run 4:02.0 with bizarre pacemaking assistance in 1953, who became the first sub-four-minute miler on the evening of 6 May 1954. It is the 50th anniversary this year of his 3:59.4 at the Iffley Road track which he had come to know so well as an Oxford University undergraduate, and perhaps the proof that the four-minute "barrier" had really been no more than an attitude of mind was provided even before the following month was out when Landy ran 3:57.9 in Finland. Bannister's achievement, with the help of Chris Brasher and Chris Chataway, remains one of the most celebrated single races in the history of athletics, though within a year the British athletics authorities had passed legislation regarding pacing which would have rendered the time unacceptable. Even the tendency to rewrite history and claim that the reaction to Bannister's mile, and in particular the comparisons drawn with the previous year's conquest of Everest, were all rather overblown is put into different perspective by John Walker's frank admission more than 20 years later that breaking 3:50 did not compare with being the first to beat four minutes.

But then, had Walter George run 4:09 in competition, Nurmi 4:04, Lovelock a conservative four minutes, and Hägg 3:57, as was claimed or surmised for all of them, we would have been celebrating 50 years of four-minute miling almost a decade ago. Now, instead, we think of a mile in 3:40 ... but even that doesn't have quite the same ring to it as 'the first four minutes', does it?

1 Mile Statistics by Peter Matthews

NEW PEAKS for number of sub-4 performances were set with 111 in 1975, 161 in 1979, 213 in 1981 and 219 in 1982, since when numbers have declined as nowadays just a few top-class miles are run annually, and the USA is the only nation that stages many races at the distance. Although 55 men ran sub-4 minute miles in 2003, that number is far fewer than those who ran the equivalent time over the standard distance of 1500m. Britain changed from Imperial to metric distances in 1969.

The 500th sub 4-minute mile came in 1972 at which time the most had been run by Jim Ryun USA 27 and Kipchoge Keino KEN 23.

The 100th man to sub sub-4 was Ben Jipcho KEN on 31 Aug 1968.

968 men have run sub-4 times to the end of 2003, and the number of performances is nearly 4800.

The most men per nation: USA 257, GBR 157, KEN 92, RSA 50, AUS 36, CAN 32, GER (all) 32, IRL 30, NZL 28, MAR 26.

39 juniors have run sub-4 timeJohn Walker NZL was the first man to sub 50 sub-4s (in 1981) and the first to run 100 (on 17 Feb 1985).

Steve Scott USA has run most sub-4s with 141 to 130 by John Walker, 101 by Marcus O'Sullivan IRL.

Progressive record of most men running sub-4

2	7 Aug 54	Vancouver	1. Roger Bannister 3:58.8, 2. John Landy 3:59.6
3	28 May 55	London (WC)	1. László Tábori 3:59.0, 2. Chris Chataway 3:59.8, 6. Brian Hewson 3:59.8
4	19 Jul 57	London (WC)	1. Derek Ibbotson 3:57.2, 2. Ron Dalany 3:58.8, 3, Stanislav Jungwirth 3:59.1, 4. Ken Wood 3:59.3
5	6 Aug 58	Dublin (S)	1. Herb Elliott 3:54.5, 2. Mervyn Lincoln 3:55.9, 3. Ron Delany 3:57.5, 4. Murray Halberg 3:57.5, 5. Albert Thomas 3:58.6
6	7 Jun 63	Compton	1. Peter Snell 3:55.0, 2. Jim Beatty 3:55.5, 3. Dyrol Burleson 3:55.6, 4. Jim Grelle 3:56.4, 5. Cary Weisiger 3:56.6, 6. Bob Seaman 3:59.1
8	5 Jun 64	Compton	1. Dyrol Burleson 3:57.4, 2. Tom O'Hara 3:57.6, 3. Archie San Romani 3:57.6, 4. Morgan Groth 3:57.9, 5. Jin Grelle 3:58.5, 6. Bob Day 3:58.9, 7. Cary Weisiger 3:58.9, 8. Jim Ryun 3:59.0
9	25 Jun 77	London (CP)	1. Steve Ovett 3:54.69
10	3 Jul 78	Stockholm	1. Steve Scott USA 3:55.96
13	8 Aug 80	Berlin	1. Thomas Wessinghage FRG 3:55.04

First from each continent:

Europe	Roger Bannister GBR	3:59.4	Oxford	6 May 1954
Australia	John Landy AUS	3:57.9	Turku	21 Jun 1954
North America	Don Bowden USA	3:58.7	Stockton	1 Jun 1957
Africa	Terence Sullivan RHO	3:59.8	Dublin (Santy)	23 Sep 1960
Asia	Takashi Ishii JPN	3:59.7	Melbourne	10 Dec 1977
South America	Joaquim Cruz BRA	3:53.00	Los Angeles (Ww)	13 May 1954
Indoors	Jim Beatty USA	3:58.9	Los Angeles	10 Feb 1962
Professional	Harry Downes AUS	3:59.7	Bendigo	10 Mar 1963
Teenager	Herb Elliott AUS (19yr 334 d)	3:59.9	Melbourne	25 Jan 1958
Junior	Jim Ryun USA (17yr 37d)	3:59.0	Compton	5 Jun 1964
M40	Eamonn Coghlan IRL	3:58.15i	Allston	20 Feb 1994
Brothers	Ian (3:57.3) and Peter (3:58.7) Stewart in same race at Reading on 11 Jun 1969			
Twins	Paul (3:57.21) and John (3:58.05) Carig in same race at Berlin 8 Aug 1980			
Father & son	Kipchoge (best 3:53.1, 1967) and Martin (best 3:52.33, 1996) Keino KEN			
4:00.0	Derek Ibbotson (4) and Michael Blagrove (5) at London (White City) 3 Sep 1958			

The First 20 Years of the Sub-4 Era

Year	*Best*		*Times under 4 minutes*	*Perfs*	*Indoor*
1954	3:58.8	Roger Bannister GBR	2	4	
1955	3:59.0	Lászlo Tábori HUN	3	3	
1956	3:58.6	John Landy AUS, Jim Bailey AUS	6	9	
1957	3:57.2	Derek Ibbotson GBR	9	14	
1958	3:54.5	Herb Elliott AUS	7	19	
1959	3:56.5	Siegfried Valentin GDR	3	4	
1960	3:57.0	Herb Elliott AUS	7	13	
1961	3:57.6	Dyrol Burleson USA	3	4	
1962	3:54.4	Peter Snell NZL	14	23	3
1963	3:54.9	Peter Snell NZL	15	29	7
1964	3:54.1	Peter Snell NZL	21	32	4
1965	3:53.6	Michel Jazy FRA	24	55	1
1966	3:51.3	Jim Ryun USA	22	36	3
1967	3:51.1	Jim Ryun USA	20	32	3
1968	3:53.8	Bodo Tümmler FRG	25	31	1
1969	3:55.9	Jim Ryun USA	20	28	0
1970	3:56.3	Roscoe Divine USA	28	36	0
1971	3:54.4	Kipchoge Keino KEN	37	53	7
1972	3:52.8	Jim Ryun USA	34	44	2
1973	3:52.0	Ben Jipcho KEN	41	68	3
1974	3:53.2	Tomy Waldrop USA	53	69	21

1 Mile World Record Progression in the IAAF era

4:14.4	John Paul Jones USA	Cambridge, MA	31 May 1913
4:12.6	Norman Taber USA	Cambridge, MA	16 Jul 1915
4:10.4	Paavo Nurmi FIN	Stockholm	23 Aug 1923
4:09.2	Jules Ladoumègue FRA	Paris	4 Oct 1931
4:07.6	Jack Lovelock NZL	Princeton	15 Jul 1933
4:06.8	Glenn Cunningham USA	Princeton	16 Jun 1934
4:06.4	Sydney Wooderson GBR	London	28 Aug 1937
4:06.2	Gunder Hägg SWE	Göteborg	1 Jul 1942
4:06.2	Arne Andersson SWE	Stockholm	10 Jul 1942
4:04.6	Gunder Hägg SWE	Stockholm	4 Sep 1942
4:02.6	Arne Andersson SWE	Göteborg	1 Jul 1943
4:01.6	Arne Andersson SWE	Malmö	18 Jul 1944
4:01.3	Gunder Hägg SWE	Malmö	17 Jul 1945
3:59.4	Roger Bannister GBR	Oxford	6 May 1954
3:57.9	John Landy AUS	Turku	21 Jun 1954
3:57.2	Derek Ibbotson GBR	London	19 Jul 1957
3:54.5	Herb Elliott AUS	Dublin	6 Aug 1958
3:54.4	Peter Snell NZL	Wanganui	27 Jan 1962
3:54.1	Peter Snell NZL	Auckland	17 Nov 1964
3:53.6	Michel Jazy FRA	Rennes	9 Jun 1965
3:51.3	Jim Ryun USA	Berkeley	17 Jul 1966
3:51.1	Jim Ryun USA	Bakersfield	23 Jun 1967
3:51.0	Filbert Bayi TAN	Kingston	17 May 1975
3:49.4	John Walker NZL	Göteborg	12 Aug 1975
3:48.95	Sebastian Coe GBR	Oslo	17 Jul 1979
3:48.8	Steven Ovett GBR	Oslo	1 Jul 1980
3:48.53	Sebastian Coe GBR	Zürich	19 Aug 1981
3:48.40	Steven Ovett GBR	Koblenz	26 Aug 1981
3:47.33	Sebastian Coe GBR	Bruxelles	28 Aug 1981
3:46.32	Steve Cram GBR	Oslo	27 Jul 1985
3:44.39	Noureddine Morceli ALG	Rieti	5 Sep 1993
3:43.13	Hicham El Guerrouj MAR	Roma	7 Jul 1999

Roger BANNISTER

Roger Gilbert Bannister.
b. 23 Mar 1929 Harrow, London.

On 6 May 1954 Bannister achieved one of the most celebrated deeds in the history of sport, with the first sub four-minute mile, running 3:59.4 at Iffley Road, Oxford. Six weeks later John Landy (Australia) improved the mile record to 3:57.9, but Bannister in this, his last season before concentrating on his medical career, beat Landy in a race dubbed 'The Mile of the Century' to win the Empire Games title at 1 mile in Vancouver. Bannister ran 3:58.8 and Landy 3:59.6, the first time two men had beaten four minutes in one race. Bannister then added the European title at 1500m.

He set four British records at 1500m to 3:42.2 in 1954 and four at 1 mile, his first being 4:03.6 in 1953. He had been 3rd in the European 800m in 1950 and a disappointed 4th at 1500m in the 1952 Olympics. AAA champion at 880y 1952, 1 mile 1951, 1953-4. Best time for 880y 1:50.7 (1953).

He studied medicine at Oxford University and at St. Mary's Hospital Medical School in London, becoming a distinguished neurologist. He was awarded the CBE in 1955 and was knighted in 1975 for his services to medicine. He was Chairman of the Sports Council 1971-4, and was Master of Pembroke College, Oxford 1985-93.

THE OLYMPIC GAMES OF 1904

By Bill Mallon

PAULA RADCLIFFE will likely arrive in Athens in early August 2004, preparing for what many assume will be her ascendance to the title of Olympic Marathon champion. She will be accompanied by her entourage. It will include her agent, who will look for financial deals that will accrue to the Olympic champion; her trainer, who will oversee her workouts, ensuring that her fine-tuning reaches its peak on the day of the race; her massage therapist, who will help her recover from workouts leading up to the competition; and her therapists, chiropractors, and doctors, who will be certain her health is at the optimum necessary to run the requisite 42 kilometres at top speed. She will be able to pay salaries for this entourage because of the high six-figure annual income her running provides her.

On the day of the race she will present herself in a skimpy, almost risqué, uniform of high-quality materials, allowing her to dissipate heat carefully during the 135-140 minute run. Her running shoes will be specially made for her, so that they fit her feet, and her feet only, precisely. They will be extremely lightweight, so she need not carry extra mass during the race, and very soft, to avoid blistering.

During the race, she will receive frequent reports of her pace, so that she knows where she stands in terms of her pre-race plan. With the other runners, she will frequently pass aid stations, where she will drink from her own pre-made refreshment. It will consist of fluids specially developed to help her replenish what she loses during the effort, and help avoid dehydration, which would likely end her goal of becoming Olympic champion.

If Radcliffe wins, she will be escorted to the drug testing area, where she will provide two urine samples, to be tested for virtually every combination of drugs known to administrative bastions. She will then meet the press, who will recount the tale of her victory to billions of people world-wide, via the print media, radio, television, and the Internet. She will become even more of a national hero in Britain.

Generosity of strangers

It was not quite the same in August 1904. Marathon runner Félix Carbajal arrived from Cuba, having earned the money for the trip by staging exhibitions, and running the entire length of the island nation for fund-raising. In July he arrived in the United States, via New Orleans, where he lost all his money in a crap game. He was able to get to St. Louis only by hitch-hiking and the generosity of strangers.

On 30 August 1904, the day of the first '04 Olympic Marathon, Carbajal arrived at the starting line, wearing heavy boots, full-length trousers, a long-sleeve shirt, and with a certain élan, a beret. The outfit was made the more ludicrous by the searing mid-America summer heat of a 32ºC. (90ºF.) day, with the race starting at the height of the mid-day sun, 3 pm (15:00).

The diminutive Carbajal (154cm/5ft) was helped by the redoubtable American weight thrower, Martin Sheridan. Somehow, Sheridan found a pair of scissors and cut the Cuban's trousers into shorts, giving him some respite from the oppressive heat. During the race, Carbajal ran over dirt-covered country roads. A few motor vehicles led the way, but they made things more difficult by kicking up the dirt as a fine dust that fell directly into the faces of the runners. There were no aid stations to be found. He was able to drink once, when he passed a water tower, where several runners partook of the cool fluid. Carbajal found some sustenance along the way, by picking a few green apples from a tree and eating them. But the apples caused him stomach cramps, and made him fall off the pace. He later saw two spectators eating peaches, and asked for some, but was refused. But he grabbed two from them, and ran off, eating them as he ran. Still, despite all these obstacles, Felix Carbajal finished fourth in the 1904 Olympic Marathon.

After the race there was no drug testing to concern him. The winner was Tom Hicks, an American who had been born in Birmingham, England. Had there been drug testing, Hicks might not be considered Olympic champion. Hicks did have some help during the race, being attended by Charles Lucas, who rode ahead of him in a car, and later wrote a report of the 1904 Olympics. Lucas described the pharmacologic assistance that he gave Hicks, "Ten miles from the finish, Hicks began to show positive signs of collapse. When he asked for a drink of water, it was refused him, and his mouth was sponged out with distilled water. He managed up well, until seven miles from the Stadium, and then the author was forced to administer one-sixtieth grain of sulphate of strychnine, by the mouth, besides the white of an egg. Although French brandy was in the possession of the party, it was deemed best to abstain from further stimulants so long as possible. As Hicks passed the twenty-mile post, his color began to become ashen pale, and then another tablet of one-sixtieth grain strychnine was administered him, and two more eggs, besides a sip of brandy."

Hicks was not disqualified, but Fred Lorz was. Though there were no timing clocks to help the runners, Lorz cared not. He flagged badly during the race, and stopped. One of the support cars picked him up and carried him near the stadium. There, he got out, and ran into the Olympic Stadium, crossing the finishing line, where at first he was feted as the Olympic champion, before his ruse was outed. The American AAU officials reacted immediately, disqualifying him for "life," for his modern-day Rosie Ruiz-like feat. Seems like a strong punishment, but not when realizes he was later allowed to compete in, and win, the 1905 Boston Marathon. One imagines this could never happen in a modern Olympic marathon, but recall that in 1972, Norbert Sudhaus, a West German student posing as a runner, preceded Frank Shorter into the Olympic Stadium.

The day after the 1904 St. Louis Olympic marathon, the newspapers contained accounts of the race. There were no radio reports, no television to be had, no official film of the race, and Bud Greenspan was not there to make Carbajal a hero. Two small reports of the 1904 Olympic Games were produced, one by Lucas, and one edited by James Sullivan, the US President of the AAU. Félix Carbajal returned to Havana. He was never heard from again as an athlete. His agent, whose name has not been left to us, did not do a very good job.

Winds of Olympic History

And so it was a little different in St. Louis in 1904 than it will be in Athens in 2004. The 1904 Olympic Games were held there because St. Louis was celebrating a great world's fair, the Louisiana Purchase International Exposition, in honour of the 'centenary' of the Louisiana Purchase from the French, which doubled the landmass of the new American nation in 1803. The Exposition was originally planned for 1903, as that should have been the centenary, but the planners did not meet the schedule and it was postponed until 1904. The 1904 Olympic Games were originally awarded to Chicago. But when St. Louis decided to hold an 'opposing' athletic festival during the Exposition, Chicago eventually ceded its rights to the Games.

The track and field events in 1904 were conducted on the campus of Washington University, a major university in St Louis. A state-of-the-art track, for 1904, was built for the competition, and the stadium and athletic field was called Francis Field, after David Francis, the President of the Louisiana Purchase Exposition. The track was a cinder affair, 1/3rd of a mile in length.It was somewhat triangular in shape, with one very long straightaway. Next to the field, the fair organizers built the Physical Culture Gymnasium, which contained all sorts of sporting and gymnastics equipment, and where many of the indoor Olympic events were conducted.

Francis Field still exists, and is the football (American) stadium for Washington University. The original track is gone, but it lasted until the early 1990s, and the author had the opportunity to walk on the old cinders in 1982, the winds of Olympic history wafting there still. It has been replaced by a modern 400m synthetic surface.

The 1904 Olympic track and field athletics events took place from 29 August to 3 September 1904 (mostly – see below). In addition to the standard Olympic programme, a series of handicap events were conducted concurrently. All through the summer, the Fair organizers held sporting events, many of them that they termed 'Olympic.' Conducted on the same track that summer, were the Olympic Interscholastic Meet, the Olympic Open Handicap Meeting, the Olympic Athletic Meet for Schools in the Louisiana Purchase Exposition Territory, the Olympic Elementary School Championship for St. Louis, the AAU Handicap Meet, the AAU Junior Championships, the AAU Championships, the Olympic Collegiate Championships, the Olympic Interscholastic Handicap Meet, the Interscholastic Championships, the Olympic Irish Sports, the Olympic Championships of the Public Schools Athletic League, the Western AAU Handicap Meeting, the Western AAU Championships, the YMCA Handicap Track and Field Meet, and the YMCA Track and Field Championships.

The actual Olympic competition consisted of the now standard programme, and a number of now-defunct events were also contested. Thus, Archie Hahn, of Milwaukee, a superb, though very small, sprinter, did not precisely become the first sprinter to win the Olympic double. He actually won the Olympic triple – 60m, 100m, and 200m. Other Olympic events we no longer see were the 200m hurdles, the 4-mile team race, standing high jump, standing long jump, and standing triple jump, and the 56lb (25.4kg.) weight throw.

There was also 'sort of' a decathlon, but it was held on one day, and that was on 4 July. It was the All-Around Championship an event that was popular in America and Ireland, but was held in one day. It was actually contested during the Olympic gymnastics competitions and some demur that it should not be considered part of the Olympic track and field programme. There is some confusion here concerning classification of events, as both weightlifting events and tug-of-war were conducted as part of the track and field athletics competition, which was common in that era.

The All-Around was won by Tom Kiely, an Irish weight-thrower and all-around champion, who represented... well, we are not really certain! There were three Irish nationals competing in 1904 – Kiely, John Holloway in the All-Around (who shortly thereafter emigrated to the USA), and John Daly, a distance runner. The athletes themselves insisted that they represented Ireland, which was not yet a free state. In fact, the English AAA offered to pay their expenses in exchange for the three to represent Great Britain, but they refused and raised their own money, to compete under an Irish flag. The fact that Ireland was not free should not automatically disqualify them from competing under that flag, as currently Puerto Rico and the British Virgin Islands represent 'national' entities that are governed under another flag. And in the early Olympic era, Bohemia competed independently, though it was a part of the Austro-Hungarian Empire, and Finland competed on its own, though it was part of Russia. Being of Irish descent, I won't get into it any further.

Repeat triple

Of the 117 known track and field athletes in 1904, fully 88 competed for the United States, winning almost all the Olympic events. There were just 10 nations competing in 1904 Olympic track and field and the only non-American champions were Kiely in the All-Around, and the Montréal policeman, Étienne Desmarteau, who won the 56lb weight throw.

Besides Archie Hahn, James Lightbody starred on the track. A Chicago runner, he won the 800m, 1500m, and the 2590m steeplechase (the distance is not a typo). Ray Ewry won all three of the standing jumps, repeating his triple from the 1900 Paris Olympics, and he would win the standing high and long jumps again in 1906 and 1908, eventually retiring with 10 Olympic gold medals. (The standing triple jump was discontinued after 1904.)

Harry Hillman won the 200 and 400m hurdle races. In both races, the bronze medalist was George Poage, a young African-American runner from Milwaukee. Long considered the first Olympic black medalist, this is probably not true. In 1904, Cleveland's Joseph Stadler won a silver medal behind Ewry in the standing high jump. Until the early 1980s, he was never mentioned as African-American, but during my research on the 1904 Olympics, a photo of Stadler at the Missouri Historical Society confirms his race beyond doubt. In addition, it is now known that Constantin Henriquez de Zubiera, a black Frenchman of North African descent, won a gold medal in 1900 rugby football.

Two dominant American weight-throwers made their Olympic débuts. Ralph Rose won the shot put, setting a new world record in the process. He tied for first in the discus throw with the aforementioned Martin Sheridan, but Sheridan trumped him in a throw-off, defeating him by 7'-3½" (2.22m.). Both athletes competed twice more at the Olympics.

In 1906, Sheridan won five Olympic medals, three of them gold. In 1908 he won the discus throw for the third consecutive Olympics and also won the classical discus throw. He ended his Olympic career with five gold medals and nine Olympic medals – don't even begin to argue with me that the 1906 competition was not an Olympic Games! Rose skipped the 1906 Games, but won the shot put again in 1908. In 1912, he fell to silver in the shot put, but added a gold medal in the shot put (both hands) competition. Rose and Sheridan died before 1920, both men dead of pneumonia, while still in the prime of life.

And there was one other major difference between 1904 and 2004 Olympic track and field. Félix Carbajal could run in 1904, but Paula Radcliffe could not have as there were no events for women. Track and field athletics would not allow women to compete at the Olympic Games until 1928. In 1904, women competed at the Olympics only in archery.

And so it was. Is it better now? Were we the worse because Félix Carbajal ran in heavy boots, or are we the better because sprinters run on an unmarred synthetic surface? The world has moved on and we will never go back to the way it was. Nobody tries to classify the 1904 St. Louis Olympic Games among the great sporting festivals – in fact, one author has called 1900 and 1904 "The Farcical Olympics."

But I've sat in the stands of Francis Field several times and looked down over the track, both the original cinder one, and the new synthetic one, devoid of flaws, yet equally devoid of feeling. The ghosts of Sheridan, Hahn, Lightbody and Carbajal linger there still and whisper in the distance, if you listen closely enough. I like that old track better.

World Records Set At 1904 Games

1500m	4:05.4	James Lightbody (USA)
Shot	14.81m	Ralph Rose (USA)
Standing LJ	3.47m	Ray Ewry (USA)

ATHLETICS REFERENCE BOOKS

Reviewed by Peter Matthews

The Toughest Race in the World – A look at 30 Years of the IAAF World Cross Country Championships. A4 370p. This massive book by Mark Butler includes full results and a comprehensive index of all competitors at the IAAF CC Champs from 1973 to 2002 – not forgetting all medallists from the preceding International CC Championships and Olympic medallists 1912-24. Details from the IAAF (see later).

Weltrekorde und Weltrekordler – Dreisprung, Stabhochsprung. A4 147 pages. Manfred Holzhausen continues his series of splendidly detailed surveys (in German) of world records and world record holders in the IAAF-era (i.e. from 1912). This tenth book in his series is an excellent reference source, giving profiles (and illustrations) of all world-record-holders at the triple jump and pole vault, with detailed surveys of their careers and a table of annual yearly world bests. Previous works in this series have been for: Price 10 euros each from Manfred Holzhausen, Dresdener Str. 4, 41516 Grevenbroich, Germany, Tel: 49 21823049, Fax: 49 2182811849 (m.holzhausen@planet- interkom.de).

Leichtathletik im 19.Jahrhundert (1891-1900) by Hubert G.Hamacher. 552 pages. Written in German, this book includes a short history of athletics in the leading countries of the 19th Century, such as Britain, United States, Ireland and France, summary descriptions of the Olympic Games of 1896 and 1900 and careers of the leading athletes of the time. Statistics include 50 best athletes per year and event results and there are over 250 photographs. Price 25 euros or equivalent in £ or $ in cash or remittance to "Postbank Berlin No, 530 474-105 (BLZ 100 100 10)" to DGLG, Hans Waynberg, Grefrather Weg 100, D41464 NEUSS/Rhl, Germany.

Olympic Track & Field History by Mel Watman. 206 pages. Revised, updated and expanded version of the 2000 edition, containing reports, trivia and results (up to top 8) of each Games 1896-2000 plus features on numerous Olympic heroes from Jim Thorpe and Paavo Nurmi to Michael Johnson and Marion Jones. £12 or 20 euros or $25 inc. airmail postage from Mel Watman, 13 Garden Court, Marsh Lane, Stanmore, Middx HA7 4TE, England; payment by cash or by cheque (in pounds sterling only).

Docathlé 2003 – Le meilleur de l'Athlétisme Français. A5 640p. Gérard Dupuy and Gilbert Rosillo head a team that have compiled a magnificent book, packed with statistical information on French athletics. Following current records there is a chronology of French senior records from the 1940s. Then, after details of French Championships, complete details are given with athlete indexes of all French performances at Olympics, World and European Championships. There are top 20 lists for all ages 16-27 for all events, all-time lists 100 deep outdoors and 30 deep indoors, an extensive directory with over 2000 top athletes and a complete record of all French international athletes. Interwoven are one-page essays on all-time greats. Price 30 euros from the FFA, 33 avenue Pierre de Coubertin, 75640 Paris CEDEX 13, France. See also their web site http://www.athle.com.

3:59.4: The Quest for the Four Minute Mile" by Bob Phillips, 255 pp. The history of the mile from the 18th Century to Bannister's first sub-four minutes based on contemporary sources and first-hand accounts, plus a detailed summary of the development of the event since. The Reverend George Dole, who ran in Bannister's historic race, tells his own story of the memorable day. More than 50 photographs and in-depth statistics. Published by The Parrswood Press, St Wilfrid's Enterprise Centre, Royce Road, Manchester M15 5BJ, Manchester, £12.95 plus postage £2 in Europe, £4 elsewhere For overseas orders visit the website: www.parrswoodpress.com.

Combined Events Annual 2003 by Hans van Kuijen. A5, 216pp. The 11th edition of this attractively produced annual includes top 200 men's decathlon and women's heptathlon lists for 2003 with 150-deep all-time world lists. There are also results of major events, profiles and complete career details for 100 of the world's top multi-eventers, records etc. In Europe: 25 Euro by international money order or cash (add 7.5 Euro for bank charges for cheques or payments to bank account 52.31.27.898 of ABN-AMRO, Helmond); or £20 sterling. Outside Europe: US $35 cash or $40 cheques. From Hans van Kuijen, de Bergen 66, 5706 RZ Helmond, Netherlands. email: hvankuijen@wxs.nl.

Balkan All-Time Lists. Compiled by Karolos Sargologos for the Association of Balkan Athletic Federations. 50-deep performers and 20-deep performance lists for all events for the Balkan nations (to 15 June 2003). Contact Karolos Sargologos, 1, Erifilis Str - Pagrati, Athens P.C.116 34, Greece.

Eesti kümnevvoistlus läbi aegade by Erlend Teemägi. 244x167mm 288 pp. A detailed history (in Estonian) of Estonian decathletes with plenty of statistics. The athletes profiled with career records include such great names as Aleksander Klumberg, Heino Lipp, Uno Palu, Rein Aun and Erki Nool. 20 euros (plus postage) from Erlend Teemägi, Mooni 105-7, 13 424 Tallinn, Estonia.

Livre d'Or 1928-2003. The 75th anniversary of the Luxembourg Federation is celebrated with this weighty and most comprehensive A5 350pp book edited by Georges Klepper. Heavily illustrated, it includes profiles of the nation's Olympic champions Michel Théato and Josy Barthel in a history of athletics in the country, with complete lists of national champions and progressive records, details of all LUX performances in major events and 75-deep all-time lists. 31 euros in Europe, 37 euros elsewhere to account no. LU32 1111 0200 0321 0000. See www.fla.lu; e-mail: fla@fla.lu.

Polscy Lekkoatleci na Listach Swiatowyc 1921-2002. 240 x 162 mm. 146pp. Janusz Wasko has produced a fascinating statistics book with a difference. To commemorate the 85th anniversary of the PZLA, he details all Polish athletes to have made the world top 100 at all men's and women's events in this period – and the best mark if outside the limits which have been gained from ATFS publications, extrapolating 100th bests from the 50-deep lists (or 10 for women) in the Performances Through the Year series. There are extensive tables for all events and athletes are scored for their annual placings (the top scorers for any event, 100 for 1st to 1 for 100th are: Men: Janusz Sidlo JT 1932, Wladyslaw Komar SP 1566, Józef Schmidt TJ 1460; women: Irena Szewinska 200m 1598 and 100m 1569). The final summary tables clearly show Poland's golden age in athletics to have been the 20 years from 1958 (when they suddenly had 6.97% of the world's top ten men and 7.16% of the women, double the previous bests) to 1977. In 2002 they had 1.67% and 1.52%. Contact the author at Aleje Wyszynskiego 28/48, 22-400 Zamosc, Poland. email: jwasko@zke.com.pl

Campionii României. 233 x 164mm 181pp. By Alexandru Boriga and the late Vladimir Simionescu. This is a second volume following the "Evolution of the National Records of Romania 1912-97, which it updates, this one giving lists of champions in the U23, U20, U18, U16, U14, U12 age groups. Details from Alexandru Boriga, Bd.Unirii, bl.68, sc.A, et.2, ap.9, Targoviste – Jud. Dambovita, Cod 0200, Romania.

Prvenstva Jugoslavije u Atletici Yugoslav Athletics Championships 1920-2002. 235 x 165mm, 176pp. By Ljubisa Gajic. Perhaps fittingly with the end of the old Yugoslavia, the author details Yugoslav champions at all age groups. There are also lists of annual best performances for all events 1919-2001, top ten lists for the Kingdom of Yugoslavia 1919-44 and biographies of top athletes from this era. Cash only, 20 euros and $20 for the author at Vukasina Stefanovica 9, YU – 2500 Jagodina.

Najbolji Rezultati Jugoslovenskih Atleticara. Yugoslav All-time Performance Lists Part One – men. 234 x 159mm. 162pp. Deep performance lists to 2003, varying in length according to standard up to the 570 shot put marks over 19m. Price 20 Euros (postage included), cash only from the author, Ozren Karamata, Karamatina 17, YU-11080 Zemun, Srbija i Crna Gora.

Enrique Figuerola. Basilio Fuentes has written a biography of the Cuban sprinter who was the 1964 Olympic silver medallist at 100m. His races 1956-68 are detailed with mini-biographies of the eight top Cuban sprinters and Cuban progressive men's sprint records. £15, $20 US or 20 euros from Ivis M. Fernandez Pita, 14964 SW 60th St, Miami, Florida 33193, USA. email: ivistour99@hotmail.com.

The First Four-Minute Mile and Tom Hullatt of Tibshelf. A5 138pp. By Peter and Paul Stanley. The authors tell of their hunt for details of the third placer (in 4:16.0) in Roger Bannister's first sub-four-minute mile. They reveal the tale of the man from a Derbyshire mining community who ran for the AAA team that day, having won the Northern mile title in 1953. Tom died in 1990 but the authors talked to his sister and many who knew him. £7.99 plus postage (50p UK) from Descartes Publishing, 83 Park Road, Peterborough, PE1 2TN, England.

Funny Running Shorts. A5 122pp. By Geoff Wightman and Dave Bedford. Two of British athletics' most jokey characters have collected 101 amusing true stories from the world of running, mostly from fellow stars. £9.99 plus postage (50p UK & Ireland) from Descartes Publishing, as above.

Listas Mundiais de Sempre (World All-Time Lists). 232 pp A4. 300 deep for men and 200 deep for women. Luís Leite has updated his lists to the end of 2003. From Luís at: Av. Alm. Gago Coutinho 154, 1700-033 Lisboa, Portugal for 20 euro within Europe, 25 elsewhere.

National Athletics Records for all countries in the world (2003 edition). 208 pages. National records of 230 countries and territories, from Afghanistan to Zimbabwe, from Greenland to the Falklands. Price: 20 euro or £15 (Payment in advance – cash or international money order) from: Winfried Kramer, Kohlrodweg 12, 66539 Neunkirchen-Kohlhof, Germany.

IAAF Handbooks

These and a long list of other productions from the IAAF, 17 rue Princesse Florestine, BP 359, MC 98007, Monaco. All prices (by Visa, Master Card or Eurocard) include postage by airmail. e-mail to: headquarters@iaaf.org. Payment by credit card (Visa, Mastercard or Eurocard only), quoting name on card, number of card, expiry date, name and address to which book should be sent, and signature.

IAAF Statistics Handbook, Paris 2003. A5 616pp. Edited by Mark Butler. About one-third of this book is devoted to the history of the World Championships 1983-01 – a report of each event, full results and tables of multiple medallists, most appearances, youngest and oldest, national placings, performance trends and more. The winners at every other IAAF World Championship event (indoor, junior, youth, cross country, road races) are listed, followed by all Olympic medallists and gold medallists at the World University Games. Commonwealth Games and major continental championships. There are world and continental records plus world junior, world youth and world over-40. World teenage bests by age come next, then 30-deep world all-time lists, Winfried Kramer's national records and a concise progression of official world records, complete results of the 2003 World Indoor and Cross Country Champs, and biographies of around 1000 current world class athletes. Truly a monumental work of reference. 20 euros.

IAAF Statistics Handbook, Budapest 2004. A5 300pp. This further superb work by Mark Butler covers similar ground to the above, except for indoor athletics, being a guide for the 10th IAAF World Indoor championships,

Progression of World Best Performances & Official IAAF World Records (2003 edition). A5 548pp. Richard Hymans has revised and brought up to date his indispensable evolution of world bests and records in the fifth edition of this book. Listed performances date back as far as 1827 and wherever possible the marks are fleshed out with such additional information as intermediate times, field event series and the complete result. There is an index of all the record breakers with dates of birth and height and weight where available, and the youngest and oldest record holders by event. $32 or 32 euros.

IAAF Magazine/Newsletter. The quarterly magazine is a top-quality colour production (A4, 60 plus pages) with reports and results of major competitions and articles by leading authorities. The regular newsletters are generally 16 pages. $80 subscription for text in English and French.

IAAF Handbook 2004-05. 169 x114mm. 212pp. Rules and regulations in English, French or Spanish editions. Each $10.

IAAF Directory and Calendar 2004. A5, 258 pages. Contact details for officials, organisations and national federations, with calendar and lists of champions. $16.

IAAF World Rankings Yearbook 2003. A5 578pp. This handbook includes comprehensive details of the rankings, with 100 deep lists and season's records for the top 20 athletes at each event in 2003. $20.

Note that the IAAF also sells videos of highlights of its World Series meetings, including all World Championships from 1991.

Annuals

For most Annuals below referring to 2002/03, there will be new issues covering 2003/04.

L'Athlétisme Africain/African Athletics 2003. A5, 152p. By Yves Pinaud. 100 deep men's and women's lists for Africa for 2002, with all-time lists, national championships and major meetings results. 21 euro including postage from La Mémoire du Sport, 103 rue de Paris, 94220 Charenton le Pont, France. (Previous annuals 1979-2002 available at various prices).

Asian Athletics 2002 rankings. A5 89 pages. By Heinrich Hubbeling. Top 30s for 2002 for athletes from Asian nations, together with continuation lists for countries other than China and Japan and all new national records set during the year, with Asian records. Euro 15/US $15 in Europe, Euro 20/US $20 outside Europe in cash or by International Money Order from the author, Haydnstrasse 8, 48691 Vreden, Germany (or for £10 from Tony Isaacs, 11 Manton Close, Trowbridge, Wiltshire BA14 0RZ, England.). Copies also available for Asia 1993, 1997, 1998, 2000 and 2001 at Euro 10 each, and the ASIA All-time Rankings as at 31.12.2000 for Euro 15.

Athletics Australia 2004 Season Guide. A5 440p. The usual comprehensive annual includes records, results and lists for 2003 with all-time lists (c. 40 deep per event) compiled by Paul Jenes. There are profiles of 124 top Australian athletes by David Tarbotton and Neil Fuller and all top 3 finishers in Australian Champs 1987-2003,. Details from the publishers Athletics Australia (athletics@athletics.org.au).

British Athletics 2003. The NUTS Annual, edited by Rob Whittingham and Peter Matthews. 416 pages including 16 of colour photographs. Contents include deep UK ranking lists for all age groups in 2002, top 12 merit rankings, all-time lists, results etc. £15 UK, £17 rest of Europe, £18 outside Europe; from Umbra Athletics Ltd, Unit 1, Bredbury Business Park, Bredbury Park Way, Stockport, SK6 2SN, England. All orders by credit card to www.umbraathletics.com will be sent worldwide post-free for £15.

Caribbean Athletics Annual 2003 A5, 136pp. By Bernard Linley. Results of major meetings in the Caribbean in 2003 with 20-deep CAC year lists and c.40-deep all-time lists. All medallists at the CAC Junior Championships 1980-2002 are listed, with Trinidad & Tobago all-time lists. 15 euros from A.LeClainche-Bramucci, Viale di Focene 160, I - 00054 Fiumicino (RM), Italy.

DAF 2002 I tal. A5 276p. The Danish athletics annual, edited by Erik Laursen, provides most comprehensive lists of records for all age groups with basic 2002 and all-time lists. Price 125 DKr excl. post and packing from the Dansk Athletic Federation, Idrattens Hus, 2605 Brondby, Denmark or on-line at www.dansk-atletik.dk.

Laursens Lille Lommebog 2002 A5 85p. This is Erik Laursen's annual compilation of Danish indoor and outdoor lists for 2002 giving more detail than in the above annual. He also includes all-time top 30s and a special feature of annual Danish lists for men's 1500m 1960-9. Price 50 DK plus postage (14 in Nordic lands, 24 in Europe, 38 elsewhere). Both these Danish books from Erik Laursen, Sandbakken 95, 8270 Høbjerg, Denmark. Or email erik.laursen@privat.dk.

Eesti Kergejõustiku Aastraamat 2003. 264pp. Edited by Erlend Teemägi and Ants Teder. Estonian ranking lists for 2002, with results and records. From Eesti Kergejõustikuliit, Regati pst. 1, 11911 Tallinn, Estonia.

Deutsche Bestenliste 2002 A5 200 pp. 30 DM or US $20. Edited by Klaus Amrhein for the Deutschen Gesellschaft für Leichtathletik-Dokumentation (DGLD). Deep performance and performer year lists, indoors and out, for Germany for 2002. See DGLD details.

DLV Leichtathletik Jahrbuch 2003. A5 384pp. The official yearbook of the German Federation. Directory and review, with articles on top athletes, detailed results of 2003 meetings, records and top tens, also many illustrations in colour. Euro 18 plus postage, from Deutsche Leichtathletik Marketing GmbH, Postfach 10 04 63, 64219 Darmstadt, Germany.

DLV Leichtathletik Bestenliste 2003. A5 432pp. The DLV's ranking lists for 2003 for all events compiled by Eberhard Vollmer, generally 50-deep for seniors and Jugend-A, 30-deep for other age groups. Also German records.

European Athletics Yearbook 2003-04. A5 530pp. The EAA's splendidly informative review of 2003 and look ahead to 2004 includes 100-deep European lists for 2003, plus under-23s and juniors, all-time lists and results of the major EAA events. Price 22 euro (for buyers in Europe) or 27 euro elsewhere from Ph. Reinheimer, Druckerei GmbH & Co. KG, c/o EAA, Alsfelder Strasse 27, 64289 Darmstadt, Germany. Payment by cash or by bank transfer to – account: Justus von Liebig Verlag Darmstadt, bank: Postgiroamt Ffm, BLZ: 500 100 60, account no: 51 889-604.

Yleisurheilu 2003. A5 640pp. The Finnish annual, by Juhani and Mirko Jalava published in December 2003 includes the usual very deep Finnish lists for all age groups – down to 9! – with results of championships and international matches. It also contains indoor and outdoor world lists for 2003 with information received as at mid-November. 25 euro or £17 in Europe, rest of world $30 from Tilastopaja Oy, Raskinpolku 9 E 88, 20360 Turku, Finland. Can be ordered by email from juhani@tilastopaja.fi – there is also a credit card facility.

Athlérama 2002. The French Annual, edited by Jean Gilbert and Patricia Doilin with a strong team of compilers, is again a superb reference book. A5, 672pp. Packed with information on French athletics – deep year lists for 2002, profiles, results, all-time lists for all age groups, and French top ten lists for 1952 and top marks for 1902. Also many colour photos. Price 25 euros from the FFA, 33 avenue Pierre de Coubertin, 75640 Paris CEDEX 13, France.

DLV-Jahrbuch 2002. A5 378pp. The official yearbook of the German Federation. Directory and review, with articles on top athletes, detailed results of 2002 meetings, records and top tens, also many illustrations in colour. Euro 17.90 plus postage, from Deutsche Leichtathletik Marketing GmbH, Postfach 10 04 63, 64219 Darmstadt, Germany.

DLV-Bestenliste 2002. A5 432pp. The DLV's ranking lists for 2002 for all events compiled by Eberhard Vollmer, generally 50-deep for seniors and Jugend-A, 30-deep for other age groups.

Greek Athletics Annual 2002. A5 288pp. Published by SEGAS. 50 deep performers and 20 deep performances for 2002, with 10 deep all-time lists and biographical profiles of leading Greek athletes, records and results. In Greek characters. Also published was a 616 page annual covering **2000 and 2001**.

Israeli Athletics 2003/4 Annual compiled by David and Arik Cooks. 235 x 168mm 48pp. $6 US or 5 Euro from David Eiger, 10 Ezra Hozsofer Str, Herzliya 46 371, Israel. Records, championship results, 2003 top ten and all-time lists, and profiles of leading Israeli athletes.

Japan Athletics Annual 2003. A5 296pp. The Japan AAF Annual has 100-deep lists for 2002 and 50-deep senior and junior all-time lists with championship results and articles on the top ten Japanese athletes of the year (in English). From Yoshimasa Noguchi, Track & Field Magazine, BBM Co. Ltd., 3-10-10 Misaki-cho, Chiyoda-ku, Tokyo 101-8381, Japan.

Latvijas Vieglatletikas Gadagramata 2004. A5 324 pp. Comprehensive coverage of Latvian athletics, including 2003 and records, all-time lists, results and biographies, compiled by Andris Stagis. From the Latvian Athletic Association, Augsiela 1, Riga LV-1009, Latvia.

Annuare FLA 2003. A4 120p. The Luxembourg Annual, edited by Georges Klepper, has every possible detail for this nation. 14 euros in Europe, 18 euros elsewhere to account no. LU32 1111 0200

0321 0000. See www.fla.lu; e-mail: fla@fla.lu.

KNAU Statistisch jaarboek 2003. A5 348pp. The Netherlands yearbook provides a chronology of top events, results, records and detailed year lists for seniors and A/B category juniors in 2003 with all-time top tens. EUR 25 in Europe and 30 outside Europe. Further **Netherlands Statistical Yearbooks** include 2002 juniors CD [i.e. born 87-90] (52pp): Europe EUR 8; outside Europe EUR 9; Indoor 1999/2000 to 2002/03: each year: Europe EUR 8; outside Europe EUR 9.. Send cash (euros only) to: KNAU, Afdeling Verkoop, Postbox 230, 3400 AE IJsselstein, The Netherlands.

Pacific Statistics –Tony Isaacs continues his great series. Available for £5 sterling or Euros 10 in banknotes from Tony Isaacs, 11 Manton Close, Trowbridge, Wiltshire, BA14 0RZ, England. E-mail: tony.isaacs2@tinyworld.co.uk. Previous editions also available at the same price.

No. 23 included detailed ranking lists for 2002 for Melanesia with performances in international and national championships. There are also South Pacific all-time lists for the javelin, the star event for the islanders of the region.

No. 24 (56pp) included top 20 Melanesian performances 2003, with details of Melanesian athletes at international championships and matches, national championships and complete results of the Oceania Cup and South Pacific Games in 2003.

Scottish Athletics Yearbook 2003. A5 268p. Edited by Arnold Black for the SATS, this is the usual very comprehensive review of Scottish athletics. There are articles, deep Scottish lists for all age groups, records, event reviews and championship results for the year 2002 with lists of Scottish champions over the past 20 years and all-time lists. There is a 4-page section of colour photographs and the book remains remarkable value at £5 (£6.50 including postage in the UK, £7.50 Europe, £8.50 elsewhere), sterling cheques only, payable to S.A.T.S. From Arnold Black, 19 Millbrae Crescent, Langside, Glasgow G42 9UW, UK.

El Atletismo Sudamericano 2003. A5 160pp. By Edgardo Fontana and Luis Vinker. South American records and lists (40 performers and 10 performances) for 2002. Details from Confederación Sudamericana de Atletismo, Avda. 7 de Setembro 874/3° andar Manaus, Brazil CEP 69005-140. email: consudatle@consudatle.org.br

Spanish Winter Annual 2002/2003 gives most comprehensive details for the first time of both Spanish cross country and indoor seasons. 392 pages, A5. It is available for 14 euros from: Spanish Athletics Federation (Publications Department), Avda. Valladolid, 81, 28008 Madrid, SPAIN.

Spanish Athletics Annual 2002/2003. This is an amazing book, a massive 792 pages – not only an annual, with immense depth of results and annual lists for 2003, but all with much of historical record, such as all-time lists, details of all Spanish champions, lists of Spanish international matches and all Spanish performances at major championships, with biographies of current stars, features and colour photographs. Price 22 euros including postage from: Federación Española de Atletismo, Avda. Valladolid 81 - 1° - 28.008 Madrid SPAIN. E-mail: publicaciones@rfea.es. Details at: http://www.sportec.es/rfea/revista/libros/ranking.htm.

Annuario 2002/2003 – Pista Cubierta y Campo a Través. A5 392pp. Another amazing book from the Spanish federation, covering indoor and cross-country. See www.rfea.es.

Friidrott 2002. A5 384pp. The tenth edition of this attractive annual by Göran Lenz covering world and Scandinavian athletics. Detailed championships results with narrative and world outdoor top 50 year and all-time lists, top 25 Scandinavian year and all-time lists plus indoor top tens. $49 Europe, $52 rest of the world. 355 kr. Details from Gordons Förlag, Bärnstensvägen 2, 226 51 Lund, Sweden. email: goran.lenz@swipnet.se

Swiss Athletics 2002. A5 338p. The 29th edition of this Annual provides the usual comprehensive compilation of Swiss records, results, year lists and all-time top tens. While without the extra details of the 2001 edition, there are also statistical profiles of 18 top athletes. From the Schweizerischer Leichtathletik Verband (SLV), Postfach 8222, CH 3001, Bern.

2003 USA Track & Field Media Guide & FAST Annual (general editors: Jill M Geer & Scott S Davis). A5 625pp. The 25th edition of the FAST Annual is again combined with the USATF Media Guide (first 192 pages of this edition) and includes 16 pages of colour photographs. Packed with US statistics and extensive index material including annual progressions etc. for all top American athletes (with distances in Imperial only!). The US lists for 2002 and the senior all-time lists are 50-deep, with 12-deep all-time junior and college lists. Price $20 ($24 sea-mail, $32 airmail to Europe) from Scott Davis, 4432 Snowbird Circle, Cerritos, CA 90703, USA.

Welsh Athletics Annual 2003. A5 278pp. Compiled and edited by Ken Bennett for the Athletics Association of Wales, The Manor, Coldra Woods, Newport, NP18 1WA, from whom the book can be obtained at £7.50 including postage. The Welsh Annual contains detailed reviews and results of the sport in Wales in 2002 with records and ranking lists for 2002 and all-time. The end piece contains a career review of the greatest ever Welsh athlete – Colin Jackson.

World Junior Athletics Annual 2002/2003, by Lionel Peters. A5, 84pp. Results of World and

Continental Junior Championships in 2002, 30-deep world junior lists for 2002, World junior records progressions 1950-2003 and age bests 12-19. Price (inc postage; payment by cash or UK cheque): UK/Europe £10, elsewhere £12. Non-UK cheque add £8. From World Junior Athletics News, 40 Berkeley Road, London NW9 9DG, England. email lionel@wjan.org.

World Junior Indoor Handbook 2003/2004, by Lionel Peters. 54pp. Includes world all-time lists (at 31.12.03), 'world record' progression, area records, junior placings at previous World Indoor Champs, and world junior results and lists for 2003. UK/Europe £8 (15 euro), elsewhere £10 ($20).

World Junior Cross Country Annual 2003/2004, by Lionel Peters. 40pp. UK/Europe £5 (10 euro), elsewhere £6 ($12); orders as above. Both books ordered together: UK/Europe £12 (20 euro), elsewhere £15 ($30).

Track Stats Historical Series: Women's Hurdles (men and women) by Stuart Mazdon. A5 88pp. The seventh in the NUTS series of event reviews for British includes: progressive UK records, senior and U20, indoors and out, age bests and very deep UK performer and performance all-time lists, best performances for each decade, results of all British internationals, national and area champions, and biographies. Previous issues on 400m (men), 1500m/1M (men), and men's and women's combined booklets on TJ, DT and JT are also available, with that for the long jump imminent.

Statistical bulletins

The **DGLD – German** statistical group, the Deutschen Gesellschaft für Leichtathletik-Dokumentation, was founded in 1990. Its members produce annual national ranking lists (see **Deutsche Bestenliste**) for Germany and most impressive bulletins of up to 268 pages, packed with historical articles and statistical compilations. Each issue (three per year) includes statistical profiles of athletes born in that quarter 70 years ago, 75, 80, 85, 90 etc. In 2003 bulletins no. 36-38 were published.

No. **37** was the **Jahrbuch der Leichtathletik 1945/6** by Otto Verhoeven. 208 A5 pages. This book includes articles, records, results and year lists for 1945 (naturally very thin for the last War year) and 1946.

No. **38** of 228 pages continued the detailed documentation of German athletics prior to 1945, and also has the first part of a series of deep (250-300) performers for the GDR with the men's 100m, 200m and 400m, German all-time lists for the imperial distances of 2, 3 and 6 miles, and the usual profiles of athletes.

Membership, with free Deutsche Bestenliste costs Euro 45 per year. Details from Hans Waynberg, Grefrather Weg 100, 41464 Neuss/Rh, Germany. Website: www.ladgld.de

Track Stats. The NUTS quarterly bulletin, edited by Bob Phillips, includes a wealth of fascinating statistics and articles. A5, generally about 80 pages. Annual subscription (4 issues) is £17 (UK), £21 (rest of Europe) or £26 (elsewhere); contact Liz Sissons, 9 Fairoak Lane, Chessington, Surrey KT9 2NS, UK.

March 2003 included a review of the Chinese women's distance records from 1993 including a career record of Wang Junxia, how Horace Ashenfelter prepared for his 1952 Olympic steeplechase victory, the careers of Maurice Herriott, Ernie Pomfret and Barney Ewell, and a list of every sub-8:30 2 miles (more than 450 of them).

June 2003 included reports and photos of the first sub-1:46 800m (1955), features on little known American 400m stars Alan Helffrich and Elmore Harris, Colin Jackson's career record, Eric Liddell's races in 1923... and the truth about Johnny Mathis's high jumping achievements.

December 2003 covered the miling scene in the 1960s and 1970s with articles on Peter Snell, Jim Ryun, Kip Keino, Filbert Bayi and John Walker. David Thurlow interviews Don Seaman, who ran on the British world 4 x 1 mile relay team in 1953. With Peter Matthews' UK indoor lists for 2003 and a career record for Sergey Bubka by Giuseppe Mappa.

February 2004. In anticipation of the 50th anniversary celebrations, this included an alphabetical list of 964 sub-4 min milers, plus various statistical compilations. Among other features: the careers of Derek Johnson, Valerie Winn and Phyl Perkins, the 1938 Germany v USA match in Berlin and Eric Liddell in 1924.

The **Spanish group**, the **AEEA** continues to produce magnificent statistical publications, with four A5 bulletins each year packed with statistical items. AEEA secretary is Ignacio Mansilla – imansilla2000@hotmail.com.

AEEA bulletin No. 66 February 2003 A5 234pp. The main sections were: a). deep Spanish all-time lists for all sprints events indoors and out with tables of best all-round sprinters; b). Spanish Lists for 2002; c). European U23 records; d). World and European records for over 30s and over 35s set 1996-2002; e). Deep men's and women's all-time lists for 1000 metres.

An annual subscription is 55 euros, £32 or $45 in Europe (or 61 euros, £35, $50 for the rest of the world) payable in cash or international money order to Asociación Española de Estadisticos de Atletismo. Orders and enquiries to: José Luis Hernández, C/Carril 21 – 28530 Morata de Tajuña. Madrid, Spain.

No. 68 October 2003 is a splendid 350-page publication featuring biographies of the top 500 World Women Athletes of All-time (in Spanish) by Enric Pla. This follows the previous three issues that covered the selection of the top 1000 Men of all-time.

No. 69 December 2003 included world indoor lists for 2003, career details for Valentín Massana, and details of the San Silvestre de São Paulo road race. Price: 20 euros and orders to José Luis Hernández or Ignacio Mansilla (AEEA General Secretary), C/Encinar del Rey, nº 18, 28.450 Collado Mediano (Madrid), Spain. E-mail: imc987@terra.es

Polymédias, 103 rue de Paris, 94220 Charenton le Pont, France will handle subscriptions for the major athletics magazines including their own **la letter de l'athlétisme** (42 euro outside France), **Leichtathletik** (Germany), **Track and Field News** (USA), and **Athletics International** (UK). www.polymedias.fr. Their catalogue of athletics books and magazine **la mémoire du sport** includes a large list of publications (including rare historical items) available.

Umbra Athletics have a wealth of invaluable books for the statistician. list from: Unit 1, Bredbury Business Park, Bredbury Park Way, Stockport, SK6 2SN, England (email: julie@umbra.co.uk). These include books that Rob Whittingham (Treasurer) holds for the ATFS. Included are: IAAF Statistics Handbooks produced for many events 1990-2001, ATFS Annuals for 1975 (£5), 1976 (£8), 1979 (£5), 1984 (£7.95), 1987 (£9.95), 1992 (£13.95). Also: National Athletics records – various editions 1975-98, Race Walking World Statistics (many in the 1980s), British Athletics Annuals 1988-2004, and other national publications. ATFS Track & Field Performances Through The Years Volumes 2, 3 and 4 (£20 each).

General

Athens to Athens – The Official History of the Olympic Games and the IOC 1894-2004. 280x230mm. 528pp. David Miller, who has covered 16 Summer and Winter Olympic Games as a journalist, was commissioned by the IOC to write their history and he does this skilfully, alternating chapters on the evolution of the IOC with descriptions of each Games. Each of these begins with a personal reminiscence by a leading figure. The major stories on Olympic history are well known from many works, but all are covered here by an expert who had produced an outstanding book; The appendices include lists of all medal winners and medal tables for each Games. Published by Mainstream Publishing, 7 Albany Street, Edinburgh EH1 3UG. www.mainstreampublishing.com at £35.

Whitaker's Olympic Almanack 2004, 228x147mm, 299 pp. By Stan Greenberg, This is an updated version of a comprehensive reference book covering all sports, with concise yet highly informative and entertaining accounts of each Games in chronological order. The extensive statistical section includes the first three in every event, with such facts as the youngest and oldest medallists and a table of medals won by nation. Price £16.99. Publishers: A & C Black Ltd, 317 Soho Square, London W1D 3QZ; e-mail: enquiries@acblack.com

To be published in June:

Arthur Lydiard Master Coach. Garth Gilmour, a close friend to Arthur Lydiard, possibly the most successful and influential running coach of the 20th century, tells for the first time the full story of the coach's amazing career, often in Lydiard's own words. Lydiard burst into prominence at the 1960 Olympics when two of his protégés, Peter Snell and Murray Halberg, won gold medals on the same day. He had turned unpromising athletes into Olympic champions, and he said he could repeat the feat if only his methods, which involved building stamina and fitness through endurance running, were followed. In the next few years thousands of people heeded his word as the jogging boom took hold. While Lydiard's abrasive personality upset athletics officials in New Zealand, his methods spread through many countries and even now, at the age of 86, he still travels to the United States every year to lecture. £17.99 in UK, Europeans add £2.00, rest of world add £4 for postage; from SportsBooks.

MARIA MUTOLA

In 2003 Maria Mutola enjoyed the unique success of being the sole winner of the $1 million IAAF Golden League Jackpot for winning all her races in the series. To that she added her fifth World Indoor title and her third World outdoor title and was unbeaten in 18 finals. That was a superb record, but a look at her career shows marvellous success ever since she first emerged as a world-class runner in 1991.

She ran 2:04.36 for 800m in the heats of the Olympic Games in Seoul in 1988 a month before her 16th birthday and then was then enabled to attend school in Eugene, Oregon, USA by a grant from the Olympic Solidarity Committee. She had season's bests of 2:05.7 in 1989 and 2:13.54 in 1990.

Career summary 1991-2003

Year	*800m*			*1000m*		*1500m/1M*		*400m*	
	Best	*wins*	*sub 2*	*Best*	*wins*	*Best*	*wins*	*Best*	*wins*
1991	1:57.63	5/6	3	–		4:12.72	0/2	–	
1992	1:57.49	8/12	8	–		4:02.60	4/5	52.69	1/1
1993	1:55.43	17/17	13	2:32.57	1/1	4:04.97	2/3	51.44	1/1
1994	1:55.19	11/11	8	2:33.02	2/2	4:13.93	2/2	51.46	0/1
1995	1:55.72	16/17*	14	2:29.34	3/3	4:01.6	1/1		
1996	1:57.07	4/5	7	2:29.66	3/4	4:01.63	1/5		
1997	1:55.29	13/14	13	–		4:09.1	1/1	52.3	2/2
1998	1:56.11	17/18	18	2:31.55	1/1			52.38	2/2
1999	1:56.04	13/18	18	2:30.94i	2/3			–	
2000	1:56.15	6/7	8	2:35.68i	1/1	4:02.39	0/2	–	
2001	1:56.85	8/15	16	2:33.53	1/1			–	
2002	1:56.16	11/16	13	2:30.12	2/2	4:01.50	1/1	51.55	2/2
2003	1:55.55	15/15	16	2:33.15	2/2	–		–	
TOTAL		144/171	155		18/20		12/22		6/9

Other distances: 200m: 2/2, 600m 2/2, 1200m 1/1, 1 mile road 1/2, 2000m 0/1

* Disqualified when winning her semi-final at the World Championships (included in sub-2 numbers as she ran 1:58.20), the only blemish on an otherwise run of 50 successive 800m wins from 2nd to Ellen van Langen in Berlin on 21 Aug 1992 to the Olympic final in Atlanta on 29 Aug 1996, when she was 3rd behind Svetlana Masterkova 1:57.73 and Ana Quirot 1:58.11.

Mutola's domination of her event can readily be seen – the only rival to gain a substantial edge for a while was Steffi Graf who beat Mutola six times in 2001 and three times indoors in 2002. Importantly, also, Svetlana Masterkova beat her to win the 1996 Olympic 800m title and gave Mutola her only losses at 1000m in 1996 (when Masterkova set the world record of 2:28.98) and in 1999.

Mutola's tally of sub-2 minute 800m times includes three during 1000m races (1 each in 1995, 1999 and 2002)

Mutola has started 2004 with 3 wins in 3 meetings at 800m and 4 more sub2 minute times, but she fell and did not finish in her one race at 1000m.

Athletes to have won World Youth, Junior and Senior Titles

World Youth (U18) Championships were first held in 1999, so the opportunity to achieve world titles at three age groups is a very new one. But within four years it had been achieved:

Jana Pittman AUS won WY 400mh 1999, WJ 400m & 400mh 2000, WCh 400mh 2003.

Jacques Freitag RSA won WY 1999, WJ 2000 and WCh 2003 at high jump.

Yelena Isinbayeva RUS won WY 1999, WJ 2000 and WI 2004 at pole vault.

Note that Kamila Skolimowska POL was the World Youth hammer champoion in 1999 and won the Olympic title in 2000 – but failed to make the final at two World Junior Championships.

HALL OF FAME 2004

WE INTRODUCED the Hall of Fame in the 2001 – and made five selections that year and in 2002. After a reader's poll we then added another 27 names in 2003. The list of selections thus stood as:

Men

Abebe Bikila ETH, Valeriy Brumel RUS, Sergey Bubka UKR, Sebastian Coe GBR, Jonathan Edwards GBR, Haile Gebrselassie ETH, Vladimir Golubnichiy RUS, Colin Jackson GBR, Michael Johnson USA, Robert Korzeniowski POL, Carl Lewis USA, Edwin Moses USA, Paavo Nurmi FIN, Parry O'Brien USA, Al Oerter USA, Jesse Owens USA, Viktor Saneyev RUS, Yuriy Sedykh RUS, Peter Snell NZL, Daley Thompson GBR, Lasse Viren FIN, Cornelius Warmerdam USA, Emil Zátopek CZE, Jan Zelezny CZE

Women

Iolanda Balas ROM, Fanny Blankers-Koen NED, Nadezhda Chizhova RUS, Gail Devers USA, Heike Drechsler GER, Ruth Fuchs GDR, Jackie Joyner-Kersee USA, Tatyana Kazankina RUS, Marita Koch GDR, Faina Melnik RUS, Maria Mutola MOZ, Gabriela Szabo ROM, Irena Szewinska POL

Having established many of the great names of our sport we now revert to five additions per year. And our five 2004 additions are:

Herb Elliott (Australia) (b. 25 Feb 1938) – Elliott had just two years, 1958 and 1960, at the head of world middle distance running, yet in that short time he established such a reputation that he remains many experts' selection as the greatest ever. Undefeated at 1500m or 1 mile in 49 races from 1954 to 1960 he set world records for the former with 3:36.0 in 1958, 2.1 secs off the old mark, and 3:35.6 when he won the Olympic title in 1960 by the huge margin of 2.8 secs. At 1 mile he improved Derek Ibbotson's 1957 record of 3:57.2 to 3:54.5 in Dublin in 1958, shortly after winning the Commonwealth Games double at 880y and 1 mile.

Kip Keino (Kenya) (b. 17 Jan 1940) – Keino was the pioneer of the great Kenyan running tradition, and a great crowd-pleaser with his long stride and huge talent. At the 1968 Olympics he won the 1500m and was second at 5000m, and in 1972 won the 3000m steeplechase and was second at 1500m. He won Commonwealth titles at 1 mile and 3 miles in 1966 and at 1500m in 1970, when he was third at 5000m. In 1965 he, Ron Clarke and Michel Jazy rewrote the record books for the distance events, Keino setting world records at 3000m (7:39.6) and 5000m (13:24.2) as well as claiming a 1500m/5000m double at the first African Games.

Ingrid Kristiansen (Norway) (b. 21 Mar 1956) – Kristiansen was the only athlete to hold world records at 5000m, 10,000m and marathon and the first to win world titles at track (10,000m 1987), road (15km 1987 and 1988) and cross-country (1988). She set a European best 2:24:26 in winning the 1984 London marathon and a world best there of 2:21:06 in 1985. She reached her peak form in 1986, when she won her first gold medal, the European 10,000m about half a lap ahead of the runner-up. She set her third world record for 5000m, 14:37.33, and improved her own record at 10,000m from 30:59.42 to 30:13.74 (Bislett Games in Oslo 1985 and 1986). Her world records lasted for 9, 7 and 13 years respectively. She had won bronze medals in the World 3000m in 1980, European marathon in 1982 and World Cross-country 1985 and 1987.

Noureddine Morceli (Algeria) – Morceli was world champion at 1500m indoors in 1991 and outdoors in 1991, 1993 and 1995 and Olympic champion in 1996. As well as many near misses, Morceli set world records for 1500m with 3:28.86 in Rieti 1992 and 3:27.37 at Nice in 1993,1 mile 3:44.39 at Rieti in 1993, 2000m 4:47.88 at Paris in 1995 and 3000m 7:25.11 at Monaco 1995, as well as indoors at 1000m (2:15.26 in 1992) and 1500m (3:34.16 in 1991). He was overall Grand Prix champion and the World Cup winner in 1994, but the end of the era of his supremacy as king of 1500m/1M came as after 45 successive wins at 1500m/1M from 1992 when he was second to Hicham El Guerrouj at the 1996 Grand Prix Final.

Paula Radcliffe (Great Britain) – Radcliffe's sensational running in 2002 and 2003 have propelled her into the Hall of Fame. She had a superb London marathon win in 2002, when her 2:18:56 was the second fastest ever run, over three minutes faster than the previous best in a women's only race and over four minutes better than the previous fastest debut marathon. She followed with her first major championships track titles with extraordinary runs in the European 10,000m and Commonwealth 5000m and she capped it all by taking 1:29 off the world record for the marathon in Chicago and another 1:53 improvement to 2:15:25 in London 2003. She has won five world titles: CC 2001 and 2002, Half Marathon 2000, 2001 and 2003, as well as the Junior CC 1992.

Herb Elliott (photo courtesy of Track & Field News)

Ingrid Kristiansen

Kip Keino

Noureddine Morceli

Paul Radcliffe seals her place in the Hall of Fame by winning the London Marathon in a world record time

Kenenisa Bekele leads fellow Ethiopian Gebre Gebremariam in the 2003 IAAF World Cross Country Championships

Saif Saaeed Shaheen (formerly Stephen Cherono) wins the IAAF World Championship steeplechase

Allen Johnson (right) beats beats Terrence Trammell (left, 2nd) and Liu Xiang (centre, 3rd) to retain his world 110m hurdles crown

Roger Bannister achieves the first sub four-minute mile (photo courtesy of Track & Field News)

NATIONAL CHAMPIONS 2003 and BIOGRAPHIES OF LEADING ATHLETES

By Peter Matthews

THIS SECTION incorporates biographical profiles of 746 of the world's top athletes, 400 men and 346 women, listed by nation. Also listed are national champions at standard events in 2003 for the leading countries prominent in athletics.

Those profiled have, as usual, changed quite considerably from the previous year, not only that all entries have been updated, but also that many newcomers have been included to replace those who have retired or faded a little from the spotlight. The choice of who to include is always invidious, but I have concentrated on those who are currently in the world's top 10-15 per event, those who have the best championship records and some up-and-coming athletes who I consider may make notable impact during the coming year.

Since this section was introduced in the 1985 Annual, biographies have been given for a total of 3088 athletes (1801 men and 1287 women).

The continuing high turnover in our sport is relected in the fact that there are 131 newcomers (79 men, 51 women) to this section, with 21 (7 men, 15 women) reinstated from previous Annuals. As in the 2002 and 2003 Annuals, there is just one athlete who has been profiled every year – Heike Drechsler.

No doubt some of those dropped from this compilation will also again make their presence felt; the keen reader can look up their credentials in previous Annuals, and, of course, basic details may be in the athletes' index at the end of this book.

Athletes included in these biographies are identified in the index by * for those profiled in this Annual and by ^ for those included in previous Annuals.

When I started this section in the 1985 Annual the 578 athletes included 98 from USA, 94 USSR, 63 GDR, 31 FRG, 41 GBR and (all men) just 13 KEN and 5 ETH. The 746 in this Annual include 105 USA, 93 RUS, 26 UKR, 31 GER, 25 GBR, 69 KEN and 21 ETH. Quite a change.

The biographical information includes:

a) Name; date and place of birth; height (in metres); weight (in kilograms).
b) Previous name(s) for married women; club or university; occupation.
c) Major championships record – all placings in such events as the Olympic Games, World Championships, European Championships, Commonwealth Games, World Cup and European Cup Super League; leading placings in finals of the World Indoor Championships, European or World Junior Championships, European Under-23 Championships and other Continental Championships; and first three to six in European Indoors or World University Games.
IAAF Grand Prix first three at each event or overall.
World Athletics Final (WAF) winners
d) National (outdoor) titles won or successes in other major events.
e) Records set: world, continental and national; indoor world records/bests (WIR/WIB).
f) Progression of best marks over the years at each athlete's main event(s).
g) Personal best performances at other events.
h) Other comments.

See Introduction to this Annual for lists of abbreviations used for events and championships.

Note that for comparison purposes decathlons and heptathlons made before the introduction of the current tables have been rescored using the 1984 IAAF Tables, except those marked *, for which event breakdowns were unavailable. Women's pentathlons (p) have not been rescored.

Information given is as known at 4 April 2004 (to include performances at the World Indoor Championships and the World Cross-country Championships as well as some early outdoor events).

I am most grateful to various ATFS members who have helped check these details. Additional information or corrections would be welcomed for next year's Annual. **Peter Matthews**

ALGERIA

Governing body: Fédération Algerienne d'Athlétisme, BP n°61, Dely-Ibrahim, Alger. Founded 1963.

Abderahmane HAMMAD b. 27 May 1977 1.89m 70kg.

At HJ: OG: '00- 3; WCh: '99- 10=, '01- 10=, '03- dnq 22=; WJ: '96- dnq 22=; AfG: '99- 2; AfCh: '98- 1, '00- 1, '02- 1, Af-J: '95- 1; WCp: '98- 6=, '02- 4; won MedG 2001, 3rd GP 2002.

Three African high jump records 1999-2000.

Progression at HJ: 1993- 2.00, 1994- 2.10, 1995- 2.12, 1996- 2.16, 1997- 2.24, 1998- 2.21, 1999- 2.32, 2000- 2.34, 2001- 2.29, 2002- 2.31, 2003- 2.30.

Djabir SAÏD-GUERNI b. 29 Mar 1977 Algers 1.87m 70kg. Army sergeant.

At 800m: OG: '00- 3; WCh: '99- 3, '03- 1; WJ: '96- h; AfCh: '98- 3, '00- 1/1R, '02- 1; WUG: '99- 4; WCp: '02- 2.

Two Algerian 800m records 1999.

Progression at 800m: 1997- 1:46.84, 1998- 1:45.72, 1999- 1:43.09, 2000- 1:43.25, 2001- 1:44.55, 2002- 1:44.03, 2003- 1:44.60. pbs: 400m 46.15 '00, 46.1 '03; 1000m 2:14.52 '99.

Made huge breakthrough at 1999 World Champs, when he reduced his pb of 1:45.72 to 1:45.65, 1:45.17 and 1:44.18 in successive rounds to the bronze medal. Then 3rd in Brussels in 1:43.09. In 2001 he married Wassila Rédoune, African champion who competed for ALG at the 2000 Olympic Games at fencing. His older brother Chakib ran on the team that was 2nd at 4x100m in the 1994 African Junior Champs.

Ali SAÏDI SIEF b. 15 Mar 1978 Constantine 1.80m 68kg. ENA d'Angers, France.

At 1500m: WCh: '97- h, '99- sf; WJ: '96- 7; AfCh: '98- 3. At 3000m: WI: '99- 9; 2nd GP 2000. At 5000m: OG: '00- 2; WCh: '01- dq 2; AfCh: '00- 1. World CC: '97- 17J, '00- 16 (4k).

World junior 2000m record 1997. Algerian records 3000m and 5000m 2000, 2000m 2001.

Progression at 1500m, 5000m: 1996- 3:41.6, 1997- 3:37.47, 1998- 3:35.87, 1999- 3:30.91, 13:39.5; 2000- 3:30.82, 12:50.86; 2001- 3:29.51, 13:02.16; 2003- 3:40.22. pbs: 1M 3:48.23 '01, 2000m 4:46.88 '01, 3000m 7:25.02 '00.

Tested positive for Nandrolene after taking second place in World 5000m 2001 and served two-year drugs ban, On his return in 2003 had a major win at 3000m in Brussels in 7:30.79.

Women

Baya RAHOULI b. 27 Jul 1979 1.76m 58kg.

At TJ(/LJ): OG: '00- 5; WCh: '99- 10, '03- 11; WJ: '96- 10, '98- 1; WI: '03- 7, '04- 10; WCp: '98- 6; AfG:'95- 4, '99- 2/6; AfCh: '98- 1/3, '00- 1; Af-J: '94- 1, '95- 1/2, '97- 1/2 (1 100mh); WUG: '99- 4; won MedG 2001.

Six African triple jump records 1998-9. ALG LJ records 1998-9.

Progression at TJ: 1993- 11.76, 1994- 12.05, 1995- 13.09, 1996- 13.48, 1997- 13.55, 1998- 14.04, 1999- 14.64A/14.30, 2000- 14.30/14.42w, 2001- 13.88/14.30w, 2002- 14.02, 2003- 14.48, 2004- 14.31i. pbs: 100m 11.1/11.62/11.51w '99, 100mh 13.50 '98, LJ 6.70 '99.

Brother Hamimed Rahouli set African 50km walk record of 4:19:15 in 1987.

ARGENTINA

Governing body: Confederación Argentina de Atletismo, 21 de Noviembre No. 207. 3260 Concepción del Uruguay, Entre Ríos.

National Championships first held in 1920 (men), 1939 (women). **2003 Champions: Men**: 100m/200m: Matías Usandivaras 10.55/21.47, 400m: Gustavo Aguirre 47.27, 800m/1500m: Sebastián González Cabot 1:52.74/3:47.56, 5000m: José Mansilla 14:42.38 (Cristian Rosales URU 14:33.41), 10000m: Juan Suárez 29:52.03, HMar: Oscar Cortnez 65:28, Mar: Daniel Simbrón 2:18:44, 3000mSt: Mariano Mastromarino 8: 58.48, 110mh: Leandro Peyrano 14.65, 400mh: José Pignataro 52.76, HJ: Erasmo Jara 2.09, PV: Javier Benítez 5.31, LJ: Eric Kerwitz 7.23, TJ: Mariano Sala 15.45, SP: Adrián Marzo 15.63, DT: Marcelo Pugliese 58.42, HT: Juan Cerra 74.29, JT: Pablo Pietrobelli 66.32, Dec: Enrique Aguirre 6599, 20000mW: Jorge Loréfice 1:37:47.0. **Women**: 100m: Vanesa Wohlgemuth 11.81, 200m: Daniela Lebreo 24.36, 400m/800m: Andrea Rossotti 55.16/2:11.61, 1500m: Natalia Siviero 4:43.79 (Elena Guerra URU 4:35.84; Valeria Rodríguez 4:23.56 doping dq), 5000m: Karina Córdoba 17: 34.97, 10000m: Sandra Torres Álvarez 36:03.62, HMar/Mar: Verónica Páez 77:55/2:49:57, 3000mSt: María de los Ángeles Peralta 10:33.71, 100mh: María de la Paz Azzato 14.60, 400mh: Verónica Barraza 66.83, HJ: Claudia Casals 1.76, PV: Alejandra García 4.10, LJ: Andrea Morales 5.93, TJ: Silvia Sastre URU 12.22w, SP: Paola Cheppi 14.56, DT: Natalia Ortiz 43.47, HT: Karina Moya 59.15, JT: Romina Maggi 52.40, Hep: Daniela Crespo 4388, 20000mW: Lidia Carriego 2:09:30.0.

AUSTRALIA

Governing body: Athletics Australia, Suite 22, Fawkner Tower, 431 St.Kilda Rd, Melbourne, Victoria 3004. Founded 1897.

National Championships first held in 1893 (men) (Australasian until 1927), 1930 (women). **2003 Champions**: **Men**: 100m/200m: Patrick Johnson 10.25/20.50, 400m: Clinton Hill 45.50, 800m: Kris McCarthy 1:48.20, 1500m: Alastair Stevenson 3:42.99, 3000m/5000m: Michael Power 8:00.45/13:55.99, 10000m: Shaun Creighton 29: 27.56, HMar: Scott Westcott 64:44, Mar: Paul Arthur 2:31:27, 3000mSt: Peter Nowill 8:41.61, 110mh: Kyle VanderKuyp 13.98, 400mh: Michael Hazel 50.50, HJ: Joshua Lodge 2.21, PV: Dmitri

Markov 5.50, LJ: Peter Burge 7.82w, TJ: Andrew Murphy 16.73, SP: Justin Anlezark 20.96, DT: Peter Elvy 58.42, HT: Stuart Rendell 76.61, JT: Andrew Currey 80.56, Dec: Matt McEwen 7724, 20kmW: Luke Adams 1:23:22, 30kmW: Frank Bertei 2:27:21, 50kmW: Duane Cousins 3:59:33. **Women**: 100m/200m: Sharon Cripps 11.50/23.39, 400m: Cathy Freeman 51.66, 800m: Tamsyn Lewis 2:00.13, 1500m: Suzy Walsham 4:12.96, 3000m/10000m/HMar: Anna Thompson 9:21.79/33:55.75/72:27, 5000m: Benita Johnson 15:21.55, Mar: Helen Verity-Tolhurst 2:58:57, 3000mSt: Melissa Rollison 9:56.92, 100mh: Jacquie Munro 13.37, 400mh: Jana Pittman 53.95, HJ: Petrina Price 1.81, PV: Rosanna Ditton 4.20, LJ: Bronwyn Thompson 6.55, TJ: Jeanette Bowles 12.72, SP: Belinda Johnson 14.26, DT: Debbie Pickersgill 58.92, HT: Brooke Krueger 66.41, JT: Rebecca Noy 52.26, Hep: Kylie Wheeler 5838, 10kmW: Simone Wolowiec 47:45, 20kmW: Jane Saville 1:31:47.

Luke ADAMS b. 22 Oct 1976 Tanzania 1.89m 70kg. Bankstown. Studied indutsrial design.
At 20kmW: WCh: '03- 5; CG: '02- 2. At 10000mW: WJ: '94- 24. Won AUS 30kmW 1998.
Progression at 20kmW: 1995- 1:30:21, 1996- 1:25:27, 1999- 1:23:52, 2000- 1:24:18, 2001- 1:26:31, 2002- 1:23:56, 2003- 1:19:35. pbs: 3000mW 11:48.4 '95. 5000mW 19:34.68 '00, 30kmW 2:17:33 '02, 50kmW 4:04:03 '02.

Justin ANLEZARK b. 14 Aug 1977 Katherine, NT 1.88m 127kg. Toowoomba Glennie.
At SP (DT): OG: '00- dnq 29; WCh: '01- dnq 27, '03- 5; CG: '98- 7, '02- 1; WJ: '94- 12 (dnq), '96- 2 (dnq); WI: '03- 5; WCp: '98- 7, '02- 2. AUS champion 1998, 2000-04.
Six Oceania shot records 2000-03.
Progression at SP: 1993- 14.75, 1994- 16.10, 1995- 17.25, 1996- 18.21, 1997- 18.56, 1998- 19.36, 1999- 18.49, 2000- 20.35, 2001- 20.14, 2002- 20.91, 2003- 20.96. pb DT 54.45 '01.

Nathan DEAKES b. 17 Aug 1977 Geelong 1.83m 66kg. Bellarine, AIS.
At 20kmW(/50kmW): OG: '00- 8/6; WCh: '99- 7, '01- 4/dq; CG: '98- 3, '02- 1/1. At 10000mW: WJ: '96- 3. Won GWG 20000mW 2001, AUS 20kmW 2000-02, 2004; 50kmW 1999 (t).
Commonwealth walk records at 20km, 20,000m track (1:19:48.1) 2001, 50km 2003.
Progression at 20kmW, 50kmW: 1996- 1:26:27, 1997- 1:23:58, 1998- 1:23:25, 1999- 1:20:15, 3:52:53; 2000- 1:21:03, 3:47:29; 2001- 1:18:14, 3:43:43; 2002- 1:21:07, 3:52:40; 2003- 3:39:42. pbs: 3000mW 11:17.0 '98, 5000mW 19:27.4 '97, 10000m 38:44.87 '02, 30kmW 2:11:10 '98, 35kmW 2:35:05 '00.

Patrick JOHNSON b. 26 Sep 1972 near Cairns 1.77m 73kg. AIS. Was at Australian National University. Administrative officer with the Department of Foreign Affairs and Trade.
At 100m/(200m)/4x100mR: OG: '00- qf (qf); WCh: '97- (h), '03- qf (qf); CG: '02- 3R. Won AUS 100m 2003, 200m 2001, 2003.
Oceania 100m record 2003.
Progression at 100m: 1996- 10.47w, 1997- 10.39/10.27w, 1998- 10.43, 1999- 10.17, 2000- 10.10, 2001- 10.25/10.13w, 2002- 20.91, 2003- 9.93/9.88w. pb 200m 20.50/20.25w '03.
Aboriginal mother, Irish father.

Dmitri MARKOV b. 14 Mar 1975 Vitebsk, Belarus 1.82m 85kg. WAIS.
At PV: OG: '96- 6, '00- 5=; WCh: '97- nh, '99- 2, '01- 1, '03- 4; CG: '02- 4=; EI: '96- 1; WJ: '94- 2; EJ: '93- 6. 3rd GP 1999. AUS champion 1998, 2001, 2003-04.
Commonwealth pole vault record 2001, four BLR records 1996-8, four AUS 1999-2001.
Progression at PV: 1991- 4.80, 1992- 5.10, 1993- 5.42, 1994- 5.50, 1995- 5.65, 1996- 5.86, 1997- 5.95, 1998- 6.00, 1999- 5.95, 2000- 5.85, 2001- 6.05, 2002- 5.65, 2003- 5.86. pb LJ 7.31w/7.24 '03.
Became an Australian citizen in May 1999, a month after his wife Valentina, who was granted citizenship as a result of spending two consecutive years in Australia after becoming a permanent resident in April 1997.

Craig MOTTRAM b. 18 Jun 1980 Frankston, Victoria 1.88m 73kg. Deakin. Degree from Deakin University
At 1500m: WCh: '01- sf. At 3000m: WI: '01- 8, '04- 10; WCp: '02- 1. At 5000m: OG: '00- h; CG: '02- 6. World CC: '99- 18J, 4k: '01-02-04: 8/5/9; 12k: '04- 13. Won AUS 1500m 2002, 5000m 2002, 2004; 10000m 2001.
Oceania 3000m & 5000m records 2002.
Progression at 5000m: 1999- 13:40.48, 2000- 13:26.20, 2001- 13:23.94, 2002- 13:12.04, 2003- 13:17.81. pbs: 800m 1:52.90, 1500m: 3:35.40 '01, 1M 3:52.90 '02, 2000m 5:06.97 '01, 3000m 7:37.30 '02, 10000m 27:50.55 '03.
Former AUS junior triathlon champion. British parents, his father Brian played football for Wimbledon.

Women

Bronwyn EAGLES b. 23 Aug 1980 Camden, New South Wales 1.78m 100kg. Campbelltown Collegians.
At HT: WCh: '01- 3, '03- dnq 16; CG: '02- 2; WJ: '98- 8; WCp: '02- 7. Won AUS 2000-02, 2004; E.Asian 2001. Six Oceania and Commonwealth hammer records (68.83 & 68.87) 2001, (69.38, 69.65, 69.65) 2002, 2003.
Progression at HT: 1995- 50.74; 1996- 52.08, 1997- 54.88, 1998- 59.79, 1999- 62.02, 2000- 66.55, 2001- 70.19, 2002- 69.65, 2003- 71.12. pb SP 12.51 '99.

Benita JOHNSON b. 6 May 1979 Mackay, QLD 1.66m 50kg. née Willis. University of Queensland.
At 3000m: WI: '01- 6, '03- 7. At 5000m (1500m): OG: '00- h; WCh: '01- 12; CG: '02- 6 (h); WJ: '98- (7); WUG: '99- (5); WCp: '02- 4. At 10000m:

WC: '03- 8. World HMar: '03- 3; CC: 4km: '01-02-03: 6/4/5; 8km: '04- 1. Won AUS 5000m 2003, 10000M 2004.
Oceania records: 3000m (2) 2001-03, 5000m (3) 2001-02, 2000m & 10000m 2003.
Progression at 5000m, 10000m: 1997- 16:11.57, 1998- 16:31.2, 2000- 15:21.37, 2001- 15:04.18, 2002- 14:47.60, 2003- 14:54.52, 30:37.68. pbs: 800m 2:05.41 '00, 1500m 4:07.05 '00, 2000m 5:37.71 '03, 3000m 8:38.06 '03, HMar 69:26 '03.
Became Australia's first World CC champion in 2004. Under-18 international at hockey. Married Cameron Johnson 2 Feb 2002.

Jana PITTMAN b. 9 Nov 1982 Sydney 1.81m 70kg. Baulkham Hills. Student.
At 400mh(/400m): OG: '00- h; WCh: '03- 1; CG: '02- 1/1R; WJ: '00- 1/1; WY: '99- 1/7; WCp: '02- 3. AUS champion 2001-03.
Equalled world junior record 400mh 2000. Oceania 300m best 2003.
Progression at 400mh: 1998- 59.75, 1999- 56.23, 2000- 55.20A/55.63, 2001- 55.93, 2002- 54.14, 2003- 53.22. pbs: 100m 11.77 '03, 200m 23.52 '03, 300m 36.34 '03, 400m 50.43 '03, 100mh 13.92 '00.
Won the 400m/400mh double at the 2000 World Juniors, the first woman to achieve this feat at an IAAF/IOC event. Named the IAAF Rising Star for 2000. World Champ at Yth, Jnr, Snr.

Jane SAVILLE b. 5 Nov 1974 Sydney 1.64m 53kg. Randwick Botany H.
At 20kmW: OG: '00- dq: WCh: '99- 7, '01- dq, '03- 11; CG: '02- 1. At 10kmW: OG: '96- 26; WCh: '97- h; CG: '94- 8, '98- 1. At 5000mW: WJ: '92- 2. Won AUS 5000mW 1997, 10kmW 1991-2, 1997-8, 20kmW 2000, 2002-04.
Commonwealth 20km walk record 2000.
Progression at 10kmW, 20kmW: 1990- 52:24, 1991- 47:10, 1992- 46:02, 1993- 47:29.1, 1994- 46:04, 1995- 45:10, 1996- 45:22, 1997- 42:59, 1998- 43:38, 1:37:53; 1999- 42:15, 1:31:58; 2000- 44:06, 1:28:56; 2001- 44:40, 1:31:20; 2002- 1:34:18, 2003- 44:43, 1:30:51. pbs: 3000mW 12:27.74 '93, 5000mW 21:32.26 '97.
Disqualified when leading just outside stadium at Sydney Olympics. Married to Matt White, who competed at cycling for Australia at the 1998 Commonwealth Games. Her sister **Natalie** (b. 7 Sep 1978) has represented AUS at WJ, WCp and CG, pbs: 10kmW 45:10 '97, 20kmW 1:35:55 '03.

Bronwyn THOMPSON b. 29 Jan 1978 Rockhampton, Queensland 1.77m 68kg. Southern Suburbs. Physiotherapist.
At LJ: WCh: '03- 7; OG: '00- dnq 16; CG: '02- 6. Australian champion 2002-03.
Oceania long jump records 2001 & 2003.
Progression at LJ: 1992- 5.42, 1993- 5.60, 1994- 6.04/6.14w, 1995- 6.10; 1996- 6.10/6.15w, 1997- 5.95, 2000- 6.56/6.64w, 2001- 6.88, 2002- 7.00, 2003- 6.73/6.75w, pbs: 100m 11.95 '02, 200m 24.19 '03.

AUSTRIA

Governing body: Österreichischer Leichtathletik Verband, 1040 Vienna, Prinz Eugenstrasse 12. Founded 1902.

National Championships first held in 1911 (men), 1918 (women). **2003 Champions**: **Men**: 100m: Martin Lachkovics 10.41, 200m: Thomas Scheidl 20.97, 400: Ralf Hegny 47.94, 800m: Sebastian Resch 1:52.79, 1500m: Daniel Spitzl 3:50.23, 5000m: Martin Pröll 14:10.94, 10000m/3000mSt: Günther Weidlinger 31:22.76/8:30.20, HMar: Harald Steindorfer 66:55, Mar: Michael Buchleitner 2:16:31, 110mh: Leonard Hudec 13.93, 400mh: Karl Lang 53.04, HJ: Pavel Vanicek 2.05, PV: Thomas Agar 4.80, LJ: Roland Schwarzl 7.34, TJ: Klaus Biberauer 15.17, SP: Erwin Pirklbauer 17.18, DT: Gerhard Mayer 59.58, HT: Walter Edletitisch 64.81, JT: Gregor Högler 76.07, Dec: Roland Schwarzl 7491, 20kmW/50kmW: Stephan Wögerbauer 1:36:21/4:46:12. **Women**: 100m/200m: Karin Mayr-Krifka 11.15/23.05, 400m: Stephanie Graf 53.20, 800m: Brigitte Mühlbacher 2:09.36, 1500m: Susanne Pumper 4:19.17, 5000m: Helene Eidenberger 16:58.07, 10000m/3000mSt: Andrea Mayr 36:05.80/11:16.18, HMar/Mar: Eva-Maria Gradwohl 76:38/2:39:48, 100mh: Elke Wölfling 13.15, 400mh: Sabine Gasselseder 59.52, HJ: Andrea Dreier 1.74, PV: Carmen Klausbruckner 3.70, LJ/TJ: Olivia Wöckinger 6.60/13.35, SP: Valentina Fedyushina 15.33, DT: Sonja Spendelhofer 50.73, HT: Claudia Stern 51.86, JT: Veronika Rösing 45.09, Hep: Elisabeth Plazotta 5145, 10kmW: Viera Toporek 52:18.

Günther WEIDLINGER b. 5 Apr 1978 Braunau 1.69m 54kg. SU IGLA Harmonie Linz. Soldier.
At 3000mSt: OG: '00- 8; WCh: '99- 9, '03- h; EC: '98- h, '02- 12; WJ: '96- 4; EU23: '99- 1; EJ: '95- 8, '97- 1. At 3000m: WI: '03- 10. Eur CC: '97-8-02-03: 2J/4/10/11. Won World Univs CC 2000. Won AUT 1500m 1999-2000, 10000m 2003, 3000mSt 1998-9, 2003; CC 2001-02.
Austrian records: 1500m 2000, 3000mSt (3) 1999.
Progression at 3000mSt, 1995- 9:02.15, 1996- 8:38.97, 1997- 8:31.43, 1998- 8:23.13, 1999- 8:10.83, 2000- 8:11.51, 2001- 8:23.62, 2002- 8:23.91, 2003- 8:17.90. pbs: 1500m 3:34.69 '00, 3000m 7:44.19i '03, 5000m 14:32.58 '97, 10000m 29:03.64 '02.

Women

Stephanie GRAF b. 26 Apr 1973 Klagenfurt 1.70m 60kg. LCC Wien.
At 800m: OG: '00- 2; WCh: '97- h, '99- 7, '01- 2, '03- dns; EC: '98- 3; WI: '99-01-03: 6/2/2; EI: '96-8-00-02: 5/6/1/2; 3rd GP 2001. Won AUT 400m 1997-2000, 2003; 800m 1994-7, 1500m 1993-4.
Austrian records 800m (5) 1998-2000, 1000m 2000.
Progression at 800m: 1985- 2:28.50, 1996- 2:24.59, 1987- 2:18.46, 1988- 2:16.11, 1989- 2:12.72, 1990- 2:10.72, 1991- 2:12.80, 1992- 2:09.20, 1993- 2:06.22, 1994- 2:05.36, 1995- 2:05.06, 1996- 2:01.54, 1997- 2:00.27, 1998- 1:57.97, 1999- 1:57.07, 2000- 1:56.64,

2001- 1:57.20, 2002- 1:55.85i, 2003- 1:57.99. pbs: 200m 25.42 '96, 400m 52.69 '99, 600m 1:26.8i '02, 1000m 2:34.47 '98, 1500m 4:13.58 '96, 3000m 9:58.78 '95.
Broke WIR 800m by 0.55 at European Indoors 2002, but beaten by Jolanda Ceplak, one of her five major champs silver medals. Benign tumour removed from her hip in July 2002. Withdrew from World 800m final in 2003 after accident. Surprisingly announced retirement in early 2004. Her mother Rita Graf (née Merva) was Austrian 800m champion in 1974, pb 2:09.4 '71.

BAHAMAS

Governing body: Bahamas Amateur Athletic Association, P.O.Box SS 5517, Nassau. F'd 1952.
National Champions 2003: **Men**: 100m/200m: Dominic Demeritte 10.26/20.61, 400m: Avard Moncur 45.62, 800m: Alexis Roberts 1:53.32, 1500m: Alex Sawyer 4:07.25, 5000m: Delroy Boothe 16:06.63, 110mh: Rhenardo Forbes 14.99, HJ: James Rolle 2.13, PV: Kenny Moxey 4.42, LJ: Leevan Sands 7.80, SP: Bernard Newbold 8.88, DT: Eljin Morrison 40.09, JT: Jermaine Curry 57.54. **Women**: 100m: Chandra Sturrup 11.01, 200m: Debbie Ferguson 22.95, 400m/100mh: Neketa Sears 56.42/14.46, 800m/1500m: Christina Badmus 2:28.47/5:04.56, LJ: Jackie Edwards 6.59, TJ: Daphne Saunders 12.84, SP/DT: Dorisa Thompson 12.78/45.07, JT: Lavern Eve 60.92.

Dominic DEMERITTE b. 22 Feb 1978 1.80m 67kg. Studied economics at University of North Carolina, USA.
At 200m/4x100mR (100m): OG: '00- h; WCh: '99- h, '01- qf, '03- sf; CG: '02- 4 (3 4x400mR); WJ: '96- qf (qf); WI: '03- 3, '04- 1; WCp: '02- 5/2R; Won BAH 1999-2003, 100m 2002-03; CAC 200m 2003. Bahamas 200m record 2002.
Progression at 200m: 1998- 21.21, 1999- 20.67/20.61w, 2000- 20.53/20.42w, 2001- 20.46, 2002- 20.21, 2003- 20.35/20.29w. pb 100m 10.26 '03.

Avard MONCUR b. 2 Nov 1978 Nassau 1.96m 82kg. Was at University of Auburn.
At 400m/4x400mR: OG: '00- sf; WCh: '01- 1/2R, '03- sf; CG: '02- 3; WJ: '96- sf; PAm: '99- 7; PAmJ: '97- 2; won NCAA 400m 2000-01, BAH 1999-2001, 2003.
Three Bahamas 400m records 2000-01.
Progression at 400m: 1995- 47.40, 1996- 47.09, 1997- 46.46, 1998- 46.45, 1999- 45.09, 2000- 44.72, 2001- 44.45, 2002- 44.85, 2003- 45.00A/45.02.

Leevan SANDS b. 16 Aug 1981 1.90m 73kg. Student at Barton County CC
At TJ: WCh: '03- 3; CG: '02- 3; WJ: '98- dnq, '00- 5; PAm: '99- 6; won CAC 2003, CAm-J 1998, 2000; NCAA & BAH LJ 2003.
Bahamas triple jump record 2002.
Progression at TJ: 1998- 15.??, 1999- 16.00/16.02w, 2000- 16.22, 2001- 16.39, 2002- 17.50, 2003- 17.40. pb LJ 8.10i '04, 8.01, 8.28w '03.

Women

Christine AMERTIL b. 18 Aug 1979 Nassau 1.68m 53kg. Was at Southeastern Louisiana University, USA
At 400m: OG: '00- h; WCh: '03- sf; CG: '02- 8; WI: '03- 2.
Progression at 400m: 1999- 52.99, 2000- 52.00, 2001- 52.70, 2002- 50.82, 2003- 51.11i/51.25. pbs: 60m 7.50i '03, 100m 11.63 '03, 200m 22.88/22.86w '03.

Lavern EVE b. 16 Jun 1965 Nassau 1.79m 77kg. Louisiana State TC, was at Louisiana State University.
At JT: OG: '88- dnq 16, '96- dnq 17, '00- dnq 16; WCh: '91/5/7/9/01- dnq 22/15/16/18/17, '03- 8; CG: '94- 7, '02- 1; PAm: '87- 5, '95- 2, '99- 3, '03- 2; CAG: '98- 3; WCp: '89- 3. At SP: CAG: '93- 3. Won NCAA 1987, TAC 1989, CAC 1989, 1991, 1999, 2001, 2003; PAm-J shot 1984.
Bahamas records for shot, discus and javelin. New javelin Commonwealth best 1999.
Progression at JT: 1982- 48.62, 1983- 50.22, 1984- 53.50, 1986- 53.54, 1987- 62.42, 1988- 60.02, 1989- 64.78, 1990- 59.12, 1991- 58.06, 1992- 56.74, 1993- 56.90, 1994- 57.26, 1995- 63.24, 1996- 58.48, 1997- 60.42. 1998- 60.66; new 1999- 62.94, 2000- 63.73, 2001- 60.26, 2002- 58.46, 2003- 62.89. pbs: SP 16.20i '93, 15.82 '94; DT 52.52 '90, HT 54.90 '99, Hep 5197w '94.

Debbie FERGUSON b. 16 Jan 1976 1.70m 57kg. Was at University of Georgia, USA.
At 100m/4x100mR (/200m): OG: '96- sf/res (2)R, '00- 8/5/1R; WCh: '95- 4R (h), '97- sf, '99- sf/5/1R, '01- 6/2, '03- sf/qf; CG: 94- (sf), '02- 1/1/1R; WJ: '92- qf/sf, '94- 5/4; PAm: '99- (1); WCp: '02- 1/1R. Won CAC 100m 1997, 200m 1995, NCAA 100m & 200m 1998, PAm-J 100m & 200m 1995, CAC-J 100m 1994, GWG 200m 2001. 3rd GP 200m 2001, 2nd 100m 2002.
Bahamas 200m record 1999.
Progression at 100m, 200m: 1991- 11.75, 24.26; 1992- 11.79, 23.97w; 1993- 23.82/23.32w, 1994- 11.48/11.1, 23.32/23.1; 1995- 11.19/10.9w, 22.86/22.7; 1996- 11.26/11.07Aw, 22.92; 1997- 11.20, 1998- 10.97/10.94w, 22.53; 1999- 10.98/10.91w, 22.19; 2000- 10.96, 22.37; 2001- 11.04, 22.39; 2002- 10.91, 22.20; 2003- 10.97, 22.50A/22.65. pbs: 55m 6.71i '99, 60m 7.20i '04, 400m 54.68 '92.
Won three gold medals at 2002 CG, winning both 100m and 200m in Games records.

Savatheda FYNES b. 17 Oct 1974 Abaco 1.65m 58kg. Was at Michigan State University, USA.
At 100m/4x100mR: OG: '96- 2R (qf), '00- 7/1R; WCh: '95- qf (h), '97- 3, '99- sf/1R. '03- qf; CG: '02- 3/1R; PAm: '03- 6; PAm-J: '91- 3, '93- 2 (2, 3 4x400), '03- 6; won NCAA 100m 1997, 200m 1995, 1997. Won GP 200m 1999, 100m: 2nd 1998, 3rd 2000. At 60m: WI: '99-01-03: 4/4/dns.
Bahamas 100m record 1999.
Progression at 100m, 200m: 1991- 11.58, 24.49;

1992- 11.52w, 23.49w; 1993- 11.55, 23.43A; 1994- 11.42/11.2w, 23.38/23.10w; 1995- 11.12/10.7w, 22.63; 1996- 11.24, 23.01; 1997- 11.03/11.00w, 22.60/22.51w; 1998- 11.02, 1999- 10.91, 22.32; 2000- 11.03, 22.87; 2001- 11.17, 23.02; 2002- 11.07, 23.43; 2003- 11.36. pbs: 50m 6.05i '00, 55m 6.65i '97, 60m 7.01i '99, 400m 53.40 '95.

Chandra STURRUP b. 12 Sep 1971 1.63m 55kg. Was at Norfolk State University, USA.
At 100m(/200m/4x100mR): OG: '96- 4/6/2R, '00- 6/qf/1R; WCh: '99- 7/sf/1R, '01- 4, '03- 4; CG: '98- 1, '02- 1R; PAm: '99- 1; CAG: '93- 3/5, '98- 1; WJ: '88- sf/sf, '90- sf/6; WCp: '98- 2/2R. At 60m: WI: '97- 2, '01- 1.
BAH records 100m (3) 1996-2000, 200m 1996.
Progression at 100m, 200m: 1987- 11.75, 1988- 11.93/11.70w, 23.96w; 1989- ?, 1990- 11.62, 23.77; 1992- 11.54, 23.55; 1993- 11.20, 22.85; 1994- 11.75, 1995- 11.39/11.35w/11.1w, 23.31/23.14w; 1996- 11.00, 22.33; 1997- 11.26, 22.77; 1998- 10.95, 23.52/22.64w; 1999- 10.96/10.94w, 22.75; 2000- 10.86, 22.57; 2001- 10.95, 22.99; 2002- 11.01, 2003- 10.89/10.88w, 23.56. pbs: 50m 6.11+ '99, 55m 6.73i '96, 60m 7.05i '01, 300m 37.95 '01, 400m 54.77 '00, LJ 6.70 '00, 6.80w '95.

Tonique WILLIAMS b. 17 Jan 1976 1.68m 59kg. At 400m: OG: '00- h; WCh: '97- qf, '99- h, '03- 5; PAm: '99- h; CAC: '99- 2; WI: '04- 3. At 200m: CAC: '03- 3.
Progression at 400m: 1994- 53.72, 1995- 52.40, 1996- 52.42, 1997- 52.15, 1998- 51.99, 1999- 52.01, 2000- 52.35, 2003- 50.24, 2004- 50.87i. pbs: 200m 22.80 '03, 300m 36.6+ '03.

BAHRAIN

MUCHIR Salim Jawher formerly Leonard MUCHERU (KEN) b. 13 Jun 1978 Kenya 1.82m 66kg.
At 3000m: WI: '01- 7. World 4km CC: '01- 4.
Progression at 5000m: 2000- 13:21.14, 2001- 13:14.94; 2002- 13:21.68; 2003- 13:01.76. pbs: 1500m 3:33.79 '01, 1M 3:49.75 '01, 3000m 7:35.05 '01.

BARBADOS

Governing body: Amateur Athletic Association of Barbados, P.O.Box 46, Bridgetown. Fd. 1947.
National Champions 2003: **Men**: 100m/200m: Andrew Hinds 10.49/20.91, 400m: Jason Hunte 47.50, 800m: Hugh Reid 1:56.74, 1500m: Ryan Ross 4:13.18, 110mh: Hugh Henry 13.80, 400mh: Ryan Smith 51.08, HJ: Damon Thompson 2.16, LJ: Kevin Bartlett 7.47, TJ: Gregory Hughes 15.39, SP: Ivorn McKnee 15.14, DT: Jason Barnett 48.43, JT: Jamal Forde 58.81. **Women**: 100m/200m: Genna Williams 11.92/24.56, 800/1500m: Sheena Gooding 55,45/2:07.64, 1500m: Najuma Commissiong 5:28.43, 100mh: Andrea Blackett 13.67, 400mh: Sheena Hurdles 64.63, LJ: Keitha Moseley 6.16, TJ: Seidre Ford 12.21, SP: Keisha Wallace 12.25, DT: Angela Hinds 38.51, JT: Kyann Maynard 39.71.

Women

Andrea BLACKETT b. 24 Jan 1976 London, GBR 1.60m 54kg. Was at Rice University, USA.
At 400mh/4x400mR: OG: '00- sf; WCh: '97- 8, '99- 4, '01- h, '03- 6; CG: '98- 1, '02- h; PAm: '99- 2/3R, '03- 3; CAG: '98- 2/3R; WJ: '94- h; WCp: '98- 2R; 2nd GP 1999; won CAC 1997 (3rd 100mh), 1999; 2nd 1998.
BAR 400mh records 1994-9, 100mh 1997-2003.
Progression at 400mh: 1994- 58.75, 1995- 58.59, 1996- 57.35A, 1997- 54.74, 1998- 53.74, 1999- 53.36, 2000- 54.41, 2001- 55.68, 2002- 56.95, 2003- 53.71. pbs: 200m 23.73 '00, 800m 2:10.47 '99, 55mh 7.65i '97, 60mh 8.37i '03, 100mh 13.39 '03, 13.2 '98.

BELARUS

Governing body: Belarus Athletic Federation, 2 Surganov Street, Minsk 220012. Founded 1991.
National Champions 2003. **Men**: 100m: Yuriy Bagatka 10.63, 200m: Maksim Piskunov 21.70, 400m: Sergey Kozlov 46.97, 800m: Mark Romanchuk 1:50.33, 1500m: Aleksandr Donchenko 3:48.81, 5000m: Igor Tetserukov 14:25.16, 10000m: Viktor Lomonosov 30:15.07; 110mh: Maksim Lynsha 14.05, 400mh: Leonid Vershinin 50.43, HJ: Aleksandr Veryutin 2.20, PV: Stanislav Tivonchik 4.80, LJ: Andrey Shablovskiy 7.36, TJ: Aleksandr Furso 16.41, SP: Dmitriy Goncharuk 19.40, DT: Vasiliy Kaptyukh 63.28, HT: Ivan Tikhon 83.64, JT: Vladimir Sasimovich 79.43, Dec: Aleksandr Parkhomenko 7954, 20kmW: Andrey Makarov 1:22:09, **Women**: 100m/200m: Yelena Nevmerzhitskaya 11.41/23.70, 400: Irina Khlyustova 53.13, 800: Natalya Dukhnova 2:04.23, 1500m: Svetlana Klimkovich 4:19.75, 5000m: Tatsyana Belkina 16:23.54, 10000m: Yelena Mazovka 34:13.45, 100mh: Yevgeniya Likhuta 13.30, 400mh: Inna Kalinina 59.54, HJ: Olga Klimova 1.75, PV: Yekaterina Arkhiova 3.90, LJ: Irina Chernushenko 6.41, TJ: Natalya Safronova 13.84, SP: Yelena Ivanenko 18.29 (Yanina Korolchik 18.88 drugs dq), DT: Irina Yatchenko 66.57, HT: Olga Tsander 68.82, JT: Marina Novik 52.00, 20kmW: Lyudmila Dolgopolova 1:33:24.

Igor ASTAPKOVICH b. 4 Jan 1963 Minsk 1.91m 118kg. Minsk. Sports instructor.
At HT: OG: '92- 2, '96- 7, '00- 3; WCh: '91- 2, '93- 2, '95- 2, '97- 5, '99- 9, '01- 7, '03- dnq; EC: '90- 1, '94- 2, '98- 7; WUG: '87- 1, '89- 1; ECp: '89- 2, '91- 1. Won GWG 1990. USSR champion 1989-90, CIS 1992, BLR 2000. Won GP 1992, 2nd 1988, 1994, 1996. BLR hammer record 1992.
Progression at HT: 1981- 66.56, 1982- 68.08, 1983- 75.02, 1984- 79.98, 1985- 80.16, 1986- 80.68, 1987- 82.96, 1988- 83.44, 1989- 82.52, 1990- 84.14, 1991- 84.26, 1992- 84.62, 1993- 82.28, 1994- 83.14, 1995- 82.60, 1996- 81.76, 1997- 82.44, 1998- 83.62, 1999- 80.12, 2000- 82.58, 2001- 82.76, 2002- 81.97, 2003- 81.35.
World number one in 1990, when he lost just once, and won the Goodwill Games (84.12)

and European titles with pbs. Since then he has won five major silver medals. Set world masters record with 81.35 in 2003. Married to Irina Yatchenko (qv). Brother **Konstantin** (b. 23 Oct 1970) has a best of 79.08 '99 and was BLR champion 1995 and 1998-9.

Vadim DEVYATOVSKIY b. 20 Mar 1977 1.94m 120kg.
At HT: WCh: '03- 7; WJ: '96- 2; EU23: '99- 4. BLR champion 2000.
Progression at HT: 1994- 67.20, 1995- 68.82, 1996- 74.18, 1997- 69.64, 1998- 75.00, 1999- 76.77, 2000- 81.36, 2003- 79.90.
Two year drugs ban from positive on 18 Sep 2000.

Viktor GINKO b. 7 Dec 1965 Sharkovshchina 1.86m 77kg. Sports instructor.
At 50kmW: OG: '96- 5, '00- dq; WCh: '93- 11, '95- dq, '97/9- dnf; WCp: '95-7-9-02: 6/12/7/18; EC: '94 & '98- dq; ECp: '98- 8, '01- 7. BLR champion 50kmW 1993, 20kmW 1995-6.
World bests for 100km walk: 8:43.30 (2000), 8:38.07 (2002).
Progression at 50kmW: 1988- 4:09:16, 1990- 3:50:45, 1991- 3:51:35, 1992- 3:48:42/3:40:46sh, 1993- 3:53:41, 1994- 3:45:34, 1995- 3:42:20, 1996- 3:42:52, 1997- 3:44:45, 1998- 3:48:27, 1999- 3:43:15, 2000- 3:47:53, 2001- 3:50:28, 2002- 3:57:31, 2003- 4:06:36. pb 20kmW 1:20:03sh '93, 1:20:31 '98; 30kmW 2:05:36 '93, 35kmW 2:31:58 '93.

Aleksandr GLAVATSKIY b. 2 May 1970 Soligarsk 1.85m 72kg.
At LJ (TJ): OG: '96- 7; WCh: '93- 7, '95- dnq 22, '97- 6, '01- (dnq 16), '03- (11); EC: '94- 10, '98- dnq 13 (4), '02- (6); WI: '97-01-03: 9/(8)/(7); EI: '02- (3); WUG: '95- 5. Won BLR LJ 1998, TJ 1998, 2001.
Progression at LJ, TJ: 1988- 7.57, 1989- 7.55, 1990- 8.10, 1991- 7.97, 1992- 7.88/7.97w, 16.28i; 1993- 8.05, 1994- 8.21, 17.12i/16.94; 1995- 8.22, 1996- 8.33A/8.30, 1997- 8.20/8.29w, 16.46; 1998- 8.26, 17.53; 2000- 16.68, 2001- 7.61i/7.43, 17.06i/17.00; 2002- 17.09, 2003- 17.19i/16.71.

Vasiliy KAPTYUKH b. 27 Jun 1967 Molodechno 1.97m 120kg. Minsk TR. Sports instructor.
At DT: OG: '96- 3, '00- 4; WCh: '91- dns, '93- 7, '95- 3, '97- 11, '01- 6, '03- 3; EC: '90- 4; WJ: '86- 3; EJ: '85- 3. BLR champion 1992, 2003.
Progression at DT: 1985- 57.18, 1986- 60.24, 1988- 61.60, 1989- 62.92, 1990- 63.72, 1991- 62.88, 1992- 63.34, 1993- 66.18, 1994- 58.86, 1995- 66.30, 1996- 66.92, 1997- 65.52, 2000- 67.59, 2001- 67.48, 2003- 66.51. pb SP 17.26 '00.
Father Boris (1950s) and aunt Vera Kaptyukh (1960s, Pen) were prominent athletes.

Andrey MIKHNEVICH b. 12 Jul 1976 2.02m 115kg.
At SP: OG: '03- 9; WCh: '01- dq 10, '03- 1; EC: '98- dnq 17; WUG: '97- 6, '03- 1; WI: '99- 8, '04- 6. BLR champion 2000.
Progression at SP: 1994- 16.74, 1995- 17.36, 1996- 19.24, 1997- 19.27, 1998- 20.07i/19.90, 1999- 20.52i/20.30, 2000- 20.48i/20.12, 2001- 20.92, 2003- 21.69.
Two year drugs ban from positive test on 4 Aug 2001, when he lost 10th place at the World Champs. He threw 21.66 four days after return from ban in August 2003, and won the world title two weeks later.

Gennadiy MOROZ b. 27 May 1978 2.00m 77kg.
At HJ: WCh: '99- dnq 24; 03- dnq 14; EC: '98/02- dnq 18=/16=; EJ: '97- 1; EU23: '99- 5=; WUG: '01- 2; WI: '03- 3, '04- 6.
Progression at HJ: 1997- 2.23, 1998- 2.25, 1999- 2.28i, 2000- 2.25, 2001- 2.33, 2002- 2.30i/2.28, 2003- 2.30.

Ivan TIKHON b. 24 Jul 1976 Slonim 1.86m 110kg.
At HT: OG: '00- 4; WCh: 97- nt (12), '01- dnq 22, '03- 1; EC: '98- dnq 30, '02- 9; EU23: 97- 1; EJ: '95- 9; WUG: '03- 1. BLR champion 2001-03.
Progression at HT: 1994- 62.66, 1995- 66.84, 1996- 75.32, 1997- 77.46, 1998- 78.03, 1999- 70.37, 2000- 79.85, 2001- 78.73, 2002- 79.04, 2003- 84.32.

Ivan TROTSKIY b. 27 May 1976 1.67m 50 kg.
At 20kmW: WCh: 99- 9, '01- 15, '03- 6; EC: '98- 6, '02- 5; WCp: '99/02- 13/13. At 10000mW: EJ: '95- 8.
Progression at 20kmW: 1996- 1:25:07, 1997- 1:23:36, 1998- 1:19:48, 1999- 1:20:45, 2001- 1:19:45, 2002- 1:20:52, 2003- 1:19:40. pbs: 5000mW 19:49.17i '03, 10000mW 39:34.99 '03.

Dmitriy VALYUKEVICH b. 31 May 1981 1.86m 78kg. Slavia UK Bratislava, SVK.
At TJ: WCh: '03- dnq 16; EU23: '03- 1; WI: '04- 4. BLR champion 2002.
Progression at TJ: 1998- 15.52, 2000- 16.39, 2001- 16.62, 2002- 16.68i/16.53, 2003- 17.57, 2004- 17.31i. pb LJ 7.60i '04.
Improved from 16.81 to 16.83 in qualifying and then 17.16, 17.51 and 17.57 in the final of the European U23s in 2003. His father Gennadiy had best of 17.53 in 1986, won the 1979 EI title (2nd 1982 and 1983) and set world indoor bests that year at 17.19 and 17.29. His mother Irina had a long jump best of 7.17 '87 and was WUG champion in 1985.

Women

Nadezhda OSTAPCHUK b. 12 Oct 1980 1.80m 78kg.
At SP: WCh: '99- dnq 17, '01- 7, '03- 2; EC: '02- 5; WJ: '98- 1; EJ: '99- 1; EU23: '01- 1; WI: '01-03-04: 2/2/8, EI: '00- 6; 2nd GP 2001. BLR champion 1999-2000.
Progression at SP: 1997- 14.23, 1998- 18.23, 1999- 18.73, 2000- 19.13i/18.83, 2001- 19.73, 2002- 19.40, 2003- 20.56i/20.12.

Natalya SAFRONNIKOVA b. 28 Feb 1973 1.68m 56kg. née Vinogradova.

At (100m)/200m: OG: '96- sf; WCh: '95/7- h, '99- sf/sf, '01- qf/sf, '03- 7; EC: '98- sf/sf, '02- h; WI: '01- 3, '03- 6, '04- 2 (8 60m); WUG: '01- 3; ECp: 95-6-7-01: 100m 6/6/3/2, 200m 6/6/4/1. Won Belarus 100m 1994-8, 200m 1995-8, 2002. Belarus 100m record 2003.
Progression at 100m, 200m: 1992- 11.68, 1994- 11.54, 23.54; 1995- 11.32/11.30w, 23.15/22.86w; 1996- 11.40, 22.98; 1997- 11.33, 23.12; 1998- 11.19/10.9, 23.29/22.3; 1999- 11.17/10.9, 22.74; 2000- 11.35i/11.37, 23.10; 2001- 11.30/11.26w/10.9, 22.68/22.4; 2002- 11.24, 22.92; 2003- 11.05, 22.71. pb 60m 7.04 '01.

Natalya SAZANOVICH b. 15 Aug 1973 Baranovich 1.79m 65kg. Gomel. Sports instructor.
At Hep: OG: '96- 2, '00- 3; WCh: '97- 5, '01- 2, '03- 3; EC: '98- 3, '02- 3; ECp: '95- 7, '96- 1, '00- 1B; WJ: '92- 1; EJ: '91- 1. At Pen: WI: '01- 1, '03- 2. Won BLR LJ & Hep 1996.
Progression at Hep: 1989- 5431, 1990- 5725, 1991- 5896, 1992- 6036, 1995- 6020, 1996- 6563, 1997- 6442, 1998- 6410, 2000- 6527, 2001- 6539, 2002- 6341, 2003- 6524. pbs: 200m 23.62 '96, 800m 2:16.41 '00, 60mh 8.23i '03, 100mh 13.28 '01, HJ 1.84 '95, LJ 6.86 '96, SP 16.81 '03, JT 47.13 '02, Pen 4850i '96.

Olga TSANDER b. 18 May 1976 1.74m 83kg.
At HT: OG: '00- dnq; WCh: '01- 10, '03- dnq; EC: '02- dnq 22; WUG: '01- 4; ECp: '01- 1; BLR champion 2002-03. At DT: WJ: '94- 5; EJ: '95- 2. BLR hammer record 2002.
Progression at HT: 1998- 58.88, 1999- 64.56, 2000- 69.81, 2001- 68.94, 2002- 70.11. 2003- 70.02. pbs: SP 15.18 '94, DT 59.82 '97.

Valentina TSYBULSKAYA b. 19 Feb 1968 Rostov-na-Donu, RUS 1.63m 54kg.
At 20kmW: OG: '00- 28; WCh: '01- 2, '03- 3; WCp: '02- 7; ECp: '00- 8; At 10kmW: OG: '96- 8; WCh: '95- 12, '97- 3; EC: '94- 12, '98- 15; WCp: '95-7-9: 13/11/25; ECp: '96- 6. Won BLR 10000mW 1999. BLR walk records: 10km 1999, 20km 2003, 20,000m track (1:38:25.5) 2001, 3000m 1995.
Progression at 10kmW, 20kmW: 1987- 46:07, 1988- 46:15, 1989- 45:15, 1991- 46:26, 1992- 45:13, 1993- 43:50, 1994- 43:16, 1995- 42:35, 1996- 43:05, 1997- 42:21, 1998- 43:47, 1:32:25; 1999- 42:06, 1:29:20; 2000- 43:35, 1:30:19; 2001- 43:51, 1:28:49; 2002- 43:27, 1:30:37; 2003- 44:11, 1:28:10. pbs: 3000mW 12:27.97 '95, 5000mW: 21:11.09i '99, 20: 33R '01.

Alesya TUROVA b. 6 Dec 1979 1.80m 64kg.
At 1500m: WCh: '01- 7, '03- sf; EC: '02- 7; WJ: '98- h; EU23: '99- 5, '01- 1; EJ: '97- 11; WI: '01-03-04: 6/7/7; EI: '02- 3; ECp: '01- 4.
Two world 3000m steeple records 2002; BLR records: 2000m & 3000m (3), 5000m 2000-01.
Progression at 1500m, 5000m, 3000mSt: 1997- 4:24.64, 1998- 4:21.53, 1999- 4:12.8, 2000- 4:05.99, 15:23.84; 2001- 4:07.25, 15:30.63; 2002- 3:59.89, 9:16.51; 2003- 4:03.32, 9:20.28. pbs: 800m 2:02.11i '03, 2:04.52 '99; 1M 4:33.88i '02, 2000m 5:42.55 '01, 3000m 8:32.89 '01.
Sister Rita (b. 28 Dec 1980) was 3rd in 1999 EJ 5000m walk.

Irina YATCHENKO b. 31 Oct 1965 Gomel 1.87m 96kg. Grodno. Sports instructor.
At DT: OG: '92- 7, '96- 12, '00- 3; WCh: '91- 7, '95- 9, '97- 5, '99- 9, '01- 10, '03- 1; EC: '90- 5, '98- 8; ECp: '95- 3, '96- 3. 2nd GP 1992. BLR champion 1997, 2003.
Progression at DT: 1982- 50.72, 1983- 57.04, 1984- 59.54, 1985- 60.56, 1986- 57.58, 1987- 63.00, 1988- 67.44, 1989- 62.38, 1990- 68.60, 1991- 64.92, 1992- 68.94, 1993- 58.74, 1995- 66.14, 1996- 65.80, 1997- 68.32, 1998- 64.00, 1999- 66.18, 2000- 66.51, 2001- 66.65, 2002- 64.23, 2003- 67.32.
Oldest ever world champion at 37y 298d in 2003. Married to hammer thrower Igor Astapkovich.

BELGIUM

Governing bodies: Ligue Royale Belge d'Athlétisme, Stade Roi Baudouin, avenue du Marathon 199B, 1020 Bruxelles (KBAB/LRBA). Vlaamse Atletiekliga (VAL); Ligue Belge Francophone d'Athlétisme (LBFA). Original governing body founded 1889.
National Championships first held in 1889 (women 1921). **2003 Champions**: **Men**: 100m: Xavier De Baerdemaker 10.51, 200m: Cédric Van Branteghem 20.52w, 400m: Christophe Lumen 47.39, 800m: Joeri Jansen 1:48.16, 1500m: Tim Clerbout 3:58.65, 5000m: Christian Nemeth 14: 30.56, 10000m: Hans Janssens 29:22.56, Mar: Rik Ceulemans 2:18:56, 3000mSt: Krijn Van Koolwyk 8:47.46, 110mh: Damien Broothaerts 14.14, 400mh: Piet Deveughele 51.27, HJ: Benoit Braconnier 2.11, PV: Thibaut Duval 5.40, LJ: Jan Guns 7.53, TJ: Michael Velter 16.25, SP: Wim Blondeel 17.65, DT: Jo Van Daele 62.19, HT: Walter De Wyngaert 62.29, JT: Marc Van Mensel 72.57, Dec: Frédéric Xhonneux 6917, 20000mW: Christophe Hune 1:32:33.6. **Women**: 100m: Kim Gevaert 11.39, 200m: Audrey Rochtus 23.69, 400m: Marleen Baggerman 54.88, 800m: Sandra Stals 2:06.11, 1500m: Veerle Dejaeghere 4:24.93, 5000m/3000mSt: Sigrid Vanden Bempt 16:31.23/9:46.60, 10000m: Marleen Renders 33:01.71, Mar: M Guillemyn 2:54:45, 100mh: Myriam Tschomba 13.24, 400mh: Nele Van Doninck 59.07, HJ: Tia Hellebaut 1.87, PV: Karen Pollefeyt 3.65, LJ/TJ: Sandra Swennen 6.26/13.66, SP/DT: Veerle Blondeel 16.58/55.11, HT: Jennifer Petit 50.52, JT: Cindy Stas 54.08, Hep: Isabel Poelmans 4880, 5000mW: Liesbet Desmet 31:11.9.

Cédric VAN BRANTEGHEM b. 13 Mar 1979 1.82m 72kg. STAX.
At 400m (200m): WCh: '03- sf (qf); EC: '02- 6; WI: '03- sf. Won BEL 200m 2002-03, 400m 2001. Belgian 400m record 2003.
Progression at 400m: 1998- 48.58, 1999- 46.85,

2000- 46.66, 2001- 46.35, 2002- 45.94, 2003- 45.02. pbs: 100m 10.54 '03, 200m 20.60, 20.52w '03; 300m 32.53 '03.
Younger sister Gaëlle competed at 2001 World Youth Championships. Their father Jacques was Belgian U17 200m champion in 1967.

Women

Kim GEVAERT b. 5 Aug 1978 1.70m 60kg. VAC.
At (100m/)200m): OG: '00- dnq 15; WCh: '99- qf/qf, '01- qf/sf, '03- sf/sf; EC: '98- h/sf, '02- 2/2; WJ: '96- sf/7; EU23: '99- 3/5; EJ: '95- (6), '97- 5; WUG: '99- 4/1, '01- 2; WCp: '02- (8). At 60m: WI: '04- 2; EI: '00- 6, '02- 1. Won BEL 100m 1996, 1998-2003, 200m 1995-2001.
Belgian records: 100m (6) 1998-2002, 200m (6) 1999-2002.
Progression at 100m, 200m: 1994- 12.02, 1995- 11.63, 23.92; 1996- 11.68/11.60w, 23.59; 1997- 11.52, 23.84/23.58w; 1998- 11.40, 23.10; 1999- 11.17, 23.03; 2000- 11.34, 23.09; 2001- 11.26, 22.94; 2002- 11.15, 22.53; 2003- 11.21, 22.64. pbs: 60m 7.12i '04, 400m 52.33 '02, TJ 11.67 '03.
'La Gazelle de Kampenhout', who was an award-winning classical pianist, set ten Belgian records in 2002. Member of EAA Athletes Commission 2002-06.

Marleen RENDERS b. 24 Dec 1968 1.66m 47kg. AVT.
At Mar: OG: '96- 25, '00- dnf; WCh: '01- 18; EC: '98- 5, '02- dnf. At 10000m: WCh: '87- 12, '95- 17, '97- dnf, '99- 9; EC: '94- 10; WJ: '86- 3. World HMar: '94- 7, '95- 13, '02- 8. Won BEL 3000m 1987, 5000m 1995-6, 10000m 1988, 1994, 1998-2000; HMar 1994-5, 1998.
World junior 10000m record 1987. Belgian records: 10000m 2000, marathon (5) 1997-2002.
Progression at 10000m, Mar: 1986- 33:41.13, 1987- 32:12.51, 1988- 32:11.49, 1991- 32:04.2mx, 1994- 32:11.18, 1995- 32:33.38, 2:28:57; 1996- 32:02.55, 2:27:42; 1997- 31:57.87, 2:25:56; 1998- 32:01.80, 2:25:22; 1999- 31:51.21, 2:23:58; 2000- 31:03.60, 2:23:43; 2001- 2:28:31, 2002- 2:23:05, 2003- 2:28:31. pbs: 1500m 4:18.07 '87, 3000m 9:03.64 '97, 5000m 15:19.20 '89, HMar 68:56 '02.
Won Antwerp marathon 1995, Paris 2000, 2002; 2nd Rotterdam 1997, Amsterdam 2001. Berlin: 3rd 1997, 1st 1998, 2nd 1999.

BRAZIL

Governing body: Confederação Brasileira de Atletismo (CBAT), Avenida Sete de Setembro 874, 4° andar, Manaus, Amazonas 69005-140. Founded 1914 (Confederação 1977).
2003 National Champions: Men: 100m: Édson Ribeiro 10.20, 200m: André da Silva 20.56, 400m: Anderson J. dos Santos 45.69, 800m: Osmar dos Santos 1:45.94, 1500m: Fabiano Peçanha 3:40.29, 5000m/10000m: Marílson dos Santos 13:48.52/ 28:35.67, Mar: Genílson da Silva 2:16:41, 3000mSt: Fernando Fernandes 8:48.06, 110mh: Redelen dos Santos 13.68, 400mh: Eronilde de Araújo 49.40, HJ: Jessé de Lima 2.27, PV: Gustavo Rehder 5.20 (Luke Walker USA 5.25), LJ: Thiago J.C. Dias 7.90w (John Thornell AUS 7.99w), TJ: Jadel Gregório 17.05, SP: Daniel F. Freire 17.35, DT: João Joaquim dos Santos 52.69, HT: Mário Luis Leme 63.32, JT: Luiz Fernando da Silva 77.16, Dec: Édson Bindilatti 7331, 20000mW: Sérgio Galdino 1:23:51.9, 50kmW: Cláudio dos Santos 4:33:55. **Women:** 100m/200m: Lucimar de Moura 11.57/23.29, 400m: Geisa Coutinho 51.55, 800m: Luciana Mendes 2:03.31, 1500m: Juliana Paula de Azevedo 4:19.16, 5000m: Maria Cristina Rodrigues 16:13.85, 10000m: Ednalva da Silva 33:58.91, Mar: Maria do Carmo Guimarães 2:39:02, 3000mSt: Michelle Costa 10:30.86, 100mh: Gilvaneide Parrela 13.60, 400mh: Lucimar Teodoro 56.28, HJ: Luciane Dambacher 1.81, PV: Karla da Silva 4.02, LJ/TJ: Keila Costa 6.32 (Prov. DQ Maurren Maggi 6.75)/13.68; SP/DT: Elisângela Adriano 18.56/58.97; HT: Katiuscia de Jesus 60.37, JT: Alessandra Resende 53.06 (Leryn Franco PAR 53.09), Hep: Elizete G. da Silva 5202, 20000mW: Cisiane Lopes 1:42:52.4.

Jadel GREGÓRIO b. 16 Sep 1980 Jandaia do Sul, Paraná 2.02m 102kg. BM&F Atletismo.
At TJ: WCh: '03- 5; PAm: '03- 2; SACh: '01- 1, 03- 1; WI: '03- 6, '04- 2; WUG: '01- 3. Won Ib-Am 2002; BRA 2001-02 (LJ 2002), BRA 2003.
Soth American indoor triple jump records 2002 & 2004.
Progression at TJ: 1999- 16.07, 2000- 16.48, 2001- 17.13, 2002- 17.35i/17.08, 2003- 17.11/17.37w, 2004- 17.46i. pb LJ 8.02 '02.

Women

Elisângela Maria ADRIANO b. 27 Jul 1972 São Paulo, SP 1.80m 95kg. BM&F Atletismo.
At SP/(DT). OG: '96- dnq 21; WCh: '97- dnq 19/dnq 18, '01- 11, '03- 9/dnq 18; PAm: '95- 4, '99- 4dq/1dq, '03- 2/5; WI: '97- 11; SACh: '93- 1/2, '95- 1, '97-99-01-03: 1/1; WUG: '97- 5/5, '99- 3/3dq; Won IbAm SP 1990, 1998; DT 2002; SAm-J SP & DT 1990.
14 BRA & South American shot records 1990-2001 and 5 South American discus records 1996-8.
Progression at SP, DT: 1989- 14.62, 1990- 16.65, 50.10, 1991- 16.84, 53.48; 1992- 17.36, 52.16; 1993- 17,11, 53.94; 1994- 16.77, 55.28; 1995- 17.50, 55.44; 1996- 18.47, 59.64; 1997- 18.90, 61.04; 1998- 18.38, 61.96; 1999- 19.02, 60.27A/62.23dq, 2000- 17.21, 58.63, 2001- 19.30, 59.68; 2002- 18.46, 60.68; 2003- 18.59, 60.03.
Drugs disqualification at 1999 WUG (DT), but reinstated 2000. Has a women's record ten gold medals at South American championships, and 14 outdoor Brazilian and South American records in SP, and 5 South American in DT.

Maurren Higa **MAGGI** b. 25 Jun 1976 São Carlos, São Paulo 1.78m 66kg. BM&F Atletismo.

At LJ (/100mh): OG: '00- dnq 25; WCh: '99- 8/qf, '01- 7/h; PAm: '99- 1/2; SACh: '97- 2/1, 99- 1/1, '01- 1/1; WUG: '99- 3, '01- 1/2/2R; WI: '03- 3. Won GP 2002, GWG 2001, IbAm 2000, 2002; SA-J 100mh 1994, BRA 100mh 1997-2000, LJ 1999-2002, TJ 2002.
South American (BRA) records: LJ 1 (3) 1999, 100mh 4 (6) 1999-2001, TJ 2002-03 (3).
Progression at 100mh, LJ: 1994- 14.13, 5.86; 1995- 14.46/14.3w, 5.75/6.02w; 1996- 13.99, 6.47; 1997- 13.67/13.53w, 6.54; 1998- 13.60, 6.42; 1999- 12.86, 7.26A/6.79/6.81w, 2000- 6.93, 2001- 12.71, 6.94/6.98w, 13.60; 2002- 7.02/7.17w, 14.32; 2003- 7.06, 14.53. pbs: 60mh 8.12i '00 (S.Am rec).
Formerly a gymnast, made huge breakthrough in 1999 with her 7.26 LJ at the high altitude of Bogotá from a previous best of 6.79. Two year ban for positive drugs test 14 Jun 2003, later reversed by CBAT but not by IAAF.

BULGARIA

Governing body: Bulgarian Athletic Federation, 75 bl. Vassil Levski, Sofia 1000. F'd 1924.
National Championships first held in 1926 (men), 1938 (women). **2003 Champions**: **Men**: 100m: Marco Jankovic SCG 10.57, 200m: Iliya Dzhivondov 21.2, 400m: Plamen Ignatov 47.28, 800m: Marin Minchev 1:51.92, 1500m: Stanislav Lambev 3:51.45, 5000m: Khristo Khristov 15:14.08, 10000m/HMar/Mar: Petko Stefanov 32:17.10/ 72:34/2:29:17, 3000mSt. Georgi Georgiev 9:04.41, 110mh: Kosta Angelov 14.42, 400mh: Stanislav Petkov 52.45, HJ: Georgi Getov 2.12, PV: Iliyan Efremov 5.50, LJ: Petar Dachev 7.97, TJ: Ivaylo Rusenov 16.85, SP: Galin Kostadinov 18.66, DT: Encho Shterev 53.70, HT: Rosen Zhelev 66.98, JT: Mikhail Kostov 70.96, Dec: Kaloyan Kirov 5905, 20kmW: Ivaylo Minkov 1:37:46. **Women**: 100m/200m: Monika Gachevska 11.63/24.04, 400m Nedyalka Nedkova 53.36, 800m: Ralitsa Atanasova 2:09.24, 1500m: Dobrinka Shalamanova 4:24.71, 5000m/10000m/HMar: Milka Mikhaylova 16:23.7/34:43.67/82:21, Mar: Rumyana Panovska 3:03:03, 3000mSt: Rumyana Panovska 10:43.33, 100mh: Desislava Mutafchieva 13.88, 400mh: Mariyana Dimitrova 60.34, HJ: Mariya Nikolova 1.75, PV: Vera Chavdarova 4.00, LJ: Antoniya Yordanova 6.34, TJ: Nina Serbezova 13.76, SP: Aneliya Yordanova 17.29, DT: Venera Getova 53.55, HT: Aneliya Yordanova 55.09, JT: Rumyana Karapetrova 51.66, Hep: Mariya Nikolova 4523, 20kmW: Nevena Mineva 1:41:34.

Petar DACHEV b. 15 Jun 1979 Troyan 1.81m 77kg. CSKA Sofia.
At LJ: OG: '00- 11; WCh: '03- dnq 29; EC: '98- 3, '02- dnq; WJ: '98- 1; WI: '03- 6; EI: '00- 1, '02- 3. BUL champion 2000, 2002-03; Balkan 2000, 2002.
Progression at LJ: 1995- 7.34, 1996- 7.41, 1998- 8.14, 1999- 7.76, 2000- 8.30, 2001- 8.02i/7.75, 2002- 8.27i/8.25/8.29w, 2003- 8.10i/8.08. pb 100m 10.54 '99, 10.5 '01.
Sister Petya TJ best of 13.26 '03.

Ivaylo RUSENOV b. 9 Sep 1979 Pleven 1.78m 65kg.
At TJ: OG: '00- dnq 22; WCh: '03- 10; EU23: '99- 6, '01- 8. Balkan champion 2000, 2002, Bulgarian 2000-01, 2003.
Progression at TJ: 1996- 15.35/15.36w, 1997- 15.88, 1998- 16.65, 1999- 16.34, 2000- 16.91, 2001- 16.95, 2002- 15.97, 2003- 17.02/17.12w. pb LJ 7.95 '03.
Younger brother Atanas Rusenov LJ 7.81 '03.

Women

Tereza MARINOVA b. 5 Sep 1977 Pleven 1.73m 56kg. Chendini.
At TJ: OG: '00- 1; WCh: '97- 6, '01- 3; EC: '98- 3; WJ: '94- dnq 15, '96- 1; EJ: '95- 1; WI: '97-9-01: 8/ 4/1; EI: '02- 1; E23: '94- 6; won GP 2001. Balkan champion 1996, 2000; BUL 1998.
Two world junior triple jump records (one unofficial) 1996. Bulgarian TJ record 2000.
Progression at TJ: 1993- 12.18, 1994- 13.23/13.51w, 1995- 13.90, 1996- 14.62, 1997- 14.34/14.53w, 1998- 14.67, 1999- 14.76i/14.64, 2000- 15.20, 2001- 14.91i/14.77, 2002- 14.81i, 2003- 14.40i/14.27. pb LJ 6.53i '02, 6.46 '00, 6.63w '01.
Smashed personal bests when winning European (1995) and World (1996) Junior gold medals and again to win 2000 Olympic title. Had surgery on left Achilles in April 2002. Her father Moncho Marinov set a Bulgarian 800m record of 1:47.7 in 1974 and brother Tsvetomir (b. 10 Jul 1976) was 3rd in the 1995 EJ 400m.

Venelina VENEVA b. 13 Jun 1974 Ruse 1.79m 61kg. Elit Vratsa.
At HJ: OG: '96- dnq 29=, '00- 9=; WCh: '91-5-9: dnq 21=/14/14=, '01- 4, '03- 4; EC: '98- 5; EJ: '91- 2; WI: '01- 3, '04- 7; EI: '00- 4. BUL champion 1995, Balkan 2003.
Progression at HJ: 1987- 1.68, 1988- 1.80, 1989- 1.86, 1990- 1.93i/1.90, 1991- 1.91, 1992- 1.91, 1993- 1.89i/1.85, 1994- 1.90, 1995- 1.94, 1996- 1.94i/1.88, 1998- 2.03, 1999- 1.90, 2000- 2.01, 2001- 2.04, 2002- 2.02i, 2003- 2.01. pbs: LJ 6.17 '90, TJ 12.51 '95.
Daughter Neapola born in 1997. World age-15 best of 1.93i in 1990.

Daniela YORDANOVA b. 8 Mar 1976 Slivnitsa 1.65m 52kg. Chendini.
At 1500m/(5000m): OG: '00- (10); WCh: '01- sf/h, '03- 7; EC: '02- 5; WI: '04- 4; EI: '02- 5. At 3000m: EI: '00- 5. Won BUL 1500m 1999, 5000m 1998.
Three Bulgarian 5000m records 2000.
Progression at 1500m, 5000m: 1994- 4:48.94, 19:10.48; 1995- 4:39.59, 17:42.73; 1996- 4:43.26i, 17:50.77; 1997- 17:13.25, 1998- 4:08.83, 16:16.46; 1999- 4:11.93, 16:07.28; 2000- 4:03.83, 14:56.95; 2001- 4:01.68, 2002- 4:00.65, 2003- 4:01.83. pbs: 800m 2:03.02 '01, 3000m 8:45.26 '00, 10000m 37:30.21 '95.
Had surgery on both tendons in May 2003, but three months later reached World 1500m final.

CAMEROON

Governing body: Fédération Camerounaise d'Athlétisme, BP 353, Yaoundé. Founded 1957.

Françoise MBANGO Etone b. 14 Apr 1976 1.72m 63kg.
At TJ(/LJ): OG: '00- 10; WCh: '99- dnq 13, '01- 2, '03- 2; CG: '98- 2/10, '02- 2, AfG: '99- 1/2; AfCh: '96-8-00-02: 3/2/1/1 (02- 1); WI: '03- 2, '04- 6; WCp: '02- 1/8. French champion 1999, 2001-02.
Eight African triple jump records 1999-2003, CMR records LJ from 1993, TJ from 1997.
Progression at TJ: 1994- 12.18, 1995- 11.92, 1996- 12.59, 1997- 13.75A, 1998- 14.02, 1999- 14.70A/14.65, 2000- 14.18, 2001- 14.65, 2002- 14.95, 2003- 15.05. pbs: 100m 12.18/11.5w '00, LJ 6.55A/6.43 '99, 6.68w '02.
First athlete from CMR to win World and Commonwealth medals.

CANADA

Governing body: Athletics Canada, Suite 300-2197 Riverside Drive, Ottawa, Ontario K1H 7X3. Formed as Canadian AAU in 1884.

National Championships first held in 1884 (men), 1925 (women). **2003 champions: Men**: 100m/200m: Nicolas Macrozonaris 10.13/20.85, 400m: Shane Niemi 46.13, 800m: Gary Reed 1:48.19, 1500m: Kevin Sullivan 3:43.66, 5000m: Sean Kaley 13:43.42, 10000m: Jeff Schiebler 28:42.24, 3000mSt: Matthew Kerr 8:30.00, 110mh: Charles Allen 13.76, 400mh: Adam Kunkel 50.15, HJ: Mark Boswell 2.23, PV: John Zubyck 5.00, LJ: Craig Cavanagh 7.74, TJ: Patrick Massok 15.70, SP: Brad Snyder 20.24, DT: Jason Tunks 62.70, HT: Derek Woodske 68.68, JT: Scott Russell 73.09, Dec: Mike Nolan 7432, 20kmW: Tim Berrett 1:29:58. **Women**: 100m/200m: Eric Witter 11.44/23.34w, 400m: Foy Williams 53.15, 800m: Diane Cummins 2:01.01, 1500m: Carmen Douma-Hussar 4:12.20, 5000m: Emilie Mondor 15:08.90, 10000m: Courtney Babcock 33:36.23, 3000mSt: Tanya Vander Muelen 11:02.80, 100mh: Perdita Felicien 12.83, 400mh: Tawa Babatunde 57.56, HJ: Wanita May 1.85, PV: Stephanie McCann 4.20, LJ: Alice Falaiye 6.27, TJ: Althea Williams 13.38w, SP: Georgette Reed 16.24, DT: Tina McDonald 50.06, HT: Jennifer Joyce 63.39, JT: Dominique Bilodeau 52.43, Hep: Nicole Haynes 5894, 20000mW: Karen Foan 1:42:53.

Mark BOSWELL b. 28 Jul 1977 Mandeville, Jamaica 1.89m 77kg. Lightning T&F. Student at University of Texas.
At HJ: OG: '00- 6=; WCh: '99- 2, '01- 7=, '03- 3; WJ: '96: 1; CG: '02- 1; PAm: '99- 1=; WUG: '99- 2; WI: '03- 5; WCp: '02- 2; Won NCAA 1999-2000, Canadian 1997, 2000-03.
Five Canadian high jump records 1999-2002.
Progression at HJ: 1994- 2.10, 1995- 2.00, 1996- 2.24, 1997- 2.28, 1998- 2.29, 1999- 2.35, 2000- 2.35, 2001- 2.33, 2002- 2.35, 2003- 2.32.
Moved to Canada in 1988.

Brad SNYDER b. 8 Jan 1976 Windsor, Ontario 1.96m 129kg. Windsor Legion. Studied criminal justice at University of South Carolina, USA.
At SP: OG: '96- dnq 30, '00- dnq 13; WCh: '97- dnq 21, '01- 8, '03- 11; WJ: '94- dnq 14; CG: '02- 4; PAm: '99- 3, '03- 3; WUG: '99- 4; WCp: '02- 8. Won Pan-Am J 1995, NCAA 1998, Canadian 1996, 1998-9, 2001-03.
Canadian shot record 2001.
Progression at SP: 1994- 16.73, 1995- 17.34, 1996- 19.70, 1997- 19.68i/19.51, 1998- 20.40, 1999- 20.51, 2000- 20.24, 2001- 20.79, 2002- 20.59, 2003- 20.70. pb DT 58.65 '99.
Younger brother Trevor has JT pb 74.59 '01, mother Beth Hosowich was a relay reserve at 1972 Olympics.

Jason TUNKS b. 7 May 1975 London, Ontario 2.00m 122kg. London Western. Was at Southern Methodist University, USA.
At DT (SP): OG: '96- dnq 33, '00- 6; WCh: '97- 9, '99- dnq 20, '01- 9, '03- 11; WJ: '94- 8 (10); CG: '98- 3, '02- 2; PAm: '99- 3 (5), '03- 1; WCp: '02- 5. Won NCAA 1997; Canadian SP 1997, DT 1995, 1997-2003.
Commonwealth & 2 CAN discus records 1998.
Progression at DT: 1992- 48.38, 1993- 51.52, 1994- 58.76, 1995- 58.66, 1996- 63.86, 1997- 65.20, 1998- 67.88, 1999- 65.54, 2000- 66.28, 2001- 67.70, 2002- 66.50, 2003- 65..84/66.55dh. pb SP 19.06 '97.
Was married to Teri Steer (USA, pb SP 19.21 '01). Now married to Lieja Koeman (NED, b. 10 Mar 1976, pb 18.82 '03, 3 EI 02}.

Women

Diane CUMMINS b. 19 Jan 1974 Durban, South Africa 1.65m 50kg. Pacific Sport.
At 800m/4x400m (1500m): WCh: '01- 5, '03- 6; CG: '98- sf/3R, '02- 2 (9); PAm: '99- 5; won CAN 800m 1998, 2000-03.
Canadian records: 800m 2001, 1000m 2002.
Progression at 800m: 1997- 2:08.65, 1998- 2:03.45, 1999- 2:02.14, 2000- 2:01.95, 2001- 1:58.39, 2002- 1:58.79, 2003- 1:58.89. pbs: 400m 53.89 '01, 1000m 2:34.14 '02, 1500m 4:05.02 '01, 1M 4:42.42i '02.
Came to Canada from South Africa in November 1994.

Perdita FELICIEN b. 29 Aug 1980 Oshawa, Ontario 1.65m 57kg. Phoenix TC. Studying kinesociology at University of Illinois.
At 100mh: WCh: '01- sf, '03- 1; PAm: '03- 2. At 60mh: WI: '04- 1. Won FrancG 2001, CAN 2002-03, NCAA 2002-03.
Canadian 100mh record 2003.
Progression at 100mh: 1997-, 1998- 13.69/13.47w, 1999- 13.69, 2000- 12.91, 2001- 12.73, 2002- 12.83/12.77w, 2003- 12.53. pbs: 60m 7.47i '03, 100m 11.78 '03, 200m 24.97i/23.43w '03, 50mh 6.80i '04, 60mh 7.75i '04.

Improved her best from 12.68 to 12.53 to win World 100mh in 2003 and from 7.90 to 7.75 to win World Indoor 60mh in 2004.

CAYMAN ISLANDS

Governing Body: Cayman Islands Amateur Athletic Association, PO Box 527, George Town, Grand Cayman. Founded 1980.

Kareem **STREETE-THOMPSON** b. 30 Mar 1973 Ithaca, New York 1.83m 84kg. Nike. Degree in political science from Rice University, USA.
At LJ (100m): OG: '92- dnq (h), '00- dnq 13; WCh: '91- dnq, '95- 14, '99- dnq 24 (8), '01- 5, '03- dnq 15; WI: '01- 2; CG: '90- 11 (qf), '02- 3; WJ: '88- dnq; '90- 3; PAm: '99- 2, '03- 4; WUG: '93- 1. Won CAC Jnr 1990 and 1992, NCAA 1995, CAC 2001, 2003. 2nd GP 1995.
Cayman Islands records 100m 1991-9, 200m 1991-2, LJ 1990-2000.
Progression at 100m, LJ: 1988- 6.84, 1989- 10.88, 7.83; 1990- 7.95, 1991- 10.59/10.50w, 8.09/8.40w; 1992- 10.57, 8.12/8.39w; 1993- 10.30/10.19Aw, 8.36A; 1994- 10.21A/10.29, 8.63/8.64w; 1995- 10.16, 8.56; 1996- 10.23, 8.34; 1997- 9.96, 8.08A/8.30Aw; 1998- 10.07, 8.17; 1999- 10.14, 8.15/8.22Aw; 2000- 10.22Aw, 8.31; 2001- 8.20, 2002- 7.89/8.14w, 2003- 10.33, 8.21. pbs: 50m 5.76i '97, 55m 6.16i '94, 60m 6.53i '98, 200m 20.3 '97, 21.34 '93.
Until 1992 he represented the Cayman Islands, where he lived for the first 18 years of his life, apart from his first month as he was born in the USA of Jamaican parents while his mother was visiting friends. He became a US citizen in 1994, and won the US indoor LJ in 1994 and 1999, but in 1999 reverted to the Cayman Islands.

Women

Cydonie MOTHERSILL b. 19 Mar 1978 Kingston, Jamaica 1.70m 54kg. Was at Clemson University.
At 200m(/100m): OG: '96- (h), '00- qf/qf; WCh: '97- (h), '01- 5, '03- sf; WJ: '96- sf/6; CG: '02- 5; PAm: '99- 5, '03- 2; PAmJ: '97- 3/3; WI: '03- 5; won CAC 2001, 2003. Cayman Islands records 100m 1994-2003. 200m 1994-03, 400m 1998-9.
Progression at 200m: 1994- 24.31, 1995- 23.83, 1996- 23.65, 1997- 23.80, 1998- 23.48, 1999- 22.81, 2000- 22.66, 2001- 22.54, 2002- 22.76, 2003- 22.45/22.41w. pbs: 60m 7.36i '03, 100m 11.26 '03, 11.21w '00; 300m 35.82 '00, 400m 53.13 '99.

CHILE

Governing body: Federación Atlética de Chile, Calle Santo Toribio No 660, Ñuñoa, Santiago de Chile. Founded 1917.
2003 National Champions: **Men**: 100m/200m: Pablo Colville 10.64/21.48, 400m: Mauricio Mery 47.89, 800m: Nelson Maldonado 1:51.70, 1500m: Ronny Bravo 3:49.85, 5000m: Jonathan Monje 14:14.64, 10000m: Carlos Jaramillo 30:05.1, 3000mSt: Sebastián Pino 8:57.52, 110mh: Cristóbal Lyon 14.97, 400mh: Carlos Zbinden 51.34, HJ: Francisco Castro 1.95, PV: José Francisco Nava 5.00, LJ: Juan Gallardo 7.01, TJ: Felipe Apablaza 15.43, SP: Daniel Muñoz 16.55, DT: Andrés Solo de Zaldívar 49.31, HT: Patricio Palma 67.18 light, JT: Diego Moraga 70.73, 20kmW: Cristián Muñoz 1:27:44. **Women**: 100m: María Isabel Coloma 11.98, 200m: María José Echevarría 24.82, 400m: Roxana González 56.33, 800m: Liliana Farfal 2:13.84, 1500m: Clara Morales 4:27.77, 5000m: Luz Silva 16:37.74, 10000m: Francisca Peregrín 47:09.89, 3000mSt: Anahí Soto 10:23.82, 100mh: Francisca Guzmán 13.79, 400mh: Minerva Navarrete 64.91, HJ: Kerstin Weiss 1.70, PV: Pamela Barnert 3.80, LJ: Marianne Hartard 5.38, SP/DT: Marianne Berndt 15.50/46.79, HT: Odette Palma 55.96, JT: Paula Palma 44.89, 20kmW: Marcela Pacheco 1:44.28.9.

CHINA

Governing body: Athletic Association of the People's Republic of China, 9 Tiyuguan Road, Beijing 100763.
National Championships first held in 1910 (men), 1959 (women). **2003 Champions**. **Men**: 100m: Chen Haijian 10.17, 200m: Yang Yaozu 20.93, 400m: Xu Zizhou 46.29, 800m: Li Huiquan 1:49.41, 1500m: Dou Zhaobo 3:45.03, 5000m: Han Gang 13:54.73, 10000m: Gong Ke 29:51.89, 3000mSt: Sun Wenli 8:42.44, Mar: Liu Zhuhong 2:14:39, 110mh: Shi Dongpeng 13.40, 400mh: Shao Yi 49.75, HJ: Wang Zhouzhou 2.21, PV: Zhang Hongwei 5.40, LJ: Huang Le 8.10, TJ: Gu Junjie 16.83, SP: Wang Zhiyong 18.86, DT: Wu Tao 61.84, HT: Ye Kuigang 68.99, JT: Li Rongxiang 78.75, Dec: Qi Haifeng 7503, 20kmW: Zhu Hongjun 1:18:43, 50kmW: Yu Chaohong 3:44:12. **Women**: 100m/200m: Qin Wangping 11.39/23.26, 400m: Sun Hongfeng 51.64, 800m: Liu Xiaoping 2:01.75, 1500m: Xing Huina 4:09.01, 5000m/10000m: Sun Yingjie 15:10.78/31:49.33, Mar: Zhou Chunxiu 2:34:16, 3000mSt: Chen Xiaofang 9:50.88, 100mh: Su Yiping 13.21, 400mh: Huang Xiaoxiao 56.37, HJ: Jing Xuezhu 1.84, PV: Zhao Yingying 4.20, LJ: Liang Shuyan 6.65w, TJ: Huang Qiuyan 14.03, SP: Li Fengfeng 18.39. DT: Song Aimin 61.59, HT: Gu Yuan 72.03, JT: Ma Ning 58.86, Hep: Shen Shengfei 5983, 10kmW: Gao Kelian 43:23, 20kmW: Song Hongjuan 1:27:16.
National Games 2003: Men: 100m/200m: He Jun 10.46/21.19, 400m: Tan Biao 46.19, 800m: Li Xiangyu 1:49.97, 1500m: Dou Zhaobo 3:36.49, 5000m: Yang Weize 14:02.41, 10000m: Zhang Yunzhan 29:01.85, 3000mSt: Meng Fei 8:49.47, 110mh: Liu Xiang 13.31, 400mh: Zhang Shibao 50.80, HJ: 1, Zheng Ting 2.24, PV: Liu Feiliang 5.20, LJ: Cai Peng 7.88, TJ: Gu Junjie 16.92, SP: Zhang Qi 18.36, DT: Wu Tao 60.72, HT: Ma Liang 71.01, JT: Liu Yanhong 79.23, Dec: Qi Haifeng 7649, 20,000W: Xu Xingde 1:23:34.7. **Women**: 100m/200m: Zou Yiting 11.53/23.31, 400m: Huang Xiaoxiao 51.93, 800m: Yang Wei 2:01.68,

1500m: Xie Sainan 4:11.68, 5000m/10000m: Xing Huina 16:00.00/32:36.24, 100mh: Zhang Rong 13.14, 400mh: Huang Xiaoxiao 55.10, HJ: Li Shan 1.85, PV: Zhao Yingying 4.20, LJ: Xu Bei 6.61, TJ: Qiu Huijing 13.78, SP: Zhang Xiaoyu 17.76, DT: Ma Xuejun 60.20, HT: Zhang Wenxiu 70.22, JT: , Hep: Liu Haili 5621.

LIU Xiang b. 15 Jul 1983 Shanghai 1.89m 82kg.
At 110mh: WCh: '01- sf, '03- 3; WJ: '00- 4; WUG: '01- 1; AsiG: '02- 1; AsiC: '02- 1; WCp: '02- dnf. Won CHN 2002, E.Asian 2001. At 60mh: WI: '03- 3, '04- 2.
World junior records 110mh 2002, indoors 50mh (6.53 and 6.52) & 60mh (7.61 and 7.55). Six Asian indoor 60mh records 2002-04.
Progression at 110mh: 1999- 14.19, 2000- 13.75, 2001- 13.32, 2002- 13.12, 2003- 13.17. pbs: 50mh 6.52i '02, 60mh 7.43i '04, HJ 2.04 '98.

SHI Dongpeng b. 6 Jan 1984 1.92m 75kg.
At 110mh: WCh: '03- 7; WJ: '02- 2; AsiG: '02- 4; AsiC: '03- 1; Won CHN 2003.
World U18 110mh record 2001.
Progression at 110mh: 2000- 14.10, 2001- 13.43, 2002- 13.50, 2003- 13.40. pb 60mh 7.75i '04.

Women

GAO Shuying b. 28 Oct 1979 1.80m 63kg.
At PV: OG: '00- 10; WCh: '01- 5, '03- 9; WJ: '98- 8; AsiG: '02- 1; AsiC: '02- 1, '03- 4; WUG: '01- 1; WCp: '02- 4. Won CHN 2000-02, E.Asian 2001, CHN NG 2001.
Seven Asian pole vault records 2000-01.
Progression at PV: 1996- 3.30, 1997- 3.70, 1998- 3.90, 1999- 4.10, 2000- 4.35, 2001- 4.52, 2002- 4.45i/4.43, 2003- 4.40.

GU Yuan b. 9 May 1982 1.68 70kg.
At HT: WCh: '03- 4; AsiG: '02- 1; AsiC: '98-02-03: 1/1/1; WCp: '02- 1. Won CHN 2003, NG 2001.
Ten CHN hammer records 1998-2003, five Asian 2001-03, five Asian junior 1999-2001.
Progression at HT: 1998- 62.28, 1999- 63.38, 2000- 64.72, 2001- 66.97, 2002- 71.10, 2003- 72.03.

GUAN Yingnan b. 25 Apr 1977 Shanghai 1.77m 60kg.
At LJ: OG: '00- dnq 19; WCh: '99- dnq 17, '01- 9, '03- dnq 13; WJ: '96- 1; AsiG: '98- 1; AsiC: '98- 1; WI: '99-01-04: 6/7/4; WUG: '01- 2; WCp: '98- 3. Won Asi-J 1996, CHN 1998-2000, E.Asian 2001.
Progression at LJ: 1994- 6.11, 1995- 6.48, 1996- 6.68, 1997- 6.86, 1998- 6.91, 1999- 6.80, 2000- 6.95, 2001- 6.77, 2003- 6.72, 2004- 6.80i. pbs: 100mh 14.53 '95, HJ 1.80 '94, JT 39.64 '95, Hep 5637 '95.

HUANG Qiuyan b. 25 Jan 1980 1.68m 60kg.
At TJ: WCh: '03- 13; AsiG: '02- 1; AsiC: '03- 1; Won CHN NG 1997, 2001; CHN 2002-03, Af-AsG 2003.
Asian triple jump record 2001.
Progression at TJ: 1997- 14.57, 1998- 14.36, 1999- 13.68, 2000- 13.76, 2001- 14.72, 2002- 14.60, 2003- 14.39. World age-17 best in 1997.

LI Meiju b. 23 Jan 1981 1.73m 85kg.
At SP: WCh: '03- 11; WJ: '00- 2; AsiG: '02- 1, AsiC: '03- 1; WI: '04- 6. Won CHN 2002, NG 2001, Af-AsG 2003.
Progression at SP: 1998- 15.89, 1999- 16.62, 2000- 17.48, 2001- 18.92, 2002- 18.95, 2003- 18.96.

SONG Aimin b. 4 Jul 1984.
At 20kmW: WCh: '03- dq; Chinese champion 2003-04.
Progression at 20kmW: 2001- 1:40:38, 2004- 1:27:16, 2004- 1:26:46. pb 10kmW 44:22 03.

SONG Hongjuan b. 15 Mar 1978 1.76m 67kg.
At DT: WCh: '03- 7; AsiG: '02- 2. Won CHN 2001-03.
Progression at DT: 1997- 55.84, 1998- 56.64, 1999- 60.50, 2000- 60.39, 2001- 62.34, 2002- 62.28, 2003- 65.33.

SUN Yingjie b. 3 Oct 1977 1.65m 50kg.
At 5000m/10000m: WCh: '03- 9/3. AsiG: '02- 1/1; AsiC: '03- 1/1. At Mar: WCh: '99- 12. Won CHN 5000m & 10000m 2002-03, Mar 1998.
Asian marathon record 2003.
Progression at 5000m, 10000m, Mar: 1997- 2:30:10, 1998- 15:47.87, 32:34.48, 2:25:45; 1999- 15:32.14, 32:12.7, 2:30:12; 2000- 2:26:36, 2001- 15:02.70, 31:49.47, 2:29:16; 2002- 14:40.41, 30:28.26, 2:21:21; 2003- 14:46.73, 30:07.20, 2:19:39. pbs: 1500m 4:16.01 '03, 3000m 8:50.34 '03, HMar 70:22 '99.
Four wins in 16 marathons: Tianjin and Dalian 1998, Tianjin and Beijing 2003.

WANG LIPING – see end of Biogs section.

XING Huina b. 25 Feb 1984. 1.66m 50kg.
At (5000m)/10000m: WCh: '03- 6; AsiG: '02- 4/3. Won CHN 1500m 2003.
World junior 10000m record 2003.
Progression at 5000m, 10000m: 2000- 16:11.09, 2001- 14:56.15, 36:38.91; 2002- 15:42.99, 31:42.58; 2003- 15:00.02, 30:31.55. pb 1500m 4:09.01 '03.

COLOMBIA

Governing body: Federación Colombiana de Atletismo, Calle 28 No. 25-18, Apartado Aéreo 6024, Santafé de Bogotá. Founded 1937.

2003 Champions: Men: 100m: Jimmy Pino 10.61, 200m: John Jairo Córdoba 21.21w, 400m: Julio César Rojas 47.51, 800m: José Bermúdez 1:50.00, 1500m: Mauricio Ladino 3:53.16, 5000m: Jacinto López 14:56.20, 10000m: William Naranjo 30:55.14, 3000mSt: John Vargas 9:35.14, 110mh: Paulo Villar 13.74, 400mh: Alexander Mena 51.77, HJ: Gilmar Mayo 2.05, PV: David Rojas 4.60, LJ: Daimnler Griego 7.49, TJ: Leigner Aragón 15.99, SP: Johnny Rodríguez 18.87, DT: Julián Angulo 54.70, HT: Freimar Arias 51.94, JT: Noraldo Palacios 74.23, Dec: Robinson Urrutia 6316. **Women:** 100m: Melisa Murillo 11.44w, 200m: Digna Murillo 23.18w, 400m/800m: Rosibel García 53.46/2:05.53, 1500m/5000m/10000m: Bertha Sánchez 4:36.08/17:51.95/37:29.50, Mar:, 3000mSt: Diana Alzate 11:31.4, 100mh/400mh:

Princesa Oliveros 13.63/59.24, HJ/LJ/TJ: Katherina Ibargüen 1.80/5.89/13.23, PV: Milena Agudelo 3.80, SP/DT: Luz Dary Castro 15.23/53.65, HT: Yaiza Córdoba 56.17, JT: Sabina Moya 54.52, Hep: Yolanda Mina 4488, 20000mW: Sandra Zapata 1:40:14.9.

DEMOCRATIC REPUBLIC OF CONGO

Governing Body: Fédération d'Athlétisme du Congo, BP 1527 Kinshasa 1. Founded 1949.

Gary KIKAYA b. 4 Feb 1978 Congo 1.84m 75kg. Sociology student at University of Tennessee.
At 400m: WCh: '03- sf; WI: '04- 3; Won NCAA 2002. COD records 200m & 400m 2001-03.
Progression at 400m: 2000- 46.51A, 2001- 45.58A, 2002- 44.53, 2003- 44.99. pbs: 55m 6.27i '04, 200m 20.73 '03.
Lived in South Africa for a decade as his father was Congo's ambassador there.

CROATIA

Governing body: Hrvatski Atletski Savez, Tg Sportova 11, 10000 Zagreb. Founded 1912.
2003 Champions: **Men**: 100m: Dejan Vojnovic 10.47, 200m: Josip Soprek 21.48, 400m: Branimir Peitel 47.38, 800m: Dalibor Balgac 1:52.43, 1500m: Jure Bozinovic 4:11.81, 3000m/5000m: Dario Nemec 9:00,64/15:21.09, 10000m/HMar: Drazen Dinjar 31:32.45/69:22, Mar: Janez Maroevic 2:32:49 3000mSt: Sasa Ljubojevic 9:43.48, 110mh: Zoran Miljus 13.94, 400mh: Milan Kotur 53.03, HJ: Goran Subotic 2.11, PV: Bosko Trisovic 4.60, LJ: Marijo Bakovic 7.80, TJ: Vedran Zoricic 15.05, SP: Nedzad Mulabegovic 20.15, DT: Drazen Prskalo 57.37, HT: Sasa Novoselec 62.50, JT: Edi Ponos 72.46, 10kmW: Bojan Puaca 1:14:09. **Women**: 100m: Ria Rukavina 11.84, 200m/400m: Danijela Grgic 24.23/55.06, 800m: Petra Pticek 2:08.81, 1500m: Vanja Perisic 4:40.29, 3000m: Ljiljana Culibrk 10:15.34, 5000m: Ivancica Cvitkovic 18:52.43, 10000m: Veronika Jurisic 39:03.06, HMar: Lidija Rajcic 84:16, Mar: Marija Trosic 2:58:01, 100mh: Andrea Ivancevic 13.88, 400mh: Nikolina Horvat 62.59, HJ: Nevena Lendjel 1.75, PV: Ivona Jerkovic 3.60, LJ/TJ: Sandra Petricevic 6.03/12.91, SP: Martina Masic 13.46, DT: Vera Begic 56.48, HT: Sanja Gavrilovic 64.96, JT: Jelena Jurlina 45.15.

Sinisa ERGOTIC b. 14 Sep 1968 Osijek 1.79m 63kg.
At LJ: OG: '96/00- dnq; WCh: '95- dnq, '03- dnq 14; EC: '98- dnq, '02- 2. Won MedG 2001, YUG 1987, 1989-90. CRO LJ records 1990-2003.
Progression at LJ: 1987- 7.73, 1988- 7.90, 1989- 7.88, 1990- 8.00/8.04w, 1991- 7.87, 1992- 7.95ex, 1994- 8.00, 1995- 7.93, 1996- 8.06, 1998- 7.86/7.90w, 1999- 7.93, 2000- 8.01, 2001- 7.98/8.09w/8.08dq, 2002- 8.23/8.25w, 2003- 8.23. pbs: 100m 10.76 '91, TJ 15.67 '89.

Women

Blanka VLASIC b. 8 Nov 1983 Split 1.92m 75kg. ASK PK Split.
At HJ: OG: '00- dnq 17; WCh: '01- 6, '03- 7; EC: '02- 5=; WJ: '00- 1, '02- 1; WY: '99- 8; EU23: '03- 1; EJ: '01- 7; WI: '03- 4, '04- 3. Won MedG 2001, CRO 2001-02.
Two Croatian high jump records 2003.
Progression at HJ: 1998- 1.68, 1999- 1.80, 2000- 1.93, 2001- 1.95, 2002- 1.96, 2003- 2.01.
Her father Josko set the Croatian decathlon record with 7659 (1983).

CUBA

Governing body: Federación Cubana de Atletismo, Calle 13 y C Vedado 601, Zone Postal 4, La Habana 10400. Founded 1922.
National Champions 2003: **Men**: 100m: Luis Reyes 10.54, 200m: Juan Pita 21.38, 400m: Yeimar López 45.95, 800m: José Ricoll 1:51.04, 1500m: Maury Castillo 3:45.48, 5000m/10000m: Norbert Gutiérrez 14:18.80/29:37.42, Mar: Yosbel Arboláez 2:32:40, 3000mSt: Yandri Caraballo 8:54.72, 110mh: Yuniel Hernández 13.69, 400mh: Sergio Hierrezuelo 49.46, HJ: Lisvani Pérez 2.21, PV: Frank Céspedes 5.10, LJ: Yoelmis Pacheco 7.72, TJ: Yoandri Betanzos 16.94, SP: Alexis Paumier 19.65, DT: Frank Casañas 59.78, HT: Iosvany Suárez 71.85, JT: Isbel Luaces 80.62, Dec: Yonelvis Águila 7543, 20kmW: Jorge Luis Pino 1:28:18. **Women**: 100m/200m: Roxana Díaz 11.60/23.45, 400m: Libania Grenot 52.20, 800m/1500m: Adriana Muñoz 2:01.07/4:15.43, 5000m/10000m: Yudelkis Martínez 16:15.91/34:45.38, Mar: Emperatriz Wilson 2:46:20, 100mh: Anay Tejeda 13.13, 400mh: Dayani Lara 59.65, HJ: Yarianny Argüelles 1.88, PV: Katiuska Pérez 4.20, LJ: Yudelkis Fernández 6.53, TJ: Mabel Gay 14.25, SP: Yumileidi Cumbá 18.89, DT: Anaelys Fernández 59.14, HT: Yipsi Moreno 72.47, JT: Osleidys Menéndez 63.96, Hep: Magalys García 5842, 20kmW: Yaimara Pérez 1:41:35.

Yoandri BETANZOS b. 15 Feb 1982 Ciego de Ávila 1.79m 71kg.
At TJ: WCh: '03- 2; WJ: '00- 2; WY: '99- 2; PAm: '03- 1; WUG: '01- 5; WI: '04- 3; Won PAm-J 2001, Cuban 2002-03,
Progression at TJ: 1999- 15.94/16.07w, 2000- 16.82, 2001- 16.84/16.86w, 2002- 17.29, 2003- 17.28, 2004- 17.39i.

Anier Octavio **GARCÍA** b. 9 Mar 1976 Santiago de Cuba 1.89m 85kg.
At 110mh: OG: '96- qf, '00- 1; WCh: '97- sf, '99- 2, '01- 2; WJ: '94- 5; PAm: '99- 1, '03- h; CAG: '98- 1; WCp: '98- 3, '02- 1. Won GP 2001, PAm-J 1995, IbAm 1996, Cuban 1997-2000. At 60mh: WI: '97-9-01-03: 1/6/2/2.
Five CAC & Cuban 110mh records 1997-2000. CAC indoor records at 50mh & 60mh 2000.
Progression at 110mh: 1993- 14.61, 1994- 13.91,

1995- 13.63/13.6, 1996- 13.39A/13.43, 1997- 13.11, 1998- 13.14A/13.24, 1999- 13.07, 2000- 13.00, 2001- 13.07, 2002- 13.03, 2003- 13.55. pb 50mh 6.36i '00, 60mh 7.37i '00.
Worod number one in 2002. His father Pedro was an international 400mh runner and his mother Barbara Ortíz was a heptathlete.

David GIRALT b. 26 Aug 1984 Santiago de Cuba 1.82m 72kg.
At TJ: WCh: '03- 4; WJ: '02- 1. Won PAm-J 2003 (2 LJ).
Progression at TJ: 2000- 15.23, 2001- 16.33, 2002- 16.84, 2003- 17.31. pb LJ 7.70 '02.
Father (also David) had LJ pbs 8.22/8.32w and was third in the World Cupin 1979.

Emeterio GONZÁLEZ b. 11 Apr 1973 San Juan y Martínez, Pinar del Río 1.84m 105kg.
At JT: OG: '96- dnq 18, '00- 8; WCh: '95- dnq 17, '97- 7, '99- 7, '01/03- dnq 18/16; WJ: '92- 6; '94- 7; PAm: '95- 1, '99- 1, '03- 1; CAG: '93- 3, '98- 1; WUG: '97- 2, '99- 4; WCp: '98- 5, '02- 3. Won CUB 1996-2002, CAC 1997, Ib-Am 2000.
Nine CAC & Cuban javelin records 1995-2000.
Progression at JT: 1989- 60.36, 1990- 67.40, 1991- 65.78, 1992- 73.56, 1993- 74.14, 1994- 78.18, 1995- 82.64, 1996- 82.10, 1997- 83.56, 1998- 84.20, 1999- 84.32, 2000- 87.12, 2001- 82.77, 2002- 82.63, 2003- 81.72.

Yoel HERNÁNDEZ b. 12 Dec 1977 Manacas, Villa Clara 1.84m 77kg.
At 110mh: OG: '00- sf; WCh: '99- 6, '01- 4, '03- 8; WJ: '94- sf, '96- 1; PAm: '99- 2; Won Cuban 2002. At 60mh: WI: '01- 5, '03- 7.
Progression at 110mh: 1994- 14.20, 1995- 13.81, 1996- 13.81/13.72w, 1997- 13.70, 1998- 13.45, 1999- 13.24, 2000- 13.24/13.20w, 2001- 13.30, 2002- 13.30, 2003- 13.49. pbs: 100m 10.69 '99, 200m 21.10 '02, 50mh 6.42i '00, 60mh 7.40i '00.

Yuniel HERNÁNDEZ b. 28 Mar 1981 Caimito 1.82m 76kg.
At 110mh: WCh: '01- sf; WJ: '00- 1; PAm: '03- 1. Cuban champion 2003. At 60mh: WI: '04- 5.
At 110mh: 1997- 14.78, 1998- 14.17, 1999- 13.99/13.81w, 2000- 13.60/13.5, 2001- 13.26, 2002- 13.63, 2003- 13.35. pbs: 100m 10.43 '01, 50mh 6.56i '01, 60mh 7.54i '02.

Alexander MARTÍNEZ b. 23 Aug 1977 Nueva Gerona, Isla de al Junentud 1.84m 82kg.
At TJ: 3rd GP 2002.
Progression at TJ: 1995- 15.53, 1996- 15.88, 1998- 16.67, 1999- 16.50, 2000- 16.80, 2001- 17.06, 2002- 17.32, 2003- 17.06.
Lives in Zürich, has a Swiss wife Marion (with whom he has won international salsa dancing competitions) and is seeking Swiss citizenship.

Luis Felipe **MÉLIZ** b. 11 Aug 1979 Santa Clara, Villa Clara 1.77m 76kg.
At LJ: OG: '00- 7; WCh: '99/01- dnq 18/17, '03- 11; WI: '01- 9, '03- 4; WJ: '98 - 3; PAm: '99- 3, '03- 2; WUG: '99- 2.
Progression at LJ: 1997- 7.65, 1998- 8.05, 1999- 8.14/8.23 irreg, 2000- 8.43, 2001- 8.11i/8.10, 2002- 8.27, 2003- 8.20.

Iván Lázaro **PEDROSO** b. 17 Dec 1972 Guanabacoa, La Habana 1.76m 70kg. Adidas.
At LJ: OG: '92- 4, '96- 12, '00- 1; WCh: '93- nj, '95- 1, '97- 1, '99- 1, '01- 1, '03- nj; WI: '93-5-7-9-01-04: 1/1/1/1/1/8; WJ: '90- 4; WUG: '97- 1; PAm: '91-5-9-03: 3/1/1/1; CAG: '98- 1; WCp: '92- 1, '98- 1, '02- 2. Won GP 1995, 1997, 1999; GWG 1998, 2001; PAm J 1991, IbAm 1992, CAC 1997, Cuban 1992-3, 1995, 1997-8, 2000.
Three CAC & Cuban long jump records 1992-5.
Progression at LJ: 1988- 7.43, 1989- 7.43, 1990- 8.06, 1991- 8.22, 1992- 8.53/8.79w, 1993- 8.49, 1994- 8.26i/8.16, 1995- 8.71/8.96Aw, 1996- 8.46i/8.32, 1997- 8.63, 1998- 8.54, 1999- 8.62i/8.60, 2000- 8.65, 2001- 8.43i/8.40, 2002- 8.30, 2003- 8.31. pb TJ 16.05 '91.
Won fifth successive World Indoor title and fourth successive outdoor title in 2001. Clearly the world top long jumper in 1995, when he had a narrow foul at 9.03 at the Pan-American Games and jumped 8.96 at Sestriere. This was shown to have a wind of just 1.2 m/s, but allegations were made of interference by an official standing in front of the gauge and the mark was not recognised. Unbeaten in 26 LJ competitions 1995 to Jan 1996. Hamstring surgery in 1996 meant that he was not fully fit at the Olympics, but he was back at the top in 1997, and won 84/99 competitions in 1997-2001. Cousin of Aliuska López (Pedroso).

Yoelbi Luis **QUESADA** b. 4 Aug 1973 Trinidad, Sancti Spíritus 1.81m 71kg. Adidas.
At TJ: OG: '92- 6, '96- 3, '00- 4; WCh: '91- 7, '93- 12, '95- 4, '97- 1, '99- 10, '03- 9; WI: '93-5-9-03: 5/2/4/3; WJ: '90- 2, '92- 1; WUG: '97- 1, '99- 1; WCp: '94- 1, '98- 3; PAm: '91-5-9-03: 1/1/1/3; CAG: '93- 1, '98- 1. Won CAC-J 1990, PAmJ 1991, IbAm 1992, Cuban 1991-5, 1997-8, 2002. 2nd GP 1996. Cuban triple jump record 1997.
Progression at TJ: 1989- 16.11, 1990- 16.68, 1991- 17.13, 1992- 17.23, 1993- 17.68, 1994- 17.61, 1995- 17.67/17.97w, 1996- 17.75, 1997- 17.85, 1998- 17.43i/17.27, 1999- 17.40, 2000- 17.37, 2001- 16.55, 2002- 17.42, 2003- 17.27i/16.97. pb LJ 7.88 '94.
World age bests for each age 15-19 in 1989-93.

Women

Sonia BISSET b. 1 Apr 1971 Palma Soriano, Santiago de Cuba 1.71m 69kg.
At JT: OG: '00- 5; WCh: '97- 6, '99- 6, '01- 3, '03- 6; PAm: '03- 5; CAG: '98- 1; WUG: '97- 2; WCp: '98- 2. CAC champion 1995, IbAm 1996, Cuban 1998, GP 2000.
Progression at JT: 1987- 50.40, 1988- 58.28, 1989- 55.94, 1990- 55.20, 1991- 57.64, 1992- 58.38, 1993- 59.52, 1994- 61.42, 1995- 62.52, 1996- 64.54, 1997- 68.24, 1998- 67.59; new: 1999- 63.52, 2000- 65.87, 2001- 66.54, 2002- 65.52. 2003- 60.75, 2004- 64.33.

Yunaika CRAWFORD b. 2 Nov 1982 La Habana 1.65m 75kg.
At HT: WCh: '03- dnq 20; WJ: '00- 3; WY: '99- 2; PAm: '03- 2; Won PAm-J 2001, CAC 2001.
Progression at HT: 1995- 38.86, 1997- 48.98, 1998- 58.92, 1999- 62.71, 2000- 65.88, 2001- 65.67, 2002- 70.62, 2003- 70.69, 2004- 71.62.

Yumileidi CUMBÁ b. 11 Feb 1975 Guantánamo 1.83m 100kg. PE student.
At SP: OG: '96- dnq 13, '00- 6; WCh: '99- 6, '01- 8, '03- dnq 13; PAm: '95- 3, '99- 2, '03- 1; CAG: '93- 2, '98- 1; WJ: '92- 4, '94- 2; WI: '99-01-03-04: 6/5/6/3; WUG: '99- 1, '01- 1; WCp: '98- 4, '02- 2. Won Cuban 1994-5, 1998, 2000-03; IbAm 2002.
Progression at SP: 1990- 14.53, 1991- 15.84, 1992- 17.44, 1993- 17.70, 1994- 18.78, 1995- 19.11, 1996- 18.57, 1998- 19.20, 1999- 19.29, 2000- 19.48, 2001- 19.10i/19.00, 2002- 19.39, 2003- 19.31, 2004- 19.31i. pb DT 42.84 '93.

Mabel GAY b. 5 May 1983 Santiago de Cuba 1.85m 71kg.
At TJ: WCh: '03- 5; WJ: '02- 1; WY: '99- 1; PAm: '03- 1; WI: '04- 9; Won CAC-J 2002, IbAm 2002, Cuban 2003.
Progression at TJ: 1997- 13.00, 1998- 13.48, 1999- 13.82, 2000- 14.02, 2001- 14.05, 2002- 14.29, 2003- 14.52, 2004- 14.57i.

Osleidys MENÉNDEZ b. 14 Nov 1979 Martí, Matanzas 1.78m 80kg.
At JT: OG: '00- 3; WCh: '97- 7, '99- 4, '01- 1, '03- 5; WJ: '96- 1, '98- 1; WUG: '01- 1; PAm: '99- 1, '03- 3; CAG: '98- 2; WCp: '02- 1. Won GWG 2001, PAm-J 1995, 1997; Cuban 1997, 1999-2002; CAC 1997, GP 2002 (3rd 2000).
Word javelin record 2001, Eight CAC bests and one world (66.45 '99) new javelin 1999-2001.
Progression at JT: 1994- 53.98, 1995- 54.30, 1996- 62.54, 1997- 66.92, 1998- 68.17, 1999- 67.59; new 1999- 66.49, 2000- 67.83, 2001- 71.54, 2002- 67.40, 2003- 63.96, 2004- 68.23.
On 1 July 2001 she became the first Cuban woman to set a world record in athletics.

Yipsi MORENO b. 19 Nov 1980 Camagüey 1.68m 70kg.
At HT: OG: '00- 4; WCh: '99- 18, '01- 1, '03- 1; WJ: '98- 4; PAm: '99- 2, '03- 1; WUG: '01- 2; WCp: '02- 2. Won PAm-J 1997, Cuban 2000-03.
World junior hammer record 1999, 19 CAC records 1999-2003.
Progression at HT: 1996- 53.94, 1997- 61.96, 1998- 61.00, 1999- 66.34, 2000- 69.36, 2001- 70.65, 2002- 71.47, 2003- 75.14, 2004- 74.43.

Daimí PERNÍA b. 27 Dec 1976 La Palma, Pinar del Rio 1.73m 59kg. PE student.
At 400mh/4x400mR: OG: '00- 4; WCh: '99- 1, '01- 3; PAm: '99- 1/1R, '03- 2; WUG: '97- 3/2R, '99- 1. Won Cuban 400mh 1997, 1999, 2001.
Seven Cuban 400mh records 1997-9.
Progression at 400mh: 1996- 59.2, 1997- 55.51, 1998- 57.40, 1999- 52.89, 2000- 53.68, 2001- 53.81, 2002- 54.54, 2003- 55.10. pbs: 200m 23.43 '99, 400m 51.10 '01.
Formerly a basketball player.

Anay TEJEDA b. 3 Apr 1983 La Habana 1.65m 59kg.
At 100mh: WJ: '00- 7, '02- 1; WY: '99- 3; PAm: '03- 8. Cuban champion 2003.
Progression at 100mh: 1998- 14.00, 1999- 13.56, 2000- 13.38, 2001- 13.20/13.07w, 2002- 12.89/12.6/12.81w, 2003- 12.99. pbs: 100m 12.12 '03, 200m 24.2 '02, 50mh 6.93i '04, 60mh 8.03i '04.

CZECH REPUBLIC

Governing body: Cesky atleticky svaz, Diskarská 100, 169 00 Praha 6 -Strahov, PO Box 40. AAU of Bohemia founded in 1897.

National Championships first held in 1907 (Bohemia), 1919 (Czechoslovakia), 1993 CZE.

2003 Champions: **Men**: 100m/200m: Jirí Vojtik 10.38w/20.82, 400m: Václav Bláha 46.46, 800m: Roman Oravec 1:53.97, 1500m: Petr Mlatecek 3:53.32, 5000m/3000mSt: Michael Nejedly 14:13.27/8:42.33, 10000m/Mar: Jan Blaha 30:24.04/2:22:21, HMar: Pavel Faschingbauer 67:18, 110mh: Stanislav Sajdok 13.97, 400mh: Stepan Tesarik 49.49, HJ: Jaroslav Baba 2.27, PV: Adam Ptácek 5.60, LJ/TJ: Petr Hnízdil 7.66/16.06, SP: Petr Stehlík 20.33, DT: Libor Malina 61.11, HT: Lukás Melich 74.72, JT: Miroslav Guzdek 75.65, Dec: Vít Zákoucky 7133, 20kmW/50kmW: Milos Holusa 1:26:19/4:04:40. **Women**: 100m: Tereza Kosková 11.73, 200m: Hana Benesová 24.08, 400m: Eva Follnerová 54.34, 800m: Petra Lochmanová 2:06.70, 1500m: Andrea Suldesová 4:14.57, 5000m: Michaela Mannová 15:54.10, 10000m: Petra Kamínková 33:58.20, HMar: Irena Sádková 79:40, Mar: Ivana Martincová 2:50:42, 3000mSt: Jana Biolková 9:49.40, 100mh: Lucie Martincová 13.22, 400mh: Lucie Sichertová 59.44, HJ: Zuzana Hlavonová 1.92, PV: Pavla Hamacková 4.55, LJ: Lucie Komrsková 6.34w, TJ: Martina Darmovzalová 12.72, SP: Jana Kárníková 15.10, DT: Vera Pospísilová 65.86, HT: Lucie Vrbenská 67.86, JT: Barbora Spotáková 52.20, Hep: Jana Klecková 5601, 20kmW: Barbora Dibelková 1:39:46.

Jaroslav BÁBA b. 2 Sep 1984 Karviná 1.96m 82kg. SSK Vitkovice.
At HJ: WCh: '03- 11; WJ: '02- 8; WY: '01- 10=; EJ: '03- 1; WI: '03- 9, '04- 3=. Won CZE 2003.
Progression at HJ: 1997- 1.72i, 1998- 1.81i/1.75, 1999- 1.93i/1.92, 2000- 1.95, 2001- 2.16i/2.15, 2002- 2.27/2.28et, 2003- 2.32i/2.30, 2004- 2.34i. pb TJ 15.43 '03.

Tomás DVORÁK b. 11 May 1972 Gottwaldov (now Zlin) 1.86m 88kg. Dukla Praha. Soldier.
At Dec: OG: '96- 3 (h 110mh), '00- 6; WCh: '93- 10, '95- 5, '97- 1, '99- 1, '01- 1, '03- 4; EC: '94- 7, '98- 5, '02- dnf; ECp: '94- 3, '95- 1, '99- 1; WJ: '90- 17; EJ: '91- 2; won GWG 2001. At Hep: WI: '95-7-9-03: 2/dnf/4/5; EI: '94-6-8-00-02: 4/2/4/1/2.

Charles Dumas (photo courtesy of Track & Field News)

Fanny Blankers Koen winning the 200m at the 1948 London Olympics, one of four golds.
(photo courtesy of Track & Field News)

Tom Pappas

Jefferson Pérez

Berhane Adere

Jana Pittman

Hestrie Cloete

Yelena Isinbayeva

The winning French relay team in Paris - from left: Sylviane Félix, Christine Arron, Patricia Girard and Muriel Hurtis

Tyree Washington - World Indoor 400m champion 2003

Won Czech 110mh 1994-2001, Dec 1991.
World decathlon record 1999, three Czech 1996-9. European indoor heptathlon record 2000.
Progression at Dec: 1989- 6999, 1990- 7251w/7138, 1991- 7748, 1992- 7392, 1993- 8054, 1994- 8313, 1995- 8347, 1996- 8664, 1997- 8837, 1998- 8592, 1999- 8994, 2000- 8900, 2001- 8902, 2002- 8226, 2003- 8242. pbs: 60m 6.90i '97, 100m 10.54 '99, 200m 21.39 '98, 400m 47.56 '97, 1000m 2:34.60i '98, 1500m 4:27.63 '03, 50mh 6.59i '96, 60mh 7.76i '00, 110mh 13.61/13.6 '97, HJ 2.09 '00, PV 5.00 '97, LJ 8.07 '01, SP 16.88 '00, DT 50.28 '00, JT 72.32 '99, Hep 6424i '00.
Set four pbs en route to Olympic bronze in 1996 and six pbs when he won World gold in 1997. In 1999 he won all his four decathlons and added 103 points to Dan O'Briens' world record, missing 9000 by just six points and setting five pbs in this supreme effort. After 2nd 1996-8, won at Götzis 1999 and 2000 and Talence 2000 before injury held him back to sixth in Sydney. Won the IAAF Combined Events Challenge in 1999 and 2001. Has 31 decathlons over 8000 points 1993-2003. Married Gabriela Vánová (pb LJ 6.28/6.30w '93, daughter of his ex-coach).

Tomás JANKU b. 27 Dec 1974 Jablonec nad Nisou 1.91m 75kg. Dukla Praha.
At HJ: OG: '96- 14; WCh: '97/03- dnq 28/16=; EC: '98- 12, '02- 5; WI: '99- 6=, '03- 6; EI: '98- 3, '02- 6; WJ: '92- 7; EJ: '93- 3; WUG: '97- 4; ECp: '93-8-9: 8/3/3. Won CZE 1992-4, 1996, 1998-2000, 2002.
Progression at HJ: 1988- 1.63, 1989- 1.77, 1990- 1.86, 1991- 2.05, 1992- 2.21, 1993- 2.20, 1994- 2.21, 1995- 2.22i/2.20, 1996- 2.29, 1997- 2.29, 1998- 2.31i/2.28, 1999- 2.32, 2000- 2.25, 2001- 2.16, 2002- 2.30, 2003- 2.30. pb TJ 15.56 '96.
Brother of Jan Janku (b. 10 Aug 1971) pb 2.30 '96, 2.29 '97. They set a world record for synchronised high jumping, clearing 2.18m in May 1997. Coached by his father Jan (pb 2.11 '71).

Jirí MUZÍK b. 1 Sep 1976 Plzen 1.81m 75kg. Dukla Praha.
At 400mh (400m): OG: '00- sf; WCh: '97- 8, '99- sf, '01- 7, '03- sf; EC: '98- 7, '02- 2; EU23: '97- 4/2R; WUG: '97- 4; ECp: '99- 7 (7). At 400m: EJ: '95- h; EI: '00- 1R, '02- 5. Won CZE 400mh 1997, 2001-02. Three Czech 400mh records 1997.
Progression at 400mh: 1997- 48.27, 1998- 48.83, 1999- 49.15, 2000- 48.71, 2001- 48.53, 2002- 48.43, 2003- 48.63. pbs: 100m 10.72 '03, 200m 21.06 '03, 400m 45.78 '98, 800m 1:52.73i '04, LJ 7.26 '93, TJ 15.55 '96.
Ran first 400mh race on 1 June 1997 and reached World final three months later. His father Jirí had LJ best of 7.75 '75.

Adam PTÁCEK b. 8 Oct 1980 Ostrava 1.78m 65kg. Dukla Praha.
At PV: WCh: '03- dnq 19; EC: '02- 6=; WJ: '98- 3=; EU23: '01- 7; EJ: '99- nh; WI: '04-2. Czech champion 2002.
Two Czech pole vault records 2002.
Progression at PV: 1994- 3.52, 1995-4.21, 1996- 4.75, 1997- 5.07, 1998- 5.40i/5.35, 1999- 5.60, 2000- 5.61, 2001- 5.62, 2002- 5.80, 2003- 5.81i/ 5.62. pbs: 100m 10.4 '98, 200m 21.63 '98, PV: 5.80 '02 , LJ 7.49 '98.

Roman SEBRLE b. 26 Nov 1974 Lanskroun 1.86m 88kg. Dukla Praha. Soldier.
At Dec: OG: '00- 2; WCh: '97- 9, '99- dnf, '01- 10, '03- 2; EC: '98- 6, '02- 1; WUG: '97- 1; ECp: '97-8-9: 1/2/2. At Hep: WI: '99- 01-03: 3/1/3; EI: '00- 2, '02- 1. At 110mh: ECp: '99- 6. Won Czech Dec 1996, LJ 1998.
World decathlon record 2001, European indoor heptathlon record 2004.
Progression at Dec: 1991- 5187, 1992- 6541, 1993- 7066, 1994- 7153, 1995- 7642, 1996- 8210, 1997- 8380, 1998- 8589, 1999- 8527, 2000- 8757, 2001- 9026, 2002- 8800, 2003- 8807. pbs: 60m 6.87i '02, 100m 10.64 '01, 200m 21.83 '00, 400m 47.76 '99, 1000m 2:37.86i '01, 1500m 4:21.98 '01, 60mh 7.84i '02, 110mh 13.79 '99, 13.68w '01; HJ 2.15 '00, PV 5.20 '03, LJ 8.11 '01, SP 16.28i '04, 15.96 '02; DT 49.37 '03, JT 70.16 '01, Hep 6438i '04.
Married Eva Kasalová (b. 4 Dec 1976, pb 800m 2:02.79 '98), on 14 Oct 2000. At Götzis in 2001 he became the first decathlete to exceed 9000 points with the current scoring tables, setting five personal bests. Unfortunately he then sustained a groin injury which held him back at the Worlds. Won again at Götzis 2003. Has 12 decathlons over 8500 and 27 over 8000.

Jan ZELEZNY b. 16 Jun 1966 Mladá Boleslav 1.86m 88kg. Dukla Praha.
At JT: OG: '88- 2, '92- 1, '96- 1, '00- 1; WCh: '87- 3, '91- dnq 18, '93- 1, '95- 1, '97- 9, '99- 3, '01- 1, '03- 4; EC: '86- dnq 18, '90- dnq 13, '94- 3, '02- nt; EJ: '83- 6, '85- 4; WCp: '92- 1; ECp: '87-89-91-3: 3/2/1/1. Won GP JT 1991, 1993, 1995, 1997 (2nd overall first 3 years), 2001; 2nd 1999. Won CS 1986, 1990, CZE 1992, 1994, 1996.; GWG 2001.
Five world javelin records 1987-96, eight CS records 1986-93, five CZE records 1992-6.
Progression at JT: 1979- 44.44, 1982- 57.22, 1983- 74.34, 1984- 80.32, 1985- 84.68, new: 1986- 82.48, 1987- 87.66, 1988- 86.88, 1989- 84.74, 1990- 89.66, 1991- 90.72, 1992- 94.74, 1993- 95.66, 1994- 91.82, 1995- 92.28, 1996- 98.48, 1997- 94.02, 1999- 89.06, 2000- 90.59A, 2001- 92.80, 2002- 87.77, 2003- 89.06.
His third successive Olympic gold in 2000 surely sealed Zelezny's place as the greatest ever javelin thrower. He won 114 of 148 competitions 1991-2003. In his career with the new javelin 1986-2003 his competition bests average 85.50, with 59 throws over 90m and 142 in all over 88m. His 100 best throws average 90.71m, 200 best 89.27, 300 best 88.17 and 500 best 86.08. His 94.74 throw in 1992 was made with a new 'Németh' javelin, later ruled illegal by the IAAF. In 1993 he added 4.08m to Steve Backley's world record with 95.54 at Pietersburg, RSA in April, and threw 95.56 at

Sheffield in August. Suffered a fractured vertebra at the end of 1989, but recovered to regain the world record in 1990. In 1991 he was most unlucky not to qualify for the World final, when he fell, perhaps over the line, on a long throw. Serious injury cost him the 1998 season amid fears that he might not compete again, but he was back training by the end of the year. His father, Jaroslav, threw the javelin 68.46m in 1969 and his mother Jana 43.23 in 1959.

Women

Pavla HAMÁCKOVÁ b. 20 May 1978 Chomutov 1.70m 68kg. Dukla Praha.
At PV: OG: '00- dnq 22=; WCh: '99- 6=, '01- 8; EC: '98- 12=; EJ: '97- 5; EU23: '99- 7=; WUG: '99- 1; WI: '99- 7, '01- 1; EI: '00- 1, '02- 6; ECp: '99- 3, '01- 3. Czech champion 1999, 2003.
Czech pole vault record 2003.
Progression at PV: 1993- 2.40i, 1994- 3.20, 1995- 3.21i/3.28i exh, 1997- 3.95, 1998- 4.15, 1999- 4.40, 2000- 4.45, 2001- 4.56i/4.47, 2002- 4.56i/4.30A, 2003- 4.60.

Zuzana HLAVONOVÁ b. 16 Apr 1973 Sala, SVK 1.78m 60kg. née Kovácikova. USK Praha.
At HJ: OG: '96- 12, '00- 11=; WCh: '95- dnq 24=, '97- dnq 21, '99- 4=; EC: '94- 11, '98- 11; WJ: '92- 12; EJ: '91- 11; WI: '99- 2; EI: '00- 2; ECp: '98- 1, '99- 3; E23Cp: '94- 1; 2= GP 1999; Czech champion 1992, 1994-7, 1999-2000, 2002-03.
Four Czech high jump records 1997-2000.
Progression at HJ: 1986- 1.57, 1987- 1.63, 1988- 1.71, 1989- 1.73, 1990- 1.77, 1991- 1.83, 1992- 1.88, 1993- 1.89, 1994- 1.94, 1995- 1.92, 1996- 1.94, 1997- 1.96, 1998- 1.98, 1999- 1.99, 2000- 2.00, 2002- 1.91, 2003- 1.92, 2004- 1.95i.
Gave birth to son Ondrej on 28 August 2001.

Sárka KASPÁRKOVÁ b. 20 May 1971 Karviná 1.87m 68kg. USK Praha. Was at Masaryks University. Sports instructor.
At TJ: OG: '96- 3, '00- nj (12); WCh: '93- 7, '95- dnq 13, '97- 1, '99- 6, '03- dnq 24; EC: '94- 6, '98- 2; WI: '93- 7, '95- 4, '97- 3, '99- 3; EI: '92- 4, '94- 4, '96- 2, '98- 2; WUG: '93- 2, '95- 1; ECp: '98- 2; E23Cp: '92- 1; 2nd GP 1997. At HJ: OG: '92- dnq; WJ: '88- 6; EJ: '89- 3. Won CS HJ 1988, CZE TJ 1993-4, 1996-8, 2000.
Ten Czech triple jump records 1992-7.
Progression at HJ, TJ: 1983- 1.42, 1984- 1.59, 1985- 1.71, 1986- 1.77, 1987- 1.80, 1988- 1.89, 1989- 1.91, 1990- 1.81, 1991- 1.78, 1992- 1.92, 14.00; 1993- 1.95i/1.84, 14.16; 1994- 1.82, 14.46i/14.14/14.20w; 1995- 1.82, 14.38; 1996- 1.80i/1.79, 14.98; 1997- 15.20, 1998- 1.81, 14.98; 1999- 14.87i/14.54, 2000- 14.34, 2002- 13.72/13.84w, 2003- 14.10. pbs: 100mh 14.72 '94, LJ 6.56 '98.
Daughter Terezka born on 7 June 2001 to her and her coach M.Pogány.

Véra POSPÍSILOVÁ b. 19 Nov 1978 Litomerice 1.78m 78kg. PSK Olymp Praha.
At (SP/)DT: WCh: '01- 7, '03- 5; EC: '02- 4; EU23: '99- 3; EJ: '97- 12/8; ECp: '01- 7/4; Won WAF 2003, 2nd GP 2002. Won CZE SP 2001-02, DT 2003.
Progression at DT: 1992- 28.24, 1993- 34.28, 1994- 39.48, 1995- 40.24, 1996- 45.72, 1997- 50.00, 1998- 54.67, 1999- 58.17, 2000- 58.28, 2001- 63.20, 2002- 64.10, 2003- 67.71. pb SP 16.92 '01.
Married wrestler Jakub Cechl on 17 Oct 2003.

DENMARK

Governing body: Dansk Athletik Forbund, Idraettens Hus, Brøndby Stadion 20, DK-2605 Brøndby. Founded 1907.

National Championships first held in 1894. **2003 Champions**: **Men**: 100m: Morten Jensen 10.40, 200m: Mads Bangsø 21.88, 400m: Christian Birk 46.82, 800m: Klint Wescom 1:53.34, 1500m: Robert K.Andersen 3:48.51, 5000m: Dennis Jensen 13:59.07, 10000m: Claus Bugge Hansen 29:16.63, HMar: Steen Walter 65:26, Mar: Jørgen Garnborg 2:23:20, 3000mSt: Morten Tjalve 9:07.50, 110mh: Anders Sækmose 14.87, 400mh: Henrik Vincentsen 53.12, HJ/Dec: Anders Black 2.05/7361, PV: Piotr Buciarski 5.40, LJ: Jesper Aabo 7.27, TJ: Anders Møller 15.74w, SP/DT: Joachim B Olsen 20.85/56.17, HT: Jan Bielecki 70.08, JT: Richard A Knudsen 71.70, 10000mW/20kmW/30kmW/50kmW: Jacob Sørensen 45:31.2/1:37:54/2:20:19/4:12:09. **Women**: 100m: Rikke Sørensen 12.05, 200m: Sofie Abildtrup 24.19, 400m: Rikke Rønholt 54.65, 800m/1500m: Heide Jensen 2:03.56/4:16.20, 5000m/10000m: Dorte Vibjerg 15:52.05/32:43.19, HMar/Mar: Gitte Karlshøj 76:13/2:34:59, 100mh: Mette Svarrer 14.68w, 400mh: Sara Petersen 64.57, HJ: Donata Jancewicz 1.74, PV: Anita Tørring 4.00, LJ/TJ: Lotte Thiesen 5.46/12.40, SP/JT: Christina Scherwin 14.64/55.44, DT: Anne Marie Gausel 44.41, HT: Vanessa Mortensen 54.08, Hep: Signe Vest 4740, 5000mW: Pia M.Christensen 29:59.2, 10kmW/20kmW: Nilda M.Christensen 64:22/2:10:39.

Wilson KIPKETER b. 12 Dec 1970 Kenya 1.72m 62kg. Sparta. Studied electronic engineering.
At 800m: OG: '00- 2; WCh: '95- 1, '97- 1, '99- 1, '03- 4; EC: '98- 8, '02- 1; WI: '97- 1, '99- 2, '03- 2; WJ: '88- dq, '90- 4. Won GP 1997 (and overall), 1999 (3rd overall), 2nd 1995; Danish 1993-4.
Three world 800m records 1997. WIR: 800m (2) 1997, 1000m (2) 2000 (2:15.25 & 2:14.96). 12 Danish 800m records 1995-7, 1000m 1995.
Progression at 800m: 1985- 1:49.6, 1986- 1:50.3, 1987- c.1:52, 1988- 1:47.0, 1989- 1:47.2, 1990- 1:45.7, 1991- 1:46.19, 1992- 1:45.62, 1993- 1:45.46, 1994- 1:43.29, 1995- 1:42.87, 1996- 1:41.83, 1997- 1:41.11, 1998- 1:43.18, 1999- 1:42.27, 2000- 1:43.35, 2002- 1:42.32, 2003- 1:43.28. pbs: 400m 46.85 '94, 1000m 2:14.96i '00, 2:16.29 '95; 1500m 3:42.80 '93, 1M 3:59.57 '93.
Went to live in Denmark in 1990, moving to Monaco in 1997. Competed for Kenya in World Juniors with year of birth 1972, but back in 1985

he was shown as second fastest African junior at 1:49.6 and born 1968! World no.1 at 800m in 1994 and allowed by the IAAF to compete for Denmark although not yet a citzizen in 1995, when he was seemingly a class apart from the rest of the world at 800m. In 1996 his Olympic entry was blocked by the Kenyan Federation, but he was again the world no. 1, with five successive 1:42 times followed by a 1:43.43 and then just missing the world record with 1:41.83. Took the world indoor record from 1:44.84 to 1:43.96 in his heat and 1:42.67 in the final of the 1997 World Indoors. In 1997 he tied Seb Coe's WR for 800m at 1:41.73 in Stockholm and after retaining his world title, improved it to 1:41.24 in Zürich and 1:41.11 in Köln. Unbeaten in 27 800m races in 1996 and 1997. In 1999 won third world title and a half share of the $1m Golden League jackpot.

Joachim B OLSEN b. 31 May 1977 Aalborg 1.84m 120kg. Studied history at the University of Idaho, USA. Århus 1900.

At SP: OG: '00- dnq 17; WCh: '99- dnq 22, 01- 10, '03- dns; EC: '02- 2; EU23: '99- 2; WI: '03- 8, '04- 3; EI: '02- 2. At DT: WJ: '96- dnq. Won DEN SP 1997-2003, DT 1999-03, NCAA SP 2000.

Five Danish shot records 2000-02 (and 14 indoor 1999-2004).

Progression at SP: 1994- 13.27, 1995- 14.54, 1996- 14.89, 1997- 17.11, 1998- 18.40, 1999- 19.75, 2000- 20.88, 2001- 20.43, 2002- 21.57, 2003- 20.85, 2004- 21.63i. pb DT 60.67 '02.

DOMINICAN REPUBLIC

Governing body: Federación Dominicana de Asociaciones de Atletismo. Avenida J.F. Kennedy, esquina Ortega y Gasset. Centro Olímpico "Juan Pablo Duarte". Santo Domingo. Fd. 1953.

2003 National Champiosn: Men: 100m: Juan Sainfleur 10.3, 200m: Arismendi Peguero 20.8, 400m: Carlos Santa 45.1, 800m: Isidro Pimentel 1:51.6, 1500m: Juan Almonte 3:52.1, 5000m/10000m: Franklin Sánchez 14:50.7/31:36.8, Mar: Joel Martínez 2:36:36, 3000mSt: José Jiménez 9:42.1, 110mh: Carlos Jorge 14.2, 400mh: Miguel García 52.3, HJ: Ubaldo Torres 2.06, PV: Natanael Semeis 4.10, LJ: Carlos Jorge 7.40, TJ: Wilkin Ruiz 15.12, SP/DT: Expedi Peña 16.55/51.14, HT: Santiago Helena 55.62, JT: Daniel Alonzo 65.65, Dec: Juan Severino 6262, 20kW: José Henriquez 1:42:34. **Women**: 100m: María Carmona 11.6, 200m/400m: Clara Hernández 24.2/53.9, 800m: Claudia Rosa Vargas 2:09.4, 1500m: Sonny García Trujillo 4:34.2, 3000m/5000m: Fanny González 10:04.0/17:51.5, 10km: Francisca Contreras 38:50, Mar: Pascuala Beras 3:15:13, 100mh: Awilda Mieses 14.4, 400mh: Jazmín Rodríguez 61.6, HJ: Juana Arrendel 1.74, PV: Leidy Araujo 3.15, LJ/TJ: María Espencer 6.10/13.03, SP: Fior Vásquez 16.88, DT: Mary Mercedes 44.47, HT: Annerys Méndez 51.59, JT: Judith Méndez 46.64, Hep: Juana Castillo 5195.

Félix SÁNCHEZ b. 30 Aug 1977 New York, USA 1.78m 73kg. Was at University of Southern California.

At 400mh: OG: '00- sf; WCh: '99- ht, '01- 1, '03- 1; PAm: '99- 4, '03- 1/3R; CAG: '02- 1R; WCp: '02- 1R. Won NCAA 2000, GWG 2001, GP 2002 (3rd overall), WAF 2003.

Three CAC 400mh records 2001-03. DOM records: 400mh (11) 1997-2003, 400m (3) 2001-02.

Progression at 400m, 400mh: 1995- 51.33, 1996- 51.19, 1997- 46.36, 50.01; 1998- 51.30, 1999- 48.60, 2000- 48.33, 2001- 44.90, 47.38; 2002- 45.14, 47.35; 2003- 45.22A/45.33, 47.25. pbs: 100m 10.63 '01, 200m 20.87 '01, 800m 1:50.33 '03.

Born in New York and raised in California, he first competed for the Dominican Republic, where his parents were born, in 1999 after placing 6th in US 400mh. Unbeaten in nine 400mh races in 2002 including GP Final and a share of the Golden League jackpot, and in eleven 400mh competions in 2003 to take his winning streak to 33 races (including 5 heats) from loss to Dai Tamesue on 2 Jul 2001.

Women

Juana Rosario ARRENDEL b. 16 Jun 1978 La Romana 1.91m 60kg.

At HJ: WCh: '01- dnq 18, '03- 8; WCp: '98- 8; PAm: '03- 1; CAG: '98- 1, '02- 1. Won IbAm 2002, NACAC U-25 2002.

Progression at HJ: 1996- 1.83, 1997- injured, 1998- 1.90, 1999- 1.93dq/1.85, 2001- 1.88, 2002- 1.97, 2003- 1.95.

Disqualified due to a doping offence, and suspended for 2 years when first at the 1999 Pan American Games.

ECUADOR

Governing body: Federación Ecuatoriana de Atletismo, Casilla 01-01-736, Cuenca. F'd 1925.

Jefferson PÉREZ b. 1 Jul 1974 Cuenca 1.74m 59kg. Graduate of business management from University of Azuay.

At 20kmW: OG: '92- dnf, '96- 1, '00- 4; WCh: '95- 32, '97- 14, '99- 2, '01- 8, '03- 1; WCp: '97- 1, '02- 1; PAm: '95- 1, '99- 3, '03- 1; SAmCh: '93- 1. Won IbAm 2002, SAm Cup 1994-5, 1997-8; PAm Cup 2003. At 10kmW: WJ: '90- 3, '92- 1; won SAm-J 1989-93, PAm-J 1993. At 50km: WCp: '99- dnf.

World best 20km walk 2003, South American record 1997 & 2003, 9 Ecuador records 20kmW 1992-2003, 50kmW 2003.

Progression at 20kmW: 1992- 1:25:50.5, 1993- 1:24:03, 1994- 1:23:27, 1995- 1:22:53, 1996- 1:20:07/1:20:55.4t, 1997- 1:18:24, 1998- 1:19:19, 1999- 1:20:46, 2000- 1:20:18, 2001- 1:22:20, 2002- 1:19:08, 2003- 1:17:21. pbs: 5000mW 19:49.54i '90, 10000mW 39:50.73 '93. 10kmW 38:24 '02, 50kmW 3:56:04 '03.

In 1996 he became the youngest ever Olympic walking champion and Ecuador's first medallist at any sport. He then walked 459km from Quito, along the Pan-American Freeway at an altitude of 2500 to 4800m, to his home-town of Cuenca, as a religious promise. The Ecuador postal authorities issued a stamp with his picture.

ERITREA

Zersenay TADESSE b 8 Feb 1982 1.58m 52kg.. At 5000m: WCh: '03- 8. At 10,000m: AfG: '02- 6. World CC: 2002-03-04: 30/9/6; HMar: '02-03: 21/7.
Eritean records 5000m and HMar 2003.
Progress at 5000m: 2002- 13:48.79, 2003- 13:05.57. pbs: 3000m 7:43.89 '03, 10000m 28:42.79 '03, Road: 15km 43:27 '03. HMar 61:26 '03.

ESTONIA

Governing body: Eesti Kergejôustikuliit, Pirita tee 12, Tallinn 10127. Founded 1920.

National Championships first held in 1917. **2003 Champions**: **Men**: 100m: Argo Golberg 10.40, 200m: Henri Sool 21.13, 400m: Lauri Birkan 48.40, 800m: Sergo Treufeld 1:52.51, 1500m: Rainis Mitt 3:53.10, 5000m/HMar: Pavel Loskutov 14:19.06/64:55, 10000m: Margus Pirksaar 31:25.78, Mar: Toomas Tarm 2:27:15, 3000mSt: Kaupo Tiislär 9:07.57, 110mh: Tarmo Jallai 14.08w, 400mh: Andrei Oll 50.74, HJ: Marko Aleksejev 2.23, PV: Erki Nool 5.10, LJ: Ilja Tumorin 7.80, TJ: Lauri Leis 16.46, SP: Taavi Peetre 18.43, DT: Aleksander Tammert 66.63, HT: Märt Israel 57.02, JT: Andrus Värnik 73.26, Dec: Indrek Kaseorg 7804, 20000mW/50kmW: Magnus Luik 1:36:56.58/4:45:15. **Women**: 100m: Kadri Viigipuu 12.05, 200m: Seidi Luik 24.89, 400m: Jekaterina Duman 55.18, 800m/1500m: Maile Mangusson 2:07.32/4:30.80, 5000m: Kadri Kelve 17:15.10, 3000mSt: Anastasia Gerassimova 11:09.18, 100mh: Mirjam Liimask 13.62, 400mh: Julia Krasnova 58.78, HJ: Kart Siilats 1.73, PV: Kristin Karu 3.50, LJ: Larisa Netseporuk 6.31, TJ: Sirkka-Liisa Kivine 13.65, SP/DT: Eha Rünne 14.99/51.11, HT: Maris Röngelep 52.49, JT: Jana Trakmann 51.01, Hep: Rutti Luksepp 5287, 10000mW: Jekaterina Jutkina 51:19.38, 20kmW: Kerly Lillemets 2:11:03.

Gerd KANTER b. 6 May 1979 Tallinn 1.96m 114kg. Altius, Pärnu.
At DT: WCh: '03- dnq 25; EC: '02- 12; EU23: '01- 5.
Progression at DT: 1998- 47.37, 1999- 49.65, 2000- 57.68, 2001- 60.47, 2002- 66.31, 2003- 67.13. pb SP 17.31i '04, 16.11 '00.

Erki NOOL b. 25 Jun 1970 Vôru 1.84m 84kg. Elite Sport Tallinn.
At Dec: OG: '92- dnf, '96- 6, '00- 1; WCh: '95- 4, '97- 6, '99- 14, '01- 2, '03- dnf; EC: '94- 10, '98- 1, '02- 2; ECp: '94-6-7-8-03: 1C/1B/2/1/1B. At Hep: WI: '95-7-9-01-04: 7/2/2/5/5; EI: '94-6-00-02: 5/1/3/3. Won EST 100m 1999, 110mh 1998-9, PV 1989, 1994, 1996-7, 2003; Dec 1990, 1992.
Estonian records: 200m and LJ 1995, Decathlon (4) 1995-2001.
Progression at Dec: 1988- 6662, 1989- 7351, 1990- 7771, 1992- 8001, 1993- 7425, 1994- 8093, 1995 - 8575, 1996- 8543, 1997- 8534, 1998- 8672, 1999- 8664, 2000- 8742, 2001- 8815, 2002- 8438, 2003- 8281. pbs: 60m 6.72i '96, 100m 10.43 '95, 10.34w '97; 200m 21.03A '95, 300m 33.97A '97, 400m 46.23 '01, 1000m 2:38.62i '99, 1500m 4:29.48 '00, 60mh 8.02i '01, 110mh 14.37 '00, HJ 2.05i '91, 2.03 '98; PV 5.60 '98, LJ 8.10 '95, 8.22w '96; SP 15.11 '00, DT 45.28 '03, JT 71.91 '98, Hep 6374i '99.
Won Götzis decathlon 1995 and 1998, IAAF Combined Events Challenge 1998 and 2000. Failed opening height (5.10) in 1999 Worlds; with 5.30 or higher he would have come 2nd. Became Estonia's first-ever Olympic athletics champion at Sydney, although very fortunate to avoid three no throws in the discus. Has 12 decathlons over 8500 and 27 over 8000.

Aleksander TAMMERT b. 2 Feb 1973 Tartu 1.96m 120kg. Audentes, Tallinn. Was at Southern Methodist University, USA.
At DT: OG: '96- dnq 25, '00- 9; WCh: '95- dnq 23, '97- 12, '99- 10, '01- dnq 16, '03- 7; EC: '98- dnq 20, '02- 5; WUG: '97- 5, '99- 4, '01- 1. Won EST SP 2002, DT 1993-5, 1997-2003.
Six Estonian discus records 1998-2004.
Progression at DT: 1990- 42.06, 1991- 48.24, 1992- 51.12, 1993- 54.54, 1994- 55.50, 1995- 60.24, 1996- 64.80, 1997- 64.78, 1998- 65.35, 1999- 66.95, 2000- 67.41, 2001- 67.10, 2002- 67.75, 2003- 66.63, 2004- 68.48. pbs: SP 18.41 '01, HT 47.01 '02.
Father (also Aleksander) was 1966 European Junior shot champion, pb 19.41 '76.

Andrus VÄRNIK b. 27 Sep 1977 Tallinn 1.82m 94kg. Lõunalõvi, Võru.
At JT: OG: '00- dnq 15; WCh: '03- 2; EC: '02- dnq 21. EST champion 1999-2000, 2003.
Two Estonian javelin records 2002-03.
Progression at JT: 1994- 65.22, 1995- 62.28, 1996- 68.36, 1997- 72.20, 1998- 69.96, 1999- 77.19, 2000- 82.16, 2001- 80.83, 2002- 85.47, 2003- 87.83. pb SP: 14.20 '03.

Women

Larisa NETSEPORUK b. 24 Dec 1970 Ukraine 1.71m 59kg. née Teteryuk. Formerly Ukraine.
At Hep: WCh: '03- 7; OG: '00- 20; EC: '94- 13, '02- 12; ECp: '03- 3. At Pen: WI: '01- 2, '04- 7; EI: '02- 8. Won EST LJ 2002.
Estonian heptathlon record 2000.
Progression at Hep: 1989- 5122, 1991- 5706, 1992- 5725, 1993- 5675, 1994- 6274, 1996- 5761, 1997- 5556, 1998- dnf, 2000- 6331, 2003- 6215. pbs: 200m 24.76 '94, 24.72w '00; 800m 2:14.44 '94, 60mh 8.61i '02, 100mh 13.91 '03, HJ 1.87 '94, LJ 6.39 '01, 6.40w '00; SP 14.38 '91, JT 53.24 '03, Pen 4382i '95.

ETHIOPIA

Governing body: Ethiopian Athletic Federation, Addis Ababa Stadium, PO Box 3241, Addis Ababa. Founded 1961.

2003 Champions: **Men**: 100m: Tadele Alemu 10.8, 200m: Negussie Getchamo 21.9, 400m: Alemayehu Adebo 46.5, 800/1500m: Berhane Alemu 1:47.7/3:47.6, 5000m/10000m: Sileshi Sihine 13:35.3/28:24.8, HMar: Dereje Adere 61:59, 3000mSt: Gulte Bekele 8:40.8, 110mh: Ubang Abaya 15.4, 400mh: Ubang Abaya 52.5, HJ: Jemal Ahmed 1.75, LJ/TJ: Gezenew Meteku ?/14.86, SP: Tsegaye Woldesenbet 13.20, DT: Tsegaye Woldesenbet 36.93, HT: Sisay Mekonnen 23.83, JT: Abdella Taddesse 64.74, 20kmW: Ashenafi Mercha 1:36.05. **Women**: 100m/200m: Leaynet Alemu 12.3/24.9, 400: Netsanet Getu 55.1, 800m/1500m: Meskerem Legesse 2:03.4/4:13.7, 3000m: Meseret Defar 9:37.9, 5000m: Tirunesh Dibaba 16:01.5, 10000m: Werknesh Kidane 32:52.6, HMar: Teyba Erkesso 73:09, 100mh: Netsanet Bekele 16.1, 400mh: Fekerte Dagne 61.5, HJ: Haymanot Bekele 1.46, LJ: Emebet Tilahun 5.33, TJ: Tadelech Erwero 11.56, SP: Roman Abera 11.60, DT: Meseret Gebregziabher 33.36, JT: Aynalem Tekabe 42.12, 10kmW: Amsale Yacob 57:09, 10kmW: Netsanet Getu 55:10.

Abiyote ABATE b. 20 Nov 1980 1.74m 56kg.
At 5000m: WCh: '01- 7, '03- 11. At 3000m: WI: '03- 5, '04- 11. World CC (4k): '99-00-02: 4J/11/15. Won ETH 5000m 2001, 4k CC 1998.
Progression at 5000m: 1999- 13:23.41, 2000- 13:10.7, 2001- 13:00.36, 2002- 13:11.80, 2003- 13:05.13. pbs: 3000m 7:32.38 '01, 2M 8:14.77i '04, 10kmRd 28:14 '99.

Gezahegne ABERA b. 23 Apr 1978 1.68m 57kg.
At Mar: WCh: '99- 11, '01- 1, '03- dnf; OG: '00- 1. World 4k CC: '00- 14.
Progression at Mar: 1999- 2:07:54, 2000- 2:09:47, 2001- 2:09:25, 2002- 2:09:13, 2003- 2:07:56. pbs: HMar 60:30 '00.
Six wins with sprint finish in 12 marathons from debut 4th at LA 1999 in 2:13:59. Won Fukuoka 1999, 2001-02; London 2003. He was 2nd in Boston 2000, before becoming the first man to win both Olympic and World marathons.

Kenenisa BEKELE b. 13 Jun 1982 near Bekoji, Arsi Province 1.60m 54kg.
At 5000m(/10000m): WCh: '03- 3/1; WJ: '00- 2; AfG: '03- 1. At 3000m: WY: '99- 2. World CC: '99- 9J, 4k: '01- 1J/2 4k, '02-03-04: all 1/1. Won WAF 3000m 2003.
World junior record 3000m 2001, World indoor 5000m record 2004.
Progression at 5000m, 10000m: 2000- 13:20.57, 2001- 13:13.33, 2002- 13:26.58, 2003- 12:52.26, 26:49.57; 2004- 12:49.60i. pbs: 2000m 5:00.32i '04. 3000m 7:30.67 '01, Rd: 10km 27:40 '01, 15km 42:42 '01.
Had record winning margin of 33 seconds for the World Junior CC title in 2001, a day after coming second in senior 4km. A year later he became the first man to win both World CC races in the same year. He then missed the track season through an Achilles injury but was back in 2003 to repeat his sensational double World CC success. Brilliant run to beat Haile Gebrselassie on track debut at 10000m at Hengelo in June 2003 and then won world title in second race at the distance. He ran 3000m in 7:30.77 on his indoor debut in 2004 to win in Stuttgart and then broke the world record for 5000m in Birmingham before his third double CC triumph.
His younger brother Tariku won the 2003 World Youth silver medal at 3000m.

Dejene BERHANU b. 1980 1.82m 64kg.
At 10000m: AfCh: '00- 2, '02- 5; AfG: '03- 3. World CC: '03- 20. Won ETH CC 2001, E.Afr 4k 2004.
Progression at 5000m, 10000m: 2000- 13:36.58, 28:41.11; 2002- 13:26.74, 28:46.21; 2003- 13:14.05, 27:47.61; 2004- 13:11.47i.

Gebre-egziabher GEBREMARIAM b. 10 Sep 1984 Tsenkanet, Tigray region 1.78m 54kg.
At 10000m (5000m): WCh: '03- (6); WJ: '02- 1 (3); AfG: '03- 2. World CC: '02- 1J, '03- 3, 04- 2/2. Won ETH CC 2003. E.Afr 2004.
Progression at 5000m, 10000m: 2001- 14:13.74A, 31:04.61A; 2002- 13:12.14, 27:25.61; 2003- 12:58.08, 28:03.03. pbs: 3000m 7:55.40 '03, 3000mSt 8:57.7A '02.

Haile GEBRSELASSIE b. 18 Apr 1973 Arssi 1.64m 53kg.
At 10000m (5000m): OG: '96- 1, '00- 1; WCh: '93- 1 (2), '95- 1, '97- 1, '99- 1, '01- 3, '03- 2; WJ: '92- 1 (1); AfG: '93- 3 (2). At 3000m: WI: '97- 1, '99- 1 (1 1500m), '03- 1. Won GP 3000m 1995, 1998. World CC: '91-2-3-4-5-6: 8J/2J/7/3/4/5; HMar: '00- 1; Rd Rly team: '94- 2.
World records 5000m (4) 1994-8, 10000m (3) 1995-8, 10km road (27:02) 2002; Indoors 2000m 1998, 3000m (7:30.72 '96, 7:26.15 '98), 5000m (13:10.98 '96, 12:59.04 '97, 12:50.38 '99). World best 2M 1995 (8:07.46) & 1997, indoor 8:04.69 (2003). ETH records 1993-9: 1500m (2), 1M (1), 3000m (6), 5000m (5), 10000m (3).
Progression at 5000m, 10000m: 1992- 13:36.06, 28:03.99; 1993- 13:03.17, 27:30.17; 1994- 12:56.96, 27:15.00; 1995- 12:44.39, 26:43.53; 1996- 12:52.70, 27:07.34; 1997- 12:41.86, 26:31.32; 1998- 12:39.36, 26:22.75; 1999- 12:49.64, 27:57.27; 2000- 12:57.95, 27:18.20; 2001- 27:54.41, 2002- 28:16.50+, 2003- 12:54.36, 26:29.22. pbs: 800m 1:49.35i '97, 1000m 2:20.3+i '98, 1500m 3:31.76i '98, 3:33.73 '99; 1M 3:52.39 '99, 2000m 4:52.86i '98, 4:56.1 '97; 3000m 7:25.09 '98, 2M 8:01.08 '97; Road: 15km 41:38 '01, HMar 59:41 '02, Mar 2:06:35 '02.
A beautifully smooth runner, perhaps the greatest ever. After finishing a place behind Ismael Kirui at two successive World Junior CC championships, he outkicked his rival for a brilliant double at the 1992 World Juniors.
He set the first of his 18 world records in Hengelo in 1994 at 5000m and in 1995 he took 8.7 secs off the 10,000m WR and regained the 5000m record by taking 10.91 secs off Kiptanui's mark. Between these feats he won the World

10,000m, with 25.1 for the last 200m!. He ran the second 5000m in c.13:11.6 to win the 1996 Olympic 10,000m and in 1997 took 6.76 secs off the world 10,000m record in Oslo. In 1998 he regained both the 5000m and 10000m world records.

Has 13 wins in 17 competitions at 10,000m (his only losses 3rd in the 1993 African Champs, the 2001 Worlds and twice to Bekele in 2003), with 24 wins at 3000m/2M from 2nd to Noureddine Morceli at Monaco in 1994 to 2003, and 16 successive wins at 5000m 1996 to 2000. In 1997 and 1998 he lost just indoors once at 1500m in 1997 and once each at 800m in 1997 and 1998. Unbeaten in 20 finals 1999-2000. He has 3/3 wins at half marathon 2001-02.

He had run c.2:48 for the marathon at the age of 15, but made his debut at the distance as a senior at London 2002, when he was third in 2:06:35. He missed the summer season through injury but returned with a world 10km road best of 27:02 at Doha, Qatar in December for a reward of $1 million.

Based during the summer in the Netherlands. His brother Tekeye has marathon pb 2:11:45 '94 andwas 13th in 1991 World Cup.

Markos GENETI b. 30 May 1984 1.75m 55kg.
At 5000m: WJ: '02- 2; AfG: '03- 4. At 3000m: WY: '01- 1; WI: '04- 3.
Progress at 5000m: 2001- 13:50.14, 2002- 13:28.83, 2003- 13:11.87. pbs: 3000m 7:37.0i '04, 7:50.05 '03; 2M 8:08.39i '04.

Hailu MEKONNEN b. 4 Apr 1980 1.72m 61kg.
At 5000m: WCh: '99- 7, '01- 9; WJ: '98- 6; AfG: '03- 2; AfCh: '98- 2 (4 3000m); won Af-AsG 2003. At 1500m: OG: '00- sf; WI: '01- 7; AfG: '99- 1. World CC J & 4k: '97- 12J, '98-3J, '99- 1J/3, '00-01-02: 6/10/3.
WIB 2 miles 2000. World junior record 3000m 1999. ETH 1500m record 2000.
Progression at 1500m, 5000m: 1998- 13:36.61, 1999- 3:35.63, 13:10.98; 2000- 3:33.14, 2001- 3:38.41i, 12:58.57; 2002- 13:24+, 2003- 13:10.16. pbs: 1M 3:53.40 '00, 2000m 5:02.06 '98, 3000m 7:30.53 '01, 2M 8:09.66i '00, 10000m 28:01.10 '02, 10kmRd 27:39 '02.
Placed third in the 4km race at the 1999 World CC Championships and returned the next day to win the junior race.

Assefa MEZGEBU b. 19 Jun 1978 1.75m 55kg.
At 10000m (5000m): OG: '96- (sf), '00- 3; WCh: '95/7/9/01- 14/5/3/2; WJ: '96- 1 (1); AfG: '95- 8, '99- 1 (5). World CC: '95-6-7-8-9-00-02: 1J/2J/13/3/11/2/12. Won ETH 10000m 2001, GWG 10000m 2001.
Progression at 5000m, 10000m: 1995- 13:33.82, 27:56.06, 1996- 13:17.68, 28:27.78; 1997- 13:05.48, 27:25.01; 1998- 12:53.84, 1999- 13:13.77, 27:18.28; 2000- 13:06.13, 27:19.75; 2001- 13:00.86, 27:22.30; 2002- 13:04.15, 26:49.90, 2003- 13:14.60. pb 3000m 7:28.45 '98.
Began running in 1994, and in 1995 won the World Junior CC at the age of 16. His brother **Ayele** (b. 6 Jan 1973) was 2nd at the 1992 World Junior 3000mSt and in the 1998 World Road relay team; pbs: 5000m 13:21.21 '94, 10000m 28:22.06 '97, 3000mSt 8:32.43 '92.

Silkeshi SIHINE b. 29 Jan 2003 Sheno 1.71m 55kg.
At 10000m: WCh: '03- 3; WJ: '02- 2; AfG: '03- 1. World CC: '02-03-04: 6J/7/3. Won Ethiopian 5000m & 10000m 2003, Af-AsG 10,000m 2003.
Progression at 5000m, 10000m: 2002- 13:21.81, 27:26.12; 2003- 13:06.53, 26:58.76. pbs: 3000m 7:41.18i '04, 7:45.7+ '03.

Women

Berhane ADERE b. 21 Jul 1973 Shewa District 1.70m 48kg.
At 10000m (5000m): OG: '96- 18, '00- 12; WCh: '95- h, '97- 4, '99- 7, '01- 2, '03- 1 (10); AfCh: '93- 1 (5 3000m). At 5000m: AfCh: '98- 1, '02- 1; WCp: '98- 3. At 3000m: WI: '03- 1, '04- 2; WCp: '02- 1; 3rd GP 2002. World CC: '96-7-00: 10/14/14; HMar: '01-02-03: 3/1/2. Won Rd Rly team '96, ETH 3000m & 10000m 1993.
Records: African 5000m and 10000m 2003, World indoor 3000m (8:29.15) 2002, 5000m 2004, African indoor 5000m 2003; Ethiopian 2000m 2003, 3000m 1997 and 2001, HMar 2003.
Progression at 5000m, 10000m: 1992- 34:13.3, 1993- 32:48.52, 1995- 15:44.46, 32:02.94; 1996- 14:59.17, 32:21.09; 1997- 15:08.22, 31:48.95; 1998- 15:22.34, 32:06.42; 1999- 14:54.88, 31:32.51; 2000- 14:52.61, 30:51.30; 2001- 14:51.67, 31:32.70; 2002- 14:33.65, 2003- 14:29.32, 30:04.18; 2004- 14:39.29i. pbs: 1500m 4:05.54i, 4:06.46 '02; 2000m 5:35.62 '03; 3000m 8:25.62 '01; road: 15km 48:11 '01, 10M 53:16 '98, HMar 67:32 '03, Mar 2:41:50 '01.
Married to Lemme Erpassa (five team medals at World CC 1988-97), son Aleme born in 1994.

Elfenesh ALEMU b. 10 Jun 1975 1.71m 57kg.
At Mar: OG: '00- 6; WCh: '99- 5, '01- dnf, '03- 6; WCp: '95- 18; AfG: '95- 3.
Progression at Mar: 1993- 2:57:32A, 1994- 3:08:05, 1995- 2:40:04, 1996- 2:36:29, 1997- 2:37:37, 1998- 2:30:19; 1999- 2:28:52, 2000- 2:24:47, 2001- 2:24:29, 2002- 2:26:01, 2003- 2:24:47. pb HMar 69:46 '00.
Broke 2:25 twice in 2000: 4th Osaka, 1st Nagano before 2:26:45 at Olympics. Won Nagano 2001 when also 5th London and 2nd Chicago. 3rd Boston 2002, won Tokyo 2003. Married Gezahegne Abera in June 2003.

Meseret DEFAR b. 19 Nov 1983 Addis Ababa 1.55m 42kg.
At 5000m: WCh: '03- h; WJ: '00- 2, '02- 1; AfG: '03- 1; AfCh: '00- 2.At 3000m: WJ: '02- 1; WY: '99- 2; WI: '03- 3, '04- 1; World CC: '02- 13J.
Progression at 3000m, 5000m: 1999- 9:02.08, 2000- 8:59.90, 15:08.36; 2001- 8:52.47, 15:08.65; 2002- 8:40.28, 15:26.45; 2003- 8:38.31, 14:40.34; 2004- 8:33.44i. pb 2000m 5:44.1i '04.

Merima DENBOBA b. 21 Aug 1974 1.68m 48kg. At 5000m: OG: '96- h; WCh: '97- 10, '01- 13; AfG: '95- 5, '99- 4; AfCh: '98- 3, '00- 3. At 10000m: WJ: '92- 5. World CC: '91-2-3-4-5: 18/20/19/4/7, '97-8-9-00-01-02-03: 6/4/2/8/8 & 4 4k/6/3 & 6 4k; Rd Rly team: '98- 1. Won ETH 10000m 1995, 2001; CC 1995, 1998 and 1997/8 World CC challenge.
Progression at 5000m, 10000m: 1992- 33:57.21, 1993- 35:15.5A, 1994- 15:47.86, 32:16.50; 1995- 15:47.12, 34:20.6A; 1996- 15:19.86, 1997- 15:11.71, 32:10.36; 1998- 15:30.06, 32:04.89; 1999- 15:08.52, 31:32.63; 2000- 15:15.17, 31:43.2; 2001- 15:06.08, 31:57.10; 2002- 15:17.24, 33:36.5A; 2003- 15:07.46, 31: 47.53. pbs: 1500m 4:14.60 '94, 3000m 8:44.21 '99.
Ten top ten placings in World Cross, with 13 team medals (six gold, six silver and one bronze).

Ejagayou DIBABA b. 21 Mar 1982.
At 10000m: WCh: '03- 9; AfG: '03- 1; won Af-AsG 2003. At 5000m: AfCh: '02- 3. World CC 4k: '03-04: 9/2 (10 8k).
Progression at 5000m, 10000m: 2001- 15:32.31, 32:24.20; 2002- 15:56.02, 2003- 14:41.67, 31:01.07. pbs: 2000m 5:49.5+ '03, 3000m 8:48.7 '03.
Older sister of Tirunesh Dibaba.

Tirunesh DIBABA b. 2 Jun 1985. 1.54m 44kg. At 5000m: WCh: '03- 1; WJ: '02- 2; AfG: '03- 4. World CC: '01-02-03-04: 5J/2J/1J/2 4k. Won ETH 4km CC & 5000m 2003.
World junior 5000m record 2003.
Progression at 5000m: 2002- 14:49.90, 2003- 14:39.94. pbs: 2000m 5:44.8i+ '04, 3000m 8:33.56i '04, 8:41.86 '02
In 2003 she became, at 18 years 90 days, the youngest ever world champion at an individual event.

Kutre DULECHA b. 22 Aug 1978 1.68m 48kg. At 1500m (800m): OG: '96- sf (h), '00- 4; WCh: '97- 9, '99- 3, '03- sf; WI: '97-9-03-04: 8/8/9/1; WJ: '94- 5 (3), '96- 1; AfG: '95- 1 (3), '99- 1, '03- 1; Af-J: '94- 2 (2); 2nd GP 1998, 2000. World CC: '96- 1J, 4k: '98-9-00: 3/12/1.
Ethiopian records: 1500m (5) 1997-8, 800m & 1000m 1999. World junior indoor 1500m 1997.
Progression at 1500m: 1994- 4:15.59, 1995- 4:08.70, 1996- 4:07.69, 1997- 4:05.67, 1998- 3:58.38, 1999- 4:00.96, 2000- 3:59.02, 2001- 4:05.75i, 2003- 4:02.74, 2004- 4:01.90i. pbs: 800m 1:59.17i/1:59.37 '99, 1000m 2:37.82 '99, 1M 4:23.33i '01, 4:39.04 '97; 10kmRd 32:29 '02.
Son Hailegebrale born 30 Nov 2001.

Werknesh KIDANE b. 21 Nov 1981 Mayshie district, Tigray region 1.58m 42kg.
At 10000m: WCh: '03- 2; AfG: '03- 2; At 5000m: OG: '00- 7; WCh: '01- h; WJ: '98- 6; AfG: '99- 4. At 3000m: WI: '01- 9. World CC: '97-8-9-00-01-03-04: 13J/3J/1J/9J/1/3; 4k: '01-02-03-04: 5/2/2/4. Won ETH 10000m 2003, 4k CC 2001-02, E.Afr 4k & 8k 2004.
Progression at 5000m, 10000m: 1998- 15:50.10, 1999- 15:24.56, 2000- 14:47.40, 33:48.7A; 2001- 15:29.96, 31:43.41; 2002- 14:43.53, 2003- 14:33.04, 30:07.15. pbs: 1500m 4:18.00 '01, 3000m 8:39.51 '03.

Derartu TULU b. 21 Mar 1972 Bejoki, Arusi province 1.55m 45kg. Employed by the prison police in Addis Ababa.
At 10000m (3000m): OG: '92- 1, '96- 4, '00- 1; WCh: '91- 8, '95- 2, '97- h, '01- 1, '03- dnf; WJ: '90- 1; AfG: '91- 1; AfCh: '90- 1 (1), '92- 1 (1); WCp: '92- 1 (1). World CC: '89-90-1-5-6-7-00-04: 23/15/2/1/4/1/1/16; HMar: '99- 14. Won GWG 10000m 2001.
Three African 10000m records 1992-2000. World junior 10000m record 1991 (32:08.74), Ethiopian records 1500m, 5000m (4), 10000m (5) 1991-2000, HMar 1995 & 2000.
Progression at 5000m, 10000m, Mar: 1990- 16:56.7, 32:56.26; 1991- 15:21.29, 31:45.95; 1992- 15:36.5, 31:06.02; 1994- 15:40.29, 31:48.93; 1995- 14:57.65, 31:08.10; 1996- 14:50.88, 31:10.46; 1997- 33:25.99, 2:30:28; 1999- 2:40:55, 2000- 14:44.57, 30:17.49, 2: 26:09; 2001- 31:48.19, 2:23:57; 2002- 15:26.73, 2: 28:37; 2003- 14:44.22, 2:26:33. pbs: 1500m 4:12.08 '92, 3000m 8:46.32 '00, HMar 67:03 '01.
Married decathlete Zewde Deboba in 1988, daughter Tsion born 1998. Returned to road racing in 1999 and to a third world CC title and second Olympic title in 2000. 5th Boston on marathon debut 1997; 6th London and 3rd Tokyo in 2000, won London and Tokyo marathons 2001.

Getenesh WAMI b. 11 Dec 1974 Debre Birhan 1.54m 45kg.
At 10000m (5000m): OG: '96- 3, '00- 2 (3); WCh: '95- 18, '97- dnf, '99- 1, '01- 3; WJ: '92- 2; AfG: '95- 3, '99- 1; AfCh: '92- 4. Won GP 3000m 1998, 2nd 5000m 1996. World CC: '91-2: 5J/9J, '95-6-7-8-9-00-01: 5/1/3/3/1/2/2 &1 4k; Rd Rly team: '96/8- 1/1.
African records 5000m 2000, 10000m 1999. ETH 3000m 1998, 5000m (4) 1996-8, Mar 2002.
Progression at 5000m, 10000m: 1992- 32:34.68, 1994- 36:15.0A, 1995- 15:28.65, 32:17.41; 1996- 14:46.45, 31:06.65; 1997- 14:54.05, 32:05.73; 1998- 14:36.08, 34:23.4A; 1999- 15:25.5, 30:24.56; 2000- 14:30.88, 30:22.48; 2001- 14:31.69, 31:49.98. pbs: 1500m 4:01.47 '98, 2000m 5:39.9 '01, 3000m 8: 27.62 '01, Mar 2:22:20 '02.
After missing 2002 track season, she became the second fastest ever marathon debutante when winning at Amsterdam. Married Geteneh Tessema Nov 1999, daughter born Aug 2003.

Ayelech WORKU b. 12 Jun 1979 1.65m 47kg.
At 5000m: OG: '96- 12, '00- 4; WCh: '97- 12, '99- 3, '01- 3; WJ: '96- 1 (3000m 4); AfG: '95- 2, '99- 1. World CC: '95-6-7-8-9-00-01-02: 11J/11J/3J/9/4/9/18/13. Rd Rly team: '98- 1. Won ETH 5000m 1995, 2001.
Progression at 5000m: 1995- 15:48.3A, 1996- 15:16.74, 1997- 15:18.19, 1998- 15:12.43, 1999-

14:44.22; 2000- 14:41.23, 2001- 14:54.00, 2002- 14:48.99, 2003- 15:10.85. pbs: 1500m 4:15.93 '98, 3000m 8:32.80 '02, 10000m 31:38.08 '01.

FINLAND

Governing body: Suomen Urheiluliitto, Radiokatu 20, SF-00240 Helsinki. Founded 1906.

National Championships first held in 1907 (men), 1913 (women). **2003 Champions**: **Men**: 100m: Markus Pöyhönen 10.32, 200m: Samsa Tuikka 21.13, 400m: Abdelghani Nouidra 47.39, 800m: Juha Kukkamo 1:51.86, 1500m/3000mSt: Jukka Keskisalo 3:42.10/8:34.03, 5000m: Jari Matinlauri 13:49.49, 10000m: Janne Holmén 28:48.87; HMar: Francis Kirwa 63:45, Mar: Yrjö Pesonen 2:24:14, 110mh: Matti Niemi 13.93, 400mh: Ari-Pekka Lattu 49.52, HJ: Mika Polku 2.14, PV: Matti Mononen 5.50, LJ: Tommi Evilä 7.93, TJ: Johan Meriluoto 16.05, SP: Tepa Reinikainen 20.30, DT: Timo Tompuri 58.19, HT: Olli-Pekka Karjalainen 75.19, JT: Aki Parviainen 82.91, Dec: Henri Kokkonen 7553, 20kmW: Jani Lehtinen 1:28:17, 50kmW: Antti Kempas 4:18:40. **Women**: 100m/200m: Johanna Manninen 11.35/ 23.19, 400m: Kirsi Mykkänen 54.09, 800m: Minna Järvenpää 2:03.43, 1500m: Johanna Risku 4:23.35, 5000m/10000m: Kirsi Valasti 15:56.47/34:25.97, HMar: Minna Myllkoski 76:45, Mar: Pauliina Rasmus 3:00:40, 3000mSt: Maria Söderström 10:36.46, 100mh/LJ: Johanna Halkoaho 13.49/ 6.65w, 400mh: Manuela Bosco 58.76, HJ: Hanna Mikkonen 1.89, PV: Hanna Palamaa 4.00, TJ: Heli Koivula-Kruger 14.02, SP: Niina Kelo 14.96, DT: Tiina Kankaanpää 54.94, HT: Sini Pöyry 65.98, JT: Paula Huhtaniemi 64.90, Hep: Tiia Hautala 5816, 20kmW: Outi Sillanpää 1:47:16.

Mika HALVARI b. 13 Feb 1970 Kemi 1.91m 135kg. Kemin Kunto.
At SP: OG: '96- dnq 14; WCh: '95- 2, '97- 5, '99- dnq 15; WI: '95- 1, '97- 6; EC: '94- 4, '98- 6; EI: '98- 2; WJ: '88- 7; EJ: '89- 5; ECp: '98- 1. Finnish champion 1994-5, 1997.
Progression at SP: 1986- 14.64, 1987- 16.06, 1988- 17.62, 1989- 17.96, 1990- 18.65, 1991- 18.71, 1992- 18.60i/18.45, 1993- 20.08, 1994- 19.93i/19.87, 1995- 21.50, 1996- 20.81i/20.42, 1997- 21.11, 1998- 20.79, 1999- 21.00, 2000- 22.09i/21.04, 2001- 19.89, 2002- 20.18. pbs: DT 47.72 '88, HT 42.16 '89.
A 'spinner', he ruptured his Achilles tendon in February 1996, which meant that he was below par in Atlanta. He produced a startling 22.09 indoors in February 2000, but suffered another Achilles rupture in August 2000.

Arsi HARJU b. 18 Mar 1974 Kurikka 1.83m 125kg. Perhon Kiri.
At SP: OG: '96- dnq, '00- 1; WCh: '95- dnq 17, '97- dnq 15, '99- nt (12), '01- 3; EC: '98- 9, '02- 4; WI: '97-9-03: 8/5/4; EI: '98- 3; WJ: '92- 11; EJ: '93- 3. Finnish champion 1998, 2000.
Progression at SP: 1989- 11.82, 1990- 15.65, 1991- 16.27, 1992- 17.60, 1993- 18.40, 1994- 18.74, 1995- 19.58, 1996- 19.84, 1997- 20.66, 1998- 21.04, 1999- 20.60, 2000- 21.39, 2001- 20.98, 2002- 21.11, 2003- 21.00i/19.76.
A 'spinner' since 1996, he improved his pb by 35cm in the 2000 Olympic qualifying to 21.39, and then threw 21.29 to win the gold medal.

Olli-Pekka KARJALAINEN b. 7 Mar 1980 Töysä 1.94m 110kg. Töysän Veto.
At HT: OG: '00- dnq 34; WCh: '99- 11, '01- 10, '03- dnq 14; EC: '02- 8; WJ: '98- 1; EJ: '97- 3, '99- 1; EU23: '01- 2; ECp: '02- 1. Finnish champion 1998-2003.
World junior hammer record 2000, Finnish 2002.
Progression at HT: 1995- 48.26, 1996- 58.80, 1997- 69.84, 1998- 75.08, 1999- 78.33, 2000- 80.55, 2001- 80.54, 2002- 81.70, 2003- 80.20.

Conny KARLSSON b. 30 Dec 1975 Dragsfjärd 1.95m 120kg. Pargas IF.
At SP: WCh: '01- 7, '03- dnq 24; EC: '02- dnq 14; WJ: '94- 6; EU23: '97- 1. Finnish champion 2001-02.
Progression at SP: 1993- 15.62, 1994- 17.08, 1995- 17.94, 1996- 18.59, 1997- 19.48, 1998- 19.21i/ 18.76, 1999- 19.31, 2000- 19.46, 2001- 20.78, 2002- 20.50, 2003- 20.60. pb DT 52.30 '97.
Raised pb from 20.49 to 20.72 (q) and 20.78 at 2001 Worlds.

Aki PARVIAINEN b. 26 Oct 1974 Helsinki 1.92m 100kg. Joensuun Kataja.
At JT: OG: '00- 5; WCh: '95- 9, '97- 8, '99- 1, '01- 2, '03- 5; EC: '98- 9, '02- 8; WJ: '92- 1; EJ: '91- 3; ECp: '98- 3. Finnish champion 1998-2003.
Finnish javelin records 1998 and 1999.
Progression at JT: 1990- 63.50, 1991- 79.96, 1992- 80.94, 1993- 78.18i/69.94, 1994- 78.76, 1995- 85.60, 1996- 84.96, 1997- 87.48, 1998- 90.88, 1999- 93.09, 2000- 90.97, 2001- 92.41, 2002- 82.48, 2003- 83.30. pbs: SP 12.26 '96, DT 36.78 '96.
Set world age records at 14-16-17. The first Finn to win world titles at junior and senior level. Missed most of 1993-4 seasons through an arm injury and had to have knee and elbow operations at the end of the 2003 season. Older brother Mika threw 80.26 in 1992.

Tepa REINIKAINEN b. 16 Mar 1976 Kangasniemi 1.98m 145kg. Kangasniemen Kalske. Was at UTEP, USA.
At SP: WCh: '03- 7; EJ: '95- 1; WI: '03- 6; EI: '00- 7. Finnish champion 2003.
Progression at SP: 1993- 13.70, 1994- 16.16, 1995- 17.69, 1996- 17.74, 1997- 17.68, 1998- 18.87, 1999- 19.53, 2000- 20.11, 2001- 20.88, 2002- 20.43, 2003- 20.69i/20.55.

Ville TIISANOJA b. 24 Dec 1975 Vantaa 1.92m 119kg. Kenttäurheilijat-58 Vantaa.
At SP: OG: '00- dnq 15; WCh: '99- 8, '01- 9, '03- 8; EC: '02- 6; WJ: '94- 3 (10 DT); EU23: '97- 4; EJ: '93- 7; EI: '02- 4; ECp: '02- 2. FIN champion 1999.
Progression at SP: 1992- 16.41, 1993- 17.35,

1994- 17.90, 1995- 19.10, 1996- 18.29, 1997- 19.40, 1998- 19.13, 1999- 20.49, 2000- 20.76, 2001- 20.78, 2002- 21.09, 2003- 20.37, 2004- 20.59i. pbs: DT 54.10 '94, HT 51.36 '94.
Reveived a suspension to 30 June 2003 after a small qualtity of illegal drugs were found by Fench police near Lyon in 2002 in the car of he and discus thrower Timo Tompuri.

Women

Mikaela INGBERG b. 29 Jul 1974 Vaasa 1.74m 75kg. Vasa Idrottssällskap.
At JT: OG: '96- 7, '00- 9; WCh: '95- 3, '97- 4, '99- 9, '01- 6, '03- 4; EC: '94- dnq 16, '98- 3, '02- 3; EJ: '91- 15, '93- 1; WCp: '98- 3, '02- 3; 2nd GP 2002. Finnish champion 1994, 1999-2000, 2002.
Finnish record new javelin 2000
Progression at JT: 1987- 33.70, 1988- 41.78, 1989- 43.92, 1990- 51.96, 1991- 52.30, 1992- 54.00, 1993- 58.26, 1994- 58.70, 1995- 65.16, 1996- 65.66, 1997- 67.32, 1998- 66.43; new 1999- 61.50, 2000- 64.03, 2001- 63.13, 2002- 63.50, 2003- 63.55. pbs: HJ 1.57 '88, SP 12.67 '99, DT 39.56 '95.

Heli KOIVULA-KRUGER b. 27 Jun 1975 Kauhajoki 1.74m 60kg. née Koivula. Kauhajoen Karhu.
At TJ (LJ): OG: '96- dnq 24 (dnq); WCh: '97-9-01-03: dnq 19/dnq 23/5/dnq 15; EC: '98- dnq 21 (dnq 23), '02- 2; EU23: '97- 3 (4). At LJ: WCh: '95-7: dnq nj/13; WJ: '92- 4, '94- 2; EJ: '91- 7. Won FIN LJ 1995-6, 1998, 2002; TJ 1996, 1998, 2000-02.
Eight Finnish triple jump records 1996-2003.
Progression at TJ: 1994- 13.20 1995- 13.47/13.79w, 1996- 13.74/13.89w, 1997- 13.92, 1998- 14.04, 1999- 14.34, 2000- 13.68, 2001- 14.28, 2002- 14.38/14.83w, 2003- 14.39. pbs: 100m 11.72 '95, 200m 25.20 '93, 100mh 15.16 '93, HJ 1.56 '90, LJ 6.59 '98, 6.61w '02.
Married South African discus thrower Frantz Kruger on 28 June 2003.

Taina KOLKKALA b. 24 Oct 1976 Pori 1.73m 74kg. née Uppa. Porin Tarmo.
At JT: OG: '96- dnq 19, '00- dnq 20; WCh: '95- dnq 24, '97- dnq 20, '99- 10, '01 12, '03- 10; EC: '94- 10, '98- dnq 14, '02- 7; EU23: '94- 4Cp, '97- 1; WJ: '94- 1; EJ: '95- 1.
Finnish record new javelin 2000.
Progression at JT: 1990- 39.58, 1991- 49.78, 1992- 54.78, 1993- 52.08, 1994- 61.78, 1995- 66.00, 1996- 63.78, 1997- 61.00, 1998- 62.31; new 1999- 63.63, 2000- 64.06, 2001- 60.55, 2002- 62.86, 2003- 61.96.

FRANCE

Governing body: Fédération Française d'Athlétisme, 33 avenue Pierre de Coubertin, 75640 Paris cedex 13. Founded 1920.
National Championships first held in 1888 (men), 1918 (women). **2003 Champions: Men**: 100m/200m: Aimé-Issa Nthepé 10.09/20.65, 400m: Marc Raquil 45.89, 800m: Nicolas Aïssat 1:47.76, 1500m: Fouad Chouki 3:37.09, 5000m: Drtiss El Himer 13:34.97, 10000m: Loic Letellier 28:33.45, HMar: Abdelgani Lahlahli 62:11, 3000mSt: Vincent Le Dauphin 8:25.68, 110mh: Sébastien Denis 13.57, 400mh: Naman Keita 49.60, HJ: Joan Charmant 2.24, PV: Romain Mesnil 5.60, LJ: Salim Sdiri 8.29w, TJ: Julien Kapek 17.24w, SP: Yves Niaré 19.07, DT: Erik Boès 56.11, HT: Christophe Épalle 77.38, JT: Dominique Pausé 74.66, Dec: Laurent Hernu 8184, 20kmW: Denis Langlois 1:27:59, 50kmW: Eddy Riva 3:55:31. **Women**: 100m: Christine Arron 10.95, 200m: Katia Benth 23.65, 400m: Marie-Louise Bévis 52.43, 800m: Virginie Fouquet 2:01.56, 1500m: Latifa Essarokh 4:10.84, 5000m: Christelle Daunay 16:10.03, 10000m: Fatima Yvelain 32:37.50, HMar: Corinne Raux 71:55, 3000mSt: Céline Rajot 9:57.41, 100mh: Patricia Girard 12.74, 400mh: Sylvanie Morandais 57.08, HJ: Gaëlle Niaré 1.89, PV: Vanessa Boslak 4.50, LJ: Aurélie Félix 6.55, TJ: Amy Zongo 13.60, SP: Laurence Manfrédi 17.95, DT: Mélina Robert-Michon 59.14, HT: Manuèla Montebrun 70.89, JT: Sarah Walter 61.05, Hep: Julie Martin 5694, 10kmW: Fatiha Ouali 46:46.

Mehdi BAALA b. 17 Aug 1978 Strasbourg 1.83m 65kg. ASPTT Strasbourg.
At 1500m (800m): OG: '00- 4; WCh: '01- 12, '03- 2; EC: '02- 1; WJ: '96- h; EU23: '99- 3; EJ: '97- 7; EI: '00- 3; WCp: '02- 3; ECp: '00-01-02: 1 (1)/2/1. Won FRA 800m 2001, 1500m 2002.
French records 800m 2002. 1000m (2) 2002-03, 1500m (2) 2003.
Progression at 800m, 1500m: 1994- 1:56.5, 4:08.1; 1995- 1:53.76, 3:48.74; 1996- 1:49.62, 3:43.50; 1997- 1:50.08, 3:45.34; 1998- 1:49.57, 3:41.86; 1999- 1:46.41, 3:34.83; 2000- 1:46.24, 3:32.05; 2001- 1:46.94, 3:31.97; 2002- 1:43.15, 3:32.03; 2003- 1:44.17, 3:28.98. pbs: 1000m 2:13.96 '03, 3000m 8:08.06i '98, 8:23.69 '98.
Married Hanane Sabri (ht WC 1500m '01, FRA champion 2001) in September 2000. His elder brother Samir won 2002 French marathon.

Romain BARRAS b. 1 Aug 1980 Calais 1.93m 84kg. SO Calais.
At Dec: EU23: '01- 4; WUG: '01- 5, 03- 1; ECp: '03- 1.
Progression at Dec: 1998- 6505, 1999- 7147, 2000- 7609, 2001- 7876, 2002- 7835, 2003- 8196. pbs: 100m 11.02 '03, 400m 48.80 '03, 1500m 4:24.99 '02, 60mh 8.14i '01, 110mh 14.24 '02, HJ 2.01 '03, PV 4.75i/4.70 '01, LJ 7.18 '03, SP 15.14 '03, DT 45.58 '03, JT 64.08 '03, Hep 5746i '03.

Stéphane DIAGANA b. 23 Jul 1969 Saint-Affrique, Aveyron 1.84m 75kg. EA Franconville.
At 400mh/4x400mR: OG: '92- 4; WCh: '93- 4, '95- 3, '97- 1, '99- 2, '03- sf/2R; EC: '90- 5, '94- 3/2R, '98- sf, '02- 1; EI: '02- 2R; WCp: '92- 3, '94- 3R; ECp: '93-4-9-01-02: 1/3/6/3/2 (3R 93-4-02). Won GP 1998 (2nd 2002, 3rd 1994). Won French 400m 1992-5, 1997, 2001; 400mh 1990.
European 400mh record 1995, eight French 1990-5.
Progression at 400mh: 1987- 54.1, 1989- 51.60, 1990- 48.92, 1992- 48.13, 1993- 47.64, 1994- 48.22, 1995- 47.37, 1997- 47.70, 1998- 48.04, 1999- 48.12,

2000- 48.70, 2001- 48.08, 2002- 47.58, 2003- 48.64. pbs: 100m 10.94 '88, 200m 20.81i '92, 20.95 '93; 300m 33.25 '99, 400m 45.18 '92, 60mh 8.10i '88, 110mh 14.56 '87, 200mh 22.94 '94, 22.9 '99.
Big advance in 1990, when he ran 50.11 to win the French title, then 49.26 and 48.92 at the Europeans. In 1992 he ran 48.55 and then French records in each round at Olympics. In 1995 he took the European record, which had stood at 47.48 to Harald Schmid since 1982. Missed most of 1996 season through stress fracture in foot and was restricted by injury to just one hurdles race in 2000. Elected president of the French athletes' association in October 1996, member of EAA Athletes Commission 2002-06. In 1999 he completed a set of World Champs 1-2-3-4.

Leslie DJHONE b. 18 Mar 1981 Abibjan, CIV 1.87m 72kg. Neuilly Plaisance.
At 400m/4x400m: WCh: '03- 5/2R; EC: '02- 3R; EU23: '03- 1. At LJ/4x100m: WJ: '98- dnq; EU23: '01- 4/4R, '03- 2R; EJ: '99- 1/1R. At 200m: ECp: '03- 5.
Progression at 400m: 2001- 47.01, 2002- 45.63, 2003- 44.83. pbs: 100m 10.52 '03, 200m 20.51i/ 20.68 '03; 300m 32.18 '03, LJ: 7.92/8.06w '01.

Ladji DOUCOURÉ b. 28 Mar 1983 Juvisy-sur-Orge 1.83m 75kg. Viry Nord Sud Evry Essonne.
At 110mh/4x100mR: WCh: '03- sf; WJ: '00- 3/2R; EU23: '03- 1; ECp: '01- 7, '03- 1. At 100mh: WY: '99- 1. At 60mh: WI: '03- 4. At Dec: EJ: '01- 1/2R.
Progression at 110mh: 2000- 13.75, 2001- 13.58, 2002- 13.87/13.73w, 2003- 13.23. pbs: 60m 6.78i '00, 100m 10.48 '01, 200m 20.75 '01, 400m 46.82 '01, 50mh 6.48i '04, 55mh 7.14i '04, 60mh 7.55i '04, PV 4.45 '01, LJ 7.82i '01, 7.57/7.73w '01, Dec 7794 '01.
Improved from 7.64 to 7.61 and 7.58 (for surprise fourth place) at 60mh at 2003 World Indoors.

Driss EL HIMER b. 4 Apr 1974 Rabat, Morocco 1.78m 58kg. Ol. Marseille.
At 5000m: WCh: '01- 12; EC: '98- 7. World CC: '99- 13 4k, '01- 6 12k; Eur CC: '98-00-03: 3/3/10. Won French 5000m 1998, 2000, 2003; 10000m 2000, CC 1998-9, 2003.
French records: 3000m 1998, marathon 2001.
Progression at 5000m, 10000m, Mar: 1997- 2:27:08, 1998- 13:15.67, 1999- 13:20.94, 2000- 13:10.99, 28:11.26; 2001- 13:15.10, 2:07:02; 2002- 13:16.31, 27:48.00, 2:11:51; 2003- 13:34.97, 2:06:48. pbs: 1500m 3:37.01 '99, 3000m 7:34.46 '98, 2M 8:23.53 '99, HMar 62:08 '01.
Gained French citizenship by joining the French Foreign Legion.

Nicolas FIGÈRE b. 19 May 1979 Moulins 1.77m 91kg. Viry Nord Sud Evry Essonne.
At HT: WCh: '01- 12, '03- 11; EC: '02- 12; WJ: '98- 6; EJ: '97- dnq 14; EU23: '01- 1, ECp: '02- 4. French champion 2001-02.
Progression at HT: 1995- 51.36, 1996- 58.70, 1997- 62.16, 1998- 68.48, 1999- 75.13, 2000- 79.01, 2001- 80.88, 2002- 80.41, 2003- 79.07. pbs: HJ 1.86 '94, PV 3.30 '94, SP 13.34 '00, DT 42.45 '00.

Laurent HERNU b. 22 Aug 1976 Creil 1.90m 85kg. Stade Nogent-sur-Oise.
At Dec: OG: '00- 19; WCh: '01- 8, '03- 5; EC: '02- 7; ECp: '00-01-02: 2/3/6. French champion 2000, 2002-03. At Hep: WI: '03- 7.
Progression at Dec: 1996- 6277, 1997- 5975, 1998- 7566w/7390, 1999- 7937, 2000- 8178, 2001- 8280, 2002- 8108, 2003- 8219. pbs: 60m 7.11i '03, 100m 10.97 '01, 400m 48.95 '03, 1000m 2:41.83i '03, 1500m 4:27.49 '00, 60mh 7.96i '00, 110mh 14.01/ 13.94w '01, HJ 2.10 '00, PV 5.15 '01, LJ 7.56 '03, SP 14.80 '01, DT 47.88 '02, JT 60.14 '01, Hep 6102i '02. Won Talence decathlon 2003.

Driss MAAZOUZI b. 15 Oct 1969 Meknès, Morocco 1.80m 65kg. Coquelicot 42 St-Etienne.
At 1500m: OG: '96- 10, '00- 11; WCh: '97- sf, '99- 8, '01- 3; WI: '03- 1. At 3000m: ECp: '99-00-01-02: 3/1/1/1. World 4k CC: '02-03: 10/14. Won FRA 1500m 1997-2001, 4k CC 1998-2000; MedG 1500m 1997.
French records 1000m (2), 1500m (3) 1998-2002, 2000m 2001.
Progression at 1500m: 1990- 3:45.8, 1991- 3:42.12, 1993- 3:43.3, 1994- 3:37.04, 1995- 3:35.45, 1996- 3:34.08, 1997- 3:35.26, 1998- 3:31.59, 1999- 3:31.51, 2000- 3:32.01, 2001- 3:31.54, 2002- 3:31.45, 2003- 3:36.93i. pbs: 800m 1:46.3 '96, 1000m 2:15.26 '99, 1M 3:51.79 '00, 2000m 4:55.55 '01, 3000m 7:36.21 '98, 2M 8:28.26i '03, 5000m 13:30.34 '02, 10km Rd 29:42 '01, HMar 64:44 '95, 3000mSt 9:08.6 '91.
Competed for Morocco to 1997, then switched allegiance (naturalised for France 23/7/96), but unable to compete for France until clearance granted by Morocco for 1999.

Romain MESNIL b. 13 Jul 1977 Plessis Bouchard 1.88m 79kg. ECLA Albi. Engineering student.
At PV: OG: '00- dnq 31; WCh: '99- nh, '01- 5, '03- dnq; EC: '02- dnq; EU23: '99-1; WJ: '96- dnq 13=; WI: '99-01-03-04: 6=/3/7/7; ECp: '00-03: 5/1. French champion 2000-03.
Progression at PV: 1993- 4.30, 1994- 4.65, 1995- 5.15, 1996- 5.30, 1997- 5.40, 1998- 5.80, 1999- 5.93, 2000- 5.75, 2001- 5.86i/5.85, 2002- 5.75, 2003- 5.95. pb Dec 5724 '98. Former gymnast.

Marc RAQUIL b. 2 Apr 1977 Créteil 1.91m 81kg. Neuilly Plaisance.
At 400m/4x400mR: OG: '00- qf; WCh: '99- 5R, '01- sf, '03- 3/2R; EC: '02- sf; EU23: '97- 4R, '99- 3; EI: '00- 3; ECp: '99-01-03: 6/1/1. French champion 2002-03.
Three French records 2001-03.
Progression at 400m: 1995- 49.12, 1996- 47.92, 1997- 47.13, 1998- 46.39, 1999- 45.82, 2000- 45.31, 2001- 44.95, 2002- 45.39, 2003- 44.79. pbs: 200m 21.03 '01, 300m 32.60 '99, 800m 1:50.90 '03.

Ismaïl SGHYR b. 16 Mar 1972 Douar Aïn Chaib Ould Teima, Morocco 1.68m 50kg. Individuel Aquitaine.

At 5000m: OG: '96- 11; WCh: '95- 4, '97- 4, '01- 5; EC: '02- 2; WCp: '02- 3; ECp: '01-02-03: 1/3/1. At 10000m: WCh: '99- 15, '03- 10. At 3000m: WI: '97- 3. World CC: '96-7-02-03: 8/8/13/9 4k. Won MedG 10000m 1997.
French 5000m record 2000.
Progression at 5000m, 10000m: 1993- 14:05.03, 28:42.76; 1994- 13:13.47, 1995- 13:04.19, 1996- 12:58.99, 1997- 13:00.62, 28:05.74; 1999- 13:03.69, 27:12.39; 2000- 12:58.83, 27:33.20; 2001- 13:01.64, 2002- 13:05.80; 2003- 13:10.79, 27:45.14. pbs: 1500m 3:36.20 '95, 1M 3:54.2 '95, 2000m 4:52.88 '95, 3000m 7:30.09 '95, 2M 8:11.73 '96, HMar 62:24 '04, Mar: 2:11:27 '03, 3000mSt 8:42.49 '01.
Switched nationality from Morocco in 2000. Won European Challenge 10000m 2003.

Bouabdellah TAHRI b. 20 Dec 1978 Metz 1.90m 65kg. ASPTT Metz.
At 3000mSt: OG: '00- h; WCh: '99- 12, '01- 5, '03- 4; EC: '98- 10, '02- 4; WJ: '96- 7; ECp: '00-01-02: 1/1/1. At 5000m: EJ: '97- 1. At 1500m: ECp: '03- 4. World CC: '97-04: 22J/15 4k. Won FRA 3000mSt 1998.
European record 3000mSt 2003, best 2000mSt 2002.
Progression at 3000mSt: 1996- 8:44.65, 1998- 8:19.75, 1999- 8:12.24, 2000- 8:16.14, 2001- 8:09.23, 2002- 8:10.83, 2003- 8:06.91. pbs: 800m 1:48.96 '01, 1000m 2:20.79i '02, 2:23.26 '97; 1500m 3:34.85 '02, 1M 3:52.95 '02. 2000m 4:57.58 '02, 3000m 7:41.41i '02, 7:46.7 '03; 5000m 13:24.05 '99, 10km Rd 30:32 '96, HMar 66:12 '03, 2000mSt 5:15.96 '02.

Benoit ZWIERZCHIEWSKI b. 19 Aug 1976 Mouscron, Belgium 1.71m 57kg. Sco. Ste-Marguerite Marseille.
At 5000m/(10000m): WJ: '94- 7; EJ: '95- 1/1. At Mar: WCh: '01- 13; EC: '02- 14. World CC: '94-5: 14J/14J. Won FRA marathon 2000.
Equalled European marathon record 2003.
Progression at 10000m, Mar: 1994- 29:06.54, 1995- 28:30.80, 1998- 2:10:51, 2000- 2:10:47, 2001- 2:18:29; 2002- 2:08:18, 2003- 2:06:36. pbs: 1500m 3:52.2 '95, 3000m 8:10.9 '93, 5000m 13:35.73 '98, 10km 28:29 '00, HMar 61:41 '97.
French junior records at 5000m and 10000m 1994 and 1995. Third in Reims on marathon debut 1998. Won marathons in Reims 2000, Paris 2002. Tied European record when 2nd Paris 2003.

Women

Christine ARRON b. 13 Sep 1973 Abymes, Guadeloupe 1.77m 64kg. Neuilly Plaisance.
At 100m/4x100m (200m): OG: '00- sf/4R; WCh: '97- 4/3R, '99- 6/2R, '03- 6/1R; EC: '98- 1/1R, ECp: '97- (1)/2R, '98- 2/3R, '99- 1/1R, '00- 2/1R, '03- 1/1R; WJ: '92- sf. At 60m: WI: '04- 7. Won French 100m 2000, 2003; 200m 1997. MedG 200m 1997.
European and four French 100m records 1998.
Progression at 100m, 200m: 1988- 12.04, 1989- 11.64/11.6, 25.43; 1990- 12.41/12.3/12.0w, 1991- 11.97, 24.4; 1992- 11.51, 23.75; 1993- 11.93/11.92w, 1994- 24.18, 1995- 23.92, 1996- 23.26, 1997- 11.03, 22.62/22.57w, 1998- 10.73, 22.95i; 1999- 10.97, 22.26; 2000- 10.99/10.89w, 2001- 11.15, 23.42/23.14w; 2003- 11.01/10.95w, 22.92. pbs: 50m 6.05+ '99, 60m 7.00+ '99, 7.08i '04; 400m 53.76 '95.
The superstar of the 1998 European Championships followed a majestic 100m victory in a European record 10.73 with an awesome final sprint relay leg to take France to gold. She first set French age records at 14 in 1988 (for 80m and 150m). Made great breakthrough in 1997, setting a French indoor 200m record (23.13), stepping in for Marie-José Pérec to win European Cup 200m and placing 4th in World 100m. Son Ethan born 28 Jun 2002.

Eunice BARBER b. 17 Nov 1974 Freetown, Sierra Leone 1.75m 68kg. EFS Reims.
At Hep (100mh): OG: '92- 26 (h), '96- 5 (dnq LJ), '00- dnf; WCh: '93- dnf, '95- 4, '97- dnf, '99- 1 (qf), '01- dnf. '03- 2 (1 LJ); WJ: '92- 14. At Pen: WI: '97- 6. At LJ: AfG: '95- 1; ECp: '99-01-03: 1/2/1; won WAF 2003.
French records: LJ 1999 & 2003, heptathlon records 1999. African heptathlon record 1996. SLE records 100mh, HJ, LJ, SP, JT, Hep 1992-8.
Progression at LJ, Hep: 1990- 5.47, 1991- 5.66, 1992- 6.02, 5048; 1993- 5.94, 5308; 1994- 5.93, 5378; 1995- 6.57/6.70Aw, 6340; 1996- 6.59/6.66w, 6416; 1997- 6.70, 1998- 6.86i/6.75/6.90w, 1999- 7.01, 6861; 2000- 6.85, 6842; 2001- 6.97, 6736; 2003- 7.05, 6755. pbs: 60m 7.36i '00, 100m 11.90 '99, 200m 23.53 '99, 800m 2:10.55 '01, 60mh 8.11i '00, 100mh 12.78 '01, 200mh 27.47 '99, HJ 1.93 '99, SP 13.99 '03, JT 52.44 '95, new: 51.91 '00; Pen 4558i '97.
Became a French citizen in February 1999, having previously represented Sierra Leone, but living in Reims from 1992. After concentrating on the long jump for a couple of years and taking the French record to 7.01, she returned in 1999 to the heptathlon where she had wins at 6461 (Arles) and 6505 (European Cup) before adding 356 points to her pb in Seville to take the world title. Another win at Talence (6514) secured her the IAAF Combined Events Challenge award. Won at Götzis with world's best score of 2000, but then held back by injuries; returned for Olympics but unable to continue beyond long jump in heptathlon. In 2001 she won again at Götzis, and started the World Championships heptathlon in great form with a clear lead after two events, but then made the terrible of error of having three no throws in the shot and withdrew. Silver and gold at 2003 Worlds.

Vanessa BOSLAK b. 11 Jun 1982 Lesquin 1.69m 56kg. ASPTT Lille. Physiotherapy student.
At PV: WCh: '03- dnq 18=; EC: '02- 11=; WJ: '98- 6; '00- 3=; EU23: '03- 2; EJ: '01- 3; WI: '04- 5=; ECp: '01-02- 5/3. French champion 2001, 2003.
Five French pole vault records 2002-03.
Progression at PV: 1995- 3.25, 1996- 3.76, 1997- 3.90, 1998- 4.10, 1999- 4.15i/4.11, 2000- 4.32, 2001-

4.33i/4.30, 2002- 4.46, 2003- 4.50, 2004- 4.50i. pb JT 44.27 '99.

Linda FERGA-KHODADIN b. 24 Dec 1976 Paris 1.69m 51kg. née Ferga. Bayard Argentan. At 100mh (/LJ): OG: '00- 7/4R; WCh: '97- (dnq), '01- 7, '03- sf; EC: '98- 8/7, '02- sf; EJ: '95- 3/1; EI: '98- (3); ECp: '97- (5), '98- (3), '00- 1/1R, '01- 2. At 60mh: WI: '99-01-03-04: 5/6/5/3; EI: '00- 1, '02- 1. Won FRA LJ 1997.

Progression at 100mh: 1994- 14.12, 1995- 13.61, 1996- 13.32/13.2, 1997- 13.34/13.02w, 1998- 12.95, 1999- 12.98/12.84w, 2000- 12.81/12.77w, 2001- 12.67, 2002- 12.84, 2003- 12.86/12.84w. pbs: 60m 7.23i '97, 100m 11.35 '98, 50mh 6.82i '00, 60mh 7.82i '04, LJ 6.80 '97, 6.82w '98.

Patricia GIRARD b. 8 Apr 1968 Pointe-à-Pitre, Guadeloupe 1.62m 48kg. Neuilly Plaisance Sports. At 100mh/4x100m (100m): OG: '88- 7R (h), '92- 4R (sf), '96- 3/6R, '00- qf; WCh: '93- sf/4R, '95- sf/5R, '97- dq/3R, '99- 8/2R, '01- sf, '03- 7/1R; EC: '94- (sf), '98- 5, '02- 4; ECp: '93-5-7-8-9-02-03: 2R/3R/2&2R/2&3R/1&1R/1&1R/3&1R; Won FRA 1993, 1995, 1997, 1999, 2001-03; MedG 1997, 2001. At 60m: WI: '93- 8, '03- 8; EI: '90- 4, '94- 3. At 60mh: WI: '93- 3, '95- dnf, '97- 3=; EI: '94-6-8-00-02: 6/1/1/2/3.

Progression at 100mh: 1985- 14.4, 1986- 14.54/ 13.82w, 1987- 13.45, 1988- 13.42, 1989- 13.53, 1992- 12.91, 1993- 12.91, 1994- 12.93, 1995- 12.87, 1996- 12.59, 1997- 12.67, 1998- 12.80, 1999- 12.73, 2000- 12.88, 2001- 12.82/12.77w/12.62 irreg, 2002- 12.64, 2003- 12.74/12.69w. pbs: 50m 6.27i '95, 60m 7.16i '94, 100m 11.11 '94, 11.10w '03, 10.9w '96; 200m 23.40 '95, 400m 56.55 '93, 50mh 6.76i '00, 60mh 7.84i '95, 200mh 25.82 '99, 25.6 '01 (both world bests); 400mh 63.86 '85. LJ 5.72 '93, JT 37.94 '85.

Two year drugs ban from 17 Mar 1990. Formerly married (1995) to European kick-boxing champion Eddy Léno.

Muriel HURTIS b. 25 Mar 1979 Bondy 1.80m 68kg. AC Bobigny.

At (100m)/200m/4x100m: OG: '00- sf/4R; WCh: '99- sf/2R, '03- 4/1R; EC: '02- 1/1R; WJ: '98- 1/2R; EJ: '97- 2/4R; EU23: '99- 2/1R; WI: '01- 5, '03- 2; EI: '00- 1, '02- 1; WCp: '02- 2; ECp: '00- 1/1R, '02- 1/1/1R, '03- 3/1R. At 60m: WI: '04- 5. Won French 200m 2000, 2002.

Progression at 100m, 200m: 1995- 11.95, 23.91/ 23.76w; 1996- 11.89/11.8, 23.92; 1997- 11.80, 23.79; 1998- 11.43, 22.76/22.72w, 1999- 11.33/11.3, 22.31; 2000- 11.36/11.28w, 22.70; 2001- 11.51, 23.06i/ 23.35/23.14w; 2002- 10.96, 22.43/22.35w, 2003- 11.08/10.97w, 22.41. pbs: 50m 6.14i '03, 60m 7.09i '03, 400m 54.44 '98, LJ 6.04i '97, 5.86 '95.

Manuèla MONTEBRUN b. 13 Nov 1979 Laval 1.75m 92kg. Stade Laval. Student.

At HT: OG: '00- dnq 24; WCh: '99- 12, '01- 5, '03- 3; EC: '98- dnq 26, '02- 3; WJ: '98- 5; EU23: '99- 4, '01- 1; WUG: '99- 3, '01- 1; ECp: '00-01-02-03: 3/4/2/1. French champion 2000-03.

Nine French hammer records 1999-2003.

Progression at HT: 1996- 47.34, 1997- 52.58, 1998- 62.79, 1999- 68.11, 2000- 71.18, 2001- 70.28, 2002- 72.54, 2003- 74.50/75.20dh. pb SP 13.99 '99.

Nicole RAMALALANIRINA b. 5 Mar 1972 Soavinandriana, Madagascar 1.64m 57kg. Married name Válerie. Neuilly Plaisance Sports. At 100mh: OG: '92- h, '96- sf, '00- 6; WCh: '93/ 95/99/01- sf, '97- ht; EC: '98- 4; AfG: '91- 3/3R, '95- 4; AfC: '90- 6, '92- 4/3R, '93- 1/2R; WCp: '94- 4, '98- dnf; WSG: '93- 3, '95- 1. At 60mh: WI: '01- 3, '04- 8; EI: '02- 4. Won FRA 100mh 1998, 2000.

African record 60mh indoors 1996.

Progression at 100mh: 1990- 13.91, 1991- 13.69, 1992- 13.40, 1993- 13.11/12.92w, 1994- 13.11, 1995- 12.92, 1996- 12.90, 1997- 13.02, 1998- 12.85/12.76w, 1999- 12.84, 2000- 12.76, 2001- 12.91/12.84w/12.87 irreg, 2002- 13.04, 2003- 13.00/12.99w. pbs: 50m 6.53i '96, 60m 7.40i '94, 100m 11.56 '96, 11.53w '95; 200m 24.3A '91, 24.34w '00; 400m 56.13 '02, 50mh 6.82i '04, 60mh 7.89i '96, 200mh 26.70 '98, 400mh 59.88 '94. LJ 5.54 '94.

Changed citizenship from Madagascar (for whom she was also a basketball international) to France in February 1998.

GERMANY

Governing body: Deutscher Leichtathletik Verband (DLV), Alsfelder Str. 27, 64289 Darmstadt. Founded 1898.

National Championships first held in 1891. **2003 Champions: Men**: 100m: Alexander Kosenkow 10.25, 200m: Tobias Unger 20.80, 400m: Ingo Schultz 45.29, 800m: René Herms 1:47.62, 1500m: Franek Haschke 3:49.97, 5000m/10000m: Dieter Baumann 13:41.22/28:28.47, HMar: Carsten Eich 64:24, Mar: Michael Fietz 2:23:17, 30000mSt: Christian Knoblich 8:34.76, 110mh: Jerome Crews 13.54, 400mh: Christian Duma 50.01, HJ: Roman Fricke 2.25, PV: Tim Lobinger 5.75, LJ: Nils Winter 7.89, TJ: Rudolf Helpling 16.78, SP: Ralf Bartels 20.22, DT: Lars Riedel 66.60, HT: Karsten Kobs 77.98, JT: Boris Henry 84.92, Dec: Matthias Spahn 7814, 10000mW: Andreas Erm 40:58.79, 20kmW: Mail Berger 1: 28:24, 50kmW: Andrea Erm 3:43:53. **Women**: 100m: Melanie Paschke 11.41, 200m: Gabi Rockmeier 23.01, 400m: Claudia Marx 52.00, 800m: Claudia Gesell 2:01.07, 1500m: Kathleen Friedrich 4:21.86, 5000m/10000m: Sabrina Mockenhaupt 15:51.73/ 32:11.95, 3000mSt: Katrin Engelen 10:34.13, HMar: Luminita Zaituc 74:08, Mar: Sylvia Renz 2:42:00, 100mh: Nadine Hentschke 13.14, 400mh: Stephanie Kampf 56.03, HJ: Melanie Skotnik 1.90, PV: Yvonne Buschbaum 4.70, LJ: Bianca Kappler 6.44, TJ: Katja Demut 13.45, SP: Astrid Kumbernuss 19.36, DT: Franke Dietzsch 62.86, HT: Susanne Keil 71.15, JT: Steffi Nerius 64.42, Hep: Andrea Tittmann 5638, 5000mW/

20kmW: Melanie Seeger 20:56.19/1:29:44.

Ralf BARTELS b. 21 Feb 1978 Malchin 1.86m 125kg. SC Neubrandenburg. Soldier.
At SP: WCh: '01- dnq 17, '03- 6; EC: '02- 3; WJ: '96- 1; EU23: '99- 6; EJ: '95- 4, '97- 1; WCp: '02- 3; ECp: '01-02-03: 4/4/5. German champion 2002-03.
Progression at SP: 1995- 17.63, 1996- 18.71, 1997- 18.35, 1998- 18.50, 1999- 18.95, 2000- 19.34, 2001- 20.30, 2002- 20.85, 2003- 20.67.

Peter BLANK b. 10 Apr 1962 Frankfurt-am-Main 1.95m 103kg. Eintracht Frankfurt.
At JT: OG: '96- 9; WCh: '91- 11, '93/9/01- dnq 29/13/17, '03- 8; EC: '90- dnq, '94- dnq 20, '98- 7; ECp: '91- 3. FRG champion 1988, 1990; GER 2001.
Progression at JT: 1978- 58.42, 1979- 64.92, 1980- 65.76, 1981- 72.84, 1982- 76.04, 1983- 78.22, 1984- 81.98, 1985- 82.34, new: 1986- 71.02, 1987- 77.94, 1988- 80.84, 1989- 79.60, 1990- 82.82R, 1991- 82.62, 1992- 81.12, 1993- 80.76, 1994- 82.56, 1995- 83.18, 1996- 88.12, 1997- 86.84, 1998- 86.99, 1999- 87.11, 2000- 85.45, 2001- 88.70, 2002- 82.24, 2003- 84.08. pbs: HJ 2.23 '83, LJ 7.41 '88, Dec 7651 '90.
Set a world decathlon javelin best 79.80 in 1992. World M40 javelin records 2002 & 2003.

Lars BÖRGELING b. 16 Apr 1979 Neuss 1.87m 86kg. Bayer Leverkusen. Student.
At PV: WCh: '03- dnq 13; EC: '02- 2; WJ: '96- 8=, '98- 2; EU23: '99- 2, '01- 1; EJ: '97- 1; EI: '02- 3; WCp: '02- 3; ECp: '03- 3. German champion 2002.
Progression at PV: 1993- 3.83, 1994- 4.30, 1995- 4.60, 1996- 5.20, 1997- 5.50, 1998- 5.62, 1999- 5.80, 2000- 5.75ex/5.70, 2001- 5.80, 2002- 5.85, 2003- 5.80. pbs: Dec 6478 '99.

Danny ECKER b. 21 Jul 1977 Leverkusen 1.92m 78kg. Bayer Leverkusen.
At PV: OG: '00- 8; WCh: '99- 4=, '01- 11; EC: '98- 4; WI: '99- 3; EI: '98- 3; WJ: '96- 3; ECp: '98- 4.
Progression at PV: 1990- 2.90, 1991- 3.30, 1992- 3.80, 1993- 4.40, 1994- 4.70, 1995- 5.12, 1996- 5.61, 1997- 5.72i/5.71, 1998- 5.93, 1999- 5.90, 2000- 5.90, 2001- 6.00i/5.85, 2002- 5.82i/5.70. pbs: HJ 2.00 '99, LJ 6.83 '99.
Son of Heide Rosendahl, 1972 Olympic LJ champion (and 2nd Pen) (WR 6.84 '70), and US basketball player John Ecker.

Andreas ERM b. 12 Mar 1976 Berlin 1.84m 70kg. SC Potsdam. Soldier.
At 20kmW: OG: '96- 24, '00- 5; WCh: '97- dq, '99/01- dnf, '03- 3; EC: '98- 4; EU23: '97- 5; ECp: '98-00-01 4/2/3. At 10000mW: WJ: '94- 9; EJ: '95- 1. Won GER 20kmW 1998-2002, 10000mW 2000-01, 50kmW 2002-03.
German records 20km walk 2000, 50km 2003; world best indoor 3000m walk 2001.
Progression at 20kmW, 50kmW: 1994- 1:26:41, 1995- 1:23:20, 1996- 1:22:16, 1997- 1:21:05, 1998- 1:20:57, 1999- 1:19:24, 2000- 1:18:42, 2001- 1:19:32, 2002- 1:22:04, 3:45:28; 2003- 1:28:49, 3:37:46. pbs: 3000mW 10:31.42i '01, 11:10.20 '01; 5000mW 18:22.25i '01, 10000mW 39:54.23 '00.

Charles-Michael FRIEDEK b. 26 Aug 1971 Giessen 1.84m 80kg. Bayer Leverkusen. Law student.
At TJ: OG: '00- nj (12); WCh: '97- 11, '99- 1; EC: '98- 6, '02- 2; WJ: '90- 12; EJ: '89- dnq; WI: '97- 4, '99- 1, '01- 4; EI: '98- 2, '00- 1; WUG: '97- 5, '99- 2; WCp: '98- 1, '02- 4; ECp: '96-7-8-01-02: 4/3/3/8/3. Won GP 1998, GER 1996-2000, 2002.
Progression at TJ: 1987- 13.67, 1988- 15.13, 1989- 15.85, 1990- 16.34, 1991- 15.77, 1992- 16.10, 1993- 16.32i/16.26/16.51w, 1994- 16.31, 1995- 16.34/16.60w, 1996- 17.10, 1997- 17.59, 1998- 17.42A/17.38, 1999- 17.59, 2000- 17.41, 2001- 17.13i/16.90, 2002- 17.33, 2003- 16.53, 2004- 16.78i. pbs: 100m 11.01 '92, 200m 22.23 '89, LJ 7.66 '97.

Raymond HECHT b. 11 Nov 1968 Gardelegen 1.91m 95kg. SG Magdeburg. Mechanical engineer.
At JT: OG: '96- 4, '00- 4; WCh: '91- 12, '93- dnq 23, '95- 4, '97- dnq 13, '99- 5, '01- 5; EC: '90- 10, '94- 5, '98- 3, '02- 5; WCp: '94- 2, '98- 3; ECp: '93-4-5-6-9-01: 4/2/1/1/3; EJ: '87- 3. GER champion 1993-4, 1996, 1999, 2002. 2nd GP 1993, 1995.
Five German javelin records 1991-5.
Progression at JT: 1984- 66.20, 1985- 69.32; new: 1986- 71.08 (71.14 old), 1987- 75.90, 1990- 83.24, 1991- 90.84R, 1992- 79.58, 1993- 88.90, 1994- 90.06, 1995- 92.60, 1996- 92.28, 1997- 87.32, 1998- 88.08, 1999- 88.67, 2000- 87.76, 2001- 88.88, 2002- 87.87, 2003- 86.22.

Boris HENRY b. 14 Dec 1973 Völklingen 1.93m 108kg. SV Saar 05 Saarbrücken. Army staff sergeant.
At JT: OG: '96- 5, '00- 7; WCh: '93- dnq, '95- 3, '97- 6, '99- 6, '01- 6, '03- 3; EC: '94- 11, '02- 3; WJ: '92- 2; EJ: '91- 4; WCp: '02- 2; ECp: '97-8-00-02: 3/1/3/3. 2nd/3rd GP 1997/99. GER champion 1995, 1997-8, 2000, 2003.
Progression at JT: 1989- 58.20, 1990- 65.86, 1991- 74.78, 1992- 76.92, 1993- 84.12, 1994- 82.02, 1995- 88.46, 1996- 88.00, 1997- 90.44, 1998- 89.21, 1999- 88.62, 2000- 86.65, 2001- 86.53, 2002- 86.67, 2003- 88.10. pbs: SP 14.37 '94, DT 46.24 '94, Pen 3503 '93.
For several years wore a red baseball cap given to him as an 18th birthday present, now sports a white one. World teenage best 84.12 '93.

Karsten KOBS b. 16 Sep 1971 Dortmund 1.96m 125kg. Bayer Leverkusen.
At HT: OG: '96/00- dnq 18/31; WCh: '93-95-03: dnq 16/16/17, '97- 9, '99- 1; EC: '94- 10, '98- 3, '02- dnq 14; WJ: '90- 4; EJ: '89- 10; WCp: '02- 3; ECp: '93-5-6-9-00-01-02-03: 7/3/1/3/3/5/5/1; E23Cp: '92- 2. German champion 1996, 1999-2003. 3rd GP 2000.
Progression at HT: 1988- 59.80, 1989- 65.02, 1990- 70.02, 1991- 71.82, 1992- 74.36, 1993- 75.94, 1994- 76.30, 1995- 76.80, 1996- 78.92, 1997- 79.08, 1998- 81.21, 1999- 82.78, 2000- 80.21, 2001- 79.15, 2002- 81.49, 2003- 80.63. pb SP 15.53 '98.
Improved every year of his career until he reached the world number one ranking in 1999. His father, Reiner, had HT pb of 58.90 (1974).

Tim LOBINGER b. 3 Sep 1972 Rheinbach 1.93m 87kg. ASV Köln.
At PV: OG: '96- 7, '00- 13; WCh: '93- dnq, '95- 11, '97- 4, '99- 6, '03- 5; EC: '94- dnq 21=, '98- 2. '02- 3; WI: '97-03-04: 5/1/5; EI: '98- 1, '02- 1; WJ: '90- dnq; EJ: '91- 3; WCp: '98- 2; ECp: '93-4-5-6-7-00-02: 5/3/nh/2/3/2/1; E23Cp: '92- 1, '94- 4. Won WAF 2003, GP 2000, 3rd 1997, 2002; German champion 1993-4, 1997-2000, 2003.
Three German pole vault records 1997-9.
Progression at PV: 1986- 3.46, 1987- 3.90, 1988- 4.60, 1989- 4.85, 1990- 5.32, 1991- 5.35, 1992- 5.50, 1993- 5.55, 1994- 5.60, 1995- 5.70, 1996- 5.91, 1997- 6.00, 1998- 5.92, 1999- 6.00, 2000- 5.95i/5.85, 2001- 5.80, 2002- 5.90, 2003- 5.91. pbs: 110mh 14.78 '99, HJ 1.97 '99, DT 42.76 '99, Dec 7346 '99.
Set (then) world decathlon PV best of 5.75 in 7346 decathlon at Leverkusen 1999.

Michael MÖLLENBECK b. 12 Dec 1969 Wesel 2.00m 120kg. TV Wattenscheid. Businessman.
At DT: OG: '96- dnq, '00- 10; WCh: '95- dnq 16, '99- 6, '01- 3, '03- 5; EC: '02- 3; WJ: '88- 9; EJ: '87- 6; WCp: '02- 4; ECp: '02-03: 1/2. Won GER 2002.
Progression at DT: 1988- 53.00, 1989- 59.26, 1990- 60.16, 1991- 58.86, 1992- 62.12, 1993- 62.82, 1994- 58.26, 1995- 65.78, 1996- 67.44, 1997- 66.66, 1998- 67.18, 1999- 67.00, 2000- 65.49, 2001- 67.61, 2002- 67.64, 2003- 67.42. pb SP 16.78 '95.
Threw pb in first round of 2001 World DT final. Married discus thrower Anja Gündler (1 EJ 91, 5 WCh 93, pb 64.63 '98) in 1996.

Christian NICOLAY b. 4 Mar 1976 Bassenheim 1.88m 90kg. TV Wattenscheid. Economics graduate.
At JT: WCh: '03- 6; WJ: '94- 5; EU23: '97- 3; EJ: '95- 1; ECp: '03- 2.
Progression at PV: 1993- 68.34, 1994- 73.80, 1995- 76.88, 1996- 79.96, 1997- 78.36, 1998- 75.71, 1999- 78.23, 2000- 80.19, 2001- 71.41, 2002- 81.90, 2003- 84.54.

Lars RIEDEL b. 28 Jun 1967 Zwickau 1.99m 110kg. LAC Chemnitz. Computer salesman.
At DT: OG: '92- dnq 14, '96- 1, '00- 2; WCh: '91-3-5-7-9-01-03: 1/1/1/1/3/1/4; EC: '90- dnq 15, '94- dns, '98- 1; WJ: '86- 4; WUG: '93- 1; WCp: '98- 2; ECp: '93-5-7-00-01: 1/1/1/1/1. GER champion 1992-8, 2000-01, 2003. Won GP 1993, 1995, 1997 (2nd overall), 1999; 2nd 1991.
Progression at DT: 1985- 52.02, 1986- 58.66, 1988- 62.26, 1989- 60.84, 1990- 64.86, 1991- 67.78, 1992- 68.66, 1993- 68.42, 1994- 66.08, 1995- 69.08, 1996- 71.06, 1997- 71.50, 1998- 68.21, 1999- 69.18, 2000- 69.72, 2001- 69.72, 2002- 66.72, 2003- 69.50. pbs: SP 15.93 '91, JT 61.14 '93, Dec 6087 '93.
The top discus thrower of the 1990s with four world titles (and a fifth in 2001) and the 1996 Olympic gold. In 1992 improved to 67.90, but failed at the Olympics before making a fine comeback with four throws over 68m at the ISTAF meeting. In 1994 a bad back caused his withdrawal from European final. He exceeded 70m for the first time in Zürich in 1995.

Ingo SCHULTZ b. 26 Jul 1975 Lingen/Ems 2.01m 96kg. TSG Bergedorf. Studying for PhD in electrical engineering.
At 400m/4x400mR: WCh: '01- 2, '03- sf; EC: '02- 1; EI: '00- 2R; WCp: '02- 2; ECp: '01-02-03: 4&2R/2/2&3R. Won GER 2002-03.
Progression at 400m: 1999- 45.99, 2000- 45.79, 2001- 44.66, 2002- 44.97, 2003- 45.06. pbs: 100m 10.57 '01, 200m 20.65 '02, 300m 33.02i '02.
While in the army in 1997 he ran the Hamburg Marathon in 3:37, and started track racing after that. He ran 52.45 for his first 400m in May 1998. Suffered from glandular fever in 2003.

Nils SCHUMANN b. 20 May 1978 Bad Frankenhausen 1.92m 77kg. SC Magdeburg.
At 800m: OG: '00- 1; WCh: '99- 8, '01- 5; EC: '98- 1, '02- 3; WJ: '96- 5; EJ: '97- 1; EU23: '99- 1; EI: '98- 1, '00- 2; WCp: '98- 1, '02- 5; ECp: '00- 2, '02- 2. German champion 1999-2000.
Progression at 800m: 1988- 2:26.5, 1989- 2:21.0, 1990- 2:18.3, 1991- 2:14.0, 1994- 2:03.6, 1995- 1:52.96, 1996- 1:48.35, 1997- 1:46.61, 1998- 1:44.89, 1999- 1:44.47, 2000- 1:44.22, 2001- 1:44.32, 2002- 1:44.16, 2003- 1:45.57i. pbs: 400m 46.62 '99, 1000m 2:17.44 '99, 1500m 3:38.51 '02.
Burst to the fore with an astonishing sequence of championship victories.

Michael STOLLE b. 17 Dec 1974 Buxtehude 1.92m 85kg. Bayer Leverkusen.
At PV: OG: '96- 9=, '00- 4; WCh: '99- 7=, '01- 4; WI: '97-01-03: 8=/9=/2; EI: '98- 2; WJ: '90- dnq; EJ: '91- dnq; ECp: '99- 1, '01- 1. German champion 1996.
Progression at PV: 1989- 3.70, 1990- 4.20, 1991- 4.75, 1992- 5.05, 1993- 5.10i/5.05, 1994- 5.41, 1995- 5.50, 1996- 5.71i/5.70, 1997- 5.70i/5.60, 1998- 5.83, 1999- 5.91, 2000- 5.95, 2001- 5.85, 2003- 5.75i. pb Dec 5817 '99.

Women

Annika BECKER b. 12 Nov 1981 Rotenburg/Fulda 1.70m 67kg. Team Erfurt. Student.
At PV: WCh: '01- dnq 14, '03- 2; EC: '02- 5; WJ: '00- 2; EU23: '01- 2; EJ: '97- 1, '99- 2; WI: '03- 5; EI: '02- 4; WCp: '02- 1; ECp: '03- 1. German champion 2001-02.
European pole vault record 2002, two German 2001-02.
Progression at PV: 1996- 3.40, 1997- 4.01, 1998- 4.15, 1999- 4.30, 2000- 4.22, 2001- 4.55, 2002- 4.77, 2003- 4.70, 2004- 4.68i. pb LJ 6.15 '03.

Grit BREUER b. 16 Feb 1972 Röbel 1.66m 63kg. SC Magdeburg.
At 400m/4x400mR: OG: '88- res (3)R, '96- 8/3R; WCh: '91- 2/3R (3 4x100mR), '97- 4/1R, '99- 7/3R, '01- 4/2R, '03- 4R; EC: '90- 1/1R, '98- 1/1R, '02- 2/1R; WJ: '88- 1 (1R & 1 4x100mR); WI: '91- 1R (3 200m), '97- 6/3R, '99- 1, '03- 3; EI: '96- 1, '98- 1; WCp: '89- 2/2R, '98- 2/1R; ECp: '89-91-6-7-01: 1/2/1/1/1 (1R/2R/1R/-/1R). Won GDR 400m

1989-90, GER 200m 1997, 400m 1996-7, 1999-2001. World junior records 400m 1990 and 1991, 4x100m and 4x400m 1988, indoor 200m 1991. WIR 4x400m 1991.
Progression at 200m, 400m: 1985- 56.21, 1986- 55.7/55.5i, 1987- 24.03, 52.59; 1988- 23.04, 51.14; 1989- 22.82, 50.48; 1990- 22.49, 49.50; 1991- 22.45, 49.42; 1992- 22.71i, 1995- 23.63, 51.68; 1996- 50.22, 1997- 22.73, 49.98; 1998- 22.95i, 49.51; 1999- 23.02, 50.16; 2000- 23.46, 51.06; 2001- 22.79, 49.78; 2002- 23.32, 50.70; 2003- 22.67i, 51.13i/52.26. pbs: 50m 6.36i '91, 60m 7.33i '90, 100m 11.13 '90, 300m 36.51+ '99.
World age records for 400m at 16-17-18-19. Olympic bronze medal at age 16 as she ran in heats of 4x400m. She did not contest the European or World Juniors 1989-91, but concentrated successfully on senior competition. Drugs ban in 1992 for allegedly tampering with sample was lifted by the DLV, but she was then caught again for use of Clenbuterol. She returned to competition when her three-year ban ended in August 1995. Ran a brilliant final leg of 48.69 to come from behind and take the gold medal for Germany in the 1997 World 4x400m. She withdrew from the 2000 Olympic team and underwent surgery for back and knee problems, but made a fine comeback in 2001.

Yvonne BUSCHBAUM b. 14 Jul 1980 Ulm 1.70m 57kg. VfB Stuttgart.
At PV: OG: '00- 6; WCh: '99- 14=, '01- 7, '03- 6; EC: '98- 3, '02- 3; WJ: '98- 4; WI: '01- 6; EI: '02- 2; ECp: '99-00-02: 1/2/2. Won GER 1999-2000, 2003.
PV records: Four world junior 1999, German 1999 & 2002. Three German indoor 2002.
Progression at PV: 1994- 2.81, 1995- 3.30, 1996- 3.55, 1997- 4.00, 1998- 4.31, 1999- 4.42/4.45ex, 2000- 4.45, 2001- 4.46, 2002- 4.65i/4.64, 2003- 4.70. pbs: 100mh 14.54 '98, HJ 1.75 '98, LJ 5.81 '98.

Franka DIETZSCH b. 22 Jan 1968 Wolgast 1.83m 95kg. SC Neubrandenburg. Bank employee.
At DT: OG: '92- 12, '96- 4, '00- 6; WCh: '91- dnq 13, '93- 8, '95- 7, '97- dnq, '99- 1, '01- 5, '03- dnq 14; EC: '94- 9, '98- 1; WJ: '86- 2; WUG: '89- 4; WCp: '98- 1; ECp: '97-9-01-02-03: 2/3/1/3/4; Won GP 2000, 2nd 1998. GER champion 1997-2001, 2003.
Progression at DT: 1981- 27.70, 1982- 43.80, 1983- 50.04, 1984- 51.16, 1985- 56.94, 1986- 64.34, 1987- 66.34, 1988- 65.56, 1989- 68.26, 1990- 67.42, 1991- 61.22, 1992- 64.64, 1993- 62.06, 1994- 62.76, 1995- 62.26, 1996- 66.66, 1997- 67.66, 1998- 68.91, 1999- 69.51, 2000- 68.06, 2001- 65.87A, 2002- 64.12, 2003- 66.00. pb SP 15.02 '85.

Heike DRECHSLER b. 16 Dec 1964 Gera 1.81m 68kg. née Daute. LG Karlsruhe.
At LJ/R- 4x100mR: OG: '88- 2 (3 100m & 200m), '92- 1, '00- 1; WCh: '83- 1, '87- 3 (2 100m), '91- 2/3R, '93- 1, '95- 9 (dnf Hep), '97- 4, '01- dnq; EC: '82- 4, '86- 1 (1 200m), '90- 1 (2 200m), '94- 1, '98- 1, '02- 5; WI: '87- 1 (1 200m), '91- 2, '97- 7, '01- 5; EI: '83- 3, '85- 3, '86- 1, '87- 1, '88- 1, '94- 1, '00- 2; EJ: '81- 1; WCp: '85- 1, '92- 1, '98- 1; ECp: '83- 1, '85- 2, '87- 1/1R (2 4x400mR), '91- 1/2R, '93-4-5-2001: 1/1/1/1. Won GDR LJ 1981, 1983-8, 1990; 200m 1986, 1988; GER LJ 1991-2, 1994-5, 1998-2002; 100m 1992; GWG LJ 1994. Won GP LJ 1990, 1992, 2000 (2nd 1996, 3rd 1994); won overall 1992 (2nd 1990).
World records: three LJ 1985-6, two 200m 1986. WIB: LJ (6): 6.88 '83, 6.99 '84 & '85, 7.25 & 7.29 '86, 7.37 '88; 100y: 10.24 '86, 10.24 & 10.15 '87; 200m: 22.27 '87. World junior LJ records 1981 and 1982, heptathlon 1981. 8 GDR LJ records 1983-8, GER record 1992.
Progression at 100m, 200m, LJ, Hep: 1977- 13.1, 4.40; 1978- 5.69, 1979- 12.3, 6.07; 1980- 6.64/6.70w, 5780; 1981- 11.75, 24.16, 6.91/7.01w, 5812; 1982- 6.98, 1983- 7.14/7.27w, 1984- 7.40, 1985- 23.19, 7.44; 1986- 10.91/10.80w, 21.71, 7.45; 1987- 10.95, 22.18, 7.40; 1988- 10.91/10.85w, 21.84, 7.48; 1990- 11.14, 22.19, 7.30; 1991- 11.09, 22.58/22.4, 7.37/7.39w; 1992- 11.24, 7.48/7.63Aw; 1993- 11.36, 23.16, 7.21; 1994- 11.38, 22.84, 7.29/7.39Aw, 6741; 1995- 23.02i/23.04, 7.09i/7.07, 6375; 1996- 23.17i, 6.96i/6.75/6.87w; 1997- 11.70, 6.95i/6.89/7.02w; 1998- 11.82w, 7.16; 1999- 6.91, 2000- 6.99/7.07w, 2001- 6.79, 2002- 6.85, 2003- 6.07. pbs: 60m 7.23i '92, 800m 2:11.53 '94, 100mh 13.34 '94, HJ 1.88i '92, TJ 13.94i '97, 13.35 '93; SP 13.88 '95, JT 40.64 '94.
World age records for long jump each age 15-19. The youngest gold medallist of the 1983 Worlds, at LJ she had 27 successive wins until injured at the 1987 World Champs and from 1982 to 2001 won 247 of 340 competitions. and has 159 competitions (and at least 409 jumps) over 7m (100th was at the 1992 Olympics). Her 7.63w/2.1 at the high altitude of Sestriere in 1992 was the first 25 ft jump by a woman. Missed 1996 Olympics and 1999 Worlds through injury, but came back in triumph in 2000 to regain her Olympic title. In all she has won 33 GDR/GER LJ titles – 16 indoors (1981, 1983-4, 1986-8, 1991-5, 1997, 1999-2002) 17 out. She made a sensational breakthrough in 1986 into a great sprinter, winning the GDR indoor 100y title in 10.24, and equalling Marita Koch's world 200m record and she ran a 50.0 400m relay leg in the 1987 European Cup. In her first heptathlon since her world junior record in 1981, she scored 6741 points to win at Talence in 1994.
Son, Toni Drechsler, born 1 Nov 1989. Her partner and coach is French decathlete Alain Blondel.

Claudia GESELL b. 18 Dec 1977 Tirschenreuth 1.70m 59kg. Bayer Leverkusen. Student.
At 800m: OG: '00- sf; WCh: '99- sf, '03- 5; EC: '02- 5; WJ: '96- 1 (1R); EU23: '97- 4, '99- 1; WCp: '02- 6; ECp: '03- 1. Won GER 1998-2000, 2002-03.
Progression at 800m: 1993- 2:12.16, 1994- 2:18.61, 1995- 2:07.20, 1996- 2:02.67, 1997- 2:02.52, 1998- 2:01.28, 1999- 1:59.87, 2000- 1:58.34, 2002- 2:00.51,

2003- 1:58.93. pbs: 400m 54.37 '96, 1000m 2:36.84 '02. Won a German Universities title at triathlon.

Susanne KEIL b. 18 May 1978 Frankfurt-am-Main 1.72m 66kg. LG Eintracht Frankfurt.
At HT: WCh: '01- dnq 14, '03- 5; EC: '02- 10; EJ: '97- 3; WUG: '01- 6; WCp: '02- 6; ECp: '03- 5. German champion 2002-03.
Two German hammer records 2003.
Progression at HT: 1994- 47.56, 1995- 52.00, 1996- 58.16, 1997- 60.94, 1998- 64.50, 1999- 64.40, 2000- 64.04, 2001- 68.07, 2002- 68.17, 2003- 71.93.
Her sister Alexandra has 100mh best of 13.4 '97, 13.65 '00.

Sonja KESSELSCHLÄGER b. 20 Jan 1978 Finsterwalde 1.79m 66kg. SC Neubrandenburg. Outdoor pbs:
At Hep: WCh: '03- 8; EC: '02- 9; WJ: '96-7; EJ: '97- 3; EU23: '99- 3; WUG: '01- 3; ECp: '01- 2, '02- 3. At Pen: WI: '03- 4; EI: '00- 6, '02- 5.
Progression at Hep: 1994- 5005, 1995- 5236, 1996- 5620, 1997- 5753, 1998- 5763, 2000- 6039, 2001- 6064, 2002- 6205, 2003- 6175. pbs: 200m 24.52 '02, 800m 2:16.23 '03, 60mh 8.37i '03, 100mh 13.34 '03, HJ 1.85 '00, LJ 6.37 '03, SP 14.28i '00, 14.28 '03; JT 46.06 '96, Pen 4531i '03.

Nadine KLEINERT b. 20 Oct 1975 Magdeburg 1.90m 90kg. SC Magdeburg.
At SP: OG: '00- 8; WCh: '97- 7, '99- 2, '01- 2, '03- 7; EC: '98- 6, '02- 6; WJ: '92- 12, '94- 6; EU23: '94- 3 Cp, '97- 1; EJ: '93- 2; WI: '99- 01-04: 5/4/4; EI: '00- 2; ECp: '99- 2, '01- 1. Won GP 1999. German champion 1998, 2000-01.
Progression at SP: 1990- 13.85, 1991- 15.08, 1992- 16.32, 1993- 17.07, 1994- 17.44, 1995- 17.13, 1996- 18.37, 1997- 18.91, 1998- 19.22, 1999- 19.61, 2000- 19.81, 2001- 19.86, 2002- 19.24, 2003- 19.33i/ 19.14, 2004- 19.05i. pb DT 50.99 '01.

Astrid KUMBERNUSS b. 5 Feb 1970 Grevesmühlen 1.86m 90kg. SC Neubrandenburg.
At SP (DT): OG: '96- 1, '00- 3; WCh: '93- 6, '95- 1, '97- 1, '99- 1, '01- 6, '03- dnq 15; EC: '90- 1, '94- 2, '02- 4; WI: '97- 2, '03- 3; EI: '90-2-4-6-00: 4/3/1/ 1/3; WJ: '88- (2); EJ: '87- (2), '89- 1 (1); WCp: '94- 3, '02- 3; ECp: '91-4-5-6-7-00-02-03: 2/1/1/1/1/ 1/2/1. Won GP 1995, 1997 (and Overall), 2001; 2nd 1993, 1999; 3rd 1991. Won GER SP 1995-7, 1999, 2002-03.
Progression at SP, DT: 1983- 11.16, 33.48; 1984- 13.44/14.01i, 44.00; 1985- 14.23, 46.96; 1986- 15.39, 53.92; 1987- 18.20, 63.88; 1988- 18.73, 66.60; 1989- 20.54, 64.74; 1990- 20.77, 65.42; 1991- 19.67, 60.88; 1992- 20.03i/19.69, 1993- 19.92, 59.64; 1994- 20.06, 1995- 21.22, 59.90; 1996- 20.97, 1997- 21.22, 1999- 19.85, 2000- 20.23, 2001- 19.87, 2002- 19.86, 2003- 19.91. World junior shot record 1989.
Unbeaten in 53 competitions 1995-6. In 1995 she had eight GP wins prior to the final, and won the world title by 1.18m, the largest ever margin of victory at World/Olympic level. She had knee surgery in November 1997 and missed the 1998 season; her son Philipp was born on 7 July 1998. Returned to take third world title in 1999.

Irina MIKITENKO b. 23 Aug 1972 Bakankas, Kazakhstan 1.58m 49kg. née Volynskaya. LG Eintracht Frankfurt.
At 5000m: OG: '96- h, '00- 5; WCh: '99- 4, '01- 5, '03- h; ECp: '99-00-03: 2/2/4. At 10000m: EC: '98- 8; WCp: '98- 5. 3rd GP 3000m 1999. World 4k CC: '00- 19. Won Central Asian 1500m 1995; German 10000m 1998, 5000m 1999-2000.
German records 3000m 2000, 5000m (3) 1999.
Progression at 5000m, 10000m: 1995- 15:47.85, 1996- 15:49.59, 1997- 15:48.29, 1998- 15:18.86, 32:10.61; 1999- 14:42.03, 31:38.68; 2000- 14:43.59; 2001- 14:53.00, 31:29.55; 2003- 14:56.64, 31:38.48. pbs: 800m 2:09.97 '98, 1500m 4:06.08 '01, 2000m 5:40.6 '01, 3000m 8:30.39 '00.
German parents; changed nationality from KAZ to Germany in March 1998. Son Alexander.

Steffi NERIUS b. 1 Jul 1972 Bergen/Rügen 1.78m 72kg. Bayer Leverkusen. PE teacher.
At JT: OG: '96- 9, '00- 4; WCh: '93- 9, '95- 11, '99- dnq 16, '01- 5, '03- 3; EC: '98- 6, '02- 2; EJ: '91- 3; WUG: '97- 5; WCp: '92- 6, '02- 4; ECp: '95-01-02-03: 1/2/3/1. 2nd GP 1996. German champion 2001, 2003.
Progression at JT: 1985- 30.12, 1987- 45.16, 1988- 48.00, 1989- 56.88, 1990- 56.14, 1991- 60.02, 1992- 59.46, 1993- 63.88, 1995- 68.42, 1996- 69.42, 1997- 64.58, 1998- 67.33; new: 1999- 61.56. 2000- 65.76, 2001- 63.72, 2002- 64.55, 2003- 64.42.
Was a GDR youth volleyball champion.

Sonja OBEREM b. 24 Feb 1973 Rheydt 1.71m 50kg. née Krolik. Bayer Leverkusen.
At Mar: OG: '96- 8, '00- 24; WCh: '95- 8, '97- 7, '99- 6, '01- 5; EC: '98- 12, '02- 3. Won GER 10000m 1997, HMar 1998.
Progression at Mar: 1993- 2:38:02, 1994- 2:31:35, 1995- 2:32:17sh, 1996- 2:29:24, 1997- 2:28:02, 1998- 2:29:30, 1999- 2:28:55, 2000- 2:27:25, 2001- 2:26:13, 2002- 2:26:21. pbs: 5000m 16:08.37 '95, 10000m 32:39.50 '97, HMar 70:13 '96.
At triathlon was World Junior champion 1990 and 1992 and European champion at Olympic (short) distance 1992 and 1994. Has four wins in 23 marathons, her first at Hamburg 2001 in her 17th race at the distance; also Athens 2001-02 and Hamburg 2002. She completed a remarkable sequence of 8-7-6-5 in World Champs marathons. 2nd Amsterdam 1998, 4th Boston 1996, London 1997.

Daniela RATH b. 6 May 1977 Willich 1.79m 60kg. TSV Bayer Leverkusen.
At HJ: WCh: '97- dnq, '03- dnq 16; EC: '98- dnq; WJ: '96- dnq; EU23: '97- 3; WI: '04- 5; ECp: '03- 1.
Progression at HJ: 1989- 1.60, 1990- 1.76, 1991- 1.78, 1992- 1.80, 1993- 1.77, 1994- 1.76, 1995- 1.85, 1996- 1.94, 1997- 1.91, 1998- 1.92, 1999- 1.88, 2002- 1.86, 2003- 2.00, 2004- 2.00i. pb TJ 12.77 '03.
Her 1.97 in May 2003 bettered her previous best

of 1.94 set in 1996, and a month later she cleared 2.00 to win at the European Cup.

Anastasija 'Nastja' **RYSHICH** b. 19 Sep 1977 Omsk, Russia 1.70m 59kg. ABC Ludwigshafen.
At PV: WCh: '99- nh; EC: '98- 4=; WI: '99- 1, '04- 8; EU23: '99- 2.
Pole vault records: four World junior and five European junior 1996, three German 1999.
Progression at PV: 1992- 2.90, 1993- 3.50, 1994- 3.71, 1995- 3.80, 1996- 4.15, 1997- 4.10, 1998- 4.32/ 4.42ex, 1999- 4.50i/4.44, 2000- 4.31, 2001- 4.30i/ 4.11, 2002- 4.40, 2003- 4.32, 2004- 4.50i.
Her family left Omsk in Siberia in 1992 to live in Ulm. Her mother Yekaterina Ryzhikh (b. 20 Jan 1959) had a high jump best of 1.91i in 1985 and her father, Vladimir, is a pole vault coach. Her sister Elisaveta 'Lisa' won the 2003 World Youth pole vault title, pb 4.10 '03.

GHANA

Governing body: Ghana Athletic Association, National Sports Council, PO Box 1272, Accra. Founded 1944.

Ignisious GAISAH b. 20 Jun 1983. 1.86m 70kg. Formerly known as Anthony Essuman. Based in Germany.
At LJ: WCh: '03- 4.
Five Ghana long jump records 2003.
Progression at LJ: 1998- 7.35, 1999- 7.42, 2000- 7.40, 2002- 8.12, 2003- 8.30.

Abdul **Aziz ZAKARI** b. 2 Sep 1976 Accra 1.78m 73kg.
At 100m(/200m): OG: '00- dnf; WCh: '97- qf, '01- 8, '03- h; CG: '98- sf/sf, '02- sf/5; AfG: '03- 7/3; AfCh: '98- (4), '00-1/1/1R, '02- -/sf; WCp: '02- 3R.
Progression at 100m, 200m: 1995- 10.4, 21.36/ 21.0; 1996- 10.30, 20.90; 1997- 10.26, 20.88; 1998- 10.29, 20.62; 1999- 10.35/10.08w, 20.84; 2000- 10.06, 20.23; 2001- 10.04, 20.27; 2002- 10.15/10.13w, 20.29; 2003- 10.07/9.98w, 20.34. pb 60m 6.63i '03.
Was at 1996 Olympics, but 4x100m team not permitted to race due to an ineligible runner.

Women

Margaret Esi **SIMPSON** b. 31 Dec 1981 Kumasi 1.61m 53kg.
At Hep: WCh: '01- 13, '03- dnf; CG: '02- 3; WJ: '00- dnf; AfG: '03- 1; AfCh: '00- 5, '02- 1. Won Af-J 1999.
Ghana records at HJ, JT and seven Heptathlon 1999-2003.
Progression at Hep: 1999- 5366, 2000- 5543, 2001- 5836, 2002- 6105w/6004, 2003- 6152. pbs: 200m 24.72/24.62w '02; 800m 2:20.60 '99, 100mh 13.47 '03, HJ 1.84 '02, LJ 6.11 '03, 6.13w '02; SP 12.62 '03, JT 53.86 '01.

GREECE

Governing body: Hellenic Amateur Athletic Association (SEGAS), 137 Siggroú Avenue, 171 21 Nea Smirni, Athens. Founded 1897.
National Championships first held in 1896 (men), 1930 (women). **2003 Champions**: **Men**: 100m: Aristotélis Gavélas 10.50, 200m: Panayiótis Sarrís 20.81, 400m: Stilianós Dimótsios 45.70, 800m: Sotírios Papadéas 1:49.46, 1500m: Konstadínos Karakatsánis 3:46.65, 5000m: Panayiótis Papoúlias 13:45.64, 10000m: Mihaíl Yelasákis 29:42.77, Mar: Nikólaos Poliás 2:23:16, 3000mSt: Hristóforos Meroúsis 8:56.18, 110mh: Dimítrios Piétris 13.94, 400mh: Periklís Iakovákis 49.51, HJ: Yiannis Constantinou CYP 2.21, PV: Stávros Kouroupákis 5.32, LJ: Loúis Tsátoumas 8.24, TJ: Hrístos Melétoglou 16.92, SP: Panayiótis Baharídis 18.75, DT: Aléxandros Ganotákis 59.86, HT: Aléxandros Papadimitríou 77.90, JT: Yeóryios Íltsios 77.71, Dec: Pródromos Korkízoglou 7705, 20kmW: Theódoros Stamatópoulos 1:28:03, 50kmW: Yeóryios Aryirópoulos 3:58:41. **Women**: 100m: Marína Vasarmídou 11.61, 200m: Olga Kaidantzí 23.45, 400m/400mh: Hrísa Goudenoúdi 52.77/56.85, 800m: Anny Christofidou CYP 2:04.08, 1500m: Konstadína Efedáki 4:12.69, 5000m: María Protópappa 16:25.20, 10000m/Mar: Yeoryía Abatzídou 34:44.37/2:46:47, 3000mSt: Pagóna Sakellári 10:54.33, 100mh: Hristiána Tabáki 13.10, HJ: Nikolía Mitropoúlou 1.87, PV: Anna Fitidou CYP 4.30, LJ: Níki Xánthou 6.63, TJ: Hrisopiyí Devetzí 14.00, SP: Iríni-Hrisovaládo Terzóglou 19.10, DT: Ekateríni Vóggoli 65.01, HT: Alexándra Papayeoryíou 66.32, JT: Líka Sávva 56.78, Hep: Aryiró Stratáki 6116, 20kmW: Athanasía Tsoumeléka 1:31:55.

Konstadínos '**Kostas**' **GATSIOUDIS** b. 17 Dec 1973 Didimótiho 1.89m 97kg. Panellínios (Athens). Officer of the Fire Brigade.
At JT: OG: '96- 10, '00- 6; WCh: '93- dnq 17, '97- 3, '99- 2, '01- 3; EC: '94- dnq 14; WJ: '90- 6, '92- 3; EJ: '91- 9; ECp: '97-9-00-01: 2/3/2/1; E23Cp: '94- 1. Won GP 1999 (2nd overall), Greek champion 1992-4, 1999-2001; Balkan 1992, MedG 1997.
Eleven Greek javelin records 1992-2000. World junior record 1992.
Progression at JT: 1990- 70.20, 1991- 72.58, 1992- 80.30, 1993- 78.44, 1994- 83.82, 1995- 82.70, 1996- 87.12, 1997- 89.22, 1998- 88.13, 1999- 89.84, 2000- 91.69, 2001- 91.27, 2002- 91.23.
Threw Greek record 87.12 in qualifying at 1996 Olympics, but only 81.46 in the final. Over 84m in all 50 competitions in 1999-2002. Only one competition in 2002 and none in 2003.

Periklis IAKOVAKIS b. 24 Mar 1979 Pátra 1.85m 67kg. AE Lehenon.
At 400mh/4x400mR: OG: '00- h; WCh: '99- h, '01- sf, '03- 3; EC: '02- 5; WJ: '98- 1; EJ: '97- 2/2R; EU23: '99- 3, '01- 2; WUG: '01- 4; ECp: '99-00-03: 6/4/2. Greek champion 1998-2003, Med.Games 2001. At 400m: ECp: '97- 8.
Four Greek 400mh records 2002-03.
Progression at 400mh: 1997- 51.6, 1998- 49.82, 1999- 49.53, 2000- 49.35, 2001- 48.87, 2002- 48.66, 2003- 48.17. pbs: 400m 46.35 '02.

Konstadínos **'Kostas' KEDÉRIS** b. 11 Jul 1973 Mitilíni 1.80m 78kg. Olympiakós Piraeus. Air Force officer. PE graduate of Thessaloníki University.
At 200m: OG: '00- 1; WCh: '99- qf, '01- 1; EC: '02- 1; WJ: '92- 6; EI: '00- 5; ECp: '00-01-03: 3/1/1 (2 100m '01). At 400m: EC: '98- sf; EJ: '91- 4; ECp: '99- 3; WCp: '98- 7R. Won MedG 400m 1993, Greek champion 100m 2001, 200m 1999, 2002; 400m 1991-3, 1998.
Greek records 200m (5) 2000-02, 400m 1993, 1998.
Progression at 200m: 1991- 21.63, 1992- 21.05, 1993- 20.76, 1994- 20.93i, 1995- 20.89, 1996- 21.17, 1997- 20.83/20.64w, 1999- 20.50, 2000- 20.09, 2001- 20.03, 2002- 19.85, 2003- 20.30. pbs: 100m 10.15 '01, 300m 32.99i '99, 400m 45.60 '98.
First man to win 200m treble of European, Olympic and World titles. After running a Greek record of 20.25, became the most surprising gold medallist of the Olympic Games in Sydney, where he improved to 20.14 and 20.09. He had been considered a rare talent with big potential in both 200m/400m. However a series of injuries from the 1994 indoor season held him back. In March 2000 he decided to leave Thessaloníki due to its poor training facilities, relocate to Athens and concentrate on 200m.

Aléxandros PAPADIMITRÍOU b. 18 Jun 1973 Lárisa 1.85m 115kg, Iraklís Thessaloníki. MSc in kinesiology at UTEP, Texas, USA.
At HT: OG: '96- dnq 16; '00- 12; WCh: '97-9-01- dnq 19/27/16, '03- 8; EC: '98- dnq 27, '02- 3; WJ: '92- 6; EJ: '91- 7; ECp: '97-00-03: 3/2/3; E23Cp: '94- 2. Greek champion 1994-7, 2000, 2002-03; Balkan 1997, 2000-01, 2003.
Three Greek hammer records 1996-2000.
Progression at HT: 1990- 61.72, 1991- 65.82, 1992- 69.48, 1993- 70.74, 1994- 73.74, 1995- 74.80, 1996- 77.84, 1997- 76.72, 1998- 77.60, 1999- 78.88, 2000- 80.45, 2001- 79.52, 2002- 80.21, 2003- 79.52.

Hrístos POLÍHRONÍOU b. 31 Mar 1972 Athína 1.86m 107kg. Olympiakós Piraeus. Harbour guard officer. Studied PE at Athens University.
At HT: OG: '96- dnq, '00- dnq 24; WCh: '95/97- dnq, '99- 6, '01- dnq 26; EC: '98- 6; WJ: '90- 9; EJ: '91- 5; WUG: '99- 2; ECp: '99- 1, '01- 3. Greek champion 1998-9, 2001.
Five Greek hammer records 1995-9.
Progression at HT: 1989- 60.00, 1990- 63.52, 1991- 67.74, 1992- 67.50, 1993- 73.16, 1994- 73.04, 1995- 76.68, 1996- 77.36, 1997- 75.58, 1998- 78.92, 1999- 79.83, 2000- 79.57, 2001- 78.34, 2002- 80.08.

Women

Hrisopiyí DEVETZÍ b. 2 Jan 1976 Alexandroupli 1.70m 60kg. Panathinaikos.
At TJ: WCh: '03- 8; EC: '02- 7; WI: '04- 3; EI: '02- dnq 16; ECp: '03- 4. Greeck champion 2002-03.
Progression at TJ: 1993- 12.48, 1994- 12.52, 1995- 12.52, 1996- 12.69, 1997- 12.59, 1998- 13.44, 1999- 13.61/13.66w, 2000- 13.48, 2001- 14.00/14.12w, 2002- 14.15, 2003- 14.84i/14.34, 2004- 14.81i. pb LJ 6.21 '99.

Anastasía KELESÍDOU b. 28 Nov 1972 Hamburg, Germany 1.92m 86kg. Iraklís Thessaloníki. Navy Officer. PE graduate of Thessaloniki University.
At DT: OG: '96- dnq 18, '00- 2; WCh: '95- 11, '97- dnq 15, '99- 2, '01- 4, '03- 2; EC: '94- dnq 22, '98- 7, '02- 3; EU23: '94- 2; EJ: '91- 11; ECp: '00- 3. Won MedG 1997, Balkan 2001, Greek 1991, 1993-7, 1999-2000, 2002.
Eight Greek discus records 1994-9.
Progression at DT: 1987- 41.82, 1988- 45.00, 1989- 48.36/49.74u, 1990- 47.90, 1991- 50.90, 1992- 54.34, 1993- 57.44, 1994- 60.50, 1995- 60.92, 1996- 62.76, 1997- 66.18, 1998- 66.18, 1999- 67.70, 2000- 67.12, 2001- 65.52, 2002- 65.08, 2003- 67.14. pb SP 12.68 '92.

Miréla MANJANI b. 21 Dec 1976 Dirráhio (Durrás), Albania 1.65m 64kg, Olympiakós Piraeus. Navy Officer.
At JT: OG: '96- dnq 24, '00- 2; WCh: '95- 12, '97- 11, '99- 1, '01- 2, '03- 1; EC: '94- dnq 22, '98- 9, '02- 1; WJ: '94- 8; EJ: '95- 2; ECp: '00- 3, '03- 2. Greek champion 1999, 2001; Balkan 1994, 1997.
Two World records (64.99 and 67.09) new javelin 1999. Six Greek records 1999-2000.
Progression at JT: 1993- 54.86, 1994- 57.20, 1995- 62.40, 1996- 62.46, 1997- 63.50, 1998- 65.14, new spec: 1999- 67.09, 2000- 67.51, 2001- 66.70, 2002- 67.47, 2003- 66.52.
Switched from Albania to become Greek citizen in 1997. Married to weightlifter Yeóryios Tzelílis (4th 1996 Olympics 64kg, 2nd 1999 Worlds 69kg) from November 1996 until late 2001.

Ekateríni **'Katerina' THÁNOU** b. 1 Feb 1975 Athína 1.65m 61kg. Olympiakós Piraeus. Air Force Officer. Was at University of Athens.
At 100m: OG: '96- qf, '00- 2; WCh: '95- sf, '97- sf, '99- 3, '01- 3, '03- 5; EC: '94- qf, '98- 3, '02- 1; WJ: '94- 4; WUG: '95- 2, '97- 1. At 60m: WI: '99- 1; EI: '96- 1, '98- 4, '00- 1. Won GRE 100m 1995, 2000-02; MedG 100m 1997.
Seven Greek 100m records 1995-9.
Progression at 100m: 1993- 12.09/12.07w, 1994- 11.43, 1995- 11.09, 1996- 11.28, 1997- 11.13, 1998- 10.87/10.8w, 1999- 10.83/10.77w, 2000- 10.91/10.84w, 2001- 10.91, 2002- 11.05, 2003- 11.03. pbs: 50m 6.01+ '99, 60m 6.96i/6.96+ '99, 200m 24.46/23.93w '94.
Brilliant run to win 1999 World Indoor 60m; Greek records in semi and final 1998 Europeans and in quarter and semi at 1999 Worlds.

Stilianí **'Stella' TSIKOÚNA** b. 19 Oct 1972 Halkída 1.71m 88kg. ASE Doúka (Athens). Navy officer. Was at University of Texas, El Paso, USA. PE student at Athens University.
At DT: OG: '96- dnq 31, '00- 5; WCh: '95- dnq 29, '97- 7, '99- 8, '01-03- dnq 13/15; EC: '98- 12. Greek champion 1992, Balkan 2000, 2003.
Two Greek records 1992.

Progression at DT: 1987- 41.84, 1988- 44.18, 1989- 43.90, 1990- 45.38, 1991- 52.10, 1992- 56.48, 1993- 55.48, 1994- 56.98, 1995- 61.02, 1996- 61.30A, 1997- 63.30, 1998- 65.00, 1999- 64.16, 2000- 65.13, 2001- 63.18, 2002- 62.48, 2003- 64.14. pb SP 14.78i '95, 14.66 '01.

Ólga-Anastasia VASDÉKI b. 26 Sep 1973 Vólos 1.74m 59kg. Panellínios (Athens). Harbour guard officer. PE graduate of Athens University.
At TJ: OG: '96- 5, '00- 7; WCh: '97- 4, '99- 3, '03- 12; EC: '98- 1; EI: '96- 3, '98- 4; WCp: '98- 1. Won GRE 1993, 1995-6, 1998; MedG 1997.
Eleven Greek triple jump records 1993-8.
Progression at TJ: 1992- 12.77, 1993- 13.37, 1994- 13.25i, 1995- 13.45/13.73w, 1996- 14.48/14.51w, 1997- 14.62, 1998- 14.64A/14.59, 1999- 14.67, 2000- 14.26, 2002- 13.82, 2003- 14.50. pb LJ 6.60 '98, 6.66w '99.
Her brother Spirídon Vasdékis (b. 23 Jan 1970) had LJ best of 8.19 '95 and 8.29Aw '96, 3 EI '96, 8 WI '97, 16 OG '92, 14 OG '96.

Ekateríni 'Katerina' **VÓGGOLI** b. 30 Oct 1970 Lárisa 1.73m 89kg. Olympiakós Piraeus. PE graduate of Thessaloniki University.
At DT: OG: '96- dnq 22, '00- 9; WCh: '99- 11, '01- dnq 14, '03- 3; EC: '98- 5, '02- 1; WJ: '88- 10; WCp: '02- 2; ECp: '03- 1. Greek champion 1989-90, 1998, 2001, 2003; Balkan 1994.
Four Greek discus records 1992-4.
Progression at DT: 1985- 39.84, 1986- 46.10, 1987- 46.74, 1988- 51.18, 1989- 51.96, 1990- 51.94, 1991- 53.24, 1992- 57.86, 1993- 59.70, 1994- 62.32, 1996- 60.34, 1997- 61.24, 1998- 64.78, 1999- 64.82, 2000- 64.35, 2001- 63.47, 2002- 64.94, 2003- 66.73. pb SP 13.91 '02.

Níki XÁNTHOU b. 11 Oct 1973 Rhodos 1.74m 56kg. Olympiakós Piraeus. Harbour guard officer.
At LJ: OG: '96- 4, '00- dnq 18; WCh: '95- dnq 15, '97- 2, '99- dnq 26, '01- 6, '03- dnq 17; EC: '94- 10, '02- dnq 18; WJ: '92- 8, WI: '95-7-9-03: 9/5/4/5; EI: '98-00-02- 5/8/1; EU23: '94- 1; ECp: '03- 5. Greek champion 1992, 1995, 1997, 1999, 2003; MedG 1997. 9 Greek long jump records 1994-7.
Progression at LJ: 1987- 5.32, 1988- 5.42, 1989- 5.60/5.73w, 1990- 5.96, 1991- 5.90/5.99w, 1992- 6.60, 1993- 6.09, 1994- 6.74, 1995- 6.94/7.12Aw, 1996- 7.01, 1997- 7.03, 1998- 6.83/6.84w, 1999- 6.98/7.01w, 2000- 6.81, 2001- 6.80, 2002- 6.85, 2003- 6.76.
In 1997 she married her coach Dimítrios Hatzópoulos (pb LJ 8.07 '94, 8.08w '89).

GRENADA

Governing body: Grenada Amateur Athletic Federation, PO Box 419, St George's. Fd. 1924.

Alleyne FRANCIQUE b. 13 Feb 1979 Grenada 1.88m 75kg. was at Louisiana State University.
At 400m: OG: '96- hR; WCh: '99- h, '01- 7, '03- 8; CG: '02- 5; PAm: '03- 3; WI: '04- 1. Won CAC 2003, NCAA indoor 400m 2002.
Four Grenada 400m records 2001-02. Commonwealth indoor 400m record 45.35 '02.
Progression at 400m: 1998- 47.30, 1999- 46.46, 2000- 47.14, 2001- 44.91, 2002- 44.72, 2003- 44.78. pb 200m 20.83 '03.

GUYANA

Governing body: Amateur Athletic Association of Guyana, PO Box 10133, Georgetown. Founded 1948.

Aliann POMPEY b. 9 Mar 1978 Guyana 1.65m 55kg. Business administration graduate of Manhattan College, USA.
At 400m: OG: '00- qf; WCh: '01- sf, '03- h; CG: '02- 1; PAm: '99- dnf, '03- 3.
Guyana records 200m 1997, 400m 2002.
Progression at 400m: 1995- 54.1, 1997- 53.04, 1998- 53.73i/53.75, 1999- 52.65, 2000- 52.21i/52.52, 2001- 51.96, 2002- 51.34, 2003- 51.48. pbs: 200m 23.59 '97, 500m 69.23i '00, 800m 2:04.80 '00.
Parents emigrated to the USA when she was 14.

HAITI

Governing body: Fédération Haitienne d'Athlétisme Amateur, BP 2405, Port-au-Prince. Founded 1969.

Dudley DORIVAL b. 1 Sep 1975 Elizabeth, New Jersey, USA 1.85m 77kg. Sales consultant, studied sociology at University of Connecticut,
At 110mh: OG: '00- 7; WCh: '99- sf, '01- 3, '03- sf; WJ: '94- 2; PAm: '03- 5; CAG: '02- 1; WUG: '97- 3. At 60mh: WI: '01- 7.
Six Haitian 110mh records from three at 13.42 in 1999 to 2001.
Progression at 110mh: 1994- 13.79/13.65w, 1995- 13.53A, 1996- 13.60/13.59w, 1997- 13.48, 1998- 13.30, 1999- 13.38/13.29w, 2000- 13.33, 2001- 13.25, 2002- 13.50, 2003- 13.41. pbs: 100m 10.45 '98, 200m 20.64w '98, 50mh 6.50i '01, 55mh 7.16i '96, 60mh 7.55i '01.
Switched from USA to Haiti (the land of his parents) from July 1999. At the 2001 Worlds he won Haiti's first global medal since Silvio Cator won the Olympic long jump in 1928.

HUNGARY

Governing body: Magyar Atlétikai Szövetség, 1146 Budapest, Hermina ut 17. Founded 1897.
National Championships first held in 1896 (men), 1932 (women). **2003 Champions**. **Men**: 100m: Gabor Dobos 10.34, 200m: Géza Pauer 21.19, 400m: Zsolt Szeglet 45.67, 800m: István Kerékjártó 1:50.93, 1500m/5000m/10000m: Olivér Bodor 3:48.12/14:24.41/29:53.72: HMar: Miklós Zatykó 65:53, Mar: László Nagy 2:24:39, 3000mSt: Máté Németh 8:58.66, 110mh: Balázs Kovács 13.95, 400mh: Ákos Dezsö 51.37, HJ: László Boros 2.24, PV: János Váczi 5.10, LJ: Imre Lörincz 7.98w, TJ: Péter Tölgyesi 16.30w, SP: Zsolt Biber

19.26, DT: Róbert Fazekas 67.94, HT: Adrián Annus 81.97, JT: Gergely Horváth 81.55, Dec: Kürtösi 7651, 20kmW: Gyula Dudás 1:31:14, 50kmW: Zoltán Czukor 4:02:26. **Women**: 100m/ 200m: Enikö Szabó 11.69/23.77, 400m: Barbara Petráhn 54.46, 800m: Judit Varga 2:04.06, 1500m: Krisztina Papp 4:21.13, 5000m/HMar: Anikó Kálovics 16:03.69/71:08, 10000m: Simona Staicu 33:08.70, Mar: Judit Földing-Nagy 2:41:56, 3000mSt: Lívia Tóth 10:28.29, 100mh: Edit Vári 13.25, 400mh: Dóra Horváth 59.82, HJ: Dóra Györffy 1.90, PV: Zsuszanna Szabó 4.20, LJ: Tünde Vaszi 6.59, TJ: Éva Miklós 13.66w, SP/DT: Eva Kürti 15.80/54.10, HT: Katalin Divós 66.26, JT: Nikolett Szabó 59.27, Hep: Katalin Deák 5122, 10kmW: Ildikó Ilyés 49:50, 20kmW: Katalin Varró 1:48:47.

Adrián ANNUS b. 28 Jun 1973 Szeged 1.94m 110kg. Haladás VSE.
At HT: OG: '96- dnq 28, '00- dnq 17; WCh: '01- 9, '03- 2; EC: '98- 8, '02- 1; WJ: '92- 11; WUG: '01- 3; WCp: '02- 1; won WAF 2003, 2nd GP 2002. HUN champion 1996, 2002-03.
Hungarian hammer record 2003.
Progression at HT: 1990- 50.80, 1991- 57.42, 1992- 68.50, 1993- 69.26, 1994- 72.56, 1995- 74.68, 1996- 76.48, 1997- 76.62, 1998- 81.22, 1999- 81.73, 2000- 78.15, 2001- 83.39, 2002- 82.97, 2003- 84.19. pbs: SP 17.01 '02, DT 50.16 '95.

Róbert FAZEKAS b. 18 Aug 1975 Szombathely 1.93m 105kg. Haladás VSE.
At DT: OG: '00- dnq 16; WCh: '99- 11, '01- dnq 26, '03- 2; EC: '98- 4, '02- 1; EU23: '97- 6; WJ: '94- 6 (dnq 18 HT); WCp: '02- 1. HUN champion 1998, 2000, 2002-03.
Three Hungarian discus records 2002.
Progression at DT: 1992- 40.08, 1993- 53.48, 1994- 58.00, 1995- 60.34, 1996- 55.08, 1997- 59.32, 1998- 66.61, 1999- 64.92, 2000- 66.11, 2001- 68.09, 2002- 71.70, 2003- 70.78. pbs: SP 14.07 '02, HT 75.33 '98.
His 71.25 at the 2002 World Cup was the longest ever discus throw at a major international event.

Balázs KISS b. 21 Mar 1972 Veszprém 1.92m 115kg. VEDAC. Was at University of Southern California, USA.
At HT: OG: '96- 1; WCh: '95- 4, '97- 4, '99- dnq 20, '01- 6; EC: '94- 12, '98- 2, '02- 4; WUG: '93- 2, '95- 1, '97- 1; EJ: '91- 3. 2nd GP 1998 (3rd 2002), HUN champion 1995, 1998, 2000; NCAA 1993-6 (5th 4-time winner).
Five Hungarian hammer records 1995-8.
Progression at HT: 1988- 56.24, 1989- 61.24, 1990- 62.82, 1991- 70.66, 1993- 77.18, 1994- 77.74, 1995- 82.56, 1996- 81.76, 1997- 82.90, 1998- 83.00, 1999- 80.87, 2000- 79.22, 2001- 81.36, 2002- 80.78, 2003- 77.46. pb DT 39.72 '91.

Zoltán KÖVAGÓ b. 10 Apr 1979 Szolnok 2.04m 127kg. Budapesti Honvéd SE.
At DT: OG: '00- dnq; WCh: '01-03: dnq 20/19; EC: '02- 7; WJ: '96- 4, '98- 1; EJ: '97- 3; EU23: '99- 6, '01- 1. HUN champion 2001.
Progression at DT: 1995- 49.78, 1996- 59.70, 1997- 62.16, 1998- 60.27, 1999- 63.23, 2000- 66.76, 2001- 66.93, 2002- 65.98, 2003- 66.03. pb SP 15.93 '01.

Zsolt NÉMETH b.9 Nov 1971 Szombathely 1.90m 110kg. Dobó SE.
At HT: OG: '96- dnq 22, '00- dnq 25; WCh: '97- dnq 26, '99- 2; WJ: '90- 6; WUG: '99- 1. HUN champion 1997.
Progression at HT: 1986- 41.00, 1987- 51.02, 1988- 56.60, 1989- 61.60, 1990- 67.66, 1991- 68.32, 1992- 71.14, 1993- 68.88, 1994- 73.14, 1995- 75.22, 1996- 77.48, 1997- 76.04, 1998- 80.19, 1999- 81.56, 2000- 80.02, 2001- 77.87, 2002- 72.59, 2003- 78.06. pbs: SP 18.51 '00, DT 54.33 '98.

Roland VARGA b. 22 Oct 1977 1.97m 102kg. Újpesti TE.
At DT: WCh: '01- 7; EC: '02- dnq 13; WJ: '96- 2; EU23: '99- 2; WUG: '01- 4, '03- 4.
Progression at DT: 1993- 43.60, 1994- 48.18, 1995- 52.88, 1996- 55.20, 1997- 58.70, 1998- 60.33, 1999- 62.78, 2000- 65.39, 2001- 65.86, 2002- 67.38, 2003- 61.71. pbs: 100m 11.2 '94, 11.46 '95; 400m 50.65 '95, 1500m 4:54.31 '95, 110mh 17.14 '95, HJ 1.84 '95, PV 3.90 '94, LJ 6.64w/6.49 '95; SP 16.33 '02, HT 53.70 '96, Dec 6782 '95.

Attila ZSIVOCZKY b. 29 Apr 1977 Budapest 1.93m 82kg. Debreceni AK. Was at Kansas State University, USA.
At Dec: OG: '00- 8; WCh: '99- 10, '01- 4, '03- dnf; EC: '98- 16; WJ: '96- 1; EU23: '97- 4, '99- 1; ECp: '98-9-01: 5/5/2. At Hep: EI: '00- 4, '02- 5.
Hungarian decathlon record 2000.
Progression at Dec: 1995- 7242, 1996- 7582, 1997- 7804, 1998- 8103, 1999- 8379, 2000- 8554, 2001- 8371, 2002- 8175, 2003- 7923. pbs: 60m 7.11i '00, 100m 10.97 '01, 10.64w '00; 400m 47.93 '00, 1000m 2:34.79i '98, 1500m 4:20.94 '99, 60mh 8.31i '03, 110mh 14.86/14.81w '01; HJ 2.23i '98, 2.22 '94; PV 4.91i '02, 4.90 '01; LJ 7.31 '99, SP 15.72 '00, DT 47.43 '00, JT 65.87 '00, Hep 6033i '00.
Son of Gyula Zsivótzky (OG: 60- 2, 64- 2, 68- 1, 72- 5; EC: 58- 3, 62- 1, 66- 2, 69- 4) who set two world hammer records – 73.74 '65 and 73.76 '68.

Women

Dóra GYÖRFFY b. 23 Feb 1978 Budapest 1.76m 58kg. BEAC. Was at Harvard University, USA.
At HJ: OG: '00- 18=; WCh: '01- 7=; EC: '98- dnq 19, '02- 12; WJ: '94- 7=, '96- 2; EJ: '95- 5=, '97- 5; EU23: '99- 5; WUG: '03- 1; WI: '01- 5=; EI: '02- 2=. HUN champion 1998-2003.
Two Hungarian high jump records 2001.
Progress at HJ: 1991- 1.69, 1992- 1.76, 1993- 1.71, 1994- 1.84, 1995- 1.87, 1996- 1.92, 1997- 1.93, 1998- 1.92, 1999- 1.94, 2000- 1.97i/1.95, 2001- 2.00, 2002- 1.97i/1.91, 2003- 1.96i/1.94. pbs: LJ 5.88 '95, TJ 13.05 '01.

Anikó KÁLOVICS b. 13 May 1977 Szombathely 1.75m 60kg. Haladás VSE.
At 10000m: OG: '00- h; WCh: '03- 20; EC: '98- 12,

'02- 14; EU23: '97- 4; EJ: '95- 6. At 3000m/5000m: WJ: '96- h/11. Eur CC: '01-02-03: 15/4/3. Won HUN 5000m 2001-03, HMar 2003.
Hungarian records HMar 2002, 10000m 2003.
Progression at 10,000m: 1993- 40:56.30. 1994- 35:21.46, 1995- 35:49.59, 1996- 35:29.07, 1997- 33:06.56, 1998- 32:53.32; 2000- 32:16.4, 2001- 32:48.76, 2002- 32:22.61, 2003- 31:40.31. pbs: 800m 2:18.89 '96, 1500m 4:29.01 '97, 3000m 9:19.0 '03, 5000m 15:18.45 '03, HMar 69:16 '02.

Nikolett SZABÓ b. 3 Mar 1980 Budapest 1.68m 65kg. FTC.
At JT: OG: '00- dnq 14; WCh: '97- dnq 19, '01- dnq 14, '03- 12; EC: '98- 8, '02- 8; WJ; '96- 2, '98- 4; EU23: '01- 1; EJ: '95- 7, '97- 1, '99- 1. HUN champion 1997-2001, 2003.
Three Hungarian records new javelin 1999-2001.
Progression at JT: 1993- 45.28, 1994- 49.78, 1995- 55.32, 1996- 58.88, 1997- 61.76, 1998- 65.10; new: 1999- 61.79, 2000- 61.23, 2001- 64.62, 2002- 63.25, 2003- 62.88. pbs: SP 12.92 '95, DT 36.43 '98.

Judit VARGA b. 16 Apr 1976 Szombathely 1.69m 49kg. Haladás VSE.
At (800m)/1500m: WCh: '99- h/h, '03- sf/sf; EC: '98- h/12, '02- 4; EI: '98- (3). Won HUN 800m 1995-2003.
Hungarian records: 800m 2003, 1500m (2) 2002.
Progression at 1500m: 1990- 4:51.31, 1991- 4:40.97, 1992- 4:27.13, 1993- 4:36.74, 1994- 4:37.0, 1995- 4:26.8, 1996- 4:27.25, 1997- 4:19.17, 1998- 4:08.83, 1999- 4:08.60, 2000- 4:13.01, 2001- 4:12.99i/4:18.88, 2002- 4:01.26, 2003- 4:02.19. pbs: 400m 54.82 '98, 800m 1:59.46 '03, 1000m 2:37.36 '03.

Tünde VASZI b. 18 Apr 1972 Piskolt, Romania 1.70m 60kg. Budapesti Honvéd SE
At LJ: OG: '96- 8, '00- 8; WCh: '95/97/99- dnq, '01- 4, '03- 6; EC: '98- 4, '02- 3; WI: '97-9-03: 9/5/8; EI: '00- 5; WCp: '98- 5; 3rd GP 2002. Won HUN 100m 1999, LJ 1996-9, 2001-03; TJ 1995.
Hungarian long jump record 2001.
Progression at LJ: 1990- 5.80, 1991- 6.05, 1992- 6.22, 1993- 5.81/6.04w, 1994- 6.43/6.46w, 1995- 6.58, 1996- 6.73/6.82Aw, 1997- 6.76/6.78w, 1998- 6.77/6.82w, 1999- 6.82i/6.66, 2000- 6.70, 2001- 6.86, 2002- 6.78, 2003- 6.76. pbs: 60m 7.49i '97, 100m 11.50 '96, 200m 24.11 '96, 400m 58.31 '96, 100mh 13.84 95, HJ 1.63 '96, PV 4.30i '02, 4.15 '99; TJ 13.39i '97, 13.38 '95.

ICELAND

Governing body: Frjálsíthróttasamband Islands, Sport Centre Laugardalur, Engjavegur 6, 104 Reykjavik. Founded 1947.

Jón Arnar MAGNUSSON b. 28 Jul 1969 Selfoss 1.83m 87kg. Teacher.
At Dec: OG: '96- 12, '00- dnf; WCh: '95/97/99/01/03- dnf; EC: '98- 4, '02- 4; WJ: '87- dnf. At Hep: WI: '97-9-01-03-04: 3/5/2/4/7; EI: '96-8-02: 3/5/4. Won ISL 100m 1994-5, 2000; 200m 1998-2000, 2002; 110mh 1994, 1998-2002; PV 1998-9, 2001; LJ 1995, 1999-2002; SP 2001, Dec 1992.
Icelandic records: 100m 1997, 110mh 1994-7, LJ 1994, decathlon 1994-8.
Progression at Dec: 1987- 6232, 1988- 6975, 1989- 7351, 1992- 7570, 1994- 7896, 1995- 8248, 1996- 8274, 1997- 8470, 1998- 8583w/8573, 1999- 6813, 2000- 8206, 2001- 7938, 2002- 8390, 2003- 8222. pbs: 60m 6.76i '99, 6.6i '97; 100m 10.56 '97, 10.2w '95; 200m 21.17 '96, 300m 33.86 '94, 400m 46.49 '98, 1000m 2:39.55i '99, 1500m 4:32.23 '98, 50mh 6.76i '00, 60mh 7.98i '00, 7.8 '97; 110mh 13.91 '97, HJ 2.07 '98, PV 5.20 '98, LJ 8.00 '94, 8.01w '00; SP 16.61 '98, DT 51.30 '96, HT 40.02 '97, JT 64.16 '98, Hep 6293i '99.
His uncle Einar Vilhjalmsson was 6th in 1984 Olympic javelin.

Women

Thórey Edda ELISDOTTIR b. 30 Jun 1977 1.81m 64kg. Was at University of Georgia, USA.
At PV: OG: '00- dnq 22=; WCh: '99- 13, '01- 6, '03- nh; EC: '98- dnq 22, '02- 11=; EU23: '97- 9, '99- 5. ISL champion 2001-02.
Progression at PV: 1997- 3,80, 1998- 4.21, 1999- 4.37i/4.22, 2000- 4.30, 2001- 4.51i/4.45, 2002- 4.41, 2003- 4.50i/4.48, 2004- 4.50i.
Member of EAA Athletes Commission 2002-06.

INDIA

Governing body: Amateur Athletic Federation of India, Room No.1148, Gate No 28, East Block, Jawaharlal Nehru Stadium, Lodi Complex, New Delhi 110003. Founded 1946.
National Championships first held as Indian Games in 1924. **2003 National Champions: Men**: 100m: Vilas Nilgund 10.70, 200m: Pityush Kumar 21.29, 400m: K J Manoj Lal 46.04, 800m: P.S.Primesh 1:49.61, 1500m/5000m: Gulab Chand 3:56.11/15:15.5, 10000m: I Shivananda 33:34.33, 3000mSt: Arun D'Souza 9:07.77, 110mh: Naunidh Singh 14.12; 400mh: V.Prasad Reddy 51.54, HJ: Hari Shankar Roy 2.12, PV: Jitendra Singh 4.90, LJ: Sanjay Rai 7.58, TJ: Sanjai Dewadi 15.50w, SP: Bahadur Singh 19.59, DT: Anil Kumar 60.07, HT: Pramod Tiwari 67.70, JT: Fazal Ansari 72.74, Dec: Kulwinder Singh 7094, 20000mW: Sita Ram 1:32:22.5. **Women**: 100m/200m: Saraswati Saha 11.70/23.75, 400m: Pinki Pramanik 54.19, 800m: Sunita Khanojia 2:07.65, 1500m: Sunita Rani 4:17.57, 5000m: Madhuri Gurnule 17:13.91, 10000m: L.Aruna Devi 36:07.03, 3000mSt: B. Hemalatha 11:07.65, 100mh: K.N.Priya 14.02, 400mh: Chithra Soman 59.31, HJ: Sahana Kumari 1.75, PV: V.S.Sureka 3.51, LJ/Hep: J.J.Shobha 6.10/5733, TJ: Manisha Dey 13.16, SP: N Latha 15.82, DT: Neelam J Singh 61.17, HT: Hardeep Kaur 57.80, JT: Gurmeet Kaur 51.64, 20kmW: Jasmine Kaur 1:48:28.8.

Anju Bobby GEORGE b. 19 Apr 1977 Cheeranchira, Kerala 1.85m 62kg. née Markose. Customs & Excise officer.

At LJ: WCh: '03- 3; CG: '02- 3, AsiG: '02- 1 (4 TJ); WI: '03- 7; won Af-AsG 2003.
Indian records LJ (5) 1999–2002, TJ 2001.
Progression at LJ: 1996- 6.13, 1997- 6.20, 1998- 6.12, 1999- 6.37, 2000- 6.59, 2001- 6.74, 2002- 6.74, 2003- 6.70. pb TJ 13.67 '02.
Married triple jumper Bobby George in 2001.

IRELAND

Governing Body: The Athletic Association of Ireland (AAI), 11 Prospect Road, Glasnevin, Dublin 9. Founded in 1999. Original Irish AAA founded in 1885.

National Championships first held in 1873. **2003 champions**: **Men**: 100m: Gary Ryan 10.29w, 200m: Paul Brizzel 21.01, 400m: Paul McKee 46.43, 800m: Daniel Caulfield 1:48.99, 1500m: Gareth Turnbull 3:40.32, 5000m: Cathal Lombard 13:51.33, 10000m: Tom Carey 31:08.91, HMar: Cian McLoughlin 66:14, Mar: Gary Crossan 2:20:26, 3000mSt: Eugene O'Neill 9:09.19; 110mh: Peter Coghlan 14.01, 400mh: Brian Liddy 53.06, HJ: Aidan O'Dwyer 2.10, PV: Ruairi O'Briain 4.70; LJ: Ciaran McDonagh 7.95, TJ: Patrick Shannon 14.52, SP: John Leahy 16.32, DT: John Menton 52.67, HT: Roman Linscheid 66.02, JT: Tery McHugh 71.45, Dec: John Kierans 5402, 10000mW/20kmW: Jamie Costin 42:29.53/1:28:46, 35kmW: Robert Heffernan 2:35:58. **Women**: 100m/200m: Ciara Sheehy 11.54/23.58, 400m: Karen Shinkins 52.58, 800m: Kelly McNeice 2:13.22, 1500m: Roisin McGettigan 4:22.74, 5000m: Sonia O'Sullivan 15:20.68, 10000m/HMar: Rosemary Ryan 34:24.7/74:53, Mar: Annette Kealy 2:43:04, 100mh: Carine Soulabail 14.80, 400mh: Michelle Carey 59.59, HJ: Rose Mary Daniels 1.73, PV: Erin Kinnear 3.70, LJ: Antoinette Furlong 6.05, TJ: Taneisha Robinson-Scanlon 12.83, SP: Eva Massey GBR 15.51, DT: Renata Katewiiz 46.70, HT: Eileen O'Keefe 60.47, JT: Jennifer O'Sullivan 47.95, Hep: Sharon Gallen 5099, 5000mW/20kmW: Gillian O'Sullivan 20:13.13/1:29:22.

Women

Gillian O'SULLIVAN b. 21 Aug 1976 Killarney 1.63m 61kg. Graduate of University College, Cork. Farranfore/Maine Valley. History teacher.
At 20kmW: OG: '00- 10; WCh: '99- 32, '01- dq, '03- 2; EC: '02- 4; ECp: '01- 9. At 10kmW: EU23: '97- 9. At 5000mW: WJ: '94- 22; EJ: '95- 9. Won Irish 5000mW 1998, 2001-03, 20kmW 1999-2003.
World 5000m walk record 2002, WIR 3000m walk 2003. Irish walks records: 5000m (5) 1998-2002, 10000m 1998, 10km 2000, 20km (8) 1999-2003.
Progression at 20kmW: 1999- 1:36:44, 2000- 1:31:31, 2001- 1:29:57, 2002- 1:28:46, 2003- 1:27:22. pbs: 3000mW 11:35.34i '03, 12:18.19 '00; 5000mW 20:02.60 '02, 10kmW 43:29 '00.
Winner of inaugural IAAF Walks Challenge 2003.

Sonia O'SULLIVAN b. 28 Nov 1969 Cobh 1.73m 53kg. Ballymore Cobh/Reebok RC. Studied accountancy at Villanova University, USA.
At 5000m (1500m): OG: '96- dnf (h), '00- 2 (6 10000m); WCh: '95- 1, '97- h (8), '03- 15; EC: '98- 1 (1 10000m), '02- 2 (2 10000m); WCp: '98- 1. At 3000m (/1500m): OG: '92- 4/sf; WCh: '93- 4/2; WI: '97- 2, '01- 7/9; EC: '90- 11, '94- 1; WJ: '88- h; WUG: '91- 2/1; WCp: '94- (5). World CC (4k): '92-7-8-00-02: 7/9/1 (1)/7 (15)/(7); HMar: '02- 14; Eur CC: '03- 4. Won overall GP 1993 (3rd 1994), 3000m 1993, 1995, 2000; 5000m 1992, 1994; NCAA 3000m 1990-1, CC 1990; Irish CC 1987, 4k CC 2002, 800m 1992, 1500m 1987, 1990, 1995-6, 2000; 5000m 1990, 1998, 2003.
Records: WIR 5000m 15:17.28 '91, World 2000m & European 3000m 1994, World best 2 miles 1998, road 10 miles 2002. Irish 1990-2002: 800m, 1000m, 1500m (6), 1M (2), 2000m (3), 3000m (6), 5000m (4), 10000m (2), HMar.
Progression at 1500m, 3000m, 5000m, 10000m: 1986- 10:02.7, 1987- 9:01.52, 1988- 9:13.6, 1989- 9:10.62, 1990- 4:08.49, 8:52.65, 15:26.9; 1991- 4:05.81, 8:54.16, 15:17.28i; 1992- 4:01.23, 8:39.67, 14:59.11; 1993- 3:59.60, 8:28.74, 14:45.92; 1994- 3:59.10, 8:21.64, 15:06.18; 1995- 3:58.85, 8:27.57, 14:41.40; 1996- 3:59.91, 8:35.32, 14:48.36; 1997- 4:05.31, 8:46.19i/8:53.53, 15:10.98; 1998- 4:01.05, 8:28.82, 14:51.61, 31:29.33; 2000- 4:01.70, 8:27.58, 14:41.02, 30:53.37; 2001- 4:06.34, 8:43.51; 2002- 4:05.94mx, 8:33.62, 14:46.97, 30:47.59; 2003- 4:09.86, 8:37.55, 14:55.50. pbs: 800m 2:00.69 '94, 1000m 2:34.66 '93, 1M 4:17.25 '94, 2000m 5:25.36 '94, 2M 9:19.56 '98; Road: 15km 47:36 '02, 10M 51:00 '02, HMar 67:19 '02, Mar 2:32:06 '02.
She became the first Irish woman to win a European title in 1994. In 1998 she took both World CC titles and then won a double at the Europeans, including her track debut at 10k. She also won the Great North Run in her first half marathon (70:05). She gave birth to daughter Ciara on 10 July 1999, and was soon back in action, setting a world road best for 5 miles with 24:27 on 16 October. In 2000 she set her first Irish records for five years – both 5000m and 10000m (taking 36 secs off her previous best) at the Olympics. Her second daughter Sophie was born in December 2001, and in 2002 she set Irish records at 10,000m and half marathon (winning Great North Run in 67:19).

ISRAEL

Governing body: Israeli Athletic Association, PO Box 24190, Tel Aviv 61241. Founded as Federation for Amateur Sport in Palestine 1931.

National Championships first held in 1935. **2003 Champions**: 100m: Gidon Jablonka 10.55, 200m: Tal Mor 21.24, 400m: Avil Shaposhnik 48.97, 800m: Gezachw Yossef 1:52.39, 1500m: Itai Maggidi 3:45.68, 5000m: Tzahi Cohen 14:49.42, 10000m: Haile Satayin 30:01.4, HMar: Vodage

Zvadya 65:54, Mar: Asaf Bimro 2:15:46, 3000mSt: Mohamed Khattib 9:51.35, 110mh: Yevgeniy Minenko 15.19, 400mh: Yochai Avital 54.06, HJ: Yoav Shuster 2.06, PV: Yevgeniy Olkhovskiy 4.70, LJ: Eldad Khagashi 6.86, TJ: Avi Tayari 15.97, SP: Shai Shalev 18.11, DT: Lior Peretz 55.75, HT: Shlomi Ben-Shoshan 59.80, JT: Vadim Bavikin 75.96, Dec: Udi Karni 6134. **Women**: 100m: Moran Katz 12.77, 200m: Talila Carter 26.09, 400m: Anat Morad 55.48, 800m/1500m: Noah Beitler 2:06.06/4:25.61, 5000m: Lital Azulay 17:38.5, 10000m: Svetlana Bkahmand 37:40.5, HMar/Mar: Eti Einer 1:20:33/2:51:06, 3000mSt: Irina Agapov 10:55.03, 100mh: Irina Lenskiy 13.74, 400mh/PV: Olga Dogadko 59.57/3.95, HJ: Olga Kurakulin 1.62, LJ/Hep: Svetlana Gnezdilov 6.00/5722, TJ: Khagit Salomon 12.52, SP: Sivan Jean 14.91, DT: Sivan Abali 37.42, HT: Tzila Ben-Atar 43.48, JT: Marina Servitz 37.54.

Alex AVERBUKH b. 1 Oct 1974 Irkutsk. Siberia 1.78m 76kg. Maccabi Tel-Aviv.

At PV: OG: '00- 10=; WCh: '99- 3, '01- 2, '03- dnq; EC: '02- 1. WI: '01- 4; EI: '00- 1; EJ: '93- dnq; WUG: '01- 1; 2nd GP 2002. EI Hep: '98- 6. Won ISR PV 2000-02, RUS Dec 1997.

Six ISR pole vault records 1999-2003 (from 5.80).

Progression at PV, Dec: 1991- 4.95, 1993- 5.30, 1994- 5.20, 1995- 5.50, 7598w; 1996- 5.40, 7716; 1997- 5.60, 8084; 1998- 5.70, 7658; 1999- 5.81, 2000- 5.85, 2001- 5.91, 2002- 5.85, 2003- 5.93. pbs: 60m 6.89i '98, 6.6i '97; 100m 10.64 '00, 400m 48.74 '98, 1500m 4:33.79 '97, 60mh 8.36i '98, 8.2i '97; 110mh 14.14 '97, HJ 2.06 '95, LJ 7.53i/7.50 '97, SP 15.12 '98, DT 41.51 '00, JT 53.26 '97, Hep 6144i '98.

His father Valeriy had a decathlon best of 7557 points and his brother Yevgeniy (died 1996 in a car crash) an 800m best of 1:48.18. Emigrated from Russia to Israel, and became a citizen on 3 August 1999, just in time to compete at World Championships. In Munich 2002 he became Israel's first European outdoor champion.

ITALY

Governing Body: Federazione Italiana di Atletica Leggera (FIDAL), Via Flaminia Nuova 830, 00191 Roma. Constituted 1926. First governing body formed 1896.

National Championships first held in 1897 (one event)/1906 (men), 1927 (women). **2003 champions**: **Men**: 100m: Francesco Scuderi 10.48, 200m: Alessandro Cavallaro 20.60, 400m: Andrea Barberi 45.79, 800m: Livio Sciandra 1:48.33, 1500m: Christian Obrist 3:44.22, 5000m: Salvatore Vincenti 13:55.26, 10000m: Marco Bartoletti 28:55.86, HMar: Michele Gamba 62:48, Mar: Angelo Carosi 2:15:54, 3000mSt: Angelo Iannelli 8:31.96, 110mh: Emiliano Pizzoli 13.87, 400mh: Gianni Carabelli 49.51, HJ: Andrea Bettinelli 2.31, PV: Fabio Pizzolato 5.40, LJ: Nicola Trentin 8.12w, TJ: Paolo Camossi 16.42, SP: Paolo Dal Soglio 19.48, DT: Cristiano Andrei 61.08, HT: Nicola Vizzoni 77.24, JT: Francesco Pignata 76.71, Dec: Paolo Casarsa 7877, 10000mW: Giovanni De Benedictis 41:12.19, 20kmW: Ivano Brugnetti 1:22:01. 50kmW: Marco Giungi 3:59:20. **Women**: 100m/200m: Daniela Graglia 11,70/23.67, 400m: Virna De Angeli 52.34, 800m: Claudia Salvarani 2:03.11, 1500m: Sara Palmas 4:15.26, 5000m: Agata Balsamo 15:44.79, 10000m: Gloria Marconi 33:05.25, HMar: Rosaria Console 71:22, Mar: Anna Incerti 2:34:40, 3000mSt: Marzena Michalska 10:21.68, 100mh: Margaret Macchiut 13.38, 400mh: Monika Niederstätter 55.41, HJ: Antonella Bevilacqua 1.88, PV: Arianna Farfalletti 4.10, LJ: Thaimi O'Reilly 6.32, TJ: Barbara Lah 14.34w, SP: Assunta Legnante 18.18, DT: Agnese Maffeis 58.24, HT: Clarissa Claretti 66.59, JT: Claudia Coslovich 61.44, Hep: Gertrud Bacher 6133, 5000W: Elisabetta Perrone 20:12.41, 20kmW: Elisa Rigaudo 1:35:21.

Stefano BALDINI b. 25 May 1971 Castelnovo di Sotto, Reggio Emilia 1.76m 60kg. Works for Corradini Excelsior Rubiera.

At Mar: OG: '00- dnf; WCh: '01- 3, '03- 3; EC: '98- 1. At 10,000m (5000m): OG: '96- 18 (sf); WCh: '95- 18, '97- 9; EC: '94- 20, '02- 4; WJ: '90- (6); EJ: '89- (9); ECp: '95- 1. World HMar: '96- 1, '97- 9. Eur CC: '99- 10. Won ITA 10,000m 1993-6, 2001-02; HMar 1995, 1998, 2001.

Italian records: half marathon 1997 & 2000, marathon 1997 & 2002.

Progression at 10,000m, Mar: 1990- 29:48.5, 1992- 28:50.16, 1993- 28:25.98, 1994- 27:57.86, 1995- 27:50.17, 2:11:01sh; 1996- 27:43.98; 1997- 28:07.81, 2:07:57; 1998- 27:55.92, 2:09:33; 2000- 2:09:45, 2001- 28:21.38, 2:08:51; 2002- 27:50.98, 2:07:29; 2003- 2:07:56. pbs: 1500m 3:45.7 '91, 3000m 7:43.14 '96, 5000m 13:23.43 '96, HMar 60:50w '00, 60:56 '97.

Three wins in 15 marathons: Rome and EC 1998, Madrid 2001; 2nd London 1997 & 2003, 3rd New York 1997. On 9 Oct 1999 married **Virna De Angeli** (b. 27 Feb 1976) (2 WJ 400mh 1994, ITA record 400m 51.31 '97). Brother Marco (b. 14 May 1968) has marathon best of 2:16:32 sh '95.

Paolo DAL SOGLIO b. 29 Jul 1970 Schio, Vicenza 1.90m 125kg. Carabinieri Bologna.

At SP: OG: 96- 4, '00- dnq 19; WCh: '93- dnq, '95- 9, '97- 9, '99/01- dnq 16/13; EC: '94- 8, '98- 5; WJ: '88- dnq; EJ: '89- 6; WUG: '93- 2, '97- 2; WI: '93/5/9/01- 5/7/6/5; EI: '96- 1; ECp: '93-4-5-6-9-00-01-02-03: 2/1/2/1/2/1/3/3/6; E23Cp: '92- 5. 3rd GP 1996. Won ITA 1994-6, 1998-2003; MedG 1993.

Progression at SP: 1988- 17.69, 1989- 18.23, 1990- 18.48, 1991- 18.60, 1992- 19.76, 1993- 20.43/20.65i, 1994- 20.68, 1995- 20.57, 1996- 21.23, 1997- 21.03i/20.69, 1998- 20.65, 1999- 20.46i/20.39, 2000- 20.75, 2001- 20.86, 2002- 20.86, 2003- 20.15i/19.72. pb DT 53.80 '89.

Fabrizio DONATO b. 14 Aug 1976 Latina 1.89m 82kg. Fiamme Galle.

At TJ: OG: '00- dnq 25; WCh: '03- dnq 13; EC:

'02- 4; EJ: '95- 5; WI: '01- 6; EI: '02- 4; ECp: '00-02-03: 2/2/1. Won MedG 2001, Italian 2000.
Italian triple jump record 2000.
Progression at TJ: 1992- 12.88, 1993- 14.36, 1994- 15.27, 1995- 15.81, 1996- 16.35, 1997- 16.40A, 1998- 16.73, 1999- 16.66i/16.53w, 2000- 17.60, 2001- 17.05, 2002- 17.17, 2003- 17.16. pb LJ 7.79i '01, 7.74/ 7.88w '00.
He married Patrizia Souri (400m pb 51.74 '98, 8 EC 98) on 27 Sep 2003.

Giuseppe GIBILISCO b. 5 Jan 1979 Siracusa 1.83m 79kg. Fiamme Galle.
At PV: OG: '00- 10=; WCh: '01- dnq, '03- 1; EC: '02- 10; WJ: '98- 3=; EU23: '99- 9, '01- 3; EJ: '97- nh; WI: '04- 6; EI: '00- 10; ECp: '00-02-03: 4/2=/2.
Four Italian records 2003.
Progression at PV: 1993- 3.50, 1994- 3.80, 1995- 4.80, 1996- 5.05, 1997- 5.30, 1998- 5.30, 1999- 5.60, 2000- 5.70, 2001- 5.60i/5.50, 2002- 5.70, 2003- 5.90, 2004- 5.82i.
Set two Italian vault records in 2003 at both Golden Gala (5.77 & 5.82) and World Champs (5.85 & 5.90).

Andrea LONGO b. 26 Jun 1975 Piove di Sacco, Padova 1.91m 82kg. Fiamme Oro Padova. Policeman.
At 800m: OG: '00- dq; WCh: '97- qf, '99- 6, '03- 5; EC: '98- 7; WJ: '94- sf; EU23: '97- 1; ECp: '98- 1, '00- 4, '01- dq 2. Italian champion 1998-2000.
Italian 800m record 2000, European best 600m 2000.
Progression at 800m: 1992- 1:58.8, 1993- 1:51.92, 1994- 1:48.87, 1995- 1:48.82, 1996- 1:45.23, 1997- 1:44.40, 1998- 1:43.86, 1999- 1:43.93, 2000- 1:43.74, 2001- 1:44.55, 2003- 1:44.96. pbs: 400m: 46.65 '00, 600m 1:14.41 '00, 1000m 2:15.83 '97, 1500m 3:45.15.
Two -year drugs disqualification 2001-03, then given special dispensation to qualify for 2003 Worlds after closing date.

Fabrizio MORI b. 28 Jun 1969 Livorno 1.75m 68kg. Fiamme Gialle.
At 400mh: OG: '92- h, '96- 6, '00- 7; WCh: '91- sf, '93- sf, '95- sf, '97- 4, '99- 1, '01- 2; EC: '94- sf, '98- 3, '02- 4; WJ: '88- sf; ECp: '89-91-4-6-7-8-9-00-01-02-03: 8/3/4/1/1/2/1/3/1/1/6 (2R 95 & 98). Won ITA 400mh 1989, 1991, 1996.
Seven Italian 400mh records 1996-2001.
Progression at 400mh: 1987- 52.55, 1988- 51.46, 1989- 49.86, 1990- 52.00, 1991- 48.92, 1992- 49.16, 1993- 49.23, 1994- 49.24, 1995- 49.27, 1996- 48.33, 1997- 47.79, 1998- 48.36, 1999- 47.72, 2000- 48.40, 2001- 47.54, 2002- 48.23, 2003- 50.18. pbs: 100m 10.6, 200m 21.8, 400m 46.19 '96, 300mh 35.7 '96.
Survived an initial disqualification in the semis to win the World title in Seville.

Nicola VIZZONI b. 4 Nov 1973 Pietrasanta, Lucca 1.93m 122kg. Fiamme Gialle.
At HT: OG: '00- 2; WCh: '97- dnq 22, '99- 7, '01- 4, '03- dnq 15; EC: '98- dnq 17, '02- dnq 13; WJ: '92- 5; EJ: '91- 8; WUG: '97- 5, '99- 5, '01- 1; ECp: '99-01-02-03: 4/2/7/5; E23Cp: '92- 5. Won ITA 1998, 2000-03.
Progression at HT: 1991- 66.62, 1992- 69.32, 1993- 70.76, 1994- 71.78, 1995- 74.48, 1996- 75.30, 1997- 77.10, 1998- 77.89, 1999- 79.59, 2000- 79.64, 2001- 80.50, 2002- 78.80, 2003- 77.69. Left-hander.

Women

Erika ALFRIDI b. 22 Feb 1968 Tregnago, Verona 1.68m 52kg. A.S.Camelot.
At 20kmW: OG: '00- 4; WCh: '99- 6, '01- 4; EC: '02- 3; WCp: '02- 1; ECp: '00- 4, '01- 4. At 10kmW: WCh: '97- 5; WCp: '97- 4; EC: '98- 2; ECp: '96- 7, '98- 9. Won ITA 5000mW 1998, 10kmW 1988, 1997, 2002; 20kmW 1996-7, 1999.
European 20km walk record 1997.
Progression at 10kmW, 20kmW: 1985- 55:30, 1987- 53:36, 1988- 46:57.5t, 1989- 44:34, 1993- 46:11.7t, 1995- 43:54, 1996- 43:27, 1:32:53; 1997- 42:15, 1:28:13; 1998- 42:54, 1999- 43:19.8, 1:31:52; 2000- 43:09, 1:28:06; 2001- 43:23, 1:27:29; 2002- 43:05, 1:28:33. pbs: 3000mW 11:57.80 '01, 5000mW 20:53.43 '02, 10000mW 43:19.8 '99.

Gertrud BACHER b. 28 Feb 1971 Merano 1.81m 67kg. SV Lana Raika.
At Hep: OG: '00- 14; WCh: '99- 14, '01- 9, '03- 6; EC: '98- 10, '02- 20; ECp: '01- 4; Italian champion 1997-8, 2001-03. At Pen: EI: '00- 9.
Progression at Hep: 1988- 4040, 1989- 4523, 1990- 4891, 1991- 5352, 1992- 5491, 1993- 5628, 1994- 5586, 1996- 5837, 1997- 5895, 1998- 6091, 1999- 6185, 2000- 5990, 2001- 6062, 2002- 5962, 2003- 6166. pbs: 200m 24.23 '99, 400m 55.9, 800m 2:08.09 '99, 60mh 8.70i '00, 100mh 13.65 '99, HJ 1.78 '93, LJ 6.11 '02, SP 14.03 '01, JT 48.14 '03, Hep 4314i '00.

Ester BALASSINI b. 20 Oct 1977 Bologna 1.73m 70kg. Fiamme Gialle.
At HT: OG: '00- dnq; WCh: '01- dnq; EC: '98- dnq 20, '02- 6; EU23: '97- 10, '99- 5; ECp: '98-9-00-01-02-03: 4/7/6/5/4/4; Won ITA 1998-2002.
15 Italian hammer records 1998-2003.
Progression at HT: 1996- 46.64, 1997- 56.04, 1998- 61.73, 1999- 64.44, 2000- 66.17, 2001- 68.50, 2002- 68.54, 2003- 70.43. pb DT 38.52.
Formerly a rollerskate dancer.

Claudia COSLOVICH b. 26 Apr 1972 Trieste 1.70m 74kg. Fondiaria Sai.
At JT: OG: '00- 12; WCh: '01- 11, '03- 7; EC: '94- dnq, '98- 7, '02- dnq 13; WUG: '99- 6; ECp: '93-5-7-8-9-00-01-02-03: 9/8/6/4/7/4/3/8/3.
Italian champion 1993-2003, MedG 2001.
Three Italian javelin records 1999-2000.
Progression at JT: 1988- 41.70, 1989- 49.62, 1990- 47.38, 1991- 51.20, 1992- 51.80, 1993- 53.88, 1994- 60.32, 1995- 60.98, 1996- 60.76, 1997- 57.82, 1998- 65.55, new: 1999- 60.12, 2000- 65.30, 2001- 64.30, 2002- 63.27, 2003- 62.70.

Rossella GIORDANO b. 1 Dec 1972 Asti 1.70m 51kg. Fiamme Azzurre Roma.
At 20kmW: WCh: '99- 27, '03- 6; WCp: '02- 9; ECp: '03- 12. At 10kmW: OG: '96- 5; WCh: '95- 6;

WCp: '95- 7, '97- 5; ECp: '96- 2; WUG: '93- 4, '95- 2, '97- 2, '99- 2. At 5000mW: WJ: '90- 18; EJ: '89- 7, '91- 6. Won ITA 10kmW 1996, 1998.
World record 20,000m track walk (1:30:48.3) 2000.
Progression at 10kmW, 20kmW: 1988- 50:42, 1989- 50:02, 1990- 48:22, 1991- 48:07, 1992- 46:35.2, 1:37:06; 1993- 45:28.1, 1994- 44:20, 1995- 42:26, 1996- 42:20, 1997- 41:38, 1:29:12; 1998- 43:21, 1999- 43:14, 1:31:02; 2000- 43:36, 1:29:47; 2001- 45:18, 1:36:13; 2002- 43:14, 1:31:10; 2003- 43:36.82t, 1:29:14. pbs: 3000mW 12:18.16 '96, 5000mW 20:48.11 '97, 10000mW 42:56.9 '96.

Magdelin MARTINEZ b. 10 Feb 1976 Camagüey, Cuba 1.78m 63kg. Atletica 2000 Milano.
At TJ: WCh: '01- 4, '03- 3; EC: '02- 6; WJ: '94- 9; PAm: '99- 3; WI: '03- 5, '04- 5; ECp: '02- 3, '03- 2. Italian champion 2002.
Four Italian triple jump records 2002-03.
Progression at TJ: 1992- 12.82, 1993- 13.07, 1994- 13.60, 1995- 13.74, 1996- 14.13/14.17w, 1997- 13.78/ 14.96w, 1998- 14.26, 1999- 14.14/14.18w, 2000- 14.40, 2001- 14.59, 2002- 14.73, 2003- 14.90, 2004- 14.81i. pb LJ 6.28 '02.
Changed nationality from Cuba to Italy in 2001 after marrying an Italian.

Fiona MAY b. 12 Dec 1969 Slough, GBR 1.81m 60kg. AS Camelot. Economics graduate of Leeds University. Married to Gianni Iapichino (PV 5.70 ITA rec '94).
At LJ: OG: '88- 6, '92- dnq, '96- 2, '00- 2; WCh: '91- dnq 19, '93- dnq 14, '95- 1, '97- 3, '99- 2, '01- 1. '03- 9; EC: '90- 7, '94- 3, '98- 2; CG: '90- 3; WJ: '86- 8, '88- 1; EJ: '87- 1; WI: '97-01-04: 1/4/6; EI: '98- 1; WUG: '91- 2; ECp: '89-91-3-5-7-8-9-00-01-03: 3/3/3/2/1/1/1/3/3/3 (TJ '98-9: 1/3). 3rd GP 1996, 1998. Won UK 1989, 1991, 1993; AAA 1989-92, Italian 1994, 1996.
Italian records: eight LJ 1994-8, three TJ 1998.
Progression at LJ, TJ: 1982- 5.34, 1983- 5.91, 1984- 6.30, 1985- 6.22/6.23w, 1986- 6.27/6.47w, 1987- 6.53/6.64w, 1988- 6.82/6.88w, 1989- 6.98w/6.80, 1990- 6.88, 1991- 6.77/6.91w, 1992- 6.73/6.76w, 1993- 6.86, 1994- 6.95A/6.90/7.00wA, 1995- 6.96/ 7.23Aw, 1996- 7.02/7.12w, 1997- 6.97/6.98w, 1998- 7.11, 14.65; 1999- 7.04, 14.39; 2000- 7.09, 2001- 6.97/7.02w, 2003- 6.67. pbs: 60m 7.7i '92, 100m 11.94 '97, 11.88w '89; 200m 25.4 '89, HJ 1.72 '83.
Competed for Britain to 1993, Italy from 1994; now lives in Firenze. In her first ever triple jump competition in 1998, she smashed the Italian indoor record with 14.56. Member of EAA Athletes Commission 2002-06. Daughter Larissa born on 14 July 2002.

Elisabetta PERRONE b. 9 Jul 1968 Camburzano, Vercelli 1.68m 55kg. Forestale.
At 20kmW: OG: '00- dq; WCh: '99- 21, '01- 3, '03- dnf; EC: '02- 6; WCp: '99- 20; ECp: '00-01-03: 2/3/2. At 10kmW: OG: '92- 19, '96- 2; WCh: '93- 4, '95- 2, '97- 10; EC: '94- 7, '98- 11; WCp: '93- 10, '95- 6, 97- 25; ECp: '96- 5. Won ITA 5000mW 1994, 1996-7, 2003; 10kmW 1994-5, 20kmW 2001; MedG 10kmW 1997.
ITA walk records 20km2000 & 2001, 5000m 2003.
Progression at 10kmW, 20kmW: 1988- 53:08, 1989- 51:18, 1990- 48:23, 1991- 46:19, 1992- 44:19, 1993- 43:26/41:56sh/44:01.6t, 1:33:37; 1994- 42:15/ 43:27.6t, 1995- 42:16, 1996- 42:09, 1997- 42:39, 1998- 44:04, 1:34:32; 1999- 42:45, 1:32:21; 2000- 43:15, 1:27:42; 2001- 43:07, 1:27:09; 2002- 43:28, 1:30:25; 2003- 43:43, 1:27:58. pbs: 3000mW 11:56.40 '93, 2MW 13:03.87 '96, 5000mW 20:12.41 '03.

JAMAICA

Governing body: Jamaica Amateur Athletic Association, PO Box 272, Kingston 5. Founded 1932. **2003 Champions**: **Men**: 100m: Asafa Powell 10.13w, 200m: Usain Bolt 20.28, 400m: Michael Blackwood 44.74, 800m: Jermaine Myers 1:49.42, 1500m: Mario Smith 3:52.38, 5000m/ 10000m: Andrew Gutzmore 16:56.32/35:05.02, 110mh: Maurice Wignall 13.54, 400mh: Danny McFarlane 48.94, HJ: Germaine Mason 2.10, PV: Jaban Ennis 4.80, LJ: Aundre Edwards 8.07, TJ: Benaud Shirley 15.74w, SP: Dorian Scott 17.64, DT: Claston Bernard 45.21, HT: Richard Wright 54.17, JT: Robert Barnes 68.97. **Women**: 100m/ 200m: Aleen Bailey 11.08/22.59, 400m: Lorraine Fenton 50.71, 800m: Michelle Ballentine 2:03.52, 3000m: Anieta Martin 11:43.27, 100mh: Brigitte Foster 12.69, 400mh: Allison Beckford 55.37, HJ: Peaches Roach 1.84, LJ: Elva Goulbourne 6.67, TJ: Suzette Lee 14.26w, SP: Kim Barrett 15.39, DT: Kesheila Reid 40.31, HT: Natalie Grant 62.12, JT: Kateema Riettie 48.44.

James BECKFORD b. 9 Jan 1975 St Mary 1.83m 73kg. Was a PE student at Blinn JC, USA.
At LJ (TJ): OG: '96- 2, '00- dnq 14; WCh: '95- 2 (6/4R), '97- 4, '01- 7, '03- 3; CG: '02- nj; WI: '97-9-04: 5/5/2; CAG: '98- 1. 2nd GP LJ 1997, 1999 (3rd 1995). Won JAM LJ 1995-8, 2000, 2002; TJ 1995.
Commonwealth records: LJ 1995 & 1997, TJ 1995, Jamaican records: LJ (5), TJ (4) 1994-7.
Progression at LJ, TJ: 1993- 7.53, 15.70; 1994- 8.13/8.29w, 17.29; 1995- 8.45/8.68w, 17.92; 1996- 8.52, 16.43i; 1997- 8.62, 1998- 8.60/8.61w, 16.09; 1999- 8.50, 2000- 8.42, 2001- 8.41, 2002- 8.21/ 8.25w, 2003- 8.28, 2004- 8.31i. pb 60m 6.79i '04.
An outstanding long/triple jumper, now concentrating on the long jump. After positive test for ephedrine on 25 June 1997 was re-admitted to competition with the IAAF new warning procedure and thus competed at the World Champs.

Michael BLACKWOOD b. 29 Aug 1976 1.90m 79kg. Was at Oklahoma University, USA.
At 400m/4x400mR: OG: '00- 3R; WCh: '01- res 3R, '03- 4/3R; CG: '02- 1; WI: '03- 2R; WCp: '02- 1/1R. Won GP 2002, JAM 400m 2002-03.
Progression at 400m: 1996- 47.04, 1997- 46.25, 1998- 45.45, 1999- 45.33, 2000- 44.69, 2001- 45.66, 2002- 44.60, 2003- 44.74.
His sister, Catherine Scott (b. 27 Aug 1973) won 2000 OG silver and 2001 World gold at 4x400m.

Usain BOLT b. 21 Aug 1986 Trelawny 1.96m 86kg. Student.
At 200m/4x100mR: WJ: 02- 1/2R/2R; WY: '01- sf, '03- 1; PAm-J: '03- 1.
World U18 200m record 2003.
Progression at 200m, 400m: 2001- 21.81, 48.28; 2002- 20.58, 47.12; 2003- 20.13, 45.35.
In 2002, after running 20.61 to win the CAC U17 title, he became the youngest ever male world junior champion at 15y 332d and set a world age best with 20.58 for 200m. Won IAAF 'Rising Star' award for men in 2002.

Deon GRIFFITHS b. 27 Jan 1980 1.80m 72kg. Student at Auburn University.
At 400mh: WCh: '03- sf; PAm: '03- 3. Won NCAA 2003.
Progression at 400mh: 1999- 51.87, 2000- 51.75, 2001- 51.21, 2002- 49.90, 2003- 48.55.

Gregory HAUGHTON b. 10 Nov 1973 St Mary 1.85m 79kg. Was at George Mason University, USA.
At 400m/4x400mR: OG: '96- 3R, '00- 3/3R; WCh: '93- 6, '95- 3/2R, '97- 3R, '99- 7/3R, '01- 3/3R; CG: '98- 6/1R; PAm: '99- 1/1R; CAG: '98- 2R; WI: '97- 2R, '04- 1R; WJ: '92- sf/2R. Won GWG 2001, CAC 400m 1993, 1999; Jamaican 1994-5, 1999-2000; NCAA 1995; 2nd GP 2002.
Progression at 400m: 1991- 47.30, 1992- 46.88, 1993- 44.78, 1994- 44.93, 1995- 44.56, 1996- 45.07, 1997- 45.18, 1998- 45.24, 1999- 44.59, 2000- 44.70, 2001- 44.58, 2002- 44.75, 2003- 45.21. pbs: 200m 20.64 '96, 300m 32.25+ '99.

Danny McFARLANE b. 14 Feb 1972 1.85m 81kg. Was at University of Oklahoma, USA.
At 400m/4x400mR: OG: '00- 8/3R; WCh: '93- 7R, '95- sf/2R, '97- 3R, '99- sf/3R, '01- 3R; CG: '02- dnf R; WI: '01- 3, '03- 2R; PAm: '99- 1R. Won CAC 1997, 2001. At 400mh: WCh: '03- 4/3R. Won JAM 400mh 2003.
Progression at 400m, 400mh: 1993- 45.82, 1994- 45.74, 1995- 44.90, 1996- 46.18i/46.23, 1997- 45.47, 1998- 45.61, 1999- 45.37, 2000- 45.26, 2001- 45.20A/ 45.59, 2002- 45.66, 2003- 45.72, 48.30. pb 200m 21.17 '95.

Germaine MASON b. 20 Jan 1983 1.95m 80kg. Studying sports medicine at Kingston University of Technology.
Six Jamaican high jump records 2002-03.
At HJ: WCh: '03- 5; CG: '02- 5; PAm: '03- 1; WJ: '00- 2, '02- 3; WI: '04- 3=; won CAC-J 2000 & 2002.
Progression at HJ: 1998- 2.08, 1999- 2.09, 2000- 2.24, 2002- 2.27, 2003- 2.34.

Asafa POWELL b. 11 Nov 1982 1.88m 87kg. Student at Kingston University of Technology.
At 100m/4x100mR: WCh: '03- dq; CG: '02- sf/ 2R; PAm-J: '01- 2R. Won JAM 100m 2003.
Progression at 100m: 2001- 10.50, 2002- 10.12, 2003- 10.02/9.9. pbs: 60m 6.56i '04, 200m 20.48 '02.
Disqualified for false start in World quarters 2003 after fastest time (10.05) in heats.

Kemel THOMPSON b. 25 Sep 1974 Kingston 1.80m 75kg. Student at Loughborough University, UK, was at South Florida University.
At 400mh: OG: '00- h; WCh: '99- sf, '03- 5; CG: '98- 6; Jamaican champion 1999-2000, 2002.
Progression at 400mh: 1996- 50.52, 1997- 49.71, 1998- 49.39, 1999- 48.82, 2000- 48.56, 2002- 48.57, 2003- 48.05. pb 400m 46.97 '99.

Maurice WIGNALL b. 17 Apr 1976 1.86m 75kg.
At 110mh (LJ): WCh: '97- (nj), '01- h; CG: '02- 3; PAm: '99- 7 (6); WUG: '01- 5. At 60mh: WI: '04- 3. Won JAM 110mh 1997, 1999, 2001-03; LJ 1999.
Three Jamaican records 110mh 2002-03.
Progession at 110mh: 1993- 14.56, 1994- 14.59/ 14.2, 1995- 13.93, 1996- 13.98, 1997- 13.75, 1999- 13.66, 2000- 13.71, 2001- 13.70, 2002- 13.49, 2003- 13.28. pbs: 60mh 7.48i '04, LJ 8.09 '97.

Women

Aleen BAILEY b. 25 Nov 1980 1.70m 64g. Student at University of Southern California.
At 100m: WCh: '03- 7. Won NCAA 100m & 200m (and indoor 200m) 2003, Jamaican 100m 2001, 2003; 200m 2003.
Progresion at 100m, 200m: 1995- 12.10, 1996- 11.67, 23.99; 1997- 11.60/11.55w, 23.65; 1998- 11.37, 23.96/23.16w, 1999- 11.41, 23.37; 2000- 11.47/ 11.38w, 23.45/22.86w; 2001- 11.14, 22.59; 2002- 11.33, 22.54; 2003- 11.07, 22.59.

Juliet CAMPBELL b. 17 Mar 1970 St Thomas 1.78m 62kg. Was at Auburn University, USA (business education).
At 200m/4x100mR: OG: '00- qf; WCh: '93- 3R, '97- sf, '99- 8, '01- 6; CG: '98- 2/2R, '02- 2/2R, CAG: '98- 2; WI: '99- 5, '01- 1/2 4x400mR, '03- 4; WCp: '02- 1R. At 400m/4x400mR: OG: '92- qf, '96- sf/4R; WCh: '93- 7/4R (3 4x100m). Won NCAA 400m 1993, JAM 400m 1993, 1996; 200m 2003.
Progression at 200m, 400m: 1987- 23.71w, 1988- 24.25, 1989- 24.20/23.7, 53.1; 1990- 23.52, 53.01; 1991- 53.59, 1992- 23.06, 51.11; 1993- 22.80/22.66w, 50.11; 1994- 23.69, 51.65; 1995- 22.77, 51.4/52.00; 1996- 22.71/22.55w, 50.11; 1997- 22.61, 52.30; 1998- 22.69/22.63w, 51.09; 1999- 22.50, 52.77; 2000- 22.70i/22.86, 2001- 22.64i/22.68, 2002- 22.54, 2003- 22.69. pbs: 60y 6.72i '90, 60m 7.16i '02, 100m 11.15 '02, 11.0 '95; 150m 17.08 '96, 300m 36.59 '92, 500m 1:12.05i '94.
Lives in Auburn, USA.

Veronica CAMPBELL b. 15 May 1982 Trelawny 1.63m 61kg. Student at University of Arkansas, USA.
At 100m/4x100mR (200m): OG: '00- 2R; CG: '02- 2/2R; WJ: '98- qf, '00- 1/2R (1); WY: '99- 1/ 1R. Won CAC-J 100m 2000, JAM 100m 2002.
Progression at 100m, 200m: 1999- 11.49, 23.73; 2000- 11.12/11.1, 22.87; 2001- 11.13/22.92; 2002- 11.00, 22.39; 2004- 22.43i. pb 60m 7.17i '02.
In 2000 became the first woman to become World Junior champion at both 100m and 200m.

Vonette DIXON b. 26 Nov 1975 1.70m 62kg. Was at Auburn University, USA.
At 100mh: WCh: '01- 8, '03- sf; CG: '02- 2.
Progression at 100mh: 1994- 15.13/15.0, 1995- 14.29, 1996- 13.52/13.30w, 1997- 13.26, 1998- 13.52, 1999- 13.40, 2000- 12.90, 2001- 12.83, 2002- 12.83/ 12.82w, 2003- 12.72. pbs: 55m 6.79i '00, 60m 7.33i '00, 100m 11.47/11.40w '00, 200m 23.57/ 23.48w '00, 50mh 6.85i '02, 55mh 7.55i '00, 60mh 7.92i '02.

Delloreen ENNIS-LONDON b. 5 Mar 1975 St Catherine 1.78m 67kg. née Ennis. Business management graduate of Abilene Christian University, USA.
At 100mh: OG: '00- 4; WCh: '99- 7; WJ: '92- sf. 3rd GP 2000. Jamaican champion 1999-2001, CAC 2003. CAC 100mh record 2000.
Progression at 100mh: 1992- 13.81, 1994- 13.96, 1996- 13.53/13.30w, 1997- 13.60/13.51w, 1998- 13.27/13.1w, 1999- 12.71/12.60w, 2000- 12.52, 2001- 12.57, 2003- 12.70. pbs: 100m 11.50 '99, 11.30w '04; 55mh 7.56i '99, 60mh 7.92i '04, 400mh 400mh 62.75 '98.

Lorraine FENTON b. 8 Sep 1973 Mandeville 1.74m 59kg. née Graham. Graduated in criminal justice from Lincoln University, USA.
At 400m/4x400mR: OG: '00- 2/2R; WCh: '97- sf/3R, '99- 3, '01- 2/1R, '03- 2/3R; CG: '02- dnf R. Won JAM 400m 1997, 1999-2003. Won GP 2000 (2nd 2002).
Progression at 400m: 1994- 53.31, 1995- 53.63, 1996- 51.85, 1997- 50.69, 1998- 50.23, 1999- 49.92, 2000- 49.58, 2001- 49.88, 2002- 49.30, 2003- 49.43. pbs: 100m 11.73 '99, 200m 22.63 '01, 300m 36.00+ '00.

Brigitte FOSTER b. 7 Nov 1974 St Elizabeth 1.70m 62kg. Was at Southwest Texas State University, USA.
At 100mh: OG: '00- 8; WCh: '01- sf, '03- 2; CG: '98- 5/2R, '02- dns; PAm: '03- 1; WCp: '02- 2; 2nd GP 2002. JAM champion 2002-03. At 60mh: WI: '03- 6.
Three CAC 100mh records 2002-03.
Progression at 100mh: 1993- 14.22, 1996- 13.34, 1998- 13.19/13.13w/12.9w, 1999- 13.35, 2000- 12.70, 2001- 12.70, 2002- 12.49, 2003- 12.45. pbs: 60m 7.32i '04; 100m 11.17 '03, 200m 23.51/ 23.35w '98, 400m 55.71 '02, 60mh 7.96i '03, 400mh 64.62 '93.

Lacena GOLDING-CLARKE b. 20 Mar 1975 1.68m 57kg. Was at Portland College, USA.
At 100mh/4x100mR: WCh: '03- 8; CG: '02- 1; PAm: '03- 3/3R.. At LJ: OG: '96- dnq WCh: '95- dnq 20, '97- dnq 18; CG: '98- 4; WJ: '92- 6, '94- 8; CAG: '98- 1; CAC: '99- 1; PAm-J '93- 1. At 60mh: WI: '01-03-04: 8/4/6; Won JAM LJ 1994, 1996-9.
Progression at 100mh: 1994- 13.98, 1995- 13.22/ 13.19w/13.0w, 1997- 13.05/13.04w, 1998- 13.00, 1999- 13.11, 2000- 12.93, 2001- 12.97, 2002- 12.74/ 12.70w, 2003- 12.72. pbs: 100m 11.69/11.64w '97, 200m 23.99 '98, 50mh 6.83i '00, 55mh 7.37Ai '98, 60mh 7.86i '04, HJ 1.71i '94, 1.70 '95; LJ 6.87 '98, TJ 12.03 '98, JT 41.02 '95, Hep 5750 '98.
Married to **Davian Clarke** (b. 30 Apr 1976) (400m 44.87 '96; OG: '96- 7; WI: '04- 2; 4x400m: OG: '96- 3; WCh: '95- 2, '97/9/03- 3; CG: '98- 1; PAm: '99- 1; WJ: '92/4- 2; WI: '03- 2, '04- 1).

Elva GOULBOURNE b. 21 Jan 1980 St Ann 1.70m 50kg. Student at Auburn University, USA.
At LJ/4x100mR: OG: '00- 10; WCh: '01- 10, '03- dnq 20; CG: '02- 1/2R; PAm: '99- 3. Won PAm-J 1997/99, CAC-J 1998, CAC 2001, 2003; JAM 2000-03, NCAA 2002-03.
Commonwealth indoor LJ record 2002.
Progression at LJ: 1997- 6.10, 1998- 6.47, 1999- 6.49, 2000- 6.74/6.79w, 2001- 6.86/6.90w, 2002- 6.91i/6.82/6.87w, 2003- 6.83/6.96w. pbs: 55m 6.73i '03, 60m 7.23i '03, 100m 11.20 '03, 200m 22.98 '03, TJ 13.78i '03.

Tayna LAWRENCE b. 17 Sep 1975 St Catherine's 1.63m 61kg. Was at Florida International University, USA.
At 100m/4x100mR: OG: '00- 3/2R; CAG: '98- 3; WCp: '02- 2/1R; 3rd GP 2002.
Progression at 100m: 1997- 11.61, 1998- 11.30/ 11.23w, 1999- 11.37/11.36w, 2000- 11.07, 2002- 10.93. pbs: 55m 6.77i '99, 60m 7.21i '99, 200m 22.84/ 22.78w '00.

Beverley McDONALD b. 15 Feb 1970 St Mary 1.69m 59kg. Was at Texas Christian University, USA.
At 100m/4x100mR (200m): OG: '00- sf/2R (4); WCh: '91- sf/1R, '93- sf, '95-sf/2R (sf), '97- qf/ 2R, '99- (2)/3R, '01- (sf), '03- 6; CG: '02- (dns); PAm: '91- 3/1R; CAG: '98- 2 (2); WJ: '88- 7; WCp: '98- 2R (4), '02- 1R. At 60m: WI: '95- 5. 3rd GP 200m 1999. Won JAM 100m 1998, 200m 1998-2000, 2002.
Progression at 100m, 200m: 1987- 11.2, 23.40/ 23.3; 1988- 11.61, 24.15/23.7; 1990- 11.52/11.27w, 23.20w; 1991- 11.37/11.29w/11.2w, 23.48/23.31w; 1992- 11.43/11.19w, 23.31; 1993- 11.22/11.05w, 22.67; 1994- 11.47, 23.02w; 1995- 11.20/11.17w, 22.56; 1996- 11.16, 23.04; 1997- 11.13A/11.11w, 22.62; 1998- 10.99, 22.24; 1999- 11.10, 22.22; 2000- 11.11, 22.35; 2001- 11.27/11.1, 22.57; 2002- 11.24, 22.75A/22.85; 2003- 11.24, 22.67. pbs: 50m 6.17i '96, 60m 7.16i '95, 300y 34.67i '91.
Her brother Michael (b. 17 Mar 1975) was World Junior 400m champion in 1994, pb 44.64A '96.

Debbie Ann **PARRIS** b. 24 Mar 1973 Trelawny 1.62m 52kg. Was at Louisiana State University, USA.
At 400mh/4x400mR: OG: '96- 4; WCh: '93- sf, '95- h, '97- 5, '99- 8, '01- 5/1R; CG: '94- 3, '02- 2; PAm: '03- 7; CAG: '98- 3; WJ: '92- 8/2R; WUG: '93- 2; WCp: '02- 6. NCAA champion 1993-4, CAC 1993, JAM 2001-02.
Progression at 400mh: 1992- 57.34, 1993- 55.80, 1994- 55.17, 1995- 54.29, 1996- 53.97, 1997- 54.19,

1998- 54.49, 1999- 54.55, 2000- 55.90, 2001- 53.88, 2002- 54.72, 2003- 55.51. pbs: 200m 23.50 '98, 400m 51.42 '01, 800m 2:13.35 '99, 100mh 13.51 '93.

Trecia-Kaye SMITH b. 5 Nov 1975 1.85m 66kg. Studied physiotherapy at University of Pittsburgh, USA.
At TJ: WCh: '97- dnq 31, '01- 8; CG: '02- 3; WI: '04- 4; WCp: '02- 4. At LJ: WJ: '94- 11. Won NCAA LJ 1997, 1999; TJ 1998.; JAM TJ 2001-02
Jamaican TJ record 1997 & 2002.
Progression at TJ: 1996- 13.55/13.58w, 1997- 14.22, 1998- 14.05i/13.98, 1999-14.02i/13.91/13.95w, 2000- 13.76/13.92w, 2001- 14.12A/14.88w, 2002- 14.32, 2003- 13.96i/13.55/13.89w, 2004- 14.71i. pbs: 200m 24.39 '97, 100mh 14.48 '97, 14.36w '99; HJ 1.81 '97, LJ 6.74 '01, 6.84w '97; SP 14.74 '98, DT 44.20 '98, JT 44.52 '98, Hep 5931 '97.
At 2004 World Indoors set national records of 14.57 in qualifying and 14.70 and 14.71 in final.

JAPAN

Governing body: Nippon Rikujo-Kyogi Renmei, 1-1-1 Jinnan, Shibuya-Ku, Tokyo 150-8050. Founded 1911.
National Championships first held in 1914 (men), 1925 (women). **2003 Champions**: **Men**: 100m/200m: Shingo Suetsugu 10.13/20.03, 400m: Mitsuhiro Sato 45.63, 800m: Hiroshi Sasano 1:47.55, 1500m: Jun Tsuji 3:48.61, 5000m: Kazuyoshi Tokumoto 13:40.68, 10000m: Toshihiro Iwasa 28:17.95, Mar:, 3000mSt: Yoshitaka Iwamizu 8:25.56, 110mh: Satoru Tanigawa 13.82, 400mh: Dai Tamesue 48.94, HJ: Naoyuki Daigo 2.18, PV: Daichi Sawano 5.75, LJ: Shin-ichi Terano 7.92, TJ: Takanori Sugibayashi 16.96, SP: Yasutada Noguchi 17.73, DT: Shigeo Hatakeyama 53.88, HT: Koji Murofushi 83.29, JT: Yukifumi Murakami 75.38, Dec: Takuro Hirata 7630, 20kmW: Toshihito Fujinohara 1:20:31, 50kmW: Fumio Imamura 3:59:20. **Women**: 100m/200m: Motoka Arai 11.53/23.82, 400m/400mh: Makiko Yoshida 53.20/55.89, 800m: Miki Nishimura 2:02.10, 1500m: Kayo Sugihara 4:17.41, 5000m: Mari Ozaki 15:12.76, 10000m: Kayoko Fukushi 31:47.15, Mar: Mizuki Noguchi 2:21:18, 100mh: Yvonne Kanazawa 13.06, HJ: Miki Imai 1.92, PV: Masumi Ono 4.21, LJ: Kumiko Ikeda 6.64, TJ: Fumiyo Yoshida 13.50, SP: Chinatsu Mori 17.48, DT: Yuka Murofushi 54.24, HT: Masumi Aya 62.79, JT: Takako Miyake 52.96, Hep: Yuki Nakada 5910, 20kmW: Ryoko Tadamasa 1:33:34.

Shigeru ABURAYA b. 6 Feb 1977 Yamaguchi pref. 1.63m 52kg. Chuguko Electric.
At Mar: WCh: '01- 5, '03- 5; JPN champion 2001. At HMar: WCh: '99- 23.
Progression at Mar: 2000- 2:10:48, 2001- 2:07:52, 2003- 2:09:26. pbs: 5000m 13:40.87 '99, 10000m 28:13.76 '00, HMar 61:54 '02.
2nd Tokyo marathon 2003.

Koji MUROFUSHI b. 8 Oct 1974 Shizuoka 1.87m 97kg. Was at Chukyo Univ. Mizuno.
At HT: OG: '00- 9; WCh: '95- dnq, '97- 10, '99- dnq 14, '01- 2, '03- 3; WJ: '92- 8; AsiG: '94- 2, '98- 1, '02- 1; AsiC: '93- 2, '95- 2, '98- 2, '02- 1; WCp: '02- 2 (9 DT). Won GWG 2001, GP 2002 (2nd 2000). Won E.Asian 1997, 2001. Japanese 1995-2003.
18 Japanese hammer records 1998-2003, Asian records 2001 & 2003.
Progression at HT: 1991- 61.76, 1992- 66.30, 1993- 68.00, 1994- 69.54, 1995- 72.32, 1996- 73.82, 1997- 75.72, 1998- 78.57, 1999- 79.17, 2000- 81.08, 2001- 83.47, 2002- 83.33, 2003- 84.86. pb DT 41.93 '02.
His father Shigenobu Murofushi won a record five Asian Games gold medals 1970-86 and held the Japanese hammer record with 75.96 (Los Angeles 1984) until Koji broke it for the first time on 26 Apr 1998. His mother was a Romanian javelin thrower. His sister Yuka (b. 11 Feb 77) was Japanese discus champion and record setter (56.84) 1999 and 6th World Juniors 1996 and has a hammer pb of 62.24 '03.

Shingo SUETSUGU b. 2 Jun 1980 Kumamoto pref. 1.78m 68kg. Mizuno. Studied at Tokai University.
At 200m/4x100m: OG: '00- sf; WCh: '01- sf, '03- 3; AsiG: '02- 1/2R. Won E.Asian 2001, JPN 100m 2003; 200m 2001, 2003. Asian 200m record 2003.
Progression at 200m: 1996- 21.62, 1997- 21.37, 1998- 21.08, 1999- 21.36, 2000- 20.26, 2001- 20.30, 2002- 20.37, 2003- 20.03. pbs: 100m 10.03 '03, 400m 45.99 '02.

Toshinari TAKAOKA b. 24 Sep 1970 Yamashiro, Kyoto 1.86m 64kg. Kanebo. Graduate of Ryukoku University.
At 10000m (/5000m): OG: '96- h, '00- 7/15; WCh: '93- (h), '97- dns, '99- 12/h, '01- 15; AsiG: '94- 1/1, AsiC: '98- (1); WUG: '93- (3). Won E.Asian 5000m 2001, JPN 10000m 1996, 1999.
Asian records 5000m 1998, 10,000m 2001, marathon 2002. Japanese records: 3000m 1999, 5000m 1992 (13:20.43) and 1998
Progression at 5000m, 10000m, Mar: 1986- 14:53.7, 1987- 14:58.4, 1988- 15:00.09, 1989- 14:40.6, 1990- 14:25.55, 30:50.15; 1991- 13:57.4, 1992- 13:20.43, 1993- 13:23.98, 28:28.1; 1994- 13:33.31, 27:59.72; 1995- 13:54.66, 1996- 13:45.52, 27:49.89; 1997- 13:27.56, 27:53.03; 1998- 13:13.40, 27:50.08; 1999- 13:21.08, 27:53.37; 2000- 13:15.34, 27:40.44; 2001- 13:38.87, 27:35.09, 2:09:41; 2002- 13:29.77, 28:17.29, 2:06:16; 2003- 13:24.66, 28:03.62, 2:07:59. pbs: 1500m 3:40.20 '99, 3000m 7:41.87 '99, HMar 61:07 '03, 30000m 1:29:23 '01.
After a successful track career, he was third in his debut marathon at Fukuoka in 2001 and was then third at Chicago 2002.

Dai TAMESUE b. 3 May 1978 Hiroshima pref. 1.70m 67kg. Graduate of Hosei University.
At 400mh: OG: '00- h; WCh: '01- 3, '03- sf; AsiG: '02- 3. Japanese champion 2001-03. At 400m: WJ: '96- 4/2R.

Two Japanese records 2001.
Progression at 400mh: 1996- 49.09, 1998- 49.19, 1999- 49.12, 2000- 48.47, 2001- 47.89, 2002- 48.69, 2003- 48.94. pbs: 200m 21.23 '96, 400m 45.94 '96.
One of the shortest ever top-class 400m hurdlers.

Women

Masako CHIBA b. 18 Jul 1976 Uji City, Kyoto pref. 1.56m 39kg. Sakura AC.
At 10000m: OG: '96- 5; WCh: 97- 3. At Mar: '03- 3. World CC: '95- 16J. Won E.Asian 10000m 1997.
World half marathon record 1999, Japanese 10000m record 1996.
Progression at 5000m, 10000m. Mar: 1993- 16:15.6, 1994- 16:01.1, 1995- 15:52.4, 31:43.7; 1996- 15:20.13, 31:20.46; 1997- 15:20.58, 31:31.85; 1998- 2:37:44, 1999- 15:29.65, 31:38.02, 2:29:00; 2001- 2:30:39, 2002- 2:25:11, 2003- 2:21:45. pbs: 3000m 9:20.50 '95, HMar 66:43 '97.
Ran a 30:55 leg for 10k in the International Chiba Ekiden 1996. Her 66:43 half marathon at Tokyo in January 1997 was just 4 secs off the fastest ever mark, by Ingrid Kristiansen, which was not able to be accepted as a world best. Chiba passed 20km in a world best 63:14. 2nd Rotterdam marathon 2002 and at Osaka 2003.

Kayoko FUKUSHI b. 25 Mar 1982 Aiomori Pref. 1.61m 45kg. Wacoal.
At 5000m/(10000m): WCh: '03- h/11; WJ: '00- 4. AsiG: '02- 2/2; World CC: '02- 15. Won JPN 5000m 2002, 10000m 2002-03.
Japanese records: 3000m, 5000m (3) 2002.
Progression at 5000m, 10,000m: 1998 - 16:56.35, 1999 - 16:38.69, 35:37.54; 2000- 15:29.70, 2001- 15:10.23, 31:42.05; 2002- 14:55.19, 30:51.81; 2003- 15:09.02, 31:10.57. pb 3000m 8:44.40 '02.
Set Japanese junior records at 3000m, 5000m and 10000m in 2001.

Harumi HIROYAMA b. 2 Sep 1968 Tokushima pref. 1.60m 47kg. née Suzuki. Graduate of Kokushikan University. Shiseido.
At 10000m: OG: '00- 20; WCh: '99- 4. At 5000m: OG: '96- h; WCh: '97- 8. At 3000m: WCh: '93- h (h 1500m); AsiG: '94- 2. At Mar: AsiG: '02- 2. Won E.Asian 5000m 1997, JPN 1500m & 3000m 1992, 10000m 1997, 1999, Mar 2000.
Japanese records: 1500m 1992 and 1994, 3000m (2) 1994, 5000m 1997 and 1998.
Progress at 5000m, 10000m, Mar: 1990- 17:18.21, 1991- 16:55.0, 2:51:36; 1993- 15:30.78, 1994- 15:33.53, 1995- 15:28.17, 32:03.35; 1996- 15:09.69, 31:43.99; 1997- 15:07.75, 31:22.72; 1998- 15:03.67, 2:28:12; 1999- 15:21.04, 31:26.84; 2000- 15:20.36, 31:59.60, 2:22:56; 2001- 15:29.73, 31:39.80, 2:29:01; 2002- 2:24:34, 2003- 15:31.78, 31:32.27. pbs: 800m 2:06.19 '94, 1500m 4:11.10 '94, 3000m 8:50.40 '94, HMar 69:41 '01.
Third in Nagoya marathon 1998, and 2nd at Osaka in 2000 and 2001. Married to Tsutomu Hiroyama (b. 22 Oct 1966, Mar pb 2:11:37 '90).

Mizuki NOGUCHI b. 3 Jul 1978 Ise, Mie pref. 1.50m 41kg. Globary.
At 10000m: WCh: '01- 13. At Mar: WCh: '03- 2. World HMar: '99-00-01-02: 2/4/4/9. Won Asian CC 1999, E.Asian HMar 2001, JPN Mar 2003.
Progression at 10000m, Mar: 1999- 33:09.98, 2000- 32:05.23, 2001- 31:51.13, 2002- 31:50.18, 2:25:35; 2003- 31:59.28, 2:21:18. pbs: 3000m 9:34.47 '97, 5000m 15:34.36 '99, Rd: 15km 48:11 '01, HMar 67:47 '04.
Won Nagoya marathon on debut 2002 and won again at Osaka in January 2003.

Naoko SAKAMOTO b. 14 Nov 1980 Hyogo Pref. 1.60m 44kg. Tenmaya.
At Mar: WCh: '03- 4.
Progression at Mar: 2003- 2:21:51, 2004- 2:25:29. pbs: 3000m 9:33.93 '98, 5000m 15:45.75 '02, HMar 69:27 '01.
Ran 2:21:51 for third on debut at Osaka 2003 and won at Osaka 2004 in her third marathon.

Yoko SHIBUI b. 14 Mar 1979 Kuroiso, Tochigi pref. 1.64m 46kg. Mitsui.
At Mar: WCh: '01- 4. At 10000m: WCh: '03- 14.
Japanese 10000m record 2002.
Progression at 10000m, Mar: 1997- 33:53.20, 1999- 32:43.02, 2000- 31:48.89, 2001- 31:48.73, 2:23:11; 2002- 30:48.89, 2:21:22; 2003- 31:42.01, 2004- 2:33:02. pbs: 3000m 9:11.37 '96, 5000m 15:18.92 '02, 15km 49:07 '02, HMar 69:17+ '02.
Ran the fastest ever debut marathon by a woman with 2:23:11 to win at Osaka in January 2001. This came after a series of fast ekiden relay 10km legs in 2000. She was third in the 2002 Chicago Marathon.

Naoko TAKAHASHI b. 6 May 1972 Gifu 1.63m 46kg. Sekisui Chemical. Graduate of Osaka Gakuin University.
At Mar: OG: '00- 1; AsiG: '98- 1. At 5000m: WCh: '97- 13. Won JPN marathon 1998.
World marathon record 2001, Asian and two Japanese records 1998.
Progression at 10000m, Mar: 1994- 34:02.02, 1996- 31:48.23, 1997- 32:34.50, 2:31:32; 1998- 31:55.95, 2:21:47; 2000- 2:22:19, 2001- 2:19:46, 2002- 2:21:49, 2003- 2:27:21. pbs: 800m 2:13.09 '90, 1500m 4:22.89 '94, 3000m 9:13.00 '94, 5000m 15:21.15 '98, HMar 68:55 '00.
Made her marathon debut with 7th at Osaka in 1997 and then had six successive marathon wins until second in Tokyo 2003. After graduating from University she joined the Recruit team coached by Yoshio Koide and later followed him to the Sekisui team. In 1998 she set national records, 2:25:48 at Nagoya in March, and then a superb 2:21:47, on her own all the way and despite slowing in intense heat and humidity, to win the Asian Games gold medal in December. Withdrew, injured, from 1999 World Champs on the eve of the race, but returned with 2:22:19 (69:39 second half) to win at Nagoya in March 2000 and later took the Olympic gold in great

style. She won at Berlin in 2001, when she became the first women to break 2:20, and in 2002.

Reiko TOSA b. 11 Jun 1976 Ehime pref. 1.67m 45kg. Mitsui. Graduate of Matsuyama University. At Mar: WCh: '01- 2. At HMar: WCh: '99- 6. Progression at Mar: 1998- 2:54:57, 2000- 2:24:36, 2001- 2:26:06, 2002- 2:22:46, 2004- 2:23:57. pbs: 3000m 9:43.00 '98, 5000m 15:37.08 '00, 10000m 32:15.63 '00, HMar 69:36 '99.
Won Nagoya Marathon 2004, 2nd Nagoya (2:24:36) and Tokyo (2:24:47) 2000; 4th London 2002.

KAZAKHSTAN

Governing body: Athletic Federation of the Republic of Kazakhstan, Abai Street 48, 480072 Almaty. Founded 1959.

2003 National Champions: Men: 100m: Gennadiy Chernovol 10.29, 200m: Dmitriy Karpov 21.65, 400m/400mh: Yevgeniy Meleshenko 46.87/49.96, 800m/1500m: Mikhail Kolganov 1:48.29/3:53.50, 5000m: Sergey Milytin 14:53.52, HMar: Sergey Milyutin 66:30, 110mh: Nazar Mukhamedzhan 15.09, HJ: Yuriy Pakhlyayev 2.12, PV: Aleksandr Akhmetov 5.00, LJ: Andrey Pakhomov 7.34, TJ: Denis Sauranbayev 15.77, SP/DT: Dmitriy Kondratenko 15.31/52.28; JT:, Dec: Pavel Dubitskiy 7469. **Women**: 100m/200m: Viktoriya Koviyreva 11.73/24.15, 400m: Svetlana Bodritskaya 52.83, 800m: Tatyana Roslanova 2:00.98, 1500m: Svetlana Lukashova 4:18.40, HMar: Yekaterina Shatnaya 80:18, 100mh: Irina Naumenko 14.39, 400mh: Natalya Torshina 55.86, HJ: Marina Korzhova 1.88, PV: Yelena Reznik 3.90, LJ: Yelena Kashcheyeva 6.30, TJ: Tatyana Bocharova 14.07, SP: Iolanta Ulyeva 17.39, DT: Yekaterina Mitina 49.18, JT: Svetlana Kazanina 46.72.

Dmitriy KARPOV b. 23 Jul 1981 Karaganda 1.98m 89kg.
At Dec: WCh: '03- 4; WJ: '00- 4; AsiG: '02- 2; won E.Asian 2001. At Hep: WI: '04- 4. At 110mh: AsiC: '02- 5. Won KAZ 200m 2003, Dec 1999.
Progression at Dec: 1999- 7105, 2000- 7620, 2001- 7567, 2002- 7995, 2003- 8374. pbs: 60m 7.04i "04, 100m 10.72 '03, 400m 47.33 '03, 1000m 2:42.34i '04, 1500m 4:34.49 '01, 60mh 7.87i '04, 110mh 13.93 '02, HJ 2.12 '03, PV 4.80 '03, LJ 8.05 '02, SP 15.51 '03, DT 50.18 '03, JT 50.53 '03, Hep 6155i '04 (Asian record).
National record of 8253 to win at Desenzano in 2003 from previous best of 7995. Then three pbs en route to world bronze and another KAZ record.

Sergey KOREPANOV b. 9 May 1964 Almaty 1.70m 61kg. State Unversity, Izhevsk. Sports teacher.
At 50kmW: OG: '96- 8, '00- 15; WCh: '93-5-7-9-0-1-3: 10/9/12/dnf/20/9; WCp: '95-9-02: 9/1/7; AsiG: '94- 1, '98- 2. At 20kmW: AsiC: '93- 3.
Asian 50km record 1999. KZK 50km walk records 1993-9.
Progression at 50kmW: 1989- 3:58:13, 1990- 3:56:33, 1991- 3:55:47, 1992- 4:08:02sh, 1993- 3:52:50, 1994- 3:54:37, 1995- 3:48:06, 1996- 3:48:42, 1997- 3:42:16, 1998- 3:45:15, 1999- 3:39:22, 2000- 3:53:05, 2001- 3:59:57, 2002- 3:52:20, 2003- 3:47:42. pbs: 5000mW 19:14.00i '95, 20kmW 1:20:34 '95.
His World Cup win at 50km walk in 1999 was the first world medal for Kazakhstan.

Women

Natalya TORSHINA b. 4 Oct 1968 Kemerovo 1.72m 60kg. Sports teacher.
At 400mh: OG: '96- h, '00- sf; WCh: '93- 8, '95- 8, '97- h, '99/01/03- sf; AsiG: '94- 3, '98- 1/3R, '02- 1; AsiC: '93-8-02-03: 1/2/1/2; WCp: '94- 6, '02- 5. Won Central Asian 1995, 1997, 2003; E.Asian 1997, Af-AsG 2003.
Three KAZ 400mh records 1992-2000.
Progression at 400mh: 1990- 59.53, 1991- 55.77, 1992- 55.43, 1993- 54.53, 1994- 55.81, 1995- 56.23, 1996- 55.94, 1997- 55.90, 1998- 55.33, 1999- 54.70, 2000- 54.50, 2001- 55.37, 2002- 55.07, 2003- 55.24. pb 100mh 14.00 '98.

KENYA

Governing body: Kenya Amateur Athletic Association, PO Box 46722, 00100 Nairobi. Founded 1951.

2003 National Champions: **Men**: 200m: Vincent Mumo 20.65, 400m: Ezra Sambu 45.26, 800m: Joseph Mwengi Mutua 1:45.97, 1500m: Isaac Songok 3:38.6, 5000m: Sammy Kipketer 13:35.65, 10000m: John C Korir 28:12.0, 3000mSt: Ezekiel Kemboi 8:21.7, 400mh: Vincent Mumo 49.9, 20kmW: Julius Sawe 1:22:53. **Women**: 800m: J Busienei 2:07.44, 1500m: Jackline Maranga 4:14.1, 5000m: Edith Masai 15:23.8, 10000m: Salina Kosgei 32:51.4, 2000mSt: Salome Jepchumba 6:27.4, JT: Cecilia Kiplangat 52.79, 20kmW: Grace Wanjiru 1:42:14

Bernard BARMASAI b. 6 May 1974 Keiyo 1.73m 55kg. Keiyo.
At 3000mSt: OG: '00- 4; WCh: '97- 3, '99- 5, '01- 3; CG: '98- 1; AfG: '95- 1; AfCh: '98- 1; WCp: '98- 2. Won GWG 1998, GP (and overall) 1999 (3rd 1997). Kenyan champion 1998-9, 2001. World CC: '97- 6.
World 3000m steeplechase record 1997.
Progress at 3000mSt: 1994- 8:14.18, 1995- 8:08.56, 1996- 8:10.84, 1997- 7:55.72, 1998- 8:00.67, 1999- 7:58.98, 2000- 8:02.76, 2001- 8:05.00, 2002- 8:16.69. pbs: 1500m 3:37.24 '00, 3000m 7:36.40 '97, 5000m 13:23.23, 2000mSt 5:28.31 '95, 10km road 28:08 '97, HMar 62:05 '04, Mar 2:14:49 '04.
After his WR in 1997, Barmasai was world no. one in 1998 and 1999. Won six of seven Golden League steeplechases in 1999, just losing to Ali Ezzine in the last, at Berlin. However, he had lost his chance of sharing the Jackpot when the IAAF determined that he had brought the sport into disrepute by apparently telling Christopher Kosgei not to beat him in Zürich.

Mark BETT b. 22 Dec 1976 1.80m 64kg.
At 5000m: AfCh: 02- 11. 3rd GP 3000m 2002. World CC: '95- 8J. World indoor 10000m best 2002.
Progression at 5000m, 10000m: 1997- 13:15.97, 27:41.14; 1998- 13:22.36, 27:18.66; 1999- 13:14.27, 27:38.64; 2000- 12:55.63, 28:15.98; 2001- 12:58.72, 27:24.68; 2002- 13:00.38, 27:50.29i; 2003- 13:16.42. pbs: 3000m 7:36.66 '01, 2M 8:35.23i '03.

Paul BITOK b. 26 Jun 1970 Kilibwoni 1.73m 58kg. Nandi. Airman (SPTE).
At 5000m: OG: '92- 2, '96- 2; WCh: '93- 8, '97- 13; WJ: '88- 9; AfG: '93- 4; AfCh: '02- 1. At 3000m: WI: '97- 2, '99- 2; WCp: '02- 4. Won GP 5000m 1992, 3000m 2001 (2nd 1999, 2002); GWG 5000m 2001. World Rd Rly team: '92- 1.
Progression at 5000m: 1988- 14:08.8, 1992- 13:08.89, 1993- 13:08.68, 1994- 13:07.30, 1995- 13:16.39, 1996- 13:04.48, 1997- 13:04.74, 1998- 13:14.26, 1999- 13:15.22i/13:31.01; 2000- 13:04.15, 2001- 13:00.10, 2002- 12:58.94, 2003- 13:14.03. pbs: 1500m 3:31.96 '01, 1M 3:56.39i '00, 3:59.6 '96; 2000m 4:54.36 '99, 3000m 7:28.41 '96, 2M 8:13.28i '01, 8:16.44 '99; 10000m 28:20.31i '02, 28:51.6 '95; Rd 10km 28:31 '93.
Ten years after winning his first GP title, he at last broke 13 minutes for 5000m in 2002. Won the Paavo Nurmi Challenge 1997 with 1500m in 3:36.87 followed by 5000m in 13:26.25. Married to **Pauline Konga** (b. 10 Apr 1970), 2nd Olympic 5000m 1996, pbs 3000m 8:37.76 '96 (then KEN record), 5000m 14:47.51 '96, HMar 69:33 '96.

Simon BIWOTT b. 3 Mar 1970.
At Mar: WCh: '99- 9, 01- 2.
Progression at Mar: 1998- 2:12:14, 1999- 2:07:41, 2000- 2:07:42, 2001- 2:09:40, 2002- 2:06:49, 2003- 2:20:54. road pbs: 10km 28:33A '99, HMar 61:27 '99.
6 wins in 14 marathons from 5th in Rome 1998 on debut: Mexico City and Cancun 1998, Berlin (when he was a pacemaker but kept on to win in 2:07:42) and Milan 2000, Paris 2001, Rotterdam 2002. Best 2:07:41 when 4th at Rotterdam 1999 and then 2:06:49 for 2nd at Berlin 2002.

Wilson BOIT KIPKETER b. 6 Oct 1973 1.67m 52kg. Keiyo.
At 3000mSt: OG: '00- 2; WCh: '97- 1, '99- 2; AfG: '99- 2; AfCh: '02- 2; WCp: '02- 1. 2nd GP 1999. World CC: '98- 5.
World 3000m steeplechase record 1997.
Progression at 3000mSt: 1993- 8:39.0A, 1994- 8:27.90A, 1995- 8:33.6A, 1996- 8:11.29, 1997- 7:59.08, 1998- 8:01.05, 1999- 8:07.10, 2000- 8:07.33, 2001- 8:01.73, 2002- 8:00.56, 2003- 8:09.16. pbs: 1500m 3:40.29 '00, 2000m 5:02.1e '97, 3000m 7:33.96 '97, 10000m 28:43.89A '97.

Wilfred Kipkemboi **BUNGEI** b. 24 Jul 1980 Kabirisang, near Kapsabet 1.72m 60kg. Nandi (Kalenjin).
At 800m: WCh: '01- 2; WJ: '98- 2; WI: '03- 3. Won WAF 2003.
Progression at 800m: 1998- 1:47.21, 1999- 1:45.14, 2000- 1:44.23, 2001- 1:42.96, 2002- 1:42.34, 2003- 1:42.52. pbs: 600m 1:14.94 '99, 1000m 2:18.60 '02.

Abrahim Kosgei **CHEBII** b. 23 Dec 1979 Kaptabuk, near Kapsowar 1.72m 63kg. Keiyo.
At 5000m: WCh: '03- 5; Won GP 3000m 2002. World 4k CC: '00- 5, '04- 19.
Progression at 5000m, 10000m: 1999- 13:30.41, 2000- 13:01.9, 2001- 13:12.53, 27:04.20; 2002- 12:58.98, 2003- 12:52.99. pbs: 1500m 3:39.76 '00, 1M 3:55.31 '00, 3000m 7:36.11 '02.
Won 2002 GP 3000m final with 50.68 last lap and outsprinted Gebrselassie in Paris and both Geb and Bekele in Rome in 2003 5000m races.

Abraham CHERONO b. 21 Jul 1980 Iten 1.74m 62kg.
At 3000mSt: WCh: '03- 5; CG: '02- 3; WJ: '98- 2; Af-J: '97- 2. World CC: '98-00-03: 11J/11/12.
Progression at 3000mSt: 1996- 8:51.0A, 1997- 8:43.0A, 1998- 8:32.24, 1999- 8:22.96, 2000- 8:13.22, 2001- 8:16.57, 2002- 8:19.26A, 2003- 8:10.33. pbs: 3000m 7:51.17 '00, 5000m 13:15.7 '00.
Bother of Christopher Kosgei (1 WCh 99) and Saif Saeed Shaheen (1 WCh 03, now Qatar).

Cornelius CHIRCHIR b. 7 Oct 1983 Bomet 1.72m 58kg. Kipsigis.
At 1500m: WJ: '00- 1; WY: '99- 1; WI: '03- 4; 3rd GP 2002. World junior 1500m record 2002.
Progression at 1500m: 1999- 3:44.02, 2000- 3:35.16, 2001- 3:34.53, 2002- 3:30.24, 2003- 3:31.17. pbs: 800m 1:44.98 '01, 1000m 2:18.24i '03, 1M 3:50.40 '03.
Younger brother of William Chirchir. World age-16 best in 2000 (& 1M 3:59.3), improving to 3:34.53 in 2001, when he also ran 1:44.98 for 800m.

William CHIRCHIR b. 6 Feb 1979 Bomet 1.75m 55kg. Kipsigis.
At 800m: WJ: '98- 1. At 1500m: OG: '00- h; WCh: '01- 4; CG: '02- 2; 3rd GP 2001. Won Kenyan 1500m 2001.
Ratified world junior 1500m record 1998.
Progression at 800m, 1500m: 1997- 1:47.08, 3:35.44; 1998- 1:44.69, 3:33.24; 1999- 1:43.33, 3:36.22; 2000- 1:43.84, 3:31.02; 2001- 1:44.02, 3:29.29; 2002- 3:30.88, 2003- 1:45.14, 3:31.70. pbs: 100m 11.1 '97, 1000m 2:14.99 '99, 1M 3:47.94 '00, 3000m 7:55.78 '97, HJ 1.90 '97.
Won Kenyan Schools decathlon in 1997.

Patrick Mutuku **IVUTI** b. 30 Jun 1978 Machakos 1.65m 52kg.
At 10000m: OG: '00- 4. World CC: '96-7-9-00-01-03: 9J/6J/2/4/7/2.
Progression at 5000m, 10000m: 1999- 28:48.0A, 2000- 13:02.68, 27:09.79; 2001- 13:24.48, 28:53.7A; 2002- 13:21.91, 27:05.88. pbs: 3000m 7:38.69 '02, HMar 59:31 '00.

Charles KAMATHI b. 18 May 1978 Mathari, Nyeri 1.65m 51kg. Police corporal.
At 10000m: WCh: '01- 1, '03- 7. World CC: '00-01-02-04: 7/3/5/5; HMar: '02- 9. Won KEN 10000m 2001.

Progression at 5000m, 10000m: 1999- 13:05.29, 26:51.49; 2000- 13:23.24; 2001- 13:05.16, 27:22.58; 2002- 13:02.51, 28:20.98A; 2003- 13:15.33, 27:29.12. pbs: 1500m 3:41.6? '99, 3000m 7:41.89 '03, road: 10M 46:01 '03, HMar 60:22 '02.

Made a sensational debut in European competition when he won at 10000m in 26:51.49 in Brussels in September 1999. He had won in India in July at 3000m 7:56.56 and 5000m 13:45.91 in his only previous races outside Kenya, where he had been 2nd at 5000m and 10,000m in the Kenyan Police Championships (c. 14:01 and 28:57) and had a 5000m best of c.13:43.

Ezekiel KEMBOI Cheboi b. 25 May 1982 Matira, near Kapsowar, Marakwet 1.75m 62kg.
At 3000mSt: WCh: '03- 2; CG: '02- 2; AfG: '03- 1; AfCh: '02- 4; Afr-J: '01- 1. KEN champion 2003.
Progression at 3000mSt: 2001- 8:23.66, 2002- 8:06.65, 2003- 8:02.49. pb 3000m 7:57.11 '01.

Nicholas KEMBOI b. 24 Nov 1983 1.63m 50kg.
At World CC: 2001- 4J, 2002- 7J.
Progression at 5000m, 10000m: 2000- 13:41.5A, 2001- 13:26.36, 2003- 13:01.14, 26:30.03. pb 3000mSt 8:53.5A '02.
After 28:19.77 in June improved to 26:30.03 for second at Brussels in September 2003.

John Kemboi **KIBOWEN** b. 21 Apr 1969 Changach 1.75m 64kg. Nandi. Air Force corporal.
At 5000m: WCh: '01- 4, '03- 4; AfG: '03- 3. At 1500m: WCh: '97- h; CG: '98- 4. World CC 4k: '98-00-01-03-04: 1/1/7/2/32; Rd Rly team: '98- 1. Won KEN 1500m 1998, 4k CC 2003.
Commonwealth 2000m record 1998.
Progression at 1500m, 5000m: 1996- 3:38.6, 13:48.5; 1997- 3:30.44, 1998- 3:30.18, 2000- 3:33.04, 2001- 12:59.97, 2002- 12:58.61, 2003- 12:54.07. pbs: 1M 3:47.88 '97, 2000m 4:48.74 '98, 3000m 7:29.09 '98.
Trained as an aircraft technician 1992-5 before concentrating on running. Missed 1999 season through injury.

Japheth KIMUTAI Butia b. 20 Dec 1978 Lelmokwo, Nandi 1.73m 55kg.
At 800m: OG: '00- sf; WCh: '99- 5, '03- sf; CG: '98- 1, '02- 5; AfG: '99- 1; AfCh: '98- 1; WJ: '94- 2, '96- 4; WCp: '98- 4; AfJ: '95- 1 (1 1500m). 3rd GP 1999. Kenyan champion 1999.
World junior 800m record 1997.
Progression at 800m: 1994- 1:47.6, 1995- 1:47.0, 1996- 1:45.4, 1997- 1:43.64, 1998- 1:42.76, 1999- 1:42.69, 2000- 1:43.87, 2001- 1:45.75, 2002- 1:43.15, 2003- 1:43.71A. pbs: 1000m 2:14.28 '00, 1500m 3:34.14 '00.
A product of St Patrick's High School and the renowned coach Brother Colm O'Connell. Broke Joaquim Cruz's 16 year-old 800m WJR in 1997 and while still a teenager in 1998, ranked as world no.1 and in Zürich broke the three year unbeaten run of Wilson Kipketer. Trains in Iten, but based during the European summer in Tubingen, Germany.

Alex KIPCHIRCHIR b. 26 Nov 1984 1.88m 63kg.
At 800m: WJ: '02- 1.
World junior 1 mile record 2003.
Progression at 1500m: 2002- 3:32.95, 2003- 3:31.42. pbs: 800m 1:45.5A '02, 1M 3:50.25 '03.
World age 18 1500m best 2003.

Eliud KIPCHOGE b. 5 Nov 1984 Kapsisiywa, Nandi 1.67m 52kg.
At 5000m: WCh: '03- 1. World CC: '02-03-04: 5J/1J/4. Won WAF 5000m 2003.
World junior 5000m record 2003.
Progression at 5000m: 2002- 13:13.03, 2003- 12:52.61. pbs: 1500m 3:36.17 '03, 2000m 5:01.1 '03, 3000m 7:30.91 '03.
Kenyan Junior CC champion 2002-03, followed World Junior CC win by winning the World 5000m title, becoming at 18 years 298 days the second youngest world champion.

Sammy KIPKETER b. 29 Sep 1981 Keiyo 1.66m 52kg.
At 5000m: WCh: '01- 7; CG: '02- 1. At 10000m: AfG: '03- 6. 3rd GP 3000m 2000. World CC: '99- 6J, 4k: '00-01-02: 2/4/4; '03- 14. Won KEN 4k CC 2002.
Official world junior record 3000m 1999. World road bests 5km 13:00 2000 & 2001, 10km 27:18 '01, 27:11 '02.
Progression at 5000m, 10000m: 1999- 12:58.10, 2000- 12:54.07, 2001- 12:59.34, 2002- 12:56.99, 26:49.38; 2003- 12:52.33, 27:13.42. pbs: 1500m 3:40.0A '01, 2000m 5:00.0e '99, 3000m 7:33.62 '01.
World age-17 bests at 3000m and 5000m 1999.

Raymond KIPKOECH Chemwelo b. 19 Apr 1978 Marakwet.
Progression at Mar: 1999- 2:16:43, 2000- 2:10:52, 2001- 2:12:41, 2002- 2:06:47, 2003- 2:09:21.
In 2002 he won his sixth and seventh marathons: Enschede and Berlin, when he improved his best by 4 minutes.

Luke KIPKOSGEI b. 27 Nov 1975 Iten 1.76m 57kg.
At 3000m: WI: '03- 3. Won GWG 5000m 1998, GP 3000m 2000 (3rd 2001). World 4kCC: '02- 2.
Progression at 5000m, 10000m: 1996- 13:15.00, 27:26.12; 1997- 13:22.68, 27:29.44; 1998- 12:57.32, 27:22.54; 1999- 13:00.83, 2000- 12:56.50, 27:57.11; 2001- 13:02.25, 27:12.37; 2002- 13:10.41, 27:47.69; 2003- 13:06.92. pbs: 1500m 3:35.48 '98, 1M 3:56.4+ '98, 2000m 4:52.82 '98, 3000m 7:27.59 '98, 2M 8:16.57i '03, 8:17.53 '98.
Ran 27:26.12 on track debut at 10000m in Melbourne, December 1996.

Benjamin KIPKURUI b. 28 Dec 1980 Molo 1.74m 57kg. Kipsigis.
At 1500m (/800m): WJ: '98- 2; AfG: '99- (4), '03- 3; Af-J: '97- 1/1.
World junior records 1000m and 1500m 1999.
Progression at 800m, 1500m: 1997- 1:49.3, 3:44.17; 1998- 1:44.71, 3:35.35, 1999- 1:44.56, 3:33.16; 2000- 1:46.30, 3:30.73; 2001- 1:44.80, 3:30.67; 2002- 3:37.17,

2003- 3:32.42. pbs: 1000m 2:15.00 '99, 1M 3:49.34 '00, 2000m 5:00.21 '03.
World age-17 bests at 800m and 1500m in 1998.

William KIPLAGAT b. 21 Jun 1972.
At Mar: WCh: '03- dnf.
Progression at Mar: 1998- 2:17:14, 1999- 2:06:50, 2000- 2:09:06, 2001- 2:09:55, 2002- 2:11:25, 2003- 2:07:42. pbs: road 10km 28:02 '99, HMar 59:51 '00.
Improved from 2:14:10 to 2:06:50 when third at Amsterdam 1999. Won Rotterdam marathon 2003. Started running seriously at age 25 in 1997.

Josephat KIPRONO b. 12 Dec 1973 Eldoret 1.72m 52kg. FILA, Italy.
At Mar: WCh: '01- dnf. At HMar: WCh: '96- 2.
Kenyan marathon record to win at Berlin 1999.
Progression at Mar: 1998- 2:07:27, 1999- 2:06:44, 2000- 2:07:29, 2001- 2:06:50, 2002- 2:09:51, 2003- 2:07:53. pbs: 5000m 13:50.37 '95, 10000m 28:57.1 '93, Road: 10km 28:39 '96, 15km 43:46 '96, HMar 60:27 '98, 59:46sh '96; 3000mSt 8:42.2 '95.
Second in 1996 Stramilano half marathon, when course was short by 49m. Marathon debut with 4th at Rotterdam (2:09:11), then 2nd Berlin 1998. He won the Milennium Marathon in Rome on 1 Jan 2000 and was second in Chicago 2000. He won at Rotterdam 2001 in 2:06:50 to become the first man to run two sub 2:07s and his 2nd at Amsterdam 2001 in 2:07:06 was the fastest third best. He was second at Rotterdam in 2003 in 2:07:53. His half-brother **Isaac Kiprono** has a marathon pb of 2:09:59 '01 and another brother **Luke Kibet** 2:10:18 '01.

Vincent KIPSOS b. 22 Jun 1976.
Progression at Mar: 2001- 2:13:51, 2002- 2:06:52, 2003- 2:09:42.
Won Rome Marathon 2002, 3rd at Reims 2001 and Berlin 2002.

Justus KOECH b. 7 Apr 1980 1.75m 60kg.
At 800m: WCh: '03- 6; AfG: '03- 3.
Progression at 800m: 2002- 1:46.10A, 2003- 1:44.16A. pb 1000m 2:19.83 '03.

Paul Kipsiele **KOECH** b. 10 Nov 1981 1.70m 60kg.
At 3000mSt: AfG: '03- 2.
Progression at 3000mSt: 2001- 8:15.92, 2002- 8:05.44, 2003- 7:57.42. pbs: 1500m 3:38.87 '01, 3000m 7:42.14 '01, 5000m 13:46.06 '01.

Paul Kipsilgich **KOECH** b. 25 Jun 1969 Burnt Forest, Uasin Gishu 1.70m 60kg. Army captain.
At 10000m: OG: '96- 6; WCh: '97- 4; AfG: '95- 3.
At 5000m: AfCh: '96- 1. 3rd GP 5000m 1996 & 1997. World CC: '95-6-7-8-9-00-03: 29/4/4/2/6/6/5; HMar: '98- 1; Rd Rly team: '98- 1. Won Kenyan 10000m 1997, CC 1997-8.
World road best 10M 1997.
Progression at 5000m, 10000m: 1995- 13:45.27, 27:50.06; 1996- 13:00.22, 26:56.78; 1997- 12:56.29, 26:36.26; 1998- 13:02.61, 26:47.89; 1999- 13:01.72, 27:10.38. pbs: 2000m 5:00.8+ '97, 3000m 7:33.79 '97, 2M 8:17.01 '99; Road: 10M 44:45 '97, HMar 60:01 '98, Mar 2:07:07 '03.
Uncle of Sally Barsosio. Triple World Champs gold in 1998 with half marathon, and team road and cross-country. Knee injury 2001-02. Second Chicago 2003 on marathon debut.

Daniel Kipngetich **KOMEN** b. 17 May 1976 Mwen 1.70m 60kg. Keiyo.
At 5000m (10000m): WCh: '97- 1, '99- 5; CG: '94- (9), '98- 1; AfCh: '98- 1; WJ: '94- 1 (1); WCp: '98- 1. Won overall & 5000m GP 1996. World CC: '94- 2J, '98- 2 4k. Won Kenyan 5000m 1997.
World records: 3000m 1996, 5000m 1997, world best 2 miles 1996 (8:03.54) and 1997. WIR 3000m 7:24.90 '98 and 5000m 12:51.48 '98. World junior records 1500m, 5000m 1995. Commonwealth & Kenyan records 2000m 1998, 3000m 1996, 5000m (4) 1996-7, Kenyan 1500m & 1M 1997.
Progression at 1500m, 5000m, 10000m: 1993- 13:58.30, 1994- 13:31.10, 28:29.74; 1995- 3:34.63, 12:56.15, 28:12.79; 1996- 3:34.17, 12:45.09; 1997- 3:29.46, 12:39.74; 1998- 3:30.49, 12:51.48i/12:54.82; 1999- 3:35.42, 12:55.16; 2000- 3:43.5A, 13:01.78; 2001- 13:01.98, 2002- 27:38.32, 2003- 13:28.56. pbs: 1M 3:46.38 '97, 2000m 4:51.30 '98, 3000m 7:20.67 '96, 2M 7:58.61 '97, 3000mSt 8:54.5 '94.
After a series of near misses at world records, took 4.44 sec off Noureddine Morceli's 3000m record, running under 60 secs for each 400m, at Rieti on 1 Sep 1996. In 1997 he ran first sub-8 minute 2 miles at Hechtel and lopped 2.12 secs off Gebrselassie's 9-day old 5000m world record at Brussels. Former high jumper and soccer goalkeeper.

John Cheruiyot **KORIR** b. 13 Dec 1981 Kiramwok, Bomet district 1.72m 57kg. Army private.
At 10000m: OG: '00- 5; WCh: '01- 8, '03- 5; CG: '02- 4; AfCh: '02- 2. World CC: '00-01-03-04: 3J/28/6/11; HMar: '03- 4. Won Kenyan 10000m 2000, 2003; CC 2001, 2003.
Progression at 5000m,10000m: 1999- 13:24.22, 27:38.86; 2000- 13:09.58, 27:24.75; 2001- 13:19.58, 27:49.34A; 2002- c.13:24+, 26:52.87; 2003- 13:17.7, 27:17.24. pbs: 3000m 7:43.35 '00, HMar 61:02 '03.
Ran fastest ever 10,000m at high altitude, 27:48.42, to win 2000 Kenyan title.

Paul Kipketer **KORIR** b. 15 Jul 1977 Kipkoror, Nandi District 1.80m 64kg. Nandi.
At 1500m: WCh: '03- 2; AfG: '03- 1; WI: '04- 1.
Won WAF 1500m 2003, Kenyan 800m 2001
Progression at 800m, 1500m: 1999- 1:47.6, 2000- 1:44.21, 3:41.3A; 2001-1:45.02, 3:41.3A; 2002- 1:45.55, 3:39.18; 2003- 3:30.72. pbs: 1000m 2:17.07i '04, 2:18.2 '03; 1M 3:48.17 '03.

Sammy KORIR b. 12 Dec 1971. FILA Milan.
At HMar: WCh: '99- 11.
Progression at Mar: 1996- 2:12:33, 1997- 2:08:02, 1998- 2:08:13, 1999- 2:08:27, 2001- 2:08:14, 2002- 2:08:10, 2003- 2:04:56. pb HMar 60:15 '98.
Second, just one second behind Paul Tergat's world record at Berlin 2003. Before that he had

won seven of his 14 marathons: Florence and Cancun 1996, Amsterdam 1997 and 1998, Turin 1999; Beppu and San Diego 2002; 3rd Rotterdam Marathon and Great North Run 1997.

Japhet KOSGEI b. 28 Dec 1968. 1.65m 52kg. FILA, Milan.
Progression at Mar: 1998- 2:09:59, 1999- 2:07:09, 2000- 2:07:15. 2001- 2:09:19, 2003- 2:07:39. pb HMar 60:01 '99.
Won first four marathons: Turin and Venice 1998, Rotterdam 1999, Tokyo 2000; then dnf London and 2nd New York 2000 & 2001, 5th London 2001. Returned to win Lake Biwa marathon 2003. Also won 1999 Lisbon half marathon in 60:01.

Paul KOSGEI Malakwen b. 22 Apr 1978 Marakwet 1.75m 57kg.
At 3000mSt: WCh: '99- 7. At 10000m: WCh: '01- 7; CG: '02- 2; AfCh: '02- 1. At 5000m: WCp: '02- 2. World CC: '97- 3J, 4k: '98-9-00: 3/2/3; 12k: '01- 5; HMar: '02- 1; Rd Rly team: '98- 1. Won KEN 10000m 2002, 4km CC 1999.
World junior record 3000m steeplechase 1997.
Progression at 5000m, 10000m, 3000mSt: 1997- 8:07.69, 1998- 8:07.86, 1999- 8:07.13, 2000- 13:05.44, 27:38.22, 8:29.57; 2001- 13:06.29, 27:51.87A; 2002- 13:20.92, 27:44.14A; 2003- 27:21.56. pbs: 1500m: 3:42.7A '00, 2000m 5:03.1+ '00, 3000m 7:39.15 '00, HMar 59:58 '02, 2000mSt 5:19.78 '98.
Won his heat at 1999 World Champs in 8:10.34, the fastest ever time in a preliminary round, but stopped steeplechasing in 2000 due to a knee injury. Ran world road best 10km 27:03 in 2000, and won the World Half marathon title in his first major race at the distance followed by the fastest ever 10000m at high altitude, 27:44.14 to win the Kenyan title, and Great North Run half marathon win in 59:58 in 2002.

Reuben KOSGEI b. 2 Aug 1979 Kapsabet 1.70m 55kg.
At 3000mSt: OG: '00- 1; WCh: '01- 1, '03- dnf; WJ: '98- 1; Afr-J: '97- 1. Kenyan champion 2000.
Progression at 3000mSt: 1998- 8:23.76, 1999- 8:12.33, 2000- 8:03.92, 2001- 7:57.29, 2002- 8:05.87, 2003- 8:09.65. pbs: 1500m 3:37.24 '00, 3000m 7:41.86i '00, 10000m 29:09.6A '02.
After his World Championship success in 2001, he improved his best ever time to 8:03.22 at Zürich and to 7:57.29, fourth fastest of all-time at the event, at Brussels, behind Brahim Boulami.

James KWALIA b. 12 Jun 1984 1.71m 59kg.
At 3000m: WY: '01- 3.
World junior 1 mile record 2003.
Progression at 5000m: 2001- 13:44.3, 2002- 13:14.34, 2003- 12:54.58. pbs: 1500m 3:38.67 '03, 1M 3:50.39 '03, 2000m 4:59.11 '03, 3000m 7:35.53 '03.

Bernard LAGAT b. 12 Dec 1974 Kapsabet 1.75m 61kg. Studied business management at Washington State University, USA. Nandi.
At 1500m: OG: '00- 3; WCh: '01- 2; WI: '03- 2; AfCh: '02- 1; WUG: '99- 1; WCp: '02- 1; 2nd GP 1999-2000-02. At 3000m: WI: '01- 6, '04- 1. Won KEN 1500m 2002, NCAA 5000m 1999 (and indoor 1M/3000m).
Commonwealth and KEN 1500m record 2001.
Progression at 1500m: 1996- 3:37.7A, 1997- 3:41.19, 1998- 3:34.48, 1999- 3:30.56, 2000- 3:28.51, 2001- 3:26.34, 2002- 3:27.91, 2003- 3:30.55. pbs: 800m 1:46.00 '03, 1000m 2:18.70 '00, 1M 3:47.28 '01, 2000m 4:55.49 '99, 3000m 7:33.51 '00, 5000m 13:19.14 '02.
After impressive results he gave up his final year of scholastic eligibility (as under NCAA rules no payments can be received) at his university in order to compete (for money) in the 1999 Grand Prix Final, in which he was 2nd. He was 2nd to Hicham El Guerrouj six times in 2001, including his 3:26.34 at Brussels for 2nd on the world all-time list, and six times in 2002. Withdrew from 2003 Worlds after testing positive for EPO, but this was later repudiated.

Martin LEL b. 29 Oct 1978.
World HMar: '03- 1.
Progression at Mar: 2002- 2:10:02, 2003- 2:10:30. pbs: 15km 43:26 '03, HMar 60:10 '03.
Second in Venice on marathon debut 2003, 3rd Boston and 1st New York 2003. Ran exclusively on the roads in 2003, and winning all three half marathons.

Benjamin LIMO b. 23 Aug 1974 Kaptagat, Keiyo 1.78m 65kg. Army engineer.
At 5000m: WCh: '99- 2; CG: '02- 2; AfG: '03- 7; AfCh: '02- 2. Won GP 3000m 1999. World 4k CC: '98-9-01-03: 4/1/3/3; Rd Rly team: '98- 1. Won KEN 5000m 2002.
Progression at 5000m: 1998- 13:07.38, 1999- 12:55.86, 2000- 12:55.82, 2001- 12:59.53, 2002- 12:57.24, 2003- 12:54.99. pbs: 1500m 3:37.59 '99, 2000m 4:59.2e '99, 3000m 7:28.67 '99; road 10km 28:00 '02.
Only began running seriously in November 1997. Has great finishing speed.

Felix LIMO b. 22 Aug 1980 Nandi 1.74m 58kg.
World best for 15km road with 41:29 at Nijmegen 2001.
Progression at 10000m, Mar: 1998- 28:48A, 1999- 28:23.30, 2000- 27:04.54, 2001- 27:26.86, 2003- 2:06:42, 2004- 2:06:14. pbs: 3000m 7:40.67 '01, 5000m 13:16.42 '01, HMar 61:15 '02, Mar 2:06:42 '03.
Made second fastest ever marathon debut when 2nd at Amsterdam in 2003. Won Rotterdam 2004.

Richard Kipkemei **LIMO** b. 18 Nov 1980 Cheptigit 1.67m 53kg. Kalenjin.
At 5000m: OG: '00- 10; WCh: '01- 1, '03- 7; CG: '98- 3; AfG: '99- 6. At 3000mSt: AfCh: '98- 2. World CC: '98-9-02-03-04: 2J/2J/4/4/32. Won KEN 5000m 2001, CC 2002.
World junior records 3000m 1998, 2M 1999.
Progression at 5000m, 10000m: 1998- 13:21.59, 1999- 12:58.15, 2000- 12:58.70, 2001- 12:56.72,

27:25.27; 2002- 12:57.52, 26:50.20; 2003- 13:01.13, 26:56.63. pbs: 1500m 3:43.3A '02, 2000m 5:00.6 '99, 3000m 7:32.23 '01, 2M 8:13.47 '99, 3000mSt 8:20.67 '98.

Simon MAINA Munyi b. 18 Mar 1978 Nyeri 1.77m 52kg. Kikuyu. Lives in Japan.
At 10000m: CG: '98- 1; AfG: '99- 4. Won JPN 5000m 1997-8, KEN 10000m 1998.
Progression at 5000m, 10000m: 1997- 13:33.1, 27:36.5; 1998- 13:10.71, 27:21.14; 1999- 13:15.88, 27:18.74; 2000- 13:19.60, 27:18.95; 2001- 13:15.92, 27:56.82; 2002- 13:19.44, 27:35.58; 2003- 13:24.68, 27:22.29. Rd pbs: 10M 45:29 '01; HMar 60:48 '00.
Married to **Anne Wamucii** (b. 29 Sep 1978) pbs: 5000m 15:20.33 '99, 10000m 32:11.28 '99, HMar 69:21 '97.

Benjamin MAIYO b. 6 Oct 1978 Trans Nzoia 1.75m 58kg.
At 10000m: WCh: '99- 7; AfG: '99- 5; AfCh: '02- 3.
Progression at 5000m, 10000m: 1998- 13:18.98, 27:34.38; 1999- 13:02.38, 28:01.8A; 2000- 13:02.28, 28:28.7A; 2001- 13:05.43, 27:07.55; 2002- 13:02.95, 28:06.0A; 2003- 13:14.75. pbs: 1500m 3:42.30 '99, 2000m 5:01.9+ '00; 3000m 7:32.36 '00, HMar 61:59 '02.

Kipkirui MISOI b. 23 Dec 1978 Bomet 1.77m 59kg.
At 3000mSt: CG: '98- 3; WJ: '96- 2; AfG: '99- 1. World CC: '98- 8 4k.
World junior record 3000m steeplechase 1998.
Progression at 3000mSt: 1995- 8:56.0A, 1996- 8:33.31, 1997- 8:16.76, 1998- 8:09.46, 1999- 8:08.62, 2000- 8:07.21, 2001- 8:01.69, 2002- 8:13.47, 2003- 8:07.74. pbs: 1500m 3:39.17 '98, 1M 4:01.12 '01, 3000m 7:40.93 '00, 5000m 13:26.83 '98.

Joseph Mwengi MUTUA b. 10 Dec 1978 1.70m 58kg.
At 800m: OG: '00- h; WJ: '96- 1; CG: '02- 2; WI: '04- 6. Won KEN 800m 2002-03.
Progression at 800m: 1995- 1:48.3A, 1996- 1:46.3A, 1997- 1:48.0A, 1998- 1:47.81, 1999- 1:48.8A, 2000- 1:45.49A, 2001- 1:43.63, 2002- 1:43.33, 2003- 1:43.52. pbs: 400m 46.6A '02, 600m 1:13.72 '03, 1000m 2:17.55 '02, 1500m 3:43.17 '99.

Noah Kiprono **NGENY** b. 2 Nov 1978 Kabenas 1.82m 68kg.
At 1500m: OG: '00- 1; WCh: '99- 2; WI: '01- 3; WJ: '96- 8 (tripped on final lap). Won GP 1999-2000, KEN 1500m 1999-2000, GWG 1M 2001.
Records: World and two records 1000m 1999, Commonwealth: 1500m (3), 1M 1999-2000.
Progression at 1500m: 1996- 3:42.44, 1997- 3:32.91, 1998- 3:30.34, 1999- 3:28.73/3:28.6+u, 2000- 3:28.12, 2001- 3:31.94, 2002- 3:33.02, 2003- 3:33.96. pbs: 800m 1:44.49 '00, 1000m 2:11.96 '99, 1M 3:43.40 '99, 2000m 4:50.08 '99, 3000m 7:35.46 '00.
Tripped on the first lap in the final of the 1996 World Juniors, sprinted to the front and led for three laps before being tripped again with 200m to go and losing his rhythm. Came through in 1997 to run world junior records. Although beaten three times by Hicham El Guerrouj, he had a wonderful season in 1999, following his World silver medal at 1500m, with the world record for 1000m (beating Seb Coe's 1981 mark) and a win in the Grand Prix Final 1500m. Then he ended El Guerrouj's winning run with Olympic gold in 2000. Brother of **Philip Kibitok** (b. 23 Mar 1971) pb 800m 1:43.55 '96.

Daniel NJENGA b. 7 May 1976 1.76m 61kg.
World Junior record when winning Japanese 3000m steeplechase title in 1994.
Progression at 3000mSt, Mar: 1993- 8:41.46, 1994- 8:19.21, 1995- 8:27.03, 2:20:28; 1996- 8:28.67, 1997- 8:30.50, 1998- 8:32.14, 1999- 2:11:49, 2001- 2:20:58, 2002- 2:06:16, 2003- 2:07:41, 2004- 2:08:43. pbs: 1500m 3:43.43 '94, 5000m 13:36.55 '96, 10000m 27:51.83 '02, HMar 60:39 '96.
Based in Japan. Huge breakthough when 2nd at Chicago 2002 in his seventh marathon, and was third there a year later. Won Tokyo 2004.

Julius NYAMU b. 1 Dec 1977 Nyeri 1.78m 66kg.
Progression at 3000mSt: 2001- 8:07.59, 2002- 8:11.13, 2003- 8:09.06. pb 2000mSt 5:25.47 '03.

Robert RONO b. 11 Oct 1974 1.72m 60kg
At 1500m: AfG: '03- 2. World Military 1500m champion 2002.
Progression at 1500m: 2000- 3:45.2A, 2001- 3:31.49, 2002- 3:30.99, 2003- 3:31.33. pbs: 800m 1:47.73 '02, 1M 3:50.98 '03, 2000m 4:57.76 '03.

Rodgers ROP b. 16 Feb 1976.
Progression at Mar: 2001- 2:09:51, 2002- 2:08:07, 2003- 2:11:11. Road pbs: 10km 28:01 '01, 10M 45:56 '01, HMar 60:45 '02, 25k 1:13:44 '01 (world best).
After third in New York 2001, achieved a unique double in 2002 by being first to win Boston (2:09:02) and New York (2:08:07) in the same year. 2nd New York 2003.

Laban ROTICH 20 Jan 1969 Mosoriot 1.63m 45kg. Fireman in Kenyan Air Force. Nandi.
At 1500m: OG: '96- 4; WCh: '97- 11, '99- 6, '01- sf; CG: '98- 1; AfCh: '98- 1, '02- 2; WI: '99-01-04: 2/4/3; WCp: '98- 1. 2nd GP 1998, 3rd 1996 & 1999. Won Kenyan 1500m 1997.
KEN records 1500m (3) 1996-7, 1000m & 1M 1997.
Progression at 800m, 1500m: 1995- 3:39.85, 1996- 1:45.8A, 3:31.06; 1997- 1:44.47, 3:30.13; 1998- 1:43.65, 3:29.91; 1999- 3:31.60, 2000- 1:48.14, 3:32.93; 2001- 3:31.38, 2002- 1:48.40, 3:32.82; 2003- 3:33.91. pbs: 1000m 2:14.43 '97, 1M 3:47.65 '97, 2000m 4:56.09i '99, 4:57.63 '96, 3000m 7:47.97i '04, 2M 8:28.25i '03.
World high altitude best 1500m 3:33.1 '98.

Michael Kosgei **ROTICH** b. 26 Oct 1982.
At Mar: WCh: '03- 8.
Progression at Mar: 2002- 2:08:59, 2003- 2:06:33, 2004- 2:09:07. pbs: 5000m 13:53.0 '01, 10km 28:38A '02, HMar 61:30 '03.

Second in Milan marathon in December 2002 and then won the Paris half marathon in March and the Paris marathon in April 2003 to move to eighth on the world all-time list.

Evans RUTTO b. 8 Apr 1978 Marakwet 1.68m 56kg.
World CC: 1999- 5; HMar: '01- 6.
Progression at 5000m, 10000m, Mar: 1999- 13:24.84, 28:06.60; 2000- 13:02.71, 27:21.32; 2001- 13:28.25, 2003- 2:05:50. pbs: 2000m 5:02.3+ '99; 3000m 7:36.38 '00; Road: 10km 28:19 '02, 15km 43:15 '01; 10M 46:26 '01, HMar 60:30 '01.
Ran fastest ever debut marathon when he won at Chicago 2003.

Isaac Kiprono **SONGOK** b. 5 Apr 1984 Kaptel, near Kapasbet, Nadi region 1.70m 54kg.
At 1500m: WCh: '03- 9; WJ: '02- 7; WY: '01- 1; Kenyan champion 2003. World 4k CC: '04- 7.
World U18 records 1M (3:54.56) & 2000m (4:56.86, also U20 record) 2001.
Progression at 1500m: 2001- 3:35.55, 2002- 3:34.20, 2003- 3:31.54. pbs: 1M 3:54.56 '01, 2000m 4:56.86 '01, 5000m 13:37.3 '01.

Wilberforce Kapkeny **TALEL** b. 10 Jan 1980 1.70m 65kg. Kenyan Navy.
At 10000m: WCh: '03- 8; CG: '02- 1. World CC: '00-02-04: 5/3/10.
Progression at 5000m, 10000m: 1999- 29:33.4A, 2000- 13:13.15, 27:36.48; 2001- 13:25.59, 28:02.30; 2002- 27:45.39, 2003- 27:33.60. pbs: 3000m 7:55.82 '02, HMar 61:17 '02.

Paul TERGAT b. 17 Jun 1969 Kabarnet, Barango 1.82m 62kg. Air Force sergeant (SPTE). Tugen.
At 10000m: OG: '96- 2, '00- 2; WCh: '95- 3, '97- 2, '99- 2. World HMar: '92-4-9-00: 5/11/1/1. World CC: '93-4-5-6-7-8-9-00: 10/4/1/1/1/1/1/3. Won Kenyan CC 1992, 1995-6.
World records: 10,000m 1997, marathon 2003. World road best 15km 1994 (42:13), half marathon 59:17 '98 and 59:06 '00 (40m dh at Lisbon). 58:51 at Milano 1996 was on a course 49m short. Two Kenyan marathon record 2002-03.
Progression at 5000m, 10000m, Mar: 1991- 29:46.8A, 1992- 13:48.64, 1993- 13:20.16, 27:18.43; 1994- 13:15.07, 27:23.89; 1995- 13:07.49, 27:14.08; 1996- 12:54.72, 26:54.41; 1997- 12:49.87, 26:27.85; 1998- 12:58.74, 26:44.44; 1999- 12:55.37, 27:10.08; 2000- 12:55.18, 27:03.87; 2001- 2:08:15, 2002- 2:05:48, 2003- 2:04:55. pbs: 1500m 3:42.3 '96, 1M 3:58.4 '96, 2000m 4:57.4 '96, 3000m 7:28.70 '96, HMar 59:06 '00, 58:51sh '96.
A former basketball player, he made a sensational impact when he won the Kenyan CC title in 1992; he had however to miss his first run outside Kenya at the World CC Champs through injury. Now has a record five successive World Cross-country titles. Won the Stramilano half marathon each year 1994-9 and unbeaten at that distance 1995-2000. On the track he has won four silver medals and a bronze behind the great Haile Gebrselassie in global 10,000m races. He was second in his first three marathons: London (2:08:15), Chicago (2:08:56) 2001 and London (2:05:48) 2002 and then fourth at Chicago (2:06:18) 2002 and London 2003, before his world record 2:04:55 at Berlin 2003.

William Oloonkishu **YIAMPOY** b. 17 May 1974 Emarti, near Kilgoris 1.83m 70kg. Masai.
At 800m: OG: '00- sf; WCh: '01- 4; AfCh: '02- 2; WI: '04- 5. Kenyan & GWG champion 2001.
Progression at 800m: 1999- 1:44.38, 2000- 1:44.23, 2001- 1:43.00, 2002- 1:42.91, 2003- 1:45.01A. pbs: 1000m 2:14.41 '99, 1500m 3:34.12 '01.
Joined Kenya Police 1990, began running 1996.

Women

Joyce CHEPCHUMBA Koech b. 6 Nov 1970 Kericho 1.60m 52kg. Kenyan postal service.
At Mar: OG: '96- dnf, '00- 3; WCh: '03- 7. World HMar: '97-8-9-01: 4/6/5/18; CC: '94- 18.
Kenyan marathon record 1997.
Progression at Mar: 1995- 2:33:51, 1996- 2:29:38, 1997- 2:26:51, 1998- 2:23:57, 1999- 2:23:22, 2000- 2:24:02, 2001- 2:24:12, 2002- 2:25:56, 2003- 2:26:06. pbs: 800m 2:11.2 '94, 1500m 4:36.3A '91, 3000m 9:23.26 '95, 5000m 15:26.19 '00, 10000m 32:07.50 '99, road 5km 15:52 '94, 10km 32:19 '96, 15km 49:21 '97, 10M 54:27 '95, HMar 68:18 '00.
Six major wins in 20 marathons: London 1997 and 1999 (when she won the then biggest ever prize of $230,000) (also 2nd 1996, 3rd 1998, 2000-01, 6th 2002), Chicago 1998 and 1999, Tokyo 2000 (2nd 1997), New York 2002 (4th on marathon debut 1995, 3rd 1996, 4th 2001, 6th 2003). Last 16 marathons all under 2:30. Won Great North Run 1999. Has a training base in Dettmond, Germany. Son born in 1991.

Susan CHEPKEMEI Kapkama b. 25 Jun 1975 West Pokot Region 1.64m 48kg.
At 5000m: WCp: '02- 5; at 10000m: CG: '02- 2; AfCh: '02- 1. World HMar: '00-01-02-03: 2/2/2/8; CC: '98-9-00-01: 12/5/3/3; Rd Rly team: '98- 2. Won Kenyan 10,000m 2001-02.
Progression at 10000m, Mar: 1995- 34:57.40A, 1996- 34:21.0A, 1997- 34:27.2A, 1998- 33:30.6A, 2:28:19, 1999- 33:01.2A, 2:26:38; 2000- 33:20.6A, 2001- 33:03.7A, 2:25:12; 2002- 31:32.04, 2:23:19; 2003- 2:23:12. pbs: 1500m 4:20.6A '01, 3000m 8:43.95 '01, 5000m 14:55.27 '01; Road: 10km 31:52 '01, 15km 47:54 '01, 10M 51:23 '01, HMar 65:44 '01.
Second in her first two marathons: Berlin 1998 and Rotterdam 1999; then won Rotterdam and 2nd New York 2001, 4th London 2002 and 2003. World best for half marathon on the slightly downhill Lisbon course in 2001; also won Great North Run 2001. Made big improvement on the track in 2001. Based in the Netherlands.

Salina KOSGEI b. 16 Nov 1976 Simotwo, Keiyo district 1.62m 58kg. Corporal in Kenya Prisons Service.
At 10000m: WCh: '03- 19; CG: '02- 1. At 800m:

CG: '94- 5. Won Kenyan 10000m 2003.
Progression at 5000m, 10000m: 1998- 15:50.43, 2002- 15:20.17, 31:27.83; 2003- 15:01.79, 32:09.15. pbs: 800m 2:03.38 '94, 1500m 4:19.9 '98, 3000m 9:34.35 '02, HMar 71:56 '03, Mar 2:24:32 '04.
Won four successive Kenyan Schools titles at heptathlon, as well as 200m, 800m and on both winning relay teams in her final year. Married (1995) Barnabas Kinyor (3rd Commonwealth 400mh 1994). Children born 1996 and 2001.

Tegla LOROUPE Chepkite b. 9 May 1973 Kapsoit, West Pokot 1.56m 48kg. Pokot. Kenyan Post & Telecommunication Corporation.
At 10000m (Mar): OG: '92- 17, '96- 6, '00- 5 (13); WCh: '93- 4, '95- 3, '97- 6, '99- 3. World HMar: '93-7-8-9: 3/1/1/1; CC: '89- 28J, '90- 16J. Won GWG 10000m 1994, 1998; KEN 10000m 1995, 2000.
World records: marathon 1998 and 1999, 1 hour 1998, 20000m 2000, 25000m 2002, 30000m 2003; three African marathon records 1997-9, KEN records: 3000m 1999, 5000m 2000, 10000m 1993 & 1999, Marathon (3) 1994-8.
Progress at 5000m, 10000m, Mar: 1989- 34:36.1A, 1990- 35:06.0A, 1991- 35:02.8A, 1992- 31:34.30mx/ 32:34.07, 1993- 15:08.03, 31:21.20; 1994- 15:22.54, 31:52.39, 2:27:37; 1995- 15:08.86, 31:17.66, 2:28:06; 1996- 15:08.79, 31:23.22, 2:28:37; 1997- 15:19.78, 31:20.53, 2:22:07; 1998- 14:47.77, 32:15.44, 2:20:47; 1999- 14:49.12, 30:32.03, 2:20:43; 2000- 14:45.95, 30:37.26, 2:24:33; 2001- 15:09.31, 31:50.97, 2:26:10; 2002- 15:04.48, 2:29:04, 2003- 15:32.22, 32:47.59, 2:33:48. pbs: 1500m 4:29.39 '90, 3000m 8:30.95 '00, 1Hr 18340m '98, 20000m 1:05:26.6 '00, 25000m 1:27:05 '02, 30000m 1:45:50.0 '03; road 15km 48:52 '95, HMar 67:12 '96.
Ten wins in 22 marathons. She won on début in New York in 1994 and again in 1995; 2nd Boston 1996 and won at Rotterdam each year 1997-9, the first was the second fastest ever, and the second a new world best time although she was controversially paced throughout by men. She was also illegally paced by a lapped runner in a 1 hour race at Borgholzhausen in 1998 but this was ratified by the IAAF as a world record. In 1999 she won a World bronze at 10,000m and showed her speed by improving her pre-season 3000m pb of 9:01.62 to 8:33.36. Then she had an amazing 22 days in September-October, in which she ran on successive weekends: won HMar 69:20, world marathon record 2:20:43 in Berlin, won World HMar 68:48, 2nd Great North Run 69:35. Won London Marathon 2000.

Faith MACHARIA b. 9 Feb 1976 Nyeri 1.65m 55kg.
At 800m: WCh: '01- 4, '03- sf; CG: '02- sf; AfG: '03- 4; won KEN 800m 2001-02.
Kenyan 1000m record 2001.
Progression at 800m, 1500m: 1996- 2:05.51, 1997- 2:03.01, 4:18.96; 1998- 2:04.4, 1999- 2:01.33, 4:08.04; 2000- 2:01.09, 4:09.57; 2001- 1:58.34, 4:16.96; 2002- 2:00.74, 2003- 1:59.23. pb 1000m 2:35.39 '01.

Leah MALOT b. 7 Jun 1972 Keiyo 1.68m 46kg. Telkom Kenya.
At 10000m: WCh: '87- h, 99- dnf; AfG: '87-99-03: 1/3/3; AfCh: '02- 2. World CC: '98-9-00-01-02: 8/9/6/6/11; HMar: '98- 10; Rd Rly team: '98- 2. 2nd GP 3000m 2000.
Kenyan records: 3000m 1999, 5000m 2000.
Progression at 5000m, 10000m: 1987- 33:58.15, 1988- 38:09.8A, 1989- 36:40.4A, 1994- 35:53.2A, 1996- 16:20.91A, 1997- 15:10.12, 32:09.37, 1998- 15:09.75, 32:04.64; 1999- 15:03.75, 31:31.73; 2000- 14:39.83, 30:57.70; 2001- 14:56.95, 31:41.74; 2002- 15:00.88, 32:00.78; 2003- 15:13.26, 32:12.91. pbs: 800m 2:04.07 '00, 1000m 2:42.77 '99, 1500m 4:10.17 '99, 3000m 8:35.74 '99; Rd: 15km 49:06 '99, 10M 53:11 '98, HMar 69:43 '01.
Won African 10,000m title at age 15 in 1987. Ran for Kenyan World CC team in 1987 and 1994 before emerging in world class in 1997. Daughter Sheila born August 1995.

Jackline MARANGA b. 16 Dec 1977 Kisii 1.65m 51kg.
At 1500m: WCh: '99- 11, '03- 5; CG: '94- 6, '98- 1, '02- 4; WJ: '92- 2, 96- 2; AfG: '99- 3, '03- 2; AfCh: '98- 1, '02- 1; WCp: '98- 2, '02- 5; 3rd GP 1999. At 800m: WJ: '94- 2. World CC: '98- 5, '99- 1 4k; Rd Rly team: '98- 2. Kenyan champion CC 1998, 1500m 1999, 2002-03.
Commonwealth 1500m record 1998, Kenyan records: 1500m (3) 1997-8, 1M (2) 1997-8.
Progression at 1500m: 1992- 4:08.79, 1993- 4:22.5, 1994- 4:12.84, 1995- 4:24.3A, 1996- 4:08.98, 1997- 4:02.35, 1998- 3:57.41, 1999- 4:03.65, 2002- 4:03.43, 2003- 4:01.22. pbs: 800m 2:00.60 '97, 1M 4:24.00 '98, 3000m 8:38.02 '98, HMar 72:46 '95, 400mh 64.0 '92.
Uniquely has won silver medals at three successive World Junior Championships. World age-14 best for 1500m in 1992. Married to Tom Nyariki (qv), their daughter Mokera was born in October 2000. Her brother **Edwin** (b. 15 Aug 1971) has 1500m pb 3:35.62 '98.

Edith Chewanjel **MASAI** b. 4 Apr 1967 Chepkoya, Mt Elgon 1.68m 55kg. Sergeant in police service.
At 5000m: WCh: '01- 7, '03- 3; CG: '02- 2; AfG: '03- 6. World 4km CC: '01-02-03-04: 3/1/1/1. Won WAF 3000m 2003, KEN 5000m 2001-02, 4km CC 2002.
African 3000m record 2002.
Progression at 5000m: 2001- 14:45.86, 2002- 14: 48.14, 2003- 14:45.35. pbs: 2000m 5:40.3 '01, 3000m 8:23.03 '02; Road: 10km 31:27 '01, 15km 48:37 '01, 10M 52:45 '02, HMar 67:53 '01.
Son born 1990. Ran successfully in primary school, but only started running seriously after she separated from her husband in 1999. Won third successive World 4k CC title in 2004.

Naomi Wanjiku **MUGO** b. 2 Jan 1977 Nyahururu 1.63m 50kg.
At 1500m: OG: '96- dns, '00- h; WCh: '03- sf; CG:

'98- 4, '02- 7; AfG: '03- 3; AfCh: '96- 1 (1 800m). Won Kenyan 1500m 1996-7. World CC: '94-6-7-8: 6J/3/8/11, 4k: '01- 11; Rd Rly team: '98- 2.
Kenyan 1500m record 1996 (also African Junior).
Progression at 1500m: 1993- 4:29.6, 1995- 4:19.0A, 1996- 4:04.29, 1997- 4:10.07, 1998- 3:58.12, 1999- 4:10.59, 2000- 4:01.64, 2001- 4:05.10, 2002- 4:05.52, 2003- 4:01.80. pbs: 800m 2:02.13 '96, 1M 4:24.43 '98, 2000m 5:37.05 '02, 3000m 8:43.30+ '02, 5000m 15:25.13 '00.

Catherine NDEREBA b. 21 Jul 1972 Nyeri 1.60m 45kg.
At Mar: WCh: '03- 1. At HMar: WCh: '99- 3.
Progression at Mar: 1999- 2:27:34, 2000- 2:21:33, 2001- 2:18:47, 2002- 2:19:26, 2003- 2:19:55. pbs: 1500m 4:22.1A '01, 3000m 9:25.10 '99, 5000m 15:27.84 '00, 10000m 32:17.58 '00; Road 5km 15:07 '98, 10km 31:02 '01, 15km 48:06 '01, 10M 52:25 '98, HMar 67:54 '01.
World marathon record 2001.
Married to Anthony Maina. Has had great success on the US road running circuit, where she was top ranked in 1996 and 1998, having had a baby, Jane, in 1997. Sixth in Boston on her debut, five wins in eleven marathons: Boston and Chicago in both 2000 and 2001 before 2003 Worlds. 2nd in New York 1999 and 2003 (2:23:03), in Boston (2:21:12) and Chicago 2002 and London 2003. Her sister **Anastasha** (b. 27 Sep 1974) won marathons in 2002 at Turin in 2:29:27 and Venice in 2:29:03, making them the fastest marathoning sisters.

Isabella OCHICHI b. 28 Oct 1979 Keroka, Kisii. Police constable.
At 5000m: WCh: '03- 6; AfG: '03- 3. World 4k CC: '02-03-04: 3/4/5; HMar: '01- 8. Won Kenyan CC 2003.
Progression at 5000m: 1997- 16:24.46, 2000- 16:54.1A, 2001- 16:34.0A, 2002- 15:01.42, 2003- 14:47.70. pbs: 800m 2:09.1A '02, 1500m 4:20.6A '02, 3000m 8:37.66 '02, Road: 10km 30:53 '02, 15km 47:54 '01, 10M 51:46 '01, HMar 68:38 '01.
Married to marathoner David Maina.

Margaret OKAYO b. 30 May 1976 Kisii 1.50m 39kg.
At HMar: WCh: '99- 14.
Progression at Mar: 1999- 2:26:00, 2000- 2:26:36, 2001- 2:24:21, 2002- 2:20:43, 2003- 2:22:31. pb: 5000m 15:30.0A '01, Road: 10km 32:32 '99, 15km 49:09 '99, HMar 67:23 '03.
Six wins in eleven marathons. Made a brilliant debut with 2:26:00 for 2nd at Chicago 1999, and won at San Diego 2000 and 2001, New York 2001 and 2003 (3rd 2000, 6th 2002) and Boston and Milan 2002.

KOREA

Governing body: Korea Amateur Athletic Federation, 10 Chamshil Dong, Songpa-Gu, Seoul. Founded 1945. **National Champions 2003**: **Men:** 100m: Kang Tae-suk 10.48, 200m: Cho Young-wook 21.53, 400m: Choi Myong-joon 47.49, 800m: Lee Jae-hoon 1:47.63, 1500m: Kim Nam-jin 3:54.31, 5000m: Lee Du-haeng 14:20.54, 10000m: Jung Hyo-suk 30:11.02, HMar: Lee Hong-kuk 65:40, Mar: Cho Keun-hyung 2:17:04, 3000mSt: Kim Jong-dong 9:03.70, 110mh: Jang Seung-han 14.35, 400mh: Kim Man-kyum 54.89, HJ: Bae Kyung-ho 2.23, PV: Kim Do-kyun 5.20, LJ: Shon Il-shik 7.69, TJ: Lee Kang-min 16.17, SP: Kim Jae-il 18.09, DT: Choi Jong-bum 51.82, HT: Lee Jun-chul 65.95, JT: Park Jae-myong 77.86, Dec: Kim Keun-woo 7426, 20kmW: Lee Dae-ro 1:21:52. **Women**: 100m: Oh Hyung-mi 11.92, 200m: Kim Dong-hyun 24.39, 400m: Lee Yun-kyong 56.08, 800m/1500m: Nam Sun-Ha 2:12.69/4:29.87, 5000m: Bae Hae-jin 16:33.29, 10000m: Nam Mi-sun 35:07.73, HMar: Lee Soo-hee 77:04, Mar: Oh Mi-ja 2:39:41; 100mh: Lee Yeon-kyung 13.69, 400mh: Choi Hae-nam 58.24, HJ: Shon Yang-mi 1.75, PV: Choi Yun-hee 3.30, LJ: Cho Eun-jung 6.19, TJ: Chung Hye-kyong 13.11, SP: Lee Myung-sun 16.76, DT: Kim Bu-young 47.38, HT: Chang Bok-shim 54.22, JT: Chang Jung-yeon 53.91, Hep: Chung So-hee 4532, 20kmW: Kim Mi-jung 1:33:03.

LEE Bong-ju b. 11 Oct 1970 1.68m 56kg. Samsung Electronics.
At Mar: OG: '96- 2, '00- 24; WCh: '95- 22, '01- dnf, '03- 11; AsiG: '98- 1, '02- 1. Korean champion 1992-3.
Korean marathon records 1998 and 2000.
Progression at Mar: 1992- 2:13:32, 1993- 2:13:16, 1994- 2:09:57, 1995- 2:10:58, 1996- 2:08:26, 1997- 2:10:33, 1998- 2:07:44, 1999- 2:12:11, 2000- 2:07:20, 2001- 2:09:11, 2002- 2:10:30, 2003- 2:08:10.
Seven wins in 26 marathons: Kwangju and Honolulu 1993, Gyeongju 1995, Fukuoka 1996, Boston 2001 and twice at Asian Games. 2nd Rotterdam 1998, Tokyo and Fukuoka 2000.

KOREA (People's Republic)

Governing body: Amateur Athletics Association of the D.P.R. of Korea, PO Box 56, Pyongyang. Founded 1955.

HAM Bong-sil b. 8 Jul 1974 1.55m 44kg.
At Mar: OG: '00- 8; WCh: '03- 5; AsiG: '02- 1. At 5000m: AsiC: '02- 1
PRK marathon record 2003.
Progression at Mar: 1999- 2:35:05; 2000- 2:27:07, 2001- 2:29.44, 2002- 2:26:23, 2003- 2:25:31. pbs: 5000m 15:42.88 '02, 10000m 34:44.92 '02.
Won Pyongyang Marathon 2002-03.

KUWAIT

Governing body: Kuwait Amateur Athletic Federation, PO Box 5499, 1305 Safat, Kuwait. Founded 1957.

Fawzi Dahesh **AL-SHAMMARI** b. 13 Feb 1979 1.85m 65kg.
At 400m (/200m): OG: '00- h; WCh: '03- sf; WJ: '98- 3; AsiG: '98- 4, '02- 1/1; AsiC: '00- 8, '02- 1/2, '03- 1/1; WCp: '02- 3. Won 200m/400m: Arab

2003, Junior 200m/400m 1998, West Asian 2002, Gulf 2002-03.
Kuwait 400m records from 1998, 200m 2002-03.
Progression at 400m: 1997- 47.05, 1998- 45.89/45.7, 1999- 47.70, 2000- 45.95, 2001- 46.18, 2002- 44.93, 2003- 44.93. pb 200m 20.41 '03.

LATVIA

Governing body: Latvian Athletic Association, 1 Augsiela Str, Riga LV-1009. Founded 1921.
National Championships first held in 1920 (men), 1922 (women). **2003 Champions**: **Men**: 100m: Sandis Sabajevs 10.84, 200m: Vadims Abdejevs 21.98, 400m/800m: Egils Tebelis 48.48/1:50.84, 1500m: Girts Azis 3:56.33, 3000m: Rolands Kaimins 8:36.25, 5000m/HMar: Ivo Zigadlo 14:48.21/69:19, 10000m.Mar: Dmitrijs Slesarjonoks 30:56.2/2:32:44:, 3000mSt: Sandis Bralitis 9:11.56, 110mh: Janis Kovals 15.14, 400mh: Marians Zigmunds 52.34, HJ: Karlis Valdmanis 2.13, PV: Atis Vaisjuns 4.60, LJ: Arturs Abolins 7.22, TJ: Marcis Klepermanis 15.03, SP: Janis Podnieks 17.07, DT: Andris Smocs 49.15, HT: Igors Sokolovs 68.56, JT: Eriks Rags 76.20, Dec: Janis Karlivans 7512, 20kmW: Aivars Kadaks 1:28:10, 50kmW: Juris Konisevs 4:18:03. **Women**: 100m/200m: Anita Kozica 12.11/24.79, 400m: Anna Anfinogentova 56.16, 800m: Jelena Stina 2:07.85, 1500m/10000m/HMar: Jelena Prokopcuka 4:19.78/32:49.3/73:12, 3000m/5000m: Inna Poluskina 8:50.69/15:22.43, Mar: Svetlana Ivanova 3:11:56, 3000mSt: Irina Stula-Pankoka 10:48.42, 100mh: Jesenija Volzankina 14.83, 400mh: Ieva Zunda 57.16, HJ: Natalija Cakova 1.75, PV: Elina Ringa 3.40, LJ: Valentina Gotovska 6.71, TJ: Antonina Antonova 12.31, SP: Liga Klavina 12.94, DT: Dace Ruskule 50.42, HT: Vaira Godmane 44.57, JT: Inga Kozarenoka 53.75, Hep: Iveta Grunte 4834, 10kmW/20kmW: Anita Líepina 49:05/1:44:58.

Aigars FADEJEVS b. 27 Dec 1975 Valmiera 1.75m 59kg. ASK.
At 20kmW (50kmW): OG: '96- 6, '00- 14 (2); WCh: '97- dnf, '99- dnf (dq), '01- dnf (4), '03 (dq); EC: '94- 17, '98- 2, '02- (dq); EU23: '97- 1; WCp: '97- 15, '99- (9); ECp: '98-00-01: 3/6/8. At 10kmW: EJ: '93- 11; WJ: '94- dq. Won LAT 50kmW 1998.
Latvian records 10000mW (2) 1998-2002, 20kmW (3) 1996-2002, 30kmW 2002, 50kmW 1998.
Progression at 20kmW, 50kmW: 1993- 1:36:19, 1994- 1:23:41, 4:02:18; 1995- 1:22:56, 1996- 1:20:40, 1997- 1:19:36, 1998- 1:19:44, 3:43:18; 1999- 1:20:31, 3:46:36; 2000- 1:20:18, 3:43:40; 2001- 1:19:53, 3:46:20; 2002- 1:19:25; 2003- 1:20:56, 3:46:03. pbs: 5000mW 18:48.30 '98, 10000mW 39:00.42 '02, 30kmW 2:06:01 '02, 35kmW 2:34:36 '02, Mar (run) 2:27:20 '01.

Stanislav(s) OLIJAR(S) b. 22 Mar 1979 Chelyabinsk, Russia 1.90m 80kg. ASK.
At 110mh: OG: '00- sf; WCh: '97- qf, '99- sf, '03- h; EC: '98- sf, '02- 2; WJ: '96- h (dnq LJ), '98- 1; EJ: '97- 2; EU23: '99- 2; WCp: '02- 3. At 60mh: WI: '01-03-04: 8/6/4; EI: '00- 1, '02- 4. Won LAT 100m 1999, 110mh 2002.
Five Latvian 110mh records 2002-03.
Progression at 110mh: 1996- 14.52, 1997- 13.62, 1998- 13.49, 1999- 13.28, 2000- 13.25, 2001- 13.29, 2002- 13.15A/13.22, 2003- 13.08. pbs: 60m 6.70i '98, 6.6i '01; 100m 10.42/10.33w '02, 200m 20.91A '03, 20.95 '02; 400m 46.66 '00, 50mh 6.48i '01, 60mh 7.49i '02, LJ 7.94i '00, 7.57A '97.
Hamstring injury caused him to pull up in heats of Worlds, but ranked world number two in 2003 at 110mh. His mother (and coach) Ludmila Olijar (b. 5 Feb 1958) set the Latvian record holder for 100mh 12.90 (1989).

Eriks RAGS b. 1 Jun 1975 Ventspils 1.83m 93kg. Ventspils.
At JT: OG: '00- dnq 26; WCh: '97- dnq 22, '99- 10, '01- 8, '03- dnq 17; EC: '98- dnq 21, '02- 4; WJ: '94- dnq 28; EU23: '97- 4; WUG: '99- 1, '01- 1. 2nd GP 2001. Latvian champion 1997, 1999-2003.
Five Latvian javelin records 1999-2001.
Progression at JT: 1991- 63.50, 1992- 60.90, 1993- 65.22, 1994- 68.42, 1995- 75.32, 1996- 76.92, 1997- 79.04, 1998- 80.50, 1999- 83.78, 2000- 83.61, 2001- 86.47, 2002- 86.44, 2003- 86.32A.

Women

Valentina GOTOVSKA b. 3 Sep 1965 Kraslava 1.76m 63kg. née Tolstik. Arkadija. Hairdresser.
At HJ: OG: '92- 13=; WCh: '93- 8, '03- 11; EC: '90- 7, '94- dnq 26. At LJ: OG: '96- dnq 28, '00- dnq 20; WCh: '95- dnq 26, '97 dnq 29, '99- dnq 15, '01- 5; EC: '98- dnq 15, '02- 12; WI: '04- 5. Won Latvian HJ 1982, 1989-96, 100m 1995, LJ 1995-9, 2003; Hep 1994, 1996.
LAT records: high jump 1990, long jump (3) 2000.
Progression at HJ, LJ: 1980- 1.50, 4.53; 1981- 1.65, 4.94; 1982- 1.82i/1.78, 5.41; 1988- 1.90, 1989- 1.95, 1990- 1.97, 1991- 1.92, 1992- 1.92, 1993- 1.95, 1994- 1.94, 6.18; 1995- 1.88, 6.66; 1996- 1.86i/1.84, 6.41/6.67w; 1997- 1.90, 6.67; 1998- 1.85, 6.70; 1999- 6.73, 2000- 6.91, 2001- 6.88, 2002- 6.67, 2003- 6.71, 2004- 6.72i. pbs: 100m 11.76 '95, 200m 24.77 '97, 24.75w '96; 100mh 14.54w '96, 14.81 '98; TJ 12.11i '98, Hep 5786w/5575 '96.
Married to Yuriy Gotovskis (HJ 2.21 '89). Son born June 1986.

Inna POLUSKINA b. 7 Jul 1984 1.74m 56kg.
At 5000m (/3000m): EJ: '99- 8, '03- 2/1. At 1500m (/3000m): WJ: '02- 9/6; WY: '01- 4; EJ: '01- 5. Won LAT 1500m 2001-02, 3000m 2001, 2003; 5000m, 4km CC 2003.
World junior best 2000m steeplechase 2003.
Progression at 1500m, 5000m: 1998- 4:42.3, 1999- 4:24.14, 16:47.90; 2000- 4:23.79, 2001- 4:15.29, 16:15.77; 2002- 4:16.80, 2003- 4:10.85, 15:22.43. pbs: 3000m 8:50.69 '03, 10000m 33:22.7 (2003), HMar 74:05 '03, 2000mSt 6:19.8 '03.

Jelena PROKOPCUKA b. 21 Sep 1976 Riga 1.68m 51kg. née Chelnova. Arkadija.
At 5000m (/10000m): OG: '96- h, '00- 9/19; WCh: '97- h, '03- (10); EC: '98- 16, '02- (5); EU23: '97- 5/6. At 3000m (/10000m): WJ: '94: h/13; EJ: '95- 5/4; EI: '98- 4, '00- 4. W HMar: '00- 5, '02- 3. Won LAT 1500m 1994, 1997-8, 2003, 3000m 1992-3, 1998-9, 2002; 5000m 1995-7, 2002; 10000m 2003, HMar 1995, 1999, 2003; CC 2001-02.
Latvian records 3000m 2000, 5000m (4) 1997-2000, 10000m (3) 2000-03, 1 Hour 2003, HMar 2001, Mar (2) 2002-03.
Progression at 5000m, 10000m, Mar: 1994- 35:22.44, 1995- 16:20.7, 34:21.84; 1996- 15:59.00, 33:59.9; 1997- 15:40.68, 33:41.51; 1998- 15:30.76, 33:29.04; 1999- 16:09.22, 2000- 14:47.71, 31:27.86; 2001- 15:14.73, 32:02.96; 2002- 15:08.28, 31:17.72, 2:29:36; 2003- 15:02.04, 31:06.14, 2:24:01. pbs: 400m 60.46 '98, 800m 2:05.82 '00, 1500m 4:12.36 '00, 3000m 8:44.66i/8:46.97 '00, 15km 48:47 '01, 1 Hour 17,776m '03, HMar 68:43 '01.
Married to Aleksandrs Prokopchuks (Latvian marathon record 2:15:56 '95). 3rd Chicago 2003.

LITHUANIA

Governing body: Athletic Federation of Lithuania, Statybininku Vilnius LT 03201. Founded 1921.

2003 National Champions: Men: 100m: Andrius Kacenas 10.78, 200m/400m: Raimondas Turla 21.14/47.10, 800m: Mindaugas Norbutas 1:50.39, 1500m: Egidijus Rupsys 3:57.53, 5000m: Linas Salkauskas 15:18.71, 10000m: Tomas Venckunas 30:50.88, HMar: Pavelas Fedorenko 69:13, Mar: Arunas Balciunas 2:31:07. 3000mSt: Karolis Levickis 9:20.92, 110mh: Vytautas Kancleris 14.29, 400mh: Ridas Karaska 53.96, HJ: Aurelijus Eirosius 2.12, PV: Vytautas Zukaitis 4.10, LJ: Tomas Bardauskas 7.82, TJ: Audrius Raizgys 15.53, SP: Tomas Keinys 16.64, DT: Virgilijus Alekna 67.71, HT: Zydrunas Vasiliauskas 62.84, JT: Arunas Jurksas 70.15, Dec: Mindaugas Serepka 7225, 20kmW: Linas Bubnelis 1:28:13, 50kmW: Anatolijus Launikonis 4:13:45. **Women**: 100m: Agne Visockaite-Eggerth 11.37, 200m: Edita Lingyte 24.82, 400m: Kristina Osipova 55.52, 800m: Rasa Drazdauskaite 2:05.90 (could lose title if drugs dq confirmed), 1500m: Aina Valatkeviciute 4:49.05, 5000m: Inga Juodeskiene 16:46.45, HMar: Ausra Kavaliauskiene 1:30:10, Mar: Modesta Drungiliene 3:04:00 2000mSt: Odeta Sidlauskaite 7:09.54, 100mh: Viktorija Zemaityte 14.73, 400mh: Kristina Osipova 1:03.15, HJ: Viktorija Zemaityte 1.80, PV: Edita Grigelionyte 3.50, LJ: Zivile Siksnelyte 6.21, TJ: Zivile Pukstiene 12.78, SP: Rasa Austyte 14.89, DT: Zinaida Sendriute 47.00, HT: Lina Kraskauskaite 48.49, JT: Rita Ramanauskaite 56.04, Hep: Enrika Baliutaviciute 4778, 10kmW/20kmW: Kristina Saltanovic 46:20/1:31:09.

Virgilijus ALEKNA b. 13 Feb 1972 Terpeikiai, Kupiskis 2.00m 130kg. PE student and (from 1995) guard of the Lithuanian president.
At DT: OG: '96- 5, '00- 1; WCh: '95- dnq 19, '97- 2, '99- 4, '01- 2. '03- 1; EC: '98- 3, '02- 2; WCp: '98- 1. Won WAF 2003, GP 2001 (2nd 1999). LTU champion 2000-03.
Four Lithuanian discus records 2000.
Progression at DT: 1990- 52.84, 1991- 57.16, 1992- 60.86, 1993- 62.84, 1994- 64.20, 1995- 62.78, 1996- 67.82, 1997- 67.70, 1998- 69.66A, 1999- 68.25, 2000- 73.88, 2001- 70.99, 2002- 66.90, 2003- 69.69. pb SP: 19.99 '97.
His 72.35 and 73.88 at the 2000 LTU Championships were the second and third longest ever and he thre 69.30 to win Olympic gold. On 4 Mar 2000 he married Kristina Sablovskyte (pb LJ 6.14 '96, TJ 12.90 '97, sister of Remigija Nazaroviene).

Women

Austra SKUJYTE b. 12 Aug 1979 Birzai 1.88m 75kg. Graduate of Kansas State University, USA (now assistant coach).
At Hep: OG: '00- 12; WCh: '01- 6, '03- 10; EC: '02- 4; WJ: '98- 6; EU23: '99- 6, '01- 3. At Pen: WI: '04- 3. Won NCAA 2001-02; LTU 100mh 2000, SP 2001-02, Hep 1997.
Progression at Hep: 1997- 4930, 1998- 5606, 1999- 5724, 2000- 6104, 2001- 6150w, 2002- 6275, 2003- 6213, 2004- 6345. pbs: 200m 25.01 '02, 24.98w '01; 800m 2:17.79 '03, 60mh 8.69i '04, 100mh 14.08 '02, 13.83w '04; HJ 1.85 '00, LJ 6.38i/6.32 '04, 6.40w '01; SP 17.03 '02, DT 51.30 '02, JT 51.02 '02, Pen 4679i '04.

LUXEMBOURG

Governing body: Fédération Luxembourgeoise d'Athlétisme, BP 503, L-2015 Luxembourg. Founded 1928.

2003 National Champions: **Men**: 100m/200m: Pacsal berchem 11.42/23.07, 400m/800m: Jeff Reuter 49.30/1:55.84, 1500m/HMar: Vincent Nothum 3:58.41/68:29, 5000m: Pascal Groben 15:05.23, 10000m: Alain Kieffer 33:11.06, Mar: Christian Krombach 2:33:34, 3000mSt: Romain Possing 10:16.37, 110mh/HJ: Claude Schaeffer 16.12/1.90, PV: Fabian Mores 4.80, LJ: Patrick Hansen 7.04, TJ/Dec: Frank Krier 14.12/6022, SP: Fernand Heintz 14.97, DT: Marco Oliva 36.99, HT: Charles De Ridder 63.81, JT: Antoine Collette 68.93. **Women**: 100m/200m/400mh: Chantal Hayen 12.42/25.84/65.72, 400m: Martinez Nobili 57.69, 800m: Christine Majerus 2:21.21, 1500m/3000m: Maryse Scheller 4:47.93/10:25.36, 10000m/HMar: Pascale Schmoetten 37:31.01/ 83:03, Mar: Danielle Lentz 3:13:06, 100mh: Linda Rippinger 17.41, HJ: Carole Kieffer 1.68, PV: Stephanie Vieillevoye 3.20, LJ/JT: Mirjam Hess 5.80/36.42, TJ: Benedicte Herr 11.33, SP: Chantal Lenertz 11.20, DT: Vanessa Bignoli 35.30, HT: Tessy Biver 37.37, Hep: Tammy Kieffer 3637.

MAURITIUS

Governing body: Mauritius Amateur Athletic Association, Nebiolo House, Maryse Justin Stadium, Réduit. Founded 1952.

Stéphane BUCKLAND b. 20 Jan 1977 Floréal 1.87m 73kg.
At (100m)/200m: OG: '00- qf/sf; WCh: '99- (qf), '01- 6, '03- 5; CG: '02- sf; AfG: '99- (8); AfCh: '00- (2).
MRI records: 100m from 1997, 200m from 1996.
Progression at 100m, 200m: 1994- 10.5, 1995- 10.61/10.4, 1996- 10.49/10.4, 21.14/21.0; 1997- 10.47, 1998- 10.47, 1999- 10.22/10.0A, 2000- 10.16, 20.31; 2001- 10.13, 20.15; 2002- 10.13, 20.29; 2003- 10.20, 20.06. pbs: 60m 6.72i '04, 300m 33.41 '01.

Éric MILAZAR b. 1 Jun 1975 Rodrigue Island 1.92m 80kg.
At 400m: OG: '00- qf; WCh: '01- 5, '03- 7; CG: '02- 6; AfG: '98- 7; AfCh: '98-00-02: 7/1/1; WCp: '02- 4/3R. At 200m: CG: '98- qf. Won French 400m 1998.
MRI records: 200m 1998, 400m from 1998.
Progression at 400m: 1994- 47.25, 1995- 46.53A, 1996- 46.54, 1997- 46.43, 1998- 45.31, 1999- 45.53A/ 45.54/45.5, 2000- 44.87, 2001- 44.69, 2002- 45.04, 2003- 44.75. pbs: 200m 20.72, 20.2w '98; 300m 33.21/33.0 '99.

MEXICO

Governing body: Federación Mexicana de Atletismo, Anillo Periférico y Av. del Conscripto, 11200 México D.F. Founded 1933.

2003 National Champions: Men: 100m: Jesús Domínguez 10.55, 200m: Juan Pedro Toledo 21.46, 400m/400mh: Oscar Juanz 47.00/50.23, 800m: Heliodoro Navarro 1:50.04, 1500m: Alejandro Suárez 3:42.85, 5000m: Teodoro Vega 13:52.16, 10000m: Eduardo Rojas 29:30.60, 3000mSt: Salvador Miranda 8:49.00, 110mh: Roberto Carvajal 14.08, HJ: Gerardo Martín 2.08, PV: Robinson Pratt 5.52, LJ: Abel Orozco 7.35, TJ: Gerardo Carrasco 15.91, SP: Francisco Guzmán 18.62, DT: Gonzalo May 47.19, HT: Carlos Valencia 63.63, JT: Juan Gerardo de la Garza 68.30, Dec: Juan Pedro Santarosa 6525, 20kmW: Claudio Vargas 1:25:34. **Women:** 100m/200m: Liliana Allen 11.36/23.57, 400m: Mayra González 53.06, 800m: Gabriela Medina 2:07.47, 1500m: Dulce Rodríguez 4:20.97, 5000m: Angélica Sánchez 16:24.37, 10000m: Madaí Pérez 32:59.70, 100mh: Lucilia Contreras 14.03, 400mh: Berenice Meza 60.29, HJ/LJ: Romary Rifka 1.90/6.30w, PV: Alejandra Meza 3.90, TJ: Mariela Martínez 12.22, SP: Tamara Lechuga 13.58, DT: Brenda Lozano 43.63, HT: Violeta Guzmán 57.67, JT: Ana Erika Gutiérrez 50.83, Hep: Kytzzia Vasquez 4701, 20kmW: Aura Morales 1:38:04 (Ariana Quino BOL 1:37:27).

Edgar HERNÁNDEZ b. 8 Jun 1977 Ciudad de México 1.74m 57kg.
At 50kmW: WCh: '01- 3. Won MEX 20kmW 2000, PAmCup 20kmW 2001.
Progression at 50kmW: 2000- 3:56:36, 2001- 3:46:12, 2002- 3:56:58A. pbs: 10000mW 19:33.37 '01, 20kmW 1:21:30 '00.
Improved pb by over ten minutes to take World bronze in 2001.

Noé HERNÁNDEZ b. 15 Mar 1978 Chimalhuacán, Estado de México 1.75m 64kg.
At 20kmW: OG: '00- 2; WCh: '01- dq, '03- 4; WCp: '02- 4. Won CAC 1999, IbAm 2000, 2nd PAm Cup 2000, MEX 2001.
Progression at 20kmW: 1998- 1:26:17, 1999- 1:20:12, 2000- 1:19:03, 2001- 1:23:03, 2002- 1:21:46A, 2003- 1:18:14. pb 50kmW 4:11:35 02.

Alejandro LÓPEZ b. 9 Feb 1975 Guadalajara 1.73m 61kg.
At 20kmW: WCh: '99- 12, '01- 11, '03- 10; WCp: '95-99-02 18/22/3; PAm: '03- 3; WUG: '97- 2, '99- 1; CAG: '02- 1. Won IbAm 1998, PAm Cup 2001, MEX 1996, 2002. At 10000mW: WJ: '92- dq, '94- 6.
Progress at 20kmW: 1995- 1:23:28, 1996- 1:19:23, 1997- 1:26:00, 1998- 1:19:52, 1999- 1:17:56, 2000- 1:20:09, 2001- 1:20:49, 2002- 1:21:36A, 2003- 1:19:49. pb 10000mW 18:47.08 '01 (MEX record).

Germán SÁNCHEZ Cruz b. 15 Sep 1966 Zimatlan 1.73m 63kg. Ejército de México.
At 50kmW: OG: '92- dq, '96- 18, '00- dq; WCh: '93- 12, '95- dnf, '97- dq, '03- 12; WCp: '91-3-5-7: 29/3/11/22; PAm: '03- 1; CAG: '93- 2. Won America's Cup 1992, 1996.
Progression at 50kmW: 1991- 4:03:40, 1992- 3:51:02, 1993- 3:54:07, 1994- 3:56:00, 1995- 3:49:29, 1996- 3:52:59, 1997- 3:53:09, 1998- 3:53:49dq, 2000- 3:48:06, 2001- 3:44:50, 2002- 3:55:32, 2003- 3:53:24, 2004- 3:48:12. pb 20kmW 1:26:30 '96, 1:25:05dq '98.
Drugs disqualification April 1998.

Bernardo SEGURA Rivera b. 11 Feb 1970 San Mateo Atenco, Estado de México. 1.75m 62kg.
At 20kmW: OG: '96- 3, '00- dq; WCh: '93/03- dq, '95/9- dnf; WCp: '95- 3, '99- 1; PAm: '95- dq, '99- 1, '03- 2; CAG: '98- 2; WUG: '93- 3. Won America's Cup 1992, PAmCp 1994, 2000; GWG 1994.
World record 20,000m track walk 1994.
Progression at 20kmW: 1991- 1:22:01, 1992- 1:24:09, 1993- 1:19:39, 1994- 1:17:25.6t, 1995- 1:19:09, 1996- 1:19:05, 1997- 1:23:19, 1998- 1:19:46, 1999- 1:20:17, 2000- 1:22:47, 2002- 1:22:46, 2003- 1:19:06. pbs: 3000mW 19:05.5 91, 10,000mW 38:24.0 '94, 1HrW: 15,577.3m '94, 50kmW 4:03:51 '94.
Disqualified after 'winning' the Olympic 20km walk in 2000 and taking his lap of honour. Director of the National Sports Institute. He has named his son Jefferson Daniel Segura after the last two 20kmW Olympic gold medallists. His brother **Jorge** (b. 23 Apr 1975) won the world junior 10,000m walk title in 1994 and at 20km was CAC champion 1995, pb 1:22:50 '95.

Women

Adriana FERNÁNDEZ b. 4 Apr 1971 Ciudad de México 1.63m 59kg.
At Mar: OG: '96- 51, '00- 16. At 5000m (10000m): WCh: '95- h, '97: h (h), '99- h; PAm: '95- 1, '99- 1, '03- 1/1; CAG: '98- (1). At 1500m/3000m: CAC: '93- 2/2, '95- 2/1. Won IbAm 5000m 2002.
Records: CAC 5000m 2003, 10000m 1996 & 2000, Mar 1998 & 1999. MEX 5000m 1995-7, 3000m 2000.
Progress at 5000m, 10000m, Mar: 1995- 15:46.32, 33:06.66; 1996- 31:53.36, 2:31:59; 1997- 15:23.8, 33:09.22; 1998- 34:06.16, 2:26:33; 1999- 15:14.33, 32:39.05, 2:24:06; 2000- 15:16.45, 31:10.12, 2:25:42; 2001- 15:43.73, 2:26:22; 2002- 15:23.09, 32:18.19, 2:24:11; 2003- 15:04.32, 31:13.75, 2:29:54. pbs: 1500m: 4:18.02 '00, 3000m 8:53.53 '00; Road: 10km 31:56 '02, HMar 69:28 '03.
Completed five years of study for a law degree before taking up running seriously. Three major marathon 2nd places: Houston 1996 (debut), New York 1998, London 1999, followed by win in New York 1999. 2nd Berlin 2002. Son Daniel born 21 Nov 2001. Coached by Rodolfo Gómez (2:09:12 marathon in 1983).

Ana Gabriela **GUEVARA** b. 4 Mar 77 Nogales, Sonora. 1.73m 61kg.
At 400m/4x400m (800m): OG: '00- 5; WCh: '99- sf, '01- 3, '03- 1; WI: '99- 4. WJ: '96- sf; PAm: '99- 1, '03- 1; CAG: '98- 2 (2), '02- 1/1R; WUG: '97- (6); WCp: '02- 1. Won WAF 2003, GP 2002 (3rd overall), GWG 2001, IbAm 1998.
Four CAC 400m records 2002-03, MEX records 400m (9) 1998-2003, 800m (2) 1998. World best 300m 2003.
Progression at 400m, 800m: 1996- 54.75A, 2:09.80; 1997- 52.46A, 2:02.90; 1998- 50.65, 2:01.12; 1999- 50.70, 2:03.69, 2000- 49.70A/49.96, 2:02.88; 2001- 49.97; 2002- 49.16, 2003- 48.89. pb 200m: 23.78A '98, 300m 35.30A '03, 35.92 '01.
She became the first Mexican woman to win a medal at any IAAF World Championship in track when 3rd in Edmonton 400m. Unbeaten in 23 successive 400m finals from then to end of 2003, with 12 in 2002, when she shared the Golden League jackpot, and 8 in 2003. Played semi-professional basketball to December 1995.

MOROCCO

Governing Body: Fédération Royale Marocaine d'Athlétisme, Complex Sportif Prince Moulay Abdellah, PO Box 1778 R/P, Rabat. Fd. 1957.

Mohammed AMYN b. 25 Mar 1976 1.68m 53kg.
At 5000m: WCh: '01- 12; AfCh: '02- 3 (1500m 11). At 3000m: WI: '04- 8. World CC: '95- 17J, 99- 10 4k.
Progression at 5000m: 1997- 13:29.2, 1998- 13:33.19, 2000- 13:40.89, 2001- 13:05.44, 2002- 13:01.98, 2003- 13:25.34. pbs: 1500m 3:34.81 '99, 1M 3:52.66 '99, 2000m 4:59.91i '99, 3000m 7:35.35 '01, 2M 8:19.57i '02.

Hicham EL GUERROUJ b. 14 Sep 1974 Berkane 1.76m 58kg.
At 1500m (5000m): OG: '96- 12, '00- 2; WCh: '95- 2, '97- 1, '99- 1, '01- 1, '03- 1 (2); WJ: '92- (3). WI: '95- 1, '97- 1. At 3000m: WI: '01- 1. World Rd Rly team: '94- 1. World CC: '92- 14J. Won GP 1500m 1996, 1998 and 2001-02 (2nd 1M 1997), 2nd overall 2002.
World records: 1500m 1998, 1M and 2000m 1999. World indoor records 1500m (3:31.18) and 1M (3:48.45) 1997. Moroccan records: 1500m & 1M 1997 and 1998, 2000m 1998.
Progression at 1500m, 1M, 5000m: 1992- 13:46.79, 1994- 3:33.61, 3:53.71; 1995- 3:31.16, 3:48.69; 1996- 3:29.05, 1997- 3:28.91, 3:44.90; 1998- 3:26.00, 3:44.60; 1999- 3:27.65, 3:43.13; 2000- 3:27.21, 3:45.96; 2001- 3:26.12, 3:44.95; 2002- 3:26.89, 3:48.28; 2003- 3:28.40, 3:50.20, 12:50.24. pbs: 1000m 2:16.85 '95, 2000m 4:44.79 '99, 3000m 7:23.09 '99, 2M 8:06.61i '03.
He won 80 of 83 races at 1500m or 1M 1996-2003. His only losses were when he fell just before the bell in the 1996 Olympic 1500m final, in his last race of 1997 to Robert Andersen at 1M in the GP Final, and to Noah Ngeny in the 2000 Olympics. In 1998 he took 1.37 secs off Morceli's 1500m WR with a majestic run at Rome, and a year later added world records at 1M and 2000m and a superb World Championships win at 1500m. His unbeaten record in 1999 also included the second best ever 3000m time of 7: 23.09 at Brussels in 1999, from a previous best of 7:49.84 (1994) and a time-trial 7:39.74 in 1996.
Made a great breakthrough in 1994 to run 3: 33.61 for 1500m at Nice with no known form at this event before, although he had taken the 5000m bronze medal at the 1992 World Juniors. At Stuttgart on 2 Feb 1997 he took 2.98 secs off Morceli's world indoor 1500m record.

Abdelkader EL MOUAZIZ b. 1 Jan 1969 Settat 1.72m 58kg.
At Mar: OG: '96- 44, '00- 7; WCh: '97- dnf, '01- 6.
Progression at Mar: 1994- 2:15:45, 1995- 2:14:45, 1996- 2:09:50, 1997- 2:09:50, 1998- 2:08:07, 1999- 2:07:57, 2000- 2:07:33, 2001- 2:07:11, 2002- 2:06:46, 2003- 2:08:03. pb HMar 61:49 '96.
Eight wins in 23 marathons. He had won at Marrakech in 1996 and 1997 in the same time of 2:09:50 and again in 1999 in 2:08:15. Won London 1999 and 2001, 2nd 1998 and 2000, won New York 2000. Twice improved pb in 2002: 4th London 2:06:52, 5th Chicago 2:06:46. Spent four years 1990-4 in Granada, Spain.
Younger brother **Hamid** (b. 17 Feb 1979) has 1500m pb 3:38.04 '01.

Ali EZZINE b. 3 Sep 1978 1.75m 57kg.
At 3000mSt: OG: '00- 3; WCh: '99- 3, '01- 2, '03- 10; WJ: '96- 3. World CC: '97- 11J; 4k: '98- 12, '00- 13.
Three MAR 3000m steeple records 1999-2000.

Progression at 3000mSt: 1996- 8:34.2, 1997- 8:23.18, 1998- 8:15.85, 1999- 8:06.70, 2000- 8:03.57, 2001- 8:10.23, 2002- 8:27.98, 2003- 8:13.31. pbs: 1500m 3:43.8 '98, 2000m 5:00.84 '98, 3000m 7:51.6 '098, 7:47.17i '04, 5000m 13:32.56 '97.
Became the then fastest ever non-Kenyan steeplechaser in 1999 with 8:07.31 and 8:06.70..

Jaouad GHARIB b. 22 May 1972 1.67m 60kg.
At Mar: WCh: '03- 1. At 10000m: WCh: '01- 11; AfCh: '02- 8. At 3000m: WI: '03- 12. World HMar: '01- 9, '02- 2; CC: '02- 10. Won MedG 10000m 2001.
Progress at 5000m, 10000m, Mar: 2001- 13:19.69, 27:29.51; 2002- 13:20.59, 28:02.09i/28:57.12; 2003- 2:08:31. pbs: 3000m 7:39.22 '01, 15km 43:08 '01, HMar 60:42 '02.
Made sudden emergence into top class in 2001. Sixth in 2:09:15 at Rotterdam 2003 on marathon debut and won world title in next marathon.

Abderrahim GOUMRI b. 21 May 1976 1.67m 60kg.
At 10000m: WCh: '01- 16; AfCh: '02- 4. At 5000m: WCh: '03- 10; At 3000m: WI: '03- 9. World CC: '95-02-03-04: 25J/7/15 (10 4k)/14; HMar: '03- 12.
Progression at 5000m, 10000m: 1999- 13:20.70, 2001- 13:03.60, 27:26.01; 2002- 13:00.76, 27:52.62i/ 28:45.92; 2003- 13:05.81. pbs: 1500m 3:39.80 '98, 2000m 5:04.8 '02, 3000m 7:32.36 '01, HMar 61:19 '01.

Abdelkader HACHLAF b. 3 July 1979 1.82m 68kg.
At 1500m: WCh: '01- 8; AfCh: '02- 3; WI: '03- 3, '04- 4. At 3000mSt: WCh: '03- 13. World 4k CC: '03- 16.
Progression at 1500m, 3000mSt: 2000- 3:39.28, 2001- 3:33.59, 2002- 3:33.66, 8:20.64; 2003- 3:35.03, 8:15.33. pbs: 1M 3:52.20 '02, 2000m 4:57.97 '01.

Salah HISSOU b. 16 Jan 1972 Kasba Tadla 1.76m 62kg.
At 5000m: WCh: '99- 1, '03- h; WJ: '90- h; AfCh: '02- 5. At 10000m: OG: '96- 3; WCh: '95- 4, '97- 3. 2nd GP 5000m 1996. Won Pan-Arab 10000m & CC, 2nd 5000m 1992, Moroccan 5000m 1991. World CC: '90-1-4-5-6-7: 12J/14J/11/3/2/2; HMar: '94- 18, '01- 11; Rd Rly team: '94- 1.
World 10000m record 1996, Moroccan records: 5000m 1996, 10000m 1995-6, 3000m 1999.
Progession at 5000m, 10000m: 1989- 14:15.0, 1990- 14:05.9, 1991- 13:37.40, 1992- 13:41.55, 28:31.62; 1993- 13:49.5, 1994- 13:04.93, 27:21.75; 1995- 13:02.25, 27:09.30; 1996- 12:50.80, 26:38.08; 1997- 12:52.39, 27:09.07; 1998- 12:57.73; 1999- 12:52.53, 2000- 13:00.06, 2002- 12:55.85, 2003- 12:59.15. pbs: 1500m 3:33.95 '96, 1M 3:52.54 '99, 2000m 4: 58.4 '99, 3000m 7:28.93 '99, 2M 8:15.60i '02; 20km 58:20 '94 (world best), HMar 61:56 '01, Mar 2:12:45 '04.
Great breakthrough in 1994. 3rd World Cross Challenge 1994/5. Withdrew from 2000 Olympics with an ankle injury and had surgery in June 2001.

Women

Amina AÏT HAMMOU b. 18 Jul 1978 1.65m 49kg.
At 800m: OG: '00- h; WCh: '03- 4; AfCh: '02- 3; WUG: '97- 7; At 3000m: WJ: '98- 12. Won World Miltary 800m 2001.
Progression at 800m: 1999- 2:03.76, 2000- 2:03.16, 2001- 2:00.47, 2002- 2:01.03; 2003- 1:57.82. pbs: 400m 53.7 '02, 1000m 2:39.80i '03, 3000m 8:59.2 '98.
Younger sister **Seltana** (b. 21 May 1980) won Med. Games 800m in 2001, pb 1:59.74 '03.

Hasna BENHASSI b. 1 Jun 1978 1.66m 55kg. Panellínios, Greece.
At 800m: OG: '00- 8; WCh: '97- sf; AfCh: '98- 2, '00- 1; WJ: '96- sf; WI: '99- 5; won MedG 1997, Moroccan 1996. At 1500m: WI: '01- 1, '03- 8; AfCh: '02- 3.
MAR records 800m (3), 1000m, 1500m (2) 1998-9.
Progression at 800m, 1500m: 1995- 2:11.0, 1996- 2:04.6, 4:31.4; 1997- 2:00.48, 4:27.1; 1998- 1:58.47, 4:05.15; 1999- 1:57.45, 4:05.29; 2000- 1:58.47, 4:14.28; 2001- 1:59.86i, 4:04.48i; 2002- 4:05.28, 2003- 2:01.08, 4:02.54. pbs: 400m 54.04 '00, 1000m 2:33.15 '99, 1M 4:32.99 '98.

Zhor EL KAMCH b. 15 Mar 1973.
At 5000m: OG: '00- h, WCh: '99- h, '03- 14. At 3000m: WI: '03- 5. At World 4km CC: '98-9-00-01-02-03: 13/24/9/29/14. Won WMil 5000m & 10000m and FrancG 10000m 2001.
Progress at 5000m: 1998- 15:15.57, 1999- 15:28.40, 2000- 15:12.23, 2001- 15:28.17, 2002- 15:01.34, 2003- 14:42.53. pbs: 1500m 4:08:09 '99, 2000m 5:37.6 '02, 3000m 8:34.85 '03, HMar 70:56 '02, Mar 2:26:10.

Zahra OUAZIZ b. 20 Dec 1969 Oulmes 1.66m 50kg. Based in France.
At 5000m: OG: '96- h; WCh: '95- 3, '97- h, '99- 2, '03- 13. At 3000m: AfCh: '98- 1; WI: '95-9-03: 7/2/4; WCp: '98- 2; 2nd GP 1998-9. World CC: '95- 12, 4k: '98-00-04: 2/2/12. Won French CC 1994, Arab 5000m 1997, Moroccan 3000m 1992, 5000m 1994.
African records: 3000m (5) and 5000m 1998-9. Moroccan 1995-8: 1500m, 3000m (6), 5000m (6).
Progression at 3000m, 5000m: 1989- 9:40.0, 1990- 9:28.3, 1991- 9:59.9, 1992- 9:32.07, 16:19.03; 1993- 9:00.55; 1994- 8:54.40, 15:50.1; 1995- 8:43.19, 14:53.77; 1996- 8:54.86, 15:18.15; 1997- 8:46.56, 15:11.10; 1998- 8:27.26, 14:32.08; 1999- 8:26.48, 14:41.34; 2000- 8:47.18, 2002- 8:45.09, 2003- 8:42.01i, 14:47.45. pbs: 800m 2:06.6+ '98, 1500m 4:00.60 '98, 2000m 5:37.55 '99, 10000m 34:04.64 '94, 10kmRd 32:54 '02.
Sisters: **Nadia** 3000m pb 9:08.58 '88, and **Seloua** (b. 27 Jul 1974) 24th in 1998 World 4k CC and at 1500m in 2000 ran a pb 4:08.18 and reached the Olympic semis, with 3000m pb 8:50.96 '02.

MOZAMBIQUE

Governing body: Federaçao Moçambicana de Atletismo,Parque dos Continuardores, CP 1094, Maputo. Founded 1978.

Maria de Lurdes **MUTOLA** b. 27 Oct 1972 Maputo 1.62m 61kg.

At 800m (1500m): OG: '88- h, '92- 5 (9), '96- 3, '00- 1; WCh: '91- 4, '93- 1, '95 dq sf, '97- 3, '99- 2, '01- 1; WI: '93-5-7-9-01-03-04: 1/1/1/2/1/1/1; CG: '98- 1, '02- 1; AfCh: '88-90-3-8-02: 2/1/1/1/1 (1 1500m 90); AfG: '91- 1, '95- 1, '99- 1; WCp: '92- 1/3R, '94- 1, '98- 1, '02- 1. Won WAF 2003, GWG 1994, 2001; GP 1993, 1995 (won overall), 1999 (2nd overall), 2001; 2nd 1997.

Records: World 1000m 1995, two WIR 1000m (2:32.08 '96 and 2:30.94 '99). African: 800m (8) 1991-4, 1000m (4) 1993-5; Commonwealth 800m 1997. African junior 800m (3) and 1500m 1991. MOZ 200m to 3000m.

Progression at 800m, 1500m: 1988- 2:04.36, 1989- 2:05.7, 4:31.5; 1990- 2:13.54, 4:25.27; 1991- 1:57.63, 4:12.72; 1992- 1:57.49, 4:02.60; 1993- 1:55.43, 4:04.97; 1994- 1:55.19, 4:13.93; 1995- 1:55.72, 4:01.6mx; 1996- 1:57.07, 4:01.63; 1997- 1:55.29, 4:09.1mx; 1998- 1:56.11, 1999- 1:56.04, 2000- 1:56.15, 4:02.39; 2001- 1:56.85, 2002- 1:56.16, 4:01.50; 2003- 1:55.55. pbs: 200m 23.86 '94, 300m 37.16mx '94, 400m 51.37 '94, 600m 1:22.87 '02, 1000m 2:29.34 '95, 1M 4:36.09 '91, 2000m 6:03.84 '92, 3000m 9:27.37 '91, 5000m 18:15.1 '90; Rd 1M 4:32.4 '95.

In 2003, she won World titles indoors and out and was the sole winner of the Golden League jackpot of £1 million and in 2004 won her sixth World indoor title for 35 successive wins at 800m including 12 heats from 19 Jul 2002 and a total of 160 sub-2 minute times from 1991. In 2002 she became the first athlete ever to win four individual World Cup titles. She became Mozambique's first ever CG champion in 1998, following her country's admittance to the Commonwealth. Star soccer player at school in Maputo; enabled to attend school in Eugene, Oregon, USA by a grant from the Olympic Solidarity Committee. 50 successive wins in 800m finals 1992-6, excluding her disqualification for stepping out of her lane after finishing first in her World Championship semi-final, ending with her Olympic bronze in 1996. Her 1:56.36 for 800m in 1998 was disallowed as a world indoor record as she ran inside the lane. Eleven successive wins at Zürich to 2003.

NAMIBIA

Governing body: Namibia AAU, PO Box 195, Swakopmund. Founded 1990.

Frank FREDERICKS b. 2 Oct 1967 Windhoek 1.80m 73kg. Graduate of Brigham Young University, USA.

At 100m/200m: OG: '92- 2/2, '96- 2/2; WCh: '91- 5/2, '93- 6/1, '95- 4/2, '97- 4/2, '99- sf, dns, '03- -/7; CG: '94- 3/1, '98- 2/-, '02- -/1; AfG: '91- 1/1, '99- 3/-, '03- -/2; AfCh: '98- 2/1, '02- 1/1. At 200m: WI: '99- 1; WCp: '94- 1, '98- 1/3R, '02- 2/3R. At 60m: WI: '93- 2. Won NCAA 100m & 200m 1991, South African 200m 1987, Af-AsG 2003. Won GP 100m 1998, 200m 1993, 1997 (2nd 1991, 1995).

WIR 100m (10.05), 200m (19.92) 1996. African records: 100m 1991 & 1996 (2), 200m (9) 1989-96.

Progression at 100m, 200m: 1985- 10.73, 21.68; 1986- 10.1, 20.6A; 1987- 10.36A, 20.58/20.41Aw; 1988- 10.32A, 20.57; 1989- 10.02A, 20.31A/20.09Aw; 1990- 10.16A/10.14Aw, 20.32/20.20Aw; 1991- 9.95/9.89w; 20.08/20.0/19.90w; 1992- 10.02/9.91w, 19.97; 1993- 10.03, 19.85; 1994- 10.04/10.00w, 19.97; 1995- 10.03A, 19.93A; 1996- 9.86, 19.68; 1997- 9.90, 19.81; 1998- 9.93, 19.97A/19.99; 1999- 9.94, 19.87; 2000- 20.79, 2001- 10.06, 20.64; 2002- 9.94A/10.06/9.85Aw, 19.99; 2003- 10.00, 20.23. pbs: 50m 5.59+ '97, 55m 6.13Ai '93, 60m 6.45+ '97, 300m 32.26i '03; 400m 46.28 '89, LJ 7.57i '91, 7.46A '90.

Fredericks has won all four Namibian Olympic medals and was the first to win a world title for his country. A former soccer player, he was sent to the USA by the Rossing Uranium Mine to study computer science. He became the first non-US sprinter to win the NCAA double. Able to compete internationally once Namibia gained independence in 1990 and IAAF affiliation 1991. At Oslo in 1996 he ended Michael Johnson's 2-year undefeated run at 200m. He ran a season's record nine sub-20 sec 200m times in 1996, and at 100m had a record nine legal sub-10.00 times in 1997 with 27 in all. He has a record 25 sub 20-sec 'legal' times for 200m.

NETHERLANDS

Governing body: Koninklijke Nederlandse Atletiek Unie (KNAU), Postbus 230, 3400 AE IJsselstein. Founded 1901.

National Championships first held in 1910 (men), 1921 (women). **2003 Champions**: **Men**: 100m: Timothy Beck 10.45, 200m: Patrick van Balkom 20.89, 400m: Rikkert van Rhee 47.08, 800m: Bram Som 1:46.98; 1500m: Marko Koers 3:47.60, 5000m/Mar: Kamiel Maase 14:01.14/2:10:28, 10000m: Jeroen van Damme 28:53.60, HMar: Koen Raymaekers 63:22, 3000mSt: Simon Vroemen 8:51.29, 110mh: Gregory Sedoc 13.85, 400mh: Thomas Kortbeek 50.99, HJ: Wilbert Pennings 2.24, PV: Rens Blom 5.70, LJ: Jurgen Cools 7.90w, TJ: Randy Sedoc 15.00, SP/DT: Rutger Smith 20.47/60.76, HT: Ronald Gram 68.24, JT: Elliott Thijssen 70.57, Dec: Eugene Martineau 7238, 20kmW:, 50kmW: Pedro Huitjens 5:02:40. **Women**: 100m/200m: Jacqueline Poelman 11.55/23.50, 400m: Annemarie Schulte 54.24, 800m: Najla Jaber 2:06.16, 1500m: Anjolie Wisse 4.19.14, 5000m: Miranda Boonstra 16:36.88, 10000m/HMar: Annelieke van der Sluijs 34:44.71/73:51, Mar: Anne van Schuppen 2:35:52, 100mh: Judith Vis 13.30, 400mh: Tamara Ruben 59.61, HJ: Frenke Bolt 1.78, PV: Sandra van der Geer 3.90, LJ: Karin Ruckstuhl 6.14, TJ: Anja Mulder 12.30, SP/DT: Lieja Tunks-Koeman 18.59/51.85,

HT: Debby van der Schilt 59.91, JT: Inge Hoogeveen 48.85, Hep: Yvonne Wisse 5785.

Rens BLOM b. 1 Mar 1977 Munstergeleen 1.78m 75kg. Unitas & Bayer Leverkusen, GER.
At PV: OG: '00- dnq 15; WCh: '01- nh, '03- dnq 14; EU23: '97- 10, '99- 5=; WI: '03- 3; EI: '00- 3; WUG: '97- 4. Dutch champion 2001-03.
Dutch pole vault record 1997.
Progression at PV: 1990- 3.41, 1991- 3.90, 1992- 4.05, 1993- 4.70, 1994- 5.10i, 1995- 5.00, 1996- 5.40, 1997- 5.62, 1998- 5.60i/5.55, 1999- 5.70i, 2000- 5.75, 2001- 5.70, 2002- 5.65, 2003- 5.75, 2004- 5.75i.

Gert-Jan LIEFERS b, 26 Sep 1978 Apeldoorn 1.87m 71kg. AV '34.
At 1500m: WCh: '97- sf, '01- 9, '03- 7; WJ: '96- 4; EU23: '99- 2; EJ: '95- 3, '97- 1. At 3000m: WI: '03- 6, '04- 6. Eur CC: '97- 1J. Won Dutch 1500m 1998-9.
Dutch records: 1500m & 2000m 2001, 1M 2003, 3000m 2002.
Progression at 1500m: 1992- 4:05.35, 1993- 3:57.2, 1994- 3:53.4, 1995- 3:46.6, 1996- 3:40.47, 1997- 3:38.07, 1998- 3:34.27, 1999- 3:35.20, 2000- 3:42.77, 2001- 3:32.89, 2002- 3:37.77, 2003- 3:33.99. pbs: 800m 1:45.47 '98, 1M 3:51.39 '03, 2000m 4:56.56 '01, 3000m 7:42.95 '02.
Younger brother Arnoud was Dutch 400m junior champion in 2000. His mother Marjon Dekker was a Dutch CC champion.

Kamiel MAASE b. 20 Oct 1971 Nijmegen 1.91m 71kg. Graduate of Universities of Texas and Leiden. Leiden.
At 10000m: WCh: '97- 11, '99- 8, '01- 10, '03- 8; EC: '98- 8, '02- 9 (5 5000m); WUG: '97- 1. At Mar: OG: '00- 13. World HMar: '99- 13. Eur CC '96-00-01-02: 20/7/2/11. Won NED 5000m 1995-7, 1999-2001, 2003; Mar 2003, CC 1997-8, 2001, 2003.
Dutch 10,000m records 1999 & 2002, 5000m 2000 & 2002, Marathon 2003.
Progress at 5000m, 10000m, Mar: 1992- 14:44.90, 1993- 13:48.85; 1994- 13:45.38; 1995- 28:52.99; 1996- 13:39.33, 28:01.4; 1997- 13:30.38, 27:35.72; 1998- 13:29.20, 27:51.42; 1999- 13:25.17, 27:34.02, 2:10:08; 2000- 13:14.13, 27:56.94; 2001- 13:19.86, 28:02.37; 2002- 13:13.06, 27:26.29; 2003- 13:29.46, 27:45.46, 2:08:31. pbs: 1500m 3:42.84 '01, 3000m 7:45.44 '99, Road: 10M 46:47 '03, HMar 62:08 '00, 30km 1:30:20 '03.

Bram SOM b. 20 Feb 1980 Terborg 1.79m 66kg. Atletico '73. Sergeant in Dutch army.
At 800m: OG: '00- h; WCh: '01/03- sf; EC: '02- 6; WJ: '98- 5; EJ: '99- 3; EU23: '01- 6; WI: '03- 5. Dutch champion 2000-01, 2003.
Progression at 800m: 1995- 2:01.27, 1996- 1:53.31, 1997- 1:49.55, 1998- 1:47.99, 1999- 1:46.58, 2000- 1:44.01, 2001- 1:43.98, 2002- 1:45.86, 2003- 1:44.22. pbs: 200m 21.56 '01, 400m 46.87 '01, 1000m 2:17.81i '03, 2:20.18 '99; 1500m 3:48.86 '01.

Simon VROEMEN b. 11 May 1969 Delft 1.89m 68kg. Oil company reservoir engineer, PhD in microbiology. av Sprint, Breda
At 3000mSt: OG: '00- 12; WCh: '97- sf, '99/01- h, '03- 7; EC: '02- 2. Won NED 1500m 1991, 1994; 3000mSt 1995, 1997, 1999-2003.
European 3000m steeplechase record 2002, Dutch records 2000 and 2002.
Progression at 3000mSt: 1994- 8:36.61; 1995- 8:33.52; 1996- 8:37.36, 1997- 8:19.16, 1998- 8:45.70, 1999- 8:19.52, 2000- 8:13.45, 2001- 8:20.67, 2002- 8:06.91, 2003- 8:09.18. pbs: 800m 1:48.87 '94, 1000m 2:20.9 '91, 1500m 3:39.19 '94, 1M 4:04.19 '92, 3000m 7:58.38 '01, 2M 8:46.10 '95, 5000m 13:50.77 '97, 2000mSt 5:26.08 '02.
Twin brother Casper has 3000mSt pb 8:35.18 '96.

Women

Lornah KIPLAGAT b. 20 Mar 1974 Kabeimit, Kenya 1.67m 49kg. AV Hylas. Married to Pieter Langerhorst NED.
At 10000m: WCh: '03- 4. World CC: '04- 6.
World road best 10 miles 2002.
Progression at 10000m, Mar: 1997- 2:33:50, 1998- 2:34:03, 1999- 2:25:29, 2000- 2:22:36, 2001- 2:27:56, 2002- 2:23:55, 2003- 30:12.53, 2:22:22. pbs: 3000m 8:52.82 '00, 5000m 14:51.95mx '02, 14:56.43 '03; Road: 5M 25:09 '97 (former world best), 10km 30:32 '02, 15km 47:28 '02, 10M 50:54 '02, HMar 66:34 '01.
Four wins in 13 marathons: Los Angeles 1997 and 1998, Amsterdam 1999, Osaka 2002. Capped a brilliant series of road runs with second in Chicago marathon 2000. Fourth Boston 2001, 4th Osaka and 3rd New York 2003. Switched from Kenyan to Dutch (citizen from 23 July 2003). Won 2004 San Juan 10km in 30:41.

NEW ZEALAND

Governing body: Athletics New Zealand, PO Box 741, Wellington.
National Championships first held in 1887 (men), 1926 (women). **2003 Champions: Men**: 100m: Donald MacDonald 10.73, 200m: Dallas Roberts 21.09, 400m: Tim Hawkes 46.86, 800m: Mark Rodgers 1:48.26, 1500m: Paul Hamblyn 3:53.54, 3000m: Rees Buck 8:08.65, 5000m/HMar: Phil Costley 14:02.80/66:44, 10000m: Jonathan Wyatt 27:56.80 (Lee Troop AUS 27:51.27), Mar: Todd Stevens 2:30:09, 3000mSt: Kim Hogarth 9:02.69, 110mh: James Mortimer 14.70, 400mh: Matthew Stratton 53.65, HJ: Glen Howard 2.11, PV: Paul Gibbons 4.75, LJ: Nigel Park 7.04, TJ: Tim Hawkes 14.47, SP/DT: Shaka Sola 16.83/55.67, HT: Philip Jensen 69.52, JT: Stuart Farquhar 76.41, Dec: Scott McLaren 6762, 3000mW/10kmW/20kmW/50kmW: Craig Barrett 12:05:51/45:07/1:27:07/4:03:42. **Women**: 100m: Caro Hunt 11.73, 200m/400m: Jane Arnott 24.11/54.42, 800m/1500m: Toni Hodgkinson 2:03.58/4:24.53, 3000m/5000m/10000m: Nyla Carroll 9:21.31/15:48.46/33:13.70, HMar: Shireen Crumpton 78:59, 3000mSt: Jane Nalder 10:59.02, 100mh/LJ/TJ: Kelera Nacewa 15.33/5.72/12.88, 400mh: Rebecca Wardell 56.25, HJ: Angela McKee 1.84, PV:

Melina Hamilton 4.20, SP/HT: Valerie Adams 18.91/55.43, DT: Beatrice Faumuina 63.40, JT: Ana Po'uhila TON 41.05, Hep: Kelera Nacewa 4533, 3000mW/10kmW/20kmW: Gabrielle Gorst 13:51.93/47:01/1:35:59.

Women

Valerie ADAMS b. 6 Oct 1984 1.93m 123kg. Auckland City.
At SP: WCh: '03- 5; CG: '02- 2; WJ: '02- 1; WY: '99- 10, '01- 1; WCp: '02- 6. Won NZ SP 2001-04, HT 2003. Ten NZ shot records 2002-04.
Progression at SP: 1999- 14.83, 2000- 15.72, 2001- 17.08, 2002- 18.40, 2003- 18.93, 2004- 18.96. pbs: DT 54.34 '02, HT 58.75 '02.
The massive Adams has so far matched her age with metres for her shot best.

Beatrice FAUMUINA b. 23 Oct 1974 Auckland 1.80m 115kg. Auckland City.
At DT (SP): OG: '96- dnq 23, '00- 12; WCh: '95- dnq 28, '97- 1, '99- 5, '03- 13; CG: '94- 2 (9), '98- 1 (4), '02- 1; WJ: '92- 5; WCp: '98- 4, '02- 1. 3rd GP 2000. Won NZ DT 1993-2000, 2002-04; SP 1994, 1997-9; AUS SP 1998, DT 1997-8, 2003.
Eleven NZ discus records 1993-7.
Progression at DT: 1990- 45.06, 1991- 46.04, 1992- 53.02, 1993- 55.20, 1994- 57.94, 1995- 60.28, 1996- 64.04, 1997- 68.52, 1998- 67.58, 1999- 64.62, 2000- 65.41A, 2001- 61.54, 2002- 65.05, 2003- 65.53 irreg/ 65.35, 2004- 66.08. pbs: SP 16.96 '98, HT 44.24 '95.
Had 37 successive wins at discus Jan 1997 - June 1998. Parents came from Western Samoa. Her first important success was winning the discus at the Pacific Schools Games in 1992.

NIGERIA

Governing body: The Athletic Federation of Nigeria, P.O.Box 211, Marina, Lagos. F'd 1944.
2003 National Champions: **Men**: 100m: Deji Aliu 9.98, 200m: Uchenna Emedolu 20.79, 400m: Saul Weigopwa 46.12, 800m: Osagie Osazuwa 1: 52.96, 1500m: Mba Uduma 3:56.20, 5000m: Wilfred Saleh 14:56.31, 10000m: Kilobas Isah 33: 28.35, HMar: Gideon Hagak 72:18, 110mh: William Erese 13.3, 400mh: Victor Okorie 49.77, HJ: Obiora Arinze 2.15, PV: Hassan Sambo 3.70, LJ: Olushola Anota 7.47, TJ: Dominic Ukwome 16.15, SP/DT: Chima Ugwu 18.48/57.08, JT: James Ayewoh 66.90, Dec: Lee Okoroafor 6707, 20kmW: Kaseem Adeyemi 1:46:51. **Women**: 100m: Endurance Ojokolo 11.27, 200m: Mary Onyali 22.4, 400m: Bisi Afolabi 51.69, 800m: Grace Ebor 2:02.21, 1500m: Tawa Adedigba 4:24.97, 5000m/ 10000m: Christiana Augustine 16:24.59/34:05.04, HMar: Laraba Joseph 1:24:32, 100mh: Angela Atede 12.96, 400mh: Kate Obilor 57.19, HJ: Nneka Ukuh 1.80, PV: Victoria Itodo 2.80, LJ: Esther Aghatise 6.27, TJ: Salamotu Alimi 13.68, SP/DT: Vivian Chukwuemeka 17.84/54.16, HT: Susan Adeoye Olufunke 57.07, JT: Sorochukwu Ihuefo 52.54, Hep: Oluchi Elechi 5409, 20kmW: Kafayat Babalola 2:13:24.

Deji ALIU b. 22 Nov 1975 1.87m 75kg.
At 100m/4x100m (200m): OG: '96- qf, '00- sf; WCh: '95- qf, '97- (sf), '99- qf/3R, '03- 7; CG: '94- qf, '02- 4=; WJ: '92- 3R, '94- 1 (2); AfG: '99- 4/1R, '03- 1/2R; WUG: '95- 4; Af-J: '94- 1 (1). At 60m: WI: '99-01-03: 5/dq/8. Won NGR 100m 2002-03.
Two African indoor 60m records 1999.
Progression at 100m: 1993- 10.64, 1994- 10.17/ 10.0, 1995- 10.02, 1996- 10.12/10.11w/9.9, 1997- 10.15/10.09w, 1998- 10.20/10.08w, 1999- 10.11A/ 10.15/10.07w, 2000- 10.15/10.10w, 2001- 10.07, 2002- 10.03, 2003- 9.95. pbs: 50m 5.61i '99, 60m 6.48i '99, 200m 20.25 '02.

Uchenna EMEDOLU b. 17 Sep 1976 1.83m 79kg. Woodford Green, UK; now lives in Italy.
At 100m/(200m): OG: '00- (qf); WCh: '01- sf/sf, '03- 8/8; CG: '02- 2/qf; AfG: '03- 2/1; AfCh: '02- 2; WCp: '02- 1/3R. Won NGR 200m 2001-03.
Progression at 100m, 200m: 1999- 21.08, 2000- 10.54/10.2, 20.69, 2001- 10.11/10.06w, 20.34; 2002- 10.06/10.00w, 20.31; 2003- 9.97, 20.38. pb 60m 6.66i '02.

Women

Olabisi AFOLABI b. 31 Oct 1975 1.71m 62kg.
At 400m/4x400mR: OG: '96- sf/2R, '00- qf/4R; WCh: '95- h, '97/99/03- sf; WJ: '94- 1; CG: '94- 7, '02- 3R; AfG: '95- 3, '99- 2/1R; WUG: '95- 1; Af-J: '94- 1. Nigerian champion 1995-6, 2003.
Two African 4x400m records 1996.
Progression at 400m: 1993- 53.42, 1994- 51.97, 1995- 50.50, 1996- 50.49/50.4, 1997- 50.41A/50.58, 1998- 50.85, 1999- 50.34A/50.40, 2000- 50.45A, 2001- 51.52, 2002- 51.94, 2003- 50.91. pbs: 100m 11.68 '96, 200m 23.37 '96, 600m 1:27.99 '95, 800m 2:06.92 '96.

NORWAY

Governing body: Norges Fri-Idrettsforbund, Serviceboks 1, Ullevaal Stadium, 0840 Oslo. Founded 1896.
National Championships first held in 1897 (men), 1947 (women). **2003 Champions**: **Men**: 100m: Aham Okeke 10.35, 200m: John Ertzgaard 21.27, 400m: Morten Sand 46.89, 800m: Stig Vervik Ellingsen 1:51.38, 1500m/5000m: Marius Bakken 3:49.40/13:46.74, 10000m: Karl Johan Rasmussen 30:03.63, HMar : Henrik Sandstad 66:41, Mar: Kristen Aaby 2:29:55, 3000mSt: Jim Svenøy 8:43.95 (11th successive), 110mh: Tom Erik Olsen 14.35, 400mh: Ragnar Bergheim 51.09, HJ: Jon Sigurd Utgårdsløkken 2.13, PV: Ketil Rønneberg 5.10, LJ: Thomas Mellin Olsen 7.68w, TJ: Trond Erik Nilsen 15.48, SP/DT: Gjøran Sørli 19.11/60.75, HT: Bjørn Henning Bøe 60.27, JT: Andreas Thorkildsen 76.04, Dec: Ove Lindekleiv 6479, 10000mW/20kmW: Erik Tysse 41:50.0/1:22:49. **Women**: 100m: Ann Helen Rinden 12.00, 200m: Sigvor Melve 24.13w, 400m/ 400mh: Margit Katrine Strand 55.37/59.18, 800m: Ingvill Måkestad 2:13.09, 1500m/3000mSt: Hanne Lyngstad 4:21.68/9:54.91, 5000m/10000m: Bente

Landøy 16:02.54/33:08.27, HMar: Susanne Wigene 75:01, Mar: Britt Helgesen 3:03:44, 100mh: Kamilla Brandt 13.87w, HJ: Anne Gerd Eieland 1.90, PV: Elin Dolør 3.25, LJ: Margrethe Renstrøm 6.26w, TJ: Cecilie Rise 13.26, SP: Tania Longe 13.79, DT: Grete Etholm 56.96, HT: Eva Danielsen 56.70, JT: Grethe Kleggetveit 48.03, Hep: Rannveig Kvalvik 5094, 5000mW/10kmW: Johanna Ellefsen Rostad 24:41.7/50.38

Trond NYMARK b. 28 Dec 1976 Bergen 1.80m 64kg. TIF Viking, Bergen.
At 50kmW: WCh: '99/01- dnf, '03- 8; EC: '02- 5. At 20kmW: EC: '98- 19; EU23: '97- 14. Won NOR 10000m W 1997-8, 20kmW 1997, 2000l 50kmW 1998-9.
NOR record 30km walk 2000.
Progression at 50kmW: 1998- 3:57:52, 1999- 3:54:36, 2000- 3:53:10, 2002- 3:49:27, 2003- 3:46:14. pbs: 3000mW 11:47.0 '00, 5000mW 19:53.44i '02, 20:07.11 '00; 10000mW: 42:17.2 '02, 20kmW 1:22:56 '02, 30kmW 2:12:56 '00, 35kmW 2:37:25 '02.

Women

Kjersti TYSSE PLÄTZER b. 18 Jan 1972 Os, Bergen 1.74m 54kg. née Tysse. IL Norna-Salhus, Bergen.
At 20kmW: OG: '00- 2; WCh: '99- 9, '01/03- dq; EC: '94- 16, '98- 9, '02- dq; WCp: '02- 5; ECp: '00- 3, '03- 6. At 5000mW: WJ: '86- 5. Won NOR 3000mW 2002, 5000mW 1985-7, 1992, 1994-6, 1998-2002, 10kmW 1994-5, 1998, 2000-02; 20kmW 1998-9.
World bests 1M walk 2001, 1500m walk 2002, 3km road (11:41) 2003. NOR walks records: 3000m (3), 5000m (4), 10km (6), 10000m, 20km (4) 1996-2002.
Progression at 10kmW, 20kmW: 1986- 48:01, 1987- 45:45, 1994- 46:10, 1995- 45:12, 1996- 44:40, 1:39:36; 1998- 42:44, 1:32:55; 1999- 41:54, 1:28:35; 2000- 43:21.1t, 1:27:53; 2001- 42:23, 1:29:55, 2002- 41:16, 1:28:55; 2003- 43:59, 1:28:49. pbs: 1500mW 5:47.03 '02, 1MW 6:16.45 '01, 3000mW 11:59.3i '04, 12:01.91 '02; 5kmW 20:08R '03, 20:37.83t '01; 15kmW 1:05:12 '00; running: 3000m 10:43.19 '01, 5000m 17:57.55 '01.
Married to Stephan Plätzer GER (b. 12 Sep 66), pbs 800m 1:46.53 '89, 1500m 3:40.26 '89. Daughter Kiara Lea born 13 Oct 1997.

POLAND

Governing body: Polski Zwiazek Lekkiej Atletyki (PZLA), 01-809 Warszawa, ul. Ceglowska 68/70. Founded 1919.
National Championships first held in 1920 (men), 1922 (women). **2003 Champions**: **Men**: 100m/200m: Marcin Jedrusinski 10.07w/ 20.38w, 400m: Rafal Wieruszewski 46.41, 800m: Miroslaw Formela 1:51.82. 1500m: Zbigniew Graczyk 3:42.07, 5000m: Radoslaw Poplawski 13:55.98, 10000m: Dariusz Kruczkowski 29:26.7, HMar/Mar: Waldemar Glinka 63:22/2:14:48, 3000mSt: Rafal Wójcik 8:32.49, 110mh: Artur Kohutek 13.74w, 400mh: Marek Plawgo 49.93, HJ: Aleksander Walerianczyk 2.32, PV: Adam Kolasa 5.60, LJ: Tomasz Mateusiak 8.15w, TJ: Robert Michniewski 16.54, SP: Tomasz Majewski 19.63, DT: Andrzej Krawczyk 60.16, HT: Wojciech Kondratowicz 76.03, JT: Dariusz Trafas 81.98, Dec: Krzysztof Andrzejak 7595, 20kmW: Robert Korzeniowski 1:22:21 (14th successive), 50kmW: Rafal Fedaczynski 4:06:39. **Women**: 100m: Daria Onysko 11.50w, 200m: Anna Pacholak 22.87, 400m: Monika Bejnar 52.89, 800m: Anna Zagórska 2:05.55, 1500m: Justyna Lesman 4:16.38, 5000m/Mar: Grazyna Syrek 16:04.69/2:32:09, 10000m/3000mSt: Patrycja Wlodarczyk 34:16.77/ 10:02.67, HMar: Dorota Gruca-Giezek 73:20, 100mh: Aurelia Trywianska 12.75, 400mh: Anna Jesien 55.90, HJ: Anna Ksok 1.92, PV: Agnieszka Wrona 4.10, LJ/TJ: Liliana Zagacka 6.61w/13.88, SP: Krystyna Zabawska 18.82, DT: Marzena Wysocka 62.70, HT: Kamila Skolimowska 65.07, JT: Barbara Madejczyk 55.57, Hep: Magdalena Szczepanska 6001, 20kmW: Sylwia Korzeniowska 1:35:26.

Pawel CZAPIEWSKI b. 30 Mar 1978 Stargard Szczecinski 1.78m 57kg. LKS Lubusz Slubice.
At 800m: WCh: '01- 3; EC: '98- h, '02- 4; WI: '01- 6; WJ: '96- h; EU23: '99- 3; EJ: '97- 8; EI: '02- 1; ECp: '01-02: 1/3. At 1500m: ECp: '02- 3. Won POL 800m 1998, 2001; 1500m 2002.
Polish records: 800m 2001, 1000m 2002.
Progression at 800m: 1995- 1:52.93, 1996- 1:49.66, 1997- 1:48.28, 1998- 1:46.57, 1999- 1:46.71, 2000- 1:46.07, 2001- 1:43.22, 2002- 1:44.32, 2003- 1:47.05. pbs: 400m 48.21 '99, 600m 1:17.24 '02, 1000m 2:17.22 '02, 1500m 3:38.96i '02, 3:43.80 '01.

Pawel JANUSZEWSKI b. 2 Jan 1972 Pyrzyce 1.78m 68kg. Wawel Kraków.
At 400mh (4x400mR): OG: 96- h, '00- 6; WCh: '95- h, '97- sf, '99- 5, '01- 6; EC: '94- sf, '98- 1, '02- 3; EJ: '91- 2R; WUG: '99- 1; WCp: '98- 4; ECp: '95-9-02: 7/3/4. Polish champion 1995, 1997, 1999-2000, 2002.
Three Polish 400mh records 1997-8.
Progression at 400mh: 1991- 52.96, 1992- 51.71, 1993- 51.88, 1994- 49.95, 1995- 49.43, 1996- 49.63, 1997- 48.94, 1998- 48.17, 1999- 48.19, 2000- 48.42, 2001- 48.40, 2002- 48.46, 2003- 50.06. pbs: 200m 21.64 '96, 400m 46.14 '02.
Survived a serious car crash in September 1997 (at first reported dead).

Robert KORZENIOWSKI b. 30 Jul 1968 Lubaczów 1.68m 60kg. US Tourcoing, France & Wawel Kraków. PE teacher.
At (20kmW/)50kmW: OG: '92- dnf/dq, '96- 8/1, '00- 1/1; WCh: '91- 10/dnf, '93- dq, '95- 3, '97- 1, '99- dq, '01- 1, '03- 1; EC: '90- (4), '94- dq/5, '98- 1, '02- 1. At 20kmW: WCp: '89- 40, '91- 7, '93- 4, '95- 9, '99- 4; ECp: '96- 1, '98- 2, '00- 1; WUG: '91- 1, '93- 1. At 10kmW: EJ: '87- dq. At 5000mW: WI: '93- 2. Won Polish 20kmW 1990-2003, 50kmW 1993.
World bests: 5km road walk (18:21 '90), 5000mW

1997, 50km 2002 & 2003. Polish records 1990-2002: 5000mW (5), 10kmW (4), 20kmW (5), 50kmW (4).
Progression at 20kmW, 50kmW: 1986- 1:32:33, 1987- 1:29:48, 1988- 1:26:04, 1989- 1:23:19, 1990- 1:19.32, 1991- 1:21:19, 1992- 1:19:14, 3:46:42; 1993- 1:20:55, 3:44:24; 1994- 1:20:55, 3:45:57; 1995- 1:20:52, 3:45:57; 1996- 1:20:51, 3:42:40; 1997- 1:19:43, 3:44:46; 1998- 1:19:36, 3:43:51; 1999- 1:18:40, 2000- 1:18:22, 3:41:50; 2001- 1:19:52, 3:42:08; 2002- 1:19:40, 3:36:39; 2003- 1:19:11, 3:36:03. pbs: 3000mW 11:05.20 '97, 5000mW 18:17.22 '92, 10000mW 38:26.53 '02, 1 Hr 14,794m '92; road 35kmW 2:28:30 (world best) '93.
Disqualified in 2nd place in the stadium just before finish of the 1992 Olympic 50km walk, but won this event in 1996. In 2000 won a unique Olympics walks double and became the first man ever to retain the 50km title. Set world bests to win 2002 Europeans and 2003 Worlds (his sixth global title). Winner of inaugural IAAF Walks Challenge 2003. His sister **Sylwia** was Polish 20km walk champion in 2000 and 2003 and 5th in the 2001 European U23 Champs . pb 1:32:40 in 2004.

Tomasz LIPIEC b. 10 May 1971 Warszawa 1.85m 72kg. Polonia Warszawa. Director of Warsaw Centre of Sports & Recreation.
At 50kmW (20kmW): OG: '00- dnf; WCh: '97- 5, '99- dq, '01- 9, '03- dq; EC: '98- 5, '02- dq; WCp: '93-7-9-02: 13/5/2/3; ECp: '98- 1, '00- (7). At 10kmW: EJ: 89- 10. Won POL 50kmW 1992, 1996, 1999.
Polish 50km walk records 1997 and 1999.
Progression at 50kmW: 1992- 4:01:13, 1993- 4:03:09, 1996- 3:49:30, 1997- 3:41:58, 1998- 3:42:57, 1999- 3:40:08, 2001- 3:48:51, 2002- 3:45:37. pbs: 5000mW 19:11.85 '01, 10000mW 39:56.00 '00, 20kmW 1:20:48 '00, 35kmW 2:34:00 '97.

Roman MAGDZIARCZYK b. 5 Jul 1977 Walbrzych 1.80m 72kg. AZS-AWF Gdansk.
At 50kmW: OG: '00- 8; WCh: '99- 19, '01- dq, '03- 7; WCp: '02- 12. At 20kmW: EC: '02- 14. Won POL 50km 1998.
Progression at 50kmW: 1998- 4:06:42, 1999- 3:51:20, 2000- 3:48:17, 2002- 3:51:15, 2003- 3:44:53. pbs: 5000mW 19:34.15 '00, 20kmW 1:22:54 '02.

Marek PLAWGO b. 25 Feb 1981 Ruda Slaska 1.83m 72kg. Warszawianka. Student of tourism.
At 400mh: WCh: '01- sf; WJ: '00- 1/3R; EU23: '03- 1/1R; EJ: '99- 4; ECp: '01: 2. Won POL 2001, 2003. At 400m/4x400m: EC: '02- 4; EI: '02- 1/1R; ECp: '02- 3.
Polish 400mh record 2001.
Progression at 400mh: 1999- 51.97, 2000- 49.23, 2001- 48.16, 2002- 48.25, 2003- 48.45. pbs: 100m 10.60 '01, 200m 20.61 '02, 300m 32.77 '02, 400m 45.35 '02.
Ran Polish indoor records 45.49 and 45.39 at 2002 European Indoors.

Grzegorz SPOSÓB b. 12 Feb 1976 Swidnik 2.00m 87kg. Start Lublin.
At HJ: WCh: '01- dnq 22=, '03- 6; EC: '02- dns; WUG: '01- 4; ECp: '01-02-03: 2/3/3. Polish champion 2001-02.
Progression at HJ: 1998- 2.05, 1999- 2.16, 2000- 2.25, 2001- 2.30, 2002- 2.30, 2003- 2.30.

Dariusz TRAFAS b. 16 May 1972 Kolobrzeg 1.88m 94kg. Medicolux Katowice Namyslow. Studied finance at University of Florida, USA.
At JT: OG: '00- 10; WCh: '99- dnq 18, '01- dnq 16; EC: '98- 11, '02- 5; WJ: '90- 2; EJ: '91- 6; ECp: '02-03: 5/3. Polish champion 1996, 1998-9, 2001-03. Five Polish javelin records 1999-2002 (and unratified 87.17 in 2000).
Progression at JT: 1988- 60.08, 1989- 69.12, 1990- 75.00, 1991- 73.84, 1992- 76.38, 1993- 77.38, 1994- 78.66, 1995- 76.60, 1996- 78.06, 1997- 77.46, 1998- 81.90, 1999- 83.23, 2000- 87.17, 2001- 85.78, 2002- 86.77, 2003- 81.98.
He lost the forefinger of his throwing hand in a sawmill accident in 1990. Coached by Uwe Hohn (104.80m WR with 'old' javelin 1984).

Aleksander WALERIANCZYK b. 1 Sep 1982 Kraków 1.95m 78kg. Wawel Kraków.
At HJ: WCh: '03- 10; EC: '02- 13=; EU23: '03- 1. Polish champion 2003.
Progression at HJ: 1999- 2.04, 2000- 2.10i/2.06, 2001- 2.15i/2.14, 2002- 2.27, 2003- 2.36.
World best mark of 2003. His brother Tomasz (b. 1981) has 400mh pb 53.26 '03.

Szymon ZIÓLKOWSKI b. 1 Jul 1976 Poznan 1.88m 104kg. AZS Poznan.
At HT: OG: '96- 10, '00- 1; WCh: '95- dnq 22, '99- dnq 23, '01- 1; EC: '98- 5, '02- dnq 15; WJ: '94- 1; EJ: '93- 7, '95- 1; EU23: '97- 2; ECp: '95/6/2001-6/2/1. Polish champion 1996-7, 1999-2002.
Six Polish hammer records 2000-01.
Progression at HT: 1991- 55.96, 1992- 63.84, 1993- 67.34, 1994- 72.48, 1995- 75.42, 1996- 79.52, 1997- 79.14, 1998- 79.58, 1999- 79.01, 2000- 81.42, 2001- 83.38, 2002- 79.78, 2003- 76.97. pbs: SP 15.25 '95, DT 49.44 '97
His sister Michalina (b. 1983) was second in the 2000 Polish U18 Championships, pb 56.64 '02. Married javelin thrower (50.90 '98) Joanna Domagala in December 2000.

Women

Lidia CHOJECKA-OKNINSKA b. 25 Jan 1977 Siedlce 1.63m 51kg. née Chojecka. Pogon Siedlce.
At 1500m (3000m): OG: '00- 5; WCh: '99- 9, '01- 5; EC: '98- 6, '02- 9; WJ: '94- 7, '96- 5; EJ: '95- 1; EU23: '97- 2, '99- 1; WUG: '97- 3; WI: '97- 9-04: 3/3/8; EI: '98- 2, '00- (2); ECp: '99- (2), '02- 2 (3). Eur CC: '02- 13. Won POL 800m 1996, 1500m 1999-2000, 2002.
POL records: 1500m 2000, 3000m (4) 1999-2002, 5000m 2002.
Progression at 1500m: 1993- 4:40.84, 1994- 4:18.70, 1995- 4:15.27, 1996- 4:11.36, 1997- 4:05.74, 1998- 4:03.32, 1999- 4:01.36, 2000- 3:59.22, 2001- 4:03.51, 2002- 4:04.84, 2003- 4:03.58i/4:08.73. pbs: 800m 1:59.97 '99, 1000m 2:36.97i '03, 2:40.49 '98; 1M 4:

24.44i '00, 4:25.18 '98; 2000m 5:48.15 '02, 3000m 8:31.69 '02, 5000m 15:04.88 '02.
Married 12 May 2001.

Anna JESIEN b. 10 Dec 1978 Sokolow Podlaski 1.68m 56kg. née Olichwierczuk. Skra Warszawa. Student.
At 400mh: OG: '00- h; WCh: '01- sf, '03- h; EC: '02- 3; ECp: '99- 7, '02- 2/3R. Polish champion 1999-2000, 2002-03.
Progression at 400mh: 1995- 66.84, 1996- 61.34, 1997- 58.97, 1998- 58.21, 1999- 56.43, 2000- 55.75, 2001- 55.61, 2002- 55.11, 2003- 55.38. pbs: 100m 12.14 '01, 200m 24.19 '00, 300m 38.33 '02, 400m 52.65 '02, 100mh 14.49 '99.
Married Pawel Jesien (400mh pb 51.08 '00) on 8 Oct 2001.

Monika PYREK b. 11 Aug 1980 Gdynia 1.69m 52kg. MKL Szczecin.
At PV: OG: '00- 7; WCh: '01- 3, '03- 4=; EC: '98- 7, '02- dnq 13=; WJ: '98- 2=; EU23: '01- 1; EJ: '97- 10, '99- 4; WI: '03- 3, '04- 5=; EI: '02- 3; ECp: '02- 4. POL champion 1999-2002 and indoors 1998-2003.
40 Polish pole vault records 1996-2002 and 27 indoors 1966-2004), European record 2001.
Progression at PV: 1995- 2.30, 1996- 3.60, 1997- 3.83, 1998- 4.15, 1999- 4.21i/4.16, 2000- 4.40, 2001- 4.61, 2002- 4.62, 2003- 4.60, 2004- 4.65i. pb HJ 1.70 '97.

Anna ROGOWSKA b. 21 May 1981 Gdynia 1.71m 54kg. SKLA Sopot.
At PV: WCh: '03- 7; EC: '02- 7=; EU23: '03- 3; WI: '03- 6=, '04- 7.
Progression at PV: 1996- 2.80, 1997- 2.60m 1998- 2.90, 1999- 3.40, 2000- 3.60, 2001- 3.90, 2002- 4.40, 2003- 4.47i/4.45, 2004- 4.52i.

Kamila SKOLIMOWSKA b. 4 Nov 1982 Warszawa 1.80m 112kg. Warszawianka.
At HT: OG: '00- 1; WCh: '99- 21, '01- 4, '03- 8; EC: '98- 7, '02- 2; WJ: '98- dnq, '00- dnq 20; WY: '99- 1; EU23: '03- 1; EJ: '97- 1, WCp: '02- 5; ECp: '99- 4, '02- 6; Won GPF & GWG 2001. Polish champion 1996-7, 1999-2003.
Five World junior hammer records 1999-2001, 13 Polish hammer records 1996-2002.
Progression at HT: 1996- 47.66, 1997- 63.48, 1998- 62.72, 1999- 66.62, 2000- 71.16, 2001- 71.71, 2002- 72.60, 2003- 71.38.
Youngest ever Polish champion and record holder (at 13y 229d), won European Junior title at 14y 264d and became the youngest Olympic champion in Sydney 2000 at 17y 331d. Father, Robert, was junior world champion at weightlifting in 1976 and 7th at super-heavyweight at the 1980 Olympics (his weight 155kg). Mother, Teresa Wenta, had DT pb 40.32 '77 as a junior.

Aurelia TRYWIANSKA b. 9 May 1976 Szczecin 1.74m 60kg. AZS-AWF Warszawa. Political science graduate of Iowa State University, USA.
At 100mh: WCh: '03- 5; EC: '02- sf; EU23: '97- 4; EJ: '95- h/3R; ECp: '02- 6. Won POL 2002-03.
Progression at 100mh: 1992- 14.79, 1993- 14.25, 1994- 13.80, 1995- 13.84, 1996- 13.68, 1997- 13.50, 1998- 13.68, 1999- 13.70, 2000- 13.36/13.32w, 2001- 13.49, 2002- 12.97, 2003- 12.74. pbs: 60m 7.36i '03, 100m 11.59 '03, 200m 24.07, 60mh 8.10i '03, LJ 6.22i '00, 6.15 '02; TJ 12.49i '00.
Married her coach, Korey Kollasch, on 1 Jun 2002.

Krystyna ZABAWSKA b. 14 Jan 1968 Dabrowa Bialostocka 1.83m 92kg. née Danilczyk. Podlasie Bialystok. Storekeeper.
At SP: OG: '92- 10, '00- 5; WCh: '91- 12, '93 dnq 17, '97- 8, '99- 8, '01- 10, '03- 6; EC: '94- 9, '98- 11, '02- 7; WI: '99-01-04: 2/8/5; EI: '94-8-00: 6/4/5; ECp: '91-3-9-02: 5/5/1/3. Polish champion 1991-4, 1996-2003.
Progression at SP: 1985- 10.98, 1986- 12.20, 1987- 14.48, 1988- 15.70, 1989- 16.22, 1990- 18.31, 1991- 19.03, 1992- 19.42, 1993- 18.31, 1994- 19.23, 1995- 16.38, 1996- 18.62, 1997- 19.06, 1998- 19.24, 1999- 19.26i/19.23, 2000- 19.18, 2001- 19.10, 2002- 18.73, 2003- 18.95, 2004- 19.00i.
Married to Przemyslaw Zabawski, Polish shot champion 1997 & 2000, pb 19.63 '01.

PORTUGAL

Governing body: Federação Portuguesa de Atletismo, Largo da Lagoa, 15-8, 2795 Linda-a-Velha. Founded in 1921.
National Championships first held in 1910 (men), 1937 (women). **2003 Champions**: **Men**: 100m: Ricardo Alves 10.47, 200m: Francis Obikwelu 21.12, 400m: Vítor Moreno 47.69, 800m: Rui Silva 1:49.00, 1500m: Adelino Monteiro 3: 56.65, 5000m: Bruno Saramago 14:24.36, 10000m: Alberto Chaiça 29:04.50, HMar: Eduardo Henriques 62:35; Mar: Luis Jesús 2:15:31, 3000mSt: Manuel Silva 8:44.16, 110mh: Luis Sá 14.12, 400mh: Edivaldo Monteiro 50.17, HJ: Paulo Gonçalves 2.04, PV: João André 5.45, LJ: Gaspar Araújo 8.10w, TJ: Nelson Evora 15.57, SP: Marco Fortes 18.57, DT: Paulo Bernardo 57.58, HT: Vítor Costa 73.19, JT: André Medeiros 66.80, Dec: Mario Aníbal 6179, 20000mW: João Vieira 1:27:58.8, 50kmW: Pedro Martins 3:56:27. **Women**: 100m: Severina Cravid 12.05, 200m: Carmo Tavares 24.28, 400m/800m: Sandra Teixeira 54.77/2:05.33, 1500m: Ines Monteiro 4:18.29, 5000m: Fernanda Ribeiro 15:27.17, 10000m/HMar: Inês Monteiro 33:20.73/74:13, Mar: Anabela Pereira 3:07:01, 3000mSt: Analidia Torre 10:03.62, 100mh: Isabel Abrantes 13.95, 400mh: Patrícia Lopes 60.31, HJ: Liliana Viana 1.81, PV: Elisabete Tavares 4.10, LJ/TJ: Susana Costa 5.68/12.55, SP/DT: Teresa Machado 14.76/61.37, HT: Vânia Silva 65.87, JT: Cristina Ferreira 52.52, Hep: Marisa Vieira 4724, 10000mW/20kmW: Susana Feitor 44:07.80/1:31:12.

Francis Obiorah **OBIKWELU** b. 22 Nov 1978 Nigeria 1.95m 74kg. Sporting Clube de Portugal.
At (100m/)200m: OG: '96- sf, '00- sf; WCh: '97- 2R (sf), '99- 3/3R, '03- h; EC: '02- 2/2; WI:

'97- 3, '99- 4; WJ: '96- 1/1; AfG: '99- 2/1/1R; WCp: 3/1. 3rd GP 200m 1999, 2001. At 400m: WJ: '94- sf; Af-J: '94- 2. At 60m: WI: '04- 6. Won NGR 100m 1999-200m, 200m 1997, 1999; POR 200m 2002-03.
Two Nigerian 200m records 1999; POR records: 100m (3), 200m (3) 2002.
Progression at 100m, 200m: 1994- 21.16, 1995- 10.31, 21.22; 1996- 10.12, 20.24; 1997- 10.10, 20.53/ 20.27Aw; 1998- 10.01, 20.17; 1999- 10.01A/10.13/ 10.11w, 19.84; 2000- 9.97, 20.01; 2001- 9.98, 20.33; 2002- 10.01, 20.18; 2003- 10.11, 20.41. pbs: 50m 5.79i '04, 60m 6.56i '04, 400m 46.29 '98.
An Ibo, and thus in an ethnic minority group in Nigeria, he emigrated to Portugal in 1994 and became a Portuguese citizen on 26 Oct 2001.

António PINTO b. 22 Mar 1966 Amarante 1.71m 61kg. Maratona CP.
At 10000m: OG: '88- 13, WCh: '95- 19, '99- 5; EC: '90- 14, '98- 1. At Mar: OG: '92- dnf, '96- 14, '00- 11; WCh: '97- dnf; EC: '94- 9. Eur CC: '94- 8. Won POR CC 1992, 5000m 1994, 1999.
World best half marathon 1998, European records: 10000m 1999, Marathon 2000; POR 5000m 1998.
Progression at 10000m, Mar: 1986- 31:13.3, 1987- 28:28.73, 1988- 28:01.00, 1989- 28:30.11, 1990- 28:14.32; 1991- 28:30.3, 2:12:39; 1992- 28:59.02, 2:10:02; 1994- 27:48.1, 2:08:31; 1995- 28:06.18, 2:08:48; 1996- 2:08:38, 1997- 2:07:55, 1998- 27:15.76, 2:08:13; 1999- 27:12.47, 2:09:00; 2000- 2:06:36, 2001- 2:09.36, 2002- 27:51.01, 2:09:10. pbs: 1500m 3:39.25 '98, 3000m 7:41.33 '99, 5000m 13:02.86 '98, HMar 59:43 '98.
Previously a cyclist, started running in 1986. He has a great record in the London marathon with wins in 1992, 1997 and 2000, 2nd 1999 and 3rd 1995, 1998 and 2001. He has run 19 marathons from 7th at Carpi 1991 on his début and won Berlin 1994; 2nd Paris 1994, Tokyo 1996; 3rd Berlin 1995. Had four in succession under 2:09 in 1994-6 and after the Olympics ran 2:07:55, to win his second London marathon. Had a poor record in championships until his European 10,000m title during a sensational season in 1998, when his times ranged from 3:39.25 for 1500m to 2:08:13 for marathon.

Rui SILVA b. 3 Aug 1977 Vila Chã de Ourique 1.75m 65kg. Sporting Club de Portugal.
At 1500m:OG: '00- h; WCh: '99- sf (fell), '01- 7, '03- 5; EC: '98- 2, '02- 3; WJ: '96- 6; EJ: '95- 8; EU23: '99- 1; WI: '99- 5. '01- 1; EI: '98- 1, '02- 1; WCp: '98- 2. At 3000m: WI: '04- 2; EI: '00- 2. Won POR 800m 2002-03, 1500m 1999, 2001; CC sh 2000-02.
Portuguese records 1998-2002: 800m, 1500m (6), 1000m, 1M (2), 2000m.
Progression at 1500m: 1994- 3:50.9, 1995- 3:44.8, 1996- 3:40.09, 1997- 3:44.6, 1998- 3:34.00, 1999- 3:30.88, 2000- 3:32.60, 2001- 3:30.36, 2002- 3:30.07, 2003- 3:32.97. pbs: 800m 1:44.91 '02, 1000m 2:16.30 '99, 1M 3:49.50 '02, 2000m 4:54.66 '99, 3000m 7:39.44i '00, 7:51.28 '02; 5000m 13:36.56 '01.

Women

Susana FEITOR b. 28 Jan 1975 Alcobertas 1.60m 52kg. C Natação Rio Maior.
At 20kmW: OG: '00- 14; WCh: '99- 4, '01- dq, '03- 9; EC: '02- dnf; WCp: '99- 9, '02- 14; ECp: '03- 5. At 10kmW: OG: '92- dq, '96- 13; WCh: '91- 13, '93- 11, '95- 17, '97- h; EC: '94- 8, '98- 3; EU23: '97- 3; WUG: '95- 4, '97- 4, '01- 2; WCp: '93- 8, '95- 15; ECp: '96- 3. At 5000mW: WJ: '90- 1, '92- dq, 94- 2; EJ: '89- 6, '91- 2, '93- 1. Won POR 10kmW 1992, 1994-2000, 2002-03, 20kmW 1998-9, 2001-04.
POR walks records 1989-2001: 3000m (10), 5000m (9), 10km (9), 20km (3), 20,000m track (1:29:36.4 WR '01). World junior 5000m best (21:01.8) 1993.
Progression at 10kmW, 20kmW: 1991- 45:37, 1992- 45:24, 1993- 43:44, 1994- 43:30, 1995- 44:05, 1996- 43:37, 1997- 44:26, 1998- 42:55, 1:31:03, 1999- 44:36, 1:30:13; 2000: 43:55, 1:28:19; 2001- 42:39, 1:27:55; 2002- 44:24, 1:31:12; 2003- 44:07.80t, 1:29:08; 2004- 1:29:32. Track pbs: 3000mW 12:08.30 '01, 5000mW 20:40.24 '01, 10000mW 44:07.80 '03.
Had a hugely successful junior career to her world silver medal in front of her home crowd in 1994, four years after she had won this title.

Enezenaide **'Naide' GOMES** b. 10 Nov 1979 São Tome e Principe 1.81m 70kg. Sporting Club de Portugal.
At Hep (LJ): EC: '02- 18 (10); AfrG: '99- 5. At Pen: WI: '03- 5, '04- 1; EI: '02- 2. At 100mh: OG: '00- h. Won POR Hep 2001, HJ and LJ 2002.
Portuguese records LJ (2), Heptathlon (2) 2002.
Progression at Hep: 1997- 4578, 1999- 4964, 2000- 5671, 2001- 5606w, 2002- 6160, 2003- 6120. 60m 7.84i '04, 200m 24.96 '02, 400m 58.13i '03, 800m 2:19.57 '03, 60mh 8.44i '04, 100mh 13.65 '03, 13.62w '02; HJ 1.88i '04, 1.86 '02; LJ 6.57 '02, TJ 11.73 '99, SP 15.08i '04, 13.54 '02, JT 42.86 '00, Pen 4759i '04.
Changed nationality from São Tome e Principe to Portugal in 2001. Set pbs at HJ (Portuguese record) and SP en route to winning WI gold in 2004.

Fernanda RIBEIRO b. 23 Jun 1969 Penafiel 1.61m 48kg. FC Porto,
At 10000m (5000m): OG: '96- 1, '00- 3; WCh: '93- 10, '95- 1 (2), '97- 2 (3), '99/03- dnf; EC: '90- dnf, '94- 1, '98- 2, '02- dnf; WCp: '94- 2; won E.Chall '98, '03. At 3000m: OG: '88- h, '92- h; WCh: '87- h, '91- h; WI: '97- 3; EC: '86- h, '90- h; EI: '94- 1, '96- 1, '98- 2; WJ: '86- 4, '88- 2; EJ: '83- 11, '85- 4, '87- 1. World CC: '94- 10, '96- 6, '00- 10 (4k); Rd Rly team: '92- 1. Eur CC: '94- 6, '98- 4. Won IbAm 5000m 2000, POR 1500m 1989-90, 1995, 1998-9; 3000m 1985, 1993; 5000m 2000, 2002-03, 10000m 1992, 1996; CC 1996-9, 2003, 4k CC 2003.
World 5000m record 1995. Portuguese records: 3000m (3), 5000m (3), 10000m (4) 1994-2000.
Progression at 3000m, 5000m, 10000m: 1982- 9:53.7, 1983- 9:21.71, 1984- 9:11.62, 1985- 9:14.19, 1986- 9:09.39, 1987- 8:56.33, 1988- 9:00.38, 1989-

9:04.33, 32:38.07; 1990- 9:03.35, 32:39.34; 1991- 8:57.64, 33:45.45; 1992- 8:56.10, 32:22.70; 1993- 8:51.91, 31:50.51; 1994- 8:42.13, 15:06.91, 31:04.25; 1995- 8:41.99, 14:36.45, 31:04.99; 1996- 8:39.49i/ 8:45.56, 14:41.07, 31:01.63; 1997- 8:37.14, 14:53.25, 31:39.15; 1998- 8:42.95, 15:22.8, 30:48.06; 1999- 8:30.66, 14:52.59; 2000- 8:34.99, 15:01.49, 30:22.88; 2001- 8:53.41i, 2002- 8:56.51i, 15:17.62, 31:40.80; 2003- 8:49.39i, 15:16.8+, 31:13.42. pbs: 800m 2:05.83 '94, 1000m 2:44.8 '92, 1500m 4:05.97 '97, 1M 4:32.66 '99, 2000m 5:37.34i '96, HMar 68:23 '00, Mar 2:37:04 '02.

At 11 was second in a half marathon in 1:24:02, just 4 secs behind Rosa Mota. Made international debut at 13 and set national age records each age 13-22 at 3000m and 14-18 and 20 at 1500m. She fulfilled her long-time promise in 1994 with brilliant performances to win European titles indoors and out, and has added World and Olympic titles in the following years.

Carla SACRAMENTO b. 10 Dec 1971 Lisboa 1.68m 53kg. Maratona CP.

At 1500m (800m): OG: '92- sf (sf), '96- 6, '00- 10; WCh: '93- 11 (h), '95- 3, '97- 1, '99- 5, '01- 4, '03- sf; EC: '94- 6 (6), '98- 2, '02- 12; WI: '93/5/7/01- 7/ 2/5/4; EI: '92- (4), '94- (3), '96- 1; WJ: '90- 4 (4); EJ: '89- (4); WUG: '97- 2; WCp: '98- 3. At 3000m: EI: '02- 2. World 4k CC: '98-00-01-02: 19/7/7/24; Eur CC: '94- 11. Won GP 1M 1997 (1500m 3rd 1998, 2nd 2001), Ib-Am 1500m 1998, POR 800m 1986-7, 1993-5, 2002; 1500m 1991, 2001; CC 2000-2.

Portuguese records 1989-99: 800m (7), 1500m (9), 1M (4), 1000m (2), 2000m and 3000m (1)

Progression at 800m, 1500m: 1985- 2:15.15/2:13.56 dq, 1986- 2:10.48, 1987- 2:09.3, 4:35.96; 1988- 2:04.27, 4:29.41; 1989- 2:03.89, 4:21.92; 1990- 2:04.83, 4:15.06; 1991- 2:04.94, 4:20.43; 1992- 2:00.57, 4:04.10; 1993- 1:59.42, 4:06.33; 1994- 1:59.39, 4:06.05; 1995- 1:59.78, 4:03.79; 1996- 2:00.24, 4:02.64; 1997- 1:58.94, 4:01.86; 1998- 2:02.3, 3:57.71; 1999- 1:59.54, 4:01.29; 2000- 2:00.22, 4:00.35; 2001- 4:00.32, 2002- 2:03.06, 4:01.35; 2003- 4:06.64. pbs: 200m 25.49 '92, 400m 54.29 '96, 500m 1:10.83 '96, 1000m 2:34.85 '95, 1M 4:23.00i '02, 4:23.41 '98; 2000m 5:40.25 '96, 3000m 8:30.22 '99, 5000m 15:52.54 '00, 400mh 61.05 '91.

11 consecutive major champs finals 1993-2002.

QATAR

Governing body: Qatar Association of Athletics Federation, PO Box 8139, Doha. Founded 1963.

Khamis Seif (Safeildin) ABDULLAH b. 1 Dec 1976 Sudan 1.81m 64kg.

At 3000mSt (/5000m): OG: '00- 10; WCh: '99- h, '01- 7, '03- 12; AsiG: '02- 1/3; AsiC: '00- 1, '02- 1/1, '03- 1; WUG: '99- 2; WCp: '02- 3. Won Arab 2001, 2003; Gulf 200203 (& 5000m 2003).

Five Qatar records 1999-2002.

Progression at 3000mSt: 1999- 8:18.58, 2000- 8:17.56, 2001- 8:14.38, 2002- 8:13.45, 2003- 8:18.51. pbs: 1500m 3:41.2 '00, 5000m 13:36.93 '99.

Mubarak Sultan Faraj Al-NUBI b. 30 Dec 1977 1.85m 72kg.

At 400mh: OG: '96- h; WCh: '97/03- sf; WJ: '96- 1; AsiG: '02- 2; AsiC: '95-8-02-03: 1/1/1/1; WUG: '97- 3; WCp: '98- 2, '02- 2. Won Asi-J 400m 1996, 400mh 1994 & 1996, Arab 400mh 1997, 2001, 2003; Gulf 2003.

Asian 400mh record 1998, five QAT records 1996-8.

Progression at 400mh: 1994- 51.21, 1995- 50.03, 1996- 49.07, 1997- 48.84, 1998- 48.17A/48.71, 2001- 49.36, 2002- 48.41, 2003- 48.53. pbs: 400m 47.15 '96.

Brother **Abdulrahman** (b. 17 Oct 1979) was 3rd in Asian LJ 1996 and set pbs of 8.11 for 2nd in 1998 World Juniors and 8.12 and 8.13 in 2003.

Abdullah Ahmad HASSAN b. 4 Apr 1981 Keiyo 1.70m 54kg. **(ex Albert CHEPKURUI** KEN)

At 10000m: WCh: '03- 4; AsiC: '03- 1. World CC: '99-01-02-04: 5J/6 4k/6/4 4k.

Asian records 5000m (13:04.65), 10000m (2) 2003.

Progression at 5000m, 10000m: 1998- 13:49.48, 1999- 13:25.18, 2000- 12:59.90, 2001- 13:18.71, 28:06.86; 2002- 13:12.22, 26:50.67; 2003- 12:56.27, 26:38.36. pbs: 1500m 3:42.42 '00, 3000m 7:43.01 '99.

Three Asian records in month after transferring from Kenya to Qatar on 9 Aug 2003. He had been 4th in Kenyan 10,000m Trials on 26 July 2003!

Saif Saaeed SHAHEEN b. 15 Oct 1982 Keiyo 1.77m 64kg. **(ex Stephen CHERONO** KEN)

At 3000mSt: WCh: '03- 1; CG: '02- 1; AfCh: '02- 3; won WAF 2003, 3rd GP 2001. At 2000mSt: WY: '99- 1. Won KEN 3000mSt 2002. At 1500m/ 5000m: AsiC: '03- 2/2. World 4k CC: '04- 5.

World junior record 3000m steeplechase 2001; three Asian records 2003.

Progression at 5000m, 3000mSt: 1997- 8:43.0A, 1999- 8:19.12, 2001- 7:58.66, 2002- 13:11.55, 7:58.10, 2003- 12:48.81, 7:57.38. pbs: 1500m 3:35.15 '03, 2000m 5:03.06 '01, 3000m 7:38.0e+ '03, 2M 8:18.80 '99.

Controversially transferred allegiance to Qatar and set first Asian record (3000mSt 8:02.48) nine days after citizenship granted (9 Aug 2003). Brother of Abraham Cherono and **Christopher Kosgei** (b. 14 Aug 1974): WCh: 95- 2, 99- 1; pb 8:05.43 '99.

ROMANIA

Governing body: Federatia Romana de Atletism, Str. Dr Primo Nebiolo nr.2, Bucuresti 71331. Founded 1912.

National Championships first held in 1914 (men), 1925 (women). **2003 Champions**: **Men**: 100m: Leonard Gherghiceanu 10.68, 200m: Adrian Stefan 20.89 400m: Ioan Vieru 46.06, 800m: Ionut Zaizan 1:47.90, 1500m: Ciprian Borz 3:44.66, 5000m: Adrian Maghiar 14:24.38, 10000m: Hugues-Aymar Moutsinga 30:27.55, HMar: Arthur-Janos Miklos 67:21, Mar: Petre Lazarescu 2:25:03, 3000mSt: Marius Cozmanciuc 8.45.05, 110mh: Alexandru Mihailescu 14.47, 400mh: Marian Neacsu 51.87, HJ: Stefan Vasilache

2.22, PV: Tiberiu Agoston 5.40, LJ: Bogdan Tarus 8.21, TJ: Marian Oprea 17.23, SP: Gheorghe Guset 19.40, DT: Sergiu Ursu 61.72, HT: Cosmin Sorescu 72.50, JT: Levente Bartha 74.77, Dec: Mihai Timofte 7237, 20kmW: Costica Balan 1:28:43, '50'kmW: Ciprian Deac 3:57:56 short, **Women**: 100m: Ramona Popovici 11.91, 200m: Angela Morosanu 24,21, 400m/400mh: Maria Rus 53.13/ 58.38, 800m/1500m: Maria Cioncan 2:00.63/ 4:06.73, 5000m: Mihaela Botezan 15:15.13, 10000m: Rodica Chirita 32:35.48, HMar: Iulia Olteanu 74:17, Mar: Ana Lupan 2:50:11, 2000mSt: Cristina Casandra 9:40.49, 100mh: Carmen Zamfir 13.32, HJ: Oana Pantelimon 1.92, PV: Andrea Imre 3.40, LJ: Alina Militaru 6.55, TJ: Adelian Gavrila 14.50, SP: Elena Hila 17.95, DT: Ileana Brîndusoiu 56.61, HT: Mihaela Melinte 70.80, JT: Ana-Mirela Termure 61.91, Hep: Madalina Stefan 4900, 10kmW: Claudia Stef 44:45, 20kmW: Daniela Cîrlan 1:32:41

Marian OPREA b. 6 Jun 1982 1.90m 80kg. Rapid Bucuresti & CSM-PAB Arad. Student.
At TJ: WCh: '01- dnq 13, '03- dnq 17; EC: '02- dnq 14; WJ: '00- 1, WY: '99- 4; EU23: '03- 2; EJ: '99- 3, '01- 1; WI: '03- 8, '04- 5; EI: '02- 2; WUG: '01- 2. ROM champion 2001, 2003; Balkan 2001-03. Romanian TJ record 2003.
Progression at TJ: 1997- 14.37, 1998- 14.78, 1999- 15.98, 2000- 16.49, 2001- 17.11/17.13w, 2002- 17.29i/17.11/17.39w, 2003- 17.63. pb LJ 7.62i '03.

Bogdan TARUS b. 1 Aug 1975 Pietra-Neamt 1.90m 77kg. ADCO Bacau.
At LJ: OG: '96- dnq 15, '00- 9; WCh: '95-7-9-01: -dnq 23/19/26/27, '03- 10; EC: '94- dnq 15, '98- 2; WJ: '94- 2; EU23: '97- 4; EJ: '93- 7; WI: '99-03-04: 6/dq/4; EI: '96- 2, '00- 2; ECp: '94- 1, '95- 1; ROM champion 1996-9, 2001, 2003 (100m 2000); Balkan 1997, 2003.
Progression at LJ: 1992- 7.48, 1993- 7.66, 1994- 8.01, 1995- 8.05, 1996- 8.29, 1997- 8.27, 1998- 8.21, 1999- 8.26i/8.20, 2000- 8.30i/8.12, 2001- 8.15, 2002- 7.92, 2003- 8.21, 2004- 8.26i. pb 100m 10.66 '00.

Women

Mihaela BOTEZAN b. 21 Nov 1976 Ocna Murec 1.60m 46kg. CSU Cluj-Napoca & Steaua Bucuresti. Sports teacher.
At (5000m)/10000m: WCh: '01- 5, '03- 13 (51 Mar); EC: '02- 6/4; ECp: '01-02-03: (3)/(6)/(3) & 4 3000m. World HMar: '00-01-02: 6/10/4. Eur CC: 2001- 11. Won ROM 5000m 2003, 10000m 2001.
Romanian 10000m record 2002.
Progression at 5000m, 10000m: 1995- 16.29.14, 1996- 16.34.72, 1997- 17.05.6, 34.58.83; 1998- 17.16.6, 35.26.45; 1999- 15:54.86, 34.33.01; 2000- 34.00.27; 2001- 15.08.78, 31.45.06; 2002- 15:19.12, 31:13.96; 2003- 15:10.69, 31:28.72. pbs: 1500m 4:26.18 '95, 3000m 9:02.61 '03; Rd: 15km 49:35 '01, HMar 69: 24 '02, Mar 2:25:32 '03, 3000mSt 10:08.46 '99.
Smashed her best when she won the European 10,000m Challenge 2002.

Cristina CASANDRA b. 1 Feb 1977 Zalau 1.68m 50kg. née Iloc. CSM Suceava. Sports teacher.
At 3000mSt: ECp: '02-03: 2/2. At 5000m: WJ: '96- 3. Won ROM 3000mSt 2000-03; Balkan 2002-03.
World 3000m steeplechase best 2000, Four ROM records 2002.
Progress at 3000mSt: 2000- 9:40.20, 2001- 9:45.12, 2002- 9:33.16, 2003- 9:40.49. pbs: 1500m 4:20.46 '96, 2000m 5:56.82 '00, 5000m 15:22.64 '99.

Norica CÎMPEAN b. 22 Mar 1972 Teius 1.64m 58kg. CSM Unirea Alba Iulia. Civil servant.
At 20kmW: OG: '00- 6; WCh: '99- dnf, '01- 6, '03- dq; EC: '02- dq; WCp: '99- 3, '02- 10; ECp: '00-01-03: 6/6/7. At 10kmW: OG: '96- 29; WCh: '95- 20; EC: '98- dq; WCp: '97- 17; ECp: '98- 12. Won ROM 10kmW 1993-7, 1999-2000, 2002; 20kmW 1995-8, 2000-02; Balkan 1994, 1999.
ROM walks records: 10km (4), 20km (2) 1995-9.
Progression at 10kmW, 20kmW: 1990- 53:45, 1991- 51:51, 1992- 46:05, 1993- 45:42, 1994- 45:10.4, 1995- 43:48, 1:37:14; 1996- 42:55, 1997- 43:21, 1:35:20; 1998- 42:57, 1:35:44, 1999- 42:16, 1:27:46; 2000- 43:51, 1:28:59; 2001- 43:39, 1:29:25; 2002- 42:31/42:54.86t, 1:30:50; 2003- 44:22, 1:30:27. pbs: 3000mW 11:41.85 '99, 5kmW 21:34.20/21:05R '98.

Maria CIONCAN b. 19 Jun 1977 Maieru 1.72m 51kg. CSU Cluj-Napoca & Siderurgica Hunedoara. Student.
At 1500m (800m): WCh: '03- 9 (sf); EU23: '99- 7; ECp: '02- 1, '03- 4 (2). Won ROM 800m & 1500m 2003.
Progression at 1500m: 1998- 4:13.36, 1999- 4:11.18, 2000- 4:06.20, 2001- 4:07.89i/4:12.24, 2002- 4:02.10, 2003- 4:02.80. pbs: 800m 1:59.68 '03, 2000m 5:56.82 '00, 3000m 8:57.71 '02.

Constantina DITA-TOMESCU b. 23 Jan 1970 Turburea 1.65m 48kg. née Dita. Pandurii Tg. Jiu. Sports teacher.
At Mar: WCh: '99- 19, '01- 10, '03- dnf. World CC: '98- 16; HMar: 99- 13, '03- 5; Eur CC: '99- 2. Won ROM 10000m 1998, HMar 2002; Balkan 5000m 2002, 10000m 1997-8.
Progression at Mar: 1997- 2:35:32, 1998- 2:34: 35, 1999- 2:36:28, 2000- 2:37:57, 2001- 2:26:39, 2002- 2:23:54, 2003- 2:23:35. pbs: 5000m 15:28.91 '00, 10000m 32:26.24 '98, Road: 10km: 32:17 '01, 15km 49:11 01, HMar 68:10 '02.
Led World marathon by almost 2 mins at 20k in 2001 and by 32sec at 5k in 2003. 2nd Chicago 2003.

Adelina GAVRILA b. 26 Nov 1978 Braila 1.74m 55kg. CSM Braila & Farul Constanta. Student.
At TJ: WCh: '99- 11, '01- dnq 15. '03- 9; EC: '98- 11; WI: '01-03-04: 8/8/7; WJ: '96- 3; EJ: '97- 1; WUG: '99- 3; ECp: '03- 3. Won Balkan 1999, 2001, ROM 2000, 2003.
Progression at TJ: 1995- 13.69: 1996- 13.50, 1997- 13.62, 1998- 14.53, 1999- 14.71, 2000- 14.44, 2001- 14.18, 2002- 14.29i/14.13w, 2003- 14.76i/14.75. pb LJ 6.24 '01.

Nicoleta GRASU b. 11 Sep 1971 Secuieni 1.76m 88kg. née Gradinaru. Administration officer. Dinamo Bucuresti.
At DT: OG: '92- dnq 13, '96- 7, '00- dnq 19; WCh: '93- 7, '95- dnq 18, '97- 10, '99- 3, '01- 3; EC: '94- 4, '98- 3; WJ: '90- 6; WUG: '97- 3, '99- 1; WCp: '98- 2; ECp: '97-9-00-01-02: 4/2/1/3/2; E23Cp: '92- 1. Won Balkan 1992, 1997, 1999; ROM 1992-3, 1995-7, 1999-2002. 3rd GP 1996.
Progression at DT: 1985- 36.02, 1986- 43.56, 1987- 50.82, 1988- 51.06, 1989- 52.54, 1990- 56.02, 1991- 59.90, 1992- 65.66, 1993- 65.16, 1994- 64.40, 1995- 64.62, 1996- 65.26, 1997- 64.68, 1998- 67.80, 1999- 68.80, 2000- 68.70, 2001- 68.31, 2002- 64.90. pb SP 15.00i '92, 14.56 '91.
Married her coach Costel Grasu (b. 5 Jul 1967) DT pb 67.08 '92; 4 OG 1992.

Monica IAGAR b. 2 Apr 1973 Sighetul Marmatiei 1.86m 68kg. Dinamo Bucuresti. Sports teacher. Former married name Dinescu.
At HJ: OG: '00- 9=; WCh: '95- dnq 17=, '97- 13, '99- 10=, '01- 7=; EC: '94- dnq, '98- 1; WI: '97-9-01: 9=/4/8; EI: '96- 5, '98- 1; WUG: '97- 2, '99- 1; WCp: '98- 1; ECp: '94-7-9-00: 2/5/2/1; E23Cp: '94- 4; 3rd GP 1997, ROM champion 1995-8, 2000; Balkan 1997.
Four Romanian high jump records 1997-2000.
Progression at HJ: 1987- 1.70, 1988- 1.78, 1989- 1.64, 1990- 1.78, 1992- 1.78, 1993- 1.87i/1.84, 1994- 1.91, 1995- 1.97i/1.92, 1996- 1.96i/1.95dq/1.93, 1997- 2.00, 1998- 2.02, 1999- 2.03i/2.01, 2000- 2.02, 2001- 1.97i/1.92, 2003- 1.85, 2004- 1.95i.
World number one high jumper of 1998. Six months drugs suspension 1996. Coached by Viorica Viscopoleanu.

Mihaela MELINTE b. 27 Mar 1975 Bacau 1.74m 92kg. SC Bacau. Student.
At HT: WCh: '99- 1, '03- 6; EC: '98- 1; WUG: '97- 1, '99- 1; EU23: '97- 1; ECp: '97-9-00-03: 2/1/dq/2; ROM champion 1992-2000, 2003; Balkan 2003.
Eight world hammer records 1995-9, 21 ROM records 1992-9, three world junior records 1992-4.
Progression at HT: 1991- 37.76, 1992- 58.70, 1993- 62.52, 1994- 65.48, 1995- 66.86, 1996- 69.42, 1997- 71.24, 1998- 73.14, 1999- 76.07, 2000- 72.90/74.80 dq, 2003- 71.15. pbs: SP 13.98 '94, DT 43.12 '97.
Won 42 successive hammer competitions between losses to Olga Kuzenkova on 27 Jun 1997 and 25 Jun 2000. Positive drugs test (on 7 June 2000) announced just as she was about to compete at the 2000 Olympic Games. Returned to competition in 2003.

Felicia MOLDOVAN b. 29 Sep 1967 Mîgura Ilvei 1.69m 70kg. née Tilea. Teacher. Rapid Bucuresti. Sports teacher.
At JT: OG: '96- 10, '00- dnq 15; WCh: '93- 8, '95- 2, '97- 5, '99- 11, '01- dnq 16; EC: '90- dq (9), '94- 3, '98- 10, '02- 9; WUG: '95- 1; ECp: '93-4-6-7-02: 1/3/1B/2/2. ROM champion 1990, 1994, 1996-8.
Romanian JT record 1996, new spec (2) 2000.
Progression at JT: 1981- 36.62, 1982- 44.00, 1983- 48.40, 1984- 46.80, 1985- 47.74, 1986- 51.42, 1987- 51.44, 1988- 47.42, 1989- 59.54, 1990- 64.02, 1993- 65.62, 1994- 66.40, 1995- 65.22, 1996- 69.26, 1997- 65.76, 1998- 65.10, 1999- 65.27; new: 60.97, 2000- 63.12, 2001- 62.27, 2002- 63.89.
Two-year drugs ban after positive test for steroids when 9th at 1990 European Champs.

Cristina NICOLAU b. 8 Aug 1977 Bucuresti 1.84m 66kg. Steaua Bucuresti. Civil Servant.
At TJ (/LJ): OG: '00- 6; WCh: '97- dnq 34, '99- 8, '01- 6, '03- dnq 26; EC: '02- 5/dnq 14; WJ: '94- (9), '96- 2/2; EJ: '95- (2); EU23: '97- 1 (2), '99- 1/4; WI: '01- 6; EI: '00- 2, '02- 5; WUG: '97- 5/3; ECp: '99- 1, '01- 3, '02- 5/2. At LJ: WJ: '96- 2; EJ: '93- 3, '95- 2; E23Cp: '94- 3. Won ROM LJ 1996, 1999, 2002; TJ 1999, 2001; Balkan TJ 2003.
Progression at TJ: 1996- 13.89, 1997- 14.22/14.23i, 1998- 14.20, 1999- 14.70, 2000- 14.94i/14.19/14.22w, 2001- 14.62, 2002- 14.40, 2003- 14.31. pbs: HJ 1.82 '95, LJ 6.65 '02, 6.69w '99.
Set European age-14 LJ best (6.19 '91). Her father Mihai Nicolau won the ROM decathlon in 1975 and 1977, pb 7465 '75.

Oana PANTELIMON b. 27 Sep 1972 Tecuci 1.78m 61kg. née Musunoi. Steaua Bucuresti. Administration officer.
At HJ: OG: '00- 3=; WCh: '01- 9, '03- dnq 14; EC: '02- 4; WJ: '90- dnq, WI: '03- 9; ECp: '01-02-03: 5/2/6=; E23Cp: '92- 3. Romanian champion 1999, 2001, 2003; Balkan 2000, 2002.
Progression at HJ: 1987- 1.78, 1988- 1.86, 1989- 1.90, 1990- 1.85, 1991- 1.87i/1.86, 1992- 1.94, 1993- 1.91i/1.87, 1994- 1.88, 1995- 1.92, 1996- 1.92, 1997- 1.93, 1999- 1.80+, 2000- 1.99, 2001- 1.93, 2002- 1.94, 2003- 1.95i/1.92.
Her bronze medal at the 2000 Olympics was a startling accomplishment, as this was her first major championship and after matching her pb of 1.94 to qualify she raised it with 1.96 and 1.99 in the final.

Lidia SIMON b. 4 Sep 1973 Târgu Cârbunesti 1.57m 44kg. née Slavuteanu. Dinamo Bucuresti. Administration officer.
At Mar: OG: '96- 6, '00- 2; WCh: '95- 10, '97- 3, '99- 3, '01- 1; EC: '94- 10; WCp: '95- 2; won Balkan 1994. At 10000m: EC: '98- 3. World HMar: '96-7-8-00: 2/3/3/3.
Romanian marathon records 1997 and 1999, half marathon 2000.
Progression at 10000m, Mar: 1990- 2:58:18, 1991- 34:23.52, 2:52:20; 1993- 2:56:10, 1994- 2:32:38, 1995- 2:31:46, 1996- 2:30:13, 1997- 2:27:04, 1998- 31:32.64, 2:28:31; 1999- 2:23:24, 2000- 2:22:54, 2001- 2:24:15, 2003- 2:40:54. pbs: 1500m 4:22.57 '91, 3000m 9:25.84 '91, HMar 68:34 '00.
Won marathons at Kastoria and Lyon 1994. Took over 3 minutes off her pb for 3rd in Osaka (2:27:04), almost matched that when 3rd in London (2:27:11) and had third 3rd of

1997 at the Worlds. Won Osaka 1998, 1999 (in a brilliant ROM record 2:23:24, the then fastest ever in a women's only race on an out and back course), and in 2000, when she moved to eighth on world all-time list with 2:22:54. 2nd London 2000 and 4th 2001. Married to her coach Liviu Simon, their son Cristian born 24 Dec 2002.

Claudia STEF b. 25 Feb 1978 Craiova 1.60m 48kg. née Iovan. CSM Craiova. Student.
At 20kmW: WCh: '99- 11, '03- 5; EC: '02- 5; WCp: '99-, '02- 6; EU23: '99- 1. At 10kmW: EC: 98- 12; ECp: '98- 3; WUG: '99- 1. At 5000mW: WJ: '98- 3; EJ: '97- 1. Won ROM 10kmW 1998.
World indoor best 3000mW 1999.
Progression at 10kmW, 20kmW: 1996- 44:52, 1997- 43:52, 1998- 43:11, 1999- 42:37, 1:29:39; 2000- 44:35dq/4:52, 1:29:39; 2002- 42:35, 1:29:57; 2003- 44:12, 1:29:09. pbs: 3000mW 12:24.47 '97, 11:40.33i '99; 5000mW 20:30.8 '98.
Two year drugs ban from 20 May 2000.

Gabriela SZABO b. 14 Nov 1975 Bistrita 1.58m 42kg. Sports teacher. Rapid Bucuresti.
At 5000m (1500m): OG: '96- h (2), '00- 1 (3); WCh: '95- 4, '97- 1, '99- 1, '01- 8 (1), '03- 11; EC: '98- 2, '02- (2); WUG: '95- 1 (1), '97- (1); ECp: '95- 1B, '97- 1 (2), '99- (1 1500 & 3000). At 3000m: EC: '94- 3; WJ: '92- 2, '94- 1; EJ: '91- 1, '93-1; WI: '95- 1, '97- 1, '99- 1 (1), '01- 2; EI: '98- 1, '00- 1; WCp: '94-8-02: 3/1/1; ECp: '00- 1, '02- 1; E23Cp: '92- 2, '94- 1. Won GP 3000m 1999 (and overall), 2002. World CC: '94- 4J, '95- 10, '96- 9. Won ROM 3000m 1993.
Records: World indoor 2000m 1998, 5000m (14:47.35) 1999, 3000m (8:32.88) 2001; European 3000m 2002, 5000m 1998, European junior 3000m 1994. ROM 3000m 1998 and 2001, 5000m (4) 1995-8.
Progress at 1500m, 3000m, 5000m: 1991- 4:17.07, 9:19.28; 1992- 4:12.57, 8:48.28; 1993- 4:10.32, 8:50.97; 1994- 4:14.43, 8:40.08; 1995- 4:11.73, 8:30.03, 14:53.91; 1996- 4:01.54, 8:36.07, 14:41.12; 1997- 4:06.14i/4:06.25, 8:27.78, 14:42.43; 1998- 3:56.97, 8:24.31, 14:31.48; 1999- 4:03.23i/4:13.61, 8:25.03, 14:40.59; 2000- 4:00.73, 8:26.35, 14:40.61; 2001- 4:00.57, 8:24.19, 14:46.92; 2002- 3:58.78, 8:21.42, 14:34.29; 2003- 8:33.95, 14:41.35. pbs: 1000m 2:36.74 '89, 1M 4:19.30 '98, 2000m 5:30.53i '98, 5:36.88 '97.
Is taking a year out from her brilliant career. In 1999 she won 1500m and 3000m at the World Indoors and went on outdoors to annex the World title at 5000m, a European Cup 1500m/3000m double, a half-share of the $1 million jackpot for her seven wins at 3000m/5000m in Golden League meetings and the overall IAAF Grand Prix title. She has not raced in Romania since 1994. Married her coach Zsolt Gyöngyössy on 2 October 1999.

Ionela TÎRLEA b. 9 Feb 1976 Horezu 1.69m 54kg. CSM-PAB Arad. Sports teacher.
At 400mh/4x400mR (200m): OG: '96- 7, '00- 6; WCh: '95- 7, '01- 6, '03- 4; EC: '94- 7, '98- 1/4. '02- 1; WJ: '94- 1/3R; EJ: '93- 1, '95- 1; WUG: '95- 2; WCp: '98- 4, '02- 4; ECp: '93- (7), '94- 7 (8), '97- 8, '99- 3R (4, 1-400, 4-100), '01- 2 (2), '02 (5), '03- 1 (2); WI: '97- 4, '99- (1); E23Cp: '94- 1 (2). At 400m: WUG: '99- 1; WJ: '92- 3/1R; WI: '97- 4, '04- 4/3R; EI: '94- 4, '96- 4, '98- 2; E23Cp: '92- 2 (4). Won ROM 100m 1998, 2001; 200m 1998-9, 2002; 400m 1996, 1999; 400mh 1994-6; Balkan 200m 2002.
Romanian records: 100m (2) 1998-9, 200m (3) 1998-9, 400m (2) 1998-9, 400mh (6) 1996-9. European Junior 400mh record 1995.
Progression at 200m, 400m, 400mh: 1991- 24.51, 1992- 23.84, 52.13; 1993- 23.49, 56.30H; 1994- 23.60, 56.25H; 1995- 23.54, 55.26H; 1996- 54.40, 1997- 23.07, 52.06i, 55.04; 1998- 22.65/22.5A, 50.32, 53.37; 1999- 22.35, 49.88, 53.25; 2000- 51.84, 54.35; 2001- 22.77, 52.64i, 54.65; 2002- 23.04, 54.61; 2003- 22.78, 52.19, 53.87. pb 100m 11.30 '99.

RUSSIA

Governing body: All-Russia Athletic Federation, Luzhnetskaya Nab. 8, Moscow 119992. Founded 1911.

National Championships first held 1908, USSR women from 1922. **2003 Champions**: **Men**: 100m: Aleksandr Smirnov 10.55, 200m: Yevgeniy Vorobyev 21.18, 400m: Anton Galkin 45.90, 800m: Dmitriy Bogdanov 1:46.76, 1500m: Vyacheslav Shabunin 3:38.86, 5000m: Mikhail Yeginov 13:57.90, 10000m: Dmitroy Maksimov 28:54.75, HMar:, Mar:, 3000mSt: Roman Usov 8:33.08, 110mh: Sergey Chepiga 13.72, 400mh: Boris Gorban 49.30, HJ: Yaroslav Rybakov 2.28, PV: Vadim Strogalyov 5.60, LJ: Vitaliy Shkurlatov 8.23, TJ: Vitaliy Moskalenko 17.17, SP: Pawel Chumachenko 20.51, DT: Dmitriy Shevchenko 65.16, HT: Ilya Konovalov 82.28, JT: Sergey Makarov 85.46, Dec: Sergey Nikitin 7916, 20kmW: Viktor Burayev 1:20:56, 50kmW: Denis Nizhegorodov 3:43:27. **Women**: 100m: Yuliya Tabakova 11.23, 200m: Yelena Bolsun 23.23, 400m: Natalya Nazarova 49.78, 800m: Natalya Khrushchelyova 1:58.07, 1500m: Tatyana Tomashova 4:01.19, 5000m/3000mSt: Gulnara Samitova 15:04.58/9:08.33, 10000m: Galina Bogomolova 30:46.48, Mar:, 100mh: Natalya Shekhodanova 13.02, 400mh: Yuliya Pechonkina 52.34, HJ: Marina Kuptsova 1.98, PV: Yelena Belyakova 4.60, LJ: Olga Rublyova 6.89, TJ: Nadezhda Bazhenova 14.35, SP: Svetlana Krivelyova 20.77, DT: Natalya Sadova 63.58, HT: Olga Kuzenkova 71.70, JT: Tatyana Shikolenko 66.00, Hep: Natalya Roshchupkina 6170, 20kmW: Tatyana Gudkova 1:28:37.
Note: Clubs abbreviations: Dyn – Dynamo, TU – Trade Union sports society, VS – Army, YR – Yunest Rossii.

Vladimir ANDREYEV b. 7 Sep 1966 Yamanchurino, Chuvashiya 1.70m 58kg. Cheboksary VS. Electrician.
At 20kmW: OG: '92- 13, '00- 3; WCh: '93- 19, '97- dnf, '99/01/03- dq; EC: '02- 2; WCp: '93-7-9-02:

11/10/3/2; ECp: '01- 5, '03- 3. USSR champion 1989, CIS 1992, Russian 1993-4.
Progression at 20kmW: 1989- 1:20:08, 1990- 1:19:21, 1991- 1:19:17, 1992- 1:19:53, 1993- 1:19:43, 1994- 1:21:53, 1995- 1:18:32, 1996- 1:19:11, 1997- 1:18:39, 1998- 1:18:40, 1999- 1:19:57, 2000- 1:18:16, 2001- 1:20:14, 2002- 1:19:18, 2003- 1:20:56. pbs: 5000mW 18:31.63i '92, 19:15.0 '02; 10000mW 39:27.0i '95, 1HrW 14,735m '92, 30kmW 2:09:07 '01, 35kmW 2:29:31 '01. Won Russian winter 20km 1995-8.

Yuriy BORZAKOVSKIY b. 12 Apr 1981 Kratovo, Moskva reg. 1.81m 70kg. Zhukovskiy Dyn. Student.
At 800m/4x400mR: OG: '00- 6; WCh: '03- 2; EC: '02- 2R; EJ: '99- 1; WI: '01- 1; EI: '00- 1; ECp: '99- 1, '02- 1; 2nd GP 2001. At 400m: EC: '02- sf; EU23: '01- 1.
Records: Two world junior indoor 800m 2000, European Junior 800m (2) & 1000m 2000; four Russian 800m 2001.
Progression at 800m: 1997- 1:52.8i/1:53.69, 1998- 1:47.71, 1999- 1:46.13, 2000- 1:44.33, 2001- 1:42.47, 2002- 1:44.20, 2003- 1:43.68. pbs: 200m 22.56 '99, 400m 45.84 '00, 1000m 2:17.40 '00, 1500m 3:43.24 '03.
He won at the World Youth Games in 1998, and at the age of 18 had a startling victory when he sprinted to victory in the European Cup 800m. In Jan 2000 he set a hugely impressive Russian senior and world junior record 1:44.38 in Dortmund. He typically leaves himself a tremendous amount to do on the second lap of his 800m races and curiously did not compete at the 2001 Worlds or 2002 Europeans at this event, although he ran a 44.75 last leg in the European 4x400m.

Viktor BURAYEV b. 23 Aug 1982 Zarechnyi, Penza Reg. 1.76m 58kg. Saransk VS.
At 20kmW: WCh: '01- 3, '03- dq; EC: '02- 4; ECp: '01- 1. At 10kmW: WJ: '00- 3; WY: '99- 1. Won RUS 20kmW 2002-03.
World junior walks records 10000m 2000, 20km 2001.
Progression at 20kmW: 1999- 1:28:18, 2001- 1:18:06, 2002- 1:20:36, 2003- 1:20:56. pbs: 5000mW 19:12.0 '02, 10000mW 38:46.4 '00.
At 18 years 264 days he became the youngest ever men's walk medallist at the World Championships – and he was the only junior to win a medal in 2001.

Danila BURKENYA b. 20 Jul 1978 Ashkhabad, Turkmenistan 1.98m 82kg. Luch Moskva
At LJ: OG: '00- dnq 26; WCh: '01/03- dnq 19/30; EC: '03- 5; EJ: '97- 5 (9 TJ); EI: '98- 4; ECp: '01- 1, '02- 4. At TJ: WI: '04- 7. Won RUS LJ 2000, 2002.
Progression at LJ, TJ: 1997- 7.81, 16.29; 1998- 7.68, 16.36/16.40w; 1999- 8.07i/8.00, 16.30i; 2000- 8.12, 16.14; 2001- 8.31, 2002- 8.19/8.35w '02, 2003- 8.23, 16.58i; 2004- 17.41i. pb 100m 10.98 '97.

Pavel GERASIMOV b. 29 May 1979 Aleksin, Tula reg. 1.90m 80kg. Luch Moskva.
At PV: OG: '00- dnq 26=; WCh: '03- dnq 17; EC: '02- 12; WJ: '98- 1; EJ: '97- 2; WI: '01- 5, EI: '02- 6. Russian champion 2000.
Progression at PV: 1995- 4.40, 1996- 5.10i/5.00, 1997- 5.30, 1998- 5.55, 1999- 5.65/5.70ex, 2000- 5.90, 2001- 5.81i/5.50, 2002- 5.80i/5.60, 2003- 5.67, 2004- 5.77i.

Vasiliy GORSHKOV b. 5 Feb 1977 Moskva. 1.83m 78kg. Luch Moskva.
At PV: WCh: '01- dnq 21; EC: '02- 8; WI: '03- 4; ECp: '01-02: 3/4. Russian champion 2001-02.
Progression at PV: 1992- 4.20, 1993- 4.60, 1994- 5.00, 1995- 5.20, 1997- 5.50?, 1998- 5.70, 1999- 5.60, 2000- 5.60i/5.55/5.70ex, 2001- 5.75/5.81ex, 2002- 5.80, 2003- 5.73i/5.60.

Aleksandr IVANOV b. 25 May 1982 Leningrad 1.94m 110kg. St-Peterburg VS.
At JT: WCh: '01- 10, '03- 12; EC: '02- 6; EU23: '03- 1; EJ: '01- 1; WJ: '00- 6; WY: '99- 3. Russian champion 2002.
Progression at JT: 1998- 67.97, 1999- 71.76, 2000- 77.11, 2001- 83.55, 2002- 87.62, 2003- 88.90.

Vadim KHERSONTSEV b. 8 Jul 1974 Kursk region 1.92m 106kg. Luch Moskva.
At HT: OG: '96- dnq 15; WCh: '97- 7, '99- 8; EC: '02- 16; EJ: '93- 3; WUG: '97- 4; ECp: '97- 2, '02- 6. Russian champion 1996.
Progression at HT: 1990- 56.72, 1991- 61.80, 1992- 68.58, 1993- 72.72, 1994- 76.78, 1995- 76.94, 1996- 80.68, 1997- 78.58, 1998- 79.10, 1999- 78.82, 2000- 78.16, 2001- 81.26, 2002- 78.80, 2003- 78.89.

Sergey KIRMASOV b. 25 Mar 1970 Mcensk Oryol region 1.80m 115kg. Mcensk VS. Soldier.
At HT: WCh: '01/03- dnq 15/20; EC: '98- dnq 18; EJ: '89- 1; ECp: '99- 7, '00- 5. Russian champion 1992, 1998, 2001.
Progression at HT: 1988- 71.20, 1989- 75.52, 1990- 77.66, 1991- 81.14, 1992- 79.92, 1993- 82.54, 1994- 79.20dq, 1998- 82.62, 1999- 79.55, 2000- 78.44, 2001- 80.07, 2002- 79.19, 2003- 79.62.
Four year drugs ban 1994.

Sergey KLYUGIN b. 24 Mar 1974 Kineshma, Ivanova region 1.92m 82kg. Luch Moskva. Teacher.
At HJ: OG: '00- 1; WCh: '97- 11, '99- dnq 24, '01- 5=; EC: '98- 3; WJ: '92- 5=, EJ: '91- 2; EU23Cp: '94- 2; ECp: '97-8-00: 2/1/3=. Russian champion 2000-01.
Progression at HJ: 1986- 1.55, 1987- 1.65, 1988- 1.80, 1989- 1.98, 1990- 2.16, 1991- 2.27, 1992- 2.28i/2.24, 1993- 2.26i/2.24, 1994- 2.28i/2.26, 1995- 2.26, 1996- 2.28, 1997- 2.31i/2.30, 1998- 2.36, 1999- 2.33, 2000- 2.35, 2001- 2.31, 2002- 2.24, 2003- 2.25, 2004- 2.28i.
Two knee operations in winter 2001/02.

Ilya KONOVALOV b. 4 Mar 1971 Efrosimovka, Kursk region 1.92m 110kg. Kursk VS. Soldier.
At HT: OG: '96- 6, '00- 5; WCh: '95- 7, '97- 6, '99- 10, '01- 3, '03- 6; EC: '98- 9, '02- dnq 20; WUG: '97- 3; ECp: '95- 1, '98- 2. Won RUS 1995, 1999, 2002-03.

Progression at HT: 1988- 63.10, 1989- 71.30, 1990- 74.66, 1991- 76.26, 1992- 77.04, 1993- 77.44, 1994- 78.30, 1995- 79.66, 1996- 79.46, 1997- 78.92, 1998- 79.82, 1999- 80.51, 2000- 81.93, 2001- 80.27, 2002- 81.81, 2003- 82.28.

Lev LOBODIN b. 1 Apr 1969 Rossosh, Voronezh reg. 1.88m 93kg. Luch Moskva. Teacher.
At Dec: OG: '96- dnf, '00- 13; WCh: '95- 7, '97- dnf, '99- 5, '01- 5, '03- 6; EC: '94- 3, '98- 3, '02- 3; ECp: '94- 2, '95- 6. UKR champion 1991. At Hep: WI: '93-9-01-03-04: 4/6/3/2/3; EI: '92- 6, '98- 3.
Progression at Dec: 1988- 7091h, 1991- 8018, 1992- 7998, 1993- 8156, 1994- 8201, 1995- 8286, 1996- 8315, 1997- 8184, 1998- 8571, 1999- 8494, 2000- 8071, 2001- 8465, 2002- 8433, 2003- 8198. pbs: 60m 6.83i '98, 100m 10.66 '01, 10.65w '94; 400m 48.39 '96, 1000m 2:43.59i '01, 1500m 4: 29.95 '91, 60mh 7.79i '98, 110mh 13.94 '99, HJ 2.10 '91, PV 5.30i '03, 5.20 '98; LJ 7.56/7.68i/ 7.74w '99, SP 16.67i '03, 16.30 '02; DT 50.72 '99, JT 59.00 '95, Hep 6412i '03.
Changed nationality UKR to RUS after 1996. 24 decathlons over 8000 points 1991-2003.

Sergey MAKAROV b. 19 Mar 1973 Lyubertsy 1.92m 100kg. Moskva Dyn.
At JT: OG: '96- 6, '00- 3; WCh: '97- 5, '99- 9, '01- 7. '03- 1; EC: '98- 4, '02- 2; WCp: '98- 2, '02- 1; ECp: '96-7-8-9-00-01-02-03: 2/4/2/2/2/2/1/1; E23Cp: '94- 2. Won GWG 1998, WAF 2003, RUS 1996-7, 2000-01, 2003.
Six Russian records 1996-2002.
Progression at JT: 1991- 73.48, 1992- 76.08, 1993- 75.78, 1994- 82.54, 1995- 84.42, 1996- 88.86, 1997- 88.54, 1998- 86.96, 1999- 89.93, 2000- 89.92, 2001- 88.42, 2002- 92.61, 2003- 90.11.
Married to Oksana Ovchinnikova (b. 21 Jul 1971, Russian 'old' javelin record 68.72 '96. 2 WJ 1990). His father Aleksandr Makarov (b. 11 Feb 1951) was 2nd in the 1980 Olympic JT with a pb 89.64 (old javelin).

Ilya MARKOV b. 19 Jun 1972 Asbest, Sverdlovsk reg. 1.74m 65kg. Asbest VS. Soldier.
At 20kmW: OG: '96- 2, '00- 15; WCh: '95- 4, '97- dq, '99- 1, '01- 2, '03- 8; EC: '94- 18, '98- 1; WUG: '97- 1; WCp: '95-3-9: 30/3/7; ECp: '03- 5. Won RUS 1995, GWG 1998. At 10kmW: WJ: '90- 1; EJ: '91- 1.
Progression at 20kmW: 1991- 1:33:46, 1992- 1:23:27, 1993- 1:20:19, 1994- 1:24:07, 1995- 1:18:53, 1996- 1:18:48, 1997- 1:18:30, 1998- 1:19:46, 1999- 1:18:50, 2000- 1:20:53, 2001- 1:19:36, 2003- 1:20:05, 2004- 1:19:25. pbs: 3000mW 11:08.2i '92, 5000mW 18:36.71i '99, 18:46.96 '01; 10000mW 39:15.6 '98.

Nikolay MATYUKHIN b. 13 Dec 1968 Zhukovskiy, Moskva region 1.79m 68kg. Moskva Dyn. Teacher.
At 50kmW: OG: '96- 25, '00- 5; WCh: '95- 10, '97- 15, '99- 2, '01- dq; EC: '98- 16; WCp: '95-7-9-02: 17/4/3/4; ECp: '01- 2. Russian champion 1995.
Progression at 20kmW, 50kmW: 1990- 1:23:52, 4:10.04; 1991- 1:22:36, 1992- 1:21:16, 1993- 1:19:43, 1994- 3:45:34, 1995- 3:51:13, 1996- 1:22:18, 3:42:30; 1997- 1:24:51, 3:41:36; 1998- 1:20:12, 3:45:29; 1999- 3:40:13, 2000- 3:42:02, 2001- 1:22:13, 3:45:48; 2002- 3:47:06. 2003- 3:47:36. pbs: 10000mW 41:46.30t '94, 30kmW 2:06:36 '97, 35kmW 2:27:29 '97.

Denis NIZHEGORODOV b. 26 Jul 1980 Saransk 1.80m 61kg. Saransk TU
At 50kmW: WCh: '03- 5; Russian champion 2003. At 20kmW: EU23: '01- 5; WUG: '01- 4; ECp: '00- 17, '01- 7.
Progression at 20kmW, 50kmW: 2000- 1:21:47, 2001- 1:18:20; 2003- 1:23:23, 3:38:23. pbs: 30kmW 2:12:27 '03, 35kmW 2:33:48 '03.

Igor PAVLOV b. 18 Jul 1979 Moskva 1.87m 78kg. Moskva VS.
At PV: WI: '04- 1; WUG: '03- 2.
Progression at PV: 1998- 5.10, 1999- 5.30i, 2000- 5.55/5.70sq, 2001- 5.60i, 2002- 5.40, 2003- 5.65, 2004- 5.80i.

Aleksandr POGORELOV b. 10 Jan 1980 Zheleznogorsk, Kursk region 2.01m 95kg. Bryansk Dyn.
At Dec: WCh: '03- dnf; EC: '02- 8; EJ: '99- dnf; ECp: '02- 5, '03- 2. At Hep: WI: '03-04: 6/6.
Progression at Dec: 1997- 5750, 1998- 6356, 1999- 6895, 2001- 7354, 2002- 8163, 2003- 8072. pbs: 60m 6.94i '04, 100m 11.05 '02, 400m 50.49 '03, 1000m 2:52.30i '03, 1500m 4:48.89 '02, 60mh 8.03i '03, 110mh 14.28 '03, HJ 2.15 '02, PV 5.00i '03, 4.95 '02; LJ 7.74 '02, SP 15.67i '04, 15.37 '03; DT 44.64 '02, JT 60.72 '03, Hep 6163i '04.

Vladimir POTEMIN b. 15 Jan 1980 Insar, Morodoviya 1.77m 69kg. Saransk VS.
At 50kmW: WCh: '01- 5; WCp: '02- 17; ECp: '01- 3. At 20kmW: OG: '00- 26. 10000mW: EJ: '99- 2.
World U23 best 50km walk 2000.
Progress at 50kmW: 2000- 3:39:21, 2001- 3:46.12, 2002- 3:57:18, 2003- 3:45:27. pbs: 10000mW 40: 28.26 '99, 20kmW 1:23:37 '03, 30kmW 2:08:05 '01, 35kmW 2:29:03 '01.

Roman RASSKAZOV b. 28 Apr 1979 Kovylkino (Mordoviya) 1.86m 64kg. Saransk VS. Student.
At 20kmW: OG: '00- 6; WCh: '99- dnf, 01- 1, '03- 3. RUS champion 1999-2001. At 10000mW: WJ: '98- 1.
World best and two RUS records 20km walk 2000.
Progression at 20kmW: 1997- 1:31:24, 1999- 1:19:36, 2000- 1:17:46, 2001- 1:20:31, 2002- 1:21:01, 2003- 1:18:07, 2004- 1:18:35. pbs: 5000mW 19:02.1i '00, 19:11.5 '02; 10kmW 37:11 (world best) '00.

Yaroslav RYBAKOV b. 22 Nov 1980 Mogilyev, Belarus 1.98m 84kg. Luch Moskva.
At HJ: WCh: '01- 2=, '03- 9; EC: '02- 1; WJ: '98- 5; EJ: '99- 3; WI: '01-03-04: 7/2/2; EI: '02- 3; WCp: '02- 1; ECp: '01-02-03: 1/2/1; Won WAF 2003, 2nd GP 2002. Russian champion 2002-03.
Progression at HJ: 1997- 2.10i/2.09, 1998- 2.20, 1999- 2.19i/2.18, 2000- 2.28, 2001- 2.33, 2002- 2.31, 2003- 2.34.

Vyacheslav SHABUNIN b. 27 Sep 1969 Kamyshlov, Sverdlovsk region 1.71m 56kg. Luch Moskva. Teacher.
At 1500m: OG: '96/00- h; WCh: '95- sf, '97/99- h, '03- 8; EC: '94- 5, '98- 9; WI: '95- 5; EI: '94- 5, '00- 5; ECp: '94-5-7-8-00-02: 6/2/3/7 (5 5000)/ 3/6. At 5000m: WCp: '92- 8. At 3000m: ECp: '99-03: 2/3. Won RUS 1500m 1992, 1994-6, 2002-03.
Russian records 1500m (3) 1997-2000, 1M (4) 1994-2001, 2000m, 3000m 1994-5.
Progression at 1500m/1M: 1988- 4:12.7, 1990- 3;54.6, 1991- 3:44.68, 1992- 3:40.49, 1993- 3:36.59, 1994- 3:38.61/3:53.54M, 1995- 3:34.79/3:51.02M, 1996- 3:34.50, 1997- 3:33.47, 1998- 3:33.30/3:53.30M, 1999- 3:34.01/3:52.23M, 2000- 3:32.28/3:50.54M, 2001- 3:33.01/3:49.83M, 2002- 3:32.37/3:52.49M, 2003- 3:32.63/3:53.74M. pbs: 800m 1:47.00 '96, 2000m 4:57.18 '97, 3000m 7:39.24 '95, 5000m 13:43.39 '94, HMar 61:29 '96.

Dmitriy SHEVCHENKO b. 13 May 1968 Taganrog, Rostov-na-Donu 2.00m 140kg. Krasnodar Dyn. Teacher.
At DT: OG: '92- 8, '00- 11; WCh: '91- 7, '93- 2, '95- 8, '99- dnq 19, '01- 4, '03- 10; EC: '94- 2, '98- dnq, '02- 6; ECp '93-4-8-01-02-03: 2/1/1/3/2/1; won GP 1995. USSR champion 1991, CIS 1992, Russian 1992-3, 1999-2001, 2003; GWG 1994.
Progression at DT: 1986- 57.30, 1987- 60.34, 1988- 59.68, 1989- 59.38/61.62?, 1990- 64.10, 1991- 63.70, 1992- 67.30, 1993- 66.90, 1994- 64.74, 1995- 68.04dq/ 66.74, 1998- 65.14, 1999- 65.68, 2000- 66.66, 2001- 67.57, 2002- 70.54, 2003- 65.39. pb SP 17.94 '99.
Four year drugs ban for positive test at Cologne 18 Aug 1995, so disqualified from his GP Final win three weeks later; reinstated 1998.

Vitaliy SHKURLATOV b. 25 May 1979 Volgograd 1.82m 76kg. Volgograd VS.
At LJ: WCh: '01- 12, '03- dnq 18; WJ: '98- 8; EU23: '99- 2; EJ: '97- 4; WI: '01- 8, '04- 3; EI: '00- 3, '02- 7; ECp: '00- 1. Russian champion 2003.
Progression at LJ: 1995- 6.84, 1996- 7.64, 1997- 7.92, 1998- 7.79i, 1999- 8.06, 2000- 8.38i/8.22, 2001- 8.18, 2002- 8.15i/8.13, 2003- 8.23, 2004- 8.28i. pb 60m 6.4/6.78i '02.

German SKURYGIN b. 15 Sep 1963 Vutno, Udmurtiya 1.65m 63kg. Izhevsk TU. Teacher.
At 50kW: WCh: '93- 23, '99- dq, '03- 2; EC: '94- 6, '02- 4; WCp: '95-9-02: 18/5/2; ECp: '03- 1. RUS champion 1994.
Russian 50km walk record 2003.
Progression at 50kmW: 1989- 3:50:25, 1990- 3:51:04, 1991- 3:53:33, 1992- 3:59:42, 1993- 3:56:19, 1994- 3:46:30, 1995- 3:51:44, 1996- 3:44:33, 1997- 3:52:57, 1998- 3:47:44, 1999- 3:40:54, 2002- 3:42:08, 2003- 3:36:42. pbs: 20kmW 1:22:12 '88, 30kmW 2:05:37 '98, 35kmW 2:25:58 '98.
Took the gold medal in Seville at the 1999 World Championships, but lost this after a two-year investigation by the Russian Federation resulted in a two-year ban for a positive test for human chorionic gonadotropin.

Kirill SOSUNOV b. 1 Nov 1975 Ryazan 1.90m 86kg. Ryazan TU.
At LJ: OG: '00- dnq 16; WCh: '97- 3; EC: '98- 1; WUG: '95- 1; WJ: '94- dnq; EU23: '97- 2; WI: '97- 2; EI: '02- 5; WCp: '98- 4; ECp: '96-7-8-9-03: 4/1/1/7/6.
Progression at LJ: 1990- 6.70, 1991- 6.85, 1992- 7.11, 1993- 7.66, 1994- 7.96, 1995- 8.28/8.48w, 1996- 8.27i/8.17, 1997- 8.41i/8.30, 1998- 8.38, 1999- 7.98, 2000- 8.34, 2001- 7.82, 2002- 8.03, 2003- 8.01/8.13w, 2004- 8.16i. pb 60m 6.5i '98.
Married to **Olga Kaliturina** (qv).

Igor SPASOVKHODSKIY b. 1 Aug 1979 Moskva 1.91m 91kg. Luch Moskva.
At TJ: OG: '00- dnq 32; WCh: '01- 3, '03- dnq 20; EC: '02- dnq 16; EU23: '01- 2; EI: '02- 7; WUG: '01- 4; ECp: '02- 5.
Progression at TJ: 1997- 14.42, 1998- 15.37, 1999- 16.32, 2000- 16.86, 2001- 17.44, 2002- 17.39/17.42w, 2003- 16.95. pb LJ 7.58 '03.

Andrey STADNICHUK b. 14 Dec 1973 1.76m 64kg.
At 20kmW: EC: '02- 10; WCp: '02- 6; ECp: '03- 10.
Progress at 20kmW: 1994- 1:26:05, 1995- 1:23:15, 1996- 1:24:42, 1997- 1:22:27, 1998- 1:22:03, 1999- 1:23:58, 2000- 1:23:34, 2001- 1:21:44.2t, 2002- 1:19:02, 2003- 1:20:28, 2004- 1:20:05. pb 3000mW 19:33.5i '00, 30kmW 2:06:54 '00, 35kmW 2:29:14 '00.

Vladimir STANKIN b. 2 Jan 1974 1.84m 71kg.
Russian 20km walk record 2004.
Progression at 20kmW: 1992- 1:23:58, 1995- 1:21:43, 1996- 1:20:22, 1998- 1:22:06, 1999- 1:20:21, 2000- 1:20:31, 2001- 1:19:14. 2002- 1:22:07, 2003- 1:21:32. pbs: 10kmW 38:50 '01, 10000mW 40:35.20 '92, 30kmW 2:06:51 '97, 35kmW 2:29:26 '97.
His sister **Irina** became, at 18 years 135 days, the youngest ever world champion (at 10km walk) in 1995 and was World Junior 5000m walk champion in 1994 and 1996.

Vadim STROGALYOV b. 9 Feb 1975 Moskva 1.84m 77kg. Luch Moskva.
At PV: WCh: 97- 7, '99- dnq 19=, '03- 9=. Russian champion 1997, 2003.
Progression at PV: 1992- 4.80, 1993- 5.00, 1994- 5.20, 1995- 5.75i/5.70, 1996- 5.80, 1997- 5.80, 1998- 5.85, 1999- 5.80, 2000- 5.75, 2001- 5.60, 2002- 5.71, 2003- 5.73.

Mikhail TSVETKOV b. 4 May 1980 Ryazan 1.94m 74kg. Ryazan VS.
At HJ: WCh: '03- 4.
Progression at HJ: 1999- 2.10, 2000- 2.20, 2001- 2.25i, 2002- 2.30i/2.25, 2003- 2.30.

Aleksey VOYEVODIN b. 9 Aug 1970 Marat, Penza Reg. 1.78m 65kg. Luch Moskva.
At 50kmW: WCh: '95- 15, '97- 10, '01- dnf, '03- 4; EC: '02- 2; WCp: '95- 10, '02- 1; ECp: '98-01-03: 4/6/2. Won RUS 50kmW 2001-02.
Progression at 50kmW: 1993- 4:04:44, 1994- 3:52:36, 1995- 3:48:55, 1996- 3:45:37, 1997- 3:41:33, 1998-

3:46:31, 1999- 3:51:43, 2000- 3:50:27, 2001- 3:44:32, 2002- 3:40:16, 2003- 3:38:01. pbs: 5000mW 19:19.0 '02, 10000mW 39:22.0i '01, 20kmW 1:19:31 '98, 30kmW 2:06:30 '98, 35kmW 2:26:51 '02.

Aleksey ZAGORNYY b. 31 May 1978 Yaroslavl 1.97m 130kg. Luch Moskva.
At HT: OG: '00- dnq 22; WCh: '03- dnq 22; EC: '02- 11; EJ: '97- 5; EU23: '99- 7; WUG: '01- 4.
Progression at HT: 1994- 59.90, 1995- 71.00, 1996- 71.94, 1997- 71.30, 1998- 77.03, 1999- 77.20, 2000- 79.68, 2001- 80.80, 2002- 83.43, 2003- 80.13.

Women

Natalya ANTYUKH b. 26 Jun 1981 Leningrad 1.81m 66kg. St-Peterburg VS.
At 400m/4x400mR: EC: '02- 2R; WI: '03- 1R, '04- GR; EI: '02- 1; ECp: '01- 3/1R.
Progression at 400m: 2000- 54.79, 2001- 51.19, 2002- 51.17i/51.24, 2003- 51.73i/52.28, 2004- 50.87i. pbs: 200m 23.54 '03, 300m 37.35i '03, 400mh 58.30 '00.

Nadezhda BAZHENOVA b. 22 Sep 1978 Vladimir 1.76m 63kg. Luch Moskva.
At TJ: WCh: '03- dnq 23; EI: '02- 4. Russian champion 2003.
Progression at TJ: 1997- 13.21, 1998- 13.04, 1999- 14.25, 2000- 14.13, 2001- 14.60, 2002- 14.65i/14.31, 2003- 14.35. pb LJ 6.58 '01.

Yelena BELYAKOVA b. 7 Apr 1976 Dolgoprudniy, Moskva reg. 1.77m 56kg. Luch Moskva. Teacher.
At PV: OG: '00- dnq; WCh: '99- 8, '03- 8; EC: '98- nh, '02- 4; EI: '00- 2=, '02- 8; ECp: '98- nh, '99- 4; Won GWG 1998, RUS 1998-9, 2003.
Three Russian pole vault records 1998-2000.
Progression at PV: 1995- 3.40, 1996- 3.90, 1997- 4.15, 1998- 4.38, 1999- 4.46, 2000- 4.50, 2001- 4.55i/4.42, 2002- 4.52, 2003- 4.60.

Lyudmila BIKTASHEVA b. 25 Jul 1974 Kamensk-Uralskiy 1.53m 41kg. Kamensk-Uralskiy TU.
At 10000m: OG: '00- 13; WCh: '01- 10; EC: '02- 3; EJ: '93- 3. World HMar: '99- 10, '03- 7. Won RUS 10000m 2001-02.
Three Russian pole vault records 1998-2000.
Progression at 10000m: 1993- 34:28.04, 1994- 33:52.75, 1996- 33:13.7, 1997- 33:28.78, 1998- 32:29.27, 1999- 32:29.83, 2000- 31:33.58, 2001- 31:30.6, 2002- 31:04.00, 2003- 31:31.87. pbs: 5000m 15:22.98 '00, HMar 70:31 '01.

Galina BOGOMOLOVA b. 15 Oct 1977 Beloretsk, Bashkorstan 1.59m 43kg.
At 10000m (5000m): OG: '00- h; WCh: '03- 6; WJ: '96- 12 (h 3000m); EU23: '97- 7/7. At 3000m: WI: '03- 6; ECp: '00- 2. Eur CC: '02- 2, '03- 10. Won RUS 10000m 2000, 2003.
Russian 10000m record (30:46.48) 2003.
Progression at 5000m. 10000m: 1996- 16:29.56, 1997- 15:53.45, 33:34.44; 1998- 16:18.06, 33:56.04; 1999- 15:52.72, 2000- 15:08.61, 31:29.66; 2002- 15:39.14, 2003- 15:13.08, 30:26.20. pbs: 1500m 4:11.72 '00, 3000m 8:43.45 '00.

Anna CHICHEROVA b. 22 Jul 1982 Yerevan 1.80m 56kg. Moskva VS.
At HJ: WCh: '03- 6; WJ: '00- 4; WY: '99- 1; EJ: '01- 2; WI: '04- 2.
Progression at HJ: 1998- 1.80, 1999- 1.89, 2000- 1.90, 2001- 1.92, 2002- 2.00i/1.89, 2003- 2.04i/2.00, 2004- 2.04i.

Alla DAVYDOVA b. 21 May 1966 Frunze, Kirgizstan 1.67m 86kg. née Fyodorova. Luch Moskva. Teacher
At HT: OG: '00- dnq 18; WCh: '03- dnq 32; EC: '98- 8, '02- 9; ECp: '01- 6. RUS champion 1996.
Two world hammer records 1991.
Progression at HT: 1989- 58.30, 1990- 59.66, 1991- 64.44, 1992- 60.80, 1994- 61.84, 1995- 63.20, 1996- 67.48, 1998- 64.61, 1999- 66.06, 2000- 68.47, 2001- 65.81, 2002- 67.40, 2003- 69 17.

Natalya FEDOSKINA b. 25 Jun 1980 Saransk 1.67m 52m. Saransk.
At 20kmW: WCh: '99/01/03- dq; EC: '02- dnf; WCp: '99- 2, '02- 3; ECp: '01- 2, '03- 4.
Two world junior 20km walk records 1999.
Progression at 10kmW, 20kmW: 1998- 44:59, 1999- 43:58, 1:27:35; 2000- 43:56, 1:28:52; 2001- 43:20, 1:26:50; 2002- 44:03+, 1:27:45; 2003- 44:34, 1:28:17; 2004- 1:28:38. pb 3000mW 12:18.29 '00, 5000mW 20:56.7 '02.

Svetlana FEOFANOVA b. 16 Jul 1980 Moskva 1.63m 52kg. Luch Moskva.
At PV: OG: '00- dnq; WCh: '01- 2, '03- 1; EC: '02- 1; WI: '01-03-04: 2/1/3; EI: '02- 1, WCp: '02- 2; ECp: '00-02: 1/1; 2nd GP 2001. Russian champion 2001.
Eight European pole vault records 2001-02, 10 Russian 2000-02, 9 world indoor 2002-04 (4.71-4.85), 12 European indoor 2001-03.
Progression at PV: 1998- 3.90, 1999- 4.10, 2000- 4.50, 2001- 4.75, 2002- 4.78, 2003- 4.80i/4.75, 2004- 4.85i.
Was a top gymnast, winning Russian titles at youth, junior and U23 level at assymetric bars and floor exercises. Set five indoor world records in a month in 2002.

Lyudmila GALKINA b. 20 Jan 1972 Saratov 1.72m 59kg. Saratov TU.
At LJ (TJ): OG: '96- dnq, '00- 9; WCh: '93- 5, '95- dnq 17, '97- 1, '99- 4, '01- 8, '03- 10; EC: '94- dnq 16, '98- 3; WJ: '90- (7); EJ: '89- 3, '91- 2 (1); WI: '95- 1, '01- 6; EI: '02- 3; WUG: '95- 3; WCp: '98- 4; ECp: '98-99-03: 2/3/4; E23Cp: '94- 1. Won RUS LJ 1997.
Progression at LJ: 1985- 5.52, 1986- 5.85, 1987- 6.14, 1988- 6.34, 1989- 6.52/6.62w, 1990- 6.63, 1991- 6.62, 1992- 6.60, 1993- 6.75, 1994- 6.78, 1995- 6.95i/6.71/6.85w, 1996- 6.88, 1997- 7.05, 1998- 6.99/7.06w, 1999- 6.95/7.08w, 2000- 6.89, 2001- 7.00i/6.70, 2002- 6.77i/6.65/6.69w, 2003- 6.74. pb TJ 13.76i '04, 13.67 '91.
Set pb to win 1995 World Indoor title and 1997 World outdoor win was her first time over 7m.

Natalya GORELOVA b. 18 Apr 1973 Moskva 1.73m 56m. née Zaytseva. Luch Moskva. Teacher.
At 800m: WCh: '99- 6. At 1500m: OG: '00- h; WCh: '01- 3; WI: '01- 3, '03- 4; 3rd GP 2001. Won Russian 800m 1999.
Progression at 800m, 1500m: 1997- 2:02.44, 1998- 2:02.21, 4:13.43; 1999- 1:57.90, 4:05:12; 2000- 2:00.24, 4:01.50; 2001- 1:58.7, 3:59.70; 2002- 4:02.33; 2003- 2:00.65, 4:00.72i/4:03.83. pb 1000m 2:34.25 '01.

Lidiya GRIGORYEVA b. 21 Jan 1974 Smychka, Chuvashiya 1.64m 58kg. Novocheboksarsk VS.
At 10000m: OG: '00- 9; WCh: '03- 16. World HMar: '01- 11, '03- 4. Won Russian CC 1998.
Progress at 10000m: 1997- 34:32.08, 1999- 32:49.64, 2000- 31:21.27, 2001- 32:36.6, 2003- 30:57.83. pbs: 3000m 8:50.21i '04, 5000m 15:18.3 '03, HMar 69:32 '03, Mar 2:32:40 '00.

Tatyana GUDKOVA b. 23 Jan 1978 Magnitogorsk 1.70m 60kg. Magnitogorsk TU. Teacher.
At 20kmW: OG: '00- 8; WCh: '03- 4. Russian champion 2000, 2002 (track), 2003.
World best 20km walk 2000.
Progression at 10kmW, 20kmW: 1996- 47:07, 1997- 45:46, 1998- 44:42, 1999- 42:51, 1:33:05; 2000- 42:42, 1:25:18; 2001- 43:17, 1:30:12; 2002- 43:20, 1:30:20.1t; 2003- 44:01, 1:28:37.

Yelena ISINBAYEVA b. 3 Jun 1982 Volgograd 1.74m 66kg. Volgograd VS.
At PV: OG: '00- dnq; WCh: '03- 3; EC: '02- 2; WJ: '98- 9, '00- 1, WY: '99 – 1; EU23: '03- 1; EJ: '99- 5, '01- 1; WI: '01-03-04: 7/2/1. RUS champion 2002.
World pole vault record 2003, WIR (3) 2004, world junior indoor records 2000 and 2001.
Progression at PV: 1997- 3.30, 1998- 4.00, 1999- 4.20, 2000- 4.45i/4.40, 2001- 4.47i/4.46, 2002- 4.60/4.65ex, 2003- 4.82, 2004- 4.86i.
Former gymnast. World titles as Youth, junior and senior.

Yekaterina IVAKINA b. 4 Dec 1964 Stavropol 1.68m 70kg. née Slyadneva, later Krasnikova. Stavropol SA. Servicewoman.
At JT: OG: '00- dnq 24; WCh: '93- 5, '95- 8; EC: '94- dnq 15; ECp: '93-4-5: 3/4/3. Russian champion 1993, 1995.
Progression at JT: 1985- 53.02, 1986- 57.92, 1987- 60.42, 1988- 64.04, 1989- 63.08, 1990- 61.90, 1992- 64.10, 1993- 65.36, 1994- 64.04, 1995- 65.34, 1996- 61.40, 1997- 62.10, 1998- 59.78; new – 1999- 62.94, 2000- 64.89, 2001- 64.54, 2002- 64.23, 2003- 63.19.

Olimpiada IVANOVA b. 5 May 1970 Munsyuty Chuvashiya 1.68m 54kg. Cheboksary Dyn.
At 20kmW: WCh: '03- dnf; EC: '02- 1; WCp: '02- 2; ECp: '00- 1. At 10kmW: WCh: '97- drugs dq (2); WCp: '93- 12, '97- 2; won GWG 1994. At 5000mW: EJ: '85- 9.
World best 20km walk 2001.
Progression at 10kmW, 20kmW: 1987- 45:15, 1992- 45:18, 1993- 42:24, 1994- 42:30.31t, 1995- 41:30, 1996- 41:46, 1:30:58; 1997- 41:24, 1999- 43:31, 1:28:21; 2000- 42:43, 1:26:08; 2001- 42:34, 1:24:50; 2002- 43:26, 1:26:42. pbs: 3000mW 12:02.2 '95, 2MW 12:54.98i '96, 5000mW 20:50.6i '97, 20:56.10 '94, 20:51R '97.
Lost her 1997 World silver medal when she tested positive for Stanozolol, receiving a two-year ban. World best 20km walk time when she won Russian winter championship in March 2001.

Olga KALITURINA b. 9 Mar 1976 Moskva 1.80m 57kg. Moskva VS.
At HJ: WCh: '97- 2=, '03- 11=; EC: '02- 3; WJ: '94- 1; EI: '00- 3; ECp: '01- 3=. RUSc hampion 1997.
Progression at HJ: 1991- 1.77, 1992- 1.85, 1993- 1.86, 1994- 1.89, 1995- 1.95i/1.92, 1996- 1.85, 1997- 1.96, 1999- 1.90, 2000- 1.96i/1.94, 2001- 1.96, 2002- 1.97i/1.95, 2003- 1.95.
Married to Kirill Sosunov (qv).

Anastasiya KAPACHINSKAYA b. 21 Nov 1979 Moskva 1.76m 60kg. Luch Moskva.
At 200m: WCh: '03- 2; WI: '03- 3, '04- 1; ECp: '03- 1. At 400m/4x400R : WCh: '01- sf/3R, '03- 2R; EC: '02- 5/2R.
Progression at 400m. 800m: 1999- 23.85, 2000- 23.66, 53.32; 2001- 23.24i/22.6, 50.97; 2002- 23.41, 51.39; 2003- 22.38, 50.59. pbs: 100m 11.79 '99, 300m 36.61 '02.

Natalya KHRUSHCHELYOVA b. 30 May 1973 Tavda, Sverdlovsk reg. 1.72m 55kg. Yekaterinburg Dyn.
At 400m/4x400mR: EC: '98- 2R; WJ: '92- 8R; WUG: '95- 1R, '99- 2R, '01- 7; EU23Cp: '94- 2; WCp: '98- 3R; ECp: '97-8- 1R/1R. At 800m: WCh: '03- 3; ECp: '03- 4. Won RUS 800m 2003.
Progression at 400m, 800m: 1992- 53.56, 1994- 51.73, 1995- 52.43/52.3, 1996- 51.74, 1997- 52.66, 1998- 51.87, 1999- 23.85, 2000- 51.49, 2001- 52.06, 2002- 52.90, 1:59.77; 2003- 1:58.05. pbs: 200m 23.28 '94, 22.8 '96; 500m 1:10.50i '02, 600m 1:25.15i '04.

Irina KHUDOROSHKINA b. 13 Oct 1968 Tonarskiy Karaganda reg, Kazakhstan. 1.82m 100kg. Moskva Dyn.
At SP: OG: '96- 3; EI: '96- 2. Russian champion 1994, 1996, 1997 (disq).
Progression at SP: 1986- 15.01i/14.34, 1987- 16.82, 1988- 17.52, 1989- 18.53, 1990- 19.16, 1991- 18.53, 1992- 18.61i/18.21, 1993- 18.89, 1994- 19.81, 1995- 19.54, 1996- 20.32, 1997- 18.54/18.95dq, 2000- 18.56, 2001- 18.67, 2002- 18.92, 2003- 19.31i/18.81.
Two-year drugs ban June 1997.

Irina KORZHANENKO b. 16 May 1974 Azov, Rostov/Don reg. 1.78m 85kg. Rostov/Don VS.
At SP: OG: '96- 8; WCh: '95- 12, '97- dnq 16, '01- 5, '03- 4; EC: '98- 2, '02- 1; EJ: '93- 7; WI: '97- 3, '99- dq (2), '03- 1; EI: '98- 1; WUG: '97- 1; WCp: '98- 2, '02- 1; ECp: '95-8-01: 2/2/2; E23Cp: '94- 1. 3rd GP 1997. Russian champion 1995.
Progression at SP: 1991- 15.58, 1992- 15.92, 1993- 17.92i/17.02, 1994- 18.36, 1995- 20.06, 1996- 19.46, 1997- 19.69, 1998- 20.82, 1999- 21.15i, 2001- 19.37, 2002- 20.64, 2003- 20.55i/20.17.

After Vita Pavlysh was disqualified, she stepped up to take gold at the 1999 World Indoors – but lost that when she also was disqualified for drugs.

Olga KOTLYAROVA b. 12 Apr 1976 Sverdlovsk 1.80m 65kg. Student. Yekaterinburg TU.
At 400m/4x400mR: OG: '96- qf/5R, '00- 8/3R; WCh: '97- sf, '99- 8/1R; EC: '98- 3/2R; WJ: '94- 4R; EJ: '95- 1/2R; EU23: '97- 2R; WI: '97- 1R, '99- 1R, '01- 2/1R, '04- 1R; EI: '96- 2; WUG: '97- 2/1R; WCp: '98- 3R; ECp: '96- 4/3R, '97- 3/1R, '99- 2/1R. Russian champion 1998.
World indoor 4x400m record 1997, 1999 & 2004.
Progression at 400m: 1994- 53.67, 1995- 52.03/ 51.8, 1996- 51.17, 1997- 50.63, 1998- 50.38, 1999- 50.32, 2000- 49.95, 2001- 50.42i/50.81A, 2003- 52.86, 2004- 50.64i. pbs: 200m 23.35A '98, 300m 36.91+ '99, 500m 1:07.68i '03, 800m 2:05.17 '00.
Gave birth to daughter Tatyana in 2002.

Tatyana KOTOVA b. 11 Dec 1976 Kokand, Uzbekistan 1.82m 59kg. Luch Moskva.
At LJ: OG: '00- 4; WCh: '99- dnq 13, '01- 2, '03- 2; EC: '02- 1; WI: '99-01-03-04: 1/2/1/2; EU23: '97- 1; WCp: '02- 1; ECp: '02- 1; 2nd GP 2002. Russian champion 1999-2001.
Progression at LJ: 1994- 6.32, 1995- 6.32, 1996- 6.65, 1997- 6.76, 1998- 6.82/6.97w, 1999- 6.99/ 7.01w, 2000- 7.04 (7.05iu), 2001- 7.12, 2002- 7.42, 2003- 6.94, 2004- 6.93i. pbs: HJ 1.75 '95, TJ 13.69i/13.64 '98.
Born in Uzbekistan, she moved to Taboshari (Tajikistan) and now lives in Central Siberia. Her father came from Cherkassy in the Ukraine. Shared Golden League jackpot 2000. Achieved the world's best long jump for eight years in 2002.

Olesya KRASNOMOVETS b. 8 Jul 1979 Nizhniy Tagil, Sverdlovsk 1.71m 60kg. St-Peterburg VS.
At 400m/4x400mR: WI: '04- 2/1R.
World indoor 4x400m record 2004.
Progression at 400m: 2001- 53.31, 2003- 53.77, 2004- 50.65i. pbs- 200m 23.8 '01, 300m 36.62i '04, 500m 1:08.84i '04.
Great breakthrough in 2004 indoor season to win EI Cup and take silver and gold at World Indoors.

Svetlana KRIVELYOVA b. 13 Jun 1969 Bryansk 1.84m 94kg. Moskva Dyn. Teacher.
At SP: OG: '92- 1, '96- dnq 15, '00- 4; WCh: '91- 3, '93- 2, '97- 10, '99- 3, '01- 9, '03- 1; EC: '98- 4, '02- 3; WJ: '88- 4; WI: '91-3-9-01-03-04: 8/1/1/3/5/2; EI: '00- 4; WUG: '91- 1; ECp: '96-9-02-03: 3/3/1/ 2; 3rd GP 2001. USSR champion 1991, Russian 1992, 1998-2000, 2002-03. Won GP 1993.
Progression at SP: 1985- 15.18, 1986- 16.76, 1987- 17.51, 1988- 18.35, 1989- 18.36, 1990- 19.70, 1991- 20.36, 1992- 21.06, 1993- 20.84, 1996- 18.97, 1997- 19.32i/19.18, 1998- 20.53, 1999- 20.69i/20.26, 2000- 20.72, 2001- 20.17, 2002- 20.53, 2003- 20.77.
Took World Student Games gold medal in 1991 after Sui Xinmei disqualified, and World Indoor gold in 1999 after both Pavlysh and Korzhanenko disqualified.

Marina KUPTSOVA b. 22 Dec 1981 Moskva 1.85m 68kg. Luch Moskva.
At HJ: OG: '00- dnq 26=; WCh: '03- 2; EC: '02- 2; WJ: '98- 1, '00- 2; EU23: '01- 2=; EJ: '97- 2, '99- 3; EI: '02- 1; WCp: '02- 2; ECp: '02-03: 4=/3. Russian champion 2000, 2002-03.
Progression at HJ: 1995- 1.78i, 1996- 1.89, 1997- 1.90, 1998- 1.95i/1.90, 1999- 1.94, 2000- 1.96, 2001- 1.91i/1.90, 2002- 2.03i/2.00, 2003- 2.02.
Was a talented swimmer and basketball player. Her 2.03i in 2002 is the best ever by a 20 year-old woman. Her father and coach Gennadiy was a decathlete and discus thrower,

Olga KUZENKOVA b. 4 Oct 1970 Smolensk 1.76m 76kg. Smolensk Dyn. Army Officer, has a diploma in physical education.
At HT: OG: '00- 2; WCh: '99- 2, '01- 2, '03- 2; EC: '98- 2, '02- 1; WUG: '97- 2; ECp: '97-8-9-00-02-03: 1/1/2/1/1/3; 3rd GP 2001. RUS champion 1992-4, 1997-2003; CIS 1992.
Eleven world hammer records 1992-8 (six officially ratified), inc. unratified 69.46 '96 and 73.80 '98 due to no drugs testing procedures; 66.84 in 1994 was the first record for the event accepted by the IAAF. 14 Russian records 1993-2000.
Progression at HT: 1990- 59.50, 1991- 61.52, 1992- 65.40, 1993- 64.64, 1994- 66.84, 1995- 68.16, 1996- 69.46, 1997- 73.10, 1998- 73.80, 1999- 74.30, 2000- 75.68, 2001- 73.62, 2002- 73.07, 2003- 74.98.
Became the first 70-m hammer thrower in 1997. After five championship silver medals at last won gold at the 2002 Europeans.

Svetlana LAPINA b. 12 Apr 1978 Makhachkala 1.80m 59kg. Makhachkala VS. Student.
At HJ: OG: '00- dnq 15; WCh: '99- 3; WJ: '96- 3; EJ: '97- 3; EU23: '99- 1; WUG: '99- 2.
Progression at HJ: 1990- 1.55, 1991- 1.76, 1992- 1.78, 1993- 1.82, 1994- 1.83, 1995- 1.89, 1996- 1.92, 1997- 1.90, 1998- 1.92i/1.90, 1999- 1.99, 2000- 1.94, 2002- 1.80, 2003- 2.00i/1.96.

Tatyana LEBEDEVA b. 21 Jul 1976 Sterlitamsk, Bashkortostan 1.71m 60kg. Volgograd VS.
At TJ (LJ): OG: '00- 2; WCh: '99- 4, '01- 1, '03- 1; EC: '98- 5; WJ: '94- 3 (10); EJ: '95- 2 (6); WI: '01- 2; EI: '00- 1; WUG: '01- 1; WCp: '98- 2; ECp: '00-01: 1/1. GP: 3rd 1999, 2nd 2001. Won WAF 2003, GWG 2001, Russian 1998-2001.
Two Russian triple jump records 2000.
Progression at LJ, TJ: 1991- 12.91, 1992- 13.03, 1993- 6.17, 13.13i/12.94; 1994- 6.65, 13.69; 1995- 13.88, 1996- 13.62, 1997- 13.89i/13.56, 1998- 14.45/ 14.58w, 1999- 14.89, 2000- 15.32, 2001- 6.71i, 15.25; 2003- 6.82, 15.18; 2004- 6.98i, 15.36i.
Won 2001 World gold by massive margin of 65cm. Son born in August 2002. Set three world indoor records (15.16, 15,25, 15.36) at WI 2004, and next day completed unique double with LJ gold.

Irina MISTYUKEVICH b. 17 Jun 1977 Kurgan region 1.82m 69kg. Kurgan VS. Teacher.

At 800m: OG: '00- sf; WCh: '01- h; EC: '02- h; EU23: '99- 7; EJ: '95- 2R; ECp: 00-01-02: 1/1/1.
Progression at 800m: 1995- 2:06.40, 1996- 2:03.8, 1997- 2:03.85, 1998- 2:01.93, 1999- 1:58.33, 2000- 1:57.49, 2001- 1:58.02, 2002- 1:58.90, 2003- 2:03.08. pbs: 400m 51.87 '00, 600m 1:27.82i '00, 1000m 2:34.52 '01.

Natalya NAZAROVA b. 26 May 1979 Moskva 1.65m 56kg. Luch Moskva. Student.
At 400m/4x400mR: OG: '00- sf/3resR; WCh: '99- 6/1R, '03- 4/2R; EC: '02- 2R; WJ: '98- 1/2R; WI: '99- 1R, '03- 1/1R, '04- 1/1R; EI: '00- 2; EJ: '97- 7; WCp: '02- 3R; ECp: '99- 1R. Russian champion 1999-2000, 2003.
World indoor 4x400m world records 1999 & 2004.
Progression at 400m: 1995- 55.79, 1996- 54.59, 1997- 52.94, 1998- 51.50, 1999- 50.48, 2000- 50.10, 2002- 51.15, 2003- 49.78, 2004- 49.68i. pbs: 100m 11.57 '99, 200m 23.01/22.9 '99, 300m 36.3+ '03, 500m 1:07.36i '04 (world best), 600m 1:26.35i '00.
Plays violin and piano.

Yelena NIKOLAYEVA b. 1 Feb 1966 Akshiki Chuvashia 1.64m 58kg. née Kuznetsova. Cheboksary Dyn. Member of the state parliament in Cheboksary.
At 20kmW: WCh: '99- 12, '01- dq, '03- 1; WCp: '99- 4, '02- 4; ECp: '01- 5, '03- 1. At 10kmW: OG: '92- 2, '96- 1; WCh: '87- 5, '93- 7, '95- 3, '97- 9; EC: '94- 3, '02- 2; WCp: '87-93-5: 5/3/2. Won GWG 1998, USSR champion 1987-8, CIS 1992, RUS 1996. Won RUS 2001-02. At 3000mW: WI: '91- 5, '93- 1; EI: '94- 4.
Three world 10km track walk records 1986-8, road best 1996, European records 3000m 1992, 5000m: 21:32.4 '87, 21:08.65 '88.
Progression at 10kmW, 20kmW: 1984- 48:29.1, 1985- 46:37, 1986- 44:32.50t, 1987- 43:57, 1988- 43:36.41t, 1991- 43:25, 1992- 42:40, 1993- 43:11, 1994- 42:43, 1995- 42:20, 1996- 41:04, 1997- 41:41, 1998- 43:51.97t, 1999- 42:04, 1:28:01; 2000- 45:55, 2001- 42:55, 1:27:49.3t; 2002- 43:20, 1:27:02; 2003- 43:26, 1:26:22. pbs: 3000mW 11:49.73i '93, 11:57.68 '96; 5000mW 20:54.65 '02, 20:48R '94.

Yelena OLEYNIKOVA b. 9 Dec 1976 Zernograd, Rostov-na-Donu reg. 1.78m 56kg. Luch Moskva.
At TJ: WCh: '01- dnq 14, '03- 14; EC: '02- 3; EI: '02- 3; WUG: '01- 3; WCp: '02- 6.
Progression at TJ: 1995- 12.79, 1996- 13.22, 1997- 13.38, 1998- 13.58, 1999- 13.85, 2000- 14.25, 2001- 14.59, 2002- 14.83, 2003- 14.56/14.70w.

Yuliya PECHONKINA b. 21 Apr 1978 Krasnoyarsk 1.80m 66kg. née Nosova. Moskva reg. VS.
At 400mh/4x400mR: OG: '00- sf; WCh: '01- 2/3R, '03- 3/2R; EC: '98- h; WJ: '96- h; EJ: '97- 6; WI: '01- 1R; WCp: '02- 1/3R; ECp: '01- 1/2R, '02- 1. RUS champion 1999, 2001, 2003. At 400m: WI: '03- 1R; EI: '01- 5.
World record 400m hurdles 2003.
Progression at 400mh: 1993- 63.47, 1994- 60.86, 1995- 60.30, 1996- 57.04, 1997- 57.53, 1998- 56.13, 1999- 53.98, 2000- 54.31, 2001- 53.84, 2002- 53.10, 2003- 52.34. pbs: 300m 37.49i '02, 400m 51.00i '03, 500m 1:09.69i '03.
Married **Yevgeniy Pechonkin** (b. 9 Oct 1973, 110mh: 1 WJ 92, 2 EJ 91, pb 13.38 '96) on 15 Aug 2001.

Lyudmila PETROVA b. 7 Oct 1968 Novocheboksary 1.60m 44kg.
At 10000m: OG: '96- 14; WCh: '01- 6. At Mar: EC: '98- 9. World HMar: '97- 7, '02- 13. Won RUS 10000m 1996.
Progression at 10000m, Mar: 1995- 33:41.40, 1996- 31:58.84, 1997- 32:14.39, 2:39:26; 1998- 2:30:26, 1999- 2:29:13, 2000- 31:52.75, 2:25:45; 2001- 32:04.94, 2:26:18; 2002- 2:22:33, 2003- 31:36.76, 2:23:14. pbs: 3000m 8:59.15i/9:00.2 '96, 5000m 15:20.44 '96, Rd 15km 48:31 '98, HMar 69:26 '00.
Two wins in 15 marathons: Moscow 1998, New York 2000. 3rd London 2002. Did not run 1987-94, when her two children were born.

Tatyana POLNOVA b. 20 Apr 1979 Krasnodar 1.79m 62kg. née Zaykova.
At PV: WJ: '98- 10; WUG: '03- 1; ECp: '03- 2. Won WAF 2003.
Progression at PV: 1995- 3.00, 1996- 3.75, 1997- 3.85, 1998- 4.10i/3.90, 2000- 4.20, 2001- 4.20, 2002- 4.60, 2003- 4.70, 2004- 4.71i.
Former gymnast, coached by her husband Sergey Polnov. She changed nationality to Turkish and competed for Turkey 1998-2000, but has now reverted to Russia.

Svetlana POSPELOVA b. 24 Dec 1979 Leningrad 1.69m 58kg. St Petersburg YR.
At 400m/4x400mR: OG: '00- dq h; WCh: '03- 8/res (2)R; WJ: '98- h/2R; EU23: '99- 1R; EI: '00- 1/1R; ECp: '00- 1, '03- 1/1R. Won Russian 200m 2000.
Progression at 400m: 1996- 56.50, 1997- 55.17, 1998- 53.80, 1999- 52.58, 2000- 50.47, 2003- 50.70. pbs: 100m 11.42 '00, 200m 22.80 '00.
Drugs disqualification announced after elimination in Olympic 400m heat 2000.

Yelena PROKHOROVA b. 16 Apr 1978 Kemerovo 1.71m 59kg. Kemerovo TU. Student.
At Hep: OG: '00- 2; WCh: '01- 1, '03- 4; EU23: '99- 2; ECp: '99- 6, '03- 1. At Pen: WI: '01- 2; EI: '00- 5, '02- 1. Won RUS Hep 2000.
Progression at Hep: 1994- 4919, 1995- 4621, 1996- 5152, 1997- 5600, 1998- 5776, 1999- 6132, 2000- 6765, 2001- 6694, 2003- 6452. pbs: 200m 23.37 '00, 400m 54.25 '03, 800m 2:04.27 '00, 60mh 8.46i '01, 100mh 13.54 '00, HJ 1.88 '01, LJ 6.72 '00, SP 14.30 '00, JT 50.73 '01, Pen 4711i '01.
Won IAAF Combined Events Challenge in 2001. Missed 2002 outdoor season with a knee injury.

Yekaterina PUZANOVA b. 1 Jan 1979 Vyksa, Gorkiy reg. 1.67m 54kg. Moskva Dyn.
At 1500m: EC: '02- h; EI: '02- 1. At 800m: WI: '03- 6.

Progression at 800m, 1500m: 1997- 2:08.89, 1998- 2:07.62, 1999- 2:05.44, 2000- 2:01.86, 2001- 2:01.29, 4:11.28; 2002- 2:01.14, 4:05.42; 2003- 1:59.91i, 4:04.77i. pb 1000m 2:42.05i '02.

Anna PYATYKH b. 4 Apr 1981 Moskva 1.76m 63kg. Luch Moskva.
At TJ: WCh: '03- 4; EC: '02- 8; WJ: '00- 2; EJ: '99- 3; WI: '03- 4; ECp: '02- 1, '03- 1.
Progression at TJ: 1998- 12.98, 1999- 13.59, 2000- 14.19, 2001- 14.21/14.22w, 2002- 14.67, 2003- 14.79. pb LJ 6.46 '00.

Olga RASPOPOVA b. 27 Dec 1978 Barabinsk, Novosibirsk reg 1.76m 62kg. Novosibirsk Dyn. Student.
At 800m: OG: '00- h; EC: '02- sf; WI: '04- 6. Russian champion 2002.
Progression at 800m: 1997- 2:12.0, 1999- 2:03.88, 2000- 1:56.85, 2001- 1:58.77, 2002- 1:58.63, 2003- 1:59.94. pb 1000m 2:34.68i '04, 2:34.77 '01.

Oksana ROGOVA b. 7 Oct 1978 Tambov 1.80m 60kg. Tambov Sp. Student, Tambov University.
At TJ: OG: '00- 8; WCh: '99- 9; WJ: '96- 4; EU23: '99- 2; WI: '01- 5; EI: '00- 5; WUG: '03- 1.
Progression at TJ: 1993- 11.52, 1994- 12.48, 1995- 13.14, 1996- 13.49, 1997- 13.31, 1998- 14.14, 1999- 14.59/14.65w, 2000- 14.28i/14.27, 2001- 14.37i/ 14.20/14.23w; 2002- 14.70i/14.59, 2003- 14.16. pb LJ 6.79 '02.

Natalya ROSHCHUPKINA b. 13 Jan1978 Lipetsk 1.82m 70kg. Lipetsk Dyn. Teacher.
At Hep: OG: '00- 6; WCh: '99- 10, '01- 4, '03- 13; EC: '98- 9; WJ: '96- 5; EU23: '99- 1; ECp: '98- 2, '00- 1; Russian champion 2003, won GWG 2001. At Pen: WI: '99- 7, '01- 4.
World junior indoor heptathlon record (4513) 1997.
Progression at Hep: 1993- 4772, 1994- 5191, 1995- 5383, 1996- 5767, 1997- 5920, 1998- 6370h, 1999- 6219, 2000- 6633, 2001- 6551, 2002- 6029, 2003- 6170. pbs: 200m 23.27/22.84w '01, 800m 2:06.67 '01, 60mh 8.60i '01, 100mh 13.70 '00, HJ 1.91 '00, LJ 6.45 '00, SP 14.96 '01, JT 45.65 '01, Pen 4664i '01.

Yekaterina ROZENBERG b. 14 Nov 1981 Khabarovsk 1.69m 60kg. née Noskova. Moskva Dyn.
At 1500m: WCh: '03- 4; EJ: '99- 3; WI: '03- 3; ECp: '03- 5.
Progression at 1500m: 1998- 4:24.84, 1999- 4: 16.56, 2000- 4:16.33, 2003- 4:00.07. pb 800m 1: 59.98 '03. Baby born 2002.

Olga RUBLYOVA b. 28 Oct 1974 Volgograd 1.76m 65kg. Volgograd VS.
At LJ: OG: '96- dnq 19, '00- 5; WCh: '95- 4, '99- 11, '01- dnq 19, '03- 5; EC: '94- 11, '02- 7; WJ: '92- 17; EJ: '93- 2; WI: '03- 4; EI: '00- 4, '02- 2; ECp: '94-4-00-01: 2/4/1/4 (8 TJ '91). Russian champion 1995-6, 1998, 2003.
Progression at LJ: 1988- 5.77, 1989- 6.10, 1990- 6.29, 1991- 6.17, 1992- 6.46, 1993- 6.74, 1994- 6.76, 1995- 6.90/7.01w, 1996- 6.87, 1998- 6.88, 1999- 6.82, 2000- 6.90i/6.89, 2001- 6.86, 2002- 6.76, 2003- 6.89. pb TJ 14.45i/14.21 '00.
Married to Viktor Sotnikov (b. 12 Sep 1974) TJ 17.11 '96, 9th OG 1996.

Nadezhda RYASHKINA b. 22 Jan 1967 Sokol 1.60m 47kg. Chelyabinsk Sp.
At 20kmW: WCp: '02- 11. At 10kmW: EC: '90- dq, '98- 7; WCp: '91- 8; ECp: '98- 1. Won GWG 1990; USSR champion 1990, Russian 1997. 3000mW: WI: '89- 4.
World 10km track walk records 1989 and 1990, equalled world best for 20km road walk 1999.
Progression at 10kmW, 20kmW: 1988- 44:07.97t, 1:32:33; 1989- 43:08.4t, 1990- 41:56.23t, 1991- 44:29, 1:33:13; 1992- 44:30, 1994- 44:15.76t, 1997- 44:29, 1998- 42:25, 1999- 42:45, 1:27:30; 2000- 42:42, 1:28:06; 2002- 43:52+, 1:28:18l 2003- 44:22, 1:28:52. pbs: 3000mW 12:07.82 '00, 5000mW 20:49.4 '90.
Previously a runner, took up walking in 1987.

Natalya SADOVA b. 15 Jun 1972 Gorkiy 1.80m 100kg. née Koptyukh. Nizhniy Novgorod TU. Teacher.
At DT: OG: '96- 2, '00- 4; WCh: '95- 5, '97- 3, '99- 4, '01- 1, '03- 8; EC: '94- 11, '98- 2, '02- 2; WJ: '90- 1; EJ: '89- 5; WUG: '95- 1, '97- 1; WCp: '98- 3, '02- 3; ECp: '95-7-8-9-01-02-03: 1/1/1/1/2/1/3; E23Cp: '94- 1. Won GP 1998, 2002; Russian champion 1995-6, 1999-2001, 2003.
Progression at DT: 1988- 53.02, 1989- 55.34, 1990- 61.44, 1991- 59.10, 1992- 57.82, 1993- 58.14, 1994- 62.12, 1995- 66.86, 1996- 67.22, 1997- 67.72, 1998- 68.50, 1999- 70.02, 2000- 67.33, 2001- 68.57, 2002- 67.73, 2003- 69.38. pb SP 14.21 '99.
Has a daughter Viktoriya.

Gulnara SAMITOVA b 9 Jul 1978 Naberezhnye Chelny, Tatarstan 1.74m 55kg. Naberezhnye Chelny TU.
At 1500m: WI: '04- 3; At 5000m: WCh: '03- 7. At 3000mSt: ECp: '03- 1. Won RUS 5000m & 3000mSt 2003, indoor 1500m & 3000m 2004.
World record and three Russian records 3000m steeplechase 2003.
Progression at 5000m, 3000mSt: 2003- 14:54.38, 9:08.33. pbs: 1000m 2:35.91i '04, 1500m 4:05.91i '04, 4:15.78 '03, 3000m 8:41.72i '04.
Great breakthrough in 2003, starting with world indoor 3000mSt indoor best of 9:29.54. Won Russian indoor 1500m and 3000m in 2004.

Viktoriya SERYOGINA b. 22 May 1973 Bryansk 1.80m 60kg. Bryansk Dyn.
At HJ: EC: '02- 10; WI: '99- 7.
Progression at HJ: 1992- 1.75, 1993- 1.84, 1994- 1.88, 1995- 1.91, 1996- 1.95, 1997- 1.85i, 1998- 1.97, 1999- 1.98i/1.96/1.97sq, 2000- 1.97i/1.93, 2001- 1.96i/ 1.90, 2002- 2.00, 2003- 2.00i/1.97. pb LJ 6.65 '98.

Tatyana SHIKOLENKO b. 10 May 1968 Gelenjik, Krasnodar reg.1.77m 74kg. Gelenjik Krasnodar TU.
At JT: OG: '00- 7; WCh: '93- 4, '97- 8, '99- 2, '01- 9, '03- 2; EC: '98- 2, '02- 4; WJ: '86- 4; EJ: '85- 5; WUG: '91- 1; WCp: '98- 4, '02- 2; ECp: '00-01-02:

2/4/1; Won WAF 2003, 2nd GP 1998 (3rd 2002), Russian champion 1997-2001, 2003.
Russian javelin record 2000
Progression at JT: 1984- 59.40, 1985- 59.90, 1986- 55.70, 1987- 59.74, 1988- 64.70, 1989- 60.74, 1990- 64.98, 1991- 63.56, 1992- 62.20, 1993- 65.18, 1994- 64.94, 1996- 60.94, 1997- 67.34, 1998- 67.84; new: 1999- 66.37, 2000- 67.20, 2001- 66.09, 2002- 65.08, 2003- 66.00.
Belarus prior to 1996. Younger sister of Natalya (1 WCh '95, 2 OG '92, pb 71.40 '94).

Irina SIMAGINA b. 25 May 1982 Ryazan 1.71m 56kg. Luch Moskva.
At LJ: WJ: '00- 6; WY: '99- 5; EU23: '03- 2; WUG: '03- 1; EI: '02- 4.
Progression at LJ: 1999- 6.32i/6.12, 2000- 6.38, 2001- 6.41i/6.11, 2002- 6.74i/6.58, 2003- 6.83, 2004- 6.95i.

Yelena SLESARENKO b. 28 Feb 1982 Volgograd 1.79m 55kg. née Sivushenko. Volgograd TU.
At HJ: EU23: '03- 2; EJ: '01- 4; WUG: '03- 3; WI: '04- 1; EI: '02- 5=.
Progression at HJ: 1999- 1.82, 2000- 1.88, 2001- 1.94i/1.88, 2002- 1.97, 2003- 1.98i/1.96, 2004- 2.04i.
Tied Russian indoor record to win gold at 2004 World Indoors.

Tatyana TOMASHOVA b. 1 Jul 1975 Perm 1.68m 58kg. Perm TU.
At 1500m: WCh: '03- 1; EC: '02- 3; WCp: '02- 2; ECp: '02- 3. At 5000m: OG: '00- 13; WCh: '01- 10; ECp: '00- 1. Won GP 3000m 2001 (2nd 2002), RUS 1500m 2001-03, 5000m 2000.
Progress at 1500m, 5000m: 1996- 4:17.97, 15:48.13; 1997- 4:16.39, 1998- 4:13.50, 1999- 4:08.5?, 15:26.67; 2000- 4:04.80, 14:53.00; 2001- 4:03.31, 14:39.22; 2002- 4:01.28, 14:47.85; 2003- 3:58.52. pbs: 800m 2:04.0 '99, 1M 4:38.13 '01, 2000m 5:43.3 '01, 3000m 8:25.56 '01, road 10km 32:48 '99.

Olga YEGOROVA b. 28 Mar 1972 Novocheboksarsk, Chuvashiya 1.60m 48kg. Cheboksary VS. Economist.
At 5000m: OG: '00- 8; WCh: '99- h, '01- 1, '03- h; EC: '98- 11, '02- 4; WCp: '02- 1; ECp: '02- 1; won RUS 1999, GWG 2001. At 3000m: WI: '97/9/01- 6/6/1; EI: '00- 6; ECp: '98-9-03: 1/3/1. At 1500m: WJ: '90- 9; EJ: '91- 3.
European 5000m record 2001, 2 Russian records 2000-01.
Progression at 3000m, 5000m: 1996- 16:00.07, 1997- 15:42.47, 1998- 15:32.74, 1999- 8:33.02, 15:22.80; 2000- 8:49.18i/8:53.76, 14:42.91; 2001- 8:23.26, 14:29.32; 2002- 8:46.24i, 14:48.29; 2003- 8:38.00, 14:55.19. pbs: 1500m 4:02.76 '01, 1M 4:25.54i '00, 2000m 5:39.30i '00, 5:39.9 '01.
Daughter Yevgeniya born June 1994.

Yelena YELESINA b. 4 Apr 1970 Chelyabinsk 1.83m 64kg. Moskva VS.
At HJ: OG: '00- 1; WCh: '91- 2, '99- 2, '01- dnq 13=; EC: '90- 3; WJ: '88- 2; EJ: '87- 3=, '89- 1; WUG: '91- 4; WI: '03- 2; EI: '92- 3, '98- 3. Won GWG & USSR 1990, Russian 1999.
Progression at HJ: 1983- 1.55, 1984- 1.65, 1985- 1.70, 1986- 1.83, 1987- 1.89, 1988- 1.98, 1989- 1.95, 1990- 2.02, 1991- 1.98, 1992- 1.94i/1.93, 1993- 1.91, 1994- 1.95, 1997- 1.95, 1998- 1.98i/1.94, 1999- 2.01, 2000- 2.01, 2001- 1.95, 2002- 1.96, 2003- 2.02i/1.98.
She has a son, Boris. Married to Agvan Grigoryan ARM who planned to represent Australia at wrestling.

Valeriya ZABRUSKOVA b. 29 Jul 1975 Germany 1.68m 65kg. née Antonova. Stravropol TU.
At JT: WCh: '03- 9; ECp: '03- 4.
Progression at JT: 1995- 51.70, 1996- 51.64, 1997- 58.08, 1998- 59.55, 1999- 63.87, new: 1999- 62.04, 2000- 60.49, 2001- 58.18, 2002- 62.69, 2003- 64.49.

Yelena ZADOROZHNAYA b. 3 Dec 1977 Ust-Kut, Irkutsk reg. 1.57m 42kg. Irkutsk VS.
At 5000m (1500m): WCh: '01- 6, '03- 4 (8); EC: '02- 3; ECp: '01- 1, '03- 1. At 3000m: WI: '01- 3, '04- 6; EI: '02- 3; WCp: '02- 3; ECp: '02- 2. At 1500m: EU23: '99- 2; ECp: '00- 2; won GP 2002.
Russian 5000m record 2001.
Progression at 1500m, 5000m: 1998- 4:12.70, 1999- 4:09.3, 2000- 4:03.32, 2001- 4:02.16, 14:40.47; 2002- 3:59.94, 15:15.22; 2003- 4:00.12, 14:51.61. pbs: 800m 2:01.74 '98, 1M 4:24.11i '01, 2000m 5:41.61i '02, 5:43.38 '03; 3000m 8:25.40 '01.

Svetlana ZAKHAROVA b. 15 Sep 1970 Atayeva, Chuvashiya 1.58m 48kg. née Vasilyeva.
At Mar: OG: '00- 3; WCh: '03- 9. World HMar: '98-9-02: 10/13/12.
Two Russian marathon records 2002.
Progression at Mar: 1994- 2:46+, 1995- 2:40:11, 1996- 2:35:36, 1997- 2:33:14, 1998- 2:36:44, 1999- 2:27:08, 2000- 2:28:11, 2001- 2:24:04, 2002- 2:21:31, 2003- 2:23:07. pbs: 10000m 32:49.01 '97, HMar 69:48 '02.
Won Honolulu Marathon 1997 and 2002 (2nd 1998-2000), Boston & Chicago 2003, 2nd Los Angeles 1999, London 2001-02; 3rd New York 2001, 4th Chicago 2002. Her husband Nikolay Zakharov was an international cross-country skier.

Alla ZHILYAYEVA b. 5 Feb 1969 Verkhniy Dubovets, Kursk reg. 1.62m 47kg. née Shumakova. Kursk TU. Teacher.
At 10000m: WCh: '95- 7, '03- 5; EC: '98- dnf; ECp: '95- 3. At Mar: OG: '96- dnf. World HMar: '94-5-6-03: 14/5/18/6; 4k CC: '03- 8. Eur CC: '94- 4, '95- 5. Won RUS 10,000m & HMar 1998.
Russian 10000n record 2003.
Progression at 10000m, Mar: 1995- 31:52.15, 2: 27:38; 1996- 2:32:32, 1997- 2:31:55, 1998- 31:45.02, 2000- 2:28:27, 2001- 2:33:21, 2002- 2:36:32, 2003- 30:23.07, 2:37:00. pbs: 3000m 8:54.00i '03, 8:58.75 '95; 5000m 15:14.3+ '03, 15:14.73 '96; HMar 69:43 '98, 10kmW 45:19 '90.
Former race walker. Ran 2:27:38 to win at Reims on her marathon début, also won Monaco and Reims marathons 1999

Olesya ZYKINA b. 7 Oct 1980 Kaluga 1.70m 60kg. Tula TU.
At 400m/4x400m: OG: '00- res (3)R; WCh: '01- 6/3R, '03- 6/2R; EC: '02- 1/2R; WJ: '98- 2R (8 100m); EJ: '99- 1/1R; WI: '01- 3/1R. '04- GR, '03- 1R; WCp: '02- 3/3R; ECp: '00- 1R. Russian champion 2001-02.
Progression at 400m: 1999- 51.31, 2000- 50.36, 2001- 50.15, 2002- 50.44, 2003- 50.39. pbs: 60m 7.47i '04, 100m 11.84 '98, 200m 22.78 '00, 22.3 '99; 300m 36.6+ '03, 36.69i '04, 36.70 '00.

SAINT KITTS & NEVIS

Governing body: Saint Kitts Amateur Athletic Association, Church Street, PO Box 932, Basseterre, St Kitts. Founded 1961.

Kim COLLINS b. 5 Apr 1976 1.75m 64kg. Studied sociology at Texas Christian University, USA.
At 100m (/200m): OG: '96- qf, 00- 7/sf; WCh: '97- h, 99- h/h, '01- 6/3=, '03- 1; CG: '02- 1; CAC: '99- 2, '01- 1/1, '03- 1; WCp: '02- 2/2R. At 60m: WI: '03- 2. Won NCAA indoor 60m & 200m 2001.
SKN records: 100m from 1996, 200m from 1998, 400m 2000.
Progression at 100m, 200m: 1995- 10.63, 21.85; 1996- 10.27, 21.06; 1998- 10.18/10.16w, 20.88/20.78w; 1999- 10.21, 20.43, 2000- 10.13A/10.15/10.02w, 20.31A/20.18w; 2001- 10.04A/10.00?/9.99w, 20.20/20.08w; 2002- 9.98, 20.49; 2003- 9.99/9.92w, 20.40w. pbs: 60m 6.53i '00, 400m 46.93 '00.
The first athlete from his country to make Olympic and World finals and in 2003 the first to win a World Indoor medal and a World title.

SAUDI ARABIA

Governing body: Saudi Arabian Amateur Athletic Federation, PO Box 5802, Riyadh 11432. Founded 1963.

Saad Shaddad AL-ASMARI b. 24 Sep 1968 Bal Asmari 1.85m 72kg. Navy sergeant.
At 3000mSt: WCh: '95- 3, '97- 4; WCp: '94- 2, '98- 3; AsiG: '94- 2; AsiC: '93-5-8-00-02: 1/1 (1 5000m)/1/2/2. Arab champion 1993, 1999; Gulf 5000m & 10000m 2002.
Six Asian 3000m steeplechase records 1994-2002. Saudi 1500m records 1992-4, 3000m 1995.
Progress at 3000mSt: 1992- 9:08.86, 1993- 8:29.38, 1994- 8:15.95, 1995- 8:09.67, 1996- 8:22.23, 1997- 8:08.26, 1998- 8:22.83, 1999- 8:22.28, 2000- 8:32.48, 2001- 8:15.01, 2002- 8:08.14, 2003- 8:27.82. pbs: 1500m 3:41.1 '94, 2000m 5:03.52 '95, 3000m 7:45.43 '95, 5000m 13:40.52 '96, 10000m 30:05.56 '02.
Lives in Abha at an altitude of c.2000m in southern Saudi Arabia. He was a member of the national junior volleyball team before taking up athletics in 1989. Won his nation's first major championships medal. His cousin Hassan Al-Asmari was 2nd in the 2000 Asian Champs 3000mSt.

Hamdan Odha **AL-BISHI** b. 5 May 1981 1.80m 70kg.
At 400mh: OG: '00- sf; WCh: '01- 6, '03- sf; WJ: '98- sf, '00- 1; AsiG: '02- 2; AsiC: '00-02-03: 2/2/2; Asi-J: '97/99- 2.
Four Asian junior 400m records 2000. Six KSA 400m records 1998-2000.
Progression at 400m: 1996- 47.74, 1997- 46.51A, 1998- 46.2, 1999- 45.98, 2000- 44.66, 2001- 45.00, 2002- 44.95, 2003- 44.99. pbs: 200m 20.55 '03, 33.42 '00.

Hussein Taher **Al-SABEE** b. 14 Nov 1979 1.86m 82kg.
At LJ: OG: '00- dnq 18; WCh: '99- 12, '01- 10, '03- 5; AsiG: '02- 1; AsiC: '00-02=-3: 1/1/1; WI: '01- 11; WCp: '02- 4. Arab champion 1997, 1999, 2003; Gulf 2000, 2003.
Six KSA long jump records 1997-2000.
Progression at LJ: 1996- 7.25, 1997- 7.73A/8.01Aw, 1998- 7.70, 1999- 8.06, 2000- 8.33, 2001- 8.31, 2002- 8.14, 2003- 8.30. pbs: 200m 21.04 '02, 21.1 '00; 300m 33.42 '00.

Hadi Soua'an AL-SOMAILY b. 30 Dec 1976 Taïf 1.91m 72kg. Teacher.
At 400mh: OG: '96- h, '00- 2; WCh: '95/99- h, '01- 4, '03- sf; WJ: '94- sf; AsiG: '94- 6, '02- 1; AsiC: '00- 1. Pan-Arab champion 1995, 1999; Gulf 1996, 2002. 2nd GP 2000.
Two Asian 400mh records 2000. Six KSA records 1994-2000.
Progression at 400mh: 1993- 52.28, 1994- 50.58, 1995- 49.30, 1996- 49.48, 1998- 51.1, 1999- 49.14/49.1A, 2000- 47.53, 2001- 47.99, 2002- 48.11, 2003- 48.97. pb 400m 47.10 '95.

SENEGAL

Governing body: Fédération Sénégalaise d'Athlétisme, BP 1737, Stade Iba Mar DIOP, Dakar. Founded 1960.

Women

Kène NDOYE b. 20 Nov 1978 1.64m 58kg.
At TJ (/LJ): OG: '00- dnq 14; WCh: '99- dnq 17, '03- 10; AfG: '99- 3, '03- 1/4; AfCh: '96- 1/3, '98- 3, '00- 3/1, '02- 2/2; WJ: '98- dnq; WI: '03- 3.
SEN records LJ 1999-2003, TJ 1996-2002.
Progression at TJ: 1996- 12.99, 1997- 13.03, 1998- 13.39, 1999- 14.08A/13.99, 2000- 14.03, 2002- 14.28, 2003- 14.91. pbs: 60mh 8.50i '04, 100mh 13.79/13.72w '02, LJ 6.54/6.62w '03, Pen 3795i '04.

Amy Mbacké THIAM b. 10 Nov 1976 1.83m 70kg. Racing Club de France.
At 400m: OG: '00- sf; WCh: '99- sf, '01- 1, '03- 3; Af G: '99- 3; AfCh: '98- 4. French champion 1998-2000. Eight SEN 400m records 1999-2001.
Progression at 400m: 1996- 54.40, 1997- 53.25, 1998- 51.60, 1999- 50.77, 2000- 50.88, 2001- 49.86, 2002- 50.96, 2003- 49.95. pbs: 100m 11.84 '98, 200m 23.20, 23.0A '99; 300m 36.0+ '03, 36.37 '00.
In 2001 she became the first athlete to win a world title for Senegal in any sport.

SERBIA & MONTENEGRO (CRNA GORA)

Governing body: Athletic Federation of Serbia & Montenegro, Strahinjica Bana 73a, 11000 Beograd. Founded in 1921.

National Championships first held in 1920 (men) and 1923 (women). **2003 champions**: **Men**: 100m/ 200m: Marko Jankovic 10.61/21.38, 400m: Zarko Mandic 48.81, 800m: Aleksandar Siladji 1:54.57, 1500m: Mirko Petrovic 3:52.11, 5000m: Velibor Radojevic 14:59.70, 10000m: Ramiz Taipi 30:40.94, HMar: Edin Zukovic 65:54 short, Mar: Sreten Ninkovic 2:19:43, 3000mSt: Dejan Bogicevic 9:28.57, 110mh: Miroslav Novakovic 13.84, 400mh: Zdenko Zec 57.08, HJ: Dejan Vreljakovic 2.15, PV: Igor Sarcevic 4.60, LJ: Danial Jahic 7.45, TJ: Zoran Rankovic 15.37w, SP/DT: Dragan Peric 20.34/ 60.39, HT: Zoran Loncar 59.11, JT: Jovan Djukic 67.20, 10000mW/20kmW: Predrag Filipovic 40: 54.8/1:21:50. **Women**: 100m/200m/400m: Elvira Pancic 11.58/24.00/54.02, 800m: Marija Papic 2:07.78, 1500m: Sonja Stolic 4:21.26, 5000m/Mar: Vesna Stevanovic 17:34.18/2:44:34, HMar: Snezana Kostic 62:21 short, 100mh: Jelena Jotanovic 14.01, 400mh: Ivana Novakovic 63.44, HJ: Marija Plazinic 1.75, PV: Jelena Radinovic-Vasic 3.55, LJ: Ana Stankovic 6.16, TJ: Marija Martinovic 12.75, SP/DT: Dragana Tomasevic 13.87/55.37, HT: Milka Djordjevic 52.00, JT: Jelena Cudanov 44.50, 10kmW: Ivana Acimovic 61:26.

Dragan PERIC b. 8 May 1964 Zivinice 1.86m 115kg. Crvena Zvezda, Beograd.
At SP: OG: '92- 7, '96- 8, '00- dnq 16; WCh: '91- 7, '93- 5, '97- dnq 19, '99- 6, '01- 5, '03- dnq 18; EC: '90- 13, '94- 6, '98- 4; WI: '95- 3; EI: '94- 2, '98- 4. Won YUG SP 1990-4, 1996-2001, 2003; DT 1992-4, 1997, 2003; Balkan SP 1996, 1998, 2003.
Yugoslav records: shot (3) 1993-8, discus 1991.
Progression at SP: 1980- 11.35, 1981- 12.23, 1982- 14.88, 1983- 17.24, 1985- 16.89, 1986- 17.70, 1987- 18.86, 1988- 19.92, 1989- 20.42, 1990- 20.06, 1991- 20.47, 1992- 20.91, 1993- 21.26, 1994- 20.64i/20.57, 1995- 20.36i/20.14, 1996- 20.90, 1997- 20.78, 1998- 21.77, 1999- 20.74, 2000- 19.88, 2001- 20.91/21.27 light, 2002- 19.47, 2003- 20.48. pb DT 61.94 '91.

Dragutin TOPIC b. 12 Mar 1971 Belgrade 1.97m 77kg. AK Vojvodina. Was at Belgrade University of PE.
At HJ: OG: '92- 8=, '96- 4, '00- dnq 21=; WCh: '91- 9, '93- dnq, '95- 8=, '97- dnq, '99- 4; EC: '90- 1, '94- 5=, '98- 9=; WJ: '90- 1; EJ: '89- 4; WI: '97- 3, '03- 4; EI: '92- 3=, '96- 1, '00- 3; WUG: '95- 1. 3rd GP 1994, 2000. Yugoslav champion 1993, 1996, 1999-2000; Balkan 1998.
World junior high jump record 1990, five Yugoslav records 1990-3.
Progression at HJ: 1985- 1.85, 1986- 1.95, 1987- 1.95, 1988- 2.06, 1989- 2.23, 1990- 2.37, 1991- 2.32/ 2.34i, 1992- 2.35, 1993- 2.38, 1994- 2.32, 1995- 2.29, 1996- 2.35, 1997- 2.32i/2.31, 1998- 2.33, 1999- 2.32, 2000- 2.34i/2.33, 2001- 2.27i/2.32i drugs dq, 2003- 2.33i/2.31. pbs: LJ 7.48i '93, TJ 15.66 '92, Dec 6155h '93.
Won World Junior and European senior HJ titles in 1990. Was at high school in Illinois, USA for a year in 1987/8, but played basketball while there and did not compete as a high jumper. Drugs ban for positive test on 2 Feb 2001 and played basketball while serving his two year ban.

Women

Olivera JEVTIC b. 24 Jul 1977 Titovo Uzice 1.74m 52kg. Mladost-Niskogradnja, Uzice.
At 10000m (/5000m): OG: '00- 11/dnf; WCh: '97- h/h, '99- 10, '01- 12/h; EC: '98- 4/4, '02- 6/dnf; EU23: '97- 1, '99- 1/3; WJ: '94- (3000m 10), 96- - /2 (3000m 5); EJ: '95- 2 (3000m 3). At Mar: WCh: '03- 8. World HMar: '98-99-01-02: 4/21/7/6; CC: '95-00-01-04: 17J/15/9/12; Eur CC: '96-7-8-9-00-01-03: 13/3/3/3/3/4/6. Won YUG 1500m & 5000m 1996, HMar 1998-9, 2002; CC 1994-7, 1999; Balkan 5000m 1998, CC 2002.
Yugoslav records: 5000m (7) 1995-2000, 10000m (2) 1998-2000, HMar (3) 1998-2002, Mar 2003.
Progress at 5000m, 10000m, Mar: 1995- 16:03.34, 33:48.61; 1996- 15:40.59, 32:38.0; 1997- 15:34.65, 32:43.42; 1998- 15:16.61, 31:34.26; 1999- 15:19.08, 31:57.67; 2000- 15:11.25, 31:29.65; 2001- 15:26.84, 31:33.08; 2002- 15:40.24, 31:47.82, 2:26:44dq; 2003- 2:25:23. pbs: 800m 2:12.41 '93, 1500m 4:16.16 '98, 3000m 8:59.21 '98, Road: 10km 31:31 '01, 15km 49:06 '01, HMar 69.18 '02.
Third in New York on marathon debut 2002, but disqualified (public warning) for positive test for ephedrine, won Rotterdam marathon 2003.

SLOVAKIA

Governing body: Slovak Athletic Federation, Junácka 6, 832 80 Bratislava. Founded 1939.

National Championships first held in 1939. **2003 Champions: Men**: 100m: Kristian Cupak 10.99, 200m: Ján Gajdos 21.9, 400m: Peter Znava 47.63, 800m: Matús Lajcák 1:53.6, 1500m: Roman Hanzel 3:53.14, 5000m/HMar: Marcel Matanin 14:48.13/67:06, 10000m: Róbert Stefko 29:34.7, Mar: Peter Behún 2:29:44, 3000mSt: Imrich Magyar 9:27.70, 110mh: Michal Zdravecky 14.95, 400mh: Frantisek Pitonák 54.76, HJ: Peter Horák 2.15, PV: Rudolf Haraksim 4.90, LJ/TJ: Martin Malovec 7.34/5.54, SP: Milan Haborák 20.24, DT: Daniel Vanek 55.97, HT: Libor Charfreitag 78.75, JT: Marián Bokor 71.12, 20kmW: Milos Bátovsky 1:27:29, 50kmW: Marek Janek 3:59:37. **Women**: 100m: Lucia Ivanova 11.99, 200m: Michaela Briatková 24.9, 400m/400mh: Miriam Hrdlicková 53.94/59.28, 800m: Barbora Bronisová 2:13.0, 1500m: Jana Styková 5:04.25, 5000m/10000m/ HMar: Dana Janecková 17:25.95/35:35.16/80:52, Mar: Andrea Béresová 3:00:31, 3000mSt: Kristina Proticová 10:51.57, 100mh/TJ: Dana Veldákova 14.52/13.58, HJ: Diana Láznicková 1.84, PV:

Slavomíra Slúková 3.60, LJ: Jana Veldáková 6.27, SP: Martina Danisová 14.40, DT: Ivona Tomanová 52.44, HT: Magda Veresová 49.36, JT: Silvia Strasíková 40.68, 10kmW/20kmW: Zuzana Malikova 47:44/1:39:22.

Libor CHARFREITAG b. 10 Nov 1976 Trnava 1.91m 117kg. Studied at Southern Methodist University, USA (now assistant coach there). ASK Slavia Trnava.
At HT: OG: '00- dnq 30; WCh: '99-01-03: dnq 32/18/13; EC: '02- 7; WJ: '96- dnq 13. NCAA champion 1998, 2000; SVK 1998-9, 2002-03.
12 SVK hammer records 1996-2003, four European indoor bests 35lb weight 2003.
Progression at HT: 1993- 49.42, 1994- 54.32, 1995- 56.90, 1996- 66.82, 1997- 66.44, 1998- 72.30, 1999- 75.18, 2000- 77.22, 2001- 77.65, 2002- 79.20, 2003- 81.81. pbs: SP 17.27i/16.69 '00, DT 51.88 '00; 35lb Wt 25.03i '03.

Milan HABORÁK b. 11 Jan 1973 Presov 1.91m 106kg. Dukla Banská Bystrica.
At SP: OG: '00- 11; WCh: '97-9-01-03: dnq 30/ 28/16/13; EC: '98- dnq 22, '02- 10; WJ: '92- 4; EJ: '91- 4. Won Slovak SP 1996-8, 2001-03, DT 2000.
Sloavk shot record 2002.
Progression at HT: 1989- 15.36, 1990- 16.95, 1991- 16.95, 1992- 17.97, 1993- 17.59, 1994- 18.77, 1995-18.97, 1996- 19.12i/18.42, 1997- 19.59, 1998- 19.71, 1999- 19.86, 2000- 20.35, 2001- 20.58, 2002- 20.82, 2003- 20.39i/20.28. pb DT 56.20 '96.
Married to Michaela Knopková, sister of throwers Mikulas and Miroslav Konopka.

SLOVENIA

Governing body: Atletska Zveza Slovenije, Vodnikova cesta 155, 1000 Ljubljana. Current organisation founded 1945.

2003 National Champions: **Men**: 100m/200m: Matic Osovnikar 10.44/20.88, 400m: Matija Sestak 46.99, 800m: Tomaz Vuk 1:51.60, 1500m: Boris Spes 3:52.12, 3000m/5000m: Pavel Pori 8:39.20/ 14:52.89, 10000m/HMar: Roman Kejzar 30:15.67/ 66:51, Mar: Zdravko Volkar 2:29:20, 3000mSt: Bostjan Buc 8:43.74, 110mh: Tevz Korent 14.31, 400mh: Damjan Zlatnar 51.74, HJ: Rozle Prezelj 2.20, PV: Jurij Rovan 5.40, LJ: Gregor Cankar 7.86, TJ: Bostjan Simunic 16.54, SP: Miran Vodovnik 19.62, DT: Igor Primc 58.20, HT: Primoz Kozmus 76.48, JT: Peter Zupanc 75.73, Dec: Damjan Sitar 7248. **Women**: 100m: Sasa Aleksandra Prokofjev 11.41, 200m: Merlene Ottey 22.89, 400m/400mh: Meta Macus 55.20/58.46, 800m: Petra Stosic 2:13.65, 1500m: Janja Bucar 4:50.63, 3000m: Darja Kokalj 10:31.28, 5000m/10000m/HMar: Helena Javornik 16:18.10/33:24.04/72:50, Mar: Ida Surbek 2:49:57, 3000mSt: Tamara Golenac 11:16.83, 100mh: Marina Tomic 13.30,: HJ: Maja Mlinaric 1.65, PV: Teja Melink 4.00, LJ: Kristina Zumer 5.99, TJ: Snezana Vukmirovic 13.24, SP/DT: Mojca Crnigoj 15.06/ 42.70, HT: Ana Susec 50.34, JT: Petra Novak 44.78, Hep: Klavdija Halimic 5055.

Primoz KOZMUS b. 30 Sep 1979 Novo Mesto 1.88m 106kg. FIT Brezice.
At HT: OG: '00- dnq 38; WCh: '03- 5; EC: '02- dnq 25; EU23: '99- 12, '01- 14; WJ: '98- dnq. SLO champion 1999-2003.
Eight SLO hammer records 2000-03.
Progression at HT: 1995- 45.82, 1996- 54.10, 1997- 61.08, 1998- 66.28, 1999- 70.11, 2000- 76.84, 2001- 71.17, 2002- 75.87, 2003- 81.21.
Older sister Simona holds Slovenian women's hammer record (58.60 '01).

Women

Jolanda CEPLAK b. 12 Sep 1976 Celje 1.68m 55kg. née Steblovnik. Velenje.
At 800m: OG: '00- h 4x400mR; WCh: 97- h, '01- sf; EC: '02- 1; EJ: '93- 4; WI: '01-03-04: 6/4/2; EI: '00- 4, '02- 1; WCp: '02- 3; ECp: '98- 8. At 1500m: WCh: '03- 12; EJ: '95- 3. Won SLO 800m 2000, 1500m 1993, 1996, 1999; 3000m 1996.
WIR 800m 2002, Slovenian records: 800m (3) 1997-2002, 1000m 2002, 1500m (2) 2002-03.
Progress at 800m, 1500m: 1989- 2:17.65, 4:48.08; 1990- 2:10.55, 4:34.03; 1991- 2:10.15, 4:33.76; 1992- 2:10.41, 4:31.90; 1993- 2:07.91, 4:31.97; 1994- 2:06.53, 4:25.80; 1995- 2:06.43, 4:20.22; 1996- 2:04.94, 4:17.82; 1997- 2:00.94, 1998- 2:02.71, 4:20.89; 1999- 2:02.53, 2000- 2:00.80, 2001- 1:58.71, 4:13.19; 2002- 1:55.19, 4:05.44i/4:05.59; 2003- 1:57.44, 4:02.44. pbs: 400m 54.67 '00, 600m 1:26.68i '02, 1000m 2:31.66 '02, 1M 5:06.6 '98, 3000m 9:50.15 '96, HMar 83:55 '97, 400mh 63.81 '95.
Broke WIR 800m by 0.58 at European Indoors 2002, front-running to 600m and reclaiming lead from Steffi Graf in one of the great races of all-time. Had set SLO age-15 records at all distances from 400m to1500m.

Helena JAVORNIK b. 26 Mar 1966 Celje 1.63m 52kg. Zrece.
At 1500m: OG: '00- h (h 800m); WI: '01- 8. At 5000m: EC: '02- 14. At 10000m: WCh: '03- 18. At Mar: OG: '96- 53. World HMar: '03- 11. Eur CC: '02- 1. Won SLO 1500m 1997, 2000, 2002; 3000m 1997-8, 2001-02; 5000m 1995, 1998, 2003; 10000m 1994, 1997-2000, 2003; HMar 1994, 1998, 2002-03; Mar 1993-5.
SLO records: 1500m (2), 1M, 2000m (2), 3000m, 5000m (3), 10000m (4), HMar (7), Mar (6) 1992-2003.
Progression at 5000m, 10000m, Mar: 1991- 2:49:30, 1992- 35:53.82, 2:37:09; 1993- 34:51.75, 2:37:27; 1994- 34:29.02, 2:34:50; 1995- 17:33.19, 2:34:29; 1996- 16:25.01, 2:34:41; 1997- 15:35.18, 33:02.79, 2:40:05; 1998- 15:27.50, 32:52.28, 2:32:33; 1999- 15:15.40, 34:07.64, 2:39:50; 2000- 15:27.68, 32:44.40; 2001- 15:23.45, 2002- 15:32.90, 2:28:15; 2003- 15: 36.81, 31:56.90, 2:28:13. pbs: 1500m 4:06.22i '01, 4:06.77 '00; 1M 4:29.35i '02, 2000m 5:44.93i '02, 3000m 8:50.71 '00, 8:47.49i '02; HMar 71:03 '03.
Won Firenze Marathon 2002 two weeks before her unexpected European CC Championships success.

Brigita LANGERHOLC b. 23 Jul 1976 Kranj 1.70m 56kg. Triglav, Kranj. Was at University of Southern California, USA. Marketing and finance manager.
At 800m: OG: '00- 4; WCh: '99- sf, '01- h, '03- sf; EC: '02- sf; WUG: '99- 2, '01- 1; won NCAA 2001. At 400m: EJ: '93- 7, '95- 5; EU23: '97- 5; ECp: '98- 8. Won SLO 400m 1996-8, 2000-02; 800m 1996, 1998-9.
SLO records: 400m, 800m (3) 1999-2000.
Progression at 800m: 1991- 2:12.69, 1992- 2:23.52, 1993- 2:17.81, 1994- 2:17.54, 1995- 2:11.36, 1996- 2:06.57, 1998- 2:04.16, 1999- 1:59.87, 2000- 1:58.51, 2001- 1:59.86, 2002- 1:58.97, 2003- 2:00.47. pbs: 100m 12.01 '00, 200m 24.32 '00, 400m 52.02 '00, 1000m 2:39.20i '03, 2:40.71 '02.

SOUTH AFRICA

Governing body: Athletics South Africa, PO Box 2712, Houghton 2041. Original body founded 1894.
National Championships first held in 1894 (men), 1929 (women). **2003 Champions**: **Men**: 100m/200m: Sherwin Vries 10.44/20.82, 400m: Paul Gorries 45.47, 800m: Mbulaeni Mulaudzi 1:46.44, 1500m: Johan Pretorius 3:40.52, 5000m: Frank Lekhwi 14:00.90, 10000m: Elias Modise 28:47.77, 3000mSt: Petrus Sithole 8:32.66, 110mh: Shaun Bownes 13.96, 400mh: Louis van Zyl 49.84, HJ: Ramsay Carelse 2.15, PV: Okkert Brits 5.40, LJ: Martin McClintock 7.55, TJ: Simeon Mars 15.93w, SP: Burger Lambrechts 18.47, DT: Frantz Kruger 66.70, HT: Chris Harmse 77.04, JT: Hardus Pienaar 74.95, Dec: Jannie Botha 7052, 20kmW: Thami Hlatswayo 1:34:07. **Women**: 100m/200m: Janice Josephs 11.43/23.26, 400m: Heide Seyerling 51.87, 800m/1500m: Rene Kalmer 2:03.63/4:11.24, 5000m/10000m: Poppy Mlambo 16:07.11/34:51.65, 3000mSt: Promise Mathonsi 10:22.45, 100mh/400mh: Surita Febbraio 13.57/55.92, HJ: Hestrie Cloete 1.90, PV: Samantha Dodd 3.60, LJ: Delia Visser 6.17, TJ: Theresa de Vries 12.29, SP: Maranelle du Toit 16.68, DT: Elizna Naude 53.75, HT: Elmarie Knoetzen 52.37, JT: Sunette Viljoen 54.32, Hep: Justine Robbeson 5761, 20000mW: Nicolene Cronje 1:45:12.6.

Shaun BOWNES b. 24 Oct 1970 Johannesburg 1.94m 90kg. Liberty-Nike, Potchefstroom.
At 110mh: OG: '00- sf; WCh: '99- qf, '01- 8, '03- sf; CG: '98- 3, '02- 1; AfG: '99- 5; AfCh: '98- 1, '02- 1; WCp: '02- 4; Won SA 1994, 1998, 2000, 2002-03. At 60mh: WI: '01- 3, '03- 8.
Records: African 110mh (7) 1998-2001, indoors: 50mh (2) & 60mh (3) 2000-01. Nine SA 110mh 1998-2001.
Progression at 110mh: 1989- 14.5A, 1990- 15.00A, 1991- 14.43A, 1992- 13.97A, 1993- 14.19A, 1994- 13.98A, 1995- 14.21A/14.19Aw, 1997- 13.97A/13.5A, 1998- 13.53/13.2A, 1999- 13.39, 2000- 13.41/13.38w, 2001- 13.26, 2002- 13.31A/13.34, 2003- 13.50. pbs: 100m 10.68A '03, 200m 21.35A '00, 50mh 6.48i '01, 60mh 7.52i '01, 7.53A '03.
Received four-year drugs ban for steroid use in 1995, commuted to two years.

Okkert BRITS b. 22 Aug 1973 Uitenhage 1.98m 84kg. Maties AC, Stellenbosch.
At PV: OG: '96- dnq, '00- 7; WCh: '93- dnq 16=, '95- 4, '97- dnq, '99- 10, '03- 2; CG: '94- nh, '02- 1; WJ: '92- 3; WI: '95- 3=, '97- 6, '01- 7; AfG: '95- 1, '99- 1; AfCh: '92-3-8: 1/1/1; WCp: '92-4-02: 3/1/1. Won GP 1995, 3rd 2000. SA champion 1993-5, 1998, 2000, 2002-03.
23 SA (1992-5), 19 African (1993-5) and 9 Commonwealth (1994-5) pole vault records.
Progression at PV: 1989- 4.50, 1990- 4.80, 1991- 5.25, 1992- 5.46, 1993- 5.71, 1994- 5.90, 1995- 6.03, 1996- 6.01, 1997- 5.92, 1998- 5.90, 1999- 5.75A, 2000- 5.85/5.90ex, 2001- 5.70i/5.60A, 2002- 5.81, 2003- 5.86. pb 100m 10.96 '96.
Younger brother Pieter (b. 14 Oct 1975) has PV best of 5.50 '97.

Jacques FREITAG b. 11 Jun 1982 Warrenton 2.07m 83kg. Rentmeester-Tuks.
At HJ: WCh: '01- dnq 24, '03- 1; WJ: '00- 1; WY: '99- 1. RSA champion 2000, 2002.
Two African and seven South African high jump records 2000-02 (three African Junior 2000-01).
Progression at HJ: 1998- 2.08, 1999- 2.25A; 2000- 2.30A, 2001- 2.31, 2002- 2.37, 2003- 2.35.
First athlete to win gold medals at World Youth, Junior and Senior Champs. RSA sportsman of the year 2003. Will miss 2004 season through injury. Mother, Hendrina Pieters was SA high jump champion and set a pb of 1.74 in 1973.

Llewellyn HERBERT b. 21 Jul 1977 Bethal 1.85m 80kg. Rentmeester-Tuks, Pretoria.
At 400mh: OG: '96- h, '00- 3; WCh: '97- 2, '01- h, '03- 8; WJ: '96- 2; AfCh: '02- 1; WUG: '97- 1; WCp: '02- 7. Won SA 110mh 1996-7, 400mh 1996-2002.
Seven SA 400mh records 1997-2000.
Progression at 400mh: 1995- 51.25, 1996- 48.76A, 1997- 47.86, 1998- 48.43A/48.76, 1999- 47.83A/48.28, 2000- 47.81, 2001- 48.52A/48.77, 2002- 48.02A/48.83, 2003- 48.50. pbs: 100m 10.30A/10.20Aw '99; 200m 20.50wA/21.06 '99, 400m 46.15A '02, 110mh 13.91A '98, 13.7A '97.
Customarily faces away from direction of running before taking his marks. Season cut short by injury in 1998, 1999 and 2001.

Frantz KRUGER b. 22 May 1975 Kempton Park 2.03m 125kg. Former medical student at Free State University, Bloemfontein. Rentmeester-Tuks.
At DT: OG: '00- 3; WCh: '99- dnq 17, '01- 8, '03- 6; CG: '98- 2, '02- 1; WJ: '94- 1; AfG: '99- 1; AfCh: '98- 1; WUG: '97- 6, '99- 1; WCp: '98- 3. Won GWG 2001, SA DT 1996, 1999-2003; Af-J SP & DT 1994.
Three African and Commonwealth discus records 2000-02.

Progression at DT: 1993- 58.28, 1994- 58.52, 1995- 60.06, 1996- 60.66, 1997- 61.64, 1998- 65.73, 1999- 67.38, 2000- 69.75A, 2001- 69.96, 2002- 70.32, 2003- 66.70.
Set RSA U13 record for 200m individual medley swimming. Married Heli Koivula (2 EC TJ 2002 for Finland) on 28 June 2003.

Mbulaeni MULAUDZI b. 8 Sep 1980 Muduluni Village, Limpopo Province 1.71m 62kg. Vaal Technikon. Student.
At 800m: WCh: '01- 6, '03- 3; CG: '02- 1; AfG: '03- 2; AfCh: '00- 2, '02- 3; WI: '04- 1; Won AfrJ 1999, RSA 2001-03.
Progress at 800m: 1998- 1:50.33A, 1999- 1:48.33A; 2000- 1:45.55, 2001- 1:44.01, 2002- 1:43.81, 2003- 1:42.89. pbs: 400m 47.20A '99, 1000m 2:18.45A '03, 1500m 3:39.70 '02.

Hendrick RAMAALA b. 2 Feb 1972 GaMalepo, Pietersburg 1.72m 58kg. Law graduate of Wits University. Mr Price AC.
At 10000m: OG: '96- h; WCh: '95- 17, '97- 14, '99- 11; AfG: '99- 7. At Mar: OG: '00- 12; WCh: '03- 9. World HMar: '97-8-9-01-02: 4/2/2/4/15. Won SA 5000m 1995, 1999; 10000m 1995, 1999-2001; HMar 1997.
SA records 10000m (3) 1997-9, HMar 1997, 2000.
Progression at 10000m, Mar: 1995- 27:54.59, 1996- 27:57.8, 1997- 27:36.30, 1998- 27:30.57, 1999- 27:29.94, 2000- 27:46.38, 2:09:43; 2001- 27:38.36, 2:11:18; 2002- 28:02.37, 2:10:06; 2003- 27:43.07, 2:08:58. pbs: 1500m 3:52.14 '03, 3000m 8:10.38 '95, 5000m 13:24.43 '98, HMar 59:20 '00.
Won Great North Run half marathon 1997 & 2003. Partner of French distance runner Rodica Moroianu.

Janus ROBBERTS b. 10 Mar 1979 Louis Trichardt 1.96m 130kg. Student at Southern Methodist University, USA.
At SP (/DT): OG: '00- 7; WCh: '99- dnq 20, '01- 11, '03- dnq 26; CG: '98- 5, '02- 2/7; WJ: '98- 2/7; AfG: '99- 2; AfCh: '02- 1/1; WCp: '02- 4. Won NCAA SP 1999, 2001-02; DT 2002; Afr-J SP/DT 1997.
Three African and one Commonwealth shot records 2001. Official world junior record 1998, four African indoors 2000-01.
Progression at SP: 1997- 18.61, 1998- 20.39, 1999- 20.10, 2000- 20.34, 2001- 21.97, 2002- 21.60, 2003- 20.27. pb DT 62.37 '02.
Led the qualifying at the 2001 Worlds with 21.26, but 20.18 for 11th in the final.

Hezekiél SEPENG b. 30 Jun 1974 Potchefstroom 1.82m 70kg. Mr Price AC, Potchefstroom.
At 800m: OG: '96- 2, '00- 4; WCh: '93- 5, '95- sf, '97- sf, '99- 2, '01- 8, '03- 7; CG: '94- 2, '98- 2; WJ: '92- 5; AfG: '95-9-03: 6/3/8; AfCh: '93- 4; WUG: '95- 1, '97- 2. 2nd GP 1999. Won SA 800m 1993-4, 1997-8; 1500m 2001.
Three SA 800m records 1996-9.
Progression at 800m: 1992- 1:47.51, 1993- 1:45.46, 1994- 1:45.32, 1995- 1:45.36, 1996- 1:42.74, 1997- 1:43.19, 1998- 1:44.44, 1999- 1:42.69, 2000- 1:43.98, 2001- 1:43.57, 2002- 1:44.39, 2003- 1:43.12. pbs: 400m 46.50A '03, 1000m 2:16.47 '00, 1500m 3:38.24 '96, 1M 3:57.33 '96, 3000m 8:21.58A '01.
Lost to Wilson Kipketer by just 0.02 in 1999 World Champs.

Women

Hestrie CLOETE b. 26 Aug 1978 Germiston 1.85m 68kg. née Storbeck. Mr Price AC.
At HJ: OG: '00- 2; WCh: '97- 10=, '99- dnq 14=, '01- 1, '03- 1; WJ: '96- 6=; CG: '98- 1, '02- 1; AfG: '95- 1, '99- 1; AfCh: '98- 1, '02- 1; WCp: '98- 2, '02- 1. Won WAF 2003, GP 1999, 2001; GWG 2001, RSA 1996-2003, African Jnr 1997.
High jump records: 14 African 1998-2003, six Commonwealth and four South African 1999-2003, African Junior 1996.
Progression at HJ: 1993- 1.75, 1994- 1.79, 1995- 1.91, 1996- 1.92, 1997- 1.94, 1998- 1.96, 1999- 2.04, 2000- 2.01, 2001- 2.01, 2002- 2.02, 2003- 2.06. pbs: 400m 56.0A '94, 800m 2:11.9 '95, LJ 5.75A '95.
Top world ranked in 1999, but had a lapse of concentration in failing to qualify for world final. Top junior in the world in 1997. IAAF Female Athlete of the Year 2003.

Surita FEBBRAIO b. 27 Dec 1973 Springs 1.68m 58kg. née Loots. Rentmeester-Tuks. Policewoman.
At 400mh: WCh: '01- h, '03- 8; AfG: '99- 2. Won RSA 400mh 1998, 2000-03; 100mh 2000-03.
Progression at 400mh: 1995- 58.33, 1997- 57.63A; 1998- 56.64A; 1999- 56.50A, 2000- 55.22A/55.77, 2001- 54.10A/54.48, 2002- 54.45A, 2003- 54.05A/54.31. pbs: 100m 11.49A/11.1A '99; 200m 23.32A '00, 22.9A '99; 400m 52.22A/52.43 '03; 100mh 13.10 '01.

Heide SEYERLING b. 19 Aug 1976 Port Elizabeth 1.68m 55kg. Mr Price AC, Durban.
At 400m: OG: '00- 6; AfG: '99- 7; WCh: '01/03- sf; CG: '02- 5. At 200m: WCh: '95- h, '99- h; CG: '98- 5; WJ: '94- 1; AfG: '03- 6 (2 4x100m); AfCh: '98- 3, Af-J: '94- 1 (100m 2). Won SA 100m 1998-9, 200m 1995, 1998-2002, 400m 2000-01, 2003.
SA 400m record 2000.
Progression at 200m, 400m: 1991- 24.4, 1992- 23.8, 1993- 24.08A/23.94Aw, 1994- 23.22A/22.80w, 1995- 23.36, 1996- 23.28, 1997- 24.19A, 1998- 22.89, 53.8; 1999- 22.88A, 51.33A; 2000- 22.87A/22.59Aw, 50.05; 2001- 22.63, 50.36; 2002- 23.26A/22.9, 51.51A; 2003- 23.10, 51.30. pbs: 100m 11.35 '99, 11.33Aw '01, 11.1w '97; 300m 37.02 '00.
Married sprinter Matthew Quinn (pb 100m 10.08A '99, WC 01 2nd 4x100m) on 4 May 2002.

SPAIN

Governing body: Real Federación Española de Atletismo, Avda. Valladolid, 81 - 1°, 28008 Madrid, Spain. Founded 1918.
National Championships first held in 1917 (men), 1931 (women). **2003 Champions**: **Men**: 100m: Orkatz Beitia 10.45, 200m: Jordi Mayoral

21.16, 400m: David Canal 45.01, 800m: Antonio M Reina 1:46.87, 1500m: Juan Carlos Higuero 3:39.71, 5000m: Jesús España 13:34.60, 10000m: José Rios 27:29.60, HMar: Alejandro Gómez 64:40, 3000mSt: Eliseo Martín 8:15.22, 110mh: Felipe Vivancos 13.75, 400mh: Iván Rodríguez 49.39, HJ: Javier Bermejo 2.20, PV: Montxu Miranda 5.31, LJ: Yago Lamela 8.06, TJ: Raúl Chapado 16.56w, SP: Manuel Martínez 20.55, DT: Mario Pestano 61.02, HT: Moisés Campeny 72.42, JT: Gustavo Dacal 74.96, Dec: Oscar González 7660, 20kmW: Francisco Fernández 1:24:10, 50kmW: Mikel Odriozola 3:42:03. **Women**: 100m: Carme Blay 11.6, 200m: Cristina Sanz 23.95, 400m: Julia Alba 53.28, 800m: Marlén Estévez 2:04.32, 1500m: Natalia Rodríguez 4:09.63, 5000m: Marta Domínguez 15:28.53, 10000m: Yesenia Centeno 31:49.58, HMar: Faustina María 75:38, 3000mSt: Rosa Morató 10:06.01, 100mh: Aliuska López 12.90, 400mh: Cora Olivero 56.17, HJ: Ruth Beitia 1.97, PV: Naroa Agirre 4.30, LJ: Concepción Montaner 6.35, TJ: Carlota Castrejana 14.03w, SP: Irache Quintanal 16.91, DT: Alice Matejková 55.23, HT: Berta Castells 64.25, JT: Mercedes Chilla 55.47, Hep: María Peinado 5629, 10,000W/20kmW: Maria Vasco 44:30.46/1:31:16.

Réyes ESTÉVEZ b. 2 Aug 1976 Barcelona 1.87m 70kg. Nike Bowerman.
At 1500m: OG: '96- sf; WCh: '97- 3, '99- 3, '01- 5, '03- 6; EC: '98- 1, '02- 2; WJ: '94- 4; EJ: '93- 1, '95- 1; EU23: '97- 1; WI: '01- 2; WCp: '02- 2; ECp: '98- 2. World CC: '94- 8J. Won Spanish 1500m 1997-8.
European Junior 1500m record 1995.
Progression at 1500m: 1992- 3:54.7, 1993- 3:42.36, 1994- 3:39.28, 1995- 3:35.51, 1996- 3:34.86, 1997- 3:33.40, 1998- 3:30.87, 1999- 3:30.57, 2000- 3:40.64, 2001- 3:32.34, 2002- 3:32.93, 2003- 3:32.86. pbs: 800m 1:46.90 '96, 1000m 2:17.45 '00, 1M 3:51.82 '02, 2000m 5:09.60 '03, 3000m 7:44.87 '99, 5000m 14:08.8 '96.

Francisco Javier **FERNÁNDEZ** b. 5 Mar 1977 Guadix, Granada 1.75m 60kg. Agropaejido.
At 20kmW: OG: '00- 7; WCh: '99- 15, '01- dnf, '03- 2; EC: '98- 3, '02- 1; WCp: '97- 47, '99- 12; EC: '98- 3; EU23: '97- 2; ECp: '98-00-01-03: 1/3/4/1. Spanish champion 1998-2003. At 10kmW: WJ: '96- 1; EJ: '95- 2.
World 20km walk best 2002. Spanish walks records 1999-2002: 5000m (2), 10000m, 10km (3), 20km (2).
Progression at 20kmW: 1997- 1:21:59, 1998- 1:20:31, 1999- 1:21:55, 2000- 1:18:56, 2001- 1:19:47, 2002- 1:17:22, 2003- 1:18:00. pb 5000mW 18:48.23 '02, 10000mW 38:42.38 '99, 10kmRd 37:52 '02 (all Spanish records).

Jesús Ángel GARCÍA b. 17 Oct 1969 Madrid 1.71m 62kg. Canal de Isabel II.
At 50kmW: OG: '92- 10, '96- dnf, '00- 12; WCh: '93-5-7-9-01-03: 1/5/2/dnf/2/6; EC: '94- 4, '98- dq, '02- 3; WCp: '93-5-7-9-02: 2/2/1/4/dq; ECp: '96-8-00-01: 1/2/1/1. At 20kmW: WUG: '91- 5. Won SPA 50kmW 1997, 2000.
Progression at 50kmW: 1991- 4:05:10, 1992- 3:48:24, 1993- 3:41:41, 1994- 3:41:28, 1995- 3:41:54, 1996- 3:46:59, 1997- 3:39.54, 1998- 3:43:17, 1999- 3:40:40, 2000- 3:42:51, 2001- 3:43:07, 2002- 3:44:33, 2003- 3:43:56. pbs: 5000mW 19:33.3 '01, 10000mW 41:38.8 '01, road: 10kmW 40:38 '91, 20kmW 1:23:34 '01, 30kmW 2:08:47 '01.
In 1997 he married Carmen Acedo, who won a rhythmic gymnastics world title in 1993.

Juan Carlos HIGUERO b. 3 Aug 1978 Aranda de Duero 1.79m 60kg. FC Barcelona.
At 1500m: OG: '00- 8; WCh: '03- 11; EC: '02- 5; EU23: '99- h; WI: '01- 9, '03- 8; EI: '00- 6, '02- 2; ECp: '03- 1. At 5000m: EJ: '97- 3. Eur CC: '96-97: 3J/4J. Won Spanish 1500m 2000, 2002-03.
Progress at 1500m: 1997- 3:50.90, 1998- 3:41.24, 1999- 3:39.57, 2000- 3:36.63, 2001- 3:32.30, 2002- 3:33.72, 2003- 3:31.61. pbs: 800m 1:46.00 '03, 1M 3:52.49 '02, 3000m 7:51.56i '04, 7:59.76 '99; 5000m 14:08.35 '97, 10kmRd 28:37 '03.

Antonio David **JIMENEZ** b. 18 Feb 1977 Sevilla 1.78m 61kg. Reebok RC
At 3000mSt: WCh: '01- 6, EC: '02- 1; ECp: '01-03: 2/4, EU23: '99- 3; Won MedG '01, ESP 1999, 2001. At 3000m: WI: '04- 4; EI: '02- 2. World 4k CC: '02- 7. Eur CC: '01- 3. Won Spanish 4k CC& 3000mSt 2002.
Progress at 3000mSt: 1995- 9:24.74, 1996- 9:17.93, 1997- 9:19.3, 1998- 8:54.90, 1999- 8:37:29, 2000- 8:20:34, 2001- 8:11.52, 2002- 8:17.77, 2003- 8:15.82. pbs: 1500m 3:43.23 '02, 2000m 5:04.91 '02, 3000m 7:46.49i '02, 7:50.30 '00; 2000mSt 5:20.07 '01 (Spanish record).

Yago LAMELA b. 24 Jul 1977 Avilés, Asturias 1.78m 68kg. Computer engineering student at University of Oviedo. Areia.
At LJ (TJ): OG: '00- dnq 19; WCh: '99- 2, '03- 3; EC: '98- 8, '02- 3; WJ: '94- (dnq 14), '96- 4; EU23: '99- 1; EJ: '95 (12); WI: '99- 2, '03- 2; EI: '98- 5, '02- 2; WCp: '02- 3; ECp: '98-01-03: 7/8/2. Won IbAm LJ 1998, Spanish LJ 1998-2000, 2003.
Five Spanish long jump records 1999.
Progression at LJ: 1991- 5.91, 1992- 6.62, 1993- 6.89/7.09w, 1994- 7.27, 1995- 7.75i/7.66, 1996- 7.80/8.04w, 1997- 7.87/7.90w, 1998- 8.14/8.20w, 1999- 8.56, 2000- 8.22, 2001- 8.07, 2002- 8.21/8.25w, 2003- 8.53. pbs: 100m, 10.93 '99, TJ 16.72 '98.
In 1999, after setting Spanish indoor records at 8.20 and 8.22 in Jan-Feb, had a superb World Indoors, with successive records of 8.29, 8.42 and 8.56, when second to Iván Pedroso, as he was also at the outdoor World Champs. Outdoors he also jumped 8.56.

David MÁRQUEZ b. 13 Oct 1977 Barcelona 1.70m 51kg. F.C.Barcelona.
At 20kmW: OG: '00- 20; WCh: '01- 5, '03- 7; EU23: '99- 1; ECp: '03- 6. At 10000mW: WJ: '96- 2.
Spanish 30km walk record 2001.

Progression at 20kmW: 1997- 1:25:14, 1998- 1:24:07, 1999- 1:23:42, 2000- 1:21:44, 2001- 1:21:09, 2003- 1:19:46. pbs: 5000mW 19:30.4 '00, 10000mW 41:03.73 '96, 30kmW 2:06:45 '01, 10kmRd 39:56 '03.

Eliseo MARTÍN b. 5 Nov 1973 Monzón, Huesca 1.73m 62kg. Transbaso Monzón Polidux.
At 3000mSt: OG: '00- 6; WCh: '99- 6, '01- 12, '03- 3; EC: '98- 7, '02- 5. At 10000m: WJ: '92- 7. Won Spanish 3000mSt 1999, 2003.
Progress at 3000mSt: 1992- 9:02.55, 1993- 8:45.77, 1994- 8:32.89, 1995- 8:31.27, 1996- 8:31.99, 1997- 8:30.50, 1998- 8:25.92, 1999- 8:13.59, 2000- 8:13.63, 2001- 8:19.20, 2002- 8:19.09, 2003- 8:09.09. pbs: 1500m 3:40.96 '00, 3000m 7:50.71 '03, 5000m 13:47.77 '01, 10000m 28:39.11 '99, 2000mSt 5:22.93 '01.

Luis Miguel MARTÍN b. 11 Jan 1972 Madrid 1.80m 69kg. Nike Bowerman.
At 3000mSt: OG: '00- 5; WCh: '99- h, '01- 4, '03- 6; EC: '98- 4, '02- 3; WCp: '02- 2; won IbAm 1998, Spanish 2000. At 1500m: WJ: '90- h; EJ: '91- h.
Four Spanish records 3000mSt 1999-2002.
Progression at 3000mSt: 1998- 8:20.54, 1999- 8:11.18, 2000- 8:09.77, 2001- 8:08.74, 2002- 8:07.44, 2003- 8:13.52. pbs: 1500m 3:36.11 '02, 2000m 5:10.63 '03, 3000m 7:50.27 '00, 5000m 13:54.35 '02, 2000mSt 5:20.52 '02.

José Manuel 'Chema' **MARTINEZ** b. 22 Oct 1971 Madrid 1.76m 63kg. Nike Bowerman.
At 10000m: WCh: '99- 19, '01- 12, EC: '02- 1; WUG: '99- 1. At Mar: WCh: '03- 16. Eur CC: '00- 9, '02- 15. Won Spanish CC 2002.
Progression at 10000m, Mar: 1993- 29:22.72, 1994- 29:19.42, 1995- 29:15.8, 1996- 28:51.97, 1997- 28:11.67, 1998- 28:16.39, 1999- 27:51.82, 2000- 27:53.9, 2001- 27:54.81, 2002- 27:41.76, 2:09:55; 2003- 27:30.56, 2:08:09. pbs: 1500m 3:48.49 '97, 2000m 5:11.14 '03, 3000m 7:41.25 '02, 5000m 13:13.57 '02, HMar 63:20 '03.
Third in Rotterdam on marathon debut 2002 and again in 2003. Won the European 10000m with a 56.6 last lap. Wife Nuria Moreno is an international hockey player.

Manuel MARTÍNEZ b. 7 Dec 1974 León 1.85m 140kg. León C.A.
At SP: OG: '96- dnq 15, '00- 6; WCh: '93- 11, '95- dnq 21, '97- dnq 13, '01- 4, '03- dnq 15; EC: '94- dnq 14, '98- 7, '02- 5; WI: '95-7-9-01-03-04: 4/5/4/3/1/5; EI: '94-00-02: 4/2/1; WJ: '92- 2; EJ: '93- 1; WUG: '01- 1; WCp: '02- 6; ECp: '93-5-6-7-8-01-03: 7/4/4/3/3/1/1; E23Cp: '94- 1. Won Spanish 1993-8, 2000-03; IbAm 1998, 2000; MedG 2001. 16 Spanish shot records 1993-2002.
Progression at SP: 1991- 15.57, 1992- 18.14, 1993- 19.53, 1994- 20.16, 1995- 19.97i/19.69, 1996- 20.12, 1997- 20.37i/20.27, 1998- 20.50i/20.08; 1999- 20.79i/20.04, 2000- 20.55, 2001- 21.35, 2002- 21.47, 2003- 21.24i/21.08. pb DT 48.04 '98.

Juan Manuel MOLINA b. 15 Mar 1979 Cieza, Murcia 1.80m 58kg. Cofrucieza.
At 20kmW: EC: '02- 3; EU23: '99- 4, '01- 1; WUG: '01- 2; WCp: '02- 8; ECp: '01- 10. At 10kmW: WJ: '96- 4; EJ: '97- 6.
Progress at 20kmW: 1999- 1:23:39, 2000- 1:22:43, 2001- 1:21:51, 2002- 1:20:18, 2003- 1:21:57. pbs: 10000mW 40:38.32 '02, 30kmW 2:11:05 '00.

Mikel ODRIOZOLA b. 25 May 1973 San Sebastián 1.80m 62kg. Real Sociedad Krafft.
At 20kmW: WCh: '99- 18, '03- 14. At 50kmW: OG: '00- 24; WCh: '01- 15, '03- 14; EC: '98- 4, '02- dq. Won Spanish 50kmW 2003.
Spanish record 30km walk 2003.
Progression at 50kmW: 1996- 4:11:45, 1997- 3:57:15, 1998- 3:47:24, 1999- 3:51:01, 2000- 3:45:57, 2001- 3:45:22, 2002- 3:47:55, 2003- 3:42:03. pbs: 5000mW 19:28.9 '00, 10000mW 42:43.1 '96, 10kmW 41:25 '00, 20kmW 1:22:29 '00, 30kmW 2:05:28 '03.

Antonio PEÑA b. 26 Aug 1970 Felanitx, Mallorca 1.75m 60kg. Nike Bowerman.
At Mar: WCh: '99- dnf, '01- 24; EC: '94- 32, '98- 6. Won Spanish Mar 1997, HMar 2000-01. World HMar: '92- 13.
Progression at Mar: 1992- 2:11:35, 1993- 2:13:06, 1994- 2:17:19, 1996- 2:13:39, 1997- 2:10:49dh, 1998- 2:13:53, 2000- 2:07:47, 2001- 2:07:34, 2002- 2:08:08, 2003- 2:07:59. pbs: 5000m 13:52.70 '92, 10000m 28:02.1 '00, HMar 61:48 '92.
Five wins in 18 marathons, including Lake Biwa 2001; 2nd Berlin 2000.

Mario PESTANO b. 8 Apr 1978 Tenerife 1.93m 105kg. C.A.Arena.
At DT: WCh: '99/01- dnq 30/22, '03- 8; EC: '02- 4; EU23: '99- 3; EJ: '97- 11; WCp: '02- 3; ECp: '02-03: 2/5. Spanish champion 2001-03.
Four Spanish discus records 2001.
Progression at DT: 1995- 49.36, 1996- 50.56, 1997- 53.68, 1998- 54.96, 1999- 61.73, 2000- 61.63, 2001- 67.92, 2002- 67.46, 2003- 64.99. pb SP 18.75i '00, 18.64 '02.

Antonio Manuel REINA b. 13 Jun 1981 Osuna, Seville 1.86m 72kg. Reebok RC.
At 800m: WCh: '01- h/7R, '03- sf/6R; EC: '02- sf; WJ: '00- 3; EU23: '01- 1; WI: '03- 4; EI: '02- 3; WCp: '02- 1; ECp: '03- 1. Won Spanish 800m 2001-03. Two Spanish 800m records 2002
Progression at 800m: 1998- 1:54.44, 1999- 1:51.75, 2000- 1:47.33, 2001- 1:46.00, 2002- 1:43.83, 2003- 1:44.37. pbs: 200m 22.64 '01, 400m 46.26 '02, 1000m 2:20.50 '01, 1500m 3:59.6 '00.
Improved in 2002 from a best of 1:45.25 (3rd in European Indoors) to a Spanish outdoor record 1:44.11 at San Sebastián and then 1:43.83 in a thrilling World Cup victory in Madrid.

Julio REY b. 13 Jan 1972 Toledo 1.66m 54kg. Adidas.
At Mar: WCh: '01- 37; EC: '02- 3. At 10000m: WCh: '97- 8; EC: '98- dnf. World HMar: '02- 11. World CC: '97- 9; Eur CC: '97-8: 7/9.
Progression at 10000m, Mar: 1995- 28:18.6, 1996- 28:00.79, 1997- 27:55.19, 1998- 27:47.33, 2:08:33;

1999- 2:07:37dq, 2001- 2:07:46, 2002- 27:51.59, 2:11:14; 2003- 2:07:27. pbs: 3000m 7:54.40 '97, 5000m 13:22.13 '98, HMar 62:10 '02.
Two year-drugs ban after third in Rotterdam marathon 1999. Won Hamburg marathon 2001 and 2003.

José RIOS b. 15 Mar 1974 Premià de Dalt (Barcelona) 1.70m 50kg. Adidas.
At 10,000m: OG: '00- 18; WCh: '01- 6; EC: '02- 3. Spanish champion 2000-03, EChall 2001.
Progression at 5000m, 10000m: 1991- 15:04.82, 31:15.89; 1992- 14:26.50, 31:24.50; 1993- 14:25.76, 29:48.44, 1994- 14:23.37, 29:35.2; 1995- 14:03.30, 29:03.6; 1996- 13:49.44, 29:00.34; 1997- 13:51.32, 28:37.52; 1998- 14:11.52, 28:56.51; 1999- 13:41.03, 28:30.53; 2000- 13:07.59, 27:22.20; 2001- 13:09.83, 27:38.57; 2002- 13:08.60, 27:35.13; 2003- 13:19.58, 27:29.60. pbs: 1500m 3:51.11 '01, 3000m 7:42.08 '02, HMar: 63:43 '04, Mar 2:07:42 '04.
Was a butcher, massive breakthrough in 2000. Won at Lake Biwa on marathon debut 2004.

Women

Glory ALOZIE b. 30 Dec 1977 Amator, Nigeria 1.55m 51kg. Valencia Terra i Mar.
At 100mh (100m): OG: '00- 2; WCh: '99- 2, '03- 4; EC: '02- 1 (4); WJ: '96- 2; AfG: '99- 1/1R; AfCh: '96- 1, '98- 1, '00- 1; Af-J: '95- 2; WCp: '98- 1, '02- 3 (5); ECp: '03- 1. 2nd GP 2000, 3rd 1998. At 60mh: WI: '99- 2, '03- 2; EI: '02- 1g. Won NGR 100mh 1999-2000, ESP 100mh 2001-02.
Records: African: 100m 1999, 100mh (5) 1998-9; indoor 50mh (2) 2001, 60mh (2) 1999; two Commonwealth 100mh 1998-9, six Spanish 2001-02 (from 12.87).
Progression at 100mh: 1993- 14.99, 1994- 14.25, 1995- 13.86, 1996- 13.30, 1997- 12.96, 1998- 12.44/12.4w, 1999- 12.44, 2000- 12.54, 2001- 12.69, 2002- 12.60, 2003- 12.66. pbs: 50m 6.3i exh '02, 60m 7.20i '99, 100m 10.90 '99; 200m 23.09 '01, 22.91w '98; 50mh 6.76i '01, 60mh 7.82i '99.
Based in Spain since January 1997, she became a Spanish citizen on 7 July 2001, but not allowed to retain European Indoor 60mh title in 2002, as ruled ineligible for international competition until later that year. Won 17 of 19 finals in 1998 at 100mh. Her fiancée, 400m runner Hyginus Anugo, was killed in a road accident in Sydney just prior to the 2000 Games.

Ruth BEITIA b.1 Apr 1979 Santander 1.86m 63kg. Valencia Terra i Mar.
At HJ: WCh: '03- 11=; EC: '02- 11; WJ: '96- dnq, '98- 8, EU23: '01- 1; EJ: '97- 9; WI: '03- 5=; WCp: '02- 6=; ECp: '03- 2. Spanish champion 2003.
Five Spanish HJ records 2002-03.
Progression at HJ: 1991- 1.50, 1992- 1.55, 1993- 1.66, 1994- 1.74, 1995- 1.80, 1996- 1.85, 1997- 1.86, 1998- 1.89, 1999- 1.83, 2000- 1.86i/1.85, 2001- 1.93i/1.91, 2002- 1.94, 2003- 2.00, 2004- 2.00i. pbs: 200m 25.26 '03, 100mh 14.95 '97, 14.93w '00; LJ 6.04 '03, TJ 10.93 '99.

Marta DOMÍNGUEZ b. 3 Nov 1975 Palencia 1.63m 52kg. Nike International.
At 5000m: OG: '00- h; WCh: '99- 9, '01- 2, '03- 2; EC: '98- 3, '02- 1; EU23: '97- 3 (1500m 5); WCp: '02- 2. At 3000m: WI: '95-7-01-03-04: 6/5/4/2/4; EI: '96-8-00-02: 3/3/3/1; ECp: '96- 3. At 1500m: OG: '96- h; WCh: '95- sf; WJ: '94- 2; EJ: '93- 1. World 4k CC: '00- 14. Won Spanish 1500m 1996, 5000m 1998-2003.
Spanish record 3000m 2000.
Progression at 3000m, 5000m: 1990- 10:15.0, 1991- 9:47.03, 1993- 9:35.16, 1994- 9:24.10, 1995- 9:01.79i, 1996- 8:53.34i/9:06.27, 1997- 8:52.74i/9:01.96, 15:41.91; 1998- 8:44.10, 14:59.49; 1999- 8:46.14, 15:16.93; 2000- 8:28.80, 15:26.00; 2001- 8:36.33, 14:58.12; 2002- 8:47.93, 15:10.67; 2003- 8:41.14i/8:50.6+, 14:48.33. pbs: 800m 2:06.1 '95, 1000m 2:50.1 '91, 1500m 4:06.08 '00, 2000m 5:49.55i '98, 10kmRd 31:35dh '03.

Mayte MARTINEZ b. 17 May 1976 Valladolid 1.68m 56kg. Adidas.
At 800m: OG: '00- sf; WCh: '01- 7, EC: '02- 2, WJ: '94- h; EJ: '95- 6; WI: '03- 3; EI: '02- 4; WCp: '02- 2; ECp: '03- 3. Won Spanish 800m 2000-02.
Progression at 800m: 1991- 2:14.48, 1992- 2:13.09, 1993- 2:07.99, 1994- 2:05.68, 1995- 2:05.00, 1996- 2:08.81i, 1997- 2:06.84, 1998- 2:05.49i, 2000- 1:59.60, 2001- 1:59.76, 2002- 1:58.29, 2003- 1:59.53i/1:59.62, 2004- 1:59.52i. pbs: 400m 53.67 '03, 1000m 2:47.20 '01. Married her coach Juan Carlos Granado on 20 Sep 2003.

Concepción MONTANER b.14 Jan 1981 L'Eliana, Valencia 1.70m 56kg. Valencia Terra i Mar.
At LJ: OG: '00- dnq, WCh: '03- 12; EC: '02- 4; WJ: '98- h 4x100m, '00- 1, EU23: '01- 2; EJ: '99- 2; WI: '03- 9, '04- 7; WCp: '02- 3; ECp: '03- 2. Spanish champion 2003.
Progression at LJ: 1996- 5.62/5.75w, 1997- 5.43/5.51w, 1998- 5.95/5.96w, 1999- 6.47, 2000- 6.64/6.79w, 2001- 6.61i/6.57/6.67w, 2002- 6.89, 2003- 6.78i/6.69/6.70w. pbs: 60m 7.47i '01, 100m 11.71 '01, 200m 25.12i '00, TJ 11.98 '97.

Natalia RODRIGUEZ b. 2 Jun 1979 Tarragona 1.67m 49kg. Adidas.
At 1500m: OG: '03- h; WCh: '01- 6, '03- sf, EC: '02- 6; EU23: '99- 4, '01- 2, WJ: '98- 6, EJ: '97- 5; ECp: '03- 1. At 800m: WJ: '96- h. Won Spanish 1500m 2000-03.
Progression at 800m, 1500m: 1995- 4:42.4, 1996- 2:06.23, 1997- 2:04.15, 4:17.28; 1998- 2:02.78, 4:16.20; 1999- 2:01.66, 4:10.65; 2000- 2:05.76, 4:04.24; 2001- 2:01.35, 4:06.32; 2002- 2:01.76, 4:02.84; 2003- 2:01.54, 4:01.30. pb 3000m 9:01.40i '03.

María VASCO b. 26 Dec 1975 Barcelona 1.56m 47kg. Ptayas de Jandia.
At 20kmW: OG: '00- 3; WCh: '99- 10, '01- 5, '03- dnf; EC: '02- dnf; WCp: '99- 23, '02- 8; ECp: '01- 7, '03- 3. At 10kmW: OG: '96- 28; WCh: '95- 26; EC: '98- 5; EU23: '97- 2; WCp '95- 26, '97- 22. At 5000mW: WJ: '90- 15, '92- 6, '94- 4; EJ: '93- 4.

Won Spanish 10kmW 1996 10000mW (t) 1997-9, 2001-03; 20kmW 1998-2004.
Spanish records 5000m 1997, 10,000m track (3) 1997-2001, 10km 1998, 20km (5) 1998-2003.
Progression at 10kmW, 20kmW: 1993- 47:11, 1994- 47:05, 1995- 44:53, 1996- 44:51.60t, 1997- 43:54, 1998- 43:02, 1:34:11; 1999- 43:35, 1:32:38; 2000- 43:33.92t, 1:30:20; 2001- 43:02.04t, 1:30:09; 2002- 43:51, 1:28:47; 2003- 44:22, 1:28:10; 2004- 1:29:51. pb 3000mW 12:42.72 '97, 5000mW 21:36.22 '97, 21:19R '04.

SRI LANKA

Governing body: Amateur Athletic Association of Sri Lanka, n°33 Torrington Avenue, Colombo 7. Founded 1922.

National Champions 2003: **Men:** 100m/200m: S.P.N. Hemantha 10.67/21.28, 400m: Sugath Thilakaratne 45.70, 800m: J.M.H Sifrath 1:49.34, 1500m: T.V. Thilashantha Nishantha 3:50.77, 5000m: K.Chandradasa 14:31.09, 10000m: R.M.Y.G. Asela Bandara 30:38.57, Mar:, 3000mSt: G.Shantha Mendis 8:55.07, 110mh: Indika Kumara Silva 14.43, 400mh: Harijan Ratnayake 52.11, HJ: A.A.D. Nalin Priyadharshana 2.11, PV: Ruwan Pradeep Perera 4.80, LJ: Lalith Ravindra 7.48, TJ: Sampath Weerasinghe 15.82, SP/DT: Talavou Alaileema 15.47/52.79, JT: Pradeep Nishantha 69.49, Dec: Ravi Ratheesan 5999, 20kmW: B.M.N.Nayanananda 1:38:22. **Women**: 100m/200m: Susanthika Jayasinghe 11.37/23.16, 400m: Menaka Wickramesinghe 53.93, 800m: D.H.Mangala Priyadharshani 2:08.23, 1500m: Wimal Chandrani 4:27.60, 5000m/10000m: Sujeewa Nilmini Jayasena 16:21.18/33:57.96, 100mh: Sriyani Kulawansa 13.57, 400mh: S.V.A. Kusumawathi 62.53, HJ: Priyangika Maduwanthi 1.71, LJ/TJ: N.C.D. Priyadharshani 5.76/12.67, SP: N.M.D. Muthunayake 12.64, DT: Padma Wijesundara 42.04, JT: Anne Maheshi De Silva 51.28, Hep: D.C.A.Dahanayake 3634, 20kmW: G.G. Nandana 1:47:21.

Women

Susanthika JAYASINGHE b. 17 Dec 1975 1.70m 62kg. Married Dhammika Nandakumara 1994.
At 200m (/100m): OG: '96- (qf); '00- sf/3; WCh: '95- h/qf, '97- 2, '99- (qf), '01- h, '03- qf; CG: '02- 4/dq h; WI: '01- 4; AsiG: '94- 2, '02- /1; AsiC: '95- 1/2, '02- 1/1; WCp: '02- 3/4; Won Asi-J 200m 1994, S.Asian 100m/200m 1995.
Two Asian 200m records 1997, SRI records: 100m (4) 1995-2000, 200m (6) 1993-2000. Asian indoor records 60m 1999, 200m 2001.
Progression at 100m, 200m: 1992- 12.36, 25.67; 1993- 12.17, 24.56; 1994- 11.49, 23.16; 1995- 11.30, 22.95; 1996- 11.18, 23.18; 1997- 11.25+/11.38, 22.33; 1998- 11.27, 23.28; 1999- 11.17, 22.74; 2000- 11.04, 22.28; 2001- 11.37, 22.63; 2002- 11.08, 22.82; 2003- 11.20, 23.16. pbs: 50m 6.31i '01, 60m 7.09i '99.
Suspended after random doping test in April 1998, but cleared by Sri Lankan AAA; she claimed she was the victim of a conspiracy.

SUDAN

Yamilé ALDAMA b. 14 Aug 1972 La Habana 1.73m 62kg. married name Dodds. Shaftesbury Barnet Harriers, GBR.
At TJ: OG: '00- 4; WCh: '97- dnq 13, '99- 2; PAm: '99- 1; CAG: '98- 1; WI: '97-9-04: 6/7/2; WCp: '98- 3. Won IbAm 1996, 1998; Cuban 1997-2000, AAA 2003.
Nine CAC triple jump records 1999-2003 (if still eligible), CAC indoor (14.65 and 14.88) 2003.
Progression at TJ: 1994- 13.92, 1995- 13.84, 1996- 14.43, 1997- 14.46, 1998- 14.55, 1999- 14.77, 2000- 14.47, 2001- 13.85i, 2002- 14.40/14.54w, 2003- 15.29, 2004- 14.90i. pbs: 100mh 14.97/14.8 '92, HJ 1.88 '92, LJ 6.13 '95, Hep 5246 '93.
Aldama, who last competed for Cuba in 2000, was immediately free to compete for Sudan after being accepted as a citizen in January 2004. She had moved to London with Scottish husband Andrew Dodds in 2001, in which year her son Amil was born, and hoped to be eligible for Britain but a three-year waiting period meant that she was unable to gain a passport in sufficient time to compete at the 2003 Worlds (or 2004 Olympics).

SWEDEN

Governing body: Svenska Friidrottsförbundet, Box 11, 171 18 Solna. Founded 1895.

National Championships first held in 1896 (men), 1927 (women). **2003 Champions**: **Men**: 100m: Johan Engberg 10.59, 200m: Johan Wissman 21.01, 400m: Jimisola Laursen 46.57, 800m: Rickard Pell 1:50.91, 1500m: Patrik Johansson 3:51.08, 5000m: Erik Sjöqvist 14:19.94, 10000m/HMar: Saïd Regraugui 30:46.11/64:25:, Mar:, 3000mSt: Mustafa Mohamed 8:49.05, 110mh: Robert Kronberg 13.63, 400mh: Mikael Jakobsson 49.86, HJ: Stefan Holm 2.31, PV: Patrik Kristiansson 5.80, LJ: David Frykholm 7.59w, TJ: Christian Olsson 17.54, SP: Magnus Lohse 18.25, DT: Mattias Borrman 56.68, HT: Bengt Johansson 68.24, JT: Daniel Ragnvaldsson 75.86, Dec: Andrus Klaar 7062, 10kmW: Bengt Bengtsson 43:26, 20kmW/50kmW: Fredrik Svensson 1:29:25/3:58:04. **Women**: 100m: Carolina Klüft 11.57, 200m: Jenny Ljunggren 23.67, 400m: Ellinor Stuhrmann 53.23, 800m: Camilla Nyqvist 2:07.47, 1500m: Kristin Ahlepil 4:24.32, 5000m/3000mSt: Ida Nilsson 16:51.78/10:14,22, 10000m: Lena Gavelin 34:04.34, HMar: Marie Söderström-Lundberg 74:33, Mar:, 100mh: Susanna Kallur 12.96, 400mh: Erica Mårtensson 57.05, HJ: Kajsa Bergqvist 1.86, PV: Linda Persson 3.98, LJ: Daniela Lincoln-Saavedra 6.45, TJ: Camilla Johansson 14.01, SP: Helena Engman 16.27, DT: Anna Söderberg 57.21, HT: Cecilia Nilsson 60.80, JT: Katarina Eklöf 50.62, Hep: Jessica Samuelsson 5017, 5kmW/10kmW/20kmW: Monica Svensson 23:51/50:09/1:37:29

Stefan HOLM b. 25 May 1976 Forshaga 1.81m 70kg. Kils AIK.
At HJ: OG: '00- 4; WCh: '99- 10=, '01- 5=, '03- 2; EC: '98- 7, '02- 2; WJ: '94- 7=; EJ: '93- 11, '95- 6; WI: '97-9-01-03-04: 8=/6=/1/1/1; EI: '00- 4, '02- 2; WUG: '99- 4; ECp: '00- 1. Won GP 2002, GWG 2001, Swedish 1998-2003.
Progression at HJ: 1987- 1.40, 1988- 1.51, 1989- 1.61, 1990- 1.83, 1991- 1.94, 1992- 2.09i/2.06, 1993- 2.14, 1994- 2.18, 1995- 2.21, 1996- 2.26, 1997- 2.30i/ 2.22, 1998- 2.33, 1999- 2.32, 2000- 2.34, 2001- 2.34i/ 2.33, 2002- 2.35, 2003- 2.36i/2.34, 2004- 2.37i. pbs: 60m 7.33i '03, 100m 11.42 '99, 110mh 16.23 '99, LJ 7.18 '99; TJ 12.35i '91.
One of the smallest top high jumpers. Maintains on his web site (www.scholm.com) a complete record of his clashes with Staffan Strand – from 1989 to March 2004, score is 72-47 to Holm. Won 8/8 indoors in both 2003 and 2004. 62 meetings over 2.30 1997-2004.

Patrik KRISTIANSSON b. 3 Jun 1977 Göteborg 1.92m 85kg. KA 2 IF.
At PV: OG: '00- dnq 20=; WCh: '99- dnq 29=, '01- dnq 14, '03- 3; EC: '98- nh, '02- 4; WJ: '96- 2; EJ: '95- 6; WI: '04- 4; EI: '02- 2; ECp: '00- 3. Swedish champion 1998, 2001-03.
Two Swedish pole vault records 2001-02.
Progression at PV: 1989- 2.20, 1990- 3.08, 1991- 3.50, 1992- 4.40, 1993- 4.70/4.80ex, 1994- 5.06/ 5.10ex, 1995- 5.30, 1996- 5.31, 1997- 5.51i/5.45, 1998- 5.77, 1999- 5.71, 2000- 5.70, 2001- 5.83, 2002- 5.85, 2003- 5.85. pbs: 110mh 15.96 '99, HJ 1.88 '99, LJ 6.64 '01, Dec 6412 '99.

Robert KRONBERG b. 15 Aug 1976 Göteborg 1.81m 82kg. Kville.
At 110mh: OG: '00- 8; WCh: '97/99- qf, '01- 5, '03- sf; EC: '02- 7; WJ: '94- sf; EJ: '95- 2; WUG: '01- 3; ECp: '00- 3. At 60mh: WI: '01-03-04: 4/7/6; EI: '00-02: 6/6. Won Swedish 110mh 1997-2003.
Three Swedish 110mh records 2001.
Progression at 110mh: 1993- 15.09, 1994- 14.21, 1995- 14.06, 1996- 13.97, 1997- 13.63, 1998- 13.61, 1999- 13.58, 2000- 13.36, 2001- 13.35, 2002- 13.42, 2003- 13.46. pbs: 60m 6.77i '04, 100m 10.73 '98, 200m 22.31 '98, 50mh 6.46i '01, 60mh 7.54i '01, HJ 1.90 '95, LJ 7.52 '97, TJ 14.23 '94.

Christian OLSSON b. 25 Jan 1980 Göteborg 1.92m 74kg. Örgryte IS.
At TJ (/HJ): OG: '00- dnq 17; WCh: '01- 2, '03- 1; EC: '02- 1; EU23: '01- 1; EJ: '99- 2/1; WI: '03- 1, '04- 1; EI: '02- 1; WCp: '02- 3; ECp: '00- 4. Won WAF 2003, GP 2002, Swedish TJ 2000-01, 2003.
Five Swedish triple jump records 2001-03. WIR 2004.
Progression at TJ: 1995- 12.20w, 1996- 12.44, 1998- 14.48, 1999- 16.30/16.59w, 2000- 16.97, 2001- 17.49, 2002- 17.80i/17.64, 2003- 17.77/17.92w, 2004- 17.83i. pbs: 110mh 16.21 '98, HJ 2.28i '02, 2.28 '03; PV 4.04 '99, LJ 7.71 '02, 7.84w '03.
Considered himself a high jumper, but took his TJ best from 14.48 to 16.27w in his first competition of 1999 and had a superb season at his new event in 2001 when he was the only man to defeat Jonathan Edwards (and did so twice). He challenged Edwards again in 2002, losing 4-5, and was easily the world number one in 2003, when unbeaten outdoors. First jumped 17m on 14 June 2001, and from then has been under that just twice in 61 meetings to WI 2004, with 162 17m jumps in all.

Staffan STRAND b. 18 Apr 1976 Upplands-Väsby 1.88m 75kg. Hässelby SK. Was at University of Minnesota, USA.
At HJ: OG: '00- 6=; WCh: '97- dnq, '99- 5, '01- 7=, '03- dnq 22=; EC: '98- 8, '02- 3; EU23: '97- 1; EJ: '95- 5; WI: '99-01-03: 5/3/7; EI: '02- 1. Won Swedish 1995-7.
Progression at HJ: 1987- 1.45i, 1988- 1.60i, 1989- 1.65i/1.63, 1990- 1.70, 1991- 1.71, 1992- 1.80, 1993- 1.91i/1.88, 1994- 2.11, 1995- 2.22, 1996- 2.27, 1997- 2.28, 1998- 2.31, 1999- 2.30, 2000- 2.32, 2001- 2.34i/ 2.31, 2002- 2.35i/2.30, 2003- 2.32i/2.26. pbs: PV 3.40 '95, LJ 6.90 '96, TJ 15.16 '96, 15.23w '00; Dec 5022 '95.
Working on PhD in computer engineering.

Women

Kajsa BERGQVIST b. 12 Oct 1976 Sollentuna 1.75m 59kg. Turebergs FK. Was at Southern Methodist University, USA.
At HJ: OG: '96- dnq 14, '00- 3=; WCh: '95- dnq 17=, 97- 5=, '99- 4=, '01- 3, '03- 3; EC: '98- dnq 14, '02- 1; WJ: '94- 2; EU23: '97- 2; EJ: '93- 8, '95- 2; WI: '97-01-03: 8/1/1; EI: '00- 1, '02- 2=; WCp: '02- 2. Swedish champion 1997-2003, NCAA 1997, 1999.
Ten Swedish high jump records 1997-2003.
Progression at HJ: 1988- 1.38, 1989- 1.56, 1990- 1.61i/1.56, 1991- 1.61, 1992- 1.77, 1993- 1.84, 1994- 1.90, 1995- 1.92i/1.90, 1996- 1.93, 1997- 1.95, 1998- 1.93, 1999- 1.98A, 2000- 2.01, 2001- 2.00, 2002- 2.05, 2003- 2.06. pbs: 100mh 14.98/14.8w '94, LJ 5.73 '95, TJ 11.74 '98, SP 11.95 '96, JT 36.60 '99, Hep 4952 '94.
Her father Gunnar had a 110mh best of 15.0 (1972).

Susanna KALLUR b. 16 Feb 1981 Huntington, New York, USA 1.70m 62kg. Falu IK. Student at University of Illinois, USA.
At 100mh: WCh: '01/03- sf; WJ: '98- 3, '00- 1/3R; EC: '02- 7; EU23: '01- 1, '03- 1; EJ: '99- 5. Won SWE 1998, 2000, 2002-03. At 60mh: WI: '03- 7, '04- 5.
Progression at 100mh: 1997- 14.11, 1998- 13.48, 1999- 13.41, 2000- 13.02, 2001- 12.74, 2002- 12.94, 2003- 12.88. pbs: 50m 6.56i '00, 60m 7.36i '04, 100m 11.53 '03, 200m 24.11 '01, 50mh 6.83i '03, 60mh 7.88i '04, HJ 1.72 '98, PV 3.00i '98, LJ 6.11 '01, TJ 11.67i '97, 11.22 '98; SP 10.80i '02, Pen 3917i '02, Hep 5282 '98.
Twin sister **Jenny** was 2nd in European U23s 2001, 6th WJ 2000, pbs: 60mh 8.02i '04 (sf WI),

100mh 13.04 '03. Their father Anders played for the New York Islanders at ice hockey, winning Stanley Cup four times.

Carolina KLÜFT b. 2 Feb 1983 Borås 1.78m 65kg. IFK Växjö.
At Hep: WCh: '03- 1; EC: '02- 1; WJ: '00- 1, '02- 1; EJ: '01- 1. At Hep: WI: '03- 1; EI: '02- 3. At LJ: EU23: '03- 1; WI: '04- 3. Won SWE 100m 2003, LJ 2001-02, Hep 2001.
Two world junior heptathlon records 2002, six Swedish records 2002-03.
Progression at LJ, Hep: 1998- 5.75, 1999- 6.13, 5162; 2000- 6.23, 6056; 2001- 6.26/6.33w, 6022; 2002- 6.48/6.59w, 6542; 2003- 6.86, 7001; 2004- 6.92i. pbs: 60m 7.46i '04, 100m 11.53 '03, 200m 22.98 '03, 400m 53.17 '02, 800m 2:12.12 '03, 60mh 8.19i '03, 100mh 13.18 '03, HJ 1.94 '03, PV 3.16 '01, SP 14.48i '03, 14.19 '03; DT 33.96 '00, JT 50.24 '03, Pen 4933i '03.
Seven gold medals and two bronze in nine major chapionship competitions. Won IAAF 'Rising Star' award for women in 2002, when she was the world's top heptathlete while still a junior. Added 398 points to her Swedish indoor record when she won 2003 World Indoor title with 4933, setting pbs at first four events. Won Götzis and the IAAF Combined Events Challenge and set five pbs en route to winning World title (for third on world all-time list) in 2003. Set Swedish record at 6.92 twice at World indoors 2004. Her mother Ingalill had long jump pb 6.09/6.20w (1979).

SWITZERLAND

Governing body: Schweizerischer Leichtathletikverband (SLV), 43/Postfach 45, 3250 Lyss. Formed 1905 as Athletischer Ausschuss des Schweizerischen Fussball-Verbandes.
National Championships first held in 1906 (men), 1934 (women). **2003 Champions**: **Men**: 100m: Daniel Dubois 10.36, 200m: Markus Lüthi 20.84, 400m: Christian Oggenfuss 47.70, 800m: Christian Niederberger 1:52.11, 1500m: Stefan Gerber 3:54.41, 5000m: Christian Belz 13:52.69, 10000m/HMar: Ivan Gisler 30:50.77/66:22, Mar: Jörg Hafner 2:22:22, 3000mSt: Markus Hagmann 8:57.22, 110mh: Raphaël Monachon 13.92, 400mh: Cédric El-Idrissi 49.10, HJ: Martin Stauffer 2.11, PV: Boris Zengaffinen 5.10, LJ: Julien Fivaz 7.68, TJ: Michael Wyss 14.95, SP: Roger Srasser 16.25, DT: Christoph Wasem 49.43, HT: Samuele Dazio 71.57, JT: Stefan Müller 77.95, Dec: Xavier Weibel 7550, 20kmW: , 50kmW: Nicolas Perrier 4:29:37. **Women**: 100m/200m: Martina Feusi 11.60/23.79, 400m: Laura Gerber 53.42, 800m: Anita Brägger 2:04.81, 1500m: Christina Carruzzo 4:25.64, 5000m: Vera Notz-Umberg 15:55.84, 10000m: Chantal Dällenbach 34:31.60, HMar: Vera Notz-Umberg 75:15, Mar:Elisabeth Krieg 2:41:24, 100mh: Sabrina Altermatt 13.68, 400mh: Regina Sonderegger 60.29, HJ: Corinne Müller 1.86, PV: Nadine Rohr 4.15, LJ: Barbara Leuthard 5.88, TJ: Laura Imberti 13.24, SP/DT: Karin Hagmann 14.40/52.56, HT: Céline Neuenschwander 54.07, JT: Inka Schade 46.83, Hep: Simone Oberer 5765, 20kmW: Marie Polli 1:44:32.

André BUCHER b. 19 Oct 1976 Neudorf 1.85m 75kg. LR Beromünster. History graduate of Bern University. Teacher.
At 800m: OG: '96- sf, '00- 5; WCh: '97/99/03- sf, '01- 1; EC: '98- 2, '02- 2; EU23: '97- 2; EJ: '95- 2; WI: '01- 3; EI: '02- 2; WUG: '99- 2; WCp: '02- 4; won GP 2001. At 1500m: WJ: '94- 2. Won Swiss 800m 1995, 1997-9, 1500m 1994, 1996.
Swiss records 800m (5), 1000m (2) 1998-2001.
Progression at 800m: 1993- 1:56.40, 1994- 1:48.32, 1995- 1:45.71, 1996- 1:46.41, 1997- 1:45.33, 1998- 1:44.96, 1999- 1:42.92, 2000- 1:43.12, 2001- 1:42.55, 2002- 1:43.93, 2003- 1:44.23. pbs: 200m 22.18w '01. 400m 46.32 '00, 600m 1:14.72 (European best) '99, 1000m 2:15.63 '01, 1500m 3:38.44 '96, 3000m 8:16.9 '98, 5000m 14:06.77 '98, 10000m 30:40.5 '95, 3000mSt 9:09.73 '95.
He had a glorious year in 2001, when he became world champion, shared the Golden League jackpot, and won the overall Grand Prix title; he won 12 of 14 races at 800m and two at 1000m.

TANZANIA

Governing body: Tanzania Amateur Athletic Association, PO Box 2172, Dar es Salaam. Founded 1954.

Fabian JOSEPH b. 24 Dec 1985 Babati, Mbulu district 1.58m 48kg. Iraqw.
At 10000m: WCh: '03- 13; won AAA 2003. World HMar: '03- 2; CC: 2003-04: 19/7.
Progression at 10000m: 2002- 29:04.7, 2003- 27:32.63. pbs: 5000m 13:22.89 '03, HMar 60:52 '03.

John YUDA Msuri b. 9 Jun 1979 Dodoma 1.62m 53kg.
At 10000m: WCh: '03- 12; CG: '02- 3. At 5000m: AfG: '03- 5. World HMar: 01- 3, '02- 3, '03- 5; CC: '01- 14 (4k), '02- 2. Won TAN HMar 2001.
Tanzanian records 5000m & 10000m 2002.
At 5000m, 10000m: 2002- 13:03.62, 27:06.17; 2003- 13:18.0, 27:09.83. pbs: HMar 60:02 '02.

TRINIDAD & TOBAGO

Governing body: National Amateur Athletic Association of Trinidad & Tobago, PO Box 605, Port of Spain, Trinidad. Founded 1945, reformed 1971.
2003 National Champions: **Men**: 100m/200m: Jacey Harper 10.19/21.13w, 400m: Damion Barry 45.67, 800m: Sheridan Kirk 1:48.13, 1500m: Carlan Arthur 4:01.55, 5000m: Denzil Ramirez 16:02.76, 110mh: Karriem Pierre 14.62, 400mh: Natakki Dasent 53.85, HJ: Kerry Edwards 2.00, PV: Lyndon Knights 3.50, LJ: Melvin Nero 7.32, SP: Dave Stoute 17.62, DT: Hubert Maingot 40.35, JT: Emmanuel Morris 56.17, Dec: Mickey Ruben

6121, 3000mW: Noel Husbands BAR 15:43.79. **Women**: 100m/200m: Fana Ashby 11.23/23.05w, 400m: Adia McKinnon 54.17, 800m: Melissa de Leon 2:04.78, 1500m: Pilar McShine 4:46.81, 100mh: Kelly Charles 14.1, 400mh: Desiree John 64.97, HJ: Rhonda Watkins 1.76, LJ: Monique Peters 6.04, TJ: Sheron Mark 12.35, SP: Candace Scott 15.89, DT: Loktoya McShine 40.58, JT: Natalie Dixon 41.43, Hep: Cuquie Melville 4147.

Ato BOLDON b. 30 Dec 1973 Port of Spain 1.76m 75kg. Studied engineering at San José City College and at UCLA, USA.
At 100m/200m: OG: '92- h/h, '96- 3/3, '00- 2/3; WCh: '93- qf/-, '95- 3/qf, '97- 5/1, '01- 4/3R, '03- sf/-; WI: '97- dnf 200m; CG: '94- 4/sf, '98- 1/-; WJ: '92- 1/1; PAm: '03- 2R. Won GWG 200m 1998, NCAA 200m 1995, 100m 1996; TRI 100m 1993-4, 200m 1992.
CAC records: 100m (9), 200m (3) 1996-9; TRI records: 100m (13) 1995-9, 200m (3) 1996-7.
Progression at 100m, 200m: 1990- 10.8, 21.3; 1991- 10.54/10.44w, 21.07; 1992- 10.22, 20.63/20.6; 1993- 10.23/10.0, 20.59; 1994- 10.07, 20.53; 1995- 10.03/ 10.01w, 20.08; 1996- 9.90, 19.80; 1997- 9.87, 19.77; 1998- 9.86, 19.88; 1999- 9.86, 19.86; 2000- 9.95, 19.97; 2001- 9.88, 20.24; 2002- 10.23, 2003- 10.09, 20.77. pbs: 50m 5.58+ '97, 55m 6.04Ai '97, 60m 6.45+ '97, 400m 47.1 '94.
Moved with mother and young brother to USA at age 14, living in New York and Los Angeles, until resettling in Trinidad late 2001. Best ever one-day sprint double, 9.90 and 19.77 in Stuttgart 1997. Missed 1999 World Championships through injury, but made a big hit with his knowledgeable interviewing.

Darrel BROWN b. 11 Oct 1984 Arima 1.84m 70kg. Nike. Student at Southern Union CC, Alabama, USA.
At 100m/4x100mR: WCh: '01- 3R, '03- 2; WJ: '00- 4; 02- 1/3R; WY: '01- 1; PAm: '03- 2R; CAC: '03- 2. Won CAC-J 100m 2000, 2002; 200m 2000; TRI 100m 2001.
World junior 100m record 2003.
Progression at 100m, 200m: 1998- 10.79, 22.41; 1999- 10.67, 21.20; 2000- 10.34, 21.14/20.76w; 2001- 10.24, 20.41; 2002- 10.09, 20.97; 2003- 10.01. pb 55m 6.15i '03, 60m 6.59i '04.
World's fastest ever for 100m at age 15, 16, 17 and 18, the last a WJR 10.01 in the quarter-finals before his silver medal in the final; the youngest 100m medallist in World Championship history.

TURKEY

Governing body: Türkiye Amator Atletizm Federasyonu, Ulus Ishani A Blok Kat 3, Ankara. Founded 1922.
National Champions 2003: **Men**: 100m: Resat Oguz 10.70, 200m: Ibrahim Erkusak (82) 21.71, 400m: Ercan Sunu 48.45, 800m: Ihsan Alptekin 1:51.27, 1500m: Metin Sazak 3:52.90, 3000m: Furkan Boyan 8:29.16, 5000m: Halil Akkas 14:28.04, 3000mSt: Hakan Yüksel 9:22.92, 110mh: Demirhan Cemberci 14.86, 400mh: Ömer Yalciner 52.46, HJ: Kemal Güner 2.10, PV: Sevket Kilic 4.60, LJ: Murat Ayaydin 7.63w, TJ: Berk Tuna 16.67, SP: Fatih Yazici 17.71, DT: Ulas Ögünc 45.57, HT: Esref Apak 76.79, JT: Gürbüz Cam 69.45. **Women**: 100m/200m: Burcu Sentürk 11.64w/24.68, 400m: Gülay Kirsan 55.73, 800m: Sinem Atman 2:14.10, 1500m: Yaprak Kalemoglu 4:23.49,100mh: Esen Kizildag 13.84, 400mh: Özge Gürler 58.19, HJ: Candeger Oguz-Kilincer 1.83, PV: Songül Kilic 3.30, LJ: Fatma Dulkan 6.17, TJ: Aysegül Baklaci 13.37, SP: Filiz Kadogan 17.09, DT: Ahu Sulak 44.39, HT: Zübeyde Yildiz 62.07, JT: Berna Demirci 48.52, 10kmW: Yeliz Ay 47:46.0.

Women

Elvan ABEYLEGASSE b. 11 Sep 1982 1.59m 40kg.
At (3000m)/5000m: WCh: '03- 5; EC: '02- 7; WJ: '00- 6/6; WY: '99- (5); EU23: '03- 1; EJ: '99- 2, '01- 1/1. Won WAF 5000m 2003. World CC: '99- 9J; Eur CC: '00-01-02-03: 3J/1J/3/2.
Turkish records 2000m 2003, 3000m 2002.
Progress at 5000m: 1999- 16:06.40, 2000- 16:33.77, 2001- 15:21.12, 2002- 15:00.49, 2003- 14:53.56. pbs: 1500m 4:07 25 '03, 2000m 5:33.83 '03, 3000m 8:31.94 '02, 10000m 33:29.20 '01.
Previously known as Hewan Abeye ETH, then as Elvan Can on move to Turkey.

Süreyya AYHAN b. 6 Sep 1978 Korgun, Çankiri 1.63m 52kg. Sports student.
At 1500m: OG: '00- sf; WCh: '01- 8, '03- 2; EC: '02- 1; WCp: '02- 1; EJ: '97- 8; EU23: '99- h; WUG: '01- 1. Won WAF 2003.
TUR records: 800m 2000, 1500m (6) 1999-2002.
Progression at 800m, 1500m: 1992- 4:50.50, 1993- 2:14.61, 4:33.71; 1995- 2:16.34, 4:37.23; 1996- 2:11.0, 4:28.6; 1997- 2:11.86, 4:25.51; 1998- 2:09.83, 4:22.81; 1999- 2:06.4, 4:14.8; 2000- 2:00.64, 4:03.02; 2001- 2:05.48, 4:06.91; 2002- 2:05.92, 3:57.75; 2003- 3:55.33. pbs: 3000m 9:56.04 '98.
Front runner, who won all four competitions at 1500m in 2002 and five of six in 2003.

Ebru KAVAKLIOGLU b. 14 Mar 1970 1.67m 58kg. Was Yelena Kopytova RUS.
At 5000m: OG: '00- h; WCh:'99- 5; EC: '98- h; won Russian 1997, Med G 2001. At 3000m: OG: '92- 6; WCh: '93- 11. Road relay team gold 1994.
Turkish records 1500m, 3000m (4), 5000m (2) 1999-2001.
Progression at 3000m, 5000m: 1991- 9:05.44, 1992- 8:47.21, 1993- 8:50.49, 1995- 15:39.59, 1997- 9:11.36, 15:37.19; 1998- 15:34.06, 1999- 8:38.98, 14:51.69; 2000- 8:56.13i, 15:49.15; 2001- 8:35.26, 15:02.62; 2002- 8:38.76, 15:00.45; 2003- 8:53.13, 15:04.22. pbs: 1500m 4:08.45 '99, 1M 4:34.40 '00, 2000m 5:45.73 '99.
Ran for Russia prior to 1998. In November 1998 she married her coach Anatoliy Bychkov, who had moved to Turkey in 1997.

UGANDA

Governing body: Uganda Amateur Athletic Federation, PO Box 22726, Kampala. Fd. 1925.

Boniface KIPROP b. 12 Oct 1985 Kabchorwa 1.67m 53kg. Kalenjin.
At 5000m (/10000m): WCh: '03- h; AfG: '03- 6/4; Af-J: '01- 1/2, '03- 1/1; World CC: '00-02-03-04: 27J/3J/2J/2J.
Ugandan 5000m & 10000m records 2003.
Progression at 5000m, 10000m: 2001- 14:06.93, 28:45.76; 2002-13:55.5, 2003- 13:16.21, 27:15.88. pbs: 3000m 7:47.16 '03.
Previously known as Boniface Toroitich Tirop. Brother Martin Toroitich (11 WJ CC 2002).

UKRAINE

Governing body: Ukrainian Athletic Federation, Esplanadnaya Str. 42, Kiev 23. Founded 1991.
National Champions 2003: **Men**: 100m: Kostyantyn Rurak 10.18, 200m: Yevheniy Zyukov 21.38, 400m: Andriy Tverdostup 46.23, 800m/1500m: Ivan Heshko 1:45.98/3:42.39, 5000m/10000m: Serhiy Lebid 13:35.87/28:12.62, HMar: Mykola Rudyk 64:49, Mar: Olexander Holovnytsky 2:24:48, 3000mSt: Vadym Slobodenyuk 8:34.00, 110mh: Serhiy Demydyuk 14.04, 400mh: Hennadiy Gorbenko 49.81, HJ: Andriy Sokolovskiy 2.30, PV: Denys Yurchenko 5.50, LJ: Volodymyr Zyuskov 8.21, TJ: Mykola Savolajnen 16.85, SP/DT: Yuriy Bilonog 21.81/60.29, HT: Andriy Skvaruk 81.74, JT: Oleg Statsenko 72.19, Dec: Fedir Lauhin 7358, 20kmW/50kmW: Aleksey Shelest 1:28:18/3:57:12. **Women**: 100m: Olena Pastushenko 11.27, 200m: Maryna Maydanova 22.86, 400m: Antonina Yefremova 51.70, 800m: Tamara Volkova 2:02.64, 1500m: Iryna Lishchynska 4:10.48, 5000m: Nataliya Sydorenko 15:52.28, 10000m: Nataliya Berkut 33:01.67, HMar: Maryna Dubrova 77:52, Mar: Tetyana Bulyshchenko 2:40:29, 3000mSt: Valentina Horpynych 10:00.73, 100mh: Olena Krasovska 13.33, 400mh: Anastasiya Rabchenyuk 56.52, HJ: Vita Palamar 2.00, PV: Natalya Kushch 4.40, LJ: Nataliya Sorokina 6.56, TJ: Olena Govorova 14.11, SP: Vita Pavlysh 19.31, DT: Olena Antonova 60.67, HT: Iryna Sekachova 71.91, JT: Hanna Slastina 57.07, Hep: Hanna Melnychenko 5523, 20kmW: Vera Zolulya 1:32:37.

Note that the names above use Ukrainian language spellings/transliterations, although at present we continue to use mostly Russian transliterations in lists in this Annual.

Yuriy BELONOG (Bilonog) b. 9 Mar 1974 2.00m 132kg. Odessa Dyn.
At SP (DT): OG: '00- 5; WCh: '97- 4, '99- 5, '01- 6, '03- 3 (dnq); EC: '98- 3, '02- 1; WI: '95-7-9-01-03-04: 5/1/3/8/3/8; WJ: '92- 1; WUG: '95- 1, '97- 1, '01- 2; WCp: '02- 5; ECp: '96- 3, '02- 1. 2nd GP 1998, 2002; 2nd overall 2000. Won UKR SP & DT 2001, 2003.
UKR shot records 2000 & 2003.
Progression at SP: 1990- 15.60, 1991- 17.91, 1992- 19.02, 1993- 18.39, 1994- 18.72, 1995- 20.05, 1996- 21.20i/20.05, 1997- 21.02i/20.75, 1998- 20.92, 1999- 20.89i/20.65, 2000- 21.64, 2001- 20.98, 2002- 21.37, 2003- 21.81. pb DT 65.53 '03.
Mother-in-law Valentina Korsak: DT 63.92 '84.

Ivan GESHKO (Heshko) b. 19 Aug 1979 1.81m 70kg
At 1500m (/800m): OG: '00- h; WCh: '03- 3; EC: '02- h; WJ: '98- 11/h; EU23: '99- 4, '01- 2; WI: '03- 5, '04- 2; ECp: '02- 5/8. Won UKR 800m 2003, 1500m 2000-03.
Progression at 1500m: 1996- 3:54.94, 1997- 3:46.21, 1998- 3:43.56, 1999-3:42.33, 2000- 3:38.48, 2001- 3:37.10, 2002- 3:37.07, 2003- 3:32.01. pb 800m 1:45.41 '03.

Aleksandr KRYKUN b. 1 Mar 1968 Leipzig, GDR 1.94m 125kg. Kolos Uman.
At HT: OG: '96- 3, '00- dnq 20; WCh: '95- 10, '97- 8, '01/03- dnq 23/21; EC: '94- 6, '98- 11, '02- dnq 18; EJ: '87- 2; WUG: '95- 2. UKR champion 2002.
Progression at HT: 1986- 68.34, 1987- 71.74, 1988- 71.40, 1989- 71.36, 1990- 70.52, 1991- 73.32, 1992- 75.12, 1993- 80.36, 1994- 79.02, 1995- 77.06, 1996- 80.02, 1997- 79.34, 1998- 76.23, 2000- 79.52, 2001- 80.38, 2002- 81.59, 2003- 79.35.

Sergey LEBED (Sergiy Lebid) b. 15 Jul 1975 1.80m 65kg. Based in Italy.
At 5000m: OG: '00- 7; WCh: '99/01- h; EC: '98- 13, '02- 3; WUG: '99- 1, '01- 1. '03- 1; EU23: '97- 7 (10000m 2). At 3000m: EI: '98- 5; WCp: '02- 7. World CC: '00- 8 (10 4k), '01- 2; Eur CC: '95-7-8-9-00-01-02-03: 11/3/1/7/2/1/1/1. Won UKR 1500m 1998, 5000m 1995-6, 1999-2001, 2003; 10000m 2003.
UKR records 3000m 2002, 5000m (2) 2001-02, HMar (2) 2003.
Progress at 5000m: 1993- 14:23.54, 1994- 14:11.27, 1995- 13:52.39, 1996- 13:39.31, 1997- 13:50.51, 1998- 13:30.23, 1999- 13:18.18, 2000- 13:27.53, 2001- 13:14.51, 2002- 13:10.78, 2003- 13:15.15. pbs: 1500m 3:39.95 '98, 3000m 7:35.06 '02, 10000m 28:12.62 '03, HMar 61:49 '03.
Has run in all ten European CC Championships, tying record with four wins. Married Yelena Gorodnichova (1500m 4:05.78 '99) on 23 Apr 2003.

Olexiy (Aleksey) **LUKASHEVICH** b. 11 Jan 1977 Dnepropetrovsk 1.75m 70kg.
At LJ: OG: '00- 4; WCh: '97/99/03: dnq 16/22/17, '01- 6; EC: '98- dnq 20, '02- 1; WJ: '96- 1; EU23: '97- 3; EI: '98-00-02: 1/4/4; WUG: '99- 1; WCp: '02- 7. 3rd GP 2001. UKR champion 2000.
Progression at LJ: 1994- 7.68, 1995- 7.57, 1996- 7.91/8.10w, 1997- 7.95/8.09w, 1998- 8.06i/8.03, 1999- 8.16/8.17w, 2000- 8.27, 2001- 8.20, 2002- 8.26, 2003- 8.19.

Vladislav PISKUNOV b. 7 Jun 1978 Novaya Kavhokva 1.83m 108kg.
At HT: OG: '00- dnq 14; WCh: '99- 3, '01/03- dnq

14/16; EC: '98- 10, '02- 2; WJ: '94- dq; EU23: '99- 1; WUG: '99- 3, '01- 2. UKR champion 1998-2000.
Progression at HT: 1993- 68.96, 1994- 73.66, 1998- 78.66, 1999- 80.00, 2000- 81.56, 2001- 79.60, 2002- 82.23, 2003- 78.57.
Used five turns when gaining 1999 World bronze medal. Threw the hammer 73.64 in June 1994 at 16 years 4 days, but disqualified for drugs use after winning (71.66) at the World Junior Championships a month later. Returned to competition in 1998 after four-year ban.
His brother Eduard had a hammer best of 75.64 '88 and threw 75.10 as a junior in 1986.

Andrey SKVARUK b. 9 Mar 1967 Brodivski 1.86m 108kg. Rovno ZS.
At HT: OG: '96- 4, '00- 10; WCh: '93- nt, '97- 2, '99- 5, '01- 5, '03- 4; EC: '94- 11, '98- dnq 14, '02- 5; ECp: '93-4-00-02: 3/2/10/2. Won GP 2000. UKR champion 1992, 1994-6, 2001, 2003.
Progression at HT: 1985- 65.42, 1986- 72.54, 1989- 73.60, 1990- 77.24, 1991- 71.60, 1992- 80.22, 1993- 80.80, 1994- 81.72, 1995- 78.00, 1996- 80.52, 1997- 81.46, 1998- 78.96, 1999- 80.75, 2000- 81.43, 2001- 82.34, 2002- 82.62, 2003- 81.74.

Andriy (Andrey) **SOKOLOVSKIY** b. 16 Jul 1978 Moskva, Russia 1.96m 80kg. Sports instructor.
At HJ: OG: '00- dnq 16=; WCh: '99/01- dnq 27=/22=, '03- 8; WI: '99-01-03-04: 6=/2/8/7; EU23: '99- 2; EI: '02- 4; ECp: '02- 4. UKR champion 2000-01, 2003.
Progression at HJ: 1997- 2.10, 1998- 2.22, 1999- 2.32, 2000- 2.28, 2001- 2.35i/2.34, 2002- 2.36, 2003- 2.33.

Roman VIRASTYUK b. 20 Apr 1968 Ivano Frankovsk 1.89m 137kg. Ivano Frankovsk ZS.
At SP: OG: '96- 6, '00- dnq 20; WCh: '95- 7, '97- 6, '99- dnq 13, '03- 10; ECh: '94- 3, '02- 9; EI: '98- 5, '00- 5; ECp: '94- 2. UKR champion 2000, 2002.
Progression at SP: 1986- 16.69, 1987- 18.53, 1988- 18.47i/18.25, 1989- 19.62, 1990- 20.03, 1991- 20.04i, 1993- 19.48, 1994- 20.00, 1995- 20.71, 1996- 21.23, 1997- 20.66, 1998- 20.63i/20.37, 1999- 20.59, 2000- 21.34, 2001- 20.08, 2002- 20.05, 2003- 20.78.
Two-year drugs ban 1991. Brother **Vasiliy** (b. 22 Apr 1974) has pb 19.75 '00 (EC: '98- dnq 13).

Denis YURCHENKO b. 27 Jan 1978 1.74m 74kg.
At PV: OG: '00- dnq; WCh: '03- 6=; EC: '02- 6=; EJ: '97- nh; WI: '03- 3; ECp: '02- 2=. Won UKR 2000, 2002-03.
Progression at PV: 1997- 5.20, 1998- 5.50, 1999- 5.59, 2000- 5.72, 2001- 5.70i/5.65/5.71ex, 2002- 5.75, 2003- 5.81, 2004- 5.75i.

Aleksandr YURKOV b. 21 Jul 1975 Prosyanaya 1.83m 84kg. Dnepropetrovsk Dyn. Sports instructor.
At Dec: OG: '00- 16; WCh: '01- 9; EC: '98- 13, '02- dnf; WJ: '94- dnf; EU23: '97-2, WUG: '97- 4; ECp: '00-01: 1/1. UKR champion 1997. At Hep: WI: '01- 6.
Progression at Dec: 1994- 7161, 1995- 7617, 1996- 7676, 1997- 7888, 1998- 8034, 1999- 8215, 2000- 8574, 2001- 8408, 2002- 8509. pbs: 60m 6.94i '01, 100m 10.69 '00, 400m 48.66 '00, 1000m 2:45.04i '01, 1500m 4:32.49 '00, 60mh 8.13i '00, 110mh 14.41 '01, 14.26w '02; HJ 2.06 '99, PV 5.40i '01, 5.40 '02; LJ 7.93 '00, SP 15.76 '02, DT 50.44 '99, JT 60.06 '01, Hep 6160i '01. Won at Talence 2001.

Volodomyr (Vladimir) **ZYUSKOV** b. 29 Aug 1981 1.87m 71kg.
At LJ: WCh: '03- 6; EC: '02- dnq; WJ: '00- 2; EU23: '01- 2, '03- 2; WI: '03- 5, '04- 5; EI: '02- 6; WUG: '01- 4. UKR champion 2001-03.
Progression at LJ: 1998- 6.97, 1999- 7.69, 2000- 7.84, 2001- 8.13, 2002- 8.10, 2003- 8.22, 2004- 8.23i. pb 100m 10.4 '03.

Women

Olena (Yelena) **ANTONOVA** b. 16 Jun 1972 Nikipol 1.82m 95kg. Elektrometallurg Nikipol.
At DT: OG: '96- dnq 29, '00- dnq 13; WCh: '97- dnq 13, '99- 7, '01- dnq 16, '03- 4; EC: '98- 11; EJ: '91- 3; WUG: '97- 4; ECp: '97-8-00: 3/3/6. UKR champion 1995-7, 1999-2003.
Progression at HJ: 1989- 55.84, 1990- 57.30, 1991- 57.12, 1992- 61.94, 1993- 58.34, 1994- 59.80, 1995- 61.54, 1996- 63.60, 1997- 61.62, 1998- 65.44, 1999- 64.32, 2000- 66.67, 2001- 64.20, 2002- 63.40, 2003- 65.90. pb HT 54.82 '95.

Inha (Inga) **BABAKOVA** b. 27 Jun 1967 Ashkabad, Turkmenistan 1.80m 60kg. née Butkus.
At HJ: OG: '96- 3, '00- 5; WCh: '91-5-7-9-01-03- 3/3/2/1/2/dnq 15; EC: '94- 4; WI: '93-7-01-03: 3/2/2/8; ECp: '93- 4=. Won GP 1995, 1997; 2= 1999, 3rd 1991. UKR champion 1991-2.
Three UKR high jump records 1995. World W35 high jump record 2003.
Progression at HJ: 1987- 1.89, 1988- 1.92, 1989- 1.89i, 1991- 2.02, 1992- 2.00, 1993- 2.00i/1.96, 1994- 2.00, 1995- 2.05, 1996- 2.03, 1997- 2.02, 1999- 2.01, 2000- 2.00, 2001- 2.03, 2002- 1.96, 2003- 2.01.
Born in Turkmenistan, Lithuanian by family and lives in Ukraine. Improved 10cm in 1991, with no previous international experience. After four World/Olympic silver and bronze medals, won gold at the 1999 Worlds. 13 competitions at 2.00 or higher in 1995 and 10 in 1996. Coached by her husband Sergey Babakov, their first son Georgiy was born in June 1990 and a second son was born prior to her World success in 1999.

Anzhela BALAKHONOVA b. 18 Dec 1972 1.62m 55kg. Kiev Dyn.
At PV: OG: '00- nh (12=); WCh: '99- 2, '01- dnq 13; EC: '98- 1; WI: '97- 9; EI: '98- 1; WUG: '97- 4=. UKR champion 1996-7, 1999-2001.
PV Records: WIR and two European indoor 1998, 8 European 1997-2000, 18 UKR 1996-2000.
Progression at PV: 1996- 3.98/4.05sq, 1997- 4.36/4.45ex, 1998- 4.45i/4.40, 1999- 4.55, 2000- 4.56, 2001- 4.52, 2003- 4.32. pbs: 100m 11.60/11.2 '95, 200m 23.63 '94, 23.4 '95; LJ 6.40 '96.
Started as a sprinter and rhythmic gymnast.

Zhanna BLOCK b. 6 Jul 1972 Nezhin, near Chernigov 1.64m 62kg. née Tarnopolskaya, then Pintusevich. Kiev Dyn.
At 100m (/200m): OG: '96- 8/qf, '00- 5/8; WCh: '93- sf, '95- 5/h, '97- 2/1, '99- 4/qf, '01- 1, '03- 3/5; EC: '94- 2/2/4R, '98- 4/2; EJ: '91- 1/1/4R/2 4x400mR; WCp: '98- 4/3; ECp: '93- 3/4, '94- 1/1R. At 60m: WI: '93- 3, '03- 1; EI: '92- 1. Won UKR 100m 1994-5.
WIR 50m at 6.09 for a few minutes in 1993. UKR records: 100m (5) 1994-2001, 200m 1997.
Progress at 100m, 200m: 1987- 11.8, 1988- 11.75/11.5, 23.75; 1989- 11.64/11.5, 24.03; 1990- 11.99, 1991- 11.29/11.0, 23.56; 1992- 11.17, 1993- 11.08, 22.79; 1994- 10.99, 22.66; 1995- 11.01, 22.71/22.64w; 1996- 11.07, 23.15; 1997- 10.85/10.6, 22.17A/22.32; 1998- 10.92/10.9A, 22.35A/22.46; 1999- 10.94, 22.42; 2000- 10.93, 22.66; 2001- 10.82, 22.74; 2002- 10.83, 22.24; 2003- 10.99, 22.61. pbs: 50m 6.03+ '97, 60m 6.97+ '97, 7.04i '03.
She won the 1997 World title at 200m in 22.32, five days after she thought that she had won the 100m, only for the photo-finish to show that Marion Jones had held on to beat her 10.83 to 10.85. Four years later it was the other way round, as she beat Jones 10.82 to 10.85. Married athletics agent Mark Block in January 1999. Formerly married to Igor Pintsuvich (3rd WJ 110mh 1992).

Natalya DOBRINSKAYA b. 29 May 1982 1.82m 77kg.
At Hep: EU23: '03- 5; EJ: '01- 10. At Pen: WI: '04- 2.
Progression at Hep: 1999- 5226, 2000- 5322, 2001- 5742, 2002- 5936, 2003- 5877. pbs: 100m 11.60/11.2 '95, 200m 25.56 '02, 800m 2:19.45i '04, 60mh 8.48i '04, 100mh 13.95/13.7 '03, HJ 1.82i '04, 1.80 '02, LJ 6.43i '04, 6.20 '02, SP 15.95 '03, JT 43.23 '01, Pen 4727i '04.
Four pbs en route to UKR pentathlon record 4727 and WI silver medal 2004.

Olena (Yelena) GOVOROVA b. 18 Sep 1973 Izmail 1.75m 63kg. Odessa ZS.
At TJ: OG: '96- 9, '00- 3; WCh: '95- 10, '97- 3, '99- 7, '01- 10, '03- 7; EC: '98- 6, '02- dnq 13; WJ: '92- 3; WI: '95-7-04: 7/7/7; EI: '00- 4; WUG: '97- 1, '99- 1; ECp: '96-8-00-02: 2/3/2/4. UKR champion 1997-2002-03.
Progression at TJ: 1990- 12.70, 1991- 13.19i/13.10, 1992- 13.43, 1993- 13.14i, 1994- 14.22, 1995- 14.08i/14.07, 1996- 14.60/14.75w, 1997- 14.67, 1998- 14.51/14.70w, 1999- 14.66/14.99w, 2000- 14.96, 2001- 14.33/14.48w, 2002- 14.54, 2003- 14.81. pb LJ 6.43 '02.

Inessa KRAVETS b. 5 Oct 1966 Dnipropetrovsk 1.78m 60kg. née Shulyak. Kiev U. Married to Sergey Izvachuk.
At LJ (TJ): OG: '88- 10, '92- 2, '96- nj (1); WCh: '95- 10 (1); EC: '90- 6, '94- 2 (3); WI: '03- 2; EI: '94- 3; WUG: '91- 1; WCp: '94- 1. At TJ: WI: '93- 1; EI: '92- 1; ECp: '93- 3. Won GWG 1990, USSR LJ 1988, 1990; TJ 1991; CIS LJ 1992, UKR TJ 1995. Won GP LJ 1996 (2nd 1990, 1992, 1994); TJ 1995. World triple jump records 1991 and 1995, three WIR 1991-3.
Progression at LJ, TJ: 1982- 6.19, 1983- 6.27, 1984- 6.44, 1985- 6.45i/6.39, 1986- 6.61, 1987- 6.72, 1988- 7.27, 1989- 6.88i/6.86, 1990- 7.10, 14.08; 1991- 6.95, 14.95; 1992- 7.37, 14.41; 1993- 6.87/7.02w, 14.70; 1994- 7.09, 14.91; 1995- 6.97, 15.50; 1996- 7.05/7.07w, 15.33; 1997- 14.04, 1999- 14.17, 2000- 7.00/7.10w, 14.57; 2003- 6.79i/6.76, 14.44i/14.42. pbs: 200m 24.0 '90, HJ 1.75 '83.
Added 41cm to world triple jump record to win 1995 World title. Had an operation in the USA in 1997 on serious right thigh injury, not returning to competition until 1999. Three month drugs ban for stimulants 1993 and further positive test 25 Jul 2000 led to two-year ban. She returned to competition indoors in 2003.

Irina LISHCHINSKAYA b. 15 Jan 1976 1.65m 53kg. née Nedelenko.
At 800m: WCh: '99- h; EC: '98- h; WUG: '97- 1; EU23: '97- 1; ECp: '97- 2, '98- 2. At 1500m: WCh: '03- sf; EC: '02- 10; WJ: '94- 6; WI: '03- 5; ECp: '02- 5. Won UKR 800m 1999, 1500m 2001-02.
Progression at 800m, 1500m: 1993- 2:07.04, 1994- 2:02.6, 1996- 2:05.03, 1997- 2:00.16, 1998- 1:59.15, 1999- 2:00.01, 2001- 2:03.36, 4:05.38; 2002- 2:00.45, 4:03.78; 2003- 2:01.22, 4:02.60. pbs: 400m 53.88 '98, 1M 4:28.31 '02, 3000m 9:04.24i '03.

Irina MIKHALCHENKO b. 20 Jan 1972 1.79m 60kg.
At HJ: OG: '00- dnq 29; WCh: '99- dnq 14=; EC: '98- dnq, '02- 9; WI: '03- 5=; ECp: '02- 1. UKR champion 1998, 2000, 2002.
Progression at HJ: 1988- 1.80, 1989- 1.86i/1.85, 1990- 1.90, 1991- 1.86, 1992- 1.93, 1993- 1.86, 1994- 1.96i/1.95, 1995- 1.91, 1996- , 1997- 1.94/1.90, 1998- 1.94, 1999- 1.96, 2000- 1.98, 2001- 1.94, 2002- 2.00, 2003- 1.99.

Viktoriya PALAMAR b. 12 Oct 1977 1.87m 64kg.
At HJ: OG: '00- 7; WCh: '01- 5, '03- 5; WJ: '96- 6=; WI: '01- 5=, '03- 4; EI: '00- 5; WUG: '01- 1. UKR champion 2001.
Progression at HJ: 1992-, 1993- 1.83, 1994- 1.91, 1995- 1.88, 1996- 1.89, 1997- 1.88, 1998- 1.89, 1999- 1.93, 2000- 1.98, 2001- 1.99, 2002- 1.95, 2003- 2.01, 2004- 2.00i.

Viktoriya PAVLYSH b. 15 Jan 1969 Kharkov 1.74m 85kg. Kharkov Dyn.
At SP: OG: '92- 8, '96- 4; WCh: '93- dnq, '95- 11, '97- 2, '01- 3, '03- 3; EC: '94- 1, '98- 1, '02- 2; EJ: '87- 6; WI: '97- 9-03-04:1/dq/4/1; EI: '98- 2, '02- 1; WCp: '94- 4, '98- 1, '02- 4. 2nd GP 1997, 3rd 1993. Won WAF 2003, UKR champion 1993, 1995-6, 2001, 2003.
Ukrainian shot record 1998.
Progression at SP: 1986- 15.73, 1987- 16.48, 1988- 16.28, 1989- 17.28, 1990- 17.86, 1991- 18.76, 1992-

19.66, 1993- 19.22, 1994- 19.61, 1995- 19.30, 1996- 19.79, 1997- 20.73, 1998- 21.69, 1999- 21.43idq, 2001- 19.62, 2002- 20.34i/20.07, 2003- 20.44i/20.08, 2004- 20.73i.
Married Aristotle Mavridis on 22 Jul 1995. Her 21.69 to win the 1998 European title was the longest SP in the world for ten years, although she said afterwards that she had thrown 21.73 in a practice session in Kharkov. Disqualified and received two-year drugs ban after 'winning' at 1999 World Indoors with 21.43. Returned to win European Throws Challenge SP in March 2001.

Vita STYOPINA b. 21 Feb 1976 Zaporozhye 1.75m 58kg.
At HJ: OG: '96- dnq 19=, WCh: '99- 7, '03- 9=; EC: '98- 7; WJ: '94- 6; EJ: '95- 1; WI: '04- 8; ECp: '97-8: 4/4. UKR champion 1996, 1999.
Progression at HJ: 1992- 1.83, 1993- 1.89, 1994- 1.86, 1995- 1.92, 1996- 1.92, 1997- 1.93, 1998- 1.94, 1999- 1.96, 2000- 1.96, 2001- 1.94, 2002- 1.92, 2003- 2.00, 2004- 1.98i.

Tetyana TERESHCHUK b. 11 Oct 1969 1.85m 63kg. Lugansk Dyn.
At 400mh: OG: '96- sf, '00- 5; WCh: '95- 5, '97- 4, '99- 7, '03- 5; EC: '94- 6, '98- 2; WUG: '97- 1; ECp: '94-5-6-8-00: 2/3/4/1/1. Won GWG 2001, 3rd/2nd GP 1997/2000. UKR champion 1994, 1996, 1999, 2001.
Four UKR 400mh records 1997.
Progression at 400mh: 1989- 57.58, 1990- 57.98, 1991- 57.19, 1993- 58.20/57.9, 1994- 54.96, 1995- 54.88, 1996- 54.68, 1997- 53.64, 1998- 53.40, 1999- 53.46, 2000- 53.98, 2001- 53.89A/54.01, 2002- 54.28A, 2003- 54.26. pbs: 200m 24.03 '97, 100mh 12.8 '95, 13.12A '98, 13.14 '97.
Set UKR 400mh records in four successive races in 12 days in 1997: World semi and final, then Zürich and Monaco. Missed 2001 Worlds & 2002 Europeans through injury.

Antonina YEFREMOVA b. 19 Jul 1981 1.76m 58kg. Business student at Donetsk Academy.
At 400m: WCh: '03- sf; EC: '02- 6; WJ: '00- sf; EU23: '01- 1 (2 4x100mR); WCp: '02- 5R; ECp: '02- 1. UKR champion 2002-03.
Progression at 400m- 1999- 54.85, 2000- 51.95, 2001- 52.29, 2002- 50.70, 2003- 51.36. pb 200m 23.4 '03.

UNITED KINGDOM

Governing body: UK Athletics, Athletics House, 10 Harborne Road, Edgbaston, Birmingham B15 3AA. Founded 1999 (replacing British Athletics, founded 1991, which succeeded BAAB, founded 1932). The Amateur Athletic Association was founded in 1880 and the Women's Amateur Athletic Association in 1922.
National Championships (first were English Championships 1863-79). **AAA Championships** first held in 1880 (women 1922). **2003 Champions**: 100m: Dwain Chambers 10.08, 200m: Julian Golding 20.37 400m: Daniel Caines 45.56, 800m: Ricky Soos 1:47.51, 1500m: Michael East 3:42.29, 5000m: Andrew Graffin 13:56.59, 10000m: Fabiano Joseph TAN 27:32.81, HMar*: Ian Hudspith 63:32, Mar: Chris Carriss 2:17:57, 3000mSt: Stuart Stokes 8:40.10, 110mh: Damien Greaves 13.66, 400mh: Chris Rawlinson 49.24, HJ: Ben Challenger 2.24, PV: Nick Buckfield 5.50, LJ: Darren Ritchie 7.74, TJ: Larry Achike 16.55, SP: Carl Myerscough 21.55, DT: Emeka Udechuku 57.26, HT: Bill Beauchamp 69.33, JT: Mick Hill 76.35, Dec: Paul Tohill 6962, 5000mW: Steve Hollier 20:59.46. **Women**: 100m: Joice Maduaka 11.31, 200m: Abi Oyepitan 22.95, 400m: Helen Karagounis 52.51, 800m: Lucy Vaughan 2:03.70, 1500m: Hayley Tullett 4:08.12, 5000m: Hayley Yelling 15:53.30, 10000m: Anikó Kalovics HUN 31:40.31, HMar*: Bev Jenkins 73:08. Mar: Paula Radcliffe 2:15:25, 100mh: Rachel King 13.07, 400mh: Liz Fairs 57.06, HJ: Susan Jones 1.86, PV: Tracey Bloomfield 4.15, LJ: Jade Johnson 6.49, TJ: Yamilé Aldama ex-CUB 14.98, SP: Joanne Duncan 16.19, DT: Shelley Newman 58.16, HT: Lorraine Shaw 65.93, JT: Goldie Sayers 56.29, Hep: Fiona Harrison 5517, 5000mW: Lisa Kehler 23:10.15. * also UK champions.
National Road Walk Champions: Men: 20kmW: Andrew Penn 1:28:52, 35kmW: Andrew Drake 2:54:36, 50kmW: Michael Smith 5:00:41. Women: 5km: Katie Stones 26:49, 10km: Estle Viljoen RSA 50:46, 20km: Joanne Hesketh 1:47:50.

Onochie '**Larry**' **ACHIKE** b. 31 Jan 1975 Islington, London 1.88m 75kg. Shaftesbury Barnet.
At TJ: OG: '00- 5; WCh: '99- 11, '01- 7; EC: '98- dnq 21; CG: '98- 1; WJ: '92- 11, '94- 1; EJ: '93- 3; ECp: '00- 1. 3rd GP 2000. AAA champion 2003.
Progression at TJ: 1989- 13.71, 1990- 14.18, 1991- 15.28, 1992- 15.97, 1993- 16.49, 1994- 16.53/16.67w, 1995- 15.91/15.94w, 1996- 16.36, 1997- 15.77, 1998- 17.10, 1999- 16.96, 2000- 17.30/17.31w, 2001- 17.21, 2002- 16.71, 2003- 16.55. pbs: 100m 10.95 '94, 200m 21.68 '97, 21.6 '96; LJ 7.46 '93.
Over 17m for the first time in June 1998 with 17.07, improving to 17.10 for Commonwealth title. Lifetime best 17.31w to win the European Cup in 2000, and maintained that form with 17.30 (q) and 17.29 for fifth at the Olympics.

Stephen BACKLEY b. 12 Feb 1969 Sidcup 1.96m 100kg. Cambridge H.
At JT: OG: '92- 3, '96- 2, '00- 2; WCh: '91- dnq 15, '93- 4, '95- 2, '97- 2, '99- 8, '01- dnq 14, '03- 9; EC: '90- 1, '94- 1, '98- 1, '02- 1; CG: '90- 1, '94- 1, '98- 2, '02- 1; WJ: '88- 2; EJ: '87- 1; WCp: '89-94-8-02: 1/1/1/4; ECp: '89-95-97-02: 1/3/1/2; WUG: '89- 1, '91- 1. Won GP 1989 (3rd overall), 3rd 1995, UK 1988-90, 1997; AAA 1989, 1992, 1998-2000.
Javelin records: Three world 1990-2, world junior 1988. Eight UK and Commonwealth 1989-92.
Progression at JT (old): 1985- 64.34, new: 1986- 64.98 (69.74), 1987- 78.16, 1988- 79.50, 1989- 85.90,

1990- 90.98, 1991- 91.36, 1992- 91.46, 1993- 85.10, 1994- 85.20, 1995- 88.54, 1996- 87.44, 1997- 89.02, 1998- 89.89, 1999- 87.59, 2000- 89.85, 2001- 90.81, 2002- 88.54, 2003- 85.69.
The first British male thrower to set a world record: 89.58 in Stockholm with a Sandvik javelin, and 90.98 at Crystal Palace on his second throw with a Németh model, both 1990. When these were banned at the end of 1991 his 89.58 was reinstated as the world record and in New Zealand in 1992 he achieved the first 90m throw with the revised javelin specification. In 2000 he became the first Briton in any athletics event to win an Olympic medal in three Games. Tied the record in 2002 with his fourth successive European title.

Daniel CAINES b. 15 May 1979 Solihull 1.78m 74kg. Birchfield H. Law graduate of Swansea University.
At 400m/4x400mR: OG: '00- sf/6R; WCh: '03- sf; EC: '02- 3/1R; CG: '02- 4/1R; WJ: '98- 5R; WI: '01- 1, '03- 2/3R; EI: '00-6; ECp: '02- 1/1R; won AAA 2003. At 200m: EI: '02- 4.
Progression at 400m: 1998- 47.13, 1999- 47.29i, 2000- 45.37, 2001- 45.58, 2002- 44.98, 2003- 45.29. pbs: 60m 6.99i '98, 200m 20.62i '02, 20.84 '03; 300m 32.7i '02.
His mother, Blondelle Thompson, set a British record at 13.0 for 100mh in 1974 and his father Joe Caines was a British junior international in 1970-1 with a 400m best of 48.2 at age 19 in 1971.

Darren CAMPBELL b. 12 Sep 1973 Manchester 1.85m 83kg. Belgrave H.
At 100m/4x100mR (200m): OG: '96- ht R, '00- 6 (2); WCh: '97- sf/3R, '99- sf/2R, '03- 3/4/2R; EC: '98- 1/1R, '02- 3/qf/1R; CG: '98- 5/1R, '02- (3)/1R; WJ: '92- 2/1R (2); EJ: '91- 1/2R (1); ECp: '96-8-9-00-03: 3R/1R/1R/1&1R/3R; Won AAA 100m 1998, 200m 2000; GP 100m 2000.
Progression at 100m, 200m: 1988- 11.39, 23.2; 1989- 10.78w/11.0, 21.8/21.72w; 1990- 10.81, 21.51; 1991- 10.37/10.28w, 20.89/20.61w; 1992- 10.37, 20.87/20.68w; 1993- 10.39/10.29w, 20.86/20.69w; 1994- 10.54, 21.23i; 1995- 10.34, 1996- 10.17, 20.98; 1997- 10.13, 20.84; 1998- 10.04, 20.48; 1999- 10.12/10.11w, 21.05/20.51w; 2000- 10.06, 20.13; 2001- 10.16, 20.41; 2002- 10.11, 20.21; 2003- 10.08, 20.34. pbs: 50m 5.77i '99, 60m 6.59i '03, LJ 6.63w? '89.
After junior successes played football for two years 1993-5.

Marlon DEVONISH b. 1 Jun 1976 Coventry 1.83m 76kg. Coventry Godiva.
At 200m/4x100mR (100m): OG: '00- hR; WCh: '97- (qf), '99- sf/2R, '01- 8, '03- 2R; EC: '98- res 1R (5), '02- 3/1R; CG: '98- 1R (8), '02- 2/1R; WJ: '94- res 1R; EJ: '95- 1/1R; EU23: '97- 1R (3); WI: '03- 1; WCp: '98- 1R, '02- 3; ECp: '97-9-00-01-02-03: 3R/1R/1R/2&2R/1&1R/3R. Won AAA 1997, 2001-02.
Progression at 200m: 1993- 21.94/21.8w, 1994- 21.25/21.20w, 1995- 20.94/20.88w, 1996- 20.86, 1997- 20.65/20.61w, 1998- 20.92, 1999- 20.25, 2000- 20.59, 2001- 20.29, 2002- 20.19/20.18w, 2003- 20.50. pbs: 60m 6.71i '00, 100m 10.13 '98, 400m 46.83 '00.

Jason GARDENER b. 18 Sep 1975 Bath 1.78m 70kg. Bath & Wessex.
At 100m/4x100mR: OG: '00- qf; WCh: '95- sf R, '99- 7/2R; EC: '02- sf; CG: '98- res (1)R, '02- 6/1R; WJ: '94- 2/1R; ECp: '95-7-9: 1R/3R/1R. At 60m: WI: '99-03-04: 3/3/1; EI: '98-00-02: 2/1/1. Won AAA 100m 1997, 1999.
Progression at 100m: 1992- 11.0, 1993- 10.62/10.46w, 1994- 10.25, 1995- 10.33, 1996- 10.5/10.41w, 1997- 10.31/10.17w, 1998- 10.30/10.17w/10.0w, 1999- 9.98, 2000- 10.09/10.04w, 2001- 10.23, 2002- 10.13/10.11w, 2003- 10.17/10.11w. pbs: 50m 5.61i '00 (= European record), 60m 6.46i '99 & '04 (European record), 200m 20.65 '99.
Broke Linford Christie's European record for 60m with 6.46 for 3rd in World Indoors 1999, and outdoors became the third European to break 10 seconds for 100m.

Phillips IDOWU b. 30 Dec 1978 Hackney, London 1.92m 87kg. Belgrave H.
At TJ: OG: '00- 6; WCh: '01- 9; EC: '02- 5; CG: '02- 2; EU23: '99-5; EJ: '97- 4. Won AAA 2000, 2002.
Progression at TJ: 1995- 13.90, 1996- 15.12/15.53w, 1997- 15.86/16.34w, 1998- 16.35, 1999- 16.41, 2000- 17.12, 2001- 17.33/17.38w, 2002- 17.68. pbs: 60m 6.81i '04, 100m 10.81 '01, 10.71w '03; LJ 7.83 '00.

Mark LEWIS-FRANCIS b. 4 Sep 1982 1.83m 85kg. Birchfield H.
At 100m/4x100mR: WCh: '01- sf, '03- sf/res (2)R; CG: '02- 7; WJ: '00- 1/1R; WY: '99- 1; EJ: '99- 2, '01- 1/1R; ECp: '01- 1/2R, '03- 1. At 60m: WI: '01- 3, '03- 4; EI: '02- 2. Won AAA 100m 2002. World junior record 60m indoors 2001.
Progression at 100m: 1996- 11.37/11.31w, 1997- 10.93, 1998- 10.49/10.36w, 1999- 10.31/10.26w, 2000- 10.10, 2001- 10.12/9.97w?, 2002- 10.04/9.97w, 2003- 10.07. pbs: 50m 5.73i '02, 60m 6.51i '01, 200m 20.94 '02.
Improved his pb of 6.65 to successive British junior records of 6.61, 6.56 and 6.51 in 2001 World Indoor 60m. After wins at the European Cup and European Juniors, he ran 9.97 in the quarter-finals at the World Championship, but was denied a possible World Junior record as the wind gauge did not function correctly.

Dean MACEY b. 12 Dec 1977 Rochford, Essex 1.96m 92kg. Harrow.
At Dec: OG: '00- 4; WCh: '99- 2, '01- 3; WJ: '96- 2; EU23: '97/99- dnf.
Progression at Dec: 1994- 5648, 1995- 6662, 1996- 7480, 1999- 8556, 2000- 8567, 2001- 8603. pbs: 100m 10.69/10.65w '99, 400m 46.21 '01, 1500m 4:23.45 '00, 110mh 14.34 '01, HJ 2.15 '01, PV 4.80 '00, LJ 7.77 '00, TJ 14.26/14.53w '94, SP 15.77 '01,

DT 47.77 '99, JT 64.03 '99.
In 1999 he set six individual event personal bests in his score of 8556 on his senior international debut for Britain at the 1999 Worlds, having earlier won at Arles with 8347, a huge improvement on his pb from his last completed decathlon, 7480 for 2nd at the 1996 World Juniors. Despite only one competition pre-Sydney in 2000, he excelled to take fourth at the Olympics, and in 2001 he improved his best again for bronze at the Worlds, despite a groin injury. Did not compete in 2002 or 2003 through injury.

Christian MALCOLM b. 3 Jun 1979 Cardiff 1.74m 67kg. Cardiff AAC.
At 200m/4x100mR (100m): OG: '00- 5; WCh: '01- 5 (7), '03- sf/2R; EC: '02- 4/1R; CG: '98- 2/4R, '02- 8; WJ: '96- sf, '98- 1 (1); EJ: '97- 1/1R (2); EU23: '99- 2/1R (2=); WI: '01- 2; EI: '00- 1, '02- 2; WCp: '02- 6R; ECp: '00-01-02-03: 1&1R/2R/1R/2&3R.
European Junior 200m record 1998.
Progression at 100m, 200m: 1993- 11.74, 1994- 10.88, 22.36/22.2; 1995- 10.85, 21.58/21.41w; 1996- 10.60/10.5, 21.27; 1997- 10.24, 20.83/20.48w; 1998- 10.12/10.10w, 20.29; 1999- 10.22/10.20w, 20.47; 2000- 10.29, 20.19; 2001- 10.11/10.09w?, 20.08; 2002- 10.29, 20.30/20.29w; 2003- 10.22, 20.25. pbs: 50m 5.81i '02, 60m 6.64i '01.

Carl MYERSCOUGH b. 21 Oct 1979 2.09m 149kg. Blackpool & Fylde. Student at University of Nebraska, USA.
At SP(/DT): WCh: '03- dnq 19; CG: '02- 3; WJ: '96- dnq 22, '98- 3/6; EJ: '97- dnq/6; EU23: '99- 8/9; WI: '04- 7; WCp: '02- 7; ECp: '03- 2/7; Won AAA 2003, (dq 1999), NCAA 2003.
British shot record 2003.
Progression at SP: 1995- 13.20, 1996- 17.30, 1997- 17.66, 1998- 19.46, 1999- 18.97, 2002- 21.26i/20.72, 2003- 21.92. pb DT 63.14 '02.
Immediately after serving a two-year drugs ban, he took Geoff Capes's 26-year old British indoor record with 21.08 at Lincoln, Nebraska on 23 Feb 2002. Two weeks later he improved to 21.26 to win the NCAA indoor title. Third UK indoor record to win 2003 NCAA indoor shot and took Geoff Capes's 23-year-old outdoor record when he won NCAAs with 21.92. Married Melissa Price (USA) in July 2003 after she had won the US hammer title with a pb 70.34.

Chris RAWLINSON b. 19 May 1972 Rotherham 1.85m 82kg. Trafford, Panellínios GRE, Loughborough University.
At 400mh/4x400mR: OG: '00- sf; WCh: '97- h, '01- 5, '03- 6; EC: '98- h, '02- dnf; CG: '02- 1/1R; WUG: '97- (res 3R), '99- 5/2R; WCp: '02- 3; ECp: '97-99-00-01-02-03: 5/5/1&2R/5/3/1&1R. Won AAA 1999-2003, UK 1997.
Progression at 400mh: 1992- 54.6, 1993- 52.9/53.62, 1994- 52.0/52.32, 1995- 50.90, 1996- 50.36, 1997- 49.69, 1998- 49.81, 1999- 48.14, 2000- 48.22, 2001- 48.27, 2002- 48.21, 2003- 48.44. pbs: 100m 10.9 '00, 200m 21.21 '02, 300m 32.5 '02, 400m 46.03 '02, 60mh 8.17i '97, 110mh 14.2/14.25w '97, 300mh 34.48 '02 (world best), PV 4.40 '92, Dec 6291 '95 (6562u).

Chris TOMLINSON b. 15 September 1981 Middlesbrough 1.96m 70kg. Newham & Essex Beagles.
At LJ: WCh: '03- 9; EC: '02- 6; CG: '02- 6; WJ: '00- 12; WI: '04- 6; WCp: '02- 6; ECp: '01-02-03: 2/1/5. British long jump record 2002.
Progression at LJ: 1996- 5.91/6.09w, 1997- 6.82w/6.44, 1998- 7.23i, 1999- 7.44i/7.40, 2000- 7.62, 2001- 7.75, 2002- 8.27, 2003- 8.16, 2004- 8.17i. pbs: 100m 10.69 '02, 10.61w/10.6 '01; 200m 21.73 '02, TJ 15.35 '01.
When he jumped 8.27 at Tallahassee in April 2002, from a previous best of 7.87 (and 8.19w), he broke the 34-year-old British record set by Lynn Davies.

Women

Natasha DANVERS b. 19 Sep 1977 London 1.75m 61kg. Shaftesbury Barnet, was at University of Southern California, USA. Married her coach Darrel Smith Jnr on 1 November 2003.
At 400mh/4x400mR: OG: '00- 8; WCh: '99/01- h, '03- sf; CG: '02- 7; EC: '98: h/3R res, '02- 7; CG: '98- 5; EU23: '99- 1; ECp: '00-01-02-03- 2: 3R/8/3; WUG: '99- 5/3R, '01- 1/2R; AAA 1998, 2002; NCAA 2000. At 100mh: WJ: '96- 6; EJ: '95- 2; ECp: '03- 7.
Progression at 400mh: 1993- 66.9, 1997- 56.84, 1998- 55.69, 1999- 55.75, 2000- 54.95, 2001- 54.94, 2002- 55.68, 2003- 54.02. pbs: 200m 24.99 '00, 300m 37.80 '00, 400m 53.26 '98, 60mh 8.32i '96, 100mh 12.96 '03, 12.8w '99; HJ 1.82 '98.

Joanne FENN b. 19 October 1974 Leytonstone 1.72m 55kg. née Mersh. Woodford Green and Essex Ladies.
At 800m: WCh: '03- sf; EC: '02- sf; CG: '02- 7; WI: '03- 5, '04- 3.
Progression at 800m: 1989- 2:16.49, 1996- 2:11.3, 1997- 2:05.63, 1998- 2:05.2, 2000- 2:04.19, 2001- 2:02.81, 2002- 2:00.24, 2003- 1:59.74i/2:00.56, 2004- 1:59.50i. pbs: 400m 55.0 '01, 1000m 2:34.73i '04, 1500m 4:11.71i '03, 4:15.42 '03; 100mh 15.0 '92, 400mh 63.10 '91, JT 39.14 '93, Hep 4220 '93.

Ashia HANSEN b. 5 Dec 1971 Evansville, Indiana, USA 1.70m 63kg. Shaftesbury Barnet.
At TJ: OG: '96- 4, '00- 11; WCh: '95- dnq 21, '97- 5, '99- 12, '01- 7; EC: '94- dnq 15, '02- 1; CG: '98- 1, '02- 1; WI: '97- 2, '99- 1, '03- 1; EI: '98- 1, '02- 1; WCp: '02- 2; ECp: '95-6-7-9-02: 1/1/3/2/2. Won GP 1997, 1999; AAA 1996, 2001-02; UK 1997.
Records: 10 UK & Commonwealth triple jump 1994-7 and 1 unratified (no wind gauge) 1994. WIR 1998, 9 UK & Commonwealth indoor 1994-8.
Progression at TJ: 1990- 10.84, 1991- 12.68, 1992- 13.31, 1993- 13.48i/13.25/13.55w, 1994- 14.22, 1995- 14.66, 1996- 14.78, 1997- 15.15, 1998- 15.16i/14.32, 1999- 15.02i/14.96, 2000- 14.29, 2001-

14.51, 2002- 14.86/15.00w, 2003- 15.01i. pbs: 60m 7.51i '98, 100m 11.7 '95, 11.95 '96, 11.81w '94; 200m 24.57i '95, 25.1 '92; LJ 6.47A '96.

Born in the USA, original name Ashia Nana Koramdina, she was adopted at three months by an English woman and her Ghanaian husband, They lived in Ghana for six years before settling in London.

Kelly HOLMES b. 19 Apr 1970 Pembury, Kent 1.64m 55kg. Middlesex Ladies.

At 1500m (800m): OG: '96- 11 (4), '00- 7 (3); WCh: '93- (sf), '95- 2 (3), '97- h, '99- (sf), '01- (6), '03- (2); EC: '94- 2, '01- h (3); CG: '94- 1, '98- 2, '02- 1; WI: '03- 2, '04- 9; WCp: '94- 3; ECp: '94-5-6-7-02: 2/1/(2)/1/(4). 2nd GP 800m 1995 and 2001. Won UK 800m 1993, 1995, 1997; AAA 800m 1993, 1995-6, 1999-2001; 1500m 1994, 1996, 2002.

Commonwealth 1500m record 1997. UK records 800m (2) 1995, 1000m 1995 & 1997.

Progression at 800m, 1500m: 1984- 2:15.1, 4:35.3; 1985- 2:13.1, 4:41.4; 1986- 2:11.0, 4:26.9; 1987- 2:09.45, 4:26.10; 1989- 2:12.1, 1991- 2:11.8, 1992- 2:03.94, 4:27.7; 1993- 1:58.64, 4:17.3; 1994- 1:59.43, 4:01.41; 1995- 1:56.21, 4:03.04; 1996- 1:57.84, 4:01.13; 1997- 1:57.14, 3:58.07; 1998- 4:06.10; 1999- 1:58.24, 4:04.58; 2000- 1:56.80, 4:05.35; 2001- 1:57.88, 2002- 1:59.83, 4:01.91; 2003- 1:58.69, 4:01.96. pbs: 200m 25.29 '95, 400m 53.8 '96, 600m 1:25.41 '03, 1000m 2:32.55 '97, 1M 4:28.04 '98, 3000m 9:01.91 '03, 10km Rd 34:54 '96.

The winner of the English Schools Junior 1500m in 1983, she hardly competed for four years after being a Junior International in 1987, and joining the Army at 18. Made a breakthrough to world class in 1993. In 1997 she left the Army, for whom she had played at volleyball and been judo champion. Great suceess despite injuries.

Jade JOHNSON b. 7 Jun 1980 London 1.85m 72kg. Herne Hill H.

At LJ: WCh: '03- 4; EC: '02- 2; CG: '02- 2; EJ: '99- dnq 14; EU23: '01- 1; ECp: '00-01-02-03: 7/5/5/6. Won AAA 2002-03.

Progression at LJ: 1994- 5.68, 1995- 6.13/6.24w, 1996- 6.08, 1999- 6.52, 2000- 6.58, 2001- 6.59/6.68w, 2002- 6.73, 2003- 6.69/6.77w. pbs: 60m 7.43i '04, 100m 12.0/11.72w '98, 12.09 '00; 200m 24.31 '98, TJ 13.11 '01.

Denise LEWIS b. 27 Aug 1972 West Bromwich 1.73m 64kg. Birchfield H.

At Hep (LJ): OG: '96- 3 (dnq 24), '00- 1; WCh: '95- 7, '97- 2, '99- 2, '03- 5; EC: '94- (dnq 19), '98- 1; CG: '94- 1 (8), '98- 1; EJ: '91- 5; ECp: '94- 12 (5), '95- 1 (8), '96- (4), '97- (4). Won AAA LJ 1996, 1998.

Three UK and two Commonwealth heptathlon records 1996-2000.

Progression at Hep: 1989- 5277, 1990- 5193, 1991- 5484, 1992- 5812, 1993- 5774, 1994- 6325, 1995- 6299, 1996- 6645, 1997- 6736, 1998- 6559, 1999- 6724, 2000- 6831, 2003- 6282. pbs: 200m 24.10 '97, 24.01w '00; 800m 2:12.20 '00, 60mh 8.30i/8.2i '97, 100mh 13.13 '00, HJ 1.87 '99, LJ 6.69 '00, 6.77w '97; SP 16.12 '99, JT 56.50 '96, new 51.13 '00.

Returned to heptathlon competition in 2003 for the first time since Olympic gold in 2000. Daughter Lauren born to her and partner Patrick Stevens (Belgian sprinter) in April 2002.

Lee McCONNELL b. 9 Oct 1978 Glasgow 1.78m 64kg. Shaftesbury Barnet.

At 400m/4x400m (HJ): WCh: '01- 5R, '03- 7; EC: '02- 3/4R; CG: '02- 2/4R; WUG: '99- 3R (14=), '01- 6/2R; WCp: '02- 4/5R; ECp: '02-03: 1R/2&2R. Won AAA 2002.

Progression at 400m: 1996- 56.4, 1997- 57.0, 1998- 54.74, 1999- 53.81, 2001- 52.05, 2002- 50.82, 2003- 51.06. pbs: 100m 12.2 '95, 12.19w '94; 200m 23.66 '01, 23.48w '02; HJ 1.88 '00.

Former high jumper set 400m pbs at AAA, CG, EC and WCp in 2002.

Katharine MERRY b. 21 Sep 1974 Dunchurch 1.70m 61kg Birchfield H.

At 400m: OG: '00- 3; WCh: '99- 5. At 200m/4x100mR (100m): OG: '96- qf/8R; WCh: '93- qf; EC: '94- sf/5R; WJ: '90- (8)/2R; '92- 5/4R (6); EJ: '89- 5 (7 100m), '91- 3/2R, '93- 1/1R (2); ECp: '93-4-6-9-01: 6-2-3-8-6, 2 100m 94, 2R '94, '03. Won UK 200m 1993 & 1997, AAA 100m & 200m 1994, 200m 1998, 400m 1999.

Progression at 200m, 400m: 1987- 25.4, 1988- 24.9, 1989- 23.94/23.54w/23.9, 1990- 23.65, 1991- 23.50/23.41w, 1992- 23.38, 1993- 23.20, 1994- 22.85, 54.0; 1995- 1996- 22.88, 1997- 22.77, 1998- 22.93, 51.01; 1999- 22.83i/22.90, 50.21; 2000- 22.76, 49.72; 2001- 23.12, 49.59; 2003- 52.35. pbs: 60m 7.34i '94, 100m: 11.34/11.27w '94, 300m 36.00 '00, HJ 1.74 '88, LJ 5.55 '87, 6.05w '88.

Unable to compete at the 2001 Worlds or at all in 2002 because of injury. Ran numerous UK age records and still holds the British best at under-13 for 70m and 75m hurdles, high jump and pentathlon and at under-15 for 100m, 200m and pentathlon. In 1989 she won the AAA girls (U15) indoor 60m with a stunning 7.35. Six years as a British junior international, with 11 national age-group titles. Engaged to Olivier-Jean Théodore FRA, who has a 400mh best of 49.21 (2001).

Joanne PAVEY b. 20 Sep 1973 Honiton 1.62m 51kg. née Davis. Bristol.

At 5000m: OG: '00- 12; EC: '02- 5; CG: '02- 5; WCp: '02- 3; ECp: '02-03: 2/2. At 3000m: WI: '04- 5. At 1500m: WCh: '97- sf, '03- 10. Won UK 1500m 1997, AAA 5000m 2001.

Progress at 1500m, 3000m, 5000m: 1988- 4:27.9, 1989- 4:30.91, 1990- 4:26.7, 1993- 9:56.1, 1994- 4:23.36, 1995- 4:28.46, 1996- 4:21.14, 9:37.6; 1997- 4:07.28, 9:05.87; 1998- 8:58.2, 2000- 8:36.70, 14:58.27; 2001- 8:36.58, 15:00.56; 2002- 4:11.16, 8:31.27, 14:48.66; 2003- 4:01.79, 8:37.89, 15:09.04; 2004- 8:34.55i. pbs: 800m 2:09.68 '90, 1M 4:30.77 '97, 2000m 5:42.5 '02.

Set a British under-15 record at 1500m with 4:27.9 in 1988 and won four national titles at U15/U17 level, but did not compete much in the early 1990s, also missing two years through injury 1998-2000. Married to middle-distance runner Gavin Pavey.

Paula RADCLIFFE b. 17 Dec 1973 Northwich 1.73m 54kg. Bedford & County. Degree in European languages from Loughborough University.
At 10000m: OG: '00- 4; WCh: '99- 2, '01- 4; EC: '98- 5, '02- 1; At 5000m: OG: '96- 5; WCh: '95- 5, '97- 4; CG: '02- 1; ECp: '98-9-01: 1-1-2 (2 1500m '98); 3rd GP 1997. At 3000m: WCh: '93- 7; WJ: '92- 4; EJ: '91- 4; ECp: '97- 3. World HMar: '00-01-03: 1/1/1; CC: '91- 15J, '92- 1J, '93-5-6-7-8-9-00-01-02: 18/18/19/2/2/3/5 (4 4k)/1 (2 4k)/1. Eur CC: '98- 1, '03- 1. Won AAA 5000m 1996, 2000; Mar 2002-03; UK 5000m 1997, CC 1994-5.
Records: World marathon 2002 & 2003; half marathon 2003; Commonwealth & UK 1998-2002: 3000m (3), 5000m (3), 10000m (5); UK 5000m (4) 1996-2001. European 10000m 2002, HMar 2000 & 2001, Marathon 2002.
Progression at 1500m, 3000m, 5000m, 10000m, Mar: 1988- 4:41.0, 1989- 4:34.9, 1990- 4:31.3, 9:41.4; 1991- 4:23.68, 9:23.29; 1992- 4:16.82, 8:51.78, 16:16.77i; 1993- 4:11.6, 8:40.40; 1994- 4:23.84, 1995- 4:06.84, 8:40.82, 14:49.27; 1996- 4:08.42, 8:37.07, 14:46.76; 1997- 4:06.93, 8:35.28, 14:45.51; 1998- 4:05.81, 8:38.84, 14:51.27, 30:48.58; 1999- 4:06.71, 8:27.40, 14:43.54, 30:27.13; 2000- 4:11.45, 8:28.85, 14:44.36, 30:26.97; 2001- 4:05.37, 8:26.97, 14:32.44, 30:55.80; 2002- 8:22.20, 14:31.42, 30:01.09, 2:17:18; 2003- 2:15:25. pbs: 400m 58.9 '92, 800m 2:05.22 '95, 1000m 2:47.17 '93, 1M 4:24.94 '96, 2000m 5:37.1 '02, 2M 9:27.5e (1998), 9:32.07 (1999); Road: 15km 46:41 '03, 10M 50:01 '03, HMar 65:40 '03, 30km 1:36:36 '03, 20M 1:43:33 '03.
Phenomenal year in 2002, with World CC, Commonwealth and European track gold medals, national records at 3000m, 5000m and 10000m and improving the world marathon record by 1:27 with 2:17:18 in Chicago after winning the London marathon in 2:18:56, beating the women's only world record by over three minutes and by over four minutes the fastest debut marathon. She ran a world road best of 30:21 in San Juan in February and then a sensational world record 2:15:25 at the 2003 London Marathon, but missed the track season through illness and injury. Returned with world 5km road best of 14:51 in September and then fastest ever half marathon, 65:40 to win Great North Run before third world half marathon and second European CC titles. Fastest ever track debut for 10,000m, 30:48.58, 2nd in 1998 European Challenge, and improved this Commonwealth record to 30:40.70 to win this race in 1999 and in Seville to 30:27.13. There, forcing the pace throughout, despite searing heat; she was passed on the last lap by Gete Wami, but won a glorious silver medal. She set an even faster pace at the 2000 Olympics, but was outkicked and finished fourth. Followed that with European half marathon record to win Great North Run and won the World Half marathon by 33 seconds.
Her great aunt Charlotte Radcliffe won an Olympic swimming silver medal at 4x100m freestyle relay in 1920. Married 3:34.76 1500m man Gary Lough on 15 April 2000 but continues to race under her maiden name.

Lorraine SHAW b. 2 Apr 1968 Gloucester 1.71m 90kg. Sale H Manchester.
At HT: OG: '00- 9; WCh: '01- 6, '03- 10; EC: '98-11, '02- dnq 20; CG: '98- 2, '02- 1; ECp: '98-9-00-01-02-03: 5/6/4/3/7/6. Won UK 1993, AAA 1994, 1998, 2000-03. At DT: CG: '94- 10. Won Irish DT 1990-2, HT 1992.
16 British hammer records 1994-2003, Commonwealth records 1995 and 2000.
Progression at HT: 1991- 35.52, 1992- 44.40/45.24 lt, 1993- 56.56, 1994- 59.94, 1995- 64.90, 1996-61.34, 1998- 63.30, 1999- 67.10, 2000- 67.44, 2001-68.15, 2002- 66.83, 2003- 68.93. pbs: SP 14.21 '94, DT 55.04 '94.
Having competed for Ireland at discus in 1992, opted for British nationality in 1993.

Hayley TULLETT b. 17 Feb 1973 Swansea 1.66m 58kg. née Parry. Swansea H.
At 1500m (800m): OG: '00- 11; WCh: '99- h, '01-sf, '03- 3; CG: '02- 2; EC: '02- h; WUG: '97- 4 (5); ECp: '97- (7), '99- 4. At 3000m: WI: '01- 8, '03- 10; ECp: '00- 3, '03- 2. Eur CC: '02- 5, '03- 11. Won AAA 1500m 1999-2000, 2003.
Progression at 1500m: 1988- 4:52.9, 1990- 5:01.4, 1994- 4:43.9, 1995- 4:25.51, 1996- 4:16.9, 1997-4:08.98, 1999- 4:05.72, 2000- 4:01.23, 2001- 4:03.54, 2002- 4:07.52, 2003- 3:59.95. pbs: 400m 55.6 '97, 800m 2:00.49 '03, 1000m 2:45.41i '01, 1M 4:26.50i '00, 4:48.88 '95; 3000m 8:45.36i '01, 8:45.39 '00; 2M 9:49.73 '99.
Married pole vaulter Ian Tullett (b. 15 Aug 1969, pb 5.35 '98, 2 CG 90) in 1999.

USA

Governing body: USA Track and Field, P.O. Box 120, Indianapolis, Indiana 46206-0120. Founded 1979, when it replaced the AAU (founded 1888) as the governing body.
National Championships first held in 1876 (men), 1923 (women). **2003 Champions**: **Men**: 100m: Bernard Williams 10.11, 200m: Darvis Patton 20.15, 400m: Tyree Washington 44.33, 800m: David Krummenacker 1:45.53, 1500m: Jason Lunn 3:44.00, 5000m: Tim Broe 13:35.23, 10000m: Alan Culpepper 27:55.36, HMar/Mar: Ryan Shay 64:13/2:14:29, 3000mSt: Steve Slattery 8:23.58, 110mh: Allen Johnson 13.37, 400mh: Eric Thomas 48.76, HJ: Jamie Nieto 2.30, PV: Jeff Hartwig 5.70, LJ: Dwight Phillips 8.24, TJ: Kenta Bell 17.59, SP: Kevin Toth 21.22, DT: Carl Brown

66.66, HT: James Parker 73.04, JT: Breaux Greer 79.37, Dec: Tom Pappas 8784, 20000mW: Kevin Eastler 1:23:52.20, 50kmW: Curt Clausen 4:29:32. **Women**: 100m/200m: Kelli White 10.93/22.21, 400m: Sanya Richards 51.01, 800m: Jearl Miles Clark 1:58.84, 1500m: Regina Jacobs 4:01.63, 5000m: Marla Runyan 15:16.18, 10000m: Deena Drossin 31:28.97, HMar: Coleen De Reuck 70:00, Mar: Sara Wells 2:35:37, 3000mSt: Brianna Shook 9:44.71, 100mh: Gail Devers 12.61, 400mh: Raasin McIntosh 54.62, HJ: Amy Acuff 1.95, PV: Stacy Dragila 4.50, LJ: Grace Upshaw 6.64, TJ: Yuliana Perez 14.23, SP: Kristin Heaston 18.33, DT: Aretha Hill 63.98, HT: Melissa Price 70.34, JT: Erica Wheeler 56.85, Hep: Shelia Burrell 6159, 10kmW/20000mW: Michelle Rohl 48:01/1:34:31.06.

NCAA Championships first held in 1921 (men), 1982 (women). **2003 champions**: **Men**: 100m: Mardy Scales 10.25, 200m: Leo Bookman 20.47, 400m: Adam Steele 44.57, 800m: Sam Burley 1:46.50, 1500m: Grant Robison 3:40.39, 5000m: Alistair Cragg IRL 13:47.87, 10000m/3000mSt: Daniel Lincoln 28:20.20/8:26.65, 110mh: Ryan Wilson 13.35, 400mh: Dean Griffiths JAM 48.55, HJ: Dawid Jaworski POL 2.28, PV: Eric Eshbach 5.45, LJ: Leevan Sands BAH 8.05w, TJ: Julien Kapek FRA 17.12, SP: Carl Myerscough GBR 21.92, DT: Hannes Hopley RSA 61.25, HT: Lucais MacKay 70.19, JT: Brian Chaput 78.69, Dec: Stephen Harris 8061. **Women**: 100m/200m: Aleen Bailey JAM 11.18/22.65, 400m: Sanya Richards 50.58, 800m: Alice Schmidt 2:01.16, 1500m: Tiffany McWilliams 4:06.75, 5000m: Lauren Fleshman 15:24.06, 10000m: Alicia Craig 32:40.03, 3000mSt: Kassi Andersen 9:44.95, 100mh: Perdita Felicien CAN 12.74, 400mh: Sheena Johnson 54.24, HJ: Whitney Evans CAN 1.86, PV: Becky Holliday 4.41, LJ: Elva Goulbourne JAM 6.76, TJ: Ineta Radevica LAT 13.93, SP: Becky Breisch 17.76, DT: Deshaya Williams 55.40, HT: Candice Scott TRI 69.79, JT: Irina Kharun UKR 61.82, Hep: Hyleas Fountain 5999.

Kenwood '**Kenta**' **BELL** b. 16 Mar 1977 Henderson, Texas 1.83m 77kg. Studied criminology at Northwestern State Louisiana University.
At TJ: WCh: '03- 6; WI: '01- 9; WUG: '01- 1 (6 LJ); US champion 2003.
Progression at 110mh: 1998- 15.85i/16.02w, 1999- 16.52/16.67w, 2000- 17.22, 2001- 17.22, 2002- 17.63, 2003- 17.59, 2004- 17.49. pbs: LJ 8.05 '00.

Andy BLOOM b. 11 Aug 1973 Stamford, Ct. 1.85m 125kg. Nike. Mathematics graduate of Wake Forest University.
At SP (/DT): OG: '00- 4; WCh: '97- (dnq 16), '99- 4/nt, '01- (dnq 23); WJ: '92- 9/6; WI: '99- 9; WUG: '97- (2), '99- 1/2. Won GP SP 2000, NCAA SP & DT 1996.
Progression at SP, DT: 1991- 16.44, 48.66; 1992- 17.52, 53.50; 1993- 18.21, 55.34; 1994- 18.31, 54.28; 1995- 18.56, 63.48; 1996- 19.82, 64.86; 1997- 20.19i/19.96, 65.30; 1998- 20.45, 66.42; 1999- 21.27, 67.46; 2000- 21.82, 67.25/68.46d; 2001- 20.94, 66.17dh/65.64; 2002- 20.24, 61.20; 2003- 61.48.
Second best ever SP/DT combination thrower (after John Godina).

Ron BRAMLETT b. 22 Oct 1979 Antioch, Tennessee 1.81m 68kg. University of Alabama, formerly Middle Tennessee State.
At 110mh: WUG: '01- 4; won NCAA 2001-02.
Progression at 110mh: 1998- 14.01/13.93w, 1999- 13.72, 2000- 13.47, 2001- 13.43/13.39w, 2002- 13.35, 2003- 13.27. pbs: 100m 10.45 '03, 55mh 7.03i '02, 60mh 7.52i '02.

Derrick BREW b. 28 Dec 1977 Houston 1.85m 82kg. Nike. Studied business management at Louisiana State University.
At 4x400mR: WCh: '01/03- 1R; WUG: '99- 1R; WI: '03- res (1)R.
Progression at 400m: 1995- 47.40, 1996- 46.67, 1997- 45.21, 1998- 44.53, 1999- 44.29, 2000- 44.70, 2001- 44.80, 2002- 46.02A, 2003- 44.83A/45.02. pb 200m 20.42, 20.38Aw '99.

Christian CANTWELL b. 30 Sep 1980 1.98m 141kg. Studied hotel and restaurant management at University of Missouri.
At SP: WI: '04- 1; won WAF 2003. DT: PAm-J: '99- 2.
Progression at SP: 1999- 15.85, 2000- 19.67, 2001- 19.71, 2002- 21.45, 2003- 21.62, 2004- 21.95i. pbs: DT 59.32 '01, HT 57.18 '01, Wt 21.31i '03.

John CAPEL b. 27 Oct 1978 Brooksville, Florida 1.80m 82kg. Was at University of Florida.
At 200m/4x100mR (100m): OG: 00- 8; WCh: '03- 1/1R; WUG: '99- (2)/1R. Won US 200m 2000, NCAA 200m 1999 (2nd 100m).
Progression at 100m, 200m: 1997- 10.46/10.2, 21.01; 1998- 10.40, 1999- 10.03, 19.87; 2000- 10.12, 19.85, 2003- 9.97, 20.17. pbs: 55m 6.14i '03, 60m 6.48i '03.
Promising footballer (wide receiver) at University of Florida, but withdrew in April 2000 to concentrate on trying for Olympic success. After running the fastest time in the semis (20.10), moved too early, then settled back onto his blocks and was virtually left at start of Olympic 200m final. He was drafted by the Chicago Bears in 2001, but cut before training camp; and then tried out for the Kansas City Chiefs. He returned to track in 2003, but had to withdraw from WI team. However, he took two gold medals outdoors.

James CARTER b. 7 May 1978 Baltimore 1.86m 77kg. Nike. Was at Hampton College.
At 400mh: OG: 00- 4; WCh: '01- sf; WCp: '02- 1/2R; 3rd GP 2002. US champion 2002.
Progression at 400mh: 1998- 50.17, 1999- 49.45, 2000- 48.04, 2001- 48.44, 2002- 47.57, 2003- 48.88. pbs: 200m 21.03i '04, 400m 46.21 '01, LJ 7.25 '99.

Bryan CLAY b.3 Jan 1980 Austin, Texas 1.80m 79kg. Was at Azusa Pacific University.
At Dec: WCh: '01/03- dnf, PAm-J: '99- 1.

Progression at Dec: 1999- 7312, 2000- 7373, 2001- 8169, 2002- 8230, 2003- 8482 '03. pbs: 60m 6.65i '04, 100m 10.43 '03, 400m 47.85 '03, 1000m 2:49.41i '04, 1500m 4:38.93 '01, 60mh 7.77i '04, 110mh 13.91 '03, HJ 2.08i '04, 2.04 '02; PV 5.05 '03?, LJ 7.81 '03, SP 15.08i '04, 15.05 '03; DT 50.86 '03, JT 67.77 '03, Hep 6365i '04.
Moved from Texas to Hawaii at age five. Brilliant breakthrough with four pbs in 2004 World Indoor heptathlon.

Ramon CLAY b. 29 Jun 1975 Memphis 1.86m 77kg. Nike. Was at Norfolk State University.
At 200m: WCh: '01- qf. 400m/4x400mR: WJ: '94- 2/1R; WCp: '02- 4. US champion 2002.
Progression at 200m: 1993- 21.30/21.0w, 1994- 21.48/21.1, 1995- 20.81/20.36w, 1996- 20.08/19.99w, 1997- 20.49, 1998- 20.06/20.0A, 1999- 20.26, 2000- 20.30, 2001- 20.05, 2002- 20.27, 2003- 20.27. pbs: 50m 5.69i '03, 55m 6.20i '97, 60m 6.56i '03, 100m 10.21 '03, 400m 45.48 '95.
Suffered hamstring injury at 2001 Worlds. Reserve on US teams for 1996 Olympics and 1997 Worlds after 4th at US Champs each year. His wife Julian (b. 2 Nov 1977, née Reynolds) ran 800m at WJ 1994, won PAm 4x400m gold in 2003 and was 5th at 400m at 2004 WI.

Charles CLINGER b. 28 Dec 1976 Jackson Hole, Wyoming 2.06m 100kg. Nike. Was at Weber State University, previously Bosie State.
At HJ: WCh: '99- dnq 27=; PAm: '99- 3; NCAA champion 2001.
Progression at HJ: 1995- 2.13, 1996- 2.16i, 1999- 2.29A, 2000- 2.31A, 2001- 2.35A, 2002- 2.35, 2003- 2.34i/2.25. pbs: LJ 7.62i '01, 7.58 '00; TJ 16.24i '01, 16.10 '00.
Went on church mission to Australia 1997-8.

Shawn CRAWFORD b. 14 Jan 1978 Van Wyck, SC 1.81m 75kg. Mizuno. Was at Clemson University.
At 200m: WCh: '01- 3=; WI: '01- 1; Won US, GWG & GP 2001, NCAA 2000. At 60m: WI: '04- 2.
Progression at 100m, 200m: 1996- 10.62, 21.57; 1997- 10.51w, 20.83; 1998- 10.34/10.15w, 20.44A/ 20.12w; 1999- 10.41, 20.39; 2000- 10.16, 20.09; 2001- 10.09, 20.17; 2002- 9.94, 19.85A/20.29; 2003- 10.07, 20.02. pb 60m 6.47i '04.
US indoor record 20.26 to win NCAA indoor 200m 2000. Disqualified in 2003 WI semis. Calls himself 'The Cheetah Man' after racing against a zebra and a cheetah on Fox TV in 2003.

Mark CREAR b. 2 Oct 1968 San Francisco 1.86m 79kg. Godwin. Sociology degree from University of Southern California.
At 110mh: OG: '96- 2, '00- 3; WCh: '93- sf, '97- 7, '99- qf. Won GP 110mh 1995, 1997, 1999; 3rd overall 1995, 1997; NCAA champion 1992, US 1994, 1999; GWG 1998.
Progression at 110mh: 1990- 13.65/13.51w, 1992- 13.33, 1993- 13.26/13.22w/12.9w, 1994- 13.07, 1995- 13.02, 1996- 13.05, 1997- 13.03, 1998- 13.00, 1999- 12.98, 2000- 13.11/13.10w, 2001- 13.26, 2002- 13.36, 2003- 13.55/13.37w. pbs: 50mh 6.41Ai '95, 55mh 7.17i '00, 60mh 7.38i '98.
Ordained as a minister after finishing his Masters degree in theology. World's top high hurdler of 1995, but he went out in the semi-finals of the US Champs. Disqualified for two false starts in his quarter-final at the Worlds, but ranked no.1 in the world on his overall record in 1999. Formerly married to Keisha Marvin (2nd 1994 NCAA 400mh in pb 56.62).

Walter DAVIS b. 2 Jul 1979 LaFayette, Louisiana 1.88m 83kg. Studied sociology at Louisiana State University.
At TJ/(LJ): OG: '00- 11; WCh: '01- 5. '03- dnq 15 (7); WI: '03- 2; WCp: '02- 2. Won US 2002, NCAA 2001-02 (& LJ 2002).
Progression at LJ, TJ: 1997- 15.67, 1998- 15.29w, 1999- 7.88i/7.70, 16.38/16.47w; 2000- 8.16, 17.07/ 17.08w, 2001- 8.14i/8.13/8.19w, 17.22; 2002- 8.15i/ 8.12/8.15w, 17.59; 2003- 8.24, 17.55. pb 200m 20.98 '96, 20.87w '95, 20.6w '94.
All-state basketball player in high school.

Kevin DILWORTH b. 14 Feb 1974 Jacksonville, Texas 1.80m 76kg. Adidas, Was at Abilene Christian University.
At LJ: WCh: '97- 8, '99- 8; WI: '01- 6; PAm: '03- 6; WUG: '97- 5. US champion 1999.
Progression at LJ: 1992- 7.52/7.73w, 1993- 7.66/ 7.87w, 1994- 7.73; 1995- 7.83/7.90w; 1996- 8.47, 1997- 8.29, 1998- 8.30, 1999- 8.09/8.12w, 2000- 8.28, 2001- 8.30, 2002- 8.20i/8.13/8.51w, 2003- 8.09/8.12w. pbs:100m 10.51 '02, 200m 20.98 '96, 20.87w '95, 20.6w '94.

Jon DRUMMOND b. 9 Sep 1968 Philadelphia 1.75m 75kg. Nike/HSI. Was at Texas Christian University.
At 200m/4x100mR (100m): OG: '96- 2R (sf), '00- 1R (5); WCh: '93- 1R, '95- hR, '97- 7, '99- 1R. '01- 1R (res), '03- dq qf; WUG: '91- 1/1R; WCp: '02- 4/1R. Won US 200m 1997. 3rd GP 100m 1994, 2002; 200m 1997. At 60m: WI: '93- 4.
World record 4x100m relay 1993.
Progression at 100m, 200m: 1986- 10.5, 21.24; 1987- 10.28/10.23w, 20.64; 1988- 10.25/10.0w, 20.79i; 1989- 10.21, 20.82; 1990- 10.10, 1991- 10.19/10.03w, 20.58; 1992- 10.12, 20.37; 1993- 10.03/9.92w, 21.05i; 1994- 9.99; 1995- 10.10/10.08w, 20.49/20.10w; 1996- 9.98, 20.05; 1997- 9.92, 20.03; 1998- 9.94, 20.15; 1999- 10.04, 20.29/20.24w; 2000- 9.96, 20.17; 2001- 10.09/10.04w, 20.44; 2002- 9.97, 2003- 10.07A/10.10. pbs: 50m 5.63i '99, 55m 6.11i '03, 60m 6.46i '98, 100y 9.33 '94, 300y 29.75i '88, 400m 45.55 '00.
Self-styled 'Crown Prince of Track'. Sings with the gospel group 'Kirk Franklin & The Family'; their first album reached No.1 on the *Billboard* gospel chart in 1993. Having won three relay gold medals, made his sixth World Champs team in 2003, but disgraced himself with long protest after dq for false start in 100m qf.

Justin GATLIN b. 10 Feb 1982 Brooklyn, NY 1.85m 79kg. Nike. Was at University of Tennessee.
At 60m: WI: '03- 1. Won NCAA 100m & 200m 2001-02 (& indoor 60m/200m 2002).
Progression at 100m, 200m: 2000- 10.36, 2001- 10.08, 20.29/19.86w; 2002- under international suspension: 10.05/10.00w, 19.86; 2003- 9.97, 20.04. pbs: 60m 6.45i '03, 55mh 7.39i '02, 60mh 7.86i '01, 110mh 13.41dq '02, LJ 7.21 '00.
Top hurdler in high school (110mh 13.66 and 300mh 36.74 on junior hurdles), now concentrating on sprints. He retained his NCAA sprint titles while ineligible for international competition in 2002 after failing a drugs test in 2001 (when he won 100m, 200m and 110mh at the US Junior Championships). Reinstated by IAAF in July 2002.

John GODINA b. 31 May 1972 Fort Sill, Oklahoma 1.93m 129kg. Adidas. Studied biology at UCLA.
At SP/(DT): OG: '96- 2/dnq 14, '00- 3/dnq 17; WCh: '95- 1/10, '97- 1/5, '99- 7/dnq 16, '01- 1/dnq 21, '03- 9; WI: '97-9-01-03: 3/2/1/2; WCp: '98- 1/4. Won GP SP 1996 (3rd 2000), 3rd DT 1997. Won US SP 1998-9, 2001; DT 1997-8, NCAA SP 1995, DT 1994-5, PAm-J SP & DT 1991; GWG SP 1998.
Progression at SP, DT: 1990- 53.58, 1991- 17.75, 58.60; 1992- 19.68, 61.52; 1993- 20.03, 60.48; 1994- 20.03, 62.24; 1995- 22.00, 64.92; 1996- 21.25, 64.58; 1997- 21.75, 67.40; 1998- 21.78, 69.91; 1999- 22.02, 69.05; 2000- 21.51, 68.32; 2001- 21.95, 67.66; 2002- 21.91, 64.71; 2003- 21.23i/21.08, 64.03/66.38dh.
Four world shot gold medals. Undefeated in 24 shot competitions July 1997 to February 1999. 4th in the US trials shot in 1997, but gained World place with a 'wild card' entry for a defending champion; came second but took gold after the disqualification of Aleksandr Bagach. He achieved the best ever one day SP-DT double with 21.58 and 69.91 at Salinas in 1998. He stepped into the US Olympic shot team after the withdrawal of CJ Hunter in 2000 and took bronze.

Maurice GREENE b. 23 Jul 1974 Kansas City, Kansas 1.76m 80kg. Adidas/HSI.
At 100m(/200m)/4x100mR: OG: '00- 1/1R; WCh: '95- qf, '97- 1, '99- 1/1/1R, '01- 1, '03- sf; Won US 100m 1997, 2000, 2002; 200m 1999; GWG 100m 1998. 2nd GP 200m 1999. At 60m: WI: '95- 4, '99- 1.
World 100m record 1999; three world indoor 60m records 1998-2001.
Progression at 100m, 200m: 1993- 10.43, 21.00; 1995- 10.19/9.88w, 1996- 10.08, 1997- 9.86, 19.86; 1998- 9.90/9.79w, 20.03/19.88w; 1999- 9.79, 19.90; 2000- 9.86, 20.02/19.93w, 2001- 9.82, 2002- 9.89/9.88w, 2003- 9.94, 20.16. pbs: 50m 5.55+ '97, 55m 6.15i '96, 60m 6.39i/6.39+ '98.
Moved from Kansas to train with John Smith in Los Angeles in September 1996. In 1997 ran 100m in 9.90 to win US Champs and twice in Athens before 9.86 to win World 100m title. Took 0.05 off world record for 100m at Athens in June 1999, and confirmed his place as world's fastest man with World Champs treble (the first man to win 100m and 200m at World Champs). Despite hobbling at the finish, he ran 9.82 to win the 2001 world title at 100m with a wind of –0.2. His elder brother Ernest was a former US junior college champion at 200m (20.60 '92).

Breaux GREER b. 19 Oct 1976 Houston 1.88m 102kg. Adidas. Was at Northeast Louisiana University.
At JT: OG: '00- 12; WCh: '01- 4, '03- dnq 14; PAm: '03- 3. US champion 2000-03.
Progression at JT: 1995- 70.92, 1996- 79.98, 1997- 78.12, 1998- 79.68, 2000- 82.63, 2001- 87.00, 2002- 81.78, 2003- 82.10.
Set five pbs in 2001, including to win US title (85.23) and in first round of World final.

Mickey GRIMES b. 10 Oct 1976 1.85m 84kg. Nike. Was at Abilene Christian University.
At 100m/4x100mR: WCh: '01- 1R; PAm: '03- dq (1).At 60m: WI: '04- 4.
Progression at 100m: 1996- 10.46, 1998- 10.32, 1999- 10.30/10.19A/10.18Aw, 2000- 10.20/10.17w, 2001- 10.18, 2002- 10.18, 2003- 9.99.pbs: 60m 6.55 '04, 200m 20.48 '03. 400mh 52.79 '96, LJ 7.23 '96.
Lost Pan-American 100m gold in 2003 with a public warning disqualification for positive test for the stimulant ephedrine. Won California State HS 300mh title in 1995. Played wide receiver and later defensive back at American Football at Riverside College and ACU.

Rickey HARRIS b. 29 Sep 1981 Virginia 1.76m 73kg. Student at University of Florida.
At 400mh: Won PAm-J 1999, NCAA 2002.
Progression at 400m, 400mh: 1998- 49.15i, 51.62; 1999- 50.28, 2000- 46.21, 50.07; 2001- 45.22, 49.65; 2002- 44.84, 48.16; 2003- 45.42, 48.83. pb 110mh 14.01 '03, 13.85w '01.

Alvin HARRISON b. 20 Jan 1974 Orlando, Florida 1.88m 80kg. Nike.
At 400m/4x400mR: OG: '96- 4/1R, '00- 2/1R; PAm: '99- 3R; PAm-J: '93- 3/1R; WCp: '02- 5. Won US 400m 2002.
Progression at 400m: 1993- 46.25, 1996- 44.09, 1997- 45.37, 1998- 44.19, 1999- 45.17, 2000- 44.18, 2002- 44.48, 2003- 46.07. pbs: 100m 10.52 '99, 200m 20.41 '96, 300m 32.00 '96.
The twins Alvin and Calvin, who both ran at the Pam Juniors in 1993, were homeless in 1995 and sleeping in an old Ford Mustang. Returning to the sport in 1996 Alvin made a huge breakthrough when he ran sub-45 seconds for the first time at the 1996 US Trials – running successively 44.93, 44.66, 44.43 and 44.09 in the four rounds.

Calvin HARRISON b. 20 Jan 1974 Orlando, Florida 1.86m 75kg. Nike.
At 400m/4x400mR: OG: '00- 1R; WCh: '03- 6/1R.

Progression at 400m: 1993- 45.25/45.07dq, 1994- 46.26, 1996- 44.70, 1997- 45.59, 1998- 44.68A/45.13, 2000- 44.64, 2001- 44.97, 2002- 44.93A/45.55, 2003- 44.62. pb 200m 20.57 '93, 300m 32.74 '02.
Tested positive for pseudoephedrine at 1993 US Junior Championships in 45.07 and this cost hjim two golds at the subsequent Pan-Am Juniors. Dropped out of school, Hartnell Junior College, Salinas, in 1994 and returned to Florida. Came back to California and to the sport in 1996.

Jeff HARTWIG b. 25 Sep 1967 St Louis 1.90m 82kg. Nike. Was at Arkansas State University.
At PV: OG: '96- 11=; WCh: '99- dnq 14=; WI: '99- 2; WCp: '98- 3, '02- 2. Won GWG 1998, US 1998-9, 2002-03; GP 2002 (2nd 1999).
Four US pole vault records 1998-2000.
Progression at PV: 1983- 3.35, 1984- 3.81, 1985- 4.42, 1986- 4.57, 1987- 4.90, 1988- 5.10, 1989- 5.34, 1990- 5.40i/5.35, 1991- 5.35, 1992- 5.60i/5.50, 1993- 5.35, 1994- 5.63, 1995- 5.72, 1996- 5.80, 1997- 5.85, 1998- 6.01, 1999- 6.02, 2000- 6.03, 2001- 5.90, 2002- 6.02i/5.90, 2003- 5.80i/5.70, 2004- 5.88i.
The first 6m-vaulter from the USA, Hartwig is also a snake rancher, with a herd of pythons and boa constrictors. Clearly headed world rankings in 2000, but failed to clear his opening height in the qualifying round of the US Trials, when he had problems with his eyes.

Matt HEMINGWAY b. 24 Oct 1972 San Pedro, California 2.01m 81kg. US West. Was at University of Arkansas. Sales manager.
At HJ: WCh: '03- 12; won NCAA 1996.
Progression at HJ: 1990- 2.08, 1991- 2.23, 1992- 2.10, 1993- 2.25, 1994- 2.17, 1995- 2.25i/2.21, 1996- 2.30, 1997- 2.21i/2.20, 2000- 2.38i/2.30, 2002- 2.32, 2003- 2.34.
Having been out for the sport for two and a half years 'tired of everything about track', but keeping fit playing basketball, he returned in sensational style in the 2000 indoor season, jumping a pb 2.32 in January, 2.36 in February and winning the US indoor title with 2.38 in March. He had been 2nd in the NCAA and 4th in the US Trials in 1996. He is a distant relative of author Ernest Hemingway.

Rees HOFFA b. 8 Oct 1977 Evans, Georgia 1.83m 115kg. New York AC. Was at University of Georgia.
At SP: WCh: '03- dnq; PAm: '03- 1; WI: '04- 2; WUG: '01- 9.
Progression at SP: 1998- 19.08, 1999- 19.35, 2000- 19.79, 2001- 20.22, 2002- 20.47, 2003- 20.95, 2004- 21.07i. pbs: DT 60.05 '02, HT 58.58 '01.

Nick HYSONG b. 9 Dec 1971 Winslow, Arizona 1.83m 77kg. Nike. Marketing degree from Arizona State University.
At PV: OG: '00- 1; WCh: '99- 4=, '01- 3; WJ: '90- 6; WI: '95- 5=, '99- 8. Won NCAA 1994. 2nd GP 2000.
Progression at PV: 1989- 4.87, 1990- 5.30, 1991- 5.45, 1992- 5.52, 1993- 5.57i/5.50, 1994- 5.70, 1995- 5.85i/5.70, 1996- 5.71A, 1997- 5.67A, 1998- 5.70, 1999- 5.85i/5.80, 2000- 5.90, 2001- 5.85, 2002- 5.75, 2003- 5.78.

Bershawn JACKSON b. 8 May 1983 Miami 1.73m 69kg. Studying accountancy at St Augustine's University, Raleigh.
At 400mh: WCh: '03- h (dq); WJ: '02- 3/1R; 2nd US Champs 2003.
Progression at 400mh: 2000- 52.17, 2001- 50.86, 2002- 50.00, 2003- 48.23, 2004- 48.48. pbs: 200m 21.29 '03, 400m 46.25 '03.

Allen JOHNSON b. 1 Mar 1971 Washington DC 1.78m 70kg. Nike. Was at University of North Carolina.
At 110mh: OG: '96- 1, '00- 4; WCh: '95- 1, '97- 1 (gold 4x400mR), '99- sf, '01- 1, '03- 1; WCp: '94- 2, '98- 2R, '02- 2; 2nd GP 1995 & 2001. Won WAF 2003, GWG 2001, US 1996-7, 2000-03. At 60mh: WI: '95-03-04: 1/1/1.
US 110mh record 1996 and indoor 60mh 2004.
Progression at 110mh: 1990- 14.4, 1991- 14.11, 1992- 13.63, 1993- 13.47/13.34w, 1994- 13.25/13.23Aw, 1995- 12.98, 1996- 12.92, 1997- 12.93, 1998- 12.98, 1999- 13.01, 2000- 12.97, 2001- 13.04, 2002- 13.04, 2003- 12.97. pbs: 60m 6.62i '98, 100m 10.41/10.10w '99, 200m 20.26 '97, 400m 48.27 '96, 50mh 6.47i '95, 55mh 7.03i '94, 60mh 7.36i '04, 400mh 52.00 '91, HJ 2.11 '89, LJ 8.14i/7.91w '93, 7.85 '91; TJ 14.83 '89.
Having leapt into world class in 1994, on 8 Feb 1995 in Madrid he ended Colin Jackson's string of 44 sprint hurdles victories. He went on to win world titles indoors and out, adding Olympic gold in 1996, when he missed the world record by just 0.01 at the US Trials, and another world gold in 1997. Had to withdraw from the 1999 World semis through injury, but came back to take his third title in 2001. Won his third World Indoor 60mh title in 2004 in 7.36 to tie the US record and improve his pb of 7.38 '95.

Joshua J JOHNSON b. 10 May 1976 Dallas 1.91m 91kg. Pioneer TC.
At 200m/4x100mR: OG: '00- res (1)R; WCh: '03- 6/1R. Won WAF 200m 2003.
Progression at 100m, 200m: 2000- 10.24/10.19w, 20.60; 2001- 10.22/10.11w, 19.88; 2002- 9.95, 20.74; 2003- 10.05, 20.05. pb 60m 6.55i '02.
Played basketball at Oklahoma Panhandle State University and after failing to make professional leagues joined IBM. Then trained with coach Nicholson Scott of the Pioneer Track Club in Arlington, Texas and in 2000 was 7th in US 100m and ran in heats of World Champs. Made a sensational improvement from 20.48 to 19.88 at Brussels in 2001 and ran brilliant last leg to bring US to gold in World 4x100m 2003. He tried out as a receiver with American Football team, the Oakland Raiders in 2002 but was let go at the final cut.

Lawrence JOHNSON b. 7 May 1974 Norfolk, Virginia 1.85m 86kg. Adidas. Was at University of Tennessee. Pianist and composer.
At PV: OG: '96- 8, '00- 2; WCh: '97- dnq; WI: '97- 2, '01- 1; WUG: '95- 2. US champion 1996-7, 2000-01; NCAA 1995-6, PAm-J 1993.
US pole vault record 1996.
Progression at PV: 1991- 4.87, 1992- 5.33, 1993- 5.71, 1994- 5.83i/5.80, 1995- 5.70, 1996- 5.98, 1997- 5.90, 1998- 5.80, 1999- 5.85, 2000- 5.90, 2001- 5.96i/ 5.90, 2002- 5.80i/5.70, 2003- 5.41. pbs: 400m 49.55 '93, 110mh 14.60 '93, HJ 1.99 '93, Dec 7576 '93.
Broke an ankle in a motorcycle accident in 1999. Had to withdraw from 2001 Worlds team due to tress fracture of the right fibula.

Meb(rahtom) **KEFLEZIGHI** b. 5 May 1975 Asmara, Eritrea 1.70m 58kg. Nike. Was at UCLA.
At 10000m: OG: '00- 12; WCh: '01- 23, '03- 16; PAm: '99- 5. At 5000m: WCp: '02- 4. World CC: '01-02-03: 13/14/11. Won US 10000m 2000, 2002; CC 2001-02; NCAA 5000m, 10000m & CC 1997.
US 10000m record 2001.
Progress at 10000m: 1995- 30:41.24, 1996- 29:55.75, 1997- 28:26.55, 1998- 28:16.79, 1999- 28:29.27, 2000- 27:53.63, 2001- 27:13.98, 2002- 27:20.15, 2003- 27:57.59. pbs: 1500m 3:42.29 '98, 1M 4:02.24i/ 4:02.86 '98, 3000m 7:48.81 '03, 2M 8:27.2 '01, 5000m 13:11.77 '00, Road: 15km 42:48 '02, Mar 2: 10:03 '03.
Emigrated from war-torn Eritrea at age of 10, first to Italy and then to San Diego, USA in 1987. Became US citizen on 2 July 1998.

Khalid KHANNOUCHI b. 22 Dec 1971 Meknès, Morocco 1.65m 57kg. New Balance.
At Mar: WCh: '01- dnf. At 5000m: WUG: '93- 1. World best for the marathon 1999 and 2002. World best road 20km 1998 (57:37). Moroccan records HMar and Mar 1997, US marathon records 2000 and 2002.
Progression at Mar: 1997- 2:07:10, 1998- 2:07:19, 1999- 2:05:42, 2000- 2:07:01, 2002- 2:05:38. pbs: 3000m 8:01.89i '96, 5000m 13:41.6 '95, 10000m 29:00.8 sh '89; Rd: 5km 13:24 '97, 10km 27:47 '98, 15km 42:57 '98, HMar 60:27 '97.
Showed great form on the roads in 1997 before running the fastest ever debut marathon to win at Chicago, just 20 seconds off the world record. A year later he was 2nd in Chicago and in 1999 returned to earn $165,000 for his win in a new world best time of 2:05:42. After 3rd in London, won again in Chicago 2000. In 2002 he improved his world record with 2:05:38 at London and had his fourth Chicago win in 2:05:56 for five wins in eight marathons. Won 1993 WUG 5000m in Buffalo, New York, USA. Feeling that he was not appreciated in his home country, he returned to Buffalo a few months later and eventually settled in Brooklyn, becoming a US citizen in 2000. He is coached and managed by his wife Sandra Natal, who ran for the Dominican Republic in the 1991 World marathon.

David KRUMMENACKER b. 24 May 1975 El Paso 1.90m 79kg. Adidas. Was at Georgia Tech University.
At 800m: WCh: '01/03- sf; WJ: '94- 7; WI: '03- 1; WCp: '02- 3. At 1500m: WCh: '99- sf. Won US 800m 2001-03.
Progression at 800m, 1500m: 1992- 1:52.02, 3:58.46; 1993- 1:51.73, 1994- 1:47.68, 1996- 1:46.73, 3:50.56; 1997- 1:46.30, 3:39.99; 1998- 1:45.99, 3:37.27; 1999- 1:44.57, 3:36.20; 2000- 1:46.62, 3:36.15; 2001- 1:45.44, 2002- 1:43.92, 3:31.93; 2003- 1:44.30, 3:35.15. pbs: 1000m 2:15.97 '02, 1M 3:54.23 '98.
Has a German mother and Nigerian father.

Tim MACK b. 15 Sep 1972 Cleveland 1.88m 78kg. Nike. Graduate of University of Tennessee.
At PV: WCh: '01- 9, '03- 6=. Won GWG 2001.
Progression at PV: 1993- 5.31, 1994- 5.52, 1995- 5.60, 1996- 5.65, 1998- 5.70, 1999- 5.70i/5.43, 2000- 5.81, 2001- 5.81, 2002- 5.85i/5.84, 2003- 5.76.

Derek MILES b. 28 Sep 1972 Sacramento 1.91m 82kg. Bell Athletics. History graduate of University of South Dakota. Academic advisor at Arkansas State University.
At PV: WCh: '03- 6=, WI: '03- 5.
Progression at PV: 1997- 5.50, 1998- 5.35, 1999- 5.40Ai/5.35, 2000- 5.65, 2001- 5.82, 2002- 5.82i/ 5.74, 2003- 5.81.

Coby MILLER b. 19 Oct 1976 Ackermann, Miss. 1.68m 68kg. Nike. Studied criminal justice at Auburn University.
At 200m/4x100m: OG: '00- 7; WUG: '99- 1/1R; WCp: '02- 1R.
Progression at 100m, 200m: 1997- 10.24/10.19w, 20.73; 1998- 10.32/10.23w, 20.64; 1999- 10.03, 20.04; 2000- 9.98/9.88w, 19.96; 2001- 20.31i, 2002- 9.98, 20.07; 2003- 10.07A/10.10, 20.04. pbs: 50m 5.67i '03, 55m 6.11i '99, 60m 6.49i '03.
All-American at both football and track in high school and played football for a year in junior college before concentrating on sprinting. Broke his leg at the 2001 US Indoor Championships.

Tim MONTGOMERY b. 28 Jan 1975 Gaffney, SC 1.78m 73kg. Nike. Was at Norfolk State University.
At 100m/4x100m: OG: '96- res (2)R, '00- res (1)R; WCh: '97- 3, '99- 6/1R, '01- 2/1R, '03- 5; US champion 2001, Won GP (and overall) 2002 (2nd 2000). At 60m: WI: '01- 2.
World 100m record 2002.
Progression at 100m: 1992- 10.45w, 1993- 10.61/ 10.3, 1994- 10.11/9.96 irreg, 1995- 10.27/9.95w, 1996- 10.08, 1997- 9.92, 1998- 10.00/9.99w, 1999- 10.01/10.00w, 2000- 10.01/9.96w, 2001- 9.84, 2002- 9.78, 2003- 10.04. pbs: 50m 5.57+ '97, 60m 6.43+ '97, 200m 20.52 '99, 20.44w '97.
Ran 100m in 9.96 to win the Junior Colleges title in 1994; but the wind gauge (+1.7) illegally placed on the outside of the track prevented ratification as world junior record; the track

was also reported to have measured 99.96m. Ran in heat and semi on US 4x100m team at 1996 Olympics and in heat in 2000.

Adam NELSON b. 7 Jul 1975 Atlanta 1.81m 115kg. Nike. Was at Dartmouth University. Training as a financial consultant.
At SP: OG: '00- 2; WCh: '01- 2, '03- 2; WI: '01- 2; WJ: '94- 1; WUG: '99- 2; WCp: '02- 1. GP 2002 (2nd 2000 and 3rd overall). Won PAm-J 1993, GWG 2001, NCAA 1997, US 2000, 2002.
Progression at SP: 1993- 16.56, 1994- 18.34, 1995- 18.27, 1996- 19.14, 1997- 19.62, 1998- 20.61, 1999- 20.64, 2000- 22.12, 2001- 21.53, 2002- 22.51, 2003- 21.29. pb DT 56.18 '96.
Had a great season in 2000, when he improved his best from 20.64 to 21.70 and then the wortd's longest throw for four years, 22.12 (to take the US title) in July. Further improvement as world number one in 2002. Small for a shot putter, but very fast and dynamic in the circle. Played American Football at high school and college.

Jamie NIETO b. 2 Nov 1976 Seattle 1.93m 79kg. HPTC. Business administration graduate of Eastern Michigan University
At HJ: WCh: '03- 7; PAm: '03- 2; WI: '03- 9; US champion 2003.
Progression at HJ: 1994- 1.93, 1995- 2.06, 1996- 2.14, 1997- 2.15, 1998- 2,25, 1999- 2.30, 2000- 2.23, 2001- 2.27, 2002- 2.30, 2003- 2.31, 2004- 2.32i.

Tom PAPPAS b. 6 Sep 1976 Azalea, Oregon 1.93m 93kg. Nike. Was at University of Tennessee.
At Dec: OG: '00- 5; WCh: '99- dnf, '03- 1. Won PAm-J 1995, NCAA 1999, US 2000, 2002-03. At Hep: WI: '03- 1.
Progression at Dec: 1995- 7198, 1996- 7499, 1997- 7677, 1999- 8463, 2000- 8467, 2001- 8323, 2002- 8583, 2003- 8784. pbs: 60m 6.89i '03, 100m 10.65 '03, 400m 47.58 '03, 1000m 2:49.32i '04, 1500m 4:35.14 '95, 55mh 7.27i '03, 60mh 7.80i '03, 110mh 13.93 '02, HJ 2.21 '00, PV 5.20 '02, LJ 7.96 '03, SP 16.48 '03, DT 52.18 '03, JT 66.56 '00, Hep 6361i '03.
Won Talence decathlon 2002 and IAAF Combined Events Challenge in 2003. Set four pbs in World Indoor heptathlon win 2003. Grandfather was a professional wrestler, father (Nick) set a world motor speed record. Younger brother Billy (b. 22 Feb 1979) has decathlon best of 7745 '03.

Miguel PATE b. 13 Jun 1979 St Francisville, Louisiana 1.88m 84kg. Nike. Studying criminal justice at University of Alabama.
At LJ: WCh: '01- 4; WI: '03- 3; WUG: '01- 1. Won US 2001, NCAA 2000-01.
Progression at LJ: 1997- 7.28, 1998- 7.68/7.73w, 1999- 7.63, 2000- 8.26, 2001- 8.20/8.48w, 2002- 8.59i/8.45, 2003- 8.46A/8.27. pbs: 100m 10.51 '03, 200m 21.48i '03, HJ 2.18i '00, 2.13 '97; TJ 16.48 '01.
2003 season cut short by ruptured ligament in left knee in May.

Darvis PATTON b. 4 Oct 1977 Dallas 1.83m 75kg. adidas. Was at Texas Christian University.
At 200m/4x100m: WCh: '03- 2/1R. Won US 200m 2003.
Progression at 100m, 200m: 1998- 10.3, 20.49w; 2000- 10.22w/10.09w, 20.29; 2001- 10.16/10.14w, 20.31; 2002- 10.14, 20.12; 2003- 10.00/9.97w, 20.03. pbs: 60m 6.58i '03, LJ 8.12 '01, TJ 16.17i '98.
Versatile performer came into his own at 200m in 2002, when he was 2nd in the US Champs indoors and out. Turned to athletics after dislocating his hip playing American football as a teenager. Improved to 9.89w in March 2004.

Chris PHILLIPS b. 24 Jul 1972 Crosset, Arizona 1.83m 77kg. Was at University of Arkansas, now an assistant coach there.
At 110mh: WCh: '03- 5. Won PAm-J 1991.
Progression at 110mh: 1991- 13.81/13.79w, 1992- 13.94, 1993- 13.58, 1994- 13.61, 1998- 13.88, 1999- 13.32A/13.43, 2000- 13.27, 2001- 13.32, 2002- 13.53, 2003- 13.26. pbs: 50mh 6.51i '99, 55mh 7.08Ai '98, 60mh 7.44i '03, 400mh 50.82 '95.

Dwight PHILLIPS b. 1 Oct 1977 Decatur, Georgia 1.81m 82kg. Nike. Was at University of Kentucky, then Arizona State University.
At LJ: OG: '00- 8; WCh: '01- 8, '03- 1; WI: '03- 1; PAm: '99- 7. Won WAF 2003, US 2003.
Progression at LJ: 1999- 8.18, 2000- 8.21/8.30w, 2001- 8.13/8.23w, 2002- 8.38, 2003- 8.44. pbs: 60m 6.59i '03, 100m 10.16 '02, 10.11w '00, 200m 20.68 '02, 400m 46.80 '97, TJ 16.41 '99.

Mitch POTTER b. 16 Sep 1980 1.88m 80kg. Student at University of Minnesota.
At 400m/4x400mR: WCh: 03- res (1)R; PAm: '03- 1/2R.
Progress at 400m: 2001- 45.40, 2002- 45.96i/46.38, 2003- 44.58. pbs: 60m 6.96i '01, 200m 20.96 '03.

Duane ROSS b. 5 Dec 1972 Shelby, North Carolina 1.83m 78kg. GWE. Financial adviser. Graduate of Clemson University.
At 110mh: WCh: '99- 3; Won NCAA 1995. At 60mh: WI: '97- 4, '99- 4.
Progression at 110mh: 1992- 13.97/13.61w, 1993- 13.74, 1994- 13.48, 1995- 13.32, 1996- 13.45, 1997- 13.50, 1998- 13.24, 1999- 13.12, 2000- 13.53, 2001- 13.54, 2002- 13.20, 2003- 13.17. pbs: 200m 21.35w '95, 50mh 6.36i '99, 55mh 7.12i '93, 60mh 7.43i '99.
Only 4th at US Trials, but top US 110m hurdler at 1999 Worlds. Injured at 2004 World Indoors.

Tim RUSAN b. 25 Jun 1977 St Louis, Missouri 1.90m 84kg. Nike. Business degree from St. Augustine's College.
At WI: '03- 5.
Progression at TJ: 1995- 14.93, 1996- 16.14, 1997- 16.29i, 2000- 16.52, 2001- 16.56/16.74w, 2002- 17.34, 2003- 17.45i/17.24. pb LJ 7.69 '01.
Was star basketball player in high school.

Adam SETLIFF b. 15 Dec 1969 El Dorado, Arizona 1.93m 125kg. Nike. Was at University of Washington.

At DT: OG: '96- 12, '00- 5; WCh: '97- 7, '01- 5; WCp: '02- 6. 2nd GP 1997. US champion 2000-02.
Progression at DT: 1990- 55.46, 1991- 59.40, 1992- 61.54, 1993- 64.08, 1994- 62.08, 1995- 64.96, 1996- 66.86, 1997- 66.14, 1998- 66.43/68.45dh, 2000- 66.86/68.51dh, 2001- 68.94/69.44dh, 2002- 63.74, 2003- 62.92.
Portrayed Mac Wilkins in Steve Prefontaine movie 1998. Missed 1999 season due to a hernia.

Adam STEELE b. 8 Oct 1980 1.88m 79kg. Student at University of Minnesota.
At 400m/4x400mR: WCh: '03- res G R; PAm: '03- 4/1R. NCAA champion 2003.
Progression at 400m: 2001- 46.93, 2002- 46.15, 2003- 44.57. pbs: 200m 21.12 '03 '02, 600m 1:18.86i '01, 800m 1:56.25 '01.

Toby STEVENSON b. 19 Nov 1976 Odessa, Texas 1.86m 79kg. ZMA. Economics graduate of Stanford University.
At PV: PAm: '03- 1, won NCAA 1998.
Progression at PV: 1994- 4.87, 1995- 5.18, 1997- 5.40i/5.37, 1998- 5.55, 1999- 5.55, 2000- 5.73A, 2001- 5.40, 2002- 5.74, 2003- 5.75, 2004- 5.81i.

Savanté STRINGFELLOW b. 6 Nov 1978 Jackson, Miss. 1.91m 84kg. Nike. Studied sociology at University of Mississippi.
At LJ: OG: '00- dnq 22; WCh: '99- dnq 39, '01- 2, '03- dnq 19; PAm: '99- 8; WI: '04- 1WCp: '02- 1. 2nd GP 2001. Won US 2001-02, NCAA 2000-01.
Progression at LJ: 1998- 7.32, 1999- 8.12, 2000- 8.30, 2001- 8.38/8.47w, 2002- 8.52, 2003- 8.46, 2004- 8.41i. pbs: 100m 10.53 '03, 10.43w '01; 200m 20.66 '01, HJ 2.14 '99, 2.18i '99?.

Angelo TAYLOR b. 29 Dec 1978 Albany, Georgia 1.88m 77kg. Nike. Was at Georgia Tech University, plans to enrol at Morris Brown College.
At 400mh/4x400mR: OG: '00- 1/res (1)R; WCh: '99- h/1R, '01- sf/1R; WJ: '96- 3; won GP 2000 (and overall), PAm-J 1997, NCAA 1998, US 1999-2001, US indoor 400m 1999
Progression at 400m, 400mh: 1995- -, 52.76, 1996- 46.7, 50.18; 1997- 46.19i/46.81, 48.72; 1998- 45.14, 47.90; 1999- 45.50i, 48.15; 2000- 44.89, 47.50; 2001- 44.68, 47.95; 2002- 44.85, 48.87; 2003- 46.32, 48.94. pbs: 200m 20.67 '97, 300m 32.67 '02, TJ 14.76 '96.
Brilliant year in 1998, with fastest ever time by a 19 year-old and losing just twice, both to Bryan Bronson, at 400mh. Went out in his heat (misjudging the finish) when favourite for the 400mh at 1999 Worlds, but made amends with relay gold, and, after winning Olympic gold in 2000, stumbled off the last hurdle in 2001 World 400mh semi.

Dan TAYLOR b. 12 May 1982 1.98m 145kg. Student at Ohio State University.
At SP: PAm: '03- 4. Won NCAA indoor 2004.
Progression at SP: 2001- 18.31, 2002- 20.01i/19.15, 2003- 21.33i/20.44, 2004- 20.45i. pbs: DT 59.00 '03, HT 67.79 '04, Wt 24.01i '04.

Paul TEREK b. 20 Oct 1979 1.86m 83kg. Was at Michigan State University.
At Dec: WCh: '03- 12. Won US indoor hepathlon 2003-04.
Progression at Dec: 1998- 7206, 1999-7225, 2001- 7695, 2002- 8041, 2003- 8275. pbs: 60m 7.04i '04, 100m 10.83 '02, 400m 48.71 '02, 1000m 2:42.97i '04, 1500m 4:24.92 '01, 60mh 8.48i '04, 110mh 15.35 '02, 15.26w '02; HJ 2.08 '03, PV 5.70i '03, 5.50 '02; LJ 7.14/7.38w '03, SP 15.51 '03, DT 46.19 '03, JT 61.14 '03, Hep 6040i '04.
Disqualified for pushing over hurdles in World Champs decathlon 2003; if his time had been allowed he would have scored 8253 for 4th.

Eric THOMAS b. 1 Dec 1973 Carthage, Texas 1.90m 88kg. ZMA. Was at Abilene Christian University.
At 400mh: OG: '00- sf; WCh: '03- sf; PAm: '99- 2, '03- 2. US champion 2003.
Progression at 400mh: 1993- 49.83, 1994- 49.29, 1995- 49.14, 1996- 48.20, 1997- 48.57, 1998- 48.45, 1999- 48.40, 2000- 47.94, 2001- 48.53, 2002- 48.27, 2003- 48.46. pbs: 300m 33.28 '02, 400m 46.33 '97.

Terrrence TRAMMELL b. 23 Nov 1978 Atlanta 1.88m 84kg. Mizuno. Was at University of South Carolina.
At 110mh/4x100m: OG: '00- 2; WCh: '01- sf, '03- 2; WUG: '99- 1/1R; Won NCAA 1999-2000.
At 60mh: WI: '01- 1.
Progression at 110mh: 1997- 13.87, 1998- 13.32, 1999- 13.28, 2000- 13.16, 2001- 13.23, 2002- 13.17, 2003- 13.17. pbs: 55m 6.12i '99, 60m 6.45Ai '00, 6.46i '03; 100m 10.04 '00, 200m 20.74 '98, 20.45w '99; 55mh 6.94i '99, 60mh 7.42i '03.
Injured in heats of World Indoor 60m 2003.

Larry WADE b. 22 Nov 1974 Giddings, Texas 1.87m 83kg. Nike. Was at Texas A&M University.
At 110mh: WCh: '03- 4; PAm: '03- 2. Won NCAA 1998, 3rd GP 1999.
Progression at 110mh: 1994- 14.06/13.74w, 1995- 13.41, 1997- 13.38, 1998- 13.37, 1999- 13.01, 2000- 13.26, 2001- 13.12, 2002- 13.15, 2003- 13.23. pbs: 50mh 6.51i '99, 55mh 7.08Ai '98, 60mh 7.44i '03, 400mh 50.82 '95.
Moved from Elgin, Texas to Los Angeles in October 1998 to train with John Smith's group.

Dawane WALLACE b. 30 Dec 1976 1.90m 79kg. Nike. Was at University of Tennessee.
At 110mh: WCh: '01- 7; WUG: '99- 3.
Progression at 110mh: 1996- 14.04w, 1997- 13.88/13.73w, 1998- 13.79/13.65w, 1999- 13.57/13.34w, 2000- 13.22, 2001- 13.22, 2002- 13.22, 2003- 13.32. pbs: 50mh 6.50i '02, 55mh 7.13i '00, 60mh 7.58i '02, LJ 7.19 '95.

Tyree WASHINGTON b. 28 Aug 1976 Riverside, California 1.85m 84kg. Was at San Bernardino Valley CC.
At 400m/4x400mR: WCh: '97- 3/1R. '03- 2/1R; WI: '03- 1/1R. US champion 2003.
World record 4x400m 1998.

Progression at 200m, 400m: 1994- 47.49, 1995- 46.34, 1996- 20.88w, 46.00; 1997- 20.10, 44.38; 1998- 20.29, 44.29; 1999- 20.09, 45.50; 2000- 44.72, 2001- 44.28, 2003- 44.33. pbs: 500y 55.6i '98. LJ 7.39 '95.
Made substantial breakthrough in 1997. Started as sprinter and won 1994 California prep LJ title. Ran world's fastest time for 400m but suffered hamstring injury at US Championships in 2001. Great comeback after missing 2002 season.

Bernard WILLIAMS b. 19 Jan 1978 Baltimore 1.83m 81kg. Nike. Was at University of Florida, moving to UCLA.
At 100m/4x100mR: OG: '00- 1R; WCh: '01- 3/1R, '03- 6/1R; PAm: '99- 1/4R. Won NCAA 2000, USA 2003, WAF 2003. 2nd GP 200m 2001.
Progression at 100m, 200m: 1997- 10.45, 21.13; 1998- 10.03, 20.46w; 1999- 10.08, 20.69Ai/20.71; 2000- 9.99, 20.03; 2001- 9.94, 20.01; 2002- 9.99, 20.19; 2003- 10.04/10.0, 20.01. pbs: 55m 6.08Ai '98, 60m 6.56iA '99, 6.59i '01.
Performs as a stand-up comedian using the name "Hollywood Williams".

Joey WOODY b. 22 May 1973 Iowa City 1.88m 78kg. Adidas. Degree in public relations from Northern Iowa University, where he is now assistant coach.
At 400mh/4x400mR: WCh: '97- sf, '99- 6/res (1)R, '03- 2; WUG: '97- 5; WCp: '98- 5/1R. NCAA champion 1997. WIR 4x800m 2000.
Progression at 400mh: 1993- 50.76, 1994- 50.42, 1995- 49.97, 1996- 48.62, 1997- 48.18, 1998- 47.97, 1999- 48.22, 2000- 48.72, 2001- 49.03, 2002- 48.24, 2003- 48.18. pbs: 400m 46.04 '99, 800m 1:47.75i '96, 1:48.41 '94; 110mh 13.98/13.63w '97.

Jerome YOUNG b. 14 Aug 1976 Jamaica 1.81m 79kg. adidas. Was at Wallace State CC.
At 400m/4x400mR: OG: '00- res (1)R; WCh: '97- 5/1R, '99- 4, '01- sf/res (1)R, '03- 1/1R; WI: '01- 2R, '03- 1R; WCp: '98- 2/1R; PAm-J: '95- 2/1R (2 4x100R). US champion 1998-9, WAF 2003.
World record 4x400m 1998.
Progression at 400m: 1993- 47.25, 1994- 46.31, 1995- 45.01, 1996- 44.96, 1997- 44.50, 1998- 44.09, 1999- 44.24, 2000- 44.70, 2001- 45.32, 2002- 45.51, 2003- 44.50. pbs: 200m 20.41 '98, 20.31w '00; 300m 31.95+ '99.
Ex-Jamaican, raised in Hartford, Connecticut, became US citizen in May 1995. Revealed in 2003 to have tested postive in 1999, but passed by USATF to compete at 2000 Olympics; case being reviewed by IAAF.

Women

Amy ACUFF b. 14 Jul 1975 Port Arthur, Texas 1.88m 66kg. Asics. Biology graduate of UCLA. Part-time model, now studying at Academy of Oriental Medicine, Austin, Texas.
At HJ: OG: '96- dnq 24=, '00- dnq 31; WCh: '95- 8=, '97- dnq 14, '99- 9, '01- 10=, '03- 9=; WI: '01- 4, '03- 10; WJ: '92- 9, '94-3=; WUG: '97- 1. 3rd GP 2001. Won PAm-J 1993, NCAA 1995-6, US 1995, 1997, 2001, 2003.
Progression at HJ: 1988- 1.73, 1990- 1.83, 1991- 1.89, 1992- 1.90, 1993- 1.93, 1994- 1.89, 1995- 1.98, 1996- 1.94, 1997- 2.00, 1998- 1.94, 1999- 1.95, 2000- 1.91, 2001- 1.98, 2002- 1.95, 2003- 2.01.
Engaged to **Tye Harvey** (b. 25 Sep 1974, PV: 2 WI 03, 5.93i '01, 5.80 '00).

Jenny ADAMS b. 8 Jul 1978 Tomball, Texas 1.65m 55kg. Nike. Corporate communications graduate of University of Houston.
At 100mh: WCh: '01- 5 (nj LJ), '03- 6. Won US LJ 2001, NCAA LJ 2000.
Progression at 100mh: 1995- 14.45w, 1996- 13.98/13.93w, 1997- 13.47, 1998- 13.25/13.22w, 1999- 12.98/12.86w, 2000- 12.86, 2001- 12.63/12.61w, 2002- 12.80/12.71w, 2003- 12.67. pbs: 200m 23.51 '03, 60mh 7.95i '03, LJ 6.68i/6.75w '01, 6.64 '00.

Shelia BURRELL b. 15 Jan 1972 Albuquerque 1.73m 64kg. Nike. Was at UCLA.
At Hep: OG: '00- 26 (nh HJ); WCh: '99- 11, '01- 3; PAm: '99- 2. US champion 1999, 2002-03.
Progression at Hep: 1991- 4720, 1995- 5735, 1996- 5601, 1998- 6294w/6270, 1999- 6261, 2000- 6422, 2001- 6472, 2002- 6363, 2003- 6159. pbs: 100m 11.63 '95, 200m 22.92?w/23.25 '01, 400m 55.89i '03, 56.1 '90; 800m 2:10.29 '00, 60mh 8.26i '03, 100mh 13.05 '01, HJ 1.76 '99, LJ 6.57 '02, SP 15.02 '02, JT 50.31 '00.
Won Talence heptathlon 2001.

Michelle COLLINS b. 12 Feb 1971 Canal Zone, Panama 1.77m 62kg. Nike. Graduate of University of Houston.
At 200m: WI: '03- 1; WUG: '91- 3. At 400m/4x400mR: OG: '00- h; WCh: '93- sf/res (1)R, '97- res (2)R, '99- sf/2R, '01- sf; WI: '99- 3R; PAm: '99- 2/2R; WCp: '94- 5R, '02- 2R; WUG: '93- 1/1R; 3rd GP 2002.
Progression at 200m, 400m: 1987- 24.2w, 1989- 24.27w, 1990- 23.75/23.44w, 1991- 23.35/23.03w, 1992- 22.80, 1993- 22.88/22.87w, 51.59; 1994- 22.74, 51.19; 1995- 23.63A, 50.84A; 1996- 23.19i/23.32, 51.84; 1997- 23.08, 50.77; 1998- 51.17, 1999- 23.58, 50.67; 2000- 22.57, 50.11; 2001- 23.05, 50.66; 2002- 22.82w, 50.43; 2003- 22.18i. pbs: 60m 7.31i '03, 100m 11.19 '00.
Limited by a right hip stress fracture at the 2000 Olympics. Has concentrated on 400m in recent years, but ran 200m indoors in 2003, with her 22.18 triumph at the World Indoors making her third all-time indoors.

Lashinda DEMUS b. 10 Mar 1983 Palmdale, California 1.70m 62kg. Student at University of South Carolina.
At 400mh/4x400mR: WJ: '02- 1/1R. Won PAm-J 1999, NCAA 2002.
Two world junior records 400mh 2002.
Progression at 400mh: 1998- 64.61, 1999- 57.04, 2001- 55.76, 2002- 54.70, 2003- 55.65. pbs: 50m 6.64i '01, 60m 7.73i '01, 100m 11.5 '01, 200m 23.84w/24.0 '01, 400m 51.24 '02, 500y 1:05.8i '01,

800m 2:09.16 '04, 55mh 7.65i '04, 60mh 8.11i '04, 100mh 13.61/13.39w '01.
Her mother, Yolanda Rich, had a 400m best of 52.19 in 1980.

Gail DEVERS b. 19 Nov 1966 Seattle 1.60m 55kg. Nike International. Studied sociology at UCLA. Married to Ron Roberts 1988-92.
At 100mh/4x100mR (100m): OG: '88- sf; '92- 5 (1), '96-4/1R (1), '00- sf; WCh: '91- 2, '93- 1/2R (1), '95- 1, '97- 1R, '99- 1 (5), '01- 2, '03- sf (8); PAm: '87- (1)/1R; WCp: '02- 1/2R. At 60mh: WI: '03- 1, '04- 2. At 60m: WI: '93- 97-99-04: 1/1/2/1. Won NCAA 100m 1988, US 100m 1993-4, 100mh 1991-2, 1995-6, 1999-2001, 2003. Won GWG 100mh 2001; WAF 100mh 2003, GP 100mh 2000, 2002 (2nd 1992), 2nd 100m 1996. overall: 3rd 2000, 2nd 2002.
US records 100mh (6) 1988-2000, indoor 60m 1993, 60mh 2003.
Progression at 100m, 100mh: 1983- 11.69; 1984- 11.51/11.34w, 14.32; 1985- 11.19, 13.16/13.15w; 1986- 11.12/10.96w, 13.08; 1987- 10.98/10.85w, 13.28/13.1w; 1988- 10.97/10.86w, 12.61; 1991- 11.29, 12.48; 1992- 10.82, 12.55; 1993- 10.82, 12.46; 1994- 11.12/10.77w; 1995- 11.04/10.8w, 12.61; 1996- 10.83, 12.62; 1997- 10.88; 1999- 10.94, 12.37; 2000- 10.99, 12.33; 2001- 12.53, 2002- 11.45, 12.40/ 12.29w; 2003- 11.11, 12.45. pbs: 50m 6.00+ '99, 55m 6.74i '89, 60m 6.95i '93, 200m 22.71/22.55w '87, 400m 52.66 '87, 800m 2:11.07 '82, 55mh 7.58i '92, 60mh 7.74i '03, 400mh 59.26 '85, LJ 6.77 '88, TJ 12.97/13.31w '86.
The fastest ever woman sprinter-hurdler. A serious thyroid disorder (Graves's Disease) caused her to miss competition in 1989-90, but after being close to having to have a foot amputated she made an astonishingly speedy return to the top in 1991 to win the TAC 100mh, World silver and set a US record in Berlin. In 1992 she was a surprise winner of the Olympic 100m but tripped over the last hurdle when well clear of the field in the 100mh. Won 16 successive 100mh finals from June 1993 to Olympic 4th 1996, after she had become only the second woman to retain Olympic 100m title. She won the 1999 World outdoor title at 100mh with her first US record for six years. She was a clear favourite to take the 2000 Olympic gold at 100mh, but, feeling a hamstring problem, pulled up after four hurdles in her semi final. She was also unable to run in the sprint relay, but started, heavily strapped, in the GP Final 100mh a week later to ensure a huge payday with a share of the Golden League jackpot and third in the overall Grand Prix. Set US records for 60mh at 7.78 and 7.74 in 2003 before winning the World Indoor title. Her World Indoor win at 60m in 2004 was her 11th global gold medal.

Stacy DRAGILA b. 25 Mar 1971 Auburn, California 1.72m 62kg. née Mikaelson. Nike. Graduate of Idaho State University.
At PV: OG: '00- 1; WCh: '99- 1, '01- 1, '03- 4=; WI: '97-8-01-03-04: 1/8/4/nh/2. Won GWG 2001, GP 2001, US 1996-7, 1999-2001, 2003.
Seven world pole vault records 1999-2001, ten WIR 1997-2003. 17 US records 1996-2001 (and 24 indoors 1995-2004).
Progression at PV: 1995- 3.70, 1996- 4.20, 1997- 4.45, 1998- 4.48i/4.42A, 1999- 4.60, 2000- 4.70b/ 4.63. 2001- 4.81, 2002- 4.72, 2003- 4.78i/4.62, 2004- 4.81i. pbs: 55mh 8.30i '03, 100mh 13.88A '98, HJ 1.70 '97, LJ 5.89/6.07w '02; SP 10.80 '02, JT 44.28A '98, Hep 5488A '98.
Won first women's world vault titles both indoors (1997) and outdoors (1999), and both in world records; also won inaugural Olympic title.

Torri EDWARDS b. 31 Jan 1977 Fontana, Cal. 1.63m 52kg. Nike/HSI. Was at University of Southern California.
At 100m/(200m)/4x100mR: OG: '00- qf/sf/3R; WCh: '01- 1 resR, '03- 2/3/2R; PAm: '99- 2R; WUG: '99- 5/1R. At 60m: WI: '03- 3, '04- 4.
Progression at 100m, 200m: 1994- 24.52, 1995- 11.84w, 23.94/23.60w; 1996- 11.48, 23.60/23.1; 1997- 11.55A/11.35w, 23.43; 1998- 11.11/11.05w, 22.88/22.87w; 1999- 11.10/11.05w, 22.89/22.84w; 2000- 11.06/10.92w, 22.65; 2001- 11.11/11.09w, 2002- 11.11, 2003- 10.93, 22.28. pbs: 50m 6.31i '02, 60m 7.12i '04.

Dawn ELLERBE b. 3 Apr 1974 Brooklyn, New York 1.86m 111kg. New York AC. Graduate of University of South Carolina and masters degree in marketing from Wyoming.
At HT: OG: '00- 7; WCh: '99- 10, '01/03- dnq 13/30; PAm: '99- 1, '03- 5; WUG: '97- 6. US champion 1995-7, 1999-2001, NCAA 1996-7.
Nine US hammer records 1996-2001. Eight WIB 20lb weight from 21.86 '97 to 23.60 '00.
Progression at HT: 1994- 51.72, 1995- 58.00, 1996- 63.76, 1997- 64.22, 1998- 63.56, 1999- 70.16, 2000- 70.46, 2001- 70.62, 2002- 68.05, 2003- 68.33. pbs: SP 16.83i '98, 16.70 '97; DT 59.56 '00.

Suzy FAVOR HAMILTON b. 8 Aug 1968 Stevens Point, Wisconsin 1.60m 50kg. née Favor. Nike. Graphic design graduate of University of Wisconsin.
At 1500m (800m): OG: '92- h, '96- (h), '00- 12; WCh: '91- h, '95/97/99- sf; WUG: '89- 2; WJ: '86- 9; WCp: '98- 4. 2nd GP 2002. Won PAm-J 1984 & 1986. US champion 1990-1, 1998, and record nine NCAA titles: 800m 1990, 1500m 1987-90, indoor 1M 1987, 1989-90; 3000m 1990. World 4k CC: '02- 5. US 1000m record 1995.
Progression at 1500m: 1983- 4:55.23 1M, 1984- 4:19.46, 1985- 4:19.43, 1986- 4:18.62, 1987- 4:09.20, 1988- 4:13.91, 1989- 4:09.7, 1990- 4:08.00, 1991- 4:06.13, 1992- 4:04.53, 1993- 4:10.69, 1994- 4:04.57, 1995- 4:05.14, 1996- 4:08.18, 1997- 4:03.50, 1998- 3:58.43, 1999- 4:13.96i, 2000- 3:57.40, 2001- 4:00.38, 2002- 3:59.10, 2003- 4:01.69. pbs: 800m 1:58.10 '00, 1000m 2:33.93 '95, 1M 4:22.93 '98, 2000m 5:42.86 '94, 3000m 8:46.16 '00, 5000m 15:06.48 '00.
Won 21 individual and two relay Big 10

conference titles. Married Mark Hamilton, former baseball player, in 1991. Broke 4 minutes for 1500m for the first time on her 30th birthday.

Allyson FELIX b. 18 Nov 1985 Los Angeles 1.68m 57kg. addas. Student at University of Southern California.
At 200m: WCh: '03- qf; WJ: '02- 2; PAm: '03- 3. At 100m: WY: '01- 1 (1 Medley R).
Unratified (no doping test) world junior record 200m 2003.
Progression at 200m: 2000- 23.90, 2001- 23,31/ 23.27w, 2002- 22.83/22.69w, 2003- 22.11A/22.51. pbs: 60m 7.32i '04, 100m 11.29/11.12w '03; 400m 52.26 '03.
Older brother Wes Felix won World Junior bronze at 200m and gold at 4x100m in 2002.

Chryste GAINES b. 14 Sep 1970 Lawton, Oklahoma 1.70m 57kg. Nike. Psychology degree from Stanford University.
At 100m/4x100mR (200m): OG: '96- 1R, '00- sf/3R; WCh: '95- 1R, '97- 8/1R, '01- 5/1R, '03- 2R; PAm: '91- 2/3R, '95- 1/1R; WUG: '91- 1/1R, '93- 5/1R; PAm-J: '89- 2/1R; WCp: '94- 8, '98- 1R, '02- 2R; 2nd GP 2000. At 60m: WI: '95- 7, '01- 3. Won WAF 100m 2003, US 100m 2001, NCAA 100m 1992.
Progression at 100m, 200m: 1985- 24.11/23.7, 1986- 11.76/11.4w, 23.68y; 1987- 11.50, 23.56/23.3; 1988- 11.50, 23.30y; 1989- 11.44, 24.24; 1990- 11.31, 23.71; 1991- 11.27/11.09w, 23.21/22.96w; 1992- 11.16/10.90w, 23.00; 1993- 11.25, 22.81; 1994- 11.32/11.2/10.99w, 23.32; 1995- 11.02, 22.92; 1996- 10.96, 22.82; 1997- 11.06, 22.91/22.53w; 1998- 10.89/10.8A, 23.08; 1999- 11.56A, 2000- 10.97, 23.04/22.83w, 2001- 10.98/10.89w, 23.50/23.01w; 2002- 10.94, 2003- 10.86, 22.67. pbs: 50m 6.16i '99, 55m 6.68i '92, 60m 7.12i '01, LJ 5.84w '86.
1992 Olympic relay reserve, but did not compete. Won first US titles in 2001 – at 60m indoors and 100m outdoors. Formerly married to Darnell Miller.

Sandra GLOVER b. 30 Dec 1968 Palestine, Texas 1.72m 57kg. née Cummings. Nike. Teacher, graduate of University of Houston.
At 400mh: OG: '00- sf; WCh: '99- 5, '01- 8, '03- 2; WCp: '02- 2; Won WAF 2003, US 1999-2002. 3rd GP 1999, 2001.
Progression at 400mh: 1988- 61.08, 1989- 59.99, 1990- 57.68, 1991- 56.97, 1992- 55.77, 1993- 56.76, 1994- 56.66, 1995- 57.39, 1996- 56.31mx/56.92, 1997- 55.63, 1998- 55.11, 1999- 53.65, 2000- 53.33, 2001- 54.30, 2002- 54.40, 2003- 53.34. pbs: 200m 23.73 '00, 100mh 13.79/13.62w '91.
Made huge improvement in 1999 at the age of 30. Coached by her husband, Don Glover.

Joanna HAYES b. 23 Dec 1976 Williamsport, Pa. 1.65m 58kg. Was at UCLA.
At 400mh: WCh: '99- h, '03- sf; PAm: '99- 5, '03- 1; WUG: '99- 2; won NCAA 1999. At 100mh: PAmJ: '95- 1. At 60mh: '04- 4.
Progression at 100mh, 400mh: 1994- 14.02/13.80w, 59.12; 1995- 13.38/13.06w, 59.02; 1996- 13.15, 58.32; 1997- 13.04, 56.38; 1998- 12.93, 57.09; 1999- 12.89, 54.57; 2000- 12.67, 54.97; 2003- 12.83/12.65w, 54.66. pbs: 100m 11.66 '97.60mh 7.83i '04.
After just missing Olympics in 2000 (4th at 400mh and 5th at 100mh in US Trials), did not compete in 2001-02 while working at the Jackie Joyner-Kersee Youth Center in East St. Louis. Then returned to LA.

Monique HENNAGAN b. 26 May 1976 Columbia, SC 1.73m 57kg. Adidas. Degree in psychology from University of North Carolina.
At 400m/4x400mR: OG: '00- qf/1R; WCh: '01- sf; WI: '99- 3R, '01- 5/4R, '03- 5/3R; WJ: '92- sf/ 4R, '94- 2/1R; PAm-J: '93- 2/2R; WCp: '02- 2R. Won NCAA 800m 1996.
Progression at 400m: 1992- 53.58, 1993- 52.30, 1994- 52.19, 1995- 52.32, 1996- 51.44, 1997- 52.00, 1998- 51.11, 1999- 51.05, 2000- 50.82, 2001- 50.98, 2002- 51.04, 2003- 51.46. pbs: 60m 7.51i '03, 100m 11.86 '92, 11.3 '93, 11.69w '94; 200m 23.23 '01, 300m 36.52 '01, 800m 2:02.5 '96.

Aretha HILL b14 Aug 1976 Seattle 1.81m 98kg. Was at University of Washington.
At DT: OG: '96- dnq 34; WCh: '99- dnq 24, '03- dnq 20; PAm: '99- 1, '03- 1; WUG: '97- 6. US champion 2003.
Progression at DT: 1992- 43.38, 1993- 47.48, 1994- 50.52, 1995- 54.84, 1996- 60.50, 1997- 59.92, 1998- 65.62dh/63.68, 1999- 62.15, 2000- 62.91, 2001- 61.64, 2002- 65.21, 2003- 65.10/66.23dh. pb SP 15.91i/15.67 '98.
Withdrew due to a collapsed lung from 1999 WUG and Worlds after 2nd in US 200m.

LaTasha JENKINS b. 19 Dec 1977 Calumet Park, Illinois 1.70m 56kg. Nike. Was at Ball State University.
At 200m: WCh: '01- 4; WI: '01- 2; Won NCAA 1999. World record 4x200m 2000.
Progression at 100m, 200m: 1996- 11.79/11.70w, 24.00/23.63w; 1997- 11.93/11.47w, 23.13/ 23.09w; 1998- 11.62/11.24w, 22.93; 1999- 11.08, 22.29/22.22w; 2000- 11.14, 22.86/22.54w; 2001- 11.02, 22.39; 2002- 11.05, 22.59; 2003- 11.21A/ 11.27/11.04w, 22.31A/22.56. pbs: 55m 6.86i '98, 60m 7.35i '99, 300m 37.87i '01, 400m 52.95 '02.
Withdrew due to a collapsed lung from 1999 WUG and Worlds after 2nd in US 200m.

Marion JONES b. 12 Oct 1975 Los Angeles 1.78m 68kg. Nike. Studied journalism at University of North Carolina at Chapel Hill.
At 100m/4x100m (200m): OG: '00- 1/3R (1, 3 LJ, 1 4x400); WCh: '97- 1/1R (10 LJ), '99- 1 (sf, 3 LJ); '01- 2/1R (2); WJ: '92- 5/2R (7); WCp: '98- 1 (1, 2 LJ), '02- 1/2R. Won GP 100m 1998, 2000, 2002; 200m 1997; won overall 1998 & 2002. 2nd 2000. Won US 100m 1997-8, 2002; 200m 1998-9, 2001-02; LJ 1997-8; GWG 100m/200m 1998, 100m 2001.
World record 4x200m 2000.

Progression at 100m, 200m, 400m, LJ: 1988- 13.0, c.59.0; 1989- 12.01, 24.46/24.06w/23.8w, 56.73; 1990- 11.62, 23.70, 54.21; 1991- 11.17, 22.76, 52.91; 1992- 11.14, 22.58, 54.44; 1993- 11.28/11.2, 23.01/22.79w, 6.71/6.75w; 1994- 11.40, 23.32, 6.75; 1995- 11.68, 23.96w, 6.64; 1997- 10.76, 21.76, 6.93; 1998- 10.65A/10.71, 21.62A/21.80, 50.36, 7.31; 1999- 10.70, 21.81, 50.79, 7.01; 2000- 10.75/10.68w, 21.84, 49.59, 7.02; 2001- 10.84, 22.23; 2002- 10.84, 22.11, 50.46. pbs: 50m 5.93+ '97, 60m 6.85+ '99, 300m 35.68 '01.

Won 59 of 60 100m finals 1997-2002, 42 successive then a loss to Zhanna Pintusevich-Block at the 2001 Worlds and 17 more to end 2002. The woman athlete of 1998, when she won 34 individual events until her 2nd to Heike Drechsler in World Cup LJ. Had another brilliant season in 1999, with 5 wins at 100m to World gold and 10 at 200m until pulled up with back spasms in her semi at the Worlds. In 2000 she won a record five medals at the Olympic Games, including three golds, in 2001 she won two golds and a silver at the Worlds, and in 2002 was unbeaten at ndividual events – 14 at 100m, 3 at 200m and 1 at 400m. Had dual nationality as mother was born in Belize, but opted for the USA. US junior champion at 100m & 200m 1991-2. 5th at 100m and 4th at 200m in 1992 US Olympic Trials, but declined Olympic relay reserve place. World 100m age bests for age 14-15-16 and 200m 15-16. She played point guard on the North Carolina basketball team that won the NCAA Division 1 title 1994, but broke her left foot in August and December 1995. Married C J Hunter (1999 World SP champ) on 3 Oct 1998, but separated in 2001. Now partner of Tim Montgomery, their son Tim was born on 28 June 2003.

Deena KASTOR b. 14 Feb 1973 Waltham, Mass. née Drossin. 1.63m 48kg.Asics. Graduate of University of Arkansas.

At 10000m: OG: '00- h; WCh: '99- 11, '01- 11, '03- 12; WUG: '97- 1. World CC: '99-00-01-02-03: 10/12/12/2/2; Won US 10000m 2000-01, 2003; CC 1997, 1999-2003.

N.American records: 10000m 2002, Mar 2003.

Progression at 5000m, 10000m, Mar: 1992- 16:21.47, 1993- 15:52.80i/16:07.73, 1994- 16:39.62, 34:10.89; 1996- 16:29.17, 34:13.75; 1997- 15:43.63, 32:47.44; 1998- 15:07.83, 1999- 14:56.84, 32:00.72; 2000- 14:51.62, 31:51.05; 2001- 15:08.02, 32:05.14, 2:26:58; 2002- 15:13.93, 30:50.32, 2:26:53; 2003- 15:08.14, 31:17.86. 2:21:16. pbs: 1500m 4:07.82 '00, 2000m 5:42.76 '01, 3000m 8:42.59 '00, 2M 9:35.89 '02; Road: 15km 49:09 01, HMar 70:08 '01.

Seventh in New York on marathon debut 2001. Married her massage therapist Andrew Kastor on 14 September 2003.

Anjanette KIRKLAND b. 24 Feb 1974 Pineville, Louisiana 1.72m 66kg. Nike. Degree in agricultural education from Texas A & M University.

At 100mh: WCh: '97- sf, '01- 1, '03- h; 3rd GP 2002. At 60mh: WI: '01- 1.

Progression at 100mh: 1992- 13.99, 1993- 13.49/13.47w, 1994- 13.22, 1995- 13.09/12.89w, 1996- 13.24, 1997- 12.74/12.70w, 1998- 12.83, 1999- 12.91/12.68w, 2000- 12.63, 2001- 12.42, 2002- 12.62, 2003- 13.80. pbs: 50mh 6.83i '01, 55mh 7.61i '96, 60mh 7.85i '01, 400mh 57.75 '97.

Partner of Bernard Williams, gave birth to daughter Jadin Williams on 4 May 2003.

Muna LEE b. 30 Oct 1981 1.73m 50kg. Student at Louisiana State University.

Progression at 100m, 200m: 1998- 24.72, 1999- 11.66, 24.08; 2000- 11.36, 23.83; 2001- 11.17/11.13w, 23.04i/23.12/22.53w; 2002- 11.19, 22.66/22.33w; 2003- 11.04/10.97w, 22.49i/22.74. pbs: 55m 6.73i 03, 60m 7.15i '03.

NCAA indoor champion 60m 2003, 200m 2002-03.

Raasin McINTOSH b. 29 Apr 1982 Houston 1.70m 61kg. Student at University of Texas.

At 400mh: WCh: '03- sf; US champion 2003. At 4x100m: WY: '99- 2R.

Progression at 400mh: 1998- 60.10, 2000- 59.46, 2001- 57.19, 2002- 55.70, 2003- 54.60. pbs: 200m 23.62 '04, 400m 52.23i '04, 53.78 '01; 60mh 7.95i '04, 100mh 12.90 '03.

Miesha McKELVY JONES b. 26 Jul 1976 Torrance, Cal. 1.73m 64kg. Nike. Was at San Diego State University.

At 100mh: WCh: '99- qf, '03- 3; PAm: '99- 3.

Progression at 100mh: 1994- 14.37/14.29w, 1997- 13.05, 1998- 12.91, 1999- 12.82/12.67w, 2000- 12.78, 2002- 12.60/12.51w, 2003- 12.51. pbs: 100m 11.40 '00, 200m 23.66 '97, 23.28Aw '99, 50mh 6.83i '02, 55mh 7.59i '00, 60mh 7.96i '02.

Anna MAHON b. 19 Dec 1974 Stamford, Connecticut 1.80m 75kg. née Norgren. Nike. Graduate of Vermont University. English teacher.

At HT: WCh: '01- dnq 1, '03- 7; PAm: '03- 4; WCp: '02- 4. US champion 2002.

Three US hammer records 2002.

Progression at HT: 1994- 41.76, 1995- 51.16, 1996- 55.66, 1997- 57.60, 1998- 63.64, 1999- 64.72, 2000- 65.88, 2001- 66.88, 2002- 72.01, 2003- 71.33. pb 20lb WT 23.56i '02.

Married Sean Mahon (2.16m high jumper) in July 2001.

Donica MERRIMAN b. 24 Jan 1979 1.78m 65kg. Was at Ohio State University

Progression at 100mh: 1994- 13.95, 1995- 13.99, 1996- 13.74, 1997- 13.84, 1998- 13.27, 1999- 12.84, 2000- 12.70, 2001- 12.82/12.73w, 2002- 12.74, 2003- 12.65. pbs: 100m 11.40 '99, 11.35w '00; 200m 23.08/22.75w '00; 60mh 7.95 '01.

Jearl MILES CLARK b. 4 Sep 1966 Gainesville 1.70m 60kg. New Balance. Was at Alabama A&M University.

At 400m (800m): OG: '92- sf/2R, '96- 5/1R, '00-

1R (sf); WCh: '91- 5/2R, '93- 1/1R, '95- 3/1R, '97- 3/2R, '99- (4)/2R, '01- 4R, '03 (h)/1R; WI: '91- 5/2R, '93- 3, '95- 5, '97- 1/2R, '99- 3; PAm: '91- 3; WUG: '89- 2/1R; WCp: '89- 4R, '92- 1, '94- 3, '98- (4), '02- 2. Won US 400m 1993, 1995, 1997, 2002; 800m 1998-9, 2003; GWG 400m 1994.
Three US 800m records 1997-9. WIR 500y 60.61 '00. World W35 400m record 2002.
Progression at 400m, 800m: 1986- 52.41, 1987- 52.36, 1988- 51.28, 1989- 51.52, 1990- 51.76, 1991- 50.19, 1992- 50.30, 2:04.78; 1993- 49.82, 1994- 50.11, 1995- 50.00, 2:00.86; 1996- 49.55, 1:58.91; 1997- 49.40, 1:56.78; 1998- 50.11, 1:56.43; 1999- 49.98, 1:56.40; 2000- 50.04, 1:59.12; 2001- 50.80, 2:00.96i; 2002- 50.27, 1:58.41; 2003- 50.53, 1:58.61. pbs: 100m 11.78/11.50w '93, 200m 23.03 '97, 300m 36.0 '95, 36.07 '00; 500m 1:08.71i '04, LJ 6.45 '86, 6.47w '88.
Tied record with five World Cup appearances. Married long-time coach J J Clark, who had a 1500m pb of 3:41.5 (1988) and is brother of Joetta and Hazel Clark, on 30 Nov 1996.

Inger MILLER b. 12 Jun 1972 Los Angeles 1.63m 55kg. Nike/HSI. Degree in biological sciences from University of Southern California.
At 200m/4x100m (100m): OG: '96- 4/1R; WCh: '97- 5/1R (5), '99- 1 (2), '01- sf/1R, '03- 2R; WUG: '95- 1R; WCp: '98- 1R, '02- 2R. Won US 100m 1999, 200m 1997. At 60m: WI: '99- 3dq.
Progression at 100m, 200m: 1988- 11.64/11.43w, 23.69; 1989- 11.53/11.38w, 23.62; 1990- 11.48, 23.57; 1991- 11.64/11.52w, 1992- 11.16/10.9w, 23.19/22.8/22.43w; 1993- 11.11, 22.33; 1994- 11.32/10.99w, 22.73/22.47w; 1995- 11.47; 1996- 10.96, 22.25; 1997- 11.04, 22.37/22.27w; 1998- 11.01/10.84w, 22.20; 1999- 10.79, 21.77; 2000- 10.91, 22.09; 2001- 11.34/11.09w, 22.82; 2002- 11.22, 2003- 11.16/11.04w, 22.67. pbs: 50m 6.00+ '99, 60m 6.94+ '99, 400m 52.76 '94.
Her father Lennox Miller (Jam) won Olympic silver in 1968 and bronze in 1972 at 100m; they are the first ever father-daughter Olympic medallists at individual events in athletics. Improved her pb at 100m of 10.96 to 10.86, 10.81 and 10.79 (2nd) and at 200m from 22.10 to 21.77 when winning at the 1999 World Champs. Ran on a wild card in 200m and won a gold medal at 4x100m at 2001 Worlds. In October 2001 USATF announced that she was disqualified from her bronze medal at the 1999 World Indoor 60m for a positive test for caffeine.

Melissa MORRISON b. 9 Jul 1971 Mooresville, NC 1.64m 56kg. Adidas. Psychology graduate of Appalachian State University .
At 100mh: OG: '00- 3; WCh: '97- h; US champion 1997. At 60mh: WI: '97-9-03: 5/6/3.
Progression at 100mh: 1988- 14.37, 1989- 14.09, 1991- 13.63w, 1992- 13.24, 1993- 13.24, 1994- 13.24, 1995- 13.05A, 1996- 12.92/12.81w, 1997- 12.61, 1998- 12.53, 1999- 12.67/12.55w, 2000- 12.57, 2001- 13.00/12.82w, 2002- 12.79, 2003- 12.70. pbs: 100m 11.45A '93, 200m 23.98 '02, 50mh 6.81i '99, 55mh 7.64i '96, 60mh 7.83i '98, LJ 6.23 '93, TJ 12.55 '93.

LeShundra '**DeDee' NATHAN** b. 20 Apr 1968 Fort Wayne 1.80m 75kg. Indiana Invaders. Was at Indiana University.
At Hep: OG: '00- 9; WCh: '93- 17, '95- 8, '97- 7, '01- 7; PAm: '91- 1, '95- 3; US champion 2000-01. At Pen: WI: '97- 7, '99- 1.
Progression at Hep: 1990- 5855, 1991- 5998, 1992- 6162, 1993- 6038, 1994- 6189, 1995- 6283, 1996- 6327, 1997- 6317, 1998- 6479, 1999- 6577, 2000- 6343, 2001- 6275, 2002- 5995. pbs: 200m 24.11 '98, 800m 2:13.82 '96, 60mh 8.26i '99, 100mh 13.10 '96, 400mh 57.39A '89, 57.78 '88; HJ 1.86i '99, 1.83 '96; LJ 6.59/6.65w '98, SP 16.06 '01, JT 50.08 '99, Pen 4753i '99.
Added 230 points to pb when taking the 1999 World Indoor heptathlon gold. Won at Götzis but then missed Worlds after no height in the high jump in US heptathlon.

Suzy POWELL b. 3 Sep 1976 Modesto 1.78m 63kg. Asics. Was at UCLA.
At DT: OG: '96- dnq 33, '00- dnq 15; WCh: '97- dnq 21, '01- dnq 18, '03- 9; WJ: '92- 10, '94- 3; PAm: '03- 4; US champion 1996, PAm-J 1995.
Progression at DT: 1990- 46.31, 1991- 49.66, 1992- 51.72, 1993- 55.06, 1994- 57.40, 1995- 58.06, 1996- 60.58, 1997- 65.22, 1998- 65.05, 1999- 60.89, 2000- 65.30, 2001- 64.50, 2002- 69.44dh/65.48, 2003- 65.38. pb JT 54.62 '97.
Her 69.44 at la Jolla in 2002 was acclaimed as a US discus record but throwing area was later found to be downhill.

Sanya RICHARDS b. 26 Feb 1985 Kingston, Jamaica 1.73m 61kg. University of Texas.
At (200m)/400m/4x400m: WCh: '03- sf/1R; WJ: '02- 3/2. Won US & NCAA 2003.
World indoor bests 200m, 400m (2) 2004.
Progression at 200m, 400m: 1999- 23.84, 2000- 23.57, 54.34; 2001- 23.09, 53.49; 2002- 23.01, 50.69; 2003- 22.80i/22.86, 50.58; 2004- 22.49i, 50.82i. pbs: 60m 7.21i '04, 100m 11.28 '03. LJ 6.08 '01.
Left Jamaica at the age of 12 and gained US citizenship on 20 May 2002.

Marla RUNYAN b. 4 Jan 1969 Santa Maria, California 1.70m 60kg. Asics. Was at San Diego State University.
At 1500m: OG: '00- 8; WCh: '99- 10; PAm: '99- 1. At 5000m: WCh: '01- h. Won US 5000m 2001-03.
Progression at 1500m, 5000m: 1999- 4:05.27, 2000- 4:06.14, 15:07.66; 2001-4:06.31, 15:05.48; 2002- 4:02.95, 15:07.19; 2003- 15:16.18. pbs: 800m 2:03.18 '99, 3000m 8:39.36 '02, Rd 10km 31:46 '02, 10M 53:37 '02, HMar 71:19 '02, Mar 2:27:10 '02, 100mh 13.79 '95, HJ 1.80 '95, Hep 5761 '96.
Registered as legally blind, having suffered from a degenerative eye condition (Stargardt's Disease) from the age of 9. Won 100m, 200m, 400m & LJ at 1992 Paralympics and 100m & Hep

in 1996. Switched from heptathlon to 1500m in 1999. In 2000 became first athlete to have competed in both Paralympics and Olympics. 4th in New York on marathon debut 2002. She married Adam Lonergan in 2002.

Jillian SCHWARTZ b. 19 Sep 1979 1.73m 62 kg. Nike. Was at Duke University.
At PV: WCh: '03- dnq 18=; WI: '04- 4
Progression at PV: 1999- 3.56, 2000- 4.10, 2001- 4.20, 2002- 4.50, 2003- 4.45, 2004- 4.60i.

Seilala SUA b. 25 Feb 1978 1.87m 109kg. Nike. Studied sociology at UCLA.
At DT/(SP): OG: '00- 10; WCh:'99- 6, '01- 6/dnq 17; WJ: '96- 2/8; PAm-J: '95- 2/1, '97- 1/1. Won US DT 1998-2001, SP 2001; NCAA SP 1999-2000, DT 1997-2000.
Progression at DT: 1994- 44.22, 1995- 53.84, 1996- 56.78, 1997- 63.44, 1998- 64.67, 1999- 64.89, 2000- 65.90, 2001- 65.64, 2002- 62.89, 2003- 61.93. pbs: SP 18.51 '02, HT 60.60 '00, JT 49.12 '99, 20lb Wt 20.52i '99.
With the discus 1997-2000, Sua is only the second woman ever to win four successive NCAA titles at the same event (after Suzy Hamilton 1500m 1987-90). Her 107 points at shot, discus and weight indoors (38) and out (69) is a new NCAA record for any athlete.

Kellie SUTTLE b. 9 May 1973 St Peters, Missouri 1.70m 59kg. Nike. Was at Arkansas State University.
At PV: OG: '00- 11; WCh: '99- 9; WI: '01- 2=, '03- 4; PAm: '99- 2, '03- 4. Won US 1998.
Progression at PV: 1995- 3.71i/3.67, 1996- 3.85i/3.66, 1997- 3.90, 1998- 4.27, 1999- 4.46i/4.35, 2000- 4.53, 2001- 4.60, 2002- 4.50, 2003- 4.58. pb LJ 5.86 '93.
Started pole vaulting in 1994 while working as a gymnastics instructor.

Brenda TAYLOR b. 9 Feb 1979 St.Louis 1.74m 63kg. Psychology/biology graduate of Harvard University.
At 400mh: WCh: '01- sf; PAm: '03- 4. NCAA champion 2001.
Progression at 400mh: 1997- 60.80, 1999- 57.29, 2000- 56.64, 2001- 55.46, 2002- 55.03, 2003- 54.92. pbs: 400m 52.56 '03, 100mh 13.44 '02.

Nicole TETER b. 8 Nov 1973 San Diego 1.72m 57kg. Nike Farm Team. Merchandising manager. Was at University of Arkansas.
At 800m: PAm-J: '91- 2. US champion 2002.
Progression at 800m: 1989- 2:11.15, 1990- 2:10.27, 1991- 2:05.61, 1992- 2:04.1, 1993- 2:04.13, 1994- 2:07.35, 1995- 2:03.71, 1996- 2:02.55, 1998- 2:02.56, 2000- 2:01.59, 2001- 2:01.32, 2002- 1:57.97, 2003- 1:59.91. pbs: 400m 55.49 '89, 1500m 4:04.19 '02, 1M 4:32.71i '02, 2M 9:49.09 '02.
US junior champion in 1991, she made a great breakthrough in 2002 when she broke the American indoor 800m record to win US title in 1:58.71 and improved outdoors to 1:58.83 to win US title and 1:57.97.

Jennifer TOOMEY b. 19 Dec 1971 New Haven, CT 1.65m 51kg Nike. née Lincoln. Biology graduate of Tufts University.
At 800m: WCh: '03- sf; WI: '04- 4. Won US indoor 800m & 1500m 2004.
Progression at 800m: 1998- 2:14, 1999- 2:06.12, 2000- 2:03.58, 2001- 2:00.38, 2002- 2:00.12, 2003- 1:59.75, 2004- 1:59.64i. pbs: 1000m 2:34.19i 04, 1500m 4:10.11 '02, 4:09.11i '04; 1M 4:39.85 '02, 4:30.9i mx '04.
Was a state champion diver in high school and did not start running seriously until 1998. Married Michael Toomey 12 Sep 1998.

Grace UPSHAW b. 22 Sep 1975 Berkeley 1.78m 65kg. Graduated in American studies from University of California, Berkeley.
At LJ: WCh: '03- 8. US champion 2003 (2nd 2001-02), indoors 2002.
Progression at LJ: 1994- 5.80, 1995- 5.79, 1996- 5.98/6.19w, 1997- 6.24, 2000- 6.47A/6.38, 2001- 6.62/6.70w, 2002- 6.60/6.75w, 2003- 6.73/6.99w.
After graduating she did not compete in 1998-9, returning in 2000. Daughter of Monte Upshaw, who set a US high school long jump record of 7.72 in 1954 (second best in the world that year).

Tisha WALLER b. 1 Dec 1970 South Boston, Virginia 1.83m 61kg. Nat Page. Was at University of North Carolina. Schoolteacher.
At HJ: OG: '96- 9=; WCh: '91- dnq 20, '93- dnq 17=, '99- 4=; WUG: '91- 3; WI: '99- 3, '03- 7; WCp: '98- 3, '02- 4. Won GWG 1998, US 1996, 1998-9, 2002.
Progression at HJ: 1986- 1.65, 1987- 1.65, 1988- 1.78, 1989- 1.78, 1990- 1.83, 1991- 1.93i/1.92, 1992- 1.92, 1993- 1.94, 1994- 1.96, 1995- 1.98, 1996- 1.99i/1.98, 1997- 1.84, 1998- 2.01i/1.98, 1999- 2.00, 2000- 1.96i/1.94, 2002- 1.96, 2003- 1.98. pb LJ 5.61 '88, TJ 12.74 '92.
US indoor record to win US indoor HJ 1998.

Kelli WHITE b. 1 Apr 1977 Oakland, California 1.63m 52kg. Nike. Was at University of Tennessss.
At (100m)/200m/4x100mR: WCh: '01- 7/3/1R, '03- 1/1; PAm-J: '95-2/1R; WCp: '02- 7. Won US 100m 2003, 200m 2002-03; WAF 200m 2003, 2nd GP 2001.
Progression 100m, 200m: 1993- 11.81w, 24.09w; 1994- 11.87/11.68w, 23.80; 1995- 11.55/11.43w, 23.49/23.33w; 1996- 11.60/11.45w, 23.85i/23.60w; 1997- 11.42/11.39w, 23.30/23.28w; 1998- 11.27/11.21w, 22.58; 1999- 11.20/10.96w, 22.65/22.49w; 2000- 11.19, 23.08/22.94w; 2001- 10.99/10.93w, 22.38; 2002- 11.16/11.03w, 22.50; 2003- 10.85/10.79w, 22.05. pbs: 55m 6.76i '99, 60m 7.14i '02, 300m 36.61 '01, 400m 53.94A '95.
Tested positive for modafinil, a stimulant, when winnng 100m/200m double at 2003 World Champs. Her father Willie White was a top sprinter with pbs 100y 9.4 '57 and 100m 10.3 '58, and her mother Debbie Byfield ran for Jamaica at 4x100m at the 1972 Olympics, pb 100y 10.7 '73.

Angela WILLIAMS b. 30 Jan 1980 Bellflower, California 1.56m 52kg. Nike/HSI. Graduate of University of Southern California.
At 100m/4x100mR: WCh: '01- sf/res (1)R, '03- 2R; WJ: '98- 2/1R; PAm: '99- 2/2R, '03- 2/1R; WUG: '99- 1/1R; PAm-J: '95- 2, '97- 1/1R; Won NCAA 1999-2002. At 60m: WI: '01- 2, '03- 2.
Progression at 100m: 1990- 12.85, 1992- 12.10, 1993- 11.79, 1994- 11.78, 1995- 11.24, 1996- 11.73/ 11.4w, 1997- 11.14/10.98w, 1998- 11.11/11.10w, 1999- 11.04/10.96w, 2000- 11.12/11.1/11.01w, 2001- 11.18/11.01w, 2002- 11.06, 2003- 11.15/ 11.08w. pbs: 50m 6.17i '01, 55m 6.73i '03, 60m 7.09i '01, 200m 23.02 '98, 22.78w '00; 400m 53.40 '95, 800m 2:16.78 '92, LJ 6.00/6.06w '98.
Became just the third woman ever to win four NCAA titles at one event.

URUGUAY

Governing body: Federación Atletica del Uruguay, Casilla Correo 10538 (Sucursal Pluna), 11100 Montevideo. Founded 1918.

National Champions 2003: **Men**: 100m: Rubén Techeira 10.6, 200m: Heber Viera 22.1, 400m/ 800m: Andrés Silva 48.5/1:57.7, 1500m: Marcos Silva 3:57.9, 5000m: Ernesto Zamora 14:45.2, 10000m: Oscar Fernández 32:51.6, 110mh: Nelson González 15.2, 400mh: Sebastián Queirolo 61.4, 3000mSt: Marcos Silva 9:06.9, HJ: Carlos Rudeli 1.80, PV: Jorge Manuel Díaz 4.10, LJ/TJ: Leandro Castro 6.34/13.08, SP: Gustavo Grinspan 10.95, DT/HT: Rodolfo Casanova 42.35/40.72, JT: Fabián Cabrera 54.45. **Women**: 100m/200m: Camila Pérez 12.3/25.8, 400m: Marcela Valeria Britos 59.0, 800m: Malvina Masdeu 2:21.3, 1500m: Camila de Mello 4:41.4, 5000m/10000m: Merceditas Cuevas 18:23.3/39:07.2, 100mh: Alejandra Monza 16.5, HJ: Irene Armand Pilon 1.55, PV: Aliusha Díaz 3.40, LJ/TJ: Adriana Manzilla 5.03/10.75, SP: Silvana Avila 10.75, DT/HT: Stefanía Zoryez 33.03/54.78; JT: Virginia Espiñeira 28.31.

VENEZUELA

Governing body: Federación Venezolana de Atletismo, Apartado Postal 29059, Caracas. Founded 1948.

National Champions 2003: **Men**: 100m: Omar Cortez 10.56, 200m: Hely Ollarves 21.49, 400m: William Hernández 47.38, 800m: Simoncito Silvera 1:50.50, 1500m: Manuel González 3:51.47, 5000m: Luis Fonseca 14:33.08, 10000m: Alejandro Semprún 30:30.87, 3000mSt: Néstor Nieves 8:48.62, 110mh: Marleán Reina 14.12w, HJ: Daniel Rodríguez 2.06, PV: Ricardo Diez 5.30, LJ: Esteban Copland 7.30, TJ: Johnny Rodríguez 15.65, SP: Yojer Medina 19.21, DT: Héctor Hurtado 52.20, HT: Aldo Bello 61.38, JT: Manuel Fuenmayor 77.64, Dec: Juan Jaramillo 6555, 20000mW: Raúl Moreno 1:35:07.8. **Women**: 100m: Wilmary Álvarez 11.81, 200m/400m: Eliana Pacheco 23.89/52.73, 800m/1500m: Yenny Mejías 2:11.57/4:43.38, 5000m/10000m: Norelys Lugo 17:35.02/36:34.05, 3000mSt: Yuli Mancilla 11:38.82, 100mh: Ada Hernández 14.37, HJ: Marierlis Rojas 1.75, PV: Zurita Ivanova 3.30, LJ/TJ: Jennifer Arveláez 5.45/12.66. SP/DT: Rosario Ramos 15.20/48.20, HT: Dubraska Rodríguez 56.50, HT: Adriana Benaventa 59.64, JT: Carolina Castillo 49.90, Hep: Thaimara Rivas 5280.

Additional Biography

WANG Liping (China) b. 8 Jul 1976 Liaoning Prov. 1.65m 48kg.
At 20kmW: OG: '00- 1. CHN champion 2000. At 10kmW: WCp: '97- 10; WUG: '01- 3.
Progression at 10kmW, 20kmW: 1994- 1:35:09, 1995- 46:19.83t, 1:29:26; 1997- 42:53, 1:36:22; 1998- 45:12, 2000- 44:55, 1:28:33; 2001- 44:01, 1:26:23; 2003- 1:32:40, 2004- 1:28:58.
Married to Zeng Menghui (pb 50kmW 3:48:12 '97), baby born November 2002.

Monika Pyrek – 67 National Records!

Surely Monika Pyrek, the Polish pole vaulter, has set more national records at one event than any other athlete.
Her latest, at the time of going to press, came on 21 February 2004 when she cleared 4.65m indoors at Spala.
Her first record was indoors – 3.10 at Gdansk on 31 March 1996, although she did not win on that occasion as she was one of three Polish women to set a record at this height with Anna Wilegus going on to win at 3.20. Outdoors Pyrek first took the record from Anna Szyranska (3.10 in 1995) with 3.20 and 3.30 at Wroclaw on 18 May 1996.
Wielgus was to go on to set seven more Polish records indoors up to 3.81 in 1998 and seven outdoors in 1997-8 from 3.70 to 4.00, alternating with Pyrek, but from then it has been all Pyrek. Including tied marks Pyrek's tally is as follows:

Years	Indoors (27)		Outdoors (40)	
1996	1	3.10	7	3.20 to 3.60
1997	3	3.40 to 3.60	3	3.80 to 3.83
1998	6	3.61 to 3.91	14	3.85 to 4.15
1999	6	3.92 to 4.21	1	4.16
2000	–		8	4.25 to 4.40
2001	4	4.30 to 4.36	6	4.40 to 4.61
2002	5	4.37 to 4.60	1	4.62
2003	–		–	
2004	2	4.61 to 4.65		

INTRODUCTION TO WORLD LISTS AND INDEX

Records

World, World U20 and U18, Olympic, Continental and Area records are listed for standard events. In running events up to and including 400 metres, only fully automatic times are shown. Marks listed are those which are considered statistically acceptable by the ATFS, and thus may differ from official records where, for instance the performance was set indoors. These are followed by road bests and bests by masters/veterans.

World All-time and Year Lists

These lists are presented in the following format: Mark, Wind reading (where appropriate), Name, Nationality (abbreviated), Date of birth, Position in competition, Meeting name (if significant), Venue, Date of performance.

In standard events the best 30 or so performances are listed followed by the best marks for other athletes. Position, meet and venue details have been omitted for reasons of space beyond 100th in year lists.

In the all-time lists performances which have been world records (or world bests, thus including some unratified marks) are shown with WR against them – outdoor records only.

Indexes

These lists contain the names of all athletes ranked with full details in the world year lists for standard events (and others such as half marathon). The format of the index is as follows:

Family name, First name, Nationality, Birthdate, Height (cm) and Weight (kg), 2003 best mark, Lifetime best (with year) as at the end of 2002.

* before the name indicates an athlete who is profiled in the Biographies section, and a ^ symbol one who has been profiled in previous editions.

General Notes

Altitude aid

Marks set at an altitude of 1000m or higher have been suffixed by the letter "A".

Although there are no separate world records for altitude assisted events, it is understood by experts that in all events up to 400m in length (with the possible exclusion of the 110m hurdles), and in the horizontal jumps, altitude gives a material benefit to performances. For events beyond 800m, however, the thinner air of high altitude has a detrimental effect.

Supplementary lists are included in relevant events for athletes with seasonal bests at altitude who have low altitude marks qualifying for the main list.

Some leading venues over 1000m

Addis Ababa ETH	2365m
Air Force Academy USA	2194
Albuquerque USA	1555
Antananarivo MAD	1350
Bloemfontein RSA	1392
Bogotá COL	2644
Boulder USA	1655
Bozeman USA	1467
Calgary CAN	1045
Cali COL	1046
Ciudad de Guatemala GUA	1402
Ciudad de México MEX	2247
Cochabamba BOL	2558
Colorado Springs USA	1823
Cuenca ECU	2561
Denver USA	1609
El Paso USA	1187
Flagstaff USA	2107
Font-Romeu FRA	1850
Fort Collins USA	1521
Germiston RSA	1661
Guadalajara MEX	1567
Harare ZIM	1473
Johannesburg RSA	1748
Krugersdorp RSA	1740
Logan USA	1372
Medellín COL	1541
Monachil ESP	2320
Nairobi KEN	1675
Pietersberg RSA	1230
Pocatello USA	1361
Potchefstroom RSA	1351
Pretoria RSA	1400
Provo USA	1380
Reno USA	1369
Roodepoort RSA	1720
Rustenburg RSA	1157
Salt Lake City USA	1321
Secunda RSA	1628
Segovia ESP	1000
Sestriere ITA	2050
Soría ESP	1056
South Lake Tahoe USA	1909
Toluca MEX	2700
Tsakhkadzor ARM	1980
Windhoek NAM	1725

Some others over 500m

Almaty KZK	847
Ankara TUR	902
Bern SUI	555
Blacksburg USA	634
Boise USA	818
Canberra AUS	581
La Chaux de Fonds SUI	997
Caracas VEN	922
Edmonton CAN	652
Jablonec CZE	598
Las Vegas USA	619

Lubbock USA	988
Madrid ESP	640
Magglingen SUI	751
Malles ITA	980
Moscow, Idaho USA	787
München GER	520
Nampa, Idaho USA	760
Osaka JPN	579
Salamanca ESP	806
Santiago de Chile CHI	520
(Apoquindo)	950
São Paulo BRA	725
Sofia BUL	564
Spokane USA	576
Taiyuan CHN	780
Tucson USA	728
350m-500m	
Annecy FRA	448
Banská Bystrica SVK	362
Fayetteville USA	407
Genève SUI	385
Götzis AUS	448
Johnson City USA	499
Lausanne SUI	375
Rieti ITA	402
Sindelfingen GER	440
Stuttgart GER	415
Tashkent UZB	477
Zürich SUI	410

Automatic timing

In the main lists for sprints and hurdles, only times recorded by fully automatic timing devices are included.

Hand timing

In the sprints and hurdles supplementary lists are included for races which are hand timed. Any athlete with a hand timed best 0.01 seconds or more better than his or her automatically timed best has been included, but hand timed lists have been terminated close to the differential levels considered by the IAAF to be equivalent to automatic times, i.e. 0.24 sec. for 100m, 200m, 100mh, 110mh, and 0.14 sec. for 400m and 400mh. It should be noted that this effectively recognises bad hand timekeeping, for there should be no material difference between hand and auto times, but what happens is that badly trained timekeepers anticipate the finish, having reacted to the flash at the start.

In events beyond 400m, auto times are integrated with hand timed marks, the latter identifiable by times being shown to tenths. All-time lists also include some auto times in tenths of a second, but these are identified with the symbol '.

Indoor marks

Indoor marks are included in the main lists for field events and straightway track events, but not for other track events. This is because track sizes vary in circumference (200m is the international standard) and banking, while outdoor tracks are standardised at 400m. Outdoor marks for athletes whose seasonal bests were set indoors are shown in a supplemental list.

Mixed races

For record purposes athletes may not, except in road races, compete in mixed sex races. Statistically there would not appear to be any particular logic in this, and women's marks set in such races are shown in our lists - annotated with mx. In such cases the athlete's best mark in single sex competition is appended.

Field event series

Field event series are given (where known) for marks in the top 30 performances lists. .

Tracks and Courses

As well as climatic conditions, the type and composition of tracks and runways will affect standards of performance, as will the variations in road race courses.

Wind assistance

Anemometer readings have been shown where available in the lists for sprints and horizontal jumps in metres per second to one decimal place. If the figure was given to two decimal places, it has been rounded to the next tenth upwards, e.g. a wind reading of +2.01m/s, beyond the IAAF legal limit of 2.0, is rounded to +2.1; or -1.22m/s is rounded up to -1.2.

For multi-events a wind-assisted mark in one in which an event is aided by a wind over 4.0m/s and the average of the three wind-measured events is > 2m/s.

Drugs bans

The IAAF have determined that its Council may decertify an athlete's records, titles and results if he or she is found to have used a banned substance before those performances. Performances at or after such a positive finding are shown in footnotes. Such athletes are shown with ¶ after their name in year lists, and in all-time lists if at any stage of their career they have served a drugs suspension of a year or more (thus not including athletes receiving 3 month bans (now public warnings) for stimulants etc., which for that year only are indicated with a #). This should not be taken as implying that the athlete was using drugs at that time. Nor have those athletes who have subsequently unofficially admitted to using banned substances been indicated; the ¶ is used only for those who have been caught.

Venues

From time to time place names are changed. Our policy is to use names in force at the time that the performance was set. Thus Leningrad prior to 1991, Sankt-Peterburg from its re-naming.

Amendments

Keen observers may spot errors in the lists. They are invited to send corrections as well as news and results for 2004.

Peter Matthews

Amendments to ATHLETICS 2003

p.50 CC Champions: Luxembourg women (LD) was Line Dupont
p.70 Mary Carew died at Framingham
p.81 The drugs ban on Romas Ubartas was rescinded.
p.126 World Youth Championships: 2001 in Debrecen HUN
p.188 Italian champions 2002: 100m: Levorato 11.3 (not /22.98)
p.205 Luxembourg champions 2002: **Men 1500m**: Thielen 4:02.45, **Women 800m**: Hansen 2:21.86, **HT:** Biver 40.94
p.607 **World Indoor Championships. Women 3000m**: Tsirba was dq, so 8. Cristina Grosu ROM 8:58.65.

WORLD LISTS – MEN 2002

100m: 10.00 Miller 2 at Zürich; hand: 10.1 Francis Saire TAN 11 Nov; Jnrs: 10.38 Gabrilla Bangura SLE 19.9.85 1 Bakau 25 May
200m: 20.89 Malik Louahla ALG 19.12.77 29 Jul
400m: 46.25 Malik Louahla ALG 19.12.77 29 Jul; Hand: 45.9A Lewis Banda ZIM-J 16.9.83 29 Jul, 46.1A Johnson Kubisa BOT 23.4.72 26 Apr
800m: 1:46.27 Khouia 9.11.79
1500m: 3:35.47 Nyaga 8.11.79 (& 3000m 7:49.25), 3:41.1A Timothy Kiptanui KEN-J 1 Eldoret 29 Jun, 3:41.5A Sammy Kiplagat KEN .73 29 Jun; delete 3:41.4 Izquierdo
3000m: 7:46.13 Kiprop 4.6.82 (& 5k 13:05.81, 10k 27:36.78), 7:48.82 Denis Kipkurui Keter b. 24.3.84 (& 5000m 13:32.71), 7:52.15 Harroufi .81
5000m: 13:21.81 Sileshi Sihene b, 29.1.83 (also 10k 27:26.12 etc).
Mar: 2:07:26 Benjamin Kimutai Kosgei 5.9.71 (& HMar 61:33), Boston times should be marked D, Juniors: delete 2:14:22 Inagaki (b.1979)
3000mSt: 8:34.04 Potapovich 26.11.80, delete 8:36.7 Lasri (see 8:33.09)
110mh: 13.14 0.0 García 1 GL Saint-Denis 5 Jul (not Rethímno 7 Jul), 13.15A Olijar 1 Pretoria 12 Apr (his best low altitude correctly shown at 13.22); 13.87/13.73w Doucouré, 13.92w Takagi 11.7.78
LJ: 8.12 Ignisious Gaisah GHA, 7.99 Al-Waleed 7.5.84, 7.88 Adamou 7 Aug (delete at 7.96 – was wa), 7.84 Ayodeji Ajijo NGR 12 Apr
SP: 20.02 Emelianov confirmed as national record, 19.61i Shapran 21.7.72 (189/97, 18.10- 91), 19.13 Adams 2.6.78
DT: 60.82 MacKay 13.4.81, Jnr 57.69 Al-Dawoodi at Busan
HT: delete the unconfirmed marks
JT: Series for Kassel 14 Jun: Makarov 86.74, 84,14, x, x, x, x,; Henry 82.97, 85.90, 83.15, 82.90, 86.67, 81.50; 77.11 Novácek 23.6.68, 76.50 Dejan Angelovski MKD 15 Jul
Dec: Jnr 7693 Andreyev 6.11.83
4x400m: add hand timed: 3:04.8A KEN Armed Forces 1 Nairobi 26 Jun
20kmW: 1:23:49 Kuzmin 4th

WORLD LISTS – WOMEN 2002

100m: 11.52 Ogundana .80
400m: 51.84 Okpanachi to drugs dq; 100th best 52.55, 53.21 Reddy .81, drugs dq: 53.22 Silifat Williams NGR 27 Apr
800m: 2:00.0mx/2:01.06 Andrews 26.5.71, 2:03.60 Julia Sakara ZIM 12.7.69 21 Apr; add indoor perfs: 1:56.85 Graf & 1:57.18 Ceplak 1/2 Gent 10 Feb, 1:57.61 Graf 1 & 1:58.20 Mutola 2 Birmingham 17 Feb, 1:57.79 Ceplak 1 Boston 27 Jan
1500m: 4:09.65/4:09.50i Yevdokimova (& 800m 2:03.15
2000m: 5:45.0+ Edith Masai KEN & 5:45.5+ Isabella Ochichi KEN 16 Aug
5000m: 15:37.5 Ham Pong-sil PRK 24.7.74 30 Apr
10km Rd: 33:05 Ionela Vasile ROM 29 Dec
100km: 7:36:12 Sakurai 20.4.71
24 Hours: 200.958k Sandra Powell b.10.6.57
100mh: 12.91 Rose-Henley
400mh: delete unconfirmed 56.69 Piskunova
LJ: 6.74 George 19.4.77 (also TJ 13.67)
TJ: 13.85 Qiu Huijing 4.2.85, 13.27 Nguyen Thi Bich Van VIE 21.2.75 6 Jul
HT: Gu Yuan – also 70.50 1 Jinan 17 Aug
JT: 54.57 Ravina
Hep: 5888 Shobha with 45.59 JT
10kmW: 44:27 Korzeniowska was short – replace by 46:16 15 Sep
50kmW: 4:43:24 Liepina

WORLD INDOOR LISTS 2003

200m: 20.72 o/s Davis not needed; **400m**: Mar 16, New York, 46.11 Witherspoon & 46.15 Gonzales run with 3-turn stagger, which turns race into “oversized track”; **1000m**: 2:18.33 Aïssat, 2:18.52 Sepeng; **2000m** (heading not 3000m): 5:01.37+ Gert-Jan Liefers NED 26.9.78 1 in 2M Birmingham 21 Feb; **3000m**: 7:42.70 España 4 WI Birmingham 10 Mar; **50mh**: 6.53+ Ladji Doucouré 1s2, 6.57+ Cédric Lavanne 1, Sébastian Denis 2s2 all at Aubière 1 Mar; **60mh**: 7.66 Niemi on 27 May (from 7.69); **HJ**: 2.30 (2) and 2.31 extra trial Harris on 2 Mar; **SP**: 20.35 Guset 1 Bucuresti 1 Feb; **Wt**: 22.25 Kruger 18.2.79. **Women 300m**: 37.18 Nadjina Kaltouma CHA 1 Winnipeg 1 Feb; **400m**: 52.36 o/s Washington not needed; **1500m**: 4:12.50 drugs dq Hendricken; **3000m**: 8:52.21 drugs dq Tsirba; **60mh**: 7.84 drugs dq Cherry (add 8.05 15 Feb); **PV**: delete 4.27A Jerz; **LJ**: delete 6.86 Akulenko (was 6.26); **TJ**: 14.32 Alna Dinu 1 Bucuresti 1 Mar (from 13.98); **Wt**: 21.17 Tara Loper USA 12.8.77 1 Findlay 12 Dec 02; **Pen**: 4398 Hellebaut 1 NC Gent 9 Mar, 4292A Schiemenz.

PREVIOUS WORLD LISTS

2001: Men: SP: 18.77 Nate DeSomber 26.10.78; **JT**: 76.40 Dejan Angelovski MKD Skopje 29 Sep
2000: Men: PV: 5.40i Yuriy Blonskiy 9.7.79
1994: Men: 4x100m: 40.26 (not 40.25 or 40.17) RSA Juniors 8 Apr
1984: Men: SP: 19.53 Trent Eddings USA 30.5.61 (193/107)

La Jolla

The throwing area for hammer and javelin at La Jolla was found to be downhill in 2003. This invalidates marks made this year, but also in previous years. Thus amend leading marks in year for:
1995: DT: 61.84 Meyer to 58.88 Q NC Sacramento 14 Jun, 60.48 Kirchhoff, 58.30 Presser; **Women DT**: 60.86 Weis to 59.48 Q NC Sacramento 17 Jun
1996: DT: 61.14 Kirchhoff to 58.42 (16 Mar), 58.72 Nuti, **Women DT**: 63.56 Barnes-Mileham to 63.04 (3 Jenner San Jose 1 Jun), 60.24 Dumble to 58.88 (4 MSR Walnut 21 Apr), 59.20 Noble to 54.24 (23 Mar), 58.92 Garrett to 56.86 (5 Modesto 11 May), 56.06 Kawar to 54.68 (13 Apr), 54.28 Apiafi
1997: DT: 65.28 Fitzpatrick to 63.66 (2 Salinas 22 May), 62.80 G Smith to 60.38 (1 CAU Bedford 25 May), 62.54 Walsh to 59.66 (6 MSR Walnut 20 Apr), 62.10 Kirchhoff to 61.96 (1 Claremont 18 Apr), 58;00 Erdkamp; **Women DT:** 60.80 Drew to 58,16 (2 CAU Bedford 26 May), 60.14 Dumble to 59.16 (2 MSR Walnut 20 Apr), 55.62 Noble, 54.78 Jurásková
1998: DT: 69.79 Washington to 68.38, 68.45 Setliff to 66.43 (2 NC Orleans 19 Jun), 64.96 Fitzpatrick to 63.21 (4 Salinas 19 May), 62.52 C Brown to 61.12 (4 NC Orleans 19 Jun), 61.75 Lindsey to 60.19 (1 Seattle 16 May), 60.92 Mielke to 59.29 (19 Apr), 59.67 San Filippo; **Women DT**: 65.62 Hill to 63.68 (1 Stanford 21 May), 61.37 Dumble to 58.96 (5 Modesto 9 May), 60.11 Kawar to 56.22 (19 May), 57.30 Hicks to 55.43 (16 Apr)
1999: DT: 63.74 Winchester to 63.40 (1 Antelope Valley 15 Apr), 61.06 Sullivan to 59.37 (2 Jun), 59.28 O'Neil, 58.26 Dumble to 57.88 (18 Apr), 58.16 Moser, (61.16 Lindsey was at Chula Vista); **Women DT**: 55.24 Pierson to 54.68 (10 Apr);
2000: DT: 68.51 Setliff to 66.96 (2 MSR Walnut 16 Apr), 68.46 Bloom to 67.25 (2 Salinas 23 May), 66.91 Máté to 66.54 (3 MSR Walnut 16 Apr), 63.67 White to 61.64 (Q NC Sacramento 22 Jun), 63.11 Dumble to 61.90 (3 San Diego 24 Apr), 62.34 Thurmond to 62.06 (3 NCAA 3 Durham 31 May), 60.16 Sullivan to 58.68 (6 May), 59.78 Moser to 59.32 (1 Apr), 59.59 Stuke to 58.30 (6 May), 59.14 Walsh; **Women HT**: Sua 58.62 to 58.38 (1 May)
2001: DT: 69.44 Setliff to 68.94, 66.17 Bloom to 65.64 (1 Indianapolis 23 Jul), 65.20 Reynolds to 63.19 (7 Stanford 9 Jun), 63.00 Moser to 62.83 (3 Salinas 22 May), 61.98 Fitzpatrick to 60.89 (3 Salinas 22 May), 59.63 Jauron
2002: DT: 65.92 Petrucci to 65.17 (1 Modesto 11 May), 64.71 Godina to 63.22 (1 Eagle Rock 11 May), 63.10 G Smith to 61.87 (1 Long Beach 20 Apr), 62.86 C Brown to 61.64 (3 Fresno 6 Apr), 61.48 O'Neil to 60.23 (1 Emmitsburg 5 May), 60.53 Inan to 58.92 (10 May), 60.45 Ames to 59.90 (8 Salinas 21 May), 59.00 Hart; 100th best 59.62. **Women DT**: 69.44 Powell to 65.48, 65.21 Hill to 65.10, 54.94 Saye to 54.75 (11 May), 54.33 Joyce

ATHLETICS 2002

P.55: We wrongly published the 2000 results (which had been in ATHLETICS 2001) under the heading of European Cross-country Championships 2001. Here for the record are the results that should have been published.

European Cross-Country Championships 2001

At Thun, Switzerland, 9 December
Senior Men (9.15k)
1. Sergey Lebed UKR 27:52, 2. Kamiel Maase NED 28:05, 3. Antonio Jiménez ESP 28:10, 4. Gabriele De Nard ITA 28:11, 5. Christian Belz SUI 28:12, 6. Sam Haughian GBR 28:12, 7. Carlos Adán ESP 28:13, 8. Mustapha El Ahmadi FRA 28:13, 9. Claes Nyberg SWE 28:14, 10. Paulo Guerra POR 28:15, 11. Augustus Gomes FRA 28:17, 12. José García ESP 28:18, 13. Umberto Pusterla ITA 28:20, 14. Tom Van Hooste BEL 28:20, 15. Laurent Vapaille FRA 28:23, 75 finished. Teams: 1. ESP 40, 2. FRA 50, 3. POR 72, 4. ITA 74, 5. GBR 92, 6. BEL 135, 7. NED 143, 8. RUS 160, 9. SUI 171, 10. IRL 172, 11. GER 211, 12. FIN 227.
Junior Men (6.15k)
1. Vasyl Matvichuk UKR 19:29, 2. Mohammed Farah GBR 19:38, 3. Stefano Scaini ITA 19:39, 4. Mircea Bogdan ROM 19:39, 5. Cosmin Suteu ROM 19:43, 6. Adam Bowden GBR 19:43, 7. Bruno Saramago POR 19:44, 8. Jeremy Pierrat FRA 19:45, 9. Javier Guerra ESP 19:46, 10. Benoit Charpentier FRA 19:52, 86 finished. **Teams**: 1. GBR 54, 2. POR 67, 3. FRA 68, 4. ITA 79, 5. ESP 98, 6. IRL 118, 7. BEL 140, 8. BLR 147, 9. GER 172, 10. TUR 175, 11. AUT 232, 12. HUN 280, 13. SUI 289.
Senior Women (4.65k)
1. Yamna Belkacem FRA 15:48, 2. Olga Romanova RUS 15:49, 3.Justyna Bak POL 15:51, 4. Olivera Jevtic YUG 15:54, 5. Liz Yelling GBR 15:55, 6. Helena Sampaio POR 15:55, 7. Ines Monteiro POR 15:56, 8. Hayley Yelling GBR 15:58, 9. Anastasiya Zubova RUS 16:01, 10. Analídia Torre POR 16:03, 11. Mihaela Botezan ROM 16:05, 12. Kathy Butler GBR 16:08, 13. Anne Keenan IRL 16:08, 14. Beáta Rakonczai HUN 16:10, 15. Anikó Kalovics HUN 16:11, 80 finished. **Teams**: 1. POR 41, 2. GBR 49, 3. FRA 66, 4. RUS 71, 5. IRL 116, 6. ROM 137, 7. ESP 138, 8. HUN 140, 9. ITA 145, 10. POL 165, 11. BEL 217, 12. SUI 232, 13. AUT 269.
Junior Women (3.15k)
1. Elvan Abeylegesse TUR 10:35, 2. Tatyana Chulakh RUS 10:53, 3. Snezana Kostic YUG 10:54, 4. Inga Abitova RUS 11:02, 5. Charlotte Dale GBR 11:07, 6. Mieke Geens BEL 11:09, 7. Turkan Erismis TUR 11:11, 8. Elina Lindgren FIN 11:11, 9. Julie Coulaud FRA 11:11, 10. Marina Ivanova RUS 11:12, 83 finished. **Teams**: 1. RUS 35, 2. GBR 54, 3. TUR 79, 4. FIN 96, 5. FRA 115, 6. ESP 129, 7. GER 147, 8. ROM 154, 9. POR 158, 10. YUG 164, 11. BEL 166, 12. HUN 167, 13. ITA 175, 14. SUI 221, 15. IRL 303.

WORLD & CONTINENTAL RECORDS

As at end of 2003. Key: W = World, Afr = Africa, Asi = Asia, CAC = Central America & Caribbean, Eur = Europe, NAm = North America, Oce = Oceania, SAm = South America, Com = Commonwealth, W20 = World Junior (U20), W18 = World Youth (U18, not officially ratified by IAAF).
Successive columns show: World or Continent, performance, name, nationality, venue, date.
A altitude over 1000m, + timing by photo-electric-cell, * awaiting ratification, § not officially ratified

100 METRES

W, NAm	9.78	Tim MONTGOMERY	USA	Paris (C)	14 Sep 2002
Com	9.84	Donovan BAILEY	CAN	Atlanta	27 Jul 1996
	9.84	Bruny SURIN	CAN	Sevilla	22 Aug 1999
Afr	9.86	Frank FREDERICKS	NAM	Atlanta	27 Jul 1996
CAC	9.86	Ato BOLDON	TRI	Walnut	19 Apr 1998
	9.86	BOLDON also at Athína 17 Jun 1998, Athína 16 Jun 1999 and Lausanne			2 Jul 1999
Eur	9.87	Linford CHRISTIE	GBR	Stuttgart	15 Aug 1993
	9.87	Dwain CHAMBERS	GBR	Paris (C)	14 Sep 2002
SAm	10.00A	Róbson da SILVA	BRA	Ciudad de México	22 Jul 1988
Asi	10.00	Koji ITO	JPN	Bangkok	13 Dec 1998
Oce	9.93	Patrick JOHNSON	AUS	Mito	5 May 2003
W20	10.01	Darrel BROWN	TRI	Saint-Denis	24 Aug 2003
W18	10.24	Darrel BROWN	TRI	Bridgetown	14 Apr 2001
	10.23 ?	Tamunoski ATORUDIBO	NGR	Enugu	23 Mar 2002

200 METRES

W, NAm	19.32	Michael JOHNSON	USA	Atlanta	1 Aug 1996
Afr	19.68	Frank FREDERICKS	NAM	Atlanta	1 Aug 1996
Eur	19.72A	Pietro MENNEA	ITA	Ciudad de México	12 Sep 1979
CAC	19.77	Ato BOLDON	TRI	Stuttgart	13 Jul 1997
Com	19.68	Frank FREDERICKS	NAM	Atlanta	1 Aug 1996
SAm	19.89	Claudinei da SILVA	BRA	München	11 Sep 1999
Oce	20.06A	Peter NORMAN	AUS	Ciudad de México	16 Oct 1968
Asi	20.03	Shingo SUETSUGU	JPN	Yokohama	7 Jun 2003
W20	20.07 §	Lorenzo DANIEL	USA	Starkville	18 May 1985
	20.13	Roy MARTIN	USA	Indianapolis	16 Jun 1985
	20.13	Usain BOLT	JAM	Bridgetown	20 Jul 2003
W18	20.13	Usain BOLT	JAM	Bridgetown	20 Jul 2003

400 METRES

W, NAm	43.18	Michael JOHNSON	USA	Sevilla	26 Aug 1999
CAC	44.14	Roberto HERNÁNDEZ	CUB	Sevilla	30 May 1990
Afr, Com	44.17	Innocent EGBUNIKE	NGR	Zürich	19 Aug 1987
SAm	44.29	Sanderlei PARRELA	BRA	Sevilla	26 Aug 1999
Eur	44.33	Thomas SCHÖNLEBE	GER	Roma	3 Sep 1987
Oce	44.38	Darren CLARK	AUS	Seoul	26 Sep 1988
Asi	44.56	Mohamed AL-MALKY	OMN	Budapest	12 Aug 1988
W20	43.87	Steve LEWIS	USA	Seoul	28 Sep 1988
W18	45.14	Obea MOORE	USA	Santiago de Chile	2 Sep 1995

800 METRES

W, Eur	1:41.11	Wilson KIPKETER	DEN	Köln	24 Aug 1997
Com	1:41.73	Sebastian COE	GBR	Firenze	10 Jun 1981
SAm	1:41.77	Joaquim CRUZ	BRA	Koln	26 Aug 1984
Afr	1:42.28	Sammy KOSKEI	KEN	Koln	26 Aug 1984
NAm	1:42.60	Johnny GRAY	USA	Koblenz	28 Aug 1985
CAC	1:42.85	Norberto TELLEZ	CUB	Atlanta	31 Jul 1996
Asi	1:44.14	LEE Jin-il	KOR	Seoul	17 Jun 1994
Oce	1:44.3 m	Peter SNELL	NZL	Christchurch	3 Feb 1962
W20	1:43.64	Japheth KIMUTAI	KEN	Zürich	13 Aug 1997
W18	1:46.48	Mohammed AL-SALHI	KSA	Saint-Denis	28 Aug 2003

1000 METRES

W, Afr, Com	2:11.96	Noah NGENY	KEN	Rieti	5 Sep 1999
Eur	2:12.18	Sebastian COE	GBR	Oslo	11 Jul 1981
NAm	2:13.9	Rick WOHLHUTER	USA	Oslo	30 Jul 1974
SAm	2:14.09	Joaquim CRUZ	BRA	Nice	20 Aug 1984
Oce	2:16.57	John WALKER	NZL	Oslo	1 Jul 1980
CAC	2:17.0	Byron DYCE	JAM	København	15 Aug 1973
Asi	2:18.91	Mohamed SULEIMAN	QAT	Lindau	28 Jul 1995
W20	2:15.00	Benjamim KIPKURUI	KEN	Nice	17 Jul 1999
W18	2:17.59	Japheth KIMUTAI	KEN	København	23 Aug 1995

1500 METRES

W, Afr	3:26.00	Hicham EL GUERROUJ	MAR	Roma	14 Jul 1998
Com	3:26.34	Bernard LAGAT	KEN	Bruxelles	24 Aug 2001
Eur	3:28.95	Fermin CACHO	ESP	Zürich	13 Aug 1997
NAm	3:29.77	Sydney MAREE	USA	Köln	25 Aug 1985
Oce	3:31.96	Simon DOYLE	AUS	Stockholm	3 Jul 1991
Asi	3:32.10	Mohammed SULEIMAN	QAT	Zürich	13 Aug 1997
SAm	3:33.99	Hudson Santos de SOUZA	BRA	Zagreb	2 Jul 2001
CAC	3:36.60	Stephen AGAR (later CAN)	DMN	Abbotsford	2 Jun 1996
W20	3:30.24	Cornelius CHIRCHIR	KEN	Monaco	19 Jul 2002
W18	3:35.16	Cornelius CHIRCHIR	KEN	Rieti	3 Sep 2000

1 MILE

W, Afr	3:43.13	Hicham El GUERROUJ	MAR	Roma	7 Jul 1999
Com	3:43.40	Noah NGENY	KEN	Roma	7 Jul 1999
Eur	3:46.32	Steve CRAM	GBR	Oslo	27 Jul 1985
NAm	3:47.69	Steve SCOTT	USA	Oslo	7 Jul 1982
Oce	3:49.08	John WALKER	NZL	Oslo	7 Jul 1982
Asi	3:51.12	Mohammed SULEIMAN	QAT	Zürich	16 Aug 1995
SAm	3:52.97	Hudson Santos de SOUZA	BRA	Roma	12 Jul 2002
CAC	3:57.34	Byron DYCE	JAM	Stockholm	1 Jul 1974
W20	3:50.25	Alex KIPCHIRCHIR	KEN	Rieti	7 Sep 2003
W18	3:54.56	Isaac SONGOK	KEN	Linz	20 Aug 2001

2000 METRES

W, Afr	4:44.79	Hicham EL GUERROUJ	MAR	Berlin	7 Sep 1999
Com	4:48.74	John KIBOWEN	KEN	Hechtel	1 Aug 1998
Eur	4:51.39	Steve CRAM	GBR	Budapest	4 Aug 1985
Oce	4:51.52	John WALKER	NZL	Oslo	30 Jun 1976
NAm	4:52.44	Jim SPIVEY	USA	Lausanne	15 Sep 1987
Asi	4:55.57	Mohammed SULEIMAN	QAT	Roma	8 Jun 1995
W18, W20	4:56.86	Issac SONGOK	KEN	Berlin	31 Aug 2001
SAm	5:03.34	Hudson Santos de SOUZA	BRA	Manaus	6 Apr 2002
CAC	5:03.4	Arturo BARRIOS	MEX	Nice	10 Jul 1989

3000 METRES

W, Afr, Com	7:20.67	Daniel KOMEN	KEN	Rieti	1 Sep 1996
Eur	7:26.62	Mohammed MOURHIT	BEL	Monaco	18 Aug 2000
NAm	7:30.84	Bob KENNEDY	USA	Monte Carlo	8 Aug 1998
CAC	7:35.71	Arturo BARRIOS	MEX	Nice	10 Jul 1989
Oce	7:37.30	Craig MOTTRAM	AUS	Monaco	19 Jul 2002
Asi	7:38.20	Mohammed SULEIMAN	QAT	Berlin	27 Aug 1993
SAm	7:39.70	Hudson Santos de SOUZA	BRA	Lausanne	2 Jul 2002
W20	7:30.67	Kenenisa BEKELE	ETH	Bruxelles	24 Aug 2001
W18	7:39.22	Hiillary CHENONGE	KEN	Bruxelles	30 Aug 2002

5000 METRES

W, Afr	12:39.36	Haile GEBRSELASSIE	ETH	Helsinki	13 Jun 1998
Com	12:39.74	Daniel KOMEN	KEN	Bruxelles	22 Aug 1997
Eur	12:49.71	Mohammed MOURHIT	BEL	Bruxelles	25 Aug 2000
NAm	12:58.21	Bob KENNEDY	USA	Zürich	14 Aug 1996
CAC	13:07.79	Arturo BARRIOS	MEX	London	14 Jul 1989
Oce	13:12.04	Craig MOTTRAM	AU	Melbourne	7 Mar 2002
Asi	13:04.65	Abdullah Ahmad HASSAN	QAT	Zürich	15 Aug 2003
SAm	13:19.64	Antonio SILIO	ARG	Roma	17 Jul 1991
W20	12:52.61	Eliud KIPCHOGE	KEN	Oslo	27 Jun 2003
W18	13:06.47	Hiillary CHENONGE	KEN	Zürich	16 Aug 2002

10,000 METRES

W, Afr	26:22.75	Haile GEBRSELASSIE	ETH	Hengelo	1 Jun 1998
Com	26:27.85	Paul TERGAT	KEN	Bruxelles	22 Aug 1997
Eur	26:52.30	Mohammed MOURHIT	BEL	Bruxelles	3 Sep 1999
CAC	27:08.23	Arturo BARRIOS	MEX	Berlin	18 Aug 1989
NAm	27:13.98	Mebrahtom KEFLEZIGHI	USA	Palo Alto	4 May 2001
Oce	27:31.92	Shaun CREIGHTON	AUS	Melbourne	25 Nov 1996
Asi	26:38.76	Abdullah Ahmad HASSAN	QAT	Bruxelles	5 Sep 2003
SAm	27:38.72	Antonio SILIO	ARG	Bruxelles	3 Sep 1993
W20	27:11.18	Richard CHELIMO	KEN	Hengelo	25 Jun 1991

MARATHON

W. Afr, Com	2:04:55	Paul TERGAT	KEN	Berlin	28 Sep 2003
NAm	2:05:38	Khalid KHANNOUCHI (ex MAR)	USA	London	14 Apr 2002
SAm	2:06:05	Ronaldo da COSTA	BRA	Berlin	20 Sep 1998
Asi	2:06:16	Toshinari TAKAOKA	JPN	Chicago	13 Oct 2002
Eur	2:06:36	António PINTO	POR	London	16 Apr 2000
	2:06:36	Benoît ZWIERZCHLEWSKI	FRA	Paris	6 Apr 2003
CAC	2:07:19	Andrés ESPINOSA	MEX	Boston	18 Apr 1994
Oce	2:07:51	Rob DE CASTELLA	AUS	Boston	21 Apr 1986
W20	2:10:46	LI Zhuhong	CHN	Beijing	14 Oct 2001

Boston course has an overall net drop of 139m (0.33%), and in 1994 there was a strong following wind.

3000 METRES STEEPLECHASE

W, Afr	7:55.28	Brahim BOULAMI	MAR	Bruxelles	24 Aug 2001
Com	7:55.72	Bernard BARMASAI	KEN	Köln	24 Aug 1997
Asi	7:57.38	Saif Saaeed SHAHEEN	QAT	Monte Carlo	14 Sep 2003
Eur	8:06.91	Simon VROEMEN	NED	Monaco	19 Jul 2002
	8:06.91	Bouabdallah TAHRI	FRA	Saint-Denis	4 Jul 2003
NAm	8:09.17	Henry MARSH	USA	Koblenz	28 Aug 1985
Oce	8:14.05	Peter RENNER	NZL	Koblenz	29 Aug 1984
SAm	8:14.41	Wander MOURA	BRA	Mar del Plata	22 Mar 1995
CAC	8:25.69	Salvador MIRANDA	MEX	Barakaldo	9 Jul 2000
W20	7:58.66	Stephen CHERONO	KEN	Bruxelles	24 Aug 2001
W18	8:19.12	Stephen CHERONO	KEN	Zürich	11 Aug 1999

110 METRES HURDLES

W, Eur, Com	12.91	Colin JACKSON	GBR	Stuttgart	20 Aug 1993
NAm	12.92	Roger KINGDOM	USA	Zürich	16 Aug 1989
	12.92	Allen JOHNSON	USA	Atlanta	23 Jun 1996
	12.92	Allen JOHNSON	USA	Bruxelles	23 Aug 1996
CAC	13.00	Anier GARCIA	CUB	Sydney	25 Sep 2000
Asi	13.12	LIU Xiang	CHN	Lausanne	2 Jul 2002
Afr	13.26	Shaun BOWNES	RSA	Heusden	14 Jul 2001
Oce	13.29	Kyle VANDER-KUYP	AUS	Göteborg	11 Aug 1995
SAm	13.34	Redelen DOS SANTOS	BRA	São Paulo	6 Sep 2003
W20	13.12	LIU Xiang	CHN	Lausanne	2 Jul 2002
W18	13.43	SHI Dongpeng	CHN	Shanghai	5 May 2001

400 METRES HURDLES

W, NAm	46.78	Kevin YOUNG	USA	Barcelona	6 Aug 1992
Afr, Com	47.10	Samuel MATETE	ZAM	Zürich	7 Aug 1991
CAC	47.25	Felix SÁNCHEZ	DOM	Saint-Denis	29 Aug 2003
Eur	47.37	Stéphane DIAGANA	FRA	Zürich	16 Aug 2002
Asi	47.53	Hadi Sou'an AL-SOMAILY	KSA	Sydney	27 Sep 2000
SAm	48.04	Eronilde de ARAUJO	BRA	Nice	12 Jul 1995
Oce	48.28	Rohan ROBINSON	AUS	Atlanta	31 Jul 1996
W20	48.02	Danny HARRIS	USA	Los Angeles	17 Jun 1984
W18	48.89	Louis VAN ZYL	RSA	Kingston	19 Jul 2002

HIGH JUMP

W, CAC	2.45	Javier SOTOMAYOR	CUB	Salamanca	27 Jul 1993
Eur	2.42	Patrik SJÖBERG	SWE	Stockholm	30 Jun 1987
	2.42 i§	Carlos THRÄNHARDT	GER	Berlin	26 Feb 1988
NAm	2.40 i§	Hollis CONWAY	USA	Sevilla	10 Mar 1991
		Charles AUSTIN	USA	Zürich	7 Aug 1991
Asi	2.39	ZHU Jianhua	CHN	Eberstadt	10 Jun 1984
Com	2.38i	Steve SMITH	GBR	Wuppertal	4 Feb 1994
	2.38	Troy KEMP	BAH	Nice	12 Jul 1995
Afr	2.37	Jacques FREITAG	RSA	Durban	23 Mar 2002
Oce	2.36	Tim FORSYTH	AUS	Melbourne	2 Mar 1997
SAm	2.33	Gilmar MAYO	COL	Pereira	17 Oct 1994
W20	2.37	Dragutin TOPIC	YUG	Plovdiv	12 Aug 1990
		Steve SMITH	GBR	Seoul	20 Sep 1992
W18	2.33	Javier SOTOMAYOR	CUB	La Habana	19 May 1984

POLE VAULT

W, Eur	6.15 i§	Sergey BUBKA	UKR	Donetsk	21 Feb 1993
	6.14 A	Sergey BUBKA	UKR	Sestriere	31 Jul 1994
Oce, Com	6.05	Dmitriy MARKOV	AUS	Edmonton	9 Aug 2001
Afr	6.03	Okkert BRITS	RSA	Köln	18 Aug 1995

NAm	6.03	Jeff HARTWIG	USA	Jonesboro	14 Jun 2000
Asi	5.92i	Igor POTAPOVICH	KAZ	Stockholm	19 Feb 1998
	5.90	Grigoriy YEGOROV	KAZ	Stuttgart 19 Aug 1993 & London	10 Sep 1993
	5.90	Igor POTAPOVICH	KAZ	Nice	10 Jul 1996
SAm	5.76	Tom HINTNAUS	BRA	Zürich	21 Aug 1985
CAC	5.70A	Dominic JOHNSON	LCA	El Paso	26 Aug 2000
	5.72A §	Paul BENAVIDES	MEX	El Paso	18 Jun 1994
W20	5.80	Maksim TARASOV	RUS	Bryansk	14 Jul 1989
W18	5.50	István BAGYULA	HUN	Milano	19 Jun 1986

LONG JUMP

W, NAm	8.95	Mike POWELL	USA	Tokyo	30 Aug 1991
Eur	8.86 A	Robert EMMIYAN	ARM	Tsakhkadzor	22 May 1987
CAC	8.71	Iván PEDROSO	CUB	Salamanca	18 Jul 1995
Com	8.62	James BECKFORD	JAM	Orlando	5 Apr 1997
Oce	8.49	Jai TAURIMA	AUS	Sydney	28 Sep 2000
Afr	8.46	Cheikh TOURÉ	SEN	Bad Langensalza	15 Jun 1997
SAm	8.40	Douglas de SOUZA	BRA	São Paulo	15 Feb 1995
Asi	8.40	LAO Jianfeng	CHN	Zhaoqing	28 May 1997
W20	8.34	Randy WILLIAMS	USA	München	8 Sep 1972
W18	8.25	Luis Alberto BUENO	CUB	La Habana	28 Sep 1986

TRIPLE JUMP

W, Eur, Com	18.29	Jonathan EDWARDS	GBR	Göteborg	7 Aug 1995
NAm	18.09	Kenny HARRISON	USA	Atlanta	27 Jul 1996
CAC	17.92	James BECKFORD	JAM	Odessa, Texas	20 May 1995
SAm	17.89 A	João Carlos de OLIVEIRA	BRA	Ciudad de México	15 Oct 1975
Oce	17.46	Ken LORRAWAY	AUS	London	7 Aug 1982
Asi	17.35	Oleg SAKIRKIN	KAZ	Moskva	5 Jun 1994
Afr	17.34	Ndabezinhle MDHLONGWA	ZIM	Lafayette	28 Mar 1998
W20	17.50	Volker MAI	GER	Erfurt	23 Jun 1985
W18	16.89	GU Junjie	CHN	Dalian	5 May 1985

SHOT

W, NAm	23.12	Randy BARNES	USA	Westwood	20 May 1990
Eur	23.06	Ulf TIMMERMANN	GER	Hania	22 May 1988
Afr, Com	21.97	Janus ROBBERTS	RSA	Eugene	2 Jun 2001
SAm	20.90	Gert WEIL	CHL	Wirges	17 Aug 1986
CAC	20.78	Alexis PAUMIER	CUB	La Habana	29 Jul 2000
Asi	20.60	Shakti SINGH	IND	Bangalore	5 Jul 2000
Oce	20.96	Justin ANLEZARK	AUS	Brisbane	5 Apr 2003
W20	21.05 i§	Terry ALBRITTON	USA	New York	22 Feb 1974
	20.65 §	Mike CARTER	USA	Boston	4 Jul 1979
	20.39	Janus ROBBERTS	RSA	Germiston	7 Mar 1998
W18	18.73	Karsten STOLZ	GER	Essen	2 Sep 1981
W20 6kg	21.96	Edis ELKASEVIC	CRO	Zagreb	20 Jun 2002

DISCUS

W, Eur	74.08	Jürgen SCHULT	GER	Neubrandenburg	6 Jun 1986
NAm	72.34 ¶	Ben PLUCKNETT	USA	Stockholm	7 Jul 1981
	71.32 §	Ben PLUCKNETT	USA	Eugene	4 Jun 1983
CAC	71.06	Luis DELIS	CUB	La Habana	21 May 1983
Afr, Com	70.32	Frantz KRUGER	RSA	Salon-de-Provence	26 May 2002
Oce	65.62 §	Werner REITERER	AUS	Melbourne	15 Dec 1987
	65.06	Wayne MARTIN	AUS	Newcastle	3 Jan 1979
Asi	65.16	LI Shaojie	CHN	Nanjing	7 May 1996
SAm	64.30	Ramón JIMÉNEZ-GAONA	PAR	Eugene	23 May 1992
W20	65.62 §	Werner REITERER	AUS	Melbourne	15 Dec 1987
	63.64	Werner HARTMANN	GER	Strasbourg	25 Jun 1978
W18	62.36	NU Ermaimaiti Tulake	CHN	Guangzhou	21 Nov 2001
W20 1.75kg	65.88	Omar Ahmed EL GHAZALI	EGY	Cairo	7 Nov 2003

¶ Disallowed by the IAAF following retrospective disqualification for drug abuse, but ratified by the AAU/TAC

HAMMER

W, Eur	86.74	Yuriy SEDYKH	UKR/RUS	Stuttgart	30 Aug 1986
Asi	84.86	Koji MUROFUSHI	JPN	Praha	29 Jun 2003
NAm	82.52	Lance DEAL	USA	Milano	7 Sep 1996

Afr, Com	80.19	Chris HARMSE	RSA	Pretoria	12 Apr 2002
Oce	79.29	Stuart RENDELL	AUS	Varazdin	6 Jun 2002
CAC	77.78	Alberto SÁNCHEZ	CUB	La Habana	15 May 1998
SAm	76.42	Juan CERRA	ARG	Trieste	25 Jul 2001
W20	78.33	Olli-Pekka KARJALAINEN	FIN	Seinäjoki	5 Aug 1999
W18	73.66	Vladislav PISKUNOV	UKR	Live	11 Jun 1994
W20 6kg	81.34	Krisztian PARS	HUN	Szmobathely	2 Sep 2001

JAVELIN

W, Eur	98.48	Jan ZELEZNY	CZE	Jena	25 May 1996
Com	91.46	Steve BACKLEY	GBR	Auckland (NS)	25 Jan 1992
NAm	89.16 §	Tom PETRANOFF	USA	Potchefstroom	1 Mar 1991
	87.12	Tom PUKSTYS	USA	Jena	25 May 1997
Afr	88.75	Marius CORBETT	RSA	Kuala Lumpur	21 Sep 1998
Oce	88.20	Gavin LOVEGROVE	NZL	Oslo	5 Jul 1996
Asi	87.60	Kazuhiro MIZOGUCHI	JPN	San José	27 May 1989
CAC	87.12	Emeterio GONZALEZ	CUB	Jena	3 Jun 2000
SAm	84.70	Edgar BAUMANN	PAR	San Marcos	17 Oct 1999
W20	83.87	Andreas THORKILDSEN	NOR	Fana	7 Jun 2001
W18	79.96	Aki PARVIAINEN	FIN	Pyhäselkä	12 Sep 1991

DECATHLON

W,Eur	9026	Roman SEBRLE	CZE	Götzis	27 May 2001
NAm	8891	Dan O'BRIEN	USA	Talence	5 Sep 1992
Com	8847	Daley THOMPSON	GBR	Los Angeles	9 Aug 1984
Oce	8490	Jagan HAMES	AUS	Kuala Lumpur	18 Sep 1998
Asi	8445	Ramil GANIYEV	UZB	Athína	6 Aug 1997
CAC	8252	Raúl DUANY	CUB	La Habana	24 Jul 2000
SAm	8291 m	Tito STEINER	ARG	Provo	23 Jun 1983
	8266	Pedro da SILVA	BRA	Walnut	24 Apr 1987
Afr	7965	Hamdi DHOUIBI	TUN	Tunis	9 Aug 2002
W20	8397	Torsten VOSS	GER	Erfurt	7 Jul 1982
W18	8104h	Valter KÜLVET	EST	Viimsi	23 Aug 1981
	7829	Valter KÜLVET	EST	Stockholm	13 Sep 1981

20 KILOMETRES WALK

W, SAm	1:17:21	Jefferson PÉREZ	ECU	Saint-Denis	23 Aug 2003
Eur	1:17:22	Francisco FERNÁNDEZ	ESP	Turku	28 Apr 2002
CAC	1:17:25.6 t	Bernardo SEGURA	MEX	Fana	7 May 1994
Asi	1:18:04	BO Lingtang	CHN	Beijing	7 Apr 1994
Oce, Com	1:18:14	Nathan DEAKES	AUS	Dublin	16 Jun 2001
Afr	1:19:02	Hatem GHOULA	TUN	Eisenhüttenstadt	10 May 1997
NAm	1:21:03	Arturo HUERTA	CAN	Etobicoke	7 Jul 2000
W20	1:18:06 §	Viktor BURAYEV	RUS	Adler	4 Mar 2001
W18	1:21:12	LIU Yunfeng	CHN	Wajima	14 Apr 1996

20,000 METRES TRACK WALK

W, CAC	1:17:25.6	Bernardo SEGURA	MEX	Fana	7 May 1994
Eur	1:18:35.2	Stefan JOHANSSON	SWE	Fana	15 May 1992
Oce, Com	1:19:48.1	Nathan DEAKES	AUS	Brisbane	4 Sep 2001
Asi	1:20:24.4	LI Mingcai	CHN	Jinan	15 Mar 1992
SAm	1:20:55.4	Jefferson PÉREZ	ECU	Fana	4 May 1996
NAm	1:22:27.0	Tim BERRETT	CAN	Edmonds, WA	9 Jun 1996
Afr	1:22:51.84	Hatem GHOULA	TUN	Leutkirch	8 Sep 1994
W20	1:21:29.2	Viktor BURAYEV	RUS	Brisbane	4 Sep 2001
W18	1:24:28.3	ZHU Hongjun	CHN	Xian	15 Sep 1999

50 KILOMETRES WALK

W, Eur	3:36:03	Robret KORZENIOWSKI	POL	Saint-Denis	27 Aug 2003
Asi	3:39:22	Sergey KOREPANOV	KAZ	Mézidon-Canon	2 May 1999
Oce, Com	3:39:43	Nathan DEAKES	AUS	Melbourne	7 Dec 2003
CAC	3:41:20	Raúl GONZÁLEZ	MEX	Praha-Podebrady	11 Jun 1978
NAm	3:47:48	Marcel JOBIN	CAN	Québec	20 Jun 1981
SAm	3:52:16	Héctor MORENO	COL	Naumberg	25 May 1997
Afr	3:59:56	Hatem GHOULA	TUN	Naumburg	5 May 2002
W20	3:43:41	ZHANG Huiqiang	CHN	Zhuhai	12 Mar 1996
W18	3:45:46	YU Guoping	CHN	Guangzhou	23 Nov 2001

50,000 METRES TRACK WALK

W, Eur	3:40:57.9	Thierry TOUTAIN	FRA	Héricourt	29 Sep 1996

CAC	3:41:38.4	Raúl GONZÁLEZ	MEX	Fana	25 May 1979
Oce, Com	3:43:50.0	Simon BAKER	AUS	Melbourne	9 Sep 1990
Asi	3:48:13.7	ZHAO Yongshen	CHN	Fana	7 May 1994
NAm	3:56:13.0	Tim BERRETT	CAN	Saskatoon	21 Jul 1991
SAm	4:14:28.5	Jorge LOREFICE	ARG	Buenos Aires	9 May 1993
	4:14:28.5	Benjamin LOREFICE	ARG	Buenos Aires	9 May 1993
Afr	4:21:44.5	Abdelwahab FERGUÈNE	ALG	Toulouse	25 Mar 1984

4 X 100 METRES RELAY

W, NAm	37.40	USA (Marsh, Burrell, Mitchell, C.Lewis)	Barcelona	8 Aug 1992
	37.40	USA (Drummond, Cason, Mitchell, Burrell)	Stuttgart	21 Aug 1993
Com	37.69	CAN (Esmie, Gilbert, Surin, Bailey)	Atlanta	3 Aug 1996
Eur	37.73	GBR (Gardener, Campbell, Devonish, Chambers)	Sevilla	29 Aug 1999
SAm	37.90	BRA (V Lima, Ribeiro, A da Silva, Cl da Silva)	Sydney	30 Sep 2000
Afr	37.91	NGR (Asonze, Obikwelu, Effiong, Aliu)	Sevilla	29 Aug 1999
CAC	38.00	CUB (Simón, Lamela, Isasi, Aguilera)	Barcelona	8 Aug 1992
Oce	38.17	AUS (Henderson, Jackson, Brimacombe, Marsh)	Göteborg	12 Aug 1995
Asi	38.31	JPN (Inoue, K Ito, Tsuchie, Asahara)	Athína	9 Aug 1997
	38.31	JPN (Kawabata, K ito, Suetsugu, Asahara)	Sydney	29 Sep 2000
W20	38.92	USA (Collins, Felix, Williams, Hordge)	Kingston	21 Jul 2002
W18	40.03	JAM (W Smith, M Frater, Spence, O Brown)	Bydgoszcz	18 Jul 1999

4 X 400 METRES RELAY

W, NAm	2:54.20	USA (Young, Pettigrew, Washington, Johnson)	Uniondale, NY	22 Jul 1998
Eur	2:56.60	GBR (Thomas, Baulch, Richardson, Black)	Atlanta	3 Aug 1996
CAC, Com	2:56.75	JAM (McDonald, Haughton, McFarlane, Clarke)	Athína	10 Aug 1997
SAm	2:58.56	BRA (C da Silva, A J dos Santos, de Araújo, Parrela)	Winnipeg	30 Jul 1999
Afr	2:58.68	NGR (Chukwu, Monye, Nada, Udo-Obong)	Sydney	30 Sep 2000
Oce	2:59.70	AUS (Frayne, Clark, Minihan, Mitchell)	Los Angeles	11 Aug 1984
Asi	3:00.76	JPN (Karube, K Ito, Osakada, Omori)	Atlanta	3 Aug 1996
W20	3:01.90	USA (Campbell, Rish, Waddle, Reed)	Athína	20 Jul 1986
W18	3:12.05	POL (Zrada, Kedzia, Grzegorczyk, Kowalski)	Kaunas	5 Aug 2001

World Records at other men's events recognised by the IAAF

20km	56:55.6	Arturo BARRIOS (now USA)	MEX	La Flèche	30 Mar 1991
1 Hour	21,101 m	Arturo BARRIOS (now USA)	MEX	La Flèche	30 Mar 1991
25km	1:13:55.8	Toshihiko SEKO	JPN	Christchurch	22 Mar 1981
30km	1:29:18.8	Toshihiko SEKO	JPN	Christchurch	22 Mar 1981
4 x 200m	1:18.68	Santa Monica Track Club	USA	Walnut	17 Apr 1994
		(Michael Marsh, Leroy Burrell, Floyd Heard, Carl Lewis)			
4 x 800m	7:03.89	United Kingdom Team	GBR	London	30 Aug 1982
		(Peter Elliott, Garry Cook, Steve Cram, Sebastian Coe)			
4 x l500m	14:38.8 m	F.R.Germany Team	GER	Köln	17 Aug 1977
		(Thomas Wessinghage, Harald Hudak, Michael Lederer, Karl Fleschen)			
Track Walking					
2 Hours	29,572m	Maurizio DAMILANO	ITA	Cuneo	4 Oct 1992
30km	2:01:44.1	Maurizio DAMILANO	ITA	Cuneo	4 Oct 1992

WOMEN

100 METRES

W, NAm	10.49	Florence GRIFFITH JOYNER	USA	Indianapolis	16 Jul 1988
Eur	10.73	Christine ARRON	FRA	Budapest	19 Aug 1998
CAC, Com	10.74	Merlene OTTEY	JAM	Milano	7 Sep 1996
Asi	10.79	LI Xuemei	CHN	Shanghai	18 Oct 1997
Afr	10.90	Glory ALOZIE	NGR	La Laguna	5 Jun 1999
	10.84 §	Chioma AJUNWA	NGR	Lagos	11 Apr 1992
Oce	11.12A	Melinda GAINSFORD/TAYLOR	AUS	Sestriere	31 Jul 1994
SAm	11.17A	Lucimar de MOURA	BRA	Bogotá (sf)	25 Jun 1999
	11.17A	Lucimar de MOURA	BRA	Bogotá	25 Jun 1999
W20	10.88	Marlies OELSNER/GÖHR	GER	Dresden	1 Jul 1977
W18	11.13	Chandra CHEESEBOROUGH	USA	Eugene	21 Jun 1976

200 METRES

W, NAm	21.34	Florence GRIFFITH JOYNER	USA	Seoul	29 Sep 1988
CAC, Com	21.64	Merlene OTTEY	JAM	Bruxelles	13 Sep 1991
Eur	21.71	Marita KOCH	GER	Chemnitz	10 Jun 1979
	21.71 §	Marita KOCH	GER	Potsdam	21 Jul 1984
	21.71	Heike DRECHSLER	GER	Jena	29 Jun 1986
	21.71 §	Heike DRECHSLER	GER	Stuttgart	29 Aug 1986

Asi	22.01	LI Xuemei	CHN	Shanghai	22 Oct 1997
Afr	22.06 A§	Evette DE KLERK	RSA	Pietersburg	8 Apr 1989
	22.07	Mary ONYALI	NGR	Zürich	14 Aug 1996
Oce	22.23	Melinda GAINSFORD-TAYLOR	AUS	Stuttgart	13 Jul 1997
SAm	22.60A	Lucimar de MOURA	BRA	Bogotá	26 Jun 1999
W20	22.11A	Allyson FELIX	USA	Ciudad de México	3 May 2003
W18	22.58	Marion JONES	USA	New Orleans	28 Jun 1992

400 METRES

W, Eur	47.60	Marita KOCH	GER	Canberra	6 Oct 1985
Oce, Com	48.63	Cathy FREEMAN	AUS	Atlanta	29 Jul 1996
NAm	48.83	Valerie BRISCO	USA	Los Angeles	6 Aug 1984
CAC	48.89	Ana GUEVARA	MEX	Saint-Denis	27 Aug 2003
Afr	49.10	Falilat OGUNKOYA	NGR	Atlanta	29 Jul 1996
SAm	49.64	Ximena RESTREPO	COL	Barcelona	5 Aug 1992
Asi	49.81	MA Yuqin	CHN	Beijing	11 Sep 1993
W20	49.42	Grit BREUER	GER	Tokyo	27 Aug 1991
W18	50.01	LI Jing	CHN	Shanghai	18 Oct 1997

800 METRES

W, Eur	1:53.28	Jarmila KRATOCHVÍLOVÁ	CZE	München	26 Jul 1983
CAC	1:54.44	Ana Fidelia QUIROT	CUB	Barcelona	9 Sep 1989
Afr	1:55.19	Maria Lurdes MUTOLA	MOZ	Zürich	17 Aug 1994
Com	1:55.29	Maria Lurdes MUTOLA	MOZ	Köln	24 Aug 1997
Asi	1:55.54	LIU Dong	CHN	Beijing	9 Sep 1993
NAm	1:56.40	Jearl MILES CLARK	USA	Zürich	11 Aug 1999
SAm	1:56.68	Letitia VRIESDE	SUR	Göteborg	13 Aug 1995
Oce	1:58.25	Toni HODGKINSON	NZL	Atlanta	27 Jul 1996
W20, W18	1:57.18	WANG Yuan	CHN	Beijing	8 Sep 1993

1000 METRES

W, Eur	2:28.98	Svetlana MASTERKOVA	RUS	Bruxelles	23 Aug 1996
Afr	2:29.34	Maria Lurdes MUTOLA	MOZ	Bruxelles	25 Aug 1995
Com	2:29.66	Maria Lurdes MUTOLA	MOZ	Bruxelles	23 Aug 1996
NAm	2:31.80	Regina JACOBS	USA	Brunswick	3 Jul 1999
SAm	2:32.25	Letitia VRIESDE	SUR	Berlin	10 Sep 1991
CAC	2:33.21	Ana Fidelia QUIROT	CUB	Jerez de la Frontera	13 Sep 1989
Asi	2:33.6 §	Svetlana ULMASOVA	UZB	Podolsk	5 Aug 1979
Oce	2:38.54	Alison WRIGHT	NZL	Berlin	17 Aug 1979
W20	2:35.4a	Irina NIKITINA	RUS	Podolsk	5 Aug 1979
	2:35.4	Katrin WÜHN	GDR	Potsdam	12 Jul 1984
W18	2:38.58	Jo WHITE	GBR	London (CP)	9 Sep 1977

1500 METRES

W, Asi	3:50.46	QU Yunxia	CHN	Beijing	11 Sep 1993
Eur	3:52.47	Tatyana KAZANKINA	RUS	Zürich	13 Aug 1980
Afr	3:55.30	Hassiba BOULMERKA	ALG	Barcelona	8 Aug 1992
NAm	3:57.12	Mary DECKER/SLANEY	USA	Stockholm	26 Jul 1983
Com	3:57.41	Jackline MARANGA	KEN	Monaco	8 Aug 1998
Oce	4:01.34	Margaret CROWLEY	AUS	Oslo	5 Jul 1996
CAC	4:01.84	Yvonne GRAHAM	JAM	Monaco	25 Jul 1995
SAm	4:05.67	Letitia VRIESDE	SUR	Tokyo	31 Aug 1991
W20	3:51.34	LANG Yinglai	CHN	Shanghai	18 Oct 1997
W18	3:54.52	ZHANG Ling	CHN	Shanghai	18 Oct 1997

1 MILE

W, Eur	4:12.56	Svetlana MASTERKOVA	RUS	Zürich	14 Aug 1996
NAm	4:16.71	Mary SLANEY	USA	Zürich	21 Aug 1985
Com	4:17.57	Zola BUDD	GBR	Zürich	21 Aug 1985
Afr	4:20.79	Hassiba BOULMERKA	ALG	Oslo	6 Jul 1991
CAC	4:24.64	Yvonne GRAHAM	JAM	Zürich	17 Aug 1994
Oce	4:25.84	Margaret CROWLEY	AUS	Monaco	10 Aug 1996
SAm	4:30.05	Soraya TELLES	BRA	Praha	9 Jun 1988
Asi	4:34.81	Ikuko TAMURA	JPN	Amagasaki	15 Jun 2002
W20	4:17.57	Zola BUDD	GBR	Zürich	21 Aug 1985
W18	4:30.81	Gelete BURIKA	ETH	Heusden	2 Aug 2003

2000 METRES

W, Eur	5:25.36	Sonia O'SULLIVAN	IRL	Edinburgh	8 Jul 1994
Com	5:26.93	Yvonne MURRAY	GBR	Edinburgh	8 Jul 1994
Asi	5:29.43 §	WANG Junxia	CHN	Beijing	12 Sep 1993

NAm	5:32.7	Mary SLANEY	USA	Eugene	3 Aug 1984
Afr	5:35.62	Berhane ADERE	ETH	Ostrava	12 Jun 2003
Oce	5:37.71	Benita JOHNSON	AUS	Ostrava	12 Jun 2003
W20	5:33.15	Zola BUDD	GBR	London (CP)	13 Jul 1984
W18	5:46.5+	Sally BARSOSIO	KEN	Zürich	16 Aug 1995

3000 METRES

W, Asi	8:06.11	WANG Junxia	CHN	Beijing	13 Sep 1993
Eur	8:21.42	Gabriela SZABO	ROM	Monaco	19 Jul 2002
Com	8:22.20	Paula RADCLIFFE	Eng	Monaco	19 Jul 2002
Afr	8:23.23	Edith MASAI	KEN	Monaco	19 Jul 2002
NAm	8:25.83	Mary SLANEY	USA	Roma	7 Sep 1985
CAC	8:37.07	Yvonne GRAHAM	JAM	Zürich	16 Aug 1995
Oce	8:38.06	Benita JOHNSON	AUS	Gateshead	13 Jul 2003
SAm	9:02.37	Delirde BERNARDI	BRA	Linz	4 Jul 1994
W20	8:28.83	Zola BUDD	GBR	Roma	7 Sep 1985
W18	8:36.45	MA Ningning	CHN	Jinan	6 Jun 1993

5000 METRES

W, Asi	14:28.09	JIANG Bo	CHN	Shanghai	23 Oct 1997
Eur	14:29.32	Olga YEGOROVA	RUS	Berlin	31 Aug 2001
Afr	14:29.32	Berhane ADERE	ETH	Oslo	27 Jun 2003
Com	14:31.42	Paula RADCLIFFE	Eng	Manchester	28 Jul 2002
NAm	14:45.35	Regina JACOBS	USA	Sacramento	21 Jul 2000
Oce	14:47.60	Benita JOHNSON	AUS	Berlin (P)	6 Sep 2002
CAC	15:04.32	Adriana FERNÁNDEZ	MEX	Gresham	17 May 2003
SAm	15:22.01	Carmen de OLIVEIRA	BRA	Hechtel	31 Jul 1993
W20	14:39.94	Tirunesh DIBABA	ETH	Oslo	27 Jun 2003
W18	14:45.71	SONG Liqing	CHN	Shanghai	21 Oct 1997

10,000 METRES

W, Asi	29:31.78	WANG Junxia	CHN	Beijing	8 Sep 1993
Eur, Com	30:01.09	Paula RADCLIFFE	GBR/Eng	München	6 Aug 2002
Afr	30:04.18	Berhane ADERE	ETH	Saint-Denis	23 Aug 2003
Oce	30:37.68	Benita JOHNSON	AUS	Saint-Denis	23 Aug 2003
NAm	30:50.32	Deena DROSSIN	USA	Stanford	3 May 2002
CAC	31:10.12	Adriana FERNANDEZ	MEX	Brunswick	1 Jul 2000
SAm	31:47.76	Carmen de OLIVEIRA	BRA	Stuttgart	21 Aug 1993
W20	30:31.55	XING Huina	CHN	Saint-Denis	23 Aug 2003
W18	31:11.26	SONG Liqing	CHN	Shanghai	19 Oct 1997

MARATHON

W, Eur, Com	2:15:25	Paula RADCLIFFE	GBR/Eng	London	13 Apr 2003
Afr	2:18:47	Catherine NDEREBA	KEN	Chicago	7 Oct 2001
Asi	2:19:39	SUN Yingjie	CHN	Beijing	19 Oct 2003
NAm	2:21:16	Deena DROSSIN	USA	London	13 Apr 2003
Oce	2:23:51	Lisa MARTIN/ONDIEKI	AUS	Osaka	31 Jan 1988
CAC	2:24:06	Adriana FERNANDEZ	MEX	London	18 Apr 1999
SAm	2:27:41	Carmen de OLIVEIRA	BRA	Boston (dh 139m & wa)	18 Apr 1994
W20	2:23:37	LIU Min	CHN	Beijing	14 Oct 2001

3000 METRES STEEPLECHASE

W, Eur	9:08.33	Gulnara SAMITOVA	RUS	Tula	10 Aug 2003
W20, Oce, Com	9:30.70	Melissa ROLLISON	AUS	Brisbane	4 Sep 2001
Afr	9:39.51	Dorcus INZIKURU	UGA	Ostrava	12 Jun 2003
NAm	9:44.71	Briana SHOOK	USA	Stanford	22 Jun 2003
Asi	9:50.88	CHEN Xiaofang	CHN	Shanghai	14 Sep 2003
CAC	9:58.9	Korene HINDS	JAM	Walnut	19 Apr 2002
SAm	10:20.75	Michelle COSTA	BRA	Rio de Janeiro	23 May 2003
W18	10:10.73	Melissa ROLLISON	AUS	Sydney	25 Feb 2000

100 METRES HURDLES

W, Eur	12.21	Yordanka DONKOVA	BUL	Stara Zagora	20 Aug 1988
NAm	12.33	Gail DEVERS	USA	Sacramento	23 Jul 2000
Asi	12.44	Olga SHISHIGINA	KAZ	Luzern	27 Jun 1995
Afr, Com	12.44	Glory ALOZIE	NGR	Monaco	8 Aug 1998
	12.44	Glory ALOZIE	NGR	Bruxelles	28 Aug 1998

	12.44	Glory ALOZIE	NGR	Sevilla	28 Aug 1999
CAC	12.45	Brigitte FOSTER	JAM	Eugene	24 May 2003
SAm	12.71	Maurren MAGGI	BRA	Manaus	19 May 2001
Oce	12.93	Pam RYAN	AUS	München	4 Sep 1972
W20	12.84	Aliuska LÓPEZ	CUB	Zagreb	16 Jul 1987
W18	12.95	Candy YOUNG	USA	Walnut	16 Jun 1979

400 METRES HURDLES

Eur, W	52.34	Yuliya PECHONKINA	RUS	Tula	8 Aug 2003
NAm	52.61	Kim BATTEN	USA	Göteborg	11 Aug 1995
Com	52.74	Sally GUNNELL	GBR	Stuttgart	19 Aug 1993
CAC	52.82	Deon HEMMINGS	JAM	Atlanta	31 Jul 1996
Afr	52.90	Nezha BIDOUANE	MAR	Sevilla	25 Aug 1999
Oce	53.17	Debbie FLINTOFF-KING	AUS	Seoul	28 Sep 1988
Asi	53.96	HAN Qing	CHN	Beijing	9 Sep 1993
	53.96	SONG Yinglan	CHN	Guangzhou	22 Nov 2001
SAm	56.05	Ximena RESTREPO	ECU	Valencia, VEN	26 Nov 1994
W20	54.70	Lashinda DEMUS	USA	Kingston	19 Jul 2002
W18	55.15	HUANG Xiaoxiao	CHN	Guangzhou	22 Nov 2001

HIGH JUMP

W, Eur	2.09	Stefka KOSTADINOVA	BUL	Roma	30 Aug 1987
Afr, Com	2.06	Hestrie CLOETE	RSA	Saint-Denis	31 Aug 2003
CAC	2.04	Silvia COSTA	CUB	Barcelona	9 Sep 1989
NAm	2.03	Louise RITTER	USA	Austin	8 Jul 1988
	2.03	Louise RITTER	USA	Seoul	30 Sep 1988
Oce	1 98	Vanessa WARD	AUS	Perth	12 Feb 1989
	1.98	Alison INVERARITY	AUS	Ingolstadt	17 Jul 1994
Asi	1.97	JIN Ling	CHN	Hamamatsu	7 May 1989
	1.97*	Svetlana ZALEVSKAYA	KAZ	Pierre-Benité	14 Jun 1996
	1.97	Svetlana ZALEVSKAYA	KAZ	Lausanne	5 Jul 2000
	1.97	Tatyana EFIMENKO	KGZ	Roma	11 Jul 2003
SAm	1.96	Solange WITTEVEEN	ARG	Oristano	8 Sep 1997
W20	2.01	Olga TURCHAK	KAZ	Moskva	7 Jul 1986
	2.01	Heike BALCK	GER	Chemnitz	18 Jun 1989
W18	1.96A	Charmaine GALE	RSA	Bloemfontein	4 Apr 1981
	1.96	Olga TURCHAK	KAZ	Donetsk	7 Sep 1984

POLE VAULT

W, Eur	4.82	Yelena ISINBAYEVA	RUS	Gateshead	13 Jul 2003
NAm	4.81	Stacy DRAGILA	USA	Palo Alto	9 Jun 2001
Oce, Com	4.60	Emma GEORGE	AUS	Sydney	20 Feb 1999
Asi	4.52	GAO Shuying	CHN	Beijing	29 Aug 2001
SAm	4.42	Alejandra GARCIA	ARG	Sydney	20 Feb 2000
Afr	4.42	Elmarie GERRYTS	RSA	Wesel	12 Jun 2000
CAC	4.20	Katiuska PÉREZ	CUB	La Habana	30 May 2003
W20	4.46 §	Yelena ISINBAYEVA	RUS	Berlin	31 Aug 2001
	4.47i	Yelena ISINBAYEVA	RUS	Budapest (OH)	10 Feb 2001
W18	4.31	Monika GÖTZ	GER	Troisdorf	9 May 1998

LONG JUMP

W, Eur	7.52	Galina CHISTYAKOVA	RUS	Sankt-Peterburg	11 Jun 1988
NAm	7.49	Jackie JOYNER-KERSEE	USA	New York	22 May 1994
	7.49A*	Jackie JOYNER-KERSEE	USA	Sestriere	31 Jul 1994
SAm	7.26A	Maurren MAGGI	BRA	Bogotá	26 Jun 1999
Afr	7.12	Chioma AJUNWA	NGR	Atlanta	1 Aug 1996
Asi	7.01	YAO Weili	CHN	Jinan	5 Jun 1993
Oce, Com	7.00	Bronwyn THOMPSON	AUS	Melbouren	7 Mar 2002
CAC	6.99	Lissette CUZA	CUB	Jena	3 Jun 2000
W20	7.14	Heike DAUTE/Drechsler	GER	Bratislava	4 Jun 1983
W18	6.91	Heike DAUTE/Drechsler	GDR	Jena	9 Aug 1981

TRIPLE JUMP

W, Eur	15.50	Inessa KRAVETS	UKR	Göteborg	10 Aug 1995
CAC	15.29	Yamilé ALDAMA	CUB	Roma	11 Jul 2003
Com	15.16i	Ashia HANSEN	GBR	Valencia	26 Feb 1998
	15.16	Ashia HANSEN	GBR	Fukuoka	13 Sep 1997
Afr	14.82	Françoise MBANGO Etone	CMR	Manchester	31 Jul 2002
Asi	14.72	HUANG Qiuyan	CHN	Guangzhou	22 Nov 2001
SAm	14.53	Maurren MAGGI	BRA	São Caetano do Sul	27 Apr 2003

NAm	14.41	Sheila HUDSON	USA	Stockholm	8 Jul 1996
Oce	14.04	Nicole MLADENIS	AUS	Perth	7 Dec 2003
W20	14.62	Tereza MARINOVA	BUL	Sydney	25 Aug 1996
W18	14.57	HUANG Qiuyan	CHN	Shanghai	19 Oct 1997

SHOT

W, Eur	22.63	Natalya LISOVSKAYA	RUS	Moskva	7 Jun 1987
Asi	21.76	LI Meisu	CHN	Shijiazhuang	23 Apr 1988
CAC	20.96	Belsy LAZA	CUB	Ciudad de México	2 May 1992
NAm	20.18	Ramona PAGEL	USA	San Diego	25 Jun 1988
Oce, Com	19.74	Gael MARTIN	AUS	Berkeley	14 Jul 1984
SAm	19.30	Elisângela ADRIANO	BRA	Tunja	14 Jul 2001
Afr	18.43	Vivianne CHUKWUEMEKA	NGR	Walnut	19 Apr 2003
W20	20.54	Astrid KUMBERNUSS	GER	Orimattila	1 Jul 1989
W18	19.08	Ilke WYLUDDA	GDR	Chemnitz	9 Aug 1986

DISCUS

W, Eur	76.80	Gabriele REINSCH	GER	Neubrandenburg	9 Jul 1988
Asi	71.68	XIAO Yanling	CHN	Beijing	14 Mar 1992
CAC	70.88	Hilda RAMOS	CUB	La Habana	8 May 1992
Oce, Com	68.72	Daniela COSTIAN	AUS	Auckland	22 Jan 1994
NAm	66.10	Carol CADY	USA	San José	31 May 1986
SAm	61.98	Elisângela ADRIANO	BRA	São Leopoldo	21 May 1999
Afr	61.74	Monia KARI	TUN	Tunis	1 May 1996
W20	74.40	Ilke WYLUDDA	GER	Berlin	13 Sep 1988
W18	65.86	Ilke WYLUDDA	GDR	Neubrandenburg	1 Aug 1986

HAMMER

W, Eur	76.07	Mihaela MELINTE	ROM	Rüdlingen	29 Aug 1999
CAC	75.14	Yipsi MORENO	CUB	Savona	17 Jul 2003
Asi	72.03	GU Yuan	CHN	Shanghai	12 Sep 2003
NAm	72.01	Anna NORGREN-MAHON	USA	Walnut	27 Jul 2002
Oce, Com	71.12	Bronwyn EAGLES	AUS	Adelaide	6 Feb 2003
Afr	65.26	Marwa Ahmed HUSSEIN	EGY	Szombathely	10 Aug 2003
SAm	62.16	Karina MOYA	ARG	Santa Fé	9 Jun 2001
W20	71.71	Kamila SKOLIMOWSKA	POL	Melbourne	9 Sep 2001
W18	70.60	ZHANG Wenxiu	CHN	Nanning	5 Apr 2003

JAVELIN

W, CAC	71.54	Osleidys MENÉNDEZ	CUB	Réthymno	1 Jul 2001
Eur	69.48	Trine HATTESTAD	NOR	Oslo	28 Jul 2000
Oce, Com	66.80	Louise CURREY	AUS	Gold Coast	5 Aug 2000
Asi	63.92	WEI Jianhua	CHN	Beijing	18 Aug 2000
SAm	62.62A	Sabina MOYA	COL	Ciudad de Guatemala	12 May 2002
Afr	61.59A	Sunette VILJOEN	RSA	Potchefstroom	5 Dec 2003
NAm	60.86	Kim KREINER	USA	Santo Domingo	7 Aug 2003
W20, W18	62.93	XUE Juan	CHN	Changsha	27 Oct 2003

HEPTATHLON

W, NAm	7291	Jackie JOYNER-KERSEE	USA	Seoul	24 Sep 1988
Eur	7007	Larisa NIKITINA	RUS	Bryansk	11 Jun 1989
Asi	6942	Ghada SHOUAA	SYR	Götzis	26 May 1996
Com	6831	Denise LEWIS	GBR	Talence	30 Jul 2000
Oce	6695	Jane FLEMMING	AUS	Auckland	28 Jan 1990
CAC	6527	Diane GUTHRIE-GRESHAM	JAM	Knoxville	3 Jun 1995
Afr	6416	Eunice BARBER	SLE	Talence	15 Sep 1996
SAm	6017	Conceição GEREMIAS	BRA	Caracas	25 Aug 1983
W20	6542	Carolina KLÜFT	SWE	München	10 Aug 2002
W18	6185	SHEN Shengfei	CHN	Shanghai	18 Oct 1997

10 KILOMETRES WALK

W, Eur	41:04	Yelena NIKOLAYEVA	RUS	Sochi	20 Apr 1996
Asi	41:16	WANG Yan	CHN	Eisenhüttenstadt	8 May 1999
Oce, Com	41:30	Kerry SAXBY-JUNNA	AUS	Canberra	27 Aug 1988
CAC	42:42	Graciella MENDOZA	MEX	Naumburg	25 May 1997
NAm	44:17	Michelle ROHL	USA	Göteborg	7 Aug 1995
SAm	45:03	Geovana IRUSTA	BOL	Podebrady	19 Apr 1997
Afr	45:06A	Susan VERMEULEN	RSA	Bloemfontein	17 Apr 1999
W20	41:55	Irina STANKINA	RUS	Adler	11 Feb 1995

10,000 METRES TRACK WALK

W, Eur	41:56.23	Nadyezhda RYASHKINA	RUS	Seattle	24 Jul 1990
Oce	41:57.22	Kerry SAXBY-JUNNA	AUS	Seattle	24 Jul 1990
Asi	42:30.13	GAO Hongmiao	CHN	Nanjing	24 Oct 1995
NAm	44:30.1 m	Alison BAKER	CAN	Fana	15 May 1992
	44:06 no kerb	Michelle ROHL	USA	Kenosha	2 Jun 1996
CAC	44:51.81	Graciela MENDOZA	MEX	Athína	4 Aug 1997
SAm	45:59.95	Geovana IRUSTA	BOL	Rio de Janeiro	20 May 2000
Afr	51:11.2 m	Sabeha MANSOURI	ALG	Cairo	26 Aug 1995
W20	42:49.7 §	GAO Hongmiao	CHN	Jinan	15 Mar 1992
	43:35.2	Lyudmila YEFIMKINA	RUS	Msokva	20 May 2000
W18	42:56.09t	GAO Hongmiao	CHN	Tangshan	27 Sep 1991

20,000 METRES TRACK WALK

W, Eur	1:26:52.3	Olimpiada IVANOVA	RUS	Brisbane	6 Sep 2001
Oce,Com	1:33:40.2	Kerry SAXBY-JUNNA	AUS	Brisbane	6 Sep 2001
CAC	1:34:56.7	Maria del Rosario SÁNCHEZ	MEX	Xalapa	16 Jul 2000
NAm	1:34:31.08	Michelle ROHL	USA	Stanford	21 Jun 2003
Asi	1:36:18.2	LI Yuxin	CHN	Qufu	27 Sep 1999
SAm	1:37:32.0	Geovanna IRUSTA	BOL	Ciudad de Guatamala	12 May 2003
W20	1:29:32.4 #	SONG Hongjuan	CHN	Changsha	24 Oct 2003
W18	1:37:33.9	GAO Kelian	CHN	Xian	18 Sep 1999

20 KILOMETRES WALK

W, Eur	1:24:50	Olimpiada IVANOVA	RUS	Adler	4 Mar 2001
Asi	1:26:22	WANG Yan	CHN	Guangzhou	19 Nov 2001
Oce, Com	1:28:56	Jane SAVILLE	AUS	Vallansbæk	6 May 2000
CAC	1:30:03	Graciela MENDOZA	MEX	Mézidon-Canon	2 May 1999
NAm	1:31:51	Michelle ROHL	USA	Kenosha	13 May 2000
SAm	1:33:42	Geovana IRUSTA	BOL	Saint-Denis	24 Aug 2003
Afr	1:36:18	Susan VERMEULEN	RSA	Mézidon-Canon	2 May 1999
W20	1:27:16	SONG Hongjuan	CHN	Yangzhou	14 Apr 2003
W18	1:30:52	JIANG Kun	CHN	Dandong	13 Apr 2001

4 X 100 METRES RELAY

W, Eur	41.37	GDR (Gladisch, Rieger, Auerswald, Göhr)	Canberra	6 Oct 1985
NAm	41.47	USA (Gaines, Jones, Miller, Devers)	Athína	9 Aug 1997
CAC, Com	41.92	BAH (Fynes, Sturrup, Davis-Thompson, Ferguson)	Sevilla	29 Aug 1999
Asi	42.23	CHN (Sichuan) (Xiao Lin, Li Yali, Liu Xiaomei, Li Xuemei)	Shanghai	23 Oct 1997
Afr	42.39	NGR (Utondu, Idehen, Opara-Thompson, Onyali)	Barcelona	7 Aug 1992
Oce	42.99A	AUS (Massey, Broadrick, Lambert, Gainsford-Taylor)	Pietersburg	18 Mar 2000
SAm	43.42	COL (Mera, Palacios, Rodríguez, Brock)	Göteborg	12 Aug 1995
W20	43.33 §	GDR (Breuer, Krabbe, Dietz, Henke)	Berlin	20 Jul 1988
	43.38	USA (A Joyce, Aleah Williams, Robinson, Buchanan)	Tampa	11 Jul 1999
W18	44.05	GDR (Koppetsch, Oelsner, Sinzel, Brehmer)	Athína	24 Aug 1975

4 X 400 METRES RELAY

W, Eur	3:15.17	URS (Ledovskaya, Nazarova, Pinigina, Bryzgina)	Seoul	1 Oct 1988
NAm	3:15.51	USA (D.Howard, Dixon, Brisco, Griffith Joyner)	Seoul	1 Oct 1988
Afr	3:21.04	NGR (Bisi Afolabi, Yusuf, Opara, Ogunkoya)	Atlanta	3 Aug 1996
Com	3:21.21	CAN (Crooks, Richardson, Killingbeck, Payne)	Los Angeles	11 Aug 1984
CAC	3:21.30	JAM (Turner, L Graham, Hemmings, Richards)	Athína	10 Aug 1997
Oce	3:23.81	AUS (Peris, Lewis, Gainsford-Taylor, Freeman)	Sydney	30 Sep 2000
Asi	3:24.28	CHN / Hebei (An, Bai, Cao, Ma)	Beijing	13 Sep 1993
SAm	3:28.07	BRA (Almirão, Tito, Teodoro, Coutinho)	Santo Domingo	9 Aug 2003
W20	3:28.39	GDR (Derr, Fabert, Wöhlk, Breuer)	Sudbury	31 Jul 1988
W18	3:36.98	GBR (Ravenscroft, E McMeekin, Kennedy, Pettett)	Duisburg	26 Aug 1973

World Records at other events recognised by the IAAF

1 Hour	18,340 m	Tegla LOROUPE	KEN	Borgholzhausen	7 Aug 1998
20km	1:05:26.6	Tegla LOROUPE	KEN	Borgholzhausen	3 Sep 2000
25km	1:27:05.84	Tegla LOROUPE	KEN	Mengerskirchen	21 Sep 2002
30km	1:45:50.0	Tegla LOROUPE	KEN	Warstein	6 Jun 2003
4x200m	1:28.15	GDR (Göhr, R Müller, Wöckel, Koch)		Jena	9 Aug 1980
4x800m	7:50.17	USSR (Olizarenko, Gurina, Borisova, Podyalovskaya)		Moskva	5 Aug 1984

WORLD BESTS AT NON-STANDARD EVENTS

50m	5.53	Bruny Surin	CAN	Sevilla (in 100m)	22 Aug 1999
	5.53	Ben Johnson ¶	CAN	Rome (in 100m)	30 Aug 1987
	drugs dq 5.52	Ben Johnson		Seoul (in 100m)	24 Sep 1988
60m	6.38	Ben Johnson ¶	CAN	Roma (in 100m)	30 Aug 1987
drugs dq	6.37	Ben Johnson	CAN	Seoul (in 100m)	24 Sep 1988
150m	14.8	Pietro Mennea	ITA	Cassino	22 May 1983
	14.93	John Regis	GBR	Stuttgart (in 200m)	20 Aug 1993
300m	30.85A	Michael Johnson	USA	Pretoria	24 Mar 2000
	31.48	Danny Everett	USA	Jerez de la Frontera	3 Sep 1990
	31.48	Roberto Hernández	CUB	Jerez de la Frontera	3 Sep 1990
500m	1:00.08	Donato Sabia	ITA	Busto Arsizio	26 May 1984
600m	1:12.81	Johnny Gray	USA	Santa Monica	24 May 1986
2 miles	7:58.61	Daniel Komen	KEN	Hechtel	19 Jul 1997
2000m Steeple	5:14.43	Julius Kariuki	KEN	Rovereto	21 Aug 1990
200mh	22.55	Laurent Ottoz	ITA	Milano	31 May 1995
(hand time)	22.5	Martin Lauer	FRG	Zürich	7 Jul 1959
220yh straight	21.9	Don Styron	USA	Baton Rouge	2 Apr 1960
300mh	34.59	Chris Rawlinson	GBR	Loughboroigh	30 Jul 2000
35lb weight	25.41	Lance Deal	USA	Azusa	20 Feb 1993
Pentathlon	4282 points	Bill Toomey	USA	London (CP)	16 Aug 1969
(1985 tables)		(7.58, 66.18, 21.3, 44.52, 4:20.3)			
Double decathlon	14185 points	Kip Janvrin	USA	Turku	7/8 Sep 2002

11.42, 6.79, 200mh 25.31, 13.63, 5k 18:23.97, 2:02.46, 1.87, 400m 50642, HT 34.27, 3kSt 11:22.96
15.23, DT 40.91, 200m 22.56, 4.93, 10:13.16, 400mh 54.40, 58.31, 4:45.76, TJ 13.18, 10k 42:37.71

3000m walk	10:47.11	Giovanni De Benedictis	ITA	San Giovanni Valdamo	19 May 1990
5000m walk	18:05.49	Hatem Ghoula	TUN	Tunis	1 May 1997
10000m walk	38:02.60	Josef Pribilinec	SVK	Banská Bystrica	30 Aug 1985
5 km road walk	18:21	Robert Korzeniowski	POL	Hildesheim	16 Sep 1990
10 km road walk	37:11	Roman Rasskazov	RUS	Saransk	28 May 2000
100 km road walk	8:38:07	Viktor Ginko	BLR	Scanzorosciate	27 Oct 2002

Women

50m	5.93	Marion Jones	USA	Sevilla (in 100m)	22 Aug 1999
60m	6.85	Marion Jones	USA	Sevilla (in 100m)	22 Aug 1999
150m	16.10	Florence Griffith-Joyner	USA	Seoul (in 200m)	29 Sep 1988
300m	34.1	Marita Koch	GDR	Canberra (in 400m)	6 Oct 1985
500m	1:05.9	Tatána Kocembová	CZE	Ostrava	2 Aug 1984
600m	1:22.63	Ana Fidelia Quirot	CUB	Guadalajara	25 Jul 1997
2 miles	9:11.97 mx	Regina Jacobs	USA	Los Gatos	12 Aug 1999
2000m Steeple	6:11.84	Marina Pluzhnikova	RUS	Sankt Peterburg	25 Jul 1994
200mh	25.6	Patricia Girard	FRA	Nantes	23 Aug 2001
	25.82	Patricia Girard	FRA	Nantes	22 Sep 1999
Double heptathlon	10798 pts	Milla Kelo	FIN	Turku	8 Sep 2002

100mh 14.89, HJ 1.51, 500m 5:03.74, 400mh 62.18, SP 12.73, 200m 25.16, 100m 12.59
LJ 5.73w, 400m 56.10, JT 32.69, 800m 2:23.94, 200mh 28.72, DT 47.86, 3000m 11:48.68

Decathlon	7885	Mona Steigauf	GER	Ahlen	20/21Sep 1997

12.15, 5.93, 12.49, 1.73, 55.34, 13.75, 34.68, 3.10, 42.24, 5:07.95

3000m walk	11:48.24	Ileana Salvador	ITA	Padova	29 Aug 1993
5000m walk	20:02.60	Gillian O'Sullivan	IRL	Dublin	13 Jul 2002
50 km road walk	4:19:13	Yelena Ginko	BLR	Scanzorosciate	27 Oct 2002
100 km road walk	10:13:56	Kora Boufflert	FRA	Roubaix	9 Oct 1994

LONG DISTANCE WORLD BESTS – MEN TRACKI

	hr:min:sec	*Name*	*Nat*	*Venue*	*Date*
15 km	0:42:34.0	Arturo Barrios	MEX	La Flèche	30 Mar 1991
10 miles	0:45:57.6	Jos Hermens	NED	Papendal	14 Sep 1975
15 miles	1:11:43.1	Bill Rodgers	USA	Saratoga, Cal.	21 Feb 1979
20 miles	1:39:14.4	Jack Foster	NZL	Hamilton, NZ	15 Aug 1971
30 miles	2:42:00	Jeff Norman	GBR	Timperley, Cheshire	7 Jun 1980
50 km	2:48:06	Jeff Norman	GBR	Timperley, Cheshire	7 Jun 1980
40 miles	3:48:35	Don Ritchie	GBR	London (Hendon)	16 Oct 1982
50 miles	4:51:49	Don Ritchie	GBR	London (Hendon)	12 Mar 1983
100 km	6:10:20	Don Ritchie	GBR	London (CP)	28 Oct 1978
150 km	10:34:30	Denis Zhalybin	RUS	London (CP)	20 Oct 2002
100 miles	11:28:03	Oleg Kharitonov	RUS	London (CP)	20 Oct 2002
200 km	15:10:27	Yiannis Kouros	AUS	Adelaide	4-5 Oct 1997
200 miles	27:48:35	Yiannis Kouros	GRE	Montauban	15-16 Mar 1985
500 km	60:23.00	Yiannis Kouros	GRE	Colac, Aus	26-29 Nov 1984
500 miles	105:42:09	Yiannis Kouros	GRE	Colac, Aus	26-30 Nov 1984

1000 km	136:17:00	Yiannis Kouros	GRE	Colac, Aus	26-31 Nov 1984
1500 km	10d 17:28:26	Petrus Silkinas	LTU	Nanango, Qld	11-21 Mar 1998
1000 mile	11d 13:54:58	Petrus Silkinas	LTU	Nanango, Qld	11-22 Mar 1998
2 hrs	37.994 km	Jim Alder	GBR	Walton-on-Thames	17 Oct 1964
12 hrs	162.400 km	Yiannis Kouros	GRE	Montauban	15 Mar 1985
24 hrs	303.506 km *	Yiannis Kouros	AUS	Adelaide	4-5 Oct 1997
48 hrs	473.797 km	Yiannis Kouros	AUS	Surgères	3-5 May 1996
6 days	1030.000 indoor	Jean-Gilles Bousiquet	FRA	La Rochelle	16-23 Nov 1992
Outdoors	1023.200 km *	Yiannis Kouros	GRE	Colac, Aus	26 Nov-1 Dec 1984
	1022.068 km	Yiannis Kouros	GRE	New York	2-8 Jul 1984

 # Running watch time, no stopped times known.

LONG DISTANCE ROAD RECORDS & BESTS – MEN

Where superior to track bests and run on properly measured road courses. (I) Official IAAF recognition.

	hr:min:sec	*Name*	*Nat*	*Venue*	*Date*
10 km (I)	0:27:02	Haile Gebrselassie	ETH	Doha	11 Dec 2002
15 km (I)	0:41:29	Felix Limo	KEN	Nijmegen	11 Nov 2001
10 miles	0:44:45	Paul Koech	KEN	Amsterdam-Zaandam	21 Sep 1997
20 km (I)	0:56:18+	Paul Tergat	KEN	Milano	4 Apr 1998
Half mar (I)	0:59:17	Paul Tergat	KEN	Milano	4 Apr 1998
	0:59:06 #	Paul Tergat	KEN	Lisboa (downhill 40m)	26 Mar 2000
25 km (I)	1:13:14	Rodgers Rop	KEN	Berlin	6 May 2001
30 km (I)	1:28:36	Takayuki Matsumiya	JPN	Kumamoto	14 Feb 2003
20 miles	1:35:22+	Steve Jones	GBR	Chicago	10 Oct 1985
30 miles	2:37:31+	Thompson Magawana	RSA	Claremont-Kirstenbosch	12 Apr 1988
50km	2:43:38	Thompson Magawana	RSA	Claremont-Kirstenbosch	12 Apr 1988
40 miles	3:45:39	Andy Jones	CAN	Houston	23 Feb 1991
50 miles	4:50:21	Bruce Fordyce	RSA	London-Brighton	25 Sep 1983
100 km (I)	6:13:33	Takahiro Sunada	JPN	Yubetsu	21 Jun 1998
1000 miles	10d:10:30:35	Yiannis Kouros	GRE	New York	21-30 May 1988
Ekiden (5 stages)	1:55:59	(I)	ETH	Chiba	24 Nov 2003
	Birhanu Dejene, Hailu Mekonnen, Gebre. Gebremariam, Markos Geneti, Sileshi Sihine				
12 hrs	162.543 km	Yiannis Kouros	GRE	Queen's, New York	7 Nov 1984
6 days	1028.370 km	Yiannis Kouros	GRE	New York	21-26 May 1988

LONG DISTANCE WORLD BESTS – WOMEN TRACK

	hr:min:sec	*Name*	*Nat*	*Venue*	*Date*
15 km	0:49:44.0	Silvana Cruciata	ITA	Roma	4 May 1981
10 miles	0:54:21.8	Lorraine Moller	NZL	Auckland	9 Jan 1993
20 miles	1:59:09 !	Chantal Langlacé	FRA	Amiens	3 Sep 1983
30 miles	3:12:25	Carolyn Hunter-Rowe	GBR	Barry, Wales	3 Mar 1996
50 km	3:18:52	Carolyn Hunter-Rowe	GBR	Barry, Wales	3 Mar 1996
40 miles	4:26:43	Carolyn Hunter-Rowe	GBR	Barry, Wales	7 Mar 1993
50 miles	5:55:41	Valentina Lyakhova	RUS	Nantes	28 Sep 1996
100 km	7:14:05.8	Norimi Sakurai	JPN	San Giovanni Lupatoto	27 Sep 2003
150 km	13:45:54	Hilary Walker	GBR	Blackpool	5-6 Nov 1988
100 miles	14:25:45	Edit Bérces	HUN	San Giovanni Lupatoto	22 Sep 2002
200 km	18:31:43	Edit Bérces	HUN	San Giovanni Lupatoto	22 Sep 2002
200 miles	39:09:03	Hilary Walker	GBR	Blackpool	5-7 Nov 1988
500 km	77:53:46	Eleanor Adams	GBR	Colac, Aus.	13-16 Nov 1989
500 miles	130:59:58	Sandra Barwick	NZL	Campbelltown, AUS	18-23 Nov 1990
1000 km	8d 00:27:06	Eleanor Robinson	GBR	Nanango, Qld	11-19 Mar 1998
1500 km	12d 06:52:12	Eleanor Robinson	GBR	Nanango, Qld	11-23 Mar 1998
1000 miles	13d 02:16:49	Eleanor Robinson	GBR	Nanango, Qld	11-24 Mar 1998
2 hrs	32.652 km	Chantal Langlacé	FRA	Amiens	3 Sep 1983
12 hrs	147.600 km	Ann Trason	USA	Hayward, Cal	3-4 Aug 1991
24 hrs	250.106 km	Edit Bérces	HUN	San Giovanni Lupatoto	22 Sep 2002
48 hrs	377.892 km	Sue Ellen Trapp	USA	Surgères	2-4 May 1997
6 days	883.631 km	Sandra Barwick	NZL	Campbelltown, AUS	18-24 Nov 1990

! Timed on one running watch only, * lap recorded by computer

LONG DISTANCE ROAD BESTS - WOMEN

	hr:min:sec	*Name*	*Nat*	*Venue*	*Date*
10 km (I)	0:30:21	Paula Radcliffe	GBR	San Juan	23 Feb 2003
15 km (I)	0:46:57	Elana Meyer	RSA	Cape Town	2 Nov 1991
	0:46:411+ dh	Paula Radcliffe	GBR	Newcastle	21 Sep 2003
10 miles	0:50:54	Lornah Kiplagat	KEN	Zaandam	22 Sep 2002
	0:50:01+ dh	Paula Radcliffe	GBR	Newcastle	21 Sep 2003
20 km (I)	1:03:26+	Paula Radcliffe	GBR	Bristol	6 Oct 2001

	1:02:21+ dh	Paula Radcliffe	GBR	London	13 Apr 2003
Half mar (l)	1:06:44	Elana Meyer	RSA	Tokyo	15 Jan 1999
	1:05:40 dh	Paula Radcliffe	GBR	South Shields	21 Sep 2003
25 km (l)	1:22:31+	Naoko Takahashi	JPN	Berlin	30 Sep 2001
	1:21:21+ dh	Ingrid Kristiansen	NOR	London	10 May 1987
30 km (l)	1:39:02+	Naoko Takahashi	JPN	Berlin	30 Sep 2001
	1:36:36+ dh	Paula Radcliffe	GBR	London	13 Apr 2003
20 miles	1:43:33+	Paula Radcliffe	GBR	London	13 Apr 2003
30 miles	3:01:16+	Frith van der Merwe	RSA	Claremont-Kirstenbosch	25 Mar 1989
50 km	3:08:39	Frith van der Merwe	RSA	Claremont-Kirstenbosch	25 Mar 1989
40 miles	4:26:13+	Ann Trason	USA	Houston	23 Feb 1991
50 miles	5:40:18	Ann Trason	USA	Houston	23 Feb 1991
100 km (l)	6:33:11	Tomoe Abe	JPN	Yubetsu	25 Jun 2000
100 miles	13:47:41	Ann Trason	USA	Queen's, New York	4 May 1991
200 km	19:00:31	Eleanor Adams	GBR	Milton Keynes (indoor)	3-4 Feb 1990
1000 km	7d 01:11:00	Sandra Barwick	NZL	New York	16-23 Sep 1991
1000 miles	12d 14:38:40	Sandra Barwick	NZL	New York	16-29 Sep 1991
Ekiden (6 stages)	2:11:22	(l)	ETH	Chiba	24 Nov 2003
Berhane Adere, Tirunesh Dibaba, Eyerusalem Kuma, Ejegayou Dibaba, Meseret Defar, Werknesh Kidane					
12 hours	144.840 km	Ann Trason	USA	Queen's, New York	4 May 1991
24 hours	243.657 km	Sigrid Lomsky	GER	Basel	1-2 May 1993

100 KILOMETRES CONTINENTAL RECORDS

W, Asi	6:13:33	Takahiro SUNADA	JPN	Yubetsu	21 Jun 1998
Eur	6:16:41	Jean-Paul PRAET	BEL	Torhout	24 Jun 1989
SAm	6:18:09	Valmir NUNES	BRA	Winschoten	16 Sep 1995
Afr	6:25:07	Bruce FORDYCE	RSA	Stellenbosch	4 Feb 1989
Oce	6:29:23	Tim SLOAN	AUS	Ross-Richmond	23 Apr 1995
NAm	6:30:11	Tom JOHNSON	USA	Winschoten	16 Sep 1995
WOMEN					
W, Asi	6:33:11	Tomoe ABE	JPN	Yubetsu	25 Jun 2000
NAm	7:00:48	Ann TRASON	USA	Winschoten	16 Sep 1995
Eur	7:18:57	Birgit LENNARTZ	GER	Hanau	28 Apr 1990
SAm	7:20:22	Maria VENANCIO	BRA	Cubatão	8 Aug 1998
Afr	7:31:47	Helena JOUBERT	RSA	Winschoten	16 Sep 1995
Oce	7:40:58	Linda MEADOWS	AUS	North Otago	18 Nov 1995

WORLD INDOOR RECORDS

Men					to March 2003
50 metres	5.56A	Donovan Bailey	CAN	Reno	9 Feb 1996
	5.56r	Maurice Greene	USA	Los Angeles	13 Feb 1999
	5.55 §	Ben Johnson ¶	CAN	Ottawa	31 Jan 1987
60 metres	6.39	Maurice Greene	USA	Madrid	3 Feb 1998
	6.39	Maurice Greene	USA	Atlanta	3 Mar 2001
200 metres	19.92	Frank Fredericks	NAM	Liévin	18 Feb 1996
400 metres	44.63	Michael Johnson	USA	Atlanta	4 Mar 1995
800 metres	1:42.67	Wilson Kipketer	KEN	Paris (Bercy)	9 Mar 1997
1000 metres	2:14.96	Wilson Kipketer	KEN	Birmingham	20 Feb 2000
1500 metres	3:31.18	Hicham El Guerrouj	MAR	Stuttgart	2 Feb 1997
1 mile	3:48.45	Hicham El Guerrouj	MAR	Gent	12 Feb 1997
2000 metres #	4:52.86	Haile Gebrselassie	ETH	Birmingham	16 Feb 1998
3000 metres	7:24.90	Daniel Komen	KEN	Budapest	6 Feb 1998
2 miles #	8:04.69	Haile Gebrselassie	ETH	Birmingham	21 Feb 2003
5000 metres	12:50.38	Haile Gebrselassie	ETH	Birmingham	14 Feb 1999
10000 metres #	27:50.29	Mark Bett	KEN	Gent	10 Feb 2002
50 m hurdles	6.25	Mark McKoy	CAN	Kobe	5 Mar 1986
60 m hurdles	7.30	Colin Jackson	GBR	Sindelfingen	6 Mar 1994
High jump	2.43	Javier Sotomayor	CUB	Budapest	4 Mar 1989
Pole vault	6.15	Sergey Bubka	UKR	Donetsk	21 Feb 1993
Long jump	8.79	Carl Lewis	USA	New York	27 Jan 1984
Triple jump	17.83	Aliecer Urrutia	CUB	Sindelfingen	1 Mar 1997
	17.83	Christian Olsson	SWE	Budapest	7 Mar 2004
Shot	22.66	Randy Barnes	USA	Los Angeles	20 Jan 1989
Javelin #	85.78	Matti Närhi	FIN	Kajaani	3 Mar 1996
35 lb weight #	25.86	Lance Deal	USA	Atlanta	4 Mar 1995
5000m walk	18:07.08	Mikhail Shchennikov	RUS	Moskva	14 Feb 1995
4 x 200m	1:22.11	United Kingdom		Glasgow	3 Mar 1991
		(Linford Christie, Darren Braithwaite, Ade Mafe, John Regis)			
4 x 400m	3:02.83	USA		Maebashi	7 Mar 1999

		(Andre Morris, Desmond Johnson, Deon Minor, Milton Campbell))			
4 x 800m	7:13.94	USA/Global Athletics & Marketing		Boston (Roxbury)	6 Feb 2000
		(Joey Woody, Karl Paranya, Rich Kenah, David Krummenacker)			
Heptathlon	6476 points	Dan O'Brien	USA	Toronto	13/14 Mar 1993
		(6.67 60m, 7.84 LJ, 16.02 SP, 2.13 HJ, 7.85 60mh, 5.20 PV, 2:57.96 1000m)			
Women					
50 metres	5.96	Irina Privalova	RUS	Madrid	9 Feb 1995
60 metres	6.92	Irina Privalova	RUS	Madrid 11 Feb 1993 &	11 Feb 1993
200 metres	21.87	Merlene Ottey	JAM	Liévin	13 Feb 1993
400 metres	49.59	Jarmila Kratochvílová	CZE	Milano	7 Mar 1982
800 metres	1:55.82	Jolanda Ceplak	SLO	Wien	3 Mar 2002
1000 metres	2:30.94	Maria Lurdes Mutola	MOZ	Stockholm	25 Feb 1999
1500 metres	3:59.98	Regina Jacobs	USA	Boston (Roxbury)	1 Feb 2003
1 mile	4:17.14	Doina Melinte	ROM	East Rutherford	9 Feb 1990
2000 metres #	5:30.53	Gabriela Szabo	ROM	Sindelfingen	8 Mar 1998
3000 metres	8:29.15	Berhane Adere	ETH	Stuttgart	3 Feb 2002
2 miles #	9:23.38	Regina Jacobs	USA	Boston (Roxbury)	27 Jan 2002
5000 metres	14:39.29	Berhane Adere	ETH	Stuttgart	31 Jan 2004
50 m hurdles	6.58	Cornelia Oschkenat	GDR	Berlin	20 Feb 1988
60 m hurdles	7.69	Lyudmila Narozhilenko	RUS	Chelyabinsk	4 Feb 1990
High jump	2.07	Heike Henkel	GER	Karlsruhe	8 Feb 1992
Pole vault	4.86	Yelena Isinbayeva	RUS	Budapest	6 Mar 2004
Long jump	7.37	Heike Drechsler	GDR	Wien	13 Feb 1988
Triple jump	15.35	Tatyana Lebedeva	RUS	Budapest	5 Mar 2004
Shot	22.50	Helena Fibingerová	CZE	Jablonec	19 Feb 1977
Javelin #	60.83	Mikaela Ingberg	FIN	Mustasaari	28 Feb 1999
20 lb weight #	23.11	Dawn Ellerbe	USA	New York	4 Feb 2000
3000m walk	11:35.34	Gillian O'Sullivan	IRL	Belfast	15 Feb 2003
5000m walk #	20:42.33	Yelena Gruzinova	RUS	Samara	1 Mar 1997
4 x 200m	1:32.55	SC Eintracht Hamm	FRG	Dortmund	20 Feb 1988
		(Helga Arendt, Silke-Beate Knoll, Mechthild Kluth, Gisela Kinzel)			
	1:32.55	LG Olympia Dortmund	GER	Karlsruhe	21 Feb 1999
		(Esther Möller, Gabi Rockmeier, Birgit Rockmeier, Andrea Philipp)			
4 x 400m	3:23.88	Russia		Budapest	7 Mar 2004
		(Olesya Krasnomovets, Olga Kotlyarova, Tatyana Levina, Natalya Nazarova)			
4 x 800m	8:18.71	Russia		Moskva	4 Feb 1994
		(Yelena Zaytseva, Olga Kuznetsova, Yelena Afanasyeva, Yekaterina Podkopayeva)			
Pentathlon	4991 points	Irina Belova	RUS	Berlin	14/15 Feb 1992
		(8.22 60mh, 1.93 HJ, 13.25 SP, 6.67 LJ, 2:10.26 800m)			

 # events not officially recognised by the IAAF

¶ The IAAF stripped Johnson of his records in January 1990, after he had admitted long-term steroid use.

WORLD VETERANS/MASTERS RECORDS

MEN - Aged 40 or over at time of performances

100 metres	10.29	Troy Douglas (30.11.62)	NED	Leiden	7 Jun 2003
200 metres	20.64	Troy Douglas (30.11.62)	NED	Utrecht	9 Aug 2003
400 metres	47.86	Eric Roeske (26.9.60)	NED	Potsdam	21 Aug 2002
	47.5u	Lee Evans (25.2.47)	USA		Apr 1989
800 metres	1:50.69	Colin Rothery (28.1.60)	IRL	Stretford	5 Sep 2000
	1:48.81i	Johnny Gray (19.6.60)	USA	Atlanta	3 Mar 2001
1000 metres	2:26.71i	Eamonn Coghlan (21.11.52)	IRL	Gainesville	21 Jan 1994
1500 metres	3:44.89	Luiz José Gonçalves (4.12.58)	BRA	Rio de Janeiro	4 Jun 1999
1 mile	4:02.53	David Moorcroft (10.4.53)	GBR	Belfast	19 Jun 1993
	3:58.15i	Eamonn Coghlan (21.11.52)	IRL	Boston	20 Feb 1994
3000 metres	8:05.08	Martti Vainio (30.12.50)	FIN	Mikkeli	12 Jun 1991
5000 metres	13:43.15	Mohamed Ezzher (26.4.60)	FRA	Sotteville	3 Jul 2000
10000 metres	28:30.88	Martti Vainio (30.12.50)	FIN	Hengelo	25 Jun 1991
Marathon	2:08:46	Andrés Espinosa (4.2.63)	MEX	Berlin	28 Sep 2003
3000m steeple	8:41.5	Gaston Roelants (5.2.37)	BEL	Oslo	6 Jul 1977
110m hurdles	14.16	Carlos Sala (20.3.60)	ESP	Castellón	16 Aug 2000
400m hurdles	52.62	Antônio Eusébio Dias Ferreira (2.3.60)	BRA	Rio de Janeiro	23 Jul 2000
High jump	2.15	Glen Conley (9.1.57)	USA	Troy, New York	2 Aug 1997
Pole vault	5.50A ?	Larry Jessee (31.3.52)	USA	El Paso	24 Aug 1996
Long jump	7.68A	Aaron Sampson (20.9.61)	USA	Cedar City	21 Jun 2001
	7.57	Hans Schicker (3.10.47)	FRG	Kitzingen	16 Jul 1989
Triple jump	16.58	Ray Kimble (19.4.53)	USA	Edinburgh	2 Jul 1993
Shot	21.41	Brian Oldfield (1.6.45)	USA	Innsbruck	22 Aug 1985
Discus	69.46	Al Oerter (19.9.36)	USA	Wichita	31 May 1980
Hammer	81.35	Igor Astapkovich (4.1.63)	BLR	Brest	11 Jul 2003

Javelin	84.08	Peter Blank (10.4.62)	GER	Ulm	29 Jun 2003
Pentathlon	3510 pts	Werner Schallau (8.9.38)	FRG	Gelsenkirchen	24 Sep 1978
		6.74, 59.20, 23.0, 43.76, 5:05.7			
Decathlon	6642 pts	Greg Richards (25.4.56)	GBR	Enfield	4 Aug 1996
		12.02, 6.81, 13.71, 1.86, 54.51, 15.63, 44.86, 4.00, 50.84, 5:18.14			
20 km walk	1:21:36	Willi Sawall (7.11.41)	AUS	Melbourne	4 Jul 1982
50 km walk	3:49:06	José Marín (21.1.50)	ESP	Badalona	22 Mar 1992
4x100m	42.79	Austin, Collins, Mitchell, Hartfield	USA		5 Feb 1992
4x400m	3:20.83	S Allah, K Morning, E Gonera, R Blackwell	USA	Philadelphia	27 Apr 2001

WOMEN – aged 35 or more

100 metres	10.74	Merlene Ottey (10.5.60)	JAM	Milano	7 Sep 1996
200 metres	21.93	Merlene Ottey (10.5.60)	JAM	Bruxelles	25 Aug 1995
400 metres	50.27	Jearl Miles Clark (4.9.66)	USA	Madrid	20 Sep 2002
800 metres	1:56.53	Lyubov Gurina (6.8.57)	RUS	Hechtel	30 Jul 1994
1000 metres	2:31.5	Maricica Puica (29.7.50)	ROM	Poiana Brasov	1 Jun 1986
1500 metres	3:57.73	Maricica Puica (29.7.50)	ROM	Bruxelles	30 Aug 1985
1 mile	4:17.33	Maricica Puica (29.7.50)	ROM	Zürich	21 Aug 1985
2000 metres	5:28.69	Maricica Puica (29.7.50)	ROM	London	11 Jul 1986
3000 metres	8:23.23	Edith Masai (4.4.67)	KEN	Monaco	19 Jul 2002
5000 metres	14:45.35	Regina Jacobs (28.8.63)	USA	Sacramento	21 Jul 2000
10000 metres	31:20.28	Ingrid Kristiansen (21.3.56)	NOR	Hechtel	10 Aug 1991
Marathon	2:24:35	Katrin Dörre-Heinig (6.10.61)	GER	Hamburg	25 Apr 1999
3000m steeple	9:51.21	Natalya Cherepanova (9.3.67)	RUS	Cheboksary	11 Jul 2002
100m hurdles	12.40	Gail Devers (19.11.66)	USA	Lausanne	2 Jul 2002
400m hurdles	52.94	Marina Styepanova (1.5.50)	RUS	Tashkent	17 Sep 1986
High jump	2.01	Inga Babakova (27.6.67)	UKR	Oslo	27 Jun 2003
Pole vault	4.22	Gabriela Mihalcea (27.1.64)	ROM	Dreux	11 Jun 1999
	4.25i	Gabriela Mihalcea (27.1.64)	ROM	Pireas	13 Feb 1999
Long jump	6.99	Heike Drechsler (16.12.64)	GER	Sydney	29 Sep 2000
Triple jump	14.42	Inessa Kravets (5.10.66)	UKR	Waszawa	15 Jun 2003
	14.44i	Inessa Kravets (5.10.66)	UKR	Moskva	30 Jan 2003
Shot	21.46	Larisa Peleshenko (29.2.64)	RUS	Moskva	26 Aug 2000
	21.47i	Helena Fibingerová (13.7.49)	CZE	Jablonec	9 Feb 1985
Discus	69.60	Faina Melnik (9.7.45)	RUS	Donetsk	9 Sep 1980
Hammer	69.17	Alla Davydova (21.5.66)	RUS	Valencia	24 May 2003
Javelin	64.89	Yekaterina Ivakina (4.12.64)	RUS	Oslo	28 Jul 2000
Heptathlon	6533 pts	Jane Frederick (7.4.52)	USA	Talence	27 Sep 1987
		13.60, 1.82, 15.50, 24.73; 6.29, 49.70, 2:14.88			
5000m walk	20:54.65	Yelena Nikolayeva (1.2.66)	RUS	Tivoli	6 Sep 2002
10km walk	42:42+	Tamara Kovalenko (5.6.64)	RUS	Moskva	19 May 2000
20km walk	1:25:59	Tamara Kovalenko (5.6.64)	RUS	Moskva	19 May 2000
4x100m	48.63	Desmier, Sulter, Andreas, Apavou	FRA	Eugene	8 Jun 1989
4x400m	3:50.80	Mitchell, Mathews, Beadnall, Gabriel	GBR	Gateshead	8 Aug 1999

WOMEN – aged 40 or more

100 metres	10.99	Merlene Ottey (10.5.60)	JAM	Thessaloniki	30 Aug 2000
200 metres	22.89	Merlene Ottey (10.5.60)	JAM	Nova Gorica	10 Aug 2003
400 metres	53.68A	Sara Montecinos (8.3.54)	CHI	Cali	19 Mar 1994
	53.73	Sara Montecinos (8.3.54)	CHI	Santiago de Chile	12 Nov 1994
800 metres	1:59.25	Yekaterina Podkopayeva (11.6.52)	RUS	Luxembourg	30 Jun 1994
1000 metres	2:36.16	Yekaterina Podkopayeva (11.6.52)	RUS	Nancy	14 Sep 1994
	2:36.08i	Yekaterina Podkopayeva (11.6.52	RUS	Liévin	13 Feb 1993
1500 metres	3:59.78	Yekaterina Podkopayeva (11.6.52)	RUS	Nice	18 Jul 1994
1 mile	4:23.78	Yekaterina Podkopayeva (11.6.52)	RUS	Roma	9 Jun 1993
3000 metres	9:11.2	Joyce Smith (26.10.37)	GBR	London	30 Apr 1978
	9:02.83i	Lyubov Kremlyova (21.12.61)	RUS	Moskva	22 Jan 2002
5000 metres	15:20.59	Elena Fidatov (24.7.60)	ROM	Bucuresti	7 Aug 2000
10000 metres	32:12.07	Nicole Lévêque (27.1.51)	FRA	Helsinki	13 Aug 1994
Marathon	2:26:51	Priscilla Welch (22.11.44)	GBR	London	10 May 1987
3000m steeple	10:38.98	Soraya Telles (15.9.58)	BRA	Rio de Janeiro	5 Jun 1999
100 m hurdles	13.55	Clova Court (10.2.60)	GBR	Bedford	19 Aug 2000
400 m hurdles	58.3	Gowry Retchakan (21.6.60))	GBR	Hoo	3 Sep 2000
	58.88	Maria José dos Santos (12.9.59)	BRA	Americana	3 Jun 2000
High jump	1.76	Debbie Brill (10.3.53) #	CAN	Gateshead	6 Aug 1999
Pole vault	3.50	Dawn Hartigan (13.11.56)	AUS	Melbourne	19 Mar 2001
	3.50	Alison Davies (6.4.61)	GBR	Birmingham	13 Jul 2002
Long jump	6.41	Vera Olenchenko (21.3.59)	RUS	Rostov-na-Donu	26 Jun 2000
Triple jump	12.49	Dana Urnánková (8.4.62)	CZE	Turnov	19 May 2002
Shot	19.05	Antonina Ivanova (25.12.32)	RUS	Oryol	28 Aug 1973
	19.16i	Antonina Ivanova	RUS	Moskva	24 Feb 1974

Discus	67.10	Ellina Zvereva (16.11.60)	BLR	Edmonton	11 Aug 2001
Hammer	59.29	Oneithea Lewis (11.6.60)	USA	Princetom	10 May 2003
Javelin (old)	64.06	Tessa Sanderson (14.3.56)	GBR	London (CP)	12 Jul 1996
Heptathlon	4359 pts	Conceição Geremias (23.7.56)	BRA	São Caetano do Sul	7 Sep 1997
		15.61, 1.57, 12.14, 28.26, 5.49, 32.08, 2:56.10			
5000m walk	22:49.06	Suzanne Griesbach (22.4.45)	FRA	Annecy	9 Aug 1987
10km walk	45:09+	Kerry Saxby-Junna (2.6.61)	AUS	Edmonton	9 Aug 2001
20km walk	1:33:40.2t	Kerry Saxby-Junna (2.6.61)	AUS	Brisbane	6 Sep 2001
4x100m	50.07	Horwedel, Fritsche, Grissmer, Stopka	GER	Gateshead	8 Aug 1999
4x400m	3:58.70	Foreman, Thompson, Board, Libal	GBR	Eugene	24 Aug 1996

 # W45 record

WORLD AND CONTINENTAL RECORDS SET IN 2003

OUTDOORS - MEN

100m	Oce	9.93	Patrick JOHNSON	AUS	Mito	5 May 2003
	W20	10.01	Darrel BROWN	TRI	Saint-Denis	24 Aug 2003
200m	W18	20.25	Usain BOLT	JAM	Kingston	5 Apr 2003
	Asi	20.03	Shingo SUETSUGU	JPN	Yokohama	7 Jun 2003
	W20=,W18	20.13	Usain BOLT	JAM	Bridgetown	20 Jul 2003
800m	W18	1:46.48	Mohammed AL-SALHI	KSA	Saint-Denis	28 Aug 2003
1M	W20	3:50.39	James KWALIA	KEN	Hengelo	1 Jun 2003
	W20	3:50.25	Alex KIPCHIRCHIR	KEN	Rieti	7 Sep 2003
5000m	W20	12:52.61	Eliud KIPCHOGE	KEN	Oslo	27 Jun 2003
	Asi	13:04.65	Abdullah Ahmad HASSAN	QAT	Zürich	15 Aug 2003
10000m	Asi	27:18.28	Abdullah Ahmad HASSAN	QAT	Saint-Denis	24 Aug 2003
	Asi	26:38.76	Abdullah Ahmad HASSAN	QAT	Bruxelles	5 Sep 2003
30km Rd	W	1:28:36	Takayuki MATSUMIYA	JPN	Kumamoto	16 Feb 2003
Mar	Eur=	2:06:36	Benoît ZWIERZCHLEWSKI	FRA	Paris	6 Apr 2003
	W,Afr,Com	2:04:55	Paul TERGAT	KEN	Berlin	28 Sep 2003
2000mSt	W18	5:27.64	Ronald KIPCHUMBA	KEN	Naimette-Xhovémont	2 Sep 2003
3000mSt	Eur=	8:06.91	Bouabdallah TAHRI	FRA	Saint-Denis	4 Jul 2003
	Asi	8:02.48	Saif Saaeed SHAHEEN	QAT	Zürich	15 Aug 2003
	Asi	8:00.06	Saif Saaeed SHAHEEN	QAT	Bruxelles	5 Sep 2003
	Asi	7:57.38	Saif Saaeed SHAHEEN	QAT	Monte Carlo	14 Sep 2003
110mh	SAm	13.34	Redelen DOS SANTOS	BRA	São Paulo	6 Sep 2003
400mh	CAC	47.25	Félix SÁNCHEZ	DOM	Saint-Denis	29 Aug 2003
SP	Oce	20.96	Justin ANLEZARK	AUS	Brisbane	5 Apr 2003
SP (5kg)	W18	21.45	LIU Feng	CHN	Sherbrooke	10 Jul 2003
DT (1.75kg)	W20	65.88	Omar Ahmed EL GHAZALI	EGY	Cairo	7 Nov 2003
HT	Asi	84.86	Koji MUROFUSHI	JPN	Praha	29 Jun 2003
Oct (U18)	W18	6456	Andrés SILVA	URU	Sherbrooke	11 Jul 2003
20kmRW	W,SAm	1:17:21	Jefferson PÉREZ	ECU	Saint-Denis	23 Aug 2003
50kmRW	W,Eur	3:36:03	Robert KORZENIOWSKI	POL	Saint-Denis	27 Aug 2003
	Oce,Com	3:39:43	Nathan DEAKES	AUS	Melbourne	7 Dec 2003

OUTDOORS - WOMEN

200m	W20	22.11A	Allyson FELIX	USA	Ciudad de México	3 May 2003
300m	W	35.30A	Ana GUEVARA	MEX	Ciudad de México	3 May 2003
400m	CAC	49.11	Ana GUEVARA	MEX	Zürich	15 Aug 2003
	CAC	48.89	Ana GUEVARA	MEX	Saint-Denis	27 Aug 2003
1M	W18	4:30.81	Gelete BURIKA	ETH	Heusden	2 Aug 2003
2000m	Afr	5:35.62	Berhane ADERE	ETH	Ostrava	12 Jun 2003
	Oce	5:37.71	Benita JOHNSON	AUS	Ostrava	12 Jun 2003
3000m	Oce	8:38.06	Benita JOHNSON	AUS	Gateshead	13 Jul 2003
5000m	CAC	15:04.32	Adriana FERNÁNDEZ	MEX	Gresham	17 May 2003
	Afr	14:29.32	Berhane ADERE	ETH	Oslo	27 Jun 2003
	W20	14:39.94	Tirunesh DIBABA	ETH	Oslo	27 Jun 2003
10000m	Afr	30:04.18	Berhane ADERE	ETH	Saint-Denis	23 Aug 2003
	W20	30:31.55	XING Huina	CHN	Saint-Denis	23 Aug 2003
	Oce	30:37.68	Benita JOHNSON	AUS	Saint-Denis	23 Aug 2003
30000m	W	1:45:50.0	Tegla LOROUPE	KEN	Warstein	6 Jun 2003
10km Rd	W	30:21	Paula RADCLIFFE	GBR	San Juan	23 Feb 2003
HMar	W,Eur,Com	1:05:40	Paula RADCLIFFE	Eng	South Shields	21 Sep 2003
Mar	W,Eur,Com	2:15:25	Paula RADCLIFFE	Eng	London	13 Apr 2003
	NAm	2:21:16	Deena DROSSIN	USA	London	13 Apr 2003
	Asi	2:19:39	SUN Yingjie	CHN	Beijing	19 Oct 2003
2000mSt	W18,W20	6:21.78	Catalina OPREA	ROM	Tampere	27 Jul 2003
	W20	6:19.8	Inna POLUSKINA	LAT	Kaunas	10 Aug 2003
3000mSt	SAm	10:20.75	Michelle COSTA	BRA	Rio de Janeiro	23 May 2003
	NAm	9:46.30	Lisa AGUILERA	USA	Stanford	31 May 2003

	Afr=	9:39.51	Dorcus INZIKURU	UGA	Ostrava	12 Jun 2003
	NAm	9:44.95	Kassi ANDERSEN	USA	Sacramento	13 Jun 2003
	NAm	9:44.71	Briana SHOOK	USA	Stanford	22 Jun 2003
	W,Eur	9:08.33	Gulnara SAMITOVA	RUS	Tula	10 Aug 2003
	Asi	9:50.88	CHEN Xiaofang	CHN	Shanghai	13 Sep 2003
100mh	CAC	12.45	Brigitte FOSTER	JAM	Eugene	24 May 2003
400mh	W,Eur	52.34	Yuliya PECHONKINA	RUS	Tula	8 Aug 2003
HJ	Asi=	1.97	Tatyana EFIMENKO	KGZ	Roma	11 Jul 2003
	Afr,Com	2.05	Hestrie CLOETE	RSA	Berlin	10 Aug 2003
	Afr,Com	2.06	Hestrie CLOETE	RSA	Saint-Denis	31 Aug 2003
PV	CAC	4.10 & 4.20	Katiuska PÉREZ	CUB	La Habana	29 May 2003
	W,Eur	4.82	Yelena ISINBAYEVA	RUS	Gateshead	13 Jul 2003
TJ	CAC	14.85A	Yamilé ALDAMA	CUB	Germiston	24 Jan 2003
	SAm	14.53	Maurren MAGGI	BRA	São Caetano do Sul	27 Apr 2003
	CAC	14.85 & 14.98	Yamilé ALDAMA	CUB	Florø	31 May 2003
	CAC	15.00	Yamilé ALDAMA	CUB	Ostrava	12 Jun 2003
	CAC=	15.00	Yamilé ALDAMA	CUB	Trikala	24 Jun 2003
	CAC	15.11	Yamilé ALDAMA	CUB	Oslo	27 Jun 2003
	CAC	15.29	Yamilé ALDAMA	CUB	Roma	11 Jul 2003
	Afr	15.03	Françoise MBANGO Etone	CMR	Lapeenranta	3 Aug 2003
	Afr	15.05	Françoise MBANGO Etone	CMR	Saint-Denis	26 Aug 2003
	Oce	14.04	Nicole MLADENIS	AUS	Perth	7 Dec 2003
SP	Afr	18.41	Vivianne CHUKWUEMEKA	NGR	Azusa	12 Apr 2003
	Afr	18.43	Vivianne CHUKWUEMEKA	NGR	Walnut	19 Apr 2003
HT	Oce,Com	71.12	Bronwyn EAGLES	AUS	Adelaide	6 Feb 2003
	CAC	72.00	Yipsi MORENO	CUB	La Habana	14 Feb 2003
	W18	70.60	ZHANG Wenxiu	CHN	Nanning	5 Apr 2003
	CAC	72.47	Yipsi MORENO	CUB	La Habana	29 May 2003
	CAC	74.07	Yipsi MORENO	CUB	La Habana	31 May 2003
	Afr	64.77	Marwa Ahmed HUSSEIN	EGY	Szombathely	12 Jul 2003
	CAC	75.14	Yipsi MORENO	CUB	Savona	17 Jul 2003
	Afr	64.83 & 65.26	Marwa Ahmed HUSSEIN	EGY	Szombathely	10 Aug 2003
	Asi	72.03	GU Yuan	CHN	Shanghai	12 Sep 2003
JT	Afr	58.62	Aïda SELLAM	TUN	Kladno	8 Jun 2003
	Afr	60.57A	Sunette VILJOEN	RSA	Potchefstroom	15 Jul 2003
	NAm	60.86	Kim KREINER	USA	Santo Domingo	7 Aug 2003
	W18	61.06	XUE Juan	CHN	Changsha	25 Oct 2003
	W20,W18	62.93	XUE Juan	CHN	Changsha	27 Oct 2003
	Afr	61.59A	Sunette VILJOEN	RSA	Potchefstroom	5 Dec 2003
20000mW	NAm	1:34:31.08	Michelle ROHL	USA	Stanford	21 Jun 2003
	W20	1:29:32.4	SONG Hongjuan	CHN	Changsha	24 Oct 2003
20kmRW	W20	1:27:16	SONG Hongjuan	CHN	Yangzhou	14 Apr 2003
	SAm	1:33:42	Geovana IRUSTA	BOL	Saint-Denis	24 Aug 2003
4x400m	SAm	3:28.64	BRA (Almirão, da Silva, Teodoro, Coutinho)		Barquisimeto	22 Jun 2003
	SAm	3:28.07	BRA (Almirão, Tito, Teodoro, Coutinho)		Santo Domingo	9 Aug 2003

INDOORS - MEN

60m	SAm=	6.63	Vicente DE LIMA	BRA	Birmingham	14 Mar 2003
400m	Oce	46.40	Daniel BATMAN	AUS	Birmingham	1 Mar 2003
	Oce	45.93	Daniel BATMAN	AUS	Birmingham	2 Mar 2003
3000m	W20	7:46.59	Markos GENETI	ETH	Boston (R)	1 Feb 2003
	Eur	7:32.98	Alberto GARCÍA	ESP	Sevilla	22 Feb 2003
	W20	7:40.83	Markos GENETI	ETH	Karlsruhe	28 Feb 2003
2M	W	8:04.69	Haile GEBRSELASSIE	ETH	Birmingham	21 Feb 2003
5000m	Eur	13:11.39	Alberto GARCÍA	ESP	Gent	9 Feb 2003
50mh	SAm	6.60+	Márcio DE SOUZA	BRA	Zuidbroek	25 Jan 2003
60mh	SAm	7.73	Márcio DE SOUZA	BRA	Zuidbroek	25 Jan 2003
	SAm	7.72	Márcio DE SOUZA	BRA	Erfurt	31 Jan 2003
	SAm	7.67	Márcio DE SOUZA	BRA	Tampere	13 Feb 2003
	Asi	7.51	LIU Xiang	CHN	Wien	9 Mar 2003
PV	W20	5.66	Artyom KUPTSOV	RUS	Donetsk	16 Feb 2003
	Oce=	5.60	Viktor CHISTIAKOV	AUS	Birmingham	1 Mar 2003
	Oce=	5.60	Viktor CHISTIAKOV	AUS	Birmingham	14 Mar 2003
	Oce=	5.60	Viktor CHISTIAKOV	AUS	Birmingham	15 Mar 2003
SP	Oce	20.21 & 20.69	Justin ANLEZARK	AUS	Wien	9 Mar 2003
	Com	21.49	Carl MYERSCOUGH	Eng	Fayetteville	15 Mar 2003
Hept	Afr	5733	Hamdi DHOUIBI	TUN	Aubière	1 Mar 2003
			6.98, 7.39, 12.58, 1.95, 8.11, 4.50, 2:44.68			
	Oce	4842	Sean GOURLEY	NZL	Cardiff	23 Mar 2003
			7.55, 6.63, 11.27, 1.78, 8.78, 4.05, 2:44.88			
5000TW	W20	19:04.5	Andrey YURIN	UKR	Brovary	18 Jan 2003
4x400	CAC,Com	3:04.21	JAM (Colquhoun, McFarlane, Blackwood, Clarke)		Birmingham	16 Mar 2003

INDOORS - WOMEN

200m	NAm	22.31	Michelle COLLINS	USA	Birmingham	14 Mar 2003
	NAm	22.18	Michelle COLLINS	USA	Birmingham	15 Mar 2003
400m	W20	51.94	Sanya RICHARDS	USA	Fayetteville	14 Mar 2003
	W20	51.87	Sanya RICHARDS	USA	Fayetteville	15 Mar 2003
800m	Asi	2:02.89	Miho SUGIMORI	JPN	Tianjin	18 Feb 2003
	Asi	2:00.78	Miho SUGIMORI	JPN	Yokohama	22 Feb 2003
1500m	W,NAm	3:59.98	Regina JACOBS	USA	Boston (R)	1 Feb 2003
	Com	4:02.66	Kelly HOLMES	Eng	Birmingham	16 Mar 2003
3000m	CAC	9:08.55	Korene HINDS	JAM	Boston (R)	1 Feb 2003
5000m	CAC	16:51.89	Talis APUD-MARTINEZ	MEX	Lincoln, NE	28 Feb 2003
	W20	15:40.68	Tirunesh DIBABA	ETH	Boston	25 Jan 2003
	Afr	14:48.21	Berhane ADERE	ETH	Dortmund	5 Feb 2003
3000mSt	W	9:29.54	Gulnara SAMITOVA	RUS	Moscow	27 Feb 2003
60mh	NAm	7.78	Gail DEVERS	USA	New York	7 Feb 2003
	NAm	7.74	Gail DEVERS	USA	Boston (R)	1 Mar 2003
PV	CAC	3.90	Alejandra MEZA	MEX	Houston	18 Jan 2003
	SAm=	3.80	Déborah GYURCSEK	URU	Valencia	25 Jan 2003
	SAm=	3.80	Déborah GYURCSEK	URU	Valencia	1 Feb 2003
	NAm	4.71	Stacy DRAGILA	USA	Boston (R)	1 Feb 2003
	W,Eur	4.76	Svetlana FEOFANOVA	RUS	Glasgow	2 Feb 2003
	NAm	4.72	Stacy DRAGILA	USA	New York	7 Feb 2003
	W,Eur	4.77	Svetlana FEOFANOVA	RUS	Birmingham	21 Feb 2003
	SAm	4.10	Carolina TORRES	CHI	Magglingen	2 Mar 2003
		note: presumably set other marks between 3.80 and 4.10 in competition				
	W,NAm	4.78	Stacy DRAGILA	USA	Boston (R)	2 Mar 2003
	W,Eur	4.80	Svetlana FEOFANOVA	RUS	Birmingham	16 Mar 2003
LJ	SAm	6.70	Maurren MAGGI	BRA	Birmingham	16 Mar 2003
TJ	Afr	14.26	Françoise MBANGO Etone	CMR	Tampere	13 Feb 2003
	CAC	14.65	Yamilé ALDAMA	CUB	Tampere	13 Feb 2003
	Afr	14.49 & 14.56	Françoise MBANGO Etone	CMR	Birmingham	21 Feb 2003
	CAC	14.88	Yamilé ALDAMA	CUB	Karlsruhe	28 Feb 2003
	Afr	14.88	Françoise MBANGO Etone	CMR	Birmingham	15 Mar 2003
SP	Afr	17.97 & 18.03	Vivianne CHUKWUEMEKA	NGR	Johnson City	8 Mar 2003
3000mW	W,Eur	11:35.34	Gillian O'SULLIVAN	IRL	Belfast	15 Feb 2003
4x200m	W20	1:35.86	Speed City, USA (?, ?, ?, Solomon)		New York (A)	16 Mar 2003
4x400m	Asi	3:38.17	CHN (Ni, Bu, Chen, Zhang)		Yokohama	22 Feb 2003
	W20	3:41.54	Speed City, USA (Lee, Harris, Woods, Solomon)		New York (A)	16 Mar 2003

Split Times in World Records

			400m	800m	1200m	1600m	2000m	2400m	2800m
Men									
800m	1:41.11	Kipketer 1997	49.3	1:41.11		*(200m 23.8, 600m 1:14.6)*			
1000m	2:11.96	Ngeny 1999	49.66	1:44.62		*(200m 24.12, 600m 1:17.14)*			
1500m	3:26.00	El Guerrouj 1998	53.6	1:50.5	2:46.4	*(1000m 2:18.5)*			
1M	3:43.13	El Guerrouj 1999	55.2	1:51.2	2:47.0	*(1000m 2:19.2)*			
2000m	4:44.79	El Guerrouj 1999	57.1	1:55.4	2:52.4	3:49.60			
3000m	7:20.67	Komen 1996	57.6	1:57.0	2:54.9	3:53.6	4:53.4	5:51.3	6:51.2
2M	7:58.61	Komen 1997	58.6	2:00.4		3:58.4	4:58.2	5:56.7	6:57.5
5000m	12:39.36	H.Gebr' 1998	kms: 2:34.2, 5:06.0, 7:39.3, 10:12.1, 12:39.36 (last 400m 56.5)						
10000m	26:22.75	H.Gebr' 1998	kms: 2:36.0, 5:16.0, 7:53.6, 10:31.3, 13:11.8, 15:51.1, 18:32.5, 21:12.9, 23:51.5						
Women									
800m	1:53.28	Kratochvílová 1983	56.1	1:53.28					
1000m	2:28.98	Masterkova 1996	58.3	1:59.8		*(200m 28.4, 600m 1:29.1)*			
1500m	3:50.46	Qu Yunxia 1993	57.2	2:00.8	3:05.2				
1M	4:12.56	Masterkova 1996	62.0	2:06.7	3:12.2	*(1000m 2:39.5)*			
2000m	5:25.36	O'Sullivan 1994	64.9	2:07.8	3:14.8	4:23.5	5:25.36		
3000m	8:06.11	Wang Junxia 1993	1km 2:42.0		2km 5:29.7	*(last 400m 62.7)*			
5000m	14:28.09	Jiang Bo 1997	kms: 2:53.4, 5:45.95, 8:41.09, 11:40.6, 14:28.09						
10000m	29:31.78	Wang Junxia 1993	kms: 2:54.7, 5:56.6, 8:59.2, 12:02.8, 15:05.7, 18:10.1, 21:14.4, 23:59.9, 26:44.8						

WORLD MEN'S ALL-TIME LISTS

100 METRES

Mark	Wind	Name		Nat	Born	Pos	Meet	Venue	Date
9.78 WR	2.0	Tim	Montgomery	USA	28.1.75	1	GPF	Paris (C)	14 Sep 02
9.79 WR	0.1	Maurice	Greene	USA	23.7.74	1rA	GP II	Athína	16 Jun 99
9.80	0.2		Greene			1	WCh	Sevilla	22 Aug 99
9.82	-0.2		Greene			1	WCh	Edmonton	5 Aug 01
9.84 WR	0.7	Donovan	Bailey	CAN	16.12.67	1	OG	Atlanta	27 Jul 96
9.84	0.2	Bruny	Surin	CAN	12.7.67	2	WCh	Sevilla	22 Aug 99
9.84	2.0		Montgomery			1	Bisl	Oslo	13 Jul 01
9.85 WR	1.2	Leroy	Burrell	USA	21.2.67	1rA	Athl	Lausanne	6 Jul 94
9.85	0.8		Greene			1	GGala	Roma	7 Jul 99
9.85	-0.2		Montgomery			2	WCh	Edmonton	5 Aug 01
9.86 WR	1.2	Carl	Lewis	USA	1.7.61	1	WCh	Tokyo	25 Aug 91
9.86	-0.4	Frank	Fredericks	NAM	2.10.67	1rA	Athl	Lausanne	3 Jul 96
9.86	0.2		Greene			1	WCh	Athína	3 Aug 97
9.86	1.8	Ato	Boldon	TRI	30.12.73	1rA	MSR	Walnut	19 Apr 98
9.86	-0.4		Boldon			1		Athína	17 Jun 98
9.86	0.1		Boldon			2rA	GP II	Athína	16 Jun 99
9.86	0.4		Boldon			1rA	Athl	Lausanne	2 Jul 99
9.86	-0.2		Greene			1	ISTAF	Berlin	1 Sep 00
9.87	0.3	Linford	Christie ¶	GBR	2.4.60	1	WCh	Stuttgart	15 Aug 93
9.87	1.9		Fredericks			1	WG	Helsinki	25 Jun 96
9.87	1.3		Boldon			1q1	WCh	Athína	2 Aug 97
9.87A	-0.2	Obadele	Thompson (10)	BAR	30.3.76	1	WCp	Johannesburg	11 Sep 98
9.87	0.6		Greene			1	DNG	Stockholm	30 Jul 99
9.87	-0.3		Greene			1	OG	Sydney	23 Sep 00
9.87	2.0	Dwain	Chambers ¶	GBR	5.4.78	2	GPF	Paris (C)	14 Sep 02
9.88	1.2		Burrell			2	WCh	Tokyo	25 Aug 91
9.88	-0.1		Boldon			1	CG	Kuala Lumpur	17 Sep 98
9.88	2.0		Boldon			2	Bisl	Oslo	13 Jul 01
9.89	0.7		Fredericks			2	OG	Atlanta	27 Jul 96
9.89	0.8		Boldon			1r2	ModR	Modesto	10 May 97
9.89	1.5		Surin			1	NC	Montreal	1 Aug 98
9.89	0.9		Greene			1rA	GGala	Roma	12 Jul 02
		(32 performances by 11 athletes)							
9.91	1.2	Dennis	Mitchell ¶	USA	20.2.66	3	WCh	Tokyo	25 Aug 91
9.92	0.3	Andre	Cason	USA	20.1.69	2	WCh	Stuttgart	15 Aug 93
9.92	0.8	Jon	Drummond	USA	9.9.68	1h3	NC	Indianapolis	12 Jun 97
9.92A	-0.2	Seun	Ogunkoya	NGR	28.12.77	2	WCp	Johannesburg	11 Sep 98
9.92	1.0	Tim	Harden	USA	27.1.74	1		Luzern	5 Jul 99
9.93AWR	1.4	Calvin	Smith	USA	8.1.61	1	USOF	USAF Academy	3 Jul 83
9.93	-0.6	Michael	Marsh	USA	4.8.67	1	MSR	Walnut	18 Apr 92
9.93	1.8	Patrick	Johnson	AUS	26.9.72	1		Mito	5 May 03
9.94	0.2	Davidson	Ezinwa ¶	NGR	22.11.71	1	Gugl	Linz	4 Jul 94
		(20)							
9.94	-0.2	Bernard	Williams	USA	19.1.78	3	WCh	Edmonton	5 Aug 01
9.94	1.8	Shawn	Crawford	USA	14.1.78	1	GP	Suita	11 May 02
9.95AWR	0.3	Jim	Hines	USA	10.9.46	1	OG	Ciudad de México	14 Oct 68
9.95A	1.9	Olapade	Adeniken	NGR	19.8.69	1A		El Paso	16 Apr 94
9.95	0.8	Vincent	Henderson	USA	20.10.72	1		Leverkusen	9 Aug 98
9.95	1.8	Joshua 'J.J.'	Johnson	USA	10.5.76	1r6	MSR	Walnut	21 Apr 02
9.95	0.6	Deji	Aliu	NGR	22.11.75	1	Afr G	Abuja	12 Oct 03
9.96	0.1	Mel	Lattany	USA	10.8.59	1r1		Athens, Ga.	5 May 84
9.96	1.2	Ray	Stewart	JAM	18.3.65	6	WCh	Tokyo	25 Aug 91
9.96	0.8	Kareem	Streete-Thompson	CAY/USA	30.3.73	2h3	NC	Indianapolis	12 Jun 97
		(30)							
9.97	1.0	Francis	Obikwelu	NGR	22.11.78	2	Athl	Lausanne	5 Jul 00
9.97	1.3	John	Capel	USA	27.10.78	1=rA	WK	Zürich	15 Aug 03
9.97	1.3	Justin	Gatlin ¶	USA	10.2.82	1=rA	WK	Zürich	15 Aug 03
9.97	0.6	Uchenna	Emedolu	NGR	17.9.76	2	Afr G	Abuja	12 Oct 03
9.98A	0.6	Silvio	Leonard	CUB	20.9.55	1	WPT	Guadalajara	11 Aug 77
9.98	0.3	Daniel	Effiong ¶	NGR	17.6.72	2s1	WCh	Stuttgart	15 Aug 93
9.98	1.4	Percy	Spencer	JAM	24.2.75	1	NC	Kingston	20 Jun 97
9.98	1.6	Leonard	Myles-Mills	GHA	9.5.73	1	NCAA	Boise	5 Jun 99
9.98	0.4	Jason	Gardener	GBR	18.9.75	3rA	Athl	Lausanne	2 Jul 99
9.98	0.4	Coby	Miller	USA	19.10.76	1s1	NCAA	Durham	2 Jun 00
		(40)							
9.98	0.2	Kim	Collins	SKN	5.4.76	1	CG	Manchester	27 Jul 02

Mark	Wind	Name		Nat	Born	Pos	Meet	Venue	Date
9.99	0.5	Brian	Lewis	USA	5.12.74	1		Cayenne	4 May 02
9.99	1.5	Mickey	Grimes	USA	10.10.76	1rB	WK	Zürich	15 Aug 03
10.00	2.0	Marian	Woronin	POL	13.8.56	1	Kuso	Warszawa	9 Jun 84
10.00	1.0	Chidi	Imo ¶	NGR	27.8.63	1	ISTAF	Berlin	15 Aug 86
10.00#A	1.6	Robson	da Silva	BRA	4.9.64	1h3	IbAm	Ciudad de México	22 Jul 88
		May not have been with auto-timing							
10.00	1.9	Koji	Ito	JPN	29.1.70	1s2	AsiG	Bangkok	13 Dec 98
10.00	1.1	Eric	Nkansah	GHA	12.12.74	3		Nürnberg	13 Jun 99
10.00	1.5	Darvis	Patton	USA	4.12.79	2rB	WK	Zürich	15 Aug 03
10.01A	0.9	Pietro	Mennea	ITA	28.6.52	1		Ciudad de México	4 Sep 79
10.01A	1.9	Bode	Osagiobare	NGR	1.12.70	2A		El Paso	16 Apr 94
10.01	0.6	Jeff	Laynes ¶	USA	3.10.70	1		Tempe	6 Apr 96
10.01	0.0	Darrel	Brown	TRI-J	11.10.84	1q3	WCh	Saint-Denis	24 Aug 03
		(53)	100th man 10.07, 200th man 10.13, 300th man 10.18						
Faulty wind gauge – possibly wind assisted									
9.88			Greene			1q2	WCh	Edmonton	4 Aug 01
9.97		Mark	Lewis-Francis	GBR	4.9.82	1q3	WCh	Edmonton	4 Aug 01
Doubtful wind reading									
9.91	-2.3	Davidson	Ezinwa ¶	NGR	22.11.71	1		Azusa	11 Apr 92
Low altitude marks for athletes with lifetime bests at high altitude									
9.94	0.1	Ogunkoya				1	AfCh	Dakar	19 Aug 98
9.97	1.6	C Smith				1	WK	Zürich	24 Aug 83
9.96	0.6	O Thompson				2	DNG	Stockholm	30 Jul 99
9.97	1.2	Adeniken				1	TexR	Austin	4 Apr 92
Wind-assisted – 15 performances to 9.86, performers listed to 9.96									
9.69A	5+	Obadele	Thompson	BAR	30.3.76	1		El Paso	13 Apr 96
9.78	5.2	Carl	Lewis	USA	1.7.61	1	OT	Indianapolis	16 Jul 88
9.79	5.3	Andre	Cason	USA	20.1.69	1h4	NC	Eugene	16 Jun 93
9.79	4.5		Cason			1s1	NC	Eugene	16 Jun 93
9.79	2.9	Maurice	Greene	USA	23.7.74	1	Pre	Eugene	31 May 98
9.80	4.3		Lewis			1q2	WCh	Tokyo	24 Aug 91
9.83	7.1	Leonard	Scott	USA	19.1.80	1r1	Sea Ray	Knoxville	9 Apr 99
9.84	3.3		Greene			1h2	NC	New Orleans	19 Jun 98
9.84	3.5		Greene			1	Pre	Eugene	30 May 99
9.85	5.3		Burrell			2h4	NC	Eugene	16 Jun 93
9.85	4.8		Cason			1	NC	Eugene	17 Jun 93
9.85	4.8	Dennis	Mitchell ¶	USA	20.2.66	2	NC	Eugene	17 Jun 93
9.85A	3.0	Frank	Fredericks	NAM	2.10.67	1		Nairobi	18 May 02
9.86	5.2		Mitchell			2	OT	Indianapolis	16 Jul 88
9.86	2.5		Burrell			1rA	TexR	Austin	9 Apr 94
9.87	11.2	William	Snoddy	USA	6.12.57	1		Dallas	1 Apr 78
9.87	4.9	Calvin	Smith	USA	8.1.61	1s2	OT	Indianapolis	16 Jul 88
9.87	2.4	Michael	Marsh	USA	4.8.67	1rA	MSR	Walnut	20 Apr 97
9.88	2.3	James	Sanford	USA	27.12.57	1		Westwood	3 May 80
9.88	5.2	Albert	Robinson	USA	28.11.64	4	OT	Indianapolis	16 Jul 88
9.88	4.9	Tim	Harden	USA	27.1.74	1	NC	New Orleans	20 Jun 98
9.88	4.5	Coby	Miller	USA	19.10.76	1		Auburn	1 Apr 00
9.88	3.6	Patrick	Johnson	AUS	26.9.72	1		Perth	8 Feb 03
9.89	4.2	Ray	Stewart	JAM	18.3.65	1s1	PAm	Indianapolis	9 Aug 87
9.90	5.2	Joe	DeLoach	USA	5.6.67	5	OT	Indianapolis	16 Jul 88
9.90	7.1	Kenny	Brokenburr	USA	29.10.68	2r1	Sea Ray	Knoxville	9 Apr 99
9.91	5.3	Bob	Hayes	USA	20.12.42	1s1	OG	Tokyo	15 Oct 64
9.91	4.2	Mark	Witherspoon	USA	3.9.63	2s1	PAm	Indianapolis	9 Aug 87
9.91	3.7	Nicolas	Macrozonaris	CAN	22.8.80	1	NC	Edmonton	22 Jun 02
9.92A	4.4	Chidi	Imo ¶	NGR	27.8.63	1s1	AfG	Nairobi	8 Aug 87
9.92A	2.8	Olapade	Adeniken	NGR	19.8.69	1rA		Sestriere	29 Jul 95
9.92	2.8	Kim	Collins	SKN	5.4.76	1rA	Tex R	Austin	5 Apr 03
9.93	7.5	Pablo	Montes	CUB	23.11.47	1s1	CAC	Panama City	1 Mar 70
9.93	5.3	Erick	Wilson	USA	10.1.82	1	JUCO	Levelland	10 May 03
9.94	2.7	Vitaliy	Savin	KZK	23.1.66	1	CIS Ch	Moskva	22 Jun 92
9.94	2.5	Daniel	Effiong ¶	NGR	17.6.72	2	TexR	Austin	9 Apr 94
9.94	7.0	Ousmane	Diarra	MLI	30.9.66	1		La Laguna	13 Jul 96
9.94	5.2	Osmond	Ezinwa	NGR	22.11.71	1		Pula	4 Sep 96
9.94	3.9	Vincent	Henderson	USA	20.10.72	1s1	WUG	Catania	29 Aug 97
9.94	2.8	Bryan	Howard	USA	7.10.76	2r7	MSR	Walnut	16 Apr 00
9.95	8.9	Willie	Gault	USA	5.9.60	1		Knoxville	2 Apr 83
9.95	2.4	Mel	Lattany	USA	10.8.59	1		Athens, Ga	7 May 83
9.95	7.1	Anthony	Jones	USA	12.12.71	3r1	Sea Ray	Knoxville	9 Apr 99
9.96	8.5	Anthony	Barnes	USA	23.12.65	1		Fresno	1 Apr 95
9.96	3.2	Percy	Spencer	JAM	24.2.75	1		Arlington	2 May 98
9.96	3.4	Brian	Lewis	USA	5.12.74	1h1	Conseil	Fort-de-France	29 Apr 00

Mark	Wind	Name		Nat	Born	Pos	Meet	Venue	Date
Disqualified for drug abuse									
9.79	1.1	Ben	Johnson ¶	CAN	30.12.61	-	OG	Seoul	24 Sep 88
9.83	1.0		Johnson			(1)	WCh	Roma	30 Aug 87
10.02	1.9	Horace	Dove-Edwin ¶	SLE	10.2.67	(2)	CG	Victoria	23 Aug 94
Rolling start									
9.89w	3.7	Patrick	Jarrett ¶	JAM	2.10.77	1	Pre	Eugene	27 May 01
Hand timing									
9.7	1.9	Donovan	Powell ¶	JAM	31.10.71	1rA		Houston	19 May 95
9.7	1.9	Carl	Lewis	USA	1.7.61	2rA		Houston	19 May 95
9.7	1.9	Olapade	Adeniken	NGR	19.8.69	3rA		Houston	19 May 95
9.7w	3.8	Osvaldo	Lara	CUB	13.7.55	1		Santiago de Cuba	24 Feb 82
9.7w	6.6	Rod	Mapstone	AUS	19.11.69	1r1		Perth	21 Dec 96
9.7w	8.1	Sayon	Cooper	LBR	24.4.74	1		Abilene	28 Mar 98
Drugs dq: 9.7w	3.5		Ben Johnson ¶	CAN	30.12.61	1		Perth	24 Jan 87

MEN All-time

200 METRES

Mark	Wind	Name		Nat	Born	Pos	Meet	Venue	Date
19.32 WR	0.4	Michael	Johnson	USA	13.9.67	1	OG	Atlanta	1 Aug 96
19.66 WR	1.7		Johnson			1	NC	Atlanta	23 Jun 96
19.68	0.4	Frank	Fredericks	NAM	2.10.67	2	OG	Atlanta	1 Aug 96
19.71A	1.8		Johnson			1rA		Pietersburg	18 Mar 00
19.72AWR	1.8	Pietro	Mennea	ITA	28.6.52	1	WUG	Ciudad de México	12 Sep 79
19.73	-0.2	Michael	Marsh	USA	4.8.67	1s1	OG	Barcelona	5 Aug 92
19.75	1.5	Carl	Lewis	USA	1.7.61	1	TAC	Indianapolis	19 Jun 83
19.75	1.7	Joe	DeLoach	USA	5.6.67	1	OG	Seoul	28 Sep 88
19.77	0.6		Johnson			1	DNG	Stockholm	8 Jul 96
19.77	0.7	Ato	Boldon	TRI	30.12.73	1rA		Stuttgart	13 Jul 97
19.79	1.7		Lewis			2	OG	Seoul	28 Sep 88
19.79	1.0		Johnson			1	OT	New Orleans	28 Jun 92
19.79	0.5		Johnson			1	WCh	Göteborg	11 Aug 95
19.80	-0.9		Lewis			1	OG	Los Angeles	8 Aug 84
19.80	0.4		Boldon			3	OG	Atlanta	1 Aug 96
19.81	0.3		Fredericks			1	GPF	Fukuoka	13 Sep 97
19.82A	2.0		Lewis			1		Sestriere	11 Aug 88
19.82	1.1		Fredericks			1	Bisl	Oslo	5 Jul 96
19.82	1.6		Boldon			1rA	DNG	Stockholm	7 Jul 97
19.83AWR	0.9	Tommie	Smith	USA	12.6.44	1	OG	Ciudad de México	16 Oct 68
19.83	1.7		Johnson			1	GP I	Atlanta	18 May 96
19.84	0.2		Lewis			1q3	OT	Los Angeles	19 Jun 84
19.84	1.7	Francis	Obikwelu	NGR	22.11.78	1s2	WCh	Sevilla	25 Aug 99
19.85	0.4		Johnson			1	IAC	Edinburgh	6 Jul 90
19.85	0.3		Fredericks			1	WCh	Stuttgart	20 Aug 93
19.85	-0.9		Boldon			1	Athl	Lausanne	3 Jul 96
19.85	1.1		Johnson			2	Bisl	Oslo	5 Jul 96
19.85	-0.3	John	Capel (10)	USA	27.10.78	1	NC	Sacramento	23 Jul 00
19.85A	0.0	Shawn	Crawford	USA	14.1.78	1		Pretoria	12 Apr 02
19.85	-0.5	Konstadínos (30/12)	Kedéris	GRE	11.7.73	1	EC	München	9 Aug 02
19.86A	1.0	Don	Quarrie	JAM	25.2.51	1	PAm	Cali	3 Aug 71
19.86	1.6	Maurice	Greene	USA	23.7.74	2rA	DNG	Stockholm	7 Jul 97
19.87	0.8	Lorenzo	Daniel	USA	23.3.66	1	NCAA	Eugene	3 Jun 88
19.87A	1.8	John	Regis	GBR	13.10.66	1		Sestriere	31 Jul 94
19.87	1.2	Jeff	Williams	USA	31.12.65	1		Fresno	13 Apr 96
19.88	-0.3	Floyd	Heard	USA	24.3.66	2	NC	Sacramento	23 Jul 00
19.88	0.1	Joshua 'J.J'	Johnson	USA	10.5.76	1	VD	Bruxelles	24 Aug 01
19.89	-0.8	Claudinei (20)	da Silva	BRA	19.11.70	1	GPF	München	11 Sep 99
19.92AWR	1.9	John	Carlos	USA	5.6.45	1	FOT	Echo Summit	12 Sep 68
19.96	-0.9	Kirk	Baptiste	USA	20.6.63	2	OG	Los Angeles	8 Aug 84
19.96	0.4	Robson	da Silva	BRA	4.9.64	1	VD	Bruxelles	25 Aug 89
19.96	-0.3	Coby	Miller	USA	19.10.76	3	NC	Sacramento	23 Jul 00
19.97	-0.9	Obadele	Thompson	BAR	30.3.76	1	Super	Yokohama	9 Sep 00
19.98	1.7	Marcin	Urbas	POL	17.9.76	2s2	WCh	Sevilla	25 Aug 99
19.99	0.6	Calvin	Smith	USA	8.1.61	1	WK	Zürich	24 Aug 83
20.00	0.0	Valeriy	Borzov	UKR	20.10.49	1	OG	München	4 Sep 72
20.01	-1.0	Michael	Bates	USA	19.12.69	3rA	WK	Zürich	19 Aug 92
20.01	0.1	Bernard (30)	Williams	USA	19.1.78	2	VD	Bruxelles	24 Aug 01
20.02	1.7	Christopher	Williams	JAM	15.3.72	1r5	MSR	Walnut	16 Apr 00
20.03	1.6	Clancy	Edwards	USA	9.8.55	1		Westwood	29 Apr 78

Mark	Wind		Name	Nat	Born	Pos	Meet	Venue	Date
20.03	1.5	Larry	Myricks ¶	USA	10.3.56	2	TAC	Indianapolis	19 Jun 83
20.03	1.2	Jon	Drummond	USA	9.9.68	1	VD	Bruxelles	22 Aug 97
20.03	0.6	Shingo	Suetsugu	JPN	2.6.80	1	NC	Yokohama	7 Jun 03
20.03	0.6	Darvis	Patton	USA	4.12.79	1s1	WCh	Saint-Denis	29 Aug 03
20.04	1.7	Kenny	Brokenburr	USA	29.10.68	2r5	MSR	Walnut	16 Apr 00
20.04	-0.1	Justin	Gatlin ¶	USA	10.2.82	1	VD	Bruxelles	5 Sep 03
20.05	1.0	Roy	Martin	USA	25.12.66	3	OT	Indianapolis	20 Jul 88
20.05	1.0	Albert	Robinson	USA	28.11.64	4	OT	Indianapolis	20 Jul 88
		(40)							
20.05	-0.1	Ramon	Clay	USA	29.6.75	1	Athl	Lausanne	4 Jul 01
20.06A	0.9	Peter	Norman	AUS	15.6.42	2	OG	Ciudad de México	16 Oct 68
20.06	1.7	Silvio	Leonard	CUB	20.9.55	1	Kuso	Warszawa	19 Jun 78
20.06	0.7	Stéphane	Buckland	MRI	20.1.77	1q3	WCh	Saint-Denis	27 Aug 03
20.07		James	Mallard	USA	29.11.57	1		Tuscaloosa	20 Apr 79
20.08	0.9	LaMonte	King	USA	18.12.59	1	TAC	Walnut	15 Jun 80
20.08A	1.6	Dwayne	Evans	USA	13.10.58	1		Albuquerque	13 Jun 87
20.08	0.3	Danny	Everett	USA	1.11.66	2	TAC	Norwalk	16 Jun 90
20.08	1.7	Aaron	Armstrong	USA	14.10.77	1		Norman	10 Apr 99
20.08	1.0	Christian	Malcolm	GBR	3.6.79	1s1	WCh	Edmonton	8 Aug 01
		(50)	100th man 20.21, 200th man 20.35, 300th man 20.43						

Wind-assisted 5 performances to 19.83, performers listed to 20.05

Mark	Wind		Name	Nat	Born	Pos	Meet	Venue	Date
19.61	>4.0	Leroy	Burrell	USA	21.2.67	1	SWC	College Station	19 May 90
19.70	2.7		Johnson			1s1	NC	Atlanta	22 Jun 96
19.79A	4.0		Marsh			1		Sestriere	21 Jul 92
19.83	3.5		Johnson			1	NC	Sacramento	18 Jun 95
19.83	9.2	Bobby	Cruse	USA	20.3.78	1r2	Sea Ray	Knoxville	9 Apr 99
19.86	4.6	Roy	Martin	USA	25.12.66	1	SWC	Houston	18 May 86
19.86	4.0	Justin	Gatlin ¶	USA	10.2.82	1h2	NCAA	Eugene	30 May 01
19.91		James	Jett	USA	28.12.70	1		Morgantown	18 Apr 92
19.93	2.4	Sebastián	Keitel	CHI	14.2.73	1		São Leopoldo	26 Apr 98
19.94	4.0	James	Sanford	USA	27.12.57	1s1	NCAA	Austin	7 Jun 80
19.94	3.7	Chris	Nelloms	USA	14.8.71	1	Big 10	Minneapolis	23 May 92
19.94	2.3	Kevin	Little	USA	3.4.68	1s3	NC	Sacramento	17 Jun 95
19.95	3.4	Mike	Roberson	USA	25.3.56	1h3	NCAA	Austin	5 Jun 80
19.96	2.2	Rohsaan	Griffin	USA	21.2.74	1s1	NC	Eugene	26 Jun 99
19.99	2.7	Ramon	Clay	USA	29.6.75	2s1	NC	Atlanta	22 Jun 96
20.00A	3.4	Olapade	Adeniken	NGR	19.8.69	1		USAF Academy	23 May 92
20.01	2.5	Derald	Harris	USA	5.4.58	1		San José	9 Apr 77
20.03	6.5	Alvis	Whitted	USA	4.9.74	1		College Park	20 Apr 96
20.05A	3.8	Cyprean	Enweani	CAN	19.3.64	1		Calgary	3 Jul 88

Low altitude marks for athletes with lifetime bests at high altitude

Mark	Wind	Name	Pos	Meet	Venue	Date
19.94	0.3	Regis	2	WCh	Stuttgart	20 Aug 93
19.96	0.0	Mennea	1		Barletta	17 Aug 80
20.02	0.8	Crawford	2	GGala	Roma	11 Jul 03
20.06	0.4	Quarrie	1	WK	Zürich	16 Aug 74

Suspended under IAAF rules

Mark	Wind		Name	Nat	Born	Pos	Meet	Venue	Date
19.86	1.5	Justin	Gatlin ¶	USA	10.2.82	1	SEC	Starkville	12 May 02

Hand timing *" during 220 yards race, * 220 yards less 0.1 seconds*

Mark	Wind		Name	Nat	Born	Pos	Meet	Venue	Date
19.7A		James	Sanford	USA	27.12.57	1		El Paso	19 Apr 80
19.7A	0.2	Robson C.	da Silva	BRA	4.9.64	1	AmCp	Bogotá	13 Aug 89
19.8"	WR1.3	Don	Quarrie	JAM	25.2.51	1	Pre	Eugene	7 Jun 75
19.8*	WR1.3	Steve	Williams	USA	13.11.53	2	Pre	Eugene	7 Jun 75
19.8	1.6	James	Mallard	USA	29.11.57	1	SEC	Tuscaloosa	13 May 79
19.8*w		Carl	Lawson	JAM	27.10.47	1		Moscow	19 May 73
19.8*w	3.4	James	Gilkes	GUY	21.9.52	1	NCAA	Austin	8 Jun 74
19.8w	4.4	Desmond	Ross	USA	30.12.61	1	Big8	Manhattan	11 May 85

300 METRES

In 300m races only, not including intermediate times in 400m races

Mark		Name	Nat	Born	Pos	Meet	Venue	Date
30.85A	Michael	Johnson	USA	13.9.67	1		Pretoria	24 Mar 00
31.48	Danny	Everett	USA	1.11.66	1		Jerez de la Frontera	3 Sep 90
31.48	Roberto	Hernández	CUB	6.3.67	2		Jerez de la Frontera	3 Sep 90
31.56		Johnson			1		Salamanca	22 Jul 94
31.56	Doug	Walker ¶	GBR	28.7.73	1		Gateshead	19 Jul 98
31.61	Anthuan	Maybank	USA	30.12.69	1		Durham	13 Jul 96
31.67	John	Regis	GBR	13.10.66	1	Vaux	Gateshead	17 Jul 92
31.70	Kirk	Baptiste	USA	20.6.63	1	Nike	London (CP)	18 Aug 84
31.73	Thomas	Jefferson	USA	8.6.62	1	DCG	London (CP)	22 Aug 87
31.74	Gabriel	Tiacoh	CIV	10.9.63	1		La Coruña	6 Aug 86
31.82	Steve	Lewis (10)	USA	16.5.69	2	Vaux	Gateshead	17 Jul 92
31.87	Mark	Richardson	GBR	26.7.72	2		Gateshead	19 Jul 98
31.88	Darren	Clark	AUS	6.9.65	1	UlstG	Belfast	30 Jun 86
31.96	Marc	Foucan	FRA	14.10.71	1r1		Strasbourg	29 Jun 99
31.97	Innocent	Egbunike	NGR	30.11.61	1	IAC	London (CP)	8 Aug 86

400 METRES

Mark Wind	Name		Nat	Born	Pos	Meet	Venue	Date
43.18 WR	Michael	Johnson	USA	13.9.67	1	WCh	Sevilla	26 Aug 99
43.29 WR	Butch	Reynolds ¶	USA	8.6.64	1	WK	Zürich	17 Aug 88
43.39		Johnson			1	WCh	Göteborg	9 Aug 95
43.44		Johnson			1	NC	Atlanta	19 Jun 96
43.49		Johnson			1	OG	Atlanta	29 Jul 96
43.50	Quincy	Watts	USA	19.6.70	1	OG	Barcelona	5 Aug 92
43.65		Johnson			1	WCh	Stuttgart	17 Aug 93
43.66		Johnson			1	NC	Sacramento	16 Jun 95
43.66		Johnson			1rA	Athl	Lausanne	3 Jul 96
43.68		Johnson			1	WK	Zürich	12 Aug 98
43.68		Johnson			1	NC	Sacramento	16 Jul 00
43.71		Watts			1s2	OG	Barcelona	3 Aug 92
43.74		Johnson			1	NC	Eugene	19 Jun 93
43.75		Johnson			1		Waco	19 Apr 97
43.76		Johnson			1	GWG	Uniondale, NY	22 Jul 98
43.81	Danny	Everett	USA	1.11.66	1	OT	New Orleans	26 Jun 92
43.83		Watts			1	WK	Zürich	19 Aug 92
43.84		Johnson			1	OG	Sydney	25 Sep 00
43.86A WR	Lee	Evans	USA	25.2.47	1	OG	Ciudad de México	18 Oct 68
43.86		Johnson			1	Bisl	Oslo	21 Jul 95
43.87	Steve	Lewis	USA	16.5.69	1	OG	Seoul	28 Sep 88
43.88		Johnson			1	WK	Zürich	16 Aug 95
43.90		Johnson			1		Madrid	6 Sep 94
43.91		Reynolds			2	NC	Atlanta	19 Jun 96
43.92		Johnson			1	Athl	Lausanne	2 Jul 99
43.92		Johnson			1	Pre	Eugene	24 Jun 00
43.93		Reynolds			1	OT	Indianapolis	20 Jul 88
43.93		Reynolds			2	OG	Seoul	28 Sep 88
43.94		Johnson			1	ISTAF	Berlin	27 Aug 93
43.95		Johnson			1s1	WCh	Sevilla	24 Aug 99
	(30/6)							
43.97A	Larry	James	USA	6.11.47	2	OG	Ciudad de México	18 Oct 68
44.09	Alvin	Harrison	USA	20.1.74	3	NC	Atlanta	19 Jun 96
44.09	Jerome	Young	USA	14.8.76	1	NC	New Orleans	21 Jun 98
44.13	Derek	Mills	USA	9.7.72	1	Pre	Eugene	4 Jun 95
	(10)							
44.14	Roberto	Hernández	CUB	6.3.67	2		Sevilla	30 May 90
44.15	Anthuan	Maybank	USA	30.12.69	1rB	Athl	Lausanne	3 Jul 96
44.17	Innocent	Egbunike	NGR	30.11.61	1rA	WK	Zürich	19 Aug 87
44.18	Samson	Kitur	KEN	25.2.66	2s2	OG	Barcelona	3 Aug 92
44.20A	Charles	Gitonga	KEN	5.10.71	1	NC	Nairobi	29 Jun 96
44.21	Ian	Morris	TRI	30.11.61	3s2	OG	Barcelona	3 Aug 92
44.21	Antonio	Pettigrew	USA	3.11.67	1		Nassau	26 May 99
44.26	Alberto	Juantorena	CUB	3.12.50	1	OG	Montreal	29 Jul 76
44.27	Alonzo	Babers	USA	31.10.61	1	OG	Los Angeles	8 Aug 84
44.28	Andrew	Valmon	USA	1.1.65	4	NC	Eugene	19 Jun 93
	(20)							
44.28	Tyree	Washington	USA	28.8.76	1		Eagle Rock	12 May 01
44.29	Derrick	Brew	USA	28.12.77	1	SEC	Athens, Ga	16 May 99
44.29	Sanderlei	Parrela	BRA	7.10.74	2	WCh	Sevilla	26 Aug 99
44.30	Gabriel	Tiacoh	CIV	10.9.63	1	NCAA	Indianapolis	7 Jun 86
44.30	Lamont	Smith	USA	11.12.72	4	NC	Atlanta	19 Jun 96
44.31	Alejandro	Cárdenas	MEX	4.10.74	3	WCh	Sevilla	26 Aug 99
44.33	Thomas	Schönlebe	GDR	6.8.65	1	WCh	Roma	3 Sep 87
44.34	Darnell	Hall	USA	26.9.71	1	Athl	Lausanne	5 Jul 95
44.36	Iwan	Thomas	GBR	5.1.74	1	NC	Birmingham	13 Jul 97
44.37	Roger	Black	GBR	31.3.66	2rA	Athl	Lausanne	3 Jul 96
	(30)							
44.37	Davis	Kamoga	UGA	17.7.68	2	WCh	Athína	5 Aug 97
44.37	Mark	Richardson	GBR	26.7.72	1	Bisl	Oslo	9 Jul 98
44.38	Darren	Clark	AUS	6.9.65	3s1	OG	Seoul	26 Sep 88
44.40	Fred	Newhouse	USA	8.11.48	2	OG	Montreal	29 Jul 76
44.41A	Ron	Freeman	USA	12.6.47	3	OG	Ciudad de México	18 Oct 68
44.43A	Ezra	Sambu	KEN	4.9.78	1	WCT	Nairobi	26 Jul 03
44.45A	Ronnie	Ray	USA	2.1.54	1	PAm	Ciudad de México	18 Oct 75
44.45	Darrell	Robinson	USA	23.12.63	2	Pepsi	Westwood	17 May 86
44.45	Avard	Moncur	BAH	2.11.78	1		Madrid	7 Jul 01

Mark	Wind	Name		Nat	Born	Pos	Meet	Venue	Date
44.45		Leonard	Byrd	USA	17.3.75	1	GP	Belém	5 May 02
		(40)							
44.47		Michael	Franks	USA	23.9.63	1	WCp	Canberra	5 Oct 85
44.47		David	Grindley	GBR	29.10.72	4s2	OG	Barcelona	3 Aug 92
44.48		Roddie	Haley	USA	6.12.65	1	SWC	Houston	18 May 86
44.49		Roxbert	Martin	JAM	5.11.69	1	NC	Kingston	21 Jun 97
44.50		Erwin	Skamrahl	FRG	8.3.58	1r1		München	26 Jul 83
44.50		Derek	Redmond	GBR	3.9.65	1s2	WCh	Roma	1 Sep 87
44.50		Bert	Cameron	JAM	16.11.59	4s1	OG	Seoul	26 Sep 88
44.51		Jerome	Davis	USA	20.8.77	5s1	WCh	Sevilla	24 Aug 99
44.53		Gary	Kikaya	COD	4.2.80	1	NCAA	Baton Rouge	1 Jun 02
44.56		Mohamed	Al Malky	OMN	1.12.62	1	BGP	Budapest	12 Aug 88
44.56		Greg	Haughton	JAM	10.11.73	3	WCh	Göteborg	9 Aug 95
		(51)	100th man 44.75, 200th man 45.07						

Hand timing

Mark	Wind	Name		Nat	Born	Pos	Meet	Venue	Date
44.1		Wayne	Collett	USA	20.10.49	1	OT	Eugene	9 Jul 72
44.2*		John	Smith	USA	5.8.50	1	AAU	Eugene	26 Jun 71
44.2		Fred	Newhouse	USA	8.11.48	1s1	OT	Eugene	7 Jul 72
44.4A WR		Vince	Matthews	USA	16.12.47	1		Echo Summit	31 Aug 68

600 METRES

Mark	Wind	Name		Nat	Born	Pos	Meet	Venue	Date
1:12.81		Johnny	Gray	USA	19.6.60	1		Santa Monica	24 May 86
1:13.2 + ?		John	Kipkurgat	KEN	16.3.44	1		Pointe-à-Pierre	23 Mar 74
1:13.49		Joseph	Mutua	KEN	10.12.78	1		Liège (NX)	27 Aug 02
1:13.80		Earl	Jones	USA	17.7.64	2		Santa Monica	24 May 86
1:14.15		David	Mack	USA	30.5.61	3		Santa Monica	24 May 86
1:14.3 A		Lee	Evans	USA	25.2.47	1		Echo Summit	31 Aug 68
1:14.41		Andrea	Longo ¶	ITA	26.6.75	1		Rovereto	30 Aug 00
1:14.48		Trinity	Gray	USA	3.4.78	2		Rovereto	30 Aug 00

800 METRES

Mark	Wind	Name		Nat	Born	Pos	Meet	Venue	Date
1:41.11 WR		Wilson	Kipketer	DEN	12.12.70	1	ASV	Köln	24 Aug 97
1:41.24 WR			Kipketer			1rA	WK	Zürich	13 Aug 97
1:41.73! WR		Sebastian	Coe	GBR	29.9.56	1		Firenze	10 Jun 81
1:41.73			Kipketer			1rA	DNG	Stockholm	7 Jul 97
1:41.77		Joaquim	Cruz	BRA	12.3.63	1	ASV	Köln	26 Aug 84
1:41.83			Kipketer			1	GP II	Rieti	1 Sep 96
1:42.17			Kipketer			1	TOTO	Tokyo	16 Sep 96
1:42.20			Kipketer			1	VD	Bruxelles	22 Aug 97
1:42.27			Kipketer			1	VD	Bruxelles	3 Sep 99
1:42.28		Sammy	Koskei	KEN	14.5.61	2	ASV	Köln	26 Aug 84
1:42.32			Kipketer			1	GP II	Rieti	8 Sep 02
1:42.33 WR			Coe			1	Bisl	Oslo	5 Jul 79
1:42.34			Cruz			1r1	WK	Zürich	22 Aug 84
1:42.34		Wilfred	Bungei	KEN	24.7.80	2	GP II	Rieti	8 Sep 02
1:42.41			Cruz			1	VD	Bruxelles	24 Aug 84
1:42.47		Yuriy	Borzakovskiy	RUS	12.4.81	1	VD	Bruxelles	24 Aug 01
1:42.49			Cruz			1		Koblenz	28 Aug 85
1:42.51			Kipketer			1	Nik	Nice	10 Jul 96
1:42.52			Bungei			1	VD	Bruxelles	5 Sep 03
1:42.54			Cruz			1	ASV	Köln	25 Aug 85
1:42.55		André	Bucher	SUI	19.10.76	1rA	WK	Zürich	17 Aug 01
1:42.57			Kipketer			1	Herc	Monaco	4 Aug 99
1:42.58		Vebjørn	Rodal	NOR	16.9.72	1	OG	Atlanta	31 Jul 96
1:42.59			Kipketer			1	Herc	Monaco	10 Aug 96
1:42.60		Johnny	Gray	USA	19.6.60	2r1		Koblenz	28 Aug 85
1:42.61			Kipketer			1rA	WK	Zürich	14 Aug 96
1:42.61			Kipketer			1rA	Athl	Lausanne	2 Jul 97
1:42.62		Patrick	Ndururi	KEN	12.1.69	2rA	WK	Zürich	13 Aug 97
1:42.65			Gray			1	WK	Zürich	17 Aug 88
1:42.69		Hezekiél	Sepeng	RSA	30.6.74	2	VD	Bruxelles	3 Sep 99
1:42.69		Japheth	Kimutai	KEN	20.12.78	3	VD	Bruxelles	3 Sep 99
		(31/12)							
1:42.79		Fred	Onyancha	KEN	25.12.69	3	OG	Atlanta	31 Jul 96
1:42.81		Jean-Patrick	Nduwimana	BDI	9.5.78	2rA	WK	Zürich	17 Aug 01
1:42.85		Norberto	Téllez	CUB	22.1.72	4	OG	Atlanta	31 Jul 96
1:42.88		Steve	Cram	GBR	14.10.60	1rA	WK	Zürich	21 Aug 85
1:42.89		Mbulaeni	Mulaudzi	RSA	8.9.80	2	VD	Bruxelles	5 Sep 03
1:42.91		William	Yiampoy	KEN	17.5.74	3	GP II	Rieti	8 Sep 02

Mark Wind	Name		Nat	Born	Pos	Meet	Venue	Date
1:42.97	Peter	Elliott	GBR	9.10.62	1		Sevilla	30 May 90
1:42.98	Patrick	Konchellah	KEN	20.4.68	2	ASV	Köln	24 Aug 97
	(20)							
1:43.03	Kennedy/Kenneth	Kimwetich	KEN	1.1.73	2		Stuttgart	19 Jul 98
1:43.06	Billy	Konchellah	KEN	20.10.62	1	WCh	Roma	1 Sep 87
1:43.08	José Luiz	Barbosa	BRA	27.5.61	1		Rieti	6 Sep 91
1:43.09	Djabir	Saïd Guerni	ALG	29.3.77	5	VD	Bruxelles	3 Sep 99
1:43.15	Mehdi	Baala	FRA	17.8.78	5	GP II	Rieti	8 Sep 02
1:43.16	Paul	Ereng	KEN	22.8.67	1	WK	Zürich	16 Aug 89
1:43.17	Benson	Koech	KEN	10.11.74	1		Rieti	28 Aug 94
1:43.20	Mark	Everett	USA	2.9.68	1rA	Gugl	Linz	9 Jul 97
1:43.22	Pawel	Czapiewski	POL	30.3.78	5rA	WK	Zürich	17 Aug 01
1:43.26	Sammy	Langat (Kibet)	KEN	24.1.70	1rB	WK	Zürich	14 Aug 96
	(30)							
1:43.30	William	Tanui	KEN	22.2.64	2		Rieti	6 Sep 91
1:43.31	Nixon	Kiprotich	KEN	4.12.62	1		Rieti	6 Sep 92
1:43.33	Robert	Chirchir	KEN	26.11.72	3		Stuttgart	19 Jul 98
1:43.33	William	Chirchir	KEN	6.2.79	6	VD	Bruxelles	3 Sep 99
1:43.33	Joseph Mwengi	Mutua	KEN	10.12.78	1rA	WK	Zürich	16 Aug 02
1:43.35	David	Mack	USA	30.5.61	3r1		Koblenz	28 Aug 85
1:43.38	David (Singoei)	Kiptoo	KEN	26.6.65	2	Herc	Monaco	10 Aug 96
1:43.38	Rich	Kenah	USA	4.8.70	3rA	WK	Zürich	13 Aug 97
1:43.38	Arthémon	Hatungimana	BDI	21.1.74	3	VD	Bruxelles	24 Aug 01
1:43.44 WR	Alberto	Juantorena	CUB	3.12.50	1	WUG	Sofiya	21 Aug 77
	(40)							
1:43.50	Mahjoub	Haïda	MAR	1.7.70	2	GGala	Roma	14 Jul 98
1:43.5* WR	Rick	Wohlhuter	USA	23.12.48	1		Eugene	8 Jun 74
1:43.54	William	Wuyke	VEN	21.5.58	2		Rieti	7 Sep 86
1:43.55	Philip	Kibitok	KEN	23.3.71	3	GP II	Rieti	1 Sep 96
1:43.56	Rob	Druppers	NED	29.4.62	4	ASV	Köln	25 Aug 85
1:43.57	Mike	Boit	KEN	6.1.49	1	ISTAF	Berlin	20 Aug 76
1:43.57	Joseph	Tengelei	KEN	8.12.72	3rB	WK	Zürich	16 Aug 95
1:43.60	Abdi	Bile	SOM	28.12.62	3	WK	Zürich	16 Aug 89
1:43.62	Earl	Jones	USA	17.7.64	2r1	WK	Zürich	13 Aug 86
1:43.63	Agberto	Guimarães	BRA	18.8.57	3		Koblenz	29 Aug 84
	(50)	100th man 1:44.3, 200th man 1:45.09						
Indoors			*! photo-electric cell time*					
1:42.67		Kipketer			1	WI	Paris (B)	9 Mar 97

1000 METRES

Mark Wind	Name		Nat	Born	Pos	Meet	Venue	Date
2:11.96 WR	Noah	Ngeny	KEN	2.11.78	1	GP II	Rieti	5 Sep 99
2:12.18 WR	Sebastian	Coe	GBR	29.9.56	1	OsloG	Oslo	11 Jul 81
2:12.66		Ngeny			1	Nik	Nice	17 Jul 99
2:12.88	Steve	Cram	GBR	14.10.60	1		Gateshead	9 Aug 85
2:13.40 WR		Coe			1	Bisl	Oslo	1 Jul 80
2:13.56	Kenneth	Kimwetich	KEN	1.1.73	2	Nik	Nice	17 Jul 99
2:13.73	Noureddine	Morceli	ALG	28.2.70	1	BNP	Villeneuve d'Ascq	2 Jul 93
2:13.9 WR	Rick	Wohlhuter	USA	23.12.48	1	King	Oslo	30 Jul 74
2:13.96	Mehdi	Baala	FRA	17.8.78	1		Strasbourg	26 Jun 03
2:14.09	Joaquim	Cruz	BRA	12.3.63	1	Nik	Nice	20 Aug 84
2:14.28	Japheth	Kimutai	KEN	20.12.78	1	DNG	Stockholm	1 Aug 00
2:14.41	William	Yampoy (10)	KEN	19.5.74	2	GP II	Rieti	5 Sep 99
2:14.43	Laban	Rotich	KEN	20.1.69	1	Nik	Nice	16 Jul 97
2:14.50	Abdi	Bile	SOM	28.12.62	1		Jerez de la Frontera	13 Sep 89
2:14.52	Djabir Saïd	Guerni	ALG	29.3.77	3	GP II	Rieti	5 Sep 99
2:14.53	Willi	Wülbeck	FRG	18.12.54	2	Bisl	Oslo	1 Jul 80

1500 METRES

Mark Wind	Name		Nat	Born	Pos	Meet	Venue	Date
3:26.00 WR	Hicham	El Guerrouj	MAR	14.9.74	1	GGala	Roma	14 Jul 98
3:26.12		El Guerrouj			1	VD	Bruxelles	24 Aug 01
3:26.34	Bernard	Lagat	KEN	12.12.74	2	VD	Bruxelles	24 Aug 01
3:26.45		El Guerrouj			1 rA	WK	Zürich	12 Aug 98
3:26.89		El Guerrouj			1	WK	Zürich	16 Aug 02
3:26.96		El Guerrouj			1	GP II	Rieti	8 Sep 02
3:27.21		El Guerrouj			1	WK	Zürich	11 Aug 00
3:27.34		El Guerrouj			1	Herc	Monaco	19 Jul 02
3:27.37 WR	Noureddine	Morceli	ALG	28.2.70	1	Nik	Nice	12 Jul 95
3.27.52		Morceli			1	Herc	Monaco	25 Jul 95
3:27.65		El Guerrouj			1	WCh	Sevilla	24 Aug 99
3:27.91		Lagat			2	Herc	Monaco	19 Jul 02

Mark Wind	Name		Nat	Born	Pos	Meet	Venue	Date
3:28.12	Noah	Ngeny	KEN	2.11.78	2	WK	Zürich	11 Aug 00
3:28.21+		El Guerrouj			1	in 1M	Roma	7 Jul 99
3.28.37		Morceli			1	GPF	Monaco	9 Sep 95
3:28.37		El Guerrouj			1	Herc	Monaco	8 Aug 98
3:28.38		El Guerrouj			1	GP	Saint-Denis	6 Jul 01
3:28.40		El Guerrouj			1	VD	Bruxelles	5 Sep 03
3:28.51		Lagat			3	WK	Zürich	11 Aug 00
3:28.57		El Guerrouj			1rA	WK	Zürich	11 Aug 99
3:28.6+		Ngeny			2	in 1M	Roma	7 Jul 99
3:28.73		Ngeny			2	WCh	Sevilla	24 Aug 99
3:28.84		Ngeny			1	GP	Paris (C)	21 Jul 99
3:28.86 WR		Morceli			1		Rieti	6 Sep 92
3:28.91		El Guerrouj			1rA	WK	Zürich	13 Aug 97
3:28.92		El Guerrouj			1	VD	Bruxelles	22 Aug 97
3:28.93		Ngeny			1	GPF	München	11 Sep 99
3:28.95	Fermín	Cacho	ESP	16.2.69	2rA	WK	Zürich	13 Aug 97
3:28.98	Mehdi	Baala	FRA	17.8.78	2	VD	Bruxelles	5 Sep 03
3:29.05		El Guerrouj			1	VD	Bruxelles	23 Aug 96
	(30/6)							
3:29.18	Vénuste	Niyongabo	BUR	9.12.73	2	VD	Bruxelles	22 Aug 97
3:29.29	William	Chirchir	KEN	6.2.79	3	VD	Bruxelles	24 Aug 01
3:29.46 WR	Saïd	Aouita	MAR	2.11.59	1	ISTAF	Berlin	23 Aug 85
3:29.46	Daniel	Komen	KEN	17.5.76	1	Herc	Monaco	16 Aug 97
	(10)							
3:29.51	Ali	Saïdi-Sief ¶	ALG	15.3.78	1	Athl	Lausanne	4 Jul 01
3:29.67 WR	Steve	Cram	GBR	14.10.60	1	Nik	Nice	16 Jul 85
3:29.77	Sydney	Maree	USA	9.9.56	1	ASV	Köln	25 Aug 85
3:29.77	Sebastian	Coe	GBR	29.9.56	1		Rieti	7 Sep 86
3:29.91	Laban	Rotich	KEN	20.1.69	2rA	WK	Zürich	12 Aug 98
3:30.07	Rui	Silva	POR	3.8.77	3	Herc	Monaco	19 Jul 02
3:30.18	John	Kibowen	KEN	21.4.69	3rA	WK	Zürich	12 Aug 98
3:30.24	Cornelius	Chirchir	KEN-J	5.6.83	4	Herc	Monaco	19 Jul 02
3:30.55	Abdi	Bile	SOM	28.12.62	1		Rieti	3 Sep 89
3:30.57	Reyes	Estévez	ESP	2.8.76	3	WCh	Sevilla	24 Aug 99
	(20)							
3:30.58	William	Tanui	KEN	22.2.64	3	Herc	Monaco	16 Aug 97
3:30.67	Benjamin	Kipkurui	KEN	28.12.80	2	Herc	Monaco	20 Jul 01
3:30.72	Paul	Korir	KEN	15.7.77	3	VD	Bruxelles	5 Sep 03
3:30.77 WR	Steve	Ovett	GBR	9.10.55	1		Rieti	4 Sep 83
3:30.83	Fouad	Chouki ¶	FRA	15.10.78	3	WK	Zürich	15 Aug 03
3:30.92	José Luis	González	ESP	8.12.57	3	Nik	Nice	16 Jul 85
3:30.94	Isaac	Viciosa	ESP	26.12.69	5	Herc	Monaco	8 Aug 98
3:30.99	Robert	Rono	KEN	11.10.74	3	VD	Bruxelles	30 Aug 02
3:31.01	Jim	Spivey	USA	7.3.60	1	R-W	Koblenz	28 Aug 88
3:31.13	José Manuel	Abascal	ESP	17.3.58	1		Barcelona	16 Aug 86
	(30)							
3:31.17	Robert K.	Andersen	DEN	12.12.72	5rA	WK	Zürich	13 Aug 97
3:31.21	José Antonio	Redolat	ESP	17.2.76	1	DNG	Stockholm	17 Jul 01
3:31.28	Enock	Koech	KEN	4.4.81	3rA	WK	Zürich	17 Aug 01
3:31.40	William	Kemei	KEN	22.2.69	2	Nik	Nice	12 Jul 95
3:31.42	Alex	Kipchirchir	KEN	26.11.84	5	VD	Bruxelles	5 Sep 03
3:31.45	Driss	Maazouzi	FRA	15.10.69	6	Herc	Monaco	19 Jul 02
3:31.48	Azzedine	Sediki	MAR	21.5.70	3rA	ASV	Köln	18 Aug 95
3:31.48	Andrés	Díaz	ESP	12.7.69	2	Herc	Monaco	18 Aug 00
3:31.52	Steve	Holman	USA	2.3.70	6	VD	Bruxelles	22 Aug 97
3:31.53	David	Lelei	KEN	10.5.71	3		Stuttgart	19 Jul 98
	(40)							
3:31.54	Isaac	Songok	KEN	25.4.84	1	NA	Heusden	2 Aug 03
3:31.58	Thomas	Wessinghage	FRG	22.2.52	2		Koblenz	27 Aug 80
3:31.61	Juan Carlos	Higuero	ESP	3.8.78	6	VD	Bruxelles	5 Sep 03
3:31.70	Ali	Hakimi	TUN	24.4.76	7	VD	Bruxelles	22 Aug 97
3:31.71	Kevin	Sullivan	CAN	20.3.74	4	GGala	Roma	30 Jun 00
3:31.75	Pierre	Délèze	SUI	25.9.58	1	WK	Zürich	21 Aug 85
3:31.76	Steve	Scott	USA	5.5.56	4	Nik	Nice	16 Jul 85
3:31.86	John	Mayock	GBR	26.10.70	8	VD	Bruxelles	22 Aug 97
3:31.87	Stephen	Kipkorir	KEN	24.10.70	2	Athl	Lausanne	3 Jul 96
3:31.89	Sammy	Rono	KEN	74	4		Stuttgart	19 Jul 98
	(50)	100th man 3:33.68, 200th 3:35.26, 300th 3:36.2						
Indoors:								
3:31.76	Haile	Gebrselassie	ETH	18.4.73	1		Stuttgart	1 Feb 98

1 MILE

Mark Wind	Name		Nat	Born	Pos	Meet	Venue	Date
3:43.13 WR	Hicham	El Guerrouj	MAR	14.9.74	1	GGala	Roma	7 Jul 99
3:43.40	Noah	Ngeny	KEN	2.11.78	2	GGala	Roma	7 Jul 99
3:44.39 WR	Noureddine	Morceli	ALG	28.2.70	1		Rieti	5 Sep 93
3:44.60		El Guerrouj			1	Nik	Nice	16 Jul 98
3:44.90		El Guerrouj			1	Bisl	Oslo	4 Jul 97
3:44.95		El Guerrouj			1	GGala	Roma	29 Jun 01
3:45.19		Morceli			1	WK	Zürich	16 Aug 95
3:45.64		El Guerrouj			1	ISTAF	Berlin	26 Aug 97
3:45.96		El Guerrouj			1	BrGP	London (CP)	5 Aug 00
3:46.24		El Guerrouj			1	Bisl	Oslo	28 Jul 00
3:46.32 WR	Steve	Cram	GBR	14.10.60	1	Bisl	Oslo	27 Jul 85
3:46.38	Daniel	Komen	KEN	17.5.76	2	ISTAF	Berlin	26 Aug 97
3:46.70	Vénuste	Niyongabo	BUR	9.12.73	3	ISTAF	Berlin	26 Aug 97
3:46.76	Saïd	Aouita	MAR	2.11.59	1	WG	Helsinki	2 Jul 87
3:46.78		Morceli			1	ISTAF	Berlin	27 Aug 93
3:46.92		Aouita			1	WK	Zürich	21 Aug 85
3:47.10		El Guerrouj			1	BrGP	London (CP)	7 Aug 99
3:47.28	Bernard	Lagat	KEN	12.12.74	2	GGala	Roma	29 Jun 01
3:47.30		Morceli			1	VD	Bruxelles	3 Sep 93
3:47.33 WR	Sebastian	Coe	GBR	29.9.56	1	VD	Bruxelles	28 Aug 81
3:47.65	Laban	Rotich	KEN	20.1.69	2	Bisl	Oslo	4 Jul 97
	(21/10)							
3:47.69	Steve	Scott	USA	5.5.56	1	OsloG	Oslo	7 Jul 82
3:47.79	José Luis	González	ESP	8.12.57	2	Bisl	Oslo	27 Jul 85
3:47.88	John	Kibowen	KEN	21.4.69	3	Bisl	Oslo	4 Jul 97
3:47.94	William	Chirchir	KEN	6.2.79	2	Bisl	Oslo	28 Jul 00
3:48.17	Paul	Korir	KEN	15.7.77	1	GP	London (CP)	8 Aug 03
3:48.23	Ali	Saïdi-Sief ¶	ALG	15.3.78	1	Bisl	Oslo	13 Jul 01
3:48.38	Andrés	Díaz	ESP	12.7.69	3	GGala	Roma	29 Jun 01
3:48.40 WR	Steve	Ovett	GBR	9.10.55	1	R-W	Koblenz	26 Aug 81
3:48.80	William	Kemei	KEN	22.2.69	1	ISTAF	Berlin	21 Aug 92
3:48.83	Sydney	Maree	USA	9.9.56	1		Rieti	9 Sep 81
	(20)							
3:49.08	John	Walker	NZL	12.1.52	2	OsloG	Oslo	7 Jul 82
3:49.20	Peter	Elliott	GBR	9.10.62	2	Bisl	Oslo	2 Jul 88
3:49.22	Jens-Peter	Herold	GDR	2.6.65	3	Bisl	Oslo	2 Jul 88
3:49.31	Joe	Falcon	USA	23.6.66	1	Bisl	Oslo	14 Jul 90
3:49.34	David	Moorcroft	GBR	10.4.53	3	Bisl	Oslo	26 Jun 82
3:49.34	Benjamin	Kipkurui	KEN	28.12.80	3	VD	Bruxelles	25 Aug 00
3:49.40	Abdi	Bile	SOM	28.12.62	4	Bisl	Oslo	2 Jul 88
3:49.45	Mike	Boit	KEN	6.1.49	2	VD	Bruxelles	28 Aug 81
3:49.50	Rui	Silva	POR	3.8.77	3	GGala	Roma	12 Jul 02
3:49.56	Fermín	Cacho	ESP	16.2.69	2	Bisl	Oslo	5 Jul 96
	(30)							
3:49.60	José Antonio	Redolat	ESP	17.2.76	4	GGala	Roma	29 Jun 01
3:49.75	Leonard	Mucheru	KEN	13.6.78	5	GGala	Roma	29 Jun 01
3:49.77	Ray	Flynn	IRL	22.1.57	3	OsloG	Oslo	7 Jul 82
3:49.77	Wilfred	Kirochi	KEN	12.12.69	2	Bisl	Oslo	6 Jul 91
3:49.80	Jim	Spivey	USA	7.3.60	3	Bisl	Oslo	5 Jul 86
3:49.83	Vyacheslav	Shabunin	RUS	27.9.69	6	GGala	Roma	29 Jun 01
3:49.91	Simon	Doyle	AUS	9.11.66	4	Bisl	Oslo	6 Jul 91
3:49.98	Thomas	Wessinghage	FRG	22.2.52	3	ISTAF	Berlin	17 Aug 83
3:50.25	Alex	Kipchirchir	KEN	26.11.84	2	GP II	Rieti	7 Sep 03
3:50.26	Kevin	Sullivan	CAN	20.3.74	4	Bisl	Oslo	28 Jul 00
	(40)							
3:50.32	John	Mayock	GBR	26.10.70	3	Bisl	Oslo	5 Jul 96
3:50.33	Eric	Dubus	FRA	28.2.66	3	WK	Zürich	16 Aug 95
3:50.34	Todd	Harbour	USA	24.3.59	5	OsloG	Oslo	11 Jul 81
3:50.38	Pierre	Délèze	SUI	25.9.58	4	R-W	Koblenz	25 Aug 82
3:50.39	James	Kwalia	KEN	12.6.84	1	FBK	Hengelo	1 Jun 03
3:50.40	Steve	Holman	USA	2.3.70	5	Bisl	Oslo	4 Jul 97
3:50.40	Cornelius	Chirchir	KEN	7.10.83	2	GP	London (CP)	8 Aug 03
3:50.52	Hauke	Fuhlbrügge	GER	21.3.66	6	Bisl	Oslo	6 Jul 91
3:50.54	José Manuel	Abascal	ESP	17.3.58	2	GP-GG	Roma	10 Sep 86
3:50.57	William	Tanui	KEN	22.2.64	5	ISTAF	Berlin	26 Aug 97
3:50.57	Ali	Hakimi	TUN	24.4.76	6	ISTAF	Berlin	26 Aug 97
	(51)	100th man 3:52.39, 200th man 3:54.68						

Mark	Wind	Name		Nat	Born	Pos	Meet	Venue	Date
Indoors									
3:49.78		Eamonn	Coghlan	IRL	24.11.52	1		East Rutherford	27 Feb 83

2000 METRES

Mark	Wind	Name		Nat	Born	Pos	Meet	Venue	Date
4:44.79	WR	Hicham	El Guerrouj	MAR	14.9.74	1	ISTAF	Berlin	7 Sep 99
4:46.88		Ali	Saïdi-Sief ¶	ALG	15.3.78	1		Strasbourg	19 Jun 01
4:47.88	WR	Noureddine	Morceli	ALG	28.2.70	1		Paris	3 Jul 95
4:48.36			El Guerrouj			1		Gateshead	19 Jul 98
4:48.69		Vénuste	Niyongabo	BUR	9.12.73	1	Nik	Nice	12 Jul 95
4:48.74		John	Kibowen	KEN	21.4.69	1		Hechtel	1 Aug 98
4:49.00			Niyongabo			1		Rieti	3 Sep 97
4:49.55			Morceli			1	Nik	Nice	10 Jul 96
4:50.08		Noah	Ngeny	KEN	2.11.78	1	DNG	Stockholm	30 Jul 99
4:50.81	WR	Saïd	Aouita	MAR	2.11.59	1	BNP	Paris	16 Jul 87
4:51.17			El Guerrouj			1	ISTAF	Berlin	31 Aug 01
4:51.30		Daniel	Komen	KEN	17.5.76	1		Milano	5 Jun 98
4:51.39	WR	Steve	Cram	GBR	14.10.60	1	BGP	Budapest	4 Aug 85
4:51.52	WR	John	Walker	NZL	12.1.52	1	Bisl	Oslo	30 Jun 76
		(14/10)							
4:52.20		Thomas	Wessinghage	FRG	22.2.52	1		Ingelheim	31 Aug 82
4:52.40		José Manuel	Abascal	ESP	17.3.58	1		Santander	7 Sep 86
4:52.44		Jim	Spivey	USA	7.3.60	1	Athl	Lausanne	15 Sep 87
4:52.53		Moses	Kiptanui	KEN	1.10.70	1	ISTAF	Berlin	21 Aug 92
4:52.82		Peter	Elliott	GBR	9.10.62	2	Athl	Lausanne	15 Sep 87
4:52.82		Luke	Kipkosgei	KEN	27.11.75	2	Slovn	Bratislava	9 Jun 98
4:52.88		Ismaïl	Sghyr	MAR/FRA	16.3.72	2	Nik	Nice	12 Jul 95
4:53.06		Jack	Buckner	GBR	22.9.61	3	Athl	Lausanne	15 Sep 87
4:53.69		Gary	Staines	GBR	3.7.63	4	Athl	Lausanne	15 Sep 87
4:53.7+		John	Kosgei (20)	KEN	13.7.73	2	in 3k	Rieti	1 Sep 96
Indoors									
4:52.86		Haile	Gebrselassie	ETH	18.4.73	1	BUPA	Birmingham	15 Feb 98

3000 METRES

Mark	Wind	Name		Nat	Born	Pos	Meet	Venue	Date
7:20.67	WR	Daniel	Komen	KEN	17.5.76	1		Rieti	1 Sep 96
7:23.09		Hicham	El Guerrouj	MAR	14.9.74	1	VD	Bruxelles	3 Sep 99
7:25.02		Ali	Saïdi-Sief ¶	ALG	15.3.78	1	Herc	Monaco	18 Aug 00
7:25.09		Haile	Gebrselassie	ETH	18.4.73	1	VD	Bruxelles	28 Aug 98
7:25.11	WR	Noureddine	Morceli	ALG	28.2.70	1	Herc	Monaco	2 Aug 94
7:25.16			Komen			1	Herc	Monaco	10 Aug 96
7:25.54			Gebrselassie			1	Herc	Monaco	8 Aug 98
7:25.87			Komen			1	VD	Bruxelles	23 Aug 96
7:26.02			Gebrselassie			1	VD	Bruxelles	22 Aug 97
7:26.03			Gebrselassie			1	GP II	Helsinki	10 Jun 99
7:26.5 e			Komen			1	in 2M	Sydney	28 Feb 98
7:26.62		Mohammed	Mourhit ¶	BEL	10.10.70	2	Herc	Monaco	18 Aug 00
7:27.18		Moses	Kiptanui	KEN	1.10.70	1	Herc	Monaco	25 Jul 95
7:27.3+			Komen			1	in 2M	Hechtel	19 Jul 97
7:27.42			Gebrselassie			1	Bisl	Oslo	9 Jul 98
7:27.50			Morceli			1	VD	Bruxelles	25 Aug 95
7:27.59		Luke	Kipkosgei	KEN	27.11.75	2	Herc	Monaco	8 Aug 98
7:27.67			Saïdi-Sief			1	Gaz	Saint-Denis	23 Jun 00
7:27.75		Tom	Nyariki	KEN	27.9.71	2	Herc	Monaco	10 Aug 96
7.28.04			Kiptanui			1	ASV	Köln	18 Aug 95
7:28.28			Kipkosgei			2	Bisl	Oslo	9 Jul 98
7:28.41		Paul	Bitok (10)	KEN	26.6.70	3	Herc	Monaco	10 Aug 96
7:28.45		Assefa	Mezegebu	ETH	19.6.78	3	Herc	Monaco	8 Aug 98
7:28.67		Benjamin	Limo	KEN	23.8.74	1	Herc	Monaco	4 Aug 99
7:28.70		Paul	Tergat	KEN	17.6.69	4	Herc	Monaco	10 Aug 96
7:28.92			Komen			3	Herc	Monaco	18 Aug 00
7:28.93		Salah	Hissou	MAR	16.1.72	2	Herc	Monaco	4 Aug 99
7:28.94		Brahim	Lahlafi	MAR	15.4.68	3	Herc	Monaco	4 Aug 99
7:28.96	WR		Kiptanui			1	ASV	Köln	16 Aug 92
7:29.09		John	Kibowen	KEN	21.4.69	3	Bisl	Oslo	9 Jul 98
		(30/16)							
7:29.34		Isaac	Viciosa	ESP	26.12.69	4	Bisl	Oslo	9 Jul 98
7:29.45	WR	Saïd	Aouita	MAR	2.11.59	1	ASV	Köln	20 Aug 89
7:30.09		Ismaïl	Sghyr	MAR/FRA	16.3.72	2	Herc	Monaco	25 Jul 95
7:30.36		Mark	Carroll	IRL	15.1.72	5	Herc	Monaco	4 Aug 99
		(20)							

Mark Wind	Name		Nat	Born	Pos	Meet	Venue	Date
7:30.50	Dieter	Baumann ¶	GER	9.2.65	6	Herc	Monaco	8 Aug 98
7:30.53	El Hassan	Lahssini	MAR	1.1.74	6	Herc	Monaco	10 Aug 96
7:30.53	Hailu	Mekonnen	ETH	4.4.80	1	VD	Bruxelles	24 Aug 01
7:30.67	Kenenisa	Bekele	ETH	13.6.82	2	VD	Bruxelles	24 Aug 01
7:30.78	Mustapha	Essaïd	FRA	20.1.70	7	Herc	Monaco	8 Aug 98
7:30.84	Bob	Kennedy	USA	18.8.70	8	Herc	Monaco	8 Aug 98
7:30.91	Eliud	Kipchoge	KEN	5.11.84	2	VD	Bruxelles	5 Sep 03
7:30.99	Khalid	Boulami	MAR	7.8.69	1	Nik	Nice	16 Jul 97
7:31.13	Julius	Gitahi	KEN	29.4.78	6	Bisl	Oslo	9 Jul 98
7:31.14	William	Kalya	KEN	4.8.74	3	Herc	Monaco	16 Aug 97
	(30)							
7:31.59	Manuel	Pancorbo	ESP	7.7.66	7	Bisl	Oslo	9 Jul 98
7:32.1 WR	Henry	Rono	KEN	12.2.52	1	Bisl	Oslo	27 Jun 78
7:32.23	Richard	Limo	KEN	18.11.80	5	VD	Bruxelles	24 Aug 01
7:32.32	Enrique	Molina	ESP	25.2.68	5	Bisl	Oslo	4 Jul 97
7:32.36	Million	Wolde	ETH	17.3.79	3	Gaz	Saint-Denis	23 Jun 00
7:32.36	Benjamin	Maiyo	KEN	6.10.78	2	GPII	Athína	28 Jun 00
7:32.36	Abderrahim	Goumri	MAR	21.5.76	6	VD	Bruxelles	24 Aug 01
7:32.38	Abiyote	Abate	ETH	20.11.80	7	VD	Bruxelles	24 Aug 01
7:32.79	David	Moorcroft	GBR	10.4.53	1		London (CP)	17 Jul 82
7:33.13	Shem	Kororia	KEN	25.9.72	7	Herc	Monaco	10 Aug 96
	(40)							
7:33.37	Sydney	Maree	USA	9.9.56	2		London (CP)	17 Jul 82
7:33.42	Salah	El Ghazi	MAR	2.11.75	4	Herc	Monaco	20 Jul 01
7:33.51	Bernard	Lagat	KEN	12.12.74	5	Herc	Monaco	18 Aug 00
7:33.62	Sammy	Kipketer	KEN	29.9.81	3	Athl	Lausanne	4 Jul 01
7:33.79	Paul	Koech	KEN	25.6.69	5	Herc	Monaco	16 Aug 97
7:33.96	Wilson	Kipketer (Boit)	KEN	6.10.73	7	Nik	Nice	16 Jul 97
7:34.03	Vénuste	Niyongabo	BUR	9.12.73	3	ASV	Köln	16 Aug 96
7:34.18	Yobes	Ondieki	KEN	21.2.61	3	ASV	Köln	16 Aug 92
7:34.46	Driss	El Himer	FRA	4.4.74	5	GP	Paris	29 Jul 98
7:34.67	Mohamed Saïd	El Wardi	MAR	19.4.72	4	Gaz	Saint-Denis	23 Jun 00
	(50)	100th man 7:38.20, 200th man 7:42.73, 300th 7:45.29						
Indoors								
7:24.90		Komen			1		Budapest	6 Feb 98
7:26.15		Gebrselassie			1		Karlsruhe	25 Jan 98
7:26.80		Gebrselassie			1		Karlsruhe	24 Jan 99
7:28.29		Gebrselassie			1		Karlsruhe	28 Feb 03
7:32.98	Alberto	García ¶	ESP	22.2.71	1		Sevilla	22 Feb 03

2 MILES

Mark Wind	Name		Nat	Born	Pos	Meet	Venue	Date
7:58.61 WR	Daniel	Komen	KEN	17.5.76	1		Hechtel	19 Jul 97
7:58.91		Komen			1		Sydney	28 Feb 98
8:01.08 WR	Haile	Gebrselassie	ETH	18.4.73	1	APM	Hengelo	31 May 97
8:01.72		Gebrselassie			1	BrGP	London (CP)	7 Aug 99
8:01.86		Gebrselassie			1	APM	Hengelo	30 May 99
8:03.54 WR		Komen			1		Lappeenranta	14 Jul 96
8:07.46 WR		Gebrselassie			1		Kerkrade	28 May 95
8:09.01 WR	Moses	Kiptanui	KEN	10.10.70	1		Hechtel	30 Jul 94
8:10.98	Khalid	Boulami	MAR	7.8.69	1		Hechtel	6 Jul 96
8:11.59	Bob	Kennedy	USA	18.8.70	2		Hechtel	19 Jul 97
8:11.73	Ismaïl	Sghyr	MAR/FRA	16.3.72	2		Hechtel	6 Jul 96
Indoors								
8:04.69		Gebrselassie			1	GP	Birmingham	21 Feb 03
8:06.61	Hicham	El Guerrouj	MAR	14.9.74	1		Liévin	23 Feb 03
8:09.66	Hailu	Mekonnen	ETH	4.4.80	1		Birmingham	20 Feb 00

5000 METRES

Mark Wind	Name		Nat	Born	Pos	Meet	Venue	Date
12:39.36WR	Haile	Gebrselassie	ETH	18.4.73	1	GP II	Helsinki	13 Jun 98
12:39.74WR	Daniel	Komen	KEN	17.5.76	1	VD	Bruxelles	22 Aug 97
12:41.86WR		Gebrselassie			1	WK	Zürich	13 Aug 97
12:44.39WR		Gebrselassie			1	WK	Zürich	16 Aug 95
12:44.90		Komen			2	WK	Zürich	13 Aug 97
12:45.09		Komen			1	WK	Zürich	14 Aug 96
12:48.81	Stephen	Cherono	KEN	15.10.82	1	GS	Ostrava	12 Jun 03
	(Saïf Saaeed Shaheen QAT from August)							
12:48.98		Komen			1	GGala	Roma	5 Jun 97
12:49.28	Brahim	Lahlafi	MAR	15.4.68	1	VD	Bruxelles	25 Aug 00
12:49.64		Gebrselassie			1	WK	Zürich	11 Aug 99
12:49.71	Mohammed	Mourhit ¶	BEL	10.10.70	2	VD	Bruxelles	25 Aug 00
12:49.87	Paul	Tergat	KEN	17.6.69	3	WK	Zürich	13 Aug 97

Mark Wind	Name		Nat	Born	Pos	Meet	Venue	Date
12:50.24	Hicham	El Guerrouj	MAR	14.9.74	2	GS	Ostrava	12 Jun 03
12:50.80	Salah	Hissou	MAR	16.1.72	1	GGala	Roma	5 Jun 96
12:50.86	Ali	Saïdi-Sief ¶	ALG	15.3.78	1	GGala	Roma	30 Jun 00
12:51.60		Komen			1	DNG	Stockholm	8 Jul 96
12:52.26	Kenenisa	Bekele (10)	ETH	13.6.82	1	Bisl	Oslo	27 Jun 03
12:52.33	Sammy	Kipketer	KEN	29.9.81	2	Bisl	Oslo	27 Jun 03
12:52.38		Komen			1	GPF	Milano	7 Sep 96
12:52.39		Hissou			2	GGala	Roma	5 Jun 97
12:52.53		Hissou			1		Milano	9 Jun 99
12:52.61	Eliud	Kipchoge	KEN	5.11.84	3	Bisl	Oslo	27 Jun 03
12.52.70		Gebrselassie			2	WK	Zürich	14 Aug 96
12:52.79		Kipchoge			1	WCh	Saint-Denis	31 Aug 03
12:52.83		El Guerrouj			2	WCh	Saint-Denis	31 Aug 03
12:52.99	Abraham	Chebii	KEN	23.12.79	4	Bisl	Oslo	27 Jun 03
12:53.12		Bekele			3	WCh	Saint-Denis	31 Aug 03
12.53.19		Gebrselassie			1	ISTAF	Berlin	1 Sep 95
12:53.37		Chebii			1	Gaz	Saint-Denis	4 Jul 03
12:53.41	Khalid	Boulami	MAR	7.8.69	4	WK	Zürich	13 Aug 97
	(30/14)							
12:53.72	Philip	Mosima	KEN	2.1.77	2	GGala	Roma	5 Jun 96
12:53.84	Assefa	Mezegebu	ETH	19.6.78	1	VD	Bruxelles	28 Aug 98
12:54.07	John	Kibowen	KEN	21.4.69	4	WCh	Saint-Denis	31 Aug 03
12:54.58	James	Kwalia	KEN	12.6.84	5	Bisl	Oslo	27 Jun 03
12:54.70	Dieter	Baumann ¶	GER	9.2.65	5	WK	Zürich	13 Aug 97
12:54.85	Moses	Kiptanui	KEN	1.10.70	3	GGala	Roma	5 Jun 96
	(20)							
12:54.99	Benjamin	Limo	KEN	23.8.74	3	Gaz	Saint-Denis	4 Jul 03
12:55.63	Mark	Bett	KEN	22.12.76	2	Bisl	Oslo	28 Jul 00
12:55.94	Tom	Nyariki	KEN	27.9.71	1	DNG	Stockholm	7 Jul 97
12:56.27	Albert	Chepkurui	KEN	4.4.81	6	Bisl	Oslo	27 Jun 03
	(lAbdullah Hassan QAT from August 2003)							
12:56.29	Paul	Koech	KEN	25.6.69	6	WK	Zürich	13 Aug 97
12:56.50	Luke	Kipkosgei	KEN	27.11.75	5	Bisl	Oslo	28 Jul 00
12:56.72	Richard	Limo	KEN	18.11.80	1	WK	Zürich	17 Aug 01
12:57.23	Worku	Bikila	ETH	6.5.68	3	GGala	Roma	8 Jun 95
12:57.79	David	Chelule	KEN	7.7.77	5	GGala	Roma	7 Jul 99
12:58.08	Gebre-egziabher	Gebremariam	ETH	10.9.84	6	WCh	Saint-Denis	31 Aug 03
	(30)							
12:58.21	Bob	Kennedy	USA	18.8.70	5	WK	Zürich	14 Aug 96
12:58.39WR	Saïd	Aouita	MAR	2.11.59	1	GGala	Roma	22 Jul 87
12:58.57	Hailu	Mekonnen	ETH	4.4.80	1	GGala	Roma	29 Jun 01
12:58.83	Ismaïl	Sghyr	MAR/FRA	16.3.72	7	Bisl	Oslo	28 Jul 00
12:58.94	Paul	Bitok	KEN	26.6.70	4	Bisl	Oslo	28 Jun 02
12:59.39	Million	Wolde	ETH	17.3.79	5	WK	Zürich	12 Aug 98
13:00.36	Abiyote	Abate	ETH	20.11.80	5	GGala	Roma	29 Jun 01
13:00.41WR	David	Moorcroft	GBR	10.4.53	1	OsloG	Oslo	7 Jul 82
13:00.54	Khalid	Skah	MAR	29.1.67	1	BNP	Villeneuve d'Ascq	8 Jul 94
13:00.76	Abderrahim	Goumri	MAR	21.5.76	1	DNG	Stockholm	16 Jul 02
	(40)							
13:01.14	Nicholas	Kemboi	KEN	25.11.83	2	WK	Zürich	15 Aug 03
13:01.15	Sydney	Maree	USA	9.9.56	2	Bisl	Oslo	27 Jul 85
13:01.41	Brahim	Jabbour	MAR	2.10.70	1	GP II	Saint-Denis	3 Jul 99
13:01.76	Leonard	Mucheru	KEN	13.6.78	4	WK	Zürich	15 Aug 03
	(later Mushir Salem Jawher BRN)							
13:01.82	Yobes	Ondiekl	KEN	21.2.61	1	WK	Zürich	7 Aug 91
13:01.89	Julius	Gitahi	KEN	29.4.78	5	DNG	Stockholm	5 Aug 98
13:01.98	Mohamed	Amyn	MAR	25.5.76	3	DNG	Stockholm	16 Jul 02
13:02.15	Mustapha	Essaïd	FRA	20.1.70	4	VD	Bruxelles	28 Aug 98
13:02.28	Benjamin	Maiyo	KEN	6.10.78	2	Athl	Lausanne	5 Jul 00
13:02.51	Charles	Kamathi	KEN	18.5.78	6	WK	Zürich	16 Aug 02
	(50)	100th man 13:10.06, 200th man 13:17.04, 300th man 13:20.19						

Indoors

12:50.38		Gebrselassie			1	BUPA	Birmingham	14 Feb 99
12:51.48		Komen			1		Stockholm	19 Feb 98

10,000 METRES

26:22.75WR	Haile	Gebrselassie	ETH	18.4.73	1	APM	Hengelo	1 Jun 98
26:27.85WR	Paul	Tergat	KEN	17.6.69	1	VD	Bruxelles	22 Aug 97
26:29.22		Gebrselassie			1	VD	Bruxelles	5 Sep 03
26:30.03	Nicholas	Kemboi	KEN	25.11.83	2	VD	Bruxelles	5 Sep 03

Mark Wind	Name		Nat	Born	Pos	Meet	Venue	Date
26:31.32WR		Gebrselassie			1	Bisl	Oslo	4 Jul 97
26:36.26	Paul	Koech	KEN	25.6.69	2	VD	Bruxelles	22 Aug 97
26:38.08WR	Salah	Hissou	MAR	16.1.72	1	VD	Bruxelles	23 Aug 96
26:38.76	Abdullah	Hassan	QAT	4.4.81	3	VD	Bruxelles	5 Sep 03
	(Formerly Albert Chepkurui KEN)							
26:43.53WR		Gebrselassie			1	APM	Hengelo	5 Jun 95
26:46.44		Tergat			1	VD	Bruxelles	28 Aug 98
26:47.89		Koech			2	VD	Bruxelles	28 Aug 98
26:49.38	Sammy	Kipketer	KEN	29.9.81	1	VD	Bruxelles	30 Aug 02
26:49.57	Kenenisa	Bekele	ETH	13.6.82	1	WCh	Saint-Denis	24 Aug 03
26:49.90	Assefa	Mezegebu	ETH	19.6.78	2	VD	Bruxelles	30 Aug 02
26:50.20	Richard	Limo (10)	KEN	18.11.80	3	VD	Bruxelles	30 Aug 02
26:50.67		Chepkurui			4	VD	Bruxelles	30 Aug 02
26:50.77		Gebrselassie			2	WCh	Saint-Denis	24 Aug 03
26:51.49	Charles	Kamathi	KEN	18.5.78	1	VD	Bruxelles	3 Sep 99
26:52.23WR	William	Sigei	KEN	11.10.69	1	Bisl	Oslo	22 Jul 94
26:52.30	Mohammed	Mourhit ¶	BEL	10.10.70	2	VD	Bruxelles	3 Sep 99
26:52.87	John Cheruiyot	Korir	KEN	13.12.81	5	VD	Bruxelles	30 Aug 02
26:53.70		Bekele			1	FBK	Hengelo	1 Jun 03
26:54.41		Tergat			2	VD	Bruxelles	23 Aug 96
26:54.58		Gebrselassie			2	FBK	Hengelo	1 Jun 03
26:56.63		R Limo			4	VD	Bruxelles	5 Sep 03
26:56.78		Koech			3	VD	Bruxelles	23 Aug 96
26:58.38WR	Yobes	Ondieki	KEN	21.2.61	1	Bisl	Oslo	10 Jul 93
26:58.76	Sileshi	Sihine	ETH	29.1.83	3	FBK	Hengelo	1 Jun 03
27:01.44		Sihine			3	WCh	Saint-Denis	24 Aug 03
27:03.87		Tergat			1	VD	Bruxelles	25 Aug 00
	(30/16)							
27:04.20	Abraham	Chebii	KEN	23.12.79	1		Palo Alto	4 May 01
27:04.54	Felix	Limo	KEN	22.8.80	2	VD	Bruxelles	25 Aug 00
27:05.88	Patrick	Ivuti	KEN	30.6.78	6	VD	Bruxelles	30 Aug 02
27:06.17	John	Yuda	TAN	9.6.79	7	VD	Bruxelles	30 Aug 02
	(20)							
27:06.44	Worku	Bikila	ETH	6.5.68	1	VD	Bruxelles	25 Aug 95
27:06.45	Habte	Jifar	ETH	29.1.76	1	APM	Hengelo	30 May 99
27:06.59	Ismael	Kirui	KEN	20.2.75	2	VD	Bruxelles	25 Aug 95
27:07.55	Benjamin	Maiyo	KEN	6.10.78	2		Palo Alto	4 May 01
27:07.91WR	Richard	Chelimo	KEN	21.4.72	1	DNG	Stockholm	5 Jul 93
27:08.23WR	Arturo	Barrios	MEX	12.12.63	1	ISTAF	Berlin	18 Aug 89
27:10.34	Josphat	Machuka	KEN	12.12.73	4	VD	Bruxelles	25 Aug 95
27:11.17	Julius	Gitahi	KEN	29.4.78	1		Kobe	26 Apr 98
27:11.62	John	Ngugi ¶	KEN	10.5.62	1	VD	Bruxelles	13 Sep 91
27:12.37	Luke	Kipkosgei	KEN	27.11.75	3		Palo Alto	4 May 01
	(30)							
27:12.39	Ismaïl	Sghyr	MAR/FRA	16.3.72	2	DNG	Stockholm	30 Jul 99
27:12.47	António	Pinto	POR	22.3.66	3	DNG	Stockholm	30 Jul 99
27:13.38	Girma	Tola	ETH	13.10.75	2	APM	Hengelo	30 May 99
27:13.66	Moses	Mosop	KEN	17.7.85	7	VD	Bruxelles	5 Sep 03
27:13.81WR	Fernando	Mamede	POR	1.11.51	1	DNG	Stockholm	2 Jul 84
27:13.98	Mebrahtom	Keflezighi	USA	5.5.75	4		Palo Alto	4 May 01
27:14.26	Fita	Bayissa	ETH	15.12.72	1	Bisl	Oslo	4 Jul 92
27:14.44	Fabián	Roncero	ESP	19.10.70	1rA	EChall	Lisboa	4 Apr 98
27:14.53	Khalid	Skah	MAR	29.1.67	2	WCh	Göteborg	8 Aug 95
27:14.61	Berhanu	Dejene	ETH	.80	8	VD	Bruxelles	5 Sep 03
	(40)							
27:15.88	Boniface	Kiprop	UGA	12.10.85	9	VD	Bruxelles	5 Sep 03
27:16.50	Salvatore	Antibo	ITA	7.2.62	1	WG	Helsinki	29 Jun 89
27:17.20	William	Kiptum	KEN	30.3.71	2	Bisl	Oslo	22 Jul 94
27:17.48	Carlos	Lopes	POR	18.2.47	2	DNG	Stockholm	2 Jul 84
27:17.82	Addis	Abebe	ETH	5.9.70	2	WG	Helsinki	29 Jun 89
27:18.02	Shem	Kororia	KEN	25.9.72	6	VD	Bruxelles	25 Aug 95
27:18.14	Jon	Brown	GBR	27.2.71	4	VD	Bruxelles	28 Aug 98
27:18.32	Moses	Tanui	KEN	20.8.65	2	VD	Bruxelles	3 Sep 93
27:18.59	Armando	Quintanilla	MEX	19.4.68	3	Bisl	Oslo	22 Jul 94
27:18.66	Mark	Bett	KEN	22.12.76	5	VD	Bruxelles	28 Aug 98
	(50)	100th man 27:31.50, 200th 27:43.98, 300th 27:53.41						

20,000m 1 HOUR

56:55.6+	21 101m	Arturo	Barrios	MEX	12.12.63	1	La Flèche	30 Mar 91

MEN All-time

HALF MARATHON

Included are the slightly downhill courses: Newcastle to South Shields 30.5m, Tokyo 33m. Lisboa 40m (69m 2000-03)

Mark	Wind	Name		Nat	Born	Pos	Meet	Venue	Date
59:06		Paul	Tergat	KEN	17.6.69	1		Lisboa	26 Mar 00
59:17			Tergat			1		Milano	4 Apr 98
59:20		Hendrick	Ramaala	RSA	2.2.72	2		Lisboa	26 Mar 00
59:22			Tergat			1	Stra	Milano	17 Apr 99
59:31		Patrick	Ivuti	KEN	30.6.78	3		Lisboa	26 Mar 00
59:38		Faustin	Baha	TAN	30.5.82	4		Lisboa	26 Mar 00
59:41		Haile	Gebrselassie	ETH	18.4.73	1		Lisboa	24 Mar 02
59:42			Ramaala			2		Lisboa	24 Mar 02
59:43		António	Pinto	POR	22.3.66	1		Lisboa	15 Mar 98
59:45			Ivuti			1	NC	Udine	29 Sep 02
59:46			Tergat			3		Lisboa (dh 69m)	24 Mar 02
59:47		Moses	Tanui	KEN	20.8.65	1		Milano	3 Apr 93
59:51		William	Kiplagat	KEN	21.6.72	5		Lisboa	26 Mar 00
59:51	w	Tesfaye	Tola	ETH	19.10.74	1		Malmö	12 Jun 00
59:52		Fabián	Roncero (10)	ESP	19.10.70	1		Berlin	1 Apr 01
59:53		Philip	Rugut	KEN	18.5.77	2	NC	Udine	29 Sep 02
59:56			Tergat			1		Milano	1 Apr 95
59:56		Shem	Kororia	KEN	25.9.72	1	WCh	Kosice	4 Oct 97
59:58			Tanui			2	WCh	Kosice	4 Oct 97
59:58		Paul	Kosgei	KEN	22.4.78	1	GNR	South Shields	6 Oct 02
60:00		Kenneth	Cheruiyot	KEN	2.8.74	3	WCh	Kosice	4 Oct 97
60:00	w		Rugut			2		Malmö	12 Jun 00
60:01		Paul	Koech	KEN	25.6.69	1	WCh	Uster	27 Sep 98
60:01		Japhet	Kosgei	KEN	68	1		Lisboa	21 Mar 99
60:01			Ramaala			1	GNR	South Shields	21 Sep 03
60:02		Benson	Masya	KEN	14.5.70	1	GNR	South Shields	18 Sep 94
60:02		Darren	Wilson	AUS	9.8.68	1		Tokyo	19 Jan 97
60:02		John	Yuda	TAN	9.6.79	2	GNR	South Shields	6 Oct 02
60:03			Tanui			2	GNR	South Shields	18 Sep 94
60:03			Gebrselassie			1	WCh	Bristol	7 Oct 01
60:04		Joseph	Kimani	KEN	21.9.72	2		Lisboa	15 Mar 98
60:04		Tesfaye	Jifar	ETH	23.4.76	2	WCh	Bristol	7 Oct 01
		(32/21)							
60:05		Jackson	Koech	KEN	26.12.78	2	GNR	South Shields	21 Sep 03
60:06		Steve	Moneghetti	AUS	26.9.62	1		Tokyo	24 Jan 93
60:06		Robert K	Cheruiyot	KEN	26.9.78	1		Roma-Ostia Lido	24 Feb 02
60:09	Sh?	Paul	Evans	GBR	13.4.61	1		Marrakesh	15 Jan 95
60:10		Martin	Lel	KEN	29.10.78	1		Lisboa	16 Mar 03
60:11		Matthews	Temane	RSA	14.12.60	1	NC	East London	25 Jul 87
60:11		Zithulele	Sinqe	RSA	9.6.63	2	NC	East London	25 Jul 87
60:11		Todd	Williams	USA	7.3.69	2		Tokyo	24 Jan 93
60:12	Sh?	Laban	Chege	KEN	70	2		Marrakesh	15 Jan 95
		(30)							
60:14		Armando	Quintanilla	MEX	19.4.68	1		Tokyo	21 Jan 96
60:14		Daniel	Rono	KEN	13.7.78	1		Groningen	11 May 02
60:15		Sammy	Korir	KEN	12.12.71	1	RdVin	Grevenmacher	27 Sep 98
60:17		Dionicio	Cerón	MEX	9.10.65	3		Tokyo	24 Jan 93
60:18		Mohamed	Mourhit ¶	BEL	10.10.70	5	WCh	Kosice	4 Oct 97
60:20		Rachid	Berradi	ITA	29.8.75	1	Stram	Milano	13 Apr 02
60:21		David	Kosgei	KEN	.77	1		Gargnano	29 Sep 02
60:21		Zakayo	Ngatho	KEN	18.3.78	1		Marugame	2 Feb 03
60:22		Charles	Kamathi	KEN	18.5.78	2	Stram	Milano	13 Apr 02
60:23		Vincent	Rousseau	BEL	29.7.62	1		Tokyo	23 Jan 94
		(40)							
60:23		Gert	Thys	RSA	12.11.71	6	WCh	Kosice	4 Oct 97
60:24		Philip	Tarus	KEN	11.9.74	2		Milano	4 Apr 98
60:24		Khalid	Skah	MAR	29.1.67	3	WCh	Uster	27 Sep 98
60:24		Elijah	Lagat	KEN	72	1		Grevenmacher	26 Sep 99
60:24		Marco	Mazza	ITA	25.6.77	3	Stram	Milano	13 Apr 02
60:26		Simon	Lopuyet	KEN	24.12.72	1		Lisboa	12 Mar 95
60:26		Tendai	Chimusasa	ZIM	28.1.71	1		Grevenmacher	24 Sep 95
60:26		Zebedayo	Bayo	TAN	20.5.76	3		Lisboa	15 Mar 98
60:27		Joseph	Kibor	KEN	22.12.72	2		Gualtieri	31 Mar 97
60:27		Khalid	Khannouchi	MAR/USA	22.12.71	1		Philadelphia	28 Sep 97
60:27		Josephat	Kiprono	KEN	12.12.73	4		Lisboa	15 Mar 98
60:27		Titus	Munji	KEN	79	2		Berlin	1 Apr 01
		(52)	100th man 60:53, 200th 61:17, 300th 61:32						

Mark	Wind	Name		Nat	Born	Pos	Meet	Venue	Date
Short courses									
58:51		Paul	Tergat	KEN	17.6.69	1	Stra	Milano 49m sh	30 Mar 96
59:24		Sammy	Lelei	KEN	14.8.64	1		Lisboa 97m	13 Mar 93
59:46		Josephat	Kiprono	KEN	12.12.73	2	Stra	Milano 49m	30 Mar 96

MARATHON

Note Boston marathon is downhill overall (139m) and, as a point-to-point course, in some years, such as 1994, has been strongly wind-aided - next bests are shown if to standard as a supplement.
In second column: L = loop course or start and finish within 30%, P = point-to-point or start and finish more than 30% apart, D = point-to-point and downhill over 1/1000

Mark	Wind	Name		Nat	Born	Pos	Meet	Venue	Date
2:04:55	L WR	Paul	Tergat	KEN	17.6.69	1		Berlin	28 Sep 03
2:04:56	L	Sammy	Korir	KEN	12.12.71	2		Berlin	28 Sep 03
2:05:38	L WR	Khalid	Khannouchi	MAR/USA	22.12.71	1		London	14 Apr 02
2:05:42	L WR		Khannouchi			1		Chicago	24 Oct 99
2:05:48	L		Tergat			2		London	14 Apr 02
2:05:50	L	Evans	Rutto	KEN	8.4.78	1		Chicago	12 Oct 03
2:05:56	L		Khannouchi			1		Chicago	13 Oct 02
2:06:05	L WR	Ronaldo da	Costa	BRA	7.6.70	1		Berlin	20 Sep 98
2:06:15	L	Titus	Munji	KEN	.79	3		Berlin	28 Sep 03
2:06:16	L	Moses	Tanui	KEN	20.8.65	2		Chicago	24 Oct 99
2:06:16	L	Daniel	Njenga	KEN	7.5.76	2		Chicago	13 Oct 02
2:06:16	L	Toshinari	Takaoka	JPN	24.9.70	3		Chicago	13 Oct 02
2:06:18	L		Tergat			4		Chicago	13 Oct 02
2:06:33	L	Gert	Thys (10)	RSA	12.11.71	1		Tokyo	14 Feb 99
2:06:33	L	Michael	Rotich	KEN	26.10.82	1		Paris	6 Apr 03
2:06:35	L	Haile	Gebrselassie	ETH	18.4.73	3		London	14 Apr 02
2:06:36	L	António	Pinto	POR	22.3.66	1		London	16 Apr 00
2:06:36	L	Benoit	Zwierzchlewski	FRA	19.8.76	2		Paris	6 Apr 03
2:06:39	L	William	Kipsang	KEN	.77	1		Amsterdam	19 Oct 03
2:06:42	L	Felix	Limo	KEN	22.8.80	2		Amsterdam	19 Oct 03
2:06:44	L	Josephat	Kiprono	KEN	12.12.73	1		Berlin	26 Sep 99
2:06:46	L	Abdelkader	El Mouaziz	MAR	1.1.69	5		Chicago	13 Oct 02
2:06:47	L	Fred	Kiprop	KEN	3.6.74	1		Amsterdam	17 Oct 99
2:06:47	L	Raymond	Kipkoech (20)	KEN	.75	1		Berlin	29 Sep 02
2:06:47	L	Wilson	Onsare	KEN	15.6.76	3		Paris	6 Apr 03
2:06:48	L	Driss	El Himer	FRA	4.4.74	4		Paris	6 Apr 03
2:06:49	L	Tesfaye	Jifar	ETH	23.4.76	2		Amsterdam	17 Oct 99
2:06:49	L	Simon	Biwott	KEN	3.3.70	2		Berlin	29 Sep 02
2:06:50	L WR	Belayneh	Dinsamo	ETH	28.6.65	1		Rotterdam	17 Apr 88
2:06:50	L	William	Kiplagat	KEN	21.6.72	3		Amsterdam	17 Oct 99
2:06:50	L		Kiprono			1		Rotterdam	22 Apr 01
		(31/26)							
2:06:51	L	Atsushi	Fujita	JPN	6.11.76	1		Fukuoka	3 Dec 00
2:06:52	L	Vincent	Kipsos	KEN	22.6.76	3		Berlin	29 Sep 02
2:06:54	L	Ondoro	Osoro	KEN	3.12.67	1		Chicago	11 Oct 98
2:06:57	L	Takayuki	Inubishi	JPN	11.8.72	2		Berlin	26 Sep 99
		(30)							
2:06:57	L	Tesfaye	Tolla	ETH	19.10.74	4		Amsterdam	17 Oct 99
2:07:02	L	Sammy	Lelei	KEN	14.8.64	1		Berlin	24 Sep 95
2:07:06	L	Ian	Syster	RSA	20.1.76	5		London	14 Apr 02
2:07:07	L	Ahmed	Salah	DJI	31.12.56	2		Rotterdam	17 Apr 88
2:07:07	L	Paul	Koech	KEN	25.6.69	2		Chicago	12 Oct 03
2:07:09	L	Japheth	Kosgei	KEN	28.12.68	1		Rotterdam	18 Apr 99
2:07:12	L WR	Carlos	Lopes	POR	18.2.47	1		Rotterdam	20 Apr 85
2:07:13	L	Steve	Jones	GBR	4.8.55	1		Chicago	20 Oct 85
2:07:15	D	Cosmas	Ndeti	KEN	24.11.71	1		Boston	18 Apr 94
2:07:18	L	Kenneth	Cheruiyot	KEN	2.8.74	2		Rotterdam	22 Apr 01
		(40)							
2:07:19	D	Andrés	Espinosa	MEX	4.2.63	2		Boston	18 Apr 94
2:07:20	L	Vincent	Rousseau	BEL	29.7.62	2		Berlin	24 Sep 95
2:07:20	L		Lee Bong-ju	KOR	11.10.70	2		Tokyo	13 Feb 00
2:07:23	L	Fabián	Roncero	ESP	19.10.70	2		Rotterdam	18 Apr 99
2:07:26	L	Benjamin Kimutai	Kosgei	KEN	5.9.71	1		Amsterdam	20 Oct 02
2:07:27	L	Julio	Rey ¶	ESP	13.1.72	1		Hamburg	27 Apr 03
2:07:28	L	Josiah	Thugwane	RSA	15.4.71	1		Fukuoka	7 Dec 97
2:07:29	L	Stefano	Baldini	ITA	25.5.71	6		London	14 Apr 02
2:07:34	L	Antonio	Peña	ESP	26.8.70	1	L.Biwa	Otsu	4 Mar 01
2:07:35	L	Taisuke	Kodama	JPN	26.7.58	1		Beijing	19 Oct 86
2:07:35	L	Abebe	Mekonnen	ETH	9.1.64	1		Beijing	16 Oct 88
		(51)	100th man 2:08:17, 200th 2:09:12, 300th 2:10:04, 400th 2:10:38, 500th 2:11:01						

2000 METRES STEEPLECHASE

Mark	Wind	Name		Nat	Born	Pos	Meet	Venue	Date
5:14.43		Julius	Kariuki	KEN	12.6.61	1		Rovereto	21 Aug 90
5:15.96		Bouabdallah	Tahri	FRA	20.12.78	1		Tomblaine	19 Jun 02
5:16.22		Phillip	Barkutwo	KEN	6.10.66	2		Rovereto	21 Aug 90
5:16.85		Eliud	Barngetuny	KEN	20.5.73	1		Parma	13 Jun 95
5:18.28		Richard	Kosgei	KEN	29.12.70	2		Parma	13 Jun 95
5:18.36		Alessandro	Lambruschini	ITA	7.1.65	1		Verona	12 Sep 89
5:18.38		Azzedine	Brahmi	ALG	13.9.66	1		Verona	17 Jun 92
5:18.51		John	Langat	KEN	27.11.74	1		Rovereto	29 Aug 01
5:18.60		Stanley	Kibiwott	KEN	8.8.69	2		Rovereto	29 Aug 01

3000 METRES STEEPLECHASE

Mark	Wind	Name		Nat	Born	Pos	Meet	Venue	Date
7:55.28	WR	Brahim	Boulami ¶	MAR	20.4.72	1	VD	Bruxelles	24 Aug 01
7:55.72	WR	Bernard	Barmasai	KEN	6.5.74	1	ASV	Köln	24 Aug 97
7:56.16		Moses	Kiptanui	KEN	1.10.70	2	ASV	Köln	24 Aug 97
7:57.29		Reuben	Kosgei	KEN	2.8.79	2	VD	Bruxelles	24 Aug 01
7:57.38		Saïf Saaeed	Shaheen	QAT	15.10.82	1	WAF	Monaco	14 Sep 03
		(Formerly Stephen	Cherono KEN)						
7:57.42		Paul Kipsiele	Koech	KEN	10.11.81	2	WAF	Monaco	14 Sep 03
7:58.09			Boulami			1	Herc	Monaco	19 Jul 02
7:58.10		Stephen	Cherono	KEN	15.10.82	2	Herc	Monaco	19 Jul 02
7:58.50			Boulami			1	WK	Zürich	17 Aug 01
7:58.66			S Cherono			3	VD	Bruxelles	24 Aug 01
7:58.98			Barmasai			1	Herc	Monaco	4 Aug 99
7:59.08	WR	Wilson	Boit Kipketer	KEN	6.10.73	1	WK	Zürich	13 Aug 97
7:59.18	WR		Kiptanui			1	WK	Zürich	16 Aug 95
7.59.52			Kiptanui			1	VD	Bruxelles	25 Aug 95
8:00.06			Shaheen			1	VD	Bruxelles	5 Sep 03
8:00.35			Barmasai			2	WK	Zürich	13 Aug 97
8:00.42			Koech			2	VD	Bruxelles	5 Sep 03
8:00.54			Kiptanui			1		Rieti	3 Sep 97
8:00.56			Boit Kipketer			1	DNG	Stockholm	16 Jul 02
8:00.67			Barmasai			1	Herc	Monaco	8 Aug 98
8:00.77			Boulami			2	DNG	Stockholm	16 Jul 02
8:00.78			Kiptanui			3	WK	Zürich	13 Aug 97
8:01.05			Boit Kipketer			1		Stuttgart	19 Jul 98
8:01.53			Barmasai			1	Nik	Nice	16 Jul 98
8:01.65			S Cherono			3	DNG	Stockholm	16 Jul 02
8:01.69		Kipkirui	Misoi	KEN	23.12.78	4	VD	Bruxelles	24 Aug 01
8:01.73			Boit Kipketer			1	Herc	Monaco	20 Jul 01
8:01.80			Kiptanui			1	DNG	Stockholm	7 Jul 97
8:01.98			Barmasai			1	WK	Zürich	12 Aug 98
8:02.08	WR		Kiptanui			1	WK	Zürich	19 Aug 92
		(30/8)							
8:02.49		Ezekiel	Kemboi	KEN	25.5.82	2	WK	Zürich	15 Aug 03
8:03.41		Patrick	Sang	KEN	11.4.64	3	ASV	Köln	24 Aug 97
		(10)							
8:03.57		Ali	Ezzine	MAR	3.9.78	1	Gaz	Saint-Denis	23 Jun 00
8:03.74		Raymond	Yator	KEN	7.4.81	3	Herc	Monaco	18 Aug 00
8:03.89		John	Kosgei	KEN	13.7.73	3	Herc	Monaco	16 Aug 97
8:05.01		Eliud	Barngetuny	KEN	20.5.73	1	Herc	Monaco	25 Jul 95
8:05.35	WR	Peter	Koech	KEN	18.2.58	1	DNG	Stockholm	3 Jul 89
8:05.37		Philip	Barkutwo	KEN	6.10.66	2		Rieti	6 Sep 92
8:05.4	WR	Henry	Rono	KEN	12.2.52	1		Seattle	13 May 78
8:05.43		Christopher	Kosgei	KEN	14.8.74	2	WK	Zürich	11 Aug 99
8:05.44		Paul Kipsiele	Koech	KEN	10.11.81	2	WK	Zürich	16 Aug 02
8:05.51		Julius	Kariuki	KEN	12.6.61	1	OG	Seoul	30 Sep 88
		(20)							
8:05.99		Joseph	Keter	KEN	13.6.69	1	Herc	Monaco	10 Aug 96
8:06.77		Gideon	Chirchir	KEN	24.2.66	2	WK	Zürich	16 Aug 95
8:06.88		Richard	Kosgei	KEN	29.12.70	2	GPF	Monaco	9 Sep 95
8:06.91		Simon	Vroemen	NED	11.5.69	3	Herc	Monaco	19 Jul 02
8:06.91		Bouabdallah	Tahri	FRA	20.12.78	3	Gaz	Saint-Denis	4 Jul 03
8:07.13		Paul	Kosgei	KEN	22.4.78	2	GP II	Saint-Denis	3 Jul 99
8:07.44		Luis Miguel	Martín	ESP	11.1.72	2	VD	Bruxelles	30 Aug 02
8:07.59		Julius	Nyamu	KEN	1.12.77	5	VD	Bruxelles	24 Aug 01
8:07.62		Joseph	Mahmoud	FRA	13.12.55	1	VD	Bruxelles	24 Aug 84
8:07.96		Mark	Rowland	GBR	7.3.63	3	OG	Seoul	30 Sep 88
		(30)							

Mark	Wind	Name		Nat	Born	Pos	Meet	Venue	Date
8:08.02	WR	Anders	Gärderud	SWE	28.8.46	1	OG	Montreal	28 Jul 76
8:08.12		Matthew	Birir	KEN	5.7.72	3	GGala	Roma	8 Jun 95
8:08.14		Sa'ad Shaddad	Al-Asmari	KSA	24.9.68	4	DNG	Stockholm	16 Jul 02
8:08.57		Francesco	Panetta	ITA	10.1.63	1	WCh	Roma	5 Sep 87
8:08.78		Alessandro	Lambruschini	ITA	7.1.65	3	WCh	Stuttgart	21 Aug 93
8:09.02		Abdelaziz	Sahere	MAR	18.9.67	5	GGala	Roma	8 Jun 95
8:09.03		Elarbi	Khattabi	MAR	16.5.67	3	GGala	Roma	7 Jul 99
8:09.09		Eliseo	Martín	ESP	5.11.73	3	WCh	Saint-Denis	26 Aug 03
8:09.11		Bronislaw	Malinowski	POL	4.6.51	2	OG	Montreal	28 Jul 76
8:09.17		Henry	Marsh	USA	15.3.54	1	R-W	Koblenz	28 Aug 85
		(40)							
8:09.18		Boguslaw	Maminski	POL	18.12.55	2	VD	Bruxelles	24 Aug 84
8:09.37		Abel	Cheruiyot Yagut	KEN/BRN	26.12.84	2	NA	Heusden	2 Aug 03
		(now Abel Yagoot Jowhar Salem)							
8:09.48		Damian	Kallabis	GER	10.6.73	4	WK	Zürich	11 Aug 99
8:09.54		Johnstone	Kipkoech	KEN	20.12.68	2	VD	Bruxelles	25 Aug 95
8:09.76		Mark	Croghan	USA	8.1.68	5	WCh	Stuttgart	21 Aug 93
8:10.01		William	van Dijck	BEL	24.1.61	1	VD	Bruxelles	5 Sep 86
8:10.10		Hicham	Bouaouiche	MAR	16.6.74	3	Nik	Nice	16 Jul 98
8:10.23		Laïd	Bessou	ALG	5.2.76	8	Herc	Monaco	18 Aug 00
8:10.32		Hagen	Melzer	GDR	16.6.59	2	WCh	Roma	5 Sep 87
8:10.33		Abraham	Cherono	KEN	21.7.80	6	GS	Ostrava	12 Jun 03
		(50)	100th man 8:15.33, 200th man 8:21.90						
Drugs disqualification									
7:53.17		Brahim	Boulami ¶	MAR	20.4.72	1	WK	Zürich	16 Aug 02

110 METRES HURDLES

Mark	Wind	Name		Nat	Born	Pos	Meet	Venue	Date
12.91 WR	0.5	Colin	Jackson	GBR	18.2.67	1	WCh	Stuttgart	20 Aug 93
12.92 WR	-0.1	Roger	Kingdom	USA	26.8.62	1	WK	Zürich	16 Aug 89
12.92	0.9	Allen	Johnson	USA	1.3.71	1	NC	Atlanta	23 Jun 96
12.92	0.2		Johnson			1	VD	Bruxelles	23 Aug 96
12.93 WR	-0.2	Renaldo	Nehemiah	USA	24.3.59	1	WK	Zürich	19 Aug 81
12.93	0.0		Johnson			1	WCh	Athína	7 Aug 97
12.94	1.6	Jack	Pierce	USA	23.9.62	1s2	NC	Atlanta	22 Jun 96
12.95	0.6		Johnson			1	OG	Atlanta	29 Jul 96
12.97A	2.0		Kingdom			1		Sestriere	11 Aug 88
12.97A	-1.6		Jackson			1A		Sestriere	28 Jul 93
12.97	-0.5		Johnson			1		Stuttgart	13 Jul 97
12.97	1.5		Johnson			1	NC	Sacramento	23 Jul 00
12.97	0.0		Johnson			1	Gaz	Saint-Denis	4 Jul 03
12.98	1.5		Kingdom			1	OG	Seoul	26 Sep 88
12.98	0.2		Jackson			1	TOTO	Tokyo	15 Sep 94
12.98	0.2		Johnson			1	ASV	Köln	18 Aug 95
12.98	-0.3		Johnson			1rA	WK	Zürich	12 Aug 98
12.98	0.6	Mark	Crear	USA	2.10.68	1		Zagreb	5 Jul 99
12.99	1.2		Jackson			1	VD	Bruxelles	3 Sep 93
12.99	-0.3		Jackson			1		Madrid	6 Sep 94
13.00 WR	0.9		Nehemiah			1	Pepsi	Westwood	6 May 79
13.00	0.5	Anthony	Jarrett	GBR	13.8.68	2	WCh	Stuttgart	20 Aug 93
13.00	-0.1		Johnson			1	WCh	Göteborg	12 Aug 95
13.00	-0.3		Crear			2rA	WK	Zürich	12 Aug 98
13.00	0.6	Anier	García	CUB	9.3.76	1	OG	Sydney	25 Sep 00
13.01	0.3	Larry	Wade	USA	22.11.74	1rA	Athl	Lausanne	2 Jul 99
13.01	0.8		Johnson			1	GGala	Roma	7 Jul 99
13.02	0.6		Kingdom			1	ISTAF	Berlin	18 Aug 89
13.02	0.9		Jackson			1A	ISTAF	Berlin	30 Aug 94
13.02	1.5		Crear			1		Luzern	27 Jun 95
13.02	1.9		Jackson			1s1	EC	Budapest	22 Aug 98
13.02	1.5		Jackson			1	EC	Budapest	22 Aug 98
		(32/9)							
13.03	-0.2	Greg	Foster (10)	USA	4.8.58	2	WK	Zürich	19 Aug 81
13.03	1.0	Reggie	Torian	USA	22.4.75	1	NC	New Orleans	21 Jun 98
13.05	1.4	Tony	Dees ¶	USA	6.8.63	1		Vigo	23 Jul 91
13.05	-0.8	Florian	Schwarthoff	GER	7.5.68	1	NC	Bremen	2 Jul 95
13.08	1.2	Mark	McKoy	CAN	10.12.61	1	BNP	Villeneuve d'Ascq	2 Jul 93
13.08	0.0	Stanislav	Olijar	LAT	22.3.79	2	Athl	Lausanne	1 Jul 03
13.11	1.4	Dominique	Arnold	USA	14.9.73	2		Leverkusen	20 Aug 00
13.12	1.5	Falk	Balzer ¶	GER	14.12.73	2	EC	Budapest	22 Aug 98
13.12	1.0	Duane	Ross	USA	5.12.72	3	WCh	Sevilla	25 Aug 99
13.12	1.6		Liu Xiang	CHN	13.7.83	1rB	Athl	Lausanne	2 Jul 02

Mark	Wind	Name		Nat	Born	Pos	Meet	Venue	Date
13.13	1.6	Igor	Kovác	SVK	12.5.69	1	DNG	Stockholm	7 Jul 97
		(20)							
13.15	0.3	Robin	Korving	NED	29.7.74	5rA	Athl	Lausanne	2 Jul 99
13.16	0.6	Terrence	Trammell	USA	23.11.78	2	OG	Sydney	25 Sep 00
13.17	-0.4	Sam	Turner	USA	17.6.57	2	Pepsi	Westwood	15 May 83
13.17	0.0	Tonie	Campbell	USA	14.6.60	3	WK	Zürich	17 Aug 88
13.17	0.5	Courtney	Hawkins	USA	11.7.67	1		Ingolstadt	26 Jul 98
13.17	0.4	Mike	Fenner	GER	24.4.71	1		Leverkusen	9 Aug 98
13.18	0.5	Emilio	Valle	CUB	21.4.67	3s1	OG	Atlanta	29 Jul 96
13.19	1.9	Steve	Brown	USA/TRI	6.1.69	1h4	NC	Atlanta	21 Jun 96
13.20	2.0	Stéphane	Caristan	FRA	31.5.64	1	EC	Stuttgart	30 Aug 86
13.20	1.8	Aleksandr	Markin ¶	RUS	8.9.62	1	Znam	Leningrad	11 Jun 88
		(30)							
13.20	1.7	Larry	Harrington	USA	24.11.70	2s1	NC	Atlanta	22 Jun 96
13.21 WR	0.6	Alejandro	Casañas	CUB	29.1.54	1	WUG	Sofiya	21 Aug 77
13.21	1.8	Vladimir	Shishkin	RUS	12.1.64	2	Znam	Leningrad	11 Jun 88
13.21	0.9	Eugene	Swift	USA	14.9.64	3	NC	Atlanta	23 Jun 96
13.22	-0.2	Terry	Reese	USA	20.6.67	2	ASV	Köln	24 Aug 97
13.22	1.5	Dawane	Wallace	USA	30.12.76	4	NC	Sacramento	23 Jul 00
13.23	1.9	Ladji	Doucouré	FRA	28.3.83	1s1	EU23	Bydgoszcz	20 Jul 03
13.24 WR	0.3	Rod	Milburn	USA	18.5.50	1	OG	München	7 Sep 72
13.24	2.0	Arthur	Blake	USA	19.8.66	2	Athl	Lausanne	24 Jun 88
13.24	1.1	Yoel	Hernández	CUB	12.12.77	2	PAm	Winnipeg	30 Jul 99
		(40)							
13.25	0.1	Andre	Phillips	USA	5.9.59	1	USOF	Baton Rouge	28 Jul 85
13.25	-0.1		Li Tong	CHN	6.5.67	2rA	Gugl	Linz	4 Jul 94
13.25	1.9	Jonathan	N'senga	BEL	21.4.73	3s1	EC	Budapest	22 Aug 98
13.25	-0.3	Dudley	Dorival	HAI	1.9.75	3	WCh	Edmonton	9 Aug 01
13.26	1.6	Willie	Gault	USA	5.9.60	1	USOF	Indianapolis	25 Jul 82
13.26	0.0	Igor	Kazanov	LAT	24.9.63	2s1	WCh	Stuttgart	19 Aug 93
13.26	1.7	Erik	Batte	CUB	10.12.74	4s2	OG	Atlanta	29 Jul 96
13.26	0.0	Dan	Philibert	FRA	6.8.70	5	WCh	Athína	7 Aug 97
13.26	0.6	Yuniel	Hernández	CUB	28.3.81	1		Salamanca	13 Jul 01
13.26	1.4	Shaun	Bownes	RSA	24.10.70	1	NA	Heusden	14 Jul 01
13.26	0.5	Chris	Phillips	USA	24.7.72	1h5	WCh	Saint-Denis	28 Aug 03
		(51)	100th man 13.40, 200th 13.52, 300th 13.60						

Rolling start but accepted by race officials

Mark	Wind	Name		Nat	Born	Pos	Meet	Venue	Date
13.10A	2.0	Falk	Balzer ¶	GER	14.12.73	1	WCp	Johannesburg	13 Sep 98

Doubtful timing

Mark	Wind	Name		Nat	Born	Pos	Meet	Venue	Date
13.06	1.3	Mike	Fenner	GER	24.4.71	1		Scheessel	4 Jun 95
13.08	1.3	Eric	Kaiser ¶	GER	7.3.71	2		Scheessel	4 Jun 95

Wind-assisted marks

Mark	Wind	Name		Nat	Born	Pos	Meet	Venue	Date
12.87	2.6	Roger	Kingdom	USA	26.8.62	1	WCp	Barcelona	10 Sep 89
12.91	3.5	Renaldo	Nehemiah	USA	24.3.59	1	NCAA	Champaign	1 Jun 79
12.94A	2.8		Jackson			1rA		Sestriere	31 Jul 94
12.95	2.6		Jackson			2	WCp	Barcelona	10 Sep 89
12.99	2.7		Jackson			1	v3N	Birmingham	23 Jun 89
13.00	3.5		Nehemiah			1	USOF	Syracuse	26 Jul 81
13.00	2.7		Kingdom			1		Sacramento	21 Jul 84
13.00	3.8		Johnson			1s1	NC	Sacramento	17 Jun 95
13.06	2.1	Mark	McKoy	CAN	10.12.61	1	Gugl	Linz	13 Aug 92
13.14	2.9	Igor	Kazanov	LAT	24.9.63	1r1	Znam	Leningrad	8 Jun 86
13.15	2.1	Courtney	Hawkins	USA	11.7.67	1		Salamanca	10 Jul 98
13.18	4.7	Robert	Reading	USA	9.6.67	1		Azusa	23 Apr 94
13.20	2.4	Arthur	Blake	USA	19.8.66	2	IAC	Edinburgh	6 Jul 90
13.20	3.1	Yoel	Hernández	CUB	12.12.77	2		Camagüey	10 Mar 00
13.21A	2.5	Eric	Cannon	USA	2.3.67	2	NCAA	Provo	3 Jun 89
13.24	2.4	Glenn	Terry	USA	10.2.71	1s2	WUG	Buffalo	18 Jul 93
13.25	2.7	Tomasz	Scigaczewski	POL	18.11.78	1		Grudziadz	20 Jun 98
13.26A	2.6	Antti	Haapakoski	FIN	6.2.71	1rB		Sestriere	31 Jul 94
13.26	7.8		Chen Yanhao	CHN	7.2.72	1		Maebashi	27 Apr 96

Hand timing

Mark	Wind	Name		Nat	Born	Pos	Meet	Venue	Date
12.8	1.0	Renaldo	Nehemiah	USA	24.3.59	1		Kingston	11 May 79
13.0 WR	1.8	Guy	Drut	FRA	6.12.50	1	ISTAF	Berlin	22 Aug 75
13.0	1.0	Greg	Foster	USA	4.8.58	2		Kingston	11 May 79
13.0	0.8	Mark	McKoy	CAN	10.12.61	1	Nik	Nice	16 Jul 85
13.0		Stéphane	Caristan	FRA	25.1.64	1		Creteil	3 May 86
13.0		Vladimir	Shishkin	RUS	12.1.64	1		Stayki	7 May 88
13.0* WR	2.0	Rod	Milburn	USA	18.5.50	1s1	AAU	Eugene	25 Jun 71
13.0	0.4	Tomasz	Scigaczewski	POL	18.11.78	1	NC	Wroclaw	28 Jun 98

Mark	Wind	Name		Nat	Born	Pos	Meet	Venue	Date
Wind-assisted									
12.8	2.4	Colin	Jackson	GBR	18.2.67	1		Sydney	10 Jan 90
12.9	4.1	Mark	Crear	USA	2.10.68	1rA	S&W	Modesto	8 May 93
13.0		Alejandro	Casañas	CUB	29.1.54	1	Barr	La Habana	22 May 77
13.0		Tonie	Campbell	USA	14.6.60	1		Los Angeles	16 Jul 86
13.0		Keith	Talley	USA	28.1.64	1		Tuscaloosa	26 Mar 88
13.0	4.1		Li Tong	CHN	6.5.67	2rA	S&W	Modesto	8 May 93

400 METRES HURDLES

Mark		Name		Nat	Born	Pos	Meet	Venue	Date
46.78	WR	Kevin	Young	USA	16.9.66	1	OG	Barcelona	6 Aug 92
47.02	WR	Edwin	Moses	USA	31.8.55	1		Koblenz	31 Aug 83
47.03		Bryan	Bronson	USA	9.9.72	1	NC	New Orleans	21 Jun 98
47.10		Samuel	Matete	ZAM	27.7.68	1rA	WK	Zürich	7 Aug 91
47.13	WR		Moses			1		Milano	3 Jul 80
47.14			Moses			1	Athl	Lausanne	14 Jul 81
47.17			Moses			1	ISTAF	Berlin	8 Aug 80
47.18			Young			1	WCh	Stuttgart	19 Aug 93
47.19		Andre	Phillips	USA	5.9.59	1	OG	Seoul	25 Sep 88
47.23		Amadou	Dia Bâ	SEN	22.9.58	2	OG	Seoul	25 Sep 88
47.25		Félix	Sánchez	DOM	30.8.77	1	WCh	Saint-Denis	29 Aug 03
47.27			Moses			1	ISTAF	Berlin	21 Aug 81
47.32			Moses			1		Koblenz	29 Aug 84
47.35			Sánchez			1rA	WK	Zürich	16 Aug 02
47.37			Moses			1	WCp	Roma	4 Sep 81
47.37			Moses			1	WK	Zürich	24 Aug 83
47.37			Moses			1	OT	Indianapolis	17 Jul 88
47.37			Young			1	Athl	Lausanne	7 Jul 93
47.37		Stéphane	Diagana	FRA	23.7.69	1	Athl	Lausanne	5 Jul 95
47.38			Moses			1	Athl	Lausanne	2 Sep 86
47.38		Danny	Harris ¶	USA	7.9.65	1	Athl	Lausanne	10 Jul 91
47.38			Sánchez			1rA	WK	Zürich	17 Aug 01
47.40			Young			1	WK	Zürich	19 Aug 92
47.42			Young			1	ASV	Köln	16 Aug 92
47.43			Moses			1	ASV	Köln	28 Aug 83
47.45	WR		Moses			1	AAU	Westwood	11 Jun 77
47.46			Moses			1	WCh	Roma	1 Sep 87
47.48		Harald	Schmid	FRG	29.9.57	1	EC	Athína	8 Sep 82
47.48			Harris			2	WCh	Roma	1 Sep 87
47.48			Schmid			3	WCh	Roma	1 Sep 87
		(30/10)							
47.50		Angelo	Taylor	USA	29.12.78	1	OG	Sydney	27 Sep 00
47.53		Hadi Soua'an	Al-Somaily	KSA	30.12.76	2	OG	Sydney	27 Sep 00
47.54		Derrick	Adkins	USA	2.7.70	2	Athl	Lausanne	5 Jul 95
47.54		Fabrizio	Mori	ITA	28.6.69	2	WCh	Edmonton	10 Aug 01
47.57		James	Carter	USA	7.5.78	2rA	WK	Zürich	16 Aug 02
47.60		Winthrop	Graham	JAM	17.11.65	1	WK	Zürich	4 Aug 93
47.75		David	Patrick	USA	12.6.60	4	OT	Indianapolis	17 Jul 88
47.81		Llewellyn	Herbert	RSA	21.7.77	3	OG	Sydney	27 Sep 00
47.82	WR	John	Akii-Bua	UGA	3.12.49	1	OG	München	2 Sep 72
47.82		Kriss	Akabusi	GBR	28.11.58	3	OG	Barcelona	6 Aug 92
		(20)							
47.89		Dai	Tamesue	JPN	3.5.78	3	WCh	Edmonton	10 Aug 01
47.91		Calvin	Davis	USA	2.4.72	1s2	OG	Atlanta	31 Jul 96
47.92		Aleksandr	Vasilyev	BLR	26.7.61	2	ECp	Moskva	17 Aug 85
47.94		Eric	Thomas	USA	1.12.73	1	GGala	Roma	30 Jun 00
47.97		Maurice	Mitchell	USA	14.5.71	2rA	WK	Zürich	14 Aug 96
47.97		Joey	Wo0ody	USA	22.5.73	3	NC	New Orleans	21 Jun 98
47.98		Sven	Nylander	SWE	1.1.62	4	OG	Atlanta	1 Aug 96
48.04		Eronilde	de Araújo	BRA	31.12.70	2	Nik	Nice	12 Jul 95
48.05		Ken	Harnden	ZIM	31.3.73	1	GP	Paris	29 Jul 98
48.05		Kemel	Thompson	JAM	25.9.74	1	GP	London (CP)	8 Aug 03
		(30)							
48.06		Oleg	Tverdokhleb	UKR	3.11.69	1	EC	Helsinki	10 Aug 94
48.06		Ruslan	Mashchenko	RUS	11.11.71	1	GP II	Helsinki	13 Jun 98
48.09		Alwyn	Myburgh	RSA	13.10.80	1	WUG	Beijing	31 Aug 01
48.12A	WR	David	Hemery	GBR	18.7.44	1	OG	Ciudad de México	15 Oct 68
48.13		Dinsdale	Morgan	JAM	19.11.72	2	GGala	Roma	14 Jul 98
48.13		Marcel	Schelbert	SUI	26.2.76	3	WCh	Sevilla	27 Aug 99
48.14		Chris	Rawlinson	GBR	19.5.72	1rB	WK	Zürich	11 Aug 99

Mark	Wind	Name		Nat	Born	Pos	Meet	Venue	Date
48.16		Tony	Rambo	USA	30.5.60	3s1	OT	Los Angeles	17 Jun 84
48.16		Marek	Plawgo	POL	25.2.81	1	GP	Osaka	12 May 01
48.16		Rickey	Harris	USA	29.9.81	1	NCAA	Baton Rouge	31 May 02
		(40)							
48.17		Pawel	Januszewski	POL	2.1.72	1	EC	Budapest	20 Aug 98
48.17A		Mubarak	Al-Nubi	QAT	30.12.77	2	WCp	Johannesburg	11 Sep 98
48.17		Periklis	Iakovákis	GRE	24.3.79	1s1	WCh	Saint-Denis	27 Aug 03
48.18		Torrance	Zellner	USA	6.1.70	4rA	WK	Zürich	14 Aug 96
48.23		Bershawn	Jackson	USA	8.5.83	1	GP	Madrid (C)	19 Jul 03
48.24		Erick	Keter	KEN	22.7.66	2s2	WCh	Stuttgart	17 Aug 93
48.26		Kazuhiko	Yamazaki	JPN	10.5.71	3	GP	Osaka	8 May 99
48.27		Jirí	Muzík	CZE	1.9.76	3s3	WCh	Athína	3 Aug 97
48.28		Tranel	Hawkins	USA	17.9.62	3	OT	Los Angeles	18 Jun 84
48.28		Everson	Teixeira	BRA	23.11.74	2s2	OG	Atlanta	31 Jul 96
48.28		Rohan	Robinson	AUS	15.11.71	4s2	OG	Atlanta	31 Jul 96
		(51)	100th man 48.69, 200th man 49.21						
48.1	**Hand**	Jim	Bolding	USA	24.3.49	1		Milano	2 Jul 74
Drugs Disqualification		47.15	Bronson			1	GWG	Uniondale, NY	19 Jul 98

HIGH JUMP

Mark		Name		Nat	Born	Pos	Meet	Venue	Date
2.45	WR	Javier	Sotomayor	CUB	13.10.67	1		Salamanca	27 Jul 93
2.44	WR		Sotomayor			1	CAC	San Juan	29 Jul 89
2.43	WR		Sotomayor			1		Salamanca	8 Sep 88
2.43i			Sotomayor			1	WI	Budapest	4 Mar 89
2.42	WR	Patrik	Sjöberg	SWE	5.1.65	1	DNG	Stockholm	30 Jun 87
2.42i	WR	Carlo	Thränhardt	FRG	5.7.57	1		Berlin	26 Feb 88
2.42			Sotomayor			1		Sevilla	5 Jun 94
2.41	WR	Igor	Paklin	KGZ	15.6.63	1	WUG	Kobe	4 Sep 85
2.41i			Sjöberg			1		Pireás	1 Feb 87
2.41i			Sotomayor			1	WI	Toronto	14 Mar 93
2.41			Sotomayor			1	NC	La Habana	25 Jun 94
2.41			Sotomayor			1	TSB	London (CP)	15 Jul 94
2.40	WR	Rudolf	Povarnitsyn	UKR	13.6.62	1		Donetsk	11 Aug 85
2.40i			Thränhardt			1		Simmerath	16 Jan 87
2.40i			Sjöberg			1		Berlin	27 Feb 87
2.40			Sotomayor			1	NC	La Habana	12 Mar 89
2.40			Sjöberg			1	ECp-B	Bruxelles	5 Aug 89
2.40			Sotomayor			1	AmCp	Bogota	13 Aug 89
2.40		Sorin	Matei	ROM	6.7.63	1	PTS	Bratislava	20 Jun 90
2.40i		Hollis	Conway	USA	8.1.67	1	WI	Sevilla	10 Mar 91
2.40			Sotomayor			1		Saint Denis	19 Jul 91
2.40		Charles	Austin	USA	19.12.67	1	WK	Zürich	7 Aug 91
2.40			Sotomayor			1	Barr	La Habana	22 May 93
2.40			Sotomayor			1	TSB	London (CP)	23 Jul 93
2.40			Sotomayor			1	WCh	Stuttgart	22 Aug 93
2.40i			Sotomayor			1		Wuppertal	4 Feb 94
2.40i			Sotomayor			1	TSB	Birmingham	26 Feb 94
2.40			Sotomayor			1		Eberstadt	10 Jul 94
2.40			Sotomayor			1	Nik	Nice	18 Jul 94
2.40			Sotomayor			1	GWG	Sankt-Peterburg	29 Jul 94
2.40			Sotomayor			1	WCp	London (CP)	11 Sep 94
2.40			Sotomayor			1	PAm	Mar del Plata	25 Mar 95
2.40		Vyacheslav	Voronin	RUS	5.4.74	1	BrGP	London (CP)	5 Aug 00
		(33/9)							
2.39	WR		Zhu Jianhua	CHN	29.5.63	1		Eberstadt	10 Jun 84
2.39i		Dietmar	Mögenburg	FRG	15.8.61	1		Köln	24 Feb 85
2.39i		Ralf	Sonn	GER	17.1.67	1		Berlin	1 Mar 91
2.38i		Gennadiy	Avdeyenko	UKR	4.11.63	2	WI	Indianapolis	7 Mar 87
2.38		Sergey	Malchenko	RUS	2.11.63	1		Banská Bystrica	4 Sep 88
2.38		Dragutin	Topic ¶	YUG	12.3.71	1		Beograd	1 Aug 93
2.38i		Steve	Smith	GBR	29.3.73	2		Wuppertal	4 Feb 94
2.38i		Wolf-Hendrik	Beyer	GER	14.2.72	1		Weinheim	18 Mar 94
2.38		Troy	Kemp	BAH	18.6.66	1	Nik	Nice	12 Jul 95
2.38		Artur	Partyka	POL	25.7.69	1		Eberstadt	18 Aug 96
2.38i		Matt	Hemingway	USA	24.10.72	1	NC	Atlanta	4 Mar 00
		(20)							
2.37		Valeriy	Sereda	RUS	30.6.59	1		Rieti	2 Sep 84
2.37		Tom	McCants	USA	27.11.62	1	Owens	Columbus	8 May 88
2.37		Jerome	Carter	USA	25.3.63	2	Owens	Columbus	8 May 88

Mark Wind	Name		Nat	Born	Pos	Meet	Venue	Date
2.37	Sergey	Dymchenko	UKR	23.8.67	1		Kiyev	16 Sep 90
2.37i	Dalton	Grant	GBR	8.4.66	1	EI	Paris	13 Mar 94
2.37	Jacques	Freitag	RSA	11.6.82	1	NC	Durban	23 Mar 02
2.36 WR	Gerd	Wessig	GDR	16.7.59	1	OG	Moskva	1 Aug 80
2.36	Sergey	Zasimovich	KZK	6.9.62	1		Tashkent	5 May 84
2.36	Eddy	Annys	BEL	15.12.58	1		Ghent	26 May 85
2.36i	Jim	Howard	USA	11.9.59	1		Albuquerque	25 Jan 86
	(30)							
2.36i	Jan	Zvara	CZE	12.2.63	1	vGDR	Jablonec	14 Feb 87
2.36i	Gerd	Nagel	FRG	22.10.57	1		Sulingen	17 Mar 89
2.36	Nick	Saunders	BER	14.9.63	1	CG	Auckland	1 Feb 90
2.36	Doug	Nordquist	USA	20.12.58	2	TAC	Norwalk	15 Jun 90
2.36	Georgi	Dakov	BUL	21.10.67	2	VD	Bruxelles	10 Aug 90
2.36	Lábros	Papakóstas	GRE	20.10.69	1	NC	Athína	21 Jun 92
2.36i	Steinar	Hoen	NOR	8.2.71	1		Balingen	12 Feb 94
2.36	Tim	Forsyth	AUS	17.8.73	1	NC	Melbourne	2 Mar 97
2.36	Sergey	Klyugin	RUS	24.3.74	1	WK	Zürich	12 Aug 98
2.36	Konstantin	Matusevich	ISR	25.2.71	1		Perth	5 Feb 00
	(40)							
2.36	Martin	Buss	GER	7.4.76	1	WCh	Edmonton	8 Aug 01
2.36	Andrey	Sokolovskiy	UKR	16.7.78	1		Berdichev	7 Sep 02
2.36i	Stefan	Holm	SWE	25.5.76	1		Arnstadt	8 Feb 03
2.36	Aleksander	Walerianczyk	POL	1.9.82	1	EU23	Bydgoszcz	20 Jul 03
2.35i	Vladimir	Yashchenko	UKR	12.1.59	1	EI	Milano	12 Mar 78
2.35 WR	Jacek	Wszola	POL	30.12.56	1		Eberstadt	25 May 80
2.35i	Aleksandr	Kotovich	UKR	6.11.61	1		Vilnius	13 Jan 85
2.35i	Brent	Harken	USA	1.12.61	1		Moscow	15 Feb 91
2.35	Darrin	Plab	USA	26.9.70	2	NC	New Orleans	28 Jun 92
2.35i	Jean-Charles	Gicquel	FRA	24.2.67	2	EI	Paris	13 Feb 94
2.35	Mark	Boswell	CAN	28.7.77	2	WCh	Sevilla	23 Aug 99
2.35	Nathan	Leeper	USA	13.6.77	1		Sacramento	21 May 00
2.35A	Charles	Clinger	USA	28.12.76	1		Pocatello	19 May 01
2.35i	Staffan	Strand	SWE	18.4.76	1	Globen	Stockholm	6 Feb 02
		(54)	100th man 2.32, 200th man 2.30, 300th man 2.28					

Best outdoor marks for athletes with indoor bests

Mark	Name	Pos	Meet	Venue	Date
2.39	Conway	1	USOF	Norman	30 Jul 89
2.38	Avdeyenko	2=	WCh	Roma	6 Sep 87
2.37	Thranhärdt	2		Rieti	2 Sep 84
2.37	Smith	1	WJ	Seoul	20 Sep 92
2.36	Mögenburg	3		Eberstadt	10 Jun 84
2.36	Howard	1		Rehlingen	8 Jun 87
2.36	Zvara	1		Praha	23 Aug 87
2.36	Grant	4	WCh	Tokyo	1 Sep 91
2.36	Hoen	1		Oslo	1 Jul 97
2.35	Nagel	1		Forbach	7 Aug 88
2.35	Holm	1	WK	Zürich	16 Aug 02

Ancillary jumps – en route to final marks

2.40 Sotomayor 8 Sep 88 2.40 Sotomayor 29 Jul 89 2.40 Sotomayor 5 Jun 94

POLE VAULT

Mark Wind	Name		Nat	Born	Pos	Meet	Venue	Date
6.15i	Sergey	Bubka	UKR	4.12.63	1		Donetsk	21 Feb 93
6.14i		Bubka			1		Liévin	13 Feb 93
6.14A WR		Bubka			1		Sestriere	31 Jul 94
6.13i		Bubka			1		Berlin	21 Feb 92
6.13 WR		Bubka			1	TOTO	Tokyo	19 Sep 92
6.12i		Bubka			1	Mast	Grenoble	23 Mar 91
6.12 WR		Bubka			1		Padova	30 Aug 92
6.11i		Bubka			1		Donetsk	19 Mar 91
6.11 WR		Bubka			1		Dijon	13 Jun 92
6.10i		Bubka			1		San Sebastián	15 Mar 91
6.10 WR		Bubka			1	MAI	Malmö	5 Aug 91
6.09 WR		Bubka			1		Formia	8 Jul 91
6.08i		Bubka			1	NC	Volgograd	9 Feb 91
6.08 WR		Bubka			1	Znam	Moskva	9 Jun 91
6.07 WR		Bubka			1	Super	Shizuoka	6 May 91
6.06 WR		Bubka			1	Nik	Nice	10 Jul 88
6.05 WR		Bubka			1	PTS	Bratislava	9 Jun 88
6.05i		Bubka			1		Donetsk	17 Mar 90
6.05i		Bubka			1		Berlin	5 Mar 93
6.05		Bubka			1	GPF	London (CP)	10 Sep 93
6.05i		Bubka			1	Mast	Grenoble	6 Feb 94
6.05		Bubka			1	ISTAF	Berlin	30 Aug 94
6.05		Bubka			1	GPF	Fukuoka	13 Sep 97
6.05	Maksim	Tarasov	RUS	2.12.70	1	GP II	Athína	16 Jun 99
6.05	Dmitriy	Markov (ex BLR)	AUS	14.3.75	1	WCh	Edmonton	9 Aug 01

MEN All-time

Mark Wind	Name		Nat	Born	Pos	Meet	Venue	Date
6.03 WR		Bubka			1	Ros	Praha	23 Jun 87
6.03i		Bubka			1		Osaka	11 Feb 89
6.03	Okkert	Brits	RSA	22.8.73	1	ASV	Köln	18 Aug 95
6.03	Jeff	Hartwig	USA	25.9.67	1		Jonesboro	14 Jun 00
6.02i	Rodion	Gataullin	RUS	23.11.65	1	NC	Gomel	4 Feb 89
6.02		Bubka			1	GP	Atlanta	18 May 96
6.02		Hartwig			1	NC	Eugene	27 Jun 99
6.02		Tarasov			1	WCh	Sevilla	26 Aug 99
6.02i		Hartwig			1	IHS	Sindelfingen	10 Mar 02
	(34/6)							
6.01	Igor	Trandenkov	RUS	17.8.66	1	NC	Sankt Peterburg	4 Jul 96
6.00	Tim	Lobinger	GER	3.9.72	1	ASV	Köln	24 Aug 97
6.00i	Jean	Galfione	FRA	9.6.71	1	WI	Maebashi	6 Mar 99
6.00i	Danny	Ecker	GER	21.7.77	1		Dortmund	11 Feb 01
	(10)							

Most competitions at 6 metres or more: S Bubka 44, Hartwig 8, Gataullin & Tarasov 7, Brits 3, Markov & Lobinger 2

Mark Wind	Name		Nat	Born	Pos	Meet	Venue	Date
5.98	Lawrence	Johnson	USA	7.5.74	1		Knoxville	25 May 96
5.97	Scott	Huffman	USA	30.11.64	1	NC	Knoxville	18 Jun 94
5.96	Joe	Dial	USA	26.10.62	1		Norman	18 Jun 87
5.95	Andrei	Tivontchik	GER	13.7.70	1	ASV	Köln	16 Aug 96
5.95	Michael	Stolle	GER	17.12.74	1	Herc	Monaco	18 Aug 00
5.95	Romain	Mesnil	FRA	13.7.77	1		Castres	6 Aug 03
5.94i	Philippe	Collet	FRA	13.12.63	1	Mast	Grenoble	10 Mar 90
5.93i	Billy	Olson	USA	19.7.58	1		East Rutherford	8 Feb 86
5.93i	Tye	Harvey	USA	25.9.74	2	NC	Atlanta	3 Mar 01
5.93	Aleksandr	Averbukh	ISR	1.10.74	1	GP	Madrid (C)	19 Jul 03
	(20)							
5.92	István	Bagyula	HUN	2.1.69	1	Gugl	Linz	5 Jul 91
5.92	Igor	Potapovich	KZK	6.9.67	2		Dijon	13 Jun 92
5.92	Dean	Starkey	USA	27.3.67	1	Banes	São Paulo	21 May 94
5.91 WR	Thierry	Vigneron	FRA	9.3.60	2	GGala	Roma	31 Aug 84
5.91i	Viktor	Ryzhenkov	UZB	25.8.66	2		San Sebastián	15 Mar 91
5.91A	Riaan	Botha	RSA	8.11.70	1		Pretoria	2 Apr 97
5.90	Pierre	Quinon	FRA	20.2.62	2	Nik	Nice	16 Jul 85
5.90i	Ferenc	Salbert	FRA	5.8.60	1	Mast	Grenoble	14 Mar 87
5.90	Miroslaw	Chmara	POL	9.5.64	1	BNP	Villeneuve d'Ascq	27 Jun 88
5.90i	Grigoriy	Yegorov	KZK	12.1.67	1		Yokohama	11 Mar 90
	(30)							
5.90	Denis	Petushinskiy ¶	RUS	29.1.67	1	Znam	Moskva	13 Jun 93
5.90i	Pyotr	Bochkaryov	RUS	3.11.67	1	EI	Paris	12 Mar 94
5.90	Jacob	Davis	USA	29.4.78	1	Tex R	Austin	4 Apr 98
5.90	Viktor	Chistiakov	RUS/AUS	9.2.75	1		Salamanca	15 Jul 99
5.90	Pavel	Gerasimov	RUS	29.5.79	1		Rüdlingen	12 Aug 00
5.90	Nick	Hysong	USA	9.12.71	1	OG	Sydney	29 Sep 00
5.90	Giuseppe	Gibilisco	ITA	5.1.79	1	WCh	Saint-Denis	28 Aug 03
5.89	Kory	Tarpenning ¶	USA	27.2.62	1	OT	Indianapolis	21 Jul 88
5.87	Earl	Bell	USA	25.8.55	1		Jonesboro	14 May 88
5.87	Oscar	Janson	SWE	22.7.75	1		Somero	29 Jun 03
	(40)							
5.86	Vasiliy	Bubka	UKR	26.11.60	1		Chelyabinsk	16 Jul 88
5.86	Bill	Payne	USA	21.12.67	1	SWC	Houston	19 May 91
5.86	Valeri	Bukrejev	EST	15.6.64	1		Somero	3 Jul 94
5.86A	Pavel	Burlachenko	RUS	7.4.76	1		Pretoria	23 Mar 01
5.85	Konstantin	Volkov	RUS	28.2.60	1	Izv	Kiyev	22 Jun 84
5.85	Pat	Manson	USA	29.11.67	2	TOTO	Tokyo	15 Sep 94
5.85	Alain	Andji	FRA	20.11.74	1		Bonneuil-sur-Marne	18 May 97
5.85	Yevgeniy	Smiryagin	RUS	17.5.76	1	Nurmi	Turku	12 Jun 97
5.85	Vadim	Strogalyov	RUS	9.2.75	2		Hania	27 May 98
5.85	Richard	Spiegelburg	GER	12.8.77	1	NC	Stuttgart	30 Jun 01
5.85i	Tim	Mack	USA	15.9.72	2		Donetsk	24 Feb 02
5.85	Lars	Börgeling	GER	16.4.79	1		Leverkusen	27 Jul 02
5.85	Patrik	Kristiansson	SWE	3.6.77	1	vFIN	Helsinki	23 Aug 02
	(53)	100th man 5.76, 200th man 5.66, 300th man 5.60						

Best outdoor marks for athletes with lifetime bests indoors

6.00	Gataullin	1	Tokyo	16 Sep 89	5.90	Yegorov	2	WCh	Stuttgart	19 Aug 93
5.98	Galfione	1	Amiens	23 Jul 99	5.86	Bochkaryov	5	OG	Atlanta	2 Aug 96
5.93	Ecker	1	Ingolstadt	26 Jul 98	5.85	Collet	2		Paris	22 Jul 86

Ancillary jump: 6.05i Bubka 13 Feb 93

Outdoors on built-up runway

5.90	Pyotr	Bochkaryov	RUS	3.11.67	1	Karlskrona	28 Jun 96
5.86	Denis	Petushinskiy	RUS	28.6.67	1	Karlskrona	23 Jul 94

Mark	Wind	Name		Nat	Born	Pos	Meet	Venue	Date
Exhibition or Market Square competitions									
6.00		Jean	Galfione	FRA	9.6.71	1		Besançon	23 May 97
5.95		Viktor	Chistyakov	AUS	9.2.75	1		Chiari	8 Sep 99
5.86		Gennadiy	Sukharev	BLR	3.2.65	1		Bisceglie	23 Jul 91
5.86i		Larry	Jessee	USA	31.3.52	1		Newcastle	16 Oct 85

LONG JUMP

Mark	Wind	Name		Nat	Born	Pos	Meet	Venue	Date
8.95 WR	0.3	Mike	Powell	USA	10.11.63	1	WCh	Tokyo	30 Aug 91
8.90A WR	2.0	Bob	Beamon	USA	29.8.46	1	OG	Ciudad de México	18 Oct 68
8.87	-0.2	Carl	Lewis	USA	1.7.61	*	WCh	Tokyo	30 Aug 91
8.86A	1.9	Robert	Emmiyan	ARM	16.2.65	1		Tsakhkadzor	22 May 87
8.79	1.9		Lewis			1	TAC	Indianapolis	19 Jun 83
8.79i	-		Lewis			1		New York	27 Jan 84
8.76	1.0		Lewis			1	USOF	Indianapolis	24 Jul 82
8.76	0.8		Lewis			1	OT	Indianapolis	18 Jul 88
8.75	1.7		Lewis			1	PAm	Indianapolis	16 Aug 87
8.74	1.4	Larry	Myricks ¶	USA	10.3.56	2	OT	Indianapolis	18 Jul 88
8.74A	2.0	Erick	Walder	USA	5.11.71	1		El Paso	2 Apr 94
8.72	-0.2		Lewis			1	OG	Seoul	26 Sep 88
8.71	-0.4		Lewis			1	Pepsi	Westwood	13 May 84
8.71	0.1		Lewis			1	OT	Los Angeles	19 Jun 84
8.71	1.9	Iván	Pedroso	CUB	17.12.72	1		Salamanca	18 Jul 95
8.70	0.8		Myricks			1	TAC	Houston	17 Jun 89
8.70	0.7		Powell			1		Salamanca	27 Jul 93
8.70	1.6		Pedroso			1	WCh	Göteborg	12 Aug 95
8.68	1.0		Lewis			Q	OG	Barcelona	5 Aug 92
8.68	1.6		Pedroso			1		Lisboa	17 Jun 95
8.67	0.4		Lewis			1	WCh	Roma	5 Sep 87
8.67	-0.7		Lewis			1	OG	Barcelona	6 Aug 92
8.66	0.8		Lewis			*	MSR	Walnut	26 Apr 87
8.66	1.0		Myricks			1		Tokyo	23 Sep 87
8.66	0.9		Powell			1	BNP	Villeneuve d'Ascq	29 Jun 90
8.66A	1.4		Lewis			*		Sestriere	31 Jul 94
8.66	0.3		Pedroso			1		Linz	22 Aug 95
8.65	0.2		Lewis			1	VD	Bruxelles	24 Aug 84
8.65	0.7		Lewis			1	TAC	San José	26 Jun 87
8.65	1.5		Pedroso			1	OD	Jena	3 Jun 00
		(30/7)							
8.63	0.5	Kareem	Streete-Thompson	CAY/USA	30.3.73	1	GP II	Linz	4 Jul 94
8.62	0.7	James	Beckford	JAM	9.1.75	1		Orlando	5 Apr 97
8.59i		Miguel	Pate (10)	USA	13.6.79	1	NC	New York	1 Mar 02
8.56i	-	Yago	Lamela	ESP	24.7.77	2	WI	Maebashi	7 Mar 99
8.54	0.9	Lutz	Dombrowski	GDR	25.6.59	1	OG	Moskva	28 Jul 80
8.53	1.2	Jaime	Jefferson	CUB	17.1.62	1	Barr	La Habana	12 May 90
8.52	0.7	Savanté	Stringfellow	USA	6.11.78	1	NC	Stanford	21 Jun 02
8.51	1.7	Roland	McGhee	USA	15.10.71	2		São Paulo	14 May 95
8.50	0.2	Llewellyn	Starks	USA	10.2.67	2		Rhede	7 Jul 91
8.49	2.0	Melvin	Lister	USA	29.8.77	1	SEC	Baton Rouge	13 May 00
8.49	0.6	Jai	Taurima	AUS	26.6.72	2	OG	Sydney	28 Sep 00
8.48	0.8	Joe	Greene	USA	17.2.67	3		São Paulo	14 May 95
8.47	1.9	Kevin	Dilworth	USA	14.2.74	1		Abilene	9 May 96
		(20)							
8.46	1.2	Leonid	Voloshin	RUS	30.3.66	1	NC	Tallinn	5 Jul 88
8.46	1.6	Mike	Conley	USA	5.10.62	2		Springfield	4 May 96
8.46	1.8	Cheikh Tidiane	Touré	SEN	25.1.70	1		Bad Langensalza	15 Jun 97
8.45	2.0	Nenad	Stekic	YUG	7.3.51	1	PO	Montreal	25 Jul 75
8.44	1.7	Eric	Metcalf	USA	23.1.68	1	TAC	Tampa	17 Jun 88
8.44	1.0	Dwight	Phillips	USA	1.10.77	1	GP	Tríkala	24 Jun 03
8.43	0.8	Jason	Grimes	USA	10.9.59	-	TAC	Indianapolis	16 Jun 85
8.43	1.8	Giovanni	Evangelisti	ITA	11.9.61	1		San Giovanni Valdarno	16 May 87
8.43i	-	Stanislav	Tarasenko	RUS	23.7.66	1		Moskva	26 Jan 94
8.43	0.1	Luis	Meliz	CUB	11.8.79	2	OD	Jena	3 Jun 00
		(30)							
8.41	1.5	Craig	Hepburn	BAH	10.12.69	1	NC	Nassau	17 Jun 93
8.41i	-	Kirill	Sosunov	RUS	1.11.75	2	WI	Paris (B)	8 Mar 97
8.40	1.4	Douglas de	Souza	BRA	6.8.72	1		São Paulo	15 Feb 95
8.40	0.4	Robert	Howard	USA	26.11.75	1	SEC	Auburn	17 May 97
8.40	2.0	Gregor	Cankar	SLO	25.1.75	1		Celje	18 May 97
8.40	0.0		Lao Jianfeng	CHN	24.5.75	1	NC	Zhaoqing	28 May 97
8.39	0.8	Dion	Bentley	USA	26.8.71	2	NCAA	New Orleans	3 Jun 93

MEN All-time

Mark	Wind	Name		Nat	Born	Pos	Meet	Venue	Date
8.38	0.4	Konstantin	Semykin	RUS	26.5.60	1	Drz	Moskva	17 Aug 84
8.38	1.1		Huang Geng	CHN	10.7.70	1	NC	Taiyuan	18 May 95
8.38i	–	Vitaliy	Shkurlatov	RUS	25.5.79	1		Samara	30 Jan 00
		(40)							
8.37A	0.4	Leroy	Burrell	USA	21.2.67	2	NCAA	Provo	2 Jun 89
8.37	1.5	Bogdan	Tudor	ROM	1.2.70	2		Bad Cannstatt	9 Jul 95
8.36	1.0	João Carlos	de Oliveira	BRA	28.5.54	1		Rieti	21 Jul 79
8.36	1.6	Frank	Paschek	GDR	25.6.56	1	OD	Berlin	28 May 80
8.36	1.5		Chen Zunrong	CHN	20.10.62	*		Shizuoka	5 May 92
8.36	1.6	Konstadinos	Koukodímos	GRE	14.9.69	1		Hania	5 Jun 94
8.36A	0.8	Nelson	Ferreira Jr	BRA	1.1.73	*	IbAm	Medellín	10 May 96
8.36	1.2	Carlos	Calado	POR	5.10.75	1		Lisboa	20 Jun 97
8.35 WR	0.0	Ralph	Boston	USA	9.5.39	1	CalR	Modesto	29 May 65
8.35AWR	0.0	Igor	Ter-Ovanesyan	RUS	19.5.38	1	PreO	Ciudad de México	19 Oct 67
8.35		six more men	(56)	100th man 8.27, 200th 8.18, 300th 8.12					

Sand layer insufficient: 8.37i		Sean Robbins	USA	9.10.72	1		Bowling Green	10 Feb 96
Irregular conditions: 8.39	1.2	Joan Lino Martínez	CUB	17.1.78	1		La Habana	5 Feb 99

Wind-assisted marks performances to 8.70, performers to 8.39

Mark	Wind	Name		Nat	Born	Pos	Meet	Venue	Date
8.99A	4.4	Mike	Powell	USA	10.11.63	1		Sestriere	21 Jul 92
8.96A	1.2+	Iván	Pedroso	CUB	17.12.72	1		Sestriere	29 Jul 95
8.95A	3.9		Powell			1		Sestriere	31 Jul 94
8.91	2.9	Carl	Lewis	USA	1.7.61	2	WCh	Tokyo	30 Aug 91
8.90	3.7		Powell			1	S&W	Modesto	16 May 92
8.79	3.0		Pedroso			1	Barr	La Habana	21 May 92
8.77	3.9		Lewis			1	Pepsi	Westwood	18 May 85
8.77	3.4		Lewis			1	MSR	Walnut	26 Apr 87
8.73	4.6		Lewis			Q	TAC	Sacramento	19 Jun 81
8.73	3.2		Lewis			Q	TAC	Indianapolis	17 Jun 83
8.73A	2.6		Powell			1		Sestriere	31 Jul 91
8.73	4.8		Pedroso			1		Madrid	20 Jun 95
8.72	2.2		Lewis			1	NYG	New York	24 May 92
8.72A	3.9		Lewis			2		Sestriere	31 Jul 94
8.70	2.5		Pedroso			1		Padova	16 Jul 95
8.68	4.9	James	Beckford	JAM	9.1.75	1	JUCO	Odessa, Tx	19 May 95
8.66A	4.0	Joe	Greene	USA	17.2.67	2		Sestriere	21 Jul 92
8.64	3.5	Kareem	Streete-Thompson	CAY/USA	30.3.73	2	NC	Knoxville	18 Jun 94
8.63	3.9	Mike	Conley	USA	5.10.62	2	TAC	Eugene	20 Jun 86
8.57	5.2	Jason	Grimes	USA	10.9.59	1	vFRG,AFR	Durham	27 Jun 82
8.53	4.9	Kevin	Dilworth	USA	14.2.74	1		Fort-de-France	27 Apr 02
8.49	2.6	Ralph	Boston	USA	9.5.39	1	FOT	Los Angeles	12 Sep 64
8.49	4.5	Stanislav	Tarasenko	RUS	23.7.66	2		Madrid	20 Jun 95
8.48	2.8	Kirill	Sosunov	RUS	1.11.75	1		Oristano	18 Sep 95
8.48	3.4	Peter	Burge	AUS	3.7.74	1		Gold Coast (RB)	10 Sep 00
8.48	5.6	Miguel	Pate	USA	13.6.79	1		Fort Worth	21 Apr 01
8.46	3.4	Randy	Williams	USA	23.8.53	1		Eugene	18 May 73
8.46		Vernon	George	USA	6.10.64	1		Houston	21 May 89
8.44		Keith	Talley	USA	28.1.64	Q		Odessa, Tx	16 May 85
8.42		Anthony	Bailous	USA	6.4.65	Q		Odessa, Tx	16 May 85
8.42A	4.5	Milan	Gombala	CZE	29.1.68	3		Sestriere	21 Jul 92
8.41	4.3	Shamil	Abbyasov	KGZ	16.4.57	2	vUSA	Indianapolis	3 Jul 82
8.41	3.3	Andre	Ester	USA	27.4.65	1	TexR	Austin	4 Apr 87
8.41A	3.2	Nelson	Ferreira Jr	BRA	1.1.73	1	IbAm	Medellín	10 May 96
8.40	4.3	Henry	Hines	USA	12.2.49	1	CalR	Modesto	27 May 72
8.40	2.1	Anthuan	Maybank	USA	30.12.69	1	DrakeR	Des Moines	24 Apr 93
8.40	3.4	Konstadínos	Koukodímos	GRE	14.9.69	1	ECp I	Valencia	11 Jun 94
8.39	6.2	Gary	Honey	AUS	26.7.59	2		Sacramento	21 Jul 84
8.39	3.5	Edrick	Floreal	CAN	5.10.66	1		Fayetteville	22 Apr 89
8.39	5.7	Yusuf	Alli	NGR	28.7.60	1	CG	Auckland	1 Feb 90
8.39	2.4		Chen Zunrong	CHN	20.10.62	1		Shizuoka	5 May 92
Exhibition: 8.46		Yuriy	Naumkin	RUS	4.11.68	1		Iglesias	6 Sep 96

Best outdoors

8.56 1.3 Lamela 1 Torino 24 Jun 99 8.38 1.1 Sosunov 1 ECp Sankt-Peterburg 27 Jun 98

8.46A 0.0 Pate 1 Cd. de México 3 May 03 and 8.45 1.5 2 NC Stanford 21 Jun 02, 8.48w 5.6 1 Fort Worth 21 Apr 01

Ancillary marks – other marks during series (to 8.66/8.71w)

Mark	Wind	Name	Date
8.84	1.7	Lewis	30 Aug 91
8.71	0.6	Lewis	19 Jun 83
8.68	0.3	Lewis	18 Jul 88
8.68	0.0	Lewis	30 Aug 91
8.67	-0.2	Lewis	5 Sep 87
8.66		Lewis	26 Apr 87
8.84Aw	3.8	Powell	21 Jul 92
8.83w	2.3	Lewis	30 Aug 91
8.80Aw	4.0	Powell	21 Jul 92
8.78Aw		Powell	21 Jul 92
8.75w	2.1	Lewis	16 Aug 87
8.75A	3.4	Powell	21 Jul 92
8.73w	2.4	Lewis	18 May 85
8.73w		Powell	16 May 92
8.71Aw		Powell	31 Jul 91
8.68w	3.7	Lewis	16 Aug 87
8.68w	4.1	Lewis	16 Aug 87

TRIPLE JUMP

Mark	Wind	Name		Nat	Born	Pos	Meet	Venue	Date
18.29 WR	1.3	Jonathan	Edwards	GBR	10.5.66	1	WCh	Göteborg	7 Aug 95
18.09	-0.4	Kenny	Harrison	USA	13.2.65	1	OG	Atlanta	27 Jul 96
18.01	0.4		Edwards			1	Bisl	Oslo	9 Jul 98
18.00	1.3		Edwards			1	McD	London (CP)	27 Aug 95
17.99	0.5		Edwards			1	EC	Budapest	23 Aug 98
17.98 WR	1.8		Edwards			1		Salamanca	18 Jul 95
17.97 WR	1.5	Willie	Banks	USA	11.3.56	1	TAC	Indianapolis	16 Jun 85
17.93	1.6		Harrison			1	DNG	Stockholm	2 Jul 90
17.92	1.6	Khristo	Markov	BUL	27.1.65	1	WCh	Roma	31 Aug 87
17.92	1.9	James	Beckford	JAM	9.1.75	1	JUCO	Odessa, Tex	20 May 95
17.92	0.7		Edwards			1	WCh	Edmonton	6 Aug 01
17.90	1.0	Vladimir	Inozemtsev	UKR	25.5.64	1	GPB	Bratislava	20 Jun 90
17.89A WR	0.0	João Carlos	de Oliveira	BRA	28.5.54	1	PAm	Ciudad de México	15 Oct 75
17.88	0.9		Edwards			2	OG	Atlanta	27 Jul 96
17.87	1.7	Mike	Conley	USA	5.10.62	1	TAC	San José	27 Jun 87
17.86	1.3	Charles	Simpkins	USA	19.10.63	1	WUG	Kobe	2 Sep 85
17.86	0.3		Conley			1	WCh	Stuttgart	16 Aug 93
17.86	0.7		Edwards			1	CG	Manchester	28 Jul 02
17.85	0.9	Yoelbi	Quesada (10)	CUB	4.8.73	1	WCh	Athína	8 Aug 97
17.84	0.7		Conley			1		Bad Cannstatt	4 Jul 93
17.83i	-	Aliecer	Urrutia	CUB	22.9.74	1		Sindelfingen	1 Mar 97
17.82	1.6		Edwards			1	WG	Helsinki	25 Jun 96
17.81	2.0		Markov			1	Nar	Sofia	31 May 87
17.80	0.6		Markov			1	BGP	Budapest	11 Aug 86
17.80i		Christian	Olsson	SWE	25.1.80	1		Göteborg	5 Mar 02
17.79	-0.8		Harrison			1	OD	Berlin	4 Jul 90
17.79	-0.7		Edwards			1	WK	Zürich	14 Aug 96
17.78	1.0	Nikolay	Musiyenko	UKR	16.12.59	1	Znam	Leningrad	7 Jun 86
17.78	0.6	Lázaro	Betancourt ¶	CUB	18.3.63	1	Barr	La Habana	15 Jun 86
17.78	-0.8		Harrison			1	WCh	Tokyo	26 Aug 91
17.78	0.7		Edwards			1	DNG	Stockholm	16 Jul 02
		(31/14)							
17.77	1.0	Aleksandr	Kovalenko	RUS	8.5.63	1	NC	Bryansk	18 Jul 87
17.77	1.4		Markov			1	NC	Sofia	3 Sep 88
17.77i	-	Leonid	Voloshin	RUS	30.3.66	1		Grenoble	6 Feb 94
17.75	0.3	Oleg	Protsenko	RUS	11.8.63	1	Znam	Moskva	10 Jun 90
17.72i		Brian	Wellman	BER	8.9.67	1	WI	Barcelona	12 Mar 95
17.69	1.5	Igor	Lapshin	BLR	8.8.63	1		Stayki	31 Jul 88
17.68	1.2	Phillips	Idowu	GBR	30.12.78	2	CG	Manchester	28 Jul 02
		(20)							
17.66	1.7	Ralf	Jaros	GER	13.12.65	1	ECp	Frankfurt-am-Main	30 Jun 91
17.65	1.0	Aleksandr	Yakovlev	UKR	8.9.57	1	Znam	Moskva	6 Jun 87
17.65	0.8	Denis	Kapustin	RUS	5.10.70	2	Bisl	Oslo	9 Jul 98
17.63	0.9	Kenta	Bell	USA	16.3.77	1c2	MSR	Walnut	21 Apr 02
17.63	0.4	Marian	Oprea	ROM	6.6.82	1	RomIC	Bucuresti	7 Jun 03
17.62i	-	Yoel	García	CUB	25.11.73	2		Sindelfingen	1 Mar 97
17.60	0.6	Vladimir	Plekhanov	RUS	11.4.58	2	NC	Leningrad	4 Aug 85
17.60	1.9	Fabrizio	Donato	ITA	14.8.76	1		Milano	7 Jun 00
17.59i	-	Pierre	Camara	FRA	10.9.65	1	WI	Toronto	13 Mar 93
17.59	0.3	Vasiliy	Sokov	RUS	7.4.68	1	NC	Moskva	19 Jun 93
		(30)							
17.59	0.8	Charles	Friedek	GER	26.8.71	1		Hamburg	23 Jul 97
17.59	1.8	Walter	Davis	USA	2.7.79	1	NC	Stanford	23 Jun 02
17.58	1.5	Oleg	Sakirkin	KZK	23.1.66	2	NC	Gorkiy	23 Jul 89
17.57A	0.0	Keith	Connor	GBR	16.9.57	1	NCAA	Provo	5 Jun 82
17.57	0.2	Dmitriy	Valyukevich	BLR	31.5.81	1	EU23	Bydgoszcz	19 Jul 03
17.56	1.9	Maris	Bruziks	LAT	25.8.62	1		Riga	3 Sep 88
17.55	0.3	Vasiliy	Grishchenkov	RUS	23.1.58	1	Spart	Moskva	19 Jun 83
17.55	0.9	Serge	Hélan	FRA	24.2.64	2	EC	Helsinki	13 Aug 94
17.53	1.0	Aleksandr	Beskrovniy	RUS	5.4.60	2	Spart	Moskva	19 Jun 83
17.53	1.6	Zdzislaw	Hoffmann	POL	27.8.59	1		Madrid	4 Jun 85
		(40)							
17.53	1.0	Gennadiy	Valyukevich	BLR	1.6.58	1		Erfurt	1 Jun 86
17.53	1.6	Al	Joyner	USA	19.1.60	Q	TAC	San José	26 Jun 87
17.53	0.9	Milán	Mikulás	CZE	1.4.63	1	NC	Praha	17 Jul 88
17.53	1.9	Oleg	Denishchik	BLR	10.11.69	2	NC	Kiyev	12 Jul 91
17.53	0.5	Aleksandr	Glavatskiy	BLR	2.5.70	2	WK	Zürich	12 Aug 98
17.50	0.4	Volker	Mai	GDR	3.5.66	1	vURS	Erfurt	23 Jun 85

Mark	Wind	Name		Nat	Born	Pos	Meet	Venue	Date
17.50	0.4	Leevan	Sands	BAH	16.8.81	1	JUCO	Odessa	18 May 02
17.49	1.4	Rostislav	Dimitrov	BUL	29.12.74	2	WCh	Sevilla	25 Aug 99
17.48	1.9	Jorge	Reyna	CUB	10.1.63	1		Santiago de Cuba	27 Feb 87
17.48	1.6	Jerome	Romain	DMN	12.6.71	Q	WCh	Göteborg	5 Aug 95
		(50)	100th man 17.28, 200th man 17.04						

Wind-assisted marks – performances to 17.80, performers to 17.53

Mark	Wind	Name		Nat	Born	Pos	Meet	Venue	Date
18.43	2.4	Jonathan	Edwards	GBR	10.5.66	1	ECp	Villeneuve d'Ascq	25 Jun 95
18.20	5.2	Willie	Banks	USA	11.3.56	1	OT	Indianapolis	16 Jul 88
18.17	2.1	Mike	Conley	USA	5.10.62	1	OG	Barcelona	3 Aug 92
18.08	2.5		Edwards			1	BUPA	Sheffield	23 Jul 95
18.03	2.9		Edwards			1	GhG	Gateshead	2 Jul 95
18.01	3.7		Harrison			1	NC	Atlanta	15 Jun 96
17.97	7.5	Yoelbi	Quesada	CUB	4.8.73	1		Madrid	20 Jun 95
17.93	5.2	Charles	Simpkins	USA	19.10.63	2	OT	Indianapolis	16 Jul 88
17.92	3.4	Christian	Olsson	SWE	25.1.80	1	GP	Gateshead	13 Jul 03
17.91	3.2		Simpkins			1	TAC	Eugene	21 Jun 86
17.86	3.9		Simpkins			1	OT	New Orleans	21 Jun 92
17.86	5.7	Denis	Kapustin	RUS	5.10.70	1		Sevilla	5 Jun 94
17.84	2.3		Conley			2	TAC	Eugene	21 Jun 86
17.82	3.6		Banks			1	Jen	San José	31 May 86
17.81	4.6	Keith	Connor	GBR	16.9.57	1	CG	Brisbane	9 Oct 82
17.75		Gennadiy	Valyukevich	BLR	1.6.58	1		Uzhgorod	27 Apr 86
17.75	7.1	Brian	Wellman	BER	8.9.67	2		Madrid	20 Jun 95
17.73	4.1	Vasiliy	Sokov	RUS	7.4.68	1		Riga	3 Jun 89
17.63	4.3	Robert	Cannon	USA	9.7.58	3	OT	Indianapolis	16 Jul 88
17.59	2.1	Jerome	Romain	DMN	12.6.71	3	WCh	Göteborg	7 Aug 95
17.58	5.2	Al	Joyner	USA	19.1.60	5	OT	Indianapolis	16 Jul 88
17.56	3.7	Ron	Livers	USA	20.7.55	1	AAU	Walnut	17 Jun 79
17.55	3.6	Zdzislaw	Hoffmann	POL	27.8.59	1	Kuso	Warszawa	9 Jun 84
17.54	3.2	Ken	Lorraway	AUS	6.2.56	2	CG	Brisbane	9 Oct 82
17.53	4.8	Ray	Kimble	USA	19.4.53	7	OT	Indianapolis	16 Jul 88

Best outdoor marks for athletes with indoor bests

Mark	Wind	Name	Pos	Meet	Venue	Date
17.77	0.2	Olsson	1	Veniz	Haniá	9 Jun 03
17.75	1.0	Voloshin	2	WCh	Tokyo	26 Aug 91
17.70	1.7	Urrutia	1	GP II	Sevilla	6 Jun 96
17.62A		Wellman	1		El Paso	15 Apr 95
17.47	1.8	García	1		Bad Cannstatt	9 Jul 95

Ancillary marks – other marks during series (to 17.78/17.84w)

Mark	Wind	Name	Date
18.16 WR	1.3	Edwards	7 Aug 95
17.99	0.1	Harrison	27 Jul 96
18.39	3.7	Edwards	25 Jun 95
18.06	4.9	Banks	16 Jul 88
17.90	2.5	Edwards	25 Jun 95
17.84	2.1	Edwards	23 Aug 98

SHOT

Mark	Name		Nat	Born	Pos	Meet	Venue	Date
23.12 WR	Randy	Barnes ¶	USA	16.6.66	1		Westwood	20 May 90
23.10		Barnes			1	Jen	San José	26 May 90
23.06 WR	Ulf	Timmermann	GDR	1.11.62	1		Hania	22 May 88
22.91 WR	Alessandro	Andrei	ITA	3.1.59	1		Viareggio	12 Aug 87
22.86	Brian	Oldfield	USA	1.6.45	1	ITA	El Paso	10 May 75
22.75	Werner	Günthör	SUI	1.6.61	1		Bern	23 Aug 88
22.67	Kevin	Toth	USA	29.12.67	1	Kans R	Lawrence	19 Apr 03
22.66i		Barnes			1	Sunkist	Los Angeles	20 Jan 89
22.64 WR	Udo	Beyer	GDR	9.8.55	1		Berlin	20 Aug 86
22.62 WR		Timmermann			1		Berlin	22 Sep 85
22.61		Timmermann			1		Potsdam	8 Sep 88
22.60		Timmermann			1	vURS	Tallinn	21 Jun 86
22.56		Timmermann			1		Berlin	13 Sep 88
22.55i		Timmermann			1	NC	Senftenberg	11 Feb 89
22.52	John	Brenner	USA	4.1.61	1	MSR	Walnut	26 Apr 87
22.51		Timmermann			1		Erfurt	1 Jun 86
22.51	Adam	Nelson	USA	7.7.75	1		Gresham	18 May 02
22.47		Timmermann			1		Dresden	17 Aug 86
22.47		Günthör			1	WG	Helsinki	2 Jul 87
22.47		Timmermann			1	OG	Seoul	23 Sep 88
22.45		Oldfield			1	ITA	El Paso	22 May 76
22.43		Günthör			1	v3-N	Lüdenscheid	18 Jun 87
22.42		Barnes			1	WK	Zürich	17 Aug 88
22.40		Barnes			1		Rüdlingen	13 Jul 96
22.39		Barnes			2	OG	Seoul	23 Sep 88
22.36 @		Timmermann			1		Athína	16 May 88
22.31		Beyer			1	NC	Potsdam	20 Aug 87
22.28		Oldfield			1	ITA	Edinburgh	18 Jun 75
22.28		Barnes			1	MSR	Walnut	22 Apr 90

Mark	Wind		Name	Nat	Born	Pos	Meet	Venue	Date
22.26i			Günthör			1	NC	Magglingen	8 Feb 87
22.26			Brenner			1		Westwood	18 Apr 87
		(31/9)							
22.24		Sergey	Smirnov	RUS	17.9.60	2	vGDR	Tallinn	21 Jun 86
		(10)							
22.10		Sergey	Gavryushin	RUS	27.6.59	1		Tbilisi	31 Aug 86
22.09		Sergey	Kasnauskas	BLR	20.4.61	1		Stayki	23 Aug 84
22.09i		Mika	Halvari	FIN	13.2.70	1		Tampere	7 Feb 00
22.02i		George	Woods	USA	11.2.43	1	LAT	Inglewood	8 Feb 74
22.02		Dave	Laut	USA	21.12.56	1		Koblenz	25 Aug 82
22.02		John	Godina	USA	31.5.72	1	NC	Eugene	27 Jun 99
22.00	WR	Aleksandr	Baryshnikov	RUS	11.11.48	1	vFRA	Colombes	10 Jul 76
21.98		Gregg	Tafralis ¶	USA	9.4.58	1		Los Gatos	13 Jun 92
21.97		Janus	Robberts	RSA	10.3.79	1	NCAA	Eugene	2 Jun 01
21.96		Mikhail	Kostin	RUS	10.5.59	1		Vitebsk	20 Jul 86
		(20)							
21.93		Remigius	Machura ¶	CZE	3.7.60	1		Praha	23 Aug 87
21.92		Carl	Myerscough ¶	GBR	21.10.79	1	NCAA	Sacramento	13 Jun 03
21.87		C.J.	Hunter ¶	USA	14.12.68	2	NC	Sacramento	15 Jul 00
21.85	WR	Terry	Albritton	USA	14.1.55	1		Honolulu	21 Feb 76
21.83i		Aleksandr	Bagach ¶	UKR	21.11.66	1		Brovary	21 Feb 99
21.82	WR	Al	Feuerbach	USA	14.1.48	1		San José	5 May 73
21.82		Andy	Bloom	USA	11.8.73	1	GPF	Doha	5 Oct 00
21.81		Yuriy	Belonog	UKR	9.3.74	1	NC	Kiev	3 Jul 03
21.78	WR	Randy	Matson	USA	5.3.45	1		College Station	22 Apr 67
21.77i		Mike	Stulce ¶	USA	21.7.69	1	v GBR	Birmingham	13 Feb 93
		(30)							
21.77		Dragan	Peric	YUG	8.5.64	1		Bar	25 Apr 98
21.76		Mike	Carter	USA	29.10.60	2	NCAA	Eugene	2 Jun 84
21.74		Janis	Bojars	LAT	12.5.56	1		Riga	14 Jul 84
21.73		Augie	Wolf ¶	USA	3.9.61	1		Leverkusen	12 Apr 84
21.69		Reijo	Ståhlberg	FIN	21.9.52	1	WCR	Fresno	5 May 79
21.69		Andrey	Mikhnevich ¶	BLR	12.7.76	1	WCh	Saint-Denis	23 Aug 03
21.68		Geoff	Capes	GBR	23.8.49	1	4-N	Cwmbrân	18 May 80
21.68		Edward	Sarul	POL	16.11.58	1		Sopot	31 Jul 83
21.67		Hartmut	Briesenick	GDR	17.3.49	1		Potsdam	1 Sep 73
21.62		Christian	Cantwell	USA	30.9.80	1		Salamanca	15 Jul 03
		(40)							
21.61		Kevin	Akins	USA	27.1.60	1	S&W	Modesto	14 May 83
21.60		Jim	Doehring ¶	USA	27.1.62	2		Los Gatos	13 Jun 92
21.58		Vladimir	Kiselyov	UKR	1.1.57	3	Drz	Moskva	17 Aug 84
21.57		Joachim	Olsen	DEN	31.5.77	2	NCAA	Baton Rouge	1 Jun 02
21.53		Yevgeniy	Mironov ¶	RUS	1.11.49	1	NC	Kiyev	24 Jun 76
21.51		Ralf	Reichenbach	FRG	31.7.50	1	ISTAF	Berlin	8 Aug 80
21.47		Brent	Noon ¶	USA	29.8.71	1	SEC	Tuscaloosa	21 May 95
21.47i		Oliver-Sven	Buder	GER	23.6.66	1	EI	Valencia	28 Feb 98
21.47		Manuel	Martínez	ESP	7.12.74	2		Salamanca	10 Jul 02
21.44		Mikhail	Domorosov	BLR	5.3.55	2		Stayki	23 Aug 84
		(50) 100th man 20.96, 200th 20.47		@ competitive meeting but unsanctioned by GDR federation					

Not recognised by GDR authorities

22.11	Rolf	Oesterreich	GDR	24.8.49	1		Zschopau	12 Sep 76

Drugs disqualification

22.84		Barnes			1		Malmö	7 Aug 90
21.82	Mike	Stulce ¶	USA	21.7.69	1		Brenham	9 May 90

Best outdoor marks for athletes with lifetime bests indoors

21.70	Stulce ¶	1	OG	Barcelona	31 Jul 92	21.50	Halvari	1			Hämeenkyrö	9 Jul 95
21.63	Woods	2	CalR	Modesto	22 May 76	21.47	Bagach ¶	1	Veniz		Haniá	31 May 97

Ancillary marks – other marks during series (to 22.42)

22.84 WR	Andrei	12 Aug 87	22.72 WR	Andrei	12 Aug 87	22.55	Barnes	20 May 90
22.76	Barnes	20 May 90	22.70	Günthör	23 Aug 88	22.45	Timmermann	22 May 88
22.74	Andrei	12 Aug 87	22.58	Beyer	20 Aug 86	22.44	Barnes	20 May 90

DISCUS

Mark	Wind		Name	Nat	Born	Pos	Meet	Venue	Date
74.08	WR	Jürgen	Schult	GDR	11.5.60	1		Neubrandenburg	6 Jun 86
73.88		Virgilijus	Alekna	LTU	13.2.72	1	NC	Kaunas	3 Aug 00
71.86	WR	Yuriy	Dumchev	RUS	5.8.58	1		Moskva	29 May 83
71.70		Róbert	Fazekas	HUN	18.8.75	1		Szombathely	14 Jul 02
71.50		Lars	Riedel	GER	28.6.67	1		Wiesbaden	3 May 97
71.32		Ben	Plucknett ¶	USA	13.4.54	1	Pre	Eugene	4 Jun 83
71.26		John	Powell	USA	25.6.47	1	TAC	San José	9 Jun 84

Mark	Wind	Name		Nat	Born	Pos	Meet	Venue	Date
71.26		Rickard	Bruch	SWE	2.7.46	1		Malmö	15 Nov 84
71.26		Imrich	Bugár	CZE	14.4.55	1	Jen	San José	25 May 85
71.25			Fazekas			1	WCp	Madrid (C)	21 Sep 02
71.18		Art	Burns	USA	19.7.54	1		San José	19 Jul 83
71.16	WR	Wolfgang	Schmidt	GDR	16.1.54	1		Berlin	9 Aug 78
71.14			Plucknett			1		Berkeley	12 Jun 83
71.14		Anthony	Washington	USA	16.1.66	1eA		Salinas	22 May 96
71.12			Alekna			1	WK	Zürich	11 Aug 00
71.06		Luis M.	Delís ¶	CUB	6.12.57	1	Barr	La Habana	21 May 83
71.06			Riedel			1	WK	Zürich	14 Aug 96
71.00			Bruch			1		Malmö	14 Oct 84
70.99			Alekna			1		Stellenbosch	30 Mar 01
70.98		Mac	Wilkins	USA	15.11.50	1	WG	Helsinki	9 Jul 80
70.98			Burns			1	Pre	Eugene	21 Jul 84
70.92			Schmidt	FRG		1		Norden	9 Sep 89
70.86	WR		Wilkins			1		San José	1 May 76
70.82			Plucknett			1		Salinas	1 Jun 83
70.78			Fazekas			1		Budapest	10 May 03
70.72			Bugár			1	vHUN,AUT	Schwechat	18 Jun 83
70.66			Wilkins			1	AAU	Walnut	16 Jun 79
70.60			Riedel			1	ISTAF	Berlin	30 Aug 96
70.58			Delís			1		Salinas	19 May 82
70.54		Dmitriy	Shevchenko ¶	RUS	13.5.68	1		Krasnodar	7 May 02
		(30/15)	53 performances over 70m						
70.38	WR u	Jay	Silvester	USA	27.8.37	1		Lancaster	16 May 71
70.32		Frantz	Kruger	RSA	22.5.75	1		Salon-de-Provence	26 May 02
70.06		Romas	Ubartas ¶	LIT	26.5.60	1		Smalininkay	8 May 88
70.00		Juan	Martínez ¶	CUB	17.5.58	2	Barr	La Habana	21 May 83
69.91		John	Godina	USA	31.5.72	1		Salinas	19 May 98
		(20)							
69.70		Géjza	Valent	CZE	3.10.53	2		Nitra	26 Aug 84
69.62		Knut	Hjeltnes ¶	NOR	8.12.51	2	Jen	San José	25 May 85
69.62		Timo	Tompuri	FIN	9.6.69	1		Helsingborg	8 Jul 01
69.46		Al	Oerter	USA	19.9.36	1	TFA	Wichita	31 May 80
69.44		Georgiy	Kolnootchenko	BLR	7.5.59	1	vUSA	Indianapolis	3 Jul 82
69.40		Art	Swarts ¶	USA	14.2.45	1		Scotch Plains	8 Dec 79
69.36		Mike	Buncic	USA	25.7.62	1		Fresno	6 Apr 91
69.28		Vladimir	Dubrovshchik	BLR	7.1.72	1	NC-w	Stayki	3 Jun 00
69.26		Ken	Stadel	USA	19.2.52	2	AAU	Walnut	16 Jun 79
68.94		Adam	Setliff	USA	15.12.69	1		Atascadero	25 Jul 01
		(30)							
68.90		Jean-Claude	Retel	FRA	11.2.68	1		Salon-de-Provence	17 Jul 02
68.88		Vladimir	Zinchenko	UKR	25.7.59	1		Dnepropetrovsk	16 Jul 88
68.64		Dmitriy	Kovtsun ¶	UKR	29.9.55	1		Riga	6 Jul 84
68.58		Attila	Horváth	HUN	28.7.67	1		Budapest	24 Jun 94
68.52		Igor	Duginyets	UKR	20.5.56	1	NC	Kiyev	21 Aug 82
68.50		Armin	Lemme	GDR	28.10.55	1	vUSA	Karl-Marx-Stadt	10 Jul 82
68.48	WR	John	van Reenen	RSA	26.3.47	1		Stellenbosch	14 Mar 75
68.44		Vaclovas	Kidykas	LIT	17.10.61	1		Sochi	1 Jun 88
68.30		Stefan	Fernholm	SWE	2.7.59	1		Västerås	15 Jul 87
68.12		Markku	Tuokko ¶	FIN	24.6.51	1	WCR	Fresno	5 May 79
		(40)							
68.12		Iosif	Nagy	ROM	20.11.46	2		Zaragoza	22 May 83
68.12		Erik	de Bruin ¶	NED	25.5.63	1		Sneek	1 Apr 91
68.08		Hein-Direck	Neu ¶	FRG	13.2.44	1		Bremerhaven	27 May 77
68.00		Svein Inge	Valvik	NOR	20.9.56	1		Juarez	31 May 82
67.92		Mario	Pestano	ESP	8.4.78	1	NC	Valencia	22 Jul 01
67.90		Vitaliy	Sidorov	UKR	23.3.70	1		Kiev	3 May 98
67.89		Nick	Sweeney	IRL	26.3.68	1		Helsingborg	4 Sep 98
67.88		Jason	Tunks	CAN	7.5.75	1		Abilene	14 May 98
67.82		Velko	Velev ¶	BUL	4.1.48	1		Riga	13 Aug 78
67.80		Alwin	Wagner	FRG	11.8.50	1		Melsungen	1 Jul 87
		(50)	100th man 66.38, 200th man 64.56						
Subsequent to or at drugs disqualification				! recognised as US record					
72.34!		Ben	Plucknett ¶	USA	13.4.54	1	DNG	Stockholm	7 Jul 81
71.20			Plucknett			1	CalR	Modesto	16 May 81
70.84		Kamy	Keshmiri ¶	USA	23.1.69	1		Salinas	27 May 92
Sloping ground									
72.08		John	Powell	USA	25.6.47	1		Klagshamn	11 Sep 87
69.80		Stefan	Fernholm	SWE	2.7.59	1		Klagshamn	13 Aug 87

Mark	Wind	Name		Nat	Born	Pos	Meet	Venue	Date
69.44		Adam	Setliff	USA	15.12.69	1		La Jolla	21 Jul 01
68.46		Andy	Bloom	USA	11.8.73	2cA		La Jolla	25 Mar 00

Ancillary marks – other marks during series (to 70.66)

72.35	Alekna	3 Aug 00	70.84	Riedel	3 May 97	71.08	Plucknett 4 Jun 83

HAMMER

Mark	Wind	Name		Nat	Born	Pos	Meet	Venue	Date
86.74	WR	Yuriy	Sedykh	RUS	11.6.55	1	EC	Stuttgart	30 Aug 86
86.66	WR		Sedykh			1	vGDR	Tallinn	22 Jun 86
86.34	WR		Sedykh			1		Cork	3 Jul 84
86.04		Sergey	Litvinov	RUS	23.1.58	1	OD	Dresden	3 Jul 86
85.74			Litvinov			2	EC	Stuttgart	30 Aug 86
85.68			Sedykh			1	BGP	Budapest	11 Aug 86
85.60			Sedykh			1	PTG	London (CP)	13 Jul 84
85.60			Sedykh			1	Drz	Moskva	17 Aug 84
85.20			Litvinov			2		Cork	3 Jul 84
85.14			Litvinov			1	PTG	London	11 Jul 86
85.14			Sedykh			1	Kuts	Moskva	4 Sep 88
85.02			Sedykh			1	BGP	Budapest	20 Aug 84
84.92			Sedykh			2	OD	Dresden	3 Jul 86
84.88			Litvinov			1	GP-GG	Roma	10 Sep 86
84.86		Koji	Murofushi	JPN	8.10.74	1	Odlozil	Praha	29 Jun 03
84.80			Litvinov			1	OG	Seoul	26 Sep 88
84.72			Sedykh			1	GWG	Moskva	9 Jul 86
84.64			Litvinov			2	GWG	Moskva	9 Jul 86
84.62		Igor	Astapkovich	BLR	4.1.63	1	Expo	Sevilla	6 Jun 92
84.60			Sedykh			1	8-N	Tokyo	14 Sep 84
84.58			Sedykh			1	Znam	Leningrad	8 Jun 86
84.48		Igor	Nikulin	RUS	14.8.60	1	Athl	Lausanne	12 Jul 90
84.46			Sedykh			1		Vladivostok	14 Sep 88
84.40		Jüri	Tamm	EST	5.2.57	1		Banská Bystrica	9 Sep 84
84.36			Litvinov			2	vGDR	Tallinn	22 Jun 86
84.32		Ivan	Tikhon	BLR	24.7.76	1		Staiki	8 Aug 03
84.26			Sedykh			1	Nik	Nice	15 Jul 86
84.26			Astapkovich			1		Reims	3 Jul 91
84.19		Adrián	Annus	HUN	28.6.73	1		Szombathely	10 Aug 03
84.16			Tamm			1		Kharkov	19 Jun 88
		(30/8)							
83.68		Tibor	Gécsek ¶	HUN	22.9.64	1		Zalaegerszeg	19 Sep 98
83.46		Andrey	Abduvaliyev	TJK/ UZB	30.6.66	1		Adler	26 May 90
		(10)	Haber: @ competitive meeting but unsanctioned by GDR federation						
83.43		Aleksey	Zagornyy	RUS	31.5.78	1		Adler	10 Feb 02
83.40	@	Ralf	Haber	GDR	18.8.62	1		Athína	16 May 88
		82.54				1		Potsdam	9 Sep 88
83.38		Szymon	Ziólkowski	POL	1.7.76	1	WCh	Edmonton	5 Aug 01
83.04		Heinz	Weis	GER	14.7.63	1	NC	Frankfurt	29 Jun 97
83.00		Balázs	Kiss	HUN	21.3.72	1	GP II	Saint-Denis	4 Jun 98
82.78		Karsten	Kobs	GER	16.9.71	1		Dortmund	26 Jun 99
82.64		Günther	Rodehau	GDR	6.7.59	1		Dresden	3 Aug 85
82.62		Sergey	Kirmasov ¶	RUS	25.3.70	1		Bryansk	30 May 98
82.62		Andrey	Skvaruk	UKR	9.3.67	1		Koncha-Zaspa	27 Apr 02
82.54		Vasiliy	Sidorenko	RUS	1.5.61	1		Krasnodar	13 May 92
		(20)							
82.52		Lance	Deal	USA	21.8.61	1	GPF	Milano	7 Sep 96
82.40		Plamen	Minev	BUL	28.4.65	1	NM	Plovdiv	1 Jun 91
82.38		Gilles	Dupray	FRA	2.1.70	1		Chelles	21 Jun 00
82.28		Ilya	Konovalov	RUS	4.3.71	1	NC	Tula	10 Aug 03
82.24		Benjaminas	Viluckis	LIT	20.3.61	1		Klaipeda	24 Aug 86
82.24		Vyacheslav	Korovin	RUS	8.9.62	1		Chelyabinsk	20 Jun 87
82.23		Vladislav	Piskunov ¶	UKR	7.6.78	2		Koncha-Zaspa	27 Apr 02
82.22		Holger	Klose	GER	5.12.72	1		Dortmund	2 May 98
82.16		Vitaliy	Alisevich	BLR	15.6.67	1		Parnu	13 Jul 88
82.08		Ivan	Tanev	BUL	1.5.57	1	NC	Sofia	3 Sep 88
		(30)							
82.00		Sergey	Alay	BLR	11.6.65	1		Stayki	12 May 92
81.88		Jud	Logan ¶	USA	19.7.59	1		State College	22 Apr 88
81.81		Libor	Charfreitag	SVK	11.9.77	3	Odlozil	Praha	29 Jun 03
81.79		Christophe	Épalle	FRA	23.1.69	1		Clermont-Ferrand	30 Jun 00
81.78		Christoph	Sahner	FRG	23.9.63	1		Wemmetsweiler	11 Sep 88
81.70		Aleksandr	Seleznyov	RUS	25.1.63	2		Sochi	22 May 93
81.70		Olli-Pekka	Karjalainen	FIN	7.3.80	1		Lahti	16 Jun 02

Mark	Wind	Name		Nat	Born	Pos	Meet	Venue	Date
81.64		Enrico	Sgrulletti	ITA	24.4.65	1		Ostia	9 Mar 97
81.59		Aleksandr	Krykun	UKR	1.3.68	3		Szombathely	14 Jul 02
81.56		Sergey	Gavrilov	RUS	22.5.70	1	Army	Rostov	16 Jun 96
		(40)							
81.56		Zsolt	Németh	HUN	9.11.71	1		Veszprém	14 Aug 99
81.52		Juha	Tiainen	FIN	5.12.55	1		Tampere	11 Jun 84
81.44		Yuriy	Tarasyuk	BLR	11.4.57	1		Minsk	10 Aug 84
81.36		Vadim	Devyatovskiy ¶	BLR	20.3.77	1	NC	Brest	1 Aug 00
81.35		Wojciech	Kondratowicz	POL	18.4.80	1		Bydgoszcz	13 Jul 03
81.32		Klaus	Ploghaus	FRG	31.1.56	1		Paderborn	25 May 86
81.28		Vladimir	Maska	CZE	6.2.73	1		Pacov	25 Sep 99
81.26		Vadim	Khersontsev	RUS	8.7.74	1		Bryansk	3 Jul 01
81.21		Primoz	Kozmus	SLO	30.9.79	1	NC	Zagreb	3 Aug 03
81.20		Igor	Grigorash	RUS	18.8.59	1		Kiyev	23 Aug 84
		(50)	100th man 79.22, 200th man 76.46						

Ancillary marks – other marks during series (to 84.85)

86.68	Sedykh	30 Aug 86	85.52	Sedykh	13 Jul 84	85.26	Sedykh	11 Aug 86
86.62	Sedykh	30 Aug 86	85.46	Sedykh	30 Aug 86	85.24	Sedykh	11 Aug 86
86.00	Sedykh	3 Jul 84	85.42	Sedykh	11 Aug 86	85.20	Sedykh	3 Jul 84
86.00	Sedykh	22 Jun 86	85.42	Litvinov	3 Jul 86	85.04	Sedykh	13 Jul 84
85.82	Sedykh	22 Jun 86	85.28	Sedykh	30 Aug 86	84.98	Sedykh	4 Sep 88
						84.92	Litvinov	3 Jul 86

JAVELIN

Mark	Wind	Name		Nat	Born	Pos	Meet	Venue	Date
98.48	WR	Jan	Zelezny	CZE	16.6.66	1		Jena	25 May 96
95.66	WR		Zelezny			1	McD	Sheffield	29 Aug 93
95.54A	WR		Zelezny			1		Pietersburg	6 Apr 93
94.64			Zelezny			1	GS	Ostrava	31 May 96
94.02			Zelezny			1		Stellenbosch	26 Mar 97
93.09		Aki	Parviainen	FIN	26.10.74	1		Kuortane	26 Jun 99
92.80			Zelezny			1	WCh	Edmonton	12 Aug 01
92.61		Sergey	Makarov	RUS	19.3.73	1		Sheffield	30 Jun 02
92.60		Raymond	Hecht	GER	11.11.68	1	Bisl	Oslo	21 Jul 95
92.42			Zelezny			1	GS	Ostrava	28 May 97
92.41			Parviainen			1	ECp-1A	Vaasa	24 Jun 01
92.28			Zelezny			1	GPF	Monaco	9 Sep 95
92.28			Hecht			1	WK	Zürich	14 Aug 96
92.12			Zelezny			1	McD	London (CP)	27 Aug 95
92.12			Zelezny			1	TOTO	Tokyo	15 Sep 95
91.82			Zelezny			1	McD	Sheffield	4 Sep 94
91.69		Kostadínos	Gatsioúdis	GRE	17.12.73	1		Kuortane	24 Jun 00
91.68			Zelezny			1	GP	Gateshead	1 Jul 94
91.50			Zelezny			1	Kuso	Lublin	4 Jun 94
91.50A			Zelezny			1		Pretoria	8 Apr 96
91.50			Hecht			1		Gengenbach	1 Sep 96
91.46	WR	Steve	Backley	GBR	12.2.69	1		Auckland	25 Jan 92
91.40			Zelezny			1	BNP	Villeneuve d'Ascq	2 Jul 93
91.34			Zelezny			1		Cape Town	8 Apr 97
91.31			Parviainen			2	WCh	Edmonton	12 Aug 01
91.30			Zelezny			1	ISTAF	Berlin	1 Sep 95
91.28			Zelezny			1	BNP	Villeneuve d'Ascq	8 Jul 94
91.27			Gatsioúdis			1	ECCp	Madrid	26 May 01
91.23			Zelezny			1		Poznan	8 Jun 01
91.23			Gatsioúdis			1		Thessaloníki	24 Jul 02
		(30/6)	59 performances over 90m, further 15 by Zelezny, 5 Parviainen, 3 Hecht, 3 Makarov, 1 Backley						
90.60		Seppo	Räty	FIN	27.4.62	1		Nurmijärvi	20 Jul 92
90.44		Boris	Henry	GER	14.12.73	1	Gugl	Linz	9 Jul 97
89.16A		Tom	Petranoff	USA	8.4.58	1		Potchefstroom	1 Mar 91
89.10	WR	Patrik	Bodén	SWE	30.6.67	1		Austin	24 Mar 90
		(10)							
88.90		Aleksandr	Ivanov	RUS	25.5.82	1	Znam	Tula	7 Jun 03
88.75		Marius	Corbett	RSA	26.9.75	1	CG	Kuala Lumpur	21 Sep 98
88.70		Peter	Blank	GER	10.4.62	1	NC	Stuttgart	30 Jun 01
88.24		Matti	Närhi	FIN	17.8.75	1		Soini	27 Jul 97
88.22		Juha	Laukkanen	FIN	6.1.69	1		Kuortane	20 Jun 92
88.20		Gavin	Lovegrove	NZL	21.10.67	1	Bisl	Oslo	5 Jul 96
88.00		Vladimir	Ovchinnikov	RUS	2.8.70	1		Tolyatti	14 May 95
87.83		Andrus	Värnik	EST	27.9.77	1		Valga	19 Aug 03
87.82		Harri	Hakkarainen	FIN	16.10.69	1		Kuortane	24 Jun 95
87.60		Kazuhiro	Mizoguchi	JPN	18.3.62	1	Jen	San José	27 May 89
		(20)							

Mark	Wind	Name		Nat	Born	Pos	Meet	Venue	Date
87.40		Vladimir	Sasimovich	BLR	14.9.68	2		Kuortane	24 Jun 95
87.34		Andrey	Moruyev	RUS	6.5.70	1	ECp	Birmingham	25 Jun 94
87.20		Viktor	Zaytsev	UZB	6.6.66	1	OT	Moskva	23 Jun 92
87.17		Dariusz	Trafas	POL	16.5.72	1		Gold Coast (RB)	17 Sep 00
87.12		Tom	Pukstys	USA	28.5.68	2	OD	Jena	25 May 97
87.12		Emeterio	González	CUB	11.4.73	1	OD	Jena	3 Jun 00
87.00		Breaux	Greer	USA	19.10.76	4	WCh	Edmonton	12 Aug 01
86.98		Yuriy	Rybin	RUS	5.3.63	1		Nitra	26 Aug 95
86.94		Mick	Hill	GBR	22.10.64	1	NC	London (CP)	13 Jun 93
86.80		Einar	Vihljálmsson	ISL	1.6.60	1		Reykjavik	29 Aug 92
		(30)							
86.74		Pål Arne	Fagernes	NOR	8.6.74	q	OG	Sydney	22 Sep 00
86.67		Andrew	Currey	AUS	7.2.71	1		Wollongong	22 Jul 01
86.64		Klaus	Tafelmeier	FRG	12.4.58	1	NC	Gelsenkirchen	12 Jul 87
86.63		Harri	Haatainen	FIN	5.1.78	2	GP II	Gateshead	19 Aug 01
86.50		Tapio	Korjus	FIN	10.2.61	1		Lahti	25 Aug 88
86.47		Eriks	Rags	LAT	1.6.75	2	BrGP	London	22 Jul 01
85.96		Kimmo	Kinnunen	FIN	31.3.68	3	NC	Seinäjoki	8 Aug 99
85.74		Dmitriy	Polyunin ¶	UZB	6.4.69	2	OT	Moskva	23 Jun 92
85.74A		Miroslav	Guzdek	CZE	3.8.75	1		Germiston	5 Apr 02
85.72		Andreas	Thorkildsen	NOR	1.4.82	1		Ventspils	14 Jun 03
		(40)							
85.70		Andrey	Shevchuk	RUS	8.3.70	2	Slovn	Bratislava	1 Jun 93
85.67		Mark	Roberson	GBR	13.3.67	2		Gateshead	19 Jul 98
85.60		Peter	Esenwein	GER	7.12.67	1		Riederich	25 May 97
85.42		Andreas	Linden	GER	20.2.65	2		Mülheim-Kärlich	17 Sep 95
85.28		Donald-Aik	Sild	EST	3.10.68	2		St Denis	10 Jun 94
85.21		Björn	Lange	GER	15.6.79	4	GP II	Gateshead	19 Aug 01
85.18		Ari	Pakarinen	FIN	14.5.69	Q		Lapua	22 Jul 95
85.16		Viktor	Yevsyukov	KZK	6.10.56	1	vGDR	Karl-Marx-Stadt	21 Jun 87
85.09		Nick	Nieland	GBR	31.1.72	2	NC	Birmingham	13 Aug 00
85.02		Dag	Wennlund	SWE	9.10.63	1		Alvesta	28 May 95
		(50)	100th man 82.38, 200th man 79.86						

Ancillary marks – other marks during series (to 91.40)

95.34	Zelezny	29 Aug 93	92.26	Zelezny	26 Mar 97	91.44	Zelezny	25 May 96
92.88	Zelezny	25 May 96	91.88	Zelezny	27 Aug 95	91.44	Zelezny	26 Mar 97
92.30	Zelezny	26 Mar 97	91.48	Zelezny	15 Sep 95			

Javelins with roughened tails, now banned by the IAAF

Mark	Wind	Name		Nat	Born	Pos	Meet	Venue	Date
96.96	WR	Seppo	Räty	FIN	27.4.62	1		Punkalaidun	2 Jun 91
94.74	Irreg		Zelezny			1	Bisl	Oslo	4 Jul 92
91.98	WR		Räty			1	Super	Shizuoka	6 May 91
91.36			Backley			1	McV	Sheffield	15 Sep 91
90.82		Kimmo	Kinnunen	FIN	31.3.68	1	WCh	Tokyo	26 Aug 91
87.00		Peter	Borglund	SWE	29.1.64	1		Stockholm	13 Aug 91
85.52		Dag	Wennlund	SWE	9.10.63	1	NC	Helsingborg	27 Jul 91
85.08		Radoman	Scekic	YUG	1.10.67	1		Zagreb	12 Jun 91

DECATHLON

Mark		Name		Nat	Born	Pos	Meet	Venue	Date
9026	WR	Roman	Sebrle	CZE	26.11.74	1		Götzis	27 May 01
10.64/0.0	8.11/1.9	15.33	2.12	47.79	13.92/-0.2	47.92	4.80	70.16	4:21.98
8994	WR	Tomás	Dvorák	CZE	11.5.72	1	ECp	Praha	4 Jul 99
10.54/-0.1	7.90/1.1	16.78	2.04	48.08	13.73/0.0	48.33	4.90	72.32	4:37.20
8902			Dvorák			1	WCh	Edmonton	7 Aug 01
10.62/1.5	8.07/0.9	16.57	2.00	47.74	13.80/-0.4	45.51	5.00	68.53	4:35.13
8900			Dvorák			1		Götzis	4 Jun 00
10.54/1.3	8.03/0.0	16.68	2.09	48.36	13.89/-1.0	47.89	4.85	67.21	4:42.33
8891	WR	Dan	O'Brien	USA	18.7.66	1		Talence	5 Sep 92
10.43w/2.1	8.08/1.8	16.69	2.07	48.51	13.98/-0.5	48.56	5.00	62.58	4:42.10
8847	WR	Daley	Thompson	GBR	30.7.58	1	OG	Los Angeles	9 Aug 84
10.44/-1.0	8.01/0.4	15.72	2.03	46.97	14.33/-1.1	46.56	5.00	65.24	4:35.00
8844w			O'Brien			1	TAC	New York	13 Jun 91
10.23	7.96	16.06	2.08	47.70	13.95W/4.2	48.08	5.10	57.40	4:45.54
8837			Dvorák			1	WCh	Athína	6 Aug 97
10.60/0.8	7.64/-0.7	16.32	2.00	47.56	13.61/0.8	45.16	5.00	70.34	4:35.40
8832	WR	Jürgen	Hingsen	FRG	25.1.58	1	OT	Mannheim	9 Jun 84
10.70w/2.9	7.76/	16.42	2.07	48.05	14.07/0.2	49.36	4.90	59.86	4:19.75
8825	WR		Hingsen			1		Bernhausen	5 Jun 83
10.92/0.0	7.74	15.94	2.15	47.89	14.10	46.80	4.70	67.26	4:19.74
8824			O'Brien			1	OG	Atlanta	1 Aug 96
10.50/0.7	7.57/1.4	15.66	2.07	46.82	13.87/0.3	48.78	5.00	66.90	4:45.89

Mark Wind	Name			Nat	Born	Pos Meet	Venue			Date
8817		O'Brien				1 WCh	Stuttgart			20 Aug 93
	10.57/0.9	7.99/0.4	15.41	2.03	47.46	14.08/0.0	47.92	5.20	62.56	4:40.08
8815	Erki	Nool		EST	25.6.70	2 WCh	Edmonton			7 Aug 01
	10.60/1.5	7.63/2.0	14.90	2.03	46.23	14.40/0.0	43.40	5.40	67.01	4:29.58
8812		O'Brien				1 WCh	Tokyo			30 Aug 91
	10.41/-1.6	7.90/0.8	16.24	1.91	46.53	13.94/-1.2	47.20	5.20	60.66	4:37.50
8811		Thompson				1 EC	Stuttgart			28 Aug 86
	10.26/2.0	7.72/1.0	15.73	2.00	47.02	14.04/-0.3	43.38	5.10	62.78	4:26.16
8807		Sebrle				1	Götzis			1 Jun 03
	10.78/-0.2	7.86/1.2	15.41	2.12	47.83	13.96/0.0	43.42	4.90	69.22	4:28.63
8800		Sebrle				1	Götzis			2 Jun 02
	10.95/0.5	7.79/1.8	15.50	2.12	48.35	13.89/1.6	48.02	5.00	68.97	4:38.16
8800		Sebrle				1 EC	München			8 Aug 02
	10.83/1.3	7.92/0.8	15.41	2.12	48.48	14.04/0.0	46.88	5.10	68.51	4:42.94
8792	Uwe	Freimuth		GDR	10.9.61	1 OD	Potsdam			21 Jul 84
	11.06/	7.79/	16.30	2.03	48.43	14.66/	46.58	5.15	72.42	4:25.19
8784	Tom	Pappas		USA	6.9.76	1 NC	Stanford			22 Jun 03
	10.78/0.2	7.96/1.4	16.28	2.17	48.22	14.13/1.7	45.84	5.20	60.77	4:48.12
8774 WR		Thompson				1 EC	Athína			8 Sep 82
	10.51/0.3	7.80/0.8	15.44	2.03	47.11	14.39/0.9	45.48	5.00	63.56	4:23.71
8762	Siegfried	Wentz		FRG	7.3.60	2	Bernhausen			5 Jun 83
	10.89	7.49/	15.35	2.09	47.38	14.00	46.90	4.80	70.68	4:24.90
8757		Sebrle				2	Götzis			4 Jun 00
	10.64/1.3	7.88/1.6	15.19	2.15	49.05	13.99/-1.0	47.21	4.75	67.23	4:35.06
8755		O'Brien				1 GWG	Uniondale, NY			20 Jul 98
	10.71/-2.3	7.78w/2.2	15.67	2.11	48.04	13.67/0.4	48.87	5.20	66.31	5:08.77
8750		Pappas				1 WCh	Saint-Denis			27 Aug 03
	10.80/-0.5	7.62/1.1	16.11	2.09	47.58	13.99/0.0	46.94	5.10	65.90	4:44.31
8744		Dvorák				1 WCh	Sevilla			25 Aug 99
	10.60/0.1	7.98/0.1	16.49	2.00	48.42	13.75/0.7	46.26	4.60	70.11	4:39.87
8742		Nool				3	Götzis			4 Jun 00
	10.69/1.3	7.78/1.8	14.14	1.97	47.18	14.37/-0.1	44.16	5.55	69.10	4:35.59
8741 WR		Hingsen				1 NC	Ulm			15 Aug 82
	10.74w	7.85	16.00	2.15	47.65	14.64	44.92	4.60	63.10	4:15.13
8738		Dvorák				1	Götzis			30 May 99
	10.71/-1.2	7.77/-0.9	16.43	2.00	48.21	13.85/-0.9	46.54	4.80	68.66	4:33.99
8735	Eduard	Hämäläinen		FIN/BLR	21.1.69	1	Götzis			29 May 94
	10.50w/2.1	7.26/1.0	16.05	2.11	47.63	13.82/-3.0	49.70	4.90	60.32	4:35.09
	(30/10)									
8727w/8705	Dave	Johnson		USA	7.4.63	1	Azusa			24 Apr 92
	10.96/0.4	7.52W/4.5 (7.43)	14.61	2.04	48.19	14.17/0.3	49.88	5.28	66.96	4:29.38
8709	Aleksandr	Apaychev		UKR	6.5.61	1 vGDR	Neubrandenburg			3 Jun 84
	10.96/	7.57/	16.00	1.97	48.72	13.93/	48.00	4.90	72.24	4:26.51
8706	Frank	Busemann		GER	26.2.75	2 OG	Atlanta			1 Aug 96
	10.60/0.7	8.07/0.8	13.60	2.04	48.34	13.47/0.3	45.04	4.80	66.86	4:31.41
8698	Grigoriy	Degtyaryov		RUS	16.8.58	1 NC	Kiyev			22 Jun 84
	10.87/0.7	7.42/0.1	16.03	2.10	49.75	14.53/0.3	51.20	4.90	67.08	4:23.09
8694	Chris	Huffins		USA	15.4.70	1 NC	New Orleans			20 Jun 98
	10.31w/3.5	7.76w/2.5	15.43	2.18	49.02	14.02/1.0	53.22	4.60	61.59	4:59.43
8680	Torsten	Voss		GDR	24.3.63	1 WCh	Roma			4 Sep 87
	10.69/-0.3	7.88/1.2	14.98	2.10	47.96	14.13/0.1	43.96	5.10	58.02	4:25.93
8667 WR	Guido	Kratschmer		FRG	10.1.53	1	Bernhausen			14 Jun 80
	10.58w/2.4	7.80/	15.47	2.00	48.04	13.92/	45.52	4.60	66.50	4:24.15
8644	Steve	Fritz		USA	1.11.67	4 OG	Atlanta			1 Aug 96
	10.90/0.8	7.77/0.9	15.31	2.04	50.13	13.97/0.3	49.84	5.10	65.70	4:38.26
8634 WR	Bruce	Jenner		USA	28.10.49	1 OG	Montreal			30 Jul 76
	10.94/0.0	7.22/0.0	15.35	2.03	47.51	14.84/0.0	50.04	4.80	68.52	4:12.61
8627	Robert	Zmelík		CZE	18.4.69	1	Götzis			31 May 92
	10.62w/2.1	8.02/0.2	13.93	2.05	48.73	13.84/1.2	44.44	4.90	61.26	4:24.83
	(20)									
8626	Michael	Smith		CAN	16.9.67	1	Götzis			26 May 96
	11.23/-0.6	7.72/0.6	16.94	1.97	48.69	14.77/-2.4	52.90	4.90	71.22	4:41.95
8603	Dean	Macey		GBR	12.12.77	3 WCh	Edmonton			7 Aug 01
	10.72/-0.7	7.59/0.4	15.41	2.15	46.21	14.34/0.0	46.96	4.70	54.61	4:29.05
8583w	Jón Arnar	Magnússon		ISL	28.7.69	1 ECp-2	Reykjavik			5 Jul 98
	10.68/2.0	7.63/2.0	15.57	2.07	47.78	14.33W/5.2	44.53	5.00	64.16	4:41.60
8574	Christian	Plaziat		FRA	28.10.63	1 EC	Split			29 Aug 90
	10.72/-0.6	7.77/1.1	14.19	2.10	47.10	13.98/0.7	44.36	5.00	54.72	4:27.83
8574	Aleksandr	Yurkov		UKR	21.7.75	4	Götzis			4 Jun 00
	10.69/0.9	7.93/1.8	15.26	2.03	49.74	14.56/-0.9	47.85	5.15	58.92	4:32.49

Mark Wind	Name		Nat	Born	Pos	Meet	Venue	Date
8571	Lev	Lobodin	RUS	1.4.69	3	EC	Budapest	20 Aug 98
	10.66w/2.2 7.42/0.2 15.67		2.03 48.65		13.97/0.9		46.55 5.20 56.55	4:30.27
8566	Sebastian	Chmara	POL	21.11.71	1		Alhama de Murcia	17 May 98
	10.97w/2.9 7.56/1.2 16.03		2.10 48.27		14.32/1.8		44.39 5.20 57.25	4:29.66
8554	Attila	Zsivóczky	HUN	29.4.77	5		Götzis	4 Jun 00
	10.64w/2.1 7.24/-1.0 15.72		2.18 48.13		14.87/-0.9		45.64 4.65 63.57	4:23.13
8548	Paul	Meier	GER	27.7.71	3	WCh	Stuttgart	20 Aug 93
	10.57/0.9 7.57/1.1 15.45		2.15 47.73		14.63/0.0		45.72 4.60 61.22	4:32.05
8547	Igor	Sobolevskiy	UKR	4.5.62	2	NC	Kiyev	22 Jun 84
	10.64/0.7 7.71/0.2 15.93		2.01 48.24		14.82/0.3		50.54 4.40 67.40	4:32.84
	(30)							
8534	Siegfried	Stark	GDR	12.6.55	1		Halle	4 May 80
	11.10w 7.64 15.81		2.03 49.53		14.86w		47.20 5.00 68.70	4:27.7
8534w/8478	Antonio	Peñalver	ESP	1.12.68	1		Alhama	24 May 92
	10.76w/3.9 7.42W/6.2 16.50 (7.19w/4.0)		2.12 49.50		14.32/0.8		47.38 5.00 59.32	4:39.94
8526	Francisco Javier	Benet	ESP	25.3.68	2		Alhama de Murcia	17 May 98
	10.72w/2.9 7.45/-1.2 14.57		1.92 48.10		13.83/1.8		46.12 5.00 65.37	4:26.81
8524	Sébastien	Levicq	FRA	25.6.71	4	WCh	Sevilla	25 Aug 99
	11.05/0.2 7.52/-0.4 14.22		2.00 50.13		14.48/0.6		44.65 5.50 69.01	4:26.81
8519	Yuriy	Kutsenko	RUS	5.3.52	3	NC	Kiyev	22 Jun 84
	11.07/0.5 7.54/-0.1 15.11		2.13 49.07		14.94/0.3		50.38 4.60 61.70	4:12.68
8506	Valter	Külvet	EST	19.2.64	1		Stayki	3 Jul 88
	11.05/-1.4 7.35/0.4 15.78		2.00 48.08		14.55/-0.8		52.04 4.60 61.72	4:15.93
8500	Christian	Schenk	GER	9.2.65	4	WCh	Stuttgart	20 Aug 93
	11.22/-0.9 7.63/0.0 15.72		2.15 48.78		15.29/0.0		46.94 4.80 65.32	4:24.44
8491	Aleksandr	Nevskiy	UKR	21.2.58	2		Götzis	20 May 84
	10.97/-1.6 7.24/1.2 15.04		2.08 48.44		14.67/1.0		46.06 4.70 69.56	4:19.62
8490	Jagan	Hames	AUS	31.10.75	1	CG	Kuala Lumpur	18 Sep 98
	10.77/0.0 7.64/0.8 14.73		2.19 49.67		14.07/0.4		46.40 5.00 64.67	5:02.68
8485	Konstantin	Akhapkin	RUS	19.1.56	1	NC	Moskva	2 Aug 82
	11.10/0.2 7.72/0.2 15.25		2.02 49.14		14.38/1.8		45.68 4.90 62.42	4:19.60
	(40)							
8485	Stefan	Schmid	GER	6.5.70	1	OT	Ratingen	23 Jul 00
	10.82/0.0 7.59/-0.6 14.14		2.01 48.99		14.20/-1.6		44.24 5.06 67.63	4:31.76
8482	Bryan	Clay	USA	3.1.80	2	NC	Stanford	22 Jun 03
	10.43/1.7 7.71/-1.3 14.01		2.02 47.85		14.12/1.7		43.51 4.70 67.77	4:42.19
8466 WR	Nikolay	Avilov	UKR	6.8.48	1	OG	München	8 Sep 72
	11.00/ 7.68/ 14.36		2.12 48.45		14.31/		46.98 4.55 61.66	4:22.82
8462w	Kip	Janvrin	USA	8.7.65	1	vGER	Edwardsville	18 Jul 96
	10.61W/4.1 7.34w/3.1 14.64		1.96 48.20		14.48W/5.7		45.84 5.00 61.82	4:20.12
8461	Mike	Maczey	GER	28.9.72	7		Götzis	4 Jun 00
	10.99/0.9 7.59/0.3 14.75		2.06 49.83		14.16/-1.0		44.56 5.15 62.27	4:29.93
8453	Alain	Blondel	FRA	7.12.62	1	EC	Helsinki	13 Aug 94
	11.12/0.6 7.50w/3.2 13.78		1.99 48.91		14.18/0.9		45.08 5.40 60.64	4:20.48
8447	Robert	de Wit	NED	7.8.62	1	NC	Eindhoven	22 May 88
	11.07/0.5 6.98/0.2 15.88		2.04 48.80		14.32/0.7		46.20 5.00 63.94	4:20.98
8445	Ramil	Ganiyev	UZB	23.9.68	5	WCh	Athína	6 Aug 97
	10.94/0.2 7.58/0.7 14.76		2.06 48.34		14.34/-0.1		46.04 5.30 55.14	4:36.78
8437	Richardas	Malakhovskis	LIT	28.4.65	2		Stayki	3 Jul 88
	10.93/0.6 7.04/0.6 14.94		2.09 47.77		14.34/-0.9		44.04 4.90 59.58	4:13.67
8436	Dezsö	Szabó	HUN	4.9.67	2	EC	Split	29 Aug 90
	11.06/-0.2 7.49/1.1 13.65		1.98 47.17		14.67/0.0		40.78 5.30 61.94	4:11.07
	(50)	100th man 8256, 200th man 8099						

4 x 100 METRES RELAY

Mark	Nat	Team	Pos	Meet	Venue	Date
37.40 WR	USA	Marsh, Burrell, Mitchell, C Lewis	1	OG	Barcelona	8 Aug 92
37.40 WR	USA	Drummond, Cason, D Mitchell, L Burrell	1s1	WCh	Stuttgart	21 Aug 93
37.48	USA	Drummond, Cason, D Mitchell, L Burrell	1	WCh	Stuttgart	22 Aug 93
37.50 WR	USA	Cason, Burrell, Mitchell, C Lewis	1	WCh	Tokyo	1 Sep 91
37.59	USA	Drummond, Montgomery, B Lewis, Greene	1	WCh	Sevilla	29 Aug 99
37.61	USA	Drummond, Williams, B Lewis, Greene	1	OG	Sydney	30 Sep 00
37.65	USA	Drummond, Williams, C Johnson, Greene	1	ISTAF	Berlin	1 Sep 00
37.67 WR	USA	Marsh, Burrell, Mitchell, C Lewis	1	WK	Zürich	7 Aug 91
37.69	CAN	Esmie 10.47, Gilbert 9.02, Surin 9.25, Bailey 8.95	1	OG	Atlanta	3 Aug 96
37.73	GBR	Gardener, Campbell, Devonish, Chambers	2	WCh	Sevilla	29 Aug 99
37.75	USA	Cason, Burrell, Mitchell, Marsh	1h2	WCh	Tokyo	31 Aug 91
37.77	GBR	Jackson, Jarrett, Regis, Christie	2	WCh	Stuttgart	22 Aug 93
37.77	USA A	Drummond, B Williams, Patton, Greene	1	ISTAF	Berlin (P)	10 Aug 03
37.79 WR	FRA	Morinière, Sangouma, Trouabal, Marie-Rose	1	EC	Split	1 Sep 90

Mark	Wind	Name	Nat	Born	Pos	Meet	Venue	Date
37.79	WR	Santa Monica TC/USA Marsh, Burrell, Heard, C Lewis			1	Herc	Monaco	3 Aug 91
37.79		USA - Santa Monica TC Marsh, Burrell, Heard, C Lewis			1	MSR	Walnut	17 Apr 94
37.82		USA Drummond, Williams, B.Lewis, Greene			1s1	OG	Sydney	29 Sep 00
37.83	WR	USA Graddy, R Brown, C Smith, C Lewis			1	OG	Los Angeles	11 Aug 84
37.83		CAN Esmie, Gilbert, Surin, Mahorn			3	WCh	Stuttgart	22 Aug 93
37.86	WR	USA E King, Gault, C Smith, C Lewis			1	WCh	Helsinki	10 Aug 83
37.86		CAN Esmie, Gilbert, Surin, Bailey			1	WCh	Athína	10 Aug 97
37.87		FRA Morinière, Sangouma, Trouabal, Marie-Rose			2	WCh	Tokyo	1 Sep 91
37.88		USA (HSI) Drummond, B Williams, C.Johnson, Greene			1	TexR	Austin	7 Apr 01
37.89		Santa Monica TC (USA) Marsh, Burrell, Heard, C Lewis			1	TexR	Austin	9 Apr 94
37.90		USA McRae, L McNeill, Glance, C Lewis			1	WCh	Roma	6 Sep 87
37.90		USA Drummond, Harden, Mitchell, Greene			1	GWG	Uniondale, NY.	22 Jul 98
37.90		BRA de Lima, Ribeiro, A da Silva, Cl da Silva			2	OG	Sydney	30 Sep 00
37.91		NGR Asonze, Obikwelu, Effiong, Aliu			3	WCh	Sevilla	29 Aug 99
		(28 by 6 nations) Further bests by nations:						
38.00		CUB Simón, Lamela, Isasi, Aguilera			3	OG	Barcelona	8 Aug 92
38.02		URS Yevgenyev, Bryzgin, Muravyov, Krylov			2	WCh	Roma	6 Sep 87
38.12		GHA Duah, Nkansah, Zakari, Tuffour			1s1	WCh	Athína	9 Aug 97
38.17		AUS Henderson, Jackson, Brimacombe, Marsh			1s2	WCh	Göteborg	12 Aug 95
		(10)						
38.20		JAM L Frater, D Thomas, C Williams, Bredwood			4	OG	Sydney	30 Sep 00
38.29		GDR Schröder, Kübeck, Prenzler, Emmelmann			2	vUSA	Karl-Marx-Stadt	9 Jul 82
38.31		JPN Inoue, K Ito, Tsuchie, Asahara			5s2	WCh	Athína	9 Aug 97
38.33		POL Zwolinski, Licznerski, Dunecki, Woronin			2	OG	Moskva	1 Aug 80
38.37		ITA Tilli, Simionato, Pavoni, Mennea			2	WCh	Helsinki	10 Aug 83
38.46		URS/RUS Zharov, Krylov, Fatun, Goremykin			4	EC	Split	1 Sep 90
38.47		RSA Nagel, du Plessis, Newton, Quinn			2	WCh	Edmonton	12 Aug 01
38.53		UKR Rurak, Osovich, Kramarenko, Dologodin			1	ECp	Madrid	1 Jun 96
38.53		TRI Alexander, Burns, Boldon, Brown			2	PAm	Santo Domingo	9 Aug 03
38.54		FRG Heer, Haas, Klein, Schweisfurth			1	R-W	Koblenz	28 Aug 88
38.60		ESP Feo, José, Mayoral, Berlanga			3s1	WCh	Athína	9 Aug 97
		(20, with RUS and UKR for USSR)						
38.60		CIV Meité, Douhou, Sonan, N'Dri			3s1	WCh	Edmonton	12 Aug 01
38.61		GRE Séggos, Alexópoulos, Panayiotópoulos, Hoídis			2	ECp	Paris (C)	19 Jun 99
38.63		SWE Karlsson, Mårtensson, Hedner, Strenius			3s2	OG	Atlanta	2 Aug 96
38.63		NED Beck, T Douglas, van Balkom, C Douglas			5s1	WCh	Saint-Denis	30 Aug 03
38.67		HUN Karaffa, Nagy, Tatár, Kovács			1	BGP	Budapest	11 Aug 86
38.80		THA Natenee, Sophanich, Janthana, Suwonprateep			1	AsiC	Jakarta	31 Aug 00
38.81		CHN Li Xiaoping, Lin Wei, Huang Danwei, Chen Wenzhong			2h3	WCh	Göteborg	12 Aug 95
38.81		ISR Jaar, Jablonka, Kafri, Porkhomovskiy			3h2	WCh	Sevilla	28 Aug 99
38.82		TCH/CZE Matousek, Demec, Kynos, Bohman			4	OG	München	10 Sep 72
38.91		SLE Lisk, Ganda, Jos. Thomas, Turay			5s1	OG	Atlanta	2 Aug 96
Multi-nation teams								
37.82		Drummond/USA, Jarrett/GBR, Regis/GBR, Mitchell/USA			2	MSR	Walnut	17 Apr 94
37.93		HSI (USA) Drummond, B Williams, Bolden TRI, Greene			1	BrGP	London (CP)	22 Jul 01

4 x 200 METRES RELAY

1:18.68	WR	USA - Santa Monica TC Marsh, Burrell, Heard, Lewis	1	MSR	Walnut	17 Apr 94
1:19.10		World All-Stars	2	MSR	Walnut	17 Apr 94
		Drummond/USA, Mitchell/USA, Bridgewater/USA, Regis/GBR				
1:19.11	WR	Santa Monica TC/USA M.Marsh, L Burrell, Heard, C Lewis	1	Penn	Philadelphia	25 Apr 92
1:19.16		USA Red Team Crawford, Clay, Patton, Gatlin	1	PennR	Philadelphia	26 Apr 03
1:19.38	WR	Santa Monica TC/USA Everett, Burrell, Heard, C Lewis	1	R-W	Koblenz	23 Aug 89
1:19.39		USA Blue Drummond, Crawford, B Williams, Greene	1	PennR	Philadelphia	28 Apr 01
1:19.45		Santa Monica TC/USA DeLoach, Burrell, C.Lewis, Heard	1	Penn	Philadelphia	27 Apr 91
1:19.47		Nike Int./USA Brokenburr, A Harrison, Greene, M Johnson	1	Penn	Philadelphia	24 Apr 99
Best non-US nations						
1:20.79		Central Arizona DC/Jamaica	1		Walnut	24 Apr 88
		Bucknor, Campbell, O'Connor, Davis)				
1:21.10		ITA Tilli, Simionato, Bongiorno, Mennea	1		Cagliari	29 Sep 83
1:21.22		POL Tulin, Balcerzak, Pilarczyk, Urbas	2		Gdansk	14 Jul 01
1:21.29		GBR Adam, Mafe, Christie, Regis	1		Birmingham	23 Jun 89
1:21.32		UKR Vanyaykin, Tverdokhleb, Streltsov, Dologodin	1	EurR	Portsmouth	5 Jun 93

4 x 400 METRES RELAY

2:54.20	WR	USA Young 44.3, Pettigrew 43.2, Washington 43.5, M Johnson 43.2	1	GWG	Uniondale, NY	22 Jul 98
2:54.29	WR	USA Valmon 44.43, Watts 43.59, Reynolds 43.23, Johnson 42.94	1	WCh	Stuttgart	22 Aug 93
2:55.74	WR	USA Valmon 44.6, Watts 43.00, M.Johnson 44.73, S Lewis 43.41	1	OG	Barcelona	8 Aug 92
2:55.99		USA L Smith 44.62, A Harrison 43.84, Mills 43.66, Maybank 43.87	1	OG	Atlanta	3 Aug 96
2:56.16A	WR	USA Matthews 45.0, Freeman 43.2, James 43.9, Evans 44.1	1	OG	Ciu. México	20 Oct 68

Mark Wind	Nat	Name	Pos	Meet	Venue	Date
2:56.16 WR	USA	Everett 44.0, S Lewis 43.6, Robinzine 44.74, Reynolds 43.94	1	OG	Seoul	1 Oct 88
2:56.35	USA	A Harrison 44.36, Pettigrew 44.17, C Harrison 43.53, Johnson 44.29	1	OG	Sydney	30 Sep 00
2:56.45	USA	J Davis 45.2, Pettigrew 43.9, Taylor 43.92, M Johnson 43.49	1	WCh	Sevilla	29 Aug 99
2:56.47	USA	Young 44.6, Pettigrew 43.1, Jones 44.80, Washington 44.80	1	WCh	Athína	10 Aug 97
2:56.60	GBR	I Thomas 44.92, Baulch 44.19, Richardson 43.62, Black 43.87	2	OG	Atlanta	3 Aug 96
2:56.60	USA Red	Taylor 45.0, Pettigrew 44.2, Washington 43.7, Johnson 43.7	1	PennR	Philadelphia	29 Apr 00
2:56.65	GBR	Thomas 44.8, Black 44.2, Baulch 44.08, Richardson 43.57	2	WCh	Athína	10 Aug 97
2:56.75	JAM	McDonald 44.5, Haughton 44.4, McFarlane 44.37, Clarke 43.51	3	WCh	Athína	10 Aug 97
2:57.29	USA	Everett 45.1, Haley 44.0, McKay 44.20, Reynolds 44.00	1	WCh	Roma	6 Sep 87
2:57.32	USA	Ramsey 44.9, Mills 44.6, Reynolds 43.74, Johnson 44.11	1	WCh	Göteborg	13 Aug 95
2:57.53	GBR	Black 44.7, Redmond 44.0, Regis 44.22, Akabusi 44.59	1	WCh	Tokyo	1 Sep 91
2:57.54	USA	Byrd 45.9, Pettigrew 43.9, Brew 44.03, Taylor 43.71	1	WCh	Edmonton	12 Aug 01
2:57.57	USA	Valmon 44.9, Watts 43.4, D.Everett 44.31, Pettigrew 44.93	2	WCh	Tokyo	1 Sep 91
2:57.87	USA	L Smith 44.59, Rouser 44.33, Mills 44.32, Maybank 44.63	1s2	OG	Atlanta	2 Aug 96
2:57.91	USA	Nix 45.59, Armstead 43.97, Babers 43.75, McKay 44.60	1	OG	Los Angeles	11 Aug 84
2:57.97	JAM	McDonald , Haughton , McFarlane, D Clarke	1	PAm	Winnipeg	30 Jul 99
2:58.00	POL	Rysiukiewicz 45.6, Czubak 44.2, Haczek 44.0, Mackowiak 44.2	2	GWG	Uniondale, NY	22 Jul 98
2:58.19	BAH	Moncur 45.1, C Brown 44.5, McIntosh 44.42, Munnings 44.13	2	WCh	Edmonton	12 Aug 01
2:58.22	GBR	Sanders 45.85, Akabusi 44.48, Regis 43.93, Black 43.96	1	EC	Split	1 Sep 90
2:58.23	USA	Ramsey 44.6, Mills 44.0, Lyles 44.41, Hall 45.22	1h1	WCh	Göteborg	12 Aug 95
2:58.29	JAM	McDonald 45.1, D Clarke 43.8, Blake 44.80, McFarlane 44.60	2h1	WCh	Göteborg	12 Aug 95
2:58.33	JAM	Haughton, M McDonald, Blackwood, D Clarke	3	GWG	Uniondale, NY	22 Jul 98
2:58.39	JAM		3	WCh	Edmonton	12 Aug 01
		Simpson 45.71, C Williams 44.50, Haughton 43.88, McFarlane 44.30				
2:58.42	JAM	McDonald 44.54, Blake 44.75, Haughton 44.60, Martin 44.53	2s2	OG	Atlanta	2 Aug 96
2:58.56	BRA	Parrela, da Silva, dos Santos, de Araújo	2	PAm	Winnipeg	30 Jul 99
	(30/6)	Further bests by nations:				
2:58.68	NGR	Chukwu 45.18, Monye 44.49, Bada 44.70, Udo-Obong 44.31	2	OG	Sydney	30 Sep 00
2:58.96	FRA	Djhone 45.4, Keita 44.7, Diagana 44.69, Raquil 44.15	2	WCh	Saint-Denis	31 Aug 03
2:59.13	CUB	Martínez 45.6, Herrera 44.38, Tellez 44.81, Hernández 44.34	1h2	OG	Barcelona	7 Aug 92
2:59.63	KEN	D Kitur 45.4, S Kitur 45.13, Kipkemboi 44.76, Kemboi 44.34	3h2	OG	Barcelona	7 Aug 92
	(10)					
2:59.70	AUS	Frayne 45.38, Clark 43.86, Minihan 45.07, Mitchell 45.39	4	OG	Los Angeles	11 Aug 84
2:59.86	GDR	Möller 45.8, Schersing 44.8, Carlowitz 45.3, Schönlebe 44.1	1	vURS	Erfurt	23 Jun 85
2:59.95	YUG	Jovkovic, Djurovic, Macev, Brankovic 44.3	2h3	WCh	Tokyo	31 Aug 91
2:59.96	FRG	Dobeleit 45.7, Henrich 44.3, Itt 45.12, Schmid 44.93	4	WCh	Roma	6 Sep 87
3:00.16	URS	Lovachov, Lomtyev, Kurochkin, Markin 43.9	1	Drz	Moskva	18 Aug 84
3:00.20	RSA		4	WCh	Sevilla	29 Aug 99
		van Oudtshoorn 46.5, Mokganyetsi 44.5, A Botha 45.43, Malherbe 43.78				
3:00.44	RUS	Kliger 45.72, Kosov 45.09, Vdovin 44.73, Golovastov 44.90	5	WCh	Stuttgart	22 Aug 93
3:00.64	SEN	Diarra 46.53, Dia 44.94, Ndiaye 44.70, Faye 44.47	4	OG	Atlanta	3 Aug 96
3:00.76	JPN	Karube 45.88, Ito 44.86, Osakada 45.08, Omori 44.94	5	OG	Atlanta	3 Aug 96
3:00.79	ZIM	Chiwira 46.2, Mukomana 44.6, Ngidhi 45.79, Harnden 44.20	2h3	WCh	Athína	9 Aug 97
3:01.05	TRI	Delice, A Daniel, De Silva, Morris	1h1	OG	Barcelona	7 Aug 92
	(20 inc. RUS/URS)					
3:01.12	FIN	Lönnqvist 46.7, Salin 45.1, Karttunen 44.8, Kukkoaho 44.5	6	OG	München	10 Sep 72
3:01.37	ITA	Bongiorni 46.2, Zuliani 45.0, Petrella 45.3, Ribaud 44.9	4	EC	Stuttgart	31 Aug 86
3:01.42	ESP	I Rodríguez 46.0, Canal 44.1, Andrés 45.88, Reina 45.48	4h1	WCh	Edmonton	11 Aug 01
3:01.60	BAR	Louis 46.67, Peltier 44.97, Edwards 45.04, Forde 44.92	6	OG	Los Angeles	11 Aug 84
3:01.61	BUL	Georgiev 45.9, Stankulov 46.0, Raykov 45.07, Ivanov 44.66	2h1	WCh	Stuttgart	21 Aug 93
3:02.02	DOM	Peguero, Santa, Vidal, Sánchez	3	PAm	Santo Domingo	9 Aug 03
3:02.09	UGA	Govile 46.72, Kyeswa 44.60, Rwamu 46.40, Okot 44.37	7	OG	Los Angeles	11 Aug 84
3:02.11	MAR	Kasbane, Dahane, Belcaid, Lahlou 44.5	1h2	WCh	Tokyo	31 Aug 91
3:02.24	BOT	Molefe, Kilego, Moseki, Kubisa	1	AfG	Abuja	15 Oct 03
3:02.31	GRE	Dimótsios 46.7, Goúsis 45.6, Sarrís 45.08, Iakovákis 44.93	2h2	WCh	Saint-Denis	30 Aug 03
Multi-nation team						
2:58.52	Adidas	McDonaldJAM, Pettigrew, Campbell, Young	1	PennR	Philadelphia	24 Apr 99

4 x 800 METRES RELAY

7:03.89 WR	GBR	Elliott 1:49.14, Cook 1:46.20, Cram 1:44.54, Coe 1:44.01	1		London (CP)	30 Aug 82
7:04.70	RSA		1		Stuttgart	6 Jun 99
		G van Oudtshoorn 1:46.9, Sepeng 1:45.2, J Kotze 1:48.3, J, Botha 1:44.3				
7:04.89	KEN/ex-St Patrick's School		2		Stuttgart	6 Jun 99
		D Kiptoo 1:46.4, Tengelei 1:48.2, W Chirchir 1:45.7, Kimutai 1:44.6				
7:06.5	Santa Monica TC/USA)		1	MSR	Walnut	26 Apr 86
		J Robinson 1:49.8, Mack 1:46.7, E Jones 1:45.2, Gray 1:44.8				
7:07.40	URS	Masunov, Kostetskiy, Matvetev, Kalinkin	1		Moskva	5 Aug 84

4 x 1500 METRES RELAY

Mark Wind	Team	Name	Pos	Meet	Venue	Date
14:38.8 WR	FRG		1		Köln	16 Aug 77
		Wessinghage 3:38.8, Hudak 3:40.2, Lederer 3:42.6, Fleschen 3:37.3				
14:40.4 WR	NZL	Polhill 3:42.9, Walker 3:40.4, Dixon 3:41.2, Quax 3:35.9	1		Oslo	22 Aug 73
14:45.63	URS	Kalutskiy, Yakovlev, Legeda, Lotarev	1		Leningrad	4 Aug 85
14:46.16	Larios, ESP		1		Madrid	5 Sep 97
		Jiménez 3:40.9, Pancorbo 3:41.2, A García 3:43.9, Viciosa 3:40.2				
14:46.3	USA	Aldridge, Clifford, Harbour, Duits	1	Int	Bourges	23 Jun 79
14:48.2	FRA	Begouin, Lequement, Philippe, Dien	2	Int	Bourges	23 Jun 79

4 x 1 MILE RELAY

Mark Wind	Team	Name	Pos	Meet	Venue	Date
15:49.08	IRL	Coghlan 4:00.2, O'Sullivan 3:55.3, O'Mara 3:56.6, Flynn 3:56.98	1		Dublin	17 Aug 85

3000 METRES TRACK WALK

Mark Wind	Name		Nat	Born	Pos	Meet	Venue	Date
10:47.11	Giovanni	De Benedictis	ITA	8.1.68	1		S.Giovanni Valdarno	19 May 90
10:56.22	Andrew	Jachno	AUS	13.4.62	1		Melbourne	7 Feb 91
10:56.34+	Roman	Mrázek	SVK	21.1.62	1k	PTS	Bratislava	14 Jun 89
11:00.2+	Jozef	Pribilinec	SVK	6.7.60	1k		Banská Bystrica	30 Aug 85
11:00.56	David	Smith	AUS	24.7.55	1		Perth	24 Jan 87
Indoors								
10:31.42	Andreas	Erm	GER	12.3.76	1		Halle	4 Feb 01
10:54.61	Carlo	Mattioli	ITA	23.10.54	1		Milano	6 Feb 80
10:56.88	Reima	Salonen	FIN	19.11.55	1		Turku	5 Feb 84

5000 METRES TRACK WALK

Mark Wind	Name		Nat	Born	Pos	Meet	Venue	Date
18:05.49	Hatem	Ghoula	TUN	7.6.73	1		Tunis	1 May 97
18:17.22	Robert	Korzeniowski	POL	30.7.68	1		Reims	3 Jul 92
18:28.80	Roman	Mrázek	SVK	21.1.62	1	PTS	Bratislava	14 Jun 89
18:30.43	Maurizio	Damilano	ITA	6.4.57	1		Caserta	11 Jun 92
18:31.76	Frants	Kostyukevich	BLR	4.4.63	1	BNP	Villeneuve d'Ascq	2 Jul 93
18:33.16	João	Vieira	POR	20.2.76	1		Rio Maior	10 May 00
ndoors								
18:07.08	Mikhail	Shchennikov	RUS	24.12.67	1		Moskva	14 Feb 95
18:11.41	Ronald	Weigel	GDR	8.8.59	1mx		Wien	13 Feb 88
18:15.25	Grigoriy	Kornev	RUS	14.3.61	1		Moskva	7 Feb 92
18:16.54 ?	Frants	Kostyukevich	BLR	4.4.63	2	NC	Gomel	4 Feb 89
18:19.97	Giovanni	De Benedictis	ITA	8.1.68	1	EI	Genova	28 Feb 92
18:22.25	Andreas	Erm	GER	12.3.76	1	NC	Dortmund	25 Feb 01
18:23.18	Rishat	Shafikov	RUS	23.1.70	1		Samara	1 Mar 97
18:27.15	Alessandro	Gandellini	ITA	30.4.73	1	NC	Genova	12 Feb 00
18:27.80	Jozef	Pribilinec	SVK	6.7.60	2	WI	Indianapolis	7 Mar 87
18:27.95	Stefan	Johansson	SWE	11.4.67	3	EI	Genova	28 Feb 92
18:31.63	Vladimir	Andreyev	RUS	7.9.66	2		Moskva	7 Feb 92
18:32.32	Mikhail	Orlov	RUS	25.6.67	3	CISCh	Moskva	2 Feb 92

10,000 METRES TRACK WALK

Mark Wind	Name		Nat	Born	Pos	Meet	Venue	Date
38:02.60	Jozef	Pribilinec	SVK	6.7.60	1		Banská Bystrica	30 Aug 85
38:06.6	David	Smith	AUS	24.7.55	1		Sydney	25 Sep 86
38:12.13	Ronald	Weigel	GDR	8.8.59	1		Potsdam	10 May 86
38:18.0+	Valdas	Kazlauskas	LTU	23.2.58	1		Moskva	18 Sep 83
38:24 0+	Bernardo	Segura	MEX	11.2.70	1	SGP	Fana	7 May 94
38:24.31	Hatem	Ghoula	TUN	7.6.73	1		Tunis	30 May 98
38:26.4	Daniel	García	MEX	28.10.71	1		Sdr Omme	17 May 97
38:26.53	Robert	Korzeniowski	POL	30.7.68	1		Riga	31 May 02
38:37.6+	Jefferson	Pérez	ECU	1.7.74	1	in 20k	Fana	9 May 98
38:38.0	Walter	Arena	ITA	30.5.64	1		Catania	13 Apr 90
Indoors								
38:31.4	Werner	Heyer	GDR	14.11.56	1		Berlin	12 Jan 80

20 KILOMETRES WALK

Mark Wind	Name		Nat	Born	Pos	Meet	Venue	Date
1:17:21 WR	Jefferson	Pérez	ECU	1.7.74	1	WCh	Saint-Denis	23 Aug 03
1:17:22 WR	Francisco Javier	Fernández	ESP	5.3.77	1		Turku	28 Apr 02
1:17:25.6t	Bernardo	Segura	MEX	11.2.70	1	SGP	Fana	7 May 94
1:17:46	Julio	Martínez	GUA	27.9.73	1		Eisenhüttenstadt	8 May 99
1:17:46	Roman	Rasskazov	RUS	28.4.79	1	NC	Moskva	19 May 00
1:17:56	Alejandro	López	MEX	9.2.75	2		Eisenhüttenstadt	8 May 99
1:18:00		Fernández			2	WCh	Saint-Denis	23 Aug 03
1:18:04 WR		Bo Lingtang	CHN	12.8.70	1	NC	Beijing	7 Apr 94
1:18:05	Dmitriy	Yesipchuk	RUS	17.11.74	1	NC-w	Adler	4 Mar 01
1:18:06	Viktor	Burayev	RUS	23.2.82	2	NC-w	Adler	4 Mar 01

Mark	Wind	Name		Nat	Born	Pos	Meet	Venue	Date
1:18:07			Rasskazov			1	NC-w	Adler	20 Feb 00
1:18:07			Rasskazov			3	WCh	Saint-Denis	23 Aug 03
1:18:12		Artur	Meleshkevich (10)	BLR	11.4.75	1		Brest	10 Mar 01
1:18:13	WR	Pavol	Blazek	SVK	9.7.58	1		Hildesheim	16 Sep 90
1:18:14		Mikhail	Khmelnitskiy	BLR	24.7.69	1	NC	Soligorsk	13 May 00
1:18:14		Nathan	Deakes	AUS	17.8.77	1		Dublin	16 Jun 01
1:18:14		Noé	Hernández	MEX	15.3.78	4	WCh	Saint-Denis	23 Aug 03
1:18:16		Vladimir	Andreyev	RUS	7.9.66	2	NC	Moskva	19 May 00
1:18:18		Yevgeniy	Misyulya	BLR	13.3.64	1		Eisenhüttenstadt	11 May 96
1:18:20	WR	Andrey	Perlov	RUS	12.12.61	1	NC	Moskva	26 May 90
1:18:20		Denis	Nizhegorodov	RUS	26.7.80	3	NC-w	Adler	4 Mar 01
1:18:22		Robert	Korzeniowski	POL	30.7.68	1		Hildesheim	9 Jul 00
1:18:23		Andrey	Makarov (20)	BLR	2.1.71	2	NC	Soligorsk	13 May 00
1:18:24			Pérez			1	WCp	Podebrady	19 Apr 97
1:18:27		Daniel	García	MEX	28.10.71	2	WCp	Podebrady	19 Apr 97
1:18:29			Korzeniowski			1	ECp	Eisenhüttenstadt	17 Jun 00
1:18:30		Ilya	Markov	RUS	19.6.72	3	WCp	Podebrady	19 Apr 97
1:18:32			Andreyev			1	NC-w	Adler	11 Feb 95
1:18:32			Li Zewen	CHN	5.12.73	4	WCp	Podebrady	19 Apr 97
1:18:35.2t		Stefan	Johansson	SWE	11.4.67	1	SGP	Fana	15 May 92
		(30/24)							
1:18:36		Mikhail	Shchennikov	RUS	24.12.67	1	NC	Sochi	20 Apr 96
1:18:37		Aleksandr	Pershin	RUS	4.9.68	2	NC	Moskva	26 May 90
1:18:37		Ruslan	Shafikov	RUS	27.6.75	1	NC-w23	Adler	11 Feb 95
1:18:40.0t	WR	Ernesto	Canto	MEX	18.10.59	1	SGP	Fana	5 May 84
1:18:41		Igor	Kollár	SVK	26.6.65	3		Eisenhüttenstadt	11 May 96
1:18:42		Andreas	Erm	GER	12.3.76	2	ECp	Eisenhüttenstadt	17 Jun 00
		(30)							
1:18:43			Zhu Hongjun	CHN	18.8.83	1	NC	Yangzhou	12 Apr 03
1:18:46			Tan Mingjun	CHN	17.7.70	2	NC	Beijing	7 Apr 94
1:18:48		Rishat	Shafikov	RUS	23.1.70	2		Cheboksary	30 Aug 98
1:18:49	WR?	Daniel	Bautista	MEX	4.8.52	1	LT	Eschborn	29 Sep 79
1:18:51		Frants	Kostyukevich	BLR	4.4.63	3	NC	Moskva	26 May 90
1:18:54		Maurizio	Damilano	ITA	6.4.57	1	7N	La Coruña	6 Jun 92
1:18:56		Grigoriy	Kornev	RUS	14.3.61	4	NC	Moskva	26 May 90
1:18:56			Yu Chaohong	CHN	12.12.76	2	NC	Yangzhou	12 Apr 03
1:19:00		Joel	Sánchez	MEX	15.9.66	3		Eisenhüttenstadt	8 May 99
1:19:02		Hatem	Ghoula	TUN	7.6.73	2		Eisenhüttenstadt	10 May 97
		(40)							
1:19:02		Andrey	Stadnichuk	RUS	14.12.73	1	NC-w	Sochi	17 Feb 02
1:19:12		Axel	Noack	GDR	23.9.61	1	vURS	Karl-Marx-Stadt	21 Jun 87
1:19:14		Vladimir	Stankin	RUS	2.1.74	4	NC-w	Adler	4 Mar 01
1:19:14			Xu Xingde	CHN	12.6.84	3	NC	Yangzhou	12 Apr 03
1:19:16			Chen Shaoguo	CHN	20.1.71	3	NC	Beijing	7 Apr 94
1:19:18		Jirí	Malysa	CZE	14.8.66	4	ECp	Eisenhüttenstadt	17 Jun 00
1:19:18.3t		Ronald	Weigel	GDR	8.8.59	1	SGP	Fana	26 May 90
1:19:19		Mikhail	Orlov	RUS	25.6.67	4	NC-w	Adler	11 Feb 95
1:19:22		David	Smith	AUS	24.7.55	1		Hobart	19 Jul 87
1:19:22.5t		Aleksey	Pershin	RUS	23.9.62	1	SGP	Fana	7 May 88
		(50)	100th man 1:20:13, 200th man 1:21:36						

Probable short course: 1:18:33 Mikhail Shchennikov RUS 24.12.67 1 4-N Livorno 10 Jul 93

Mark	Wind	Name		Nat	Born	Pos	Meet	Venue	Date
1:19:08		Yuriy	Kuko	BLR	23.1.68	2	4-N	Livorno	10 Jul 93

30 KILOMETRES WALK

Mark	Wind	Name		Nat	Born	Pos	Meet	Venue	Date
2:01:44.1t		Maurizio	Damilano	ITA	6.4.57	1		Cuneo	4 Oct 92
2:02:41		Andrey	Perlov	RUS	12.12.61	1	NC-w	Sochi	19 Feb 89
2:02:45		Yevgeniy	Misyulya	BLR	13.3.64	1		Mogilyov	28 Apr 91
2:03:06		Daniel	Bautista	MEX	4.8.52	1		Cherkassy	27 Apr 80
2:03:56.5t		Thierry	Toutain	FRA	14.2.62	1		Héricourt	24 Mar 91
2:04:00		Aleksandr	Potashov	BLR	12.3.62	1		Adler	14 Feb 93
2:04:24		Valeriy	Spitsyn	RUS	5.12.65	1	NC-w	Sochi	22 Feb 92
2:04:30		Vitaliy	Matsko	RUS	8.6.60	2	NC-w	Sochi	19 Feb 89

50 KILOMETRES WALK

Mark	Wind	Name		Nat	Born	Pos	Meet	Venue	Date
3:36:03	WR	Robert	Korzeniowski	POL	30.7.68	1	WCh	Saint-Denis	27 Aug 03
3:36:39	WR		Korzeniowski			1	EC	München	8 Aug 02
3:36:42		German	Skurygin ¶	RUS	15.9.63	2	WCh	Saint-Denis	27 Aug 03
3:37:26	WR	Valeriy	Spitsyn	RUS	5.12.65	1	NC	Moskva	21 May 00
3:37:41	WR	Andrey	Perlov	RUS	12.12.61	1	NC	Leningrad	5 Aug 89
3:37:46		Andreas	Erm	GER	12.3.76	3	WCh	Saint-Denis	27 Aug 03

Mark	Wind	Name		Nat	Born	Pos	Meet	Venue	Date
3:38:01		Aleksey	Voyevodin	RUS	9.8.70	4	WCh	Saint-Denis	27 Aug 03
3:38:17	WR	Ronald	Weigel	GDR	8.8.59	1	IM	Potsdam	25 May 86
3:38:23		Denis	Nizhegorodov	RUS	26.7.80	5	WCh	Saint-Denis	27 Aug 03
3:38:29		Vyacheslav	Ivanenko	RUS	3.3.61	1	OG	Seoul	30 Sep 88
3:38:31	WR		Weigel			1		Berlin	20 Jul 84
3:38:43		Valentin	Massana (10)	ESP	5.7.70	1	NC	Orense	20 Mar 94
3:38:56			Weigel			2	OG	Seoul	30 Sep 88
3:39:21		Vladimir	Potemin	RUS	15.1.80	2	NC	Moskva	21 May 00
3:39:22		Sergey	Korepanov	KAZ	9.5.64	1	WCp	Mézidon-Canon	2 May 99
3:39:34		Valentin	Kononen	FIN	7.3.69	1		Dudince	25 Mar 00
3:39:43		Nathan	Deakes	AUS	17.8.77	1		Melbourne	7 Dec 03
3:39:45		Hartwig	Gauder	GDR	10.11.54	3	OG	Seoul	30 Sep 88
3:39:47			Perlov			1		Leningrad	3 Aug 85
3:39:54		Jesús Angel	García	ESP	17.10.69	1	WCp	Podebrady	20 Apr 97
3:40:02		Aleksandr	Potashov	BLR	12.3.62	1	NC	Moskva	27 May 90
3:40:07			Perlov			1		Kharkov	5 Sep 87
3:40:07		Andrey	Plotnikov	RUS	12.8.67	2	NC	Moskva	27 May 90
3:40:08		Tomasz	Lipiec ¶	POL	10.5.71	2	WCp	Mézidon-Canon	2 May 99
3:40:12		Oleg	Ishutkin	RUS	22.7.75	2	WCp	Podebrady	20 Apr 97
3:40:13		Nikolay	Matyukhin	RUS	13.12.68	3	WCp	Mézidon-Canon	2 May 99
3:40:16		Aleksey	Voyevodin	RUS	9.8.70	2	EC	München	8 Aug 02
3:40:40			J A García			4	WCp	Mézidon-Canon	2 May 99
3:40:42			Voyevodin			1	NC	Cheboksary	26 May 02
3:40:46	WR	José	Marin	ESP	21.1.50	1		Valencia	13 Mar 83
		(30/22)							
3:40:57.9t		Thierry	Toutain	FRA	14.2.62	1		Héricourt	29 Sep 96
3:41:20	WR	Raul	González	MEX	29.2.52	1		Podebrady	11 Jun 78
3:41:20			Zhao Yongsheng	CHN	16.4.70	1	WCp	Beijing	30 Apr 95
3:41:28.2t		René	Piller	FRA	23.4.65	1	SGP	Fana	7 May 94
3:41:51		Venyamin	Nikolayev	RUS	7.10.58	2		Leningrad	3 Aug 85
3:41:56		Yevgeniy	Shmalyuk	RUS	14.1.76	6	WCp	Mézidon-Canon	2 May 99
3:42:00		Stanislav	Vezhel	BLR	11.10.58	3	NC	Moskva	27 May 90
3:42:03		Carlos	Mercenario	MEX	3.5.67	1	WCp	San José	2 Jun 91
		(30)							
3:42:03		Mikel	Odriozola	ESP	25.5.73	1	NC	Orense	16 Feb 03
3:42:04		Yevgeniy	Yevsyukov	RUS	2.1.50	3		Leningrad	3 Aug 85
3:42:06		Yuriy	Andronov	RUS	6.11.71	2	NC	Cheboksary	26 May 02
3:42:20		Pavel	Szikora	SVK	26.3.52	1		Dudince	4 Apr 87
3:42:20		Viktor	Ginko	BLR	7.12.65	2		Palma	5 Mar 95
3:42:36		Reima	Salonen	FIN	19.11.55	1	NC	Vantaa	24 May 86
3:42:37		Valeriy	Suntsov	RUS	10.7.55	4		Leningrad	3 Aug 85
3:42:45		Miguel Angel	Rodríguez	MEX	15.1.67	6	WCp	Podebrady	20 Apr 97
3:42:52		Stepan	Yudin	RUS	3.4.80	3	NC	Cheboksary	26 May 02
3:43:13		Simon	Baker	AUS	6.2.58	1	LT	L'Hospitalet	28 May 89
		(40)							
3:43:14		Dietmar	Meisch	GDR	10.2.59	3	LT	New York	2 May 87
3:43:16			Zhou Yongshen	CHN	15.10.72	1	NC	Beijing	10 Apr 94
3:43:18		Aigars	Fadejevs	LAT	27.12.75	1	NC	Ogre	6 Jun 98
3:43:36		Martín	Bermúdez	MEX	19.7.58	1	LT	Eschborn	30 Sep 79
3:43:41			Zhang Huiqiang	CHN	14.10.77	2	NC	Zhuhai	12 Mar 96
3:43:46		Mikhail	Shchennikov	RUS	24.12.67	2	OG	Atlanta	2 Aug 96
3:43:50		Axel	Noack	GER	23.9.61	4	WCh	Stuttgart	21 Aug 93
3:43:55		Giovanni	Perricelli	ITA	25.8.67	3	EC	Helsinki	13 Aug 94
3:43:57		Vitaliy	Matsko	RUS	8.6.60	2	NC	Leningrad	5 Aug 89
3:43:57		Vitaliy	Popovich	UKR	22.10.62	3	NC	Leningrad	5 Aug 89
		(50)	100th man 3:47:54						

100 KILOMETRES WALK

8:38.07		Viktor	Ginko	BLR	7.12.65	1		Scanzorosciate	27 Oct 02
8:43:30			Ginko			1		Scanzorosciate	29 Oct 00
8:44:28			Ginko			1		Scanzoroscaite	19 Oct 03
8:48:28		Modris	Liepins	LAT	3.8.66	1		Scanzorosciate	28 Oct 01
8:54:35		Aleksey	Rodionov	RUS	5.3.57	1		Scanzorosciate	15 Nov 98
8:55:12		Pascal	Kieffer	FRA	6.5.61	1		Besançon	18 Oct 92
8:55:40		Vitaliy	Popovich	UKR	22.10.62	1		Scanzorosciate	31 Oct 99
8:58:12		Gérard	Lelievre	FRA	13.11.49	1		Laval	7 Oct 84
8:58:47		Zóltan	Czukor	HUN	18.12.62	2		Scanzorosciate	27 Oct 02
9:01:29		Sten	Reichel	GER	16.5.75	3		Scanzorosciate	29 Oct 00
9:02:00		Peter	Tichy	SVK	12.3.69	3		Scanzorosciate	27 Oct 02

JUNIOR MEN'S ALL-TIME LISTS

100 METRES

Mark	Wind	Name		Nat	Born	Pos	Meet	Venue	Date
10.01	0.0	Darrel	Brown	TRI	11.10.84	1q3	WCh	Saint-Denis	24 Aug 03
10.05		Davidson	Ezinwa	NGR	22.11.71	1		Bauchi	4 Jan 90
10.06	2.0	Dwain	Chambers	GBR	5.4.78	1	EJ	Ljubljana	25 Jul 97
10.07	2.0	Stanley	Floyd	USA	23.6.61	1		Austin	24 May 80
10.07	1.1	DaBryan	Blanton	USA	3.7.84	1h2	NCAA-r	Lincoln, NE	30 May 03
10.08	0.0	Andre	Cason	USA	13.1.69	1	TAC-j	Tallahassee	24 Jun 88
10.08	0.0	Justin	Gatlin	USA	10.2.82	1	NCAA	Eugene	2 Jun 01
10.08A	1.9	Obadele	Thompson	BAR	30.3.76	3		El Paso	16 Apr 94
10.09A	1.8	Mel	Lattany	USA	10.8.59	2r2	USOF	USAF Academy	30 Jul 78
10.10	1.9	Stanley	Kerr	USA	19.6.67	1	TAC-j	Towson	28 Jun 86
10.10	1.2	Francis	Obikwelu	NGR	22.11.78	1		Lisboa	20 Jun 97
10.10	1.9	Mark	Lewis-Francis	GBR	4.9.82	1B	BrGP	London (CP)	5 Aug 00
Wind assisted to 10.08									
9.83	7.1	Leonard	Scott	USA	19.1.80	1		Knoxville	9 Apr 99
9.97	??	Mark	Lewis-Francis	GBR	4.9.82	1q3	WCh	Edmonton	4 Aug 01
10.07	2.9	Lee	McRae	USA	23.1.66	2h5	NCAA	Austin	30 May 85
10.08	4.0	Johnny	Jones	USA	4.4.58	1		Austin	20 May 77
10.08	2.2	Billy	Fobbs	USA	29.2.76	1r3		Houston	19 May 95

200 METRES

Mark	Wind	Name		Nat	Born	Pos	Meet	Venue	Date
20.07	1.5	Lorenzo	Daniel	USA	23.3.66	1	SEC	Starkville	18 May 85
20.13	1.7	Roy	Martin	USA	25.12.66	1		Austin	11 May 85
20.13	0.0	Usain	Bolt	JAM	21.8.86	1	PAm-J	Bridgetown	20 Jul 03
20.16A	-0.2	Riaan	Dempers	RSA	4.3.77	1	NC-j	Germiston	7 Apr 95
20.22	1.7	Dwayne	Evans	USA	13.10.58	2	OT	Eugene	22 Jun 76
20.23	0.5	Michael	Timpson	USA	6.6.67	1		State College	16 May 86
20.24	0.2	Joe	DeLoach	USA	5.6.67	3		Los Angeles	8 Jun 85
20.24	0.2	Francis	Obikwelu	NGR	22.11.78	2rB		Granada	29 May 96
20.29	1.5	Clinton	Davis	USA	17.8.65	1	TAC-j	State College	26 Jun 83
20.29	-0.2	Christian	Malcolm	GBR	3.6.79	2	CG	Kuala Lumpur	19 Sep 98
20.29	0.6	Justin	Gatlin	USA	10.2.82	1	SEC	Columbia, SC	11 May 01
20.29	0.6	Yusuke	Omae	JPN	6.4.82	1	NC-j	Matsumoto	30 Jun 01
Wind assisted									
19.86	4.0	Justin	Gatlin	USA	10.2.82	1h2	NCAA	Eugene	30 May 01
20.01	2.5	Derald	Harris	USA	5.4.58	1		San José	9 Apr 77
20.08	9.2	Leonard	Scott	USA	19.1.80	2r2		Knoxville	9 Apr 99
20.10	4.6	Stanley	Kerr	USA	19.6.67	2r2	SWC	Houston	18 May 86
Hand timing									
19.9		Davidson	Ezinwa	NGR	22.11.71	1		Bauchi	18 Mar 89

400 METRES

Mark	Name		Nat	Born	Pos	Meet	Venue	Date
43.87	Steve	Lewis	USA	16.5.69	1	OG	Seoul	28 Sep 88
44.66	Hamdam	Al-Bishi	KSA	5.5.81	1	WJ	Santiago de Chile	20 Oct 00
44.69	Darrell	Robinson	USA	23.12.63	2	USOF	Indianapolis	24 Jul 82
44.73A	James	Rolle	USA	2.2.64	1	USOF	USAF Academy	2 Jul 83
44.75	Darren	Clark	AUS	6.9.65	4	OG	Los Angeles	8 Aug 84
44.75	Deon	Minor	USA	22.1.73	1s1	NCAA	Austin	5 Jun 92
45.01	Thomas	Schönlebe	GDR	6.8.65	1		Berlin	15 Jul 84
45.01	Jerome	Young	USA	14.8.76	1	NC-j	Walnut	24 Jun 95
45.04A	Wayne	Collett	USA	20.10.49	1q2	OT	Echo Summit	13 Sep 68
45.04	Brandon	Couts	USA	17.2.79	1	DrakeR	Des Moines	25 Apr 98
45.05	Roberto	Hernández	CUB	6.3.67	2		Santiago de Cuba	21 Feb86
44.9+A	Steve	Williams	USA	13.11.53	1	WAC	El Paso	13 May 72

800 METRES

Mark	Name		Nat	Born	Pos	Meet	Venue	Date
1:43.64	Japheth	Kimutai	KEN	20.12.78	3rB	WK	Zürich	13 Aug 97
1:44.3*	Jim	Ryun	USA	29.4.47	1	USTFF	Terre Haute	10 Jun 66
1:44.3	Joaquim	Cruz	BRA	12.3.63	1		Rio de Janeiro	27 Jun 81
1:44.33	Yuriy	Borzakovskiy	RUS	12.4.81	2s2	OG	Sydney	25 Sep 00
1:44.46	Nicholas	Wachira	KEN	19.11.82	5	GP II	Rieti	2 Sep 01
1:44.56	Benjamin	Kipkurui	KEN	28.12.80	2		Rehlingen	24 May 99
1:44.69	William	Chirchir	KEN	6.2.79	6	Herc	Monaco	8 Aug 98
1:44.77	Benson	Koech	KEN	10.11.74	1	WJ	Seoul	19 Sep 92
1:44.98	Cornelius	Chirchir	KEN	5.6.83	4		Rovereto	29 Aug 01
1:45.14	Wilfred	Bungei	KEN	24.7.80	3		Pátra	1 Aug 99
1:45.3A	Emmanuel	Kemboi	KEN	.81	1		Kakamega	9 Apr 00

Mark	Wind	Name		Nat	Born	Pos	Meet	Venue	Date

1000 METRES

2:15.00	Benjamin	Kipkurui	KEN	28.12.80	5	Nik	Nice	17 Jul 99
2:16.84	Ali	Hakimi	TUN	24.4.76	1		Lindau	28 Jul 95
2:16.86	Japheth	Kimutai	KEN	20.12.78	1	VD	Bruxelles	22 Aug 97
2:17.10	Julius	Achon	UGA	12.12.76	1		Rhede	30 Jul 95

1500 METRES

3:30.24	Cornelius	Chirchir	KEN	5.6.83	4	Herc	Monaco	19 Jul 02
3:31.42	Alex	Kipchirchir	KEN	26.11.84	5	VD	Bruxelles	5 Sep 03
3:31.54	Isaac	Songok	KEN	25.4.84	1	NA	Heusden	2 Aug 03
3:32.91	Noah	Ngeny	KEN	2.11.78	9	Herc	Monaco	16 Aug 97
3:33.16	Benjamin	Kipkurui	KEN	28.12.80	1rB	WK	Zürich	11 Aug 99
3:33.24	William	Chirchir	KEN	6.2.79	8rA	WK	Zürich	12 Aug 98
3:34.17	Michael	Too	KEN	3.8.83	4	GP	Doha	15 May 02
3:34.63	Daniel	Komen	KEN	17.5.76	2	Znam	Moskva	5 Jun 95
3:34.92	Kipkoech	Cheruiyot	KEN	2.12.64	1		München	26 Jul 83
3:35.47	Stephen	Cherono	KEN	15.10.82	5	GP II	Zagreb	2 Jul 01
3:35.51	Reyes	Estévez	ESP	2.8.76	2	WK	Zürich	16 Aug 95
3:35.63	Hailu	Mekonnen	ETH	4.4.80	3		Arnhem	10 Jul 99

1 MILE

3:50.25	Alex	Kipchirchir	KEN	26.11.84	2	GP II	Rieti	7 Sep 03
3:50.39	James	Kwalia	KEN	12.6.84	1	FBK	Hengelo	1 Jun 03
3:50.41	Noah	Ngeny	KEN	2.11.78	2	Nik	Nice	16 Jul 97
3:50.69	Cornelius	Chirchir	KEN	5.6.83	5	GGala	Roma	12 Jul 02
3:51.3	Jim	Ryun	USA	29.4.47	1		Berkeley	17 Jul 66

2000 METRES

4:56.86	Isaac	Songok	KEN	25.4.84	6	ISTAF	Berlin	31 Aug 01
4:59.11	James	Kwalia	KEN	12.6.84	5		Naimette	2 Sep 03
4:59.14	Ali	Saïdi-Sief	ALG	15.3.78	9	Gaz	Villeneuve d'Ascq	29 Jun 97
5:00.0+	Sammy	Kipketer	KEN	29.9.81	8	in3k	Monaco	4 Aug 99

3000 METRES

7:30.67	Kenenisa	Bekele	ETH	13.6.82	2	VD	Bruxelles	24 Aug 01
7:30.91	Eliud	Kipchoge	KEN	5.11.84	2	VD	Bruxelles	5 Sep 03
7:33.00	Hailu	Mekonnen	ETH	4.4.80	2		Stuttgart	6 Jun 99
7:34.32	Richard	Limo	KEN	18.11.80	4	VD	Bruxelles	3 Sep 99
7:34.58	Sammy	Kipketer	KEN	29.9.81	5	VD	Bruxelles	3 Sep 99
7:35.52	Philip	Mosima	KEN	2.1.77	1	GP	London (CP)	12 Jul 96
7:35.53	James	Kwalia	KEN	12.6.84	5	VD	Bruxelles	5 Sep 03
7:38.09	Daniel	Komen	KEN	17.5.76	7	GPF	Monaco	9 Sep 95
7:39.22	Hillary	Chenonge	KEN	30.5.85	7	VD	Bruxelles	30 Aug 02
7:39.82	Ismael	Kirui	KEN	20.2.75	3	ISTAF	Berlin	27 Aug 93

5000 METRES

12:52.61	Eliud	Kipchoge	KEN	5.11.84	3	Bisl	Oslo	27 Jun 03
12:53.72	Philip	Mosima	KEN	2.1.77	2	GGala	Roma	5 Jun 96
12:54.07	Sammy	Kipketer	KEN	29.9.81	2	GGala	Roma	30 Jun 00
12:54.58	James	Kwalia	KEN	12.6.84	5	Bisl	Oslo	27 Jun 03
12:56.15	Daniel	Komen	KEN	17.5.76	2	GG	Roma	8 Jun 95
12:58.08	Gebre-egziabher	Gebremariam	ETH	10.9.84	6	WCh	Saint-Denis	31 Aug 03
12:58.15	Richard	Limo	KEN	18.11.80	6	GGala	Roma	7 Jul 99
12:59.39	Million	Wolde	ETH	17.3.79	5	WK	Zürich	12 Aug 98
12:59.90	Albert	Chepkirui	KEN	4.4.81	8	Bisl	Oslo	28 Jul 00
13:02.75	Ismael	Kirui	KEN	20.2.75	1	WCh	Stuttgart	16 Aug 93
13:05.48	Assefa	Mezegebu	ETH	19.6.78	4	GGala	Roma	5 Jun 97

10,000 METRES

27:11.18	Richard	Chelimo	KEN	21.4.72	1	APM	Hengelo	25 Jun 91
27:13.66	Moses	Mosop	KEN	17.7.85	7	VD	Bruxelles	5 Sep 03
27:15.88	Boniface	Kiprop	UGA	12.10.85	9	VD	Bruxelles	5 Sep 03
27:17.82	Addis	Abebe	ETH	5.9.70	2	WG	Helsinki	29 Jun 89
27:24.75	John Cheruiyot	Korir	KEN	13.12.81	5	OG	Sydney	25 Sep 00
27:25.01	Assefa	Mezegebu	ETH	19.6.78	1	APM	Hengelo	31 May 97
27:25.55	Robert	Kipchumba	KEN	24.2.84	2	VD	Bruxelles	24 Aug 01
27:25.61	Gebregziabher	Gebremariam	ETH	10.9.84	8	VD	Bruxelles	30 Aug 02
27:26.12	Sileshi	Sihen	ETH	29.1.83	9	VD	Bruxelles	30 Aug 02
27:27.87	Elijah H.	Korir	KEN	15.4.78	5	VD	Bruxelles	22 Aug 97
27:28.60	Julius	Gitahi	KEN	29.4.78	1		Konosu	5 Oct 96

Mark	Wind	Name		Nat	Born	Pos	Meet	Venue	Date

3000 METRES STEEPLECHASE

Mark	Wind	Name		Nat	Born	Pos	Meet	Venue	Date
7:58.66		Stephen	Cherono	KEN	15.10.82	3	VD	Bruxelles	24 Aug 01
8:03.74		Raymond	Yator	KEN	7.4.81	3	Herc	Monaco	18 Aug 00
8:07.69		Paul	Kosgei	KEN	22.4.78	5	DNG	Stockholm	7 Jul 97
8:09.37		Abel	Cheruiyot/Yugut	KEN	26.12.84	2	NA	Heusden	2 Aug 03
8:12.91		Thomas	Kiplitan	KEN	15.6.83	7	GP	Doha	15 May 02
8:16.76		Kipkirui	Misoi	KEN	23.10.78	2		Dortmund	8 Jun 97
8:18.71		Julius	Chelule	KEN	25.12.78	4	Slovn	Bratislava	10 Jun 97
8:19.21		Daniel	Njenga	KEN	7.5.76	1	JPN Ch	Tokyo	12 Jun 94
8:20.07		Christopher	Soget	KEN	15.5.80	2	Afr-J	Tunis	23 Jul 99
8:20.67		Richard	Limo	KEN	18.11.80	2	AfrC	Dakar	20 Aug 98
8:20.73		Paul	Chemase	KEN	24.8.76	10	Herc	Monaco	25 Jul 95

110 METRES HURDLES

Mark	Wind	Name		Nat	Born	Pos	Meet	Venue	Date
13.12	1.6		Liu Xiang	CHN	13.7.83	1rB	Athl	Lausanne	2 Jul 02
13.23	0.0	Renaldo	Nehemiah	USA	24.3.59	1r2	WK	Zürich	16 Aug 78
13.40	-1.0		Shi Dongpeng	CHN	6.1.84	1	NC	Shanghai	14 Sep 03
13.44	-0.8	Colin	Jackson	GBR	18.2.67	1	WJ	Athína	19 Jul 86
13.46	1.8	Jon	Ridgeon	GBR	14.2.67	1	EJ	Cottbus	23 Aug 85
13.47	1.9	Holger	Pohland	GDR	5.4.63	2	vUSA	Karl-Marx-Stadt	10 Jul 82
13.49	0.6	Stanislav	Olijar	LAT	22.3.79	1		Valmiera	11 Jul 98
13.51!	1.2	Tomasz	Scigaczewski	POL	18.11.78	1		Lodz	7 Sep 97
13.52	0.6	Ubeja	Anderson	USA	30.3.74	1		Knoxville	16 May 93
13.53	0.5	Kenneth	Ferguson	USA	22.3.84	2	SEC	Knoxville	18 May 03
Wind assisted									
13.42	4.5	Colin	Jackson	GBR	18.2.67	2	CG	Edinburgh	27 Jul 86
13.42	2.6	Antwon	Hicks	USA	12.3.83	1	WJ	Kingston	21 Jul 02
13.47	2.1	Frank	Busemann	GER	26.2.75	1	WJ	Lisboa	22 Jul 94

400 METRES HURDLES

Mark	Wind	Name		Nat	Born	Pos	Meet	Venue	Date
48.02		Danny	Harris	USA	7.9.65	2s1	OT	Los Angeles	17 Jun 84
48.68		Bayano	Kamani	USA	17.4.80	1	NCAA	Boise	4 Jun 99
48.72		Angelo	Taylor	USA	29.12.78	2	NCAA	Bloomington	6 Jun 97
48.74		Vladimir	Budko	BLR	4.2.65	2	DRZ	Moskva	18 Aug 84
48.76A		Llewellyn	Herbert	RSA	21.7.77	1		Pretoria	7 Apr 96
		49.15				2	WJ	Sydney	23 Aug 96
48.79		Kenneth	Ferguson	USA	22.3.84	1	SEC	Knoxville	18 May 03
48.89		Louis	van Zyl	RSA	20.7.85	1	WJ	Kingston	19 Jul 02
49.07		Mubarak	Al-Nubi	QAT	30.12.77	1	WJ	Sydney	23 Aug 96
49.09		Dai	Tamesue	JPN	3.5.78	1		Hiroshima	14 Oct 96
49.10		Yoshihiko	Saito	JPN	12.2.72	1		Kanazawa	17 Oct 91
49.23		Marek	Plawgo	POL	25.2.81	1	WJ	Santiago de Chile	21 Oct 00

HIGH JUMP

Mark	Wind	Name		Nat	Born	Pos	Meet	Venue	Date
2.37		Dragutin	Topic	YUG	12.3.71	1	WJ	Plovdiv	12 Aug 90
2.37		Steve	Smith	GBR	29.3.73	1	WJ	Seoul	20 Sep 92
2.36		Javier	Sotomayor	CUB	13.10.67	1		Santiago de Cuba	23 Feb 86
2.35i		Vladimir	Yashchenko	UKR	12.1.59	1	EI	Milano	12 Mar 78
		2.34				1	Prv	Tbilisi	16 Jun 78
2.35		Dietmar	Mögenburg	FRG	15.8.61	1		Rehlingen	26 May 80
2.34		Tim	Forsyth	AUS	17.8.73	1	Bisl	Oslo	4 Jul 92
2.33			Zhu Jianhua	CHN	29.5.63	1	AsiG	New Delhi	1 Dec 82
2.33		Patrik	Sjöberg	SWE	5.1.65	1	OsloG	Oslo	9 Jul 83
2.32i		Jaroslav	Bába	CZE	2.9.84	3		Arnstadt	8 Feb 03
2.31		Jörg	Freimuth	GDR	10.9.61	3	OG	Moskva	1 Aug 80
2.31		Lochsley	Thomson	AUS	20.8.73	3	NC	Adelaide	8 Mar 92
2.31i		Andrey	Chubsa	BLR	29.11.82	1		Vitebsk	12 Jan 01
2.31		Jacques	Freitag	RSA	11.6.82	1		Rehlingen	4 Jun 01
2.31		Andra	Manson	USA	30.4.84	1	WJ	Kingston	18 Jul 02

POLE VAULT

Mark	Wind	Name		Nat	Born	Pos	Meet	Venue	Date
5.80		Maksim	Tarasov	RUS	2.12.70	1	vGDR-j	Bryansk	14 Jul 89
5.71		Lawrence	Johnson	USA	7.5.74	1		Knoxville	12 Jun 93
5.70		Viktor	Chistyakov	RUS	9.2.75	1		Leppävirta	7 Jun 94
5.70		Artyom	Kuptsov	RUS	22.4.84	1	Znam	Tula	7 Jun 03
5.65		Radion	Gataullin	UZB	23.11.65	2	NC	Donetsk	8 Sep 84
5.65		István	Bagyula	HUN	2.1.69	1	WJ	Sudbury	28 Jul 88
5.65i		Jacob	Davis	USA	29.4.78	1	Big 12	Lincoln	21 Feb 97
		5.62				2		Austin	5 Apr 97
5.62		Gérald	Baudouin	FRA	15.11.72	1	NC-j	Dreux	7 Jul 91

Mark	Wind	Name		Nat	Born	Pos	Meet	Venue	Date
5.62		Lars	Börgeling	GER	16.4.79	1		Mannheim	13 Jun 98
5.61		Thierry	Vigneron	FRA	9.3.60	1		Longwy	30 Sep 79
5.61i		Grigoriy	Yegorov	KZK	12.1.67	1	vGDR-j	Moskva	16 Feb 86
5.61		Danny	Ecker	GER	21.7.77	1		Ljubljana	28 Sep 96
5.61		Vasiliy	Petrov	RUS	5.2.83	1		Bebra	8 Sep 01

LONG JUMP

Mark	Wind	Name		Nat	Born	Pos	Meet	Venue	Date
8.34	0.0	Randy	Williams	USA	23.8.53	Q	OG	München	8 Sep 72
8.28	0.8	Luis A	Bueno	CUB	22.5.69	1		La Habana	16 Jul 88
8.24	0.2	Eric	Metcalf	USA	23.1.68	1	NCAA	Indianapolis	6 Jun 86
8.24	1.8	Vladimir	Ochkan	UKR	13.1.68	1	vGDR-j	Leningrad	21 Jun 87
8.22		Larry	Doubley	USA	15.3.58	1	NCAA	Champaign	3 Jun 77
8.22		Ivan	Pedroso	CUB	17.12.72	1		Santiago de Cuba	3 May 91
8.21A	2.0	Vance	Johnson	USA	13.3.63	1	NCAA	Provo	4 Jun 82
8.20	1.5	James	Stallworth	USA	29.4.71	Q	WJ	Plovdiv	9 Aug 90
8.18		LaMonte	King	USA	18.12.59	2	CalR	Modesto	20 May 78
8.18		Petr	Lampart	CZE	31.3.83	1		Brno	15 Sep 02
Wind assisted									
8.40	3.2	Kareem	Streete-Thompson	CAY	30.3.73	1		Houston	5 May 91
8.35	2.2	Carl	Lewis	USA	1.7.61	1	NCAA	Austin	6 Jun 80
8.29	2.3	James	Beckford	JAM	9.1.75	1		Tempe	2 Apr 94
8.23	4.4	Peller	Phillips	USA	23.6.70	1		Sacramento	11 Jun 88
8.21	2.8	Masaki	Morinaga	JPN	27.3.72	1		Hamamatsu	7 Sep 91

TRIPLE JUMP

Mark	Wind	Name		Nat	Born	Pos	Meet	Venue	Date
17.50	0.4	Volker	Mai	GDR	3.5.66	1	vURS	Erfurt	23 Jun 85
17.42	1.3	Khristo	Markov	BUL	27.1.65	1	Nar	Sofiya	19 May 84
17.40A	0.4	Pedro	Pérez	CUB	23.2.52	1	PAm	Cali	5 Aug 71
17.31	-0.2	David	Giralt Jr.	CUB	26.8.84	Q	WCh	Saint-Denis	23 Aug 03
17.29	1.3	James	Beckford	JAM	9.1.75	1		Tempe	2 Apr 94
17.27		Aliecer	Urrutia	CUB	22.9.74	1		Artemisa	23 Apr 93
17.23	0.2	Yoelbi	Quesada	CUB	4.8.73	1	NC	La Habana	13 May 92
17.11	1.4	Marian	Oprea	ROM	6.6.82	2	WUG	Beijing	31 Aug 01
17.03	0.6	Osiris	Mora	CUB	3.10.73	2	WJ	Seoul	19 Sep 92
17.00		Gustavo	Plá	CUB	29.7.54	1		La Habana	5 May 73
17.00		Yevgeniy	Timofeyev	RUS	22.2.74	1		Krasnodar	26 May 93
17.13w	4.1	Marian	Oprea	ROM	6.6.82	1	ECp-1B	Budapest	24 Jun 01

SHOT

Mark	Wind	Name		Nat	Born	Pos	Meet	Venue	Date
21.05i		Terry	Albritton	USA	14.1.55	1	AAU	New York	22 Feb 74
		20.38				2	MSR	Walnut	27 Apr 74
20.65		Mike	Carter	USA	29.10.60	1	vSU-j	Boston	4 Jul 79
20.39		Janus	Robberts	RSA	10.3.79	1	NC	Germiston	7 Mar 98
20.20		Randy	Matson	USA	5.3.45	2	OG	Tokyo	17 Oct 64
20.20		Udo	Beyer	GDR	9.8.55	2	NC	Leipzig	6 Jul 74
20.13		Jeff	Chakouian	USA	20.4.82	2		Atlanta	18 May 01
19.99		Karl	Salb	USA	19.5.49	4	OT	Echo Summit	10 Sep 68
19.95		Edis	Elkasevic	CRO	18.2.83	1		Velenje	15 Jun 02
19.74		Andreas	Horn	GDR	31.1.62	2	vSU-j	Cottbus	24 Jun 81
19.71		Vladimir	Kiselyov -1	UKR	1.1.57	1		Yalta	15 May 76
19.69		Mikulás	Konopka	SVK	23.1.79	2	NC	Nitra	11 Jul 98

DISCUS

Mark	Wind	Name		Nat	Born	Pos	Meet	Venue	Date
65.62		Werner	Reiterer	AUS	27.1.68	1		Melbourne	15 Dec 87
63.64		Werner	Hartmann	FRG	20.4.59	1	vFRA	Strasbourg	25 Jun 78
63.26		Sergey	Pachin	UKR	24.5.68	2		Moskva	25 Jul 87
63.22		Brian	Milne	USA	7.1.73	1		State College	28 Mar 92
62.52		John	Nichols	USA	23.8.69	1		Baton Rouge	23 Apr 88
62.36		Nuermaimaiti	Tulake	CHN	8.3.84	2	NG	Guangzhou	21 Nov 01
62.16		Zoltán	Kövágó	HUN	10.4.79	1		Budapest	9 May 97
62.04		Kenth	Gardenkrans	SWE	2.10.55	2		Helsingborg	11 Aug 74
62.04			Wu Tao	CHN	3.10.83	1	NGP	Shanghai	18 May 02
61.84		Attila	Horváth	HUN	28.7.67	2		Budapest	18 May 85
61.84		Andreas	Seelig	GDR	6.7.70	1		Halle	15 May 88

HAMMER

Mark	Wind	Name		Nat	Born	Pos	Meet	Venue	Date
78.33		Olli-Pekka	Karjalainen	FIN	7.3.80	1	NC	Seinäjoki	5 Aug 99
78.14		Roland	Steuk	GDR	5.3.59	1	NC	Leipzig	30 Jun 78
78.00		Sergey	Dorozhon	UKR	17.2.64	1		Moskva	7 Aug 83
76.54		Valeriy	Gubkin	BLR	3.9.67	2		Minsk	27 Jun 86
76.42		Ruslan	Dikiy	TJK	18.1.72	1		Togliatti	7 Sep 91

Mark	Wind	Name		Nat	Born	Pos	Meet	Venue	Date
75.52		Sergey	Kirmasov	RUS	25.3.70	1		Kharkov	4 Jun 89
75.42		Szymon	Ziolkowski	POL	1.7.76	1	EJ	Nyíregyhazá	30 Jul 95
75.24		Christoph	Sahner	FRG	23.9.63	1	vPOL-j	Göttingen	26 Jun 82
75.22		Yaroslav	Chmyr	UKR	29.11.66	1		Kiyev	9 Sep 85
75.20		Igor	Nikulin	RUS	14.8.60	2		Leselidze	1 Jun 79

JAVELIN

83.87	Andreas	Thorkildsen	NOR	1.4.82	1		Fana	7 Jun 01
83.55	Aleksandr	Ivanov	RUS	25.5.82	2	NC	Tula	14 Jul 01
82.52	Harri	Haatainen	FIN	5.1.78	4		Leppävirta	25 May 96
81.80	Sergey	Voynov	UZB	26.2.77	1		Tashkent	6 Jun 96
80.94	Aki	Parviainen	FIN	26.10.74	4	NC	Jyväskylä	5 Jul 92
80.57	Teemu	Wirkkala	FIN	14.1.84	1		Espoo	14 Sep 03
80.43	Tero	Järvenpää	FIN	2.10.84	3	NC	Helsinki	11 Aug 03
80.30	Konstadínos	Gatsioúdis	GRE	17.12.73	1	NC	Athína	20 Jun 92
80.26	Vladimir	Ovchinnikov	RUS	2.8.70	Q	OG	Seoul	24 Sep 88
79.58	Gavin	Lovegrove	NZL	21.10.67	2		Nouméa	26 Oct 86

DECATHLON

8397	Torsten	Voss	GDR	24.3.63	1	NC	Erfurt			7 Jul 82
	10.76	7.66	14.41	2.09	48.37	14.37	41.76	4.80	62.90	4:34.04
8114	Michael	Kohnle	FRG	3.5.70	1	EJ	Varazdin			26 Aug 89
	10.95	7.09/0.1	15.27	2.02	49.91	14.40	45.82	4.90	60.82	4:49.43
8104	Valter	Külvet	EST	19.2.64	1		Viimsi			23 Aug 81
	10.7	7.26	13.86	2.09	48.5	14.8	47.92	4.50	60.34	4:37.8
8082	Daley	Thompson	GBR	30.7.58	1	ECp/s	Sittard			31 Jul 77
	10.70/0.8	7.54/0.7	13.84	2.01	47.31	15.26/2.0	41.70	4.70	54.48	4:30.4
8041		Qi Haifeng	CHN	7.8.83	1	AsiG	Busan			10 Oct 02
	11.09/0.2	7.22/0.0	13.05	2.06	49.09	14.54/0.0	43.16	4.80	61.04	4:35.17
8036	Christian	Schenk	GDR	9.2.65	5		Potsdam			21 Jul 84
	11.54	7.18	14.26	2.16	49.23	15.06	44.74	4.20	65.98	4:24.11
7938	Frank	Busemann	GER	26.2.75	1		Zeven			2 Oct 94
	10.68/1.6	7.37/1.1	13.08	2.03	50.41	14.34/-1.1	39.84	4.40	63.00	4:37.31)
7913	Raul	Duany	CUB	4.1.75	2		La Habana			26 May 94
	11.50	7.13	13.99	2.10	49.70	14.77	37.76	4.50	65.58	4:24.03
7906	Mikhail	Romanyuk	UKR	6.2.62	1	EJ	Utrecht			21 Aug 81
	11.26/1.8	7.11w/3.7	13.50	1.98	49.98	14.72w/4.0	42.94	4.90	59.74	4:30.63
7897	Dennis	Leyckes	GER	20.4.82	1	WJ	Santiago de Chile			19 Oct 00
	10.98/1.6	7.22/0.4	13.46	1.95	47.59	14.61/-0.1	39.52	4.80	54.76	4:33.10

10,000 METRES WALK

38:46.4	Viktor	Burayev	RUS	23.8.82	1	NC-j	Moskva	20 May 00
38:54.75	Ralf	Kowalsky	GDR	22.3.62	1		Cottbus	24 Jun 81
39:44.71	Giovanni	De Benedictis	ITA	8.1.68	1	EJ	Birmingham	7 Aug 87
39:49.22		Pei Chuang	CHN	5.12.81	2	NSG	Chengdu	8 Sep 00
39:50.73	Jefferson	Pérez	ECU	1.7.74	1	PAmJ	Winnipeg	15 Jul 93
39:55.52	Ilya	Markov	RUS	19.6.72	1	WJ	Plovdiv	10 Aug 90
39:56.49	Alberto	Cruz	MEX	6.6.72	2	WJ	Plovdiv	10 Aug 90
39:59.58	Sergey	Tyulenyev	RUS	14.3.71	1		Kharkov	4 Jun 90
40:05.62	Michele	Didoni	ITA	7.3.74	1	EJ	San Sebastián	30 Jul 93
40:13.11	Yevgeniy	Shmalyuk	RUS	14.1.76	1		Sankt-Peterburg	28 May 94

4 x 100 METRES RELAY

38.92	USA	Collins, Felix, I.Williams, Hordge	1	WJ	Kingston	21 Jul 02
39.05	GBR	Edgar, Grant, Benjamin, Lewis-Francis	1	WJ	Santiago de Chile	22 Oct 00
39.15	JAM	Hutton, Nicely, Plummer, Bolt	2	WJ	Kingston	21 Jul 02
39.17	TRI	Simpson, Burns, Holder, Brown	3	WJ	Kingston	21 Jul 02
39.25	FRG	Dobeleit, Klameth, Evers, Lübke	1	EJ	Schwechat	28 Aug 83
39.30	JPN	Matsumaga, Noda, Takahira, Aikawa	1	AsiC-j	Bangkok	28 Oct 02
39.33	FRA	Pognon, Calligny, Doucoure, Djhone	2	WJ	Santiago de Chile	22 Oct 00
39.47	JPN	Mogi, Kitamura, Omaer, Miyazaki	3	WJ	Santiago de Chile	22 Oct 00

4 x 400 METRES RELAY

3:01.90	USA	Campbell, Rish, Waddle, Reed	1	WJ	Athína	20 Jul 86
3:03.80	GBR	Grindley, Patrick, Winrow, Richardson	2	WJ	Plovdiv	12 Aug 90
3:04.06	JAM	S Clarke, Bolt, Myers, Gonzales	2	WJ	Kingston	21 Jul 02
3:04.22	CUB	Cadogan, Mordoche, González, Hernández	2	WJ	Athína	20 Jul 86
3:04.58	GDR	Preusche, Löper, Trylus, Carlowitz	1	EJ	Utrecht	23 Aug 81
3:04.74	AUS	McFarlane, Batman, Thom, Vincent	1	WJ	Annecy	2 Aug 98
3:05.60	URS	Angelov, Oleynikov, Belikov, Golovastov	4	WJ	Plovdiv	12 Aug 90
3:05.77	FRG	Grüber, Seybold, Mikisch, Just	2	EJ	Schwechat	28 Aug 83

WOMEN'S ALL-TIME WORLD LISTS

100 METRES

Mark	Wind	Name		Nat	Born	Pos	Meet	Venue	Date
10.49WR	0.0	Florence	Griffith-Joyner	USA	21.12.59	1q1	OT	Indianapolis	16 Jul 88
		@ Probably strongly wind-assisted, but recognised as a US and world record							
10.61	1.2		Griffith-Joyner			1	OT	Indianapolis	17 Jul 88
10.62	1.0		Griffith-Joyner			1q3	OG	Seoul	24 Sep 88
10.65A	1.1	Marion	Jones	USA	12.10.75	1	WCp	Johannesburg	12 Sep 98
10.70	1.6		Griffith-Joyner			1s1	OT	Indianapolis	17 Jul 88
10.70	-0.1		Jones			1	WCh	Sevilla	22 Aug 99
10.71	0.1		Jones			1		Chengdu	12 May 98
10.71	2.0		Jones			1s2	NC	New Orleans	19 Jun 98
10.72	2.0		Jones			1	NC	New Orleans	20 Jun 98
10.72	0.0		Jones			1	Herc	Monaco	8 Aug 98
10.72	0.0		Jones			1	Athl	Lausanne	25 Aug 98
10.73	2.0	Christine	Arron	FRA	13.9.73	1	EC	Budapest	19 Aug 98
10.74	1.3	Merlene	Ottey	JAM	10.5.60	1	GPF	Milano	7 Sep 96
10.75	0.6		Jones			1	GGala	Roma	14 Jul 98
10.75	-0.4		Jones			1	OG	Sydney	23 Sep 00
10.76WR	1.7	Evelyn	Ashford	USA	15.4.57	1	WK	Zürich	22 Aug 84
10.76	0.9		Jones			1	VD	Bruxelles	22 Aug 97
10.76	0.3		Jones			1q4	WCh	Sevilla	21 Aug 99
10.77	0.9	Irina	Privalova	RUS	22.11.68	1rA	Athl	Lausanne	6 Jul 94
10.77	-0.9		Jones			1rA	WK	Zürich	12 Aug 98
10.78A	1.0	Dawn	Sowell	USA	27.3.66	1	NCAA	Provo	3 Jun 89
10.78	1.7		Ottey			1	Expo	Sevilla	30 May 90
10.78	0.4		Ottey			1	GPF	Paris	3 Sep 94
10.78	1.1		Jones			1	BrGP	London (CP)	5 Aug 00
10.78	0.1		Jones			1	ISTAF	Berlin	1 Sep 00
10.79AWR	0.6		Ashford			1	USOF	USAF Academy	3 Jul 83
10.79	1.7		Ottey			1		Vigo	23 Jul 91
10.79	0.0		Li Xuemei	CHN	5.1.77	1	NG	Shanghai	18 Oct 97
10.79	-0.6		Jones			1		Osaka	9 May 98
10.79	-0.1	Inger	Miller	USA	12.6.72	2	WCh	Sevilla	22 Aug 99
		(30 performances by 9 athletes)							
10.81WR	1.7	Marlies	Göhr' (10)	GDR	21.3.58	1	OD	Berlin	8 Jun 83
10.82	-1.0	Gail	Devers	USA	19.11.66	1	OG	Barcelona	1 Aug 92
10.82	0.4	Gwen	Torrence	USA	12.6.65	2	GPF	Paris	3 Sep 94
10.82	-0.3	Zhanna	Pintusevich-Block	UKR	6.7.72	1	WCh	Edmonton	6 Aug 01
10.83	1.7	Marita	Koch	GDR	18.2.57	2	OD	Berlin	8 Jun 83
10.83	0.0	Sheila	Echols	USA	2.10.64	1q2	OT	Indianapolis	16 Jul 88
10.83	-1.0	Juliet	Cuthbert	JAM	9.4.64	2	OG	Barcelona	1 Aug 92
10.83	0.1	Ekateríni	Thánou	GRE	1.2.75	2s1	WCh	Sevilla	22 Aug 99
10.84	1.3	Chioma	Ajunwa ¶	NGR	25.12.70	1		Lagos	11 Apr 92
10.85	2.0	Anelia	Nuneva	BUL	30.6.62	1h1	NC	Sofiya	2 Sep 88
10.85	0.9	Kelli	White	USA	1.4.77	1	WCh	Saint-Denis	24 Aug 03
		(20)							
10.86	0.6	Silke	Gladisch/Möller	GDR	20.6.64	1	NC	Potsdam	20 Aug 87
10.86@	0.0	Diane	Williams	USA	14.12.60	2q1	OT	Indianapolis	16 Jul 88
		10.94A	0.6			2	USOF	USAF Academy	3 Jul 83
10.86	0.1	Chandra	Sturrup	BAH	12.9.71	1	NC	Nassau	21 Jul 00
10.86	1.2	Chryste	Gaines	USA	14.9.70	1	WAF	Monaco	14 Sep 03
10.89	1.8	Katrin	Krabbe ¶	GDR	22.11.69	1		Berlin	20 Jul 88
10.89	0.0		Liu Xiaomei	CHN	11.1.72	2	NG	Shanghai	18 Oct 97
10.90	1.4	Glory	Alozie	NGR/ESP	30.12.77	1		La Laguna	5 Jun 99
10.91	0.2	Heike	Drechsler'	GDR	16.12.64	2	GWG	Moskva	6 Jul 86
10.91	1.1	Savatheda	Fynes	BAH	17.10.74	2	Athl	Lausanne	2 Jul 99
10.91	1.5	Debbie	Ferguson	BAH	16.1.76	1	CG	Manchester	27 Jul 02
		(30)							
10.92	0.0	Alice	Brown	USA	20.9.60	2q2	OT	Indianapolis	16 Jul 88
10.92	1.1	D'Andre	Hill	USA	19.4.73	3	NC	Atlanta	15 Jun 96
10.93	1.8	Ewa	Kasprzyk	POL	7.9.57	1	NC	Grudziadz	27 Jun 86
10.93	1.0	Tayna	Lawrence	JAM	17.9.75	3	VD	Bruxelles	30 Aug 02
10.93	0.9	Torri	Edwards	USA	31.1.77	2	WCh	Saint-Denis	24 Aug 03
10.94	1.0	Carlette	Guidry	USA	4.9.68	1	TAC	New York	14 Jun 91
10.95	1.0	Bärbel	Wöckel'	GDR	21.3.55	2	NC	Dresden	1 Jul 82
10.96	1.2	Marie-José	Pérec	FRA	9.5.68	1	NC	Dijon	27 Jul 91
10.96	2.0	Galina	Malchugina	RUS	17.12.62	2	CIS Ch	Moskva	22 Jun 92
10.96	1.0	Eldece	Clarke-Lewis	BAH	13.2.65	1	Conseil	Fort-de-France	29 Apr 00
		(40)							

Mark	Wind	Name		Nat	Born	Pos	Meet	Venue	Date
10.96	0.4	Muriel	Hurtis	FRA	25.3.79	1	ECp-S	Annecy	22 Jun 02
10.97	0.0	Angella	Issajenko' ¶	CAN	28.9.58	3	ASV	Köln	16 Aug 87
10.97	0.2	Mary	Onyali	NGR	3.2.68	1q2	WCh	Stuttgart	15 Aug 93
10.97	0.1	Pauline	Davis-Thompson	BAH	9.7.66	3	NC	Nassau	21 Jul 00
10.98	0.1	Marina	Zhirova	RUS	6.6.63	2	ECp	Moskva	17 Aug 85
10.98	0.8	Angela	Bailey	CAN	28.2.62	2	BGP	Budapest	6 Jul 87
10.98	1.6	Natalya	Pomoshchnikova'	RUS	9.7.65	2q2	OG	Seoul	24 Sep 88
10.98	0.6	Léonie Myriam	Mani	CMR	21.5.77	2rA	GP	Athína	11 Jun 01
10.99	1.3	Valerie	Brisco-Hooks	USA	6.7.60	1	Pepsi	Westwood	17 May 86
10.99	0.7	Beverly	McDonald	JAM	15.2.70	1	GP II	Doha	7 May 98
		(50)	100th women 11.09, 200th 11.20, 300th 11.28						
Probably semi-automatic timing									
10.87	1.9	Lyudmila	Kondratyeva	RUS	11.4.58	1		Leningrad	3 Jun 80
10.99	1.9	Natalya	Bochina	RUS	4.1.62	2		Leningrad	3 Jun 80
Low altitude best: 10.91	1.6		Sowell			1	TAC	Houston	16 Jun 89
Wind-assisted to 10.78 performances and 10.96 performers									
10.54	3.0		Griffith-Joyner			1	OG	Seoul	25 Sep 88
10.60	3.2		Griffith-Joyner			1h1	OT	Indianapolis	16 Jul 88
10.68	2.2		Jones			1	DNG	Stockholm	1 Aug 00
10.70	2.6		Griffith-Joyner			1s2	OG	Seoul	25 Sep 88
10.75	4.1		Jones			1h3	NC	New Orleans	19 Jun 98
10.77	2.3	Gail	Devers	USA	19.11.66	1	Jen	San José	28 May 94
10.77	2.1		Jones			1	Pre	Eugene	31 May 98
10.77	2.3	Ekateríni	Thánou	GRE	1.2.75	1		Rethymno	28 May 99
10.78	3.1		Ashford			1		Modesto	12 May 84
10.78	5.0	Gwen	Torrence	USA	12.6.65	1q3	OT	Indianapolis	16 Jul 88
10.78	2.3		Ottey			1s2	WCh	Tokyo	27 Aug 91
10.79	3.3	Marlies	Göhr'	GDR	21.3.58	1	NC	Cottbus	16 Jul 80
10.79	2.3	Kelli	White	USA	1.4.77	1		Carson/Los Angeles	1 Jun 03
10.80	2.9	Pam	Marshall	USA	16.8.60	1	TAC	Eugene	20 Jun 86
10.80	2.8	Heike	Drechsler'	GDR	16.12.64	1	Bisl	Oslo	5 Jul 86
10.82	2.2	Silke	Gladisch/Möller	GDR	20.6.64	1s1	WCh	Roma	30 Aug 87
10.84	2.9	Alice	Brown	USA	20.9.60	2	TAC	Eugene	20 Jun 86
10.89	3.1	Kerstin	Behrendt	GDR	2.9.67	2		Berlin	13 Sep 88
10.91	4.6	Carlette	Guidry	USA	4.9.68	1s1	NCAA	Eugene	31 May 91
10.92	3.3	Bärbel	Wöckel'	GDR	21.3.55	2	NC	Cottbus	16 Jul 80
10.92	3.4	Angella	Taylor' ¶	CAN	28.9.58	1s2	CG	Brisbane	4 Oct 82
10.92	3.4	Torri	Edwards	USA	31.1.77	1	MAI	Malmö	7 Aug 00
10.93	3.8	Sonia	Lannaman	GBR	24.3.56	1	ECp/sf	Dublin	17 Jul 77
10.93	3.3	Ingrid	Auerswald'	GDR	2.9.57	3	NC	Cottbus	16 Jul 80
10.93	4.2	Holli	Hyche	USA	6.9.71	2h2	NC	Eugene	16 Jun 93
10.94	3.9	Jackie	Washington	USA	17.7.62	1		Houston	18 May 86
10.94A	3.0	Evette	de Klerk'	RSA	21.8.65	1h	NC	Germiston	20 Apr 90
10.96	2.9	Brenda	Morehead	USA	5.10.57	1s2	AAU	Walnut	16 Jun 79
10.96	4.2	Olga	Naumkina'	RUS	20.5.64	1	Znam	Volgograd	11 Jun 89
10.96A	2.5	Michelle	Finn	USA	8.5.65	1		Sestriere	8 Aug 90
10.96	3.7	Angela	Williams	USA	30.1.80	1		Las Vegas	3 Apr 99
Hand timing									
10.6	0.1	Zhanna	Pintusevich	UKR	6.7.72	1		Kiev	12 Jun 97
10.7		Merlene	Ottey	JAM	10.5.60	1h		Kingston	15 Jul 88
10.7	1.1	Juliet	Cuthbert	JAM	9.4.64	1	NC	Kingston	4 Jul 92
10.7		Mary	Onyali	NGR	3.2.68	1	NC	Lagos	22 Jun 96
10.7	-0.2	Svetlana	Goncharenko	RUS	28.5.71	1		Rostov	30 May 98
10.7w	2.6	Savatheda	Fynes	BAH	17.10.74	1		Nassau	22 Jun 95

200 METRES

Mark	Wind	Name		Nat	Born	Pos	Meet	Venue	Date
21.34WR	1.3	Florence	Griffith-Joyner	USA	21.12.59	1	OG	Seoul	29 Sep 88
21.56WR	1.7		Griffith-Joyner			1s1	OG	Seoul	29 Sep 88
21.62A	-0.6	Marion	Jones	USA	12.10.75	1	WCp	Johannesburg	11 Sep 98
21.64	0.8	Merlene	Ottey	JAM	10.5.60	1	VD	Bruxelles	13 Sep 91
21.66	-1.0		Ottey			1	WK	Zürich	15 Aug 90
21.71WR	0.7	Marita	Koch	GDR	18.2.57	1	v Can	Karl-Marx-Stadt	10 Jun 79
21.71WR	0.3		Koch			1	OD	Potsdam	21 Jul 84
21.71WR	1.2	Heike	Drechsler'	GDR	16.12.64	1	NC	Jena	29 Jun 86
21.71WR	-0.8		Drechsler			1	EC	Stuttgart	29 Aug 86
21.72	1.3	Grace	Jackson	JAM	14.6.61	2	OG	Seoul	29 Sep 88
21.72	-0.1	Gwen	Torrence	USA	12.6.65	1s2	OG	Barcelona	5 Aug 92
21.74	0.4	Marlies	Göhr'	GDR	21.3.58	1	NC	Erfurt	3 Jun 84
21.74	1.2	Silke	Gladisch'	GDR	20.6.64	1	WCh	Roma	3 Sep 87
21.75	-0.1	Juliet	Cuthbert (10)	JAM	9.4.64	2s2	OG	Barcelona	5 Aug 92

Mark	Wind	Name		Nat	Born	Pos	Meet	Venue	Date
21.76	0.3		Koch			1	NC	Dresden	3 Jul 82
21.76	0.7		Griffith-Joyner			1q1	OG	Seoul	28 Sep 88
21.76	-0.8		Jones			1	WK	Zürich	13 Aug 97
21.77	-0.1		Griffith-Joyner			1q2	OT	Indianapolis	22 Jul 88
21.77	1.0		Ottey			1	Herc	Monaco	7 Aug 93
21.77	-0.3		Torrence			1	ASV	Köln	18 Aug 95
21.77	0.6	Inger	Miller	USA	12.6.72	1	WCh	Sevilla	27 Aug 99
21.78	-1.3		Koch			1	NC	Leipzig	11 Aug 85
21.79	1.7		Gladisch			1	NC	Potsdam	22 Aug 87
21.80	-1.1		Ottey			1	Nik	Nice	10 Jul 90
21.80	0.4		Jones			1	GWG	Uniondale, NY	20 Jul 98
21.81	-0.1	Valerie	Brisco	USA	6.7.60	1	OG	Los Angeles	9 Aug 84
21.81	0.4		Ottey			1	ASV	Köln	19 Aug 90
21.81	-0.6		Torrence			1	OG	Barcelona	6 Aug 92
21.81	0.0		Torrence			1	Herc	Monaco	25 Jul 95
21.81	1.6		Jones			1	Pre	Eugene	30 May 99
		(30/12)							
21.83	-0.2	Evelyn	Ashford	USA	15.4.57	1	WCp	Montreal	24 Aug 79
21.85	0.3	Bärbel	Wöckel'	GDR	21.3.55	2	OD	Potsdam	21 Jul 84
21.87	0.0	Irina	Privalova	RUS	22.11.68	2	Herc	Monaco	25 Jul 95
21.93	1.3	Pam	Marshall	USA	16.8.60	2	OT	Indianapolis	23 Jul 88
21.95	0.3	Katrin	Krabbe ¶	GDR	22.11.69	1	EC	Split	30 Aug 90
21.97	1.9	Jarmila	Kratochvílová	CZE	26.1.51	1	PTS	Bratislava	6 Jun 81
21.99	0.9	Chandra	Cheeseborough	USA	10.1.59	2	TAC	Indianapolis	19 Jun 83
21.99	1.1	Marie-José	Pérec	FRA	9.5.68	1	BNP	Villeneuve d'Ascq	2 Jul 93
		(20)							
22.01	-0.5	Anelia	Nuneva'	BUL	30.6.62	1	NC	Sofiya	16 Aug 87
22.01	0.0		Li Xuemei	CHN	5.1.77	1	NG	Shanghai	22 Oct 97
22.04A	0.7	Dawn	Sowell	USA	27.3.66	1	NCAA	Provo	2 Jun 89
22.05	-0.3	Kelli	White	USA	1.4.77	1	WCh	Saint-Denis	28 Aug 03
22.06A	0.7	Evette	de Klerk'	RSA	21.8.65	1		Pietersburg	8 Apr 89
22.07	-0.1	Mary	Onyali	NGR	3.2.68	1	WK	Zürich	14 Aug 96
22.10	-0.1	Kathy	Cook'	GBR	3.5.60	4	OG	Los Angeles	9 Aug 84
22.11A	-0.5	Allyson	Felix	USA	18.11.85	1		Ciudad de México	3 May 03
22.13	1.2	Ewa	Kasprzyk	POL	7.9.57	2	GWG	Moskva	8 Jul 86
22.14	-0.6	Carlette	Guidry	USA	4.9.68	1	NC	Atlanta	23 Jun 96
		(30)							
22.17A	-2.3	Zhanna	Pintusevich	UKR	6.7.72	1		Monachil	9 Jul 97
		22.24	-0.3			2	VD	Bruxelles	30 Aug 02
22.18	-0.6	Dannette	Young-Stone	USA	6.10.64	2	NC	Atlanta	23 Jun 96
22.18	0.9	Galina	Malchugina	RUS	17.12.62	1s2	NC	Sankt Peterburg	4 Jul 96
22.18	0.5	Merlene	Frazer	JAM	27.12.73	1s2	WCh	Sevilla	25 Aug 99
22.19	1.5	Natalya	Bochina	RUS	4.1.62	2	OG	Moskva	30 Jul 80
22.19	0.0	Debbie	Ferguson	BAH	16.1.76	1	GP II	Saint-Denis	3 Jul 99
22.22	0.6	Beverly	McDonald	JAM	15.2.70	2	WCh	Sevilla	27 Aug 99
22.21 WR	1.9	Irena	Szewinska'	POL	24.5.46	1		Potsdam	13 Jun 74
22.22	-0.9	Falilat	Ogunkoya	NGR	12.5.68	1	AfCh	Dakar	22 Aug 98
22.23	0.8	Melinda	Gainsford-Taylor	AUS	1.10.71	1		Stuttgart	13 Jul 97
		(40)							
22.24	0.3	Gesine	Walther	GDR	6.10.62	2	NC	Dresden	3 Jul 82
22.24	0.1	Maya	Azarashvili	GEO	6.4.64	1		Kiyev	16 Aug 88
22.25A	0.8	Angella	Taylor'	CAN	28.9.58	1		Colorado Springs	20 Jul 82
22.25	1.3	Cathy	Freeman	AUS	16.2.73	1	CG	Victoria	26 Aug 94
22.25	1.8	Andrea	Philipp	GER	29.7.71	2s1	WCh	Sevilla	25 Aug 99
22.26	0.0	Christine	Arron	FRA	13.9.73	2	GP II	Saint-Denis	3 Jul 99
22.27	1.2	Elvira	Barbashina'	UZB	25.2.63	3	GWG	Moskva	8 Jul 86
22.27	0.7	Pauline	Davis-Thompson	BAH	9.7.66	2	OG	Sydney	28 Sep 00
22.28	1.1	Fatima	Yusuf	NGR	2.5.71	2q2	WCh	Sevilla	24 Aug 99
22.28	0.7	Susanthika	Jayasinghe	SRI	17.12.75	3	OG	Sydney	28 Sep 00
22.28	0.5	Torri	Edwards	USA	31.1.77	1	GGala	Roma	11 Jul 03
		(51)	100th woman 22.49, 200th woman 22.76						
Indoors									
22.18i		Michelle	Collins	USA	12.2.71	1	WI	Birmingham	15 Mar 03
Wind-assisted									
21.82	3.1	Irina	Privalova	RUS	22.11.68	1	Athl	Lausanne	6 Jul 94
22.16	3.1	Dannette	Young-Stone	USA	6.10.64	2	Athl	Lausanne	6 Jul 94
22.16	3.2	Nanceen	Perry	USA	19.4.77	1		Austin	6 May 00
22.18A	2.8	Melinda	Gainsford-Taylor	AUS	1.10.71	1		Pietersburg	18 Mar 00
22.19A	3.1	Angella	Taylor'	CAN	28.9.58	1		Colorado Springs	21 Jul 82
22.22	2.7	LaTasha	Jenkins	USA	19.12.77	1s1	NCAA	Boise	4 Jun 99

Mark	Wind	Name		Nat	Born	Pos	Meet	Venue	Date
22.25	3.8	Peta-Gaye	Dowdie	JAM	18.1.77	1		Baton Rouge	17 Apr 99
Hand timing									
21.9	-0.1	Svetlana	Goncharenko	RUS	28.5.71	1		Rostov-na-Donu	31 May 98
22.0	-0.6	Marina	Molokova	RUS	24.8.62	1	Ros	Praha	23 Jun 87
21.6w	2.5	Pam	Marshall	USA	16.8.60	1	TAC	San José	26 Jun 87

300 METRES

Times in 300m races

35.30A	Ana Gabriela	Guevara	MEX	4.3.77	1		Ciudad de México	3 May 03
35.46	Kathy	Cook'	GBR	3.5.60	1	Nike	London (CP)	18 Aug 84
35.46	Chandra	Cheeseborough	USA	10.1.59	2	Nike	London (CP)	18 Aug 84
35.68	Marion	Jones	USA	12.10.75	1	MSR	Walnut	22 Apr 01

Indoors

35.45		Irina	Privalova	RUS	22.11.68	1		Moskva	17 Jan 93
35.48	#	Svetlana	Goncharenko	RUS	28.5.71	1		Tampere	4 Feb 98

400 METRES

47.60 WR	Marita	Koch	GDR	18.2.57	1	WCp	Canberra	6 Oct 85
47.99 WR	Jarmila	Kratochvílová	CZE	26.1.51	1	WCh	Helsinki	10 Aug 83
48.16 WR		Koch			1	EC	Athína	8 Sep 82
48.16		Koch			1	Drz	Praha	16 Aug 84
48.22		Koch			1	EC	Stuttgart	28 Aug 86
48.25	Marie-José	Pérec	FRA	9.5.68	1	OG	Atlanta	29 Jul 96
48.26		Koch			1	GO	Dresden	27 Jul 84
48.27	Olga	Vladykina'	UKR	30.6.63	2	WCp	Canberra	6 Oct 85
48.45		Kratochvílová			1	NC	Praha	23 Jul 83
48.59	Tatána	Kocembová'	CZE	2.5.62	2	WCh	Helsinki	10 Aug 83
48.60 WR		Koch			1	ECp	Torino	4 Aug 79
48.60		Vladykina			1	ECp	Moskva	17 Aug 85
48.61		Kratochvílová			1	WCp	Roma	6 Sep 81
48.63	Cathy	Freeman	AUS	16.2.73	2	OG	Atlanta	29 Jul 96
48.65		Bryzgina'			1	OG	Seoul	26 Sep 88
48.73		Kocembová			2	Drz	Praha	16 Aug 84
48.77		Koch			1	v USA	Karl-Marx-Stadt	9 Jul 82
48.82		Kratochvílová			1	Ros	Praha	23 Jun 83
48.83	Valerie	Brisco	USA	6.7.60	1	OG	Los Angeles	6 Aug 84
48.83		Pérec			1	OG	Barcelona	5 Aug 92
48.85		Kratochvílová			2	EC	Athína	8 Sep 82
48.86		Kratochvílová			1	WK	Zürich	18 Aug 82
48.86		Koch			1	NC	Erfurt	2 Jun 84
48.87		Koch			1	VD	Bruxelles	27 Aug 82
48.88		Koch			1	OG	Moskva	28 Jul 80
48.89 WR		Koch			1		Potsdam	29 Jul 79
48.89		Koch			1		Berlin	15 Jul 84
48.89	Ana Gabriela	Guevara	MEX	4.3.77	1	WCh	Saint-Denis	27 Aug 03
48.94 WR		Koch			1	EC	Praha	31 Aug 78
48.96		Vladykina			1	NC	Leningrad	3 Aug 85
	(30/8)							
49.05	Chandra	Cheeseborough	USA	10.1.59	2	OG	Los Angeles	6 Aug 84
49.10	Falilat	Ogunkoya	NGR	12.5.68	3	OG	Atlanta	29 Jul 96
	(10)							
49.11	Olga	Nazarova ¶	RUS	1.6.65	1s1	OG	Seoul	25 Sep 88
49.19	Mariya	Pinigina'	UKR	9.2.58	3	WCh	Helsinki	10 Aug 83
49.24	Sabine	Busch	GDR	21.11.62	2	NC	Erfurt	2 Jun 84
49.28 WR	Irena	Szewinska'	POL	24.5.46	1	OG	Montreal	29 Jul 76
49.28	Pauline	Davis	BAH	9.7.66	4	OG	Atlanta	29 Jul 96
49.29	Charity	Opara ¶	NGR	20.5.72	1	GGala	Roma	14 Jul 98
49.30	Petra	Müller'	GDR	18.7.65	1		Jena	3 Jun 88
49.30	Lorraine	Fenton'	JAM	8.9.73	2	Herc	Monaco	19 Jul 02
49.40	Jearl	Miles-Clark	USA	4.9.66	1	NC	Indianapolis	14 Jun 97
49.42	Grit	Breuer ¶	GER	16.2.72	2	WCh	Tokyo	27 Aug 91
	(20)							
49.43	Kathy	Cook'	GBR	3.5.60	3	OG	Los Angeles	6 Aug 84
49.43A	Fatima	Yusuf	NGR	2.5.71	1		Harare	15 Sep 95
49.47	Aelita	Yurchenko	UKR	1.1.65	2	Kuts	Moskva	4 Sep 88
49.56	Bärbel	Wöckel'	GDR	21.3.55	1		Erfurt	30 May 82
49.57	Grace	Jackson	JAM	14.6.61	1	Nik	Nice	10 Jul 88
49.58	Dagmar	Rübsam'	GDR	3.6.62	3	NC	Erfurt	2 Jun 84
49.59	Marion	Jones	USA	12.10.75	1r6	MSR	Walnut	16 Apr 00
49.59	Katharine	Merry	GBR	21.9.74	1	GP	Athína	11 Jun 01
49.61	Ana Fidelia	Quirot	CUB	23.3.63	1	PAm	Habana	5 Aug 91

Mark	Wind	Name		Nat	Born	Pos	Meet	Venue	Date
49.64		Gwen	Torrence	USA	12.6.65	2	Nik	Nice	15 Jul 92
		(30)							
49.64		Ximena	Restrepo	COL	10.3.69	3	OG	Barcelona	5 Aug 92
49.66		Christina	Lathan'	GDR	28.2.58	3	OG	Moskva	28 Jul 80
49.66		Lillie	Leatherwood	USA	6.7.64	1	TAC	New York	15 Jun 91
49.67		Sandra	Myers	ESP	9.1.61	1	Bisl	Oslo	6 Jul 91
49.74		Anja	Rücker	GER	20.12.72	2	WCh	Sevilla	26 Aug 99
49.75		Gaby	Bussmann	FRG	8.10.59	4	WCh	Helsinki	10 Aug 83
49.78		Natalya	Nazarova	RUS	26.5.79	1	NC	Tula	9 Aug 03
49.79		Sandie	Richards	JAM	6.11.68	2	WCh	Athína	4 Aug 97
49.79		Donna	Fraser	GBR	7.11.72	4	OG	Sydney	25 Sep 00
49.81			Ma Yuqin	CHN	11.9.72	1	NG	Beijing	11 Sep 93
		(40)							
49.84		Diane	Dixon	USA	23.9.64	3s1	OG	Seoul	25 Sep 88
49.86		Ami Mbacké	Thiam	SEN	10.11.76	1	WCh	Edmonton	7 Aug 01
49.87		Denean	Howard/Hill	USA	5.10.64	4s1	OG	Seoul	25 Sep 88
49.87		LaTasha	Colander-Richardson	USA	23.8.76	1	NC	Sacramento	16 Jul 00
49.88		Ionela	Tîrlea	ROM	9.2.76	1	WUG	Palma de Mallorca	12 Jul 99
49.89		Irina	Privalova	RUS	22.11.68	1	Kuts	Moskva	30 Jul 93
49.91		Marita	Payne'	CAN	7.10.60	4	OG	Los Angeles	6 Aug 84
49.91		Jillian	Richardson	CAN	10.3.65	5s1	OG	Seoul	25 Sep 88
49.95		Olga	Kotlyarova	RUS	12.4.76	1	Super	Yokohama	9 Sep 00
49.98		Tatyana	Alekseyeva	RUS	7.10.63	1	NC	Tula	8 Jul 97
		(50)	100th woman 50.60, 200th woman 51.12						
Low altitude best: 49.77			Yusuf			6	OG	Atlanta	29 Jul 96
Hand timing									
48.9		Olga	Nazarova ¶	RUS	1.6.65	1	NP	Vladivostok	13 Sep 88
49.2A		Ana Fidelia	Quirot	CUB	23.3.63	1	AmCp	Bogotá	13 Aug 89

600 METRES

Mark	Wind	Name		Nat	Born	Pos	Meet	Venue	Date
1:22.63		Ana Fidelia	Quirot	CUB	23.3.63	1		Guadalajara	25 Jul 97
1:22.87		Maria Lurdes	Mutola	MOZ	27.10.72	1		Liège (NX)	27 Aug 02
1:23.5		Doina	Melinte	ROM	27.12.56	1		Poiana Brasov	27 Jul 86
1:23.78		Natalya	Khrushchelyova	RUS	30.5.73	2		Liège (NX)	2 Sep 03

800 METRES

Mark	Wind	Name		Nat	Born	Pos	Meet	Venue	Date
1:53.28	WR	Jarmila	Kratochvílová	CZE	26.1.51	1		München	26 Jul 83
1:53.43	WR	Nadezhda	Olizarenko'	UKR	28.11.53	1	OG	Moskva	27 Jul 80
1:54.44		Ana Fidelia	Quirot	CUB	23.3.63	1	WCp	Barcelona	9 Sep 89
1:54.68			Kratochvílová			1	WCh	Helsinki	9 Aug 83
1:54.81		Olga	Mineyeva	RUS	1.9.52	2	OG	Moskva	27 Jul 80
1:54.82			Quirot			1	ASV	Köln	24 Aug 97
1:54.85	WR		Olizarenko			1	Prav	Moskva	12 Jun 80
1:54.94	WR	Tatyana	Kazankina ¶	RUS	17.12.51	1	OG	Montreal	26 Jul 76
1:55.04			Kratochvílová			1	OsloG	Oslo	23 Aug 83
1:55.05		Doina	Melinte	ROM	27.12.56	1	NC	Bucuresti	1 Aug 82
1:55.1 '			Mineyeva			1	Znam	Moskva	6 Jul 80
1:55.19		Maria Lurdes	Mutola	MOZ	27.10.72	1	WK	Zürich	17 Aug 94
1:55.19		Jolanda	Ceplak	SLO	12.9.76	1rA	NA	Heusden	20 Jul 02
1:55.26		Sigrun	Wodars/Grau	GDR	7.11.65	1	WCh	Roma	31 Aug 87
1:55.29			Mutola			2	ASV	Köln	24 Aug 97
1:55.32		Christine	Wachtel (10)	GDR	6.1.65	2	WCh	Roma	31 Aug 87
1:55.41			Mineyeva			1	EC	Athína	8 Sep 82
1:55.42		Nikolina	Shtereva	BUL	25.1.55	2	OG	Montreal	26 Jul 76
1:55.43			Mutola			1	WCh	Stuttgart	17 Aug 93
1:55.46		Tatyana	Providokhina	RUS	26.3.53	3	OG	Moskva	27 Jul 80
1:55.5			Mineyeva			1	Kuts	Podolsk	21 Aug 82
1:55.54		Ellen	van Langen	NED	9.2.66	1	OG	Barcelona	3 Aug 92
1:55.54			Liu Dong	CHN	24.12.73	1	NG	Beijing	9 Sep 93
1:55.55			Mutola			1	GP	Madrid (C)	19 Jul 03
1:55.56		Lyubov	Gurina	RUS	6.8.57	3	WCh	Roma	31 Aug 87
1:55.60		Elfi	Zinn	GDR	24.8.53	3	OG	Montreal	26 Jul 76
1:55.62			Mutola			1A	WK	Zürich	4 Aug 93
1:55.68		Ella	Kovacs	ROM	11.12.64	1	RomIC	Bucuresti	2 Jun 85
1:55.69		Irina	Podyalovskaya	RUS	19.10.59	1	Izv	Kiyev	22 Jun 84
1:55.70			Wodars			2	WCp	Barcelona	9 Sep 89
		(30/18)							
1:55.74		Anita	Weiss'	GDR	16.7.55	4	OG	Montreal	26 Jul 76
1:55.87		Svetlana	Masterkova	RUS	17.1.68	1	Kuts	Moskva	18 Jun 99
		(20)							

Mark	Wind	Name		Nat	Born	Pos	Meet	Venue	Date
1:55.96		Lyudmila	Veselkova	RUS	25.10.50	2	EC	Athína	8 Sep 82
1:55.96		Yekaterina	Podkopayeva'	RUS	11.6.52	1		Leningrad	27 Jul 83
1:55.99		Liliya	Nurutdinova ¶	RUS	15.12.63	2	OG	Barcelona	3 Aug 92
1:56.0	WR	Valentina	Gerasimova	KAZ	15.5.48	1	NC	Kiyev	12 Jun 76
1:56.0		Inna	Yevseyeva	UKR	14.8.64	1		Kiyev	25 Jun 88
1:56.09		Zulia	Calatayud	CUB	9.11.79	1	Herc	Monaco	19 Jul 02
1:56.1		Ravilya	Agletdinova'	BLR	10.2.60	2	Kuts	Podolsk	21 Aug 82
1:56.2 '		Totka	Petrova ¶	BUL	17.12.56	1		Paris	6 Jul 79
1:56.2		Tatyana	Mishkel	UKR	10.6.52	3	Kuts	Podolsk	21 Aug 82
1:56.21		Martina	Kämpfert'	GDR	11.11.59	4	OG	Moskva	27 Jul 80
		(30)							
1:56.21		Zamira	Zaytseva	UZB	16.2.53	2		Leningrad	27 Jul 83
1:56.21		Kelly	Holmes	GBR	19.4.70	2	GPF	Monaco	9 Sep 95
1:56.24			Qu Yunxia	CHN	25.12.72	2	NG	Beijing	9 Sep 93
1:56.40		Jearl	Miles-Clark	USA	4.9.66	3	WK	Zürich	11 Aug 99
1:56.42		Paula	Ivan	ROM	20.7.63	1	Balk	Ankara	16 Jul 88
1:56.44		Svetlana	Styrkina	RUS	1.1.49	5	OG	Montreal	26 Jul 76
1:56.51		Slobodanka	Colovic	YUG	10.1.65	1		Beograd	17 Jun 87
1:56.53		Patricia	Djaté	FRA	3.1.71	3	GPF	Mpnaco	9 Sep 95
1:56.56		Ludmila	Formanová	CZE	2.1.74	4	WK	Zürich	11 Aug 99
1:56.57		Zoya	Rigel	RUS	15.10.52	3	EC	Praha	31 Aug 78
		(40)							
1:56.60		Natalya	Tsyganova	RUS	7.2.71	1	NC	Tula	25 Jul 00
1:56.6		Tamara	Sorokina'	RUS	15.8.50	5	Kuts	Podolsk	21 Aug 82
1:56.61		Yelena	Afanasyeva	RUS	1.3.67	3	WK	Zürich	13 Aug 97
1:56.62		Tina	Paulino	MOZ	7.7.73	2	NYG	New York	22 May 93
1:56.64		Nadezhda	Loboyko	KAZ	30.6.61	1	NC	Kiyev	7 Jul 90
1:56.64		Stephanie	Graf	AUT	26.4.73	2	OG	Sydney	25 Sep 00
1:56.67		Fita	Lovin'	ROM	14.1.51	2	Prav	Moskva	12 Jun 80
1:56.68		Letitia	Vriesde	SUR	5.10.64	2	WCh	Göteborg	13 Aug 95
1:56.7		Dalia	Matuseviciene	LTU	12.11.62	2		Kiyev	25 Jun 88
1:56.78		Lyudmila	Borisova	RUS	30.7.59	3	Izv	Kiyev	22 Jun 84
		(50)	100th woman 1:57.90, 200th woman 1:59.07						
Indoors									
1:55.85		Stephanie	Graf	AUT	26.4.73	2	EI	Wien	3 Mar 02

1000 METRES

Mark	Wind	Name		Nat	Born	Pos	Meet	Venue	Date
2:28.98	WR	Svetlana	Masterkova	RUS	17.1.68	1	VD	Bruxelles	23 Aug 96
2:29.34	WR	Maria Lurdes	Mutola	MOZ	27.10.72	1	VD	Bruxelles	25 Aug 95
2:30.6	WR	Tatyana	Providokhina	RUS	26.3.53	1		Podolsk	20 Aug 78
2:30.67	WR	Christine	Wachtel	GDR	6.1.65	1	ISTAF	Berlin	17 Aug 90
2:30.85		Martina	Kämpfert'	GDR	11.11.59	1		Berlin	9 Jul 80
2:31.50		Natalya	Artyomova ¶	RUS	5.1.63	1	ISTAF	Berlin	10 Sep 91
2:31.5		Maricica	Puica	ROM	29.7.50	1		Poiana Brasov	1 Jun 86
2:31.51		Sandra	Gasser ¶	SUI	27.7.62	1		Jerez de la Frontera	13 Sep 89
2:31.6 '		Beate	Liebich	GDR	21.2.58	2		Berlin	9 Jul 80
2:31.65		Olga	Dvirna	RUS	11.2.53	1		Athína	1 Sep 82

1500 METRES

Mark	Wind	Name		Nat	Born	Pos	Meet	Venue	Date
3:50.46	WR		Qu Yunxia	CHN	25.12.72	1	NG	Beijing	11 Sep 93
3:50.98			Jiang Bo	CHN	13.3.77	1	NG	Shanghai	18 Oct 97
3:51.34			Lang Yinglai	CHN	22.8.79	2	NG	Shanghai	18 Oct 97
3:51.92			Wang Junxia	CHN	9.1.73	2	NG	Beijing	11 Sep 93
3:52.47	WR	Tatyana	Kazankina ¶	RUS	17.12.51	1	WK	Zürich	13 Aug 80
3:53.91			Yin Lili ¶	CHN	11.11.79	3	NG	Shanghai	18 Oct 97
3:53.96		Paula	Ivan'	ROM	20.7.63	1	OG	Seoul	1 Oct 88
3:53.97			Lan Lixin	CHN	14.2.79	4	NG	Shanghai	18 Oct 97
3:54.23		Olga	Dvirna	RUS	11.2.53	1	NC	Kiyev	27 Jul 82
3:54.52			Zhang Ling (10)	CHN	13.4.80	5	NG	Shanghai	18 Oct 97
3:55.0 '	WR		Kazankina ¶			1	Znam	Moskva	6 Jul 80
3:55.01			Lan Lixin			1h2	NG	Shanghai	17 Oct 97
3:55.07			Dong Yanmei	CHN	16.2.77	6	NG	Shanghai	18 Oct 97
3:55.30		Hassiba	Boulmerka	ALG	10.7.68	1	OG	Barcelona	8 Aug 92
3:55.33		Süreyya	Ayhan	TUR	6.9.78	1	VD	Bruxelles	5 Sep 03
3:55.38			Qu Yunxia			2h2	NG	Shanghai	17 Oct 97
3:55.47			Zhang Ling			3h2	NG	Shanghai	17 Oct 97
3:55.60			Ayhan			1	WK	Zürich	15 Aug 03
3:55.82			Dong Yanmei			4h2	NG	Shanghai	17 Oct 97
3:56.0	WR		Kazankina ¶			1		Podolsk	28 Jun 76

Mark	Wind	Name		Nat	Born	Pos	Meet	Venue	Date
3:56.14		Zamira	Zaytseva	UZB	16.2.53	2	NC	Kiyev	27 Jul 82
3:56.22			Ivan			1	WK	Zürich	17 Aug 88
3:56.31			Liu Dong	CHN	24.12.73	5h2	NG	Shanghai	17 Oct 97
3:56.50		Tatyana	Pozdnyakova	RUS	4.3.56	3	NC	Kiyev	27 Jul 82
3:56.56			Kazankina ¶			1	OG	Moskva	1 Aug 80
3:56.63		Nadezhda	Ralldugina	UKR	15.11.57	1	Drz	Praha	18 Aug 84
3:56.65		Yekaterina	Podkopayeva'	RUS	11.6.52	1		Rieti	2 Sep 84
3:56.7 '		Lyubov	Smolka	UKR	29.11.52	2	Znam	Moskva	6 Jul 80
3:56.7		Doina	Melinte (20)	ROM	27.12.56	1		Bucuresti	12 Jul 86
3:56.77+		Svetlana	Masterkova	RUS	17.1.68	1	WK	Zürich	14 Aug 96
		(30/21)							
3:56.8 '		Nadezhda	Olizarenko'	UKR	28.11.53	3	Znam	Moskva	6 Jul 80
3:56.91		Lyudmila	Rogachova	RUS	30.10.66	2	OG	Barcelona	8 Aug 92
3:56.97		Gabriela	Szabo	ROM	14.11.75	1	Herc	Monaco	8 Aug 98
3:57.03			Liu Jing	CHN	.2.71	6h2	NG	Shanghai	17 Oct 97
3:57.05		Svetlana	Guskova	MDA	19.8.59	4	NC	Kiyev	27 Jul 82
3:57.12		Mary	Decker/Slaney	USA	4.8.58	1	vNord	Stockholm	26 Jul 83
3:57.22		Maricica	Puica	ROM	29.7.50	1		Bucuresti	1 Jul 84
3:57.40		Suzy	Favor Hamilton	USA	8.8.68	1	Bisl	Oslo	28 Jul 00
3:57.4 '		Totka	Petrova ¶	BUL	17.12.56	1	Balk	Athína	11 Aug 79
		(30)							
3:57.41		Jackline	Maranga	KEN	16.12.77	3	Herc	Monaco	8 Aug 98
3:57.46			Zhang Linli	CHN	6.3.73	3	NG	Beijing	11 Sep 93
3:57.71		Christiane	Wartenberg'	GDR	27.10.56	2	OG	Moskva	1 Aug 80
3:57.71		Carla	Sacramento	POR	10.12.71	4	Herc	Monaco	8 Aug 98
3:57.72		Galina	Zakharova	RUS	7.9.56	1	NP	Baku	14 Sep 84
3:57.92		Tatyana	Dorovskikh ¶	UKR	12.8.61	4	OG	Barcelona	8 Aug 92
3:58.07		Kelly	Holmes	GBR	19.4.70	1		Sheffield	29 Jun 97
3:58.12		Naomi	Mugo	KEN	2.1.77	5	Herc	Monaco	8 Aug 98
3:58.20		Anita	Weyermann	SUI	8.12.77	6	Herc	Monaco	8 Aug 98
3:58.2 '		Natalia	Marasescu' ¶	ROM	3.10.52	1	NC	Bucuresti	13 Jul 79
		(40)							
3:58.29		Violeta	Szekely' ¶	ROM	26.3.65	1	Herc	Monaco	18 Aug 00
3:58.37		Tatyana	Providokhina	RUS	26.3.53	1	Kuts	Podolsk	22 Aug 82
3:58.38		Kutre	Dulecha	ETH	22.8.78	7	Herc	Monaco	8 Aug 98
3:58.40		Ravilya	Agletdinova'	BLR	10.2.60	1	ECp	Moskva	18 Aug 85
3:58.5 '		Ileana	Silai ¶	ROM	14.10.41	2	NC	Bucuresti	13 Jul 79
3:58.52		Tatyana	Tomashova	RUS	1.7.75	1	WCh	Saint-Denis	31 Aug 03
3:58.64			Wang Renmei	CHN	5.7.70	4	NG	Beijing	11 Sep 93
3:58.65		Gabriella	Dorio	ITA	26.6.57	2		Tirrenia	25 Aug 82
3:58.67		Hildegard	Körner'	GDR	20.12.59	2	WCh	Roma	5 Sep 87
3:58.71		Lyubov	Kremlyova ¶	RUS	21.12.61	1	WK	Zürich	19 Aug 92
		(50)	100th woman 4:01.00, 200th woman 4:04.29						

1 MILE

Mark	Wind	Name		Nat	Born	Pos	Meet	Venue	Date
4:12.56 WR		Svetlana	Masterkova	RUS	17.1.68	1	WK	Zürich	14 Aug 96
4:15.61 WR		Paula	Ivan'	ROM	20.7.63	1	Nik	Nice	10 Jul 89
4:15.8		Natalya	Artyomova ¶	RUS	5.1.63	1		Leningrad	5 Aug 84
4:16.71 WR		Mary	Slaney (Decker)	USA	4.8.58	1	WK	Zürich	21 Aug 85
4:17.25		Sonia	O'Sullivan	IRL	28.11.69	1	Bisl	Oslo	22 Jul 94
4:17.33		Maricica	Puica	ROM	29.7.50	2	WK	Zürich	21 Aug 85
4:17.57		Zola	Budd'	GBR	26.5.66	3	WK	Zürich	21 Aug 85
4:18.13		Doina	Melinte	ROM	27.12.56	1	Bisl	Oslo	14 Jul 90
Indoors									
4:17.14		Doina	Melinte	ROM	27.12.56	1		East Rutherford	9 Feb 90

2000 METRES

Mark	Wind	Name		Nat	Born	Pos	Meet	Venue	Date
5:25.36 WR		Sonia	O'Sullivan	IRL	28.11.69	1	TSB	Edinburgh	8 Jul 94
5:26.93		Yvonne	Murray	GBR	4.10.64	2	TSB	Edinburgh	8 Jul 94
5:28.69 WR		Maricica	Puica	ROM	29.7.50	1	PTG	London (CP)	11 Jul 86
5:28.72 WR		Tatyana	Kazankina ¶	RUS	17.12.51	1		Moskva	4 Aug 84
5:29.43+			Wang Junxia	CHN	9.1.73	1h2	NG	Beijing	12 Sep 93
5:29.64		Tatyana	Pozdnyakova	UKR	4.3.56	2		Moskva	4 Aug 84
5:30.19		Zola	Budd'	GBR	26.5.66	3	PTG	London (CP)	11 Jul 86
5:30.92		Galina	Zakharova	RUS	7.9.56	3		Moskva	4 Aug 84
Indoors									
5:30.53		Gabriela	Szabo	ROM	14.11.75	1		Sindelfingen	8 Mar 98

3000 METRES

Mark	Wind	Name		Nat	Born	Pos	Meet	Venue	Date
8:06.11 WR			Wang Junxia	CHN	9.1.73	1	NG	Beijing	13 Sep 93
8:12.18			Qu Yunxia	CHN	25.12.72	2	NG	Beijing	13 Sep 93

Mark	Wind	Name		Nat	Born	Pos	Meet	Venue	Date
8:12.19	WR		Wang Junxia			1h2	NG	Beijing	12 Sep 93
8:12.27			Qu Yunxia			2h2	NG	Beijing	12 Sep 93
8:16.50			Zhang Linli	CHN	6.3.73	3	NG	Beijing	13 Sep 93
8:19.78			Ma Liyan	CHN	6.9.68	3h2	NG	Beijing	12 Sep 93
8:21.26			Ma Liyan			4	NG	Beijing	13 Sep 93
8:21.42		Gabriela	Szabo	ROM	14.11.75	1	Herc	Monaco	19 Jul 02
8:21.64		Sonia	O'Sullivan	IRL	28.11.69	1	TSB	London (CP)	15 Jul 94
8:21.84			Zhang Lirong	CHN	3.3.73	5	NG	Beijing	13 Sep 93
8:22.06	WR		Zhang Linli			1h1	NG	Beijing	12 Sep 93
8:22.20		Paula	Radcliffe	GBR	17.12.73	2	Herc	Monaco	19 Jul 02
8:22.44			Zhang Lirong			2h1	NG	Beijing	12 Sep 93
8:22.62	WR	Tatyana	Kazankina ¶	RUS	17.12.51	1		Leningrad	26 Aug 84
8:23.23		Edith	Masai (10)	KEN	4.4.67	3	Herc	Monaco	19 Jul 02
8:23.26		Olga	Yegorova	RUS	28.3.72	1	WK	Zürich	17 Aug 01
8:23.75			Yegorova			1	GP	Saint-Denis	6 Jul 01
8:23.96			Yegorova			1	GGala	Roma	29 Jun 01
8:24.19			Szabo			2	WK	Zürich	17 Aug 01
8:24.31			Szabo			1	GP	Paris	29 Jul 98
8:25.03			Szabo			1	WK	Zürich	11 Aug 99
8:25.40		Yelena	Zadorozhnaya	RUS	3.12.77	2	GGala	Roma	29 Jun 01
8:25.56		Tatyana	Tomashova	RUS	1.7.75	3	GGala	Roma	29 Jun 01
8:25.59			Szabo			1	GP	Paris (C)	21 Jul 99
8:25.62		Berhane	Adere	ETH	21.7.73	3	WK	Zürich	17 Aug 01
8:25.82			Szabo			1	VD	Bruxelles	3 Sep 99
8:25.83		Mary	Slaney	USA	4.8.58	1	GGALA	Roma	7 Sep 85
8:26.14			Adere			1	VD	Bruxelles	30 Aug 02
8:26.15			Szabo			2	VD	Bruxelles	30 Aug 02
8:26.35			Szabo			1	WK	Zürich	11 Aug 00
		(30/15)							
8:26.48		Zahra	Ouaziz	MAR	20.12.69	2	WK	Zürich	11 Aug 99
8:26.53		Tatyana	Samolenko' ¶	UKR	12.8.61	1	OG	Seoul	25 Sep 88
8:26.78	WR	Svetlana	Ulmasova	UZB	4.2.53	1	NC	Kiyev	25 Jul 82
8:27.12	WR	Lyudmila	Bragina	RUS	24.7.43	1	v USA	College Park	7 Aug 76
8:27.15		Paula	Ivan'	ROM	20.7.63	2	OG	Seoul	25 Sep 88
		(20)							
8:27.62		Gete	Wami	ETH	11.12.74	4	WK	Zürich	17 Aug 01
8:27.83		Maricica	Puica	ROM	29.7.50	2	GGALA	Roma	7 Sep 85
8:28.80		Marta	Domínguez	ESP	3.11.75	3	WK	Zürich	11 Aug 00
8:28.83		Zola	Budd'	GBR	26.5.66	3	GGALA	Roma	7 Sep 85
8:29.02		Yvonne	Murray	GBR	4.10.64	3	OG	Seoul	25 Sep 88
8:29.14		Lydia	Cheromei	KEN	11.5.77	5	WK	Zürich	11 Aug 00
8:29.36		Svetlana	Guskova	MDA	19.8.59	2	NC	Kiyev	25 Jul 82
8:30.18		Mariya	Pantyukhova	RUS	14.8.74	4	WK	Zürich	11 Aug 99
8:30.22		Carla	Sacramento	POR	10.12.71	2	Herc	Monaco	4 Aug 99
8:30.39		Irina	Mikitenko	GER	23.8.72	6	WK	Zürich	11 Aug 00
		(30)							
8:30.45		Yelena	Romanova	RUS	20.3.63	4	OG	Seoul	25 Sep 88
8:30.59		Daniela	Yordanova	BUL	8.3.76	5	GP	Saint-Denis	6 Jul 01
8:30.66		Fernanda	Ribeiro	POR	23.6.69	3	Herc	Monaco	4 Aug 99
8:30.95		Tegla	Loroupe	KEN	9.5.73	2	Herc	Monaco	18 Aug 00
8:31.27		Joanne	Pavey	GBR	20.9.73	4	VD	Bruxelles	30 Aug 02
8:31.67		Natalya	Artyomova ¶	RUS	5.1.63	5	OG	Seoul	25 Sep 88
8:31.69		Lidia	Chojecka	POL	25.1.77	5	VD	Bruxelles	30 Aug 02
8:31.75		Grete	Waitz'	NOR	1.10.53	1	OsloG	Oslo	17 Jul 79
8:31.94		Elvan	Abeylegesse	TUR	11.9.82	6	VD	Bruxelles	30 Aug 02
8:32.00		Elana	Meyer'	RSA	10.10.66	1		Durban	29 Apr 91
		(40)							
8:32.0		Tatyana	Pozdnyakova	UKR	4.3.56	1		Ryazan	11 Aug 84
8:32.17		Angela	Chalmers	CAN	6.9.63	1	CG	Victoria	23 Aug 94
8:32.70		Katalin	Szentgyörgyi	HUN	1.1.79	6	GP	Saint-Denis	6 Jul 01
8:32.80		Ayelech	Worku	ETH	12.6.79	7	VD	Bruxelles	30 Aug 02
8:32.89		Alesya	Turova	BLR	6.12.79	7	GP	Saint-Denis	6 Jul 01
8:33.07			Dong Yanmei	CHN	16.2.77	1	GP	Athína	28 Jun 00
8:33.40		Galina	Zakharova	RUS	7.9.56	3	NC	Kiyev	25 Jul 82
8:33.53		Natalia	Marasescu' ¶	ROM	3.10.52	2	EC	Praha	29 Aug 78
8:33.53		Yelena	Sipatova	RUS	7.6.55	1		Moskva	12 Jul 80
8:33.85		Asmae	Leghzaoui ¶	MAR	30.8.76	3	Herc	Monaco	18 Aug 00
		(50)	100th woman 8:39.94, 200th 8:47.04						
Indoors:	8:33.82	Elly	van Hulst	NED	9.6.59	1	WI	Budapest	4 Mar 89

Mark	Wind	Name		Nat	Born	Pos	Meet	Venue	Date

5000 METRES

Mark	Wind	Name		Nat	Born	Pos	Meet	Venue	Date
14:28.09	WR		Jiang Bo	CHN	13.3.77	1	NG	Shanghai	23 Oct 97
14:29.32		Olga	Yegorova	RUS	28.3.72	1	ISTAF	Berlin	31 Aug 01
14:29.32		Berhane	Adere	ETH	21.7.73	1	Bisl	Oslo	27 Jun 03
14:29.82			Dong Yanmei	CHN	16.2.77	2	NG	Shanghai	23 Oct 97
14:30.88		Gete	Wami	ETH	11.12.74	1	NA	Heusden	5 Aug 00
14:31.27	WR		Dong Yanmei			1h1	NG	Shanghai	21 Oct 97
14:31.30			Jiang Bo			2h1	NG	Shanghai	21 Oct 97
14:31.42		Paula	Radcliffe	GBR	17.12.73	1	CG	Manchester	28 Jul 02
14:31.48		Gabriela	Szabo	ROM	14.11.75	1	ISTAF	Berlin	1 Sep 98
14:31.69			Wami			2	ISTAF	Berlin	31 Aug 01
14:32.08		Zahra	Ouaziz	MAR	20.12.69	2	ISTAF	Berlin	1 Sep 98
14:32.33			Liu Shixiang ¶	CHN	13.1.71	3h1	NG	Shanghai	21 Oct 97
14:32.44			Radcliffe			3	ISTAF	Berlin	31 Aug 01
14:33.04		Werknesh	Kidane (10)	ETH	21.11.81	2	Bisl	Oslo	27 Jun 03
14:33.65			Adere			1	BrGP	London (CP)	23 Aug 02
14:34.29			Szabo			2	BrGP	London (CP)	23 Aug 02
14:36.08			Wami		4	3	ISTAF	Berlin	1 Sep 98
14:36.45	WR	Fernanda	Ribeiro	POR	23.6.69	1		Hechtel	22 Jul 95
14:37.33	WR	Ingrid	Kristiansen'	NOR	21.3.56	1		Stockholm	5 Aug 86
14:38.14			Liu Shixiang			3	NG	Shanghai	23 Oct 97
14:39.22		Tatyana	Tomashova	RUS	1.7.75	4	ISTAF	Berlin	31 Aug 01
14:39.83		Leah	Malot	KEN	7.6.72	1	ISTAF	Berlin	1 Sep 00
14:39.94		Tirunesh	Dibaba	ETH	2.6.85	3	Bisl	Oslo	27 Jun 03
14:39.96			Yin Lili ¶	CHN	11.11.79	4	NG	Shanghai	23 Oct 97
14:40.19			Ouaziz			1	DNG	Stockholm	5 Aug 98
14:40.34		Meseret	Defar	ETH	19.11.83	1	GGala	Roma	11 Jul 03
14:40.41			Sun Yingjie	CHN	3.10.77	1	AsiG	Busan	12 Oct 02
14:40.47		Yelena	Zadorozhnaya	RUS	3.12.77	1	ECp-S	Bremen	24 Jun 01
14:40.59			Szabo			1	ISTAF	Berlin	7 Sep 99
14:40.61			Szabo			2	ISTAF	Berlin	1 Sep 00
		(30/19)							
14:41.02		Sonia	O'Sullivan	IRL	28.11.69	2	OG	Sydney	25 Sep 00
14:41.23		Ayelech	Worku	ETH	12.6.79	1	BrGP	London (CP)	5 Aug 00
14:41.67		Ejagayou	Dibaba	ETH	21.3.82	3	GGala	Roma	11 Jul 03
14:42.03		Irina	Mikitenko	GER	23.8.72	3	ISTAF	Berlin	7 Sep 99
14:44.05		Elana	Meyer	RSA	10.10.66	2		Hechtel	22 Jul 95
14:44.22		Derartu	Tulu	ETH	21.3.72	1	VD	Bruxelles	5 Sep 03
14:44.50		Roberta	Brunet	ITA	20.5.65	2	ASV	Köln	16 Aug 96
14:44.95		Julia	Vaquero	ESP	18.9.70	3	Bisl	Oslo	5 Jul 96
14:45.33			Lan Lixin	CHN	14.2.79	2h2	NG	Shanghai	21 Oct 97
14:45.35		Regina	Jacobs	USA	28.8.63	1	NC	Sacramento	21 Jul 00
		(30)							
14:45.35		Edith	Masai	KEN	4.4.67	1h1	WCh	Saint-Denis	26 Aug 03
14:45.71			Song Liqing ¶	CHN	.1.80	3h2	NG	Shanghai	21 Oct 97
14:45.95		Tegla	Loroupe	KEN	9.5.73	3	BrGP	London (CP)	5 Aug 00
14:46.41		Rose	Cheruiyot	KEN	21.7.76	3	ASV	Köln	16 Aug 96
14:46.71		Sally	Barsosio	KEN	21.3.78	3	VD	Bruxelles	22 Aug 97
14:46.72		Lydia	Cheromei	KEN	11.5.77	2	ISTAF	Berlin	26 Aug 97
14:47.20			Dong Zhaoxia	CHN	13.11.74	5	NG	Shanghai	23 Oct 97
14:47.51		Pauline	Konga	KEN	10.4.70	6	ASV	Köln	16 Aug 96
14:47.60		Benita	Johnson	AUS	6.5.79	3	ISTAF	Berlin (P)	6 Sep 02
14:47.70		Isabella	Ochichi	KEN	28.10.79	2	VD	Bruxelles	5 Sep 03
		(40)							
14:47.71		Jelena	Prokopcuka	LAT	21.9.76	5	DNG	Stockholm	1 Aug 00
14:47.79		Yamna	Belkacem	FRA	20.2.74	6	DNG	Stockholm	1 Aug 00
14:48.07	WR	Zola	Budd'	GBR	26.5.66	1	McV	London (CP)	26 Aug 85
14:48.31		Asmae	Leghzaoui ¶	MAR	30.8.76	4	ISTAF	Berlin	1 Sep 00
14:48.33		Marta	Domínguez	ESP	3.11.75	4h1	WCh	Saint-Denis	26 Aug 03
14:48.45			Wang Dongmei	CHN	3.12.72	6	NG	Shanghai	23 Oct 97
14:48.66		Joanne	Pavey	GBR	20.9.73	4	ISTAF	Berlin (P)	6 Sep 02
14:49.40		Catherina	McKiernan	IRL	30.11.69	7	ASV	Köln	16 Aug 96
14:51.62		Deena	Drossin	USA	14.2.73	9	DNG	Stockholm	1 Aug 00
14:51.69		Ebru	Kavaklioglou	TUR	14.3.70	5	WCh	Sevilla	27 Aug 99
		(ex Yelena	Kopytova	RUS)					
		(50)	100th woman 15:06.08, 200th woman 15:18.01						

1 HOUR

Mark	Wind	Name		Nat	Born	Pos	Meet	Venue	Date
18,340	WR	Tegla	Loroupe	KEN	9.5.73	1		Borgholzhausen	7 Aug 98
18,084	WR	Silvana	Cruciata	ITA	15.2.53	1		Roma	2 May 81

Mark	Wind	Name		Nat	Born	Pos	Meet	Venue	Date

10,000 METRES

Mark	Wind	Name		Nat	Born	Pos	Meet	Venue	Date
29:31.78	WR		Wang Junxia	CHN	9.1.73	1	NG	Beijing	8 Sep 93
30:01.09		Paula	Radcliffe	GBR	17.12.73	1	EC	München	6 Aug 02
30:04.18		Berhane	Adere	ETH	21.7.73	1	WCh	Saint-Denis	23 Aug 03
30:07.15		Werknesh	Kidane	ETH	21.11.81	2	WCh	Saint-Denis	23 Aug 03
30:07.20			Sun Yingjie	CHN	3.10.77	3	WCh	Saint-Denis	23 Aug 03
30:12.53		Lornah	Kiplagat (KEN)	NED	20.3.74	4	WCh	Saint-Denis	23 Aug 03
30:13.37			Zhong Huandi	CHN	28.6.67	2	NG	Beijing	8 Sep 93
30:13.74	WR	Ingrid	Kristiansen'	NOR	21.3.56	1	Bisl	Oslo	5 Jul 86
30:17.49		Derartu	Tulu	ETH	21.3.72	1	OG	Sydney	30 Sep 00
30:22.48		Gete	Wami	ETH	11.12.74	2	OG	Sydney	30 Sep 00
30:22.88		Fernanda	Ribeiro	POR	23.6.69	3	OG	Sydney	30 Sep 00
30:23.07		Alla	Zhilyayeva	RUS	5.2.69	5	WCh	Saint-Denis	23 Aug 03
30:23.25			Kristiansen			1	EC	Stuttgart	30 Aug 86
30:24.56			Wami			1	WCh	Sevilla	26 Aug 99
30:26.20		Galina	Bogomolova	RUS	15.10.77	6	WCh	Saint-Denis	23 Aug 03
30:26.97			Radcliffe			4	OG	Sydney	30 Sep 00
30:27.13			Radcliffe			2	WCh	Sevilla	26 Aug 99
30:28.26			Sun Yingjie			1	AsiG	Busan	8 Oct 02
30:31.55			Xing Huina	CHN	25.2.84	7	WCh	Saint-Denis	23 Aug 03
30:32.03		Tegla	Loroupe	KEN	9.5.73	3	WCh	Sevilla	26 Aug 99
30:37.26			Loroupe			5	OG	Sydney	30 Sep 00
30:37.68		Benita	Johnson	AUS	6.5.79	8	WCh	Saint-Denis	23 Aug 03
30:38.09			Dong Yanmei	CHN	16.2.77	1	NG	Shanghai	19 Oct 97
30:39.41			Lan Lixin	CHN	14.2.79	2	NG	Shanghai	19 Oct 97
30:39.98			Yin Lili ¶	CHN	11.11.79	3	NG	Shanghai	19 Oct 97
30:40.70			Radcliffe			1rA	EChall	Barakaldo	10 Apr 99
30:41.40			Kidane			1	GP II	Stanford	7 Jun 03
30:46.48			Bogomolova			1	NC	Tula	3 Aug 03
30:47.22			Dong Zhaoxia	CHN	13.11.74	4	NG	Shanghai	19 Oct 97
30:47.59		Sonia	O'Sullivan	IRL	28.11.69	2	EC	München	6 Aug 02
30:47.72			Wang Dongmei	CHN	3.12.72	5	NG	Shanghai	19 Oct 97
		(32/22)							
30:48.89		Yoko	Shibui	JPN	14.3.79	1		Stanford	3 May 02
30:50.32		Deena	Drossin	USA	14.2.73	2		Stanford	3 May 02
30:51.81		Kayoko	Fukushi	JPN	25.3.82	2	AsiG	Busan	8 Oct 02
30:52.51		Elana	Meyer	RSA	10.10.66	1	WCp	London (CP)	10 Sep 94
30:55.83			Liu Shixiang ¶	CHN	13.1.71	6	NG	Shanghai	19 Oct 97
30:57.07		Liz	McColgan	GBR	24.5.64	1	APM	Hengelo	25 Jun 91
30:57.21		Olga	Bondarenko'	RUS	2.6.60	2	EC	Stuttgart	30 Aug 86
30:57.70		Leah	Malot	KEN	7.6.72	2	NA	Heusden	5 Aug 00
		(30)							
30:57.83		Lydia	Grigoryeva	RUS	21.1.74	3	NC	Tula	3 Aug 03
30:59.92		Merima	Hashim	ETH	.81	3	NA	Heusden	5 Aug 00
31:01.07		Ejagayou	Dibaba	ETH	21.3.82	9	WCh	Saint-Denis	23 Aug 03
31:03.60		Marleen	Renders	BEL	24.12.68	4	NA	Heusden	5 Aug 00
31:03.62		Kathrin	Ullrich'	GER	14.8.67	1	ECp	Frankfurt-am-Main	30 Jun 91
31:04.00		Lyudmila	Biktasheva	RUS	25.7.74	3	EC	München	6 Aug 02
31:05.57		Maura	Viceconte	ITA	3.10.67	5	NA	Heusden	5 Aug 00
31:06.14		Jelena	Prokopcuka	LAT	21.9.76	10	WCh	Saint-Denis	23 Aug 03
31:06.20		Lucy	Wangui	KEN	24.3.84	1rA		Okayama	27 Sep 03
31:06.94			Li Ji ¶	CHN	19.9.79	7	OG	Sydney	30 Sep 00
		(40)							
31:07.88		Jill	Hunter	GBR	14.10.66	2	ECp	Frankfurt-am-Main	30 Jun 91
31:08.41		Catherina	McKiernan	IRL	30.11.69	1		Villeneuve d'Ascq	17 Jun 95
31:09.25			Zhang Lirong	CHN	3.3.73	3	NG	Beijing	8 Sep 93
31:09.40		Yelena	Zhupiyova'	UKR	18.4.60	2	WCh	Roma	4 Sep 87
31:09.46		Yuko	Kawakami	JPN	1.8.75	2		Brunswick	1 Jul 00
31:10.12		Adriana	Fernández	MEX	4.4.71	3		Brunswick	1 Jul 00
31:10.46			Ma Liyan	CHN	6.9.68	4	NG	Beijing	8 Sep 93
31:11.26			Song Liqing ¶	CHN	.1.80	7	NG	Shanghai	19 Oct 97
31:11.72		Lisa	Ondieki'	AUS	12.5.60	1	WG	Helsinki	30 Jun 92
31:12.58			Wang Mingxia	CHN	6.6.71	8	NG	Shanghai	19 Oct 97
		(50)	100th woman 31:40.56, 200th woman 31:56.00, 300th 32:12.45						

20,000 METRES

Mark	Wind	Name		Nat	Born	Pos	Meet	Venue	Date
1:05:26.6	WR	Tegla	Loroupe	KEN	9.5.73	1		Borgholzhausen	3 Sep 00
1:06:48.8	WR	Izumi	Maki	JPN	10.12.68	1		Amagasaki	19 Sep 93
1:06:55.5	WR	Rosa	Mota	POR	29.6.58	1		Lisboa	14 May 83

HALF MARATHON

Included are the slightly downhill courses: Newcastle to South Shields 30.5m, Tokyo 33m (to 1998), Lisboa 40m

Mark	Wind	Name		Nat	Born	Pos	Meet	Venue	Date
65:40		Paula	Radcliffe	GBR	17.12.73	1	GNR	South Shields	21 Sep 03
65:44		Susan	Chepkemei	KEN	25.6.75	1		Lisboa (60m dh)	1 Apr 01
66:34		Lornah	Kiplagat	KEN	20.3.74	2		Lisboa	1 Apr 01
66:40*		Ingrid	Kristiansen	NOR	21.3.56	1	NC	Sandnes	5 Apr 87
66:43		Masako	Chiba	JPN	18.7.76	1		Tokyo	19 Jan 97
66:44		Elana	Meyer	RSA	10.10.66	1		Tokyo	15 Jan 99
66:47			Radcliffe			1	WCh	Bristol	7 Oct 01
66:49		Esther	Wanjiru	KEN	27.3.77	2		Tokyo	15 Jan 99
66:56			L Kiplagat			1	City-Pier	Den Haag	25 Mar 00
67:03		Derartu	Tulu	ETH	21.3.72	3		Lisboa	1 Apr 01
67:07			Radcliffe			1	GNR	South Shields	22 Oct 00
67:11		Liz	McColgan	GBR	24.5.64	1		Tokyo	26 Jan 92
67:12		Tegla	Loroupe (10)	KEN	9.5.73	1		Lisboa	10 Mar 96
67:19		Sonia	O'Sullivan	IRL	28.11.69	1	GNR	South Shields	6 Oct 02
67:22			Meyer			1		Tokyo	24 Jan 93
67:23		Margaret	Okayo	KEN	30.5.76	1		Udine	28 Sep 03
67:24			Loroupe			1		Lisboa	26 Mar 00
67:29			Meyer			1		Kyoto	8 Mar 98
67:32			Loroupe			1		Den Haag	28 Mar 98
67:32		Berhane	Adere	ETH	21.7.73	2	GNR	South Shields	21 Sep 03
67:33			Meyer			1		Tokyo	10 Jan 00
67:35			Radcliffe			1	WCh	Vilamoura	4 Oct 03
67:36			Meyer			1		Kyoto	9 Mar 97
67:36			Chepkemei			2	WCh	Bristol	7 Oct 01
67:37			Kiplagat			1		Zaandam	17 Sep 00
67:41			Wanjiru			2		Tokyo	10 Jan 00
67:43			Loroupe			2		Tokyo	19 Jan 97
67:48		Kerryn	McCann	AUS	2.5.67	3		Tokyo	10 Jan 00
67:50		Catherina	McKiernan	IRL	30.11.69	1		Lisboa	15 Mar 98
67:51			Chepkemei			3	GNR	South Shields	21 Sep 03
		(30/15)							
67:53		Edith	Masai	KEN	4.4.67	1		Nice	22 Apr 01
67:54		Catherine	Ndereba	KEN	21.7.72	1		Den Haag	24 Mar 01
67:56		Susie	Power	AUS	26.3.75	2	GNR	South Shields	6 Oct 02
67:58		Uta	Pippig ¶	GER	7.9.65	1		Kyoto	19 Mar 95
67:59	w	Restituta	Joseph	TAN	30.7.71	1		Malmö	12 Jun 00
		(20)							
68:09		Cristina	Pomacu	ROM	15.9.73	2		Lisboa	15 Mar 98
68:10		Constantina	Tomescu'	ROM	23.1.70	1	NC	Turnu-Severin	14 Sep 02
68:18		Izumi	Maki	JPN	10.12.68	2		Tokyo	21 Jan 96
68:18		Yoshiko	Ichikawa	JPN	18.4.76	3		Tokyo	19 Jan 97
68:18	w	Joyce	Chepchumba	KEN	6.11.70	2		Malmö	12 Jun 00
68:21		Albertina	Dias	POR	26.4.65	3		Lisboa	10 Mar 96
68:22		Mizuki	Noguchi	JPN	3.7.78	1		Miyazaki	6 Jan 02
68:23		Fernanda	Ribeiro	POR	23.6.69	3		Lisboa	26 Mar 00
68:30		Maria	Guida	ITA	23.1.66	4		Lisboa	10 Mar 96
68:32		Mikie	Takanaka	JPN	6.10.80	2		Miyazaki	6 Jan 02
		(30)							
68:33		Lisa	Ondieki	AUS	12.5.60	2		Tokyo	26 Jan 92
68:34		Joan	Benoit	USA	16.5.57	1		Philadelphia	16 Sep 84
68:34		Olga	Appell	MEX	2.8.63	2		Tokyo	24 Jan 93
68:34		Asmae	Leghzaoui ¶	MAR	30.8.76	1		Marrakech	31 Jan 99
68:34		Lidia	Simon	ROM	4.9.73	4		Tokyo	10 Jan 00
68:35		Takako	Kotorida	JPN	2.4.77	2		Yamaguchi	9 Mar 03
68:38		Colleen	de Reuck	RSA	13.4.64	1	NC	Durban	23 Jul 89
68:38		Isabella	Ochichi	KEN	79	2		Nice	22 Apr 01
68:41		Junko	Kataoka	JPN	13.6.70	1		Tokyo	23 Jan 94
68:43		Jelena	Prokopcuka	LAT	21.9.76	5	WCh	Bristol	7 Oct 01
		(40)							
68:45	w	Lyubov	Morgunova	RUS	14.1.71	3		Malmö	12 Jun 00
68:48	w	Abebe	Tola	ETH	3.6.77	4		Malmö	12 Jun 00
68:49		Grete	Waitz	NOR	1.10.53	1	GNR	South Shields	24 Jul 88
68:54		Miwako	Yamanaka	JPN	24.5.78	1		Kobe	16 Dec 01
68:54		Lenah	Cheruiyot	KEN	1.3.73	1		Den Haag	23 Mar 02
68:54		Ines	Chenonge	KEN	1.2.82	4		Lisboa (dh 69m)	24 Mar 02
68:55		Naoko	Takahashi	JPN	6.5.72	1		Chiba	23 Jan 00
68:55		Yasuko	Hashimoto	JPN	12.8.75	2		Kobe	16 Dec 01

Mark	Wind	Name		Nat	Born	Pos	Meet	Venue	Date
68:56		Carla	Beurskens	NED	10.2.52	1		Grevenmacher	21 Sep 86
68:56		Marleen	Renders	BEL	24.12.68	2		Den Haag	23 Mar 02
		(50)	100th woman 69:34, 200th 70:28, 300th 71:07						

Downhill * uncertain course measurement

Mark	Wind	Name		Nat	Born	Pos	Meet	Venue	Date
68:12		Claudia	Metzner	GER	5.5.66	1		Las Vegas (260m)	4 Feb 95
68:13		Petra	Wassiluk	GER	27.10.69	1		Las Vegas	9 Feb 97

Drugs disqualification: 68:50 Yasuko Kimura # JPN 6.1.76 (3) Tokyo 21 Jan 96

MARATHON

Note Boston times included, but course is downhill overall (139m) and sometimes, as in 1994, strongly wind-aided
In second column: first character: L = loop course or start and finish within 30%, P = point-to-point or start and finish more than 30% apart, D + point-to-point and downhil over 1/1000
Second character: M mixed marathon (men and women), W women only race or separated start by time

Mark	Wind	Name		Nat	Born	Pos	Meet	Venue	Date
2:15:25	LM	Paula	Radcliffe	GBR	17.12.73	1		London	13 Apr 03
2:17:18	LM		Radcliffe			1		Chicago	13 Oct 02
2:18:47	LM	Catherine	Ndereba	KEN	21.7.72	1		Chicago	7 Oct 01
2:18:56	LW		Radcliffe			1		London	14 Apr 02
2:19:26	LM		Ndereba			2		Chicago	13 Oct 02
2:19:39	LM		Sun Yingjie	CHN	3.10.77	1		Beijing	19 Oct o3
2:19:46	LM	Naoko	Takahashi	JPN	6.5.72	1		Berlin	30 Sep 01
2:19:55	LM		Ndereba			2		London	13 Apr 03
2:20:43	LM	Tegla	Loroupe	KEN	9.5.73	1		Berlin	26 Sep 99
2:20:43	DM	Margaret	Okayo	KEN	30.5.76	1		Boston	15 Apr 02
2:20:47	LM		Loroupe			1		Rotterdam	19 Apr 98
2:21:06	LM	Ingrid	Kristiansen	NOR	21.3.56	1		London	21 Apr 85
2:21:12	DM		Ndereba			2		Boston	15 Apr 02
2:21:16	LM	Deena	Drossin	USA	14.2.73	3		London	13 Apr 03
2:21:18	LW	Mizuki	Noguchi	JPN	3.7.78	1		Osaka	26 Jan 03
2:21:21	LM	Joan	Benoit' (10)	USA	16.5.57	1		Chicago	20 Oct 85
2:21:21	LM		Sun Yingjie			2		Beijing	20 Oct 02
2:21:22	LM	Yoko	Shibui	JPN	14.3.79	3		Chicago	13 Oct 02
2:21:31	LM	Svetlana	Zakharova	RUS	15.9.70	4		Chicago	13 Oct 02
2:21:33	LM		Ndereba			1		Chicago	22 Oct 00
2:21:45	DM	Uta	Pippig ¶	GER	7.9.65	1		Boston	18 Apr 94
2:21:45	LW	Masako	Chiba	JPN	18.7.76	2		Osaka	26 Jan 03
2:21:47	PW		N Takahashi			1	AsiG	Bangkok	6 Dec 98
2:21:49	LM		N Takahashi			1		Berlin	29 Sep 02
2:21:51	LW	Naoko	Sakamoto	JPN	14.11.80	3		Osaka	26 Jan 03
2:22:07	LM		Loroupe			1		Rotterdam	20 Apr 97
2:22:12	LW	Eri	Yamaguchi	JPN	14.1.73	1		Tokyo	22 Nov 99
2:22:19	LW		N Takahashi			1		Nagoya	12 Mar 00
2:22:20	LM	Gete	Wami	ETH	11.12.74	1		Amsterdam	20 Oct 02
2:22:22	LW	Lornah	Kiplagat	KEN	20.3.74	4		Osaka	26 Jan 03
2:22:23	LM	Catherina	McKiernan	IRL	30.11.69	1		Amsterdam	1 Nov 98
		(31/19)							
2:22:33	LW	Lyudmila	Petrova	RUS	7.10.68	3		London	14 Apr 02
2:22:46	LW	Reiko	Tosa	JPN	11.6.76	4		London	14 Apr 02
2:22:54	LW	Lidia	Simon	ROM	4.9.73	1		Osaka	30 Jan 00
2:22:56	LW	Harumi	Hiroyama	JPN	2.9.68	2		Osaka	30 Jan 00
2:23:05	LM	Marleen	Renders	BEL	24.12.68	1		Paris	7 Apr 02
2:23:12	LM	Susan	Chepkemei	KEN	25.6.75	4		London	13 Apr 03
2:23:17	LM		Zhang Shujing	CHN	13.9.78	3		Beijing	20 Oct 02
2:23:21	DM	Fatuma	Roba	ETH	18.12.73	1		Boston	20 Apr 98
2:23:22	LW	Joyce	Chepchumba	KEN	6.11.70	1		London	18 Apr 99
2:23:29	LM	Rosa	Mota	POR	29.6.58	3		Chicago	20 Oct 85
2:23:30	LW	Mari	Ozaki	JPN	16.7.75	5		Osaka	26 Jan 03
		(30)							
2:23:31	LW	Esther	Wanjiru	KEN	27.3.77	3		Osaka	30 Jan 00
2:23:33	DM	Valentina	Yegorova	RUS	16.2.64	2		Boston	18 Apr 94
2:23:35	LM	Constantina	Dita/Tomescu	ROM	23.1.70	2		Chicago	12 Oct 03
2:23:37	LM		Liu Min	CHN	29.11.83	1		Beijing	14 Oct 01
2:23:43	DM	Olga	Markova	RUS	6.8.68	1		Boston	20 Apr 92
2:23:43	LM	Takami	Ominami	JPN	15.11.75	1		Rotterdam	21 Apr 02
2:23:47	LM	Maura	Viceconte	ITA	3.10.67	1		Wien	21 May 00
2:23:51	LW	Lisa	Martin/Ondieki	AUS	12.5.60	1		Osaka	31 Jan 88
2:23:57	LW	Derartu	Tulu	ETH	21.3.72	1		London	22 Apr 01
2:23:57	LM		Zhu Xiaolin	CHN	20.4.84	4		Beijing	20 Oct 02
		(40)							
2:24:01	LM	Jelena	Prokopcuka	LAT	21.9.76	7		London	13 Apr 03
2:24:02	LM		Wei Yanan¶	CHN	6.12.81	2		Beijing	14 Oct 01

Mark	Wind	Name		Nat	Born	Pos	Meet	Venue	Date
2:24:06	LW	Adriana	Fernández	MEX	4.4.71	2		London	18 Apr 99
2:24:07	LW		Wang Junxia	CHN	9.1.73	1		Tianjin	4 Apr 93
2:24:18	DM	Wanda	Panfil	POL	26.1.59	1		Boston	15 Apr 91
2:24:22	LM		Ren Xiujuan	CHN	14.9.74	3		Beijing	14 Oct 01
2:24:29	LW	Elfenesh	Alemu	ETH	10.6.75	5		London	22 Apr 01
2:24:32	LW		Qu Yunxia	CHN	25.12.72	2		Tianjin	4 Apr 93
2:24:33	LM	Rie	Matsuoka	JPN	9.3.77	2		Paris	7 Apr 02
2:24:35	PM	Katrin	Dörre-Heinig	GER	6.10.61	1		Hamburg	25 Apr 99
		(50)	100th woman 2:26:20, 200th 2:28:14, 300th 2:29:44, 400th 2:31:13, 500th 2:32:25						
Drugs dq:	2:20:23 LM		Wei Yanan ¶	CHN	6.12.81	1		Beijing	20 Oct 02

2000 METRES STEEPLECHASE

6:11.84	Marina	Pluzhnikova	RUS	25.2.63	1	GWG	Sankt-Peterburg	25 Jul 94
6:14.52	Svetlana	Rogova	RUS	4.8.67	1	Znam	Moskva	11 Jun 92
6:16.49	Yelena	Motalova	RUS	28.1.71	1	NC	Moskva	2 Aug 98
6:17.80	Irina	Mozharova	RUS	19.7.58	1	NC	Gorkiy	23 Jul 89
6:18.2	Svetlana	Vinogradova	RUS	71	1	Army	Rostov	16 Jun 96
6:19.00	Irene	Limika	KEN	28.8.79	1		Loughborough	20 May 01

3000 METRES STEEPLECHASE

$ short water jump (3.06m, standard is now 3.66m)

9:08.33	WR	Gulnara	Samitova	RUS	9.7.78	1	NC	Tula	10 Aug 03
9:16.51	WR	Alesya	Turova	BLR	6.12.79	1		Gdansk	27 Jul 02
9:20.28			Turova			1	GS	Ostrava	12 Jun 03
9:21.72	WR		Turova			1	GS	Ostrava	12 Jun 02
9:22.29	WR	Justyna	Bak	POL	1.8.74	1		Milano	5 Jun 02
9:23.91			Turova			1	NA	Heusden	20 Jul 02
9:24.78		Lyubov	Ivanova	RUS	2.3.81	2	NC	Tula	10 Aug 03
9:25.31	WR$		Bak			1	Nik	Nice	9 Jul 01
9:25.87			Samitova			1		Réthimno	6 Jul 03
9:30.70		Melissa	Rollison	AUS	13.4.83	1	GWG	Brisbane	4 Sep 01
9:32.05			Samitova			1	Znam	Tula	7 Jun 03
9:32.26			Bak			2	GS	Ostrava	12 Jun 02
9:32.31		Yekaterina	Volkova	RUS	16.2.78	3	NC	Tula	10 Aug 03
9:32.80			Turova			2		Réthimno	6 Jul 03
9:33.12		Élodie	Olivarès	FRA	22.5.76	2	NA	Heusden	20 Jul 02
9:33.16		Cristina	Casandra	ROM	1.2.77	1	NC	Bucuresti	27 Jul 02
9:33.69			Casandra			3	NA	Heusden	20 Jul 02
9:34.41			Samitova			1	GP	Tríkala	24 Jun 03
9:37.04			Olivarès			1	NC	Saint-Étienne	13 Jul 02
9:38.31		Melanie	Schulz	GER	27.8.79	1	NC	Wattenscheid	6 Jul 02
9:39.51	$	Irene	Limika	KEN	28.8.79	2	Nik	Nice	9 Jul 01
9:39.51		Dorcus	Inzikuru	UGA	2.2.82	2	GS	Ostrava	12 Jun 03
9:39.65	$		Limika			2	GWG	Brisbane	4 Sep 01
		(23/11)							
9:41.94	$	Elizabeth	Jackson	USA	27.10.77	4	GWG	Brisbane	4 Sep 01
9:42.01		Michaela	Mannová	CZE	11.1.82	2	EU23	Bydgoszcz	19 Jul 03
9:42.04		Sigrid	Vanden Bempt	BEL	10.2.81	3	EU23	Bydgoszcz	19 Jul 03
9:43.89		Laurence	Duquénoy	FRA	29.9.69	3	GS	Ostrava	12 Jun 02
9:44.71		Brianna	Shook	USA	6.1.81	1	NC	Stanford	21 Jun 03
9:44.95		Kassi	Andersen	USA	25.6.83	1	NCAA	Sacramento	13 Jun 03
9:46.30		Lisa	Aguilera	USA	30.11.79	1	NCAA-r	Stanford	31 May 03
9:46.74		Ida	Nilsson	SWE	8.2.81	2	NCAA	Sacramento	13 Jun 03
9:46.76		Alina	Proca	ROM	24.10.83	3		Pírgos	27 Jul 03
		(20)							
9:47.87		Anália	Rosa	POR	28.2.76	4	NA	Heusden	20 Jul 02
9:48.88	WR	Yelena	Motalova	RUS	28.1.71	1	NC	Tula	31 Jul 99
9:49.14		Lisa	Nye	USA	17.11.68	3	NC	Stanford	21 Jun 03
9:49.40		Jana	Biolková	CZE	18.5.74	1	NC	Olomouc	12 Jul 03
9:49.51		Malika	Assahssah	MAR	24.9.82	1	NC	Rabat	6 Jul 03
9:50.12		Roisin	McGettigan	IRL	23.8.80	3	NCAA	Sacramento	13 Jun 03
9:50.29		Natalya	Cherepanova	RUS	9.3.67	4	NC	Tula	10 Aug 03
9:50.88			Chen Xiaofang	CHN	28.10.81	1	NC	Shanghai	13 Sep 03
9:51.16		Carol	Henry	CAN	20.6.82	3	NCAA	Baton Rouge	1 Jun 02
9:51.38		Lívia	Tóth	HUN	7.1.80	1	ECp-1A	Banská Bystrica	22 Jun 02
		(30)		50th best 9:57.67					
9:52.13		Patrycja	Wlodarczyk	POL	9.6.80	5	GS	Ostrava	12 Jun 03
9:52.71	$	Tara	Krzywicki	GBR	9.3.74	2	v2N	Glasgow	1 Jul 01
9:52.77		Julia	Budniak	POL	4.3.81	2		Gdansk	27 Jul 02
9:52.98		Letiwe	Marakurwa	ZIM	2.6.78	4	NCAA	Sacramento	13 Jun 03
9:54.01			Ju Yinglan	CHN	10.10.84	2	NC	Shanghai	13 Sep 03

100 METRES HURDLES

Mark	Wind	Name		Nat	Born	Pos	Meet	Venue	Date
12.21	WR 0.7	Yordanka	Donkova	BUL	28.9.61	1		Stara Zagora	20 Aug 88
12.24	0.9		Donkova			1h		Stara Zagora	28 Aug 88
12.25	WR 1.4	Ginka	Zagorcheva	BUL	12.4.58	1	v TCH,GRE	Drama	8 Aug 87
12.26	WR 1.5		Donkova			1	Balk	Ljubljana	7 Sep 86
12.26	1.7	Lyudmila	Narozhilenko ¶	RUS	21.4.64	1rB		Sevilla	6 Jun 92
		(now Ludmila Engquist SWE)							
12.27	-1.2		Donkova			1		Stara Zagora	28 Aug 88
12.28	1.8		Narozhilenko			1	NC	Kiyev	11 Jul 91
12.28	0.9		Narozhilenko			1rA		Sevilla	6 Jun 92
12.29	WR -0.4		Donkova			1	ASV	Köln	17 Aug 86
12.32	1.6		Narozhilenko			1		Saint-Denis	4 Jun 92
12.33	1.4		Donkova			1		Fürth	14 Jun 87
12.33	-0.3	Gail	Devers	USA	19.11.66	1	NC	Sacramento	23 Jul 00
12.34	-0.5		Zagorcheva			1	WCh	Roma	4 Sep 87
12.35	WR 0.1		Donkova			1h2	ASV	Köln	17 Aug 86
12.36	WR 1.9	Grazyna	Rabsztyn	POL	20.9.52	1	Kuso	Warszawa	13 Jun 80
12.36	WR -0.6		Donkova			1	NC	Sofiya	13 Aug 86
12.36	1.1		Donkova			1		Schwechat	15 Jun 88
12.37	1.4		Donkova			1	ISTAF	Berlin	15 Aug 86
12.37	0.7		Devers			1	WCh	Sevilla	28 Aug 99
12.38	0.0		Donkova			1	BGP	Budapest	11 Aug 86
12.38	-0.7		Donkova			1	EC	Stuttgart	29 Aug 86
12.38	0.2		Donkova			1	OG	Seoul	30 Sep 88
12.39	1.5	Vera	Komisova'	RUS	11.6.53	1	GGala	Roma	5 Aug 80
12.39	1.5		Zagorcheva			2	Balk	Ljubljana	7 Sep 86
12.39	1.8	Natalya	Grigoryeva ¶	UKR	3.12.62	2	NC	Kiyev	11 Jul 91
12.39	-0.7		Devers			1	WK	Zürich	11 Aug 00
12.40	0.4		Donkova			1	GWG	Moskva	8 Jul 86
12.40	1.2		Devers			1rA	Athl	Lausanne	2 Jul 02
12.42	1.8	Bettine	Jahn	GDR	3.8.58	1	OD	Berlin	8 Jun 83
12.42	1.0		Zagorcheva			1		Sofiya	14 Aug 85
12.42	-0.2		Donkova			1	VD	Bruxelles	5 Sep 86
12.42	0.2		Narozhilenko			1	GGala	Roma	9 Jun 92
12.42	2.0	Anjanette	Kirkland	USA	24.2.74	1	WCh	Edmonton	11 Aug 01
12.42	1.1		Devers			1	DNG	Stockholm	16 Jul 02
12.42	0.0		Devers			1	Herc	Monaco	19 Jul 02
		(35/9)							
12.43	-0.9	Lucyna	Kalek (Langer)	POL	9.1.56	1		Hannover	19 Aug 84
12.44	-0.5	Gloria	Uibel (-Siebert)	GDR	13.1.64	2	WCh	Roma	4 Sep 87
12.44	-0.8	Olga	Shishigina ¶	KAZ	23.12.68	1		Luzern	27 Jun 95
12.44	0.4	Glory	Alozie	NGR/ESP	30.12.77	1	Herc	Monaco	8 Aug 98
12.45	1.3	Cornelia	Oschkenat'	GDR	29.10.61	1		Neubrandenburg	11 Jun 87
12.45	1.4	Brigitte	Foster	JAM	7.11.74	1	Pre	Eugene	24 May 03
12.47	1.1	Marina	Azyabina	RUS	15.6.63	1s2	NC	Moskva	19 Jun 93
12.50	0.0	Vera	Akimova'	RUS	5.6.59	1		Sochi	19 May 84
12.51	1.4	Miesha	McKelvy	USA	26.7.76	2	Pre	Eugene	24 May 03
12.52	-0.4	Michelle	Freeman	JAM	5.5.69	1s1	WCh	Athína	10 Aug 97
12.52	1.9	Delloreen	Ennis-London	JAM	5.3.75	1	NC	Kingston	22 Jul 00
		(20)							
12.53	0.2	Tatyana	Reshetnikova	RUS	14.10.66	1rA	GP II	Linz	4 Jul 94
12.53	-0.4	Svetla	Dimitrova ¶	BUL	27.1.70	1	Herc	Stara Zagora	16 Jul 94
12.53	1.0	Melissa	Morrison	USA	9.7.71	1	DNG	Stockholm	5 Aug 98
12.53	-0.2	Perdita	Felicien	CAN	29.8.80	1	WCh	Saint-Denis	27 Aug 03
12.54	0.4	Kerstin	Knabe	GDR	7.7.59	3	EC	Athína	9 Sep 82
12.54	0.9	Sabine	Paetz/John'	GDR	16.10.57	1		Berlin	15 Jul 84
12.56	1.2	Johanna	Klier'	GDR	13.9.52	1		Cottbus	17 Jul 80
12.56	1.2	Monique	Ewanje-Epée	FRA	11.7.67	1	BNP	Villeneuve d'Ascq	29 Jun 90
12.59	WR -0.6	Anneliese	Ehrhardt	GDR	18.6.50	1	OG	München	8 Sep 72
12.59	0.0	Natalya	Shekhodanova ¶	RUS	29.12.71	1	NC	Sankt Peterburg	3 Jul 96
		(30)							
12.59	1.0	Patricia	Girard ¶	FRA	8.4.68	2s2	OG	Atlanta	31 Jul 96
12.59	0.2	Brigita	Bukovec	SLO	21.5.70	2	OG	Atlanta	31 Jul 96
12.61	0.3	Svetlana	Gusarova	KAZ	29.5.59	2	NC	Leningrad	3 Aug 85
12.61	0.2	Jackie	Joyner-Kersee	USA	3.3.62	1	Jenn	San José	28 May 88
12.61	1.4	Katie	Anderson	CAN	9.1.68	1		Villeneuve d'Ascq	13 Jun 99
12.62	1.2	Mihaela	Pogacian'	ROM	27.1.58	2	BNP	Villeneuve d'Ascq	29 Jun 90
12.62	1.1	Yuliya	Graudyn	RUS	13.11.70	1A	ISTAF	Berlin	30 Aug 94
12.63	1.8	Zofia	Bielczyk	POL	22.9.58	1h1	Kuso	Warszawa	18 Jun 79

Mark	Wind	Name		Nat	Born	Pos	Meet	Venue	Date
12.63	1.4	Heike	Terpe/Theele	GDR	4.10.64	2	NC	Jena	27 Jun 86
12.63	0.0	Angie	Vaughn	USA	4.11.76	1	GP	Edwardsville	25 Jul 98
		(40)							
12.63	2.0	Jenny	Adams	USA	8.7.78	5	WCh	Edmonton	11 Aug 01
12.64	0.4	Paraskeví	Patoulídou	GRE	29.3.65	1	OG	Barcelona	6 Aug 92
12.64	0.1		Zhang Yu	CHN	8.4.71	1	NG	Beijing	9 Sep 93
12.64	1.0	Dionne	Rose-Henley	JAM	7.11.69	4s2	OG	Atlanta	31 Jul 96
12.65A	0.0	Danuta	Perka	POL	22.6.56	1h3	WUG	Ciudad de México	9 Sep 79
12.65	0.0	Nadezhda	Korshunova'	UKR	18.5.61	2		Sochi	19 May 84
12.65	1.4	Donica	Merriman	USA	24.1.79	3	Pre	Eugene	24 May 03
12.66	0.0	Yelena	Biserova	RUS	24.3.62	3		Sochi	19 May 84
12.66	0.7	Lidiya	Yurkova '	BLR	15.1.67	1s2	NC	Kiyev	5 Jul 90
12.66	2.0	Gillian	Russell	JAM	28.9.73	2	CAG	Maracaibo	16 Aug 98
		(50)	100th woman 12.80, 200th 12.96, 300th 13.10						

Wind assisted performances to 12.39, performers to 12.65

Mark	Wind	Name		Nat	Born	Pos	Meet	Venue	Date
12.28	2.7	Cornelia	Oschkenat'	GDR	29.10.61	1		Berlin	25 Aug 87
12.29	3.5		Donkova			1	Athl	Lausanne	24 Jun 88
12.29	2.7	Gail	Devers	USA	19.11.66	1	Pre	Eugene	26 May 02
12.35	2.4	Bettine	Jahn	GDR	3.8.58	1	WCh	Helsinki	13 Aug 83
12.37	2.7	Gloria	Uibel/Siebert'	GDR	13.1.64	2		Berlin	25 Aug 87
12.39	2.8		Rabsztyn			1	4-N	Bremen	24 Jun 79
12.40	2.1	Michelle	Freeman	JAM	5.5.69	1	GPF	Fukuoka	13 Sep 97
12.41	2.2	Olga	Shishigina ¶	KAZ	23.12.68	1rA	Athl	Lausanne	5 Jul 95
12.42	2.4	Kerstin	Knabe	GDR	7.7.59	2	WCh	Helsinki	13 Aug 83
12.50	2.7	Svetla	Dimitrova ¶	BUL	27.1.70	1		Saint-Denis	10 Jun 94
12.51	3.2	Johanna	Klier'	GDR	13.9.52	1	NC	Cottbus	17 Jul 80
12.51	3.6	Sabine	Paetz/John'	GDR	16.10.57	1		Dresden	27 Jul 84
12.51A	3.3	Yuliya	Graudyn	RUS	13.11.70	1		Sestriere	31 Jul 94
12.53	2.2	Mihaela	Pogacian	ROM	27.1.58	1	IAC	Edinburgh	6 Jul 90
12.61	4.0	Jenny	Adams	USA	8.7.78	1h1	NC	Eugene	23 Jun 01
12.63	2.8	Eva	Sokolova	RUS	25.3.62	1s1	NC	Moskva	19 Jun 93
12.64	5.0	Anne	Piquereau	FRA	15.6.64	3		Dijon	12 Jun 94
12.65	3.2	Dawn	Bowles	USA	12.11.68	1q1	NC	Atlanta	22 Jun 96
12.65	2.6	Sharon	Couch-Jewell	USA	13.9.69	1		Hechtel	7 Aug 99

Probably hand timed

Mark	Wind	Name		Nat	Born	Pos	Meet	Venue	Date
12.4	0.7	Svetla	Dimitrova ¶	BUL	27.1.70	1		Stara Zagora	9 Jul 97
		Officially 12.36, but subsequent investigations showed this unlikely to have been auto-timed							
12.63		Angela	Atede	NGR	8.2.72	1	NC	Lagos	28 Jun 97

Hand timed

Mark	Wind	Name		Nat	Born	Pos	Meet	Venue	Date
12.3 WR	1.5	Anneliese	Ehrhardt	GDR	18.6.50	1	NC	Dresden	22 Jul 73
12.3		Marina	Azyabina	RUS	15.6.63	1		Yekaterinburg	30 May 93
12.0w	2.1	Yordanka	Donkova	BUL	28.9.61	1		Sofiya	3 Aug 86
12.1w	2.1	Ginka	Zagorcheva	BUL	12.4.58	2		Sofiya	3 Aug 86

400 METRES HURDLES

Mark	Name		Nat	Born	Pos	Meet	Venue	Date
52.34 WR	Yuliya	Pechonkina'	RUS	21.4.78	1	NC	Tula	8 Aug 03
52.61 WR	Kim	Batten	USA	29.3.69	1	WCh	Göteborg	11 Aug 95
52.62	Tonja	Buford-Bailey	USA	13.12.70	2	WCh	Göteborg	11 Aug 95
52.74 WR	Sally	Gunnell	GBR	29.7.66	1	WCh	Stuttgart	19 Aug 93
52.74		Batten			1	Herc	Monaco	8 Aug 98
52.79	Sandra	Farmer-Patrick	USA	18.8.62	2	WCh	Stuttgart	19 Aug 93
52.82	Deon	Hemmings	JAM	9.10.68	1	OG	Atlanta	31 Jul 96
52.84		Batten			1	WK	Zürich	12 Aug 98
52.89	Daimí	Pernía	CUB	27.12.76	1	WCh	Sevilla	25 Aug 99
52.90		Buford			1	WK	Zürich	16 Aug 95
52.90	Nezha	Bidouane	MAR	18.9.69	2	WCh	Sevilla	25 Aug 99
52.94 WR	Marina	Styepanova'	RUS	1.5.50	1s	Spart	Tashkent	17 Sep 86
52.96A		Bidouane			1	WCp	Johannesburg	11 Sep 98
52.97		Batten			1	NC	Indianapolis	14 Jun 97
52.97		Bidouane			1	WCh	Athína	8 Aug 97
52.98		Hemmings			1rA	WK	Zürich	13 Aug 97
52.99		Hemmings			1s1	OG	Atlanta	29 Jul 96
53.02	Irina	Privalova (10)	RUS	22.11.68	1	OG	Sydney	27 Sep 00
53.03A		Hemmings			2	WCp	Johannesburg	11 Sep 98
53.05		Bidouane			1	GGala	Roma	7 Jul 99
53.06		Batten			1	Herc	Monaco	16 Aug 97
53.06		Batten			1	Gaz	Paris	29 Jul 98
53.08		Batten			2	OG	Atlanta	31 Jul 96
53.08		Bidouane			1	Athl	Lausanne	2 Jul 99

Mark Wind	Name		Nat	Born	Pos	Meet	Venue	Date
53.09		Hemmings			2	WCh	Ath'na	8 Aug 97
53.10		Pechonkina			1	Znam	Tula	9 Jun 02
53.11	Tatyana	Ledovskaya	BLR	21.5.66	1	WCh	Tokyo	29 Aug 91
53.16		Gunnell			2	WCh	Tokyo	29 Aug 91
53.16		Hemmings			3	WCh	Sevilla	25 Aug 99
53.17	Debbie	Flintoff-King	AUS	20.4.60	1	OG	Seoul	28 Sep 88
53.17		Batten			1	Nik	Nice	16 Jul 98
53.17A		Batten			1	WCp	Johannesburg	11 Sep 98
	(32/12)							
53.21	Marie-José	Pérec	FRA	9.5.68	2	WK	Zürich	16 Aug 95
53.22	Jana	Pittman	AUS	9.11.82	1	WCh	Saint-Denis	28 Aug 03
53.24	Sabine	Busch	GDR	21.11.62	1	NC	Potsdam	21 Aug 87
53.25	Ionela	Tîrlea	ROM	9.2.76	2	GGala	Roma	7 Jul 99
53.33	Sandra	Glover	USA	30.12.68	1	NC	Sacramento	17 Jul 00
53.36	Andrea	Blackett	BAR	24.1.76	4	WCh	Sevilla	25 Aug 99
53.40	Tatyana	Tereshchuk	UKR	11.10.69	2		Villeneuve d'Ascq	11 Jul 98
53.47	Janeene	Vickers	USA	3.10.68	3	WCh	Tokyo	29 Aug 91
	(20)							
53.48	Margarita	Ponomaryova'	RUS	19.6.63	3	WCh	Stuttgart	19 Aug 93
53.58	Cornelia	Ullrich'	GDR	26.4.63	2	NC	Potsdam	21 Aug 87
53.63	Ellen	Fiedler'	GDR	26.11.58	3	OG	Seoul	28 Sep 88
53.65A	Myrtle	Bothma'	RSA	18.2.64	mx		Pretoria	12 Mar 90
	53.74A				1		Johannesburg	18 Apr 86
53.88	Debbie-Ann	Parris	JAM	24.3.73	3s1	WCh	Edmonton	6 Aug 01
53.96		Han Qing ¶	CHN	4.3.70	1	NG	Beijing	9 Sep 93
53.96		Song Yinglan	CHN	14.9.75	1	NG	Guangzhou	22 Nov 01
54.02 WR	Anna	Ambraziené'	LTU	14.4.55	1	Znam	Moskva	11 Jun 83
54.02A	Judit	Szekeres ¶	HUN	18.11.66	1		Roodepoort	23 Jan 98
54.02	Natasha	Danvers	GBR	19.9.77	2	GGala	Roma	11 Jul 03
	(30)							
54.03	Heike	Meissner	GER	29.1.70	5	OG	Atlanta	31 Jul 96
54.04	Gudrun	Abt	FRG	3.8.62	6	OG	Seoul	28 Sep 88
54.05A	Surita	Febbraio	RSA	27.12.73	1		Pretoria	4 Apr 03
54.11	Anna	Knoroz	RUS	30.7.70	3	Nik	Nice	18 Jul 94
54.14	Yekaterina	Fesenko/Grun	RUS	10.8.58	1	WCh	Helsinki	10 Aug 83
54.15	Ann-Louise	Skoglund	SWE	28.6.62	4	EC	Stuttgart	30 Aug 86
54.15	Michelle	Johnson	USA	12.4.74	5	WK	Zürich	11 Aug 99
54.17	Tonya	Williams	USA	5.10.74	3	Athl	Lausanne	3 Jul 96
54.21	Ryan	Tolbert	USA	16.6.76	3	NC	Indianapolis	14 Jun 97
54.22A	Silvia	Rieger	GER	14.11.70	5	WCp	Johannesburg	11 Sep 98
	(40)							
54.23	Judi	Brown King	USA	14.7.61	1	PAm	Indianapolis	12 Aug 87
54.24	Susanne	Losch	GDR	12.2.66	1	v FRG	Düsseldorf	19 Jun 88
54.24	Sheena	Johnson	USA	1.10.82	1	NCAA	Sacramento	13 Jun 03
54.25	Anita	Protti	SUI	4.8.64	6	WCh	Tokyo	29 Aug 91
54.27	Genowefa	Blaszak'	POL	22.8.57	1	DNG	Stockholm	2 Jul 85
54.28 WR	Karin	Rossley	GDR	5.4.57	1		Jena	17 May 80
54.31	Susan	Smith	IRL	14.9.71	7	WK	Zürich	12 Aug 98
54.34	Tatyana	Pavlova'	UZB	12.12.58	1h1	NC	Leningrad	2 Aug 85
54.35	Petra	Krug	GDR	9.11.63	1	vSU	Bryansk	14 Jul 89
54.36	LaTanya	Sheffield	USA	11.10.63	3s1	OG	Seoul	26 Sep 88
	(50)	100th woman 55.11, 200th woman 55.89						

Low altitude bests 54.27 Rieger 2s2 OG Atlanta 29 Jul 96
54.31 Febbraio 1 Poznan 29 Jun 03

Drugs disqualification

53.38		Jiang Limei ¶	CHN	.3.70	(1)	NG	Shanghai	22 Oct 97

HIGH JUMP

2.09 WR	Stefka	Kostadinova	BUL	25.3.65	1	WCh	Roma	30 Aug 87
2.08 WR		Kostadinova			1	NM	Sofiya	31 May 86
2.07 WR	Lyudmila	Andonova ¶	BUL	6.5.60	1	OD	Berlin	20 Jul 84
2.07 WR		Kostadinova			1		Sofiya	25 May 86
2.07		Kostadinova			1		Cagliari	16 Sep 87
2.07		Kostadinova			1	NC	Sofiya	3 Sep 88
2.07i	Heike	Henkel'	GER	5.5.64	1	NC	Karlsruhe	8 Feb 92
2.06		Kostadinova			1	ECp	Moskva	18 Aug 85
2.06		Kostadinova			1		Fürth	15 Jun 86
2.06		Kostadinova			1		Cagliari	14 Sep 86
2.06		Kostadinova			1		Wörrstadt	6 Jun 87
2.06		Kostadinova			1		Rieti	8 Sep 87

Mark	Wind	Name		Nat	Born	Pos	Meet	Venue	Date
2.06i			Kostadinova			1		Pireás	20 Feb 88
2.06		Kajsa	Bergqvist	SWE	12.10.76	1		Eberstadt	26 Jul 03
2.06		Hestrie	Cloete	RSA	26.8.78	1	WCh	Saint-Denis	31 Aug 03
2.05	WR	Tamara	Bykova	RUS	21.12.58	1	Izv	Kiyev	22 Jun 84
2.05			Kostadinova			1		Wörrstadt	14 Jun 86
2.05			Kostadinova			1		Rieti	7 Sep 86
2.05i			Kostadinova			1	WI	Indianapolis	8 Mar 87
2.05			Kostadinova			1	Bisl	Oslo	4 Jul 87
2.05			Kostadinova			1		Padova	13 Sep 87
2.05			Kostadinova			1	BGP	Budapest	12 Aug 88
2.05			Henkel			1	WCh	Tokyo	31 Aug 91
2.05i			Kostadinova			1	NC	Sofiya	1 Feb 92
2.05			Kostadinova			1		San Marino	4 Jul 92
2.05			Kostadinova			1	Toto	Fukuoka	18 Sep 93
2.05		Inga	Babakova	UKR	27.6.67	1		Tokyo	15 Sep 95
2.05			Kostadinova			1	OG	Atlanta	3 Aug 96
2.05			Bergqvist			1		Poznan	18 Aug 02
2.05			Claoete			1	ISTAF	Berlin (P)	10 Aug 03
		(30/7)							
2.04		Silvia	Costa	CUB	4.5.64	1	WCp	Barcelona	9 Sep 89
2.04i		Alina	Astafei	GER	7.6.69	1		Berlin	3 Mar 95
2.04		Venelina	Veneva	BUL	13.6.74	1		Kalamáta	2 Jun 01
		(10)							
2.04i		Anna	Chicherova	RUS	22.7.82	1		Yekaterinburg	7 Jan 03
2.03	WR	Ulrike	Meyfarth	FRG	4.5.56	1	ECp	London (CP)	21 Aug 83
2.03		Louise	Ritter	USA	18.2.58	1		Austin	8 Jul 88
2.03		Tatyana	Motkova	RUS	23.11.68	2		Bratislava	30 May 95
2.03		Níki	Bakoyiánni	GRE	9.6.68	2	OG	Atlanta	3 Aug 96
2.03i		Monica	Iagar/Dinescu	ROM	2.4.73	1		Bucuresti	23 Jan 99
2.03i		Marina	Kuptsova	RUS	22.12.81	1	EI	Wien	2 Mar 02
2.02i		Susanne	Beyer'	GDR	24.6.61	2	WI	Indianapolis	8 Mar 87
2.02		Yelena	Yelesina	RUS	4.4.70	1	GWG	Seattle	23 Jul 90
2.01	WR	Sara	Simeoni	ITA	19.4.53	1	v Pol	Brescia	4 Aug 78
2.01		Olga	Turchak	UKR	5.3.67	2	GWG	Moskva	7 Jul 86
		(20)							
2.01		Desiré	du Plessis	RSA	20.5.65	1		Johannesburg	16 Sep 86
2.01i		Gabriele	Günz	GDR	8.9.61	2		Stuttgart	31 Jan 88
2.01		Heike	Balck	GDR	19.8.70	1	vSU-j	Karl-Marx-Stadt	18 Jun 89
2.01i		Ioamnet	Quintero	CUB	8.9.72	1		Berlin	5 Mar 93
2.01		Hanne	Haugland	NOR	14.12.67	1	WK	Zürich	13 Aug 97
2.01i		Tisha	Waller	USA	1.12.70	1	NC	Atlanta	28 Feb 98
2.01		Yelena	Gulyayeva	RUS	14.8.67	2		Kalamata	23 May 98
2.01		Vita	Palamar	UKR	12.10.77	2=	WK	Zürich	15 Aug 03
2.01		Blanka	Vlasic	CRO	8.11.83	2=	WK	Zürich	15 Aug 03
		(30)							
2.01		Amy	Acuff	USA	14.7.75	4	WK	Zürich	15 Aug 03
2.00	WR	Rosemarie	Ackermann'	GDR	4.4.52	1	ISTAF	Berlin	26 Aug 77
2.00i		Coleen	Sommer'	USA	6.6.60	1		Ottawa	14 Feb 82
2.00		Charmaine	Gale/Weavers	RSA	27.2.64	1		Pretoria	25 Mar 85
2.00i		Emilia	Dragieva'	BUL	11.1.65	3	WI	Indianapolis	8 Mar 87
2.00		Lyudmila	Avdyeyenko'	UKR	14.12.63	1	NC	Bryansk	17 Jul 87
2.00		Svetlana	Isaeva/Leseva	BUL	18.3.67	2	v TCH,GRE	Drama	8 Aug 87
2.00i		Larisa	Kositsyna	RUS	14.12.63	2	NC	Volgograd	11 Feb 88
2.00		Jan	Wohlschlag'	USA	14.7.58	1	Bisl	Oslo	1 Jul 89
2.00		Yolanda	Henry	USA	2.12.64	1	Expo	Sevilla	30 May 90
		(40)							
2.00		Biljana	Petrovic ¶	YUG	28.2.61	1		St. Denis	22 Jun 90
2.00		Tatyana	Shevchik ¶	BLR	11.6.69	1		Gomel	14 May 93
2.00i		Britta	Bilac'	SLO	4.12.68	1		Frankfurt	9 Feb 94
2.00i		Yuliya	Lyakhova	RUS	8.7.77	1		Wuppertal	5 Feb 99
2.00		Zuzana	Hlavonová	CZE	16.4.73	1	Odlozil	Praha	5 Jun 00
2.00		Dóra	Györffy	HUN	23.2.78	1	NC	Nyíregyháza	26 Jul 01
2.00		Irina	Mikhalchenko	UKR	20.1.72	1	OC	Kiev	25 May 02
2.00		Viktoriya	Seryogina	RUS	22.5.73	1	Univ Ch	Bryansk	11 Jun 02
2.00i		Svetlana	Lapina	RUS	12.4.78	3=	NC	Moskva	26 Feb 03
2.00		Viktoria	Styopina	UKR	21.2.76	1		Kiev	26 May 03
2.00		Daniela	Rath	GER	6.5.77	1	ECp-S	Firenze	22 Jun 03
2.00		Ruth	Beitia	ESP	1.4.79	1		Avilés	26 Jul 03
		(52)	100th woman 1.96, 200th woman 1.93						

Mark Wind	Name		Nat	Born	Pos	Meet	Venue	Date

Best outdoor marks

2.02	Iagar/Dinescu	1		Budapest	6 Jun 98	2.00	Kositsyna	1		Chelyabinsk	16 Jul 88
2.02	Kuptsova	1	FBK	Hengelo	1 Jun 03	2.00	Bilac	1	EC	Helsinki	14 Aug 94
2.01	Astafei	2		Wörrstadt	27 May 95	2.00	Waller	1	MSR	Walnut	18 Apr 99
2.00	Quintero	1	Herc	Monaco	7 Aug 93	2.00	Chicherova	1		Moskva	15 Jul 03

Ancillary jumps – en route to final marks

2.06 Kostadinova 30 Aug 87 2.05i Henkel 8 Feb 92

POLE VAULT

Mark Wind	Name		Nat	Born	Pos	Meet	Venue	Date
4.82 WR	Yelena	Isinbayeva	RUS	3.6.82	1	GP	Gateshead	13 Jul 03
4.81 WR	Stacy	Dragila	USA	25.3.71	1	GP	Palo Alto	9 Jun 01
4.80i	Svetlana	Feofanova	RUS	16.7.80	1	WI	Birmingham	16 Mar 03
4.78		Feofanova			1	DNG	Stockholm	16 Jul 02
4.78i		Dragila			1	NC	Boston (R)	2 Mar 03
4.78		Isinbayeva			1	GP	London (CP)	8 Aug 03
4.77	Annika	Becker	GER	12.11.81	1	NC	Wattenscheid	7 Jul 02
4.77i		Feofanova			1	GP	Birmingham	21 Feb 03
4.76		Feofanova			1		Villeneuve d'Ascq	16 Jun 02
4.76i		Feofanova			1	v4N	Glasgow	2 Feb 03
4.75		Dragila			1	WCh	Edmonton	6 Aug 01
4.75		Feofanova			2	WCh	Edmonton	6 Aug 01
4.75i		Feofanova			1	EI	Wien	3 Mar 02
4.75		Feofanova			1	WCh	Saint-Denis	25 Aug 03
4.74i		Feofanova			1		Liévin	24 Feb 02
4.73i		Feofanova			1		Gent	10 Feb 02
4.73		Isinbayeva			1		Poznan	29 Jun 03
4.73		Feofanova			2	GP	London (CP)	8 Aug 03
4.72		Dragila			1	GGala	Roma	29 Jun 01
4.72		Dragila			1		Rethimnó	1 Jul 01
4.72		Dragila			1	DNG	Stockholm	17 Jul 01
4.72		Dragila			1	BrGP	London (CP)	22 Jul 01
4.72i		Feofanova			1		Stockholm	6 Feb 02
4.72		Dragila			1	Pre	Eugene	26 May 02
4.72		Dragila			1		Rovereto	28 Aug 02
4.72i		Dragila			1	Mill	New York	7 Feb 03
4.72iA		Dragila			1		Pocatello	8 Mar 03
4.72		Feofanova			1	GP	Villeneuve-d'Ascq	15 Jun 03
4.71i		Feofanova			1		Stuttgart	3 Feb 02
4.71i		Dragila			1		Boston (R)	1 Feb 03
	(30/4)							
4.70i	Tatyana	Polnova	RUS	20.4.79	1		Moskva	11 Feb 03
4.70	Yvonne	Buschbaum	GER	14.7.80	1	NC	Ulm	29 Jun 03
4.66i	Christine	Adams	GER	28.2.74	1	IHS	Sindelfingen	10 Mar 02
EI Wien	3 Mar 02							
4.65	Mary	Sauer	USA	31.10.75	2		Madrid (C)	3 Jul 02
4.62	Monika	Pyrek	POL	11.8.80	2	BrGP	London (CP)	23 Aug 02
4.60 WR	Emma	George	AUS	1.11.74	1		Sydney	20 Feb 99
	(10)							
4.60	Kellie	Suttle	USA	9.5.73	1	Mod R	Modesto	12 May 01
4.60Ai	Mel	Mueller	USA	16.11.72	1		Flagstaff	9 Feb 02
4.60	Pavla	Hamácková	CZE	20.5.78	1	ECp-1B	Velenje	21 Jun 03
4.60	Yelena	Belyakova	RUS	7.4.76	1	NC	Tula	10 Aug 03
4.56i	Nicole	Rieger/Humbert	GER	5.2.72	1		Stockholm	25 Feb 99
4.56	Anzhela	Balakhonova	UKR	18.12.72	1	Gugl	Linz	8 Aug 00
4.56	Tatiana	Grigorieva	AUS	8.10.75	1		Yokohama	15 Sep 01
4.53i	Amy	Linnen	USA	15.7.82	1	NCAA	Fayetteville	8 Mar 02
4.53	Krisztina	Molnár	HUN	8.4.76	3	GP II	Rieti	8 Sep 02
4.52		Gao Shuying	CHN	28.10.79	1	WUG	Beijing	29 Aug 01
	(20)							
4.51	Daniela	Bártová	CZE	6.5.74	1	Slovn	Bratislava	9 Jun 98
4.51i	Zsuzsanna	Szabó	HUN	6.5.73	1		Budapest	4 Feb 99
4.51i	Thórey Edda	Elísdottír	ISL	30.6.77	1	NCAA	Fayetteville	10 Mar 01
4.51	Kirsten	Belin	SWE	2.5.81	1		Göteborg	27 Aug 02
4.51	Carolin	Hingst	GER	18.9.80	3		Salamanca	15 Jul 03
4.50i	Nastja	Ryshich	GER	19.9.77	1	WI	Maebashi	5 Mar 99
4.50	Vala	Flosadóttir	ISL	16.2.78	3	OG	Sydney	25 Sep 00
4.50	Alicia	Warlick	USA	11.10.77	1		Houston	24 Mar 01
4.50	Jillian	Schwartz	USA	19.9.79	2		Jonesboro	16 Jun 02
4.50	Vanessa	Boslak	FRA	11.6.82	1	NC	Narbonne	26 Jul 03
	(30)							

Mark	Wind	Name		Nat	Born	Pos	Meet	Venue	Date
4.47i		Anna	Rogowska	POL	21.5.81	1		Praha	19 Feb 03
4.47		Becky	Holliday	USA	12.3.80	1	NCAA-r	Stanford	30 May 03
4.46		Marie	Poissonnier	FRA	4.5.79	1	NC	Saint-Étienne	13 Jul 02
4.45		Tracy	O'Hara	USA	20.7.80	1	USTCA	Austin	22 Apr 00
4.45		Kym	Howe	AUS	12.6.80	1		Perth	16 Mar 02
4.45i		Monique	de Wilt	NED	21.3.76	1	NC	Gent	15 Feb 03
4.45i		Lacy	Janson	USA	20.2.83	1	NCAA	Fayetteville	15 Mar 03
4.45		Tanya	Koleva	BUL	8.3.72	2	ECp-1B	Velenje	21 Jun 03
4.45		Naroa	Agirre	ESP	15.5.79	1		Arona	26 Jul 03
4.44i		Doris	Auer	AUT	10.5.71	2		Glasgow	18 Mar 01
		(40)							
4.44i		Janine	Whitlock ¶	GBR	11.8.73	4	BrGP	Birmingham	17 Feb 02
4.43 sq		Sabine	Schulte	GER	29.1.76	2		Recklinghausen	24 May 02
		4.40				4		Kassel	14 Jun 02
4.42		Alejandra	García	ARG	13.6.73	1		Sydney	20 Feb 00
4.42		Elmarie	Gerryts	RSA	25.8.72	1		Wesel	12 Jun 00
4.42		Martina	Strutz	GER	4.11.81	1		Schwerin	24 Jun 01
4.41		Floé	Kühnert	GER	6.3.84	1		Mannheim	15 Jun 02
4.41		Stephanie	McCann	CAN	22.4.77	2		Atascadero	9 Jul 03
4.40sq		Anna	Wielgus	POL	27.10.81	1		Ustron	11 May 03
4.40i		Agnès	Livebardon	FRA	31.5.80	1		Aubière	18 Jan 03
4.40i		Natalya	Kushch	UKR	5.3.83	1		Donetsk	15 Feb 03
44.40		Melina	Hamilton	NZL	15.6.76	1		Gold Coast (RB)	12 Apr 03
4.40		Yeoryía	Tsiliggíri	GRE	21.6.72	9	GP	Tríkala	24 Jun 03
.40		Anastasiya	Ivanova	RUS	3.5.79	1		Moskva	14 Jul 03
		(53)	100th woman 4.25, 200th 4.10						

Outdoor best

Mark	Name	Pos	Meet	Venue	Date
4.70	Polnova	1	GP	Ostrava	12 Jun 03
4.60	Mueller	1		Atascadero	9 Jul 03
4.51	Humbert	1		Salamanca	13 Jul 01
4.48sq	Elisdóttir	1		Recklinghausen	30 May 03
	4.45	6	WCh	Edmonton	6 Aug 01
4.45	Rogowska	1		Bydgoszcz	13 Jul 03
4.44	Ryshich	3	Nik	Nice	17 Jul 99
4.40	Szabó	4	WCh	Sevilla	21 Aug 99
4.40	Isinbayeva	2	NC	Tula	24 Jul 00
4.40	Auer	2		Gold Coast (RB)	17 Sep 00
4.40	Whitlock	1	NC	Birmingham	14 Jul 01
4.40	Adams	2		Cottbus	1 Jun 02
4.40	Kushch	3	ECp1B	Velenje	21 Jun 03
4.40	de Wilt	6	EC	München	9 Aug 02
4.40	Linnen	1		Atascadero	23 Jul 03

Ancillary jumps – en route to final marks

4.75i Feofanova 16 Mar 03, 4.74 Isinbayeva 13 Jul 03, 4.73 Feofanova 16 Jul 02, 4.72 Becker 7 Jul 02

Street competition, raised runway, slightly uphill

Mark	Name		Nat	Born	Pos	Venue	Date
4.62	Melissa	Mueller	USA	16.11.72	1	Clovis	4 Aug 01

Exhibition or 'town square' meetings under questionable conditions

Mark	Name		Nat	Born	Pos	Venue	Date
4.40	Andrea	Müller	GER	29.6.74	1	Zweibrücken	8 Oct 95

LONG JUMP

Mark	Wind	Name		Nat	Born	Pos	Meet	Venue	Date
7.52 WR	1.4	Galina	Chistyakova	RUS	26.7.62	1	Znam	Leningrad	11 Jun 88
7.49	1.3	Jackie	Joyner-Kersee	USA	3.3.62	1	NYG	New York	22 May 94
7.49A	1.7		Joyner-Kersee			1		Sestriere	31 Jul 94
7.48	1.2	Heike	Drechsler	GER	16.12.64	1	v ITA	Neubrandenburg	9 Jul 88
7.48	0.4		Drechsler			1	Athl	Lausanne	8 Jul 92
7.45 WR	0.9		Drechsler'			1	v URS	Tallinn	21 Jun 86
7.45 WR	1.1		Drechsler			1	OD	Dresden	3 Jul 86
7.45 WR	0.6		Joyner-Kersee			1	PAm	Indianapolis	13 Aug 87
7.45	1.6		Chistyakova			1	BGP	Budapest	12 Aug 88
7.44 WR	2.0		Drechsler			1		Berlin	22 Sep 85
7.43 WR	1.4	Anisoara	Cusmir/Stanciu	ROM	28.6.62	1	RomIC	Bucuresti	4 Jun 83
7.42	2.0	Tatyana	Kotova	RUS	11.12.76	1	ECp-S	Annecy	23 Jun 02
7.40	1.8		Daute' (Drechsler)			1		Dresden	26 Jul 84
7.40	0.7		Drechsler			1	NC	Potsdam	21 Aug 87
7.40	0.9		Joyner-Kersee			1	OG	Seoul	29 Sep 88
7.39	0.3		Drechsler			1	WK	Zürich	21 Aug 85
7.39	0.5	Yelena	Byelevskaya'	BLR	11.10.63	1	NC	Bryansk	18 Jul 87
7.39			Joyner-Kersee			1		San Diego	25 Jun 88
7.37i	-		Drechsler			1	v2N	Wien	13 Feb 88
7.37A	1.8		Drechsler			1		Sestriere	31 Jul 91
7.37		Inessa	Kravets ¶	UKR	5.10.66	1		Kiyev	13 Jun 92
7.36	0.4		Joyner			1	WCh	Roma	4 Sep 87
7.36	1.8		Byelevskaya			2	Znam	Leningrad	11 Jun 88
7.36	1.8		Drechsler			1		Jena	28 May 92
7.35	1.9		Chistyakova			1	GPB	Bratislava	20 Jun 90
7.34	1.6		Daute'			1		Dresden	19 May 84
7.34	1.4		Chistyakova			2	v GDR	Tallinn	21 Jun 86

Mark	Wind	Name		Nat	Born	Pos	Meet	Venue	Date
7.34			Byelevskaya			1		Sukhumi	17 May 87
7.34	0.7		Drechsler			1	v URS	Karl-Marx-Stadt	20 Jun 87
7.33	0.4		Drechsler			1	v URS	Erfurt	22 Jun 85
7.33	2.0		Drechsler			1		Dresden	2 Aug 85
7.33	-0.3		Drechsler			1	Herc	Monaco	11 Aug 92
		(32/7)							
7.31	1.5	Yelena	Kokonova'	UKR	4.8.63	1	NP	Alma-Ata	12 Sep 85
7.31	1.9	Marion	Jones	USA	12.10.75	1	Pre	Eugene	31 May 98
7.26A	1.8	Maurren	Maggi ¶	BRA	25.6.76	1	SACh	Bogotá	26 Jun 99
		(10)							
7.24	1.0	Larisa	Berezhnaya	UKR	28.2.61	1	Blanc	Granada	25 May 91
7.21	1.6	Helga	Radtke	GDR	16.5.62	2		Dresden	26 Jul 84
7.20 WR	-0.5	Valy	Ionescu	ROM	31.8.60	1	NC	Bucuresti	1 Aug 82
7.20	2.0	Irena	Ozhenko'	LTU	13.11.62	1		Budapest	12 Sep 86
7.20	0.8	Yelena	Sinchukova'	RUS	23.1.61	1	BGP	Budapest	20 Jun 91
7.20	0.7	Irina	Mushayilova	RUS	6.1.67	1	NC	Sankt-Peterburg	14 Jul 94
7.17	1.8	Irina	Valyukevich	BLR	19.11.59	2	NC	Bryansk	18 Jul 87
7.16		Iolanda	Chen	RUS	26.7.61	1		Moskva	30 Jul 88
7.14	1.8	Niole	Medvedyeva ¶	LTU	20.10.60	1		Riga	4 Jun 88
7.14	1.2	Mirela	Dulgheru	ROM	5.10.66	1	Balk G	Sofiya	5 Jul 92
		(20)							
7.12	1.6	Sabine	Paetz/John'	GDR	16.10.57	2		Dresden	19 May 84
7.12	0.9	Chioma	Ajunwa ¶	NGR	25.12.70	1	OG	Atlanta	2 Aug 96
7.11	0.8	Fiona	May	ITA	12.12.69	2	EC	Budapest	22 Aug 98
7.09 WR	0.0	Vilma	Bardauskiene	LTU	15.6.53	Q	EC	Praha	29 Aug 78
7.09	1.5	Ljudmila	Ninova	AUT	25.6.60	1	GP II	Sevilla	5 Jun 94
7.08	0.5	Marieta	Ilcu ¶	ROM	16.10.62	1	RumIC	Pitesti	25 Jun 89
7.07	0.0	Svetlana	Zorina	RUS	2.2.60	1		Krasnodar	15 Aug 87
7.06	0.4	Tatyana	Kolpakova	KGZ	18.10.59	1	OG	Moskva	31 Jul 80
7.06	-0.1	Niurka	Montalvo	CUB/ESP	4.6.68	1	WCh	Sevilla	23 Aug 99
7.06		Tatyana	Ter-Mesrobyan	RUS	12.5.68	1		Sankt Peterburg	22 May 02
		(30)							
7.05	0.6	Lyudmila	Galkina	RUS	20.1.72	1	WCh	Athína	9 Aug 97
7.05	-0.4	Eunice	Barber	FRA	17.11.74	1	WAF	Monaco	14 Sep 03
7.04	0.5	Brigitte	Künzel/Wujak	GDR	6.3.55	2	OG	Moskva	31 Jul 80
7.04	0.9	Tatyana	Proskuryakova'	RUS	13.1.56	1		Kiyev	25 Aug 83
7.04	2.0	Yelena	Yatsuk	UKR	16.3.61	1	Znam	Moskva	8 Jun 85
7.04	0.3	Carol	Lewis	USA	8.8.63	5	WK	Zürich	21 Aug 85
7.03	0.6	Níki	Xánthou	GRE	11.10.73	1		Bellinzona	18 Aug 97
7.03i	-	Dawn	Burrell	USA	1.11.73	1	WI	Lisboa	10 Mar 01
7.01	-0.4	Tatyana	Skachko	UKR	18.8.54	3	OG	Moskva	31 Jul 80
7.01	-0.3	Eva	Murková	SVK	29.5.62	1	PTS	Bratislava	26 May 84
		(40)							
7.01	-1.0	Marina	Kibakina'	RUS	2.8.60	1		Krasnoyarsk	10 Aug 85
7.01	1.4		Yao Weili	CHN	6.5.68	1	NC	Jinan	5 Jun 93
7.01	1.1	Shana	Williams	USA	7.4.72	Q	NC	Atlanta	21 Jun 96
7.00	2.0	Jodi	Anderson	USA	10.11.57	1	OT	Eugene	28 Jun 80
7.00		Margarita	Butkiene	LTU	19.8.49	1		Vilnius	25 May 83
7.00	-0.2	Birgit	Grosshennig	GDR	21.2.65	2		Berlin	9 Jun 84
7.00	0.6	Silvia	Khristova'	BUL	22.8.65	1		Sofiya	3 Aug 86
7.00		Susen	Tiedtke ¶	GER	23.1.69	2		Seoul	18 Aug 91
7.00	1.8	Bronwyn	Thompson	AUS	29.1.78	1	GP II	Melbourne	7 Mar 02
6.99 WR	2.0	Sigrun	Thon/Siegl	GDR	29.10.54	1	OD	Dresden	19 May 76
6.99	0.4	Lissette	Cuza	CUB	26.2.75	1	OD	Jena	3 Jun 00
6.99	1.9	Erica	Johansson	SWE	5.2.74	*	Athl	Lausanne	5 Jul 00
		(52)	100th woman 6.86, 200th woman 6.76						
Drugs dq: 7.03	0.1		Xiong Qiying	CHN	14.10.67	Q	NG	Shanghai	21 Oct 97
Wind assisted									
7.63A	2.1	Heike	Drechsler	GER	16.12.64	1		Sestriere	21 Jul 92
7.45	2.6		Joyner-Kersee			1	OT	Indianapolis	23 Jul 88
7.39	2.6		Drechsler			1		Padova	15 Sep 91
7.39	2.9		Drechsler			1	Expo	Sevilla	6 Jun 92
7.39A	3.3		Drechsler			2		Sestriere	31 Jul 94
7.36	2.2		Chistyakova			1	Znam	Volgograd	11 Jun 89
7.35	3.4		Drechsler			1	NC	Jena	29 Jun 86
7.23A	4.3	Fiona	May	ITA	12.12.69	1		Sestriere	29 Jul 95
7.19A	3.7	Susen	Tiedtke ¶	GER	23.1.69	1		Sestriere	28 Jul 93
7.17	3.6	Eva	Murková	SVK	29.5.62	1		Nitra	26 Aug 84
7.14A	4.5	Marieke	Veltman	USA	18.9.71	2		Sestriere	29 Jul 95
7.12A	5.8	Níki	Xánthou	GRE	11.10.73	3		Sestriere	29 Jul 95

Mark	Wind	Name		Nat	Born	Pos	Meet	Venue	Date
7.12A	4.3	Nicole	Boegman	AUS	5.3.67	4		Sestriere	29 Jul 95
7.09	2.9	Renata	Nielsen	DEN	18.5.66	2		Sevilla	5 Jun 94
7.08	2.2	Lyudmila	Galkina	RUS	20.1.72	1		Thessaloniki	23 Jun 99
7.07A	5.6	Valentina	Uccheddu	ITA	26.10.66	5		Sestriere	29 Jul 95
7.07A	2.7	Sharon	Couch	USA	13.9.67	1		El Paso	12 Apr 97
7.07A	w	Erica	Johansson	SWE	5.2.74	1		Vygieskraal	15 Jan 00
7.06	3.4		Ma Miaolan	CHN	18.1.70	1	NG	Beijing	10 Sep 93
7.01	2.2	Olga	Rublyova	RUS	28.10.74	1	NC	Moskva	16 Jun 95
7.00	3.8	Ramona	Neubert'	GDR	26.7.58	1	v GBR	Dresden	14 Jun 81
7.00	4.2	Sue	Hearnshaw'	GBR	26.5.61	1	NC	Cwmbran	27 May 84

Best at low altitude:

7.06 0.8 Maggi ¶ 1 Milano 3 Jun 03 7.12w 3.4 May 1 NC Bologna 25 May 96

7.17w 2.6 1 São Paulo 13 Apr 02

Ancillary marks – other marks during series (to 7.34/7.36w)

7.45 1.0 Chistyakova 11 Jun 88 | 7.47Aw 3.1 Drechsler 31 Jul 94 | 7.38w 2.2 Chistyakova 11 Jun 88

7.37 Drechsler 9 Jul 88 | 7.39Aw 3.1 Drechsler 31 Jul 94 | 7.36w Joyner-Kersee 31 Jul 94

TRIPLE JUMP

Mark	Wind	Name		Nat	Born	Pos	Meet	Venue	Date
15.50 WR	0.9	Inessa	Kravets ¶	UKR	5.10.66	1	WCh	Göteborg	10 Aug 95
15.33	-0.1		Kravets			1	OG	Atlanta	31 Jul 96
15.32	0.5	Tatyana	Lebedeva	RUS	21.7.76	1	Super	Yokohama	9 Sep 00
15.29	0.3	Yamilé	Aldama	CUB/SUD	14.8.72	1	GGala	Roma	11 Jul 03
15.27	1.3		Aldama			1	GP	London (CP)	8 Aug 03
15.25	-0.8		Lebedeva			1	WCh	Edmonton	10 Aug 01
15.20	0.0	Sarka	Kaspárková	CZE	20.5.71	1	WCh	Athína	4 Aug 97
15.20	-0.3	Tereza	Marinova	BUL	5.9.77	1	OG	Sydney	24 Sep 00
15.18	0.3	Iva	Prandzheva ¶	BUL	15.2.72	2	WCh	Göteborg	10 Aug 95
15.18	-0.2		Lebedeva			1	WCh	Saint-Denis	26 Aug 03
15.16	0.1	Rodica	Mateescu ¶	ROM	13.3.71	2	WCh	Athína	4 Aug 97
15.16i	-	Ashia	Hansen	GBR	5.12.71	1	EI	Valencia	28 Feb 98
15.15	1.7		Hansen			1	GPF	Fukuoka	13 Sep 97
15.14	-0.1		Mateescu			1	RomIC	Bucuresti	14 Jun 97
15.14	0.3		Lebedeva			1	VD	Bruxelles	5 Sep 03
15.13	0.1		Lebedeva			1	WAF	Monaco	13 Sep 03
15.12	2.0		Prandzheva			1	TOTO	Tokyo	19 Sep 98
15.12	-0.9		Lebedeva			1	GL	Saint-Denis	4 Jul 03
15.11	0.1		Aldama			1	Bisl	Oslo	27 Jun 03
15.09 WR	0.5	Anna	Biryukova	RUS	27.9.67	1	WCh	Stuttgart	21 Aug 93
15.09	-0.5	Inna	Lasovskaya (10)	RUS	17.12.69	1	ECCp-A	Valencia	31 May 97
15.08	1.4		Biryukova			3	WCh	Göteborg	10 Aug 95
15.08	0.7		Lasovskaya			1		Madrid	12 Jun 96
15.08	0.3		Aldama			2	GL	Saint-Denis	4 Jul 03
15.07	-0.6	Paraskeví	Tsiamíta	GRE	10.3.72	Q	WCh	Sevilla	22 Aug 99
15.05	-0.7	Françoise	Mbango	CMR	14.4.76	2	WCh	Saint-Denis	26 Aug 03
15.04	0.9		Prandzheva			1	NC	Sofia	17 Jun 00
15.03i		Iolanda	Chen	RUS	26.7.61	1	WI	Barcelona	11 Mar 95
15.03	0.0		Biryukova			1	WK	Zürich	16 Aug 95
15.03	1.3		Mbango			1		Lappeenranta	3 Aug 03
		(30/13)							
14.98	1.8	Sofiya	Bozhanova ¶	BUL	4.10.67	1		Stara Zagora	16 Jul 94
14.96	0.7	Yelena	Govorova	UKR	18.9.73	4	OG	Sydney	24 Sep 00
14.94i	–	Cristina	Nicolau	ROM	9.8.77	1	NC	Bucuresti	5 Feb 00
14.91	1.7	Kène	Ndoye	SEN	20.11.78	1		Villeneuve d'Ascq	15 Jun 03
14.90	-0.2	Magdelin	Martinez	ITA	10.2.76	3	WCh	Saint-Denis	26 Aug 03
14.84i		Hrisopiyí	Devetzí	GRE	2.1.76	1	Balk	Athína (P)	4 Mar 03
14.83i	-	Yelena	Lebedenko	RUS	16.1.71	1		Samara	1 Feb 01
		(20)							
14.83	0.5	Yelena	Oleynikova	RUS	9.12.76	1	Odlozil	Praha	17 Jun 02
14.79	1.7	Irina	Mushayilova	RUS	6.1.67	1	DNG	Stockholm	5 Jul 93
14.79	-0.7	Anna	Pyatykh	RUS	4.4.81	1	ECp-S	Firenze	21 Jun 03
14.76	0.9	Galina	Chistyakova	RUS	26.7.62	1		Luzern	27 Jun 95
		later Cistjaková SVK							
14.76	1.1	Gundega	Sproge	LAT	12.12.72	3		Sheffield	29 Jun 97
14.76i		Adelina	Gavrila	ROM	26.11.78	1	NC	Bucuresti	22 Feb 03
14.72	1.8		Huang Qiuyan	CHN	25.1.80	1	NG	Guangzhou	22 Nov 01
14.70i		Oksana	Rogova	RUS	7.10.78	1		Volgograd	6 Feb 02
14.69	1.2	Anja	Valant	SLO	8.9.77	3		Kalamáta	4 Jun 00
14.67	1.2	Ólga	Vasdéki	GRE	26.9.73	1		Haniá	28 Jul 99
		(30)							
14.66	1.9		Ren Ruiping	CHN	1.2.76	1	Oda	Hiroshima	29 Apr 97

Mark	Wind	Name		Nat	Born	Pos	Meet	Venue	Date
14.65	0.3	Fiona	May	ITA	12.12.69	1	ECp	Sankt-Peterburg	27 Jun 98
14.65	2.0	Natalya	Safronova	BLR	11.4.74	1	NCp	Stayki	3 Jun 00
14.65i		Nadezhda	Bazhenova	RUS	22.9.78	1		Pireás	20 Feb 02
14.64A	0.2	Baya	Rahouli	ALG	27.7.79	2	AfG	Johannesburg	18 Sep 99
14.60	0.7	Niurka	Montalvo	CUB/ESP	4.6.68	1	NC	La Habana	24 Jun 94
14.58	0.3	Yelena	Donkina	RUS	15.3.73	2	NC	Tula	10 Jul 97
14.57		Irina	Vasilyeva	RUS	9.4.79	2		Moskva	23 Jun 01
14.55	0.9		Li Huirong	CHN	14.4.65	1	Nambu	Sapporo	19 Jul 92
14.55	-0.3	Jelena	Blazevica	LAT	11.5.70	1	NC	Riga	8 Jun 96
		(40)							
14.54i	-	Mariya	Sokova	RUS	2.9.70	1	NC	Volgograd	24 Feb 95
14.53	0.7	Maurren	Maggi ¶	BRA	25.6.76	1		São Caetano do Sul	27 Apr 03
14.52	0.6	Anastasiya	Ilyina	RUS	16.1.82	Q	WJ	Santiago de Chile	20 Oct 00
14.52	0.0	Mabel	Gay	CUB	5.5.83	5	WCh	Saint-Denis	26 Aug 03
14.51		Natalya	Kayukova	RUS	10.12.66	1		Vladivostok	29 May 99
14.51	0.8	Carlota	Castrejana	ESP	25.4.73	1	ECp-1B	Sevilla	22 Jun 02
14.50	-0.1	Betty	Lise	FRA	5.9.72	Q	WCh	Athína	2 Aug 97
14.47	1.8	Olga	Yershova	RUS	13.8.76	4	Veniz	Haniá	14 Jun 00
14.46	1.0	Helga	Radtke	GER	16.5.62	1	NC	Erfurt	3 Jul 94
14.46			Peng Fengmei	CHN	2.7.79	1		Chengdu	19 Apr 98
		(50)	100th woman 14.17, 200th woman 13.84						

Wind assiste7

Mark	Wind	Name		Nat	Born	Pos	Meet	Venue	Date
15.07	2.5		Marinova			1		Réthimno	10 Jun 00
15.05	2.7		Lasovskaya			1		Sevilla	3 Jun 95
14.99	6.8	Yelena	Govorova	UKR	18.9.73	1	WUG	Palma de Mallorca	11 Jul 99
14.88	3.8	Trecia	Smith	JAM	5.11.75	1	Kans R	Lawrence	21 Apr 01
14.84	4.1	Galina	Chistyakova	RUS	26.7.62	1		Innsbruck	28 Jun 95
14.83	8.3		Ren Ruiping	CHN	1.2.76	1	NC	Taiyuan	21 May 95
14.83	2.2	Heli	Koivula	FIN	27.6.75	2	EC	München	10 Aug 02
14.75	4.2	Jelena	Blazevica	LAT	11.5.70	1	v2N	Kaunas	23 Aug 97
14.66	3.2	Sheila	Hudson	USA	30.6.67	1	NC	Sacramento	17 Jun 95
14.65	2.6	Oksana	Rogova	RUS	7.10.78	2	EU23	Göteborg	1 Aug 99
14.55	5.5		Wu Lingmei	CHN	16.2.73	2	WUG	Palma de Mallorca	11 Jul 99

Best outdoor mark for athlete with all-time best indoors

14.97WR 0.9 Chen 1 NC Moskva 18 Jun 93
14.50 Sokova 2 Znam Moskva 5 Jun 99
14.75 1.1 Gavrila 3 GP II Rieti 7 Sep 03
14.70 1.3 Nicolau 1 EU23 Göteborg 1 Aug 99
14.41 -0.2 Lebedenko 1 ECCp-A Vilamoura 30 May 98
14.60 Bazhenova 1 Moskva 23 Jun 01
14.59 1.1 Rogova * EU23 Göteborg 1 Aug 99
14.65w 2.6 2 EU23 Göteborg 1 Aug 99

Best low altitude:: 14.48 0.7 Rahouli 5 ISTAF Berlin (P) 10 Aug 03

Ancillary marks – other marks during series (to 14.99)

15.16 Lebedeva 9 Sep 00 | 15.16 -0.2 Ledebeva 26 Aug 03 | 15.15 Lebedeva 9 Sep 00
15.15 Lebedeva 9 Sep 00 | 15.12 1.6 Aldama 8 Aug 03 | 15.11 -1.1 Lebedeva 10 Aug 01

SHOT

Mark		Name		Nat	Born	Pos	Meet	Venue	Date
22.63 WR		Natalya	Lisovskaya	RUS	16.7.62	1	Znam	Moskva	7 Jun 87
22.55			Lisovskaya			1	NC	Tallinn	5 Jul 88
22.53 WR			Lisovskaya			1		Sochi	27 May 84
22.53			Lisovskaya			1		Kiyev	14 Aug 88
22.50i		Helena	Fibingerová	CZE	13.7.49	1		Jablonec	19 Feb 77
22.45 WR		Ilona	Slupianek' ¶	GDR	24.9.56	1		Potsdam	11 May 80
22.41			Slupianek			1	OG	Moskva	24 Jul 80
22.40			Slupianek			1		Berlin	3 Jun 83
22.38			Slupianek			1		Karl-Marx-Stadt	25 May 80
22.36 WR			Slupianek			1		Celje	2 May 80
22.34			Slupianek			1		Berlin	7 May 80
22.34			Slupianek			1	NC	Cottbus	18 Jul 80
22.32 WR			Fibingerová			1		Nitra	20 Aug 77
22.24			Lisovskaya			1	OG	Seoul	1 Oct 88
22.22			Slupianek			1		Potsdam	13 Jul 80
22.19		Claudia	Losch	FRG	10.1.60	1		Hainfeld	23 Aug 87
22.14i			Lisovskaya			1	NC	Penza	7 Feb 87
22.13			Slupianek			1		Split	29 Apr 80
22.06			Slupianek			1		Berlin	15 Aug 78
22.06			Lisovskaya			1		Moskva	6 Aug 88
22.05			Slupianek			1	OD	Berlin	28 May 80
22.05			Slupianek			1		Potsdam	31 May 80
22.04			Slupianek			1		Potsdam	4 Jul 79
22.04			Slupianek			1		Potsdam	29 Jul 79
21.99 WR			Fibingerová			1		Opava	26 Sep 76

Mark Wind		Name	Nat	Born	Pos	Meet	Venue	Date
21.98		Slupianek			1		Berlin	17 Jul 79
21.96		Fibingerová			1	GS	Ostrava	8 Jun 77
21.96		Lisovskaya			1	Drz	Praha	16 Aug 84
21.96		Lisovskaya			1		Vilnius	28 Aug 88
21.95		Lisovskaya			1	IAC	Edinburgh	29 Jul 88
	(30/4)							
21.89 WR	Ivanka	Khristova	BUL	19.11.41	1		Belmeken	4 Jul 76
21.86	Marianne	Adam	GDR	19.9.51	1	v URS	Leipzig	23 Jun 79
21.76		Li Meisu	CHN	17.4.59	1		Shijiazhuang	23 Apr 88
21.73	Natalya	Akhrimenko	RUS	12.5.55	1		Leselidze	21 May 88
21.69	Viktoriya	Pavlysh ¶	UKR	15.1.69	1	EC	Budapest	20 Aug 98
21.66		Sui Xinmei ¶	CHN	29.1.65	1		Beijing	9 Jun 90
	(10)							
21.61	Verzhinia	Veselinova	BUL	18.11.57	1		Sofiya	21 Aug 82
21.60i	Valentina	Fedyushina	UKR	18.2.65	1		Simferopol	28 Dec 91
21.58	Margitta	Droese/Pufe	GDR	10.9.52	1		Erfurt	28 May 78
21.57 @	Ines	Müller'	GDR	2.1.59	1		Athína	16 May 88
	21.45				1		Schwerin	4 Jun 86
21.53	Nunu	Abashidze ¶	UKR	27.3.55	2	Izv	Kiyev	20 Jun 84
21.52		Huang Zhihong	CHN	7.5.65	1	NC	Beijing	27 Jun 90
21.46	Larisa	Peleshenko ¶	RUS	29.2.64	1	Kuts	Moskva	26 Aug 00
21.45 WR	Nadezhda	Chizhova	RUS	29.9.45	1		Varna	29 Sep 73
21.43	Eva	Wilms	FRG	28.7.52	2	HB	München	17 Jun 77
21.42	Svetlana	Krachevskaya'	RUS	23.11.44	2	OG	Moskva	24 Jul 80
	(20)	*@ competitive meeting, but unsanctioned by GDR federation*						
21.31 @	Heike	Hartwig'	GDR	30.12.62	2		Athína	16 May 88
	21.27				1		Haniá	22 May 88
21.27	Liane	Schmuhl	GDR	29.6.61	1		Cottbus	26 Jun 82
21.22	Astrid	Kumbernuss	GER	5.2.70	1	WCh	Göteborg	5 Aug 95
21.21	Kathrin	Neimke	GDR	18.7.66	2	WCh	Roma	5 Sep 87
21.19	Helma	Knorscheidt	GDR	31.12.56	1		Berlin	24 May 84
21.15i	Irina	Korzhanenko ¶	RUS	16.5.74	1	NC	Moskva	18 Feb 99
21.10	Heidi	Krieger	GDR	20.7.65	1	EC	Stuttgart	26 Aug 86
21.06	Svetlana	Krivelyova	RUS	13.6.69	1	OG	Barcelona	7 Aug 92
21.05	Zdenka	Silhavá' ¶	CZE	15.6.54	2	NC	Praha	23 Jul 83
21.01	Ivanka	Petrova-Stoycheva	BUL	3.2.51	1	NC	Sofiya	28 Jul 79
	(30)							
21.00	Mihaela	Loghin	ROM	1.6.52	1		Formia	30 Jun 84
21.00	Cordula	Schulze	GDR	11.9.59	4	OD	Potsdam	21 Jul 84
20.96	Belsy	Laza	CUB	5.6.67	1		Ciudad de México	2 May 92
20.95	Elena	Stoyanova ¶	BUL	23.1.52	2	Balk	Sofiya	14 Jun 80
20.91	Svetla	Mitkova	BUL	17.6.64	1		Sofiya	24 May 87
20.80	Sona	Vasícková	CZE	14.3.62	1		Praha	2 Jun 88
20.72	Grit	Haupt/Hammer	GDR	4.6.66	3		Neubrandenburg	11 Jun 87
20.61	María Elena	Sarría	CUB	14.9.54	1		Habana	22 Jul 82
20.61	Yanina	Korolchik ¶	BLR	26.12.76	1	WCh	Edmonton	5 Aug 01
20.60	Marina	Antonyuk	RUS	12.5.62	1		Chelyabinsk	10 Aug 86
	(40)							
20.56i	Nadezhda	Ostapchuk	BLR	12.10.80	1		Minsk	21 Feb 03
20.54		Zhang Liuhong	CHN	16.1.69	1	NC	Beijing	5 Jun 94
20.53	Iris	Plotzitzka	FRG	7.1.66	1	ASV	Köln	21 Aug 88
20.50i	Christa	Wiese	GDR	25.12.67	2	NC	Senftenberg	12 Feb 89
20.47	Nina	Isayeva	RUS	6.7.50	1		Bryansk	28 Aug 82
20.47		Cong Yuzhen	CHN	22.1.63	2	IntC	Tianjin	3 Sep 88
20.44	Tatyana	Orlova	BLR	19.7.55	1		Staiki	28 May 83
20.40		Zhou Tianhua ¶	CHN	10.4.66	1		Beijing	5 Sep 91
20.34	Stephanie	Storp	FRG	28.11.68	1		Wolfsburg	1 Jul 90
20.32	Irina	Khudorozhkina	RUS	13.10.68	1		Sochi	25 May 96
	(50)	100th woman 19.43, 200th woman c.18.58						

Best outdoor marks

21.08 Fedyushina 1 Leselidze 15 May 88 — 20.82 Korzhanenko ¶ 1 Rostov na Donu 30 May 98

Ancillary marks – other marks during series (to 22.09)

22.60	Lisovskaya (WR)	7 Jun 87	22.20	Slupianek	13 Jul 80	22.12	Slupianek	13 Jul 80
22.40	Lisovskaya	14 Aug 88	22.19	Lisovskaya	5 Jul 88	22.11	Slupianek	7 May 80
22.34	Slupianek	11 May 80	22.14	Slupianek	25 May 80	22.10	Slupianek	25 May 80
22.33	Slupianek	2 May 80	22.14	Slupianek	13 Jul 80	22.09	Slupianek	7 May 80

DISCUS

Mark Wind		Name	Nat	Born	Pos	Meet	Venue	Date
76.80 WR	Gabriele	Reinsch	GDR	23.9.63	1	v ITA	Neubrandenburg	9 Jul 88
74.56 WR	Zdenka	Silhavá' ¶	CZE	15.6.54	1		Nitra	26 Aug 84
74.56	Ilke	Wyludda	GDR	28.3.69	1	NC	Neubrandenburg	23 Jul 89

Mark	Wind	Name		Nat	Born	Pos	Meet	Venue	Date
74.44			Reinsch			1		Berlin	13 Sep 88
74.40			Wyludda			2		Berlin	13 Sep 88
74.08		Diana	Gansky'	GDR	14.12.63	1	v URS	Karl-Marx-Stadt	20 Jun 87
73.90			Gansky			1	ECp	Praha	27 Jun 87
73.84		Daniela	Costian ¶	ROM	30.4.65	1		Bucuresti	30 Apr 88
73.78			Costian			1		Bucuresti	24 Apr 88
73.42			Reinsch			1		Karl-Marx-Stadt	12 Jun 88
73.36	WR	Irina	Meszynski	GDR	24.3.62	1	Drz	Praha	17 Aug 84
73.32			Gansky			1		Neubrandenburg	11 Jun 87
73.28		Galina	Savinkova'	RUS	15.7.53	1	NC	Donetsk	8 Sep 84
73.26	WR		Savinkova			1		Leselidze	21 May 83
73.26			Sachse/Gansky			1		Neubrandenburg	6 Jun 86
73.24			Gansky			1		Leipzig	29 May 87
73.22		Tsvetanka	Khristova ¶	BUL	14.3.62	1		Kazanlak	19 Apr 87
73.10		Gisela	Beyer	GDR	16.7.60	1	OD	Berlin	20 Jul 84
73.04			Gansky			1		Potsdam	6 Jun 87
73.04			Wyludda			1	ECp	Gateshead	5 Aug 89
72.96			Savinkova			1	v GDR	Erfurt	23 Jun 85
72.94			Gansky			2	v ITA	Neubrandenburg	9 Jul 88
72.92		Martina	Opitz/Hellmann	GDR	12.12.60	1	NC	Potsdam	20 Aug 87
72.90			Costian			1		Bucuresti	14 May 88
72.78			Hellmann			2		Neubrandenburg	11 Jun 87
72.78			Reinsch			1	OD	Berlin	29 Jun 88
72.72			Wyludda			1		Neubrandenburg	23 Jun 89
72.70			Wyludda			1	NC-j	Karl-Marx-Stadt	15 Jul 88
72.54			Gansky			1	NC	Rostock	25 Jun 88
72.52			Hellmann			1		Frohburg	15 Jun 86
72.52			Khristova			1	BGP	Budapest	11 Aug 86
		(31/10)							
72.14		Galina	Murashova	LTU	22.12.55	2	Drz	Praha	17 Aug 84
71.80	WR	Maria	Vergova/Petkova	BUL	3.11.50	1	NC	Sofiya	13 Jul 80
71.68			Xiao Yanling ¶	CHN	27.3.68	1		Beijing	14 Mar 92
71.58		Ellina	Zvereva' ¶	BLR	16.11.60	1	Znam	Leningrad	12 Jun 88
71.50	WR	Evelin	Schlaak/Jahl	GDR	28.3.56	1		Potsdam	10 May 80
71.30		Larisa	Korotkevich	RUS	3.1.67	1	RusCp	Sochi	29 May 92
71.22		Ria	Stalman	NED	11.12.51	1		Walnut	15 Jul 84
70.88		Hilda	Ramos ¶	CUB	1.9.64	1		Habana	8 May 92
70.80		Larisa	Mikhalchenko	UKR	16.5.63	1		Kharkov	18 Jun 88
70.68		Maritza	Martén	CUB	16.8.63	1	Ib Am	Sevilla	18 Jul 92
		(20)							
70.50	WR	Faina	Melnik	RUS	9.6.45	1	Znam	Sochi	24 Apr 76
70.34	@	Silvia	Madetzky	GDR	24.6.62	3		Athína	16 May 88
		69.34				1		Halle	26 Jun 87
70.02		Natalya	Sadova	RUS	15.6.72	1		Thessaloniki	23 Jun 99
69.86		Valentina	Kharchenko	RUS	.49	1		Feodosiya	16 May 81
69.72		Svetla	Mitkova	BUL	17.6.64	2	NC	Sofiya	15 Aug 87
69.68		Mette	Bergmann	NOR	9.11.62	1		Florø	27 May 95
69.51		Franka	Dietzsch	GER	22.1.68	1		Wiesbaden	8 May 99
69.50		Florenta	Craciunescu'	ROM	7.5.55	1	Balk	Stara Zagora	2 Aug 85
69.08		Carmen	Romero	CUB	6.10.50	1	NC	Habana	17 Apr 76
69.08		Mariana	Ionescu/Lengyel	ROM	14.4.53	1		Constanta	19 Apr 86
		(30)							
68.94		Irina	Yatchenko	BLR	31.10.65	1	Nik	Nice	15 Jul 92
68.92		Sabine	Engel	GDR	21.4.54	1	v URS,POL	Karl-Marx-Stadt	25 Jun 77
68.80		Nicoleta	Grasu	ROM	11.9.71	1		Poiana Brasov	7 Aug 99
68.64		Margitta	Pufe'	GDR	10.9.52	1	ISTAF	Berlin	17 Aug 79
68.62			Yu Hourun	CHN	9.7.64	1		Beijing	6 May 88
68.62			Hou Xuemei	CHN	27.2.62	1	IntC	Tianjin	4 Sep 88
68.60		Nadezhda	Kugayevskikh	RUS	19.4.60	1		Oryol	30 Aug 83
68.58		Lyubov	Zverkova	RUS	14.6.55	1	Izv	Kiyev	22 Jun 84
68.52		Beatrice	Faumuiná	NZL	23.10.74	1	Bisl	Oslo	4 Jul 97
68.38		Olga	Burova'	RUS	17.9.63	2	RusCp	Sochi	29 May 92
		(40)							
68.18		Tatyana	Lesovaya	KAZ	24.4.56	1		Alma-Ata	23 Sep 82
68.18		Irina	Khval	RUS	17.5.62	1		Moskva	8 Jul 88
68.18		Barbara	Hechevarría	CUB	6.8.66	2		Habana	17 Feb 89
67.96		Argentina	Menis	ROM	19.7.48	1	RomIC	Bucuresti	15 May 76
67.90		Petra	Sziegaud	GDR	17.10.58	1		Berlin	19 May 82
67.82		Tatyana	Belova	RUS	12.2.62	1		Irkutsk	10 Aug 87

Mark	Wind	Name		Nat	Born	Pos	Meet	Venue	Date
67.80		Stefenia	Simova ¶	BUL	5.6.63	1		Stara Zagora	27 Jun 92
67.71		Vera	Pospísilová	CZE	19.11.78	1		Réthimno	6 Jul 03
67.70		Anastasía	Kelesídou	GRE	28.11.72	2		Réthimno	29 May 99
67.54		Svetlana	Petrova	BLR	19.12.51	1		Brest-Litovsk	20 Sep 78
		(50)	100th woman 65.32, 200th woman c.63.00						
Unofficial meeting									
78.14		Martina	Hellmann	GDR	12.12.60	1		Berlin	6 Sep 88
75.36		Ilke	Wyludda	GDR	28.3.69	2		Berlin	6 Sep 88
Downhill									
69.44		Suzy	Powell	USA	3.9.76	1		La Jolla	27 Apr 02

Ancillary marks – other marks during series (to 72.92)

73.32	Reinsch	13 Sep 88	73.28	Gansky	27 Jun 87	73.10	Reinsch	9 Jul 88
73.28	Gansky	11 Jun 87	73.16	Wyludda	13 Sep 88	73.06	Gansky	27 Jun 87
						72.92	Hellmann	20 Aug 87

HAMMER

Mark	Wind	Name		Nat	Born	Pos	Meet	Venue	Date
76.07	WR	Mihaela	Melinte ¶	ROM	27.3.75	1		Rüdlingen	29 Aug 99
75.97	WR		Melinte			1		Clermont-Ferrand	13 May 99
75.68		Olga	Kuzenkova	RUS	4.10.70	1	NCp	Tula	4 Jun 00
75.21			Melinte			1c1		Rüdlingen	28 Aug 99
75.20			Melinte			1	WCh	Sevilla	24 Aug 99
75.14		Yipsi	Moreno	CUB	19.11.80	1		Savona	17 Jul 03
74.98			Kuzenkova			1	NC	Tula	9 Aug 03
74.90			Melinte			1		Bucuresti	4 Jul 99
74.77			Melinte			1		Nürnberg	13 Jun 99
74.50		Manuéla	Montebrun	FRA	13.11.79	1		Villeneuve d'Ascq	15 Jun 03
74.48			Melinte			1	ECp	Paris (C)	20 Jun 99
74.43			Montebrun			1	ECpS	Firenze	22 Jun 03
74.30			Kuzenkova			1	Znam	Moskva	4 Jun 99
74.25			Moreno			1	PAm	Santo Domingo	5 Aug 03
74.24			Melinte			1	WUG	Palma de Mallorca	9 Jul 99
74.22			Melinte			1		Bucuresti	29 May 99
74.20			Melinte			1		Poiana Brasov	7 Aug 99
74.07			Moreno			1	Barr	La Habana	31 May 03
74.00			Kuzenkova			1	Kuts	Moskva	26 Aug 00
73.91			Moreno			1		Padova	5 Jul 03
73.85			Kuzenkova			1		Togliatti	14 May 00
73.80	UWR		Kuzenkova			1		Tolyatti	15 May 98
73.74			Montebrun			1		Saumur	4 May 03
73.62			Kuzenkova			1	NC-w	Adler	24 Feb 01
73.60			Melinte			1		Bugeat	28 Jun 99
73.42			Moreno			1	WAF	Szombathely	7 Sep 03
73.40			Kuzenkova			1	NC	Tula	13 Jul 01
73.40			Montebrun			1		Kuortane	20 Jul 03
73.33			Moreno			1	WCh	Saint-Denis	28 Aug 03
73.31			Montebrun			1	GP II	Zagreb	7 Jul 03
		(30/4)							
72.96		Irina	Sekachova	UKR	21.7.76	1		Koncha-Zaspa	23 May 03
72.60		Kamila	Skolimowska	POL	4.11.82	1		Bydgoszcz	8 Jun 02
72.09		Tatyana	Konstantinova	RUS	18.11.70	2	Znam	Moskva	4 Jun 99
72.03			Gu Yuan	CHN	9.5.82	1	NC	Shanghai	12 Sep 03
72.01		Anna	Norgren-Mahon	USA	19.12.74	1		Walnut	27 Jul 02
71.93		Susanne	Keil	GER	18.5.78	1		Fränkisch-Crumbach	8 Jun 03
		(10)							
71.12		Bronwyn	Eagles	AUS	23.8.80	1		Adelaide	6 Feb 03
70.79		Katalin	Divós ¶	HUN	11.5.74	2	GP	Doha	18 May 01
70.69		Yunaika	Crawford	CUB	2.11.82	2	NC	La Habana	27 May 03
70.67			Zhao Wei	CHN	27.1.79	1		Nanning	5 Apr 03
70.62		Dawn	Ellerbe	USA	3.4.74	1	Penn R	Philadelphia	28 Apr 01
70.60			Zhang Wenxiu	CHN	22.3.86	2		Nanning	5 Apr 03
70.43		Ester	Balassini	ITA	20.10.77	2		Padova	5 Jul 03
70.42		Betty	Heidler	GER	14.10.83	1		Mannheim	21 Jun 03
70.34		Melissa	Price	USA	5.9.79	1	NC	Stanford	19 Jun 03
70.11		Olga	Tsander	BLR	18.5.76	2		Bydgoszcz	8 Jun 02
		(20)							
69.98		Alexándra	Papayeoryíou	GRE	17.12.80	1	ROM Ch	Bucuresti	9 Aug 03
69.92		Lyudmila	Gubkina	BLR	13.8.73	1		Staiki	19 Aug 00
69.79		Candace	Scott	TRI	17.9.80	1	NCAA	Sacramento	14 Jun 03
69.72		Aldenay	Vasallo	CUB	25.2.77	1		La Habana	21 Jun 03
69.63		Mia	Strömmer	FIN	26.2.74	1		Potchefstroom	24 Mar 01

Mark	Wind	Name	Nat	Born	Pos	Meet	Venue	Date
69.59		Yelena Konevtsova (Tauryanina)	RUS	11.3.81	2	NC	Tula	9 Aug 03
69.33		Andrea Bunjes	GER	5.2.76	1		Schönau	21 Jun 03
69.28		Kirsten Münchow/Klose	GER	21.1.77	3	OG	Sydney	29 Sep 00
69.24		Lisa Misipeka	ASA	3.1.75	1	Jerome	Burnaby	8 Jun 03
69.17		Alla Davydova	RUS	21.5.66	1	ECCp	Valencia	24 May 03
		(30)						
69.05		Liu Yinghui	CHN	29.6.79	1	WUG	Daegu	26 Aug 03
68.93		Lorraine Shaw	GBR	2.4.68	1		Loughborough	8 Jun 03
68.92		Gulfiya Khanafeyeva	RUS	12.6.82	1		Moskva	14 Jun 03
68.55		Svetlana Sudak	BLR	20.3.71	2	NC	Minsk	11 Jul 03
68.50		Martina Danisová ¶	SVK	21.3.83	1		Kladno	16 Jun 01
68.43		Vânia Silva	POR	8.6.80	4		Madrid (C)	3 Jul 02
68.40		Bianca Achilles	GER	17.4.81	1		Dortmund	25 Sep 99
68.28		Amy Palmer	USA	20.4.75	2	PennR	Philadelphia	29 Apr 00
68.28		Sini Pöyry	FIN	3.2.80	1		Helsinki	12 Jun 02
68.23		Clarissa Claretti	ITA	7.10.80	1	v2N-23	Macerata	28 Jul 02
		(40)						
68.18		Ivana Brkljacic	CRO	25.1.83	1		Pula	28 Apr 00
68.12		Evdokía Tsámoglou	GRE	15.12.78	3		Nikíti	1 Aug 03
68.03		Florence Ezeh	FRA	29.12.77	4	EC	München	9 Aug 02
67.98		Agnieszka Pogroszewska	POL	20.2.77	2		Poznan	8 Jun 01
67.98		Bethany Hart	USA	10.4.77	1		New Haven	6 Jul 03
67.95		Debbie Sosimenko	AUS	5.4.74	5	OG	Sydney	29 Sep 00
67.87		Brooke Krueger	AUS	9.7.80	4		Szombathely	14 Jul 02
67.86		Lucie Vrbenská	CZE	12.5.77	1	NC	Olomouc	13 Jul 03
67.72		Sanja Gavrilovic	CRO	20.9.82	1		Split	11 May 03
67.58		Oksana Menkova	BLR	28.3.82	2	EU23	Bydgoszcz	20 Jul 0
		(50) 100th woman 64.30, 200th 61.04						

Downhill

Mark	Wind	Name	Nat	Born	Pos	Meet	Venue	Date
75.20		Manuéla Montebrun	FRA	13.11.79	1		Vineuil	18 May 03

Ancillary marks – other marks during series

76.05	Melinte	29 Aug 99	74.58	Melinte	29 Aug 99	74.21	Melinte	28 Aug 99
75.29	Melinte	13 May 99	74.57	Kuzenkova	9 Aug 03	74.15	Kuzenkova	9 Aug 03
75.16	Kuzenkova	4 Jun 00	74.47	Melinte	28 Aug 99	74.10	Melinte	9 Jul 99
74.65	Melinte	28 Aug 99	74.21	Melinte	24 Aug 99	74.02	Melinte	29 Aug 99

Drugs disqualification

74.80	Melinte	1		Rüdlingen	12 Aug 00	73.75	Melinte	1	NC Bucuresti	6 Aug 00
74.32	Melinte	1		Nitra	26 Aug 00	73.74	Melinte	1	Noisy-le-Grand	20 Jun 00

JAVELIN

Mark	Wind	Name	Nat	Born	Pos	Meet	Venue	Date
71.54	WR	Osleidys Menéndez	CUB	14.11.79	1		Réthimno	1 Jul 01
69.82		Menéndez			1	WUG	Beijing	29 Aug 01
69.53		Menéndez			1	WCh	Edmonton	7 Aug 01
69.48	WR	Trine Hattestad	NOR	18.4.66	1	Bisl	Oslo	28 Jul 00
68.91		Hattestad			1	OG	Sydney	30 Sep 00
68.40		Menéndez			1		Tartu	19 Jun 01
68.32		Hattestad			1	ISTAF	Berlin	1 Sep 00
68.22	WR	Hattestad			1	GGala	Roma	30 Jun 00
68.19	WRu	Hattestad			1		Fana	28 Jul 99
67.92		Hattestad			1	DNG	Stockholm	1 Aug 00
67.83		Menéndez			2	ISTAF	Berlin	1 Sep 00
67.76		Hattestad			1	VD	Bruxelles	25 Aug 00
67.51	WR	Miréla Manjani/Tzelíli	GRE	21.12.76	2	OG	Sydney	30 Sep 00
67.47		Manjani			1	EC	München	8 Aug 02
67.40		Menéndez			1	Athl	Lausanne	2 Jul 02
67.34		Menéndez			Q	OG	Sydney	29 Sep 00
67.20		Tatyana Shikolenko	RUS	10.5.68	1	Herc	Monaco	18 Aug 00
67.14		Menéndez			1	NC	La Habana	10 Mar 02
67.09		Tzelíli			1	WCh	Sevilla	28 Aug 99
66.96		Hattestad			1	ECp1A	Nadderud	8 Jul 00
66.91		Tanja Damaske	GER	16.11.71	1	NC	Erfurt	4 Jul 99
66.80		Louise Currey	AUS	24.1.69	1		Gold Coast (RB)	5 Aug 00
66.74		Menéndez			1	GPII	Helsinki	14 Jun 01
66.73		Damaske			1	NC	Braunschweig	29 Jul 00
66.73		Hattestad			2	Herc	Monaco	18 Aug 00
66.70		Manjani			1	NC	Athína	16 Jun 01
66.55		Tzelíli			1	NC	Athína	7 Aug 99
66.54		Hattestad			1		Fana	27 Jun 00
66.54		Sonia Bisset	CUB	1.4.71	1		Madrid	7 Jul 01

Mark	Wind	Name		Nat	Born	Pos	Meet	Venue	Date
66.52			Manjani			1	WCh	Saint-Denis	30 Aug 03
		(30/7)							
65.76		Steffi	Nerius	GER	1.7.72	Q	OG	Sydney	29 Sep 00
65.71		Nikola	Tomecková	CZE	25.6.74	Q	WCh	Edmonton	4 Aug 01
65.30		Claudia	Coslovich	ITA	26.4.72	1		Ljubljana	10 Jun 00
		(10)							
65.29		Xiomara	Rivero	CUB	22.11.68	1		Santiago de Cuba	17 Mar 01
65.17		Karen	Forkel	GER	24.3.70	2	NC	Erfurt	4 Jul 99
65.08		Ana Mirela	Termure ¶	ROM	13.1.75	1	NC	Bucuresti	10 Jun 01
64.90		Paula	Huhtaniemi	FIN	17.2.73	1	NC	Helsinki	10 Aug 03
64.89		Yekaterina	Ivakina	RUS	4.12.64	4	Bisl	Oslo	28 Jul 00
64.87		Kelly	Morgan	GBR	17.6.80	1	NC	Birmingham	14 Jul 02
64.62		Joanna	Stone	AUS	4.10.72	2		Gold Coast (RB)	5 Aug 00
64.62		Nikolett	Szabó	HUN	3.3.80	1		Pátra	22 Jul 01
64.61		Oksana	Makarova	RUS	21.7.71	2	ECp	Paris (C)	19 Jun 99
64.49		Valeriya	Zabruskova	RUS	29.7.75	1	Znam	Tula	7 Jun 03
		(20)							
64.46		Dörthe	Friedrich	GER	21.6.73	1	NC	Wattenscheid	7 Jul 02
64.06		Taina	Uppa/Kolkkala	FIN	24.10.76	1		Pihtipudas	23 Jul 00
64.03		Mikaela	Ingberg	FIN	29.7.74	6	ISTAF	Berlin	1 Sep 00
63.92			Wei Jianhua	CHN	23.3.79	1		Beijing	18 Aug 00
63.89		Felicia	Tilea-Moldovan ¶	ROM	29.9.67	2	WK	Zürich	16 Aug 02
63.73		Laverne	Eve	BAH	16.6.65	1		Nashville	22 Apr 00
63.69			Li Lei	CHN	4.5.74	1	OT	Jinzhou	8 Jun 00
63.32		Khristina	Georgieva	BUL	3.1.72	3	GP	Athína	28 Jun 00
63.14		Aggelikí	Tsiolakoúdi	GRE	10.5.76	5	EC	München	8 Aug 02
62.93			Xue Juan	CHN	10.2.86	1	NG	Changsha	27 Oct 03
		(30)	50th best 61.12						

Ancillary marks – other marks during series (to 66.70)

69.42	Menéndez	7 Aug 01	67.51	Tzelíli	30 Sep 00	66.83	Menéndez	19 Jun 01
67.61	Hattestad	28 Jul 99	67.04	Hattestad	28 Jul 99	66.70	Menéndez	7 Aug 01

Specification changed from 1 May 1999. See ATHLETICS 2000 for Old specification all-time list. Top 10:

Mark	Wind	Name		Nat	Born	Pos	Meet	Venue	Date
80.00	WR	Petra	Felke	GDR	30.7.59	1		Potsdam	9 Sep 88
77.44	WR	Fatima	Whitbread	GBR	3.3.61	Q	EC	Stuttgart	28 Aug 86
74.76	WR	Tiina	Lillak	FIN	15.4.61	1		Tampere	13 Jun 83
74.20	WR	Sofía	Sakorafa	GRE	29.4.57	1	NC	Haniá	26 Sep 82
73.58		Tessa	Sanderson	GBR	14.3.56	1		Edinburgh	26 Jun 83
72.70		Anna	Veroúli ¶	GRE	13.11.56	1		Haniá	20 May 84
72.16		Antje	Kempe-Zöllkau	GDR	23.6.63	2		Celje	5 May 84
72.12		Trine	Hattestad'	NOR	18.4.66	1	Bisl	Oslo	10 Jul 93
71.88	WR	Antoaneta	Todorova'	BUL	8.6.63	1	ECp	Zagreb	15 Aug 81
71.82		Ivonne	Leal	CUB	27.2.66	1	WUG	Kobe	30 Aug 85

HEPTATHLON

Mark	Wind	Name		Nat	Born	Pos	Meet	Venue	Date
7291	WR	Jackie	Joyner-Kersee	USA	3.3.62	1	OG	Seoul	24 Sep 88
		12.69/0.5	1.86	15.80	22.56/1.6	7.27/0.7		45.66	2:08.51
7215	WR		Joyner-Kersee			1	OT	Indianapolis	16 Jul 88
		12.71/-0.9	1.93	15.65	22.30/ 0.0	7.00/-1.3		50.08	2:20.70
7158	WR		Joyner-Kersee			1	USOF	Houston	2 Aug 86
		13.18/-0.5	1.88	15.20	22.85/1.2	7.03/2.9		50.12	2:09.69
7148	WR		Joyner-Kersee			1	GWG	Moskva	7 Jul 86
		12.85/0.2	1.88	14.76	23.00/0.3	7.01/-0.5		49.86	2:10.02
7128			Joyner-Kersee			1	WCh	Roma	1 Sep 87
		12.91/0.2	1.90	16.00	22.95/1.2	7.14/0.9		45.68	2:16.29
7044			Joyner-Kersee			1	OG	Barcelona	2 Aug 92
		12.85/-0.9	1.91	14.13	23.12/0.7	7.10/1.3		44.98	2:11.78
7007		Larisa	Nikitina ¶	RUS	29.4.65	1	NC	Bryansk	11 Jun 89
		13.40/1.4	1.89	16.45	23.97/1.1	6.73/4.0		53.94	2:15.31
7001		Carolina	Klüft	SWE	2.2.83	1	WCh	Saint-Denis	24 Aug 03
		13.18/-0.4	1.94	14.19	22.98/1.1	6.68/1.0		49.90	2:12.12
6985		Sabine	Braun	GER	19.6.65	1		Götzis	31 May 92
		13.11/-0.4	1.93	14.84	23.65/2.0	6.63/2.9		51.62	2:12.67
6979			Joyner-Kersee			1	TAC	San José	24 Jun 87
		12.90/2.0	1.85	15.17	23.02/0.4	7.25/2.3		40.24	2:13.07
6946	WR	Sabine	Paetz'	GDR	16.10.57	1	NC	Potsdam	6 May 84
		12.64/0.3	1.80	15.37	23.37/0.7	6.86/-0.2		44.62	2:08.93
6942		Ghada	Shouaa	SYR	10.9.72	1		Götzis	26 May 96
		13.78/0.3	1.87	15.64	23.78/0.6	6.77/0.6		54.74	2:13.61
6935	WR	Ramona	Neubert	GDR	26.7.58	1	v URS	Moskva	19 Jun 83
		13.42/1.7	1.82	15.25	23.49/0.5	6.79/0.7		49.94	2:07.51

Mark	Wind	Name		Nat	Born	Pos	Meet	Venue	Date
6910			Joyner			1	MSR	Walnut	25 Apr 86
		12.9/0.0	1.86	14.75	23.24/2.8	6.85/2.1		48.30	2:14.11
6897			John'			2	OG	Seoul	24 Sep 88
		12.85/0.5	1.80	16.23	23.65/1.6	6.71/ 0.0		42.56	2:06.14
6878			Joyner-Kersee			1	TAC	New York	13 Jun 91
		12.77	1.89	15.62	23.42	6.97/0.4		43.28	2:22.12
6875			Nikitina			1	ECp-A	Helmond	16 Jul 89
		13.55/-2.1	1.84	15.99	24.29/-2.1	6.75/-2.5		56.78	2:18.67
6861		Eunice	Barber	FRA	17.11.74	1	WCh	Sevilla	22 Aug 99
		12.89/-0.5	1.93	12.37	23.57/0.5	6.86/-0.3		49.88	2:15.65
6859		Natalya	Shubenkova	RUS	25.9.57	1	NC	Kiyev	21 Jun 84
		12.93/1.0	1.83	13.66	23.57/-0.3	6.73/0.4		46.26	2:04.60
6858		Anke	Vater/Behmer (10)	GDR	5.6.61	3	OG	Seoul	24 Sep 88
		13.20/0.5	1.83	14.20	23.10/1.6	6.68/0.1		44.54	2:04.20
6847			Nikitina			1	WUG	Duisburg	29 Aug 89
		13.47	1.81	16.12	24.12	6.66		59.28	2:22.07
6845	WR		Neubert			1	v URS	Halle	20 Jun 82
		13.58/1.8	1.83	15.10	23.14/1.4	6.84w/2.3		42.54	2:06.16
6845		Irina	Belova ¶	RUS	27.3.68	2	OG	Barcelona	2 Aug 92
		13.25/-0.1	1.88	13.77	23.34/0.2	6.82/0.0		41.90	2:05.08
6842			Barber			1		Götzis	4 Jun 00
		12.97/0.2	1.88	12.23	23.84/0.5	6.85/-0.1		51.91	2:11.55
6841			Joyner			1		Götzis	25 May 86
		13.09/-1.3	1.87	14.34	23.63/-0.8	6.76/-0.3		48.88	2:14.58
6837			Joyner-Kersee			1	WCh	Stuttgart	17 Aug 93
		12.89/0.1	1.81	14.38	23.19/0.0	7.04/1.4		43.76	2:14.49
6831		Denise	Lewis	GBR	27.8.72	1		Talence	30 Jul 00
		13.13/1.0	1.84	15.07	24.01w/3.6	6.69/-0.4		49.42	2:12.20
6813			Paetz			1	OD	Potsdam	21 Jul 84
		12.71/0.4	1.74	16.16	23.23w	6.58		41.94	2:07.03
6805			Behmer			1		Götzis	19 Jun 88
		13.28/1.6	1.84	14.38	22.73/4.0	6.62/1.1		40.48	2:04.64
6803		Jane	Frederick	USA	7.4.52	1		Talence	16 Sep 84
		13.27/1.2	1.87	15.49	24.15/1.6	6.43/0.2		51.74	2:13.55
		(30/13)							
6765		Yelena	Prokhorova	RUS	16.4.78	1	NC	Tula	23 Jul 00
		13.54/-2.8	1.82	14.30	23.37/-0.2	6.72/1.0		43.40	2:04.27
6750			Ma Miaolan	CHN	18.1.70	1	NG	Beijing	12 Sep 93
		13.28/1.5	1.89	14.98	23.86/	6.64/		45.82	2:15.33
6741		Heike	Drechsler	GER	16.12.64	1		Talence	11 Sep 94
		13.34/-0.3	1.84	13.58	22.84/-1.1	6.95/1.0		40.64	2:11.53
6703		Tatyana	Blokhina	RUS	12.3.70	1		Talence	11 Sep 93
		13.69/-0.6	1.91	14.94	23.95/-0.4	5.99/-0.3		52.16	2:09.65
6702		Chantal	Beaugeant ¶	FRA	16.2.61	2		Götzis	19 Jun 88
		13.10/1.6	1.78	13.74	23.96/3.5	6.45/0.2		50.96	2:07.09
6695		Jane	Flemming	AUS	14.4.65	1	CG	Auckland	28 Jan 90
		13.21/1.4	1.82	13.76	23.62/2.4	6.57/1.6		49.28	2:12.53
6660		Ines	Schulz	GDR	10.7.65	3		Götzis	19 Jun 88
		13.56/0.4	1.84	13.95	23.93/2.8	6.70/0.7		42.82	2:06.31
		(20)							
6658		Svetla	Dimitrova ¶	BUL	27.1.70	2		Götzis	31 May 92
		13.41/-0.7	1.75	14.72	23.06/2.4	6.64/1.9		43.84	2:09.60
6646		Natalya	Grachova	UKR	21.2.52	1	NC	Moskva	2 Aug 82
		13.80	1.80	16.18	23.86	6.65/3.5		39.42	2:06.59
6635		Sibylle	Thiele	GDR	6.3.65	2	GWG	Moskva	7 Jul 86
		13.14/0.6	1.76	16.00	24.18	6.62/1.0		45.74	2:15.30
6635		Svetlana	Buraga	BLR	4.9.65	3	WCh	Stuttgart	17 Aug 93
		12.95/0.1	1.84	14.55	23.69/	6.58/-0.2		41.04	2:13.65
6633		Natalya	Roshchupkina	RUS	13.1.78	2	NC	Tula	23 Jul 00
		14.05/-2.8	1.88	14.28	23.47/-0.2	6.45/0.4		44.34	2:07.93
6623		Judy	Simpson'	GBR	14.11.60	3	EC	Stuttgart	30 Aug 86
		13.05/0.8	1.92	14.73	25.09/0.0	6.56/2.5		40.92	2:11.70
6619		Liliana	Nastase	ROM	1.8.62	4	OG	Barcelona	2 Aug 92
		12.86/-0.9	1.82	14.34	23.70/0.2	6.49/-0.3		41.30	2:11.22
6616		Malgorzata	Nowak'	POL	9.2.59	1	WUG	Kobe	31 Aug 85
		13.27/4.0	1.95	15.35	24.20/0.0	6.37/3.9		43.36	2:20.39
6604		Remigija	Nazaroviene'	LTU	2.6.67	2	URSCh	Bryansk	11 Jun 89
		13.26/1.4	1.86	14.27	24.12/0.7	6.58/0.9		40.94	2:09.98
6604		Irina	Tyukhay	RUS	14.1.67	3		Götzis	28 May 95
		13.20/-0.7	1.84	14.97	24.33/1.7	6.71/0.5		43.84	2:17.64

WOMEN All-time

Mark Wind	Name		Nat	Born	Pos	Meet	Venue		Date
	(30)								
6598	Svetlana	Moskalets	RUS	22.1.69	1	NC	Vladimir		17 Jun 94
	13.20/0.8	1.82	13.78	23.56/0.1		6.74/0.8	42.48	2:14.54	
6577	DeDee	Nathan	USA	20.4.68	1		Götzis		30 May 99
	13.28/-0.1	1.76	14.74	24.23/0.2		6.59/1.6	50.08	2:16.92	
6573	Rita	Ináncsi	HUN	6.1.71	3		Götzis		29 May 94
	13.66/2.0	1.84	13.94	24.20/2.5		6.78/1.4	46.28	2:16.02	
6572	Heike	Tischler	GDR	4.2.64	2	EC	Split		31 Aug 90
	14.08/-0.9	1.82	13.73	24.29/0.9		6.22/-0.7	53.24	2:05.50	
6563	Natalya	Sazanovich	BLR	15.8.73	2	OG	Atlanta		28 Jul 96
	13.56/-1.6	1.80	14.52	23.72/-0.3		6.70/1.1	46.00	2:17.92	
6552	Nadezhda	Vinogradova'	RUS	1.5.58	2	NC	Kiyev		21 Jun 84
	13.92/1.0	1.80	15.19	23.84/0.2		6.67/0.1	38.60	2:06.80	
6551	Yelena	Martsenyuk	RUS	21.2.61	2		Staiki		2 Jul 88
	13.54/-0.4	1.82	15.32	24.25/0.3		6.25/0.7	47.56	2:12.72	
6546	Mona	Steigauf	GER	17.1.70	1	WUG	Catania		27 Aug 97
	13.13/1.6	1.85	12.83	24.14/1.7		6.56/1.3	43.86	2:11.15	
6542	Urszula	Wlodarczyk	POL	22.12.65	4	WCh	Athína		4 Aug 97
	13.55/0.3	1.81	14.16	24.48/0.1		6.63/0.6	44.18	2:09.59	
6541	Mila	Kolyadina	RUS	31.12.60	4	v GDR	Moskva		19 Jun 83
	14.05	1.82	16.28	24.81		6.48/0.8	48.26	2:15.26	
	(40)								
6539	Tatyana	Shpak	UKR	17.11.60	3		Staiki		2 Jul 88
	13.57/-0.4	1.76	15.30	23.61/0.5		6.52/-0.6	39.28	2:07.25	
6536	Yekaterina	Smirnova	RUS	22.10.56	3	v GDR	Moskva		19 Jun 83
	13.41	1.82	14.82	24.84		6.56/1.1	45.66	2:13.38	
6531	Peggy	Beer	GDR	15.9.69	3	EC	Split		31 Aug 90
	13.27/-0.2	1.82	13.46	23.99/0.4		6.38/0.9	42.10	2:05.79	
6527	Diane	Guthrie-Gresham	JAM	24.10.71	1	NCAA	Knoxville		3 Jun 95
	13.86w/2.5	1.86	13.80	24.91/-1.3		6.92w/2.5	49.04	2:20.82	
6523	Sabine	Everts	FRG	4.3.61	1	v URS	Mannheim		10 Jun 82
	13.45	1.89	12.39	23.73		6.75	36.02	2:07.73	
6500	Birgit	Clarius	GER	18.3.65	1	NC	Vaterstetten		20 Jun 93
	13.61/1.3	1.81	15.22	24.69w/2.1		6.08/-0.6	50.20	2:11.29	
6493	Svetlana	Filatyeva '	RUS	3.4.64	1		Kiyev		14 Aug 88
	13.77	1.89	13.89	24.94		6.30	48.44	2:11.89	
6487	Birgit	Dressel	FRG	4.5.60	4	EC	Stuttgart		30 Aug 86
	13.56/-1.6	1.92	14.12	24.68/0.0		6.28/1.1	45.70	2:15.78	
6474	Marianna	Maslennikova	RUS	17.5.61	2	NC	Kiyev		2 Aug 88
	13.37/0.4	1.83	13.68	24.07/0.0		6.28/0.2	40.42	2:05.60	
6472	Shelia	Burrell	USA	15.1.72	3	WCh	Edmonton		5 Aug 01
	13.05/0.5	1.67	12.87	22.92		6.45/0.4	48.74	2:14.24	
	(50)	100th woman 6308, 200th woman 6089							

DECATHLON

Mark	Name				Nat	Born	Pos		Venue		Date
7885	Mona	Steigauf			GER	17.1.70	1		Ahlen		21 Sep 97
	12.15/1.2	5.93	12.49	1.73	55.34	13.75/0.2	34.68	3.10	42.24	5:07.95	
7731	Marie	Collonvillé			FRA	23.11.73	1		Lage		10 Sep 00
	12.61	6.03	11.55	1.75	56.48	14.28	31.91	3.40	43.94	5:13.70	
7577	Tiffany	Lott-Hogan			USA	1.8.75	2		Lage		10 Sep 00
	12.31	5.77	13.86	1.69	58.01	13.57	38.39	3.00	46.93	6:01.24	

4 x 100 METRES RELAY

Mark	Nat	Team	Pos	Meet	Venue	Date
41.37 WR	GDR	Gladisch, Rieger, Auerswald, Göhr	1	WCp	Canberra	6 Oct 85
41.47	USA	Gaines, Jones, Miller, Devers	1	WCh	Athína	9 Aug 97
41.49	RUS	Bogoslovskaya, Malchugina, Voronova, Privalova	1	WCh	Stuttgart	22 Aug 93
41.49	USA	Finn, Torrence, Vereen, Devers	2	WCh	Stuttgart	22 Aug 93
41.52	USA	Gaines, Jones, Miller, Devers	1h1	WCh	Athína	8 Aug 97
41.53 WR	GDR	Gladisch, Koch, Auerswald, Göhr	1		Berlin	31 Jul 83
41.55	USA	Brown, Williams, Griffith, Marshall	1	ISTAF	Berlin	21 Aug 87
41.58	USA	Brown, Williams, Griffith, Marshall	1	WCh	Roma	6 Sep 87
41.60 WR	GDR	Müller, Wöckel, Auerswald, Göhr	1	OG	Moskva	1 Aug 80
41.61A	USA	Brown, Williams, Cheeseborough, Ashford	1	USOF	USAF Academy	3 Jul 83
41.63	USA	Brown, Williams, Cheeseborough, Ashford	1	v GDR	Los Angeles	25 Jun 83
41.65	USA	Brown, Bolden, Cheeseborough, Ashford	1	OG	Los Angeles	11 Aug 84
41.65	GDR	Gladisch, Koch, Auerswald, Göhr	1	ECp	Moskva	17 Aug 85
41.68	GDR	Möller, Krabbe, Behrendt, Günther	1	EC	Split	1 Sep 90
41.69	GDR	Gladisch, Koch, Auerswald, Göhr	1	OD	Potsdam	21 Jul 84
41.71	USA	White, Gaines, Miller, Jones	1	WCh	Edmonton	11 Aug 01
41.73	GDR	Möller, Behrendt, Lange, Göhr	1		Berlin	13 Sep 88

Mark	Wind	Name	Nat	Born	Pos	Meet	Venue	Date
41.76	GDR	Gladisch, Koch, Auerswald, Göhr			1	WCh	Helsinki	10 Aug 83
41.78	FRA	Girard, Hurtis, Félix, Arron			1	WCh	Saint-Denis	30 Aug 03
41.79	GDR	Gladisch, Drechsler, Auerswald, Göhr			1	v URS	Karl-Marx-Stadt	20 Jun 87
		(20 performances by 3 nations) from here just best by nation						
41.92	BAH	Fynes, Sturrup, Davis-Thompson, Ferguson			1	WCh	Sevilla	29 Aug 99
41.94	JAM	Duhaney, Cuthbert, McDonald, Ottey			1	WCh	Tokyo	1 Sep 91
42.08mx	BUL	Pavlova, Nuneva, Georgieva, Ivanova			mx		Sofiya	8 Aug 84
	42.29	Pencheva, Nuneva, Georgieva, Donkova			1		Sofiya	26 Jun 88
42.23	CHN	(Sichuan) Xiao Lin, Li Yali, Liu Xiaomei, Li Xuemei			1	NG	Shanghai	23 Oct 97
42.39	NGR	Utondu, Idehen, Opara-Thompson, Onyali			2h2	OG	Barcelona	7 Aug 92
42.43	GBR	Hunte, Smallwood, Goddard, Lannaman			3	OG	Moskva	1 Aug 80
	(10)							
42.59	FRG	Possekel, Helten, Richter, Kroniger			2	OG	Montreal	31 Jul 76
42.71	POL	Tomczak, Pakula, Pisiewicz, Kasprzyk			3	ECp	Moskva	17 Aug 85
42.77	CAN	Bailey, Payne, Taylor, Gareau			2	OG	Los Angeles	11 Aug 84
42.89	CUB	Ferrer, López, Duporty, Allen			6	WCh	Stuttgart	22 Aug 93
42.96	UKR	Tkalich, Kravchenko, Pastushenko, Maydanova			1		Kiev	6 Jul 03
42.98	CZE/TCH	Sokolová, Soborová, Kocembová, Kratochvilová			1	WK	Zürich	18 Aug 82
42.99A	AUS	Massey, Broadrick, Lambert, Gainsford-Taylor			1		Pietersburg	18 Mar 00
43.07	GRE	Tsóni, Kóffa, Vasarmídou, Thánou			2	MedG	Bari	18 Jun 97
43.11	BLR	Nesterenko, Dragun, Nevmerhytskaya, Safronnikova			3h1	WCh	Saint-Denis	29 Aug 03
43.19	GHA	Akoto, Twum, Anim, Nsiah			5s1	OG	Sydney	29 Sep 00
	(20)							
43.22	BEL	De Caluwe, Callaerts, Ouedraogo, Gevaert			4	EC	München	11 Aug 02
43.25A	RSA	Hartman, Moropane, Holtshausen, Seyerling			2		Pietersburg	18 Mar 00
43.35	KAZ	Aleksandrova, Kvast, Miljauskiene, Sevalnikova			2	SPART	Taskent	16 Sep 86
43.37	FIN	Pirtimaa, Hanhijoki, Hernesniemi, Salmela			7	WCh	Stuttgart	22 Aug 93
43.42	COL	Mera, Palacios, Rodriguez, Brock			4h2	WCh	Göteborg	12 Aug 95
43.44A WR	NED	van den Berg, Sterk, Hennipman, Bakker			4	OG	Ciudad de México	20 Oct 68
43.44	ITA	Pistone, Graglia, Grillo, Levorato			1		Barletta	26 Jul 00
43.61	MAD	Rahanitraniriana, Ratsimbazafy, Rakotozafy, Rakotondrabé			4h4	OG	Sydney	29 Sep 00
43.75	SWE	S Kallur, Klüft, J Kallur, Ljunggren			1	v FIN	Helsinki	5 Sep 03
43.78	ESP	Blay, Reinares, Montaner, Alozie			2	ECp1B	Sevilla	22 Jun 02
	(30)							
Best at low altitude								
43.18	AUS	Wilson, Wells, Robertson, Boyle			5	OG	Montreal	31 Jul 76
43.48	NED	Cooman, Tromp, Olyslager, Vader			5s1	OG	Seoul	1 Oct 88

4 x 200 METRES RELAY

Mark	Team	Name	Pos	Meet	Venue	Date
1:27.46 WR	USA Blue	Jenkins, Colander-Richardson, Perry, Jones	1	Penn	Philadelphia	29 Apr 00
1:28.15 WR	GDR	Göhr, R.Müller, Wöckel, Koch	1		Jena	9 Aug 80
1:29.24	Nike International USA	Roberts, Miller, Green, M Jones	1	Penn	Philadelphia	25 Apr 98
1:29.78	Louisiana State University USA	Davy, Hall, Durst, Lee	1	PennR	Philadelphia	26 Apr 03
1:30.07	Louisiana State University USA	Davy, Hall, Durst, Lee	1	TexR	Austin	5 Apr 03
1:30.20	Nike International USA	Mondie-Milner, Green, Gaines, Miller	1	Penn	Philadelphia	26 Apr 97
1:30.23	JAM	McDonald, Frazier, V Campbell, A Walker	1	Penn	Philadelphia	28 Apr 01

4 x 400 METRES RELAY

Mark	Team	Name	Pos	Meet	Venue	Date
3:15.17 WR	URS		1	OG	Seoul	1 Oct 88
		Ledovskaya 50.12, O.Nazarova 47.82, Pinigina 49.43, Bryzgina 47.80				
3:15.51	USA		2	OG	Seoul	1 Oct 88
		D.Howard 49.82, Dixon 49.17, Brisco 48.44, Griffith-Joyner 48.08				
3:15.92 WR	GDR	G.Walther 49.8, Busch 48.9, Rübsam 49.4, Koch 47.8	1	NC	Erfurt	3 Jun 84
3:16.71	USA		1	WCh	Stuttgart	22 Aug 93
		Torrence 49.0, Malone 49.4, Kaiser-Brown 49.48, Miles 48.78				
3:16.87	GDR	Emmelmann 50.9, Busch 48.8, Müller 48.9, Koch 48.3	1	EC	Stuttgart	31 Aug 86
3:18.29	USA		1	OG	Los Angeles	11 Aug 84
		Leatherwood 50.50, S.Howard 48.83, Brisco-Hooks 49.23, Cheeseborough 49.73				
3:18.29	GDR	Neubauer 50.58, Emmelmann 49.89, Busch 48.81, Müller 48.99	3	OG	Seoul	1 Oct 88
3:18.38	RUS		2	WCh	Stuttgart	22 Aug 93
		Ruzina 50.8, Alekseyeva 49.3, Ponomaryova 49.78, Privalova 48.47				
3:18.43	URS		1	WCh	Tokyo	1 Sep 91
		Ledovskaya 51.7, Dzhigalova 49.2, Nazarova 48.87, Bryzgina 48.67				
3:18.58	URS	I.Nazarova, Olizarenko, Pinigina, Vladykina	1	ECp	Moskva	18 Aug 85
3:18.63	GDR	Neubauer 51.4, Emmelmann 49.1, Müller 48.64, Busch 49.48	1	WCh	Roma	6 Sep 87
3:19.04 WR	GDR	Siemon' 51.0, Busch 50.0, Rübsam 50.2, Koch 47.9	1	EC	Athína	11 Sep 82
3:19.12	URS	Baskakova, I.Nazarova, Pinigina, Vladykina	1	Drz	Praha	18 Aug 84
3:19.23 WR	GDR	Maletzki, Rohde, Streidt, Brehmer	1	OG	Montreal	31 Jul 76
3:19.49	GDR	Emmelmann, Busch, Neubauer, Koch	1	WCp	Canberra	4 Oct 85
3:19.50	URS	Yurchenko, O.Nazarova, Pinigina, Bryzgina	2	WCh	Roma	6 Sep 87
3:19.60	USA	Leatherwood, S.Howard, Brisco-Hooks, Cheeseborough	1		Walnut	25 Jul 84

Mark	Wind	Name	Nat	Born	Pos	Meet	Venue	Date
3:19.62		GDR Kotte, Brehmer, Köhn, Koch			1	ECp	Torino	5 Aug 79
3:19.66		GDR Busch, Emmelmann, Neubauer, Müller			1	v FRG	Düsseldorf	20 Jun 88
3:19.73		GDR K.Walther, Busch, Koch, Rübsam			1	WCh	Helsinki	14 Aug 83
		(20/4 with USSR and Russia counted separately)						
3:20.32		CZE/TCH Kocembová, Matejkovicová, Moravcíková, Kratochvílová			2	WCh	Helsinki	14 Aug 83
3:20.65		JAM Richards 50.9, Scott 50.1, Parris 49.70, Fenton 49.95			1	WCh	Edmonton	12 Aug 01
3:21.04		NGR Afolabi 51.13, Yusuf 49.72, Opara 51.29, Ogunkoya 48.90			2	OG	Atlanta	3 Aug 96
3:21.21		CAN Crooks, Richardson, Killingbeck, Payne			2	OG	Los Angeles	11 Aug 84
3:21.94		UKR Dzhigalova, Olizarenko, Pinigina, Vladykina			1	URSCh	Kiyev	17 Jul 86
3:22.01		GBR Hanson, Smith, Gunnell, Keough			4	WCh	Tokyo	1 Sep 91
		(10)						
3:22.34		FRA Landre 51.3, Dorsile 51.1, Elien 50.54, Pérec 49.36			1	EC	Helsinki	14 Aug 94
3:22.49		FRG Thimm, Arendt, Thomas, Abt			4	OG	Seoul	1 Oct 88
3:23.81		AUS Peris-Kneebone, Lewis, Gainsford-Taylor, Freeman			5	OG	Sydney	30 Sep 00
3:24.23		CUB Bonne, Duporty, Morales, Quirot			2h2	OG	Atlanta	2 Aug 96
3:24.28		CHN (Hebei) An X, Bai X, Cao C, Ma Y			1	NG	Beijing	13 Sep 93
3:24.65		POL Kasprzyk, Wojdecka, Kapusta, Blaszak			3	EC	Stuttgart	31 Aug 86
3:25.68		ROM Ruicu, Rîpanu, Barbu, Tîrlea			2	ECp	Paris (C)	20 Jun 99
3:25.7a		FIN Eklund, Pursiainen, Wilmi, Salin			2	EC	Roma	8 Sep 74
3:25.81		BUL Ilieva, Stamenova, Penkova, Damyanova			1	v Hun,Pol	Sofiya	24 Jul 83
3:26.31		BLR Sologub, Budnik, Khlyustova, Kozak			3h1	OG	Sydney	29 Sep 00
		(20)						
3:26.69		ITA Perpoli, Spuri, Carbone, De Angeli			5	ECp	Paris (C)	20 Jun 99
3:27.08		CMR			7	WCh	Saint-Denis	31 Aug 03
		Nguimgo 51.7, Kaboud 52.1, Atangana 51.98, Bewouda 51.35						
3:27.54		LTU Navickaite, Valiuliene, Mendzoryte, Ambraziene			3	SPART	Moskva	22 Jun 83
3:27.57		ESP Merino, Lacambra, Myers, Ferrer			7	WCh	Tokyo	1 Sep 91
3:27.86		HUN Orosz, Forgács, Tóth, Pál			5	OG	Moskva	1 Aug 80
3:28.02		SEN Diop, M T Diouf, A Diouf, Thiam			4h3	OG	Sydney	29 Sep 00
3:28.07		BRA Almirão, Tito, Teodoro, Coutinho			3	PAm	Santo Domingo	9 Aug 03
3:28.11		IND Kuriakose, Philip, P Kaur, Beenamol			1	NC	Chennai	31 Jul 00
3:28.23		MEX Allen, Medina, González, Guevara			4	PAm	Santo Domingo	9 Aug 03
3:28.34		BLR Bobrik, Khlustova, Kozak, Usovich			1	ECp-IA	Lappeenranta	22 Jun 03

5000 METRES WALK (TRACK)

Mark	Wind	Name	Nat	Born	Pos	Meet	Venue	Date
20:02.60	WR	Gillian O'Sullivan	IRL	21.8.76	1	NC	Dublin (S)	13 Jul 02
20:03.0	WR	Kerry Saxby-Junna	AUS	2.6.61	1		Sydney	11 Feb 96
20:07.52	WR	Beate Anders/Gummelt	GDR	4.2.68	1	vURS	Rostock	23 Jun 90
20:12.41		Elisabetta Perrone	ITA	9.7.68	1	NC	Rieti	2 Aug 03
20:21.69		Annarita Sidoti	ITA	25.7.69	1	NC	Cesenatico	1 Jul 95
20:27.59	WR	Ileana Salvador	ITA	16.1.62	1		Trento	3 Jun 89
20:28.62		Sari Essayah	FIN	21.2.67	1	NC	Tuusula	9 Jul 94
20:29.63		Claudia Iovan ¶	ROM	25.2.78	1		Istanbul	19 Jun 99
20:31.4		Irina Stankina	RUS	25.3.77	1	NC-wj	Adler	10 Feb 96
20:37.7		Jin Bingjie	CHN	1.4.71	1	NC	Hefei	3 Mar 90

10 KILOMETRES WALK

Mark	Wind	Name	Nat	Born	Pos	Meet	Venue	Date
41:04	WR	Yelena Nikolayeva	RUS	1.2.66	1	NC	Sochi	20 Apr 96
41:16		Wang Yan	CHN	3.5.71	1		Eisenhüttenstadt	8 May 99
41:16		Kjersti Plätzer (Tysse)	NOR	18.1.72	1	NC	Os	11 May 02
41:17		Irina Stankina	RUS	25.3.77	1	NC-w	Adler	9 Feb 97
41:24		Olimpiada Ivanova ¶	RUS	5.5.70	2	NC-w	Adler	9 Feb 97
41:29	WR	Larisa Ramazanova	RUS	23.9.71	1	NC	Izhevsk	4 Jun 95
41:30	WR	Kerry Saxby-Junna	AUS	2.6.61	1	NC	Canberra	27 Aug 88
41:30		O Ivanova			2	NC	Izhevsk	4 Jun 95
41:31		Yelena Gruzinova	RUS	24.12.67	2	NC	Sochi	20 Apr 96
41:38		Gao Hongmiao	CHN	17.3.74	1	NC	Beijing	7 Apr 94
41:38		Rossella Giordano (10)	ITA	1.12.72	1		Naumburg	25 May 97
41:41		Nikolayeva			2		Naumburg	25 May 97
41:45		Liu Hongyu	CHN	11.1.75	2		Eisenhüttenstadt	8 May 99
41:46		Annarita Sidoti	ITA	25.7.69	1		Livorno	12 Jun 94
41:46		O Ivanova			1	NC/w	Adler	11 Feb 96
41:47		Saxby-Junna			1		Eisenhüttenstadt	11 May 96
41:48		Li Chunxiu	CHN	13.8.69	1	NG	Beijing	8 Sep 93
41:49		Ramazanova			3	NC	Sochi	20 Apr 96
41:49		Nikolayeva			1	OG	Atlanta	29 Jul 96
41:50		Yelena Arshintseva	RUS	5.4.71	1	NC-w	Adler	11 Feb 95
41:51		Beate Anders/Gummelt	GER	4.2.68	2		Eisenhüttenstadt	11 May 96
41:52		Stankina			1	WCp	Podebrady	19 Apr 97
41:54		Plätzer			3		Eisenhüttenstadt	8 May 99

Mark Wind	Name		Nat	Born	Pos	Meet	Venue	Date
41:55		Stankina			1	NC-wj	Adler	11 Feb 95
41:56	Yelena	Sayko	RUS	24.12.67	2	NC/w	Adler	11 Feb 96
41:56		Khmelnitskaya	(Ramazanova)		1		Eisenhüttenstadt	10 May 97
41:56		Plätzer			1		Hildesheim	25 Aug 02
41:56.23t	Nadezhda	Ryashkina	RUS	22.1.67	1	GWG	Seattle	24 Jul 90
41:57		Gao Hongmiao			2	NG	Beijing	8 Sep 93
41:57.22t		Saxby-Junna			2	GWG	Seattle	24 Jul 90
	(30/17)							
42:01	Tamara	Kovalenko	RUS	5.6.64	3	NC-w	Adler	11 Feb 95
42:01	Olga	Panfyorova	RUS	21.8.77	1	NC-23	Izhevsk	16 May 98
42:06	Valentina	Tsybulskaya	BLR	19.2.68	4		Eisenhüttenstadt	8 May 99
	(20)							
42:07	Ileana	Salvador	ITA	16.1.62	1		Sesto San Giovanni	1 May 92
42:09	Elisabetta	Perrone	ITA	9.7.68	4		Eisenhüttenstadt	11 May 96
42:11	Nina	Alyushenko	RUS	29.5.68	3	NC	Izhevsk	4 Jun 95
42:13	Natalya	Misyulya	BLR	16.4.66	5		Eisenhüttenstadt	8 May 99
42:13.7t	Madelein	Svensson	SWE	20.7.69	2	SGP	Fana	15 May 92
42:15		Gu Yan	CHN	17.3.74	3	WCp	Podebrady	19 Apr 97
42:15	Erica	Alfridi	ITA	22.2.68	5		Naumburg	25 May 97
42:15	Jane	Saville	AUS	5.11.74	6		Eisenhüttenstadt	8 May 99
42:16	Alina	Ivanova	RUS	16.3.69	1		Novopolotsk	27 May 89
42:16	Norica	Cîmpean	ROM	22.3.72	1		Calella	9 May 99
	(30)							
42:17	Katarzyna	Radtke	POL	31.8.69	5		Eisenhüttenstadt	11 May 96
42:20	Sari	Essayah	FIN	21.2.67	4	WCh	Göteborg	7 Aug 95
42:29	Olga	Kardopoltseva	BLR	11.9.66	4		Eisenhüttenstadt	10 May 97
42:31	Vera	Nacharkina'	RUS	17.2.66	1	NC	Izhevsk	16 May 98
42:32	Maya	Sazonova	KAZ	28.5.68	4	Rus Ch	Sochi	20 Apr 96
42:34	Mária	Rosza/Urbaník	HUN	12.2.67	7	WCh	Göteborg	7 Aug 95
42:35	Claudia	Iovan/Stef ¶	ROM	25.2.78	2	NC	Alba Iulia	15 Sep 02
42:37	Olga	Lukyanchuk	UKR	7.12.76	1		Mukachevo	21 Oct 00
42:39	Susana	Feitor	POR	28.1.75	1		Lanciano	11 Mar 01
42:40	Yuliya	Odzilyayeva	RUS	17.10.71	5		Livorno	12 Jun 94
	(40)							
42:40.37t		Feng Haixia	CHN	23.2.75	3		Nanjing	24 Oct 95
42:42	Graciela	Mendoza	MEX	22.3.63	11		Naumburg	25 May 97
42:42+	Tatyana	Gudkova	RUS	23.1.78	1=	in 20k	Moskva	19 May 00
42:43+	Olga	Polyakova	RUS	23.9.80	4=	in 20k	Moskva	19 May 00
42:44	Irina	Strakhova	RUS	4.3.59	3		Sochi	17 Feb 91
42:44		Long Yuwen	CHN	1.8.75	3		Shenzhen	18 Feb 93
42:45		Li Yuxin	CHN	4.12.74	4		Shenzhen	18 Feb 93
42:46.7t		Cui Yingzi	CHN	26.1.71	1	NC	Jinan	15 Mar 92
42:46.7t		Chen Yueling	CHN	1.4.68	2	NC	Jinan	15 Mar 92
42:48	M del Rosario	Sánchez	MEX	26.10.73	8		Eisenhüttenstadt	8 May 99
	(50)	100th woman 43:41, 200th woman 44:42						
Probable short course								
41:30	Ileana	Salvador	ITA	16.1.62	1	4-N	Livorno	10 Jul 93
41:56	Elisabeta	Perrone	ITA	9.7.68	2	4-N	Livorno	10 Jul 93
Best track times								
41:57.22	Kerry	Saxby-Junna	AUS	2.6.61	2	GWG	Seattle	24 Jul 90
42:11.5	Beate	Anders/Gummelt	GER	4.2.68	1	SGP	Fana	15 May 92
42:23.7	Ileana	Salvador		16.1.62	2	SGP	Fana	8 May 93
42:30.13		Gao Hongmiao	CHN	17.3.74	1		Nanjing	24 Oct 95
42:30.31	Olimpiada	Ivanova ¶	RUS	5.5.70	1	GWG	Sankt-Peterburg	26 Jul 94
42:37.0	Sari	Essayah	FIN	21.2.67	3	SGP	Fana	8 May 93
42:38.24		Liu Hongyu	CHN	11.1.75	2		Nanjing	24 Oct 95
42:43.23	Yelena	Sayko	RUS	16.2.68	2	GWG	Sankt-Peterburg	26 Jul 94
42:45.0	Elisabetta	Perrone	ITA	9.7.68	1		Catania	30 May 99
42:47.4	Katarzyna	Radtke	POL	31.8.69	4	SGP	Fana	8 May 93

20 KILOMETRES WALK

Mark Wind	Name		Nat	Born	Pos	Meet	Venue	Date
1:24:50 WR	Olimpiada	Ivanova ¶	RUS	5.5.70	1	NC-w	Adler	4 Mar 01
1:25:18 WR	Tatyana	Gudkova	RUS	23.1.78	1	NC	Moskva	19 May 00
1:25:20	Olga	Polyakova	RUS	23.9.80	2	NC	Moskva	19 May 00
1:25:29	Irina	Stankina	RUS	25.3.77	3	NC	Moskva	19 May 00
1:25:59	Tamara	Kovalenko	RUS	5.6.64	4	NC	Moskva	19 May 00
1:26:08		Ivanova			5	NC	Moskva	19 May 00
1:26:22		Wang Yan	CHN	3.5.71	1	NG	Guangzhou	19 Nov 01
1:26:22	Yelena	Nikolayeva	RUS	1.2.66	1	ECp	Cheboksary	18 May 03
1:26:23		Wang Liping	CHN	8.7.76	2	NG	Guangzhou	19 Nov 01

Mark Wind		Name	Nat	Born	Pos	Meet	Venue	Date
1:26:35		Liu Hongyu	CHN	11.1.75	3	NG	Guangzhou	19 Nov 01
1:26:42		O Ivanova			1	EC	München	7 Aug 02
1:26:48		Ivanova			1	ECp	Eisenhüttenstadt	17 Jun 00
1:26:48		Ivanova			1	ECp	Dudince	19 May 01
1:26:50	Natalya	Fedoskina (10)	RUS	25.6.80	2	ECp	Dudince	19 May 01
1:26:52		Nikolayeva			1	WCh	Saint-Denis	24 Aug 03
1:26:52.3 t		Ivanova			1	GWG	Brisbane	6 Sep 01
1:27:02		Nikolayeva			1	NC	Cheboksary	25 May 02
1:27:09	Elisabetta	Perrone	ITA	9.7.68	3	ECp	Dudince	19 May 01
1:27:14	Antonina	Petrova	RUS	25.1.77	1	NC-w	Adler	1 Mar 03
1:27:16		Song Hongjuan	CHN	4.7.84	1	NC	Yangzhou	14 Apr 03
1:27:22	Gillian	O'Sullivan	IRL	21.8.76	1		Sesto San Giovanni	1 May 03
1:27:23	Larisa	Yemelyanova (Safronova)	RUS	6.1.80	2	NC-w	Adler	1 Mar 03
1:27:25		Nikolayeva			1		La Coruña	7 Jun 03
1:27:29	Erica	Alfridi	ITA	22.2.68	4	ECp	Dudince	19 May 01
1:27:30 WR		Liu Hongyu			1		Beijing	1 May 95
1:27:30 WR	Nadezhda	Ryashkina	RUS	22.1.67	1	NC-w	Adler	7 Feb 99
1:27:32		Liu Hongyu			1	WCp	Mézidon-Canon	2 May 99
1:27:33	Tatyana	Sibilyeva	RUS	17.5.80	2	NC-w	Adler	4 Mar 01
1:27:34		O'Sullivan			2	WCh	Saint-Denis	24 Aug 03
1:27:35		Fedoskina			2	WCp	Mézidon-Canon	2 May 99
1:27:35		Fedoskina			3	NC-w	Adler	4 Mar 01
	(31/18)							
1:27:46	Norica	Cîmpean	ROM	22.3.72	1		Békéscsaba	28 Mar 99
1:27:51	Lyudmila	Yefimkina	RUS	22.8.81	2	NC	Cheboksary	25 May 02
	(20)							
1:27:53	Kjersti	Tysse Plätzer	NOR	18.1.72	3	ECp	Eisenhüttenstadt	17 Jun 00
1:27:54		Song Lijuan	CHN	9.2.75	2		Beijing	1 May 95
1:27:55	Susana	Feitor	POR	28.1.75	1		Rio Maior	7 Apr 01
1:28:10	María	Vasco	ESP	26.12.75	3	ECp	Cheboksary	18 May 03
1:28:10	Valentina	Tsybulskaya	BLR	19.2.68	3	WCh	Saint-Denis	24 Aug 03
1:28:18		Kong Yan	CHN	6.7.73	3		Beijing	1 May 95
1:28:19	Vera	Zozulya	UKR	31.8.70	1	NC-w	Yevpatoriya	23 Feb 03
1:28:24	Natalya	Misyulya	BLR	16.4.66	1	NC	Soligorsk	13 May 00
1:28:24	Margarita	Nazarova	RUS	1.10.76	6	NC	Cheboksary	25 May 02
1:28:38	Annarita	Sidoti	ITA	25.7.69	5	ECp	Eisenhüttenstadt	17 Jun 00
	(30)							
1:28:38	Svetlana	Tolstaya	KAZ	9.8.71	7	NC	Cheboksary	25 May 02
1:28:39		Gu Yan	CHN	17.3.74	4		Beijing	1 May 95
1:28:45		Gao Hongmiao	CHN	17.3.74	1	NC	Dandong	13 Apr 01
1:28:51	Olga	Kardopoltseva	BLR	11.9.66	2		Brest	4 Jun 99
1:28:52	Valentina	Savchuk	UKR	19.1.75	2	NC-w	Yevpatoriya	23 Feb 03
1:28:56	Jane	Saville	AUS	5.11.74	1		København	6 May 00
1:28:56	Larisa	Khmelnitskaya	BLR	23.9.71	2	NC	Soligorsk	13 May 00
1:29:08	Olga	Lukyanchuk	UKR	7.12.76	5	RUS-w	Adler	4 Mar 01
1:29:09	Claudia	Iovan/Stef ¶	ROM	25.2.78	5	WCh	Saint-Denis	24 Aug 03
1:29:12	Rossella	Giordano	ITA	1.12.72	2	NC	Cassino	9 Mar 97
	(40)							
1:29:12	Tatyana	Korotkova	RUS	24.4.80	8	NC	Cheboksary	25 May 02
1:29:15		Feng Haixia	CHN	23.2.75	1	NC	Zhuhai	12 Mar 96
1:29:23	Lyudmila	Dolgopolova	BLR	11.8.69	3	NC	Soligorsk	13 May 00
1:29:31	Margarita	Turova	BLR	28.12.80			Brest	10 Mar 01
1:29:31		Jian Xingli	CHN	4.12.83	3	NG	Guangzhou	19 Nov 01
1:29:34	Athanasia	Tsoumeléka	GRE	2.1.82	7	WCh	Saint-Denis	24 Aug 03
1:29:36	Kerry	Saxby-Junna	AUS	2.6.61	2		Naumburg	30 Apr 00
1:29:36	Maya	Sazonova	KAZ	28.5.65	1		Almaty	31 Mar 01
1:29:39	Yuliya	Voyevodina	RUS	17.10.71	7	NC	Moskva	19 May 00
1:29:39		Gao Kelian	CHN	15.8.83	5	NG	Guangzhou	19 Nov 01
	(50)	100th best woman 1:31:38, 200th c.1:34:35						

50 KILOMETRES WALK

4:19:13	Yelena	Ginko	BLR	30.7.76	1		Scanzorosciate	27 Oct 02
4:22:00		Ginko			1		Scanzoroscaite	19 Oct 03
4:29:56	Natalia	Bruniko	ITA	23.2.73	2		Scanzorosciate	27 Oct 02
4:32:22	Evaggelía	Xinoú	GRE	22.11.81	2		Scanzoroscaite	19 Oct 03
4:36:45	Yelena	Krivokhizha	UKR	10.3.79	3		Scanzorosciate	28 Oct 01
4:39:45	Susan	Armenta	USA	19.9.73	1	NC	Chula Vista	17 Feb 02
4:41:57	Kora	Boufflért	FRA	23.4.66	1		Ay-Champagne	17 Sep 95
4:43:24	Anita	Lipeina	LAT	17.11.67	3		Scanzorosciate	27 Oct 02

Mark	Wind	Name		Nat	Born	Pos	Meet	Venue	Date

JUNIOR WOMEN'S ALL-TIME LISTS

Based on the age regulations introduced for 1988, that is under 20 in year of competition.

100 METRES

10.88	2.0	Marlies	Oelsner	GDR	21.3.58	1	NC	Dresden	1 Jul 77
10.89	1.8	Katrin	Krabbe	GDR	22.11.69	1rB		Berlin	20 Jul 88
11.03	1.7	Silke	Gladisch	GDR	20.6.64	3	OD	Berlin	8 Jun 83
11.04	1.4	Angela	Williams	USA	30.1.80	1	NCAA	Boise	5 Jun 99
11.08	2.0	Brenda	Morehead	USA	5.10.57	1	OT	Eugene	21 Jun 76
11.11	0.2	Shakedia	Jones	USA	15.3.79	1		Los Angeles (Ww)	2 May 98
11.11	1.1	Joan Uduak	Ekah	NGR	16.12.80	5	Athl	Lausanne	2 Jul 99
11.12	2.0	Veronica	Campbell	JAM	15.5.82	1	WJ	Santiago de Chile	18 Oct 00
11.13	2.0	Chandra	Cheeseborough	USA	10.1.59	2	OT	Eugene	21 Jun 76
11.13	-1.0	Grit	Breuer	GDR	16.2.72	1		Jena	6 Jun 90
Uncertain timing: 10.99	1.9	Natalya	Bochina	RUS	4.1.62	2		Leningrad	3 Jun 80
Wind assisted to 11.11									
10.96	3.7	Angela	Williams	USA	30.1.80	1		Las Vegas	3 Apr 99
10.97	3.3	Gesine	Walther	GDR	6.10.62	4	NC	Cottbus	16 Jul 80
11.02	2.1	Nikole	Mitchell	JAM	5.6.74	1	Mutual	Kingston	1 May 93
11.06	2.2	Brenda	Morehead	USA	5.10.57	1s	OT	Eugene	21 Jun 76
11.09		Angela	Williams	TRI	15.5.65	1		Nashville	14 Apr 84

200 METRES

22.11A	-0.5	Allyson	Felix	USA	18.11.85	1		Ciudad de México	3 May 03
		22.51	1.3			1	MSR	Walnut	19 Apr 03
22.19	1.5	Natalya	Bochina	RUS	4.1.62	2	OG	Moskva	30 Jul 80
22.37	1.3	Sabine	Rieger	GDR	6.11.63	2	vURS	Cottbus	26 Jun 82
22.42	0.4	Gesine	Walther	GDR	6.10.62	1		Potsdam	29 Aug 81
22.45	0.5	Grit	Breuer	GER	16.2.72	2	ASV	Köln	8 Sep 91
22.51	2.0	Katrin	Krabbe	GDR	22.11.69	3		Berlin	13 Sep 88
22.52	1.2	Mary	Onyali	NGR	3.2.68	6	WCh	Roma	3 Sep 87
22.58	0.8	Marion	Jones	USA	12.10.75	4	TAC	New Orleans	28 Jun 92
22.70		Marita	Koch	GDR	18.2.57	1		Halle	16 May 76
22.70A	1.9	Kathy	Smallwood	GBR	3.5.60	2	WUG	Ciudad de México	12 Sep 79
Wind assisted									
22.34	2.3	Kathrin	Krabbe	GDR	22.11.69	1	WJ	Sudbury	30 Jul 88
22.49	2.3	Brenda	Morehead	USA	5.10.57	1	OT	Eugene	24 Jun 76
22.53	2.5	Valerie	Brisco	USA	6.7.60	2	AAU	Walnut	17 Jun 79
22.64	2.3	Chandra	Cheeseborough	USA	16.1.59	2	OT	Eugene	24 Jun 76
22.65	3.5	Shakedia	Jones	USA	15.3.79	1	NC-j	Edwardsville IL	27 Jun 98
22.66	5.0	Lauren	Hewitt	AUS	25.11.78	3	NC	Melbourne	2 Mar 97
22.70	2.5	Kinshasa	Davis	USA	10.7.79	1		Long Beach	30 May 97

400 METRES

49.42		Grit	Breuer	GER	16.2.72	2	WCh	Tokyo	27 Aug 91
49.77		Christina	Brehmer	GDR	28.2.58	1		Dresden	9 May 76
50.01			Li Jing	CHN	14.2.80	1	NG	Shanghai	18 Oct 97
50.19		Marita	Koch	GDR	18.2.57	3	OD	Berlin	10 Jul 76
50.58		Sanya	Richards	USA	26.2.85	1	NCAA	Sacramento	14 Jun 03
50.59		Fatima	Yusuf	NGR	2.5.71	1	HGP	Budapest	5 Aug 90
		50.5 hand				1	NC	Lagos	25 Aug 90
50.74		Monique	Henderson	USA	18.2.83	1		Norwalk	3 Jun 00
50.86		Charity	Opara	NGR	20.5.72	2		Bologna	7 Sep 91
50.87		Denean	Howard	USA	5.10.64	1	TAC	Knoxville	20 Jun 82
50.87		Magdalena	Nedelcu	ROM	12.5.74	1	NC-j	Bucuresti	31 Jul 92
50.90		Sheila	Ingram	USA	23.3.57	3s1	OG	Montreal	28 Jul 76

800 METRES

1:57.18			Wang Yuan	CHN	8.4.76	2h2	NG	Beijing	8 Sep 93
1:57.45		Hildegard	Ullrich	GDR	20.12.59	5	EC	Praha	31 Aug 78
1:57.62			Lang Yinglai	CHN	22.8.79	1	NG	Shanghai	22 Oct 97
1:57.63		Maria	Mutola	MOZ	27.10.72	4	WCh	Tokyo	26 Aug 91
1:57.77			Lu Yi	CHN	10.4.74	4	NG	Beijing	9 Sep 93
1:57.86		Katrin	Wühn	GDR	19.11.65	1		Celje	5 May 84
1:58.16			Lin Nuo	CHN	.1.80	3	NG	Shanghai	22 Oct 97
1:58.18		Marion	Hübner	GDR	29.9.62	2		Erfurt	2 Aug 81
1:58.24		Christine	Wachtel	GDR	6.1.65	3		Potsdam	25 May 84
1:58.37		Gabriela	Sedláková	SVK	2.3.68	4	ISTAF	Berlin	21 Aug 87
1:59.01			Liu Qifang	CHN	.2.79	4h3	NG	Shanghai	21 Oct 97

Mark	Wind	Name		Nat	Born	Pos	Meet	Venue	Date

1500 METRES

3:51.34			Lang Yinglai	CHN	22.8.79	2	NG	Shanghai	18 Oct 97
3:53.91			Yin Lili	CHN	11.11.79	3	NG	Shanghai	18 Oct 97
3:53.97			Lan Lixin	CHN	14.2.79	4	NG	Shanghai	18 Oct 97
3:54.52			Zhang Ling	CHN	13.4.80	5	NG	Shanghai	18 Oct 97
3:59.81			Wang Yuan	CHN	8.4.76	7	NG	Beijing	11 Sep 93
3:59.96		Zola	Budd	GBR	26.5.66	3	VD	Bruxelles	30 Aug 85
4:00.05			Lu Yi	CHN	10.4.74	8	NG	Beijing	11 Sep 93
4:01.71			Li Ying	CHN	24.6.75	4h2	NG	Beijing	10 Sep 93
4:03.45		Anita	Weyermann	SUI	8.12.77	1	Athl	Lausanne	3 Jul 96
4:03.5		Svetlana	Guskova	MOL	19.8.59	3	Kuts	Podolsk	13 Aug 78

1 MILE: 4:17.57 Zola Budd GBR 26.5.66 3 WK Zürich 21 Aug 85

2000 METRES: 5:33.15 Zola Budd GBR 26.5.66 1 London 13 Jul 84

3000 METRES

8:28.83		Zola	Budd	GBR	26.5.66	3	GG	Roma	7 Sep 85
8:35.89		Sally	Barsosio	KEN	21.3.78	2	Herc	Monaco	16 Aug 97
8:36.45			Ma Ningning	CHN	1.6.76	4	NC	Jinan	6 Jun 93
8:40.08		Gabriela	Szabo	ROM	14.11.75	3	EC	Helsinki	12 Aug 94
8:40.28		Meseret	Defar	ETH	19.11.83	10	VD	Bruxelles	30 Aug 02
8:41.86		Tirunesh	Dibaba	ETH	2.6.85	11	VD	Bruxelles	30 Aug 02
8:42.39			Li Ying	CHN	24.6.75	8	NG	Beijing	13 Sep 93
8:44.1mx		Donna	Gould	AUS	10.6.66	-		Eugene	13 Jul 84
8:44.14		Worknesh	Kidane	ETH	21.11.81	6		Milano	7 Jun 00
8:44.57		Ayelech	Worku	ETH	12.6.79	3	APM	Hengelo	1 Jun 98

5000 METRES

14:39.94		Tirunesh	Dibaba	ETH	2.6.85	3	Bisl	Oslo	27 Jun 03
14:39.96			Yin Lili	CHN	11.11.79	4	NG	Shanghai	23 Oct 97
14:45.33			Lan Lixin	CHN	14.2.79	2h2	NG	Shanghai	21 Oct 97
14:45.71			Song Liqing	CHN	20.1.80	3h2	NG	Shanghai	21 Oct 97
14:45.90			Jiang Bo	CHN	13.3.77	1		Nanjing	24 Oct 95
14:46.71		Sally	Barsosio	KEN	21.3.78	3	VD	Bruxelles	22 Aug 97
14:47.40		Worknesh	Kidane	ETH	21.11.81	7	OG	Sydney	25 Sep 00
14:48.07		Zola	Budd	GBR	26.5.66	1	McV	London (CP)	26 Aug 85
14:53.44		Lydia	Cheromei	KEN	11.5.77	3	ISTAF	Berlin	1 Sep 95
14:53.99		Sentayehu	Ejigu	ETH	.85	7	ISTAF	Berlin (P)	6 Sep 02
14:56.15			Xing Huina	CHN	25.2.84	2	NG	Guangzhou	23 Nov 01

10,000 METRES

30:31.55			Xing Huina	CHN	25.2.84	7	WCh	Saint-Denis	23 Aug 03
30:39.41			Lan Lixin	CHN	14.2.79	2	NG	Shanghai	19 Oct 97
30:39.98			Yin Lili	CHN	11.11.79	3	NG	Shanghai	19 Oct 97
30:59.92		Merima	Hashim	ETH	.81	3	NA	Heusden	5 Aug 00
31:06.20		Lucy	Wangui	KEN	24.3.84	1rA		Okayama	27 Sep 03
31:11.26			Song Liqing	CHN	20.1.80	7	NG	Shanghai	19 Oct 97
31:15.38		Sally	Barsosio	KEN	21.3.78	3	WCh	Stuttgart	21 Aug 93
31:32.15			Feng Wenhui	CHN	21.1.74	9	NG	Beijing	8 Sep 93
31:40.42		Annemari	Sandell	FIN	2.1.77	6h2	OG	Atlanta	27 Jul 96
31:40.56		Delillah	Asiago	KEN	24.2.72	1	JPN Ch	Tokyo	15 Jun 91
31:41.09		Lydia	Cheromei	KEN	11.5.77	2	AfrCh	Belle Vue Mauricia	27 Jun 92

HALF MARATHON

69:05		Delillah	Asiago	KEN	24.2.72	1	GWR	Exeter	5 May 91
69:21		Ann	Wamuchi	KEN	29.9.78	5		Tokyo	19 Jan 97
69:48		Yuka	Hata	JPN	3.2.79	4		Lisboa	15 Mar 98
70:05		Hiromi	Fujii	JPN	7.2.83	5		Yamaguchi	10 Mar 02
70:19		Snezana	Kostic	YUG	5.8.84	2		Novi Sad	31 Mar 02
70:35		Iress	Chenonge	KEN	1.2.82	1		Aveiro	1 Dec 01

MARATHON

2:23:37			Liu Min	CHN	29.11.83	1		Beijing	14 Oct 01
2:23:57			Zhu Xiaolin	CHN	20.4.84	4		Beijing	20 Oct 02
2:25:48			Jin Li	CHN	29.5.83	6		Beijing	14 Oct 01
2:26:34			Wei Yanan	CHN	6.12.81	1		Beijing	15 Oct 00
2:27:30			Ai Dongmei	CHN	15.10.79	3	NG	Beijing	4 Oct 97
2:27:37			Lu Cui	CHN	26.3.85	10		Beijing	20 Oct 02
2:29:12		Chika	Horie	JPN	15.2.81	4		Nagano	9 Apr 00
2:29:33			Wang Linan	CHN	26.11.85	4		Beijing	19 Oct 03

Mark	Wind	Name		Nat	Born	Pos	Meet	Venue	Date

3000 METRES STEEPLECHASE

Mark	Wind	Name		Nat	Born	Pos	Meet	Venue	Date
9:30.70		Melissa	Rollison	AUS	13.4.83	1	GWG	Brisbane	4 Sep 01
9:54.01			Ju Yinglan	CHN	10.10.84	2	NC	Shanghai	13 Sep 03
10:01.56		Galina	Yegorova	RUS	5.8.83	1		Cheboksary	27 Jul 02
10:02.07			Zhang Chong	CHN	.84	2	NGPF	Tiantai	27 Oct 02
10:04.99		Ulla	Tuimala	FIN	27.4.82	1	vSWE	Göteborg	2 Sep 01

100 METRES HURDLES

Mark	Wind	Name		Nat	Born	Pos	Meet	Venue	Date
12.84	1.5	Aliuska	López	CUB	29.8.69	2	WUG	Zagreb	16 Jul 87
12.88	1.5	Yelena	Ovcharova	UKR	17.6.76	2	ECp	Villeneuve d'Ascq	25 Jun 95
12.89	1.3	Anay	Tejeda	CUB	3.4.83	1		Padova	1 Sep 02
12.92	0.0		Sun Hongwei	CHN	24.11.79	6	NG	Shanghai	18 Oct 97
12.95	1.5	Candy	Young	USA	21.5.62	2	AAU	Walnut	16 Jun 79
12.95A	1.5	Cinnamon	Sheffield	USA	8.3.70	2	NCAA	Provo	3 Jun 89
13.00	0.7	Gloria	Kovarik	GDR	13.1.64	3h2	NC	Karl-Marx-Stadt	16 Jun 83
13.00	2.0	Lyudmila	Khristosenko	UKR	14.10.66	1	NC-j	Krasnodar	16 Jul 85
13.02	-1.7	Susanna	Kallur	SWE	16.2.81	1	WJ	Santiago de Chile	19 Oct 00
13.02	0.5	Gergana	Stoyanova	BUL	3.1.82	1h3	NC-j	Sofia	15 Jun 01
Wind assisted to 13.00									
12.81	3.4	Anay	Tejeda	CUB	3.4.83	1	WJ	Kingston	21 Jul 02
12.90	3.0	Adrianna	Lamalle	FRA-J	27.9.82	1		Fort-de-France	28 Apr 01
13.00	3.5	Gergana	Stoyanova	BUL	3.1.82	1h1	EJ	Grosseto	20 Jul 01

400 METRES HURDLES

Mark	Wind	Name		Nat	Born	Pos	Meet	Venue	Date
54.70		Lashinda	Demus	USA	10.3.83	1	WJ	Kingston	19 Jul 02
54.93			Li Rui	CHN	22.11.79	1	NG	Shanghai	22 Oct 97
55.15			Huang Xiaoxiao	CHN	15.2.85	2	NG	Guangzhou	22 Nov 01
55.20		Lesley	Maxie	USA	4.1.67	2	TAC	San Jose	9 Jun 84
55.20A		Jana	Pittman	AUS	9.11.82	1		Pietersburg	18 Mar 00
		55.63				1		Sydney	13 Feb 00
55.22		Tiffany	Ross	USA	5.2.83	2	NCAA	Baton Rouge	31 May 02
55.26		Ionela	Tîrlea	ROM	9.2.76	1	Nik	Nice	12 Jul 95
55.43			Li Shuju	CHN	20.7.81	1h2	NG	Shanghai	21 Oct 97
55.53		Radostina	Dimitrova	BUL	1.6.66	3	OD	Potsdam	21 Jul 84
55.62		Melanie	Walker	JAM	1.1.83	1		Bridgetown	19 May 01
55.65		Schowonda	Williams	USA	3.12.66	3	NCAA	Austin	31 May 85
Drugs disqualification: 54.54			Peng Yinghua ¶	CHN	21.2.79	(2)	NG	Shanghai	22 Oct 97

HIGH JUMP

Mark	Wind	Name		Nat	Born	Pos	Meet	Venue	Date
2.01		Olga	Turchak	KZK	5.3.67	2	GWG	Moskva	7 Jul 86
2.01		Heike	Balck	GDR	19.8.70	1	vURS-j	Karl-Marx-Stadt	18 Jun 89
2.00		Stefka	Kostadinova	BUL	25.3.65	1		Sofiya	25 Aug 84
2.00		Alina	Astafei	ROM	7.6.69	1	WJ	Sudbury	29 Jul 88
1.98		Silvia	Costa	CUB	4.5.64	2	WUG	Edmonton	11 Jul 83
1.98		Yelena	Yelesina	RUS	5.4.70	1	Druzh	Nyiregyháza	13 Aug 88
1.97		Svetlana	Isaeva	BUL	18.3.67	2		Sofiya	25 May 86
1.96A		Charmaine	Gale	RSA	27.2.64	1	NC-j	Bloemfontein	4 Apr 81
1.96i		Desislava	Aleksandrova	BUL	27.10.75	2	EI	Paris	12 Mar 94
1.96		Marina	Kuptsova	RUS	22.12.81	1	NC	Tula	26 Jul 00
1.96		Blanka	Vlasic	CRO	8.11.83	1	WJ	Kingston	20 Jul 02

POLE VAULT

Mark	Wind	Name		Nat	Born	Pos	Meet	Venue	Date
4.47i		Yelena	Isinbayeva	RUS	3.6.82	1		Budapest	10 Feb 01
		4.46				2	ISTAF	Berlin	31 Aug 01
4.42		Yvonne	Buschbaum	GER	14.7.80	1		Rheinau-Freistett	27 Jun 99
4.41		Floé	Kühnert	GER	6.3.84	1		Mannheim	15 Jun 02
4.35		Yuliya	Golubchikova	RUS	27.3.83	2	Mos Ch	Moskva	28 Jun 02
4.33i		Vanessa	Boslak	FRA	11.6.82	5		Liévin	25 Feb 01
		4.32				1		La Roche-sur-Yon	23 Sep 00
4.31		Monika	Götz	GER	15.6.81	1		Troisdorf	9 May 98
4.31		Amandine	Homo	FRA	24.12.80	3	GP-II	Saint-Denis	3 Jul 99
4.30		Annika	Becker	GER	12.11.81	2		Mannheim	18 Jun 99
4.30		Katerina	Badurová	CZE	18.12.82	3		Turnov	11 Jun 00
4.30		Natalya	Belinskaya	RUS	21.1.83	1	NC-j	Kazan	25 Jun 02
4.30			Wu Sha	CHN	21.10.87	2		Shijiazhuang	3 Aug 03

LONG JUMP

Mark	Wind	Name		Nat	Born	Pos	Meet	Venue	Date
7.14	1.1	Heike	Daute	GDR	16.12.64	1	PTS	Bratislava	4 Jun 83
7.00	-0.2	Birgit	Grosshennig	GDR	21.2.65	2		Berlin	9 Jun 84
6.94	-0.5	Magdalena	Khristova	BUL	25.2.77	2		Kalamata	22 Jun 96

Mark	Wind	Name		Nat	Born	Pos	Meet	Venue	Date
6.91	0.0	Anisoara	Cusmir	ROM	29.6.62	1		Bucuresti	23 May 81
6.90	1.4	Beverly	Kinch	GBR	14.1.64	*	WCh	Helsinki	14 Aug 83
6.88	0.6	Natalya	Shevchenko	RUS	28.12.66	2		Sochi	26 May 84
6.84		Larisa	Baluta	UKR	13.8.65	2		Krasnodar	6 Aug 83
6.82	1.8	Fiona	May	GBR	12.12.69	*	WJ	Sudbury	30 Jul 88
6.81	1.6	Carol	Lewis	USA	8.8.63	1	TAC	Knoxville	20 Jun 82
6.81	1.4	Yelena	Davydova	KZK	16.11.67	1	NC-j	Krasnodar	17 Jul 85
Wind assisted									
7.27	2.2	Heike	Daute	GDR	16.12.64	1	WCh	Helsinki	14 Aug 83
6.93	4.6	Beverly	Kinch	GBR	14.1.64	5	WCh	Helsinki	14 Aug 83
6.88	2.1	Fiona	May	GBR	12.12.69	1	WJ	Sudbury	30 Jul 88
6.84	2.8	Anu	Kaljurand	EST	16.4.69	2		Riga	4 Jun 88

TRIPLE JUMP

14.62	1.0	Teresa	Marinova	BUL	5.9.77	1	WC	Sydney	25 Aug 96
14.57	0.2		Huang Qiuyan	CHN	25.1.80	1	NG	Shanghai	19 Oct 97
14.52	0.6	Anastasiya	Ilyina	RUS	16.1.82	q	WJ	Santiago de Chile	20 Oct 00
14.46	1.0		Peng Fengmei	CHN	2.7.79	1		Chengdu	18 Apr 98
14.37i	-		Ren Ruiping	CHN	1.2.76	3	WI	Barcelona	11 Mar 95
		14.36	0.0			1	NC	Beijing	1 Jun 94
14.32	-0.1	Yelena	Lysak ¶	RUS	19.10.75	1		Voronezh	18 Jun 94
14.29	1.2	Mabel	Gay	CUB	5.5.83	1		La Habana	5 Apr 02
14.23			Li Jiahui	CHN	8.8.79	1	Asi-J	Bangkok	6 Nov 97
14.22	1.2	Yusmay	Bicet	CUB	8.12.83	2		La Habana	23 Feb 02
14.19	2.0	Anna	Pyatkh	RUS	4.4.81	1		Lapinlahti	16 Jul 00
Wind assisted									
14.83A	8.3		Ren Ruiping	CHN	1.2.76	1	NC	Taiyuan	21 May 95
14.43	2.7	Yelena	Lysak ¶	RUS	19.10.75	1	WJ	Lisboa	21 Jul 94

SHOT

20.54	Astrid	Kumbernuss	GDR	5.2.70	1	vFIN-j	Orimattila	1 Jul 89
20.51i	Heidi	Krieger	GDR	20.7.65	2		Budapest	8 Feb 84
	20.24				5		Spilt	30 Apr 84
20.23	Ilke	Wyludda	GDR	28.3.69	1	NC-j	Karl-Marx-Stadt	16 Jul 88
20.12	Ilona	Schoknecht	GDR	24.9.56	2	NC	Erfurt	23 Aug 75
20.02		Cheng Xiaoyan	CHN	30.11.75	3	NC	Beijing	5 Jun 94
19.90	Stephanie	Storp	FRG	28.11.68	1		Hamburg	16 Aug 87
19.63		Wang Yawen	CHN	23.8.73	1		Shijiazhuang	25 Apr 92
19.57	Grit	Haupt	GDR	4.6.66	1		Gera	7 Jul 84
19.48	Ines	Wittich	GDR	14.11.69	5		Leipzig	29 Jul 87
19.42	Simone	Michel	GDR	18.12.60	3	vSU	Leipzig	23 Jun 79

DISCUS

74.40	Ilke	Wyludda	GDR	28.3.69	2		Berlin	13 Sep 88
67.38	Irina	Meszynski	GDR	24.3.62	1		Berlin	14 Aug 81
67.00	Jana	Günther	GDR	7.1.68	6	NC	Potsdam	20 Aug 87
66.80	Svetla	Mitkova	BUL	17.6.64	1		Sofiya	2 Aug 83
66.60	Astrid	Kumbernuss	GDR	5.2.70	1		Berlin	20 Jul 88
66.34	Franka	Dietzsch	GDR	22.1.68	2		St Denis	11 Jun 87
66.30	Jana	Lauren	GDR	28.6.70	1	vURS-j	Karl-Marx-Stadt	18 Jun 89
66.08		Cao Qi	CHN	15.1.74	1	NG	Beijing	12 Sep 93
65.96	Grit	Haupt	GDR	4.6.66	3		Leipzig	13 Jul 84
65.22	Daniela	Costian	ROM	30.4.65	3		Nitra	26 Aug 84

HAMMER

71.71	Kamila	Skolimowska	POL	4.11.82	1	GPF	Melbourne	9 Sep 01
70.60		Zhang Wenxiu	CHN	22.3.86	2		Nanning	5 Apr 03
68.50	Martina	Danisová	SVK	21.3.83	1		Kladno	16 Jun 01
68.40	Bianca	Achilles	GER	17.4.81	1		Dortmund	25 Sep 99
68.18	Ivana	Brkljacic	CRO	25.1.83	1		Pula	28 Apr 00
67.08	Mariya	Smolyachkova	BLR	10.2.85	3	Klim	Staiki	28 Jun 03
66.97		Gu Yuan	CHN	9.5.82	1	NG	Guangzhou	22 Nov 01
66.34	Yipsi	Moreno	CUB	19.11.80	1		Ciudad de México	29 May 99
66.08	Katarzyna	Kita	POL	4.7.84	1	EJ	Tampere	26 Jul 03
65.88	Yunaika	Crawford	CUB	2.11.82	1		Las Tunas	3 Mar 00

JAVELIN

62.93		Xue Juan	CHN	10.2.86	1	NG	Changsha	27 Oct 03
61.99		Wang Yaning	CHN	4.1.80	1	NC	Huizhou	14 Oct 99
61.79	Nikolett	Szabó	HUN	3.3.80	1		Schwechat	23 May 99
61.49		Liang Lili	CHN	16.11.83	1	NC	Benxi	1 Jun 02

Mark	Wind	Name		Nat	Born	Pos	Meet	Venue	Date
Pre 1999 specification									
71.88		Antoaneta	Todorova	BUL	8.6.63	1	ECp	Zagreb	15 Aug 81
71.82		Ivonne	Leal	CUB	27.2.66	1	WUG	Kobe	30 Aug 85
70.12		Karen	Forkel	GDR	24.9.70	1	EJ	Varazdin	26 Aug 89
68.94		Trine	Solberg	NOR	18.4.66	1	vURS	Oslo	16 Jul 85
68.38		Antje	Kempe	GDR	23.6.63	Q	EC	Athína	8 Sep 82
68.17		Osleidys	Menéndez	CUB	14.11.79	1	WJ	Annecy	29 Jul 98

HEPTATHLON

6542	Carolina	Klüft	SWE	2.2.83	1	EC	München	10 Aug 02
	13.33/-0.3	1.89	13.16	23.71/-0.3	6.36/1.1	47.61	2:17.99	
6465	Sibylle	Thiele	GDR	6.3.65	1	EJ	Schwechat	28 Aug 83
	13.49	1.90	14.63	24.07	6.65	36.22	2:18.36	
6436	Sabine	Braun	FRG	19.6.65	1	vBUL	Mannheim	9 Jun 84
	13.68	1.78	13.09	23.88	6.03	52.14	2:09.41	
6428	Svetla	Dimitrova ¶	BUL	27.1.70	1	NC	Sofiya	18 Jun 89
	13.49/-0/7	1.77	13.98	23.59/-0.2	6.49/0.7	40.10	2:11.10	
6403	Emilia	Dimitrova	BUL	13.11.67	6	GWG	Moskva	7 Jul 86
	13.73	1.76	13.46	23.17	6.29	43.30	2:09.85	
6276	Larisa	Nikitina	RUS	29.4.65	8	URS Ch	Kiyev	21 Jun 84
	13.87/1.6	1.86	14.04	25.26/-0.7	6.31/0.1	48.62	2:22.76	
6218	Jana	Sobotka	GDR	3.10.65	6	OD	Potsdam	21 Jul 84
	14.40	1.74	13.28	24.19	6.27	43.64	2:06.83	
6198	Anke	Schmidt	GDR	5.2.68	7		Götzis	24 May 87
	13.80/0.9	1.72	13.32	23.82/0.3	6.63/2.0	35.78	2:12.44	
6194	Camelia	Cornateanu	ROM	23.1.67	2	NC	Pitesti	8 Aug 86
	14.35	1.86	14.70	24.97	6.15	38.94	2:11.93	
6187	Ionica	Domniteanu	ROM	8.1.69	1	Bal-j	Pitesti	26 Jul 87
	13.51	1.77	14.56	24.66	6.00	43.86	2:17.60	
Disqualified for positive drugs test								
6534	Svetla	Dimitrova	BUL	27.1.70	H	ECp	Helmond	16 Jul 89
	13.30/1.0	1.84	14.35	23.33/-2.2	6.47/-1.4	39.20	2:13.56	

10 KILOMETRES WALK

41:55	Irina	Stankina	RUS	25.3.77	1	NCw-j	Adler	11 Feb 95
41:57		Gao Hongmiao	CHN	17.3.74	2	NG	Beijing	8 Sep 93
42:44		Long Yuwen	CHN	1.8.75	3	NC	Shenzen	18 Feb 93
42:45		Li Yuxin	CHN	4.12.74	4		Shenzhen	18 Feb 93
42:47		Liu Hongyu	CHN	1.12.75	5	NC	Shenzen	18 Feb 93
42:50		Gu Yan	CHN	17.3.74	4	NG	Beijing	8 Sep 93
42:53.9t		Tan Lihong	CHN	13.2.73	6	NC	Jinan	15 Mar 92
43:07		Song Lijuan	CHN	1.2.76	6	NG	Beijing	8 Sep 93
43:10.4		Zhang Qinghua	CHN	6.3.73	8	NC	Jinan	15 Mar 92
43:15		Li Hong	CHN	1.6.79	7	NC	Zhuhai	10 Mar 96

20 KILOMETRES WALK

1:27:16		Song Hongjuan	CHN	4.7.84	1	NC	Yangzhou	14 Apr 03
1:27:35	Natalya	Fedoskina	RUS	25.6.80	2	WCp	Mézidon-Canon	2 May 99
1:29:09	Olga	Polyakova	RUS	23.9.80	5	NC-w	Adler	7 Feb 99
1:29:26		Wang Liping	CHN	8.7.76	6		Beijing	1 May 95
1:29:31		Jian Xingli	CHN	4.12.83	3	NG	Guangzhou	19 Nov 01
1:29:39		Gao Kelian	CHN	15.8.83	5	NG	Guangzhou	19 Nov 01

4 X 100 METRES RELAY

43.38	USA	Joyce, A.Williams, Robinson, Buchanan	1	PAm-J	Tampa	11 Jul 99
43.40	JAM	Simpson, Stewart, McLaughlin, Facey	1	WJ	Kingston	20 Jul 02
43.44A	NGR	Utondu, Iheagwam, Onyali, Ogunkoya	1	AfrG	Nairobi	9 Aug 87
43.48	GDR	Breuer, Krabbe, Dietz, Henke	1	WJ	Sudbury	31 Jul 88
	Unsanctioned race 43.33	Breuer, Krabbe, Dietz, Henke	1		Berlin	20 Jul 88
43.87	URS	Lapshina, Doronina, Bulatova, Kovalyova	1	vGDR-j	Leningrad	20 Jun 87
44.04	CUB	Riquelme, Allen, López, Valdivia	2	WJ	Sudbury	31 Jul 88
44.07	FRA	Thélamon, Hurtis, Imalouan, Rapp	2	WJ	Annecy	2 Aug 98

4 X 400 METRES RELAY

3:28.39	GDR	Derr, Fabert, Wöhlk, Breuer	1	WJ	Sudbury	31 Jul 88
3:29.66	JAM	Stewart, Morgan, Walker, Hall	1	PennR	Philadelphia	28 Apr 01
3:29.95	USA	Hardeman, Henderson, Ross, Demus	1	WJ	Kingston	21 Jul 02
3:30.38	AUS	Scamps, R Poetschka, Hanigan, Andrews	1	WJ	Plovdiv	12 Aug 90
3:30.46	GBR	Wall, Spencer, James,. Miller	2	WJ	Kingston	21 Jul 02
3:30.72	BUL	Kireva, Angelova, Rashova, Dimitrova	3	v2N	Sofiya	24 Jul 83
3:30.72	RUS	Migunova, Dryakhlova, Gushkhina, Popova	3	WJ	Kingston	21 Jul 02

Mark Name Nat Born Pos Meet Venue Date

CHANGES IN NATIONAL ALLEGIANCE

Men
Richard Alleyne BAR to GBR
Saud al-Thubaiti MAR to KSA
Bolota Asmeron ERI to USA
Mickaël Conjungo CAF to FRA
Attila Farkas ISR to HUN (back again)
Christophe Fernandes FRA to POR
Bayano Kamani USA to PAN
Abdulkabir Louraibi MAR to BRN
Paddy McGrath IRL to USA
Hassan Mourhit MAR to BEL
Lamberte Nyabamikazi BUR to RWA
Jorge Paula CPV to POR
Rachid Ramzi MAR to BRN
Philipp Rist SUI to CAN.
Yared Shegumo ETH to POL

Women
Yamilé Aldama CUB to SUD
Jolene Elizabeth Byrne USA to IRL
Yesenia Centeno CUB to ESP
Jessica DeFreitas USA to GUY
Antoinette Djimou CMR to FRA
Du Xianhiu CHN to SIN
Najia Ejjafini MAR to BRN
Nolle Graham JAM to USA
Natalie Harvey AUS to GBR (2004)
Lornah Kiplagat KEN to NED
Marina Lapina RUS to AZE
Magdalena Lewy POL to USA
Aliuska López CUB to ESP
Marzena Michalska POL to ITA
Teresa Nzola Meso ANG to FRA
Cora Olivero ARG to ESP
Elodie Ouédraogo BUR to BEL
Sandrine Thiébaud-Kangni FRA to TOG
Zhang Guirong CHN to SIN

CHANGES IN ALLEGIANCE AND NAME

Men
Albert Chepkurui KEN to Abdullah Ahmad Hassan KEN to QAT
Stephen Cherono KEN to Saif Saaeed Shaheen QAT
Abel Cheruiyot KEN to Abel Yagut BRN
Abdelhak El Gorche MAR to Abdulhak Zakaria BRN
Rachid Khouya MAR to Rachid Mohamed BRN
Gregory Konchellah KEN to Yousef Saïd Kamel BRN
Todd Matthews USA to Todd Matthews Jouda SUD
Leonard Mucheru KEN to Mushir Salem Jawher BRN
Onèsphore Nkunzimana BDI to Sultan Khamis Zaman QAT

Women
Gergana Stoyanova BUL to Yeoryía Syoyiannídou GRE

In March 2004 the IAAF discussed the cases of two former Kenyan athletes, who have changed allegiance to Bahrain and are now known as Abel Yagoot Jowhar Salem (Abel Cheruiyot) and Mucheru Salem Jawhar Salem (Leonard Mucheru). Mucheru last competed for Kenya on 16 Mar 2003 and although not eligible for Bahrain until 16 Mar 2006, competed for them on 7 Feb 2004 at the Asian Indoor Champs. Cheruiyot competed for Kenya at the World Cross on 24 Mar 2002 and is not eligible to represent Bahrain until 24 Mar 2005. However, he allegedly competed on 8 Sep 2003 at the Arab Champs. Council agreed that both athletes had competed for their new country before they were eligible to do so, the relevant results would be annulled and that a letter of warning would be sent to Bahrain.

ATHLETE MARRIAGES IN 2003

Gezahegne Abera to Elefenesh Alemu ETH on 8 June
Jared Deacon GBR to Susan Burnside on 6 Sep
Fabrizio Donato ITA to Patrizia Spuri on 27 Sep
Mark Grant GBR to Tracey Bloomfield in August
Frantz Kruger RSA to Heli Koivula FIN on 28 June
Sergey Lebed to Yelena Gorodnichova UKR on 23 April.
Dan Lincoln USA to Jennifer Culp USA on 12 July
Romain Mesnil FRA to Karine Bénézech (pb 3.75i in 1999)
Carl Myerscough GBR to Melissa Price USA on 27 June
Fabio Pizzolato ITA to Maria Carla Bresciani on 4 Oct
Jon Sinclair USA to Kim Jones USA in August
Brad Snyder CAN to Grete Etholm SWE in September
Natasha Danvers GBR to Darrell Smith jr USA on 1 Nov
Vera Pospisilová CZE to wrestler Jakub Cechl on 17 Oct
Jai Taurima AUS to Kerrie Perkins on 8 Nov

FURTHER RECENT WOMEN'S NAME CHANGES

Oksana Andrusina to Tuchak
Liliana Barbulescu to Popescu
Yuliya Bartsevich to Nesterenko
Stacey Bowers to Smith
Marina Bryukhach to Brezgina
Susan Burnside to Deacon
Jelena Celnova to Prokopcuka
Lidia Chojecka to Okninska
Michelle Clayton to Boswell
Gina Curtis to Rickert
Karol Damon (Jenkins) to Rovelto
Saraswati Dey to Saha
Constantina Dita to Tomescu
Deena Drossin to Kastor
Maranelle du Toit to Bell
Carey Easton to Marshall
Debbie Edwards to Shulstad
Dana Ellis to Buller
Kim Fitchen to Young
Wioletta Frankiewicz to Jankowska
Jill Gaitenby to Boaz
G.Pramila Ganapathy to Aiyappa
Adrija Grociebe to Parsukova
Yuliya Gurtovenko to Krevsun
Wendy Hartman to Seegers
Nora Ivanova - back from Güner
Karol Jenkins/Damon to Revolto
Candeger Kilinçer to Oguz
Lieja Koeman to Tunks
Tanya Koleva to Stefanova
Irina Korotya to Shevchenko
Tiffany Lott to Hogan
Miesha McKelvy to Jones
Marie McMahon to Davenport
Marsha Mark to Baird
Elva Martinez to Dryer
Sheryl Morrow to Purcell
Kirsten Münchow to Klose
Tatyana Nikolayeva to Shchurenko
Anna Norgren to Mahon
Yekaterina Noskova to Rozenberg
Yuliya Nosova to Pechonkina
Anna Olichwierczuk to Jesien
Yoko Ota to Hunnicutt
Yelena Ovcharova to Krasovskaya
Helen Pattinson to Clitheroe
Karyne Perkins to Di Marco
Vivian Peters to Chukwuemeka
Zhanna (Tarnopolskaya) Pintusevich to Block
Marina Pirog to Rezanova
Lyudmila Prikhodko to Vaylenko
Blake Russell to Phillips
Larisa Safronova to Yemelyanova
Yevgeniya Savina to Katkova
Nina Serbezova to Mitkova
Heide Seyerling to Quinn
Natalya Sidorenko to Tobias
Yelena Sivushenko to Slesarenko
Lucie Skrobáková to Martincová
Julianne Sprenger to Afflerbach
Ryoko Tadamasa to Sakamoto
Liz Talbot to Yelling
Yelena Tauryanina to Konevtsova
Helen Thieme to Karagounis
Ryan Tolbert to Jackson
Anna Tolokina to Omarova
Kjersti Tysse to Plätzer
Anca Vilceanu to Heltne
Natalya Vinogradova to Safronnikova
Lilia Volkova to Shobukova
Tamara Volkova to Tverdostup
Benita Willis to Johnson
Oksana Yelyasova to Gulumyan
Irina Yermoleyeva to Porfiriadi
Aneliya Yordanova to Kumanova
Firiya Zhdanova to Sultanova

MEN'S WORLD LISTS 2003

100 METRES

Mark	Wind		Name	Nat	Born	Pos	Meet	Venue	Date
9.93	1.8	Patrick	Johnson	AUS	26.9.72	1		Mito	5 May
9.94	1.4	Maurice	Greene	USA	23.7.74	1		Carson/Los Angeles	1 Jun
9.95	0.6	Deji	Aliu	NGR	22.11.75	1	Afr G	Abuja	12 Oct
9.97	1.3	John	Capel	USA	27.10.78	1=rA	WK	Zürich	15 Aug
9.97	1.3	Justin	Gatlin	USA	10.2.82	1=rA	WK	Zürich	15 Aug
9.97	0.6	Uchenna	Emedolu	NGR	17.9.76	2	Afr G	Abuja	12 Oct
9.98	0.0		Aliu			1	NC	Abuja	19 Jul
9.99	1.5	Mickey	Grimes	USA	10.10.76	1rB	WK	Zürich	15 Aug
9.99	1.3	Kim	Collins	SKN	5.4.76	3rA	WK	Zürich	15 Aug
10.00	1.3	Frank	Fredericks	NAM	2.10.67	1		Durban	11 Apr
10.00	0.5		Collins			1	Pre	Eugene	24 May
10.00	0.0		Aliu			1	GP	Tríkala	24 Jun
10.00	1.5	Darvis	Patton (10)	USA	4.12.79	2rB	WK	Zürich	15 Aug
10.01	0.0	Darrel	Brown	TRI-J	11.10.84	1q3	WCh	Saint-Denis	24 Aug
10.02	1.9		Capel			1		Réthimno	6 Jul
10.02	0.6		Collins			1q4	WCh	Saint-Denis	24 Aug
10.02	0.8	Asafa	Powell	JAM	11.11.82	1	VD	Bruxelles	5 Sep
10.03A	0.0	Nicolas	Macrozonaris	CAN	22.8.80	1		Ciudad de México	3 May
10.03	1.8	Shingo	Suetsugu	JPN	2.6.80	2		Mito	5 May
10.03	0.0		Aliu			1h1	GP	Tríkala	24 Jun
10.03	0.0	Dwain	Chambers ¶	GBR	5.4.78	2	GP	Tríkala	24 Jun
10.03	0.6	Leonard	Myles-Mills	GHA	9.5.73	3	Afr G	Abuja	12 Oct
10.04A	0.0	Tim	Montgomery	USA	28.1.75	2		Ciudad de México	3 May
10.04	-0.3		Montgomery			1	GP	Osaka	10 May
10.04	1.0		Montgomery			1h4	NC	Stanford	19 Jun
10.04	-0.1		Aliu			1	Athl	Lausanne	1 Jul
10.04	-0.3		Capel			1	GGala	Roma	11 Jul
10.04	0.9		Aliu			1h1	GP	London (CP)	8 Aug
10.04	0.6		Montgomery			1q1	WCh	Saint-Denis	24 Aug
10.04	0.6		Greene			3q4	WCh	Saint-Denis	24 Aug
10.04	0.6		Aliu			4q4	WCh	Saint-Denis	24 Aug
10.04	1.9	Bernard (32/18)	Williams	USA	19.1.78	1	WAF	Monaco	13 Sep

Note video evidence indicated times of 9.96 Chambers ¶ (dq), 9.98 Collins, 10.00 Aliu for 10.0s London (CP) 8 Aug

Mark	Wind		Name	Nat	Born	Pos	Meet	Venue	Date
10.05	0.0	Joshua 'J.J'	Johnson	USA	10.5.76	1		Abuja	17 May
10.07A	0.0	Shawn	Crawford	USA	14.1.78	1		Pretoria	4 Apr
10.07	2.0	Marcus (20)	Brunson	USA	24.4.78	1h1		Fort-de-France	26 Apr
10.07A	0.0	Jon	Drummond	USA	9.9.68	3		Ciudad de México	3 May
10.07A	0.0	Coby	Miller	USA	19.10.76	4		Ciudad de México	3 May
10.07	0.0	Abdul Aziz	Zakari	GHA	2.9.76	2		Abuja	17 May
10.07	1.1	DaBryan	Blanton	USA-J	3.7.84	1h2	NCAA-r	Lincoln, NE	30 May
10.07	0.0	Mark	Lewis-Francis	GBR	4.9.82	1	GS	Ostrava	12 Jun
10.08	1.3	Sherwin	Vries	RSA	22.3.80	2		Durban	11 Apr
10.08	0.9	Obadele	Thompson	BAR	30.3.76	1rA		Walnut	12 Jul
10.08	0.0	Darren	Campbell	GBR	12.9.73	3	WCh	Saint-Denis	25 Aug
10.09	1.2	Matt	Shirvington	AUS	25.10.78	1		Gold Coast (RB)	12 Apr
1		(30)							
0.09	1.0	Rae	Edwards	USA	7.5.81	2h4	NC	Stanford	19 Jun
10.09	-0.6	Julien	Dunkley	JAM	20.12.75	1		La Chaux-de-Fonds	17 Aug
10.09	0.7	Ato	Boldon	TRI	30.12.73	1q2	WCh	Saint-Denis	24 Aug
10.11	0.0	Kenny	Brokenburr	USA	29.10.68	3		Abuja	17 May
10.11	1.5	Francis	Obikwelu	POR	22.11.78	5rB	WK	Zürich	15 Aug
10.12	-1.5	Eric	Nkansah	GHA	12.12.74	1		Córdoba	6 Sep
10.13	1.3	Morné	Nagel	RSA	23.2.78	3		Durban	11 Apr
10.13	0.9	Marquis	Davis	USA	14.8.80	1	SEC	Knoxville	18 May
10.13	1.1	Michael (40)	Frater	JAM	6.10.82	2h2	NCAA-r	Lincoln, NE	30 May
10.13	0.0	Ronald	Pognon	FRA	16.11.82	1		Castres	6 Aug
10.14	1.4	Kaaron	Conwright	USA	8.8.76	1rA	MSR	Walnut	19 Apr
10.14	0.4	Alexander	Kosenkow	GER	14.3.77	1		Leverkusen	3 Aug
10.15	1.1	Brian	Lewis	USA	5.12.74	2h2	NC	Stanford	19 Jun
10.15	-0.5	Freddy	Mayola	CUB	1.11.77	1		Castellón	18 Aug
10.15	-0.6	Olusoji	Fasuba	NGR-J	9.7.84	1	Af-AsG	Hyderabad	30 Oct
10.16	0.9	Pierre	Browne	CAN	14.1.80	2	SEC	Knoxville	18 May

Mark	Wind	Name		Nat	Born	Pos	Meet	Venue	Date
10.17	0.4	Hristóforos	Hoídis	GRE	10.9.78	2	Veniz	Haniá	9 Jun
10.17	0.4	Aristotélis	Gavélas	GRE	10.11.78	3	Veniz	Haniá	9 Jun
10.17	1.0	Salem Mubarak	Al-Yami	KSA	9.2.82	1		Eurajoki	25 Jun
		(50)							
10.17	1.3	Aaron	Armstrong	USA	14.10.77	1rB		Nuoro	9 Jul
10.17	0.0	Jason	Gardener	GBR	18.9.75	2	Gugl	Linz	31 Jul
10.17	0.7	Yeóryios	Theodoridis	GRE	12.12.72	2h1	WCh	Saint-Denis	24 Aug
10.17	0.4		Chen Haijan	CHN	5.4.80	1	NC	Shanghai	12 Sep
10.18	0.9	Samie	Parker	USA	24.5.81	1h1	Pac-10	Los Angeles	17 May
10.18	-0.1	Konstantin	Rurak	UKR	9.4.74	1	NC	Kiev	3 Jul
10.19	0.9	Bennie	Chatman	USA	24.1.79	2h1	Pac-10	Los Angeles	17 May
10.19	2.0	Eddy	De Lépine	FRA-J	30.3.84	1		Fort-de-France	7 Jun
10.19	1.5	Jacey	Harper	TRI	20.5.80	1	NC	Port of Spain	20 Jun
10.19	1.8	Prodromos	Katsantonis	CYP	20.10.75	1	ECp-2B	Istanbul	21 Jun
		(60)							
10.19	0.6	Dwight	Thomas	JAM	23.9.80	5s2	WCh	Saint-Denis	25 Aug
10.20	0.7	Édson	Ribeiro	BRA	8.12.72	1	NC	São Paulo	15 Jun
10.20	-0.1	Gábor	Dobos	HUN	21.2.76	4	Odlozil	Praha	29 Jun
10.20	-0.8	Ricardo	Williams	JAM	29.9.76	3		San Sebastián	10 Aug
10.20	-0.6	Stéphane	Buckland	MRI	20.1.77	2		La Chaux-de-Fonds	17 Aug
10.20	-0.6	Tamunosiki	Atorudibo	NGR-J	21.3.85	2	Af-AsG	Hyderabad	30 Oct
10.21	2.0	Lindel	Frater	JAM	13.11.77	1	Oda	Hiroshima	29 Apr
10.21	-1.6	Ramon	Clay	USA	29.6.75	1		Sainte-Anne	8 May
10.21	0.7	Jarbas	Mascarenhas	BRA	25.8.80	2	NC	São Paulo	15 Jun
10.21	0.8	Sheldon	Morant	JAM	21.6.80	1h3	CAC	St George's	4 Jul
		(70)							
10.21	0.9	Jerome	Avery	USA	18.4.78	2rA		Walnut	12 Jul
10.21	1.8	Aimé-Issa	Nthépé	FRA	26.6.73	1s2	NC	Narbonne	25 Jul
10.22	1.7	Christie	van Wyk	NAM	12.10.77	1		Abilene	22 Mar
10.22	1.1	Ernest	Wiggins	USA	18.6.82	1h2		Clemson	10 May
10.22	1.4	Jabari	Fields	USA	10.9.81	1h3	NCAA-r	Lincoln, NE	30 May
10.22	1.6	Yuta	Kanno	JPN	13.12.80	1h2	NC	Yokohama	8 Jun
10.22	1.7	Christian	Malcolm	GBR	3.6.79	1		Riga	12 Jun
10.22	1.5	Niconnor	Alexander	TRI	4.2.77	3	NC	Port of Spain	20 Jun
10.22	0.8	Fabrice	Calligny	FRA	4.11.81	1h5	CAC	St George's	4 Jul
10.22	1.4	Matic	Osovnikar	SLO	19.1.80	1		Wolfsberg	26 Jul
		(80)							
10.22	0.7	Mardy	Scales	USA	10.9.81	2	PAm	Santo Domingo	6 Aug
10.22	-1.0	Aaron	Egbele	NGR	29.1.79	2s3	Afr G	Abuja	12 Oct
10.23	2.0	Hiroyasu	Tsuchie	JPN	14.6.74	2	Oda	Hiroshima	29 Apr
10.23A	-0.4	Vicente L	de Lima	BRA	4.6.77	1h2		Cochabamba	11 May
10.23	0.7	Olan	Coleman	USA	29.7.80	1	NCAA II	Edwardsville	24 May
10.23	0.9	Tyrone	Edgar	GBR	29.3.82	6h1	GP	London (CP)	8 Aug
10.23	0.8	Nobuharu	Asahara	JPN	21.6.72	4h2	WCh	Saint-Denis	24 Aug
10.24	1.1	Tesfa	Latty	JAM-J	9.11.84	1	N.Sch	Kingston	4 Apr
10.24	0.2	Marvin	Anderson	JAM	12.5.82	1rB		Tempe	12 Apr
10.24A	0.6	Taiwo	Ajibade	NGR	17.6.82	2		El Paso	12 Apr
		(90)							
10.24	2.0	Dwight	Phillips	USA	1.10.77	4rA	Mod R	Modesto	10 May
10.24	1.8	Anthony	Buchanan	USA	10.9.81	1h2	Pac-10	Los Angeles	17 May
10.24	1.5	Chris	Stewart	USA	6.3.80	1		San Marcos	19 May
10.24	0.4	Ronny	Ostwald	GER	7.4.74	3		Leverkusen	3 Aug
10.24	1.7	Patrick	Jarrett	JAM	2.10.77	1h1		Fribourg	23 Aug
10.25	2.0	Kazuki	Ishikura	JPN	1.10.80	3	Oda	Hiroshima	29 Apr
10.25	0.6	Brendan	Christian	ANT	11.12.83	1h2	Big12	Austin	18 May
10.25	1.3	Cláudio R	Sousa	BRA	14.10.73	1		São Caetano do Sul	31 May
10.25	1.0	Shingo	Kawabata	JPN	15.5.78	1	NG	Fukuroi	27 Oct
10.26A	1.8	Mike	Appelhans	USA	24.8.80	1		Alamosa	3 May
		(100)							
10.26	1.1	Kevin	Bartlett	BAR	20.1.81	1		Emporia	9 May
10.26	1.9	Greg	Saddler	USA	29.6.74	1rB	Mod R	Modesto	10 May
10.26		Dominic	Demeritte	BAH	22.2.78	1	NC	Freeport	20 Jun
10.26	1.0	Jamal	Al-Saffar	KSA	24.10.71	2		Eurajoki	25 Jun
10.26	0.9	Bobby	Williams	USA	3.2.78	4rA		Walnut	12 Jul
10.26	1.2	Markus	Pöyhönen	FIN	25.10.78	1		Turku	23 Jul

10.27A	0.0	Matthew	Quinn	RSA	17.4.76	4 Apr
10.27	1.9	Anson	Henry	CAN	9.3.79	12 Apr
10.27	1.6	Guy	McGowan	USA		19 Apr
10.27		Lowell	Fernander	BAH		19 Jun
10.27	0.0	Gennadiy	Chernovol	KAZ	6.6.76	21 Sep
10.28	1.1	Steve	Mullings	JAM	29.11.82	4 Apr
10.28	0.0	E.J.	Jackson	USA	3.2.78	10 May
10.28	0.5	Marc	Blume	GER	28.12.73	28 Jun
10.28	1.2	Argo	Golberg	EST	16.12.82	19 Jul
10.28	1.8		Shen Yunbao	CHN	28.7.76	2 Aug
10.28	-0.6	Marc	Burns	TRI	7.1.83	24 Aug
10.29	0.6	Curtis	Coleman	USA	10.3.79	28 Mar

Mark	Wind	Name		Nat	Born	Date
10.29	1.5	Carlos	Moore	USA-J	8.5.84	11 Apr
10.29	1.3	Idrissa	Sanou	BUR	12.6.77	11 Apr
10.29	1.2	Adam	Basil	AUS	14.4.75	12 Apr
10.29	1.9	Earvin	Parker	USA-J	6.4.84	10 May
10.29	0.9	Tre	Gardner	USA	25.10.79	18 May
10.29	0.8	Airese	Currie	USA	16.11.82	31 May
10.29	1.9	Troy	Douglas	NED	30.11.62	7 Jun
10.29	1.7	Tim	Harden	USA	27.1.74	19 Jun
10.29	0.8	Churandy	Martina	AHO-J	3.7.84	4 Jul
10.29	0.3	Musa	Deji	NGR	22.11.75	12 Jul
10.29	1.9	Aristídis	Petrídis	GRE	6.12.79	12 Jul
10.29	1.7	Francesco	Scuderi	ITA	4.10.77	2 Aug
10.29A	1.5	Hisashi	Miyazaki	JPN	19.3.81	3 Aug
10.29	0.6	Abdolghafar	Saghar	IRI	22.3.74	8 Aug
10.30	-2.2	Sean	Lambert	GRN	16.8.82	5 Apr
10.30	0.0	Kwesi	Frimpong-Boateng	GHA	25.5.80	4 May
10.30A	0.6	Claudinei	da Silva	BRA	19.11.70	11 May
10.30	0.9	LaTonel	Williams	JAM	3.6.78	17 May
10.30	0.7	Jason	Smoots	USA	13.7.80	24 May
10.30	-1.9	Antoine	Boussombo	GAB	18.5.68	25 May
10.30	0.9	André D	da Silva	BRA	26.11.72	4 Jun
10.30		Derrick	Atkins	BAH-J	5.1.84	19 Jun
10.30	1.0	Panayiótis	Sarris	GRE	14.9.75	6 Jul
10.30	0.9	Shomari	Wilson	USA	6.6.76	12 Jul
10.30	0.4	Roger	Anguono-Moké	CGO	20.11.81	12 Jul
10.30	1.8	Éric	Pacôme N'Dri	CIV	24.3.78	23 Jul
10.30	1.3	Simone	Collio	ITA	27.12.79	2 Aug
10.31	1.3	Clinton	Venter	RSA	3.2.80	11 Apr
10.31	2.0	Ryo	Matsuda	JPN	26.12.79	29 Apr
10.31	1.8	Nobuhiro	Tajima	JPN	7.11.80	5 May
10.31	1.6	Kazuhiro	Tamura	JPN	3.7.78	8 Jun
10.31	0.3	Tommi	Hartonen (150)	FIN	12.5.77	15 Jun
10.31		Stanley	Egbor	NGR	19.3.77	6 Jul
10.31	1.9	Ággelos	Pavlákakis	GRE	7.11.76	12 Jul
10.31		Ibrahim	Tanko Braimah	GHA	12.5.79	12 Jul
10.31	1.1	Aleksandr	Smirnov	RUS	25.2.74	14 Jul
10.31	0.0	Jérôme	Éyana	FRA	5.7.77	6 Aug
10.31	0.8	Chris	Lambert	GBR	6.4.81	25 Aug
10.31	1.3	Shigeyuki	Kojima	JPN	25.9.79	28 Sep
10.32	1.5	Tyree	Gailes	USA	24.2.83	12 Apr
10.32		Surya	Agung Wibowo	INA	8.10.83	19 Apr
10.32	1.5	Tatsuro	Yoshino	JPN	11.9.82	16 May
10.32	1.9	Rashaad	Allen	USA	19.2.83	17 May
10.32	0.7	Clement	Campbell	JAM	19.2.75	24 May
10.32	1.0	Nick	Smith	GBR	6.12.82	25 May
10.32	0.0	Tobias	Unger	GER	10.7.79	31 May
10.32	1.5	Rubin	Williams	USA	9.7.83	8 Jun
10.32		Christopher	Williams	JAM	15.3.72	9 Jun
10.32	1.9	Kristof	Beyens	BEL	13.7.83	14 Jun
10.32		James	Harden	USA		12 Jul
10.32	0.9	Ja'Warren	Hooker	USA	24.9.78	12 Jul
10.32	0.0	Lukasz	Chyla	POL	31.3.81	17 Jul
10.32	1.5	Naoki	Tsukahara	JPN-J	10.5.85	30 Jul
10.32	0.2	Marcin	Krzywanski	POL	29.8.75	3 Aug
10.33	0.5	Ambrose	Ezenwa	NGR	10.4.77	22 Feb
10.33	1.3	Douglas	Bignall	GBR	20.10.74	5 Apr
10.33	1.9	Bruce	Swan	GRN	4.5.77	3 May
10.33A	1.5	Vitaliy	Medvedev	KAZ	6.1.77	3 May
10.33	1.8	Wesley	Felix	USA	21.7.83	17 May
10.33	1.4	Gentry	Bradley	USA	19.1.74	1 Jun
10.33	1.4	Kareem	Streete-Thompson	CAY	30.3.73	1 Jun
10.33	1.1	Llewelyn	Bredwood	JAM	30.4.76	7 Jun
10.33		Konstantin	Vasyukov	UKR	10.1.81	12 Jun
10.33	-1.2	Erick	Wilson	USA	20.1.82	19 Jun
10.33	1.2	Heber	Viera	URU	29.4.79	20 Jun
10.33	1.7	Andrea	Rabino	ITA	23.4.78	2 Aug
10.33	0.3	Luca	Verdecchia	ITA	24.5.78	4 Sep
10.34		Andre	Blackman	GUY	3.11.80	6 Apr
10.34	-0.2	Kendrick	Triggs	USA	27.8.82	19 Apr
10.34		Dan	Tutskey	USA	3.9.79	9 May
10.34	1.2	Jimmie	Hackley	USA	11.9.75	10 May
10.34	1.9	Aaron	Thigpen	USA	18.9.64	10 May
10.34	0.9	Ahmad	Carroll	USA	4.8.83	18 May
10.34	0.0	Dejan	Vojnovic	CRO	23.3.75	7 Jun
10.34	1.1	Marko	Jankovic	SCG	29.2.76	13 Jun
10.34	0.1	Oumar	Loum	SEN	31.12.73	1 Jul
10.34	1.0	Aléxandros	Terzián	GRE	24.6.68	6 Jul
10.34	1.3	Maurizio	Checcucci (196)	ITA	26.2.74	9 Jul

Wind assisted

Mark	Wind	Name		Nat	Born	Pos	Meet	Venue	Date
9.88	3.6	Patrick	Johnson	AUS	26.9.72	1		Perth	8 Feb
9.90	5.7		P Johnson			1h1		Perth	8 Feb
9.92	2.8	Kim	Collins	SKN	5.4.76	1rA	Tex R	Austin	5 Apr
9.93	5.3	Erick	Wilson	USA	10.1.82	1	JUCO	Levelland	10 May
9.96	5.2	Olan	Coleman	USA	29.7.80	1		Abilene	3 May
9.97	2.9	Darvis	Patton	USA	4.12.79	1		Fort Worth	19 Apr
9.97	3.4	Kenny	Brokenburr	USA	29.10.68	1		Abilene	8 May
9.97	2.5		Collins			1h2	GP	London (CP)	8 Aug
9.98	3.5	Abdul Aziz	Zakari	GHA	2.9.76	1		Dakar	4 Apr
10.00	5.3	Steve	Mullings	JAM	29.11.82	2	JUCO	Levelland	10 May
10.01	5.3	Tyson	Gay	USA	9.9.82	3	JUCO	Levelland	10 May
10.02	5.2	Mardy	Scales	USA	10.9.81	1	NCAA-r	Columbus	31 May
10.03	5.3	Tyree	Gailes	USA	24.2.83	4	JUCO	Levelland	10 May
10.03	2.5		Gatlin			2h2	GP	London (CP)	8 Aug
10.04	5.3	Tyrone	Edgar	GBR	29.3.82	5	JUCO	Levelland	10 May
10.04	2.8	Patrick	Jarrett	JAM	2.10.77	1		Fribourg	23 Aug
10.06	5.2	Niconnor	Alexander	TRI	4.2.77	2		Abilene	3 May
10.07	3.4	Marcin	Jedrusinski	POL	28.9.81	1	NC	Bielsko-Biala	5 Jul
10.09	2.8	Pierre	Browne	CAN	14.1.80	2rA	Tex R	Austin	5 Apr
10.09	2.3	Aimé-Issa	Nthépé	FRA	26.6.73	1	NC	Narbonne	25 Jul
10.10	3.0	Marquis	Davis	USA	14.8.80	1rB	Tex R	Austin	5 Apr
10.10	2.9	Lindel	Frater	JAM	13.11.77	2		Fort Worth	19 Apr
10.10	3.7	Anthony	Buchanan	USA	10.9.81	1	Pac-10	Los Angeles	18 May
10.10	2.4	Brian	Lewis	USA	5.12.74	1	ECCp	Valencia	24 May
10.11	2.8	Konstantin	Rurak	UKR	9.4.74	1h3		Kiev	27 May
10.11	2.5	Jason	Gardener	GBR	18.9.75	5h2	GP	London (CP)	8 Aug
10.12	3.7	Bennie	Chatman	USA	24.1.79	2	Pac-10	Los Angeles	18 May
10.12	3.0	Ronald	Pognon	FRA	16.11.82	1s3	CAC	St George's	4 Jul
10.13	3.6	Ambrose	Ezenwa	NGR	10.4.77	2		Perth	8 Feb
10.13	2.9	Ricardo	Williams	JAM	29.9.76	4		Fort Worth	19 Apr
10.15	2.3	Idrissa	Sanou	BUR	12.6.77	3		Dakar	4 Apr
10.15	3.8	Jason	Smoots	USA	13.7.80	3h2	NCAA II	Edwardsville	22 May
10.16	3.5	Oumar	Loum	SEN	31.12.73	4		Dakar	4 Apr
10.16	5.2	Christie	van Wyk	NAM	12.10.77	3		Abilene	3 May

Mark	Wind	Name		Nat	Born	Pos	Meet	Venue	Date
10.16	3.2	Ivory	Williams	USA-J	2.5.85	1		Austin	10 May
10.16	2.2	Clement	Campbell	JAM	19.2.75	1h1	NCAA II	Edwardsville	22 May
10.17	3.0	Vicente	de Lima	BRA	4.6.77	1h1		São Caetano do Sul	31 May
10.18	4.6	Robert	Foster	USA	15.5.81	1		Houston	29 Mar
10.18	2.5	Abdolghafar	Saghar	IRI	22.3.74	1		Sari	13 Jun
10.19	2.1	Francesco	Scuderi	ITA	4.10.77	1		Roma	17 May
10.20	3.0	Nick	Johnson	USA	12.11.83	3rB	Tex R	Austin	5 Apr
10.20	5.3	Andre	Summers	USA-J	.85	6	JUCO	Levelland	10 May
10.20	2.2	Daniel	Dubois	SUI	24.12.71	1		Genève	14 Jun
10.20	3.4	Marcin	Krzywanski	POL	29.8.75	2	NC	Bielsko-Biala	5 Jul
10.21	4.3	Takayuki	Kon	JPN	15.7.77	1rB	Oda	Hiroshima	29 Apr
10.21	5.4	Aulton	Kohn	USA-J	.84	1		Beaufort, SC	10 May
10.21	3.0	Cláudio	Sousa	BRA	14.10.73	2h1		São Caetano do Sul	31 May
10.21	4.9	Ryosuke	Igumi	JPN-J	6.7.84	1	NC-j	Maebashi	29 Jun
10.21	2.3	Tim	Harden	USA	27.1.74	1rC		Walnut	12 Jul
10.22	2.8	E.J. (Ephion)	Jackson	USA	3.2.78	1		Sacramento	8 Jun
10.22	3.4	Piotr	Balcerzak	POL	25.6.75	3	NC	Bielsko-Biala	5 Jul
10.22	2.9	Jonathan	Barbour	GBR	3.11.80	2		Fribourg	23 Aug
10.23	3.6	Paul	Di Bella	AUS	12.2.77	3		Perth	8 Feb
10.23	5.0	Shomari	Wilson	USA	6.6.76	4		Arlington	29 Mar
10.23	2.8	Desmond	Bynum	USA	.80	1		Austin	3 May
10.23	3.8	Lerone	Clarke	JAM	.81	3h2	NCAA II	Edwardsville	22 May
10.23	2.6	Roger	Anguono-Moké	CGO	20.11.81	1		Argentan	9 Jun
10.23	5.1	Shingo	Kawabata	JPN	15.5.78	1		Maebashi	21 Jun
10.24	2.1	Wesley	Felix	USA	21.7.83	1		Los Angeles	26 Apr
10.24	2.8	Brendan	Christian	ANT	11.12.83	1h1	NCAA-r	Lincoln, NE	30 May
10.24	5.2	Sean	Lambert	GRN	16.8.82	3	NCAA-r	Columbus	31 May
10.24	5.2	Marc	Burns	TRI	7.1.83	4	NCAA-r	Columbus	31 May
10.24	2.2	Marc	Blume	GER	28.12.73	1h1		Zeven	8 Jun
10.24	2.3	Gentry	Bradley	USA	19.1.74	2rC		Walnut	12 Jul
10.24A	3.2	Adam	Basil	AUS	14.4.75	1		Terminillo	6 Aug
10.24	2.9	Dwayne	Grant	GBR	17.7.82	3		Fribourg	23 Aug
10.24	2.6	Leigh	Julius	RSA-J	25.3.85	1		Durban	5 Dec

10.25	3.5	Joseph	Batangdon	CMR	29.7.78	4 Apr
10.25	3.0	Patrik	Lövgren	SWE	12.10.75	13 Jul
10.25	2.3	Marcin	Nowak	POL	2.8.77	9 Sep
10.26	4.3	Akihiro	Yasui	JPN	2.10.77	29 Apr
10.26	2.1	Simone	Collio	ITA	27.12.79	17 May
10.26	2.9	Nick	Smith	GBR	6.12.82	26 May
10.26	2.2	Stéphane	Cali	FRA	26.4.72	14 Jun
10.26	2.4	Churandy	Martina	AHO-J	3.7.84	28 Jun
10.27	2.8	Tre	Gardner	USA	25.10.79	5 Apr
10.27	2.6	Clement	Taylor	BAH	5.6.82	3 May
10.27	2.8	Adam	Wooten	USA	18.3.82	30 May
10.27	2.8	Bryan	Howard	USA	7.10.76	8 Jun
10.27	2.6	Vitaliy	Medvedev	KAZ	6.1.77	9 Jun
10.27	3.4	Lukasz	Chyla	POL	31.3.81	5 Jul
10.27	3.1	Ággelos	Pavlakákis	GRE	7.11.76	19 Jul
10.27	2.3	Jérôme	Éyana	FRA	5.7.77	26 Jul
10.28	2.8	Brian	Johnson	USA	25.3.80	4 Apr
10.28	2.3	LaTonel	Williams	JAM	3.6.782	25 Apr
10.28	2.8	Ahmad	Carroll	USA	4.8.83	30 May
10.29	3.0	Ernest	Simms	USA	19.7.80	5 Apr
10.29	2.2	Kyle	Farmer	USA	15.4.83	3 May
10.29		Chris	Lambert	GBR	6.4.81	3 May
10.29	4.8	Lewis	Turner	USA	77	8 May
10.29		Walter	Dix	USA-Y	31.1.86	10 May
10.29	3.0	Gary	Ryan	IRL	12.6.72	10 Aug
10.29	2.7	Adel Mohamed	Farhan	BRN	25.12.79	7 Sep
10.30	4.3	Toshiyuki	Fujimoto	JPN	25.6.79	29 Apr
10.30	2.6	Daniel	McLemore	USA	1.11.82	3 May
10.30	2.1	Massimiliano	Donati	ITA	16.6.79	24 May
10.30	2.7	Tommi	Hartonen	FIN	12.5.77	2 Jul
10.31	3.9	Monu	Miah	GBR-J	10.1.84	28 Jun
10.31	2.2	Anthony	Ferro	BEL	12.12.80	15 Aug
10.31	5.0	Yusuke	Nii	JPN-J	16.4.84	23 Aug
10.32		Rubin	Williams	USA	9.7.83	10 May
10.32	2.4	Graham	Beasley	GBR	24.10.77	24 May
10.32	2.6	Nathan	Bongelo	BEL	2.12.73	9 Jun
10.32	2.7	Luca	Verdecchia	ITA	24.5.78	2 Jul
10.32	3.1	Vasílios	Séggos	GRE	24.10.76	19 Jul
10.32	2.3	Fréderic	Krantz	FRA	13.9.78	26 Jul
10.33	3.2	Adrian	Peterson	USA-J	21.3.85	9 May
10.33	3.2	Anthony	Aldridge	USA-J		9 May
10.33	5.3	Marquel	Russell	USA-J	19.7.84	10 May
10.33	2.9	Daniel	Plummer	GBR	4.1.81	25 May
10.34	4.6	Fred	Day	USA	22.5.81	29 Mar
10.34A	3.4	Nate	Soelberg	USA	19.3.81	17 May
10.34	2.2	Johan	Wissman	SWE	2.11.82	13 Jul

Low altitude bests

10.07	1.5	Crawford	3rB	WK	Zürich	15 Aug
10.10	-0.1	Miller	1	Neb	Torino	6 Jun
10.10	-0.1	Drummond	1	Odl	Praha	29 Jun
10.13	1.3	Macrozonaris	1	NC	Victoria	19 Jul
10.28	1.3	Quinn				11 Apr
10.30	1.8	Miyazaki				5 May

Hand timing

9.9	1.4	Asafa	Powell	JAM	11.11.82	1		Spanish Town	30 Mar
9.9	-0.6	Gary	Ryan	IRL	12.6.72	1		Jambes	26 Jul
10.0		Guy	McGowan	USA		1		Los Gatos	3 Jul
10.0	0.1	Anatoliy	Dovgal	UKR	29.1.76	1		Kiev	29 Jul
10.0	0.9	Bernard	Williams	USA	19.1.78	4	GP	London (CP)	8 Aug
10.0	1.8	Vicente	de Lima	BRA	4.6.77	1h1		São Paulo	6 Sep

10.1	1.4	Winston	Smith	JAM	22.11.82	30 Mar
10.1	-1.5	Steve	Mullings	JAM	29.11.82	27 Mar
10.1		Juan Antonio	Pita	CUB	29.7.79	15 May
10.1		Jamial	Rolle	BAH	16.4.80	19 Jun
10.1		Jérôme	Éyana	FRA	5.7.77	28 Jun
10.1	-0.6	Anthony	Ferro	BEL	12.12.80	26 Jul
10.1	1.8	Eliezer	de Almeida	BRA	31.3.83	6 Sep
10.1	1.8	Jarbas	Mascarenhas	BRA	25.8.80	6 Sep
10.1		Terrance	Wheatley	USA		29 Mar

Wind assisted

10.0		Maurice	Hewitt	USA		1		Lindsborg	15 Mar

Mark	Wind	Name		Nat	Born	Pos	Meet	Venue	Date
10.0		E.J. (Ephion)	Jackson	USA	3.2.78	1		Fresno	26 Apr
10.0		Terry	Bowen	USA	15.9.71	2		Fresno	26 Apr

10.1 Clayton Latham CAN 18.4.80 15 Mar | 10.1A 3.6 Luis Morán ECU 24.5.80 22 May
10.1 5.9 Tim Williams AUS 9.12.81 15 Nov

Drugs disqualification

10.03	0.6		Chambers ¶			2q4	WCh	Saint-Denis	24 Aug
		hand: 10.0 0.9	(9.96 on video)			1 GP		London (CP)	8 Aug

JUNIORS

See main list for top 6 Juniors. 10 performances by 4 men to 10.19. Additional marks and further juniors:

Brown 10.08 0.5 2 Pre Eugene 24 May | 10.11 0.6 2s2 WCh Saint-Denis 25 Aug
10.08 0.0 2 WCh Saint-Denis 25 Aug | 10.17 0.6 2 CAC St George's 4 Jul
10.10 1.7 2h5 WCh Saint-Denis 24 Aug | 10.17 0.0 3 Gugl Linz 31 Jul

10.29	1.5	Carlos	Moore	USA	8.5.84	1	MSR	Walnut	11 Apr
10.29	1.9	Earvin	Parker	USA	6.4.84	1B		Austin	10 May
10.29	0.8	Churandy	Martina	AHO	3.7.84	2h5	CAC	St George's	4 Jul
10.30		Derrick	Atkins (10)	BAH	5.1.84	1h3	NC	Freeport	19 Jun
10.35	2.0	Jorge Célio	Sena	BRA	31.1.85	1	NC-j	Londrina	17 May
10.37	1.8	Adrian	Durant	ISV	10.10.84	1r1		Clemson	10 May
10.37	1.4	Demi	Omole	USA	29.7.85	1s2		Ypsilanti	28 Jul
10.38	1.2	Xavier	Carter	USA	8.12.85	1		Arcadia	12 Apr
10.38	0.0	Oluwole	Ogunde	NGR-Y	13.5.86	1s1		Enugu	24 May
10.39	1.2	Adam	Miller	AUS	22.6.84	2		Canberra	16 Mar
10.39	-2.2	Jonathan	Wade	USA	27.3.84	2		Columbia, SC	5 Apr
10.40		Marcus	Julien	GRN	.86	1		St. George's	2 Apr
10.40	1.7	Sebastian	Ernst	GER	11.10.84	1		Zeven	7 Jun
10.40	0.0	Kenny	O'Neal (20)	USA-Y	2.5.86	2	NC-j	Stanford	22 Jun
10.40	2.0	Yahya Saed	Al-Kahes	KSA-Y	19.2.86	1		Jämsänkoski	29 Jun

Wind assisted – see main list for five juniors. Additional men:

10.26	2.4	Churandy	Martina	AHO	3.7.84	1	NED-j	Lisse	28 Jun
10.29		Walter	Dix	USA-Y	31.1.86	1		Coral Springs	10 May
10.31	3.9	Monu	Miah	GBR	10.1.84	1s1	NC-j	Bedford	28 Jun
10.31	5.0	Yusuke	Nii	JPN	16.4.84	1h2		Sapporo	23 Aug
10.33	3.2	Adrian	Peterson	USA	21.3.85	2A		Austin	9 May
10.33	3.2	Anthony	Aldridge	USA		3A		Austin	9 May
10.33	5.3	Marquel	Russell	USA	19.7.84	7	JUCO	Levelland	10 May
10.36	3.7	Jerald	Watson	USA	11.12.85	1r1		Baton Rouge	9 May
10.36	2.7	Yahya Saeed	Al-Kahes	KSA-Y	19.2.86	5rA		Lahti	2 Jul
10.39	2.2	Hank	Palmer	CAN	16.3.85	1s2	NC-j	Saskatoon	5 Jul
10.39	2.5	Reia	Chinen	JPN-Y	11.7.86	1		Oita	18 Oct

Hand timed

10.1		Bryan	Hendricks	USA		1		Round Rock	8 Mar
10.1		Bradley	Reed	USA	.85	1		Greenville	29 Mar
10.1		Andrew	Alexander	USA		1		Edmond	10 May

200 METRES

20.01	0.8	Bernard	Williams	USA	19.1.78	1	GGala	Roma	11 Jul
20.02	0.8	Shawn	Crawford	USA	14.1.78	2	GGala	Roma	11 Jul
		note – ran out of lane							
20.03	0.6	Shingo	Suetsugu	JPN	2.6.80	1	NC	Yokohama	7 Jun
20.03	0.6	Darvis	Patton	USA	4.12.79	1s1	WCh	Saint-Denis	29 Aug
20.04	0.0	Coby	Miller	USA	19.10.76	1	Athl	Lausanne	1 Jul
20.04	-0.1	Justin	Gatlin	USA	10.2.82	1	VD	Bruxelles	5 Sep
20.05	0.0	Joshua 'J.J'	Johnson	USA	10.5.76	1		Abuja	17 May
20.06	0.7	Stéphane	Buckland	MRI	20.1.77	1q3	WCh	Saint-Denis	27 Aug
20.08A	-0.5		Crawford			1		Pretoria	4 Apr
20.10	-0.6		Crawford			1		Zagreb	7 Jul
20.11	0.6		Buckland			2s1	WCh	Saint-Denis	29 Aug
20.13A	0.0		Miller			1		Ciudad de México	3 May
20.13	0.0	Usain	Bolt	JAM-Y	21.8.86	1	PAm-J	Bridgetown	20 Jul
20.14	0.0		Patton			2	Athl	Lausanne	1 Jul
20.15A	-0.4	André D	da Silva (10)	BRA	26.11.72	1		Cochabamba	11 May
20.15	0.1		Patton			1	NC	Stanford	22 Jun
20.16	0.0	Maurice	Greene	USA	23.7.74	1	MSR	Walnut	19 Apr
20.17	0.1	John	Capel	USA	27.10.78	2	NC	Stanford	22 Jun
20.17	-0.1		Williams			2	VD	Bruxelles	5 Sep
20.18	0.0		Johnson			1s2	NC	Stanford	22 Jun
20.18	0.0		Capel			1s2	WCh	Saint-Denis	29 Aug
20.18	-0.1		Crawford			3	VD	Bruxelles	5 Sep
20.20A	-0.5	Sherwin	Vries	RSA	22.3.80	2		Pretoria	4 Apr
20.21	0.5		Capel			1	Gaz	Saint-Denis	4 Jul

Mark	Wind	Name		Nat	Born	Pos	Meet	Venue	Date
20.21	1.2		Capel			1		Réthimno	6 Jul
20.21	0.2		Johnson			1		Thessaloníki	3 Aug
20.22	0.1		Johnson			3	NC	Stanford	22 Jun
20.22	0.7		Johnson			2q3	WCh	Saint-Denis	27 Aug
20.22	0.0		Suetsugu			2s2	WCh	Saint-Denis	29 Aug
20.23	0.8	Frank	Fredericks	NAM	2.10.67	1		Villeneuve d'Ascq	15 Jun
		(30/14)							
20.24A	-0.4	Cláudio R	Sousa	BRA	14.10.73	2		Cochabamba	11 May
20.25	0.1	Kenny	Brokenburr	USA	29.10.68	4	NC	Stanford	22 Jun
20.25	1.3	Christian	Malcolm	GBR	3.6.79	1	GP	London (CP)	8 Aug
20.27	0.1	Ramon	Clay	USA	29.6.75	5	NC	Stanford	22 Jun
20.29	-0.6	Brendan	Christian	ANT	11.12.83	1	Big 12	Austin	19 May
20.30A	-0.4	Claudinei	da Silva	BRA	19.11.70	3		Cochabamba	11 May
		(20)							
20.30	0.0	Konstadinos	Kedéris	GRE	11.7.73	1	GP	Tríkala	24 Jun
20.32	1.9	Jimmie	Hackley	USA	11.9.75	1h4		Tallahassee	10 May
20.34	0.8	Abdul Aziz	Zakari	GHA	2.9.76	2		Villeneuve d'Ascq	15 Jun
20.34	0.7	Chris	Lambert	GBR	6.4.81	1	EU23	Bydgoszcz	20 Jul
20.34	0.0	Darren	Campbell	GBR	12.9.73	3s2	WCh	Saint-Denis	29 Aug
20.35	0.8	Dominic	Demeritte	BAH	22.2.78	1	GP	Belém	4 May
20.37A	-0.5	Morné	Nagel	RSA	23.2.78	4		Pretoria	4 Apr
20.37	-0.6	Leo	Bookman	USA	3.1.82	2	Big 12	Austin	19 May
20.37	2.0	Julian	Golding	GBR	17.2.75	1	NC	Birmingham	27 Jul
20.38	0.6	Uchenna	Emedolu	NGR	17.9.76	2s3	Afr G	Abuja	14 Oct
		(30)							
20.39	0.7	Marcin	Jedrusinski	POL	28.9.81	2	EU23	Bydgoszcz	20 Jul
20.40	1.7	Erick	Wilson	USA	10.1.82	1		Overland Park	26 Apr
20.40	0.2	LaTonel	Williams	JAM	3.4.78	2	NC	Kingston	21 Jun
20.41	1.7	Tobias	Unger	GER	10.7.79	1		Oberkirch	1 Jun
20.41	1.5	Francis	Obikwelu	POR	22.11.78	1	ECp-1B	Velenje	22 Jun
20.41	0.2	Fawzi	Al-Shammari	KUW	13.2.79	1	Arab C	Amman	9 Sep
20.42	-0.5	Alessandro	Cavallaro	ITA	22.2.80	2h4	WCh	Saint-Denis	27 Aug
20.42	0.4	Ricardo	Williams	JAM	29.9.76	2	GP II	Rieti	7 Sep
20.43	0.7	Johan	Wissman	SWE	2.12.82	3	EU23	Bydgoszcz	20 Jul
20.43	1.1	Bobby	Williams	USA	3.2.78	1		Dublin (S)	15 Aug
		(40)							
20.45A	0.0	Clinton	Venter	RSA	3.2.80	2		Roodepoort	28 Mar
20.48	-0.6	Mickey	Grimes	USA	10.10.76	1		Basse-Terre	30 Apr
20.48A	-0.4	Heber	Viera	URU	29.4.79	4		Cochabamba	11 May
20.48	-0.9	Jerome	Mathis	USA	26.7.83	2	NCAA	Sacramento	14 Jun
20.48	1.1	Dwight	Thomas	JAM	23.9.80	2		Dublin (S)	15 Aug
20.48	-0.3	Joseph	Batangdon	CMR	29.7.78	1		Nantes	3 Sep
20.49	0.8	Deji	Aliu	NGR	22.11.75	4		Villeneuve d'Ascq	15 Jun
20.49	-0.7	Leigh	Julius	RSA-J	25.3.85	1	WUG	Daegu	28 Aug
20.50	-1.4	Patrick	Johnson	AUS	26.9.72	1	NC	Brisbane	5 Apr
20.50	-1.7	Marquis	Davis	USA	14.8.80	1	SEC	Knoxville	18 May
		(50)							
20.50	0.0	Marlon	Devonish	GBR	1.6.76	4	GP	Tríkala	24 Jun
20.51	0.5	Ryan	Shields	USA	12.5.83	1		Lubbock	3 May
20.51	-1.0	Stanford	Routt	USA	23.7.83	1s2	NCAA	Sacramento	12 Jun
20.52	1.4	Steve	Mullings	JAM	29.11.82	2		Fayetteville	12 Apr
20.53	0.6	Hisashi	Miyazaki	JPN	19.3.81	1h2	NC	Yokohama	6 Jun
20.53	1.2	Panayiótis	Sarrís	GRE	14.9.75	3		Réthimno	6 Jul
20.53	2.0	Anastásios	Goúsis	GRE	7.7.79	1	Balk G	Thíva	13 Jul
20.54	1.6	Ronald	Pognon	FRA	16.11.82	2rA		Fort-de-France	26 Apr
20.54	0.6	Christopher	Williams	JAM	15.3.72	2	PAm	Santo Domingo	8 Aug
20.55	2.0	Marcin	Urbas	POL	17.9.76	1h3	NC	Bielsko-Biala	6 Jul
		(60)							
20.55	-1.8	Hamed Hamadan	Al Bishi	KSA	3.3.82	1		Hamburg	20 Jul
20.55	-0.1	Marcus	Brunson	USA	24.4.78	5	VD	Bruxelles	5 Sep
20.56	-0.6	DaBryan	Blanton	USA-J	3.7.84	3	Big 12	Austin	19 May
20.56	0.1	Paul	Brizzel	IRL	3.10.76	5q4	WCh	Saint-Denis	27 Aug
20.57	1.6	Allen	Johnson	USA	1.3.71	3rA		Fort-de-France	26 Apr
20.57	1.2	Kendrick	Triggs	USA	27.8.82	1		Oxford, MS	3 May
20.57	2.0	Olan	Coleman	USA	29.7.80	1	NCAA II	Edwardsville	24 May
20.57	0.0	Julian	Raeburn	TRI	18.9.78	2	CAC	St George's	6 Jul
20.58A	1.6	Rae	Edwards	USA	7.5.81	1		El Paso	12 Apr
20.58	1.6	Dwayne	Grant	GBR	17.7.82	2		Szombathely	10 Aug
		(70)							
20.59	1.6	Anninos	Marcoullides	CYP	8.2.71	1	ECp-2B	Istanbul	22 Jun
20.60	1.6	Aaron	Armstrong	USA	14.10.77	4rA		Fort-de-France	26 Apr

Mark	Wind	Name		Nat	Born	Pos	Meet	Venue	Date
20.60	0.6	Yusuke	Omae	JPN	6.4.82	2h2	NC	Yokohama	6 Jun
20.60	0.4	Cédric	Van Branteghem	BEL	13.3.79	1h2	NC	Jambes	9 Aug
20.61	0.9	Kelly	Willie	USA	7.9.82	1		Baton Rouge	3 May
20.61	0.0	Kyle	Farmer	USA	15.4.83	2	NCAA-r	Fairfax	31 May
20.62	1.8	Ambrose	Ezenwa	NGR	10.4.77	1h3		Sydney	9 Mar
20.62	0.9	Troy	McIntosh	BAH	29.3.73	2		Baton Rouge	3 May
20.62	0.8	Vicente	de Lima	BRA	4.6.77	4	GP	Belém	4 May
20.62	0.6	Ryo	Matsuda	JPN	26.12.79	3h2	NC	Yokohama	6 Jun
		(80)							
20.63	-0.6	Kaaron	Conwright	USA	8.8.76	3		Basse-Terre	30 Apr
20.63	0.8	Jorge Célio	Sena	BRA-J	31.1.85	5	GP	Belém	4 May
20.63	0.0	David	Neville	USA-J	1.6.84	2	PAm-J	Bridgetown	20 Jul
20.63	1.0	Sebastian	Ernst	GER-J	11.10.84	1	EJ	Tampere	27 Jul
20.63	1.5	Julien	Dunkley	JAM	20.12.75	2		La Chaux-de-Fonds	17 Aug
20.63	0.2	Shinji	Takahira	JPN-J	18.7.84	1		Maebashi	12 Oct
20.64	1.3	Troy	Douglas	NED	30.11.62	1		Utrecht	9 Aug
20.65	2.0	Brian	Johnson	USA	25.3.80	1		Beaumont	29 Mar
20.65	1.0	Chris	Stewart	USA	6.3.80	1h4		San Marcos	18 May
20.65	2.0	Clement	Campbell	JAM	19.2.75	2	NCAA II	Edwardsville	24 May
		(90)							
20.65	0.0	Airese	Currie	USA	16.11.82	3	NCAA-r	Fairfax	31 May
20.65A		Vincent	Mumo	KEN	3.8.82	1	NC	Nairobi	12 Jul
20.65	-2.7	Aimé-Issa	Nthépé	FRA	26.6.73	2	NC	Narbonne	26 Jul
20.66	1.7	Lindel	Frater	JAM	13.11.77	1h3		Shizuoka	3 May
20.66	0.3	Gentry	Bradley	USA	19.1.74	1		Eagle Rock	10 May
20.66		Stanley	Egbor	NGR	19.3.77	1		New Haven	7 Jul
20.67	0.2	Tatsuro	Yoshino	JPN	11.9.82	1h3	NC	Yokohama	6 Jun
20.68	0.8	Milton	Campbell	USA	15.5.76	1		Atlanta	7 Jun
20.68	-2.3	Leslie	Djhone	FRA	18.3.81	5	ECp-S	Firenze	22 Jun
20.69	1.1	Xavier	Carter	USA-J	8.12.85	1		Gainesville	16 May
		(100)							
20.69	1.7	Aaron	Collins	USA-J	18.2.84	2	NCAA-r	Lincoln, NE	31 May
20.69	0.4	Géza	Pauer	HUN	7.1.76	1		Budapest	12 Jul
20.69	-0.6	James	Dolphin	NZL	17.6.83	4h1	WCh	Saint-Denis	27 Aug
20.70	1.3	Earvin	Parker	USA-J	6.4.84				10 May
20.70	1.1	Rubin	Williams	USA	9.7.83				8 Jun
20.70	-0.3	Prodromos	Katsantonis	CYP	20.10.75				6 Jul
20.71	0.6	Tomoyuki	Arai	JPN	14.6.81				7 Jun
20.71	0.0	Churandy	Martina	AHO-J	3.7.84				20 Jul
20.72	0.0	Brian	Dzingai	ZIM	29.4.81				30 May
20.72	0.6	Tatsuya	Ito	JPN	21.12.76				7 Jun
20.72	0.3	Marcin	Nowak	POL	2.8.77				9 Sep
20.73	-0.1	Gary	Kikaya	COD	4.2.78				5 Apr
20.73	0.3	Derrick	Brew	USA	28.12.77				12 Apr
20.73	1.9	Angelo	Taylor	USA	29.12.78				3 May
20.73	0.9	Gary	Ryan	IRL	12.6.72				5 Jul
20.73	0.7	Oumar	Loum	SEN	31.12.73				27 Aug
20.74	1.7	Andre	Ammons	USA	12.11.78				26 Apr
20.74	1.4	Corey	Nelson	USA	9.10.77				10 May
20.74	1.0	Roger	Anguono-Moké	CGO	20.11.81				29 May
20.74	0.4		Yang Yaozu	CHN	9.1.81				20 Jun
20.74	0.2	Shingo	Kawabata	JPN	15.5.78				12 Oct
20.75		Dwain	Chambers ¶	GBR	5.4.78				13 Jul
20.76	0.1	Jabari	Fields	USA	10.9.81				16 May
20.76	1.8	Jirí	Vojtík	CZE	2.7.81				31 May
20.76	1.6	Thomas	Scheidl	AUT	20.11.79				26 Jul
20.77	1.7	Kazuhiro	Tamura	JPN	3.7.78				3 May
20.77	0.0	Ato	Boldon	TRI	30.12.73				1 Jul
20.77	1.0	David	Canal	ESP	7.12.78				26 Jul
20.77	-0.5	Graham	Beasley	GBR	24.10.77				16 Aug
20.78	0.0	Floyd	Heard	USA	24.3.66				19 Apr
20.78	1.4	Jeremy	Wariner	USA-J	31.1.84				3 May
20.78	1.3	Mardy	Scales	USA	10.9.81				11 May
20.79	0.8	Jonathan	Wade	USA-J	27.3.84				22 Mar
20.79	0.5	Wesley	Felix	USA	21.7.83				26 Apr
20.79	2.0	Albert	Booker	USA	10.1.82				8 May
20.79	1.1	Tre	Gardner	USA	25.10.79				18 May
20.79	0.9	Ingo	Schultz	GER	26.7.75				13 Jun
20.79	0.5	Hamdan	Odha Al-Bishi	KSA	5.5.81				20 Jun
20.79	-0.3	Éric	Milazar	MRI	1.6.75				29 Jun
20.79	0.5	Jamahl	Alert-Khan	GBR-Y	12.9.86				7 Sep
20.80	1.7	Tyree	Gailes	USA	24.2.83				26 Apr
20.80	0.3	Jerome	Davis	USA	20.8.77				10 May
20.80	0.4	Anson	Henry	CAN	9.3.79				1 Jul
20.80	0.0	Jacey	Harper	TRI	20.5.80				6 Jul
20.80	0.2	Paul	Hession	IRL	27.1.83				28 Aug
20.81	1.0	Jason	Gardener	GBR	18.9.75				8 Jun
20.81	-0.8	Gennadiy	Chernovol	KAZ	6.6.76				29 Oct
20.82	1.6	Ahmad	Jasmine	USA	6.12.82				3 May
20.82	0.8	Jerry	Harris	USA	29.10.81				16 May
20.82A	-0.1	Chris	Riggs (150)	USA					17 May
20.82		Jamial	Rolle	BAH	16.4.80				29 Jun
20.82		Byron	Campbell	JAM	10.7.75				6 Jul
20.82	-1.0	Gábor	Dobos	HUN	21.2.76				6 Sep
20.83A	0.8	Mike	Appelhans	USA	24.8.80				2 May
20.83A	-0.4	Ricardo	Roach	CHI	12.10.72				11 May
20.83	0.0	Robert	Foster	USA	15.5.81				16 May
20.83	0.0	Sheldon	Morant	JAM	21.6.80				30 May
20.83		Alleyne	Francique	GRN	7.6.76				21 Jun
20.83	0.7	Johan	Engberg	SWE	11.10.81				20 Jul
20.83	0.0	Adrian	Durant	ISV-J	10.10.84				20 Jul
20.83	0.0	Malik	Louahla	ALG	19.12.77				2 Aug
20.83A	1.4	Paul	Di Bella	AUS	12.2.77				6 Aug
20.84	-2.4	Daniel	Batman	AUS	20.3.81				28 Jan
20.84		Andrew	Rock	USA	23.1.82				3 May
20.84	1.6	Rohsaan	Griffin	USA	21.2.74				3 May
20.84	1.4	Desmond	Bynum	USA	80				3 May
20.84	1.3	Jamey	Sperle	USA	28.11.79				24 May
20.84	1.0	Kristof	Beyens	BEL	13.7.83				29 May
20.84	0.4	Ronny	Ostwald	GER	7.4.74				29 Jun
20.84	-0.3	Marco	Cuneo	ITA	2.7.80				29 Jun
20.84	1.0	Markus	Lüthi	SUI	14.2.80				6 Jul
20.84	-0.5	Daniel	Caines	GBR	15.5.79				16 Aug
20.84	-0.1	Tommi	Hartonen	FIN	12.5.77				6 Sep
20.85		LeShaunte	Edwards	USA	26.7.79				26 Apr
20.85	0.6	Hirofumi	Nakagawa	JPN	3.1.80				6 Jun
20.85	-0.4	Brian	Lewis	USA	5.12.74				19 Jul
20.85	1.6	Nicolas	Macrozonaris	CAN	22.8.80				20 Jul
20.86A	1.0	Marcus	la Grange	RSA	12.12.77				24 Jan
20.86	-0.2	DeRico	Tilley	USA	10.2.77				12 Apr
20.86	1.7	Toshiyuki	Fujimoto	JPN	25.6.79				3 May
20.86A	-0.5	Jairo	Duzant	AHO	1.8.79				17 May
20.86	0.5	Hiroyuki	Noda	JPN-J	25.1.85				6 Jun
20.86	0.4	Alexander	Kosenkow	GER	14.3.77				29 Jun
20.86	0.0	Ainsley	Waugh	JAM	81				6 Jul
20.86	1.0	Roman	Smirnov	RUS-J	2.9.84				27 Jul

Mark	Wind	Name		Nat	Born	Date
20.86	1.0	Till	Helmke	GER-J	6.5.84	27 Jul
20.86A	0.0	Hiroyasu	Tsuchie	JPN	14.6.74	3 Aug
20.87	1.1	Lancford	Davis	JAM	11.10.78	12 Apr
20.87A	1.3	Leo	Settle	USA	19.10.75	12 Apr
20.87	-0.3	Craphonso	Thorpe	USA	27.6.83	19 Apr
20.87	-1.1	Christopher	Tyler	CAN	3.10.83	19 Apr
20.87	0.4	Benjamin	Henderson	USA	5.4.83	16 May
20.87	1.3	Derrick	Atkins	BAH-J	5.1.84	24 May
20.87	1.2	Lionel	Larry	USA-Y	14.9.86	30 May
20.87	1.3	Lukasz	Chyla (195)	POL	31.3.81	27 Jun
20.87	0.8	Salem Mubarak	Al Yami	KSA	9.2.82	24 Jul

Wind assisted

Mark	Wind	Name		Nat	Born	Pos	Meet	Venue	Date
20.15	2.8	Marquis	Davis	USA	14.8.80	1		Fort Worth	19 Apr
20.19	4.2	Erick	Wilson	USA	10.1.82	1	JUCO	Levelland	10 May
20.19	2.3		Crawford			1	Super	Yokohama	23 Sep
20.20	2.8	Ricardo	Williams	JAM	29.9.76	2		Fort Worth	19 Apr
20.25	2.6	Patrick	Johnson	AUS	26.9.72	1		Sydney (C)	15 Feb
20.28	2.4	Stanford	Routt	USA	23.7.83	1h1	NCAA-r	Lincoln, NE	30 May
20.29	2.7	Dominic	Demeritte	BAH	22.2.78	1h1	CAC	St George's	5 Jul
20.31	4.2	Tyson	Gay	USA	9.9.82	2	JUCO	Levelland	10 May
20.38	2.9	Marcin	Jedrusinski	POL	28.9.81	1	NC	Bielsko-Biala	6 Jul
20.38	2.9	Dwayne	Grant	GBR	17.7.82	1		Fribourg	23 Aug
20.40	2.2	Kim	Collins	SKN	5.4.76	1rA	Mod R	Modesto	10 May
20.40	2.4	Chris	Stewart	USA	6.3.80	2h1	NCAA-r	Lincoln, NE	30 May
20.46	3.6	Ambrose	Ezenwa	NGR	10.4.77	1		Sydney	9 Mar
20.51	3.6	Tatsuro	Yoshino	JPN	11.9.82	2		Shizuoka	3 May
20.52	2.6	Alvin	Harrison	USA	20.1.74	3		Sydney (C)	15 Feb
20.52	2.5	Cédric	Van Branteghem	BEL	13.3.79	1	NC	Jambes	10 Aug
20.53	w	Earvin	Parker	USA-J	6.4.84	1		Lubbock	26 Apr
20.53	3.1	Elston	Cawley	JAM	24.6.76	1		Arlington	3 May
20.56	2.5	Adam	Wooten	USA	18.3.82	2h3	NCAA-r	Lincoln, NE	30 May
20.57	3.6	Lindel	Frater	JAM	13.11.77	3		Shizuoka	3 May
20.57	4.2	Rodney	Martin	USA	22.12.82	3	JUCO	Levelland	10 May
20.57	4.2	Tyrone	Edgar	GBR	29.3.82	4	JUCO	Levelland	10 May
20.57	4.2	Tyree	Gailes	USA	24.2.83	5	JUCO	Levelland	10 May
20.57	2.7	Ainsley	Waugh	JAM	.81	2h1	CAC	St George's	5 Jul
20.59	2.8	Pierre	Browne	CAN	14.1.80	3		Fort Worth	19 Apr
20.59	4.2	Danny	Johnson	USA	11.5.83	6	JUCO	Levelland	10 May
20.59	2.7	Jabari	Fields	USA	10.9.81	1		Charlotte	17 May
20.62	2.5	Aaron	Collins	USA-J	18.2.84	3h3	NCAA-r	Lincoln, NE	30 May
20.63	2.8	Carlos	Moore	USA-J	8.5.84	1	MSR	Walnut	11 Apr
20.63A	2.2	Mike	Appelhans	USA	24.8.80	1		Alamosa	3 May
20.64	2.2	Bryan	Bronson	USA	9.9.72	1		College Station	12 Apr
20.64	3.5	Greg	Carter	USA	5.8.80	1		Itta Bena	3 May
20.67	3.6	Salem Mubarak	Al-Yami	KSA	9.2.82	2	Kuso	Warszawa	15 Jun
20.67	2.3	Oumar	Loum	SEN	31.12.73	5q1	WCh	Saint-Denis	27 Aug
20.68	2.7	Jacey	Harper	TRI	20.5.80	3h1	CAC	St George's	6 Jul

Mark	Wind	Name		Nat	Born	Date
20.70	2.4	Christian	Nsiah	GHA	25.12.75	12 Apr
20.71	3.0	Kendrick	Campbell	USA	16.12.77	19 Apr
20.71	4.1	LeShaunte	Edwards	USA	26.7.79	3 May
20.71	2.4	Curtis	Johnson	USA	8.2.80	30 May
20.72	2.4	Chauncey	Harris	USA	21.9.83	12 Apr
20.74	2.8	Ricardo	Roach	CHI	12.10.72	21 Jun
20.77	2.5	Mardy	Scales	USA	10.9.81	19 Apr
20.77	2.8	LaChristophe	Lewis	USA	28.10.82	19 Apr
20.77	3.7	Dennis	Darling	BAH	6.5.75	8 May
20.78	2.6	David	Geddes	AUS	26.1.82	15 Feb
20.78	3.9	Michael	Mitchell	USA	16.5.81	12 Apr
20.78		Jairo	Duzant	AHO	1.8.79	30 May
20.78	2.8	Stilianós	Dimótsios	GRE	13.11.74	7 Jun
20.80	4.4	Chris	Riggs	USA		30 May
20.81	2.3	Tyler	Christopher	CAN	3.10.83	18 Apr
20.81	3.8	Robert	Parham	USA	2.6.82	31 May
20.82	2.6	Luke	Mansfield	AUS-J	13.5.85	15 Feb
20.83	2.5	DeRico	Tilley	USA	10.2.77	19 Apr
20.83	4.9	Raheem	Travis	USA		8 May
20.84	2.2	Jerome	Young	USA	14.8.76	29 Mar
20.84	2.8	Yuji	Ishikawa	JPN	11.1.80	3 May
20.85	2.5	Ivory	Williams	USA-J	2.5.85	10 May
20.85	3.9	Lionel	Larry	USA-Y	14.9.86	24 May
20.85	2.2	Shomari	Wilson	USA	6.6.76	13 Jul
20.86	3.0	Steve	Slowly	JAM	18.4.79	19 Apr
20.86	2.1	Kenneth	Baxter	USA	17.4.82	11 May
20.86	2.2	Ja'Warren	Hooker	USA	24.9.78	13 Jul

Indoors

Mark	Name		Nat	Born	Pos	Meet	Venue	Date
20.47	Joseph	Batangdon	CMR	29.7.78	1	FRA Ch	Aubière	2 Mar
20.51	Leslie	Djhone	FRA	18.3.81	2	NC	Aubière	2 Mar
20.69	Allyn	Condon	GBR	24.8.74	1	NC	Birmingham	2 Mar

Mark	Name		Nat	Born	Date
20.77	Matic	Osovnikar	SLO	19.1.80	14 Mar
20.78	Marco	Torrieri	ITA	14.5.78	2 Mar
20.78	Kenneth	Baxter	USA	17.4.82	14 Mar
20.82	Robert	Foster	USA	15.5.81	14 Mar

Low altitude bests

Mark	Wind	Name	Pos	Meet	Venue	Date
20.35	0.7	Vries	1		Durban	11 Apr
20.56	0.4	A da Silva	1	NC	São Paulo	13 Jun
20.60	0.8	Sousa	3	GP	Belém	4 May
20.60	-0.9	H Viera	1	SACh	Barquisimeto	22 Jun
20.63	-0.9	Cl. da Silva	2	SACh	Barquisimeto	22 Jun
20.62w	2.8		1		São Caetano do Sul	23 Apr
20.68	0.7	Venter	2		Durban	11 Apr

20.84 2.0 Appelhans 24 Ma 20.86 0.7 Tsuchie 27 Sep 20.88 -2.3 Nagel 26 Apr

Hand timing

Mark	Wind	Name		Nat	Born	Date
20.5		Badaway	Goma'amin	EGY	9.12.79	4 Apr
20.5A		Vincent	Mumo	KEN	3.8.82	11 Jul
20.6		Winston	Smith	JAM	22.11.82	30 Mar
20.6	-0.7	Oumar	Loum	SEN	31.12.73	12 Apr
20.6	-0.1	Kris	Neofytou	AUS-J	3.5.84	20 Dec

Wind assisted

Mark	Name		Nat	Born	Date
20.6w	Maurice	Hewitt	USA		15 Mar
20.6w	Theodore	Ginn	USA-J	12.4.85	17 May

JUNIORS

See main list for top 9 Juniors. 12 performances by 7 men to 20.63. Additional marks and further juniors:

Bolt 20.25 1.9 1 N.Sch Kingston 5 Apr | 20.43 -1.1 1 Carifta Port of Spain 21 Apr
20.28 0.2 1 NC Kingston 21 Jun | 20.3 h 1 Montego Bay 18 Feb
20.40 -1.1 1 WY Sherbrooke 13 Jul

Blanton 20.60 1.1 1h4 Big12 Austin 18 May

Mark	Wind		Name	Nat	Born	Pos	Meet	Venue	Date
20.70	1.3	Earvin	Parker (10)	USA	6.4.84	1		Austin	10 May
20.71	0.0	Churandy	Martina	AHO	3.7.84	2h1	PAm-J	Bridgetown	20 Jul
20.78	1.4	Jeremy	Wariner	USA	31.1.84	1r3		Austin	3 May
20.79	0.8	Jonathan	Wade	USA	27.3.84	1		Tallahasse	22 Mar
20.79	0.5	Jamahl	Alert-Khan	GBR-Y	12.9.86	1		Derby	7 Sep
20.83	0.0	Adrian	Durant	ISV	10.10.84	5	PAm-J	Bridgetown	20 Jul
20.86	0.5	Hiroyuki	Noda	JPN	25.1.85	3h1	NC	Yokohama	6 Jun
20.86	1.0	Roman	Smirnov	RUS	2.9.84	2	EJ	Tampere	27 Jul
20.86	1.0	Till	Helmke	GER	6.5.84	3	EJ	Tampere	27 Jul
20.87	1.3	Derrick	Atkins	BAH	5.1.84	3	NAIA	Olathe	24 May
20.87	1.2	Lionel	Larry (20)	USA-Y	14.9.86	1		Norwalk	30 May

Wind assisted – see main list for three juniors. Additional men:

Mark	Wind		Name	Nat	Born	Pos	Meet	Venue	Date
20.82	2.6	Luke	Mansfield	AUS	13.5.85	5		Sydney (C)	15 Feb
20.85	2.5	Ivory	Williams	USA	2.5.85	1B		Austin	10 May
20.85	3.9	Lionel	Larry	USA-Y	14.9.86	1		Norwalk	24 May

Hand timed

Mark	Wind		Name	Nat	Born	Pos	Meet	Venue	Date
20.6	-0.1	Kris	Neofytou	AUS	3.5.84	1		Sydney (C)	20 Dec
20.6w		Theodore	Ginn	USA	12.4.85	1		Cleveland	17 May

300 METRES

Mark		Name	Nat	Born	Pos	Venue	Date
32.18	Leslie	Djhone	FRA	18.3.81	1	Nancy	16 Sep
32.26		Djhone			1	Strasbourg	26 Jun
32.27	Marcus	la Grange	RSA	12.12.77	1	Brasschaat	13 Aug
32.40	Johan	Wissman	SWE	2.12.82	1	Göteborg	1 Sep
32.53	Cédric	Van Branteghem	BEL	13.3.79	1	Woluwe	14 Jun
32.58	Dennis	Darling	BAH	6.5.75	1A	Bondoufle	16 Aug
32.59	Stilianós	Dimótsios	GRE	13.11.74	2	Brasschaat	13 Aug
32.71	Markus	Malucha	GER	5.12.83			18 May
32.76	Tyler	Christopher	CAN	3.10.83			16 Aug
32.77	Ingo	Schultz	GER	26.7.75			9 Jun
32.83	Sofiane	Labidi	TUN	29.9.77			13 Aug

Times in World 400m 26 Aug: Young 32.2, C Harrison 32.4, Blackwood, Milazar & Washington 32.5

Indoors: 32.36 Frank Fredericks NAM 2.10.67 1 Karlsruhe 28 Feb

400 METRES

Mark		Name	Nat	Born	Pos	Meet	Venue	Date
44.33	Tyree	Washington	USA	28.8.76	1	NC	Stanford	21 Jun
44.42		Washington			1	GGala	Roma	11 Jul
44.43A	Ezra	Sambu	KEN	4.9.78	1	WCT	Nairobi	26 Jul
44.50	Jerome	Young	USA	14.8.76	1	WCh	Saint-Denis	26 Aug
44.57	Adam	Steele	USA	8.10.80	1	NCAA	Sacramento	14 Jun
44.57	Otis	Harris	USA	30.6.82	2	NCAA	Sacramento	14 Jun
44.58	Mitch	Potter	USA	16.9.80	3	NCAA	Sacramento	14 Jun
44.60		Washington			1s2	WCh	Saint-Denis	24 Aug
44.62	Calvin	Harrison	USA	20.1.74	2	NC	Stanford	21 Jun
44.70		Washington			1	Pre	Eugene	24 May
44.70		Young			1s1	WCh	Saint-Denis	24 Aug
44.71		Young			2	GGala	Roma	11 Jul
44.71		Harrison			2s1	WCh	Saint-Denis	24 Aug
44.74	Michael	Blackwood	JAM	29.8.76	1	NC	Kingston	21 Jun
44.75	Éric	Milazar	MRI	1.6.75	3s1	WCh	Saint-Denis	24 Aug
44.77		Washington			2	WCh	Saint-Denis	6 Aug
44.78	Alleyne	Francique (10)	GRN	7.6.76	1rA	GP II	Madrid (C)	19 Jul
44.79		Young			3	NC	Stanford	21 Jun
44.79	Marc	Raquil	FRA	2.4.77	3	WCh	Saint-Denis	26 Aug
44.80		Raquil			1	GP II	Sevilla	7 Jun
44.80		Blackwood			4	WCh	Saint-Denis	6 Aug
44.81		Francique			4s1	WCh	Saint-Denis	24 Aug
44.83A	Derrick	Brew	USA	28.12.77	1		Ciudad de México	3 May
44.83	Leslie	Djhone	FRA	18.3.81	5	WCh	Saint-Denis	26 Aug
44.84	Brandon	Simpson	JAM	6.9.81	2	NC	Kingston	21 Jun
44.85		Blackwood			1	GP	Gateshead	13 Jul
44.86		Djhone			1	WK	Zürich	15 Aug
44.87		Blackwood			1		Réthimno	6 Jul
44.87		Simpson			3	GGala	Roma	11 Jul
44.88		Raquil			1	ECp-S	Firenze	21 Jun

Mark	Name		Nat	Born	Pos	Meet	Venue	Date
44.88		Raquil			1s3	WCh	Saint-Denis	24 Aug
	(31/14)							
44.93	Fawzi	Al-Shammari	KUW	13.2.79	1	Arab C	Amman	7 Sep
44.94A	Chris	Brown	BAH	14.10.79	1		Roodepoort	28 Mar
44.95	Darold	Williamson	USA	19.2.83	2	NCAA-r	Lincoln, NE	31 May
44.99	Hamdan Odha	Al Bishi	KSA	5.5.81	5s1	WCh	Saint-Denis	24 Aug
44.99	Gary	Kikaya	COD	4.2.78	3s3	WCh	Saint-Denis	24 Aug
45.00A	Corey	Nelson	USA	9.10.77	2		Ciudad de México	3 May
	(20)							
45.00A	Avard	Moncur	BAH	2.11.78	3		Ciudad de México	3 May
45.01	David	Canal	ESP	7.12.78	1	NC	Jerez de la Frontera	3 Aug
45.02	Daniel	Batman	AUS	20.3.81	1		Canberra	22 Feb
45.02	Cédric	Van Branteghem	BEL	13.3.79	1	VD	Bruxelles	5 Sep
45.06	Ingo	Schultz	GER	26.7.75	5	GGala	Roma	11 Jul
45.08	Leonard	Byrd	USA	17.3.75	1rB	GP II	Madrid (C)	19 Jul
45.11	Yeimar	López	CUB	20.8.82	4s3	WCh	Saint-Denis	24 Aug
45.13	Jeremy	Wariner	USA-J	31.1.84	1		Tempe	12 Apr
45.14	Kelly	Willie	USA	7.9.82	3s1	NCAA	Sacramento	13 Jun
45.16	Sanjay	Ayre	JAM	19.6.80	1s2	NCAA	Sacramento	13 Jun
	(30)							
45.18	Davian	Clarke	JAM	30.4.76	3	NC	Kingston	21 Jun
45.18	Yuki	Yamaguchi	JPN-J	22.2.84	1	NG	Fukuroi	29 Oct
45.21	Greg	Haughton	JAM	10.11.73	6	GGala	Roma	11 Jul
45.22A	Félix	Sánchez	DOM	30.8.77	4		Ciudad de México	3 May
45.22	Shane	Niemi	CAN	2.6.78	1		Nuoro	9 Jul
45.22	Nagmeldin	El Abubakr	SUD-Y	22.2.86	2	Afr G	Abuja	13 Oct
45.27	Tim	Benjamin	GBR	2.5.82	2-23	WK	Zürich	15 Aug
45.28	Obra	Hogans	USA	29.6.82	1h1		Storrs	3 May
45.28	Jun	Osakada	JPN	2.4.74	1		Osaka	29 Jun
45.29A	Marcus	la Grange	RSA	12.12.77	3		Roodepoort	28 Mar
	(40)							
45.29	Andrew	Rock	USA	23.1.82	1	NCAA-3	Canton, NY	24 May
45.29	Clinton	Hill	AUS	19.4.80	2		Nuoro	9 Jul
45.29	Daniel	Caines	GBR	15.5.79	3s2	WCh	Saint-Denis	24 Aug
45.30A	Paul	Gorries	RSA	28.2.81	4		Roodepoort	28 Mar
45.32A	Vincent	Mumo	KEN	3.8.82	2	WCT	Nairobi	26 Jul
45.33	James	Davis	USA	19.3.76	1		Walnut	12 Jul
45.35	Usain	Bolt	JAM-Y	21.8.86	1	N.Sch	Kingston	5 Apr
45.35	Sofiane	El Abidi	TUN	29.9.77	1		Córdoba	6 Sep
45.42	Rickey	Harris	USA	29.9.81	2		Austin	3 May
45.43	Calfornia	Molefe	BOT	2.5.80	1		Bordeaux	11 Jun
	(50)							
45.43	Carlos	Santa	DOM	7.1.78	7s1	WCh	Saint-Denis	24 Aug
45.46	Michael	McDonald	JAM	17.3.75	2		Réthimno	6 Jul
45.48	Michael	Campbell	JAM	11.9.78	5	NC	Kingston	21 Jun
45.49	Chris	Lloyd	DMA	10.10.80	1	SWAC	Itta Bena	4 May
45.49	Zsolt	Szeglet	HUN	4.5.77	1rB		San Sebastián	10 Aug
45.50	Mitsuhiro	Sato	JPN	8.1.80	1h3	NC	Yokohama	7 Jun
45.50A	Victor	Kibet	KEN	.81	3	WCT	Nairobi	26 Jul
45.51	Lloyd	Zvasiya	ZIM	20.5.81	1s2	AfG	Abuja	12 Oct
45.52	Jerry	Harris	USA	29.10.81	5s1	NC	Stanford	20 Jun
45.54	Anton	Galkin	RUS	20.2.79	1h3	NC	Tula	8 Aug
	(60)							
45.56	Sugath	Thilakeratne	SRI	30.7.73	1		Colombo	3 Aug
45.57	Otto	Spain	USA	27.2.81	2		Clemson	10 May
45.57	Anastásios	Goúsis	GRE	7.7.79	1		Pírgos	27 Jul
45.58	Iwan	Thomas	GBR	5.1.74	4	ECp-S	Firenze	21 Jun
45.58	Ian	Mackie	GBR	27.2.75	5	GP	Gateshead	13 Jul
45.59	Ashton	Collins	USA-J	18.2.84	1	PAm-J	Bridgetown	19 Jul
45.61	Ato	Modibo	TRI	19.6.79	1		Auburn	4 May
45.61	Tyler	Christopher	CAN	3.10.83	2		Seattle	14 Jun
45.62	Dmitriy	Forshev	RUS	30.5.76	4	ECp-S	Firenze	21 Jun
45.62	Rafal	Wieruszewski	POL	24.2.81	5	ECp-S	Firenze	21 Jun
	(70)							
45.62	Anthuan	Maybank	USA	30.12.69	7	NC	Stanford	21 Jun
45.62	Anderson Jorge	Santos	BRA	23.4.72	4h1	WCh	Saint-Denis	23 Aug
45.63	Adem	Hecini	ALG	13.12.75	3	Arab C	Amman	7 Sep
45.63	Tomohiro	Ito	JPN	16.8.82	2	NG	Fukuroi	29 Oct
45.66	Richard	James	JAM	1.12.79	5s2	NCAA	Sacramento	13 Jun
45.67	Damion	Barry	TRI	3.3.82	1	NC	Port of Spain	20 Jun
45.67	Jimisola	Laursen	SWE	13.7.77	4rB	GP II	Madrid (C)	19 Jul

Mark	Name		Nat	Born	Pos	Meet	Venue	Date
45.67	Pat	Dwyer	AUS	3.11.77	1		Canberra	29 Nov
45.68	Lewis	Banda	ZIM	16.4.82	2	DrakeR	Des Moines	26 Apr
45.70	Stilianós	Dimótsios	GRE	13.11.74	1	NC	Tríkala	14 Jun
	(80)							
45.71	Ibrahima	Wade	FRA	6.9.68	2		Malles	12 Jul
45.72	Albert	Booker	USA	10.1.82	1		Abilene	8 May
45.72	Danny	McFarlane	JAM	14.2.72	1		Cottbus	4 Jun
45.72	Ja'Warren	Hooker	USA	24.9.78	1h2	NC	Stanford	19 Jun
45.73	Milton	Campbell	USA	15.5.76	1		Atlanta	7 Jun
45.75	Andre	Ammons	USA	12.11.78	2		Basse-Terre	30 Apr
45.75	Mohammed	Al-Salhi	KSA-Y	11.5.86	2		Bondoufle	17 Aug
45.76	Andrey	Rudnitskiy	RUS	12.11.79	1s1	NC	Tula	8 Aug
45.77	Felix	Anderson	USA	13.5.83	1		Carbondale	17 May
45.77	Ioan	Vieru	ROM	4.1.79	2		Alger	17 Jul
	(90)							
45.78	Hideo	Togashi	JPN	21.7.81	1		Machida	12 Apr
45.79	Andrea	Barberi	ITA	15.1.79	1	NC	Rieti	3 Aug
45.80	Johan	Wissman	SWE	2.12.82	4	DNG	Stockholm	5 Aug
45.81	William	Hernández	VEN	18.2.81	1	SACh	Barquisimeto	21 Jun
45.81	Sanderlei	Parrela	BRA	7.10.74	4		Nuoro	9 Jul
45.81	Malik	Louahla	ALG	19.12.77	2		Castres	6 Aug
45.82	LaChristopher	Lewis	USA	28.10.82	3	SEC	Knoxville	18 May
45.82	Brandon	Couts	USA	17.2.79	5		Walnut	12 Jul
45.82	Yukihiro	Mukai	JPN	24.4.80	3	NG	Fukuroi	29 Oct
45.83	Dennis	Darling	BAH	6.5.75	2s1	NC	Freeport	19 Jun
	(100)							

Mark	Name		Nat	Born	Date
45.85	Stéphane	Diagana	FRA	23.7.69	5 Sep
45.86	Godfrey	Herring	USA	18.5.78	7 Jun
45.86	Glauder	Garzón	CUB	13.2.82	4 Jul
45.87	Takahiro	Yamamura	JPN	13.8.79	29 Jun
45.87	Sean	Baldock	GBR	3.12.76	8 Aug
45.88	Xavier	Carter	USA-J	8.12.85	5 Apr
45.88	DeWayne	Barrett	JAM	26.9.81	31 May
45.88	Bastian	Swillims	GER	9.12.82	29 Jun
45.88	Kenji	Tabata	JPN	24.9.74	29 Jun
45.88	Darnell	Hall	USA	26.9.71	19 Jul
45.91	Marco	Salvucci	ITA	25.4.76	3 Aug
45.92	Carnell	Coleman	USA		10 May
45.93	Du'aine	Ladejo	GBR	14.2.71	27 Jul
45.94	Joe	Mendel	USA	4.2.81	31 May
45.95	Paul	Pearce	AUS	8.1.77	22 Feb
45.95	Rohan Pradeep Kumara		SRI	10.3.75	28 May
45.95	Johnson	Kubisa	BOT	23.4.72	31 May
45.95	Paul	McKee	IRL	15.11.77	7 Jun
45.95	Salvador	Rodríguez	ESP	13.11.80	19 Jul
45.96	Bryan	Swarn	USA	19.11.79	30 May
45.97	Lancford	Spence	JAM	15.12.82	4 Jul
45.98	Peter	Coley	JAM	21.2.81	12 Jun
45.98	Sebastian	Gatzka	GER	19.5.82	29 Jun
45.98	Musa	Audu	NGR	18.6.80	13 Oct
45.99	Jonathan	Fortenberry	USA	19.7.83	28 Mar
46.00	Jason	Barton	USA	9.4.82	22 Mar
46.01	Yoshihiro	Horigome	JPN	2.1.81	4 Jul
46.01	Hamed Hamadan Al Bishi		KSA	3.3.82	13 Jul
46.01	Shinji	Takahira	JPN-J	18.7.84	29 Oct
46.02	Luis Eduardo	Ambrósio	BRA	28.1.83	13 Jun
46.03A	Matthew	Elias	GBR	25.4.79	3 May
46.03	Flávio	Godoy	BRA	13.12.69	13 Jun
46.04	Brandon	Matlock	USA	1.10.83	26 Apr
46.04	Naman	Keita	FRA	9.4.78	26 Jun
46.04	K.J.	Manoj Lal	IND	16.5.78	29 Sep
46.05	Prasanna	Amarasekara	SRI	21.3.81	2 Mar
46.05	David	McCarthy	IRL	16.7.83	18 Jul
46.05	Vladimir	Demchenko	UKR	16.4.81	18 Jul
46.06	Casey	Vincent	AUS	17.3.79	22 Feb
46.06	Tomas	Coman	IRL	10.11.79	4 Jun
46.07	John	Steffensen	AUS	30.8.82	8 Feb
46.07	Alvin	Harrison	USA	20.1.74	20 Jun
46.08	Seth	Amoo	USA	20.3.83	18 May
46.08	Fernando	Augustin	MRI	25.4.80	9 Jul
46.08	Ahmed	Douhou	FRA	14.12.76	25 Jul
46.08	Andrey	Tverdostup	UKR	18.6.77	27 Aug
46.10	Wilan	Louis	BAR	1.3.83	8 May
46.10A	Richard	Petty	BAH	5.5.81	17 May
46.11A	Arnaud	Malherbe	RSA	20.11.72	4 Apr
46.11	Jirí	Muzík (150)	CZE	1.9.76	31 May
46.11	Aleksandr	Yelistratov	BLR	15.8.81	19 Jul
46.11	Yevgeniy	Lebedyev	RUS	19.2.81	8 Aug
46.11	Oleg	Mishukov	RUS	31.8.80	8 Aug
46.12	Yoshiaki	Kitaoka	JPN	30.9.81	8 Jun
46.12	Saul	Weigopwa	NGR-J	14.6.84	19 Jul
46.14A	Sammy	Rono	KEN-J	.84	12 Jul
46.14	D'Marcus	Williams	USA		12 Jul
46.15	Mark	Teter	USA-J	23.9.84	10 May
46.16	Ruwen	Faller	GER	22.7.80	29 Jun
46.16	Masayuki	Okusako	JPN	2.4.79	23 Aug
46.18	Ryuji	Muraki	JPN	29.12.79	29 Jun
46.19	Talkmore	Nyongani	ZIM	2.9.83	6 Apr
46.19	Branimir	Peitel	CRO	12.4.80	12 Apr
46.19	Iván	Rodríguez	ESP	7.4.78	7 Jun
46.19	Igor	Vasilyev	RUS	20.4.77	15 Jul
46.19		Tan Biao	CHN-J	3.2.84	24 Oct
46.20	Jonathan	Johnson	USA	5.3.82	8 May
46.20	Mauricio	Mery	CHI	22.2.80	21 Jun
46.22	Dirk	Homewood	USA	21.1.82	3 May
46.22	Jerome	Davis	USA	20.8.77	24 May
46.22	Artur	Gasiewski	POL	1.11.73	4 Jul
46.22	Andrey	Semyonov	RUS	16.8.77	17 Jul
46.22		Liang Chao	CHN	21.6.83	24 Oct
46.23	Nathaniel	McKinney	BAH	.82	19 Jun
46.23	Andrés	Silva	URU-Y	27.3.86	21 Jun
46.24	Chris	Jones	USA	8.10.73	8 Jun
46.25A	Jopie	van Oudtshoorn	RSA	5.2.76	15 Mar
46.25	Reggie	Witherspoon	USA-J	31.5.85	3 May
46.25	Bershawn	Jackson	USA	8.5.83	6 Jul
46.27	Wágner	Souza	BRA	27.2.76	28 Jun
46.28	Kenneth	Telemaque	ISV	24.10.82	10 May
46.28	Sékou	Clarke	JAM	7.10.83	30 May
46.28	Aleksandr	Usov	RUS	2.3.76	31 May
46.29	Troy	McIntosh	BAH	29.3.73	3 May
46.29	Suguru	Matsumoto	JPN	3.5.78	7 Jun
46.29		Xu Zizhou	CHN	8.1.81	12 Sep
46.29	Yasuaki	Sagawa (187)	JPN	26.1.82	29 Oct

Indoors

Mark	Name		Nat	Born	Date
45.93	Jonathan	Fortenberry	USA	19.7.83	14 Mar
45.99	Jamie	Baulch	GBR	3.5.73	16 Mar
46.11	# Reggie	Witherspoon	USA-J	31.5.85	16 Mar
46.15	# Jermaine	Gonzales	JAM-J	26.11.84	16 Mar
46.17	# Dirk	Homewood	USA	21.1.82	15 Feb
46.24	Marek	Plawgo	POL	25.2.81	23 Feb
46.29	Quentin	Bowens	USA-J	28.11.84	9 Mar

Note: A made at an altitude of 1000m or more, h made in a heat, q quarter-final, s semi-final, -J Juniors, -Y Youths

MEN 2003

Mark	Name		Nat	Born	Pos	Meet	Venue	Date
Hand timing								
44.7		Washington			1	GP	London (CP)	8 Aug
44.8		Blackwood			2	GP	London (CP)	8 Aug
45.1	Carlos	Santa	DOM	7.1.78	1	NC	Santo Domingo	4 Sep
45.2	Arismendi	Peguero	DOM	7.8.80	2	NC	Santo Domingo	4 Sep
45.6	Patrick	Dwyer	AUS	3.11.77	1		Canberra	13 Dec

45.9	Talkmore	Nyangani	ZIM	2.9.83	12 Apr
46.1	Djabir	Saïd-Guerni	ALG	29.3.77	14 Jul
46.1	Julio	Vidal	DOM	13.6.82	28 Jul

Low altitude bests

44.98	Sambu	1 Afr G	Abuja		13 Oct
45.02	Moncur	4 GGala	Roma		11 Jul
45.03	Brew	2rA GP II	Madrid (C)		19 Jul
45.16	C Brown	2	Thessaloníki		3 Aug
45.23	Sánchez	3 GP II	Sevilla		7 Jun
45.38	la Grange	1	Castres		6 Aug
45.47	Gorries	1 NC	Port Elizabeth		26 Apr
45.55	Nelson	1 MSR	Walnut		19 Apr
45.63	Mumo	4 Afr G	Abuja		13 Oct

JUNIORS

See main list for top 6 Juniors. 13 performances by 6 men to 45.80. Additional marks and further juniors:

Wariner	45.58	4		Austin	3 May	45.63	2	PAm-J	Bridgetown	19 Jul
N El Abubakr	45.35	1		Budapest	8 Aug	45.44	2	Af-AsG	Hyderabad	28 Oct
	45.43	1	Arab	Amman	7 Sep					
Collins	45.64	1	NC-J	Stanford	22 Jun	45.80	7	NCAAr	Lincoln, NE	31 May

Mark	Name		Nat	Born	Pos	Meet	Venue	Date
45.88	Xavier	Carter	USA	8.12.85	1		Mobile	5 Apr
46.01	Shinji	Takahira	JPN	18.7.84	5	NG	Fukuroi	29 Oct
46.12	Saul	Weigopwa	NGR	14.6.84	1	NC	Abuja	19 Jul
46.14A	Sammy	Rono (10)	KEN	.84	3	NC	Nairobi	12 Jul
46.15	Mark	Teter	USA	23.9.84	1		Austin	10 May
46.19		Tan Biao	CHN	3.2.84	1	NG	Changsha	24 Oct
46.23	Andrés	Silva	URU-Y	27.3.86	4	SACh	Barquisimeto	21 Jun
46.25	Reggie	Witherspoon	USA	31.5.85	1		Marietta	3 May
46.35	Cedric	Goodman	USA-Y	17.3.86	1	G.West	Sacramento	15 Jun
46.42	Ricardo	Chambers	USA	7.10.84	1		Gainesville	17 May
46.43	Aaron	Collins	USA	18.2.84	2h1	Big 12	Austin TX	18 May
46.46	Arthur	Davis	USA		1		Mobile	19 Apr
46.47	Andre	Johnson	USA	29.9.84	2		Gainesville	17 May
46.47	Michael	Mathieu (20)	BAH	24.6.84	3	PAm-J	Bridgetown	19 Jul
Best European: 46.54	Dimítrios	Grávalos	GRE	18.4.84	1	EJ	Tampere	26 Jul
Indoors								
46.11 #	Reggie	Witherspoon	USA	31.5.85	1r2	NSch	New York (A)	16 Mar
46.15 #	Jermaine	Gonzales	JAM	26.11.84	2r2	NSch	New York (A)	16 Mar
46.29	Quentin	Bowens	USA	28.11.84	2r2	IC4A	Boston	9 Mar

600 METRES

1:13.72	Joseph	Mutua	KEN	10.12.78	1		Naimette	2 Sep
1:14.72	Gary	Reed	CAN	25.10.81	2		Naimette	2 Sep
1:16.01	Gregory	Konchellah	KEN	.83	3		Naimette	2 Sep
	(now Yousef Saïd Kamel		BRN)					
1:16.13	Ezra	Sambu	KEN	4.9.78	4		Naimette	2 Sep

800 METRES

1:42.52	Wilfred	Bungei	KEN	24.7.80	1	VD	Bruxelles	5 Sep
1:42.89	Mbulaeni	Mulaudzi	RSA	8.9.80	2	VD	Bruxelles	5 Sep
1:43.05		Bungei			1	FBK	Hengelo	1 Jun
1:43.12	Hezekiél	Sepeng	RSA	30.6.74	3	VD	Bruxelles	5 Sep
1:43.24		Bungei			1	GS	Ostrava	12 Jun
1:43.25		Mulaudzi			1		Rehlingen	9 Jun
1:43.28	Wilson	Kipketer	DEN	12.12.70	4	VD	Bruxelles	5 Sep
1:43.52	Joseph	Mutua Mwengi	KEN	10.12.78	5	VD	Bruxelles	5 Sep
1:43.62		Bungei			1	GP II	Sevilla	7 Jun
1:43.68	Yuriy	Borzakovskiy	RUS	12.4.81	6	VD	Bruxelles	5 Sep
1:43.71A	Japheth	Kimutai	KEN	20.12.78	1	WCT	Nairobi	26 Jul
1:43.93		Borzakovskiy			2	GP II	Sevilla	7 Jun
1:43.94		Borzakovskiy			1	Gaz	Saint-Denis	4 Jul
1:43.97		Borzakovskiy			1	GP	Tríkala	24 Jun
1:44.00		Mulaudzi			1	GGala	Roma	11 Jul
1:44.04		Mutua			1		Abuja	17 May
1:44.11		Mulaudzi			1	Bisl	Oslo	27 Jun
1:44.12		Mulaudzi			2	Gaz	Saint-Denis	4 Jul
1:44.12		Mulaudzi			1rA	WK	Zürich	15 Aug
1:44.15		Bungei			2	Bisl	Oslo	27 Jun
1:44.16A	Justus	Koech	KEN	19.3.80	2	WCT	Nairobi	26 Jul

Mark	Name		Nat	Born	Pos	Meet	Venue	Date
1:44.17	Mehdi	Baala	FRA	17.8.78	1		Villeneuve d'Ascq	15 Jun
1:44.18		Sepeng			3	GP II	Sevilla	7 Jun
1:44.19		Mulaudzi			2		Villeneuve d'Ascq	15 Jun
1:44.21		Sepeng			2	GGala	Roma	11 Jul
1:44.21		Mutua			1rA	NA	Heusden	2 Aug
1:44.22	Bram	Som (10)	NED	20.2.80	4	GP II	Sevilla	7 Jun
1:44.23	André	Bucher	SUI	19.10.76	7	VD	Bruxelles	5 Sep
1:44.25		Bucher			3	Gaz	Saint-Denis	4 Jul
1:44.26		Sepeng			2rA	WK	Zürich	15 Aug
	(30/11)							
1:44.30	David	Krummenacker	USA	24.5.75	4	Gaz	Saint-Denis	4 Jul
1:44.34A	Nicholas	Wachira	KEN	19.11.82	3	WCT	Nairobi	26 Jul
1:44.37	Antonio M	Reina	ESP	13.6.81	5	Gaz	Saint-Denis	4 Jul
1:44.60	Djabir	Saïd-Guerni	ALG	29.3.77	1rB	WK	Zürich	15 Aug
1:44.61	Florent	Lacasse	FRA	21.1.81	1	Nebiolo	Torino	6 Jun
1:44.75	Michael	Rotich	KEN	14.7.78	2rA	NA	Heusden	2 Aug
1:44.95	Joeri	Jansen	BEL	28.5.79	4	GS	Ostrava	12 Jun
1:44.96	Andrea	Longo	ITA	26.6.75	2	GP II	Rieti	7 Sep
1:44.98	Graham	Davidson	RSA	14.10.78	2		Rehlingen	9 Jun
	(20)							
1:45.01A	William	Yiampoy	KEN	17.5.74	2		Roodepoort	28 Mar
1:45.03	Khadevis	Robinson	USA	19.7.76	1		Luzern	25 Jun
1:45.05	Ashraf	Tadili	CAN	8.7.80	1	PAm	Santo Domingo	6 Aug
1:45.08	Abdoulaye	Wagne	SEN	30.1.81	1		Castres	6 Aug
1:45.14	William	Chirchir	KEN	6.2.79	7	Bisl	Oslo	27 Jun
1:45.20	Vincent	Kemboi	KEN	29.5.82	2		Luzern	25 Jun
1:45.20	Amine	Laalou	MAR	13.5.82	1		Alger	17 Jul
1:45.28	Dmitriy	Bogdanov	RUS	11.4.79	6	GP II	Sevilla	7 Jun
1:45.30	James	McIlroy	GBR	30.12.76	5rB	WK	Zürich	15 Aug
1:45.31	Nicolas	Aïssat	FRA	24.7.80	8	Gaz	Saint-Denis	4 Jul
	(30)							
1:45.32	Khalid	Tighazouine	MAR	18.6.77	1		Cuxhaven	19 Jul
1:45.33	Werner	Botha	RSA	31.1.78	1		Arnhem	25 Jun
1:45.34	Gary	Reed	CAN	25.10.81	3		Luzern	25 Jun
1:45.35	Osmar	dos Santos	BRA	20.10.68	1h1	NC	São Paulo	14 Jun
1:45.39	René	Herms	GER	17.7.82	2		Dortmund	15 Jun
1:45.41	Ivan	Geshko	UKR	19.8.79	3		Dortmund	15 Jun
1:45.44	Arthémon	Hatungimana	BDI	21.1.74	3		Castres	6 Aug
1:45.45	Rizak	Dirshe	SWE	5.1.72	2		Cuxhaven	19 Jul
1:45.46	Bryan	Woodward	USA	3.3.74	1		Budapest	8 Aug
1:45.48	Rui	Silva	POR	3.8.77	6	GP	Madrid (C)	19 Jul
	(40)							
1:45.51	Jean-Patrick	Nduwimana	BDI	9.5.78	9	GS	Ostrava	12 Jun
1:45.54A	Henry	Rotich	KEN	5.12.81	6	WCT	Nairobi	26 Jul
1:45.56	Jimmy	Lomba	FRA	30.6.78	4		Rehlingen	9 Jun
1:45.57	Manuel	Olmedo	ESP	17.5.83	7	GP II	Sevilla	7 Jun
1:45.63	Berhanu	Alemu	ETH	16.7.82	1h2	WCh	Saint-Denis	28 Aug
1:45.68	Kenneth	Kimwetich	KEN	1.1.73	6	GP	Tríkala	24 Jun
1:45.69	Derrick	Peterson	USA	28.11.77	1		Brunswick	5 Jul
1:45.73	Mouhsin	Chehibi	MAR	28.1.78	3		Alger	17 Jul
1:45.75	Tom	Omey	BEL	24.4.75	5		Rehlingen	9 Jun
1:45.77	Fouad	Chouki ¶	FRA	15.10.78	1		Sotteville	8 Jul
	(50)							
1:45.81A	Neil	Speaight	GBR	9.9.78	1		Potchefstroom	8 Apr
1:45.86	Kris	McCarthy	AUS	15.10.79	5rA	NA	Heusden	2 Aug
1:45.88	Gregory	Konchellah	KEN	.83	4	Nebiolo	Torino	6 Jun
	(now Yousef Saïd Kamel		BRN)					
1:45.89	David	Lelei	KEN	10.5.71	7	GP	Tríkala	24 Jun
1:45.93	Alex	Kipchirchir	KEN-J	26.11.84	6	Athl	Lausanne	1 Jul
1:45.94	Samwel	Mwera	TAN-J	3.6.85	1rB		Rovereto	10 Sep
1:45.96	Anthony	Kabara	KEN	9.3.78	2		Brunswick	5 Jul
1:46.00	Juan Carlos	Higuero	ESP	3.8.78	4		San Sebastián	10 Aug
1:46.00	Bernard	Lagat	KEN	12.12.74	8	ISTAF	Berlin (P)	10 Aug
1:46.03	Timothy	Kiptanui	KEN	5.1.80	1		Napoli	10 Jun
	(60)							
1:46.06	Ricky	Soos	GBR	28.6.83	4	GP	London (CP)	8 Aug
1:46.15	Ahmed	Ismail	SUD-J	10.9.84	3		Budapest	8 Aug
1:46.17	Sam	Burley	USA	13.2.81	2rB	NA	Heusden	2 Aug
1:46.20	Fabiano	Peçanha	BRA	5.6.82	2	NC	São Paulo	15 Jun
1:46.20	Adam Abdou	Adam	QAT	15.6.83	1	AsiC	Manila	23 Sep
1:46.21	Anthony	Whiteman	GBR	13.11.71	2		Lappeenranta	3 Aug

Mark	Name		Nat	Born	Pos	Meet	Venue	Date
1:46.25A	Bonolo	Maboa	RSA-J	24.8.85	3		Roodepoort	28 Mar
1:46.31	Sylas	Kimutai	KEN	12.10.83	3		Arnhem	25 Jun
1:46.35	Christian	Obrist	ITA	20.11.80	6	Nebiolo	Torino	6 Jun
1:46.37	João	Pires	POR	10.6.79	4		Funchal	26 Jul
	(70)							
1:46.38	Eugenio	Barrios	ESP	3.11.76	8	GP II	Sevilla	7 Jun
1:46.41	Jackson	Langat	KEN	15.12.80	1h1	NCAA	Sacramento	11 Jun
1:46.45	Jess	Strutzel	USA	4.1.78	4	PAm	Santo Domingo	6 Aug
1:46.48	Mohammed	Al-Salhi	KSA-Y	11.5.86	3h8	WCh	Saint-Denis	28 Aug
1:46.50	Rickard	Pell	SWE	24.3.79	4		Arnhem	25 Jun
1:46.50	Wilson	Kirwa	FIN	28.12.74	3		Lappeenranta	3 Aug
1:46.51	Jonathan	Johnson	USA	5.3.82	2	NCAA	Sacramento	14 Jun
1:46.51	Abdulrahman	Sulaiman	QAT-J	10.1.84	4		Castres	6 Aug
1:46.55	Adem	Hecini	ALG	13.12.75	6		Alger	17 Jul
1:46.56	Marc	Sylvester	USA	21.11.82	1	SEC	Knoxville	18 May
	(80)							
1:46.57	Glody	Dube	BOT	2.7.78	5		Arnhem	25 Jun
1:46.60	Abdelsalam	Kennouche	ALG	7.10.80	5		Castres	6 Aug
1:46.62	Robbie	Stevens	RSA	18.2.81	2	SEC	Knoxville	18 May
1:46.63	Salem Amer	Al-Badri	QAT-J	12.12.85	1		Nivelles	15 Aug
1:46.64	Mindaugas	Norbutas	LTU	24.8.76	6		Cuxhaven	19 Jul
1:46.64A	Maswi	Nthambe	KEN	.71	2h1	WCT	Nairobi	25 Jul
1:46.65	Michael	East	GBR	20.1.78	3	v2N	Glasgow (S)	29 Jun
1:46.70	John	Litei	KEN	.83	7	Nebiolo	Torino	6 Jun
1:46.71	Norberto	Téllez	CUB	22.1.72	1		Alcalá de Henares	28 Jun
1:46.72	Jebreh	Harris	USA	22.9.78	5		Cottbus	4 Jun
	(90)							
1:46.72	Gert-Jan	Liefers	NED	26.9.78	8		Arnhem	25 Jun
1:46.78	Floyd	Thompson	USA	22.11.79	4	NC	Stanford	22 Jun
1:46.79	Eliud	Njubi	KEN	27.7.79	1		Amagasaki	14 Jun
1:46.83	Ramil	Aritkulov	RUS	1.3.78	2	NC	Tula	8 Aug
1:46.84	Grzegorz	Krzosek	POL	10.1.76	8		Poznan	29 Jun
1:46.87	Willy	Rotich	KEN	23.3.76	2		Tallinn	30 Jul
1:46.88	Peter	Etoot	KEN-J	17.4.84	3	SEC	Knoxville	18 May
1:46.89	Yassine	Bensghir	MAR	3.1.83	2		Leuven-Heverlee	7 Jun
1:46.91	Rachid	Mohamed (Khouya)	BRN	9.11.79	2		La Roche-sur-Yon	16 Jul
1:46.92	Fernando	Almeida	POR	22.6.81	2		Alcalá de Henares	28 Jun
	(100)							
1:46.92	Chris	Moss	GBR	17.6.79	5		Budapest	8 Aug

1:46.93	Sergey	Kozhevnikov	RUS	12.5.70	31 May
1:46.95	Christian	Neunhäuserer	ITA	21.6.78	11 Jul
1:47.01	Pávlos	Faroúggias	GRE	6.6.77	24 Jun
1:47.03	Daniel	Caulfield	IRL	16.10.72	5 Jul
1:47.04	Nathan	Brannen	CAN	8.9.82	11 Jun
1:47.05	Otukile	Lekote	BOT	19.10.78	31 May
1:47.05	Moise	Joseph	USA	27.12.81	14 Jun
1:47.05	Pawel	Czapiewski	POL	30.3.78	9 Aug
1:47.09	Toby	Henkels	USA	25.8.79	11 Jun
1:47.09	Juha	Kukkamo	FIN	1.4.76	3 Aug
1:47.09	Siakha	Bamba	FRA	24.5.75	6 Aug
1:47.15	Pascar	Owor	UGA	22.12.80	26 Jun
1:47.15	Nabil	Madi	ALG	81	17 Jul
1:47.15A	Joel	Marwa	KEN	30.8.74	25 Jul
1:47.15	Antoine	Martiak	FRA	28.1.83	6 Aug
1:47.16	Sotírios	Papadeás	GRE	4.5.82	31 May
1:47.22	Jean	Balan	USA	14.8.81	18 May
1:47.22A	Julius	Koech	KEN		6 Jun
1:47.22	Christian	Köhler	GER	14.10.80	19 Jul
1:47.23	Stephan	Frosch	GER	4.1.77	3 Aug
1:47.24A	Lulu	Basinyi	BOT	30.6.76	8 Apr
1:47.24	Arnoud	Okken	NED	20.4.82	24 May
1:47.24	Roman	Hanzel	SVK	15.1.77	30 Jul
1:47.26	Maksim	Adamovich	RUS	24.6.80	8 Jun
1:47.26	Torsten	Kühn	GER	1.8.76	3 Aug
1:47.27	Hudson	de Souza	BRA	25.2.77	25 Jul
1:47.30	Ricardo	Etheridge	PUR	12.5.78	12 Jul
1:47.30	Panayiótis	Stroubákos	GRE	8.9.72	3 Aug
1:47.31	Sadjad	Moradi	IRI	30.3.83	8 Aug
1:47.32	Andrey	Zadorozhniy	RUS	3.9.73	8 Jun
1:47.32	Hiroshi	Sasano	JPN	23.9.78	23 Jul
1:47.33	James	Karanu	KEN	5.1.76	12 Apr
1:47.34	Isaac	Sang	KEN	78	4 Jun
1:47.38A	Robert	Rono	KEN	11.10.74	7 Jun
1:47.38A	Francis	Marwa	KEN	4.12.76	25 Jul
1:47.38	Juan de Dios	Jurado	ESP	9.4.81	3 Aug
1:47.39	Timothy	Dunne	USA	22.5.79	11 Jun
1:47.39	Juan Carlos	Esteso	ESP	13.10.76	6 Sep
1:47.40	Paul	Korir	KEN	15.7.77	9 Jun
1:47.40	Toni	Mohr	GER	7.5.83	13 Jun
1:47.40	Miroslaw	Formela	POL	31.10.78	12 Aug
1:47.41A	Dedan	Maina	KEN	.78	7 Jun
1:47.42	Zbigniew	Graczyk	POL	4.7.78	31 May
1:47.43	Abdelkebir	Louraibi	BRN	9.2.81	23 Jul
1:47.44A	Juan	van Deventer	RSA	26.3.83	31 Jan
1:47.44	Mohd Khalaf	Al-Azimi	KUW	16.6.82	8 Aug
1:47.45	Ehsan	Mohajershojaei	IRI	23.3.83	10 Aug
1:47.46	Daniel	Ruiz	ESP	30.10.81	7 Jun
1:47.46	Lluis Francisco	Martín (150)	ESP	13.7.79	15 Aug
1:47.48	Peter	Roko Ashak	SUD-J	84	30 Oct
1:47.50	Farid	Essaki	MAR	2.3.80	16 Jul
1:47.50	Sheridan	Kirk	TRI	11.2.81	6 Aug
1:47.50	James	Nolan	IRL	27.1.77	10 Sep
1:47.52	Michael	Stember	USA	30.1.78	19 Apr
1:47.55	Edward Kibet	Mutai	KEN-J	84	7 Jun
1:47.56	Jesse	O'Connell	USA	20.3.82	14 Jun
1:47.56	Rachid	Ramzi	BRN	17.7.80	7 Sep
1:47.57	Aldwyn	Sappleton	JAM	21.12.81	12 Jun
1:47.57	Matthew	Shone	GBR	10.7.75	8 Aug
1:47.63	Stefan	Beumer	NED	28.4.81	24 May
1:47.63		Lee Jae-hoon	KOR	28.11.76	5 Jun
1:47.63	Mounir	Yemmouni	FRA	12.10.83	6 Jul
1:47.66	Reyes	Estévez	ESP	2.8.76	15 Jul
1:47.67	Alexandre	Padovani	FRA	11.1.81	6 Jul
1:47.68	Nahashon	Ruto	KEN		27 Jul
1:47.69	Yuriy	Koldin	RUS	1.11.83	8 Jun
1:47.69A	Evans	Ndungu	KEN	22.2.79	12 Jul
1:47.70	Roman	Oravec	CZE	5.4.78	8 Aug
1:47.72	Jacob	Koczman	USA	21.11.78	19 Jul
1:47.72	Gareth	Hyett	NZL	13.2.80	2 Aug

Mark	Name		Nat	Born	Date
1:47.73	Miguel	Quesada	ESP	18.9.79	13 Aug
1:47.75	Thomas	Planque	FRA	26.4.79	26 Jun
1:47.76A	Michael	Chepkonga	KEN		12 Jul
1:47.77	Bryan	Berryhill	USA	15.12.77	5 Jul
1:47.78	Zachary	Whitmarsh	CAN	5.4.77	17 May
1:47.78	Fabio	Lettieri	ITA	10.7.80	10 Jun
1:47.80	Márcio	de Oliveira	BRA	1.2.73	15 Jun
1:47.81	Jason	Stewart	NZL	21.11.81	15 Jun
1:47.81	Oleg	Lobanov	UKR-J	2.11.84	22 Jun
1:47.82	Alibey	Sükürov	AZE	2.5.77	10 Aug
1:47.83	Nick	Brunet	BEL	14.4.83	17 May
1:47.85	Franek	Haschke	GER	28.3.80	10 Aug
1:47.87	Elkana	Chepsiror	KEN		23 Aug
1:47.89	Michael	Taylor	USA	5.1.82	18 Apr
1:47.89	Mike	Inge	USA-J	31.1.84	22 Jun
1:47.89	Gezahegn	Alemu	ETH-J	85	5 Jul
1:47.89	Artyom	Mastrov	RUS	12.11.76	8 Aug
1:47.9	Vladimir	Kovalik	UKR	25.5.76	27 May
	1:47.91				4 Jul
1:47.90	Ionut	Zaizan	ROM	21.7.83	10 Aug
1:47.91	Nathan	Kahan	BEL	12.2.71	13 Aug
1:47.93	Andrew	Neugebauer	USA	5.5.77	26 Apr
1:47.93	Peter	Biwott	KEN	22.8.76	15 Jun
1:47.93	Sergio	Gallardo	ESP	22.3.79	19 Jul
1:47.94	Yeimar	López	CUB	20.8.82	6 Jul
1:47.96	Grant	Robison	USA	27.9.78	12 Jul
1:47.97A	Francis	Maina	KEN		7 Jun
1:47.99A	Isaiah	Nkuna ¶ (199)	RSA	5.3.77	18 Jan

Indoors

Mark		Name		Nat	Born	Pos	Meet	Venue	Date
1:45.57		Nils	Schumann	GER	20.5.78	3	Spark	Stuttgart	2 Feb
1:46.88	#	Otukile	Lekote	BOT	19.10.78	1		Lexington	25 Jan

Mark	Name		Nat	Born	Date
1:47.38 #	Zachary	Whitmarsh	CAN	5.4.77	15 Feb
1:47.40 #	David	Freeman	USA	28.4.82	25 Jan
1:47.53 #	Fred	Sharpe	USA	21.8.78	8 Mar
1:47.64	Cornelius	Chirchir	KEN	7.10.83	21 Feb
1:47.75	Joseph	Lee	USA	4.5.82	14 Mar

Drugs Disqualification

Mark	Name		Nat	Born	Date
1:47.62	Isaiah	Nkuna ¶	RSA	5.3.77	14 Feb

JUNIORS

See main list for top 8 Juniors. 17 performances by 7 men to 1:46.7. Additional marks and further juniors:

Mwera	1:46.13	1	Afg	Abuja	13 Oct	1:46.41	1	Pergine Valsug.	25 Jul
Al-Salhi	1:46.62	4		Lappeenranta	3 Aug				
Ismail	1:46.6	1		Bangor	1 Aug				

Mark	Name		Nat	Born	Pos	Meet	Venue	Date
1:47.48	Peter	Roko Ashak	SUD	84	1	Af-AsG	Hyderabad	30 Oct
1:47.55	Edward Kibet	Mutai (10)	KEN	84	3		Leuven-Heverlee	7 Jun
1:47.81	Oleg	Lobanov	UKR	2.11.84	2	ECp-1B	Velenje	22 Jun
1:47.89	Mike	Inge	USA	31.1.84	1	NC	Stanford	22 Jun
1:47.89	Gezahegn	Alemu	ETH	85	3		Uden	5 Jul
1:48.01A	Johnny	Shuping	RSA	10.9.84	5		Potchefstroom	8 Apr
1:48.28	Simeon	Bovell	TRI	.85	2	NC	Port-of-Spain	21 Jun
1:48.3	Chris	Reynolds	GBR	23.1.85	1		Brighton	13 Aug
1:48.31	P.W.Manoi	Pushpakumara	SRI	11.1.85	3		Colombo	1 Jun
1:48.45	Cosmas Kipkorir	Rono	KEN	12.12.84	1	AfrC-j	Garoua	1 Aug
1:48.5A	Abraham Kipngetich	Ngeno	KEN-Y	6.5.86			Nairobi	18 Jun
1:48.55	Kleberson	Davide (20)	BRA	20.7.85	3h1	NC	São Paulo	14 Jun

1000 METRES

Mark	Name		Nat	Born	Pos	Meet	Venue	Date
2:13.96	Mehdi	Baala	FRA	17.8.78	1		Strasbourg	26 Jun
2:16.19	Timothy	Kiptanui	KEN	5.1.80	1		Réthimno	6 Jul
2:16.43	David	Lelei	KEN	10.5.71	1	GP II	Stanford	7 Jun
2:16.83	Japheth	Kimutai	KEN	20.12.78	2		Réthimno	6 Jul
2:17.10	David	Krummenacker	USA	24.5.75	2	GP II	Stanford	7 Jun
2:17.25	Abdelsalam	Kennouche	ALG	7.10.80	2		Strasbourg	26 Jun
2:17.34	Florent	Lacasse	FRA	21.1.81	1		St-Florentin	14 Sep
2:17.40	Abdelkader	Chékhémani	FRA	18.7.71	3		Strasbourg	26 Jun
2:17.73	Michael	Rotich	KEN	14.7.78	3		Réthimno	6 Jul
2:17.85	Samwel	Mwera	TAN-J	3.6.85	1		Oristano	6 Sep
2:18.03	Guillaume	Éraud	FRA	1.7.81	4		Strasbourg	26 Jun
2:18.10	Jean-Patrick	Nduwimana	BDI	9.5.78	4		Réthimno	6 Jul
2:18.2+	Paul	Korir	KEN	15.7.77	1	in 1500	Roma	11 Jul
2:18.4+	Hicham	El Guerrouj	MAR	14.9.74	2	in 1500	Roma	11 Jul

Mark	Name		Nat	Born	Date
2:18.45A	Mbulaeni	Mulaudzi	RSA	8.9.80	28 Mar
2:18.8+	Benjamin	Kipkurui	KEN	28.12.80	11 Jul
2:19.06	Kevin	Sullivan	CAN	20.3.74	7 Jun
2:19.26	Joseph	Mutua Mwengi	KEN	10.12.78	11 Apr
2:19.38A	Juan	van Deventer	RSA	26.3.83	28 Mar
2:19.41A	Graham	Davidson	RSA	14.10.78	28 Mar
2:19.41	Michael	Stember	USA	30.1.78	7 Jun
2:19.51A	Johan	Pretorius	RSA	23.9.82	28 Mar
2:19.53A	Glody	Dube	BOT	2.7.78	28 Mar
2:19.54A	Johan	Cronje	RSA	13.4.82	4 Apr

Indoors

Mark	Name		Nat	Born	Pos	Meet	Venue	Date
2:17.81	Bram	Som	NED	20.2.80	1	Spark	Stuttgart	2 Feb
2:18.02	Glody	Dube	BOT	2.7.78	2	Spark	Stuttgart	2 Feb
2:18.15	William	Yiampoy	KEN	17.5.74	2	Spark	Stuttgart	2 Feb
2:18.24	Cornelius	Chirchir	KEN	7.10.83	2		Liévin	23 Feb
2:18.33	Nicolas	Aïssat	FRA	24.7.80	3		Liévin	23 Feb
2:18.36	Wilson	Kipketer	DEN	12.12.70	4	Spark	Stuttgart	2 Feb

Mark	Name		Nat	Born	Date
2:18.52	Hezekiél	Sepeng	RSA	30.6.74	23 Feb
2:19.01	Joseph	Mutua Mwengi	KEN	10.12.78	23 Feb

1500 METRES

Mark	Name		Nat	Born	Pos	Meet	Venue	Date
3:28.40	Hicham	El Guerrouj	MAR	14.9.74	1	VD	Bruxelles	5 Sep
3:28.98	Mehdi	Baala	FRA	17.8.78	2	VD	Bruxelles	5 Sep
3:29.13		El Guerrouj			1	WK	Zürich	15 Aug

Mark	Name		Nat	Born	Pos	Meet	Venue	Date
3:29.76		El Guerrouj			1	GGala	Roma	11 Jul
3:30.55	Bernard	Lagat	KEN	12.12.74	2	WK	Zürich	15 Aug
3:30.72	Paul	Korir	KEN	15.7.77	3	VD	Bruxelles	5 Sep
3:30.83	Fouad	Chouki ¶	FRA	15.10.78	3	WK	Zürich	15 Aug
3:30.97		Baala			1	Gaz	Saint-Denis	4 Jul
3:31.17	Cornelius	Chirchir	KEN	7.10.83	1	GS	Ostrava	12 Jun
3:31.33	Robert	Rono	KEN	11.10.74	4	VD	Bruxelles	5 Sep
3:31.40		Lagat			2	Gaz	Saint-Denis	4 Jul
3:31.42	Alex	Kipchirchir	KEN-J	26.11.84	5	VD	Bruxelles	5 Sep
3:31.54	Isaac	Songok	KEN-J	25.4.84	1	NA	Heusden	2 Aug
3:31.61	Juan Carlos	Higuero (10)	ESP	3.8.78	6	VD	Bruxelles	5 Sep
3:31.70	William	Chirchir	KEN	6.2.79	2	GS	Ostrava	12 Jun
3:31.77		El Guerrouj			1	WCh	Saint-Denis	27 Aug
3:32.01	Ivan	Geshko	UKR	19.8.79	3	GS	Ostrava	12 Jun
3:32.31		Baala			2	WCh	Saint-Denis	27 Aug
3:32.35		Kipchirchir			3	WK	Zürich	15 Aug
3:32.42	Benjamin	Kipkurui	KEN	28.12.80	2	NA	Heusden	2 Aug
3:32.44		Korir			3	Gaz	Saint-Denis	4 Jul
3:32.58		Kipkurui			7	VD	Bruxelles	5 Sep
3:32.59		Kipkurui			2	GGala	Roma	11 Jul
3:32.60		Kipchirchir			4	GS	Ostrava	12 Jun
3:32.61		C Chirchir			1	GP	Tríkala	24 Jun
3:32.63	Vyacheslav	Shabunin	RUS	27.9.69	8	VD	Bruxelles	5 Sep
3:32.67		Kipchirchir			2	GP	Tríkala	24 Jun
3:32.73		Geshko			3	GP	Tríkala	24 Jun
3:32.86	Reyes	Estévez	ESP	2.8.76	3	GGala	Roma	11 Jul
3:32.93		W Chirchir			4	GP	Tríkala	24 Jun
3:32.97	Rui	Silva	POR	3.8.77	5	GP	Tríkala	24 Jun
3:32.99		Lagat			1	DNG	Stockholm	5 Aug
	(32/16)							
3:33.91	Laban	Rotich	KEN	20.1.69	6	Gaz	Saint-Denis	4 Jul
3:33.96	Noah	Ngeny	KEN	2.11.78	7	GP	Tríkala	24 Jun
3:33.99	Gert-Jan	Liefers	NED	26.9.78	7	WCh	Saint-Denis	27 Aug
3:34.07	Timothy	Kiptanui	KEN	5.1.80	3		Milano	3 Jun
	(20)							
3:34.57	Tarek	Boukensa	ALG	19.11.81	2		San Sebastián	10 Aug
3:34.60	Kevin	Sullivan	CAN	20.3.74	2	GP II	Gresham	17 May
3:35.02	Roberto	Parra	ESP	6.4.76	11	WCh	Saint-Denis	27 Aug
3:35.03	Abdelkader	Hachlaf	MAR	3.7.78	2	GP	Madrid (C)	19 Jul
3:35.09	David	Kiplak	KEN	27.12.81	2		Dortmund	15 Jun
3:35.10	Álvaro	Fernández	ESP	7.4.81	3		San Sebastián	10 Aug
3:35.15	Stephen	Cherono	KEN	15.10.82	5	Athl	Lausanne	1 Jul
	(later Saïf Saaeed Shaheen QAT)							
3:35.15	David	Krummenacker	USA	24.5.75	3	GP	Gateshead	13 Jul
3:35.17	Youssef	Baba	MAR	7.8.79	4		San Sebastián	10 Aug
3:35.24	Sergio	Gallardo	ESP	22.3.79	6	Athl	Lausanne	1 Jul
	(30)							
3:35.35	Anas	Selmouni	MAR	15.3.79	4	GP	Gateshead	13 Jul
3:35.49	Anthony	Whiteman	GBR	13.11.71	10	Gaz	Saint-Denis	4 Jul
3:35.49	Michael	East	GBR	20.1.78	3	GP	Madrid (C)	19 Jul
3:35.50	Wolfram	Müller	GER	8.7.81	5		Milano	3 Jun
3:35.69	James	Nolan	IRL	27.1.77	5	NA	Heusden	2 Aug
3:35.73	Job	Tanui	KEN	26.8.74	1	Gugl	Linz	31 Jul
3:35.74	Bert	Leenaerts	BEL	1.7.80	6	NA	Heusden	2 Aug
3:35.75	Grant	Robison	USA	27.9.78	7	NA	Heusden	2 Aug
3:35.84	Manuel	Damião	POR	4.7.78	6		Milano	3 Jun
3:35.85	Richard	Geemi	KEN	23.8.73	1	MAI	Malmö	12 Aug
	(40)							
3:36.12	Mohamed	Khaldi	ALG	3.5.75	5	GP II	Zagreb	7 Jul
3:36.13	Paul	Mwangi	KEN	19.11.73	2	Gugl	Linz	31 Jul
3:36.17	Eliud	Kipchoge	KEN-J	5.11.84	2		Rehlingen	9 Jun
3:36.35	Youcef	Abdi	AUS	7.12.77	10	NA	Heusden	2 Aug
3:36.36	Christian	Obrist	ITA	20.11.80	8		Milano	3 Jun
3:36.40	Samwel	Mwera	TAN-J	3.6.85	1-23	WK	Zürich	15 Aug
3:36.41	Hudson	de Souza	BRA	25.2.77	6	GP II	Zagreb	7 Jul
3:36.49		Dou Zhaobo	CHN	23.9.83	1	NG	Changsha	24 Oct
3:36.55	Bouabdellah	Tahri	FRA	20.12.78	5	GP II	Sevilla	7 Jun
3:36.57	Adrian	Blincoe	NZL	4.11.79	11	NA	Heusden	2 Aug
	(50)							

Mark	Name		Nat	Born	Pos	Meet	Venue	Date
3:36.58	Nick	Willis	NZL	25.4.83	7	GP II	Zagreb	7 Jul
3:36.60	Gareth	Turnbull	IRL	14.5.79	1		Cuxhaven	19 Jul
3:36.66	Abdelkader	Chékhémani	FRA	18.7.71	12	Gaz	Saint-Denis	4 Jul
3:36.68	Bryan	Berryhill	USA	15.12.77	8	GP II	Zagreb	7 Jul
3:36.76	Yassine	Bensghir	MAR	3.1.83	3		Rehlingen	9 Jun
3:36.82	David	Lelei	KEN	10.5.71	4	GP II	Gresham	17 May
3:36.86	Pedro Antonio	Esteso	ESP	13.10.76	8	GP II	Sevilla	7 Jun
3:36.93	Abdelsalam	Kennouche	ALG	7.10.80	2		Cuxhaven	19 Jul
3:36.96	Ali Nabil	Maataoui	MAR	11.12.80	4		Rehlingen	9 Jun
3:36.97		Yang Weize	CHN	10.2.83	2	NG	Changsha	24 Oct
	(60)							
3:36.98	Suleiman	Simotwo	KEN	21.4.80	1		Leverkusen	3 Aug
3:36.99	Jason	Lunn	USA	19.9.74	9	GP II	Zagreb	7 Jul
3:37.04	Charles	Kiplangat Bett	KEN-J	21.7.84	6		Rehlingen	9 Jun
3:37.09	Zbigniew	Graczyk	POL	4.7.78	8	GS	Ostrava	12 Jun
3:37.10	Michal	Sneberger	CZE	23.6.78	9	GS	Ostrava	12 Jun
3:37.19	David	Nyaga	KEN	8.11.79	1		Arnhem	25 Jun
3:37.46	Kamel	Boulahfane	ALG	1.7.76	10	GP II	Zagreb	7 Jul
3:37.48	Augustine	Kiprono Choge	KEN-Y	21.1.87	2-23	WK	Zürich	15 Aug
3:37.51	Michael	Too	KEN	3.8.83	10	GP II	Sevilla	7 Jun
3:37.58	Branko	Zorko	CRO	1.7.67	11	GP II	Zagreb	7 Jul
	(70)							
3:37.58	Edward	Mutai Kibet	KEN-J	.84	3		Cuxhaven	19 Jul
3:37.59	John	Mayock	GBR	26.10.70	11	GP II	Sevilla	7 Jun
3:37.65	Panayiótis	Stroubákos	GRE	8.9.72	12	GP	Tríkala	24 Jun
3:37.67	José Manuel	Cerezo	ESP	23.6.73	9		San Sebastián	10 Aug
3:37.73	Graham	Davidson	RSA	14.10.78	4		Dortmund	15 Jun
3:37.92	Shadrack	Korir	KEN	14.12.78	3		Kalamáta	31 May
3:38.18	Ralf	Assmus	GER	28.1.77	5		Dortmund	15 Jun
3:38.18	Tom	Mayo	GBR	2.5.77	7	Odlozil	Praha	29 Jun
3:38.32	Tim	Clerbout	BEL	13.10.81	12	NA	Heusden	2 Aug
3:38.34	Dalibor	Balgac	CRO	22.9.77	13	GP II	Zagreb	7 Jul
	(80)							
3:38.36	José Antonio	Redolat	ESP	17.2.76	12	GP II	Sevilla	7 Jun
3:38.47	Marko	Koers	NED	3.11.72	2		Arnhem	25 Jun
3:38.47	Ridouane	Es-Saadi	BEL	1.1.76	13	NA	Heusden	2 Aug
3:38.54	Mounir	Yemmouni	FRA	12.10.83	7		Poznan	29 Jun
3:38.54	Andrés	Díaz	ESP	12.7.69	1		Barakaldo	5 Jul
3:38.67	James	Kwalia	KEN-J	12.6.84	1		Abuja	17 May
3:38.81	Andrey	Zadorozhniy	RUS	3.9.73	4		Kalamáta	31 May
3:38.87	Juan	van Deventer	RSA	26.3.83	1		Durban	7 Mar
3:38.88	Franek	Haschke	GER	28.3.80	8		Dortmund	15 Jun
3:38.96	Lorenzo	Perrone	ITA	26.9.81	12		Milano	3 Jun
	(90)							
3:39.03	Guillaume	Éraud	FRA	1.7.81	9		Rehlingen	9 Jun
3:39.04	Miroslaw	Formela	POL	31.10.78	9	Odlozil	Praha	29 Jun
3:39.09	Carles	Castillejo	ESP	18.8.78	8	GP	Madrid (C)	19 Jul
3:39.15	Fumikazu	Kobayashi	JPN	21.3.78	1rB	NA	Heusden	2 Aug
3:39.17	Johan	Pretorius	RSA	23.9.82	3		Durban	7 Mar
3:39.20	Abdulrahman	Sulaiman	QAT-J	10.1.84	8	Gugl	Linz	31 Jul
3:39.24	Alistair	Cragg	IRL	13.6.80	1		Fayetteville	12 Apr
3:39.30	Rachid	Ramzi	BRN	17.7.80	1		Rabat	31 May
3:39.46	António	Travassos	POR	24.9.71	2rB	GP	Madrid (C)	19 Jul
3:39.49	Hillary	Chenonge	KEN-J	30.5.85	10		Rehlingen	9 Jun
	(100)							

3:39.60	Jun	Tsuji	JPN	6.12.81	2 Aug
3:39.61	Antonio	Martínez	ESP	20.12.78	5 Jul
3:39.61	Philmon	Kibet	KEN	20.11.82	15 Aug
3:39.62	Daniel	Zegeye	ETH	13.3.79	31 Jul
3:39.63	Saïd	Chébili	FRA	6.5.73	9 Jun
3:39.67	Samuel	Dadi	ETH-J	.85	7 Jun
3:39.72	Andrew	Graffin	GBR	20.12.77	14 Jun
3:39.74	Charlie	Gruber	USA	6.8.78	17 May
3:39.74	Fabiano	Peçanha	BRA	5.6.82	20 Jun
3:39.75	Graham	Hood	CAN	2.4.72	7 Jun
3:39.79	Darko	Radomirovic	SCG	5.8.77	2 Jun
3:39.91	Abdulaziz	Al-Ameeri	QAT	.82	12 Aug
3:39.92	Joseph Mwengi	Mutua	KEN	10.12.78	27 Jul
3:39.94	Jess	Strutzel	USA	4.1.78	1 Jun
3:40.0A	James	Geemi	KEN		12 Jul
3:40.11	Matthieu	Vandiest	BEL	10.2.81	2 Aug
3:40.12	Jared	Shegumo	ETH/POL	10.1.83	29 Jun
3:40.16	Seneca	Lassiter	USA	12.3.77	17 May
3:40.17	Abdallah	Abdelkadir	SUD-Y	87	29 Oct
3:40.21	Josephat	Muchiri Ndambiri	KEN-J	12.2.85	30 Jul
3:40.21	Peter	Roko Ashak	SUD-J	84	29 Oct
3:40.22	Ali	Saidi-Sief	ALG	15.3.78	23 Aug
3:40.25	Toni	Mohr	GER	7.5.83	4 Jun
3:40.30	Mark	Fountain	AUS	10.3.82	17 May
3:40.33	Khalid	Lamri	MAR	20.3.77	31 May
3:40.40	Kazuyoshi	Tokumoto	JPN	22.6.79	2 Aug
3:40.43	Abdallah	Lemgharbi	MAR		14 Jun
3:40.44	Chris	Mulvaney	GBR	25.5.81	14 Jun
3:40.49	Fabio	Lettieri	ITA	10.7.80	3 Jun
3:40.5A	Daniel	Wambogo	KEN	,83	29 Mar
3:40.59	Tom	Van Rooy	BEL	30.1.82	2 Aug
3:40.60	Xavier	Areny	ESP	20.1.81	10 Aug
3:40.66	Roman	Tarasov	RUS	9.4.77	10 Aug
3:40.7A	Simon	Solonei	KEN		3 Jul
3:40.78	Keith	Kelly	IRL	1.10.77	6 Aug
3:40.87	Michael	Power	AUS	9.5.76	22 Mar

MEN 2003

Mark	Name		Nat	Born	Pos	Meet	Venue	Date
3:40.87	Konstadínos	Karakatsánis	GRE	29.11.74				24 Jun
3:40.89	Frans	Leenaerts	BEL	29.3.77				2 Aug
3:41.01	Miguel Ángel	García	VEN	7.11.76				20 Jun
3:41.1A	Frederick	Cheruiyot	KEN	20.9.70				12 Jul
3:41.11	Joel	Atwater	USA	18.8.80				14 Jun
3:41.14	Isaac	Sang	KEN	78				13 Jun
3:41.17	Seifu	Nefsie	ETH-J	85				2 Aug
3:41.21	Onésphore	Nkunzimana	BDI-J	23.7.85				23 Jul
3:41.28	Kader	Mahmoudi	FRA	16.1.83				6 Jul
3:41.28	Samson	Kiplangat Ngetich	KEN-Y	10.11.86				15 Aug
3:41.30	Mattias	Norling	SWE	1.6.77				12 Aug
3:41.32	Francois	Pretorius	RSA-J	11.2.84				26 Apr
3:41.33	Boujemaa	Stouti	MAR	74				27 Jun
3:41.34	Joseph Koskei	Kipkemboi	KEN	25.8.74				28 Jun
3:41.36	Ali Abubaker	Kamal	QAT	83				13 Jul
3:41.36	Aléxis	Abraham	FRA	14.2.76				26 Jul
3:41.37	Jonas	Stifel	GER	5.9.80				15 Jun
3:41.38A	Sammy	Mutai	KEN	20.12.74				7 Jun
3:41.41	Michael	Stember	USA	30.1.78				1 Jun
3:41.45	Ryan	Hayden	CAN	27.1.82				17 May
3:41.46	Simon	Vroemen	NED	11.5.69				13 Aug
3:41.47	Dmitriy	Onufriyenko	RUS	12.8.80				10 Aug
3:41.49	Daniel	Wilson	USA	19.2.79				2 May
3:41.49	Neil	Speaight (160)	GBR	9.9.78				31 May

Indoors

Mark	Name		Nat	Born	Pos	Meet	Venue	Date
3:34.66	Roberto	Parra	ESP	6.4.76	1		Sevilla	22 Feb
3:36.93	Driss	Maazouzi	FRA	15.10.69	2		Athína	6 Mar
3:38.87	Antonio	Martínez	ESP	20.12.78	3		Sevilla	22 Feb
3:41.03	Berhanu	Alemu	ETH	16.7.82				1 Feb
3:41.18	James	Thie	GBR	27.6.78				14 Mar

JUNIORS

See main list for top 10 Juniors. 17 performances by 4 men to 3:37.0. Additional marks and further juniors:

Athlete	Mark	Pos	Meet	Venue	Date	Mark	Pos	Meet	Venue	Date
Kipchirchir 4+	3:33.40	2	DNG	Stockholm	5 Aug	3:34.70	8	Gaz	Saint-Denis	4 Jul
	3:34.15	1		San Sebastián	10 Aug	3:34.77	4		Milano	3 Jun
Songok	3:33.52	1		Dortmund	15 Jun	3:34.39	10	WCh	Saint-Denis	27 Aug
	3:33.71	2		Milano	3 Jun	3:34.85	12	VD	Bruxelles	5 Sep
	3:33.74	3	DNG	Stockholm	5 Aug	3:35.01	1		Rehlingen	9 Jun

Mark	Name		Nat	Born	Pos	Meet	Venue	Date
3:39.67	Samuel	Dadi	ETH	.85	2		Rennes	7 Jun
3:40.17	Abdallah	Abdelkadir	SUD-Y	87	1	Af-AsG	Hyderabad	29 Oct
3:40.21	Josephat Muchiri	Ndambiri	KEN	12.2.85	1		Nagasaki	30 Jul
3:40.21	Peter	Roko Ashak	SUD	84	2	Af-AsG	Hyderabad	29 Oct
3:41.17	Seifu	Nefsie	ETH	85	6B	NA	Heusden	2 Aug
3:41.21	Onésphore	Nkunzimana	BDI	23.7.85	3		Gent	23 Jul
3:41.28	Samson	Kiplangat Ngetich	KEN-Y	10.11.86	8B		Zurich	15 Aug
3:41.32	Francois	Pretorius	RSA	11.2.84	3	NC	Port Elizabeth	26 Apr
3:42.59	John	Kariuki	KEN-Y	10.11.86	2		Nagasaki	30 Jul
3:42.6	Tesfu	Bikila (20)	ETH-Y	.86	1	Afr-j	Garoua	2 Aug

Best European: 3:44.35 Patrick Schulz GER 28.5.84 1 Mannheim 21 Jun

1 MILE

Mark	Name		Nat	Born	Pos	Meet	Venue	Date
3:48.17	Paul	Korir	KEN	15.7.77	1	GP	London (CP)	8 Aug
3:50.20	Hicham	El Guerrouj	MAR	14.9.74	1	GP II	Rieti	7 Sep
3:50.21	Bernard	Lagat	KEN	12.12.74	1	Pre	Eugene	24 May
3:50.25	Alex	Kipchirchir	KEN-J	26.11.84	2	GP II	Rieti	7 Sep
3:50.39	James	Kwalia	KEN-J	12.6.84	1	FBK	Hengelo	1 Jun
3:50.40	Cornelius	Chirchir	KEN	7.10.83	2	GP	London (CP)	8 Aug
3:50.98	Robert	Rono	KEN	11.10.74	3	GP II	Rieti	7 Sep
3:51.39	Gert-Jan	Liefers	NED	26.9.78	2	FBK	Hengelo	1 Jun
3:51.98	Rui	Silva	POR	3.8.77	4	GP II	Rieti	7 Sep
3:52.18	William (10/10)	Chirchir	KEN	6.2.79	5	GP II	Rieti	7 Sep
3:52.34	Tarek	Boukensa	ALG	19.11.81	6	GP II	Rieti	7 Sep
3:52.66	Anas	Selmouni	MAR	15.3.79	3	FBK	Hengelo	1 Jun
3:52.89	Benjamin	Kipkurui	KEN	28.12.80	4	FBK	Hengelo	1 Jun
3:53.29	Hillary	Chenonge	KEN-J	30.5.85	5	FBK	Hengelo	1 Jun
3:53.34	Kevin	Sullivan	CAN	20.3.74	2	Pre	Eugene	24 May
3:53.69	Michael	Too	KEN	3.8.83	6	FBK	Hengelo	1 Jun
3:53.74	Vyacheslav	Shabunin	RUS	27.9.69	7	FBK	Hengelo	1 Jun
3:53.86	Graham	Davidson	RSA	14.10.78	8	FBK	Hengelo	1 Jun
3:54.07	Laban	Rotich	KEN	20.1.69	1		Victoria	11 Jun
3:54.26	David (20)	Lelei	KEN	10.5.71	4	Pre	Eugene	24 May
3:54.39	Hudson	de Souza	BRA	25.2.77	5	Pre	Eugene	24 May
3:54.40	Adrian	Blincoe	NZL	4.11.79	8	GP II	Rieti	7 Sep
3:54.43	Jason	Lunn	USA	19.9.74	6	Pre	Eugene	24 May
3:54.62	James	Nolan	IRL	27.1.77	9	GP II	Rieti	7 Sep
3:54.93	John	Mayock	GBR	26.10.70	9	FBK	Hengelo	1 Jun
3:54.94	Anthony	Whiteman	GBR	13.11.71	4	GP	London (CP)	8 Aug
3:55.37	Tom	Mayo	GBR	2.5.77	5	GP	London (CP)	8 Aug
3:56.02	Graham	Hood	CAN	2.4.72	2		Victoria	11 Jun
3:56.23	Youcef	Abdi	AUS	7.12.77	8	Pre	Eugene	24 May
3:56.78	Sergio (30)	Gallardo	ESP	22.3.79	10	GP II	Rieti	7 Sep
3:56.97	Luke	Kipkosgei	KEN	27.11.75	4		Victoria	11 Jun

Mark	Name		Nat	Born	Pos	Meet	Venue	Date
3:57.07	Adam	Goucher	USA	18.2.75	5		Victoria	11 Jun

Mark	Name		Nat	Born	Date
3:58.59	Mike	Power	AUS	9.5.76	4 Jun
3:58.79	Noah	Ngeny	KEN	2.11.78	24 May
3:58.81	Marco	Koers	NED	3.11.72	1 Jun
3:58.84	Alan	Webb	USA	13.1.83	24 May
3:58.99	David	Kiplak	KEN	27.12.81	15 Aug
3:59.49	Ibrahim	Aden	USA	11.11.82	24 May
3:59.61	Boaz	Cheboiywo	KEN	2.8.78	26 Apr
3:59.64	Mark	Fountain	AUS	10.3.82	24 May
3:59.69	Michael	Stember	USA	30.1.78	26 Apr
3:59.83	Dan	Wilson	USA	19.2.79	5 Jul
3:59.94	Abdelkader	Hachlaf (43)	MAR	3.7.78	8 Aug

Indoors

Mark	Name		Nat	Born	Pos	Meet	Venue	Date
3:55.70	Graham	Hood	CAN	2.4.72	3		Fayetteville	15 Feb

Mark	Name		Nat	Born	Date
3:57.71	James	Thie	GBR	27.6.78	15 Feb
3:57.83 #	Luke	Watson	USA	20.8.80	8 Feb
3:57.96 #	Nathan	Brannen	CAN	8.9.82	8 Feb
3:58.07 #	Boaz	Cheboiywo	KEN	2.8.78	8 Feb
3:58.15 #	Nick	Willis	NZL	25.4.83	8 Feb
3:58.24 #	Ian	Connor	USA	30.8.79	8 Feb
3:58.40 #	Michael	Stember	USA	30.1.78	15 Feb
3:58.64 #	Rob	Myers	USA	5.8.80	8 Feb
3:58.72	Eliud	Njubi	KEN	27.7.79	15 Feb
3:58.94	Chris	Mulvaney	GBR	25.5.81	15 Feb
3:58.95 #	Grant	Robison	USA	27.9.78	8 Mar
3:59.72	Ryan	Hayden	CAN	27.1.82	15 Feb
3:59.94	Alistair	Cragg	IRL	13.6.80	2 Mar
3:59.99	Jason	Long	USA	23.10.78	15 Feb

JUNIORS

See main list for top 3 Juniors. 4 performances by 3 men to 3:54.0. Additional marks and further juniors:

Kipchirchir 3:53.73 3 Pre Eugene 24 May

Mark	Name		Nat	Born	Pos	Meet	Venue	Date
4:00.84	Abdallah	Abdelkadir	SUD-Y	.87	3		Dublin (S)	15 Aug
4:01.02	Steve	Magness	USA	11.10.84	14	Pre	Eugene	24 May

2000 METRES

Mark	Name		Nat	Born	Pos	Meet	Venue	Date
4:57.76	Robert	Rono	KEN	11.10.74	1		Naimette	2 Sep
4:58.22	Isaac	Songok	KEN-J	25.4.84	2		Naimette	2 Sep
4:58.72	Adrian	Blincoe	NZL	4.11.79	3		Naimette	2 Sep
4:59.06	Suleiman	Simotwo	KEN	21.4.80	4		Naimette	2 Sep
4:59.11	James	Kwalia	KEN-J	12.6.84	5		Naimette	2 Sep
4:59.52	Timothy	Kiptanui	KEN	5.1.80	6		Naimette	2 Sep
5:00.21	Benjamin	Kipkurui	KEN	28.12.80	7		Naimette	2 Sep
5:00.64	Samwel	Mwera	TAN-J	3.6.85	8		Naimette	2 Sep
5:00.82+	Benjamin	Limo	KEN	23.8.74	1	in 3k	Bruxelles	5 Sep
5:01.1+	Eliud	Kipchoge	KEN-J	5.11.84	2	in 3k	Bruxelles	5 Sep

Mark	Name		Nat	Born	Date
5:01.48	Marius	Bakken	NOR	27.3.78	31 May
5:01.7+	John	Kibowen	KEN	21.4.69	5 Sep
5:01.8+	Ali	Saïdi Sief	ALG	15.3.78	5 Sep
5:03.13	Ali Nabil	Maataoui	MAR	11.12.80	31 May

Indoors

Mark	Name		Nat	Born	Pos	Meet	Venue	Date
4:58.53i+	Laban	Rotich	KEN	20.1.69	1	in 3k	Karlsruhe	28 Feb
4:58.6+i	Haile	Gebrselassie	ETH	18.4.73	2	in 3k	Karlsruhe	28 Feb
5:01.31+i	Hicham	El Guerrouj	MAR	14.9.74	1	in 2M	Liévin	23 Feb

Mark	Name		Nat	Born	Date
5:01.37i+	Gert-Jan	Liefers	NED	26.9.78	21 Feb
5:02.82i	Alberto	García ¶	ESP	22.2.71	22 Feb

JUNIORS

See main list for top 4 Juniors. 5 performances by 4 men to 5:02.0. Additional mark and further junior:

Kwalia 5:01.4 3+ in 3k Bruxelles 5 Sep

Mark	Name		Nat	Born	Pos	Meet	Venue	Date
5:05.26	Ken Koima	Komen	KEN	.84	3		Florø	31 May

3000 METRES

Mark	Name		Nat	Born	Pos	Meet	Venue	Date
7:30.23	Hicham	El Guerrouj	MAR	14.9.74	1	Nebiolo	Torino	6 Jun
7:30.79	Ali	Saïdi Sief	ALG	15.3.78	1	VD	Bruxelles	5 Sep
7:30.91	Eliud	Kipchoge	KEN-J	5.11.84	2	VD	Bruxelles	5 Sep
7:32.01	John	Kibowen	KEN	21.4.69	3	VD	Bruxelles	5 Sep
7:33.13	Benjamin	Limo	KEN	23.8.74	4	VD	Bruxelles	5 Sep
7:35.53	James	Kwalia	KEN-J	12.6.84	5	VD	Bruxelles	5 Sep
7:36.98	Kenenisa	Bekele	ETH	13.6.82	1	WAF	Monaco	13 Sep
7:37.64	Luke	Kipkosgei	KEN	27.11.75	6	VD	Bruxelles	5 Sep
7:37.65+	Paul	Bitok	KEN	26.6.70	1	in 5k	Ostrava	12 Jun
7:38.0+	Stephen	Cherono (10)	KEN	15.10.82	-	in 5k	Ostrava	12 Jun
	(later Saïd Saaeed Shaheen QAT)							
7:38.21		Kibowen			2	WAF	Monaco	13 Sep
7:38.36	Leonard	Mucheru	KEN	13.6.78	1	ISTAF	Berlin (P)	10 Aug
	(later Mushir Salem Jawher BRN)							
7:38.48	Paul Kipsiele	Koech	KEN	10.11.81	1	GP II	Rieti	7 Sep
7:39.23		Kwalia			2	ISTAF	Berlin (P)	10 Aug
7:39.28	Abraham	Chebii	KEN	23.12.79	2	WAF	Monaco	13 Sep
	(15/13)							
7:40.82	Pius	Muli	KEN	15.12.82	4	GP II	Rieti	7 Sep
7:41.41	Abiyote	Abate	ETH	20.11.80	2	GP II	Sevilla	7 Jun
7:41.83	Saïd	Bérioui	MAR	3.6.75	3	Nebiolo	Torino	6 Jun
7:41.89	Charles	Kamathi	KEN	18.5.78	4	Nebiolo	Torino	6 Jun
7:42.82	Elijah	Maru	KEN	12.6.76	5	Nebiolo	Torino	6 Jun
7:43.04	Hillary	Chenonge	KEN-J	30.5.85	6	Nebiolo	Torino	6 Jun

Mark	Name		Nat	Born	Pos	Meet	Venue	Date
7:43.09	Mohamed Saïd	El Wardi	MAR	19.4.72	7	Nebiolo	Torino	6 Jun
	(20)							
7:43.24	Carles	Castillejo	ESP	18.8.78	4	GP II	Sevilla	7 Jun
7:43.57	Juan Carlos	de la Ossa	ESP	25.11.76	5	GP II	Sevilla	7 Jun
7:43.63	Khoudir	Aggoune	ALG	5.1.81	5	ISTAF	Berlin (P)	10 Aug
7:43.89	Zersenay	Tadesse	ERI	8.2.82	6	GP II	Sevilla	7 Jun
7:43.93	Dieter	Baumann	GER	9.2.65	6	ISTAF	Berlin (P)	10 Aug
7:44.57+	Shadrack	Korir	KEN	14.12.78	1	in 5k	London (CP)	5 Aug
7:44.62+	Haile	Gebrselassie	ETH	18.4.73	1	in 5k	Saint-Denis	4 Jul
7:44.70	Joseph	Kosgei	KEN	25.8.74	5	GP II	Rieti	7 Sep
7:45.05	Wolfram	Müller	GER	8.7.81	1		Dessau	30 May
7:45.07	Solomon	Bushendich	KEN-J	10.1.84	8	Nebiolo	Torino	6 Jun
	(30)							
7:45.1+	Sammy	Kipketer	KEN	29.9.81	+	in 5k	London (CP)	5 Aug
7:45.35	Manuel Ángel	Penas	ESP	9.11.77	7	GP II	Sevilla	7 Jun
7:45.41	Mohammed	Amyn	MAR	25.3.76	1		Rabat	14 Jun
7:45.59	Moses	Kigen	KEN	22.4.73	2		Dessau	30 May
7:45.70	Moses	Mosop	KEN-J	17.7.85	2		Luzern	25 Jun
7:45.7+	Sileshi	Sihine	ETH	29.1.83	3	in 5k	Oslo	27 Jun
7:45.9+	Salah	Hissou	MAR	16.1.72	6+	in 5k	Oslo	27 Jun
7:45.94	Mourad	Maaroufit	MAR	.82	2		Rabat	14 Jun
7:45.96	Shadrack	Kosgei	KEN-J	.84	2	GP II	Gresham	17 May
7:46.0	José Antonio	Redolat	ESP	17.2.76	1		Burjassot	21 May
	(40)							
7:46.21	Bernard	Barmasai	KEN	6.5.74	6	GP II	Rieti	7 Sep
7:46.22	Jan	Fitschen	GER	2.5.77	3		Dessau	30 May
7:46.34	Jesús	España	ESP	21.8.78	8	GP II	Sevilla	7 Jun
7:46.36	M Abdelhak	Zakaria	BRN	20.7.74	1		Arras	28 Jun
7:46.49	Abel	Cheruiyot	KEN-J	26.12.84	10	Nebiolo	Torino	6 Jun
	(later Abel Yagut BRN)							
7:46.57	Tim	Broe	USA	20.6.77	3	GP II	Gresham	17 May
7:46.7	Bouabdellah	Tahri	FRA	20.12.78	2		Burjassot	21 May
7:46.7+	Albert	Chepkurui	KEN	4.4.81	9+	in 5k	Oslo	27 Jun
	(later Abdullah Hassan QAT)							
7:46.72	Abderrahim	Goumri	MAR	21.5.76	3		Rabat	14 Jun
7:46.8+	Gebre-egziabher	Gebremariam	ETH-J	10.9.84	7	in 5k	Saint-Denis	31 Aug
	(50)							
7:46.95	Michael	Power	AUS	9.5.76	4	GP II	Gresham	17 May
7:47.0+ ?	Francis	Kiprop	KEN	4.6.82	10+	in 5k	Oslo	27 Jun
7:47.16	Boniface	Kiprop	UGA-J	12.10.85	3		Luzern	25 Jun
7:47.36	David	Kiplak	KEN	27.12.81	7	ISTAF	Berlin (P)	10 Aug
7:47.38	Pablo	Villalobos	ESP	20.5.78	9	GP II	Sevilla	7 Jun
7:47.46	Adrian	Blincoe	NZL	4.11.79	4	GP II	Helsinki	18 Aug
7:47.47	John	Mayock	GBR	26.10.70	5	GP II	Helsinki	18 Aug
7:47.68	Jonathon	Riley	USA	29.12.78	5	GP II	Gresham	17 May
7:48.38	Suleiman	Simotwo	KEN	21.4.80	8	ISTAF	Berlin (P)	10 Aug
7:48.50	Onésphore	Nkunzimana	BDI-J	23.7.85	1		Oordegem	16 Aug
	(60)							
7:48.53	Martin	Keino	KEN	20.6.72	3	GP II	Stanford	7 Jun
7:48.6+	Ismaïl	Sghyr	FRA	16.3.72		in 5k	Saint-Denis	4 Jul
7:48.72	Adam	Goucher	USA	18.2.75	4	GP II	Stanford	7 Jun
7:48.76	Craig	Mottram	AUS	18.6.80	8	WAF	Monaco	13 Sep
7:48.78	Abdelhalim	Zahraoui	MAR	18.2.83	4		Rabat	14 Jun
7:48.81	Mebrahtom	Keflezighi	USA	5.5.75	9	ISTAF	Berlin (P)	10 Aug
7:49.09	Sergey	Lebed	UKR	15.7.75	10	ISTAF	Berlin (P)	10 Aug
7:49.26	Monder	Rizki	BEL	16.8.79	2		Oordegem	16 Aug
7:49.36	Erik	Sjöqvist	SWE	4.12.72	6	GP II	Helsinki	18 Aug
7:49.41	Wilson Kipkoskei	Chemweno	KEN	.78/79	4		Rehlingen	9 Jun
	(70)							
7:49.48	Khalid	Zoubaa	FRA	27.4.77	7	GP II	Helsinki	18 Aug
7:49.55	David	Chemweno	KEN	18.12.81	8	GP II	Helsinki	18 Aug
7:49.67	Mario	Kröckert	GER	2.3.78	4		Dessau	30 May
7:49.75	Ridha	Amri	TUN	16.12.76	6		Rehlingen	9 Jun
7:49.8	Hicham	Bellani	MAR	15.9.79	1		Meknès	24 May
7:49.88	Freddy	González	VEN	7.10.77	4	GP	Madrid (C)	19 Jul

7:50.05	Markos	Geneti	ETH-J	30.5.84	17 May
7:50.05	Salah	El Ghazi	MAR	2.11.75	19 Jul
7:50.09	Richard	Geemi	KEN	23.8.73	19 Jul
7:50.14	Ridouane	Es-Saadi	BEL	1.1.76	16 Aug
7:50.44	Michael	May	GER	21.8.79	30 May
7:50.54	Jari	Matinlauri	FIN	5.2.78	18 Aug
7:50.71	Eliseo	Martín	ESP	5.11.73	19 Jul
7:50.76	Steve	Slattery	USA	14.8.80	7 Jun
7:50.76	Saud	Al-Thubaiti	KSA	15.7.80	14 Jun
7:50.80	Abraham	Tandoi	KEN	12.12.74	9 Jun
7:51.32	Christian	Belz	SUI	11.9.74	7 Sep
7:51.52	Augustine	Kiprono Choge	KEN-Y	21.1.87	10 Aug

Mark	Name		Nat	Born	Date
7:51.57	Chris	Thompson	GBR	17.4.81	13 Jul
7:52.09	William	Kirui	KEN	5.8.82	17 May
7:52.15	Jorge	Torres	USA	22.8.80	18 Aug
7:52.26	Michael	Aish	NZL	24.7.76	7 Jun
7:52.26	Andrew	Graffin	GBR	20.12.77	13 Jul
7:52.40	José Manuel	Martínez	ESP	22.10.71	7 Jun
7:52.46	James	Getanda	KEN	5.7.82	30 Jul
7:52.52	Daniel	Komen	KEN	17.5.76	25 Jun
7:52.67	Mike	Donnelly	USA	2.2.75	7 Jun
7:52.79	Philip	Mosima	KEN	2.1.77	9 Jun
7:53.27	Barnabas	Kosgei	KEN-Y	20.8.86	30 Jul
7:53.52	Takayuki	Matsumiya	JPN	21.2.80	30 Jul
	(100)				
7:53.58	Kazuyoshi	Tokumoto	JPN	22.6.79	18 Jun
7:53.75	Toshinari	Takaoka	JPN	24.9.70	18 Jun
7:53.77	Laban	Chege	KEN	10.9.69	18 May
7:53.84	David	Galván	MEX	6.4.73	17 May
7:53.90	Dalibor	Balgac	CRO	22.9.77	25 Jun
7:53.96	Mark	Bett	KEN	22.12.76	6 Jun
7:54.00	Sebastian	Hallmann	GER	7.1.77	18 May
7:54.2	Abderrahim	Hadji	MAR		10 May
7:54.24	Thorsten	Gombert	GER	12.5.78	30 May
7:54.27	Rui	Silva	POR	3.8.77	25 May
7:54.30	Zouhaïr	El Ouardi	MAR	15.2.77	16 Jul
7:54.31	Youcef	Abdi	AUS	7.12.77	19 Jul
7:54.34	Filmon	Ghirmai	GER	25.1.79	18 May
7:54.34	Sammy	Kiplagat	KEN	.73	19 Jul
7:54.69	Sander	Schutgens	NED	31.12.75	16 Aug
7:54.70	Joseph Koskei	Kipkemboi	KEN	25.8.74	16 Jul
7:54.71	Tariku	Bekele	ETH-Y	21.1.87	12 Jul
7:54.72	Tessema	Abshero	ETH-Y	9.12.86	16 Jul
7:54.81	Bob	Kennedy	USA	18.8.70	13 Jul
7:54.82	Antonio	Martínez	ESP	20.12.78	19 Jul
7:54.89	Moses	Waweru (121)	KEN	78	5 Jul

Indoors

Mark	Name		Nat	Born	Pos	Meet	Venue	Date
7:28.29	Haile	Gebrselassie	ETH	18.4.73	1		Karlsruhe	28 Feb
7:32.9+		Gebrselassie			1	in 2M	Birmingham	21 Feb
7:32.98	Alberto	García ¶	ESP	22.2.71	1		Sevilla	22 Feb
7:33.73		El Guerrouj			1	in 2M	Liévin	23 Feb
7:40.75	Abiyote	Abate	ETH	20.11.80	2		Karlsruhe	28 Feb
7:40.83	Markos	Geneti	ETH-J	30.5.84	3		Karlsruhe	28 Feb
7:40.85	Abderrahim	Goumri	MAR	21.5.76	2	Spark	Stuttgart	2 Feb
7:42.55	Rui	Silva	POR	3.8.77	1		Stockholm	18 Feb
7:42.70	Jesús	España	ESP	21.8.78	3	WI	Birmingham	16 Mar
7:44.19	Günther	Weidlinger	AUT	5.4.78	3		Stockholm	18 Feb
7:44.27	Hailu	Mekonnen	ETH	4.4.80	4	Spark	Stuttgart	2 Feb
7:44.34	Gert-Jan	Liefers	NED	26.9.78	5	WI	Birmingham	16 Mar
7:45.22	Alistair	Cragg	IRL	13.6.80	1		Boston (R)	1 Feb
7:45.32	John	Mayock	GBR	26.10.70	7	WI	Birmingham	16 Mar
7:46.21	Noah	Ngeny	KEN	2.11.78	2		Boston (R)	1 Feb
7:47.77	Isaac	Viciosa	ESP	26.12.69	3		Sevilla	22 Feb
7:47.96	Vyacheslav	Shabunin	RUS	27.9.69	4		Boston (R)	1 Feb
7:49.35	Mark	Bett	KEN	22.12.76	5		Stockholm	18 Feb
7:49.40	Yusef	El Nasri	ESP	28.7.79	4		Gent	9 Feb
7:49.68 #	Bolote	Asmeron	USA	12.10.78	1		Seattle	1 Feb

Mark	Name		Nat	Born	Date
7:50.44	Lorenzo	Perrone	ITA	26.9.81	2 Mar
7:50.65	Michael	Aish	NZL	24.7.76	1 Feb
7:50.94	Luís	Feiteira	POR	21.4.73	18 Feb
7:51.34	Sergio	Gallardo	ESP	22.3.79	22 Feb
7:51.39	Daniel	Lincoln	USA	22.10.80	1 Feb
7:51.59	Jaouad	Gharib	MAR	22.5.72	14 Mar
7:51.74	Tom	Mayo	GBR	2.5.77	18 Feb
7:52.40	Boaz	Cheboiywo	KEN	2.8.78	15 Feb
7:52.40 #	Kip	Kangogo	KEN	20.7.79	8 Mar
7:53.33	Mohamed	Khaldi	ALG	3.5.75	14 Mar
7:54.13 #	Jeremy	Park	USA	8.12.79	15 Feb
7:54.35 #	Lyle	Weese	USA	26.10.79	8 Mar
7:54.41	Girma	Tola	ETH	13.10.75	31 Jan
7:54.67	Martin	Pröll	AUT	21.3.81	18 Feb
7:54.70	Salvatore	Vincenti	ITA	5.3.72	2 Mar
7:54.78	Antonio	Martínez	ESP	20.12.78	1 Mar
7:54.92	Reuben	Kosgei	KEN	2.8.79	5 Feb
7:54.93	Berhanu	Adane	ETH	7.9.75	1 Feb

MEN 2003

JUNIORS

See main list for top 10 juniors. 16 performances by 8 men to 7:47.0 (plus 2 indoors). Additional marks and further juniors:

Kipchoge 7:45.1+ 4 in 5k Saint-Denis 4 Jul; 7:45.6+ 2 in 5k Saint-Denis 31 Aug
7:45.8+ 5 in 5k Oslo 27 Jun
Kwalia 2+ 7:41.40 5 WAF Monaco 13 Sep; 7:46.1+ 7 in 5k Oslo 27 Jun
7:42.20 3 GP Sevilla 7 Jun
Chenonge 7:46.37 7 Rieti 7 Sep
Geneti 7:46.59i 3 Boston (R) 1 Feb

Mark	Name		Nat	Born	Pos	Meet	Venue	Date
7:50.05	Markos	Geneti	ETH	30.5.84	6	GP II	Gresham	17 May
7:51.52	Augustine	Kiprono Choge	KEN-Y	21.1.87	11		Berlin	10 Aug
7:53.27	Barnabas	Kosgei	KEN-Y	20.8.86	2		Tallinn	30 Jul
7:54.71	Tariku	Bekele	ETH-Y	21.1.87	2	WY	Sherbrooke	12 Jul
7:54.72	Tessema	Abshero	ETH-Y	9.12.86	4		Reims	16 Jul
7:55.12	Shimelis	Girma	ETH-Y	12.6.87	3	WY	Sherbrooke	12 Jul
7:55.39	Denis Keter	Kipkirui	KEN	24.3.84	2r1	Kuso	Warszawa	15 Jun
7:56.30	William Kimeli	Tarus	KEN-Y	7.6.87	4	WY	Sherbrooke	12 Jul
7:57.17	Jean-Claude	Nduwingoma	BDI-Y	10.7.88	3h1	WY	Sherbrooke	10 Jul
7:58.03	Yassine	Mandour (20)	MAR	21.1.85	7		Rabat	14 Jun

Best European: 8:05.94 Jérémy Pierrat FRA 7.2.84 9 Pézenas 31 May

2 MILES

Indoors

Mark	Name		Nat	Born	Pos	Meet	Venue	Date
8:04.69	Haile	Gebrselassie	ETH	18.4.73	1	GP	Birmingham	21 Feb
8:06.61	Hicham	El Guerrouj	MAR	14.9.74	1		Liévin	23 Feb
8:16.57	Luke	Kipkosgei	KEN	27.11.75	2	GP	Birmingham	21 Feb
8:16.59	Hailu	Mekonnen	ETH	4.4.80	3	GP	Birmingham	21 Feb
8:19.08	Abiyote	Abate	ETH	20.11.80	4	GP	Birmingham	21 Feb

Mark	Name		Nat	Born	Pos	Meet	Venue	Date
8:22.52	John	Mayock	GBR	26.10.70	5	GP	Birmingham	21 Feb

8:28.25	Laban	Rotich	KEN	20.1.69	23 Feb	8:29.75	Khoudir	Aggoune	ALG	5.1.81	23 Feb
8:28.26	Driss	Maazouzi	FRA	20.10.69	23 Feb	8:30.08	Kevin	Sullivan	CAN	20.3.74	23 Feb
8:28.28	Mohamed	Amyn	MAR	25.5.76	23 Feb	8:31.57	Saïd	Chébili	FRA	6.5.73	23 Feb
8:29.13	Martin	Keino	KEN	20.6.72	21 Feb	8:33.01	Luís	Feiteira	POR	21.4.73	21 Feb

JUNIORS

8:36.59	Onésphore	Nkunzimana	BDI	23.7.85	1		Woluwe	14 Jun

5000 METRES

12:48.81	Stephen	Cherono	KEN	15.10.82	1	GS	Ostrava	12 Jun
	(Saïf Saaeed Shaheen QAT from August)							
12:50.24	Hicham	El Guerrouj	MAR	14.9.74	2	GS	Ostrava	12 Jun
12:52.26	Kenenisa	Bekele	ETH	13.6.82	1	Bisl	Oslo	27 Jun
12:52.33	Sammy	Kipketer	KEN	29.9.81	2	Bisl	Oslo	27 Jun
12:52.61	Eliud	Kipchoge	KEN-J	5.11.84	3	Bisl	Oslo	27 Jun
12:52.79		Kipchoge			1	WCh	Saint-Denis	31 Aug
12:52.83		El Guerrouj			2	WCh	Saint-Denis	31 Aug
12:52.99	Abraham	Chebii	KEN	23.12.79	4	Bisl	Oslo	27 Jun
12:53.12		Bekele			3	WCh	Saint-Denis	31 Aug
12:53.37		Chebii			1	Gaz	Saint-Denis	4 Jul
12:54.07	John	Kibowen	KEN	21.4.69	4	WCh	Saint-Denis	31 Aug
12:54.36	Haile	Gebrselassie	ETH	18.4.73	2	Gaz	Saint-Denis	4 Jul
12:54.58	James	Kwalia	KEN-J	12.6.84	5	Bisl	Oslo	27 Jun
12:54.99	Benjamin	Limo (10)	KEN	23.8.74	3	Gaz	Saint-Denis	4 Jul
12:55.52		Kipchoge			4	Gaz	Saint-Denis	4 Jul
12:56.27	Albert	Chepkurui	KEN	4.4.81	6	Bisl	Oslo	27 Jun
	(lAbdullah Hassan QAT from August)							
12:57.14		Chebii			1	GGala	Roma	11 Jul
12:57.23		Gebrselassie			1	GP	London (GP)	8 Aug
12:57.34		Bekele			2	GGala	Roma	11 Jul
12:57.74		Chebii			5	WCh	Saint-Denis	31 Aug
12:58.08	Gebre-egziabher	Gebremariam	ETH-J	10.9.84	6	WCh	Saint-Denis	31 Aug
12:59.13		Kipketer			2	GP	London (GP)	8 Aug
12:59.15	Salah	Hissou	MAR	16.1.72	5	Gaz	Saint-Denis	4 Jul
12:59.74		Kibowen			3	GP	London (GP)	8 Aug
13:00.32		Gebrselassie			3	GGala	Roma	11 Jul
13:00.63		Kipchoge			1	DNG	Stockholm	5 Aug
13:01.01		Kibowen			1	WK	Zürich	15 Aug
13:01.13	Richard	Limo	KEN	18.11.80	7	WCh	Saint-Denis	31 Aug
13:01.14	Nicholas	Kemboi	KEN	25.11.83	2	WK	Zürich	15 Aug
13:01.44		Kipketer			3	WK	Zürich	15 Aug
13:01.76	Leonard	Mucheru	KEN	13.6.78	4	WK	Zürich	15 Aug
	(later Mushir Salem Jawher BRN)							
13:02.44		Mucheru			2	DNG	Stockholm	5 Aug
	(32/16)							
13:03.19		Gebremariam			6	Gaz	Saint-Denis	4 Jul
13:03.79		Kwalia			5	WK	Zürich	15 Aug
13:04.20		Hassan			3	DNG	Stockholm	5 Aug
13:04.39		Chebii			6	WK	Zürich	15 Aug
13:04.65		Hassan	QAT		7	WK	Zürich	15 Aug
13:04.72		Kwalia			3	GS	Ostrava	12 Jun
13:05.13	Abiyote	Abate	ETH	20.11.80	4	GS	Ostrava	12 Jun
13:05.57	Zersenay	Tadesse	ERI	8.2.82	8	WCh	Saint-Denis	31 Aug
13:05.81	Abderrahim	Goumri	MAR	21.5.76	4	DNG	Stockholm	5 Aug
	(20)							
13:06.53	Sileshi	Sihine	ETH	29.1.83	6	GGala	Roma	11 Jul
13:06.92	Luke	Kipkosgei	KEN	27.11.75	7	Gaz	Saint-Denis	4 Jul
13:10.16	Hailu	Mekonnen	ETH	4.4.80	8	GGala	Roma	11 Jul
13:10.79	Ismaïl	Sghyr	FRA	16.3.72	8	Gaz	Saint-Denis	4 Jul
13:11.75	Moses	Mosop	KEN-J	17.7.85	4	Athl	Lausanne	1 Jul
13:11.87	Markos	Geneti	ETH-J	30.5.84	6	DNG	Stockholm	5 Aug
13:12.16	Christian	Belz	SUI	11.9.74	2	NA	Heusden	2 Aug
13:12.24	Shadrack	Kosgei	KEN-J	.84	3	Pre	Eugene	24 May
13:12.83	Solomon	Bushendich	KEN-J	10.1.84	2		Milano	3 Jun
13:14.03	Paul	Bitok	KEN	26.6.70	1		Villeneuve d'Ascq	15 Jun
	(30)							
13:14.05	Dejene	Berhanu	ETH	.80	1		San Sebastián	10 Aug
13:14.60	Assefa	Mezgebu	ETH	19.6.78	10	GGala	Roma	11 Jul

Mark	Name		Nat	Born	Pos	Meet	Venue	Date
13:14.75	Benjamin	Maiyo	KEN	6.10.78	3		Milano	3 Jun
13:15.03	Hicham	Bellani	MAR	15.9.79	4		San Sebastián	10 Aug
13:15.07	Dieter	Baumann	GER	9.2.65	9	WK	Zürich	15 Aug
13:15.09	Pius	Muli	KEN	15.12.82	1		Rovereto	10 Sep
13:15.11	Joseph	Kosgei	KEN	25.8.74	2		Rovereto	10 Sep
13:15.15	Sergey	Lebed	UKR	15.7.75	9	DNG	Stockholm	5 Aug
13:15.33	Charles	Kamathi	KEN	18.5.78	6	GS	Ostrava	12 Jun
13:15.91	Khoudir	Aggoune	ALG	5.1.81	4		Villeneuve d'Ascq	15 Jun
	(40)							
13:16.21	Boniface	Kiprop	UGA-J	12.10.85	8	GS	Ostrava	12 Jun
13:16.42	Mark	Bett	KEN	22.12.76	5		San Sebastián	10 Aug
13:16.71	David	Kilel	KEN-J	21.5.84	2		Sotteville	8 Jul
13:16.92	Shadrack	Korir	KEN	14.12.78	5		Villeneuve d'Ascq	15 Jun
13:17.54	Francis	Kiprop	KEN	4.6.82	11	Bisl	Oslo	27 Jun
13:17.7+	John Cheruiyot	Korir	KEN	13.12.81	9	in 10k	Bruxelles	5 Sep
	13:22.78				14	DNG	Stockholm	5 Aug
13:17.81	Craig	Mottram	AUS	18.6.80	3		Rovereto	10 Sep
13:18.0+	John	Yuda	TAN	9.6.79	10	in 10k	Bruxelles	5 Sep
13:18.13	Alejandro	Suárez	MEX	30.11.80	2		Victoria	11 Jun
13:18.19	M Abdelhak	Zakaria	BRN	20.7.74	3		Sotteville	8 Jul
	(50)							
13:19.22	Cathal	Lombard	IRL	12.2.76	5	NA	Heusden	2 Aug
13:19.29	Moses	Kigen	KEN	22.4.73	1		Naimette	2 Sep
13:19.58	José	Ríos	ESP	15.3.74	2		Barakaldo	5 Jul
13:19.95	Robert	Kipngetich	KEN		5		Milano	3 Jun
13:20.08	Augustine	Kiprono Choge	KEN-Y	21.1.87	6	NA	Heusden	2 Aug
13:20.46	Juan Carlos	de la Ossa	ESP	25.11.76	3		Barakaldo	5 Jul
13:20.50	Mebrahtom	Keflezighi	USA	5.5.75	12	DNG	Stockholm	5 Aug
13:20.91	Enock	Mitei	KEN	26.11.80	7	NA	Heusden	2 Aug
13:21.11	Moukhled	Al-Outaibi	KSA	30.4.80	13	DNG	Stockholm	5 Aug
13:21.85	Bob	Kennedy	USA	18.8.70	8	NA	Heusden	2 Aug
	(60)							
13:21.97	Hassan	Mourhit	BEL	2.1.82	9	NA	Heusden	2 Aug
13:22.23	Hillary	Chenonge	KEN-J	30.5.85	4		Naimette	2 Sep
13:22.40	Teodoro	Vega	MEX	14.7.76	3		Victoria	11 Jun
13:22.89	Fabiano	Joseph	TAN-J	24.12.85	8	Athl	Lausanne	1 Jul
13:22.89	El Hassan	Lahssini	FRA	1.1.75	13	Gaz	Saint-Denis	4 Jul
13:23.23	Bernard	Barmasai	KEN	6.5.74	5		Naimette	2 Sep
13:23.24	Erik	Sjöqvist	SWE	4.12.72	1		Kassel	13 Jun
13:23.25	Abdi	Abdirahman	USA	1.1.77	10	NA	Heusden	2 Aug
13:23.68	Loïc	Letellier	FRA	1.10.76	4		Sotteville	8 Jul
13:24.17	Jorge	Torres	USA	22.8.80	11	NA	Heusden	2 Aug
	(70)							
13:24.45	William	Kirui	KEN	5.8.82	5	GP	Osaka	10 May
13:24.51	Julius	Maina	KEN	14.10.77	1	Super	Yokohama	23 Sep
13:24.66	Toshinari	Takaoka	JPN	24.9.70	6	GP	Osaka	10 May
13:24.68	Simon	Maina Munyi	KEN	18.3.78	1	Jpn Ch	Yokohama	8 Jun
13:24.88	José Manuel	Martínez	ESP	22.10.71	14	Gaz	Saint-Denis	4 Jul
13:25.34	Mohammed	Amyn	MAR	25.3.76	15	Gaz	Saint-Denis	4 Jul
13:25.34	Abel	Cheruiyot/Yagut	KEN/BRN-J	26.12.84	6		Naimette	2 Sep
13:25.57	Carles	Castillejo	ESP	18.8.78	3		Barakaldo	5 Jul
13:25.59	Alistair	Cragg	IRL	13.6.80	1	MSR	Walnut	17 Apr
13:26.19	Kazuyoshi	Tokumoto	JPN	22.6.79	9	GP	Osaka	10 May
	(80)							
13:26.68	Jan	Fitschen	GER	2.5.77	3		Kassel	13 Jun
13:26.73	Wondimu	Mulugeta	ETH-J	.85	1		Chiba	24 Nov
13:26.78	Toshihiro	Iwasa	JPN	18.5.76	12	NA	Heusden	2 Aug
13:26.84	Tomohiro	Seto	JPN	19.10.76	10	GP	Osaka	10 May
13:26.87	Dennis	Jensen	DEN	11.9.69	13	NA	Heusden	2 Aug
13:27.18	John	Kariuki	KEN-Y	10.11.86	11	GP	Osaka	10 May
13:27.59	Khalid	El Amri	MAR	20.3.77	17	GGala	Roma	11 Jul
13:27.72	Julius	Gitahi	KEN	29.4.78	1		Sapporo	2 Jul
13:28.24	Manuel Angel	Penas	ESP	9.11.77	14	Bisl	Oslo	27 Jun
13:28.37	Jeff	Schiebler	CAN	1.6.73	3	MSR	Walnut	17 Apr
	(90)							
13:28.50	Ridha	Amri	TUN	16.12.76	1B	NA	Heusden	2 Aug
13:28.56	Daniel	Komen	KEN	17.5.76	10		Villeneuve d'Ascq	15 Jun
13:28.61	Justus	Kiprono Kipchirchir	KEN-Y	28.2.87	4		Rovereto	10 Sep
13:29.15	Marco	Mazza	ITA	25.6.77	5		Rovereto	10 Sep
13:29.16	Freddy	González	VEN	7.10.77	5		Barakaldo	5 Jul
13:29.19	James	Getanda	KEN	5.7.82	1		Cork	5 Jul

Mark	Name		Nat	Born	Pos	Meet	Venue	Date
13:29.24	Jesús	España	ESP	21.8.78	15	Bisl	Oslo	27 Jun
13:29.46	Kamiel	Maase	NED	20.10.71	2		Cork	5 Jul
13:29.55	Dema	Woyessa	ETH-Y	.86	6		Barakaldo	5 Jul
13:29.77	Boaz (100)	Cheboiywo	KEN	2.8.78	4	MSR	Walnut	17 Apr

13:30.06	Barnabas	Kosgei	KEN-Y	20.8.86	5 Jul
13:30.31	Mohamed Saïd	El Ouardi	MAR	19.4.72	12 Jun
13:30.52	Denis	Keter Kipkurui	KEN-J	24.3.84	5 Jul
13:30.65	Laban	Kagika	KEN	17.7.78	29 Apr
13:30.93	Philip	Korir	KEN	.83	2 Aug
13:31.24	James	Ndungu	KEN	30.4.79	10 May
13:31.46	Tsuyoshi	Ogata	JPN	11.5.73	10 May
13:31.64	Andrew	Graffin	GBR	20.12.77	5 Jul
13:31.67	Yuki	Nakamura	JPN	21.6.81	22 Jun
13:31.79	John	Mayock	GBR	26.10.70	8 Aug
13:31.80	Louis	Luchini	USA	24.5.81	17 Apr
13:31.80	Ignacio	Cáceres	ESP	18.6.76	10 Aug
13:31.95	Hosea	Kogo	KEN	11.8.72	13 Jun
13:32.30	Onésphone	Nkunzimana	BDI-J	23.7.85	2 Aug
13:32.53	Matthew	Kerr	CAN	3.5.76	11 Jun
13:32.76	Samuel	Kabiru	KEN	6.6.83	8 Jun
13:32.76	Ridouane	Es-Saadi	BEL	1.1.76	23 Aug
13:33.03	Mark	Tucker	AUS	15.8.79	20 Nov
13:33.09	David	Galván	MEX	6.4.73	24 May
13:33.09	James	Kosgei	KEN	.78	23 Aug
13:33.18	Abdulaziz	Al-Ameeri	QAT	.82	2 Aug
13:33.22	Ali	Al-Dawoodi	QAT-J		2 Aug
13:33.78	Marius	Bakken	NOR	27.3.78	27 Jun
13:34.93	Chris	Thompson	GBR	17.4.81	14 Jun
13:34.97	Driss	El Himer	FRA	4.4.74	24 Jul
13:35.23	Tim	Broe	USA	20.6.77	20 Jun
13:35.46	Pablo	Olmedo	MEX	8.5.75	17 Apr
13:35.67	Adam	Goucher	USA	18.2.75	20 Jun
13:36.0A	Philip	Kirui	KEN	11.9.73	10 Jul
13:36.14	Josephat	Muchiri Ndambiri	KEN-J	12.2.85	1 Aug
13:36.15	Martin	Keino	KEN	20.6.72	11 Jun
13:36.20	Satoshi	Irifune	JPN	14.12.75	22 Jun
13:36.33	Joseph Koskei	Kipkemboi	KEN	25.8.74	23 Aug
13:36.89	Chad	Johnson	USA	20.4.76	17 Apr
13:36.89	Yoshinari	Horikawa	JPN	19.6.75	2 Jul
13:36.96	Million	Wolde	ETH	17.3.79	27 Jun
13:37.08	Jonathon	Riley	USA	29.12.78	20 Jun
13:37.10	Rachid	Chékhémani	FRA	1.10.73	2 Aug
13:37.31	Daniel	Lincoln	USA	22.10.80	2 May
13:37.51	Jim	Svenøy	NOR	22.4.72	23 Aug
13:37.60	Mohamed	Khaldi	ALG	3.5.75	10 Aug
13:37.71	Ali Abdallah	Afringi	ERI	2.11.82	31 Jul
13:37.76	Dalibor	Balgac	CRO	22.9.77	17 Apr
13:37.79	Michael	Power	AUS	9.5.76	11 Jul
13:38.32	Hendrick	Ramaala	RSA	2.2.72	14 Feb
13:38.36	Dmitriy	Baranovskiy	UKR	28.7.79	3 Jul
13:38.41	Mohamed	Farah	GBR	23.3.83	8 Aug
13:38.57	Monder	Rizki	BEL	16.8.79	25 Jun
13:38.70	Daniel	Mwangi Muchunu	KEN-J	.84	29 Apr
13:38.73	Luke	Watson (150)	USA	20.8.80	17 Apr
13:38.81	Tomoaki	Kunichika	JPN	22.7.73	2 Jul
13:38.94	Brett	Cartwright	AUS	25.1.73	6 Feb
13:38.96	Masayuki	Obata	JPN	5.4.80	2 Jul
13:38.98	Samuel	Wanjiru	KEN-J	10.11.86	1 Aug
13:39.00	James	Mwangi	KEN-J	23.6.84	1 Aug
13:39.17	Dathan	Ritzenhein	USA	30.12.82	17 Apr
13:39.23	Ken-ichiro	Setoguchi	JPN	12.12.80	2 Jul
13:39.35	Nobuya	Matsunaga	JPN	8.11.74	10 May
13:39.56	Pablo	Villalobos	ESP	20.5.78	3 Aug
13:39.83	Abiyote	Endale	ETH		5 Jul
13:39.86	Mohamed	Awol	ETH-J	21.6.85	12 Apr
13:39.91	Linus	Maiyo	KEN	83	24 Apr
13:40.13	Koichiro	Nagata	JPN	19.12.78	2 Jul
13:40.17	Driss	Siguini	MAR		31 May
13:40.25	Koen	Raymakers	NED	31.1.80	23 Aug
13:40.29	Azzeddine	Zardouny	ALG		31 May
13:40.38	Takashi	Matsuyama	JPN	15.1.74	10 May
13:40.46	Mike	Donnelly	USA	2.2.75	17 Apr
13:40.48	Atsushi	Sato	JPN	8.5.78	29 Apr
13:40.72	Ramiro	Morán	ESP	17.5.69	5 Jul
13:40.92	Takayuki	Matsumiya	JPN	21.2.80	12 Apr
13:41.33	Ombeche	Mokamba	KEN	6.4.82	12 Apr
13:41.36	Christopher	Graff	USA	5.10.75	17 Apr
13:41.36	Yoji	Yamaguchi	JPN	12.6.75	22 Jun
13:41.53	Tatsumi	Morimasa	JPN	3.4.76	10 May
13:41.61	Christopher	Davies	GBR	19.10.76	14 Jun
13:41.61A	Albert	Okemwa	KEN	66	12 Jul
13:41.63	Ronald	Kipchumba Rutto	KEN-Y	8.10.87	10 Sep
13:41.74	Dean	Cavuoto	AUS	4.6.75	6 Feb
13:41.75	Obed	Mutanya	ZAM	10.8.81	17 Apr
13:41.81	David	Kariuki	KEN	23.5.80	29 Apr
13:41.82	Grant	Robison	USA	27.9.78	2 May
13:41.88	Matt	Gabrielson	USA	28.7.78	17 Apr
13:41.99	Spencer	Barden (184)	GBR	31.3.73	5 Jul

Indoors

13:11.39	Alberto	García ¶	ESP	22.2.71	1		Gent	9 Feb
13:29.26	Boaz	Cheboiywo	KEN	2.8.78	2	NCAA	Fayetteville	14 Mar

13:41.25	Richard	Kiplagat	KEN	5.1.81	14 Feb
13:41.74	Ben	Dawson	USA	29.12.79	14 Mar

JUNIORS

See main list for top 17 Juniors. 34 performances by 12 men to 13:24.0. Additional marks and further juniors:

Kipchoge 4+	13:11.01	1		Milano	3 Jun					
Kwalia	13:03.79	5	WK	Zürich	15 Aug	13:11.57	5	DNG	Stockholm	5 Aug
	13:04.72	3	GS	Ostrava	12 Jun					
Gebremariam	13:03.19	6	Gaz	Saint-Denis	4 Jul	13:14.54	9	Bisl	Oslo	27 Jun
	13:05.47	4		Reims	11 Jul	13:23.57	3	GP	Osaka	10 May
Mosop	13:16.53	1		Sevilla	8 Jul	13:18.36	4		Milano	3 Jun
	13:17.73	7		Villeneuve d'Ascq	15 Jun					
Geneti	13:13.27	4	Pre	Eugene	24 May	13:21.92	12	Bisl	Oslo	27 Jun
	13:20.38	12	GGala	Roma	11 Jul					
S Kosgei	13:16.47	1	PennR	Philadelphia	25 Apr	13:19.82	8		Villeneuve d'Ascq	15 Jun
Bushendich	13:16.02	7	GS	Ostrava	12 Jun					
Kilel	13:17.45	4	NA	Heusden	2 Aug	13:19.88	7	Athl	Lausanne	8 Jul

13:30.06	Barnabas	Kosgei	KEN-Y	20.8.86	3		Cork	5 Jul
13:30.52	Denis	Keter Kipkurui	KEN	24.3.84	5		Cork	5 Jul
13:32.30	Onésphone	Nkunzimana (20)	BDI	23.7.85	2B	NA	Heusden	2 Aug

Best European: 14:05.38 Jérémy Pierrat FRA 7.2.84 1 Carquefou 6 Jun

10,000 METRES

26:29.22	Haile	Gebrselassie	ETH	18.4.73	1	VD	Bruxelles	5 Sep
26:30.03	Nicholas	Kemboi	KEN	25.11.83	2	VD	Bruxelles	5 Sep
26:38.76	Abdullah (Formerly Albert Chepkurui KEN)	Hassan	QAT	4.4.81	3	VD	Bruxelles	5 Sep

Mark	Name		Nat	Born	Pos	Meet	Venue	Date
26:49.57	Kenenisa	Bekele	ETH	13.6.82	1	WCh	Saint-Denis	24 Aug
26:50.77		Gebrselassie			2	WCh	Saint-Denis	24 Aug
26:53.70		Bekele			1	FBK	Hengelo	1 Jun
26:54.58		Gebrselassie			2	FBK	Hengelo	1 Jun
26:56.63	Richard	Limo	KEN	18.11.80	4	VD	Bruxelles	5 Sep
26:58.76	Sileshi	Sihine	ETH	29.1.83	3	FBK	Hengelo	1 Jun
27:01.44		Sihine			3	WCh	Saint-Denis	24 Aug
27:09.83	John	Yuda	TAN	9.6.79	5	VD	Bruxelles	5 Sep
27:13.42	Sammy	Kipketer	KEN	29.9.81	6	VD	Bruxelles	5 Sep
27:13.66	Moses	Mosop	KEN-J	17.7.85	7	VD	Bruxelles	5 Sep
27:14.61	Dejene	Berhanu (10)	ETH	.80	8	VD	Bruxelles	5 Sep
27:15.88	Boniface	Kiprop	UGA-J	12.10.85	9	VD	Bruxelles	5 Sep
27:17.24	John Cheruiyot	Korir	KEN	13.12.81	10	VD	Bruxelles	5 Sep
27:18.28		Hassan			4	WCh	Saint-Denis	24 Aug
27:19.94		Korir			5	WCh	Saint-Denis	24 Aug
27:21.56	Paul	Kosgei	KEN	22.4.78	11	VD	Bruxelles	5 Sep
27:22.29	Simon	Maina Munyi	KEN	18.3.78	12	VD	Bruxelles	5 Sep
27:29.12	Charles	Kamathi	KEN	18.5.78	1	ESP Ch	Pontevedra	20 Jul
27:29.47		Kamathi			13	VD	Bruxelles	5 Sep
27:29.60	José	Ríos	ESP	15.3.74	2	NC	Pontevedra	20 Jul
27:30.56	José Manuel	Martínez	ESP	22.10.71	3	NC	Pontevedra	20 Jul
27:32.63	Fabiano	Joseph	TAN-J	24.12.85	14	VD	Bruxelles	5 Sep
27:32.81		Joseph			1	AAA	Watford	5 Jul
27:33.60	Wilberforce	Talel Kapkeny	KEN	10.1.80	6	WCh	Saint-Denis	24 Aug
27:37.49	Teodoro	Vega (20)	MEX	14.7.76	4	ESP Ch	Pontevedra	20 Jul
27:40.87	Julius	Gitahi	KEN	29.4.78	1		Okayama	27 Sep
27:40.9	Gilbert	Okari	KEN	2.7.78	1		Haverford	6 Aug
	(30/22)							
27:41.90	Alan	Culpepper	USA	15.9.72	1		Stanford	2 May
27:42.81	Julius	Maina	KEN	14.10.77	2		Okayama	27 Sep
27:43.07	Hendrick	Ramaala	RSA	2.2.72	1		Port Elizabeth	28 Feb
27:43.12	Gebre-egziabher	Gebremariam	ETH-J	10.9.84	2	Afr G	Abuja	12 Oct
27:43.16	Martin	Irungu Mathathi	KEN-J	25.12.85	1		Shizuoka	11 Oct
27:44.33	Shadrack	Hoff	RSA	19.5.73	2		Port Elizabeth	28 Feb
27:44.85	David	Galván	MEX	6.4.73	2		Stanford	2 May
27:45.14	Ismaïl	Sghyr	FRA	16.3.72	1	EChall	Athína (E)	12 Apr
	(30)							
27:45.20	Francis	Kipkoech-Bowen	KEN	12.10.73	2	NC	Watford	5 Jul
27:45.46	Kamiel	Maase	NED	20.10.71	8	WCh	Saint-Denis	24 Aug
27:46.47	Boaz	Cheboiywo	KEN	2.8.78	3		Stanford	2 May
27:46.53	David	Kariuki	KEN	23.5.80	3		Okayama	27 Sep
27:46.87	John	Kanyi	KEN	6.9.80	4		Okayama	27 Sep
27:47.89	Karl	Keska	GBR	7.5.72	9	WCh	Saint-Denis	24 Aug
27:50.55	Craig	Mottram	AUS	18.6.80	1	Zat	Melbourne	4 Dec
27:50.97	Takayuki	Matsumiya	JPN	21.2.80	3		Kobe	20 Apr
27:51.06	Bob	Kennedy	USA	18.8.70	15	VD	Bruxelles	5 Sep
27:51.27	Lee	Troop	AUS	22.3.73	1	NC	Inglewood	15 Feb
	(40)							
27:52.24	Abdi	Abdirahman	USA	1.1.77	4		Stanford	2 May
27:54.82	Dean	Cavuoto	AUS	4.6.75	2	NC	Inglewood	15 Feb
27:54.88	Kenta	Oshima	JPN	29.6.79	5		Okayama	27 Sep
27:56.80	Jonathan	Wyatt	NZL	20.12.72	3	NC	Inglewood	15 Feb
27:57.59	Mebrahtom	Keflezighi	USA	5.5.75	2	NC	Stanford	19 Jun
27:58.92	Philemon	Kemei	KEN	12.2.82	1		Rabat	14 Jun
27:58.98	Tomoo	Tsubota	JPN	16.6.77	1rA		Fukagawa	25 Jun
28:00.54	Jeff	Schiebler	CAN	1.6.73	5		Stanford	2 May
28:01.19	Michael	Aish	NZL	24.7.76	7		Stanford	2 May
28:01.88	Laban	Kagika	KEN	17.7.78	6		Okayama	27 Sep
	(50)							
28:02.09	Josphat Muchiri	Ndambiri	KEN-J	12.2.85	5		Kobe	20 Apr
28:02.34	Michael	Donnelly	USA	2.2.75	9		Stanford	2 May
28:02.72	John	Kariuki	KEN-Y	10.11.86	6		Kobe	20 Apr
28:02.80	Ahmed Ibrahim	Warsama	QAT	4.2.66	1	NC	Doha	16 Jun
28:03.48	Dan	Browne	USA	24.6.75	3	NC	Stanford	19 Jun
28:03.62	Toshinari	Takaoka	JPN	24.9.70	1		Shizuoka	3 May
28:03.63	Samuel	Mutsuri	KEN-Y	2.5.86	2		Shizuoka	11 Oct
28:05.09	Eduardo	Henriques	POR	24.3.68	2	EChall	Athína (E)	12 Apr
28:05.27	Cathal	Lombard	IRL	12.2.76	4	AAA	Watford	5 Jul
28:05.38	Tomoaki	Kunichika	JPN	22.7.73	7		Okayama	27 Sep
	(60)							

Mark	Name		Nat	Born	Pos	Meet	Venue	Date
28:05.99	Solomon	Bushendich	KEN-J	10.1.84	5	Esp Ch	Pontevedra	20 Jul
28:06.58	Weldon	Johnson	USA	24.7.73	4	NC	Stanford	19 Jun
28:06.93	Satoshi	Irifune	JPN	14.12.75	2rA		Fukagawa	25 Jun
28:07.18	Samuel	Kabiru	KEN	6.6.83	1		Sendai	17 May
28:07.19	Juan Carlos	de la Ossa	ESP	25.11.76	3	EChall	Athína (E)	12 Apr
28:07.92	Khalid	El Amri	MAR	20.3.77	2		Rabat	14 Jun
28:08.19	Blair	Martin	NZL	25.4.75	4	NC	Inglewood	15 Feb
28:09.94	Janne	Holmén	FIN	26.9.77	1	PNG	Turku	15 Jun
28:10.66	Kazuhiro	Maeda	JPN	19.4.81	8		Okayama	27 Sep
28:11.23	Toshihiro	Iwasa	JPN	18.5.76	3		Shizuoka	3 May
	(70)							
28:12.62	Sergey	Lebed	UKR	15.7.75	1	NC	Kiev	5 Jul
28:13.23	Kazuyoshi	Tokumoto	JPN	22.6.79	9		Okayama	27 Sep
28:13.34	Daniel	Mwangi Muchunu	KEN-J	.84	1		Konosu	27 Sep
28:13.63	Kenji	Noguchi	JPN	23.2.75	10		Okayama	27 Sep
28:15.03	José	Ramos	POR	28.7.68	4	EChall	Athína (E)	12 Apr
28:15.24	Nobuyuki	Sato	JPN	8.8.72	4		Shizuoka	3 May
28:15.54	Jackson	Gachiuri	KEN	15.4.77	11		Okayama	27 Sep
28:15.66	Marco	Mazza	ITA	25.6.77	5	EChall	Athína (E)	12 Apr
28:15.73	Atsushi	Sato	JPN	8.5.78	8		Kobe	20 Apr
28:15.82	Yoshinori	Oda	JPN	5.12.80	12		Okayama	27 Sep
	(80)							
28:16.15	Koichiro	Nagata	JPN	19.12.78	13		Okayama	27 Sep
28:16.80	Toshihide	Kato	JPN	4.7.73	14		Okayama	27 Sep
28:17.3A	Enock	Mitei	KEN	26.11.80	2	NC	Nairobi	12 Jul
28:17.84	Shigeru	Aburaya	JPN	6.2.77	10		Kobe	20 Apr
28:17.91	Kenji	Takao	JPN	23.3.75	11		Kobe	20 Apr
28:18.30	Suehiro	Ishikawa	JPN	27.9.79	2		Sendai	17 May
28:18.43	Yuki	Nakamura	JPN	21.6.81	3rA		Fukagawa	25 Jun
28:18.79	Takeshi	Hamano	JPN	30.7.74	12		Kobe	20 Apr
28:19.16	Francis	Mwihia	KEN	27.2.78	5		Shizuoka	3 May
28:19.57	Wataru	Okutani	JPN	9.1.75	4		Sendai	17 May
	(90)							
28:20.06	Samuel	Wanjiru	KEN-Y	10.11.86	3		Konosu	27 Sep
28:20.20	Dan	Lincoln	USA	22.10.80	1	NCAA	Sacramento	12 Jun
28:20.29	Alistair	Cragg	IRL	13.6.80	2	NCAA	Sacramento	12 Jun
28:20.51	Ian	Dobson	USA	6.2.82	6	NC	Stanford	19 Jun
28:21.16	Tsuyoshi	Ogata	JPN	11.5.73	13		Kobe	20 Apr
28:21.41	Christopher	Graff	USA	5.10.75	7	NC	Stanford	19 Jun
28:21.46	Ed	Torres	USA	22.8.80	8	NC	Stanford	19 Jun
28:21.51	James	Ndungu	KEN	30.4.79	14		Kobe	20 Apr
28:22.22	Francis	Kiprop	KEN	4.6.82	7	FBK	Hengelo	1 Jun
28:22.29	Michitaka	Hosokawa	JPN	26.4.76	17		Okayama	27 Sep
	(100)							

28:22.58	Marílson	dos Santos	BRA	6.8.77	28 Mar
28:22.5A	Salim	Kipsang	KEN	22.12.79	12 Jul
28:22.97	Terukazu	Omori	JPN	3.9.79	29 Nov
28:23.05	Ken-ichiro	Setoguchi	JPN	12.12.80	27 Sep
28:23.16	Silas	Sang	KEN	21.8.78	15 Jun
28:23.29	Ryan	Kirkpatrick	USA	10.9.78	19 Jun
28:23.40	Yu	Mitsuya	JPN-J	18.12.84	29 Nov
28:23.52	Dave	Davis	USA	13.9.78	2 May
28:23.67	Adam	Tenforde	USA	9.8.80	19 Jun
28:23.73	Hélder	Ornelas	POR	6.5.74	12 Apr
28:24.11	Nick	Rogers	USA	2.5.75	2 May
28:24.73	Yoshinari	Horikawa	JPN	19.6.75	10 May
28:25.71	Atsushi	Fujita	JPN	6.11.76	17 May
28:25.73	Alejandro	Suárez	MEX	30.11.80	20 Jul
28:25.88	Tomonori	Watanabe	JPN	9.6.76	10 May
28:26.04	Takashi	Ota	JPN	27.4.76	29 Nov
28:26.11	Enrique	Molina	ESP	25.2.68	12 Apr
28:26.75	Isaac	Viciosa	ESP	26.12.69	20 Jul
28:26.88	Matt	Gonzalez	USA	9.10.81	12 Jun
28:27.01	Ramiro	Morán	ESP	17.5.69	20 Jul
28:27.09	Daisuke	Isomatsu	JPN	17.12.73	17 May
28:27.12	Ken-ichi	Shiraishi	JPN	6.4.82	10 May
28:27.20	Mekubo	Mogusu	KEN-Y	25.12.86	29 Nov
28:27.39	Yuichiro	Ueno	JPN-J	29.7.85	29 Nov
28:27.82	Masayuki	Kobayashi	JPN	4.4.74	17 May
28:28.47	Dieter	Baumann	GER	9.2.65	17 May
28:28.54	Saïd	Bérioui	MAR	3.6.75	14 Jun
28:28.78	Yuko	Matsumiya	JPN	21.2.80	29 Nov
28:29.01	Toshinari	Suwa	JPN	29.1.77	25 Jun
28:31.04	Kenneth	Korir Kiprono	KEN	.83	18 Sep
28:31.19	Tatsumi	Morimasa	JPN	3.4.76	17 May
28:31.71	Phil	Costley	NZL	16.3.70	15 Feb
28:31.73	Yoshitaka	Iwamizu	JPN	20.6.79	29 Nov
28:31.96	Jason	Hartman	USA	21.3.81	12 Jun
28:32.24	Alejandro	Gómez	ESP	11.4.67	20 Jul
28:32.37	Sammy	Kipkoech Tum	KEN	18.5.78	14 Jun
28:32.45	Erik	Sjöqvist	SWE	4.12.72	12 Apr
28:32.85	Tadayuki	Ojima	JPN	22.11.76	18 Oct
28:33.03	James	Wainaina	KEN	16.6.81	11 Oct
28:33.45	Loic	Letellier	FRA	1.10.76	30 May
28:33.76	Giuliano	Battocletti	ITA	1.8.75	18 Sep
28:33.81	Joep	Tigchelaar	NED	9.2.81	29 Mar
28:33.98	Shuichi	Fujii	JPN	14.2.82	20 Apr
28:34.16	Brett	Cartwright	AUS	25.1.73	15 Feb
28:34.4	Demissie	Girma	ETH	15.12.83	29 Apr
28:34.63	Satoshi	Osaki	JPN	4.6.76	29 Nov
28:35.2A	Elisha	Birgen Kipkorir	KEN	80	25 Jul
28:35.23	Chad	Johnson	USA	20.4.76	2 May
28:35.55	Koji	Ueoka	JPN	20.7.77	29 Nov
28:35.64	Mingaudas	Pukstas (150)	LTU	3.8.78	29 Mar
28:36.60	Michitane	Noda	JPN	25.3.75	17 May
28:37.0	Martin	Sulle	TAN	28.12.82	4 Jul
28:37.48	Ryuichi	Hashinokuchi	JPN	25.1.82	16 May
28:37.69	Dieudonné	Disi	RWA	24.4.78	12 Oct
28:38.56	Aleksandr	Vasilyev	RUS	6.12.70	12 Apr
28:38.67	Peter	Riley	GBR	6.7.79	12 Jun
28:38.85	Ryuji	Ono	JPN-J	27.1.85	18 Oct
28:38.88	Tomohiro	Seto	JPN	19.10.76	3 May
28:39.16	Tomoyuki	Honda	JPN	20.1.83	10 May
28:39.20	Robert	Kipngetich	KEN		14 Jun

Mark	Name		Nat	Born	Date
28:39.31	Enoch	Skosana	RSA	20.2.74	28 Feb
28:39.60	Ridha	Amri	TUN	16.12.76	30 May
28:40.07	Hisashi	Yotsuji	JPN	24.12.82	20 Apr
28:40.09	Iván	Galán	ESP	5.9.79	20 Jul
28:40.36	Koji	Watanabe	JPN	20.2.78	16 May
28:40.84	Gert	Thys	RSA	12.11.71	28 Feb
28:41.0	Hicham	Lamalem	MAR	4.4.79	22 Mar
28:41.00	Yoji	Yamaguchi	JPN	12.6.75	29 Nov
28:41.13	Louis	Luchini	USA	24.5.81	29 Mar
28:41.40	Adam	Wallace	USA	16.4.80	29 Mar
28:41.42	Hidemori	Noguchi	JPN	22.2.80	25 Jun
28:41.9	José Antonio	Ramallos	ESP	24.9.76	22 Mar
28:41.95	Westly	Keating (173)	USA	13.1.82	29 Mar

JUNIORS

See main list for top 11 juniors. 18 performances by 10 men to 28:10.0. Additional marks and further juniors:

Mosop	27:56.56	5	AfG	Abuja	12 Oct					
B Kiprop	27:53.37	4	AfG	Abuja	12 Oct					
Joseph 2+	28:06.36	13	WCh	Saint-Denis	24 Aug					
Geb'mariam	28:03.03	4	FBK	Hengelo	1 Jun	28:08.79	2	Af-AsG	Hyderbad	30 Oct
Irungu Math.	27:48.86	2		Kobe	20 Apr	28:05.31	2		Shizuoka	3 May

Mark	Name		Nat	Born	Pos	Meet	Venue	Date
28:23.40	Yu	Mitsuya	JPN-J	18.12.84	1		Isahaya	29 Nov
28:27.20	Mekubo	Mogusu	KEN-Y	25.12.86	2		Isahaya	29 Nov
28:27.39	Yuichiro	Ueno	JPN-J	29.7.85	3		Yokohama	29 Nov
28:38.85	Ryuji	Ono	JPN-J	27.1.85	2		Nobeoka	18 Oct
28:47.96	Pharis	Irungu Kimani	KEN	11.1.84	4r11		Konosu	27 Sep
28:55.49	Satoru	Kitamura	JPN-Y	4.2.86	1		Kobe	6 Apr
29:00.12	Haile	Gelalcha Tafa	ETH	4.5.84	10		Hachioji	29 Nov
29:00.5A	Andrew	Limo	KEN	15.3.84	1		Nairobi	24 May
29:02.4	Yusuke	Ichinoi (20)	JPN	6.1.84	12r1		Yokohama	16 May

Best European: 29:25.96 Aleksey Reunkov RUS 28.1.84 1 NC-j Kazan 1 Jul

10 KILOMETRES ROAD

Mark	Name		Nat	Born	Pos	Venue	Date
27:28	Gilbert	Okari	KEN	2.8.78	1	Cape Elizabeth	2 Aug
27:36	Linus	Maiyo	KEN	.83	1	Mobile	22 Mar
27:40	John	Kibowen	KEN	21.4.69	1	Brunssum	6 Apr
27:41	Thomas	Nyariki	KEN	27.9.71	2	Mobile	22 Mar
27:47		Okari			3	Mobile	22 Mar
27:48	Moses	Kigen	KEN	22.4.73	1	Würzburg	27 Apr
27:50	Valentine	Orare	KEN	14.2.83	2	Würzburg	27 Apr
27:51	John	Korir	KEN	15.12.75	2	Cape Elizabeth	2 Aug
27:52	Benson	Barus	KEN	4.7.80	1	Gualtieri	21 Apr

Others where superior to track bests

Mark	Name		Nat	Born	Pos	Venue	Date
28:02	Wilson	Onsare	KEN	15.6.76	1	La Courneuve	23 Mar
28:04	Enock	Mitei	KEN	26.11.80	2	La Courneuve	23 Mar
28:05	Moses	Macharia	KEN	.74	4	Mobile	22 Mar
28:06	Benson	Ogato	KEN	.80	1	Masimba	30 Dec
28:08	James	Mbote	KEN	.77	2	Brunssum	6 Apr
28:08	Elijah	Nyabuti	KEN	10.10.79	2	Gualtieri	21 Apr
28:09	James	Koskei	KEN	23.11.68	3	Cape Elizabeth	2 Aug
28:11	Wilson Kipkoskei	Chemweno	KEN	.79	3	Würzburg	27 Apr
28:11	Paul	Koech	KEN	25.6.69	4	Cape Elizabeth	2 Aug
28:12	Peter	Kiprotich	KEN	.79	2	Zevenaar	31 Aug
28:15	Yevgeniy	Bozhko	UKR	1.6.75	3	Zevenaar	31 Aug
28:16	Douglas	Momanyi	KEN		2	Masimba	30 Dec
28:17	John	Itati	KEN	26.12.73	5	Mobile	22 Mar
28:17	Richard	Yatich	KEN	2.12.80	1	Alphen	12 Jul
28:17	Paul	Biwott	KEN	18.4.78	4	Zevenaar	31 Aug
28:18	Luke	Kibet	KEN	12.4.83	3	La Courneuve	23 Mar
28:18	Marílson	dos Santos	BRA	6.8.77	1	Santos	25 May
28:19	Wilfred	Kigen	KEN	23.2.75	6	Würzburg	27 Apr
28:19	George	Morara Nchoga	KEN	.79	1	Langueux	15 Jun
28:21	Jimmy	Thimoty	ERI	.78	2	Langueux	15 Jun
28:22	Vincent	Kropp	KEN	.81	2	Düsseldorf	7 Sep
28:22	Obed	Gisemba	KEN		3	Masimba	30 Dec

Mark	Name		Nat	Born	Date
28:23	Robert K	Cheruiyot	KEN	26.9.78	23 Feb
28:23	David	Karanja	KEN	.76	23 Feb
28:23	Girma	Assefa	ETH-J	12.10.84	19 Apr
28:23	Thomas	Kiplitan	KEN	15.6.83	1 May
28:23	Abraham	Tandoi	KEN	12.12.74	7 Sep
28:23	James Kiplagat	Kosgei	KEN	.78	7 Sep
28:24	David	Kipngetich	KEN	15.4.75	22 Mar
28:24	James	Kipketer	KEN	.75	23 Mar
28:24	Jeroen	van Damme	NED	29.9.72	12 Sep
28:26	Philip	Korir	KEN	.83	23 Mar
28:26	Simon	Kasimili	KEN	12.12.80	27 Apr
28:27	Dennis	Musembi Ndiso	KEN	.83	14 Sep
28:28	Redouane	El Harroufi	MAR	30.7.81	21 Apr
28:28	Lazarus	Nyakeraka	KEN	22.11.75	10 May
28:29	Jacob	Losian	KEN	6.6.71	19 Apr
28:30	Gilbert	Koech	KEN	1.9.80	22 Mar
28:30	Francis	Komu	KEN	5.5.74	6 Jun
28:31	Paul	Tergat	KEN	17.6.69	23 Feb
28:31	Simon	Kiilu	KEN	.82	21 Sep
28:32	David	Kilel	KEN-J	21.5.84	1 Mar
28:32	Jamal	Baligha	MAR	11.12.73	12 Sep
28:32	Daniel	Rono	KEN	13.7.78	21 Sep
28:34+	Zakayo	Ngatho	KEN	18.3.78	2 Feb
28:34	Isaac	Macharia	KEN	.78	6 Jun
28:34+	John	Kipchumba	KEN	9.12.74	7 Sep
28:34	Carsten	Eich	GER	9.1.70	14 Sep
28:34	Martin	Sulle	TAN	28.12.82	18 Oct
28:35	Andrew	Limo	KEN-J	15.3.84	27 Aug

Mark	Name		Nat	Born	Pos	Meet	Venue	Date
28:37	Kebede	Tekeste	ETH	.74				22 Mar
28:37	Wesley	Ochoro	KEN	.78				23 Mar
28:37	David	Ndungu	KEN	.78				10 May
28:37	Paul	Kirui	KEN	5.2.80				8 Jun
28:37	Robert	Kipchumba	KEN-J	24.2.84				18 Oct
28:37	Juan Carlos	Higuero	ESP	3.8.78				23 Nov
28:37A	Stephen	Kiogora	KEN	29.11.76				6 Dec
28:38	Evans	Rutto	KEN	8.4.78				4 Jul
28:38A		Kimutia	KEN					6 Dec
28:39	Glynn	Tromans	GBR	17.3.69				23 Mar
28:39	Hosea	Kogo	KEN	11.8.72				27 Apr
28:39	Benjamin	Maiyo	KEN	6.10.78				1 May
28:39	Martin	Lel	KEN	29.10.78				4 Jul
28:39A	Denis	Kipkurui Keter	KEN-J	24.3.84				6 Dec

Qustionable distance

Mark	Name		Nat	Born	Date
28:32	David	Tuwei	KEN	22.2.79	30 Mar

Downhill to 28:30

4 May, Toronto: 1. Peter Ntabo KEN 28:02, 2, Joseph Nderitu KEN 28:05
24 Jul, Salt Lake City (A) 157m: 1. Patrick Nthiwa KEN 27:16, 2. Julius Kimati KEN 27:52, 3. John Gwako KEN 28:08, 4. Teren Jamesen USA 28:14. 26 Oct, East London: 1. Lusapho April RSA 24.5.82 28:25

JUNIORS

Mark	Name		Nat	Born	Pos	Meet	Venue	Date
28:23	Girma	Assefa	ETH	12.10.84	4		Paderborn	19 Apr
28:32	David	Kilel	KEN	21.5.84	4		Marseille	1 Mar
28:35	Andrew	Limo	KEN	15.3.84	1		Port Elizabeth	27 Aug
28:37	Robert	Kipchumba	KEN	24.2.84	3		Trento	18 Oct
28:39A	Denis	Kipkurui Keter	KEN	24.3.84	3		Kisumu	6 Dec
28:48	Damian Paul	Chopa	TAN-Y	.86	4		Madrid	23 Nov
28:53	Dehe	Woyesa	ETH-Y	.86	3		Basel	29 Nov

15 KILOMETRES ROAD

Mark	Name		Nat	Born	Pos	Meet	Venue	Date
42:43+	Zakayo	Ngatho	KEN	18.3.78	1	in HMar	Marugame	2 Feb
42:43	Richard	Yatich	KEN	2.12.80	1		Nijmegen	16 Nov
43:20		Yatich			1		's Heerenberg	7 Dec
43:23	John	Korir	KEN	15.12.75	1		Utica	13 Jul
43:24	Evans	Rutto	KEN	8.4.78	2		Utica	13 Jul
43:26+	Fabiano	Joseph	TAN-J	24.12.85	1=	in HMar	Vilamoura	4 Oct
43:26+	Martin	Lel	KEN	29.10.78	1=	in HMar	Vilamoura	4 Oct
43:26+	Martin Hhaway	Sulle	TAN	28.12.82	1=	in HMar	Vilamoura	4 Oct
43:26+	John Cheruiyot	Korir	KEN	13.12.81	1=	in HMar	Vilamoura	4 Oct
43:26+	John	Yuda	TAN	9.6.79	1=	in HMar	Vilamoura	4 Oct
43:27+	Yusuf	Songoka	KEN	5.2.79	6=	in HMar	Vilamoura	4 Oct
43:27+	Jackson	Koech	KEN	26.12.78	6=	in HMar	Vilamoura	4 Oct
43:27+	Tesfaye	Tola	ETH	19.10.74	6=	in HMar	Vilamoura	4 Oct
43:27+	Zersenay	Tadesse	ERI	8.2.82	6=	in HMar	Vilamoura	4 Oct
43:27+	Jackson	Koech	KEN	26.12.78	6=	in HMar	Vilamoura	4 Oct
43:28	Shadrack	Hoff	RSA	19.5.73	3		Utica	13 Jul
43:31	Mebrahtom	Keflezighi	USA	5.5.75	1	NC	Jacksonville	8 Mar
43:31	Paul	Koech	KEN	26.6.69	4		Utica	13 Jul
43:41	Kipchumba	Cherono	KEN					21 Jun
43:44+	James	Wainaina	KEN	16.6.81				24 Nov
43:44+	Alene	Emere	ETH	25.6.82				24 Nov
43:49	Marílson	dos Santos	BRA	6.8.77				31 Dec
43:50	Philemon	Kemei	KEN	12.2.82				21 Jun
43:51	Paul	Tergat	KEN	17.6.69				16 Nov
43:57	Romulo	da Silva	BRA	26.5.77				31 Dec
43:54+	Shin-ichiro	Okuda	JPN	4.1.80				2 Feb
43:54+	Shuichi	Fujii	JPN	14.2.82				2 Feb
43:54	Paulo	Catarino	POR	30.9.63				21 Jun
43:54	Joseph	Kimani	KEN	21.9.72				13 Jul
43:56	Nicholas	Kemboi	KEN	25.11.83				1 May
43:57	Patrick	Ivuti	KEN	30.6.78				1 May
42:36+ dh	Jackson	Koech	KEN	26.12.78	1	in HMar	South Shields	21 Sep

10 MILES ROAD

Mark	Name		Nat	Born	Pos	Meet	Venue	Date
45:30	Martin	Irungu Mathathi	KEN-J	25.12.85	1		Kosa	14 Dec
45:46	Francis	Kibiwott	KEN	15.9.78	1		Zaandam	21 Sep
45:49	Julius	Maina	KEN	14.10.77	2		Kosa	14 Dec
46:01	Charles	Kamathi	KEN	18.5.78	2		Zaandam	21 Sep
46:10	Luke	Kibet	KEN	12.4.83	3		Zaandam	21 Sep
46:23	John	Korir	KEN	15.12.75	1		Flint	23 Aug
46:24	James	Koskei	KEN	23.11.68	2		Flint	23 Aug
46:25	Wilson	Kigen	KEN	15.9.80	3		Flint	23 Aug
46:29	John	Kipchumba	KEN	9.12.74	2		Tilburg	7 Sep
46:32	Laban	Kipkemboi	KEN	30.12.77	4		Flint	23 Aug
46:35	John	Yuda	TAN	9.6.79	1		Portsmouth	12 Oct
46:37	Paul	Biwott	KEN	18.4.78	3		Tilburg	7 Sep
46:43	Girma	Tola	ETH	13.10.75	1		Bern	10 May
46:45	James	Kipketer	KEN	.75	4		Zaandam	21 Sep
46:47	Tomoaki	Kunichika	JPN	22.7.73	1		Himeji	11 Feb
46:47	Kamiel	Maase	NED	20.10.71	5		Zaandam	21 Sep
46:50	Tomoyuki	Sato	JPN	31.1.81	3		Kosa	14 Dec
46:52	Jackson	Gachiuri	KEN	15.4.77	4		Kosa	14 Dec
46:53	Kazuhiro	Maeda	JPN	19.4.81	1		Karatsu	9 Feb
46:53	Koichiro	Nagata	JPN	19.12.78	5		Kosa	14 Dec
46:53	Yukinobu	Nakazaki	JPN	4.4.79	6		Kosa	14 Dec

Mark		Name		Nat	Born	Pos	Meet	Venue	Date
46:54		Jeff	Schiebler	CAN	1.6.73	7		Kosa	14 Dec
46:55		Toshinari	Suwa	JPN	29.1.77	2		Karatsu	9 Feb
46:56		Tomo	Tsubota	JPN	16.6.77				11 Feb
46:57		Mitsuru	Irifune	JPN	23.6.79				9 Feb
46:57		Yoshihiro	Yamamoto	JPN	20.4.83				14 Dec
46:58		Kenji	Takao	JPN	23.3.75				9 Feb
46:58		Yoshinori	Oda	JPN	5.12.80				9 Feb
46:58		Tsuyoshi	Nakano	JPN	12.3.73				14 Dec
Downhill									
45:19		Simon	Wangai	KEN	12.11.78	1		Philadelphia (48/3m)	4 May
45:41+		Jackson	Koech	KEN	26.12.78	1	in HMar	South Shields	21 Sep

HALF MARATHON

Mark		Name		Nat	Born	Pos	Meet	Venue	Date
60:01	dh	Hendrick	Ramaala	RSA	2.2.72	1	GNR	South Shields	21 Sep
60:05	dh	Jackson	Koech	KEN	26.12.78	2	GNR	South Shields	21 Sep
60:10	dh	Martin	Lel	KEN	29.10.78	1		Lisboa	16 Mar
60:14	dh		Ramaala			2		Lisboa	16 Mar
60:21		Zakayo	Ngatho	KEN	18.3.78	1		Marugame	2 Feb
60:24	dh	Robert K	Cheruiyot	KEN	26.9.78	3		Lisboa	16 Mar
60:25		John	Yuda	TAN	9.6.79	1		Milano	5 Apr
60:31	dh	Nicholas	Kemboi	KEN	25.11.83	4		Lisboa	16 Mar
60:33	dh	Christopher	Cheboiboch	KEN	3.3.77	5		Lisboa	16 Mar
60:38		James	Kwambai	KEN	.76	1		Udine	28 Sep
60:49			Lel			1	WCh	Vilamoura	4 Oct
60:50	dh	Rodgers	Rop (10)	KEN	16.2.76	6		Lisboa	16 Mar
60:51	dh	Paul	Tergat	KEN	17.6.69	7		Lisboa	16 Mar
60:51		John	Kyalo	KEN-J	.84	1		Vitry-sur-Seine	27 Apr
60:52		Paul	Kirui	KEN	5.2.80	2		Vitry-sur-Seine	27 Apr
60:52		Wilson	Onsare	KEN	15.6.76	1		Lille	6 Sep
60:52		Fabiano	Joseph	TAN-J	24.12.85	2	WCh	Vilamoura	4 Oct
60:53		Patrick	Ivuti	KEN	30.6.78	2		Milano	5 Apr
60:56		Joseph	Ngolepus	KEN	.75	1		Den Haag	29 Mar
60:56		Martin Hhaway	Sulle	TAN	28.12.82	3	WCh	Vilamoura	4 Oct
60:58		Yusuf	Songoka	KEN	5.2.79	2		Den Haag	29 Mar
61:01		Ridouane	El Harroufi (20)	MAR	30.7.81	1		Casablanca	19 Oct
61:02		Salim	Kipsang	KEN	22.12.79	3		Den Haag	29 Mar
61:02		John Cheruiyot	Korir	KEN	13.12.81	4	WCh	Vilamoura	4 Oct
61:05			P Kirui			1		Berlin	6 Apr
61:07		Toshinari	Takaoka	JPN	24.9.70	1		Yamaguchi	9 Mar
61:10		Luke	Kibet	KEN	19.6.73	4		Den Haag	29 Mar
61:12		Khalid	El Boumlili	MAR		2		Casablanca	19 Oct
61:13		Boniface	Usisivu	KEN	5.9.74	1		Ostia Lido	23 Feb
61:13			Yuda			5	WCh	Vilamoura	4 Oct
61:15		Philip	Manyim	KEN	24.3.78	1		Merano	27 Apr
		(31/27)							
61:16		Moulay	Tahar	MAR	.69	3		Casablanca	19 Oct
61:16		Abderrahim	Hajji	MAR		4		Casablanca	19 Oct
61:18		Barnabas	Koech	KEN		1		Los Palacios	14 Dec
		(30)							
61:19		Elijah	Nyabuti	KEN	10.10.79	2		Merano	27 Apr
61:19		James	Moiben	KEN	20.4.77	2		Los Palacios	14 Dec
61:21		Philmon	Kipkering Meto	KEN	10.8.74	2		Ostia Lido	23 Feb
61:24		Dennis	Musembi Ndiso	KEN	.83	1		Montbéliard	28 Sep
61:26		Zersenay	Tadesse	ERI	8.2.82	7	WCh	Vilamoura	4 Oct
61:26		Aziz	Driouche	MAR	15.11.77	5		Casablanca	19 Oct
61:29		Laban	Kipkemboi	KEN	30.12.77	1		Philadelphia	21 Sep
61:30		Michael	Rotich	KEN	26.10.82	1		Paris	9 Mar
61:32		Abdellatif	Meftah	MAR		6		Casablanca	19 Oct
61:32		Hassan	Loukhili	MAR		7		Casablanca	19 Oct
		(40)							
61:33		**Mohamed Saïd**	**El Wardi**	**MAR**	**19.4.72**	**8**		**Casablanca**	**19 Oct**
61:34		Takayuki	Matsumiya	JPN	21.2.80	2		Yamaguchi	9 Mar
61:34		Simon	Kiilu	KEN	.82	2		Udine	28 Sep
61:34		Mohammed	El Hattab	MAR	.76	9		Casablanca	19 Oct
61:35	dh	Rachid	Ziar	ALG	15.11.73	8		Lisboa	16 Mar
61:35		Christopher	Soget	KEN	15.5.80	3		Lille	6 Sep
61:35		Joseph	Ngeny	KEN		3		Udine	28 Sep
61:35		Tesfaye	Tola	ETH	19.10.74	9	WCh	Vilamoura	4 Oct
61:37		Kamal	Saïdou	MAR	9.12.64	10		Casablanca	19 Oct
61:38	dh	Paulo	Gomes	POR	15.5.73	9		Lisboa	16 Mar
		(50)							
61:39		Stefano	Baldini	ITA	25.5.71	3		Ostia Lido	23 Feb

Mark		Name		Nat	Born	Pos	Meet	Venue	Date
61:39		Daniel	Rono	KEN	13.7.78	5		Milano	5 Apr
61:39		Elarbi	Khattabi	MAR	16.5.67	2		Philadelphia	21 Sep
61:40		Ottaviano	Andriani	ITA	4.1.74	4		Ostia Lido	23 Feb
61:41		James	Wainaina	KEN	16.6.81	1		Nagoya	24 Nov
61:42		Benson	Cherono	KEN	.82	1		Córdoba	30 Nov
61:43		Sergio	Chiesa	ITA	7.9.72	5		Ostia Lido	23 Feb
61:44		Hicham	Bellani	MAR	15.9.79	1		Marrakech	19 Jan
61:44		Samson	Loywapet	KEN	24.12.72	5		Den Haag	29 Mar
61:46		Alene	Emere	ETH	25.6.82	2		Nagoya	24 Nov
		(60)							
61:48		Fabio	Rinaldi	ITA	15.7.73	6		Ostia Lido	23 Feb
61:48		Kenta	Oshima	JPN	29.6.79	3		Yamaguchi	9 Mar
61:49		Kazuyuki	Maeda	JPN	10.2.80	4		Yamaguchi	9 Mar
61:49		Peter	Kiprotich	KEN	.79	1		Glasgow	7 Sep
61:49		Jason	Mbote	KEN	.79	2		Glasgow	7 Sep
61:49	dh	Sergey	Lebed	UKR	15.7.75	3	GNR	South Shields	21 Sep
61:50		Francis	Kibiwott	KEN	15.9.78	6		Den Haag	29 Mar
61:51		Abdelkebir	Lamachi	MAR	.80	7		Ostia Lido	23 Feb
61:52		Kazushi	Hara	JPN	16.11.80	5		Yamaguchi	9 Mar
61:52	dh	Benjamin	Kimutai Koskei	KEN	5.9.71	10		Lisboa	16 Mar
		(70)							
61:53	dh	Paulo	Catarino	POR	30.9.63	11		Lisboa	16 Mar
61:54		Barnabas	Rutto	KEN	19.4.77	1		Torino	9 Mar
61:55		Robert	Cheboror	KEN		2		Berlin	6 Apr
61:55		Abner	Chipu	RSA	2.1.72	3		Glasgow	7 Sep
61:57		Paul	Koech	KEN	25.6.69	2		Virginia Beach	31 Aug
61:58		Haron	Toroitich	KEN	.78	2		Paris	9 Mar
61:58		Jimmy	Muindi	KEN	14.8.73	4		Glasgow	7 Sep
61:59A		Dereje	Adere	ETH-J	.85	1	NC	Addis Ababa	21 Sep
62:00		Francis	Robert Naali	TAN	1.4.71	1		Moshi	15 Jun
62:00	dh	Paul	Kosgei	KEN	22.4.78	4	GNR	South Shields	21 Sep
		(80)							
62:02		Shin-ichiro	Okuda	JPN	4.1.80	2		Marugame	2 Feb
62:02	dh	Alberto	Chaíça	POR	17.9.73	13		Lisboa	16 Mar
62:02A		Tariku	Jifar	ETH-J	.84	2	NC	Addis Ababa	21 Sep
62:04		Abdelfatah	Aïtzouri	MAR	6.6.70	7		Den Haag	29 Mar
62:04		Tendai	Chimusasa	ZIM	28.1.71	1		Paderborn	19 Apr
62:05		George	Morara Nchoga	KEN	.79	3		Paris	9 Mar
62:05		Tesfaye	Girma	ETH		2		Paderborn	19 Apr
62:05		Gilbert	Koech	KEN	1.9.80	3		Philadelphia	21 Sep
62:06		Japhet	Kosgei	KEN	20.12.68	3		Virginia Beach	31 Aug
62:06		Sammy	Kipruto	KEN	22.11.78	1		Breda	5 Oct
		(90)							
62:06		Girma	Tola	ETH	13.10.75	2		Breda	5 Oct
62:07		Samson	Ramadhani	TAN	25.12.82	2		Moshi	15 Jun
62:08		David	Makori	KEN	6.11.73	4		Paris	9 Mar
62:08		Musa	Cherotich	KEN	.75	.8		Den Haag	29 Mar
62:08		Barnabas	Kenduiywo	KEN	.74	4		Paderborn	19 Apr
62:08		John	Kanyi	KEN	6.9.80	1		Sapporo	6 Jul
62:08		Evans	Rutto	KEN	8.4.78	4		Virginia Beach	31 Aug
62:09		Shuichi	Fujii	JPN	14.2.82	3		Marugame	2 Feb
62:09		Luke	Kibet	KEN	12.4.83	3		Breda	5 Oct
62:11		Yoji	Yamaguchi	JPN	12.6.75	4		Marugame	2 Feb
		(100)							
62:11		Takashi	Tokunaga	JPN	6.6.81	5		Marugame	2 Feb
62:11		Wesley	Ochoro	KEN	.78	5		Paris	9 Mar
62:11		Hatsuo	Kitada	JPN	31.1.77	6		Yamaguchi	9 Mar
62:11		Joseph	Kahugu	KEN	7.6.71	1		Maracaibo	7 Sep
62:11		Abdelgani	Lahlali	FRA	11.9.77	1	NC	Chassieu	14 Sep
62:11		David	Kosgei	KEN	.77	4		Udine	28 Sep
62:11		Eliud	Kurgat	KEN	20.8.73	4		Breda	5 Oct

62:12	Yuki	Abe	JPN	14.10.75	9 Mar
62:12	Thomas	Chemitei	KEN	.78	9 Mar
62:12	Robert	Cheruiyot	KEN	20.12.74	28 Sep
62:13	Laban	Kagika	KEN	17.7.78	6 Jul
62:13	John	Korir	KEN	15.12.75	28 Sep
62:13	Wilson	Kiprotich	KEN	.75	5 Oct
62:14	Shota	Nakai	JPN	8.4.83	2 Feb
62:15	Khalid	Khannouchi	USA	22.12.71	9 Mar
62:15A	Enock	Keter	KEN	28.2.82	18 May
62:15	Atsushi	Sato	JPN	8.5.78	6 Jul
62:15	Tsuyoshi	Ogata	JPN	11.5.73	6 Jul
62:15	Tarik	Bouzid	FRA	24.2.77	14 Sep
62:15A	Hailu	Mesfin	ETH	.81	21 Sep
62:15	Moses	Kibor	KEN		28 Sep
62:15	Vasiliy	Matviychuk	UKR	13.1.82	1 Nov
62:16	Luís	Jesus	POR	19.11.68	26 Jan
62:16	Ombeche	Mokamba	KEN	6.4.82	2 Feb
62:16	Erustus	Limo	KEN		19 Apr
62:16	Sammy	Korir	KEN	12.12.71	4 May
62:16	Solomon	Tsege	ETH	.82	21 Sep
62:16	Benjamin	Kiplimo Mutai	KEN	13.7.82	28 Sep
62:16	John	Kanda	KEN	.71	4 Oct

Mark	Name		Nat	Born	Date
62:17 dh	Joseph	Kimani	KEN	21.9.72	16 Mar
62:17	Christopher	Isegwe	TAN		15 Jun
62:20	John	Ngeny	KEN	12.9.77	19 Oct
62:21	Yoichiro	Akiyama	JPN	25.12.79	2 Feb
62:21	Oscar	Fernández	ESP	23.10.74	16 Feb
62:21	Peter	Kipkasi	KEN	70	4 May
62:21	Daniel	Andrew	TAN-J	30.6.84	15 Jun
62:21	Luke	Metto	KEN	76	16 Nov
62:23	Suehiro	Ishikawa	JPN	27.9.79	9 Mar
62:23	Julius	Kibet	KEN		23 Mar
62:24	Masato	Wada	JPN	25.8.79	2 Feb
62:24	Kenji	Takao	JPN	23.3.75	23 Feb
62:24A	Jaouad	Gharib	MAR	22.5.72	20 Jul
62:24	Ronald	Mogaka	KEN	17.4.78	21 Sep
62:25	Masaya	Shimizu	JPN	12.11.80	9 Mar
62:26	Wilson	Chelal	KEN	15.11.82	29 Mar
62:26	Hassan	Laajili	MAR		19 Oct
62:27	Barnabas	Cheruiyot	KEN	75	29 Mar
62:27	Rachid	Boulenouar	ALG	13.6.74	16 May
62:27	Saïd	Belhout	ALG	16.4.75	16 May
62:27	Saïd	Hank	ALG	72	16 May
62:27	James	Koskei (150)	KEN	23.11.68	31 Aug
62:28	Danilo	Goffi	ITA	3.12.72	23 Feb
62:28	Peter	Raburu	KEN	78	29 Mar
62:28	El Hassan	Lahssini	FRA	1.1.75	14 Sep
62:28	Tom	Van Hooste	BEL	23.9.72	5 Oct
62:29	Ken	Konishi	JPN	29.3.79	2 Feb
62:29	David Siya	Cherui	KEN	12.8.77	28 Sep
62:30	Kamel	Kohil	ALG	25.12.71	19 Jan
62:30	William	Kiplagat	KEN	21.6.72	9 Mar
62:30	Paul	Wakou	UGA	17.10.83	28 Sep
62:30	Samson	Kirwa Tuiyange	KEN-J	84	28 Sep
62:30	Wilfred	Kibet Kigen	KEN	23.2.75	16 Nov
62:31	Masahiko	Takeyasu	JPN	12.11.80	2 Feb
62:31	Giacomo	Leone	ITA	10.4.71	29 Mar
62:32	Matthew	Sigei	KEN		14 Sep
62:33	Atsushi	Fujita	JPN	6.11.76	6 Jul
62:33	Paul	Lekuraa	KEN		21 Sep
62:34	Charles	Tangus	KEN	4.6.74	9 Mar
62:35	Eduardo	Henriques	POR	24.3.68	2 Nov
62:36	Isaac	Macharia	KEN	78	6 Apr
62:36	Paul	Kangogo Kanda	KEN	12.12.74	28 Sep
62:37	Tomonori	Onitsuka	JPN	21.3.80	9 Mar
62:37	Zebedaya	Bayo	TAN	20.5.76	15 Jun
62:38	Benjamin	Pseret	KEN		27 Apr
62:38	Raymond	Kipkoech	KEN	75	31 Aug
62:38	Takayuki	Nishida	JPN	26.4.77	24 Nov
62:39	Nobuaki	Nagai	JPN	26.5.78	9 Mar
62:40	Cuthbert	Nyasango	ZIM	17.9.82	6 Apr
62:41	Hiroyuki	Suzuki	JPN	9.4.71	9 Mar
62:41	Hamisi	Mori	TAN		15 Jun
62:41	Simon	Wangai	KEN	12.11.78	22 Jun
62:41	Enock	Mitei	KEN	26.11.80	28 Sep
62:42	David	Kariuki	KEN	23.5.80	2 Feb
62:42	David	Ngeny Cheruiyot	KEN	5.5.81	28 Sep
62:43	Yoshiro	Tanigawa	JPN	20.10.79	9 Mar
62:43	Koji	Kimura	JPN	2.1.78	9 Mar
62:43	Simon	Kasimili	KEN	12.12.80	28 Sep
62:44	Koji	Kannan	JPN	8.11.81	9 Mar
62:45	Luc	Krotwaar	NED	25.1.68	26 Jan
62:45	Stephen	Rerimoi (190)	KEN	22.12.73	9 Nov

Slightly downhill courses: Lisboa 69m, South Shields 30.5m

JUNIORS

See main list for top 4 juniors. 5 performances by 3 men to 62:00. Additional marks and further juniors:

Joseph 61:34 4 Stra Milano 5 Apr 61:41 3 Vitry-sur-Seine 27 Apr

Mark	Name		Nat	Born	Pos	Venue	Date
62:21	Daniel	Andrew	TAN	30.6.84	4	Moshi	15 Jun
62:30	Samson	Kirwa Tuiyange	KEN	.84	3	Gargnano	28 Sep
62:55	Hiroyuki	Saito	JPN	27.1.84	3	Fuchu	23 Nov
63:13	Tsuyoshi	Ueno	JPN	16.8.84	13	Marugame	2 Feb
63:16	Daniel	Mwangi Muchunu	KEN	.84	8	Sapporo	6 Jul
63:50	Makoto	Nozaki (10)	JPN	7.3.84	52	Yamaguchi	9 Mar
63:52	Pharis Irungu	Kimani	KEN	11.1.84	13	Sapporo	6 Jul
63:57	Takaaki	Koda	JPN	27.3.84	15	Kyoto	9 Mar

MARATHON

L = loop course, P = point-to-point, D =downhill over 1/1000

Mark		Name		Nat	Born	Pos	Meet	Venue	Date
2:04:55	L	Paul	Tergat	KEN	17.6.69	1		Berlin	28 Sep
2:04:56	L	Sammy	Korir	KEN	12.12.71	2		Berlin	28 Sep
2:05:50	L	Evans	Rutto	KEN	8.4.78	1		Chicago	12 Oct
2:06:15	L	Titus	Munji	KEN	.79	3		Berlin	28 Sep
2:06:33	L	Michael	Rotich	KEN	26.10.82	1		Paris	6 Apr
2:06:36	L	Benoit	Zwierzchlewski	FRA	19.8.76	2		Paris	6 Apr
2:06:39	L	William	Kipsang	KEN	.77	1		Amsterdam	19 Oct
2:06:42	L	Felix	Limo	KEN	22.8.80	2		Amsterdam	19 Oct
2:06:47	L	Wilson	Onsare	KEN	15.6.76	3		Paris	6 Apr
2:06:48	L	Driss	El Himer (10)	FRA	4.4.74	4		Paris	6 Apr
2:07:07	L	Paul	Koech	KEN	25.6.69	2		Chicago	12 Oct
2:07:27	L	Julio	Rey	ESP	13.1.72	1		Hamburg	27 Apr
2:07:39	L	Japhet	Kosgei	KEN	28.12.68	1	L.Biwa	Otsu	2 Mar
2:07:39	L	Benjamin	Kimutai Koskei	KEN	5.9.71	3		Amsterdam	19 Oct
2:07:41	L	Daniel	Njenga	KEN	7.5.76	3		Chicago	12 Oct
2:07:42	L	William	Kiplagat	KEN	21.6.72	1		Rotterdam	13 Apr
2:07:49	L	Ian	Syster	RSA	20.1.76	1		Beijing	19 Oct
2:07:51	L		Kiplagat			4		Amsterdam	19 Oct
2:07:52	L	Tomoaki	Kunichika	JPN	22.7.73	1		Fukuoka	7 Dec
2:07:53	L	Josephat	Kiprono	KEN	12.12.73	2		Rotterdam	13 Apr
2:07:55	L	Toshinari	Suwa (20)	JPN	29.1.77	2		Fukuoka	7 Dec
2:07:56	L	Gezahegne	Abera	ETH	23.4.78	1		London	13 Apr
2:07:56	L	Stefano	Baldini	ITA	25.5.71	2		London	13 Apr
2:07:57	L	Joseph	Ngolepus	KEN	.75	3		London	13 Apr
2:07:59	L	Antonio	Peña	ESP	26.8.70	2	L.Biwa	Otsu	2 Mar
2:07:59	L		Tergat			4		London	13 Apr
2:07:59	L	Toshinari	Takaoka	JPN	24.9.70	3		Fukuoka	7 Dec
2:08:01	L	Samson	Ramadhani	TAN	25.12.82	5		London	13 Apr

Mark		Name		Nat	Born	Pos	Meet	Venue	Date
2:08:03	L	Abdelkader	El Mouaziz	MAR	1.1.69	6		London	13 Apr
2:08:09	L	José Manuel	Martínez	ESP	22.10.71	3		Rotterdam	13 Apr
2:08:10	L		Lee Bong-ju	KOR	11.10.70	7		London	13 Apr
2:08:10	L		Peña			4		Fukuoka	7 Dec
2:08:12	L	Masakazu	Fujiwara (30)	JPN	6.3.81	3	L.Biwa	Otsu	2 Mar
2:08:13	L	Robert	Cheruiyot	KEN	20.12.74	5		Amsterdam	19 Oct
2:08:21	L	David	Rutto	KEN	.80	5		Paris	6 Apr
2:08:21	L	Hailu	Negussie	ETH	16.4.78	5		Fukuoka	7 Dec
2:08:28	L	Koji	Shimizu	JPN	17.10.69	4	L.Biwa	Otsu	2 Mar
2:08:31	L	Jaouad	Gharib	MAR	22.5.72	1	WCh	Saint-Denis	30 Aug
2:08:31	L	Kamiel	Maase	NED	20.10.71	6		Amsterdam	19 Oct
2:08:34	L	Haron	Toroitich	KEN	.78	6		Paris	6 Apr
2:08:37	L	Tsuyoshi	Ogata	JPN	11.5.73	6		Fukuoka	7 Dec
2:08:38	L		Rey			2	WCh	Saint-Denis	30 Aug
2:08:42	L	Gert	Thys	RSA	12.11.71	1		Seoul	16 Mar
2:08:43	L	(40)	Ji Young-joon	KOR	15.10.81	2		Seoul	16 Mar
2:08:43	L	Peter	Chebet	KEN	24.6.76	4		Chicago	12 Oct
2:08:46	L	Andrés	Espinosa	MEX	4.2.63	4		Berlin	28 Sep
2:08:47	L	Frederick	Cherono	KEN	23.11.77	1		Roma	23 Mar
2:08:48	L	Noah	Bor	KEN	18.7.77	5		Roma	23 Mar
2:08:48	L	Tadayuki	Ojima	JPN	22.11.76	7		Fukuoka	7 Dec
2:08:50	L	Atsushi (50/46)	Sato	JPN	8.5.78	5	L.Biwa	Otsu	2 Mar
2:08:53	L	Jimmy	Muindi	KEN	14.8.73	3		Seoul	16 Mar
2:08:53	L	Alberico	Di Cecco	ITA	19.4.74	3		Roma	23 Mar
2:08:53	L	David	Kirui	KEN	29.12.77	7		Paris	6 Apr
2:08:54	L	Zebedayo (50)	Bayo	TAN	20.5.76	8		Paris	6 Apr
2:08:58	L	Hendrick	Ramaala	RSA	2.2.72	8		London	13 Apr
2:09:05	L	Willy	Cheruiyot	KEN	67	1		Eindhoven	12 Oct
2:09:06	L	Wilson	Chelal Cheruiyot	KEN	15.11.82	2		Eindhoven	12 Oct
2:09:08	L	John	Birgen	KEN	.74	1		Milano	30 Nov
2:09:11	L	Boniface	Usisivu	KEN	5.9.74	4		Roma	23 Mar
2:09:14	L	Fred	Kiprop	KEN	3.6.74	4		Rotterdam	13 Apr
2:09:14	L	Ashebir	Demissie	ETH	.77	5		Rotterdam	13 Apr
2:09:15	L	Pavel	Loskutov	EST	2.12.69	1		Seoul	2 Nov
2:09:17	L	Matthew	Sigei	KEN		1		Brescia	9 Mar
2:09:21	L	Raymond (60)	Kipkoech	KEN	.75	5		Berlin	28 Sep
2:09:23	L	Grzegorz	Gajdus	POL	16.1.67	4		Eindhoven	12 Oct
2:09:24	L	Philip	Tarus	KEN	11.9.74	2		Milano	30 Nov
2:09:25	L	Alberto	Chaíça	POR	17.9.73	4	WCh	Saint-Denis	30 Aug
2:09:26	L	Shigeru	Aburaya	JPN	6.2.77	5	WCh	Saint-Denis	30 Aug
2:09:28	L	Boaz	Kimaiyo	KEN	10.12.76	1		Frankfurt am Main	26 Oct
2:09:29	L	Takeshi	Hamano	JPN	30.7.74	6	L.Biwa	Otsu	2 Mar
2:09:29	L	Daniele	Caimmi	ITA	17.12.72	6	WCh	Saint-Denis	30 Aug
2:09:31	L	Stephen	Cheptot Matebo	KEN	30.3.74	7		Rotterdam	13 Apr
2:09:33	L	Joseph	Kahugu	KEN	7.6.71	1		Dubai	10 Jan
2:09:33	L	Leonid (70)	Shvetsov	RUS	28.3.69	2		Frankfurt am Main	26 Oct
2:09:34	L	Tadesse	Hailemariam	ETH	17.9.72	.7		Amsterdam	19 Oct
2:09:38	D	Ondoro	Osoro	KEN	3.12.67	1		San Diego (76m)	1 Jun
2:09:42	L	Vincent	Kipsos	KEN	22.6.76	8		Fukuoka	7 Dec
2:09:45	L	Patrick	Chumba	KEN	24.7.74	5		Eindhoven	12 Oct
2:09:49	L	Lee	Troop	AUS	22.3.73	7	L.Biwa	Otsu	2 Mar
2:09:49	L	Kazuhiro	Matsuda	JPN	24.6.74	6		Berlin	28 Sep
2:09:52	L	Mark	Yatich	KEN	4.12.76	1		Los Angeles	2 Mar
2:09:52	L	Kurao	Umeki	JPN	30.9.75	7		Berlin	28 Sep
2:09:54	L	Stephen	Ndungu	KEN	1.6.67	2		Los Angeles	2 Mar
2:09:55	L	Ernest (80)	Kipyego	KEN	6.10.78	6		Eindhoven	12 Oct
2:09:57	L	Mbarak	Hussein	KEN	4.4.65	4		Seoul	16 Mar
2:09:58	L	André Luiz	Ramos	BRA	20.1.70	8		Berlin	28 Sep
2:09:58	L	Michitane	Noda	JPN	25.3.75	9		Fukuoka	7 Dec
2:09:59	L	Oscar	Fernández	ESP	23.10.74	10		Fukuoka	7 Dec
2:10:03	L	Mebrahtom	Keflezighi	USA	5.5.75	7		Chicago	12 Oct
2:10:05	L	Tesfaye	Eticha	ETH	16.9.74	1		Lausanne	26 Oct
2:10:07	L	Henry	Serem	KEN		.7		Eindhoven	12 Oct
2:10:11	L	Noriaki	Igarashi	JPN	28.10.72	3		Tokyo	9 Feb

Mark	Name		Nat	Born	Pos	Meet	Venue	Date
2:10:11 D	Robert Kipkoech	Cheruiyot	KEN	26.9.78	1		Boston	21 Apr
2:10:13 L	Mark (90)	Saina	KEN	10.11.70	9		Rotterdam	13 Apr
2:10:13 L	John	Nada Saya	TAN	8.8.78	2		Seoul	2 Nov
2:10:13 L	Luc	Krotwaar	NED	25.1.68	11		Fukuoka	7 Dec
2:10:16 L	Makhosonke	Fika	RSA	20.1.72	9		Berlin	28 Sep
2:10:18 L	Tefere	Wodajo	ETH	.83	2	Beppu	Oita	2 Feb
2:10:21 L	Charles E	Kibiwott	KEN		1		Reims	26 Oct
2:10:22 L	Nick	Harrison	AUS	18.10.70	3		Oita	2 Feb
2:10:26 L	Thomas	Chemitei	KEN	.78	.8		Amsterdam	19 Oct
2:10:30 P	Martin	Lel	KEN	29.10.78	1		New York	2 Nov
2:10:33 L	Naoki	Mishiro	JPN	16.3.77	4		Tokyo	9 Feb
2:10:38 L	Dawit (100)	Terefa	ETH	.77	1		Padova	27 Apr
2:10:38 L	Isaac	Kiprono	KEN	5.9.76	2		Reims	26 Oct
2:10:38 L	Vanderlei	de Lima	BRA	11.8.69	12		Fukuoka	7 Dec

Mark			Nat	Born	Date
2:10:39 L	Francisco Javier Cortés		ESP	25.10.71	13 Apr
2:10:40 L	Gashaw	Melesse Asfaw	ETH	.78	10 Jan
2:10:42 L	Habtamu	Bekele	ETH	.78	23 Mar
2:10:43 L	Yohei	Sato	JPN	31.8.76	2 Feb
2:10:43 L	Laban	Kagika	KEN	17.7.78	9 Feb
2:10:44 L	Javier	Caballero	ESP	24.3.72	28 Sep
2:10:44 L	Johnstone	Chepkwony	KEN	.79	26 Oct
2:10:46 L	Peter	Korir	KEN		23 Nov
2:10:48 L	Migidio	Bourifa	ITA	31.1.69	27 Apr
2:10:50 L	Francesco	Ingargiola	ITA	15.2.73	27 Apr
2:10:53 L	Tadayuki	Tsutsumi	JPN	12.8.77	2 Feb
2:10:53 P	Alberto	Juzdado	ESP	20.8.66	16 Mar
2:10:53 L	Ruggero	Pertile	ITA	8.8.74	27 Apr
2:10:55 L	Yasuaki	Yamamoto	JPN	5.8.72	28 Sep
2:10:56 L	Rachid	El Ghanmouni	MAR	.78	30 Aug
2:10:57 L	Sergey	Lukin	RUS	3.1.75	12 Oct
2:10:58 L	Benjamin	Itok	KEN	.72	16 Mar
2:11:01 P	El Hassan	Lahssini	FRA	1.1.75	26 Oct
2:11:05 L	Viktor	Röthlin	SUI	14.10.74	13 Apr
2:11:06 L	Robert	Cheboror	KEN		19 Oct
2:11:07 L	Daniel	Kirwa Too	KEN	21.11.76	12 Oct
2:11:08 L	Sisay	Bezabeh	AUS	9.9.77	12 Oct
2:11:11 P	Rodgers	Rop	KEN	16.2.76	2 Nov
2:11:12 L	Benson	Mbithi	KEN	22.3.78	2 Mar
2:11:12 L	Paul	Kiptanui	KEN	69	26 Oct
2:11:12 L	Ambese	Tolossa	ETH	28.8.77	30 Nov
2:11:18 L	Satoshi	Watanabe	JPN	27.2.77	2 Mar
2:11:22 P	Joseph	Kamau	KEN	21.9.72	21 Jun
2:11:23 L	Charles	Seronei	KEN	74	2 Mar
2:11:23 L	Frederick	Chumba	KEN	24.7.74	23 Mar
2:11:23 P	Christopher	Cheboibok	KEN	3.3.77	2 Nov
2:11:23 L	Danilo	Goffi	ITA	3.12.72	30 Nov
2:11:25 L	Tsutomu	Sassa	JPN	26.7.74	2 Feb
2:11:26 L	Ibrahim	Mitei Kipkirui	KEN	15.8.78	4 May
2:11:27 L	Ismaïl	Sghyr	FRA	16.3.72	19 Oct
2:11:28 D	Timothy	Cherigat	KEN	29.12.76	21 Apr
2:11:30 P	Sergio	Chiesa	ITA	7.9.72	26 Oct
2:11:31 P	Elly	Rono	KEN	5.5.70	2 Nov
2:11:33 L	David	Kosgei	KEN	77	6 Apr
2:11:34 L	Elijah	Yator	KEN	20.10.82	30 Nov
2:11:38 L	Wilson	Kibet	KEN	18.2.72	25 May
2:11:42 L	Daisuke	Isomatsu	JPN	17.12.73	7 Dec
2:11:51 L	Samson	Loywapet	KEN	24.12.72	26 Oct
2:11:53 P	Paul	Kangogo Kanda	KEN	12.12.74	26 Oct
2:11:54 L	Ottaviano	Andriani	ITA	4.1.74	13 Apr
2:11:55 L	Ryuji	Takei	JPN	18.5.71	16 Mar
2:11:55 L	Henry	Cherono	KEN	17.7.78	27 Apr
2:11:58 L	Rachid	Ziar	ALG	15.11.73	30 Aug
2:11:59 L	Barnabas	Rutto	KEN	19.4.77	27 Apr
2:12:03 L	Benjamin	Rotich	KEN	75	5 Oct
2:12:04 L	Wilson	Musto	KEN	18.2.76	6 Apr
2:12:05 L	Juan	Camacho	MEX	5.9.72	4 May
2:12:06 L	Takashi	Horiguchi	JPN	26.9.79	2 Mar
2:12:07 L	Samuel	Kemboi	KEN		30 Nov
2:12:07 L	Satoshi	Osaki	JPN	4.6.76	28 Sep
2:12:09 L	José Alirio	Carrasco	COL	22.2.76	12 Oct
2:12:10 L	Janne	Holmén	FIN	26.9.77	28 Sep
2:12:11 D	David	Mutua	KEN	76	1 Jun
2:12:13 P	Philemon	Rotich	KEN		12 Oct
2:12:15 L	Abdelfattah	Aïtzouri	MAR	6.6.70	19 Jan
2:12:17 P	Francis	Kipketer	KEN	17.4.76	12 Oct
2:12:18 L	Andrew	Sambu	TAN	5.10.72	5 Oct
2:12:23 L	Julius	Sugut	KEN	78	23 Mar
2:12:24 L	Otavio	Pinheiro	BRA	11.5.73	2 Feb
2:12:24 L	Moses	Tanui	KEN	20.8.65	19 Oct
2:12:25 L	Koichi	Inagaki	JPN	26.6.79	2 Feb
2:12:25 L	Lucian Desdery	Hombo	TAN		26 Oct
2:12:29 L	Stephen	Kiogora	KEN	29.11.76	5 Oct
2:12:32 L	John	Rotich	KEN	68	14 Sep
2:12:37 L	Elijah	Mutai Chemwolo	KEN	1.4.78	16 Mar
2:12:37 L	David	Simukwo	KEN	69	5 Oct
2:12:39 L	Agustine	Kavutu Mbusya	KEN	77	2 Mar
2:12:42 L	Henry	Tarus	KEN	6.12.78	27 Apr
2:12:45 L	Moges	Taye	ETH	12.11.73	9 Jan
2:12:45 L	Andrew	Letherby	AUS	19.9.73	7 Dec
2:12:46 L	Eddy	Hellebuyck	USA	22.1.61	5 Oct
2:12:47 L	Dmitriy	Baranovskiy	UKR	28.7.79	26 Oct
2:12:50 P	Nelson	Lebo	KEN	27.12.77	26 Oct
2:12:51 P	Michael	Kapkiai	KEN	27.12.68	12 Oct
2:12:52 L	John	Kiprono	KEN	68	23 Mar
2:12:53 L	Luke	Kibet	KEN	19.6.73	23 Mar
2:12:53 L	Dickson	Marwa	KEN	83	6 Jul
2:12:53 L	Eric	Gerome	BEL	4.2.69	12 Oct
2:12:54 L	Yoshiteru	Morishita	JPN	26.5.71	9 Feb
2:12:54 L	Angelo	Carosi	ITA	20.1.64	27 Apr
2:12:56 L	Jomo Godwin	Kororia	KEN	81	26 Apr
2:12:57 L	Kamel	Ziani	ESP	20.2.72	13 Apr
2:12:58 L	Dale	Warrender	NZL	8.9.73	7 Dec
2:13:00 L	Jonathon	Wyatt	NZL	20.12.72	27 Apr
2:13:02 L	Tomoyuki	Sato	JPN	31.1.81	23 Feb
2:13:03 L	Julius	Rutto	KEN	26.12.71	26 Oct
2:13:05 L		Kim Yi-yong	KOR	20.9.73	2 Nov
2:13:11 L	Toshiya	Katayama	JPN	23.4.73	2 Mar
2:13:11 L	Lukas	Cherono	KEN	30.12.76	9 Mar
2:13:12 L	Barnabas	Kenduiywo	KEN	74	5 Oct
2:13:13 L	Erick	Wainaina	KEN	19.12.73	31 Aug
2:13:15 L	Mukhamet	Nazipov (199)	RUS	10.9.61	26 Apr

Downhill

Mark			Nat	Born	Date
2:12:00 D	Erick	Wainaina	KEN	19.12.73	20 Apr
2:12:41 D	Andrzej	Krzyscin	POL	16.8.67	16 Feb
2:12:51 D	Jimmy	Hearld	USA	5.3.68	16 Feb

600m short:

Mark			Nat	Born	Date
2:11:46 L	Nikolay Kerimov		RUS	13.11.67	21 Jun

100 KILOMETRES

Mark	Name		Nat	Born	Pos	Meet	Venue	Date
6:26:38	Jorge	Aubeso	ESP	5.12.66	1	NC	Madrid	16 May
6:28:27	Farit	Ganiyev	RUS	13.12.64	1	EC	Chernogolovka	19 Apr
6:29:41	Grigoriy	Murzin	RUS	23.1.70	2	EC	Chernogolovka	19 Apr
6:33:22	Mario	Ardemagni	ITA	2.4.63	3	EC	Chernogolovka	19 Apr
6:33:42	Oleg	Rudenko	RUS	14.10.72	4	EC	Chernogolovka	19 Apr
6:36:32	Igor	Tyazhkorov	RUS	4.12.67	1		Torhout	19/20 Jun

Mark	Name		Nat	Born	Pos	Meet	Venue	Date
6:37:07	Anatoliy	Kruglikov	RUS	9.10.57	5	EC	Chernogolovka	19 Apr
6:38:06	Yoshiaki	Kobayashi	JPN	7.11.72	1		Yubetsu	29 Jun
6:39:32		Ganiyev			2		Torhout	19/20 Jun
6:39:40		Murzin			1		Santa Cruz de Bezana	4 Oct
6:40:22		Murzin			3		Torhout	19/20 Jun
	(11/7)							
6:41:39	Jaroslaw	Janicki	POL	6.7.66	2		Madrid	16 Mar
6:43:36	Jun-ichi	Nomura	JPN	5.1.77	2		Yubetsu	29 Jun
6:46:48	Ildar	Akhmetshin (10)	RUS	.70	7	EC	Chernogolovka	19 Apr
6:47:38	Hideo	Nojo	JPN	24.12.76	3		Yubetsu	29 Jun
6:47:45	Valeriy	Sinyushkin	RUS	31.3.67	8	EC	Chernogolovka	19 Apr
6:48:10	Dmitriy	Radyuchenko	RUS	27.11.70	9	EC	Chernogolovka	19 Apr
6:48:38.8 t	Vladimir	Netreba	RUS	21.10.67	2		S.Giovanni Lupatoto	27 Sep

6:50:00	Stefano	Sartori	ITA	28.5.65	19 Apr
6:51:40	Stanislav	Lazyuta	UKR	24.10.72	19 Apr
6:53:00	Michael	Sommer	GER	2.3.64	19 Apr
6:53:07	Marc	Vanderlinden	BEL	3.12.58	20 Jun
6:54:03	Aleksandr	Vishnyagov	RUS	76	19 Apr
6:54:03	Mario	Fattore (20)	ITA	16.6.75	25 May

Best track times

6:41:48.6 t	Ardemagni	1	S.Giovanni Lupatoto	27 Sep
6:49:52.7 t	Tyazhkorov	3	S.Giovanni Lupatoto	27 Sep

24 HOURS

273.828 km t	Valmir	Nunes	BRA	16.1.64	1		Soochow	10-11 Mar
270.087	Paul	Beckers	BEL	22.8.62	1	EC	Uden	11-12 Oct
267.510t	Yiannis	Kouros	GRE	13.2.56	1	in 48hr	Surgères	3-4 May
267.427	Ewald	Eder	AUT	27.12.56	1		Worschach	19-20 Jul
267.223	Ryoichi	Sekiya	JPN	12.2.67	2	EC	Uden	11-12 Oct
264.967	Etienne	Van Acker	BEL	2.3.52	3	EC	Uden	11-12 Oct
264.901	Günter	Klammer	AUT	.59	1		Worschach	19-20 Jul
261.640t		Sekiya			2		Soochow	10-11 Mar
261.030t	Joseph	Gaebler	USA	.78	1	NC	San Diego	8-9 Nov
258.037	Andrey	Kazantsev	RUS	16.11.62	4	EC	Uden	11-12 Oct
256.847	Lucien	Taelman	BEL	9.7.57	5	EC	Uden	11-12 Oct
255.302	Dmitriy	Tishin	RUS	1.5.82	6	EC	Uden	11-12 Oct
	(12/11)							
254.992	Valeriy	Kanarski	BLR		7	EC	Uden	11-12 Oct
254.278	Anatoliy	Kruglikov	RUS	9.10.57	1		St Petersburg	6-7 Sep
252.014	Vladimir	Bychkov	RUS	.67	2		St Petersburg	6-7 Sep
251.572	Wim	Epskamp	NED	8.1.54	8	EC	Uden	11-12 Oct
251.046	Alan	Prual	FRA	24.9.59	1		Brive	29-30 May

248.864t	John	Geesler	USA	2.9.59	9 Nov
248.170	Mohammed	Magroun	FRA	15.7.59	12 Oct
244.835t		Chen Chen-yun	TPE	16.6.56	11 Mar
243.634	Jirí	Krejci	CZE	10.4.66	25 Jul
241.561t	Tatsuya	Maeda (21)	JPN	9.10.65	-6 Jul

Further best track time

247.705t	Dmitriy	Tishin	RUS	1.5.82	11 May

2000 METRES STEEPLECHASE

5:23.04	José Luis	Blanco	ESP	3.6.75	1	v2N	Barcelona (M)	11 Jul
5:25.47	Julius	Nyamu	KEN	1.12.77	1		Naimette	2 Sep
5:26.08	Kipkirui	Misoi	KEN	23.12.78	2		Naimette	2 Sep
5:27.64	Ronald	Kipchumba Rutto	KEN-Y	8.10.87	3		Naimette	2 Sep
5:28.45	Francisco Javier	Munuera	ESP	7.7.72	2	v2N	Barcelona (M)	11 Jul
5:28.56	John	Langat	KEN	27.11.74	4		Naimette	2 Sep
5:28.78	Justus Kiprono	Kipchirchir	KEN-Y	28.2.87	5		Naimette	2 Sep
5:29.51	Jakub	Czaja	POL	12.9.80	1		Gdansk	24 May

JUNIORS

5:34.52	Jonas	Monaheng	RSA	4.5.84	1		Potchefstroom	25 Jun
5:35.36	Ruben	Schwarz	GER	31.1.84	1	NC-j	Fulda	5 Jul
5:37.68	David	Kirwa	KEN	1.8.85	2		Torrevieja	26 Apr
5:39.31	Siyaya	Khosa	RSA	12.6.87	1		Durban	13 Apr
5:40.28	Lukhanyo	Mabinza	RSA	9.9.86	2		Durban	13 Apr

3000 METRES STEEPLECHASE

7:57.38	Saïf Saaeed	Shaheen	QAT	15.10.82	1	WAF	Monaco	14 Sep
	(Formerly Stephen Cherono KEN)							
7:57.42	Paul Kipsiele	Koech	KEN	10.11.81	2	WAF	Monaco	14 Sep
8:00.06		Shaheen			1	VD	Bruxelles	5 Sep
8:00.42		Koech			2	VD	Bruxelles	5 Sep
8:02.48		Shaheen			1	WK	Zürich	15 Aug
8:02.49	Ezekiel	Kemboi	KEN	25.5.82	2	WK	Zürich	15 Aug
8:04.39		Shaheen			1	WCh	Saint-Denis	26 Aug
8:04.75		Cherono/Shaheen			1	DNG	Stockholm	5 Aug

Mark	Name		Nat	Born	Pos	Meet	Venue	Date
8:05.11		Kemboi			2	WCh	Saint-Denis	26 Aug
8:05.28		Koech			2	DNG	Stockholm	5 Aug
8:05.68		Cherono/Shaheen			1	GP	Tríkala	24 Jun
8:06.19		Kemboi			1	GS	Ostrava	12 Jun
8:06.37		Kemboi			1	Athl	Lausanne	1 Jul
8:06.41		Cherono/Shaheen			1	Gaz	Saint-Denis	4 Jul
8:06.63		Koech			2	Gaz	Saint-Denis	4 Jul
8:06.68		Koech			1	FBK	Hengelo	1 Jun
8:06.91	Bouabdellah	Tahri	FRA	20.12.78	3	Gaz	Saint-Denis	4 Jul
8:07.74	Kipkirui	Misoi	KEN	23.12.78	4	Gaz	Saint-Denis	4 Jul
8:07.98		Koech			2	GS	Ostrava	12 Jun
8:09.06	Julius	Nyamu	KEN	1.12.77	1	NA	Heusden	2 Aug
8:09.09	Eliseo	Martín	ESP	5.11.73	3	WCh	Saint-Denis	26 Aug
8:09.16	Wilson	Boit Kipketer	KEN	6.10.73	3	GS	Ostrava	12 Jun
8:09.18	Simon	Vroemen	NED	11.5.69	3	VD	Bruxelles	5 Sep
8:09.34		Nyamu			4	GS	Ostrava	12 Jun
8:09.37	Abel	Cheruiyot/Yagut	KEN-J	26.12.84	2	NA	Heusden	2 Aug
	(now Abel Yagoot Jowhar Salem BRN) (10)							
8:09.45		Nyamu			2	GP	Tríkala	24 Jun
8:09.54		Koech			3	WK	Zürich	15 Aug
8:09.65	Reuben	Kosgei	KEN	2.8.79	2	FBK	Hengelo	1 Jun
8:09.79		Misoi			5	GS	Ostrava	12 Jun
8:10.22		Misoi			3	GP	Tríkala	24 Jun
8:10.33	Abraham	Cherono	KEN	21.7.80	6	GS	Ostrava	12 Jun
8:10.33		Nyamu			4	VD	Bruxelles	5 Sep
8:10.65		Tahri			4	WCh	Saint-Denis	26 Aug
8:10.83		Misoi			2	Athl	Lausanne	1 Jul
8:11.79		Kemboi			3	WAF	Monaco	14 Sep
	(35/12)							
8:13.02	Michael	Kipyego	KEN	2.10.83	3	FBK	Hengelo	1 Jun
8:13.31	Ali	Ezzine	MAR	3.9.78	6	VD	Bruxelles	5 Sep
8:13.52	Luis Miguel	Martín	ESP	11.1.72	6	WCh	Saint-Denis	26 Aug
8:13.86	José Luis	Blanco	ESP	3.6.75	3		San Sebastián	10 Aug
8:14.14	David	Chemweno	KEN	18.12.81	4	GP II	Sevilla	7 Jun
8:14.81	Zouhaïr	El Ouardi	MAR	15.2.77	8	VD	Bruxelles	5 Sep
8:15.33	Abdelkader	Hachlaf	MAR	3.7.78	6	Gaz	Saint-Denis	4 Jul
8:15.54	Pavel	Potapovich	RUS	26.11.80	7	Gaz	Saint-Denis	4 Jul
	(20)							
8:15.82	Antonio	Jiménez	ESP	18.2.77	5	GP II	Sevilla	7 Jun
8:16.96	Bostjan	Buc	SLO	13.4.80	7	GS	Ostrava	12 Jun
8:17.48	Vincent	Le Dauphin	FRA	28.6.76	9	Gaz	Saint-Denis	4 Jul
8:17.72	Jukka	Keskisalo	FIN	27.3.81	9	WCh	Saint-Denis	26 Aug
8:17.90	Günther	Weidlinger	AUT	5.4.78	8	GS	Ostrava	12 Jun
8:18.27	John	Langat	KEN	27.11.74	4	NA	Heusden	2 Aug
8:18.51	Khamis Seif	Abdullah	QAT	1.12.76	1	GP II	Zagreb	7 Jul
8:18.79	Lotfi	Turki	TUN	6.3.75	5	NA	Heusden	2 Aug
8:18.93	Yoshitaka	Iwamizu	JPN	20.6.79	4h1	WCh	Saint-Denis	23 Aug
8:19.26	Linus	Chumba	KEN	9.2.80	2	GP II	Zagreb	7 Jul
	(30)							
8:19.31	Martin	Pröll	AUT	21.3.81	9	GS	Ostrava	12 Jun
8:19.35	Antonio	Martínez	ESP	20.12.78	7	GP II	Sevilla	7 Jun
8:19.82	César	Pérez	ESP	7.4.75	4	NC	Jerez de la Frontera	2 Aug
8:19.92	Gaël	Pencréach	FRA	5.8.77	10	GS	Ostrava	12 Jun
8:20.50	Filmon	Ghirmai	GER	25.1.79	2		Luzern	25 Jun
8:21.15	Damian	Kallabis	GER	10.6.73	3	GP II	Zagreb	7 Jul
8:21.30	Luleseged	Wale	ETH	.82	7h1	WCh	Saint-Denis	23 Aug
8:21.92	Radoslaw	Poplawski	POL	16.1.83	1	Mal M	Grudziadz	9 Jun
8:22.32	Steve	Slattery	USA	14.8.80	5h3	WCh	Saint-Denis	23 Aug
8:22.39	Francisco Javier	Munuera	ESP	7.7.72	6	NC	Jerez de la Frontera	2 Aug
	(40)							
8:22.95	Frédéric	Denis	FRA	3.3.75	1		Albertville	10 Jul
8:23.35	Mustafa	Mohamed	SWE	1.3.79	12	DNG	Stockholm	5 Aug
8:23.41	Tewodros	Shiferaw	ETH	.80	6h3	WCh	Saint-Denis	23 Aug
8:23.80	Adil	El Ouadili	FRA	3.9.81	3		Strasbourg	26 Jun
8:23.85	Philip	Manyim	KEN	24.3.78	5	GP II	Zagreb	7 Jul
8:24.10	Dan	Lincoln	USA	22.10.80	2	NC	Stanford	21 Jun
8:24.12	Hicham	Guermoud	MAR	.79	4		Rabat	14 Jun
8:24.54	Ronald	Kipchumba Rutto	KEN-Y	8.10.87	3	Gugl	Linz	31 Jul
8:24.57	Ralf	Assmus	GER	28.1.77	1		Rehlingen	9 Jun

Mark	Name		Nat	Born	Pos	Meet	Venue	Date
8:24.60	Hakim	Maazouz	ALG	28.8.75	7h2	WCh	Saint-Denis	23 Aug
	(50)							
8:24.82	Robert	Gary	USA	5.4.73	3	NC	Stanford	21 Jun
8:25.04	Daba	Maru Girma	ETH	12.12.80	2		Rennes	7 Jun
8:25.46	Irba	Lakhal	FRA	12.12.75	7	GP II	Zagreb	7 Jul
8:25.55	Henrik	Skoog	SWE	17.4.79	8	GP II	Zagreb	7 Jul
8:25.61	Vincent	Zouaoui Dandrieux	FRA	12.10.80	1		Paris (C)	1 Jun
8:25.65	Angelo	Iannelli	ITA	27.7.76	9	GP II	Zagreb	7 Jul
8:25.73	Merzak Ould	Bouchiba	ALG	27.4.75	1		Casablanca	12 Aug
8:25.92	Sammy	Kiplagat	KEN	.73	4		Rehlingen	9 Jun
8:26.13	Peter	Nowill	AUS	15.6.79	6		Luzern	25 Jun
8:26.18	Jakub	Czaja	POL	12.9.80	4	Odlozil	Praha	29 Jun
	(60)							
8:26.46	Rafal	Wójcik	POL	18.9.72	10	GP II	Zagreb	7 Jul
8:26.65	Raphael	Schäfer	GER	6.3.81	5		Rehlingen	9 Jun
8:26.91	Stéphane	Desaulty	FRA	8.1.72	1		Saint-Maur	16 Jul
8:27.82	Sa'ad Shaddad	Al-Asmari	KSA	24.9.68	11	GS	Ostrava	12 Jun
8:28.36	Christian	Knoblich	GER	1.10.76	6		Rehlingen	9 Jun
8:28.53	Jan	Zakrzewski	POL	21.12.70	12	GS	Ostrava	12 Jun
8:28.64	Vadim	Slobodenyuk	UKR	17.3.81	8h3	WCh	Saint-Denis	23 Aug
8:28.72	Christian	Belz	SUI	11.9.74	7		Rehlingen	9 Jun
8:28.76	Roman	Usov	RUS	4.6.78	1		Moskva	15 May
8:29.39	Alexander	Motone	RSA	26.6.78	1		Port Elizabeth	28 Feb
	(70)							
8:29.44	Jordan	Desilets	USA	5.12.80	2	NCAA	Sacramento	13 Jun
8:29.54	Sivuyile	Dlongwana	RSA	21.8.81	2		Port Elizabeth	28 Feb
8:29.8A	Mark	Tanui	KEN		3	NC	Nairobi	12 Jul
8:29.94	Matthew	Kerr	CAN	3.5.76	1	Jerome	Burnaby	8 Jun
8:29.96	Julius	Kiptoo	KEN	4.9.77	1		Dreux	13 Jun
8:30.52	Yasunori	Uchitomi	JPN	29.10.72	2	NC	Yokohama	7 Jun
8:30.67	Manuel	Núñez	ESP	16.6.74	10		San Sebastián	10 Aug
8:30.74	Tom	Kloos	USA	.78	2h2	NC	Stanford	19 Jun
8:30.99	Thomas	Chorny	USA	23.11.76	4	NC	Stanford	21 Jun
8:31.03	Anthony	Famiglietti	USA	8.11.78	2h1	NC	Stanford	19 Jun
	(80)							
8:31.23	Jared	Cordes	USA	22.7.77	3h1	NC	Stanford	19 Jun
8:31.50	Jim	Svenøy	NOR	22.4.72	2	ECp-1A	Lappeenranta	22 Jun
8:31.57	Sergio	Martín	ESP	25.3.78	11		San Sebastián	10 Aug
8:31.64	Badre Din	Zioini	FRA	25.3.76	2		Pezenas	31 May
8:31.71	Bashir Omer	Ibrahim	SUD	14.3.79	3	NCAA	Sacramento	13 Jun
8:31.85	Thomas	Kiplitan	KEN	15.6.83	8	GP	Tríkala	24 Jun
8:31.93	Sergey	Redko	UKR	24.1.73	3	MalM	Grudziadz	9 Jun
8:31.97	Barnabas	Kosgei	KEN-Y	20.9.86	1		Karlstad	24 Jul
8:32.05	Michael	Nejedly	CZE	1.10.69	12	GP II	Zagreb	7 Jul
8:32.18	Isaiah	Festa	USA	10.3.80	4	NCAA	Sacramento	13 Jun
	(90)							
8:32.66	Petrus	Sithole	RSA	29.3.76	1	NC	Port Elizabeth	26 Apr
8:33.0A	Luke	Kibet	KEN	12.4.83	5	NC	Nairobi	12 Jul
8:33.01	José María	González	ESP	3.3.73	7	NC	Jerez de la Frontera	2 Aug
8:33.02	Ahmed	Hamzaoui	MAR	23.3.80	6		Rabat	14 Jun
8:33.12	Alexander	Greaux	PUR	22.9.77	12	GP II	Sevilla	7 Jun
8:33.14	Dave	Cullum	USA	26.10.73	5h2	NC	Stanford	19 Jun
8:33.26	Manuel	Silva	POR	8.10.78	8	Odlozil	Praha	29 Jun
8:33.35	Lyle	Weese	USA	26.10.79	6h2	NC	Stanford	19 Jun
8:33.54	Carlos	Blackhurst	USA	2.9.77	5h1	NC	Stanford	19 Jun
8:33.58	Yoshio	Sekikawa	JPN	16.2.79	3	NC	Yokohama	7 Jun
	(100)							

8:33.61	Mustafa Ahmed	Shebto	QAT-Y	4.7.86	12 Aug
8:33.68	Halil	Akkas	TUR	1.7.83	19 Jul
8:33.70	Mário	Teixeira	POR	20.9.74	5 Jul
8:33.79	Joël	Bourgeois	CAN	25.4.71	29 Jun
8:33.8A	Nathan	Naibei	KEN-Y	10.11.86	18 Jun
8:33.88	Sandy	Rebenciuc	USA	26.5.69	8 Jun
8:33.90	Aziz	Driouche	MAR	15.11.77	16 Jul
8:34.26	Néstor	Nieves	VEN	29.12.74	7 Aug
8:34.36	Yuri	Floriani	ITA	25.12.81	1 Jun
8:34.37	Andy	Smith	USA		19 Jun
8:34.5A	Brimin	Kipruto	KEN-J	31.7.85	18 Jun
8:34.52	Nordine	Gezzar	FRA	17.2.80	13 Jun
8:34.68	Ion	Luchianov	MDA	31.1.81	17 Jul
8:34.72	David	Kirwa	KEN-J	1.8.85	11 May
8:34.74	Hassan	Oubassour	MAR	20.7.80	16 Jul
8:34.97	David	Gerych	CZE	3.5.77	12 Jun
8:35.10	Joaquín	Torres	ESP	14.8.77	5 Jul
8:35.1A	Amon	Kipchirchir	KEN-J	.85	18 Jun
8:35.26	Andrey	Olshanskiy	RUS	15.6.78	10 Aug
8:35.65	David	Milne	CAN	12.9.79	2 May
8:35.81	Kevin	Barra	USA	19.12.80	13 Jun
8:36.04	Hamid	Ezzine	MAR	5.10.83	6 Jul
8:36.12	Koen	Wilssens	BEL	15.3.81	2 Aug
8:36.25	Christian	Klein	GER	19.9.83	17 Jul
8:36.50	Jakub	Wisniewski	POL	3.11.77	9 Jun
8:36.79	Steffen	Preuk	GER	2.6.82	9 Jun
8:36.92	Itai	Maggidi	ISR	9.1.81	13 Jun
8:37.19	Gulte	Bekele	ETH-J	84	20 Jul
8:37.36	Eric	Segura	ESP	9.6.79	5 Jul
8:37.43	Hamid	Jaouane	FRA	3.4.72	13 Jun

Mark	Wind	Name		Nat	Born	Pos	Meet	Venue	Date

Mark	Name		Nat	Born	Date
8:37.53	Máté	Németh	HUN	9.2.81	2 May
8:37.55	Stuart	Stokes	GBR	5.12.76	31 May
8:37.60	Mohamed	Abdellaoui	ALG	22.4.79	13 Jun
8:37.65	Marc	Cepeda	ESP	1.7.74	10 Aug
8:37.79	Titus	Chepkwony	KEN		20 Jul
8:37.87	Mohammed Ali	Al-Banai	KSA-J	13.9.85	17 Jul
8:37.93	José Salvador	Miranda	MEX	22.8.71	17 Apr
8:37.99	Kim	Bergdahl	FIN	5.3.78	10 Aug
8:38.34	Rubén	Palomeque	ESP	14.8.80	5 Jul
8:38.41	Mourad	Benslimani	ALG	19.2.74	9 Jun
8:38.5A	Eric	Rotich	KEN		12 Jul
8:38.68	Krijn	Van Koolwijk	BEL	30.8.81	2 Aug
8:38.90	Kevin	Paulsen	FRA	28.3.80	31 May
8:39.08	Antonio	Lagares	ESP	26.12.82	22 Jul
8:39.09	Andrew	Franklin	GBR	13.9.80	31 May
8:39.10	Ben	Bruce	USA		11 Jun
8:39.24	Mark	Croghan	USA	8.1.68	2 May
8:39.3A	Richard	Matelong	KEN	.82	10 Jul
8:39.38	Francisco Javier	Lara	ESP	24.6.76	5 Jul
8:39.4	Jaroslav	Muschinschi	MDA	8.8.76	31 May
8:39.70	Richard	Jeremiah	AUS	3.12.82	2 May
8:39.90	Abraham	Kebeto	ETH-Y	86	3 Aug
8:39.93	Tuomo	Lehtinen	FIN	2.2.79	12 Jul
8:39.97	Pieter	Desmet (154)	BEL	7.6.83	2 Aug

JUNIORS

See main list for top 3 juniors. 11 performances by 5 men to 8:34.0. Additional marks and further juniors:

Cher't/Yugut	8:16.96	4	San Sebastián	10 Aug	8:19.24	8	WK	Zürich	15 Aug
	8:18.43	2	Rabat	14 Jun	8:19.94	3	Odl	Praha	29 Jun
	8:18.70	1	Luzern	25 Jun	8:24.23	1	Gaz	Saint-Denis	4 Jul

8:33.61	Mustafa Ahmed	Shebto	QAT-Y	4.7.86	2		Casablanca	12 Aug
8:33.8A	Nathan	Naibei	KEN-Y	10.11.86	1		Nairobi	18 Jun
8:34.5A	Brimin	Kipruto	KEN	31.7.85	2		Nairobi	18 Jun
8:34.72	David	Kirwa	KEN	1.8.85	2		Gavá	11 May
8:35.1A	Amon	Kipchirchir	KEN	.85	3		Nairobi	18 Jun
8:37.19	Gulte	Bekele	ETH	84	5		Hamburg	20 Jul
8:37.87	Mohammed Ali	Al-Banai (10)	KSA	13.9.85	6		Alger	17 Jul
8:39.90	Abraham	Kebeto	ETH-Y	86	1	Af-J	Garoua	3 Aug
8:42.86	Anthony	Godongwana	RSA	24.9.84	3		Port Elizabeth	28 Feb
8:43.26	Mandla	Maseko	RSA	12.9.85	4		Port Elizabeth	28 Feb
8:45.17	Cyrus	Njui	KEN-Y	11.2.86	1		Maebashi	16 Jun
8:45.53	Marcel	Ionascu	ROM	4.8.84	2	NC	Bucuresti	10 Aug
8:46.21	Ruben	Schwarz	GER	31.1.84	1	EJ	Tampere	27 Jul
8:47.06		Lin Xiangqian	CHN	27.1.87	2		Shanghai	13 Sep
8:49.47		Meng Fei	CHN	1.8.85	1	NG	Changsha	26 Oct
8:50.75	Mark	Christie	IRL	12.1.85	1	NC	Dublin (S)	10 Aug
8:51.25	Norbert	Löwa (20)	GER	2.1.84	17		Rehlingen	9 Jun

110 METRES HURDLES

Mark	Wind	Name		Nat	Born	Pos	Meet	Venue	Date
12.97	0.0	Allen	Johnson	USA	1.3.71	1	Gaz	Saint-Denis	4 Jul
13.06	0.0		Johnson			1	Athl	Lausanne	1 Jul
13.08	0.0	Stanislav	Olijar	LAT	22.3.79	2	Athl	Lausanne	1 Jul
13.08	-0.4		Johnson			1	GGala	Roma	11 Jul
13.11	-1.5		Johnson			1	WAF	Monaco	13 Sep
13.12	0.3		Johnson			1	WCh	Saint-Denis	30 Aug
13.14	0.2		Olijar			1	Bisl	Oslo	27 Jun
13.15	-0.8		Olijar			1	GS	Ostrava	12 Jun
13.16	0.3		Johnson			1	VD	Bruxelles	5 Sep
13.17	0.0		Liu Xiang	CHN	13.7.83	3	Athl	Lausanne	1 Jul
13.17	0.5	Duane	Ross	USA	5.12.72	1	GP II	Zagreb	7 Jul
13.17	-1.5	Terrence	Trammell	USA	23.11.78	2	WAF	Monaco	13 Sep
13.19	0.0		Johnson			1s2	WCh	Saint-Denis	29 Aug
13.19	0.3		Liu Xiang			2	VD	Bruxelles	5 Sep
13.20	0.4		Olijar			1	GP	Tríkala	24 Jun
13.20	-0.4		Liu Xiang			2	GGala	Roma	11 Jul
13.20	0.3		Trammell			1	WCh	Saint-Denis	30 Aug
13.21	0.0		Liu Xiang			1r2		Guangzhou	8 Apr
13.21	1.4		Ross			1s1	NC	Stanford	21 Jun
13.21	0.0		Ross			2	Gaz	Saint-Denis	4 Jul
13.22	0.5		Liu Xiang			2	GP II	Zagreb	7 Jul
13.22	-0.5		Ross			1	WK	Zürich	15 Aug
13.22	-0.5		Olijar			2	WK	Zürich	15 Aug
13.23	1.4	Larry	Wade	USA	22.11.74	1	Mod R	Modesto	10 May
13.23	1.9	Ladji	Doucouré	FRA	28.3.83	1s1	EU23	Bydgoszcz	20 Jul
13.23	0.3		Liu Xiang			3	WCh	Saint-Denis	30 Aug
13.24	1.0		Wade			1	Pre	Eugene	24 May
13.24	-0.4		Ross			3	GGala	Roma	11 Jul
13.25	-0.6		Ross			1		Dortmund	15 Jun
13.25	0.6		Doucouré			1	EU23	Bydgoszcz	20 Jul
13.25	-1.5		Olijar			3	WAF	Monaco	13 Sep
		(31/7)							
13.26	0.5	Chris	Phillips	USA	24.7.72	1h5	WCh	Saint-Denis	28 Aug
13.27	0.8	Ron	Bramlett	USA	22.10.79	1	Odlozil	Praha	29 Jun

Mark	Wind	Name		Nat	Born	Pos	Meet	Venue	Date
13.28	0.4	Maurice	Wignall	JAM	17.4.76	1	Gugl	Linz	31 Jul
		(10)							
13.32	0.5	Jabari	Greer	USA	11.2.82	1	SEC	Knoxville	18 May
13.32	-0.3	Dawane	Wallace	USA	30.12.76	1		Fribourg	23 Aug
13.34	1.5	Redelen	dos Santos	BRA	24.4.76	1h1		São Paulo	6 Sep
13.35	-0.1	Ryan	Wilson	USA	19.12.80	1	NCAA	Sacramento	14 Jun
13.35	1.0	Dominique	Arnold	USA	14.9.73	1		Walnut	13 Jul
13.35	-0.2	Yuniel	Hernández	CUB	28.3.81	1	PAm	Santo Domingo	9 Aug
13.36	1.3	Robert	Newton	GBR	10.5.81	1		Loughborough	31 Jul
13.36	0.4	Elmar	Lichtenegger	AUT	25.5.74	2	Gugl	Linz	31 Jul
13.38	0.8	Chris	Pinnock	JAM	26.3.79	1	Big 12	Austin	19 May
13.40i	-	Colin	Jackson	GBR	18.2.67	1		Tampere	13 Feb
		(20)							
13.40A	0.5	Márcio de	Souza	BRA	24.1.75	1		Cochabamba	11 May
13.40	-1.0		Shi Dongpeng	CHN-J	6.1.84	1	NC	Shanghai	14 Sep
13.41	0.5	Dudley	Dorival	HAI	1.9.75	3h5	WCh	Saint-Denis	28 Aug
13.42A	0.5	Mateus	Inocêncio	BRA	17.5.81	2		Cochabamba	11 May
13.42	0.0	Josh	Walker	USA	6.5.82	1	NCAA-r	Fairfax	31 May
13.42	1.7	William	Erese	NGR	12.9.76	2		Malles	12 Jul
13.43	1.4	Micah	Harris	USA	30.4.79	2	Mod R	Modesto	10 May
13.44	0.1	Anwar	Moore	USA	5.3.79	1h2	PennR	Philadelphia	25 Apr
13.46	1.1	Arend	Watkins	USA	23.5.79	1h1	NC	Stanford	20 Jun
13.46	0.0	Jerome	Crews	GER	20.2.77	1		Cuxhaven	19 Jul
		(30)							
13.46	0.2	Robert	Kronberg	SWE	15.8.76	1h1	WCh	Saint-Denis	28 Aug
13.47	0.4	Greg	Richardson	USA	27.12.76	2		Dudelange	24 May
13.47	1.0	Masato	Naito	JPN	31.7.80	1		Nagoya	20 Jul
13.49	0.2	Antwon	Hicks	USA	12.3.83	1		Oxford, MS	19 Apr
13.49	0.0	Aubrey	Herring	USA	19.9.78	2		Holmdel	11 Jun
13.49	0.6	Andrea	Giaconi	ITA	11.4.74	1		Bellinzona	26 Jul
13.49	0.0	Yoel	Hernández	CUB	12.12.77	3s2	WCh	Saint-Denis	29 Aug
13.50	0.2	Michael	Thomas	USA	21.12.81	2h1	SEC	Knoxville	17 May
13.50	0.6	Philip	Nossmy	SWE	6.12.82	2	EU23	Bydgoszcz	20 Jul
13.50	0.1	Shaun	Bownes	RSA	24.10.70	3h2	WCh	Saint-Denis	28 Aug
		(40)							
13.51	1.6	Tim	Bogdanof	USA	9.11.79	1h1	NCAA-r	Stanford	30 May
13.51	1.1	Todd	Matthews Jouda	USA/SUD	28.6.79	3h1	NC	Stanford	20 Jun
13.52	1.6	Anselmo G	da Silva	BRA	22.3.81	1rB		São Paulo	6 Jul
13.53	0.5	Kenneth	Ferguson	USA-J	22.3.84	2	SEC	Knoxville	18 May
13.53	0.5	Karl	Jennings	CAN	14.5.79	4	SEC	Knoxville	18 May
13.53	0.0	Mike	Fenner	GER	24.4.71	1h1		Dessau	30 May
13.53	-0.1	David	Payne	USA	24.7.82	3	NCAA	Sacramento	14 Jun
13.54	1.9	Jurica	Grabusic	CRO	28.3.83	2s1	EU23	Bydgoszcz	20 Jul
13.55	-0.5	Mark	Crear	USA	2.10.68	4h3	NC	Stanford	20 Jun
13.55	0.4	Anier	García	CUB	9.3.76	4	GP	Tríkala	24 Jun
		(50)							
13.55	0.6	Gregory	Sedoc	NED	16.10.81	3	EU23	Bydgoszcz	20 Jul
13.57	1.2	Matti	Niemi	FIN	15.11.76	1		Lahti	2 Jul
13.57	1.9	Sébastien	Denis	FRA	4.5.71	1	NC	Narbonne	25 Jul
13.58	-0.6	Falk	Balzer	GER	14.12.73	2	NC	Ulm	28 Jun
13.58	0.7	Charles	Allen	CAN	29.3.77	4h2	PAm	Santo Domingo	8 Aug
13.59	1.5	Jackson	Quiñónez	ECU	12.6.80	2	SACh	Barquisimeto	21 Jun
13.60	0.3	Ricardo	Moody	USA	24.9.80	1	NCAA-2	Edwardsville	24 May
13.60	1.4	Jan	Schindzielorz	GER	8.8.78	1		Zeven	8 Jun
13.60	-0.1	David	Oliver	USA	24.4.82	4	NCAA	Sacramento	14 Jun
13.60	1.9	Nenad	Loncar	SCG	6.3.81	3s1	EU23	Bydgoszcz	20 Jul
		(60)							
13.60	1.9	Jonathan	N'senga	BEL	21.4.73	2	FRA Ch	Narbonne	25 Jul
13.60	0.6	Satoru	Tanigawa	JPN	5.7.72	1		Kitakyushu	2 Nov
13.63	0.6	Sergey	Chepiga	RUS	6.3.82	6	EU23	Bydgoszcz	20 Jul
13.64	1.9	Joseph-Berlioz	Randriamihaja	MAD	30.11.75	3	NC	Narbonne	25 Jul
13.65	1.6	Emiliano	Pizzoli	ITA	29.6.74	2		Milano	28 Jun
13.65	-1.0		Cao Jing	CHN	31.1.78	2	NC	Shanghai	14 Sep
13.66A	1.7	Frikkie	van Zyl	RSA	30.7.81	2		Potchefstroom	31 Jan
13.66	0.6	Andrew	Turner	GBR	19.9.80	1		Loughborough	8 Jun
13.66	0.0	Sultan	Tucker	LBR	24.10.78	3		Holmdel	11 Jun
13.66	-0.9	Damien	Greaves	GBR	19.9.77	1	NC	Birmingham	26 Jul
		(70)							
13.66	0.3	Thomas	Blaschek	GER	5.4.81	1		Sondershausen	3 Sep
13.67	1.3	Kyle	Vander-Kuyp	AUS	30.5.71	1	Oda	Hiroshima	29 Apr
13.67	0.8	Sebastian	Siebert	GER	23.6.82	3		Zeulenroda	29 May

Mark	Wind	Name		Nat	Born	Pos	Meet	Venue	Date
13.67	1.7	Florian	Seibold	GER	27.6.79	4		Malles	12 Jul
13.68	0.0		Wu Youjia	CHN	6.5.83	3r2		Guangzhou	8 Apr
13.68	-0.2	Dimítrios	Piétris	GRE	24.10.79	4	ECp-S	Firenze	22 Jun
13.69	1.8	Robby	Hughes	USA	10.10.78	2r1		Clemson	10 May
13.70	1.1	Corey	Taylor	USA	2.5.81	1h2	NCAA-r	Fairfax	30 May
13.70	0.6	Igor	Peremota	RUS	14.1.81	7	EU23	Bydgoszcz	20 Jul
13.70	1.6	Marcel	van de Westen	NED	1.8.76	2h1		Leverkusen	3 Aug
		(80)							
13.71	0.0	Adrian	Ray	USA	9.10.81	1		San Marcos	19 May
13.71	2.0	Pawel	Didkowski	POL	7.7.77	1		Biala Podlaska	31 May
13.71	1.9	Chris	Stokes	USA	1.2.79	1		Sacramento	8 Jun
13.71	-0.1	David	Davis	USA	23.1.80	7	NCAA	Sacramento	14 Jun
13.71	0.2	Artur	Kohutek	POL	1.5.71	5		Königs Wusterhausen	6 Aug
13.71	-0.7		Park Tae-kyong	KOR	30.7.80	2	AsiC	Manila	21 Sep
13.72	0.9	Ivan	Bitzi	SUI	4.8.75	4=		Luzern	25 Jun
13.73	1.6	Dexter	Faulk	USA-J	14.4.84	1h3		Fayetteville	12 Apr
13.73	0.0	Paul	Whitty	CAN	1.10.82	2		San Marcos	19 May
13.73	1.8	Kelvin	Harris	USA	22.6.81	2h1	NCAA-r	Columbus	30 May
		(90)							
13.73	-0.6	Claude	Edorh	GER	27.2.72	4	NC	Ulm	28 Jun
13.73	0.0	Andreas	Dengler	GER	22.12.80	3=		Cuxhaven	19 Jul
13.73	0.0	Leonard	Hudec	AUT	13.6.73	3=		Cuxhaven	19 Jul
13.73A	1.2	Paulo	Villar	COL	28.7.78	1		Medellín	26 Jul
13.74	0.4	Dominique	DeGrammont	USA/HAI	13.3.79	2		Azusa	12 Apr
13.74	1.7	Reggie	Harrell	USA	28.11.81	1		Charlotte	17 May
13.74	-0.2	Joel	Brown	USA	31.1.80	5s1	NCAA	Sacramento	12 Jun
13.74	0.5	Cedric	Lavanne	FRA	13.11.80	2h1		Fribourg	23 Aug
13.75	1.8	Terry	Reese	USA	20.6.67	3r1		Clemson	10 May
13.75	1.1	Eric	Mitchum	USA-J	2.8.84	1h2	Pac-10	Los Angeles	17 May
		(100)							
13.75	0.6	David	Ilariani	GEO	20.1.81	5s2	EU23	Bydgoszcz	20 Jul
13.75	0.8	Felipe	Vivancos	ESP	16.6.80	1	NC	Jerez de la Frontera	2 Aug
13.76	0.1	Luis André	Balcers	BRA	18.10.73	29	Mar		

13.76	1.3	Tasuku	Tanonaka	JPN	23.9.78	29 Apr
13.76	1.1	Jeff	Hunter	USA	19.2.83	17 May
13.76	1.0	Philippe	Lamine	FRA	4.10.76	31 May
13.76	0.2	Shannon	Armstrong	USA	2.9.82	11 Jun
13.76	-0.4	Andrey	Kislykh	RUS	24.11.76	22 Jun
13.76	0.6	Zhivko	Videnov	BUL	23.5.77	13 Jul
13.76	1.3	Peter	Coghlan	IRL	27.3.75	31 Jul
13.78	0.0	Charles	Ryan	USA	10.2.81	17 May
13.78	1.2	Mubarak Ata	Mubarak	KSA	17.12.81	2 Jul
13.78	2.0	Dominic	Girdler	GBR	6.3.82	5 Jul
13.79	0.5	Virgil	Spier	NED	8.1.81	18 Jul
13.79	1.1	Muhammed	Sillah-Freckleton	GBR	11.9.80	31 Jul
13.80	0.7	Stephen	Jones	BAR	25.7.78	5 Apr
13.80	0.9	Eddie	Jackson	USA	19.12.80	19 Apr
13.80	1.9	Eugene	Swift	USA	14.9.64	8 Jun
13.80	-2.4	Walmes	da Silva	BRA	14.9.74	12 Jun
13.80		Hugh	Henry	BAR	.79	21 Jun
13.80	1.5	David	Filpowski	GER	25.10.83	22 Jun
13.80	0.7	Devis	Favaro	ITA	14.7.72	25 Jul
13.81	2.0	Marcin	Kuszewski	POL	19.5.77	6 Jul
13.82	1.3	Ricardo	Melbourne	JAM	26.2.82	19 Apr
13.82	0.8	Dirk	Riekmann	GER	14.4.72	7 Jun
13.82	0.6	Duncan	Malins	GBR	12.6.78	8 Jun
13.82	0.5	Luca	Giovannelli	ITA	29.9.75	9 Aug
13.83	0.0		Wang Hui	CHN	12.6.83	8 Apr
13.83	-1.5	Yuriy	Volkov	RUS	1.8.77	31 May
13.84	-0.6	Wenston	Riley	USA	24.4.77	28 Mar
13.84	0.1	Montrell	Person	USA	28.11.81	12 Apr
13.84	0.6	Chris	Baillie	GBR	21.4.81	8 Jun
13.84	-1.3	Daniel	Kiss	HUN	12.2.82	28 Jun
13.84	0.6	Balázs	Kovács	HUN	14.6.77	26 Jul
13.84	2.0	Miroslav	Novakovic	SCG	14.9.76	8 Aug
13.86	2.0	Vincent	Clarico	FRA	8.1.66	3 Jul
13.86	1.9	Thomas	Martin	FRA	19.2.80	25 Jul
13.86	1.9		Liu Zhu	CHN	30.4.83	26 Aug
13.86	0.9	Luis	Sá	POR	17.3.81	26 Aug
13.87A		Luis	López	MEX	21.2.82	17 May
13.87		Gabriel	Burnett	BAR	20.9.75	21 Jun
13.87	0.5	Douhou	Félou Sow	SEN	1.1.76	24 Jul
13.88	1.2	Chris	Carswell	USA	13.2.79	10 May
13.88	0.0	Deworski	Odom	USA	11.4.77	11 Jun
13.89	0.1	Tommy	Moore	USA		21 Mar
13.89	0.9	Yuji	Ohashi	JPN	5.9.83	5 Jul
13.89	2.0	Nicola	Comencini	ITA	7.5.78	12 Jul
13.89	0.7	Brandon	Hon	USA	7.7.79	19 Jul
13.90A	0.2	Ryan	Dowling	RSA	15.5.79	1 Mar
13.90	1.6	Lewis	Edmonson (150)	USA	26.2.79	12 Apr
13.90	1.7	Kenji	Yahata	JPN	4.11.80	18 May
13.90	1.3	Danyne	Brown	USA	14.4.81	30 May
13.90	0.0	Andrea	Alterio	ITA	11.6.73	14 Jun
13.90	0.8	Bartolomiej	Szymanski	POL	8.3.82	18 Jul
13.90	0.4	Raphaël	Monachon	SUI	8.2.73	6 Aug
13.91	0.4	Gregory	Hines	JAM	16.9.75	19 Apr
13.91	1.3	Gergely	Palágyi	HUN	19.4.79	20 Jun
13.91		Bryan	Clay	USA	3.1.80	13 Jul
13.92	0.8	Ivo	Burkhardt	GER	7.12.77	29 May
13.92	1.8	Artur	Budzillo	POL	21.7.79	11 Jun
13.92	0.0	Antonio	De Sanctis	ITA	18.10.72	12 Jul
13.92	1.9	Sergey	Demidyuk	UKR	5.6.82	20 Jul
13.92	2.0	Juha	Sonck	FIN	15.4.81	17 Aug
13.92	1.9	Suphan	Wongsriphuck	THA	31.5.77	8 Dec
13.93	1.5	Jonathon	Williams	USA	29.8.83	17 May
13.93	1.5	Terry	Ellis	USA	10.3.81	17 May
13.93	0.0	Shamar	Sands	BAH-J	30.4.85	17 May
13.93	0.5	Amadou	Bâ	SEN	28.7.79	24 Jul
13.93	0.5	Thiago	Castelo Branco	BRA	4.11.79	13 Oct
13.94	1.3	Kimihiro	Asami	JPN	8.11.72	29 Apr
13.94	1.5	Paul	Brown	USA	21.1.80	9 May
13.94	0.0	Richard	Phillips	JAM	26.1.83	31 May
13.94	-0.5	Tsuyoshi	Tsutsumi	JPN	27.9.76	6 Jun
13.94		Decosmo	Wright	JAM	82	14 Jun
13.94	1.7	Marko	Ritola	FIN	29.1.79	26 Jun
13.94	0.3	Andrea	Putignani	ITA	31.12.70	19 Jul
13.94	0.6	Zoran	Miljus	CRO	26.5.76	2 Aug
13.95	1.5	Ben	Clark	USA		22 Mar
13.95	-0.7	Selim	Nurudeen	USA	1.2.83	4 May
13.95	1.3	Willie	Powell	USA		30 May
13.95	-0.5	Paul	Gray	GBR	25.5.69	1 Jun
13.95	1.5	Krzysztof	Mehlich	POL	2.8.74	6 Jul
13.95	1.2	Bano	Traoré	FRA-J	25.4.85	13 Jul
13.95	-0.6	Dmitriy	Karpov	KAZ	23.7.81	27 Aug
13.95	0.0		Ji Wei	CHN-J	5.2.84	13 Sep
13.95	0.3		Liu Lilu (186)	CHN-J	6.2.85	24 Oct
13.96 to 13.99			25 men			

MEN 2003

Mark	Wind	Name		Nat	Born	Pos	Meet	Venue	Date
Wind assisted									
13.15	2.1		Olijar			1	ISTAF	Berlin (P)	10 Aug
13.19	2.1		Ross			2	ISTAF	Berlin (P)	10 Aug
13.20	2.6		Johnson			1		Carson/Los Angeles	1 Jun
13.21	2.1		Johnson			1		Fort-de-France	26 Apr
13.21	2.1		Johnson			3	ISTAF	Berlin (P)	10 Aug
13.37	2.6	Mark	Crear	USA	2.10.68	3		Carson/Los Angeles	1 Jun
13.46	2.3	Antwon	Hicks	USA	12.3.83	1rA	Tex R	Austin	5 Apr
13.46	2.1	Greg	Richardson	USA	27.12.76	3		Fort-de-France	26 Apr
13.47	3.2	Cédric	Lavanne	FRA	13.11.80	1		Saint-Brieuc	29 May
13.57	3.7	Shannon	Armstrong	USA	2.9.82	1h3	NCAA-r	Lincoln, NE	30 May
13.58	5.0	Dexter	Faulk	USA-J	14.4.84	1	JUCO	Levelland	10 May
13.58	4.3	Joel	Brown	USA	31.1.80	2	NCAA-r	Columbus	31 May
13.58	2.1	Dimítrios	Piétris	GRE	24.10.79	3	Veniz	Haniá	9 Jun
13.58	2.1	Jonathan	N'senga	BEL	21.4.73	4	Veniz	Haniá	9 Jun
13.59	5.0	Derrick	Williams	USA	25.3.82	2	JUCO	Levelland	10 May
13.59	2.9	Sergey	Chepiga	RUS	6.3.82	3h1	EU23	Bydgoszcz	18 Jul
13.62	2.6	Dominique	DeGrammont	USA/HAI	13.3.79	7		Carson/Los Angeles	1 Jun
13.63	2.1	Zhivko	Videnov	BUL	23.5.77	5	Veniz	Haniá	9 Jun
13.65	4.3	Kelvin	Harris	USA	22.6.81	4	NCAA-r	Columbus	31 May
13.68	3.9	David	Davis	USA	23.1.80	1h4	NCAA-r	Lincoln, NE	30 May
13.71	4.0	Ryan	Harlan	USA	25.4.81	2		College Station	8 May
13.71	2.9	Mubarak Ata	Mubarak	KSA	17.12.81	1	Arab C	Amman	7 Sep
13.72	2.4	Bashir	Ramzy	USA	4.5.79	1rB	Tex R	Austin	5 Apr
13.73	3.8	Eric	Mitchum	USA-J	2.8.84	2	Pac-10	Los Angeles	18 May

Mark	Wind	Name		Nat	Born	Date
13.75	3.2	Luis André	Balcers	BRA	18.10.73	31 May
13.79	2.2	Krzysztof	Mehlich	POL	2.8.74	6 Jul
13.80	2.9	Daniel	Kiss	HUN	12.2.82	18 Jul
13.82	2.1	Gregory	Hines	JAM	16.9.75	3 May
13.84	4.3	Selim	Nurudeen	USA	1.2.83	31 May
13.85	5.7	Milton	Manson	USA	4.12.82	30 Mar
13.85	4.5	Ben	Clark	USA		2 May
13.86		Clement	Owunna	NGR		29 Mar
13.86	2.2	Anson	Jackson	USA	12.2.81	12 Apr
13.86	3.3	Kenji	Yahata	JPN	4.11.80	6 Jun
13.88	2.1	Joey	Scott	USA	12.5.78	3 May
13.89	2.5	Franz	Petzold	GER	21.5.79	8 May
13.89	2.2	Willie	Powell	USA		16 May
13.90	2.8	Damien	Broothaerts	BEL	13.3.83	9 Jun
13.91	2.8	Justin	Wickard	USA	21.3.82	26 Apr
13.92	2.8	Andy	Long	USA	30.11.78	9 May
13.92	3.4	Tarmo	Jallai	EST	30.1.79	4 Aug
13.93	2.8	Sean	Temple	USA		9 May
13.94	4.9	0.	Nemba	USA		18 Apr
13.94	2.3	Esteban	Guzman	USA-J	2.5.84	25 Apr
13.94	3.2	Thierry	Herbé-Groleau	FRA	27.1.71	30 May

Low altitude bests

Mark	Wind	Name	Pos	Venue	Date
13.40	1.7	de Souza	1	Malles	12 Jul
13.43	0.5	Inocêncio	1	Cubatão	13 Oct
13.80	0.9	van Zyl			4 Feb
13.81	0.9	Villar			8 Aug
13.90	1.3	Dowling			1 Apr

Hand Timing

Mark	Wind	Name		Nat	Born	Pos	Venue	Date
13.2	1.1	Greg	Richardson	USA	27.12.76	1	Argentan	9 Jun
13.3	1.1	William	Erese	NGR	12.9.73	2	Argentan	9 Jun
13.3	1.1	Joseph-Berlioz	Randriamihaja	MAD	30.11.75	3	Argentan	9 Jun
13.5	-1.8	Anselmo G	da Silva	BRA	22.3.81	1	São Caetano do Sul	29 Mar
13.5	1.1	Sébastien	Denis	FRA	4.5.71	4	Argentan	9 Jun
13.5A	1.1	Ryan	Dowling	RSA	15.5.79	1	Germiston	20 Sep

Mark	Wind	Name		Nat	Born	Date
13.6	0.2	Miroslav	Novakovic	SCG	14.9.76	19 May
13.6		Chinedu	Elekwa	NGR-J	6.4.84	19 Jul
13.6	1.5	Yuji	Ohashi	JPN	5.9.83	13 Oct
13.7	1.5	Tasuku	Tanonaka	JPN	23.9.78	12 Apr
13.7	1.1	Yann	Dien	FRA	24.9.75	9 Jun
13.7		Deinma	Afesimana	NGR-J	14.6.84	19 Jul
13.7w	3.2	Ryan	Purcell	AUS	24.1.83	18 Oct

JUNIORS

See main list for top 4 juniors. 12 performances by 2 men to 13.65. Additional marks and further juniors:

Name	Mark	Wind	Pos	Meet	Venue	Date	Mark	Wind	Pos	Meet	Venue	Date
Shi D	13.48	0.2	4h5	WCh	Saint-Denis	28 Aug	13.53	0.4	1s1	WCh	Saint-Denis	29 Aug
	13.50	-0.7	1	AsiC	Manila	21 Sep	13.55	0.3	7	WCh	Saint-Denis	30 Aug
	13.50	0.0	2	NG	Changsha	25 Oct	13.57	0.0	2r2		Guangzhou	8 Apr
	13.51	-0.4	2		Shijiazhuang	4 Aug	13.63	0.0	2r1		Guangzhou	8 Apr
Ferguson	13.60	-0.4	1	NC-j	Stanfird	22 Jun	13.60	0.0	1	PAm-J	Bridgetown	18 Jul

Mark	Wind	Name		Nat	Born	Pos	Meet	Venue	Date
13.93	0.0	Shamar	Sands	BAH	30.4.85	4h3	SEC	Knoxville	17 May
13.95	1.2	Bano	Traoré	FRA	25.4.85	1	NC-j	Vénissieux	13 Jul
13.95	0.0		Ji Wei	CHN	5.2.84	1h1	NC	Shanghai	13 Sep
13.95	0.3		Liu Lilu	CHN	6.2.85	1h2	NG	Changsha	24 Oct
13.96	-0.3		Chen Ming	CHN	8.3.84	2h3	NC	Shanghai	13 Sep
13.98	0.5	Willi	Mathiszik (10)	GER	17.6.84	1		Rostock	28 May
13.98	-1.0	Yevgeniy	Borisov	RUS	7.3.84	4	Znam	Tula	8 Jun
13.99	-0.3	Yoichi	Iwafune	JPN	12.6.85	1		Nagasaki	2 Aug
14.00	-0.5	Kai	Doskoczynski	GER	15.7.84	1h3	EJ	Tampere	25 Jul
14.03	1.3	Thiago Carahyba	Dias	BRA	2.3.84	3h1		São Caetano do Sul	12 Feb
14.03	-1.0		Wang Yin	CHN	17.2.84	5	NC	Shanghai	14 Sep
14.04	0.7	Petr	Svoboda	CZE	10.10.84	3	Danek	Turnov	18 May
14.04	2.0	Mubarak	Al-Mabadi	KSA-Y	2.5.86	1		Lappeenranta	3 Aug
14.05	-0.1	Maksim	Lynsha	BLR	6.4.85	1	NC	Brest	11 Jul
14.08	0.5	Hideki	Nomoto	JPN	13.3.84	3=		Yokohama	5 Jul
14.10	1.3	Obiamlam	Ikwuakor (20)	USA	13.8.84	3h1	Big 12	Austin	18 May

Mark		Name		Nat	Born	Pos	Meet	Venue	Date
Wind assisted – see main list for two juniors. Additional men:									
13.94	2.3	Esteban	Guzman	USA	2.5.84	1h4	DrakeR	Des Moines	25 Apr
13.99	2.9	Mubarak Mabr.	Al-Mabadi	KSA-Y	2.5.86	2	ArabC	Amman	7 Sep
14.00	2.6	Eddy	De Lépine	FRA	30.3.84			Fort-de-France	5 Apr
14.05	3.2	Hideki	Nomoto	JPN	13.3.84	1h1	NC-j	Maebashi	29 Jun
Hand timed									
13.6		Chinedu	Elekwa	NGR	6.4.84	2	NC	Abuja	19 Jul
13.7		Deinma	Afesimana	NGR	14.6.84	3	NC	Abuja	19 Jul

300 METRES HURDLES

Mark	Name		Nat	Born	Pos	Meet	Venue	Date
35.54	Yoshihiro	Chiba	JPN	29.4.79	1		Nanao	27 Jul
35.80A	Llewellyn	Herbert	RSA	21.7.77	1		Parow	19 Dec
35.8	Christian	Duma	GER	5.2.82	1r2		Pliezhausen	18 May
35.9	Jan	Schneider	GER	24.1.76	1r3		Pliezhausen	18 May
35.91	Cédric	El-Idrissi	SUI	24.3.77	1		Langenthal	29 May

400 METRES HURDLES

Mark	Name		Nat	Born	Pos	Meet	Venue	Date
47.25	Félix	Sánchez	DOM	30.8.77	1	WCh	Saint-Denis	29 Aug
47.80		Sánchez			1	Athl	Lausanne	1 Jul
47.80		Sánchez			1	WAF	Monaco	14 Sep
47.82		Sánchez			1rA	WK	Zürich	15 Aug
48.05	Kemel	Thompson	JAM	25.9.74	1	GP	London (CP)	8 Aug
48.07		Sánchez			1	GP	Tríkala	24 Jun
48.10		Sánchez			1	GS	Ostrava	12 Jun
48.15		Sánchez			1	GGala	Roma	11 Jul
48.16		Sánchez			1s2	WCh	Saint-Denis	27 Aug
48.17	Periklis	Iakovákis	GRE	24.3.79	1s1	WCh	Saint-Denis	27 Aug
48.18	Joey	Woody	USA	22.5.73	2	WCh	Saint-Denis	29 Aug
48.19		Sánchez			1	PAm	Santo Domingo	6 Aug
48.23	Bershawn	Jackson	USA	8.5.83	1	GP	Madrid (C)	19 Jul
48.24		Thompson			1	GP II	Zagreb	7 Jul
48.24		Woody			2s1	WCh	Saint-Denis	27 Aug
48.24		Iakovákis			3	WCh	Saint-Denis	29 Aug
48.25		Iakovákis			2rA	WK	Zürich	15 Aug
48.28		Thompson			1		Poznan	29 Jun
48.30		Sánchez			1	Gaz	Saint-Denis	4 Jul
48.30	Danny	McFarlane	JAM	14.2.72	4	WCh	Saint-Denis	29 Aug
48.33		Thompson			1s3	WCh	Saint-Denis	27 Aug
48.35		McFarlane			3s1	WCh	Saint-Denis	27 Aug
48.42		Woody			2	GP	London (CP)	8 Aug
48.43		Woody			1	GP II	Helsinki	18 Aug
48.43		Sánchez			1h4	WCh	Saint-Denis	26 Aug
48.44	Chris	Rawlinson	GBR	19.5.72	1	v2N	Glasgow (S)	29 Jun
48.45		Rawlinson			1	ECp-S	Firenze	21 Jun
48.45		Woody			2	GP II	Zagreb	7 Jul
48.45	Marek	Plawgo	POL	25.2.81	1	EU23	Bydgoszcz	19 Jul
48.46		Woody			3rA	WK	Zürich	15 Aug
48.46	Eric	Thomas	USA	1.12.73	4rA	WK	Zürich	15 Aug
	(31/9)							
48.50	Llewellyn	Herbert (10)	RSA	21.7.77	2	GGala	Roma	11 Jul
48.53	Mubarak	Al-Nubi	QAT	30.12.77	4s1	WCh	Saint-Denis	27 Aug
48.54	Matthew	Douglas	GBR	26.11.76	1s1	WUG	Daegu	28 Aug
48.55	Dean	Griffiths	JAM	27.1.80	1	NCAA	Sacramento	13 Jun
48.55	Ian	Weakley	JAM	24.2.74	2	GP	Tríkala	24 Jun
48.61A	Ockert	Cilliers	RSA	21.4.81	1		Pretoria	4 Apr
48.61	Alwyn	Myburgh	RSA	13.10.80	2		Poznan	29 Jun
48.63	Jirí	Muzík	CZE	1.9.76	2	GS	Ostrava	12 Jun
48.64	Stéphane	Diagana	FRA	23.7.69	5s1	WCh	Saint-Denis	27 Aug
48.79	Kenneth	Ferguson	USA-J	22.3.84	1	SEC	Knoxville	18 May
48.83	Rickey	Harris	USA	29.9.81	2	NCAA	Sacramento	13 Jun
	(20)							
48.84	Yevgeniy	Meleshenko	KAZ	19.1.81	4s2	WCh	Saint-Denis	27 Aug
48.86	Fred	Sharpe	USA	21.8.78	2	SEC	Knoxville	18 May
48.86	Naman	Keïta	FRA	9.4.78	1		Clermont-Ferrand	9 Aug
48.88	James	Carter	USA	7.5.78	4	GP	London (CP)	8 Aug
48.92	Marnus	Kritzinger	RSA	10.2.82	2		Durban	11 Apr
48.93	Boris	Gorban	RUS	28.9.78	3rB	WK	Zürich	15 Aug
48.94	Angelo	Taylor	USA	29.12.78	1	Nebiolo	Torino	6 Jun
48.94	Dai	Tamesue	JPN	3.5.78	1	NC	Yokohama	7 Jun

Mark	Name		Nat	Born	Pos	Meet	Venue	Date
48.95	Thomas	Kortbeek	NED	2.4.81	1	WUG	Daegu	30 Aug
48.97	Bennie	Brazell	USA	2.6.82	2s2	NCAA	Sacramento	12 Jun
	(30)							
48.97	Hadi Soua'an	Al-Somaily	KSA	30.12.76	4h3	WCh	Saint-Denis	26 Aug
49.07	Neil	Gardner	JAM	8.12.74	1		Luzern	25 Jun
49.09	Stepán	Tesarík	CZE	6.7.78	1		Szombathely	10 Aug
49.10	Sébastien	Maillard	FRA	2.5.81	1		Genève	14 Jun
49.10	Cédric	El-Idrissi	SUI	24.3.77	1	NC	Frauenfeld	6 Jul
49.12	Anthony	Borsumato	GBR	13.12.73	6rB	WK	Zürich	15 Aug
49.19	Victor	Okorie	NGR	10.8.81	3s2	NCAA	Sacramento	12 Jun
49.22	Louis	van Zyl	RSA-J	20.7.85	3		Durban	11 Apr
49.23	Sherman	Armstrong	USA	22.9.78	1		Tucson	24 May
49.23	Yoshihiro	Chiba	JPN	29.4.79	2	NC	Yokohama	7 Jun
	(40)							
49.30	Ken	Garrett	USA	9.11.76	3s2	NC	Stanford	21 Jun
49.33	Ryan	Wilson	USA	19.12.80	1	Pac-10	Los Angeles	18 May
49.35	Hennie	Botha	RSA	20.2.75	2s1	WUG	Daegu	28 Aug
49.36	Ari-Pekka	Lattu	FIN	22.6.78	2		Lahti	2 Jul
49.36	Edivaldo	Monteiro	POR	28.4.76	1		Vitoria	13 Jul
49.37	Torrance	Zellner	USA	6.1.70	4		Luzern	25 Jun
49.37	Iván	Rodríguez	ESP	7.4.78	6h2	WCh	Saint-Denis	26 Aug
49.40	Eronilde	de Araújo	BRA	31.12.70	1	NC	São Paulo	15 Jun
49.40	Mikael	Jakobsson	SWE	9.1.81	6h3	WCh	Saint-Denis	26 Aug
49.42	Masahira	Yoshikata	JPN	23.8.82	1h2	NC	Yokohama	6 Jun
	(50)							
49.43	Ruslan	Mashchenko	RUS	11.11.71	3	ECp-S	Firenze	21 Jun
49.46	Sergio	Hierrezuelo	CUB	15.3.82	1	NC	La Habana	29 May
49.49	Adam	Kunkel	CAN	21.2.81	1		Iowa City	3 May
49.49	Gennadiy	Gorbenko	UKR	22.9.75	1s2	WUG	Daegu	28 Aug
49.50	Dwight	Ruff	USA	31.3.83	3s1	NCAA	Sacramento	12 Jun
49.51	Gianni	Carabelli	ITA	30.5.79	1	NC	Rieti	3 Aug
49.53	Christian	Duma	GER	5.2.82	2	EU23	Bydgoszcz	19 Jul
49.54	Aleksandr	Derevyagin	RUS	24.3.79	2s2	WUG	Daegu	28 Aug
49.56	Ferdana	Johnson	USA	6.10.72	3		Tucson	24 May
49.59	Eric	Dudley	USA	18.4.80	2	Pac-10	Los Angeles	18 May
	(60)							
9.60	Vladislav	Shiryayev	RUS	30.10.73	2h3	NC	Tula	8 Aug
49.62	Matthew	Elias	GBR	25.4.79	3	v2N	Glasgow (S)	29 Jun
49.63	José María	Romera	ESP	2.9.80	1h1	NC	Jerez de la Frontera	2 Aug
49.66	Roman	Matveyev	RUS	7.11.82	4	WUG	Daegu	30 Aug
49.67	Hideaki	Kawamura	JPN	15.9.74	1	NG	Fukuroi	28 Oct
49.70	Regan	Nichols	USA	26.7.73	3s1	NC	Stanford	21 Jun
49.71	Yacnier	Luis	CUB	24.1.82	1		La Habana	18 Jul
49.72	Brian	Derby	USA	18.2.81	1	Big 10	Minneapolis	18 May
49.73	Derrick	Adkins	USA	2.7.70	1		Atlanta	5 Apr
49.74	Olivier	Jean-Théodore	FRA	13.11.74	1rB	GP	Madrid (C)	19 Jul
	(70)							
49.75		Shao Yi	CHN	20.3.79	1	NC	Shanghai	14 Sep
49.78	Kyle	Erickson	USA	11.1.81	1		Eagle Rock	10 May
49.79	Ken	Yoshizawa	JPN	7.7.78	2		Matto	20 Jul
49.81A	Greg	Flint	USA	16.4.79	1		Albuquerque	17 May
49.82	Bayano	Kamani	USA/PAN	17.4.80	4		Fort-de-France	26 Apr
49.88	Pieter	de Villiers	RSA	13.7.82	3		Durban	7 Mar
49.90	Nic	O'Brien	NZL	3.1.80	1		Storrs	4 May
49.90	Cleverson	da Silva	BRA	5.9.73	2	NC	São Paulo	15 Jun
49.91	Naohiro	Kawaklta	JPN	18.11.80	3s2	WUG	Daegu	28 Aug
49.94	Ibrahim	Al-Hamaidi	KSA-J	28.8.85	2	Gulf	Al-Kuwait	9 Oct
	(80)							
49.99A	Vincent	Mumo	KEN	3.8.82	1	NC	Nairobi	12 Jul
50.02	Aaron	Lacy	USA	1.4.71	5	GP	Osaka	10 May
50.04	Sérgio	Duro	POR	14.2.80	2		V.R. de St.António	10 Jun
50.04	Tiago	Bueno	BRA	21.2.83	3	NC	São Paulo	15 Jun
50.04	Gregory	Little	JAM	20.2.83	1	CAC	St George's	5 Jul
50.05A	Wouter	le Roux	RSA-Y	17.1.86	1		Pretoria	8 Nov
50.06	Pawel	Januszewski	POL	2.1.72	6	GP II	Thessaloníki	3 Aug
50.08	Lueroy	Colquhoun	JAM	1.3.80	5	NC	Kingston	20 Jun
50.08	Ibou	Faye	SEN	13.12.69	2	Af-AsG	Hyderabad	28 Oct
50.09	LaRon	Bennett	USA	25.11.82	2	NCAA-r	Fairfax	31 May
	(90)							
50.09	Aleksandr	Borshchenko	RUS	8.6.82	5	EU23	Bydgoszcz	19 Jul
50.11	Quinton	Milner	USA	20.12.74	2		Bloomington	19 Jul

Mark	Name		Nat	Born	Pos	Meet	Venue	Date
50.13	Kerron	Clement	TRI-J	31.10.85	1		Miami	3 Aug
50.14	James	Graham	USA	3.3.81	2		Knoxville	11 Apr
50.14	Derrick	Williams	USA	25.3.82	1		Fayetteville	12 Apr
50.15		Tan Chunhua	CHN	13.3.77	2	NC	Shanghai	14 Sep
50.18	Burke	Bockman	USA	2.9.79	2	NCAA-r	Lincoln, NE	31 May
50.18	Fabrizio	Mori	ITA	28.6.69	6	ECp-S	Firenze	21 Jun
50.19	Jaime	Juan	ESP	28.8.77	2rB	GP	Madrid (C)	19 Jul
50.20	Derek (100)	Toshner	USA	.80	1		La Crosse	9 May
50.20	Yevgeniy	Mikheyko	BLR	24.4.81	3s2	EU23	Bydgoszcz	18 Jul
50.20		Meng Yan	CHN	30.9.80	3	NC	Shanghai	14 Sep

50.21		Lu Xiaobing	CHN	13.1.79	14 Sep
50.22	Yosuke	Tsushima	JPN	24.12.81	7 Jun
50.23	Oscar	Juanz	MEX	17.9.73	13 Jul
50.25A	Marcel	Lopuchovsky	SVK	2.5.77	28 Mar
50.25	Osita	Okeagu	NGR	29.11.78	14 Oct
50.28	Martin	Leiser	SUI	17.6.78	30 Aug
50.29	Adrian	Findlay	USA	1.10.82	26 Apr
50.30	Mike	King	USA	21.2.79	10 May
50.30	Teppei	Suzuki	JPN-J	10.5.85	28 Jun
50.30	Ashraf	Saber	ITA	2.4.73	3 Aug
50.31	Corrado	Agrillo	ITA	31.10.74	10 Jun
50.31A	Roberto	Carvajal	MEX	23.9.79	29 Jun
50.31A	Daniel	Kibet	KEN	15.10.83	12 Jul
50.32	Jeff	Ellis	CAN	18.10.78	7 Jun
50.33	Jamal	Collier	USA		12 Jun
50.34A	Pieter	Koekemoer	RSA	12.1.82	31 Jan
50.34	Ben	Clark	USA		5 Apr
50.35	Jan	Schneider	GER	24.1.76	26 Jul
50.36	Jorge Josué	Moreno	CUB	25.5.77	29 May
50.37	Yuta	Otsuki	JPN	12.2.82	18 May
50.38	Leonid	Vershinin	BLR	23.6.77	8 Aug
50.39	Tom	Clark	USA		31 May
50.39	Laurent	Claudel	FRA	12.3.78	20 Jun
50.44	Ryan	Smith	BAR	31.3.81	12 Apr
50.44	Henning	Kuschewitz	GER	9.4.81	29 Jun
50.44		Zhang Shibao	CHN-J	12.3.84	14 Sep
50.45		Chen Tien-Wen	TPE	1.6.78	6 Sep
50.46	Loïc	Clément	FRA	5.3.81	15 Jun
50.47	Michael	Hazel	AUS	12.12.76	22 Mar
50.47	Jeff	Hunter	USA	19.2.83	18 May
50.47	Mikhail	Lipskiy	RUS	6.3.82	9 Aug
50.47	Kamel	Tabbal	TUN	13.2.78	13 Aug
50.48	Ahmad	Wright	USA	2.12.80	8 Jun
50.49	Asoka Kumara	Jayasundara	SRI	17.1.78	2 Mar
50.49	Ondrej	Danek	CZE	26.11.81	14 Sep
50.51	Jonathon	Williams	USA	29.8.83	31 May
50.51	Henning	Hackelbusch	GER	23.2.82	22 Jun
50.51	Kirill	Sedykh	RUS	20.7.79	9 Aug
50.53	Andrew	Carruthers	USA	8.3.83	5 Apr
50.53A	Francois	Malan	RSA	11.5.81	6 Apr
50.53	Kenji	Narisako	JPN-J	25.7.84	28 Sep
50.54	Jindrich	Simánek	CZE	27.5.79	13 Jul
50.55	De'Juan	Spann	USA	11.11.80	5 Apr
50.57	Pablo	Martínez	ESP	22.7.81	6 Jul
50.58	Jaroslav	Ruza	CZE	26.9.83	14 Sep
50.59	Luca	Bortolaso	ITA	23.1.81	3 Aug
50.59	Johan	Koen	RSA	13.7.83	6 Dec
50.60	Carlos	Silva	POR	8.6.74	17 May
50.60	Heni	Kéchi	TUN	31.8.80	9 Jun
50.60	Yuki	Arakawa	JPN	17.11.83	28 Oct
50.61	Andrey	Kozlovskiy	BLR	29.12.83	17 Jul
50.61	Bradley	Yiend	GBR	25.10.80	27 Jul
50.62	Kota	Ito	JPN	22.11.80	19 Jul
50.63A	Martin	Willemse	RSA	23.4.75	28 Mar
50.63	Maurice	Bridges	USA	19.11.80	18 May
50.64	Osiris	Martínez	CUB	31.12.79	26 Jun
50.65	Yvon	Rakotoarimiandry	MAD	5.1.76	9 Jun
50.66	John	Barbieri	USA	14.5.81	31 May
50.66	Sanderson	dos Santos	BRA	14.7.76	14 Jun
50.66	Ibrahima	Maiga	MLI	14.3.79	17 Aug
50.67	Atle	McAdam	NOR	18.6.77	31 May
50.68	Iñigo	Monreal	ESP	26.9.74	10 Aug
50.69	Danyne	Brown	USA	14.4.81	30 May
50.70A	Brett	Guymon	USA	9.1.77	26 Apr
50.70	John	Karanja	KEN	81	24 May
50.71	Yuki	Iwataki	JPN-J	29.11.86	26 Oct
50.72	Jin	Sakiyama	JPN	17.4.81	18 May
50.72	Jason	Richardson	USA-Y	4.4.86	6 Jul
50.72	Markus	Crepaz	ITA	16.12.81	3 Aug
50.74	Andrei	Oll	EST	23.7.81	3 Aug
50.75	Ryan	King	BAR	20.4.77	4 Jul
50.76A	Billy	Threets	USA	19.12.79	17 May
50.76A	Hillary	Maritim	KEN	5.2.73	7 Jun
50.77	Monte	Raymond	CAN	18.11.73	9 Aug
50.77		Xiao Junhui	CHN-J	7.10.84	13 Sep
50.78	Christian	Grossenbacher	SUI	28.1.80	10 Aug
50.78	Piet	Deveughele	BEL	3.6.77	17 Aug
50.79A	Henk	Meyer	RSA	26.3.81	4 Apr
50.79	Brandon	Holliday	USA	15.4.82	31 May
50.80	Luis Alejandro	Montenegro	CHI	5.10.81	11 May
50.80	Marqueth	Tard	BAH	15.5.80	11 Jun
50.82	Naoki	Ihara	JPN	22.4.82	6 Jul
50.84	Panayiótis	Liopíris	GRE	26.5.78	2 Jul
50.85	Andreas	Wickert	GER	15.2.80	6 Jun
50.85	Michal	Uhlík (187)	CZE	9.3.80	29 Jun

Low altitude bests

48.88 Cilliers 2rB WK Zürich 15 Aug

50.77 Carvajal 17 May | 50.82 Flint 20 Jun | 50.84 Willemse 11 Apr

Hand Timing

49.4	Yacnier	Luis	CUB	24.1.82	1		La Habana	4 Jul
49.8	Jorge Josué	Moreno	CUB	25.5.77	1r2		La Habana	14 Jun
50.7A	Julius	Bungei	KEN-J	16.6.84	2	WCT	Nairobi	26 Jul

JUNIORS

See main list for top 5 Juniors. 11 performances by 4 men to 50.05. Additional marks and further juniors:

Ferguson	49.27	1	FlaR	Gainesville	28 Mar	49.81	1h1	SEC	Knoxville	16 May
	49.63	1	PennR	Philadelphia	26 Apr	49.89	1		Knoxville	11 Apr
van Zyl	49.80A	1	NC-j	Pretoria	6 Apr	49.84	1	NC	Port Elizabeth	26 Apr
Al-Hamaidi	50.05	2	Arab	Amman	9 Sep					

50.30	Teppei	Suzuki	JPN	10.5.85	1	NC-j	Maebashi	28 Jun
50.44		Zhang Shibao	CHN	12.3.84	5	NC	Shanghai	14 Sep
50.53	Kenji	Narisako	JPN	25.7.84	1		Kumagawa	28 Sep
50.71	Yuki	Iwataki	JPN	29.11.86	1h1	NG	Fukuroi	26 Oct
50.72	Jason	Richardson (10)	USA-Y	4.4.86	1		Amherst	6 Jul
50.77		Xiao Junhui	CHN	7.10.84	2h2	NC	Shanghai	13 Sep
50.93	Kimani	Williams	JAM	27.3.84	1	N.Sch	Kingston	4 Apr
50.95	Isa	Phillips	JAM	22.4.84	2	PAm-J	Bridgetown	20 Jul
51.10	Javier	Culson	PUR	25.7.84	3	PAm-J	Bridgetown	20 Jul

Mark	Name		Nat	Born	Pos	Meet	Venue	Date
51.10	Susumu	Saito	JPN	5.5.84	1h1		Kumagaya	28 Sep
51.11	Raphael	Fernandes	BRA	8.11.84	1		Cubatão	12 Oct
51.15	Rhys	Williams	GBR	27.2.84	1	EJ	Tampere	26 Jul
51.16A	Dieter	Viljoen	RSA	21.2.84	2	NC-j	Pretoria	6 Apr
51.19	Atsushi	Ogawa	JPN	19.4.85	1-18	NG	Fukuroi	27 Oct
51.33	Go	Tanabe (20)	JPN-Y	21.3.86	2	NC-j	Maebashi	28 Jun

HIGH JUMP

Mark	Name		Nat	Born	Pos	Meet	Venue	Date
2.36i	Stefan	Holm	SWE	25.5.76	1		Arnstadt	8 Feb
			2.20/1 2.24/1 2.27/1 2.30/1 2.32/1 2.34/2 2.36/1 2.38/xxx					
2.35i	1 WI	Birmingham	15 Mar	2.20/1 2.25/1 2.30/1 2.33/3 2.35/2 2.37/xx 2.40/x				
2.34i	1	Banská Bystrica	25 Feb	2.20/1 2.25/1 2.28/1 2.30/1 2.32/1 2.34/2 2.37/xxx				
2.34i	1	Tallinn	5 Mar	2.23/3 2.27/1 2.30/1 2.34/3 2.37/xxx				
2.34	1	Réthimno	6 Jul	2.18/1 2.21/1 2.24/1 2.27/1 2.30/2 2.32/3 2.34/3 2.37/xxx				
2.32i	1 NC	Sätra	2 Mar	2.20/1 2.24/2 2.28/1 2.30/1 2.32/2 2.38/xxx				
2.32	1	Kil	19 Jul	2.14/1 2.20/1 2.24/1 2.28/1 2.32/3 2.37/xxx				
2.32	1 MAI	Malmö	12 Aug	2/20/1 2.26/2 2.29/3 2.32/1 2.37/xxx				
2.32	2 WCh	Saint-Denis	25 Aug	2.20/1 2.25/1 2.29/1 2.32/2 2.35/xxx				
2.32	et (1)	Göteborg	2 Sep	2.16/1 2.20/1 2/24/1 2.28/1 2.32/4				
2.36	Aleksander	Walerianczyk	POL	1.9.82	1	EU23	Bydgoszcz	20 Jul
			2.15/1 2.21/1 2.25/1 2.27/1 2.29/1 2.34/1 2.36/2 2.39/xxx					
2.32	1 NC	Bielsko-Biala	6 Jul	2.10/1 2.18/2 2.22/1 2.25/2 2.28/2 2.30/1 2.32/1 2.34/xxx				
2.35	Jacques	Freitag	RSA	11.6.82	1	GGala	Roma	11 Jul
			2.15/1 2.20/1 2.25/1 2.31/2 2.33/2 2.35/2 2.38/x					
2.35	1 WCh	Saint-Denis	25 Aug	2.20/1 2.25/2 2.29/1 2.32/1 2.35/2				
2.34i	Charles	Clinger	USA	28.12.76	1		Nampa	1 Feb
				2.18/1 2.23/1 2.29/1 2.34/1 2.39/xxx				
2.34i	Yaroslav	Rybakov	RUS	22.11.80	2		Arnstadt	8 Feb
				2.20/1 2.24/1 2.27/1 2.30/2 2.32/2 2.34/3 2.36/xxx				
2.34	1 ECpS	Firenze	21 Jun	2.20/1 2.24/1 2.27/1 2.30/2 2.32/1 2.34/3 2.36/xxx				
2.33i	2 WI	Birmingham	15 Mar	2.20/1 2.25/1 2.30/3 2.33/3 2.35/x 2.37/xx				
2.32i	2	Tallinn	5 Mar	2.19/1 2.23/1 2.27/1 2.30/1 2.32/1 2.34/xxx				
2.32	1 GP	Villeneuve-d'Ascq	15 Jun	2.20/1 2.24/1 2.27/1 2.30/1 2.32/2 2.35/xxx				
2.32	2	Réthimno	6 Jul	2.21/1 2.27/2 2.30/3 2.32/2 2.34/xxx				
2.34	Matt	Hemingway	USA	24.10.72	1	Mod R	Modesto	10 May
				2.18/1 2.23/1 2.28/1 2.34/3 2.37/xx 2.41/x				
2.34	Germaine	Mason	JAM	20.1.83	1	PAm	Santo Domingo	9 Aug
				2.16/1 2.20/2 2.24/1 2.28/1. 2.32/2 2.34/2				
2.32	1 DNG	Stockholm	5 Aug	2.15/2 2.20/3 2.24/1 2.27/1 2.32/3				
2.33i	Andrey	Sokolovskiy	UKR	16.7.78	1		Athína (NI)	5 Feb
				2.15/1 2.10/1 2.24/1 2.30/1 2.33/1 2.37/xxx				
2.33	1	Langen	14 Jun	2.17/1 2.21/1 2.25/1 2.28/1 2.30/1 2.33/2 2.37/xxx				
2.32	1	Bästad	29 Jun	2.17/1 2.21/1 2.25/1 2.28/2 2.30/2 2.32/3 2.37/xxx				
2.33i	Dragutin	Topic	SCG	12.3.71	1	Balk C	Athína (P)	4 Mar
				2.20/1 2.28/1 2.33/2				
2.32i	Jaroslav	Bába (10)	CZE-J	2.9.84	3		Arnstadt	8 Feb
			2.15/1 2.20/1 2.24/1 2.27/2 2.30/xx 2.32/1 2.34/xx					
2.32i	Staffan	Strand	SWE	18.4.76	2	NC	Satra	2 Mar
				2.20/1 2.24/2 2.28/3 2.30/x 2.32/2 2.38/xxx				
2.32	Mark	Boswell	CAN	28.7.77	3	WCh	Saint-Denis	25 Aug
				2.25/1 2.32/3 2.35/xxx				
	(30/12)							
2.31	Andrea	Bettinelli	ITA	6.10.78	1	NC	Rieti	3 Aug
2.31	James	Nieto	USA	2.11.76	1	Super	Yokohama	23 Sep
2.30i	Mikhail	Tsvetkov	RUS	4.5.80	2		Brno	11 Feb
2.30i	Gennadiy	Moroz	BLR	27.5.78	3		Brno	11 Feb
2.30i	Tomás	Jankú	CZE	27.12.74	4		Banská Bystrica	25 Feb
2.30i	Charles	Austin	USA	19.12.67	1	NC	Boston (R)	2 Mar
2.30i	Tora	Harris	USA	21.9.78	2=	NC	Boston (R)	2 Mar
	2.31i extra trial				-		Boston	2 Mar
2.30	Pyotr	Brayko	RUS	27.3.77	1		Tula	31 May
	(20)							
2.30	Alessandro	Talotti	ITA	7.10.80	2	ECp-S	Firenze	21 Jun
2.30	Michal	Bieniek	POL-J	17.5.84	1	NC-j	Zamosc	29 Jun
2.30	Stefan	Vasilache	ROM	9.5.79	1	Balk G	Thíva	12 Jul
2.30	Abderahmane	Hammad	ALG	27.5.77	1		Alger	14 Jul
2.30	Nicola	Ciotti	ITA	5.10.76	1		Viersen	20 Jul
2.30	Grzegorz	Sposób	POL	12.2.76	1		Pírgos	27 Jul
2.30	Aleksey	Lesnichiy	BLR	3.2.78	2		Staiki	8 Aug

Mark	Name		Nat	Born	Pos	Meet	Venue	Date
2.30	Linus	Thörnblad	SWE-J	6.3.85	1		Vellinge	16 Aug
2.28i	Aleksey	Dmitrik	RUS-J	12.4.84	2		Samara	26 Jan
2.28i	Pavel	Fomenko	RUS	29.6.76	1		Moskva	30 Jan
	(30)							
2.28	Andrey	Chubsa	BLR	29.11.82	2	GP II	Bratislava	10 Jun
2.28	Dawid	Jaworski	POL	31.1.78	1	NCAA	Sacramento	14 Jun
2.28	Shaun	Kologinczak	USA	13.10.79	2	NCAA	Sacramento	14 Jun
2.28	Christian	Olsson	SWE	25.1.80	5		Båstad	29 Jun
2.28	Emilian	Kaszczyk	POL	21.4.80	3	NC	Bielsko-Biala	6 Jul
2.28	Oskari	Frösén	FIN	24.1.76	1		Lapinlahti	13 Jul
2.27	Cedric	Norman	USA	5.10.81	1		Charlotte	17 May
2.27A	Fabrício	Romero	BRA	13.5.78	1		Tunja	17 May
2.27	Martin	Stauffer	SUI	7.7.75	2		Herzogenbuchsee	7 Jun
2.27	Rozle	Prezelj	SLO	26.9.79	1		Velenje	8 Jun
	(40)							
2.27	Jessé	de Lima	BRA	16.2.81	1	NC	São Paulo	15 Jun
2.27	Grégory	Gabella	FRA	22.6.80	7		Villeneuve d'Ascq	15 Jun
2.27	Terrance	Woods	USA	18.4.79	3	NC	Stanford	20 Jun
2.27	Wilbert	Pennings	NED	23.2.75	2	ECp-1B	Velenje	21 Jun
2.27	Andrey	Tereshin	RUS	15.12.82	2	EU23	Bydgoszcz	20 Jul
2.27	Wojciech	Borysiewicz	POL	18.10.82	3	EU23	Bydgoszcz	20 Jul
2.27	Roman	Fricke	GER	23.3.77	2=		Viersen	20 Jul
2.27A	Alfredo	Deza	PER	24.8.79	1		Lima	26 Jul
2.26i	Giulio	Ciotti	ITA	5.10.76	1		Genova	22 Feb
2.26i	Joe	Squittieri	USA	15.12.81	1		Gainesville	2 Mar
	(50)							
2.26	Jimmy	Baxter	USA	17.11.81	1		Tampa	4 Apr
2.26	Ruslan	Glivinskiy	UKR	7.2.75	2	NC	Kiev	5 Jul
2.26	Viktor	Shapoval	UKR	17.10.79	2		Fribourg	23 Aug
2.26i	Kyle	Lancaster	USA	15.8.83	1		Manhattan, KS	12 Dec
2.25i	Aleksey	Krysin	RUS	25.11.76	1		Yekaterinburg	7 Jan
2.25i	Kenny	Evans	USA	6.4.79	1		Fayetteville	14 Feb
2.25i	Dalton	Grant	GBR	8.4.66	1	NC	Birmingham	1 Mar
2.25	Sergey	Ivanov	BLR-J	28.3.84			Minsk	17 May
2.25	Robert	Wolski	POL	8.12.82	1		Poznan	24 May
2.25		Cui Kai	CHN	26.3.82	1		Shanghai	20 Jun
	(60)							
2.25	Andrea	Lemmi	ITA-J	12.5.84	3	NC	Rieti	3 Aug
2.25	Sergey	Klyugin	RUS	24.3.74	4	NC	Tula	9 Aug
2.25	Shuhei	Manabe	JPN	31.8.82	2	Super	Yokohama	23 Sep
2.25	Nick	Moroney	AUS	3.8.72	1		Sydney (H)	15 Nov
2.24i	Aleksandr	Veryutin	BLR	18.11.79	1		Minsk	24 Jan
2.24i	Javier	Bermejo	ESP	23.12.78	1		Valencia	25 Jan
2.24i	Ivan	Bernasconi	ITA	19.10.74	1		Firenze	25 Jan
2.24i	Vyacheslav	Voronin	RUS	5.4.74	2		Moskva	2 Mar
2.24i	Nathan	Leeper	USA	13.6.77	5	NC	Boston (R)	2 Mar
2.24i	Michael	Morrison	USA-J	4.3.84	1		Landover	16 Mar
	(70)							
2.24		Wang Zhouzhou	CHN	20.4.77	2		Guangzhou	8 Apr
2.24	Henry	Patterson	USA	27.5.75	1		Akron	10 May
2.24	Jesse	Williams	USA	27.12.83	1		Clemson	10 May
2.24	Lisvany	Pérez	CUB	24.1.82	2	Barr	La Habana	31 May
2.24	Aleksandr	Kravtsov	RUS	18.3.74	2		Tula	31 May
2.24	Jan	Jankú	CZE	10.8.71	3		Herzogenbuchsee	7 Jun
2.24	Filippo	Campioli	ITA	21.2.82	2		Milano	29 Jun
2.24	Ben	Challenger	GBR	7.3.78	1	NC	Birmingham	26 Jul
2.24	Joan	Charmant	FRA	4.6.78	1	NC	Narbonne	26 Jul
2.24	Mickaël	Hanany	FRA	25.3.83	2	NC	Narbonne	26 Jul
	(80)							
2.24	Sergey	Dymchenko	UKR	23.8.67	3		Pírgos	27 Jul
2.24	László	Boros	HUN	3.2.82	1	NC	Nyíregyháza	2 Aug
2.24		Liu Yang	CHN-Y	4.1.86	1		Shijiazhuang	4 Aug
2.24		Zheng Ting	CHN-J	15.2.85	1	NG	Changsha	26 Oct
2.23i	Kwaku	Boateng	CAN	30.6.74	4		New York	7 Feb
2.23i	Toni	Riepl	GER	28.2.69	3=		Siegen	14 Feb
2.23i	Peter	Horák	SVK	7.12.83	1	NC	Bratislava	22 Feb
2.23i	Einar Karl	Hjartarson	ISL	28.10.80	1		Nampa	28 Feb
2.23i	Henderson	Dottin	BAR	4.1.80	2		Nampa	28 Feb
2.23i	Jerrick	Holmes	USA	.81	1dq	NCAA	Fayetteville	15 Mar
	(90)							
2.23	Dejan	Vreljakovic	SCG	24.1.77	1		Bar	1 May

Mark	Name		Nat	Born	Pos	Meet	Venue	Date
2.23	Teak	Wilburn	USA	22.12.83	2	Pac-10	Los Angeles	18 May
2.23		Bae Kyung-ho	KOR	16.3.76	1	NC	Daegu	5 Jun
2.23	Marius	Hanniske	GER-J	17.6.85	2	NC	Ulm	28 Jun
2.23	Eike	Onnen	GER	3.8.82	5	EU23	Bydgoszcz	20 Jul
2.23	Sandro	Finesi	ITA	5.4.80	4	NC	Rieti	3 Aug
2.23	Marko	Aleksejev	EST	14.2.79	1	NC	Tallinn	4 Aug
2.23		Lee Jin-taek	KOR	13.4.72	1		Busan	27 Sep

Mark	Name		Nat	Born	Date
2.22i	Gregory	Roberts	USA	16.7.76	15 Feb
2.22i		Zhu Wannan	CHN	15.2.83	22 Feb
	(100)				
2.22i	Luke	Crawley	GBR	5.9.81	1 Mar
2.22	Chris	Peoples	USA	18.7.82	17 May
2.22	Adam	Shunk	USA	29.8.79	30 May
2.22	Jan Peter	Larsen	NED	18.3.79	7 Jun
2.22	Artyom	Kozbanov	UKR	18.7.83	8 Jun
2.22	Artyom	Zaytsev	BLR-J	4.3.84	8 Jun
2.22	Yuriy	Krymarenko	UKR	11.8.83	8 Jun
2.22	Scott	Sellers	USA-Y	16.8.86	14 Jun
2.22	Jean	Hughens	HAI	81	14 Jun
2.22	Andra	Manson	USA-J	30.4.84	20 Jun
2.22	Adrian	O'Dwyer	IRL	1.12.83	6 Jul
2.22	Thomas	Bipella	SWE-J	24.4.84	16 Aug
2.22i	Dmitriy	Demanyuk	UKR	30.6.83	27 Dec
2.21i	Shaun	Guice	USA	11.8.80	18 Jan
2.21i	Jirí	Krehula	CZE	17.7.82	9 Feb
2.21i	Ryan	Fitzpatric	USA	1.3.80	22 Feb
2.21i	Aleksandr	Plisko	BLR-J	28.10.84	1 Mar
2.21i	Sergey	Bochmago	RUS-J	;84	1 Mar
2.21	Joshua	Lodge	AUS	14.9.81	5 Apr
2.21		Liu Jianmin	CHN	27.10.78	8 Apr
	(2.24 2 Claremont 18 Apr?)				
2.21	Dailén	Ortega	CUB	24.7.83	28 May
2.21	Yunier	Carrillo	CUB	1.10.81	28 May
2.21	Raúl	Touset	CUB	14.7.78	28 May
2.21	Igor	Savenkov	RUS	73	31 May
2.21	Yiannis	Constantinou	CYP	23.3.78	15 Jun
2.21	Lábros	Papakóstas	GRE	20.10.69	6 Jul
2.21	Mika	Polku	FIN	19.7.75	9 Jul
2.21	Vladimir	Chubsa	BLR	29.11.82	18 Jul
2.21		Xu Xin	CHN	20.10.83	4 Aug
2.21	Jean-Claude	Rabbath	LIB	12.7.77	9 Sep
2.21	Erasmo	Jara	ARG	25.3.76	15 Nov
2.20i	Metin	Durmusoglu	TUR	11.1.74	18 Jan
2.20i	Ignacio	Pérez	ESP	12.4.73	1 Feb
2.20i	Dimitrios	Sirrákos	GRE	26.1.74	5 Feb
2.20i	Christian	Rhoden	GER	27.3.74	14 Feb
2.20		Fan Enliang	CHN	19.8.79	22 Feb
2.20	Jason	Cornelius	USA	4.6.78	29 Mar
2.20	Mark	Dillon	CAN-J	6.10.84	29 Mar
2.20	Jesse	Sims	USA	22.9.82	12 Apr
2.20	Stilianós	Kesídis	GRE	23.1.81	3 May
2.20	Olavi	Paavo	EST	31.5.77	3 May
2.20	Mihaíl	Tomarás	GRE	3.9.81	4 May
2.20	Jaron	Van Maanen	USA-Y	17.2.86	8 May
2.20	Donovan	Kilmartin	USA-J	11.6.84	9 May
2.20	Daikichi	Takao	JPN	12.8.81	15 May
2.20	Branko	Djuricic	SCG	5.1.81	18 May
2.20	Chad	Pharis	USA	13.7.83	18 May
2.20	Whit	Smith	USA		23 May
2.20	Vladimir	Sitarskiy	UKR	22.4.81	27 May
2.20	Sergey	Shapoval	RUS	.78	27 May
2.20		Kim Jong-pyo	KOR-J	28.3.84	5 Jun
2.20	Jesse	Lipscombe	CAN	4.4.80	8 Jun
2.20	Aurelijus	Eirosius	LTU	21.2.82	9 Jun
2.20	Dimitrios	Kokótis	GRE	12.4.72	21 Jun
2.20	Jan	Titze	GER	6.2.81	22 Jun
2.20	Nikólaos	Giósis	GRE	22.9.80	24 Jun
2.20	Kemal	Güner	TUR	1.10.74	29 Jun
2.20	Ylannis	Stokkos	CYP	23.3.83	2 Jul
2.20	Kirill	Shimanskiy	UKR-J	23.10.85	5 Jul
2.20	Román	Fehér	HUN	11.2.81	6 Jul
2.20	Keith	Moffatt	USA-J	14.10.84	19 Jul
2.20	Dusty	Jonas (2.21?)	USA-Y	19.4.86	27 Jul
2.20		Liu Shuai	CHN	31.7.83	27 Aug
2.20		Dong Hui	CHN-J	18.1.85	27 Aug
2.20	Fábio	Baptista	BRA-J	19.10.84	7 Sep
2.20		Nguyen Duy Bang	VIE	4.7.82	11 Oct
2.20	Ramsay	Carelse (167)	RSA-J	30.10.85	19 Dec

Best outdoor marks

Mark	Name	Pos	Meet	Venue	Date
2.31	Topic	1		Istanbul	7 Jun
2.30	Bába	2		Villeneuve d'Ascq	15 Jun
2.30	T Jankú	1	ECp1B	Velenje	21 Jun
2.30	Tsvetkov	2	GP	Madrid (C)	19 Jul
2.30	Moroz	1		Staiki	8 Aug
2.28	Dmitrik	1	Znam	Tula	7 Jun
2.27	Austin	1	Tex R	Austin	5 Apr
2.27	Harris	1		Herzogenbuchsee	7 Jun
2.26	Strand	4	MAI	Malmö	12 Aug
2.25	Lancaster	1		Lincoln	3 May
2.25	G Ciotti	1		Pavia	4 May
2.25	Clinger	2=	GP	Belém	4 May
2.23	Grant	6	GP	Gateshead	13 Jul

Mark	Name	Date
2.22	Roberts	19 Apr
2.22	Horák	8 Jun
2.22	Bermejo	14 Jun
2.22	Morrison	14 Jun
2.21	Guice	17 May
2.21	Voronin	31 May
2.21	Bernasconi	3 Aug
2.20	Veryutin	9 Jun
2.20	Plisko	14 Jun
2.20	Fomenko	17 Jul
2.20	Krysin	9 Aug
2.20	Dottin	28 Aug
2.20	Romero	15 Jun

JUNIORS

See main list for top 10 Juniors. 13 performances by 4 men to 2.28. Additional marks and further juniors:

Name	Mark	Pos	Meet	Venue	Date
Bába 2+	2.31i	1		Wuppertal	31 Jan
	2.30i	1		Hustopece	18 Jan
	2.30i	2=		Banská Bystrica	25 Feb
	2.30i	1	NC	Bratislava	2 Mar
	2.30	1	GP II	Thessaloniki	3 Aug
	2.29	Q	WCh	Saint-Denis	23 Aug
	2.28i	3		Stockholm	18 Feb
	2.28	1	EJ	Tampere	26 Jul
	2.28	4		Bratislava	10 Jun
Dmitrik	2.28i	2		Samara	26 Jan

Mark	Name		Nat	Born	Pos	Meet	Venue	Date
2.22	Artyom	Zaytsev	BLR	4.3.84	2		Bydgoszcz	8 Jun
2.22	Scott	Sellers	USA-Y	16.8.86	1	N.Sch	Raleigh	14 Jun
2.22	Andra	Manson	USA	30.4.84	6	NC	Stanford	20 Jun
2.22	Thomas	Bipella	SWE	24.4.84	2		Vellinge	16 Aug
2.21i	Aleksandr	Plisko	BLR	28.10.84	1		Minsk	1 Mar
	2.20				2		Wroclaw	14 Jun
2.21i	Sergey	Bochmago	RUS-J	.84	2		Minsk	1 Mar
2.20	Mark	Dillon	CAN	6.10.84	2	FlaR	Gainesville	29 Mar
2.20	Jaron	Van Maanen	USA-Y	17.2.86	1		Sully	8 May
2.20	Donovan	Kilmartin	USA	11.6.84	1		Eagle ID	9 May
2.20	(20)	Kim Jong-pyo	KOR	28.3.84	2	NC	Daeju	5 Jun
2.20	Kirill	Shimanskiy	UKR	23.10.85	5	NC	Kiev	5 Jul
2.20	Keith	Moffatt	USA	14.10.84	1	PAm-J	Bridgetown	19 Jul
2.20	Dusty	Jonas	USA-Y	19.4.86	1		Ypsilanti	27 Jul
	2.21					?		30 Ju;l

Mark	Name		Nat	Born	Pos	Meet	Venue	Date
2.20		Dong Hui	CHN	18.1.85	3		Chengdu	27 Aug
2.20	Fábio	Baptista	BRA-	19.10.84	1		São Paulo	7 Sep
2.20	Ramsay	Carelse	RSA-	30.10.85	1		Parow	19 Dec
Best out: 2.22	Michael	Morrison	USA	4.3.84	2	N.Sch	Raleigh	14 Jun

POLE VAULT

Mark	Name		Nat	Born	Pos	Meet	Venue	Date	Series
5.95	Romain	Mesnil	FRA	13.7.77	1		Castres	6 Aug	5.70/x 5.75/1 5.95/3
5.92					1	GGala	Roma	11 Jul	5.62/1 5.72/1 5.82/3 5.92/1 6.00/xxx
5.93	Alex	Averbukh	ISR	1.10.74	1	GP	Madrid (C)	19 Jul	5.53/1 5.73/1 5.83/3 5.93/3
5.91	Tim	Lobinger	GER	3.9.72	1	WAF	Monaco	13 Sep	5.60/2 5.76/1 5.81/2 5.86/xx 5.91/1 5.96/xx 6.01/x
5.86					1		Kassel	13 Jun	5.86/3
5.85					1	Veniz	Haniá	9 Jun	5.40/1 5.60/1 5.70/1 5.80/2 5.85/3 5.95/xxx
5.82i					1		Stockholm	18 Feb	5.64/2 5.82/3 5.87/xxx
5.81i					1		Chemnitz	7 Feb	5.50/2 5.60/1 5.70/3 5.81/1 5.86/xxx
5.81i					1		Donetsk	16 Feb	5.60/1 5.71/1 5.81/3 5.91/xxx
5.81					1		Albershausen	1 May	5.40/1 5.55/1 5.65/3 5.75/1 5.81/2 5.86/xxx
5.90	Giuseppe	Gibilisco	ITA	5.1.79	1	WCh	Saint-Denis	28 Aug	5.60/1 5.75/xx 5.80/1 5.85/1 5.90/1
5.82					2	GGala	Roma	11 Jul	5.52/1 5.72/3 5.77/2 rec 5.82/3 5.92/x
5.81					1	GP II	Rieti	7 Sep	5.60/2 5.81/3 5.91/xxx
5.87	Oscar	Janson	SWE	22.7.75	1		Somero	29 Jun	5.20/1 5.40/2 5.50/1 5.60/1 5.76/3 5.82/3 5.87/3
5.86	Dmitri	Markov	AUS	14.3.75	1	ISTAF	Berlin (P)	10 Aug	5.55/3 5.76/3 5.86/2 5.96/xxx
5.85					1	Athl	Lausanne	1 Jul	5.50/1 5.70/x 5.75/2 5.85/1 5.90/xx 5.92/x
5.85					4	WCh	Saint-Denis	28 Aug	5.60/2 5.75/2 5.85/3 5.90/xx 5.95/x
5.86	Okkert	Brits	RSA	22.8.73	2	WAF	Monaco	13 Sep	5.60/2 5.76/2 5.81/2 5.86/2 5.96/xxx
5.85					2	WCh	Saint-Denis	28 Aug	5.60/2 5.75/2 5.85/2 5.90/x 5.95/xx
5.85	Patrik	Kristiansson	SWE	3.6.77	3	WCh	Saint-Denis	28 Aug	5.60/2 5.75/1 5.80/1 5.85/3 5.90/xxx
5.81i	Adam	Ptácek	CZE	8.10.80	2		Chemnitz	7 Feb	5.30/1 5.50/1 5.60/1 5.70/2 5.81/3 5.86/xxx
5.81	Derek	Miles (10)	USA	28.9.72	1		Jonesboro	28 May	5.44/2 5.54/2 5.71/1 5.81/2 5.86/xxx
5.81	Denis	Yurchenko	UKR	27.1.78	2	GP II	Rieti	7 Sep	5.60/2 5.70/2 5.81/3 5.86/xxx
	(23/11) with further 20 performances at 5.80								
5.80i	Brad	Walker	USA	21.6.81	1	NCAA	Fayetteville	14 Mar	
5.80i	Jeff	Hartwig	USA	25.9.67	1		Jonesboro	1 Jun	
5.80	Lars	Börgeling	GER	16.4.79	3	Veniz	Haniá	9 Jun	
5.78	Nick	Hysong	USA	9.12.71	2	GP	Madrid (C)	19 Jul	
5.76	Tim	Mack	USA	15.9.72	4	Gaz	Saint-Denis	4 Jul	
5.75i	Aleksandr	Korchmyd	UKR	22.1.82	1		Brovary	8 Feb	
5.75i	Michael	Stolle	GER	17.12.74	2	NC	Leipzig	22 Feb	
5.75i	Rens	Blom	NED	1.3.77	3	WI	Birmingham	15 Mar	
5.75	Toby	Stevenson	USA	19.11.76	1		Stanford	29 Mar	
	(20)								
5.75	Russ	Buller	USA	10.9.78	1	MSR	Walnut	19 Apr	
5.75	Daichi	Sawano	JPN	16.9.80	1	NC	Yokohama	8 Jun	
5.75sq	Ilian	Efremov	BUL	2.8.70	1		Ostrava	11 Jun	
	Not included by some statisticians, next: 5.70				2	ECp-1B	Velenje	22 Jun	
5.75	Alexandre	Barbaud	FRA	15.2.80	1		Sotteville	8 Jul	
5.73i	Vasiliy	Gorshkov	RUS	5.2.77	1		Sindelfingen	8 Mar	
5.73i	Richard	Spiegelburg	GER	12.8.77	2		Sindelfingen	8 Mar	
5.73	Vadim	Strogalyov	RUS	9.2.75	3	GP	Madrid (C)	19 Jul	
5.72i	Björn	Otto	GER	16.10.77	1		Potsdam	8 Feb	
	Not included by some statisticians, next: 5.70i				1		Cottbus	29 Jan	
5.71	Viktor	Chistiakov	AUS	9.2.75	2		Napoli	10 Jun	
5.70Ai	Tye	Harvey	USA	25.9.74	3		Reno	17 Jan	
	(30)								

In these lists some marks are shown as "not included by some statisticians". The pole vault held in Ostrava is a case in point. This was, according to the meeting organiser, a genuine compeition held under "normal rules". But the Czech Federation deems it to have been an exhibition, and this attitude affects similar events in Germany and elsewhere. However other governing bodies look on such events, held outside "normal" athletics meetings, in a different way. For instance the `annual indoor Reno pole vault competitions are held on specially laid-down runways and are accepted in the USA. My concern for these lists is to adopt a consistent approach, and I prefer to include all marks in genuine competition provided that competition rules have been followed, relegating to a footnote others as "exhibitions". PJM.

Mark	Name		Nat	Born	Pos	Meet	Venue	Date
5.70i	Paul	Terek	USA	20.10.79	1		Seattle	1 Feb
5.70i	Dmitriy	Kuptsov	RUS	9.11.82	2	NC	Moskva	27 Feb
5.70i	Stepán	Janácek	CZE	12.6.77	2	NC	Bratislava	1 Mar
5.70i	Jeremy	Scott	USA	1.5.81	2	NC	Boston (R)	1 Mar
5.70A	Christian	Tamminga	NED	30.4.74	2		Pretoria	4 Apr
5.70	Spas	Bukhalov	BUL	14.11.80	1		Plovdiv	31 May
5.70	Nick	Buckfield	GBR	5.6.73	2		Cottbus	4 Jun
5.70	Artyom	Kuptsov	RUS-J	22.4.84	1	Znam	Tula	7 Jun
5.70	Yevgeniy	Smiryagin	RUS	17.5.76	1		Sankt Peterburg	17 Jun
5.70sq	Martin	Kysela	CZE	25.3.74	2		Ostrava	11 Jun
	Not included by some statisticians, next: 5.55				1		Praha	24 May
	(40)							
5.70	Adam	Kolasa	POL	2.8.75	4	ECp-S	Firenze	22 Jun
5.70	Pierre-Charles	Peuf	FRA	27.4.79	2		Castres	6 Aug
5.70	Pavel	Gerasimov	RUS	29.5.79	2		Rovereto	10 Sep
5.70	Paul	Burgess	AUS	14.8.79	1		Perth	20 Dec
5.66	Scott	Slover	USA	9.7.75	1		Los Gatos	10 Aug
5.65	Igor	Alekseyev	RUS	7.4.83	1		Moskva	14 Jul
5.65	Igor	Pavlov	RUS	18.7.79	2		Moskva	14 Jul
5.65	Matti	Mononen	FIN	25.11.83	1		Lappeenranta	3 Aug
5.63i	Ruslan	Yeremenko	UKR	31.7.78	3		Karlsruhe	28 Feb
5.61	Thibaut	Duval	BEL	1.2.79	1		Nancy	16 Sep
	(50)							
5.60i	Nicolas	Guigon	FRA	10.10.80	1		Aubière	18 Jan
5.60	Martin	Eriksson	SWE	15.6.71	1		Perth	2 Feb
5.60i	Aleksey	Khanafin	RUS	12.4.81	4=		Chemnitz	7 Feb
5.60i	Vladislav	Revenko	UKR-J	15.11.84	1		Donetsk	15 Feb
5.60Ai	Piotr	Buciarski	DEN	22.11.75	1		Reno	22 Feb
5.60	Jim	Davis	USA	15.6.78	1		Irvine	3 May
5.60	Kurt	Hanna	USA	23.4.75	1		Abilene	8 May
5.60	Pavel	Burlachenko	RUS	7.4.76	1		Almaty	21 Jun
5.60	Fanie	Jacobs	RSA	21.4.76	1		Rheinau-Freistett	6 Jul
5.60	Vesa	Rantanen	FIN	2.12.75	2		Lappeenranta	3 Aug
	(60)							
5.58i	Eric	Eshbach	USA	4.2.81	2	NCAA	Fayetteville	14 Mar
5.56i	Alhaji	Jeng	SWE	13.12.81	1H		Göteborg	9 Mar
5.56	Róbison	Pratt	MEX	25.2.80	1	NCAA-r	Stanford	31 May
5.56	Tommy	Skipper	USA-J	14.4.84	1	G.West	Sacramento	15 Jun
5.56i	Jérôme	Clavier	FRA	3.5.83	1		Aulnay-sous-Bois	14 Dec
5.55i	Stávros	Kouroupákis	GRE	17.5.83	1		Athína (E)	8 Feb
5.55	Dean	Starkey	USA	27.3.67	3		Stanford	29 Mar
5.55A	Adam	Keul	USA	27.1.80	2		El Paso	3 May
5.55		Kim Yoo-suk	KOR	19.1.82	2	Pac-10	Los Angeles	17 May
5.55	Laurens	Looije	NED	12.1.73	2	ECCp	Valencia	25 May
	(70)							
5.55	Damiel	Dossevi	FRA	3.2.83	1	NC-23	Vénissieux	14 Jul
5.55	Yevgeniy	Mikhaylichenko	RUS	13.2.79	3		Moskva	14 Jul
5.54	Daniel	Ryland	USA	6.8.79	1		Jonesboro	15 Jun
5.51i	Tom Erik	Olsen	NOR	20.10.74	1		Oslo	10 Feb
5.51	Marvin	Osei-Tutu	GER	22.4.81	1		Regensburg	19 Jun
5.51i	Alain	Andji	FRA	20.11.74	2		Aulnay-sous-Bois	14 Dec
5.50i	Pat	Manson	USA	29.11.67	1		Air Force Academy	11 Jan
5.50Ai	Steve	Deming	USA	17.10.73	5eC		Reno	17 Jan
5.50Ai	Paul	Litchfield	USA	.81	1eC		Reno	17 Jan
5.50Ai	Justin	Norberg	USA	18.7.77	1eB		Reno	17 Jan
	(80)							
5.50i	Fabio	Pizzolato	ITA	16.3.75	1		Reggio Emilia	6 Feb
5.50i	Jacob	Pauli	USA	15.6.79	1		Cedar Falls	8 Feb
5.50i	Dennis	Kholev	ISR	21.10.75	2		Los Angeles	15 Feb
5.50i	Artyom	Matiyenko	UKR	30.8.82	2		Donetsk	15 Feb
5.50i	Maksim	Mazurik	UKR	2.4.83	9		Donetsk	16 Feb
5.50i	Yuriy	Yeliseyev	RUS	27.5.75	5=	NC	Moskva	27 Feb
5.50	Bobby	Most	USA	13.12.82	1eB	Tex R	Austin	5 Apr
5.50	Satoru	Yasuda	JPN	27.7.75	1		Shizuoka	3 May
5.50	Giovanni	Lanaro	MEX	27.9.81	1		Eagle Rock	10 May
5.50	Kevin	Rans	BEL	19.8.82	6	FBK	Hengelo	1 Jun
	(90)							
5.50	Montxu	Miranda	ESP	27.12.76	1		Zaragoza	7 Jun
5.50	Tiberiu	Agoston	ROM	25.12.76	4		Pierre Bénite	13 Jun
5.50	Vincent	Favretto	FRA-J	5.4.84	6		Pierre Bénite	13 Jun
5.50		Kim Se-in	KOR	29.7.74	1		Atascadero	25 Jun

Mark	Name		Nat	Born	Pos	Meet	Venue	Date
5.50	Sergey	Chemovskoy	RUS	13.7.83	2	NC-23	Cheboksary	27 Jun
5.50	Tim	Thomas	GBR	18.11.73	2		Cork	5 Jul
5.50	Guillaume	Savary	FRA	11.2.81	2	NC-23	Dijon	14 Jul
5.50	Mathieu	Boisrond	FRA	8.1.77	1		Reims	20 Jul
5.50	Yuriy	Blonskiy	UKR	9.7.79	1		Kiev	29 Jul
5.50		Liu Feiliang	CHN-J	27.3.85	1		Shijiazhuang	4 Aug
	(100)							
5.50	Przemyslaw	Czerwinski	POL	28.7.83	1	NC-23	Biala Podlaska	13 Sep

Mark	First	Last	Nat	Born	Date	Mark	First	Last	Nat	Born	Date
5.45	Steve	Hooker	AUS	16.7.82	18 Jan	5.40i	Roger	Noguera	ESP	27.2.82	8 Mar
5.45i	Toni	Latvala	FIN	6.7.77	23 Feb	5.40	David	Grijalva	MEX	3.1.79	22 Mar
5.45	Jeff	Ryan	USA	8.12.80	17 May	5.40	Mark	Vinci	USA		22 Mar
5.45i	Mark	Calvin	USA	17.11.74	4 Jun	5.40	Jon	Takahashi	USA	21.10.82	22 Mar
5.45	Trent	Powell	USA	25.6.78	13 Jun	5.40	Brian	Hunter	USA	28.3.79	5 Apr
5.45	Brian	DaCunha	USA	20.5.80	13 Jun	5.40	Trevor	Woods	USA	12.10.81	5 Apr
5.45	Javier	Gazol	ESP	27.10.80	22 Jun	5.40A	Cristian	Sánchez	MEX	12.7.83	12 Apr
5.45	Fabian	Schulze	GER-J	7.3.84	22 Jun	5.40	Filippos	Sgoúros	GRE	26.9.81	3 May
5.45	Mikko	Latvala	FIN	8.7.80	20 Jul	5.40	Jean	Galfione	FRA	9.6.71	4 May
5.45	João	André	POR	28.5.76	3 Aug	5.40	Michael	Westlund	USA	24.3.80	19 May
5.44	Bubba	McLean	USA	2.9.79	28 May	5.40i	Fumiaki	Kobayashi	JPN	10.12.74	25 May
5.43i	David	Stephens	USA	81	22 Feb	5.40	Pavel	Chernov	RUS	13.7.83	14 Jun
5.42i	Chris	Steddum	USA	21.5.80	9 Feb	5.40	Vyacheslav	Ostapenko (150)	RUS	28.4.82	14 Jun
5.42i	Joël	Soler	FRA	25.2.82	15 Feb	5.40	Dmitriy	Zakharchuk	RUS	78	14 Jun
5.41i	Pooh	Williams	USA	20.12.79	22 Feb	5.40	Mikael	Westö	FIN	3.4.82	29 Jun
5.41i		Zhang Hongwei	CHN	26.4.75	21 Mar	5.40	Sébastien	Homo	FRA	27.4.82	6 Jul
5.41	Lawrence	Johnson	USA	7.5.74	12 Apr	5.40	Alberto	Martínez	ESP	4.4.82	10 Jul
5.41	Ray	Scotten	USA	20.5.83	12 Apr	5.40	Nicolas	Jolivet	FRA	24.3.77	20 Jul
5.41	Brad	Tyler	USA	14.7.80	15 Jun	5.40	Jurij	Rovan	SLO	23.1.75	9 Aug
5.41	Ashley	Swain	GBR	3.10.80	27 Jul	5.40	Oliver	Frey	SUI	11.2.79	11 Aug
5.41	Rudolf	Haraksim	SVK	23.12.81	23 Aug	5.40	Giorgio	Piantella	ITA	6.7.81	14 Sep
5.41	Georgi	Wassilew	GER	16.2.80	23 Aug	5.38i	Fredrik	Skoglund	SWE	11.3.81	1 Mar
5.40i	Grigoriy	Yegorov	KAZ	12.1.67	11 Jan	5.36i	Jeremy	Kemp	USA	4.2.78	1 Mar
5.40i	Fabrice	Fortin	FRA	2.2.80	18 Jan	5.36	Pooh	Williams	USA	20.12.79	31 May
5.40i	Rocky	Danners	USA	21.6.81	25 Jan	5.36	Austin	Landreth	USA	5.2.83	31 May
5.40i	Maurilio	Mariani	ITA	22.4.73	26 Jan	5.36	Scott	Simpson	GBR	21.7.79	9 Aug
5.40	Luke	Vedelago	AUS	13.6.80	1 Feb	5.35Ai	Michael	McNamara	USA	27.3.79	17 Jan
5.40i	Matt	Phillips	USA	28.12.77	1 Feb	5.35Ai	Brian	McLaughlin	USA	25.7.77	8 Feb
5.40i	Dominic	Johnson	LCA	31.10.75	9 Feb	5.35i	Daniel	Trosclair	USA	22.1.82	21 Feb
5.40i	Sergey	Kucheryanu	RUS-J	30.6.85	12 Feb	5.35i	John	Russell	USA	9.10.83	1 Mar
5.40i	Paul	Condron	USA	2.7.81	14 Feb	5.35	Hans	Schmidt	USA		25 Apr
5.40i	Ketil	Rønneberg	NOR	9.12.76	15 Feb	5.35	José Francisco	Nava	CHI	19.1.83	26 Apr
5.40i	Andrey	Afonin	UKR	22.7.78	15 Feb	5.35	Andrea	Giannini	ITA	18.12.76	25 May
5.40i	Tobias	Ulrich	GER	6.4.79	22 Feb	5.35	Mark	Beharrel	GBR	10.1.81	29 Jun
5.40i	André	Niklaus	GER	30.8.81	22 Feb	5.35	Javier	Benítez	ARG	30.6.76	8 Aug
5.40i	Khalid	Lachheb	FRA	16.1.75	1 Mar	5.35	Hideji	Suzuki (173)	JPN	10.3.74	28 Oct

Best outdoor marks

Mark	Name	Pos	Meet	Venue	Date	Mark	Name	Pos	Meet	Venue	Date
5.75	Blom	1	ECp1B	Velenje	22 Jun	5.55	Eshbach	7=	NC	Stanford	22 Jun
5.75	Korchmyd	1	WUG	Daegu	28 Aug	5.50	Terek	1		San Luis Obispo	22 Mar
5.70	Hartwig	1		Jonesboro	24 May	5.50	Kholev	4	MSR	Walnut	19 Apr
5.70	Spiegelburg	2	FBK	Hengelo	1 Jun	5.50	Guigon	1		Aix-les-Bains	4 May
5.70	Otto	3	NC	Ulm	28 Jun	5.50	Deming	3	ModR	Modesto	10 May
5.65	Walker	2		Stanford	29 Mar	5.50	Norberg	4		Phoenix	16 May
5.62	Ptácek	7=	GGala	Roma	11 Jul	5.50	Revenko	4		Kiev	27 May
5.60	Gorshkov	6=	Bisl	Oslo	27 Jun	5.50	Pizzolato	1		Salerno	31 May
5.60	Buciarski	3	GP II	Helsinki	18 Aug	5.50	Clavier	1		Mannheim	22 Jun
5.60	D Kuptsov	1		Oristano	6 Sep	5.50	Andji	2		La Roche-sur-Yon	16 Jul

Mark	Name	Date	Mark	Name	Date	Mark	Name	Date	Mark	Name	Date
5.46	Litchfield	31 May	5.40	Danners	29 Mar	5.40	Mariani	25 Jun	5.40	Yegorov	11 Aug
5.45	Calvin	4 Jun	5.40	Zhang Hongwei	19 Apr	5.40	Latvala	29 Jun	5.40	Jeng	6 Sep
5.45	Kouroupákis	22 Jun	5.40	Soler	1 Jun	5.40	Fortin	1 Jul	5.36	Pauli	26 Apr
5.45	Mazurik	20 Jul	5.40	Olsen	12 Jun	5.40	Johnson	8 Aug	5.36	P Williams	31 May
5.40	Condron	29 Mar	5.40	Khanafin	14 Jun	5.40	Kobayashi	8 Jun	5.35	Phillips	10 May

Exhibition

Mark	Name		Nat	Born	Pos	Venue	Date
5.75	Igor	Pavlov	RUS	18.7.79	1	Treviso	7 Sep

JUNIORS

See main list for top 5 Juniors. 9 performances by 3 men to 5.51. Additional marks and further juniors:

A Kuptsov	5.66i	4		Donetsk	16 Feb	5.55i	1		Moskva 10 Feb
	5.60	1		Krasnodar	28 May	5.55	4=	Kuts	Moskva 14 Jul
	5.60	4		Haniá	9 Jun	5.51i	1		Moskva 12 Feb

Mark	Name		Nat	Born	Pos	Meet	Venue	Date
5.45	Fabian	Schulze	GER	7.3.84	1		Mannheim	22 Jun
5.40i	Sergey	Kucheryanu	RUS	30.6.85	2		Moskva	12 Feb
5.32	Germán	Chiaraviglio	ARG-Y	16.4.87	1	NC-j	Mar del Plata	2 Nov
5.30	Donovan	Kilmartin	USA	11.6.84	1c2	MSR	Walnut	19 Apr
5.30	Denis	Fedas (10)	UKR	24.8.85	5		Kiev	20 Jun
5.26	Ty	Barrington	USA	27.2.85	1		Lubbock	26 Apr
5.25	Guillermo	González	ESP	10.12.84	2		Zaragoza	7 Jun

Mark	Wind	Name		Nat	Born	Pos	Meet	Venue	Date
5.25		Nikólaos	Sidihákis	GRE	3.10.84	2		Kastoriá	28 Jun
5.22		Konstadínos	Filippídis	GRE-Y	26.11.86	2	NC	Trikala	14 Jun
5.20	(17-1)	Chase	Shealy	USA	9.5.85	1		Summerville	13 Jun
5.20		Chip	Heuser	USA	9.2.85	1	TexR	Austin	4 Apr
5.20		Gable	Baldwin	USA	9.1.85	3	NC-j	Stanford	21 Jun
5.20		Charles	Andureu	FRA	13.2.85	2		Mannheim	22 Jun
5.20		Masafumi	Moribe	JPN	29.1.84	1	NC-j	Maebashi	28 Jun
5.20			Zhao Yu (20)	CHN	28.4.85	2		Shijiazhuang	4 Aug
Best out: 5.20		Sergey	Kucheryanu	RUS	30.6.85	2	NC-j	Kazan	3 Jul

LONG JUMP

Mark	Wind	Name		Nat	Born	Pos	Meet	Venue	Date	Series
8.53	1.3	Yago	Lamela	ESP	24.7.77	1		Castellón	18 Aug	8.12/1.8 8.12/0.6 8.26/1.2 8.19/0.9 8.28/1.2 8.53
8.44	0.6					1		Bad Langensalza	15 Jun	8.11 6.98 8.05 x 8.19 8.44
8.43i						1		Sevilla	22 Feb	8.15 8.07 8.21 7.82 8.43 8.33
8.36	1.3					1		Castellón	12 Aug	8.23/1.7 8.33/0.9 8.36/1.2 8.30/1.6 8.35/1.0 8.35/1.4
8.33	0.2					1		Córdoba	6 Sep	x 8.30/0.0 8.05 8.00 x 8.33
8.28i						1	NC	Valencia	2 Mar	x x 7.75 8.28 x x
8.28i						2	WI	Birmingham	15 Mar	7.99 8.13 x 8.20 8.11 8.28
8.26i						1		Athína (P)	6 Mar	7.48 8.24 7.96 8.10 8.26 8.25
8.39w	3.3					1		Rivas	12 Jun	8.14w/ 2.8 8.39w x x x 7.44w
8.46	1.0	Savanté	Stringfellow	USA	6.11.78	1		Oxford, MS	12 Apr	8.46 8.41 x p p p
8.29i						1		Fayetteville	15 Feb	8.29 x x x p 8.09
8.28	0.3					3	GP	Tríkala	24 Jun	x 8.00 8.28 8.25/0.0 8.09 x
8.46A	0.0	Miguel	Pate	USA	13.6.79	1		Ciudad de México	3 May	8.46 8.33 p p 6.44 p
8.27i						2		Fayetteville	15 Feb	x 7.89 8.01 8.27 p x
8.27	0.8					1	Pre	Eugene	24 May	x 8.19w/2.2 8.15w 8.27 x x
8.44	1.0	Dwight	Phillips	USA	1.10.77	1	GP	Tríkala	24 Jun	x 8.26/1.2 x 8.44 7.95 p
8.32	0.5					1	WCh	Saint-Denis	29 Aug	8.09 x 8.22/0.4 x 8.32 x
8.31	0.1					1	WAF	Monaco	13 Sep	x 8.27/0.4 8.31 8.02 four only
8.29i						1	WI	Birmingham	15 Mar	7.97 8.23 8.14 x x 8.29
8.34	1.4	Loúis	Tsátoumas	GRE	12.2.82	2	GP	Tríkala	24 Jun	8.01 8.34 8.03 x p p
8.33	1.8	Yahya	Berrabah	MAR	13.10.81	1		Casablanca	12 Aug	
8.31	1.7	Iván	Pedroso	CUB	17.12.72	1		Padova	6 Jul	7.91/-0.9 8.31/1.7 x x x x
8.31	0.4	Nikolay	Atanasov	BUL	11.12.74	1		Pírgos	27 Jul	8.00 8.06 7.83 8.12 8.00 8.31
8.30	2.0	Dimitrios	Filíndras	GRE	9.2.73	1	Veniz	Haniá	9 Jun	x 7.94w 8.30 p p x
8.30	0.4	Hussein	Al-Sabee (10)	KSA	14.11.79	2	WAF	Monaco	13 Sep	7.82 8.30 7.81 8.16/0.0 four only
8.30w	2.4					1	Arab	Amman	6 Sep	
8.30	0.1	Ignisious	Gaisah	GHA	20.6.83	1	Afr G	Abuja	14 Oct	
8.26	0.1					3	WAF	Monaco	13 Sep	8.01 7.94 8.23/ -0.1 8.26 four only
8.28i		Brian	Johnson	USA	25.3.80	1	NCAA	Fayetteville	14 Mar	8.28 x x x 8.15 8.15
8.28	0.1	James	Beckford	JAM	9.1.75	2	WCh	Saint-Denis	29 Aug	x 7.99 8.16/1.0 8.12 8.28 8.14
8.27w						1		Leverkusen	3 Aug	7.92 7.96 6.60 8.27w x 7.95
8.27	1.3	Julien	Fivaz	SUI	9.1.79	1		Ebensee	2 Aug	8.01 x 8.11 8.03 x 8.27
8.26A	1.9	Jonathan	Chimier	MRI	6.8.82	1		Sestriere	19 Jul	7.73w 7.95w 8.12w 8.14w 8.29w/3.3 8.26
8.26	1.2	Nathan	Morgan	GBR	30.6.78	1		Hamburg	20 Jul	7.70 8.26 p p p p
		(31/16)								
8.24	1.7	Walter	Davis	USA	2.7.79	2	NC	Stanford	20 Jun	
8.23	0.0	Vitaliy	Shkurlatov	RUS	25.5.79	1	NC	Tula	10 Aug	
8.23	0.4	Danila	Burkenya	RUS	20.7.78	2	NC	Tula	10 Aug	
8.23	0.0	Sinisa	Ergotic	CRO	14.9.68	2		Córdoba	6 Sep	
		(20)								
8.22i		Vladimir	Zyuskov	UKR	29.8.81	1		Zaporozhye	2 Mar	
8.21	0.7	Kareem	Streete-Thompson	CAY	30.3.73	2		Bad Langensalza	15 Jun	
8.21	1.4	Dimítrios	Serélis	GRE	5.5.80	1		Athína (K)	6 Aug	
8.21	0.0	Bogdan	Tarus	ROM	1.8.75	1	NC	Bucuresti	10 Aug	

Mark	Wind	Name		Nat	Born	Pos	Meet	Venue	Date
8.20	1.8	Nicola	Trentin	ITA	20.6.74	3		Padova	6 Jul
8.20	0.8	Joan Lino	Martínez	CUB	17.1.78	1	GP	Madrid (C)	19 Jul
8.20	0.7	Luis Felipe	Méliz	CUB	11.8.79	2	PAm	Santo Domingo	6 Aug
8.19i		Valeriy	Vasilyev	UKR	21.4.76	2		Zaporozhye	2 Mar
8.19	1.3	Aleksey	Lukashevich	UKR	11.1.77	4	GP	Tríkala	24 Jun
8.16i		Salim	Sdiri	FRA	26.10.78	1	NC	Aubière	2 Mar
		(30)							
8.16	0.1	Stephan	Louw	NAM	26.2.75	1		Bad Camberg	7 Jun
8.16	0.6	Dmitriy	Mitrofanov	RUS	7.9.75	3		Pírgos	27 Jul
8.16	0.7	Chris	Tomlinson	GBR	15.9.81	Q	WCh	Saint-Denis	27 Aug
8.14	0.5	Gable	Garenamotse	BOT	28.2.77	4		Bad Langensalza	15 Jun
8.13	0.1	Aleksandr	Patselya	UKR	3.7.83	1		Kharkov	17 May
8.13A	1.8	Arnaud	Casquette	MRI	16.4.78	2		Sestriere	19 Jul
8.13	0.9	Abdulrahman	Al-Nubi	QAT	17.10.79	Q	AsiC	Manila	21 Sep
8.12	0.0	Danut Marian	Simion	ROM	25.1.83	2	NC	Bucuresti	10 Aug
8.12	0.6	Andrey	Bragin	RUS	20.9.79	3	NC	Tula	10 Aug
8.12i		Viktor	Kuznetsov	UKR-J	14.7.86	1		Brovary	20 Dec
		(40)							
8.11i		Ruslan	Gataullin	RUS	1.12.79	1		Moskva	30 Jan
8.11	1.9	Yann	Doménech	FRA	17.3.79	*		Bron	29 May
8.11	0.3	Nils	Winter	GER	27.3.77	1		Wesel	9 Jun
8.11	1.8	Antonio	Adsuar	ESP	4.7.78	1		Castellón	23 Jul
8.11	1.8		Zhou Can	CHN	20.5.79	2	AsiC	Manila	23 Sep
8.10i		Petar	Dachev	BUL	15.6.79	1		Sofia	9 Feb
8.10	1.8	Konstadínos	Vasiliádis	GRE	9.3.77	1		Thessaloníki	31 May
8.10	1.7	Konstadínos	Koukodímos	GRE	14.9.69	2		Thessaloníki	31 May
8.10	-0.4		Huang Le	CHN	25.9.77	1	NC	Shanghai	14 Sep
8.09	1.7	Kevin	Dilworth	USA	14.2.74	3	GP	Gateshead	13 Jul
		(50)							
8.08i		John	Moffitt	USA	12.12.80	1		Gainesville	1 Mar
8.08i		Frank	Tolen	USA	17.7.82	2dq	NCAA	Fayetteville	14 Mar
8.08		Tomasz	Mateusiak	POL	5.12.80	2		Königs Wusterhausen	6 Aug
8.07	0.5	Aundre	Edwards	JAM	11.12.80	1	NC	Kingston	21 Jun
8.06	1.4	Kader	Klouchi	FRA	1.6.69	*		Pierre Bénite	13 Jun
8.06A	1.4	Raúl	Fernández	ESP	8.3.78	1		Monachil	9 Jul
8.06	1.5	Gregor	Cankar	SLO	25.1.75	3		Malles	12 Jul
8.05	1.6	Younes	Moudrik	MAR	1.10.77	2		Casablanca	12 Aug
8.04i		Leevan	Sands	BAH	16.8.81	3	NCAA	Fayetteville	14 Mar
8.04i		Tony	Allmond	USA	8.10.82	4	NCAA	Fayetteville	14 Mar
		(60)							
8.04	0.4	Petr	Lampart	CZE	31.3.83	2	GS	Ostrava	12 Jun
8.04	1.8	Shin-ichi	Terano	JPN	10.7.79	3	AsiC	Manila	23 Sep
8.03i		Vladimir	Malyavin	RUS	4.3.73	2		Moskva	30 Jan
8.02	-0.3	Yoelmis	Pacheco	CUB	9.6.82	1		La Habana	21 Feb
8.02	1.0	Allen	Simms	USA	26.7.82	1		Los Angeles	1 Mar
8.02	1.2	Mohamed Salim	Al-Khuwalidi	KSA	19.6.81	2		Hamburg	20 Jul
8.01		Kirill	Sosunov	RUS	1.11.75	1		Moskva	15 May
8.01	0.7	Anastásios	Makrinikólas	GRE	21.7.77	3	NC	Tríkala	15 Jun
8.00i		Schahriar	Bigdeli	GER	26.3.80	1	NC	Leipzig	23 Feb
8.00	1.9	Konstadínos	Papadópoulos	GRE	7.6.74	3		Thessaloníki	31 May
		(70)							
8.00	0.7	Osbourne	Moxey	BAH	27.8.78	4		Pírgos	27 Jul
8.00	0.6	Rémi	Robert	FRA	21.1.76	1		Bondoufle	16 Aug
7.99	0.0	Juaune	Armon	USA	6.5.82	1	NCAA-r	Stanford	30 May
7.99	1.1	Denis	Sinyavskiy	RUS	13.8.79	1	Znam	Tula	8 Jun
7.99	1.8	Marijo	Bakovic	CRO	11.4.82	1		Tarvisio	27 Jul
7.98	1.9	Peter	Burge	AUS	3.7.74	*		Perth	8 Feb
7.98		Amrit	Pal Singh	IND	6.10.83	1		Chennai	4 Mar
7.98i		Carlos	Calado	POR	5.10.75	1	vESP	Espinho	8 Mar
7.98	1.1	Víctor	Castillo	VEN	8.6.81	3	PAm	Santo Domingo	6 Aug
7.98A		Armen	Martirosyan	ARM	6.8.69	1		Artashat	19 Aug
		(80)							
7.97i		Okoineme	Giwa-Agbomeirele	USA	30.11.78	1		Blacksburg	15 Feb
7.97	1.0	Leandro	de Jesus	BRA	2.3.81	1		São Caetano do Sul	27 Apr
7.97	0.9	Roland	McGhee	USA	15.10.71	2	Mod R	Modesto	10 May
7.97	0.0	Grzegorz	Marciniszyn	POL	22.5.77	1		Biala Podlaska	31 May
7.97	0.9	Morten	Jensen	DEN	2.12.82	Q	EU23	Bydgoszcz	19 Jul
7.96	1.4	Tom	Pappas	USA	6.9.76	D	NC	Stanford	21 Jun
7.96	0.4	Jan	Zumer	SLO	9.6.82	2		Ebensee	2 Aug
7.96	0.3	Tommy	Evilä	FIN	6.4.80	1		Lappeenranta	3 Aug
7.95	0.6	Ivaylo	Rusenov	BUL	9.9.79	1		Plovdiv	31 May

Mark	Wind	Name		Nat	Born	Pos	Meet	Venue	Date
7.95	0.0	Hatem (90)	Mersal	EGY	20.1.75	2	RomIC	Bucuresti	8 Jun
7.95	1.8	Ahmad	Al-Dosari	KSA-J	3.7.85	1	W.Pol	Barcelona	31 Jul
7.95	1.3	Ciaran	McDonagh	IRL	20.5.76	1	NC	Dublin (S)	9 Aug
7.94i		Luka	Aracic	CRO	13.3.81	3		Ljubljana	16 Feb
7.94	0.7	Tim	Parravicini	AUS	25.4.81	1		Canberra	22 Feb
7.94	1.7	Ramon	Washington	USA	23.6.81	1		Fayetteville	12 Apr
7.94	1.8	Tarik	Bouguétaib	MAR	30.4.81	3		Casablanca	12 Aug
7.93i		Bogdan	Tudor	ROM	1.2.70	2	NC	Bucuresti	23 Feb
7.93	0.4	Arvidas	Nazarovas	LTU	17.4.81	4	EU23	Bydgoszcz	20 Jul
7.93	0.0	Nabil	Adamou	ALG	8.4.75	1	Af-AsG	Hyderabad	29 Oct
7.92	0.7	Niklas (100)	Rorarius	FIN	7.6.78	*		Lapinlahti	13 Jul
7.92	0.9	Ivan	Pucelj	CRO	11.7.81	1		Ljubljana	30 Jul
7.92	-0.8	Yevgeniy	Tretyak	RUS	18.7.71	6	NC	Tula	10 Aug
7.92	0.8	Ndiss Kaba	Badji	SEN	21.9.83	2	Afr G	Abuja	14 Oct

7.91	1.8	Mike	Bragg	USA	13.12.81	8 May
7.91A	1.1	Emmanuel	Bangué	FRA	21.7.71	3 Aug
7.90	0.1	Wilfredo	Martínez	CUB-J	9.1.85	21 Feb
7.90	0.3	Milton	Little	USA	13.6.81	19 Apr
7.90	0.0	Darren	Ritchie	GBR	14.2.75	16 Aug
7.90	0.8	Wayne	Peppin	IND	9.2.83	6 Sep
7.90	0.6		Cai Peng	CHN	28.3.83	13 Sep
7.89	0.3	Aarik	Wilson	USA	25.10.82	29 Mar
7.89	1.4	Erick	Walder	USA	5.11.71	3 May
7.89	0.0	George	Kitchens	USA	16.11.83	16 May
7.89	1.6	Jadel	Gregório	BRA	16.9.80	12 Jun
7.88	0.2	Nelson Carlos	Ferreira	BRA	1.1.73	29 Mar
7.87i		Mesut	Yavas	TUR	14.4.78	8 Mar
7.87	0.9	Daisuke	Arakawa	JPN	19.9.81	8 Jun
7.87	1.7	Matthias	Eifert	GER	10.9.77	9 Jun
7.87	1.9	Thiago Carahyba	Dias	BRA-J	2.3.84	12 Jun
7.87	1.9	Naohiro	Shinada	JPN-Y	10.2.86	17 Jun
7.87	-2.6	Tamás	Margl	HUN	18.6.76	2 Aug
7.87	2.0	Jürgen	Cools	NED	16.9.75	3 Aug
7.87	0.8	Tomas	Bardauskas	LTU	22.3.75	9 Aug
7.86	1.2	Roman	Sebrle	CZE	26.11.74	31 May
7.86	1.1	Sérgio Muniz	dos Santos	BRA	13.5.76	12 Jun
7.86	0.7	Marco	Kummle	GER	19.7.73	2 Aug
7.86	0.5		Su Suk-kyun	KOR-J	2.11.85	11 Oct
7.85	-1.9	Brandon	Parker	USA	3.6.82	16 May
7.85	0.7	Jon Arnar	Magnusson	ISL	28.7.69	31 May
7.85	0.0	Kafétien	Gomis	FRA	23.3.80	1 Jun
7.85	1.5	Mickael	Loria	FRA	9.6.73	25 Jul
7.85	0.8	Kazushige	Inadomi	JPN	4.5.78	12 Oct
7.84A	1.3	Godfrey Khotso	Mokoena	RSA-J	6.3.85	31 Jan
7.84	0.0	Dmitriy	Sapinskiy	RUS	23.10.83	28 Jun
7.83	2.0	Fukurato	Shimakawa	JPN	80	24 May
7.83		Vytautas	Seliuskas	LTU	21.4.82	20 Jun
7.83	0.7	Nelson	Évora	POR-J	20.4.84	25 Jul
7.82i		Richard	Smith	USA	16.7.80	25 Jan
7.82	0.8	Murat	Ayaydin	TUR	19.11.65	17 May
7.82		Sergey	Seliverstov	UKR	12.3.80	17 May
7.82	0.4	Melvin	Lister	USA	29.8.77	20 Jun
7.82	1.4	Eroni	Tuivanuavou	FIJ	2.5.83	11 Jul
7.82	-1.9	Gaspar	Araújo	POR	17.12.81	2 Aug
7.82	1.4		Chou Chien-Cheng	TPE	10.9.77	22 Oct
7.81i		LeJuan	Simon	USA	7.2.81	31 Jan
7.81	1.5	Bryan	Clay	USA	3.1.80	1 Jun
7.81	1.2	John	Thornell	AUS-J	22.4.85	12 Jun
7.81	1.1	Atanas	Rusenov	BUL	30.8.81	15 Jun
7.81	0.8	Gabriel	Gui	ROM	3.6.75	9 Jul
7.81	1.8	Dimítrios	Koukourdís	GRE	20.10.83	19 Jul
7.81	1.2	Christian	Kaczmarek	GER-J	17.6.84	25 Jul
7.81	1.0	Wolfgang	Ebner	SUI	19.6.76	2 Aug
7.80	1.5	Ferdinando	Lucolano	ITA	7.8.80	17 May
7.80	-0.5	Povilas	Mykolaitis	LTU	22.2.83	6 Jun
7.80	-0.7	Sascha	Müller	GER	10.8.76	28 Jun
7.80	0.7	Todor	Georgiev	BUL	10.7.80	5 Jul
7.80	1.8	Frédéric	Miyoupo	CMR	20.11.82	5 Jul
7.80	1.3	Ilja	Tumorin (157)	EST	17.3.79	4 Aug

Wind assisted

Mark	Wind	Name		Nat	Born	Pos	Meet	Venue	Date
8.32	2.1	Joan Lino	Martínez	CUB	17.1.78	1		Arona	26 Jul
8.29A	3.3	Jonathan	Chimier	MRI	6.8.82	1		Sestriere	19 Jul
8.29	3.1	Salim	Sdiri	FRA	26.10.78	1	NC	Narbonne	25 Jul
					8.17w/2.8	8.29w	x	x x	x
8.28	3.0	Leevan	Sands	BAH	16.1.81	1	NCAA-r	Columbus	31 May
					7.55	7.93w	x	7.81w 7.99w	8.28w
8.26	2.2	Kader	Klouchi	FRA	1.6.69	1		Pierre Bénite	13 Jun
8.24	3.6	Peter	Burge	AUS	3.7.74	1		Perth	8 Feb
8.23	2.8	Arnaud	Casquette	MRI	16.4.78	2	FRA Ch	Narbonne	25 Jul
8.19	2.2	Yann	Doménech	FRA	17.3.79	1		Bron	29 May
8.15	3.3	Younes	Moudrik	MAR	1.10.77	1		Dakar	4 Apr
8.15	2.1	Tomasz	Mateusiak	POL	5.12.80	1	NC	Bielsko-Biala	4 Jul
8.15	4.9	Shane	Hair	AUS	24.10.75	1		Perth	29 Nov
8.13	6.5	Kirill	Sosunov	RUS	1.11.75	1	ECCp	Valencia	24 May
8.12	2.7	Kevin	Dilworth	USA	14.2.74	2	v2N	Glasgow (S)	29 Jun
8.10		Víctor	Castillo	VEN	8.6.81	Q	CAC	St George's	5 Jul
8.10		Osbourne	Moxey	BAH	27.8.78	Q	CAC	St George's	5 Jul
8.10	3.2	Gaspar	Araújo	POR	17.12.81	1	NC	Seia	2 Aug
8.08	6.2	Darren	Ritchie	GBR	14.2.75	3	v2N	Glasgow (S)	29 Jun
8.07	2.6	Gregor	Cankar	SLO	25.1.75	1		Celje	24 May
8.07	3.4	Nabil	Adamou	ALG	8.4.75	2	Arab C	Amman	6 Sep
8.05	2.7	Stefano	Dacastello	ITA	17.2.80	1		Milano	28 Jun
8.03	3.9	Thiago Carahyba	Dias	BRA-J	2.3.84	1	NC-j	Londrina	17 May
8.03	3.5	Ferhat	Çiçek	TUR	13.6.81	1		Istanbul	7 Jun
8.02	5.2	Tim	Parravicini	AUS	25.4.81	2		Perth	8 Feb
8.01	3.2	Drew	Carter	USA	5.9.81	2	NCAA-r	Columbus	30 May
7.99	4.2	Nelson Carlos	Ferreira	BRA	1.1.73	1		São Caetano do Sul	29 Mar
7.99	3.7	Leonard	Cobb	USA	20.1.75	3	Tex R	Austin	4 Apr
7.99	5.2	John	Thornell	AUS-J	22.4.85	1	BRA Ch	São Paulo	14 Jun

Mark	Wind	Name		Nat	Born	Pos	Meet	Venue	Date
7.98	2.7	Imre	Lörincz	HUN	12.3.82	1	NC	Nyíregyháza	2 Aug
7.97	3.3	Tyrone	Ward	USA	.81	1		San Luis Obispo	22 Mar
7.97	2.1	Niklas	Rorarius	FIN	7.6.78	1		Lapinlahti	13 Jul
7.96	2.8	Jason	Ward	USA	6.4.81	1		Austin	3 May
7.96	2.3	Mickaël	Loria	FRA	9.6.73	6	NC	Narbonne	6 Jul
7.95	9.0	Clayton	Latham	CAN	18.4.80	1	JUCO	Levelland	8 May
7.94	4.7	Felix	Coetzee	RSA	30.7.75	1		Wanganui	19 Jan
7.93	3.8	Cleavon	Dillion	TRI	5.10.82	2		Fort Worth	19 Apr

7.92	3.8	Deandre	Free	USA	15.1.81	8 May
7.92	2.6	Tommy	Oleksy	USA	26.3.81	30 May
7.92	2.7	Jonathan	Moore	GBR-J	31.5.84	13 Jul
7.90	3.0	Jürgen	Cools	NED	16.9.75	13 Jul
7.89	4.6	Tarrant	Fuller	USA		2 May
7.89	3.1	Kazushige	Inadomi	JPN	4.5.78	27 Sep
7.88		Jeff	Billing	USA		8 Jun
7.88	2.3	Vladimir	Yashin	RUS	1.2.81	28 Jun
7.87	3.6	Stephen	Moore	USA	13.8.75	3 May
7.87A	2.8	Dominic	Zeigler	USA-J	84	24 May
7.87	2.9	Scott	Mayle	USA		30 May
7.87	4.9	Kenneth	Kastrén	FIN	8.11.75	8 Jun
7.87	4.3	Gabriel	Gui	ROM	3.6.75	6 Jul
7.87	2.4	Dimítrios	Koukourdís	GRE	20.10.83	20 Jul
7.86	2.2	Cheikh Tidiane	Touré	FRA	25.1.70	4 Apr
7.85	4.1	Fabrice	Lapierre	AUS	17.10.83	30 May
7.84	3.2	Vytautas	Seliuskas	LTU	21.4.82	4 Jul
7.84	2.3	Christian	Olsson	SWE	25.1.80	6 Sep
7.82	2.1	Naoki	Saito	JPN	3.3.83	19 Apr
7.82	3.5	Ronald	Hill	USA-J	17.5.84	16 May
7.82	2.8	Daniel	Kaczmarczyk	POL	28.6.81	4 Jul
7.81	2.7	Andrejs	Tolstiks	LAT	19.1.77	7 Jun
7.81	3.7	Todor	Georgiev	BUL	10.7.80	5 Jul
7.80	3.8	José Antonio	Giralde	ESP	27.11.72	3 May

Best outdoor marks

8.22	0.0	Zyuskov	1		Kalamáta	31 May
8.11	0.3	Vasilyev	2		Rivas	12 Jun
8.10	0.3	Sdiri	1		Pierrelatte	31 May
8.09	0.6	Gataullin	4	NC	Tula	10 Aug
8.08	-0.4	Dachev	1		Sofia	2 Jul
8.05	1.1	Johnson	1	Tex R	Austin	4 Apr
8.02	1.8	Moffitt	2	Tex R	Austin	4 Apr
8.02	1.6	Allmond	2	NCAA	Sacramento	13 Jun
8.01	1.3	Sands	*	NCAA	Sacramento	13 Jun
7.94	0.8	Bigdeli	7		Bad Langensalza	15 Jun

7.88 0.0 Aracic 7 Jun | 7.85 Malyavin 15 May | 7.82 1.9 Yavas 7 Jun
7.86 0.0 Calado 24 May | 7.83 -0.8 Giwa-Agbomeirele 9 Jun

Low altitude best

8.08	1.8	JChimier	1		Marseille (L)	21 Jun
8.05	1.7	Casquette	*	Fra Ch	Narbonne	26 Jul
7.83	0.2	Mokoena	3	AfG	Abuja	14 Oct

JUNIORS

See main list for top 2 juniors. 11 performances by 9 men to 7.81. Additional marks and further juniors:

Al-Dosari 7.85 0.0 2 Bangkok 5 Jun Dias 7.90w/2.1 2 NC São Paulo 12 Jun

7.90	0.1	Wilfredo	Martínez	CUB-J	9.1.85	2		La Habana	21 Feb
7.87	1.9	Thiago Carahyba	Dias	BRA-J	2.3.84	*	NC	São Paulo	12 Jun
7.87	1.9	Naohiro	Shinada	JPN-Y	10.2.86	1		Obihiro	17 Jun
7.86	0.5		Su Suk-kyun	KOR-J	2.11.85	1	NG	Chunju	11 Oct
7.84A	1.3	Godfrey Khotso	Mokoena	RSA-J	6.3.85	1		Potchestroom	31 Jan
		7.83 0.2 3 Afg Abuja 14 Oct							
7.83	0.7	Nelson	Évora	POR-J	20.4.84	1	EJ	Tampere	25 Jul
7.81	1.2	John	Thornell	AUS-J	22.4.85	*	NC	São Paulo	12 Jun
7.81	1.2	Christian	Kaczmarek (10)	GER-J	17.6.84	2	EJ	Tampere	25 Jul
7.79	0.3	Luis	Tristán	PER	1.5.84	2		Santiago de Chile	26 Apr
7.79	0.0	Shota	Abe	JPN	9.3.84	3	NC	Yokohama	8 Jun
7.77i			Wang Minsheng	CHN	7.4.85	1		Tianjin	17 Feb
7.77	0.0	J.J.	Sturm	USA	17.1.84	3		Atlanta	16 May
7.76	1.9	Jonathan	Moore	GBR	31.5.84	*		Merksem	6 Sep
7.74	0.2	Ibrahim Abdulla	Al-Waleed	QAT	7.5.84	4	Gulf	Al-Kuwait	8 Oct
7.74	0.8		Kuang Li	CHN	13.8.84	Q	NG	Changsha	25 Oct
7.71	0.6	Dimítrios	Diamadáras	GRE	18.7.84	6	NC	Trikala	15 Jun
7.71	0.0		Jin Zutao	CHN-Y	9.1.87	3		Shijiazhuang	4 Aug
7.70	-1.1	Yuki	Imai (20)	JPN	12.8.85	1	N.Sch	Nagasaki	31 Jul

Wind assisted – see main list for 2 juniors. Additional men:

7.92	2.7	Jonathan	Moore	GBR	31.5.84	5	GP	Gateshead	13 Jul
7.87A	2.8	Dominic	Zeigler	USA	84	1		Albuquerque	24 May
7.82	3.5	Ronald	Hill	USA	17.5.84	1		Hayward	16 May
7.77	3.3	Derrell	Hutsona	USA	.84	1		Norwalk	7 Jun
7.76	2.1	Ibrahim Abdulla	Al-Waleed	QAT	7.5.84	6	AsiC	Manila	23 Sep
7.71	2.7	Greig	Cryer	USA	25.9.84	3		Clemson	10 May

TRIPLE JUMP

17.77	0.2	Christian	Olsson	SWE	25.1.80	1	Veniz	Haniá	9 Jun

16.77/1.2 17.77/1.6 x p x 17.27/0.2

17.74	1.9	*	GP	Gateshead	13 Jul	17.69/1.6 17.74/1.9 17.92w 17.61/1.4 x p
17.72	-0.3	1	WCh	Saint-Denis	25 Aug	17.72 17.52/-0.2 17.50/-0.3 17.52/0.0 17.34/0.0 15.33
17.70i		1	WI	Birmingham	16 Mar	16.95 16.64 x 17.28 17.31 17.70
17.56	-0.2	Q	WCh	Saint-Denis	23 Aug	17.56 only jump
17.55	0.8	1		Réthimno	6 Jul	17.54/-0.4 17.25/1.0 16.97/0.0 17.55 17.11/0.0 x
17.55	-0.1	1	WAF	Monaco	14 Sep	17.09/0.3 17.55 17.48/-0.3 x four only
17.54	0.4	1	NC	Norrtälje	1 Aug	17.08/0.0 17.22/0.5 p 17.54 17.42/ 0.5 17.43/0.0
17.51	0.9	1	vFIN	Helsinki	5 Sep	16.95 x 17.51 p p 17.21/0.7

MEN 2003

Mark	Wind	Name		Nat	Born	Pos	Meet	Venue	Date
17.43	0.9	1	Karlstad	24 Jul	15.46 17.22/0.5 15.35 17.10/1.6 17.43 17.09/0.0				
17.40i		1	Stockholm	18 Feb	17.11 17.40 17.32 15.54 x 17.07				
17.38	1.1	1 ECp1A	Lappeenranta	22 Jun	17.01 17.07 17.38 17.08 four only				
17.37i		1	Sätra	2 Mar	17.13 x 17.16 17.11 p 17.37				
17.36	-0.2	1 DNG	Stockholm	5 Aug	x 17.27 17.36 17.01 17.32 17.09				
17.36	0.8	1 MAI	Malmö	12 Aug	17.36/0.8 x 17.04/0.4 17.28/-0.4 p 17.14/1.5				
17.34	0.0	1	Moskva	20 Sep	17.27/0.0 17.34 x x four only				
17.57w	2.5	1	Göteborg	1 Sep	17.01 17.57w p 17.13/0.2 x x				
17.63	0.4	Marian	Oprea	ROM	6.6.82	1	RomIC	Bucuresti	7 Jun
					17.63 17.11/0.9p p p p				
17.50	0.8	2 Veniz	Haniá	9 Jun	17.50 x p x p x				
17.34	0.0	2 DNG	Stockholm	5 Aug	17.21/0.8 17.34 16.47 x p 17.13				
17.32	0.9	1 Athl	Lausanne	1 Jul	17.19/-0.5 17.32 p 17.05/-1.1 p 16.76				
17.61	1.1	Jonathan	Edwards	GBR	10.5.66	2	GP	Gateshead	13 Jul
					17.61 x x p p p				
17.44i		1 GP	Birmingham	21 Feb	17.44 x p p p p				
17.59	1.0	Kenta	Bell	USA	16.3.77	1	NC	Stanford	22 Jun
					16.45w 16.73 17.40/-1.4 17.08/0.4 17.59 x				
17.33	0.2	1	Tucson	24 May					
17.31A	1.3	1	El Paso	12 Apr	16.45w x 17.13w 16.81 x 17.31				
17.31	1.3	1 MSR	Walnut	19 Apr	17.23 17.31 16.93 x p x				
17.57	0.2	Dmitriy	Valyukevich	BLR	31.5.81	1	EU23	Bydgoszcz	19 Jul
					17.16/0.6 17.51/0.5 x 17.57 16.91 x				
17.55	1.1	Walter	Davis	USA	2.7.79	2	NC	Stanford	22 Jun
					16.89 17.04/0.8 17.32/1.8 15.80w 17.55 16.89				
17.35i		2 WI	Birmingham	16 Mar	16.74 16.44 16.52 16.85 16.92 17.35				
17.46w	2.2	1 Neb	Torino	6 Jun	x 17.46w p p p p				
17.45i		Tim	Rusan	USA	25.6.77	1	NC	Boston (R)	1 Mar
					16.67 17.45 p p p p				
17.40	0.3	Leevan	Sands	BAH	16.8.81	1	GP	London (CP)	8 Aug
					16.98 16.96 17.40 17.22/0.3 p p				
17.31	-0.2	David	Giralt Jr.	CUB-J	26.8.84	Q	WCh	Saint-Denis	23 Aug
					x 17.31 two jumps				
		(32/9)							
17.28	0.2	Yoandri	Betanzos (10)	CUB	15.2.82	2	WCh	Saint-Denis	25 Aug
17.27i		Yoelbi	Quesada	CUB	4.8.73	3	WI	Birmingham	16 Mar
17.26i		Allen	Simms	USA	26.7.82	1	NCAA	Fayetteville	15 Mar
17.19i		Aleksandr	Glavatskiy	BLR	2.5.70	2		Gent	9 Feb
17.17		Vitaliy	Moskalenko	RUS	30.6.74	1	NC	Tula	9 Aug
17.16	0.5	Fabrizio	Donato	ITA	14.8.76	1	ECp-S	Firenze	22 Jun
17.12	1.7	Julien	Kapek	FRA	12.1.79	1	NCAA	Sacramento	14 Jun
17.11	0.4	Jadel	Gregório	BRA	16.9.80	3	Nebiolo	Torino	6 Jun2
17.06	1.3	Alexander	Martínez	CUB	23.8.77	1		Tallinn	30 Jul
17.03	0.0	Viktor	Yastrebov	UKR	13.1.82	1		Kharkov	17 May
17.03	0.3	Nikolay	Savolainen	UKR	25.3.80	1		Kiev	29 Jul
		(20)							
17.02	-0.6	Ivaylo	Rusenov	BUL	9.9.79	1	ECp-1B	Velenje	22 Jun
16.99i		Aarik	Wilson	USA	25.10.82	2	NCAA	Fayetteville	15 Mar
16.99A	1.3	Jérôme	Romain	FRA	12.6.71	2		El Paso	12 Apr
16.96	1.0	Takanori	Sugibayashi	JPN	14.3.76	1	NC	Yokohama	7 Jun
16.96	0.5	Karl	Taillepierre	FRA	13.8.76	2		Strasbourg	26 Jun
16.95	0.9	Momchil	Karailiev	BUL	21.5.82	1	NC-23	Sofia	14 Jun
16.95	0.0	Sébastien	Pincemail	FRA	21.2.79	2	NA	Heusden	2 Aug
16.95		Igor	Spasovkhodskiy	RUS	1.8.79	2	NC	Tula	9 Aug
16.92	0.3	Hrístos	Melétoglu	GRE	2.1.72	1	NC	Tríkala	14 Jun
16.92	0.0		Gu Junjie	CHN-J	5.5.85	1	NG	Changsha	24 Oct
		(30)							
16.91i		Viktor	Gushchinskiy	RUS	12.8.78	2	NC	Moskva	27 Feb
16.91	1.3	Olivier	Sanou	BKF	2.1.75	1		Castres	6 Aug
16.89i		Sergey	Izmailov	UKR	1.5.75	1	NC	Sumy	23 Feb
16.88	0.5	Andrew	Owusu	GHA	8.7.72	Q	WCh	Saint-Denis	23 Aug
16.85i		Maksim	Molokov	RUS	.77	2		Samara	26 Jan
16.84	0.7	Kazuyoshi	Ishikawa	JPN	16.11.82	1	NG	Fukuroi	29 Oct
16.82i		Gregor	Cankar	SLO	25.1.75	1		Ljubljana	16 Feb
16.82		Sergey	Bochkov	AZE	20.8.79	1		Moskva	23 May
16.82	0.9	Arius	Filet	FRA	17.12.77	6	Nebiolo	Torino	6 Jun
16.82	-0.2	Yevgeniy	Plotnir	RUS	26.6.77	3	WUG	Daegu	30 Aug
		(40)							
16.81	-0.1	Andrew	Murphy	AUS	18.12.69	1		Leverkusen	3 Aug
16.80	1.6	Randy	Lewis	GRN	14.10.80	1	DrakeR	Des Moines	26 Apr
16.80	0.9	Aleksandr	Sergeyev	RUS	29.7.83	1	Znam	Tula	7 Jun

Mark	Wind	Name		Nat	Born	Pos	Meet	Venue	Date
16.78	1.7	Rudolph	Helpling	GER	23.2.81	1	NC	Ulm	29 Jun
16.78	0.4		Zhu Shujing	CHN-J	24.5.85	2	NG	Changsha	24 Oct
16.76	1.2	Denis	Kapustin	RUS	5.10.70	2	Znam	Tula	7 Jun
16.74	0.5	Péter	Tölgyesi	HUN	9.6.81	2	ECp-1A	Lappeenranta	22 Jun
16.73i		LeVar	Anderson	USA	26.3.77	1		Baton Rouge	25 Jan
16.71	1.5	Johan	Meriluoto	FIN	22.3.74	1		Lahti	2 Jul
16.71	0.9	Daniel	Donovici	ROM	5.3.80	5	WUG	Daegu	30 Aug
		(50)							
16.70	0.7	Aleksandr	Aseledchenko	RUS	10.10.73	3	Znam	Tula	7 Jun
16.67	0.5	Berk	Tuna	TUR	7.5.76	1	NC	Ankara	1 Jun
16.67	0.7		Wu Ji	CHN	14.8.78	3	AsiC	Manila	22 Sep
16.66	-0.6	Jefferson	Sabino	BRA	4.11.82	2		São Caetano do Sul	27 Apr
16.65	1.8	Takashi	Komatsu	JPN	30.12.67	1	Afr-As	Hyderabad	30 Oct
16.61		Osniel	Tosca	CUB-J	30.6.84	2		Santa Clara	28 Feb
16.61i		Tosin	Oke	GBR	1.10.80	1	NC	Birmingham	1 Mar
16.61	0.1	Andrey	Trots	UKR	17.1.78	2		Kharkov	17 May
16.61		Yevgeniy	Inozemtsev	RUS	14.4.74	5	NC	Tula	9 Aug
16.60	0.9	Anisio	Silva	BRA	16.6.69	3		São Caetano do Sul	27 May
		(60)							
16.59i		Dimítrios	Tsiámis	GRE	12.1.82	4	Balk	Athína (P)	4 Mar
16.59	1.3	Brandon	Evans	USA	30.10.79	1		Austin	3 May
16.58A	0.7	Raúl	Chapado	ESP	4.5.70	1		Ávila	12 Aug
16.58i		Danila	Burkenya	RUS	20.7.78	1		Moskva	24 Dec
16.57	1.6	Rostislav	Dimitrov	BUL	26.12.74	2	Balk G	Thíva	13 Jul
16.56	0.9	Leonard	Cobb	USA	20.1.75	1	Tex R	Austin	5 Apr
16.56	1.8	Marcelo	da Costa	BRA	1.5.81	4	NC	São Paulo	14 Jun
16.56	1.4	Yuri	Litvinski	BUL	25.11.81	Q	EU23	Bydgoszcz	17 Jul
16.55i		Konstantin	Pozatsidi	RUS	23.1.83	5	NC	Moskva	27 Feb
16.55	-0.7	Larry	Achike	GBR	31.1.75	1	NC	Birmingham	26 Jul
		(70)							
16.55	-0.6	Mohammed	Hamdi Awadh	QAT	4.12.81	1	Arab C	Amman	8 Sep
16.54	1.1	Robert	Michniewski	POL	16.2.74	1	NC	Bielsko-Biala	5 Jul
16.54	0.0	Bostjan	Simunic	SLO	28.12.74	1	NC	Nova Gorica	10 Aug
16.53	0.0	John	Moffitt	USA	12.12.80	2	SEC	Knoxville	18 May
16.53	1.5	Charles	Friedek	GER	26.8.71	4		Dortmund	15 Jun
16.52	1.4	Yevgeniy	Semenenko	UKR-J	17.7.84	2	NC	Kiev	6 Jul
16.52	2.0	António	da Costa	BRA	8.2.73	1		Sertãozinho	21 Sep
16.52			Wu Bo	CHN-J	17.6.84	2		Guangzhou	27 Sep
16.50	0.4	Avi	Tayari	ISR	25.10.73	*		Tel Aviv	7 Jun
16.48	w?	Von	Ware	USA	30.6.75	1		Fresno	5 Apr
		16.29	-1.0			1		Irvine	3 May
		(80)							
16.48			Li Xin	CHN-J	21.11.85	3		Guangzhou	27 Sep
16.48	0.6	Mohamed	Hazouri	SYR	.83	5	AsiC	Manila	22 Oct
16.47	0.0	Jacob	McReynolds	AUS	8.12.78	1		Canberra	21 Jan
16.47i		Vladimir	Letnicov	MDA	7.10.81	4	Ukr C	Sumy	23 Feb
16.47A	1.5	Quincy	Howe	TRI	11.1.79	1		Greeley	5 Apr
16.46i		Aleksandr	Petrenko	RUS	8.2.83	4		Moskva	11 Feb
16.46	0.7	Sergio Muniz	dos Santos	BRA	13.5.76	1		São Caetano do Sul	4 Jun
16.46	0.2	Denis	Saurambayev	KAZ	30.6.77	1		Tashkent	13 Jun
16.46	1.9	Djeke	Mambo	BEL	4.3.77	7	FRA Ch	Narbonne	26 Jul
16.46	0.5	Lauri	Leis	EST	7.10.78	1	NC	Tallinn	3 Aug
		(90)							
16.46	0.0		Li Yanxi	CHN-J	26.6.84	2	NC	Shanghai	14 Sep
16.45	-0.2	Alassane	Diarra	FRA	22.1.81	1		Lamentin	30 Apr
16.45		Pavel	Kalinin	RUS	21.8.79	1		Sankt Peterburg	22 May
16.44i		Thomas	Moede	GER	26.7.77	1	NC	Leipzig	22 Feb
16.44	1.7	Lawrence	Willis	USA		1		Baton Rouge	3 May
16.44	2.0	Femi	Akinsaya	GBR	29.11.69	1		Celle Ligure	1 Jul
16.44	0.8	Nick	Thomas	GBR	4.4.79	2	NC	Birmingham	26 Jul
16.44	0.3	Sergey	Lebedev	RUS	.82	7	NC	Tula	8 Aug
16.43	0.4	LeJuan	Simon	USA	7.2.81	3	SEC	Knoxville	18 May
16.43	0.8	Oleg	Sakirkin	KAZ	23.1.66	1		Almaty	21 Jun
		(100)							
16.43	0.4	Nelson	Évora	POR-J	20.4.84	1	EJ	Tampere	27 Jul

16.42A		Rashid	Al-Rumani	KSA	23.3.82	20 Mar
16.42	0.0		Lao Jianfeng	CHN	24.5.75	8 Apr
16.42	1.7	Paolo	Camossi	ITA	6.1.74	3 Aug
16.41	2.0	Aleksandr	Furso	BLR	.79	11 Jul
16.40	0.0	Petr	Hnizdil	CZE	20.6.81	7 Jun
16.40A	1.7	Leigner	Aragón	COL	8.3.76	26 Jul
16.40	0.5	Anton	Andersson	SWE	12.3.81	1 Aug
16.39	0.6	Mohamed	Hamimid	FRA	16.11.73	6 Aug
16.38	0.7	Davy	Manga	FRA	6.5.83	14 Jul
16.37	0.9	Colomba	Fofana	FRA	11.4.77	1 Jun
16.36i		Jaanus	Uudmäe	EST	24.12.80	15 Mar
16.36	0.4	Stávros	Yeoryíou	GRE	23.4.80	14 Jun

Mark	Wind	Name		Nat	Born	Pos	Meet	Venue	Date
16.34i		Rafeeq	Curry	USA	10.8.83				9 Feb
16.34	1.4	Alexis	Copello	CUB-J	12.8.85				5 Aug
16.33	1.8	Gregory	Hughes	BAR	18.3.79				9 May
16.32i		Andreas	Pohle	GER	6.4.81				22 Feb
16.32i		Viktor	Kuznetsov	UKR-J	14.7.86				12 Dec
16.31A		Salem Mouled	Al Ahmadi	KSA	12.9.69				20 Mar
16.31	1.7	Édson	C. dos Santos	BRA	29.10.74				22 Mar
16.30i		Gregory	Yeldell	USA	5.8.83				15 Feb
16.30i		Frank	Tolen	USA	17.7.82				1 Mar
16.30	0.3	François	Dofén	GRE	17.8.77				14 Jun
16.30	1.6	Marcus	Jones	USA	13.8.76				22 Jun
16.30	0.5	Nathan	Douglas	GBR	4.12.82				29 Jun
16.29	-1.0	Von	Ware	USA	30.6.75				3 May
16.29	0.1	Ayata	Joseph	ANT-J	10.8.85				20 Jul
16.28	1.7	Fabrizio	Schembri	ITA	27.1.81				3 Aug
16.28	0.3	Godfrey Khotso	Mokoena	RSA-J	6.3.85				11 Oct
16.28			Lin Mujie	CHN-J	25.9.85				14 Oct
16.27i		Richard	Smith	USA	16.7.80				7 Mar
16.27			Shang Yapeng	CHN	3.1.83				19 Apr
16.27		Ibrahim	Mohd Abubaker	QAT	10.12.82				5 May
16.27	1.3	Jacek	Kazimierowski	POL	2.7.74				31 May
16.27	1.0	Andrej	Batagelj	SLO	9.9.80				10 Aug
16.27	0.3		Song Jian	CHN	7.5.83				12 Sep
16.26i		Samuel	Okantey	IRL	3.11.74				23 Feb
16.25	1.0	Michael	Perry	AUS	30.9.77				5 Apr
16.25	0.5	Michaël	Velter (139)	BEL	21.3.80				10 Aug

Wind assisted

17.92	3.4	Christian	Olsson	SWE	25.1.80	1	GP	Gateshead	13 Jul
17.37	2.1	Jadel	Gregório	BRA	16.9.80	3	GP	Gateshead	13 Jul
					17.37w	x	x	x 16.56	16.80w
17.24	2.5	Julien	Kapek	FRA	12.1.79	1	NC	Narbonne	26 Jul
17.12	2.1	Ivaylo	Rusenov	BUL	9.9.79	2		Réthimno	6 Jul
17.02	2.2	Colomba	Fofana	FRA	11.4.77	2	NC	Narbonne	26 Jul
17.00	4.1	Anísio	Silva	BRA	16.6.69	2	NC	São Paulo	14 Jun
16.99	2.5	Karl	Taillepierre	FRA	13.8.76	3	NC	Narbonne	26 Jul
16.89	3.7	Jacob	McReynolds	AUS	8.12.78	1		Sydney (H)	22 Mar
16.82	3.3	Andrew	Murphy	AUS	18.12.69	2		Sydney (H)	22 Mar
16.75	3.9	Bostjan	Simunic	SLO	28.12.74	1		Ljubljana	18 May
16.72	2.9	Johan	Meriluoto	FIN	22.3.74	1		Hanko	12 Jul
16.71	2.5	Rostislav	Dimitrov	BUL	26.12.74	2		Sofia	2 Jul
16.70	2.4	LeJuan	Simon	USA	7.2.81	2	PennR	Philadelphia	26 Apr
16.62	3.9	John	Moffitt	USA	12.12.80	1	Tex R	Austin	5 Apr
16.58	2.1	Avi	Tayari	ISR	25.10.73	1		Tel Aviv	7 Jun
16.58	2.9	Leonardo	dos Santos	BRA-J	7.5.84	3	NC	São Paulo	14 Jun
16.55	3.7	Mark	Dzradosi	GHA	29.3.78	2	DrakeR	Des Moines	26 Apr
16.53	2.7	Sérgio	Muniz dos Santos	BRA	13.5.76	5	NC	São Paulo	14 Jun
16.49	3.3	Richard	Smith	USA	16.7.80	1	NCAA-r	Columbus	31 May
16.42	2.2	Salvatore	Morello	ITA	5.9.74				3 Aug
16.41	2.7	Rafeeq	Curry	USA	19.8.83				12 Jun
16.40	4.5	Masashi	Watanabe	JPN	10.12.80				29 Apr
16.37	2.5	Emanuele	Sardano	ITA	16.2.79				3 Aug
16.34	3.1	Charles	Burton	USA	4.8.79				12 Jun
16.31	5.4	Brian	Wellman	BER	8.9.67				18 Apr
16.31	3.7	Desmond	Kapofu	ZIM	6.2.78				12 Jun
16.31	2.3	François	Dofén	GRE	17.8.77				1 Jul
16.28	2.3	Vladislav	Gorbenko	UKR	6.8.83				27 May
16.25	2.2	Arvidas	Nazarovas	LTU	17.4.81				7 Jun

Best outdoor marks

17.24	0.9	Rusan	2	Neb	Torino	6 Jun
17.17	0.6	Simms	1		Los Angeles	26 Apr
16.97	1.2	Quesada	Q	WCh	Saint-Denis	23 Aug
16.87		Gushchinskiy	3	NC	Tula	9 Aug
16.79	0.7	Izmailov	1		Kiev	27 May
16.71	0.7	Glavatskiy	Q	WCh	Saint-Denis	23 Aug
16.69	0.0	Wilson	1	Fla R	Gainesville	29 Mar
16.63	0.4	Anderson	3	GP	Osaka	10 May
16.59	-0.4	Oke	1	BIG	Bedford	1 Jun
16.38		Petrenko				9 Aug
16.36	-0.1	Molokov				7 Jun
16.32	1.3	Tsiámis				14 Jun
16.30		Pozatsidi				17 May
16.30		Letnicov				1 Jun
16.27	0.4	Pohle				29 Jun

Best at low altitude

16.67	-0.3	Romain	1		Saint-Denis	4 Jul
16.56w	4.7	Chapado	1	NC	Jerez	3 Aug
16.34	1.3	Chapado				26 Jul
16.30	0.5	Al-Rumani				2 Jul

JUNIORS

See main list for top 9 Juniors. 12 performances by 4 men to 16.57. Additional marks and further juniors:

Giralt	17.24	1.3	1	NC-j	Santiago de C	5 Aug
	17.23	0.1	4	WCh	Saint-Denis	25 Aug
	17.06	1.2	1		La Habana	13 Jun
	16.93	-0.5	1	PAm-J	Bridgetown	20 Jul
Gu Junjie	16.90	1.0	1	WUG	Daeju	30 Aug
	16.83	0.3	1	NC	Shanghai	14 Sep
	16.68	-0.4	2	AsiC	Manila	22 Sep
	16.57		1		Guangzhou	27 Sep

16.34	1.4	Alexis	Copello I10)	CUB	12.8.85	3	NC-j	Santiago de Cuba	5 Aug
16.32i		Viktor	Kuznetsov	UKR	14.7.86	1		Kiev	12 Dec
16.29	0.1	Ayata	Joseph	ANT	10.8.85	2	PAm-J	Bridgetown	20 Jul
16.28	0.3	Godfrey Khotso	Mokoena	RSA	6.3.85	2	AfG	Abuja	11 Oct
16.28			Lin Mujie	CHN	25.9.85	1		Fuzhou	14 Oct
16.17			Wang Zilong	CHN	26.11.84	3		Deyang	19 Apr
16.16	1.0	Alwyn	James	AUS	28.2.85	1		Adelaide	26 Oct
16.15	-0.1		Kim Duk-hyung	KOR	8.12.85	1		Daegu	15 Jun
16.14	1.9	Stéphane	Grèze	FRA	12.11.84	1	NC-j	Vénissieux	13 Jul
16.10i			Wang Minsheng	CHN	7.4.65	1		Tianjin	17 Feb
16.09		Teymur	Abbasov (20)	AZE	12.3.85	1		Baku	25 Jun
16.09	1.5	Yandri	Herrera	CUB	12.7.84	4	NC-j	Santiago de Cuba	5 Aug
16.09	0.0		Hu Xiong	CHN-Y	18.1.86	5	NG	Changsha	24 Oct

Wind assisted – see main list for 1 junior. Additional man:

16.13	2.4	Dmitriy	Detsuk	BLR	9.4.85	2	EJ	Tampere	27 Jul

Mark	Name		Nat	Born	Pos	Meet	Venue		Date

SHOT

Mark	Name		Nat	Born	Pos	Meet	Venue		Date
22.67	Kevin	Toth	USA	29.12.67	1	Kans R	Lawrence		19 Apr
				x	x	x	21.62	22.67	x
21.76	1 Pre	Eugene	24 May	x	21.76	x	x	x	x
21.70i	1	Kent	11 Jan	20.28	19.50	x	21.46	f	21.70
21.69	1	Carson	1 Jun	20.89	21.02	x	x	20.72	21.69
21.30i	1 NC	Boston (R)	2 Mar	21.30	x	x	x	x	x
21.24	1 ModR	Modesto	10 May	21.24	x	x	x	x	x
21.22	1 NC	Stanford	21 Jun	21.22	20.32	x	20.05	21.14	20.92
21.21	1 GP II	Gresham	17 May	20.34	20.36	20.52	x	21.21	x
21.17i	1	Kent	8 Feb						
21.92	Carl	Myerscough	GBR	21.10.79	1	NCAA	Sacramento		13 Jun
				20.67	x	20.85	19.78	20.30	21.92
21.55	1 NC	Birmingham	27 Jul	x	20.27	21.55	x	20.75	x
21.50	1 GP	London (CP)	8 Aug	18.42	20.11	21.50	20.78	x	x
21.49i	1 NCAA	Fayetteville	19 Mar	20.44	21.49	20.35	x	19.84	x
21.16	1 NCAAr	Lincoln, NE	31 May	19.59	20.50	x	21.16	20.49	20.31
21.81	Yuriy	Belonog	UKR	9.3.74	1	NC	Kiev		3 Jul
				21.23	21.81	x	x	20.57	p
21.46i	1	Sumy	21 Feb	20.64	x	20.20	20.79	21.46	x
21.15	1	Rivas	12 Jun	20.38	21.15	x	20.74	20.52	20.86
21.13i	3 WI	Birmingham	14 Mar	21.13	20.92	21.07	x	20.83	x
21.10	1	Kiev	27 May	21.10	20.57	p	x	x	x
21.10	3 WCh	Saint-Denis	23 Aug	x	20.82	21.10	20.95	x	20.72
21.09	1 GP II	Helsinki	18 Aug	20.78	21.09	x	x	x	x
21.69	Andrey	Mikhnevich	BLR	12.7.76	1	WCh	Saint-Denis		23 Aug
				21.24	21.69	21.36	21.45	x	21.44
21.66	1	Minsk	8 Aug						
21.62	Christian	Cantwell	USA	30.9.80	1		Salamanca		15 Jul
				21.02	x	x	21.62	x	21.01
21.56	2 NCAA	Sacramento	13 Jun	19.67	x	20.04	20.93	21.56	21.11
21.47	2 Pre	Eugene	24 May	21.47	21.27	x	20.59	x	21.21
21.16	1 Drake	Des Moines	26 Apr	20.44	x	x	20.47	21.16	x
21.33i	Dan	Taylor	USA	12.5.82	2	NCAA	Fayetteville		15 Mar
				19.61	21.33	19.97	19.40	19.84	x
21.29	Adam	Nelson	USA	7.7.75	1		Kuortane		20 Jul
				20.55	x	x	x	20.10	21.29
21.26	WCh	Saint-Denis	23 Aug	20.00	x	x	21.26	20.65	20.53
21.10		Salamanca	15 Jul	20.95	21.10	x	x	x	x
21.24i	Manuel	Martínez	ESP	7.12.74	1	WI	Birmingham		14 Mar
				20.73	21.14	21.07	21.01	20.70	21.24
21.08	1 ECpS	Firenze	21 Jun	19.66	21.08	20.89	20.70		four only
21.23i	John	Godina	USA	31.5.72	2	WI	Birmingham		14 Mar
				x	x	21.23	x	x	20.66
21.08	Q WCh	Saint-Denis	23 Aug	21.08		one throw			
21.14	Yuriy	Belov	BLR	20.3.81	1		Minsk		21 May
	(36/10)								
21.00i	Arsi	Harju	FIN	18.3.74	1		Mustasaari		10 Feb
20.96	Justin	Anlezark	AUS	14.8.77	1	NC	Brisbane		5 Apr
20.95	Reese	Hoffa	USA	8.10.77	1	PAm	Santo Domingo		5 Aug
20.86	Pavel	Lyzhin	BLR	24.3.81	1	Klim	Staiki		28 Jun
20.85	Joachim	Olsen	DEN	31.5.77	1	NC	Hvidovre		9 Aug
20.78	Roman	Virastyuk	UKR	20.4.68	2	NC	Kiev		3 Jul
20.70	Brad	Snyder	CAN	8.1.76	2	Mod R	Modesto		10 May
20.69i	Tepa	Reinikainen	FIN	16.3.76	1	NC	Kuortane		23 Feb
20.67	Ralf	Bartels	GER	21.2.78	2		Neuwied-Engers		28 May
20.64	Jamie	Beyer	USA	29.12.76	3	GP II	Stanford		7 Jun
	(20)								
20.60	Conny	Karlsson	FIN	30.12.75	1		Lahti		2 Jul
20.56	Yuriy	Parkhomenko	UKR	7.7.73	1		Kiev		29 Jul
20.52	Rutger	Smith	NED	9.7.81	1	EChall	Gioia Tauro		1 Mar
20.51	Pavel	Chumachenko	RUS	5.4.71	1	NC	Tula		7 Aug
20.48	Gheorghe	Guset	ROM	28.5.68	1		Bucuresti		24 May
20.48	Dragan	Peric	SCG	8.5.64	1	Balk G	Thíva		12 Jul
20.46	Miran	Vodovnik	SLO	11.9.77	1		Varazdin		5 Jul
20.39i	Milan	Haborák	SVK	11.1.73	1	NC	Bratislava		22 Feb
20.38	Marco Antonio	Verni	CHI	27.2.76	1		Santiago de Chile		26 Apr
20.37	Ville	Tiisanoja	FIN	24.12.75	Q	WCh	Saint-Denis		23 Aug
	(30)								
20.33	Petr	Stehlík	CZE	15.4.77	1	NC	Olomouc		13 Jul

Mark	Name		Nat	Born	Pos	Meet	Venue	Date
20.33	Pavel	Sofin	RUS	4.9.81	2	EU23	Bydgoszcz	20 Jul
20.28	Ivan	Yushkov	RUS	15.1.81	1		Irkutsk	15 Aug
20.27	Janus	Robberts	RSA	10.3.79	2	MSR	Walnut	19 Apr
20.16	Tonyo	Sylvester	USA	17.12.67	7	NC	Stanford	21 Jun
20.15i	Paolo	Dal Soglio	ITA	29.7.70	1	NC	Genova	22 Feb
20.15	Nedzad	Mulabegovic	CRO	4.2.81	1	NC	Zagreb	2 Aug
20.12	Detlef	Bock	GER	15.8.74	2		Gotha	14 Jun
20.09	Tomasz	Majewski	POL	30.8.81	4	ECp-S	Firenze	21 Jun
20.08	Ivan	Emelianov	MDA	19.2.77	1		Chisinau	31 May
	(40)							
20.08	Sergey	Rubtsov	KAZ	4.9.65	1		Bishkek	28 Jun
20.04	Richard	Harrison	USA	13.5.70	1		Santa Monica	16 May
20.02	John	Davis	USA	19.2.77	3	MSR	Walnut	19 Apr
20.02	Chima	Ugwu	NGR	19.7.73	1		Halle	24 May
19.97	Dmitriy	Goncharuk	BLR	17.7.70	3		Minsk	21 May
19.96i	Peter	Sack	GER	27.7.79	2	NC	Leipzig	22 Feb
19.91i	Sergio	Mottin	ITA	15.6.76	1		Schio	1 Feb
19.89i	Scott	Wiegand	USA	26.9.80	1		Nampa	21 Feb
19.88	Grigoriy	Panfilov	RUS	17.5.80	2		Irkutsk	15 Aug
19.87i	Alexis	Paumier	CUB	21.1.75	2		Athína	6 Mar
	(50)							
19.87	Andrey	Borodkin	UKR	18.4.78	3		Koncha-Zaspa	23 May
19.87	Zsolt	Bíber	HUN	31.5.76	1		Kiskunhalas	24 May
19.81i	Pavel	Pankúch	SVK	20.2.75	1		Bratislava	22 Jan
19.81i	Dmitriy	Gorshkov	RUS	8.3.82	1		Moskva	24 Dec
19.79	Gjøran	Sørli	NOR	3.6.78	1		Oslo (S)	12 Aug
19.77i	Karl	Erickson	USA	1.6.82	2		Ames	8 Mar
19.75 ?	Mark	Proctor	GBR	15.1.63	1		Loughborough	21 May
19.75	Rene	Sack	GER	14.7.76	2	NC	Ulm	28 Jun
19.73i	Dan	Ames	USA	16.1.81	2		Nampa	21 Feb
19.71	Sergiu	Ursu	ROM	26.4.80	2		Bucuresti	24 May
	(60)							
19.68	Jani	Illikainen	FIN	26.1.76	1		Övertorneå	2 Jul
19.62	Chris	Adams	USA	2.6.78	1		Akron	10 May
19.59	Bahadur	Singh	IND	7.5.73	1	NC	Bangalore	30 Sep
19.58i	Sean	Shields	USA	10.2.83	2		Nampa	8 Feb
19.58	Anton	Savkin	RUS	15.9.80	1	Znam	Tula	7 Jun
19.57	Zlatan	Zmirak	CRO	20.9.73	2	NC	Zagreb	2 Aug
19.52	Jon	O'Neil	USA	23.3.79	1		La Jolla	26 Apr
19.50	Jesse	Roberge	USA	2.10.78	1		Stanford	9 May
19.50	Andy	Dittmar	GER	5.7.74	4		Neuwied-Engers	28 May
19.47	Tomasz	Chrzanowski	POL	12.7.81	6	EU23	Bydgoszcz	20 Jul
	(70)							
19.45i	Yevgeniy	Kozlov	RUS	.78	3		Moskva	30 Jan
19.44	Dmitriy	Lopatin	RUS	80	1		Krasnodar	17 May
19.43	Dorian	Scott	JAM	1.2.82	2	PennR	Philadelphia	25 Apr
19.41	Timo	Aaltonen	FIN	11.4.69	1		Saarijärvi	21 Jun
19.41	Bilal Saad	Mubarak	QAT	18.12.72	1	AsiC	Manila	23 Sep
19.40	Michael	Mertens	GER	27.12.65	5		Neuwied-Engers	28 May
19.39	Jaroslaw	Cichocki	POL	28.7.82	1		Bydgoszcz	28 Aug
19.38	Jarkko	Haukijärvi	FIN	10.6.77	1		Valkeakoski	8 Jun
19.35	Tony	Thompson	USA	12.3.80	1		Fresno	26 Apr
19.33	Vince	Mosca	USA	23.1.80	3	NCAA-r	Stanford	31 May
	(90)							
19.18i	Simon	Stewart	USA	28.1.80	1		Cheney	11 Jan
19.15i	Andrey	Sinyakov	BLR	6.1.82	4		Minsk	6 Feb
19.14	Hamza	Alic	BIH	20.1.79	3	Balk G	Thíva	12 Jul
19.13i	Marco	Dodoni	ITA	5.9.72	2		Genova	2 Mar
19.10	Burger	Lambrechts	RSA	3.4.73	1		Pretoria	8 Nov
19.09	Antonín	Zalsky	CZE	7.8.80	2		Kladno	8 Jun
19.06	Panayiótis	Baharídis	GRE	31.5.81	5	Balk G	Thíva	12 Jul
19.05	Shakti	Singh	IND	14.5.62	1	Af-AsG	Hyderabad	30 Oct
19.04	Clay	Cross	AUS	26.11.77	2		Riese Pio X	20 Jul
19.02i	Igor	Tuchak	RUS	10.2.77	1		Shakhty	18 Jan
	(100)							
19.02	Taavi	Peetre	EST	4.7.83	1	NC-23	Valga	29 Jun

19.01i	Gunnar	Pfingsten	GER	24.3.75	14 Feb
18.99i	Hannes	Hopley	RSA	26.1.81	8 Feb
18.96	Edhem	Kacevic	BIH	18.5.70	1 May
18.95	Eric	van Vreumingen	NED	15.6.78	26 Apr
18.90	Rhuben	Williams	USA	14.2.82	22 Mar
18.90	Robert	Sadler	USA	26.1.76	16 May
18.89	Yevgeniy	Korotkov	RUS	80	31 May
18.88	Roelie	Potgieter	RSA	20.3.80	15 Mar
18.86i	Robert	Häggblom	FIN	9.8.82	6 Feb
18.86		Wang Zhiyong	CHN	3.1.79	11 Sep

Mark	Name		Nat	Born	Date
18.85i	Pávlos	Atmatsídis	GRE	12.5.80	25 Jan
18.85	Jon	Kalnas	USA	18.4.80	12 Apr
18.85	Sven-Eric	Hahn	GER	17.10.80	22 Jun
18.81	Scott	Martin	AUS	12.10.82	30 Jan
18.81	Galin	Kostadinov	BUL	25.12.79	30 Mar
18.81	Navpreet	Singh	IND	15.6.79	30 Oct
18.80i	Steve	Manz	USA	19.9.81	1 Mar
18.79	Amin	Nikfar	IRI	2.1.81	31 May
18.78	Gaute	Myklebust	NOR	29.4.79	16 May
18.77i	Gábor	Máté	HUN	9.2.79	14 Feb
18.77	Jaiveer	Singh	IND	1.10.70	17 Jul
18.74	Mihail	Stamatóyiannis	GRE	20.5.82	1 Jun
18.74	Borivoje	Stanic	SCG	2.10.74	13 Jun
18.73	Dirk	Urban	GER	14.1.69	29 May
18.72i	Michal	Oertelt	CZE	13.4.79	19 Feb
18.72	Michal	Hodun	POL	17.2.83	27 Jun
18.71i	Thomas	Keinys	LTU	8.4.81	22 Jan
18.71	Ahmad Hassan	Gholoum	KUW	31.5.80	12 May
18.71	Kevin	Bookout	USA	12.2.83	13 Jun
18.69	Paolo	Capponi	ITA	25.3.76	25 Jun
18.69	Anton	Lyuboslavskiy	RUS-J	26.6.84	15 Jul
18.67i	Ioánnis	Vasilópoulos	GRE	16.1.75	1 Feb
18.67i	Váios	Tíggas	GRE	16.10.78	8 Feb
18.65	Jaroslav	Zitnansky	SVK	18.2.71	1 Jun
18.62	Brian	Hallett	USA	20.5.79	31 May
18.62	? John	Newell	USA	20.5.79	7 Jun
18.62	Francisco	Guzmán	MEX	2.8.78	13 Jul
18.61i	Jimmy	Nordin	SWE	19.10.79	10 Feb
18.61	Mika	Vasara	FIN	22.10.83	16 Aug
18.57i		Wen Jili	CHN	11.7.73	18 Feb
18.57	Jeremy	Silverman	USA	28.1.83	26 Apr
18.57	Marco	Fortes	POR	26.9.82	2 Aug
18.57	Khalid Habas	Al Suwaidi	QAT-J	84	23 Sep
18.56	Stefan	Blomqvist	SWE	7.2.65	15 May
18.55	Brad	Johnson	USA	14.7.81	17 May
18.55	Stuart	Gyngell	AUS	25.11.63	3 Nov
18.54i	Marius	Vornicu	ROM	18.1.77	1 Feb
18.54	Edis	Elkasevic	CRO	18.2.83	2 Aug
18.52i	Mikhail	Zabruskov	RUS	26.1.74	1 Mar
18.52	Kevin	Robinson	USA	21.5.75	29 Mar
18.51	Sultan Mubarak	Al Habashi	KSA-J	31.1.85	23 Sep
18.50i	Josh	Sides	USA	14.4.81	21 Feb
18.50	Kuldeep	Singh Mann	IND	16.10.82	10 Jul
18.49	Shai	Shalev	ISR	20.8.75	27 Jul
18.49	Ronny	Jiménez	VEN	15.1.79	11 Dec
18.48	Maris	Urtans	LAT	9.2.81	16 May
18.46i	Krasimir	Aleksandrov	BUL	26.5.68	8 Feb
18.46	Chris	Figures	USA		26 Apr
18.46	Wim	Blondeel	BEL	25.12.73	25 May
18.44	Chris	Meisner	CAN	22.2.83	18 Jul
18.42	Rhys	Jones	AUS	19.3.81	12 Apr
18.42	Hrístos	Sarákoglou	GRE	5.5.79	17 May
18.41	Magnus	Lohse	SWE-J	28.7.84	29 Jun
18.41	Noah	Bryant	USA-J	11.5.84	12 Jul
18.41	Tuomo	Tihinen	FIN	12.12.77	3 Aug
18.39	Krzysztof	Krzywosz	POL	1.10.83	4 Jul
18.39i	Ken	Kemeny	USA	16.4.82	10 Dec
18.38i	Mike	D'Andrea	USA-J	7.2.84	22 Feb
18.37	Aleksandr	Kotov	RUS	.81	17 May
18.37	Anton	Dubinin	RUS	7.7.81	28 Jun
18.36		Zhang Qi	CHN-J	24.12.84	27 Oct
18.34i	Blake	Jackson	USA		8 Mar
18.34	Dmitriy	Dobrotolyubov	RUS	23.11.76	7 Jun
18.34	Tilman	Northoff	GER	18.6.69	16 Aug
18.33i	Jeff	Rubenstein	USA	18.5.81	1 Mar
18.33	Antonio	Lora	ESP	13.4.76	10 Jun
18.31		Tian Yingchun	CHN	29.5.79	11 Sep
18.30i	Manuel	Brändeborn	SWE	7.4.73	1 Mar
18.29	Tucker	Woolsey	USA	.79?	9 May
18.29	Ivan	Napreyevko	UKR	27.11.81	17 May
18.28	Scott	Hecht	USA	29.9.80	11 Apr
18.28	Jeremy	Hoff	USA	20.11.80	12 Apr
18.27	Quint	Melius	USA	19.5.80	12 Apr
18.26		Li Wenkui	CHN	3.7.74	11 Sep
18.25	Andy	Paulsen (186)	USA		26 Apr

Exhibition

Mark	Name		Nat	Born	Date
18.60	Antonio	Lora	ESP	13.4.76	5 Sep

Best outdoor marks

Mark	Name	Pos	Meet	Venue	Date
20.55	Reinikainen	Q	WCh	Saint-Denis	23 Aug
20.44	Taylor	1	JO	Columbus	3 May
20.28	Haborák	1		Bratislava	12 Jul
19.87	P Sack	6	FBK	Hengelo	1 Jun
19.76	Harju	3	PNG	Turku	15 Jun
19.72	Dal Soglio	5		Padova	6 Jul
19.70	Ames	Q		San Diego	11 Apr
19.70	Paumier	1		La Habana	25 Jul
19.40	Erickson	1		Tempe	21 Mar
19.60	Wiegand	Q		San Diego	11 Apr
19.51	Gorshkov	1		Moskva	15 Jul
19.34	Shields	2	NCAA-r	Stanford	31 May
19.29	Niaré	1		Saint-Maur	11 Jun
19.19	Pankúch	1		Dubnica	20 Jul
19.10	Sliwa	1		Bydgoszcz	8 Jun
19.09	Mottin	4	E.Chall	Gioia Tauro	1 Mar

Mark	Name	Date
18.95	Stewart	14 Jun
18.87	Johnson	29 Mar
18.85	Dodoni	25 Apr
18.82	Atmatsídis	14 May
18.82	Pfingsten	22 Jun
18.74	Sinyakov	28 Jun
18.73	Kozlov	15 Jul
18.72	Máté	3 Aug
18.62	Häggblom	14 Jun
18.60	Vasilópoulos	14 May
18.58	Manz	12 Apr
18.50	Tíggas	31 May
18.48	Wen Jili	11 Sep
18.47	Hopley	16 May
18.46	Keinys	6 Jun
18.41	Vornicu	3 May
18.35	Tuchak	31 May
18.34	Oertelt	5 Jul
18.33	Zabruskov	14 Jul
18.26	Sides	19 Apr

JUNIORS

9 performances by 4 juniors to 18.50

Mark	Name		Nat	Born	Pos	Meet	Venue	Date
19.26i	Garrett	Johnson	USA-J	24.5.84	8	NC	Boston (R)	2 Mar
	18.87				2	FlaR	Gainesville	29 Mar
	18.68				4	PennR	Philadelphia	25 Apr
	18.83				1		Atlanta	5 Apr
	18.57				Q	NCAA	Sacramento	11 Jun
	18.68				1		Raleigh	18 Apr
18.69	Anton	Lyuboslavskiy	RUS	26.6.84	3	Kuts	Moskva	15 Jul
18.57	Khalid Habas	Al Suwaidi	QAT	84	3	AsiC	Manila	23 Sep
18.51	Sultan Mubarak	Al Habashi	KSA	31.1.85	4	AsiC	Manila	23 Sep
18.41	Magnus	Lohse	SWE	28.7.84	2		Bottnaryd	29 Jun
18.41	Noah	Bryant	USA	11.5.84	2		Walnut	12 Jul
18.38i	Mike	D'Andrea	USA	7.2.84	2		Columbus	22 Feb
18.36		Zhang Qi	CHN	24.12.84	1	NG	Changsha	27 Oct
18.21i		Jia Peng	CHN	12.1.84	1		Beijing	22 Feb
	18.17				Q	NC	Shanghai	11 Sep
18.17	Ranvijay	Singh (10)	IND	2.10.84	3		Nagercoil	10 Jul
18.08		Sun Ke	CHN	18.5.85	1		Chengdu	27 Aug
18.05	Brian	Ruziecki	USA	10.3.84	3		Northridge	22 Mar
18.02i	Georgi	Ivanov	BUL	13.3.85	1		Sofia	2 Feb
18.02	Milan	Jotanovic	SCG	11.1.84	4		Bar	1 May
17.96	Yasser	Ibrahim	EGY	2.5.84	3	AfrG	Abuja	15 Oct
17.78	Will	Denbo	USA	24.2.84	5		Northridge	22 Mar
17.68	Soslan	Tsirikhov	RUS	24.11.84	2		Krasnodar	17 May

Mark	Name		Nat	Born	Pos	Meet	Venue	Date	Series
17.57i	Gavin	Ball	USA	14.10.84	1		Manhattan, KS	12 Dec	
17.46	Dane	Miller	USA	.84	6	NCAAr	Fairfax	31 May	
17.44	Jaroslav	Pittner (20)	SVK	20.4.84	2		Nové Mesto	9 Aug	
6kg Shot									
21.11	Magnus	Lohse	SWE	28.7.84	1		Lerum	19 Jun	
	20.86				1		Göteborg	5 Jul	
	20.28				1	EJ	Tampere	25 Jul	
20.69	Milan	Jotanovic	SCG	11.1.84	1		Senta	30 Aug	
20.25i	Georgi	Ivanov	BUL	13.3.85	1		Sofia	15 Feb	
	20.01				1	NC-w	Sofia	30 Mar	
20.10	Anton	Lyuboslavskiy	RUS	26.6.84	2	EJ	Tampere	25 Jul	
19.95	Garrett	Johnson	USA	24.5.84	1	PAm-J	Bridgetown	18 Jul	
19.72	Jaroslav	Pittner	SVK	20.4.84	1	NC-j	Bratislava	13 Jul	
19.42	Reynaldo	Proenza	CUB	20.11.84	1	NC-j	Santiago de Cuba	6 Aug	
19.41	Soslan	Tsirikhov	RUS	24.11.84	2		Krasnodar	27 May	
19.40	Noah	Bryant	USA	11.5.84	2	PAm-J	Bridgetown	18 Jul	
19.24	Gustavo	de Mendonça (10)	BRA	10.4.84	3	PAm-J	Bridgetown	18 Jul	
19.20	Aleksandr	Grekov	RUS	6.5.85	Q	EJ	Tampere	24 Jul	
18.92	Nikolay	Umrikhin	RUS	.84			Krasnodar	17 May	
18.92	Luka	Rujevic	SCG	14.10.85	2	NC-j	Kragujevac	4 Jul	

DISCUS

Mark	Name		Nat	Born	Pos	Meet	Venue	Date	Series
70.78	Róbert	Fazekas	HUN	18.8.75	1		Budapest	10 May	64.77 68.56 70.78 68.78 69.34 x
	70.00				1		Réthimno	6 Jul	x 60.83 67.01 x 70.00 x
	69.62				1	GP II	Sevilla	7 Jun	66.48 66.80 x 69.31 x 69.62
	69.39				1		Salon-de-Provence	29 May	69.39 66.00 x x 67.30 67.30
	69.14				1	WK	Zürich	15 Aug	66.08 69.14 67.01 68.57 66.18 67.30
	69.06				1		Szombathely	10 Aug	66.70 67.62 68.36 66.95 x 69.06
	69.01				2	WCh	Saint-Denis	26 Aug	66.86 69.01 x 64.94 65.63 68.78
	67.94				1	NC	Nyíregyháza	3 Aug	64.12 65.45 66.71 67.94 x 64.22
	67.16				1	GP II	Rieti	7 Sep	x 66.06 x 67.16 x x
	67.07				1	GP	Madrid (C)	19 Jul	63.01 x x 64.26 67.07 65.84
69.69	Virgilijus	Alekna	LTU	13.2.72	1	WCh	Saint-Denis	26 Aug	69.69 x 66.14 68.75 x x
	68.95				2	WK	Zürich	15 Aug	68.95 68.61 68.54 67.15 67.25 x
	68.86				1		Vilnius	26 Apr	65.25 66.94 64.08 68.86 x 65.91
	68.72				1	Sule	Tartu	17 Jun	67.88 67.01 67.54 65.32 p 68.72
	68.31				1		Tallinn	30 Jul	68.12 67.56 68.31 66.79 66.54 66.78
	68.30				1	WAF	Monaco	13 Sep	68.30 x 66.95 67.96 four only
	68.29				Q		Paris	24 Aug	68.29 only throw
	67.73				1	ECp2A	Århus	22 Jun	66.47 67.73 x 67.35 four only
	67.71				1	NC	Kaunas	1 Aug	66.32 65.74 66.52 67.71 x x
	67.48				2		Salon-de-Provence	29 May	65.42 67.19 x 64.28 67.08 67.48
	67.36				1		Jurbarkas	20 Sep	
69.50	Lars	Riedel	GER	28.6.67	1eA		Halle	24 May	64.20 66.86 68.04 69.50 67.30 65.71
	67.56				1		Wiesbaden	17 May	66.89 x 67.56 66.40 x 67.12
	67.37				1		Cuxhaven	19 Jul	x 67.09 x 67.39 67.36 66.56
	66.64				1		Sondershausen	3 Sep	
	66.60				1	NC	Ulm	28 Jun	64.00 64.58 x 66.60 x 63.67
67.42	Michael	Möllenbeck	GER	12.12.69	1		Dortmund	15 Jun	66.38 66.18 63.62 67.42 66.72 p
	67.20				2		Cuxhaven	19 Jul	x 66.85 x 65.62 66.00 67.20
	66.81				2		Wiesbaden	17 May	63.52 65.44 x 64.80 65.04 66.81
67.13	Gerd	Kanter	EST	6.5.79	1		Tallinn	5 Sep	x 63.70 64.91 63.97 67.13 p
66.70	Frantz	Kruger	RSA	22.5.75	1	NC	Port Elizabeth	26 Apr	64.66 66.70 64.43 x x x
66.66	Carl	Brown	USA	11.2.70	1	NC	Stanford	19 Jun	62.75 63.56 66.66 63.79 58.65 58.96
66.63	Aleksander	Tammert	EST	2.2.73	1	NC	Tallinn	3 Aug	65.12 66.05 66.36 65.03 66.63 63.57
	(33/8)								
66.51	Vasiliy	Kaptyukh	BLR	27.6.67	2	WCh	Saint-Denis	26 Aug	
66.35	Nick	Petrucci	USA	10.11.75	1		Walnut	13 Jul	
	(10)								
66.03	Zoltán	Kövágó	HUN	10.4.79	2		Szombathely	10 Aug	
65.84	Jason	Tunks	CAN	7.5.75	1		Huntington	22 Apr	
65.53	Yuriy	Belonog	UKR	9.3.74	1		Kiev	26 May	
65.39	Dmitriy	Shevchenko	RUS	13.5.68	1	ECp-S	Firenze	22 Jun	

Mark	Name		Nat	Born	Pos	Meet	Venue	Date
65.08	Frank	Casañas	CUB	18.10.78	1		La Habana	16 May
65.05	Gábor	Máté	HUN	9.2.79	1	NCAA-r	Columbus	30 May
64.99	Mario	Pestano	ESP	8.4.78	1		Jaén	23 Feb
64.73	Leonid	Cherevko	BLR	21.4.74	1		Staiki	8 Aug
64.70	Aleksandr	Borichevskiy	RUS	25.6.70	1		Moskva	26 Jul
64.62	Lois Maikel	Martínez	CUB	3.6.81	1		La Habana	30 Jul
	(20)							
64.56	Doug	Reynolds	USA	11.8.75	1		College Station	22 Mar
64.49	Cristiano	Andrei	ITA	14.5.73	1		Lucca	6 May
64.43A	Casey	Malone	USA	6.4.77	1		Fort Collins	26 Apr
64.26	Torsten	Schmidt	GER	9.12.74	3		Wiesbaden	17 May
64.23	Libor	Malina	CZE	14.6.73	3	Danek	Turnov	18 May
64.03	John	Godina	USA	31.5.72	2	MSR	Walnut	19 Apr
63.92	Kirill	Chuprinin	UKR	22.7.75	2		Kiev	26 May
63.91A	Chima	Ugwu	NGR	19.7.73	1		El Paso	12 Apr
63.88	Jo	Van Daele	BEL	6.4.72	2		Leverkusen	3 Aug
63.78	Sergiu	Ursu	ROM	26.4.80	1		Bucuresti	30 Jul
	(30)							
63.68		Wu Tao	CHN	3.10.83	1		Shijiazhuang	4 Aug
63.65	Diego	Fortuna	ITA	14.2.68	1		Clermont-Ferrand	9 Aug
63.51	Michael	Lischka	GER	23.12.73	4		Zeulenroda	29 May
63.24	Mikko	Kyyrö	FIN	12.7.80	1		Järvenpää	5 Jun
63.20	Ercüment	Olgundeniz	TUR	7.7.76	1	NC-w	Izmir	16 Feb
63.08	Timo	Tompuri	FIN	9.6.69	1		Valkeakoski	8 Jun
62.94	Marcelo	Pugliese	ARG	2.9.68	1		Mar del Plata	13 Apr
62.92	Adam	Setliff	USA	15.12.69	2	NC	Stanford	19 Jun
62.79	Andrzej	Krawczyk	POL	11.4.76	1		Biala Podlaska	13 Jul
62.70	Rutger	Smith	NED	9.7.81	1		Arnhem	25 Jun
	(40)							
62.67	Ionel	Oprea	ROM	12.10.70	1	NC-w	Bucuresti	22 Feb
62.66	Josh	Ralston	USA	1.9.80	4	NC	Stanford	19 Jun
62.60	Abbas	Samimi	IRI	9.6.77	1		Bangkok	5 Jun
62.55	Ian	Waltz	USA	15.4.77	2		Salinas	20 May
62.55	Jaroslav	Zitnansky	SVK	18.2.71	1		Wien	24 Jun
62.34	Magnus	Hallgrímsson	ISL	23.3.76	1		Hafnarfjördur	11 May
62.24	Jarred	Rome	USA	21.12.76	1		Boise	5 Jun
62.19	Scott	Martin	AUS	12.10.82	1c2		Geelong	8 Nov
61.97	Aleksandr	Malashevich	BLR	7.4.77	3		Staiki	8 Aug
61.93	Jean-Claude	Retel	FRA	11.2.68	5		Salon-de-Provence	29 May
	(50)							
61.90	Timo	Sinervo	FIN	5.8.75	2		Ikaalinen	20 Jun
61.85	Carl	Myerscough	GBR	21.10.79	1		Lincoln	3 May
61.81	Gerhard	Mayer	AUT	1.1.80	1B		Halle	24 May
61.71	Roland	Varga	HUN	22.10.77	3		Szombathely	10 Aug
61.56	Jason	Young	USA	27.5.81	1	NCAA-r	Lincoln, NE	30 May
61.52	Gaute	Myklebust	NOR	29.4.79	1		Oslo (S)	12 Aug
61.49	Hannes	Hopley	RSA	26.1.81	1		Arlington	29 Mar
61.48	Andy	Bloom	USA	11.8.73	3		Salinas	20 May
61.46	Rolf	Mordhorst	GER	11.5.73	1eB		Wiesbaden	17 May
61.40	Petri	Hakala	FIN	21.2.79	2	PNG	Turku	15 Jun
	(60)							
61.37i	Mika	Loikkanen	FIN	20.2.74	1	NC-i	Helsinki	22 Feb
	61.07				3		Jalasjärvi	4 Jul
61.33	Reedus	Thurmond	USA	15.12.79	1		Marietta	8 Jun
61.29	Marco	Jakobs	GER	30.5.74	2eB		Wiesbaden	17 May
61.24	Olgierd	Stanski	POL	4.4.73	1		Suwalki	10 Aug
61.20	Dan	Ames	USA	16.1.81	Q		San Diego	11 Apr
60.91	Brian	Trainor	USA	14.3.80	2	NCAA-r	Lincoln, NE	30 May
60.91	Gjøran	Sørli	NOR	3.6.78	1		Oslo (S)	2 Sep
60.89	Jorge	Balliengo	ARG	5.1.78	1		Rosario	12 Oct
60.75	Stefano	Lomater	ITA	23.4.74	3		Donnas	15 Jul
60.70	Yuriy	Seskin	RUS	7.7.66	2		Moskva	26 Jul
	(70)							
60.68	Anil	Kumar	IND	20.6.75	1	Af-AsG	Hyderabad	29 Oct
60.66	Matthias	Thriene	GER	28.12.71	1		Vellmar	11 Jul
60.66	Emeka	Udechuku	GBR	10.7.79	1		Loughborough	31 Jul
60.58	Paulo	Bernardo	POR	21.11.74	1		Lisboa (U)	8 Jun
60.56	Stéfanos	Kónstas	GRE	16.5.77	1		Iráklio	1 Jun
60.50	Aléxandros	Ganotákis	GRE	3.12.74	2		Iráklio	1 Jun
60.38	Kevin	Fitzpatrick	USA	26.9.69	1		Athens	3 May

Mark	Name		Nat	Born	Pos	Meet	Venue	Date
60.35	Cameron	Bolles	USA	24.3.76	3		Fresno	5 Apr
60.34	Graham	Hicks	AUS	14.12.78	2		Ballarat	15 Nov
60.33	Mike	van der Bilt	NED	23.10.76	2eB		Halle	24 May
	(80)							
60.28	Peter	Elvy	AUS	3.6.80	1		Sydney (H)	22 Mar
60.19	Einar Kristian	Tveitå	NOR	22.2.73	1		Ski	28 Jul
60.18	Michael	Robertson	USA	19.12.83	3		College Station	22 Mar
60.16	Janne	Hummastenniemi	FIN	4.10.79	1		Oulu	17 May
60.04	Drew	Loftin	USA	15.9.80	1		Albuquerque	17 May
60.02	Stéphane	Nativel	FRA	4.4.75	1		Salon-de-Provence	18 Jun
59.99	Karl	Erickson	USA	1.6.82	1		Iowa City	3 May
59.95	Sergey	Lyakhov	RUS	1.3.68	2	Kuts	Moskva	14 Jul
59.92	Johannes	van Wyk	RSA	16.3.80	2		Loughborough	31 Jul
59.89	Daniel	Vanek	SVK	18.1.83	1		Nitra	3 Jul
	(90)							
59.85	Heinrich	Seitz	GER	6.4.80			Eppstein	17 Jun
59.85	Eric	Forshaw	CAN	14.9.68	2	NC	Victoria	19 Jul
	60.40 unconfirmed							
59.83	Scott	Wiegand	USA	26.9.80	6		Salinas	20 May
59.82A	Niklas	Arrhenius	SWE	10.9.82	1		Provo	23 Oct
59.77	Omar	El-Ghazaly	EGY-J	9.2.84	3	Af-As	Hyderabad	29 Oct
59.72	Ilya	Kostin	RUS	1.4.79	2		Tula	1 Jun
59.70	Hannes	Kirchler	ITA	22.12.78	1		Vado Ligure	18 Jun
59.66	Sultan M.	Al-Dawoodi	KSA-J	16.3.85	2		Colombo	1 Jun
59.62	Patrik	Stang	GER	17.5.78	3eB		Wiesbaden	17 May
59.62	Mike	Ransky	CAN	26.10.70	2		London, Ont.	20 Sep
	(100)							

59.57	Vyacheslav	Ivashkin	RUS	6.3.74	18 May
59.54	Robert	Harting	GER-J	18.10.84	15 Jun
59.50	Dave	Smith	USA		13 May
59.48	Mattias	Borrman	SWE	20.6.72	20 May
59.48	Aleksey	Semyonov	UKR	27.6.82	26 May
59.48	Nuermaimaiti	Tulake	CHN	8.3.82	20 Sep
59.34	Kibwe	Johnson	USA	17.8.81	20 May
59.32	Vikas	Gowda	IND	5.7.83	4 Apr
59.20	Drazen	Prskalo	CRO	15.1.70	7 Jun
59.19	Rashid Shafik	Al Dosari	QAT	8.5.81	16 Apr
59.08	Igor	Primc	SLO	8.1.66	25 May
59.03	Sam	Segond	USA	4.4.83	16 May
59.02	Ivan	Emilianov	MDA	19.2.77	25 Apr
59.00	Daniel	Taylor	USA	12.5.82	30 May
59.00	Michal	Hodun	POL	17.2.83	6 Jul
58.92	Joe	Erdkamp	USA	10.1.76	13 May
58.84		Zhang Cunbiao	CHN	11.2.69	12 Sep
58.66	Gregg	Hart	USA	21.8.70	20 May
58.65	Sean	Shields	USA	10.2.83	20 May
58.59	Julián	Angulo	COL	24.5.80	25 Apr
58.53	Glen	Smith	GBR	21.5.72	31 May
58.49	Jon	O'Neil	USA	23.3.79	16 Apr
58.43	Spirídon	Arabatzís	GRE	2.6.78	1 Jun
58.38	Stanislav	Alekseyev	RUS	10.2.82	18 May
58.37	Frank	Vicet	CUB	13.11.71	26 Jun
58.25	John	Davis	USA	19.2.77	8 Jun
58.21	Derek	Randall	USA	15.6.83	29 Mar
58.20	Khalid Habas	Al Suwaidi	QAT-J	84	20 Sep
58.17	Kris	Coene	BEL	29.9.83	17 Jul
58.15	Kyle	Bookout	USA	1.5.79	19 Apr
58.02	Henrik	Wennberg	SWE	11.3.66	13 Sep
58.00	Dmitriy	Sivakov	BLR	15.2.83	19 Jul
58.00	Joachim	Olsen	DEN	31.5.77	4 Aug
57.99	Pavel	Lyzhin	BLR	24.3.81	28 Jun
57.96	Sam	Johnson	USA	26.4.81	8 May
57.90	Vadim	Hronovschi	MDA	14.2.83	25 Apr
57.89	Juha	Lahdenranta	FIN	12.6.76	20 Jun
57.88	Omer	Inan	TUR	20.10.81	3 May
57.86	Sergey	Pruglo	UKR	18.11.83	26 May
57.83	Piotr	Malachowski (140)	POL	7.6.83	6 Sep

Note 1.75kg discus at African C (Abuja 13 Oct): 1. Al-Ghazali EGY-J 63.61; 2. Hopley RSA 62.86; 3. J van Wyk RSA 62.43

Downhill

67.86	Carl	Brown	USA	11.2.70	1		La Jolla	26 Apr
66.99	Gábor	Máté	HUN	9.2.79	2		La Jolla	26 Apr
66.55	Jason	Tunks	CAN	7.5.75	3		La Jolla	26 Apr
66.49	Doug	Reynolds	USA	11.8.75	1		La Jolla	28 Mar
66.38	John	Godina	USA	31.5.72	4		La Jolla	26 Apr
66.35	Chima	Ugwu	NGR	19.7.73	5		La Jolla	26 Apr
61.80	Aléxandros	Ganotákis	GRE	3.12.74	7		La Jolla	26 Apr
60.55	Jon	O'Neil	USA	23.3.79	9		La Jolla	26 Apr
60.39	Dragan	Peric	SCG	8.5.64	1	NC	Kragujevac	9 Aug
59.96	James	Dennis	USA	25.2.76	10		La Jolla	26 Apr
59.13	Omer	Inan	TUR	20.10.81	11		La Jolla	26 Apr

JUNIORS

See main list for top 2 juniors. 6 performances by 4 men to 58.00. Additional marks and further juniors:

El Ghazaly	58.30	1 Arab	Amman	7 Sep				
59.54	Robert	Harting	GER-J	18.10.84	6		Dortmund	15 Jun
	59.07	1	Potsdam	14 Jun				
58.20	Khalid Habas	Al Suwaidi	QAT-J	84	5	AsiC	Manila	20 Sep
57.39		Xu Yongyi	CHN	28.7.84	1		Nantong	5 Jun
55.63		Liu Jian	CHN	5.3.85	3	NG	Changsha	24 Oct
55.23	Garrett	Johnson	USA	24.5.84	1		Tallahassee	11 Apr
55.08	Andreas	Porth	GER	21.3.84			Fulda	27 Aug
54.74		Wu Jian	CHN-Y	25.5.86	4	NG	Changsha	24 Oct
54.40	Ehsan	Haddodi (10)	IRI	21.1.85	8	AsC	Manila	20 Sep

Mark		Name		Nat	Born	Pos	Meet	Venue	Date
54.36		Stefan	Keller	GER	26.10.85	1		Dortmund	13 Jul
54.05	?	Vladimir	Meliksetyan	ARM-Y	10.9.86			Artashat	11 May
54.05		Erik	Cadee	NED	15.2.84	1		Amsterdam	15 Jun
54.02		Martin	Maric	CRO	19.4.84	3	NC	Zagreb	3 Aug
53.97		Sultan Mubarak	Al-Habash	KSA	31.1.85	2	Gulf	Al-Kuwait	9 Oct
53.87A		Leif	Arrhenius	SWE-Y	15.7.86	2		Orem	23 Oct
53.74			Dai Wenbin	CHN	8.1.85	2		Chengdu	27 Aug
53.32		Yevgeniy	Labutov	KAZ	17.11.84	1		Bishkek	29 Jun
53.14		Adam	Kuehl	USA	19.1.84	4c1	MSR	Walnut	18 Apr
53.01		Roman	Ryzhiy (20)	UKR	17.1.85	8		Kiev	26 May
1.75kg Discus									
65.88		Omar	El-Ghazaly	EGY	9.2.84	1		Cairo	7 Nov
		63.61	1 AfG Abuja		13 Oct				
64.05		Robert	Harting	GER	18.10.84	1		Halle	25 May
		63.70	1 Zeulenroda		29 May				
		63.00	1 Mannheim		22 Jun				
		63.54	1 Berlin		1 Jun				
		62.99	1 Wiesbaden		17 May				
62.37		Erik	Cadee	NED	15.2.84	1	NC-j	Lisse	28 Jun
62.29		Gustavo	de Mendonça	BRA	10.4.84	1	SAm-j	Guayaquil	8 Jun
61.00		Maksim	Zuyevich	RUS	23.9.84	1	NC-j	Kazan	1 Jul
60.90		Martin	Maric	CRO	19.4.84	1		Maribor	31 May
59.90		Stefan	Keller	GER	26.10.85	2	NC-j	Fulda	5 Jul
59.44		Tobias	Obermaier	GER	3.2.84	2		Erdng	11 May
		60.16 ?				2		Wiesbaden	17 May
59.12		Andreas	Porth	GER	21.3.84	3	NC-j	Fulda	5 Jul
59.02		Ronnie	Buckley (10)	AUS-Y	15.8.86	1		Melbourne	6 Dec
58.92		Bartosz	Ratajzak	POL	18.3.85	1		Poznan	8 Jun
58.79		Tim	Driesen	AUS	27.3.84	1	NC	Brisbane	5 Apr
58.44		Konrad	Szuster	POL	21.1.84	1	NC-j	Zamosc	29 Jun
58.16		Adam	Kuehl	USA	19.1.84	1	NC-j	Stanford	21 Jun

HAMMER

Mark	Name		Nat	Born	Pos	Meet	Venue	Date	1	2	3	4	5	6
84.86	Koji	Murofushi	JPN	8.10.74	1	Odlozil	Praha	29 Jun	81.76	x	81.82	82.13	84.86	84.80
83.29					1	NC	Yokohama	8 Jun	78.60	81.22	81.04	80.97	81.98	83.29
82.95					1		Osaka	10 May	81.45	82.06	82.64	81.55	82.65	82.95
82.67					1		Toyota	24 May	78.81	80.62	81.07	82.64	82.67	82.04
82.57					1		Réthimno	6 Jul	82.57	x	82.25	x	x	80.72
82.36					1		Toyota	26 Apr	80.29	80.69	82.36	81.06	81.49	81.66
84.32	Ivan	Tikhon	BLR	24.7.76	1		Staiki	8 Aug						
83.64					1	NC	Minsk	10 Jul						
83.05					1	WCh	Saint-Denis	25 Aug	80.69	81.77	x	x	83.05	
82.77					1	WUG	Daegu	30 Aug						
81.04					1	Znam	Tula	8 Jun	79.44	x	81.04	x	73.75	x
80.84					3	WAF	Szombathely	7 Sep	78.84	78.14	80.84	x	78.26	80.83
84.19	Adrián	Annus	HUN	28.6.73	1		Szombathely	10 Aug	80.45	81.10	82.54	82.15	83.37	84.19
82.73					2	Odlozil	Praha	29 Jun	x	79.43	77.41	82.73	81.68	82.49
82.10					1	WAF	Szombathely	7 Sep	79.68	81.11	82.10	x	p	p
81.97					1	NC	Nyíregyháza	2 Aug	76.44	x	x	x	79.08	81.97
81.94					2		Réthimno	6 Jul	77.79	79.67	77.79.	81.10	81.94	80.22
80.94					1		Szombathely	26 Apr						
82.28	Ilya	Konovalov	RUS	4.3.71	1	NC	Tula	10 Aug	81.19	81.33	x	p	81.07	82.28
81.61					1		Moskva	26 Jul	80.05	81.02	79.39	78.23	81.43	81.61
80.83					1	Kuts	Moskva	14 Jul	80.39	79.12	80.83	79.83	p	p
81.81	Libor	Charfreitag	SVK	11.9.77	3	Odlozil	Praha	29 Jun	79.27	81.81	x	80.02	79.49	x
81.22					2	WAF	Szombathely	7 Sep	x	x	x	78.19	x	81.22
81.74	Andrey	Skvaruk	UKR	9.3.67	1	NC	Kiev	4 Jul	78.71	79.99	78.42	80.62	81.74	x
81.35	Igor	Astapkovich	BLR	4.1.63	2	NC	Minsk	11 Jul						
80.83					2		Staiki	8 Aug						
81.35	Wojciech	Kondratowicz	POL	18.4.80	1		Bydgoszcz	13 Jul	81.35	77.45	x	x	x	p
81.21	Primoz	Kozmus	SLO	30.9.79	1	NC	Zagreb	3 Aug	79.95	79.26	81.21	80.49	80.37	80.21
80.89	Maciej	Palyszko (10)	POL	4.1.78	2		Bydgoszcz	13 Jul	80.89	x	78.48	x	x	p
80.83	Karsten	Kobs	GER	16.9.71	1		Nikiti	1 Aug	80.44	80.42	80.83	78.46	x	x
	(30/11)													

Mark	Name		Nat	Born	Pos	Meet	Venue	Date
80.67	Péter	Botfa	HUN	30.6.79	1		Zalaegerszeg	14 Jun
80.51	Patric	Suter	SUI	17.5.77	1		Löffingen	17 Sep
80.44	Christophe	Épalle	FRA	23.1.69	1		Saint-Etienne	10 May
80.20	Olli-Pekka	Karjalainen	FIN	7.3.80	1	NC	Helsinki	9 Aug
80.13	Aleksey	Zagorniy	RUS	31.5.78	2	NC	Tula	10 Aug
79.90	Vadim	Devyatovskiy	BLR	20.3.77	3		Staiki	8 Aug
79.62	Sergey	Kirmasov	RUS	25.3.70	2		Moskva	26 Jul
79.52	Aléxandros	Papadimitríou	GRE	18.6.73	2		Nikiti	1 Aug
79.35	Aleksandr	Krykun	UKR	1.3.68	1		Koncha-Zaspa	11 May
	(20)							
79.20	Stuart	Rendell	AUS	30.6.72	1		Canberra	22 Feb
79.07	Nicolas	Figère	FRA	19.5.79	1		Chelles	1 Oct
78.89	Vadim	Khersontsev	RUS	8.7.74	3		Moskva	26 Jul
78.83	David	Söderberg	FIN	11.8.79	1		Lahti	2 Jul
78.81	Krisztián	Pars	HUN	18.2.82	1		Szombathely	13 Sep
78.80	Pavel	Sedlácek	CZE	5.4.68	1		Kladno	21 Aug
78.69	Yuriy	Voronkin	RUS	18.5.79	3	Znam	Tula	8 Jun
78.64	Chris	Harmse	RSA	31.5.73	1		Durban	11 Apr
78.57	Vladislav	Piskunov	UKR	7.6.78	1		Yalta	30 Jan
78.53	Andrey	Vorontsov	BLR	24.7.75	4		Staiki	8 Aug
	(30)							
78.44	Miloslav	Konopka	SVK	23.1.79	1		Szombathely	12 Jul
78.34	Vladimír	Maska	CZE	6.2.73	1		Jablonec	10 May
78.21	Holger	Klose	GER	5.12.72	3		Nikiti	1 Aug
78.16	András	Haklits	CRO	23.9.77	1		Athens, GA	21 Aug
78.13	Markus	Esser	GER	3.2.80	1		Fränkisch-Crumbach	8 Jun
78.06	Zsolt	Németh	HUN	9.11.71	1B		Szombathely	7 Sep
77.69	Nicola	Vizzoni	ITA	4.11.73	1		Viareggio	13 Aug
77.57	Esref	Apak	TUR	3.1.82	1		Istanbul	6 Jul
77.46	Balázs	Kiss	HUN	21.3.72	4	GP	Osaka	10 May
77.35	Artyom	Rubanko	UKR	21.3.74	4	NC	Kiev	4 Jul
	(40)							
76.97	Szymon	Ziólkowski	POL	1.7.76	2		Poznan	24 May
76.62	Roman	Rozna	MDA	25.3.76	4	Klim	Staiki	28 Jun
76.46	Cosmin	Sorescu	ROM	11.7.75	1	RomIC	Bucuresti	7 Jun
76.38	Lukás	Melich	CZE	16.9.80	2		Reims	16 Jul
76.32	Juan Ignacio	Cerra	ARG	16.10.76	2		Trieste	19 Jul
76.24	Igor	Tugay	UKR	22.3.75	1		Kiev	29 Jul
75.76	Aleksandr	Vashchilo	BLR	30.8.81	2		Minsk	3 Jun
75.56	Dilshod	Nazarov	TJK	6.5.82	1		Dushanbe	25 May
75.42	Moisés	Campeny	ESP	27.5.79	1		Jaén	23 Feb
75.32	James	Parker	USA	3.12.75	1		Walnut	12 Jul
	(50)							
74.97	Marco	Lingua	ITA	4.6.78	1		Genève	14 Jun
74.78	Vítor	Costa	POR	28.5.74	2	FRA Ch	Narbonne	26 Jul
74.73	John	McEwen	USA	5.3.74	2	MSR	Walnut	19 Apr
74.70	Vadim	Grabovoy	UKR	5.4.73	4		Kiev	27 May
74.34	Viktor	Ustinov	UZB	20.7.74	1	NC	Tashkent	5 Sep
74.29	Jarkko	Paljakka	FIN	7.2.79	3		Lahti	2 Jul
74.07	Kevin	McMahon	USA	26.5.72	1		Berkeley	11 Apr
73.82	Ioánnis	Barlís	GRE	26.11.79	2		Iráklio	1 Jun
73.76	Loris	Paoluzzi	ITA	14.5.74	2	NC	Rieti	3 Aug
73.69	Iosvani	Suárez	CUB	20.12.72	1		La Habana	16 May
	(60)							
73.64	Samuele	Dazio	SUI	16.1.75	2		Genève	14 Jun
73.40	Paddy	McGrath	USA	1.7.71	1		New Haven	6 Jul
73.33	Hiroaki	Doi	JPN	2.12.78	2	NC	Yokohama	8 Jun
73.33	Stefan	Paukner	GER	16.8.76	1		Wilhelmshaven	10 Aug
73.16	Mick	Jones	GBR	23.7.63	1	BIG	Bedford	1 Jun
72.79	Denis	Kulagin	RUS	23.5.80	9	Znam	Tula	8 Jun
72.79	Giovanni	Sanguin	ITA	14.5.69	4	NC	Rieti	3 Aug
72.79	William	Beauchamp	GBR	9.9.70	1		Peterborough	25 Aug
72.70	Ali Mohamed	Al-Zankawi	KUW-J	27.2.84	1	Arab C	Amman	8 Sep
72.65	Vitaliy	Alisevich	BLR	15.6.67	5	NC	Minsk	11 Jul
	(70)							
72.42	Vyacheslav	Svyatokho	BLR	20.7.81	7	Klim	Staiki	28 Jun
72.18	Roland	Ciofani	FRA	29.9.71	4		Clermont-Ferrand	9 Aug
72.14	Kazimierz	Boulge	POL	13.2.76	1		Bydgoszcz	28 Aug
71.87	Bengt	Johansson	SWE	7.7.73	2		Magglingen	7 Jun
71.84	Kristóf	Páli	HUN	29.12.80	2		Veszprém	28 Jun
71.72	Jacob	Freeman	USA	5.11.80	3		Walnut	12 Jul

Mark	Name		Nat	Born	Pos	Meet	Venue	Date
71.71	Andrey	Vikhrov	RUS	.73	1		Krasnodar	17 May
71.65	Steve	Harnapp	GER	30.7.75	1		Schönau	21 Jun
71.58	Ronald	Gram	NED	31.3.74	1		Leiden	20 Aug
71.55	Fatih (80)	Eryildirim	TUR	1.3.79	2		Izmir	11 May
71.51	Dylan	Armstrong	CAN	15.1.81	5	MSR	Walnut	19 Apr
71.33	Michael	Mai	USA	27.9.77	1B	MSR	Walnut	19 Apr
71.33	Dorian	Collaku	ALB	2.6.77	1		Tirana	19 Sep
71.28	Pellegrino	Delli Carri	ITA	4.8.76	1		Spoleto	12 Jul
71.10	Yamine Hussein Abdel Moneim		EGY	19.6.78	2		Bloemfontein	15 Mar
71.09	Marco	Felice	ITA	20.10.79	1		Matera	3 May
71.03	Jens	Rautenkrantz	GER	11.4.82	4		Fränkisch-Crumbach	8 Jun
71.02	Werner	Smit	RSA-J	14.9.84	1		Parow	19 Feb
71.02	Jan	Bielecki	DEN	20.2.71	1		Aix-les-Bains	4 May
71.02	Claus (90)	Dethloff	GER	24.9.68	1		Neulussheim	14 Jun
71.01	Drew	Loftin	USA	15.9.80	1		Albuquerque	16 May
71.01		Ma Liang	CHN	22.7.83	1	NG	Changsha	26 Oct
71.00	Nasser	Al-Jarallah	KUW	26.11.73	2	Arab C	Amman	8 Sep
70.87	Mohd Faraj	Al-Kaabi	QAT-J	31.12.84	1		Doha	8 Apr
70.87	Scott	Boothby	USA	9.4.73	1		Vancouver	6 Jun
70.85	Samir	Haouam	ALG	20.6.68	3	Arab C	Amman	8 Sep
70.84	Aleksey	Yeliseyev	RUS	12.3.82	1	NC-23	Cheboksary	28 Jun
70.81	Saber	Souid	TUN	9.3.81	2	Al AfrG	Abuja	11 Oct
70.76	Alberto	Sánchez	CUB	3.2.73	1		La Habana	4 Jul
70.63	Derek (100)	Woodske	CAN	22.10.76	3		Kamloops	5 Jun

70.53	A.G.	Kruger	USA	18.2.79	10 May
70.51	Travis	Nutter	USA	9.2.75	11 Apr
70.45	Panayiótis	Mavragánis	GRE	27.5.79	16 May
70.37	Sergey	Karpovich	UKR	23.4.81	4 Jul
70.36	Harálabos	Arsoníádis	GRE	19.1.78	15 Jun
70.31	Jerry	Ingalls	USA	24.9.74	19 Apr
70.22	Mats	Granö	FIN	6.9.81	9 Aug
70.19	Lucais	MacKay	USA	13.4.81	13 Jun
70.16	Rakesh	Kumar Yadav	IND	1.12.81	17 Jul
70.14	Raphaël	Piolanti	FRA	14.11.67	1 Jun
70.05	Krzysztof	Kaliszewski	POL	9.8.72	5 Jul
70.04	Aleksey	Korolyov	RUS	5.4.82	15 May
70.00	Markus	Kahlmeyer	GER	20.1.82	16 Aug
69.98	Benjamin	Boruschewski	GER	23.4.80	29 Jun
69.88	Janne	Vartia	FIN	18.3.77	3 May
69.74	Iain	Park	GBR	16.7.74	7 Sep
69.61	Spirídon	Zoullién	GRE	21.6.81	4 May
69.53	Petri	Rautio	FIN	28.6.82	19 Jul
69.52	Phil	Jensen	NZL	8.11.67	23 Mar
69.34	Matko	Tesija	CRO-J	4.3.85	11 May
69.30	Bernard	Reibel	FRA	13.8.67	14 Oct
69.12	Daniel	Abramovic	GER	10.12.82	25 May
69.11	Kibwe	Johnson	USA	17.8.81	22 Mar
69.09	Athanásios	Koukouzíkis	GRE	24.9.76	12 Jul
69.06	Vitaliy	Baukh	RUS	29.1.83	28 Jun
69.05	Riaan	Smit	RSA	1.12.82	14 Feb
68.99		Ye Kuigang	CHN	4.1.75	11 Sep
68.87	Andrey	Mezhevov	RUS	11.1.82	28 Jun
68.84	Aleksandr	Kozulko	BLR	8.12.83	28 Jun
68.79	Mohsen Anani Youssef		EGY-J	21.5.85	18 Sep
68.65	Samu-Petri	Simo	FIN	22.6.78	11 Jul
68.65	Adrián	Marzo	ARG	24.1.68	7 Aug
68.64	Mohd Nasser	Al Husaini	KUW	24.8.82	21 Sep
68.58	Erik	Jiménez	CUB	17.9.81	28 Feb
68.56	Igors	Sokolovs	LAT	17.8.74	2 Aug
68.29	Stamátios	Papadoníou	GRE-J	3.5.84	15 Jun
68.28		Zhang Dapeng	CHN	6.8.83	26 Oct
68.26	Marco	Quintarelli	ITA	20.6.73	3 Aug
68.21	Takashi	Usui	JPN	15.5.77	20 Jun
68.21	Norbert	Horváth	HUN	13.6.75	26 Jul
68.19	Ralf	Jossa	GER	2.11.66	14 Jun
68.12	Yuriy	Kravchuk	BLR	.81	10 Jun
68.09	Adam	Judge	USA	24.1.80	16 May
68.09	Rosen	Zhelev	BUL	80	17 May
68.08	Noleysi	Vicet	CUB	6.2.81	14 Feb
68.07	Luke	Woydziak	USA	13.4.77	7 Jun
68.00	Ignacio	Calderón (147)	ESP	23.6.76	13 Jul

Downhill

68.52	Bjørnar	Halvorsen	NOR	12.11.73	5 Oct

JUNIORS

See main list for top 3 Juniors. 10 performances by 4 men to 69.65. Additional marks and further juniors:

Al Zankawi	70.62	1	AsiC	Manila	21 Sep	69.79	1	Al-Kuwait	18 Feb
Smit	70.99	1		Bellville	22 Feb	70.02	1	Parow	10 Jan
	70.73	1		Bellville	22 Mar	69.67	3	Durban	11 Apr

69.34	Matko	Tesija	CRO	4.3.85	1		Split	11 May
68.79	Mohsen Anani Youssef		EGY	21.5.85	1	NC	Cairo	18 Sep
68.29	Stamátios	Papadoníou	GRE	3.5.84	4	NC	Tríkala	15 Jun
67.74	Aleksey	Sokirskiy	UKR	16.3.85	1		Simferapol	24 May
66.72	Massimo	Marussi	ITA	5.4.84	1		Macerata	18 May
65.60	James	Steacy	CAN	29.5.84	1		Kamloops	5 Jun
65.25		Zheng Leilei (10)	CHN	16.4.84	3	NG	Changsha	26 Oct
64.82		Li Xiangkui	CHN	15.2.84	2		Nanchang	6 Jun
64.44	Mohamed Jassem	Abdulkarim	KUW	27.8.84	1		Al Kuwait	21 Oct
64.42	Lorenzo	Povegliano	ITA	11.11.84	2		Rosà	1 Jun
64.27	Michal	Fiala	CZE	22.6.85	1	NC-23	Litomysl	13 Sep
64.19	Kamilius	Bethke	GER	21.2.85			Hahnenbruch	26 Sep
63.56		Zhao Yihai	CHN	29.3.85	2		Chengdu	26 Aug
63.20	Yeóryios	Papadópoulos	GRE	24.1.84	6	NC	Trikala	15 Jun
63.09	Igor	Vinichenko	RUS	11.4.84	8		Moskva	26 Jul

6kg Hammer

Mark	Name		Nat	Born	Pos	Meet	Venue	Date
81.04	Werner	Smit	RSA	14.9.84	1		Bellville	29 Mar
	79.88	1 NC-j Pretoria		6 Apr	78.76	1	Bellville	25 Nov
	79.45	1 Bellville		22 Mar	78.51	1	Bellville	15 Mar
78.41	Ali Mohamed	Al-Zankawi	KUW	27.2.84	1		Al-Kuwait	2 Mar
76.90	Matko	Tesija	CRO	4.3.85	1		Pula	26 Apr
76.70	Massimo	Marussi	ITA	5.4.84	1	NC-j	Grosseto	13 Jun
75.85	Kirill	Ikonnikov	RUS	5.3.84	1	NC-w	Adler	22 Feb
75.71	Mohsen Anani Youssef		EGY	21.5.85	1		Cairo	22 Aug
75.30	Yevgeniy	Vinogradov	UKR	30.4.84	1	NC-j	Koncha-Zaspa	3 Jun
74.86	Stamátios	Papadoníou ¶	GRE	3.5.84	1		Haniá	11 May
	75.10 drugs dq				(1)		Kórinthos	5 Jul
74.68	Kamilius	Bethke	GER	21.2.85	1		Hahnenbach	27 Sep
74.34	József	Horváth (10)	HUN	3.4.84	1		Szombathely	26 Apr
74.09	James	Steacy	CAN	29.5.84	1		Edmonton	22 Jun
73.94	Andrey	Azarenkov	RUS	26.9.85	1	NC-j	Kazan	3 Jul
73.24	Pavel	Krivitskiy	BLR	17.4.84	1		Brest	20 Jun
72.72	Lorenzo	Povegliano	ITA	11.11.84	1	EJ	Tampere	27 Jul
71.98	Aleksey	Sokirskiy	UKR	16.3.85	1		Yalta	30 Jan
71.52	Leonid	Konchits	UKR	2.1.84	1		Kiev	13 Jun
71.37	Andreas	Sahner	GER	27.1.85	2		Hahnenbach	27 Sep
71.31	Igor	Vinichenko	RUS	11.4.84	2		Adler	15 Feb

JAVELIN

Mark	Name		Nat	Born	Pos	Meet	Venue		Date
90.11	Sergey	Makarov	RUS	19.3.73	1		Dessau		30 May
				76.05	83.99	86.18	84.68	83.77	90.11
88.61	1	Kassel	13 Jun						
87.69	2 GL	Saint-Denis	4 Jul	85.90	x	87.69	85.62	85.04	82.05
86.40	3 WK	Zürich	15 Aug	86.17	85.49	84.83	84.37	86.40	83.29
86.34	1 GP	Tríkala	24 Jun	86.34	83.04	85.28	85.25	80.96	83.26
85.86	1 ECpS	Firenze	22 Jun	84.64	85.86	p	p		four only
85.66	1 WAF	Monaco	14 Sep	74.08	85.66	81.70	x		four only
85.61	1 Bisl	Oslo	27 Jun	85.61	83.69	84.59	84.16	85.37	84.61
85.46	1 NC	Tula	9 Aug	78.41	85.46	x	x	x	p
85.44	1 WCh	Saint-Denis	31 Aug	85.44	x	x	82.72	82.11	85.31
89.06	Jan	Zelezny	CZE	16.6.66	1	Gaz	Saint-Denis		4 Jul
			x	89.06	84.10	84.91	x. 83.63		
88.99	1 GP	Ostrava	12 Jun	84.45	x	87.90	87.35	88.99	85.25
87.95	1 WK	Zürich	15 Aug	82.81	83.73	x	87.95	x	84.97
87.92	1	Halle	24 May	81.52	83.12	84.57	87.07	81.16	87.92
85.47	2 GP	Tríkala	24 Jun	85.24	x	x	82.69	x	85.47
88.90	Aleksandr	Ivanov	RUS	25.5.82	1	Znam	Tula		7 Jun
				83.63	85.37	84.81	88.69	88.90	x
85.53	1 ECCp	Valencia	25 May	85.53	76.35	x	81.40		four only
85.01	2 DNG	Stockholm	5 Aug	85.01	81.18	x	80.27	80.61	p
88.10	Boris	Henry	GER	14.12.73	1		Rehlingen		9 Jun
				83.14	84.58	84.10	86.57	88.10	84.50
86.98	2 WK	Zürich	15 Aug	86.56	82.93	84.41	x	86.98	x
85.77	1 GP	London (CP)	8 Aug	81.96	84.21	85.77	81.72	81.10	84.95
85.26	1 DNG	Stockholm	5 Aug	81.95	83.60	85.26	x	82.50	83.42
84.92	1 NC	Ulm	29 Jun	84.92	81.67	83.08	84.86	x	x
87.83	Andrus	Värnik	EST	27.9.77	1		Valga		19 Aug
85.17	2 WCh	Saint-Denis	31 Aug	85.17	x	x	81.98	x	77.78
86.32A	Eriks	Rags	LAT	1.6.75	1		Potchefstroom		22 Apr
				x	x	86.32	p	p	p
85.55A	1	Potchefstroom	15 Apr	x	x	81.31	81.95	82.01	85.55
86.22	Raymond	Hecht	GER	11.11.68	4	WK	Zürich		15 Aug
				82.85	x	x	78.75	x	86.22
85.72	Andreas	Thorkildsen	NOR	1.4.82	1		Ventspils		14 Jun
				85.72	x	p	p	p	p
85.69	Steve	Backley	GBR	12.2.69	1	GP	Gateshead		13 Jul
				85.69	80.14	x	80.03	80.39	85.27
	(30/9)								
84.54	Christian	Nicolay (10)	GER	4.3.76	3		Dessau		30 May
84.50	Hardus	Pienaar	RSA	10.8.81	1	Af-AsG	Hyderabad		29 Oct
84.19	Voldemars	Lusis	LAT	7.12.74	1		Riga		12 Jun
84.08	Peter	Blank	GER	10.4.62	3	NC	Ulm		29 Jun
83.71	Miroslav	Guzdek	CZE	3.8.75	1		Olomouc		8 May
83.30	Aki	Parviainen	FIN	26.10.74	1		Joensuu		11 Jun

Mark	Name		Nat	Born	Pos	Meet	Venue	Date
83.03	Peter	Esenwein	GER	7.12.67	1		Herborn	12 Jul
82.97	Nick	Nieland	GBR	31.1.72	2	Sule	Tartu	17 Jun
82.54	Igor	Janik	POL	12.1.83	2	EU23	Bydgoszcz	20 Jul
82.29	Andrew	Currey	AUS	7.2.71	1		Sydney (H)	22 Mar
82.10	Breaux	Greer	USA	19.10.76	1		Brasschaat	13 Aug
	(20)							
82.02	Esko	Mikkola	FIN	14.2.75	1		Tucson	21 Mar
81.98	Dariusz	Trafas	POL	16.5.72	1	NC	Bielsko-Biala	5 Jul
81.96	Stephan	Steding	GER	29.1.82	1		Mannheim	21 Jun
81.82	William	Hamlyn-Harris	AUS	14.1.78	1		Sydney (H)	9 Mar
81.76		Li Rongxiang	CHN	8.1.72	Q	WCh	Saint-Denis	29 Aug
81.72	Emeterio	González	CUB	11.4.73	1	PAm	Santo Domingo	6 Aug
81.66	Isbel	Luaces	CUB	20.7.75	1		Nuoro	9 Jul
81.56	Scott	Russell	CAN	16.1.79	1		Brunswick	5 Jul
81.55	Gergely	Horváth	HUN	5.6.75	1	NC	Nyíregyháza	2 Aug
81.46		Park Jae-myong	KOR	15.12.81	1		Chunju	23 Apr
	(30)							
81.46	Jarko	Koski-Vähälä	FIN	21.11.78	1		Kuortane	20 Jul
81.38A	Brian	Erasmus	RSA	23.2.80	1		Potchefstroom	5 Nov
80.95	Vadim	Bavikin	ISR	4.10.70	1		Bottnaryd	28 Jun
80.82	Rajmund	Kólko	POL	1.3.71	1		Wróclaw	10 May
80.75	Ainars	Kovals	LAT	21.11.81	1	v2N	Kaunas	10 Aug
80.57	Teemu	Wirkkala	FIN-J	14.1.84	1		Espoo	14 Sep
80.55	Mark	Frank	GER	21.6.77	1		Neustrelitz	21 Jun
80.45	Tero	Pitkämaki	FIN	19.12.82	2	NC	Helsinki	11 Aug
80.43	Tero	Järvenpää	FIN-J	2.10.84	3	NC	Helsinki	11 Aug
80.32A	Gerbrandt	Grobler	RSA	26.1.83	1		Potchefstroom	24 Oct
	(40)							
80.15	Denis	Davydov	RUS	25.9.82	2		Adler	15 Feb
80.04	Laurent	Dorique	FRA	10.7.76	1		Alès	28 Jun
79.62	Latrell	Frederick	USA	7.9.80	1	NCAA-r	Columbus	31 May
79.57	Vladimir	Sasimovich	BLR	14.9.68	1	Klim	Staiki	28 Jun
79.50	Luiz Fernando	da Silva	BRA	2.7.71	1	SACh	Barquisimeto	21 Jun
79.44	Oleg	Statsenko	UKR	22.10.80	1		Yalta	30 Jan
79.42	Stefan	Wenk	GER	13.3.81	1		Rheinau-Freistett	6 Jul
79.40	Tim	Werner	GER	25.9.80	1		Pliezhausen	18 May
79.33	Ronny	Nilsen	NOR	7.5.71	1		Florø	31 May
79.31	David	Brisseault	FRA	7.3.69	1		Lons-le-Saunier	10 May
	(50)							
79.31	Tom	Pukstys	USA	28.5.68	1	Mod R	Modesto	10 May
79.28	Manuel	Nau	GER	2.7.77	4		Dessau	30 May
79.23		Liu Yanhong	CHN	20.4.83	1	NG	Changsha	23 Oct
79.06	Sergey	Voynov	UZB	26.2.77	1		Colombo	1 Jun
78.98	Yukifumi	Murakami	JPN	23.12.79	1		Mito	5 May
78.73	Mick	Hill	GBR	22.10.64	4	GP	London (CP)	8 Aug
78.69	Brian	Chaput	USA	9.4.81	1	NCAA	Sacramento	13 Jun
78.60	Dominique	Pausé	FRA	11.1.76	3		Gioia Tauro	2 Mar
78.40	Francesco	Pignata	ITA	14.2.78	1		Reggio Calabria	5 Apr
78.39	Vladislav	Shkurlatov	RUS	30.3.83	2	NC-w	Adler	22 Feb
	(60)							
78.30	Chris	Clever	USA	10.8.78	2eA		Saarbrücken	25 Jul
78.25	Pekka	Alaräisänen	FIN	27.12.75	1		Äänekoski	28 Jul
78.05	Pavel	Stasyuk	BLR	14.6.77	5	DNG	Stockholm	5 Aug
77.95	Stefan	Müller	SUI	20.9.79	1	NC	Frauenfeld	6 Jul
77.93	Andis	Anskins	LAT	25.1.79	3		Ventspils	14 Jun
77.86	Gustavo	Dacal	ESP	30.3.77	1		Pontevedra	20 Jul
77.81	Vadims	Vasilevskis	LAT	5.1.82	2	WMilG	Catania	8 Dec
77.71	Yeóryios	Íltsios	GRE	28.11.81	1	NC	Tríkala	14 Jun
77.66	Rinat	Tarzumanov	UZB-J	26.3.84	1	NC	Tashkent	5 Sep
77.64	Manuel	Fuenmayor	VEN	3.12.80	1	NC	Maracaibo	25 May
	(70)							
77.56	Gregor	Högler	AUT	27.6.72	1	ECp-2A	Århus	22 Jun
77.54	Mark	Roberson	GBR	13.3.67	2		Loughborough	8 Jun
77.52	Harri	Hakkarainen	FIN	16.10.69	1		Keitele	7 Jun
77.42	Marcel	Plautz	GER	1.7.80	5		Gioia Tauro	2 Mar
77.34	Rob	Minnitti	USA	6.9.79	2		Pihtipudas	6 Jul
77.33		Huh Hee-sun	KOR	13.4.81	4		Busan	27 Sep
77.32		Chen Qi	CHN	10.3.82	2	NC	Shanghai	14 Sep
77.30	Oscar	Duncan	USA	5.3.75	1		Boise	19 Apr
77.30	Matti	Närhi	FIN	17.8.75	Q	NC	Helsinki	10 Aug
77.30	Walid Abderrazak	Mohamed	EGY	4.4.73	1	Arab C	Amman	9 Sep

Mark	Name		Nat	Born	Pos	Meet	Venue	Date
	(80)							
77.29	Matthias	Rau	GER	21.12.74	7	NC	Ulm	29 Jun
77.27	Tino	Häber	GER	6.10.82			Lauf	6 Sep
77.20	Máximo	Rigondeaux	CUB	17.10.76	1		La Habana	4 Jul
77.20	Janis	Liepa	LAT	14.3.81	2		Kaunas	10 Aug
77.03	Tomasz	Damszel	POL	25.3.72	6	Kuso	Warszawa	15 Jun
76.97	Vladimir	Chizhov	RUS	5.8.75	3	NC	Tula	9 Aug
76.92	Ramandeep	Singh	IND	.78	2		Hyderabad	28 May
76.91	Elefthérios	Karasmanákis	GRE	16.8.78	6	GP	Tríkala	24 Jun
76.81	Noraldo	Palacios	COL	8.7.80	2	SACh	Barquisimeto	21 Jun
76.80	Ari	Pakarinen	FIN	14.5.69	3		Äänekoski	28 Jul
	(90)							
76.74		Shin Kyung-ha	KOR-J	18.8.84	2		Chunan	11 Apr
76.72	Igor	Sukhomlinov	RUS	13.2.77	3		Adler	15 Feb
76.71	Daniel	Ragnvaldsson	SWE	3.1.76	1		Nyköping	31 May
76.65	Mats	Nilsson	SWE	16.7.75	3	v FIN	Helsinki	6 Sep
76.42A	Willie	Human	RSA	8.3.82	2		Potchefstroom	31 Jan
76.41	Stuart	Farquhar	NZL	15.3.82	1	NC	Dunedin	22 Mar
76.31	Kirt	Thompson	TRI	13.12.67	1		Bloomington	19 Jul
76.23	Justin	St Clair	USA	17.5.79	5		Kuortane	20 Jul
76.21	Viktor	Mishchuk	UKR	12.5.80	2		Koncha-Zaspa	29 Mar
76.17	Mikael	Snällfot	SWE	23.5.80			Gävle	11 May
	(100)							

Mark	Name		Nat	Born	Date
76.16	Josh	Johnson	USA	6.4.75	21 Jun
76.11	Edi	Ponos	CRO	10.4.76	17 Sep
76.09	Marián	Bokor	SVK	17.4.77	1 Sep
76.02	Dimítrios	Polimérou	GRE	17.5.74	14 Jun
75.96	Marko	Kantanen	FIN	17.4.78	11 Aug
75.80		Qin Qiang	CHN	18.4.83	23 Oct
75.73	Peter	Zupanc	SLO	8.1.82	9 Aug
75.69	Johan	Kloeck	BEL	4.12.75	29 May
75.68	Arunas	Jurksas	LTU	3.5.72	7 Jun
75.60	Kazuki	Yamamoto	JPN	8.10.83	27 Apr
75.53	Nery	Kennedy	PAR	28.5.73	21 Jun
75.35	Guillermo	Martínez	CUB	24.8.74	27 Jun
75.34	Jagdish	Singh Bishnoi	IND	20.5.72	29 Oct
75.21	Mariusz	Roszkowski	POL	16.11.75	6 Sep
75.18	Diego	Moraga	CHI	6.10.76	13 Apr
75.13	Richard	Knudsen	DEN	28.7.72	9 Jun
75.10	Alberto	Desiderio	ITA	26.3.73	16 Feb
75.07	Mohd Fazal	Ansari	IND	1.2.78	28 Jul
75.04	Mehdi	Ravaei	IRI	15.8.80	10 Aug
75.00	Stuart	Faben	GBR	28.2.75	10 May
74.98	Csongor	Olteán	HUN-J	8.4.84	20 Sep
74.95	Pauli	Piiparinen	FIN	21.8.79	21 Jun
74.86A	Mohd Ibrahim	Al-Khalifa	QAT	25.12.82	5 Mar
74.82	Pål Arne	Fagernes	NOR	8.6.74	27 Jun
74.80	Heiko	Väät	EST	25.8.75	14 May
74.77	Marko	Hyytiainen	FIN	27.11.66	24 Jul
74.77	Levente	Bartha	ROM	8.3.77	10 Aug
74.76	Trevor	Snyder	CAN	2.6.82	12 Apr
74.67	Ty	Sevin	USA	17.6.71	10 May
74.65	Dimítrios	Martátos	GRE	21.5.74	3 May
74.62	Saku	Kuusisto	FIN	9.3.82	3 Jul
74.58	Teemu	Pasanen	FIN	24.5.77	2 Jul
74.54	Kimmo	Kinnunen	FIN	31.3.68	28 Jul
74.45	Michal	Safár	CZE	14.3.79	12 Jul
74.43	Raldu	Potgieter	RSA-Y	3.4.86	19 Dec
74.42	Mikhail	Oleynikov	RUS	24.4.81	7 Jun
74.37	Vadim	Yeftukhovich	BLR	24.5.81	11 Jun
74.28	Nick	Bennett	AUS	1.6.82	22 Mar
74.27	Pradeep	Nishanta	SRI	28.9.73	1 Jun
74.27	Bill	Neumann	CAN	22.9.82	13 Jun
74.23	Michael	Allen	GBR	7.3.80	1 Aug
74.20	Raimundo	Fernández	ESP	5.6.70	31 May
74.08	Seppo	Hirvonen	FIN	1.11.82	3 Jul
74.08	Robi	Tersek	SLO	1.7.70	9 Aug
74.04	Yasutaka	Fujiwara	JPN	14.7.81	6 Jun
74.04	Juhani	Virrankoski	FIN	18.10.81	3 Jul
74.02	Roald	Bradstock (147)	USA	24.4.62	22 Mar

Unknown irregularity

Mark	Name		Nat	Born	Date
78.88	Gustavo	Dacal	ESP	30.3.77	5 Apr

JUNIORS

See main list for top 4 Juniors. 10 performances by 3 men to 77.50. Additional marks and further juniors:

Wirkkala	80.07	3		Kuortane	20 Jul	78.49	2		Rovaniemi	30 Aug
	80.07	1	vSWE	Helsinki	6 Sep	78.39	2		Østerbro	2 Jun
	79.90	1	EJ	Tampere	26 Jul	77.69	1	v3N	Odense	24 Aug
Järvenpää	79.57	Q	NC	Helsinki	10 Aug					

Mark	Name		Nat	Born	Pos	Meet	Venue	Date
74.98	Csongor	Olteán	HUN-J	8.4.84	1		Koper	20 Sep
74.43	Raldu	Potgieter	RSA-Y	3.4.86	2		Parow	19 Dec
73.00		Lim Chang-man	KOR	2.2.84	3		Chunju	23 Apr
72.87	Antti	Ruuskanen	FIN	21.2.84	3	EJ	Tampere	26 Jul
72.52	Júlio César	de Oliveira	BRA	4.2.86	2	NC	São Paulo	15 Jun
72.28	Jonas	Baseda (10)	GER	15.5.84	1		Buxtehude	27 Aug
71.77	Robert	Bober	POL	12.1.84	1		Bielsko-Biala	25 May
71.28	Avtar	Singh	IND	3.1.84	3		Patiala	14 Oct
71.26	Tom	Goyvaerts	BEL	20.3.84	2		Merksem	6 Sep
71.11	Joshua	Robinson	AUS	4.10.85	5	NC	Brisbane	5 Apr
71.06		Hou Xingliang	CHN	5.1.84	3	NG	Changsha	23 Oct
70.90	Aleksey	Tovarnov	RUS	20.1.85	2		Koper	20 Sep
70.75A	Wimpie	du Plessis	RSA	23.7.84	6		Potchefstroom	15 Apr
70.65	Kazunori	Onizuka	JPN	16.11.85	1		Kitakyushu	2 Nov
70.56		Guo Jie	CHN	16.3.84	7	NC	Shanghai	14 Sep
70.27	Tomasz	Roginski (20)	POL	5.2.85	1		Gdansk	4 Oct

Mark	Name		Nat	Born	Pos	Meet	Venue	Date

PENTATHLON

3602	7.27w	50.60	23.09	41.58	4:44.40	Anders	Black	DEN	11.6.79	1	(NC) Glostrup	24 Ma
3574	6.61	61.57	23.70	38.12	4:30.16	André	Röttger	GER	26.3.79	1	Regensburg	13 Sep
3501	6.48	66.91	24.56	44.41	4:58.74	Helmut	Maryniak	GER	14.6.68		Erding	14 Jun

DECATHLON

8807	Roman	Sebrle		CZE	26.11.74	1		Götzis		1 Jun
	10.78/-0.2	7.86/1.2	15.41	2.12	47.83	13.96/0.0	43.42	4.90	69.22	4:28.63
8784	Tom	Pappas		USA	6.9.76	1	NC	Stanford		22 Jun
	10.78/0.2	7.96/1.4	16.28	2.17	48.22	14.13/1.7	45.84	5.20	60.77	4:48.12
8750		Pappas				1	WCh	Saint-Denis		27 Aug
	10.80/-0.5	7.62/1.1	16.11	2.09	47.58	13.99/0.0	46.94	5.10	65.90	4:44.31
8634		Sebrle				1	WCh	Saint-Denis		27 Aug
	11.00/-0.5	7.64/-0.9	15.47	2.06	47.90	14.25/0.0	47.47	4.80	69.79	4:34.45
8606		Sebrle				1		Ratingen		13 Jul
	10.93/1.6	7.60/0.5	15.41	2.09	48.59	14.30/-1.2	47.31	5.10	63.14	4:35.37
8585		Pappas				2		Götzis		1 Jun
	10.65/-0.2	7.42/1.3	16.48	2.18	48.74	14.09/0.0	46.71	5.00	62.06	5:00.25
8482	Bryan	Clay		USA	3.1.80	2	NC	Stanford		22 Jun
	10.43/1.7	7.71/-1.3	14.01	2.02	47.85	14.12/1.7	43.51	4.70	67.77	4:42.19
8374	Dmitriy	Karpov		KAZ	23.7.81	3	WCh	Saint-Denis		27 Aug
	10.72/-0.6	7.75/0.1	15.51	2.12	47.33	13.95/-0.6	47.38	4.40	47.53	4:37.70
8281	Erki	Nool		EST	25.6.70	1	ECp-1	Tallinn		6 Jul
	10.79/1.3	7.56w/2.2	13.98	1.97	48.18	14.55/1.7	42.96	5.30	56.09	4:35.86
8275	Paul	Terek		USA	20.10.79	3	NC	Stanford		22 Jun
	10.90/1.7	7.38w/2.3	15.51	2.08	49.26	15.78/1.0	46.19	5.20	58.79	4:37.25
8253		Karpov				1		Desenzano del Gardo		11 May
	10.91/0.0	7.77/-0.5	14.53	2.12	48.65	14.12/0.6	48.48	4.62	50.53	4:48.79
8242	Tomás	Dvorák		CZE	11.5.72	4	WCh	Saint-Denis		27 Aug
	11.03/-0.5	7.28/-0.5	15.95	1.94	50.04	14.15/0.0	45.47	4.50	67.10	4:27.63
8225		Clay				1		Berkeley		10 May
	10.46w/2.5	7.33/0.3	14.02	1.99	49.43	14.26w/2.1	49.33	4.80	58.45	4:49.64
8222	Jón Arnar	Magnússon		ISL	28.7.69	3		Götzis		1 Jun
	10.79/-0.2	7.85/0.7	15.81	2.00	48.47	14.40/-0.8	42.08	4.90	60.24	5:08.72
8219	Laurent	Hernu		FRA	22.8.76	1		Talence		21 Sep
	11.23/-0.9	7.56/0.6	14.77	2.00	49.15	14.32/-1.2	47.14	5.02	58.06	4:44.06
8218		Hernu				5	WCh	Saint-Denis		27 Aug
	11.20/-0.6	7.22/0.1	13.99	2.03	48.95	14.15/-0.6	46.13	4.90	59.63	4:28.38
8203	Kristjan	Rahnu (10)		EST	29.8.79	1		Tartu		20 Jul
	10.79/-0.4	7.38/0.8	15.64	2.00	49.81	14.20/0.5	50.70	4.50	65.02	5:05.75
8198	Lev	Lobodin		RUS	1.4.69	6	WCh	Saint-Denis		27 Aug
	10.99/-0.5	7.08/-0.6	15.43	1.97	49.54	14.36/0.0	48.36	5.00	56.50	4:34.63
8196	Romain	Barras		FRA	1.8.80	1	WUG	Daegu		30 Aug
	11.18/1.3	7.15/-0.2	14.51	2.01	48.84	14.35/0.1	45.58	4.70	63.60	4:27.19
8184		Hernu				1	NC	Narbonne		25 Jul
	11.12/0.0	7.43/1.5	14.37	2.06	49.31	14.05/2.0	45.63	4.75	58.21	4:39.79
8126		Qi Haifeng		CHN	7.8.83	7	WCh	Saint-Denis		27 Aug
	11.30/-0.6	7.39/-0.7	12.85	2.00	48.73	14.40/-0.6	46.72	4.80	59.98	4:25.40
8122	Indrek	Turi		EST	30.7.81	2	WUG	Daegu		30 Aug
	11.05/0.1	7.07w/2.9	14.31	2.10	49.72	14.36/1.6	40.23	5.00	62.84	4:39.69
8103w	Stephen	Harris		USA	5.12.80	1		College Station		21 Mar
	10.69w/4.3	7.66w/3.5	12.63	2.14	48.32	14.53w/2.3	39.86	4.50	56.72	4:35.98
8072	Aleksandr	Pogorelov		RUS	10.1.80	1		Arles		8 Jun
	11.22/-0.7	7.57w/3.4	15.28	2.11	51.50	14.54/-1.6	44.31	4.91	59.42	4:57.10
8061		Harris				1	NCAA	Sacramento		12 Jun
	10.87/-1.2	7.50/2.0	12.60	2.05	47.96	14.50/-3.0	39.96	4.70	58.69	4:33.73
8060	Chiel	Warners		NED	2.4.78	2	ECp-1	Tallinn		6 Jul
	10.76/1.3	7.69/0.8	14.53	1.97	47.91	14.34/1.7	41.79	4.60	56.96	4:53.28
8060		Barras				2		Talence		21 Sep
	11.42/-1.9	7.18/1.9	14.89	2.00	48.80	14.49/-1.2	42.67	4.62	63.07	4:26.77
8023		Magnússon				2		Ratingen		13 Jul
	10.93/1.6	7.45/-1.6	15.24	2.03	49.27	14.64/-1.2	42.56	4.90	62.51	5:15.47
8021	Vitaliy	Smirnov		UZB	25.10.78	1	AsiC	Manila		23 Sep
	10.91/0.8	7.18/1.4	13.80	2.03	48.82	14.69/1.2	42.72	4.60	62.23	4:37.18
8020	André	Niklaus		GER	30.8.81	8	WCh	Saint-Denis		27 Aug
	11.19/0.3	7.21/0.1	13.87	1.97	49.95	14.50/-0.6	42.68	5.10	57.55	4:28.84
8019	Rolf	Schläfli		SUI	15.3.71	4		Götzis		1 Jun
	11.07/0.4	7.28/1.3	15.53	1.88	48.69	14.80/-1.2	42.94	4.70	65.14	4:42.29
	(31/20)									

MEN 2003

Mark	Name			Nat	Born	Pos Meet	Venue			Date
8010	Stephen	Moore		USA	13.8.75	4 NC	Stanford			22 Jun
	10.80/1.7	7.33/-0.8	12.87	2.02	47.18	14.44/1.7	42.28	4.60	54.34	4:35.44
8000	Claston	Bernard		JAM	22.3.79	8 WCh	Saint-Denis			27 Aug
	10.91/0.3	7.22/-0.9	15.39	2.03	49.31	14.76/-0.6	43.47	4.30	59.47	4:34.49
7980	Klaus	Ambrosch		AUT	23.5.73	5	Götzis			1 Jun
	11.03/1.3	7.23/-1.0	14.43	1.94	50.04	14.56/-0.8	38.34	4.80	68.29	4:37.78
7964	Sébastien	Levicq		FRA	25.6.71	4	Arles			8 Jun
	11.43/-0.4	7.26/1.7	13.81	1.96	51.26	15.24/-0.9	42.62	5.21	66.86	4:33.28
7958	Sebastian	Knabe		GER	13.10.78	7	Götzis			1 Jun
	11.02/1.3	7.65/0.8	13.94	2.00	48.89	14.35/0.0	43.34	4.70	52.02	4:47.26
7954	Aleksandr	Parkhomenko		BLR	22.3.81	1 NC	Staiki			11 Jun
	11.29/1.0	7.18/1.5	15.14	1.97	51.11	15.18/-2.3	40.24	4.80	69.88	4:32.52
7925w	Maurice	Smith		JAM	28.9.80	1 Tex R	Austin			3 Apr
	10.79w/4.5	7.40w/4.8	14.46	1.95	50.10	14.42w/3.3	49.81	4.10	55.71	4:40.64
7923	Attila	Zsivóczky		HUN	29.4.77	5	Arles			8 Jun
	11.35/-0.4	7.02/1.3	14.76	2.14	50.21	15.13/-0.9	43.23	4.51	60.85	4:32.32
7918	Kip	Janvrin		USA	8.7.65	5 NC	Stanford			22 Jun
	11.10/1.7	6.83w/2.1	14.45	1.84	48.35	14.86/0.8	40.80	4.90	58.00	4:12.91
7916	Sergey	Nikitin		RUS	13.5.73	1 NC	Tula			3 Aug
	11.26	6.99	16.27	2.03	51.15	14.85	44.28	4.70	61.64	4:46.86
	(30)									
7911w	Santiago	Lorenzo		ARG	4.4.78	2 Tex R	Austin			3 Apr
	10.87w/5.0	7.25w/4.9	12.82	1.92	50.11	14.83w/3.1	44.40	4.80	60.72	4:32.58
7911	Nikolay	Tishchenko		RUS	4.2.77	3 WUG	Daegu			30 Aug
	11.02/1.3	7.70w/2.2	13.20	1.95	50.01	14.66/1.6	43.55	4.70	53.47	4:32.00
7894	Will	Thomas		USA	11.8.81	2 NCAA	Sacramento			12 Jun
	11.39/-0.4	6.92/1.6	15.45	2.05	48.99	15.20/-1.0	42.12	5.00	54.09	4:36.56
7877	Paolo	Casarsa		ITA	2.7.75	1 NC	Rieti			2 Aug
	11.35/0.4	6.85/-0.9	14.81	1.94	51.20	14.69/1.0	49.72	4.80	64.32	4:49.18
7868	Nikolay	Averyanov		RUS	4.2.80	4 WUG	Daegu			30 Aug
	10.82/0.1	7.52/1.9	14.07	1.95	50.11	14.71/0.1	39.90	4.80	50.42	4:31.69
7851	Hamdi	Dhouibi		TUN	24.1.82	4	Desenzano del Gardo			11 May
	10.74/0.0	7.25/0.0	13.91	1.91	47.67	14.76/0.6	42.64	4.82	45.33	4:34.65
7842	Oscar	González		ESP	8.8.76	1 NC	Alhama de Murcia			8 Jun
	10.91w/3.5	7.47/2.0	13.48	2.08	49.37	14.58/-2.3	40.69	4.30	47.50	4:24.55
7841	Joe	Cebulski		USA	25.10.76	2	Berkeley			10 May
	11.24	6.75	13.85	2.02	49.91	15.06	48.51	4.80	57.23	4:38.15
7835	Michal	Modelski		POL	16.4.75	3 ECp-1	Tallinn			6 Jul
	11.15/2.0	7.39/0.5	14.32	2.00	49.59	14.81/1.9	39.39	4.80	53.06	4:35.76
7815	Aleksandr	Shtepa		RUS	15.5.79	9	Götzis			1 Jun
	11.33/-1.3	6.91/1.2	15.43	1.94	51.28	14.73/0.4	48.79	4.50	61.15	4:41.58
	(40)									
7814	Matthias	Spahn		GER	3.1.79	1 NC	Wesel			24 Aug
	11.01/0.8	7.02/-1.5	14.47	1.94	49.17	14.86/1.4	43.95	4.60	60.61	4:48.06
7809	David	Lemen		USA	13.11.79	6 NC	Stanford			22 Jun
	11.22/1.7	7.38w/2.3	12.75	1.90	50.94	14.58/0.8	40.12	5.30	65.83	5:00.58
7804	Andy	Giesler		USA	24.2.78	3	Berkeley			10 May
	11.26	7.08	15.23	1.84	51.09	15.19	47.63	4.80	60.93	4:38.78
7804	Indrek	Kaseorg		EST	16.12.67	1 NC	Kärdla			10 Aug
	11.37/1.3	7.12/0.9	13.47	1.95	50.10	14.62/2.0	40.92	4.80	63.50	4:37.02
7799	Dmitriy	Ivanov		RUS	23.3.77	6	Arles			8 Jun
	11.10/-0.7	7.20/0.5	13.78	1.90	48.44	15.18/-1.6	43.87	4.81	60.32	4:50.63
7788	Lionel	Marceny		FRA	17.7.74	4 ECp	Bressanone			6 Jul
	11.13/0.0	7.36/1.7	13.31	1.93	49.84	14.40/-1.3	41.62	4.90	51.98	4:38.72
7788	Florian	Schönbeck		GER	13.1.74	2 NC	Wesel			24 Aug
	11.25/0.7	7.03/-0.8	13.81	1.85	50.28	14.65/1.4	44.97	4.80	58.25	4:28.73
7762	Philipp	Huber		SUI	18.2.74	4 ECp-1	Tallinn			6 Jul
	11.46/1.3	7.38w/2.7	14.24	1.85	50.01	15.60/1.7	41.98	4.90	59.38	4:25.13
7754	Bevan	Hart		USA	1.8.77	7 NC	Stanford			22 Jun
	11.20/1.7	6.81/1.0	13.53	1.96	50.00	14.83/0.8	42.16	5.00	54.10	4:29.45
7745	Billy	Pappas		USA	22.2.79	4	Berkeley			10 May
	11.14	6.97	13.73	1.96	50.46	14.55	44.45	4.50	61.04	4:43.01
	(50)									
7745	Sergey	Blonskiy		UKR	7.1.73	2	Staiki			10 Jun
	11.23	7.04	15.59	1.91	51.67	14.75	44.60	5.00	59.89	5:03.64
7739	Cristian	Gasparro		ITA	15.12.74	2 NC	Rieti			2 Aug
	11.40/-1.4	6.92/-0.3	13.88	1.97	50.79	14.86/1.0	44.67	4.90	56.56	4:36.80
7739	Trond	Høiby		NOR	24.1.73	4	Talence			21 Sep
	11.62/-1.9	6.88w/2.7	14.53	1.97	50.93	15.42/-2.0	44.39	4.62	64.67	4:27.66
7729	Travis	Geopfert		USA	20.8.78	1	Fargo			6 Jun
	11.02	7.24	14.56	1.87	48.81	15.58	43.22	4.30	55.34	4:21.48

Mark	Name		Nat	Born	Pos	Meet	Venue	Date
7724	Matt	McEwen	AUS	16.10.71	1	NC	Brisbane	4 Apr
	11.09/0.0 7.23/1.3 14.51 1.94 50.07 15.09/-0.7 39.20 4.80 60.50 4:50.97							
7721	Jukka	Väkeväinen	FIN	12.9.78	12		Götzis	1 Jun
	11.30/1.3 7.26w/2.1 13.02 2.00 48.89 15.04/0.4 38.78 4.80 55.17 4:34.63							
7717	Jamie	Cook	USA	21.7.76	1		Princeton	19 Apr
	10.8w/3.3 7.47w/3.0 13.87 1.96 51.3 15.08/1.1 45.70 4.27 56.34 4:36.18							
7715	Stefan	Drews	GER	12.2.79	6	ECp	Bressanone	6 Jul
	11.02/0.0 7.01/0.9 12.32 1.90 48.21 14.29/-1.3 38.17 5.00 51.97 4:34.97							
7712	Luca	Ceglie	ITA	24.10.79	7	ECp	Bressanone	6 Jul
	10.98/0.6 7.25/0.0 13.33 1.96 48.88 14.65/-1.3 39.67 4.60 56.76 4:49.22							
7705	Pródromos	Korkízoglou	GRE	27.2.75	1	NC	Athína (E)	1 Jun
	10.7/1.8 7.07w/3.6 14.36 1.92 51.02 14.79/1.5 48.41 4.80 54.25 5:03.57							
	(60)							
7704	Luiggy	Llanos	PUR	22.8.78	2	PAm	Santo Domingo	6 Aug
	11.02/1/7 7.47/0.3 14.62 1.86 50.27 14.29w/2.4 43.93 4.50 59.78 5:11.24							
7696	Krzysztof	Andrzejak	POL	10.1.75	6	ECp-1	Tallinn	6 Jul
	10.98/1.3 7.32w/2.1 14.73 2.06 49.13 14.94/1.3 36.87 4.80 50.92 5:02.76							
7693	Pavel	Dubitskiy	KAZ	27.8.82	7	WUG	Daegu	30 Aug
	11.15/0.1 7.27/0.0 12.69 2.13 51.18 15.04/1.6 41.84 4.80 52.69 4:48.14							
7685w	Knut	Sommerfeldt	NOR	13.7.79	1	Big12	Austin	18 May
	11.12w/2.3 7.18w/4.2 14.42 1.77 51.69 15.01/0.4 43.69 4.90 62.62 4:44.11							
7681	Atis	Vaisjuns	LAT	27.9.82	3	EU23	Bydgoszcz	18 Jul
	11.29/1.0 7.08/-0.3 13.46 2.03 49.87 15.12/1.2 40.57 4.60 58.48 4:38.72							
7675		Kim Kun-woo	KOR	29.2.80	7	WUG	Daegu	30 Aug
	11.36/1.3 7.45/2.0 12.25 1.98 49.10 15.41/0.1 38.85 4.60 52.13 4:13.72							
7673	Steve	Keller	USA	23.7.76	2		Fargo	6 Jun
	11.42 6.73 14.96 1.96 50.69 15.25 46.84 4.10 58.82 4:17.79							
7669	Josef	Karas	CZE/CAN	20.8.78	2	Big12	Austin	18 May
	11.00w/2.3 7.52w/3.4 12.68 2.01 49.52 15.80/0.4 42.76 4.60 49.25 4:32.90							
7662	Xavier	Weibel	SUI	21.1.80	7	ECp-1	Tallinn	6 Jul
	11.09/2.0 7.61/1.2 13.41 1.94 50.81 15.35/1.9 38.06 4.50 61.53 4:39.17							
7651	Zsolt	Kürtösi	HUN	21.3.71	1	NC	Budapest	14 Sep
	11.39/0.5 7.01/1.4 14.93 2.01 51.33 15.02/-1.1 43.22 4.60 62.10 4:58.13							
	(70)							
7649	Bruno	Lambèse	FRA	11.4.69	8		Arles	8 Jun
	11.21/-0.7 7.23w/2.2 15.10 1.90 50.51 14.56/-0.6 45.38 4.51 46.63 4:39.28							
7646	Gaëtan	Blouin	FRA	4.1.74	1		Evian	22 Jun
	11.29/0.8 7.11/-0.5 12.90 1.98 49.97 15.07/0.0 40.41 4.70 59.66 4:39.95							
7642	Lars	Albert	GER	9.2.82	13		Götzis	1 Jun
	11.26/0.4 7.14/0.1 14.92 1.94 51.91 15.07/0.4 43.43 4.50 61.38 4:47.63							
7633	Eugene	Martineau	NED	14.5.80	6		Talence	21 Sep
	11.34/-1.9 7.21/1.9 12.36 1.94 50.02 15.41/-2.0 41.54 4.72 61.27 4:34.79							
7630w	Pávlos	Kouromihalákis	GRE	16.2.76	2	NC	Athína (E)	1 Jun
	11.1/1.8 7.48w/4.2 14.32 2.04 52.95 15.36/1.5 41.45 4.90 51.29 4:44.34							
	7504 points with 6.96w/2.6							
7630	Takuro	Hirata	JPN	4.7.80	1	NC	Yokohama	7 Jun
	11.00/0.3 7.37/1.5 12.06 1.90 48.52 15.11/0.6 40.46 4.60 60.06 4:50.00							
7616	Marc	Magrans	ESP	26.9.76	2	NC	Alhama de Murcia	8 Jun
	11.01w/3.5 7.24w/3.5 12.78 1.90 49.52 15.14/-2.3 37.35 4.70 53.16 4:24.14							
7615	Christopher	Hallmann	GER	6.6.83	5	EU23	Bydgoszcz	18 Jul
	10.79/0.3 7.22/-0.3 11.48 1.91 47.76 14.94/-2.1 36.04 4.50 55.90 4:30.10							
7601	Philipp	Grimm	GER	18.10.78	3	NC	Wesel	24 Aug
	10.81/0.8 6.97/-1.3 13.64 1.88 48.52 15.57/1.4 44.29 4.50 60.04 4:57.64							
7596	Marzio	Viti	ITA	10.8.73	4	NC	Rieti	2 Aug
	11.33/0.3 7.37/-0.8 14.46 1.97 51.91 14.94/1.0 43.68 4.40 55.62 4:46.15							
	(80)							
7593	Vladimir	Mikhaylenko	UKR	27.8.73	9		Arles	8 Jun
	11.22/-0.7 7.17/-0.5 13.33 1.96 48.97 14.77/-0.6 41.71 4.91 44.69 4:46.53							
7593	Yonelvis	Aguila	CUB	1.8.75	3	PAm	Santo Domingo	6 Aug
	11.16/1.7 7.06/0.2 13.77 2.01 50.24 14.89w/2.4 47.04 3.70 63.01 4:49.93							
7587	Hans Olav	Uldal	NOR	16.12.82	1	Fla R	Gainesville	27 Mar
	11.24/1.7 7.25/1.0 13.66 1.86 50.87 15.33/0.4 46.44 4.50 56.02 4:37.25							
7584	David	Gómez	ESP	13.2.81	1		Salamanca	6 Jul
	11.42/0.5 7.05/0.6 13.56 1.98 49.17 14.61/-1.0 41.72 4.00 60.06 4:37.38							
7581	Phil	McMullen	USA	3.2.75	7		Talence	21 Sep
	11.91/-1.9 6.33/0.4 14.21 1.85 50.81 15.28/-2.0 50.35 4.92 56.26 4:21.41							
7569	Pavel	Havlícek	CZE	3.11.81	2		Maribor	1 Jun
	11.39/-0.9 7.29/1.0 13.65 2.05 50.22 14.98/-0.1 41.21 4.80 56.54 5:15.61							
7562	Henri	Kokkonen	FIN	11.8.78	10	ECp	Bressanone	6 Jul
	11.38/0.0 6.78/0.8 15.00 1.93 50.70 15.09/0.0 42.02 4.50 62.31 4:47.95							

Mark	Name			Nat	Born	Pos	Meet	Venue		Date
7561	Eric	Kerwitz		ARG	29.1.80	1		Rosario		7 Dec
	10.6/1.5	7.77/0.6	13.15	1.91	50.1,	14.8	35.06	4.10	58.60	4:38.9
7560	Ryan	Harlan		USA	25.4.81	11	NC	Stanford		22 Jun
	11.06/0.2	6.89/-0.5	14.81	2.05	51.13	14.08/1.7	38.40	4.50	51.65	4:59.06
7557	Masatoshi	Ishizawa		JPN	13.3.79	2	NC	Yokohama		7 Jun
	11.01/1.0	7.11/2.0	11.39	1.93	48.23	14.51/1.2	34.68	4.50	58.64	4:35.71
	(90)									
7551	Ireneusz	Zurawicz		POL	24.1.78	9	ECp-1	Tallinn		6 Jul
	11.36/1.6	7.04/0.4	13.98	1.88	50.04	14.91/0.7	42.77	4.80	51.66	4:42.10
7544	Trey	Hardee		USA-J	7.2.84	3	SEC	Knoxville		16 May
	10.68/1.0	6.69/0.0	11.57	1.92	49.26	14.59w/2.4	40.38	5.00	49.94	4:46.57
7536	Aleksey	Drozdov		RUS	3.12.83	1		Krasnodar		24 May
	11.31/-0.9	7.35/0.7	14.97	1.93	51.98	15.93/-0.3	44.94	4.40	54.84	4.38.11
7535	Stéphane	Bamboux		FRA	28.2.74	10		Arles		8 Jun
	10.99/-0.7	7.38w/3.4	13.61	1.87	50.12	14.63/-0.6	41.72	4.61	50.93	4:56.99
7528	Mikk	Joorits		EST	12.2.81	6		Desenzano del Gardo		11 May
	10.82/-0.2	7.06/1.2	13.21	1.82	47.35	15.64/0.0	40.99	4.42	50.04	4:29.39
7528	Francisco José	Caro		ESP	23.10.78	2	NC	Valencia		20 Jul
	11.05/0.3	7.36/0.0	13.87	1.92	52.12	15.70/0.4	38.38	4.90	60.04	4:54.61
7526	Kevin	Thompson		USA	24.3.80	4	SEC	Knoxville		16 May
	11.13/0.5	6.91/0.0	14.33	1.98	49.96	14.96/0.2	42.52	4.50	50.00	4:47.60
7522	Casey	Thom		USA	16.8.79	3	Big 12	Austin		16 May
	11.15w/3.5	6.83w/2.8	11.97	2.01	47.98	15.74w/2.2	42.37	4.30	55.80	4:30.58
7513	Nate	Schmidt		USA	13.8.81	1		Fargo		29 Apr
	10.99/2.0	7.29w/3.6	11.90	2.00	48.98	14.70w/2.8	40.61	4.66	44.88	4:49.93
7512	Janis	Karlivans		LAT	2.6.82	1	NC	Riga		31 May
	11.68/-1.3	7.66/0.5	13.52	2.10	50.23	15.05	44.70	4.20	51.09	5:03.21
	(100)									

Mark	Name		Nat	Born	Date
7511	Darion	Powell	USA	14.6.82	12 Jun
7491	Roland	Schwarzl	AUT	10.12.80	27 Jul
7487	Pavel	Andreyev	UZB	24.11.78	23 Sep
7475	Markus	Walser	AUT	15.12.79	1 Jun
7473	Sergey	Ryabchun	UKR	8.2.78	19 May
7466	Mustafa	Abdur-Rahim	USA	29.9.82	12 Jun
7458	Sergey	Dudnik	UKR	30.3.77	1 Jun
7458	Hiromasa	Tanaka	JPN	28.9.81	5 Jul
7455	Paolo	Mottadelli	ITA	7.6.79	6 Jul
7466	Ivan	Vdovin	RUS	3.12.83	24 May
7445	Andrey	Kharlamov	RUS	80	3 Aug
7443	Kenny	Beele	GER	11.4.80	13 Jul
7436	Mihail	Papaioánnou	GRE	9.10.82	18 Jul
7435w	Paul	Speer	USA	20.9.81	21 Mar
7433w	Allen	Bulick	USA	21.10.81	21 Mar
7432	Michael	Nolan	CAN	22.9.73	19 Jul
7426	Mikko	Halvari	FIN	4.3.83	6 Jul
7424	J.T.	Kuretich	USA	5.11.79	16 May
7420	Mark	Schumacher	GER	27.6.76	24 Aug
7419	John	Heanley	GBR	25.9.80	6 Jul
7418	Alvaro	Contreras	ESP	27.1.82	8 Jun
7413	Stephan	Zeyen	GER	11.9.78	8 Jun
7412	Alberto	Juantorena Jr	CUB	27.6.77	28 May
7410	Rubén	Delgado	ESP	20.9.76	20 Jul
7408	Ivan	Caetano da Silva	BRA	30.7.82	11 May
7405	Víctor	Ruiz	ESP	24.10.74	20 Jul
7403	Ryan	Tremelling	USA	9.8.80	16 May
7402	Rudy	Bourguignon	FRA	16.7.79	8 Jun
7401	Clifford	Caines	CAN	18.1.79	15 Jun
7400	Mustafa	Taha Hussein (130)	EGY	26.7.80	12 Oct

Best with 'legal' wind

Mark	Name			Nat	Born	Pos	Meet	Venue		Date
7854	Maurice	Smith		JAM	28.9.80	3	NCAA	Sacramento		12 Jun
	10.93/-0.6	7.17w/2.3	15.18	1.90	49.38	14.50/-3.0	46.50	4.30	56.51	4:41.63
7564	Santiago	Lorenzo		ARG	4.4.78	1	Pac-10	Los Angeles		11 May
	11.09/0.5	7.00/0.8	13.71	1.80	48.96	14.97/0.3	40.39	4.75	57.11	4:44.02
7506	Knut	Sommerfeldt		NOR	13.7.79	2	FlaR	Gainesville		25 Mar

Drugs disqualification

Mark	Name			Nat	Born	Pos	Meet	Venue		Date
7711	Georgios	Andreou ¶		CYP	26.7.74	1	ECp-2	Maribor		6 Jul
	10.75/0.6	7.18/1.6	14.32	1.98	50.64	14.94/0.0	45.46	4.80	53.50	5:11.45

JUNIORS

Mark	Name			Nat	Born	Pos	Meet	Venue		Date
7333	Aleksandr	Korzun		BLR	17.3.85	1		Staiki		11 Jun
	10.71/1.0	6.72/+0.9	13.67	1.88	49.65	15.53/-0.5	41.16	4.50	51.97	4:58.01
7307	Dimitriy	Sobolev		BLR	19.4.84	2		Staiki		11 Jun
	11.12/+1.5	6.91/1.4	15.44	1.91	50.83	14.46/-0.5	31.34	4.60	47.93	4:52.27
7149	Mikhail	Logvynenko		RUS	.84	10	NC	Tula		3 Aug
	11.44	6.87	11.61	2.00	49.44	15.02	31.98	4.60	40.18	4:23.47
7132		Yu Bin		CHN	26.11.85	2	NG	Changsha		26 Oct
	11.08/0.0	7.05/0.2	13.16	1.89	49.85	15.27/0.0	28.29	4.30	60.32	4:58.91
7106	Marian	Geisler		GER	10.8.84	6	vUSA	Filderstadt		3 Aug
	11.64/0.0	7.08/00.0	11.61	2.00	51.63	15.48/-0.6	37.06	4.40	46.38	4:27.71
7069	Nikolay	Shubenok		BLR	.85	3		Staiki		11 Jun
	11.45/1.5	6.58/1.5	14.40	1.88	53.02	15.78	38.02	4.40	51.66	4:31.60
7048		Lu Baoyun		CHN	20.1.84	5	NC	Shanghai		14 Sep
	11.22	6.92	12.69	1.89	51.93	15.05	38.63	4.10	54.70	4:57.30
7022	Jason	Dudley (8)		AUS	10.11.84	2		Brisbane		16 Feb
	11.85/-2.0	6.71/0.2	13.40	1.91	52.61	15.34/0.0	40.12	4.20	60.76	4:55.91

For multi-events a wind-assisted mark in one in which an event is aided by a wind over 4.0m/s and the average of the three wind-measured events (100m, 110mh, LJ) is greater than 2m/s.

Mark	Name		Nat	Born	Pos	Meet	Venue	Date
Deactahlon – Juniors with ith 6kg SP, 1.75kg DT								
7604	Nicklas	Wiberg	SWE	16.4.85	1	EJ	Tampere	25 Jul
	11.68/-0.4 6.85/0.6 14.51 2.05 49.58 15.89/-0.9 38.58 4.00 65.38 4:14.38							
7531	Aleksey	Sysojev	RUS	8.3.85	2	EJ	Tampere	25 Jul
	11.33/-1.9 6.60/1.3 14.98 1.99 50.88 15.69/0.1 51.58 4.20 55.34 4:44.27							
7497	Steffen	Willwacher	GER	17.5.84	3	EJ	Tampere	25 Jul
	11.40/-0.5 6.61/0.2 14.66 1.84 49.77 15.22/-1.2 44.10 4.50 53.47 4:25.54							
7490	Robert	Gindera	POL	26.2.84	4	EJ	Tampere	25 Jul
	11.60/-1.0 6.86/1.5 15.73 2.02 52.58 15.39/0.0 39.43 4.30 65.50 4:46.26							
7486	Donovan	Kilmartin	USA	11.6.84	1	PAm-J	Bridgetown	19 Jul
	11.21/0.0 6.92/-2.5 13.63 1.81 50.42 15.00/-1.6 43.03 5.30 42.75 4:40.33							
7478	Tim	Golemski	GER	4.2.84	1		Filderstadt	8 Jun
	11.42/-2.0 7.36/0.4 14.40 2.03 51.95 14.66/0.0 41.11 4.40 49.16 4:50.88							
7461	Jason	Dudley	AUS	10.11.84	1	NC-j	Brisbane	4 Apr
	11.58/0.0 6.80/0.3 14.86 1.91 51.28 15.31/-1.3 47.66 4.20 64.18 4:55.11							
7456	Pascal	Behrenbruch	GER	19.1.85	1	NC-j	Wesel	24 Aug
	11.58/0.6 6.40/0.2 15.65 1.90 51.53 14.87/-0.2 44.61 4.40 58.48 4:39.12							
7441	Stephen	Cain	AUS	23.7.84	2	NC-j	Brisbane	4 Apr
	11.14/0.0 6.78/-0.3 13.92 2.00 50.37 14.96/-1.3 40.29 4.40 54.92 4:51.78							
7402	Stephan	Hommel (10)	GER	3.9.84	1		Alzenau	11 May
	11.25/-0.3 7.05/-0.1 16.20 1.88 50.15 15.43/0.0 49.69 4.10 42.34 4:50.00							
7390	Pelle	Rietveld	NED	4.2.85	5	EJ	Tampere	25 Jul
	11.18/-1.9 6.71/-0.4 13.07 1.81 49.09 15.I0/-0.9 37.61 4.70 55.15 4:31.74							
7341	Brent	Nedwick	NZL	31.1.85	1		Hastings	2 Nov
	11.13/1.9 6.81/0.0 14.93 1.85 49.98 15.56/-0.9 45.96 4.30 50.28 4:52.41							
7334	Norman	Müller	GER	7.8.85	3	Nc-j	Wesel	24 Aug
	11.51/0.6 6.96/0.8 14.89 1.96 51.37 15.35/-0.2 40.07 4.30 56.07 4:49.45							
7320	Tobias	Otterbring	SWE	14.3.85	7	EJ	Tampere	25 Jul
	11.44/-0.5 6.64/0.8 15.71 1.84 49.88 15.32/0.0 40.57 4.00 50.72 4:20.40							
7297	Simon	Ruckdeschel	GER	14.10.84	1		Vaterstetten	3 Aug
	11.44/-0.8 6.49/-0.1 14.12 2.00 52.22 15.32/0.1 42.08 4.70 54.59 4:54.97							
7275	Jannis	Bäcker	GER	1.1.85	1		Bad Oeynhausen	20 Jul
	11.46/0.5 6.90/0.1 13.53 2.02 50.12 15.70/-2.1 36.30 3.90 55.80 4:25.96							
7266	Jürgen	Aschenbroich	GER	24.3.84	1		Wesel	11 May
	11.16/1.5 6.72 14.20 1.92 49.99 15.92/1.0 42.29 4.00 54.28 4:39.34							
7231	Sergey	Petrov	RUS	.84	2		Krasnodar	29 May
	11.43/-0.9 7.22/0.2 13.56 1/87 50.57 15.38/-1.7 38.06 4.50 51.00 4:48.37							
7230	Marian	Geisler	GER	10.8.85	5		Filderstadt	8 Jun
	11.66/0.1 7.33/0.0 13.29 1.97 51.56 15.76/-0.6 38.02 4.40 43.06 4:20.10							
7208	Olivier	Jehannet (20)	FRA	17.10.84	8	EJ	Tampere	25 Jul
	11.28/-1.0 6.85/0.2 14.01 1.87 51.78 16.03/0.1 39.99 4.90 51.66 4:53.89							

4 x 100 METRES RELAY

Mark	Nat	Team	Pos	Meet	Venue	Date
37.77	USA	ADrummond, B Williams, Patton, Greene	1	ISTAF	Berlin (P)	10 Aug
37.99	USA	Capel, B Williams, Patton, JJ Johnson	1s1	WCh	Saint-Denis	30 Aug
38.06	USA	Capel, B Williams, Patton, JJ Johnson	1	WCh	Saint-Denis	31 Aug
38.15	USA B	Capel, Gatlin, Miller, JJ Johnson	2	ISTAF	Berlin (P)	10 Aug
38.26	BRA	de Lima, Ribeiro, A.da Silva, Sousa	3	WCh	Saint-Denis	31 Aug
38.28	USA	Capel, B Williams, Patton, JJ Johnson	1h1	WCh	Saint-Denis	30 Aug
38.42	ITA	Scuderi, Collio, Donati, Cavallaro	1	ECp-S	Firenze	21 Jun
38.44	BRA	de Lima, Ribeiro, A da Silva, Sousa	1	PAm	Santo Domingo	9 Aug
38.45	POL	Krzywanski, Chyla, Jedrusinski, Urbas	2	ECp-S	Firenze	21 Jun
38.45	JAM	R Williams, Thomas, M Frater, A Powell	2s1	WCh	Saint-Denis	30 Aug
38.50	POL	Krzywanski, Chyla, Nowak, Jedrusinski	3s1	WCh	Saint-Denis	30 Aug
38.50	BRA	de Lima, Ribeiro, A da Silva, Sousa	2s2	WCh	Saint-Denis	30 Aug
38.52	USA Red	Avery, Miller, A Armstrong, JJ Johnson	1	MSR	Walnut	19 Apr
38.52	POL	Krzywanski, Chyla, Nowak, Jedrusinski	1h3	WCh	Saint-Denis	30 Aug
38.53	TRI	Alexander, Burns, Boldon, Brown	2	PAm	Santo Domingo	9 Aug
38.53	BRA	de Lima, Ribeiro, A da Silva, Sousa	1h2	WCh	Saint-Denis	30 Aug
38.56	JPN	Kawabata, Suetsugu, Matsuda, Asahara	1	GP	Osaka	10 May
	(17 performances by teams from 7 nations)					
38.58	NGR	Deji, Emedolu, Fasuba, Aliu	3s2	WCh	Saint-Denis	30 Aug
38.60	GBR	Malcolm, Campbell, Devonish, Golding	3	ECp-S	Firenze	21 Jun
38.61	FRA	Pognon, Nthépé, Krantz, Eyana	2h1	WCh	Saint-Denis	30 Aug
	(10)					
38.63	NED	Beck, T Douglas, van Balkom, C Douglas	5s1	WCh	Saint-Denis	30 Aug
38.63	GHA	Nsiah, Nkansah, Zakari, Myles-Mills	1	Afr G	Abuja	13 Oct
38.66	CAN	Allen, Henry, Joseph, Browne	4s2	WCh	Saint-Denis	30 Aug
38.70	GER	Unger, M Blume, Kosenkow, Ostwald	1		Leverkusen	3 Aug
38.76	AUS	Shirvington, Johnson, Di Bella, Basil	4h4	WCh	Saint-Denis	30 Aug

Mark	Nat	Name	Pos	Meet	Venue	Date
39.01	DOM	Encarnación, Morillo, Sainfleur, Báez	5h1	WCh	Saint-Denis	30 Aug
39.05	BEL	Bongelo, Ferro, Beyens, de Baerdemaker	4h2	WCh	Saint-Denis	30 Aug
39.09	CUB	César, Peña, Reyes, Pita	3	PAm	Santo Domingo	9 Aug
39.11	UKR	Vasyukov, Rurak, Dovgal, Glushchenko	1		Tel Aviv	14 Jul
39.19	AHO	Goeloe, Raffaela, Duzant, Martina	4	PAm	Santo Domingo	9 Aug
	(20)					
39.22	CHN	Shen Yunbao, He Jun, Yang Yaozu, Chen Haijian	1	AsiC	Manila	23 Sep
39.23	MRI	Victoire, Milazar, Augustin, Buckland	1		Bambous	4 Sep
39.25	NZL	Roberts, Donaldson, Dolphin, MacDonald	5h3	WCh	Saint-Denis	30 Aug
39.30	RUS	Yepishin, Ryabov, A Smirnov, R Smirnov	6	ECp-S	Firenze	21 Jun
39.34	CIV	Loua, Meité, Sonan, N'Dri	5h4	WCh	Saint-Denis	30 Aug
39.40	RSA	Vries, Gorries, la Grange, Quinn	1		Tampere	9 Jul
39.47	SWE	Lövgren, Wahn, Wissman, Engberg	1	ECp1A	Lappeenranta	21 Jun
39.47	ESP	Dorrego, A Rodríguez, Santos, Berlanga	7	ECp-S	Firenze	21 Jun
39.51	HUN	Ágoston, Pauer, Dobos, Gyulai	2	ECp1A	Lappeenranta	21 Jun
39.53	ISR	Mor, Kafri, Jablonka, Bar-Yeoshua	1		Tel Aviv	5 Jul
	(30)					

39.57	THA	23 Sep	39.70	IRL	21 Jun	39.88	SKN	5 Jul	40.07	HKG	23 Sep	40.31	AUT	18 Jul
39.58	SEN	29 Oct	39.70	BAH	5 Jul	39.94A	KEN	12 Jul	40.08	LBR	30 Aug	40.32	PUR	5 Jul
39.59	KSA	9 Jul	39.73	FIN	7 Jul	39.94	CMR	13 Oct	40.10	QAT	9 Sep	40.42	OMN	9 Sep
39.62	CYP	21 Jun	39.75	QAT	9 Oct	39.96	GRE	12 Jul	40.13	GRN	5 Jul	40.45	DEN	21 Jun
39.64	IND	29 Oct	39.81	SLO	21 Jun	39.99	CZE	21 Jun	40.29	CAY	5 Jul	40.48	DMA	5 Jul
39.69	SUI	14 Jun	39.81	POR	21 Jun	40.04	CHI	21 Jun	40.29	SRI	23 Sep	**Hand timed**		
39.69	EST	22 Jul	39.85	VEN	21 Jun	40.06	CRO	21 Jun	40.31	SCG	21 Jun	39.5	POR	17 May

Disqualified (one athlete subsequently drugs dq)

Mark	Nat	Name	Pos	Meet	Venue	Date
38.08	GBR	Malcolm, Campbell, Devonish, Chambers ¶	2	WCh	Saint-Denis	31 Aug
38.24	GBR	Malcolm, Chambers ¶, Devonish, Lewis-Francis	1h4	WCh	Saint-Denis	30 Aug
38.26	GBR	Malcolm, Campbell, Devonish, Chambers ¶	1s2	WCh	Saint-Denis	30 Aug
38.27	USA	Grimes #, Smoots, Brokenburr, Coleman)	(1)	PAm	Santo Domingo	9 Aug

JUNIORS

Mark	Nat	Name	Pos	Meet	Venue	Date
39.29	USA	C Moore, Aaron Collins, Ashton Collins, Hordge	1	PAm-J	Bridgetown	20 Jul
39.40	JAM	Hutton, Latty, Cephas, Bolt	2	PAm-J	Bridgetown	20 Jul
39.43	JAM	Hutton, Nicely, Latty, Bolt	1	Carifta	Port of Spain	20 Apr
39.99	FRA	Fagris, Fernandez, G Wallard, De Lépine	1h2	EJ	Tampere	28 Jul
40.04	ITA	La Naia, Anceschi, Marin, Howe	2h2	EJ	Tampere	28 Jul
40.09	GER	Hemke, Lohmann, Ernst, Doskoczynski	1		Mannheim	21 Jun
40.12	GBR	Matthews, Oboh, Ellington, Miah	1	vITA-J	Nove	5 Jul
40.55	POL	Olszanski, Kaska, Majchrzak, Badurek	3		Bydgoszcz	8 Jun
40.59	NED	Heisen, Mathew, Raat, Davis	3		Leiden	7 Jun
40.61	BRA	(Rio de Janeiro) Sena, André, da Costa Terto, Rodrigues	1	NC-j	Londrina	17 May
40.64	TRI	Duncan, Rodriguez, Phillip, D Brown	2	Carifta	Port of Spain	20 Apr
40.67	JPN	Imai, Fujimitsu, Suzuki, Tsukahara	1	v2N	Jeju-Do	25 Aug

4 x 200 METRES RELAY

Mark	Team	Pos	Meet	Venue	Date
1:19.16	USA Red Team Crawford, Clay, Patton, Gatlin	1	PennR	Philadelphia	26 Apr
1:20.79	Univ of Texas USA Gardner, Aa. Collins, As. Collins, Christian ANT	1	TexR	Austin	5 Apr
1:21.43	USA Blue Team Miller, Brokenburr, Williams, Johnson	2	PennR	Philadelphia	26 Apr
1:21.73	JAM (U.Tech) Waugh, W Smith, O Thompson, A Powell	1r2	PennR	Philadelphia	26 Apr

4 x 400 METRES RELAY

Mark	Team	Pos	Meet	Venue	Date
2:58.40	USA Blue Brew 45.4, Young 43.6, Nelson 44.7, James Davis 44.7	1	PennR	Philadelphia	26 Apr
2:58.88	USA C Harrison 45.2, Washington 44.6, Brew 44.75, Young 44.31	1	WCh	Saint-Denis	31 Aug
2:58.96	FRA Djhone 45.4, Keita 44.7, Diagana 44.69, Raquil 44.15	2	WCh	Saint-Denis	31 Aug
2:59.60	JAM	3	WCh	Saint-Denis	31 Aug
	Simpson 45.4, McFarlane 45.1 Clarke 44.04, Blackwood 45.06				
3:00.53	BAH Moncur 44.6, Darling 46.1, McKinney 45.54, Brown 44.36	4	WCh	Saint-Denis	31 Aug
3:00.66	USA BlueTeam	1	Tex R	Austin	5 Apr
	James Davis 45.6, Young 44.7 Nelson 45.0, Campbell 45.4				
3:00.72	USA High Performance	2	PennR	Philadelphia	26 Apr
	Campbell 45.6, Jerome Davis 45.1, Maybank 45.4, B Jackson 44.6				
3:00.98	USA C Harrison 44.9, Potter 44.4, Steele 45.54 Brew 46.08	1h1	WCh	Saint-Denis	30 Aug
3:01.00	GBR Mackie 46.4, Baldock 44.8, Rawlinson 45.01, Caines 44.72	5	WCh	Saint-Denis	31 Aug
3:01.33	BAH Moncur 45.2, McKinney 45.4, Oliver 45.96, Brown 44.79	2h1	WCh	Saint-Denis	30 Aug
3:01.37	JAM Campbell 45.0, Simpson 45.7, Spence 45.78, Clarke 44.92	1h2	WCh	Saint-Denis	30 Aug
3:01.68	USA Red Team	4	PennR	Philadelphia	26 Apr
	Carter 46.2, Washington 44.5, A.Harrison 46.0, C.Harrison 45.0				
3:01.79	FRA Douhou 46.8, Keita 44.1, Diagana 45.84 Raquil 44.98	1h3	WCh	Saint-Denis	30 Aug
3:01.81	JAM Campbell , Ayre, Spence, Clarke	1	PAm	Santo Domingo	9 Aug
3:01.87	USA Potter, Hooker, Steele, Davi	1	PAm	Santo Domingo	9 Aug

Mark		Name	Nat	Born	Pos	Meet	Venue	Date
3:01.99	USA	Red Hooker 45.6, Ammons 44.9, Couts 45.2, Maybank 46.2			2	Tex R	Austin	5 Apr
3:02.02	DOM	Peguero, Santa, Vidal, Sánchez			3	PAm	Santo Domingo	9 Aug
3:02.22	GBR	Benjamin 45.9, Baldock 45.5, Mackie 46.00, Caines 44.84			2h3	WCh	Saint-Denis	30 Aug
3:02.24	BOT	Molefe, Kilego, Moseki, Kubisa			1	AfG	Abuja	15 Oct
3:02.26	ESP	I Rodríguez 46.3, Canal 44.7, S Rodríguez 45.41, Reina 45.88			3h1	WCh	Saint-Denis	30 Aug
		(20 performances by teams from 8 nations) See below for mixed-nation teams						
3:02.31	GRE	Dimótsios 46.7, Goúsis 45.6, Sarrís 45.08, Iakovákis 44.93			2h2	WCh	Saint-Denis	30 Aug
3:02.35	JPN	Yamaguchi 45.8, Yamamura 45.5, Osakada 45.98, Sato 45.09			3h2	WCh	Saint-Denis	30 Aug
	(10)							
3:02.83	GER	Schultz 46.2, Gatzka 45.7, Faller 45.76, Swillims 45.26			3	ECp-S	Firenze	22 Jun
3:02.89	AUS	Steffenson 46.8, Hill 44.3, Pearce 45.49, Ormrod 46.22			4h1	WCh	Saint-Denis	30 Aug
3:02.97	CAN	Christopher 46.1, Niemi 45.1, Reed 45.35, Nelson 46.39			4h2	WCh	Saint-Denis	30 Aug
3:03.05	RSA	La Grange 46.3, Cilliers 45.6, Myburgh 45.72, Gorries 45.47			3h3	WCh	Saint-Denis	30 Aug
3:03.05	SRI	Kumara, Wimalawansa, Amarasekera, Thilakaratne			1	AsiC	Manila	23 Sep
3:03.15	UKR	Demchenko, Zyukov, Gorbenko, Tverdostup			1	WUG	Daegu	30 Aug
3:03.32	POL	Wieruszewski, Skalski, Dabrowski, Plawgo			1	EU23	Bydgoszcz	20 Jul
3:03.40	RUS	Usov 46.3, Semyonov 45.4, Forshev 46.80, Borzakovskiy 44.91			6	ECp-S	Firenze	22 Jun
3:04.16	NED	van Rhee, Som, van Balkom, Lathouwers			1	ECp1B	Velenje	22 Jun
3:04.31	IRL	McKee 46.6, Ryan 45.8, McCarthy 45.72, Gillick 46.19			5h3	WCh	Saint-Denis	30 Aug
	(20)							
3:04.32	QAT	Al-Haj, Al-Akbar, Moussa, Safi			3	AsiC	Manila	23 Sep
3:04.48	TRI	Barry, Raeburn, Bovell, Kirk			3	CAC	St George's	6 Jul
3:04.49	NGR	Agunbiade, Godday, Lawal, Audu			2	AfG	Abuja	15 Oct
3:04.76	CZE	Tesarik, Bláha, Klvana, Mazanec			3	ECp1B	Velenje	22 Jun
3:04.93	ITA	Barberi 46.9, Galletti 46.1, Salvucci 45.93, Amanfu 46.07			8	ECp-S	Firenze	22 Jun
3:05.0 A	KEN	(Armed Forces)			1	NC	Nairobi	12 Jul
3:05.22	IND	B Singh, S Singh, Shankar, A Kumar			4	AsiC	Manila	23 Sep
3:05.28	BRA	Ambrósio, de Araújo, Godoy, A J Santos			1	SACh	Barquisimeto	22 Jun
3:05.35	ZIM	Mutakanyi, Ncube, Nyongai, Wilson			3	Af-AsG	Hyderbad	30 Oct
3:05.44	VEN	Palma, Silvera, Luna, Hernández			4	CAC	St George's	6 Jul
	(30)							

3:05.54 KSA 10 Oct	3:06.70 TUN 25 Jun	3:07.00 HUN 22 Jun	3:08.73 FIN 6 Sep	3:09.48 COL 22 Jun
3:05.59 POR 22 Jun	3:06.71 SWE 22 Jun	3:07.27 PHI 23 Sep	3:08.86 SUD 9 Sep	3:09.64 DEN 22 Jun
3:06.15 CHN 27 Pct	3:06.84 MAR 25 Jun	3:07.85 SEN 15 Oct	3:09.18 SVK 22 Jun	3:09.78 ARG 22 Jun
3:06.19 ROM 13 Jul	3:06.94 THA 30 Oct	3:08.12 BEL 22 Jun	3:09.23 SLO 22 Jun	3:09.79 IRI 22 Jun
3:06.27 CUB 9 Aug	3:06.98 NOR 22 Jun	3:08.29 CRO 22 Jun	3:09.32 SUI 22 Jun	3:09.9A ETH 10 May
3:06.29 BLR 22 Jun	3:06.98 GRN 6 Jul	3:08.62 PUR 6 Jul	3:09.34 KUW 9 Sep	

Mixed nation teams

3:01.09	Caribbean All-Stars	3	PennR	Philadelphia	26 Apr
	Brown/BAH 45.2, Demeritte/BAH 45.8, Moncur/BAH 44.9, Francique/GRN 45.2				
3:02.01	Louisiana State University	1	NCAA	Sacramento	14 Jun
	Parham/USA 46.4, Brazell/USA 45.9, Coley/JAM 45.1, Willie/USA 44.6				

JUNIORS

3:02.88	USA	E Coleman, Wariner, Fergusson, Ashton Collins	1	PAm-J	Bridgetown	20 Jul
3:08.31	GER	Förster, Wilhelm, Gernand, Gaba	1	EJ	Tampere	27 Jul
3:08.32	JPN	(Narita HS)	2s2		Maebashi	12 Oct
3:08.62	POL	Pryga, Grzegorczyk, Blocian, Kedzia	2	EJ	Tampere	27 Jul
3:08.81	RUS	Svechkar, Aleksandrenko, Kozhukhar, Shubin	3	EJ	Tampere	27 Jul
3:09.02	CHN	(Wamg Youxin)	2	NG	Changsha	27 Oct
3:09.36	GBR	Davenport, R Williams, Charlton, Preddy	4	EJ	Tampere	27 Jul
3:09.70	JAM	D Brown, K Williams, Phillips, Bolt	1	Carifta	Port of Spain	21 Apr
3:11.56A	SUD	U18	1		Addis Ababa	21 May
3:11.56	CAN	Adjetey-Nelson, Dugal, Suddaby, Vadeboncoeur	2	PAm-J	Bridgetown	20 Jul
3:11.71	KEN	Leting, Rono Kipkorir, Polonet, Oabone	1	Af-J	Garoua	2 Aug
3:11.82	FRA	Venel, Atig, R Wallarde, Alerte	5	EJ	Tampere	27 Jul
3:12.27	ESP	Montero, Albalat, A Fernández, Testa	1		Almería	19 Jul
3:12.46	TRI	Pile, Francis, Charles, James	2	Carifta	Port of Spain	21 Apr

4 x 800 METRES RELAY

7:16.09	University of Arkansas	1	PennR	Philadelphia	26 Apr
	Mulvaney GBR 1:50.3, Hatch USA 1:48.2, Stevens USA 1:48.1, Taylor USA 1:49.5				
7:18.61	Georgetown Univ. USA LaGrenade, Najjar, Welsh, O'Connell	2	PennR	Philadelphia	26 Apr

4 x 1500 METRES RELAY

15:11.07	University of Arkansas	1	TexR	Philadelphia	5 Apr
	Taylor 3:50.6, Lincoln 3:47.4, Mulvaney GBR 3:47.3, Cragg IRL 3:45.8				

4 x 1 MILE RELAY

16:16.22	University of Arkansas	1	PennR	Philadelphia	26 Apr
	Ahmed 4:0.90, Lincoln 3:58.4, Mulvaney GBR 4:05.5, Cragg IRL 4:03.3				

4 x 110 METRES HURDLES

Mark	Name	Pos	Meet	Venue	Date
53.94	Univ. of South Carolina USA Taylor, Townsend, Ryan, Ferguson	1	PennR	Philadelphia	25 Apr
54.78	University of Florida USA Brown, Carswell, Walker, Ruff	1	FlaR	Gainesville	29 Mar
55.17	Univ. of Tennessee USA Boulware, Campbell, Greer, Jennings	1		Knoxville	12 Apr

3000 METRES WALK

Mark	Name		Nat	Born	Pos	Meet	Venue	Date
11:15.88	Alessandro	Gandellini	ITA	30.4.73	1		Castelfidardo	6 Sep
11:17.35	Matej	Tóth	SVK	10.2.83	1		Dubnica	7 Sep
11:17.69	Zdeno	Babik	SVK-J	9.1.84	2		Dubnica	7 Sep
11:17.91	Nathan	Deakes	AUS	17.8.77	1		Melbourne	6 Nov
11:19.51+	Robert	Korzeniowski	POL	30.7.68	1	in 5k	Warszawa	6 Sep

11:35.34	Giovanni	De Benedictis	ITA	8.1.68	6 Sep	11:37.88	Radovan	Elko	SVK	4.4.80	7 Sep
11:37.0	Maik	Berger	GER	17.2.79	13 Sep	11:39.57	Peter	Korcok	SVK	12.8.74	7 Sep

Indoors

11:03.65+	Alessandro	Gandellini	ITA	30.4.73	1	in 5k	Genova	1 Mar
11:04.52	Robert	Korzeniowski	POL	30.7.68	1		Mondeville	1 Feb
11:13.9	Matej	Tóth	SVK	10.2.83	1		Hlohovec	28 Nov
11:13.94+	Andreas	Erm	GER	12.3.76	1	in 5k	Leipzig	22 Feb

11:35.90	Tim	Seaman	USA	14.5.72	28 Dec	11:39.7	Kazimir	Verkin	SVK	27.3.72	28 Nov

5000 METRES WALK

18:55.33	Robert	Korzeniowski	POL	30.7.68	1		Warszawa	6 Sep
18:57.32	Hatem	Ghoula	TUN	7.6.73	1		Radès	28 Jun
19:06.2		Korzeniowski			1		Villeneuve d'Ascq	4 May
19:22.1	João	Vieira	POR	20.2.76	1		Lisboa (U)	24 May
	(4/3)							
19:28.09	Denis	Langlois	FRA	10.10.68	1		Reims	16 Jul
19:28.66	Tim	Seaman	USA	14.5.72	1		San Diego	7 Jun
19:28.86	Erik	Tysse	NOR	4.12.80	1	NC	Fredrikstad	9 Aug

19:33.6	Matej	Tóth	SVK	10.2.83	28 Jun	19:41.7	José David	Domínguez (10)	ESP	29.7.80	14 Jun
19:40.5	Milos	Bátovsky	SVK	26.5.79	28 Jun	19:42.92	Eiichi	Yoshizawa	JPN	5.9.80	17 May
19:40.8	Zdeno	Babik	SVK-J	9.1.84	28 Jun	19:43.24	Ivano	Brugnetti	ITA	1.9.76	9 Aug

Indoors

18:39.19	Alessandro	Gandellini	ITA	30.4.73	1	NC	Genova	1 Mar
18:42.4	Robert	Korzeniowski	POL	30.7.68	1		Liévin	9 Feb
18:45.81	Andreas	Erm	GER	12.3.76	1	NC	Leipzig	22 Feb
18:47.35	Ivano	Brugnetti	ITA	1.9.76	2	NC	Genova	1 Mar
18:58.69	Ilya	Markov	RUS	19.6.72	1		Yekaterinburg	7 Jan
18:58.89		Korzeniowski			1		Liévin	19 Jan
19:04.5	Andrey	Yurin	UKR-J	20.1.84	1		Brovary	18 Jan
19:06.57		Korzeniowski			2		Yekaterinburg	7 Jan
19:09.4	Mike	Trautmann	GER	13.3.74	1		Halle	18 Dec
19:16.95	Robert	Heffernan	IRL	28.2.78	1	NC	Belfast	15 Feb
19:19.72	Michele	Didoni	ITA	7.3.74	3	NC	Genova	1 Mar
19:21.56	Tim	Seaman	USA	14.5.72	1	NC	Boston (R)	2 Mar
19:22.0	Vasiliy	Ivanov	RUS	26.12.77	1		Cheboksary	10 Jan
19:26.43	John	Nunn	USA	3.2.78	2	NC	Boston (R)	2 Mar
19:31.0	Sergey	Petrov	RUS	26.11.80	2		Cheboksary	10 Jan

19:39.16	Enrico	Lang	ITA	31.3.72	1 Mar	19:40.39	Roman	Magdziarczyk	POL	5.7.77	1 Mar
19:39.5	Aleksandr	Yargunkin	RUS	6.1.81	7 Jan	**Indoors – Training competition**					
19:40.3	Aleksandr	Arkhipov	RUS	7.8.73	10 Jan	19:25.2	Peter	Barto	SVK	1.5.75	4 Jan

JUNIORS

19:59.6		Zhang Yuan	CHN	6.5.87	1	NC-y	Yangzhou	12 Apr
20:11.83	Chihiro	Yamane	JPN	.85	1		Hiroshima	30 May
20:20.26	Vladimir	Kanaykin	RUS	21.3.85	1	v2N	Szczecin	9 Aug
20:24.12	Luis Manuel	Corchete	ESP	14.5.84	1		Torrevieja	26 Apr

10,000 METRES WALK

39:14.16	Ivano	Brugnetti	ITA	1.9.76	1		Milano	28 Jun
39:29.45	Alessandro	Gandellini	ITA	30.4.73	1	WMilG	Catania	6 Dec
39:30.14	Hatem	Ghoula	TUN	7.6.73	1		Tunis	12 Apr
39:33.16	Ilya	Markov	RUS	19.6.72	2	WMilG	Catania	6 Dec
39:34.99	Ivan	Trotskiy	BLR	27.5.76	3	WMilG	Catania	6 Dec
39:36.95	Akinori	Matsuzaki	JPN	30.12.81	1		Tokyo	11 May
	(6/6)							
39:59.82	Akihiro	Sugimoto	JPN	20.10.81	1		Yokohama	6 Jul
40:02.06	Beniamin	Kucinski	POL	1.6.82	1		Spala	4 May
40:03.42	Takayuki	Tanii	JPN	14.2.83	2		Yokohama	6 Jul
40:04.28	Koji	Takada	JPN	31.12.83	2		Tokyo	11 May

Mark		Name	Nat	Born	Pos	Meet	Venue	Date
40:14.15	Lorenzo	Civallero	ITA	8.8.75	3		Milano	28 Jun
40:18.14		Lee Dae-ro	KOR	12.3.80	1		Bucheon	9 Apr

40:30.05 Kim Dong-young KOR 6.3.80 9 Apr | 40:33.87 Luis Fernando López COL 3.6.79 7 Dec
40:31.82 Vladimir Andreyev RUS 7.9.66 7 Dec | 40:42.39 Hwang Sang-eum KOR-J 3.3.85 13 Oct

JUNIORS

Mark		Name	Nat	Born	Pos	Meet	Venue	Date
40:42.39		Hwang Sang-jung	KOR	3.3.85	1	NG	Jeonju	13 Oct
40:52.58		Kim Hyun-sub	KOR	31.5.85	2	NG	Jeonju	13 Oct
40:58.7	Vladimir	Polyakov	RUS	2.1.85	1		Sankt-Peterburg	6 Jun
41:08.76	Kosuke	Takahashi	JPN	23.6.84	5		Yokohama	6 Jul
41:18.2		Xing Shucai	CHN	4.8.84	1	NC	Qinhangdao	28 Sep
41:20.48	Yuki	Yamazaki	JPN	16.1.84	7		Yokohama	6 Jul
41:22.8		Zhang Yuan	CHN	6.5.87	1	NC-y	Yangzhou	13 Apr
41:29.3	Ondrej	Kocúr	SVK	17.1.84	1		Banská Bystrica	12 Apr
41:33.55	Vladimir	Parvatshkin	RUS	10.10.84	1	EJ	Tampere	26 Jul
41:41.87	(10)	Byun Young-joon	KOR	20.3.84	1		Cheonan	11 Apr
41:47.0		Sun Chao	CHN-Y	8.1.87	2	NC	Qinhangdao	28 Sep
41:51.91	Satoshi	Yotsutani	JPN	15.8.84	11		Yokohama	6 Jul
41:54.66	Michal	Blazek	SVK	2.9.85	2	EJ	Tampere	26 Jul
41:55.00	Hiroshi	Okoshi	JPN	29.1.84	12		Yokohama	6 Jul
41:56.70	Francisco	Flores	MEX	18.8.84	3		Guadalajara	7 Jun
41:56.79	Gou	Kurose	JPN	21.5.84	13		Yokohama	6 Jul
41:57.8	Zdeno	Babík	SVK	9.1.84	3		Nitra	2 Mar
41:59.05		Yun Sang-bun	KOR	20.6.85	3	NG	Jeonju	13 Oct
42:03.27	Michael	Krause	GER	23.9.85	1	NC-j	Fulda	6 Jul
42:03.6	Sergey	Zemskov (20)	RUS	1.10.84	1		Cheboksary	7 Sep

20 KILOMETRES WALK

Mark		Name	Nat	Born	Pos	Meet	Venue	Date
1:17:21	Jefferson	Pérez	ECU	1.7.74	1	WCh	Saint-Denis	23 Aug
1:18:00	Francisco	Fernández	ESP	5.3.77	2	WCh	Saint-Denis	23 Aug
1:18:07	Roman	Rasskazov	RUS	28.4.79	3	WCh	Saint-Denis	23 Aug
1:18:14	Noé	Hernández	MEX	15.3.78	4	WCh	Saint-Denis	23 Aug
1:18:43		Zhu Hongjun	CHN	18.8.83	1	NC	Yangzhou	12 Apr
1:18:56		Yu Chaohong	CHN	12.12.76	2	NC	Yangzhou	12 Apr
1:19:06	Bernardo	Segura	MEX	11.2.70	1		Tijuana	8 Mar
1:19:08		Fernández			2		Tijuana	8 Mar
1:19:11	Robert	Korzeniowski	POL	30.7.68	3		Tijuana	8 Mar
1:19:14		Xu Xingde	CHN-J	12.6.84	3	NC	Yangzhou	12 Apr
1:19:25		Fernández			1		Sesto San Giovanni	1 May
1:19:35	Luke	Adams (10)	AUS	22.10.76	5	WCh	Saint-Denis	23 Aug
1:19:40	Ivan	Trotskiy	BLR	27.5.76	6	WCh	Saint-Denis	23 Aug
1:19:46	David	Márquez	ESP	13.10.77	7	WCh	Saint-Denis	23 Aug
1:19:48		Korzeniowski			2		Sesto San Giovanni	1 May
1:19:48		Fernández			1	ECp	Cheboksary	18 May
1:19:49	Alejandro	López	MEX	9.2.75	4		Tijuana	8 Mar
1:19:56		Korzeniowski			1		La Coruña	7 Jun
1:20:00		Han Yucheng	CHN	16.12.78	4	NC	Yangzhou	12 Apr
1:20:05	Ilya	Markov	RUS	19.6.72	1	NC-w	Adler	1 Mar
1:20:09		Pei Chuang	CHN	5.12.81	5	NC	Yangzhou	12 Apr
1:20:14		Markov			8	WCh	Saint-Denis	23 Aug
1:20:15	José David	Domínguez	ESP	29.7.80	9	WCh	Saint-Denis	23 Aug
1:20:24		López			10	WCh	Saint-Denis	23 Aug
1:20:28	Andrey	Stadnichuk	RUS	14.12.73	2	NC-w	Adler	1 Mar
1:20:28	Konstantin	Golubtsov	RUS	1.6.73	3	NC-w	Adler	1 Mar
1:20:30	João	Vieira (20)	POR	20.2.76	2		La Coruña	7 Jun
1:20:31	Toshihito	Fujinohara	JPN	19.9.75	1	NC	Kobe	28 Jan
1:20:31	Vasiliy	Ivanov	RUS	26.12.76	4	NC-w	Adler	1 Mar
1:20:34	Lorenzo	Civallero	ITA	8.8.75	11	WCh	Saint-Denis	23 Aug
	(30/23)							
1:20:38	Yuki	Yamazaki	JPN-J	16.1.84	2	NC	Kobe	28 Jan
1:20:38	Yevgeniy	Misyulya	BLR	13.3.64	12	WCh	Saint-Denis	23 Aug
1:20:44	Andre	Höhne	GER	10.3.78	13	WCh	Saint-Denis	23 Aug
1:20:45	Takayuki	Tanii	JPN	14.2.83	3	NC	Kobe	28 Jan
1:20:46	Akinori	Matsuzaki	JPN	30.12.81	1		Wajima	20 Apr
1:20:48		Bai Liansheng	CHN	28.7.78	6	NC	Yangzhou	12 Apr
1:20:51		Wang Shigang	CHN	22.2.81	7	NC	Yangzhou	12 Apr
	(30)							
1:20:52	Alessandro	Gandellini	ITA	30.4.73	2	ECp	Cheboksary	18 May
1:20:54		Lu Ronghua	CHN	21.2.83	8	NC	Yangzhou	12 Apr
1:20:56	Vladimir	Andreyev	RUS	7.9.66	3	ECp	Cheboksary	18 May

Mark	Name		Nat	Born	Pos	Meet	Venue	Date
1:20:56	Aigars	Fadejevs	LAT	27.12.75	5		La Coruña	7 Jun
1:20:56	Viktor	Burayev	RUS	23.2.82	1	NC	Cheboksary	16 Jun
1:21:06	Aleksey	Kronin	RUS	23.7.70	5	NC-w	Adler	1 Mar
1:21:10	Valeriy	Borisov	KAZ	18.9.66	6	NC-w	Adler	1 Mar
1:21:12	Hatem	Ghoula	TUN	7.6.73	14	WCh	Saint-Denis	23 Aug
1:21:23	Vladimir	Kanaykin	RUS-J	21.3.85	2	NC	Cheboksary	16 Jun
1:21:23	Michele	Didoni	ITA	7.3.74	16	WCh	Saint-Denis	23 Aug
	(40)							
1:21:27	Christian	Berdeja	MEX	21.6.81	6		La Coruña	7 Jun
1:21:32	Vladimir	Stankin	RUS	2.1.74	3	NC	Cheboksary	16 Jun
1:21:36	Eiichi	Yoshizawa	JPN	5.9.80	2		Wajima	20 Apr
1:21:39		Zhang Tianping	CHN	11.1.82	9	NC	Yangzhou	12 Apr
1:21:48.3t	José Alessandro	Baggio	BRA	16.4.81	1		Itajai	24 May
1:21:50	Predrag	Filipovic	SCG	5.10.78	1		Surcin	22 Mar
1:21:52		Lee Dae-ro	KOR	12.3.80	1	NC	Daegu	5 Jun
1:21:53	Jorge Ignacio	Silva	ESP	19.4.79	9		La Coruña	7 Jun
1:21:54		Liu Dashan	CHN	10.5.80	10	NC	Yangzhou	12 Apr
1:21:57	Juan Manuel	Molina	ESP	15.3.79	2		Rio Maior	5 Apr
	(50)							
1:21:59		Chang Chunhu	CHN	1.5.82	4	NC	Qinghangdao	27 Sep
1:22:01	Ivano	Brugnetti	ITA	1.9.76	1	NC	Rimini	8 Jun
1:22:06A	Julius	Sawe	KEN	21.11.71	1	WCT	Nairobi	26 Jul
1:22:07	Beniamin	Kucinski	POL	1.6.82	1	EU23	Bydgoszcz	19 Jul
1:22:07.5t	Sergey	Melentyev	RUS	5.12.76	1	NC	Izhevsk	22 Sep
1:22:09	Andrey	Makarov	BLR	2.1.71	1	NC	Brest	11 Jul
1:22:15.3t	Aleksandr	Arkhipov	RUS	7.8.73	2	NC	Izhevsk	22 Sep
1:22:20	Sergey	Lystsov	RUS	14.11.82	7	NC-w	Adler	1 Mar
1:22:25	Grigoriy	Sergeyev	RUS	27.4.76	8	NC-w	Adler	1 Mar
1:22:25	Kevin	Eastler	USA	14.10.77	18	WCh	Saint-Denis	23 Aug
	(60)							
1:22:33	Andrey	Talashko	BLR	31.5.82	2		Minsk	3 Jun
1:22:35	Andrey	Stepanchuk	BLR	12.6.79	2	NC	Brest	11 Jul
1:22:36	Akihiro	Sugimoto	JPN	20.10.81	4	AsiC	Manila	22 Sep
1:22:38		Park Chil-sung	KOR	8.7.82	2	NC	Daeju	5 Jun
1:22:39	Pyotr	Trofimov	RUS	18.12.83	9	NC-w	Adler	1 Mar
1:22:39	Alejandro	Cambil	ESP	26.1.75	1		Santa Eulalia	15 Mar
1:22:43	Erik	Tysse	NOR	4.12.80	19	WCh	Saint-Denis	23 Aug
1:22:46	Grzegorz	Sudol	POL	28.8.78	1		Zaniemysl	12 Apr
1:22:58		Xing Shucai	CHN-J	4.8.84	11	NC	Yangzhou	12 Apr
1:22:59	Yusuke	Yachi	JPN	2.1.80	4		Wajima	20 Apr
	(70)							
1:23:03		Yu Guohui	CHN	30.4.77	13	NC	Yangzhou	12 Apr
1:23:03	Robert	Heffernan	IRL	28.2.78	7		Sesto San Giovanni	1 May
1:23:09		Wang Weihua	CHN	8.1.83	7	NC	Qinghangdao	27 Sep
1:23:17	Matej	Tóth	SVK	10.2.83	1		Podebrady	5 Apr
1:23:23+	Semyon	Lovkin	RUS	14.7.77	1+	NC-w	Adler	1 Mar
1:23:23+	Denis	Nizhegorodov	RUS	26.7.80	1+	NC-w	Adler	1 Mar
1:23:23+	Stepan	Yudin	RUS	3.4.80	1+	NC-w	Adler	1 Mar
1:23:24+	Sergey	Kerdyapkin	RUS	16.1.80	5+	in 35k	Adler	1 Mar
1:23:24+	Marat	Ramazanov	RUS	5.3.64	5+	in 35k	Adler	1 Mar
1:23:24		Chang Wei	CHN	5.7.83	14	NC	Yangzhou	12 Apr
	(80)							
1:23:24	Yevgeniy	Yakovlev	RUS	17.6.79	3		Cheboksary	7 Sep
1:23:28	Denis	Langlois	FRA	10.10.68	12	ECp	Cheboksary	18 May
1:23:29	Sergey	Chernov	BLR	5.2.79	2	NC-w23	Brest	7 Mar
1:23:30	Marco	Giungi	ITA	30.10.74	9		Sesto San Giovanni	1 May
1:23:31	Trond	Nymark	NOR	28.12.76	2		Bergen	25 Jun
1:23:31	Takeaki	Akatsuma	JPN	27.11.81	2		Takahata	2 Nov
1:23:33.4t	Sérgio	Galdino	BRA	7.5.69	2		Itajai	24 May
1:23:36	Fumihiro	Kobayashi	JPN	21.7.83	3		Takahata	2 Nov
1:23:37+	Vladimir	Potemin	RUS	15.1.80	6	in 35k	Adler	1 Mar
1:23:46	Jirí	Malysa	CZE	14.8.66	14	ECp	Cheboksary	18 May
	(90)							
1:23:47	Viktor	Ginko	BLR	7.12.65	3	NC-w	Brest	7 Mar
1:23:47		Cui Zhide	CHN	11.1.83	15	NC	Yangzhou	12 Apr
1:23:49	Maik	Berger	GER	17.2.79	3		Dublin	12 Jul
1:23:51	Feodosei	Ciumacenco	MDA	27.1.73	11	RusC-w	Adler	1 Mar
1:23:57	Koji	Takada	JPN	31.12.83	5	NC	Kobe	28 Jan
1:23:57	Rafal	Dys	POL	14.1.82	3		Zaniemysl	12 Apr
1:23:58		Zhang Jianjun	CHN	4.12.78	16	NC	Yangzhou	12 Apr
1:24:00	Xavier	Moreno	ECU	15.11.79	2	NC	Portoviejo	29 Jun

Mark	Name		Nat	Born	Pos	Meet	Venue	Date
1:24:02	Tomasz	Lipiec	POL	10.5.71	3	NC	Bielsko-Biala	6 Jul
1:24:04	(100)	He Xiaodong	CHN	14.1.78	17	NC	Yangzhou	12 Apr
1:24:05		Chen Guangdong	CHN	19.1.83				12 Apr
1:24:07	Milos	Batovsky	SVK	26.5.79				6 Jul
1:24:09	Enrico	Lang	ITA	31.3.72				18 May
1:24:11	Liam	Murphy	AUS	5.6.79				26 Jul
1:24:12	Aleksey	Lopatin	RUS	30.4.77				1 Mar
1:24:12	Gyula	Dudás	HUN	20.8.66				5 Jul
1:24:14		Wang Xiaohong	CHN	15.5.83				12 Apr
1:24:15	Daniel	Andrei	ROM	26.6.71				6 Apr
1:24:17	Erick	Guevara	MEX	25.8.80				8 Mar
1:24:18	Elefthèros	Thanópoulos	GRE	22.2.75				5 Oct
1:24:20		Zhao Qingwei	CHN	17.8.83				12 Apr
1:24:21		Zhang Ronglong	CHN-J	2.11.84				12 Apr
1:24:22	Aleksey	Bakharev	RUS	10.11.79				1 Mar
1:24:23	Fumio	Imamura	JPN	5.11.66				28 Jan
1:24:23	Costica	Balan	ROM	25.8.64				13 Apr
1:24:25	Ken	Akashi	JPN	6.11.76				28 Jan
1:24:26	Nenad	Filipovic	SCG	5.10.78				18 May
1:24:29	Milos	Holusa	CZE	2.5.65				15 Jun
1:24:34	Cristian	Muñoz	CHI	15.2.81				15 Mar
1:24:35	Jésus	Sánchez	MEX	7.2.76				8 Mar
1:24:36	Aleksandr	Yargunkin	RUS	6.1.81				16 Jun
1:24:40		Wang Zhiping	CHN	11.12.83				12 Apr
1:24:41		Zeng Guoqiang	CHN-J	25.10.84				12 Apr
1:24:45		Kim Dong-young	KOR	6.3.80				20 Apr
1:24:46	Ivan	Kuznetsov	RUS	11.9.83				1 Mar
1:24:46		Dong Jimin	CHN-J	10.10.85				12 Apr
1:24:47.37t	Tim	Seaman	USA	14.5.72				20 Jun
1:24:47.7t	Martin	Pupis	SVK	19.10.78				2 Mar
1:24:48		Wang Yieying	CHN-Y	12.12.86				27 Sep
1:24:48		Shin Il-yong	KOR	17.2.79				12 Oct
1:24:49	Julio	Martínez	GUA	27.9.73				1 Jun
1:24:51	Augusto	Cardoso	POR	13.12.70				18 May
1:25:00		Gao Lianzuo	CHN-J	30.8.85				12 Apr

Best track times

1:23:34.7		Xu Xingde	CHN-J	12.6.84	1	NG	Changsha	24 Oct
1:23:52.2	Kevin	Eastler	USA	14.10.77	1	NC	Stanford	20 Jun

JUNIORS

See main list for top 4 juniors. Additional men:

1:24:21		Zhang Ronglong	CHN	2.11.84	21	NC	Yangzhou	12 Apr
1:24:41		Zeng Guoqiang	CHN	25.10.84	23	NC	Yangzhou	12 Apr
1:24:46		Dong Jimin	CHN	10.10.85	24	NC	Yangzhou	12 Apr
1:24:48		Wang Yieying	CHN-Y	12.12.86	2	NC-j	Qinghangdao	27 Sep
1:25:00		Gao Lianzuo	CHN	30.8.85	25		Yangzhou	12 Apr
1:25:12	(10)	Fang Mingbiao	CHN	3.12.84	10	NC	Qinhangdao	27 Sep
1:25:22		Sui Jiangfeng	CHN	29.5.84	29	NC	Yangzhou	12 Apr
1:25:23		Hiroshi Okoshi	JPN	29.1.84	9		Wajima	20 Apr
1:25:40		Mou Jichun	CHN	19.5.84	31	NC	Yangzhou	12 Apr
1:25:58		Sun Chao	CHN-Y	8.1.87	3	NC	Qinhangdao	27 Sep
1:26:12		Yang Jinshi	CHN	5.7.84	4	NC	Qinhangdao	27 Sep
1:26:18		Liu Wenjun	CHN-Y	8.1.87	5	NC	Qinhangdao	27 Sep
1:26:30	Yuki	Yamazaki	JPN	16.1.84	10		Wajima	20 Apr
1:26:33		Si Tianfeng	CHN	17.6.84	1	NC	Yangzhou	12 Apr
1:26:37		Li Jianbo	CHN-Y	14.11.86	12	NC	Qinhangdao	27 Sep
1:26:48	(20)	Yan Changhui	CHN-Y	20.3.87	35	NC	Yangzhou	12 Apr

30 KILOMETRES WALK

2:04:49+	Semyon	Lovkin	RUS	14.7.77	1=	in 35k	Adler	1 Mar
2:04:49+	Stepan	Yudin	RUS	3.4.80	1=	in 35k	Adler	1 Mar
2:05:06+	Sergey	Kerdyapkin	RUS	16.1.80	3	in 35k	Adler	1 Mar
2:05:28	Mikel	Odriozola	ESP	25.5.73	1		Badalona	19 Jan
2:05:39+	Aleksandr	Arkhipov	RUS	7.8.73	4	in 35k	Adler	1 Mar
2:06:21+		Kerdyapkin			1	in 35k	Cheboksary	7 Sep
2:06:33+	Marat	Ramazanov	RUS	5.3.64	5	in 35k	Adler	1 Mar
2:07:25+	Yuriy	Andronov	RUS	6.11.71	6	in 35k	Adler	1 Mar
2:10:34+	Sergey	Yerokhin	RUS	30.12.80	7	in 35k	Adler	1 Mar
2:10:47+	Aleksandr	Yargunkin	RUS	6.1.81	8	in 35k	Adler	1 Mar
2:11:01	Ivano (10)	Brugnetti	ITA	1.9.76	1		Livorno	23 Feb
2:11:02	José Antonio	González	ESP	15.6.79	2		Badalona	19 Jan
2:11:20+	Robert	Korzeniowski	POL	30.7.68	1	in 50k	Saint-Denis	27 Aug
2:11:38+	Andreas	Erm	GER	12.3.76	2	in 50k	Saint-Denis	27 Aug
2:11:41	Santiago	Pérez	ESP	15.1.72	3		Badalona	19 Jan
2:11:46+	Aleksandr	Strokov	RUS	6.1.81	9	in 35k	Adler	1 Mar
2:12:11	Robert	Heffernan	IRL	28.2.78	1	in 35k	Dublin	6 Dec
2:12:27+	Denis	Nizhegorodov	RUS	26.7.80	3=	in 50k	Saint-Denis	27 Aug
2:12:27+	German	Skurygin	RUS	15.9.63	3=	in 50k	Saint-Denis	27 Aug
2:12:30+	Aleksey	Voyevodin	RUS	9.8.70	5	in 50k	Saint-Denis	27 Aug
2:12:33	Marco	Giungi	ITA	30.10.74	2		Livorno	23 Feb
2:12:36	Jesús Ángel	García	ESP	17.10.69	4		Badalona	19 Jan
2:12:41	Sergey	Korepanov	KAZ	9.5.64				1 Mar
2:12:57	Alessandro	Mistretta	ITA	6.3.71				23 Feb
2:12:57+	Nathan	Deakes	AUS	17.8.77				7 Dec
2:13:53	Andrey	Yurin	UKR-J	20.1.84				18 Oct
2:13:54	Mario	Avellaneda	ESP	12.11.74				19 Jan
2:13:55	Diego	Cafagna (27)	ITA	9.7.75				23 Feb

35 KILOMETRES WALK

2:24:25	Semyon	Lovkin	RUS	14.7.77	1	NC-w	Adler	1 Mar
2:25:38	Stepan	Yudin	RUS	3.4.80	2	NC-w	Adler	1 Mar
2:26:31	Sergey	Kerdyapkin	RUS	16.1.80	3	NC-w	Adler	1 Mar

Mark	Name		Nat	Born	Pos	Meet	Venue	Date
2:26:54		Kerdyapkin			1		Cheboksary	7 Sep
2:28:01	Yuriy	Andronov	RUS	6.11.71	4	NC-w	Adler	1 Mar
2:28:40	Aleksandr	Arkhipov	RUS	7.8.73	5	NC-w	Adler	1 Mar
2:29:07	Marat	Ramazanov	RUS	11.11.64	6	NC-w	Adler	1 Mar
2:32:12	Sergey	Yerokhin	RUS	30.12.80	7	NC-w	Adler	1 Mar
2:32:29+	Robert	Korzeniowski	POL	30.7.68	1	in 50k	Saint-Denis	27 Aug
2:32:54+	Andreas	Erm	GER	12.3.76	2	in 50k	Saint-Denis	27 Aug
2:33:18	Vladimir	Potemin	RUS	15.1.80	8	NC-w	Adler	1 Mar
	(10)							
2:33:19+	German	Skurygin	RUS	15.9.63	3	in 50k	Saint-Denis	27 Aug
2:33:48+	Denis	Nizhegorodov	RUS	26.7.80	4	in 50k	Saint-Denis	27 Aug
2:33:56+	Aleksey	Voyevodin	RUS	9.8.70	5	in 50k	Saint-Denis	27 Aug
2:34:27	Aleksandr	Strokov	RUS	6.1.81	9	NC-w	Adler	1 Mar
2:35:02	Sergey	Korepanov	KAZ	9.5.64	10	RUS-w	Adler	1 Mar
2:35:40	Aleksandr	Yargunkin	RUS	6.1.81	11	NC-w	Adler	1 Mar
2:35:58	Robert	Heffernan	IRL	28.2.78	1	NC	Dublin	6 Dec

2:36:33+	Jesús Ángel	García	ESP	17.10.69	27 Aug
2:36:42	Andrey	Stepanchuk	BLR	12.6.79	27 Sep
2:36:42	Viktor	Ginko (20)	BLR	7.12.65	27 Sep
2:36:47+	Mikel	Odriozola	ESP	25.5.73	16 Feb
2:36:48+		Wang Yinhang	CHN	15.2.77	27 Aug
2:37:45+	Roman	Magdziarczyk	POL	5.7.77	27 Aug
2:37:53+	Denis	Langlois	FRA	10.10.68	27 Aug
2:38:24+	Aigars	Fadejevs	LAT	27.12.75	13 Apr
2:38:30+	Trond	Nymark	NOR	28.12.76	27 Aug
2:38:31	Valeriy	Spitsyn (27)	RUS	5.12.65	7 Sep

50 KILOMETRES WALK

Mark	Name		Nat	Born	Pos	Meet	Venue	Date
3:36:03	Robert	Korzeniowski	POL	30.7.68	1	WCh	Saint-Denis	27 Aug
3:36:42	German	Skurygin	RUS	15.9.63	2	WCh	Saint-Denis	27 Aug
3:37:46	Andreas	Erm	GER	12.3.76	3	WCh	Saint-Denis	27 Aug
3:38:01	Aleksey	Voyevodin	RUS	9.8.70	4	WCh	Saint-Denis	27 Aug
3:38:23	Denis	Nizhegorodov	RUS	26.7.80	5	WCh	Saint-Denis	27 Aug
3:39:43	Nathan	Deakes	AUS	17.8.77	1		Melbourne	7 Dec
3:42:03	Mikel	Odriozola	ESP	25.5.73	1	NC	Orense	16 Feb
3:43:27		Nizhegorodov			1	NC	Cheboksary	16 Jun
3:43:53		Erm			1	NC	Naumburg	13 Apr
3:43:56	Jesús Ángel	García	ESP	17.10.69	6	WCh	Saint-Denis	27 Aug
3:44:11		Yu Chaohong	CHN	12.12.76	1	NC	Yangzhou	14 Apr
3:44:53	Roman	Magdziarczyk (10)	POL	5.7.77	7	WCh	Saint-Denis	27 Aug
3:45:27	Vladimir	Potemin	RUS	15.1.80	2	NC	Cheboksary	16 Jun
3:46:03		García			2	NC	Orense	16 Feb
3:46:03	Aigars	Fadejevs	LAT	27.12.75	2		Naumburg	13 Apr
3:46:14	Trond	Nymark	NOR	28.12.76	8	WCh	Saint-Denis	27 Aug
3:46:46		García			1		Tijuana	9 Mar
3:46:49		Nymark			3		Naumburg	13 Apr
3:47:36	Nikolay	Matyukhin	RUS	13.12.68	3	NC	Cheboksary	16 Jun
3:47:42	Sergey	Korepanov	KAZ	9.5.64	9	WCh	Saint-Denis	27 Aug
3:47:49		Yu Chaohong			1	NC	Qinhangdao	29 Sep
3:47:50		Skurygin			1	ECp	Cheboksary	18 May
3:47:54	Takayuki	Tanii	JPN	14.2.83	1		Takahata	2 Nov
3:48:11		Wang Yinhang	CHN	15.2.77	2	NC	Yangzhou	14 Apr
3:48:26	Yuriy	Andronov	RUS	6.11.71	4	NC	Cheboksary	16 Jun
3:48:43		Voyevodin			2	ECp	Cheboksary	18 May
3:49:05	Denis	Langlois	FRA	10.10.68	10	WCh	Saint-Denis	27 Aug
3:49:29		Korepanov			4		Naumburg	13 Apr
3:49:35	Mario	Avellaneda (20)	ESP	12.11.74	3	NC	Orense	16 Feb
3:50:34	Craig	Barrett	NZL	16.11.71	2		Melbourne	7 Dec
	(30/21)							
3:51:36	Semyon	Lovkin	RUS	14.7.77	3	ECp	Cheboksary	18 May
3:51:37	Eiichi	Yoshizawa	JPN	5.9.80	2		Takahata	2 Nov
3:51:51		Bian Aiguo	CHN	10.6.80	3	NC	Yangzhou	14 Apr
3:52:18		Li Hongguang	CHN	10.2.80	4	NC	Yangzhou	14 Apr
3:52:45		Bai Liansheng	CHN	28.7.78	5	NC	Yangzhou	14 Apr
3:52:57	Santiago	Pérez	ESP	15.1.72	4	ECp	Cheboksary	18 May
3:53:10		Zhang Defu	CHN-J	5.6.84	6	NC	Yangzhou	14 Apr
3:53:18	Eddy	Riva	FRA	17.4.73	11	WCh	Saint-Denis	27 Aug
3:53:24	Germán	Sánchez	MEX	31.7.67	12	WCh	Saint-Denis	27 Aug
	(30)							
3:53:31	Luis F	García	GUA	13.9.74	5		Naumburg	13 Apr
3:53:58	Jamie	Costin	IRL	1.6.77	6		Naumburg	13 Apr
3:54:01	Francisco	Pinardo	ESP	15.3.75	5	ECp	Cheboksary	18 May
3:54:11	Ken	Akashi	JPN	6.11.76	3		Takahata	2 Nov
3:54:12	Peter	Korcok	SVK	12.8.74	13	WCh	Saint-Denis	27 Aug
3:54:16	Marat	Ramazanov	RUS	5.3.64	5	NC	Cheboksary	16 Jun

Mark	Name		Nat	Born	Pos	Meet	Venue	Date
3:54:21		Gadasu Alatan	CHN-J	27.1.84	2	NC	Qinhangdao	29 Sep
3:54:45		Han Yucheng	CHN	16.12.78	7	NC	Yangzhou	14 Apr
3:55:00	José Antonio	González	ESP	15.6.79	4	NC	Orense	16 Feb
3:55:13	Yoshimi	Hara	JPN	2.3.68	4		Takahata	2 Nov
	(40)							
3:55:20	José David	Domínguez	ESP	29.7.80	5	NC	Orense	16 Feb
3:55:26	Stepan	Yudin	RUS	3.4.80	6	ECp	Cheboksary	18 May
3:55:39		Chang Chunhu	CHN	1.5.82	8	NC	Yangzhou	14 Apr
3:55:40	Grzegorz	Sudol	POL	28.8.78	1		Wien	5 Oct
3:56:04	Jefferson	Pérez	ECU	1.7.74	8		Naumburg	13 Apr
3:56:26	Bengt	Bengtsson	SWE	4.9.61	9		Naumburg	13 Apr
3:56:29		Ao Xinli	CHN	26.1.81	9	NC	Yangzhou	14 Apr
3:56:31	Fredrik	Svensson	SWE	10.9.73	15	WCh	Saint-Denis	27 Aug
3:56:41	Spirídon	Kastánis	GRE	23.9.64	16	WCh	Saint-Denis	27 Aug
3:56:44		Zhang Tianping	CHN	11.1.82	3	NC	Qinhangdao	29 Sep
	(50)							
3:57:06	Zoltán	Czukor	HUN	18.12.62	2		Wien	5 Oct
3:57:12	Aleksey	Shelest	UKR	27.3.73	1	NC-w	Yevpatoria	22 Feb
3:57:42	Pedro	Martins	POR	12.1.68	1	NC	São João de Madeira	1 Mar
3:58:05	Milos	Holusa	CZE	2.5.65	9	ECp	Cheboksary	18 May
3:58:20	Aleksey	Kazanin	UKR	22.5.82	2	NC-w	Yevpatoria	22 Feb
3:58:41	Yeóryios	Aryirópoulos	GRE	20.1.70	1		Athínai	12 Oct
3:58:52		Zhao Qingwei	CHN	17.8.83	10	NC	Yangzhou	14 Apr
3:58:58	Sérgio	Galdino	BRA	7.5.69	1		Porto Alegre	26 Apr
3:58:59	Mário José	dos Santos	BRA	10.9.79	2		Porto Alegre	26 Apr
3:59:20	Fumio	Imamura	JPN	5.11.66	1	NC	Wajima	20 Apr
	(60)							
3:59:20	Marco	Giungi	ITA	30.10.74	1		Reggio Calabria	12 Oct
3:59:23		Si Tianfeng	CHN-J	17.6.84	5	NC	Qinhangdao	29 Sep
3:59:24	János	Tóth	HUN	15.4.78	11	ECp	Cheboksary	18 May
3:59:30	José Ignacio	Díaz	ESP	22.11.79	6	NC	Orense	16 Feb
3:59:33	Duane	Cousins	AUS	13.7.73	1	NC	Melbourne	18 May
3:59:37	Marek	Janek	SVK	29.1.77	2	NC	Dudince	29 Mar
3:59:37		Cui Zhide	CHN	11.1.83	11	NC	Yangzhou	14 Apr
3:59:46		Zhang Huabing	CHN	28.9.83	12	NC	Yangzhou	14 Apr
3:59:52		Pei Chuang	CHN	5.12.81	13	NC	Yangzhou	14 Apr
3:59:57		Qu Fanhua	CHN	21.2.77	14	NC	Yangzhou	14 Apr
	(70)							
4:00:05	David	Boulanger	FRA	11.12.74	2		Miramas	16 Mar
4:00:17		Dong Jimin	CHN-J	10.10.85	15	NC	Yangzhou	14 Apr
4:00:50	Valeriy	Spitsyn	RUS	5.12.65	6	NC	Cheboksary	16 Jun
4:00:51	Yuriy	Burban	UKR	18.4.80	12	ECp	Cheboksary	18 May
4:00:52	Juan Antonio	Porras	ESP	19.2.72	7	NC	Orense	16 Feb
4:01:01	Jeffrey	Cassin	IRL	15.12.71	13	ECp	Cheboksary	18 May
4:01:46		Zhao Yongsheng	CHN	16.4.70	17	NC	Yangzhou	14 Apr
4:01:58	David	Sánchez	ESP	23.8.73	1		Dublin	12 Jul
4:01:59		Wang Weijun	CHN	31.12.80	18	NC	Yangzhou	14 Apr
4:02:03	Tim	Berrett	CAN	23.1.65	19	WCh	Saint-Denis	27 Aug
	(80)							
4:02:21		Li Yi	CHN	19.1.81	19	NC	Yangzhou	14 Apr
4:02:25	Diego	Cafagna	ITA	9.7.75	15	ECp	Cheboksary	18 May
4:02:26	Hironori	Kawai	JPN	3.2.76	1		Kobe	26 Jan
4:03:08		Li Jianbo	CHN-Y	14.11.86	7	NC	Qinhangdao	29 Sep
4:03:23		Wang Shigang	CHN	22.2.81	9	NC	Qinhangdao	29 Sep
4:04:07		Sun Chao	CHN-Y	8.1.87	20	NC	Yangzhou	14 Apr
4:04:07	Birger	Fält	SWE	12.8.68	17	ECp	Cheboksary	18 May
4:04:18	Alessandro	Mistretta	ITA	6.3.71	18	ECp	Cheboksary	18 May
4:04:26	Jorge	Costa	POR	20.3.61	2		São João de Madeira	1 Mar
4:04:53		Wang Yieying	CHN-Y	12.12.86	10	NC	Qinhangdao	29 Sep
	(90)							
4:04:56	Liam	Murphy	AUS	5.6.79	2	NC	Melbourne	18 May
4:05:20	Denis	Trautmann	GER	15.8.72	19	ECp	Cheboksary	18 May
4:05:57	Aleksandr	Romanenko	UKR	26.6.81	4	NC-w	Yevpatoria	22 Feb
4:06:06	Enrico	Lang	ITA	31.3.72	1+		Scanzorosciate	19 Oct
4:06:30	Pascal	Servanty	FRA	26.5.66	3		Miramas	16 Mar
4:06:36	Viktor	Ginko	BLR	7.12.65	1		Lugano	7 Sep
4:06:37	Milos	Batovsky	SVK	26.5.79	4	NC	Dudince	29 Mar
4:06:39	Rafal	Fedaczynski	POL	3.12.80	1	NC	Zaniemysl	12 Apr
4:06:43	Andrey	Stepanchuk	BLR	12.6.79	2		Lugano	7 Sep
4:06:54	Mike	Trautmann	GER	13.3.74	10	2 NC	Naumburg	13 Apr
	(100)							

Mark		Name	Nat	Born	Date
4:06:57		He Lin	CHN	1.3.83	14 Apr
4:07:02	Yusuke	Yachi	JPN	2.1.80	2 Nov
4:07:04	Maciej	Rosiewicz	POL	31.7.77	12 Apr
4:07:22	Aleksandr	Andrushevskiy	BLR	4.3.78	7 Sep
4:07:40	Anatoliy	Malivskiy	UKR	3.3.66	22 Feb
4:07:42	Theódoros	Stamatópoulos	GRE	24.4.70	12 Oct
4:07:50		Liu Yong	CHN	1.3.83	14 Apr
4:08:02	Maik	Berger	GER	17.2.79	13 Apr
4:08:36	Curt	Clausen	USA	9.10.67	25 May
4:08:38	Akihiko	Koike	JPN	10.4.73	20 Apr
4:08:46		Gao Lianzuo	CHN-J	30.8.85	14 Apr
4:09:47	(112)	Han Guodong	CHN-J	8.5.84	14 Apr

JUNIORS

See main list for top 7 juniors. Additional men:

Mark		Name	Nat	Born	Pos	Meet	Venue	Date
4:08:46		Gao Lianzuo	CHN	30.8.85	1	NC-j	Yangzhou	14 Apr
4:09:47		Han Guodong	CHN	8.5.84	2	NC-j	Yangzhou	14 Apr
4:10:43	(10)	Zhang Jiawei	CHN-Y	27.10.86	13	NC	Qinhangdao	29 Sep
4:12:11		Bai Yun	CHN	1.4.84	26	NC	Yangzhou	14 Apr
4:17:54		Ren Zhenjiang	CHN-Y	7.1.86	28	NC	Yangzhou	14 Apr
4:19:22		Fang Mingbiao	CHN	3.12.84	19	NC	Qinhangdao	29 Sep

100 KILOMETRES WALK

Mark		Name	Nat	Born	Pos	Venue	Date
8:44:28	Viktor	Ginko	BLR	7.12.65	1	Scanzoroscaite	19 Oct
8:59:52	Zoltán	Czukor	HUN	18.12.62	2	Scanzoroscaite	19 Oct
9:04:57	Peter	Tichy	SVK	12.3.69	3	Scanzoroscaite	19 Oct
9:09:08	Sergey	Chernov	BLR	5.2.79	4	Scanzoroscaite	19 Oct
9:19:48	Andrey	Stepanchuk	BLR	12.6.79	5	Scanzoroscaite	19 Oct
9:22:55	Aleksey	Shelest	UKR	27.3.73	6	Scanzoroscaite	19 Oct
9:29:44	Róbert	Tubak	HUN	1.3.79	7	Scanzoroscaite	19 Oct
9:33:14	Yuriy	Burban	UKR	18,4,80	8	Scanzoroscaite	19 Oct
9:38:48	Aleksandr	Andrushevskiy	BLR	4.3.78	9	Scanzoroscaite	19 Oct
9:42:32	Roberto	Defendeti	ITA	30.5.68	10	Scanzoroscaite	19 Oct
9:44:46	David	Régy	FRA	1.5.69	11	Scanzoroscaite	19 Oct
9:44:47	Ferenc	Major	HUN	30.3.61	12	Scanzoroscaite	19 Oct

WOMEN'S WORLD LISTS 2003

100 METRES

Mark	Wind		Name	Nat	Born	Pos	Meet	Venue	Date
10.85	0.9	Kelli	White	USA	1.4.77	1	WCh	Saint-Denis	24 Aug
10.86	1.2	Chryste	Gaines	USA	14.9.70	1	WAF	Monaco	14 Sep
10.87	-0.1		White			1	VD	Bruxelles	5 Sep
10.88	-0.1		Gaines			2	VD	Bruxelles	5 Sep
10.89	0.0	Chandra	Sturrup	BAH	12.9.71	1	GGala	Roma	11 Jul
10.89	-0.1		Gaines			1rA	WK	Zürich	15 Aug
10.93	-1.1		White			1	NC	Stanford	20 Jun
10.93	1.3		White			1	GP	London (CP)	8 Aug
10.93	0.9	Torri	Edwards	USA	31.1.77	2	WCh	Saint-Denis	24 Aug
10.96	0.7		White			1	Pre	Eugene	24 May
10.96	0.3		Sturrup			1	Bisl	Oslo	27 Jun
10.96	0.2		White			1q3	WCh	Saint-Denis	23 Aug
10.96	0.8		White			1s1	WCh	Saint-Denis	24 Aug
10.97	1.2	Debbie	Ferguson	BAH	16.1.76	1		Durban	11 Apr
10.97	0.8		White			1rA	MSR	Walnut	19 Apr
10.97	0.3		White			2	Bisl	Oslo	27 Jun
10.97	-0.1		Sturrup			2rA	WK	Zürich	15 Aug
10.98	0.0		Sturrup			1q1	WCh	Saint-Denis	23 Aug
10.98	-0.1		Edwards			3	VD	Bruxelles	5 Sep
10.98	0.0		Gaines			1		Moskva	20 Sep
10.99	0.0		White			2	GGala	Roma	11 Jul
10.99	1.3		Gaines			1	GP	London (CP)	8 Aug
10.99	0.9	Zhanna	Block	UKR	6.7.72	3	WCh	Saint-Denis	24 Aug
11.01			Sturrup			1	NC	Freeport	19 Jun
11.01	-0.4		Sturrup			1	Gaz	Saint-Denis	4 Jul
11.01	0.8	Christine	Arron	FRA	13.9.73	2s1	WCh	Saint-Denis	24 Aug
11.01	-0.1		Sturrup			4	VD	Bruxelles	5 Sep
11.02A	-0.6		Gaines			1		Ciudad de México	3 May
11.02	0.9		Sturrup			4	WCh	Saint-Denis	24 Aug
11.02	0.8		Block			3s1	WCh	Saint-Denis	24 Aug
		(30/7)							
11.03	0.9	Ekateríni	Thánou	GRE	1.2.75	5	WCh	Saint-Denis	24 Aug
11.04	0.8	Muna	Lee	USA	30.10.81	2rA	MSR	Walnut	19 Apr
11.05	1.7	Natalya	Safronnikova	BLR	28.2.73	1		Minsk	28 Jun
		(10)							
11.07	0.9	Aleen	Bailey	JAM	25.11.80	7	WCh	Saint-Denis	24 Aug

Mark	Wind	Name		Nat	Born	Pos	Meet	Venue	Date
11.08	0.7	LaTasha	Richardson	USA	23.8.76	3	Pre	Eugene	24 May
11.08	-0.1	Muriel	Hurtis	FRA	25.3.79	4rA	WK	Zürich	15 Aug
11.09	0.8	Natasha	Mayers	VIN	10.3.79	3rA	MSR	Walnut	19 Apr
11.09	2.0	Mary	Onyali	NGR	3.2.68	1		Austin	3 May
11.11	0.2	Marina	Kislova	RUS	7.2.78	1		Luzern	25 Jun
11.11	0.9	Gail	Devers	USA	19.11.66	8	WCh	Saint-Denis	24 Aug
11.12	1.7	Lauryn	Williams	USA	11.9.83	1	PAm	Santo Domingo	6 Aug
11.14	0.7	Ivet	Lalova	BUL-J	18.5.84	1	NC-23	Sofia	14 Jun
11.15	1.5	Erica	Whipple	USA	4.12.82	2	SEC	Knoxville	18 May
		(20)							
11.15	1.6	Angela	Williams	USA	30.1.80	2	PAm	Santo Domingo	6 Aug
11.15	0.0	Karin	Mayr-Krifka	AUT	4.6.71	1	NC	Salzburg	9 Aug
11.16	1.0	Inger	Miller	USA	12.6.72	1	Mod R	Modesto	10 May
11.16	0.1	Endurance	Ojokolo	NGR	29.9.75	1s2	AfG	Abuja	11 Oct
11.17	1.8	Brigitte	Foster	JAM	7.11.74	1	Barr	La Habana	31 May
11.18	-0.2	Lyubov	Perepelova	UZB	26.2.79	1	NC	Tashkent	5 Sep
11.20	1.2	Geraldine	Pillay	RSA	25.8.77	2		Durban	11 Apr
11.20	0.4	Elva	Goulbourne	JAM	21.1.80	2	NC	Kingston	20 Jun
11.20	0.3	Yuliya	Tabakova	RUS	1.5.80	1	MAI	Malmö	12 Aug
11.20	-0.1	Susanthika	Jayasinghe	SRI	17.12.75	2h4	WCh	Saint-Denis	23 Aug
		(30)							
11.21A	-0.6	LaTasha	Jenkins	USA	19.12.77	3		Ciudad de México	3 May
11.21	1.5	Kim	Gevaert	BEL	5.8.78	1	ECCp	Valencia	24 May
11.21	1.7	Connie	Moore	USA	29.8.81	3	NCAA-r	Fairfax	31 May
11.21	0.7	Nolle	Graham	USA	12.9.81	1		Bloomington	19 Jul
11.22	1.9	Rachelle	Boone	USA	30.6.81	1h1	NCAA-r	Columbus	30 May
11.22	0.6	Merlene	Ottey	SLO	10.5.60	1		Velenje	7 Jun
11.22	-0.7	Mercy	Nku	NGR	17.7.76	2rB	GGala	Roma	11 Jul
11.22	0.1	Vida	Anim	GHA	7.12.83	1		Malles	12 Jul
11.23	1.7	Fana	Ashby	TRI	15.6.81	1	NC	Port of Spain	20 Jun
11.23	1.0	Anzhela	Kravchenko	UKR	25.1.71	1		San Sebastián	10 Aug
		(40)							
11.24	0.7	Tayna	Lawrence	JAM	17.9.75	6	Pre	Eugene	24 May
11.24	0.4	Beverly	McDonald	JAM	15.2.70	3	NC	Kingston	20 Jun
11.24	0.5	Delphine	Atangana	CMR-J	16.8.84	2s1	Afr G	Abuja	11 Oct
11.25	0.9	Tatyana	Tkalich	UKR	30.5.75	1		Kharkov	17 May
11.25	0.6	Yelena	Nevmerzhitskaya	BLR	27.7.80	1		Minsk	21 May
11.25	0.7	Yelena	Pastushenko	UKR	14.7.79	1h2		Kiev	26 May
11.25	-0.6	Esther	Möller	GER	13.9.77	1		Rehlingen	9 Jun
11.26	1.0	Cydonie	Mothersill	CAY	19.3.78	1		Auburn	4 May
11.26	1.6	Judyth	Kitson	JAM	2.11.79	2h1	SEC	Knoxville	17 May
11.28	1.5	Sanya	Richards	USA-J	26.2.85	1h2	Big 12	Austin	18 May
		(50)							
11.28	1.8	Lakadron	Ivery	USA	23.6.83	1h1	NCAA-r	Lincoln, NE	30 May
11.28	0.8	Sylviane	Félix	FRA	31.10.77	1h2		Castres	6 Aug
11.28	1.6	Liliana	Allen	MEX	24.5.70	3	PAm	Santo Domingo	6 Aug
11.28	1.6	Vírgen	Benavídes	CUB	31.12.74	4	PAm	Santo Domingo	6 Aug
11.29	1.4	Allyson	Felix	USA-J	18.11.85	1		Norwalk	7 Jun
11.29	0.9	Joice	Maduaka	GBR	30.9.73	2		Villeneuve d'Ascq	15 Jun
11.29	-1.3	Glory	Alozie	ESP	30.12.77	3	ECp-S	Firenze	21 Jun
11.29	0.0	Juliet	Campbell	JAM	17.3.70	2		Poznan	29 Jun
11.29	-0.7	Agné	Visockaite-Eggerth	LTU	4.8.78	5rB	GGala	Roma	11 Jul
11.30	0.5	Guzel	Khubbieva	UZB	2.5.76	1		Bangkok	5 Jun
		(60)							
11.31	1.3	Olga	Fyodorova	RUS	14.7.83	2h1	Znam	Tula	8 Jun
11.31	1.4	Oksana	Dragun	BLR	19.4.81	2		Minsk	28 Jun
11.31	1.8	Jessica	Onyepunuka	USA-Y	3.5.86	1	WY	Sherbrooke	11 Jul
11.31	0.1	Marion	Wagner	GER	1.2.78	2		Malles	12 Jul
11.31	0.0	Manuela	Levorato	ITA	16.3.77	1		Carbonia	5 Sep
11.33	1.4	LaShauntea	Moore	USA	31.7.83	1		Fayetteville	12 Apr
11.33	0.6	Tameka	Clarke	BAH	9.11.80	2	CAC	St George's	5 Jul
11.33	1.7	Véronique	Mang	FRA-J	15.12.84	1	NC-23	Vénissieux	12 Jul
11.33	1.3	Yeoryía	Koklóni	GRE	7.5.81	1	EU23	Bydgoszcz	19 Jul
11.33	0.8	Katia	Benth	FRA	16.11.75	1h1		Castres	6 Aug
		(70)							
11.34	1.2	Kerron	Stewart	JAM-J	16.4.84	1	N.Sch	Kingston	4 Apr
11.35	0.3	Rosa	Rakotozafy	MAD	12.11.77	1		Yaoundé	12 Apr
11.35	1.1	Shalonda	Solomon	USA-J	19.12.85	1		Norwalk	24 May
11.35	0.2	Digna	Murillo	COL	22.5.81	1	SACh	Barquisimeto	20 Jun
11.35	0.0	Patient	Edem	NGR	15.10.83	2s2	NC	Abuja	17 Jul
11.35	1.9	Johanna	Manninen	FIN	4.4.80	1	NC	Helsinki	10 Aug

Mark	Wind	Name		Nat	Born	Pos	Meet	Venue	Date
11.36	1.2	Winneth	Dube	ZIM	10.5.72	4		Durban	11 Apr
11.36	1.0	Angela	Daigle	USA	28.5.76	3	Mod R	Modesto	10 May
11.36	0.6	Abiodun	Oyepitan	GBR	30.12.79	3	Kuso	Warszawa	15 Jun
11.36	0.0	Savatheda (80)	Fynes	BAH	17.10.74	6q4	WCh	Saint-Denis	23 Aug
11.37	1.1	Sherone	Simpson	JAM-J	12.8.84	2	N.Sch	Kingston	4 Apr
11.37	1.4	Laverne	Jones	ISV	16.9.81	2h1	Big 12	Austin	18 May
11.37	1.3	LaJuana	Lovett	USA	7.5.82	1		San Marcos	19 May
11.38A	0.3	Janice	Josephs	RSA	31.3.82	1		Bloemfontein	7 Feb
11.38	1.2	Makaridja	Sanganoko	CIV	8.5.80	5		Durban	11 Apr
11.38	1.6	Melanie	Paschke	GER	29.6.70	2h2		Rehlingen	9 Jun
11.39	1.7	Gloria	Kemasuode	NGR	30.12.79	1h1		Canberra	15 Mar
11.39	0.8	Mileydis	Lazo	CUB	7.9.81	2		La Habana	27 Jun
11.39	0.0		Qin Wangping	CHN	16.6.82	1	NC	Shanghai	12 Sep
11.40	1.7	Amandi (90)	Rhett	USA	29.6.82	1		Atlanta	17 May
11.40	-0.8	Larisa	Kruglova	RUS	27.10.72	3	NC	Tula	8 Aug
11.41	1.4	Monique	Tubbs	USA	23.1.81	2h7	Tex R	Austin	4 Apr
11.41	0.7	Crystal	Cox	USA	28.3.79	2		Bloomington	19 Jul
11.41	0.0	Aleksandra	Prokofjev	SLO	28.11.71	1	NC	Nova Gorica	9 Aug
11.42	1.6	Gabrielle	Rockmeier	GER	29.11.73	3h2		Rehlingen	9 Jun
11.43	1.5	Amber	Robinson	USA	5.6.80	6	SEC	Knoxville	18 May
11.43	1.9	Ara	Towns	USA	26.3.83	3h1	NCAA-r	Columbus	30 May
11.43	-0.6	Martina	Feusi	SUI	17.6.74	4		Rehlingen	9 Jun
11.43	0.2	Lucimar	de Moura	BRA	22.3.74	2	SACh	Barquisiemto	20 Jun
11.43	1.6	Krystin (100)	Lacy	USA-Y	8.7.87	1h6	WY	Sherbrooke	10 Jul

11.44	0.0	Illia	Miles	USA	11.1.82	3 May
11.44	0.8	Shana	Robinson	USA	13.2.82	17 May
11.44	1.6	Sina	Schielke	GER	19.5.81	15 Jun
11.44	0.2	Chinedu	Odozor	NGR	24.12.77	25 Jun
11.44	0.6	Cynthia	Octavia	FRA	16.6.78	28 Jun
11.44	0.1	Maja	Nose	SLO	12.5.82	12 Jul
11.44	1.3	Erica	Witter	CAN	10.12.76	19 Jul
11.44	1.3	Priscilla	Lopes	CAN	26.8.82	19 Jul
11.45	0.3	Aida	Diop	SEN	27.4.70	12 Apr
11.45	0.8	Miesha	McKelvy	USA	26.7.76	19 Apr
11.45	1.9	Motoka	Arai	JPN	4.7.74	5 May
11.45	0.1	Oranut	Klomdee	THA	1.6.80	28 May
11.45	0.6	Yuliya	Nesterenko	BLR	15.6.79	3 Jun
11.45	1.1	Patricia	Girard	FRA	8.4.68	7 Sep
11.46	1.2	Wendy	Seegers	RSA	28.2.76	11 Apr
11.46	1.3	Natalya	Ignatova	RUS	28.12.73	8 Jun
11.46	1.3	Daria	Onysko	POL	30.7.81	19 Jul
11.47	-0.9	Sharon	Cripps	AUS	29.6.77	22 Feb
11.47	-0.5		Chen Shu-Chuan	TPE	20.4.78	23 Mar
11.47	0.3	Monica	Twum	GHA	14.3.78	17 May
11.47	1.5	Zenobia	Reed	USA-J	24.1.84	18 May
11.47	1.5	Aleah	Williams	USA	7.1.81	18 May
11.47	0.7	Irina	Kozhemyakina	UKR	16.6.80	26 May
11.47	1.8	Roxana	Díaz	CUB	17.5.81	31 May
11.47	0.3	Marina	Maydanova	UKR	22.8.82	15 Jun
11.47	0.4	Aminata	Diouf	SEN	18.2.77	6 Aug
11.48	0.3	Keenan	Gibson	TRI	3.10.78	17 May
11.48	1.3	Rikki	Holland	USA	6.8.79	19 May
11.48	1.8	Ananka	Clark	USA	18.5.81	30 May
11.48	0.5	Marilia	Gregoriou	CYP	13.2.80	3 Jun
11.48	0.5	Kelli-Ann	Baptiste	TRI-Y	14.10.86	9 Jun
11.48	0.4	Danielle	Browning	JAM	29.8.81	20 Jun
11.49	1.4	Merlene	Frazer	JAM	27.12.73	19 Apr
11.49	-0.5	Sylvie	Mballa Eloundou	FRA	21.4.77	26 Apr
11.49	1.5	Gloria	Asumnu	USA-J	22.5.85	10 May
11.49	-0.5	Oksana	Kaydash	UKR	16.6.74	12 Aug
11.49	0.8	Odiah	Sidibé	FRA	13.1.70	16 Aug
11.49	0.5	Affoué Amandine	Allou	CIV	.80	11 Oct
11.50	1.6	SaDonna	Thornton	USA	16.8.78	5 Apr
11.50	1.2	Shereefa	Lloyd	JAM	2.9.82	17 Apr
11.50	-0.5	Teneeshia	Jones	USA	28.1.79	26 Apr
11.50	1.0	Peta-Gaye	Dowdie	JAM	18.1.77	10 May
11.50A	1.8	Melinda	Smedley	USA	11.2.81	16 May
11.50A	0.8	Nina	Mayes	USA	10.8.83	17 May
11.50	0.7	Danielle	Carruthers	USA	22.12.79	18 May
11.50	1.5	Shavonda	Benjamin	USA	16.6.82	18 May
11.50	-2.1	Tarama	Perry-Self	CAN	20.11.74	4 Jun
11.50	0.2	Enikö	Szabó	HUN	10.11.79	7 Jun
11.50	1.1	Elodie	Ouédraogo	BEL	27.2.81	29 Jun
11.50	1.3	Joan	Uduak Ekah (150)	NGR	16.12.80	9 Jul
11.50	0.3	Yelena	Bolsun	RUS	25.6.82	25 Aug
11.51	0.6	Alenka	Bikar	SLO	7.1.74	7 Jun
11.52	1.5	Cheasa	Gibson	USA	14.12.80	3 May
11.52	0.2	Ginnie	Powell	USA	7.9.83	18 May
11.52	0.7	Sierra	Hauser-Price	USA	17.12.83	18 May
11.52	1.3	Irina	Khabarova	RUS	18.3.66	8 Jun
11.52	1.4	Rosemar	Coelho Neto	BRA	2.1.77	16 Jul
11.52	1.3	Asha	James	CAN	3.9.79	19 Jul
11.52	1.2	Ciara	Sheehy	IRL	12.8.80	23 Aug
11.53i		Nora	Ivanova	TUR	1.6.77	13 Feb
11.53	1.6	Lolo	Jones	USA	5.8.82	12 Apr
11.53	1.4	Kerri-Ann	Mitchell	CAN	29.3.83	12 Apr
11.53		Heather	Samuel	ANT	6.7.70	3 May
11.53	0.0	Franca	Idoko	NGR		17 May
11.53	1.8	Aisha	Morgan	USA	8.2.81	30 May
11.53	0.4	Natalya	Pigida	UKR	30.1.81	19 Jul
11.53	0.7	Daniela	Graglia	ITA	26.5.76	2 Aug
11.53	1.8	Aksel	Gürcan	TUR	2.1.73	9 Aug
11.53	1.5	Susanna	Kallur	SWE	16.2.81	5 Sep
11.53	1.5	Carolina	Klüft	SWE	2.2.83	5 Sep
11.53	0.0		Zou Yiting	CHN-Y	17.9.86	24 Oct
11.54A	1.2	Isabel	Rossouw	RSA	27.5.80	11 Apr
11.54	0.3	Kadiatou	Camara	MLI	4.5.81	12 Apr
11.54	1.8	Shandria	Brown	BAH	7.7.83	12 Apr
11.54	1.6	Pascal	van Assendeldt	NED	6.10.79	10 May
11.54	1.4	LaToya	Phelps	USA-J	30.6.84	18 May
11.54	-1.1	Jeanette	Kwakye	GBR	20.3.83	8 Jun
11.54	1.6	Katja	Wakan	GER	27.6.81	15 Jun
11.54	0.5		Sun Hongfeng	CHN-J	11.4.84	2 Aug
11.54	0.4	Delphine	Combe	FRA	6.12.74	6 Aug
11.54	0.7	Jacqueline	Poelman (181)	NED	5.10.73	9 Aug

Wind assisted

10.79	2.3	Kelli	White	USA	1.4.77	1		Carson/Los Angeles	1 Jun
10.84	2.8		White			1	ISTAF	Berlin (P)	10 Aug
10.86	2.8		Gaines			2	ISTAF	Berlin (P)	10 Aug
10.88	2.8	Chandra	Sturrup	BAH	12.9.71	3	ISTAF	Berlin (P)	10 Aug
10.95	2.5	Christine	Arron	FRA	13.9.73	1	NC	Narbonne	25 Jul
10.96	2.3		Edwards			2		Carson/Los Angeles	1 Jun
10.97	3.1	Muna	Lee	USA	30.10.81	1	Tex R	Austin	5 Apr

Mark	Wind	Name		Nat	Born	Pos	Meet	Venue	Date
10.97	3.4	Muriel	Hurtis	FRA	25.3.79	1s1	NC	Narbonne	25 Jul
10.97	2.8		Edwards			4	ISTAF	Berlin (P)	10 Aug
11.00	3.1		Edwards			1h3	NC	Stanford	19 Jun
11.00	3.1		White			2h3	NC	Stanford	19 Jun
11.00	2.5		Hurtis			2	NC	Narbonne	25 Jul
11.04	2.3	LaTasha	Jenkins	USA	19.12.77	3		Carson/Los Angeles	1 Jun
11.04	2.6	Inger	Miller	USA	12.6.72	1	GP II	Stanford	7 Jun
11.06	2.4	Fana	Ashby	TRI	15.6.81	1	JUCO	Levelland	10 May
11.08	2.3	Angela	Williams	USA	30.1.80	5		Carson/Los Angeles	1 Jun
11.10	3.1	Patricia	Girard	FRA	8.4.68	1		Genève	14 Jun
11.12	2.4	Allyson	Felix	USA-J	18.11.85	1		Norwalk	30 May
11.13	3.1	Monique	Tubbs	USA	23.1.81	2	Tex R	Austin	5 Apr
11.16	2.8	Vida	Anim	GHA	7.12.83	5	ISTAF	Berlin (P)	10 Aug
11.18	4.3	Gloria	Kemasuode	NGR	30.12.79	1h1		Perth	8 Feb
11.20	2.5	Odiah	Sidibé	FRA	13.1.70	3	NC	Narbonne	25 Jul
11.22	3.5	Manuela	Levorato	ITA	16.3.77	1		Oristano	6 Sep
11.24	4.0	Judyth	Kitson	JAM	2.11.79	1h2	NCAA-r	Columbus	30 May
11.25	2.4	Shalonda	Solomon	USA-J	19.12.85	2		Norwalk	30 May
11.25A	5.3	Digna	Murillo	COL	22.5.81	1		Medellin	26 Jul
11.26	3.6	Teneeshia	Jones	USA	28.1.79	1		Coral Gables	22 Mar
11.26	3.2	Johanna	Manninen	FIN	4.4.80	1	ECp-1A	Lappeenranta	21 Jun
11.27	2.4	LaShauntea	Moore	USA	31.7.83	2	JUCO	Levelland	10 May
11.28	2.6	Angela	Daigle	USA	28.5.76	3	GP II	Stanford	7 Jun
11.28	2.8	Marion	Wagner	GER	1.2.78	7	ISTAF	Berlin (P)	10 Aug
11.29	2.8	Monica	Twum	GHA	14.3.78	1		Fort Worth	19 Apr
11.29	4.7	Véronique	Mang	FRA-J	15.12.84	1h3	NC-23	Vénissieux	12 Jul
11.30	3.1	Danielle	Browning	JAM	29.8.81	5	Tex R	Austin	5 Apr
11.30	3.1	Martina	Feusi	SUI	17.6.74	2		Genève	14 Jun
11.31	4.2	Sharon	Cripps	AUS	29.6.77	2		Adelaide	6 Feb
11.31	4.2	Lauren	Hewitt	AUS	25.11.78	3		Adelaide	6 Feb
11.32	dt?	Janice	Davis	USA-J	27.10.84	1		Natches	3 May
11.32	3.0	Marina	Maydanova	UKR	22.8.82	4h2		Dortmund	15 Jun
11.32	2.5	Frédérique	Bangué	FRA	31.12.76	4	NC	Narbone	25 Jul
11.33	2.4	Lucia	Ivanová	SVK	8.7.80	1		Praha	31 May
11.34	2.2	Rosemary	Okafor	NGR	22.5.81	1h2		Denton	10 May
11.34A	5.3	Norma	González	COL	11.8.82	2		Medellin	26 Jul
11.35		Krystin	Lacy	USA-Y	8.7.87	1		Dallas	26 Apr
11.35	2.8	Shana	Robinson	USA	13.2.82	1h3	NCAA-r	Lincoln, NE	30 May
11.35	2.8	Nina	Mayes	USA	10.8.83	2h3	NCAA-r	Lincoln, NE	30 May
11.38	3.2	Illia	Miles	USA	11.1.82	2		Athens	29 Mar
11.38	2.2	Amandi	Rhett	USA	29.6.82	2h1		Clemson	10 May
11.38	3.1	Fabé	Dia	FRA	14.2.77	3		Genève	14 Jun
11.38A	2.3	Melissa	Murillo	COL	13.1.82	1		Bogotá	12 Jul
11.40	2.5	Gloria	Asumnu	USA-J	22.5.85	1		Humble	26 Apr
11.40	3.2	Cleo	Tyson	USA-J	27.2.85	1		Austin	9 May
11.40	2.8	Ioánna	Kafetzí	GRE	30.5.76	1		Mililíni	7 Jun
11.40	3.4	Aminata	Diouf	SEN	18.2.77	4s1	FRA Ch	Narbonne	25 Jul
11.41	2.6	Brianna	Glenn	USA	18.4.80	2		Cork	5 Jul

11.43	3.3	Carmelitta	Jeter	USA		5 Apr
11.43A	3.1	Melinda	Smedley	USA	11.2.81	17 May
11.44	3.2	Sherita	King	USA	4.8.82	29 Mar
11.45	2.1	Sueny	Oliveira	BRA	13.9.81	5 Jul
11.46A	3.4	Ashley	Owens	USA-J	19.11.85	24 May
11.46	2.6	Carima	Louami	FRA	12.5.79	9 Jun
11.46	3.1	Susan	Burnside	GBR	3.2.80	11 Jul
11.46	2.9	Gwladys	Belliard	FRA	10.11.82	12 Jul
11.47	2.5	Grace-Ann	Dinkins	LBR	13.9.66	1 Mar
11.47	3.6	Anita	Edwards	HAI	16.4.80	22 Mar
11.47	3.2	Krysha	Bayley	CAN-J	21.1.84	29 Mar
11.47A	3.1	Tonette	Dyer	USA	28.3.82	17 May
11.47	2.9	Marína	Vasarmídou	GRE	16.7.72	9 Jun
11.47		Wanda	Hutson	TRI-J	19.12.85	14 Jun
11.47	2.9	Amélie	Huyghes	FRA	31.5.82	12 Jul
11.48	3.6	India	Ransom	USA-J	24.1.84	22 Mar
11.48	2.4	Kaori	Sakagami	JPN	12.5.74	29 Apr
11.49	2.4	Nadine	Palmer	JAM	19.2.83	10 May
11.49	3.1	Halima	Decree	USA	27.7.83	17 May
11.49	3.2	Shandria	Brown	BAH	7.7.83	22 May
11.49	2.6	Danielle	Carruthers	USA	22.12.79	30 May
11.50	4.2	Caro	Hunt	NZL	10.1.78	6 Feb
11.50	3.6	Wyllesheia	Myrick	USA	21.11.79	19 Jun
11.51	4.4	Mindy	Slomka	AUS	2.5.80	6 Feb
11.51	3.5	Sierra	Hauser-Price	USA	17.12.83	3 May
11.51	3.1	Céline	Thélamon	FRA	1.3.79	14 Jun
11.51	3.4	Fabienne	Béret-Martinel	FRA	22.12.77	25 Jul
11.52	2.5	Erica	Lattin	USA	19.8.81	29 Mar
11.52	2.8	LaToya	White	USA	7.2.83	19 Apr
11.52	2.8	Andria	Lloyd	JAM?	10.8.71	19 Apr
11.52	3.2	Gyaisha	Hall	USA-Y	8.12.86	9 May
11.52	4.3	Heidi	Hannula	FIN	26.2.80	21 Jun
11.52	4.3	Dorota	Dydo	POL	4.2.82	21 Jun
11.53	2.4	Kerri-Ann	Mitchell	CAN	29.3.83	22 Mar
11.53	3.2	LaDedra	Guy	USA-J	16.11.84	9 May
11.53	3.0	Jacqueline	Poelman	NED	5.10.73	10 May
11.53		Courtney	Champion	USA-J	10.6.86	10 May
11.54	3.6	Alison	Culley	USA	1.3.80	22 Mar
11.54	2.8	Kandice	Bell	USA	7.8.83	30 May
11.54	3.5	Anna	Boyle	IRL	29.3.83	7 Jun
11.54	2.8	Haríklia	Boudá	GRE	17.8.80	7 Jun
11.54	3.1		Vu Thi Huong	VIE-Y	7.10.86	7 Dec

Low altitude bests

11.27 -0.7 Jenkins 4rB GGala Roma 11 Jul

11.46 -0.1 Josephs 1h1 NC Port Elizabeth 15 Apr

11.39w 2.5 1 Parow 10 Jan

Mark	Wind	Name		Nat	Born	Pos	Meet	Venue	Date
Hand timing									
11.1		Sherone	Simpson	JAM-J	12.8.84	1		Spanish Town	14 Jun
11.2		Kerron	Stewart	JAM-J	16.4.84	2		Spanish Town	14 Jun
11.2	0.3	Irina	Kozhemyakina	UKR	16.6.80	1		Kiev	29 Jul
11.3		Heather	Samuel	ANT	6.7.70	1			28 Mar
11.3	0.3	Natalya	Pigida	UKR	30.1.81				17 May
11.3	-0.6	Marilia	Gregoriou	CYP	13.2.80				11 Jul
11.3	1.4	Manuela	Grillo	ITA	9.5.77				14 Jul
11.3	-0.2	Preya	Carey	AUS	16.11.83	1			20 Dec
Wind assisted									
11.1		Donesha	Spivey	USA	20.8.83	1		Lindsborg	15 Mar
11.1	2.4	Gloria	Kemasuode	NGR	30.12.79	1		Canberra	13 Dec
11.2		Nickiesha	Anderson	JAM-J	15.3.85	1h3		Spanish Town	28 Feb
11.2	2.5	LaShauntea	Moore	USA	31.7.83	1		Emporia	27 Mar
11.2	4.9	Renee	Robson	AUS	3.11.78	1h4		Ballarat	15 Nov
11.3A	3.7	Ana Mariuxi	Caicedo	ECU	24.10.80				22 May
11.3		Vanesa	Wohlgemuth	ARG	12.10.76				24 May
11.3		Daniela Laura	Lebreo	ARG	13.8.71				24 May

JUNIORS

See main list for top 10 Juniors. 10 performances by 7 women to 11.34. Additional marks and further juniors:

Lalova 11.22 1.8 1 Sofia 2 Jul 11.28 1.0 1 NC-j Sofia 21 Jun
11.34 -0.3 1 Leverkusen 3 Aug

Mark	Wind	Name		Nat	Born	Pos	Meet	Venue	Date
11.47	1.5	Zenobia	Reed	USA	24.1.84	2h2	Big12	Austin	18 May
11.48	0.5	Kelli-Ann	Baptiste	TRI-Y	14.10.86	1		Bridgetown	9 Jun
11.49	1.5	Gloria	Asumnu	USA	22.5.85	2C		Austin	10 May
11.53	0.0		Zou Yiting	CHN-Y	17.9.86	1	NG	Changsha	24 Oct
11.54	1.4	LaToya	Phelps	USA	30.6.84	3h1	Big12	Austin	18 May
11.54	0.5		Sun Hongfeng	CHN	11.4.84	1h2		Shijiazhuang	2 Aug
11.55	0.0		Shu Yan	CHN	25.1.84	2	NG	Changsha	24 Oct
11.56	1.1	Jody	Powell	JAM	10.7.85	3-18	N.Sch	Kingston	4 Apr
11.56	-2.0	Wanda	Hutson	TRI	8.1.85	1		Portt of Spain	14 Jun
11.57	1.7	Sally	McLellan (20)	AUS-Y	19.9.86	1r1		Gold Coast	12 Apr
11.57		Shelly-Ann	Fraser	JAM-Y	.88	1		Spanish Town	3 Jun
11.57	0.0		Zhu Juanhong	CHN	5.12.85	3	NG	Changsha	24 Oct

Wind assisted – see main list for 7 juniors. Additional women to 11.53w and performances:

Felix 11.24w 2.7 1 MSR Walnut 18 Apr 11.29w 3.0 1 Arcadia 12 Apr
Mang 11.32w 2.7 1s1 NC-23 Vénissieux 12 Jul

Mark	Wind	Name		Nat	Born	Pos	Meet	Venue	Date
11.46A	3.4	Ashley	Owens	USA	19.11.85	1		Albuquerque	24 May
11.47	3.2	Krysha	Bayley	CAN	21.1.84	4		Athens	29 Mar
11.47		Wanda	Hutson	TRI	19.12.85	1h		Port of Spain	14 Jun
11.48	3.6	India	Ransom	USA	24.1.84	3		Coral Gables	22 Mar
11.52	3.2	Gyaisha	Hall	USA-Y	8.12.86	2B		Austin	9 May
11.53	3.2	LaDedra	Guy	USA	16.11.84	3B		Austin	9 May
11.53		Courtney	Champion	USA	10.6.86	1		Albany	10 May

200 METRES

Mark	Wind	Name		Nat	Born	Pos	Meet	Venue	Date
22.05	-0.3	Kelli	White	USA	1.4.77	1	WCh	Saint-Denis	28 Aug
22.11A	-0.5	Allyson	Felix	USA-J	18.11.85	1		Ciudad de México	3 May
22.21	0.0		White			1	NC	Stanford	22 Jun
22.28	0.5	Torri	Edwards	USA	31.1.77	1	GGala	Roma	11 Jul
22.31A	-0.5	LaTasha	Jenkins	USA	19.12.77	2		Ciudad de México	3 May
22.31	1.6		White			1	WAF	Monaco	13 Sep
22.33A	-0.5		White			3		Ciudad de México	3 May
22.38	-0.5	Anastasiya	Kapachinskaya	RUS	21.11.79	2	WCh	Saint-Denis	28 Aug
22.41	-0.2	Muriel	Hurtis	FRA	25.3.79	1s2	WCh	Saint-Denis	27 Aug
22.41	1.6		Hurtis			2	WAF	Monaco	13 Sep
22.43	0.7		White			1	Gaz	Saint-Denis	4 Jul
22.43	-0.2		Kapachinskaya			2s2	WCh	Saint-Denis	27 Aug
22.44	-0.2		Edwards			3s2	WCh	Saint-Denis	27 Aug
22.45	0.0		Edwards			2	NC	Stanford	22 Jun
22.45	0.2	Cydonie	Mothersill	CAY	19.3.78	1	CAC	St George's	6 Jul
22.47	-0.3		Edwards			3	WCh	Saint-Denis	28 Aug
22.48	1.6		Kapachinskaya			1		Villeneuve d'Ascq	15 Jun
22.50A	0.0	Debbie	Ferguson	BAH	16.1.76	1		Pretoria	4 Apr
22.50	-0.1		White			1s1	WCh	Saint-Denis	27 Aug
22.51	1.3		Felix			1	MSR	Walnut	19 Apr
22.51	0.3		Hurtis			1	NA	Heusden	2 Aug
22.51	0.3		Hurtis			1h2	WCh	Saint-Denis	26 Aug
22.52	0.8		Felix			1		Norwalk	7 Jun
22.56	2.0		Jenkins			1s2	NC	Stanford	22 Jun
22.56	1.1		Edwards			1r2		Réthimno	6 Jul
22.57	1.6		Kapachinskaya			3	WAF	Monaco	13 Sep

Mark	Wind	Name		Nat	Born	Pos	Meet	Venue	Date
22.58	1.6		Edwards			4	WAF	Monaco	13 Sep
22.59	0.0	Aleen	Bailey	JAM	25.11.80	1	NC	Kingston	21 Jun
22.59	0.0		Felix			3	NC	Stanford	22 Jun
22.59	-0.3		Hurtis			4	WCh	Saint-Denis	28 Aug
		(30/9)							
22.60	0.0	Mary	Onyali (10)	NGR	3.2.68	1		Abuja	17 May
22.61	-0.1	Zhanna	Block	UKR	6.7.72	2s1	WCh	Saint-Denis	27 Aug
22.63	0.9	Connie	Moore	USA	29.8.81	1	NCAA-r	Fairfax	31 May
22.64	1.6	Kim	Gevaert	BEL	5.8.78	2		Villeneuve d'Ascq	15 Jun
22.66	1.3	Yuliya	Tabakova	RUS	1.5.80	1	MAI	Malmö	12 Aug
22.66	-0.1	Anzhela	Kravchenko	UKR	25.1.71	3s1	WCh	Saint-Denis	27 Aug
22.67	1.8	Inger	Miller	USA	12.6.72	1s1	NC	Stanford	22 Jun
22.67	0.3	Beverly	McDonald	JAM	15.2.70	1r1		Réthimno	6 Jul
22.67	1.4	Chryste	Gaines	USA	14.9.70	1	GP II	Yokohama	23 Sep
22.69	0.0	Juliet	Campbell	JAM	17.3.70	2	NC	Kingston	21 Jun
22.69	1.3	Roxana	Díaz	CUB	17.5.81	1	PAm	Santo Domingo	8 Aug
		(20)							
22.70	0.6	Marina	Maydanova	UKR	22.8.82	1	ECp-1B	Velenje	22 Jun
22.71	0.3	Natalya	Safronnikova	BLR	28.2.73	2		Réthimno	6 Jul
22.74	0.9	Muna	Lee	USA	30.10.81	1rA		Baton Rouge	12 Apr
22.78	-0.4	Ionela	Tîrlea	ROM	9.2.76	2	ECp-S	Firenze	22 Jun
22.79	1.6	Lauren	Hewitt	AUS	25.11.78	1		Adelaide	6 Feb
22.79	0.3	Svetlana	Goncharenko	RUS	28.5.71	1		Moskva	15 Jul
22.80	0.2	Tonique	Williams	BAH	17.1.76	3	CAC	St George's	6 Jul
22.82	-0.2	Erica	Whipple	USA	4.12.82	1	SEC	Knoxville	18 May
22.83	-0.3	Mercy	Nku	NGR	17.7.76	1	GP II	Thessaloníki	3 Aug
22.84	1.6	Sharon	Cripps	AUS	29.6.77	2		Adelaide	6 Feb
		(30)							
22.86	0.9	Stephanie	Durst	USA	6.1.82	1rB		Baton Rouge	12 Apr
22.86	0.9	Sanya	Richards	USA-J	26.2.85	1h1	Big 12	Austin	18 May
22.87	1.8	Rachelle	Boone	USA	30.6.81	1	Big 10	Minneapolis	18 May
22.87	-0.4	Ivet	Lalova	BUL-J	18.5.84	1	NC-23	Sofia	15 Jun
22.87	1.3	Anna	Pacholak	POL	15.1.80	1	NC	Bielsko-Biala	6 Jul
22.88	0.2	Christine	Amertil	BAH	18.8.79	4	CAC	St George's	6 Jul
22.89A	-0.5	Demetria	Washington	USA	31.12.79	4		Ciudad de México	3 May
22.89	0.0	Merlene	Ottey	SLO	10.5.60	1	NC	Nova Gorica	10 Aug
22.90	0.7	Vida	Anim	GHA	7.12.83	2	VD	Bruxelles	5 Sep
22.92	0.0	Christine	Arron	FRA	13.9.73	2	Nebiolo	Torino	6 Jun
		(40)							
22.92	1.6	Joice	Maduaka	GBR	30.9.73	4		Villeneuve d'Ascq	15 Jun
22.93	0.0	Shalonda	Solomon	USA-J	19.12.85	1	PAm-J	Bridgetown	20 Jul
22.95	1.1	Abiodun	Oyepitan	GBR	30.12.79	1	NC	Birmingham	27 Jul
22.96	0.9	Crystal	Cox	USA	28.3.79	1		Atlanta	7 Jun
22.97	0.5	Johanna	Manninen	FIN	4.4.80	1		Lahti	2 Jul
22.98	0.0	Elva	Goulbourne	JAM	21.1.80	1		Tempe	12 Apr
22.98	1.1	Carolina	Klüft	SWE	2.2.83	1H3	WCh	Saint-Denis	23 Aug
22.99	1.2	Sylviane	Félix	FRA	31.10.77	1		Meilen	10 Aug
23.00	1.3	Natasha	Mayers	VIN	10.3.79	2	MSR	Walnut	19 Apr
23.01	0.9	Debbie	Dunn	JAM	26.3.78	2		Atlanta	7 Jun
		(50)							
23.01	-1.2	Gabrielle	Rockmeier	GER	29.11.73	1	NC	Ulm	29 Jun
23.02	-0.1	Marina	Kislova	RUS	7.2.78	1	Znam	Tula	8 Jun
23.04	0.0	Lakadron	Ivery	USA	23.6.83	2	Big 12	Austin	19 May
23.05	?	Fana	Ashby	TRI	15.6.81	2	NC	Port of Spain	21 Jun
23.05	0.3	Karin	Mayr-Krifka	AUT	4.6.71	1	NC	Salzburg	10 Aug
23.06	1.8	Lucia	Ivanová	SVK	8.7.80	1		Praha	31 May
23.07A	0.0	Geraldine	Pillay	RSA	25.8.77	3		Pretoria	4 Apr
23.08	0.0	Aleah	Williams	USA	7.1.81	3	Big 12	Austin	19 May
23.08A		Digna	Murillo	COL	22.5.81	1		Bogotá	12 Jul
23.09	1.0	LaShauntea	Moore	USA	31.7.83	1		Fayetteville	12 Apr
		(60)							
23.09	0.9	Monique	Hall	USA	9.10.80	2rB		Baton Rouge	12 Apr
23.09	1.0	Maja	Nose	SLO	12.5.82	2	EU23	Bydgoszcz	20 Jul
23.10	1.8	Geisa	Coutinho	BRA	1.6.80	1		Sao Caetano do Sul	23 Apr
23.10	1.1	Heide	Seyerling	RSA	19.8.76	1		Riga	12 Jun
23.11	0.1	Yelena	Pastushenko	UKR	14.7.79	1		Kalamáta	31 May
23.11	0.5	Lyubov	Perepelova	UZB	26.2.79	1	AsiC	Manila	23 Sep
23.13	-1.2	Melanie	Paschke	GER	29.6.70	2	NC	Ulm	29 Jun
23.15	1.9	Tatyana	Bonenko	UKR	7.6.76	2	NC	Kiev	5 Jul
23.16	-2.0	Lorraine	Fenton	JAM	8.9.73	1	Drake R	Des Moines	26 Apr
23.16	-1.7	Susanthika	Jayasinghe	SRI	17.12.75	1	NC	Colombo	26 Jul
		(70)							

Mark	Wind	Name		Nat	Born	Pos	Meet	Venue	Date
23.18	0.4	Charlette	Greggs	USA	20.10.83	1		Storrs	4 May
23.18A	1.0	Norma	González	COL	11.8.82	2		Medellin	26 Jul
23.18	0.0	Manuela	Levorato	ITA	16.3.77	4		Rovereto	10 Sep
23.19	0.6	Anneisha	McLaughlin	JAM-Y	6.1.86	1	N.Sch	Kingston	5 Apr
23.19A	0.0	Lucimar	de Moura	BRA	22.3.74	1		Cochabamba	11 May
23.19	0.3	Jacqueline	Poelman	NED	5.10.73	6	NA	Heusden	2 Aug
23.21	0.9	Danielle	Browning	JAM	29.8.81	2s1	PAm	Santo Domingo	7 Aug
23.22	0.8	Janice	Josephs	RSA	31.3.82	1h3	NC	Port Elizabeth	25 Apr
23.22	1.7	Kelliann	Baptiste	TRI-Y	14.10.86	1		Bridgetown	9 Jun
23.22		Nickiesha	Anderson	JAM-J	18.3.85	2		Spanish Town	14 Jun
		(80)							
23.23A	0.0	Winneth	Dube	ZIM	10.5.72	4		Pretoria	4 Apr
23.23	1.9	Ami Mbacké	Thiam	SEN	10.11.76	2		Sotteville	8 Jul
23.23	-1.7	Yelena	Bolsun	RUS	25.6.82	1	NC	Tula	9 Aug
23.24	0.0	Birgit	Rockmeier	GER	29.11.73	2		Dessau	30 May
23.24	0.0	Shana	Cox	USA-J	22.1.85	1	N.Sch	Raleigh	14 Jun
23.24	0.3	Larisa	Kruglova	RUS	27.10.72	2		Moskva	15 Jul
23.25	0.0	Lauryn	Williams	USA	11.9.83	1		Coral Gables	12 Apr
23.25	0.0	Irina	Lenskiy	ISR	12.6.71	1		Tel Aviv	12 May
23.26	0.0	Laverne	Jones	ISV	16.9.81	4	Big 12	Austin	19 May
23.26	-1.6		Qin Wangping	CHN	16.6.82	1	NC	Shanghai	14 Sep
		(90)							
23.27	0.3	Ebony	Floyd	USA	21.10.83	1h5		Charlotte	16 May
23.27	1.3	Shandria	Brown	BAH	7.7.83	1h2	NCAA II	Edwardsville	23 May
23.27	0.0	Jenice	Daley	JAM	13.8.78	5	NC	Kingston	21 Jun
23.27	0.0		Sun Hongfeng	CHN-J	11.4.84	1		Shijiazhuang	4 Aug
23.27	-0.5	Delphine	Atangana	CMR-J	16.8.84	2h1	Afr G	Abuja	14 Oct
23.27A	0.6	Wendy	Seegers	RSA	28.2.76	1		Pretoria	7 Nov
23.28	0.7	Sonja	Collins	USA	28.2.82	1h1		Lynchburg	8 May
23.30	1.6	Gloria	Kemasuode	NGR	30.12.79	3		Adelaide	6 Feb
23.31	0.9	Illia	Miles	USA	11.1.82	4	NCAA-r	Fairfax	31 May
23.31	-0.5		Zou Yiting	CHN-Y	17.9.86	1	NG	Changsha	26 Oct
		(100)							

Mark	Wind	Name		Nat	Born	Date
23.32	0.0	Shaunta	Pelham	USA	12.2.78	22 Jun
23.33A	2.0	Estie	Wittstock	RSA	15.9.80	24 Jan
23.33	0.5	Vronique	Wilson	USA		28 Mar
23.34	1.6	Libia Patricía	Rodrguez	COL	25.10.70	23 May
23.34	-1.0	Esther	Möller	GER	13.9.77	1 Jun
23.34	-0.1	Olga	Fyodorova	RUS	14.7.83	8 Jun
23.34	1.0	Dorota	Dydo	POL	4.2.82	20 Jul
23.35	0.4	Kim	Lyles	USA	5.10.83	4 May
23.35	0.9	Natasha	Staten	USA-J	2.12.84	18 May
23.35	0.7	Fatou Bintou	Fall	SEN	23.8.81	25 May
23.35	0.0	Amandi	Rhett	USA	6.6.82	30 May
23.35	1.6	Jenny	Ljunggren	SWE-J	2.7.84	27 Jul
23.36	1.5	Ashlee	Williams	USA-J	27.3.84	19 Apr
23.36	-0.2	DeeDee	Trotter	USA	8.12.82	18 May
23.36	0.0	Sandra	Möller	GER	16.3.80	30 May
23.36	1.6	Virginie	Michanol	FRA-J	18.6.85	27 Jul
23.37	0.3	Monique	Tubbs	USA	23.1.81	18 Apr
23.38	1.5	Merlene	Frazer	JAM	27.12.73	19 Apr
23.38	0.4	Alison	Culley	USA	1.3.80	4 May
23.38	0.3	Wyllesheia	Myrick	USA	21.11.79	12 Jul
23.38	-3.1	Yekaterina	Kondratyeva	RUS	8.4.82	27 Jul
23.38	1.5	Enikö	Szabó	HUN	10.11.79	10 Aug
23.38	-0.5	Louise	Ayétotché	CIV	3.6.75	14 Oct
23.39	0.9	Haríklía	Boudá	GRE	17.8.80	25 May
23.39	0.5	Wilmary	Álvarez	VEN-J	13.5.84	5 Jul
23.39	0.5		Chen Lisha	CHN	10.4.81	23 Sep
23.40	0.7	Jennifer	Wilson	USA	26.6.76	8 May
23.40A	0.0	Melinda	Smedley	USA	11.2.81	16 May
23.40		Yelena	Nevmerzhitskaya	BLR	27.7.80	22 May
23.40	1.3	Jenny	Kallur	SWE	16.2.81	12 Aug
23.40	1.9	Ciara	Sheehy	IRL	12.8.80	23 Aug
23.40	0.1	Monika	Bejnar	POL	10.3.81	14 Sep
23.42	-0.7	Teneeshia	Jones	USA	28.1.79	24 May
23.42	-0.3	Donita	Harmon	USA	1.3.83	11 Jun
23.42	0.6	Monika	Gachevska	BUL	30.10.74	22 Jun
23.42		Olga	Mishchenko	UKR	24.11.71	6 Aug
23.42	-1.8	Olga	Khalandyreva	RUS	13.11.81	9 Aug
23.43	0.0	LaToya	Phelps	USA-J	30.6.84	19 May
23.43	0.1	Endurance	Ojokolo	NGR	29.9.75	12 Jul
23.43	0.4	Joan	Uduak Ekah	NGR	16.12.80	14 Oct
23.43	-0.8	Saraswati	Saha	IND	23.11.79	29 Oct
23.44	1.1	Erica	Witter	CAN	10.12.76	5 Apr
23.44	0.7	Zenobia	Reed	USA-J	24.1.84	18 May
23.45	2.0	Aminata	Diouf	SEN	18.2.77	9 Jun
23.45	-0.5	Ólga	Kaidantzí	GRE	17.7.79	15 Jun
23.45	1.7	Anita	Mormand	FRA	20.2.71	28 Jun
23.45	0.5	Amy	Spencer	GBR-J	19.9.85	26 Jul
23.46	-0.5	Mikele	Barber	USA	4.10.80	12 Apr
23.46	0.0	Kiamesha	Otey	USA	28.5.81	30 May
23.46		Yuliya	Nesterenko (150)	BLR	15.6.79	3 Jun
23.46	0.0	Fabienne	Feraez	BEN	6.8.76	14 Oct
23.47	1.1	Chante	Threets	USA	19.12.79	3 May
23.47	-1.7	Daniela	Graglia	ITA	26.5.76	29 Jun
23.47	-0.4	Cristina	Sanz	ESP	6.11.78	19 Jul
23.47	-1.8	Irina	Khabarova	RUS	18.3.66	9 Aug
23.48	?	Katia	Benth	FRA	16.11.75	31 Jul
23.48	0.4	Alexandria	Anderson	USA-Y	28.1.87	3 Aug
23.49	0.2	Marion	Wagner	GER	1.2.78	24 May
23.49	-4.1	Svetlana	Pospelova	RUS	24.12.79	29 Jun
23.50	0.5	Amber	Robinson	USA	5.6.80	28 Mar
23.50	-0.1	Kerron	Stewart	JAM-J	16.4.84	5 Apr
23.50	1.1	Sherita	King	USA	4.8.82	5 Apr
23.50	0.0	Rosemary	Okafor	NGR	22.5.81	19 Apr
23.50	0.0	Rosemar	Coelho Neto	BRA	2.1.77	22 Jun
23.50	0.1	Aida	Diop	SEN	27.4.70	12 Jul
23.51		Mariya	Lisnichenko	RUS	27.12.80	16 May
23.51	-0.6	Melisa	Barber	USA	4.10.80	7 Jul
23.51	0.7	Jenny	Adams	USA	8.7.78	5 Sep
23.52	1.8	Jana	Pittman	AUS	9.11.82	15 Feb
23.52	0.0	Tonette	Dyer	USA	28.3.82	19 Apr
23.53	1.5	Solen	Désert	FRA	2.8.82	26 Apr
23.53	1.5	Glory	Alozie	ESP	30.12.77	3 May
23.53	1.2	Angela	Daigle	USA	28.5.76	10 May
23.53	0.0	Hyleas	Fountain	USA	14.1.81	13 Jun
23.53	0.0	Courtney	Champion	USA-Y	10.6.86	14 Jun
23.53	1.6	Vincenza	Cali	ITA	15.10.83	28 Jun
23.53	0.4	Wanda	Hutson	TRI-J	19.12.85	19 Jul
23.53	-1.4	Fabé	Dia	FRA	14.2.77	25 Jul
23.53	0.0		Jiao Guiyan	CHN-J	12.6.85	25 Oct
23.54	0.3	Natalya	Antyukh (180)	RUS	26.6.81	15 Jul

Wind assisted

Mark	Wind	Name		Nat	Born	Pos	Meet	Venue	Date
22.41	4.5	Cydonie	Mothersill	CAY	19.3.78	1h1	CAC	St George's	5 Jul

Mark	Wind	Name		Nat	Born	Pos	Meet	Venue	Date
22.58	4.5		Kapachinskaya			1	ECCp	Valencia	25 May
22.69	4.6	Fana	Ashby	TRI	15.6.81	1	JUCO	Levelland	10 May
22.81	4.0	LaShauntea	Moore	USA	31.7.83	2	JUCO	Levelland	10 May
22.84	2.8	Shana	Robinson	USA	13.2.82	1		Fort Worth	19 Apr
22.86	3.9	Christine	Amertil	BAH	18.8.79	1h2	CAC	St George's	5 Jul
22.87	3.1	Lakadron	Ivery	USA	23.6.83	1h3	NCAA-r	Lincoln, NE	30 May
22.93	4.3	Laverne	Jones	ISV	16.9.81	1h1	NCAA-r	Lincoln, NE	30 May
22.98	4.3	LaToya	Phelps	USA-J	30.6.84	2h1	NCAA-r	Lincoln, NE	30 May
23.05	2.8	Ashlee	Williams	USA-J	27.3.84	2		Austin	3 May
23.05	3.1	LaJuana	Lovett	USA	7.5.82	1h2	NCAA-r	Lincoln, NE	30 May
23.06	4.9	Ebony	Floyd	USA	21.10.83	1h1		College Station	8 May
23.10A	2.2	Melinda	Smedley	USA	11.2.81	1		Albuquerque	17 May
23.12	2.8	Monica	Twum	GHA	14.3.78	2		Fort Worth	19 Apr
23.15	4.2	Nicole	Ireland	USA	23.4.82	1		Northridge	5 Apr
23.16	2.1	Jacqueline	Poelman	NED	5.10.73	1		Utrecht	9 Aug
23.17	3.1	Donita	Harmon	USA	1.3.83	2h3	NCAA-r	Lincoln, NE	30 May
23.18	4.9	Allison	Beckford	JAM	8.5.79	2		College Station	8 May
23.18	2.3	Rosemary	Okafor	NGR	22.5.81	1h1		Denton	10 May
23.18	2.8	Irina	Lenskiy	ISR	12.6.71	1	ECp-2B	Istanbul	22 Jun
23.19	4.2		Nguyen Thi Tinh	VIE	20.9.81	1	SEAG	Hanoi	10 Dec
23.20	4.9	Illia	Miles	USA	11.1.82	1		Athens	3 May
23.20	3.1	Tremedia	Brice	USA		3h3	NCAA-r	Lincoln, NE	30 May
23.24	3.1	Kandice	Bell	USA	7.8.83	4h3	NCAA-r	Lincoln, NE	30 May
23.28	2.8	Natasha	Staten	USA	2.12.81	3		Austin	3 May
23.31	2.8	Naleya	Downer	JAM	27.1.80	4r1	TexR	Austin	3 May

23.34	4.6	Nadine	Palmer	JAM	19.2.83	10 May
23.34	2.3	Erica	Witter	CAN	10.12.76	20 Jul
23.36	3.8	Keenan	Gibson	TRI	3.10.78	17 May
23.38	4.5	Ólga	Kaidantzí	GRE	17.7.79	25 May
23.39	2.3	Cleo	Tyson	USA-J	27.2.85	10 May
23.45	2.1	Jasmine	Lee	USA-Y	5.4.86	30 May
23.46		Latonya	Loche	USA-J	8.10.85	13 Jul
23.48A	2.2	Tonette	Dyer	USA	28.3.82	17 May

23.48	3.1	Shyrell	Hobson	USA	30.9.81	30 May
23.49	2.1	Elizabeth	Olear	USA-Y	16.11.88	30 May
23.49	4.2	Juthamas	Thavoncharoen	THA	21.12.81	10 Dec
23.50	3.3	Lolo	Jones	USA	5.8.82	28 Mar
23.50	4.0	Courtney	Champion	USA-Y	10.6.86	11 Jul
23.52	2.8	Moushami	Robinson	USA	13.4.81	3 May
23.53	2.7	Donna	Arnett	USA	28.8.74	10 May
23.53	2.4	Monique	Henderson	USA	27.1.83	17 May

Low altitude bests

22.56	2.0	Jenkins	1s2	NC	Stanford	22 Jun
22.65		Ferguson	2	GGala	Roma	11 Jul
23.11	1.5	Pillay	1		Szombathely	10 Aug

23.13	0.0	Murillo	1	SACh	Barquisimeto	22 Jun
23.26	-1.7	de Moura	1h1	SACh	Barquisimeto	21 Jun
23.34	1.3	González				7 Aug
23.34	-0.5	Wittstock				14 Oct

Indoors

22.18	Michelle	Collins	USA	12.2.71	1	WI	Birmingham	15 Mar
22.31		Collins			1s2	WI	Birmingham	14 Mar
22.49	Muna	Lee	USA	30.10.81	1h2	NCAA	Fayetteville	14 Mar
22.49		Hurtis			1s1	WI	Birmingham	14 Mar
22.54		Hurtis			2	WI	Birmingham	15 Mar
22.59		Kapachinskaya			1	NC	Moskva	27 Feb
22.63	Veronica	Campbell	JAM	15.5.82	1		Fayetteville	14 Feb
22.76	Sylviane	Félix	FRA	31.10.77	1		Liévin	23 Feb
22.80	Sanya	Richards	USA-J	26.2.85	1h4	NCAA	Fayetteville	14 Mar
22.88	Karin	Mayr-Krifka	AUT	4.6.71	1		Wien	9 Mar
23.05	Nora	Ivanova	TUR	1.6.77	1		Wien	28 Jan
23.06	Mikele	Barber	USA	4.10.80	2h2	NCAA	Fayetteville	14 Mar
23.14	Manuela	Levorato	ITA	16.3.77	1	NC	Genova	2 Mar
23.16	Laverne	Jones	ISV	16.9.81	2h1	NCAA	Fayetteville	14 Mar
23.17	Ciara	Sheehy	IRL	12.8.80	1	UK Ch	Birmingham	2 Mar
23.20	Amy	Spencer	GBR-J	19.9.85	2	NC	Birmingham	2 Mar
23.25	Alenka	Bikar	SLO	7.1.74	1		Wien	23 Feb

23.46	Solen	Désert	FRA	2.8.82	2 Mar
23.47	Fabé	Dia	FRA	14.2.77	7 Feb
23.47	Hana	Benesová	CZE	19.4.75	22 Feb

23.49	Monique	Henderson	USA	18.2.83	21 Feb
23.49	Moushami	Robinson	USA	13.4.81	1 Mar
23.52	Natalya	Nazarova	RUS	26.5.79	11 Feb

Hand timing

22.4	Mary	Onyali	NGR	3.2.68	1	NC	Abuja	19 Jul
23.2 23.4?	Kelliann	Baptiste	TRI-Y	14.10.86				6 Apr
23.3	Damola	Osayomi	NGR-Y	26.8.86				14 Jun
22.9w	Donesha	Spivey	USA	20.8.83	1		Lindsborg	15 Mar

JUNIORS

See main list for top 11 Juniors. 15 performances (inc. 2 indoors) by 4 women to 22.94. Additional marks and further juniors:

Felix 4+	22.66	0.7	3	Gaz	Saint-Denis	4 Jul	22.88	0.4	1		Norwalk	24 May
	22.84	1.8	2s1	NC	Stanford	22 Jun	22.65w	2.1	1		Norwalk	30 May
Lalova	22.88	1.6	1	EJ	Tampere	27 Jul	22.91	0.8	1		Sovia	2 Jul
Richards 2+	22.90i		2	NCAA	Fayetteville	15 Mar	22.92	0.0	1	Big12	Austin	19 May

23.35	0.9	Natasha	Staten	USA	2.12.84	2h1	Big12	Austin	18 May

WOMEN 2003

Mark	Wind	Name		Nat	Born	Pos	Meet	Venue	Date
23.35	1.6	Jenny	Ljunggren	SWE	2.7.84	2	EJ	Tampere	27 Jul
23.36	1.5	Ashlee	Williams	USA	27.3.84	1		Austin	19 Apr
23.36	1.6	Virginie	Michanol	FRA-	18.6.85	3	EJ	Tampere	27 Jul
23.39	0.5	Wilmary	Álvarez	VEN-	13.5.84	2h3	CAC	St George's	5 Jul
23.43	0.0	LaToya	Phelps	USA	30.6.84	5	Big12	Austin	19 May
23.44	0.7	Zenobia	Reed	USA	24.1.84	1h3	Big12	Austin	18 May
23.45	0.5	Amy	Spencer	GBR	19.9.85	1h3	EJ	Tampere	26 Jul
23.48	0.4	Alexandria	Anderson (20)	USA-Y	28.1.87	1		Miami	3 Aug

Wind assisted – see main list for 2 juniors. Additional women:

Mark	Wind	Name		Nat	Born	Pos	Meet	Venue	Date
23.39	2.3	Cleo	Tyson	USA	27.2.85	1		Austin	10 May
23.45	2.1	Jasmine	Lee	USA-Y	5.4.86	3		Norwalk	30 May
23.46		Latonya	Loche	USA	8.10.85	1		Nashville	13 Jul

300 METRES

Mark	Name		Nat	Born	Pos	Venue	Date
35.30A	Ana Gabriela	Guevara	MEX	4.3.77	1	Ciudad de México	3 May
36.20A	Ionela	Tîrlea	ROM	9.2.76	2	Ciudad de México	3 May
36.34	Jana	Pittman	AUS	9.11.82	1	Sydney (C)	15 Feb
36.42A	Cathy	Freeman	AUS	16.2.73	3	Ciudad de México	3 May
36.79A	Monique	Hennagan	USA	26.5.76	4	Ciudad de México	3 May

37.05	Julian	Clay	USA	2.11.77	16 Aug
37.06	Solen	Désert	FRA	2.8.82	16 Aug
37.14	Moushami	Robinson	USA	13.4.81	16 Aug
37.43A	Barbara	Petráhn	HUN	16.9.78	3 May

Indoors

37.08	Olesya	Zykina	RUS	7.10.80	7 Jan
37.18	Nadjina	Kaltouma	CHA	16.11.76	1 Feb
37.35	Natalya	Antyukh	RUS	26.6.81	7 Jan

Times in World 400m 27 Aug: Guevara 35.7, Fenton 35.9, Thiam 36.0, Nazarova 36.3, Williams 36.4, Zykina 36.6, Pospelova 36.7, McConnell 37.0

JUNIORS

Mark	Name		Nat	Born	Pos	Venue	Date
37.59	Virginie	Michanol	FRA	18.6.85	5	Bondoufle	17 Aug

400 METRES

Mark	Name		Nat	Born	Pos	Meet	Venue	Date
48.89	Ana Gabriela	Guevara	MEX	4.3.77	1	WCh	Saint-Denis	27 Aug
49.11		Guevara			1	WK	Zürich	15 Aug
49.34		Guevara			1	Pre	Eugene	24 May
49.34		Guevara			1	WAF	Monaco	14 Sep
49.43	Lorraine	Fenton	JAM	8.9.73	2	WCh	Saint-Denis	27 Aug
49.62		Guevara			1		Carson/Los Angeles	1 Jun
49.71		Fenton			1	Athl	Lausanne	1 Jul
49.78	Natalya	Nazarova	RUS	26.5.79	1	NC	Tula	9 Aug
49.88		Fenton			1	GP	London (CP)	8 Aug
49.95	Ami Mbacké	Thiam	SEN	10.11.76	3	WCh	Saint-Denis	27 Aug
49.98		Fenton			1	ISTAF	Berlin (P)	10 Aug
49.98		Nazarova			4	WCh	Saint-Denis	27 Aug
50.09A		Guevara			1		Guadalajara	7 Jun
50.14		Thiam			2	WK	Zürich	15 Aug
50.24	Tonique	Williams	BAH	17.1.76	3	WK	Zürich	15 Aug
50.29		Fenton			2	WAF	Monaco	14 Sep
50.30		Fenton			1		Poznan	29 Jun
50.36		Guevara			1	PAm	Santo Domingo	8 Aug
50.38		Williams			5	WCh	Saint-Denis	27 Aug
50.39		Williams			2	Pre	Eugene	24 May
50.39	Olesya	Zykina	RUS	7.10.80	2	NC	Tula	9 Aug
50.43	Jana	Pittman	AUS	9.11.82	1		Sydney (H)	22 Mar
50.43		Williams			1s2	WCh	Saint-Denis	25 Aug
50.44		Nazarova			1		Moskva	15 May
50.45		Fenton			1	Nebiolo	Torino	6 Jun
50.45		Fenton			2s2	WCh	Saint-Denis	25 Aug
50.53	Jearl	Miles-Clark	USA	4.9.66	4	WK	Zürich	15 Aug
50.58	Sanya	Richards	USA-J	26.2.85	1	NCAA	Sacramento	14 Jun
50.59	Anastasiya	Kapachinskaya	RUS	21.11.79	1h6	NC	Tula	7 Aug
50.59		Zykina			6	WCh	Saint-Denis	27 Aug
	(30/10)							
50.66	Dee Dee	Trotter	USA	8.12.82	2	NCAA	Sacramento	14 Jun
50.66	Nadia	Davy	USA	24.12.80	3	NCAA	Sacramento	14 Jun
50.70	Svetlana	Pospelova	RUS	24.12.79	1		Luzern	25 Jun
50.79	Mireille	Nguimgo	CMR	7.11.76	1		La Chaux-de-Fonds	17 Aug
50.87	Maria	Lisnichenko	RUS	27.12.80	1		Tula	31 May
50.91	Olabisi	Afolabi	NGR	31.10.75	1		San Sebastián	10 Aug
50.93	Svetlana	Goncharenko	RUS	28.5.71	3	NC	Tula	9 Aug
51.01	Allison	Beckford	JAM	8.5.79	4	NCAA	Sacramento	14 Jun
51.06	Lee	McConnell	GBR	9.10.78	3s1	WCh	Saint-Denis	25 Aug

Mark	Name		Nat	Born	Pos	Meet	Venue	Date
51.12	Fatou Bintou	Fall	SEN	23.8.81	1	FRA Ch	Narbonne	25 Jul
	(20)							
51.25	Demetria	Washington	USA	31.12.79	4	GP	London (CP)	8 Aug
51.25	Christine	Amertil	BAH	18.8.79	2		La Chaux-de-Fonds	17 Aug
51.30	Heide	Seyerling/Quinn	RSA	19.8.76	2	GP	Gateshead	13 Jul
51.32	Hazel-Ann	Regis	GRN	1.2.81	5	NCAA	Sacramento	14 Jun
51.35	Ronetta	Smith	JAM	2.5.80	3	GP	Gateshead	13 Jul
51.36	Antonina	Yefremova	UKR	19.7.81	1	NC	Kiev	4 Jul
51.36	Grazyna	Prokopek	POL	20.4.77	3h5	WCh	Saint-Denis	24 Aug
51.38	Tatyana	Levina	RUS	28.2.77	4	NC	Tula	9 Aug
51.39	Svetlana	Usovich	BLR	14.10.80	2h1	WCh	Saint-Denis	24 Aug
51.41	Doris	Jacob	NGR	16.12.81	2	AfG	Abuja	13 Oct
	(30)							
51.43	Marsha	Dawkins	JAM	5.1.81	6	NCAA	Sacramento	14 Jun
51.43	Tatyana	Firova	RUS	10.10.82	5	NC	Tula	9 Aug
51.44	Geisa	Coutinho	BRA	1.6.80	1		Rio de Janeiro	26 Apr
51.46	Monique	Hennagan	USA	26.5.76	4	GP	Gateshead	13 Jul
51.48	Aliann	Pompey	GUY	9.3.78	1	Kuso	Warszawa	15 Jun
51.54	Yulia	Sotnikova	RUS	18.11.70	1h7	NC	Tula	7 Aug
51.64	Hortense	Béwouda	CMR	19.10.78	3		La Chaux-de-Fonds	17 Aug
51.64		Sun Hongfeng	CHN-J	11.4.84	1	NC	Shanghai	12 Sep
51.65	Charlette	Greggs	USA	20.10.83	1	NCAA-r	Fairfax	31 May
51.66	Cathy	Freeman	AUS	16.2.73	1	NC	Brisbane	4 Apr
	(40)							
51.66	Anna	Tkach	RUS/ISR	17.4.75	4		Moskva	26 Jul
51.68	Claudia	Marx	GER	16.9.78	1		Leverkusen	3 Aug
51.71	Estie	Wittstock	RSA	15.9.80	3h1	AfG	Abuja	12 Oct
51.78	Helen	Karagounis	GBR	28.9.81	1	EU23	Bydgoszcz	19 Jul
51.80	Moya	Thompson	JAM		1	NCAA II	Edwardsville	24 May
51.80	Sandie	Richards	JAM	6.11.68	5s3	WCh	Saint-Denis	25 Aug
51.83		Nguyen Thi Tinh	VIE	20.9.81	1	SEAG	Hanoi	8 Dec
51.84	Crystal	Cox	USA	28.3.79	1		Walnut	13 Jul
51.88	Anna	Pacholak	POL	15.1.80	3	Kuso	Warszawa	15 Jun
51.89	Libia Patricia	Rodríguez	COL	25.10.70	2	NCAA II	Edwardsville	24 May
	(50)							
51.92A	Jessica	Fox	USA		1		Albuquerque	17 May
51.92	Olga	Mishchenko	UKR	24.11.71	2	NC	Kiev	4 Jul
51.93	Novlene	Williams	JAM	26.4.82	2	NCAA-r	Fairfax	31 May
51.93	Moushami	Robinson	USA	13.4.81	4	NC	Stanford	21 Jun
51.93		Huang Xiaoxiao	CHN	3.3.83	1	NG	Changsha	24 Oct
51.94	Debbie	Dunn	JAM	26.3.78	1		Atlanta	7 Jun
51.94	Yuliya	Gushchina	RUS	4.3.83	2	NC-23	Cheboksary	28 Jun
51.96	Monique	Henderson	USA	18.2.83	2h1	NCAA	Sacramento	12 Jun
51.97	Irina	Rosikhina	RUS	11.5.75	2		Tula	31 May
51.98	Olga	Golendukhina	RUS	14.11.81	3		Tula	31 May
	(60)							
51.98	Julian	Clay	USA	2.11.77	4	v2N	Glasgow (S)	29 Jun
52.01	Natalya	Lavshuk	RUS	22.2.80	1		Florø	31 May
52.01	Olga	Stefashina	RUS	10.10.81	3	NC-23	Cheboksary	28 Jun
52.01	Makelesi	Bulikiobo	FIJ	23.10.77	4h4	WCh	Saint-Denis	24 Aug
52.03	Catherine	Scott	JAM	24.8.73	1		Houston	6 Jun
52.04	Me'Lisa	Barber	USA	4.10.80	5	NC	Stanford	21 Jun
52.04	Stephanie	Smith	USA-J	27.6.85	1	NC-j	Stanford	22 Jun
52.04	Tatyana	Roslanova	KAZ	28.9.80	1h	NC	Almaty	25 Jul
52.05	Michelle	Burgher	JAM	12.3.77	3	NC	Kingston	21 Jun
52.05	Solen	Désert	FRA	2.8.82	2	EU23	Bydgoszcz	19 Jul
	(70)							
52.06	Angel	Perkins	USA-J	10.5.84	2	NC-j	Stanford	22 Jun
52.06	Marie-Louise	Bévis	FRA	12.10.72	1		Nogent-sur-Marne	28 Jun
52.06	Karen	Shinkins	IRL	15.10.76	5h1	WCh	Saint-Denis	24 Aug
52.07	Lucimar	Teodoro	BRA	1.5.81	2	NC	São Paulo	13 Jun
52.09	Natasha	Hastings	USA-Y	23.7.86	3	NC-j	Stanford	22 Jun
52.11	Hrísa	Goudenoúdi	GRE	28.3.77	3	ECp-S	Firenze	21 Jun
52.12	Damayanthi	Dharsha	SRI	13.2.75	1		Manila	9 Jun
52.13	Birgit	Rockmeier	GER	29.11.73	2		Leverkusen	3 Aug
52.16	Ebony	Floyd	USA	21.10.83	1		Charlotte	17 May
52.19	Ionela	Tîrlea	ROM	9.2.76	2	ECCp	Valencia	24 May
	(80)							
52.20	Libania	Grenot	CUB	12.7.83	1	NC	La Habana	28 May
52.22A	Surita	Febbraio	RSA	27.12.73	2		Bloemfontein	7 Feb
52.23		Bu Fanfang	CHN	10.2.78	2	NC	Shanghai	12 Sep

Mark	Name		Nat	Born	Pos	Meet	Venue	Date
52.24	Rosemary	Hayward	AUS	10.11.80	2	NC	Brisbane	4 Apr
52.24	Monika	Bejnar	POL	10.3.81	4	Kuso	Warszawa	15 Jun
52.26	Allyson	Felix	USA-J	18.11.85	1		Pasadena	29 Mar
52.26	Grit	Breuer	GER	16.2.72	2	NC	Ulm	29 Jun
52.26	Anita	Mormand	FRA	20.2.71	1		Albertville	10 Jul
52.27	Claudia	Hoffmann	GER	10.12.82	3		Leverkusen	3 Aug
52.27	Anna	Belova	RUS	.80	4s1	NC	Tula	8 Aug
	(90)							
52.28A	Perla	dos Santos	BRA	29.1.82	1		Tunja	18 May
52.28	Natalya	Antyukh	RUS	26.6.81	3	Odlozil	Praha	29 Jun
52.30	Androula	Sialou	CYP	27.1.73	1		Kalamáta	31 May
52.30	Josiane	Tito	BRA	8.8.79	3	NC	São Paulo	13 Jun
52.30	Awatef	Benhassine	TUN	5.4.80	1		Alger	17 Jul
52.30	Shanta	Ghosh	GER	3.1.75	4		Leverkusen	3 Aug
52.31	Francine	Landre	FRA	26.7.70	2		Genève	14 Jun
52.33	Glory	Nwosu	NGR-J	24.12.84	2h3	AfG	Abuja	12 Oct
52.34	Irina	Belova	RUS	.81	2rB		Moskva	26 Jul
52.34	Virna	De Angeli	ITA	27.2.76	1	NC	Rieti	3 Aug
	(100)							

52.35	Katharine	Merry	GBR	21.9.74	13 Jul
52.36	Tonette	Dyer	USA	28.3.82	12 Jun
52.40	Natasha	Staten	USA	2.12.81	19 May
52.42	Rosemary	Okafor	NGR	22.5.81	18 Jul
52.43	Mikele	Barber	USA	4.10.80	28 Mar
52.43	Shana	Cox	USA-J	22.1.85	31 May
52.43	Eliana	Pacheco	VEN	14.1.79	21 Jun
52.44	Natalya	Ivanova	RUS	25.6.81	28 Jun
52.50	Karen	Gayle	JAM	15.10.81	26 Apr
52.50	Cassandra	Reed	USA	13.9.83	12 Jun
52.50	Sandrine	Thiébaud-Kangni	TOG	21.4.76	24 Aug
52.52	Jasmine	Lee	USA-Y	5.4.86	22 Jun
52.53	Rajwinder	Kaur Gill	IND	.80	4 Mar
52.56	Brenda	Taylor	USA	9.2.79	22 Mar
52.56	Yekaterina	Bakhvalova	RUS	8.3.72	29 Jul
52.57	Aneisha	McLaughlin	JAM-Y	6.1.86	19 Apr
52.57		Tang Xiaoyin	CHN-J	29.4.85	12 Sep
52.59	Svetlana	Bodritskaya	KAZ	7.11.71	28 May
52.61	Nedyalka	Nedkova	BUL	15.3.77	7 Jun
52.62	Mary	Danner	USA	3.1.80	11 May
52.64A	Jacinta	Wambui	KEN	.78	26 Jul
52.65	Mariya	Dryakhlova	RUS-J	24.4.84	26 Jul
52.66	Olesya	Pogorelova	RUS	30.3.79	31 May
52.67	Laura	Gerber	SUI	29.10.80	22 Mar
52.67	Jennifer	Meadows	GBR	17.4.81	29 Jun
52.68	Anna	Kozak	BLR	22.6.74	21 May
52.68	Shellene	Williams	JAM	19.2.81	21 Jun
52.69	Sheryl	Morgan	JAM	6.11.83	5 Apr
52.69		Zhang Xiaoyuan	CHN	17.8.82	12 Sep
52.69	Annabelle	Smith	AUS	8.1.83	13 Dec
52.70	Natalya	Shevtsova	RUS	17.12.74	31 May
52.70	Sophie	Smellie	JAM	6.11.79	12 Jun
52.71	Anissa	Gainey	USA	25.7.81	31 May
52.75	Ana H.	Peña	CUB	1.1.82	28 May
52.75	Danielle	Perpoli	ITA	7.3.68	3 Aug
52.76	Debbie-Ann	Parris	JAM	24.3.73	12 Apr
52.76	Tiandra	Ponteen	SKN-J	9.11.84	19 Apr
52.76	Natalya	Pigida	UKR	30.1.81	4 Jul
52.77	Jerrika	Chapple	USA-J	11.9.84	10 May
52.77	Deonna	Lawrence	USA-Y	21.3.86	22 Jun
52.78	Mariana	Dimitrova	BUL	29.7.82	12 Jul
52.78	Olga	Maksimova	RUS	9.8.76	7 Aug
52.81	Maria Laura	Almirão	BRA	20.9.77	6 Jul
52.82	Tamsyn	Lewis	AUS	20.7.78	13 Mar
52.82	Olga	Goncharova	RUS	1.1.77	8 Jun
52.82	Norfalia	Carabalí	ESP	21.1.64	28 Jun
52.83	Yvonne	Harrison	PUR	12.2.75	21 Jun
52.86	Olga	Kotlyarova	RUS	12.4.76	8 Aug
52.89	Yana	Bagnyuk	RUS	7.1.83	28 Jun
52.89	Tatyana	Movchan (150)	UKR	19.9.70	4 Jul
52.90	Yekaterina	Bobrik	BLR	15.11.83	21 May
52.91	Nicole	Ireland	USA	23.4.82	19 Apr
52.92	Catherine	Murphy	GBR	21.9.75	26 Jul
52.93	Oluyemi	Fagbamila	NGR	23.2.83	19 Jul
52.94	Tiffany	Barnes	USA		31 May
52.94	Joanne	Cuddihy	IRL-J	11.5.84	27 Aug
52.95	Sasha	Spencer	USA	4.8.79	19 Apr
52.95	Olga	Tereshkova	KAZ-J	26.10.84	21 Jun
52.95	Zhanna	Kashcheyeva	RUS	27.7.82	28 Jun
52.96		Yin Yin Khine	MYA	15.6.77	21 Sep
52.97	Julia	Alba	ESP	30.5.72	7 Jun
52.97	Yulia	Krevsun (Gurtovenko)	UKR	8.12.80	3 Jul
53.00	Patricia	Hall	JAM	16.10.82	12 Apr
53.01	Ieva	Zunda	LAT	20.7.78	3 May
53.01	Johsie	Liles	USA-J	85	10 May
53.02	Yelena	Andreyeva	RUS	9.5.69	31 May
53.02	Yekaterina	Dakhnovskaya	RUS	81	28 Jun
53.03	Shevon	Stoddart	USA	21.11.82	30 May
53.04	Naleya	Downer	JAM	27.1.80	16 Jul
53.06	Mayra	González	MEX	24.11.73	12 Jul
53.06A	Virginie	Michanol	FRA-J	18.6.85	3 Aug
53.07	Indira	Terrero	CUB-J	29.11.85	28 May
53.08	Lesley	Owusu	GBR	21.12.78	12 Apr
53.08	Nahida	Touhami	ALG	10.2.78	14 Jul
53.09	Joni	Smith	USA	2.7.81	18 May
53.09	Antonina	Krivoshapka	RUS-Y	21.7.87	29 Jul
53.10	Patrizia	Spuri	ITA	18.2.73	6 Jun
53.10	Elena	Córcoles	ESP	7.6.77	7 Jun
53.11A	Licretia	Sibley	USA	3.8.83	12 Apr
53.11	Courtnie	Ratliff	USA	30.10.80	12 Apr
53.11	Carielle	Doe	USA	10.11.80	30 May
53.12	Carole	Mebam Kaboud	CMR	17.9.78	28 Feb
53.12	Elodie	Cruchant	FRA	22.12.80	28 Jun
53.13	Miriam	Hrdlickova	SVK	4.1.76	21 Jun
53.13	Irina	Khlyustova	BLR	14.6.78	11 Jul
53.13	Maria	Rus	ROM	19.1.83	9 Aug
53.14	Susan	Andrews	AUS	26.5.71	9 Mar
53.14	Ahandrea	Allen	USA		30 May
53.15	Letitia	Davis	USA		19 Apr
53.15	Foy	Williams	CAN	27.9.73	20 Jul
53.16	Anna	Jesien	POL	10.12.78	25 May
53.16	Yudalis	Díaz	CUB	20.9.79	28 May
53.16	Carey	Marshall	GBR	19.11.79	14 Jun
53.17	Katerina	Dressler	AUS	21.9.81	22 Mar
53.17	Sashanie	Simpson	JAM	15.1.81	30 May
53.17	Dímitra	Dóva	GRE	2.7.74	12 Jul
53.18	Zuzanna	Radecka	POL	2.4.75	3 Aug
53.19	Adia	McKinnon (198)	TRI	18.4.81	31 May

Indoors

50.57		Nazarova			1	NC	Moskva	26 Feb
51.00	Yuliya	Pechonkina	RUS	21.4.78	2	NC	Moskva	26 Feb
51.11	Christine	Amertil	BAH	18.8.79	2s1	WI	Birmingham	15 Mar
51.13	Grit	Breuer	GER	16.2.72	3	WI	Birmingham	16 Mar
51.73	Natalya	Antyukh	RUS	26.6.81	4	NC	Moskva	26 Feb
51.74	Catherine	Murphy	GBR	21.9.75	2s2	WI	Birmingham	15 Mar
51.79	Lashinda	Demus	USA	10.3.83	1rA	NCAA	Fayetteville	15 Mar

Mark	Name		Nat	Born	Pos	Meet	Venue	Date
51.92	Mikele	Barber	USA	4.10.80	1h2	NCAA	Fayetteville	14 Mar

52.41	Faith	Rein	USA	7.4.81	14 Mar	52.91	Raasin	McIntosh	USA	29.4.82	14 Mar
52.52	Olesya	Pogorelova	RUS	30.3.79	1 Mar	52.94	Naleya	Downer	JAM	27.1.80	14 Mar
						53.09	Irina	Anashkina	RUS	31.1.72	30 Jan

Low altitude bests

51.93	Fox	3	Lincoln NE	31 May	52.43	Febbraio	7 Mar	52.71	dos Santos	29 Mar

Hand timing

51.8	Olga	Mishchenko	UKR	24.11.71	1		Kiev	29 Jul
52.2	Nedyalka	Nedkova	BUL	15.3.77	1	Serb Ch	Kragujevac	1 Aug
53.0	Aleksandra	Ryzhkova	UKR	9.7.80	2		Kiev	29 Jul

JUNIORS

See main list for top 7 juniors. 14 performances by 2 women to 51.90. Additional marks and further juniors:

Richards	50.63	1	NCAAr	Lincoln NE	31 May	51.32	4s1	WCh	Saint-Denis	25 Aug
	51.00	2h5	WCh	Saint-Denis	24 Aug	51.41	2s2	NCAA	Sacramento	13 Jun
	51.01	1	NC	Stanford	21 Jun	51.73	1		Austin	3 May
	51.03	3	GP	London CP)	8 Aug	51.74	1s2	NC	Stanford	20 Jun
	51.15	6	WK	Zürich	15 Aug	51.81	1h2	NC	Stanford	19 Jun
	51.26	3	ISTAF	Berlin (P)	10 Aug	51.87i	1	NCAA	Fayetteville	15 Mar

52.43	Shana	Cox	USA	22.1.85	2		Orlando	31 May
52.52	Jasmine	Lee	USA-Y	5.4.86	4	NC	Stanford	22 Jun
52.57	Aneisha	McLaughlin (10)	JAM-Y	6.1.86	1	Carifta	Port of Spain	19 Apr
52.57		Tang Xiaoyin	CHN	29.4.85	3	NC	Shanghai	12 Sep
52.65	Mariya	Dryakhlova	RUS	24.4.84	1	EJ	Tampere	26 Jul
52.76	Tiandra	Ponteen	SKN	9.11.84	2	Carifta	Port of Spain	19 Apr
52.77	Jerrika	Chapple	USA	11.9.84	1		Austin	10 May
52.77	Deonna	Lawrence	USA-Y	21.3.86	5	NC-j	Stanford	22 Jun
52.94	Joanne	Cuddihy	IRL-J	11.5.84	4	WUG	Daegu	27 Aug
52.95	Olga	Tereshkova	KAZ	26.10.84	1		Almaty	21 Jun
53.01	Johsie	Liles	USA	.85	2		Austin	10 May
53.06A	Virginie	Michanol	FRA	18.6.85	1		Font-Romeu	3 Aug
53.07	Indira	Terrero (20)	CUB	29.11.85	3	NC	La Habana	28 May

600 METRES

1:23.13	Maria	Mutola	MOZ	27.10.72	1		Naimette	2 Sep
1:23.78	Natalya	Khrushchelyova	RUS	30.5.73	2		Naimette	2 Sep
1:25.41	Kelly	Holmes	GBR	19.4.70	3		Naimette	2 Sep
1:26.75	Tina	Paulino	MOZ	7.7.73	4		Naimette	2 Sep
1:27.01	Letitia	Vriesde	SUR	5.10.64	5		Naimette	2 Sep
1:27.11	Sandra	Stals	BEL	5.6.75	6		Naimette	2 Sep

800 METRES

1:55.55	Maria	Mutola	MOZ	27.10.72	1	GP	Madrid (C)	19 Jul
1:56.57		Mutola			1	Athl	Lausanne	1 Jul
1:57.21		Mutola			1	GGala	Roma	11 Jul
1:57.44	Jolanda	Ceplak	SLO	12.9.76	2	GGala	Roma	11 Jul
1:57.58		Mutola			1	Gaz	Saint-Denis	4 Jul
1:57.76		Ceplak			1	GS	Ostrava	12 Jun
1:57.78		Mutola			1	VD	Bruxelles	5 Sep
1:57.79		Ceplak			1	GP	Tríkala	24 Jun
1:57.82	Amina	Aït Hammou	MAR	18.7.78	3	GGala	Roma	11 Jul
1:57.84		Ceplak			2	Gaz	Saint-Denis	4 Jul
1:57.98		Mutola			1	Pre	Eugene	24 May
1:57.99	Stephanie	Graf	AUT	26.4.73	4	GGala	Roma	11 Jul
1:58.05	Natalya	Khrushchelyova	RUS	30.5.73	1	Znam	Tula	8 Jun
1:58.07		Khrushchelyova			1	NC	Tula	8 Aug
1:58.26		Ceplak			1	GP II	Rieti	7 Sep
1:58.26		Ceplak			1		Rovereto	10 Sep
1:58.30		Ceplak			1	ECp-1B	Velenje	21 Jun
1:58.45		Mutola			1s2	WCh	Saint-Denis	24 Aug
1:58.47	Svetlana	Klyuka	RUS	27.12.78	1r4		Moskva	27 Jul
1:58.53		Khrushchelyova			2	VD	Bruxelles	5 Sep
1:58.61	Jearl	Miles-Clark	USA	4.9.66	2	Pre	Eugene	24 May
1:58.66		Aït Hammou			3	VD	Bruxelles	5 Sep
1:58.69	Kelly	Holmes	GBR	19.4.70	4	VD	Bruxelles	5 Sep
1:58.71	Larisa	Chzhao	RUS	4.2.71	2	Znam	Tula	8 Jun
1:58.75	Natalya	Yevdokimova	RUS	17.3.78	2	NC	Tula	8 Aug
1:58.80		Mutola			1	GP	Gateshead	13 Jul
1:58.82		Aït Hammou			3	Gaz	Saint-Denis	4 Jul
1:58.82		Mutola			1		Moskva	20 Sep

Mark	Name		Nat	Born	Pos	Meet	Venue	Date
1:58.84		Miles-Clark			1	NC	Stanford	22 Jun
1:58.86		Holmes			2s2	WCh	Saint-Denis	24 Aug
	(30/10)							
1:58.89	Diane	Cummins	CAN	19.1.74	3	Athl	Lausanne	1 Jul
1:58.93	Claudia	Gesell	GER	18.12.77	5	GGala	Roma	11 Jul
1:59.23	Faith	Macharia	KEN	9.2.76	3	Athl	Lausanne	1 Jul
1:59.28	Svetlana	Cherkasova	RUS	20.5.78	2r4		Moskva	27 Jul
1:59.35	Tamsyn	Lewis	AUS	20.7.78	4	Athl	Lausanne	1 Jul
1:59.46	Judit	Varga	HUN	16.4.76	2	GS	Ostrava	12 Jun
1:59.56	Tanya	Blake	MLT	16.1.71	4	Pre	Eugene	24 May
1:59.62	Mayte	Martínez	ESP	17.5.76	6	Gaz	Saint-Denis	4 Jul
1:59.63	Irina	Vashentseva	RUS	30.9.80	1r3		Moskva	27 Jul
1:59.68	Maria	Cioncan	ROM	19.6.77	1	RomIC	Bucuresti	8 Jun
	(20)							
1:59.74	Seltana	Aït Hammou	MAR	21.5.80	1		Alger	17 Jul
1:59.75	Jennifer	Toomey	USA	19.12.71	5	Pre	Eugene	24 May
1:59.91	Nicole	Teter	USA	8.11.73	2	NC	Stanford	22 Jun
1:59.94	Olga	Raspopova	RUS	27.12.78	3r4		Moskva	27 Jul
1:59.98	Yekaterina	Rozenberg	RUS	23.1.80	2r3		Moskva	27 Jul
2:00.01	Regina	Jacobs	USA	28.8.63	6	Pre	Eugene	24 May
2:00.06	Liliana	Barbulescu	ROM	5.2.82	1	WUG	Daegu	30 Aug
2:00.11	Anna	Zagórska	POL	26.7.80	2	WUG	Daegu	30 Aug
2:00.42	Akosua	Serwah	GHA	3.1.81	4s2	WCh	Saint-Denis	24 Aug
2:00.47	Brigita	Langerholc	SLO	23.7.76	5	Athl	Lausanne	1 Jul
	(30)							
2:00.49	Hayley	Tullett	GBR	17.2.73	3	GP	Madrid (C)	19 Jul
2:00.50	Susan	Andrews	AUS	26.5.71	1		Perth	16 Mar
2:00.50	Tina	Paulino	MOZ	7.7.73	2		Rovereto	10 Sep
2:00.52	Tatyana	Yegorova	RUS	23.10.80	6	NC	Tula	8 Aug
2:00.56	Joanne	Fenn	GBR	19.10.74	3s1	WCh	Saint-Denis	24 Aug
2:00.59	Anita	Brägger	SUI	6.10.72	2		Luzern	25 Jun
2:00.60	Lucia	Klocová	SVK	20.11.83	4	GS	Ostrava	12 Jun
2:00.62	Yuliya	Kosenkova	RUS	28.3.73	4r4		Moskva	27 Jul
2:00.65	Chantee	Earl	USA	17.7.78	4	NC	Stanford	22 Jun
2:00.65	Natalya	Gorelova	RUS	18.4.73	5r4		Moskva	27 Jul
	(40)							
2:00.69	Nelya	Neporadnaya	UKR-J	29.7.85	2	Gugl	Linz	31 Jul
2:00.76	Esther	Desviat	ESP	27.1.82	6	Athl	Lausanne	1 Jul
2:00.81	Anja	Knippel	GER	19.8.74	2		Cuxhaven	19 Jul
2:00.88	Letitia	Vriesde	SUR	5.10.64	4s1	WCh	Saint-Denis	24 Aug
2:00.90	Nouria	Mérah (Benida)	ALG	19.10.70	1		Alger	18 Aug
2:00.91	Yanelis	Lara	CUB	19.8.78	1		Getafe	10 Jul
2:00.93+	Virginie	Fouquet	FRA	9.9.75	1	in 1k	Heusden	2 Aug
2:00.94	Svetlana	Sidunova	RUS	29.5.81	1rB	NC	Tula	8 Aug
2:00.96	Tatyana	Andrianova	RUS	10.12.79	6r4		Moskva	27 Jul
2:00.96	Monika	Gradzki	GER	21.9.79	7	ISTAF	Berlin (P)	10 Aug
	(50)							
2:00.98	Christiane	Ritz dos Santos	BRA	6.10.81	1		São Paulo	28 Jun
2:00.98	Tatyana	Roslanova	KAZ	28.9.80	1	NC	Almaty	26 Jul
2:01.07	Adriana	Muñoz	CUB	16.3.82	1	NC	La Habana	28 May
2:01.07	Sandra	Stals	BEL	5.6.75	2		Tallinn	30 Jul
2:01.08	Susan	Scott	GBR	26.9.77	2	FBK	Hengelo	1 Jun
2:01.08	Hasna	Benhassi	MAR	1.6.78	5	GP	Tríkala	24 Jun
2:01.08	Yuliya	Krevsun (Gurtovenko)	UKR	8.12.80	2		Alger	17 Jul
2:01.11	Meskerem	Legesse	ETH-Y	28.9.86	2	GP II	Gresham	17 May
2:01.16	Alice	Schmidt	USA	3.10.81	1	NCAA	Sacramento	14 Jun
2:01.19	Tatyana	Rodionova	RUS	27.8.80	7r4		Moskva	27 Jul
	(60)							
2:01.2	Tamara	Tverdostup (Volkova)	UKR	17.7.79	1		Kiev	27 May
2:01.21	Charlotte	Moore	GBR-J	4.1.85	3		San Sebastián	10 Aug
2:01.22	Irina	Lishchinskaya	UKR	15.1.76	3	Gugl	Linz	31 Jul
2:01.39	Laura	Gerber	SUI	29.10.80	4	WUG	Daegu	30 Aug
2:01.51	Agnes	Samaria	NAM	11.8.72	6h2	WCh	Saint-Denis	23 Aug
2:01.54	Natalia	Rodríguez	ESP	2.6.79	4	GP	Madrid (C)	19 Jul
2:01.54	Mardrea	Hyman	JAM	22.12.72	3	GP II	Helsinki	18 Aug
2:01.56	Sasha	Spencer	USA	4.8.79	7	Pre	Eugene	24 May
2:01.62	Michelle	Ballentine	JAM	31.8.75	1	GP II	Stanford	7 Jun
2:01.65	Yelena	Sobolyeva	RUS	3.8.82	1	NC-23	Cheboksary	28 Jun
	(70)							
2:01.68		Yang Wei	CHN	24.7.83	1	NG	Changsha	26 Oct
2:01.68	Lwiza Msyani	John	TAN	18.5.80	1	Af-AsG	Hyderabad	30 Oct

Mark	Name		Nat	Born	Pos	Meet	Venue	Date
2:01.71	Hazel	Clark	USA	3.10.77	6	NC	Stanford	22 Jun
2:01.71	Marian	Burnett	GUY	22.2.76	2	GP II	Zagreb	7 Jul
2:01.73	Heidi	Jensen	DEN	14.8.66	8s2	WCh	Saint-Denis	24 Aug
2:01.75	Neisha	Bernard-Thomas	GRN	21.1.81	2	NCAA	Sacramento	14 Jun
2:01.75	Anca	Safta	ROM	9.1.78	2	NC	Bucuresti	10 Aug
2:01.75		Liu Xiaoping	CHN	4.1.78	1	NC	Shanghai	14 Sep
2:01.76	Rebecca	Lyne	GBR	4.7.82	3	NCAA	Sacramento	14 Jun
2:01.76+	Najla	Jaber	NED-J	12.5.84	1	in 1k	Heusden	2 Aug
	2:01.84	Jaber			6		San Sebastián	10 Aug
	(80)							
2:01.77	Ivonne	Teichmann	GER	11.4.77	2		Rehlingen	9 Jun
2:01.81	Nadezhda	Vorobyeva	RUS	30.5.77	3		Luzern	25 Jun
2:01.88	Josiane	Tito	BRA	8.8.79	1		São Caetano do Sul	31 May
2:01.92	Oksana	Zbrozhek	RUS	12.1.78	2rB	NC	Tula	8 Aug
2:01.96	Yin Yin	Khine	MYA	15.6.77	1	AsiC	Manila	23 Sep
2:01.97	Nahida	Touhami	ALG	10.2.78	5		Alger	17 Jul
2:02.00	Suzy	Walsham	AUS	22.11.73	3	GP II	Gresham	17 May
2:02.00	Mihaela	Olaru	ROM	7.2.82	3	NC	Bucuresti	10 Aug
2:02.01	Daniela	Cîmpanu	ROM	17.12.82	2	RomIC	Bucuresti	8 Jun
2:02.04	Grace	Ebor	NGR	8.8.77	1	AfG	Abuja	15 Oct
	(90)							
2:02.06	Luciana	Mendes	BRA	26.7.71	1	SACh	Barquisimeto	22 Jun
2:02.10	Miki	Nishimura	JPN	14.4.82	1	NC	Yokohama	8 Jun
2:02.16	Alina	Rîpanu	ROM	29.10.81	5	NC	Bucuresti	10 Aug
2:02.17	Adoración	García	ESP	19.7.76	6	GP	Madrid (C)	19 Jul
2:02.24	Rasa	Drazdauskaitė ¶	LTU	20.3.81	2		Gdansk	27 Jun
2:02.25	Lauren	Simmons	USA	1.5.79	7	NC	Stanford	22 Jun
2:02.25		Liu Qing	CHN-Y	28.4.86	2	NC	Shanghai	14 Sep
2:02.26	Lotte	Visschers	NED	2.8.79	4		Arnhem	25 Jun
2:02.31	Tatyana	Kononenko	RUS	29.3.81	4rB	NC	Tula	8 Aug
2:02.38	Alina	Cucerzan	ROM	28.7.74	3	RomIC	Bucuresti	8 Jun
	(100)							

2:02.42	Sandra	Teixeira	POR	13.3.78	29 Aug
2:02.45	Tatyana	Petlyuk	UKR	22.2.82	25 Jun
2:02.46	Olga	Komyagina	RUS	10.2.74	15 Jul
2:02.46		Xie Sainan	CHN-Y	3.11.86	26 Oct
2:02.47	Sonja	Roman	SLO	11.3.79	7 Jul
2:02.53	Vicki	Lynch-Pounds	CAN	6.6.70	6 Jul
2:02.55	Olesya	Chumakova	RUS	23.7.81	27 Jul
2:02.59	Heather	Hennigar	CAN	13.5.73	11 Jun
2:02.61	Marlén	Estévez	ESP	29.8.71	5 Jul
2:02.7	Oksana	Ilyushkina	UKR	25.5.74	27 May
2:02.70	Claudia	Salvarani	ITA	8.3.75	11 Jul
2:02.74	Tiffany	McWilliams	USA	20.10.82	18 May
2:02.76	Simona	Barcau	ROM-J	17.7.85	26 Jul
2:02.76		Wang Yuanping	CHN	8.12.76	14 Sep
2:02.79	Elisabetta	Artuso	ITA	25.4.74	31 May
2:02.79	Amechi Joy	Eze	NGR-J	.84	17 Jul
2:02.82	Zamira	Amirova	UZB	11.6.79	28 May
2:02.84	Rosibel	García	COL	13.2.81	22 Jun
2:02.88	Kathleen	Friedrich	GER	13.7.77	19 Jul
2:02.9	Yuneisy	Santiusty	CUB-J	24.12.84	20 Jun
2:02.9	Ieva	Zunda	LAT	20.7.78	28 Jun
2:02.92mx	Rikke	Rønholt	DEN	1.1.76	18 Jun
	2:03.56				16 Jul
2:03.00	Docus	Inzikuru	UGA	2.2.82	12 Jul
2:03.05	Nédia	Semedo	POR	14.11.78	19 Jul
2:03.05	Janet	Jepkosgei Busienei	KEN	13.2.83	15 Aug
2:03.06	Joanna	Kaczor	POL	27.12.81	18 Jul
2:03.07	Natalya	Lavshuk	RUS	22.2.80	15 Jun
2:03.08	Yuliya	Chizhenko	RUS	30.8.79	15 Jul
2:03.08	Irina	Mistyukevich	RUS	17.6.77	19 Jul
2:03.12	Tatyana	Buloychik	BLR	7.1.75	3 Aug
2:03.13	Debbie	Savage	AUS	18.2.80	22 Feb
2:03.14	Sarah	Ali-Khan	CAN	9.5.73	19 Jul
2:03.16	Maria Laura	Almirão	BRA	20.9.77	31 May
2:03.18	Latifa	Essarokh	FRA	11.12.73	12 Jul
2:03.19	Hayley	Ovens	GBR	5.12.75	29 Jun
2:03.19	Joanna	Buza	POL	15.4.81	29 Jun
2:03.21	Kenia	Sinclair	JAM	14.7.80	14 Jun
2:03.21	Ewelina	Setowska	POL	5.3.80	9 Jul
2:03.22	Alice	Nwosu	NGR-J	24.12.84	14 Oct
2:03.25	Freda	Davoren	IRL	16.3.73	12 Jun
2:03.27	Carmen	Douma-Hussar	CAN	12.3.77	11 Jun
2:03.31	Mary Jayne	Harrelson	USA	17.6.78	13 Jul
2:03.38	Amel	Tlili	TUN	31.7.83	22 Aug
2:03.40	Mariya	Shapayeva	RUS-Y	7.11.86	13 Jul
2:03.4	Svetlana	Chervan	UKR	19.2.81	13 Jun
2:03.41	Spéciose	Gakobwa	BDI	24.12.79	25 Jul
2:03.41	Kelly	McNeice	IRL	17.6.78	15 Aug
2:03.42	Jemma	Simpson	GBR-J	10.2.84	26 Jul
2:03.43	Mari	Järvenpää	FIN	29.11.81	11 Aug
2:03.44	Mishael	Bertrand (150)	USA	79	5 Jul
2:03.44	Ibtissam	Lakhouad	MAR	.82	5 Jul
2:03.45	Anny	Christofidou	CYP	7.1.81	29 Aug
2:03.46	Johanna	Risku	FIN	21.2.79	11 Aug
2:03.48	Hope	Sanders	USA	24.8.73	5 Jul
2:03.48	Madhuri A.	Singh	IND	15.2.71	23 Sep
2:03.50	Maura	Prendeville	IRL	27.6.75	25 Jun
2:03.5	Natalya	Sidorenko (Tobias)	UKR	22.11.80	12 Aug
2:03.5mx	Lucy	Vaughan	GBR	20.4.69	7 Sep
	2:03.70				26 Jul
2:03.51	Saïda	El Mehdi	MAR	82	31 May
2:03.55	Liliya	Bikbulatova	RUS-J	25.2.84	3 Jul
2:03.55	Alexia	Oberstolz	ITA	2.6.80	3 Aug
2:03.58	Toni	Hodgkinson	NZL	12.12.71	22 Mar
2:03.60	Nicole	Cook	USA	16.12.82	18 May
2:03.6	Oksana	Meltsayeva	UKR	16.8.75	13 Jun
2:03.63	René	Kalmer	RSA	3.11.80	26 Apr
2:03.64	Yevgeniya	Khaliullina	RUS-J	22.1.84	3 Jul
2:03.70	Natalya	Dukhnova	BLR	16.7.66	8 Aug
2:03.71	Mihaela	Stancescu	ROM	3.5.79	8 Jun
2:03.73	Anna	Katenkova	BLR	79	28 Jun
2:03.75	Tatyana	Borisova	KGZ	3.6.76	28 May
2:03.77	Svetlana	Lukashova	KAZ	2.5.77	26 Jul
2:03.78	Natalya	Shipitsyna	RUS	81	28 Jun
2:03.82	Yekaterina	Dedkova	RUS	8.3.72	15 Jun
2:03.85	Margarita	Plaksina	RUS	1.10.77	16 Jul
2:03.86	Lena	Nilsson	SWE	28.1.80	18 May
2:03.90	Yelena	Sidorchenkova	RUS	30.5.80	27 Jul
2:03.91	Sheena	Gooding	BAR	1.8.81	26 Apr
2:03.93	Rachael	Ogden	GBR	23.7.79	20 Aug
2:03.94	Irina	Krakoviak	LTU	16.11.77	12 Jun
2:03.96	Juliana Paula	de Azevedo	BRA	12.7.83	15 Jun
2:04.00	Berhane	Hirpassa	ETH	30.7.83	14 Oct
2:04.01	Kristina	Bratton	USA	7.5.81	18 May
2:04.02	Hind	Dehiba	MAR	.79	28 Jun
2:04.03	Aneta	Lemiesz	POL	17.1.81	14 Jun

Mark	Name		Nat	Born	Pos	Meet	Venue	Date
2:04.03	Kitty	Cziráki	HUN-J	16.7.84				26 Jul
2:04.04	Katrin Judit	Trauth	GER-J	21.6.84				3 Aug
2:04.05	Norica	Marafu	ROM	16.2.83				10 Aug
2:04.07	Jennifer	Ward	GBR	22.9.78				15 Aug
2:04.11	Viviane	Dorsile	FRA	1.6.67				25 Jul
2:04.12	Aleksandra	Starovoytova	BLR	4.11.82				8 Aug
2:04.14	Konstadína	Efedáki	GRE	1.10.78				15 Jun
2:04.18A	Lisa	van der Merwe	RSA	30.7.79				28 Mar
2:04.22A	Leonor	Piuza	MOZ	.78				28 Mar
2:04.22		Jiang Zhongmin	CHN-Y	5.8.86				26 Oct
2:04.24	Larisa	Mikhaylova	RUS	3.1.69				15 Jun
2:04.25	Lisbeth	Pedersen	NOR	20.11.75				9 Jun
2:04.25	Svetlana	Klimkovich (197)	BLR	26.8.80				8 Aug

Indoors

Mark	Name		Nat	Born	Pos	Meet	Venue	Date
1:58.83		Mutola			1		Gent	9 Feb
1:59.53	Mayte	Martínez	ESP	17.5.76	3	WI	Birmingham	16 Mar
1:59.74	Joanne	Fenn	GBR	19.10.74	1	NC	Birmingham	2 Mar
1:59.91	Yekaterina	Puzanova	RUS	1.1.79	1	NC	Moskva	26 Feb
2:00.52	Svetlana	Sidunova	RUS	29.5.81	1h2	NC	Moskva	25 Feb
2:00.55	Agnes	Samaria	NAM	11.8.72	4		Gent	9 Feb
2:00.59	Nadezhda	Vorobyeva	RUS	30.5.77	3	NC	Moskva	26 Feb
2:00.78	Miho	Sugimori	JPN	14.4.78	1	v CHN	Yokohama	22 Feb
2:01.11	Nédia	Semedo	POR	14.11.78	1	v ESP	Espinho	8 Mar
2:02.09	Elena	Iagar	ROM	16.1.75	1	NC	Bucuresti	22 Feb
2:02.11	Alesya	Turova	BLR	6.12.79	1	NC	Minsk	7 Feb
2:02.31	Heike	Meissner	GER	29.1.70	3	Spark	Stuttgart	2 Feb
2:02.4	Yelena	Sidorchenkova	RUS	30.5.80				16 Feb
2:04.03	Anna	Jakubczak	POL	2.2.73				15 Feb

Drugs disqualification

Mark	Name		Nat	Born	Date
2:02.92	Natalya	Dyadkova ¶	BLR	2.12.79	28 Jun

JUNIORS

See main list for top 5 juniors. 12 performances by 6 women to 2:02.65. Additional marks and further juniors:

Jaber	2:02.08	1		Arnhem	25 Jun					
Moore	2:02.45mx	1		Watford	14 May	2:02.59	4		Cottbus	4 Jun
	2:02.49	1h1	EJ	Tampere	24 Jul	2:02.65	10	GP	Gateshead	13 Jul

Mark	Name		Nat	Born	Pos	Meet	Venue	Date
2:02.46		Xie Sainan	CHN-Y	3.11.86	2	NG	Changsha	26 Oct
2:02.76	Simona	Barcau	ROM	17.7.85	1	EJ	Tampere	26 Jul
2:02.79	Amechi Joy	Eze	NGR-	.84	2	NC	Abuja	17 Jul
2:02.9	Yuneisy	Santiusty	CUB	24.12.84	3		La Habana	20 Jun
2:03.22	Alice	Nwosu (10)	NGR	24.12.84	3h3	AfG	Abuja	14 Oct
2:03.40	Mariya	Shapayeva	RUS-Y	7.11.86	1	WY	Sherbrooke	13 Jul
2:03.42	Jemma	Simpson	GBR	10.2.84	3	EJ	Tampere	26 Jul
2:03.55	Liliya	Bikbulatova	RUS	25.2.84	1	NC-j	Kazan	3 Jul
2:03.64	Yevgeniya	Khaliullina	RUS	22.1.84	2	NC-j	Kazan	3 Jul
2:04.03	Kitty	Cziráki	HUN	16.7.84	4	EJ	Tampere	26 Jul
2:04.04	Katrin Judit	Trauth	GER-J	21.6.84	6		Leverkusen	3 Aug
2:04.22		Jiang Zhongmin	CHN-Y	5.8.86	4	NG	Changsha	26 Oct
2:04.27	Diosmely	Peña	CUB	12.6.85	5	NC	La Habana	28 May
2:04.29		Liu li	CHN	2.9.84	5	NG	Changsha	26 Oct
2:04.30	Olga	Cristea (20)	MDA-Y	13.12.87	2	WY	Sherbrooke	13 Jul

1000 METRES

Mark	Name		Nat	Born	Pos	Meet	Venue	Date
2:33.15	Maria	Mutola	MOZ	27.10.72	1	DNG	Stockholm	5 Aug
2:35.56	Nelya	Neporadnaya	UKR-J	29.7.85	2	DNG	Stockholm	5 Aug
2:36.75	Seltana	Aït Hammou	MAR	21.5.80	3	DNG	Stockholm	5 Aug
2:36.94	Nouria	Mérah (Benida)	ALG	19.10.70	4	DNG	Stockholm	5 Aug
2:37.36	Judit	Varga	HUN	16.4.76	5	DNG	Stockholm	5 Aug
2:39.10	Diane	Cummins	CAN	19.1.74				5 Aug
2:39.53	Charlotte	Moore	GBR-J	4.1.85				5 Sep
2:39.58	Agnes	Samaria	NAM	11.8.72				5 Aug
2:40.20mx	Anita	Brägger	SUI	6.10.72				17 May
2:40.48	Michelle	Ballentine	JAM	31.8.75				2 Aug
2:41.38	Sonja	Roman	SLO	11.3.79				12 Sep

Indoors

Mark	Name		Nat	Born	Pos	Meet	Venue	Date
2:34.61		Mutola			1		Liévin	23 Feb
2:36.97	Lidia	Chojecka/Okninska	POL	25.1.77	2		Liévin	23 Feb
2:38.03	Jolanda	Ceplak	SLO	12.9.76	1	GP	Birmingham	21 Feb
2:38.24	Diane	Cummins	CAN	19.1.74	3		Liévin	23 Feb
2:38.45	Joanne	Fenn	GBR	19.10.74	2	GP	Birmingham	21 Feb
2:38.47	Kelly	Holmes	GBR	19.4.70	4		Liévin	23 Feb
2:38.59	Agnes	Samaria	NAM	11.8.72	5		Liévin	23 Feb
2:39.20	Brigita	Langerholc	SLO	23.7.76				21 Feb
2:39.74	Lucia	Klocová	SVK	20.11.83				16 Feb
2:39.80	Amina	Aït Hammou	MAR	18.7.78				21 Feb
2:40.00	Irina	Vashentseva	RUS	30.9.80				21 Feb
2:40.15	Tsvetelina	Kirilova	BUL	14.7.77				2 Feb

JUNIORS

Mark	Name		Nat	Born	Pos	Meet	Venue	Date
2:39.53	Charlotte	Moore	GBR	4.1.85	1-j	VD	Bruxelles	5 Sep
2:43.71i	Anna	Kutimskaya	RUS	1.7.84	2		Yekaterinburg	7 Jan
2:43.72	Georgie	Clarke	AUS	17.6.84	3		Navan	17 May

Symbols/Abbreviations

+ intermediate time in longer race, A made at an altitude of 1000m or higher, H in a heptathlon, h heat, qf quarter-final, sf semi-final, i indoors, Q qualifying round, r race number, -J juniors (b. 1984-5), Y- Youths (b. 1986 or later)

1500 METRES

Mark	Name		Nat	Born	Pos	Meet	Venue	Date
3:55.33	Süreyya	Ayhan	TUR	6.9.78	1	VD	Bruxelles	5 Sep
3:55.60		Ayhan			1	WK	Zürich	15 Aug
3:57.72		Ayhan			1	WAF	Monaco	13 Sep
3:58.52	Tatyana	Tomashova	RUS	1.7.75	1	WCh	Saint-Denis	31 Aug
3:59.04		Ayhan			2	WCh	Saint-Denis	31 Aug
3:59.58		Ayhan			1	ISTAF	Berlin (P)	10 Aug
3:59.95	Hayley	Tullett	GBR	17.2.73	3	WCh	Saint-Denis	31 Aug
4:00.07	Yekaterina	Rozenberg	RUS	23.1.80	2	WK	Zürich	15 Aug
4:00.12	Yelena	Zadorozhnaya	RUS	3.12.77	2	VD	Bruxelles	5 Sep
4:00.58		Rozenberg			3	VD	Bruxelles	5 Sep
4:00.59		Rozenberg			4	WCh	Saint-Denis	31 Aug
4:00.91		Tomashova			3	WK	Zürich	15 Aug
4:01.00	Olga	Yegorova	RUS	28.3.72	1	GGala	Roma	11 Jul
4:01.18		Tullett			4	WK	Zürich	15 Aug
4:01.19		Tomashova			1	NC	Tula	10 Aug
4:01.22	Jackline	Maranga	KEN	16.12.77	4	VD	Bruxelles	5 Sep
4:01.30	Natalia	Rodríguez	ESP	2.6.79	2	GGala	Roma	11 Jul
4:01.45		Zadorozhnaya			2	NC	Tula	10 Aug
4:01.48		Maranga			2	WAF	Monaco	13 Sep
4:01.60		Tullett			3	WAF	Monaco	13 Sep
4:01.63	Regina	Jacobs	USA	28.8.63	1		Stanford	21 Jun
4:01.64		Maranga			5	WCh	Saint-Denis	31 Aug
4:01.69	Suzy	(10) Favor Hamilton	USA	8.8.68	3	GGala	Roma	11 Jul
4:01.76		Rozenberg			3	NC	Tula	10 Aug
4:01.79	Jo	Pavey	GBR	20.9.73	4	WAF	Monaco	13 Sep
4:01.80	Naomi	Mugo	KEN	2.1.77	5	VD	Bruxelles	5 Sep
4:01.83	Daniela	Yordanova	BUL	8.3.76	6	VD	Bruxelles	5 Sep
4:01.96	Kelly	Holmes	GBR	19.4.70	4	GGala	Roma	11 Jul
4:01.99	Courtney	Babcock	CAN	30.6.72	7	VD	Bruxelles	5 Sep
4:02.03		Pavey			5	GGala	Roma	11 Jul
	(30/15)							
4:02.19	Judit	Varga	HUN	16.4.76	6	GGala	Roma	11 Jul
4:02.44	Jolanda	Ceplak	SLO	12.9.76	1	Pre	Eugene	24 May
4:02.54	Hasna	Benhassi	MAR	1.6.78	7	GGala	Roma	11 Jul
4:02.60	Irina	Lishchinskaya	UKR	15.1.76	1		Dortmund	15 Jun
4:02.74	Kutre	Dulecha	ETH	22.8.78	9	GGala	Roma	11 Jul
	(20)							
4:02.80	Maria	Cioncan	ROM	19.6.77	9	WCh	Saint-Denis	31 Aug
4:03.32	Alesya	Turova	BLR	6.12.79	10	GGala	Roma	11 Jul
4:03.57	Nuria	Fernández	ESP	16.8.76	12	GGala	Roma	11 Jul
4:03.83	Natalya	Gorelova	RUS	18.4.73	10	VD	Bruxelles	5 Sep
4:03.96	Meskerem	Legesse	ETH-Y	28.9.86	3	Pre	Eugene	24 May
4:04.24	Nelya	Neporadnaya	UKR-J	29.7.85	5s1	WCh	Saint-Denis	29 Aug
4:04.38	Yuliya	Kosenkova	RUS	28.3.73	3	GP	Madrid (C)	19 Jul
4:04.55	Maria	Martins	FRA	1.4.74	5	Gaz	Saint-Denis	4 Jul
4:04.61	Natalya	Yevdokimova	RUS	17.3.78	2	GP II	Rieti	7 Sep
4:04.77	Olga	Komyagina	RUS	10.2.74	6	NC	Tula	10 Aug
	(30)							
4:05.18	Adoración	García	ESP	19.7.76	13	GGala	Roma	11 Jul
4:05.36	Veerle	Dejaeghere	BEL	1.8.73	14	GGala	Roma	11 Jul
4:05.55	Svetlana	Cherkasova	RUS	20.5.78	7	NC	Tula	10 Aug
4:05.57	Nouria	Mérah-Benida	ALG	19.10.70	10	WK	Zürich	15 Aug
4:05.80	Alina	Cucerzan	ROM	28.7.74	1		Pírgos	27 Jul
4:06.07	Latifa	Essarokh	FRA	11.12.73	1		San Sebastián	10 Aug
4:06.36	Mardrea	Hyman	JAM	22.12.72	4	Pre	Eugene	24 May
4:06.64	Carla	Sacramento	POR	10.12.71	3		San Sebastián	10 Aug
4:06.75	Tiffany	McWilliams	USA	20.10.82	1	NCAA	Sacramento	14 Jun
4:07.16	Helen	Clitheroe (Pattinson)	GBR	2.1.74	2	GP II	Sevilla	7 Jun
	(40)							
4:07.21	Yuliya	Chizhenko	RUS	30.8.79	1		Cuxhaven	19 Jul
4:07.25	Elvan	Abeylegesse	TUR	11.9.82	1	ECCpB	Beograd	25 May
4:07.32	Johanna	Risku	FIN	21.2.79	7	Bisl	Oslo	27 Jun
4:07.38	Margaret	Ngotho	KEN	6.9.71	3	GP II	Sevilla	7 Jun
4:07.52	Trine	Pilskog	NOR	1.12.72	15	GGala	Roma	11 Jul
4:07.56	Freda	Davoren	IRL	16.3.73	2		Cuxhaven	19 Jul
4:07.69	Lena	Nilsson	SWE	28.1.80	5	Pre	Eugene	24 May
4:07.69	René	Kalmer	RSA	3.11.80	3		Dortmund	15 Jun
4:07.76	Andrea	Suldesová	CZE	11.2.75	8	Bisl	Oslo	27 Jun

Mark	Name		Nat	Born	Pos	Meet	Venue	Date
4:07.78	Suzy	Walsham	AUS	22.11.73	6	Pre	Eugene	24 May
	(50)							
4:07.78	Rasa	Drazdauskaité ¶	LTU	20.3.81	4		Poznan	29 Jun
4:07.79	Natalya	Sidorenko (Tobias)	UKR	22.11.80	3		Luzern	25 Jun
4:08.01	Berhane	Hirpassa	ETH	30.7.83	5		Poznan	29 Jun
4:08.02	Meryem	Boucetta	MAR	15.5.81	16	GGala	Roma	11 Jul
4:08.09	Carmen	Douma-Hussar	CAN	12.3.77	1	Jerome	Burnaby	8 Jun
4:08.16	Sarah	Schwald	USA	2.1.73	3		Carson/Los Angeles	1 Jun
4:08.33	Bouchra	Chaabi	MAR	22.9.80	4		San Sebastián	10 Aug
4:08.37	Leah	Pells	CAN	9.11.64	2	Jerome	Burnaby	8 Jun
4:08.73	Lidia	Chojecka/Okninska	POL	25.1.77	13	WK	Zürich	15 Aug
4:08.74	Yelena	Burykina	RUS	7.5.72	4		Moskva	26 Jul
	(60)							
4:08.90	Justyna	Lesman	POL	6.11.80	6		Poznan	29 Jun
4:08.90	Eva	Arias	ESP	1.1.80	5		San Sebastián	10 Aug
4:08.99	Oksana	Belyakova	RUS	9.9.75	5		Moskva	26 Jul
4:09.01		Xing Huina	CHN-J	25.2.84	1	NC	Shanghai	12 Sep
4:09.06	Konstadína	Efedákí	GRE	1.10.78	3	ECp-S	Firenze	22 Jun
4:09.10	Shayne	Culpepper	USA	3.12.73	4		Carson/Los Angeles	1 Jun
4:09.17	Viola	Kibiwott	KEN	22.12.83	6	ISTAF	Berlin (P)	10 Aug
4:09.25	Zulema	Fuentes-Pila	ESP	25.5.77	6		San Sebastián	10 Aug
4:09.28	Livia	Tóth	HUN	7.1.80	2		Florø	31 May
4:09.39	Anna	Zagórska	POL	26.7.80	2		Königs Wusterhausen	6 Aug
	(70)							
4:09.5	Yelena	Fadeyeva	UKR	23.6.66	1		Kiev	29 Jul
4:09.51	Anna	Jakubczak	POL	2.2.73	6	GP	Madrid (C)	19 Jul
4:09.57	Adriana	Muñoz	CUB	16.3.82	1	PAm	Santo Domingo	7 Aug
4:09.58	Mary Jayne	Harrelson	USA	17.6.78	2		Brunswick	5 Jul
4:09.67	Sonja	Roman	SLO	11.3.79	7	GP	Madrid (C)	19 Jul
4:09.77	Meselech	Melkamu	ETH-J	19.4.85	7		San Sebastián	10 Aug
4:09.86	Sonia	O'Sullivan	IRL	28.11.69	1		Cork	5 Jul
4:10.11	Jennifer	Toomey	USA	19.12.71	5		Carson/Los Angeles	1 Jun
4:10.13	Monica	Wangare	KEN-Y	4.10.86	8	GP	Madrid (C)	19 Jul
4:10.24	Marlene	Breytenbach	RSA	4.1.82	2		Durban	11 Apr
	(80)							
4:10.31	Wioletta	Janowska	POL	9.6.77	3		Königs Wusterhausen	6 Aug
4:10.34	Roisin	McGettigan	IRL	23.8.80	3		Cork	5 Jul
4:10.42	Malindi	Elmore	CAN	13.3.80	4	PAm	Santo Domingo	7 Aug
4:10.49	Christy	Wurth	USA	11.7.80	3	NCAA	Sacramento	14 Jun
4:10.62	Collette	Liss	USA	29.4.73	8	Pre	Eugene	24 May
4:10.72	Johanna	Nilsson	SWE	27.3.83	1	MSR	Walnut	19 Apr
4:10.74	Tatyana	Yegorova	RUS	23.10.80	6		Moskva	26 Jul
4:10.76	Irina	Mikitenko	GER	23.8.72	6		Dortmund	15 Jun
4:10.82	Gelete	Burika	ETH-Y	15.2.86	3		Cuxhaven	19 Jul
	4:10.8+				7	in 1M	Heusden	2 Aug
4:10.84	Maria	Protópappa	GRE	5.5.73	3		Pírgos	27 Jul
	(90)							
4:10.85	Inna	Poluskina	LAT-J	7.7.84	1	v2N	Kaunas	9 Aug
4:10.87	Irina	Krakoviak	LTU	16.11.77	7		Dortmund	15 Jun
4:10.93	Courtney	Inman	CAN	7.1.80	4	NCAA	Sacramento	14 Jun
4:10.98	Heidi	Jensen	DEN	14.8.66	4		Königs Wusterhausen	6 Aug
4:11.17	Kara	Goucher	USA	9.7.78	4		Pírgos	27 Jul
4:11.23	Marina	Muncan	SCG	6.11.82	5	NCAA	Sacramento	14 Jun
4:11.27	Zhor	El Kamch	MAR	15.3.73	1		Khémisset	28 Jun
4:11.30	Emilie	Mondor	CAN	29.4.81	3	Jerome	Burnaby	8 Jun
4:11.34	Daniela	Cîmpanu	ROM	17.12.82	2	RomIC	Bucuresti	7 Jun
4:11.37		Xie Sainan	CHN-Y	3.11.86	2	NC	Shanghai	12 Sep
	(100)							

4:11.38+	Mestawet	Tadesse	ETH-J	19.7.85	15 Jun
4:11.46	Dulce	Rodríguez	MEX	14.8.72	7 Aug
4:11.49	Lyubov	Ivanova	RUS	2.3.81	26 Jul
4:11.53	Beth	Brewster	USA	18.2.80	14 Jun
4:11.60	Shalane	Flanagan	USA	8.7.81	16 May
4:11.67	Jamie	Cottle	USA	25.6.80	14 Jun
4:11.75	Olesya	Chumakova	RUS	23.7.81	19 Jul
4:11.78	Vicky	Pounds (Lynch)	CAN	6.6.70	8 Jun
4:11.92	Aurélie	Coulaud	FRA	5.5.79	3 Jul
4:11.92	Rakhim	Rakhimkulova	RUS	5.11.79	10 Aug
4:12.00	Megan	Metcalfe	CAN	27.1.82	14 Jun
4:12.02	Yelena	Sobolyeva	RUS	3.8.82	8 Jun
4:12.03	Janet	Trujillo	USA	7.8.75	8 Jun
4:12.11	Kerry	Gillibrand	GBR	13.9.76	5 Jul
4:12.37	Emily	Morris	AUS	23.10.78	24 May
4:12.39	Amy	Mortimer	USA	16.8.81	14 Jun
4:12.44	Tatyana	Rodionova	RUS	27.8.80	26 Jul
4:12.5	Carrie	Tollefson	USA	18.1.77	7 Jun
4:12.53	Hayley	Ovens	GBR	5.12.75	5 Jul
4:12.54	Fernanda	Ribeiro	POR	23.6.69	26 Jul
4:12.54	Olga	Kharina	RUS	21.12.80	26 Jul
4:12.55	Coletta	Chepchirchir	KEN	.78	19 Jul
4:12.60	Miesha	Marzell-Arnold	USA	29.1.75	16 May
4:12.61	Anastasiya	Fesenko	RUS	17.6.82	14 Jul
4:12.66		Wang Qingqin	CHN	17.9.83	12 Sep
4:12.67	Yelena	Stina	LAT-Y	11.5.86	14 Jun
4:12.85	Tatyana	Buloychik	BLR	7.1.75	28 Jun
4:12.9	Seltana	Aït Hammou	MAR	21.5.80	24 May

Mark	Name		Nat	Born	Date
4:12.95	Lisa	Dobriskey	GBR	23.12.83	19 Jul
4:12.97	Heather	Hennigar	CAN	13.5.73	8 Jun
4:13.00	Charlotte	Moore	GBR-J	4.1.85	8 Aug
4:13.08	Yelena	Sidorchenkova	RUS	30.5.80	10 Aug
4:13.13	Mieke	Geens	BEL	10.3.82	7 Jun
4:13.15	Krisztina	Papp	HUN	17.12.82	10 Jun
4:13.16	Ibtissam	Lakhouad	MAR	.82	6 Jul
4:13.26	María	Papadopoúlou	GRE	15.12.74	3 Aug
4:13.3	Saïda	El Mehdi	MAR	82	14 Jun
4:13.31	Yekaterina	Dedkova	RUS	8.3.72	10 Aug
4:13.32	Iris	Fuentes-Pila	ESP	10.8.80	7 Jun
4:13.37	Lisbeth	Pedersen	NOR	20.11.75	7 Jun
4:13.44	Anna	Kokina	RUS	12.12.76	10 Aug
4:13.57	Florence	Djépé	CMR	31.12.78	3 Jul
4:13.57	Georgie	Clarke	AUS-J	17.6.84	4 Dec
4:13.58	Ingvill	Måkestad	NOR	7.8.81	19 Jul
4:13.78	Mihalea	Olaru	ROM	7.2.82	27 Jul
4:13.79	Christine	Bardelle	FRA	16.8.74	26 Jun
4:13.87	Lucy	Wangui	KEN-J	24.3.84	10 May
4:13.89	Margarita	Plaksina	RUS	1.10.77	9 Aug
4:14.07	Svetlana	Lukashova	KAZ	2.5.77	28 Aug
4:14.1	Katie	McGregor (150)	USA	2.9.77	7 Jun
4:14.10	Natalie	Lewis	GBR	25.5.82	17 Jul
4:14.12	Heather	Sagan	USA	28.2.80	19 Jun
4:14.25	Amane	Godana	ETH-Y	86	31 May
4:14.27	Viola	Bor	KEN	79	6 Aug
4:14.46	Jenelle	Deatherage	USA	25.9.77	19 Jun
4:14.49	Anastasia	Starovoytova	BLR	4.11.82	28 Jun
4:14.5	Nanae	Kuwashiro	JPN	16.10.82	13 Oct
4:14.56	Emmanuelle	Bossert	FRA	23.9.71	3 Jul
4:14.66	Abir	Nakhli	TUN	21.9.81	24 Jun
4:14.68	Lauren	Fleshman	USA	26.9.81	18 May
4:14.69	Alemu	Techale	ETH-Y	13.12.87	25 Jun
4:14.70	Malgorzata	Jamroz	POL	16.10.73	29 Jun
4:14.70	Anita	Weyermann	SUI	8.12.77	8 Aug
4:14.72	Lauren	King	CAN	13.9.82	16 May
4:14.73	Alla	Zhilyayeva	RUS	5.2.69	26 Jul
4:14.80	Valeria	Rodríguez	ARG	23.9.76	8 Mar
4:14.82	Rebecca	Lyne	GBR	4.7.82	5 Jul
4:14.83	Elissa	Riedy	USA	13.7.77	19 Jun
4:14.84	Tatyana	Golovchenko	UKR	13.2.80	6 Jul
4:14.88	Yelena	Baranova/Pellois	RUS	9.11.69	1 Jun
4:14.89	Fanny	Pruvost	FRA	21.5.79	3 Jul
4:14.90	Docus	Inzikuru	UGA	2.2.82	28 Jun
4:14.94	Tatyana	Rasputina	RUS-J	12.5.84	3 Jul
4:14.96	Marie	Davenport	IRL	24.1.75	1 Jul
4:14.99	Pagóna	Níka	GRE	11.7.77	27 Jul
4:15.0	Nicole	Jefferson	USA	8.3.76	7 Jun
4:15.00	Danielle	Barnes	GBR-J	8.10.85	31 May
4:15.00	Treniere	Clement	USA	27.10.81	12 Jun
4:15.03	Barbara	Jablonska	POL	23.11.77	29 Jun
4:15.1	Siham	Hilali	MAR-Y	2.5.86	14 Jun
4:15.15	Christina	Carruzzo	SUI	9.1.81	19 Jul
4:15.16	Catherine	Berry	GBR	8.10.75	24 May
4:15.24	Kathleen	Friedrich	GER	13.7.77	15 Jun
4:15.25	Zakia	Mrisho	TAN-J	19.2.84	6 Sep
4:15.26	Sara	Palmas	ITA	7.7.77	3 Aug
4:15.28	Julie	Coulaud	FRA	7.8.82	3 Jul
4:15.31	Louise	Whittaker	GBR	29.11.82	17 Jul
4:15.32	Londa	Bevins	USA	30.5.81	12 Jun
4:15.35	Peninah	Chepchumba Biwott	KEN-J	14.1.85	3 Aug
4:15.42	Joanne	Fenn	GBR	19.10.74	8 Aug
4:15.43	Irene	Alfonso	ESP	6.2.81	17 Jul
4:15.46	Akiko	Kawashima	JPN	5.8.77	27 Sep
4:15.48	Sara	Gorton (193)	USA	2.10.81	2 May

Indoors

Mark	Name		Nat	Born	Pos	Meet	Venue	Date
3:59.98	Regina	Jacobs	USA	28.8.63	1		Boston (R)	1 Feb
4:00.72	Natalya	Gorelova	RUS	18.4.73	1	NC	Moskva	27 Feb
4:01.67		Jacobs			1	WI	Birmingham	16 Mar
4:03.58	Lidia	Chojecka/Okninska	POL	25.1.77	1	GP	Birmingham	21 Feb
4:04.77	Yekaterina	Puzanova	RUS	1.1.79	3	NC	Moskva	27 Feb
4:07.44	Elena	Iagar	ROM	16.1.75	6	WI	Birmingham	16 Mar
4:08.98	Yelena	Sidorchenko	RUS	30.5.80	3		Moskva	10 Feb
4:09.08	Olesya	Chumakova	RUS	23.7.81	5	NC	Moskva	27 Feb
4:09.28	Fernanda	Ribeiro	POR	23.6.69	1		Espinho	1 Feb
4:09.42	Kathleen	Friedrich	GER	13.7.77	1		Erfurt	22 Jan
4:10.91	Berhane	Adere	ETH	21.7.73	5		Stockholm	18 Feb

Mark	Name		Nat	Born	Date
4:11.71	Joanne	Fenn	GBR	19.10.74	18 Feb
4:12.20	Cristina	Grosu	ROM	11.11.76	23 Feb
4:12.65	Galina	Bogomolova	RUS	15.10.77	10 Feb
4:12.75	Jenelle	Deatherage	USA	25.9.77	1 Feb
4:13.58	Nédia	Semedo	POR	14.11.78	1 Feb
4:13.83	Abir	Nakhli	TUN	21.9.81	15 Mar
4:13.85	Nadezhda	Trilinskaya	RUS	.79	27 Feb
4:13.91	Heather	Sagan	USA	28.2.80	1 Feb
4:14.45	Inês	Monteiro	POR	18.5.80	1 Feb
4:14.46	Irina	Vashentseva	RUS	30.9.80	6 Mar
4:14.67	Fatiha	Baouf	BEL	15.7.70	25 Jan
4:14.76	Maria	Tsírba	GRE	28.7.79	4 Mar
4:15.50	Maria	Lynch	IRL	3.9.78	16 Feb

Drugs disqualification

Mark	Name		Nat	Born	Date
4:12.50i	Geraldine	Hendricken ¶	IRL	19.4.74	16 Feb
4:13.26	Natalya	Dyadkova ¶	BLR	2.12.79	19 Jul

JUNIORS

See main list for top 8 juniors. 16 performances by 9 women to 4:11.7. Additional marks and further juniors:

Name	Mark	Pos	Meet	Venue	Date	Mark	Pos	Meet	Venue	Date
Neporadnaya	4:04.44	11	WCh	Saint-Denis	31 Aug	4:10.57i	2	NC	Sumy	22 Feb
	4:04.64	7	WK	Zürich	15 Aug	4:10.77i	5h3	WI	Birmingham	15 Mar
	4:05.37	1	GP II	Thessaloniki	3 Aug	4:11.68	3	NC	Kiev	6 Jul
Xing Huina	4:10.16	1		Beijing	18 Jul					

Mark	Name		Nat	Born	Pos	Meet	Venue	Date
4:11.38+	Mestawet	Tadesse	ETH	19.7.85	4		Villeneuve d'Ascq	15 Jun
4:12.67	Yelena	Stina (10)	LAT-Y	11.5.86	1		Ventspils	14 Jun
4:13.00	Charlotte	Moore	GBR	4.1.85	7	GP	London CP)	8 Aug
4:13.57	Georgie	Clarke	AUS	17.6.84	1		Melbourne	4 Dec
4:13.87	Lucy	Wangui	KEN	24.3.84	3	GP	Osaka	10 May
4:14.25	Amane	Godana	ETH-Y	86	1		Pézenas	31 May
4:14.69	Alemu	Techale	ETH-Y	13.12.87	2		Arnhem	25 Jun
4:14.94	Tatyana	Rasputina	RUS	12.5.84	1	NC-j	Kazan	3 Jul
4:15.00	Danielle	Barnes	GBR	8.10.85	1		Manchester (W)	31 May
4:15.1	Siham	Hilali	MAR-Y	2.5.86	3		Rabat	14 Jun
4:15.25	Zakia	Mrisho	TAN	19.2.84	1		Oristano	6 Sep
4:15.35	Peninah Chepchumba	Biwott (20)	KEN	14.1.85	1	Af-J	Garoua	3 Aug

1 MILE

Mark	Name		Nat	Born	Pos	Meet	Venue	Date
4:24.40	Natalya	Yevdokimova	RUS	17.3.78	1	NA	Heusden	2 Aug

Mark	Name		Nat	Born	Pos	Meet	Venue	Date
4:25.11	Latifa	Essarokh	FRA	11.12.73	2	NA	Heusden	2 Aug
4:25.40	Jackline	Maranga	KEN	16.12.77	3	NA	Heusden	2 Aug
4:27.12	Naomi	Mugo	KEN	2.1.77	4	NA	Heusden	2 Aug
4:28.20	Berhane	Hirpassa	ETH	30.7.83	2		Villeneuve d'Ascq	15 Jun
4:28.51	Mestawet	Tadesse	ETH-J	.85	3		Villeneuve d'Ascq	15 Jun
4:28.67	Maria	Martins	FRA	1.4.74	4		Villeneuve d'Ascq	15 Jun
4:28.68	Leah	Pells	CAN	9.11.64	5	NA	Heusden	2 Aug
4:28.86	Olga	Komyagina	RUS	10.2.74	5		Villeneuve d'Ascq	15 Jun
4:29.10	Mary Jayne	Harrelson	USA	17.6.78	1		Falmouth	9 Aug
4:29.39	Vicky	Pounds (Lynch)	CAN	6.6.70	2		Falmouth	9 Aug
4:29.93	Veerle	Dejaeghere	BEL	1.8.73	6	NA	Heusden	2 Aug
4:30.48	Lyudmila	Vasilyeva	RUS	20.10.69	3		Falmouth	9 Aug
4:30.81	Gelete	Burika	ETH-Y	15.2.86	7	NA	Heusden	2 Aug
4:31.85	Yuliya	Kosenkova	RUS	28.3.73	4		Naimette	2 Sep

4:32.65	Margaret	Ngotho	KEN	6.9.71	15 Jun
4:33.62	Carmen	Douma-Husar	CAN	12.3.77	26 Apr
4:33.94	Meselech	Melkamu	ETH-J	19.4.85	15 Jun
4:34.86	Jenelle	Deatherage	USA	25.9.77	9 Aug
4:34.88	Mieke	Geens	BEL	10.3.82	2 Aug
4:35.03	Nouria	Mérah-Benida	ALG	19.10.70	15 Jun
4:35.54	Tiffany	McWilliams	USA	20.10.82	26 Apr
4:36.05	Docus	Inzikuru	UGA	2.2.82	2 Aug

Note: Falmouth reported to have an "irregular kerb"?

Indoors

4:27.46	Hayley	Tullett	GBR	17.2.73	1		New York (A)	25 Jan
4:29.72	Lyubov	Kremlyova	RUS	21.12.61	2		New York (A)	25 Jan

4:32.49	Johanna	Nilsson	SWE	27.3.83	15 Mar
4:33.41 #	Lena	Nilsson	SWE	28.1.80	8 Mar
4:35.21	Tiffany	McWilliams	USA	20.10.82	2 Mar
4:36.08	Elena	Iagar	ROM	16.1.75	7 Feb

2000 METRES

5:33.83	Elvan	Abeylegesse	TUR	11.9.82	1		Istanbul	7 Jun
5:35.62	Berhane	Adere	ETH	21.7.73	1	GS	Ostrava	12 Jun
5:37.36	Naomi	Mugo	KEN	2.1.77	2	GS	Ostrava	12 Jun
5:37.71	Benita	Johnson	AUS	6.5.79	3	GS	Ostrava	12 Jun
5:39.18+	Gabriela	Szabo	ROM	14.11.75	1	in 3k	Zürich	15 Aug
5:41.02	Margaret	Ngotho	KEN	6.9.71	4	GS	Ostrava	12 Jun
5:43.16	Berhane	Hirpassa	ETH	30.7.83	5	GS	Ostrava	12 Jun
5:43.38+	Yelena	Zadorozhnaya	RUS	3.12.77	1	in 3k	Lausanne	1 Jul
5:44.98	Andrea	Suldesová	CZE	11.2.75	6	GS	Ostrava	12 Jun

5:46.62+	Rose	Kosgei	KEN	22.8.81	19 Jul
5:47.09+	Olga	Komyagina	RUS	10.2.74	4 Jul
5:48.53	Tatyana	Golovchenko	UKR	13.2.80	7 Jun
5:49.0+	Werknesh	Kidane	ETH	21.11.81	11 Jul
5:49.2+	Meseret	Defar	ETH	19.11.83	11 Jul
5:49.4+	Zhor	El Kamch	MAR	15.3.73	11 Jul
5:49.5+	Ejagayou	Dibaba	ETH	21.3.82	11 Jul
5:49.8+	Tirunesh	Dibaba	ETH-J	2.6.85	11 Jul

Indoors

5:46.64+	Olga	Komyagina	RUS	10.2.74	22 Feb
5:46.9+	Marta	Domínguez	ESP	3.11.75	22 Feb
5:47.37	Oksana	Belyakova	RUS	9.9.75	7 Jan
5:48.51	Lyubov	Kremlyova	RUS	21.12.61	7 Jan

3000 METRES

8:33.95	Gabriela	Szabo	ROM	14.11.75	1	WK	Zürich	15 Aug
8:34.09		Szabo			1	Gaz	Saint-Denis	4 Jul
8:34.85	Zhor	El Kamch	MAR	15.3.73	2	Gaz	Saint-Denis	4 Jul
8:35.50	Yelena	Zadorozhnaya	RUS	3.12.77	1	Athl	Lausanne	1 Jul
8:36.24		El Kamch			1	GP	Gateshead	13 Jul
8:36.25	Berhane	Adere	ETH	21.7.73	3	Gaz	Saint-Denis	4 Jul
8:36.82	Edith	Masai	KEN	4.4.67	1	WAF	Monaco	14 Sep
8:37.40		Zadorozhnaya			2	WAF	Monaco	14 Sep
8:37.55	Sonia	O'Sullivan	IRL	28.11.69	2	WK	Zürich	15 Aug
8:37.89	Jo	Pavey	GBR	20.9.73	3	WAF	Monaco	14 Sep
8:37.97		Pavey			2	GP	Gateshead	13 Jul
8:38:00	Olga	Yegorova	RUS	28.3.72	4	Gaz	Saint-Denis	4 Jul
8:38.06	Benita	Johnson	AUS	6.5.79	3	GP	Gateshead	13 Jul
8:38.31	Meseret	Defar (10)	ETH	19.11.83	4	WAF	Monaco	14 Sep
8:38.45		Johnson			1	GP	Madrid (C)	19 Jul
8:39.26		Adere			5	WAF	Monaco	14 Sep
8:39.29	Irina	Mikitenko	GER	23.8.72	3	WK	Zürich	15 Aug
8:39.51	Werknesh (18/12)	Kidane	ETH	21.11.81	5	Gaz	Saint-Denis	4 Jul
8:40.14	Viola	Kibiwott	KEN	22.12.83	4	WK	Zürich	15 Aug
8:42.29	Elvan	Abeylegesse	TUR	11.9.82	1		Izmir	11 May
8:43.6+	Tirunesh	Dibaba	ETH-J	2.6.85	3	in 5k	Oslo	27 Jun
8:44.53	Emilie	Mondor	CAN	29.4.81	6	WK	Zürich	15 Aug
8:44.65	Sabrina	Mockenhaupt	GER	6.12.80	1		Bergisch Gladbach	14 Aug
8:44.78	Tatyana	Tomashova	RUS	1.7.75	3	Athl	Lausanne	1 Jul
8:45.29	Leah	Malot	KEN	7.6.72	7	WK	Zürich	15 Aug
8:45.52	Courtney (20)	Babcock	CAN	30.6.72	8	WK	Zürich	15 Aug

Mark	Name		Nat	Born	Pos	Meet	Venue	Date
8:45.97	Isabella	Ochichi	KEN	28.10.79	2		Villeneuve d'Ascq	15 Jun
8:46.0+	Zahra	Ouaziz	MAR	20.12.69	2	in 5k	Oslo	27 Jun
8:46.29	Docus	Inzikuru	UGA	2.2.82	6	Gaz	Saint-Denis	4 Jul
8:46.38	Irene	Kwambai	KEN	25.10.78	9	WK	Zürich	15 Aug
8:46.51	Sentayehu	Ejigu	ETH-J	.85	7	Gaz	Saint-Denis	4 Jul
8:46.77	Zakia	Mrisho	TAN-J	19.2.84	6	WAF	Monaco	14 Sep
8:47.62+	Olga	Komyagina	RUS	10.2.74	1	in 5k	Roma	11 Jul
8:47.68	Merima	Denboba	ETH	21.8.74	1		Milano	3 Jun
8:48.66	Deena	Drossin	USA	14.2.73	10	WK	Zürich	15 Aug
8:48.7+	Ejagayou	Dibaba	ETH	21.3.82	8	in 5k	Roma	11 Jul
	(30)							
8:48.93	Gelete	Burika	ETH-Y	15.2.86	8	Gaz	Saint-Denis	4 Jul
8:49.10	Kayoko	Fukushi	JPN	25.3.82	9	Gaz	Saint-Denis	4 Jul
8:50.34+		Sun Yingjie	CHN	3.10.77	1h1	in 5k	Saint-Denis	26 Aug
8:50.6+	Marta	Domínguez	ESP	3.11.75	2h1	in 5k	Saint-Denis	26 Aug
8:50.68	Margaret	Ngotho	KEN	6.9.71	3		Milano	3 Jun
8:50.69	Inna	Poluskina	LAT-J	7.7.84	1	NC	Riga	3 Aug
8:51.20	Meselech	Melkamu	ETH-J	19.4.85	11	WK	Zürich	15 Aug
8:51.32	Natalya	Sidorenko (Tobias)	UKR	22.11.80	1	Odlozil	Praha	29 Jun
8:51.61	René	Kalmer	RSA	3.11.80	6	Athl	Lausanne	1 Jul
8:51.7+	Jane	Wanjiku	KEN	14.6.79	6h1	in 5k	Saint-Denis	26 Aug
	(40)							
8:52.00	Yelena	Burykina	RUS	7.5.72	2	Odlozil	Praha	29 Jun
8:52.02	Ayelech	Worku	ETH	12.6.79	4	GP	Madrid (C)	19 Jul
8:53.13	Ebru	Kavaklioglu	TUR	14.3.70	4		Villeneuve d'Ascq	15 Jun
8:53.59	Jelena	Prokopcuka	LAT	21.9.76	3	NC	Riga	2 Aug
8:53.63	Natalie	Harvey	AUS	19.1.75	3	Odlozil	Praha	29 Jun
8:54.26	Fernanda	Ribeiro	POR	23.6.69	5	GP	Madrid (C)	19 Jul
8:54.83	Etalemahu	Kidane	ETH	.83	5		Villeneuve d'Ascq	15 Jun
8:54.91	Lornah	Kiplagat	KEN/NED	20.3.74	1		Nijmegen	24 May
8:56.22	Seloua	Ouaziz	MAR	27.7.74	5		Milano	3 Jun
8:56.38	Rahab	Ndungu	KEN	19.10.78	4	Odlozil	Praha	29 Jun
	(50)							
8:56.60	Una	English	IRL	14.8.70	7		Villeneuve d'Ascq	15 Jun
8:56.63mx	Georgie	Clarke	AUS-J	17.6.84	1mx		Melbourne	9 Dec
8:56.9+	Derartu	Tulu	ETH	21.3.72	2	in 5k	London (CP)	8 Aug
8:57.14	Oksana	Belyakova	RUS	9.9.75	6		Milano	3 Jun
8:57.45	Hayley	Tullett	GBR	17.2.73	2	ECp-S	Firenze	21 Jun
8:57.76	Konstadína	Efedákí	GRE	1.10.78	5	Odlozil	Praha	29 Jun
8:58.4 mx	Gloria	Marconi	ITA	31.3.68	1		Bondeno	11 Jun
8:58.91	Silvia	Weissteiner	ITA	13.7.79	8		Milano	3 Jun

9:00.16	Meryem	Boucetta	MAR	15.5.81	5 Jul
9:00.28	Jane	Kiptoo	KEN	8.8.82	24 May
9:00.6	Yelena	Zhilkina	RUS	5.2.73	25 Jul
9:01.22	Yuliya	Chizhenko	RUS	30.8.79	5 Jul
9:01.55	Alice	Timbilil	KEN	16.6.83	10 Sep
9:01.76	Tatyana	Golovchenko	UKR	13.2.80	27 May
9:01.84	Ines	Chenonge	KEN	1.2.82	10 Sep
9:01.91	Kelly	Holmes	GBR	19.4.70	13 Jul
9:02.08	Dire	Tune	ETH-J	85	24 May
9:02.24	Agata	Balsamo	ITA	11.11.70	3 Jun
9:02.27	Breeda	Dennehy-Willis	IRL	2.3.70	5 Jul
9:02.31	Bezunesh	Bekele	ETH	83	19 Jul
9:02.5	Bouchra	Chaabi	MAR	22.9.80	24 May
9:02.61	Mihaela	Botezan	ROM	21.11.76	21 Jun
9:02.98	Christelle	Daunay	FRA	5.12.74	16 Jul
9:03.19	Inés	Monteiro	POR	18.5.80	13 Jul
9:04.73	Elodie	Olivarès	FRA	22.5.76	15 Jun
9:04.79	Marie	Davenport	IRL	24.1.75	5 Jul
9:05.05	Susan	Kirui	KEN	4.4.80	1 Aug
9:05.46mx	Sarah	Jamieson	AUS	24.3.75	9 Dec
9:05.63	Yuko	Nohara	JPN-Y	23.1.88	29 Oct
9:06.5	Natalya	Berkut	UKR	30.5.75	29 Jul
9:06.68	Trine	Pilskog	NOR	1.12.72	3 Jun
9:06.76	Jessica	Augusto	POR	8.11.81	17 May
9:06.77	Jennifer	Rhines	USA	1.7.74	5 Jul
9:06.96	Rkia	Chébili	FRA	28.2.74	5 Jul
9:07.05	Julia	Mombi	KEN-J	25.1.84	2 Aug
9:07.09	Elva	Dryer	USA	26.9.71	1 Jul
9:07.54	Yoshiko	Ichikawa	JPN	18.4.76	27 Sep
9:07.68mx	Anja	Smolders	BEL	2.6.73	29 May
9:07.85	Marzena	Michalska	ITA	20.10.75	3 Jun
9:07.87	Carrie	Tollefson (90)	USA	18.1.77	5 Jul

Indoors

8:31.73	Berhane	Adere	ETH	21.7.73	1	Spark	Stuttgart	2 Feb
8:39.27		El Kamch			2	Spark	Stuttgart	2 Feb
8:41.14	Marta	Domínguez	ESP	3.11.75	1		Sevilla	22 Feb
8:42.01	Zahra	Ouaziz	MAR	20.12.69	1		Gent	9 Feb
8:46.95	Hayley	Tullett	GBR	17.2.73	3		Gent	9 Feb
8:48.95	Lidia	Chojecka/Okninska	POL	25.1.77	1	NC	Spala	1 Mar
8:49.39	Fernanda	Ribeiro	POR	23.6.69	1		Espinho	2 Feb
8:50.62	Galina	Bogomolova	RUS	15.10.77	6	WI	Birmingham	15 Mar
8:51.07	Sarah	Schwald	USA	2.1.73	5	Spark	Stuttgart	2 Feb
8:51.23	Restituta	Joseph	TAN	30.7.71	6	Spark	Stuttgart	2 Feb
8:51.58	Cristina	Grosu	ROM	11.11.76	2h2	WI	Birmingham	14 Mar
8:52.57	Regina	Jacobs	USA	28.8.63	1	NC	Boston (R)	2 Mar
8:54.00	Alla	Zhilyayeva	RUS	5.2.69	1	NC	Moskva	25 Feb
8:55.15	Yelena	Sidorchenko	RUS	30.5.80	1		Moskva	11 Feb

Mark	Name		Nat	Born	Pos	Meet	Venue	Date
8:56.22	Bezunesh	Bekele	ETH	.83	5		Gent	9 Feb
8:56.26	Shayne	Culpepper	USA	3.12.73	2	NC	Boston (R)	2 Mar
8:57.44	Amy	Rudolph	USA	18.9.73	3	NC	Boston (R)	2 Mar
8:57.92	Brigitta	Tusai	HUN	30.6.77	6		Gent	9 Feb
8:58.08	Collette	Liss	USA	29.4.73	4	NC	Boston (R)	2 Mar
8:59.64	Katie	McGregor	USA	2.9.77	5	NC	Boston (R)	2 Mar
8:59.76	Amaia	Piedra	ESP	2.6.72	9	WI	Birmingham	15 Mar

Mark	Name		Nat	Born	Date
9:00.22	Shalane	Flanagan	USA	8.7.81	1 Feb
9:00.70	Alesya	Turova	BLR	6.12.79	24 Feb
9:00.77	Melanie	Schulz	GER	27.8.79	2 Feb
9:00.77	Wioletta	Janowska	POL	9.6.77	15 Feb
9:00.92	Maria	Martins	FRA	1.4.74	15 Feb
9:01.40	Natalia	Rodríguez	ESP	2.6.79	22 Feb
9:01.47	María	Tsírba ¶	GRE	28.7.79	15 Feb
9:01.58	Lauren	Fleshman	USA	26.9.81	15 Mar
9:01.85	Cristina	Petite	ESP	10.5.72	22 Feb
9:02.49	Galina	Aleksandrova	RUS	15.10.75	25 Feb
9:02.98	Susanne	Pumper	AUT	1.9.70	14 Mar
9:03.55	Ana	Dias	POR	15.1.74	2 Feb
9:03.68	Maria	McCambridge	IRL	10.7.75	14 Mar
9:04.21	Iris	Fuentes-Pila	ESP	10.8.80	22 Feb
9:04.24	Irina	Lishchinskaya	UKR	15.1.76	2 Feb
9:04.65	Livia	Tóth	HUN	7.1.80	2 Mar
9:04.77	Fatiha	Baouf	BEL	15.7.70	9 Feb
9:05.46	Blake	Russell/Phillips	USA	24.7.75	2 Mar
9:05.66	Krisztina	Papp	HUN	17.12.82	28 Jan
9:06.80	Tatyana	Petrova	RUS	8.4.83	25 Feb
9:07.16	Sara	Gorton	USA	2.10.81	15 Mar
9:07.72 #	Ulrike	Maisch	GER	21.1.77	5 Jan
9:07.83	Kathleen	Friedrich	GER	13.7.77	12 Jan
9:07.88 #	Alicia	Craig	USA	14.6.82	1 Feb

Drugs disqualification

Mark	Name		Nat	Born	Pos	Meet	Venue	Date
8:52.21i	María	Tsírba ¶	GRE	28.7.79	(8)	WI	Birmingham	15 Mar

JUNIORS

See main list for top 7 juniors. 12/13 performances by 6 women to 8:56.0. Additional marks and further juniors:

T Dibaba	8:49.0+	9	GGala	Roma	11 Jul
	8:50.8+	3h1 in 5k		Saint-Denis	26 Aug
	8:50.20	5	Athl	Lausanne	1 Jul
Ejigu	8:52.33	7	Athl	Lausanne	1 Jul
Melkamu	8:51.66	4		Milano	3 Jun

Mark	Name		Nat	Born	Pos	Meet	Venue	Date
9:02.08	Dire	Tune	ETH	85	3		Nijmegen	24 May
9:05.63	Yuko	Nohara	JPN-Y	23.1.88	1	NG	Fukuroi	29 Oct
9:07.05	Julia	Mombi (10)	KEN	25.1.84	1		Nagasaki	2 Aug
9:08.4A	Pasalia Chepkorir	Kipkoech	KEN-Y	22.12.88	1		Nairobi	18 Jun
9:08.50	Chiaki	Iwamoto	JPN	6.3.85	1r2		Okayama	28 Sep
9:08.53	Mariem Alaoui	Selsouli	MAR	8.4.84	1	Af-J	Garoua	31 Jul
9:08.62	Fyles	Ongori	KEN-Y	19.7.86	2		Nagasaki	2 Aug
9:09.67	Win	Fridam	KEN	16.4.85	3		Nagasaki	2 Aug

5000 METRES

Mark	Name		Nat	Born	Pos	Meet	Venue	Date
14:29.32	Berhane	Adere	ETH	21.7.73	1	Bisl	Oslo	27 Jun
14:33.04	Werknesh	Kidane	ETH	21.11.81	2	Bisl	Oslo	27 Jun
14:39.94	Tirunesh	Dibaba	ETH-J	2.6.85	3	Bisl	Oslo	27 Jun
14:40.34	Meseret	Defar	ETH	19.11.83	1	GGala	Roma	11 Jul
14:41.35	Gabriela	Szabo	ROM	14.11.75	2	GGala	Roma	11 Jul
14:41.67	Ejagayou	Dibaba	ETH	21.3.82	3	GGala	Roma	11 Jul
14:41.97		T Dibaba			4	GGala	Roma	11 Jul
14:42.53	Zhor	El Kamch	MAR	15.3.73	5	GGala	Roma	11 Jul
14:42.89		Adere			6	GGala	Roma	11 Jul
14:43.46		Defar			4	Bisl	Oslo	27 Jun
14:44.22	Derartu	Tulu	ETH	21.3.72	1	VD	Bruxelles	5 Sep
14:44.40		Kidane			7	GGala	Roma	11 Jul
14:45.35	Edith	Masai	KEN	4.4.67	1h1	WCh	Saint-Denis	26 Aug
14:45.96		T Dibaba			2h1	WCh	Saint-Denis	26 Aug
14:46.73		Sun Yingjie (10)	CHN	3.10.77	3h1	WCh	Saint-Denis	26 Aug
14:47.45	Zahra	Ouaziz	MAR	20.12.69	5	Bisl	Oslo	27 Jun
14:47.70	Isabella	Ochichi	KEN	28.10.79	2	VD	Bruxelles	5 Sep
14:48.33	Marta	Domínguez	ESP	3.11.75	4h1	WCh	Saint-Denis	26 Aug
14:50.60		Masai			1	DNG	Stockholm	5 Aug
14:50.78		Masai			1	GP	London (CP)	8 Aug
14:51.61	Yelena	Zadorozhnaya	RUS	3.12.77	8	GGala	Roma	11 Jul
14:51.72		T Dibaba			1	WCh	Saint-Denis	30 Aug
14:51.75		Szabo			2	GP	London (CP)	8 Aug
14:52.26		Domínguez			2	WCh	Saint-Denis	30 Aug
14:52.30		Masai			3	WCh	Saint-Denis	30 Aug
14:52.33		Ochichi			1	NA	Heusden	2 Aug
14:52.36		Zadorozhnaya			4	WCh	Saint-Denis	30 Aug
14:52.64		Tulu			3	GP	London (CP)	8 Aug
14:52.66		Ouaziz			5h1	WCh	Saint-Denis	26 Aug
14:53.51		Ochichi			2	DNG	Stockholm	5 Aug
14:53.56	Elvan	Abeylegesse	TUR	11.9.82	5	WCh	Saint-Denis	30 Aug
	(31/15)							
14:54.38	Gulnara	Samitova	RUS	9.7.78	7	WCh	Saint-Denis	30 Aug
14:54.52	Benita	Johnson	AUS	6.5.79	2	NA	Heusden	2 Aug

Mark	Name		Nat	Born	Pos	Meet	Venue	Date
14:54.98	Courtney	Babcock	CAN	30.6.72	8	WCh	Saint-Denis	30 Aug
14:55.19	Olga	Yegorova	RUS	28.3.72	6	Bisl	Oslo	27 Jun
14:55.50	Sonia	O'Sullivan	IRL	28.11.69	2h2	WCh	Saint-Denis	26 Aug
	(20)							
14:56.43	Lornah	Kiplagat	KEN/NED	20.3.74	3	DNG	Stockholm	5 Aug
14:56.64	Irina	Mikitenko	GER	23.8.72	9	GGala	Roma	11 Jul
14:59.68	Émilie	Mondor	CAN	29.4.81	7h1	WCh	Saint-Denis	26 Aug
15:00.02		Xing Huina	CHN-J	25.2.84	1		Beijing	18 Jul
15:00.53	Sentayehu	Ejigu	ETH-J	.85	7	Bisl	Oslo	27 Jun
15:01.79	Salina	Kosgei	KEN	16.11.76	3	NA	Heusden	2 Aug
15:02.04	Jelena	Prokopcuka	LAT	21.9.76	8	Bisl	Oslo	27 Jun
15:04.00	Jane	Wanjiku	KEN	14.6.79	8h1	WCh	Saint-Denis	26 Aug
15:04.22	Ebru	Kavaklioglu	TUR	14.3.70	9	Bisl	Oslo	27 Jun
15:04.32	Adriana	Fernández	MEX	4.4.71	4	GP II	Gresham	17 May
	(30)							
15:06.10	Irene	Kwambai	KEN	25.10.78	5	NA	Heusden	2 Aug
15:07.39	Restituta	Joseph	TAN	30.7.71	4	VD	Bruxelles	5 Sep
15:07.46	Merima	Denboba	ETH	21.8.74	5	DNG	Stockholm	5 Aug
15:08.14	Deena	Drossin	USA	14.2.73	8	GP	London (CP)	8 Aug
15:09.02	Kayoko	Fukushi	JPN	25.3.82	10	GGala	Roma	11 Jul
15:09.04	Jo	Pavey	GBR	20.9.73	9	GP	London (CP)	8 Aug
15:09.70	Eyerusalem	Kuma	ETH	4.11.81	10	Bisl	Oslo	27 Jun
15:09.80	Sabrina	Mockenhaupt	GER	6.12.80	10	GP	London (CP)	8 Aug
15:10.23	Lucy	Wangui	KEN-J	24.3.84	1	Super	Yokohama	23 Sep
15:10.69	Mihaela	Botezan	ROM	21.11.76	1	WMilG	Catania	7 Dec
	(40)							
15:10.85	Ayelech	Worku	ETH	12.6.79	7	DNG	Stockholm	5 Aug
15:12.71	Lauren	Fleshman	USA	26.9.81	11h2	WCh	Saint-Denis	26 Aug
15:12.76	Mari	Ozaki	JPN	16.7.75	3	NC	Yokohama	8 Jun
15:13.08	Galina	Bogomolova	RUS	15.10.77	1	Znam	Tula	7 Jun
	15:13.0+					in 10k	Saint-Denis	23 Aug
15:13.26	Leah	Malot	KEN	7.6.72	5	GP II	Gresham	17 May
15:14.3+	Alla	Zhilyayeva	RUS	5.2.69		in 10k	Saint-Denis	23 Aug
15:15.16	Takako	Kotorida	JPN	2.4.77	4	NC	Yokohama	8 Jun
15:15.32	Hristosomia	Iakóvou	GRE	9.4.71	6	NA	Heusden	2 Aug
15:15.40	Tatyana	Khmeleva	RUS	2.4.79	2	NC	Tula	7 Aug
15:15.75	Yelena	Samokhvalova	RUS	21.11.80	3	NC	Tula	7 Aug
	(50)							
15:15.83	Yelena	Zhilkina	RUS	5.2.73	4	NC	Tula	7 Aug
15:16.18	Marla	Runyan	USA	4.1.69	1	NC	Stanford	20 Jun
15:16.8 +	Fernanda	Ribeiro	POR	23.6.69		in 10k	Saint-Denis	23 Aug
15:17.57	Kathy	Butler	GBR	22.10.73	6	GP II	Gresham	17 May
15:18.3+	Lydia	Grigoryeva	RUS	21.1.74		in 10k	Saint-Denis	23 Aug
15:18.4+	Alevtina	Ivanova	RUS	22.5.75	1	NC	Tula	3 Aug
15:18.45	Anikó	Kálovics	HUN	13.5.77	1	ECp-1A	Lappeenranta	22 Jun
15:18.55	Elva	Dryer	USA	26.9.71	7	GP II	Gresham	17 May
15:18.76	Souad	Aït Salem	ALG	6.1.79	1		Alger	17 Jul
15:18.79	Susanne	Pumper	AUT	1.9.70	1	Gugl	Linz	31 Jul
	(60)							
15:20.54	Shalane	Flanagan	USA	8.7.81	2	NC	Stanford	20 Jun
15:20.94	Kazue	Ogoshi	JPN	2.3.81	5	NC	Yokohama	8 Jun
15:21.59	Natalya	Berkut	UKR	30.5.75	1		Kiev	26 May
15:22.39	María	Protópappa	GRE	5.5.73	8	NA	Heusden	2 Aug
15:22.43	Inna	Poluskina	LAT-J	7.7.84	1	NC	Riga	2 Aug
15:22.46		Zhou Chunxiu	CHN	8.3.79	2h1	NC	Shanghai	11 Sep
15:22.51	Terumi	Asoshina	JPN	2.5.82	2		Sapporo	2 Jul
15:23.52	Susan	Kirui	KEN	4.4.80	2	Gugl	Linz	31 Jul
15:23.55	Malika	Assahssah	MAR	24.9.82	2		Alger	17 Jul
15:23.59	Shayne	Culpepper	USA	3.12.73	3	NC	Stanford	20 Jun
	(70)							
15:24.29	Lidia	Chojecka/Okninska	POL	25.1.77	8	VD	Bruxelles	5 Sep
15:24.54	Marie	Davenport	IRL	24.1.75	2	NC	Dublin (S)	10 Aug
15:24.68	Blake	Russell/Phillips	USA	24.7.75	10	GP II	Gresham	17 May
15:24.97	Sara	Gorton	USA	2.10.81	3	MSR	Walnut	17 Apr
15:25.38	Oksana	Belyakova	RUS	9.9.75	5	NC	Tula	7 Aug
15:25.75	Alicia	Craig	USA	14.6.82	4	MSR	Walnut	17 Apr
15:27.00	Carrie	Tollefson	USA	18.1.77	11	GP II	Gresham	17 May
15:27.41	Monica	Wangare	KEN-Y	4.10.86	2		Kobe	11 Oct
15:27.81	Yelena	Burykina	RUS	7.5.72	2	Znam	Tula	7 Jun
15:27.83	Yoko	Shibui	JPN	14.3.79	6	NC	Yokohama	8 Jun
	(80)							

Mark	Name		Nat	Born	Pos	Meet	Venue	Date
15:27.93	Meselech	Melkamu	ETH-J	19.4.85	4	GP II	Sevilla	7 Jun
15:28.11	Yuki	Saito	JPN	25.9.80	3		Kobe	11 Oct
15:29.42	Katie	McGregor	USA	2.9.77	12	GP II	Gresham	17 May
15:29.56	Cristina	Petite	ESP	10.5.72	2	NC	Jerez de la Frontera	2 Aug
15:29.57	Megumi	Tanaka	JPN	4.9.75	4	Super	Yokohama	23 Sep
15:30.05	Nora	Rocha	MEX	18.12.67	13	GP II	Gresham	17 May
15:30.25	Catherine	Berry	GBR	8.10.75	14	GP II	Gresham	17 May
15:30.90	Yoshiko	Ichikawa	JPN	18.4.76	1	NG	Fukuroi	27 Oct
15:31.3	Miho	Notagashira	JPN	17.8.83	1		Takamatsu	4 Oct
15:31.49	Ruth (90)	Wanjiru	KEN	11.9.81	5	Super	Yokohama	23 Sep
15:31.69	Rocio	Ríos	ESP	13.3.69	3	NC	Jerez de la Frontera	2 Aug
15:31.78	Harumi	Hiroyama	JPN	2.9.68	1		Okayama	28 Sep
15:32.22	Tegla	Loroupe	KEN	9.5.73	14	GGala	Roma	11 Jul
15:32.87	Viola	Kibiwott	KEN	22.12.83	13	Bisl	Oslo	27 Jun
15:32.97	Hiromi	Fujii	JPN	7.2.83	1	Oda	Hiroshima	29 Apr
15:32.97	Bouchra	Chaabi	MAR	22.9.80	3		Alger	17 Jul
15:33.6mx	Agata	Balsamo	ITA	11.10.70	1		Catania	24 Apr
	15:37.85				4	Gugl	Linz	31 Jul
15:33.99	Etalemahu	Kidane	ETH	.83	6	GP II	Sevilla	7 Jun
15:34.09	Galina	Aleksandrova	RUS	15.10.75	2		Moskva	15 Jul
15:34.14	Aki (100)	Fujikawa	JPN	14.11.78	4		Okayama	28 Sep

15:34.35	Miki	Ohira	JPN	28.6.81	5 May
15:34.40	Miwako	Yamanaka	JPN	24.5.78	28 Sep
15:34.94	Yesenia	Centeno	CUB/ESP	27.6.71	7 Jun
15:35.04	Ines	Chenonge	KEN	1.2.82	5 Sep
15:35.43	Rose	Kosgei	KEN	22.8.81	5 Jul
15:35.7A	Priscila	Jepleting	KEN	26.6.80	12 Jul
15:35.76	Esther	Wanjiru	KEN	27.3.77	5 May
15:35.84	Beatriz	Santiago	ESP	28.10.68	2 Aug
15:35.97	Nicole	Jefferson	USA	8.3.76	20 Jun
15:36.32	Teresa	Recio	ESP	7.7.63	5 Jul
15:36.44	Breeda	Dennehy-Willis	IRL	2.3.70	2 Aug
15:36.81	Helena	Javornik	SLO	26.3.66	1 Jun
15:36.95	Molly	Huddle	USA-J	31.8.84	17 Apr
15:36.97	Emi	Ikeda	JPN	29.8.83	27 Oct
15:37.02	Yuko	Manabe	JPN	8.2.79	28 Sep
15:37.21	Luisa	Larraga	ESP	10.12.70	2 Aug
15:37.48	Melissa	Buttry	USA	12.12.82	17 Apr
15:37.49	Haruko	Yamamoto	JPN	31.10.81	5 May
15:38.05	Natalie	Harvey	AUS	19.1.75	7 Jun
15:38.17	Rodica	Chirita	ROM	28.10.76	10 Aug
15:38.48	Judit	Pla	ESP	2.5.78	2 Aug
15:38.61	Julia	Mombi	KEN-J	25.1.85	24 Aug
15:38.75	Akiko	Kawashima	JPN	5.8.77	11 Oct
15:38.81	Valentina	Levushkina	RUS	30.4.82	7 Jun
15:39.16	Dorte	Vibjerg	DEN	28.10.73	22 Jun
15:39.22	Miwako	Haraguchi	JPN	7.2.79	2 Jul
15:39.46	Aster	Demissie	ETH	.83	18 Jul
15:39.48	Amane	Godana	ETH-Y	.86	7 Jun
15:39.91	Makiko	Kawashima	JPN	5.8.77	18 Jun
15:39.96	Sonia	Bejarano	ESP	2.8.81	5 Jul
15:40.10	Catherine	Chikwakwa	MAW-J	24.7.85	26 Aug
15:40.1A	Fridah	Domongole	KEN-J	15.1.84	18 Jun
15:40.15		Li Helan	CHN	2.1.78	11 Sep
15:40.68	Ann Marie	Brooks	USA	14.11.78	17 Apr
15:41.02	Hayley	Yelling	GBR	3.1.74	1 Jun
15:41.15	Machi	Tanaka	JPN	21.7.83	18 Jun
15:41.2+	Lyudmila	Biktasheva	RUS	25.7.74	3 Aug
15:41.46	Nami	Kurosawa	JPN	26.12.78	2 Jul
15:41.80	Eloise	Poppett	AUS	9.11.82	20 Nov
15:42.02	Susanne	Wigene	NOR	12.2.78	2 Aug
15:42.09	Bente	Landøy	NOR	16.12.72	22 Jun
15:42.18	Maya	Nishio	JPN	19.12.78	2 Jul
15:42.40	Vicky	Gill	GBR	21.8.80	9 May
15:42.97	Kara	Goucher	USA	9.7.78	2 Aug
15:43.42	Amaia	Piedra	ESP	2.6.72	11 Jul
15:43.50	Michiko	Ogawa	JPN	30.12.83	2 Jul
15:43.74	Mika	Matsumoto	JPN-J	24.11.84	2 Jul
15:43.86	Christelle	Daunay	FRA	5.12.74	7 Jun
15:43.88	Naoko	Hashimoto	JPN	8.9.82	5 May
15:44.36	Elodie	Olivarès (150)	FRA	22.5.76	11 Jul
15:44.44	Mizuki	Noguchi	JPN	3.7.78	17 May
15:44.5	Yuko	Nohara	JPN-Y	23.1.88	29 Nov
15:44.67	Amy	Mortimer	USA	16.8.81	17 Apr
15:44.8A	Vivian	Cheruiyot	KEN	11.9.83	12 Jul
15:44.92	Mie	Ueda	JPN	9.6.82	24 May
15:44.95	Mika	Okunaga	JPN	27.10.82	8 Jun
15:45.01	Siri Merete	Alfheim	NOR	6.7.76	27 Jun
15:45.09	Haley	McGregor	AUS	27.5.79	20 Nov
15:45.17	Mirisent	Kariuki	KEN-Y	4.4.86	30 Nov
15:45.75	Rodica	Moroianu	FRA	18.11.70	2 Aug
15:45.79	Sarah	Toland	USA	12.12.78	17 Apr
15:45.87	Naomi	Sakashita	JPN	25.5.75	18 May
15:46.17	Rahab	Ndungu	KEN	19.10.78	14 Jun
15:46.24	Hiromi	Koga	JPN	28.5.82	18 May
15:46.27	Kathy	Newberry	USA	31.8.78	17 Apr
15:46.3A	Margaret	Okayo	KEN	30.5.76	12 Jul
15:46.40	Ayako	Suzuki	JPN	17.12.80	2 Jul
15:46.50	Regina	Rakhimkulova	RUS	5.11.79	7 Aug
15:46.55	Rkia	Chébili	FRA	28.2.74	7 Jun
15:46.58	Tatyana	Petrova	RUS	8.4.83	27 Jun
15:46.63	Yoshimi	Ozaki	JPN	1.7.81	8 Jun
15:46.78	Ann	McGranahan	USA	8.1.79	20 Jun
15:47.11	Yuri	Kano	JPN	27.10.78	24 May
15:47.14	Luminita	Gogîrlea	ROM	5.11.71	10 Aug
15:47.35	Rocio	Martínez	ESP	24.9.75	5 Jul
15:47.56	Ayako	Katafuchi	JPN-J	31.1.84	2 Jul
15:47.58		Zhang Yuhong	CHN	15.1.83	8 Apr
15:47.69	Hiromi	Ominami	JPN	15.11.75	11 May
15:47.75	Yumiko	Hara	JPN	9.1.82	24 May
15:47.79	Ayumi	Hashimoto	JPN	17.6.83	28 Sep
15:47.80	Tina	Connelly	CAN	16.8.70	18 Jul
15:47.83	Dire	Tune	ETH-J	85	1 Jun
15:47.90	Sarah	Hann	USA	4.1.73	17 Apr
15:47.91		Wang Yu	CHN-J	27.2.84	11 Sep
15:47.92	Kim	Smith (185)	NZL	19.11.81	24 Apr

Indoors

14:48.21		Adere			1		Dortmund	5 Feb
15:04.73	Restituta	Joseph	TAN	30.7.71	2		Dortmund	5 Feb
15:40.88	Kate	O'Neill	USA	29.7.80	2	NCAA	Fayetteville	14 Mar

JUNIORS

See main list for top 7 juniors. 13 performances by 4 women to 15:11.0. Additional marks and further juniors:

T Dibaba 4+	14:57.87	3	WAF	Monaco	13 Sep	15:01.44	2	GP II	Gresham	17 May
Ejigu	15:02.46	3	GP II	Gresham	17 May	15:08.13	6	DNG	Stockholm	5 Aug
	15:04.80	4	NA	Heusden	2 Aug					
Wangui	15:10.47	1	JPN Ch	Yokohama	8 Jun					

Mark	Name		Nat	Born	Pos	Meet	Venue	Date
15:36.95	Molly	Huddle	USA	31.8.84	5	MSR	Walnut	17 Apr
15:38.61	Julia	Mombi	KEN	25.1.85	1		Aomori	24 Aug
15:39.48	Amane	Godana (10)	ETH-Y	.86	1		Rennes	7 Jun
15:40.10	Catherine	Chikwakwa	MAW	24.7.85	13h1	WCh	Saint-Denis	26 Aug
15:40.1A	Fridah	Domongole	KEN	15.1.84	1		Nairobi	18 Jun
15:43.74	Mika	Matsumoto	JPN	24.11.84	12		Sapporo	2 Jul
15:44.5	Yuko	Nohara	JPN-Y	23.1.88	1		Fukuoka	29 Nov
15:45.17	Mirisent	Kariuki	KEN-Y	4.4.86	1r2		Yokohama	30 Nov
15:47.56	Ayako	Katafuchi	JPN	31.1.84	15		Sapporo	2 Jul
15:47.83	Dire	Tune	ETH	85	9	FBK	Hengelo	1 Jun
15:47.91		Wang Yu	CHN	27.2.84	2h2	NC	Shanghai	11 Sep
15:48.33		Bao Guiying	CHN-Y	20.1.86	5	NC	Shanghai	12 Sep
15:49.79	(20)	Jiang Chengcheng	CHN-Y	5.11.86	4h2	NC	Shanghai	11 Sep
15:49.85		Bai Xue	CHN	3.12.84	5h2	NC	Shanghai	11 Sep

10,000 METRES

Mark	Name		Nat	Born	Pos	Meet	Venue	Date
30:04.18	Berhane	Adere	ETH	21.7.73	1	WCh	Saint-Denis	23 Aug
30:07.15	Werknesh	Kidane	ETH	21.11.81	2	WCh	Saint-Denis	23 Aug
30:07.20		Sun Yingjie	CHN	3.10.77	3	WCh	Saint-Denis	23 Aug
30:12.53	Lornah	Kiplagat	NED	20.3.74	4	WCh	Saint-Denis	23 Aug
30:23.07	Alla	Zhilyayeva	RUS	5.2.69	5	WCh	Saint-Denis	23 Aug
30:26.20	Galina	Bogomolova	RUS	15.10.77	6	WCh	Saint-Denis	23 Aug
30:31.55		Xing Huina	CHN-J	25.2.84	7	WCh	Saint-Denis	23 Aug
30:37.68	Benita	Johnson	AUS	6.5.79	8	WCh	Saint-Denis	23 Aug
30:41.40		Kidane			1	GP II	Stanford	7 Jun
30:46.48		Bogomolova			1	NC	Tula	3 Aug
30:57.14		Zhilyayeva			2	NC	Tula	3 Aug
30:57.83	Lydia	Grigoryeva	RUS	21.1.74	3	NC	Tula	3 Aug
31:01.07	Ejagayou	Dibaba (10)	ETH	21.3.82	9	WCh	Saint-Denis	23 Aug
31:02.72		E Dibaba			2	GP II	Stanford	7 Jun
31:06.14	Jelena	Prokopcuka	LAT	21.9.76	10	WCh	Saint-Denis	23 Aug
31:06.20	Lucy	Wangui	KEN-J	24.3.84	1rA		Okayama	27 Sep
31:10.57	Kayoko	Fukushi	JPN	25.3.82	11	WCh	Saint-Denis	23 Aug
31:11.61		Fukushi			2rA		Okayama	27 Sep
31:13.42	Fernanda	Ribeiro	POR	23.6.69	1	EChall	Athína (E)	12 Apr
31:13.75	Adriana	Fernández	MEX	4.4.71	1		Stanford	2 May
31:14.28		Kiplagat			1		Utrecht	20 Jun
31:15.95		Adere			1		Marseille	30 May
31:17.86	Deena	Drossin	USA	14.2.73	12	WCh	Saint-Denis	23 Aug
31:24.00	Kazue	Ogoshi	JPN	2.3.81	3rA		Okayama	27 Sep
31:26.88	Elva	Dryer	USA	26.9.71	2		Stanford	2 May
31:28.41		Johnson			3		Stanford	2 May
31:28.72	Mihaela	Botezan	ROM	21.11.76	13	WCh	Saint-Denis	23 Aug
31:28.97		Drossin			1	NC	Stanford	19 Jun
31:31.87	Lyudmila	Biktasheva (20)	RUS	25.7.74	4	NC	Tula	3 Aug
31:32.10	Miwako	Yamanaka	JPN	24.5.78	4rA		Okayama	27 Sep
31:32.27	Harumi	Hiroyama	JPN	2.9.68	5rA		Okayama	27 Sep
31:35.74		Dryer			2	NC	Stanford	19 Jun
31:36.76	Lyudmila	Petrova	RUS	7.10.68	4		Stanford	2 May
31:38.48	Irina	Mikitenko	GER	23.8.72	2	EChall	Athína (E)	12 Apr
31:40.31	Anikó	Kálovics	HUN	13.5.77	1	AAA	Watford	5 Jul
31:42.01	Yoko	Shibui	JPN	14.3.79	14	WCh	Saint-Denis	23 Aug
31:43.14	Haley	McGregor	AUS	27.5.79	1	Zat	Melbourne	4 Dec
31:43.51	Yelena	Samokhvalova	RUS	21.11.80	5	NC	Tula	3 Aug
31:44.74	Courtney	Babcock	CAN	30.6.72	5		Stanford	2 May
31:45.84	Takako (40/30)	Kotorida	JPN	2.4.77	1rA		Fukagawa	25 Jun
31:46.57	Mari	Ozaki	JPN	16.7.75	2rA		Fukagawa	25 Jun
31:47.00	Megumi	Tanaka	JPN	4.9.75	15	WCh	Saint-Denis	23 Aug
31:47.53	Merima	Denboba	ETH	21.8.74	1	ESP Ch	Pontevedra	20 Jul
31:48.31	Asha	Gigi	ETH	15.10.73	3	GP II	Stanford	7 Jun
31:48.32	Ana	Dias	POR	15.1.74	3	EChall	Athína (E)	12 Apr
31:49.29	Yuki	Saito	JPN	25.9.80	7rA		Okayama	27 Sep
31:49.58	Yesenia	Centeno	ESP	27.6.71	2	ESP Ch	Pontevedra	20 Jul
31:49.59	Terumi	Asoshina	JPN	2.5.82	8rA		Okayama	27 Sep
31:51.80	Yumiko	Hara	JPN	9.1.82	4rA		Fukagawa	25 Jun
31:54.78	Katie (40)	McGregor	USA	2.9.77	3	NC	Stanford	19 Jun
31:56.21	Ruth	Wanjiru	KEN	11.9.81	3	JPN Ch	Yokohama	6 Jun

Mark	Name		Nat	Born	Pos	Meet	Venue	Date
31:56.23	Rahab	Ndungu	KEN	19.10.78	2	AAA	Watford	5 Jul
31:56.90	Helena	Javornik	SLO	26.3.66	4	EChall	Athína (E)	12 Apr
31:57.76	Makiko	Kawashima	JPN	5.8.77	9rA		Okayama	27 Sep
31:59.06	Aki	Fujikawa	JPN	14.11.78	4	NC	Yokohama	6 Jun
31:59.28	Mizuki	Noguchi	JPN	3.7.78	5	NC	Yokohama	6 Jun
32:02.09	Hayley	Yelling	GBR	3.1.74	3	NC	Watford	5 Jul
32:03.99	Rocio	Ríos	ESP	13.3.69	5	EChall	Athína (E)	12 Apr
32:08.84	Mikie	Takanaka	JPN	6.10.80	5rA		Fukagawa	25 Jun
32:09.15	Salina	Kosgei	KEN	16.11.76	19	WCh	Saint-Denis	23 Aug
	(50)							
32:11.94	Blake	Russell	USA	24.7.75	7		Stanford	2 May
32:11.95	Sabrina	Mockenhaupt	GER	6.12.80	1	NC	München	17 May
32:12.91	Leah	Malot	KEN	7.6.72	1		Shizuoka	3 May
32:13.18	Jane	Wanjiku	KEN	14.6.79	2		Shizuoka	3 May
32:13.96		Zhou Chunxiu	CHN	8.3.79	2	NC	Shanghai	14 Sep
32:16.01	Yuko	Manabe	JPN	8.2.79	10rA		Okayama	27 Sep
32:17.59	Hiromi	Ominami	JPN	15.11.75	5		Shizuoka	3 May
32:20.12	María	Abel	ESP	23.10.74	6	EChall	Athína (E)	12 Apr
32:22.21	Liz	Yelling	GBR	5.12.74	7	EChall	Athína (E)	12 Apr
32:22.53	Emi	Ikeda	JPN	29.8.83	1		Osaka	14 May
	(60)							
32:23.08	Amaia	Piedra	ESP	2.6.72	8	EChall	Athína (E)	12 Apr
32:23.61	Miho	Notagashira	JPN	17.8.83	1		Kobe	11 Oct
32:23.67	Yuri	Kano	JPN	27.10.78	8		Shizuoka	3 May
32:23.68	Natalie	Harvey	AUS	19.1.75	4	NC	Watford	5 Jul
32:24.70	Shayne	Culpepper	USA	3.12.73	8		Stanford	2 May
32:26.60	Yoshiko	Ichikawa	JPN	18.4.76	1		Kobe	20 Apr
32:26.63	Takami	Ominami	JPN	15.11.75	9		Shizuoka	3 May
32:27.01	Machi	Tanaka	JPN	21.7.83	2		Kobe	11 Oct
32:28.14	Souad	Aït Salem	ALG	6.1.79	2	FRA Ch	Marseille	30 May
32:28.23	Galina	Aleksandrova	RUS	15.10.75	6	NC	Tula	3 Aug
	(70)							
32:28.53	Yasuko	Hashimoto	JPN	12.8.75	11	NC	Yokohama	6 Jun
32:28.65	Gloria	Marconi	ITA	31.3.68	9	EChall	Athína (E)	12 Apr
32:28.91	Olga	Romanova	RUS	23.5.80	7	NC	Tula	3 Aug
32:29.07	Mika	Okunaga	JPN	27.10.82	7rA		Fukagawa	25 Jun
32:31.54	Esther	Wanjiru	KEN	27.3.77	3		Kobe	20 Apr
32:32.76	Mie	Ueda	JPN	9.6.82	1		Kitakyushu	10 May
32:33.00	Haruko	Okamoto	JPN	19.8.74	5		Kobe	20 Apr
32:33.22	Naomi	Sakashita	JPN	25.5.75	6		Kobe	20 Apr
32:33.34	Beatriz	Santiago	ESP	28.10.68	10	EChall	Athína (E)	12 Apr
32:33.66	Tomoko	Horioka	JPN-J	27.3.84	2		Yokohama	5 Jul
	(80)							
32:35.48	Rodica	Chirita	ROM	28.10.76	1	NC	Bucuresti	9 Aug
32:35.52	Naoko	Hashimoto	JPN	8.9.82	3		Kitakyushu	10 May
32:37.18	Nicole	Jefferson	USA	8.3.76	9		Stanford	2 May
32:37.50	Fatima	Yvelain	FRA	4.5.69	3	NC	Marseille	30 May
32:38.74	Miki	Ohira	JPN	28.6.81	2		Sendai	17 May
32:39.10	Kim	Fitchen-Young	USA	3.9.68	11		Stanford	2 May
32:39.11	Christelle	Daunay	FRA	5.12.74	4	NC	Marseille	30 May
32:39.41		Li Helan	CHN	2.1.78	3	NC	Shanghai	14 Sep
32:39.60		Zhu Xiaolin	CHN-J	20.4.84	2	NG	Changsha	23 Oct
32:39.98	Miki	Oyama	JPN	22.10.79	12rA		Okayama	27 Sep
	(90)							
32:40.03	Alicia	Craig	USA	14.6.82	1	NCAA	Sacramento	12 Jun
32:40.70	Rodica	Moroianu	FRA	18.11.70	12	EChall	Athína (E)	12 Apr
32:41.14		Zhang Yin	CHN-Y	6.10.86	3	NG	Changsha	23 Oct
32:41.71	Hiromi	Koga	JPN	28.5.82	11		Shizuoka	3 May
32:41.76	Magdalena	Lewy	USA	1.8.73	1		Stanford	28 Mar
32:42.42	Fumi	Murata	JPN	13.3.75	13	NC	Yokohama	6 Jun
32:42.49	Alessandra	Aguilar	ESP	1.7.78	13	EChall	Athína (E)	12 Apr
32:42.61	Nami	Kurosawa	JPN	26.12.78	10rA		Fukagawa	25 Jun
32:42.73	Dorte	Vibjerg	DEN	28.10.73	14	EChall	Athína (E)	12 Apr
32:43.75		Bao Guiying	CHN-Y	20.1.86	4	NG	Changsha	23 Oct
	(100)							

32:44.03	Albina	Ivanova	RUS	16.5.77	3 Aug
32:44.69		Shi Hongjuan	CHN-J	17.12.84	23 Oct
32:44.72	Ryoko	Kitajima	JPN	12.6.76	17 May
32:44.84	Rie	Matsuoka	JPN	9.3.77	20 Apr
32:45.2	Alice	Timbilil	KEN	16.6.83	14 Jun
32:45.70	Ai	Yamamoto	JPN	6.7.78	10 May
32:46.17		Zhu Yanmei	CHN-Y	16.10.86	23 Oct
32:46.36		Sun Jing	CHN-J	12.6.85	23 Oct
32:47.07	Kate	O'Neill	USA	29.7.80	12 Jun
32:47.59	Tegla	Loroupe	KEN	9.5.73	30 May
32:47.85	Maya	Nishio	JPN	19.12.78	25 Jun
32:47.99	Margaret	Maury	FRA	15.5.74	30 May

Mark	Name		Nat	Born	Date
32:49.00	Jenny	Crain	USA	12.2.68	19 Jun
32:49.02	Hiromi	Fujii	JPN	7.2.83	27 Jun
32:49.06	Agata	Balsamo	ITA	11.11.70	12 Apr
32:50.01	Kristin	Price	USA	25.11.81	12 Jun
32:50.06	Rkia	Chébili	FRA	28.2.74	30 May
32:50.77	Natalya	Berkut	UKR	30.5.75	8 Jun
32:50.89	Madai	Pérez	MEX	2.2.80	17 Apr
32:51.80	Akemi	Ozaki	JPN	12.10.77	20 Apr
32:52.26	Laura	O'Neill	USA	29.7.80	12 Jun
32:52.44	Teresa	Recio	ESP	7.7.63	20 Jul
32:52.51	Yoko	Manabe	JPN	8.2.79	6 Jun
32:52.60	Charlotte	Dale	GBR-J	23.3.84	12 Apr
32:52.87	Jamie	Krzyminski	USA	17.2.82	12 Jun
32:53.04	Hiroko	Miyauchi	JPN	19.6.83	10 May
32:53.38	Haruko	Yamamoto	JPN	31.10.81	17 May
32:55.69	Olesya	Lutskovskaya	RUS	19.11.80	3 Aug
32:55.73		Zhang Chong	CHN-Y	5.1.86	23 Oct
32:55.89	Leila	Aman	ETH	24.11.77	7 Jun
32:56.43	Sylvia	Weissteiner	ITA	13.7.79	12 Apr
32:56.79	Kiyomi	Ogawa	JPN	15.9.81	25 Jun
32:56.80	Luisa	Larraga	ESP	10.12.70	20 Jul
32:56.94	Ayano	Kozuka	JPN	27.10.77	25 Jun
32:58.0A	Eunice	Jepkorir	KEN	.81	11 Jul
32:58.1A	Catherine	Ndereba	KEN	21.7.72	11 Jul
32:59.63	Masayo	Kobayashi	JPN	4.2.80	27 Sep
32:59.94	Miho	Nakashima	JPN	16.12.80	27 Sep
33:00.0A	Irene	Kwambai	KEN	25.10.78	11 Jul
33:00.20	Madoka	Ogi	JPN	26.10.83	27 Sep
33:00.62	Keiko	Isogai	JPN	22.7.81	27 Sep
33:00.62	Risa	Hagiwara	JPN	22.11.82	27 Sep
33:01.71	Marleen	Renders	BEL	24.12.68	2 Jul
33:02.77	Hiroko	Shoi	JPN	18.6.80	27 Sep
33:03.22	Miho	Ichikawa	JPN	20.5.73	25 Jun
33:03.90	Alevtina	Ivanova	RUS	22.5.75	3 Aug
33:04.0A	Jane	Ekwama	KEN		11 Jul
33:06.17	Naoko	Sakamoto	JPN	14.11.80	11 Oct
33:07.00	Asuka	Maeda	JPN	4.10.78	10 May
33:07.58	Dana	Coons (150)	USA	27.9.78	2 May
33:07.6A	Joyce	Chepchumba	KEN	6.11.70	11 Jul
33:08.27	Bente	Landøy	NOR	16.12.72	8 Aug
33:08.70	Simona	Staicu	HUN	5.5.71	18 May
33:08.76	Akane	Otsuka	JPN	23.10.76	10 May
33:08.87	Sonja	Stolic	SCG	21.4.80	23 Aug
33:09.34	Mika	Watanabe	JPN	25.8.77	25 Jun
33:09.35	Vicky	Gill	GBR	21.8.80	12 Jun
33:09.41	Mako	Yagi	JPN	24.6.82	10 May
33:09.80	Sarah	Toland	USA	12.12.78	2 May
33:11.23	Siri Merete	Alfheim	NOR	6.7.76	17 May
33:11.41	Beáta	Rakonczai	HUN	25.6.77	18 May
33:11.55	Eyerusalem	Kuma	ETH	18.9.81	7 Jun
33:12.98	Soulef	Bouguerra	TUN	10.2.77	9 Aug
33:13.70	Nyla	Carroll	NZL	24.11.65	15 Feb
33:13.72	María	Protópappa	GRE	5.5.73	12 Apr
33:14.68	Megumi	Kobayashi (166)	JPN	4.8.76	11 Oct

JUNIORS

See main list for top 6 Juniors. 11 performances by 9 women to 32:50.0. Additional marks and further juniors:

Xing Huina 32:36.24 1 NG Changsha 23 Oct

Wangui 32:13.24 3 Shizuoka 3 May

Mark	Name		Nat	Born	Pos	Meet	Venue	Date
32:44.69		Shi Hongjuan	CHN	17.12.84	5	NG	Changsha	23 Oct
32:46.17		Zhu Yanmei	CHN-Y	16.10.86	6	NG	Changsha	23 Oct
32:46.36		Sun Jing	CHN	12.6.85	7	NG	Changsha	23 Oct
32:52.60	Charlotte	Dale (10)	GBR	23.3.84	16	EChall	Athína (E)	12 Apr
32:55.73		Zhang Chong	CHN-Y	5.1.86	8	NG	Changsha	23 Oct
33:22.7	Inna	Poluskina	LAT	7.7.84	2	NC	Riga	21 May
33:43.04		Wang Yu	CHN	27.2.84	5	NC	Shanghai	14 Sep
33:46.15		Yao Xuejing	CHN	22.4.85	9	NG	Changsha	23 Oct
33:55.12	Yudelkis	Martínez	CUB	28.2.85	2	PAm	Santo Domingo	8 Aug
33:56.75		Dong Xiaoqin	CHN	2.1.84	11	NG	Changsha	23 Oct
33:58.18		Xu Suyin	CHN-Y	20.11.86	1		Deyang	19 Apr

1 HOUR

Mark	Name		Nat	Born	Pos	Meet	Venue	Date
17,776m	Jelena	Prokopcuka	LAT	21.9.76	1mx		Riga	30 Aug
17,264	Sigrid	Vanden Bempt	BEL	10.2.81	1		Woluwe	18 Oct

30.000 METRES

Mark	Name		Nat	Born	Pos	Meet	Venue	Date
1:45:50.0	Tegla	Loroupe	KEN	9.5.73	1		Warstein	6 Jun
1:48:11.0	Emily	Kimuria	KEN	.75	2		Warstein	6 Jun

10 KILOMETRES ROAD

Mark	Name		Nat	Born	Pos	Meet	Venue	Date
30:21	Paula	Radcliffe	GBR	17.12.73	1		San Juan	23 Feb
30:51		Radcliffe			1		Richmond Park	7 Sep
31:13	Lornah	Kiplagat	KEN/NED	20.3.74	1		New York	7 Jun
31:13	Susan	Chepkemei	KEN	25.6.75	1		Atlanta	4 Jul
31:18+		Radcliffe			1	in HMar	Newcastle	21 Sep
31:24	Isabella	Ochichi	KEN	28.10.79	1		New Orleans	19 Apr
31:25+		Radcliffe			1	in HMar	Vilamoura	4 Oct
31:27+	Deena	Drossin	USA	14.2.73	1	in 15k	Jacksonville	8 Mar
31:28	Irina	Mikitenko	GER	23.8.72	1		Paderborn	19 Apr
31:33		Chepkemei			2		New York	7 Jun
31:34		Kiplagat			2		Atlanta	4 Jul
31:36	Asmae	Leghzaoui ¶	MAR	30.8.76	2		San Juan	23 Feb
31:37		Kiplagat			1		Glasgow	18 May
31:38	Zhor	El Kamch	MAR	15.3.73	1		Casablanca	11 May
31:39	Benita	Johnson	AUS	6.5.79	1		Kuta	2 Feb
	(15/9)							
31:49	Yelena	Burykina	RUS	7.5.72	2		Glasgow	18 May
31:50	Berhane	Adere	ETH	21.7.73	1		Manchester	26 May
31:53	Derartu	Tulu	ETH	21.3.72	2		Manchester	26 May
31:53	Catherine	Ndereba	KEN	21.7.72	1		Cape Elizabeth	2 Aug

Mark	Name		Nat	Born	Pos	Meet	Venue	Date
31:54	Luminita	Talpos	ROM	9.10.72	2		Cape Elizabeth	2 Aug
31:55	Yoko	Shibui	JPN	14.3.79	1		Hitachinaka	11 Feb
31:56	Tegla	Loroupe	KEN	9.5.73	2		Casablanca	11 May
31:58	Linah	Cheruiyot	KEN	1.3.73	2		Paderborn	19 Apr
32:00	Sonia	O'Sullivan	IRL	28.11.69	3		Manchester	26 May
Others where superior to track bests								
32:01	Christine	Chepkonga	KEN	12.12.80	3		Paderborn	19 Apr
32:02	Malika	Assahssah	MAR	24.9.82	3		Casablanca	11 May
32:05	Caroline	Kwambai	KEN	9.9.75	3		Glasgow	18 May
32:05	Yuliya	Gromova	RUS	21.5.74	1		Sankt-Peterburg	21 Jun
32:06	Constantina	Tomescu (Dita)	ROM	23.1.70	3		Cape Elizabeth	2 Aug
32:07	Jane	Kiptoo	KEN	8.8.82	1		Voorthuizen	23 Jul
32:08	Susan	Kirui	KEN	4.4.80	4		Paderborn	19 Apr
32:11	Leah	Malot	KEN	7.6.72	1		La Courneuve	23 Mar
32:12	Edna	Kiplagat	KEN	15.11.79	1		Mobile	22 Mar
32:13	Eunice	Chepkorir	KEN	.81	2		Düsseldorf	7 Sep
32:14	Luminita	Zaituc	GER	9.10.68	3		Düsseldorf	7 Sep
32:19	Jane	Omoro	KEN	12.9.74	2		La Courneuve	23 Mar
32:22	Jen	Rhines	USA	1.7.74	4		Cape Elizabeth	2 Aug
32:24	Mestawat	Tufa	ETH	14.9.83	1		Madrid	23 Nov
32:26	Lyudmila	Korchagina	RUS	26.7.71	2		Ottawa	10 May
32:26	Margaret	Okayo	KEN	30.5.76	3		New York	7 Jun
32:30	Zakia	Mrisho	TAN-J	19.2.84	3		La Courneuve	23 Mar
32:30	Salina	Kosgei	KEN	16.11.76	4		La Courneuve	23 Mar
32:31	Svetlana	Zakharova	RUS	15.9.70	7		New York	7 Jun
32:33	Eva	Sanz	ESP	4.7.73	2		Madrid	23 Nov
32:37	Tatyana	Khmeleva	RUS	2.4.79	2		Mobile	22 Mar
32:39	Aster	Demissie	ETH	.83	3		Ottawa	10 May
32:40	Petra	Kaminková	CZE	19.1.73	1		Oeide	5 Jul
32:40+	Elfenesh	Alemu	ETH	16.6.75	1=	in Mar	Tokyo	16 Nov
32:40+	Naoko	Takahashi	JPN	6.5.72	1	in Mar	Tokyo	16 Nov
32:41+	Teyiba	Erkesso	ETH	82	7	in HMar	Vilamoura	4 Oct
32:42	Dorte	Vibjerg	DEN	28.10.73	1		Hamburg	31 Aug
32:43 ?	Amina	Godana	ETH-Y	.86	1		Tourcoing	19 Oct
32:43	Emily	Chebet	KEN-Y	18.2.86	3		Madrid	23 Nov

32:44	Christine	Clifton	USA	2.8.72	7 Jun
32:44	Meselech	Melkamu	ETH-J	19.4.85	16 Nov
32:45	Silviya	Skvortsova	RUS	16.11.74	2 Aug
32:46	Chieko	Yamasaki	JPN	28.5.77	7 Dec
32:47+	Masayo	Kobayashi	JPN	4.2.80	2 Feb
32:47	Joyce	Chepchumba	KEN	6.11.70	7 Jun
32:47	Lyubov	Denisova	RUS	6.10.71	7 Jun
32:47	Kathy	Butler	GBR	22.10.73	14 Jun
32:47	Atalelech	Ketema	ETH	.83	28 Sep
32:48	Deborah	Mengich	KEN		21 Apr
32:49	Tina	Connelly	CAN	16.8.70	27 Jul
32:50	Gladys	Asiba	KEN	31.5.77	22 Mar
32:50	Beáta	Rakonczai	HUN	25.6.77	7 Sep
32:50	Emily	Samoei	KEN	.80	28 Sep
32:52	Rakiya	Quétier	FRA	12.9.67	23 Mar
32:52	Restituta	Joseph	TAN	30.7.71	23 Jul
32:53	Esther	Kiplagat	KEN	8.12.66	23 Feb
32:54	Viola	Bor	KEN	.79	9 Mar
32:54	Naoko	Sakamoto	JPN	14.11.80	7 Dec
32:56	Claudia	Dreher	GER	2.5.71	19 Apr
32:56	Lucy	Smith	CAN	27.4.67	27 Jul
32:56	Fatiha	Klilech-Fauvel	FRA	1.2.75	21 Sep
32:57	Carmen	Oliveras	FRA	29.6.71	23 Mar
32:57	Zivile	Balciunaite	LTU	3.4.79	2 Aug
32:58	Irene	Jerotich	KEN	.82	19 Apr
32:58	Poppy	Mlambo	RSA	7.12.80	22 Jun
32:58	Carrie	Tollefson	USA	18.1.77	8 Nov
32:59	Nadia	Ejjafini	BRN	8.11.80	11 May
32:59	Inês	Monteiro	POR	18.5.80	28 Dec
33:03	Junko	Kumagai	JPN	31.12.74	16 Feb
33:03	René	Kalmer	RSA	3.11.80	10 May
33:04	Nozomi	Sasaki	JPN	13.2.80	16 Feb
33:05+	Reiko	Tosa	JPN	11.6.76	6 Jul

Downhill

31:35	Marta	Domínguez	ESP	3.11.75	1		Madrid	31 Dec

4 May, Toronto: 1. Nicole Stevenson CAN 32:56

24 Jul, Salt Lake City (A): 1. Emily Jamesen USA 14.9.77 32:05, 2. Naomi Wangui KEN 32:29, 3. Susan Nielson USA 32:31, 4, Nicole Hunt USA 32:49.

30 Oct, Fukuroi – in HMar: 2. Yasuyo Iwamoto JPN 32:46, 3. Hisae Yoshimatsu JPN 33:04

Drugs disqualification

32:17	Elana	Meyer #	RSA	10.10.66	3		Kuta	2 Feb

JUNIORS

See main list for top 3 juniors. Additional juniors:

32:44	Meselech	Melkamu	ETH	19.4.85	2		Marseille	16 Nov
33:19	Irvette	van Blerk	RSA	5.7.87	2		Durban	22 Jun
33:20+	Ayako	Katafuchi	JPN	31.1.84	7	in HMar	Marugame	2 Feb
33:28	Shika	Marumo	JPN	11.1.84	5		Okayama	7 Dec

15 KILOMETRES ROAD

46:41+ dh	Paula	Radcliffe	GBR	17.12.73	1	in HMar	Newcastle	21 Sep
47:15	Deena	Drossin	USA	14.2.73	1	NC	Jacksonville	8 Mar
47:46+		Radcliffe			1	in HMar	Vilamoura	4 Oct
48:22+	Catherine	Ndereba	KEN	21.7.72	1	in HMar	Sapporo	6 Jul

Mark	Name		Nat	Born	Pos	Meet	Venue	Date
48:24	Isabella	Ochichi	KEN	28.10.79	1		Le Puy-en-Velay	1 May
48:43	Marla	Runyan	USA	4.1.69	2	NC	Jacksonville	8 Mar
48:52+	Mikie	Takanaka	JPN	6.10.80	2	in HMar	Sapporo	6 Jul
48:55	Susan	Chepkemei	KEN	25.6.75	1		Utica	13 Jul
48:59+	Lydia	Grigoryeva	RUS	21.1.74	2	in HMar	Vilamoura	4 Oct
48:59+	Berhane	Adere	ETH	21.7.73	3	in HMar	Vilamoura	4 Oct
48:59+		Chepkemei			4	in HMar	Vilamoura	4 Oct
49:02+	Yumiko	Hara	JPN	9.1.82	3	in HMar	Sapporo	6 Jul
49:06	Mestawat	Tufa	ETH	14.9.83	1		Nijmegen	16 Nov
49:08	Luminita	Talpos	ROM	9.10.72	2		Utica	13 Jul
49:14+	Naoko	Takahashi	JPN	6.5.72	1=	in Mar	Tokyo	16 Nov
49:14+	Elfenesh	Alemu	ETH	16.6.75	1=	in Mar	Tokyo	16 Nov
49:15+	Yasuko	Hashimoto	JPN	12.8.75	1	in HMar	Marugame	2 Feb
49:18+	Masayo	Kobayashi	JPN	4.2.80	2	in HMar	Marugame	2 Feb
49:20+	Mizuki	Noguchi	JPN	3.7.78	1	in HMar	Kobe	9 Nov
49:29+	Constantina	Tomescu (Dita)	ROM	23.1.70	5	in HMar	Vilamoura	4 Oct
49:29+	Benita	Johnson	AUS	6.5.79	6	in HMar	Vilamoura	4 Oct
49:30	Colleen	de Reuck	USA	13.4.64	3	NC	Jacksonville	8 Mar
49:44	Rahab	Ndungu	KEN	19.10.78	3		Utica	13 Jul
49:44+	Lyudmila	Biktasheva	RUS	25.7.74	7	in HMar	Vilamoura	4 Oct
49:49+	Akemi	Ozaki	JPN	12.10.77	3	in HMar	Marugame	2 Feb
49:51+	Kumi	Tanabe	JPN	2.4.81	1	in HMar	Osaka	23 Feb
49:57+	Lornah	Kiplagat	KEN/NED	20.3.74	1	in Mar	Osaka	26 Jan
49:58+	Naoko	Sakamoto	JPN	14.11.80		in Mar	Osaka	26 Jan
49:58+	Megumi	Tanaka	JPN	4.9.75		in Mar	Osaka	26 Jan
49:58+	Masako	Chiba	JPN	18.7.76		in Mar	Osaka	26 Jan
49:58+	Miwako	Yamanaka	JPN	24.5.78		in Mar	Osaka	26 Jan
49:59+	Alla	Zhilyayeva	RUS	5.2.69	8	in HMar	Vilamoura	4 Oct
Downhill								
49:42+	Aki	Fujikawa	JPN	14.11.78	1	in HMar	Fukuroi	30 Oct
49:43+	Yasuyo	Iwamoto	JPN	8.9.76	2	in HMar	Fukuroi	30 Oct

10 MILES ROAD

Mark	Name		Nat	Born	Pos	Meet	Venue	Date
50:01+ dh	Paula	Radcliffe	GBR	17.12.73	1		Newcastle	21 Sep
51:52	Lyudmila	Biktasheva	RUS	25.7.74	1		Flint	23 Aug
52:17	Restituta	Joseph	TAN	30.7.71	1		Zaandam	21 Sep
52:57	Leah	Malot	KEN	7.6.72	2		Flint	23 Aug
53:07	Jane	Kiptoo	KEN	8.8.82	3		Flint	23 Aug
53:16	Kathy	Butler	GBR	22.10.73	4		Flint	23 Aug
53:18	Alevtina	Ivanova	RUS	22.5.75	1		Park Forest	1 Sep
53:22	Olga	Romanova	RUS	23.5.80	5		Flint	23 Aug
53:26	Sonia	O'Sullivan	IRL	28.11.69	1		Portsmouth	12 Oct
53:39	Beáta	Rakonczai	HUN	25.6.77	2		Zaandam	21 Sep
53:46	Helena	Javornik	SLO	26.3.66	1		Bern	10 May
53:49	Asha	Gigi	ETH	15.10.73	2		Washington	6 Apr
53:49	Jane	Ekimat	KEN	12.6.74	3		Zaandam	21 Sep
53:58	Sylvia	Mosqueda	USA	8.4.66	3		Washington	6 Apr
53:58	Lyudmila	Petrova	RUS	7.10.68	6		Flint	23 Aug

HALF MARATHON

Slightly downhill courses: Lisboa 69m, South Shields 30.5m

Mark	Name		Nat	Born	Pos	Meet	Venue	Date
65:40 dh	Paula	Radcliffe	GBR	17.12.73	1	GNR	South Shields	21 Sep
67:23	Margaret	Okayo	KEN	30.5.76	1		Udine	28 Sep
67:32 dh	Berhane	Adere	ETH	21.7.73	2	GNR	South Shields	21 Sep
67:35		Radcliffe			1	WCh	Vilamoura	4 Oct
67:51 dh	Susan	Chepkemei	KEN	25.6.75	3	GNR	South Shields	21 Sep
68:02+ dh		Radcliffe			1	in Mar	London	13 Apr
68:23	Catherine	Ndereba	KEN	21.7.72	1		Sapporo	6 Jul
68:29	Mizuki	Noguchi	JPN	3.7.78	1		Yamaguchi	9 Mar
68:35	Takako	Kotorida	JPN	2.4.77	2		Yamaguchi	9 Mar
68:40 dh	Sonia	O'Sullivan	IRL	28.11.69	4	GNR	South Shields	21 Sep
68:42	Isabella	Ochichi	KEN	28.10.79	1		Nice	27 Apr
69:02		Adere			2	WCh	Vilamoura	4 Oct
69:12 dh	Derartu	Tulu (10)	ETH	21.3.72	5	GNR	South Shields	21 Sep
69:12	Margaret	Atodonyang	KEN	.78	2		Udine	28 Sep
69:17		Okayo			1		Virginia Beach	31 Aug
69:19 dh	Jelena	Prokopcuka	LAT	21.9.76	6	GNR	South Shields	21 Sep
69:20 dh		Tulu			1		Lisboa	16 Mar
69:21+ dh	Constantina	Tomescu (Dita)	ROM	23.1.70	2	in Mar	London	13 Apr
69:25	Gloria	Marconi	ITA	31.3.68	1		Ostia Lido	23 Feb
69:26	Benita	Johnson	AUS	6.5.79	3	WCh	Vilamoura	4 Oct

Mark	Name		Nat	Born	Pos	Meet	Venue	Date
69:28	Adriana	Fernández	MEX	4.4.71	1		Kyoto	9 Mar
69:30+ dh		Chepkemei			3	in Mar	London	13 Apr
69:32	Yasuko	Hashimoto	JPN	12.8.75	1		Marugame	2 Feb
69:32	Lydia	Grigoryeva	RUS	21.1.74	4	WCh	Vilamoura	4 Oct
69:37	Yumiko	Hara	JPN	9.1.82	2		Sapporo	6 Jul
69:39	Magdalene	Chemjor (20)	KEN	12.11.78	1		Lille	6 Sep
69:41	Hiromi	Ominami	JPN	15.11.75	3		Yamaguchi	9 Mar
69:42		Prokopcuka			1		Paris	9 Mar
69:42	Restituta	Joseph	TAN	30.7.71	1		Remich	28 Sep
69:45	Beáta	Rakonczai	HUN	25.6.77	1		Krems	14 Sep
69:47 dh	Leah	Malot	KEN	7.6.72	2		Lisboa	16 Mar
69:48	Anikó	Kálovics	HUN	13.5.77	3		Udine	28 Sep
69:51		Kálovics			2		Krems	14 Sep
69:52		Noguchi			1		Kobe	9 Nov
69:53 dh	Joyce	Chepchumba	KEN	6.11.70	3		Lisboa	16 Mar
69:54	Marleen	Renders	BEL	24.12.68	1		Den Haag	29 Mar
69:55	Kumi	Tanabe	JPN	2.4.81	1		Osaka	23 Feb
69:56	Rosaria	Console	ITA	17.12.79	2		Ostia Lido	23 Feb
69:59	Yesenia	Centeno (30)	CUB/ESP	27.6.71	1		Azpeitia	29 Mar
70:00	Colleen	de Reuck	USA	13.4.64	1	NC	Duluth	21 Jun
	(40/31)							
70:03+	Naoko	Takahashi	JPN	6.5.72	1=	in Mar	Tokyo	16 Nov
70:03+	Elfenesh	Alemu	ETH	16.6.75	1=	in Mar	Tokyo	16 Nov
70:06	Masako	Chiba	JPN	18.7.76	1		Miyazaki	6 Jan
70:13	Alla	Zhilyayeva	RUS	5.2.69	6	WCh	Vilamoura	4 Oct
70:14	Masayo	Kobayashi	JPN	4.2.80	2		Marugame	2 Feb
70:17	Fujiko	Takahashi	JPN	19.6.83	2		Miyazaki	6 Jan
70:19	Ruth	Wanjiru	KEN	11.9.81	3		Miyazaki	6 Jan
70:20	Tatyana	Khmeleva	RUS	2.4.79	2		Kyoto	9 Mar
70:21+	Lornah	Kiplagat	KEN/NED	20.3.74	1	in Mar	Osaka	26 Jan
	(40)							
70:21		Zheng Guixia	CHN	24.6.73	4		Yamaguchi	9 Mar
70:21	Fumi	Murata	JPN	13.3.75	5		Yamaguchi	9 Mar
70:21	Mika	Okunaga	JPN	27.10.82	6		Yamaguchi	9 Mar
70:21	Yelena	Burykina	RUS	7.5.72	1		Moskva	10 May
70:22+	Mari	Ozaki	JPN	16.7.75	3=	in Mar	Osaka	26 Jan
70:22+	Naoko	Sakamoto	JPN	14.11.80	3=	in Mar	Osaka	26 Jan
70:22+	Miwako	Yamanaka	JPN	24.5.78	3=	in Mar	Osaka	26 Jan
70:23	Yuko	Manabe	JPN	8.2.79	4		Miyazaki	6 Jan
70:23+	Megumi	Tanaka	JPN	4.9.75	6	in Mar	Osaka	26 Jan
70:23	Alice	Chelangat	KEN	.77	1		Saint-Denis	5 Oct
	(50)							
70:26	Natalya	Berkut	UKR	30.5.75	2		Den Haag	29 Mar
70:26	Hiromi	Fujii	JPN	7.2.83	1		Gold Coast	6 Jul
70:28	Yuri	Kano	JPN	27.10.78	5		Miyazaki	6 Jan
70:28	Ana	Dias	POR	15.1.74	1		Oruña de Piélagos	6 Sep
70:30	Galina	Aleksandrova	RUS	15.10.75	2		Novosibirsk	13 Sep
70:31	Akemi	Ozaki	JPN	12.10.77	3		Marugame	2 Feb
70:31	Lyudmila	Biktasheva	RUS	25.7.74	7	WCh	Vilamoura	4 Oct
70:32	Mikie	Takanaka	JPN	6.10.80	3		Sapporo	6 Jul
70:34	Irina	Safarova	RUS	19.6.69	3		NovosibirsK	13 Sep
70:36	Jane	Omoro	KEN	12.9.74	1		Peterborough	9 Mar
	(60)							
70:39	Kiyomi	Ogawa	JPN	15.9.81	8		Yamaguchi	9 Mar
70:43	Simona	Staicu	HUN	5.5.71	3		Krems	14 Sep
70:44	Jane	Ekimat	KEN	12.6.74	4		Udine	28 Sep
70:44+ dh	Mihaela	Botezan	ROM	21.11.76	6		London	13 Apr
70:45+ dh	Deena	Drossin	USA	14.2.73	7=		London	13 Apr
70:45+ dh	Lyudmila	Petrova	RUS	7.10.68	7=		London	13 Apr
70:45	Direbe	Alemu	ETH	.83	1		Reims	26 Oct
70:46+	Shitaye	Gemechu	ETH	80	1=	in Mar	Hamburg	27 Apr
70:46+	Hellen	Kimutai	KEN	28.12.77	1=	in Mar	Hamburg	27 Apr
70:50	Lyudmila	Korchagina	RUS	26.7.71	1		Vancouver	22 Jun
	(70)							
70:51	Luminita	Zaituc	GER	9.10.68	1		Frankfurt am Main	9 Mar
70:56	Caroline	Kwambai	KEN	9.9.75	1		Glasgow	7 Sep
70:57	Yoshiko	Ichikawa	JPN	18.4.76	7		Miyazaki	6 Jan
70:57	Marie	Davenport	IRL	24.1.75	1		Boston	12 Oct
70:58	Harumi	Hiroyama	JPN	2.9.68	3		Kyoto	9 Mar
70:59	Alina	Ivanova	RUS	16.3.69	10	WCh	Vilamoura	4 Oct

Mark		Name		Nat	Born	Pos	Meet	Venue	Date
71:00	dh	Esther	Kiplagat	KEN	8.12.66	4		Lisboa	16 Mar
71:03		Helena	Javornik	SLO	26.3.66	1		Praha	22 Mar
71:04		Luminita	Talpos	ROM	9.10.72	2		Okayama	7 Dec
71:07		Olivera	Jevtic	SCG	24.7.77	2		Praha	22 Mar
		(80)							
71:08		Aki	Fujikawa	JPN	14.11.78	1	NG	Fukoroi	30 Oct
71:12		Nozomi	Iijima	JPN-J	17.3.84	1		Matsue	16 Mar
71:13		Naoko	Hashimoto	JPN	8.9.82	2		Gold Coast	6 Jul
71:13		Elizabeth	Chemweno	KEN	13.7.78	2		Reims	26 Oct
71:15		Reiko	Tosa	JPN	11.6.76	5		Sapporo	6 Jul
71:15		Rose	Chepchumba	KEN		1		Arezzo	1 Nov
71:16		Salina	Kosgei	KEN	16.11.76	2		Lille	6 Sep
71:22		Sylvia	Mosqueda	USA	8.4.66	12	WCh	Vilamoura	4 Oct
71:24		Rita	Jeptoo	KEN	15.2.81	4		Praha	22 Mar
71:24+	dh	Larisa	Zyusko	RUS	27.4.69	11		London	13 Apr
		(90)							
71:24		Albina	Ivanova	RUS	16.5.77	1		Indianapolis	3 May
71:24		Ruth	Kutol	KEN	16.5.73	2		Remich	28 Sep
71:27		Emily	Kimuria	KEN	.75	1		Altötting	7 Sep
71:28		Yasuyo	Iwamoto	JPN	8.9.76	2	NG	Fukuroi	30 Oct
71:31		Susie	Power	AUS	26.3.75	1		Sydney	25 May
71:31		Christine	Clifton	USA	2.8.72	2	NC	Duluth	21 Jun
71:34	dh	Tegla	Loroupe	KEN	9.5.73	6		Lisboa	16 Mar
71:36		Annemette	Aagård (Jensen)	DEN	11.4.72	3		Den Haag	29 Mar
71:37		Makiko	Kawashima	JPN	5.8.77	10		Yamaguchi	9 Mar
71:39		Corinne	Raux	FRA	16.8.76	1		Chassieu	18 May
		(100)							

71:40		Eri	Amo	JPN	26.7.77	2 Feb
71:41		Kayoko	Obata	JPN	18.9.71	6 Jan
71:42		Esther	Wanjiru	KEN	27.3.77	15 Nov
71:43		Sakiko	Kato	JPN	8.5.79	6 Jan
71:44		Asami	Obi	JPN	22.3.76	7 Dec
71:45		Jen	Rhines	USA	1.7.74	21 Sep
71:48		Kiyoko	Shimahara	JPN	22.12.76	6 Jan
71:48		Megumi	Kobayashi	JPN	4.8.76	24 Nov
71:48		Kozue	Saito	JPN	25.9.82	7 Dec
71:50		Margaret	Maury	FRA	15.5.74	26 Oct
71:51		Eva	Sanz	ESP	4.7.73	12 Jan
71:51		Haruko	Yamamoto	JPN	31.10.81	16 Mar
71:51		Madai	Pérez	MEX	2.2.80	6 Apr
71:53		Ai	Yamamoto	JPN	6.7.78	9 Mar
71:53		Machi	Tanaka	JPN	21.7.83	16 Mar
71:55		Keiko	Isogai	JPN	22.7.81	9 Mar
71:55		Risa	Hagiwara	JPN	22.11.82	6 Jul
71:57		Debbie	Robinson	GBR	31.1.68	16 Mar
71:57+		Zinaida	Semyonova	RUS	22.12.62	13 Apr
71:58		Miriam	Wangari	KEN		16 Mar
71:58		Lidia	Simon	ROM	4.9.73	31 Aug
71:58		Mizuho	Nasukawa	JPN	22.11.79	9 Nov
71:59		Anastasia	Ndereba	KEN	27.9.74	3 May
72:00		Asuka	Maeda	JPN	4.10.78	9 Mar
72:00		Lenah	Cheruiyot	KEN	1.3.73	6 Apr
72:01		Madina	Biktagirova	RUS	20.9.64	9 Nov
72:07+		Firiya	Sultanova	RUS	29.4.61	2 Nov
72:08		Hafida	Izem	MAR	79	2 Feb
72:08		Yoshie	Hayatsu	JPN	23.12.83	9 Mar
72:08		Olga	Kovpotina	RUS	10.1.68	3 May
72:10		Naomi	Sakashita	JPN	25.5.75	9 Mar
72:10	dh	Fernanda	Ribeiro	POR	23.6.69	21 Sep
72:11+		Olga	Romanova	RUS	23.5.80	2 Nov
72:12		Galina	Bogomolova	RUS	15.10.77	4 Oct
72:12		Hisae	Yoshimatsu	JPN	13.5.79	30 Oct
72:13+		Takami	Ominami	JPN	15.11.75	9 Mar
72:14		Jennifer	Chesinon	KEN	6.8.82	21 Sep
72:15		Emi	Nakajima	JPN	8.8.80	2 Feb
72:16		Patrizia	Tisi	ITA	17.5.71	21 Sep
72:17		Caroline	Cheptanui	KEN	21.3.81	18 May
72:17		Hellen	Cherono	KEN		19 Oct
72:17		Malika	Assahssah	MAR	24.9.82	19 Oct
72:18		Anne	Chelagat	KEN	4.6.69	28 Sep
72:19		Mary	Ptikany	KEN	78	6 Jan
72:19		Yuka	Hashimoto	JPN	22.12.81	23 Feb
72:23		Miki	Oyama	JPN	22.10.79	16 Mar
72:23	dh	Fátima	Cabral	POR	14.1.72	16 Mar
72:25			Wang Hongxia	CHN	13.1.75	6 Jan
72:26		Yukari	Komatsu	JPN	13.2.74	2 Feb
72:26		Noriko	Takahashi (150)	JPN	9.11.76	16 Feb
72:27		Anna	Thompson	AUS	11.12.76	6 Jul
72:27		Emily	Samoei	KEN	80	7 Sep
72:28		Nyla	Carroll	NZL	24.11.65	1 Jun
72:29		Sayuri	Tanaka	JPN	29.8.81	9 Mar
72:33		Banwella	Mrashani	TAN	14.11.77	9 Mar
72:33		Mara	Yamauchi	GBR	13.8.73	7 Sep
72:35		Kanako	Kamikihara	JPN	28.11.81	9 Mar
72:37		Christelle	Daunay	FRA	5.12.74	14 Sep
72:38		Natalie	Harvey	AUS	19.1.75	9 Mar
72:38		Bruna	Genovese	ITA	24.9.76	4 Oct
72:39	dh	Adélia	Elias	POR	7.5.74	16 Mar
72:40		Yukari	Urashima	JPN	21.10.82	16 Mar
72:40		Eri	Hayakawa	JPN	81	6 Jul
72:40		Yelena	Orlova	RUS	3.2.70	26 Oct
72:41		Deborah	Mengich	KEN		30 Nov
72:42		Ayako	Katafuchi	JPN-J	31.1.84	2 Feb
72:43		Kyoko	Miyajima	JPN	17.10.78	6 Jan
72:43		Chieko	Yamasaki	JPN	28.5.77	2 Feb
72:43		Tomoka	Fukuda	JPN	3.6.79	5 Oct
72:43		Teyiba	Erkesso	ETH	82	4 Oct
72:43+		Svetlana	Zakharova	RUS	15.9.70	12 Oct
72:44		Nozomi	Sasaki	JPN	13.7.80	9 Mar
72:44		Nami	Kamiya	JPN	17.6.80	16 Mar
72:46		Megumi	Hasegawa	JPN	9.9.80	9 Mar
72:46+		Nuta	Olaru	ROM	28.8.70	31 Aug
72:46+			Zhang Shujing	CHN	13.9.78	31 Aug
72:46+		Stine	Larsen	NOR	5.11.75	31 Aug
72:46+			Li Helan	CHN	2.1.78	31 Aug
72:46		Ramilya	Burangulova	RUS	11.7.61	21 Sep
72:47		Minori	Hayakari	JPN	29.11.72	16 Feb
72:47+			Ham Bong-sil	PRK	24.7.74	31 Aug
72:47+		Asha	Gigi	ETH	15.10.73	31 Aug
72:47+		Jane	Salaumäe	EST	17.1.68	31 Aug
72:49		Beatrice	Omwanza	KEN	24.2.74	18 May
72:50+		Viktoria	Klimina	RUS	1.3.76	26 Jan
72:51		Yuko	Nishigaki	JPN	26.11.82	6 Jan
72:51		Deeja	Youngqvist	USA	30.3.77	21 Jun
72:52		Rakiya	Quétier	FRA	12.9.67	9 Mar
72:54		Eri	Kojima	JPN	3.3.83	9 Mar
72:54		Nicole	Stevenson	CAN	13.9.73	22 Jun
72:56		Kaori	Tanabe	JPN	30.4.75	6 Jan
72:56		Iulia	Olteanu	ROM	26.1.67	27 Apr
72:58		Shiho	Takai	JPN	6.8.80	6 Jan
72:59		Simona	Viola (194)	ITA	18.11.71	23 Feb

Drugs dq

71:49	Pamela	Chepchumba ¶	KEN	8.3.78	6 Apr
72:19	Marizete	Resende	BRA	14.12.74	31 Aug

Mark		Name		Nat	Born	Pos	Meet	Venue	Date
				JUNIORS					
71:12		Nozomi	Iijima	JPN	17.3.84	1		Matsue	16 Mar
72:42		Ayako	Katafuchi	JPN	31.1.84	7		Marugame	2 Feb
74:05		Inna	Poluskina	LAT	7.7.84	2		Riga	19 Apr
74:16A		Ashu	Kasim	ETH	.85	5	NC	Addis Ababa	21 Sep

MARATHON

Mark		Name		Nat	Born	Pos	Meet	Venue	Date
2:15:25	LM	Paula	Radcliffe	GBR	17.12.73	1		London	13 Apr
2:19:39	LM		Sun Yingjie	CHN	3.10.77	1		Beijing	19 Oct
2:19:55	LM	Catherine	Ndereba	KEN	21.7.72	2		London	13 Apr
2:21:16	LM	Deena	Drossin	USA	14.2.73	3		London	13 Apr
2:21:18	LW	Mizuki	Noguchi	JPN	3.7.78	1		Osaka	26 Jan
2:21:45	LW	Masako	Chiba	JPN	18.7.76	2		Osaka	26 Jan
2:21:51	LW	Naoko	Sakamoto	JPN	14.11.80	3		Osaka	26 Jan
2:22:22	LW	Lornah	Kiplagat	KEN/NED	20.3.74	4		Osaka	26 Jan
2:22:31	PM	Margaret	Okayo	KEN	30.5.76	1		New York	2 Nov
2:23:03	PM		Ndereba			2		New York	2 Nov
2:23:07	LM	Svetlana	Zakharova (10)	RUS	15.9.70	1		Chicago	12 Oct
2:23:12	LM	Susan	Chepkemei	KEN	25.6.75	4		London	13 Apr
2:23:14	LM	Lyudmila	Petrova	RUS	7.10.68	5		London	13 Apr
2:23:18	LM		Zhang Shujing	CHN	13.9.78	1		Seoul	16 Mar
2:23:30	LW	Mari	Ozaki	JPN	16.7.75	5		Osaka	26 Jan
2:23:35	LM	Constantina	Tomescu (Dita)	ROM	23.1.70	2		Chicago	12 Oct
2:23:41	LM		Zhou Chunxiu	CHN	8.3.79	2		Beijing	19 Oct
2:23:43	LM		Tomescu			6		London	13 Apr
2:23:43	PM		Kiplagat			3		New York	2 Nov
2:23:55	LW		Ndereba			1	WCh	Saint-Denis	31 Aug
2:24:01	LM	Jelena	Prokopcuka	LAT	21.9.76	7		London	13 Apr
2:24:14	LW		Noguchi			2	WCh	Saint-Denis	31 Aug
2:24:47	LW	Elfenesh	Alemu	ETH	10.6.75	1		Tokyo	16 Nov
2:24:53	LM		Prokopcuka			3		Chicago	12 Oct
2:24:56	LM		Alemu			8		London	13 Apr
2:25:00	PM		Petrova			4		New York	2 Nov
2:25:03	LW	Takami	Ominami	JPN	15.11.75	1		Nagoya	9 Mar
2:25:09	LW		Chiba			3	WCh	Saint-Denis	31 Aug
2:25:20	DM		Zakharova			1		Boston	21 Apr
2:25:23	LM	Olivera	Jevtic (20)	SCG	24.7.77	1		Rotterdam	13 Apr
2:25:25	LW		Sakamoto			4	WCh	Saint-Denis	31 Aug
2:25:31	LW		Ham Bong-sil	PRK	24.7.74	5	WCh	Saint-Denis	31 Aug
2:25:32	LM	Mihaela	Botezan	ROM	21.11.76	9		London	13 Apr
2:25:33	LM		Sun Yingjie			1		Tianjin	19 Apr
2:25:35	LM	Albina	Ivanova	RUS	16.5.77	4		Chicago	12 Oct
2:25:42	LM	Worknesh	Tola	ETH	3.6.77	2		Seoul	16 Mar
2:25:53	LM	Hellen	Kimutai	KEN	28.12.77	1		Hamburg	27 Apr
2:25:58	PM	Lyubov	Denisova	RUS	6.10.71	5		New York	2 Nov
2:26:06	PM	Joyce	Chepchumba	KEN	6.11.70	6		New York	2 Nov
2:26:17	LM	Hiromi	Ominami	JPN	15.11.75	2		Rotterdam	13 Apr
		(40/28)							
2:26:22	LM	Grazyna	Syrek	POL	9.1.72	5		Chicago	12 Oct
2:26:32	LM	Yasuko	Hashimoto	JPN	12.8.75	1		Berlin	28 Sep
		(30)							
2:26:33	LM	Derartu	Tulu	ETH	21.3.72	10		London	13 Apr
2:27:05	PM	Firiya	Sultanova (Zhdanova)	RUS	29.4.61	1		Duluth	21 Jun
2:27:12	LM	Stine	Larsen	NOR	5.11.75	1		Torino	13 Apr
2:27:21	LW	Naoko	Takahashi	JPN	6.5.72	2		Tokyo	16 Nov
2:27:22	LM	Ruth	Kutol	KEN	16.5.73	1		Dublin	27 Oct
2:27:26	LW	Shitaye	Gemechu	ETH	.80	10	WCh	Saint-Denis	31 Aug
2:27:32	LW	Luminita	Talpos	ROM	9.10.72	6		Osaka	26 Jan
2:27:44	LW	Beatrice	Omwanza	KEN	24.2.74	1		Paris	6 Apr
2:27.48	LW	Rosaria	Console	ITA	17.12.79	2		Paris	6 Apr
2:27:50	LM	Malgorzata	Sobanska	POL	25.4.69	6		Chicago	12 Oct
		(40)							
2:28:01	LM	Colleen	de Reuck	USA	13.4.64	7		Chicago	12 Oct
2:28:05	LM	Larisa	Zyusko	RUS	27.4.69	11		London	13 Apr
2:28:06	LM	Irina	Bogachova	KGZ	30.5.61	1		Nashville	26 Apr
2:28:06	LM	Helena	Sampaio	POR	9.10.73	1		Amsterdam	19 Oct
2:28:10	LM	Yelena	Burykina	RUS	7.5.72	2		Dublin	27 Oct
2:28:13	LM	Helena	Javornik	SLO	26.3.66	3		Hamburg	27 Apr
2:28:14	LW	Risa	Hagiwara	JPN	22.11.82	2		Nagoya	9 Mar

Mark		Name		Nat	Born	Pos	Meet	Venue	Date
2:28:15	LM	Lyudmila	Pushkina	UKR	2.10.65	1		Columbus	19 Oct
2:28:17	LM	Kiyoko	Shimahara	JPN	22.12.76	1		Hitachinaka	11 Feb
2:28:18	LM	Emily	Kimuria	KEN	.75	2		Berlin	28 Sep
		(50)							
2:28:24	LW	Nuta	Olaru	ROM	28.8.70	11	WCh	Saint-Denis	31 Aug
2:28:28	LM	Ornella	Ferrara	ITA	17.4.68	3		Berlin	28 Sep
2:28:31	LM	Marleen	Renders	BEL	24.12.68	4		Hamburg	27 Apr
2:28:33	LM	Madina	Biktagirova	RUS	20.9.64	8		Chicago	12 Oct
2:28:42	LM	Olga	Kovpotina	RUS	10.1.68	2		Nashville	26 Apr
2:28:47	LM	Caroline	Kwambai	KEN	9.9.75	2		Amsterdam	19 Oct
2:28:49	LM	Ana	Dias	POR	15.1.74	4		Berlin	28 Sep
2:28:52	LM		Jong Yong-ok	PRK	24.1.81	2		Pyongyang	13 Apr
2:28:57	LW	Eri	Amo	JPN	26.7.77	4		Nagoya	9 Mar
2:29:00	LM		Kim Chang-ok	PRK	16.4.75	3		Pyongyang	13 Apr
		(60)							
2:29:00	LM	Alina	Ivanova	RUS	16.3.69	5		Berlin	28 Sep
2:29:01	LM	Deeja	Youngquist	USA	30.3.77	10		Chicago	12 Oct
2:29:11	LM		Jo Bun-hui	PRK	29.11.79	4		Pyongyang	13 Apr
2:29:13	LM	Banwella	Mrashani	TAN	14.11.77	3		Paris	6 Apr
2:29:13	LM	Maura	Viceconte	ITA	3.10.67	2		Torino	13 Apr
2:29:17	LM	Renata	Paradowska	POL	14.6.70	5		Hamburg	27 Apr
2:29:20	LM	Margaret	Atodonyang	KEN	.78	3		Amsterdam	19 Oct
2:29:23	LM	Anne	Chelagat	KEN	4.6.69	1		Milano	30 Nov
2:29:25	LW	Beatriz	Ros	ESP	12.5.74	13	WCh	Saint-Denis	31 Aug
2:29:33	LM		Wang Linan	CHN-J	26.11.85	4		Beijing	19 Oct
		(70)							
2:29:35	LM	Gloria	Marconi	ITA	31.3.68	1		Roma	23 Mar
2:29:40	LM	Tatyana	Pozdnyakova	UKR	4.3.56	1		Los Angeles	2 Mar
2:29:41	LM	Luminita	Zaituc	GER	9.10.68	1		Frankfurt am Main	26 Oct
2:29:46	LW		Li Helan	CHN	2.1.78	14	WCh	Saint-Denis	31 Aug
2:29:53	LM	Lyudmila	Korchagina	RUS	26.7.71	1		Pittsburgh	4 May
2:29:54	LM	Adriana	Fernández	MEX	4.4.71	12		London	13 Apr
2:29:54	LM	Beáta	Rakonczai	HUN	25.6.77	4		Amsterdam	19 Oct
2:29:57	LW	Megumi	Tanaka	JPN	4.9.75	7		Osaka	26 Jan
2:29:57	LM	Monika	Drybulska	POL	15.5.80	6		Berlin	28 Sep
2:29:59	LM	Márcia	Narloch	BRA	28.3.69	6		Hamburg	27 Apr
		(80)							
2:30:13	LW	Aki	Fujikawa	JPN	14.11.78	8		Osaka	26 Jan
2:30:15	LW	María	Abel	ESP	23.10.74	15	WCh	Saint-Denis	31 Aug
2:30:15	LM	Fumi	Murata	JPN	13.3.75	7		Berlin	28 Sep
2:30:21	LM	Anastasha	Ndereba	KEN	27.9.74	11		Chicago	12 Oct
2:30:22	PM	Carolyn	Cheptanui	KEN	21.3.81	2		Venezia	26 Oct
2:30:26	DM	Fatuma	Roba	ETH	18.12.73	2		San Diego (76m)	1 Jun
2:30:28	DM	Marla	Runyan	USA	4.1.69	5		Boston	21 Apr
2:30:34	DM	Svetlana	Demidenko	RUS	16.2.76	3		San Diego	1 Jun
2:30:38	LW	Hafida	Gadi	FRA	14.7.74	4		Paris	6 Apr
2:30:39	LW	Lena	Gavelin	SWE	26.2.74	16	WCh	Saint-Denis	31 Aug
		(90)							
2:30:41	LM	Blake	Russell	USA	24.7.75	1		St Paul	5 Oct
2:30:45	LM	Zivile	Balciunaite	LTU	3.4.79	3		Dublin	27 Oct
2:30:50	LM		Chung Yun-hee	KOR	3.1.83	1		Seoul	2 Nov
2:30:57	LM		Choi Kyung-hee	KOR	13.9.81	3		Seoul	16 Mar
2:30:58	LM	Liz	Yelling	GBR	5.12.74	8		Berlin	28 Sep
2:31:01	LW	Asha	Gigi	ETH	15.10.73	19	WCh	Saint-Denis	31 Aug
2:31:12	LM	Angélica	Sánchez	MEX	11.12.75	3		Milano	30 Nov
2:31:15	LM		Wang Yu	CHN-J	27.2.84	5		Beijing	19 Oct
2:31:19	LW		Wang Hongxia	CHN	13.1.75	7		Nagoya	9 Mar
2:31:21	LW	Ulrike	Maisch	GER	21.1.77	20	WCh	Saint-Denis	31 Aug
		(100)							

2:31:23	LW	Rakiya	Quétier	FRA	12.9.67	31 Aug
2:31:25	LM	Alice	Chelangat	KEN	.77	18 May
2:31:28	LW	Yukari	Komatsu	JPN	13.2.74	9 Mar
2:31:34	LM	Madai	Pérez	MEX	2.2.80	12 Oct
2:31:38	LM	Magdalena	Lewy	USA	1.8.73	4 May
2:31:38	PM	Jennifer	Chesinon	KEN	6.8.82	12 Oct
2:31:38	LM		Chae Eun-hee	KOR	20.7.82	2 Nov
2:31:43	LW	Aiko	Nitta	JPN	18.11.75	9 Mar
2:31:45	LW	Viktoriya	Klimina	RUS	1.3.76	31 Aug
2:31:51	LW	Shiho	Takai	JPN	6.8.80	9 Mar
2:31:55	LW	Annemette	Jensen	DEN	11.4.72	31 Aug
2:31:56	LM	María Teresa	Pulido	ESP	1.10.74	13 Apr
2:31:57	LM	Eri	Hayakawa	JPN	.81	14 Dec
2:32:01	LM	Tatyana	Titova	RUS	6.8.65	26 Apr
2:32:04	LW	Mary	Ptikany	KEN	.78	6 Apr
2:32:07	LM		Oh Song-suk	PRK		13 Apr
2:32:08	LW		Ri Kum-sil	PRK	2.11.76	31 Aug
2:32:15	LM	Simona	Staicu	HUN	5.5.71	23 Mar
2:32:22	LM		Chen Ping	CHN	29.5.79	19 Oct
2:32:27	LW	M.	Söderström-Lundberg	SWE	21.10.60	31 Aug
2:32:33	LM	Irina	Safarova	RUS	19.6.69	5 Oct
2:32:37	LM	Zinaida	Semyonova	RUS	22.12.62	13 Apr
2:32:39	LM	Jenny	Spangler	USA	20.7.63	12 Oct
2:32:44	LM	Tatyana	Gladyr	UKR	17.4.75	5 Oct
2:32:55	LM	Rodica	Chirita	ROM	28.10.76	27 Apr
2:32:55	LM		Lee Eun-jung	KOR	21.4.81	2 Nov

Mark		Name		Nat	Born	Date
2:32:56	LM		Bae Hae-jin	KOR	15.3.79	2 Nov
2:32:57	LM	Fátima	Silva	POR	6.5.70	27 Apr
2:32:58	LM	Bruna	Genovese	ITA	24.9.76	13 Apr
2:32:59	LM	Larisa	Malikova	RUS	2.4.69	26 Oct
2:33:03	LM	Yelena	Fadeyeva	UKR	23.6.66	4 Apr
2:33:10	PM	Sylvia	Mosqueda	USA	8.4.66	2 Nov
2:33:12	LM		Kim Jong-sun	PRK	9.3.81	13 Apr
2:33:23	LW	Giovanna	Volpato	ITA	20.8.75	6 Apr
2:33:24	LM	Meseret	Kotu	ETH	81	30 Nov
2:33:26	LM	Ramilya	Burangulova	RUS	11.7.61	11 Oct
2:33:28	LM	Karina	Szymanska	POL	16.1.75	13 Apr
2:33:32	LM	Fátima	Cabral	POR	14.1.72	30 Nov
2:33:40	LW	Aki	Negoro	JPN	10.9.81	9 Mar
2:33:40	DM	Silviya	Skvortsova	RUS	16.11.74	1 Jun
2:33:42	LM	Tadelesh	Birra	ETH	24.4.75	4 May
2:33:43	PM	Anne	Kosgei	KEN	80	12 Oct
2:33:45	LM		Hong Ok-dan	PRK	19.1.78	13 Apr
2:33:48	LM	Abeba	Tola	ETH	3.6.77	23 Mar
2:33:48	LM	Tegla	Loroupe	KEN	9.5.73	5 Oct
2:33:49	LM	Alevtina	Ivanova	RUS	22.5.75	14 Dec
2:33:50	LM	Maria	Cocchetti	ITA	19.6.66	4 May
2:33:51	LW	Sandy	Jacobson	CAN	23.3.66	31 Aug
2:33:53	PM	Svetlana	Shepeleva	MDA	10.5.69	21 Jun
2:34:07	LM	Adélia	Elias (150)	POR	7.5.74	28 Sep
2:34:11	LM	Chihiro	Tanaka	JPN	13.11.69	31 Aug
2:34:15	LM	Aura	Buia	ROM	16.2.70	2 Mar
2:34:18	PM	Albina	Gallyamova	RUS	8.5.64	21 Jun
2:34:23	LM	Dorota	Gruca	POL	5.12.70	11 May
2:34:24	LM	Leila	Aman	ETH	24.11.77	30 Mar
2:34:25	LM		Ryung Gum-hwa	PRK		13 Apr
2:34:27	LM		Kan Yongying	CHN	20.4.79	30 Mar
2:34:27	LW		Yun Sun-sook	KOR	28.5.72	19 Oct
2:34:28	LW	Miwako	Ueki	JPN	27.6.78	9 Mar
2:34:29	PM	Carol	Howe	CAN	8.12.65	21 Jun
2:34:31	LW	Zahia	Dahmani	FRA	2.6.72	6 Apr
2:34:36	LW	Mai	Tagami	JPN	22.1.80	26 Jan
2:34:36	LM	Dagmar	Rabensteiner	AUT	15.6.63	28 Sep
2:34:37	LW	Taeko	Terauchi	JPN	19.12.72	26 Jan
2:34:40	LM	Emebet	Abossa	ETH	74	26 Oct
2:34:40	LM	Anna	Incerti	ITA	19.1.80	23 Nov
2:34:43	LW	Kaori	Tanabe	JPN	30.4.75	9 Mar
2:34:44	LW	Wioletta	Uryga	POL	18.10.68	9 Mar
2:34:47	LW	Mika	Hikita	JPN	4.8.76	9 Mar
2:34:51	DM	Tina	Connelly	CAN	16.8.70	7 Dec
2:34:54	LW	Jill	Gaitenby	USA	21.1.67	31 Aug
2:34:57	LM	Romy	Spitzmüller	GER	19.9.81	12 Oct
2:34:58	LM	Gitte	Karlshøj	DEN	14.5.59	12 Oct
2:35:00	LM	Faustina	María	ESP	28.4.71	23 Feb
2:35:03	LW	Fatima	Yvelain	FRA	4.5.69	6 Apr
2:35:13	LW	Marlene	Fortunato	BRA	8.1.70	9 Mar
2:35:13	LM	Aniela	Nikiel	POL	1.11.65	19 Oct
2:35:17	LM	Claudia	Oberlin	SUI	29.1.79	26 Oct
2:35:23	LM	Simona	Viola	ITA	18.11.71	9 Mar
2:35:23	PM	Natalya	Berkut	UKR	30.5.75	2 Nov
2:35:29	LM	Lenah	Cheruiyot	KEN	1.3.73	28 Sep
2:35:32	LM	Lucilla	Andreucci	ITA	19.12.69	25 May
2:35:37	LW	Sara	Wells	USA	19.3.79	5 Apr
2:35:38	LM	Jackline	Torori	KEN	78	2 Mar
2:35:38	LM	Stefania	Benedetti	ITA	6.9.69	19 Oct
2:35:39	LM	Sylvia	Renz	GER	6.6.69	27 Apr
2:35:39	LM	Ivana	Iozzia	ITA	18.2.73	28 Sep
2:35:44	LM	Lidiya	Vasilevskaya	RUS	1.4.73	2 Mar
2:35:45	LW	Asami	Obi	JPN	22.3.76	9 Mar
2:35:51	LM	Lale	Oztürk	TUR	1.12.71	30 Nov
2:35:52	LM		Oh Jung-hee	KOR	4.12.78	16 Mar
2:35:52	LM	Antje	van Schuppen	NED	11.10.60	13 Apr
2:35:53	PM	Irina	Permitina	RUS	3.2.68	21 Jun
2:35:53	LM	Anuta	Catuna	ROM	1.10.68	5 Oct
2:35:53	LM	Patrizia	Ritondo	ITA	18.9.74	23 Nov
2:35:58	PM	Esther	Kiplagat	KEN	8.12.66	2 Nov
2:35:59	LM		Jang Hyon-ok	PRK		13 Apr
2:36:03	LM	Chika	Horie	JPN	15.2.81	31 Aug
2:36:06	LM	Catherine	Lallemand	BEL	16.8.79	26 Oct
2:36:07	LM	Galina	Zhulyeva (200)	UKR	5.3.66	4 May

Uncertain measurement

2:35:34	LM	Tatyana	Zolotaryova	RUS	22.6.70	18 May

Downhill

2:28:24	DM	Madina	Biktagirova	RUS	20.9.64	1	Nagano (219.5m)	20 Apr
2:29:06	DM	Alevtina	Ivanova	RUS	22.5.75	2	Nagano	20 Apr
2:32:17	DM	Hiase	Yoshimatsu	JPN	13.5.79			20 Apr

JUNIORS

See main list for top 2 juniors. 4 performances by 2 women to 2:40:00. Additional marks and further juniors:

Wang Linan 2:32:40 6 Pyongyang 13 Apr

2:38:55		Sun Weiwei	CHN	6.4.85	1	Hong Kong	16 Feb
2:40:00		Sum Mei	CHN	14.5.84	8	Xiamen	30 Mar
2:40:17		Zheng Hong	CHN	.85	1	Dalian	26 Oct
2:42:57	LM	Jiang Qinghua	CHN	1.5.85	10	Beijing	19 Oct

100 KILOMETRES

7:14:05:8 t	Norimi	Sakurai	JPN	20.4.71	1		S.Giovanni Lupatoto	27 Sep
7:19:51	Tatyana	Zhyrkova	RUS	70	1	EC	Chernogolovka	19 Apr
7:20:02		Sakurai			1		Yubetsu	29 Jun
7:28:00	Monica	Casiraghi	ITA	4.4.69	2	EC	Chernogolovka	19 Apr
7:31:14	Yelena	Nurgalieva	RUS	9.1.76	3	EC	Chernogolovka	19 Apr
7:31:14	Olesya	Nurgalieva	RUS	9.1.76	4	EC	Chernogolovka	19 Apr
7:33:21	Marina	Myshlianova	RUS	16.6.66	5	EC	Chernogolovka	19 Apr
7:35:01	Nadezhda	Karaseva	RUS	18.12.60	6	EC	Chernogolovka	19 Apr
7:41:30	Magali	Maggiolini	FRA	21.5.69	7	EC	Chernogolovka	19 Apr
7:47:53	Tanja	Hooss	GER	25.9.67	1	NC	Endingen	6 Sep
7:59:42		Casiraghi			1		Faenza	24/25 May
8:02:06	Edit	Bérces	HUN	16.5.64	1		Torhout	19/20 Jun
8.04.47		Casiraghi			1	WCp	Tainan	16 Nov
	(13/10)							
8:07:01	Akiko	Sekiya	JPN	8.3.65	1		Nakamura	19 Oct
8:08:16	Elke	Hiebl	GER	12.6.64	8	EC	Chernogolovka	19 Apr
8:08:37	Christine	Billet-Denis	FRA	3.12.71	9	EC	Chernogolovka	19 Apr
8:09:49	Yekaterina	Malafeyeva	RUS	31.1.67	10	EC	Chernogolovka	19 Apr

8:11:24	Karine	Herry	FRA	2.1.68	30 May
8.15.13	Paola	Sanna	ITA	19.3.77	16 Nov
8:18:17	Maria Luisa	Costetti	ITA	31.7.61	19 Apr
8:19:20	Simone	Stöppler	GER	5.4.64	19 Apr
8:19:48	Éva	Koran	HUN	18.12.67	19 Apr
8:21:43	Nadine	Weiss-Dumarche	FRA	14.8.62	19 Apr
8:22:09	Siri	Terejesen	GBR	29.6.75	6 Jul
8.23.21	Danielle	Sanderson	GBR	26.10.62	16 Nov
8:24:05	Oksana	Ladyzhina	RUS	21.7.67	4 Oct
8.24.58	Elvira	Kolpakova	RUS	30.10.72	16 Nov

Mark	Name		Nat	Born	Pos	Meet	Venue	Date
237.645	Edit	Bérces	HUN	16.5.64	1		Worschach	19-20 Jul
237.052	Irina	Reutovich	RUS	21.01.50	1	EC	Uden	11-12 Oct
233.550		Reutovich			1		St Petersburg	6-7 Sep
232.050	Galina	Yeremina	RUS	14.2.53	2	EC	Uden	11-12 Oct
231,576		Reutovich			2		Worschach	19-20 Jul
228.906+t		Bérces			1	in 48hr	Surgères	3-4 May
227.777t		Bérces			1		Soochow	10-11 Mar
227.279	Joëlle	Semur	FRA	22.12.60	3	EC	Uden	11-12 Oct
225.710		Bérces			4	EC	Uden	11-12 Oct
224.469t	Hiroko	Okiyama	JPN	21.4.62	2		Soochow	10-11 Mar
223.634t	Pam	Reed	USA		1	NC	San Diego	8-9 Nov
222.895	Masae	Kamura	JPN	4.4.58	5	EC	Uden	11-12 Oct
220.797t	Kimie	Funada-Noto	JPN	10.1.52	3		Soochow	10-11 Mar
220.654		Reutovich			1		Apeldoorn	30-31 May
	(14/8)							
215.756	Irina	Koval	RUS	19.11.58	7	EC	Uden	11-12 Oct
215.623	Guija	Lee (10)	USA		8	EC	Uden	11-12 Oct

214.556	Lyudmila	Kalinina	RUS	30.8.68	12 Oct
212.849	Colette	Musy	FRA	11.4.59	12 Oct
212.217	Nina	Mytrofanova	UKR		12 Oct
211.990	Barbara	Szlachetka	GER	17.5.56	15 Jun
210.714	Nadezhda	Tarasova	RUS	7.4.52	12 Oct
210.520	Fumie	Sata	JPN	25.6.62	12 Oct
210.000	Stephanie	Ehret	USA	21.1.63	1 Jan 04
209.175	Véronique	Jehanno	FRA	27.12.62	12 Oct
207.889	Cornelia	Bullig	GER	20.9.59	15 Jun
207.498		Koval			7 Sep
205.865	Sharon	Gayter	GBR	30.10.63	12 Oct
203.324		Bullig			18 May
203.026	Rimma	Paltseva	RUS	10.10.48	7 Sep
202.051	Heike	Pawzik	GER	21.9.63	12 Oct
200.607t	Monica	Scholz	CAN	26.6.67	9 Nov
200.346t	Janet	Runyon	USA	.58	9 Nov

Further best track times

215.033	Irina	Reutovich	RUS	21.1.50	2		Surgeres	3-4 May
207.366t	Galina	Yeremina	RUS	14.2.53				11 May
204.302	Fumie	Sata	JPN	25.6.62				11 Mar

Indoor: 215.250 Irina Reutovich RUS 21.1.50 1 Brno 21-22 Mar

2000 METRES STEEPLECHASE

6:19.8	Inna	Poluskina	LAT-J	7.7.84	1	v2N	Kaunas	10 Aug
6:21.78	Catalina	Oprea	ROM-Y	11.4.86	1	EJ	Tampere	27 Jul
6:25.2A	Eunice	Chepkorir	KEN	.81	1		Nairobi	24 May
6:25.83	Sigrid	Vanden Bempt	BEL	10.2.81	1		Woluwe	14 Jun
6:26.92	Johanna	Risku	FIN	21.2.79	1		Turku	28 May
6:27.4A	Salome	Chepchumba	KEN-Y	29.9.89	1	NC	Nairobi	12 Jul
6:27.6A	Irene	Limika	KEN	28.8.79	2		Nairobi	24 May
6:28.07	Tara	Krzywicki	GBR	9.3.74	1	NC	Birmingham	26 Jul
6:32.03	Ancufia	Bobocel	ROM-Y	3.10.87	2	EJ	Tampere	27 Jul
6:32.85	Urszula	Necka	POL-J	28.6.84	1	v2N-j	Szczecin	9 Aug
6:33.0A	Eunice	Chepkurui	KEN-J	20.5.84	3	NC	Nairobi	12 Jul
6:33.12	Hanne	Lyngstad	NOR	5.12.75	1		Nadderud	15 Jun
6:33.15	Olga	Dereveva	RUS-J	5.4.85	1	NC-j	Kazan	3 Jul

JUNIORS

See main list for top 7 Juniors. 11 performances by 7 women to 6:35.00. Additional marks and further juniors:

Chepkorir	6:29.6A2					NC	Naorobi	12 Jul
Bobocel	6:34.021h1					EJ	Tampere	25 Jul
Necka	6:33.851					NC-j	Zamosc	29 Jun
	6:34.331						Chorzów	14 Jun
6:35.11	Yekaterina	Bespalova	RUS	.84	3	EJ	Tampere	27 Jul
6:35.19	Xénia	Kazimírova	GRE	17.9.84	1	NC-j	Kórinthos	5 Jul
6:36.05	Eva	Tománková (10)	CZE	11.9.84	4	EJ	Tampere	27 Jul
6:36.90	Mélanie	Véron	FRA	15.2.84	2	v2N	Szczecin	9 Aug
6:37.59	Türkan	Bozkürk-Erismis	TUR	5.1.84	4h1	EJ	Tampere	25 Jul
6:37.84	Angela	Marvin	USA	26.4.84	1	PAm-J	Bridgetown	20 Jul
6:37.90	Verena	Dreier	GER	15.1.85	5h1	EJ	Tampere	25 Jul
6:38.64	Irina	Orlova	RUS	28.12.85	3	NC-j	Kazan	3 Jul

3000 METRES STEEPLECHASE

9:08.33	Gulnara	Samitova	RUS	9.7.78	1	NC	Tula	10 Aug
9:20.28	Alesya	Turova	BLR	6.12.79	1	GS	Ostrava	12 Jun
9:24.78	Lyubov	Ivanova	RUS	2.3.81	2	NC	Tula	10 Aug
9:25.87		Samitova			1		Réthimno	6 Jul
9:32.05		Samitova			1	Znam	Tula	7 Jun
9:32.31	Yekaterina	Volkova	RUS	16.2.78	3	NC	Tula	10 Aug
9:32.80		Turova			2		Réthimno	6 Jul
9:34.41		Samitova			1	GP	Tríkala	24 Jun
9:39.51	Docus	Inzikuru	UGA	2.2.82	2	GS	Ostrava	12 Jun
9:40.49	Cristina	Casandra	ROM	1.2.77	1	NC	Bucuresti	10 Aug
9:40.89		Samitova			1	ECp-S	Firenze	22 Jun

Mark	Name		Nat	Born	Pos	Meet	Venue	Date
9:41.16		Ivanova			1	EU23	Bydgoszcz	19 Jul
9:42.01	Michaela	Mannová	CZE	11.1.82	2	EU23	Bydgoszcz	19 Jul
9:42.04	Sigrid	Vanden Bempt	BEL	10.2.81	3	EU23	Bydgoszcz	19 Jul
9:42.76		Inzikuru			2	GP	Tríkala	24 Jun
9:43.99		Casandra			1		Pírgos	27 Jul
9:44.44		Casandra			3		Réthimno	6 Jul
9:44.54		Mannová			2		Pírgos	27 Jul
9:44.71	Brianna	Shook	USA	6.1.81	1	NC	Stanford	21 Jun
9:44.95	Kassi	Andersen (10)	USA	25.6.83	1	NCAA	Sacramento	13 Jun
9:46.23		Casandra			1	RomIC	Bucuresti	8 Jun
9:46.30	Lisa	Aguilera	USA	30.11.79	1	NCAA-r	Stanford	31 May
9:46.30		Casandra			3	GP	Tríkala	24 Jun
9:46.60		Vanden Bempt			1	NC	Ninove	2 Jul
9:46.74	Ida	Nilsson	SWE	8.2.81	2	NCAA	Sacramento	13 Jun
9:46.76	Alina	Proca	ROM	24.10.83	3		Pírgos	27 Jul
9:47.17		Andersen			2	NC	Stanford	21 Jun
9:48.15		Proca			4	EU23	Bydgoszcz	19 Jul
9:48.19		Turova			1	ECp-1A	Lappeenranta	21 Jun
9:48.47		Casandra			2	ECp-S	Firenze	22 Jun
	(30/13)							
9:49.14	Lisa	Nye	USA	17.11.68	3	NC	Stanford	21 Jun
9:49.40	Jana	Biolková	CZE	18.5.74	1	NC	Olomouc	12 Jul
9:49.51	Malika	Assahssah	MAR	24.9.82	1	NC	Rabat	6 Jul
9:49.62	Anália	Rosa	POR	28.2.76	3	GS	Ostrava	12 Jun
9:50.12	Roisin	McGettigan	IRL	23.8.80	3	NCAA	Sacramento	13 Jun
9:50.29	Natalya	Cherepanova	RUS	9.3.67	4	NC	Tula	10 Aug
9:50.88		Chen Xiaofang	CHN	28.10.81	1	NC	Shanghai	13 Sep
	(20)							
9:52.13	Patrycja	Wlodarczyk	POL	9.6.80	5	GS	Ostrava	12 Jun
9:52.53	Elodie	Olivarès	FRA	22.5.76	6	GS	Ostrava	12 Jun
9:52.98	Letiwe	Marakurwa	ZIM	2.6.78	4	NCAA	Sacramento	13 Jun
9:52.99	Irene	Limika	KEN	28.8.79	7	GS	Ostrava	12 Jun
9:54.01		Ju Yinglan	CHN-J	10.10.84	2	NC	Shanghai	13 Sep
9:54.36	Alina	Cucerzan	ROM	28.7.74	4	GP	Tríkala	24 Jun
9:54.43	Bouchra	Chaabi	MAR	22.9.80	1		Rabat	14 Jun
9:54.91	Hanne	Lyngstad	NOR	5.12.75	1	NC	Lisleby	9 Aug
9:55.44	Johanna	Risku	FIN	21.2.79	1		Karlstad	24 Jul
9:55.71	Céline	Rajot	FRA	22.3.75	1		Pezenas	31 May
	(30)							
9:57.67	Galina	Yegorova	RUS	5.8.83	1		Tula	31 May
9:57.97	Susanne	Wigene	NOR	12.2.78	2		Karlstad	24 Jul
9:59.30	Dawn	Cleary	USA	24.11.79	5	NC	Stanford	21 Jun
10:00.44	Korine	Hinds	JAM	18.1.76	9	GS	Ostrava	12 Jun
10:00.73	Valentina	Gorpynich	UKR	12.3.83	1	NC	Kiev	4 Jul
10:00.93	Livia	Tóth	HUN	7.1.80	5	ECp-1A	Lappeenranta	21 Jun
10:01.70	Rosa María	Morató	ESP	19.6.79	1		Barcelona (CD)	31 May
10:01.75	Lydia	Kurgat	KEN	.76	1		Königs Wusterhausen	6 Aug
10:02.22	Julia	Budniak	POL	4.3.81	8	GP	Tríkala	24 Jun
10:03.20	Miranda	Boonstra	NED	29.8.72	2		Königs Wusterhausen	6 Aug
	(40)							
10:03.44	Carol	Henry	CAN	20.6.82	7	NCAA	Sacramento	13 Jun
10:03.62	Analídia	Torre	POR	10.10.76	1	NC	Seia	2 Aug
10:04.14	Brianna	Dahm	USA	13.3.82	8	NCAA	Sacramento	13 Jun
10:04.52	Jennifer	Donovan	USA	4.5.82	9	NCAA	Sacramento	13 Jun
10:05.19	Yamina	Bouchaouante	FRA	31.7.80	2	NC	Narbonne	24 Jul
10:05.53	Janet	Trujillo	USA	7.8.75	1		Stanford	9 May
10:05.70	Tatyana	Petrova	RUS	8.4.83	2	NC-23	Cheboksary	28 Jun
10:07.15	Andrea	Etter	SUI	21.1.75	1	ECp-2A	Århus	21 Jun
10:07.59	Marzena	Michalska	ITA	20.10.75	1		Ancona	5 Jul
10:07.78	Molly	Landreth	USA	27.11.82	3h2	NCAA	Sacramento	11 Jun
	(50)							
10:09.34	Svetlana	Ivanova	RUS	30.6.83	2		Moskva	15 Jul
10:09.42	Tamara	Sanfabio	ESP	14.3.78	2	NC	Jerez de la Frontera	3 Aug
10:09.52	Valeriya	Mara	UKR	22.2.83	6	EU23	Bydgoszcz	19 Jul
10:09.69	Emma	Quaglia	ITA	15.8.80	2		Ancona	5 Jul
10:10.29	Tatyana	Vilisova	RUS	.79	5	NC	Tula	10 Aug
10:10.39	Sarai	Sarmiento	ESP	3.12.78	3	NC	Jerez de la Frontera	3 Aug
10:10.61	Andrea	Kremer	USA	2.7.82	10	NCAA	Sacramento	13 Jun
10:11.29	Anzhelika	Averkova	UKR	13.3.69	2	NC	Kiev	4 Jul
10:11.52	Urszula	Necka	POL-J	28.6.84	1		Czestochowa	30 Aug

Mark	Name		Nat	Born	Pos	Meet	Venue	Date
10:12.10	Barbora	Kuncová (80)	CZE	26.4.82	2		Praha	31 May

10:13.03	Edyta	Lewandowska	POL	22.11.80	6 Jul
10:13.59	Clarisse	Cruz	POR	9.7.78	28 May
10:13.69	Barbara	Parker	GBR	8.11.82	6 Aug
10:13.98	Gwendoline	Desprès	FRA	27.11.83	19 Jul
10:14.37	Lisa	Antonelli	USA	12.3.82	13 Jun
10:14.38	Katie	Sabino	USA	23.1.79	17 Apr
10:14.46	Haingo	Rakotomalala	MAD	.81	24 Jul
10:14.80	Catalina	Oprea	ROM-Y	11.4.86	10 Aug
10:15.31	Samira	Raïf	MAR	4.4.74	24 Jun
10:15.64	Kelly	MacDonald	USA	27.9.78	2 May
10:16.41	Siri Merete	Alfheim	NOR	6.7.76	24 Jul
10:16.91	Tracey	Brauksieck	USA-J	24.4.84	11 Jun
10:17.28	Rumyana	Panovska	BUL	13.5.66	21 Jun
10:17.55	Victoria	Mitchell	AUS	25.4.82	8 Mar
10:17.68	Christin	Johansson	SWE	26.1.78	6 Sep
10:17.76	Sophie	Duarte	FRA	31.7.81	19 Jul
10:18.10	Molly	DeFrancesco	USA	17.2.80	24 Apr
10:18.64	Alba	García	ESP	23.11.83	26 Jul
10:19.22	Yamilka	González	CUB/ESP	1.8.72	3 Aug
10:19.56	Jolanda	Verstraten	NED	26.6.83	6 Aug
10:19.64	Alicia	Fernández	ESP	22.9.78	3 Aug
10:19.88	Rachel	Bennion	USA	16.9.80	11 Jun
10:19.64	Alicia	Fernández	ESP	22.9.78	3 Aug
10:19.88	Rachel	Bennion (84)	USA	16.9.80	11 Jun

Irregular water jump

10:14.19	Audrey	Giesler	USA	6.3.82	17 May
10:17.37	Sarah	Pepera	USA	1.1.81	17 May

JUNIORS

See main list for top 2 juniors. 5 performances by 5 women to 10:22.00. Further juniors:

10:21.48	Biljana	Jovic	SCG	2.3.85	4	ECp-1B	Velenje	21 Jun
10:23.73	Angela	Marvin	USA	26.4.84	2		Des Moines	25 Apr
10:25.51	Türkan	Bozkürt-Erismis	TUR	5.1.84	2	ECp-2B	Istanbul	21 Jun
10:26.98		Zhang Chong	CHN-Y	5.1.86	1		Shijiazhuang	3 Aug
10:29.87	Felicitas	Mensing	GER	14.12.84	1		Krefeld	17 Aug
10:32.04	Zenaide	Vieira	BRA	25.6.85	2		Rio de Janeiro	23 May
10:32.88	Shalice	Pugmire	USA	19.1.84	9r2	NCAA-r	Stanford	31 May
10:33.61		Zhang Jianru (10)	CHN-Y	18.10.86	4		Shijiazhuang	3 Aug
10:34.54	Kristin	Möller	GER	5.4.84	3		Krefeld	17 Aug
10:35.53	Lavinia	Rolea	ROM-Y	.86	5	NC	Bucuresti	10 Aug
10:36.68	Eva	Tománková	CZE	11.9.84	2	NC-23	Litomysl	14 Sep
10:37.03		Li Lihua	CHN-Y	7.2.86	3	NC	Shanghai	13 Sep

100 METRES HURDLES

12.45	1.4	Brigitte	Foster	JAM	7.11.74	1	Pre	Eugene	24 May
12.45	1.3	Gail	Devers	USA	19.11.66	1	WAF	Monaco	14 Sep
12.49	0.0		Devers			1rA	Gaz	Saint-Denis	4 Jul
12.50	0.0		Devers			1rA	WK	Zürich	15 Aug
12.51	1.4	Miesha	McKelvy-Jones	USA	26.7.76	2	Pre	Eugene	24 May
12.53	-0.2	Perdita	Felicien	CAN	29.8.80	1	WCh	Saint-Denis	27 Aug
12.57	1.1		Devers			1	Athl	Lausanne	1 Jul
12.57	-0.2		Foster			2	WCh	Saint-Denis	27 Aug
12.58	0.0		Foster			2rA	WK	Zürich	15 Aug
12.60	1.9		McKelvy			1	GP II	Stanford	7 Jun
12.61	-0.1		Devers			1	NC	Stanford	22 Jun
12.61	1.1		Foster			2	Athl	Lausanne	1 Jul
12.62	-0.1		McKelvy			2	NC	Stanford	22 Jun
12.62	1.7		Foster			1	GP	Madrid (C)	19 Jul
12.64	0.0		Foster			2rA	Gaz	Saint-Denis	4 Jul
12.65	1.4	Donica	Merriman	USA	24.1.79	3	Pre	Eugene	24 May
12.65	0.5		Foster			1	GS	Ostrava	12 Jun
12.65	0.6		Devers			1s2	NC	Stanford	22 Jun
12.65	-0.1		Foster			1s2	WCh	Saint-Denis	26 Aug
12.66	1.1		McKelvy			3	Athl	Lausanne	1 Jul
12.66	1.1		Foster			1h1	PAm	Santo Domingo	8 Aug
12.66	1.3	Glory	Alozie	ESP	30.12.77	2	WAF	Monaco	14 Sep
12.67	0.6		McKelvy			2s2	NC	Stanford	22 Jun
12.67	1.1	Jenny	Adams	USA	8.7.78	4	Athl	Lausanne	1 Jul
12.67	-0.3		Foster			1	PAm	Santo Domingo	9 Aug
12.67	-0.5		Felicien			1rB	WK	Zürich	15 Aug
12.67	-0.5		Foster			1h2	WCh	Saint-Denis	25 Aug
12.67	-0.2		McKelvy			3	WCh	Saint-Denis	27 Aug
12.68	1.4		Adams			4	Pre	Eugene	24 May
12.68	1.8		Felicien			1s1	NCAA	Sacramento	12 Jun
12.68	-0.1		Adams			3	NC	Stanford	22 Jun
12.68	0.4		Felicien			1s1	WCh	Saint-Denis	26 Aug
		(32/7)							
12.70	1.4	Melissa	Morrison	USA	9.7.71	5	Pre	Eugene	24 May
12.70	0.5	Delloreen	Ennis-London	JAM	5.3.75	1	CAC	St George's	5 Jul
12.72	-0.5	Lacena	Golding-Clarke	JAM	20.3.75	2rB	WK	Zürich	15 Aug
		(10)							
12.72	-0.5	Vonette	Dixon	JAM	26.11.75	3rB	WK	Zürich	15 Aug
12.74	0.0	Aurelia	Trywianska	POL	9.5.76	2	GP II	Zagreb	7 Jul

Mark	Wind	Name		Nat	Born	Pos	Meet	Venue	Date
12.74	1.8	Patricia	Girard	FRA	8.4.68	1	NC	Narbonne	25 Jul
12.78	1.1	Angela	Whyte	CAN	27.5.80	2h1	PAm	Santo Domingo	8 Aug
12.79	1.4	Danielle	Carruthers	USA	22.12.79	3s1	NC	Stanford	22 Jun
12.80	1.1	Michelle	Perry	USA	1.5.79	3h1	PAm	Santo Domingo	8 Aug
12.82	0.1	Irina	Lenskiy	ISR	12.6.71	1	Veniz	Haniá	9 Jun
12.82	0.5	Nadine	Faustin	HAI	14.4.76	2	CAC	St George's	5 Jul
12.82	1.1	Yaumara	Neira	CUB	18.4.76	4h1	PAm	Santo Domingo	8 Aug
12.83	1.4	Joanna	Hayes	USA	23.12.76	5s1	NC	Stanford	22 Jun
		(20)							
12.83	0.0	Natalya	Shekhodanova	RUS	29.12.71	1rB	Gaz	Saint-Denis	4 Jul
12.86	0.1	Linda	Ferga-Khodadin	FRA	24.12.76	3h4	WCh	Saint-Denis	25 Aug
12.87	0.0	Juliane	Sprenger	GER	22.3.77	1h1		Cuxhaven	19 Jul
12.88	1.9	Susanna	Kallur	SWE	16.2.81	1		Enskede	24 May
12.88	-0.1	Svetlana	Laukhova	RUS	7.5.73	2	ECp-S	Firenze	22 Jun
12.88	0.4	Eunice	Barber	FRA	17.11.74	1		Bondoufle	16 Aug
12.89	1.2	Aliuska	López	ESP	29.8.69	1		Oviedo	12 Jul
12.89	1.0	Nadine	Hentschke	GER	27.1.82	2	EU23	Bydgoszcz	20 Jul
12.90	2.0	Lolo	Jones	USA	5.8.82	1rA	Tex R	Austin	5 Apr
12.90	0.8	Raasin	McIntosh	USA	29.4.82	1rA		Austin	3 May
		(30)							
12.90	0.6	Yolanda	McCray	USA	11.9.76	4s2	NC	Stanford	22 Jun
12.90	1.1	Flóra	Redoúmi	GRE	11.9.76	2	GP II	Thessaloníki	3 Aug
12.92	1.7	Haydy	Aron	FRA	21.5.73	1		Malles	12 Jul
12.93	1.4	Joyce	Bates	USA	16.2.77	6s1	NC	Stanford	22 Jun
12.93	0.3	Rosa	Rakotozafy	MAD	12.11.77	1		Nuoro	9 Jul
12.94	1.0	Trecia	Roberts	THA	4.2.71	1		Manila	9 Jun
12.95	1.6	Yana	Kasova	BUL	13.8.81	1		Istanbul	7 Jun
12.95	1.0	Maria	Koroteyeva	RUS	10.11.81	3	EU23	Bydgoszcz	20 Jul
12.96	1.9	Natasha	Danvers	GBR	19.9.77	4	GP II	Stanford	7 Jun
12.96	0.9	Angela	Atede	NGR	8.2.72	1	NC	Abuja	17 Jul
		(40)							
12.96	1.0	Derval	O'Rourke	IRL	28.5.81	4	EU23	Bydgoszcz	20 Jul
12.97	0.3	Toni Ann	D'Oyley	JAM	25.10.81	2		Nuoro	9 Jul
12.98	1.1	Nichole	Denby	USA	10.10.82	1h1	Big 12	Austin	18 May
12.98	0.6	Bisa	Grant	USA	10.7.76	5s2	NC	Stanford	22 Jun
12.99	0.9	Aneta	Sosnowska	POL	10.5.74	2	NC	Bielsko-Biala	6 Jul
12.99	1.3	Anay	Tejeda	CUB	3.4.83	4h2	PAm	Santo Domingo	8 Aug
13.00	1.9	Natasha	Neal	USA	22.7.80	5	GP II	Stanford	7 Jun
13.00	1.8	Nicole	Ramalalanirina	FRA	5.3.72	3	NC	Narbonne	25 Jul
13.01	0.8	Dionne	Rose-Henley	JAM	7.11.69	3rA		Austin	3 May
13.01	1.6	Svetla	Dimitrova	BUL	27.1.70	2		Istanbul	7 Jun
		(50)							
13.01	1.3	Natalya	Kresova	RUS	12.12.80	3	Znam	Tula	8 Jun
13.01	1.0	Justyna	Oleksy	POL	19.9.83	5	EU23	Bydgoszcz	20 Jul
13.04	1.0	Reïna-Flor	Okori	FRA	2.5.80	1		Genève	14 Jun
13.04	0.4	Jenny	Kallur	SWE	16.2.81	3	MAI	Malmö	12 Aug
13.04			Feng Yun	CHN	23.2.76	1		Busan	27 Sep
13.05	2.0	Felicia	Stone	USA	10.8.77	1		Eagle Rock	8 Jun
13.05	1.2	Judith	Vis	NED	21.6.80	1	Bel Ch	Jambes	10 Aug
13.06	-0.5	Yvonne	Kanazawa	JPN	19.11.74	1	NC	Yokohama	6 Jun
13.06	0.0	Yelena	Krasovskaya	UKR	17.8.76	4	Odlozil	Praha	29 Jun5
13.06	1.1	Hristiána	Tabáki	GRE	13.1.73	3	GP II	Thessaloníki	3 Aug
		(60)							
13.06	-1.5	Damaris	Agbugba	NGR	26.12.82	2	AfG	Abuja	15 Oct
13.07	-1.6	Astia	Walker	JAM	4.4.75	1h1		Atlanta	17 May
13.07	2.0	Rachel	King	GBR	11.5.76	1		Loughborough	8 Jun
13.07	-0.4	Virginia	Powell	USA	7.9.83	6	NCAA	Sacramento	14 Jun
13.09	0.0		Su Yiping	CHN	4.8.79	2		Guangzhou	8 Apr
13.09	1.1	Kim	Jones	USA	13.6.81	1		Tallahassee	12 Apr
13.09	0.5	RaNysha	LeBlanc	USA	11.1.83	2	SEC	Knoxville	18 May
13.09	-0.4	Sheena	Johnson	USA	1.10.82	8	NCAA	Sacramento	14 Jun
13.09	1.3	Elke	Wölfling	AUT	27.11.71	1		Wolfsburg	26 Jul
13.10A	0.4	Maiía Paula	Machado	BRA	22.1.81	1		Cochabamba	11 May
		(70)							
13.11	2.0	Christina	Ohaeri	USA	30.3.79	2		Eagle Rock	8 Jun
13.12	0.0	Tiffany	Ross	USA	5.2.83	1	NCAA-r	Fairfax	31 May
13.12	0.9	Priscilla	Lopes	CAN	26.8.82	2h2	NC	Victoria	18 Jul
13.12	1.4	Sarah	Claxton	GBR	23.9.79	2	NC	Birmingham	27 Jul
13.12	0.1	Patricia	Buval	FRA	22.1.76	1h1		Castres	6 Aug
13.13	1.2	Molly	Logan	USA	28.4.81	1h2	NCAA-r	Columbus	30 May
13.13	1.5	Cécile	Michot	FRA	2.6.74	1h2		Argentan	9 Jun

Mark	Wind	Name		Nat	Born	Pos	Meet	Venue	Date
13.14	-0.8	Annette	Thimm	GER	24.11.77	1h3	NC	Ulm	28 Jun
13.14	0.2		Zhang Rong	CHN	5.1.83	1	NG	Changsha	24 Oct
13.15	1.2	Lucie (80)	Martincová	CZE	4.1.82	5s2	EU23	Bydgoszcz	20 Jul
13.15	0.4	Tiffany	Hogan (Lott)	USA	1.8.75	1H	PAm	Santo Domingo	7 Aug
13.16	0.6	Kisha	Jett	USA	11.2.75	1		Tallahassee	10 May
13.17	1.4	Jacquie	Munro	AUS	4.10.81	1		Gold Coast (RB)	24 Jun
13.17	0.1		Xu Jia	CHN	23.9.79	1h1	WUG	Daegu	26 Aug
13.18	1.2	Andrea	Bliss	JAM	5.10.80	1	Fla R	Gainesville	28 Mar
13.18	1.0	Kia	Davis	USA	23.5.78	1		Lynchburg	8 May
13.18	-1.7	Irina	Shevchenko	RUS	2.9.75	3	NC	Tula	8 Aug
13.18	-0.4	Carolina	Klüft	SWE	2.2.83	2H2	WCh	Saint-Denis	23 Aug
13.19A	1.9	Gilvaneide	de Oliveira/Parrela	BRA	31.8.76	1		Bogotá	12 Jul
13.20		Yevgeniya (90)	Likhuta	BLR	24.3.81	1		Minsk	21 May
13.21	-0.1	Carmen	Zamfir	ROM	25.11.75	5	ECp-S	Firenze	22 Jun
13.22	1.6	Tatyana	Ladovskaya	UKR	4.5.77	3		Istanbul	7 Jun
13.22	1.2	Edit	Vári	HUN	31.5.75	4	ECp-1A	Lappeenranta	22 Jun
13.23	1.9	Gi-Gi	Miller	USA	12.1.79	5		Walnut	12 Jul
13.24	1.2	Myriam	Tschomba	BEL	8.1.77	2	NC	Jambes	10 Aug
13.24	1.9	Kumiko	Ikeda	JPN	10.1.81	1		Okayama	28 Sep
13.25	1.0	Alandra	Sherman	USA-J	25.11.85	1		Austin	10 May
13.25	0.0	Sharianne	Lawson	USA	25.7.80	2	NCAA-r	Fairfax	31 May
13.25	0.1	Mirjam	Liimask	EST	25.10.83	1		Tartu	6 Jun
13.26	1.0	Ayumi (100)	Fujita	JPN	2.11.77	1h1		Mito	5 May
13.26	0.9	Margaret	Macchiut	ITA	25.7.74	1		Trento	31 May
13.26	1.9	Svetlana	Gnezdilov	ISR	20.7.69	1H	NC	Tel Aviv	12 Aug

13.27	0.7	Ashlee	Williams	USA-J	27.3.84	19 May
13.27	0.0	Marina	Tomic	SLO	30.4.83	12 Jul
13.28	-0.1	Sophie	Krauel	GER-J	2.3.85	25 Jul
13.29	1.1	Aurore	Kassambara	FRA	26.10.79	6 Jul
13.30A	0.4	Francisca	Guzmán	CHI	21.6.81	11 May
13.30	1.7	Fiona	Cullen	AUS	31.8.79	21 Jun
13.32	0.2	Sriyani	Kulawansa	SRI	1.3.70	28 May
13.32	0.6	Annika	Meyer	GER	9.6.80	22 Jun
13.32	-0.5	Vasiliki	Delinikóla	GRE	9.2.81	17 Jul
13.32	-0.5		Moh Siew Wei	MAS	30.4.78	3 Aug
13.32	0.8	Brenda	Taylor	USA	9.2.79	23 Aug
13.33	0.7	Zamyal	Jackson	USA	29.5.82	3 May
13.33	1.8	Brittany	Littlejohn	USA		18 May
13.33	0.4	Dawn	Harper	USA-J	14.6.84	18 May
13.33	1.0	Margherita	Nicolussi	ITA	23.1.76	12 Jul
13.34	0.1	Olutoyin	Augustus	NGR	24.12.79	7 Jun
13.34	1.6	Fanny	Gérance	FRA	4.1.81	18 Jul
13.34	1.2	Elodie	Ouédraogo	BEL	27.2.81	10 Aug
13.34	0.3	Michaela	Hejnová	CZE	10.4.80	16 Aug
13.34	0.0	Sonja	Kesselschläger	GER	20.1.78	23 Aug
13.34	-1.5		Tan Yali	CHN	17.1.77	12 Sep
13.35	-0.6	Lashinda	Demus	USA	10.3.83	5 Apr
13.35	-0.1	Suzanne	Dickenson	JAM	12.2.78	21 Jun
13.35	1.2	Johanna	Halkoaho	FIN	13.1.77	22 Jun
13.35	0.7	Éva	Miklós	HUN	30.7.78	5 Jul
13.35	0.2		Ji Fangqian	CHN-J	18.7.84	24 Oct
13.36	0.7	LaTasha	Pharr	USA	6.5.83	3 May
13.36	0.4	Sharifa	Jones	USA	16.11.82	18 May
13.36	1.1	Alexándra	Kómnou	GRE	4.9.79	3 Aug
13.36	1.0		He Liyuan	CHN	14.1.83	4 Aug
13.37	0.7	Joanna	Bujak	FRA	30.8.79	15 Jun
13.37	-0.4	Denise	Lewis	GBR	27.8.72	23 Aug
13.38	-0.1	Kim	Schiemenz	USA	13.4.77	3 Apr
13.38	0.0	Christy	Akinremi	NGR	29.3.72	17 May
13.39	0.1	Yeoryía	Stoyiannídou	GRE	3.1.82	9 Jun
13.39	0.5	Julie	Pratt	GBR	20.3.79	31 Jul
13.39	0.3	Andrea	Blackett	BAR	24.1.76	2 Sep
13.40	2.0	Eva	Gérard	FRA	23.1.80	25 Jul
13.42	0.7	Shelly-Ann	Brown	CAN	15.5.80	31 May
13.42	-0.2	Agnieszka	Frankowska	POL	9.3.83	20 Jul
13.43	1.1	Evaggelía	Nesoúdi	GRE	27.4.79	19 Jul
13.44	0.3	Teresa	Covert	USA		17 May
13.45	1.3	Helen	Worsey	GBR	29.8.82	5 May
13.45		Melanie	Walker	JAM	1.1.83	17 May
13.45	-0.2	Hiroe	Washizu	JPN	27.12.81	5 Jul
13.45	1.5	Micol	Cattaneo	ITA	14.5.82	9 Aug
13.45	0.0	Radmila	Vukmirovic	SLO	23.11.79	10 Aug
13.46	-0.8	Hyleas	Fountain (150)	USA	14.1.81	15 May
13.46	1.9	Alyssa	Aiken	USA	15.9.82	18 May
13.46		Mariya	Balina	RUS	.80	21 May
13.46	0.6	Tina	Klein	GER	24.4.83	1 Jun
13.47	0.5	Shaneatra	Neely	USA	11.8.82	12 Apr
13.47	0.8	Alicia	Cave	TRI	4.2.82	17 May
13.47	0.4	Hasani	Roseby	USA	5.2.82	18 May
13.47	1.8	Nadège	Joseph	FRA	12.8.73	25 Jul
13.47	1.8	Margaret	Simpson	GHA	31.12.81	13 Oct
13.48	-0.4	Lindsay	Johnson	USA	7.1.82	3 May
13.48	2.0	Stephanie	Lichtl	GER-J	12.7.85	5 Jul
13.48	0.5	Dainelky	Pérez	CUB	6.1.76	5 Jul
13.49	0.0	Yevgeniya	Snigur	UKR-J	7.3.84	6 Jul
13.49	-0.8	Ronetta	Alexander	USA-J	8.5.85	3 Aug
13.49	0.0	Katja	Hödl	GER	15.8.83	17 Aug
13.50	0.5	Kasia	Williams	JAM-J	14.12.84	12 Apr
13.50	1.2	Hanna	Korell	FIN	16.3.79	9 Aug
13.50	1.1	Tomoko	Motegi	JPN	8.8.78	29 Oct
13.51	-1.4	Bertha	Peñalver	CUB	3.10.81	8 May
13.51		Yenima	Arencibia	CUB-J	25.12.84	13 Jun
13.51	0.5	Corina	Rehwagen	GER	17.5.81	28 Jun
13.51	0.1	Maria	Conjungo	CAF	14.7.75	25 Aug
13.51	-1.5		Liu Xiaomin	CHN-J	7.7.84	12 Sep
13.52	2.0	Ellanee	Richardson	USA	18.3.80	5 Apr
13.52	0.8	Jessica	Zelinka	CAN	3.9.81	18 Jul
13.53	-0.1	Antoinette	Wilks	USA	14.10.80	15 May
13.53	0.8	Lauren	Smith	USA	27.8.81	17 May
13.53	1.0	Polina	Roslavtseva	RUS	78	7 Jun
13.53	2.0	Tamsin	Stephens	GBR	2.8.80	8 Jun
13.53	-0.2	Sayuri	Kawakami	JPN	14.4.79	5 Jul
13.53	1.4	Gnima	Faye	SEN-J	17.11.84	6 Jul
13.53	-0.1	Symone	Belle	GBR-J	12.11.84	25 Jul
13.53	1.4	Elizabeth	Fairs	GBR	1.12.77	27 Jul
13.54	0.0	Lyudmila	Blonskaya ¶	UKR	9.11.77	17 May
13.54	1.6	Séverine	Rivalin (183)	FRA	11.4.78	6 Jul

Wind assisted

12.58	2.8		McKelvy			1		Carson/Los Angeles	1 Jun
12.65	2.8	Joanna	Hayes	USA	23.12.76	2		Carson/Los Angeles	1 Jun
12.69	2.8	Patricia	Girard	FRA	8.4.68	1s1	NC	Narbonne	25 Jul
12.84	2.2	Linda	Ferga-Khodadin	FRA	24.12.76	1s2	NC	Narbonne	25 Jul
12.93	2.8	Natasha	Neal	USA	22.7.80	3		Carson/Los Angeles	1 Jun
12.93	3.7	Angela	Atede	NGR	8.2.72	1		Valencia	14 Jun

Mark	Wind	Name		Nat	Born	Pos	Meet	Venue	Date
12.99	3.2	Natalya	Kresova	RUS	12.12.80	1h1		Sankt Peterburg	15 Jul
12.99	2.3	Nicole	Ramalalanirina	FRA	5.3.72	2s1	NC	Narbonne	25 Jul
13.02	2.9	Hristiána	Tabáki	GRE	13.1.73	2	ECCp	Valencia	25 May
13.03	6.2	Molly	Logan	USA	28.4.81	3	NCAA-r	Columbus	31 May
13.03	3.7	Damaris	Agbugba	NGR	26.12.82	2		Valencia	14 Jun
13.12	3.0	Fanny	Gérance	FRA	4.1.81	1		Maurepas	4 May
13.13	4.8	Jacquie	Munro	AUS	4.10.81	1		Perth	8 Feb
13.13	6.2	Brittany	Littlejohn	USA		4	NCAA-r	Columbus	31 May
13.14	2.8	Fiona	Cullen	AUS	31.8.79	1		Argentan	9 Jun
13.20	6.2	LaTasha	Pharr	USA	6.5.83	6	NCAA-r	Columbus	31 May
13.21	2.4	Dawn	Harper	USA-J	14.6.84	1h1	NCAA-r	Stanford	30 May
13.22	2.9	Margaret	Macchiut	ITA	25.7.74	3	ECCp	Valencia	25 May
13.22	2.5	Svetlana	Gnezdilov	ISR	20.7.69	1H		Tel Aviv	28 Jul
13.23	3.2	Shelly-Ann	Brown	CAN	15.5.80	1h4		Lincoln, NE	31 May
13.23	3.0	Kumiko	Ikeda	JPN	10.1.81	1h2		Mito	5 May

Mark	Wind	Name		Nat	Born	Date
13.28	2.6	Sani	Roseby	USA	5.2.82	30 May
13.29	4.0	Yuliya	Kondakova	RUS	4.12.81	15 Jul
13.31	3.6	Seneca	Holmes	USA	21.2.81	30 May
13.32	5.0	Alicia	Cave	TRI	4.2.82	30 May
13.35	3.8	Melanie	Walker	JAM	1.1.83	10 May
13.35	2.4	Agnieszka	Frankowska	POL	9.3.83	6 Jul
13.35	2.8	Adrianna	Lamalle	FRA	27.9.82	13 Jul
13.36A	2.9	Nicole	Ireland	USA	23.4.82	17 May
13.36	2.8	Nadège	Joseph	FRA	12.8.73	25 Jul
13.41	2.7	Teresa	Covert	USA		3 May
13.41	4.5	Alyssa	Aiken	USA	15.9.82	30 May
13.41	3.0	Hanna	Korell	FIN	16.3.79	26 Jun
13.42	2.8	Robin	Landfair	USA	24.6.81	18 May
13.43	3.6	Korto	Dunbar	USA	26.10.82	30 May
13.44	3.8	Kasia	Williams	JAM-J	14.12.84	10 May
13.45	2.4	Antoinette	Wilks	USA	14.10.80	10 May
13.51	3.0	Amanda	Mullins-Hall	USA	3.10.83	19 Apr
13.51	2.3	Argiró	Stratáki	GRE	3.8.75	31 May
13.51	4.0	Svetlana	Simonchik	RUS	10.8.82	15 Jul
13.52	2.5	Tameisha	King	USA	24.8.81	3 May
13.53	3.4	Lauren	Smith	USA	27.8.81	30 Mar
13.54	2.1	Ashlee	Brown	USA-J	3.12.85	30 May

Low altitude bests

Mark	Wind	Name		Nat	Born	Pos	Meet	Venue	Date
13.13	0.0	Maíla Paula	Machado	BRA	22.1.81	2	GP	Belém	4 May
13.26		Gilvaneide	de Oliveira/Parrela	BRA	31.8.76	1		São Paulo	5 Jul

Hand timing

Mark	Wind	Name		Nat	Born	Pos	Meet	Venue	Date
12.9	1.4	Jacquie	Munro	AUS	4.10.81	1		Gold Coast (RB)	12 Apr
13.0	1.4	Fiona	Cullen	AUS	31.8.79	2		Gold Coast (RB)	12 Apr
13.0	-1.0	Tatyana	Ladovskaya	UKR	4.5.77	1		Kiev	27 May
13.1	1.4	Gilvaneide	de Oliveira/Parrela	BRA	31.8.76	1h1		São Caetano do Sul	20 May

Drugs disqualification

Mark	Wind	Name		Nat	Born	Pos	Meet	Venue	Date
12.68	1.4	Damu	Cherry ¶	USA	29.11.77	1s1	NC	Stanford	22 Jun
13.45	1.0	Lyudmila	Blonskaya ¶	UKR	9.11.77	H		Arles	7 Jun

JUNIORS

9 performances by 5 women to 13.40. Additional marks and further juniors:

Mark	Wind	Name		Nat	Born	Pos	Meet	Venue	Date
13.25	1.0	Alandra	Sherman	USA	25.11.85	1		Austin	10 May
		13.30A 1.3 1	Albuquerque	24 May					
13.27	0.7	Ashlee	Williams	USA	27.3.84	3	Big 12	Austin	19 May
		13.38 1.1 2h1	Big12 Austin	18 May					
13.28	-0.1	Sophie	Krauel	GER	2.3.85	1	EJ	Tampere	25 Jul
		13.29 2.0 1	NC-j Fulda	5 Jul	13.34w 2.2 5			Kassel	13 Jun
13.33	0.4	Dawn	Harper	USA	14.6.84	2	Pac-10	Los Angeles	18 May
		13.33 1.4 4	NCAAr Stanford	31 May	13.40 -0.6 4h3			NCAA Sacramento	11 Jun
		13.28w 2.3 1	NC-j Stanford	22 Jun					
13.35	0.2		Ji Fangqian	CHN	18.7.84	2	NG	Changsha	24 Oct
13.48	2.0	Stephanie	Lichtl	GER	12.7.85	2	NC-j	Fulda	5 Jul
13.49	0.0	Yevgeniya	Snigur	UKR	7.3.84	1h1	NC	Kiev	6 Jul
13.49	-0.8	Ronetta	Alexander	USA	8.5.85	1		Miami	3 Aug
13.50	0.5	Kasia	Williams	JAM	14.12.84	3		Fayetteville	12 Apr
13.51		Yenima	Arencibia (10)	CUB	25.12.84	1r1		La Habana	13 Jun
13.51	-1.5		Liu Xiaomin	CHN	7.7.84	6	NC	Shanghai	12 Sep
13.53	1.4	Gnima	Faye	SEN	17.11.84	2		Bondoufle	6 Jul
13.53	-0.1	Symone	Belle	GBR	12.11.84	2	EJ	Tampere	25 Jul
13.58	0.8	Ashlee	Brown	USA	3.12.85	1		Norwalk	7 Jun
13.58		Dayaní	Lara	CUB	27.10.85	2r1		La Habana	13 Jun
13.59	0.1	Sabrina	Altermatt	SUI	6.3.85	3h3		Mannheim	22 Jun
13.59	0.5	Dora	Jémaa	FRA	15.7.85	1s1	NC-j	Vénissieux	13 Jul
13.59	1.7	Gnima	Faye	SEN	17.11.84	1	Af-J	Garoua	2 Aug
13.60	-0.4	Osarhieman	Omwanghe	USA	4.5.84	2		Stanford	3 May
13.60	-2.2	Jacquelyn	Johnson (20)	USA	8.9.84	1		Tucson	17 May
13.60		Latoya	Greaves	JAM	31.5.86	3		Spanish Town	3 Jun
13.60	-0.6	Ronetta	Alexander	USA	8.5.85	1	NC-y	Amherst	6 Jul

Wind assisted

Mark	Wind	Name		Nat	Born	Pos	Meet	Venue	Date
13.21	2.4	Dawn	Harper	USA	14.6.84	1h1	NCAA-r	Stanford	30 May
13.44	3.8	Kasia	Williams	JAM	14.12.84	2	JUCO	Levelland	10 May
13.54	2.1	Ashlee	Brown	USA	3.12.85	1		Norwalk	30 May
13.59	2.3	Ashley	Lodree	USA	22.10.85	3	NC-j	Stanford	22 Jun

Mark	Name		Nat	Born	Pos	Meet	Venue	Date

300 METRES HURDLES

Mark	Name		Nat	Born	Pos	Meet	Venue	Date
39.4	Stephanie	Kampf	GER	25.4.78	1		Pliezhausen	18 May

400 METRES HURDLES

Mark	Name		Nat	Born	Pos	Meet	Venue	Date
52.34	Yuliya	Pechonkina	RUS	21.4.78	1	NC	Tula	8 Aug
53.22	Jana	Pittman	AUS	9.11.82	1	WCh	Saint-Denis	28 Aug
53.34	Sandra	Glover	USA	30.12.68	1	GP II	Rieti	7 Sep
53.43		Pechonkina			2	GP II	Rieti	7 Sep
53.49		Pechonkina			1	VD	Bruxelles	5 Sep
53.52		Pechonkina			1h2	NC	Tula	7 Aug
53.57		Pechonkina			1s2	WCh	Saint-Denis	25 Aug
53.62		Pittman			1	GGala	Roma	11 Jul
53.65		Glover			2	WCh	Saint-Denis	28 Aug
53.65		Glover			1	WAF	Monaco	13 Sep
53.71		Pechonkina			3	WCh	Saint-Denis	28 Aug
53.71	Andrea	Blackett	BAR	24.1.76	1		Rovereto	10 Sep
53.76		Pittman			1		Canberra	22 Feb
53.77		Pittman			1s1	WCh	Saint-Denis	25 Aug
53.79		Glover			2		Rovereto	10 Sep
53.87	Ionela	Tîrlea	ROM	9.2.76	1	GS	Ostrava	12 Jun
53.87		Glover			2	VD	Bruxelles	5 Sep
53.90		Glover			2s1	WCh	Saint-Denis	25 Aug
53.94		Pittman			1	ISTAF	Berlin (P)	10 Aug
53.95		Pittman			1	NC	Brisbane	5 Apr
54.01		Pechonkina			1h1	WCh	Saint-Denis	24 Aug
54.02	Natasha	Danvers	GBR	19.9.77	2	GGala	Roma	11 Jul
54.05A	Surita	Febbraio	RSA	27.12.73	1		Pretoria	4 Apr
54.10		Tîrlea			1	Nebiolo	Torino	6 Jun
54.15		Glover			3	GGala	Roma	11 Jul
54.20		Glover			2	ISTAF	Berlin (P)	10 Aug
54.24	Sheena	Johnson	USA	1.10.82	1	NCAA	Sacramento	13 Jun
54.26	Tatyana	Tereshchuk	UKR	11.10.69	3s1	WCh	Saint-Denis	25 Aug
54.27		Pechonkina			1		Moskva	27 Jul
54.28		Blackett			2	WAF	Monaco	13 Sep
	(30/9)							
54.60	Raasin	McIntosh	USA	29.4.82	1	Tex R	Austin	5 Apr
	(10)							
54.66	Joanna	Hayes	USA	23.12.76	4	Gaz	Saint-Denis	4 Jul
54.92	Brenda	Taylor	USA	9.2.79	4	WK	Zürich	15 Aug
55.00	Heike	Meissner	GER	29.1.70	4s1	WCh	Saint-Denis	25 Aug
55.03	Yvonne	Harrison	PUR	2.12.75	2		Poznan	29 Jun
55.10	Daimí	Pernía	CUB	27.12.76	2	PAm	Santo Domingo	6 Aug
55.10		Huang Xiaoxiao	CHN	3.3.83	1	NG	Changsha	26 Oct
55.12	Allison	Beckford	JAM	8.5.79	1	CAC	St George's	5 Jul
55.18	Malgorzata	Pskit	POL	25.5.76	3h4	WCh	Saint-Denis	24 Aug
55.24	Natalya	Torshina	KAZ	4.10.68	5s1	WCh	Saint-Denis	25 Aug
55.28	Maren	Schott	GER	11.2.76	1	WUG	Daegu	30 Aug
	(20)							
55.35	Stephanie	Kampf	GER	25.4.78	5s2	WCh	Saint-Denis	25 Aug
55.38	Anna	Jesien	POL	10.12.78	4		Poznan	29 Jun
55.41	Monika	Niederstätter	ITA	2.3.74	1	NC	Rieti	3 Aug
55.42	Androula	Sialou	CYP	27.1.73	2	Veniz	Haniá	9 Jun
55.51	Debbie-Ann	Parris	JAM	24.3.73	1	GP II	Bratislava	10 Jun
55.65	Lashinda	Demus	USA	10.3.83	1s2	NC	Stanford	20 Jun
55.65	Cora	Olivero	ESP	28.8.78	1		Salamanca	26 Jun
55.67	Mame Tacko	Diouf	SEN	17.10.76	2		La Chaux-de-Fonds	17 Aug
55.77	Keisha	Downer	JAM	27.1.80	3	NC	Kingston	20 Jun
55.89	Tiffany	Ross	USA	5.2.83	1	NCAA-r	Fairfax	31 May
	(30)							
55.89	Makiko	Yoshida	JPN	16.7.76	1	NC	Yokohama	8 Jun
55.94	Yekaterina	Bakhvalova	RUS	8.3.72	4	v2N	Glasgow (S)	29 Jun
55.98	Oksana	Gulumyan	RUS	8.12.82	1h3	EU23	Bydgoszcz	18 Jul
56.07	Anja	Neupert	GER	10.10.78	1		Tübingen	13 Jul
56.08	Perla	dos Santos	BRA	29.1.82	1		São Caetano do Sul	23 Apr
56.10	Nicole	Ireland	USA	23.4.82	4	NCAA	Sacramento	13 Jun
56.11	Ieva	Zunda	LAT	20.7.78	1	ECp-2	Århus	21 Jun
56.12	TaNisha	Mills	USA	2.11.74	5		Fort-de-France	26 Apr
56.21	Lucimar	Teodoro	BRA	1.5.81	4	GP	Belém	4 May

Mark	Name		Nat	Born	Pos	Meet	Venue	Date
56.24	Melinda	Sallins	USA	30.6.73	5	NC	Stanford	21 Jun
	(40)							
56.24	Irina	Anashkina	RUS	31.1.72	2		Moskva	27 Jul
56.25	Rebecca	Wardell	NZL	21.12.77	1	NC	Dunedin	23 Mar
56.25	Yevgeniya	Isakova	RUS	.78	3	NC	Tula	8 Aug
56.29		Yao Yuehua	CHN	27.8.80	2	Af-AsG	Hyderabad	30 Oct
56.30	Anastasiya	Rabchenyuk	UKR	14.9.83	3	WUG	Daegu	30 Aug
56.33	Ryan	Tolbert	USA	16.6.76	6	NC	Stanford	21 Jun
56.34	Megan	Addy	USA	22.5.78	2		San Diego	22 Mar
56.34	Maria	Rus	ROM	19.1.83	4	WUG	Daegu	30 Aug
56.38	Tawa	Babatunde	CAN	19.12.79	1		Fayetteville	12 Apr
56.40	Faní	Halkiá	GRE	2.2.79	5	GP II	Thessaloníki	3 Aug
	(50)							
56.40	Vassanee	Vinatho	THA	30.6.80	3	AsiC	Manila	23 Sep
56.43A	Carmo	Tavares	POR	27.4.74	1		Monachil	9 Jul
56.47	Irena	Zauna	LAT	16.3.81	2	EU23	Bydgoszcz	19 Jul
56.49	Benedetta	Ceccarelli	ITA	23.1.80	1	v2N	Barcelona (M)	11 Jul
56.54		Wang Xing	CHN-Y	30.11.86	2	NG	Changsha	26 Oct
56.60	Tatyana	Debelaya	UKR	28.1.70	1		Kiev	27 May
56.61	Camille	Robinson	JAM-J	30.3.84	1	Carifta	Port of Spain	20 Apr
56.62A	Sylvanie	Morandais	FRA	14.7.79	1		Font-Romeu	3 Aug
56.70	Michelle	Perry	USA	1.5.79	3		Tucson	24 May
56.70	Olesya	Pogorelova	RUS	30.3.79	5	NC	Tula	8 Aug
	(60)							
56.84	Ysanne	Williams	USA	25.9.80	6	NCAA	Sacramento	13 Jun
56.85	Hrísa	Goudenoúdi	GRE	28.3.77	1	NC	Tríkala	15 Jun
56.86	Alyssa	Aiken	USA	15.9.82	2s1	NCAA	Sacramento	12 Jun
56.89	Zhanna	Bordyugova	UKR	8.7.82	2	NC	Kiev	4 Jul
56.89	Marta	Chrust	POL	29.9.78	5	WUG	Daegu	30 Aug
56.90	Norasheela	Khalid	MAS	27.9.79	6	WUG	Daegu	30 Aug
56.97	Corinne	Tafflet	FRA	8.11.75	1h4	NC	Narbonne	24 Jul
56.98	Omolade	Akinremi	NGR	13.9.74	1	AfG	Abuja	12 Oct
57.05	Lara	Rocco	ITA	20.12.75	3		Milano	29 Jun
57.05	Erica	Mårtensson	SWE	24.6.79	1	NC	Norrtälje	3 Aug
	(70)							
57.06	Elizabeth	Fairs	GBR	1.12.77	1	NC	Birmingham	26 Jul
57.08	Mariya	Menshikova	RUS	26.2.83	1	NC-23	Cheboksary	28 Jun
57.09	Shauna	Smith	USA	10.9.83	4s1	NC	Stanford	20 Jun
57.09	Yusmelys	García	VEN	19.12.83	4	CAC	St George's	4 Jul
57.09	Alena	Rücklová	CZE	7.10.81	1		Praha	16 Aug
57.14	Luciana	França	BRA	19.5.77	2		São Caetano do Sul	27 May
57.17	Ashik	Beevi	IND	.79	1		Chennai	3 Mar
57.19	Catherine	Obilor	NGR-J	17.7.85	1	NC	Abuja	17 Jul
57.20	Althea	Thoma	USA	8.8.81	1		State College	22 Mar
57.24	Melanie	Walker	JAM	1.1.83	2	PennR	Philadelphia	24 Apr
	(80)							
57.26		Wang Wenwen	CHN-Y	15.6.86	2	NC	Shanghai	14 Sep
57.26		Zhang Rongrong	CHN-J	27.1.84	3	NG	Changsha	26 Oct
57.27	Amanda	Dias	BRA-J	11.11.84	1	NC-j	Londrina	18 May
57.28	Meta	Macus	SLO	23.3.75	2	ECp-1B	Velenje	21 Jun
57.30	Satomi	Kubokura	JPN	27.4.82	2	NC	Yokohama	8 Jun
57.31	Carole	Mebam Kaboud	CMR	17.9.78	4		La Chaux-de-Fonds	17 Aug
57.35	Karlene	Haughton	CAN	18.10.72	5	GP	Osaka	10 May
57.39	Olivia	Abderrhamanne	FRA	2.8.79	2		Bron	3 Jul
57.40	Nadja	Petersen	SWE	14.7.78	2		Göteborg	4 Jul
57.44	Princesa	Oliveros	COL	10.8.75	5h2	PAm	Santo Domingo	5 Aug
	(90)							
57.45	Shevon	Stoddart	USA	21.11.82	6s1	NCAA	Sacramento	12 Jun
57.46A	Kerryn	Hulsen	RSA	5.10.74	5		Pretoria	4 Apr
57.46	Tracey	Duncan	GBR	16.5.79	2		Cwmbran	9 Aug
57.51	Yamelis	Ortiz	PUR	26.2.78	2rB	MSR	Walnut	19 Apr
57.51	Raquel	da Costa	BRA	30.12.83	2	SACh	Barquisimeto	20 Jun
57.52	Yekaterina	Kostetskaya	RUS-Y	31.12.87	1	EJ	Tampere	26 Jul
57.53	Ewelina	Setowska	POL	5.3.80	4	NC	Bielsko-Biala	5 Jul
57.54	Zuzana	Hejnová	CZE-Y	19.12.86	1	WY	Sherbrooke	13 Jul
57.57	Elizabeth	Bayne	USA	22.7.82	1		Storrs	4 May
57.57	Irina	Obedina	RUS-J	1.7.85	2	EJ	Tampere	26 Jul
	(100)							

57.61	Mie	Osakada	JPN	20.1.74	23 Sep
57.62	Jamillah	Wade	USA	17.7.81	4 May
57.66	Le'Gretta	Smith	USA	12.1.74	8 Jun
57.66	Hristína	Hantzí-Neag	GRE	26.12.76	9 Jun
57.69	LeBren	Martin	USA		17 May
57.70	Katie	Jones	GBR	4.1.77	9 Aug

Mark	Name		Nat	Born	Pos Meet	Venue	Date
57.71	Mayumi	Yuno	JPN	23.6.81			18 May
57.72	Tina	Kron	GER	3.4.81			29 Jun
57.72		Xiao Hongfan	CHN	6.1.83			14 Sep
57.78	Nadezhda	Kopp	RUS	.76			1 Jun
57.78	Marina	Ivanova	UKR	19.8.82			3 Jul
57.80	Isabel	Rocha Silva	BRA	15.6.79			28 Jun
57.81	Josanne	Lucas	TRI-J	.84			18 May
57.84	Miriam	Hrdlicková	SVK	1.1.76			31 May
57.84	Karolina	Tlustochowska	POL	19.9.81			18 Jul
57.88	Yelena	Ildeykina	RUS	16.6.83			28 Jun
57.88	Katarzyna	Izydorek	POL	4.10.79			4 Jul
57.89	Frances	Santin	USA	27.7.80			31 May
57.89	Yekaterina	Bikert	RUS	.80			8 Jun
57.89	Andrea	Bliss	JAM	5.10.80			12 Jun
57.90	Oksana	Volosyuk	UKR	28.11.81			4 Jul
57.90		Lee Yun-kyong	KOR	15.8.77			13 Aug
57.92	Emmanuela	Baggiolini	ITA	10.6.72			3 Aug
57.92	Manuela	Bosco	FIN	11.6.82			3 Aug
57.92	Yudalis	Díaz	CUB	20.9.79			5 Aug
57.94		Ruan Zhuofen	CHN-J	21.1.85			25 Oct
57.97	Salhaté	Djamalidine	COM	23.12.78			26 Jul
57.99	Aissata	Soulama	BUR	11.2.79			30 Oct
58.01	Carrie	Damschen	USA				17 May
58.01	Ulrike	Urbansky	GER	6.4.77			1 Jun
58.04	Sapinder	Kaur	IND	8.4.82			3 Mar
58.04	Tacita	Bass	USA	28.10.79			17 May
58.04	Olga	Salnikova	RUS	19.6.71			1 Jun
58.05	Cara	Evans	USA	23.7.78			7 Jun
58.07	Marina	Shiyan	RUS	22.1.80			7 Aug
58.09	Virna	De Angeli	ITA	27.2.76			28 Jun
58.12	Danielle	Myricks	USA	25.10.83			26 Apr
58.15	Sheryl	Morgan	JAM	6.11.83			24 Apr
58.15	Vera	Simms	USA	8.3.82			8 Jun
58.15	Celia	Medina	ESP	10.7.77			2 Aug
58.16	Svetlana	Starkova	RUS	5.12.68			7 Aug
58.16		Chen Lin	CHN	22.8.81			14 Sep
58.18	Margit	Strand	NOR	22.1.78			27 Aug
58.19	Özge	Gürler	TUR-J	17.6.85			31 May
58.21	Comfort	Agara	USA				17 May
58.22	Patricia	Lopes	POR	3.3.82			10 Jun
58.24		Choi Hae-nam	KOR	17.2.76			5 Jun
58.25		Li Yun	CHN	20.7.83			27 Aug
58.26	Aleksandra	Pieluzek	POL	4.4.79			24 May
58.27	Gaia	Biella (150)	ITA	25.1.80			3 Aug
58.28	Danielle	Hobson	USA	2.1.80			4 May
58.28	Devron	Kennedy	USA				17 May
58.30	Nikki	Nelson	USA	5.8.80			3 May
58.32	Monique	Jessie	USA	4.12.82			31 May
58.33	Sinead	Dudgeon	GBR	9.7.76			1 Jun
58.33	Olga	Nikolayeva	RUS-J	30.8.84			2 Jul
58.35	Amber	Delpino	USA				17 May
58.35	Oksana	Kholodkova	UKR	24.2.82			3 Jul
58.36	Sian	Scott	GBR-J	20.3.84			29 Jun
58.38	Tawana	Watkins	USA-J	27.3.84			22 Jun
58.38	Elizabeth	Ndubueze	NGR	17.12.79			17 Jul
58.39	MacKenzie	Hill	USA-Y	5.1.86			22 Jun
58.42	Jazmín	Rodriguez	DOM	82			5 Aug
58.44	Zuzana	Bergrová	CZE-J	24.11.84			28 Jun
58.47	Carlene	Robinson	JAM-J	30.4.84			20 Apr
58.48	Chloe	Davis	USA	16.1.83			31 May
58.48	Dora	Jémaa	FRA-J	15.7.85			25 Jul
58.49	Jamillah	Bowman	USA	12.12.81			8 Jun
58.49	Laia	Forcadelli (169)	ESP	6.6.82			10 Jun

Low altitude bests

54.31	Febbraio	1		Poznan	29 Jun	
56.84	Morandais	5	GS	Ostrava	12 Jun	
57.01	Tavares	1		Pamplona	19 Jul	
57.60	Hulsen	2	NC	Port Elizabeth	26 Apr	

Hand timing

55.8	Ieva	Zunda	LAT	20.7.78	1	Valmiera	27 Jun
56.1	Irena	Zauna	LAT	16.3.81	2	Valmiera	27 Jun
57.3	Yudalis	Díaz	CUB	20.9.79	1r1	La Habana	4 Jul
57.9	Yaimara	Pérez	CUB	12.3.81	2r1	La Habana	4 Jul

JUNIORS

See main list for top 9 juniors. 8 performances by 6 women to 57.50. Additional mark and further juniors:

Wang Xing	57.14		1h2			Dalian		27 Aug
Wang W	57.36		4	NG		Changsha		26 Oct
57.81	Josanne	Lucas (10)	TRI	.84	2	SEC	Knoxville	18 May
57.94		Ruan Zhuofen	CHN	21.1.85	2h3	NG	Changsha	25 Oct
58.19	Özge	Gürler	TUR-	17.6.85	1	NC	Ankara	31 May
58.33	Olga	Nikolayeva	RUS	30.8.84	h	NC-j	Kazan	2 Jul
58.36	Sian	Scott	GBR	20.3.84	1	NC-j	Bedford	29 Jun
58.38	Tawana	Watkins	USA	27.3.84	1	NC	Stanford	22 Jun
58.39	MacKenzie	Hill	USA-Y	5.1.86	2	NC	Stanford	22 Jun
58.44	Zuzana	Bergrová	CZE	24.11.84	1	v3N	Cakovec	28 Jun
58.47	Carlene	Robinson	JAM	30.4.84	2	Carifta	Port of Spain	20 Apr
58.48	Dora	Jémaa	FRA	15.7.85	3h2	EJ	Tampere	25 Jul
58.67	Jessica	Samuelsson (20)	SWE	14.3.85	3	NC	Norrtälje	3 Aug

HIGH JUMP

2.06 Kajsa Bergqvist SWE 12.10.76 1 Eberstadt 26 Jul
1.80/1 1.84/1 1.88/1 1.92/1 1.95/1 1.98/1 2.00/1 2.02/1 2.06/2 2.10/xxx

2.03i	1		Stockholm	18 Feb	1.85/1 1.90/1 1.94/1 1.97/1 1.99/3 2.01/1 2.03/1 2.08/xxx
2.02i	2		Arnstadt	8 Feb	1.91/1 1.94/1 1.97/1 2.00/1 2.02/2 2.04/xxxx 2.02/x
2.02i	1	GP	Birmingham	21 Feb	1.93/1 1.96/1 1.99/2 2.02/1 2.04/xxx
2.01i	1	WI	Birmingham	16 Mar	1.96/1 1.99/1 2.01/1
2.01	1	GP	Ostrava	12 Jun	1.95/1 1.97/3 1.99/1 2.01/2 2.03/xxx
2.00i	2		Athína (NI)	5 Feb	1.94/1 1.96/2 2.00/3 2.02/xxx
2.00i	1		Liévin	23 Feb	1.95/1 2.00/3 2.03/xxx
2.00i	1	NC	Sätra	1 Mar	1.94/1 1.97/1 2.00/3 2.04/xxx
2.00i	1		Tallinn	5 Mar	1.84/1 1.91/1 1.94/1 1.97/1 2.00/2 2.04/xxx
2.00	3	WCh	Saint-Denis	31 Aug	1.85/1 1.90/1 1.95/1 1.98/3 2.00/2 2.02/x 2.04/xx

2.06 Hestrie Cloete RSA 26.8.78 1 WCh Saint-Denis 31 Aug
1.85/1 1.90/1 1.95/1 1.98/1 2.00/1 2.02/1 2.04/1 2.06/1 2.10/xxx

2.05	1	ISTAF	Berlin (P)	10 Aug	1.85/1 1.90/1 1.93/1 1.96/1 1.99/1 2.01/2 2.05/1 2.10/xxx
2.03	1	WK	Zürich	15 Aug	1.85/1 1.90/1 1.95/1 1.98/1 2.01/2 2.03/1 2.06/xxx
2.03	1	VD	Bruxelles	5 Sep	1.85/1 1.90/1 1.95/2 1.98/1 2.01/2 2.03/2 2.07/xxx

Mark	Name		Nat	Born	Pos	Meet	Venue	Date
	2.02 1 GP London CP) 8 Aug 1.85/1 1.90/1 1.93/1 1.96/1 2.02/2 2.05/xxx							
	2.01 1 DNG Stockholm 5 Aug 1.84/1 1.88/1 1.92/1 1.95/1 1.98/1 2.01/1 2.05/xxx							
	2.01 1 WAF Monaco 13 Sep 1.88/1 1.92/1 1.96/1 1.99/2 2.01/2 2.03/xxx							
	2.00 1 GP II Zagreb 7 Jul 1.85/1 1.90/1 1.94/1 1.97/3 2.00/1 2.02/xxx							
	2.00 1 GGala Roma 11 Jul 1.85/1 1.90/1 1.94/1 1.97/1 2.00/1 2.03/xxx							
2.04i	Anna	Chicherova	RUS	22.7.82	1		Yekaterinburg	7 Jan
	1.85/1 1.89/1 1.92/1 1.95/2 1.98/1 2.01/1 2.04/3							
	2.02i 2 Moskva 26 Feb 1.82, 1.89, 1.92, 1.94, 1.96, 1.98, 2.00/all 1 2.02/3 2.06/xx							
	2.01i 2 Stockholm 18 Feb 1.85/1 1.90/1 1.94/1 1.97/1 1.99/1 2.01/3 2.03/xxx							
	2.00i 2 Stuttgart 2 Feb 1.84/1 1.88/1 1.91/1 1.94/1 1.96/1 1.98/1 2.00/2 2.02/xxx							
	2.00 1 Moskva 15 Jul 1.85/3 1.88/1 1.90/1 1.94/1 1.97/1 2.00/2							
	2.00 1 Moskva 27 Jul 1.85/1 1.90/1 1.92/2 1.94/1 1.96/2 2.00/2							
2.02i	Marina	Kuptsova	RUS	22.12.81	1		Arnstadt	8 Feb
	1.80/1 1.85/1 1.91/1 1.94/1 1.97/1 2.00/1 2.02/2 2.04/xxxx 2.02/1							
	2.02 1 FBK Hengelo 1Jun 1.80, 1.85, 1.88, 1.91, 1.94, 1.96/1 1.98/2 2.00/1 2.02/3 2.04/xxx							
	2.00i 1 Spark Stuttgart 2 Feb 1.80/1 1.84/1 1.91/1 1.94/1 1.96/1 1.98/1 2.00/1 2.02/xxx							
	2.00i 3 Moskva 26 Feb 1.79/1 1.85/1 1.89/1 1.94/1 1.96/1 1.98/2 2.00/1 2.02/xxx							
	2.00i 1 Linz 7 Mar 1.80/1 1.85/1 1.89/1 1.92/1 1.95/1 1.98/1 2.00/3 2.05/xxx							
	2.00 2 WCh Saint-Denis 31 Aug 1.85/1 1.90/1 1.95/2 1.98/1 2.00/1 2.02/x 2.04/x 2.06/x							
2.02i	Yelena	Yelesina	RUS	4.4.70	1	NC	Moskva	26 Feb
	1.82/1 1.85/1 1.89/1 1.92/1 1.94/1 1.96/1 1.98/2 2.00/1 2.02/1 2.06/x							
	2.01i 2 Yekaterinburg 7 Jan							
2.01	Inga	Babakova	UKR	27.6.67	1	Bisl	Oslo	27 Jun
	1.80/1 1.85/1 1.89/1 1.92/1 1.95/1 1.97/1 1.99/2 2.01/3 2.03/xxx							
	2.00 1 GP II Sevilla 7 Jun 1.80/1 1.86/1 1.89/1 1.92/1 1.95/1 1.97/1 2.00/1 2.02/xxx							
2.01	Vita	Palamar	UKR	12.10.77	2=	WK	Zürich	15 Aug
	1.85/1 1.90/1 1.95/1 1.98/1 2.01/1 2.03/xxx							
	2.01 2 WAF Monaco 13 Sep 1.83/1 1.88/1 1.92/1 1.96/2 1.99/2 2.01/3 2.03/xxx							
	2.00 1 Kiev 20 Jun 1.80/1 1.83/1 1.86/1 1.90/1 1.95/1 1.98/3 2.00/2 2.03/xx							
	2.00 1 NC Kiev 6 Jul 1.80/1 1.85/1 1.90/1 1.94/1 1.96/1 1.98/1 2.00/2 2.02/xxx							
	2.00 2 Eberstadt 26 Jul 1.80/1 1.84/1 1.88/1 1.92/1 1.95/1 1.98/1 2.00/1 2.02/xxx							
2.01	Blanka	Vlasic	CRO	8.11.83	2=	WK	Zürich	15 Aug
	1.90/1 1.95/1 2.01/1 2.03/xxx							
	2.00 2 GP II Zagreb 7 Jul 1.85/1 1.90/1 1.94/3 2.00/3 2.02/							
2.01	Amy	Acuff	USA	14.7.75	4	WK	Zürich	15 Aug
	1.80/1 1.85/1 1.90/1 1.95/1 1.98/2 2.01/3 2.03/xxx							
2.01	Venelina	Veneva	BUL	13.6.74	1	GP II	Rieti	7 Sep
	1.83/1 1.88/1 1.92/1 1.95/1 1.98/1 2.01/2 2.04/xxx							
2.00i	Viktoriya	Seryogina	RUS	22.5.73	1		Athína (NI)	5 Feb
	1.80/1 1.85/1 1.91/1 1.94/1 1.96/1 1.98/1 2.00/1 2.02/xxx							
2.00i	Svetlana	Lapina	RUS	12.4.78	3=	NC	Moskva	26 Feb
	1.79/1 1.85/1 1.89/1 1.92/1 1.94/1 1.96/1 1.98/2 2.00/1 2.02/xxx							
2.00	Viktoria	Styopina	UKR	21.2.76	1		Kiev	26 May
	1.75/1 1.80/1 1.85/1 1.90/1 1.93/1 1.95/1 1.97/1 2.00/2 2.02/xxx							
2.00	Daniela	Rath	GER	6.5.77	1	ECp-S	Firenze	22 Jun
	1.85/1 1.92/1 1.95/1 1.98/1 2.00/1 2.02/xxx							
2.00	Ruth	Beitia	ESP	1.4.79	1		Avilés	26 Jul
	1.75/1 1.80/1 1.90/1 1.95/1 1.97/2 rec 2.00/2 2.02/xxx							
	(50/15)							
1.99	Irina	Mikhalchenko	UKR	20.1.72	3	Bisl	Oslo	27 Jun
1.98i	Yelena	Slesarenko	RUS	28.2.82	1		Volgograd	18 Jan
1.98	Tisha	Waller	USA	1.12.70	1	Pre	Eugene	24 May
1.97i	Melanie	Skotnik	GER	8.11.82	1		Dortmund	5 Feb
1.97	Karol	Rovelto	USA	20.12.69	1=	GP II	Stanford	7 Jun
	(20)							
1.97	Yekaterina	Aleksandrova	RUS	3.6.77	1	Kuso	Warszawa	15 Jun
1.97	Tatyana	Efimenko	KGZ	2.1.81	6	GGala	Roma	11 Jul
1.96i	Antonietta	Di Martino	ITA	1.6.78	3	GP	Birmingham	21 Feb
1.96i	Iva	Straková	CZE	4.8.80	1	NC	Bratislava	2 Mar
1.96i	Dóra	Györffy	HUN	23.2.78	1		Wien	9 Mar
1.96	Tatyana	Grigoryeva	RUS	13.5.81	1		Moskva	15 Jun
1.95i	Oana	Pantelimon	ROM	27.9.72	Q	WI	Birmingham	15 Mar
1.95	Gwen	Wentland	USA	29.4.72	3	GP II	Stanford	7 Jun
1.95	Marta	Mendía	ESP	18.5.75	2	NC	Jerez de la Frontera	2 Aug
1.95	Olga	Kaliturina	RUS	9.3.76	3	NC	Tula	10 Aug
	(30)							
1.95	Juana	Rosario Arrendel	DOM	16.6.78	8	WCh	Saint-Denis	31 Aug
1.95i	Irina	Kovalenko	UKR-Y	12.6.86	1		Lvov	26 Dec
1.94i	Elena	Herzenberg	GER	24.6.79	1	NC	Leipzig	22 Feb
1.94i	Anna	Ksok	POL	29.9.83	1	NC	Spala	2 Mar
1.94	Romary	Rifka	MEX	23.12.70	1		Xalapa	14 Jun

Mark	Name		Nat	Born	Pos	Meet	Venue	Date
1.94	Viktoriya	Slivka	RUS	28.9.80	2		Moskva	27 Jul
1.94	Carolina	Klüft	SWE	2.2.83	1H	WCh	Saint-Denis	23 Aug
1.93i	Susan	Jones	GBR	8.6.78	6	GP	Birmingham	21 Feb
1.93	Gaëlle	Niaré	FRA	12.3.82	1		Rennes	7 Jun
1.93	Anne Gerd	Eieland	NOR	28.12.82	1		Kristiansand	15 Aug
	(40)							
1.93	Petrina	Price	AUS-J	26.4.84	1		Sydney (H)	15 Nov
1.92i	Gina	Rickert-Curtis	USA	2.1.79	1		Ames	15 Feb
1.92i	Kathryn	Holinski	GER	19.7.82	3	NC	Leipzig	22 Feb
1.92i	Sophia	Sagonas	GER	18.9.81	4	NC	Leipzig	22 Feb
1.92i	Bernadett	Bódi	HUN	14.4.80	1	NC	Budapest	2 Mar
1.92	Miki	Imai	JPN	30.5.75	1		Shizuoka	3 May
1.92	Yulia	Lyakhova	RUS	8.7.77	4		Kalamáta	31 May
1.92	Zuzana	Hlavonová	CZE	16.4.73	7	GS	Ostrava	12 Jun
1.92	Candeger	Oguz (Kilinçer)	TUR	16.7.80	2	Balk G	Thíva	13 Jul
1.92	Solange	Witteveen	ARG	6.2.76	1		Vic	20 Jul
	(50)							
1.92	Antonella	Bevilacqua	ITA	15.10.71	1		Clermont-Ferrand	9 Aug
1.91i	Inna	Gliznutsa	MDA	18.4.73	5		Athína (NI)	5 Feb
1.91i	Ifoma	Jones	USA	4.9.77	3	NC	Boston (R)	2 Mar
1.91	Tia	Hellebaut	BEL	16.2.78	1=H		Götzis	31 May
1.91	Katja	Schötz	GER	22.7.81	3		Cottbus	4 Jun
1.91	Barbora	Laláková	CZE	2.5.81	1eA		Mannheim	22 Jun
1.91	Eunice	Barber	FRA	17.11.74	2H	WCh	Saint-Denis	23 Aug
1.90A	Svetlana	Zalevskaya	KAZ	14.6.73	2		Potchefstroom	31 Jan
1.90i	Kärt	Siilats	EST	7.9.80	1		Tallinn	7 Feb
1.90	Marisa	Gertenbach	RSA	20.10.82	2	NC	Port Elizabeth	26 Apr
	(60)							
1.90A	Nicole	Forrester	CAN	17.11.76	5		Ciudad de México	3 May
1.90	Miyuki	Aoyama	JPN	4.1.77	1		Amagasaki	18 May
1.90	Julia	Farmaka	CYP	20.4.78	2	ECCp	Valencia	25 May
1.90	Yelena	Kholosha-Motok	UKR	26.1.82	2		Kiev	26 May
1.90	Yelena	Fedoseyeva	RUS	18.3.83	1		Tula	1 Jun
1.90	Corinne	Müller	SUI	20.11.75	1	ECp-2A	Århus	22 Jun
1.90	Oksana	Zubkovskaya	UKR	15.7.81	5	NC	Kiev	6 Jul
1.90	Tatyana	Ivanova	RUS	22.1.76	1		Sankt Peterburg	16 Jul
1.90	Hanna	Mikkonen	FIN	15.1.81	1		Karlstad	24 Jul
1.90	Birgit	Kähler	GER	14.8.70	1		Dudelange	13 Sep
	(70)							
1.90	Yoko	Hunnicutt (Ota)	JPN	14.1.75	3	Super	Yokohama	23 Sep
1.89i	Nevena	Lendjel	CRO	18.7.79	1	NCAA	Fayetteville	14 Mar
1.89	Chaunte	Howard	USA-J	12.1.84	1	PennR	Philadelphia	24 Apr
1.89	Stacy Ann	Grant	USA	18.8.77	1		Princeton	10 May
1.89	Nikolía	Mitropoúlou	GRE	16.2.82	6=	ECp-S	Firenze	22 Jun
1.89	Bobby	Aloysius	IND	22.6.74	1		Hyderabad	30 Jul
1.89	Yariadmis	Argüelles	CUB-J	18.4.84	3	PAm	Santo Domingo	8 Aug
1.89	Marina	Korzhova-Aitova	KAZ	13.9.82	1	C.Asian	Dushanbe	18 Oct
1.88i	Inge	Jankú	CZE	1.5.74	2		Cejkovice	20 Feb
1.88i	Alina	Dinu	ROM	2.9.82	2	NC	Bucuresti	23 Feb
	(80)							
1.88	Sharon	Day	USA-J	9.6.85	1		Mission Viejo	5 Apr
1.88		Zhao Ning	CHN	26.7.81	1		Guangzhou	8 Apr
1.88A	Desiree	Crichlow	BAR-J	1.6.84	2	WAC	El Paso	17 May
1.88A	Luciane	Dambacher	BRA	10.5.76	1		Tunja	17 May
1.88	Svetlana	Shkolina	RUS-Y	9.3.86	1		Krasnodar	27 May
1.88	Yamilé	Aldama	ex CUB	14.8.72	1		London (He)	19 Jul
1.88	Ariane	Friedrich	GER-J	10.1.84	1	EJ	Tampere	27 Jul
1.88	Ramona	Pop	ROM	5.4.82	2	NC	Bucuresti	10 Aug
1.88		Bui Thi Nhung	VIE	21.1.83	1	AsiC	Manila	21 Sep
1.87i	María	Hotokourídou	GRE	22.5.77	1		Thessaloníki	18 Jan
	(90)							
1.87i	Katerina	Korcová	CZE	31.7.76	1		Otrokovice	23 Jan
1.87i	Maresa	Cadienhead	CAN	7.4.76	1		Lubbock	25 Jan
1.87i	Stefania	Cadamuro	ITA	23.2.79	1		Sempeter	26 Jan
1.87i	Cecilia	Axelsson	SWE-J	4.9.84	1	NC-j	Vasteras	23 Feb
1.87i	Alexandra	Church	AUS-J	14.1.84	2	NCAA	Fayetteville	14 Mar
1.87	Kaylene	Wagner	USA-J	15.11.84	1		Northridge	3 May
1.87	Peaches	Roach	JAM-J	21.12.84	1		Spanish Town	14 Jun
1.87	Aileen	Herrmann	GER-J	16.9.85	1		Mannheim	22 Jun
1.87i	Wanita	May (Dykstra)	CAN	30.1.75	1		Toronto	6 Aug
1.87	Irina	Glavatskikh	RUS-J	29.12.84	1		Szczecin	9 Aug
	(100)							

Mark	Name		Nat	Born	Pos	Meet	Venue	Date
1.87	Amewu	Mensah	GER	21.3.77	2		Dudelange	13 Sep

1.86i	Kristen	Matthews	CAN	3.5.82	11 Jan
1.86i	Heike	Siener	GER	19.11.80	18 Jan
1.86i	Elena	Brambilla	ITA	23.4.83	1 Feb
1.86A	Anika	Smit	RSA-Y	26.5.86	18 Feb
1.86i	Julie	Crane	GBR	26.9.76	22 Feb
1.86i	Marie	Collonvillé	FRA	23.11.73	14 Mar
1.86	Lavern	Spencer	LCA-J	23.6.84	28 Mar
1.86	Daniela	Galeotti	ITA	22.3.77	17 May
1.86	Svetlana	Stavskaya	KAZ	10.5.77	13 Jun
1.86	Whitney	Evans	CAN	10.4.80	14 Jun
1.86	Jessica	Johnson	USA	13.9.80	14 Jun
1.86	Marije	Langen	NED-Y	29.12.86	22 Jun
1.86	Diana	Láznicková	SVK	14.8.74	28 Jun
1.86	Annett	Engel	GER-Y	6.11.87	12 Jul
1.86	Emma	Green	SWE-J	8.12.84	27 Jul
1.86	Roberta	Bugarini	ITA	19.6.69	2 Aug
1.86	Anna	Visigalli	ITA	24.2.81	2 Aug
1.86	Irina	Gordeyeva	RUS-Y	9.10.86	19 Aug
1.86A	Dianie	Wondergem	RSA	2.3.82	15 Oct
1.86	Noegrothai	Chaipetch	THA	1.12.82	11 Dec
1.85i	Olga	Pinakina	RUS-J	85	26 Feb
1.85i	Yevgenia	Zhdanova	RUS	21.7.66	1 Mar
1.85i		Liang Na	CHN	5.9.78	9 Mar
1.85A	Monica	Iagar	ROM	2.4.73	3 May
1.85	Rassamee	Sumethivit	THA	12.9.71	16 May
1.85	Maria	Papayeoryíou	GRE	8.8.79	28 May
1.85	Iva	Moravcová	CZE-J	21.2.85	1 Jul
1.85	Julia	Bennett	GBR	26.3.70	19 Jul
1.85	Julie	Hollman	GBR	16.2.77	23 Aug
1.85	Sónia	Carvalho	POR	10.5.77	29 Aug
1.85		Li Shan	CHN	4.3.83	27 Oct
1.84i	Raffaella	Lamera	ITA	13.4.83	1 Feb
1.84i	Kristy	Laramee	USA		8 Feb
1.84i	Deidre	Mullen	USA	21.5.80	23 Feb
1.84i	Aura	Feniuc	ROM	26.9.80	23 Feb
1.84i	Miruna	Mataoanu	ROM	4.6.83	23 Feb
1.84	Viktoriya	Andonova	BUL-Y	19.11.86	8 Mar
1.84	Angela	McKee	NZL	11.12.74	22 Mar
1.84	Spring	Harris	USA	3.11.80	22 Mar
1.84	Kim	Schiemenz	USA	13.4.77	3 Apr
1.84	Shaunette	Davidson	JAM-J	3.8.84	21 Apr
1.84	Tatyana	Makarova	RUS-J	.84	27 May
1.84	Anett	Jambor	GER	27.7.83	31 May
1.84	Magalie	Cartal	FRA	11.1.81	1 Jun
1.84	Elena	Meuti	ITA	26.6.83	3 Jun
1.84	Alica	Javad	SVK	26.6.69	21 Jun
1.84	Irina	Naumenko	KAZ	13.2.80	21 Jun
1.84	Carri	Long	USA	23.4.77	22 Jun
1.84	Tamika	Toppin	USA	5.6.79	22 Jun
1.84	Annabella	Scherer (150)	GER-J	2.9.84	5 Jul
1.84	Irina	Butor	BLR	26.2.80	5 Jul
1.84		Jing Xuezhu	CHN	20.4.75	4 Aug
1.84	Nneka	Ukuah	NGR-Y	20.11.87	12 Oct
1.84		Lu Jieming	CHN	25.1.83	27 Oct
1.84		Li Rong	CHN	14.9.83	27 Oct
1.84	(156)	Cai Danping	CHN	21.9.83	27 Oct

Best outdoor marks

1.98	Yelesina	3	VD	Bruxelles	5 Sep
1.97	Seryogina	3	GP II	Zagreb	7 Jul
1.96	Lapina	2		Moskva	15 Jun
1.96	Slesarenko	2	EU23	Bydgoszcz	19 Jul
1.94	Györffy	1	WUG	Daegu	29 Aug
1.94	Ksok	2	WUG	Daegu	29 Aug
1.92	Kovalenko	1	WY	Sherbrooke	12 Jul
1.92	Pantelimon	1	NC	Bucuresti	10 Aug
1.91	Straková	3	Odl	Praha	29 Jun
1.91	Skotnik	1		Tettnang	5 Jul
1.90A	I Jones	3=		Ciudad de México	3 May
1.90	Herzenberg	3		Zweibrücken	29 May
1.90	Sagonas	3		Wipperfürth	14 Jun
1.90	Siilats	2=	ECp2B	Istanbul	22 Jun
1.90	Gliznutsa	5	ECp2B	Istanbul	22 Jun
1.90	Di Martino	1	v2N	Barcelona (M)	11 Jul
1.89	S Jones	5	ECp-S	Firenze	22 Jun
1.88A	Lendjel	1	WAC	El Paso	17 May
1.87	Rickert-Curtis	1		Clemson	5 Apr
1.87	Holinski	5		Zweibrücken	29 May
1.87	Cadamuro	1		Celle Ligure	1 Jul

1.86	May (Dykstra)	29 Jul
1.86	Korcová	16 Aug
1.85	Church	21 Mar
1.85	Hotokourídou	28 May
1.85	Brambilla	4 Oct
1.84	Siener	7 Jun
1.84	Crane	5 Jul
1.84	Cadienhead	21 Aug
1.84	Collonvillé	20 Sep

Drugs disqualification

1.87	Lyudmila	Blonskaya ¶	UKR	18.3.75	H	ECp	Bressanone	5 Jul

JUNIORS

See main list for top 14 juniors. 10 performances by 4 women to 1.89. Additional mark and further juniors:

Price	1.92	1		Sydney	11 Oct	1.89	3	GP	Osaka	10 May
	1.92	1	N.Sch	Brisbane	13 Dec					
Howard	1.89	4=	NC	Stanford	22 Jun	1.89i	1		Clemson	6 Dec

1.86A	Anika	Smit	RSA-Y	26.5.86	1		Krugersdorp	18 Feb
1.86	Lavern	Spencer	LCA	23.6.84	1		St George's	28 Mar
1.86	Marije	Langen	NED-Y	29.12.86	3	ECp-1B	Velenje	22 Jun
1.86	Annett	Engel	GER-Y	6.11.87	2=	WY	Sherbrooke	12 Jul
1.86	Emma	Green	SWE	8.12.84	3	EJ	Tampere	27 Jul
1.86	Irina	Gordeyeva (20)	RUS-Y	9.10.86	1		Sankt-Peterburg	19 Aug

POLE VAULT

4.82	Yelena	Isinbayeva	RUS	3.6.82	1	GP	Gateshead	13 Jul

4.30/1 4.44/2 4.54/1 4.64/2 4.74/2 4.82/2

4.78	1	GP	London (CP)	8 Aug	4.33/1 4.43/1 4.53/1 4.63/2 4.68/1 4.73/xx4.78/1 4.83/xxx
4.73	1		Poznan	29 Jun	4.23/1 4.33/1 4.43/1 4.53/1 4.63/1 4.73/3 4.82/xxx
4.65i	1		Athína (P)	6 Mar	4.10/2 4.25/1 4.40/1 4.50/1 4.65/3 4.79/xx
4.65	1	EU23	Bydgoszcz	19 Jul	4.30/2 4.40/2 4.50/1 4.65/1 4.85/x
4.65	3	WCh	Saint-Denis	25 Aug	4.35/1 4.45/1 4.55/1 4.60/2 4.65/1 4.70/xx4.75/
4.63	1	DNG	Stockholm	5 Aug	4.33/1 4.43/1 4.53/1 4.63/1 4.79/xxx

4.80i	Svetlana	Feofanova	RUS	16.7.80	1	WI	Birmingham	16 Mar

4.35/1 4.45/1 4.55/2 4.60/1 4.65/1 4.70/1 4.75/1 4.80/2

4.77i	1	GP	Birmingham	21 Feb	4.40/1 4.50/1 4.60/2 4.70/1 4.77/2 4.82/xx
4.76i	1	v4N	Glasgow	2 Feb	4.35/1 4.45/1 4.55/1 4.65/3 4.76/1 4.82/x
4.75	1	WCh	Saint-Denis	25 Aug	4.35/1 4.45/1 4.55/1 4.60/1 4.65/1 4.70/2 4.75/1
4.73	2	GP	London (CP)	8 Aug	4.33/1 4.43/1 4.53/1 4.63/3 4.73/1 4.78/x 4.83/xx

Mark	Name		Nat	Born	Pos	Meet	Venue	Date
	4.72 1 GP	Villeneuve-d'Ascq	15 Jun	4.40/1 4.52/3 4.62/2 4.72/1 4.82/xxx				
	4.70 1 GP	Tríkala	24 Jun	4.40/1 4.50/1 4.60/1 4.70/1 ?				
	4.67i 1	Dortmund	5 Feb	4.41/1 4.51/1 4.61/1 4.67/2 4.77/xxx				
	4.65i 1 EICp	Leipzig	15 Feb	4.40/1 4.50/1 4.60/1 4.65/2 4.77/xxx				
4.78i	Stacy	Dragila	USA	25.3.71	1	NC	Boston (R)	2 Mar
				4.30/1 4.35/2 4.40/1 4.60/2 4.78/2 4.88/xxx				
	4.72i 1 Mill	New York	7 Feb	4.25/1 4.35/2 4.45/1 4.55/2 4.64/2 4.72/2 4.77/xxx				
	4.72iA 1	Pocatello	8 Mar	4.27/1 4.42/1 4.57/1 4.72/3 4.81/xxx				
	4.71i 1	Boston (R)	1 Feb	4.21/1 4.31/1 4.41/1 4.51/1 4.61/2 4.71/1 4.81/x 4.76/xxx				
	4.67iA 1	Pocatello	21 Feb	4.78/xxx				
4.70i	Tatyana	Polnova	RUS	20.4.79	1		Moskva	11 Feb
	4.70 1 GP	Ostrava	12 Jun	4.32/2 4.42/1 4.52/3 4.58/1 4.64/1 4.70/2				
	4.70 1 WUG	Daegu	27 Aug					
	4.68 1 WAF	Monaco	14 Sep	4.25/1 4.40/2 4.50/2 4.60/1 4.68/2 4.73/xxx				
	4.66i 1	Stockholm	18 Feb	4.16/1 4.26/1 4.36/2 4.46/1 4.56/1 4.66/1 4.77/xx				
4.70	Yvonne	Buschbaum	GER	14.7.80	1	NC	Ulm	29 Jun
				4.25/1 4.40/1 4.55/1 4.60/1 4.70/2 4.75/xx4.78/x				
	4.66 1	Salamanca	15 Jul	4.26/1 4.51/1 4.61/2 4.66/1 4.71/xxx				
	4.63 1	Cuxhaven	19 Jul	4.43/2 4.53/1 4.63/1 4.73/xx				
4.70	Annika	Becker	GER	12.11.81	2	WCh	Saint-Denis	25 Aug
				4.35/1 4.50/2 4.60/1 4.70/2 4.75/xx4.80/x				
	4.67i 1	Chemnitz	7 Feb	4.20/1 4.40/1 4.50/1 4.60/2 4.67/2 4.77/xxx				
	4.65 2 NC	Ulm	29 Jun	4.30/1 4.45/1 4.55/1 4.65/3 4.70/x 4.75/xx				
	4.63 3 GP	London (CP)	8 Aug	4.33/1 4.43/1 4.53/3 4.63/1 4.73/xxx				
	(33/6)							
4.60	Pavla	Hamácková	CZE	20.5.78	1	ECp-1B	Velenje	21 Jun
4.60	Monika	Pyrek	POL	11.8.80	3	GP	Tríkala	24 Jun
4.60	Melissa	Mueller	USA	16.11.72	1		Atascadero	9 Jul
4.60	Yelena	Belyakova	RUS	7.4.76	1	NC	Tula	10 Aug
	(10)							
4.58	Kellie	Suttle	USA	9.5.73	2		Poznan	29 Jun
4.51	Carolin	Hingst	GER	18.9.80	3		Salamanca	15 Jul
4.50i	Thórey Edda	Elisdóttir	ISL	30.6.77	3		Athína	6 Mar
4.50	Vanessa	Boslak	FRA	11.6.82	1	NC	Narbonne	26 Jul
4.47i	Anna	Rogowska	POL	21.5.81	1		Praha	19 Feb
4.47	Becky	Holliday	USA	12.3.80	1	NCAA-r	Stanford	30 May
4.45i	Monique	de Wilt	NED	21.3.76	1	NC	Gent	15 Feb
4.45i	Jillian	Schwartz	USA	19.9.79	3		Fayetteville	15 Feb
4.45i	Lacy	Janson	USA	20.2.83	1	NCAA	Fayetteville	15 Mar
4.45	Tanya	Koleva	BUL	8.3.72	2	ECp-1B	Velenje	21 Jun
	(20)							
4.45	Naroa	Agirre	ESP	15.5.79	1		Arona	26 Jul
4.41	Stephanie	McCann	CAN	22.4.77	2		Atascadero	9 Jul
4.40sq	Anna	Wielgus	POL	27.10.81	1		Ustron	11 May
	Not included by some statisticians, next:			4.32	5=	GS	Ostrava	12 Jun
4.40i	Agnès	Livebardon	FRA	31.5.80	1		Aubière	18 Jan
4.40i	Natalya	Kushch	UKR	5.3.83	1		Donetsk	15 Feb
4.40i	Krisztina	Molnár	HUN	8.4.76	1		Budapest	15 Feb
4.40i	Marie	Poissonnier	FRA	4.5.79	2	NC	Aubière	2 Mar
4.40	Melina	Hamilton	NZL	15.6.76	1		Gold Coast (RB)	12 Apr
4.40	Tracy	O'Hara	USA	20.7.80	1	MSR	Walnut	19 Apr
4.40	Mary	Sauer	USA	31.10.75	2=		Carson/Los Angeles	1 Jun
	(30)							
4.40	Yeoryía	Tsiliggíri	GRE	21.6.72	9	GP	Tríkala	24 Jun
4.40	Kirsten	Belin	SWE	2.5.81	1		Göteborg	4 Jul
4.40	Anastasiya	Ivanova	RUS	3.5.79	1		Moskva	14 Jul
4.40	Amy	Linnen	USA	15.7.82	1		Atascadero	23 Jul
4.40		Gao Shuying	CHN	28.10.79	1		Shijiazhuang	3 Aug
4.35i	Christine	Adams	GER	28.2.74	4	NC	Leipzig	23 Feb
4.35i	April	Steiner	USA	22.4.80	3	NCAA	Fayetteville	15 Mar
4.35	Alicia	Warlick	USA	11.10.77	1		Tucson	24 May
4.35	Dana	Cervantes	ESP	18.8.78	1		Valencia	14 Jun
4.33	Zsuzsanna	Szabó	HUN	6.5.73	5		Poznan	29 Jun
	(40)							
4.32	Floe	Kühnert	GER-J	6.3.84	1		Wipperfurth	24 May
4.32	Nastja	Ryshich	GER	19.9.77	5		Weissach im Tal	19 Jun
4.32	Anzhela	Balakhonova	UKR	18.12.72	6		Weissach im Tal	19 Jun
4.31	Alejandra	García	ARG	13.6.73	1		Buenos Aires	10 Dec
4.30Ai	Niki	McEwen-Reed	USA	1.4.80	1eB		Reno	17 Jan
4.30i	Sabine	Schulte	GER	29.1.76	6	NC	Leipzig	23 Feb
4.30	Yevgeniya	Katkova (Savina)	UKR	21.4.76	2		Bydgoszcz	8 Jun

Mark	Name		Nat	Born	Pos	Meet	Venue	Date
4.30	Yuliya	Golubchikova	RUS	27.3.83	1		Moskva	14 Jun
4.30	Connie	Jerz	USA	26.4.82	2	NCAA	Sacramento	14 Jun
4.30	Anna	Fitidou	CYP	22.4.77	1	GRE Ch	Tríkala	15 Jun
	(50)							
4.30	Dana	Ellis	CAN	7.12.78	5		Atascadero	25 Jun
4.30	Vala	Flosadóttír	ISL	16.2.78	2		Karlsruhe	23 Jul
4.30		Wu Sha	CHN-Y	21.10.87	2		Shijiazhuang	3 Aug
4.30	Carolina	Torres/Maurer	CHI	16.3.79	2	PAm	Santo Domingo	9 Aug
4.30	Nadine	Rohr	SUI	29.6.77	1		Baden	9 Aug
4.30	Kym	Howe	AUS	12.6.80	1		Melbourne	4 Dec
4.25i	Sandra	van der Geer	NED	25.5.72	2	NC	Gent	15 Feb
4.25i	Evridíki	Prezerákou	GRE	8.3.75	5		Athína (P)	6 Mar
4.25	Rosanna	Ditton	AUS	7.6.79	1		Melbourne	8 Mar
4.25	Afrodíti	Skafída	GRE	20.3.82	1	Veniz	Haniá	9 Jun
	(60)							
4.25	Chelsea	Johnson	USA	20.12.83	8	NC	Stanford	21 Jun
4.25	Thália	Iakovídou	GRE	10.9.72	1		Pírgos	27 Jul
4.25	Elisabete	Tavares	POR	7.3.80	4	WUG	Daegu	27 Aug
4.23	Andrea	DuToit	USA	28.2.78	1	Kans R	Lawrence	19 Apr
4.23	Tatiana	Grigorieva	AUS	8.10.75	4	MAI	Malmö	12 Aug
4.22i	Marie	Bagger-Bohn	DEN	1.11.72	7		Bad Oeynhausen	1 Mar
4.22	Kate	Soma	USA	13.2.83	2	NCAA-r	Stanford	30 May
4.22	Sárka	Mládková	CZE	30.8.76	8	GS	Ostrava	12 Jun
4.21i	Andrea	Wildrick	USA	23.12.79	6		Boston (R)	1 Feb
4.21	Masumi	Ono	JPN	5.12.75	1	NC	Yokohama	6 Jun
	(70)							
4.20i	Aleksandra	Kiryashova	RUS-J	21.8.85	2		Sankt Peterburg	6 Jan
4.20i	Fanni	Juhász	HUN	31.3.81	1		Chapel Hill	1 Feb
4.20i	Hanna-Mia	Persson	SWE	11.2.78	1		University Park	2 Feb
4.20i	Maria Carla	Bresciani	ITA	16.7.73	1		Reggio Emilia	6 Feb
4.20i	Shannon	Gallagher	USA	10.3.75	1		Kent	8 Feb
4.20i	Tünde	Vaszi	HUN	18.4.72	2		Budapest	15 Feb
4.20i	Lyudmila	Vaylenko	UKR	18.3.74	2		Donetsk	15 Feb
4.20i	Syrine	Balti	TUN	31.10.83	1		Bordeaux	22 Feb
4.20i	Silke	Spiegelburg	GER-Y	17.3.86	7	NC	Leipzig	23 Feb
4.20	Jenny	Dryburgh	NZL	30.8.78	1	NC	Dunedin	23 Mar
	(80)							
4.20	Adigóni	Asteríou	GRE	2.11.76	3		Athína (K)	3 May
4.20	Natalya	Belinskaya	RUS	21.1.83	2		Krasnodar	23 May
4.20	Katiuska	Pérez	CUB	21.12.75	1	NC	La Habana	29 May
4.20	Vera	Chavdarova	BUL	19.11.80	1		Plovdiv	31 May
4.20	Sandra	Tavares	POR	29.5.82	1		Paris (C)	31 May
4.20	Kira	Sims	USA	1.3.82	4	NCAA	Sacramento	14 Jun
4.20	Katalin	Donáth	HUN	12.11.79	1		Budapest	21 Jun
4.20	Martina	Strutz	GER	4.11.81	1		Mannheim	21 Jun
4.20	Anna	Schultze	GER-J	26.5.85	7=	NC	Ulm	29 Jun
4.20	Róza	Kasprzak	POL	9.4.82	2		Bydgoszcz	13 Jul
	(90)							
4.20		Zhao Yingying	CHN-Y	15.2.86	3		Shijiazhuang	3 Aug
4.20	Linda	Persson	SWE	22.9.81	1	v FIN	Helsinki	5 Sep
4.20		Zhang Na	CHN	27.9.80	3	NC	Shanghai	14 Sep
4.18	Kira	Costa	USA-J	18.3.85	1	G.West	Sacramento	15 Jun
4.17i	Stacie	Manuel	USA	6.12.83	1		Gainesville	2 Mar
4.17	Kelsie	Hendry	CAN	29.6.82	1		Saskatoon	12 Jul
4.15i	Teja	Melink	SLO	23.3.80	1		Ljubljana	1 Mar
4.15i	Jennifer	Bennett	USA	1.2.82	6=	NCAA	Fayetteville	15 Mar
4.15	Arianna	Farfaletti-Casali	ITA	22.6.76	1		Rovellasca	8 Jun
4.15	Yekaterina	Yashchenko	RUS	12.1.82	1	NC-23	Cheboksary	28 Jun
	(100)							
4.15	Ana	Rebenaque	ESP	15.9.83	Q	EU23	Bydgoszcz	13 Jul
4.15	Petra	Pechstein	SUI	26.7.71	5		Karlsruhe	23 Jul
4.15	Tracey	Bloomfield/Grant	GBR	13.9.79	1	NC	Birmingham	26 Jul

4.13i	Séverine	Phélippon	FRA	19.1.81	15 Feb
4.13	Julene	Bailey	USA-J	28.2.85	21 Jun
4.12	Debbie	Samson	USA	17.10.81	30 May
4.12	Dímitra	Emmanouíl	GRE-J	13.5.84	6 Jul
4.11i	Amandine	Homo	FRA	24.12.80	22 Mar
4.11A	Beth	Hinshaw	USA	30.7.81	16 May
4.11	Michaela	Boulová	CZE	2.8.81	29 Jun
4.11	Joanna	Piwowarska	POL	4.11.83	7 Sep
4.11i	Caroline	Bocquet	FRA	22.9.76	13 Dec
4.10i	Yulia	Lukinskaya	RUS	3.5.76	7 Jan
4.10i	Antonina	Miller	RUS	79	17 Jan
4.10i	Anastasia	Kiryanova	RUS	26.7.82	17 Jan
4.10i	Yekaterina	Sultanova	RUS-J	84	18 Jan
4.10i	Gaëlle	Delcourt	FRA	31.7.79	18 Jan
4.10i	Sandrine	Toulouse	FRA	14.9.72	18 Jan
4.10i	Nadine	Sonnabend	GER	10.9.80	26 Jan
4.10i	Irena	Dufour	BEL	1.6.78	16 Feb
4.10		Chang Ko-Hsin	TPE	20.6.80	12 Apr

Mark	Name		Nat	Born	Date
4.10	Jennifer	Culp	USA	26.10.81	12 Apr
4.10	Takayo	Kondo	JPN	17.11.75	26 Apr
4.10	Anna	Giordano Bruno	ITA	13.12.80	1 May
4.10	Tara	Clack	USA	7.3.80	9 May
4.10	Elise	Genévrier	FRA	27.6.83	25 May
4.10	Julie	Vigourt	FRA	19.10.79	31 May
4.10	Elizabeth	Metzinger	USA	16.6.79	11 Jun
4.10	Melissa	Pundt	USA	8.6.80	14 Jun
4.10	Lisa	Ryshich	GER-Y	27.9.88	21 Jun
4.10	Alla	Chechelyeva	RUS	1.7.81	28 Jun
4.10	Agnieszka	Wrona	POL	5.5.82	5 Jul
4.10	Mari Mar	Sánchez	ESP	25.12.79	22 Jul
4.10	Aurore	Pignot	FRA	24.12.79	26 Jul
4.10	Natalya	Menshenina	RUS	74	10 Aug
4.10	Yayoi	Minamino	JPN-J	10.7.85	27 Oct
4.07	Jill	Starkey	USA	7.3.71	25 Jun
4.06i	Lesa	Kubishta	USA	19.4.78	17 Jan
4.06i	Christi	Lehman	USA	8.8.83	8 Mar
4.06	Irie	Hill	GBR	16.1.69	30 Jul
4.06	Fabiana	Murer	BRA	16.3.81	6 Sep
4.05	Wendy	Young	AUS-J	18.3.84	8 Feb
4.05i	Jamie	Kollar	USA	18.10.83	15 Feb
4.05i	Saara	Laaksonen	FIN	7.2.82	22 Feb
4.05i	Kirsten	Riley	USA	8.3.82	8 Mar
4.05	Anne	Latvala	FIN	5.4.82	5 Jun
4.05	Paulina	Sigg	FIN	31.8.81	15 Jun
4.05	Karla	da Silva	BRA-J	12.11.84	6 Jul
4.05	Yulia	Taratynova	BLR	25.5.83	17 Jul
4.05	Sonia	Lawrence (150)	GBR	19.1.80	19 Jul
4.05i	Erica	Bartolina	USA	15.5.80	12 Dec
4.04	Jennifer	Green	USA-J	26.6.85	15 May
4.03Ai	Bridgid	Isworth	AUS	15.10.81	28 Feb
4.03i	Jessica	Graff	USA-J	12.1.84	1 Mar
4.02i	Stepahnie	Maugham	USA	29.9.77	22 Feb
4.02i	Christie	Elwin	AUS	4.6.81	2 Mar
4.02	Erin	Curtis	USA	19.7.83	5 Apr
4.02	Samantha	Shepard	USA	11.11.83	30 May
4.02	Shayla	Balentine	USA	7.8.82	30 May
4.02	Emily	Roberts	USA		30 May
4.02	Kellie	Kern	USA		31 May
4.02	Simona	Kovacs	CAN	20.7.80	31 May
4.02	Jirina	Ptácniková	CZE-Y	20.5.86	12 Jun
4.01i	Zoë	Brown	GBR	15.9.83	9 Feb
4.01i	Céline	Poissonier	FRA	4.5.79	22 Mar
4.01	Laura	Olson	USA		16 May
4.01	Kim	Marino	USA		22 May
4.01	Adrianne	Vangool	CAN-J	30.10.85	10 Jul
4.00i	Elizabeth	Spain	GBR	23.8.82	18 Jan
4.00i	Kierney	Hiteshew	USA	12.4.83	25 Jan
4.00i	Béatrice	Denis	FRA	18.6.72	25 Jan
4.00i	Mariya	Pastukhova	RUS-J	19.4.87	28 Jan
4.00i	Michelle	Legatt	USA	13.4.82	31 Jan
4.00i	Mami	Nakano	JPN	12.3.79	22 Feb
4.00i	Jaime	Volkmer	USA	21.7.81	22 Feb
4.00i	Teija	Saari	FIN	21.3.78	22 Feb
4.00i	Mariya	Smirnova	RUS	83	26 Feb
4.00	Annelie	van Wyk	RSA-J	28.5.84	15 Mar
4.00		Qin Xia	CHN	6.12.79	5 Apr
4.00		Yang Hong	CHN	2.2.78	8 Apr
4.00		Yu Shaomei	CHN	2.7.80	8 Apr
4.00	Rachele	Viau	USA-J	23.2.84	12 Apr
4.00	Shiho	Majima	JPN	8.1.82	26 Apr
4.00	Angela	Hilgers	USA	28.2.82	9 May
4.00	Sue	DeNigris	USA		9 May
4.00 sq	Katarzyna	Wierzbicka	POL-J	30.4.84	11 May
4.00A	Alejandra	Meza	MEX	18.7.78	16 May
4.00	Sarah	Semeraro	ITA	10.10.82	25 May
4.00	Pamela	Azzolini	ITA	15.7.82	31 May
4.00	Katerina	Badurová	CZE	18.12.82	31 May
4.00	Dennise	Orengo	PUR		14 Jun
4.00	Milena	Agudelo	COL-J	15.4.85	20 Jun
4.00	Elizabeth	Hughes	GBR	9.6.77	21 Jun
4.00	Marie Emilie	Montagut	FRA-J	16.6.85	21 Jun
4.00	Simone	Langhirt	GER-J	19.1.84	21 Jun
4.00	Anna	Huculak	POL-J	31.7.84	29 Jun
4.00	Aurélie	Clerc	FRA	13.4.83	10 Jul
4.00	Lindsay	Taylor	USA	9.2.79	12 Jul
4.00	Svetlana	Makarevich	BLR-Y	5.3.86	13 Jul
4.00	Charmaine	Lucock	AUS-Y	8.4.87	13 Jul
4.00	Kim	Kühnert	GER-Y	9.5.88	13 Jul
4.00	Hanna	Palamaa	FIN	8.9.77	30 Jul
4.00	Slavica	Semenjuk	SCG-J	25.10.84	1 Aug
4.00	Anita	Tørring	DEN	19.1.79	10 Aug
4.00		Yang Jing	CHN-J	1.1.84	28 Aug
4.00		Feng Lingjian	CHN	28.4.83	26 Oct
4.00	Akane	Eguchi	JPN	20.6.76	2 Nov
4.00i	Liesbet	Van Roie (207)	BEL	20.1.81	20 Dec

Best outdoor marks

Mark	Name	Pos	Meet	Venue	Date
4.62	Dragila	1	Drake	Des Moines	26 Apr
4.48sq	Elisdóttir	1		Recklinghausen	30 May
	4.43	3		Cuxhaven	19 Jul
4.45	Schwartz	2		Jonesboro	28 May
4.45	Rogowska	1		Bydgoszcz	13 Jul
4.40	M Poissonnier	4=		Villeneuve d'Ascq	15 Jun
4.40	Kushch	3	ECp1B	Velenje	21 Jun
4.37	Janson	1	Fla R	Gainesville	29 Mar
4.30	Livebardon	6		Villeneuve d'Ascq	15 Jun
4.30	Molnár	12	GP	Tríkala	24 Jun
4.30	McEwen-Reed	4		Atascadero	25 Jun
4.30	Adams	3	NC	Ulm	29 Jun
4.27	Steiner	1	PennR	Philadelphia	24 Apr
4.25	Prezerákou	2		Athína (K)	3 May
4.21	Bagger-Bohn	4=	Odl	Praha	29 Jun
4.20	Wildrick	1		Lubbock	3 May
4.20	Juhász	3	NCAA	Sacramento	14 Jun
4.20	van der Geer	4	ECp1B	Velenje	21 Jun
4.17	Gallagher	1		Jonesboro	24 May
4.15	Spiegelburg	1	EJ	Tampere	26 Jul
4.15	Kiryashova	3	EJ	Tampere	26 Jul

Mark	Name	Date
4.12	Bennett	30 May
4.10	Manuel	12 Apr
4.10	Delcourt	3 May
4.10	Balti	13 Jun
4.10	Schulte	29 Jun
4.10	Kiryanova	14 Jul
4.05	Kubishta	16 May
4.05	Melink	10 Sep
4.02	Lehman	30 May
4.02	Elwin	31 May
4.02	H-M Persson	19 Jun
4.00	Nakano	12 Apr
4.00	Vaylenko	2 May
4.00	Phélippon	11 May
4.00	Miller	15 May
4.00	Sonnabend	29 May
4.00	Vaszi	7 Jun
4.00	C Poissonier	13 Jun
4.00	Pastukhova	19 Jun
4.00	Denis	20 Jul
4.00	Z Brown	2 Aug
4.00	Bresciani	30 Aug
	4.10 exhibition	7 Sep

JUNIORS

See main list for top 7 juniors. 7 performances by 2 women to 4.21. Additional mark and further juniors:

Kühnert	4.30i	6=		Stuuttgart	2 Feb
	4.30i	5	NC	Leipzig	23 Feb
	4.30	2		Kassel	13 Jun
	4.30	1		Mannheim	21 Jun
	4.21	9	GP	Sevilla	7 Jun

Mark	Name		Nat	Born	Pos	Meet	Venue	Date
4.13	Julene	Bailey	USA	28.2.85	1	NC-j	Stanford	21 Jun
4.12	Dímitra	Emmanouíl	GRE	13.5.84	1	NC-j	Kórinthos	6 Jul
4.10i	Yekaterina	Sultanova (10)	RUS	84	1		Ludwigshafen	18 Jan
4.10	Lisa	Ryshich	GER-Y	27.9.88	1		Mannheim	21 Jun
4.10	Yayoi	Minamino	JPN	10.7.85	1	NG	Fukuroi	27 Oct
4.05	Wendy	Young	AUS	18.3.84	2		Perth	8 Feb
4.05	Karla	da Silva	BRA	12.11.84	1		São Paulo	6 Jul
4.04	Jennifer	Green	USA	26.6.85	1		Grand Island	15 May
4.03i	Jessica	Graff	USA	12.1.84	1		Gainesville	1 Mar

Mark	Wind	Name		Nat	Born	Pos	Meet	Venue	Date
4.02		Jirina	Ptácniková	CZE-Y	20.5.86	10=	GS	Ostrava	12 Jun
4.01		Adrianne	Vangool	CAN	30.10.85	1		Saskatoon	10 Jul
4.00		13 women – see above							

LONG JUMP

Mark	Wind	Name		Nat	Born	Pos	Meet	Venue	Date
7.06	0.8	Maurren	Maggi ¶	BRA	25.6.76	1		Milano	3 Jun
					6.65 7.06 6.80/1.0 6.98/0.4 x 6.84/0.0				
6.95	0.8	1 Veniz	Haniá	9 Jun	x 6.88/0.8 6.84/0.9 p 6.85/0.2 6.95				
6.94	0.2	1 Neb	Torino	6 Jun	6.52 6.94 6.78/0.0 p p p				
6.90	1.1	1	São Caetano do Sul	27 Apr	x 6.81 6.82 6.90 p p				
6.80	0.3	1	Belém	4 May	6.69 4.45 6.62 6.80 x 6.65				
7.05	-0.4	Eunice	Barber	FRA	17.11.74	1	WAF	Monaco	14 Sep
					x 6.75/-0.5 6.80/1.1 7.05 four only				
6.99	0.4	1 WCh	Saint-Denis	30 Aug	6.52 6.74/0.1 x 6.48 x 6.99				
6.80	2.0	1H	Arles	8 Jun	6.80 p p				
6.78	0.0	Q WCh	Saint-Denis	28 Aug	6.78 only jump				
6.76	0.5	1 ECpS	Firenze	22 Jun	6.59 6.72/0.7 6.55 6.76 four only				
6.94	1.2	Tatyana	Kotova	RUS	11.12.76	1		Réthimno	6 Jul
					x 6.94 6.86/1.6 6.91/1.4 6.87/1.9 x				
6.92	-0.3	2 WAF	Monaco	14 Sep	x 6.63 6.92 x four only				
6.88	0.7	1	Luzern	25 Jun	6.71/0.7 6.88 6.60 x x p				
6.84i		1 WI	Birmingham	16 Mar	6.84 x 6.68 6.81 x x				
6.82	1.5	* v2N	Glasgow (S)	29 Jun	see below				
6.78	0.3	2 NC	Tula	9 Aug	6.78 6.77 x 5.08 x x				
6.94w	3.8	2 v2N	Glasgow	29Jun	6.85w/3.3 6.77w/3.0 x 6.61w 6.94w 6.82				
6.89	1.3	Olga	Rublyova	RUS	28.10.74	1	NC	Tula	9 Aug
					6.89 x x p x x				
6.86	0.5	Carolina	Klüft	SWE	2.2.83	1	EU23	Bydgoszcz	19 Jul
					x 6.77/0.9 x x 6.86 x				
6.77	0.2	1H	ECp-1	Tallinn 6 Jul	6.55 6.77 x				
6.83	0.0	Elva	Goulbourne	JAM	21.1.80	1	SEC	Knoxville	17 May
6.81i		1 NCAA	Fayetteville	14 Mar	6.81 p p p p p				
6.81	0.3	* CAC	St George's	5 Jul					
6.77	0.9	1 ISTAF	Berlin (P)	10 Aug	6.44 6.44 6.31 6.68w 6.77 6.41				
6.76	-0.1	1 NCAA	Sacramento	13 Jun	6.32 4.93 6.76 6.69w x 6.51				
6.83	1.2	Irina	Simagina	RUS	25.5.82	1	NC-23	Cheboksary	28 Jun
					6.77/1.9 6.61 6.83 6.25 6.57 x				
6.82	-0.5	Tatyana	Lebedeva	RUS	21.7.76	1		Moskva	20 Sep
					6.64 6.82 6.63 6.71/-0.2				
6.80i		Stilianí	Pilátou	GRE	28.3.80	1	Balk	Athína (P)	4 Mar
					x 6.80 6.54 x p p				
6.79i		Inessa	Kravets (10)	UKR	5.10.66	1	NC	Sumy	23 Feb
					6.79 p p p p p				
6.76		1	Kiev	20 Jun	6.37 6.76 p p x p				
6.76	1.1	1 GP	Madrid (C)	19 Jul	x 6.53 x 6.38 6.76 6.41				
6.78i		Concepción	Montaner	ESP	14.1.81	1	NC	Valencia	1 Mar
					x 6.78 6.69 x 5.31 6.52				
6.78	1.9	Aisha	James	TRI	12.3.81	1	DrakeR	Des Moines	26 Apr
					6.66w 6.61 6.78 6.28 x x				
6.78	2.0	Oksana	Udmurtova	RUS	.82	2	NC-23	Cheboksary	28 Jun
					6.69 6.78 x p x p				
6.76	-0.1	Irina	Melnikova- 2	RUS	12.10.75	1	Znam	Tula	8 Jun
					6.60 x 6.59 6.63 6.76 6.53				
6.76	1.8	Níki	Xánthou	GRE	11.10.73	2		Réthimno	6 Jul
					6.76 x. 6.70/1.2 6.30 6.41 x				
6.76	0.0	Tünde	Vaszi	HUN	18.4.72	1		Córdoba	6 Sep
					6.32 x 6.76 x 6.62 6.56				
		(36/16)							
6.74	0.9	Déspina	Papavasiláki	GRE	24.3.73	2	Veniz	Haniá	9 Jun
6.74	0.2	Lyudmila	Galkina	RUS	20.1.72	1		Moskva	14 Jul
6.74	2.0	Tatyana	Ter-Mesrobyan	RUS	12.5.68	3	NC	Tula	9 Aug
6.73	1.6	Bronwyn	Thompson	AUS	29.1.78	1		Brisbane	8 Mar
		(20)							
6.73	0.5	Grace	Upshaw	USA	22.9.75	1		Rovereto	10 Sep
6.72	0.4		Guan Yingnan	CHN	25.4.77	1		Nanning	20 Jun
6.71	1.1	Valentina	Gotovska	LAT	3.9.65	1	NC	Riga	2 Aug
6.70	1.8	Ineta	Radevica	LAT	13.7.81	3	EU23	Bydgoszcz	19 Jul
6.70	1.2	Anju Bobby	George	IND	19.4.77	3	WCh	Saint-Denis	30 Aug
6.69	0.7	Bianca	Kappler	GER	8.8.77	1		Dortmund	15 Jun
6.69	0.5	Anastasiya	Zhuravlyeva	UZB	9.10.81	1		Almaty	21 Jun
6.69	1.0	Yudelkis	Fernández	CUB-J	28.2.85	1		La Habana	28 Jun

Mark	Wind	Name		Nat	Born	Pos	Meet	Venue	Date
6.69	1.5	Jade	Johnson	GBR	7.6.80	2	GP	Madrid (C)	19 Jul
6.69	0.5	Olivia	Wöckinger	AUT	23.5.79	1		Ebensee	2 Aug
		(30)							
6.68	2.0	Maho	Hanaoka	JPN	3.8.76	*		Mito	5 May
6.68	0.0	Jackie	Edwards	BAH	14.4.71	1		Hamburg	20 Jul
6.67		Yelena	Shekhovtsova	UKR	31.5.72	2		Kiev	20 Jun
6.67	1.5	Fiona	May	ITA	12.12.69	3	ECp-S	Firenze	22 Jun
6.65i		Tatyana	Ivanova	RUS	16.10.81	1		Sankt-Peterburg	27 Dec
6.64	0.8	Kumiko	Ikeda	JPN	10.1.81	1	NC	Yokohama	7 Jun
6.63i		Viktoriya	Vershinina	UKR	11.6.71	2		Zaporozhye	2 Mar
6.63	0.7	Yargelis	Savigne	CUB-J	13.11.84	1		La Habana	7 Mar
6.63	1.5	Johanna	Halkoaho	FIN	13.1.77	1		Lapinlahti	13 Jul
6.62i		Adina	Anton	ROM-J	6.10.84	1	NC	Bucuresti	22 Feb
		(40)							
6.62	0.6	Yelena	Kashcheyeva	KAZ	17.2.73	1		Hyderabad	28 May
6.61i		Inna	Ivlyeva	RUS	27.6.71	1		Novocheboksarsk	18 Jan
6.61i		Liliana	Zagacka	POL	28.1.77	1	NC	Spala	1 Mar
6.61	1.3	Svetlana	Zaytseva	RUS	14.8.81	4	NC-23	Cheboksary	28 Jun
6.61	1.3		Xu Bei	CHN	2.1.83	1	NG	Changsha	25 Oct
6.60	1.2	Adrien	Sawyer	USA	13.12.75	1		College Station	12 Apr
6.60		Yelena	Donkina	RUS	15.3.73	1		Moskva	15 May
6.60	0.0	Viktoriya	Molchanova	UKR	26.5.82	1		Kharkov	17 May
6.60	1.1	Sofia	Schulte	GER	8.4.76	2		Wesel	9 Jun
6.60	-0.2	Sophie	Krauel	GER-J	2.3.85	1		Mannheim	21 Jun
		(50)							
6.60	0.0	Alina	Militaru	ROM	10.4.82	Q	EU23	Bydgoszcz	18 Jul
6.59	1.6	Brianna	Glenn	USA	18.4.80	1		Tucson	24 May
6.59	0.0	Éva	Miklós	HUN	30.7.78	1		Zalaegerszeg	14 Jun
6.59	0.3	Malgorzata	Trybanska	POL	21.6.81	Q	EU23	Bydgoszcz	18 Jul
6.58i		Livia	Pruteanu	ROM	22.12.81	1		Bucuresti	8 Feb
6.58	1.1	Ola	Sesay	USA	30.5.79	2		Sacramento	8 Jun
6.58	1.7	Kelly	Sotherton	GBR	13.11.76	2H	ECp-1	Tallinn	6 Jul
6.58	0.2	Esther	Aghatise	NGR-J	15.4.85	1	AfG	Abuja	15 Oct
6.57i		Natalya	Sazanovich	BLR	15.8.73	1P		Minsk	29 Jan
6.57	1.7	Viktoriya	Rybalko	UKR	26.10.82	2	PennR	Philadelphia	24 Apr
		(60)							
6.57	2.0	Alice	Falaiye	CAN	24.12.78	*		College Station	8 May
6.57	0.5	Aurélie	Félix	FRA	26.3.79	1		Reims	16 Jul
6.57	0.2	Kylie	Wheeler	AUS	17.1.80	H	WUG	Daegu	26 Aug
6.56	0.5	Nadezhda	Bazhenova	RUS	22.9.78	4	Znam	Tula	8 Jun
6.56		Colleen	Scott	JAM	18.8.74	2	NC	Kingston	19 Jun
6.56	1.2	Tina	Carman	SLO	8.1.78	1		Dolenjske Toplice	5 Jul
6.56	0.6	Grace	Umelo	NGR	.78	2	AfG	Abuja	15 Oct
6.55		Yuliya	Ignatkina	RUS	13.9.82	1H	NC	Tula	3 Aug
6.54i		Yelena	Shchinova	RUS	.80	2		Novocheboksarsk	18 Jan
6.54i		Irina	Porfiriadi	RUS	14.10.79	1		Samara	26 Jan
		(70)							
6.54	1.2	Kène	Ndoye	SEN	20.11.78	-		Dakar	4 Apr
6.53		Kadiatou	Camara	MLI	4.5.81	1		Bamako	6 Apr
6.53	1.1	Naide	Gomes	POR	10.11.79	2	ECCp	Valencia	25 May
6.53	1.6	Urszula	Gutowicz-Westhof	POL	13.7.77	3		Wesel	9 Jun
6.52i		Katja	Keller	GER	9.8.80	2	NC	Leipzig	22 Feb
6.52	1.7	Antoinette	Wilks	USA	14.10.80	1		Columbia	22 Mar
6.52	0.3	Keila	Costa	BRA	6.2.83	2	NC	São Paulo	15 Jun
6.52	1.7	Kristina	Zumer	SLO	2.2.80	2		Dolenjske Toplice	5 Jul
6.52	-0.9	Chinedu	Odozor	NGR	24.12.77	3	AfG	Abuja	15 Oct
6.51	0.0	Hyleas	Fountain	USA	14.1.81	2	SEC	Knoxville	17 May
		(80)							
6.51	0.2		Liang Shuyan	CHN	16.9.77	2	AsiC	Manila	21 Sep
6.51	0.8	Yelena	Prokhorova	RUS	16.4.78	H		Talence	21 Sep
6.50	1.1	Kerrie	Perkins/Taurima	AUS	2.4.79	2	NC	Brisbane	5 Apr
6.50	-0.1	Katja	Umlauft	GER	22.11.74	4		Wesel	9 Jun
6.50	-0.3	Rose	Richmond	USA	29.1.81	*	NC	Stanford	21 Jun
6.50	-0.1	Lerma Elvira	Gabito	PHI	17.10.74	3	AsiC	Manila	21 Sep
6.49i		Viktoriya	Gurova	RUS	22.5.82	2		Shakhty	19 Jan
6.49i			Huang Jianfen	CHN	10.10.78	1	vJPN	Yokohama	22 Feb
6.49	1.5	Sharifa	Jones	USA	16.11.82	2		Tucson	24 May
6.49	1.2	Natalia	Kilpeläinen	FIN	19.7.70	1		Lahti	2 Jul
		(90)							
6.49	1.1	Bianca	Dürr	AUT	12.11.76	1		Illertissen	12 Jul
6.48	0.5	Luciana	dos Santos	BRA	10.2.70	1		São Caetano do Sul	31 May

Mark	Wind	Name		Nat	Born	Pos	Meet	Venue	Date
6.48	1.1	Tameisha	King	USA	24.2.81	*	NCAA	Sacramento	13 Jun
6.48	-1.2	Antoniya	Yordanova	BUL	17.8.76	1		Plovdiv	5 Jul
6.47	0.0	Zita	Ajkler	HUN	9.6.75	1		Budapest	12 Jul
6.47	0.7	Svetlana	Semyonova	RUS	16.3.79	3		Moskva	14 Jul
6.46i		Adrija	Parsukova (Grociene)	LTU	25.7.74	1		Vilnius	15 Jan
6.46i		Anna	Kovalenko	RUS	3.2.80	1		Moskva	15 Feb
6.46	1.4	Kim	Jones	USA	13.6.81	1		Raleigh	18 Apr
6.46	0.8	Irene (100)	Charalambous	CYP	18.5.78	1		Nicosia	1 May
6.46	1.0	Asimína	Vanakára	GRE	14.7.79	1		Lárisa	3 May
6.46		Olena	Shchors	UKR-J	6.3.84	1		Belaya Tserkov	3 Jun
6.46	0.2	Akiba	McKinney	USA	9.3.79	1		Walnut	13 Jul

6.45	0.0	Cameal	Rhule	JAM	12.5.80	17 May
6.45	1.3	Tatyana	Obukhova	UKR	15.1.78	24 May
6.45		Irina	Nikolayeva	UKR-J	10.1.84	11 Jun
6.45	-1.6	Jenny	Adams	USA	8.7.78	21 Jun
6.45	0.0	Yekaterina	Chernyavskaya	UKR	31.1.83	22 Jun
6.45	0.9	Natalya	Sorokina	UKR	24.3.75	4 Jul
6.45	0.0	Laura	Gatto	ITA	4.3.77	20 Jul
6.45	1.9	Daniela	Lincoln-Saavedra	SWE-J	4.8.84	3 Aug
6.44i		Patricia	Soman	CIV	12.8.81	21 Feb
6.44i		Krysha	Bayley	CAN-J	21.1.84	1 Mar
6.44	1.6	Gina	Harris	USA	6.2.81	3 May
6.44		Zhanna	Demidova	UKR-Y	8.4.87	3 Jun
6.44	0.1	Nolle	Graham	USA	12.9.81	11 Jun
6.44	0.3	Claudia	Tonn	GER	18.4.81	18 Jul
6.43i		Kathrin	Geissler	GER-J	10.6.85	9 Feb
6.43	1.8	Françoise	Mbango	CMR	14.4.76	4 Apr
6.43	-0.5	Sirkka-Liisa	Kivine	EST	22.6.77	17 Jun
6.43	1.0	Yuliya	Akulenko	UKR	3.6.77	4 Jul
6.43i		Lyudmila	Kolchanova	RUS	1.10.79	23 Dec
6.42	1.7	Dana	Veldáková	SVK	3.6.81	19 Apr
6.42	0.1	April	Holliness	USA	27.5.82	13 Jun
6.42		Kedine	Geddes	JAM-J	28.2.84	19 Jun
6.41i		Lucie	Komrsková	CZE	24.10.77	19 Feb
6.41	1.5	Sharon	Sutherland	AUS	10.3.77	5 Apr
6.41	1.3	Shermin	Oksuz	AUS-J	24.3.84	12 Apr
6.41A	1.6	LaVada	Hill	USA	16.7.81	16 May
6.41	-0.8	Yuleidis	Limonta	CUB	14.3.82	29 May
6.41	1.0	Déborah	Grapotte	FRA	2.4.78	13 Jun
6.41	2.0	Irina	Chernushenko	BLR	9.3.79	11 Jul
6.41	1.7	Cristine	Spîtaru	ROM-Y	4.2.86	13 Jul
6.40i		Anna	Pyatykh	RUS	4.4.81	7 Jan
6.40i		Meredith	Davis	USA	9.6.79	8 Feb
6.40i		Martina	Darmovzalová	CZE	12.10.78	2 Mar
6.40i		Marie	Collonvillé	FRA	23.11.73	14 Mar
6.40	2.0	Panayióta	Koutsioumári	GRE	23.3.81	9 Jun
6.40	0.7	Kathrin	van Bühren	GER	29.5.82	9 Jun
6.40	0.1	Yelena	Bobrovskaya	KGZ	11.4.75	28 Jun
6.40	1.0	Denisa	Scerbová	CZE-Y	21.8.86	13 Jul
6.40	0.0		Wang Lina	CHN	28.2.83	25 Oct
6.39i		Katarzyna	Klisowska	POL	2.2.83	1 Mar
6.39	0.9	Monique	Freeman	USA	1.7.77	21 Jun
6.39	1.0	Susanna	Rajamäki	FIN	19.9.79	6 Jul
6.38i		Heli	Koivula-Kruger	FIN	27.6.75	10 Feb
6.38i		Yelena	Ivanova	RUS	16.3.79	1 Mar
6.38i		Angel	Heath	USA	28.1.80	1 Mar
6.38	1.5		Jin Yan	CHN	20.4.82	20 Apr
6.38	0.6	Keisha	Spencer (150)	JAM	16.2.78	26 Apr
6.38		Yekaterina	Zasemko	RUS	82	17 May
6.38	1.7	Baya	Rahouli	ALG	27.7.79	18 May
6.38	2.0	Renee	Dunn	USA		30 May
6.37i		Irina	Yermolayeva	RUS	14.10.79	18 Jan
6.37	-0.9	Chi-Chi	Aduba	USA	26.8.82	28 Mar
6.37	0.3	Pamela	Simpson	USA	28.4.77	19 Apr
6.37	1.7	Chelsea	Hammond	USA	2.8.83	25 Apr
6.37	0.8	Aldona	Wozignój	POL	13.9.81	3 May
6.37	0.9	Sonja	Kesselschläger	GER	20.1.78	1 Jun
6.37	2.0	Bozena	Trzcinska	POL	24.10.76	9 Jun
6.37		Mariya	Kirichenko	KAZ	10.7.82	13 Jun
6.36i		Stephanie	Sowell	USA		21 Feb
6.36		Hrisopiyí	Devetzí	GRE	2.1.76	4 May
6.36	-0.3	Jessica	DeFreitas	USA	11.11.80	7 Jun
6.36	0.2	Angela	Dies	GER-J	16.3.84	21 Jun
6.36	0.3		Huo Weiwei	CHN	14.1.81	4 Jul
6.36	-1.7	Olga	Zaytseva	RUS-J	10.11.84	16 Jul
6.36	-0.4	Katalin	Deák	HUN	4.3.68	27 Jul
6.36		Anastasiya	Ilyina	RUS	16.1.82	7 Aug
6.36		J.J.	Shobha	IND	14.1.78	14 Oct
6.36i		Yelena	Ivlyeva	RUS	74	20 Dec
6.35i		Tongula	Givens	USA	3.3.73	11 Jan
6.35i			Chen Yaling	CHN-J	24.2.84	17 Feb
6.35i			Guo Chunfang	CHN	4.1.79	18 Feb
6.35i		Oksana	Titenko	UKR	7.10.77	22 Feb
6.35	0.4	Larisa	Netseporuk	EST	24.12.70	6 Jul
6.35	0.2	Julie	Hollman	GBR	16.2.77	6 Jul
6.35	0.9	Yah	Koita	MLI	23.9.80	25 Jul
6.35	0.5	Olga	Salazhenkova	RUS	76	26 Jul
6.34i		Olga	Alekseyeva	KAZ-J	30.11.84	12 Feb
6.34		Manuela	Witting	AUT	9.8.80	24 May
6.34	0.0	Wacharee	Ritthiwat	THA	18.10.76	5 Jun
6.34	1.0	Tiffany	Greer	USA	8.6.81	13 Jun
6.34	0.2	Marestella	Torres	PHI	20.2.81	21 Sep
6.33i		Vesna	Kostic	SCG	15.8.79	28 Feb
6.33i		Kiamesha	Otey	USA	28.5.81	2 Mar
6.33	0.0	Sharianne	Lawson	USA	25.7.80	12 Apr
6.33	1.2	Liga	Klavina	LAT	27.1.80	1 Jun
6.33	1.9	Christelle	Préau	FRA	3.11.81	13 Jun
6.33	1.8	Denise	Lewis	GBR	27.8.72	6 Jul
6.33	0.3	Irina	Butor (191)	BLR	26.2.80	6 Jul

Wind assisted

6.99	4.9	Grace	Upshaw	USA	22.9.75	1	v2N	Glasgow (S)	29 Jun
					6.92w/4.9 6.81w/3.5 6.99w 6.73w/2.6 6.94w/3.8 6.67w/2.1				
6.96	2.6	Elva	Goulbourne	JAM	21.1.80	1	CAC	St George's	5 Jul
					& 6.81				
6.83	3.4		Upshaw			1		Sacramento	8 Jun
					6.83w 6.61w 6.51 6.54 6.61 6.69				
6.77	3.7	Jade	Johnson	GBR	7.6.80	3	v2N	Glasgow (S)	29 Jun
					6.50w x x 6.49w 6.77w 6.55w				
6.75	3.2	Bronwyn	Thompson	AUS	29.1.78	1		Melbourne	1 Mar
6.69	2.8	Maho	Hanaoka	JPN	3.8.76	1		Mito	5 May
6.68	4.0	Kelly	Sotherton	GBR	13.11.76	4	v2N	Glasgow (S)	29 Jun
6.67A	6.9	Alice	Falaiye	CAN	24.12.78	1	WAC	El Paso	17 May
6.66	3.5	Keisha	Spencer	JAM	16.2.78	1		College Station	8 May
6.65	4.2	Johanna	Halkoaho	FIN	13.1.77	1	NC	Helsinki	10 Aug
6.65	2.3		Liang Shuyan	CHN	16.9.77	1	NC	Shanghai	12 Sep
6.64	2.9	Tatyana	Ivanova	RUS	16.10.81	3	NC-23	Cheboksary	28 Jun
6.62	3.2	Kène	Ndoye	SEN	20.11.78	1		Dakar	4 Apr
6.61	2.2	Tameisha	King	USA	24.2.81	1		Storrs	3 May
6.60	3.4	Patricia	Soman	CIV	12.8.81	2	NCAA-r	Columbus	30 May

Mark	Wind	Name		Nat	Born	Pos	Meet	Venue	Date
6.56	2.6	Rose	Richmond	USA	29.1.81	2	NC	Stanford	21 Jun
6.47	2.9	April	Holliness	USA	27.5.82	1		Waco	19 Apr
6.47	2.7	Jenny	Adams	USA	8.7.78	3	DrakeR	Des Moines	26 Apr
6.47	2.1	Sunna	Gestsdóttir	ISL	27.6.76	1		Borgarnes	26 Jul

6.46	3.3	Shermin	Oksuz	AUS-J	24.3.84	15 Feb
6.46	3.1	Laura	Gatto	ITA	4.3.77	18 May
6.44	6.5	Pamela	Simpson	USA	28.4.77	10 May
6.44	4.7	Renee	Dunn	USA		30 May
6.42	4.0	Monique	Freeman	USA	1.7.77	8 May
6.42	3.5	LaVada	Hill	USA	16.7.81	30 May
6.42	2.8	Lúzia Maria	Teodoro	BRA	25.7.78	6 See
6.41	2.1	LaToya	Payne	USA	5.1.83	30 May
6.41	2.5	Carlota	Castrejana	ESP	25.4.73	19 Jul
6.40	5.9	Ychlindria	Spears	USA-J	17.7.84	30 May
6.39	2.6	Gisele	de Oliveira	BRA	1.8.80	10 May
6.37	3.9	Peta-Gaye	Beckford	JAM-J	17.4.85	28 Feb
6.37	3.9	Vesna	Kostic	SCG	15.8.79	30 May
6.37	2.6	Liga	Klavina	LAT	27.1.80	12 Jun
6.36	3.4	Shameka	Marshall	USA	9.9.83	3 May
6.36	2.3	Sachiko	Masumi	JPN-J	20.12.84	3 May
6.36	2.1	Tiffany	Greer	USA	8.6.81	17 May
6.35	3.2	Elysée	Vésanes	FRA-J	25.1.84	5 Apr
6.34	3.1	Beyonka	McDowell	USA	19.9.82	8 Jun

Best outdoor marks

6.69	0.6	Montaner	2	ECp-S	Firenze	22 Jun
		6.70w 3.4	1		Arona	26 Jul
6.60	0.0	Anton	1	RomIC	Bucuresti	8 Jun
6.57	0.3	Pilátou	2	NC	Tríkala	15 Jun
		6.63w 3.8	2		Athína (E)	17 May
6.56	0.0	Pruteanu	2	RomIC	Bucuresti	8 Jun
6.49	1.8	Ivanova	*	NC-23	Cheboksary	28 Jun
6.49	0.8	Huang Jianfen	1		Shijiazhuang	4 Aug
6.47	0.0	Sazanovich	3H	WCh	Saint-Denis	24 Aug
6.61w	2.6	Zagacka	1	NC	Bielsko-Biala	5 Jul

6.42	1.3	Ivlyeva	8 Jun
6.41	0.8	Komrsková	3 Jun
6.41		Zagacka	28 Aug
6.38	1.9	Bayley	29 Mar
6.38	2.0	Soman	26 Apr
6.38	0.6	Keller	9 Jun
6.38		Pyatykh	7 Aug
6.36	0.2	Klisowska	18 Jul
6.36	1.0	Vershinina	4 Jul
		6.44w 2.3	3 Jul
6.35	-0.7	Chen Yaling	25 Oct
6.33	1.7	Sowell	18 May
		6.34w 2.3	4 Apr

Drugs disqualification

6.51	-0.2	Lyudmila	Blonskaya ¶	UKR	18.3.75	H	ECp	Bressanone	5 Jul
6.41		Olga	Basayeva #	RUS-J	.84	1	NC-j	Kazan	2 Jul

JUNIORS

See main list for top 6 juniors. 12 performances by 5 women to 6.53 Additional marks and further juniors:

Fernández	6.59		1	NC-j	Santiago de C	7 Aug	6.53	-2.4	1	NC	La Habana	29 May
Savigne	6.54	0.6	1		La Habana	28 Feb						
Anton 2+	6.55	0.0	2	NC	Bucuresti	10 Aug						
Krauel	6.56i		1		Chemnizt	7 Feb	6.56	0.0	1		Wesel	9 Jun

6.45		Irina	Nikolayeva	UKR	10.1.84	1		Belaya Tserkov	11 Jun
6.45	1.9	Daniela	Lincoln-Saavedra	SWE	4.8.84	1	NC	Norrtälje	3 Aug
6.44i		Krysha	Bayley	CAN	21.1.84	2		Gainesville	1 Mar
		6.38	1.9			1		Athens, GA	29 Mar
6.44		Zhanna	Demidova (10)	UKR-Y	8.4.87	2		Belaya Tserkov	3 Jun
6.43i		Kathrin	Geissler	GER	10.6.85	1P	NC-j	Neubrandenburg	9 Feb
6.42		Kedine	Geddes	JAM	28.2.84	1	NC-j	Kingston	19 Jun
6.41	1.3	Shermin	Oksuz	AUS	24.3.84	3		Gold Coast (RB)	12 Apr
6.41	1.7	Cristine	Spîtaru	ROM-Y	4.2.86	1	WY	Sherbrooke	13 Jul
6.40	1.0	Denisa	Scerbová	CZE-Y	21.8.86	2	WY	Sherbrooke	13 Jul
6.36	0.2	Angela	Dies	GER	16.3.84	2		Mannheim	21 Jun
6.36	-1.7	Olga	Zaytseva	RUS	10.11.84	H		Sankt Peterburg	16 Jul
6.35i			Chen Yaling	CHN	24.2.84	2		Tianjin	17 Feb
		6.35	-0.7			3	NG	Changsha	25 Oct
6.34i		Olga	Alekseyeva	KAZ	30.11.84	1		Moskva	12 Feb
6.32A	0.0	Yuridia	Bustamante (20)	MEX	10.1.84	2		Ciudad de México	3 May
6.32	0.0	Elysée	Vésanes	FRA	25.1.84	1		Paris	5 Jun

Wind assisted

6.46	3.3	Shermin	Oksuz	AUS	24.3.84	2		Sydney (C)	15 Feb
6.40	5.9	Ychlindria	Spears	USA	17.7.84	6	NCAA-r	Lincoln, NE	30 May
6.37	3.9	Peta-Gaye	Beckford	JAM	17.4.85	1		Spanish Town	28 Feb
6.36	2.3	Sachiko	Masumi	JPN	20.12.84	1		Marugame	3 May
6.35	3.2	Elysée	Vésanes	FRA	25.1.84	1		Fort-de-France	5 Apr

TRIPLE JUMP

15.29	0.3	Yamilé	Aldama	ex-CUB	14.8.72	1	GGala	Roma	11 Jul

						14.69/0.4	x	14.90/-0.4	14.77/-0.3	x	15.29
15.27	1.3	1	GP	London (CP)	8 Aug	14.40	15.12/1.6	14.75/1.5	14.77/1.2	p	15.27
15.11	0.1	1	Bisl	Oslo	27Jun	14.63/-1.0	15.11	x	14.77/0.2	p	14.97/-0.2
15.08	0.3	2	GL	Saint-Denis	4Jul	14.87/0.3	14.96/-0.6	14.83/-0.1	15.04/0.0	14.79/0.8	15.08
15.00	0.0	1	GP	Ostrava	12 Jun	12.29	x	14.73/0.3	15.00	13.31	x
15.00	0.4	1	GP	Tríkala	24 Jun	x	x	14.98/0.0	15.00	p	14.79/0.6
15.00	0.2	2	VD	Bruxelles	5 Sep	x	x	14.03	x	14.21	15.00
14.99	0.1	2	WAF	Monaco	13 Sep	x	14.90/0.2	14.99	14.99/0.1		four only
14.98	1.1	1		Florø	31 May	14.37	14.85/1.1	14.98/1.1	p	p	p
14.98	-0.4	1	AAA	Birmingham	27 Jul	x	13.79	14.98	14.73/-1.2	14.73/0.3	14.86/-0.9
14.88i		1		Karlsruhe	28 Feb	14.58	x	14.88	x	14.54	x
14.85A	0.9	1		Germiston	24 Jan	x	14.27	14.85	p	p	p

Mark	Wind	Name		Nat	Born	Pos	Meet	Venue	Date
15.18	-0.2	Tatyana	Lebedeva	RUS	21.7.76	1	WCh	Saint-Denis	26 Aug
					14.80/0.0 14.97/-0.4 15.16/-0.2 15.18 x x				
15.14	0.3	1 VD	Bruxelles	5Sep	15.04/0.2 x 15.14 14.98/0.8 x 14.87/-0.4				
15.13	0.1	1 WAF	Monaco	13 Sep	14.71/-0.1 15.01/0.0 15.04/0.3 15.13 four only				
15.12	-0.9	1 GL	Saint-Denis	4Jul	14.80/0.3 14.93/-1.0 x x 14.85/-0.8 15.12				
15.00	0.6	2 GP	Tríkala	24Jun	14.86/0.8 14.92/0.7 x 14.48 x 15.00				
14.99	0.8	2 GP	London (CP)	8 Aug	14.73/1.5 x 14.74/1.3 14.96/1.4 p 14.99				
14.89	-2.7	1 ISTAF	Berlin (P)	10 Aug	14.52 14.88/-0.2 14.74/-0.5 14.64 x 14.89				
14.86	-0.1	3 Bisl	Oslo	27 Jun	x 14.64/0.3 14.81/0.4 14.47/0.2 14.85/-0.5 14.86				
14.86	0.5	2 GGala	Roma	11 Jul	14.35 14.52 14.46 14.86 14.51 14.81/1.0				
15.05	-0.7	Françoise	Mbango	CMR	14.4.76	2	WCh	Saint-Denis	26 Aug
					14.77/0.3 15.05 14.78/-0.1 14.85/0.5 15.02/0.0 x				
15.03	1.3	1	Lappeenranta	3 Aug	13.88 x 14.80/1.1 14.83/1.2 15.03/1.3 14.68/0.4				
14.88i		2 WI	Birmingham	15 Mar	14.88 14.35 14.57 14.24 x 14.73				
14.88	0.3	2 Bisl	Oslo	27 Jun	14.39 14.62 14.88 x 14.80/-0.9 14.81/-0.4				
14.87	0.6	1 WK	Zürich	15 Aug	14.53 x 14.87 14.77/0.0 14.56/0.3 14.50				
14.83	0.0	3 WAF	Monaco	13 Sep	14.83 x 14.82/0.2 four only				
14.82	-0.9	3 GL	Saint-Denis	4 Jul	14.16 14.31 14.63 14.82 14.58 14.51				
15.01i		Ashia	Hansen	GBR	5.12.71	1	WI	Birmingham	15 Mar
					14.77 x 14.56 14.62 15.01 x				
14.91	1.7	Kène	Ndoye	SEN	20.11.78	1		Villeneuve d'Ascq	15 Jun
					x 13.76 14.52 14.91 14.68 11.41				
14.90	-0.2	Magdelin	Martinez	ITA	10.2.76	3	WCh	Saint-Denis	26 Aug
					14.67 14.75/-0.3 14.66 14.64 14.90 14.86/0.2				
14.89	1.6	1	Milano	28 Jun	14.59 x x 14.78/1.7 14.64 14.89				
14.84	1.1	1 GP II	Rieti	7 Sep	14.76/0.9 14.88w/2.2 x 14.83/1.1 x 14.84/1.1				
14.84i		Hrisopiyí	Devetzí	GRE	2.1.76	1	Balk	Athína (P)	4 Mar
					14.37 14.50 14.53 14.84 p p				
14.81	1.2	Yelena	Govorova	UKR	18.9.73	2		Villeneuve d'Ascq	15 Jun
					14.81 x 14.42 14.49 x p				
		(35/8)							
14.79	-0.7	Anna	Pyatykh	RUS	4.4.81	1	ECp-S	Firenze	21 Jun
14.76i		Adelina	Gavrila	ROM	26.11.78	1	NC	Bucuresti	22 Feb
		(10)							
14.56	-0.1	Yelena	Oleynikova	RUS	9.12.76	5	GGala	Roma	11 Jul
14.53	0.7	Maurren	Maggi ¶	BRA	25.6.76	1		São Caetano do Sul	27 Apr
14.52	0.0	Mabel	Gay	CUB	5.5.83	5	WCh	Saint-Denis	26 Aug
14.50	1.2	Ólga	Vasdéki	GRE	26.9.73	Q	WCh	Saint-Denis	24 Aug
14.48	0.7	Baya	Rahouli	ALG	27.7.79	5	ISTAF	Berlin (P)	10 Aug
14.44i		Inessa	Kravets	UKR	5.10.66	1		Moskva	30 Jan
14.40i		Tereza	Marinova	BUL	5.9.77	4	Balk C	Athína	4 Mar
14.39	1.7	Heli	Koivula-Kruger	FIN	27.6.75	2		Lappeenranta	3 Aug
14.39			Huang Qiuyan	CHN	25.1.80	1	Asi C	Manila	20 Sep
14.38	0.6	Barbara	Lah	ITA	24.3.72	6	WCh	Saint-Denis	26 Aug
		(20)							
14.37	1.4	Viktoriya	Gurova	RUS	22.5.82	1	EU23	Bydgoszcz	20 Jul
14.35	-0.4	Nadezhda	Bazhenova	RUS	22.9.78	1	NC	Tula	10 Aug
14.32i		Alina	Dinu	ROM	2.9.82	1		Bucuresti	1 Mar
14.32i		Carlota	Castrejana	ESP	25.4.73	6	WI	Birmingham	15 Mar
14.31		Cristina	Nicolau	ROM	8.8.77	2		Bucuresti	24 May
14.31	2.0	Simona	La Mantia	ITA	14.4.83	2	EU23	Bydgoszcz	20 Jul
14.26	0.5	Yelena	Donkina	RUS	15.3.73	1		Tula	31 May
14.25	0.5	Yelena	Ivanova	RUS	16.3.79	2	Znam	Tula	8 Jun
14.24	0.6	Olga	Bolshova	MDA	16.6.68	2		Alcalá de Henares	28 Jun
14.23	1.8	Yuliana	Pérez	USA	21.7.81	1	NC	Stanford	22 Jun
		(30)							
14.22	0.9		Zhang Hao	CHN	26.2.78	1		Nanning	28 Jun
14.21	0.6	Anastasiya	Zhuravlyeva	UZB	9.10.81	1	NC	Tashkent	5 Sep
14.20	0.0	Yeoryía	Yiannakitsídou	GRE	10.2.82	1		Athína (K)	9 Jul
14.18	1.0	Natalia	Kilpeläinen	FIN	19.7.70	3		Lappeenranta	3 Aug
14.17	1.8	Mariya	Dimitrova	BUL	7.8.76	1		Kragujevac	1 Aug
14.16i		Yelena	Lebedyenko	RUS	16.1.71	2	NC	Moskva	27 Feb
14.16	1.0	Oksana	Rogova	RUS	7.10.78	2	WUG	Daegu	29 Aug
14.15	0.5	Camilla	Johansson	SWE	3.11.76	1		Halmstad	20 Jul
14.10	1.4	Sárka	Kaspárková	CZE	20.5.71	1		Praha	31 May
14.09	1.0	Mariana	Solomon	ROM	8.9.80	3	WUG	Daegu	29 Aug
		(40)							
14.08	2.0	Natalya	Safronova	BLR	11.7.74	1		Minsk	28 Jun
14.07	-0.4	Iríni	Dimitráki	GRE	8.8.80	4		Kalamáta	31 May
14.07	-1.0	Tatyana	Bocharova	KAZ	22.4.83	1	NC	Almaty	26 Jul
14.06	1.7	Yusmay	Bicet	CUB	8.12.83	6		Villeneuve d'Ascq	15 Jun

Mark	Wind	Name		Nat	Born	Pos	Meet	Venue	Date
14.06	0.7	Anastasiya	Ilyina	RUS	16.1.82	2	NC-23	Cheboksary	27 Jun
14.04	1.2	Ineta	Radevica	LAT	13.7.81	3	EU23	Bydgoszcz	20 Jul
14.04	1.8	Nicole	Mladenis	AUS	22.9.75	1		Perth	7 Dec
14.03i		Yevgeniya	Zhdanova	RUS	21.7.66	5		Moskva	30 Jan
14.03	1.4	Colleen	Scott	JAM	18.8.74	1		Atlanta	17 May
14.03	1.4	Yudelkis	Fernández	CUB-J	28.2.85	1		La Habana	20 Jun
		(50)							
14.02i		Mihaela	Gîndila	ROM	29.10.74	1		Bucuresti	1 Feb
14.02	1.0	Dana	Veldáková	SVK	3.6.81	4	EU23	Bydgoszcz	20 Jul
14.01i		Liliana	Zagacka	POL	28.1.77	1	NC	Spala	2 Mar
14.01	0.0		Wu Lingmei	CHN	16.2.73	1		Guangzhou	8 Apr
13.99	1.0	Aneta	Sadach	POL	22.4.75	3	Kuso	Warszawa	15 Jun
13.98i		Martina	Darmovzalová	CZE	12.10.78	1		Bratislava	9 Feb
13.98	1.1	Constanta	Stucan	ROM	12.7.81	4	WUG	Daegu	29 Aug
13.96i		Trecia	Smith	JAM	5.11.75	1		Blacksburg	17 Jan
13.96	0.5	Yarianna	Martínez	CUB-J	20.9.84	2	NC-J	Santiago de Cuba	5 Aug
13.94	0.8	Suzette	Lee	JAM	6.3.75	1		Houston	6 Jun
		(60)							
13.94		Galina	Sharova	RUS	30.1.79	1		Moskva	15 Jun
13.93	1.9	Anastasiya	Taranova	RUS-J	6.9.85	1	NC-j	Kazan	3 Jul
13.92	1.4	Svetlana	Semyonova	RUS	16.3.79	1		Moskva	15 Jul
13.91i		Silvia	Biondini	ITA	24.1.76	1		Modena	16 Feb
13.90	0.0	Thaimi	O'Reilly	ITA	20.7.76	1		Castres	6 Aug
13.89i		Katja	Umlauft	GER	22.11.74	1	NC	Leipzig	23 Feb
13.89	0.4		Xie Limei	CHN-Y	27.6.86	Q	NC	Shanghai	11 Sep
13.88	0.0	Rodica	Mateescu	ROM	13.3.71	4	NC	Bucuresti	9 Aug
13.87i		Irina	Vasilyeva	RUS	9.4.79	2		Moskva	11 Feb
13.86	-0.6	Cristine	Spîtaru	ROM-Y	4.2.86	1	WY	Sherbrooke	11 Jul
		(70)							
13.84A	2.0	Shakeema	Walker	USA	10.11.76	1		El Paso	12 Apr
13.83	-1.4	Luciana	dos Santos	BRA	10.2.70	1		São Paulo	28 Jun
13.82i		Theresa	Nzola	ANG	30.11.83	3	FRA Ch	Aubière	2 Mar
13.82	1.5	Maho	Hanaoka	JPN	3.8.76	1		Kumagaya	24 Aug
13.79	1.3	Shani	Marks	USA	24.8.80	1	DrakeR	Des Moines	25 Apr
13.79	2.0	Teresa	Bundy	USA	14.2.79	5	NC	Stanford	22 Jun
13.79	0.4	Sandra	Swennen	BEL	12.2.73	1		Heusden	29 Jun
13.78i		Nina	Serbezova	BUL	6.5.81	2	NC	Sofia	8 Feb
13.78i		Elva	Goulbourne	JAM	21.1.80	1	NCAA	Fayetteville	15 Mar
13.78	1.2	Rose-Lise	Retel	FRA	27.6.73	1		Dreux	13 Jun
		(80)							
13.78	0.0		Qiu Huijing	CHN-J	4.2.85	2	NC	Shanghai	13 Sep
13.77i		Virginija	Petkeviciené	LTU	12.6.71	1	NC	Kaunas	22 Feb
13.77i		Nicole	Toney	USA	19.12.82	2	NCAA	Fayetteville	15 Mar
13.77	0.9	Nicole	Gamble	USA	21.6.77	-	NC	Stanford	22 Jun
13.76	1.9	Sirkka-Liisa	Kivine	EST	22.6.77	2		Joensuu	11 Jun
13.75i		Tongula	Givens	USA	3.3.73	2		Blacksburg	17 Jan
13.75	1.2	Marina	Ogorodova	RUS	.76	1		Sankt Peterburg	16 Jul
13.75	0.6	Yekaterina	Chernyavskaya	UKR	31.1.83	Q	EU23	Bydgoszcz	18 Jul
13.74	0.3	Katja	Demut	GER	21.12.83	5	EU23	Bydgoszcz	20 Jul
13.73		Svetlana	Mameyeva	UKR	19.4.82	1		Kharkov	19 Jun
		(90)							
13.72i		Vanitta	Kinard	USA	26.7.75	1	NC	Boston (R)	1 Mar
13.72	1.4	Svetlana	Klimina	UZB	27.4.66	3		Moskva	27 Jul
13.70	1.8	Olga Lidia	Cepero	CUB	4.2.75	*		La Habana	25 Jan
13.70	2.0	Aurélie	Talbot	FRA	22.8.81	1		Argentan	9 Jun
13.70	0.0	Olivia	Wöckinger	AUT	23.5.79	1		Ebensee	15 Jun
13.69	-0.5	Alina-Elena	Popescu	ROM-J	27.10.85	1	Balk-j	Constanta	13 Sep
13.68	0.2	Keila	Costa	BRA	6.2.83	1	NC	São Paulo	13 Jun
13.68		Salamotu	Alimi	NGR	30.12.76	1	NC	Abuja	18 Jul
13.68	1.2	Tiombe	Hurd	USA	17.8.73	5	Pam	Santo Domingo	8 Aug
13.67			Niu Nana	CHN	20.5.83	1		Deyang	19 Apr
		(100)							
13.67	1.9	Chaytain	Hill	USA	13.10.82	2	NCAA-r	Lincoln, NE	31 May
13.67	1.4	Athanasía	Pérra	GRE	2.2.83	1		Spárti	19 Jul

13.66		Andreja	Ribac	SLO	14.1.76	19 Apr
13.66	0.2	Althea	Williams	CAN	4.1.75	15 Jun
13.66	1.8	Zita	Ajkler	HUN	9.6.75	30 Jul
13.66	1.8	Maráa	Espencer	DOM	1.10.82	8 Aug
13.65i	1.9	Kristina	Neyzhpapa	UKR	27.3.79	22 Feb
13.65	0.0	Biljana	Mitrovic	SCG	17.10.77	13 Jun
13.65	1.0	Betty	Lise	FRA	5.9.72	13 Jun
13.64i		Svetlana	Bolshakova	RUS-J	14.10.84	22 Feb
13.62	1.8	Monica	Cabbler	USA	15.11.74	12 Jul
13.60	0.0	Viktoriya	Molchanova	UKR	26.5.82	17 May
13.60	1.0	Amy	Zongo	FRA	4.10.80	2 Jul
13.60	1.2	Marina	Samborskaya	UKR	6.4.77	6 Jul
13.60	0.4	Irina	Beskrovnaja	SVK	28.12.82	30 Jul
13.59	0.0		Wang Ying	CHN	24.7.83	13 Sep

WOMEN 2003

Mark	Wind	Name		Nat	Born	Date
13.58	1.8	Anastasia	Nazarova	RUS	13.1.83	27 Jun
13.56	0.0	Anja	Valant	SLO	8.9.77	7 Jun
13.56	0.6	Natalya	Kayukova	RUS	10.12.66	7 Jun
13.56	1.6	Gisele	de Oliveira	BRA	1.8.80	14 Jun
13.54	1.5	Jenny	Adams	USA	8.7.78	26 Apr
13.54	0.3		Wu Xueli	CHN	5.1.78	28 Jun
13.54	0.0	Tatyana	Obukhova	UKR	15.1.78	6 Jul
13.54		Wacharee	Ritthiwat	THA	18.10.76	20 Sep
13.53i		Dimitra	Márkou	GRE	28.7.80	16 Feb
13.53		Yahyma	Kindelán	CUB	25.9.82	27 Jun
13.53	-0.3	Svetlana	Semyonova	RUS	16.3.79	10 Aug
13.52i		Keisha	Spencer	JAM	16.2.78	14 Feb
13.52	0.7	Natasha	Gibson	USA	12.7.69	4 May
13.52	1.2	Nicole	Herschmann	GER	27.10.75	30 May
13.52		Natalya	Tomashevskaya	UKR-J	12.10.84	20 Jun
13.51	0.2	Natalya	Marinina	RUS-J	85	29 May
13.51	1.0	Stéphanie	Luzieux	FRA	7.7.82	7 Jun
13.51	-1.5	Antonia	Yordanova	BUL	17.8.76	8 Jun
13.51	-0.6		Hei Na	CHN	10.2.78	13 Sep
13.51	0.0		Lee Kyung-sun	KOR	11.9.77	12 Oct
13.50	0.3	Indira	Valladares	CUB-Y	10.7.86	8 Mar
13.50	0.4	Fumiyo	Yoshida	JPN	25.4.81	6 Jun
13.50	1.3	Teija	Hannila	FIN	2.8.80	20 Jul
13.50	0.7		Lin Baohua	CHN	12.6.83	27 Oct
13.48	0.0		Yu Shaohua	CHN-J	4.1.85	8 Apr
13.48	0.0		Li Xiaoling	CHN	19.8.80	4 Aug
13.47		Jacqueline	Mau	GER	17.10.76	1 Jun
13.47	0.6	Natalya	Konovalova	RUS	23.12.83	27 Jun
13.47	0.0	Snezana	Vukmirovic	SLO	19.8.82	18 Jul
13.46i		Nicole	Whitman	USA	9.11.80	1 Feb
13.46	-0.4	Sandra	Busch	GER	1.9.77	10 May
13.46	-0.4		Nguyen Mai Quynh	VIE		10 Oct
13.45i		Chi-Chi	Aduba	USA	26.8.82	2 Mar
13.45	1.4	Laura	Tosoni (150)	ITA	10.10.79	3 Aug
13.45	0.2		Lin Nuai	CHN-J	6.1.84	28 Aug
13.44i		Olga	Rublyova	RUS	28.10.74	18 Jan
13.44i		Krisztina	Kövesi	HUN	13.9.79	15 Mar
13.44	1.0	Francesca	Brogi	ITA	10.4.76	10 Jun
13.44	1.5	M Costanza	Moroni	ITA	23.3.69	10 Jun
13.44	0.2	Nathalie	Jacques-Gustave	FRA	12.5.76	24 Jul
13.42i		Melanie	Carter	USA	14.3.82	15 Feb
13.42	1.1	Brandi	Prieto	USA	17.4.78	22 Jun
13.41	-0.9	Zivile	Pukstiene	LTU	9.11.79	19 Apr
13.41	0.0		Zhao Hanjun	CHN	8.7.83	27 Oct
13.39i		Karoline	Köhler	GER-J	20.2.84	23 Feb
13.38	0.4	Olga	Saladukha	UKR	4.6.83	17 May
13.38	0.3		Bui Thi Nhat Thanh	VIE	80	10 Oct
13.37	1.0	Aysegül	Baklaci	TUR	25.12.77	31 May
13.37	-0.3	Sara	Fabris	ITA-J	17.8.84	5 Jul
13.37	1.4	Malgorzata	Trybanska	POL	21.6.81	14 Sep
13.36	1.8	Alesya	Lyasun	BLR	18.10.82	21 Jun
13.36			Lu Bin	CHN	23.2.83	27 Oct
13.35	1.7	Silvia	Otto	GER	21.1.79	9 Jun
13.35	-0.6		Chung Hye-kyong	KOR	13.4.81	12 Oct
13.34i		Simidele	Adeagbo	CAN	29.7.81	2 Mar
13.34	0.8	Latifa	Ezziraoui	MAR-J	84	10 May
13.34		Linda	Osifo	NGR-Y	15.5.86	18 Jul
13.33i		Adrija	Parsukova	LTU	25.4.74	24 Jan
13.33i			Ren Ni	CHN	14.5.79	2 Mar
13.33	-0.7	Irina	Malkina	RUS	80	31 May
13.33		Alexandra	Zelenina	MDA-Y	21.11.86	1 Jun
13.33	0.6	Eliza	Todorova	BUL	27.6.74	7 Jun
13.33	0.0		Zhang Chunxiao	CHN	3.5.83	28 Aug
13.32	1.0	Darya	Zuyeva	RUS	83	27 Jun
13.31i		Niina	Kelo	FIN	26.3.80	23 Feb
13.31	0.1	Giovanna	Franzon	ITA	26.5.81	5 Jul
13.30			Ngew Siew Mei	MAS	4.6.83	22 Jul
13.30	0.0	(184)	Teng Hongfang	CHN-J	15.7.84	4 Aug

Wind assisted

Mark	Wind	Name		Nat	Born	Pos	Meet	Venue	Date
14.70	2.6	Yelena	Oleynikova	RUS	9.12.76	1		Pírgos	27 Jul
14.26	5.7	Suzette	Lee	JAM	6.3.75	1	NC	Kingston	20 Jun
14.24	6.1	Colleen	Scott	JAM	18.8.74	2	NC	Kingston	20 Jun
14.24	2.8	Mariya	Dimitrova	BUL	7.8.76	1		Kragujevac	8 Aug
14.22	2.4	Natalya	Kayukova	RUS	10.12.66	1		Moskva	27 Jul
14.22	6.0	Nicole	Mladenis	AUS	22.9.75	1		Perth	20 Dec
13.96	2.1	Tiombe	Hurd	USA	17.8.73	2	NC	Stanford	22 Jun
13.93	4.2	Vanitta	Kinard	USA	26.7.75	1		Emporia	9 May
13.90	2.5	Nicole	Gamble	USA	21.6.77	3	NC	Stanford	22 Jun
13.87	2.7	Shakeema	Walker	USA	10.11.76	4	NC	Stanford	22 Jun
13.80	2.1	Olga Lidia	Cepero	CUB	4.2.75	1		La Habana	25 Jan
13.69	2.9	Keila	Costa	BRA	6.2.83	2		São Caetano do Sul	22 Feb
13.69	4.9	Irina	Beskrovnaja	SVK	28.12.82	6	ECCp	Valencia	24 May

Mark	Wind	Name		Nat	Born	Date
13.66	3.1	Brandi	Prieto	USA	17.4.78	24 May
13.66	4.0	Éva	Miklós	HUN	30.7.78	2 Aug
13.64	2.3	Antonia	Yordanova	BUL	17.8.76	17 May
13.58	2.4	Teija	Hannila	FIN	2.8.80	20 Jul
13.54	2.4	Zivile	Pukstiene	LTU	9.11.79	5 Apr
13.52	3.1		Nguyen Mai Quynh	VIE		6 Sep
13.50	2.7	Chi-Chi	Aduba	USA	26.8.82	18 May
13.43	3.5	Patricia	Soman	CIV	12.8.81	31 May
13.42	3.0	Simidele	Adeagbo	CAN	29.7.81	5 Apr
13.41	3.5		Rapitsaravolazandry	MAD	.76	4 Sep
13.40	2.3	Zhanna	Melnichenko	UKR	24.4.83	6 Jul
13.40	3.4	Victoria	Mayo	ESP	9.3.77	26 Jul
13.33	5.0	LaTasha	Mosley	USA	17.3.81	3 May
13.30A	3.9	Desiree	Crichlow	BAR-J	1.6.84	17 May

Best outdoor marks

Mark	Wind	Name	Pos	Meet	Venue	Date
14.75	1.1	Gavrila	3	GP II	Rieti	7 Sep
14.42	1.0	Kravets	1	Kuso	Warszawa	15 Jun
14.34	-0.2	Devetzí	Q	WCh	Saint-Denis	24 Aug
14.27	1.7	Marinova	2		Kalamáta	31 May
14.17	0.0	Castrejana	1	GP II	Sevilla	7 Jun
14.17	0.0	Dinu	2	RomIC	Bucuresti	7 Jun
13.96		Gîndila	3		Bucuresti	24 May
13.88	1.0	Zagacka	1	NC	Bielsko-Biala	6 Jul
13.84	1.1	Vasilyeva	5	Kuso	Warszawa	15 Jun
13.76	0.8	Serbezova	1	NC	Sofia	8 Jun
13.71		Kinard	*		Emporia	9 May
13.67	1.2	Biondini	3	NC	Rieti	3 Aug
13.82w	2.8		3		Milano	28 Jun

Mark	Wind	Name	Date
13.64	1.9	Neyzhpapa	7 Jun
13.60	0.0	Umlauft	30 May
13.56		Lebedyenko	16 May
13.55	-0.3	T Smith	10 Aug
13.89w	3.8		26 Apr
13.54	1.1	Toney	14 Jun
13.58w			31 May
13.47	0.0	Niu Nana	8 Apr
13.46	1.4	Cabbler	22 Jun
13.43	1.0	Bolshakova	1 Jul
13.39	-0.6	Darmovzalová	7 Sep
13.38	1.9	Aduba	3 May
13.33	-1.0	Nzola	6 Aug
13.41w	2.6		9 Jun
13.32	1.9	Whitman	31 May
13.31	0.9	Kelo	2 Jul
13.43w	2.8	Kövesi	19 May

Low altitude best

Mark	Wind	Name	Nat	Born	Pos	Venue	Date
13.82	1.0	Shakeema Walker	USA	10.11.76	2	Eagle Rock	8 Jun

JUNIORS

See main list for top 7 juniors. 11 performances by 6 women to 13.95. Additional mark and further juniors:

Name	Mark	Wind	Pos	Meet	Venue	Date
Fernández	13.98	0.4	1	NC-j	Santiago de C	4 Aug
	13.89	0.0	1	PAm-J	Bridgetown	20 Jul
Martínez	13.80	1.2	2	NC	La Habana	27 May

Mark	Wind	Name		Nat	Born	Pos	Meet	Venue		Date
Xie Limei		13.76 0.0 3	NC Shanghai	13 Sep						
Spîtaru		13.75 0.0 6	NC Bucuresti	9 Aug						
13.64i		Svetlana	Bolshakova	RUS	14.10.84	1		Moskva		22 Feb
		13.43	1.0			2	NC-j	Kazan		1 Jul
13.52		Natalya	Tomashevskaya	UKR	12.10.84	1		Kiev		20 Jun
13.51	0.2	Natalya	Marinina (10)	RUS	85	2		Krasnodar		29 May
13.50	0.3	Indira	Valladares	CUB-Y	10.7.86	1		La Habana		8 Mar
13.48	0.0		Yu Shaohua	CHN	4.1.85	4		Guangzhou		8 Apr
13.45	0.2		Lin Nuai	CHN	6.1.84	3		Dalian		28 Aug
13.39i		Karoline	Köhler	GER	20.2.84	2	NC	Leipzig		23 Feb
13.37	-0.3	Sara	Fabris	ITA	17.8.84	1	vGBR-j	Nove		5 Jul
13.34	0.8	Latifa	Ezziraoui	MAR	84	1		Casablanca		10 May
13.34		Linda	Osifo	NGR-Y	15.5.86	2	NC	Abuja		18 Jul
13.33		Alexandra	Zelenina	MDA-Y	21.11.86	1		Chisinau		1 Jun
13.30	0.0		Teng Hongfang	CHN	15.7.84	6		Shijiazhuang		4 Aug
13.29i		Elena	Anghelescu (20)	ROM	20.6.84	2		Bucuresti		8 Mar
13.30wA	3.9	Desiree	Crichlow	BAR	1.6.84	2	WAC	El Paso		17 May

SHOT

Mark		Name		Nat	Born	Pos	Meet	Venue		Date
20.77		Svetlana	Krivelyova	RUS	13.6.69	1	NC	Tula		10 Aug
					19.32	19.33	19.92	20.77	19.55	p
	20.63	1 WCh	Saint-Denis	27 Aug	19.60	19.97	20.30	20.63	20.03	20.12
	19.94i	1 NC	Moskva	26 Feb	19.94	19.04	19.79	19.72	19.71	19.84
	19.66	2 WAF	Monaco	13 Sep	18.15	19.66	19.21	19.10		four only
	19.57i	5 WI	Birmingham	15 Mar	18.72	18.64	x	19.45	19.57	19.44
	19.57	1	Oristano	6 Sep	18.43	19.57	19.51	19.10		four only
20.56i		Nadezhda	Ostapchuk	BLR	12.10.80	1		Minsk		21 Feb
	20.31i	2 WI	Birmingham	15 Mar	19.49	20.31	19.99	19.77	20.09	19.69
	20.12	2 WCh	Saint-Denis	27 Aug	18.46	19.56	x	19.45	20.12	x
	19.75	1	Dortmund	15 Jun	x	18.51	x	x	19.22	19.75
	19.56	Q WCh	Saint-Denis	27 Aug	19.56		one throw			
	19.56	1 Super	Yokohama	23 Sep	18.42	18.81	x	18.84	18.65	19.56
	19.51	3 WAF	Monaco	13 Sep	19.28	18.86	19.51	x		four only
20.55i		Irina	Korzhanenko	RUS	16.5.74	1	WI	Birmingham		15 Mar
					20.14	20.55	x	x	x	19.86
	20.17	2 NC	Tula	10 Aug	18.64	19.90	20.17	19.67	p	p
	19.94i	2 NC	Moskva	26 Feb	19.28	19.72	19.47	x	x	19.94
	19.69	1 Kuts	Moskva	15 Jul						
20.44i		Viktoriya	Pavlysh	UKR	15.1.69	1	NC	Sumy		22 Feb
					20.44	x	19.33	x	x	p
	20.25i	1	Kiev	4 Jan						
	20.08	3 WCh	Saint-Denis	27 Aug	x	19.43	20.03	18.72	20.08	19.98
	20.00	1	Koncha Zaspa	23 May	19.27	20.00	x	19.50	18.66	18.83
	19.86	1 WAF	Monaco	13 Sep	18.69	19.86	18.32	x		four only
	19.79	1	Koncha Zaspa	11 May	18.52	19.55	19.79	19.42	19.25	19.01
	19.73i	4 WI	Birmingham	15 Mar	19.16	x	19.66	19.08	x	19.73
19.91		Astrid	Kumbernuss	GER	5.2.70	1		Eberswalde		20 Aug
					19.91	19.65	19.58	19.43	x	x
	19.86i	3 WI	Birmingham	15 Mar	19.05	19.86	19.78	x	x	19.59
	19.74	1	Rehlingen	9 Jun	19.70	19.74	x	18.78	x	x
	19.70	1	Wachsenburg	16 Aug						
	19.61	1	Iffezheim	30 Jun						
	19.58	1	Halle	24 May	18.81	x	x	19.19	19.38	19.58
	19.56	1	Cottbus	4 Jun	x	x	x	19.56	19.03	19.40
	19.55	2	Dortmund	15 Jun	19.09	x	19.04	18.96	x	19.55
	19.53	1	Neuwied-Engers	28 May						
	19.49	1	Gotha	14 Jun	19.20	x	19.49	x	x	19.28
	19.46	1 ECpS	Firenze	22 Jun	19.25	19.46	x	18.90		four only
	19.36	1 NC	Ulm	29 Jun	18.99	19.36	x	x	x	x
19.39		Yanina	Korolchik ¶	BLR	26.12.76	1		Minsk		3 Jun
		(37/6)								
19.36i		Olga	Ryabinkina	RUS	24.9.76	1		Bryansk		22 Jan
19.33i		Nadine	Kleinert	GER	20.10.75	1		Sondershausen		8 Feb
19.31i		Irina	Khudoroshkina	RUS	13.10.68	1		Moskva		10 Feb
19.31		Yumileidi (10)	Cumbá	CUB	11.2.75	1	PAm	Santo Domingo		7 Aug
19.18		Anna	Romanova	RUS	9.3.68	1		Bryansk		10 Jul
19.10		Iríni	Terzóglou	GRE	2.2.79	1	NC	Tríkala		14 Jun
18.96			Li Meiju	CHN	23.1.81	1		Shijiazhuang		6 Jun
18.96			Li Fengfeng	CHN	9.1.79	1		Hefei		27 Jun
18.95		Krystyna	Zabawska	POL	14.1.68	1		Gdansk		27 Jun

WOMEN 2003

Mark	Name		Nat	Born	Pos	Meet	Venue	Date
18.93	Valerie	Adams	NZL-J	6.10.84	1	GP	Osaka	10 May
18.82	Laura	Gerraughty	USA	29.7.83	1		Clemson	10 May
18.82	Lieja	Tunks	NED	10.3.76	1		Arnhem	25 Jun
18.73		Zhang Xiaoyu	CHN	16.3.83	1		Nanning	5 Apr
18.64i	Cristiana	Checchi ¶	ITA	8.7.77	1		Schio	13 Feb
	(20)							
18.59	Elisângela	Adriano	BRA	27.7.72	1		Santiago de Chile	26 Apr
18.59	Nadine	Beckel	GER	27.5.77	1		Mannheim	21 Jun
18.55	Kallíopi	Ouzoúni	GRE	8.2.73	1	Balk G	Thíva	13 Jul
18.43	Vivian	Chukwuemeka	NGR	4.5.77	2	MSR	Walnut	19 Apr
18.43	Assunta	Legnante	ITA	14.5.78	1		Salamanca	15 Jul
18.38		Du Xianhui	CHN/SIN	4.1.81	1		Hyderabad	28 May
18.38	Aneliya	Yordanova/Kumanova	BUL	27.4.72	1	NC-23	Sofia	14 Jun
18.33	Kristin	Heaston	USA	23.11.75	1	NC	Stanford	20 Jun
18.29	Yelena	Ivanenko	BLR	5.5.78	1	NC	Minsk	11 Jul
18.24	Lucica	Ciobanu	ROM	10.5.79	1		Craiova	10 May
	(30)							
18.15	Elena	Hila	ROM	20.5.74	3	Balk G	Thíva	13 Jul
18.14	Fior	Vásquez	DOM	27.12.77	3	PAm	Santo Domingo	7 Aug
18.11	Misleydis	González	CUB	19.6.78	2	Barr	La Habana	31 May
18.05	Natalya	Khoroneko	BLR	25.5.82	2		Minsk	3 Jun
18.01	Laurence	Manfrédi	FRA	20.5.74	1		Noisy-le-Grand	10 Jun
17.99	Adriane	Blewitt	USA	24.5.80	1		Atlanta	17 May
17.99		Zhang Guirong	CHN/SIN	5.2.78	2		Bangkok	5 Jun
17.95i	Cleopatra	Borel	TRI	3.10.79	1		Lexington	6 Dec
17.94		Cheng Xiaoyan	CHN	30.11.75	3		Guangzhou	8 Apr
17.89		Jia Lina	CHN	26.4.80	4		Guangzhou	8 Apr
	(40)							
17.86i	Oksana	Zakharchuk	UKR	3.4.80	1		Kiev	5 Feb
17.83i	Seilala	Sua	USA	25.2.78	2	NC	Boston (R)	2 Mar
17.80	Chinatsu	Mori	JPN	20.5.80	3	AsiC	Manila	20 Sep
17.79i	Oksana	Chibisova	RUS	31.3.77	6	NC	Moskva	26 Feb
17.76	Becky	Breisch	USA	16.3.83	1	NCAA	Sacramento	14 Jun
17.71		Lee Myung-sun	KOR	12.2.76	1		Chunju	10 Oct
17.66i		Song Feina	CHN	25.1.77	2		Shanghai	2 Mar
17.64	Kathleen	Kluge	GER	17.11.81	2		Thum	18 May
17.60	Olga	Ivanova	RUS	6.4.79	1		Tula	1 Jun
17.60		Lee Mi-young	KOR	19.8.79	4	AsiC	Manila	20 Sep
	(50)							
17.52	Juthaporn	Krasaeyan	THA	13.2.72	5	AsiC	Manila	20 Sep
17.49		Wang Lihong	CHN	9.1.83	6		Guangzhou	8 Apr
17.49	Jill	Camarena	USA	2.8.82	3	NCAA	Sacramento	14 Jun
17.49	Iolanta	Ulyeva	KAZ	27.7.76	1		Almaty	21 Jun
17.44	Yuliya	Leontyuk	BLR-J	31.1.84			Brest	20 Jun
17.37	Yevgeniya	Ospishcheva	RUS	.78	2		Tula	1 Jun
17.37	Stephanie	Brown	USA	1.8.79	4	NCAA	Sacramento	14 Jun
17.32		Qian Chunhua	CHN	11.2.79	1		Nantong	5 Jun
17.28i	Rebekah	Green	USA	19.9.80	1		Lawrence	24 Jan
17.28	Anna	Omarova	RUS	3.10.81	3		Tula	31 May
	(60)							
17.28	Yoko	Toyonaga	JPN	15.4.77	1	NG	Fukuroi	26 Oct
17.27i	Manuela	Frauendorf	GER	21.11.78	1		Leipzig	1 Feb
17.25		Jiang Ping	CHN	10.1.79	2		Shijiazhuang	4 Aug
17.25i	Kim	Barrett	JAM	18.11.81	1		Clemson	6 Dec
17.20	Tatyana	Nasonova	UKR	15.12.76	2	NC	Kiev	3 Jul
17.18	Veronica	Abrahamse	RSA	18.3.80	1		Roodepoort	28 Mar
17.16	Filiz	Kadogan	TUR	12.2.82	1		Sofia	2 Jul
17.12i	Katja	Kròl	GER	5.2.80	5	NC	Leipzig	23 Feb
17.09		Wang Yawen	CHN	23.8.73	2		Shijiazhuang	6 Jun
17.06	Chiara	Rosa	ITA	28.1.83	1		Clermont-Ferrand	9 Aug
	(70)							
17.04	Maranelle	du Toit	RSA	31.12.78	1		Parow	12 Apr
17.04	Olga	Shukina	UZB	6.4.77	1		Tashkent	12 Jun
17.04	Valentina	Fedyushina	AUT	18.2.65	1		Wien	15 Jun
17.01	Karen	Freberg	USA	30.9.82	1	SEC	Knoxville	18 May
17.01	Jessica	Cosby	USA	31.5.82	2		Salinas	20 May
17.01	Yelena	Dementiy	UKR	6.3.69	1		Kiev	29 Jul
17.00	Martina	de la Puente	ESP	4.4.75	1		Oviedo	12 Jul
16.91	Anna	Avdeyeva	RUS-J	6.4.85	1		Krasnodar	28 May
16.91	Aline	Schäffel	GER	15.5.80	5		Neuwied-Engers	28 May
16.91	Irache	Quintanal	ESP	18.9.78	1	NC	Jerez de la Frontera	3 Aug
	(80)							

Mark	Name		Nat	Born	Pos	Meet	Venue	Date
16.90		Zhang Chunjing	CHN	19.5.83	4		Shijiazhuang	4 Aug
16.89	Tatyana	Ilyushchenko	BLR	18.4.83	3		Minsk	21 May
16.89	Jessica	Cérival	FRA	20.1.82	2		Montgeron	25 May
16.85i	Krista	Keir	USA	19.12.79	1		University Park	15 Feb
16.85	Alina	Frunza	ROM	17.4.79	2		Craiova	10 May
16.83i		Yu Jing	CHN	7.3.83	6		Shanghai	2 Mar
16.81	Ashley	Dorsey	USA	29.1.80	1		Arlington	3 May
16.81	Natalya	Sazanovich	BLR	15.8.73	1H	WCh	Saint-Denis	23 Aug
16.76i	April	Phillips	USA	22.9.81	4	NCAA	Fayetteville	14 Mar
16.74	Candace	Scott	TRI	17.9.80	2	SEC	Knoxville	18 May
	(90)							
16.73	Michelle	Carter	USA-J	12.10.85	1		Austin	9 May
16.69	Chaniqua	Ross	USA	24.5.80	1		Northridge	22 Mar
16.67	Sumi	Ichioka	JPN	25.7.79	3	NG	Fukuroi	26 Oct
16.65	Kristen	Marten	GER	23.5.83	2	NC-23	Krefeld	17 Aug
16.63i	Aleksandra	Kopaneva	RUS	5.12.80	2		Moskva	16 Feb
16.63	L'Orangerie	Crawford	USA	2.12.81	4		Stanford	29 Mar
16.61	Ilona	Zakharchenko	UKR	16.6.67	3	NC	Kiev	3 Jul
16.60	Anja	Burkhardt	GER	13.10.81	2eB		Halle	25 May
16.59	Luz Dary	Castro	COL	30.5.78	2	SAmC	Barquisimeto	22 Jun
16.58	Eléni	Tsedemeídou	GRE	21.5.69	1		Athína (K)	25 Jun
	(100)							
16.58	Veerle	Blondeel	BEL	14.1.75	1	NC	Jambes	10 Aug

Mark	Name		Nat	Born	Date
16.56i	Leann	Boerema	USA	25.8.80	15 Feb
16.56i	Magnolia	Iglesias	ESP	25.5.79	8 Mar
16.55		Li Ling	CHN-J	7.2.85	4 Aug
16.52i	Jennifer	Gilson	USA	29.10.82	6 Dec
16.50	Andréa Maria	Pereira	BRA	8.12.73	26 Apr
16.47	Dana	Lawson	USA	13.7.79	19 Apr
16.47	Yelena	Voynova	RUS	1.7.81	17 May
16.46i	Mara	Rosolen	ITA	27.7.65	2 Mar
16.46	Mailín	Vargas	CUB	24.3.83	14 Jun
16.44	Chandra	Brewer	USA		14 Jun
16.43	Oksana	Gaus	RUS	24.7.81	31 May
16.41i	Janae	Strickland	USA	19.8.82	14 Mar
16.41	Helena	Engman	SWE		5 Sep
16.41		Yang Cui	CHN-J	15.8.84	24 Oct
16.39	Marianne	Berndt	CHI	24.12.78	22 Jun
16.35i	Nicole	Kendrick	USA	4.4.83	22 Feb
16.35	Anca	Vilceanu	ROM	1.1.78	5 Jul
16.35	Austra	Skujyte	LTU	12.8.79	23 Aug
16.33	Vera	Yepimashko	BLR	10.7.76	21 May
16.33	Joanne	Duncan	GBR	27.12.66	19 Jul
16.32i	Loree	Smith	USA	6.11.82	1 Feb
16.32i	Eva	Massey	GBR	22.12.80	16 Feb
16.32	Julia	Wiechmann	GER-J	28.3.84	5 Jul
16.29	Alean	Frawley	USA	5.11.81	8 May
16.25		Lu Ying	CHN-J	30.10.85	4 Jun
16.24i	Teresa	Machado	POR	22.7.69	8 Mar
16.24	Georgette	Reed	CAN	26.1.67	19 Jul
16.23	Petra	Lammert	GER-J	3.3.84	30 Jun
16.21i	Éva	Kürti	HUN	21.7.76	1 Mar
16.21		Zhang Juan	CHN	8.4.83	24 Oct
16.18	Linda	Nestorsson	SWE	2.12.75	12 Apr
16.16	Eliese	Mitchell	USA	20.3.80	19 Apr
16.13	Amel	Benkhaled	TUN	6.6.74	25 May
16.12	Jennifer	Brown	USA	1.9.79	8 Mar
16.12		Feng Haiying	CHN-J	3.6.85	4 Aug
16.11	Svetlana	Shevchenko	UKR	11.2.80	3 Jul
16.10i	Melinda	Ramsey	USA		14 Feb
16.10i	Johvonne	Hernandez	USA	29.12.82	23 Feb
16.06i	Anna	Söderberg	SWE	11.6.73	1 Mar
16.04i	Galina	Ivanova	BUL	27.11.74	8 Feb
16.04	Erin	Gilreath	USA	11.8.80	4 May
16.04	Ja'Nai	O'Connor	USA	30.4.82	20 Jun
16.03		Yang Dehui	CHN	28.4.83	27 Oct
16.02i	Hannah	Metzler	USA		8 Mar
16.02i	Zara	Northover	JAM-J	6.3.84	9 Mar
16.00	Kelli	Burton	USA-J	5.7.84	26 Apr
15.99	Serena	Boykin	USA	26.9.82	12 Apr
15.99	Cassandra	Lee	USA		9 May
15.98	Melissa	Bickett (150)	USA	16.4.82	20 Jun
15.98		Yu Ping	CHN-Y	8.3.86	27 Oct
15.97	Liz	Podominick	USA-J	5.12.84	21 Jun
15.96	Briona	Reynolds	USA	2.6.83	5 Apr
15.95i	Ruta	Rakstyte	LTU	28.7.80	28 Feb
15.95i		Sun Chuanna	CHN	13.5.83	2 Mar
15.95	Natalya	Dobrinskaya	UKR	29.5.82	17 May
15.95	Fotini	Kyriakídou	GRE	6.1.71	14 Jun
15.95	Wioletta	Potepa	POL	14.12.80	4 Jul
15.94	Heike	Koderisch	GER-J	27.5.85	11 May
15.92	Sabine	Noack	GER	21.6.83	30 Jul
15.91i	Dore	DeBartolo	USA	16.10.80	25 Jan
15.91i	Kortney	Ihnen	USA	26.10.80	15 Mar
15.90	Yelena	Odintsova	TJK	83	26 May
15.90	Jana	Kárníková	CZE	14.2.81	21 Jun
15.89i	Selema	Sione	FRA	18.7.82	22 Feb
15.89i	Adrienne	Moss	USA	15.11.81	8 Mar
15.89	Ana	Pouhila	TGA	12.10.79	9 Jul
15.88		Jiang Limin	CHN-Y	20.2.88	5 Jun
15.88		Feng Wanting	CHN	30.10.83	27 Aug
15.87i	Tawanna	Williams	USA		7 Mar
15.87i	Katie	McKeever	USA	7.2.83	7 Mar
15.86	(172)	Han Meng	CHN	15.4.83	27 Aug

Best outdoor marks

Mark	Name	Pos	Meet	Venue	Date
19.14	Kleinert	2		Neuwied-Engers	28 May
18.81	Khudoroshkina	2		Moskva	15 Jul
17.91	Checchi ¶	3	EChall	Gioia Tauro	1 Mar
17.82	Zakharchuk	2		Koncha-Zaspa	23 May
17.79	Borel	2	CAC	St George's	6 Jul
17.69	Sua	2	NC	Stanford	20 Jun
17.67	Chibisova	3		Moskva	15 Jul
17.34	Song Feina	7		Guangzhou	8 Apr
17.26	Frauendorf	1		Zittau	1 Jun
17.24	Green	6	NC	Stanford	20 Jun
16.94	Barrett	5	NCAA	Sacramento	14 Jun
16.66	Kròl	7	EChall	Gioia Tauro	1 Mar

Mark	Name	Date
16.52	Kopaneva	17 May
16.43	Phillips	26 Apr
16.42	Rosolen	25 Jul
16.37	Strickland	3 May
16.15	Massey	1 Aug
16.10	Boerema	5 Apr
16.08	Yu Jing	27 Aug
16.07	Iglesias	10 May
15.96	Keir	12 Apr
15.96	Kürti	18 May
15.94	Ivanova	7 Jun
15.88	Moss	12 Apr
15.86	DeBartolo	18 May
15.86	Yu Jing	4 Aug
15.85	Machado	8 Jun
15.85	Sun Chuanna	20 Jun

JUNIORS

See main list for top 4 juniors. 10 performances by 1 women to 17.65. Additional mark and further juniors:

Name	Mark	Pos	Meet	Venue	Date	Mark	Pos	Venue	Date
Adams	18.91	1	NC	Dunedin	21 Mar	18.51	1	Bondoufle	6 Jul
	18.77	Q	WCh	Saint-Denis	27 Aug	18.33	1	Albertville	10 Jul
	18.66	1	FRA Ch	Narbonne	26 Jul	18.01	1	Auckland (NS)	8 Feb

Mark	Name	Nat	Born	Pos	Meet	Venue	Date	Series
Adams	18.65 1 Bondoufle 16 Aug		17.65		Q	Vénissieux	12 Jul	
	18.65 5 WCh Saint-Denis 27 Aug							
16.55	Li Ling	CHN	7.2.85	5		Shijiazhuang	4 Aug	
16.41	Yang Cui	CHN	15.8.84	3	NG	Changsha	24 Oct	
16.32	Julia Wiechmann	GER-	28.3.84	1	NC-j	Fulda	5 Jul	
16.25	Lu Ying	CHN	30.10.85	2		Nantong	4 Jun	
16.23	Petra Lammert	GER-	3.3.84	5		Iffezheim	30 Jun	
16.12	Feng Haiying (10)	CHN	3.6.85	6		Shijiazhuang	4 Aug	
16.02i	Zara Northover	JAM	6.3.84	1		Boston	9 Mar	
16.00	Kelli Burton	USA	5.7.84	1		Eugene	26 Apr	
15.98	Yu Ping	CHN-Y	8.3.86	6	NG	Changsha	27 Oct	
15.97	Liz Podominick	USA	5.12.84	2	NC-j	Stanford	21 Jun	
15.94	Heike Koderisch	GER	27.5.85	1		Erding	11 May	
15.88	Jiang Limin	CHN-Y	20.2.88	1		Nantong	5 Jun	
15.77	Yelena Saprunova	RUS	11.6.84	2		Krasnodar	28 May	
15.75	Kamaiya Warren	USA	10.3.84	3		La Jolla	26 Apr	
15.71	Amarachi Ukabam	USA	14.3.84	4	NCAA-r	Columbus	30 May	
15.67	Jessica Pressley (20)	USA	27.12.84	1	G.West	Sacramento	15 Jun	

DISCUS

Mark	Name	Nat	Born	Pos	Meet	Venue	Date	Series
69.38	Natalya Sadova	RUS	15.6.72	1		Halle	24 May	64.43 69.38 x 63.43 63.82 65.82
65.22				6	WCh	Saint-Denis	25 Aug	65.22 x x 63.94 65.07 x
64.90				1		Salon-de-Provence	29 May	63.60 59.59 61.44 62.23 64.90 x
67.71	Vera Pospísilová	CZE	19.11.78	1		Réthimno	6 Jul	x 61.35 64.50 x x 67.71
66.66				1		Kladno	7 Jun	62.31 59.11 61.81 61.92 66.66 65.48
65.86				1	NC	Olomouc	13 Jul	60.04 x 59.61 x 65.86 64.48
65.55				5	WCh	Saint-Denis	25 Aug	62.04 61.12 63.23 64.01 65.55 61.96
65.42				1	WAF	Monaco	14 Sep	x 65.42 x 62.20 four only
65.08				1		Praha	16 Aug	
64.43				3		Halle	24 May	52.87 64.43 x 60.12 x 63.70
67.32	Irina Yatchenko	BLR	31.10.65	1	WCh	Saint-Denis	25 Aug	67.32 62.57 66.12 x x x
66.57				1	NC	Minsk	11 Jul	
64.38				1		Minsk	3 Jun	
67.14	Anastasía Kelesídou	GRE	28.11.72	2	WCh	Saint-Denis	25 Aug	65.76 63.93 67.13 65.18 x 67.14
66.73	Ekateríni Vóggoli	GRE	30.10.70	3	WCh	Saint-Denis	25 Aug	x 63.39 66.04 66.73 64.75 65.64
65.01				1	NC	Tríkala	15 Jun	64.18 65.01 x 62.50 62.90 60.76
64.78				1		Édessa	14 May	64.78 63.26 x 61.44 64.66 x
66.59	Olga Chernyavskaya	RUS	17.9.63	1		Krasnodar	18 May	
66.00	Franka Dietzsch	GER	22.1.68	2		Réthimno	6 Jul	66.00 60.30 x 63.32 x x
65.47				1	GP	Tríkala	24 Jun	59.45 60.84 x 62.87 63.88 65.47
65.42				2		Halle	24 May	65.42 x x 60.32 x 61.76
65.90	Yelena Antonova	UKR	16.6.72	4	WCh	Saint-Denis	25 Aug	64.51 60.56 x 60.70 65.90 61.72
65.15				1		Koncha Zaspa	11 May	64.01 62.00 x 60.82 63.23 65.15
65.53 irreg	Beatrice Faumuina	NZL	23.10.74	1		Auckland (NS)	8 Feb	60.53 63.02 65.53 61.14 63.98 63.00
65.35				1		Salinas	20 May	
64.32				1		Hamilton	6 Feb	
65.38	Suzy Powell (10)	USA	3.9.76	3		Réthimno	6 Jul	63.21 62.69 64.48 62.73 63.89 65.38
65.33	Song Aimin	CHN	15.3.78	1		Shijiazhuang	24 May	
65.10	Aretha Hill	USA	14.8.76	2	WAF	Monaco	14 Sep	x 65.10 63.03 64.53 four only
64.71				1		Carson	1 Jun	62.93 63.70 64.71 x 64.11 x
64.05				4		Réthimno	6 Jul	62.47 61.30 63.10 64.05 x 60.13
64.27	Melina Robert-Michon	FRA	18.7.79	1		Bron	3 Jul	inc: 60.95 60.51 64.27
64.14	Stiliani Tsikoúna	GRE	19.10.72	1	Veniz	Haniá	9 Jun	x 63.30 x x 61.42 64.14
	(33/13)							
63.65	Teresa Machado	POR	22.7.69	1	E.Chall	Gioia Tauro	2 Mar	
63.60	Marzena Wysocka	POL	17.2.69	1		Biala Podlaska	13 Jul	
63.11	Natalya Fokina	UKR	7.7.82	1	WUG	Daegu	28 Aug	
62.94	Agnese Maffeis	ITA	9.3.65	1		Lucca	15 Jun	

Mark	Name		Nat	Born	Pos	Meet	Venue	Date
62.91	Joanna	Wisniewska	POL	24.5.72	1		Siedlce	6 Jun
62.89	Philippa	Roles	GBR	1.3.78	1		Loughborough	8 Jun
62.71	María	Kolétsou	GRE	14.6.77	1		Spárti	19 Jul
	(20)							
62.09	Anaelys	Fernández	CUB	15.12.79	1		La Habana	13 Jun
62.06	Aretí	Abatzí	GRE	14.5.74	1		Athína (E)	17 May
62.03	Viktoria	Boyko	UKR	20.1.74	1		Koncha-Zaspa	24 May
62.00	Yania	Ferrales	CUB	28.7.77	1		La Habana	25 Jul
61.94	Neelam Jaswant	Singh	IND	8.1.71	1	Af-AsG	Hyderabad	30 Oct
61.93	Seilala	Sua	USA	25.2.78	2		Salinas	20 May
61.87		Li Yanfeng	CHN	15.5.79	1	AsiC	Manila	21 Sep
61.61	Anna	Söderberg	SWE	11.6.73	8	WCh	Saint-Denis	25 Aug
61.22	Shelley	Newman	GBR	8.8.73	2		Loughborough	8 Jun
61.16	Oksana	Yesipchuk	RUS	13.12.76	1		Bryansk	11 Jul
	(30)							
61.10		Huang Qun	CHN	12.4.79	1		Nantong	4 Jun
61.03	Vladimíra	Racková	CZE	15.5.67	2		Praha	16 Aug
60.97	Natalya	Ampleyeva	RUS	25.9.72	1		Moskva	26 Jul
60.80	Wioletta	Potepa	POL	14.12.80	3	NC	Bielsko-Biala	6 Jul
60.67		Cao Liping	CHN	8.11.78	2	NC	Shanghai	13 Sep
60.30	Valentina	Ivanova	RUS	1.5.63	1		Durban	7 Mar
60.20		Ma Xuejun	CHN-J	26.3.85	1	NG	Changsha	25 Oct
60.16	Alison	Lever	AUS	13.10.72	1		Brisbane	10 Jan
60.09	Kristin	Kuehl	USA	30.7.70	4	GP II	Gresham	17 May
60.02	Elisângela	Adriano	BRA	27.7.72	1		São Caetano do Sul	20 May
	(40)							
59.96	Ileana	Brîndusoiu	ROM	9.5.79	1		Bucuresti	24 May
59.91	Monique	Nacsa	AUS	26.10.76	1		Gold Coast	17 Jan
59.48	Grete	Etholm	NOR	25.1.76	1		Helsingborg	13 Jul
59.29		Wang Yu	CHN-J	4.2.85	3	NC	Shanghai	13 Sep
59.26	Gina	LoMonaco	USA	18.4.77	5	NC	Stanford	19 Jun
59.11	Debbie	Pickersgill	AUS	23.3.80	1		Brisbane	28 Mar
59.03	Olga	Ryabinkina	RUS	24.9.76	1		Bryansk	17 May
59.03	Lyudmila	Rublevskaya	RUS	7.6.77	2		Krasnodar	18 May
58.76		Xu Shaoyang	CHN	9.2.83	1		Guangzhou	8 Apr
58.69	Becky	Breisch	USA	16.3.83	1	Tex R	Austin	4 Apr
	(50)							
58.66	Roberta	Collins	USA	31.7.77	6	NC	Stanford	19 Jun
58.50	Olga	Chernogorova	BLR	30.1.82	2	Klim	Staiki	28 Jun
58.46	Monia	Kari	TUN	14.4.71	1		Radès	24 Jun
58.37	Yarelis	Barrios	CUB	12.7.83	2		La Habana	13 Jun
58.26	Jana	Tucholke	GER	20.5.81	1	NC-23	Krefeld	17 Aug
58.20	Katja	Kròl	GER	5.2.80	2	NC	Ulm	29 Jun
58.10	Katja	Schreiber	GER	30.6.78	3		Hamburg	20 Jul
57.89		Tao Hongbo	CHN	20.9.79	6	NC	Shanghai	13 Sep
57.88		Ma Shuli	CHN	20.1.78	7	NC	Shanghai	13 Sep
57.78	Stephanie	Brown	USA	1.8.79	8	NC	Stanford	19 Jun
	(60)							
57.77	Ina	Reiber	GER	12.3.80	8		Halle	24 May
57.76	Harwant	Kaur	IND	5.7.80	1		Chennai	19 Jul
57.70	Veerle	Blondeel	BEL	14.1.75	1		Knokke	17 Jul
57.44	Elizna	Naude	RSA	14.9.78	1	AfG	Abuja	12 Oct
57.25	Éva	Kürti	HUN	21.7.76	5	GS	Ostrava	12 Jun
57.12	Olga	Olshevskaya	RUS	5.7.82	2		Bryansk	17 May
57.04	Tiina	Kankanpää	FIN	16.8.76	2	vSWE	Helsinki	6 Sep
56.92	Vivian	Chukwuemeka	NGR	4.5.77	1	NAIA	Olathe	23 May
56.72	Krista	Keir	USA	19.12.79	1		Tempe	22 Mar
56.65		Lin Xiaojing	CHN-Y	8.1.86	3	NG	Changsha	25 Oct
	(70)							
56.63	Anita	Hietalahti	FIN	17.2.77	1		Turku	23 Jul
56.59	Lieja	Tunks	NED	10.3.76	1		Arnhem	25 Jun
56.48	Vera	Begic	CRO	17.3.82	1	NC	Zagreb	2 Aug
56.42	Deshaya	Williams	USA	8.7.80	4		Walnut	13 Jul
56.40	Ilona	Rutjes	NED	28.5.80	1		Tucson	6 Dec
56.39		Cheng Xianhong	CHN	24.10.68	6		Shijiazhuang	4 Aug
56.33	Ivona	Tomanová	SVK	24.10.72	1		Nitra	3 Jul
56.29	Chaniqua	Ross	USA	24.5.80	5		Salinas	20 May
56.24	Dragana	Tomasevic	SCG	4.6.82	2	RomIC	Bucuresti	7 Jun
56.21	Amarachi	Ukabam	USA-J	14.3.84	1	NC-j	Stanford	22 Jun
	(80)							
56.10	Alice	Matejková	ESP	11.1.69	1		Valencia	14 Jun

Mark	Name		Nat	Born	Pos	Meet	Venue	Date
56.05	Yuneydis	Bonne	CUB	7.3.78	4		La Habana	16 May
55.97	Agnès	Teppe	FRA	4.5.68	1		Salon-de-Provence	18 Jun
55.93	Billie Jo	Grant	USA-J	4.4.85	1		Huntington Beach	29 Mar
55.92	Ulrike	Giesa	GER-J	16.8.84	1-20		Mannheim	22 Jun
55.80	Eha	Rünne	EST	25.5.63	1	v2N	Kaunas	9 Aug
55.78	Sabine	Rumpf	GER	18.3.83	1		Halle	2 Feb
55.76	Sandy	Orsund	USA	24.9.81	1	Pac-10	Los Angeles	18 May
55.76	Ilona	Zakharchenko	UKR	16.6.67	1		Kiev	12 Jun
55.65	Luz Dary (90)	Castro	COL	30.5.78	6	PAm	Santo Domingo	5 Aug
55.56		Wang Jinxiang	CHN-J	14.8.84	4	NG	Changsha	25 Oct
55.49	Yelena	Lebusova	RUS	26.6.81	1		Moskva	14 Jun
55.48	Olga	Ivanova	RUS	6.4.79	5	Znam	Tula	7 Jun
55.43	Karin	Hagmann	SUI	9.3.74	1		Bern	28 Jun
55.35	Melissa	Bickett	USA	16.4.82	Q	NCAA	Sacramento	11 Jun
55.34	Annika	Larsson	SWE	10.7.70	3		Göteborg	2 Sep
55.31		Lan Chunyan	CHN	8.9.83	5	NG	Changsha	25 Oct
55.24	Elin	Isane	NOR	18.4.75	2		Tønsberg	12 Jun
55.20	Adriane	Blewitt	USA	24.5.80	1	NCAA II	Edwardsville	24 May
55.15	Tomoko (100)	Yamaguchi	JPN	14.2.72	1	Oda	Hiroshima	29 Apr
55.15	Rachelle	Longfors	USA	6.6.83	1	NCAA-r	Fairfax	31 May

55.14	Christelle	Bornil	FRA	9.5.78	7 Jun
55.11	Abby	Emsick	USA	18.11.83	31 May
54.98	Yuka	Murofushi	JPN	11.2.77	29 Apr
54.98		Sun Taifeng	CHN	26.8.82	13 Sep
54.95	Gia	Lewis	USA	1.4.79	19 Jun
54.81	Oksana	Tuchak (Andrusina)	RUS	26.3.73	18 May
54.80	Darya	Pishchalnikova	RUS-J	19.7.85	9 Aug
54.79	Alifatou	Djibril	TOG	13.2.80	12 Oct
54.74	Mary	Etter	USA	25.8.80	30 May
54.73	Rebecca	Roles	GBR	14.12.79	18 May
54.66	Olga	Goncharenko	BLR	13.7.81	3 Jun
54.65	Saroj	Kumari Sihag	IND	13.6.80	4 Mar
54.59	Seema	Antil	IND	27.7.83	28 Jul
54.49	Claire	Smithson	GBR	3.8.83	2 Mar
54.48	Irache	Quintanal	ESP	18.9.78	3 Aug
54.44	Laura	Bordignon	ITA	26.3.81	9 Aug
54.40	Dayana	Octavien	USA	10.6.82	31 May
54.26	Swaranjeet	Kaur	IND	7.6.76	4 Mar
54.25	Makiba	Batten	USA	26.10.80	15 Mar
54.23	Beth	Mallory	USA-J	31.5.84	29 Mar
54.18	Jill	Pedretti	USA	30.9.80	4 Apr
54.18		Zhang Yaqing	CHN	15.1.77	20 Apr
54.18	Amélie	Perrin	FRA	30.3.80	26 Apr
54.11	Tatyana	Tishchenko	UKR	24.9.80	24 Oct
54.02	Tara	Loper	USA	12.8.77	10 May
53.91	Karen	Honea	USA	27.1.81	8 May
53.88	Dace	Ruskule	LAT	20.9.81	28 Jun
53.88	Kalthoum	Saadaoui	TUN	17.9.80	12 Oct
53.87	Anna	Golub	BLR	25.2.81	28 Jun
53.82	Alina	Roman	ROM	7.7.83	9 Aug
53.72	Sonia	Godall	ESP	28.3.68	22 Jun
53.69	Hiba Necilhi	Abou Zaghari	EGY	.70	18 Aug
53.68	Krishna	Poonia	IND		19 Jul
53.67	Dore	DeBartolo	USA	16.10.80	10 May
53.67		Luo Xiaorong	CHN	4.11.83	25 Oct
53.62	Olga	Shukina	UZB	6.4.77	26 Jul
53.60	Chandra	Flinn	USA	11.7.74	5 Apr
53.60	Venera	Getova	BUL	13.12.80	14 Jun
53.54	Kate	Hutchinson	USA-J	10.6.85	12 Apr
53.52	Maria	Pettersson (141)	SWE	17.3.77	9 Jun

Downhill marks

66.23	Aretha	Hill	USA	14.8.76	1		La Jolla	26 Apr
56.74	Dragana	Tomasevic	SCG	4.6.82	1		Kargujevac	13 Jun
54.58	Chandra	Flinn	USA	11.7.74	5		La Jolla	26 Apr

JUNIORS

See main list for top 7 juniors. 11 performances by 4 women to 56.00. Additional mark and further juniors:

Ma Xuejun	56.96	4		Guangzhou	8 Apr	56.07	9	NC	Shanghai	13 Sep
	56.55	6		Nanning	5 Apr					
Wang Yu	59.08	2	NG	Changsha	25 Oct	57.63	4		Nanning	5 Apr
	58.33	2		Guangzhou	8 Apr	57.42	4		Shijiazhuang	4 Aug

54.80	Darya	Pishchalnikova	RUS	19.7.85	1		Szczecin	9 Aug
54.23	Beth	Mallory	USA	31.5.84	1	Towns	Athens, GA	29 Mar
53.54	Kate	Hutchinson (10)	USA	10.6.85	2		Arcadia	12 Apr
53.44	Nadine	Müller	GER	21.11.85	2	EJ	Tampere	25 Jul
53.22		Huang Xi	CHN-Y	15.3.86	4		Deyang	20 Apr
53.15	Valerie	Adams	NZL	6.10.84	1	NC	Dunedin	23 Mar
52.48	Yelena	Saprunova	RUS	11.6.84	2		Krasnodar	27 May
52.28	Katerina	Karsak	UKR	26.12.85	1		Kiev	29 Jul
52.08	Veronika	Watzek	AUT	13.8.85	1	v2N	Bregenz	28 Jun
51.78	Allyson	Criner	USA	2.3.84	3		Clemson	10 May
51.71	Agnieszka	Jarmusek	POL	3.2.84	4	EJ	Tampere	25 Jul
51.47	Kristina	Gehrig	GER-Y	21.6.87	1		Wiesbaden	17 May
51.38	Heike	Koderisch (20)	GER	27.5.85	2		Schönebeck	14 Jun

HAMMER

75.14	Yipsi	Moreno	CUB	19.11.80	1		Savona	17 Jul

					72.22	x	x	x	73.33	75.
74.25	1	PAm	Santo Domingo	5 Aug	x	73.75	73.05	74.25	73.89	x
74.07	1	Barr	La Habana	31 May	x	73.70	74.07	69.02	four only rain	
73.91	1		Padova	5 Jul	73.91	x	72.96	x	x	69.74

Mark	Name		Nat	Born	Pos	Meet	Venue		Date
73.42	1 WAF	Szombathely	7 Sep	71.68	73.42	70.95	70.75	x	x
73.33	1 WCh	Saint-Denis	28 Aug	71.02	73.33	72.52	69.84	64.98	x
72.47	1 NC	La Habana	28 May	x	70.72	70.95	x	72.47	70.56
72.00	1	La Habana	14 Feb	x	69.24	x	x	72.00	68.47
71.59	2	Villeneuve-d'Ascq	15 Jun	69.57	68.37	69.17	x	70.04	71.59
74.98	Olga	Kuzenkova	RUS	4.10.70	1	NC	Tula		9 Aug
				74.15	x	74.98	73.68	74.57	x
71.71	2 WCh	Saint-Denis	28 Aug	68.71	71.14	x	71.71	70.73	65.86
74.50	Manuèla	Montebrun	FRA	13.11.79	1		Villeneuve d'Ascq		15 Jun
				74.50	x	73.19	68.52	71.50	71.09
74.43	1 ECp-S	Firenze	22 Jun	71.63	73.11	72.60	74.43		four only
73.74	1	Saumur	4 May	69.20	69.96	71.19	73.53	72.50	73.74
73.40	1	Kuortane	20 Jul	72.21	71.06	68.96	73.17	73.40	72.70
73.31	1 GP II	Zagreb	7 Jul	68.70	71.51	73.31	70.16	67.70	x
73.21	1	Dreux	13 Jun	72.96	69.63	72.86	72.30	72.05	73.21
73.11	1	Forbach	1 Jun	72.43	72.36	71.71	72.21	73.11	72.03
72.18	1 EChall	Gioia Tauro	2 Mar	70.71	x	x	69.90	72.18	66.84
71.54	1 FBK	Hengelo	30 May	68.52	71.54	69.88	70.15	69.94	71.42
75.20dh	1	Vineuil	18 May	71.62	x	66.98	75.20	x	74.14
72.96	Irina	Sekachova	UKR	21.7.76	1		Koncha-Zaspa		23 May
				72.96	71.91	x	72.50	x	x
71.91	1	Koncha Zaspa	11 May	68.51	70.77	x	71.91	71.13	x
71.91	1 NC	Kiev	4 Jul	x	70.67	71.91	61.95	p	p
71.89	1	Kiev	26 May	71.30	71.09	71.89	69.00	71.28	x
71.73	1 ECp1B	Velenje	22 Jun	65.88	71.73	x	x		
72.03		Gu Yuan	CHN	9.5.82	1	NC	Shanghai		12 Sep
71.99	Mihaela	Melinte	ROM	27.3.75	2	ECp-S	Firenze		22 Jun
				69.00	70.11	71.03	71.99		
71.75	1 BalkC	Thíva	13 Jul	64.58	66.33	68.58	71.75	69.81	x
71.52	1	Izmir	8 Feb						
71.93	Susanne	Keil	GER	18.5.78	1		Fränkisch-Crumbach		8 Jun
				x	69.69	71.93	x	70.75	71.84
	(30/7)								
71.38	Kamila	Skolimowska	POL	4.11.82	1	EU23	Bydgoszcz		20 Jul
71.33	Anna	Mahon	USA	19.12.74	1	MSR	Walnut		19 Apr
71.12	Bronwyn	Eagles	AUS	23.8.80	1		Adelaide		6 Feb
	(10)								
70.69	Yunaika	Crawford	CUB	2.11.82	2	NC	La Habana		27 May
70.67		Zhao Wei	CHN	27.1.79	1		Nanning		5 Apr
70.60		Zhang Wenxiu	CHN-Y	22.3.86	2		Nanning		5 Apr
70.43	Ester	Balassini	ITA	20.10.77	2		Padova		5 Jul
70.42	Betty	Heidler	GER	14.10.83	1		Mannheim		21 Jun
70.34	Melissa	Price	USA	5.9.79	1	NC	Stanford		19 Jun
70.02	Olga	Tsander	BLR	18.5.76	1		Brest		30 Apr
69.98	Alexándra	Papayeoryíou	GRE	17.12.80	1	ROM Ch	Bucuresti		9 Aug
69.79	Candace	Scott	TRI	17.9.80	1	NCAA	Sacramento		14 Jun
69.72	Aldenay	Vasallo	CUB	25.2.77	1		La Habana		21 Jun
	(20)								
69.59	Yelena	Konevtsova (Tauryanina)	RUS	11.3.81	2	NC	Tula		9 Aug
69.33	Andrea	Bunjes	GER	5.2.76	1		Schönau		21 Jun
69.24	Lisa	Misipeka	ASA	3.1.75	1	Jerome	Burnaby		8 Jun
69.17	Alla	Davydova	RUS	21.5.66	1	ECCp	Valencia		24 May
69.05		Liu Yinghui	CHN	29.6.79	1	WUG	Daegu		26 Aug
68.93	Lorraine	Shaw	GBR	2.4.68	1		Loughborough		8 Jun
68.92	Gulfiya	Khanafeyeva	RUS	12.6.82	1		Moskva		14 Jun
68.71	Kirsten	Klose (Münchow)	GER	21.1.77	2		Fränkisch-Crumbach		8 Jun
68.55	Svetlana	Sudak	BLR	20.3.71	2	NC	Minsk		11 Jul
68.33	Dawn	Ellerbe	USA	3.4.74	1	PennR	Philadelphia		26 Apr
	(30)								
68.14	Vânia	Silva	POR	8.6.80	1		Mariunha Grande		22 Mar
68.12	Evdokía	Tsámoglou	GRE	15.12.78	3		Nikíti		1 Aug
68.03	Ivana	Brkljacic	CRO	25.1.83	4	GP II	Zagreb		7 Jul
67.98	Bethany	Hart	USA	10.4.77	1		New Haven		6 Jul
67.86	Lucie	Vrbenská	CZE	12.5.77	1	NC	Olomouc		13 Jul
67.82	Debbie	Sosimenko	AUS	5.4.74	1		Sydney		29 Nov
67.72	Sanja	Gavrilovic	CRO	20.9.82	1		Split		11 May
67.64	Sini	Pöyry	FIN	3.2.80	1	ECp-1A	Lappeenranta		22 Jun
67.58	Oksana	Menkova	BLR	28.3.82	2	EU23	Bydgoszcz		20 Jul
67.51	Florence	Ezeh	FRA	29.12.77	3	MSR	Walnut		19 Apr
	(40)								
67.43	Clarissa	Claretti	ITA	7.10.80	1		Salerno		31 May

Mark	Name		Nat	Born	Pos	Meet	Venue	Date
67.40	Brooke	Krueger	AUS	9.7.80	2	GP	Osaka	10 May
67.40	Katalin	Divós	HUN	11.5.74	1		Veszprém	26 Jul
67.36	Agnieszka	Pogroszewska	POL	20.2.77	3	Kuso	Warszawa	15 Jun
67.26	Manuela	Priemer	GER	29.11.78	3		Cottbus	4 Jun
67.19	Tatyana	Lysenko	RUS	9.10.83	2		Moskva	16 May
67.08	Mariya	Smolyachkova	BLR-J	10.2.85	3	Klim	Staiki	28 Jun
66.85	Karyne	Di Marco	AUS	14.3.78	2		Sydney (H)	22 Mar
66.69	Julianna	Tudja	HUN	13.10.79	2	NCAA	Sacramento	14 Jun
66.35	Marina	Rezanova	UKR	28.8.74	1		Kiev	20 Jun
	(50)							
66.18	Jukina	Dickerson	USA	7.8.81	Q	NCAA	Sacramento	12 Jun
66.08	Katarzyna	Kita	POL-J	4.7.84	1	EJ	Tampere	26 Jul
66.06	Jamine	Moton	USA	14.12.78	1		Clemson	12 Apr
66.06	Livia	Marx	HUN	5.4.80	2		Veszprém	26 Jul
65.93	Lyudmila	Gubkina	BLR	13.8.73	2		Staiki	8 Aug
65.92	Cari	Soong	USA	11.7.81	1	NCAA-r	Stanford	31 May
65.77	Éva	Orbán	HUN-J	29.11.84	1		Tapolca	16 Aug
65.70	Berta	Castells	ESP-J	24.1.84	1		Barcelona (CD)	31 May
65.67		Li Xiaoxue	CHN	11.1.80	1		Shanghai	13 Jun
65.66	Leslie	Coons	USA	16.7.73	1		Claremont	1 Mar
	(60)							
65.57	Tara	Loper	USA	12.8.77	1		Columbus	2 May
65.54	Bianca	Achilles	GER	17.4.81	1		Dortmund	13 Jul
65.53	Mia	Strömmer	FIN	26.2.74	1		Lappeenranta	3 Aug
65.45	Amélie	Perrin	FRA	30.3.80	2		Clermont-Ferrand	9 Aug
65.40	Evaggelia	Dervéni	GRE	2.5.80	3	NC	Tríkala	14 Jun
65.39	Simone	Mathes	GER	13.3.75	4		Halle	24 May
65.35	Michelle	Boswell (Clayton)	USA	29.10.76	3		Walnut	13 Jul
65.26	Marwa Ahmed	Hussein	EGY	19.6.78	2		Szombathely	10 Aug
65.13		Liao Xiaoyon	CHN-Y	8.1.87	2	NG	Changsha	23 Oct
65.04	Elena	Teloni	CYP	16.12.64	1		Athína (K)	24 Jul
	(70)							
64.83	Erin	Gilreath	USA	11.10.80	5	NC	Stanford	19 Jun
64.60		Yang Meiping	CHN-J	23.10.85	1		Nantong	4 Jun
64.58	Amber	Campbell	USA	5.6.81	4	NCAA	Sacramento	14 Jun
64.44	Merja	Korpela	FIN	15.5.81	6	EU23	Bydgoszcz	20 Jul
64.43	Martina	Danisová ¶	SVK	21.3.83	6	GP	Osaka	10 May
64.42	Yekaterina	Khoroshikh	RUS	21.1.83	1		Adler	8 Feb
64.38		Guo Peng	CHN-J	21.6.84	2		Xi'an	30 May
64.30		Yang Qiaoyu	CHN-J	14.9.85	3	NG	Changsha	23 Oct
64.29	Dolores	Pedrares	ESP	17.1.73	1		Madrid (I)	15 Feb
64.26	Jennifer	Joyce	CAN	25.9.80	1		Kamloops	27 Jul
	(80)							
64.16	Stéphanie	Falzon	FRA	7.1.83	3	NC	Narbonne	26 Jul
64.04	Masumi	Aya	JPN	1.1.80	3	AsiC	Manila	22 Sep
63.91	L'Orangerie	Crawford	USA	2.12.81	1		Fullerton	8 Mar
63.88	Cristina	Buzau	ROM	12.4.76	1		Bucuresti	21 Jun
63.80	Sónia	Alves	POR	3.6.79	1		A.Heroísmo	25 May
63.77	Marina	Lapina	AZE	6.3.81	2		Adler	8 Feb
63.72	Kathrin	Klaas	GER-J	6.2.84	1		Regensburg	9 Aug
63.70	Maria José	Conde	POR	26.8.80	1		Viana do Castelo	10 May
63.70	Michelle	Fournier	CAN	9.5.77	2		Victoria	11 Jun
63.61	Amalía	Láboura	GRE	16.3.68	2		Athína (K)	3 May
	(90)							
63.55	Maureen	Griffin	USA	6.10.80	1		Bozeman	17 May
63.49	Cecilia	Nilsson	SWE	22.6.79	4		Kuortane	20 Jul
63.46	Stiliani	Papadopoúlou	GRE	15.3.82	1		Thessaloníki	31 May
63.41	Indira	Salinas	CUB-J	28.10.85	2		La Habana	21 Jun
63.35	Shirley	Webb	GBR	28.9.81	6	v2N	Glasgow (S)	29 Jun
63.27	Andrea	Kéri	HUN-J	3.7.84	1		Szombathely	7 May
63.26	Nadezhda	Ovcharenko	RUS	8.12.81	4	NC-23	Cheboksary	28 Jun
63.25	Eileen	O'Keefe	IRL	31.5.81	1		Tullamore	3 Aug
63.23	Jackie	Jeschelnig	USA	19.11.79	1	NCAA II	Edwardsville	23 May
63.23	Malgorzata	Zadura	POL	3.10.82	3		Gdansk	27 Jun
	(100)							

63.19	Valentina	Srsa	CRO-Y	16.1.86	26 Jul
63.17		Yang Jie	CHN	10.12.83	23 Oct
63.14	Natalya	Zolotukhina	UKR-J	4.1.85	26 Jul
63.06	Zübeyde	Yildiz	TUR	7.9.80	11 May
62.84	Barbara	Németh	HUN	7.11.80	28 Jun
62.72	Alexandria	Earl-Givan	USA	25.4.70	20 Jul
62.68	Laura	Gerraughty	USA	29.7.83	24 Apr
62.65	Svetlana	Kovalchuk	UKR-J	3.1.84	17 May
62.62	Ramona	Jungton	GER-J	24.5.85	21 Sep
62.58	Mária	Hajnal	HUN	5.3.79	17 May
62.51	Adriane	Blewitt	USA	24.5.80	22 May
62.48	Gabrielle	Neighbour	AUS	22.11.83	29 Mar

Mark	Name		Nat	Born	Date
62.34	Larisa	Tarasyuk	RUS	14.6.70	1 Jun
62.25	Inna	Sayenko	UKR	8.3.82	29 Jul
62.24	Yuka	Murofushi	JPN	11.2.77	19 Jul
62.21	Yelena	Priyma	RUS	2.12.83	28 Jun
62.18	Natalya	Zledennaya	UKR	22.11.77	4 Jul
62.12	Nicky	Grant	JAM	25.5.81	21 Jun
62.00	Katie	McCoy	USA	10.4.79	3 May
61.99	Julie	Sorrentino	USA	25.6.80	3 May
61.90	Debby	van der Schilt	NED	24.11.81	20 Jul
61.64	Katiuscia	de Jesus	BRA	8.5.77	23 Apr
61.60	Jennifer	Dahlgren	ARG-J	27.8.84	21 Aug
61.54	Anastasia	Medvedyeva	RUS-J	5.2.84	29 May
61.45	Irina	Rusetskaya	BLR	83	11 Jul
61.40	Damisela	Aguilera	CUB-J	9.6.84	14 Mar
61.35	Orsolya	Németh	HUN-Y	14.4.86	28 May
61.24	Zoe	Derham	GBR	24.11.80	8 Jun
61.18	Yuliya	Rozenfeld	RUS-J	5.4.84	29 May
61.17	Yelena	Kiselyova	RUS	24.3.79	9 Aug
61.15	Jessica	Cosby	USA	31.5.82	17 May
60.98	Dayana	Octavien	USA	10.6.82	15 May
60.94	Erika	Melián	ARG	8.3.75	16 Nov
60.90		Shang Lina	CHN	11.3.83	4 Aug
60.90		Wei Xiaoyan	CHN	13.3.83	12 Sep
60.87		Zhao Wenjiang	CHN	10.7.81	4 Aug
60.85	Karina	Moya	ARG	28.9.73	26 Apr
60.85	Anne Laure	Grémillet	FRA	27.9.78	13 Jun
60.82	Vanda	Nickl	HUN-J	4.9.85	14 Jun
60.74	April	Phillips	USA	22.9.81	9 May
60.66	Jennifer	Allen	USA	29.6.81	17 May
60.63		Huang Chih-Feng	TPE	9.5.77	12 Apr
60.53	Karin	Engström	SWE	10.8.83	29 Jun
60.52	Hayat	El Ghazi	MAR	79	9 Mar
60.51	Nancy	Guillén	ESA	14.10.76	26 Jul
60.47	Jennifer	Folz	USA	24.12.75	11 Apr
60.40	Nadezhda	Pavlikovskaya	BLR-J	30.5.84	21 Jun
60.35	Darya	Pchelnik	BLR	20.12.81	8 Aug
60.28	Betina	Gabler	GER	22.8.71	18 May
60.18	Laura	Gibilisco (150)	ITA-Y	17.1.86	31 May
60.15	Noémi	Németh	HUN-J	7.4.86	9 Aug
60.14	Mallory	McDonald	USA	6.5.83	3 Apr
60.12	Kate	Johnston	USA	29.12.83	11 Apr
60.07	Tatyana	Chikina	UKR	16.11.82	11 May
60.04	Elizabeth	Pidgeon	GBR	27.4.77	27 Jul
60.02	Olivia	Waldet	FRA-J	23.5.84	18 Jun
59.93	Andrea	Thornton	USA	14.12.78	19 Jun
59.92	Tatyana	Konstantinova	RUS	18.11.70	8 Jun
59.90	Carol	Stevenson	CAN	15.5.81	11 Apr
59.89	Chisato	Tanaka	JPN	31.5.77	8 Jun
59.85	Katri	Räsänen	FIN	31.5.80	29 May
59.84	Mouna	Dani	MAR	79	1 Feb
59.81	Loree	Smith	USA	6.11.82	29 Mar
59.81	Erin	Wibbels	USA	3.7.78	8 Jun
59.77	Monica	Torazzi	ITA	26.2.71	17 May
59.76	Josiane	Soares	BRA	21.6.76	12 Jun
59.72		Wang Xiaoyu	CHN	25.12.81	19 Apr
59.65	Amarilis	Alméstica	PUR	12.2.81	5 Apr
59.64	Amanda	Moreley	USA	1.12.80	17 May
59.64	Adriana	Benaventa	VEN-J	19.10.84	25 May
59.62	Ibiene	Bilaya-Benibo	USA	25.12.81	3 Apr
59.62	Arasay	Thondike	CUB-Y	28.5.86	5 Aug
59.59	Oneithea	Lewis	USA	11.6.60	10 May
59.58	Daimara	Rovira	CUB-J	9.5.85	4 Jul
59.56	Alessandra	Coaccioli	ITA	11.9.75	8 Jun
59.56	Aurélie	Philippon	FRA	23.5.82	2 Aug
59.52	Keturah	Lofton	USA	24.7.82	11 Apr
59.46	Georgiana	Artenie	ROM-Y	14.8.86	16 Feb
59.33	Angela	Foster	USA	27.12.79	16 Feb
59.33	Odette	Palma	CHI	7.8.82	11 May
59.32	Tatyana	Khatantseva	RUS	18.2.81	28 Jun
59.30		Hong Mei	CHN	16.1.82	4 Aug
59.20	Violeta	Guzmán	MEX	14.5.77	13 Jun
59.14	Markéta	Hajdu	CZE	9.9.74	20 Sep
59.13	Katariina	Lahti	FIN	11.3.82	12 Jun
59.12	Svetlana	Sherina	RUS	29.4.71	15 Feb
59.11	Kim	Barrett	JAM	18.11.81	21 Jun
59.06	Celine	Neuenschwander	SUI	9.6.80	18 May
59.04	Melissa	Bickett	USA	16.4.82	31 May
59.00	Lauren	Collins	USA		17 May
58.93	Amy	Parulis	USA	7.1.82	24 Apr
58.91	Kaisa	Kiintonen	FIN	18.3.80	20 Jul
58.89	Marie	Hilmersson	SWE	14.1.81	17 Aug
58.86	Susan	Adoeye	NGR-J	.85	14 Oct
58.85	LaQuanda	Cotten	USA	30.12.80	5 Apr
58.84	Amy	Thiel	USA	4.10.79	17 May
58.84	Rachael	Beverley	GBR	23.7.79	8 Jun
58.81	Dore	DeBartolo	USA	16.10.80	29 Mar
58.77	Maris	Röngelep	EST-J	17.3.84	14 May
58.73	Abbey	Elsberry (200)	USA	5.4.81	19 Apr

Downhill marks

Mark	Name		Nat	Born	Pos	Venue	Date
75.20	Manuéla	Montebrun	FRA	13.11.79	1	Vineuil	18 May
64.50	Jennifer	Joyce	CAN	25.9.80	2	La Jolla	25 Apr

Drugs disqualification

Mark	Name		Nat	Born	Pos	Venue	Date
66.36	Martina	Danisová ¶	SVK	21.3.83	1	Kladno	7 Jun

JUNIORS

See main list for top 12 juniors. 12 performances by 5 women to 65.70. Additional mark and further juniors:

Zhang W	70.22	1	NG	Changsha	23 Oct	69.45	2	NC	Shanghai	13 Sep
	69.89	1	WMIIG	Catania	6 Dec	67.78	2		Deyang	19 Apr
	69.46	4		Padova	5 Jul		2		Guangzhou	8 Apr
Smolyachkova	66.20	3	NC	Minsk	11 Jul	65.89	2	EJ	Tampere	26 Jul

63.19	Valentina	Srsa	CRO-Y	16.1.86	4	EJ	Tampere	26 Jul
63.14	Natalya	Zolotukhina	UKR-	4.1.85	5	EJ	Tampere	26 Jul
62.65	Svetlana	Kovalchuk	UKR-	3.1.84	1		Kharkov	17 May
62.62	Ramona	Jungton	GER-	24.5.85	1		Merzig	21 Sep
61.60	Jennifer	Dahlgren	ARG-	27.8.84	1		Athens, GA	21 Aug
61.54	Anastasia	Medvedyeva	RUS-	5.2.84	1		Krasnodar	29 May
61.40	Damisela	Aguilera	CUB-	9.6.84	1		La Habana	14 Mar
61.35	Orsolya	Németh	HUN-Y	14.4.86	1c2		Szombathely	28 May

Annual number of women hammer throwers exceeding 60m: 1989- 2, 1990- 4, 1991- 5, 1992- 3, 1993- 4, 1994- 9, 1995- 14, 1996- 18, 1997- 28, 1998- 57, 1999- 84, 2000- 115, 2001- 113, 2003- 130, 2004- 156

WOMEN 2003

JAVELIN

66.52	Mirela	Manjani	GRE	21.12.76	1	WCh	Saint-Denis			30 Aug
				64.55	64.46	64.09	66.52	x		56.84
63.13	2	ECpS	Firenze	21 Jun	x	55.82	62.89	63.13		four only
66.00	Tatyana	Shikolenko	RUS	10.5.68	1	NC	Tula			10 Aug
				62.79	61.36	61.30	66.00	p		p
64.47	1	WAF	Monaco	13 Sep	63.53	64.47	x	61.48		four only
63.71	Q	WCh	Saint-Denis	28 Aug	63.71		only throw			

Mark	Name		Nat	Born	Pos	Meet	Venue		Date
63.52	2 Athl	Lausanne	1 Jul	63.52	x	x	x	x	x
63.34	1	Tallinn	30 Jul	x	61.38	62.04	62.87	63.34	x
63.28	2 WCh	Saint-Denis	30 Aug	62.76	62.99	63.28	x	60.67	59.93
64.90	Paula	Huhtaniemi	FIN	17.2.73	1	NC	Helsinki		10 Aug
				64.90	x	p	57.06	x	x
63.99	1	Lapua	14 Jun						
64.49	Valeriya	Zabruskova	RUS	29.7.75	1	Znam	Tula		7 Jun
				64.49	60.88	61.53	58.08	x	59.34
64.42	Steffi	Nerius	GER	1.7.72	1	NC	Ulm		28 Jun
				61.09	x	59.16	61.04	62.99	64.42
64.25	2 WAF	Monaco	13 Sep	64.25	63.24	63.10	63.00		four only
64.09	1	Osnabrück	6 Jun	62.39	61.80	61.02	x	x	64.09);
64.06	1	Alger	17 Jul						
63.91	1	Leverkusen	16 Feb	61.24	60.21	60.94	59.86	63.91	x
63.81	1 Athl	Lausanne	1 Jul	62.06	62.24	61.79	60.84	63.81	62.09
63.30	1 ECpS	Firenze	21 Jun	60.06	56.29	60.87	63.30		four only
63.00	1	Zeulenroda	29 May	61.26	58.32	60.34	x	63.00	x
62.87	1	Halle	24 May	x	62.87	61.58	x	62.08	60.86
62.70	3 WCh	Saint-Denis	30 Aug	59.15	62.70	60.30	x	61.81	x
63.96	Osleidys	Menéndez	CUB	14.11.79	1	NC	La Habana		28 May
				59.13	63.96	x	61.41	62.34	61.51
63.55	Mikaela	Ingberg	FIN	29.7.74	1		Lapinlahti		13 Jul
				59.14	61.61	63.55	x	60.90	60.42);
62.68	3 Athl	Lausanne	1 Jul	55.01	62.68	x	x	59.74	x
63.19	Yekaterina	Ivakina	RUS	7.12.64	2	Znam	Tula		7 Jun
				55.93	x	60.31	59.83	63.19	x
62.69	1 ECCp	Valencia	24 May	56.35	62.69	61.79.	57.78		four only
62.93		Xue Juan	CHN-Y	10.2.86	1	NG	Changsha		27 Oct
62.89	Lavern	Eve (10)	BAH	16.6.65	Q	WCh	Saint-Denis		28 Aug
				62.89		only throw			
62.88	Nikolett	Szabó	HUN	3.3.80	3	WAF	Monaco		13 Sep
				53.27	62.88	59.72	x		four only
62.70	Claudia	Coslovich	ITA	26.4.72	3	ECpS	Firenze		21 Jun
				62.70	58.43	57.83	58.98		four only
	(30/12)								
62.53	Sarah	Walter	FRA	5.5.78	1		Strasbourg		26 Jun
62.40	Nora Aïda	Bicet	CUB	29.10.77	1		La Habana		18 Jul
62.38		Ma Ning	CHN	4.11.83	1		Shijiazhuang		6 Jun
61.96	Taina	Kolkkala	FIN	24.10.76	1		Lappeenranta		3 Aug
61.91	Ana Mirela	Termure	ROM	13.1.75	1	NC	Bucuresti		10 Aug
61.82	Irina	Kharun	UKR	22.1.82	1	NCAA	Sacramento		13 Jun
61.59	Sunette	Viljoen	RSA	6.10.83	1		Durban		5 Dec
61.12	Oksana	Gromova	RUS	23.9.80	2	EChall	Gioia Tauro		1 Mar
	(20)								
60.87	Rita	Ramanauskaite	LTU	22.2.70	1	v2N	Kaunas		10 Aug
60.86	Kim	Kreiner	USA	26.7.77	1	PAm	Santo Domingo		7 Aug
60.75	Sonia	Bisset	CUB	1.4.71	2	NC	La Habana		28 May
60.54	Jarmila	Klimesová	CZE	9.2.81	1	EU23	Bydgoszcz		19 Jul
60.17	Sabina	Moya	COL	27.1.77	4	PAm	Santo Domingo		7 Aug
60.07	Sávva	Líka	GRE	27.6.70	1		Athína (K)		25 Jun
59.89	Barbara	Madejczyk	POL	30.9.76	2		Halle		24 May
59.81	Tatyana	Fedotova	RUS	19.9.80	1		Moskva		14 Jul
59.45	Monika	Aava	EST	19.6.79	1	Sule	Tartu		17 Jun
59.22	Mercedes	Chilla	ESP	19.1.80	1		Jaén		23 Feb
	(30)								
58.93		Liang Lili	CHN	16.11.83	2	NG	Changsha		27 Oct
58.82	Claudia	Isaila	ROM	17.7.73	2	NC	Bucuresti		10 Aug
58.81	Kirsi	Ahonen	FIN	8.4.76	4	GP II	Helsinki		18 Aug
58.70A	Zuleima	Araméndiz	COL	23.9.75	2		Tunja		17 May
58.62	Aïda	Sellam	TUN	13.9.77	1		Kladno		8 Jun
58.50		Yi Chunmei	CHN	15.3.83	4	NG	Changsha		27 Oct
58.31	Nadine	Auzeil	FRA	19.8.64	1		Montgeron		25 May
58.21	Jana	Woytowska	GER	7.8.77	1		Leverkusen		15 Feb
58.12	Xénia	Frajka	HUN	24.1.82	1		Szombathely		18 May
58.03		Liu Chunhua	CHN-Y	1.10.86	1		Changchun		21 Jun
	(40)								
57.97	Mariya	Yakovenko	RUS	6.1.82	1		Adler		15 Feb
57.93	Oksana	Yarygina	UZB	24.12.72	3	Znam	Tula		7 Jun
57.81	Kristina	Klishchevskaya	UKR	17.12.74	1		Koncha Zaspa		12 May
57.76	Elisabetta	Marin	ITA	5.11.77	4	EChall	Gioia Tauro		1 Mar
57.75	Julia	Zandt	GER-J	8.5.84	1	NC-j	Fulda		5 Jul

Mark	Name		Nat	Born	Pos	Meet	Venue	Date
57.64	Natalya	Shimchuk	BLR	1.10.81	1	Klim	Staiki	28 Jun
57.42	Tiziana	Rocco	ITA	2.12.78	6	EChall	Gioia Tauro	1 Mar
57.40	Christina	Obergföll	GER	22.8.81	3		Halle	24 May
57.37	Constanta	Iancu	ROM	12.9.76	1		Bucuresti	20 Feb
57.33	Indre	Jakubaitité	LTU	24.1.76	1		Ventspils	14 Jun
	(50)							
57.30		Zhang Li	CHN	19.10.78	4	NC	Shanghai	14 Sep
57.27	Lyudmila	Gamanyuk	UKR	11.10.77	1		Koncha-Zaspa	24 May
57.11	Kathryn	Mitchell	AUS	10.7.82	1		Canberra	23 Feb
57.07	Zhanna	Slastina	UKR	4.9.77	1	NC	Kiev	6 Jul
57.01	Alessandra	Resende	BRA	5.3.75	2	SACh	Barquisimeto	21 Jun
57.01	Åsa	Lindberg	FIN	12.4.79	Q	NC	Helsinki	9 Aug
57.00	Stephanie	Hessler	GER	16.3.83	1-23		Halle	25 May
56.96		Lee Young-sun	KOR	21.2.74	1		Jeonju	12 Oct
56.90		Chang Jung-yeon	KOR	6.4.77	2		Jeonju	12 Oct
56.85	Erica	Wheeler	USA	28.11.67	1	NC	Stanford	20 Jun
	(60)							
56.84	Natalya	Davydova	RUS	24.11.78	6	GP II	Bratislava	10 Jun
56.82	Tatyana	Lyakhovich	UKR	20.5.79	2		Koncha=Zaspa	12 May
56.80	Christina	Scherwin	DEN	11.7.76	1		Holte	16 Aug
56.73	Dörthe	Friedrich	GER	21.6.73	4		Halle	24 May
56.66	Aggelikí	Tsiolakoúdi	GRE	10.5.76	Q	WCh	Saint-Denis	28 Aug
56.65	Barbora	Spotáková	CZE	30.6.81	6	EU23	Bydgoszcz	19 Jul
56.50	Nadezhda	Kobrin	UKR	21.1.72	1		Koncha-Zaspa	30 Mar
56.50	Zahra	Bani	ITA	31.12.79	1		Cagliari	18 May
56.48	Mareike	Rittweg	GER-J	1.6.84	1	NC-23	Krefeld	16 Aug
56.43	Maria de la Caridad	Álvarez	CUB	30.8.75	3	NC	La Habana	28 May
	(70)							
56.40	Alexándra	Nástas	GRE	2.7.81	2		Athína (K)	25 Jun
56.38	Ilze	Gribule	LAT-J	25.1.84	Q	EJ	Tampere	26 Jul
56.29	Goldie	Sayers	GBR	16.7.82	1	NC	Birmingham	27 Jul
56.28	Marion	Bonaudo	FRA	12.9.82	1		Alès	29 Jun
56.24		Geng Aihua	CHN	29.6.83	2		Guangzhou	8 Apr
56.16	Lada	Chernova	RUS	1.1.70	5	NC-w	Adler	22 Feb
55.99	Takako	Miyake	JPN	22.7.74	1		Tsuyama	27 Jun
55.93	Nadia	Vigliano	FRA	24.6.77	2	NC-w	Rochefort	16 Feb
55.72	Bina	Ramesh	FRA	19.8.79	2	NC	Narbonne	25 Jul
55.50	Monica	Stoian	ROM	25.8.82	2	NC-w	Bucuresti	22 Feb
	(80)							
55.40	Barbara	Vontein	GER	7.6.78	5		Halle	24 May
55.31	Alana	Redfern	CAN	30.8.83	1		Iowa City	3 May
55.19	Annika	Suthe	GER-J	15.10.85	Q	EJ	Tampere	26 Jul
55.14	Yelena	Makarova	RUS	21.12.81	4		Moskva	14 Jul
54.88	Lindy	Leveaux	SEY	14.11.79	1		Victoria	8 Aug
54.79		Wu Meihong	CHN-J	5.6.84	5	NG	Changsha	27 Oct
54.78		Chu Chunxia	CHN	28.1.78	3		Guangzhou	8 Apr
54.72	Hanaa	Ramadhan Omar	EGY	3.1.83	1		Cairo	6 May
54.63	Lilya	Dusmetova	UZB	11.2.81	1	NC	Tashkent	5 Sep
54.62	Chlöe	Cozens	GBR	9.4.80	1		Grangemouth	3 Aug
	(90)							
54.56	Vivian	Zimmer	GER-Y	22.7.87	1-j		Osnabrück	6 Jun
54.55	Esther	Eisenlauer	GER	29.10.77	6	NC	Ulm	28 Jun
54.55		Ha Xiaoyan	CHN	30.1.72	5	NC	Shanghai	14 Sep
54.51		Tan Dongyun	CHN-Y	25.10.86	6	NG	Changsha	27 Oct
54.50	Inga	Kozarenoka	LAT	16.3.82	1		Riga	12 May
54.49	Linda	Brivule	LAT	9.9.83	2	ECp-2A	Århus	21 Jun
54.43	Sorochukwu	Ihuefo	NGR	20.6.79	1		Kaduna	10 May
54.30	Yuneisy	Rodríguez	CUB-J	1.5.84	1	NC-j	Santiago de Cuba	6 Aug
54.28		Yang Lina	CHN	6.3.83	1		Deyang	20 Apr
54.27	Olga	Ivankova	UKR	7.1.73	5	NC	Kiev	6 Jul
	(100)							

54.23	Inga	Stasiulionyte	LTU	29.6.81	4 Jul
54.14	Harumi	Yamamoto	JPN	8.5.74	11 Oct
54.09	Magdalena	Czenska	POL	14.6.81	19 Jul
54.08	Cindy	Stas	BEL	5.9.79	10 Aug
54.04	Monika	Mrówka (Kolodziejska)	POL	6.3.79	31 May
53.96	Romina	Maggi	ARG	27.3.76	26 Oct
53.84	Karen	Wyzykowski	USA-J	13.6.84	21 Mar
53.80	Dayamit	Delgado	CUB-J	14.3.85	28 May
53.74		Shin Bo-ra	KOR-Y	22.10.86	13 Jul
53.72	Emika	Yoshida	JPN-J	10.12.85	29 Jul
53.65		Zheng Ruixia	CHN	14.3.83	3 Aug
53.60	Trina	Rogers	USA	9.12.79	30 May
53.51	Rebecca	Noy	AUS	5.2.81	22 Mar
53.49	Daniela	Janke	GER-J	21.5.84	29 May
53.47	Galina	Kakhova	BLR	26.3.82	8 Aug
53.46	Katja	Nokelainen	FIN	16.4.79	6 Jul
53.43	Sandra	Lamrani	FRA	11.1.74	24 Jul
53.40		Zhang Cuido	CHN-J	18.3.85	27 Oct
53.38	Margaret	Simpson	GHA	31.12.81	1 Jun
53.38	Dee	O'Connell	USA	17.4.78	20 Jun

Mark	Name		Nat	Born	Pos	Meet	Venue	Date
53.37	Gurmeet	Kaur	IND	20.6.70				28 Oct
53.30	Rumyana	Karapetrova	BUL	7.2.82				12 Jul
53.24	Jeanette	Kottonau	GER	28.6.79				24 May
53.24	Larisa	Netseporuk	EST	24.12.70				6 Jul
53.23	Amber	Miller	USA					21 Mar
53.23	Buaban	Phamang-Y	THA	27.12.86				11 Dec
53.12		Park Ho-Hyun	KOR	21.3.78				5 Jun
53.10	Urszula	Jasinska	POL	26.12.83				17 May
53.09	Leryn	Franco	PAR	1.3.82				13 Jun
53.03	Hidemi	Ueki (130)	JPN	1.12.82				14 Jun

JUNIORS

See main list for top 10 juniors. 11 performances by 5 women to 56.00. Additional mark and further juniors:

Xue Juan	61.06	Q	NG	Changsha	25 Oct	56.82	1	WY	Sherbrooke	13 Jul
	57.51	3	NC	Shanghai	13 Sep	56.47	Q	NC	Shanghai	12 Sep
Zandt	56.96	1	EJ	Tampere	27 Jul					
Rittweg	56.27	2	NC-j	Fulda	5 Jul					

53.84	Karen	Wyzykowski	USA	13.6.84	1		Charlotte	21 Mar
53.80	Dayamit	Delgado	CUB	14.3.85	5	NC	La Habana	28 May
53.74		Shin Bo-ra	KOR-Y	22.10.86	2	WY	Sherbrooke	13 Jul
53.72	Emika	Yoshida	JPN	10.12.85	1	N.Sch	Nagasaki	29 Jul
53.49	Daniela	Janke	GER	21.5.84	2		Zeulenroda	29 May
53.40		Zhang Cuido	CHN	18.3.85	8	NG	Changsha	27 Oct
53.23	Buaban	Phamang	THA-Y	27.12.86	1	SEAG	Hanoi	11 Dec
52.87	Olga	Gamza	BLR	2.10.85	1		Brest	21 Jun
52.80		Xu Xin	CHN	30.8.87	Q	NC	Shanghai	13 Sep
52.74	Elodie	Masset (20)	FRA	2.7.84	1	NC-j	Vénissieux	14 Jul

7001	Carolina	Klüft	SWE	2.2.83	1	WCh	Saint-Denis	24 Aug
	13.18/-0.4 1.94 14.19 22.98/1.1			6.68/1.0		49.90	2:12.12	
6755	Eunice	Barber	FRA	17.11.74	2	WCh	Saint-Denis	24 Aug
	13.05/-0.4 1.91 12.97 23.92/1.1			6.61/0.8		49.60	2:13.68	
6694		Barber			1		Arles	8 Jun
	13.37/1.0 1.88 13.99 24.31/-1.8			6.80/2.0		46.92	2:14.84	
6692		Klüft			1	ECp-1	Tallinn	6 Jul
	13.22/1.9 1.86 13.24 23.45/1.9			6.77/0.2		44.53	2:13.03	
6602		Klüft			1		Götzis	1 Jun
	13.64/-0.2 1.91 12.84 23.69/0.9			6.62/1.0		45.34	2:13.85	
6524	Natalya	Sazanovich	BLR	15.8.73	3	WCh	Saint-Denis	24 Aug
	13.67/-0.4 1.76 16.81 24.25/1.1			6.47/0.0		44.93	2:16.53	
6452	Yelena	Prokhorova	RUS	16.4.78	4	WCh	Saint-Denis	24 Aug
	13.87/-0.4 1.82 13.36 23.99/1.1			6.46/0.7		43.60	2:08.31	
6316	Lyudmila	Blonskaya ¶	UKR	9.11.77	1		Kharkov	19 May
	13.54/0.0 1.79 12.77 23.97/0.0			6.30/0.2		46.17	2:15.81	
6313		Prokhorova			1	ECp	Bressanone	6 Jul
	13.95/0.0 1.81 13.69 24.06/0.0			6.13/0.8		44.88	2:11.82	
6282	Denise	Lewis	GBR	27.8.72	2	ECp-1	Tallinn	6 Jul
	13.80/1.9 1.74 15.54 25.39/1.9			6.33/1.8		49.57	2:20.34	
6264	Irina	Butor	BLR	26.2.80	2	ECp	Bressanone	6 Jul
	13.91/0.0 1.84 13.17 24.74/0.0			6.33/0.3		45.26	2:16.41	
6254		Lewis			5	WCh	Saint-Denis	24 Aug
	13.37/-0.4 1.64 15.25 24.55/1.1			6.19/0.1		49.88	2:19.58	
6254		Prokhorova			1		Talence	21 Sep
	14.07/-0.2 1.78 13.45 24.45/-1.4			6.51/0.8		42.92	2:14.10	
6215	Larisa	Netseporuk	EST	24.12.70	3	ECp-1	Tallinn	6 Jul
	13.94/1.9 1.74 13.32 25.17/1.9			6.35/0.2		53.24	2:20.04	
6213	Austra	Skujyté	LTU	12.8.79	2		Götzis	1 Jun
	14.25/-1.1 1.73 15.63 25.22/0.0			6.26/0.8		48.19	2:17.79	
6209A	Kim	Schiemenz (10)	USA	13.4.77	1		Greeley	5 Apr
	13.38/-0.1 1.84 13.29 24.23w/3.9			6.02/-1.0		43.86	2:21.15	
6181	Svetlana	Kazanina	KAZ	31.10.71	1		Almaty	17 May
	14.44/-1.1 1.80 13.44 24.99/-0.4			6.28/1.1		46.33	2:13.46	
6175	Sonja	Kesselschläger	GER	20.1.78	3		Götzis	1 Jun
	13.52/-0.2 1.79 13.81 25.03/0.0			6.37/0.9		39.45	2:16.23	
6170	Natalya	Roshchupkina	RUS	13.1.78	1	NC	Tula	3 Aug
	14.38 1.79 14.68 24.53			5.88		44.89	2:11.96	
6166	Gertrud	Bacher	ITA	28.2.71	6	WCh	Saint-Denis	24 Aug
	14.01/-0.2 1.76 13.32 24.91/0.7			5.99/0.6		47.11	2:09.83	
6159	Shelia	Burrell	USA	15.1.72	1	NC	Stanford	20 Jun
	14.29/-2.6 1.72 13.70 24.12/1.6			6.17w/2.4		49.36	2:18.12	
6154		Netseporuk			7	WCh	Saint-Denis	24 Aug
	13.91/-0.4 1.76 13.97 24.96/1.1			6.05/0.2		50.05	2:19.76	
6152	Margaret	Simpson	GHA	31.12.81	1	AfG	Abuja	14 Oct
	13.47/1.8 1.81 12.09 24.72/-0.3			6.11/-0.1		50.59	2:23.94	

Mark	Name		Nat	Born	Pos	Meet	Venue	Date
6140	Irina	Naumenko	KAZ	13.2.80	1		Almaty	22 Jun
	14.02/0.6 1.84 13.00 24.77w/2.2 6.19/-0.2 42.30 2:15.84							
6137	Yelena	Chernyavskaya	RUS	13.4.78	2	NC	Tula	3 Aug
	13.80 1.79 13.17 24.89 6.18 40.59 2:11.42							
6134		Kesselschläger			8	WCh	Saint-Denis	24 Aug
	13.34/0.0 1.76 13.77 24.94/0.7 6.17/0.7 41.57 2:17.19							
6133		Bacher			1	NC	Rieti	2 Aug
	14.06/0.1 1.72 13.13 24.64/0.8 5.92/0.8 48.14 2:09.01							
6120	Naide	Gomes	POR	10.11.79	4		Götzis	1 Jun
	13.65/0.3 1.82 13.49 25.33/1.6 6.45/1.3 39.18 2:19.57							
6120		Simpson			5		Götzis	1 Jun
	13.82/-0.2 1.76 12.55 24.77/0.0 6.06/1.8 53.38 2:22.6							
6119	Liga	Klavina	LAT	27.1.80	6		Götzis	1 Jun
	13.95/0.3 1.82 14.32 24.98/0.0 6.33/1.2 40.53 2:21.94							
	(30/20)							
6116	Aryiró	Stratáki	GRE	3.8.75	1	NC	Athína (E)	1 Jun
	13.51w/2.3 1.77 14.08 24.48/-0.4 5.96/0.2 44.25 2:21.32							
6064	Tiffany	Hogan (Lott)	USA	1.8.75	1	PAm	Santo Domingo	8 Aug
	13.15/0.4 1.68 13.78 24.59/1.2 6.02/0.4 49.52 2:27.74							
6059	Kelly	Sotherton	GBR	13.11.76	4	ECp-1	Tallinn	6 Jul
	13.73/1.5 1.74 12.70 24.07/0.4 6.58/1.7 32.84 2:14.94							
6033	Sylvie	Dufour	SUI	24.1.79	1	ECp-2	Maribor	6 Jul
	13.74/0.7 1.75 13.81 24.86/-0.4 5.82/1.9 41.39 2:12.27							
6031	Svetlana	Gnezdilov	ISR	20.7.69	1	NC	Tel Aviv	13 Aug
	13.26/1.9 1.68 12.38 24.28/0.0 6.31/1.1 34.92 2:10.39							
6031	Kylie	Wheeler	AUS	17.1.80	1	WUG	Daegu	26 Aug
	14.21/-0.2 1.79 12.56 24.69/-1.2 6.57/0.2 37.12 2:17.30							
6023	Tatyana	Zhevnova	BLR	17.10.77	4	ECp	Bressanone	6 Jul
	13.83/-0.2 1.81 13.37 25.29/0.0 6.00/-0.1 41.17 2:16.09							
6019	Tia	Hellebaut	BEL	16.2.78	8		Götzis	1 Jun
	14.28/-0.7 1.91 11.89 25.32/1.6 6.04/0.3 41.31 2:14.86							
6018	Julie	Hollman	GBR	16.2.77	14	WCh	Saint-Denis	24 Aug
	14.10/-0.2 1.85 12.05 24.72/0.7 6.06/0.3 41.01 2:15.83							
6017	Karin	Ruckstuhl	NED	2.11.80	7	ECp-1	Tallinn	6 Jul
	13.65/1.9 1.77 12.99 24.73/1.9 6.29/2.0 36.37 2:16.54							
	(30)							
6007	Marie	Collonvillé	FRA	23.11.73	6		Talence	21 Sep
	14.10/-0.2 1.84 11.90 25.71/-1.4 6.11/1.8 43.54 2:13.17							
6001	Magdalena	Szczepanska	POL	25.1.80	1	NC	Siedlce	7 Jun
	13.69w/3.4 1.75 13.01 25.00/0.1 5.95/0.2 41.29 2:13.03							
5999	Svetlana	Ladokhina	RUS	21.2.79	1		Krasnodar	24 May
	13.96w/3.7 1.72 15.02 24.97/1.4 6.04/1.2 41.72 2:20.14							
5999	Hyleas	Fountain	USA	14.1.81	1	NCAA	Sacramento	14 Jun
	13.82/0.2 1.83 11.65 23.53/0.0 6.16w/2.1 40.12 2:25.87							
5983		Shen Shengfei	CHN	21.1.81	1	NC	Shanghai	12 Sep
	14.12 1.75 13.49 25.89 6.31 46.63 2:21.88							
5970		Wang Hailan	CHN	6.4.76	2	NC	Shanghai	12 Sep
	14.03 1.69 13.29 24.73 6.22 41.67 2:16.07							
5969	Nicole	Haynes	CAN	18.9.74	2	PAm	Santo Domingo	8 Aug
	14.03/1.3 1.74 14.87 26.04/1.2 5.89/1.2 48.40 2:21.65							
5966	Yelena	Ivlyeva	RUS	.74	3	NC	Tula	3 Aug
	13.90 1.79 12.45 24.72 6.12 40.03 2:18.19							
5943	Svetlana	Parfyonova	RUS	14.7.73	2		Krasnodar	24 May
	13.93w/3.7 1.75 11.53 24.05/1.4 6.09/1.5 34.67 2:08.22							
5933	Simone	Oberer	SUI	8.4.80	11		Götzis	1 Jun
	14.08/-1.1 1.79 12.42 25.11/1.6 6.19w/3.2 38.89 2:15.91							
	(40)							
5918	Katja	Keller	GER	9.8.80	12		Götzis	1 Jun
	13.70/0.3 1.67 12.40 24.84/0.9 6.36/1.2 39.34 2:16.50							
5910	Yuki	Nakata	JPN	10.3.77	1	NC	Yokohama	7 Jun
	13.95/-0.9 1.75 11.84 24.74/0.9 6.12/2.0 44.14 2:20.76							
5909	Vasiliki	Delinikóla	GRE	9.2.81	7	ECp	Bressanone	6 Jul
	13.36/-0.2 1.72 12.91 24.74/0.0 6.06/-0.1 44.54 2:29.13							
5908	Jane	Jamieson	AUS	23.6.75	2	WUG	Daegu	26 Aug
	14.36/0.2 1.82 13.38 25.97/-1.0 5.89/-0.3 45.92 2:19.77							
5903	Olga	Levenkova	RUS-J	11.1.84	3		Krasnodar	24 May
	14.27/-3.9 1.77 12.09 24.79/1.1 6.14/0.1 38.70 2:13.59							
5901	Jennifer	Oeser	GER	29.11.83	1	EU23	Bydgoszcz	19 Jul
	14.11/-0.5 1.80 12.21 25.59/-1.0 6.02/-0.5 42.91 2:16.39							
5899	Sabine	Krieger	GER	4.9.73	13		Götzis	1 Jun
	14.27/-0.7 1.70 14.17 25.10/0.0 5.89/0.0 41.98 2:14.55							

Mark	Name		Nat	Born	Pos	Meet	Venue	Date
5895	Yvonne	Wisse	NED	6.6.82	2	EU23	Bydgoszcz	19 Jul
	13.69/-0.5 1.74	12.55	24.31/-0.5	5.97/0.4		33.97	2:12.51	
5884	J.J.	Shobha	IND	14.1.78	1	Af-AsG	Hyderabad	29 Oct
	13.76/-0.1 1.63	11.93	24.01/-1.6	6.23/0.4		43.36	2:20.95	
5883	Tiia	Hautala	FIN	3.4.72	2		Desenzano del Gardo	11 May
	13.89/0.4 1.76	13.17	25.42/-0.5	6.06/1.0		41.88	2:21.57	
	(50)							
5883	Susanna	Rajamäki	FIN	19.9.79	9	ECp-1	Tallinn	6 Jul
	13.80/1.5 1.65	13.86	24.54/1.3	6.39/1.0		37.27	2:23.24	
5882	Yuliya	Ignatkina	RUS	13.9.82	4	NC	Tula	3 Aug
	14.35 1.76	11.18	24.90	6.55		36.49	2:14.55	
5877	Natalya	Dobrinskaya	UKR	29.5.82	5		Arles	8 Jun
	14.02/0.8 1.73	15.23	25.70/-3.7	5.94/1.8		40.43	2:21.55	
5871	Yuleidis	Limonta	CUB	14.3.82	1		La Habana	4 Jul
	13.5/-0.9 1.77	12.69	24.6	6.39		34.82	2:24.3	
5870	Michaela	Hejnová	CZE	10.4.80	3		Hexham	3 Aug
	13.63/2.0 1.71	11.88	25.63/0.3	5.94/-0.3		48.96	2:20.41	
5864	Magalys	García	CUB	23.10.71	3	PAm	Santo Domingo	8 Aug
	13.61/1.3 1.71	13.69	24.44/1.2	5.61/1.1		45.79	2:26.26	
5858	Lyudmila	Kovalyova	UKR	18.3.75	2		Kharkov	19 May
	14.59/0.0 1.70	13.08	25.27/0.0	5.95/0.2		45.03	2:13.	
5842	Claudia	Tonn	GER	18.4.81	4	EU23	Bydgoszcz	19 Jul
	13.96/-0.5 1.71	11.66	24.77/-0.5	6.44/0.3		33.35	2:13.3	
5839	Ellanee	Richardson	USA	18.3.80	2	NCAA	Sacramento	14 Jun
	13.92/-2.2 1.74	10.36	23.95/-1.0	5.86/1.2		39.89	2:12.04	
5829	DeDee	Nathan	USA	20.4.68	4	NC	Stanford	20 Jun
	14.03/-2.6 1.69	13.66	24.98w/4.8	6.15/1.0		38.73	2:20.70	
	(60)							
5826	Marina	Brezgina (Bryukhach)	UKR	16.1.77	3		Kharkov	19 May
	13.80/0.0 1.79	12.84	25.76/0.0	6.11/0.1		36.70	2:19.42	
5818	Joanna	Grzesiak	POL	15.8.80	9	ECp	Bressanone	6 Jul
	13.98/-0.2 1.69	12.70	24.32/0.0	5.89/-0.8		35.83	2:12.07	
5815	Emilie	Boulleret	FRA	23.5.73	6		Arles	8 Jun
	14.27/0.8 1.70	13.46	25.53/-3.7	5.76/-0.6		44.88	2:15.65	
5808	Robin	Unger	USA	12.12.72	2	MSR	Azusa	17 Apr
	14.47/1.7 1.78	13.92	25.86/0.6	5.85:03.1		43.25	2:20.97	
5787	G. Pramila	Aiyappa (Ganapathy)	IND	8.5.77	1	I-State	Jamshedpur	7 Sep
	14.20 1.75	11.12	24.91	6.18		43.37	2:22.79	
5786	Niina	Kelo	FIN	26.3.80	10	ECp-1	Tallinn	6 Jul
	13.97/1.5 1.65	14.39	25.99/0.4	5.74/1.1		49.76	2:24.46	
5783	Judith	Méndez	DOM	27.7.81	4	PAm	Santo Domingo	8 Aug
	14.10/1.3 1.65	13.34	24.52/0.7	5.38/0.9		47.24	2:16.56	
5769	Anna	Kryazheva	RUS-J	17.7.84	4		Krasnodar	24 May
	14.80/-3.9 1.74	13.70	25.60/1.1	6.02/-0.2		37.80	2:13.78	
5761	Justine	Robbeson	RSA-J	15.5.85	1	NC	Port Elizabeth	26 Apr
	13.84/0.5 1.74	12.08	24.83/-0.1	6.04/-0.1		49.08	2:38.91	
5754	Missy	Vanek	USA	11.9.79	5	NC	Stanford	20 Jun
	14.23/-2.6 1.78	11.40	25.00w/2.5	5.63w/2.1		42.92	2:15.51	
	(70)							
5752	Sophie	Krauel	GER-J	2.3.85	1	NC-j	Wesel	22 Aug
	13.51w/2.1 1.69	10.06	24.37/1.9	6.29/0.3		34.70	2:16.11	
5747	Gi-Gi	Miller	USA	12.1.79	2		Berkeley	10 May
	13.36 1.64	12.01	23.9	5.85		34.13	2:14.17	
5745	Anna	Snetkova	RUS	.80	5		Krasnodar	24 May
	14.14w/3.7 1.75	12.88	25.75/1.4	5.93/0.8		38.66	2:17.20	
5745	Angela	Whyte	CAN	27.5.80	3	NCAA	Sacramento	14 Jun
	13.75/-0.4 1.68	11.98	23.78/0.0	5.80/1.6		37.79	2:19.91	
5740	Janice	Josephs	RSA	31.3.82	9		Arles	8 Jun
	13.60/1.0 1.70	10.50	23.45/-1.8	6.17/2.0		30.66	2:17.	
5736	Lidiya	Bashlykova	RUS	10.1.81	1	NC-23	Cheboksary	28 Jun
	14.64/0.0 1.73	13.38	25.37/-0.6	6.17w/3.3		39.80	2:22.92	
5735	Lilly	Schwarzkopf	GER	28.8.83	2	NC-23	Wesel	23 Aug
	14.22/0.6 1.75	12.15	25.84/-1.1	5.70/1.3		47.10	2:19.77	
5734	Kim	Vander Hoek	CAN	30.11.70	10		Arles	8 Jun
	13.83w/3.5 1.70	13.92	25.57/-3.7	5.76/0.7		40.45	2:21.84	
5726	Silvia	Dalla Piana	ITA	3.2.75	12	ECp-1	Tallinn	6 Jul
	14.10/1.5 1.71	12.49	26.42/0.4	6.03w/2.7		44.19	2:19.31	
5726		Dong Wangwei	CHN	28.6.81	3	NC	Shanghai	12 Sep
	14.09 1.69	13.18	25.47	5.85		44.68	2:23.70	
	(80)							

Mark	Name		Nat	Born	Pos	Meet	Venue	Date
5719	Julie	Martin	FRA	28.9.79	1	ECp	Perpignan	11 May
	14.36w/2.6	1.81	11.88	25.65/1.8	5.73/0.4	41.06	2:17.11	
5716	Jessica	Zelinka	CAN	3.9.81	3	NC	Victoria	19 Jul
	13.52/0.8	1.68	12.66	24.39/0.4	5.63/1.9	36.80	2:18.32	
5699	Olga	Alekseyeva	KAZ-J	30.11.84	5		Desenzano del Gardo	11 May
	14.74/0.5	1.82	12.06	25.16/-0.5	6.03/0.9	37.74	2:21.77	
5699	Christine	Schulz	GER-J	30.1.84	2	NC-j	Wesel	23 Aug
	14.15w/2.1	1.72	11.93	25.20/1.9	5.95/0.7	37.73	2:15.92	
5695	Vera	Yepimashko	BLR	10.7.76	14	ECp	Bressanone	6 Jul
	14.13/0.0	1.72	16.00	26.35/0.0	6.14/1.8	38.81	2:35.60	
5684	Michelle	Perry	USA	1.5.79	3		Azusa	17 Apr
	13.23/1.3	1.63	12.07	23.84w/2.6	5.79w/2.7	33.38	2:19.21	
5684	Christell	Préau	FRA	3.11.81	1	NC-23	Evian	22 Jun
	14.23/0.0	1.78	11.92	25.22/1.0	6.17/0.0	37.77	2:26.69	
5682	Sárka	Beránková	CZE	16.4.78	6		Desenzano del Gardo	11 May
	14.28/0.6	1.67	13.78	25.04/-0.5	6.20/-0.3	36.18	2:25.01	
5679	Irina	Tyukhay	RUS	14.1.67	6		Krasnodar	24 May
	14.06/1.9	1.66	14.17	25.51/1.4	5.90/0.9	40.82	2:25.14	
5672	Meredith	Davis	USA	9.6.79	1		Fargo	6 Jun
	(90)							
5670w	Amber	Miller	USA		1		San Angelo	11 Apr
	14.64w/3.3	1.62	12.85	26.08w/2.4	5.93/0.0	48.98	2:18.34	
5649	Sayoko	Sato	JPN	23.10.77	2	NC	Yokohama	7 Jun
	14.17/-0.9	1.63	11.53	24.68/0.9	6.18/0.1	38.87	2:19.76	
5640	Alexandra	Barlet	FRA	17.2.77	7		Desenzano del Gardo	11 May
	14.64/0.5	1.70	13.02	26.17/-0.6	5.92/0.0	44.92	2:21.99	
5638	Andrea	Tittmann	GER	1.3.76	1	NC	Wesel	24 Aug
	14.54/0.6	1.78	12.71	26.10/-1.1	5.82/-0.2	42.97	2:24.26	
5631	Kathrin	Geissler	GER-J	10.6.85	2	EJ	Tampere	27 Jul
	14.12/0.2	1.71	10.37	24.46/0.0	6.18/0.8	32.78	2:16.05	
5629	Maria	Peinado	ESP	8.2.77	1	NC	Palencia	20 Jul
	14.59/-2.2	1.70	13.07	25.84/-0.1	6.03w/3.2	39.57	2:20.53	
5627	Jana	Klecková	CZE	19.3.75	2		Maribor	1 Jun
	14.00/1.8	1.73	11.85	25.89/1.1	5.75/1.1	38.84	2:15.87	
5624	Regla M	Cárdenas	CUB	21.1.75	2	NC	La Habana	29 May
	14.48/0.2	1.64	14.61	25.62	6.18/-0.8	35.24	2:23.10	
5622	Shaina	Damm	USA	16.1.80	1		Princeton	19 Apr
5622	Thaimara	Rivas	VEN	23.7.82	1	SACh	Barquisimeto	21 Jun
	14.38/0.2	1.70	12.37	25.36/0.0	5.88/0.7	40.87	2:21.34	
	(100)							

5621		Liu Haili	CHN-J	24.12.84	24 Oct
5609	Maike	Goldkuhle	GER	10.3.80	13 Jul
5607	Inmaculada	Clopes	ESP	19.1.68	8 Jun
5602A	Leslie	Miller	USA	23.2.81	15 May
5601	Viktorija	Zemaityte	LTU-J	11.3.85	6 Jul
5598	Fiona	Harrison	GBR	30.11.81	18 Jul
5592	Laurien	Hoos	NED	18.8.83	18 Jul
5586	Olga	Kungurova	RUS	5.5.74	8 Jun
5585	Maren	Schwerdtner	GER-J	3.10.85	23 Aug
5583	Fiona	Asigbee	USA	18.5.81	18 May
5582	Rutti	Luksepp	EST	19.6.74	6 Jul
5575	Patricia	Berner	GER-J	16.12.84	27 Jul
5565	Tatyana	Alisevich	BLR	22.1.69	22 May
5564	Eva	Gérard	FRA	23.1.80	26 Jul
5557	Natalya	Germanyuk	BLR	30.3.75	22 May
5557	Kate	Brewington	GBR	15.10.81	20 Jul
5554	Natalya	Kotova	RUS	13.5.83	28 Jun
5549	Ashley	Selig	USA-J	23.2.84	18 May
5543	Saskia	Triesscheijn	GER	16.6.81	8 Jun
5538A	Jackie	Poulson	USA		15 May
5536		Chen Jing	CHN-J	16.8.84	12 Sep
5532	Soma	Biswas	IND	16.5.78	29 Oct
5527		Fu Pengcheng	CHN	15.1.80	12 Sep
5526		Shi Wei	CHN	7.7.83	24 Oct
5523	Zhanna	Melnichenko	UKR	24.4.83	4 Jul
5520		Cao Lan	CHN	25.1.82	12 Sep
5519	Lillian	Bush	USA	25.4.82	11 May
5514	Agnieszka	Falasa	POL	16.2.79	14 Sep
5512	Maija	Kovalainen	FIN	23.8.81	18 Jul
5509	Barbara	Szlendaková	CZE	6.8.78	6 Jul
5509	Gabriela	Kouassi	FRA	18.11.79	26 Jul
5506	Jennifer	Hoppe	USA	5.12.76	10 Apr
5499	Jordan	Willmann	USA	1.7.82	18 May
5498	Elisa	Trevisan	ITA	5.3.80	2 Aug
5491	Irina	Zhukovskaya	RUS	78	3 Aug
5481A	Shannon	Meyer	USA-J	20.7.84	15 May
5472		Liu Fang	CHN	23.11.83	24 Oct
5468	Francia	Manzanillo	DOM		7 Jul
5463	Annelie	Schrader	GER	19.12.79	8 Jun
5463	Yulia	Cherey	RUS	15.11.83	28 Jun
5461	Aleksandra	Kasitskaya	RUS-J	85	3 Aug
5460	Asimina	Vanakára	GRE	14.7.79	6 Jul
5454	Céline	Grout	FRA	9.2.82	1 Jun
5451	Franziska	Lakomy	GER	12.2.83	11 May
5444	Josie	Hahn	USA	17.10.83	14 Jun
5436	Patience	Okoro	NGR-J	10.7.84	14 Oct
5433	Elzbieta	Raczka	POL	19.11.70	7 Jun
5431	Kendra	Reimer	USA	7.4.80	17 Apr
5429	Ulrike	Hebestreit	GER	19.3.81	24 Aug
5428	Beth	Stroud (150)	CAN	7.4.77	15 Jun
5419	Linise	Gordon	USA	23.8.79	24 Apr
5416	Yekaterina	Butko	BLR	14.5.83	18 Jul
5414	Elizabeth	Plazotta	AUT	29.10 77	6 Jul
5413		Zhang Nina	CHN	3.3.81	12 Sep
5412	Frenke	Bolt	NED	8.6.80	25 May
5409	Oluchi	Elechi	NGR	20.7.73	18 Jul
5404	Mizuyo	Kasahara (157)	JPN-J	5.12.84	7 Jun

Drugs disqualification

6425	Lyudmila	Blonskaya ¶	UKR	9.11.77	(1)	ECp	Bressanone	6 Jul
	13.55/0.0	1.87	12.59	24.07/0.0	6.51/-0.2	44.20	2:15.68	
6418		Blonskaya ¶			2		Arles	8 Jun
	13.45/1.0	1.82	13.23	24.20/-1.8	6.42/1.5	44.49	2:13.29	

Mark		Name	Nat	Born	Pos	Meet	Venue	Date

JUNIORS

See main list for top 7 juniors. 10 performances by 6 women over 5690. Additional marks and further juniors:

Levenkova	5752	10	ECp	Bressanone	6 Jul	5748	1	EJ	Tampere	27 Jul
Robbeson	5697	2	AfG	Abuja	14 Oct					
Aleksejeva	5690	8	WUG	Daeju	26 Aug					

Mark		Name	Nat	Born	Pos	Meet	Venue	Date
5621		Liu Haili	CHN	24.12.84	1	NG	Changsha	24 Oct
	14.10/-0.7 1.78 11.88 25.28/-0.2			5.80/0.0		38.30 2:24.27		
5601	Viktorija	Zemaityte	LTU	11.3.85	13	ECp-1	Tallinn	6 Jul
	14.56/1.5 1.83 11.68 25.95/0.4			5.87w/2.3		37.83 2:21.29		
5585	Maren	Schwerdtner (10)	GER	3.10.85	3	NC-j	Wesel	23 Aug
	14.23/1.3 1.81 11.39 24.84/1.9			6.16/0.9		35.29 2:33.57		
5575	Patricia	Berner	GER	16.12.84	4	EJ	Tampere	27 Jul
	14.14/0.2 1.68 10.81 25.05/0.0			5.67w/2.1		40.90 2:15.45		
5549	Ashley	Selig	USA	23.2.84	2	Big12	Austin	18 May
	14.68/1.8 1.73 11.52 25.10w/2.6			5.65/1.5		36.99 2:13.56		
5536		Chen Jing	CHN	16.8.84	4	NC	Shanghai	12 Sep
	14.76 1.66 13.13 25.21			5.97		33.66 2:16.93		
5481A	Shannon	Meyer	USA	20.7.84	2		Albuquerque	15 May
	15.13/-1.6 1.61 12.03 24.37/0.9			5.75w/4.1		42.44 2:20.81		
5461	Aleksandra	Kasitskaya	RUS	.85	7	NC	Tula	3 Aug
	14.51 1.61 11.92 24.99			5.83		33.81 2:13.35		
5436	Patience	Okoro	NGR	10.7.84	3	AfrC	Abuja	14 Oct
	14.33/-0.8 1.72 13.67 25.59/-0.3			5.74/-0.1		38.38 2:36.58		
5404	Mizuyo	Kasahara	JPN	5.12.84	3	NC	Yokohama	7 Jun
	14.01/1.4 1.63 11.02 24.35/0.9			5.73/1.1		34.25 2:22.64		
5381	Juana	Castillo	DOM	.84	1	PAm-J	Bridgetown	20 Jul
	14.90/-0.1 1.58 12.67 25.65/0.0			5.37/-3.1		43.74 2:16.07		
5360	Antoinette	Djimou	CMR	2.8.85	4	FRA Ch	Narbonne	26 Jul
	14.18/1.4 1.63 12.01 25.45/0.0			5.82/0.9		40.12 2:32.41		
5338	Beata	Lewicka (20)	POL	21.1.84	25	ECp	Bressanone	6 Jul
	15.12/0.0 1.72 13.10 26.53/0.0			5.50/0.0		36.85 2:18.75		

4 x 100 METRES RELAY

41.78	FRA	Girard, Hurtis, Félix, Arron	1	WCh	Saint-Denis	30 Aug
41.83	USA	A.Williams, Gaines, Miller, Edwards	2	WCh	Saint-Denis	30 Aug
42.03	USA	A.Williams, Gaines, Miller, L.Williams	1h1	WCh	Saint-Denis	29 Aug
42.04	FRA	Girard, Hurtis, Félix, Arron	1h2	WCh	Saint-Denis	29 Aug
42.55		Louisiana State University (USA) Durst, Hall, Jones, Lee	1	NCAA	Sacramento	13 Jun
42.62	FRA	Girard, Hurtis, Dia, Arron	1	ECp-S	Firenze	21 Jun
42.62	RUS	Fyodorova, Tabakova, Kislova, Kruglova	2h1	WCh	Saint-Denis	29 Aug
42.63		Louisiana State University (USA) Durst, Hall, Jones, Lee	1	Tex R	Austin	5 Apr
42.66	RUS	Fyodorova, Tabakova, Kislova, Kruglova	2h1	WCh	Saint-Denis	29 Aug
42.73		Louisiana State University (USA) Durst, Hall, Jones, Lee	1	PennR	Philadelphia	26 Apr
42.76		HIS (USA) A.Williams, Edwards, Miller, Colander Richardson	1	MSR	Walnut	20 Apr
42.80		USA, Red Team Thornton, White, Daigle, Gaines	2	MSR	Walnut	20 Apr
42.86		Univ. of Texas (USA) Phelps, Richards, Staten, Al.Williams	3	NCAA	Sacramento	13 Jun
42.96	UKR	Tkalich, Kravchenko, Pastushenko, Maydanova	1		Kiev	6 Jul
43.04	NGR	Edem, Ojokolo, Odozor, Onyali	1	Afr G	Abuja	13 Oct
43.05	JAM	Golding-Clarke, Goulbourne, McDonald, Foster	2h3	WCh	Saint-Denis	29 Aug
43.06	BAH	T Clarke, Ferguson, Amertil, Brown	1	CAC	St George's	5 Jul
43.06	USA	A Williams, Moore, Daigle, L Williams	1	PAm	Santo Domingo	9 Aug
43.07	UKR	Tkalich, Kravchenko, Pastushenko, Maydanova	4	WCh	Saint-Denis	30 Aug
43.08		Louisiana State University (USA) Durst, Hall, Jones, Lee	1h3	NCAA	Sacramento	11 Jun
		(20 performances by teams from 7 nations) See below for mixed-nation team				
43.11	BLR	Nesterenko, Dragun, Nevmerhytskaya, Safronnikova	3h1	WCh	Saint-Denis	29 Aug
43.13	GER	Paschke, G.Rockmeier, Möller, Wagner	2	ECp-S	Firenze	21 Jun
43.36	BEL	De Caluwé, Rochtus, Ouédraogo, Geveart	2h2	WCh	Saint-Denis	29 Aug
	(10)					
43.40	CUB	Pérez, Díaz, Benavídes, Lazo	2	PAm	Santo Domingo	9 Aug
43.75	SWE	S Kallur, Klüft, J Kallur, Ljunggren	1	v FIN	Helsinki	5 Sep
43.81	GRE	Koklóni, Padaléon, Vasarmídou, Thánou	4h1	WCh	Saint-Denis	29 Aug
43.82	CHN	(Changsha) Zhang N, CXie R, Zou Y, Jiao G	1	NG	Changsha	27 Oct
43.90	THA	Jaksunin, Thawoncharoen, Jandang, Sukha	3	Af-AsG	Hyderabad	29 Oct
43.91	SLO	Bikar, Zumer, Nose, Ottey	1		Per.Valsugana	25 Jul
43.95	ESP	Blay, Recio, Sanz, Alozie	5	ECp-S	Firenze	21 Jun
43.96	NED	van den Akker, Poelman, van Assendelft, Kramer	5h2	WCh	Saint-Denis	29 Aug
43.97	TRI	Gibson, Ashby, Hutson, Baptiste	4	PAm	Santo Domingo	9 Aug
43.99	GBR	Burnside, Spencer, Kwakye, Oyepitan	6	ECp-S	Firenze	21 Jun
	(20)					
44.10	JPN	Ishida, Suzuki, Sakagami, Arai	1		Sapporo	26 Jul

Mark	Nat	Name	Pos	Meet	Venue	Date
44.11	AUS	Harris, Cripps, Hewitt, McLellan	6h2	WCh	Saint-Denis	29 Aug
44.16	BRA	de Moura, Coelho Neto, Ignácio, Sampaio	1	SACh	Barquisimeto	21 Jun
44.21	ITA	Marchetti, Graglia, Grillo, Cali	7	ECp-S	Firenze	21 Jun
44.36	POL	Dorobisz, Onysko, Dydo, Balcerzak	1	Kuso	Warszawa	15 Jun
44.42	FIN	Keskitalo, Manninen. Lax, Hannula	3	ECp1A	Lappeenranta	21 Jun
44.44	RSA	Moropane, Seyerling-Quinn, Wittstock, Pillay	2	AfG	Abuja	13 Oct
44.67	COL	Brock, Ararat, M Murillo, D Murillo	2	SACh	Barquisimeto	21 Jun
44.68	UZB	Zhuravlyeva, Perepelova, Dmitriadi, Khubbieva	1		Dushanbe	17 Oct
44.82	GHA		1		Saint-Etienne	18 May
	(30)					

44.86	FIJ	12 Jul	45.18	BUL	21 Jun	45.42	SEN	13 Oct	45.66	AUT	21 Jun	45.82	MAD	4 Sep
44.86	IND	29 Oct	45.29	SUI	21 Jun	45.54	EST	21 Jun	45.76	HUN	21 Jun	45.85	ISV	5 Jul
44.97	IRL	21 Jun	45.35	PUR	5 Jul	45.57	VIE	11 Dec	45.76	DOM	9 Aug	45.86	INA	11 Dec
45.13	CAN	26 Apr	45.37	CHI	21 Jun	45.60	CIV	29 Aug	45.80	CRO	21 Jun			

Mixed nations teams

Mark	Name	Pos	Meet	Venue	Date
42.83	South Carolina University (USA/JAM) Ross, Whipple, Joyce, Bailey/JAM	2	NCAA	Sacramento	13 Jun

JUNIORS

Mark	Nat	Name	Pos	Meet	Venue	Date
44.00	USA	Owens, Broaddus, Sherman, Soloman	1	PAm-J	Bridgetown	20 Jul
44.24	JAM	J Powell, Facey, McLaughlin, S Simpson	2	PAm-J	Bridgetown	20 Jul
44.42	JAM	T Powell, K Stewart, Anderson, S Simpson	1	Carifta	Port of Spain	20 Apr
44.60	FRA	Vouaux, Jacques-Sébastien, Kamga, Mang	1	EJ	Tampere	27 Jul
44.81	GBR	Any. Onuarah, Thomas, Spencer, Lucas-Reed	2	EJ	Tampere	27 Jul
44.87	GER	Köhler, Halm, Kedzierski, Sailer	1h2	EJ	Tampere	27 Jul
45.00	FIN	Pylkkä, Korjansalo, Keskitalo, Hakamäki	3	EJ	Tampere	27 Jul
45.09	TRI	Cooke, Hutson, Cabral, Baptiste	2	Carifta	Port of Spain	20 Apr
45.29	SWE	Andersson, Ljunggren, Lincoln-Saavedra, Claesson	4	EJ	Tampere	27 Jul
45.64	SUI	F Weyermann, Altermatt, Kissling, Frei	1		Bern	7 Jun
45.86	UKR	Snigur, Tonkovid, Semenova, Pilyugina	3h2	EJ	Tampere	27 Jul
45.89	NED	van den Akker, Kool, Appelman, Anpong	4h1	EJ	Tampere	27 Jul
46.02	BRA	Valentim, Krasucki, E dos Santos, Palinkas	4	PAm-J	Bridgetown	20 Jul

4 x 200 METRES RELAY

Mark	Name	Pos	Meet	Venue	Date
1:29.78	Louisiana State University USA Davy, Hall, Durst, Lee	1	PennR	Philadelphia	26 Apr
1:30.07	Louisiana State University USA Davy, Hall, Durst, Lee	1	TexR	Austin	5 Apr
1:30.67	University of Texas USA Al.Williamsm, As.Williams, Robinson, Richards	2	TexR	Austin	5 Apr
1:30.73	University of South Carolina USA Whipple, Joyce, Barber, Bailey JAM	1	FlaR	Gainesville	28 Mar
1:31.22	University of Texas USA McIntosh, Staten, Robinson, Richards	2	PennR	Philadelphia	26 Apr
1:31.26	University of South Carolina USA Whipple, Bailey JAM, Stroddart, Demus	3	PennR	Philadelphia	26 Apr
1:31.41	USA Red White, Colander-Richardson, Merriman, Cox	1	PennR	Philadelphia	26 Apr

4 x 400 METRES RELAY

Mark	Nat	Name	Pos	Meet	Venue	Date
3:22.63	USA	L.Barber 51.1, Washington 50.9, Miles-Clark 50.05, Richards 50.28	1	WCh	Saint-Denis	31 Aug
3:22.91	RUS	Zykina 50.8, Pechonkina 50.6, Kapachinskaya 50.67, Nazarova 50.93	2	WCh	Saint-Denis	31 Aug
3:22.92	JAM	Richards 52.0, Beckford 50.5, Smith 51.10, Fenton 49.38	3	WCh	Saint-Denis	31 Aug
3:24.57	USA	L.Barber 51.18, Trotter 51.1, Richards 50.89, Miles-Clark 50.75	1	WCh	Saint-Denis	31 Aug
3:26.02	RUS	Lavshuk 52.8, Ivanova 51.2, Firova 50.79, Pospelova 50.65	1	ECp-S	Firenze	22 Jun
3:26.22	JAM	Richards 53.2, Smith 50.8, Burgher 51.29, Beckford 50.99	1h1	WCh	Saint-Denis	30 Aug
3:26.25	GER	Marx 52.2, Rockmeier 51.5, Hoffmann 51.89, Breuer 50.63	4	WCh	Saint-Denis	31 Aug
3:26.40	USA	Barber, Robinson, Clay, Trotter	1	PAm	Santo Domingo	9 Aug
3:26.44	GBR	Karagounis 53.0, Meadows 51.6, Murphy 51.54, McConnell 50.36	2h1	WCh	Saint-Denis	30 Aug
3:26.52	GBR	Karagounis 52.7, Merry 51.3, Murphy 51.78, McConnell 50.67	2	ECp-S	Firenze	22 Jun
3:26.64	POL	Bejnar 52.6, Pskit 51.7, Jesien 51.46, Prokopek 50.91	5	WCh	Saint-Denis	31 Aug
3:26.65	USA, Red	Howard 52.9, Miles-Clark 50.4, ox 52.3, Washington 51.0	1rA	PennR	Philadelphia	26 Apr
3:26.66	POL	Pacholak 52.7, Bejnar 51.3, Jesien 51.71, Prokopek 50.91	3h1	WCh	Saint-Denis	30 Aug
3:26.67	GBR	McConnell 51.2, Meadows 51.8, Murphy 51.54, Danvers 52.48	6	WCh	Saint-Denis	31 Aug
3:27.08	CMR	Nguimgo 51.7, Kaboud 52.1, Atangana 51.98, Bewouda 51.35	7	WCh	Saint-Denis	31 Aug
3:27.34	JAM	Downer, Burgher, N.Williams, Beckford	2	PAm	Santo Domingo	9 Aug
3:27.76	NGR		1	AfG	Abuja	15 Oct
3:27.97	RUS	Pospelova, Goncharenko, Zykina, Nazarova	1h2	WCh	Saint-Denis	30 Aug
3:27.97	HER	Marx, B Rockmeier, Hoffmann, Breuer	2h3	WCh	Saint-Denis	30 Aug
3:28.07	BRA	Almirão, Tito, Teodoro, Coutinho	3	PAm	Santo Domingo	9 Aug
3:28.23	MEX	Allen, Medina, González, Guevara	4	PAm	Santo Domingo	9 Aug

Mark	Nat	Name	Pos	Meet	Venue	Date
		(21 performances by teams from 10 nations) See below for mixed-nation teams				
3:28.34	BLR	Bobrik, Khlustova, Kozak, Usovich	1	ECp-IA	Lappeenranta	22 Jun
3:28.37	SEN	Fall 51.7, M.Douf 53.0, A.Diouf 53.2, Thiam 50.5	3h3	WCh	Saint-Denis	30 Aug
3:28.39	FRA	Landre 52.09, Kamissoko 53.09, Désert 51.61, Bévis 51.60	3	ECp-S	Firenze	22 Jun
3:28.79	CUB	Grenot, Lara, Díaz, Muñoz	5	PAm	Santo Domingo	9 Aug
3:29.36	GRE	Boudá 52.8, Dóva 52.9, Koumnáki 52.04, Goudenoúdi 51.74	5	ECp-S	Firenze	22 Jun
3:29.65	UKR	Pigida 53.2, Mishchenko 51.3, Ryzhkova 53.3, Yefremova 51.9	4h3	WCh	Saint-Denis	30 Aug
3:31.20	KAZ	Roslanova 52.9, Torshina 52.8, Tereshkova 53.3, Bodritskaya 52.2	6h3	WCh	Saint-Denis	30 Aug
3:31.30	CHN	Chen L., Zhang X, Huang X, Bu F	1	AsiC	Manila	23 Sep
3:31.94	ROM	Florea 55.2, Ripanu 52.6, Rus 52.39, Tîrlea 51.89	6	ECp-S	Firenze	22 Jun
3:32.00	ITA	Perpoli 54.1, Niederstätter 53.1, Schutzmann 53.0, De Angeli 51.8	5h2	WCh	Saint-Denis	30 Aug
	(20)					
3:32.28	PUR	Castro, Harrison, Moya, Ortiz	6	PAm	Santo Domingo	9 Aug
3:32.77	ESP	Alba 53.9, Olivero 52.9, Carabali 51.97, Córcoles 54.07	8	ECp-S	Firenze	22 Jun
3:32.99	GRN	George, Bernard-Thomas, Morain, Regis	2	CAC	St George's	6 Jul
3:32.99	ISR	Lenskiy, Gnedzilov, Morad, Tkach	7h3	WCh	Saint-Denis	30 Aug
3:33.27	HUN	Kun, Varga, Szabó, Petráhn	3	ECp1A	Lappeenranta	22 Jun
3:33.57	BUL	Gachevska, Dimitrova, Mashova, Nedkova	1	Balk C	Thíva	13 Jul
3:33.78	IND	Parmanik, Reddy, Geetha, Philip	4	Af-AsG	Hyderabad	30 Oct
3:33.93	SWE	Dahlgren, Mårtensson, Petersen, Stuhrmann	4	ECp1A	Lappeenranta	22 Jun
3:34.30	VEN	Álvarez, Alfonso, García, Pacheco	2	SACh	Barquisimeto	22 Jun
3:34.44	IRL	McCarthy, Cuddihy, Hill, Shinkins	5	ECp1A	Lappeenranta	22 Jun
	(30)					
3:34.48	NED	Groenenboom, Jaber, Visschers, Schulte	2	ECp1B	Velenje	22 Jun

3:37.14	SUI	22 Jun	3:38.06	VIE	12 Dec	3:39.93	ALG	25 Jun	3:41.57	NZL	30 Aug	3:43.66	MYA	12 Dec
3:37.23	THA	23 Sep	3:38.09	CZE	22 Jun	3:40.03	FIJ	12 Jul	3:41.74	RSA	26 Apr	3:43.81	NOR	22 Jun
3:37.36	FIN	22 Jun	3:38.09	JPN	23 Sep	3:40.08	TRI-J	21 Apr	3:41.89	DEN	25 May	3:44.16	ARG	22 Jun
3:37.39	POR	22 Jun	3:38.12	SVK	22 Jun	3:40.29	TUR	25 May	3:42.24	MAR	25 Jun	3:44.22	MDA	22 Jun
3:37.52	EST	22 Jun	3:38.48	DOM	9 Aug	3:40.50	MAD	6 Sep	3:42.94	LTU	10 Aug	3:44.46	SRI	23 Sep
3:37.69	LAT	22 Jun	3:38.79	SLO	22 Jun	3:40.80	BEL	22 Jun	3:43.17	CAN	26 Apr	3:44.48	CYP	7 Jun
3:37.79	COL	9 Aug	3:39.65	AUS	5 Apr	3:41.19	TUN	25 Jun	3:43.31A	KEN	7 Jun	3:44.60	CRO	22 Jun

Mixed nation teams

Mark	Name	Pos	Meet	Venue	Date
3:26.76	University of Texas (USA/JAM)	1	NCAA	Sacramento	14 Jun
	Downer JAM 53.2, Robinson 51.4, McIntosh 51.0, Richards 51.2				
3:26.96	University of Texas (USA/JAM)	1	Tex R	Austin	5 Apr
	Downer JAM 52.4, Aiken 52.2, McIntosh 51.2, Richards 51.2				
3:27.64	University of Texas (USA/JAM)	1rB	PennR	Philadelphia	26 Apr
	Downer JAM 53.0, Robinson 51.7, McIntosh 51.1, Richards 51.8				
3:27.88	Louisiana State University	2	NCAA	Sacramento	14 Jun
	Davy USA, Hall JAM, Bernard-Thomas GRN, Regis GRN				

JUNIORS

Mark	Nat	Name	Pos	Meet	Venue	Date
3:33.48	RUS	T Popova, Kostetskaya, Migunova, Dryakhlova	1	EJ	Tampere	27 Jul
3:34.08	USA	J Lee, Perkins, Hastings, S Smith	1	PAm-J	Bridgetown	20 Jul
3:36.20	JAM	Prendergast, Car. Robinson, Cam. Robinson, McLaughlin	1	Carifta	Port of Spain	21 Apr
3:37.10	RUS	Nikolayeva, Migunova, Zaytseva, T Popova	1h2	EJ	Tampere	26 Jul
3:37.78	FRA	Jémaa, Sigère, Ndje, Michanol	2	EJ	Tampere	27 Jul
3:38.96	GBR	Ohurougu, Scott, Griffiths, Nicol	3	EJ	Tampere	27 Jul
3:40.08	TRI	Skeete, Davis, Lucas, Hills	2	Carifta	Port of Spain	21 Apr
3:40.48	GER	Neubert, Schwidde, Klose, Trauth	4	EJ	Tampere	27 Jul
3:40.65	TUR	Sentürk, Uslu, Saka, Gürler	1h1	EJ	Tampere	26 Jul
3:41.05	SWE	Ndiwabane, Samuelsson, Wiik, J Nilsson	5	EJ	Tampere	27 Jul
3:42.14	BLR	Tsivako, Chebotar, Koreyvo, Zholneruk	6	EJ	Tampere	27 Jul
3:42.24	BRA	S da Silva, F Tavares, M da Costa, A Dias	1	SAm-j	Guayaquil	8 Jun
3:42.52	CHN		6	NG	Changsha	27 Oct
3:42.55	VEN	Álvarez, Mejias, Londoño, Alfonso	2	SAm-j	Guayaquil	8 Jun
3:43.47	NGR	Seyi, Aveeru, Odomusu, Chigozis	1	Af-J	Garoua	2 Aug
3:43.7	CUB	(Guantánamo) Bience, Joy, Videaux, Savigne	1	NC-j	Santiago de C	7 Aug
3:44.55	CZE	Bartonicková, Buresová, Z Hejnová, Scerbová	8	EJ	Tampere	27 Jul
3:44.63	JPN	(Saitamasakae HS)	1		Nagasaki	2 Aug
3:44.73A	RSA	(Gauteng North) York, Hlongwane, Geldenhuis, Vorster	1	MC-j	Pretoria	6 Apr
3:44.82	CMR	Kemegne Fotsing, Monthe, Songwa, Atangana	2	Af-J	Garoua	2 Aug

4 x 800 METRES RELAY

Mark	Name	Pos	Meet	Venue	Date
8:26.71	University of North Carolina USA	1	PennR	Philadelphia	26 Apr
	Donohue 2:08.6, Flanagan 2:06.1, Munson 2:08.9, Schmidt 2:03.1				

4 x 1500 METRES RELAY

Mark	Name	Pos	Meet	Venue	Date
17:20.18	University of North Carolina USA	1	PennR	Philadelphia	25 Apr
	Henry CAN 4:28.8, Donohue 4:20.7, Schmidt 4:20.2, Flanagan 4:10.5				

4 x 100 METRES HURDLES

Mark	Team	Pos	Meet	Venue	Date
53.04	Louisiana State University USA – Le Blanc, Robinson, Jackson, Jones	1	PennR	Philadelphia	26 Apr
53.83	University of South Carolina USA – Demus, Wilks, Stoddard, Ross	2	PennR	Philadelphia	26 Apr
53.87	University of Miami USA – Dardden, Laeson, Wade, A Williams	1	FlaR	Gainesville	29 Mar

3000 METRES WALK

Mark	Name		Nat	Born	Pos	Meet	Venue	Date
12:06.77	Elisabetta	Perrone	ITA	9.7.68	1		Castelfidardo	6 Sep
12:07.77+		Perrone			1	in 5k	Rieti	2 Aug
12:20.50	Kjersti	Plätzer	NOR	18.1.72	1	NC	Fredrikstad	9 Aug
12:32.21	Susana	Feitor	POR	28.1.75	1		V.Real St.António	10 Jun

Mark	Name		Nat	Born	Date	Mark	Name		Nat	Born	Date
12:45.39	Sylwia	Korzeniowska	POL	25.4.80	31 May	12:48.88	Fatiha	Ouali	FRA	25.10.74	29 May

Indoors

Mark	Name		Nat	Born	Pos	Meet	Venue	Date
11:35.34	Gillian	O'Sullivan	IRL	21.8.76	1	NC	Belfast	15 Feb
11:59.96	Melanie	Seeger	GER	8.1.77	1	NC	Leipzig	22 Feb
12:06.0	Sabine	Zimmer	GER	6.2.81	1		Halle	18 Dec
12:13.00		Perrone			1	NC	Genova	1 Mar
12:31.06	Norica	Cîmpean	ROM	22.3.72	1	NC	Bucuresti	23 Feb
12:32.51	Olive	Loughnane	IRL	14.1.76	2	NC	Belfast	15 Feb
12:34.98	Daniela	Cîrlan	ROM	18.9.80	2	NC	Bucuresti	23 Feb

Mark	Name		Nat	Born	Date	Mark	Name		Nat	Born	Date
12:36.68	Ana Maria	Groza	ROM	1.6.76	23 Feb	12:45.72	Annarita	Sidoti	ITA	25.7.69	1 Mar
12:42.03	Gisela	Orsini	ITA	9.12.71	1 Mar	12:48.3	Irina	Petrova	RUS-J	26.5.85	8 Mar

JUNIORS

Mark	Name		Nat	Born	Pos	Meet	Venue	Date
12:57.6		Li Cui	CHN	18.1.87	1-17	NC	Yangzhou	12 Apr
13:06.1		Pang Yingting	CHN	28.1.87	2-17	NC	Yangzhou	12 Apr
13:06.23	Vera	Sokolova	RUS	8.6.87	1	v2N	Szczecin	9 Aug
12:48.3i	Irina	Petrova	RUS-J	26.5.85	1		Sankt-Peterburg	8 Mar

5000 METRES WALK

Mark	Name		Nat	Born	Pos	Meet	Venue	Date
20:12.41	Elisabetta	Perrone	ITA	9.7.68	1	NC	Rieti	2 Aug
20:13.13	Gillian	O'Sullivan	IRL	21.8.76	1	NC	Dublin (S)	9 Aug
20:56.19	Melanie	Seeger	GER	8.1.77	1	NC	Ulm	28 Jun
21:04.74	Sabine	Zimmer	GER	6.2.81	2	NC	Ulm	28 Jun
21:10.31	Elisa	Rigaudo	ITA	17.6.80	2	NC	Rieti	2 Aug
21:13.59	Olive	Loughnane	IRL	14.1.76	2	NC	Dublin (S)	9 Aug
21:14.7+		Liu Wenjie	CHN-Y	8.1.87	1	in 10k	Qinhangdao	28 Sep
21:21.0+		Ma Yefei	CHN-Y	6.1.87	2	in 10k	Qinhangdao	28 Sep
21:22.1+		Xu Xingyu	CHN-Y	1.12.86	3	in 10k	Qinhangdao	28 Sep
21:26.92		Perrone			1		Milano	28 Jun
21:30.4+		Wang Hongmin	CHN-Y	1.1.86	4	in 10k	Qinhangdao	28 Sep
21:34.30	Fumi	Mitsumura	JPN-J	1.3.85	1		Yokohama	6 Jul

Mark	Name		Nat	Born	Date	Mark	Name		Nat	Born	Date
21:47.87	Mayumi	Kawasaki	JPN	10.5.80	27 Sep	21:58.01	Gisela	Orsini	ITA	9.12.71	2 Aug
21:49.62	Sachiko	Konishi	JPN	4.2.82	6 Jul	22:00.63	Ryoko	Sakakura	JPN	9.5.76	29 Oct
21:49.94	Lisa	Barbieri	ITA	18.5.78	28 Jun	22:04.7+	Susana	Feitor	POR	28.1.75	2 Aug
21:52.85	Maite	Gargallo	ESP	15.10.69	26 Jul	22:04.90	Athanasia	Tsoumeléka	GRE	2.1.82	9 Apr

Indoors

Mark	Name		Nat	Born	Pos	Meet	Venue	Date
21:13.5	Marina	Smyslova	RUS	25.2.66	1		Novosibirsk	29 Jan
21:31.2	Tatyana	Korotkova	RUS	24.4.80	1		Moskva	7 Jan
21:32.0	Larisa	Yemelyanova (Safronova)	RUS	6.1.80	2		Moskva	7 Jan
21:54.2	Irina	Balakley	RUS	6.10.81	2		Novosibirsk	29 Jan

JUNIORS – ADDITIONAL

Mark	Name		Nat	Born	Pos	Meet	Venue	Date
22:07.05	Vera	Sokolova	RUS-Y	8.8.87	1		Kazan	8 Sep
22:09.29	Aleksandra	Kubasova	RUS-Y	19,8,86	2		Kazan	8 Sep
22:21.4		Sun Ronghui	CHN-Y	9.1.88	1-17	NC	Qinhangdao	28 Sep
22:26.6		Li Cui	CHN-Y	18.1.87	1-17	NC	Yangzhou	13 Apr
22:29.7		Yang Yawei	CHN-Y	1.1.86	2-17	NC	Yangzhou	13 Apr

10 KILOMETRES WALK

Mark	Name		Nat	Born	Pos	Meet	Venue	Date
43:23		Gao Kelian	CHN	15.8.83	1	NC	Yangzhou	12 Apr
43:26+	Yelena	Nikolayeva	RUS	1.2.66	1	in 20k	Saint-Denis	24 Aug
43:36		Xu Aihui	CHN	25.4.78	2	NC	Yangzhou	12 Apr
43:36.82t	Rossella	Giordano	ITA	1.12.72	1		Saluzzo	25 Jun
43:43+		Nikolayeva			1=	in 20k	Cheboksary	18 May
43:43+	Gillian	O'Sullivan	IRL	21.8.76	1=	in 20k	Cheboksary	18 May
43:43+	Elisabetta	Perrone	ITA	9.7.68	1=	in 20k	Cheboksary	18 May
43:44	Lyudmila	Yegorova	UKR	4.10.74	1		Ivano-Frankovsk	5 Oct
43:46+		O'Sullivan			1	in 20k	Sesto San Giovanni	1 May
43:46+		O'Sullivan			2=	in 20k	Saint-Denis	24 Aug
43:46+		Perrone			2=	in 20k	Saint-Denis	24 Aug

Mark	Name		Nat	Born	Pos	Meet	Venue	Date
43:48		Zang Yan	CHN	13.12.83	3	NC	Yangzhou	12 Apr
43:49		Shi Na	CHN	17.2.81	4	NC	Yangzhou	12 Apr
43:51.6t	Yelena	Ginko	BLR	30.7.76	1		Grodno	27 Sep
43:59+	Kjersti	Plätzer	NOR	18.1.72	4	in 20k	Cheboksary	18 May
	(15/11)							
44:00.8t		Liu Wenjie	CHN-Y	8.1.87	1	NC-y	Qinhangdao	28 Sep
44:01+	Tatyana	Gudkova	RUS	23.1.78	4	in 20k	Saint-Denis	24 Aug
44:02		Jiang Qiuyan	CHN	5.7.83	5	NC	Yangzhou	12 Apr
44:07.80t	Susana	Feitor	POR	28.1.75	1	NC	Seia	2 Aug
44:08	Melanie	Seeger	GER	8.1.77	1		Kleinmachnow	1 Jun
44:07.8t		Zhang Nan	CHN-Y	18.4.86	1	NC	Qinhangdao	27 Sep
44:11+	Valentina	Tsybulskaya	BLR	19.2.68	6	in 20k	Saint-Denis	24 Aug
44:11.8	Olga	Kardopoltseva	BLR	11.9.66	2		Grodno	27 Sep
44:12+	Claudia	Stef (Iovan)	ROM	25.2.78	7	in 20k	Saint-Denis	24 Aug
	(20)							
44:22+	Tatyana	Korotkova	RUS	24.4.80	1=	in 20k	Adler	1 Mar
44:22+	Antonina	Petrova	RUS	25.1.77	1=	in 20k	Adler	1 Mar
44:22+	Nadezhda	Ryashkina	RUS	22.1.67	1=	in 20k	Adler	1 Mar
44:22+	Tatyana	Sibilyeva	RUS	17.5.80	1=	in 20k	Adler	1 Mar
44:22+	Lyudmila	Yefimkina	RUS	22.8.81	1=	in 20k	Adler	1 Mar
44:22+	Larisa	Yemelyanova	RUS	6.1.80	1=	in 20k	Adler	1 Mar
44:22+	Norica	Cîmpean	ROM	22.3.72	5=	in 20k	Cheboksary	18 May
44:22+	María	Vasco	ESP	26.12.75	5=	in 20k	Cheboksary	18 May
44:22+		Song Hongjuan	CHN-J	4.7.84	11	in 20k	Saint-Denis	24 Aug
44:26		Jian Xingli	CHN	4.12.83	6	NC	Yangzhou	12 Apr
	(30)							
44:28+	Marina	Smyslova	RUS	20.2.66	8	in 20k	Adler	1 Mar
44:30	Sonata	Milusauskaité	LTU	31.8.73	1		Prat de Llobregat	23 Mar
44:30	Daniela	Cîrlan	ROM	18.9.80	2		Bucuresti	5 Jul
44:33		Jiang Jing	CHN-J	23.10.85	2	NC-j	Yangzhou	12 Apr
44:33+	Elisa	Rigaudo	ITA	17.6.80	12	in 20k	Saint-Denis	24 Aug
44:33+	Jane	Saville	AUS	5.11.74	12	in 20k	Saint-Denis	24 Aug
44:34+	Natalya	Fedoskina	RUS	25.6.80	8	in 20k	Cheboksary	18 May
44:37.2t		Ha Mingming	CHN	15.4.82	3	NC	Qinhangdao	27 Sep
44:40.62t	Athanasia	Tsoumeléka	GRE	2.1.82	1		Pírgos	3 May
44:41.71t	Mari Cruz	Díaz	ESP	24.10.69	2		Jerez de la Frontera	2 Aug
	(40)							
44:42+	Maite	Gargallo	ESP	15.10.69	7=	in 20k	La Coruña	7 Jun
44:43+	Aleksandra	Sorokina	RUS	24.2.79	9	in 20k	Adler	1 Mar
44:45+	Margarita	Nazarova	RUS	1.10.76	10	in 20k	Adler	1 Mar
44:45		Fan Haixia	CHN	10.3.82	7	NC	Yangzhou	12 Apr
44:50	Andrea	Meloni	GER	1.10.67	1		Diez	27 Apr
44:52+	Olive	Loughnane	IRL	14.1.76	11	in 20k	Cheboksary	18 May
44:53+	Svetlana	Tolstaya	KAZ	9.8.71	11	in 20k	Adler	1 Mar
44:53+	Valentina	Savchuk	UKR	19.1.75	12	in 20k	Cheboksary	18 May
44:58+	Vera	Zozulya	UKR	31.8.70	13	in 20k	Cheboksary	18 May
44:58+	Tatyana	Kozlova	RUS	2.9.83	4	in 20k	Cheboksary	15 Jun
	(50)							
45:00.5t		Shi Yong	CHN-Y	7.2.87	2	NC-y	Qinhangdao	28 Sep
45:01	Sabine	Zimmer	GER	6.2.81	1		Aschersleben	30 Mar
45:07.2t		Liu Xiaoyan	CHN-J	4.9.85	6	NC	Qinhangdao	27 Sep
45:10		Zou Ying	CHN	27.3.74	8	NC	Yangzhou	12 Apr
45:16.3t		Xu Xingyu	CHN-Y	1.12.86	3	NC-y	Qinhangdao	28 Sep
45:18.86t		Kim Mi-jung	KOR	10.6.79	1		Bucheon	10 Apr
45:22	Vera	Sokolova	RUS-Y	8.6.87	1		Adler	1 Mar
45:23	Kseniya	Ishcheykina	RUS-J	19.8.84	2		Adler	1 Mar
45:26	Irina	Petrova	RUS-J	26.5.85	3		Adler	1 Mar
45:26+	Natalya	Shiviryova	RUS	31.8.78	2	in 20k	Cheboksary	7 Sep
	(60)							
45:30	Nadezhda	Putilova	RUS	8.4.83	1		Gachina	6 Apr
45:31+	María del Rosario	Sánchez	MEX	26.10.73	21	in 20k	Saint-Denis	24 Aug
45:36		Ye Zhong	CHN-Y	12.10.87	3	NC-j	Yangzhou	12 Apr
45:36+	Olga	Lukyanchuk	UKR	7.12.76	19	in 20k	Cheboksary	18 May
45:37+	Athiná	Papayiánni	GRE	18.8.80	20	in 20k	Cheboksary	18 May
45:37+	Kristina	Saltanovic	LTU	20.2.75	24	in 20k	Saint-Denis	24 Aug
45:38.6t		Ma Yefei	CHN-Y	6.1.87	4	NC-y	Qinhangdao	28 Sep
45:44	Svetlana	Vasilyeva	RUS-J	17.8.85	4		Adler	1 Mar
45:45+	Victoria	Palacios	MEX	29.3.77	10=	in 20k	La Coruña	7 Jun
45:45+	Eva	Pérez	ESP	18.7.75	10=	in 20k	La Coruña	7 Jun
	(70)							
45:46	Zuzana	Maliková	SVK	2.8.83	1		Borsky Mikulás	31 May

Mark	Name		Nat	Born	Pos	Meet	Venue	Date
45:48+	Vera	Santos	POR	3.12.81	23	in 20k	Cheboksary	18 May
45:50+	Kathrin	Boyde	GER	4.12.70	24	in 20k	Cheboksary	18 May
45:50+	Geovanna	Irusta	BOL	26.9.75	26	in 20k	Saint-Denis	24 Aug
45:50.53t	Maribel	Gonçalves	POR	1.4.78	1		Funchal	6 Dec
45:51+	Sylwia	Korzeniowska	POL	25.4.80	25=	in 20k	Cheboksary	18 May
45:51+	Fatiha	Ouali	FRA	25.10.74	25=	in 20k	Cheboksary	18 May
45:52	Yelena	Kurochkina	RUS-J	11.5.85	5		Adler	1 Mar
45:53	Olga	Savelyeva	RUS-J	7.4.84	6		Adler	1 Mar
45:54		Cao Xue	CHN	2.3.82	9	NC	Yangzhou	12 Apr
	(80)							
45:55	Carolina	Jiménez	ESP	2.2.80	2		Prat de Lloregat	23 Mar

46:01+	Mayumi	Kawasaki	JPN	10.5.80	2 Nov
46:03+	Ryoko Sakakura (Tadamasa)		JPN	9.5.76	2 Nov
46:04+	Ana Maria	Groza	ROM	1.6.76	26 Apr
46:07+	Irina	Balakley	RUS	6.10.81	1 Mar
46:09	Lisa	Barbieri	ITA	18.5.78	9 Feb
46:09	Anna	Bragina	RUS-J	23.8.85	1 Mar
46:09+	Lyudmila	Arkhipova	RUS	12.9.78	1 Mar
46:10+	Beatriz	Pascual	ESP	9.5.82	18 May
46:13		Li Yanxia	CHN-J	21.2.87	12 Apr
46:13+	Barbora	Dibelková	CZE	26.5.83	23 Aug
46:19.4t	Natalya	Misyulya	BLR	16.4.66	27 Sep
46:19.7t		Sun Lihua	CHN	30.9.83	27 Sep
46:20+	Alena	Zenkova	RUS	1.1.82	8 Sep
46:20+	Yevdokiya	Korotkova	RUS	28.2.79	8 Sep
46:21+	Gisella	Orsini	ITA	9.12.71	18 May
46:22		He Dan	CHN-J	22.7.84	12 Apr
46:22.40t	María José	Poves	ESP	16.3.78	2 Aug
46:23	Tatyana	Matyushkina	RUS	22.1.79	1 Mar
46:23+	Takako	Terui	JPN	11.1.78	20 Apr
46:23+	Kaori	Nikaido	JPN	25.7.79	2 Nov
46:23.61t	Hristina	Kokótou	GRE	9.1.72	4 May
46:25+	Yekaterina	Lobashova	BLR	15.11.83	18 May
46:28		Li Ruibin	CHN-J	29.9.84	12 Apr
46:28+	Yuliya	Voyevodina	RUS	17.10.71	15 Jun
46:33+	Yekaterina	Yeshova	RUS	3.7.82	1 Mar
46:34		Liu Yanan	CHN-J	18.1.87	12 Apr
46:35.0+t	Joanne	Dow	USA	19.3.64	21 Jun
46:36.0+t	Michelle	Rohl	USA	12.11.65	21 Jun
46:39	Anna	Pudovkina	RUS-J	29.3.85	1 Mar
46:41.6t		Li Cui	CHN-Y	18.1.87	27 Sep
46:43+	Lyudmila	Dolgopolova	BLR	11.8.69	18 May
46:43+	Irina	Pudovkina	RUS	7.2.80	8 Sep
46:46+	Vanessa	Espinosa	ESP	4.2.79	7 Jun
46:47	Maria	Shokhorova	RUS-J	24.12.85	1 Mar
46:47		Zuo Yan	CHN	18.8.83	12 Apr
46:48		Li Yanhong	CHN-J	2.6.84	12 Apr
46:53		Wu Cuilian	CHN	27.4.81	12 Apr
46:53.5t		Hu Ming	CHN-J	8.10.84	27 Sep
46:55	Rocío	Florido	ESP	16.1.76	26 Jan
46:58.5t	Nina	Moskvina (121)	UKR	6.8.71	10 Oct

Best track times

44:14.9		Gao Kelian	CHN	15.8.83	2	NC	Qinhangdao	27 Sep
44:30.46	María	Vasco	ESP	26.12.75	1	NC	Jerez de la Frontera	2 Aug
44:46.3		Xu Aihui	CHN	25.4.78	4	NC	Qinhangdao	27 Sep
44:55.3		Jiang Qiuyan	CHN	5.7.83	5	NC	Qinhangdao	27 Sep
45:14.2		Zang Yan	CHN	13.12.83	7	NC	Qinhangdao	27 Sep
45:15.1		Jian Xingli	CHN	4.12.83	8	NC	Qinhangdao	27 Sep
45:22.4		Zou Ying	CHN	27.3.74	9	NC	Qinhangdao	27 Sep
45:24.2	Lyudmila	Yegorova	UKR	4.10.74	1		Mukachevo	10 Oct
45:42.0+	Marina	Smyslova	RUS	20.2.66	1	in 20k	Izhevsk	22 Sep

46:06.02	Vera	Santos	POR	3.12.81	2 Aug
46:23.5	Zuzana	Maliková	SVK	2.8.83	12 Apr
46:28.52+	Fatiha	Ouali	FRA	25.10.74	13 Apr
46:41.29	Beatriz	Pascual	ESP	9.5.82	2 Aug
46:42.0+	Yevdokiya	Korotkova	RUS	28.2.79	22 Sep
46:45.1	Anna	Bragina	RUS-J	23.8.85	16 Jun
46:50.0+	Lyudmila	Arkhipova	RUS	12.9.78	22 Sep
46:58.5	Nina	Moskvina	UKR	6.8.71	10 Oct
46:59.0	Yekaterina	Yeshova	RUS	3.7.82	22 Sep
46:59.1	Svetlana	Vasilyeva	RUS-J	17.8.85	16 Jun

Indoors

46:44.2	Irina	Petrova	RUS-J	26.5.85	9 Feb
46:47.54	Yekaterina	Lobashova	BLR	15.11.83	6 Feb
46:48.48	Tatyana	Zuyeva	BLR	15.11.83	6 Feb

JUNIORS

See main list for 15 top juniors. 13 performances by 12 women to 45:30. Additional mark and further juniors:

Zhang Nan 44:08 1 NC-j Qinghangdao 27 Sep

46:09	Anna	Bragina	RUS	23.8.85	7		Adler	1 Mar
46:13		Li Yanxia	CHN	21.2.87	11	NC	Yangzhou	12 Apr
46:22		He Dan	CHN	22.7.84	10		Yangzhou	12 Apr
46:28		Li Ruibin	CHN	29.9.84	5	j	Yangzhou	12 Apr
46:34		Liu Yanan (20)	CHN	18.1.87	6	j	Yangzhou	12 Apr

WOMEN 2003

20 KILOMETRES WALK

1:26:22	Yelena	Nikolayeva	RUS	1.2.66	1	ECp	Cheboksary	18 May
1:26:52		Nikolayeva			1	WCh	Saint-Denis	24 Aug
1:27:14	Antonina	Petrova	RUS	25.1.77	1	NC-w	Adler	1 Mar
1:27:16		Song Hongjuan	CHN-J	4.7.84	1	NC	Yangzhou	14 Apr
1:27:22	Gillian	O'Sullivan	IRL	21.8.76	1		Sesto San Giovanni	1 May
1:27:23	Larisa	Yemelyanova (Safronova)	RUS	6.1.80	2	NC-w	Adler	1 Mar
1:27:25		Nikolayeva			1		La Coruña	7 Jun
1:27:34		O'Sullivan			2	WCh	Saint-Denis	24 Aug
1:27:54	Tatyana	Sibilyeva	RUS	17.5.80	3	NC-w	Adler	1 Mar
1:27:58	Elisabetta	Perrone	ITA	9.7.68	2	ECp	Cheboksary	18 May
1:28:10	María	Vasco	ESP	26.12.75	3	ECp	Cheboksary	18 May
1:28:10	Valentina	Tsybulskaya	BLR	19.2.68	3	WCh	Saint-Denis	24 Aug
1:28:17	Natalya	Fedoskina (10)	RUS	25.6.80	4	ECp	Cheboksary	18 May
1:28:19	Vera	Zozulya	UKR	31.8.70	1	NC-w	Yevpatoriya	23 Feb

Mark	Name		Nat	Born	Pos	Meet	Venue	Date
1:28:20	Lyudmila	Yefimkina	RUS	22.8.81	4	NC-w	Adler	1 Mar
1:28:28		O'Sullivan			1		La Coruña	7 Jun
1:28:37	Tatyana	Gudkova	RUS	23.1.78	1	NC	Cheboksary	15 Jun
1:28:49	Kjersti	Plätzer	NOR	18.1.72	3		La Coruña	7 Jun
1:28:52	Valentina	Savchuk	UKR	19.1.75	2	NC-w	Yevpatoriya	23 Feb
1:28:52	Nadezhda	Ryashkina	RUS	22.1.67	5	NC-w	Adler	1 Mar
1:28:53		Gudkova			4	WCh	Saint-Denis	24 Aug
1:29:08	Susana	Feitor	POR	28.1.75	5	ECp	Cheboksary	18 May
1:29:09	Claudia	Stef	ROM	25.2.78	5	WCh	Saint-Denis	24 Aug
1:29:14	Rossella	Giordano	ITA	1.12.72	6	WCh	Saint-Denis	24 Aug
1:29:22		O'Sullivan			1		Dublin	12 Jul
1:29:25		Gudkova			6	NC-w	Adler	1 Mar
1:29:28		Yefimkina			2	NC	Cheboksary	15 Jun
1:29:29		Perrone			4		La Coruña	7 Jun
1:29:34	Athanasia	Tsouméléka	GRE	2.1.82	7	WCh	Saint-Denis	24 Aug
1:29:35	Tatyana	Korotkova	RUS	24.4.80	3	NC	Cheboksary	15 Jun
	(30/21)							
1:29:39		Gao Kelian	CHN	15.8.83	2	NC	Yangzhou	14 Apr
1:29:40		Xu Aihui	CHN	25.4.78	3	NC	Yangzhou	14 Apr
1:29:42		Jiang Jing	CHN-J	23.10.85	4	NC	Yangzhou	14 Apr
1:29:44	Melanie	Seeger	GER	8.1.77	1	NC	Naumburg	13 Apr
1:29:46	Olga	Kardopoltseva	BLR	11.9.66	5		La Coruña	7 Jun
1:29:54	Hristina	Kokótou	GRE	9.1.72	1		Tilburg	5 Oct
1:30:03		Jiang Qiuyan	CHN	5.7.83	5	NC	Yangzhou	14 Apr
1:30:20	Yelena	Miroshnichenko	UKR	1.3.77	3	NC-w	Yevpatoriya	23 Feb
1:30:26		Ha Mingming	CHN	15.4.82	6	NC	Yangzhou	14 Apr
	(30)							
1:30:27	Norica	Cîmpean	ROM	22.3.72	7	ECp	Cheboksary	18 May
1:30:29	Olive	Loughnane	IRL	14.1.76	8	ECp	Cheboksary	18 May
1:30:34		Jian Xingli	CHN	4.12.83	7	NC	Yangzhou	14 Apr
1:30:34	Elisa	Rigaudo	ITA	17.6.80	10	WCh	Saint-Denis	24 Aug
1:30:41	Maria Teresa	Gargallo	ESP	15.10.69	7		La Coruña	7 Jun
1:30:48	Marina	Smyslova	RUS	25.2.66	8	NC-w	Adler	1 Mar
1:30:51	Jane	Saville	AUS	5.11.74	11	WCh	Saint-Denis	24 Aug
1:30:53	Sonata	Milusauskaité	LTU	31.8.73	1	ESP Ch	Orense	16 Feb
1:30:57	Svetlana	Tolstaya	KAZ	9.8.71	9	RUS-w	Adler	1 Mar
1:31:04		Zang Yan	CHN	13.12.83	8	NC	Yangzhou	14 Apr
	(40)							
1:31:09	Kristina	Saltanovic	LTU	20.2.75	1	NC	Kaunas	1 Aug
1:31:12		Fan Haixia	CHN	10.3.82	9	NC	Yangzhou	14 Apr
1:31:14		Shi Na	CHN	17.2.81	10	NC	Yangzhou	14 Apr
1:31:18	Sabine	Zimmer	GER	6.2.81	2	NC	Naumburg	13 Apr
1:31:21	Margarita	Nazarova	RUS	1.10.76	10	NC-w	Adler	1 Mar
1:31:31	Beatriz	Pascual	ESP	9.5.82	3	NC	Orense	16 Feb
1:31:45	Olga	Lukyanchuk	UKR	7.12.76	4	NC-w	Yevpatoriya	23 Feb
1:31:55		Zhang Nan	CHN-Y	18.4.86	1	NC	Qinhangdao	29 Sep
1:32:07		Zou Ying	CHN	20.8.82	2	AsiC	Manila	23 Sep
1:32:10	Mari Cruz	Díaz	ESP	24.10.69	15	ECp	Cheboksary	18 May
	(50)							
1:32:16	Mayumi	Kawasaki	JPN	10.5.80	1		Takahata	2 Nov
1:32:17	Athiná	Papayiánni	GRE	18.8.80	17	ECp	Cheboksary	18 May
1:32:18	Natalya	Shiviryova	RUS	31.8.78	3		Cheboksary	8 Sep
1:32:20	Eva	Pérez	ESP	18.7.75	4	NC	Orense	16 Feb
1:32:25		Yuan Yufang	MAS	1.2.76	3	AsiC	Manila	23 Sep
1:32:34	Kathrin	Boyde	GER	4.12.70	3	NC	Naumburg	13 Apr
1:32:36		Liu Xiaoyan	CHN-J	4.9.85	11	NC	Yangzhou	14 Apr
1:32:40		Wang Liping	CHN	8.7.76	4	NC	Qinhangdao	29 Sep
1:32:41	Daniela	Cîrlan	ROM	18.9.80	1	RomIC	Bucuresti	8 Jun
1:32:43	Vera	Santos	POR	3.12.81	15	WCh	Saint-Denis	24 Aug
	(60)							
1:32:43	Ryoko	Sakakura (Tadamasa)	JPN	9.5.76	2		Takahata	2 Nov
1:32:49	Carolina	Jiménez	ESP	2.2.80	10		La Coruña	7 Jun
1:32:56	Aleksandra	Sorokina	RUS	24.2.79	11	NC-w	Adler	1 Mar
1:32:57	Alena	Zenkova	RUS	1.1.82	4		Cheboksary	8 Sep
1:32:58	Yelena	Kuznetsova	KAZ	4.7.77	2	LTU Ch	Kaunas	1 Aug
1:33:03		Kim Mi-jung	KOR	10.6.79	1	NC	Daejun	5 Jun
1:33:18	Lyudmila	Arkhipova	RUS	12.9.78	12	NC-w	Adler	1 Mar
1:33:24	Barbora	Dibelková	CZE	26.5.83	5	UKR-w	Yevpatoriya	23 Feb
1:33:24	Irina	Balakley	RUS	6.10.81	13	NC-w	Adler	1 Mar
1:33:24	Lyudmila	Dolgopolova	BLR	11.8.69	1	NC	Brest	11 Jul
	(70)							

Mark	Name		Nat	Born	Pos	Meet	Venue	Date
1:33:25	Fatiha	Ouali	FRA	25.10.74	21	ECp	Cheboksary	18 May
1:33:27	Aggeliki	Makrí	GRE	25.9.78	1		Lugano	7 Sep
1:33:42	Geovanna	Irusta	BOL	26.9.75	18	WCh	Saint-Denis	24 Aug
1:33:47	Sylwia	Korzeniowska	POL	25.4.80	1		Zaniemysl	12 Apr
1:33:52	Andrea	Meloni	GER	1.10.67	25	ECp	Cheboksary	18 May
1:33:56	Irina	Pudovkina	RUS	2.11.80	5		Cheboksary	8 Sep
1:34:05	Kaori	Nikaido	JPN	25.7.79	4	AsiC	Manila	23 Sep
1:34:08	Lyudmila	Yegorova	UKR	4.10.74	6	NC-w	Yevpatoriya	23 Feb
1:34:12	Yevdokiya	Korotkova	RUS	28.2.79	6		Cheboksary	8 Sep
1:34:18		Cao Xue	CHN	2.3.82	13	NC	Yangzhou	14 Apr
	(80)							
1:34:23	Nina	Moskvina	UKR	6.8.71	7	NC-w	Yevpatoriya	23 Feb
1:34:27	Gisella	Orsini	ITA	9.12.71	27	ECp	Cheboksary	18 May
1:34:28	Natalya	Misyulya	BLR	16.4.66	2	NC	Brest	11 Jul
1:34:31.06t	Michelle	Rohl	USA	12.11.65	1	NC	Stanford	21 Jun
1:34:34	Tatyana	Matyushkina	RUS	22.1.79	14	NC-w	Adler	1 Mar
1:34.34		Xue Ailing	CHN	12.2.79	7	NC	Qinhangdao	29 Sep
1:34:53	María del Rosario	Sánchez	MEX	26.10.73	7		Tijuana	8 Mar
1:34:54	Yekaterina	Yeshova	RUS	18.2.82	15	NC-w	Adler	1 Mar
1:34:55		Zuo Yan	CHN	18.8.83	14	NC	Yangzhou	14 Apr
1:34:56	Victoria	Palacios	MEX	29.3.77	12		La Coruña	7 Jun
	(90)							
1:34:56.4tmx	Christine	Guinaudeau	FRA	20.6.78	1mx		Beaune	23 Mar
	1:37:53				34	ECp	Cheboksary	18 May
1:34:57.79t	Joanne	Dow	USA	19.3.64	2	NC	Stanford	21 Jun
1:35:02		Hu Ming	CHN-J	8.10.84	15	NC	Yangzhou	14 Apr
1:35:12	Veronica	Budileanu	ROM	27.2.76	1	Balk C	Ruse	6 Apr
1:35:20	Lisa	Barbieri	ITA	18.5.78	10		Sesto San Giovanni	1 May
1:35:20		Sun Lihua	CHN	30.9.83	8	NC	Qinhangdao	29 Sep
1:35:25		Sun Chunfang	CHN	1.3.77	16	NC	Yangzhou	14 Apr
1:35:30		He Xingtong	CHN-Y	11.2.86	17	NC	Yangzhou	14 Apr
1:35:32	Maria José	Poves	ESP	16.3.78	7	NC	Orense	16 Feb
1:35:46	Ana Maria	Groza	ROM	1.6.76	2	RomIC	Bucuresti	8 Jun
	(100)							

Mark	Name		Nat	Born	Date
1:35:47	Takako	Terui	JPN	11.1.78	2 Nov
1:35:49		He Dan	CHN-J	22.7.84	14 Apr
1:35:53		Li Yanhong	CHN-J	2.6.84	14 Apr
1:35:53	Yekaterina	Lobashova	BLR	15.11.83	18 May
1:35:55	Maribel	Gonçalves	POR	1.4.78	1 Mar
1:35:55	Natalie	Saville	AUS	7.9.78	6 Apr
1:35:59	Gabrielle	Gorst	NZL	16.2.64	23 Mar
1:36:02solo	Monica	Svensson	SWE	26.12.78	20 Jul
	1:36:24				18 May
1:36:03	Inês	Henriques	POR	1.5.80	18 May
1:36:09	Marina	Koznyeva	RUS	69	15 Jun
1:36:18	Cheryl	Webb	AUS	3.10.76	23 Feb
1:36:22	Vanessa	Espinosa	ESP	4.2.79	16 Feb
1:36:22		Lu Yanmei	CHN-J	29.6.85	29 Sep
1:36.23	Larisa	Khmelnitskaya	BLR	23.9.71	6 Mar
1:36:23		Ye Zhong	CHN-Y	12.10.87	14 Apr
1:36:23.8t	Yelena	Kurochkina	RUS-J	11.5.85	28 Jun
1:36:38.38t	Teresa	Vaill	USA	20.11.62	21 Jun
1:36:44	Yuliya	Voyevodina	RUS	17.10.71	1 Mar
1:36:45		Li Cui	CHN-Y	18.1.87	29 Sep
1:36:46	Toshie	Kawatsu	JPN	17.12.81	28 Jan
1:36:51	Nadezhda	Putilova	RUS	8.4.83	1 Mar
1:36:51	Evaggelía	Xinoú	GRE	22.11.81	16 Mar
1:36:56	Tatyana	Zuyeva	BLR	15.11.83	6 Mar
1:37:09	Agnieszka	Olesz	POL	27.8.79	12 Apr
1:37:23	Yelena	Ginko	BLR	30.7.76	13 Apr
1:37:26	Mara	Ibáñez	MEX	17.12.74	7 Jun
1:37:27	Ariana	Quino	BOL	31.12.83	13 Jul
1:37:34	Sachiko	Konishi	JPN	4.2.82	25 Aug
1:37:37	Monica	Ballester	ESP	24.6.75	19 Jan
1:37:44	Anna	Szumny	POL	24.3.83	6 Jul
1:37:47	Zuzana	Blazeková	SVK	1.7.80	5 Apr
1:37:49	Svetlana	Trifonova	RUS	24.3.82	1 Mar
1:37:52	Nevena	Mineva/Dimitrova	BUL	14.6.72	6 Apr
1:38:04	Aura	Morales	MEX	7.6.82	13 Jul
1:38:05.8t		Jiang Kun	CHN-J	18.5.85	24 Oct
1:38:06	Zuzana	Malíková	SVK	2.8.83	29 Mar
1:38:08	Snezhana	Yurchenko	BLR-J	8.3.84	6 Mar
1:38:15		Chen Jiao	CHN-Y	16.2.86	14 Apr
1:38:15	Simone	Wolowiec	AUS	12.2.74	20 Jul
1:38:16	Nadezhda	Prokopuk	UKR	25.2.81	23 Feb
1:38:21	Yekaterina	Marchotenko	BLR	22.9.81	6 Mar
1:38:22	Tatyana	Metlevskaya	BLR-J	14.9.84	3 Jun
1:38:23		Deng Guocun	CHN-J	16.8.85	14 Apr
1:38:23		Yang Sha	CHN-Y	16.1.86	29 Sep
1:38:25		Pan Hailian	CHN	21.11.77	14 Apr
1:38:29	Yeliz	Ay	TUR	9.11.77	12 Jul
1:38:34	Graciela	Mendoza	MEX	22.3.63	8 Mar
1:38:39	Yelena	Ulyanova	RUS-J	4.7.85	1 Mar
1:38:45	Sandra	Zapata	COL	3.2.77	15 Mar
1:38:49	Natsuki	Kimura	JPN-J	27.7.84	20 Apr
1:38:58	Sofia	Avoila	POR	30.7.76	19 Jan
1:38:58	Carmen	Bone	ESP	20.12.80	16 Feb
1:39:16	Elzbieta	Tuwalska	POL	10.7.79	12 Apr
1:39:18	Natividad	Collado	GUA	20.11.71	6 Aug
1:39:19	Sandra	Evaristo	MEX	14.10.76	7 Jun
1:39:28	Yoko	Oura	JPN	8.4.83	2 Nov
1:39:29		Li Shuang	CHN-J	4.1.85	29 Sep
1:39:33	Masumi	Kadowaki	JPN	16.7.80	2 Nov
1:39:38.2	Galina	Kolpakova	RUS	83	22 Sep
1:39:44		Zhang Libo	CHN	4.2.82	14 Apr
1:39:48	Natalya	Karpetchenko	KAZ	22.2.82	1 Mar
1:39:49	Karen	Foan	CAN	11.6.79	4 May
1:39:50	Jolene	Moore	USA	14.3.66	17 May
1:39:55.35t	Amber	Antonia (164)	USA	4.11.79	21 Jun

Best track times

Mark	Name		Nat	Born	Pos	Meet	Venue	Date
1:29:32.4		Song Hongjuan	CHN-J	4.7.84	1	NG	Changsha	24 Oct
1:31:06.6		Jiang Jing	CHN-J	23.10.85	2	NG	Changsha	24 Oct
1:32:16.5	Marina	Smyslova	RUS	25.2.66	1	NC	Ishevsk	22 Sep
1:34:43.6	Lyudmila	Dolgopolova	BLR	11.8.69	1		Brest	6 Mar
1:34:58.0		Gao Kelian	CHN	15.8.83	3	NG	Changsha	24 Oct
1:35:02.2	Lyudmila	Arkhipova	RUS	12.9.78	2	NC	Ishevsk	22 Sep
1:35:37.6	Fatiha	Ouali	FRA	28.10.74	1		Sotteville	13 Apr

Mark		Name	Nat	Born	Pos	Meet	Venue	Date
1:36:05.6	Yevdokiya	Korotkova	RUS	28.2.79	3	NC	Ishevsk	22 Sep
1:36:28.6		Jiang Qiuyan	CHN	5.7.83	4	NG	Changsha	24 Oct
1:36:57.5	Aleksandra	Sorokina	RUS	24.2.79	4	NC	Ishevsk	22 Sep
1:37:03.8	Irina	Pudovkina	RUS	7.2.80	5	NC	Izhevsk	22 Sep
1:37:53.9	Yekaterina	Yeshova	RUS	3.7.82	6	NC	Izhevsk	22 Sep
1:38:38.0	Maribel	Gonçalves	POR	1.4.78	1	NC	Seia	2 Aug

JUNIOR

See main list for top 6 juniors.Additional women:

1:35:49		He Dan	CHN	22.7.84	18	NC	Yangzhou	14 Apr
1:35:53		Li Yanhong	CHN	2.6.84	19	NC	Yangzhou	14 Apr
1:36:22		Lu Yanmei	CHN	29.6.85	1	NC-j	Qinhangdao	29 Sep
1:36:23		Ye Zhong (10)	CHN-Y	12.10.87	1	NC-j	Yangzhou	14 Apr
1:36:23.8t	Yelena	Kurochkina	RUS	11.5.85	1		Sankt Peterburg	28 Jun
1:36:45		Li Cui	CHN-Y	18.1.87	2	NC-j	Qinhangdao	29 Sep
1:38:05.8t		Jiang Kun	CHN	18.5.85	5	NG	Changsha	24 Oct
1:38:08	Snezhana	Yurchenko	BLR	8.3.84	5	NC-w	Brest	6 Mar
1:38:15		Chen Jiao	CHN-Y	16.2.86	22		Yangzhou	14 Apr
1:38:22	Tatyana	Metlevskaya	BLR	14.9.84	2		Minsk	3 Jun
1:38:23		Deng Guocun	CHN	16.8.85	23		Yangzhou	14 Apr
1:38:23		Yang Sha	CHN-Y	16.1.86	3	NC	Qinhangdao	29 Sep
1:38:39	Yelena	Ulyanova	RUS	4.7.85	21		Adler	1 Mar
1:38:49	Natsuki	Kimura (20)	JPN	27.7.84	4	NC	Wajima	20 Apr

30 KILOMETRES WALK

2:34:36.1 t	Nadezhda	Putilova	RUS	8.4.83	1		Sankt-Peterburg	28 Jun
2:39:45+	Yelena	Ginko	BLR	30.7.76	1	in 50k	Scanzoroscaite	19 Oct
2:43:23+	Evaggelía	Xinoú	GRE	22.11.81	2	in 50k	Scanzoroscaite	19 Oct
2:43:56.8	Tatyana	Abramtseva	RUS-Y	18.7.86	2		Sankt-Peterburg	28 Jun
2:46:23+	Henrieta	Rusnáková	SVK	17.1.71	3	in 50k	Scanzoroscaite	19 Oct

50 KILOMETRES WALK

4:22:00	Yelena	Ginko	BLR	30.7.76	1		Scanzoroscaite	19 Oct
4:32:22	Evaggelía	Xinoú	GRE	22.11.81	2		Scanzoroscaite	19 Oct
4:44:09	Henrieta	Rusnáková	SVK	17.1.71	3		Scanzoroscaite	19 Oct
4:45:00+	Anita	Liepina	LAT	17.11.67	4	in 100k	Scanzoroscaite	19 Oct
4:46:35	Monica	Gardini	ITA	3.11.73	5		Scanzoroscaite	19 Oct
5:00:10+	Valentina	Setrova	BLR	19.12.71	6	in 100k	Scanzoroscaite	19 Oct
Junior: 5:05:44.7	Tatyana	Ambrazeva	RUS-Y	18.7.86	1		Sankt-Peterburg	12 Oct

100 KILOMETRES WALK

10:23:47	Anita	Liepina	LAT	17.11.67	1		Scanzoroscaite	19 Oct
10:54.19	Valentina	Setrova	BLR	19.12.71	2		Scanzoroscaite	19 Oct

WORLD LIST TRENDS – MEN

This table shows the 10th and 100th bests in the year lists for 1984, 1988, 1992, 1996 and the last six years.

Men 10th Bests	*1984*	*1988*	*1992*	*1996*	*1998*	*1999*	*2000*	*2001*	*2002*	*2003*
100m	10.14	10.06	10.07	10.01	10.00	10.00	10.03	10.05	9.99	10.00
200m	20.34	20.18	20.15	20.17	20.27	20.08	**20.03**	20.19	20.21	20.15
400m	44.83	44.61	44.52	**44.51**	44.65	44.59	44.70	44.80	44.84	44.78
800m	1:43.93	1:44.10	1:44.33	**1:43.66**	1:44.17	1:43.98	1:44.06	1:43.98	1:43.93	1:44.22
1500m	3:34.20	3:34.61	3:33.80	3:33.00	3:31.89	3:31.60	3:32.01	**3:31.49**	3:32.37	3:31.61
5000m	13:16.41	3:17.48	13:10.47	12:59.19	13:00.59	12:59.09	12:58.70	13:01.64	13:01.98	**12:54.99**
10000m	27:47.00	7:40.36	27:45.46	27:30.37	27:22.54	27:18.28	27:23.65	27:25.55	27:26.12	**27:14.61**
Marathon	2:10:05	2:08:49	2:09:30	2:09:15	2:07:57	2:07:09	2:07:47	2:07:52	2:07:06	**2:06:48**
3000mSt	8:17.27	8:16.04	8:13.65	8:12.54	8:10.67	8:10.56	8:10.23	8:09.23	**8:08.14**	8:09.37
110mh	13.45	13.36	13.33	13.24	**13.20**	13.21	13.24	13.26	13.30	13.28
400mh	48.74	48.65	48.60	48.28	48.30	**48.22**	48.40	48.40	48.25	48.50
HJ	2.33	**2.36**	2.34	2.34	2.32	2.32	2.34	2.33	2.32	2.32
PV	5.75	5.80	5.85	**5.90**	**5.90**	5.85	5.85	5.85	5.81	5.81
LJ	8.27	8.31	8.28	8.34	8.28	8.26	8.33	8.22	8.26	8.30
TJ	17.34	17.43	17.30	17.20	17.24	17.27	17.26	17.22	17.35	17.28
SP	**21.63**	21.16	20.93	20.78	20.79	20.84	21.27	20.88	21.11	21.14
DT	67.76	67.38	66.64	66.70	66.69	66.95	66.93	67.57	66.90	66.35
HT	80.50	**81.88**	80.46	79.52	80.88	80.51	81.36	80.88	81.59	80.89
JT	(90.94)	82.70	85.74	**87.12**	86.92	87.11	86.65	86.63	85.74	84.54
Decathlon	8491	8387	8237	8462	**8526**	8379	8467	8307	8175	8203
20kmW	1:21:49	1:20:10	1:20:32	1:19:31	1:19:43	1:19:55	1:19:18	1:19:45	1:20:36	1:19:35
50kmW	3:48:50	3:46:30	3:50:01	**3:44:19**	3:45:29	3:46:36	3:44:33	3:46:12	3:45:45	3:44:53

Peak years shown in bold. Other peaks: 100m 9.98 (1997), TJ 17.48 (1985), DT 68.20 (1982)

Men 100th Bests

100m	10.36	10.34	10.32	10.27	10.27	10.26	**10.24**	10.26	10.27	10.26
200m	20.78	20.79	20.78	**20.66**	20.67	20.66	20.66	20.72	20.74	20.69
400m	46.03	45.99	45.98	45.91	45.91	45.88	**45.78**	45.90	45.99	45.83
800m	1:46.97	1:46.91	1:46.95	1:46.82	1:46.87	**1:46.54**	1:46.71	1:47.00	1:47.12	1:46.92
1500m	3:38.89	3:39.46	3:39.11	3:38.66	3:39.10	3:39.05	3:38.68	3:38.94	3:39.70	3:39.49
5000m	13:35.10	13:37.20	13:31.44	13:34.29	13:34.34	13:32.94	**13:28.62**	13:30.56	13:31.61	13:29.77
10000m	28:26.10	28:27.28	28:30.42	28:20.9	28:26.4	28:19.07	**28:15.98**	28:27.33	28:27.17	28:22.29
Marathon	2:13:20	2:13:08	2:13:22	2:12:25	2:11:50	2:11:26	2:11:24	2:11:18	**2:11:08**	**2:10:38**
3000mSt	8:35.35	8:35.24	8:34.43	8:34.91	8:36.24	8:34.04	**8:33.37**	8:35.17	8:34.18	8:33.58
110mh	13.91	13.83	13.78	**13.72**	13.80	13.80	13.76	13.78	13.79	13.87
400mh	50.53	50.52	50.50	50.17	50.20	50.10	**50.06**	50.12	50.19	50.20
HJ	**2.24**	**2.24**	**2.24**	**2.24**	2.23	2.22	2.23	2.22	2.23	2.22
PV	5.41	5.50	5.50	5.50	5.50	5.50	**5.55**	5.45	5.50	5.50
LJ	7.90	7.93	7.93	**7.94**	7.90	7.92	7.93	7.89	7.90	7.92
TJ	16.41	**16.60**	16.59	16.56	16.42	16.37	16.48	16.45	16.41	16.43
SP	**19.48**	19.17	18.79	18.81	18.89	18.81	19.05	19.00	19.11	19.02
DT	**60.96**	60.84	59.80	59.82	59.98	59.87	60.16	59.60	59.72	59.62
HT	**73.08**	72.34	70.70	70.88	71.10	70.93	71.28	70.62	69.88	70.63
JT	(81.52)	76.48	76.40	76.20	76.20	75.78	76.06	76.12	76.60	76.17
Decathlon	7630	**7702**	7567	7701	7607	7592	7633	7562	7537	7512
20kmW	1:25:57	1:24:54	1:24:09	1:23:55	1:24:30	1:24:31	1:24:22	1:24:08	1:24:41	1:24:04
50kmW	4:09:40	4:06:34	4:07:33	4:06:31	4:08:00	**4:03:49**	4:04:34	4:05:45	4:07:43	4:06:54

Other peaks: HJ 2.24 (also 1989), JT 77.14 (1991), 20km W 1:23:39 (1995)

WOMEN'S WORLD LIST TRENDS

This table shows the 10th and 100th bests in the year lists for 1984, 1988, 1992, 1996 and the last six years.

10th Bests	*1984*	*1988*	*1992*	*1996*	*1998*	*1999*	*2000*	*2001*	2002	*2003*
100m	11.10	**10.92**	11.07	11.03	10.99	10.98	10.99	11.06	11.05	11.05
200m	22.36	**22.24**	22.44	22.27	22.53	22.31	22.49	22.63	22.54	22.60
400m	**49.74**	49.90	50.30	50.32	50.33	50.34	50.04	50.63	50.80	50.59
800m	1:57.20	**1:56.91**	1:57.93	1:58.22	1:58.39	1:58.24	1:58.34	1:58.60	1:58.90	1:58.86
1500m	4:00.18	4:01.02	4:01.23	4:02.38	4:00.60	4:03.14	4:01.23	4:03.20	4:01.28	4:01.69
5000m	15:30.63	15:17.89	15:19.20	14:48.36	15:03.67	14:56.00	**14:45.35**	14:51.58	14:48.29	14:46.73
10000m	32:30.91	31:42.02	31:28.06	31:24.08	31:52.98	31:32.63	31:03.60	31:38.18	31:27.83	**31:01.07**
Marathon	2:29:10	2:28:40	2:27:42	2:27:41	2:26:11	2:25:29	2:24:33	2:24:21	**2:22:33**	2:23:07
100mh	12.74	12.73	12.76	12.69	**12.67**	12.73	12.70	12.71	12.75	12.72
400mh	54.93	54.49	54.70	54.40	54.49	**54.15**	54.41	54.47	54.72	54.60
HJ	1.97	1.98	1.96	1.98	1.96	1.99	1.98	1.96	1.97	**2.01**
PV		-	3.70	4.15	4.34	4.46	4.50	4.52	**4.60**	**4.60**
LJ	7.01	**7.07**	6.92	6.92	6.91	6.93	6.93	6.87	6.79	6.79
TJ		13.07	14.07	14.55	14.53	14.70	14.52	14.57	14.56	**14.76**
SP	20.55	20.81	19.78	19.46	19.12	19.21	19.32	19.30	19.20	19.10
DT	68.56	**70.34**	67.08	64.90	65.05	64.68	65.41	65.12	64.55	65.38
HT		-	56.40	61.84	64.61	67.24	69.36	68.50	68.70	**71.12**
JT	66.56	**68.42**	65.02	66.14	66.43	63.52*	64.89	64.30	63.89	62.89
Heptathlon	6424	**6540**	6460	6406	6381	6287	6396	6270	6151	6209
20kmW	Previously 10km standard walk event					1:28:51	1:28:06	**1:27:55**	1:28:46	1:28:17

Other peaks: 1500m 3:58/07 (1997), SP 20.85 (1987). 5000m succeeded 3000m as standard from 1995.

100th Bests										
100m	11.51	11.43	11.45	11.44	11.39	11.41	**11.36**	11.43	11.43	11.43
200m	23.39	23.32	23.36	23.32	23.24	23.22	**23.21**	23.27	23.35	23.31
400m	52.63	52.50	52.60	52.29	52.40	52.46	**52.25**	52.49	52.55	52.34
800m	**2:01.50**	2:01.66	2:02.80	2:02.96	2:02.6	2:02.53	2:02..51	2:03.02	2:02.65	2:02.38
1500m	**4:10.22**	4:11.70	4:11.80	4:11.87	4:12.68	4:11.79	4:11.18	4:12.13	4:12.37	4:11.37
5000m				15:35.62	15:40.74	15:37.76	**15:29.36**	15:34.49	15:36.99	15:43.15
10000m	34:26.36	33:11.31	33:05.80	32:56.63	33:11.36	32:59.05	**32:32.47**	32:35.90	32:46.11	32:43.76
Marathon	2:37:29	2:35:29	2:36:14	2:33:24	2:33:45	2:33:05	2:32:25	**2:31:05**	2:31:29	2:31:21
100mh	13.48	13.39	13.35	13.31	13.33	13.32	**13.22**	13.31	13.33	13.26
400mh	58.07	57.50	57.60	57.63	57.74	57.59	**57.48**	57.50	57.88	57.57
HJ	1.87	**1.88**	**1.88**	1.87	1.86	1.86	1.87	1.86	1.86	1.87
PV				3.60	3.90	4.00	4.10	4.08	4.10	**4.15**
LJ	6.48	**6.53**	6.45	6.50	6.48	6.48	6.49	6.45	6.43	6.46
TJ			13.16	13.45	13.51	13.64	**13.68**	13.60	13.64	13.67
SP	17.18	17.02	16.40	16.34	16.58	16.53	16.46	16.57	16.49	16.58
DT	**58.50**	57.40	56.20	56.86	56.28	56.02	56.22	55.54	55.20	55.15
HT				53.84	57.66	59.08	60.66	61.46	61.50	**63.23**
JT	57.74	**58.14**	56.36	56.16	54.80	54.54*	55.55	54.56	54.97	54.27
Heptathlon	c.5590	**5741**	5661	5649	5604	5596	5647	5640	5580	5622
20kmW						1:36:59	**1:34:44**	1:35:15	1:37:08	1:35:46

All-time record levels indicated in bold. * Note new javelin from 1999.

Other peaks: 3000m 9:00.65 (1993), HJ 1.88 (also 1986, 1987, 1993), SP 17.19 (1987)

Name		Nat	Born	Ht/Wt	Event	2003 Mark	Pre-2003 Best

MEN'S INDEX 2003

Athletes included are those ranked in the top 100s at standard (World Championships) events (plus shorter lists for 1000m.1M, 2000m and 3000m). Those with detailed biographical profiles are indicated in first column by:
* in this year's Annual, ^ in a previous year's Annual.

^ Aaltonen	Timo	FIN	11.4.69	189/130	SP	19.41	20.70- 00
* Abate	Abiyote	ETH	20.11.80	174/56	3000	7:40.75i, 7:41.41	7:32.38- 01
					5000	13:05.13	13:00.36- 01
Abdi	Youcef	AUS	7.12.77	177/66	1500	3:36.35	3:36.35- 02
					1M	3:56.23	3:59.57- 01
Abdirahman	Abdihakim	USA	1.1.77	178/60	5000	13:23.25	13:19.82- 01
					10000	27:52.24	27:42.83- 02
* Abdullah	Khamis Seif	QAT	1.12.76	181/64	3kSt	8:18.51	8:13.45- 02
* Abera	Gezahegne	ETH	23.4.78	168/57	Mar	2:07:56	2:07:54- 99
* Aburaya	Shigeru	JPN	6.2.77	163/51	10000	28:17.84	28:13.76- 00
					Mar	2:09:26	2:07:52- 01
* Achike	Larry	GBR	31.1.75	188/75	TJ	16.55	17.30, 17.31w- 00
Adam	Adam Abdou	QAT	15.6.83	178/63	800	1:46.20	1:46.86- 02
Adamou	Nabil	ALG	8.4.75		LJ	7.93, 8.07w	7.96, 7.98w- 02
Adams	Chris	USA	2.6.78	185/126	SP	19.62	19.13- 02
* Adams	Luke	AUS	22.10.76	189/70	20kW	1:19:35	1:23:52- 99
Adere	Dereje	ETH-J	.85		HMar	61:59A	
^ Adkins	Derrick	USA	2.7.70	188/80	400H	49.73	47.54- 95
Adsuar	Antonio	ESP	4.7.78	178/79	LJ	8.11	8.03- 01, 8.06w- 00
Aggoune	Khoudir	ALG	5.1.81		3000	7:43.63	7:48.32- 02
					5000	13:15.91	13:19.75- 02
Agoston	Tiberiu	ROM	25.12.76	189/78	PV	5.50	5.61i- 01, 5.35- 00
Aguila	Yonelvis	CUB	1.8.75	197/98	Dec	7593	7844- 98
Aish	Michael	NZL	24.7.76	175/60	10000	28:01.19	28:00.96- 02
Aïssat	Nicolas	FRA	24.7.80	175/60	800	1:45.31	1:44.98- 01
					1000	2:18.33i	2:16.86- 01
Aïtzouri	Abdelfatah	MAR	6.6.70		HMar	62:04	61:26- 96
Ajibade	Taiwo	NGR	17.6.82	173/72	100	10.24A	10.18A- 02, 10.27- 01
Akashi	Ken	JPN	6.11.76	169/59	50kW	3:54:11	3:58:55- 02
Akatsuma	Takeaki	JPN	27.11.81	170/54	20kW	1:23:31	1:25:01- 02
Akinsaya	Femi	GBR	29.11.69	171/74	TJ	16.44	16.63A- 99, 16.58- 96
Alaräisänen	Pekka	FIN	27.12.75	188/111	JT	78.25	81.63- 01
* Al-Asmari	Sa'ad Shaddad	KSA	24.9.68	185/72	3kSt	8:27.82	8:08.14- 02
Al-Badri	Salem Amer	QAT-J	12.12.85	180/65	800	1:46.63	1:46.63- 02
* Al Bishi	Hamdan Odha	KSA	5.5.81	180/70	400	44.99	44.66- 00
Al Bishi	Hamed Hamadan		KSA	3.3.82	180/70	200	20.55
21.04- 02							
Albert	Lars	GER	9.2.82	197/97	Dec	7642	7893 -02
Al-Dawoodi	Sultan M.	KSA-J	16.3.85	183/95	DT	59.66	57.69- 02
Al-Dosari	Ahmad	KSA-J	3.7.85	180/75	LJ	7.95	8.12- 02
* Alekna	Virgilijus	LTU	13.2.72	200/130	DT	69.69	73.88- 00
Aleksejev	Marko	EST	14.2.79	196/78	HJ	2.23	2.26i. 2.22- 00
Alekseyev	Igor	RUS	7.4.83		PV	5.65	5.40i- 02, 5.30- 01
Alemu	Berhanu	ETH	16.7.82	178/63	800	1:45.63	1:45.35- 02
Alexander	Niconnor	TRI	4.2.77	178/68	100	10.22,10.06w	10.19, 10.0- 00, 10.13w- 99
Al-Hamaidi	Ibrahim	KSA-J	28.8.85	177/68	400H	49.94	51.46- 02
Alic	Hamza	BIH	20.1.79	192/108	SP	19.14	18.13- 02
^ Alisevich	Vitaliy	BLR	15.6.67	186/112	HT	72.65	82.16- 88
* Aliu	Deji	NGR	22.11.75	187/75	100	9.95	10.02- 95, 9.9- 96
					200	20.49	20.25- 02
Al-Jarallah	Nasser	KUW	26.11.73	178/105	HT	71.00	70.19- 01
Al-Kaabi	Mohd Faraj	QAT-J	31.12.84	188/115	HT	70.87	69.17- 02
Al-Khuwalidi	Mohamed Salim	KSA	19.6.81	177/67	LJ	8.02	7.91, 8.18w- 02
Allen	Charles	CAN	29.3.77	175/72	110H	13.58	13.53A, 13.59, 13.52w- 02
Almeida	Fernando	POR	22.6.81		800	1:46.92	1:46.54- 02
Allmond	Tony	USA	8.10.82	193/75	LJ	8.04i, 8.02	8.05w- 02
Al-Nubi	Abdulrahman	QAT	17.10.79	190/80	LJ	8.13	8.11- 98
*							
Al-Outaibi	Moukhled	KSA	30.4.80	174/67	5000	13:21.11	13:41.48- 02
* Al-Sabee	Hussein	KSA	14.11.79	186/82	LJ	8.30	8.33- 00
Al-Salhi	Mohammed	KSA-Y	11.5.86	172/66	400	45.75	47.04- 02
					800	1:46.48	1:50.95- 02
* Al-Shammari	Fawzi	KUW	13.2.79	185/65	200	20.41	20.44- 02
					400	44.93	44.93- 02
* Al-Somaily	Hadi Soua'an	KSA	30.12.76	191/72	400H	48.97	47.53- 00

Name		Nat	Born	Ht/Wt	Event	2003 Mark	Pre-2003 Best
Al-Yami	Salem Mubarak	KSA	9.2.82	175/70	100	10.17	10.13- 02
					200	20.87, 20.67w	20.42A- 02, 20.88- 99
Al-Zankawi	Ali Mohamed	KUW-J	27.2.84	183/95	HT	72.70	66.88- 02
Ambrosch	Klaus	AUT	23.5.73	187/88	Dec	7980	8122- 01
Ames	Dan	USA	16.1.81	193/109	SP	19.73i, 19.70	19.46- 01
					DT	61.20	61.00- 01
Ammons	Andre	USA	12.11.78	175/73	400	45.75	45.83- 02
Amri	Ridha	TUN	16.12.76		3000	7:49.75	7:56.62- 02
					5000	13:28.50	13:38.25- 02
* Amyn	Mohammed	MAR	25.3.76	168/53	3000	7:45.41	7:35.35- 01
					5000	13:25.34	13:01.98- 02
Anderson	Felix	USA	13.5.83		400	45.77	
Anderson	LeVar	USA	26.3.77	183/77	TJ	16.73i, 16.63	17.02- 02, 17.12w- 99
Anderson	Marvin	JAM	12.5.82	175/69	100	10.24	10.39- 01, 10.1w- 00
^ Andji	Alain	FRA	20.11.74	187/89	PV	5.51i, 5.50	5.85- 97
Andrei	Cristiano	ITA	14.5.73	198/112	DT	64.49	64.11- 02
Andreou ¶	Georgios	CYP	26.7.74	188/80	Dec	7711dq	7811- 00
* Andreyev	Vladimir	RUS	7.9.66	170/58	20kW	1:20:56	1:18:16- 00
Andriani	Ottaviano	ITA	4.1.74	172/61	HMar	61:40	62:08- 02
Andronov	Yuriy	RUS	6.11.71	180/68	50kW	3:48:26	3:42:06- 02
Andrzejak	Krzysztof	POL	10.1.75	192/79	Dec	7696	7925- 02
Anguono-Moké	Roger	CGO	20.11.81	180/80	100	10.30, 10.23w	10.37- 02
* Anlezark	Justin	AUS	14.8.77	188/127	SP	20.96	20.91- 02
* Annus	Adrián	HUN	28.6.73	194/110	HT	84.19	83.39- 01
Anskins	Andis	LAT	25.1.79	183/82	JT	77.93	78.43- 02
Ao Xinli		CHN	26.1.81		50kW	3:56:29	4:03:10- 01
Apak	Esref	TUR	3.1.82	185/97	HT	77.57	73.24- 02
Appelhans	Mike	USA	24.8.80		200	20.83A, 20.63Aw	20.89- 02
Aracic	Luka	CRO	13.3.81	184/78	LJ	7.94i	8.12- 01
^ de Araújo	Eronilde	BRA	31.12.70	182/78	400H	49.40	48.04- 95
Araújo	Gaspar	POR	17.12.81		LJ	8.10	7.85, 7.94w- 02
Aritkulov	Ramil	RUS	1.3.78	178/67	800	1:46.83	1:46.82- 02
Arkhipov	Aleksandr	RUS	7.8.73	178/69	20kW	1:22:15.3t	1:22:07- 97
Armon	Juaune	USA	6.5.82	193/84	LJ	7.99	8.00- 02
Armstrong	Aaron	USA	14.10.77	173/70	100	10.17	10.19Aw- 00, 9.8w- 99
					200	20.60	20.08- 99
Armstrong	Dylan	CAN	15.1.81	190/125	HT	71.51	70.66- 00
Armstrong	Shannon	USA	2.9.82		110H	13.76, 13.57w	
Armstrong	Sherman	USA	22.9.78	185/75	400H	49.23	48.61- 00
^ Arnold	Dominique	USA	14.9.73	185/76	110H	13.35	13.11- 00
Arrhenius	Niklas	SWE	10.9.82	194/108	DT	59.82A	59.19- 00
Aryirópoulos	Yeóryios	GRE	20.1.70		50kW	3:58:41	4:05:05- 02
Asahara	Nobuharu	JPN	21.6.72	179/73	100	10.23	10.02- 01
Aseledchenko	Aleksandr	RUS	10.10.73	190/76	TJ	16.70	17.29- 97
Asmeron	Bolote	USA	12.10.78		3000	7:49.68i	7:51.93- 02
Assmus	Ralf	GER	28.1.77	177/69	1500	3:38.18	3:38.78- 01
					3kSt	8:24.57	8:19.32- 01
* Astapkovich	Igor	BLR	4.1.63	191/118	HT	81.35	84.62- 92
Atanasov	Nikolay	BUL	11.12.74	188/72	LJ	8.31	8.20- 00
Atorudibo	Tamunosiki	NGR-J	21.3.85	179/74	100	10.20	10.23- 02
^ Austin	Charles	USA	19.12.67	184/77	HJ	2.30i, 2.27	2.40- 91
Avellaneda	Mario	ESP	12.11.74	168/58	50kW	3:49:35	3:49:50- 00
* Averbukh	Alex	ISR	1.10.74	178/76	PV	5.93	5.91- 01
Avery	Jerome	USA	18.4.78	170/68	100	10.21	10.18- 00
Averyanov	Nikolay	RUS	4.2.80	182/77	Dec	7868	7813- 02
Ayre	Sanjay	JAM	19.6.80	188/75	400	45.16	44.92- 02
* Baala	Mehdi	FRA	17.8.78	183/65	800	1:44.17	1:43.15- 02
					1000	2:13.96	2:15.17- 02
					1500	3:28.98	3:31.97- 01
Baba	Youssef	MAR	7.8.79	173/55	1500	3:35.17	3:33.92- 00
* Bába	Jaroslav	CZE-J	2.9.84	196/82	HJ	2.32i, 2.30	2.27, 2.28et- 02
* Backley	Steve	GBR	12.2.69	196/100	JT	85.69	91.46- 92
Badji	Ndiss Kaba	SEN	21.9.83	192/79	LJ	7.92	7.83, 7.90w- 02
Bae Kyung-ho		KOR	16.3.76	193/78	HJ	2.23	2.24- 01
Baggio	José Alessandro	BRA	16.4.81	172/63	20kW	1:21:48.3t	1:22:52.6t- 02
Baharídis	Panayiótis	GRE	31.5.81	185/100	SP	19.06	18.97- 02
Bai Liansheng		CHN	28.7.78	178/65	20kW	1:20:48	1:22:05- 01
					50kW	3:52:45	3:51:52- 01
Bakovic	Marijo	CRO	11.4.82	186/72	LJ	7.99	7.93- 02
Balcers	Luis André	BRA	18.10.73		110H	13.76, 13.75w	13.46- 99
Balcerzak	Piotr	POL	25.6.75	175/68	100	10.22	10.15- 99

Name		Nat	Born	Ht/Wt	Event	2003 Mark	Pre-2003 Best
* Baldini	Stefano	ITA	25.5.71	176/60	HMar	61:39	60:56- 97, 60:50w- 00
					Mar	2:07:56	2:07:29- 02
Balgac	Dalibor	CRO	22.9.77		1500	3:38.34	3:41.89- 96
Balliengo	Jorge	ARG	5.1.78		DT	60.89	55.55- 02
^ Balzer	Falk	GER	14.12.73	189/80	110H	13.58	13.12, 13.10Ar- 98
Bamboux	Stéphane	FRA	28.2.74	185/82	Dec	7535	7793- 99
Banda	Lewis	ZIM	16.4.82		400	45.68	45.92A- 02
Barbaud	Alexandre	FRA	15.2.80	194/82	PV	5.75	5.40- 02
Barberi	Andrea	ITA	15.1.79	178/64	400	45.79	46.29- 01
Barbour	Jonathan	GBR	3.11.80	184/79	100	10.22w	10.28- 00, 10.13w- 01
Barlís	Ioánnis	GRE	26.11.79	182/100	HT	73.82	72.13- 00
* Barmasai	Bernard	KEN	6.5.74	173/55	3000	7:46.21	7:36.40- 97
					5000	13:23.23	13:43.2- 94
* Barras	Romain	FRA	1.8.80	193/84	Dec	8196	7876- 01
Barrett	Craig	NZL	16.11.71	183/70	50kW	3:50:34	3:48:05- 01
Barrios	Eugenio	ESP	3.11.76	182/75	800	1:46.38	1:47.44- 02
Barry	Damion	TRI	3.3.82	188/83	400	45.67	45.75- 01
* Bartels	Ralf	GER	21.2.78	186/120	SP	20.67	20.85- 02
Basil	Adam	AUS	14.4.75	176/73	100	10.29,10.24Aw	10.34- 99,10.22Aw- 00
Batangdon	Joseph	CMR	29.7.78	180/75	100	10.25w	10.19- 02, 9.9- 00
					200	20.47i, 20.48	20.31A, 20.3- 99, 20.31- 00
Batman	Daniel	AUS	20.3.81	171/71	400	45.02	45.60, 45.4- 00
Batovsky	Milos	SVK	26.5.79	178/65	50kW	4:06:37	4:05:33- 00
^ Baumann	Dieter	GER	9.2.65	178/64	3000	7:43.93	7:30.50- 98
					5000	13:15.07	12:54.70- 97
Bavikin	Vadim	ISR	4.10.70	188/97	JT	80.95	81.68- 02
Baxter	Jimmy	USA	17.11.81	196/84	HJ	2.26	2.24- 02
Bayo	Zebedayo	TAN	20.5.76	178/64	Mar	2:08:54	2:08:51- 98
Beauchamp	William	GBR	9.9.70	196/110	HT	72.79	72.63- 99
* Beckford	James	JAM	9.1.75	183/73	LJ	8.28	8.62- 97, 8.68w- 95
* Bekele	Kenenisa	ETH	13.6.82	160/54	3000	7:36.98	7:30.67- 01
					5000	12:52.26	13:13.33- 01
					10000	26:49.57	-0-
* Bell	Kenta	USA	16.3.77	183/77	TJ	17.59	17.63- 02
Bell	Russ	USA	27.2.81	191/122	SP	19.32	19.54- 02
Bellani	Hicham	MAR	15.9.79		3000	7:49.8	
					5000	13:15.03	13:54.94- 01
					HMar	61:44	
* Belonog	Yuriy	UKR	9.3.74	200/132	SP	21.81	21.64- 00
					DT	65.53	65.32- 99
Belov	Yuriy	BLR	20.3.81	183/115	SP	21.14	19.68- 02
Belz	Christian	SUI	11.9.74	178/63	5000	13:12.16	13:34.08- 01
					3kSt	8:28.72	8:22.24- 01
Bengtsson	Bengt	SWE	4.9.61	176/65	50kW	3:56:26	3:56:27- 01, 3:49:24sh- 00
Benjamin	Tim	GBR	2.5.82	183/72	400	45.27	45.73- 02
Bennett	LaRon	USA	25.11.82	183/75	400H	50.09	51.36- 02
Bensghir	Yassine	MAR	3.1.83	170/68	800	1:46.89	1:47.8- 02
					1500	3:36.76	3:38.61- 02
Berdeja	Christian D	MEX	21.6.81		20kW	1:21:27	1:21:20- 01
Berger	Maik	GER	17.2.79	184/68	20kW	1:23:49	1:24:55- 02
* Berhanu	Dejene	ETH	.80	182/64	5000	13:14.05	13:26.74- 02
					10000	27:14.61	28:41.11- 00
Bérioui	Saïd	MAR	3.6.75	178/65	3000	7:41.83	7:42.39- 98
Bermejo	Javier	ESP	23.12.78	191/77	HJ	2.24i, 2.22	2.25- 02
Bernard	Claston	JAM	22.3.79	193/90	Dec	8000	8094- 02
Bernardo	Paulo	POR	21.11.74		DT	60.58	60.38- 99
Bernasconi	Ivan	ITA	19.10.74	193/74	HJ	2.24i	2.28- 99
Berrabah	Yahya	MAR	13.10.81		LJ	8.33	8.12- 01
^ Berrett	Tim	CAN	23.1.65	179/66	50kW	4:02:03	3:50:23- 93
Berryhill	Bryan	USA	15.12.77	183/75	1500	3:36.68	3:35.48- 01
* Betanzos	Yoandri	CUB	15.2.82	179/71	TJ	17.28	17.29- 02
* Bett	Mark	KEN	22.12.76	180/64	3000	7:49.35i	7:36.66- 01
					5000	13:16.42	12:55.63- 00
Bettinelli	Andrea	ITA	6.10.78	194/82	HJ	2.31	2.30i, 2.28- 02
Beyer	Jamie	USA	29.12.76	193/113	SP	20.64	21.00- 02
Bian Aiguo		CHN	10.6.80	178/65	50kW	3:51:51	3:58:18- 02
Bíber	Zsolt	HUN	31.5.76	194/104	SP	19.87	20.47- 01
Bielecki	Jan	DEN	20.2.71	188/103	HT	71.02	77.02- 02
Bieniek	Michal	POL-J	17.5.84	195/73	HJ	2.30	2.24- 02
Bigdeli	Schahriar	GER	26.3.80	182/71	LJ	8.00i, 7.94	8.15- 01, 8.22w- 00
Birgen	John	KEN	.74		Mar	2:09:08	?

Name		Nat	Born	Ht/Wt	Event	2003 Mark	Pre-2003 Best
* Bitok	Paul	KEN	26.6.70	173/58	3000	7:37.65+	7:28.41- 96
					5000	13:14.03	12:58.94- 02
Bitzi	Ivan	SUI	4.8.75	185/73	110H	13.72	13.59- 02
Blackhurst	Carlos	USA	2.9.77		3kSt	8:33.54	8:42.04- 02
* Blackwood	Michael	JAM	29.8.76	190/79	400	44.74	44.60- 02
Blanco	José Luis	ESP	3.6.75	175/61	3kSt	8:13.86	8:15.02- 02
* Blank	Peter	GER	10.4.62	195/103	JT	84.08	88.70- 01
Blanton	DaBryan	USA-J	3.7.84	181/77	100	10.07	10.30- 01, 10.26w- 02
					200	20.56	20.37- 01
Blaschek	Thomas	GER	5.4.81	189/82	110H	13.66	13.78- 00
Blincoe	Adrian	NZL	4.11.79	181/61	1500	3:36.57	3:41.85- 02
					1M	3:54.40	3:58.19i, 3:59.90- 02
					2000	4:58.72	
					3000	7:47.46	7:47.50i- 02
* Blom	Rens	NED	1.3.77	178/75	PV	5.75	5.75- 00
Blonskiy	Sergey	UKR	7.1.73	187/85	Dec	7745	7890- 01
Blonskiy	Yuriy	UKR	9.7.79	189/86	PV	5.50	5.40i- 00, 5.20- 99
* Bloom	Andy	USA	11.8.73	185/120	DT	61.48	67.25, 68.46dh- 00
Blouin	Gaëtan	FRA	4.1.74	190/85	Dec	7646	7998w- 98, 7909- 00
Blume	Marc	GER	28.12.73	180/68	100	10.28, 10.24w	10.13- 96, 10.12w- 02
^ Boateng	Kwaku	CAN	30.6.74	182/80	HJ	2.23i	2.34- 00
Bochkov	Sergey	AZE	20.8.79	185/74	TJ	16.82	16.70- 99
Bock	Detlef	GER	15.8.74	194/130	SP	20.12	20.47- 02
Bockman	Burke	USA	2.9.79	178/70	400H	50.18	51.37- 00
Bogdanof	Tim	USA	9.11.79		110H	13.51	14.03- 02, 14.00w- 99
Bogdanov	Dmitriy	RUS	11.4.79	190/74	800	1:45.28	1:45.72- 02
Boisrond	Mathieu	FRA	8.1.77	175/69	PV	5.50	5.51- 00
* Boit Kipketer	Wilson	KEN	6.10.73	167/52	3kSt	8:09.16	7:59.08- 97
* Boldon	Ato	TRI	30.12.73	176/75	100	10.09	9.86- 98
Bolles	Cameron	USA	24.3.76		DT	60.35	61.37- 01
* Bolt	Usain	JAM-Y	21.8.86	196/75	200	20.13	20.58- 02
					400	45.35	47.12- 02
Booker	Albert	USA	10.1.82	178/68	400	45.72	46.23- 02
Bookman	Leo	USA	3.1.82	191/95	200	20.37	20.67- 00
Boothby	Scott	USA	9.4.73	183/104	HT	70.87	70.32- 02
Bor	Noah	KEN	18.7.77		Mar	2:08:48	2:11:43- 02
* Börgeling	Lars	GER	16.4.79	192/83	PV	5.80	5.85- 02
^ Borichevskiy	Aleksandr	RUS	25.6.70	194/120	DT	64.70	65.08- 99
Borisov	Valeriy	KAZ	18.9.66	180/62	20kW	1:21:10	1:19:55- 96
Borodkin	Andrey	UKR	18.4.78	202/122	SP	19.87	19.71- 01
Boros	László	HUN	3.2.82		HJ	2.24	2.14- 02
Borshchenko	Aleksandr	RUS	8.6.82		400H	50.09	51.04- 02
Borsumato	Anthony	GBR	13.12.73	187/80	400H	49.12	48.90- 02
Borysiewicz	Wojciech	POL	18.10.82	187/65	HJ	2.27	2.18- 01
* Borzakovskiy	Yuriy	RUS	12.4.81	181/70	800	1:43.68	1:42.47- 01
* Boswell	Mark	CAN	28.7.77	189/77	HJ	2.32	2.35- 99
Botfa	Péter	HUN	30.6.79	186/126	HT	80.67	77.42- 00
Botha	Hennie	RSA	20.2.75	180/68	400H	49.35	49.02A, 49.60- 00
Botha	Werner	RSA	31.1.78	186/73	800	1:45.33	1:44.41- 00
Bouchiba	Merzak Ould	ALG	27.4.75		3kSt	8:25.73	8:26.0- 02
Bouguétaib	Tarik	MAR	30.4.81	180/75	LJ	7.94	7.84- 02
Boukensa	Tarek	ALG	19.11.81	178/62	1500	3:34.57	3:35.08- 02
					1M	3:52.34	
Boulahfane	Kamel	ALG	1.7.76	178/63	1500	3:37.46	3:33.07- 00
Boulanger	David	FRA	11.12.74	176/64	50kW	4:00:05	3:51:36- 01
Boulge	Kazimierz	POL	13.2.76	195/99	HT	72.14	76.58- 01
Bowen	Terry	USA	15.9.71	175/64	100	10.0w	10.06, 9.97w- 95
* Bownes	Shaun	RSA	24.10.70	194/90	110H	13.50	13.26- 01, 13.2A- 98
Bradley	Gentry	USA	19.1.74	183/77	100	10.24	10.26- 98, 10.23w- 00
					200	20.66	20.34, 20.20w- 96
Bragin	Andrey	RUS	20.9.79	188/81	LJ	8.12	8.16i, 7.88- 99
* Bramlett	Ron	USA	22.10.79	181/68	110H	13.27	13.35- 02
Brayko	Pyotr	RUS	27.3.77	202/92	HJ	2.30	2.31i, 2.30- 02
Brazell	Bennie	USA	2.6.82	185/77	400H	48.97	48.80- 02
* Brew	Derrick	USA	28.12.77	185/82	400	44.83A, 45.03	44.29- 99
Brisseault	David	FRA	7.3.69	185/95	JT	79.31	79.85- 00
* Brits	Okkert	RSA	22.8.73	198/84	PV	5.86	6.03- 95
Brizzel	Paul	IRL	3.10.76	186/70	200	20.56	20.54A, 20.65 - 00
Broe	Tim	USA	20.6.77	180/66	3000	7:46.57	7:39.23i- 02, 7:39.45- 01
Brokenburr	Kenny	USA	29.10.68	178/79	100	10.11, 9.97w	10.04- 97, 9.90w- 99
					200	20.25	20.04- 00

Name		Nat	Born	Ht/Wt	Event	2003 Mark	Pre-2003 Best
^ Bronson	Bryan	USA	9.9.72	183/75	200	20.64w	20.28- 92
Brown	Carl	USA	11.2.70	193/105	DT	66.66, 67.86dh	63.78- 01
Brown	Chris	BAH	14.10.79	178/68	400	44.94A, 45.16	45.08- 00
* Brown	Darrel	TRI-J	11.10.84	184/79	100	10.01	10.09- 02
Brown	Joel	USA	31.1.80		110H	13.74, 13.58w	14.04- 01
Browne	Dan	USA	24.6.75	178/67	10000	28:03.48	27:47.04- 02
Browne	Pierre	CAN	14.1.80	178/75	100	10.16, 10.09w	10.12, 9.98w- 02
					200	20.89, 20.59w	20.41- 02
^ Brugnetti	Ivano	ITA	1.9.76	175/62	20kW	1:22:01	1:21:21- 00
Brunson	Marcus	USA	24.4.78	185/79	100	10.07	10.10- 99, 10.06w- 01
					200	20.55	20.37- 01
Buc	Bostjan	SLO	13.4.80		3kSt	8:16.96	8:28.53- 02
Buchanan	Anthony	USA	10.9.81	175/77	100	10.24, 10.10w	10.23- 02
* Bucher	André	SUI	19.10.76	185/75	800	1:44.23	1:42.55- 01
Buciarski	Piotr	DEN	22.11.75	183/79	PV	5.60	5.75- 02
Buckfield	Nick	GBR	5.6.73	185/78	PV	5.70	5.80- 98, 5.81i- 02
Bucki	Gaëtan	FRA	9.5.80	195/135	SP	19.24	19.11- 02
* Buckland	Stéphane	MRI	20.1.77	187/73	100	10.20	10.13- 01, 10.0A- 99
					200	20.06	20.15- 01
Bueno	Tiago	BRA	21.2.83		400H	50.04	52.93- 02
Bukhalov	Spas	BUL	14.11.80	186/85	PV	5.70	5.55- 02
Buller	Russ	USA	10.9.78	178/72	PV	5.75	5.81- 01
* Bungei	Wilfred	KEN	24.7.80	172/60	800	1:42.52	1:42.34- 02
* Burayev	Viktor	RUS	23.2.82	176/62	20kW	1:20:56	1:18:06- 01
Burban	Yuriy	UKR	18.4.80	179/69	50kW	4:00:51	4:05:55- 02
^ Burge	Peter	AUS	3.7.74	187/80	LJ	7.98, 8.24w	8.30, 8.48w- 00
Burgess	Paul	AUS	14.8.79	183/78	PV	5.70	5.75- 02
* Burkenya	Danila	RUS	20.7.78	198/82	LJ	8.23	8.31- 01, 8.35w- 02
					TJ	16.58i	16.36, 16.40w- 98
Burlachenko	Pavel	RUS	7.4.76	184/80	PV	5.60	5.81- 98
Burley	Sam	USA	13.2.81	175/68	800	1:46.17	1:45.39- 02
Burns	Marc	TRI	7.1.83	185/79	100	10.24	10.18- 02
Bushendich	Solomon	KEN-J	10.1.84	165/58	3000	7:45.07	
					5000	13:12.83	13:36.97- 02
					10000	28:05.99	28:35.5- 02
Bynum	Desmond	USA	.80		100	10.23w	10.46- 02
Byrd	Leonard	USA	17.3.75	178/64	400	45.08	44.45- 02
Cafagna	Diego	ITA	9.7.75	173/57	50kW	4:02:25	3:57:23- 02
Caimmi	Daniele	ITA	17.12.72	180/60	Mar	2:09:29	2:08:59- 02
* Caines	Daniel	GBR	15.5.79	178/74	400	45.29	44.98- 02
Calado	Carlos	POR	5.10.75	186/80	LJ	7.98i	8.36- 97
Calligny	Fabrice	FRA	4.11.81	180/74	100	10.22	10.22- 02, 10.19w- 99
Cambil	Alejandro	ESP	26.1.75	176/66	20kW	1:22:39	1:22:28- 02
Campbell	Clement	JAM	19.2.75	184/82	100	10.32, 10.16w	10.38- 00
					200	20.65	20.90- 00
* Campbell	Darren	GBR	12.9.73	185/83	100	10.08	10.04- 98
					200	20.34	20.13- 00
Campbell	Michael	JAM	11.9.78	188/79	400	45.48	45.64- 02
^ Campbell	Milton	USA	15.5.76	178/75	200	20.68	20.47- 02
					400	45.73	44.67- 97
Campeny	Moisés	ESP	27.5.79	186/90	HT	75.42	73.65- 99
Campioli	Filippo	ITA	21.2.82	193/78	HJ	2.24	2.23- 02
Canal	David	ESP	7.12.78	183/63	400	45.01	45.04- 01
^ Cankar	Gregor	SLO	25.1.75	180/68	LJ	8.06, 8.07w	8.40- 97
					TJ	16.82i	16.51- 99
* Cantwell	Christian	USA	30.9.80	198/141	SP	21.62	21.45- 02
Cao Jing		CHN	31.1.78		110H	13.65	13.75- 02, 13.69w- 01
* Capel	John	USA	27.10.78	180/82	100	9.97	10.03- 99
					200	20.17	19.85- 00
Carabelli	Gianni	ITA	30.5.79	187/69	400H	49.51	49.92- 00
Caro	Francisco José	ESP	23.10.78	190/80	Dec.	7528	7695- 02
Carter	Drew	USA	5.9.81	193/91	LJ	8.01w	7.72- 02
Carter	Greg	USA	5.8.80	183/75	200	20.64w	21.27- 02
* Carter	James	USA	7.5.78	186/77	400H	48.88	47.57- 02
Carter	Xavier	USA-J	8.12.85	190/86	200	20.69	21.02- 02
Casañas	Frank	CUB	18.10.78	184/101	DT	65.08	64.04- 02
Casarsa	Paolo	ITA	2.7.75	194/90	Dec	7877	7918- 02
Casquette	Arnaud	MRI	16.4.78	175/70	LJ	8.13A, 8.05, 8.23w	8.05- 00
Cassin	Jeffrey	IRL	15.12.71	179/59	50kW	4:01:01	4:05:21- 00
Castillejo	Carles	ESP	18.8.78	174/52	1500	3:39.09	3:45.28- 02
					3000	7:43.24	8:04.36- 02
					5000	13:25.57	13:54.48- 02

Name		Nat	Born	Ht/Wt	Event	2003 Mark	Pre-2003 Best
Castillo	Víctor	VEN	8.6.81	180/74	LJ	7.98, 8.10w	7.71, 7.77w- 00
Catarino	Paulo	POR	30.9.63	174/55	HMar	61:53	62:09- 01
Cavallaro	Alessandro	ITA	22.2.80	180/74	200	20.42	20.48- 00, 20.46w- 99
Cavuoto	Dean	AUS	4.6.75	179/61	10000	27:54.82	27:50.73- 02
Cawley	Elston	JAM	24.6.76	184/90	200	20.53w	20.53- 97, 20.35w- 98
Cebulski	Joe	USA	25.10.76		Dec	7841	7969- 01
Ceglie	Luca	ITA	24.10.79	186/78	Dec	7712	7510- 02
Cerezo	José Manuel	ESP	23.6.73	180/57	1500	3:37.67	3:40.27- 02
Cerra	Juan Ignacio	ARG	16.10.76	180/110	HT	76.32	76.42- 01
Chaíça	Alberto	POR	17.9.73		HMar	62:02	62:20- 00
					Mar	2:09:25	2:12:02- 02
Chakouian	Jeff	USA	20.4.82	183/118	SP	19.29i	20.13- 01
Challenger	Ben	GBR	7.3.78	186/75	HJ	2.24	2.30- 99
^ Chambers ¶	Dwain	GBR	5.4.78	180/83	100	10.03/10.0dq	9.87- 02
Chang Chunhu		CHN	1.5.82		20kW	1:21:59	1:23:07- 01
					50kW	3:55:39	4:10:14- 00
Chang Wei		CHN	5.7.83		20kW	1:23:24	1:22:20- 01
Chapado	Raúl	ESP	4.5.70	194/85	TJ	16.58A, 16.56w	16.87i- 98, 16.83- 97
Chaput	Brian	USA	9.4.81		JT	78.69	71.85- 02
* Charfreitag	Libor	SVK	11.9.77	191/110	HT	81.81	79.20- 02
Charmant	Joan	FRA	4.6.78	184/71	HJ	2.24	2.25i, 2.23- 02
Chatman	Bennie	USA	24.1.79	178/82	100	10.19, 10.12w	10.33- 98
Chebet	Peter	KEN	24.6.76		Mar	2:08:43	2:09:22- 02
* Chebii	Abraham	KEN	23.12.79	172/63	3000	7:39.28	7:36.11- 02
					5000	12:52.99	12:58.98- 02
Cheboiboch	Christopher	KEN	3.3.77		HMar	60:33	60:45- 01
Cheboiywo	Boaz	KEN	2.8.78	160/54	5000	13:29.26i, 13:29.77	13:46.92- 02
					10000	27:46.47	28:29.13- 02
Cheboror	Robert	KEN			HMar	61:55	61:42- 02
Chehibi	Mouhsin	MAR	28.1.78	182/70	800	1:45.73	1:46.15- 99
Chékhémani	Abdelkader	FRA	18.7.71	180/70	1000	2:17.40	2:18.24- 99
					1500	3:36.66	3:33.10- 96
Chelal Cheruiyot	Wilson	KEN	15.11.82		Mar	2:09:06	0
Chemitei	Thomas	KEN	.78		Mar	2:10:26	0
Chemovskoy	Sergey	RUS	13.7.83		PV	5.50	5.30- 01
Chemweno	David	KEN	18.12.81	175/58	3000	7:49.55	
					3kSt	8:14.14	8:30.12- 01
Chemweno	Wilson Kipkoskei	KEN	.78/79		3000	7:49.41	8:04.18- 02
Chen Haijan		CHN	5.4.80	173/70	100	10.17	10.20- 01, 10.18w- 02
Chen Qi		CHN	10.3.82	184/79	JT	77.32	77.89- 01
Chenonge	Hillary	KEN-J	30.5.85	166/52	1500	3:39.49	
					1M	3:53.29	
					3000	7:43.04	7:39.22- 02
					5000	13:22.23	13:06.47- 02
Chepiga	Sergey	RUS	6.3.82		110H	13.63, 13.59w	14.18- 02
* Chepkurui	Albert	KEN	4.4.81	170/54	3000	7:46.7+	7:43.01- 99
(Hassan	Abdullah	QAT)	(now)		5000	12:56.27	12:59.90- 00
					10000	26:38.76	26:50.67- 02
Cheptot Matebo	Stephen	KEN	30.3.74		Mar	2:09:31	2:07:59- 02
Cherevko	Leonid	BLR	21.4.74	198/126	DT	64.73	65.56- 00
Chernov	Sergey	BLR	5.2.79		20kW	1:23:29	1:24:45- 02
* Cherono	Abraham	KEN	21.7.80	174/62	3kSt	8:10.33	8:13.22- 00
Cherono	Benson	KEN	.82		HMar	61:42	
Cherono	Frederick	KEN	23.11.77		Mar	2:08:47	2:14:25- 02
Cherono	Stephen	KEN	15.10.82	177/64	1500	3:35.15	3:35.47- 01
* (Shaheen	Saïf Saaeed	QAT(	now		3000	7:38.0+	7:46.03- 01
					5000	12:48.81	13:11.55- 02
					3kSt	7:57.38	7:58.10- 02
Cherotich	Musa	KEN	.75		HMar	62:08	63:31- 02
Cheruiyot/Yagut	Abel	KEN-J	26.12.84		3000	7:46.49	
(Jowher Salem,	Abel Yacoob	BRN)	now		5000	13:25.34	
					3kSt	8:09.37	
Cheruiyot	Robert	KEN	20.12.74		Mar	2:08:13	2:09:39- 02
Cheruiyot	Robert Kipkoech	KEN	26.9.78		HMar	60:24	60:06- 02
					Mar	2:10:11	2:08:59- 02
Cheruiyot	Willy	KEN	67		Mar	2:09:05	2:08:48- 00
Chiba	Yoshihiro	JPN	29.4.79	178/65	400H	49.23	48.65- 01
Chiesa	Sergio	ITA	7.9.72	174/62	HMar	61:43	63:41- 02
Chimier	Jonathan	MRI	6.8.82	175/75	LJ	8.26A, 8.08, 8.29Aw	7.89, 8.03w- 01
Chimusasa	Tendai	ZIM	28.1.71	180/60	HMar	62:04	60:26- 95
Chipu	Abner	RSA	2.1.72	160/57	HMar	61:55	61:50- 01

Name		Nat	Born	Ht/Wt	Event	2003 Mark	Pre-2003 Best
* Chirchir	Cornelius	KEN	7.10.83	172/58	1000	2:18.24i	
					1500	3:31.17	3:30.24- 02
					1M	3:50.40	3:50.69- 02
* Chirchir	William	KEN	6.2.79	175/55	800	1:45.14	1:43.33- 99
					1500	3:31.70	3:29.29- 01
					1M	3:52.18	3:47.94- 00
^ Chistiakov	Viktor	AUS	9.2.75	202/92	PV	5.71	5.90, 5.95ex- 99
Chizhov	Vladimir	RUS	5.8.75	184/84	JT	76.97	77.80- 97
Chorny	Thomas	USA	23.11.76	183/70	3kSt	8:30.99	8:22.16- 01
Chouki ¶	Fouad	FRA	15.10.78	183/69	800	1:45.77	1:46.54- 02
					1500	3:30.83	3:33.89- 01
Christian	Brendan	ANT	11.12.83	178/70	100	10.25, 10.24w	10.20, 10.15w, 9.9- 02
					200	20.29	20.56- 01, 20.32w, 20.1- 02
Christopher	Tyler	CAN	3.10.83	188/86	400	45.61	46.53- 02
Chrzanowski	Tomasz	POL	12.7.81	189/119	SP	19.47	19.26- 02
Chubsa	Andrey	BLR	29.11.82	191/75	HJ	2.28	2.32- 02
^ Chumachenko	Pavel	RUS	5.4.71	189/138	SP	20.51	20.91i, 20.54- 01
Chumba	Linus	KEN	9.2.80		3kSt	8:19.26	
Chumba	Patrick	KEN	24.7.74		Mar	2:09:45	2:12:10- 02
Chuprinin	Kirill	UKR	22.7.75	197/130	DT	63.92	63.54- 00
Çiçek	Ferhat	TUR	13.6.81		LJ	8.03w	7.44- 01, 7.61w- 02
Cichocki	Jaroslaw	POL	28.7.82	190/105	SP	19.39	19.70- 02
Cilliers	Ockert	RSA	21.4.81	186/76	400H	48.61A, 48.88	49.30A, 49.80- 02
Ciofani	Roland	FRA	29.9.71	181/95	HT	72.18	68.22- 01
Ciotti	Giulio	ITA	5.10.76	188/78	HJ	2.26i, 2.25	2.28- 02
Ciotti	Nicola	ITA	5.10.76	188/78	HJ	2.30	2.30i- 02, 2.27- 01
Ciumacenco	Feodosei	MDA	27.1.73	176/50	20kW	1:23:51	1:23:26- 96
Civallero	Lorenzo	ITA	8.8.75	183/64	20kW	1:20:34	1:21:12- 02
Clarke	Davian	JAM	30.4.76	178/67	400	45.18	44.87- 96
Clarke	Lerone	JAM	.81		100	10.23w	10.50, 10.49w- 02
Clavier	Jérôme	FRA	3.5.83	176/60	PV	5.56i, 5.50	5.40- 02
* Clay	Bryan	USA	3.1.80	180/79	Dec	8482	8230- 02
* Clay	Ramon	USA	29.6.75	186/77	100	10.21	10.24- 02
					200	20.27	20.05- 01, 20.0A- 98, 19.99w- 96
Clement	Kerron	TRI-J	31.10.85		400H	50.13	
Clerbout	Tim	BEL	13.10.81		1500	3:38.32	3:40.73- 02
Clever	Chris	USA	10.8.78	197/108	JT	78.30	75.86- 02
* Clinger	Charles	USA	28.12.76	206/100	HJ	2.34i, 2.25	2.35A- 01, 2.35 -02
Cobb	Leonard	USA	20.1.75	178/73	LJ	7.99w	7.94, 8.04w- 97
					TJ	16.56	16.95- 95
Coetzee	Felix	RSA	30.7.75	185/68	LJ	7.94w	7.94A- 98, 7.99Aw- 01
Coleman	Olan	USA	29.7.80	175/70	100	10.23, 9.96w	10.09w- 02
					200	20.57	20.59- 02
Collaku	Dorian	ALB	2.6.77	184/108	HT	71.33	71.88- 99
Collins	Aaron	USA-J	18.2.84	181/77	200	20.69, 20.62w	21.18, 20.8w- 02
Collins	Ashton	USA-J	18.2.84	183/78	400	45.59	45.95- 02
* Collins	Kim	SKN	5.4.76	175/64	100	9.99, 9.92w	9.98- 02
					200	20.40w	20.20, 20.08w- 01
Colquhoun	Lueroy	JAM	1.3.80	185/73	400H	50.08	48.91- 02
Condon	Allyn	GBR	24.8.74	176/74	200	20.69i	20.53i, 20.63- 97- 98
Conwright	Kaaron	USA	8.8.76	175/73	100	10.14	10.10, 10.05A- 00
					200	20.63	20.59- 02, 20.56w- 00
Cook	Jamie	USA	21.7.76		Dec	7717	7705- 02
Cordes	Jared	USA	22.7.77	183/68	3kSt	8:31.23	8:27.62- 02
da Costa	António	BRA	8.2.73		TJ	16.52	16.68, 16.92w- 02
Costa	Jorge	POR	20.3.61	170/65	50kW	4:04:26	3:56:14- 01
da Costa	Marcelo	BRA	1.5.81	180/72	TJ	16.56	16.53- 02
Costa	Vítor	POR	28.5.74	183/105	HT	74.78	76.34- 00
Costin	Jamie	IRL	1.6.77	179/72	50kW	3:53:58	3:59:02- 00
Cousins	Duane	AUS	13.7.73	177/65	50kW	3:59:33	3:54:38- 95
Couts	Brandon	USA	17.2.79	175/71	400	45.82	44.72- 00
Cragg	Alistair	IRL	13.6.80	183/59	1500	3:39.24	3:42.10- 02
					3000	7:45.22i	7:56.40+- 02
					5000	13:25.59	13:22.07- 02
					10000	28:20.29	29:33.77- 02
* Crawford	Shawn	USA	14.1.78	181/75	100	10.07	9.94- 02
					200	20.02	19.85A- 02, 20.09- 00
* Crear	Mark	USA	2.10.68	186/79	110H	13.55, 13.37w	12.98- 99
Crews	Jerome	GER	20.2.77	188/77	110H	13.46	13.41- 98
Cross	Clay	AUS	26.11.77	195/125	SP	19.04	19.15- 98
Cui Kai		CHN	26.3.82	192/60	HJ	2.25	2.24- 98

Name		Nat	Born	Ht/Wt	Event	2003 Mark	Pre-2003 Best
Cui Zhide		CHN	11.1.83		20kW	1:23:47	1:25:20- 02
					50kW	3:59:37	4:11:59- 01
Cullum	Dave	USA	26.10.73		3kSt	8:33.14	8:30.35- 02
Culpepper	Alan	USA	15.9.72	185/59	10000	27:41.90	27:33.93- 01
Currey	Andrew	AUS	7.2.71	184/95	JT	82.29	86.67- 01
Currie	Airese	USA	16.11.82	180/84	200	20.65	21.27- 02
Czaja	Jakub	POL	12.9.80	180/62	3kSt	8:26.18	8:23.00- 01
* Czerwinski	Przemyslaw	POL	28.7.83	184/60	PV	5.50	5.40- 02
Czukor	Zoltán	HUN	18.12.62	186/74	50kW	3:57:06	3:50:02- 95
Dacal	Gustavo	ESP	30.3.77	185/80	JT	77.86	77.20- 00
Dacastello	Stefano	ITA	17.2.80	183/72	LJ	8.05w	7.83i, 7.64- 01
* Dachev	Petar	BUL	15.6.79	181/77	LJ	8.10i, 8.08	8.30- 00
* Dal Soglio	Paolo	ITA	29.7.70	190/125	SP	20.15i, 19.72	21.23- 96
Damião	Manuel	POR	4.7.78		1500	3:35.84	3:37.25- 00
Damszel	Tomasz	POL	25.3.72	188/95	JT	77.03	77.60- 93
Darling	Dennis	BAH	6.5.75	183/73	400	45.83	45.82- 97
Davidson	Graham	RSA	14.10.78		800	1:44.98	1:47.70A- 00
					1500	3:37.73	3:46.27- 00
					50kW	3:53.86	4:09.00- 01
Davis	David	USA	23.1.80	188/80	110H	13.71, 13.68w	14.09- 01
Davis	James	USA	19.3.76	185/82	400	45.33	45.21- 02
Davis	Jim	USA	15.6.78	185/82	PV	5.60	5.80A- 00
Davis	John	USA	19.2.77	190/104	SP	20.02	20.53- 01
Davis	Marquis	USA	14.8.80	185/84	100	10.13, 10.10w	10.11, 9.98w-dt- 00
					200	20.50, 20.15w	20.27- 00
* Davis	Walter	USA	2.7.79	188/78	LJ	8.24	8.16- 00, 8.19w- 01
					TJ	17.55	17.59- 02
Davydov	Denis	RUS	25.9.82		JT	80.15	74.88- 01
Dazio	Samuele	SUI	16.1.75	195/102	HT	73.64	74.02- 01
De Lépine	Eddy	FRA-J	30.3.84	175/72	100	10.19	10.50- 02
de Villiers	Pieter	RSA	13.7.82	179/75	400H	49.88	49.28- 02
* Deakes	Nathan	AUS	17.8.77	183/66	50kW	3:39:43	3:43:43- 01
DeGrammont	Dominique	USA/HAI	13.3.79		110H	13.74, 13.62w	13.66, 13.63w- 02
Delli Carri	Pellegrino	ITA	4.8.76	182/97	HT	71.28	66.38- 02
* Demeritte	Dominic	BAH	22.2.78	180/67	200	20.35, 20.20w	20.21- 02
Deming	Steve	USA	17.10.73		PV	5.50	5.60- 02
Demissie	Ashebir	ETH	.77		Mar	2:09:14	2:10:45- 01
Dengler	Andreas	GER	22.12.80	186/77	110H	13.73	13.84- 00
Denis	Frédéric	FRA	3.3.75	172/57	3kSt	8:22.95	8:22.03- 01
Denis	Sébastien	FRA	4.5.71	185/71	110H	13.57, 13.5	13.63- 00, 13.59w- 97
Dennis	James	USA	25.2.76		DT	59.96dh	63.54- 00
Derby	Brian	USA	18.2.81	178/79	400H	49.72	49.77- 01
Derevyagin	Aleksandr	RUS	24.3.79	178/78	400H	49.54	49.82- 01
Desaulty	Stéphane	FRA	8.1.72	183/68	3kSt	8:26.91	8:16.00- 01
Desilets	Jordan	USA	5.12.80	175/64	3kSt	8:29.44	8:32.79- 02
Dethloff	Claus	GER	24.9.68	187/115	HT	71.02	77.68- 94
* Devonish	Marlon	GBR	1.6.76	183/76	200	20.50	20.19, 20.18w- 02
* Devyatovskiy	Vadim	BLR	20.3.77	194/120	HT	79.90	81.36- 00
Deza	Alfredo	PER	24.8.79		HJ	2.27A	2.24A- 98
Dhouibi	Hamdi	TUN	24.1.82		Dec	7851	7965w- 02
Di Bella	Paul	AUS	12.2.77	178/69	100	10.23w	10.26- 01, 10.15w- 00
Di Cecco	Alberico	ITA	19.4.74	174/62	Mar	2:08:53	2:10:27- 02
* Diagana	Stéphane	FRA	23.7.69	184/75	400H	48.64	47.37- 95
Diarra	Alassane	FRA	22.1.81	179/79	TJ	16.45	15.86- 02
Dias	Thiago Carahyba	BRA-J	2.3.84	188/71	LJ	7.87, 8.03w	7.97- 02
^ Díaz	Andrés	ESP	12.7.69	187/71	1500	3:38.54	3:31.48- 00
Díaz	José Ignacio	ESP	22.11.79	173/63	50kW	3:59:30	4:10:43- 02
Didkowski	Pawel	POL	7.7.77	184/71	110H	13.71	14.26- 00
^ Didoni	Michele	ITA	7.3.74	176/73	20kW	1:21:23	1:19:59- 95
Dillion	Cleavon	TRI	5.10.82	186/79	LJ	7.93w	7.89- 02, 8.09w- 00
* Dilworth	Kevin	USA	14.2.74	180/76	LJ	8.09, 8.12w	8.47- 96, 8.53w- 02
Dimitrov	Rostislav	BUL	26.12.74	182/80	TJ	16.57, 16.71w	17.49- 99
Dimótsios	Stilianós	GRE	13.11.74	185/85	400	45.70	45.98- 02
Dirshe	Rizak	SWE	5.1.72	182/65	800	1:45.45	1:47.00- 98
Dittmar	Andy	GER	5.7.74	196/120	SP	19.50	20.23- 02
* Djhone	Leslie	FRA	18.3.81	187/72	200	20.51i, 20.68	20.94- 01
					400	44.83	45.63- 02
Dlongwana	Sivuyile	RSA	21.8.81	168/60	3kSt	8:29.54	
Dmitrik	Aleksey	RUS-J	12.4.84	191/69	HJ	2.28	2.26- 02
Dobos	Gábor	HUN	21.2.76	178/76	100	10.20	10.17- 99, 10.13dq- 00

MEN'S INDEX

Name		Nat	Born	Ht/Wt	Event	2003 Mark	Pre-2003 Best
Dobson	Ian	USA	6.2.82	188/68	10000	28:20.51	29:06.41- 02
Dodoni	Marco	ITA	5.9.72	197/120	SP	19.13i	19.65i- 01, 19.61- 99
Doi	Hiroaki	JPN	2.12.78	180/113	HT	73.33	72.66- 02
Dolphin	James	NZL	17.6.83	187/82	200	20.69	
Doménech	Yann	FRA	17.3.79	173/61	LJ	8.11, 8.19w	8.16- 02, 8.24w- 01
Domínguez	José David	ESP	29.7.80	172/55	20kW	1:20:15	1:22:25- 01
					50kW	3:55:20	4:26:11- 01
* Donato	Fabrizio	ITA	14.8.76	189/82	TJ	17.16	17.60- 00
Dong Jimin		CHN-J	10.10.85		50kW	4:00:17	4:07:42- 01
Donnelly	Michael	USA	2.2.75		10000	28:02.34	28:24.22- 00
Donovici	Daniel	ROM	5.3.80	191/75	TJ	16.71	16.37- 00
Dorique	Laurent	FRA	10.7.76	191/99	JT	80.04	80.88- 01
* Dorival	Dudley	HAI	1.9.75	185/77	110H	13.41	13.25- 01
Dossevi	Damiel	FRA	3.2.83	182/78	PV	5.55	5.35- 02
Dottin	Henderson	BAR	4.1.80	190/79	HJ	2.23i	2.22A- 02
Dou Zhaobo		CHN	23.9.83	175/70	1500	3:36.49	3:43.13- 02
* Doucouré	Ladji	FRA	28.3.83	183/74	110H	13.23	13.58- 01
Douglas	Matthew	GBR	26.11.76	190/82	400H	48.54	49.26- 00
Douglas	Troy	NED	30.11.62	173/71	200	20.64	20.19- 01
Dovgal	Anatoliy	UKR	29.1.76	174/73	100	10.0	10.30- 99, 10.22w- 00
Dowling	Ryan	RSA	15.5.79		110H	13.5A	
Drews	Stefan	GER	12.2.79	187/72	Dec	7715	8049- 01
Driouche	Aziz	MAR	15.11.77		HMar	61:26	
Drozdov	Aleksey	RUS	3.12.83		Dec	7536	7037- 02
* Drummond	Jon	USA	9.9.68	175/75	100	10.07A, 10.10	9.92- 97
Dube	Glody	BOT	2.7.78	165/56	800	1:46.57	1:44.59- 01
					1000	2:18.02i	2:20.25i- 02
Dubitskiy	Pavel	KAZ	27.8.82	177/75	Dec	7693	7051- 02
Dubois	Daniel	SUI	24.12.71	173/73	100	10.20w	10.30- 01, 10.26w- 00
Dudley	Eric	USA	18.4.80	190/80	400H	49.59	50.13- 02
Duma	Christian	GER	5.2.82	177/74	400H	49.53	50.26- 01
Duncan	Oscar	USA	5.3.75	185/86	JT	77.30	75.35- 02
Dunkley	Julien	JAM	20.12.75	186/83	100	10.09	10.16- 01
					200	20.63	20.68- 02
Duro	Sérgio	POR	14.2.80		400H	50.04	51.13- 01
Duval	Thibaut	BEL	1.2.79	185/76	PV	5.61	5.70- 00
* Dvorák	Tomás	CZE	11.5.72	186/88	Dec	8242	8994- 99
Dwyer	Pat	AUS	3.11.77	186/80	400	45.67, 45.6	44.73A, 45.19- 00
^ Dymchenko	Sergey	UKR	23.8.67	203/80	HJ	2.24	2.37- 90
Dys	Rafal	POL	14.1.82	178/55	20kW	1:23:57	1:25:48- 01
Dzradosi	Mark	GHA	29.3.78		TJ	16.55w	16.04- 00, 16.42w- 01
East	Michael	GBR	20.1.78	187/68	800	1:46.65	1:48.30- 02
					1500	3:35.49	3:37.35- 02
Eastler	Kevin	USA	14.10.77	190/72	20kW	1:22:25	1:26:08.8t- 00
Edgar	Tyrone	GBR	29.3.82	183/73	100	10.23, 10.04w	10.28- 02, 10.17w- 01
					200	20.57w	20.96, 20.8w- 01
Edorh	Claude	GER	27.2.72	183/82	110H	13.73	13.41- 94
Edwards	Aundre	JAM	11.12.80	175/85	LJ	8.07	8.00w- 02
Edwards	Jonathan	GBR	10.5.66	182/73	TJ	17.61	18.29, 18.43w- 95
Edwards	Monzavous 'Rae'		USA	7.5.81	183/77	100	10.09
10.18- 00							
					200	20.58A	20.57- 00
Efremov	Ilian	BUL	2.8.70	191/84	PV	5.75sq, 5.70	5.70- 98
Egbele	Aaron	NGR	29.1.79	181/79	100	10.22	10.21A, 10.11Aw- 02, 10.25- 01
Egbor	Stanley	NGR	19.3.77		200	20.66	20.94- 01
El Abidi	Sofiane	TUN	29.9.77	186/69	400	45.35	45.26- 02
El Abubakr	Nagmeldin	SUD-Y	22.2.86	171/61	400	45.22	47.90A- 02
El Amri	Khalid	MAR	20.3.77		5000	13:27.59	13:39.0- 02
					10000	28:07.92	
El Boumlili	Khalid	MAR			HMar	61:12	
* El Guerrouj	Hicham	MAR	14.9.74	176/58	1000	2:18.4+	2:16.85- 95
					1500	3:28.40	3:26.00- 98
					1M	3:50.20	3:43.13- 99
					3000	7:30.23	7:23.09- 99
					5000	12:50.24	13:46.79- 02
El Harroufi	Ridouane	MAR	30.7.81		HMar	61:01	
El Hattab	Mohammed	MAR	.76		HMar	61:34	
* El Himer	Driss	FRA	4.4.74	178/58	Mar	2:06:48	2:07:02- 01
* El Mouaziz	Abdelkader	MAR	1.1.69	172/58	Mar	2:08:03	2:06:46- 02
El Nasri	Yusef	ESP	28.7.79	178/65	3000	7:49.40i	7:39.80- 99
El Ouadili	Adil	FRA	3.9.81	174/61	3kSt	8:23.80	8:31.56- 02
El Ouardi	Zouhaïr	MAR	15.2.77		3kSt	8:14.81	8:19.44- 99

	Name		Nat	Born	Ht/Wt	Event	2003 Mark	Pre-2003 Best
	El Wardi	Mohamed Saïd	MAR	19.4.72	178/65	3000	7:43.09	7:34.67- 00
						HMar	61:33	
	El-Ghazaly	Omar	EGY-J	9.2.84	199/120	DT	59.77	55.35- 00
	Elias	Matthew	GBR	25.4.79	182/62	400H	49.62	49.11- 02
	El-Idrissi	Cédric	SUI	24.3.77		400H	49.10	50.83- 98
	Elvy	Peter	AUS	3.6.80	195/100	DT	60.28	60.45- 00
*	Emedolu	Uchenna	NGR	17.9.76	183/79	100	9.97	10.06, 10.00w- 02
						200	20.38	20.31- 02
	Emelianov	Ivan	MDA	19.2.77	202/130	SP	20.08	19.05, 20.26i- 00
	Emere	Alene	ETH	25.6.82		HMar	61:46	
^	Épalle	Christophe	FRA	23.1.69	194/116	HT	80.44	81.79- 00
	Erasmus	Brian	RSA	23.2.80		JT	81.38A	81.27A- 01
	Éraud	Guillaume	FRA	1.7.81	180/62	1000	2:18.03	2:20.18- 02
						1500	3:39.03	3:41.72- 01
	Erese	William	NGR	12.9.73		110H	13.3	
*	Ergotic	Sinisa	CRO	14.9.68	179/63	LJ	8.23	8.23, 8.25w- 02
	Erickson	Karl	USA	1.6.82	191/116	SP	19.77i, 19.40	17.55- 02
						DT	59.99	56.36- 02
	Erickson	Kyle	USA	11.1.81	183/70	400H	49.78	49.62- 02
	Eriksson	Martin	SWE	15.6.71	174/77	PV	5.60	5.80A, 5.72i- 00, 5.70- 97
*	Erm	Andreas	GER	12.3.76	184/70	50kW	3:37:46	3:45:28- 02
	Ernst	Sebastian	GER-J	11.10.84	183/66	200	20.63	20.97- 02
	Eryildirim	Fatih	TUR	1.3.79		HT	71.55	68.39- 02
	Esenwein	Peter	GER	7.12.67	188/85	JT	83.03	85.60- 97
	Eshbach	Eric	USA	4.2.81	183/84	PV	5.58i, 5.55	5.55- 00
	España	Jesús	ESP	21.8.78	173/56	3000	7:42.70i, 7:46.34	7:48.08i- 02, 7:59.14- 00
						5000	13:29.24	13:22.66- 02
^	Espinosa	Andrés	MEX	4.2.63	167/55	Mar	2:08:46	2:07:19- 94
	Es-Saadi	Ridouane	BEL	1.1.76	172/57	1500	3:38.47	3:42.98- 02
	Esser	Markus	GER	3.2.80	180/92	HT	78.13	76.97- 02
	Esteso	Pedro Antonio	ESP	13.10.76	181/70	1500	3:36.86	3:36.71- 02
*	Estévez	Reyes	ESP	2.8.76	187/70	1500	3:32.86	3:30.57- 99
	Eticha	Tesfaye	ETH	16.9.74		Mar	2:10:05	2:10:14- 02
	Etoot	Peter	KEN-J	17.4.84	175/62	800	1:46.88	
	Evans	Brandon	USA	30.10.79	180/79	TJ	16.59	15.94- 01
	Evans	Kenny	USA	6.4.79	188/74	HJ	2.25i	2.31i, 2.30- 00
	Evilä	Tommy	FIN	6.4.80	194/83	LJ	7.96	8.04, 8.11w- 01
	Évora	Nelson	POR-J	20.4.84	181/64	TJ	16.43	16.15- 01
	Ezenwa	Ambrose	NGR	10.4.77		100	10.33, 10.13w	10.50, 10.44w-02
						200	20.62, 20.46w	20.85- 00
*	Ezzine	Ali	MAR	3.9.78	175/57	3kSt	8:13.31	8:03.57- 00
*	Fadejevs	Aigars	LAT	27.12.75	175/59	20kW	1:20:56	1:19:25- 02
						50kW	3:46:03	3:43:18- 98
	Fält	Birger	SWE	12.8.68	175/65	50kW	4:04:07	4:12:59- 97
	Famiglietti	Anthony	USA	8.11.78	173/57	3kSt	8:31.03	8:19.07- 02
	Farmer	Kyle	USA	15.4.83		200	20.61	20.85- 02
	Farquhar	Stuart	NZL	15.3.82	190/97	JT	76.41	78.51- 02
	Fasuba	Olusoji	NGR-J	9.7.84	182/75	100	10.15	10.1, 10.52- 02
	Faulk	Dexter	USA-J	14.4.84	187/75	110H	13.73, 13.58w	13.97- 02
	Favretto	Vincent	FRA-J	5.4.84	188/72	PV	5.50	5.50- 02
	Faye	Ibou	SEN	13.12.69	190/75	400H	50.08	48.80- 00, 48.30A- 99
*	Fazekas	Róbert	HUN	18.8.75	193/105	DT	70.78	71.70- 02
	Fedaczynski	Rafal	POL	3.12.80	160/50	50kW	4:06:39	4:17:31- 02
	Felice	Marco	ITA	20.10.79	190/105	HT	71.09	74.08- 02
	Felix	Wesley	USA	21.7.83	180/75	100	10.24	10.48- 02
	Fenner	Mike	GER	24.4.71	187/88	110H	13.53	13.17- 98, 13.06dt- 95
	Ferguson	Kenneth	USA-J	22.3.84	186/73	110H	13.53	13.85- 02
						400H	48.79	49.38- 02
	Fernández	Álvaro	ESP	7.4.81		1500	3:35.10	3:38.99- 02
*	Fernández	Francisco	ESP	5.3.77	175/60	20kW	1:18:00	1:17:22- 02
	Fernández	Oscar	ESP	23.10.74	165/60	Mar	2:09:59	2:10:33- 01
	Fernández	Raúl	ESP	8.3.78	174/64	LJ	8.06A	8.26A, 8.22i, 8.19- 02
^	Ferreira Junior	Nelson Carlos	BRA	1.1.73	188/82	LJ	7.88, 7.99w	8.36A, 8.32, 8.41Aw- 96
	Festa	Isaiah	USA	10.3.80		3kSt	8:32.18	8:39.66- 02
	Fields	Jabari	USA	10.9.81	183/75	100	10.22	10.26- 01
						200	20.59	
*	Figère	Nicolas	FRA	19.5.79	177/91	HT	79.07	80.88- 01
	Fika	Makhosonke	RSA	20.1.72		Mar	2:10:16	2:10:39- 99
	Filet	Arius	FRA	17.12.77	182/67	TJ	16.82	17.15- 01
	Filíndras	Dimitrios	GRE	9.2.73	178/68	LJ	8.30	8.06- 02
	Filipovic	Predrag	SCG	5.10.78	182/70	20kW	1:21:50	1:23:28- 02

	Name		Nat	Born	Ht/Wt	Event	2003 Mark	Pre-2003 Best
	Finesi	Sandro	ITA	5.4.80	186/77	HJ	2.23	2.12- 01
	Fitschen	Jan	GER	2.5.77	176/60	3000	7:46.22	7:48.76i- 01, 7:49.34- 02
						5000	13:26.68	13:32.18- 02
	Fitzpatrick	Kevin	USA	26.9.69	193/105	DT	60.38	64.82, 65.28dh- 97
	Fivaz	Julien	SUI	9.1.79		LJ	8.27	7.70- 98
	Flint	Greg	USA	16.4.79	188/79	400H	49.81A	50.56- 02
	Fofana	Colomba	FRA	11.4.77	186/76	TJ	16.37. 17.02w	17.00- 00
	Fomenko	Pavel	RUS	29.6.76	198/76	HJ	2.28i	2.32i, 2.31- 02
	Formela	Miroslaw	POL	31.10.78	165/69	1500	3:39.04	3:40.12- 02
	Forshaw	Eric	CAN	14.9.68	195/123	DT	59.85, 60.40u	60.53- 02
	Forshev	Dmitriy	RUS	30.5.76	183/68	400	45.62	46.38- 01
	Fortuna	Diego	ITA	14.2.68	190/116	DT	63.65	64.69- 00
	Foster	Robert	USA	15.5.81	180/82	100	10.18	10.32, 10.21w- 01
*	Francique	Alleyne	GRN	7.6.76	188/75	400	44.78	44.72- 02
	Frank	Mark	GER	21.6.77	185/90	JT	80.55	83.24- 02
	Frater	Lindel	JAM	13.11.77	170/66	100	10.21, 10.10w	10.07- 00, 9.9w- 98
						200	20.66, 20.57w	20.58- 98
	Frater	Michael	JAM	6.10.82	170/67	100	10.13	10.21, 10.05w- 02
	Frederick	Latrell	USA	7.9.80	188/84	JT	79.62	77.91- 02
*	Fredericks	Frank	NAM	2.10.67	180/73	100	10.00	9.86- 96, 9.85Aw- 02
						200	20.23	19.68- 96
	Free	Deandre	USA	15.1.81	180/84	LJ	7.92w	8.00- 00
	Freeman	Jacob	USA	5.11.80	193/129	HT	71.72	69.75- 02
*	Freitag	Jacques	RSA	11.6.82	204/83	HJ	2.35	2.37- 02
	Fricke	Roman	GER	23.3.77	191/78	HJ	2.27	2.20- 99
*	Friedek	Charles	GER	26.8.71	184/80	TJ	16.53	17.59- 97
	Frösén	Oskari	FIN	24.1.76	194/86	HJ	2.28	2.30i- 00, 2.30- 01
	Fuenmayor	Manuel	VEN	3.12.80		JT	77.64	75.72- 02
	Fujii	Shuichi	JPN	14.2.82	176/58	HMar	62:09	64:04- 02
	Fujinohara	Toshihito	JPN	19.9.75	164/56	20kW	1:20:31	1:22:39- 98
	Fujiwara	Masakazu	JPN	6.3.81	167/54	Mar	2:08:12	0
	Gabella	Grégory	FRA	22.6.80	190/70	HJ	2.27	2.30- 02
	Gachiuri	Jackson	KEN	15.4.77	165/53	10000	28:15.54	27:58.93- 02
	Gadasu Alatan		CHN-J	27.1.84		50kW	3:54:21	4:08:51- 01
	Gailes	Tyree	USA	24.2.83	170/67	100	10.32, 10.03w	10.38- 01, 10.28w- 02
						200	20.80, 20.57w	21.33- 02
*	Gaisah	Ignisious	GHA	20.6.83	186/70	LJ	8.30	8.12- 02
	Gajdus	Grzegorz	POL	16.1.67	181/70	Mar	2:09:23	2:09:45- 98
	Galdino	Sérgio	BRA	7.5.69	169/57	20kW	1:23:33.4t	1:22:41- 91
						50kW	3:58:58	4:06:54- 00
	Galkin	Anton	RUS	20.2.79	183/75	400	45.54	46.09- 00
	Gallardo	Sergio	ESP	22.3.79	178/67	1500	3:35.24	3:37.86- 02
						1M	3:56.78	
	Galván	David	MEX	6.4.73	172/60	10000	27:44.85	27:37.69- 00
^	Gandellini	Alessandro	ITA	30.4.73	180/68	20kW	1:20:52	1:20:28- 00
	Ganotákis	Aléxandros	GRE	3.12.74		DT	60.50, 61.80dh	55.98- 96
^	García ¶	Alberto	ESP	22.2.71	163/45	3000	7:32.98i	7:36.53- 01
						5000	13:11.39i	13:02.54- 01
*	García	Anier	CUB	9.3.76	189/79	110H	13.55	13.00- 00
*	García	Jesús Ángel	ESP	17.10.69	171/62	50kW	3:43:56	3:39:54- 97
	García	Luis F	GUA	13.9.74	174/62	50kW	3:53:31	3:58:44- 02
*	Gardener	Jason	GBR	18.9.75	178/70	100	10.17, 10.11w	9.98- 99
	Gardner	Neil	JAM	8.12.74	178/72	400H	49.07	48.30- 96
	Garenamotse	Gable	BOT	28.2.77	183/75	LJ	8.14	7.99, 8.26w- 01, 8.01i- 02
	Garrett	Ken	USA	9.11.76	181/75	400H	49.30	49.76- 01
	Gary	Robert	USA	5.4.73	178/68	3kSt	8:24.82	8:19.26- 96
	Gasparro	Cristian	ITA	15.12.74	180/76	Dec	7739	7616- 99
	Gataullin	Ruslan	RUS	1.12.79		LJ	8.11i, 8.09	7.81- 01
*	Gatlin	Justin	USA	10.2.82	185/79	100	9.97	10.05dq, 10.00wdq- 02, 10.08- 01
						200	20.04	20.29, 19.86w- 01, 19.86dq- 02
	Gavélas	Aristotélis	GRE	10.11.78	179/70	100	10.17	10.14- 01
	Gay	Tyson	USA	9.9.82	183/73	100	10.01w	10.27, 10.08w- 02
						200	20.31w	20.21w- 02
*	Gebremariam	Gebre-egziabher	ETH-J	10.9.84	178/56	3000	7:46.8+	
						5000	12:58.08	13:12.14- 02
						10000	27:43.12	27:25.61- 02
*	Gebrselassie	Haile	ETH	18.4.73	164/53	2000	4:58.6+i	4:52.86i- 98, 4:56.1- 98
						3000	7:28.29i, 7:44.62	7:25.09- 98
						5000	12:54.36	12:39.36- 98
						10000	26:29.22	26:22.75- 98
	Geemi	Richard	KEN	23.8.73	168/55	1500	3:35.85	3:35.07- 01

Name		Nat	Born	Ht/Wt	Event	2003 Mark	Pre-2003 Best
* Geneti	Markos	ETH-J	30.5.84	175/55	3000	7:40.83i	7:47.90i, 7:50.58- 02
					5000	13:11.87	13:28.83- 02
Geopfert	Travis	USA	20.8.78		Dec	7729	7223- 01
* Gerasimov	Pavel	RUS	29.5.79	190/80	PV	5.70	5.90- 00
* Geshko	Ivan	UKR	19.8.79	181/70	800	1:45.41	1:47.77- 02
					1500	3:32.01	3:37.07- 02
Getanda	James	KEN	5.7.82	178/66	5000	13:29.19	13:23.59- 01
* Gharib	Jaouad	MAR	22.5.72	176/66	Mar	2:08:31	0
Ghirmai	Filmon	GER	25.1.79	182/63	3kSt	8:20.50	8:24.58- 02
Ghoula	Hatem	TUN	7.6.73	180/67	20kW	1:21:12	1:19:02- 97
Giaconi	Andrea	ITA	11.4.74	184/72	110H	13.49	13.35, 13.1- 02
* Gibilisco	Giuseppe	ITA	5.1.79	183/79	PV	5.90	5.70- 00
Giesler	Andy	USA	24.2.78	188/91	Dec	7804	7671- 02
* Ginko	Viktor	BLR	7.12.65	186/77	20kW	1:23:47	1:20:31- 98, 1:20:03sc- 93
					50kW	4:06:36	3:42:20- 95
* Giralt Jr.	David	CUB-J	26.8.84	182/72	TJ	17.31	16.84- 02
Girma	Tesfaye	ETH			HMar	62:05	
^ Gitahi	Julius	KEN	29.4.78	168/52	5000	13:27.72	13:01.89- 98
					10000	27:40.87	27:11.17- 98
Giungi	Marco	ITA	30.10.74	174/60	20kW	1:23:30	1:19:49- 02
					50kW	3:59:20	3:45:55- 02
Giwa-Agbomeirele	Okoineme	USA	30.11.78		LJ	7.97i, 7.83	7.93- 01
* Glavatskiy	Aleksandr	BLR	2.5.70	185/72	TJ	17.19i, 16.71	17.53- 98
Glivinskiy	Ruslan	UKR	7.2.75	204/85	HJ	2.26	2.28- 00
* Godina	John	USA	31.5.72	193/129	SP	21.23i, 21.08	22.02- 99
					DT	64.03, 66.38dh	69.91- 98
Golding	Julian	GBR	17.2.75	183/68	200	20.37	20.18- 98
Golubtsov	Konstantin	RUS	1.6.73	172/60	20kW	1:20:28	1:22:10- 99
Gomes	Paulo	POR	15.5.73		HMar	61:38	63:24- 02
Gómez	David	ESP	13.2.81	185/85	Dec	7584	7772- 00
Goncharuk	Dmitriy	BLR	17.7.70	190/112	SP	19.97	20.33- 95
* González	Emeterio	CUB	11.4.73	184/105	JT	81.72	87.12- 00
González	Freddy	VEN	7.10.77		3000	7:49.88	7:57.91- 99
			7		5000	13:29.16	13:37.48- 99
González	José Antonio	ESP	15.6.79	177/65	50kW	3:55:00	3:54:47A- 99
González	José María	ESP	3.3.73	177/63	3kSt	8:33.01	8:22.72- 99
González	Oscar	ESP	8.8.76	193/83	Dec	7842	7949- 01
^ Gorban	Boris	RUS	28.9.78	191/78	400H	48.93	48.50, 48.27dq- 01
Gorbenko	Gennadiy	UKR	22.9.75	187/72	400H	49.49	48.40- 00
Gorries	Paul	RSA	28.2.81	184/75	400	45.30A, 45.47	45.47A- 01, 45.71- 02
* Gorshkov	Dmitriy	RUS	8.3.82		SP	19.81i, 19.51	18.34i, 18.10- 02
Gorshkov	Vasiliy	RUS	5.2.77	186/84	PV	5.73i, 5.60	5.80- 02, 5.81ex- 01
Goucher	Adam	USA	18.2.75	178/64	1M	3:57.07	3:54.17- 99
					3000	7:48.72	7:34.96- 01
* Goumri	Abderrahim	MAR	21.5.76	167/60	3000	7:40.85i, 7:46.72	7:32.36- 01
					5000	13:05.81	13:00.76- 02
Goúsis	Anastásios	GRE	7.7.79	177/75	200	20.53	20.69- 00
					400	45.57	45.55- 00
Grabovoy	Vadim	UKR	5.4.73	190/112	HT	74.70	79.82- 02
Grabusic	Jurica	CRO	28.3.83	185/75	110H	13.54	13.80- 02
Graczyk	Zbigniew	POL	4.7.78	188/64	1500	3:37.09	3:39.46- 02
Graff	Christopher	USA	5.10.75		10000	28:21.41	28:07.17- 99
Graham	James	USA	3.3.81	188/79	400H	50.14	50.48- 02
Gram	Ronald	NED	31.3.74		HT	71.58	71.77- 02
^ Grant	Dalton	GBR	8.4.66	186/76	HJ	2.25i, 2.23	2.37i- 94, 2.36- 91
Grant	Dwayne	GBR	17.7.82	183/76	100	10.24w	10.47, 10.22w- 01
					200	20.58, 20.38w	20.64, 20.4w- 01, 20.60w- 02
Greaux	Alexander	PUR	22.9.77		3kSt	8:33.12	5:42.39- 02
Greaves	Damien	GBR	19.9.77	185/95	110H	13.66	13.54- 02
* Greene	Maurice	USA	23.7.74	175/75	100	9.94	9.79- 99
					200	20.16	19.86- 97
* Greer	Breaux	USA	19.10.76	188/102	JT	82.10	87.00- 01
Greer	Jabari	USA	11.2.82	178/79	110H	13.32	13.78- 02
* Gregório	Jadel	BRA	16.9.80	202/102	TJ	17.11, 17.37w	17.13- 01, 17.35i- 02
* Griffiths	Dean	JAM	27.1.80	180/72	400H	48.55	49.90- 02
* Grimes	Mickey	USA	10.10.76	185/84	100	9.99	10.18- 01, 10.17w- 00
					200	20.48	20.57- 02
Grimm	Philipp	GER	18.10.78		Dec	7601	
Grobler	Gerbrandt	RSA	26.1.83		JT	80.32A	72.63- 02
Gu Junjie		CHN-J	5.5.85	184/60	TJ	16.92	16.89- 00
Guermoud	Hicham	MAR	.79		3kSt	8:24.12	8:25.25- 01

	Name		Nat	Born	Ht/Wt	Event	2003 Mark	Pre-2003 Best
	Guigon	Nicolas	FRA	10.10.80	181/70	PV	5.60i, 5.50	5.50- 02
	Guset	Gheorghe	ROM	28.5.68	185/110	SP	20.48	20.84- 99
	Gushchinskiy	Viktor	RUS	12.8.78	202/84	TJ	16.91i, 16.87	16.97i- 02, 16.91- 01
	Guzdek	Miroslav	CZE	3.8.75	191/93	JT	83.71	85.74A- 02
	Häber	Tino	GER	6.10.82	185/76	JT	77.27	72.26- 02
*	Haborák	Milan	SVK	11.1.73	191/106	SP	20.39i, 20.28	20.82- 02
*	Hachlaf	Abdelkader	MAR	3.7.78	182/68	1500	3:35.03	3:33.59- 01
						3kSt	8:15.33	8:20.64- 02
	Hackley	Jimmie	USA	11.9.75	175/69	200	20.32	20.64- 99
	Hailemariam	Tadesse	ETH	17.9.72		Mar	2:09:34	2:12:54- 01
	Hair	Shane	AUS	24.10.75	181/68	LJ	8.15	8.24, 8.35w- 99
	Hajji	Abderrahim	MAR			HMar	61:16	
	Hakala	Petri	FIN	21.2.79	194/95	DT	61.40	62.59- 00
^	Hakkarainen	Harri	FIN	16.10.69	194/110	JT	77.52	87.82- 95
	Haklits	András	CRO	23.9.77	189/103	HT	78.16	79.30- 02
	Hallgrímsson	Magnus	ISL	23.3.76	192/110	DT	62.34	63.09- 00
	Hallmann	Christopher	GER	6.6.83	188/84	Dec	7615	7264- 02
	Hamano	Takeshi	JPN	30.7.74	174/63	10000	28:18.79	28:08.23- 00
						Mar	2:09:29	2:09:18- 02
	Hamdi Awadh	Mohammed	QAT	4.12.81	189/80	TJ	16.55	16.51- 01
	Hamlyn-Harris	William	AUS	14.1.78	191/96	JT	81.82	79.52- 02
	Hammad	Abderahmane	ALG	27.5.77	189/70	HJ	2.30	2.34- 00
	Hamzaoui	Ahmed	MAR	23.3.80		3kSt	8:33.02	
	Han Yucheng		CHN	16.12.78		20kW	1:20:00	
						50kW	3:54:45	
	Hanany	Mickaël	FRA	25.3.83	198/78	HJ	2.24	2.23i- 02. 2.20- 00
	Hanna	Kurt	USA	23.4.75	178/73	PV	5.60	5.75- 01
	Hanniske	Marius	GER-J	17.6.85	192/75	HJ	2.23	2.01- 02
	Haouam	Samir	ALG	20.6.68	188/103	HT	70.85	71.28- 01
	Hara	Kazushi	JPN	16.11.80	170/56	HMar	61:52	61:52- 01
	Hara	Yoshimi	JPN	2.3.68	170/60	50kW	3:55:13	3:52:26- 00
	Hardee	Trey	USA-J	7.2.84	196/82	Dec	7544	
^	Harden	Tim	USA	27.1.74	178/79	100	10.21	9.92- 99, 9.88w- 98
*	Harju	Arsi	FIN	18.3.74	183/125	SP	21.00i, 19.76	21.39- 00
	Harlan	Ryan	USA	25.4.81	191/93	110H	13.71	13.96, 13.90w- 02
						Dec	7560	7948- 02
	Harmse	Chris	RSA	31.5.73	184/118	HT	78.64	80.19- 02
	Harnapp	Steve	GER	30.7.75	180/92	HT	71.65	75.14- 02
	Harper	Jacey	TRI	20.5.80	183/77	100	10.19	10.21- 01
						200	20.80, 20.68w	20.71- 01
	Harrell	Reggie	USA	28.11.81	190/93	110H	13.74	13.73- 01
	Harris	Jebreh	USA	22.9.78		800	1:46.72	1:46.76- 02
	Harris	Jerry	USA	29.10.81	182/68	400	45.52	45.62- 02
	Harris	Kelvin	USA	22.6.81	193/80	110H	13.73, 13.65w	13.97- 02
	Harris	Micah	USA	30.4.79	190/84	110H	13.43	13.67- 02
	Harris	Otis	USA	30.6.82	188/77	400	44.57	45.42- 02
*	Harris	Rickey	USA	29.9.81	176/73	400	45.42	44.84- 02
						400H	48.83	48.16- 02
	Harris	Stephen	USA	5.12.80	191/82	Dec	8103w, 8061	7955- 02
	Harris	Tora	USA	21.9.78	190/83	HJ	2.30i, 2.31iet, 2.27	2.31- 02
*	Harrison	Alvin	USA	20.1.74	188/80	200	20.52w	20.41- 96
*	Harrison	Calvin	USA	20.1.74	186/75	400	44.62	44.64- 00
	Harrison	Nick	AUS	18.10.70	172/59	Mar	2:10:22	2:15:17- 01
	Harrison	Richard	USA	13.5.70	193/139	SP	20.04	19.68- 00
	Hart	Bevan	USA	1.8.77	180/75	Dec	7754	8002- 00
*	Hartwig	Jeff	USA	25.9.67	190/82	PV	5.80i, 5.70	6.03- 00
^	Harvey	Tye	USA	25.9.74	186/73	PV	5.70Ai	5.80- 00, 5.93i- 01
	Haschke	Franek	GER	28.3.80	191/72	1500	3:38.88	3:36.99- 02
*	Hassan	Abdullah	QAT	4.4.81	170/54	see Chepkurui, Albert		
	Hatungimana	Arthémon	BDI	21.1.74	180/64	800	1:45.44	1:43.38- 01
*	Haughton	Greg	JAM	10.11.73	185/79	400	45.21	44.56- 95
	Haukijärvi	Jarkko	FIN	10.6.77	189/125	SP	19.38	20.31- 00
	Havlícek	Pavel	CZE	3.11.81	191/83	Dec	7569	7253-01
	Hazouri	Mohamed	SYR	.83		TJ	16.48	16.17- 02
	He Xiaodong		CHN	14.1.78	180/64	20kW	1:24:04	1:21:15- 01
*	Hecht	Raymond	GER	11.11.68	191/95	JT	86.22	92.60- 95
	Hecini	Adem	ALG	13.12.75	175/66	400	45.63	45.81- 02
						800	1:46.55	1:44.59- 97
	Heffernan	Robert	IRL	28.2.78	173/55	20kW	1:23:03	1:20:25- 02
	Helpling	Rudolph	GER	23.2.81	195/78	TJ	16.78	16.29- 00
*	Hemingway	Matt	USA	24.10.72	198/81	HJ	2.34	2.38i- 00, 2.32- 02

	Name		Nat	Born	Ht/Wt	Event	2003 Mark	Pre-2003 Best
	Henriques	Eduardo	POR	24.3.68	185/58	10000	28:05.09	28:06.71- 00
*	Henry	Boris	GER	14.12.73	193/108	JT	88.10	90.44- 97
*	Herbert	Llewellyn	RSA	21.7.77	185/80	400H	48.50	47.81- 00
	Herms	René	GER	17.7.82	195/80	800	1:45.39	1:45.85- 02
*	Hernández	Noé	MEX	15.3.78	175/64	20kW	1:18:14	1:19:03- 00
	Hernández	William	VEN	18.2.81	177/68	400	45.81	45.94- 00
*	Hernández	Yoel	CUB	12.12.77	184/77	110H	13.49	13.24- 99, 13.20w- 00
*	Hernández	Yuniel	CUB	28.3.81	183/76	110H	13.35	13.26- 01
*	Hernu	Laurent	FRA	22.8.76	190/85	Dec	8219	8280- 01
	Herring	Aubrey	USA	19.9.78	183/77	110H	13.49	13.36- 02
	Hewitt	Maurice	USA			100	10.0w	
	Hicks	Antwon	USA	12.3.83	187/73	110H	13.49, 13.46w	13.59, 13.42w- 02
	Hicks	Graham	AUS	14.12.78		DT	60.34	55.56- 01
	Hierrezuelo	Sergio	CUB	15.3.82	175/70	400H	49.46	49.93- 02
*	Higuero	Juan Carlos	ESP	3.8.78	178/72	800	1:46.00	1:46.42- 00
						1500	3:31.61	3:32.30- 01
	Hill	Clinton	AUS	19.4.80	186/77	400	45.29	45.41- 02
	Hill	Mick	GBR	22.10.64	190/98	JT	78.73	86.94-93
	Hirata	Takuro	JPN	4.7.80	185/84	Dec	7630	7527- 01
*	Hissou	Salah	MAR	16.1.72	176/62	3000	7:45.9+	7:28.93- 99
						5000	12:59.15	12:50.80- 96
	Hjartarson	Einar Karl	ISL	28.10.80	190/72	HJ	2.23i	2.28i, 2.25- 01
	Hoff	Shadrack	RSA	19.5.73	169/51	10000	27:44.33	27:43.89- 96
*	Hoffa	Reese	USA	8.10.77	183/115	SP	20.95	20.47- 02
	Hogans	Obra	USA	29.6.82		400	45.28	46.39- 02
	Högler	Gregor	AUT	27.6.72	181/93	JT	77.56	84.03- 99
	Höhne	Andre	GER	10.3.78	184/68	20kW	1:20:44	1:21:38- 02
	Høiby	Trond	NOR	24.1.73	194/94	Dec	7739	8085- 99
	Hoídis	Hristóforos	GRE	10.9.78	180/71	100	10.17	10.19- 99
*	Holm	Stefan	SWE	25.5.76	181/70	HJ	2.36i	2.35- 02
	Holmén	Janne	FIN	26.9.77	177/59	10000	28:09.94	28:23.84- 01
	Holmes	Jerrick	USA	.81		HJ	2.23i	2.13- 00
	Holusa	Milos	CZE	2.5.65	174/62	50kW	3:58:05	3:49:08- 96
^	Hood	Graham	CAN	2.4.72	186/68	1M	3:55.70i, 3:56.02	3:51.55- 97
	Hooker	Ja'Warren	USA	24.9.78	183/77	400	45.72	44.78- 00
	Hopley	Hannes	RSA	26.1.81	182/100	DT	61.49	63.68- 01
	Horák	Peter	SVK	7.12.83	197/83	HJ	2.23i	2.21- 02
	Horváth	Gergely	HUN	5.6.75	186/90	JT	81.55	81.14- 02
	Hosokawa	Michitaka	JPN	26.4.76	173/61	10000	28:22.29	28:31.73- 01
	Howe	Quincy	TRI	11.1.79	183/77	TJ	16.47A	16.69iA- 01, 16.58A- 02
	Huang Le		CHN	25.9.77	176/65	LJ	8.10	8.21- 99
	Huber	Philipp	SUI	18.2.74	184/82	Dec	7762	8153- 00
	Hudec	Leonard	AUT	13.6.73	185/79	110H	13.73	13.67- 00
	Hughes	Robby	USA	10.10.78		110H	13.69	13.66, 13.63A, 13.59w- 00
	Huh Hee-sun		KOR	13.4.81		JT	77.33	72.28- 02
	Human	Willie	RSA	8.3.82	181/95	JT	76.42A	78.03A- 01
	Hummastenniemi	Janne	FIN	4.10.79	196/107	DT	60.16	60.28- 01
	Hussein	Mbarak	KEN	4.4.65		Mar	2:09:57	2:09:45- 02
	Hussein Abdel Moneim	Yamine	EGY	19.6.78		HT	71.10	70.47- 02
*	Hysong	Nick	USA	9.12.71	183/77	PV	5.78	5.90- 00
*	Iakovákis	Periklis	GRE	24.3.79	185/73	400H	48.17	48.66- 02
	Iannelli	Angelo	ITA	27.7.76	175/61	3kSt	8:25.65	8:22.06- 99
	Ibrahim	Bashir Omer	SUD	14.3.79		3kSt	8:31.71	8:36.03- 02
	Igarashi	Noriaki	JPN	28.10.72	165/55	Mar	2:10:11	2:09:26- 00
	Igumi	Ryosuke	JPN-J	6.7.84		100	10.21w	10.52, 10.50w- 02
	Ilariani	David	GEO	20.1.81	195/84	110H	13.75	14.08- 01
	Illikainen	Jani	FIN	26.1.76	196/152	SP	19.68	20.56- 01
	Íltsios	Yeóryios	GRE	28.11.81	187/90	JT	77.71	75.49- 02
	Imamura	Fumio	JPN	5.11.66	178/63	50kW	3:59:20	3:49:38- 98
	Inocêncio	Mateus	BRA	17.5.81	180/65	110H	13.42A, 13.43	13.47- 02
	Inozemtsev	Yevgeniy	RUS	14.4.74		TJ	16.61	16.23- 02
	Irifune	Satoshi	JPN	14.12.75	176/59	10000	28:06.93	27:53.92- 01
	Irungu Mathathi	Martin	KEN-J	25.12.85	165/49	10000	27:43.16	
	Ishikawa	Kazuyoshi	JPN	16.11.82	178/70	TJ	16.84	16.50- 02
	Ishikawa	Suehiro	JPN	27.9.79	168/56	10000	28:18.30	28:46.19- 00
	Ishikura	Kazuki	JPN	1.10.80	173/60	100	10.25	10.24- 02, 10.17w- 01
	Ishizawa	Masatoshi	JPN	13.3.79	180/75	Dec	7557	7644- 02
	Ismail	Ahmed	SUD-J	10.9.84	191/71	800	1:46.15	1:46.36- 02
	Ito	Tomohiro	JPN	16.8.82		400	45.63	46.28- 02
*	Ivanov	Aleksandr	RUS	25.5.82	194/110	JT	88.90	87.62- 02
	Ivanov	Dmitriy	RUS	23.3.77	187/77	Dec	7799	8065- 01

Name		Nat	Born	Ht/Wt	Event	2003 Mark	Pre-2003 Best
Ivanov	Sergey	BLR-J	28.3.84	201/75	HJ	2.25	2.20- 02
Ivanov	Vasiliy	RUS	26.12.76	174/62	20kW	1:20:31	1:21:56- 98
* Ivuti	Patrick	KEN	30.6.78	165/52	HMar	60:53	59:31- 00
Iwamizu	Yoshitaka	JPN	20.6.79	174/53	3kSt	8:18.93	8:26.77- 01
Iwasa	Toshihiro	JPN	18.5.76	172/57	5000	13:26.78	13:32.09- 00
					10000	28:11.23	28:06.89- 00
Izmailov	Sergey	UKR	1.5.75	180/72	TJ	16.89i, 16.79	17.02- 96, 17.09dq- 99
* Jackson	Bershawn	USA	8.5.83	173/68	400H	48.23	50.00- 02
^ Jackson	Colin	GBR	18.2.67	182/75	110H	13.40i	12.91- 93, 12.8w- 90
Jackson	E.J. (Ephion)	USA	3.2.78	175/70	100	10.22w, 10.0w	10.35- 98, 10.29w- 00
Jacobs	Fanie	RSA	21.4.76		PV	5.60	5.40A- 01
Jakobs	Marco	GER	30.5.74	200/100	DT	61.29	64.96- 97
Jakobsson	Mikael	SWE	9.1.81	194/90	400H	49.40	49.38- 02
James	Richard	JAM	1.12.79		400	45.66	45.96- 02
Janácek	Stepán	CZE	12.6.77		PV	5.70i	5.76- 02
Janek	Marek	SVK	29.1.77	176/66	50kW	3:59:37	3:58:49- 00
Janik	Igor	POL	12.1.83	194/78	JT	82.54	78.90- 02
Jankú	Jan	CZE	10.8.71	193/79	HJ	2.24	2.30i- 96, 2.29- 97
^ Jankú	Tomás	CZE	27.12.74	191/75	HJ	2.30	2.32- 99
Jansen	Joeri	BEL	28.5.79	180/64	800	1:44.95	1:44.38- 02
Janson	Oscar	SWE	22.7.75	192/90	PV	5.87	5.64- 02
* Januszewski	Pawel	POL	2.1.72	178/68	400H	50.06	48.17- 98
^ Janvrin	Kip	USA	8.7.65	183/84	Dec	7918	8462w, 8345- 96
Jarrett	Patrick	JAM	2.10.77	186/82	100	10.24, 10.04w	10.12, 10.08dq, 9.89rw- 01
Järvenpää	Tero	FIN-J	2.10.84	186/90	JT	80.43	70.85- 02
Jaworski	Dawid	POL	31.1.78	190/74	HJ	2.28	2.25- 02
Jean-Théodore	Olivier	FRA	13.11.74	183/75	400H	49.74	49.04- 02
Jedrusinski	Marcin	POL	28.9.81	190/88	100	10.07w	10.36- 02
					200	20.39, 20.38w	20.31- 02
Jeng	Alhaji	SWE	13.12.81	186/75	PV	5.56i	5.49- 01
Jennings	Karl	CAN	14.5.79	188/82	110H	13.53	13.88- 01
Jensen	Dennis	DEN	11.9.69		5000	13:26.87	13:25.39- 00
Jensen	Morten	DEN	2.12.82	189/81	LJ	7.97	7.49- 00
de Jesus	Leandro	BRA	2.3.81		LJ	7.97	7.55- 02
Ji Young-joon		KOR	15.10.81		Mar	2:08:43	2:09:48- 02
Jifar	Tariku	ETH-J	.84		HMar	62:02A	
* Jiménez	Antonio	ESP	18.2.77	178/61	3kSt	8:15.82	8:11.52- 01
Johansson	Bengt	SWE	7.7.73	189/119	HT	71.87	76.32- 01
* Johnson	Allen	USA	1.3.71	178/70	200	20.57	20.26- 97
					110H	12.97	12.92- 96
Johnson	Brian	USA	25.3.80	186/77	200	20.65	
					LJ	8.28i, 8.05	8.07A, 8.33w- 02, 8.01- 01
Johnson	Danny	USA	11.5.83		200	20.59w	20.96- 02
Johnson	Ferdana	USA	6.10.72	183/69	400H	49.56	49.55- 00
Johnson	Garrett	USA-J	24.5.84		SP	19.26i	
Johnson	Jonathan	USA	5.3.82	177/73	800	1:46.51	1:45.81- 02
* Johnson	Joshua 'J.J'	USA	10.5.76	191/91	100	10.05	9.95- 02
					200	20.05	19.88- 01
Johnson	Nick	USA	12.11.83	175/66	100	10.20	10.29, 10.21w- 00
* Johnson	Patrick	AUS	26.9.72	177/73	100	9.93, 9.88w	10.10- 00
					200	20.50, 20.25w	20.52- 01
Johnson	Weldon	USA	24.7.73	178/71	10000	28:06.58	28:10.14- 01
Jones	Mick	GBR	23.7.63	187/119	HT	73.16	76.43- 01
Joorits	Mikk	EST	12.2.81	192/79	Dec	7528	7459- 02
* Joseph	Fabiano	TAN-J	24.12.85	158/48	5000	13:22.89	
					10000	27:32.63	
					HMar	60:52	64:00- 02
Juan	Jaime	ESP	28.8.77	186/76	400H	50.19	49.80- 02
Julius	Leigh	RSA-J	25.3.85	170/66	100	10.24	10.42A- 03, 10.24w- 03
					200	20.49	20.79A- 02
Kabara	Anthony	KEN	9.3.78	182/73	800	1:45.96	1:45.29- 01
Kabiru	Samuel	KEN	6.6.83	175/57	10000	28:07.18	27:59.61- 02
Kagika	Laban	KEN	17.7.78	164/50	10000	28:01.88	27:57.81- 00
Kahugu	Joseph	KEN	7.6.71	168/58	Mar	2:09:33	2:07:59- 98
Kalinin	Pavel	RUS	21.8.79	194/78	TJ	16.45	16.59- 02
Kallabis	Damian	GER	10.6.73	177/67	3kSt	8:21.15	8:09.48- 99
Kamani	Bayano	USA/PAN	17.4.80	188/79	400H	49.82	48.43- 00
* Kamathi	Charles	KEN	18.5.78	165/51	3000	7:41.89	7:43.50- 00
					5000	13:15.33	13:02.51- 02
					10000	27:29.12	26:51.49- 99
Kamel	Yousef Saïd	BRN			see Konchellah, Gregory		

Name		Nat	Born	Ht/Wt	Event	2003 Mark	Pre-2003 Best
Kanaykin	Vladimir	RUS-J	21.3.85	170/62	20kW	1:21:23	
Kanno	Yuta	JPN	13.12.80	173/62	100	10.22	10.32- 01, 10.24w- 02
* Kanter	Gerd	EST	6.5.79	196/114	DT	67.13	66.31- 02
Kanyi	John	KEN	6.9.80	160/50	10000	27:46.87	27:47.44- 00
					HMar	62:08	60:49- 99
Kapek	Julien	FRA	12.1.79	179/74	TJ	17.12, 17.24w	17.04- 02
* Kaptyukh	Vasiliy	BLR	27.6.67	197/120	DT	66.51	67.59- 00
^ Kapustin	Denis	RUS	5.10.70	189/86	TJ	16.76	17.65- 98, 17.86w- 94
Karailiev	Momchil	BUL	21.5.82		TJ	16.95	15.60- 02
Karas	Josef	CZE/CAN	20.8.78	191/85	Dec	7669	7360- 02
Karasmanákis	Elefthérios	GRE	16.8.78		JT	76.91	77.58- 01
Kariuki	David	KEN	23.5.80	164/53	10000	27:46.53	28:16.31- 00
Kariuki	John	KEN-Y	10.11.86	171/55	5000	13:27.18	13:37.25- 02
					10000	28:02.72	
* Karjalainen	Olli-Pekka	FIN	7.3.80	194/110	HT	80.20	81.70- 02
Karlivans	Janis	LAT	2.6.82	193/82	Dec	7512	7665- 01
* Karlsson	Conny	FIN	30.12.75	195/120	SP	20.60	20.78- 01
* Karpov	Dmitriy	KAZ	23.7.81	198/89	Dec	8374	7995- 02
Kaseorg	Indrek	EST	16.12.67	194/86	Dec	7804	8179- 98
Kastánis	Spirídon	GRE	23.9.64	176/65	50kW	3:56:41	3:54:11- 90
Kaszczyk	Emilian	POL	21.4.80	193/72	HJ	2.28	2.20i- 02, 2.18- 00
Kato	Toshihide	JPN	4.7.73	174/56	10000	28:16.80	28:31.79- 02
Katsantonis	Prodromos	CYP	20.10.75	180/72	100	10.19	10.26- 97
Kawabata	Shingo	JPN	15.5.78	175/70	100	10.25, 10.23w	10.11- 00
Kawai	Hironori	JPN	3.2.76	166/53	50kW	4:02:26	4:06:00- 02
Kawakita	Naohiro	JPN	18.11.80	181/75	400H	49.91	49.70- 01
Kawamura	Hideaki	JPN	15.9.74	175/69	400H	49.67	48.84- 00
Kazanin	Aleksey	UKR	22.5.82	170/58	50kW	3:58:20	4:10:27- 02
* Kedéris	Konstadinos	GRE	11.7.73	180/78	200	20.30	19.85- 02
* Keflezighi	Mebrahtom	USA	5.5.75	169/58	3000	7:48.81	8:09.5i- 98
					5000	13:20.50	13:11.77- 00
					10000	27:57.59	27:13.98- 01
					Mar	2:10:03	2:12:35- 02
^ Keino	Martin	KEN	20.6.72	180/67	3000	7:48.53	7:35.97- 97
Keïta	Naman	FRA	9.4.78	196/86	400H	48.86	49.60- 02
Keller	Steve	USA	23.7.76		Dec	7673	7477- 99
* Kemboi	Ezekiel	KEN	25.5.82	175/62	3kSt	8:02.49	8:06.65- 02
* Kemboi	Nicholas	KEN	25.11.83	163/50	5000	13:01.14	13:26.36- 01
					10000	26:30.03	
					HMar	60:31	
Kemboi	Vincent	KEN	29.5.82		800	1:45.20	1:44.92A- 02
Kemei	Philemon	KEN	12.2.82		10000	27:58.92	27:40.08- 00
Kenduiywo	Barnabas	KEN	.74		HMar	62:08	62:07- 02
^ Kennedy	Bob	USA	18.8.70	183/66	5000	13:21.85	12:58.21- 96
					10000	27:51.06	27:38.37- 99
Kennouche	Abdelslaam	ALG	7.10.80		800	1:46.60	1:48.69- 02
					1000	2:17.25	2:19.74- 02
					1500	3:36.93	3:39.06- 01
Kerdyapkin	Sergey	RUS	16.1.80	178/66	20kW	1:23:24+	1:24:38- 02
Kerr	Matthew	CAN	3.5.76	186/66	3kSt	8:29.94	8:32.05- 98
Kerwitz	Eric	ARG	29.1.80		Dec	7561	7305- 01
Keska	Karl	GBR	7.5.72	183/68	10000	27:47.89	27:44.09- 00
Keskisalo	Jukka	FIN	27.3.81	176/66	3kSt	8:17.72	8:36.05- 02
Keul	Adam	USA	27.1.80	193/88	PV	5.55A, 5.50	5.68i, 5.59- 01
Khaldi	Mohamed	ALG	3.5.75	172/60	1500	3:36.12	3:33.03- 01
Khanafin	Aleksey	RUS	12.4.81	190/78	PV	5.60i, 5.40	5.56i, 5.50- 00, 5.65ex- 02
Khattabi	Elarbi	MAR	16.5.67	174/61	HMar	61:39	64:16- 98
* Khersontsev	Vadim	RUS	8.7.74	192/106	HT	78.89	81.26- 01
Kholev	Dennis	ISR	21.10.75	187/80	PV	5.50	5.71- 02
Kibet	Luke	KEN	19.6.73		HMar	61:10	61:43- 98
Kibet	Luke	KEN	12.4.83		HMar	62:09	
					3kSt	8:33.0A	8:42.0A- 02
Kibet	Victor	KEN	.81		400	45.50A	45.95A- 02
Kibiwott	Charles E	KEN			Mar	2:10:21	2:12:12- 02
Kibiwott	Francis	KEN	15.9.78		HMar	61:50	62:18- 02
* Kibowen	John	KEN	21.4.69	175/64	3000	7:32.01	7:29.09- 98
					5000	12:54.07	12:58.61- 02
Kigen	Moses	KEN	22.4.73	182/68	3000	7:45.59	7:52.14- 01
					5000	13:19.29	13:41.87- 02
Kiilu	Simon	KEN	.82		HMar	61:34	64:07- 02
* Kikaya	Gary	COD	4.2.78	184/75	400	44.99	44.53- 02

Name		Nat	Born	Ht/Wt	Event	2003 Mark	Pre-2003 Best
Kilel	David	KEN-J	21.5.84	170/59	5000	13:16.71	13:17.75- 02
Kim Kun-woo		KOR	29.2.80	181/79	Dec	7675	7464- 02
Kim Se-in		KOR	29.7.74	176/70	PV	5.50	5.40- 02
Kim Yoo-suk		KOR	19.1.82	190/81	PV	5.55	5.30- 01
Kimaiyo	Boaz	KEN	10.12.76		Mar	2:09:28	2:08:45- 02
* Kimutai	Japheth	KEN	20.12.78	173/55	800	1:43.71A	1:42.69- 99
					1000	2:16.83	2:14.28- 00
Kimutai	Sylas	KEN	12.10.83		800	1:46.31	1:45.91- 02
Kimutai Koskei	Benjamin	KEN	5.9.71		HMar	61:52	63:24- 02
					Mar	2:07:39	2:07:26- 02
Kimwetich	Kenneth	KEN	1.1.73	183/73	800	1:45.68	1:43.03- 98
* Kipchirchir	Alex	KEN-J	26.11.84	188/63	800	1:45.93	1:45.5A- 02
					1500	3:31.42	3:32.95- 02
					1M	3:50.25	
* Kipchoge	Eliud	KEN-J	5.11.84	167/52	1500	3:36.17	
					3000	7:30.91	7:46.34- 02
					5000	12:52.61	13:13.03- 02
Kipchumba Rutto	Ronald	KEN-Y	8.10.87		3kSt	8:24.54	
Kipkemboi	Laban	KEN	30.12.77	172/66	HMar	61:29	60:12- 95
Kipkering Meto	Philmon	KEN	10.8.74		HMar	61:21	61:12- 02
* Kipketer	Sammy	KEN	29.9.81	166/52	3000	7:45.1+	7:33.62- 01
					5000	12:52.33	12:54.07- 00
					10000	27:13.42	26:49.38- 02
* Kipketer	Wilson	DEN	12.12.70	172/62	800	1:43.28	1:41.11- 97
					1000	2:18.36i	2:16.29- 95, 2:14.96i- 00
* Kipkoech	Raymond	KEN	.75		Mar	2:09:21	2:06:47- 02
Kipkoech-Bowen	Francis	KEN	12.10.73		10000	27:45.20	
* Kipkosgei	Luke	KEN	27.11.75	176/57	1M	3:56.97	3:56.4+- 98
					3000	7:37.64	7:27.59- 98
					5000	13:06.92	12:56.50- 00
* Kipkurui	Benjamin	KEN	28.12.80	174/57	1500	3:32.42	3:30.67- 01
					1M	3:52.89	3:49.34- 00
					2000	5:00.21	
Kiplagat	Sammy	KEN	.73		3kSt	8:25.92	8:24.22- 02
* Kiplagat	William	KEN	21.6.72		Mar	2:07:42	2:06:50- 99
Kiplak	David	KEN	27.12.81	170/60	1500	3:35.09	3:33.73- 02
					3000	7:47.36	7:58.04- 01
Kiplangat Bett	Charles	KEN-J	21.7.84		1500	3:37.04	
Kiplitan	Thomas	KEN	15.6.83	175/63	3kSt	8:31.85	8:12.91- 02
Kipngetich	Robert	KEN		165/53	5000	13:19.95	13:59.45- 02
Kiprono	Isaac	KEN	5.9.76		Mar	2:10:38	2:09:59- 01
* Kiprono	Josephat	KEN	12.12.73	172/52	Mar	2:07:53	2:06:44- 99
Kiprono Choge	Augustine	KEN-Y	21.1.87	162/53	1500	3:37.48	3:43.7A- 02
					5000	13:20.08	
Kiprono Kipchirchir	Justus	KEN-Y	28.2.87		5000	13:28.61	
* Kiprop	Boniface	UGA-J	12.10.85	167/53	3000	7:47.16	7:57.28- 02
					5000	13:16.21	13:48.6- 01
					10000	27:15.88	28:45.76- 01
Kiprop	Francis	KEN	4.6.82	172/54	3000	7:47.0+	7:46.13- 02
					5000	13:17.54	13:05.81- 02
					10000	28:22.22	27:36.78- 02
^ Kiprop	Fred	KEN	3.6.74		Mar	2:09:14	2:06:47- 99
Kiprotich	Peter	KEN	.79		HMar	61:49	
Kipruto	Sammy	KEN	22.11.78		HMar	62:06	62:23- 02
Kipsang	Salim	KEN	22.12.79	172/52	HMar	61:02	61:07- 02
Kipsang	William	KEN	.77		Mar	2:06:39	0
* Kipsos	Vincent	KEN	22.6.76		Mar	2:09:42	2:06:52- 03
Kiptanui	Timothy	KEN	5.1.80	182/60	800	1:46.03	
					1000	2:16.19	
					1500	3:34.07	3:42.7A- 02
					2000	4:59.52	
Kiptoo	Julius	KEN	4.9.77	172/60	3kSt	8:29.96	8:15.88- 98
Kipyego	Ernest	KEN	6.10.78		Mar	2:09:55	2:10:52- 02
Kipyego	Michael	KEN	2.10.83	162/58	3kSt	8:13.02	8:22.90- 02
Kirchler	Hannes	ITA	22.12.78	191/98	DT	59.70	59.85- 02
* Kirmasov	Sergey	RUS	25.3.70	180/115	HT	79.62	82.62- 98
Kirui	David	KEN	29.12.77		Mar	2:08:53	2:09:40- 01
Kirui	Paul	KEN	5.2.80		HMar	60:52	61:53- 02
Kirui	William	KEN	5.8.82	160/52	5000	13:24.45	13:18.02- 02
Kirwa	Wilson	FIN	28.12.74	183/68	800	1:46.50	1:44.69- 00
* Kiss	Balázs	HUN	21.3.72	192/115	HT	77.46	83.00- 98

Name		Nat	Born	Ht/Wt	Event	2003 Mark	Pre-2003 Best
Kloos	Tom	USA	.78		3kSt	8:30.74	8:47.95- 00
Klose	Holger	GER	5.12.72	191/104	HT	78.21	82.22- 98
Klouchi	Kader	FRA	1.6.69	177/70	LJ	8.06, 8.26w	8.30, 8.33w- 98
* Klyugin	Sergey	RUS	24.3.74	192/82	HJ	2.25	2.36- 98
Knabe	Sebastian	GER	13.10.78	184/83	Dec	7958	8151- 01
Knoblich	Christian	GER	1.10.76	177/60	3kSt	8:28.36	8:24.52- 99
Kobayashi	Fumihiro	JPN	21.7.83		20kW	1:23:36	
Kobayashi	Fumikazu	JPN	21.3.78	175/60	1500	3:39.15	3:39.86- 02
* Kobs	Karsten	GER	16.9.71	196/125	HT	80.83	82.78- 99
Koech	Barnabas	KEN			HMar	61:18	
Koech	Gilbert	KEN	1.9.80		HMar	62:05	62:26- 02
Koech	Jackson	KEN	26.12.78	173/55	HMar	60:05	61:34- 02
* Koech	Justus	KEN	19.3.80	175/60	800	1:44.16A	1:46.10A- 02
* Koech	Paul	KEN	25.6.69		HMar	61:57	60:01- 98
					Mar	2:07:07	0
* Koech	Paul Kipsiele	KEN	10.11.81	170/60	3000	7:38.48	7:33.79- 97
					3kSt	7:57.42	8:05.44- 02
^ Koers	Marko	NED	3.11.72	193/80	1500	3:38.47	3:33.05- 96
Kohn	Aulton	USA-J	.84		100	10.21w	
^ Kohutek	Artur	POL	1.5.71	190/78	110H	13.71	13.27- 97
Kokkonen	Henri	FIN	11.8.78	178/80	Dec	7562	7759- 99
Kolasa	Adam	POL	2.8.75	191/75	PV	5.70sq, 5.55	5.75- 01
Kólko	Rajmund	POL	1.3.71	186/83	JT	80.82	84.95- 01
Kologinczak	Shaun	USA	13.10.79		HJ	2.28	2.23i- 01, 2.22- 00
Komatsu	Takashi	JPN	30.12.67	181/73	TJ	16.65	16.88- 94
* Komen	Daniel	KEN	17.5.76	170/60	5000	13:28.56	12:39.74- 97
Kon	Takayuki	JPN	15.7.77	177/70	100	10.21w	10.33- 97, 10.22w- 98
Konchellah	Gregory	KEN	.83		800	1:45.88 (later Mushir Salem Jawher BRN)	
Kondratowicz	Wojciech	POL	18.4.80	196/120	HT	81.35	77.06- 01
Konopka	Miloslav	SVK	23.1.79	189/102	JT	78.44	79.98- 02
* Konovalov	Ilya	RUS	4.3.71	192/110	HT	82.28	81.93- 00
Kónstas	Stéfanos	GRE	16.5.77	198/119	DT	60.56	61.29- 02
Korchmyd	Aleksandr	UKR	22.1.82	184/75	PV	5.75	5.50, 5.60sq- 00
Korcok	Peter	SVK	12.8.74	178/64	50kW	3:54:12	3:52:49- 02
* Korepanov	Sergey	KAZ	9.5.64	170/61	50kW	3:47:42	3:39:22- 99
* Korir	John Cheruiyot	KEN	13.12.81	172/57	5000	13:17.7+	13:09.58- 00
					10000	27:17.24	26:52.87- 02
					HMar	61:02	
* Korir	Paul	KEN	15.7.77	180/64	1000	2:18.2+	
					1500	3:30.72	3:39.18- 02
					1M	3:48.17	
* Korir	Sammy	KEN	12.12.71		Mar	2:04:56	2:08:02- 97
Korir	Shadrack	KEN	14.12.78	170/54	1500	3:37.92	3:35.16- 01
					3000	7:44.57+	
					5000	13:16.92	13:14.02- 02
Korkízoglou	Pródromos	GRE	27.2.75	190/84	Dec	7705	8069- 00
Kortbeek	Thomas	NED	2.4.81	191/78	400H	48.95	49.51- 02
* Korzeniowski	Robert	POL	30.7.68	168/60	20kW	1:19:11	1:18:22- 00
					50kW	3:36:03	3:36:39- 02
Kosenkow	Alexander	GER	14.3.77	178/68	100	10.14	10.26- 99
Kosgei	Barnabas	KEN-Y	20.9.86		3kSt	8:31.97	
* Kosgei	Japhet	KEN	20.12.68	165/52	HMar	62:06	60:01- 99
					Mar	2:07:39	2:07:09- 99
Kosgei	Joseph	KEN	25.8.74	173/60	3000	7:44.70	7:39.38- 02
					5000	13:15.11	13:15.07- 02
* Kosgei	Paul	KEN	22.4.78	175/57	10000	27:21.56	27:38.22- 00
					HMar	62:00	59:58- 02
* Kosgei	Reuben	KEN	2.8.79	170/55	3kSt	8:09.65	7:57.29- 01
Kosgei	Shadrack	KEN-J	.84		3000	7:45.96	7:51.86- 02
					5000	13:12.24	13:23.44- 02
Koski-Vähälä	Jarko	FIN	21.11.78	194/97	JT	81.46	80.64- 02
Kostin	Ilya	RUS	1.4.79	192/110	DT	59.72	61.48- 02
^ Koukodímos	Konstadínos	GRE	14.9.69	186/80	LJ	8.10	8.36, 8.40w- 94
Kouromihalákis	Pávlos	GRE	16.2.76		Dec	7630w, 7504	
Kouroupákis	Stávros	GRE	17.5.83	177/68	PV	5.55i, 5.45	5.50- 02
* Kövágó	Zoltán	HUN	10.4.79	204/127	DT	66.03	66.93- 01
Kovals	Ainars	LAT	21.11.81	192/100	JT	80.75	76.58- 01
Kozlov	Yevgeniy	RUS	.78		SP	19.45i	18.47- 02
* Kozmus	Primoz	SLO	30.9.79	188/102	HT	81.21	76.84- 00
Kravtsov	Aleksandr	RUS	18.3.74		HJ	2.24	2.31- 01
Krawczyk	Andrzej	POL	11.4.76	195/100	DT	62.79	63.67- 02

Name		Nat	Born	Ht/Wt	Event	2003 Mark	Pre-2003 Best
* Kristiansson	Patrik	SWE	3.6.77	192/85	PV	5.85	5.85- 02
Kritzinger	Marnus	RSA	10.2.82		400H	48.92	49.57A- 01
Kröckert	Mario	GER	2.3.78	185/64	3000	7:49.67	7:51.93- 02
* Kronberg	Robert	SWE	15.8.76	181/82	110H	13.46	13.35- 01
Kronin	Aleksey	RUS	23.7.70	180/69	20kW	1:21:06	1:20:01- 99
Krotwaar	Luc	NED	25.1.68		Mar	2:10:13	2:10:59- 02
* Kruger	Frantz	RSA	22.5.75	203/125	DT	66.70	70.32- 02
* Krummenacker	David	USA	24.5.75	190/79	800	1:44.30	1:43.92- 02
					1000	2:17.10	2:15.97- 02
					1500	3:35.15	3:31.93- 02
* Krykun	Aleksandr	UKR	1.3.68	194/125	HT	79.35	81.59- 02
Krysin	Aleksey	RUS	25.11.76	202/80	HJ	2.25i, 2.20	2.30- 98
Krzosek	Grzegorz	POL	10.1.76	182/67	800	1:46.84	1:45.97- 01
Krzywanski	Marcin	POL	29.8.75	185/74	100	10.20w	10.23- 98
Kucinski	Beniamin	POL	1.6.82	172/51	20kW	1:22:07	1:22:25- 02
Kulagin	Denis	RUS	23.5.80		HT	72.79	75.92- 02
Kumar	Anil	IND	20.6.75	189/99	DT	60.68	62.12- 02
Kunichika	Tomoaki	JPN	22.7.73	179/60	10000	28:05.38	28:08.86- 97
					Mar	2:07:52	2:10:10- 99
Kunkel	Adam	CAN	21.2.81	180/77	400H	49.49	49.87- 01
Kuptsov	Artyom	RUS-J	22.4.84	183/64	PV	5.70	5.40- 02
Kuptsov	Dmitriy	RUS	9.11.82	184/75	PV	5.70i, 5..60	5.65- 02
Kürtösi	Zsolt	HUN	21.3.71	188/86	Dec	7651	8149- 00
Kuznetsov	Viktor	UKR-J	14.7.86	190/67	LJ	8.12i	6.89- 02
* Kwalia	James	KEN-J	12.6.84	171/59	1500	3:38.67	3:42.3A- 01
					1M	3:50.39	
					2000	4:59.11	
					3000	7:35.53	7:37.18- 02
					5000	12:54.58	13:14.34- 02
Kwambai	James	KEN	.76		HMar	60:38	
Kyalo	John	KEN-J	.84		HMar	60:51	
Kysela	Martin	CZE	25.3.74	178/66	PV	5.70x, 5.55	5.60- 96, 5.65i- 98, 5.70sq- 00
Kyyrö	Mikko	FIN	12.7.80	191/106	DT	63.24	62.35- 01
la Grange	Marcus	RSA	12.12.77	186/75	400	45.29A, 45.38	44.65A, 44.76- 02
Laalou	Amine	MAR	13.5.82	178/57	800	1:45.20	1:46.5- 02
Lacasse	Florent	FRA	21.1.81	185/65	800	1:44.61	1:45.53- 02
					1000	2:17.34	2:18.80- 02
Lacy	Aaron	USA	1.4.71	188/79	400H	50.02	49.79- 02
* Lagat	Bernard	KEN	12.12.74	175/61	800	1:46.00	1:46.02- 98
					1500	3:30.55	3:26.34- 01
					1M	3:50.21	3:47.28- 01
^ Lahssini	El Hassan	FRA	1.1.75	177/64	5000	13:22.89	13:04.32- 96
Lakhal	Irba	FRA	12.12.75	176/60	3kSt	8:25.46	8:22.09- 95
Lamachi	Abdelkebir	MAR	.80		HMar	61:51	
Lambert	Chris	GBR	6.4.81	188/80	200	20.34	20.37- 02
Lambert	Sean	GRN	16.8.82	170/70	100	10.30, 10.24w	10.17, 10.13w- 01
Lambèse	Bruno	FRA	11.4.69	190/96	Dec	7649	7756- 01
^ Lambrechts	Burger	RSA	3.4.73	200/145	SP	19.10	20.56- 00, 20.90dq- 01
* Lamela	Yago	ESP	24.7.77	178/68	LJ	8.53	8.56i, 8.56- 99
Lampart	Petr	CZE	31.3.83	191/77	LJ	8.04	8.18- 02
Lanaro	Giovanni	MEX	27.9.81	183/77	PV	5.50	5.35- 01
Lancaster	Kyle	USA	15.8.83		HJ	2.26i, 2.25	2.18- 02
Lang	Enrico	ITA	31.3.72	165/51	50kW	4:06:06	0
Langat	Jackson	KEN	15.12.80		800	1:46.41	1:47.37- 02
Langat	John	KEN	27.11.74	185/72	3kSt	8:18.27	8:15.17- 01
Langlois	Denis	FRA	10.10.68	172/60	20kW	1:23:28	1:20:35- 97
					50kW	3:49:05	3:47:38- 00
Latham	Clayton	CAN	18.4.80	188/82	LJ	7.95w	8.16- 02
Lattu	Ari-Pekka	FIN	22.6.78	192/79	400H	49.36	50.26- 02
Latty	Tesfa	JAM-J	9.11.84		100	10.24	10.71- 01, 10.52w- 02
Laursen	Jimisola	SWE	13.7.77	183/85	400	45.67	45.54- 01
Lavanne	Cedric	FRA	13.11.80	183/72	110H	13.74, 13.47w	13.58- 02
Le Dauphin	Vincent	FRA	28.6.76	190/72	3kSt	8:17.48	8:15.76- 99
le Roux	Wouter	RSA-Y	17.1.86		400H	50.05A	
* Lebed	Sergey	UKR	15.7.75	180/65	3000	7:49.09	7:35.06- 02
					5000	13:15.15	13:10.78- 02
					10000	28:12.62	28:39.71- 97
				HMar	61:49	62:09- 01	
Lebedev	Sergey	RUS	.82		TJ	16.44	16.21- 02
* Lee Bong-ju		KOR	11.10.70	168/56	Mar	2:08:10	2:07:20- 00
Lee Dae-ro		KOR	12.3.80	169/58	20kW	1:21:52	1:25:54- 00

Name		Nat	Born	Ht/Wt	Event	2003 Mark	Pre-2003 Best
^ Lee Jin-taek		KOR	13.4.72	190/72	HJ	2.23	2.34- 97
Leenaerts	Bert	BEL	1.7.80	194/74	1500	3:35.74	3:39.25- 00
^ Leeper	Nathan	USA	13.6.77	188/82	HJ	2.24i	2.35- 00
Leis	Lauri	EST	7.10.78	184/74	TJ	16.46	16.51, 16.56w -02
Lekote	Otukile	BOT	19.10.78	178/64	800	1:46.88i, 1:47.05	1:44.47- 01
* Lel	Martin	KEN	29.10.78		HMar	60:10	
					Mar	2:10:30	2:10:02- 02
^ Lelei	David	KEN	10.5.71	176/60	800	1:45.89	1:43.97- 00
					1000	2:16.43	2:17.74- 01
					1500	3:36.82	3:31.53- 98
					1M	3:54.26	3:53.14- 99
Lemen	David	USA	13.11.79	190/82	Dec	7809	7972- 02
Lemmi	Andrea	ITA-J	12.5.84	190/70	HJ	2.25	2.14- 02
Lesnichiy	Aleksey	BLR	3.2.78	195/69	HJ	2.30	2.28i- 99, 2.28- 02
Letellier	Loïc	FRA	1.10.76	168/58	5000	13:23.68	13:29.82- 02
Letnicov	Vladimir	MDA	7.10.81	185/73	TJ	16.47i, 16.30	17.06- 02
^ Levicq	Sébastien	FRA	25.6.71	186/81	Dec	7964	8524- 99
Lewis	Brian	USA	5.12.74	170/72	100	10.15, 10.10w	9.99- 02, 9.96w- 00
Lewis	LaChristopher	USA	28.10.82	183/77	400	45.82	46.20- 02
Lewis	Randy	GRN	14.10.80	188/74	TJ	16.80	16.06- 02
* Lewis-Francis	Mark	GBR	4.9.82	183/85	100	10.07	10.04- 02, 9.97w?-01
Li Hongguang		CHN	10.2.80		50kW	3:52:18	4:01:47- 02
Li Jianbo		CHN-Y	14.11.86		50kW	4:03:08	
Li Rongxiang		CHN	8.1.72	180/80	JT	81.76	84.29- 00
Li Xin		CHN-J	21.11.85		TJ	16.48	15.96- 02
Li Yanxi		CHN-J	26.6.84	176/54	TJ	16.46	16.66- 02
Li Yi		CHN	19.1.81		50kW	4:02:21	3:59:00- 01
^ Lichtenegger	Elmar	AUT	25.5.74	186/82	110H	13.36	13.33- 99
* Liefers	Gert-Jan	NED	26.9.78	185/71	800	1:46.72	1:45.47- 98
					1500	3:33.99	3:32.89- 01
					1M	3:51.39	
					3000	7:44.34i	7:42.95- 02
Liepa	Janis	LAT	14.3.81	191/96	JT	77.20	79.78- 01
de Lima	Jessé	BRA	16.2.81	186/85	HJ	2.27	2.27- 02
^ de Lima	Vanderlei	BRA	11.8.69	169/52	Mar	2:10:38	2:08:31- 98
de Lima	Vicente L	BRA	4.6.77	165/63	100	10.23A, 10.17w, 10.0	10.20A, 10.23, 10.08Aw- 02, 10.18A- 00
					200	20.62	20.56- 99
* Limo	Benjamin	KEN	23.8.74	178/65	2000	5:00.82+	4:59.2+- 99
					3000	7:33.13	7:28.67- 99
					5000	12:54.99	12:55.82- 00
* Limo	Felix	KEN	22.8.80	174/58	Mar	2:06:42	-0-
* Limo	Richard	KEN	18.11.80	167/53	5000	13:01.13	12:56.72- 01
					10000	26:56.63	26:50.20- 02
Lincoln	Dan	USA	22.10.80	190/70	10000	28:20.20	29:24.55- 02
					3kSt	8:24.10	8:22.34- 02
Lingua	Marco	ITA	4.6.78	179/98	HT	74.97	76.72- 99
* Lipiec	Tomasz	POL	10.5.71	185/72	20kW	1:24:02	1:20:48- 00
Lischka	Michael	GER	23.12.73	197/135	DT	63.51	65.04- 01
Litchfield	Paul	USA	.81		PV	5.50Ai, 5.46	5.38- 02
Litei	John	KEN	.83		800	1:46.70	
Little	Gregory	JAM	20.2.83	168/56	400H	50.04	50.46- 01
Litvinski	Yuri	BUL	25.11.81		TJ	16.56	16.32- 02
Liu Dashan		CHN	10.5.80		20kW	1:21:54	1:22:36- 01
Liu Feiliang		CHN-J	27.3.85		PV	5.50	4.90- 02
* Liu Xiang		CHN	13.7.83	186/74	110H	13.17	13.12- 02
Liu Yang		CHN-Y	4.1.86		HJ	2.24	2.16- 02
Liu Yanhong		CHN	20.4.83		JT	79.23	72.42- 02
Llanos	Luiggy	PUR	22.8.78	180/80	Dec	7704	7613- 01
Lloyd	Chris	DMA	10.10.80	178/62	400	45.49	46.20- 02
* Lobinger	Tim	GER	3.9.72	193/87	PV	5.91	6.00- 97
* Lobodin	Lev	RUS	1.4.69	188/93	Dec	8198	8571- 98
Loftin	Drew	USA	15.9.80	190/102	DT	60.04	55.92- 02
					HT	71.01	69.86- 02
Loikkanen	Mika	FIN	20.2.74	195/120	DT	61.37i/61.07	62.93- 01
Lomater	Stefano	ITA	23.4.74	190/115	DT	60.75	62.12- 02
Lomba	Jimmy	FRA	30.6.78	182/73	800	1:45.56	1:46.16- 01
Lombard	Cathal	IRL	12.2.76		5000	13:19.22	13:54.58- 01
					10000	28:05.27	0
Loncar	Nenad	SCG	6.3.81	192/79	110H	13.60	13.90- 01
* Longo	Andrea	ITA	26.6.75	191/82	800	1:44.96	1:43.74- 00

Name		Nat	Born	Ht/Wt	Event	2003 Mark	Pre-2003 Best
Looije	Laurens	NED	12.1.73	185/75	PV	5.55	5.71- 98
Lopatin	Dmitriy	RUS	80		SP	19.44	19.82 -02
* López	Alejandro	MEX	9.2.75	173/61	20kW	1:19:49	1:17:56- 99
López	Yeimar	CUB	20.8.82	184/73	400	45.11	45.42- 02
Lorenzo	Santiago	ARG	4.4.78	191/88	Dec	7911w, 7564	7889- 01
Loria	Mickaël	FRA	9.6.73	182/74	LJ	7.85,7.96w	8.23A- 98, 8.10i- 01, 7.99- 00
Lörincz	Imre	HUN	12.3.82	183/72	LJ	7.98w	7.84- 01
Loskutov	Pavel	EST	2.12.69	178/63	Mar	2:09:15	2:08:53- 02
Louahla	Malik	ALG	19.12.77	174/72	400	45.81	45.13- 01
Loukhili	Hassan	MAR			HMar	61:32	
Loum	Oumar	SEN	31.12.73	184/79	100	10.34, 10.16w	10.17- 02, 10.06Aw- 00
					200	20.73,20.67w	20.21A,20.19w -00, 20.42 -94
Louw	Stephan	NAM	26.2.75	187/76	LJ	8.16	8.17A- 99, 8.11- 01
Lövgren	Patrik	SWE	12.10.75	185/85	100	10.25w	10.26- 02
Lovkin	Semyon	RUS	14.7.77	180/67	20kW	1:23:23+	1:20:12- 00
					50kW	3:51:36	3:53:45- 01
Loywapet	Samson	KEN	24.12.72		HMar	61:44	61:23 -01
Lu Ronghua		CHN	21.2.83	174/60	20kW	1:20:54	1:22:23- 02
Luaces	Isbel	CUB	20.7.75	187/97	JT	81.66	83.63- 02
Luis	Yacnier	CUB	24.1.82	179/75	400H	49.71, 49.4	49.22- 02
* Lukashevich	Aleksey	UKR	11.1.77	175/70	LJ	8.19	8.27- 00
Lunn	Jason	USA	19.9.74	187/71	1500	3:36.99	3:36.5- 01
					1M	3:54.43	3:57.45i, 3:57.96- 02
Lusis	Voldemars	LAT	7.12.74	187/102	JT	84.19	83.08- 00
^ Lyakhov	Sergey	RUS	1.3.68	195/107	DT	59.95	66.78- 95
Lystsov	Sergey	RUS	14.11.82	177/60	20kW	1:22:20	1:23:43- 02
Lyzhin	Pavel	BLR	24.3.81	189/110	SP	20.86	20.15- 02
Ma Liang		CHN	22.7.83		HT	71.01	64.78- 02
Maaroufit	Mourad	MAR	.82		3000	7:45.94	
* Maase	Kamiel	NED	20.10.71	191/71	5000	13:29.46	13:13.06- 02
					10000	27:45.46	27:26.29- 02
					Mar	2:08:31	2:10:08- 99
Maataoui	Ali Nabil	MAR	11.12.80		1500	3:36.96	3:35.72- 02
Maazouz	Hakim	ALG	28.8.75		3kSt	8:24.60	8:22.9- 02
* Maazouzi	Driss	FRA	15.10.69	180/65	1500	3:36.93i	3:31.45- 02
Maboa	Bonolo	RSA-J	24.8.85	175/56	800	1:46.25A	1:48.21- 02
* Mack	Tim	USA	15.9.72	188/78	PV	5.76	5.85i, 5.84- 02
Mackie	Ian	GBR	27.2.75	188/82	400	45.58	0
Macrozonaris	Nicolas	CAN	22.8.80	181/78	100	10.03A, 10.13	10.19, 10.18Aw- 00
Maeda	Kazuhiro	JPN	19.4.81	166/54	10000	28:10.66	28:16.17- 01
Maeda	Kazuyuki	JPN	10.2.80	166/51	HMar	61:49	64:30- 01
* Magdziarczyk	Roman	POL	5.7.77	180/70	50kW	3:44:53	3:48:17- 00
* Magnússon	Jón Arnar	ISL	28.7.69	183/87	Dec	8222	8583w, 8573- 98
Magrans	Marc	ESP	26.9.76	185/80	Dec	7616	7783- 00
Mai	Michael	USA	27.9.77		HT	71.33	65.88- 02
Maillard	Sébastien	FRA	2.5.81	184/81	400H	49.10	50.22- 02
Maina	Julius	KEN	14.10.77	179/65	5000	13:24.51	13:22.39- 02
					10000	27:42.81	27:41.96- 02
* Maina Munyi	Simon	KEN	18.3.78	177/58	5000	13:24.68	13:10.71- 98
					10000	27:22.29	27:18.74- 99
* Maiyo	Benjamin	KEN	6.10.78	175/58	5000	13:14.75	13:02.28- 00
Majewski	Tomasz	POL	30.8.81	200/100	200	20.09	19.33- 02
Makarov	Andrey	BLR	2.1.71	181/72	20kW	1:22:09	1:18:23- 00
* Makarov	Sergey	RUS	19.3.73	192/100	Dec	90.11	92.61- 02
Makori	David	KEN	6.11.73	178/63	HMar	62:08	61:39- 01
Makrinikólas	Anastásios	GRE	21.7.77	186/76	LJ	8.01	8.05- 02
Malashevich	Aleksandr	BLR	7.4.77	200/115	DT	61.97	63.78- 99
* Malcolm	Christian	GBR	3.6.79	174/67	100	10.22	10.11, 10.09w?- 01
					200	20.25	20.08- 01
Malina	Libor	CZE	14.6.73	193/115	DT	64.23	67.13- 01
Malone	Casey	USA	6.4.77	203/106	DT	64.43A	66.58A- 02
Malyavin	Vladimir	RUS	4.3.73	188/75	LJ	8.03i, 7.85	8.25- 00
Malysa	Jirí	CZE	14.8.66	180/71	20kW	1:23:46	1:19:18- 00
Mambo	Djeke	BEL	4.3.77	182/76	TJ	16.46	16.62i- 00, 16.56- 01
Manabe	Shuhei	JPN	31.8.82	187/74	HJ	2.25	2.23- 02
^ Manson	Pat	USA	29.11.67	178/75	PV	5.50i	5.85- 94
Manyim	Philip	KEN	24.3.78	175/64	HMar	61:15	62:01- 00
					3kSt	8:23.85	8:20.03- 02
Marceny	Lionel	FRA	17.7.74	184/70	Dec	7788	8094- 00
Marciniszyn	Grzegorz	POL	22.5.77	187/82	LJ	7.97	8.28- 01
Marcoullides	Anninos	CYP	8.2.71	185/79	200	20.59	20.43- 98

	Name		Nat	Born	Ht/Wt	Event	2003 Mark	Pre-2003 Best
*	Markov	Dmitri	AUS	14.3.75	182/85	PV	5.86	6.05- 01
*	Markov	Ilya	RUS	19.6.72	174/65	20kW	1:20:05	1:18:30- 97
*	Márquez	David	ESP	13.10.77	170/51	20kW	1:19:46	1:21:09- 01
	Martin	Blair	NZL	25.4.75	174/60	10000	28:08.19	28:27.23- 01
*	Martín	Eliseo	ESP	5.11.73	173/62	3kSt	8:09.09	8:13.59- 99
*	Martín	Luis Miguel	ESP	11.1.72	180/69	3kSt	8:13.52	8:07.44- 02
	Martin	Rodney	USA	22.12.82	182/75	200	20.57w	21.13, 20.81w- 02
	Martin	Scott	AUS	12.10.82	190/115	DT	62.19	58.22- 02
	Martín	Sergio	ESP	25.3.78	175/60	3kSt	8:31.57	8:36.68- 02
	Martineau	Eugene	NED	14.5.80	176/75	Dec	7633	7681- 02
*	Martínez	Alexander	CUB	23.8.77	184/82	TJ	17.06	17.32- 02
	Martínez	Antonio	ESP	20.12.78	186/70	1500	3:39.61, 3:38.87i	
						3kSt	8:19.35	8:36.23- 02
	Martínez	Joan Lino	CUB	17.1.78	176/69	LJ	8.20, 8.32w	8.24- 02, 8.39irr- 99
*	Martínez	José Manuel	ESP	22.10.71	176/65	5000	13:24.88	13:13.57- 02
						10000	27:30.56	27:41.76- 02
						Mar	2:08:09	2:09:55- 02
	Martínez	Lois Maikel	CUB	3.6.81	185/90	DT	64.62	64.48- 02
*	Martínez	Manuel	ESP	7.12.74	185/140	SP	21.24i, 21.08	21.47- 02
	Martins	Pedro	POR	12.1.68	163/60	50kW	3:57:42	3:55:54- 01
	Martirosyan	Armen	ARM	6.8.69	187/74	LJ	7.98A	8.20A- 94
	Maru	Elijah	KEN	12.6.76	176/62	3000	7:42.82	8:02.37- 02
	Maru Girma	Daba	ETH	12.12.80	184/61	3kSt	8:25.04	8:26.52- 99
	Mascarenhas	Jarbas	BRA	25.8.80		100	10.21	10.43- 00
^	Mashchenko	Ruslan	RUS	11.11.71	193/83	400H	49.43	48.06- 98
	Maska	Vladimír	CZE	6.2.73	193/120	HT	78.34	81.28- 99
*	Mason	Germaine	JAM	20.1.83	195/80	HJ	2.34	2.27- 02
	Máté	Gábor	HUN	9.2.79	199/104	DT	65.05, 66.99dh	66.54, 66.91dh- 00
	Mateusiak	Tomasz	POL	5.12.80	170/62	LJ	8.08, 8.15w	7.92- 99
	Mathis	Jerome	USA	26.7.83		200	20.48	21.24- 01
	Matiyenko	Artyom	UKR	30.8.82	182/73	PV	5.50i	5.20- 01
	Matsuda	Kazuhiro	JPN	24.6.74	177/62	Mar	2:09:49	2:10:24- 00
	Matsuda	Ryo	JPN	26.12.79	177/70	200	20.62	20.75- 99, 20.64w- 01
	Matsumiya	Takayuki	JPN	21.2.80	163/49	10000	27:50.97	28:02.80- 00
						HMar	61:34	61:53- 00
	Matsuzaki	Akinori	JPN	30.12.81	178/65	20kW	1:20:46	1:22:21- 02
	Matthews Jouda	Todd	USA/SUD	28.6.79	193/86	110H	13.51	13.36- 02
	Matveyev	Roman	RUS	7.11.82	180/70	400H	49.66	51.77- 02
*	Matyukhin	Nikolay	RUS	13.12.68	179/68	50kW	3:47:36	3:40:13- 99
^	Maybank	Anthuan	USA	30.12.69	188/81	400	45.62	44.15- 96
	Mayer	Gerhard	AUT	1.1.80	191/93	DT	61.81	59.60- 01
	Mayo	Tom	GBR	2.5.77	194/76	1500	3:38.18	3:38.3, 3:38.34- 01
						1M	3:55.37	3:55.57- 01
^	Mayock	John	GBR	26.10.70	177/66	1500	3:37.59	3:31.86- 97
						1M	3:54.93	3:50.32- 96
						3000	7:47.47,7:45.32i	7:41.09i- 02, 7:47.28- 95
^	Mayola	Freddy	CUB	1.11.77	176/74	100	10.15	10.10- 99,10.00rw- 00,10.08w- 01
	Mazurik	Maksim	UKR	2.4.83	184/70	PV	5.50i, 5.45	5.55- 02
	Mazza	Marco	ITA	25.6.77	179/62	5000	13:29.15	13:34.12- 01
						10000	28:15.66	27:44.05- 02
	Mbote	Jason	KEN	.79		HMar	61:49	63:15- 02
	McCarthy	Kris	AUS	15.10.79	189/80	800	1:45.86	1:45.57- 00
	McDonagh	Ciaran	IRL	20.5.76		LJ	7.95	8.00- 00, 8.04w- 99
	McDonald	Michael	JAM	17.3.75	183/85	400	45.46	44.64A- 96, 44.65- 97
	McEwen	John	USA	5.3.74	190/114	HT	74.73	74.18- 02
	McEwen	Matt	AUS	16.10.71	194/88	Dec	7724	7825- 01
*	McFarlane	Danny	JAM	14.2.72	185/81	400	45.72	44.90- 95
						400H	48.30	
^	McGhee	Roland	USA	15.10.71	180/70	LJ	7.97	8.51- 95
	McGowan	Guy	USA			100	10.0	
	McGrath	Paddy	USA	1.7.71	183/120	HT	73.40	77.49- 99
	McIlroy	James	GBR	30.12.76	180/68	800	1:45.30	1:45.32- 98
^	McIntosh	Troy	BAH	29.3.73	178/75	200	20.62	20.62- 99
	McMahon	Kevin	USA	26.5.72	183/102	HT	74.07	79.26- 99
	McMullen	Phil	USA	3.2.75	188/84	Dec	7581	8220- 01
	McReynolds	Jacob	AUS	8.12.78	184/79	TJ	16.47, 16.89w	16.46, 16.74w- 02
	Medina	Yoger	VEN	5.9.73	185/108	SP	19.29	20.01- 00
	Meftah	Abdellatif	MAR			HMar	61:32	
*	Mekonnen	Hailu	ETH	4.4.80	172/61	3000	7:44.27i	7:30.53- 01
						5000	13:10.16	12:58.57- 01
	Melentyev	Sergey	RUS	5.12.76	178/68	20kW	1:22:07.5t	1:22:30- 00

Name		Nat	Born	Ht/Wt	Event	2003 Mark	Pre-2003 Best
Meleshenko	Yevgeniy	KAZ	19.1.81	185/70	400H	48.84	48.46- 01
Melétoglu	Hrístos	GRE	2.1.72	190/80	TJ	16.92	17.19- 01
Melich	Lukás	CZE	16.9.80	186/105	HT	76.38	71.47- 01
* Méliz	Luis Felipe	CUB	11.8.79	177/76	LJ	8.20	8.43- 00
Meng Yan		CHN	30.9.80		400H	50.20	50.25- 01
Meriluoto	Johan	FIN	22.3.74	187/76	TJ	16.71, 16.72w	16.95- 00, 17.04w- 01
^ Mersal	Hatem	EGY	20.1.75	186/79	LJ	7.95	8.31- 99
Mertens	Michael	GER	27.12.65	191/105	SP	19.40	20.24- 98
* Mesnil	Romain	FRA	13.7.77	188/79	PV	5.95	5.93- 99
* Mezgebu	Assefa	ETH	19.6.78	175/55	5000	13:14.60	12:53.84- 98
Michniewski	Robert	POL	16.2.74	188/76	TJ	16.54	16.02- 02
Mikhaylenko	Vladimir	UKR	27.8.73	196/84	Dec	7593	8052- 00
Mikhaylichenko	Yevgeniy	RUS	13.2.79	185/77	PV	5.55	5.70- 02
Mikheyko	Yevgeniy	BLR	24.4.81		400H	50.20	50.53- 02
* Mikhnevich	Andrey	BLR	12.7.76	202/115	SP	21.69	20.92- 01
Mikkola	Esko	FIN	14.2.75	185/94	JT	82.02	82.48- 01
* Milazar	Éric	MRI	1.6.75	192/80	400	44.75	44.69- 01
* Miles	Derek	USA	28.9.72	188/84	PV	5.81	5.82- 01
* Miller	Coby	USA	19.10.76	168/68	100	10.07A, 10.10	9.98, 9.88w- 00
					200	20.04	19.96- 00
Milner	Quinton	USA	20.12.74	180/75	400H	50.11	49.49- 97
Minnitti	Rob	USA	6.9.79		JT	77.34	73.47- 02
Miranda	Montxu	ESP	27.12.76	191/83	PV	5.50	5.81- 00
Mishchuk	Viktor	UKR	12.5.80	186/88	JT	76.21	73.18- 02
Mishiro	Naoki	JPN	16.3.77	166/52	Mar	2:10:33	2:19:59- 98
* Misoi	Kipkirui	KEN	23.12.78	177/59	3kSt	8:07.74	8:01.69- 01
Mistretta	Alessandro	ITA	6.3.71	172/58	50kW	4:04:18	3:51:33- 99
^ Misyulya	Yevgeniy	BLR	13.3.64	178/68	20kW	1:20:38	1:18:18- 96
Mitchum	Eric	USA-J	2.8.84	188/80	110H	13.75, 13.73w	
Mitei	Enock	KEN	26.11.80	172/52	5000	13:20.91	13:19.55- 00
					10000	28:17.3A	27:32.97- 00
Mitrofanov	Dmitriy	RUS	7.9.75		LJ	8.16	8.13- 02
Miyazaki	Hisashi	JPN	19.3.81	181/74	200	20.53	20.65- 02
Modelski	Michal	POL	16.4.75	186/84	Dec	7835	7729- 02
Modibo	Ato	TRI	19.6.79	188/75	400	45.61	44.87- 01
Moede	Thomas	GER	26.7.77	184/77	TJ	16.44i	16.90- 01
Moffitt	John	USA	12.12.80	185/75	LJ	8.08i, 8.02	7.83, 7.95w- 02
					TJ	16.53, 16.62w	16.22- 02, 16.42w- 01
Mohamed	Mustafa	SWE	1.3.79	172/54	3kSt	8:23.35	8:32.07- 02
Mohamed	Walid Abderrazak		EGY	4.4.73		JT	77.30
78.90- 02							
Mohamed (Khouya)	Rachid	BRN	9.11.79	186/74	800	1:46.91	1:45.38- 99
Moiben	James	KEN	20.4.77	170/58	HMar	61:19	62:03- 97
Molefe	Calfornia	BOT	2.5.80	172/62	400	45.43	45.91, 45.5- 02
* Molina	Juan Manuel	ESP	15.3.79	170/52	20kW	1:21:57	1:20:18- 02
* Möllenbeck	Michael	GER	12.12.69	200/120	DT	67.42	67.64- 02
Molokov	Maksim	RUS	.77		TJ	16.85i, 16.36	16.73- 02
* Moncur	Avard	BAH	2.11.78	196/82	400	45.00A, 45.02	44.45- 01
Mononen	Matti	FIN	25.11.83	175/75	PV	5.65	5.60- 02
Monteiro	Edivaldo	POR	28.4.76		400H	49.36	49.64- 01
* Montgomery	Tim	USA	28.1.75	178/72	100	10.04	9.78- 02
Moody	Ricardo	USA	24.9.80		110H	13.60	13.80- 00, 13.76w- 99
Moore	Anwar	USA	5.3.79		110H	13.44	13.66- 02
Moore	Carlos	USA-J	8.5.84		200	20.63w	21.12- 02
Moore	Jonathan	GBR-J	31.5.84	180/74	LJ	7.92w	8.03- 02
Moore	Stephen	USA	13.8.75	180/75	Dec	8010	8037- 99
Morant	Sheldon	JAM	21.6.80	182/80	100	10.21	10.51- 02
Morara Nchoga	George	KEN	.79		HMar	62:05	62:36- 02
Mordhorst	Rolf	GER	11.5.73	201/110	DT	61.46	59.66- 01
Moreno	Jorge Josué	CUB	25.5.77		400H	49.8	50.03- 02
Moreno	Xavier	ECU	15.11.79	168/60	20kW	1:24:00	1:24:49- 02
Morgan	Nathan	GBR	30.6.78	187/86	LJ	8.26	8.11- 98, 8.17w- 02
* Mori	Fabrizio	ITA	28.6.69	175/68	400H	50.18	47.54- 01
Moroney	Nick	AUS	3.8.72	186/75	HJ	2.25	2.25- 00
* Moroz	Gennadiy	BLR	27.5.78	200/77	HJ	2.30i	2.33- 01
Morrison	Michael	USA-J	4.3.84		HJ	2.24i, 2.22	2.14- 02
Mosca	Vince	USA	23.1.80	189/127	SP	19.33	18.21- 02
Moskalenko	Vitaliy	RUS	30.6.74	184/80	TJ	17.17	17.00i, 16.84- 99
Mosop	Moses	KEN-J	17.7.85	172/57	3000	7:45.70	
					5000	13:11.75	
					10000	27:13.66	28:38.6A- 02

Name		Nat	Born	Ht/Wt	Event	2003 Mark	Pre-2003 Best
Moss	Christopher	GBR	17.6.79		800	1:46.92	1:47.75- 00
Most	Bobby	USA	13.12.82		PV	5.50	5.40- 01
Motone	Alexander	RSA	26.6.78		3kSt	8:29.39	8:37.79- 02
Mottin	Sergio	ITA	15.6.76	186/115	SP	19.91i, 19.09	19.62i, 19.47- 01
* Mottram	Craig	AUS	18.6.80	188/72	3000	7:48.76	7:37.30- 02
					5000	13:17.81	13:12.04- 02
					10000	27:50.55	28:19.26- 01
^ Moudrik	Younes	MAR	1.10.77	176/72	LJ	8.05, 8.15w	8.34- 00
Mourhit	Hassan	BEL	2.1.82		5000	13:21.97	
Moxey	Osbourne	BAH	27.8.78		LJ	8.00, 8.01w	8.19- 02
Mubarak	Bilal Saad	QAT	18.12.72	189/110	SP	19.41	19.65- 97
Mubarak	Mubarak Ata	KSA	17.12.81	175/67	110H	13.71	
* Mucheru	Leonard	KEN	13.6.78	182/66	3000	7:38.36	7:35.35- 01
(Muchir	Salim Jawher	BRN)	now		5000	13:01.76	13:14.94- 01
Muchiri Ndambiri	Josphat	KEN-J	12.2.85		10000	28:02.09	28:45.05- 02
Muindi	Jimmy	KEN	14.8.73	171/62	HMar	61:58	61:33- 96
					Mar	2:08:53	2:08:25- 02
Mukai	Yukihiro	JPN	24.4.80	174/60	400	45.82	46.66- 02
Mulabegovic	Nedzad	CRO	4.2.81	189/100	SP	20.15	19.53i, 19.28- 02
* Mulaudzi	Mbulaeni	RSA	8.9.80	171/62	800	1:42.89	1:43.81- 02
					1000	2:18.45A	2:19.77- 01
Muli	Pius	KEN	15.12.82	169/54	3000	7:40.82	7:40.92- 02
					5000	13:15.09	13:15.16- 02
Müller	Stefan	SUI	20.9.79	190/96	JT	77.95	75.73- 02
Müller	Wolfram	GER	8.7.81	190/65	1500	3:35.50	3:37.61- 01
					3000	7:45.05	7:45.41- 01
Mullings	Steve	JAM	29.11.82	177/72	100	10.28, 10.1, 10.00w	10.47- 01, 10.1- 02
					200	20.52	20.36- 02
Mulugeta	Wondimu	ETH-J			5000	13:26.73	
Mumo	Vincent	KEN	3.8.82	163/59	200	20.65A, 20.5A	
					400	45.32A, 45.63	
					400H	49.99A	50.80A- 02
Munji	Titus	KEN	.79		Mar	2:06:15	0
Munuera	Francisco Javier	ESP	7.7.72	180/64	3kSt	8:22.39	8:22.91- 01
Murakami	Yukifumi	JPN	23.12.79	185/92	JT	78.98	80.59- 01
* Murofushi	Koji	JPN	8.10.74	187/97	HT	84.86	83.47- 01
^ Murphy	Andrew	AUS	18.12.69	185/82	TJ	16.81, 16.82w	17.32- 99
Murphy	Liam	AUS	5.6.79	174/63	50kW	4:04:56	3:54:37- 01
Mutai Kibet	Edward	KEN-J	.84		1500	3:37.58	3:41.6A- 02
Mutsuri	Samuel	KEN-Y	2.5.86		10000	28:03.63	
* Mutua Mwengi	Joseph	KEN	10.12.78	170/58	800	1:43.52	1:43.33- 02
* Muzík	Jirí	CZE	1.9.76	181/75	400H	48.63	48.27- 97
Mwangi	Paul	KEN	19.11.73	179/63	1500	3:36.13	3:34.29- 00
Mwangi Muchunu	Daniel	KEN-J	.84	176/62	10000	28:13.34	
Mwera	Samwel	TAN-J	3.6.85	175/52	800	1:45.94	1:48.96A- 02
					1000	2:17.85	
					1500	3:36.40	3:41.41- 02
					2000	5:00.64	
Mwihia	Francis	KEN	27.2.78	165/53	10000	28:19.16	28:39.66- 01
Myburgh	Alwyn	RSA	13.10.80	188/71	400H	48.61	48.09- 01
* Myerscough	Carl	GBR	21.10.79	209/149	SP	21.92	21.26i, 20.72- 02
					DT	61.85	63.14- 02
Myklebust	Gaute	NOR	29.4.79		DT	61.52	58.56- 02
Myles-Mills	Leonard	GHA	9.5.73	172/68	100	10.03	9.98- 99
Naali	Francis Robert	TAN	1.4.71		HMar	62:00	61:09- 02
Nada Saya	John	TAN	8.8.78		Mar	2:10:13	2:08:57- 01
Nagata	Koichiro	JPN	19.12.78	175/58	10000	28:16.15	27:53.19- 00
^ Nagel	Morné	RSA	23.2.78	183/77	100	10.13	10.13A, 10.17, 10.16w- 02
					200	20.37A, 20.88	20.11A, 20.34- 02
Naito	Masato	JPN	31.7.80	185/75	110H	13.47	13.50- 01
Nakamura	Yuki	JPN	21.6.81	170/52	10000	28:18.43	28:33.55- 01
Närhi	Matti	FIN	17.8.75	188/100	JT	77.30	88.24- 97
Nativel	Stéphane	FRA	4.4.75	195/95	DT	60.02	59.41- 01
Nau	Manuel	GER	2.7.77	190/90	JT	79.28	83.04- 00
Nazarov	Dilshod	TJK	6.5.82	187/100	HT	75.56	68.08- 01, 69.86uc- 02
Nazarovas	Arvidas	LTU	17.4.81	192/83	LJ	7.93	7.21- 01
Ndiso	Dennis Musembi	KEN	.83		HMar	61:24	62:27- 02
Ndungu	James	KEN	30.4.79	173/56	10000	28:21.51	28:02.06- 00
Ndungu	Stephen	KEN	1.6.67		Mar	2:09:54	2:10:24- 02
^ Nduwimana	Jean-Patrick	BDI	9.5.78	178/61	800	1:45.51	1:42.81- 01
					1000	2:18.10	2:16.98- 00

Name		Nat	Born	Ht/Wt	Event	2003 Mark	Pre-2003 Best
Negussie	Hailu	ETH	16.4.78		Mar	2:08:21	2:08:16- 02
Nejedly	Michael	CZE	1.10.69	188/72	3kSt	8:32.05	8:27.60- 00
* Nelson	Adam	USA	7.7.75	181/115	SP	21.29	22.51- 02
Nelson	Corey	USA	9.10.77	183/77	400	45.00A, 45.55	45.36- 99
* Németh	Zsolt	HUN	9.11.71	190/110	HT	78.06	81.56- 99
Neville	David	USA-J	1.6.84		200	20.63	21.21, 21.10w- 02
Newton	Robert	GBR	10.5.81	190/77	110H	13.36	13.92- 02
Ngatho	Zakayo	KEN	18.3.78	165/54	HMar	60:21	
Ngeny	Joseph	KEN			HMar	61:35	
* Ngeny	Noah	KEN	2.11.78	182/68	1500	3:33.96	3:28.12- 00
					3000	7:46.21i	7:35.46- 00
Ngolepus	Joseph	KEN	.75		HMar	60:56	62:33- 02
					Mar	2:07:57	2:08:47- 01
Niaré	Yves	FRA	20.7.77	195/106	SP	19.31i, 19.29	19.76- 01
Nichols	Regan	USA	26.7.73	183/79	400H	49.70	48.66- 98
* Nicolay	Christian	GER	4.3.76	188/90	JT	84.54	81.90- 02
Nieland	Nick	GBR	31.1.72	190/100	JT	82.97	85.09- 00
Niemi	Matti	FIN	15.11.76	196/90	110H	13.57	13.66- 99, 13.59w- 02
Niemi	Shane	CAN	2.6.78	186/80	400	45.22	44.86- 01
* Nieto	James	USA	2.11.76	193/79	HJ	2.31	2.30- 99
Nikitin	Sergey	RUS	13.5.73		Dec	7916	8012h- 98, 7862- 99
Niklaus	André	GER	30.8.81	190/78	Dec	8020	8042- 01
Nilsen	Ronny	NOR	7.5.71		JT	79.33	78.00- 97
Nilsson	Mats	SWE	16.7.75	178/85	JT	76.65	77.14- 97
* Nizhegorodov	Denis	RUS	26.7.80	180/61	20kW	1:23:23+	1:18:20- 01
					50kW	3:38:23	
* Njenga	Daniel	KEN	7.5.76	175/60	Mar	2:07:41	2:06:16- 02
Njubi	Eliud	KEN	27.7.79		800	1:46.79	1:47.17- 01
Nkansah	Eric	GHA	12.12.74	178/80	100	10.12	10.00- 99
Nkunzimana	Onésphore	BDI-J	23.7.85	175/61	3000	7:48.50	7:53.3- 02
Noda	Michitane	JPN	25.3.75	174/54	Mar	2:09:58	0
Noguchi	Kenji	JPN	23.2.75	160/50	10000	28:13.63	28:43.40- 01
Nolan	James	IRL	27.1.77	183/71	1500	3:35.69	3:36.30- 00
					1M	3:54.62	3:56.31- 99
* Nool	Erki	EST	25.6.70	184/84	Dec	8281	8815- 01
Norberg	Justin	USA	18.7.77	190/82	PV	5.50	5.30- 00
Norbutas	Mindaugas	LTU	24.8.76		800	1:46.64	1:47.82- 02
Norman	Cedric	USA	5.10.81	191/	HJ	2.27	2.14- 02
Nossmy	Philip	SWE	6.12.82	189/84	110H	13.50	13.61- 02
Nowak	Marcin	POL	2.8.77	174/71	100	10.25w	10.21- 00
Nowill	Peter	AUS	15.6.79	179/68	3kSt	8:26.13	8:33.48- 01
N'senga	Jonathan	BEL	21.4.73	188/82	110H	13.60, 13.58w	13.25- 98
Nthambe	Maswi	KEN	.71		800	1:46.64A	1:47.0A- 00
Nthépé	Aimé-Issa	FRA	26.6.73	180/70	100	10.21, 10.09w	10.11- 02
					200	20.65	20.58- 02
Núñez	Manuel	ESP	16.6.74	176/58	3kSt	8:30.67	8:36.55- 02
Nyabuti	Elijah	KEN	10.10.79	174/54	HMar	61:19	61:20- 02
Nyaga	David	KEN	8.11.79		1500	3:37.19	3:35.47- 02
* Nyamu	Julius	KEN	1.12.77	178/66	3kSt	8:09.06	8:07.59- 01
* Nymark	Trond	NOR	28.12.76	180/62	20kW	1:23:31	1:22:56- 02
					50kW	3:46:14	3:49:27- 02
* Obikwelu	Francis	POR	22.11.78	195/79	100	10.11	9.97- 00
					200	20.41	19.84- 99
O'Brien	Nic	NZL	3.1.80	191/85	400H	49.90	50.16- 02
Obrist	Christian	ITA	20.11.80	183/66	800	1:46.35	1:47.12- 02
					1500	3:36.36	3:35.74- 02
Oda	Yoshinori	JPN	5.12.80	164/49	10000	28:15.82	28:23.98- 02
* Odriozola	Mikel	ESP	25.5.73	180/62	50kW	3:42:03	3:45:22- 01
Ogata	Tsuyoshi	JPN	11.5.73	165/50	10000	28:21.16	28:13.26- 02
					Mar	2:08:37	2:09:15- 02
Ojima	Tadayuki	JPN	22.11.76	174/59	Mar	2:08:48	2:09:10- 98
Okari	Gilbert	KEN	2.7.78		10000	27:40.9	28:06.62A- 02
Oke	Tosin	GBR	1.10.80	178/77	TJ	16.61i, 16.59	16.65- 02
Okorie	Victor	NGR	10.8.81	183/79	400H	49.19	51.20, 50.7 99
Okuda	Shin-ichiro	JPN	4.1.80	178/57	HMar	62:02	62:43- 01
Okutani	Wataru	JPN	9.1.75	181/61	10000	28:19.57	28:33.5- 95
Oleksy	Tommy	USA	26.3.81	190/79	LJ	7.92w	7.89i, 7.89- 01
Olgundeniz	Ercüment	TUR	7.7.76		DT	63.20	62.90- 00
* Olijar	Stanislav	LAT	22.3.79	190/80	110H	13.08	13.15A, 13.22- 02
Oliver	David	USA	24.4.82		110H	13.60	13.92, 13.88w- 02
Olmedo	Manuel	ESP	17.5.83	173/53	800	1:45.57	1:47.27i, 1:47.64- 02

Name		Nat	Born	Ht/Wt	Event	2003 Mark	Pre-2003 Best
* Olsen	Joachim	DEN	31.5.77	184/120	SP	20.85	21.57- 02
Olsen	Tom Erik	NOR	20.10.74	198/80	PV	5.51i	5.60- 02
* Olsson	Christian	SWE	25.1.80	192/74	HJ	2.28	2.28i, 2.24- 02
					TJ	17.77, 17.92w	17.80i, 17.64- 02
Omae	Yusuke	JPN	6.4.82	176/68	200	20.60	20.29- 01
Omey	Tom	BEL	24.4.75	186/70	800	1:45.75	1:45.93- 01
O'Neil	Jon	USA	23.3.79	207/143	SP	19.52	19.32- 01
					DT	60.55dh	60.23, 61.48dh- 02
Onnen	Eike	GER	3.8.82	194/83	HJ	2.23	2.15- 02
Onsare	Wilson	KEN	15.6.76		HMar	60:52	61:33- 02
					Mar	2:06:47	0
Oprea	Ionel	ROM	12.10.70	191/120	DT	62.67	63.82- 02
* Oprea	Marian	ROM	6.6.82	190/80	TJ	17.63	17.29i, 17.39w- 02; 17.11- 01
Osakada	Jun	JPN	2.4.74	176/67	400	45.28	45.05- 00
Osei-Tutu	Marvin	GER	22.4.81	184/77	PV	5.51	5.50- 02
Oshima	Kenta	JPN	29.6.79	175/60	10000	27:54.88	28:38.41- 02
					HMar	61:48	62:27- 00
^ Osoro	Ondoro	KEN	3.12.67	167/63	Mar	2:09:38	2:06:54- 98
Osovnikar	Matic	SLO	19.1.80	177/75	100	10.22	10.34- 00, 10.21w- 01
de la Ossa	Juan Carlos	ESP	25.11.76	168/50	3000	7:43.57	8:11.92- 02
					5000	13:20.46	13:47.17- 02
					10000	28:07.19	29:06.77- 02
Ostwald	Ronny	GER	7.4.74	180/83	100	10.24	10.30- 00
Otto	Björn	GER	16.10.77	191/86	PV	5.72ix/5.70	5.65, 5.71ex- 00
Owusu	Andrew	GHA	8.7.72	180/75	TJ	16.88	17.23- 98
Pacheco	Yoelmis	CUB	9.6.82	180/74	LJ	8.02	8.18- 02
^ Pakarinen	Ari	FIN	14.5.69	184/103	JT	76.80	85.18- 95
Pal Singh	Amrit	IND	6.10.83	183/79	LJ	7.98	7.73- 02
Palacios	Noraldo	COL	8.7.80		JT	76.81	75.11- 02
Páli	Kristóf	HUN	29.12.80		HT	71.84	68.06- 02
Paljakka	Jarkko	FIN	7.2.79	186/108	HT	74.29	70.88- 02
Palyszko	Maciej	POL	4.1.78	186/112	HT	80.89	80.25- 00
Panfilov	Grigoriy	RUS	17.5.80		SP	19.88	18.16- 02
Pankúch	Pavel	SVK	20.2.75	194/130	SP	19.81i, 19.19	19.78- 99
Paoluzzi	Loris	ITA	14.5.74	191/128	HT	73.76	80.98- 99
* Papadimitríou	Aléxandros	GRE	18.6.73	183/123	HT	79.52	80.45- 00
Papadópoulos	Konstadínos	GRE	7.6.74		LJ	8.00	7.87- 02
Pappas	Billy	USA	22.2.79	183/82	Dec	7745	7532- 02
* Pappas	Tom	USA	6.9.76	193/93	LJ	7.96	7.62- 02
					Dec	8784	8583- 02
Park Chil-sung		KOR	8.7.82	173/61	20kW	1:22:38	1:35:53- 02
Park Jae-myong		KOR	15.12.81	181/88	JT	81.46	80.96- 02
Park Tae-kyong		KOR	30.7.80	181/75	110H	13.71	13.89- 02
Parker	Earvin	USA-J	6.4.84		200	20.70, 20.53w	
Parker	James	USA	3.12.75	180/107	HT	75.32	73.32- 01
Parker	Samie	USA	24.5.81	178/73	100	10.18	10.60- 01, 10.41w- 02
Parkhomenko	Aleksandr	BLR	22.3.81	182/82	Dec	7954	7676- 02
Parkhomenko	Yuriy	UKR	7.7.73	195/140	SP	20.56	19.76- 02
Parra	Roberto	ESP	6.4.76	185/66	1500	3:34.66i, 3:35.02	3:40.62- 00
Parravicini	Tim	AUS	25.4.81	189/83	LJ	7.94, 8.02w	7.94- 01, 8.00w- 02
Parrela	Sanderlei	BRA	7.10.74	194/77	400	45.81	44.29- 99
Pars	Krisztián	HUN	18.2.82	183/98	HT	78.81	74.18- 02
* Parviainen	Aki	FIN	26.10.74	192/100	JT	83.30	93.09- 99
* Pate	Miguel	USA	13.6.79	188/84	LJ	8.46A, 8.27	8.59i, 8.45- 02
Patselya	Aleksandr	UKR	3.7.83	183/83	LJ	8.13	7.73- 02
Patterson	Henry	USA	27.5.75	196/86	HJ	2.24	2.32- 99
* Patton	Darvis	USA	4.12.79	183/75	100	10.00, 9.97w	10.14- 02, 10.09w- 00
					200	20.03	20.12, 20.06w- 02
Pauer	Géza	HUN	7.1.76	179/62	200	20.69	20.93- 00, 20.91w 02
Paukner	Stefan	GER	16.8.76	188/90	HT	73.33	72.34- 02
Pauli	Jacob	USA	15.6.79	191/86	PV	5.50i	5.68i- 01, 5.65- 00
Paumier	Alexis	CUB	21.1.75	191/100	SP	19.87i, 19.70	20.78- 00
Pausé	Dominique	FRA	11.1.76	176/72	JT	78.60	79.66- 02
* Pavlov	Igor	RUS	18.7.79	187/78	PV	5.65, 5.75ex	5.70sq, 5.55- 00, 5.60i- 01
Payne	David	USA	24.7.82		110H	13.53	13.92- 02
Peçanha	Fabiano	BRA	5.6.82	186/73	800	1:46.20	1:48.68- 02
* Pedroso	Iván	CUB	17.12.72	176/70	LJ	8.31	8.71, 8.96Adw- 95, 8.79w-92
Peetre	Taavi	EST	4.7.83	192/110	SP	19.02	18.21i, 17.71- 02
Peguero	Arismendi	DOM	7.8.80		400	45.2	47.75- 02
Pei Chuang		CHN	5.12.81	176/62	20kW	1:20:09	1:20:58- 01
					50kW	3:59:52	3:56:20- 00

Name		Nat	Born	Ht/Wt	Event	2003 Mark	Pre-2003 Best
Pell	Rickard	SWE	24.3.79	180/67	800	1:46.50	1:47.27- 02
* Peña	Antonio	ESP	26.8.70	175/60	Mar	2:07:59	2:07:34- 01
Penas	Manuel Ángel	ESP	9.11.77	172/54	3000	7:45.35	8:03.63- 02
					5000	13:28.24	13:50.97- 01
Pencréach	Gaël	FRA	5.8.77	180/68	3kSt	8:19.92	8:13.16- 99
Pennings	Wilbert	NED	23.2.75	194/81	HJ	2.27	2.31i- 02, 2.30- 99,
Peremota	Igor	RUS	14.1.81	191/78	110H	13.70	13.97- 02
Pérez	César	ESP	7.4.75	172/63	3kSt	8:19.82	8:24.53- 02
* Pérez	Jefferson	ECU	1.7.74	174/59	20kW	1:17:21	1:18:24- 97
					50kW	3:56:04	0
Pérez	Lisvany A.	CUB	24.1.82	198/76	HJ	2.24	2.24- 02
Pérez	Santiago	ESP	15.1.72	179/70	50kW	3:52:57	3:45:55- 98
* Peric	Dragan	SCG	8.5.64	186/107	SP	20.48	21.77- 98
					DT	60.39dh	61.94- 91
Perrone	Lorenzo	ITA	26.9.81	183/59	1500	3:38.96	3:38.52- 01
* Pestano	Mario	ESP	8.4.78	193/105	DT	64.99	67.92- 01
Peterson	Derrick	USA	28.11.77	182/73	800	1:45.69	1:45.18- 00
Petrenko	Aleksandr	RUS	8.2.83	183/75	TJ	16.46i, 16.38	16.26- 02
Petrucci	Nick	USA	10.11.75	197/129	DT	66.35	65.17, 65.92dh- 02
Peuf	Pierre-Charles	FRA	27.4.79	187/82	PV	5.70	5.57- 02
* Phillips	Chris	USA	24.7.72	183/77	110H	13.26	13.27- 00
* Phillips	Dwight	USA	1.10.77	181/82	100	10.24	10.16- 02, 10.11w- 00
					LJ	8.44	8.38- 02
Pienaar	Hardus	RSA	10.8.81	190/88	JT	84.50	81.40- 02
Piétris	Dimítrios	GRE	24.10.79	184/79	110H	13.68, 13.58w	13.63- 02
Pignata	Francesco	ITA	14.2.78	190/81	JT	78.40	78.69- 02
Pinardo	Francisco	ESP	15.3.75	179/64	50kW	3:54:01	3:52:51- 02
Pincemail	Sébastien	FRA	21.2.79	186/84	TJ	16.95	16.73i- 02, 16.69- 00, 16.83w- 01
Pinnock	Chris	JAM	26.3.79	183/82	110H	13.38	13.54- 02
Pires	João	POR	10.6.79	175/70	800	1:46.37	1:45.59- 00
* Piskunov	Vladislav	UKR	7.6.78	183/108	HT	78.57	82.23- 02
Pitkämaki	Tero	FIN	19.12.82	193/86	JT	80.45	77.24- 02
Pizzolato	Fabio	ITA	16.3.75	177/75	PV	5.50	5.75- 97
Pizzoli	Emiliano	ITA	29.6.74	192/80	110H	13.65	13.54- 00, 13.5- 99, 13.43r- 98
Plautz	Marcel	GER	1.7.80	192/86	JT	77.42	78.02- 02
* Plawgo	Marek	POL	25.2.81	181/72	400H	48.45	48.16- 01
Plotnir	Yevgeniy	RUS	26.6.77	196/85	TJ	16.82	16.54- 00
Pognon	Ronald	FRA	16.11.82	185/75	100	10.13, 10.12w	10.24- 02
					200	20.54	20.77- 02, 20.4w- 01
* Pogorelov	Aleksandr	RUS	10.1.80	201/94	Dec	8072	8163- 02
Poplawski	Radoslaw	POL	16.1.83	176/61	3kSt	8:21.92	8:33.46- 02
Porras	Juan Antonio	ESP	19.2.72	174/65	50kW	4:00:52	3:59:10- 01
Potapovich	Pavel	RUS	26.11.80	185/74	3kSt	8:15.54	8:34.04- 02
* Potemin	Vladimir	RUS	15.1.80	177/69	20kW	1:23:37+	1:29:03- 01
					50kW	3:45:27	3:39:21- 00
* Potter	Mitch	USA	16.9.80	188/78	400	44.58	45.40- 01
* Powell	Asafa	JAM	11.11.82	188/87	100	10.02, 9.9	10.12- 02
Power	Michael	AUS	9.5.76	183/70	3000	7:46.95	7:46.22- 00
Pozatsidi	Konstantin	RUS	23.1.83		TJ	16.55i	16.48, 16.69w- 01
Pratt	Róbison	MEX	25.2.80	197/80	PV	5.56	5.60A- 00
Pretorius	Johan	RSA	23.9.82		1500	3:39.17	3:41.13- 02
Prezelj	Rozle	SLO	26.9.79	193/73	HJ	2.27	2.25- 02
Proctor	Mark	GBR	15.1.63	193/131	SP	19.75	20.85i- 98, 20.40- 99
Pröll	Martin	AUT	21.3.81	177/60	3kSt	8:19.31	8:24.59- 02
* Ptácek	Adam	CZE	8.10.80	178/65	PV	5.81i, 5.62	5.80- 02
Pucelj	Ivan	CRO	11.7.81	181/70	LJ	7.92	7.89- 02
Pugliese	Marcelo	ARG	2.9.68	191/105	DT	62.94	64.23- 02
Pukstys	Tom	USA	28.5.68	188/98	JT	79.31	87.12- 97
Qi Haifeng		CHN	7.8.83	181/75	Dec	8126	8041- 02
Qu Fanhua		CHN	21.2.77		50kW	3:59:57	3:57:59- 00
* Quesada	Yoelbi	CUB	4.8.73	181/71	TJ	17.27i, 16.97	17.85- 97, 17.97w- 95
Quiñónez	Jackson	ECU	12.6.80	186/80	110H	13.59	13.64A- 01, 13.64- 02
Raeburn	Julian	TRI	18.9.78	188/82	200	20.57	20.63, 20.61w- 00
Ragnvaldsson	Daniel	SWE	3.1.76		JT	76.71	77.34- 01
* Rags	Eriks	LAT	1.6.75	183/93	JT	86.32A	86.47- 01
Rahnu	Kristjan	EST	29.8.79	193/90	Dec	8203	8081- 02
Ralston	Josh	USA	1.9.80	193/109	DT	62.66	59.14- 01
* Ramaala	Hendrick	RSA	2.2.72	172/58	10000	27:43.07	27:29.94- 99
					HMar	60:01	59:20- 00
					Mar	2:08:58	2:09:43- 00
Ramadhani	Samson	TAN	25.12.82		HMar	62:07	
					Mar	2:08:01	0

	Name		Nat	Born	Ht/Wt	Event	2003 Mark	Pre-2003 Best
	Ramazanov	Marat	RUS	5.3.64	175/68	20kW	1:23:24+	1:23:56- 90
						50kW	3:54:16	4:15:49- 02
	Ramos	André Luiz	BRA	20.1.70		Mar	2:09:58	2:08:26- 98
	Ramos	José	POR	28.7.68	171/68	10000	28:15.03	27:56.30- 00
	Ramzi	Rachid	BRN	17.7.80		1500	3:39.30	
	Ramzy	Bashir	USA	4.5.79	185/86	110H	13.72	13.64- 02
	Randriamihaja	Joseph-Berlioz	MAD	30.11.75	188/75	110H	13.64, 13/3	13.61- 01
	Rans	Kevin	BEL	19.8.82	180/81	PV	5.50	5.60- 01
	Ransky	Mike	CAN	26.10.70		DT	59.62	57.86- 01
	Rantanen	Vesa	FIN	2.12.75	184/73	PV	5.60	5.72- 01
*	Raquil	Marc	FRA	2.4.77	191/81	400	44.79	44.95- 01
*	Rasskazov	Roman	RUS	28.4.79	179/64	20kW	1:18:07	1:17:46- 00
	Rau	Matthias	GER	21.12.74	182/86	JT	77.29	76.20- 99
	Rautenkrantz	Jens	GER	11.4.82	189/85	HT	71.03	68.24- 02
*	Rawlinson	Chris	GBR	19.5.72	185/82	400H	48.44	48.14- 99
	Ray	Adrian	USA	9.10.81	185/77	110H	13.71	14.41- 01, 13.97w- 02
	Redko	Sergey	UKR	24.1.73	184/67	3kSt	8:31.93	8:24.35- 99
^	Redolat	José Antonio	ESP	17.2.76	181/66	1500	3:38.36	3:31.21- 01
						3000	7:46.0	7:53.67- 00
	Reed	Gary	CAN	25.10.81	175/66	800	1:45.34	1:48.08- 02
^	Reese	Terry	USA	20.6.67	183/79	110H	13.75	13.22- 97
*	Reina	Antonio M	ESP	13.6.81	181/58	800	1:44.37	1:43.83- 02
*	Reinikainen	Tepa	FIN	16.3.76	198/145	SP	20.69i, 20.55	20.88- 01
	Rendell	Stuart	AUS	30.6.72	187/120	HT	79.20	79.29- 02
	Retel	Jean-Claude	FRA	11.2.68	193/100	DT	61.93	68.90- 02
	Revenko	Vladislav	UKR-J	15.11.84	177/64	PV	5.60i, 5.50	5.55- 02
*	Rey	Julio	ESP	13.1.72	168/57	Mar	2:07:27	2:07:46- 01, 2:07:37dq- 99
	Reynolds	Doug	USA	11.8.75	196/124	DT	64.56, 66.49dh	66.76- 99
	Ribeiro	Édson	BRA	8.12.72	183/80	100	10.20	10.14- 98
	Richardson	Greg	USA	27.12.76	184/77	110H	13.47, 13.2, 13.46w	13.37- 02
*	Riedel	Lars	GER	28.6.67	199/110	DT	69.50	71.50- 97
	Riepl	Toni	GER	28.2.69	175/69	HJ	2.23i	2.26- 93
	Rigondeaux	Máximo	CUB	17.10.76	182/85	JT	77.20	81.43- 00
	Riley	Jonathon	USA	29.12.78		3000	7:47.68	7:46.84i- 02, 7:57.05- 99
	Rinaldi	Fabio	ITA	15.7.73	173/57	HMar	61:48	63:52- 02
*	Ríos	José	ESP	15.3.74	170/50	5000	13:19.58	13:07.59- 00
						10000	27:29.60	27:22.20- 00
	Ritchie	Darren	GBR	14.2.75	187/77	LJ	7.90, 8.08w	7.93 -02
	Riva	Eddy	FRA	17.4.73	185/65	50kW	3:53:18	3:57:52- 02
	Rizki	Monder	BEL	16.8.79		3000	7:49.26	7:57.48- 02
*	Robberts	Janus	RSA	10.3.79	196/130	SP	20.27	21.97- 01
	Roberge	Jesse	USA	2.10.78	193/136	SP	19.50	18.24- 02
	Roberson	Mark	GBR	13.3.67	193/100	JT	77.54	85.67- 98
	Robert	Rémi	FRA	21.1.76	187/80	LJ	8.00	7.96, 8.12w- 01
	Robertson	Michael	USA	19.12.83	198/111	DT	60.18	55.23- 02
	Robinson	Khadevis	USA	19.7.76	183/74	800	1:45.03	1:44.41- 02
	Robison	Grant	USA	27.9.78	186/68	1500	3:35.75	3:41.72- 02
	Rock	Andrew	USA	23.1.82	188/75	400	45.29	46.08- 02
	Rodríguez	Iván	ESP	7.4.78	179/64	400H	49.37	49.27- 02
	Rodríguez	Jhonny	COL	11.12.79	181/114	SP	19.30	19.15- 02
	Romain	Jérôme	FRA	12.6.71	183/76	TJ	16.99A, 16.67	17.48, 17.59w- 95
	Romanenko	Aleksandr	UKR	26.6.81	168/60	50kW	4:05:57	
	Rome	Jarred	USA	21.12.76	196/145	DT	62.24	65.92- 02
	Romera	José María	ESP	2.9.80	170/62	400H	49.63	49.44- 02
	Romero	Fabrício	BRA	13.5.78	190/72	HJ	2.27	2.26A- 99, 2.25- 00
	Rono	Daniel	KEN	13.7.78		HMar	61:39	60:14- 02
*	Rono	Robert	KEN	11.10.74	172/60	1500	3:31.33	3:30.99- 02
						1M	3:50.98	3:54.05- 01
						2000	4:57.76	
*	Rop	Rodgers	KEN	16.2.76		HMar	60:50	60:45- 02
	Rorarius	Niklas	FIN	7.6.78	186/79	LJ	7.92w, 7.97	7.97, 8.05w- 02
*	Ross	Duane	USA	5.12.72	183/78	110H	13.17	13.12- 99
	Rotich	Henry	KEN	5.12.81	175/60	800	1:45.54A	1:45.25- 01
*	Rotich	Laban	KEN	20.1.69	163/45	1500	3:33.91	3:29.91- 98
						1M	3:54.07	3:47.65- 97
						2000	4:58.53i+	4:57.63- 96, 4:56.09i- 99
	Rotich	Michael	KEN	14.7.78		800	1:44.75	1:45.24- 01
						1000	2:17.73	
*	Rotich	Michael	KEN	26.10.82	174/58	HMar	61:30	63:00- 02
						Mar	2:06:33	2:08:59- 02
	Rotich	Willy	KEN	23.3.76	177/58	800	1:46.87	1:45.33- 02

Name		Nat	Born	Ht/Wt	Event	2003 Mark	Pre-2003 Best
Routt	Stanford	USA	23.7.83	185/82	200	20.51, 20.28w	20.74- 01
Rozna	Roman	MDA	25.3.76	190/105	HT	76.62	73.28- 01
Rubanko	Artyom	UKR	21.3.74	192/105	HT	77.35	80.18- 02
Rubtsov	Sergey	KAZ	4.9.65	190/154	200	20.08	20.68- 88
Rudnitskiy	Andrey	RUS	12.11.79	176/66	400	45.76	46.57- 02
Ruff	Dwight	USA	31.3.83	173/68	400H	49.50	50.37- 01
Rurak	Konstantin	UKR	9.4.74	179/79	100	10.18, 10.11w	10.17- 00,10.03dt,10.13w- 96
* Rusan	Tim	USA	25.6.77	190/84	TJ	17.45i, 17.24	17.34- 02
* Rusenov	Ivaylo	BUL	9.9.79	178/65	LJ	7.95	7.67- 00
					TJ	17.02, 17.12w	16.95- 01
Russell	Scott	CAN	16.1.79	206/122	JT	81.56	81.66- 01
Rutto	Barnabas	KEN	19.4.77		HMar	61:54	61:33- 00
Rutto	David	KEN	.80		Mar	2:08:21	2:11:38- 02
* Rutto	Evans	KEN	8.4.78	168/56	HMar	62:08	60:30- 01
					Mar	2:05:50	0
Ryan	Gary	IRL	12.6.72	175/70	100	9.9	10.45, 10.18w- 99
* Rybakov	Yaroslav	RUS	22.11.80	198/84	HJ	2.34i	2.33i, 2.33- 01
Ryland	Daniel	USA	6.8.79	185/82	PV	5.54	4.82- 02
Sabino	Jefferson	BRA	4.11.82	188/78	TJ	16.66	16.45- 02
Sack	Peter	GER	27.7.79	192/113	SP	19.96i, 19.87	19.05i- 01, 18.80- 02
Sack	Rene	GER	14.7.76	190/135	SP	19.75	19.84- 02
Saghar	Abdolghafar	IRI	22.3.74		100	10.18w	10.37- 99, 10.36w- 02
* Saïd-Guerni	Djabir	ALG	29.3.77	187/70	800	1:44.60	1:43.09- 99
* Saïdi Sief	Ali	ALG	15.3.78	170/55	3000	7:30.79	7:25.02- 00
Saïdou	Kamal	MAR	9.12.64		HMar	61:37	
Saina	Mark	KEN	10.11.70		Mar	2:10:13	2:09:00- 00
^ Sakirkin	Oleg	KAZ	23.1.66	182/72	TJ	16.43	17.58- 89
Salnikov	Aleksandr	RUS	27.9.71		SP	19.20i	19.52- 99
Sambu	Ezra	KEN	4.9.78	175/70	400	44.43A, 44.98	44.47A, 45.92- 01
Samimi	Abbas	IRI	9.6.77	203/110	DT	62.60	60.49- 02
Sánchez	Alberto	CUB	3.2.73	180/92	HT	70.76	77.78- 98
Sánchez	David	ESP	23.8.73	176/63	50kW	4:01:58	3:56:00- 99
* Sánchez	Félix	DOM	30.8.77	178/73	400	45.22A, 45.23	44.90- 01
					400H	47.25	47.35- 02
* Sánchez	Germán	MEX	31.7.67	173/63	50kW	3:53:24	3:44:50- 01
* Sands	Leevan	BAH	16.8.81	190/73	LJ	8.04i, 8.01, 8.28w	7.90- 02, 8.00w- 01
					TJ	17.40	17.50- 02
Sanguin	Giovanni	ITA	14.5.69	185/100	HT	72.79	74.52- 97
Sanou	Idrissa	BUR	12.6.77	183/80	100	10.29, 10.15w	10.14, 10.12Aw- 02
Sanou	Olivier	BKF	2.1.75		TJ	16.91	16.74A, 16.64, 17.06w- 02
Santa	Carlos	DOM	7.1.78	182/68	400	45.43, 45.1	45.69A, 45.77- 02
Santos	Anderson Jorge	BRA	23.4.72	186/75	400	45.62	45.39A- 99, 45.47- 01
dos Santos	Leonardo	BRA-J	7.5.84	183/65	TJ	16.58	16.12- 02
dos Santos	Mário José	BRA	10.9.79		50kW	3:58:59	
dos Santos	Osmar	BRA	20.10.68	175/65	800	1:45.35	1:44.87- 00
dos Santos	Redelen	BRA	24.4.76		110H	13.34	13.59- 00
dos Santos	Sergio Muniz	BRA	13.5.76		TJ	16.46, 16.53w	16.68- 00
Sarrís	Panayiótis	GRE	14.9.75	181/74	200	20.53	20.48- 02
^ Sasimovich	Vladimir	BLR	14.9.68	178/86	JT	79.57	87.40- 95
Sato	Atsushi	JPN	8.5.78	170/55	10000	28:15.73	28:13.18- 01
					Mar	2:08:50	2:09:50- 00
Sato	Mitsuhiro	JPN	8.1.80	175/62	400	45.50	46.30- 01
Sato	Nobuyuki	JPN	8.8.72	175/57	10000	28:15.24	28:16.86- 99
Saurambayev	Denis	KAZ	30.6.77		TJ	16.46	16.80- 01
Savary	Guillaume	FRA	11.2.81	183/68	PV	5.50	5.20- 02
Savkin	Anton	RUS	15.9.80	189/127	SP	19.58	19.50i, 19.08- 02
Savolainen	Nikolay	UKR	25.3.80	189/74	TJ	17.03	17.08- 02
Sawano	Daichi	JPN	16.9.80	182/67	PV	5.75	5.52- 01
Sawe	Julius	KEN	21.11.71	173/63	20kW	1:22:06A	1:21:21A- 00
Scales	Mardy	USA	10.9.81	173/73	100	10.22, 10.02w	10.33, 10.25w- 01
Schäfer	Raphael	GER	6.3.81	173/59	3kSt	8:26.65	8:30.05- 02
Schiebler	Jeff	CAN	1.6.73	171/55	5000	13:28.37	13:13.96- 98
					10000	28:00.54	27:36.01- 01
Schindzielorz	Jan	GER	8.8.78	186/82	110H	13.60	13.50- 02
Schläfli	Rolf	SUI	15.3.71	197/97	Dec	8019	7984- 00
Schmidt	Nate	USA	13.8.81		Dec	7513	7119 -02
Schmidt	Torsten	GER	9.12.74	207/105	DT	64.26	64.56- 02
Schönbeck	Florian	GER	13.1.74	190/89	Dec	7788	8127- 00
* Schultz	Ingo	GER	26.7.75	201/96	400	45.06	44.66- 01
* Schumann	Nils	GER	20.5.78	192/77	800	1:45.57i	1:44.16- 02
Scott	Dorian	JAM	1.2.82		SP	19.43	17.54- 02

Name		Nat	Born	Ht/Wt	Event	2003 Mark	Pre-2003 Best
Scott	Jeremy	USA	1.5.81	206/91	PV	5.70i	5.55- 02
Scuderi	Francesco	ITA	4.10.77	168/68	100	10.29, 10.19w	10.19- 00
Sdiri	Salim	FRA	26.10.78	185/75	LJ	8.16i, 8.10, 8.29w	8.23- 02
* Sebrle	Roman	CZE	26.11.74	186/88	Dec	8807	9026- 01
Sedlácek	Pavel	CZE	5.4.68	198/125	HT	78.80	79.56- 96
Sedoc	Gregory	NED	16.10.81	179/72	110H	13.55	13.79, 13.66w- 02
* Segura	Bernardo	MEX	11.2.70	175/62	20kW	1:19:06	1:17:25.6t- 94
Seibold	Florian	GER	27.6.79	187/74	110H	13.67	13.73- 02
Seitz	Heinrich	GER	6.4.80	190/100	DT	59.85	60.16- 02
Sekikawa	Yoshio	JPN	16.2.79	178/56	3kSt	8:33.58	8:45.94- 00
Selmouni	Anas	MAR	15.3.79	178/67	1500	3:35.35	3:39.3- 02
					1M	3:52.66	
Semenenko	Yevgeniy	UKR-J	17.7.84	178/67	TJ	16.52	15.60- 02
Sena	Jorge Célio	BRA-J	31.1.85	179/65	200	20.63	20.92- 02
* Sepeng	Hezekiél	RSA	30.6.74	178/64	800	1:43.12	1:42.69- 99
Serélis	Dimítrios	GRE	5.5.80	186/83	LJ	8.21	8.08i, 8.00, 8.04w- 00
Serem	Henry	KEN			Mar	2:10:07	2:10:39- 02
Sergeyev	Aleksandr	RUS	29.7.83	191/81	TJ	16.80	16.89i, 16.62- 02
Sergeyev	Grigoriy	RUS	27.4.76	178/69	20kW	1:22:25	1:22:19- 01
Servanty	Pascal	FRA	26.5.66	176/67	50kW	4:06:30	3:52:51- 99
Seskin	Yuriy	RUS	7.7.66	196/110	DT	60.70	64.58- 88
* Setliff	Adam	USA	15.12.69	193/125	DT	62.92	68.94, 69.44dh- 01
Seto	Tomohiro	JPN	19.10.76	169/53	5000	13:26.84	13:30.74- 99
* Sghyr	Ismaïl	FRA	16.3.72	168/50	3000	7:48.6+	7:30.09- 95
					5000	13:10.79	12:58.83- 00
					10000	27:45.14	27:12.39- 99
* Shabunin	Vyacheslav	RUS	27.9.69	171/56	1500	3:32.63	3:32.28- 00
					1M	3:53.74	3:49.83- 01
					3000	7:47.96i	7:39.24- 95
Shaheen	Saïf Saaeed	QAT	15.10.82	177/64	see	Cherono, Stephen	
Shao Yi		CHN	20.3.79		400H	49.75	51.21- 02
Shapoval	Viktor	UKR	17.10.79	199/72	HJ	2.26	2.18- 02
Sharpe	Fred	USA	21.8.78		400H	48.86	49.60- 01
Shelest	Aleksey	UKR	27.3.73	173/64	50kW	3:57:12	3:58:09- 99
* Shevchenko	Dmitriy	RUS	13.5.68	200/140	DT	65.39	70.54- 02
* Shi Dongpeng		CHN-J	6.1.84	189/75	110H	13.40	13.43- 01
Shields	Ryan	USA	12.5.83	188/82	200	20.51	
Shields	Sean	USA	10.2.83	196/117	SP	19.58i, 19.34	19.11- 02
Shiferaw	Tewodros	ETH	.80		3kSt	8:23.41	
Shimizu	Koji	JPN	17.10.69	176/52	Mar	2:08:28	2:09:00- 99
Shin Kyung-ha		KOR-J	18.8.84		JT	76.74	68.83- 02
^ Shirvington	Matt	AUS	25.10.78	184/82	100	10.09	10.03- 98
Shiryayev	Vladislav	RUS	30.10.73	176/72	400H	49.60	49.02- 00
* Shkurlatov	Vitaliy	RUS	25.5.79	182/76	LJ	8.23	8.38i, 8.22- 00
Shkurlatov	Vladislav	RUS	30.3.83	182/82	JT	78.39	74.09- 92
Shtepa	Aleksandr	RUS	15.5.79	197/84	Dec	7815	8007- 02
Shvetsov	Leonid	RUS	28.3.69	185/70	Mar	2:09:33	2:09:16- 97
Si Tianfeng		CHN-J	17.6.84		50kW	3:59:23	
Siebert	Sebastian	GER	23.6.82	192/76	110H	13.67	13.83- 01
Sigei	Matthew	KEN			Mar	2:09:17	2:10:12- 02
* Sihine	Sileshi	ETH	29.1.83	171/55	3000	7:45.7+	
					5000	13:06.53	13:21.81- 02
					10000	26:58.76	27:26.12- 02
da Silva	André D	BRA	26.11.72	187/78	200	20.15A, 20.56	20.35, 20.17A- 00
Silva	Anisio	BRA	16.6.69	185/79	TJ	16.60, 17.00w	17.32- 93
da Silva	Anselmo G	BRA	22.3.81	186/67	110H	13.52, 13.5	13.53- 02
^ da Silva	Claudinei	BRA	19.11.70	186/86	200	20.30A, 20.63, 20.62w	19.89- 99
da Silva	Cleverson	BRA	5.9.73	185/75	400H	49.90	49.10- 99
Silva	Jorge Ignacio	ESP	19.4.79	175/60	20kW	1:21:53	1:23:48- 00
da Silva	Luiz Fernando	BRA	2.7.71	186/87	JT	79.50	79.50- 00
Silva	Manuel	POR	8.10.78	179/65	3kSt	8:33.26	8:24.60- 00
* Silva	Rui	POR	3.8.77	175/65	800	1:45.48	1:44.91- 02
					1500	3:32.97	3:30.07- 02
					1M	3:51.98	3:49.50- 02
					3000	7:42.55i	7:39.44i- 00, 7:53.87- 99
Simion	Danut Marian	ROM	25.1.83	190/78	LJ	8.12	7.71- 02
Simms	Allen	USA	26.7.82	178/75	LJ	8.02	8.00- 01
					TJ	17.26i, 17.17	16.37, 16.54w- 01
Simon	LeJuan	USA	7.2.81	186/75	TJ	16.43, 16.70w	16.87, 17.39w- 02
Simotwo	Suleiman	KEN	21.4.80		1500	3:36.98	3:42.2A- 02
					2000	4:59.06	
					3000	7:48.38	

Name		Nat	Born	Ht/Wt	Event	2003 Mark	Pre-2003 Best
Simpson	Brandon	JAM	6.9.81	172/75	400	44.84	45.11- 02
Simunic	Bostjan	SLO	28.12.74	186/73	TJ	16.54, 16.75w	16.82- 02
Sinervo	Timo	FIN	5.8.75	192/103	DT	61.90	63.28- 01
Singh	Bahadur	IND	7.5.73	187/95	SP	19.59	20.01- 00
Singh	Ramandeep	IND	.78		JT	76.92	80.56- 98
Singh	Shakti	IND	14.5.62	185/100	SP	19.05	20.60- 00
Sinyakov	Andrey	BLR	6.1.82		SP	19.15i	16.92- 01?
Sinyavskiy	Denis	RUS	13.8.79		LJ	7.99	7.90- 02
Sithole	Petrus	RSA	29.3.76		3kSt	8:32.66	8:33.90- 01
Sjöqvist	Erik	SWE	4.12.72	183/72	3000	7:49.36	7:54.20- 02
					5000	13:23.24	13:32.32- 02
Skipper	Tommy	USA-J	14.4.84	186/86	PV	5.56	5.37- 02
Skoog	Henrik	SWE	17.4.79	185/71	3kSt	8:25.55	8:30.32- 01
* Skurygin	German	RUS	15.9.63	165/63	50kW	3:36:42	3:40:54- 99
* Skvaruk	Andrey	UKR	9.3.67	186/108	HT	81.74	82.62- 02
Slattery	Steve	USA	14.8.80		3kSt	8:22.32	8:23.44- 02
Sliwa	Leszek	POL	20.9.79	187/110	SP	19.19i, 19.10	20.02i, 19.78- 02
Slobodenyuk	Vadim	UKR	17.3.81	185/73	3kSt	8:28.64	8:25.52- 02
Slover	Scott	USA	9.7.75	185/79	PV	5.66	5.76- 02
Smirnov	Vitaliy	UZB	25.10.78		Dec	8021	7537- 02
^ Smiryagin	Yevgeniy	RUS	17.5.76	185/77	PV	5.70	5.85- 97
Smit	Werner	RSA-J	14.9.84	187/110	HT	71.02	69.38- 02
Smith	Maurice	JAM	28.9.80		Dec	7925w, 7854	7755A- 01
Smith	Richard	USA	16.7.80	178/79	TJ	16.27i, 16.49w	16.46- 02
Smith	Rutger	NED	9.7.81	197/125	SP	20.52	20.39- 02
					DT	62.70	64.69- 02
Smoots	Jason	USA	13.7.80	180/89	100	10.30, 10.15w	10.22, 10.07w- 02
Snällfot	Mikael	SWE	23.5.80		JT	76.17	75.38- 01
Sneberger	Michal	CZE	23.6.78	185/75	1500	3:37.10	3:39.31- 02
* Snyder	Brad	CAN	8.1.76	196/128	SP	20.70	20.79- 01
Söderberg	David	FIN	11.8.79	185/105	HT	78.83	76.51- 02
Sofin	Pavel	RUS	4.9.81	201/110	SP	20.33	19.63- 02
Soget	Christopher	KEN	15.5.80		HMar	61:35	
* Sokolovskiy	Andrey	UKR	16.7.78	196/76	HJ	2.33	2.36- 02
* Som	Bram	NED	20.2.80	177/62	800	1:44.22	1:43.98- 01
					1000	2:17.81i	2:18.23i- 01
Sommerfeldt	Knut	NOR	13.7.79		Dec	7685w, 7506	7531- 01
* Songok	Isaac	KEN-J	25.4.84	170/54	1500	3:31.54	3:34.20- 02
					2000	4:58.22	4:56.86- 01
Songoka	Yusuf	KEN	5.2.79	170/55	HMar	60:58	60:53- 02
Soos	Ricky	GBR	28.6.83	188/70	800	1:46.06	1:47.18- 02
Sorescu	Cosmin	ROM	11.7.75	188/95	HT	76.46	75.96- 02
Sørli	Gjøran	NOR	3.6.78	191/125	SP	19.79	19.59- 01
					DT	60.91	60.55- 01
* Sosunov	Kirill	RUS	1.11.75	190/86	LJ	8.01, 8.13w	8.41i- 97, 8.38- 98, 8.48w- 95
Souid	Saber	TUN	9.3.81		HT	70.81	68.40- 02
Sousa	Cláudio R	BRA	14.10.73	168/68	100	10.25, 10.21w	10.19- 02
					200	20.24A, 20.60	20.39- 02
de Souza	Hudson	BRA	25.2.77	180/65	1500	3:36.41	3:33.99- 01
					1M	3:54.39	3:52.97- 02
Souza	Márcio de	BRA	24.1.75	180/72	110H	13.40	13.38- 99
Spahn	Matthias	GER	3.1.79	189/85	Dec	7814	7814- 02
Spain	Otto	USA	27.2.81	185/81	400	45.57	46.39- 02
* Spasovkhodskiy	Igor	RUS	1.8.79	191/91	TJ	16.95	17.44- 01
Speaight	Neil	GBR	9.9.78	191/79	800	1:45.81A	1:46.92- 02
Spiegelburg	Richard	GER	12.8.77	182/77	PV	5.73i, 5.70	5.85- 01
^ Spitsyn	Valeriy	RUS	5.12.65	178/67	50kW	4:00:50	3:37:26- 00
* Sposób	Grzegorz	POL	12.2.76	200/87	HJ	2.30	2.30- 01
Squittieri	Joe	USA	15.12.81	183/77	HJ	2.26i	2.20- 02
St Clair	Justin	USA	17.5.79		JT	76.23	74.01- 02
* Stadnichuk	Andrey	RUS	14.12.73	176/64	20kW	1:20:28	1:19:02- 02
Stang	Patrik	GER	17.5.78	198/112	DT	59.62	59.29- 00
* Stankin	Vladimir	RUS	2.1.74	184/71	20kW	1:21:32	1:19:14- 01
Stanski	Olgierd	POL	4.4.73	196/98	DT	61.24	64.20- 00
Starkey	Dean	USA	27.3.67	188/84	PV	5.55	5.92- 94
Stasyuk	Pavel	BLR	14.6.77		JT	78.05	79.80- 02
Statsenko	Oleg	UKR	22.10.80	188/95	JT	79.44	78.16- 02
Stauffer	Martin	SUI	7.7.75	205/85	HJ	2.27	2.27i- 00, 2.25- 02
Steding	Stephan	GER	29.1.82	203/105	JT	81.96	78.50- 02
* Steele	Adam	USA	8.10.80	188/79	400	44.57	46.15- 02
Stehlík	Petr	CZE	15.4.77	185/102	SP	20.33	20.50- 01

Name		Nat	Born	Ht/Wt	Event	2003 Mark	Pre-2003 Best
Stepanchuk	Andrey	BLR	12.6.79	176/65	20kW	1:22:35	1:22:17- 01
					50kW	4:06:43	4:26:20- 02
Stevens	Robbie	RSA	18.2.81	184/73	800	1:46.62	1:47.76- 02
* Stevenson	Toby	USA	19.11.76	186/79	PV	5.75	5.74- 02
Stewart	Chris	USA	6.3.80	186/86	100	10.24	10.46- 00, 10.44w- 01
					200	20.65, 20.40w	21.17, 20.71w- 00
Stewart	Simon	USA	28.1.80		SP	19.18i, 18.95	19.48- 02
Stokes	Chris	USA	1.2.79	183/79	110H	13.71	13.90- 01, 13.72w- 02
* Stolle	Michael	GER	17.12.74	192/85	PV	5.75i	5.95- 00
* Strand	Staffan	SWE	18.4.76	188/75	HJ	2.32i, 2.26	2.35i- 02, 2.32- 00
* Streete-Thompson	Kareem	CAY	30.3.73	183/84	LJ	8.21	8.63, 8.64w- 94
* Stringfellow	Savanté	USA	6.11.78	191/84	LJ	8.46	8.52- 02
* Strogalyov	Vadim	RUS	9.2.75	183/77	PV	5.73	5.85- 98
Stroubákos	Panayiótis	GRE	8.9.72	187/73	1500	3:37.65	3:36.74- 97
Strutzel	Jess	USA	4.1.78	185/70	800	1:46.45	1:45.81- 99
Suárez	Alejandro	MEX	30.11.80		5000	13:18.13	13:39.08- 01
Suárez	Iosvani	CUB	20.12.72	181/95	HT	73.69	73.18- 02
Sudol	Grzegorz	POL	28.8.78	174/60	20kW	1:22:46	1:24:20- 02
					50kW	3:55:40	3:50:37- 02
* Suetsugu	Shingo	JPN	2.6.80	178/68	100	10.03	10.05- 02
					200	20.03	20.26- 00
Sugibayashi	Takanori	JPN	14.3.76	185/68	TJ	16.96	17.02- 00
Sugimoto	Akihiro	JPN	20.10.81	162/54	20kW	1:22:36	1:25:06- 02
Sukhomlinov	Igor	RUS	13.2.77	184/90	JT	76.72	79.92- 02
Sulaiman	Abdulrahman	QAT-J	10.1.84	177/65	800	1:46.51	1:47.11- 02
					1500	3:39.20	3:40.57- 02
Sulle	Martin Hhaway	TAN	28.12.82	162/52	HMar	60:56	61:25- 02
^ Sullivan	Kevin	CAN	20.3.74	180/68	1500	3:34.60	3:31.71- 00
					1M	3:53.34	3:50.26- 00
Summers	Andre	USA-J	.85		100	10.20w	10.43, 10.41w- 02
Sun Chao		CHN-Y	8.1.87		50kW	4:04:07	
Suter	Patric	SUI	17.5.77	192/100	HT	80.51	74.56- 02
Suwa	Toshinari	JPN	29.1.77	178/58	Mar	2:07:55	2:09:10- 02
^ Svenøy	Jim	NOR	22.4.72	186/70	3kSt	8:31.50	8:12.05- 97
Svensson	Fredrik	SWE	10.9.73	184/77	50kW	3:56:31	3:56:32- 02
Svyatokho	Vyacheslav	BLR	20.7.81		HT	72.42	68.02- 01
Sylvester	Marc	USA	21.11.82	186/73	800	1:46.56	1:46.21- 02
Sylvester	Tonyo	USA	17.12.67	188/99	SP	20.16	20.51- 02
Syster	Ian	RSA	20.1.76		Mar	2:07:49	2:07:06- 02
Szeglet	Zsolt	HUN	4.5.77	180/73	400	45.49	45.43- 01
* Tadesse	Zersenay	ERI	8.2.82	158/52	3000	7:43.89	8:04.83- 02
					5000	13:05.57	13:48.79- 02
					HMar	61:26	63:05- 02
Tadili	Ashraf	CAN	8.7.80	180/68	800	1:45.05	1:45.48- 01
Tahar	Moulay	MAR	.69		HMar	61:16	
* Tahri	Bouabdellah	FRA	20.12.78	190/65	1500	3:36.55	3:34.85- 02
					3000	7:46.7	7:41.41i- 02, 7:48.98- 97
					3kSt	8:06.91	8:09.23- 01
Taillepierre	Karl	FRA	13.8.76	176/64	TJ	16.96, 16.99w	17.10- 01
Takada	Koji	JPN	31.12.83	170/57	20kW	1:23:57	1:27:57- 02
Takahira	Shinji	JPN-J	18.7.84	179/62	200	20.63	20.97- 02
Takao	Kenji	JPN	23.3.75	170/57	10000	28:17.91	27:56.05- 95
* Takaoka	Toshinari	JPN	24.9.70	186/64	5000	13:24.66	13:13.40- 98
					10000	28:03.62	27:35.09- 01
					HMar	61:07	61:49- 02
					Mar	2:07:59	2:06:16- 02
Talashko	Andrey	BLR	31.5.82	173/65	20kW	1:22:33	1:21:42- 02
* Talel Kapkeny	Wilberforce	KEN	10.1.80	170/65	10000	27:33.60	27:36.48- 00
Talotti	Alessandro	ITA	7.10.80	193/79	HJ	2.30	2.27- 02
* Tamesue	Dai	JPN	3.5.78	170/67	400H	48.94	47.89- 01
* Tammert	Aleksander	EST	2.2.73	196/126	DT	66.63	67.75- 02
Tamminga	Christian	NED	30.4.74	172/67	PV	5.70A	5.76- 98
Tan Chunhua		CHN	13.3.77		400H	50.15	49.25- 98
Tanigawa	Satoru	JPN	5.7.72	185/79	110H	13.60	13.55- 99
Tanii	Takayuki	JPN	14.2.83	166/57	20kW	1:20:45	1:24:23- 02
					50kW	3:47:54	0
Tanui	Job	KEN	26.8.74		1500	3:35.73	
Tanui	Mark	KEN			3kSt	8:29.8A	
Tarus	Bogdan	ROM	1.8.75	192/76	LJ	8.21	8.30i- 00, 8.29- 96
* Tarus	Philip	KEN	11.9.74		Mar	2:09:24	2:08:33- 99
Tarzumanov	Rinat	UZB-J	26.3.84		JT	77.66	

Name		Nat	Born	Ht/Wt	Event	2003 Mark	Pre-2003 Best
Tayari	Avi	ISR	25.10.73	181/74	TJ	16.50, 16.58w	16.94, 16.95w- 97
* Taylor	Angelo	USA	29.12.78	188/77	400H	48.94	47.50- 00
Taylor	Corey	USA	2.5.81	185/77	110H	13.70	13.72- 02
* Taylor	Dan	USA	12.5.82	198/145	SP	21.33i, 20.44	20.01i, 19.15- 02
^ Téllez	Norberto	CUB	22.1.72	186/78	800	1:46.71	1:42.85- 96
Terano	Shin-ichi	JPN	10.7.79	176/67	LJ	8.04	7.99- 01, 8.08w- 00
Terefa	Dawit	ETH	.77		Mar	2:10:38	2:16:34- 00
* Terek	Paul	USA	20.10.79	186/83	PV	5.70i, 5.50	5.56i- 01, 5.50- 02
					Dec	8275	8041- 02
Tereshin	Andrey	RUS	15.12.82	196/76	HJ	2.27	2.24- 02
^ Tergat	Paul	KEN	17.6.69	183/61	HMar	60:51	59:06- 00, 58:51sh- 96
					Mar	2:04:55	2:05:48- 02
Tesarík	Stepán	CZE	6.7.78	192/75	400H	49.09	49.38- 02
Theodoridis	Yeóryios	GRE	12.12.72	181/80	100	10.17	10.20- 02
Thie	James	GBR	27.6.78	178/70	50kW	3:57.71i	3:58.24- 02
Thilakeratne	Sugath	SRI	30.7.73	170/57	400	45.56	44.61- 98
Thom	Casey	USA	16.8.79		Dec	7522	7133 -02
Thomas	Dwight	JAM	23.9.80	185/82	100	10.19	10.12- 00
					200	20.48	20.45- 02
* Thomas	Eric	USA	1.12.73	190/88	400H	48.46	47.94- 00
^ Thomas	Iwan	GBR	5.1.74	188/80	400	45.58	44.36- 97
Thomas	Michael	USA	21.12.81	188/77	110H	13.50	13.66- 02
Thomas	Nick	GBR	4.4.79		TJ	16.44	16.31- 00
Thomas	Tim	GBR	18.11.73	187/82	PV	5.50	5.40- 97
Thomas	Will	USA	11.8.81		Dec	7894	7630- 02
Thompson	Floyd	USA	22.11.79		800	1:46.78	1:47.13- 02
* Thompson	Kemel	JAM	25.9.74	180/75	400H	48.05	48.56- 00
Thompson	Kevin	USA	24.3.80	190/88	Dec	7526	7598- 02
Thompson	Kirt	TRI	13.12.67	178/80	JT	76.31	78.06- 96
Thompson	Obadele	BAR	30.3.76	175/67	100	10.08	9.87A-98, 9.96-99, 9.69Aw- 96
Thompson	Tony	USA	12.3.80	188/109	SP	19.35	18.79- 02
Thorkildsen	Andreas	NOR	1.4.82	188/90	JT	85.72	83.87- 01
Thörnblad	Linus	SWE-J	6.3.85	180/80	HJ	2.30	2.19- 02
Thornell	John	AUS-J	22.4.85	175/60	LJ	7.81, 7.99w	7.78- 02
Thriene	Matthias	GER	28.12.71		DT	60.66	59.98- 01
Thurmond	Reedus	USA	15.12.79		DT	61.33	62.06, 62.34dh- 00
Thys	Gert	RSA	12.11.71	167/55	Mar	2:08:42	2:06:33- 99
Tighazouine	Khalid	MAR	18.6.77	175/68	800	1:45.32	1:45.27- 01
* Tiisanoja	Ville	FIN	24.12.75	192/119	SP	20.37	21.09- 02
* Tikhon	Ivan	BLR	24.7.76	186/110	HT	84.32	79.85- 00
Tishchenko	Nikolay	RUS	4.2.77	195/93	Dec	7911	7858- 02
Togashi	Hideo	JPN	21.7.81	174/57	400	45.78	47.01- 02
Tokumoto	Kazuyoshi	JPN	22.6.79	173/59	5000	13:26.19	13:39.59- 02
					10000	28:13.23	28:23.16- 02
^ Tola	Girma	ETH	13.10.75	171/57	HMar	62:06	
^ Tola	Tesfaye	ETH	19.10.74	167/60	HMar	61:35	59:51w- 00, 60:24- 01
Tolen	Frank	USA	17.7.82	183/73	LJ	8.08i	7.59, 7.69w- 02
Tölgyesi	Péter	HUN	9.6.81	199/89	TJ	16.74	15.71- 02
* Tomlinson	Chris	GBR	15.9.81	196/70	LJ	8.16	8.27- 02
Tompuri	Timo	FIN	9.6.69	187/120	DT	63.08	69.62- 01
Too	Michael	KEN	3.8.83	171/60	1500	3:37.51	3:34.17- 02
					1M	3:53.69	3:54.60- 02
* Topic	Dragutin	SCG	12.3.71	197/77	HJ	2.33i, 2.31	2.38- 93
Toroitich	Haron	KEN	.78		HMar	61:58	60:49- 01
					Mar	2:08:34	0
Torres	Ed	USA	22.8.80	170/55	10000	28:21.46	28:43.28- 02
Torres	Jorge	USA	22.8.80	170/66	5000	13:24.17	13:26.00- 02
Tosca	Osniel	CUB-J	30.6.84	178/68	TJ	16.61	16.45- 02
Toshner	Derek	USA	.80		400H	50.20	51.26- 02
Tóth	János	HUN	15.4.78		50kW	3:59:24	4:01:14- 02
^ Toth	Kevin	USA	29.12.67	193/144	SP	22.67	22.19- 02
Tóth	Matej	SVK	10.2.83	185/72	20kW	1:23:17	1:29:33- 01
Trafas	Dariusz	POL	16.5.72	188/87	JT	81.98	87.17- 00
Trainor	Brian	USA	14.3.80	193/118	DT	60.91	60.38A- 02
* Trammell	Terrence	USA	23.11.78	188/84	110H	13.17	13.16- 00
Trautmann	Denis	GER	15.8.72	182/71	50kW	4:05:20	3:48:05- 99
Trautmann	Mike	GER	13.3.74	180/72	50kW	4:06:54	3:51:38- 01
Travassos	António	POR	24.9.71	174/69	1500	3:39.46	3:37.2- 97
Trentin	Nicola	ITA	20.6.74	178/70	LJ	8.20	8.15- 02, 8.32w- 96
Tretyak	Yevgeniy	RUS	18.7.71	184/75	LJ	7.92	8.29- 94
Triggs	Kendrick	USA	27.8.82		200	20.57	20.81- 01, 20.74w- 02

Name		Nat	Born	Ht/Wt	Event	2003 Mark	Pre-2003 Best
Trofimov	Pyotr	RUS	18.12.83	174/63	20kW	1:22:39	1:26:04- 02
Troop	Lee	AUS	22.3.73	176/55	10000	27:51.27	28:03.01- 02
					Mar	2:09:49	2:10:04- 01
Trots	Andrey	UKR	17.1.78	188/78	TJ	16.61	16.98i- 02, 16.73- 00
* Trotskiy	Ivan	BLR	27.5.76	167/50	20kW	1:19:40	1:19:45- 01
Tsátoumas	Loúis	GRE	12.2.82	186/76	LJ	8.34	8.17- 02
Tsiámis	Dimítrios	GRE	12.1.82	177/60	TJ	16.59i, 16.32	16.84- 02
Tsubota	Tomoo	JPN	16.6.77	175/59	10000	27:58.98	27:51.85- 02
Tsuchie	Hiroyasu	JPN	14.6.74	171/65	100	10.23	10.25- 00, 10.09w- 99
* Tsvetkov	Mikhail	RUS	4.5.80	194/73	HJ	2.30	2.30i, 2.25- 02
Tucker	Sultan	LBR	24.10.78	181/75	110H	13.66	13.69- 01
Tuchak	Igor	RUS	10.2.77	189/108	SP	19.02i, 18.35	19.23- 02
^ Tudor	Bogdan	ROM	1.2.70	187/70	LJ	7.93i	8.37- 95
Tugay	Igor	UKR	22.3.75	185/103	HT	76.24	75.74- 00
Tuna	Berk	TUR	7.5.76		TJ	16.67	16.22- 02
* Tunks	Jason	CAN	7.5.75	200/125	DT	65.84, 66.55dh	67.88- 98
Turi	Indrek	EST	30.7.81	190/84	Dec	8122	7639- 01
Turki	Lotfi	TUN	6.3.75	190/65	3kSt	8:18.79	8:21.78- 01
Turnbull	Gareth	IRL	14.5.79	185/77	1500	3:36.60	3:38.28- 01
Turner	Andrew	GBR	19.9.80		110H	13.66	13.90- 02
Tveitå	Einar Kristian	NOR	22.2.73	185/120	DT	60.19	63.64- 99
Tysse	Erik	NOR	4.12.80	184/59	20kW	1:22:43	1:21:41- 02
Uchitomi	Yasunori	JPN	29.10.72	173/62	3kSt	8:30.52	8:26.48- 97
Udechuku	Emeka	GBR	10.7.79	176/102	DT	60.66	62.07- 00
Ugwu	Chima	NGR	19.7.73	196/140	SP	20.02	20.26- 00
					DT	63.91A, 66.35dh	64.52- 02
Uldal	Hans Olav	NOR	16.12.82		Dec	7587	7443- 02
Umeki	Kurao	JPN	30.9.75	175/55	Mar	2:09:52	2:14:50- 02
Unger	Tobias	GER	10.7.79	179/70	200	20.41	20.68- 01
^ Urbas	Marcin	POL	17.9.76	179/75	200	20.55	19.98- 99
Ursu	Sergiu	ROM	26.4.80	202/127	SP	19.71	19.35- 01
					DT	63.78	61.64- 02
Usisivu	Boniface	KEN	5.9.74		HMar	61:13	61:41- 00
					Mar	2:09:11	2:07:50- 02
Usov	Roman	RUS	4.6.78	176/56	3kSt	8:28.76	8:26.96- 00
Ustinov	Viktor	UZB	20.7.74	189/110	HT	74.34	75.77- 00
Vaisjuns	Atis	LAT	27.9.82	183/80	Dec	7681	7553- 01
Väkeväinen	Jukka	FIN	12.9.78	182/76	Dec	7721	7944- 01
* Valyukevich	Dmitriy	BLR	31.5.81	186/78	TJ	17.57	16.68i- 02, 16.62- 01
* Van Branteghem	Cédric	BEL	13.3.79	182/72	200	20.60, 20.52w	20.73- 02
					400	45.02	45.94- 02
Van Daele	Jo	BEL	6.4.72	191/110	DT	63.88	64.24- 01
van de Westen	Marcel	NED	1.8.76	191/87	110H	13.70	13.71- 01, 13.70w- 02
van der Bilt	Mike	NED	23.10.76	197/115	DT	60.33	60.88- 98
van Deventer	Juan	RSA	26.3.83		1500	3:38.87	3:45.73- 02
van Wyk	Christie	NAM	12.10.77	171/65	100	10.22, 10.16w	10.27- 02, 9.99w- 01
van Wyk	Johannes	RSA	16.3.80		DT	59.92	59.02- 02
van Zyl	Frikkie	RSA	30.7.81		110H	13.66A, 13.80	13.65A, 13.70- 02
van Zyl	Louis	RSA-J	20.7.85	186/75	400H	49.22	48.89- 02
^ Vander-Kuyp	Kyle	AUS	30.5.71	192/82	110H	13.67	13.29- 95, 13.27Aw, 13.2- 94
Vanek	Daniel	SVK	18.1.83	188/110	DT	59.89	57.58- 02
* Varga	Roland	HUN	22.10.77	197/102	DT	61.71	67.38- 02
* Värnik	Andrus	EST	27.9.77	182/94	JT	87.83	85.47- 02
Vashchilo	Aleksandr	BLR	30.8.81	197/108	HT	75.76	72.70- 02
Vasilache	Stefan	ROM	9.5.79	190/70	HJ	2.30	2.28i, 2.25- 02
Vasilevskis	Vadims	LAT	5.1.82	187/82	JT	77.81	81.92- 02
Vasiliádis	Konstadínos	GRE	9.3.77		LJ	8.10	7.88- 02
Vasilyev	Valeriy	UKR	21.4.76	189/82	LJ	8.19i, 8.11	7.78- 01
Vega	Teodoro	MEX	14.7.76		5000	13:22.40	13:34.48- 01
					10000	27:37.49	27:58.35- 02
Venter	Clinton	RSA	3.2.80		200	20.45A, 20.68	20.85A- 02
Verni	Marco Antonio	CHI	27.2.76	188/114	SP	20.38	19.79- 02
Veryutin	Aleksandr	BLR	18.11.79	179/81	HJ	2.24i, 2.20	2.28i- 02, 2.25- 01
^ Viciosa	Isaac	ESP	26.12.69	176/64	3000	7:47.77i	7:29.34- 98
Videnov	Zhivko	BUL	23.5.77	193/80	110H	13.76, 13.63w	13.33- 00
Vieira	João	POR	20.2.76	174/58	20kW	1:20:30	1:20:44- 02
Viera	Heber	URU	29.4.79	180/74	200	20.48A, 20.60	20.46A, 20.52- 02
Vieru	Ioan	ROM	4.1.79	183/70	400	45.77	45.86- 02
Vikhrov	Andrey	RUS	.73		HT	71.71	75.76 -99
Villalobos	Pablo	ESP	20.5.78	178/60	3000	7:47.38	7:54.14- 02
Villar	Paulo	COL	28.7.78		110H	13.73A, 13.81	13.57A,13.78,13.55w- 02

Name		Nat	Born	Ht/Wt	Event	2003 Mark	Pre-2003 Best
* Virastyuk	Roman	UKR	20.4.68	189/137	SP	20.78	21.34- 00
Viti	Marzio	ITA	10.8.73	187/80	Dec	7596	7861- 02
Vivancos	Felipe	ESP	16.6.80	177/70	110H	13.75	13.79- 01, 13.64w- 02
* Vizzoni	Nicola	ITA	4.11.73	193/122	HT	77.69	80.50- 01
Vodovnik	Miran	SLO	11.9.77	197/115	SP	20.46	18.72- 99
Voronin	Vyacheslav	RUS	5.4.74	190/78	HJ	2.24i, 2.21	2.40- 00
Voronkin	Yuriy	RUS	18.5.79	184/83	HT	78.69	76.03- 00
Vorontsov	Andrey	BLR	24.7.75	191/105	HT	78.53	77.23- 01
* Voyevodin	Aleksey	RUS	9.8.70	178/65	50kW	3:38:01	3:40:16- 02
Voynov	Sergey	UZB	26.2.77	188/89	JT	79.06	84.80- 00
Vreljakovic	Dejan	SCG	24.1.77	195/78	HJ	2.23	2.22- 02
Vries	Sherwin	RSA	22.3.80	179/74	100	10.08	10.24A, 10.27, 10.17Aw- 02
					200	20.20A, 20.35	20.56A, 20.57, 20.50w- 02
* Vroemen	Simon	NED	11.5.69	189/68	3kSt	8:09.18	8:06.91- 02
Wachira	Nicholas	KEN	19.11.82	181/67	800	1:44.34A	1:44.44- 02
Wade	Ibrahima	FRA	6.9.68	193/82	400	45.71	45.05- 98
* Wade	Larry	USA	22.11.74	187/83	110H	13.23	13.01- 99
Wagne	Abdoulaye	SEN	30.1.81	180/75	800	1:45.08	1:49.42- 02
Wainaina	James	KEN	16.6.81	161/54	HMar	61:41	61:26- 00
Wale	Luleseged	ETH	.82		3kSt	8:21.30	8:32.57- 00
* Walerianczyk	Aleksander	POL	1.9.82	196/81	HJ	2.36	2.27- 02
Walker	Brad	USA	21.6.81	188/86	PV	5.80i, 5.65	5.64- 02
Walker	Josh	USA	6.5.82	185/73	110H	13.42	14.05- 02
* Wallace	Dawane	USA	30.12.76	190/79	110H	13.32	13.22- 00
Waltz	Ian	USA	15.4.77	186/122	DT	62.55	64.44- 98
Wang Shigang		CHN	22.2.81		20kW	1:20:51	1:22:06- 01
					50kW	4:03:23	3:55:00- 01
Wang Weihua		CHN	8.1.83		20kW	1:23:09	
Wang Weijun		CHN	31.12.80		50kW	4:01:59	
Wang Yieying		CHN-Y	12.12.86		50kW	4:04:53	
Wang Yinhang		CHN	15.2.77	170/54	50kW	3:48:11	3:44:28- 01
Wang Zhouzhou		CHN	20.4.77	190/72	HJ	2.24	2.27- 99
Wanjiru	Samuel	KEN-Y	10.11.86	163/51	10000	28:20.06	28:36.08- 02
Ward	Jason	USA	6.4.81	188/79	LJ	7.96w	7.74i- 02
Ward	Tyrone	USA	.81	183/73	LJ	7.97w	8.12- 02
Ware	Von	USA	30.6.75	175/79	TJ	16.48	16.97, 17.21w- 98
Wariner	Jeremy	USA-J	31.1.84	188/67	400	45.13	45.57- 02
Warners	Chiel	NED	2.4.78	194/85	Dec	8060	8363- 99
Warsama	Ahmed Ibrahim	QAT	4.2.66	182/62	10000	28:02.80	28:43.53- 02
Washington	Ramon	USA	23.6.81	191/73	LJ	7.94	7.82- 00
* Washington	Tyree	USA	28.8.76	185/84	400	44.33	44.28- 01
Watkins	Arend	USA	23.5.79	190/86	110H	13.46	13.44- 02
Waugh	Ainsley	JAM	.81		200	20.86, 20.57w	20.96- 02
Weakley	Ian	JAM	24.2.74	180/68	400H	48.55	48.76- 02
Weese	Lyle	USA	26.10.79	188/70	3kSt	8:33.35	8:52.40- 01
Weibel	Xavier	SUI	21.1.80		Dec	7662	7330- 02
* Weidlinger	Günther	AUT	5.4.78	169/54	3000	7:44.19i	7:47.79i- 00
					3kSt	8:17.90	8:10.83- 99
Wenk	Stefan	GER	13.3.81	192/83	JT	79.42	81.20- 02
Wenta	Sebastian	POL	4.5.75	201/126	SP	19.31	19.48- 01
Werner	Tim	GER	25.9.80	195/95	JT	79.40	82.66- 02
^ Whiteman	Anthony	GBR	13.11.71	189/72	800	1:46.21	1:45.81- 00
					1500	3:35.49	3:32.34- 97
					1M	3:54.94	3:51.90- 98
Whitty	Paul	CAN	1.10.82		110H	13.73	14.18- 01
Wiegand	Scott	USA	26.9.80	203/129	SP	19.89i, 19.60	19.70i, 19.55- 02
					DT	59.83	57.22- 02
Wieruszewski	Rafal	POL	24.2.81	181/63	400	45.62	45.76- 01
Wiggins	Ernest	USA	18.6.82		100	10.22	10.38- 02
* Wignall	Maurice	JAM	17.4.76	186/75	110H	13.28	13.49- 02
Wilburn	Teak	USA	22.12.83		HJ	2.23	2.24- 02
* Williams	Bernard	USA	19.1.78	183/81	100	10.04, 10.0	9.94- 01
					200	20.01	20.01- 01
Williams	Bobby	USA	3.2.78	170/75	200	20.43	20.77- 02
^ Williams	Christopher	JAM	15.3.72	177/68	200	20.54	20.02- 00
Williams	Derrick	USA	25.3.82		110H	13.96, 13.59w	14.24, 14.13w- 02
					400H	50.14	51.23 -01
Williams	Ivory	USA-J	2.5.85	173/77	100	10.16	10.27, 10.12w- 02
Williams	Jesse	USA	27.12.83	183/67	HJ	2.24	2.21- 02
Williams	LaTonel	JAM	3.4.78	183/82	200	20.40	21.15, 20.83w- 02

	Name		Nat	Born	Ht/Wt	Event	2003 Mark	Pre-2003 Best
	Williams	Ricardo	JAM	29.9.76	183/73	100	10.20, 10.13w	10.23- 00, 10.07w- 02
						200	20.42, 20.20w	20.33- 00
	Williamson	Darold	USA	19.2.83	188/77	400	44.95	45.23- 02
	Willie	Kelly	USA	7.9.82	177/72	200	20.61	20.49A, 20.3 02
						400	45.14	45.52- 02
	Willis	Lawrence	USA			TJ	16.44	15.39, 16.09w- 02
	Willis	Nick	NZL	25.4.83	183/68	1500	3:36.58	3:42.69- 02
	Wilson	Aarik	USA	25.10.82		TJ	16.69, 16.69	
	Wilson	Erick	USA	10.1.82	183/77	100	10.33, 9.93w	10.21, 10.14w- 02
						200	20.40, 20.19w	20.68, 20.43w- 02
	Wilson	Ryan	USA	19.12.80	188/79	110H	13.35	13.55- 02
						400H	49.33	50.82- 01
	Wilson	Shomari	USA	6.6.76	183/73	100	10.30,10.23w	10.23A,10.19Aw-00,10.49-98
	Winter	Nils	GER	27.3.77	187/84	LJ	8.11	7.84- 02
	Wirkkala	Teemu	FIN-J	14.1.84	185/84	JT	80.57	74.56- 02
	Wissman	Johan	SWE	2.12.82	180/72	200	20.43	20.51- 02
						400	45.80	46.17- 02
	Wodajo	Tefere	ETH	.83		Mar	2:10:18	2:09:51- 02
	Wójcik	Rafal	POL	18.9.72	180/66	3kSt	8:26.46	8:17.09- 00
	Wolski	Robert	POL	8.12.82	176/61	HJ	2.25	2.22- 02
	Woods	Terrance	USA	18.4.79	180/76	HJ	2.27	2.25- 02
	Woodske	Derek	CAN	22.10.76	188/107	HT	70.63	67.16- 02
	Woodward	Bryan	USA	3.3.74	190/84	800	1:45.46	1:45.23- 99
*	Woody	Joey	USA	22.5.73	188/78	400H	48.18	47.97- 98
	Wooten	Adam	USA	18.3.82	175/73	200	20.56w	20.59w- 01
	Woyessa	Dema	ETH-Y	.86		5000	13:29.55	
	Wu Bo		CHN-J	17.6.84		TJ	16.52	16.37- 02
	Wu Ji		CHN	14.8.78		TJ	16.67	17.04- 01
	Wu Tao		CHN	3.10.83	190/100	DT	63.68	62.04- 02
	Wu Youjia		CHN	6.5.83		110H	13.68	13.93- 02
	Wyatt	Jonathan	NZL	20.12.72	175/63	10000	27:56.80	28:18.07- 95
	Xing Shucai		CHN-J	4.8.84		20kW	1:22:58	
	Xu Xingde		CHN-J	12.6.84	168/54	20kW	1:19:14	1:22:36- 02
	Yachi	Yusuke	JPN	2.1.80	172/55	20kW	1:22:59	1:27:15- 01
	Yakovlev	Yevgeniy	RUS	17.6.79	176/65	20kW	1:23:24	1:21:52- 01
	Yamaguchi	Yuki	JPN-J	22.2.84	174/63	400	45.18	46.58- 02
	Yamazaki	Yuki	JPN-J	16.1.84	177/65	20kW	1:20:38	1:20:43- 02
	Yang Weize		CHN	10.2.83		1500	3:36.97	3:41.27- 01
	Yastrebov	Viktor	UKR	13.1.82	186/71	TJ	17.03	16.73- 02
	Yasuda	Satoru	JPN	27.7.75	175/66	PV	5.50	5.50- 00
	Yatich	Mark	KEN	4.12.76		Mar	2:09:52	2:10:55- 02
	Yeliseyev	Aleksey	RUS	12.3.82	188/90	HT	70.84	72.15- 02
	Yeliseyev	Yuriy	RUS	27.5.75	178/65	PV	5.50i	5.70- 96
	Yemmouni	Mounir	FRA	12.10.83	184/63	1500	3:38.54	3:43.23- 02
	Yeremenko	Ruslan	UKR	31.7.78	185/75	PV	5.63i	5.80i- 02, 5.70- 01
*	Yiampoy	William	KEN	17.5.74	183/70	800	1:45.01A	1:42.91- 02
						1000	2:18.15i	2:14.41- 99
	Yoshikata	Masahira	JPN	23.8.82	175/65	400H	49.42	50.01- 02
	Yoshino	Tatsuro	JPN	11.9.82	170/63	200	20.67, 20.51w	20.81- 01
	Yoshizawa	Eiichi	JPN	5.9.80	170/54	20kW	1:21:36	1:21:56- 02
						50kW	3:51:37	0
	Yoshizawa	Ken	JPN	7.7.78	180/71	400H	49.79	48.98- 02
	Young	Jason	USA	27.5.81	185/107	DT	61.56	61.00- 02
*	Young	Jerome	USA	14.8.76	181/79	400	44.50	44.09- 98
	Yu Chaohong		CHN	12.12.76	175/63	20kW	1:18:56	1:21:04- 01
						50kW	3:44:11	3:47:04- 01
	Yu Guohui		CHN	30.4.77	182/70	20kW	1:23:03	1:19:38- 96
*	Yuda	John	TAN	9.6.79	162/53	5000	13:18.0+	13:03.62- 02
						10000	27:09.83	27:06.17- 02
						HMar	60:25	60:02- 02
	Yudin	Stepan	RUS	3.4.80	175/61	20kW	1:23:23+	1:21:33- 01
						50kW	3:55:26	3:42:52- 02
*	Yurchenko	Denis	UKR	27.1.78	174/74	PV	5.81	5.75- 02
	Yushkov	Ivan	RUS	15.1.81	192/112	SP	20.28	19.47- 02
	Zadorozhniy	Andrey	RUS	3.9.73	184/72	1500	3:38.81	3:36.68- 98
*	Zagorniy	Aleksey	RUS	31.5.78	197/110	HT	80.13	83.43- 02
	Zahraoui	Abdelhalim	MAR	18.2.83		3000	7:48.78	
*	Zakari	Abdul Aziz	GHA	2.9.76	178/73	100	10.07, 9.98w	10.04- 01
						200	20.34	20.23- 00
	Zakaria	M Abdelhak	BRN	20.7.74	169/61	3000	7:46.36	
						5000	13:18.19	13:43.82- 02

	Name		Nat	Born	Ht/Wt	Event	2003 Mark	Pre-2003 Best
	Zakrzewski	Jan	POL	21.12.70	187/73	3kSt	8:28.53	8:22.49- 01
	Zalsky	Antonín	CZE	7.8.80	200/108	SP	19.09	19.17- 02
*	Zelezny	Jan	CZE	16.6.66	186/88	JT	89.06	98.48- 96
	Zellner	Torrance	USA	6.1.70	187/75	400H	49.37	48.18- 96
	Zhang Defu		CHN-J	5.6.84		50kW	3:53:10	4:12:46- 00
	Zhang Huabing		CHN	28.9.83		50kW	3:59:46	4:01:18- 01
	Zhang Jianjun		CHN	4.12.78		20kW	1:23:58	1:26:03- 01
	Zhang Tianping		CHN	11.1.82		20kW	1:21:39	1:22:21- 01
						50kW	3:56:44	4:06:12- 01
	Zhao Qingwei		CHN	17.8.83		50kW	3:58:52	4:07:34- 01
^	Zhao Yongsheng		CHN	16.4.70	172/62	50kW	4:01:46	3:41:20- 95
	Zheng Ting		CHN-J	15.2.85		HJ	2.24	2.18- 01
	Zhou Can		CHN	20.5.79	184/68	LJ	8.11	8.11- 99
	Zhu Hongjun		CHN	18.8.83	175/68	20kW	1:18:43	1:21:48- 02
	Zhu Shujing		CHN-J	24.5.85		TJ	16.78	16.13- 02
	Ziar	Rachid	ALG	15.11.73		HMar	61:35	61:30- 99
	Zioini	Badre Din	FRA	25.3.76	178/56	3kSt	8:31.64	8:23.97- 02
*	Ziólkowski	Szymon	POL	1.7.76	188/104	HT	76.97	83.38- 01
	Zitnansky	Jaroslav	SVK	18.2.71	190/120	DT	62.55	67.20- 02
	Zmirak	Zlatan	CRO	20.9.73		SP	19.57	19.66 -02
	Zorko	Branko	CRO	1.7.67	180/73	1500	3:37.58	3:33.30- 98
	Zouaoui Dandrieux	Vincent	FRA	12.10.80	188/72	3kSt	8:25.61	8:35.82- 02
	Zoubaa	Khalid	FRA	27.4.77	180/58	3000	7:49.48	7:57.42- 00
*	Zsivóczky	Attila	HUN	29.4.77	193/82	Dec	7923	8554- 00
	Zumer	Jan	SLO	9.6.82	189/75	LJ	7.96	7.74- 02
	Zurawicz	Ireneusz	POL	24.1.78	189/79	Dec	7551	7495- 00
	Zvasiya	Lloyd	ZIM	20.5.81		400	45.51	46.0A- 01
*	Zwierzchlewski	Benoit	FRA	19.8.76	171/57	Mar	2:06:36	2:08:18- 02
*	Zyuskov	Vladimir	UKR	29.8.81	187/71	LJ	8.22	8.13- 01

WOMEN'S INDEX 2003

Athletes included are those ranked in the top 100s at standard (World Champs) events (plus shorter lists for 1000m, 1M, 2000m, 3000m and 3000m St). Those with detailed biographical profiles are indicated in first column by:
* in this year's Annual, ^ in a previous year's Annual, # old javelin.

	Aagård (Jensen)	Annemette	DEN	11.4.72	163/52	HMar	71:36	72:37- 02
	Aava	Monika	EST	19.6.79	171/61	JT	59.45	57.98- 01
	Abatzí	Aretí	GRE	14.5.74	183/78	DT	62.06	62.95- 01
	Abderrhamanne	Olivia	FRA	2.8.79	163/48	400h	57.39	57.50- 00
	Abel	María	ESP	23.10.74	162/45	10000	32:20.12	32:03.2- 00
						Mar	2:30:15	2:26:59- 02
*	Abeylegesse	Elvan	TUR	11.9.82	159/40	1500	4:07.25	4:11.00- 02
						2000	5:33.83	
						3000	8:42.29	8:31.94- 02
						5000	14:53.56	15:00.49- 02
	Abrahamse	Veronica	RSA	18.3.80	180/117	SP	17.18	17.76- 02
^	Achilles	Bianca	GER	17.4.81	180/98	HT	65.54	68.40- 99
*	Acuff	Amy	USA	14.7.75	188/66	HJ	2.01	2.00-97
	Adams	Christine	GER	28.2.74	182/72	PV	4.35i, 4.30	4.66i, 4.40- 02
*	Adams	Jenny	USA	8.7.78	165/55	100h	12.67	12.63, 12.61w- 01
						LJ	6.45, 6.47w	
*	Adams	Valerie	NZL-J	6.10.84	196/120	SP	18.93	18.40- 02
	Addy	Megan	USA	22.5.78		400h	56.34	56.62- 02
*	Adere	Berhane	ETH	21.7.73	170/48	1500	4:10.91i	4:06.46, 4:05.54i- 02
						2000	5:35.62	5:37.3+- 02
						3000	8:31.73i, 8:36.25	8:25.62- 01
						5000	14:29.32	14:33.65- 02
						10000	30:04.18	30:51.30- 00
						HMar	67:32	68:17- 01
*	Adriano	Elisângela	BRA	27.7.72	180/95	SP	18.59	19.30- 01
						DT	60.02	62.23dq- 99, 61.96- 98
*	Afolabi	Olabisi	NGR	31.10.75	171/62	400	50.91	50.34A, 50.40- 99
	Agbugba	Damaris	NGR	26.12.82		100h	13.06, 13.03w	13.49- 00, 13.48w- 02
	Aghatise	Esther	NGR-J	15.4.85	165/58	LJ	6.58	6.50- 02
	Agirre	Naroa	ESP	15.5.79	176/64	PV	4.45	4.40- 02
	Aguilar	Alessandra	ESP	1.7.78	164/50	10000	32:42.49	32:48.89- 00
	Aguilera	Lisa	USA	30.11.79		3kSt	9:46.30	9:59.66- 02
	Ahonen	Kirsi	FIN	8.4.76	170/78	JT	58.81	59.75- 00
	Aiken	Alyssa	USA	15.9.82		400h	56.86	58.06- 99
	Aït Hammou	Amina	MAR	18.7.78	165/49	800	1:57.82	2:00.47- 01

	Name		Nat	Born	Ht/Wt	Event	2003 Mark	Pre-2003 Best
*	Aiyappa (Ganapathy)	G. Pramila	IND	8.5.77		Hep	5787	6105- 00
	Ajkler	Zita	HUN	9.6.75	170/56	LJ	6.47	6.70- 00
	Akinremi	Omolade	NGR	13.9.74	158/60	400h	56.98	55.44- 95
*	Aldama	Yamilé	ex CUB	14.8.72	172/65	HJ	1.88	1.88- 92
			(now SUD)			TJ	15.29	14.77- 99
	Aleksandrova	Galina	RUS	15.10.75		5000	15:34.09	16:05.13- 97
						10000	32:28.23	32:11.52- 02
						HMar	70:30	71:18- 99
	Aleksandrova	Yekaterina	RUS	3.6.77	181/57	HJ	1.97	1.96i- 98, 1.96- 01
	Alekseyeva	Olga	KAZ-J	30.11.84	179/53	Hep	5699	5903- 02
	Alemu	Direbe	ETH	.83		HMar	70:45	
*	Alemu	Elfenesh	ETH	16.6.75	171/57	HMar	70:03+	69:46- 00
						Mar	2:24:47	2:24:29- 01
	Alimi	Salamotu	NGR	30.12.76		TJ	13.68	13.55- 02
^	Allen	Liliana	MEX	24.5.70	170/62	100	11.28	11.10- 92, 11.09A- 99
	Aloysius	Bobby	IND	22.6.74	172/58	HJ	1.89	1.86- 98
*	Alozie	Glory	ESP	30.12.77	165/51	100	11.29	10.90- 99
						100h	12.66	12.44, 12.4w- 98
	Álvarez	Maria de la Caridad	CUB	30.8.75	165/62	JT	56.43	63.02#- 95, 61.57- 00
	Alves	Sónia	POR	3.6.79		HT	63.80	64.23- 02
*	Amertil	Christine	BAH	18.8.79	168/53	200	22.88, 22.86w	23.06- 02
						400	51.11i, 51.25	50.82- 02
	Amo	Eri	JPN	26.7.77	163/46	Mar	2:28:57	2:36:45- 02
	Ampleyeva	Natalya	RUS	25.9.72		DT	60.97	63.58- 02
	Anashkina	Irina	RUS	31.1.72		400h	56.24	
	Andersen	Kassi	USA	25.6.83		3kSt	9:44.95	
	Anderson	Nickiesha	JAM-J	15.3.85		100	11.2w	
						200	23.22	23.34- 02
	Andrews	Susan	AUS	26.5.71	173/58	800	2:00.50	2:00.32, 1:59.8mx- 00
	Andrianova	Tatyana	RUS	10.12.79	172/61	800	2:00.96	2:05.85- 01
	Anim	Vida	GHA	7.12.83	168/58	100	11.22, 11.16w	11.38- 01, 11.26w, 11.0- 02
						200	22.90	23.32- 00
	Anton	Adina	ROM-J	6.10.84	174/56	LJ	6.62i, 6.60	6.46- 02
*	Antonova	Yelena	UKR	16.6.72	182/95	DT	65.90	66.67- 00
*	Antyukh	Natalya	RUS	26.6.81	180/64	400	51.73i. 52.28	51.19- 01
	Aoyama	Miyuki	JPN	4.1.77	172/56	HJ	1.90	1.87- 02
	Araméndiz	Zuleima	COL	23.9.75	172/75	JT	58.70A	59.09A- 01, 61.72#- 96
	Argüelles	Yariadmis	CUB-J	18.4.84	173/58	HJ	1.89	1.88- 02
	Arias	Eva	ESP	1.1.80	164/49	1500	4:08.90	4:19.42- 02
	Arkhipova	Lyudmila	RUS	12.9.78	167/55	20kW	1:33:18	
	Aron	Haydy	FRA	21.5.73	170/58	100h	12.92	12.85- 02
*	Arrendel	Juana Rosario	DOM	16.6.78	191/60	HJ	1.95	1.97- 02
^	Arron	Christine	FRA	13.9.73	177/64	100	11.01, 10.95w	10.73- 98
						200	22.92	22.26- 99
	Ashby	Fana	TRI	15.6.81	163/64	100	11.23. 11.06w	11.26, 11.22w- 02
						200	23.05, 22.69w	23.43- 98
	Asoshina	Terumi	JPN	2.5.82	157/42	5000	15:22.51	15:52.08- 02
						10000	31:49.59	
	Assahssah	Malika	MAR	24.9.82	173/56	5000	15:23.55	15:52.0- 01
						3kSt	9:49.51	
	Asteríou	Adigóni	GRE	2.11.76		PV	4.20	4.05- 02
	Asumnu	Gloria	USA-J	22.5.85		100	11.49, 11.40w	11.78w- 02
	Atangana	Delphine	CMR-J	16.8.84		100	11.24	
						200	23.27	
^	Atede	Angela	NGR	8.2.72	170/66	100h	12.96, 12.93w	12.72- 98, 12.63dt- 97
	Atodonyang	Margaret	KEN	.78		HMar	69:12	69:55- 02
						Mar	2:29:20	2:34:57- 02
	Auzeil	Nadine	FRA	19.8.64	176/64	JT	58.31	62.16- 00, 64.10#- 96
	Avdeyeva	Anna	RUS-J	6.4.85	175/74	SP	16.91	15.83- 02
	Averkova	Anzhelika	UKR	13.3.69	165/50	3kSt	10:11.29	9:54.10- 00
	Axelsson	Cecilia	SWE-J	4.9.84		HJ	1.87i	1.78- 02
	Aya	Masumi	JPN	1.1.80	165/74	HT	64.04	66.27- 02
*	Ayhan	Süreyya	TUR	6.9.78	163/52	1500	3:55.33	3:57.75- 02
*	Babakova	Inga	UKR	27.6.67	180/60	HJ	2.01	2.05- 95
	Babatunde	Tawa	CAN	19.12.79	175/60	400h	56.38	56.99- 01
	Babcock	Courtney	CAN	30.6.72	163/50	1500	4:01.99	
						3000	8:45.52	8:43.18- 02
						5000	14:54.98	15:07.53- 02
						10000	31:44.74	32:14.52- 02
*	Bacher	Gertrud	ITA	28.2.71	181/67	Hep	6166	6185- 99
	Bagger-Bohn	Marie	DEN	1.11.72	178/65	PV	4.22i, 4.21	4.35- 00

Name		Nat	Born	Ht/Wt	Event	2003 Mark	Pre-2003 Best
* Bailey	Aleen	JAM	25.11.80	170/64	100	11.07	11.14- 01
					200	22.59	22.54- 02
^ Bakhvalova	Yekaterina	RUS	8.3.72	175/61	400h	55.94	54.65- 00
* Balakhonova	Anzhela	UKR	18.12.72	162/55	PV	4.32	4.56- 00
Balakley	Irina	RUS	6.10.81	171/57	20kW	1:33:24	1:41:22- 02
* Balassini	Ester	ITA	20.10.77	173/70	HT	70.43	68.54- 02
Balciunaite	Zivile	LTU	3.4.79		Mar	2:30:45	2:33:36- 02
Ballentine	Michelle	JAM	31.8.75	178/63	800	2:01.62	2:02.11- 01
Balsamo	Agata	ITA	11.10.70	169/55	5000	15:33.6mx, 15:37.85	15:14.70- 99
Balti	Syrine	TUN	31.10.83	173/57	PV	4.20i	4.10- 02
Bangué	Frédérique	FRA	31.12.76	179/61	100	11.32w	11.16- 98, 11.09w- 01
Bani	Zahra	ITA	31.12.79	173/71	JT	56.50	55.34- 02
Bao Guiying		CHN-Y	20.1.86		10000	32:43.75	
Baptiste	Kelliann	TRI-Y	14.10.86	161/55	200	23.22	24.03- 02
* Barber	Eunice	FRA	17.11.74	175/68	100h	12.88	12.78- 01
					HJ	1.91	1.93- 99
					LJ	7.05	7.01- 99
					Hep	6755	6861- 99
Barber	Me'Lisa	USA	4.10.80	160/52	400	52.04	52.18- 01
Barber	Mikele	USA	4.10.80	159/50	200	23.06i, 23.46	22.98- 00, 22.71w- 01
					400	51.92i, 52.43	
Barbieri	Lisa	ITA	18.5.78	149/43	20kW	1:35:20	1:33:13- 01
Barbulescu	Liliana	ROM	5.2.82	179/65	800	2:00.06	2:01.44- 02
Barlet	Alexandra	FRA	17.2.77	185/63	Hep	5640	5678- 02
Barrett	Kimberly	JAM	18.11.81		SP	17.25i, 16/94	15.66- 01
Barrios	Yarelis	CUB	12.7.83		DT	58.37	54.10- 02
Bashlykova	Lidiya	RUS	10.1.81	179/65	Hep	5736	5979- 00
Bates	Joyce	USA	16.2.77	163/59	100h	12.93	12.85, 12.79w- 00, 12.5w- 01
Bayne	Elizabeth	USA	22.7.82		400h	57.57	57.88- 02
* Bazhenova	Nadezhda	RUS	22.9.78	176/63	LJ	6.56	6.58- 01
				TJ	14.35	14.65i- 02, 14.60- 01	
Beckel	Nadine	GER	27.5.77	190/89	SP	18.59	18.26- 02
* Becker	Annika	GER	12.11.81	170/67	PV	4.70	4.77- 02
Beckford	Allison	JAM	8.5.79	175/60	200	23.18w	23.78- 01
					400	51.01	50.83- 02
					400h	55.12	56.22- 01
Beevi	Ashik	IND	.79		400h	57.17	
Begic	Vera	CRO	17.3.82	169/69	DT	56.48	56.38- 02
* Beitia	Ruth	ESP	1.4.79	178/56	HJ	2.00	1.94i- 01, 1.94- 02
Bejnar	Monika	POL	10.3.81	173/57	400	52.24	53.00- 02
Bekele	Bezunesh	ETH	.83		3000	8:56.22i	
Belin	Kirsten	SWE	2.5.81	175/59	PV	4.40	4.51- 02
Belinskaya	Natalya	RUS	21.1.83	176/57	PV	4.20	4.30- 02
Bell	Kandice	USA	7.8.83		200	23.24w	
Belova	Anna	RUS	.80		400	52.27	52.92- 02
Belova	Irina	RUS	.81		400	52.34	53.36- 02
Belyakova	Oksana	RUS	9.9.75	173/53	1500	4:08.99	4:10.80- 01
					3000	8:57.14	8:56.82i- 02
					5000	15:25.38	15:42.68- 02
* Belyakova	Yelena	RUS	7.4.76	177/56	PV	4.60	4.55i- 01, 4.52- 02
Benavídes	Vírgen	CUB	31.12.74	165/56	100	11.28	11.14, 11.10w- 99
* Benhassi	Hasna	MAR	1.6.78	166/55	800	2:01.08	1:57.45- 99
					1500	4:02.54	4:04.48i- 01, 4:05.15- 98
Benhassine	Awatef	TUN	5.4.80	175/65	400	52.30	52.97- 01
Bennett	Jennifer	USA	1.2.82		PV	4.15i	
Benth	Katia	FRA	16.11.75	172/56	100	11.33	11.20- 98
Beránková	Sárka	CZE	16.4.78	176/69	Hep	5682	6079- 00
* Bergqvist	Kajsa	SWE	12.10.76	175/59	HJ	2.06	2.05- 02
Berkut	Natalya	UKR	30.5.75	172/53	5000	15:21.59	15:21.95- 01
					HMar	70:26	73:55- 00
Bernard-Thomas	Neisha	GRN	21.1.81		800	2:01.75	2:06.55- 00
Berry	Catherine	GBR	8.10.75	179/57	5000	15:30.25	15:31.23- 02
Beskrovnaja	Irina	SVK	28.12.82	174/66	TJ	13.60, 13.69w	13.71- 01
^ Bevilacqua	Antonella	ITA	15.10.71	170/54	HJ	1.92	1.98, 1.99dq- 96
Bévis	Marie-Louise	FRA	12.10.72	170/58	400	52.06	51.79- 96
Béwouda	Hortense	CMR	19.10.78	171/65	400	51.64	51.74- 02
Bicet	Nora Aïda	CUB	29.10.77	178/78	JT	62.40	61.88- 02
Bicet	Yusmay	CUB	8.12.83	178/67	TJ	14.06	14.22- 02
Bickett	Melissa	USA	16.4.82	168/68	DT	55.35	56.83- 02
Bikar	Alenka	SLO	7.1.74	161/53	200	23.25i	22.76- 01
^ Biktagirova	Madina	RUS	20.9.64	158/50	Mar	2:28:33, 2:28:24dh	2:24:46- 97

Name		Nat	Born	Ht/Wt	Event	2003 Mark	Pre-2003 Best
* Biktasheva	Lyudmila	RUS	25.7.74	160/48	10000	31:31.87	31:04.00- 02
					HMar	70:31	70:31- 01
Biolková	Jana	CZE	18.5.74	179/61	3kSt	9:49.40	9:58.86- 02
Biondini	Silvia	ITA	24.1.76	166/58	TJ	13.91i, 13,67, 13.82w	14.15- 01
* Bisset	Sonia	CUB	1.4.71	171/69	JT	60.75	66.54- 01, 68.24#- 97
* Blackett	Andrea	BAR	24.1.76	160/54	400h	53.71	53.36- 99
Blake	Tanya	MLT	16.1.71	167/58	800	1:59.56	2:00.10- 98
Blewitt	Adriane	USA	24.5.80		SP	17.99	17.18- 02
					DT	55.20	
Bliss	Andrea	JAM	5.10.80		100h	13.18	13.68, 13.66w- 02
* Block	Zhanna	UKR	6.7.72	164/62	100	10.99	10.83- 02, 10.6- 97
					200	22.61	22.17A, 22.32- 97
Blondeel	Veerle	BEL	14.1.75	179/86	SP	16.58	16.54- 01
					DT	57.70	57.63- 00
Blonskaya ¶	Lyudmila	UKR	18.3.75	176/68	HJ	1.87dq	1.83- 02
					LJ	6.51dq	6.32- 02
					Hep	6316, 6425dq	6039- 02
Bloomfield/Grant	Tracey	GBR	13.9.79	168/59	PV	4.15	4.05- 02
Bocharova	Tatyana	KAZ	22.4.83	179/60	TJ	14.07	13.78- 02
Bódi	Bernadett	HUN	14.4.80	174/57	HJ	1.92i	1.86- 01
Bogachova	Irina	KGZ	30.5.61	167/52	Mar	2:28:06	2:26:27- 00
* Bogomolova	Galina	RUS	15.10.77	158/41	3000	8:50.62i	8:43.45- 00
					5000	15:13.08, 15:13.0+	15:08.61- 00
					10000	30:26.20	31:29.66- 00
Bolshova	Olga	MDA	16.6.68	174/60	TJ	14.24	14.17i, 14.15- 01
Bolsun	Yelena	RUS	25.6.82	168/60	200	23.23	24.09- 02
Bonaudo	Marion	FRA	12.9.82	174/65	JT	56.28	53.71- 01
Bonenko	Tatyana	UKR	7.6.76	164/57	200	23.15	23.06- 00, 22.8- 98
Bonne	Yuneydis	CUB	7.3.78	177/80	DT	56.05	57.62- 02
Boone	Rachelle	USA	30.6.81	163/59	100	11.22	11.33- 01
					200	22.87	22.99i- 02, 23.29, 22.94w- 01
Boonstra	Miranda	NED	29.8.72		3kSt	10:03.20	10:16.23- 02
Bordyugova	Zhanna	UKR	8.7.82	180/67	400h	56.89	58.02- 02
Borel	Cleopatra	TRI	3.10.79	170/88	SP	17.95i, 17.79	16.90, 17.50i- 02
* Boslak	Vanessa	FRA	11.6.82	169/58	PV	4.50	4.46- 02
Boswell (Clayton)	Michelle	USA	29.10.76		HT	65.35	62.96- 01
* Botezan	Mihaela	ROM	21.11.76	160/46	5000	15:10.69	15:08.78- 01
					10000	31:28.72	31:13.96- 02
					HMar	70:44+	69:24- 02
					Mar	2:25:32	0
Boucetta	Meryem	MAR	15.5.81		1500	4:08.02	4:12.37- 02
Bouchaouante	Yamina	FRA	31.7.80	164/58	3kSt	10:05.19	9:57.17- 02
Boulleret	Emilie	FRA	23.5.73	171/57	Hep	5815	5665- 01
Boyde	Kathrin	GER	4.12.70	172/62	20kW	1:32:34	1:30:42- 00
Boyko	Viktoria	UKR	20.1.74	180/85	DT	62.03	63.43- 01
Brägger	Anita	SUI	6.10.72	171/58	800	2:00.59	1:59.66- 01
Breisch	Becky	USA	16.3.83		SP	17.76	16.66- 02
					DT	58.69	55.67- 02
Bresciani	Maria Carla	ITA	16.7.73	171/64	PV	4.20i, 4.00, 4.10ex	4.20- 00
* Breuer	Grit	GER	16.2.72	166/60	400	51.13i, 52.26	49.42- 91
Breytenbach	Marlene	RSA	4.1.82		1500	4:10.24	4:16.19- 02
Brezgina (Bryukhach)	Marina	UKR	16.1.77	168/60	Hep	5826	6021- 00
Brice	Tremedia	USA			200	23.20w	23.61- 02
Brîndusoiu	Ileana	ROM	9.5.79	174/77	DT	59.96	58.33- 02
Brivule	Linda	LAT	9.9.83	185/74	JT	54.49	55.35- 02
Brkljacic	Ivana	CRO	25.1.83	170/65	HT	68.03	68.18- 00
Brown	Shandria	BAH	7.7.83		200	23.27	23.56, 23.12w- 02
Brown	Shelly-Ann	CAN	15.5.80		100h	13.42, 13.23w	13,34, 13.31w- 02
Brown	Stephanie	USA	1.8.79	196/105	SP	17.37	16.31- 01
					DT	57.78	54.11- 02
Browning	Danielle	JAM	29.8.81	170/62	100	11.48, 11.30w	11.79, 11.60w- 02
					200	23.21	24.15- 01
Bu Fanfang		CHN	10.2.78		400	52.23	51.35- 01
Budileanu	Veronica	ROM	27.2.76	179/58	20kW	1:35:12	1:37:35- 99
Budniak	Julia	POL	4.3.81	166/53	3kSt	10:02.22	9:52.77- 02
Bui Thi Nhung		VIE	21.1.83		HJ	1.88	1.83- 01
Bulikiobo	Makelesi	FIJ	23.10.77		400	52.01	
Bundy	Teresa	USA	14.2.79		TJ	13.79	13.59, 13.79w- 02
Bunjes	Andrea	GER	5.2.76	175/80	HT	69.33	67.57- 02
Burgher	Michelle	JAM	12.3.77	170/67	400	52.05	52.45- 00

Name		Nat	Born	Ht/Wt	Event	2003 Mark	Pre-2003 Best
Burika	Gelete	ETH-Y	15.2.86		1500	4:10.82, 4:10.8+	
					1M	4:30.81	
					3000	8:48.93	
Burkhardt	Anja	GER	13.10.81	187/103	SP	16.60	16.20- 02
Burnett	Marian	GUY	22.2.76	156/50	800	2:01.71	2:02.56- 02
* Burrell	Shelia	USA	15.1.72	173/64	Hep	6159	6472- 01
Burykina	Yelena	RUS	7.5.72		1500	4:08.74	4:09.93- 02
					3000	8:52.00	9:16.09- 02
					5000	15:27.81	15:28.07- 01
					HMar	70:21	71:34- 02
					Mar	2:28:10	
* Buschbaum	Yvonne	GER	14.7.80	170/57	PV	4.70	4.65i, 4.64- 02
Butler	Kathy	GBR	22.10.73	175/55	5000	15:17.57	15:10.69- 98
Butor	Irina	BLR	26.2.80	167/59	Hep	6264	6268- 02
Buval	Patricia	FRA	22.1.76	168/57	100h	13.12	13.02, 12.98w- 01
Buzau	Cristina	ROM	12.4.76	176/76	HT	63.88	63.55- 02
Cadamuro	Stefania	ITA	23.2.79	178/57	HJ	1.87	1.91- 00
Cadienhead	Maresa	CAN	7.4.76	168/55	HJ	1.87i, 1.84	1.95- 02
Camara	Kadiatou	MLI	4.5.81	180/53	LJ	6.53	6.40- 02
Camarena	Jill	USA	2.8.82	180/91	SP	17.49	16.82i, 16.79- 02
Campbell	Amber	USA	5.6.81		HT	64.58	63.76- 02
* Campbell	Juliet	JAM	17.3.70	178/62	100	11.29	11.15- 02, 11.0- 95
					200	22.69	22.50- 99
* Campbell	Veronica	JAM	15.5.82	163/61	200	22.63i	22.39- 02
Cao Liping		CHN	8.11.78		DT	60.67	56.76- 02
Cao Xue		CHN	2.3.82		20kW	1:34:18	
Cárdenas	Regla M	CUB	21.1.75	186/77	Hep	5624	6306- 95
Carman	Tina	SLO	8.1.78		LJ	6.56	6.45- 02
Carruthers	Danielle	USA	22.12.79	173/62	100h	12.79	12.68- 02
Carter	Michelle	USA-J	12.10.85		SP	16.73	16.25- 02
* Casandra	Cristina	ROM	1.2.77	168/50	3kSt	9:40.49	9:33.16- 02
Castells	Berta	ESP-J	24.1.84	174/73	HT	65.70	64.99- 02
Castrejana	Carlota	ESP	25.4.73	188/67	TJ	14.32i, 14.17	14.51- 02
Castro	Luz Dary	COL	30.5.78		SP	16.59	16.21- 00
					DT	55.65	55.37A- 01
Ceccarelli	Benedetta	ITA	23.1.80	170/51	400h	56.49	56.80- 02
Centeno	Yesenia	CUB/ESP	27.6.71	157/47	10000	31:49.58	34:48.5- 93
					HMar	69:59	74:40- 01
Cepero	Olga Lidia	CUB	4.2.75	178/66	TJ	13.70, 13.80w	14.43- 98
* Ceplak	Jolanda	SLO	12.9.76	168/55	800	1:57.44	1:55.19- 02
					1000	2:38.03i	2:31.66-02
					1500	4:02.44	4:05.44i, 4:05.59- 02
Cérival	Jessica	FRA	20.1.82	185/	SP	16.89	15.36- 02
Cervantes	Dana	ESP	18.8.78	166/63	PV	4.35	4.36- 02
Chaabi	Bouchra	MAR	22.9.80	162/50	1500	4:08.33	
					5000	15:32.97	16:28.02- 02
					3kSt	9:54.43	
Chang Jung-yeon		KOR	6.4.77	174/74	JT	56.90	56.64- 02
Charalambous	Irene	CYP	18.5.78		LJ	6.46	6.30- 01
Chavdarova	Vera	BUL	19.11.80		PV	4.20	4.03- 02
Checchi ¶	Cristiana	ITA	8.7.77	183/86	SP	18.64i, 17.91	17.48- 02
Chelagat	Anne	KEN	4.6.69		Mar	2:29:23	2:32:18- 02
Chelangat	Alice	KEN	.77		HMar	70:23	69:10- 02
Chemjor	Magdalene	KEN	12.11.78		HMar	69:39	70:32- 01
Chemweno	Elizabeth	KEN	13.7.78		HMar	71:13	
Chen Xiaofang		CHN	28.10.81		3kSt	9:50.88	
Cheng Xianhong		CHN	24.10.68		DT	56.39	66.00- 97
^ Cheng Xiaoyan		CHN	30.11.75	174/100	SP	17.94	20.02- 94
* Chepchumba	Joyce	KEN	6.11.70	160/52	HMar	69:53	68:18- 00
					Mar	2:26:06	2:23:22- 99
Chepchumba	Rose	KEN			HMar	71:15	
* Chepkemei	Susan	KEN	25.6.75	164/48	HMar	67:51	65:44- 01
					Mar	2:23:12	2:23:19- 02
Cheptanui	Carolyn	KEN	21.3.81		Mar	2:30:22	
Cherepanova	Natalya	RUS	9.3.67		3kSt	9:50.29	9:51.21- 02
Cherkasova	Svetlana	RUS	20.5.78	171/56	800	1:59.28	1:57.59- 01
					1500	4:05.55	4:12.39- 00
Chernogorova	Olga	BLR	30.1.82	182/90	DT	58.50	55.14- 02
Chernova	Lada	RUS	1.1.70		JT	56.16	58.88- 01, 61.34#- 96
^ Chernyavskaya	Olga	RUS	17.9.63	180/80	DT	66.59	68.38- 92
Chernyavskaya	Yekaterina	UKR	31.1.83	172/55	TJ	13.75	13.19- 02

Name		Nat	Born	Ht/Wt	Event	2003 Mark	Pre-2003 Best
Chernyavskaya	Yelena	RUS	13.4.78	175/67	Hep	6137	6384- 00
Cherry ¶	Damu	USA	29.11.77		100h	12.68dq	12.85- 01
* Chiba	Masako	JPN	18.7.76	155/38	HMar	70:06	66:43- 97
					Mar	2:21:45	2:25:11- 02
Chibisova	Oksana	RUS	31.3.77	177/87	SP	17.79i, 17.67	18.20- 02
* Chicherova	Anna	RUS	22.7.82	180/56	HJ	2.04i, 2.00	2.00i- 02, 1.92- 01
Chilla	Mercedes	ESP	19.1.80	165/54	JT	59.22	57.91- 00
Chirita	Rodica	ROM	28.10.76	159/45	10000	32:35.48	34:26.62- 94
Chizhenko	Yuliya	RUS	30.8.79	166/54	1500	4:07.21	4:16.79- 02
Choi Kyung-hee		KOR	13.9.81	160/46	Mar	2:30:57	2:34:21- 02
* Chojecka/Okninska	Lidia	POL	25.1.77	163/47	1000	2:36.97i	2:40.49- 98
					1500	4:03.58i, 4:08.73	3:59.22- 00
					3000	8:48.95i	8:31.69- 02
					5000	15:24.29	15:04.88- 02
Chrust	Marta	POL	29.9.78	161/51	400h	56.89	58.52- 02
Chu Chunxia		CHN	28.1.78	182/60	JT	54.78	59.85- 01, 61.91#- 98
Chukwuemeka	Vivian	NGR	4.5.77	178/90	SP	18.43	18.17- 02
					DT	56.92	56.12- 02
Chumakova	Olesya	RUS	23.7.81		1500	4:09.08i, 4:11.75	4:08.40- 02
Chung Yun-hee		KOR	3.1.83		Mar	2:30:50	2:33:22- 02
Church	Alexandra	AUS-J	14.1.84		HJ	1.87i, 1.85	1.82- 02
Chzhao	Larisa	RUS	4.2.71		800	1:58.71	1:59.85- 02
Cîmpanu	Daniela	ROM	17.12.82	164/47	800	2:02.01	2:07.62- 02
					1500	4:11.34	4:20.17- 02
* Cîmpean	Norica	ROM	22.3.72	164/58	20kW	1:30:27	1:27:46- 99
Ciobanu	Lucica	ROM	10.5.79	175/80	SP	18.24	18.94- 00
* Cioncan	Maria	ROM	19.6.77	172/51	800	1:59.68	2:04.37- 99
					1500	4:02.80	4:02.10- 02
Cîrlan	Daniela	ROM	18.9.80	162/45	20kW	1:32:41	1:31:30- 00
Claretti	Clarissa	ITA	7.10.80	170/70	HT	67.43	68.23- 02
Clark	Hazel	USA	3.10.77	178/55	800	2:01.71	1:58.75- 00
Clarke	Georgie	AUS-J	17.6.84	170/48	3000	8:56.63mx	9:01.7mx- 00
Clarke	Tameka	BAH	9.11.80		100	11.33	11.61, 11.57w- 02
Claxton	Sarah	GBR	23.9.79	165/57	100h	13.12	13.36- 01,, 13.28w- 98
Clay	Julian	USA	2.11.77	168/54	400	51.98	54.63 '95
Cleary	Dawn	USA	24.11.79		3kSt	9:59.30	10:03.13- 02
Clifton	Christine	USA	2.8.72		HMar	71:31	70:37- 01
Clitheroe (Pattinson)	Helen	GBR	2.1.74	168/57	1500	4:07.16	4:01.10- 02
* Cloete	Hestrie	RSA	26.8.78	185/68	HJ	2.06	2.04- 99
* Collins	Michelle	USA	12.2.71	176/62	200	22.18i	22.57- 00
Collins	Roberta	USA	31.7.77	170/122	DT	58.66	58.64- 01
Collins	Sonja	USA	28.2.82		200	23.28	23.67- 02
^ Collonvillé	Marie	FRA	23.11.73	163/54	Hep	6007	6350- 97
Conde	Maria José	POR	26.8.80	159/64	HT	63.70	61.30- 02
Console	Rosaria	ITA	17.12.79	160/42	HMar	69:56	72:32- 01
					Mar	2:27:48	2:30:55- 01
Coons	Leslie	USA	16.7.73	175/74	HT	65.66	66.23- 02
Cosby	Jessica	USA	31.5.82	173/77	SP	17.01	17.38- 02
* Coslovich	Claudia	ITA	26.4.72	170/70	JT	62.70	65.30- 00, 65.55#- 98
Costa	Keila	BRA	6.2.83		LJ	6.52	6.46- 02
					TJ	13.68, 13.69w	14.00, 14.15w- 01
Costa	Kira	USA-J	18.3.85	165/52	PV	4.18	3.81- 02
Coutinho	Geisa	BRA	1.6.80		200	23.10	23.47- 02
					400	51.44	51.50- 02
Cox	Crystal	USA	28.3.79	190/73	100	11.41	11.64, 11.46w- 99
					200	22.96	23.02, 22.70w- 02
					400	51.84	53.66- 98
Cox	Shana	USA-J	22.1.85		200	23.24	23.14- 02
Cozens	Chlöe	GBR	9.4.80	174/68	JT	54.62	51.79- 00
Craig	Alicia	USA	14.6.82		5000	15:25.75	
Craig	Alicia	USA	14.6.82		10000	32:40.03	
Crawford	L'Orangerie	USA	2.12.81	183/	SP	16.63	16.36- 02
					HT	63.91	62.62- 02
* Crawford	Yunaika	CUB	2.11.82	165/75	HT	70.69	70.62- 02
Crichlow	Desiree	BAR-J	1.6.84	170/57	HJ	1.88A	1.75- 98
Cripps	Sharon	AUS	29.6.77	165/56	100	11.47, 11.31w	11.38, 11.0w-02, 11.31w-98
					200	22.84	22.97- 02, 22.94w- 01
Cucerzan	Alina	ROM	28.7.74	160/42	800	2:02.38	2:05.44- 93
					1500	4:05.80	4:13.13- 99
					3kSt	9:54.36	9:59.77- 02
Cullen	Fiona	AUS	31.8.79	172/64	100h	13.30, 13.0, 13.14w	13.19- 02

	Name		Nat	Born	Ht/Wt	Event	2003 Mark	Pre-2003 Best
	Culpepper	Shayne	USA	3.12.73	165/55	1500	4:09.10	4:07.99- 00
						3000	8:56.26i	
						5000	15:23.59	15:31.49- 00
						10000	32:24.70	
*	Cumbá	Yumileidi	CUB	11.2.75	183/100	SP	19.31	19.48- 00
*	Cummins	Diane	CAN	19.1.74	165/50	800	1:58.89	1:58.39- 01
						1000	2:38.24i	
	da Costa	Raquel	BRA	30.12.83		400h	57.51	58.50- 02
	Dahm	Brianna	USA	13.3.82		3kSt	10:04.14	10:01.77- 02
	Daigle	Angela	USA	28.5.76	157/57	100	11.36, 11.28w	11.37, 11.33w- 00
	Daley	Jenice	JAM	13.8.78	176/62	200	23.27	24.15- 02
	Dalla Piana	Silvia	ITA	3.2.75	173/60	Hep	5726	5795- 00
	Dambacher	Luciane	BRA	10.5.76	176/61	HJ	1.88A	1.88- 99
	Damm	Shaina	USA	16.1.80		Hep	5622	5321- 02
	Danisová ¶	Martina	SVK	21.3.83	180/100	HT	64.43, 66.36dq	68.50- 01
*	Danvers	Natasha	GBR	19.9.77	175/61	100h	12.96	13.20- 98, 12.8w- 99
						400h	54.02	54.94- 01
	Darmovzalová	Martina	CZE	12.10.78	172/54	TJ	13.98i, 13.39	13.98- 02
	Daunay	Christelle	FRA	5.12.74	163/43	10000	32:39.11	-
	Davenport	Marie	IRL	24.1.75		5000	15:24.54	15:29.83- 02
						HMar	70:57	
	Davis	Kia	USA	23.5.78		100h	13.18	13.08, 12.94w- 02
	Davis	Meredith	USA	9.6.79		Hep	5672	
	Davoren	Freda	IRL	16.3.73		1500	4:07.56	4:10.13- 01
	Davy	Nadia	USA	24.12.80	168/55	400	50.66	53.78- 00
*	Davydova	Alla	RUS	21.5.66	167/86	HT	69.17	68.47- 00
	Davydova	Natalya	RUS	24.11.78		JT	56.84	55.31- 02
	Dawkins	Marsha	JAM	5.1.81		400	51.43	
	Day	Sharon	USA-J	9.6.85		HJ	1.88	1.80- 02
	De Angeli	Virna	ITA	27.2.76	170/56	400	52.34	51.31- 97
^	de Reuck	Colleen	USA	13.4.64	164/47	HMar	70:00	68:38- 89
						Mar	2:28:01	2:26:35- 96
	de Wilt	Monique	NED	21.3.76	170/68	PV	4.45i	4.44i, 4.40- 02
	Debelaya	Tatyana	UKR	28.1.70	174/64	400h	56.60	55.67- 99
*	Defar	Meseret	ETH	19.11.83	155/42	3000	8:38.31	8:40.28- 02
						5000	14:40.34	15:08.36- 00
	Dejaeghere	Veerle	BEL	1.8.73	164/52	1500	4:05.36	4:05.05- 02
						1M	4:29.93	4:31.59- 99
	Delinikóla	Vasiliki	GRE	9.2.81		Hep	5909	5441- 02
	Dementiy	Yelena	UKR	6.3.69	180/82	SP	17.01	18.00- 01
	Demidenko	Svetlana	RUS	16.2.76	164/54	Mar	2:30:34	2:29:56- 02
*	Demus	Lashinda	USA	10.3.83	172/62	400	51.79i	51.24- 02
						400h	55.65	54.70- 02
	Demut	Katja	GER	21.12.83	176/60	TJ	13.74	13.27- 02
*	Denboba	Merima	ETH	21.8.74	168/48	3000	8:47.68	8:44.21- 99
						5000	15:07.46	15:06.08- 01
						10000	31:47.53	31:32.63- 99
	Denby	Nichole	USA	10.10.82	163/52	100h	12.98	13.17- 02
	Denisova	Lyubov	RUS	6.10.71	152/40	Mar	2:25:58	2:26:17- 02
	Dervéni	Evaggelia	GRE	2.5.80	167/79	HT	65.40	61.35- 01
	Désert	Solen	FRA	2.8.82	178/60	400	52.05	52.78- 02
	Desviat	Esther	ESP	27.1.82	162/48	800	2:00.76	2:02.86i, 2:03.53- 02
*	Devers	Gail	USA	19.11.66	160/55	100	11.11	10.82- 92, 10.8w- 95
						100h	12.45	12.33- 00, 12.29w- 02
*	Devetzí	Hrisopiyí	GRE	2.1.76	170/60	TJ	14.84i, 14.34	14.15- 02
	Dharsha	Damayanthi	SRI	13.2.75	168/60	400	52.12	51.05- 00
	Di Marco	Karyne	AUS	14.3.78	168/77	HT	66.85	65.71- 02
	Di Martino	Antonietta	ITA	1.6.78	169/57	HJ	1.96i, 1.90	1.98- 01
	Dia	Fabé	FRA	14.2.77	173/62	100	11.38w	11.31- 98
	Dias	Amanda	BRA-J	11.11.84		400h	57.27	58.86- 02
	Dias	Ana	POR	15.1.74	169/50	10000	31:48.32	31:39.52- 99
						HMar	70:28	
						Mar	2:28:49	
^	Díaz	Mari Cruz	ESP	24.10.69	161/47	20kW	1:32:10	1:36:09- 02
	Díaz	Roxana	CUB	17.5.81	167/58	200	22.69	22.80A, 22.87, 22.8- 02
	Díaz	Yudalis	CUB	20.9.79	164/58	400h	57.3	57.24- 01
*	Dibaba	Ejagayou	ETH	21.3.82		3000	8:48.7+	9:04.86- 01
						5000	14:41.67	15:32.31- 01
						10000	31:01.07	32:24.20- 01
*	Dibaba	Tirunesh	ETH-J	2.6.85	154/44	3000	8:43.6+	8:41.86- 02
						5000	14:39.94	14:49.90- 02

	Name		Nat	Born	Ht/Wt	Event	2003 Mark	Pre-2003 Best
	Dibelková	Barbora	CZE	26.5.83	172/58	20kW	1:33:24	1:39:24- 02
	Dickerson	Jukina	USA	7.8.81	173/90	HT	66.18	63.55- 02
*	Dietzsch	Franka	GER	22.1.68	183/95	DT	66.00	69.51- 99
	Dimitráki	Iríni	GRE	8.8.80		TJ	14.07	13.19- 02
	Dimitrova	Mariya	BUL	7.8.76	170/55	TJ	14.17, 14.24w	14.28- 98
^	Dimitrova	Svetla	BUL	27.1.70	170/65	100h	13.01	12.53, 12.50w- 94, 12.4- 97
	Dinu	Alina	ROM	2.9.82	178/62	HJ	1.88i	1.86- 01
						TJ	14.32i, 14.17	14.00- 02
	Diouf	Aminata	SEN	18.2.77	172/60	100	11.47, 11.40w	11.24- 99, 10.9 98
	Diouf	Mame Tacko	SEN	17.10.76	169/57	400h	55.67	54.75- 99
	Ditton	Rosanna	AUS	7.6.79	166/63	PV	4.25	4.10- 02
	Divós	Katalin	HUN	11.5.74	180/84	HT	67.40	70.79- 01
*	Dixon	Vonette	JAM	26.11.75	169/62	100h	12.72	12.83- 01, 12.82w- 02
*	Dobrinskaya	Natalya	UKR	29.5.82	182/77	Hep	5877	5936- 02
	Dolgopolova	Lyudmila	BLR	11.8.69	160/53	20kW	1:33:24	1:29:23- 00
*	Domínguez	Marta	ESP	3.11.75	163/52	3000	8:41.14i, 8:50.6+	8:28.80- 00
						5000	14:48.33	14:58.12- 01
	Donáth	Katalin	HUN	12.11.79	161/50	PV	4.20	4.30- 00
	Dong Wangwei		CHN	28.6.81		Hep	5726	5436- 02
	Donkina	Yelena	RUS	15.3.73	180/64	LJ	6.60	6.81- 97
						TJ	14.26	14.58- 97
	Donovan	Jennifer	USA	4.5.82		3kSt	10:04.52	10:25.94- 01
	Dorsey	Ashley	USA	29.1.80		SP	16.81	16.75- 02
	Douma-Hussar	Carmen	CAN	12.3.77	170/57	1500	4:08.09	4:14.60- 02
	Dow	Joanne	USA	19.3.64	172/61	20kW	1:34:57.79t	1:33:27- 99
	Downer	Keisha	JAM	27.1.80	175/65	400h	55.77	
	D'Oyley	Toni Ann	JAM	25.10.81	180/64	100h	12.97	13.14- 01
*	Dragila	Stacy	USA	25.3.71	173/64	PV	4.78i, 4.62	4.81- 01
	Dragun	Oksana	BLR	19.4.81	170/60	100	11.31	11.54- 01
	Drazdauskaité ¶	Rasa	LTU	20.3.81	172/53	800	2:02.24	2:04.94- 01
						1500	4:07.78	4:12.35- 02
*	Drossin	Deena	USA	14.2.73	163/48	3000	8:48.66	8:42.59- 00
	(now Kastor)					5000	15:08.14	14:51.62- 00
						10000	31:17.86	30:53.02-02
						HMar	70:45+	70:08- 01
						Mar	2:21:16	2:26:53- 02
	Drybulska	Monika	POL	15.5.80	163/49	Mar	2:29:57	2:39:20- 02
	Dryburgh	Jenny	NZL	30.8.78	173/65	PV	4.20	4.35- 01
	Dryer	Elva	USA	26.9.71	165/51	5000	15:18.55	15:03.56- 01
						10000	31:26.88	
	du Toit	Maranelle	RSA	31.12.78		SP	17.04	17.30- 02
	Du Xianhui		CHN/SIN	4.1.81	188/90	SP	18.38	18.67- 02
	Dube	Winneth	ZIM	10.5.72	160/58	100	11.36	11.65- 02
						200	23.23A	23.74, 23.72w, 23.4- 02
	Dufour	Sylvie	SUI	24.1.79	176/65	Hep	6033	5502- 00
*	Dulecha	Kutre	ETH	22.8.78	168/48	1500	4:02.74	3:58.38- 98
	Duncan	Tracey	GBR	16.5.79	176/62	400h	57.46	56.53- 02
	Dunn	Debbie	JAM	26.3.78		200	23.01	23.22i- 00
						400	51.94	52.31- 00
	Dürr	Bianca	AUT	12.11.76		LJ	6.49	6.23- 98, 6.30w- 01
	Durst	Stephanie	USA	6.1.82	168/58	200	22.86	22.48, 22.46w- 02
	Dusmetova	Lilya	UZB	11.2.81		JT	54.63	54.07- 02
	DuToit	Andrea	USA	28.2.78	178/64	PV	4.23	4.25A- 02, 4.20- 01
*	Eagles	Bronwyn	AUS	23.8.80	176/95	HT	71.12	70.19- 01
	Earl	Chantee	USA	17.7.78	152/45	800	2:00.65	2:00.26- 02
	Ebor	Grace	NGR	8.8.77		800	2:02.04	2:03.12- 02
	Edem	Patient	NGR	15.10.83		100	11.35	11.60- 01, 11.1- 00
	Edwards	Jackie	BAH	14.4.71	172/64	LJ	6.68	6.80- 96, 6.89Aw- 95
*	Edwards	Torri	USA	31.1.77	163/52	100	10.93	11.06, 10.92w- 00
						200	22.28	22.65- 00
	Efedákí	Konstadína	GRE	1.10.78	162/48	1500	4:09.06	4:24.10- 96
						3000	8:57.76	9:40.51- 02
	Efimenko	Tatyana	KGZ	2.1.81	187/70	HJ	1.97	1.95- 99
	Eieland	Anne Gerd	NOR	28.12.82		HJ	1.93	1.86- 02
	Eisenlauer	Esther	GER	29.10.77	180/79	JT	54.55	54.24- 02, 56.02#- 97
	Ejigu	Sentayehu	ETH-J	.85	160/45	3000	8:46.51	8:48.30- 02
						5000	15:00.53	14:53.99- 02
	Ekimat	Jane	KEN	12.6.74		HMar	70:44	70:18- 00
*	El Kamch	Zhor	MAR	15.3.73	167/52	1500	4:11.27	4:08.09- 99
						3000	8:34.85	8:35.10- 02
						5000	14:42.53	15:01.34- 02

	Name		Nat	Born	Ht/Wt	Event	2003 Mark	Pre-2003 Best
*	Elisdóttir	Thórey Edda	ISL	30.6.77	181/64	PV	4.50i, 4.48sq, 4.43	4.51i, 4.45- 01
*	Ellerbe	Dawn	USA	3.4.74	186/111	HT	68.33	70.62- 01
	Ellis	Dana	CAN	7.12.78	163/56	PV	4.30	4.20A- 02
	Elmore	Malindi	CAN	13.3.80		1500	4:10.42	4:14.66- 01
	English	Una	IRL	14.8.70	181/61	3000	8:56.60	8:54.73- 02
*	Ennis-London	Delloreen	JAM	5.3.75	178/67	100h	12.70	12.52- 00
	Essarokh	Latifa	FRA	11.12.73	162/48	1500	4:06.07	4:17.62- 99
						1M	4:25.11	
	Etholm	Grete	NOR	25.1.76	183/72	DT	59.48	56.76- 99
	Etter	Andrea	SUI	21.1.75		3kSt	10:07.15	10:02.07- 02
*	Eve	Lavern	BAH	16.6.65	179/77	JT	62.89	64.78#- 89, 63.73- 00
^	Ezeh	Florence	FRA	29.12.77	173/96	HT	67.51	68.03- 02
	Fadeyeva	Yelena	UKR	23.6.66	168/53	1500	4:09.5	4:13.78- 00
	Fairs	Elizabeth	GBR	1.12.77	175/60	400h	57.06	58.48- 02
	Falaiye	Alice	CAN	24.12.78	168/55	LJ	6.57, 6.67Aw	6.63A, 6.46- 00, 6.51i- 01
	Fall	Fatou Bintou	SEN	23.8.81	166/67	400	51.12	52.15- 02
	Falzon	Stéphanie	FRA	7.1.83	170/66	HT	64.16	59.98- 02
	Fan Haixia		CHN	10.3.82		20kW	1:31:12	
	Farfaletti-Casali	Arianna	ITA	22.6.76	158/51	PV	4.15	4.31- 02
	Farmaka	Julia	CYP	20.4.78	176/56	HJ	1.90	1.86- 02
*	Faumuina	Beatrice	NZL	23.10.74	185/125	DT	65.53, 65.35	68.52- 97
	Faustin	Nadine	HAI	14.4.76	160/56	100h	12.82	12.80- 00
*	Favor Hamilton	Suzy	USA	8.8.68	160/44	1500	4:01.69	3:57.40- 00
*	Febbraio	Surita	RSA	27.12.73	168/58	400	52.22A, 52.43	52.40A- 02
						400h	54.05A, 54.31	54.10A, 54.48- 01
	Fedoseyeva	Yelena	RUS	18.3.83		HJ	1.90	1.84- 00
*	Fedoskina	Natalya	RUS	25.6.80	167/52	20kW	1:28:17	1:26:50- 01
	Fedotova	Tatyana	RUS	19.9.80	167/68	JT	59.81	56.08- 02
^	Fedyushina	Valentina	AUT	18.2.65	190/90	SP	17.04	21.60i- 91, 21.08- 88
*	Feitor	Susana	POR	28.1.75	160/52	20kW	1:29:08	1:27:55- 01
*	Felicien	Perdita	CAN	29.8.80	163/63	100h	12.53	12.73- 01
*	Felix	Allyson	USA-J	18.11.85	168/57	100	11.29, 11.12w	11.40- 02
						200	22.11A, 22.51	22.83, 22.69w- 02
						400	52.26	55.01- 02
	Félix	Aurélie	FRA	26.3.79	180/60	LJ	6.57	6.85- 99
	Félix	Sylviane	FRA	31.10.77	174/58	100	11.28	11.15- 98
						200	22.76i, 22.99	22.56- 97
	Feng Yun		CHN	23.2.76	170/60	100h	13.04	12.85- 99
*	Fenn	Joanne	GBR	19.10.74	172/55	800	1:59.74i, 2:00.56	1:59.86- 02
						1000	2:38.45i	0
*	Fenton	Lorraine	JAM	8.9.73	174/59	200	23.16	22.63- 01
						400	49.43	49.30- 02
*	Feofanova	Svetlana	RUS	16.7.80	162/52	PV	4.80i, 4.75	4.78- 02
*	Ferga-Khodadin	Linda	FRA	24.12.76	169/51	100h	12.86, 12.84w	12.67- 01
*	Ferguson	Debbie	BAH	16.1.76	167/59	100	10.97	10.91- 02
						200	22.50A, 22.65	22.19- 99
*	Fernández	Adriana	MEX	4.4.71	163/59	5000	15:04.32	15:14.33- 99
						10000	31:13.75	31:10.12- 00
						HMar	69:28	70:21- 02
						Mar	2:29:54	2:24:06- 99
	Fernández	Anaelys	CUB	15.12.79	180/93	DT	62.09	58.86- 02, 62.75ex- 99
	Fernández	Nuria	ESP	16.8.76	168/58	1500	4:03.57	4:03.99- 02
	Fernández	Yudelkis	CUB-J	28.2.85		LJ	6.69	6.38- 02
						TJ	14.03	
	Ferrales	Yania	CUB	28.7.77	180/86	DT	62.00	59.04- 02
	Ferrara	Ornella	ITA	17.4.68	153/40	Mar	2:28:28	2:28:01- 97
	Feusi	Martina	SUI	17.6.74	168/62	100	11.43, 11.30w	11.36- 02
	Firova	Tatyana	RUS	10.10.82	178/64	400	51.43	52.94- 01
	Fitchen-Young	Kim	USA	3.9.68	178/55	10000	32:39.10	32:14.64- 01
	Fitidou	Anna	CYP	22.4.77	160/57	PV	4.30	4.05- 02
	Flanagan	Shalane	USA	8.7.81		5000	15:20.54	16:29.68- 02
	Fleshman	Lauren	USA	26.9.81		5000	15:12.71	15:35.59- 02
^	Flosadóttír	Vala	ISL	16.2.78	180/67	PV	4.30	4.50- 00
	Floyd	Ebony	USA	21.10.83		200	23.27, 23.06w	
						400	52.16	53.80- 02
	Fokina	Natalya	UKR	7.7.82	178/80	DT	63.11	59.88- 01, 60.54irr- 02
	Forrester	Nicole	CAN	17.11.76	192/72	HJ	1.90A	1.94- 01
*	Foster	Brigitte	JAM	7.11.74	170/62	100	11.17	11.54- 00
						100h	12.45	12.49- 02
	Fountain	Hyleas	USA	14.1.81	170/60	LJ	6.51	
						Hep	5999	5673w- 02

Name		Nat	Born	Ht/Wt	Event	2003 Mark	Pre-2003 Best
Fouquet	Virginie	FRA	9.9.75	162/48	800	2:00.93+	1:59.78- 02
Fournier	Michelle	CAN	9.5.77	176/86	HT	63.70	65.63- 00
Fox	Jessica	USA		175/60	400	51.92A, 51.93	53.31A- 02
Frajka	Xénia	HUN	24.1.82	178/66	JT	58.12	56.65- 02
França	Luciana	BRA	19.5.77	167/58	400h	57.14	57.45- 99
Frauendorf	Manuela	GER	21.11.78	187/90	SP	17.27i, 17.26	16.90- 02
Freberg	Karen	USA	30.9.82	183/122	SP	17.01	16.34- 01
Freeman	Cathy	AUS	16.2.73	164/52	400	51.66	48.63- 96
Friedrich	Ariane	GER-J	10.1.84	178/60	HJ	1.88	1.86- 02
Friedrich	Dörthe	GER	21.6.73	174/68	JT	56.73	64.46- 02, 65.25#- 98
Friedrich	Kathleen	GER	13.7.77	174/57	1500	4:09.42i, 4:15.24	4:04.27- 01
Frunza	Alina	ROM	17.4.79	182/100	SP	16.85	17.56i- 01, 17.31- 99
Fuentes-Pila	Zulema	ESP	25.5.77	166/52	1500	4:09.25	4:08.39- 02
Fujii	Hiromi	JPN	7.2.83	170/46	5000	15:32.97	15:47.11- 02
					HMar	70:26	70:05- 02
Fujikawa	Aki	JPN	14.11.78	159/43	5000	15:34.14	15:34.29- 98
					10000	31:59.06	32:14.35- 98
					HMar	71:08	70:22- 98
					Mar	2:30:13	2:27:42- 99
Fujita	Ayumi	JPN	2.11.77	165/50	100h	13.26	13.43- 01, 13.30w- 99
* Fukushi	Kayoko	JPN	25.3.82	161/45	3000	8:49.10	8:44.40- 02
					5000	15:09.02	14:55.19- 02
					10000	31:10.57	30:51.81- 02
* Fynes	Savatheda	BAH	17.10.74	165/58	100	11.36	10.91- 99, 10.7w- 95
Fyodorova	Olga	RUS	14.7.83	175/67	100	11.31	11.51, 11.42w- 02
Gabito	Lerma Elvira	PHI	17.10.74	163/53	LJ	6.50	6.46 -02
Gadi	Hafida	FRA	14.7.74	167/47	Mar	2:30:38	2:52:37- 01
* Gaines	Chryste	USA	14.9.70	170/57	100	10.86	10.89- 98
					200	22.67	22.81- 93, 22.53w- 97
* Galkina	Lyudmila	RUS	20.1.72	172/58	LJ	6.74	7.05- 97, 7.08w- 99
Gallagher	Shannon	USA	10.3.75	165/59	PV	4.20i, 4.17	4.21- 02
Gamanyuk	Lyudmila	UKR	11.10.77	172/70	JT	57.27	56.67- 02
Gamble	Nicole	USA	21.6.77	163/55	TJ	13.77, 13.90w	14.05i, 14.08w- 99
Gao Kelian		CHN	15.8.83	165/55	20kW	1:29:39	1:29:39- 01
* Gao Shuying		CHN	28.10.79	180/63	PV	4.40	4.52- 01
García	Adoración	ESP	19.7.76	163/48	800	2:02.17	2:02.06- 99
					1500	4:05.18	4:04.64- 02
García	Alejandra	ARG	13.6.73	172/58	PV	4.31	4.42- 00
García	Magalys	CUB	23.10.71	178/71	Hep	5864	6352- 96
García	Yusmelys	VEN	19.12.83	165/48	400h	57.09	57.84- 02
Gargallo	Maria Teresa	ESP	15.10.69	162/46	20kW	1:30:41	
Gatto	Laura	ITA	4.3.77	170/58	LJ	6.45, 6.46w	6.48- 99
Gavelin	Lena	SWE	26.2.74		Mar	2:30:39	2:31:58- 01
* Gavrila	Adelina	ROM	26.11.78	174/55	TJ	14.76i, 14.75	14.71- 99
Gavrilovic	Sanja	CRO	20.9.82		HT	67.72	61.59- 02
* Gay	Mabel	CUB	5.5.83	185/71	TJ	14.52	14.29-02
Geissler	Kathrin	GER-J	10.6.85		Hep	5631	5318- 02
Gemechu	Shitaye	ETH	80		HMar	70:46+	71:43- 02
					Mar	2:27:26	2:26:15- 02
Geng Aihua		CHN	29.6.83		JT	56.24	56.08- 01
* George	Anju Bobby	IND	19.4.77	170/62	LJ	6.70	6.74- 01
Gérance	Fanny	FRA	4.1.81	171/61	100h	13.34, 13.12w	13.21- 00, 13.10w- 02
Gerber	Laura	SUI	29.10.80	170/58	800	2:01.39	2:06.08- 01
Gerraughty	Laura	USA	29.7.83	175/93	SP	18.82	17.57- 02
Gertenbach	Marisa	RSA	20.10.82	177/65	HJ	1.90	1.90A- 01, 1.88- 00
* Gesell	Claudia	GER	18.12.77	170/59	800	1:58.93	1:58.34- 00
Gestsdóttir	Sunna	ISL	27.6.76		LJ	6.47w	6.24- 01
* Gevaert	Kim	BEL	5.8.78	170/60	100	11.21	11.15- 02
					200	22.64	22.53- 02
Ghosh	Shanta	GER	3.1.75	168/56	400	52.30	51.25- 01
Giesa	Ulrike	GER-J	16.8.84	183/90	DT	55.92	51.99- 02
Gigi	Asha	ETH	15.10.73		10000	31:48.31	32:25.74- 02
					Mar	2:31:01	
Gilreath	Erin	USA	11.10.80		HT	64.83	54.28- 02
Gîndila	Mihaela	ROM	29.10.74	178/62	TJ	14.02i, 13.96	14.43, 14.44w- 02
* Giordano	Rossella	ITA	1.12.72	170/51	20kW	1:29:14	1:29:12- 97
* Girard	Patricia	FRA	8.4.68	162/48	100	11.45, 11.10w	11.11- 94
					100h	12.74, 12.69w	12.59- 96
Givens	Tongula	USA	3.3.73		TJ	13.75i	13.10- 01
Glavatskikh	Irina	RUS-J	29.12.84	180/56	HJ	1.87	1.85- 02
Glenn	Brianna	USA	18.4.80	168/55	100	11.41w	11.33- 00, 11.15w- 01
					LJ	6.59	6.65A, 6.47- 00, 6.56i- 01

	Name		Nat	Born	Ht/Wt	Event	2003 Mark	Pre-2003 Best
	Gliznutsa	Inna	MDA	18.4.73	184/65	HJ	1.91i, 1.90	1.95- 99
*	Glover	Sandra	USA	30.12.68	173/59	400h	53.34	53.33- 00
	Gnezdilov	Svetlana	ISR	20.7.69	170/58	100h	13.26, 13.22w	13.04- 01
						Hep	6031	5830- 02
*	Golding-Clarke	Lacena	JAM	20.3.75	168/57	100h	12.72	12.74, 12.70w- 02
	Golendukhina	Olga	RUS	14.11.81		400	51.98	53.17- 02
	Golubchikova	Yuliya	RUS	27.3.83	175/54	PV	4.30	4.35- 02
*	Gomes	Naide	POR	10.11.79	175/62	LJ	6.53	6.57- 02
						Hep	6120	6160- 02
^	Goncharenko	Svetlana	RUS	28.5.71	176/61	200	22.79	22.43i, 22.46, 21.9- 98
						400	50.93	50.23- 00
	González	Misleydis	CUB	19.6.78		SP	18.11	17.79- 02
	González	Norma	COL	11.8.82	172/53	100	11.34Aw	11.54A- 02
						200	23.18A	23.67- 01
*	Gorelova	Natalya	RUS	18.4.73	173/56	800	2:00.65	1:57.90- 99
						1500	4:00.72i. 4:03.83	3:59.70- 01
	Gorpynich	Valentina	UKR	12.3.83	160/49	3kSt	10:00.73	10:27.05- 02
	Gorton	Sara	USA	2.10.81	173/52	5000	15:24.97	15:51.55- 02
*	Gotovska	Valentina	LAT	3.9.65	176/63	LJ	6.71	6.91- 00
	Goucher	Kara	USA	9.7.78		1500	4:11.17	4:12.15- 00
	Goudenoúdi	Hrísa	GRE	28.3.77	164/54	400	52.11	51.81- 02
						400h	56.85	56.90- 00
*	Goulbourne	Elva	JAM	21.1.80	170/50	100	11.20	11.30- 01
						200	22.98	23.04- 02
						LJ	6.83, 6.96w	6.91i- 02, 6.86, 6.90w- 01
						TJ	13.78i	
*	Govorova	Yelena	UKR	18.9.73	175/53	TJ	14.81	14.96- 00, 14.99w- 99
	Gradzki	Monika	GER	21.9.79	172/59	800	2:00.96	2:02.52- 02
*	Graf	Stephanie	AUT	26.4.73	170/60	800	1:57.99	1:56.64- 00, 1:55.85i- 02
	Graham	Nolle	USA	12.9.81	167/59	100	11.21	11.47- 00, 11.45w- 01
	Grant	Billie Jo	USA-J	4.4.85		DT	55.93	53.91- 02
	Grant	Bisa	USA	10.7.76	166/61	100h	12.98	13.04, 12.95w- 00
	Grant	Stacy Ann	USA	18.8.77		HJ	1.89	1.88- 01
	Green	Rebekah	USA	19.9.80	175/86	SP	17.28i, 17.24	17.07- 01
	Greggs	Charlette	USA	20.10.83		200	23.18	
						400	51.65	54.08- 02
	Grenot	Libania	CUB	12.7.83		400	52.20	52.91- 01
	Gribule	Ilze	LAT-J	25.1.84	175/70	JT	56.38	54.46- 01
	Griffin	Maureen	USA	6.10.80	176/88	HT	63.55	64.37- 01
^	Grigorieva	Tatiana	AUS	8.10.75	172/60	PV	4.23	4.56- 01
*	Grigoryeva	Lydia	RUS	21.1.74	163/48	5000	15:18.3+	15:19.65- 00
						10000	30:57.83	31:21.27- 00
						HMar	69:32	70:48- 98
	Grigoryeva	Tatyana	RUS	13.5.81	180/62	HJ	1.96	1.88i- 01, 1.88- 02
	Gromova	Oksana	RUS	23.9.80		JT	61.12	58.36- 02
	Grosu	Cristina	ROM	11.11.76	176/58	3000	8:51.58i	8:55.22i- 02, 9:04.91- 01
	Groza	Ana Maria	ROM	1.6.76	167/53	20kW	1:35:46	1:29:59- 00
	Grzesiak	Joanna	POL	15.8.80	173/56	Hep	5818	5708- 02
*	Gu Yuan		CHN	9.5.82	168/70	HT	72.03	71.10- 02
*	Guan Yingnan		CHN	25.4.77	176/60	LJ	6.72	6.95- 00
	Gubkina	Lyudmila	BLR	13.8.73	174/76	HT	65.93	69.92- 00
*	Gudkova	Tatyana	RUS	23.1.78	170/60	20kW	1:28:37	1:25:18- 00
*	Guevara	Ana Gabriela	MEX	4.3.77	173/61	400	48.89	49.96, 49.70A- 00
	Guinaudeau	Christine	FRA	20.6.78	162/49	20kW	1:34:56.4t	1:39:19.4- 02
	Gulumyan	Oksana	RUS	8.12.82		400h	55.98	56.41- 02
	Guo Peng		CHN-J	21.6.84		HT	64.38	62.07- 02
	Gurova	Viktoriya	RUS	22.5.82	177/66	LJ	6.49i	
						TJ	14.37	14.22- 02
	Gushchina	Yuliya	RUS	4.3.83	173/59	400	51.94	53.26- 02
	Gutowicz-Westhof	Urszula	POL	13.7.77		LJ	6.53	6.12- 97
*	Győrffy	Dóra	HUN	23.2.78	175/55	HJ	1.96i, 1.94	2.00- 01
	Ha Mingming		CHN	15.4.82		20kW	1:30:26	1:33:02- 01
	Ha Xiaoyan		CHN	30.1.72		JT	54.55	59.90- 02, 65.44#- 93
	Hagiwara	Risa	JPN	22.11.82	160/44	Mar	2:28:14	
	Hagmann	Karin	SUI	9.3.74	185/80	DT	55.43	60.00, 61.22dq- 99
	Halkiá	Faní	GRE	2.2.79		400h	56.40	58.80- 02
	Halkoaho	Johanna	FIN	13.1.77	165/54	LJ	6.63, 6.65w	6.79- 98
	Hall	Monique	USA	9.10.80		200	23.09	23.41- 01, 23.28w- 01
	Ham Bong-sil		PRK	24.7.74	155/44	Mar	2:25:31	2:26:23- 02
*	Hamácková	Pavla	CZE	20.5.78	170/66	PV	4.60	4.56i- 01, 4.47
	Hamilton	Melina	NZL	15.6.76	172/64	PV	4.40	4.25- 02

	Name		Nat	Born	Ht/Wt	Event	2003 Mark	Pre-2003 Best
	Hanaoka	Maho	JPN	3.8.76	171/56	LJ	6.68, 6.69w	6.82- 01
						TJ	13.82	14.04- 99
*	Hansen	Ashia	GBR	5.12.71	170/63	TJ	15.01i	15.16i- 98, 15.15- 97
	Hara	Yumiko	JPN	9.1.82	163/45	10000	31:51.80	31:48.50- 01
						HMar	69:37	69:28- 02
	Harmon	Donita	USA	1.3.83		200	23.42, 23.17w	
	Harper	Dawn	USA-J	14.6.84		100h	13.33, 13.21w	
	Harrelson	Mary Jayne	USA	17.6.78	170/54	1500	4:09.58	4:07.37- 01
						1M	4:29.10	4:42.41- 00
	Harrison	Yvonne	PUR	2.12.75	178/64	400h	55.03	55.09- 00
	Hart	Bethany	USA	10.4.77		HT	67.98	64.69- 02
	Harvey	Natalie	AUS	19.1.75	164/50	3000	8:53.63	8:53.58mx- 00, 8:56.23- 02
			(now GBR)			10000	32:23.68	32:07.44- 00
	Hashimoto	Naoko	JPN	8.9.82	154/41	10000	32:35.52	33:35.35- 02
						HMar	71:13	
	Hashimoto	Yasuko	JPN	12.8.75	162/47	10000	32:28.53	32:04.27- 02
						HMar	69:32	68:55- 01
						Mar	2:26:32	
	Hastings	Natasha	USA-Y	23.7.86		400	52.09	43.42- 02
	Haughton	Karlene	CAN	18.10.72	165/57	400h	57.35	55.11- 97
^	Hautala	Tiia	FIN	3.4.72	171/65	Hep	5883	6369- 99
*	Hayes	Joanna	USA	23.12.76	165/58	100h	12.83, 12.65w	12.67- 00
						400h	54.66	54.57- 99
	Haynes	Nicole	CAN	18.9.74	180/75	Hep	5969	6077- 00
	Hayward	Rosemary	AUS	10.11.80	183/68	400	52.24	52.76- 02
	He Xingtong		CHN-Y	11.2.86		20kW	1:35:30	
	Heaston	Kristin	USA	23.11.75	180/127	SP	18.33	17.59- 02
	Heidler	Betty	GER	14.10.83	175/79	HT	70.42	63.38- 02
	Hejnová	Michaela	CZE	10.4.80	167/62	Hep	5870	6032- 02
	Hejnová	Zuzana	CZE-Y	19.12.86	170/54	400h	57.54	58.42- 02
	Hellebaut	Tia	BEL	16.2.78	182/66	HJ	1.91	1.89- 00
						Hep	6019	5859- 01
	Henderson	Monique	USA	18.2.83	170/54	400	51.96	50.74- 00
	Hendry	Kelsie	CAN	29.6.82	170/59	PV	4.17	4.05- 02
*	Hennagan	Monique	USA	26.5.76	173/55	400	51.46	50.82- 00
	Henry	Carol	CAN	20.6.82		3kSt	10:03.44	9:51.16- 02
	Hentschke	Nadine	GER	27.1.82	175/58	100h	12.89	13.25- 01
	Herrmann	Aileen	GER-J	16.9.85	181/60	HJ	1.87	1.83- 02
	Herzenberg	Elena	GER	24.6.79	184/62	HJ	1.94i, 1.90	1.94i- 01, 1.91- 02
	Hessler	Stephanie	GER	16.3.83	166/65	JT	57.00	54.96- 02
^	Hewitt	Lauren	AUS	25.11.78	170/60	100	11.31w	11.28- 99, 11.18w- 00
						200	22.79	22.52- 00
	Hietalahti	Anita	FIN	17.2.77	177/75	DT	56.63	56.25- 00
	Hila	Elena	ROM	20.5.74	180/98	SP	18.15	18.73i- 99, 18.73- 02
*	Hill	Aretha	USA	14.8.76	181/98	DT	65.10	65.62dh- 98, 65.10- 02
	Hill	Chaytain	USA	13.10.82		TJ	13.67	12.96- 02
	Hinds	Korine	JAM	18.1.76	163/54	3kSt	10:00.44	9:58.9- 02
	Hingst	Carolin	GER	18.9.80	170/61	PV	4.51	4.50- 01
*	Hiroyama	Harumi	JPN	2.9.68	160/47	5000	15:31.78	15:03.67- 98
						10000	31:32.27	31:22.72- 97
						HMar	70:58	69:41- 01
	Hirpassa	Berhane	ETH	30.7.83	167/47	1500	4:08.01	4:07.44- 01
						1M	4:28.20	
						2000	5:43.16	5:49.07- 01
*	Hlavonová	Zuzana	CZE	16.4.73	178/60	HJ	1.92	2.00- 00
	Hoffmann	Claudia	GER	10.12.82	168/57	400	52.27	52.91- 02
	Hogan (Lott)	Tiffany	USA	1.8.75	170/61	100h	13.15	12.72A, 12.92, 12.8- 97
						Hep	6064	6211- 97
	Holinski	Kathryn	GER	19.7.82	178/61	HJ	1.92i, 1.87	1.93- 02
	Holliday	Becky	USA	12.3.80	160/52	PV	4.47	4.37- 01
	Holliness	April	USA	27.5.82	173/60	LJ	6.42, 6.47w	
	Hollman	Julie	GBR	16.2.77	180/69	Hep	6018	6135- 02
*	Holmes	Kelly	GBR	19.4.70	164/55	800	1:58.69	1:56.21- 95
						1000	2:38.47i	2:32.55- 97
						1500	4:01.96	3:58.07- 97
	Horioka	Tomoko	JPN-J	27.3.84	160/43	10000	32:33.66	
	Hotokourídou	María	GRE	22.5.77		HJ	1.87i	1.89- 01
	Howard	Chaunte	USA-J	12.1.84		HJ	1.89	1.87- 02
	Howe	Kym	AUS	12.6.80	176/63	PV	4.30	4.45- 02
	Hu Ming		CHN-J	8.10.84		20kW	1:35:02	1:34:25- 01
	Huang Jianfen		CHN	10.10.78		LJ	6.49	6.51- 98

Name		Nat	Born	Ht/Wt	Event	2003 Mark	Pre-2003 Best
* Huang Qiuyan		CHN	25.1.80	168/60	TJ	14.39	14.72- 01
Huang Qun		CHN	12.4.79		DT	61.10	59.51- 00
Huang Xiaoxiao		CHN	3.3.83	171/51	400	51.93	52.71- 01
					400h	55.10	55.15- 01
Huhtaniemi	Paula	FIN	17.2.73	167/68	JT	64.90	63.05- 01
Hulsen	Kerryn	RSA	5.10.74		400h	57.46A, 57.60	56.19A- 02
Hunnicutt (Ota)	Yoko	JPN	14.1.75	174/51	HJ	1.90	1.95- 02
Hurd	Tiombe	USA	17.8.73	178/64	TJ	13.68, 13.96w	14.19i, 14.07- 01
* Hurtis	Muriel	FRA	25.3.79	180/68	100	11.08, 10.97w	10.96- 02
					200	22.41	22.31- 99
Hussein	Marwa Ahmed	EGY	19.6.78		HT	65.26	63.88- 02
Hyman	Mardrea	JAM	22.12.72	168/52	800	2:01.54	1:59.71- 98
					1500	4:06.36	4:05.25- 01
Iagar	Elena	ROM	16.1.75	173/54	800	2:02.09i	2:00.26- 99
					1500	4:07.44i	4:02.90- 02
Iakovídou	Thália	GRE	10.9.72	171/56	PV	4.25	4.22- 00
Iakóvou	Hristosomia	GRE	9.4.71	170/52	5000	15:15.32	15:20.46- 01
Iancu	Constanta	ROM	12.9.76	179/82	JT	57.37	56.69- 00
Ichikawa	Yoshiko	JPN	18.4.76	161/48	5000	15:30.90	15:20.53- 97
					10000	32:26.60	31:44.87- 02
					HMar	70:57	68:18- 97
Ichioka	Sumi	JPN	25.7.79	173/97	SP	16.67	16.49- 02
Ignatkina	Yuliya	RUS	13.9.82		LJ	6.55	6.12- 01
					Hep	5882	5771- 02
Ihuefo	Sorochukwu	NGR	20.6.79		JT	54.43	
Iijima	Nozomi	JPN-J	17.3.84	157/44	HMar	71:12	
Ikeda	Emi	JPN	29.8.83	158/40	10000	32:22.53	33:10.20- 02
Ikeda	Kumiko	JPN	10.1.81	166/53	100h	13.24, 13.23w	13.38- 01
					LJ	6.64	6.78- 01
Ilyina	Anastasiya	RUS	16.1.82	172/57	TJ	14.06	14.52- 00
Ilyushchenko	Tatyana	BLR	18.4.83	178/85	SP	16.89	16.66- 02
Imai	Miki	JPN	30.5.75	174/55	HJ	1.92	1.96- 01
* Ingberg	Mikaela	FIN	29.7.74	174/75	JT	63.55	67.32#- 97, 64.03- 00
Inman	Courtney	CAN	7.1.80		1500	4:10.93	4:15.14- 02
Inzikuru	Docus	UGA	2.2.82	158/47	3000	8:46.29	8:48.81- 02
					3kSt	9:39.51	
Ireland	Nicole	USA	23.4.82	178/66	200	23.15w	23.82- 02
					400h	56.10	57.43- 01
Irusta	Geovanna	BOL	26.9.75	157/48	20kW	1:33:42	1:34:37- 00
Isaila	Claudia	ROM	17.7.73	167/64	JT	58.82	66.56#- 94, 59.10- 01
Isakova	Yevgeniya	RUS	.78		400h	56.25	56.55- 01
Isane	Elin	NOR	18.4.75	178/82	DT	55.24	55.55- 99
* Isinbayeva	Yelena	RUS	3.6.82	174/65	PV	4.82	4.60- 02
* Ivakina	Yekaterina	RUS	7.12.64	168/67	JT	63.19	65.36#- 93, 64.89- 00
Ivanenko	Yelena	BLR	5.5.78	180/90	SP	18.29	19.13- 99
Ivankova	Olga	UKR	7.1.73	173/62	JT	54.27	57.75- 00, 60.94#- 96
Ivanova	Albina	RUS	16.5.77		HMar	71:24	73:54- 02
					Mar	2:25:35	2:29:53- 02
Ivanova	Alevtina	RUS	22.5.75		5000	15:18.4+?	
					Mar	2:29:06dh	2:30:25- 02
^ Ivanova	Alina	RUS	16.3.69	163/52	HMar	70:59	71:15- 99
					Mar	2:29:00	2:25:34- 01
Ivanova	Anastasiya	RUS	3.5.79	174/63	PV	4.40	4.30- 01
Ivanova	Lyubov	RUS	2.3.81		3kSt	9:24.78	10:14.60- 02
Ivanova	Nora	TUR	1.6.77	174/59	200	23.05i	22.71- 02
Ivanova	Olga	RUS	6.4.79		SP	17.60	16.30- 02
					DT	55.48	52.95- 02
Ivanova	Svetlana	RUS	30.6.83		3kSt	10:09.34	10:08.81- 02
Ivanova	Tatyana	RUS	22.1.76		HJ	1.90	1.90- 02
Ivanova	Tatyana	RUS	16.10.81		LJ	6.65i, 6.49, 6.64w	6.40- 02
Ivanova	Valentina	RUS	1.5.63	178/90	DT	60.30	65.12A- 01, 63.68- 00
Ivanova	Yelena	RUS	16.3.79		TJ	14.25	14.34i- 02, 13.83- 02
Ivanová	Lucia	SVK	8.7.80		100	11.33w	11.71- 99
					200	23.06	24.03, 24.00w- 99
Ivery	Lakadron	USA	23.6.83	170/57	100	11.28	11.68- 02
					200	23.04, 22.87w	23.92, 23.66w- 02
Ivlyeva	Inna	RUS	27.6.71		LJ	6.61i, 6.42	6.71i, 6.52, 6.59w- 01
Ivlyeva	Yelena	RUS	.74		Hep	5966	5846- 99
Iwamoto	Yasuyo	JPN	8.9.76	155/50	HMar	71:28	70:06- 01
Jaber	Najla	NED-J	12.5.84	173/56	800	2:01.76+, 2:01.84	2:05.67- 02
Jacob	Doris	NGR	16.12.81	155/55	400	51.41	51.04- 99

Name		Nat	Born	Ht/Wt	Event	2003 Mark	Pre-2003 Best
^ Jacobs	Regina	USA	28.8.63	168/51	800	2:00.01	1:58.08- 00
					1500	4:01.63	4:00.35- 00
					1500	3:59.98i	4:00.35- 99
					3000	8:52.57i	8:39.14i- 99, 8:39.56- 98
Jakubaitité	Indre	LTU	24.1.76		JT	57.33	57.88- 02
^ Jakubczak	Anna	POL	2.2.73	166/53	1500	4:09.51	4:01.43- 99
James	Aisha	TRI	12.3.81		LJ	6.78	6.30- 00
^ Jamieson	Jane	AUS	23.6.75	171/58	Hep	5908	6354- 98
Jankú	Inge	CZE	1.5.74	178/60	HJ	1.88i	1.91- 98
Janowska	Wioletta	POL	9.6.77	177/58	1500	4:10.31	4:07.84- 02
Janson	Lacy	USA	20.2.83	178/68	PV	4.45i, 4.37	4.27- 02
* Javornik	Helena	SLO	26.3.66	163/52	10000	31:56.90	32:44.40- 00
					HMar	71:03	71:45- 02
					Mar	2:28:13	2:28:15- 02
* Jayasinghe	Susanthika	SRI	17.12.75	170/62	100	11.20	11.04- 00
					200	23.16	22.28- 00
Jefferson	Nicole	USA	8.3.76		10000	32:37.18	32:12.93- 02
* Jenkins	LaTasha	USA	19.12.77	170/55	100	11.21A, 11.27, 11.04w	11.02- 01
					200	22.31A, 22.56	22.29, 22.22w- 99
Jensen	Heidi	DEN	14.8.66	173/65	800	2:01.73	2:01.11- 02
					1500	4:10.98	4:07.18- 02
Jeptoo	Rita	KEN	15.2.81		HMar	71:24	71:44- 01
Jerz	Connie	USA	26.4.82	165/62	PV	4.30	4.07- 02
Jeschelnig	Jackie	USA	19.11.79		HT	63.23	64.85- 02
* Jesien	Anna	POL	10.12.78	168/56	400h	55.38	55.11- 02
Jett	Kisha	USA	11.2.75	168/56	100h	13.16	13.03- 01
* Jevtic	Olivera	SCG	24.7.77	174/52	HMar	71:07	69:18- 02
					Mar	2:25:23	2:26:44dq- 02
Jia Lina		CHN	26.4.80		SP	17.89	18.41- 01
Jian Xingli		CHN	4.12.83		20kW	1:30:34	1:29:31- 01
Jiang Jing		CHN-J	23.10.85		20kW	1:29:42	
Jiang Ping		CHN	10.1.79		SP	17.25	18.59- 01
Jiang Qiuyan		CHN	5.7.83		20kW	1:30:03	1:30:13- 01
Jiménez	Carolina	ESP	2.2.80		20kW	1:32:49	1:37:35- 02
Jo Bun-hui		PRK	29.11.79		Mar	2:29:11	2:27:36- 02
Johansson	Camilla	SWE	3.11.76	166/52	TJ	14.15	14.14- 00, 14.17w- 01
John	Lwiza Msyani	TAN	18.5.80	156/48	800	2:01.68	1:59.58- 00
* Johnson	Benita	AUS	6.5.79	166/50	2000	5:37.71	
					3000	8:38.06	8:42.95, 8:42.75i- 01
					5000	14:54.52	14:47.60- 02
					10000	30:37.68	0
					HMar	69:26	0
Johnson	Chelsea	USA	20.12.83		PV	4.25	4.11- 02
* Johnson	Jade	GBR	7.6.80	185/72	LJ	6.69, 6.77w	6.73- 02
Johnson	Sheena	USA	1.10.82	163/53	100h	13.09	13.36- 02
					400h	54.24	55.71- 02
Jones	Ifoma	USA	4.9.77	168/60	HJ	1.91i, 1.90A	1.88i, 1.87- 99
* Jones	Kim	USA	13.6.81	163/60	100h	13.09	13.30- 02, 12.7w- 01
					LJ	6.46	6.43- 02
Jones	Laverne	ISV	16.9.81	171/59	100	11.37	11.77- 01
					200	23.16i, 23.26, 22.93w	24.30- 02
Jones	Lolo	USA	5.8.82	168/60	100h	12.90	12.84- 02, 12.7w- 01
Jones	Sharifa	USA	16.11.82		LJ	6.49	5.99- 02
Jones	Susan	GBR	8.6.78	179/62	HJ	1.93i, 1.89	1.95- 01
Jones	Teneeshia	USA	28.1.79	163/54	100	11.50, 11.26w	11.24- 00, 11.23w- 01
Jong Yong-ok		PRK	24.1.81		Mar	2:28:52	2:26:12- 02
Joseph	Restituta	TAN	30.7.71	164/56	3000	8:51.23i	8:44.28- 01
					5000	15:07.39, 15:04.73i	15:05.33- 01
					HMar	69:42	67:59- 00
Josephs	Janice	RSA	31.3.82	160/60	100	11.38A, 11.46, 11.39w	11.46- 02
					200	23.22	23.90- 02
					Hep	5740	5466A- 00
Joyce	Jennifer	CAN	25.9.80	175/80	HT	64.26, 64.50dh	65.23- 02
Ju Yinglan		CHN-J	10.10.84		3kSt	9:54.01	10:01.53- 02
Juhász	Fanni	HUN	31.3.81	169/58	PV	4.20	4.15- 01
Kadogan	Filiz	TUR	12.2.82	187/95	SP	17.16	15.80- 02
Kafetzí	Ioánna	GRE	30.5.76		100	11.40w	11.50- 01
^ Kähler	Birgit	GER	14.8.70	182/60	HJ	1.90	1.94- 91
* Kaliturina	Olga	RUS	9.3.76	180/57	HJ	1.95	1.97i- 02, 1.96- 97
Kallur	Jenny	SWE	16.2.81	171/63	100h	13.04	13.15, 13.11w- 01
* Kallur	Susanna	SWE	16.2.81	169/61	100h	12.88	12.74- 01

Name		Nat	Born	Ht/Wt	Event	2003 Mark	Pre-2003 Best
Kalmer	René	RSA	3.11.80	170/55	1500	4:07.69	4:08.94- 01
					3000	8:51.61	9:07.15- 00
* Kálovics	Anikó	HUN	13.5.77	175/60	5000	15:18.45	15:56.0- 02
					10000	31:40.31	32:16.4- 00
					HMar	69:48	69:16- 02
Kampf	Stephanie	GER	25.4.78	175/62	400h	55.35	55.86- 01
Kanazawa	Yvonne	JPN	19.11.74	173/65	100h	13.06	13.00, 12.90Aw- 00
Kankanpää	Tiina	FIN	16.8.76	178/80	DT	57.04	61.04- 99
Kano	Yuri	JPN	27.10.78	152/40	10000	32:23.67	32:25.68- 01
					HMar	70:28	71:58- 02
* Kapachinskaya	Anastasiya	RUS	21.11.79	176/64	200	22.38	22.6- 01, 23.24i- 00, 23.41- 02
					400	50.59	50.97- 01
Kappler	Bianca	GER	8.8.77	180/62	LJ	6.69	6.65- 02
Karagounis	Helen	GBR	28.9.81	170/68	400	51.78	51.97- 02
^ Kardopoltseva	Olga	BLR	11.9.66	170/56	20kW	1:29:46	1:28:51- 99
Kari	Monia	TUN	14.4.71	172/72	DT	58.46	61.74- 96
Kashcheyeva	Yelena	KAZ	17.2.73	175/58	LJ	6.62	6.76- 98
Kasova	Yana	BUL	13.8.81	174/62	100h	12.95	12.75- 02
* Kaspárková	Sárka	CZE	20.5.71	187/68	TJ	14.10	15.20- 97
Kasprzak	Róza	POL	9.4.82	174/60	PV	4.20	3.60- 82
Katkova (Savina)	Yevgeniya	UKR	21.4.76	166/50	PV	4.30	4.15- 02
Kaur	Harwant	IND	5.7.80		DT	57.76	60.10- 02
* Kavaklioglu	Ebru	TUR	14.3.70	167/58	3000	8:53.13	8:35.26- 01
					5000	15:04.22	14:51.69- 00
Kawasaki	Mayumi	JPN	10.5.80		20kW	1:32:16	1:34:45- 02
Kawashima	Makiko	JPN	5.8.77	159/41	10000	31:57.76	32:02.16- 01
					HMar	71:37	71:57- 98
Kayukova	Natalya	RUS	10.12.66	175/66	TJ	13.56, 14.22w	14.51- 99
Kazanina	Svetlana	KAZ	31.10.71	172/62	Hep	6181	6228- 99
* Keil	Susanne	GER	18.5.78	172/66	HT	71.93	68.17- 02
Keir	Krista	USA	19.12.79	178/109	SP	16.85i, 15.96	15.66- 02
					DT	56.72	56.98- 01
* Kelesídou	Anastasía	GRE	28.11.72	192/90	DT	67.14	67.70- 99
Keller	Katja	GER	9.8.80	175/62	LJ	6.52i, 6.38	6.47- 02
					Hep	5918	6082- 01
Kelo	Niina	FIN	26.3.80	178/69	Hep	5786	5728- 00
Kemasuode	Gloria	NGR	30.12.79		100	11.39, 11.18w, 11.1w	11.21- 02
					200	23.30	23.09- 02
Kéri	Andrea	HUN-J	3.7.84	178/70	HT	63.27	63.15- 02
* Kesselschläger	Sonja	GER	20.1.78	178/66	Hep	6175	6205- 02
Khalid	Norasheela	MAS	27.9.79		400h	56.90	58.70- 99
Khanafeyeva	Gulfiya	RUS	12.6.82	170/73	HT	68.92	63.26- 01, 64.50dq- 02
Kharun	Irina	UKR	22.1.82	176/73	JT	61.82	56.58- 02
Khine	Yin Yin	MYA	15.6.77		800	2:01.96	2:06.07- 02
Khmeleva	Tatyana	RUS	2.4.79		5000	15:15.40	15:35.70- 01
					HMar	70:20	71:25- 02
Kholosha-Motok	Yelena	UKR	26.1.82	183/56	HJ	1.90	1.90- 02
Khoroneko	Natalya	BLR	25.5.82	180/81	SP	18.05	17.25- 01
Khoroshikh	Yekaterina	RUS	21.1.83	172/73	HT	64.42	61.73- 02
* Khrushchelyova	Natalya	RUS	30.5.73	172/55	800	1:58.05	1:59.77- 02
Khubbieva	Guzel	UZB	2.5.76	165/59	100	11.30	11.37- 98
* Khudoroshkina	Irina	RUS	13.10.68	182/100	SP	19.31i, 18.81	20.32- 96
Kibiwott	Viola	KEN	22.12.83	157/45	1500	4:09.17	4:12.57- 02
					3000	8:40.14	8:47.59- 02
					5000	15:32.87	
Kidane	Etalemahu	ETH	.83		3000	8:54.83	9:11.55- 00
					5000	15:33.99	
* Kidane	Werknesh	ETH	21.11.81	158/42	3000	8:39.51	8:41.58- 02
					5000	14:33.04	14:43.53- 02
					10000	30:07.15	31:43.41- 01
Kilpeläinen	Natalia	FIN	19.7.70	168/59	LJ	6.49	6.46, 6.50w- 01
					TJ	14.18	14.10- 94
Kim Chang-ok		PRK	16.4.75	155/44	Mar	2:29:00	2:28:26- 02
Kim Mi-jung		KOR	10.6.79	165/56	20kW	1:33:03	1:34:47- 02
Kimuria	Emily	KEN	.75		HMar	71:27	
					Mar	2:28:18	2:34:57- 02
Kimutai	Hellen	KEN	28.12.77		HMar	70:46+	69:59- 00
					Mar	2:25:53	2:26:10- 02
Kinard	Vanitta	USA	26.7.75	178/58	TJ	13.72i, 13.71, 13.93w	13.90i, 13.88- 02
King	Rachel	GBR	11.5.76	167/57	100h	13.07	13.46- 99, 13.44w- 98
King	Tameisha	USA	24.2.81	173/64	LJ	6.48, 6.61w	6.35, 6.45w- 00

Name		Nat	Born	Ht/Wt	Event	2003 Mark	Pre-2003 Best
^ Kiplagat	Esther	KEN	8.12.66	168/50	HMar	71:00	69:55- 00
* Kiplagat	Lornah	KEN/NED	20.3.74	161/47	3000	8:54.91	8:52.82- 00
					5000	14:56.43	14:51.95- 02
					10000	30:12.53	
					HMar	70:21+	66:34- 01
					Mar	2:22:22	2:22:36- 00
Kirui	Susan	KEN	4.4.80		5000	15:23.52	16:37.5A- 02
Kiryashova	Aleksandra	RUS-J	21.8.85	162/54	PV	4.20i, 4.15	4.21- 02
Kislova	Marina	RUS	7.2.78	167/63	100	11.11	11.09- 01
					200	23.02	22.99- 00
Kita	Katarzyna	POL-J	4.7.84	168/94	HT	66.08	61.15- 02
Kitson	Judyth	JAM	2.11.79	170/67	100	11.26, 11.24w	11.59- 02
Kivine	Sirkka-Liisa	EST	22.6.77	172/56	TJ	13.76	13.69- 02
Klaas	Kathrin	GER-J	6.2.84	168/72	HT	63.72	57.74- 02
^ Klavina	Liga	LAT	27.1.80	180/69	Hep	6119	6279- 01
Klecková	Jana	CZE	19.3.75	175/55	Hep	5627	5678- 98
* Kleinert	Nadine	GER	20.10.75	190/90	SP	19.33i, 19.14	19.86- 01
Klimesová	Jarmila	CZE	9.2.81	172/78	JT	60.54	56.04- 00
Klimina	Svetlana	UZB	27.4.66		TJ	13.72	
Klishchevskaya	Kristina	UKR	17.12.74	172/70	JT	57.81	61.04- 02
Klocová	Lucia	SVK	20.11.83	176/53	800	2:00.60	2:01.59- 02
^ Klose (Münchow)	Kirsten	GER	21.1.77	172/75	HT	68.71	69.28- 00
* Klüft	Carolina	SWE	2.2.83	178/64	200	22.98	23.71- 02
					100h	13.18	13.33- 02
					HJ	1.94	1.92- 02
					LJ	6.86	6.48, 6.59w- 02
					Hep	7001	6542- 02
Kluge	Kathleen	GER	17.11.81	170/100	SP	17.64	17.37- 00
Klyuka	Svetlana	RUS	27.12.78	170/62	800	1:58.47	2:00.97- 02
Knippel	Anja	GER	19.8.74	166/57	800	2:00.81	2:00.11- 02
Kobayashi	Masayo	JPN	4.2.80	154/39	HMar	70:14	71:54- 01
Kobrin	Nadezhda	UKR	21.1.72	165/67	JT	56.50	62.04#- 98, 59.79- 00
Koga	Hiromi	JPN	28.5.82	173/50	10000	32:41.71	
* Koivula-Kruger	Heli	FIN	27.6.75	175/60	TJ	14.39	14.38, 14.83w- 02
Koklóni	Yeoryía	GRE	7.5.81	165/57	100	11.33	11.41- 02
Kokótou	Hristina	GRE	9.1.72	165/60	20kW	1:29:54	1:34:59- 00
Kolétsou	María	GRE	14.6.77		DT	62.71	61.86- 02
Koleva	Tanya	BUL	8.3.72	178/62	PV	4.45	4.43- 01
Kolkkala	Taina	FIN	24.10.76	173/74	JT	61.96	66.00#- 95, 64.06- 00
Komyagina	Olga	RUS	10.2.74	162/48	1500	4:04.77	4:02.32- 00
					1M	4:28.86	4:25.71- 99
					3000	8:47.62+	8:42.58- 99
Konevtsova (Tauryanina)	Yelena	RUS	11.3.81	183/83	HT	69.59	67.35- 02
Kononenko	Tatyana	RUS	29.3.81		800	2:02.31	
Kopaneva	Aleksandra	RUS	5.12.80		SP	16.63i	17.17- 02
Korchagina	Lyudmila	RUS	26.7.71		HMar	70:50	72:43- 01
					Mar	2:29:53	2:33:14- 02
Korcová	Katerina	CZE	31.7.76		HJ	1.87i, 1.86	1.86i -02, 1.84- 00
^ Korolchik ¶	Yanina	BLR	26.12.76	187/87	SP	19.39	20.61- 01
Koroteyeva	Maria	RUS	10.11.81	175/63	100h	12.95	12.94- 02
Korotkova	Tatyana	RUS	24.4.80	165/57	20kW	1:29:35	1:29:12- 02
Korotkova	Yevdokiya	RUS	28.2.79	166/54	20kW	1:34:12	1:34:02- 02
Korpela	Merja	FIN	15.5.81	170/74	HT	64.44	63.75- 02
Korzeniowska	Sylwia	POL	25.4.80	164/52	20kW	1:33:47	1:32:47- 01
* Korzhanenko	Irina	RUS	16.5.74	178/85	SP	20.55i	20.82- 98, 21.15i- 99
Korzhova-Aitova	Marina	KAZ	13.9.82	180/60	HJ	1.89	1.90- 00
Kosenkova	Yuliya	RUS	28.3.73	170/58	800	2:00.62	2:00.2- 01
					1500	4:04.38	4:03.66- 02
					1M	4:31.85	
* Kosgei	Salina	KEN	16.11.76	162/58	5000	15:01.79	15:20.17- 02
					10000	32:09.15	31:27.83- 02
					HMar	71:16	72:01- 99
Kostetskaya	Yekaterina	RUS-Y	31.12.87	168/59	400h	57.52	59.68- 02
Kotorida	Takako	JPN	2.4.77	169/50	5000	15:15.16	15:29.64- 01
					10000	31:45.84	31:41.32- 01
					HMar	68:35	69:04- 01
* Kotova	Tatyana	RUS	11.12.76	182/59	LJ	6.94	7.42- 02
Kovalenko	Anna	RUS	3.2.80		LJ	6.46i	6.75- 02
Kovalenko	Irina	UKR-Y	12.6.86	181/53	HJ	1.95i, 1.92	1.85- 02
Kovalyova	Lyudmila	UKR	18.3.75	174/62	Hep	5858	6230- 99
Kovpotina	Olga	RUS	10.1.68		Mar	2:28:42	2:27:37- 01

Name		Nat	Born	Ht/Wt	Event	2003 Mark	Pre-2003 Best
Kozarenoka	Inga	LAT	16.3.82	174/70	JT	54.50	57.58- 00
Kozhemyakina	Irina	UKR	16.6.80		100	11.47, 11.2	
Krakoviak	Irina	LTU	16.11.77	167/53	1500	4:10.87	4:07.99- 00
Krasaeyan	Juthaporn	THA	13.2.72	175/90	SP	17.52	19.43- 95
^ Krasovskaya	Yelena	UKR	17.8.76	176/65	100h	13.06	12.82- 00, 12.8- 97, 12.73w- 02
Krauel	Sophie	GER-J	2.3.85	166/55	LJ	6.60	6.42- 02
					Hep	5752	
Kravchenko	Anzhela	UKR	25.1.71	166/60	100	11.23	11.16- 98, 11.13w- 99
					200	22.66	23.08- 99
* Kravets	Inessa	UKR	5.10.66	178/60	LJ	6.79i, 6.76	7.37- 92
					TJ	14.44i, 14.42	15.50- 95
Kreiner	Kim	USA	26.7.77	175/76	JT	60.86	60.68- 02
Kremer	Andrea	USA	2.7.82	168/57	3kSt	10:10.61	10:12.86- 01
^ Kremlyova	Lyubov	RUS	21.12.61		1M	4:29.72i	
Kresova	Natalya	RUS	12.12.79	178/66	100h	13.01, 12.99w	13.39- 02
Krevsun (Gurtovenko)	Yuliya	UKR	8.12.80	170/54	800	2:01.08	2:00.49- 02
Krieger	Sabine	GER	4.9.73	180/64	Hep	5899	5973- 02, 6052w- 01
* Krivelyova	Svetlana	RUS	13.6.69	184/94	SP	20.77	21.06- 92
Kròl	Katja	GER	5.2.80	193/93	SP	17.12i, 16.66	17.00- 01
					DT	58.20	57.63- 02
Krueger	Brooke	AUS	9.7.80	180/125	HT	67.40	67.87- 02
Kruglova	Larisa	RUS	27.10.72	166/63	100	11.40	11.37- 01
					200	23.24	23.24- 98
Kryazheva	Anna	RUS-J	17.7.84	173/62	Hep	5769	5611- 02
Ksok	Anna	POL	29.9.83	181/68	HJ	1.94	1.94- 02
Kubokura	Satomi	JPN	27.4.82	161/51	400h	57.30	57.72- 02
^ Kuehl	Kristin	USA	30.7.70	183/89	DT	60.09	65.34- 00
Kühnert	Floe	GER-J	6.3.84	174/58	PV	4.32	4.41- 02
Kuma	Eyerusalem	ETH	4.11.81	157/45	5000	15:09.70	15:38.93- 01
* Kumbernuss	Astrid	GER	5.2.70	186/90	SP	19.91	21.22- 95
Kuncová	Barbora	CZE	26.4.82		3kSt	10:12.10	10:52.71- 02
* Kuptsova	Marina	RUS	22.12.81	185/65	HJ	2.02	2.03i, 2.00- 02
Kurgat	Lydia	KEN	.76		3kSt	10:01.75	
Kurosawa	Nami	JPN	26.12.78	162/48	10000	32:42.61	31:56.78- 01
Kürti	Éva	HUN	21.7.76	183/82	DT	57.25	57.72- 01
Kushch	Natalya	UKR	5.3.83	172/58	PV	4.40	4.20- 01
Kutol	Ruth	KEN	16.5.73		HMar	71:24	69:24- 00
					Mar	2:27:22	2:27:54- 01
* Kuzenkova	Olga	RUS	4.10.70	176/76	HT	74.98	75.68- 00
Kuznetsova	Yelena	KAZ	4.7.77	164/53	20kW	1:32:58	1:32:23- 00
Kwambai	Caroline	KEN	9.9.75	148/37	HMar	70:56	69:45- 01
					Mar	2:28:47	
Kwambai	Irene	KEN	25.10.78	170/52	3000	8:46.38	9:03.19- 00
					5000	15:06.10	15:48.06- 00
La Mantia	Simona	ITA	14.4.83	177/65	TJ	14.31	13.51, 13.63w- 01
Láboura	Amalía	GRE	16.3.68		HT	63.61	62.69- 00
Lacy	Krystin	USA-Y	8.7.87		100	11.43, 11.35w	11.87, 11.80w- 02
Ladokhina	Svetlana	RUS	21.2.79	171/67	Hep	5999	5569- 02
Ladovskaya	Tatyana	UKR	4.5.77	168/62	100h	13.22, 13.0	13.20- 02
Lah	Barbara	ITA	24.3.72	185/67	TJ	14.38	14.17, 14.18w- 95
Laláková	Barbora	CZE	2.5.81	178/58	HJ	1.91	1.94i, 1.91- 02
Lalova	Ivet	BUL-J	18.5.84	164/52	100	11.14	11.64- 02
					200	22.87	24.03- 01
Lan Chunyan		CHN	8.9.83		DT	55.31	
Landre	Francine	FRA	26.7.70	164/50	400	52.31	51.21- 94
Landreth	Molly	USA	27.11.82		3kSt	10:07.78	11:00.59- 02
* Langerholc	Brigita	SLO	23.7.76	170/56	800	2:00.47	1:58.51- 00
Lapina	Marina	AZE	6.3.81		HT	63.77	58.90- 01
* Lapina	Svetlana	RUS	12.4.78	180/58	HJ	2.00i, 1.96	1.99- 99
Lara	Yanelis	CUB	19.8.78	167/56	800	2:00.91	2:00.98- 02
Larsen	Stine	NOR	5.11.75	157/48	Mar	2:27:12	2:27:06- 02
Larsson	Annika	SWE	10.7.70		DT	55.34	57.39- 00
Laukhova	Svetlana	RUS	7.5.73	170/60	100h	12.88	12.72- 01
Lavshuk	Natalya	RUS	22.2.80	172/59	400	52.01	51.84- 02
* Lawrence	Tayna	JAM	17.9.75	163/52	100	11.24	10.93- 02
Lawson	Sharianne	USA	25.7.80		100h	13.25	13.26- 02
Lazo	Mileydis	CUB	7.9.81	162/58	100	11.39	11.51, 11.50w- 99, 11.1- 02
* Lebedeva	Tatyana	RUS	21.7.76	171/60	LJ	6.82	6.71i- 01, 6.65- 94
					TJ	15.18	15.32- 00
Lebedyenko	Yelena	RUS	16.1.71	177/63	TJ	14.16i, 13.56	14.74i- 99, 14.41- 98
LeBlanc	Ranysha	USA	11.1.83	165/55	100h	13.09	13.38- 01

Name		Nat	Born	Ht/Wt	Event	2003 Mark	Pre-2003 Best
Lebusova	Yelena	RUS	26.6.81	175/70	DT	55.49	54.51- 01
* Lee	Muna	USA	30.10.81	173/50	100	11.04, 10.97w	11.17, 11.13w- 01
					200	22.49i, 22.74	22.66, 22.33w- 02
Lee	Suzette	JAM	6.3.75	180/70	TJ	13.94, 14.26w	14.09- 99, 14.25i- 97
Lee Mi-young		KOR	19.8.79		SP	17.60	16.45- 02
Lee Myung-sun		KOR	12.2.76	168/89	SP	17.71	19.36- 00
Lee Young-sun		KOR	21.2.74	165/65	JT	56.96	58.87- 02, 63.32#- 92
Legesse	Meskerem	ETH-Y	28.9.86	160/48	800	2:01.11	2:03.34A- 02
					1500	4:03.96	4:20.29- 02
Legnante	Assunta	ITA	14.5.78	187/118	SP	18.43	19.20i, 18.23 02
Lendjel	Nevena	CRO	18.7.79	181/62	HJ	1.89i, 1.88A	1.91- 99
Lenskiy	Irina	ISR	12.6.71	176/54	200	23.25, 23.18w	23.15- 02
					100h	12.82	12.80- 02
Leontyuk	Yuliya	BLR-J	31.1.84	180/82	SP	17.44	16.47- 02
Lesman	Justyna	POL	6.11.80	168/49	1500	4:08.90	4:16.32- 02
Leveaux	Lindy	SEY	14.11.79	172/65	JT	54.88	55.83- 02
Levenkova	Olga	RUS-J	11.1.84	172/60	Hep	5903	5724- 02
Lever	Alison	AUS	13.10.72	182/85	DT	60.16	63.73- 00
Levina	Tatyana	RUS	28.2.77	173/60	400	51.38	51.46- 02
Levorato	Manuela	ITA	16.3.77	180/66	100	11.31, 11.22w	11.14- 01, 11.13w- 00
					200	23.14i, 23.18	22.60- 99
* Lewis	Denise	GBR	27.8.72	173/64	Hep	6282	6831- 00
Lewis	Tamsyn	AUS	20.7.78	168/57	800	1:59.35	1:59.21- 00
Lewy	Magdalena	USA	1.8.73		10000	32:41.76	32:52.84- 02
Li Fengfeng		CHN	9.1.79	175/100	SP	18.96	18.39- 02
Li Helan		CHN	2.1.78		10000	32:39.41	32:38.02- 01
					Mar	2:29:46	2:26:59- 02
* Li Meiju		CHN	23.1.81	173/85	SP	18.96	18.95- 02
Li Xiaoxue		CHN	11.1.80	180/70	HT	65.67	64.50- 00
Li Yanfeng		CHN	15.5.79	179/76	DT	61.87	63.67- 99
Liang Lili		CHN	16.11.83	170/75	JT	58.93	61.49- 02, 61.81#- 98
Liang Shuyan		CHN	16.9.77		LJ	6.51, 6.65w	6.70- 00
Liao Xiaoyon		CHN-Y	8.1.87		HT	65.13	54.93- 02
Liimask	Mirjam	EST	25.10.83	173/59	100h	13.25	13.45- 02
Líka	Sávva	GRE	27.6.70		JT	60.07	58.53- 01
Likhuta	Yevgeniya	BLR	24.3.81	173/59	100h	13.20	13.32- 02
Limika	Irene	KEN	28.8.79		3kSt	9:52.99	9:39.51- 01
Limonta	Yuleidis	CUB	14.3.82	174/66	Hep	5871	5593- 02
Lin Xiaojing		CHN-Y	8.1.86		DT	56.65	56.89- 02
Lindberg	Åsa	FIN	12.4.79	175/78	JT	57.01	56.36- 00
Linnen	Amy	USA	15.7.82		PV	4.40	4.53i, 4.31- 02
* Lishchinskaya	Irina	UKR	15.1.76	165/53	800	2:01.22	2:00.45- 02
					1500	4:02.60	4:03.78- 02
Lisnichenko	Maria	RUS	27.12.80	175/63	400	50.87	52.18- 02
Liss	Collette	USA	29.4.73		1500	4:10.62	4:09.10- 01
					3000	8:58.08i	8:55.51- 01
Littlejohn	Brittany	USA			100h	13.33, 13.13w	13.45, 13.42w- 02
Liu Chunhua		CHN-Y	1.10.86		JT	58.03	49.77- 02
Liu Qing		CHN-Y	28.4.86		800	2:02.25	2:04.40- 02
Liu Xiaoping		CHN	4.1.78		800	2:01.75	2:03.82- 01
Liu Xiaoyan		CHN-J	4.9.85		20kW	1:32:36	
Liu Yinghui		CHN	29.6.79	180/85	HT	69.05	68.06- 02
Livebardon	Agnès	FRA	31.5.80	167/61	PV	4.40i, 4.30	4.35- 02
Logan	Molly	USA	28.4.81		100h	13.13, 13.03w	13.88- 00
LoMonaco	Gina	USA	18.4.77		DT	59.26	55.60- 98
Longfors	Rachelle	USA	6.6.83		DT	55.15	53.09- 02
Loper	Tara	USA	12.8.77	175/86	HT	65.57	59.13- 01
Lopes	Priscilla	CAN	26.8.82		100h	13.12	13.78- 00
^ López	Aliuska	ESP	29.8.69	169/53	100h	12.89	12.67- 96
* Loroupe	Tegla	KEN	9.5.73	156/48	5000	15:32.22	14:45.95- 00
					HMar	71:34	67:12- 96
Loughnane	Olive	IRL	14.1.76	160/49	20kW	1:30:29	1:32:44- 02
Lovett	LaJuana	USA	7.5.82	168/54	100	11.37	11.51, 11.27w- 02
					200	23.05w	23.50- 02
Lukyanchuk	Olga	UKR	7.12.76	167/59	20kW	1:31:45	1:29:08- 01
Lyakhova	Yulia	RUS	8.7.77	185/60	HJ	1.92	2.00i- 99, 1.99- 97
Lyakhovich	Tatyana	UKR	20.5.79	174/75	JT	56.82	60.78- 02
Lyne	Rebecca	GBR	4.7.82	173/52	800	2:01.76	2:02.45- 02
Lyngstad	Hanne	NOR	5.12.75	160/50	3kSt	9:54.91	0
Lysenko	Tatyana	RUS	9.10.83	185/72	HT	67.19	61.65- 02
Ma Ning		CHN	4.11.83		JT	62.38	57.90- 02

Name		Nat	Born	Ht/Wt	Event	2003 Mark	Pre-2003 Best
Ma Shuli		CHN	20.1.78	178/75	DT	57.88	62.21- 01
Ma Xuejun		CHN-J	26.3.85	185/90	DT	60.20	58.85- 02
Macchiut	Margaret	ITA	25.7.74	171/48	100h	13.26, 13.22w	13.16- 02
Machado	Maiía Paula	BRA	22.1.81	167/62	100h	13.10A, 13.13	12.93- 02
^ Machado	Teresa	POR	22.7.69	170/80	DT	63.65	65.40- 98
* Macharia	Faith	KEN	9.2.76	165/55	800	1:59.23	1:58.34- 01
Macus	Meta	SLO	23.3.75	166/58	400h	57.28	56.63- 02
Madejczyk	Barbara	POL	30.9.76	179/78	JT	59.89	59.54- 01
Maduaka	Joice	GBR	30.9.73	172/65	100	11.29	11.24- 99
					200	22.92	22.83- 99
Maffeis	Agnese	ITA	9.3.65	187/84	DT	62.94	63.66- 96
* Maggi ¶	Maurren	BRA	25.6.76	178/66	LJ	7.06	7.26A- 99, 7.02, 7.17w- 02
					TJ	14.53	14.32- 02
* Mahon	Anna	USA	19.12.74	180/75	HT	71.33	72.01- 02
Maisch	Ulrike	GER	21.1.77	171/57	Mar	2:31:21	2:32:15- 02
Makarova	Yelena	RUS	21.12.81		JT	55.14	55.35- 02
Makrí	Aggeliki	GRE	25.9.78		20kW	1:33:27	1:40:43- 02
* Malot	Leah	KEN	7.6.72	168/46	3000	8:45.29	8:35.74- 99
					5000	15:13.26	14:39.83- 00
					10000	32:12.91	30:57.70- 00
					HMar	69:47	69:43- 01
Mameyeva	Svetlana	UKR	19.4.82		TJ	13.73	12.90i, 12.73- 01
Manabe	Yuko	JPN	8.2.79	158/41	10000	32:16.01	32:07.58- 00
					HMar	70:23	69:36- 02
Manfrédi	Laurence	FRA	20.5.74	175/92	SP	18.01	18.69i, 18.68- 00
Mang	Véronique	FRA-J	15.12.84	170/63	100	11.33, 11.29w	11.39- 00
* Manjani	Mirela	GRE	21.12.76	165/64	JT	66.52	67.51- 00
Manninen	Johanna	FIN	4.4.80	170/58	100	11.35, 11.26w	11.33- 01
					200	22.97	22.93- 01
Mannová	Michaela	CZE	11.1.82	163/49	3kSt	9:42.01	9:45.94- 02
Manuel	Stacie	USA	6.12.83		PV	4.17i, 4.10	4.06- 00
Mara	Valeriya	UKR	22.2.83	163/54	3kSt	10:09.52	10:33.0- 02
Marakurwa	Letiwe	ZIM	2.6.78		3kSt	9:52.98	10:44.41- 02
* Maranga	Jackline	KEN	16.12.77	165/51	1500	4:01.22	3:57.41- 98
					1M	4:25.40	4:24.00- 98
Marconi	Gloria	ITA	31.3.68	163/48	3000	8:58.4mx	9:11.37- 02
					10000	32:28.65	32:36.25- 02
					HMar	69:25	71:31- 02
					Mar	2:29:35	0
Marin	Elisabetta	ITA	5.11.77	177/75	JT	57.76	60.12- 02
* Marinova	Tereza	BUL	5.9.77	173/56	TJ	14.40i, 14.27	15.20- 00
Marks	Shani	USA	24.8.80		TJ	13.79	13.04- 02
Marten	Kristen	GER	23.5.83	184/90	SP	16.65	16.58i- 02, 16.30- 01
Mårtensson	Erica	SWE	24.6.79	165/55	400h	57.05	57.54- 01
Martin	Julie	FRA	28.9.79	175/57	Hep	5719	5773- 01
Martincová	Lucie	CZE	4.1.82	176/64	100h	13.15	13.46, 13.30w- 02
* Martinez	Magdelin	ITA	10.2.76	178/63	TJ	14.90	14.73- 02
* Martínez	Mayte	ESP	17.5.76	168/56	800	1:59.53i, 1:59.62	1:58.29- 02
Martínez	Yarianna	CUB-J	20.9.84	168/56	TJ	13.96	13.90- 02
Martins	Maria	FRA	1.4.74	162/53	1500	4:04.55	4:08.99- 02
					1M	4:28.67	
Marx	Claudia	GER	16.9.78	172/61	400	51.68	51.41- 01
Marx	Livia	HUN	5.4.80		HT	66.06	64.93- 02
* Masai	Edith	KEN	4.4.67	168/55	3000	8:36.82	8:23.23- 02
					5000	14:45.35	14:45.86- 01
^ Mateescu	Rodica	ROM	13.3.71	180/63	TJ	13.88	15.16- 97
Matejková	Alice	ESP	11.1.69	180/74	DT	56.10	62.66- 97
^ Mathes	Simone	GER	13.3.75	171/85	HT	65.39	67.13- 99
Matyushkina	Tatyana	RUS	22.1.79	165/52	20kW	1:34:34	1:33:40- 00
* May	Fiona	ITA	12.12.69	181/60	LJ	6.67	7.11- 98, 7.23Aw- 95
May (Dykstra)	Wanita	CAN	30.1.75		HJ	1.87i	1.92- 93
Maydanova	Marina	UKR	22.8.82	172/62	100	11.47, 11.32w	11.52- 02
					200	22.70	23.56, 23.1- 02
Mayers	Natasha	VIN	10.3.79	168/69	100	11.09	11.09- 02, 11.01w- 01
					200	23.00	22.80, 22.6w- 02
Mayes	Nina	USA	10.8.83		100	11.50A, 11.35w	11.85- 01
Mayr-Krifka	Karin	AUT	4.6.71	179/69	100	11.15	11.23- 02
					200	22.88i, 23.05	22.70- 02
* Mbango	Françoise	CMR	14.4.76	172/63	TJ	15.05	14.95- 02
McCann	Stephanie	CAN	22.4.77	171/59	PV	4.41	4.35- 02
* McConnell	Lee	GBR	9.10.78	178/64	400	51.06	50.82- 02

Name		Nat	Born	Ht/Wt	Event	2003 Mark	Pre-2003 Best
McCray	Yolanda	USA	11.9.76	168/60	100h	12.90	12.78, 12.77w- 99
* McDonald	Beverly	JAM	15.2.70	169/59	100	11.24	10.99- 98
					200	22.67	22.22- 99
McEwen-Reed	Niki	USA	1.4.80		PV	4.30	4.21i- 02, 4.10- 00
McGettigan	Roisin	IRL	23.8.80		1500	4:10.34	4:23.28- 01
					3kSt	9:50.12	10:08.24- 02
McGregor	Haley	AUS	27.5.79	160/46	10000	31:43.14	
McGregor	Katie	USA	2.9.77	173/54	3000	8:59.64i	9:09.30i- 00
					5000	15:29.42	15:30.15- 02
					10000	31:54.78	32:17.49- 02
* McIntosh	Raasin	USA	29.4.82	170/61	100h	12.90	13.60, 13.32w- 02
					400h	54.60	55.70- 02
* McKelvy-Jones	Miesha	USA	26.7.76	173/64	100h	12.51	12.60, 12.51w- 02
McKinney	Akiba	USA	9.3.79		LJ	6.46	6.26- 97, 6.31w- 01
McLaughlin	Anneisha	JAM-Y	6.1.86	167/59	200	23.19	22.94- 02
McWilliams	Tiffany	USA	20.10.82	178/58	1500	4:06.75	4:20.13- 02
Mebam Kaboud	Carole	CMR	17.9.78		400h	57.31	58.10- 02
^ Meissner	Heike	GER	29.1.70	173/57	800	2:02.31i	1:59.50- 98
					400h	55.00	54.03- 96
Melink	Teja	SLO	23.3.80	168/57	PV	4.15i	4.10- 02
* Melinte	Mihaela	ROM	27.3.75	174/92	HT	71.99	76.07- 99
Melkamu	Meselech	ETH-J	19.4.85	158/47	1500	4:09.77	
					3000	8:51.20	
					5000	15:27.93	
Melnikova- 2	Irina	RUS	12.10.75	169/57	LJ	6.76	6.69i- 02, 6.68- 96
Meloni	Andrea	GER	1.10.67	168/52	20kW	1:33:52	1:32:48- 02
Mendes	Luciana	BRA	26.7.71	170/55	800	2:02.06	1:58.27- 94
Méndez	Judith	DOM	27.7.81		Hep	5783	5014- 02
Mendía	Marta	ESP	18.5.75	172/58	HJ	1.95	1.94i- 01, 1.93- 00
* Menéndez	Osleidys	CUB	14.11.79	178/80	JT	63.96	71.54- 01
Menkova	Oksana	BLR	28.3.82		HT	67.58	66.42- 02
Mensah	Amewu	GER	21.3.77	182/64	HJ	1.87	1.94- 00
Menshikova	Mariya	RUS	26.2.83		400h	57.08	58.32- 02
^ Mérah (Benida)	Nouria	ALG	19.10.70	162/52	800	2:00.90	1:59.49- 99
					1000	2:36.94	2:34.60- 99
					1500	4:05.57	3:59.12- 00
* Merriman	Donica	USA	24.1.79	178/65	100h	12.65	12.70- 00
Michalska	Marzena	ITA	20.10.75	166/46	3kSt	10:07.59	10:21.61- 02
Michot	Cécile	FRA	2.6.74	170/57	100h	13.13	13.06- 02
* Mikhalchenko	Irina	UKR	20.1.72	179/60	HJ	1.99	2.00- 02
* Mikitenko	Irina	GER	23.8.72	158/49	1500	4:10.76	4:06.08- 01
					3000	8:39.29	8:30.39- 00
					5000	14:56.64	14:42.03- 99
					10000	31:38.48	31:29.55- 01
Mikkonen	Hanna	FIN	15.1.81	171/56	HJ	1.90	1.88- 02
Miklós	Éva	HUN	30.7.78	174/56	LJ	6.59	6.65- 01
Miles	Illia	USA	11.1.82		100	11.44, 11.38w	11.65w- 02
					200	23.31, 23.20w	23.59- 02, 23.31w -01
* Miles-Clark	Jearl	USA	4.9.66	170/60	400	50.53	49.40- 97
					800	1:58.61	1:56.40- 99
Militaru	Alina	ROM	10.4.82	173/53	LJ	6.60	6.42- 98
Miller	Amber	USA			Hep	5670w	5310- 02
Miller	Gi-Gi	USA	12.1.79	165/55	100h	13.23	13.36- 00, 13.11w- 01
					Hep	5747	5925- 01
* Miller	Inger	USA	12.6.72	163/55	100	11.16, 11.04w	10.79- 99
					200	22.67	21.77- 99
Mills	TaNisha	USA	2.11.74	172/62	400h	56.12	56.14- 01
Milusauskaité	Sonata	LTU	31.8.73	163/53	20kW	1:30:53	1:33:29- 99
Miroshnichenko	Yelena	UKR	1.3.77	170/52	20kW	1:30:20	1:33:36- 02
Mishchenko	Olga	UKR	24.11.71	180/67	400	51.92, 51.8	52.02- 02, 52.0- 99
^ Misipeka	Lisa	ASA	3.1.75	170/84	HT	69.24	67.55- 00
^ Misyulya	Natalya	BLR	16.4.66	157/47	20kW	1:34:28	1:28:24- 00
Mitchell	Kathryn	AUS	10.7.82	170/78	JT	57.11	54.98- 01
Mitropoúlou	Nikolía	GRE	16.2.82		HJ	1.89	1.84- 02
Miyake	Takako	JPN	22.7.74	161/62	JT	55.99	61.15- 01
Mladenis	Nicole	AUS	22.9.75	170/58	TJ	14.04, 14.22w	14.04, 14.21w- 02
Mládková	Sárka	CZE	30.8.76	171/59	PV	4.22	4.26sq- 00, 4.20- 99
Mockenhaupt	Sabrina	GER	6.12.80	156/45	3000	8:44.65	8:55.55- 02
					5000	15:09.80	15:16.32- 02
					10000	32:11.95	32:08.52- 02
Molchanova	Viktoriya	UKR	26.5.82	171/55	LJ	6.60	6.23- 02

	Name		Nat	Born	Ht/Wt	Event	2003 Mark	Pre-2003 Best
	Möller	Esther	GER	13.9.77	170/58	100	11.25	11.33- 00
	Molnár	Krisztina	HUN	8.4.76	168/51	PV	4.40i, 4.30	4.53- 02
	Mondor	Emilie	CAN	29.4.81	167/55	1500	4:11.30	4:10.9- 02
						3000	8:44.53	9:25.30- 98
						5000	14:59.68	15:42.07- 02
*	Montaner	Concepción	ESP	14.1.81	170/56	LJ	6.78i, 6.69, 6.70w	6.89- 02
*	Montebrun	Manuèla	FRA	13.11.79	175/92	HT	74.50, 75.20 dh	72.54- 02
	Moore	Charlotte	GBR-J	4.1.85	164/49	800	2:01.21	1:59.75- 02
	Moore	Connie	USA	29.8.81	165/63	100	11.21	11.31- 02
						200	22.63	23.12- 02
	Moore	LaShauntea	USA	31.7.83	170/56	100	11.33, 11.27w, 11.2w	11.47- 02
						200	23.09, 22.81w	23.13, 22.89w- 02
	Morandais	Sylvanie	FRA	14.7.79	162/50	400h	56.62A, 56.84	55.49- 01
	Morató	Rosa María	ESP	19.6.79	170/56	3kSt	10:01.70	10:57.6- 98
*	Moreno	Yipsi	CUB	19.11.80	168/70	HT	75.14	71.47- 02
	Mori	Chinatsu	JPN	20.5.80	169/88	SP	17.80	17.39- 02
	Mormand	Anita	FRA	20.2.71	175/60	400	52.26	51.94- 98
	Moroianu	Rodica	FRA	18.11.70	170/50	10000	32:40.70	32:27.81- 02
*	Morrison	Melissa	USA	9.7.71	163/50	100h	12.70	12.53- 98
	Moskvina	Nina	UKR	6.8.71	168/54	20kW	1:34:23	1:39:22- 02
	Mosqueda	Sylvia	USA	8.4.66	160/48	HMar	71:22	71:20- 00
*	Mothersill	Cydonie	CAY	19.3.78	168/53	100	11.26	11.30- 02, 11.21w- 00
						200	22.45, 22.41w	22.54- 01
	Moton	Jamine	USA	14.12.78		HT	66.06	67.21- 02
	de Moura	Lucimar	BRA	22.3.74	174/60	100	11.43	11.29, 11.17A- 99
						200	23.19A, 23.26	22.75, 22.75- 99
	Moya	Sabina	COL	27.1.77	162/70	JT	60.17	62.62A- 02
	Mrashani	Banwella	TAN	14.11.77		Mar	2:29:13	2:24:59- 02
	Mrisho	Zakia	TAN-J	19.2.84	165/45	3000	8:46.77	
^	Mueller	Melissa	USA	16.11.72	178/66	PV	4.60	4.60Ai-02, 4.47, 4.62St- 01
*	Mugo	Naomi	KEN	2.1.77	163/50	1500	4:01.80	3:58.12- 98
						1M	4:27.12	4:24.43- 98
						2000	5:37.36	5:37.02- 02
	Müller	Corinne	SUI	20.11.75		HJ	1.90	1.87- 02
	Muncan	Marina	SCG	6.11.82	164/44	1500	4:11.23	4:19.87- 01
	Muñoz	Adriana	CUB	16.3.82		800	2:01.07	2:01.25- 02
						1500	4:09.57	4:16.71- 02
	Munro	Jacquie	AUS	4.10.81	166/57	100h	13.17,12.9,13.13w	13.09- 02,13.03w- 00
	Murata	Fumi	JPN	13.3.75	152/42	10000	32:42.42	32:26.91- 01
						HMar	70:21	69:26- 00
						Mar	2:30:15	2:34:46- 01
	Murillo	Digna	COL	22.5.81	160/56	100	11.35, 11.25Aw	11.46A- 00
						200	23.08A, 23.13	23.48A- 00
	Murillo	Melissa	COL	13.1.82	157/51	100	11.38Aw	11.68A- 00
	Murphy	Catherine	GBR	21.9.75	172/60	400	51.74i, 52.92	51.36- 02
*	Mutola	Maria Lurdes	MOZ	27.10.72	162/61	800	1:55.55	1:55.19- 94
						1000	2:33.15	2:29.34- 95
	Nacsa	Monique	AUS	26.10.76	177/85	DT	59.91	58.48- 02
	Nakata	Yuki	JPN	10.3.77	167/56	Hep	5910	5862- 01
	Narloch	Márcia	BRA	28.3.69		Mar	2:29:59	2:34:18- 00
	Nasonova	Tatyana	UKR	15.12.76	183/92	SP	17.20	16.55i- 99, 16.03- 02
	Nástas	Alexándra	GRE	2.7.81		JT	56.40	51.72- 02
*	Nathan	DeDee	USA	20.4.68	180/75	Hep	5829	6577- 99
	Naude	Elizna	RSA	14.9.78	180/87	DT	57.44	60.99- 02
	Naumenko	Irina	KAZ	13.2.80	180/63	Hep	6140	6078- 00
	Nazarova	Margarita	RUS	1.10.76	167/58	20kW	1:31:21	1:28:24- 02
*	Nazarova	Natalya	RUS	26.5.79	165/55	400	49.78	50.10- 00
	Ndereba	Anastasha	KEN	27.9.74		Mar	2:30:21	2:29:03- 02
*	Ndereba	Catherine	KEN	21.7.72	160/45	HMar	68:23	67:54- 01
						Mar	2:19:55	2:18:47- 01
*	Ndoye	Kéne	SEN	20.11.78	164/58	LJ	6.54, 6.62w	6.47A- 99, 6.44, 6.45w- 02
						TJ	14.91	14.28- 02
	Ndungu	Rahab	KEN	19.10.78		3000	8:56.38	
						10000	31:56.23	
	Neal	Natasha	USA	22.7.80		100h	13.00, 12.93w	13.24, 13.19w- 01
	Necka	Urszula	POL-J	28.6.84	168/49	3kSt	10:11.52	0
	Nedkova	Nedyalka	BUL	15.3.77		400	52.2	53.48- 02
	Neira	Yaumara	CUB	18.4.76	158/50	100h	12.82	12.75, 12.7- 02, 12.70w- 01
	Neporadnaya	Nelya	UKR-J	29.7.85	163/46	800	2:00.69	2:08.78- 01
						1000	2:35.56	
						1500	4:04.24	4:12.56- 02

Name		Nat	Born	Ht/Wt	Event	2003 Mark	Pre-2003 Best
* Nerius	Steffi	GER	1.7.72	178/72	JT	64.42	69.42#- 96, 65.76- 00
* Netseporuk	Larisa	EST	24.12.70	171/59	Hep	6215	6331- 00
Neupert	Anja	GER	10.10.78	174/58	400h	56.07	57.32- 02
Nevmerzhitskaya	Yelena	BLR	27.7.80	168/55	100	11.25	11.63- 02
Newman	Shelley	GBR	8.8.73	182/84	DT	61.22	60.82- 98
Ngotho	Margaret	KEN	6.9.71		1500	4:07.38	4:10.33- 97
					2000	5:41.02	
					3000	8:50.68	9:06.55- 96
Nguimgo	Mireille	CMR	7.11.76	172/56	400	50.79	50.69- 00
Nguyen Thi Tinh		VIE	20.9.81		200	23.19w	
					400	51.83	53.86- 02
Niaré	Gaëlle	FRA	12.3.82	187/72	HJ	1.93	1.88- 01
* Nicolau	Cristina	ROM	8.8.77	186/66	TJ	14.31	14.94i- 00, 14.70- 99
Niederstätter	Monika	ITA	2.3.74	168/52	400h	55.41	55.10- 99
Nikaido	Kaori	JPN	25.7.79	162/51	20kW	1:34:05	1:32:44- 00
* Nikolayeva	Yelena	RUS	1.2.66	164/58	20kW	1:26:22	1:27:02- 02
Nilsson	Cecilia	SWE	22.6.79	177/82	HT	63.49	65.14- 02
Nilsson	Ida	SWE	8.2.81	173/60	3kSt	9:46.74	9:49.49- 02
Nilsson	Johanna	SWE	27.3.83		1500	4:10.72	4:17.99- 01
Nilsson	Lena	SWE	28.1.80	166/56	1500	4:07.69	4:09.89- 02
Nishimura	Miki	JPN	14.4.82	156/46	800	2:02.10	2:02.23- 01
Niu Nana		CHN	20.5.83		TJ	13.67	13.52- 02
^ Nku	Mercy	NGR	17.7.76	170/67	100	11.22	11.06- 01, 11.03A, 10.98w- 99
					200	22.83	22.53- 99
* Noguchi	Mizuki	JPN	3.7.78	150/41	10000	31:59.28	31:50.18 -02
					HMar	68:29	68:22 -02
					Mar	2:21:18	2:25:35- 02
Nose	Maja	SLO	12.5.82	170/55	200	23.09	23.45- 02
Notagashira	Miho	JPN	17.8.83	171/50	5000	15:31.3	15:52.93- 02
					10000	32:23.61	
Nwosu	Glory	NGR-J	24.12.84		400	52.33	52.4, 54.10- 01
Nye	Lisa	USA	17.11.68	178/60	3kSt	9:49.14	9:49.41- 01
Nzola	Theresa	ANG	30.11.83	170/48	TJ	13.82i, 13.33, 13.41w	13.49, 13.59w- 02
Obedina	Irina	RUS-J	1.7.85	170/58	400h	57.57	60.26- 02
Oberer	Simone	SUI	8.4.80	176/61	Hep	5933	5820- 01
Obergföll	Christina	GER	22.8.81	175/71	JT	57.40	60.61- 02
Obilor	Catherine	NGR-J	17.7.85		400h	57.19	59.56- 02
* Ochichi	Isabella	KEN	28.10.79	162/48	3000	8:45.97	8:37.66- 02
					5000	14:47.70	15:01.42- 02
					HMar	68:42	68:38- 01
Odozor	Chinedu	NGR	24.12.77		LJ	6.52	6.53- 98
Oeser	Jennifer	GER	29.11.83	176/58	Hep	5901	5595- 02
Ogawa	Kiyomi	JPN	15.9.81	157/46	HMar	70:39	69:39- 02
Ogorodova	Marina	RUS	.76		TJ	13.75	14.13- 02
Ogoshi	Kazue	JPN	2.3.81	161/42	5000	15:20.94	15:22.33- 02
					10000	31:24.00	31:46.31- 02
Oguz (Kilinçer)	Candeger	TUR	16.7.80	182/63	HJ	1.92	1.92- 01
Ohaeri	Christina	USA	30.3.79	175/64	100h	13.11	13.09, 13.05w- 01
O'Hara	Tracy	USA	20.7.80	165/55	PV	4.40	4.45- 00
Ohira	Miki	JPN	28.6.81	169/49	10000	32:38.74	
Ojokolo	Endurance	NGR	29.9.75	178/67	100	11.16	11.06- 01
Okafor	Rosemary	NGR	22.5.81	165/58	100	11.34w	11.66- 02
					200	23.50, 23.18w	23.77- 02
Okamoto	Haruko	JPN	19.8.74	154/40	10000	32:33.00	31:50.39- 01
* Okayo	Margaret	KEN	30.5.76	150/39	HMar	67:23	68:49- 02
					Mar	2:22:31	2:20:43- 02
O'Keefe	Eileen	IRL	31.5.81	170/80	HT	63.25	61.10- 02
Okori	Reïna-Flor	FRA	2.5.80	165/56	100h	13.04	12.96, 12.91w- 00
Oksuz	Shermin	AUS-J	24.3.84	169/62	LJ	6.41, 6.46w	6.45, 6.65w- 01
Okunaga	Mika	JPN	27.10.82	160/43	10000	32:29.07	33:02.7- 01
					HMar	70:21	
Olaru	Mihaela	ROM	7.2.82	167/52	800	2:02.00	2:04.15- 02
Olaru	Nuta	ROM	28.8.70	161/40	Mar	2:28:24	2:25:18- 01
Oleksy	Justyna	POL	19.9.83	169/57	100h	13.01	13.21- 02
* Oleynikova	Yelena	RUS	9.12.76	178/57	TJ	14.56, 14.70w	14.83- 02
Olivarès	Elodie	FRA	22.5.76	170/55	3kSt	9:52.53	9:33.12- 02
de Oliveira/Parrela	Gilvaneide	BRA	31.8.76		100h	13.19A, 13.26	13.23- 00
Olivero	Cora	ESP	28.8.78	170/54	400h	55.65	56.55- 02
Oliveros	Princesa	COL	10.8.75		400h	57.44	57.19- 01
Olshevskaya	Olga	RUS	5.7.82		DT	57.12	55.75- 02
Omarova	Anna	RUS	3.10.81	182/90	SP	17.28	17.13- 01

Name		Nat	Born	Ht/Wt	Event	2003 Mark	Pre-2003 Best
Ominami	Hiromi	JPN	15.11.75	165/48	10000	32:17.59	31:50.89- 00
					HMar	69:41	69:40- 00
					Mar	2:26:17	2:27:29- 02
Ominami	Takami	JPN	15.11.75	167/47	10000	32:26.63	32:11.64- 00
					Mar	2:25:03	2:23:43- 02
Omoro	Jane	KEN	12.9.74		HMar	70:36	72:09- 99
Omwanza	Beatrice	KEN	24.2.74		Mar	2:27:44	2:35:36- 02
Ono	Masumi	JPN	5.12.75	161/51	PV	4.21	4.30i- 02, 4.20- 99
^ Onyali	Mary	NGR	3.2.68	168/54	100	11.09	10.97- 93, 10.7- 96
					200	22.60, 22.4	22.07- 96
Onyepunuka	Jessica	USA-Y	3.5.86		100	11.31	11.47Aw- 02
Orbán	Éva	HUN-J	29.11.84	173/75	HT	65.77	62.00- 02
O'Reilly	Thaimi	ITA	20.7.76	174/60	TJ	13.90	0
O'Rourke	Derval	IRL	28.5.81	168/57	100h	12.96	13.38, 13.34w- 02
Orsini	Gisella	ITA	9.12.71	161/49	20kW	1:34:27	1:32:57- 00
Orsund	Sandy	USA	24.9.81		DT	55.76	50.00- 02
Ortiz	Yamelis	PUR	26.2.78	165/51	400h	57.51	57.26A- 01, 57.52- 02
Ospishcheva	Yevgeniya	RUS	.78		SP	17.37	15.86- 98
* Ostapchuk	Nadezhda	BLR	12.10.80	180/78	SP	20.56i	19.73- 01
* O'Sullivan	Gillian	IRL	21.8.76	163/61	20kW	1:27:22	1:28:46- 02
* O'Sullivan	Sonia	IRL	28.11.69	173/53	1500	4:09.86	3:58.85- 95
					3000	8:37.55	8:21.64- 94
					5000	14:55.50	14:41.02- 00
					HMar	68:40	67:19- 02
^ Ottey	Merlene	SLO	10.5.60	173/61	100	11.22	10.74- 96
					200	22.89	21.64- 91
Ouali	Fatiha	FRA	25.10.74	159/52	20kW	1:33:25	1:32:14- 00
Ouaziz	Seloua	MAR	27.7.74	161/45	3000	8:56.22	8:59.17- 99
* Ouaziz	Zahra	MAR	20.12.69	166/50	3000	8:42.01i, 8:46.0+	8:26.48- 99
					5000	14:47.45	14:32.08- 98
^ Ouzoúni	Kalliópi	GRE	8.2.73	183/83	SP	18.55	19.03i, 18.63- 00
Ovcharenko	Nadezhda	RUS	8.12.81		HT	63.26	57.59- 02
Oyama	Miki	JPN	22.10.79	157/41	10000	32:39.98	32:33.05- 02
Oyepitan	Abiodun	GBR	30.12.79	165/53	100	11.36	11.29, 11.17w- 01
					200	22.95	23.52- 02
Ozaki	Akemi	JPN	12.10.77	157/44	HMar	70:31	73:13- 01
Ozaki	Mari	JPN	16.7.75	162/46	5000	15:12.76	15:25.99- 98
					10000	31:46.57	31:50.56- 01
					HMar	70:22+	69:33- 02
					Mar	2:23:30	
Pacholak	Anna	POL	15.1.80	174/51	200	22.87	23.51- 02
					400	51.88	52.74- 00
Palacios	Victoria	MEX	29.3.77		20kW	1:34:56	1:32:52- 01
* Palamar	Vita	UKR	12.10.77	187/64	HJ	2.01	1.99- 01
* Pantelimon	Oana	ROM	27.9.72	179/61	HJ	1.95i, 1.92	1.99- 00
Papadopoúlou	Stiliani	GRE	15.3.82		HT	63.46	62.30- 02
Papavasiláki	Déspina	GRE	24.3.73	173/60	LJ	6.74	6.75- 01
Papayeoryíou	Alexándra	GRE	17.12.80	175/80	HT	69.98	66.49- 02
Papayiánni	Athiná	GRE	18.8.80	170/56	20kW	1:32:17	1:31:45- 02
Paradowska	Renata	POL	14.6.70	163/52	Mar	2:29:17	2:27:17- 98
Parfyonova	Svetlana	RUS	14.7.73	175/62	Hep	5943	6187- 00
* Parris	Debbie-Ann	JAM	24.3.73	162/52	400h	55.51	53.88- 01
Parsukova (Grociene)	Adrija	LTU	25.7.74		LJ	6.46i	
^ Paschke	Melanie	GER	29.6.70	168/54	100	11.38	11.04- 95, 11.01w- 96
					200	23.13	22.45- 94
Pascual	Beatriz	ESP	9.5.82	163/53	20kW	1:31:31	1:32:38- 02
Pastushenko	Yelena	UKR	14.7.79	174/59	100	11.25	11.24- 99, 11.1- 00
					200	23.11	22.85- 00
^ Paulino	Tina	MOZ	7.7.73	166/61	800	2:00.50	1:56.62- 93
* Pavey	Jo	GBR	20.9.73	162/51	1500	4:01.79	4:07.28- 97
					3000	8:37.89	8:31.27- 02
					5000	15:09.04	14:48.66- 02
* Pavlysh	Viktoriya	UKR	15.1.69	174/85	SP	20.44i, 20.08	21.69- 98
* Pechonkina	Yuliya	RUS	21.4.78	180/65	400	51.00i	52.10i- 02, 53.22- 01
					400h	52.34	53.10- 02
Pechstein	Petra	SUI	26.7.71		PV	4.15	4.20- 02
Pedrares	Dolores	ESP	17.1.73	168/69	HT	64.29	62.90- 02
Peinado	Maria	ESP	8.2.77	175/67	Hep	5629	5965w, 5860- 02
^ Pells	Leah	CAN	9.11.64	173/55	1500	4:08.37	4:03.56- 96
					1M	4:28.68	4:23.38- 96
Perepelova	Lyubov	UZB	26.2.79	163/53	100	11.18	11.04- 00
					200	23.11	22.72- 00

Name		Nat	Born	Ht/Wt	Event	2003 Mark	Pre-2003 Best
Pérez	Eva	ESP	18.7.75	165/52	20kW	1:32:20	1:31:38- 02
Pérez	Katiuska	CUB	21.12.75		PV	4.20	4.05- 01
Pérez	Yuliana	USA	21.7.81	171/70	TJ	14.23	14.20- 02, 14.29w- 01
Perkins	Angel	USA-J	10.5.84		400	52.06	52.18- 01
Perkins/Taurima	Kerrie	AUS	2.4.79	174/59	LJ	6.50	6.36- 02
* Pernía	Daimí	CUB	27.12.76	173/59	400h	55.10	52.89- 99
Pérra	Athanasía	GRE	2.2.83		TJ	13.67	13.52, 13.73w- 01
Perrin	Amélie	FRA	30.3.80	171/85	HT	65.45	63.33- 02
* Perrone	Elisabetta	ITA	9.7.68	168/55	20kW	1:27:58	1:27:09- 01
Perry	Michelle	USA	1.5.79	175/60	100h	12.80	13.15, 13.03w- 00, 12.9w- 99
					400h	56.70	56.23- 01
					Hep	5684	5759- 01
Persson	Hanna-Mia	SWE	11.2.78	177/60	PV	4.20i	4.30- 02
Persson	Linda	SWE	22.9.81	177/55	PV	4.20	4.15- 02
Petersen	Nadja	SWE	14.7.78		400h	57.40	56.95- 02
Petite	Cristina	ESP	10.5.72	163/53	5000	15:29.56	15:23.23- 01
Petkevicienė	Virginija	LTU	12.6.71	176/58	TJ	13.77i	13.73- 02
Petrova	Antonina	RUS	25.1.77	162/52	20kW	1:27:14	1:29:47- 02
* Petrova	Lyudmila	RUS	7.10.68	160/44	10000	31:36.76	31:52.75- 00
					HMar	70:45+	69:26- 00
					Mar	2:23:14	2:22:33- 02
Petrova	Tatyana	RUS	8.4.83		3kSt	10:05.70	0
Pharr	LaTasha	USA	6.5.83		100h	13.36, 13.20w	
Phelps	LaToya	USA-J	30.6.84		200	23.43, 22.98w	23.27- 02
Phillips	April	USA	22.9.81		SP	16.76i, 16.43	15.88- 02
Pickersgill	Debbie	AUS	23.3.80	176/97	DT	59.11	55.50- 02
Piedra	Amaia	ESP	2.6.72	165/50	3000	8:59.76i	8:58.67- 02
					10000	32:23.08	0
Pilátou	Stilianí	GRE	28.3.80	172/56	LJ	6.80i, 6.57, 6.63w	6.75- 02
Pillay	Geraldine	RSA	25.8.77	178/64	100	11.20	11.55- 02
					200	23.07A, 23.11	23.66- 02
Pilskog	Trine	NOR	1.12.72		1500	4:07.52	4:12.52- 02
* Pittman	Jana	AUS	9.11.82	181/68	400	50.43	51.74mx- 01, 51.76A- 00
					400h	53.22	54.14- 02
* Plätzer	Kjersti	NOR	18.1.72	174/54	20kW	1:28:49	1:27:53- 00
Poelman	Jacqueline	NED	5.10.73	171/63	200	23.19, 23.16w	23.00- 02
Pogorelova	Olesya	RUS	30.3.79		400h	56.70	59.40- 02
Pogroszewska	Agnieszka	POL	20.2.77	170/75	HT	67.36	67.98- 01
Poissonnier	Marie	FRA	4.5.79	166/58	PV	4.40	4.46- 02
* Polnova	Tatyana	RUS	20.4.79	170/62	PV	4.70	4.60- 02
* Poluskina	Inna	LAT-J	7.7.84	174/56	1500	4:10.85	4:15.29- 01
					3000	8:50.69	9:20.63- 02
					5000	15:22.43	16:15.77- 01
^ Pompey	Aliann	GUY	9.3.78	165/55	400	51.48	51.34- 02
Pop	Ramona	ROM	5.4.82	183/64	HJ	1.88	1.92- 01
Popescu	Alina-Elena	ROM-J	27.10.85	172/52	TJ	13.69	13.76- 01
Porfiriadi	Irina	RUS	14.10.79		LJ	6.54i	6.71- 00
* Pospelova	Svetlana	RUS	24.12.79	169/58	400	50.70	50.47- 00
* Pospísilová	Vera	CZE	19.11.78	178/78	DT	67.71	64.10- 02
Potepa	Wioletta	POL	14.12.80	186/86	DT	60.80	59.58- 02
Pounds (Lynch)	Vicky	CAN	6.6.70	168/59	1M	4:29.39	4:34.17- 01
Poves	Maria José	ESP	16.3.78	167/52	20kW	1:35:32	1:38:42- 02
* Powell	Suzy	USA	3.9.76	178/73	DT	65.38	65.48, 69.44dh- 02
Powell	Virginia	USA	7.9.83		100h	13.07	13.62- 02
Power	Susie	AUS	26.3.75	176/58	HMar	71:31	67:56- 02
Pöyry	Sini	FIN	3.2.80	182/86	HT	67.64	68.28- 02
^ Pozdnyakova	Tatyana	UKR	4.3.56	164/59	Mar	2:29:40	2:29:00- 02
Préau	Christell	FRA	3.11.81	166/60	Hep	5684	5212- 02
Prezerákou	Evridíki	GRE	8.3.75	171/59	PV	4.25	4.15- 02
Price	Melissa	USA	5.9.79	170/84	HT	70.34	66.81- 02
Price	Petrina	AUS-J	26.4.84	180/55	HJ	1.93	1.90- 01
Priemer	Manuela	GER	29.11.78	178/75	HT	67.26	66.30- 99
Proca	Alina	ROM	24.10.83	173/55	3kSt	9:46.76	10:35.38- 02
* Prokhorova	Yelena	RUS	16.4.78	171/59	LJ	6.51	6.72- 00
					Hep	6452	6765- 00
Prokofjev	Aleksandra	SLO	28.11.71	165/56	100	11.41	11.54, 11.52w- 97
* Prokopcuka	Jelena	LAT	21.9.76	168/51	3000	8:53.59	8:44.66i, 8:46.97- 00
					5000	15:02.04	14:47.71- 00
					10000	31:06.14	31:17.72- 02
					HMar	69:19	68:43- 01
					Mar	2:24:01	2:28:36- 02

Name		Nat	Born	Ht/Wt	Event	2003 Mark	Pre-2003 Best
Prokopek	Grazyna	POL	20.4.77	170/51	400	51.36	51.34- 02
Protópappa	Maria	GRE	5.5.73		1500	4:10.84	4:10.51- 02
					5000	15:22.39	15:43.89- 02
Pruteanu	Livia	ROM	22.12.81	177/59	LJ	6.58i, 6.56	6.40- 02
Pskit	Malgorzata	POL	25.5.76	172/56	400h	55.18	55.04- 01
Pudovkina	Irina	RUS	2.11.80	173/50	20kW	1:33:56	1:32:23- 02
de la Puente	Martina	ESP	4.4.75	180/97	SP	17.00	18.17- 99
Pumper	Susanne	AUT	1.9.70	170/50	5000	15:18.79	15:10.54- 01
Pushkina	Lyudmila	UKR	2.10.65	168/54	Mar	2:28:15	2:28:23- 02
* Puzanova	Yekaterina	RUS	1.1.79	168/52	800	1:59.91i	2:01.14- 02
					1500	4:04.77i	4:05.42- 02
* Pyatykh	Anna	RUS	4.4.81	175/64	TJ	14.79	14.67- 02
* Pyrek	Monika	POL	11.8.80	169/52	PV	4.60	4.62- 02
Qian Chunhua		CHN	11.2.79		SP	17.32	18.41- 01
Qin Wangping		CHN	16.6.82	164/53	100	11.39	11.30- 00
					200	23.26	23.08- 00
Qiu Huijing		CHN-J	4.2.85		TJ	13.78	13.85- 02
Quaglia	Emma	ITA	15.8.80	160/46	3kSt	10:09.69	10:16.61- 02
Quintanal	Irache	ESP	18.9.78	170/70	SP	16.91	16.76i- 00, 16.71- 01
Rabchenyuk	Anastasiya	UKR	14.9.83	172/53	400h	56.30	58.01- 00
Racková	Vladimíra	CZE	15.5.67	178/79	DT	61.03	65.50- 01
* Radcliffe	Paula	GBR	17.12.73	173/54	HMar	65:40	66:47- 01
					Mar	2:15:25	2:17:18- 02
Radevica	Ineta	LAT	13.7.81	173/56	LJ	6.70	6.33- 00
					TJ	14.04	13.75- 02
* Rahouli	Baya	ALG	27.7.79	176/58	TJ	14.48	14.64A, 14.30- 99, 14.42w- 00
Rajamäki	Susanna	FIN	19.9.79	177/68	Hep	5883	6021- 00
Rajot	Céline	FRA	22.3.75	162/50	3kSt	9:55.71	10:02.28- 02
Rakonczai	Beáta	HUN	25.6.77		HMar	69:45	73:04- 00, 69:27sc- 01
					Mar	2:29:54	0
Rakotozafy	Rosa	MAD	12.11.77	165/55	100	11.35	11.36- 99, 11.2- 98
					100h	12.93	12.84- 99
Ramadhan Omar	Hanaa	EGY	3.1.83	162/70	JT	54.72	51.41#?- 00
* Ramalalanirina	Nicole	FRA	5.3.72	164/57	100h	13.00, 12.99w	12.76- 00
Ramanauskaite	Rita	LTU	22.2.70	174/72	JT	60.87	65.46#- 96, 62.69- 00
Ramesh	Bina	FRA	19.8.79	176/62	JT	55.72	61.66#- 97, 57.03- 00
* Raspopova	Olga	RUS	27.12.78	176/62	800	1:59.94	1:56.85- 00
* Rath	Daniela	GER	6.5.77	179/60	HJ	2.00	1.94- 96
Raux	Corinne	FRA	16.8.76	164/50	HMar	71:39	75:02- 02
Rebenaque	Ana	ESP	15.9.83	171/48	PV	4.15	4.02- 02
Redfern	Alana	CAN	30.8.83	163/59	JT	55.31	49.90- 02
Redoúmi	Flóra	GRE	11.9.76	168/59	100h	12.90	12.90- 02
Regis	Hazel-Ann	GRN	1.2.81	165/50	400	51.32	51.86- 02
Reiber	Ina	GER	12.3.80	175/69	DT	57.77	55.96- 02
* Renders	Marleen	BEL	24.12.68	166/41	HMar	69:54	68:56- 02
					Mar	2:28:31	2:23:05- 02
Resende	Alessandra	BRA	5.3.75		JT	57.01	57.44- 02
Retel	Rose-Lise	FRA	27.6.73	179/62	TJ	13.78	13.63- 02, 13.70w- 01
Rezanova	Marina	UKR	28.8.74	180/75	HT	66.35	66.80- 02
Rhett	Amandi	USA	29.6.82	168/56	100	11.40, 11.38w	11.48- 02
* Ribeiro	Fernanda	POR	23.6.69	161/48	1500	4:09.28i	4:05.97- 97
					3000	8:49.39i, 8:54.26	8:30.66- 99
					5000	15:16.8 +	14:36.45- 95
					10000	31:13.42	30:22.88- 00
^ Richards	Sandie	JAM	6.11.68	175/67	400	51.80	49.79- 97
* Richards	Sanya	USA-J	26.2.85	173/61	100	11.28	11.39- 02
					200	22.80i, 22.86	23.01- 02
					400	50.58	50.69- 02
Richardson	Ellanee	USA	18.3.80	174/61	Hep	5839	5821- 02
Richardson	LaTasha	USA	23.8.76	168/52	100	11.08	11.68- 01
Richmond	Rose	USA	29.1.81	168/61	LJ	6.50, 6.56w	6.31- 01
Rickert-Curtis	Gina	USA	2.1.79		HJ	1.92i, 1.87	1.89i, 1.86- 02
Rifka	Romary	MEX	23.12.70		HJ	1.94	1.86A- 97
Rigaudo	Elisa	ITA	17.6.80	169/56	20kW	1:30:34	1:29:54- 01
Ríos	Rocio	ESP	13.3.69	156/46	5000	15:31.69	15:47.08- 02
					10000	32:03.99	32:00.11- 96
Rîpanu	Alina	ROM	29.10.81	180/57	800	2:02.16	2:01.96- 99
Risku	Johanna	FIN	21.2.79	170/55	1500	4:07.32	4:13.10- 02
					3kSt	9:55.44	10:09.96- 01
Rittweg	Mareike	GER-J	1.6.84	175/68	JT	56.48	51.71- 02
Ritz dos Santos	Christiane	BRA	6.10.81		800	2:00.98	2:02.80- 02

Name		Nat	Born	Ht/Wt	Event	2003 Mark	Pre-2003 Best
Rivas	Thaimara	VEN	23.7.82		Hep	5622	5063- 02
Roach	Peaches	JAM-J	21.12.84		HJ	1.87	
Roba	Fatuma	ETH	18.12.73	160/48	Mar	2:30:26	2:23:21- 98
Robbeson	Justine	RSA-J	15.5.85	167/58	Hep	5761	
Robert-Michon	Melina	FRA	18.7.79	178/87	DT	64.27	65.78- 02
Roberts	Trecia	THA	4.2.71	163/59	100h	12.94	12.73A- 98, 12.83- 99
Robinson	Amber	USA	5.6.80	165/56	100	11.43	
Robinson	Camille	JAM-J	30.3.84	165/53	400h	56.61	56.14- 02
Robinson	Moushami	USA	13.4.81	167/55	400	51.93	51.79- 01
Robinson	Shana	USA	13.2.82		100	11.44, 11.35w	11.42, 11.40w- 01
					200	23.55A, 22.84w	23.74- 02
Robson	Renee	AUS	3.11.78		100	11.2w	
Rocco	Lara	ITA	20.12.75	163/51	400h	57.05	56.43- 98
Rocco	Tiziana	ITA	2.12.78	176/78	JT	57.42	57.27#- 99, 56.88- 00
Rocha	Nora	MEX	18.12.67	168/56	5000	15:30.05	15:06.54- 98
Rockmeier	Birgit	GER	29.11.73	173/62	200	23.24	22.90- 01, 22.89i- 98
					400	52.13	51.45- 00
Rockmeier	Gabrielle	GER	29.11.73	173/59	100	11.42	11.17- 01
					200	23.01	22.68- 01
Rodionova	Tatyana	RUS	27.8.80	163/53	800	2:01.19	2:00.65- 01
Rodríguez	Libia Patricia	COL	25.10.70	158/50	400	51.89	52.95- 95
* Rodríguez	Natalia	ESP	2.6.79	167/49	800	2:01.54	2:01.35- 01
					1500	4:01.30	4:02.84- 02
Rodríguez	Yuneisy	CUB-J	1.5.84	165/56	JT	54.30	54.86- 02
* Rogova	Oksana	RUS	7.10.78	180/60	TJ	14.16	14.70i- 02, 14.59- 99
* Rogowska	Anna	POL	21.5.81	171/52	PV	4.47i, 4.45	4.40- 02
Rohl	Michelle	USA	12.11.65	150/41	20kW	1:34:31.06t	1:31:51- 00
Rohr	Nadine	SUI	29.6.77	170/56	PV	4.30	4.21- 02
Roles	Philippa	GBR	1.3.78	180/100	DT	62.89	60.00- 99
Roman	Sonja	SLO	11.3.79		1500	4:09.67	4:12.66- 02
^ Romanova	Anna	RUS	9.3.68	182/88	SP	19.18	20.24- 93
Romanova	Olga	RUS	23.5.80		10000	32:28.91	32:52.26- 02
Ros	Beatriz	ESP	12.5.74	168/54	Mar	2:29:25	2:34:57- 02
Rosa	Anália	POR	28.2.76		3kSt	9:49.62	9:47.87- 02
Rosa	Chiara	ITA	28.1.83	176/80	SP	17.06	16.96- 02
^ Rose-Henley	Dionne	JAM	7.11.69	169/57	100h	13.01	12.64- 96
* Roshchupkina	Natalya	RUS	13.1.78	182/70	Hep	6170	6633- 00
Rosikhina	Irina	RUS	11.5.75	175/65	400	51.97	50.76- 00, 50.5- 98
Roslanova	Tatyana	KAZ	28.9.80		400	52.04	54.00- 01
					800	2:00.98	
Ross	Chaniqua	USA	24.5.80	173/80	SP	16.69	16.55- 01
					DT	56.29	57.47- 02
Ross	Tiffany	USA	5.2.83	157/57	100h	13.12	13.30, 13.01w- 02
					400h	55.89	55.22- 02
Rovelto	Karol	USA	20.12.69	178/58	HJ	1.97	1.93- 99
* Rozenberg	Yekaterina	RUS	23.1.80	168/56	800	1:59.98	2:05.38- 00
					1500	4:00.07	4:16.33- 00
Rublevskaya	Lyudmila	RUS	7.6.77	186/87	DT	59.03	60.04- 99
* Rublyova	Olga	RUS	28.10.74	175/65	LJ	6.89	6.90, 7.01w- 95
Rücklová	Alena	CZE	7.10.81	165/65	400h	57.09	57.31- 02
Ruckstuhl	Karin	NED	2.11.80	181/65	Hep	6017	5858- 02
^ Rudolph	Amy	USA	18.9.73	176/55	3000	8:57.44i	8:39.86- 00
Rumpf	Sabine	GER	18.3.83	176/95	DT	55.78	54.82- 02
Rünne	Eha	EST	25.5.63	182/86	DT	55.80	63.18- 88
* Runyan	Marla	USA	4.1.69	170/60	5000	15:16.18	15:05.48- 01
					Mar	2:30:28	2:27:10- 02
Rus	Maria	ROM	19.1.83	183/60	400h	56.34	0
Russell/Phillips	Blake	USA	24.7.75	168/51	5000	15:24.68	15:21.37- 00
					10000	32:11.94	32:16.33- 00
					Mar	2:30:41	-0-
Rutjes	Ilona	NED	28.5.80	181/76	DT	56.40	56.12- 99
Ryabinkina	Olga	RUS	24.9.76	190/90	SP	19.36i, 19.07	19.36- 02
					DT	59.03	61.66- 98
* Ryashkina	Nadezhda	RUS	22.1.67	160/47	20kW	1:28:52	1:27:30- 99
Rybalko	Viktoriya	UKR	26.10.82	177/59	LJ	6.57	6.43- 99, 6.47w- 02
* Ryshich	Nastja	GER	19.9.77	170/58	PV	4.32	4.50i, 4.44- 99
* Sacramento	Carla	POR	10.12.71	173/58	1500	4:06.64	3:57.71- 98
Sadach	Aneta	POL	22.4.75	175/62	TJ	13.99	13.75- 02
* Sadova	Natalya	RUS	15.6.72	180/100	DT	69.38	70.02- 99
Safarova	Irina	RUS	19.6.69		HMar	70:34	69:55- 01

Name		Nat	Born	Ht/Wt	Event	2003 Mark	Pre-2003 Best
* Safronnikova	Natalya	BLR	28.2.73	174/60	100	11.05	11.17- 99, 10.9- 98
					200	22.71	22.68- 01, 22.3- 98
^ Safronova	Natalya	BLR	11.7.74	176/60	TJ	14.08	14.65- 00
Safta	Anca	ROM	9.1.78	175/52	800	2:01.75	2:02.12i- 01, 2:02.31- 96
Sagonas	Sophia	GER	18.9.81	175/57	HJ	1.92i, 1.90	1.88i- 00, 1.85- 99
Saito	Yuki	JPN	25.9.80	153/44	5000	15:28.11	15:38.75- 01
					10000	31:49.29	
Sakakura (Tadamasa)	Ryoko	JPN	9.5.76	164/47	20kW	1:32:43	1:33:43- 99
* Sakamoto	Naoko	JPN	14.11.80	160/44	HMar	70:22+	69:27- 01
					Mar	2:21:51	0
Sakashita	Naomi	JPN	25.5.75	158/44	10000	32:33.22	31:53.40- 96
Salinas	Indira	CUB-J	28.10.85		HT	63.41	57.76- 02
Sallins	Melinda	USA	30.6.73	178/64	400h	56.24	56.06- 97
Saltanovic	Kristina	LTU	20.2.75	162/53	20kW	1:31:09	1:30:44- 02
Samaria	Agnes	NAM	11.8.72	166/56	800	2:00.55i, 2:01.51	1:59.15- 02
					1000	2:38.59i, 2:39.58	
* Samitova	Gulnara	RUS	9.7.78	173/55	5000	14:54.38	
					3kSt	9:08.33	0
Samokhvalova	Yelena	RUS	21.11.80	165/49	5000	15:15.75	16:02.62- 00
					10000	31:43.51	32:15.98- 02
Sampaio	Helena	POR	9.10.73	159/46	Mar	2:28:06	2:29:34- 00
Sánchez	Angélica	MEX	11.12.75		Mar	2:31:12	
Sánchez	María del Rosario	MEX	26.10.73		20kW	1:34:53	1:30:52- 99
Sanfabio	Tamara	ESP	14.3.78	160/46	3kSt	10:09.42	10:39.63- 02
Sanganoko	Makaridja	CIV	8.5.80	160/58	100	11.38	11.17- 02
Santiago	Beatriz	ESP	28.10.68	160/50	10000	32:33.34	32:12.6- 00
dos Santos	Luciana	BRA	10.2.70	160/56	LJ	6.48	6.72- 00, 6.81A- 99
					TJ	13.83	14.01- 00
dos Santos	Perla	BRA	29.1.82	155/49	400	52.28A, 52.71	53.39- 00
					400h	56.08	56.52- 01
Santos	Vera	POR	3.12.81	164/59	20kW	1:32:43	1:34:46.6t- 02
Sarmiento	Sarai	ESP	3.12.78	160/50	3kSt	10:10.39	0
Sato	Sayoko	JPN	23.10.77	168/58	Hep	5649	5713- 01
^ Sauer	Mary	USA	31.10.75	164/59	PV	4.40	4.65- 02
Savchuk	Valentina	UKR	19.1.75	157/49	20kW	1:28:52	1:28:56- 01
Savigne	Yargelis	CUB-J	13.11.84	165/53	LJ	6.63	6.46- 02
* Saville	Jane	AUS	5.11.74	164/53	20kW	1:30:51	1:28:56- 00
Sawyer	Adrien	USA	13.12.75	170/57	LJ	6.60	6.87- 99
Sayers	Goldie	GBR	16.7.82	171/69	JT	56.29	58.20- 02
* Sazanovich	Natalya	BLR	15.8.73	178/63	LJ	6.57i. 6.47	6.86- 96
					SP	16.81	16.58- 02
					Hep	6524	6563- 96
Schäffel	Aline	GER	15.5.80	178/84	SP	16.91	16.70- 02
Scherwin	Christina	DEN	11.7.76	177/61	JT	56.80	59.06- 00
Schiemenz	Kim	USA	13.4.77	178/66	Hep	6209A	5840- 02
Schmidt	Alice	USA	3.10.81		800	2:01.16	2:04.35- 02
Schott	Maren	GER	11.2.76	173/62	400h	55.28	55.44- 01
Schötz	Katja	GER	22.7.81	183/57	HJ	1.91	1.90- 02
Schreiber	Katja	GER	30.6.78	182/75	DT	58.10	60.32- 01
Schulte	Sabine	GER	29.1.76	169/58	PV	4.30i, 4.10	4.40, 4.43sq- 02
Schulte	Sofia	GER	8.4.76	178/58	LJ	6.60	6.72- 00
Schultze	Anna	GER-J	26.5.85	173/61	PV	4.20	3.91- 02
Schulz	Christine	GER-J	30.1.84		Hep	5699	5393- 02
Schwald	Sarah	USA	2.1.73	165/48	1500	4:08.16	4:04.43- 01
					3000	8:51.07i	8:51.68i- 01
* Schwartz	Jillian	USA	19.9.79	173/62	PV	4.45	4.50- 02
Schwarzkopf	Lilly	GER	28.8.83	173/65	Hep	5735	5597- 02
Scott	Candace	TRI	17.9.80	180/100	SP	16.74	16.86- 02
					HT	69.79	63.26- 02
Scott	Catherine	JAM	24.8.73	174/61	400	52.03	51.65- 00
Scott	Colleen	JAM	18.8.74	183/63	LJ	6.56	6.51- 96
					TJ	14.03, 14.24w	13.83- 98
Scott	Susan	GBR	26.9.77	168/52	800	2:01.08	1:59.30- 02
Seeger	Melanie	GER	8.1.77	166/49	20kW	1:29:44	1:30:41- 01
Seegers	Wendy	RSA	28.2.76		200	23.27A	22.74A- 99
Sekachova	Irina	UKR	21.7.76	165/72	HT	72.96	69.53- 00
Sellam	Aïda	TUN	13.9.77		JT	58.62	56.20- 01
Semedo	Nédia	POR	14.11.78	160/50	800	2:01.11i, 2:03.05	2:00.54- 02
Semyonova	Svetlana	RUS	16.3.79		LJ	6.47	6.26- 02
					TJ	13.92	
Serbezova	Nina	BUL	6.5.81		TJ	13.78i, 13.76	12.95- 02

Name		Nat	Born	Ht/Wt	Event	2003 Mark	Pre-2003 Best
Serwah	Akosua	GHA	3.1.81		800	2:00.42	2:01.30- 02
* Seryogina	Viktoriya	RUS	22.5.73	170/60	HJ	2.00i, 1.97	2.00- 02
Sesay	Ola	USA	30.5.79		LJ	6.58	6.47i, 6.53w- 00; 6.40- 99
Setowska	Ewelina	POL	5.3.80	170/55	400h	57.53	58.65- 02
* Seyerling/Quinn	Heide	RSA	19.8.76	168/55	200	23.10	22.63- 01, 22.59Aw- 00
					400	51.30	50.05- 00
Sharova	Galina	RUS	30.1.79	179/59	TJ	13.94	14.21- 01
* Shaw	Lorraine	GBR	2.4.68	171/90	HT	68.93	68.15- 01
Shchinova	Yelena	RUS	.80		LJ	6.54i	
Shchors	Olena	UKR-J	6.3.84	175/60	LJ	6.46	6.13- 02
Sheehy	Ciara	IRL	12.8.80	170/59	200	23.17i, 23.40	23.21A, 23.02w- 02
Shekhodanova	Natalya	RUS	29.12.71	169/55	100h	12.83	12.59- 96
^ Shekhovtsova	Yelena	UKR	31.5.72	178/58	LJ	6.67	6.97- 96
Shen Shengfei		CHN	21.1.81	178/70	Hep	5983	6263- 01
Sherman	Alandra	USA-J	25.11.85		100h	13.25	14.12- 02
^ Shevchenko	Irina	RUS	2.9.75	175/65	100h	13.18	12.81- 01, 12.77Aw- 98
Shi Na		CHN	17.2.81	160/50	20kW	1:31:14	1:34:15- 96
* Shibui	Yoko	JPN	14.3.79	164/46	5000	15:27.83	15:18.92- 02
					10000	31:42.01	30:48.89- 02
* Shikolenko	Tatyana	RUS	10.5.68	177/74	JT	66.00	67.84#- 98, 67.20- 00
Shimahara	Kiyoko	JPN	22.12.76	153/43	Mar	2:28:17	
Shimchuk	Natalya	BLR	1.10.81	179/77	JT	57.64	57.12- 02
Shinkins	Karen	IRL	15.10.76	165/53	400	52.06	51.07- 99
Shiviryova	Natalya	RUS	31.8.78	164/54	20kW	1:32:18	1:31:51- 00
Shkolina	Svetlana	RUS-Y	9.3.86		HJ	1.88	1.84- 02
Shobha	J.J.	IND	14.1.78	167/59	Hep	5884	5870- 02
Shook	Brianna	USA	6.1.81		3kSt	9:44.71	9:58.97- 02
Shukina	Olga	UZB	6.4.77		SP	17.04	16.36- 02
Sialou	Androula	CYP	27.1.73	170/61	400	52.30	53.34i- 02, 55.11- 01
					400h	55.42	55.25- 02
Sibilyeva	Tatyana	RUS	17.5.80	164/51	20kW	1:27:54	1:27:33- 01
Sidibé	Odiah	FRA	13.1.70	176/64	100	11,49, 11.20w	11.23- 95, 10.8w- 96
Sidorchenko	Yelena	RUS	30.5.80		1500	4:08.98i, 4:13.08	
					3000	8:55.15i	
Sidorenko (Tobias)	Natalya	UKR	22.11.80	160/49	1500	4:07.79	4:10.14- 00
					3000	8:51.32	9:03.66- 02
Sidunova	Svetlana	RUS	29.5.81		800	2:00.94, 2:00.52i	2:01.46- 02
Siilats	Kärt	EST	7.9.80	184/62	HJ	1.90	1.89- 99
Silva	Vânia	POR	8.6.80		HT	68.14	68.43- 02
* Simagina	Irina	RUS	25.5.82	170/60	LJ	6.83	6.74i, 6.58- 02
Simmons	Lauren	USA	1.5.79		800	2:02.25	2:03.87- 02
* Simpson	Margaret	GHA	31.12.81	162/53	Hep	6152	6004, 6105w- 02
Simpson	Sherone	JAM-J	12.8.84	173/44	100	11.37, 11.1	11.60- 02
Sims	Kira	USA	1.3.82		PV	4.20	3.95- 02
Singh	Neelam Jaswant	IND	8.1.71	166/80	DT	61.94	64.55- 02
Skafída	Afrodíti	GRE	20.3.82		PV	4.25	4.00i, 3.95- 02
* Skolimowska	Kamila	POL	4.11.82	180/112	HT	71.38	72.60- 02
Skotnik	Melanie	GER	8.11.82	182/61	HJ	1.97i, 1.91	1.88- 02
* Skujyté	Austra	LTU	12.8.79	188/75	Hep	6213	6275- 02
Slastina	Zhanna	UKR	4.9.77	167/64	JT	57.07	55.05- 01
* Slesarenko	Yelena	RUS	28.2.82	178/54	HJ	1.98i, 1.96	1.97- 02
Slivka	Viktoriya	RUS	28.9.80	178/54	HJ	1.94	1.94- 99
Smedley	Melinda	USA	11.2.81		200	23.40A, 23.10Aw	23.32A- 02
Smith	Ronetta	JAM	2.5.80	172/60	400	51.35	51.62- 02
Smith	Shauna	USA	10.9.83	178/64	400h	57.09	58.89- 02
Smith	Stephanie	USA-J	27.6.85		400	52.04	52.11- 01
* Smith	Trecia-Kaye	JAM	5.11.75	185/66	TJ	13.96i, 13.55, 13.89w	14.32-02, 14.88w-01
Smolyachkova	Mariya	BLR-J	10.2.85	179/76	HT	67.08	60.47- 02
Smyslova	Marina	RUS	25.2.66	163/61	20kW	1:30:48	1:32:38- 91
Snetkova	Anna	RUS	.80		Hep	5745	5809- 02
^ Sobanska	Malgorzata	POL	25.4.69	165/50	Mar	2:27:50	2:26:08- 01
Sobolyeva	Yelena	RUS	3.8.82		800	2:01.65	2:04.43- 02
^ Söderberg	Anna	SWE	11.6.73	177/82	DT	61.61	64.54- 99
Solomon	Mariana	ROM	8.9.80	172/58	TJ	14.09	13.96i- 01, 13.92- 02
Solomon	Shalonda	USA-J	19.12.85	169/56	100	11.35, 11.25w	11.59- 00, 11.37w- 01
					200	22.93	23.31- 02
Soma	Kate	USA	13.2.83		PV	4.22	4.00- 02
Soman	Patricia	CIV	12.8.81		LJ	6.44i, 6.38, 6.60w	
Song Aimin		CHN	15.3.78	176/67	DT	65.33	62.34- 01
* Song Feina		CHN	25.1.77	183/95	SP	17.66i, 17.34	18.73- 01
* Song Hongjuan		CHN-J	4.7.84		20kW	1:27:16	1:40:38- 01

	Name		Nat	Born	Ht/Wt	Event	2003 Mark	Pre-2003 Best
	Soong	Cari	USA	11.7.81	173/89	HT	65.92	64.24- 01
	Sorokina	Aleksandra	RUS	24.2.79	163/54	20kW	1:32:56	1:34:31.2t- 01
^	Sosimenko	Debbie	AUS	5.4.74	170/95	HT	67.82	67.95- 00
	Sosnowska	Aneta	POL	10.5.74	170/58	100h	12.99	12.96- 02
	Sotherton	Kelly	GBR	13.11.76	180/66	LJ	6.58, 6.68w	6.23, 6.28w- 01
						Hep	6059	5794- 02
	Sotnikova	Yulia	RUS	18.11.70	164/53	400	51.54	50.73- 00
	Spencer	Amy	GBR-J	19.9.85	180/	200	23.20i, 23.45	
	Spencer	Keisha	JAM	16.2.78	176/61	LJ	6.66w	6.61- 00
	Spencer	Sasha	USA	4.8.79		800	2:01.56	2:02.34- 02
	Spiegelburg	Silke	GER-Y	17.3.86	173/62	PV	4.20i, 4.15	4.20- 02
	Spîtaru	Cristine	ROM-Y	4.2.86	171/61	TJ	13.86	13.26- 02
	Spivey	Donesha	USA	20.8.83		100	11.1w	
						200	22.9w	
	Spotáková	Barbora	CZE	30.6.81	182/80	JT	56.65	56.76- 02
	Sprenger	Juliane	GER	22.3.77	163/53	100h	12.87	13.00- 00
	Staicu	Simona	HUN	5.5.71	164/48	HMar	70:43	70:11- 00, 68:36sc- 01
	Stals	Sandra	BEL	5.6.75	170/55	800	2:01.07	1:58.31- 98
	Staten	Natasha	USA	2.12.81	165/58	200	23.28w	23.62- 00
*	Stef	Claudia	ROM	25.2.78	160/48	20kW	1:29:09	1:29:39- 99
	Stefashina	Olga	RUS	10.10.81		400	52.01	54.05- 02
	Steiner	April	USA	22.4.80		PV	4.35i, 4.27	4.15i- 02, 4.07- 01
	Stewart	Kerron	JAM-J	16.4.84	175/61	100	11.34, 11.2	11.60- 02
	Stoddart	Shevon	USA	21.11.82		400h	57.45	57.64- 02
	Stoian	Monica	ROM	25.8.82	168/67	JT	55.50	55.66- 00
	Stone	Felicia	USA	10.8.77		100h	13.05	13.21- 00, 13.15w- 02
	Straková	Iva	CZE	4.8.80		HJ	1.96i, 1.91	1.90- 02
	Stratáki	Aryiró	GRE	3.8.75	173/55	Hep	6116	5855- 02
	Strömmer	Mia	FIN	26.2.74	170/70	HT	65.53	69.63- 01
	Strutz	Martina	GER	4.11.81	160/53	PV	4.20	4.42- 01
	Stucan	Constanta	ROM	12.7.81	175/60	TJ	13.98	13.96- 00
*	Sturrup	Chandra	BAH	12.9.71	163/55	100	10.89, 10.88w	10.86- 00
*	Styopina	Viktoria	UKR	21.2.76	175/58	HJ	2.00	1.96- 99
	Su Yiping		CHN	4.8.79	174/58	100h	13.09	12.91- 99, 12.70w- 01
*	Sua	Seilala	USA	25.2.78	188/109	SP	17.83i, 17.69	18.51- 02
						DT	61.93	65.90- 00
^	Sudak	Svetlana	BLR	20.3.71	174/90	HT	68.55	68.21- 99
	Sugimori	Miho	JPN	14.4.78	156/49	800	2:00.78i	2:03.22- 02
^	Suldesová	Andrea	CZE	11.2.75	164/51	1500	4:07.76	4:06.13- 98
						2000	5:44.98	
	Sultanova (Zhdanova)	Firiya	RUS	29.4.61	166/52	Mar	2:27:05	2:27:58- 02
	Sun Chunfang		CHN	1.3.77	171/58	20kW	1:35:25	1:29:45- 00
	Sun Hongfeng		CHN-J	11.4.84		200	23.27	
						400	51.64	
	Sun Lihua		CHN	30.9.83		20kW	1:35:20	1:38:12- 02
*	Sun Yingjie		CHN	3.10.77	165/50	3000	8:50.34+	9:19.28i- 02
						5000	14:46.73	14:40.41- 02
						10000	30:07.20	30:28.26- 02
						Mar	2:19:39	2:21:21- 02
	Suthe	Annika	GER-J	15.10.85	175/68	JT	55.19	49.97- 02
*	Suttle	Kellie	USA	9.5.73	170/59	PV	4.58	4.60- 01
	Swennen	Sandra	BEL	12.2.73	163/56	TJ	13.79	13.57- 01
	Syrek	Grazyna	POL	9.1.72	180/59	Mar	2:26:22	2:35:11- 02
*	Szabo	Gabriela	ROM	14.11.75	158/43	2000	5:39.18+	5:36.88+- 97
						3000	8:33.95	8:21.42- 02
						5000	14:41.35	14:31.48- 98
*	Szabó	Nikolett	HUN	3.3.80	168/65	JT	62.88	64.62- 01
^	Szabó	Zsuzsanna	HUN	6.5.73	176/63	PV	4.33	4.51i, 4.40- 99
	Szczepanska	Magdalena	POL	25.1.80	178/62	Hep	6001	6051- 02
	Tabáki	Hristiána	GRE	13.1.73	173/59	100h	13.06, 13.02w	13.01- 02
	Tabakova	Yuliya	RUS	1.5.80	165/57	100	11.20	11.16- 02
						200	22.66	22.68- 01
	Tadesse	Mestawet	ETH-J	19.7.85		1M	4:28.51	
	Tafflet	Corinne	FRA	8.11.75	163/48	400h	56.97	57.08- 01
	Takahashi	Fujiko	JPN	19.6.83	156/43	HMar	70:17	
*	Takahashi	Naoko	JPN	6.5.72	163/46	HMar	70:03+	68:55- 00
						Mar	2:27:21	2:19:46- 01
	Takanaka	Mikie	JPN	6.10.80	163/43	10000	32:08.84	32:23.00- 01
						HMar	70:32	68:32- 02
	Talbot	Aurélie	FRA	22.8.81	176/58	TJ	13.70	13.30- 99

Name		Nat	Born	Ht/Wt	Event	2003 Mark	Pre-2003 Best
Talpos	Luminita	ROM	9.10.72	164/47	HMar	71:04	70:08- 02
					Mar	2:27:32	2:31:13- 97
Tan Dongyun		CHN-Y	25.10.86		JT	54.51	50.56- 02
Tanabe	Kumi	JPN	2.4.81	158/40	HMar	69:55	71:58- 01
Tanaka	Machi	JPN	21.7.83	153/45	10000	32:27.01	
Tanaka	Megumi	JPN	4.9.75	160/43	5000	15:29.57	15:17.92- 99
					10000	31:47.00	31:42.74- 02
					HMar	70:23+	72:43- 02
					Mar	2:29:57	2:28:10- 02
Tao Hongbo		CHN	20.9.79		DT	57.89	60.83- 99
Taranova	Anastasiya	RUS-J	6.9.85	178/61	TJ	13.93	13.18- 02
Tavares	Carmo	POR	27.4.74	168/52	400h	56.43A, 57.01	56.25- 02
Tavares	Elisabete	POR	7.3.80	170/54	PV	4.25	4.10- 02
Tavares	Sandra	POR	29.5.82	166/55	PV	4.20	4.00- 02
* Taylor	Brenda	USA	9.2.79	174/63	400h	54.92	55.46- 01
Teichmann	Ivonne	GER	11.4.77	170/50	800	2:01.77	1:58.62- 01
* Tejeda	Anay	CUB	3.4.83	164/59	100h	12.99	12.89, 12.81w, 12.6- 02
Teloni	Elena	CYP	16.12.64	171/82	HT	65.04	61.58- 02
Teodoro	Lucimar	BRA	1.5.81		400	52.07	53.61- 01
					400h	56.21	
Teppe	Agnès	FRA	4.5.68	182/78	DT	55.97	60.14- 92
* Tereshchuk	Tatyana	UKR	11.10.69	185/63	400h	54.26	53.40- 98
Ter-Mesrobyan	Tatyana	RUS	12.5.68	180/62	LJ	6.74	7.06- 02
Termure	Ana Mirela	ROM	13.1.75	175/63	JT	61.91	65.08- 01
Terzóglou	Iríni	GRE	2.2.79	176/86	SP	19.10	17.70- 02
* Teter	Nicole	USA	8.11.73	172/57	800	1:59.91	1:57.97- 02
* Thánou	Ekateríni	GRE	1.2.75	165/56	100	11.03	10.83, 10.77w- 99
* Thiam	Ami Mbacké	SEN	10.11.76	183/70	200	23.23	23.20, 23.0A- 99
					400	49.95	49.86- 01
Thimm	Annette	GER	24.11.77		100h	13.14	13.41- 01
Thoma	Althea	USA	8.8.81		400h	57.20	
* Thompson	Bronwyn	AUS	29.1.78	177/68	LJ	6.73, 6.75w	7.00- 02
Thompson	Moya	JAM			400	51.80	54.07- 02
* Tirlea	Ionela	ROM	9.2.76	169/54	200	22.78	22.35- 99
					400	52.19	49.88- 99
					400h	53.87	53.25- 99
Tito	Josiane	BRA	8.8.79		400	52.30	52.68- 02
					800	2:01.88	2:01.47- 02
Tittmann	Andrea	GER	1.3.76		Hep	5638	5622- 01
Tkach	Anna	RUS/ISR	17.4.75	168/61	400	51.66	50.67- 00
Tkalich	Tatyana	UKR	30.5.75	160/50	100	11.25	11.47- 02, 11.0- 98
Tola	Worknesh	ETH	3.6.77		Mar	2:25:42	2:29:10- 02
Tolbert	Ryan	USA	16.6.76	174/64	400h	56.33	54.21- 97
Tollefson	Carrie	USA	18.1.77	175/54	5000	15:27.00	15:21.37- 02
Tolstaya	Svetlana	KAZ	9.8.71	168/52	20kW	1:30:57	1:28:38- 02
Tomanová	Ivona	SVK	24.10.72	185/80	DT	56.33	59.24- 96
Tomasevic	Dragana	SCG	4.6.82	175/80	DT	56.24	54.41, 55.33dh- 02
* Tomashova	Tatyana	RUS	1.7.75	164/50	1500	3:58.52	4:01.28- 02
					3000	8:44.78	8:25.56- 01
* Tomescu (Dita)	Constantina	ROM	23.1.70	165/48	HMar	69:21+	68:10- 02
					Mar	2:23:35	2:23:54- 02
Toney	Nicole	USA	19.12.82		TJ	13.77i, 13.54, 13.58w	13.72i- 02
Tonn	Claudia	GER	18.4.81	182/72	Hep	5842	5696- 02
* Toomey	Jennifer	USA	19.12.71	165/51	800	1:59.75	2:00.12- 02
					1500	4:10.11	4:11.74- 02
Torre	Analídia	POR	10.10.76		3kSt	10:03.62	10:03.16- 02
Torres/Maurer	Carolina	CHI	16.3.79		PV	4.30	4.00- 02
* Torshina	Natalya	KAZ	4.10.68	172/57	400h	55.24	54.50- 00
* Tosa	Reiko	JPN	11.6.76	167/45	HMar	71:15	69:36- 99
Tóth	Livia	HUN	7.1.80	171/52	1500	4:09.28	4:11.06- 02
					3kSt	10:00.93	9:51.38- 02
Touhami	Nahida	ALG	10.2.78		800	2:01.97	2:02.93- 01
Towns	Ara	USA	26.3.83	163/	100	11.43	11.68- 02
Toyonaga	Yoko	JPN	15.4.77	164/90	SP	17.28	16.90- 02
Trotter	Dee Dee	USA	8.12.82	178/60	400	50.66	53.66- 02
Trujillo	Janet	USA	7.8.75		3kSt	10:05.53	10:09.70- 01
Trybanska	Malgorzata	POL	21.6.81	176/61	LJ	6.59	6.26- 01
* Trywianska	Aurelia	POL	9.5.76	174/59	100h	12.74	12.97- 02
Tsámoglou	Evdokía	GRE	15.12.78	174/84	HT	68.12	65.83- 01
* Tsander	Olga	BLR	18.5.76	174/83	HT	70.02	70.11- 02
Tschomba	Myriam	BEL	8.1.77	171/53	100h	13.24	13.35- 97, 12.9w- 99

Name		Nat	Born	Ht/Wt	Event	2003 Mark	Pre-2003 Best
Tsedemeídou	El'éni	GRE	21.5.69		SP	16.58	18.53- 97
* Tsikoúna	Stiliani	GRE	19.10.72	171/88	DT	64.14	65.13- 00
Tsiliggíri	Yeoryía	GRE	21.6.72	158/46	PV	4.40	4.38- 02
Tsiolakoúdi	Aggelikí	GRE	10.5.76	172/66	JT	56.66	63.14- 02, 63.32#- 97
Tsírba ¶	María	GRE	28.7.79		3000	8:52.21i dq	9:35.06- 00
Tsoumeléka	Athanasia	GRE	2.1.82	157/49	20kW	1:29:34	1:31:25- 02
* Tsybulskaya	Valentina	BLR	19.2.68	163/54	20kW	1:28:10	1:28:49- 01
Tubbs	Monique	USA	23.1.81	163/59	100	11.41, 11.13w	11.52, 11.37dt- 00
Tucholke	Jana	GER	20.5.81	185/90	DT	58.26	58.99- 02
Tudja	Julianna	HUN	13.10.79	175/77	HT	66.69	64.29- 01
* Tullett	Hayley	GBR	17.2.73	166/58	800	2:00.49	2:01.25- 00
					1500	3:59.95	4:01.23- 00
					1M	4:27.46i	4:26.50i- 01, 4:48.85- 95
					3000	8:57.45, 8:46.95i	8:45.36i-01, 8:45.39- 00
* Tulu	Derartu	ETH	21.3.72	155/45	3000	8:56.9+	8:46.32- 00
					5000	14:44.22	14:44.57- 00
					HMar	69:12	67:03- 01
					Mar	2:26:33	2:23:57- 01
Tunks	Lieja	NED	10.3.76	183/95	SP	18.82	18.56- 01
					DT	56.59	58.93- 02
* Turova	Alesya	BLR	6.12.79	180/64	800	2:02.11i	2:04.52- 99
					1500	4:03.32	3:59.89- 02
					3kSt	9:20.28	9:16.51- 02
Tusai	Brigitta	HUN	30.6.77		3000	8:57.92i	10:36.0i- 93
Tverdostup (Volkova)	Tamara	UKR	17.7.79	167/58	800	2:01.2	2:02.26- 01
Twum	Monica	GHA	14.3.78	159/58	100	11.47, 11.29w	11.31- 01, 11.29w- 99
					200	23.12w	23.21- 00, 23.20w- 01
Tyson	Cleo	USA-J	27.2.85		100	11.40w	11.54w- 02
^ Tyukhay	Irina	RUS	14.1.67	171/64	Hep	5679	6604- 95
Udmurtova	Oksana	RUS	.82		LJ	6.78	6.41- 02
Ueda	Mie	JPN	9.6.82	157/42	10000	32:32.76	
Ukabam	Amarachi	USA-J	14.3.84		DT	56.21	53.39- 02
Ulyeva	Iolanta	KAZ	27.7.76	172/85	SP	17.49	18.04i- 02, 17.82- 00
Umelo	Grace	NGR	.78		LJ	6.56	6.60- 99
Umlauft	Katja	GER	22.11.74	180/60	LJ	6.50	6.42- 99
					TJ	13.89i, 13.60	14.01i, 13.93- 01
Unger	Robin	USA	12.12.72	179/66	Hep	5808	5667- 02
* Upshaw	Grace	USA	22.9.75	178/65	LJ	6.73, 6.99w	6.62- 01, 6.75w- 02
Usovich	Svetlana	BLR	14.10.80		400	51.39	51.64- 02
Vanakára	Asimína	GRE	14.7.79		LJ	6.46	6.31- 01
Vanden Bempt	Sigrid	BEL	10.2.81		3kSt	9:42.04	9:53.20- 02
van der Geer	Sandra	NED	25.5.72		PV	4.25i, 4.20	4.34- 02
Vander Hoek	Kim	CAN	30.11.70	172/64	Hep	5734	5935- 92
Vanek	Missy	USA	11.9.79	173/60	Hep	5754	5602- 00
* Varga	Judit	HUN	16.4.76	169/49	800	1:59.46	2:01.00- 02
					1000	2:37.36	2:39.01- 02
					1500	4:02.19	4:01.26- 02
Vári	Edit	HUN	31.5.75	172/61	100h	13.22	13.17- 02
Vasallo	Aldenay	CUB	25.2.77	170/73	HT	69.72	67.36- 02
* Vasco	María	ESP	26.12.75	156/47	20kW	1:28:10	1:28:47- 02
* Vasdéki	Ólga	GRE	26.9.73	174/59	TJ	14.50	14.67- 99
Vashentseva	Irina	RUS	30.9.80	173/58	800	1:59.63	2:01.69- 02
Vasilyeva	Irina	RUS	9.4.79	168/54	TJ	13.87i, 13.84	14.57- 01
Vasilyeva	Lyudmila	RUS	20.10.69		1M	4:30.48	4:31.62- 00
Vásquez	Fior	DOM	27.12.77		SP	18.14	17.04- 02
* Vaszi	Tünde	HUN	18.4.72	170/60	PV	4.20i, 4.00	4.30i- 02, 4.15- 99
					LJ	6.76	6.86- 01
Vaylenko	Lyudmila	UKR	18.3.74	169/62	PV	4.20i	4.10- 01
Veldáková	Dana	SVK	3.6.81	178/59	TJ	14.02	13.99- 02
* Veneva	Venelina	BUL	13.6.74	179/61	HJ	2.01	2.04- 01
^ Vershinina	Viktoriya	UKR	11.6.71	178/69	LJ	6.63i	6.92- 96, 6.98sq- 95
Vibjerg	Dorte	DEN	28.10.73	173/54	10000	32:42.73	33:00.15- 99
Viceconte	Maura	ITA	3.10.67	156/47	Mar	2:29:13	2:23:47- 00
Vigliano	Nadia	FRA	24.6.77		JT	55.93	54.26- 00
Vilisova	Tatyana	RUS	.79		3kSt	10:10.29	10:12.07- 00
Viljoen	Sunette	RSA	6.10.83		JT	61.59	58.33- 02
Vinatho	Vassanee	THA	30.6.80		400h	56.40	58.67- 02
Vis	Judith	NED	21.6.80	183/72	100h	13.05	13.17- 02
Visockaite-Eggerth	Agné	LTU	4.8.78	173/60	100	11.29	11.35- 00
Visschers	Lotte	NED	2.8.79		800	2:02.26	2:03.53- 02
* Vlasic	Blanka	CRO	8.11.83	192/75	HJ	2.01	1.96- 02

Name		Nat	Born	Ht/Wt	Event	2003 Mark	Pre-2003 Best
* Vóggoli	Ekateríni	GRE	30.10.70	173/89	DT	66.73	64.94- 02
Volkova	Yekaterina	RUS	16.2.78		3kSt	9:32.31	9:41.54- 01
Vontein	Barbara	GER	7.6.78	182/64	JT	55.40	56.45- 00
Vorobyeva	Nadezhda	RUS	30.5.77		800	2:01.81, 2:00.59i	2:00.47- 02
Vrbenská	Lucie	CZE	12.5.77	180/85	HT	67.86	66.26- 02
^ Vriesde	Letitia	SUR	5.10.64	159/55	800	2:00.88	1:56.68- 95
Wagner	Kaylene	USA-J	15.11.84		HJ	1.87	1.83- 02
Wagner	Marion	GER	1.2.78	172/61	100	11.31, 11.28w	11.33- 01, 11.31w- 02
Walker	Astia	JAM	4.4.75	178/59	100h	13.07	12.82- 97
Walker	Melanie	JAM	1.1.83	165/53	400h	57.24	55.62- 01
Walker	Shakeema	USA	10.11.76		TJ	13.84A, 13.82, 13.87w	13.74- 00
* Waller	Tisha	USA	1.12.70	183/59	HJ	1.98	2.01i- 98, 2.00- 99
Walsham	Suzy	AUS	22.11.73	168/50	800	2:02.00	2:04.45- 01
					1500	4:07.78	4:11.04- 00, 4:10.7mx- 01
Walter	Sarah	FRA	5.5.78	173/64	JT	62.53	62.48- 02
Wang Hailan		CHN	6.4.76	168/59	Hep	5970	5917- 01
Wang Hongxia		CHN	13.1.75	159/47	Mar	2:31:19	2:40:03- 02
Wang Jinxiang		CHN-J	14.8.84		DT	55.56	53.05- 02
Wang Lihong		CHN	9.1.83		SP	17.49	
Wang Linan		CHN-J	26.11.85		Mar	2:29:33	2:31:51- 02
* Wang Liping		CHN	8.7.76	165/48	20kW	1:32:40	1:26:23- 01
Wang Wenwen		CHN-Y	15.6.86		400h	57.26	
Wang Xing		CHN-Y	30.11.86		400h	56.54	58.34- 02
Wang Yawen		CHN	23.8.73	187/90	SP	17.09	19.89- 93
Wang Yu		CHN-J	27.2.84		Mar	2:31:15	
Wang Yu		CHN-J	4.2.85		DT	59.29	57.17- 02
Wangare	Monica	KEN-Y	4.10.86	163/50	1500	4:10.13	4:21.6A- 01
					5000	15:27.41	
Wangui	Lucy	KEN-J	24.3.84	155/42	5000	15:10.23	15:33.03- 02
					10000	31:06.20	32:45.70- 02
Wanjiku Gakunyi	Jane	KEN	14.6.79	158/43	3000	8:51.7+	
					5000	15:04.00	15:21.68- 02
					10000	32:13.18	32:53.08 -02
Wanjiru	Esther	KEN	27.3.77	162/44	10000	32:31.54	31:52.44- 97
Wanjiru	Ruth	KEN	11.9.81	156/45	5000	15:31.49	15:43.05- 02
					10000	31:56.21	32:34.71- 02
					HMar	70:19	70:15 -02
Wardell	Rebecca	NZL	21.12.77		400h	56.25	57.02- 02
Warlick	Alicia	USA	11.10.77		PV	4.35	4.50- 01
Washington	Demetria	USA	31.12.79	178/65	200	22.89A	23.18, 22.87w- 01
					400	51.25	51.05- 01
Webb	Shirley	GBR	28.9.81	176/91	HT	63.35	59.95- 02
Weissteiner	Silvia	ITA	13.7.79	163/46	3000	8:58.91	9:01.36- 02
Wentland	Gwen	USA	29.4.72	178/64	HJ	1.95	1.96i, 1.94- 95
Wheeler	Erica	USA	28.11.67	172/68	JT	56.85	62.76#- 96, 56.81- 01
Wheeler	Kylie	AUS	17.1.80	180/73	LJ	6.57	6.27, 6.32w- 02
					Hep	6031	5962- 02
Whipple	Erica	USA	4.12.82	168/50	100	11.15	11.32- 00, 11.0- 99
					200	22.82	23.13i- 02
* White	Kelli	USA	1.4.77	163/57	100	10.85, 10.79w	10.99, 10.93w- 01
					200	22.05	22.38- 01
Whyte	Angela	CAN	27.5.80	170/57	100h	12.78	13.03- 02, 12.82w- 01
					Hep	5745	
Wielgus	Anna	POL	27.10.81	170/60	PV	4.40sq, 4.32	4.10- 00
Wigene	Susanne	NOR	12.2.78		3kSt	9:57.97	10:01.54- 00
Wildrick	Andrea	USA	23.12.79		PV	4.21i, 4.20	4.35- 02
Wilks	Antoinette	USA	14.10.80	170/55	LJ	6.52	6.60i- 01, 6.48- 02
Williams	Aleah	USA	7.1.81	173/60	200	23.08	23.23- 02, 22.81w- 00
* Williams	Angela	USA	30.1.80	156/52	100	11.15, 11.08w	11.04, 10.96w- 99
Williams	Ashlee	USA-J	27.3.84	170/54	200	23.36, 23.05w	23.48- 00
Williams	Deshaya	USA	8.7.80	173/82	DT	56.42	56.38- 02
Williams	Lauryn	USA	11.9.83	157/57	100	11.12	11.33- 02
					200	23.25	23.64, 23.63w- 02
Williams	Novlene	JAM	26.4.82	167/55	400	51.93	52.05- 02
* Williams	Tonique	BAH	17.1.76	168/59	200	22.80	23.50- 97
					400	50.24	51.99- 98
Williams	Ysanne	USA	25.9.80	168/55	400h	56.84	57.34- 01
Wisniewska	Joanna	POL	24.5.72	187/82	DT	62.91	63.97- 99
Wisse	Yvonne	NED	6.6.82	180/60	Hep	5895	5719- 02
^ Witteveen	Solange	ARG	6.2.76	171/59	HJ	1.92	1.96- 97
Wittstock	Estie	RSA	15.9.80		400	51.71	52.96A- 02

Name		Nat	Born	Ht/Wt	Event	2003 Mark	Pre-2003 Best
Wlodarczyk	Patrycja	POL	9.6.80	167/54	3kSt	9:52.13	9:59.92- 02
Wöckinger	Olivia	AUT	23.5.79	168/56	LJ	6.69	6.62- 02
					TJ	13.70	13.55- 02
Wölfling	Elke	AUT	27.11.71	168/56	100h	13.09	13.32- 99
* Worku	Ayelech	ETH	12.6.79	165/47	3000	8:52.02	8:32.80- 02
					5000	15:10.85	14:41.23- 00
Woytowska	Jana	GER	7.8.77	182/64	JT	58.21	59.55- 02
Wu Lingmei		CHN	16.2.73	168/60	TJ	14.01	14.39- 98, 14.55w- 99
Wu Meihong		CHN-J	5.6.84		JT	54.79	53.80- 02
Wu Sha		CHN-Y	21.10.87		PV	4.30	4.00- 02
Wurth	Christy	USA	11.7.80	165/52	1500	4:10.49	4:16.80- 02
Wysocka	Marzena	POL	17.2.69	176/85	DT	63.60	63.20- 99
* Xánthou	Níki	GRE	11.10.73	174/56	LJ	6.76	7.03- 97, 7.12Aw- 95
Xie Limei		CHN-Y	27.6.86		TJ	13.89	13.51- 02
Xie Sainan		CHN-Y	3.11.86		1500	4:11.37	
* Xing Huina		CHN-J	25.2.84	166/50	1500	4:09.01	4:10.43- 01
					5000	15:00.02	14:56.15- 01
					10000	30:31.55	31:42.58- 02
Xu Aihui		CHN	25.4.78	167/54	20kW	1:29:40	1:30:00- 01
Xu Bei		CHN	2.1.83		LJ	6.61	6.21- 02
Xu Jia		CHN	23.9.79	172/56	100h	13.17	13.36- 99
Xu Shaoyang		CHN	9.2.83	180/84	DT	58.76	62.54- 02
Xue Ailing		CHN	12.2.79	173/52	20kW	1:34.34	1:3145- 00
Xue Juan		CHN-Y	10.2.86		JT	62.93	57.76- 02
Yakovenko	Mariya	RUS	6.1.82	174/85	JT	57.97	57.03- 02
Yamaguchi	Tomoko	JPN	14.2.72	170/71	DT	55.15	52.52- 01
Yamanaka	Miwako	JPN	24.5.78	164/46	10000	31:32.10	31:41.33- 02
					HMar	70:22+	68:54- 01
Yang Lina		CHN	6.3.83		JT	54.28	54.23- 01
Yang Meiping		CHN-J	23.10.85		HT	64.60	65.21- 01
Yang Qiaoyu		CHN-J	14.9.85		HT	64.30	
Yang Wei		CHN	24.7.83		800	2:01.68	2:02.82- 00
Yao Yuehua		CHN	27.8.80		400h	56.29	55.58- 01
Yarygina	Oksana	UZB	24.12.72	170/65	JT	57.93	64.62#- 94, 60.02- 01
Yashchenko	Yekaterina	RUS	12.1.82		PV	4.15	3.90- 02
* Yatchenko	Irina	BLR	31.10.65	187/96	DT	67.32	68.94- 92
Yefimkina	Lyudmila	RUS	22.8.81	158/44	20kW	1:28:20	1:27:51- 02
* Yefremova	Antonina	UKR	19.7.81	176/58	400	51.36	50.70- 02
Yegorova	Galina	RUS	5.8.83		3kSt	9:57.67	10:02.42- 02
Yegorova	Lyudmila	UKR	4.10.74	164/54	20kW	1:34:08	1:32:02- 00
* Yegorova	Olga	RUS	28.3.72	160/48	1500	4:01.00	4:02.76- 01
					3000	8:38:00	8:23.26- 01
					5000	14:55.19	14:29.32- 01
Yegorova	Tatyana	RUS	23.10.80	159/48	800	2:00.52	2:05.39- 01
					1500	4:10.74	
* Yelesina	Yelena	RUS	4.4.70	183/64	HJ	2.02i, 1.98	2.02- 90
Yelling	Hayley	GBR	3.1.74	157/56	10000	32:02.09	32:29.73- 02
Yelling	Liz	GBR	5.12.74	174/56	10000	32:22.21	31:58.39- 02
					Mar	2:30:58	0
Yemelyanova (Safronova)	Larisa	RUS	6.1.80	164/52	20kW	1:27:23	1:28:03- 02
Yepimashko	Vera	BLR	10.7.76		Hep	5695	5657- 01
Yeshova	Yekaterina	RUS	18.2.82	166/51	20kW	1:34:54	1:40:20- 02
Yesipchuk	Oksana	RUS	13.12.76	183/95	DT	61.16	63.68- 00
Yevdokimova	Natalya	RUS	17.3.78	174/65	800	1:58.75	2:01.51- 00
					1500	4:04.61	4:09.19- 00
					1M	4:24.40	
Yi Chunmei		CHN	15.3.83		JT	58.50	57.72- 01
Yiannakitsídou	Yeoryía	GRE	10.2.82		TJ	14.20	13.42i- 02, 12.81- 01
Yordanova/Kumanova	Aneliya	BUL	27.4.72	175/85	SP	18.38	17.14- 95
Yordanova	Antoniya	BUL	17.8.76	170/52	LJ	6.48	6.70- 02
* Yordanova	Daniela	BUL	8.3.76	165/52	1500	4:01.83	4:00.65- 02
Yoshida	Makiko	JPN	16.7.76	164/49	400h	55.89	56.68- 02
Youngquist	Deeja	USA	30.3.77		Mar	2:29:01	
Yu Jing		CHN	7.3.83		SP	16.83i, 16.08	17.41- 01
Yuan Yufang		MAS	1.2.76	164/53	20kW	1:32:25	1:34:13- 99
Yvelain	Fatima	FRA	4.5.69	165/52	10000	32:37.50	31:43.29- 00
* Zabawska	Krystyna	POL	14.1.68	183/92	SP	18.95	19.42- 92
* Zabruskova	Valeriya	RUS	29.7.75	168/65	JT	64.49	62.69- 02, 63.87#- 99
* Zadorozhnaya	Yelena	RUS	3.12.77	157/42	1500	4:00.12	3:59.94- 02
					2000	5:43.38+	5:41.61i- 00, 5:43.4- 01
					3000	8:35.50	8:25.40- 01
					5000	14:51.61	14:40.47- 01

Name		Nat	Born	Ht/Wt	Event	2003 Mark	Pre-2003 Best
Zadura	Malgorzata	POL	3.10.82	172/75	HT	63.23	59.46- 02
Zagacka	Liliana	POL	28.1.77	168/56	LJ	6.61i, 6.41, 6.61w	6.63- 02
					TJ	14.01i, 13.88	14.22- 01
Zagórska	Anna	POL	26.7.80	174/54	800	2:00.11	2:02.04- 01
					1500	4:09.39	4:24.79- 00
^ Zaituc	Luminita	GER	9.10.68	165/47	HMar	70:51	69:50- 02
					Mar	2:29:41	2:26:01- 01
Zakharchenko	Ilona	UKR	16.6.67	178/85	SP	16.61	16.75- 86
					DT	55.76	64.80- 92
Zakharchuk	Oksana	UKR	3.4.80	180/92	SP	17.86i, 17.82	18.03- 01
* Zakharova	Svetlana	RUS	15.9.70	158/48	Mar	2:23:07	2:21:31- 02
Zalevskaya	Svetlana	KAZ	14.6.73	188/63	HJ	1.90A	1.98i, 1.97- 96
Zamfir	Carmen	ROM	25.11.75	163/50	100h	13.21	13.04- 02
Zandt	Julia	GER-J	8.5.84	178/73	JT	57.75	50.86- 00
Zang Yan		CHN	13.12.83		20kW	1:31:04	1:38:21- 00
Zauna	Irena	LAT	16.3.81	179/59	400h	56.47, 56.1	56.40- 00
Zaytseva	Svetlana	RUS	14.8.81		LJ	6.61	6.62- 02
Zbrozhek	Oksana	RUS	12.1.78	167/49	800	2:01.92	2:00.46- 01
Zelinka	Jessica	CAN	3.9.81		Hep	5716	5688- 00
Zenkova	Alena	RUS	1.1.82	167/54	20kW	1:32:57	
Zhang Chunjing		CHN	19.5.83		SP	16.90	16.38- 02
Zhang Guirong		CHN/SIN	5.2.78		SP	17.99	18.17- 02
Zhang Hao		CHN	26.2.78	172/60	TJ	14.22	14.06- 02
Zhang Li		CHN	19.10.78		JT	57.30	60.02- 00
Zhang Na		CHN	27.9.80	178/60	PV	4.20	4.10- 00
Zhang Nan		CHN-Y	18.4.86		20kW	1:31:55	
Zhang Rong		CHN	5.1.83		100h	13.14	13.31- 02, 13.03w- 01
Zhang Rongrong		CHN-J	27.1.84		400h	57.26	59.69- 02
Zhang Shujing		CHN	13.9.78	158/55	Mar	2:23:18	2:23:17- 02
Zhang Wenxiu		CHN-Y	22.3.86		HT	70.60	67.13- 02
Zhang Xiaoyu		CHN	16.3.83		SP	18.73	18.49- 01
Zhang Yin		CHN-Y	6.10.86		10000	32:41.14	
Zhao Ning		CHN	26.7.81	172/55	HJ	1.88	1.84- 00
Zhao Wei		CHN	27.1.79	185/95	HT	70.67	66.16- 01
Zhao Yingying		CHN-Y	15.2.86		PV	4.20	3.90- 02
Zhdanova	Yevgeniya	RUS	21.7.66	175/53	TJ	14.03i	14.27-01
Zheng Guixia		CHN	24.6.73	160/49	HMar	70:21	68:58- 01
Zhevnova	Tatyana	BLR	17.10.77	173/60	Hep	6023	5987- 02
Zhilkina	Yelena	RUS	5.2.73		5000	15:15.83	15:48.27- 01
* Zhilyayeva	Alla	RUS	5.2.69	163/47	3000	8:54.00i	8:57.53i- 01, 8:58.75- 95
					5000	15:14.3+	15:14.73- 96
					10000	30:23.07	31:45.02- 98
					HMar	70:13	69:43- 98
Zhou Chunxiu		CHN	8.3.79		5000	15:22.46	15:38.28- 00
					10000	32:13.96	33:24.63- 00
					Mar	2:23:41	
Zhu Xiaolin		CHN-J	20.4.84		10000	32:39.60	34:26.80- 02
Zhuravlyeva	Anastasiya	UZB	9.10.81		LJ	6.69	6.34- 00
					TJ	14.21	13.34- 02
Zimmer	Sabine	GER	6.2.81	165/48	20kW	1:31:18	0
Zimmer	Vivian	GER-Y	22.7.87	176/69	JT	54.56	48.68- 02
Zou Ying		CHN	20.8.82		20kW	1:32:07	
Zou Yiting		CHN-Y	17.9.86		200	23.31	
Zozulya	Vera	UKR	31.8.70	166/56	20kW	1:28:19	1:31:26- 00
Zubkovskaya	Oksana	UKR	15.7.81	175/60	HJ	1.90	1.83- 00
Zumer	Kristina	SLO	2.2.80		LJ	6.52	6.36, 6.50w- 02
Zunda	Ieva	LAT	20.7.78	162/54	400h	56.11, 55.8	57.09- 99
Zuo Yan		CHN	18.8.83		20kW	1:34:55	1:32:11- 01
* Zykina	Olesya	RUS	7.10.80	170/60	400	50.39	50.15- 01
Zyusko	Larisa	RUS	27.4.69	168/57	HMar	71:24+	
					Mar	2:28:05	2:29:42- 02

WORLD INDOOR LISTS 2003 – MEN

50 METRES

5.68+	Freddy	Mayola	CUB	1.11.77	1	in 60m	Liévin	28 Feb

60 METRES

6.46	Jason	Gardener	GBR	17.9.75	1		Karlsruhe	15 Feb
6.47	Shawn	Crawford	USA	14.1.78	1	NC	Boston (R)	28 Feb
6.50	Olusoji	Fasuba	NGR	9.7.84	1h1		Chemnitz	27 Feb
6.52	John	Capel	USA	27.11.78	2	NC	Boston (R)	28 Feb
6.53	Mark	Lewis-Francis	GBR	4.9.82	1h1	GP	Birmingham	20 Feb
6.54	Konstantin	Rurak	UKR	9.4.74	1		Zaporozhye	29 Jan
6.54	Yeóryios	Theodorídis	GRE	12.12.72	1r2		Athína (P)	22 Feb
6.55	Niconnor	Alexander	TRI	4.2.77	2h5	WI	Budapest	5 Mar
6.55	Mickey	Grimes	USA	10.10.76	4	WI	Budapest	5 Mar
6.56	Marcus	Brunson	USA	24.4.78	2	Spark	Stuttgart	31 Jan
6.56	Asafa	Powell	JAM	11.11.82	1r2	Mill	New York	6 Feb
6.56	Francis	Obikwelu	POR	22.11.78	2r2		Athína (P)	22 Feb
6.56	Kareem	Streete-Thompson	CAY	30.3.73	1		Leipzig	29 Feb
6.57	Eric	Nkansah	GHA	12.12.74	2		Chemnitz	27 Feb
6.57	DaBryan	Blanton	USA	3.7.84	1s1	Big 12	Lincoln NE	27 Feb
6.57	Freddy	Mayola	CUB	1.11.77	1	Gaz	Liévin	28 Feb
6.57	Tyson	Gay	USA	9.8.82	1	SEC	Lexington	29 Feb

6.58	Simone	Collio	ITA	27.12.79	29 Jan	6.61	Konstantin	Vasyukov	UKR	10.1.81	29 Jan
6.58	Brian	Lewis	USA	5.12.74	20 Feb	6.61	Jon	Drummond	USA	9.9.68	31 Jan
6.58	Matic	Osovnikar	SLO	19.1.80	5 Mar	6.61	Marc	Burns	TRI	7.1.83	6 Feb
6.59	Darrel	Brown	TRI	11.10.84	14 Feb	6.61	Dwight	Thomas	JAM	23.9.80	20 Feb
6.59	Steve	Mullings	JAM	29.11.82	6 Mar	6.61	Bernard	Williams	USA	19.1.78	27 Feb
6.60A	Tim	Harden	USA	27.1.74	17 Jan	6.61	Maurice	Greene	USA	23.7.74	28 Feb
6.60	Tyrone	Edgar	GBR	29.3.82	13 Feb	6.61	Coby	Miller	USA	19.10.76	28 Feb
6.60	Ronny	Ostwald	GER	7.4.74	27 Feb	6.61	Oliver	Williams	USA	10.5.84	6 Mar
6.61	Marc	Blume	GER	28.12.73	4 Jan	6.61	Mardy	Scales	USA	10.9.81	13 Mar

200 METRES

20.42	Leo	Bookman	USA					
20.57	Kenneth	Baxter	USA	13.4.82	1r2	NCAA	Fayetteville	12 Mar
20.57	Domenik	Peterson	USA	12.12.84	2r1	NCAA	Fayetteville	12 Mar
20.57	Kyle	Farmer	USA	15.4.83	2r2	NCAA	Fayetteville	12 Mar
20.58	Tyson	Gay	USA	9.8.82	3r2	NCAA	Fayetteville	12 Mar
20.59	Tobias	Unger	GER	10.7.79	1	NC	Dortmund	22 Feb
20.64	Allyn	Condon	GBR	24.8.74	1s1		Sheffield	31 Jan
20.65	Johan	Wissman	SWE	2.12.82	1r1	Gaz	Liévin	28 Feb
20.66	Dominic	Demeritte	BAH	22.2.78	1	WI	Budapest	7 Mar
20.69	Xavier	Carter	USA-J	8.12.85	1	N.Sch	New York (A)	14 Mar
20.71	Joseph	Batangdon	CMR	29.7.78	2r1	Gaz	Liévin	28 Feb
20.72	Steve	Mullings	JAM	29.11.82	1		Fayetteville	13 Feb
20.74	Wallace	Spearmon	USA	24.12.84	2		Fayetteville	13 Feb
20.74	Christian	Malcolm	GBR	3.6.79	1	GP	Birmingham	20 Feb

20.77	Leslie	Djhone	FRA	18.3.81	22 Feb	20.83	Kelly	Willie	USA	7.9.82	16 Jan
20.79	Frank	Fredericks	NAM	2.10.67	28 Feb	20.83	Jimmie	Hackley	USA	11.9.75	29 Feb
20.79	Marcin	Urbas	POL	17.9.76	6 Mar	20.84	Rodney	Martin	USA	22.12.82	14 Feb

Oversized track

20.40	Tyson	Gay	USA	9.8.82	1r2	SEC	Lexington	29 Feb

20.84	Gary	Kikaya	COD	4.2.80	31 Jan	20.84	Mike	Mitchell	USA	16.5.81	15 Mar
20.84	Mardy	Scales	USA	10.9.81	28 Feb						

300m: 32.95 Tyler Christopher CAN 3.10.83 1 Winnipeg 31 Jan

400 METRES

45.39	Jeremy	Wariner	USA	31.1.84	1r2	NCAA	Fayetteville	13 Mar
45.52	Jerry	Harris	USA	29.10.81	1r11		Fayetteville	13 Feb
45.56	Jason	Barton	USA	9.4.82	3r2	NCAA	Fayetteville	13 Mar
45.83	Obra	Hogans	USA	29.6.82	1	IC4A	Boston	7 Mar
45.88	Alleyne	Francique	GRN	6.6.76	1	WI	Budapest	6 Mar
45.89	Darold	Williamson	USA	19.2.83	4r2	NCAA	Fayetteville	13 Mar
45.90	Kerron	Clement	TRI-J	31.10.85	1r1	NCAA	Fayetteville	13 Mar
45.92A	Elzie	Coleman	USA	23.9.85	1		Pocatello	21 Feb
45.92	Davian	Clarke	JAM	30.4.76	2	WI	Budapest	6 Mar
45.93	Sofiane	Labidi	TUN	29.9.79	1r3		Fayetteville	13 Feb
45.94	Greg	Haughton	JAM	10.11.73	1r1		Allston	14 Feb
45.94	Kelly	Willie	USA	7.9.82	2r1	NCAA	Fayetteville	13 Mar
46.00	Mitch	Potter	USA	16.9.80	1r10		Lincoln NE	7 Feb

46.05	David	Canal	ESP	7.12.78	22 Feb	46.29	Dmitriy	Forshev	RUS	30.5.76	18 Feb

Oversized track

45.75	Gary	Kikaya	COD	4.2.80	1r1		Lexington	31 Jan
45.79	Darold	Williamson	USA	19.2.83	1r2		Ames	14 Feb
45.82A	Lewis	Banda	ZIM	16.4.82	2r1		Flagstaff	31 Jan
45.82	Andrew	Rock	USA	23.1.82	1r1		Ames	14 Feb
600m 1:15.90	Osmar	dos Santos	BRA	20.10.68	1	BIG	Boston (R)	31 Jan
1:16.21	Gary	Reed	CAN	25.10.81	1		Winnipeg	31 Jan

800 METRES

\# Oversized track

1:44.58	Yuriy	Borzakovskiy	RUS	12.4.81	1	GEG	Stockholm	12 Feb
1:44.71	Joseph	Mutua	KEN	10.12.78	1r2	Spark	Stuttgart	31 Jan
1:45.28	Wilfred	Bungei	KEN	24.7.80	2	GEG	Stockholm	12 Feb
1:45.43	Mbulaeni	Mulaudzi	RSA	8.9.80	2r3	Spark	Stuttgart	31 Jan
1:45.80	William	Yiampoy	KEN	17.5.74	2r2	Spark	Stuttgart	31 Jan
1:45.85	Berhanu	Alemu	ETH	16.7.82	1	Tyson	Fayetteville	14 Feb
1:45.96	Osmar	dos Santos	BRA	20.10.68	2	Tyson	Fayetteville	14 Feb
1:46.00	David	Krummenacker	USA	24.5.75	3	Tyson	Fayetteville	14 Feb
1:46.09	Jackson	Langat	KEN	15.12.80	1r5		Fayetteville	13 Feb
1:46.15	Rashid	Ramzi	BRN	17.7.80	2	WI	Budapest	7 Mar
1:46.35	Glody	Dube	BOT	2.7.78	3r2	Spark	Stuttgart	31 Jan
1:46.36	Bram	Som	NED	20.2.80	2r2	Flanders	Gent	8 Feb
1:46.46	Joeri	Jansen	BEL	28.5.79	4r2	Flanders	Gent	8 Feb
1:46.47	Gary	Reed	CAN	25.10.81	4	Tyson	Fayetteville	14 Feb
1:46.57	Amine	Laalou	MAR	13.5.82	4	WI	Budapest	7 Mar
1:46.62	Hezekiél	Sepeng	RSA	30.6.74	3r3	Spark	Stuttgart	31 Jan
1:46.67	Michael	Rotich	KEN	14.7.78	1		Leipzig	29 Feb
1:46.91#	Peter	Etoot	KEN	17.4.84	1	SEC	Lexington	29 Feb

1:47.09#	Dmitrijs	Milkevics	LAT	6.12.81	6 Mar
1:47.10	Florent	Lacasse	FRA	21.1.81	22 Feb
1:47.11	Ivan	Geshko	UKR	19.8.79	22 Feb
1:47.16	Youssef	Saad Kamel	BRN	.83	6 Mar
1:47.2	Dmitriy	Bogdanov	RUS	11.4.79	8 Feb
1:47.31	Derrick	Peterson	USA	28.11.77	14 Feb
1:47.33	David	Lelei	KEN	10.5.71	29 Feb
1:47.33	Antonio M	Reina	ESP	13.6.81	6 Mar
1:47.45	Mouhsin	Chehibi	MAR	28.1.78	6 Mar
1:47.47	Khalid	Tighazouine	MAR	18.6.77	27 Feb

1000 METRES

2:17.06	Mehdi	Baala	FRA	17.8.78	1	Gaz	Liévin	28 Feb
2:17.07	Paul	Korir	KEN	15.7.77	2	Gaz	Liévin	28 Feb

1500 METRES

3:35.15	Ivan	Geshko	UKR	19.8.79	1		Karlsruhe	15 Feb
3:35.83	Rui	Silva	POR	3.8.77	2	GP	Birmingham	20 Feb
3:36.02	Ali	Saïdi-Sief	ALG	15.3.78	2		Karlsruhe	15 Feb
3:36.39	Juan Carlos	Higuero	ESP	3.8.78	1		Valencia	14 Feb
3:36.42	Michael	East	GBR	20.1.78	3	GP	Birmingham	20 Feb
3:36.55	José Antonio	Redolat	ESP	17.2.76	2		Valencia	14 Feb
3:36.90	Alvaro	Fernández	ESP	7.4.81	3		Valencia	14 Feb
3:37.05	Paul	Korir	KEN	15.7.77	4	GP	Birmingham	20 Feb
3:37.17	Laban	Rotich	KEN	20.1.69	5	GP	Birmingham	20 Feb
3:37.49	Gert-Jan	Liefers	NED	26.9.78	6	GP	Birmingham	20 Feb
3:37.61	Abdelkader	Hachlaf	MAR	3.7.79	7	GP	Birmingham	20 Feb
3:37.66	Michael	Too	KEN	3.8.83	8	GP	Birmingham	20 Feb
3:37.87	Youssef	Baba	MAR	7.8.79	9	GP	Birmingham	20 Feb
3:38.28	Mounir	Yemmouni	FRA	12.10.83	4	Spark	Stuttgart	31 Jan
3:38.31	Job	Tanui	KEN	26.8.74	5	Spark	Stuttgart	31 Jan
3:38.39	Vyacheslav	Shabunin	RUS	27.9.69	4		Karlsruhe	15 Feb
3:38.69	James	Thie	GBR	27.6.78	10	GP	Birmingham	20 Feb
3:38.98	Michal	Sneberger	CZE	23.6.78	6	Spark	Stuttgart	31 Jan
3:39.21	Sergio	Gallardo	ESP	22.3.79	2r2	Flanders	Gent	8 Feb

3:39.32	Bouabdellah	Tahri	FRA	20.12.78	8 Feb
3:39.59	Marko	Koers	NED	3.11.72	15 Feb
3:40.01	Anas	Selmouni	MAR	15.3.79	15 Feb
3:40.80	Rob	Myers	USA	5.8.80	28 Feb
3:40.83	Charlie	Gruber	USA	8.8.78	28 Feb
3:40.84	Tom	Mayo	GBR	2.5.77	20 Feb

1 MILE

3:53.26	Paul	Korir	KEN	15.7.77	1	Tyson	Fayetteville	14 Feb
3:55.93	Laban	Rotich	KEN	20.1.69	2	Tyson	Fayetteville	14 Feb
3:56.55#	Nick	Willis	NZL	25.4.83	1		South Bend	7 Feb
3:56.57	Kevin	Sullivan	CAN	20.3.74	3	Tyson	Fayetteville	14 Feb

3:57.00	Boaz	Cheboiywo	KEN	2.8.78	31 Jan
3:57.52	Alan	Webb	USA	13.1.83	14 Feb
3:58.14	Hudson	de Souza	BRA	25.2.77	13 Feb
3:58.55#	Nathan	Brannen	CAN	8.9.82	7 Feb

2000 METRES

5:00.16+	Haile	Gebrselassie	ETH	18.4.73	1	in 3k	Karlsruhe	15 Feb
5:00.32+	Kenenisa	Bekele	ETH	13.6.82	1	in 3k	Stuttgart	31 Jan
5:02.80+	Hicham	El Guerrouj	MAR	14.9.74	1	in 3k	Liévin	28 Feb

3000 METRES

7:29.34	Haile	Gebrselassie	ETH	18.4.73	1		Karlsruhe	15 Feb
7:30.77	Kenenisa	Bekele	ETH	13.6.82	1	Spark	Stuttgart	31 Jan
7:34.71	Hicham	El Guerrouj	MAR	14.9.74	1	Gaz	Liévin	28 Feb
7:34.96	Bernard	Lagat	KEN	12.12.74	1		Athína (P)	22 Feb
7:37.0+	Markos	Geneti	ETH	30.5.84	2	in 2M	Birmingham	20 Feb
7:38.30	Boaz	Cheboiywo	KEN	2.8.78	1	Tyson	Fayetteville	14 Feb
7:38.43	Abiyote	Abate	ETH	20.11.80	2		Karlsruhe	15 Feb
7:38.59	Alistair	Cragg	IRL	13.6.80	2	Tyson	Fayetteville	14 Feb
7:38.86	Mark	Bett	KEN	22.12.76	2		Athína (P)	22 Feb
7:40.17	Daniel	Lincoln	USA	22.10.80	3	Tyson	Fayetteville	14 Feb
7:41.01	Sergey	Lebed	UKR	15.7.75	3		Athína (P)	22 Feb
7:41.18	Sileshi	Sihine	ETH	29.1.83	2	Spark	Stuttgart	31 Jan
7:42.55	Mushir	Salem Jawher	BRN	13.6.78	4		Athína (P)	22 Feb
7:43.09	Robert	Kipngetich	KEN	.82	2	Gaz	Liévin	28 Feb
7:43.23	Paul	Bitok	KEN	26.6.70	3	Spark	Stuttgart	31 Jan
7:43.53	Hicham	Bellani	MAR	15.9.79	4	Gaz	Liévin	28 Feb
7:43.57	Rui	Silva	POR	3.8.77	2	GEG	Stockholm	12 Feb
7:44.00	Abderrahim	Goumri	MAR	21.5.76	4	Spark	Stuttgart	31 Jan
7:44.46	Kevin	Sullivan	CAN	20.3.74	3	BIG	Boston (R)	31 Jan
7:44.90	Nick	Willis	NZL	25.4.83	5	BIG	Boston (R)	31 Jan
7:44.96	Martin	Keino	KEN	20.6.72	6	BIG	Boston (R)	31 Jan
7:45.72	Matt	Lane	USA	5.9.77	8	BIG	Boston (R)	31 Jan
7:46.08	Luke	Kipkosgei	KEN	27.11.75	5	Gaz	Liévin	28 Feb
7:46.46	Günther	Weidlinger	AUT	5.4.78	6	GEG	Stockholm	12 Feb
7:46.49	Robert	Kipchumba	KEN	24.2.84	6		Athína (P)	22 Feb

7:46.58	Hailu	Mekonnen	ETH	4.4.80	31 Jan
7:47.17	Ali	Ezzine	MAR	3.9.78	12 Feb
7:47.20	Jason	Lunn	USA	19.9.74	31 Jan
7:47.29	Mohamed	Amyn	MAR	25.3.76	22 Feb
7:47.97	Laban	Rotich	KEN	20.1.69	8 Feb
7:47.98	Gert-Jan	Liefers	NED	26.9.78	8 Feb
7:48.09	Craig	Mottram	AUS	18.6.80	5 Mar
7:48.20	Ali	Saïdi-Sief	ALG	15.3.78	31 Jan
7:48.27	Sergio	Gallardo	ESP	22.3.79	5 Mar
7:48.40	Antonio	Jiménez	ESP	18.2.77	12 Feb
7:48.59#	Bolota	Asmerom	USA	12.10.78	31 Jan
7:48.66	Manuel Angel	Penas	ESP	9.11.77	12 Feb
7:49.20	Bouabdellah	Tahri	FRA	20.12.78	15 Feb
7:49.42	Mourad	Maaroufit	MAR	.82	22 Feb
7:49.56	Luke	Watson	USA	20.8.80	31 Jan
7:50.91	John	Mayock	GBR	26.10.70	31 Jan

2 MILES

8:08.39	Markos	Geneti	ETH	30.5.84	1	GP	Birmingham	20 Feb
8:08.65	Haile	Gebrselassie	ETH	18.4.73	2	GP	Birmingham	20 Feb
8:14.77	Abiyote	Abate	ETH	20.11.80	3	GP	Birmingham	20 Feb

5000 METRES

12:49.60	Kenenisa	Bekele	ETH	13.6.82	1	GP	Birmingham	20 Feb
13:11.47	Dejene	Berhanu	ETH	.80	2	GP	Birmingham	20 Feb
13:19.30	Luke	Kipkosgei	KEN	27.11.75	3	GP	Birmingham	20 Feb

13:23.56	Robert	Kipchumba	KEN	24.2.84	20 Feb
13:28.43	Solomon	Bushendich	KEN	10.1.84	20 Feb

50mh	6.44+		Liu Xiang	CHN	13.7.83	1	in 60mh	Liévin	28 Feb
	6.48+	Ladji	Doucouré	FRA	28.3.83	1h2	in 60mh	Aubière	21 Feb
	6.56+	Charles	Allen	CAN	29.3.77	2	in 60mh	Liévin	28 Feb
	6.58+	Yoel	Hernández	CUB	12.12.77	3	in 60mh	Liévin	28 Feb
	6.60	Gregory	Sedoc	NED	16.10.81	1	Cooman	Zuidbroek	24 Jan
55mh	7.14	Ladji	Doucouré	FRA	28.3.83	1h3		Gainesville	1 Feb
	7.15	Antwon	Hicks	USA	12.3.83	1		Gainesville	25 Jan

60 METRES HURDLES

7.36	Allen	Johnson	USA	1.3.71	1	WI	Budapest	6 Mar
7.43		Liu Xiang	CHN	13.7.83	2	WI	Budapest	6 Mar
7.48	Maurice	Wignall	JAM	17.4.76	3	WI	Budapest	6 Mar
7.49	Stanislav	Olijar	LAT	22.3.79	4	WI	Budapest	6 Mar
7.53	Duane	Ross	USA	5.12.72	1h4	NC	Boston (R)	27 Feb
7.54	Ladji	Doucouré	FRA	28.3.83	1s2	NC	Aubière	21 Feb
7.57	Yuniel	Hernández	CUB	28.3.81	2		Erfurt	29 Jan
7.59	Dawane	Wallace	USA	30.12.76	2		Chapel Hill	17 Jan
7.59	Larry	Wade	USA	22.11.74	1		Houston	23 Jan
7.59	Robert	Kronberg	SWE	15.8.76	6	WI	Budapest	6 Mar
7.59	Yoel	Hernández	CUB	12.12.77	2s1	WI	Budapest	6 Mar
7.59	Dwight	Thomas	JAM	23.9.80	2s2	WI	Budapest	6 Mar
7.60	Ron	Bramlett	USA	22.10.79	3r2	Mill	New York	6 Feb
7.60	Márcio	de Souza	BRA	24.1.75	2		Karlsruhe	15 Feb
7.61	Aubrey	Herring	USA	19.9.78	1h4		State College	31 Jan
7.61	Robby	Hughes	USA	10.10.78	2h4	NC	Boston (R)	28 Feb
7.61	Antwon	Hicks	USA	12.3.83	1	NCAA	Fayetteville	12 Mar
7.64	Shaun	Bownes	RSA	24.10.70	3		Leipzig	29 Feb

7.66	Kenneth	Ferguson	USA	22.3.84	13 Feb
7.66	Charles	Allen	CAN	29.3.77	28 Feb
7.66	Arend	Watkins	USA	23.5.79	28 Feb
7.66	Joel	Brown	USA	31.1.80	28 Feb
7.66	Gregory	Sedoc	NED	16.10.81	6 Mar
7.66	Andrea	Giaconi	ITA	11.4.74	6 Mar
7.67	Josh	Walker	USA	6.5.82	13 Feb
7.67	Anier	García	CUB	9.3.76	15 Feb
7.67	Jermaine	Cooper	USA	31.8.80	12 Mar
7.68	Chris	Phillips	USA	24.7.72	16 Jan
7.68	Sébastien	Denis	FRA	4.5.71	24 Jan
7.68	Dominique	Arnold	USA	14.9.73	31 Jan
7.68	Mohammed	Sillah-Freckleton	GBR	11.9.80	7 Feb
7.68	Brandon	Hon	USA	7.7.79	7 Feb
7.68	Richard	Phillips	JAM	26.1.83	12 Mar
7.69	Robert	Newton	GBR	10.5.81	7 Feb
7.69	Damien	Greaves	GBR	19.9.77	7 Feb
7.69	Mike	Thomas	USA	21.12.81	13 Feb
7.69	Dexter	Faulk	USA	14.4.84	6 Mar
7.69	Ivan	Bitzi	SUI	4.8.75	6 Mar
7.69	Eric	Mitchum	USA	2.8.84	12 Mar
7.69	David	Oliver	USA	24.4.82	12 Mar

HIGH JUMP

2.37	Stefan	Holm	SWE	25.5.76	1	GEG	Stockholm	12 Feb
2.34	Jaroslav	Bába	CZE	2.9.84	2		Arnstadt	7 Feb
2.32	Jamie	Nieto	USA	2.11.76	2		Weinheim	11 Feb
2.32	Andrey	Sokolovskiy	UKR	16.7.78	2		Banská Bystrica	17 Feb
2.32	Yaroslav	Rybakov	RUS	22.11.80	2	WI	Budapest	6 Mar
2.31	Rozle	Prezelj	SLO	26.9.79	1		Ljubljana	24 Jan
2.31	Oskari	Frösén	FIN	24.1.76	2		Tallinn	25 Feb
2.30	Stefan	Vasilache	ROM	9.5.79	1	NC	Bucuresti	14 Feb
2.30	Aleksey	Dmitrik	RUS	12.4.84	2		Athína (P)	22 Feb
2.29	Andra	Manson	USA	30.4.84	1		New York	14 Feb
2.28	Mikhail	Tsvetkov	RUS	4.5.80	1		Moskva	7 Jan
2.28	Tomás	Jankú	CZE	27.12.74	2		Hustopece	17 Jan
2.28	Sergey	Klyugin	RUS	24.3.74	1		Moskva	1 Feb
2.28	Gennadiy	Moroz	BLR	27.5.78	4		Banská Bystrica	17 Feb
2.28	Andrey	Tereshin	RUS	15.12.82	2	NC	Moskva	19 Feb
2.28	Joan	Charmant	FRA	4.6.78	1	NC	Aubière	22 Feb
2.28	Adrian	O'Dwyer	IRL	1.12.83	1	NC	Budapest	24 Feb
2.28	Pyotr	Brayko	RUS	27.3.77	3=		Tallinn	25 Feb
2.28	Vyacheslav	Voronin	RUS	5.4.74	1		Chelyabinsk	29 Feb

2.27	Marko	Aleksejev	EST	14.2.79	15 Feb
2.27	Germaine	Mason	JAM	1.4.83	5 Mar
2.27	Scott	Sellers	USA-J	16.8.86	14 Mar
2.26	Kyle	Lancaster	USA	15.8.83	13 Dec
2.26	Terrance	Woods	USA	18.4.79	23 Jan
2.26	Linus	Thörnblad	SWE-J	6.3.85	31 Jan
2.26	Aleksander	Walerianczyk	POL	1.9.82	7 Feb
2.26	Dmitriy	Demyanyuk	UKR	30.6.83	22 Feb
2.25	Aleksey	Krysin	RUS	25.11.76	7 Jan
2.25	Tora	Harris	USA	21.9.78	23 Jan
2.25	Jacques	Freitag	RSA	11.6.82	3 Feb
2.25	Javier	Bermejo	ESP	23.12.78	12 Feb
2.25	Svatoslav	Ton	CZE	20.10.78	12 Feb
2.25	Jessé	de Lima	BRA	16.2.81	17 Feb
2.25	Ben	Challenger	GBR	7.3.78	19 Feb
2.25	Roman	Fricke	GER	23.3.77	21 Feb

POLE VAULT

5.88	Jeff	Hartwig	USA	25.9.67	1		Jonesboro	22 Feb
5.82	Giuseppe	Gibilisco	ITA	5.1.79	1	Stars	Donetsk	15 Feb
5.81	Toby	Stevenson	USA	19.11.76	1		Seattle	31 Jan
5.81	Björn	Otto	GER	16.10.77	1		Leipzig	29 Feb
5.80A	Derek	Miles	USA	28.9.72	1		Reno	10 Jan
5.80	Igor	Pavlov	RUS	18.7.79	1		Moskva	1 Feb
5.80	Alex	Averbukh	ISR	1.10.74	2		Moskva	1 Feb
5.77	Pavel	Gerasimov	RUS	29.5.79	2	Stars	Donetsk	15 Feb
5.75	Tim	Lobinger	GER	3.9.72	1	NC	Dortmund	22 Feb
5.75	Denis	Yurchenko	UKR	27.1.78	1	NC	Sumy	22 Feb
5.75	Okkert	Brits	RSA	22.8.73	1		Chemnitz	27 Feb
5.75	Rens	Blom	NED	1.3.77	2		Chemnitz	27 Feb
5.75	Russ	Buller	USA	10.9.78	2	NC	Boston (R)	28 Feb
5.73	Ilian	Efremov	BUL	2.8.70	1		Sofia	24 Jan
5.73	Patrik	Kristiansson	SWE	3.6.77	1		Tallinn	25 Feb
5.71	Tommy	Skipper	USA	14.4.84	1		Nampa	7 Feb
5.71	Romain	Mesnil	FRA	13.7.77	3	GEG	Stockholm	12 Feb
5.70A	Daichi	Sawano	JPN	16.9.80	1		Reno	10 Jan
5.70	Ruslan	Yeremenko	UKR	31.7.78	1		Potsdam	7 Feb
5.70	Tye	Harvey	USA	25.9.74	2		Potsdam	7 Feb
5.70	Michael	Stolle	GER	17.12.74	4		Chemnitz	27 Feb
5.70	Adam	Ptácek	CZE	8.10.80	Q	WI	Budapest	6 Mar
5.70	Brad	Walker	USA	21.6.81	1	NCAA	Fayetteville	13 Mar
5.70	Oscar	Janson	SWE	22.7.75	2		Bad Oeynhausen	13 Mar

5.65A	Piotr	Buciarski	DEN	22.11.75	31 Jan
5.65	Jérôme	Clavier	FRA	3.5.83	7 Feb
5.65	Yevgeniy	Mikhaylichenko	RUS	13.2.79	18 Feb
5.65	Aleksandr	Korchmyd	UKR	22.1.82	22 Feb
5.65	Bubba	McLean	USA	2.9.79	22 Feb
5.65	Dmitri	Markov	AUS	14.3.75	6 Mar
5.62	Vasiliy	Gorshkov	RUS	5.2.77	15 Feb
5.62	Tim	Mack	USA	15.9.72	15 Feb
5.61	Jim	Davis	USA	15.6.78	13 Feb
5.60A	Nick	Hysong	USA	9.12.71	17 Jan
5.60	Richard	Spiegelburg	GER	12.8.77	25 Jan
5.60	Jacob	Pauli	USA	15.6.79	14 Feb

5.60	Artyom	Kuptsov	RUS	22.4.84	18 Feb
5.60	Pierre-Charles	Peuf	FRA	27.4.79	21 Feb
5.60	Fabian	Schulze	GER	7.3.84	22 Feb
5.60	Georgi	Wassilew	GER	16.2.80	22 Feb
5.60	Lars	Börgeling	GER	16.4.79	22 Feb
5.60	Matti	Mononen	FIN	25.11.83	22 Feb
5.60	Mark	Calvin	USA	17.11.74	22 Feb
5.60	Alhaji	Jeng	SWE	13.12.81	28 Feb
5.60	Justin	Norberg	USA	18.7.77	28 Feb
5.60	Danny	Ecker	GER	21.7.77	29 Feb

LONG JUMP

8.41	Savanté	Stringfellow	USA	6.11.78	1		Fayetteville	13 Feb
8.31	James	Beckford	JAM	9.1.75	2	WI	Budapest	6 Mar
8.28	Vitaliy	Shkurlatov	RUS	25.5.79	3	WI	Budapest	6 Mar
8.27	John	Moffitt	USA	12.12.80	1		New York	13 Feb
8.26	Bogdan	Tarus	ROM	1.8.75	4	WI	Budapest	6 Mar
8.23	Vladimir	Zyuskov	UKR	29.8.81	5	WI	Budapest	6 Mar
8.17	Chris	Tomlinson	GBR	13.9.81	6	WI	Budapest	6 Mar
8.16	Kirill	Sosunov	RUS	1.11.75	7	WI	Budapest	6 Mar
8.13		Zhou Can	CHN	20.5.79	1	NGP	Tianjin	18 Feb
8.12	Viktor	Kuznetsov	UKR-J	14.7.86	1		Brovary	20 Dec
8.10	Yann	Doménech	FRA	17.3.79	1	Univ Ch	Liévin	31 Jan
8.10	Luis Felipe	Méliz	CUB	11.8.79	2		Moskva	1 Feb
8.10	Leevan	Sands	BAH	16.1.81	1	SEC	Lexington	28 Feb
8.09	Iván	Pedroso	CUB	17.12.72	8	WI	Budapest	6 Mar
8.08	Matt	Mason	USA	30.6.82	1		Seattle	27 Feb
8.08	Tony	Allmond	USA	8.10.82	2	NCAA	Fayetteville	12 Mar
8.07	Jan	Zumer	SLO	9.6.82	1		Ljubljana	7 Feb
8.07	Valeriy	Vasilyev	UKR	21.4.76	2	NC	Sumy	22 Feb
8.05	Jonathan	Chimier	MRI	6.8.82	1	FRA Ch	Aubière	22 Feb
8.04	Dmitriy	Sapinskiy	RUS	23.10.83	1		Orel	17 Jan
8.04	Yago	Lamela	ESP	24.7.77	1		Zaragoza	31 Jan
8.02	Nils	Winter	GER	27.3.77	2		Chemnitz	27 Feb

8.01	Marcin	Starzak	POL-J	20.10.85	10 Jan
8.00	Bogdan	Tudor	ROM	1.2.70	7 Feb
8.00	Ndiss Kaba	Badji	SEN	21.9.83	15 Feb
8.00	Loúis	Tsátoumas	GRE	12.2.82	22 Feb
7.99	Kafetien	Gomis	FRA	20.3.80	31 Jan
7.99	Dmitriy	Karpov	KAZ	23.7.81	8 Feb
7.98	Arvidas	Nazarovas	LTU	17.4.81	21 Jan
7.98	Marijo	Bakovic	CRO	11.4.82	21 Feb
7.98	Peter	Rapp	GER	29.5.83	22 Feb
7.98	Salim	Sdiri	FRA	26.10.78	22 Feb
7.97	Aleksey	Lukashevich	UKR	11.1.77	22 Feb
7.97	Aundre	Edwards	JAM	11.12.80	12 Mar
7.97	Juaune	Armon	USA	6.5.82	12 Mar
7.96	Joan Lino	Martínez	CUB	17.1.78	25 Jan
7.96	Nicola	Trentin	ITA	20.6.74	21 Feb
7.96	Denis	Sinyavskiy	RUS	13.8.79	23 Feb
7.96	Povilas	Mykolaitis	LTU	22.2.83	28 Feb
7.96	Roman	Sebrle	CZE	26.11.74	6 Mar
7.94	Dimítrios	Filíndras	GRE	9.2.73	24 Jan
7.94	Mohamed S	Al-Khuwailidi	KSA	19.6.81	6 Feb

TRIPLE JUMP

17.83	Christian	Olsson	SWE	25.1.80	1	WI	Budapest	7 Mar
17.46	Jadel	Gregório	BRA	16.9.80	1		Karlsruhe	15 Feb
17.41	Danila	Burkenya	RUS	20.7.78	1		Samara	29 Jan
17.39	Yoandri	Betanzos	CUB	15.2.82	2		Samara	29 Jan
17.31	Dmitriy	Valyukevich	BLR	31.5.81	3		Samara	29 Jan
17.23	Aleksandr	Sergeyev	RUS	29.7.83	1	NC	Moskva	19 Feb
17.19	Marian	Oprea	ROM	6.6.82	5	WI	Budapest	7 Mar
17.16	Nikolay	Savolainen	UKR	25.3.80	Q	WI	Budapest	5 Mar
17.09	Igor	Spasovkhodskiy	RUS	1.8.79	2		Moskva	18 Jan
17.05	Viktor	Gushchinskiy	RUS	12.8.78	2		Tallinn	25 Feb
17.05	LeJuan	Simon	USA	7.2.81	1	NCAA	Fayetteville	13 Mar
17.02	Leevan	Sands	BAH	16.1.81	1	Tyson	Fayetteville	14 Feb
16.99	LaMark	Carter	USA	23.8.70	1		Houston	17 Jan
16.96	Julien	Kapek	FRA	12.1.79	1	NC	Aubière	21 Feb
16.88	Allen	Simms	USA	26.7.82	1	NC	Boston (R)	28 Feb
16.85	Nelson	Évora	POR	20.4.84	1	NC-23	Moskva	15 Feb
16.82	Sébastien	Pincemail	FRA	21.2.79	2	NC	Aubière	21 Feb
16.82	Daniel	Donovici	ROM	5.3.80	1	BalkC	Athína (P)	28 Feb
16.79	Hrístos	Melétoglou	GRE	2.1.72	9	WI	Budapest	5 Mar
16.79	John	Moffitt	USA	12.12.80	2	NCAA	Fayetteville	13 Mar
16.78	Aleksandr	Glavatskiy	BLR	2.5.70	6		Samara	29 Jan
16.78	Charles	Friedek	GER	26.8.71	3		Göteborg	3 Feb
16.74	David	Giralt	CUB	26.1.84	4		Budapest	23 Feb

16.72	Vitaliy	Moskalenko	RUS	30.6.74	19 Feb
16.71	Viktor	Yastrebov	UKR	13.1.82	21 Feb
16.69	Fabrizio	Donato	ITA	14.8.76	22 Feb
16.68	LeVar	Anderson	USA	26.3.77	20 Feb
16.67	Andrew	Murphy	AUS	18.12.69	5 Mar
16.64	Aleksandr	Petrenko	RUS	8.2.83	29 Jan
16.62	Yevgeniy	Plotnir	RUS	26.6.77	18 Jan
16.59	Jacek	Kazimierowski	POL	2.7.74	21 Feb
16.59	Willie	Bradley	USA	18.10.82	13 Mar
16.58	Andrey	Orlov	RUS	31.1.84	15 Feb

SHOT

21.95	Christian	Cantwell	USA	30.9.80	1		Columbia MO	20 Feb
21.63	Joachim	Olsen	DEN	31.5.77	1		Tallinn	25 Feb

21.07	Reese	Hoffa	USA	8.10.77	2	WI	Budapest	7 Mar
20.91	Carl	Myerscough	GBR	21.10.79	1	Big 12	Lincoln NE	28 Feb
20.85	Andrey	Mikhnevich	BLR	12.7.76	1	NC	Minsk	30 Jan
20.83	Tomasz	Majewski	POL	30.8.81	4	WI	Budapest	7 Mar
20.81	Zsolt	Bíber	HUN	31.5.76	1		Budapest	15 Feb
20.79	Yuriy	Belonog	UKR	9.3.74	Q	WI	Budapest	6 Mar
20.79	Manuel	Martínez	ESP	7.12.74	5	WI	Budapest	7 Mar
20.75	Rutger	Smith	NED	9.7.81	1	NC	Gent	21 Feb
20.66	Ralf	Bartels	GER	21.2.78	1		Neubrandenburg	14 Feb
20.59	Ville	Tiisanoja	FIN	24.12.75	1	NC	Helsinki	21 Feb
20.49	Ivan	Yushkov	RUS	15.1.81	1		Moskva	1 Feb
20.46	Tepa	Reinikainen	FIN	16.3.76	2	NC	Helsinki	21 Feb
20.45	Dan	Taylor	USA	12.5.82	1		Columbus	21 Feb
20.42	Janus	Robberts	RSA	10.3.79	1		Lubbock	23 Jan
20.23	Dmitriy	Goncharuk	BLR	17.7.70	2	NC	Minsk	30 Jan
20.21	Miran	Vodovnik	SLO	11.9.77	1		Budapest	24 Jan
20.15	Milan	Haborák	SVK	11.1.73	1	Stars	Tampere	14 Feb
20.13	Pavel	Lyzhin	BLR	24.3.81	3	NC	Minsk	30 Jan
20.07	Khalid Habas	Al-Suwaidi	QAT	.84	1	ITA Ch	Genova	22 Feb
20.04	Pavel	Chumachenko	RUS	5.4.71	2		Moskva	1 Feb
19.98	Dan	Ames	USA	16.1.81	3	NCAA	Fayetteville	12 Mar

19.93	Detlef	Bock	GER	15.8.74	23 Jan
19.91	Mika	Halvari	FIN	13.2.70	21 Feb
19.91	Niklas	Arrhenius	SWE	10.9.82	28 Feb
19.87	Peter	Sack	GER	27.7.79	29 Feb
19.81	Dmitriy	Gorshkov	RUS	8.3.82	24 Dec
19.81	Adam	Nelson	USA	7.7.75	6 Feb
19.78	Gheorghe	Guset	ROM	28.5.68	14 Feb
19.68	Brad	Snyder	CAN	8.1.76	21 Feb
19.61	Marco Antonio	Verni	CHI	27.2.76	6 Mar
19.60	Hannes	Hopley	RSA	26.1.81	24 Jan
19.59	Galin	Kostadinov	BUL	25.12.79	1 Feb
19.59	Paolo	Dal Soglio	ITA	29.7.70	26 Feb
19.56	Ronny	Jiménez	VEN	15.1.79	28 Feb
19.55	Nedzad	Mulabegovic	CRO	4.9.81	30 Jan
19.48	Jeff	Chakouian	USA	20.4.82	17 Jan
19.43	Andy	Dittmar	GER	5.7.74	21 Feb

WEIGHT

24.48	Libor	Charfreitag	SVK	11.9.77	1		Nampa	7 Feb
24.01	Dan	Taylor	USA	12.5.82	1		Columbus	21 Feb
23.18	James	Parker	USA	3.12.75	1	NC	Boston (R)	27 Feb
23.08	Derek	Woodske	CAN	22.10.76	1		Findlay	13 Feb
22.94	John	McEwen	USA	5.3.74	1		Kent	6 Dec
22.87	A.G.	Kruger	USA	18.2.79	1		Kent	31 Jan
22.58	Mike	Mai	USA	27.9.77	1	Mill	New York (Bronx)	7 Feb
	22.61	outdoors			1		Mountain View	5 Jan

22.48	Jacob	Freeman	USA	5.11.80	7 Feb
22.23	Chris	Brown	USA	8.1.78	18 Jan
22.04	Keith	McBride	USA	15.2.81	24 Jan
22.02	James	Steacy	CAN	29.5.84	8 Feb
21.91	Bert	Sorin	USA	5.10.76	27 Feb
21.70	Dan	Ames	USA	16.1.81	13 Mar

HEPTATHLON

6438	Roman	Sebrle	CZE	26.11.74	1	WI	Budapest	7 Mar
	6.97	7.96 16.28	2.11	7.95		4.80	2:39.67	
6365	Bryan	Clay	USA	3.1.80	2	WI	Budapest	7 Mar
	6.65	7.78 14.84	2.08	7.77		4.90	2:49.41	
6203	Lev	Lobodin	RUS	1.4.69	3	WI	Budapest	7 Mar
	6.90	7.36 15.99	2.05	7.83		4.80	2:45.76	
6161	Aleksandr	Pogorelov	RUS	10.1.80	1		Orel	18 Jan
	6.94	7.64 15.67	2.09	8.14		5.00	2:55.24	
6155	Dmitriy	Karpov	KAZ	23.7.81	4	WI	Budapest	7 Mar
	7.04	7.97 14.95	1.99	7.87		4.60	2:42.34	
6136	Donovan	Kilmartin	USA	11.6.84	1	NCAA	Fayetteville	13 Mar
	7.05	7.37 14.27	2.08	8.17		5.40	2:49.44	
6123	Erki	Nool	EST	25.6.70	2		Tallinn	8 Feb
	6.96	7.68 14.62	2.01	8.25		5.05	2:44.77	
6040	Paul	Terek	USA	20.10.79	1	NC	Chapel Hill	7 Mar
	7.04	7.08 15.31	1.98	8.48		5.41	2:42.97	
5993	Jón Arnar	Magnússon	ISL	28.7.69	7	WI	Budapest	7 Mar
	7.02	7.64 15.77	1.96	8.08		4.60	2:47.52	
5989	Stephen	Harris	USA	5.12.80	2	NC	Chapel Hill	7 Mar
	7.02	7.54 13.09	2.16	8.29		4.51	2:40.28	
5928	Maurice	Smith	JAM	28.9.80	2	NCAA	Fayetteville	13 Mar
	7.02	7.22 15.33	1.99	7.96		4.50	2:43.85	
5901	Nikolay	Averyanov	RUS	4.2.80	2	NC	Moskva	9 Feb
	6.92	7.42 13.83	1.94	8.21		4.90	2:46.91	

5898	Phil	McMullen	USA	3.2.75	7 Mar
5894	Ranko	Leskovar	SLO	2.1.77	15 Feb
5893	Laurent	Hernu	FRA	22.8.76	21 Feb
5892	Kristjan	Rahnu	EST	29.8.79	8 Feb
5831	Oscar	González	ESP	8.8.76	22 Feb
5818	Tomás	Dvorák	CZE	11.5.72	8 Feb
5815	Krzysztof	Andrzejak	POL	10.1.75	22 Feb
5806	Michal	Modelski	POL	16.4.75	22 Feb

3000 METRES WALK

11:08.0+	Robert Korzeniowski		POL	30.7.68	1	in 5k	Belfast	15 Feb
11:13.9	Matej	Tóth	SVK	10.2.83	1		Hlohovec	28 Nov
11:15.27+	Andreas	Erm	GER	12.3.76	1	in 5k	Dortmund	21 Feb

5000 METRES WALK

18:34.15	Alessandro	Gandellini	ITA	30.4.73	1	NC	Genova	21 Feb
18:38.79	Robert	Korzeniowski	POL	30.7.68	1	IRL Ch	Belfast	15 Feb
18:42.80	Ivano	Brugnetti	ITA	1.9.76	2	NC	Genova	21 Feb
18:54.14	Ilya	Markov	RUS	19.6.72	1		Yekaterinburg	7 Jan
18:59.16	Andreas	Erm	GER	12.3.76	1	NC	Dortmund	21 Feb
19:05.60	Robert	Heffernan	IRL	28.2.78	2	NC	Belfast	15 Feb
19:09.4	Mike	Trautmann	GER	13.3.74	1		Halle	18 Dec
	19:09.97				2	NC	Dortmund	21 Feb

WORLD INDOOR LISTS 2004 – WOMEN

50m	6.12+	Christine	Arron	FRA	13.9.73	1	in 60m	Aubière	21 Feb
	6.22+	Muriel	Hurtis	FRA	25.3.79	1s2	in 60m	Aubière	21 Feb

60 METRES

7.06	Yuliya	Tabakova	RUS	1.5.80	1	NC	Moskva	17 Feb
7.08	Christine	Arron	FRA	13.9.73	1	NC	Aubière	21 Feb
7.08	Gail	Devers	USA	19.11.66	1	WI	Budapest	5 Mar
7.10	Yuliya	Nesterenko	BLR	15.6.79	1h	NC	Minsk	30 Jan
7.12	Torri	Edwards	USA	31.1.77	2	NC	Boston (R)	28 Feb
7.12	Kim	Gevaert	BEL	5.8.78	2	WI	Budapest	5 Mar
7.15	Tatyana	Tkalich	UKR	30.5.75	1		Zaporozhye	29 Jan
7.15	Natalya	Safronnikova	BLR	28.2.73	2		Karlsruhe	15 Feb
7.16	Irina	Kozhemyakina	UKR	16.6.80	2		Zaporozhye	29 Jan
7.16	Virgen	Benavídes	CUB	31.12.74	3		Karlsruhe	15 Feb
7.16	Marion	Jones	USA	12.10.75	2	GP	Birmingham	20 Feb
7.17	Karin	Mayr-Krifka	AUT	4.6.71	2h1		Karlsruhe	15 Feb
7.17	Muna	Lee	USA	30.10.81	1	SEC	Lexington	29 Feb
7.17	Muriel	Hurtis	FRA	25.3.79	5	WI	Budapest	5 Mar
7.18	Vida	Anim	GHA	7.12.83	1		Chemnitz	27 Feb
7.18	LaKeisha	Backus	USA	15.12.76	3	NC	Boston (R)	28 Feb
7.19A	Ashley	Owens	USA-J	19.11.85	1		Pocatello	21 Feb

7.20	Debbie	Ferguson	BAH	16.1.76	14 Feb
7.20	Angela	Daigle	USA	28.5.76	28 Feb
7.20	Veronica	Campbell	JAM	15.5.82	29 Feb
7.21	Ivet	Lalova	BUL	18.5.84	1 Feb
7.21	Manuela	Levorato	ITA	16.3.77	8 Feb
7.21	Sanya	Richards	USA-J	26.2.85	28 Feb
7.21	Merlene	Ottey	SLO	10.5.60	5 Mar
7.22	Chryste	Gaines	USA	14.9.70	28 Feb
7.23	Yuliya	Skotnikova	RUS	.76	1 Feb
7.23	Toyin	Olupona	CAN	29.1.83	29 Feb
7.24	Irina	Shtangeyeva	UKR	8.2.82	29 Jan
7.24	Lauryn	Williams	USA	11.9.83	14 Feb
7.24	Gabi	Rockmeier	GER	29.11.73	22 Feb
7.24	Laverne	Jones	ISV	16.9.81	28 Feb

200 METRES

22.43	Veronica	Campbell	JAM	15.5.82	1r2	NCAA	Fayetteville	12 Mar
22.49	Sanya	Richards	USA-J	26.2.85	2r2	NCAA	Fayetteville	12 Mar
22.60	Connie	Moore	USA	29.8.81	1r1	NCAA	Fayetteville	12 Mar
22.71	Anastasiya	Kapachinskaya	RUS	21.11.79	1s1	NC	Moskva	18 Feb
22.76	Muna	Lee	USA	30.10.81	1h2	NCAA	Fayetteville	12 Mar
22.79	Lauryn	Williams	USA	11.9.83	2r1	NCAA	Fayetteville	12 Mar
22.87	Ivet	Lalova	BUL	18.5.84	1		Sofia	1 Feb
22.88	Karin	Mayr-Krifka	AUT	4.6.71	1		Karlsruhe	15 Feb
22.96	Natalya	Safronnikova	BLR	28.2.73	2s2	WI	Budapest	6 Mar
23.08	Svetlana	Goncharenko	RUS	28.5.71	1h2	WI	Budapest	6 Mar
23.14	Gabi	Rockmeier	GER	29.11.73	1r1	Spark	Dortmund	4 Feb

23.15	Crystal	Cox	USA	28.3.79	14 Feb
23.15	Erica	Whipple	USA	4.12.82	12 Mar
23.18	Stephanie	Durst	USA	6.1.82	12 Mar
23.19	Dee Dee	Trotter	USA	8.12.82	31 Jan
23.24	Yelena	Mironova	RUS	22.3.82	15 Feb
23.29	Marina	Maydanova	UKR	22.8.82	8 Feb
Oversized track					
23.13	Erica	Whipple	USA	4.12.82	29 Feb

300m: All Moskva 1 Feb: 36.62 Olesya Krasnomovets RUS 8.7.79 1r1, 36.69 Olesya Zykina RUS 7.10.80 2r1
36.87 Svetlana Goncharenko RUS 26.7.71 1r2, 37.01 Natalya Ivanova RUS 25.6.81 3r1

400 METRES

49.68	Natalya	Nazarova	RUS	26.5.79	1	NC	Moskva	18 Feb
50.64	Olga	Kotlyarova	RUS	12.4.76	1h4	NC	Moskva	17 Feb
50.65	Olesya	Krasnomovets	RUS	8.7.79	2	WI	Budapest	6 Mar
50.82	Sanya	Richards	USA-J	26.2.85	1r1	NCAA	Fayetteville	13 Mar
50.87	Natalya	Antyukh	RUS	26.6.81	3	NC	Moskva	18 Feb
50.87	Tonique	Williams	BAH	17.1.76	3	WI	Budapest	6 Mar
51.23	Tiandra	Ponteen	SKN	9.11.84	2r1	NCAA	Fayetteville	13 Mar

51.25	Tatyana	Levina	RUS	28.2.77	4	NC	Moskva	18 Feb
51.29	Dee Dee	Trotter	USA	8.12.82	1r2	NCAA	Fayetteville	13 Mar
51.31	Hazel-Ann	Regis	GRN	1.2.81	2r2	NCAA	Fayetteville	13 Mar
51.58	Ionela	Tîrlea	ROM	9.2.76	4	WI	Budapest	6 Mar
51.59	Svetlana	Usovich	BLR	14.10.80	1	NC	Minsk	30 Jan
51.63	Lashinda	Demus	USA	10.3.83	3r2	NCAA	Fayetteville	13 Mar
51.65	Olesya	Zykina	RUS	7.10.80	6	NC	Moskva	18 Feb
51.68	Faní	Halkiá	GRE	2.2.79	2s2	WI	Budapest	6 Mar
51.79	Shauna	Smith	USA	10.9.83	3r1	NCAA	Fayetteville	13 Mar
51.80	Novlene	Williams	JAM	26.4.82	1h1	NCAA	Fayetteville	12 Mar
52.00	Nadia	Davy	USA	24.12.80	4r1	NCAA	Fayetteville	13 Mar
52.01	Claudia	Marx	GER	16.9.78	2r2	EICp	Leipzig	14 Feb
52.18	Catherine	Murphy	GBR	21.9.75	2h2	WI	Budapest	5 Mar
52.19	Nicole	Leach	USA-Y	18.7.87	1	N.Sch	New York (A)	14 Mar

52.23	Raasin	McIntosh	USA	29.4.82	28 Feb
52.28	Allyson	Felix	USA-J	18.11.85	31 Jan
52.31	Svetlana	Pospelova	RUS	24.12.79	17 Feb
52.34	Zhanna	Kashcheyeva	RUS	27.7.82	15 Feb
52.35	Julian	Clay	USA	2.11.77	6 Mar
52.40	Karen	Shinkins	IRL	15.10.76	13 Feb
52.41	Antonina	Yefremova	UKR	19.7.81	14 Feb
52.41	Rosemary	Okafor	NGR	22.5.81	12 Mar
52.43	Natalya	Pigida	UKR	30.1.81	21 Feb
52.53	Helen	Karagounis	GBR	28.9.81	6 Mar
52.55	Svetlana	Goncharenko	RUS	28.5.71	12 Feb
52.56	Grazyna	Prokopek	POL	20.4.77	22 Feb
52.57	Demetria	Washington	USA	31.12.79	14 Feb
52.59	Natalya	Ivanova	RUS	25.6.81	21 Feb
52.61	Olga	Zaytseva	RUS	10.11.84	15 Feb
52.65	Hrísa	Goudenoúdi	GRE	28.3.77	22 Feb
52.66	Irina	Rosikhina	RUS	11.5.75	17 Feb
52.72	Olga	Golendukhina	RUS	14.11.81	17 Feb

Oversized track

51.13	Hazel-Ann	Regis	GRN	1.2.81	1r2	SEC	Lexington	29 Feb
51.55	Novlene	Williams	JAM	26.4.82	2r2	SEC	Lexington	29 Feb
51.59	Lashinda	Demus	USA	10.3.83	3r2	SEC	Lexington	29 Feb

52.44	Stephanie	Smith	USA	27.6.85	29 Feb
52.56A	Geísa	Coutinho	BRA	1.6.80	7 Feb

500m:

1:07.36	Natalya	Nazarova	RUS	26.5.79	1	Moskva	7 Jan
1:07.68	Olga	Kotlyarova	RUS	12.4.76	1r2	Yekaterinburg	7 Jan
1:08.71	Jearl	Miles-Clark	USA	4.9.66	1	State College	31 Jan
1:08.84	Olesya	Krasnomovets	RUS	8.7.79	1r1	Yekaterinburg	7 Jan

600m: All Moskva 1 Feb: 1:23.44 Olga Kotlyarova RUS 12.4.76 1r2, 1:25.15 Natalya Khrushchelyova RUS 30.5.73 2r2 1:26.81 Tatyana Andrianova 10.12.79, 1:26.98 Svetlana Cherkasova 20.5.78, 1:27.31 Natalya Lavshuk 22.2.80 (RUS)

800 METRES

1:57.48	Maria	Mutola	MOZ	27.10.72	1		Karlsruhe	15 Feb
1:58.72	Jolanda	Ceplak	SLO	12.9.76	2	WI	Budapest	7 Mar
1:59.50	Jo	Fenn	GBR	19.10.74	3	WI	Budapest	7 Mar
1:59.52	Maite	Martínez	ESP	17.5.76	1	Flanders	Gent	8 Feb
1:59.64	Jen	Toomey	USA	19.12.71	4	WI	Budapest	7 Mar
1:59.71	Tatyana	Andrianova	RUS	10.12.79	5	WI	Budapest	7 Mar
2:00.02	Irina	Vashentseva	RUS	30.9.80	1h2	NC	Moskva	17 Feb
2:00.41	Olga	Raspopova	RUS	27.12.78	1	EICp	Leipzig	14 Feb
2:00.68	Natalya	Khrushchelyova	RUS	30.5.73	2		Karlsruhe	15 Feb
2:00.93	Svetlana	Cherkasova	RUS	20.5.78	2h3	NC	Moskva	17 Feb
2:01.03	Meskerem	Legesse	ETH	28.9.86	1	Tyson	Fayetteville	14 Feb
2:01.06	Hazel	Clark	USA	3.10.77	2	NC	Boston (R)	28 Feb
2:01.14	Tatyana	Petlyuk	UKR	22.2.82	3	EICp	Leipzig	14 Feb
2:01.16	Liliana	Popescu	ROM	5.2.82	3		Karlsruhe	15 Feb
2:01.40	Kelly	Holmes	GBR	19.4.70	1	NC	Sheffield	8 Feb
2:01.67	Natalya	Tsyganova	RUS	7.2.71	2	NC	Moskva	18 Feb
2:01.88	Sandra	Stals	BEL	5.6.75	2h2	WI	Budapest	5 Mar

2:01.93	Olesya	Chumakova	RUS	23.7.81	22 Feb
2:02.01	Monika	Gradzki	GER	21.9.79	14 Feb
2:02.11	Oksana	Zbrozhek	RUS	12.1.78	18 Feb
2:02.11	Judit	Varga	HUN	16.4.76	24 Feb
2:02.16	Nicole	Teter	USA	8.11.73	14 Feb
2:02.33	Seltana	Aït Hamou	MAR	21.5.80	6 Mar
2:02.56	Sandra	Teixeira	POR	13.3.78	15 Feb
2:02.62	Virginie	Fouquet	FRA	9.9.75	8 Feb
2:02.62	Heather	Hennigar	CAN	13.5.73	14 Feb
2:02.74	Natalya	Kutkina	RUS	.77	17 Feb
2:02.78	Natalya	Yevdokimova	RUS	17.3.78	31 Jan
2:02.88	Esther	Desviat	ESP	27.1.82	22 Feb
2:02.91	Larisa	Chzhao	RUS	4.2.71	17 Feb
2:02.99	Lotte	Visschers	NED	2.8.79	27 Feb

1000 METRES

2:32.96	Kelly	Holmes	GBR	19.4.70	1	GP	Birmingham	20 Feb
2:34.19	Jen	Toomey	USA	19.12.71	2	GP	Birmingham	20 Feb
2:34.68	Olga	Raspopova	RUS	27.12.78	1rA		Moskva	1 Feb
2:34.73	Jo	Fenn	GBR	19.10.74	3	GP	Birmingham	20 Feb
2:35.71	Irina	Vashentseva	RUS	30.9.80	2rA		Moskva	1 Feb
2:35.91	Gulnara	Samitova	RUS	9.7.78	3rA		Moskva	1 Feb
2:36.01	Seltana	Aït Hamou	MAR	21.5.80	4	GP	Birmingham	20 Feb
2:36.39	Natalya	Tsyganova	RUS	7.2.71	4rA		Moskva	1 Feb
2:36.70	Olesya	Chumakova	RUS	23.7.81	5rA		Moskva	1 Feb

2:37.71	Yelena	Zadorozhnaya	RUS	3.12.77	1 Feb
2:38.68	Kutre	Dulecha	ETH	22.8.78	20 Feb

1500 METRES

4:01.90	Kutre	Dulecha	ETH	22.8.78	1		Karlsruhe	15 Feb
4:04.42	Alesya	Turova	BLR	6.12.79	1	GEG	Stockholm	12 Feb
4:04.83	Kelly	Holmes	GBR	19.4.70	2	GEG	Stockholm	12 Feb
4:05.63	Hayley	Tullett	GBR	17.2.73	3	GEG	Stockholm	12 Feb
4:05.91	Gulnara	Samitova	RUS	9.7.78	1	NC	Moskva	19 Feb
4:06.04	Judit	Varga	HUN	16.4.76	3		Karlsruhe	15 Feb
4:06.61	Yelena	Zadorozhnaya	RUS	3.12.77	2	NC	Moskva	19 Feb
4:07.76	Natalya	Yevdokimova	RUS	17.3.78	3		Athína (P)	22 Feb
4:07.9	Olesya	Chumakova	RUS	23.7.81	1		Shchelkovo	8 Feb
4:07.97	Yuliya	Chizhenko	RUS	30.8.79	3	NC	Moskva	19 Feb
4:08.18	Carmen	Douma-Hussar	CAN	12.3.77	2	WI	Budapest	6 Mar
4:08.50	Daniela	Yordanova	BUL	8.3.76	3h1	WI	Budapest	5 Mar
4:08.51	Yuliya	Kosenkova	RUS	28.3.73	4	NC	Moskva	19 Feb
4:08.95	Irina	Lishchinskaya	UKR	15.1.76	4		Athína (P)	22 Feb
4:08.96	Natalya	Sidorenko	UKR	22.11.80	4h1	WI	Budapest	5 Mar
4:09.01	Lidia	Chojecka/Okninska	POL	25.1.77	5h1	WI	Budapest	5 Mar
4:09.16	Natalia	Rodríguez	ESP	2.6.79	1		Valencia	14 Feb
4:09.82	Jen	Toomey	USA	19.12.71	1	NC	Boston (R)	29 Feb
4:09.88	Konstadína	Efedáki	GRE	1.10.78	5		Karlsruhe	15 Feb

4:10.68	Andrea	Suldesová	CZE	11.2.75	28 Feb	4:11.95	Nuria	Fernández	ESP	16.8.76	5 Mar
4:11.23	Yelena	Kanales	RUS	7.2.76	19 Feb	4:12.00	Carrie	Tollefson	USA	18.1.77	31 Jan
4:11.30	Alina	Cucerzan	ROM	28.7.74	22 Feb	4:12.67	Jo	Fenn	GBR	19.10.74	8 Feb
4:11.54	Nouria	Mérah-Benida	ALG	19.10.70	22 Feb	4:12.86	Mardrea	Hyman	JAM	22.12.72	15 Feb
4:11.72	Sonja	Roman	SLO	11.3.79	5 Mar	4:12.87	Maria	Martins	FRA	1.4.74	14 Feb
4:11.93	Amy	Rudolph	USA	18.9.73	29 Feb	4:12.87	Suzy	Favor Hamilton	USA	8.8.68	29 Feb

1 MILE

4:27.28	Hayley	Tullett	GBR	17.2.73	1		New York (A)	24 Jan
4:30.61	Kim	Smith	NZL	19.11.81	1		Allston	10 Feb
4:30.9 mx	Jen	Toomey	USA	19.12.71	1		Boston	11 Jan

4:31.65	Lyubov	Kremlyova	RUS	21.12.61	24 Jan	4:32.72	Johanna	Nilsson	SWE	23.3.83	13 Mar
4:32.24	Tiffany	McWilliams	USA	20.10.82	13 Mar	4:33.20	Amy	Rudolph	USA	18.9.73	24 Jan

2000 METRES

5:39.4+	Berhane	Adere	ETH	21.7.73	1	in 3k	Dortmund	4 Feb

At Birmingham 20 Feb: 5:44.1+ Meseret Defar ETH (2), 5:44.3+ Tirunesh Dibaba ETH-J (3), 5:44.4+ Jo Pavey GBR (4)

3000 METRES

8:33.05	Berhane	Adere	ETH	21.7.73	1	Spark	Dortmund	4 Feb
8:33.44	Meseret	Defar	ETH	19.11.83	1	GP	Birmingham	20 Feb
8:33.56	Tirunesh	Dibaba	ETH-J	2.6.85	2	GP	Birmingham	20 Feb
8:34.55	Jo	Pavey	GBR	20.9.73	3	GP	Birmingham	20 Feb
8:41.72	Gulnara	Samitova	RUS	9.7.78	1	NC	Moskva	17 Feb
8:42.20	Marina	Dubrova	UKR	9.12.78	2	NC	Moskva	17 Feb
8:46.02	Sabrina	Mockenhaupt	GER	6.12.80	2	Spark	Dortmund	4 Feb
8:46.34	Irina	Mikitenko	GER	23.8.72	3	Spark	Dortmund	4 Feb
8:48.77	Hayley	Tullett	GBR	17.2.73	4	Spark	Dortmund	4 Feb
8:49.18	Kim	Smith	NZL	19.11.81	1	NCAA	Fayetteville	13 Mar
8:49.21	Galina	Bogomolova	RUS	15.10.77	3	NC	Moskva	17 Feb
8:50.21	Lidiya	Grigoryeva	RUS	21.1.74	4	NC	Moskva	17 Feb
8:50.37	Zahra	Ouaziz	MAR	20.12.69	5	Spark	Dortmund	4 Feb
8:50.73	Yelena	Zadorozhnaya	RUS	3.12.77	2h1	WI	Budapest	5 Mar
8:51.05	Marta	Domínguez	ESP	3.11.75	4h1	WI	Budapest	5 Mar

8:51.81	Lidia	Chojecka/Okninska	POL	25.1.77	8 Feb	8:55.36	Carrie	Tollefson	USA	18.1.77	14 Feb
8:53.58	Lyubov	Ivanova	RUS	2.3.81	17 Feb	8:55.42	Shayne	Culpepper	USA	3.12.73	14 Feb
8:53.73	Andrea	Suldesová	CZE	11.2.75	4 Feb	8:55.94	Sarah	Schwald	USA	2.1.73	14 Feb
8:53.90	Wioletta	Janowska	POL	9.6.77	4 Feb	8:55.97	Veerle	Dejaeghere	BEL	1.8.73	5 Mar
8:53.99	Margaret	Maury	FRA	15.5.74	21 Feb	8:56.48	Maria	McCambridge	IRL	10.7.75	14 Feb
8:54.61	Liliya	Shobukhova	RUS	13.11.77	17 Feb	8:56.62	Mestawet	Tadesse	ETH-J	19.7.85	8 Feb
8:55.14	Alla	Zhilyayeva	RUS	5.2.69	17 Feb	8:56.82	Maria	Martins	FRA	1.4.74	8 Feb
8:55.17	Sentayehu	Ejigu	ETH-J	.85	14 Feb	8:57.86	Inna	Poluskina	LAT	7.7.84	14 Feb

5000 METRES

14:39.29	Berhane	Adere	ETH	21.7.73	1	Spark	Stuttgart	31 Jan
14:53.14	Meseret	Defar	ETH	19.11.83	1	BIG	Boston (R)	31 Jan
14:53.99	Tirunesh	Dibaba	ETH-J	2.6.85	2	BIG	Boston (R)	31 Jan
14:54.73	Derartu	Tulu	ETH	21.3.72	3	BIG	Boston (R)	31 Jan
14:58.85	Sentayehu	Ejigu	ETH-J	.85	4	BIG	Boston (R)	31 Jan
15:11.15	Zahra	Ouaziz	MAR	20.12.69	2	Spark	Stuttgart	31 Jan
15:14.18	Kim	Smith	NZL	19.11.81	1	NCAA	Fayetteville	12 Mar
15:29.95	Marie	Davenport	IRL	24.1.75	2		Allston	30 Jan

50mh

6.80+	Perdita	Felicien	CAN	29.8.80	1	in 60mh	Liévin	28 Feb
6.82+	Linda	Ferga-Khodadin	FRA	24.12.76	2	in 60mh	Liévin	28 Feb
6.82+	Nicole	Ramalalanirina	FRA	5.3.72	1s1	in 60mh	Aubière	21 Feb

6.91+ Aliuska López ESP 29.8.69, 6.93+ Anay Tejeda CUB 3.4.83 both at Liévin 28 Feb

55mh

7.47	Tiffany	Lott-Hogan	USA	1.8.75	1		Ogden	24 Jan

7.57 Andrea Bliss JAM 5.10.80, 7.58 Yolanda McCray USA 11.9.76 1h1/2h1 Gainesville 6 Mar

60 METRES HURDLES

7.75	Perdita	Felicien	CAN	29.8.80	1	WI	Budapest	7 Mar
7.76	Gail	Devers	USA	19.11.66	1	Mill	New York	6 Feb
7.82	Linda	Ferga-Khodadin	FRA	24.12.76	3	WI	Budapest	7 Mar
7.83	Joanna	Hayes	USA	23.12.76	2s1	WI	Budapest	7 Mar
7.86	Lacena	Golding-Clarke	JAM	20.3.75	3s1	WI	Budapest	7 Mar
7.88	Susanna	Kallur	SWE	16.2.81	1		Tallinn	25 Feb
7.91	Flóra	Redoúmi	GRE	11.9.76	2s2	WI	Budapest	7 Mar
7.92	Delloreen	Ennis-London	JAM	5.3.75	1		Chemnitz	27 Feb
7.93	Melissa	Morrison	USA	9.7.71	1h1	NC	Boston (R)	28 Feb
7.93	Nicole	Ramalalanirina	FRA	5.3.72	2h3	WI	Budapest	7 Mar
7.94	Juliane	Sprenger-Afflerbach	GER	22.3.77	1	Spark	Dortmund	4 Feb
7.95	Raasin	McIntosh	USA	29.4.82	1s2	Big 12	Lincoln NE	27 Feb
7.96	Carmen	Zamfir	ROM	25.11.75	3h3	WI	Budapest	7 Mar
7.96	Priscilla	Lopes	CAN	26.8.82	1	NCAA	Fayetteville	12 Mar
7.97	Glory	Alozie	ESP	30.12.77	1		Valencia	25 Jan
7.97	Jenny	Adams	USA	8.7.78	3	Tyson	Fayetteville	14 Feb
7.99	Anjanette	Kirkland	USA	24.2.74	3	NC	Boston (R)	28 Feb
7.99	Tiffany	Lott-Hogan	USA	1.8.75	1P	NC	Chapel Hill	7 Mar
8.00	Natalya	Kresova	RUS	12.12.79	1		Moskva	1 Feb
8.00	Nadine	Faustin	HAI	14.4.76	1		Athína (P)	22 Feb
8.00	Lolo	Jones	USA	5.8.82	2	NCAA	Fayetteville	12 Mar
8.01	Vonette	Dixon	JAM	26.11.75	2	BIG	Boston (R)	31 Jan
8.01	Nichole	Denby	USA	10.10.82	1	Big 12	Lincoln NE	28 Feb
8.01	Aliuska	López	ESP	29.8.69	3h1	WI	Budapest	7 Mar
8.02	Jenny	Kallur	SWE	16.2.81	4h1	WI	Budapest	7 Mar
8.02	Irina	Shevchenko	RUS	2.9.75	3h4	WI	Budapest	7 Mar

8.03	Natalya	Shekhodanova	RUS	29.12.71	22 Feb
8.03	Anay	Tejeda	CUB	3.4.83	22 Feb
8.04	Yuliya	Shabanova	RUS	11.8.82	1 Feb
8.04	Dainelky	Pérez	CUB	6.1.76	22 Feb
8.05	Mariya	Koroteyeva	RUS	10.11.81	1 Feb
8.06	Nadine	Hentschke	GER	27.1.82	15 Feb
8.06	Sheena	Johnson	USA	1.10.82	27 Feb
8.07	Lucie	Martincová	CZE	4.1.82	21 Feb
8.09	Hyleas	Fountain	USA	14.1.81	29 Feb
8.10	Evaggelía	Nesoúdi	GRE	27.4.79	7 Feb
8.10	Reina-Flor	Okori	FRA	2.5.80	14 Feb
8.10	Aurelia	Trywianska	POL	9.5.76	15 Feb
8.10	Patricia	Girard	FRA	8.4.68	29 Feb
8.11	Kia	Davis	USA	23.5.76	31 Jan
8.11	Sarah	Claxton	GBR	23.9.79	8 Feb
8.11	Lashinda	Demus	USA	10.3.83	12 Mar

HIGH JUMP

2.04	Anna	Chicherova	RUS	22.7.82	1		Arnstadt	7 Feb
2.04	Yelena	Slesarenko	RUS	28.2.82	1	WI	Budapest	7 Mar
2.02	Kajsa	Bergqvist	SWE	12.10.76	2		Arnstadt	7 Feb
2.00	Daniela	Rath	GER	6.5.77	1		Wuppertal	23 Jan
2.00	Vita	Palamar	UKR	12.10.77	3		Arnstadt	7 Feb
2.00	Ruth	Beitia	ESP	1.4.79	1	NC	Valencia	21 Feb
1.99	Blanka	Vlasic	CRO	8.11.83	1		Karlsruhe	15 Feb
1.98	Viktoriya	Styopina	UKR	21.2.76	4		Arnstadt	7 Feb
1.98	Yekaterina	Aleksandrova	RUS	3.6.77	1		Chelyabinsk	29 Feb
1.96	Irina	Mikhalchenko	UKR	20.1.72	5		Arnstadt	7 Feb
1.96	Tatyana	Novoseltseva	RUS	23.6.84	2		Chelyabinsk	29 Feb
1.96	Marta	Mendía	ESP	18.5.75	Q	WI	Budapest	6 Mar
1.96	Venelina	Veneva	BUL	13.6.74	Q	WI	Budapest	6 Mar
1.95	Irina	Kovalenko	UKR-J	12.6.86	1		Kiev	26 Dec
1.95	Monica	Iagar	ROM	1.4.73	2		Wuppertal	23 Jan
1.95	Dóra	Györffy	HUN	23.2.78	1		Budapest	24 Jan
1.95	Zuzana	Hlavonová	CZE	16.4.73	1		Brno	19 Feb
1.94	Marina	Kuptsova	RUS	22.12.81	1		Moskva	18 Jan
1.94	Tia	Hellebaut	BEL	16.2.78	1P	v4N	Zuidbroek	1 Feb
1.94	Viktoriya	Seryogina	RUS	22.5.73	1P	NC	Moskva	8 Feb
1.93	Antonella	Bevilacqua	ITA	15.10.71	1	NC	Genova	21 Feb
1.93	Melanie	Skotnik	GER	8.11.82	2	NC	Dortmund	22 Feb
1.93	Amy	Acuff	USA	14.7.75	1	NC	Boston (R)	29 Feb

1.92	Viktoriya	Slivka	RUS	28.9.80	7 Jan
1.92	Ariane	Friedrich	GER	10.1.84	17 Jan
1.92	Tisha	Waller	USA	1.12.70	6 Feb
1.92	Anna	Ksok	POL	29.9.83	22 Feb
1.92	Chaunte	Howard	USA	12.1.84	13 Mar
1.91	Marina	Aitova	KAZ	13.9.82	24 Jan
1.91	Marisa	Cadienhead	CAN	7.4.76	11 Feb
1.91	Ifoma	Jones	USA	4.9.77	12 Feb
1.91	Iva	Straková	CZE	4.8.80	29 Feb
1.90	Elena	Herzenberg	GER	24.6.79	11 Jan
1.90	Olga	Kaliturina	RUS	9.3.76	17 Jan
1.90	Irina	Glavatskikh	RUS	29.12.84	27 Jan

1.90	Corinne	Müller	SUI	20.11.75	30	Jan
1.90	Oana	Pantelimon	ROM	27.9.72	7	Feb
1.90	Diana	Láznicková	SVK	14.8.74	19	Feb
1.90	Barbora	Laláková	CZE	2.5.81	19	Feb
1.90	Julie	Crane	GBR	26.9.76	28	Feb
1.89	Kaylene	Wagner	USA	15.11.84	14	Feb

POLE VAULT

4.86	Yelena	Isinbayeva	RUS	3.6.82	1	WI	Budapest	6 Mar
4.85	Svetlana	Feofanova	RUS	16.7.80	1		Athína (P)	22 Feb
4.81	Stacy	Dragila	USA	25.3.71	2	WI	Budapest	6 Mar
4.71	Tatyana	Polnova	RUS	20.4.79	1	Gaz	Liévin	28 Feb
4.68	Annika	Becker	GER	12.11.81	2	Spark	Dortmund	4 Feb
4.65	Monika	Pyrek	POL	11.8.80	1	NC	Spala	21 Feb
4.60	Jillian	Schwartz	USA	19.9.79	4	WI	Budapest	6 Mar
4.58	Kellie	Suttle	USA	9.5.73	1		Jonesboro	25 Jan
4.52	Anna	Rogowska	POL	21.5.81	4=	Stars	Donetsk	15 Feb
4.52	Yelena	Belyakova	RUS	7.4.76	6	Stars	Donetsk	15 Feb
4.50	Nastja	Ryshich	GER	19.9.77	4	Spark	Dortmund	4 Feb
4.50	Vanessa	Boslak	FRA	11.6.82	1	NC	Aubière	22 Feb
4.50	Thórey Edda	Elísdóttir	ISL	30.6.77	3		Athína (P)	22 Feb
4.47	Chelsea	Johnson	USA	20.12.83	1		Seattle	14 Feb
4.46	Dana	Cervantes	ESP	18.8.78	1		Zaragoza	31 Jan
4.42	Natalya	Kushch	UKR	5.3.83	7	Stars	Donetsk	15 Feb
4.40	Anastasiya	Ivanova	RUS	3.5.79	3	NC	Moskva	19 Feb
4.40	Carolin	Hingst	GER	18.9.80	3		Chemnitz	27 Feb
4.37A	Tracy	O'Hara	USA	20.7.80	3c1		Reno	10 Jan
4.36		Gao Shuying	CHN	28.10.79	1	NGP	Shanghai	14 Feb

4.35A	Stephanie	McCann	CAN	22.4.77	7	Feb
4.35A	April	Steiner	USA	22.4.80	7	Feb
4.35	Katerina	Badurová	CZE	18.12.82	11	Feb
4.35	Naroa	Agirre	ESP	15.5.79	21	Feb
4.35	Hanna-Mia	Persson	SWE	11.2.78	29	Feb
4.35	Lindsay	Taylor	USA	9.2.79	29	Feb
4.35	Lesa	Kubishta	USA	19.4.78	29	Feb
4.32	Anzhela	Balakhonova	UKR	18.12.72	15	Feb
4.30	Yekaterina	Sultanova	RUS	31.12.84	18	Jan
4.30	Yeoryía	Tsiliggíri	GRE	21.6.72	31	Jan
4.30	Tanya	Stefanova	BUL	8.3.72	31	Jan
4.30	Tünde	Vaszi	HUN	18.4.72	6	Feb
4.30	Afrodíti	Skafída	GRE	20.3.82	7	Feb
4.30	Mary	Sauer	USA	31.10.75	14	Feb
4.30		Zhao Yingying	CHN-J	15.2.86	21	Feb
4.30	Alicia	Warlick	USA	11.10.77	29	Feb
4.30	Niki	McEwen	USA	1.4.80	29	Feb
4.27	Erica	Bartolina	USA	15.5.80	21	Feb
4.27	Shannon	Gallagher	USA	10.3.75	22	Feb
4.27	Kira	Sims	USA	1.3.82	27	Feb
4.26	Zoë	Brown	GBR	15.9.83	21	Feb
4.25A	Dana	Buller	CAN	7.12.79	10	Jan
4.25	Martina	Strutz	GER	4.11.81	25	Jan
4.25	Vala	Flosadóttir	ISL	16.2.78	30	Jan
4.25	Aleksandra	Kiryashova	RUS-J	21.8.85	14	Feb
4.25	Sandrine	Toulouse	FRA	14.9.72	22	Feb
4.25		Zhang Na	CHN	27.9.80	22	Feb
4.25	Fanni	Juhász	HUN	31.3.81	12	Mar

LONG JUMP

6.98	Tatyana	Lebedeva	RUS	21.7.76	1	WI	Budapest	7 Mar
6.95	Irina	Simagina	RUS	25.5.82	2	NC	Moskva	19 Feb
6.93	Tatyana	Kotova	RUS	11.12.76	2	WI	Budapest	7 Mar
6.92	Carolina	Klüft	SWE	2.2.83	3	WI	Budapest	7 Mar
6.80		Guan Yingnan	CHN	25.4.77	Q	WI	Budapest	6 Mar
6.78	Olga	Rublyova	RUS	28.10.74	3	NC	Moskva	19 Feb
6.75	Marion	Jones	USA	12.10.75	1	GP	Birmingham	20 Feb
6.72	Valentina	Gotovska	LAT	3.9.65	1	NC	Riga	6 Feb
6.69	Fiona	May	ITA	12.12.69	2		Athína (P)	22 Feb
6.66	Irina	Melnikova	RUS	12.10.75	4	NC	Moskva	19 Feb
6.66	Stilianí	Pilátou	GRE	28.3.80	1	BalkC	Athína (P)	28 Feb
6.65	Concepción	Montaner	ESP	14.1.81	1	NC	Valencia	22 Feb
6.65	Antoniya	Yordanova	BUL	17.8.76	1	NC	Budapest	23 Feb
6.65	Lyudmila	Galkina	RUS	20.1.72	3	Gaz	Liévin	28 Feb
6.63	Bianca	Kappler	GER	8.8.77	1		Chemnitz	27 Feb
6.63	Adina	Anton	ROM	6.10.84	Q	WI	Budapest	6 Mar
6.62	Sophie	Krauel	GER-J	2.3.85	1		Halle	24 Jan
6.61	Denisa	Scerbová	CZE-J	21.8.86	1	NC	Praha	22 Feb
6.61	Eunice	Barber	FRA	17.11.74	4	Gaz	Liévin	28 Feb
6.60	Elva	Goulbourne	JAM	21.1.80	1		Fayetteville	13 Feb
6.58	Hyleas	Fountain	USA	14.1.81	1	NCAA	Fayetteville	12 Mar

6.57	Ioánna	Kafetzí	GRE	30.5.76	24	Jan
6.57	Martina	Darmovzalová	CZE	12.10.78	11	Feb
6.57	Tatyana	Ter-Mesrobyan	RUS	12.5.68	21	Feb
6.57	Karin	Ruckstuhl	NED	2.11.80	5	Mar
6.55	Grace	Upshaw	USA	22.9.75	14	Feb
6.55	Livia	Pruteanu	ROM	22.12.81	15	Feb
6.55	Yelena	Shekhovtsova	UKR	31.5.72	21	Feb
6.55	Tatyana	Ivanova	RUS	16.10.81	21	Feb
6.55	Niurka	Montalvo	ESP	4.6.68	22	Feb
6.54	Kumiko	Ikeda	JPN	10.1.81	21	Feb
6.54	Níki	Xánthou	GRE	11.10.73	28	Feb
6.53	Olga	Alekseyeva	KAZ	30.11.84	23	Jan
6.51	Bronwyn	Thompson	AUS	29.1.78	6	Mar
6.49		Wang Lina	CHN	28.2.83	18	Feb
6.49	Anna	Kovalenko	RUS	3.2.82	21	Feb
6.49	Alina	Militaru	ROM	10.4.82	29	Feb
6.48	Angelica	Badea	ROM	1.10.75	31	Jan
6.48	Inna	Ivlyeva	RUS	27.6.71	21	Feb

TRIPLE JUMP

15.36	Tatyana	Lebedeva	RUS	21.7.76	1	WI	Budapest	6 Mar
14.90	Yamilé	Aldama	SUD	14.8.72	2	WI	Budapest	6 Mar
14.81	Hrisopiyí	Devetzí	GRE	2.1.76	1		Athína (P)	22 Feb
14.81	Magdelin	Martinez	ITA	10.2.76	Q	WI	Budapest	5 Mar
14.71	Trecia	Smith	JAM	5.11.75	4	WI	Budapest	6 Mar
14.62	Françoise	Mbango	CMR	14.4.76	6	WI	Budapest	6 Mar
14.62	Adelina	Gavrila	ROM	26.11.78	7	WI	Budapest	6 Mar
14.59	Yelena	Govorova	UKR	18.9.73	8	WI	Budapest	6 Mar
14.57	Mabel	Gay	CUB	5.5.83	Q	WI	Budapest	5 Mar
14.47	Ashia	Hansen	GBR	5.12.71	1	GP	Birmingham	20 Feb
14.45	Simona	La Mantia	ITA	14.4.83	Q	WI	Budapest	5 Mar
14.43	Tereza	Marinova	BUL	5.9.77	2	BalkC	Athína (P)	28 Feb
14.41	Yelena	Oleynikova	RUS	9.12.76	1	NC	Moskva	18 Feb
14.37	Carlota	Castrejana	ESP	25.4.73	1	NC	Valencia	21 Feb
14.36	Anna	Pyatykh	RUS	4.4.81	2	NC	Moskva	18 Feb
14.33	Viktoriya	Gurova	RUS	22.5.82	3	NC	Moskva	18 Feb
14.31	Yelena	Ivanova	RUS	16.3.79	3		Samara	29 Jan
14.31	Baya	Rahouli	ALG	27.7.79	Q	WI	Budapest	5 Mar
14.30	Natalya	Safronova	BLR	11.7.74	Q	WI	Budapest	5 Mar
14.29	Oksana	Rogova	RUS	7.10.78	2		Moskva	1 Feb
14.28	Olga	Vasdéki	GRE	26.9.73	4		Athína (P)	22 Feb
14.24	Mariana	Solomon	ROM	8.9.80	2		Bucuresti	31 Jan
14.24		Huang Qiuyan	CHN	25.1.80	14q	WI	Budapest	5 Mar
14.08	Natalia	Kilpeläinen	FIN	19.7.70	1	Stars	Tampere	14 Feb
14.07	Heli	Koivula-Kruger	FIN	27.6.75	2	Stars	Tampere	14 Feb

14.05	Rodica	Mateescu	ROM	13.3.71	25 Jan	13.93	Yekaterina	Chernyavskaya	UKR	31.1.83	29 Jan
14.04	Cristina	Nicolau	ROM	9.8.77	14 Feb	13.93	Nina	Serbezova	BUL	6.5.81	1 Feb
14.04	Sárka	Kaspárková	CZE	20.5.71	21 Feb	13.92	Anastasiya	Zhuravlyeva	UZB	9.10.81	5 Mar
14.03	Iríni	Dimitráki	GRE	8.8.80	8 Feb	13.87	Barbara	Lah	ITA	24.3.72	22 Feb
14.03	Cristine	Spîtaru	ROM-J	4.2.86	28 Feb	13.86	Mariya	Dimitrova	BUL	7.8.76	8 Feb
13.96	Katja	Demut	GER	21.12.83	7 Feb	13.85	Constanta	Stucan	ROM	12.7.81	14 Feb
13.95	Tiombé	Hurd	USA	17.8.73	8 Feb	13.84	Kène	Ndoye	SEN	20.11.78	25 Feb
13.95	Nadezhda	Bazhenova	RUS	22.9.78	18 Feb	13.80	Silvia	Biondini	ITA	24.1.76	31 Jan
13.95	Camilla	Johansson	SWE	3.11.76	22 Feb	13.80	Yuliana	Perez	USA	21.7.81	13 Feb

SHOT

20.73	Vita	Pavlysh	UKR	15.1.69	1	NC	Sumy	22 Feb
20.13	Irina	Korzhanenko	RUS	16.5.74	1		Moskva	1 Feb
19.90	Svetlana	Krivelyova	RUS	13.6.69	2	WI	Budapest	5 Mar
19.48	Cleopatra	Borel	TRI	3.10.79	1		Blacksburg	14 Feb
19.31	Yumileidi	Cumbá	CUB	11.2.75	3	WI	Budapest	5 Mar
19.15	Laura	Gerraughty	USA	29.7.83	1	NCAA	Fayetteville	13 Mar
19.05	Nadine	Kleinert	GER	20.10.75	4	WI	Budapest	5 Mar
19.00	Krystyna	Zabawska	POL	14.1.68	5	WI	Budapest	5 Mar
18.91	Natalya	Khoroneko	BLR	25.5.82	1	NC	Minsk	30 Jan
18.76		Li Meiju	CHN	23.1.81	Q	WI	Budapest	5 Mar
18.75	Irina	Khudoroshkina	RUS	13.10.68	1	EICp	Leipzig	14 Feb
18.60	Nadezhda	Ostapchuk	BLR	12.10.80	Q	WI	Budapest	5 Mar
18.56	Misleydis	González	CUB	19.6.78	Q	WI	Budapest	5 Mar
18.44	Cristiana	Checchi	ITA	8.7.77	1		Schio	14 Feb
18.42	Oksana	Chibisova	RUS	31.3.77	2		Shakhty	17 Jan
18.39	Lieja	Tunks	NED	10.3.76	9	WI	Budapest	5 Mar
18.33	Assunta	Legnante	ITA	14.5.78	2		Schio	14 Feb
18.22	Valerie	Adams	NZL	6.10.84	11	WI	Budapest	5 Mar
18.20	Laurence	Manfrédi	FRA	2.5.74	Q	NC	Aubière	21 Feb

18.04	Kristin	Heaston	USA	23.11.75	7 Feb	17.61	Nadine	Beckel	GER	27.5.77	7 Feb
17.86	Stephanie	Brown	USA	1.8.79	7 Feb	17.57		Cheng Xiaoyan	CHN	30.11.75	18 Feb
17.81	Kim	Barrett	JAM	18.11.81	29 Feb	17.54	Vera	Yepimashko	BLR	10.7.76	30 Jan

WEIGHT

23.95	Erin	Gilreath	USA	11.8.80	1		Gainesville	25 Jan
23.14	Anna	Mahon	USA	19.12.74	1		Allston	18 Jan
23.05	Candice	Scott	TRI	17.9.80	1	NCAA	Fayetteville	12 Mar
22.95	Kim	Barrett	JAM	18.11.81	2	NCAA	Fayetteville	12 Mar
22.48	Dawn	Ellerbe	USA	3.4.74	1		Columbia SC	21 Feb
22.24	Amber	Campbell	USA	5.6.81	3	NC	Boston (R)	27 Feb
22.20	Jamine	Moton	USA	14.12.78	1		Clemson	14 Feb
22.03	Jennifer	Dahlgren	ARG	27.8.84	3	NCAA	Fayetteville	12 Mar

22.00	LaQuanda	Cotten	USA	30.12.80	17 Jan	21.27	Dayana	Octavien	USA	10.6.82	27 Feb
21.85	Jukina	Dickerson	USA	7.8.81	12 Mar	21.15	Cari	Soong	USA	11.7.81	12 Mar

Continued on page 607

WORLD INDOOR CHAMPIONSHIPS 2004

At Budapest, HUN 5-7 March

MEN

60 Metres (a)
1. Jason Gardener GBR 6.49
2. Shawn Crawford USA 6.52
3. Yeóryios Theodorídis GRE 6.54
4. Mickey Grimes USA 6.55
5. Matic Osovnikar SLO 6.58
6. Francis Obikwelu POR 6.60
7. Simone Collio ITA 6.60
8. Niconnor Alexander TRI 6.76

200 Metres (c)
1. Dominic Demeritte BAH 20.66
2. Johan Wissman SWE 20.72
3. Tobias Unger GER 21.02
4. Joseph Batangdon CMR 21.16
5. Jimmie Hackley USA 21.35
6. Marcin Urbas POL 21.49

400 Metres (b)
1. Alleyne Francique GRN 45.88
2. Davian Clarke JAM 45.92
3. Gary Kikaya COD 46.30
4. Sofiane Labidi TUN 46.48
5. Milton Campbell USA 46.74
6. Joe Mendel USA 47.34

800 Metres (c)
1. Mbulaeni Mulaudzi RSA 1:45.71
2. Rashid Ramzi BRN 1:46.15
3. Osmar dos Santos BRA 1:46.26
4. Amine Laalou MAR 1:46.57
5. William Yiampoy KEN 1:46.88
6. Joseph Mutua KEN 1:47.86

1500 Metres (c)
1. Paul Korir KEN 3:52.31
2. Ivan Heshko UKR 3:52.34
3. Laban Rotich KEN 3:52.93
4. Abdelkader Hachlaf MAR 3:53.22
5. James Thie GBR 3:53.36
6. Miroslaw Formela POL 3:53.70
7. José Antonio Redolat ESP 3:56.55
8. Youssef Baba MAR 3:57.79

dq. Michael East GBR (3:52.88)

3000 Metres (b)
1. Bernard Lagat KEN 7:56.34
2. Rui Silva POR 7:57.08
3. Markos Geneti ETH 7:57.87
4. António Jiménez ESP 7:58.23
5. Sergio Gallardo ESP 7:58.96
6. Gert-Jan Liefers NED 8:02.86
7. Kevin Sullivan CAN 8:03.34
8. Mohammed Amyn MAR 8:03.50
9. Hicham Bellani MAR 8:03.73
10. Craig Mottram AUS 8:03.82
11. Abiyote Abate ETH 8:09.71
12. Sergey Lebed UKR 8:14.32

Fastest heat: Lagat 7:47.70

60 Metres Hurdles (b)
1. Allen Johnson USA 7.36*
2. Liu Xiang CHN 7.43
3. Maurice Wignall JAM 7.48
4. Stanislav Olijar LAT 7.49
5. Yuniel Hernández CUB 7.58
6. Robert Kronberg SWE 7.59
7. Yoel Hernández CUB 7.78
8. Dwight Thomas JAM 7.87

Third title for Johnson

High Jump (a-b)

1\. Stefan Holm SWE 2.35
2\. Yaroslav Rybakov RUS 2.32
3= Jaroslav Bába CZE 2.25
3= Germaine Mason JAM 2.25
3= Stefan Vasilache ROM 2.25
6\. Gennadiy Moroz BLR 2.25
7\. Andrey Sokolovskiy UKR 2.25
8\. Adrian O'Dwyer IRL 2.25
9\. Jamie Nieto USA 2.20

Holm's third consecutive indoor title.

Pole Vault (c)
1. Igor Pavlov RUS 5.80
2. Adam Ptácek CZE 5.70
3. Denys Yurchenko UKR 5.70
4. Patrik Kristiansson SWE 5.70
5. Tim Lobinger GER 5.70
6. Giuseppe Gibilisco ITA 5.60
7. Romain Mesnil FRA 5.60

nh. Rens Blom NED –

Pavlov 5.75 and eight men (inc. 9. Okkert Brits RSA) 5.70 in qualifying

Long Jump (b)
1. Savanté Stringfellow USA 8.40
2. James Beckford JAM 8.31
3. Vitaliy Shkurlatov RUS 8.28
4. Bogdan Tarus ROM 8.26
5. Vladimir Zyuskov UKR 8.23
6. Chris Tomlinson GBR 8.17
7. Kirill Sosunov RUS 8.16
8. Iván Pedroso CUB 8.09

Best ever 7th place.

Triple Jump (c)
1. Christian Olsson SWE WR 17.83*
2. Jadel Gregório BRA 17.43
3. Yoandri Betanzos CUB 17.36
4. Dmitriy Valyukevich BLR 17.22
5. Marian Oprea ROM 17.19
6. Nikolay Savolaynen UKR 16.95
7. Danila Burkenya RUS 16.62
8. Julien Kapek FRA 16.50

Shot (b-c)
1. Christian Cantwell USA 21.49
2. Rees Hoffa USA 21.07
3. Joachim Olsen DEN 20.99
4. Tomasz Majewski POL 20.83
5. Manuel Martínez ESP 20.79
6. Andrey Mikhnevich BLR 20.50
7. Carl Myerscough GBR 20.47
8. Yuriy Bilonog UKR 20.26

Heptathlon (b-c)
1. Roman Sebrle CZE 6438 ER
2. Bryan Clay USA 6365
3. Lev Lobodin RUS 6203
4. Dmitriy Karpov KAZ 6155 AR
5. Erki Nool EST 6093
6. Aleksandr Pogorelov RUS 6022
7. Jón-Arnar Magnússon ISL 5993
8. Ranko Leskovar SLO 5612

4 x 400 Metres Relay (c)

1\. JAM 3:05.21
(Haughton 46.42, Colquhoun 46.36, M McDonald 46.49, D Clarke 45.94)

2\. RUS 3:06.23
(D Forshev 47.61, B Gorban 46.35, A Rudnitskiy 45.94, A Usov 46.33)

3\. IRL 3:10.44
(R Daly 47.79, G Ryan 48.00, D Gillick 47.74, D McCarthy 46.91)

4\. SUI 3:12.62

5\. BAH 3:17.57

dq. USA (3:06.96)
J Carter 46.64, M Campbell 46.12, J Mendel 46.39, G Herring 47.81

WOMEN

60 Metres (a)
1. Gail Devers USA 7.08
2. Kim Gevaert BEL 7.12
3. Yuliya Nesterenko BLR 7.12
4. Torri Edwards USA 7.16
5. Muriel Hurtis FRA 7.17
6. Yuliya Tabakova RUS 7.17
7. Christine Arron FRA 7.21
8. Natalya Safronnikova BLR 7.23

Devers third world indoor 60m title.

200 Metres (c)
1. Anast. Kapachinskaya RUS 22.78
2. Natalya Safronnikova BLR 23.13
3. Svetlana Goncharenko RUS 23.15
4. Karin Mayr-Krifka AUT 23.18
5. Maryna Maydanova UKR 23.64
6. Nataliya Pygyda UKR 23.80

400 Metres (b)
1. Natalya Nazarova RUS 50.19*
2. Olesya Krasnomovets RUS 50.65
3. Tonique Williams BAH 50.87
4. Ionela Tîrlea ROM 51.58
5. Julian Clay USA 52.82
6. Fani Halkiá GRE 52.90

800 Metres (c)
1. Maria Mutola MOZ 1:58.50
2. Jolanda Ceplak SLO 1:58.72
3. Jo Fenn GBR 1:59.50
4. Jen Toomey USA 1:59.64
5. Tatyana Andrianova RUS 1:59.71
6. Olga Raspopova RUS 2:00.56

Mutola became the first athlete to capture a sixth world indoor title.

1500 Metres (b)
1. Kutre Dulecha ETH 4:06.40
2. Car. Douma-Hussar CAN 4:08.18
3. Gulnara Samitova RUS 4:08.26
4. Daniela Yordanova BUL 4:08.52
5. Natalya Tobias UKR 4:09.03
6. Yuliya Kosenkova RUS 4:09.32
7. Alesya Turova BLR 4:09.81
8. Lidia Okninska POL 4:10.32
9. Kelly Holmes GBR 4:12.30

3000 Metres (c)
1. Meseret Defar ETH 9:11.22
2. Berhane Adere ETH 9:11.43
3. Shayne Culpepper USA 9:12.15
4. Marta Domínguez ESP 9:12.85
5. Joanne Pavey GBR 9:13.09
6. Yelena Zadorozhnaya RUS 9:13.70
7. Sabrina Mockenhaupt GER 9:13.70
8. Maryna Dubrova UKR 9:14.34
9. Maria McCambridge IRL 9:14.72
10. Veerle Dejaeghere BEL 9:15.21
11. Galina Bogomolova RUS 9:17.15

dns. Hayley Tullett GBR –

Fsatest heat Adere 8:49.76

60 Metres Hurdles (c)
1. Perdita Felicien CAN 7.75*
2. Gail Devers USA 7.78
3. Linda Ferga-Khodadin FRA 7.82
4. Joanna Hayes USA 7.86

5. Susanna Kallur SWE 7.89
6. Lacena Golding-Clarke JAM 7.89
7. Flóra Redoúmi GRE 7.94
8. Nicole Ramalalanirina FRA 8.01

High Jump (c)
1. Yelena Slesarenko RUS 2.04
2. Anna Chicherova RUS 2.00
3. Blanka Vlasic CRO 1.97
4. Vita Palamar UKR 1.97
5. Daniela Rath GER 1.97
6. Marta Mendía ESP 1.94
7. Venelina Veneva BUL 1.94
8. Viktoriya Styopina UKR 1.91

All eight cleared 1.96 to qualify.

Pole Vault (b)
1. Yelena Isinbayeva RUS 4.86* WR
2. Stacy Dragila USA 4.81
3. Svetlana Feofanova RUS 4.70
4. Jillian Schwartz USA 4.60

5= Vanessa Boslak FRA 4.50
5= Monika Pyrek POL 4.50

7. Anna Rogowska POL 4.40
8. Nastja Ryshich GER 4.40

Best ever marks for 1-4 after record 12 women over 4.30 in qualifying.

Long Jump (c)
1. Tatyana Lebedeva RUS 6.98
2. Tatyana Kotova RUS 6.93
3. Carolina Klüft SWE 6.92
4. Guan Yingnan CHN 6.75
5. Valentina Gotovska LAT 6.67
6. Fiona May ITA 6.64
7. Concepción Montaner ESP 6.46
8. Adina Anton ROM 6.43

Triple Jump (b)
1. Tatyana Lebedeva RUS 15.36*
2. Yamilé Aldama SUD 14.90
3. Hrysopiyí Devetzí GRE 14.73
4. Trecia Smith JAM 14.71
5. Magdelin Martínez ITA 14.67
6. Françoise Mbango CMR 14.62
7. Adelina Gavrila ROM 14.62
8. Olena Hovorova UKR 14.59
9. Mabel Gay CUB 14.49
10. Baya Rahouli ALG 14.19
11. Simona La Mantia ITA 14.14
12. Natalya Safronova BLR 14.00

Lebedeva series: 15.16 =WR, 15.25 WR. p, 15.15, p, 15.36 WR. Best ever marks for 5-9 and 10th (14.31) to 18th (14.02) in qualifying.

Shot (a)
1. Vita Pavlysh UKR 20.49
2. Svetlana Krivelyova RUS 19.90
3. Yumileidi Cumbá CUB 19.31
4. Nadine Kleinert GER 19.05
5. Krystyna Zabawska POL 19.00
6. Li Meiju CHN 18.69
7. Misleydis González CUB 18.41
8. Nadezhda Ostapchuk BLR 18.33

Pentathlon (a)
1. Naide Gomes POR 4759
2. Natalya Dobrynska UKR 4727
3. Austra Skujyte LTU 4679
4. Karin Ruckstuhl NED 4640
5. Tia Hellebaut BEL 4526
6. Irina Butor BLR 4315
7. Larisa Netseporuk EST 4227
8. Kim Schiemenz USA 4012

4 x 400 Metres Relay (c)
1. RUS 3:23.88* WR
(Krasnomovets 51.37, Kotlyarova 50.12, Levina 52.50, Nazarova 49.89)
2. BLR 3:29.96
(N Sologub 52.63, A Kozak 52.61, I Usovich 53.79, S Usovich 50.93)
3. ROM 3:30.06
(A Morosanu 54.00, A Rîpanu 52.73, M Rus 52.64, I Tîrlea 50.69)
4. POL 3:30.52
5. JAM 3:33.77
6. GRE 3:39.23

Kotlyarova & Nazarova ran first ever sub-50 splits indoors

World Indoor Lists 2004 (Continued)

PENTATHLON

4759	Naide	Gomes	POR	10.11.79	1	WI	Budapest	5 Mar
	8.48	1.88 15.08	6.45	2:21.69				
4727	Natalya	Dobrinskaya	UKR	29.5.82	2	WI	Budapest	5 Mar
	8.48	1.82 15.39	6.43	2:19.45				
4679	Austra	Skujyte	LTU	12.8.79	3	WI	Budapest	5 Mar
	8.69	1.79 16.30	6.38	2:20.24				
4640	Karin	Ruckstuhl	NED	2.11.80	4	WI	Budapest	5 Mar
	8.39	1.82 13.21	6.57	2:19.92				
4589	Tia	Hellebaut	BEL	16.2.78	1	NC	Aubière	21 Feb
	8.57	1.91 13.21	6.04	2:16.99				
4523	Anna	Snetkova	RUS	.80	2	NC	Moskva	8 Feb
	8.63	1.76 14.17	6.35	2:18.65				
4521	Marina	Brezgina	UKR	16.1.77	1	NC	Minsk	27 Jan
	8.20	1.77 12.97	6.38	2:21.57				
4505	Sonja	Kesselschläger	GER	20.1.78	1	NC	Halle	31 Jan
	8.43	1.78 13.45	6.21	2:18.22				
4500	Yuliya	Ignatkina	RUS	13.9.82	1		Novocheboksarsk	25 Jan
	8.91	1.81 13.54	6.32	2:16.75				
4483	Magdalena	Szczepanska	POL	25.6.80	1	NC	Spala	21 Feb
	8.61	1.78 13.58	6.05	2:14.06				
4467	Tatyana	Zhevnova	BLR	17.10.77	2	NC	Minsk	27 Jan
	8.40	1.80 13.99	6.06	2:22.53				
4447	Natalya	Roshchupkina	RUS	13.1.78	3	NC	Moskva	8 Feb
	8.73	1.82 12.59	6.18	2:16.50				
4447	Marie	Collonvillé	FRA	23.11.73	2	NC	Aubière	21 Feb
	8.55	1.82 12.10	6.16	2:16.54				
4428	Yelena	Ivlyeva	RUS	.74	1		Kemerovo	20 Dec
	8.56	1.78 12.80	6.36	2:22.11				
4417#	Hyleas	Fountain	USA	14.1.81	1	SEC	Lexington	27 Feb
	8.23	1.81 11.71	6.32	2:24.94				
	4412				1	NCAA	Fayetteville	13 Mar

4388	Claudia	Tonn	GER	18.4.81	31 Jan
4383	Julie	Hollman	GBR	16.2.77	1 Feb
4380	Vera	Yepimashko	BLR	10.7.76	27 Jan
4364	Joanna	Grzesiak	POL	15.8.80	21 Feb
4351	Mihaela	Gîndila	ROM	29.10.74	31 Jan
4347	Aryiró	Stratáki	GRE	3.8.75	22 Feb
4344	Olga	Alekseyeva	KAZ	30.11.84	6 Feb
4328	GiGi	Miller	USA	12.1.79	23 Jan
4315	Irina	Butor	BLR	26.2.80	5 Mar
4288	Svetlana	Sokolova	RUS	9.1.81	8 Feb
4268	Maren	Schwerdtner	GER	3.10.85	1 Feb
4263	Jackie	Johnson	USA	8.9.84	13 Mar
4260	Gertrud	Bacher	ITA	28.2.71	15 Feb
4251	Lilli	Schwarzkopf	GER	28.8.83	31 Jan
4247	Maren	Freisen	GER	15.2.82	31 Jan
4245	Anna	Kryazeva	RUS	17.7.84	8 Feb

WORLD CROSS-COUNTRY CHAMPIONSHIPS 2004

Brussels, Belgium 20-21 March

Kenenisa Bekele won both men's races in supreme style for the third successive year, Edith Masai won the women's short race for the third successive year and Benita Johnson became the first Australian World CC champion. The battle between the East African super-powers of distance running has usually gone to Kenya in recent years. but this time Ethiopia won five of the six team titles and 14 of the 18 individual medals. Kenya had taken the men's short course team title on all six previous occasions the race has been contested and they had won the men's long course title for an amazing 18 successive years before this year, when Ethiopians took the first three places in the race.

Men's 4km (20)

1. Kenenisa Bekele ETH	11:31
2. Gebre Gebremariam ETH	11:36
3. Maregu Zewde ETH	11:42
4. Abdullah Ahmad Hassan QAT	11:44
5. Saïf Saaeed Shaheen QAT	11:44
6. Eliud Kirui KEN	11:45
7. Isaac Songok KEN	11:45
8. Sultan Khamis Zaman QAT	11:50
9. Craig Mottram AUS	11:51
10. Adil El Kaouch MAR	11:56
11. Berhanu Dejene ETH	11:56
12. Tarek Boukensa ALG	11:56
13. Alejandro Suárez MEX	11:57
14. Carlos García ESP	11:58
15. Bouabdallah Tahri FRA	11:58
16. Alistair Cragg IRL	11:58
17. Kevin Sullivan CAN	11:58
18. Paul Morrison CAN	11:59
19. Abraham Chebii KEN	11:59
20. Kiplimo Muneria KEN	12:00

139 finished

Team 18 completed

1. ETH	17	6. CAN	128
2. QAT	39	7. USA	163
3. KEN	52	8. ESP	192
4. ALG	119	9. POR	206
5. MAR	119	10. FRA	210

Men's 12km (21)

1. Kenenisa Bekele ETH	35:52
2. Gebre Gebremariam ETH	36:10
3. Sileshi Sihine ETH	36:11
4. Eliud Kipchoge KEN	36:34
5. Charles Kamathi KEN	36:36
6. Tadesse Zersenay ERI	36:37
7. Fabiano Joseph TAN	36:49
8. Yibeltal Admasu ETH	36:52
9. Yonas Kifle ERI	36:53
10. Wilberforce Taleli KEN	37:01
11. John Cheruiyot Korir KEN	37:03
12. Hicham Chatt MAR	37:09
13. Craig Mottram AUS	37:10
14. Abderrahim Goumri MAR	37:17
15. Tibebu Yenew ETH	37:26
16. Saïd El Wardi MAR	37:29
17. El Hassan Lahssini FRA	37:30
18. Dieudonné Disi RWA	37:36
19. Jon Brown GBR	37:38
20. John Stephen Rogarth TAN	37:41

130 finished

Team 19 completed

1. ETH	14	6. TAN	118
2. KEN	30	7. RWA	164
3. ERI	66	8. ESP	166
4. MAR	68	9. FRA	168
5. AUS	101	10. GBR	170

Junior Men's 8km (21)

1. Meba Tadesse ETH	24:01
2. Boniface Kiprop UGA	24:03
3. Ernest Kimeli KEN	24:16
4. Barnabas Kosgei KE	24:24
5. Wondimu Mulugeta ETH	24:44
6. Hosea Macharinyang KEN	24:51
7. Ronald Rutto KEN	25:04
8. Moses Aliwa UGA	25:08
9. Tessema Absher ETH	25:12
10. Yirefu Birhanu ETH	25:18

118 finished

Team 18 completed

1. KEN	20	6. ALG	157
2. ETH	25	7. USA	175
3. UGA	33	8. RUS	179
4. MAR	61	9. EGY	187
5. JPN	105	10. ERI	213

Women's 4km (21)

1. Edith Masai KEN	13:07
2. Tirunesh Dibaba ETH	13:09
3. Teyiba Erkesso ETH	13:11
4. Werknesh Kidane ETH	13:14
5. Isabella Ochichi KEN	13:18
6. Olga Romanova RUS	13:19
7. Peninah Chepchumba KEN	13:22
8. Vivian Cheruiyot KEN	13:23
9. Jane Wanjiku KEN	13:23
10. Ejagayou Dibaba ETH	13:23
11. Amane Godana ETH	13:27
12. Zahra Ouaziz MAR	13:33
13. Émilie Mondor CAN	13:33
14. Shalane Flanagan USA	13:34
15. Sarah Jamieson AUS	13:40
16. Bouchra Chaabi MAR	13:40
17. Carmen Douma-Hussar CAN	13:41
18. Bezunesh Bekele ETH	13:42
19. Helen Clitheroe GBR	13:45
20. Kathy Butler GBR	13:47

89 finishers

Teams 12 completed

1. ETH	19	6. POR	127
2. KEN	21	7. USA	141
3. CAN	87	8. ESP	191
4. MAR	101	9. FRA	209
5. GBR	125	10. BEL	217

Women's 8km (20)

1. Benita Johnson AUS	27:17
2. Ejagayou Dibaba ETH	27:29
3. Werknesh Kidane ETH	27:34
4. Alice Timbilil KEN	27:36
5. Teyiba Erkesso ETH	27:43
6. Lornah Kiplagat NED	27:56
7. Eunice Chepkorir KEN	27:59
8. Émilie Mondor CAN	28:01
9. Fridah Domongole KEN	28:03
10. Sally Barsosio KEN	28:08
11. Kathy Butler GBR	28:13
12. Olivera Jevtic SCG	28:18
13. Liz Yelling GBR	28:25
14. Margaret Maury FRA	28:29
15. Kate O'Neill USA	28:37
16. Derartu Tulu ETH	28:39
17. Haley McGregor AUS	28:41
18. Patrizia Tisi ITA	28:45
19. Zahia Dahmani FRA	28:46
20. Jane Ngotho KEN	28:47

96 finishers

Team 14 completed

1. ETH	26	6. AUS	99
2. KEN	30	7. CAN	161
3. GBR	74	8. POR	167
4. FRA	90	9. ESP	206
5. USA	98	10. JPN	206

Junior Women's 6km (20)

1. Meselech Melkamu ETH	20:48
2. Aziza Aliyu ETH	20:53
3. Mestawat Tadesse ETH	20:56
4. Workitu Ayanu ETH	20:59
5. Chemtai Rionotukei KEN	21:04
6. Jebichi Yator KEN	21:05
7. Yemealem Ayano ETH	21:05
8. Bao Guiying CHN	21:05
9. Gladys Chemweno KEN	21:13
10. Hitomi Miyai JPN	21:15

112 finishers

Team 17 completed

1. ETH	10	6. CHN	169
2. KEN	36	7. RSA	185
3. JPN	67	8. MAR	196
4. USA	120	9. FRA	200
5. RUS	160	10. RWA	204

World Indoor Lists 2004 (Continued)

3000 METRES WALK

11:50.48	Melanie	Seeger	GER	8.1.77	1	NC	Dortmund	21 Feb
11:57.00	Elisa	Rigaudo	ITA	17.6.80	1	NC	Genova	21 Feb
11:59.3	Kjersti	Plätzer	NOR	18.1.72	1		Liévin	1 Feb
11:59.79	Gillian	O'Sullivan	IRL	21.8.76	1	NC	Belfast	15 Feb
12:00.39	Sabine	Zimmer	GER	6.2.81	2	NC	Dortmund	21 Feb
12:34.28	Andrea	Meloni	GER	1.10.67	3	NC	Dortmund	21 Feb